GREENS
ANNOTATED RULES OF THE
COURT OF SESSION
2007/2008

AUSTRALIA
Law Book Co.
Sydney

CANADA and USA
Carswell
Toronto

HONG KONG
Sweet & Maxwell Asia

NEW ZEALAND
Brookers
Wellington

SINGAPORE and MALAYSIA
Sweet & Maxwell Asia
Singapore and Kuala Lumpur

Reprinted from the *Parliament House Book*, published in looseleaf form
and updated five times a year by W. Green, the Scottish Law Publisher

The following paperback titles are also available in the series:
Sheriff Court Rules 2007/2008
Solicitors Professional Handbook 2007/8
and
Criminal Law Statutes 2007/2008
reprinted from *Renton & Brown's Criminal Procedure Legislation*

Parliament House Book consists of the following Divisions:
A Fees and Stamps
B Courts, Upper
C Rules of the Court of Session (annotated)
D Courts, Lower
E Licensing
F Solicitors
G Legal Aid
H Bankruptcy and other Mercantile Statutes
I Companies
J Conveyancing, Land Tenure and Registration
K Family Law
L Landlord and Tenant
M Succession, Trusts, Liferents and Judicial Factors

GREENS
ANNOTATED RULES
OF THE COURT OF SESSION
2007/2008

Reprinted from
Division C (Court of Session Practice)
of the *Parliament House Book*

THOMSON

W. GREEN

Published in 2007 by W. Green & Son Ltd
21 Alva Street
Edinburgh EH2 4PS

*Printed in Great Britain by William Clowes Ltd
Beccles, Suffolk*

No natural forests were destroyed to make this product;
only farmed timber was used and replanted

A CIP catalogue record for this book is available from the British Library

ISBN 9780414016842

© W. Green & Son Ltd 2007

PREFACE

The idea for this book occurred to me in about 1980. The project was delayed in 1984 when the Rules Review Group was set up to consider changes to the R.C.S. 1965.

It seemed to me that there was room for a Scottish equivalent to the English "White Book" (*The Supreme Court Practice*). When a matter concerning the application of a rule arises unexpectedly in court, for example, there is a need for a book readily to hand which might suggest, or even provide, the answer: this was the book's original purpose. The aim has been to provide a practical, everyday tool for all who work and practise in the Court of Session, and to give authorities, and guidance, on the interpretation of the rules. While it is not possible to set out the law either in detail or on every topic, some attempt has been made to point the reader in the right direction. Further annotations will be included in subsequent releases.

We would like to express our grateful thanks to all those who have assisted in bringing this work to fruition. These include Peter Nicholson and his team at W. Green & Son Ltd., who, with infinite patience and faith, have put up with late material and achieved timely publication; Margo Wright who so willingly and cheerfully deciphered many manuscript scribblings and transformed them into typed prose; Morag Armstrong who, in a moment of rash generosity, volunteered to prepare the Table of Destinations and check the Table of Derivations; Ruth Ludlam who produced an excellent index, with assistance from Peter Nicholson and David Mackay, with great expedition; and Hugo who sacrificed walks with his master to allow (if he but knew it) the work to be completed.

Nigel Morrison

CONTENTS

    [NEXT TEXT PAGE IS C ix]

CONTENTS

LIST OF ABBREVIATIONS

A.S.	Act of Sederunt.
A.S. (R.C.A. No.)	Act of Sederunt (Rules of Court Amendment No.).
A.S. (R.C.S.A. No.)	Act of Sederunt (Rules of the Court of Session Amendment No.).
C.J.J.A.	Civil Jurisdiction and Judgments Act (*i.e.* Civil Jurisdiction and Judgments Act 1982 (c. 27) or Civil Jurisdiction and Judgments Act 1991 (c. 9)).
C.S.A.	Court of Session Act.
First Div.	First Division of the Inner House of the Court of Session.
2nd Div.	Second Division of the Inner House of the Court of Session.
E.C.H.R.	European Convention on Human Rights.
Extra Div.	Extra Division of the Inner House of the Court of Session.
I.H.	Inner House of the Court of Session.
L.J.-C.	Lord Justice-Clerk.
L.P.	Lord President.
O.H.	Outer House of the Court of Session.
P.N.	Practice Note
R.C.S.	Rules of the Court of Session.
R.C.S. 1965	Rules of the Court of Session in A.S. (Rules of Court, consolidation and amendment) 1965 [S.I. 1965 No. 321].
R.C.S. 1994	Rules of the Court of Session 1994 in A.S. (Rules of the Court of Session) 1994 [S.I. 1994 No. 1443].
Bell's *Comm.*	G.J. Bell, *Commentaries on the Law of Scotland and the Principles of Mercantile Jurisprudence,* 7th ed. by G. Watson, Edinburgh 1890.
Erskine	John Erskine of Carnock, *An Institute of the Law of Scotland,* 8th ed. by J.B. Nicholson, 2 vols., dinburgh 1871.
Stair	James, Viscount of Stair, *The Institutions of the Law of Scotland,* 2nd ed. 1693, reprinted ed. by D.M. Walker, Edinburgh and Glasgow 1981.

LIST OF ABBREVIATIONS

GREENS
ANNOTATED
RULES
OF THE
COURT OF SESSION

by

NIGEL MORRISON, Q.C.
Sheriff of Lothian and Borders at Edinburgh
formerly First Counsel to the Lord President
of the Court of Session

DAVID BARTOS, LL.B., Advocate
formerly Legal Assistant to the
Lord President of the Court of Session

NEIL CRICHTON, W.S.
Auditor of the Court of Session

THOMAS HIGGINS
Depute Clerk of Session and Justiciary
and formerly Clerk to the First Division of the Court of Session

IAIN MACLEAN, LL.B., LL.M., M.Sc., Advocate
formerly Legal Assistant to the
Lord President of the Court of Session

J. HALDANE TAIT, S.S.C.
formerly Auditor of the Court of Session

MATTHEW WEIR
Depute Clerk of Session and Justiciary
and Clerk to the First Division of the Court of Session

SARAH WOLFFE, B.A., LL.B., Advocate

TABLE OF CASES

[NEXT TEXT PAGE IS C–T71]

TABLE OF STATUTES

(References in *bold type* are to a rule in the R.C.S. 1994; references in ordinary type are to annotations)

TABLE OF STATUTORY INSTRUMENTS

(References in **bold type** are to a rule in the R.C.S. 1994;
references in ordinary type are to annotations)

TABLE OF DERIVATIONS

R.C.S. 1994 rule		Derivation (r. = rule in R.C.S. 1965)
Chapter 1,	r. 1.3(2)	r. 168(3)
	r. 1.3(3)	r. 68G
Chapter 2,	r. 2.1	A.S. (Rules of Court, consolidation and amendment) 1965, para. (4)
Chapter 3,	r. 3.1	r. 12(a) (part) and (b) (part)
	r. 3.2(1)	r. 12(b) (part)
	r. 3.2(2)	r. 13(a) as amended by S.I. 1982/1679
	r. 3.2(3)	r. 15
	r. 3.3(1)	r. 12(b) (part)
	r. 3.3(2)	r. 13(b)
	r. 3.4(2)	r. 14
	r. 3.5(1)	r. 12(b) (part)
	r. 3.5(4)	A.S. (Edictal Citations, Commissary Petitions and Petitions of Service) 1971 [S.I. 1971/1165]
	r. 3.6(1)	r. 12(b) (part)
	r. 3.6(2)	r. 13(c)
Chapter 4,	r. 4.1	r. 19
	r. 4.2(1) and (7)	r. 73(a) as amended by S.I. 1991/2483
	r. 4.2(2)	r. 73(b)
	r. 4.2(3), (4) and (8)	r. 28(1) as amended by S.I. 1991/2483
	r. 4.2(3) and (4)	r. 193 as amended by S.I. 1986/514 and 1991/2483
	r. 4.2(9)	r. 28(2) inserted by S.I. 1991/2483
	r. 4.3	P.N. No. 3 of 1976, para. 3(i)
	r. 4.4(1) and (2)	r. 20
	r. 4.4(3)	r. 78(d) as amended by S.I. 1990/705, and r. 194
	r. 4.5	r. 25
	r. 4.6	r. 21
	r. 4.6(1)(b)	r. 83(d)
	r. 4.7	r. 26(b)
	r. 4.8	r. 26(a)
	r. 4.9	r. 27
	r. 4.10	r. 29
	r. 4.11(1) and (2)	r. 31(a)
	r. 4.12(1) to (4)	r. 32(a)
	r. 4.12(5)	r. 32(b)
	r. 4.14	r. 23
	r. 4.15(2) and (5)	r. 30(1) substituted by S.I. 1984/472
	r. 4.15(3)	r. 93A inserted by S.I. 1978/799 and as amended by S.I. 1984/472
	r. 4.15(4)	r. 30(3) substituted by S.I. 1984/472
	r. 4.15(6)	r. 30(2) substituted by S.I. 1984/472
	r. 4.16(2), (3) and (5)	r. 295
	r. 4.16(4)	r. 30(3) inserted by S.I. 1986/1937
	r. 4.16(6)	r. 30(1) substituted by S.I. 1984/472
	r. 4.16(7)	r. 30(2) substituted by S.I. 1984/472
Chapter 5,	r. 5.1	r. 68H inserted by S.I. 1990/2118
	r. 5.1(d)	r. 218A(1)
	r. 5.2	r. 68I inserted by S.I. 1990/2118
Chapter 6,	r. 6.1	r. 18
	r. 6.2(2)	r. 17
	r. 6.2(3)	r. 94(a)
	r. 6.2(4)	P.N. 5th May 1972
	r. 6.2(7) (part)	P.N. No. 2 of 1987, para. 5
	r. 6.2(13) and (14)	P.N. 29th May 1975
	r. 6.3(5) and (6)	r. 294C(7) and (8) inserted by S.I. 1987/1206
	r. 6.3(8)	P.N. No. 2 of 1987, para. 5
	r. 6.4	r. 16
Chapter 7,	r. 7.1	P.N. 9th July 1980, regs. 1 and 3

R.C.S. 1994 rule	Derivation (r. = rule in R.C.S. 1965)
r. 7.2(1)	r. 168(11) substituted by S.I. 1978/106
r. 7.2(2)	r. 170K inserted by S.I. 1982/1679
r. 7.2(3)	P.N. 9th July 1980, regs. 6, 7 and 8
r. 7.3	P.N. 9th July 1980, reg. 1
r. 7.4	P.N. 9th July 1980, reg. 2
r. 7.5	P.N. 9th July 1980, reg. 5A
r. 7.6	P.N. 9th July 1980, reg. 5
r. 7.7	r. 66 as amended by S.I. 1969/1819, 1974/2090, 1983/398, 1985/1178 and 1993/770
r. 7.8	r. 63A inserted by S.I. 1986/1937
r. 7.9(2) and (3)	r. 63 substituted by S.I. 1986/1937
r. 7.10	r. 64
r. 7.11(2)	r. 170D(6) inserted by S.I. 1976/1994
Chapter 8, r. 8.1	r. 36
Chapter 9, r. 9.1	r. 32A inserted by S.I. 1976/745 and as amended by S.I. 1982/1825
r. 9.2	r. 34
Chapter 10, r. 10.1(2) and (3)	r. 68B inserted by S.I. 1987/2160
r. 10.2	r. 68C inserted by S.I. 1987/2160
r. 10.3	r. 68D inserted by S.I. 1987/2160
r. 10.5	r. 68E inserted by S.I. 1987/2160
r. 10.6	r. 68F inserted by S.I. 1987/2160
Chapter 11, r. 11.1	r. 1 as amended by S.I. 1987/1206
Chapter 12, r. 12.1(1)	r. 37 as amended by S.I. 1978/955, and r. 38
r. 12.1(2)	r. 40
r. 12.1(3)	Nautical Assessors (Scotland) Act 1894 (c. 40), s. 2; r. 41
r. 12.2	r. 44(c)
r. 12.3	r. 39(a)
r. 12.4	r. 39(c)
r. 12.5	Nautical Assessors (Scotland) Act 1894, s. 4; rr. 38 and 46(a)
r. 12.6	r. 43
r. 12.7(1)	r. 146
r. 12.7(2) to (4)	r. 42
r. 12.8	Nautical Assessors (Scotland) Act 1894, s. 3; r. 45
r. 12.9	Nautical Assessors (Scotland) Act 1894, s. 5; r. 44(b)
Chapter 13, r. 13.1	r. 69 (part)
r. 13.2(1) to (3) and (5)	r. 70(1)(a) and (b) as amended by S.I. 1984/472
r. 13.2(4)	r. 70(1)(c) inserted by S.I. 1986/1941 and as amended by S.I. 1987/1206
r. 13.3	r. 71
r. 13.4(1)(a) to (c) and (3)	r. 72(1) and (3) substituted by S.I. 1986/1941
r. 13.4(1)(d)	r. 75(7) substituted by S.I. 1986/1941
r. 13.5(1) and (2)	r. 74 (preamble (part))
r. 13.5(2) to (5)	P.N. No. 3 of 1976
r. 13.6	r.74 (preamble (part)) as amended by S.I. 1986/1941
r. 13.6A	Debtors (Scotland) Act 1838 (c. 114), s. 16; r. 70(2)(b) inserted by S.I. 1984/472, and r. 74 (preamble (part)) as amended by S.I. 1986/1941
r. 13.7(2)	A.S. 8th July 1831, para. III
r. 13.8(1) and (2)	r. 74(d)
r. 13.9(1)	r. 70(2)(a) inserted by S.I. 1984/472, and r. 74(e) (as amended by S.I. 1984/472) and (f)
r. 13.9(1) and (2)	r. 74(e) (as amended by S.I. 1984/472) and (f)
r. 13.10(1) and (2)	Debtors (Scotland) Act 1838, s. 20; r. 74(g) as amended by S.I. 1990/705 and 1991/2483
r. 13.10(3)	r. 74(h) as amended by S.I. 1990/705
r. 13.11	r. 74(g) and (h), and r. 140(d) and (dd), as amended by

R.C.S. 1994 rule	Derivation (r. = rule in R.C.S. 1965)
	S.I. 1990/705
r. 13.12	r. 76 as amended by S.I. 1991/2483
r. 13.13(1) and (2)	r. 78; P.N. No. 3 of 1976, para. 3(vi)
r. 13.13(1) to (5)	r. 78(a) to (c) and (e)
r. 13.13(6)	A.S. 8th July 1831, para. III
r. 13.14	r. 80(a)
Chapter 14, r. 14.2(a) to (h)	r. 69 and r. 189(a) (preamble) (as amended by S.I. 1970/134), (i), (ii), (iii) (substituted by S.I. 1987/1206), (iv) (as amended by S.I. 1987/1206) and (xxxvii) (inserted by S.I. 1990/705)
r. 14.3(a) to (j)	r. 190 (preamble) (as amended by S.I. 1970/134), (i) (as amended by S.I. 1980/1144), (iv) (as amended by S.I. 1992/1422), (v) and (vi) (as amended by S.I. 1976/283 and 1987/1206), (vii) (as amended by S.I. 1976/283 and 1977/1621), (viii)–(x) (substituted by S.I. 1987/1206) and (xi) (inserted by S.I. 1992/1422)
r. 14.4	r. 191 as amended by S.I. 1987/1206
r. 14.5	r. 195(a) (part)
r. 14.6(1)(a) to (c)	r. 192(1) substituted by S.I. 1986/1941
r. 14.6(2)	r. 192(3) substituted by S.I. 1986/1941
r. 14.7(1)	r. 195(a) (part)
r. 14.7(2)	r. 195(c) as amended by S.I. 1986/1941
r. 14.9(1)	r. 197 (preamble) as amended by S.I. 1986/1941
r. 14.9(2)	r. 197(a) substituted by S.I. 1986/1941
r. 14.9(3)	r. 197(b) substituted by S.I. 1986/1941
r. 14.9(4)	r. 197(c) substituted by S.I. 1986/1941
r. 14.9(5)	r. 197(d)
Chapter 16, r. 16.1(1)	r. 74A(1) inserted by S.I. 1984/472 and as amended by S.I. 1985/1600, 1986/1941 and 1990/705
r. 16.1(3)	r. 74A(3) inserted by S.I. 1984/472, and r. 77
r. 16.1(4)	r. 195(d)
r. 16.2(2)	r. 74B(1) inserted by S.I. 1986/1941
r. 16.2(3)	r. 74B(4) inserted by S.I. 1986/1941
r. 16.2(4)	r. 74B(5) inserted by S.I. 1986/1941
r. 16.2(5)	r. 74B(6) inserted by S.I. 1986/1941
r. 16.3(1), (2), (3) and (5)	r. 74A(4) inserted by S.I. 1984/472 and as amended by S.I. 1990/705 and 1991/1157
r. 16.3(4)	r. 74(i)
r. 16.4(2)	r. 68A inserted by S.I. 1968/1150, and r. 74A(5) (inserted by S.I. 1984/472) and (6) (inserted by S.I. 1984/472 and as amended by S.I. 1991/2483), and r. 74B(3)(a) (part) inserted by S.I. 1986/1941 and as amended by S.I. 1991/2483
r. 16.4(3)	r. 74B(7)(b) inserted by S.I. 1986/1941
r. 16.4(4)	r. 74(a) (part), r. 74A(7) inserted by S.I. 1984/472, and r.74B(3)(b) inserted by S.I. 1986/1941
r. 16.4(6)	r. 72(2), and r. 192(2), substituted by S.I. 1986/1941
r. 16.4(7)	r. 74A(8) substituted by S.I. 1984/472
r. 16.5(1)	r. 75(1) substituted by S.I. 1986/1941 and as amended by S.I. 1987/1206, and r. 75(2) substituted by S.I. 1986/1941
r. 16.5(3)	r. 75(4) substituted by S.I. 1986/1941
r. 16.5(5)	r. 75(3) substituted by S.I. 1986/1941 and as amended by S.I. 1991/2483
r. 16.5(6)	r. 75(5) substituted by S.I. 1986/1941
r. 16.6(1)	r. 74B(7)(a) inserted by S.I. 1986/1941
r. 16.6(3)	r. 74B(4)(b), (5)(b), (6)(b) and (7)(a), inserted by S.I. 1986/1941
r. 16.6(4)	r. 74B(8) inserted by S.I. 1986/1941
r. 16.10	r. 74(b) as amended by S.I. 1991/2483
r. 16.11	r. 82
r. 16.12(4)	Court of Session Act 1825 (c. 120), s. 53

R.C.S. 1994 rule	*Derivation (r. = rule in R.C.S. 1965)*
r. 16.13(1) (part), (3) and (4)	r. 140(a)
r. 16.14	r. 140(b)
r. 16.15(2)	r. 74(c) and r. 140(c)
Chapter 17, r. 17.1(1)	r. 81(1) substituted by S.I. 1991/2483
r. 17.1(2)	r. 81(1B) inserted by S.I. 1991/2483
r. 17.1(3)	r. 86
r. 17.2	r. 81(2) inserted by S.I. 1986/1941
Chapter 18, r. 18.1(1)	r. 83(b)
r. 18.1(2)	r. 83(a)
r. 18.2	r. 83(e) inserted by S.I. 1986/1941
r. 18.3(2)	r. 196(b)
r. 18.3(3)	r. 196(a)
Chapter 19, r. 19.1(1) and (2)	r. 89(a) (part) as amended by S.I. 1984/472
r. 19.1(4)	r. 89(aa) inserted by S.I. 1984/472
r. 19.1(5)	r. 89(b) substituted by S.I. 1986/1941
r. 19.1(6)	r. 89(c) substituted by S.I. 1986/1941
r. 19.1(7)	r. 89(i) inserted by S.I. 1984/472 and as amended by S.I. 1986/1941
r. 19.2(1)	r. 89(ab) inserted by S.I. 1984/472
r. 19.2(2), (3) and (4)	r. 89(e) and (f)
r. 19.2(5)	r. 89(d) substituted by S.I. 1986/1941
Chapter 20, r. 20.1(b), (3) and (4)	r. 94(d) as amended by S.I. 1991/2483
Chapter 21, r. 21.1	r. 89B(1) inserted by S.I. 1984/499 and as amended by S.I. 1990/705
r. 21.2	r. 89B(2) to (6) inserted by S.I. 1984/499
r. 21.3(1)	r. 89B(7) inserted by S.I. 1984/499
Chapter 22, r. 22.1(3)	r. 90(2) as amended by S.I. 1980/1144
r. 22.2(2)	r. 90(3) inserted by S.I. 1980/1144
r. 22.2(3) and (4)	r. 90A(2)(a) and (3) inserted by S.I. 1980/1144
r. 22.3(1)	r. 91(2) substituted by S.I. 1982/1825 and r. 91(5) substituted by S.I. 1982/1825
r. 22.3(5)	r. 91(3) substituted by S.I. 1982/1825
r. 22.3(6)	r. 91(6) substituted by S.I. 1982/1825
Chapter 23, r. 23.2(1)	r. 93(a)
r. 23.2(2)	r. 93(b) and (c) (part), r. 198 (amended by S.I. 1978/799) and P.N. No. 8 of 1991, para. 10(3)
r. 23.2(3)	P.N. No. 8 of 1991, para. 2
r. 23.2(4)	P.N. No. 8 of 1991, para. 10(2)
r. 23.2(7)	r. 93(d) (part)
r. 23.3(1) and (3)	r. 93(c) as amended by S.I. 1980/1144
r. 23.3(4)	r. 105
r. 23.3(5)	r. 93(b) (part)
r. 23.4(1), (5) and (6)	r. 93(3) (part)
r. 23.4(4)	r. 93(e) (part) as amended by S.I. 1980/1144
r. 23.6(1)	r. 93(d) (part)
r. 23.7	P.N. 31st March 1970
r. 23.9	r. 79(1) (part) and (2), and r. 236(b) amended by S.I. 1984/499
r. 23.12	r. 93(f)
Chapter 24, r. 24.1	r. 92(1) and (3)
r. 24.2(3) and (4)	P.N. 27th March 1986 (procedure following minute of amendment)
r. 24.2(5)	P.N. 26th March 1981
r. 24.3(1)	r. 92(3)
r. 24.4	r. 92(2)
r. 24.5	r. 92(4)

R.C.S. 1994 rule		Derivation (r. = rule in R.C.S. 1965)
Chapter 25,	r. 25.1(1)	r. 84(a) (part) and (j)
	r. 25.1(2)	r. 84(a) (part)
	r. 25.1(3)	r. 84(b)
	r. 25.2	r. 84(c)
	r. 25.3	r. 84(k)
	r. 25.4(1)	r. 84(d)
	r. 25.4(2)	r. 84(f)
	r. 25.5	r. 84(g)
	r. 25.6	r. 84(h)
Chapter 26,	r. 26.1(1)	r. 85(1) (preamble (part)) as amended by S.I. 1980/1144
	r. 26.1(2)	r. 85(1)(g) and (2) as amended by S.I. 1980/1144
	r. 26.2	r. 85(1) (preamble (part)) as amended by S.I. 1980/1144
	r. 26.3	r. 85(1)(b)
	r. 26.4	r. 85(1)(a)
	r. 26.5	r. 85(1) (preamble (part)) as amended by S.I. 1980/1144
	r. 26.7(1)	r. 85(1)(c) (part) as amended by S.I. 1976/2197 and 1980/1144
	r. 26.7(3) and (4)	r. 85(1)(e)
Chapter 27,	r. 27.1	r. 134E inserted by S.I. 1990/705
Chapter 28,	r. 28.1(1) and (2)	r. 94(c) as amended by S.I. 1991/2483
	r. 28.1(4)	r. 94(e)
Chapter 29,	r. 29.1(1)(b), (2) and (3)	r. 91A inserted by S.I. 1984/472
	r. 29.2	r. 84(e)
Chapter 31,	r. 31.1	r. 106 (part)
	r. 31.2	r. 106 (part)
Chapter 32,	r. 32.1	r. 104B inserted by S.I. 1986/1955 and as amended by S.I. 1987/1206
	r. 32.2	r. 104A inserted by S.I. 1984/472
	r. 32.3	r. 274 substituted by S.I. 1980/1801
	r. 32.4(1)	r. 275(2) substituted by S.I. 1982/1825
	r. 32.4(2)	r. 275(3)
	r. 32.5	r. 275(5)(a) and (b)(i) substituted by S.I. 1982/1825
	r. 32.6	r. 275(5)(b)(ii) substituted by S.I. 1982/1825
	r. 32.7	r. 275(6) substituted by S.I. 1982/1825
Chapter 33,	r. 33.6	r. 238(a)
	r. 33.7(1)	238(c)
	r. 33.8	r. 240
	r. 33.9	r. 238(f)
	r. 33.12(1)	r. 13(d)
	r. 33.12(2)	P.N. 14th May 1970
Chapter 34,	r. 34.1	r. 91B(1) inserted by S.I. 1984/472 and as amended by S.I. 1986/1937, and r. 198A inserted by S.I. 1986/1937
	r. 35.2(1), (2) and (3)	r. 95(b) and r. 95A(b) (inserted by S.I. 1972/2021)
	r. 35.2(1)(b)	r. 95A(d)(i) substituted by S.I. 1987/1206
	r. 35.2(4)	r. 95A(b) inserted by S.I. 1972/2021
	r. 35.2(5)	r. 95(a) (part) as amended by S.I. 1992/88, and r. 95A(a) (part) inserted by S.I. 1972/2021
	r. 35.2(6)	r. 95(a) (part), r. 95A(a) (part) inserted by S.I. 1972/2021
	r. 35.3	r. 96(a) to (f)
	r. 35.4	r. 97
	r. 35.8	r. 98
	r. 35.9	r. 103(a) to ()c)
	r. 35.10	r. 104
	r. 35.11	rr. 100 and 101
	r. 35.14	A.S. 16th February 1841, s. 17
	r. 35.15	r. 102 substituted by S.I. 1976/283

R.C.S. 1994 rule	Derivation (r. = rule in R.C.S. 1965)
r. 38.19(1)	r. 294A(a) (part) inserted by S.I. 1972/2022; P.N. No. 2 of 1989, para. 2(2)
r. 38.20	r. 262(d)
r. 38.21	P.N. 26th March 1981
Chapter 39, r. 39.1(1) to (3)	r. 126(a)
r. 39.6(3)	r. 125(c) inserted by S.I. 1984/472
Chapter 40, r. 40.1	r. 267
r. 40.2(5) and (6)	P.N. 6th November 1986
r. 40.4	r. 268(1) substituted by S.I. 1990/2118 and as amended by S.I. 1991/2483
r. 40.5	r. 268(2) substituted by S.I. 1990/2118
r. 40.6	r. 268(3) and (4) as amended by S.I. 1990/2118
r. 40.7(1)	r. 269(a) as amended by S.I. 1974/845 and 1991/2483; P.N. 13th November 1969, para. 2
r. 40.7(2)	r. 269(b) (part) as amended by S.I. 1974/845
r. 40.7(3)	r. 269(c)
r. 40.8	r. 269(b) (part) as amended by S.I. 1974/845
r. 40.9(1)	r. 269(b) (part) as amended by S.I. 1974/845
r. 40.9(2) to (6)	r. 272 as amended by S.I. 1985/1600
r. 40.10(1) and (2)	r. 271
r. 40.12(1) to (3)	r. 270
r. 40.13(1)	r. 294B(1) inserted by S.I. 1987/1206
r. 40.14	r. 294B(2) to (6) inserted by S.I. 1987/1206 and as amended by S.I. 1991/1157
r. 40.16	P.N. No. 2 of 1989, para. 2(1)
r. 40.17(1)	r. 294A(a) (part) inserted by S.I. 1972/2022; P.N. No. 2 of 1989, para. 2(2)
r. 40.18	r. 262(d)
r. 40.19	P.N. 26th March 1981
Chapter 41, r. 41.1	r. 276 as amended by S.I. 1972/2021, and r. 290(a) (part) as amended by S.I. 1973/540 and 1986/1955
r. 41.2(4) and (5)	P.N. 6th November 1986
r. 41.4	r. 276 as amended by S.I. 1972/2021
r. 41.5(1) and (2)	r. 277(a) as amended by S.I. 1982/1825
r. 41.6	r. 277(b)
r. 41.7	r. 277(c) and (d)
r. 41.8	r. 278
r. 41.9(1) (part) and (2)	r. 279
r. 41.9(1) (part) and (3)	r. 277(e)
r. 41.9(4) and (5)	r. 277(f)
r. 41.9(6)	r. 277(g)
r. 41.10(1)	r. 277(h)(i)
r. 41.10(2) and (3)	r. 277(j)
r. 41.11	r. 277(h)(ii) (part) and (k)(i) (part) (as amended by S.I. 1984/499)
r. 41.12(1)	r. 277(k)(i) (part)
r. 41.12(2)	r. 277(k)(ii)
r. 41.13	r. 277(k)(i) (part)
r. 41.14	r. 277(k)(iii)
r. 41.15	r. 280(a)
r. 41.16	r. 280(b) (part)
r. 41.17(1)	r. 280(b) (part)
r. 41.18	r. 290(a) (part) as amended by S.I. 1973/540
r. 41.19(1) (part)	r. 290(a) (part) and (d)
r. 41.19(2)	r. 290(a) (part), (b) and (c)
r. 41.20(1) (part)	r. 290(a) (part) as amended by S.I. 1984/499
r. 41.20(1)(b)(iii)	r. 290(i) inserted by S.I. 1982/1825
r. 41.21(1)	r. 290(e)
r. 41.21(2)	r. 293(a) as amended by S.I. 1972/1835
r. 41.21(3)	r. 293B(5) inserted by S.I. 1980/1754 and as amended by S.I. 1992/2289

R.C.S. 1994 rule	Derivation (r. = rule in R.C.S. 1965)
r. 41.21(4)	r. 292(a) as amended by S.I. 1972/1835
r. 41.21(5)	r. 293A(a) and (b) inserted by S.I. 1976/847
r. 41.23(1)	r. 281(1) (part) substituted by S.I. 1976/1849 and as amended by S.I. 1984/499
r. 41.25	r. 282(1) substituted by S.I. 1976/1849 and as amended by S.I. 1990/705
r. 41.26(1)	r. 283(1) substituted by S.I. 1976/1849 and as amended by S.I. 1990/705
r. 41.26(2)	r. 283(7) substituted by S.I. 1976/1849 and as amended by S.I. 1990/705
r. 41.26(6)	r. 283(13) inserted by S.I. 1990/705
r. 41.26(7)	r. 283(12) substituted by S.I. 1976/1849
r. 41.27	r. 286(1)
r. 41.30	r. 289A(2) and (4) (part) inserted by S.I. 1971/203
r. 41.31	r. 289A(6) and (8) inserted by S.I. 1971/203
r. 41.32	r. 289A(7) inserted by S.I. 1971/203
r. 41.33	r. 289A(9) inserted by S.I. 1971/203
r. 41.34	r. 284 (preamble) as amended by S.I. 1980/1144
r. 41.35	r. 284 (preamble) as amended by S.I. 1980/1144
r. 41.36	r. 284(a)
r. 41.37	r. 284(b)
r. 41.38	r. 284(c)
r. 41.39	r. 291(2) (preamble)
r. 41.40	r. 291(2)(a), (b), (c) and (d) (as amended by S.I. 1985/1600)
r. 41.41	r. 288(1) substituted by S.I. 1992/2289
r. 41.42	r. 288(3) and (4) substituted by S.I. 1992/2289
Chapter 42, r. 42.1	r. 348(1) and (2) substituted by S.I. 1983/826
r. 42.2	r. 348(3) and (4) substituted by S.I. 1983/826
r. 42.3(1)(a)	r. 349(1) substituted by S.I. 1983/826
r. 42.4(1)	r. 349(2) substituted by S.I. 1992/1433
r. 42.4(2)	r. 349(3) substituted by S.I. 1983/826 and as amended by S.I. 1991/1157
r. 42.4(3) to (5)	r. 349(4) to (6) substituted by S.I. 1983/826
r. 42.5(1)	r. 347(c)
r. 42.6	r. 349(8) substituted by S.I. 1983/826; P.N. 16th January 1970
r. 42.7	r. 350 substituted by S.I. 1992/1433
r. 42.8(1)	r. 347(aa) inserted by S.I. 1984/499
r. 42.9	r. 347(a) (part) inserted by S.I. 1974/1686
r. 42.10(1)	r. 347(a) (part) inserted by S.I. 1974/1686
r. 42.10(2)	r. 347, Table of Fees, Chapter I, note 5
r. 42.10(3)	r. 347(e) (part) substituted by S.I. 1970/1746 and as amended by S.I. 1981/497
r. 42.10(4)	r. 347(e) (part) substituted by S.I. 1970/1746 and as amended by S.I. 1981/497
r. 42.10(5)	r. 347(f) substituted by S.I. 1970/1746
r. 42.11(1) and (2)	r. 347(g) substituted by S.I. 1974/1686
r. 42.12	r. 347(h) inserted by S.I. 1973/360
r. 42.13(1)	r. 347, Table of Fees, Chapter II, para. 8
r. 42.13(2) and (3)	r. 347, Table of Fees, Chapter II, para. 9
r. 42.14	r. 347(d) substituted by S.I. 1970/1746 and as amended by S.I. 1991/272
r. 42.15	r. 347(b) substituted by S.I. 1970/1746
r. 42.16	r. 347(a) (part) substituted by S.I. 1970/1746 and as amended by S.I. 1992/1433, and Table of Fees amended by S.I. 1971/1161, 1989/445, 1993/900 and 1357, 1994/1139 and 1140
r. 42.17	r. 350A inserted by S.I. 1992/1898
Chapter 43, r. 43.1(2)(part)	r. 75A(2) (part) substituted by S.I. 1984/920 and as amended by S.I. 1986/1941
r. 43.2(2)	r. 134B inserted by S.I. 1984/919

R.C.S. 1994 rule		Derivation (r. = rule in R.C.S. 1965)
	r. 43.11(1) to (8)	r. 89A(1)(a) to (g) inserted by S.I. 1974/845
	r. 43.11(9) (part)	r. 89A(1)(h) inserted by S.I. 1974/845
	r. 43.12	r. 89A(2) inserted by S.I. 1974/845
	r. 43.13	r. 134C inserted by S.I. 1984/919
	r. 43.14(1)	r. 75A(1) and (2) substituted by S.I. 1984/920 and as amended by S.I. 1986/1941
	r. 43.14(2)	r. 75A(3) substituted by S.I. 1984/920 and as amended by S.I. 1986/1941
	r. 43.15	r. 75A(6) substituted by S.I. 1984/920 and as amended by S.I. 1986/1941
	r. 43.16(1)	r. 75A(4) substituted by S.I. 1984/920 and as amended by S.I. 1986/1941
	r. 43.16(2) and (3)	r. 75A(5) substituted by S.I. 1984/920 and as amended by S.I. 1986/1941
	r. 43.17	r. 75A(7) (part) substituted by S.I. 1984/920 and as amended by S.I. 1986/1941
	r. 43.18(1)	r. 75A(9) and (10) substituted by S.I. 1984/920 and as amended by S.I. 1986/1941
	r. 43.19(1)	r. 75A(11) substituted by S.I. 1984/920 and as amended by S.I. 1986/1941
Chapter 44,	r. 44.1(2)	r. 88A inserted by S.I. 1988/2060
	r. 44.2	r. 88B inserted by S.I. 1988/2060
	r. 44.3	r. 88C inserted by S.I. 1988/2060
	r. 44.4	r. 88D inserted by S.I. 1988/2060
	r. 44.5	r. 88E inserted by S.I. 1988/2060
	r. 44.6	r. 88F inserted by S.I. 1988/2060
	r. 44.7	r. 88H inserted by S.I. 1988/2060
Chapter 46,	r. 46.1	r. 135
	r. 46.2	r. 136
	r. 46.3	r. 137(a) and (b)
	r. 46.4(1) to (3)	r. 138
	r. 46.4(4) and (5)	r. 142
	r. 46.5	r. 143
	r. 46.6	r. 144
	r. 46.7	r. 145
	r. 46.8	r. 147
	r. 46.9	r. 147A inserted by S.I. 1979/670
Chapter 47,	r. 47.2	r. 149 substituted by S.I. 1988/1521
	r. 47.3(1)	r. 148(3) substituted by S.I. 1988/1521
Chapter 48,	r. 48.1(1)	r. 153A(2) inserted by S.I. 1984/472
	r. 48.1(2)	r. 153B inserted by S.I. 1984/472
	r. 48.2	r. 153A(1) inserted by S.I. 1984/472
	r. 48.3	r. 153E inserted by S.I. 1984/472
Chapter 49,	r. 49.1(1), (2) and (3)	r. 154(1) and (2) substituted by S.I. 1976/1994 and as amended by S.I. 1986/1231
	r. 49.2	r. 157(3) substituted by S.I. 1976/1994
	r. 49.3(1)	r. 170B(11) inserted by S.I. 1988/615, and r. 260EA inserted by S.I. 1988/615; the Family Law Act 1986 (c. 55), s. 39
	r. 49.4	r. 157(1) substituted by S.I. 1976/1994
	r. 49.7(1)	r. 155A(1) inserted by S.I. 1991/1157
	r. 49.8(1)(a)	r. 155(3)(a) and (4) substituted by S.I. 1976/1994
	r. 49.8(1)(b)	r. 155(1) and (2) substituted by S.I. 1976/1994
	r. 49.8(1)(c)	r. 155(3)(b) and (4) substituted by S.I. 1976/1994
	r. 49.8(1)(d)	r. 155(5) substituted by S.I. 1976/1994
	r. 49.8(1)(e)	r. 155(6) substituted by S.I. 1976/1994, and r. 170B(6)(a) inserted by S.I. 1976/1994 and as amended by S.I. 1986/1955 and 1990/705
	r. 49.8(1)(f)	Children Act 1975 (c. 72), s. 48 as amended by the Law Reform (Parent and Child) (Scotland) Act 1986 (c. 9),

R.C.S. 1994 rule	Derivation (r. = rule in R.C.S. 1965)
	Sched. 2
r. 49.8(1)(g)	Children Act 1975, s. 49(1)(a) as amended by the Law Reform (Parent and Child) (Scotland) Act 1986, Sched. 1, para. 14
r. 49.8(1)(i)	r. 170D(9) inserted by S.I. 1986/1231
r. 49.8(1)(j)	r. 155(7) inserted by S.I. 1982/1825, and r. 170D(4)(c) substituted by S.I. 1977/1621 and as amended by S.I. 1986/1231
r. 49.8(1)(k)	r. 188D(7) and (10) inserted by S.I. 1982/1381
r. 49.8(4)	Children Act 1975, s. 49(1)(b) as amended by the Law Reform (Parent and Child) (Scotland) Act 1986, Sched. 1, para. 14
r. 49.9	r. 162 substituted by S.I. 1976/1994
r. 49.11	Children Act 1975, s. 49 as amended by the Law Reform (Parent and Child) (Scotland) Act 1986, Sched. 1, para. 14
r. 49.12	r. 159(2) substituted by S.I. 1986/1941 and as amended by S.I. 1987/1206
r. 49.13	r. 159(5) and (6) substituted by S.I. 1976/1994
r. 49.14	r. 161 substituted by S.I. 1976/1994
r. 49.15(1)	r. 164 substituted by S.I. 1976/1994
r. 49.16	r. 165 substituted by S.I. 1976/1994
r. 49.17(1) to (7)	r. 167(1) substituted by S.I. 1976/1994
r. 49.17(9)	P.N. 10th February 1983
r. 49.18	r. 167(2) substituted by S.I. 1976/1994
r. 49.19	r. 166 substituted by S.I. 1976/1994
r. 49.22(1), (4) and (5)	r. 170B(14)(c), (d), (f) and (g) inserted by S.I. 1990/705, and r. 260D(4), (5), (7) and (8) inserted by S.I. 1986/515
r. 49.22(2)(b)	P.N. 13th November 1969, para. 3
r. 49.23	r. 170B(15), and r. 260D(10), inserted by S.I. 1990/705
r. 49.24	r. 170B(12), and r. 260EB, inserted by S.I. 1988/615
r. 49.25(1) (part)	r. 170B(13), and r. 260EC, inserted by S.I. 1988/615
r. 49.25(1) (part)	r. 170C(2), and r. 260E(2) and (3), inserted by S.I. 1986/515
r. 49.26	P.N. No. 1 of 1988
r. 49.27	r. 170B(5) inserted by S.I. 1976/1994
r. 49.28(1) to (4)	r. 168(1), (2), (5) and (6) substituted by S.I. 1978/106 and as amended by S.I. 1980/1144
r. 49.29	r. 168(7) to (11) substituted by S.I. 1978/106
r. 49.30	r. 170A inserted by S.I. 1976/1994
r. 49.31	r. 170B(3) and (4) inserted by S.I. 1976/1994, r. 170D(2) inserted by S.I. 1976/1994 and as amended by S.I. 1986/1231, 1990/705 and 1991/1157, r. 170D(4)(a) substituted by S.I. 1977/1621 and as amended by S.I. 1986/1231, r. 170D(5) substituted by S.I. 1986/1231, and r. 170D(7)(b) inserted by S.I. 1986/1231
r. 49.33(5) (part)	r. 168A inserted by S.I. 1980/1144 and as amended by S.I. 1982/1381
r. 49.34	r. 169 substituted by S.I. 1976/1994
r. 49.35(1)	r. 170B(1)(b) inserted by S.I. 1976/1994
r. 49.37	r. 170B(6)(b)(i) and (7)(a)(ii) inserted by S.I. 1976/1994
r. 49.38	r. 170B(6)(b)(ii) inserted by S.I. 1976/1994
r. 49.40(1)(a) and (2)	P.N. 13th November 1969, para. 1
r. 49.42(1) to (4)	r. 170B(10) inserted by S.I. 1977/1621
r. 49.43	r. 170B(10) inserted by S.I. 1977/1621
r. 49.45(1)	r. 170D(11) inserted by S.I. 1986/1231
r. 49.46	r. 170D(1) and (2) (part) inserted by S.I. 1976/1994 and as amended by S.I. 1986/1231, r. 170D(4)(a) substituted by S.I. 1977/1621, and r. 188D(4) (part) and (5) (part) inserted by S.I. 1982/1381
r. 49.48(2)	P.N. 13th November 1969, para. 1
r. 49.49	r. 170D(3) substituted by S.I. 1977/1621 and as amended

R.C.S. 1994 rule	Derivation (r. = rule in R.C.S. 1965)
	by S.I. 1987/1206, and r. 170D(7)(a) and (8) inserted by S.I. 1986/1231
r. 49.50	r. 170D(7)(c) inserted by S.I. 1986/1231
r. 49.51(1)	r. 170D(4)(a) substituted by S.I. 1977/1621 and as amended by S.I. 1986/1231
r. 49.51(2)	r. 170D(7)(c) inserted by S.I. 1986/1231
r. 49.53	r. 170M inserted by S.I. 1986/1231
r. 49.55	r. 170N inserted by S.I. 1986/1231
r. 49.56	r. 170P inserted by S.I. 1986/1231
r. 49.57	r. 170R inserted by S.I. 1986/1231
r. 49.58(1)	r. 260C(1) inserted by S.I. 1986/515
r. 49.61(2)	P.N. 13th November 1969, para. 1
r. 49.63(1)	r. 260E(1)(b) inserted by S.I. 1986/515
r. 49.64	r. 188D(1)(c) inserted by S.I. 1982/1381
r. 49.65	r. 188D(2), (4)(b) and (5) inserted by S.I. 1982/1381
r. 49.66	r. 188D(7)(a) and (b) inserted by S.I. 1982/1381
r. 49.67(1)	r. 188D(3) inserted by S.I. 1982/1381
r. 49.67(2)	r. 188D(7) and (9) inserted by S.I. 1982/1381
r. 49.68	r. 188D(6) inserted by S.I. 1982/1381
r. 49.69	r. 188D(11) inserted by S.I. 1982/1381
r. 49.70(1)	r. 188D(12) inserted by S.I. 1982/1381 and as amended by S.I. 1991/2483
r. 49.70(2)	r. 188D(13) inserted by S.I. 1982/1381
r. 49.71(1)	r. 188D(15) inserted by S.I. 1982/1381
r. 49.72(1) to (3)	r. 170E inserted by S.I. 1982/1679
r. 49.72(4)	r. 170H(1) inserted by S.I. 1982/1679
r. 49.73	r. 170F inserted by S.I. 1982/1679
r. 49.74(1)	r. 170G inserted by S.I. 1982/1679
r. 49.74(2)	r. 170H(2) inserted by S.I. 1982/1679
r. 49.75(1)	r. 170I(1) inserted by S.I. 1982/1679
r. 49.75(2)	r. 170I(3) inserted by S.I. 1982/1679 and as amended by S.I. 1987/1206
r. 49.77	r. 170J inserted by S.I. 1982/1679
r. 49.80	r. 170L inserted by S.I. 1982/1679
Chapter 50, r. 50.1	r. 188B(1) inserted by S.I. 1978/161
r. 50.2(4)	r. 188B(3) and (4) (part) inserted by S.I. 1978/161
r. 50.2(5)	r. 188B(4) (part) and (5) inserted by S.I. 1978/161
r. 50.2(6)	r. 188B(6) inserted by S.I. 1978/161
r. 50.5(1) and (2)	r. 188B(2), (3), (5) and (6) inserted by S.I. 1978/161
r. 50.6	r. 188B(8) and (9) inserted by S.I. 1978/161
Chapter 51, r. 51.2	r. 175 substituted by S.I. 1986/1941
r. 51.3	r. 176(a) and (b) (part) as amended by S.I. 1986/1941
r. 51.4(1) (part), (2) andr. 176(b) (part) as amended by S.I. 1986/1941 (4)	
r. 51.4(1) (part)	r. 177(a) as amended by S.I. 1986/1941
r. 51.4(3)	r. 177(b) as amended by S.I. 1986/1941
r. 51.5(1) and (2)(a)	r. 182(a)
r. 51.6	r. 180
r. 51.7(1)	r. 182(c)
r. 51.7(3)	r. 179 (part) as amended by S.I. 1986/1941
r. 51.8	r. 178 (part) as amended by S.I. 1986/1941
r. 51.9	r. 178 (part) as amended by S.I. 1986/1941
r. 51.11	r. 181
r. 51.12(1)	r. 183 (part)
r. 51.12(2)	r. 185
r. 51.13	r. 183 (part)
r. 51.14	r. 184
Chapter 52, r. 52.1	r. 186
r. 52.2	r. 187
r. 52.3	r. 188
Chapter 53, r. 53.3(1)	r. 171

R.C.S. 1994 rule	Derivation (r. = rule in R.C.S. 1965)
r. 53.3(4)	r. 173 (part)
r. 53.4(1)	r. 172
r. 53.4(2)	r. 173 (part)
r. 53.7	r. 173 (part)
r. 53.8	r. 174
Chapter 54, r. 54.1	r. 188A(a) (part) inserted by S.I. 1966/868
r. 54.2	r. 188A(a) (part) and (b) inserted by S.I. 1966/868
Chapter 55, r. 55.1	r. 250 substituted by S.I. 1991/1621
r. 55.2	r. 251 substituted by S.I. 1991/1621
r. 55.3	r. 252 substituted by S.I. 1991/1621
r. 55.4	r. 253 substituted by S.I. 1991/1621
r. 55.5	r. 254 substituted by S.I. 1991/1621
r. 55.6	r. 255 substituted by S.I. 1991/1621
r. 55.7	r. 256 substituted by S.I. 1991/1621
r. 55.8	r. 257 substituted by S.I. 1991/1621
r. 55.9	r. 257A substituted by S.I. 1991/1621
r. 55.10	r. 257B substituted by S.I. 1991/1621
r. 55.11	r. 257C substituted by S.I. 1991/1621
r. 55.12	r. 257D substituted by S.I. 1991/1621
r. 55.13	r. 257E substituted by S.I. 1991/1621
r. 55.14	r. 257F substituted by S.I. 1991/1621
r. 55.15	r. 257G substituted by S.I. 1991/1621
r. 55.16	r. 257H substituted by S.I. 1991/1621
r. 55.17	r. 257I substituted by S.I. 1991/1621
r. 55.18	r. 257J substituted by S.I. 1991/1621
Chapter 57, r. 57.3(2)	r. 351 substituted by S.I. 1968/1016
Chapter 58, r. 58.3	r. 260B(1), (2) and (3) inserted by S.I. 1985/500
r. 58.4	r. 260B(4) inserted by S.I. 1985/500
r. 58.5	r. 260B(6) inserted by S.I. 1985/500
r. 58.6(1)	r. 260B(5) inserted by S.I. 1985/500 and as amended by S.I. 1990/705
r. 58.6(2) to (4)	r. 260B(8) to (10) inserted by S.I. 1985/500
r. 58.7	r. 260B(11) inserted by S.I. 1985/500
r. 58.8	r. 260B(13) and (14) inserted by S.I. 1985/500
r. 58.9	r. 260B(15) and (16) inserted by S.I. 1985/500
r. 58.10	r. 260B(17) to (20) inserted by S.I. 1985/500
Chapter 59, r. 59.1(2)	r. 68J(1) inserted by S.I. 1991/2483
r. 59.1(4)	r. 68J(2) inserted by S.I. 1991/2483
r. 59.1(5)	r. 68J(3) inserted by S.I. 1991/2483
Chapter 60, r. 60.2	r. 234 (part)
r. 60.3	r. 236(d) (part)
r. 60.4	r. 243
r. 60.5	r. 247
r. 60.6	r. 242(a)
r. 60.7	r. 242(b)
Chapter 61, r. 61.1(2)	r. 199
r. 61.6(1)	r. 200(a)
r. 61.6(2)	r. 200(b)
r. 61.8	r. 200(e) (preamble (part))
r. 61.9(2)	r. 200(c) (part)
r. 61.9(3)	r. 200(e)(i) (part)
r. 61.9(4)	r. 200(e)(ii) (part)
r. 61.9(5)	r. 200(d)
r. 61.9(6)	r. 200(e)(i) (part)
r. 61.9(7)	r. 200(e)(iii) as amended by S.I. 1985/1600
r. 61.10	r. 200(e)(i) (part) as amended by S.I. 1967/487
r. 61.12	r. 200(g)
r. 61.13	r. 200B inserted by S.I. 1990/705
r. 61.14	r. 200A inserted by S.I. 1980/1803

R.C.S. 1994 rule	Derivation (r. = rule in R.C.S. 1965)
r. 61.16	r. 201 (preamble) substituted by S.I. 1986/514
r. 61.17	r. 201(a) as amended by S.I. 1986/514
r. 61.18	r. 201(b) (part)
r. 61.19	r. 201(c) (part)
r. 61.20	r. 201(d) as amended by S.I. 1967/487
r. 61.21	r. 201(e)
r. 61.22	r. 201(f) (part) as amended by S.I. 1967/487
r. 61.23	r. 201(n)
r. 61.24	r. 201(g) (part)
r. 61.25(1)	r. 201(h)
r. 61.25(2)	r. 201(j) (part)
r. 61.26(1)	r. 201(f) (part)
r. 61.26(2) and (3)	r. 201(k)
r. 61.27	r. 201(l)
r. 61.28	r. 201(m)
r. 61.29	r. 201(g) (part)
r. 61.30	r. 201(o)
r. 61.31(1)	r. 201Z inserted by S.I. 1991/1915
r. 61.31(2)	r. 201AA inserted by S.I. 1991/1915
r. 61.31(3)	r. 201BB(1) inserted by S.I. 1991/1915
r. 61.31(4)	r. 201CC inserted by S.I. 1991/1915
r. 61.31(5)	r. 201DD inserted by S.I. 1991/1915
r. 61.31(6) and (7)	r. 201EE inserted by S.I. 1991/1915
r. 61.32	r. 201FF inserted by S.I. 1991/1915
r. 61.33	r. 201(p)
Chapter 62, r. 62.2	P.N. No. 7 of 1988
r. 62.3	r. 249E(2)(a)(v) inserted by S.I. 1986/1941
r. 62.5(1)	r. 248(a) (part)
r. 62.5(2)	r. 249.1
r. 62.6	r. 248(a) (part), and r. 249.2 as amended by S.I. 1980/891
r. 62.7(1)	r. 248(b) as amended by S.I. 1980/891, and r. 249.5(1)
r. 62.7(2) and (3)	r. 248(c) and 249.5(2) and (3)
r. 62.8(1)	r. 249.6
r. 62.8(2) and (3)	r. 248(d) as amended by S.I. 1986/1941, and r. 249.7 as amended by S.I. 1986/1941
r. 62.9	r. 248(e) as amended by S.I. 1986/1941, and r. 249.8
r. 62.10(1) and (2)	r. 249.9
r. 62.10(3)	r. 248(f) (part) and r. 249.11
r. 62.10(4)	r. 248(g)
r. 62.11	r. 248(h) and r. 249.13
r. 62.12(2)	r. 249A.1 inserted by S.I. 1971/1809
r. 62.13	r. 249A.2 and 3 inserted by S.I. 1971/1809
r. 62.14	r. 249A.5 inserted by S.I. 1971/1809
r. 62.15(1)	r. 249A.6 inserted by S.I. 1971/1809
r. 62.15(3)	r. 249A.7(3) (part) inserted by S.I. 1971/1809
r. 62.16	r. 249A.7(1) and (2) inserted by S.I. 1971/1809
r. 62.17	r. 249A.8 and 9 inserted by S.I. 1971/1809
r. 62.18	r. 296F inserted by S.I. 1972/1982
r. 62.19	r. 296G inserted by S.I. 1972/1982
r. 62.20(1)	r. 296H(i) (part) inserted by S.I. 1972/1982
r. 62.20(2)	r. 296H(iii)(a) and (b) inserted by S.I. 1972/1982
r. 62.20(3)	r. 296H(ii) (part) inserted by S.I. 1972/1982
r. 62.21(1)	r. 296H(i) (part) inserted by S.I. 1972/1982
r. 62.23	r. 296H(iv) (part) inserted by S.I. 1972/1982
r. 62.24	r. 296J inserted by S.I. 1972/1982
r. 62.25	r. 296K inserted by S.I. 1972/1982
r. 62.26(2)	r. 249D(1) (part) inserted by S.I. 1986/1941
r. 62.28(1)	r. 249E(1)(a) inserted by S.I. 1986/1941
r. 62.28(2) and (3)	r. 249E(2) and (3) inserted by S.I. 1986/1941
r. 62.29(1)	r. 249G(3) inserted by S.I. 1986/1941
r. 62.30	r. 249G(1) and (2) inserted by S.I. 1986/1941
r. 62.31	r. 249H inserted by S.I. 1986/1941
r. 62.32	r. 249I inserted by S.I. 1986/1941

R.C.S. 1994 rule	Derivation (r. = rule in R.C.S. 1965)
r. 62.33	r. 249J(1) inserted by S.I. 1986/1941
r. 62.34	r. 249K inserted by S.I. 1986/1941
r. 62.35	r. 249L inserted by S.I. 1986/1941
r. 62.36	r. 249M inserted by S.I. 1986/1941
r. 62.37	r. 249P(2), (3) and (4) inserted by S.I. 1986/1941
r. 62.38	r. 249Q(4) to (9) inserted by S.I. 1986/1941
r. 62.39	r. 249R inserted by S.I. 1986/1941
r. 62.40	r. 249N inserted by S.I. 1986/1941
r. 62.41	r. 249P(1) and (2) inserted by S.I. 1986/1941
r. 62.42	r. 249Q(1) to (3) inserted by S.I. 1986/1941
r. 62.44	r. 249B(1) to (4) inserted by S.I. 1986/799
r. 62.45	r. 249C(1) inserted by S.I. 1986/799
r. 62.46	r. 249C(2) and (3) inserted by S.I. 1986/799
r. 62.47	r. 249S(1) inserted by S.I. 1987/12 and as amended by S.I. 1990/705 and 1991/1183
r. 62.48	r. 249T(1) substituted by S.I. 1991/1157, r. 249T(1A) inserted by S.I. 1991/1157 and as amended by S.I. 1991/1183, and r. 249T(2) inserted by S.I. 1987/12
r. 62.49	r. 249U(1) inserted by S.I. 1987/12 and as amended by S.I. 1990/705 and 1991/1183
r. 62.50	r. 249U(2) inserted by S.I. 1987/12 and as amended by S.I. 1990/705 and 1991/1183, and r. 249U(3) inserted by S.I. 1987/12
r. 62.51	r. 249V inserted by S.I. 1987/12 and as amended by S.I. 1991/1183
r. 62.52	r. 249W inserted by S.I. 1987/12 and as amended by S.I. 1990/705
r. 62.53	r. 249X inserted by S.I. 1987/12 and as amended by S.I. 1991/1157
r. 62.54	r. 249Y inserted by S.I. 1987/12 and as amended by S.I. 1990/705 and 1991/1183
r. 62.55	r. 249AA inserted by S.I. 1990/705
r. 62.57	r. 249AB inserted by S.I. 1991/2213
r. 62.58	r. 249AC inserted by S.I. 1991/2213
Chapter 63, r. 63.2	r. 260(d)
r. 63.3	r. 260(c) and (e)
r. 63.4	r. 232
r. 63.5(1) and (2)	r. 233(a)
r. 63.5(3)	r. 233(b)
r. 63.6	r. 233(c)
r. 63.7(2)	r. 233A inserted by S.I. 1992/1533
r. 63.8	r. 233C inserted by S.I. 1992/1533
r. 63.10(1)	r. 233B(1) inserted by S.I. 1992/1533
r. 63.10(2)	r. 233B(2) inserted by S.I. 1992/1533
r. 63.10(4)	r. 233H(1) inserted by S.I. 1992/1533
r. 63.11	r. 233D inserted by S.I. 1992/1533
r. 63.12	r. 233E inserted by S.I. 1992/1533
r. 63.13	r. 233F inserted by S.I. 1992/1533
r. 63.14	r. 233G inserted by S.I. 1992/1533
r. 63.15	r. 233I inserted by S.I. 1992/1533
Chapter 64, r. 64.2	r. 95A(c) (part) inserted by S.I. 1972/2021, and r. 95A(d)(ii) substituted by S.I. 1987/1206
r. 64.4	r. 95A(c) (part) inserted by S.I. 1972/2021
Chapter 65, r. 65.1	r. 296A inserted by S.I. 1972/1981
r. 65.2	r. 296B inserted by S.I. 1972/1981
r. 65.4	r. 296C inserted by S.I. 1972/1981
r. 65.5	r. 296D inserted by S.I. 1972/1981
Chapter 66, r. 66.3(1)	r. 102A(2) (part) inserted by S.I. 1976/283 and as amended by S.I. 1982/1825
r. 66.5	r. 102A(5) inserted by S.I. 1990/705
r. 66.6	r. 102A(3) inserted by S.I. 1976/283

R.C.S. 1994 rule	Derivation (r. = rule in R.C.S. 1965)
r. 66.7	r. 102A(4) inserted by S.I. 1978/955
Chapter 67, r. 67.1(2)	r. 219(1) substituted by S.I. 1984/997
r. 67.2	rr. 220(2), 221(2), 222(2) and 226(2), substituted by S.I. 1984/997
r. 67.3	r. 230(6) substituted by S.I. 1984/997
r. 67.4	r. 230(8) substituted by S.I. 1984/997
r. 67.5(1)(a) and (b)	r. 222(9)(a) substituted by S.I. 1984/997
r. 67.5(1)(c)	r. 220(8)(a) substituted by S.I. 1984/997
r. 67.5(2)(a)	r. 222(9)(b) substituted by S.I. 1984/997
r. 67.5(2)(b)	r. 220(4) substituted by S.I. 1984/997
r. 67.5(2)(c)	r. 220(8)(b) substituted by S.I. 1984/997
r. 67.5(3)	r. 230(1) substituted by S.I. 1984/997
r. 67.6(1)	r. 230(5) substituted by S.I. 1984/997
r. 67.7	r. 230(7) substituted by S.I. 1984/997
r. 67.9(1)	r. 220(1) substituted by S.I. 1984/997
r. 67.9(2)	r. 220(3) substituted by S.I. 1984/997
r. 67.9(3)	r. 220(5) substituted by S.I. 1984/997
r. 67.10(1) and (2)	r. 220(6) and (7) substituted by S.I. 1984/997
r. 67.10(3) to (7)	r. 225 substituted by S.I. 1984/997
r. 67.11(1)	r. 224(1) substituted by S.I. 1984/997
r. 67.11(2)	r. 224(4) substituted by S.I. 1984/997
r. 67.11(3)	r. 220(8) substituted by S.I. 1984/997
r. 67.11(4)	r. 220(9) substituted by S.I. 1984/997
r. 67.12(1)	r. 220(8)(c) substituted by S.I. 1984/997
r. 67.12(3)	r. 220(14) substituted by S.I. 1984/997
r. 67.12(4)	r. 230(2) substituted by S.I. 1984/997
r. 67.13	r. 220(10) to (13) substituted by S.I. 1984/997
r. 67.14(1) to (4) and (6)	r. 221(1) to (5) substituted by S.I. 1984/997
r. 67.14(5)	r. 224(5) substituted by S.I. 1984/997
r. 67.15(2) to (5)	r. 221(6) to (9) substituted by S.I. 1984/997
r. 67.16	r. 221(10) substituted by S.I. 1984/997
r. 67.17	r. 226(1) substituted by S.I. 1984/997
r. 67.18	r. 227(1)(b) and (2)(b) substituted by S.I. 1984/997
r. 67.20	r. 222(3) substituted by S.I. 1984/997
r. 67.21	r. 222(7) and (8) substituted by S.I. 1984/997
r. 67.22(1)	r. 222(1) substituted by S.I. 1984/997
r. 67.22(2)	r. 222(4) substituted by S.I. 1984/997
r. 67.23(1) and (2)	r. 222(5) and (6) substituted by S.I. 1984/997
r. 67.23(3) to (7)	r. 225 substituted by S.I. 1984/997
r. 67.24(1)	r. 224(2) and (3) substituted by S.I. 1984/997
r. 67.24(2)	r. 224(6) substituted by S.I. 1984/997
r. 67.24(3) and (4)	r. 222(9) and (10) substituted by S.I. 1984/997
r. 67.25	r. 222(11) to (14) substituted by S.I. 1984/997
r. 67.26	r. 222(16) substituted by S.I. 1984/997
r. 67.27(1) and (2)	r. 223 substituted by S.I. 1984/997
r. 67.28(1)	r. 227(1)(a) and (c) substituted by S.I. 1984/997
r. 67.28(2)	r. 227(2)(a) and (c) substituted by S.I. 1984/997
r. 67.28(3) and (4)	r. 227(3) substituted by S.I. 1984/997
r. 67.29	r. 228 substituted by S.I. 1984/997
r. 67.30	r. 229 substituted by S.I. 1984/997
r. 67.31	r. 230(3) substituted by S.I. 1984/997
r. 67.32	r. 230(4) substituted by S.I. 1984/997
r. 67.33	r. 230A inserted by S.I. 1978/1373 and as amended by S.I. 1984/997
r. 67.34	r. 230B inserted by S.I. 1978/1373 and as amended by S.I. 1984/997
r. 67.35	r. 230C(1), (2) and (4) inserted by S.I. 1978/1373
r. 67.36	r. 230C(3) inserted by S.I. 1978/1373
r. 67.40	r. 230J inserted by S.I. 1978/1373 and as amended by S.I. 1984/997
r. 67.41	r. 230I inserted by S.I. 1978/1373 and as amended by S.I. 1984/997

R.C.S. 1994 rule	*Derivation (r. = rule in R.C.S. 1965)*

Chapter 68,	r. 68.2	r. 2 substituted by S.I. 1992/1422
	r. 68.3	r. 3 substituted by S.I. 1992/1422
	r. 68.4	r. 4 substituted by S.I. 1992/1422
	r. 68.5	r. 5 substituted by S.I. 1992/1422
	r. 68.6	r. 6 substituted by S.I. 1992/1422
	r. 68.7	r. 8 substituted by S.I. 1992/1422
Chapter 69,	r. 69.2	r. 298 as amended by S.I. 1979/516 and 1985/1426
	r. 69.3	r. 297(*a*) as amended by S.I. 1979/516, and r. 299(*a*) as amended by S.I. 1991/2483
	r. 69.4(1)	r. 299A inserted by S.I. 1985/1426
	r. 69.4(3)	r. 300 as amended by S.I. 1985/1426
	r. 69.5	r. 303 as amended by S.I. 1985/1426
	r. 69.6(1)(*a*) and (*b*)	r. 304(*b*)
	r. 69.6(1)(*c*)	r. 304(*c*)
	r. 69.6(2)	r. 305
	r. 69.6(3)	r. 306(*c*) (part)
	r. 69.8	r. 307 as amended by S.I. 1979/516 and 1985/1426
	r. 69.9	r. 308 as amended by S.I. 1979/516 and 1985/1426
	r. 69.10	r. 312
	r. 69.11	r. 310 as amended by S.I. 1985/1426
	r. 69.12	r. 311 as amended by S.I. 1985/1426
	r. 69.13	r. 313 as amended by S.I. 1985/1426
	r. 69.14	r. 314
	r. 69.15	r. 315
	r. 69.16	r. 317 as amended by S.I. 1979/516
	r. 69.17	r. 316
	r. 69.18	r. 318(1) as amended by S.I. 1985/1426
	r. 69.19(1), (2) and (3)	r. 320 as amended by S.I. 1985/1426
	r. 69.19(4)	r. 321
	r. 69.20	r. 322
	r. 69.21	r. 324
	r. 69.22	r. 323
	r. 69.23	r. 325 as amended by S.I. 1985/1426
	r. 69.24	r. 326
	r. 69.25	r. 327 as amended by S.I. 1985/1426
	r. 69.26	r. 328 as amended by S.I. 1979/516 and 1985/1426
	r. 69.27	r. 329 as amended by S.I. 1985/1426
	r. 69.28	r. 330
	r. 69.29(1)	r. 309
Chapter 70,	r. 70.1	r. 260H(2) inserted by S.I. 1986/1955
	r. 70.2	r. 260J(6), and 260K(9), inserted by S.I. 1986/1955
	r. 70.3	r. 260L(1) inserted by S.I. 1986/1955
	r. 70.4	r. 260L(2) inserted by S.I. 1986/1955
	r. 70.5(1)	r. 260J(1) inserted by S.I. 1986/1955 and as amended by S.I. 1991/1157
	r. 70.5(2) and (3)	r. 260J(2) and (3) inserted by S.I. 1986/1955
	r. 70.6(1) and (2)	r. 260J(4) inserted by S.I. 1986/1955, and r. 260J(5) inserted by S.I. 1986/1955 and as amended by S.I. 1991/1157
	r. 70.7	r. 260J(7) and (8) inserted by S.I. 1986/1955
	r. 70.8	r. 260J(9) to (12) inserted by S.I. 1986/1955
	r. 70.9	r. 260K(1) to (5) inserted by S.I. 1986/1955
	r. 70.10(1)	r. 260K(6) inserted by S.I. 1986/1955
	r. 70.10(2)	r. 260K(8) inserted by S.I. 1986/1955 and as amended by S.I. 1991/1157
	r. 70.11	r. 260K(10) inserted by S.I. 1986/1955
	r. 70.12	r. 260(11) and (12) inserted by S.I. 1986/1955
	r. 70.13	r. 260(13) to (16) inserted by S.I. 1986/1955
	r. 70.14	r. 260(17) and (18) inserted by S.I. 1986/1955
Chapter 71,	r. 71.1	r. 260P(1) inserted by S.I. 1988/615
	r. 71.2(1) and (2)	r. 260Q inserted by S.I. 1988/615 and as amended by S.I.

R.C.S. 1994 rule	Derivation (r. = rule in R.C.S. 1965)
	1991/2483
r. 71.2(3)	r. 260X(3) inserted by S.I. 1988/615
r. 71.3	r. 260R inserted by S.I. 1988/615 and as amended by S.I. 1990/2118 and 1991/2483
r. 71.4	r. 260S inserted by S.I. 1988/615
r. 71.5	r. 260T inserted by S.I. 1988/615 and as amended by S.I. 1990/2118
r. 71.6	r. 260U inserted by S.I. 1988/615 and as amended by S.I. 1990/2118
r. 71.7	r. 260V inserted by S.I. 1988/615
r. 71.8	r. 260W inserted by S.I. 1988/615
r. 71.9	r. 260X(1) inserted by S.I. 1988/615
r. 71.10	r. 260X(2) inserted by S.I. 1988/615
Chapter 72, r. 72.2	P.N. No. 1 of 1987, para. 1 (part)
r. 72.5	r. 201B inserted by S.I. 1986/514
r. 72.6(1), (3), (4) and (5)	r. 201A inserted by S.I. 1986/514 and as amended by S.I. 1993/899
Chapter 73, r. 73.2	r. 189(*b*) inserted by S.I. 1986/1955 and as amended by S.I. 1991/2483
Chapter 74, r. 74.1(2) and (3)	r. 202(1) (part) and (2) substituted by S.I. 1986/2298
r. 74.2	r. 202(1) (part) substituted by S.I. 1986/2298, and r. 218Q (part) inserted by S.I. 1986/2298
r. 74.3	r. 218S inserted by S.I. 1986/2298
r. 74.4	r. 203(1) to (5) substituted by S.I. 1986/2298
r. 74.5	r. 204(1) to (5) substituted by S.I. 1986/2298
r. 74.6	r. 203(6), and r. 204(6), substituted by S.I. 1986/2298
r. 74.7	r. 206 substituted by S.I. 1986/2298
r. 74.8	r. 207 substituted by S.I. 1986/2298
r. 74.9	r. 205, and r. 208, substituted by S.I. 1986/2298
r. 74.10	r. 209(1), (3) and (4) substituted by S.I. 1986/2298
r. 74.11	r. 210 substituted by S.I. 1986/2298
r. 74.12	r. 212 substituted by S.I. 1986/2298
r. 74.13	r. 213 substituted by S.I. 1986/2298
r. 74.14	r. 211(2) substituted by S.I. 1986/2298
r. 74.15(1) and (2)	r. 211(1) substituted by S.I. 1986/2298
r. 74.15(3) and (4)	r. 211(3) and (4) inserted by S.I. 1991/1157
r. 74.17	r. 214(3) substituted by S.I. 1986/2298
r. 74.18	r. 215(1), (2), (6), (7) and (8) substituted by S.I. 1986/2298
r. 74.19	r. 216 substituted by S.I. 1986/2298
r. 74.21	r. 217(3) substituted by S.I. 1986/2298
r. 74.22	r. 218(2), (6), (7) and (8) substituted by S.I. 1986/2298
r. 74.23	r. 218B inserted by S.I. 1986/2298
r. 74.24	r. 218C inserted by S.I. 1986/2298
r. 74.25	r. 218E inserted by S.I. 1986/2298
r. 74.26	r. 218D, and r. 218H, inserted by S.I. 1986/2298
r. 74.27	r. 218F inserted by S.I. 1986/2298
r. 74.28	r. 218G inserted by S.I. 1986/2298
r. 74.29	r. 218J inserted by S.I. 1986/2298
r. 74.30	r. 218K inserted by S.I. 1986/2298
r. 74.31	r. 218L(1), (3), (4) and (5) inserted by S.I. 1986/2298
r. 74.32	r. 218M inserted by S.I. 1986/2298 and as amended by S.I. 1991/1157
r. 74.33	r. 218N(1) inserted by S.I. 1986/2298
r. 74.34	r. 218N(3) substituted by S.I. 1990/705
Chapter 75, r. 75.1(2)	r. 260M inserted by S.I. 1987/2160
r. 75.2	r. 260N(1) and (2) inserted by S.I. 1987/2160
r. 75.3	r. 260N(3) inserted by S.I. 1987/2160
r. 75.4	r. 260N(4) inserted by S.I. 1987/2160
Chapter 76, r. 76.1	r. 201C inserted by S.I. 1990/705

R.C.S. 1994 rule	Derivation (r. = rule in R.C.S. 1965)
r. 76.3(1)	r. 201E(1) inserted by S.I. 1990/705
r. 76.3(2)	r. 201F(2) inserted by S.I. 1990/705
r. 76.4(1)	r. 201G(1) inserted by S.I. 1990/705
r. 76.4(2)	r. 201F(1) inserted by S.I. 1990/705
r. 76.4(3)	r. 201G(4) inserted by S.I. 1990/705
r. 76.4(4)	r. 201G(5) inserted by S.I. 1990/705
r. 76.4(6)	r. 201G(6) inserted by S.I. 1990/705
r. 76.5	r. 201G(7) inserted by S.I. 1990/705
r. 76.6	r. 201G(8) inserted by S.I. 1990/705
r. 76.7	r. 201H inserted by S.I. 1990/705
r. 76.8	r. 201J inserted by S.I. 1990/705
r. 76.9	r. 201K(2) inserted by S.I. 1990/705
r. 76.10	r. 201L inserted by S.I. 1990/705
r. 76.11(2)	r. 201M inserted by S.I. 1990/705
r. 76.13	r. 201N inserted by S.I. 1990/705
r. 76.14	r. 201P inserted by S.I. 1990/705
r. 76.15	r. 201Q inserted by S.I. 1990/705
r. 76.17	r. 201R inserted by S.I. 1990/705
r. 76.19	r. 201S inserted by S.I. 1991/1183
r. 76.21(1)	r. 201T(1) inserted by S.I. 1991/1183
r. 76.21(2)	r. 201U(1) inserted by S.I. 1991/1183
r. 76.22	r. 201V(1) to (4) inserted by S.I. 1991/1183
r. 76.23	r. 201V(5) inserted by S.I. 1991/1183
r. 76.24	r. 201W inserted by S.I. 1991/1183
r. 76.25	r. 201X inserted by S.I. 1991/1183
r. 76.26	r. 201Y inserted by S.I. 1991/1183
Chapter 77, r. 77.3	r. 231(a) (part) and (b)
r. 77.4(1) and (2)	r. 231(d) substituted by S.I. 1976/387
r. 77.4(3)	r. 231(e) substituted by S.I. 1976/387
r. 77.4(4)	r. 231(f)
r. 77.5	r. 231(j)
r. 77.6	r. 231(g)
r. 77.7	r. 231(h)
r. 77.8	r. 231(k) (part)
r. 77.9	r. 231(l)
r. 77.10	r. 231(m)
r. 77.11	r. 231(n)
Chapter 78, r. 78.2(1)	r. 265(a)
r. 78.2(2)	r. 265(b)
r. 78.3(1)	r. 265(c) inserted by S.I. 1984/472
r. 78.4	r. 266
Chapter 79, r. 79.1	r. 260Y(1) and (2) inserted by S.I. 1991/2652
r. 79.2(1) and (3)	r. 260Y(3) and (5) inserted by S.I. 2652
r. 79.3	r. 260Y(4) inserted by S.I. 1991/2652
Chapter 80, r. 80.2	r. 9 substituted by S.I. 1992/1422
r. 80.3	r. 10 substituted by S.I. 1992/1422
r. 80.4	r. 11 substituted by S.I. 1992/1422
r. 80.5(1)	r. 11B substituted by S.I. 1992/1422

[NEXT TEXT PAGE IS C ccxxi]

TABLE OF DESTINATIONS

Section, rule or paragraph	Destination in R.C.S. 1994
Court of Session Act 1825 (6 Geo.4, c.120)	
s.53	r.16.12(4)
National Assessors (Scotland) Act 1894 (57 & 58 Vict. C.40)	
s.2	r.12.1(2)
s.3	r.12.8
s.4	r.12.5
s.5	r.12.9
A.S. (Rules of Court, consolidation and amendment) 1965 (S.I. 1965/321)	
para.(4)	r.2.1
r..1	r.11.1
r..2	r.68.2
r.3	r.68.3
r.4	r.68.4
r.5	r.68.5
r.6	r.68.6
r.8	r.68.7
r.9	r.80.2
r.10	r.80.3
r.11	r.80.4
r.11B	r.80.5(1)
r.12(a)	r.3.1
r.12(b)	r.3.1, r.3.2(1), r.3.3(1), r.3.5(1) and r.3.6(1)
r.13(a)	r.3.2(2)
r.13(b)	r.3.3(2)
r.13(c)	r.3.6(2)
r.13(d)	r.33.12(1)
r.14	r.3(4)(2)
r.15	r.3.2(3)
r.16	r.6.4
r.17	r.6.2(2)
r.18	r.6.1
r.19	r.4.1
r.20	r.4.4(1) and (2)
r.21	r.4.6
r.23	r.4.14
r.25	r.4.5
r.26(a)	r.4.8
r.26(b)	r.4.7
r.27	r.4.9
r.28(1)	r.4.2(3), (4) and (8)
r.28(2)	r.4.2(9)
r.29	r.4.10
r.30(1)	r.4.15(2) and (5), and r.4.16(7)
r.30(2)	r.4.15(6) and r.4.16(6)
r.30(3)	r.4.15(4) and r.4.16(4)
r.31(a)	r.4.11(1) and (2)
r.32(a)	r.4.12(1) to (4)
r.32(b)	r.4.12(5)
r.32A	r.9.1
r.34	r.9.2
r.36	r.8.1
r.37	r.12.1(1)
r.38	r.12.1(1) and r.12.5(1)
r.39(a)	r.12.3

Section, rule or paragraph	Destination in R.C.S. 1994
r.74B(6)	r.16.2(5)
r.74B(7)(*a*)(part)	r.16.6(1)
r.74B(7)(*b*)	r.16.4(3)
r.74B(8)	r.16.6(4)
r.75(1) and (2)	r.16.5(1)
r.75(3)	r.16.5(5)
r.75(4)	r.16.5(3)
r.75(5)	r.16.5(4)
r.75(7)	r.13.4(1)(*d*)
r.75A(1)	r.43.1(1)
r.75A(2)	r.43.1(2)(part)
r.75A(3)	r.43.14(2)
r.75A(4)	r.43.16(1)
r.75A(5)	r.43.16(2) and (3)
r.75A(6)	r.43.15
r.75A(7)(part)	r.43.17
r.75A(9) and (10)	r.43.18(1)
r.75A(11)	r.43.19(1)
r.76	r.13.12
r.78(*a*) to (*c*) (*e*)	r.13.13(1) to (5)
r.78(*d*)	r.4.4(3)
r.79(1)(part) and (2)	r.23.9(part)
r.80(*a*)	r.13.14
r.81(1)	r.17.1(1)
r.81(1B)	r.17.1(2)
r.81(2)	r.17.2
r.82	r.16.11
r.83(*a*)	r.18.1(2)
r.83(*b*)	r.18.1(1)
r.83(*d*)	r.4.6(1)(*b*)
r.83(*e*)	r.18.2
r.84(*a*)	r.25.1(1)(part) and (2)
r.84(*b*)	r.25.1(3)
r.84(*c*)	r.25.2
r.84(*d*)	r.25.4(1)
r.84(*e*)	r.29.2
r.84(*f*)	r.25.4(2)
r.84(*g*)	r.25.5
r.84(*h*)	r.25.6
r.84(*j*)	r.25.1(preamble)(part)
r.84(*k*)	r.25.3
r.85(1)(preamble)	r.26.1(1), r.26.2 and r.26.5
r.85(1)(*a*)	r.26.4
r.85(1)(*b*)	r.26.3
r.85(1)(*c*)	r.26.7(1)
r.85(1)(*e*)	r.26.7(3) and (4)
r.85(1)(*g*)	r.26.1(2)
r.85(2)	r.26.1(2)
r.86	r.17.1(3)
r.88A	r.44.1(2)
r.88B	r.44.2
r.88C	r.44.3
r.88D	r.44.4
r.88E	r.44.5
r.88F	r.44.6
r.88G(3)	r.38.4(2)
r.88H	r.44.7
r.89(*a*)	r.19.1(1) and (2)
r,89(*aa*)	r.19.1(4)
r.89(*ab*)	r.19.2(1)
r.89(*b*)	r.19.1(5)
r.89(*c*)	r.19.1(6)

Section, rule or paragraph	Destination in R.C.S. 1994
r.89(*d*)	r.19.2(5)
r.89(*e*) and (*f*)	r.19.2(2), (3) and (4)
r.89(*i*)	r.19.1(7)
r.89(*j*)	r.19.2(7)
r.89A(1)(*a*) to (*g*)	r.43.1(1) to (8)
r.89A(1)(*h*)	r.43.11(9)(part)
r.89A(2)	r.43.12
r.89B(1)	r.21.1
r.89B(2) to (6)	r.21.2
r.89B(7)	r.21.3(1)
r.89B(8)	r.38.4(1)
r.90(1)	r.22.1(1)
r.90(2)	r.22.1(3)
r.90(3)	r.22.2(3)
r.90(4)	r.22.2(1)
r.90(5)	r.22.2(2)
r.90A(2)(*a*) and (3)	r.22.2(4) and (5)
r.91(1)	r.22.3(1)
r.91(2)	r.22.3(2)
r.91(3)	r.22.3(5)
r.91(5)	r.22.3(3)
r.91(6)	r.22.3(6)
r.91A	r.29.1
r.91B	r.34.1(part)
r.91C	r.6.2(5) to (11)
r.92(1) and (3)	r.24.1
r.92(2)	r.24.4
r.92(3)	r.24.3(1)
r.92(4)	r.24.5
r.93(*a*)	r.23.2(1)
r.93(*b*)(part) and (*c*)(part)	r.23.2(2)
r.93(*b*) (part)	r.23.3(5)
r.93(*c*)	r.23.3(1) and (3)
r.93(*d*)(part)	r.23.2(7) and r.23.6(1)
r.93(*e*)	r.23.4(1), (4), (5) and (6)
r.93(*f*)	r.23.12
r.93A	r.4.15(3)
r.94(*a*)	r.6.2(3)
r.94(*c*)	r.28.1(1) and (2)
r.94(*d*)	r.20.1(*b*), (3) and (4)
r.94(*e*)	r.28.1(4)
r.95(*a*)(part)	r.35.2(5) and (6)
r.95(*b*)	r.35.2(1), (2) and (3)
r.95A(*a*)(part)	r.35.2(5) and (6)
r.95A(*b*)	r.35.2(1), (2) and (3), and r.35.2(4)
r.95A(*c*)(part)	r.64.7
r.95A(*c*)(part) and (*d*)(ii)	r.64.2(1)
r.95A(*d*)	r.35.2(1)(*b*)
r.96(*a*) to (*f*)	r.35.3
r.97	r.35.4
r.98	r.35.8
r.100	r.35.11
r.101	r.35.11
r.102	r.35.15
r.102A(2)	r.66.3(1) and (2)
r.102A(3)	r.66.6
r.102A(4)	r.66.7
r.102A(5)	r.66.5
r.103(*a*) to (*c*)	r.35.9
r.104	r.35.10
r.104A	r.32.2
r.104B	r.32.1

Section, rule or paragraph	Destination in R.C.S. 1994
r.105	r.23.3(4)
r.106	r.31.1 and r.31.2
r.106A	r.36.2(2)
r.106B	r.36.2(5)
r.107	r.36.3 and r.36.5
r.108	r.36.1
r.109	r.36.7
r.110	r.36.11(2)
r.111((a) to (d)	r.36.9
r.112	r.36.13(1) to (4)
r.113(a)	r.36.11(1), (4) and (5)
r.113(b)	r.36.11(3) and (8)
r.113(c)	r.36.11(9)
r.113(d)	r.36.11(6)
r.114(1) to (5)	r.37.1(1) to (5)
r.114(6)	r.37.1(6) and (7)
r.114(7)	r.37.1(9)
r.116(b)	r.37.8
r.117	r.38.12
r.117A(1)	r.37.2(1)
r.117A(2)	r.37.2(4)
r.119(a) and (c)	r.37.3
r.119(b)	r.37.2(5)
r.121	r.37.4(part)
r.122	r.37.4(part)
r.122A(1)	r.37.6
r.122A(2)	r.36.10 and r.37.4(part)
r.123	r.37.4(part)
r.124	r.37.7
r.125(a)	r.37.9
r.125(b)	r.37.10
r.125(c)	r.39.6(3)
r.126(a)	r.93.1(1) to (3)
r.127	r.37.4(part) and r.37.5
r.134B	r.43.2(2)
r.134C	r.43.13
r.134D	r.38.3
r.134E	r.27.1
r.135	r.46.1
r.136	r.46.2
r.137(a) and (b)	r.46.3
r.138	r.46.4
r.140(a)	r.16.13(1)(part), (3) and (4)
r.140(b)	r.16.14
r.140(c)	r.16.15(2)(part)
r.140(d)	r.13.11
r.140(dd)	r.13.11
r.142	r.46.4(4) and (5)
r.143	r.46.5
r.144	r.46.6
r.145	r.46.7
r.146	r.12.7(1)
r.147	r.46.8
r.147A	r.46.9
r.148(3)	r.47.3(1)
r.149	r.47.2
r.153A(1)	r.48.2
r.153A(2)	r.48.1(1)
r.153B	r.48.1(2)
r.153C	r.48.2
r.154(1)	r.48.3
r.154(1)	r.49.1(1)

Section, rule or paragraph	Destination in R.C.S. 1994
r.170E	r.49.72(1) to (3)
r.170F	r.49.73
r.170G	r.49.74(1)
r.170H(1)	r.48.72(4)
r.170H(2)	r.49.74(2)
r.170I(1)	r.49.75(1)
r.170E(3)	r.49.75(2)
r.170J	r.49.77
r.170K	r.7.2(2)
r.170L	r.49.80
r.170M	r.49.53
r.170N	r.49.55
r.170P	r.49.56
r.170R	r.49.57
r.171	r.53.3(1)
r.172	r.53.4(1)
r.173(part)	r.53.3(4), r.53.4(2) and r.53.7
r.174	r.53.8
r.175	r.51.2
r.176(a) and (b)(part)	r.51.3(part)
r.176(b)(part)	r.51.4(1)(part), (2) and (4)
r.177(a)	r.51.4(1)(part)
r.177(b)	r.51.4(3)
r.178	r.51.8 and r.51.9
r.179	r.51.7(3)
r.180	r.51.6
r.181	r.51.11
r.182(a)(part)	r.51.5(1) and (2)(a)
r.182(c)	r.51.7(1)
r.183	r.51.12(1) and 51.13
r.184	r.51.14
r.185	r.51.12(2)
r.186	r.52.1
r.187	r.52.2
r.188	r.52.3
r.188A(a)(part)	r.54.1
r.188A(a)(part) and (b)	r.54.2
r.188B(1)	r.50.1
r.188B(2), (3), (5) and (6)	r.50.5(1) and (2)
r.188B(3) and (4)(part)	r.50.2(4)
r.188B(4)(part) and (5)	r.50.2(5)
r.188B(6)(part)	r.50.2(6)
r.188B(8) and (9)	r.50.6
r.188D(1)(c)	r.49.64
r.188D(2), (4)(b) and (5)	r.49.65
r.188D(3)	r.49.67(1)
r.188D(4)(part) and (5)(part)	r.49.46(part)
r.188D(6)	r.49.68
r.188D(7)(a) and (b)	r.49.66
r.188D(7) and (9)	r.49.67(2)
r.188D(7) and (10)	r.49.8(1)(k)
r.188D(11)	r.49.69
r.188D(12)	r.49.70(1)
r.188D(13)	r.49.70(2)
r.188D(15)	r.49.71(1)
r.188P	r.38.4(3)
r.189(a)(preamble), (i), (ii), (iii), (iv) and (xxxvii)	r.14.2
r.189(b)	r.73.2
r.190(preamble), (i) and (iv) to (xi)	r.14.3(a) to (j)
r.191	r.14.4
r.192(1)	r.14.6(1)(a) to (c)
r.192(2)	r.16.4(6)

Section, rule or paragraph	Destination in R.C.S. 1994
r.201G(5)	r.76.4(4)
r.201G(6)	r.76.4(6)
r.201G(7)	r.76.5
r.201G(8)	r.76.6
r.201H	r.76.7
r.201J	r.76.8
r.201K(2)	r.76.9
r.201L	r.76.10
r.201M	r.76.11(2)
r.201N	r.76.13
r.201P	r.76.14
r.201Q	r.76.15
r.201R	r.76.17
r.201S	r.76.19
r.201T(1)	r.76.21(1)
r.201U(1)	r.76.21(2)
r.201V(1) to (4)	r.76.22
r.201V(5)	r.76.23
r.201W	r.76.24
r.201X	r.76.25
r.201Y	r.76.26
r.201Z	r.61.31(1)
r.201AA	r.61.31(2)
r.201BB(1)	r.61.31(3)
r.201CC	r.61.31(4)
r.201DD	r.61.31(5)
r.201EE	r.61.31(6) and (7)
r.201FF	r.61.32
r.202(1)(part) and (2)	r.74.1(2) and (3)
r.202(1)(part)	r.74.2
r.203(1) to (5)	r.74.4
r.203(6)	r.74.6(part)
r.204(1) to (5)	r.74.5
r.204(6)	r.74.6(part)
r.205	r.74.9(part)
r.206	r.74.7
r.207	r.74.8
r.208	r.74.9(part)
r.209(1), (3) and (4)	r.74.10
r.210	r.74.11
r.211(1)	r.74.15(1) and (2)
r.211(2)	r.74.14
r.211(3) and (4)	r.74.15(3) and (4)
r.212	r.74.12
r.213	r.74.13
r.214(3)	r.74.17
r.215(1), (2), (6), (7) and (8)	r.74.18
r.216	r.74.19
r.217(3)	r.74.21
r.218(2), (6), (7) and (8)	r.74.22
r.218A(1)	r.5.1(*d*)
r.218B	r.74.23
r.218C	r.74.24
r.218D	r.74.26(part)
r.218E	r.74.25
r.218F	r.74.27
r.218G	r.74.28
r.218H	r.74.26(part)
r.218J	r.74.29
r.218K	r.74.30
r.218L(1), (3), (4) and (5)	r.74.31
r.218M	r.74.32

Section, rule or paragraph	Destination in R.C.S. 1994
r.218N(1)	r.74.33
r.218N(3)	r.74.34
r.218Q(2)	r.74.2
r.218S	r.74.3
r.219(1)	r.67.1(2)
r.220(1)	r.67.9(1)
r.220(2)	r.67.2(part)
r.220(3)	r.67.9(2)
r.220(4)	r.67.5(2)(*b*)
r.220(5)	r.67.9(3)
r.220(6) and (7)	r.67.10(1) and (2)
r.220(8)	r.67.11(3)
r.220(8)(*a*)	r.67.5(1)(*c*)
r.220(8)(*b*)	r.67.5(2)(*c*)
r.220(8)(*c*)	r.67.12(1)
r.220(9)	r.67.11(4)
r.220(10) to (13)	r.67.13
r.220(14)	r.67.12(3)
r.221(1) to (5)	r.67.14(1) to (4) and (6)
r.221(2)	r.67.2
r.221(6) to (9)	r.67.15(2) to (5)
r.221(10)	r.67.16
r.222(1)	r.67.22(1)
r.222(2)	r.67.2
r.222(3)	r.67.20
r.222(4)	r.67.22(2)
r.222(5) and (6)	r.67.23(1) and (2)
r.222(7) and (8)	r.67.21
r.222(9) and (10)	r.67.24(3) and (4)
r.222(11) to (14)	r.67.25
r.222(16)	r.67.26
r.223	r.67.27(1) and (2)
r.224(1)	r.67.11(1)
r.224(2) and (3)	r.67.24(1)
r.224(4)	r.67.11(2)
r.224(5)	r.67.14(5)
r.224(6)	r.67.24(2)
r.225	r.67.10(3) to (7), and r.67.23(3) to (7)
r.226(1)	r.67.17
r.226(2)	r.67.2(part)
r.227(1)(*a*) and (*c*)	r.67.28(1)
r.227(1)(*b*) and (2)(*b*)	r.67.18
r.227(2)(*a*) and (*c*)	r.67.28(2)
r.227(3)	r.67.28(3) and (4)
r.228	r.67.29
r.229	r.67.30
r.230(1)	r.67.5(3)
r.230(2)	r.67.12(4)
r.230(3)	r.67.31
r.230(4)	r.67.32
r.230(5)	r.67.6(1)
r.230(6)	r.67.3
r.230(7)	r.67.7
r.230(8)	r.67.4
r.230A	r.67.33
r.230B	r.67.34
r.230C(1), (2) and (4)	r.67.35
r.230C(3)	r.67.36
r.230E	r.67.37
r.230F	r.67.38(1) to (4), (6) and (7)
r.230G	r.67.38(5)
r.230H	r.67.39

Section, rule or paragraph	Destination in R.C.S. 1994
r.260B(17) to (20)	r.58.10
r.260B(21)	r.38.4(4)
r.260C(1)	r.49.58(1)
r.260D(4), (5), (7) and (8)(part)	r.49.22(1), (4) and (5)(part)
r.260D(10)	r.49.23(part)
r.260E(1)(b)	r.49.63(1)
r.260E(2) and (3)	r.49.25(1)(part)
r.260EA	r.49.3(1)(part)
r.260EB	r.49.24(part)
r.260EC	r.49.25(1)(part)
r.260H(2)	r.70.1
r.260J(1)	r.70.5(1)
r.260J(2) and (3)	r.70.5(2) and (3)
r.260J(4) and (5)	r.70.6(1) and (2)
r.260J(6)	r.70.2(part)
r.260J(7) and (8)	r.70.7
r.260J(9) to (12)	r.70.8
r.260K(1) to (5)	r.70.9
r.260K(6)	r.70.10(1)
r.260K(7)	r.70.10(2)
r.260K(9)	r.70.2(part)
r.260K(10)	r.70.11
r.260K(11) and (12)	r.70.12
r.260K(13) to (16)	r.70.13
r.260K(17) and (18)	r.70.14
r.260L(1)	r.70.3
r.260L(2)	r.70.4
r.260M	r.75.1(2)
r.260N(1) and (2)	r.75.2
r.260N(3)	r.75.3
r.260N(4)	r.75.4
r.260P(1)	r.71.1
r.260Q	r.71.2(1) and (2)
r.260R	r.71.3
r.260S	r.71.4
r.260T	r.71.5
r.260U	r.71.6
r.260V	r.71.7
r.260W	r.71.8
r.260X(1)	r.71.9
r.260X(2)	r.71.10
r.260X(3)	r.71.2(3)
r.260Y(1) and (2)	r.79.1
r.260Y(3) and (5)	r.79.2(1) and (3)
r.260Y(4)	r.79.3
r.261	r.38.2
r.262(a)(part)	r.38.2(part)
r.262(a) and (b)	r.38.6(1)
r.262(c)	r.38.8(1) and (3)
r.262(d)	r.38.20 and r.40.18
r.263(a)	r.38.15
r.263(b)	r.38.14(1) to (3)
r.264(a)	r.38.3(2) and r.38.8(5)
r.264(b)	r.38.3(4)
r.264(c)	r.38.3(5) and r.38.5(2), (6) and (7)
r.264(d)	r.38.7(1)
r.264(e)	r.38.11
r.264(f)	r.36.12
r.265(a)	r.78.2(1)
r.265(b)	r.78.2(2)
r.265(c)	r.78.3(1)
r.266	r.78.4

Section, rule or paragraph	Destination in R.C.S. 1994
r.293	r.41.21(2)
r.293A(a) and (b)	r.41.21(5)
r.293B(5)	r.41.21(3)
r.294A(a)(part)	r.38.19(1) and r.40.17(1)
r.294B(1)	r.38.15(1) and r.40.13(1)
r.294B(2)	r.38.16(1) and r.40.14(1)
r.294B(3)	r.38.16(2) and r.40.14(2)
r.294B(4)	r.38.16(5) and r.40.14(5)
r.294B(5)(a)	r.38.16(3) and r.40.14(3)
r.294B(6)	r.38.16(4) and r.40.14(4)
r.294C(7) and (8)	r.6.3(5) and (6)
r.295	r.4.16(2), (3) and (5)
r.296A	r.65.1
r.296B	r.65.2
r.296C	r.65.4
r.296D	r.65.5
r.296F	r.62.18
r.296G	r.62.19
r.296H(i)	r.62.20(1) and r.62.21(1)
r.296H(ii)(part)	r.62.20(3)
r.296H(iii)(a) and (b)	r.62.20(2)
r.296H(iv)(part)	r.62.23
r.296J	r.62.24
r.296K	r.62.25
r.297(a)	r.69.3(part)
r.298	r.69.2
r.299(a)	r.69.3(part)
r.299A	r.69.4(1)(part)
r.300	r.69.4(3)
r.303	r.69.5
r.304(b)	r.69.6(1) (a) and (b)
r.304(c)	r.69.6(1)(c)
r.305	r.69.6(2)
r.306(c)	r.69.6(3)
r.307	r.69.8
r.308	r.69.9
r.309	r.69.29(1)
r.310	r.69.11
r.311	r.69.12
r.312	r.69.10
r.313	r.69.13
r.314	r.69.14
r.315	r.69.15
r.316	r.69.17
r.317	r.69.16
r.318(1)	r.69.18
r.320	r.69.19(1), (2) and (3)
r.321	r.69.19(4)
r.322	r.69.20
r.323	r.69.22
r.324	r.69.21
r.325	r.69.23
r.326	r.69.24
r.327	r.69.25
r.328	r.69.26
r.329	r.69.27
r.330	r.69.28
r.347(a)	r.42.9, r.42.10(1) and r.42.16
r.347(aa)	r.42.8(1)
r.347(b)	r.42.15
r.347(c)	r.42.5(1)
r.347(d)	r.42.14

Section, rule or paragraph	Destination in R.C.S. 1994
r.347(e)	r.42.10(3) and (4)
r.347(f)	r.42.10(5)
r.347(g)	r.42.11(1) and (2)
r.347(h)	r.42.12
r.347, Table of Fees, Chapter I, note 5	r.42.10(2)
r.347, Table of Fees, Chapter II, para.8	r.42.13(1)
r.347, Table of Fees, Chapter II, para.9	r.42.13(2) and (3)
r.348(1) and (2)	r.42.1
r.348(3) and (4)	r.42.2
r.349(1)	r.42.3(1)(a)
r.349(2)	r.42.4(1)
r.349(3)	r.42.4(2)
r.349(4) to (6)	r.42.4(3) to (5)
r.349(7)	r.38.4(5)
r.349(8)	r.42.6
r.350	r.42.7
r.350A	r.42.17
r.351	r.57.3(2)

[NEXT PAGE C 1]

Act of Sederunt (Rules of the Court of Session 1994) 1994

(S.I. 1994 No. 1443)
[31st May 1994]

The Lords of Council and Session, under and by virtue of the powers conferred on them by section 5 of the Court of Session Act 1988, the provisions specified in Schedule 1 to this Act of Sederunt and of all other powers enabling them in that behalf, do hereby enact and declare:

Citation and commencement
1.—(1) This Act of Sederunt may be cited as the Act of Sederunt (Rules of the Court of Session 1994) 1994 and shall come into force on 5th September 1994.
(2) This Act of Sederunt shall be inserted in the Books of Sederunt.

Rules of the Court of Session
2. The provisions of Schedule 2 to this Act of Sederunt shall have effect for the purpose of providing new rules for the Court of Session.

Amendments, repeals, revocations and savings
3.—(1) The enactments mentioned in Schedule 3 to this Act of Sederunt shall have effect subject to the amendments there specified.
(2) The enactments mentioned in Schedule 4 to this Act of Sederunt, being enactments relating to matters in respect of which the rules specified in the fourth column of that Schedule are made, are repealed to the extent specified in the third column of that Schedule.
(3) Subject to paragraphs (5) and (6) below, the Acts of Sederunt mentioned in Schedule 5 to this Act of Sederunt are revoked to the extent specified in the third column of that Schedule.
(4) All Acts of Sederunt to the extent that they relate to practice or procedure in the Court of Session made before 10th November 1964 (being the date on which the Act of Sederunt (Rules of Court, consolidation and amendment) 1965 was made) are, in so far as still in force, revoked.
(5) No revocation, by virtue of sub-paragraph (3) above, of an Act of Sederunt relating to fees and outlays of solicitors, witnesses' fees and allowances or shorthand writers' fees shall affect fees or allowances in respect of anything done, or outlays incurred, before the date on which this Act of Sederunt comes into force.
(6) No revocation, by virtue of sub-paragraph (3) above, of an Act of Sederunt relating to interest on decrees or extracts shall affect interest included in or exigible under a decree pronounced or an extract extracted before the coming into force of this Act of Sederunt.

SCHEDULE 1 **Preamble**

POWERS UNDER AND BY VIRTUE OF WHICH THIS ACT OF SEDERUNT IS MADE

Column 1 *Relevant enactment conferring power*	Column 2 *Relevant amending enactment*	Column 3 *Relevant provision in Schedule 2*
Section 34A of the Judicial Factors Act 1849 (c.51)	Inserted by section 67 of the Law Reform (Miscellaneous Provisions) (Scotland) Act 1990 (c.40)	Rules 61.31 and 61.32
Section 40 of the Judicial Factors Act 1849	Amended by paragraph 15 of Schedule 1 to the Age of Legal Capacity (Scotland) Act 1991 (c.50)	Chapter 61

Column 1	Column 2	Column 3
Relevant enactment conferring power	*Relevant amending enactment*	*Relevant provision in Schedule 2*
Section 11B of the Judicial Factors Act 1889 (c.39)	Inserted by paragraph 4 of Schedule 7 to the Bankruptcy (Scotland) Act 1985 (c.66)	Rules 61.9 and Part II of Chapter 61
Section 21 of the Judicial Factors Act 1889		Chapter 61
Section 4 of the Court of Session Consignations (Scotland) Act 1895 (c.19)		Rule 33.12(4)
Section 11 of the Administration of Justice Act 1920 (c.81)		Part II of Chapter 62
Section 12(*b*) of the Foreign Judgments (Reciprocal Enforcement) Act 1933 (c.13)		Part II of Chapter 62
Section 1(1) of the Public Records (Scotland) Act 1937 (c.43)	Amended by section 1(3) and (7) of the Public Registers and Records (Scotland) Act 1948 (c.57)	Rule 9.1
Section 1(2) of the Public Records (Scotland) Act 1937		Rule 9.2
Section 58C of the Trade Marks Act 1938 (c.22)	Inserted by section 300 of the Copyright, Designs and Patents Act 1988 (c.48)	Rules 55.17
Section 8(4) of the Law Reform (Miscellaneous Provisions) (Scotland) Act 1966 (c.19)	Amended by section 52(5) of the Court of Session Act (c.36)	Rules 32.3 and 32.7
Section 7(*b*) of the Arbitration (International Investment Disputes) Act 1966 (c.41)		Part III of Chapter 62
Section 1(3) of the Administration of Justice (Scotland) Act 1972 (c.59)		Chapter 64
Paragraph 5 of Schedule 3 to the Domicile and Matrimonial Proceedings Act 1973 (c.45)		Rule 49.1(3)
Sections 47(6) and 102(1) and (3) of the Children Act 1975 (c.72)	Section 102 was amended by Schedule 4 to the Adoption Act 1976 (c.36)	Rule 49.20
Section 48(1) of the Children Act 1975	Amended by Schedule 2 to the Law Reform (Parent and Child) (Scotland) Act 1986 (c.9)	Rules 49.8(3)(*g*) and 49.20
Section 11 of the Divorce (Scotland) Act 1976 (c.39)		Rule 49.17
Section 15 of the Presumption of Death (Scotland) Act 1977 (c.27)		Chapter 50
Section 92(4) of the Patents Act 1977 (c.37)		Rule 66.7
Section 59(1) of the Adoption Act 1978 (c.28)		Chapter 67

Column 1	Column 2	Column 3
Relevant enactment conferring power	*Relevant amending enactment*	*Relevant provision in Schedule 2*
Section 57(4) of the Solicitors (Scotland) Act 1980 (c.46)	Amended by Schedule 2 to the Solicitors (Scotland) Act 1988 (c.42) and section 37(2) of the Law Reform (Miscellaneous Provisions) (Scotland) Act 1990	Rules 68.2(1) and 68.3
Section 4 of the Civil Jurisdiction and Judgments Act 1982 (c.27)	Extended by the Civil Jurisdiction and Judgments (Authentic Instruments and Court Settlements) Order 1993 [S.I. 1993/604]	Rule 62.28
Section 12 of the Civil Jurisdiction and Judgments Act 1982	Extended by the Civil Jurisdiction and Judgments (Authentic Instruments and Court Settlements) Order 1993	Rule 62.40
Section 48 of the Civil Jurisdiction and Judgments Act 1982		Part V of Chapter 62
Section 9(5) of the Merchant Shipping (Liner Conferences) Act 1982 (c.37)		Part VI of Chapter 62
Sections 121(3) and (4) and 185 of the Representation of the People Act 1983 (c.2)		Rules 69.2 and 69.3
Sections 136(2)–(4) and (7) and 185 of the Representation of the People Act 1983	Amended by paragraph 48 of Schedule 4 of the Representation of the People Act 1985 (c.50)	Rule 69.4
Sections 138(1) and 185 of the Representation of the People Act 1983		Rule 69.8
Sections 139(1) and 185 of the Representation of the People Act 1983		Rule 69.9
Sections 146(1) and 185 of the Representation of the People Act 1983		Rule 69.18
Sections 147(1) and (2) and 185 of the Representation of the People Act 1983		Rule 69.19
Sections 152(3) and 185 of the Representation of the People Act 1983		Rule 69.20
Sections 153(1) and 185 of the Representation of the People Act 1983		Rule 69.25
Section 10 of the Child Abduction and Custody Act 1985 (c.60)		Parts I and II of Chapter 70
Section 24 of the Child Abduction and Custody Act 1985		Parts I and III of Chapter 70

Column 1 *Relevant enactment conferring power*	Column 2 *Relevant amending enactment*	Column 3 *Relevant provision in Schedule 2*
Section 1A(1)(*b*) of the Bankruptcy (Scotland) Act 1985 (c.66)	Inserted by section 1(1) of the Bankruptcy (Scotland) Act 1993 (c.6)	Rule 72.6(1)
Section 14(4) of the Bankruptcy (Scotland) Act 1985	Amended by paragraph 3 of Schedule 1 to the Bankruptcy (Scotland) Act 1993	Rule 72.6(3)
Section 62(2) of the Bankruptcy (Scotland) Act 1985		Rule 72.5
Paragraph 2 of Schedule 5 to the Bankruptcy (Scotland) Act 1985		Rule 72.6(3) and (4)
Section 27 of the Family Law Act 1986 (c.55)		Rule 71.3
Section 28 of the Family Law Act 1986		Rule 71.6
Section 90(4) of the Debtors (Scotland) Act 1987 (c.18)		Rule 16.15(1)(*i*)
Section 102 of the Debtors (Scotland) Act 1987		Part II of Chapter 16
Section 8(4) of the Criminal Justice (Scotland) Act 1987 (c.41)		Rule 76.4(2)
Section 22 of the Criminal Justice (Scotland) Act 1987		Rules 76.10 to 76.14
Section 28(1) of the Criminal Justice (Scotland) Act 1987		Part VII of Chapter 62
Section 46 of the Criminal Justice (Scotland) Act 1987		Rules 76.3(2) and 76.7(2)
Section 7(*e*) of the Multilateral Investment Guarantee Agency Act 1988 (c.8)		Part VIII of Chapter 62
Section 91(1) and (2) of the Criminal Justice Act 1988 (c.33)		Part VII of Chapter 62
Section 6(i) of the Court of Session Act 1988		Chapter 3
Section 6(ii) of the Court of Session Act 1988		Rules 14.2 and 14.3
Section 6(iii) of the Court of Session Act 1988		Rules 46.2, 46.3 and 46.5
Section 6(iv) of the Court of Session Act 1988		Rules 46.2 and 46.4
Section 6(v) of the Court of Session Act 1988		Chapter 25
Section 6(vi) of the Court of Session Act 1988		Part II of Chapter 63

Column 1 *Relevant enactment conferring power*	Column 2 *Relevant amending enactment*	Column 3 *Relevant provision in Schedule 2*
Section 6(vii) of the Court of Session Act 1988		Rule 13.6(b)
Section 26(2) of the Court of Session Act 1988		Rule 77.10
Section 26(3) of the Court of Session Act 1988		Rule 77.3
Sections 28 and 51 of the Court of Session Act 1988		Chapter 38
Sections 29(1) and 51 of the Court of Session Act 1988		Rules 39.1 to 39.5
Sections 34 and 51 of the Court of Session Act 1988		Rule 53.1 and Chapter 60
Sections 48(2)(b) and 51 of the Court of Session Act 1988	Section 48(2)(b) was substituted by paragraph 38 of Schedule 8 to the Law Reform (Miscellaneous Provisions) (Scotland) Act 1990	Rule 23.14
Sections 49(1) and 51 of the Court of Session Act 1988		Rule 58.1(3)
Section 114(3) of the Copyright, Designs and Patents Act 1988 (c.48)		Rule 55.17(2)
Section 204(3) of the Copyright, Designs and Patents Act 1988		Rule 55.17(2)
Section 231(3) of the Copyright, Designs and Patents Act 1988		Rule 55.17(2)
Paragraph 11(2) of Schedule 4 to the Prevention of Terrorism (Temporary Provisions) Act 1989 (c.4)		Rule 76.24
Paragraph 19(1)–(3) of Schedule 4 to the Prevention of Terrorism (Temporary Provisions) Act 1989		Part VII of Chapter 62
Section 8(1) to the Access to Health Records Act 1990 (c.23)		Rule 79.3

Paragraph 2 SCHEDULE 2

THE RULES OF THE COURT OF SESSION 1994
ARRANGEMENT OF RULES

Preliminary

CHAPTER 1

CITATION, APPLICATION, ETC.

CHAPTER 2

RELIEF FROM COMPLIANCE WITH RULES

General and Administration

CHAPTER 3

OFFICES OF THE COURT

CHAPTER 4

THE PROCESS

CHAPTER 5

CAVEATS

CHAPTER 6

THE ROLLS

CHAPTER 7

EXTRACTS AND OFFICIAL CERTIFIED COPY INTERLOCUTORS

CHAPTER 8

TAXES ON FUNDS UNDER CONTROL OF THE COURT

CHAPTER 9

COURT RECORDS

CHAPTER 10

SITTINGS OF THE COURT

CHAPTER 11

VACATION JUDGE

CHAPTER 12

ASSESSORS

Initiation and Progress of Proceedings

CHAPTER 13

SUMMONSES, NOTICE, WARRANTS AND CALLING

CHAPTER 14

PETITIONS

CHAPTER 15

APPLICATIONS BY MINUTE OR NOTE

CHAPTER 16

SERVICE, INTIMATION AND DILIGENCE

PART I

SERVICE AND INTIMATION

CHAPTER 35

RECOVERY OF EVIDENCE

CHAPTER 36

PROOFS

CHAPTER 37

JURY TRIALS

CHAPTER 38

RECLAIMING

CHAPTER 39

APPLICATIONS FOR NEW TRIAL OR TO ENTER JURY VERDICTS

CHAPTER 40

APPEALS FROM INFERIOR COURTS

CHAPTER 41

APPEALS UNDER STATUTE

PART I

GENERAL PROVISIONS

PART II

APPEALS BY STATED CASE, ETC.

PART III

APPEALS IN FORM 41.19

PART IV

EXCHEQUER APPEALS

PART V

APPEALS UNDER THE PENSIONS APPEAL TRIBUNAL ACT 1943

PART VI

APPEALS UNDER SECTION 50 OF THE SOCIAL WORK (SCOTLAND) ACT 1968

PART VII

APPEALS UNDER THE REPRESENTATION OF THE PEOPLE ACT 1983

PART II

FEES OF SOLICITORS

PART III

FEES IN SPECULATIVE CAUSES

Special Provisions in Relation to Particular Proceedings

CHAPTER 43

ACTIONS OF DAMAGES FOR, OR ARISING FROM, PERSONAL INJURIES

CHAPTER 43—**OLD** *(Now revoked)*

ACTIONS OF DAMAGES

PART I

INTIMATION TO CONNECTED PERSONS IN CERTAIN ACTIONS OF DAMAGES

PART II

INTERIM PAYMENTS OF DAMAGES

PART III

PROVISIONAL DAMAGES FOR PERSONAL INJURIES

PART IV

MANAGEMENT OF MONEY PAYABLE TO CHILDREN

PART V

OPTIONAL PROCEDURE IN CERTAIN ACTIONS OF DAMAGES

PART VI

PRODUCTIONS IN CERTAIN ACTIONS OF DAMAGES

CHAPTER 43A

ACTIONS OF HARASSMENT

CHAPTER 44

TIME TO PAY DIRECTIONS

CHAPTER 45

ACTIONS OF DIVISION AND SALE

CHAPTER 45A

ACTIONS OF REMOVING

CHAPTER 46

ADMIRALTY ACTIONS

CHAPTER 47

COMMERCIAL ACTIONS

CHAPTER 48

EXCHEQUER CAUSES

Chapter 49

Family Actions

Part I

General Provisions

Part II

Undefended Family Actions

Part III

Defended Family Actions

Part IV

APPLICATIONS AND ORDERS RELATING TO CHILDREN IN CERTAIN ACTIONS

Part V

ORDERS RELATING TO FINANCIAL PROVISION, ETC.

Part VI

APPLICATIONS RELATING TO AVOIDANCE TRANSACTIONS

Part VII

FINANCIAL PROVISION AFTER OVERSEAS DIVORCE OR ANNULMENT

Part VIIA

FINANCIAL PROVISION AFTER OVERSEAS DISSOLUTION OR ANNULMENT OF A CIVIL PARTNERSHIP

Part VIII

ACTIONS OF ALIMENT

Part IX

APPLICATIONS FOR ORDERS UNDER SECTION 11 OF THE CHILDREN (SCOTLAND) ACT 1995

PART X

CAUSES UNDER THE MATRIMONIAL HOMES (FAMILY PROTECTION) (SCOTLAND) ACT 1981

PART XA

CAUSES UNDER CHAPTERS 3 AND 4 OF PART 3 OF THE CIVIL PARTNERSHIP ACT 2004

PART XI

SIMPLIFIED DIVORCE APPLICATIONS

PART XIA

SIMPLIFIED APPLICATIONS FOR DISSOLUTION OF CIVIL PARTNERSHIPS

PART XII

CHILD SUPPORT ACT 1991

PART XIII

REFERRALS TO PRINCIPAL REPORTER

PART XIV

MANAGEMENT OF MONEY PAYABLE TO CHILDREN

PART XV

MANAGEMENT OF CHILD'S PROPERTY BY VIRTUE OF SECTION 9(5)(a) OR 11(2)(g) OF THE ACT OF 1995

PART XVA

APPLICATION BY SURVIVOR FOR PROVISION ON INTESTACY

CHAPTER 50

CAUSES UNDER THE PRESUMPTION OF DEATH (SCOTLAND) ACT 1977

CHAPTER 51

ACTIONS OF MULTIPLEPOINDING

CHAPTER 52

ACTIONS OF PROVING THE TENOR

CHAPTER 53

ACTIONS OF REDUCTION

CHAPTER 54

APPLICATIONS UNDER THE DEFAMATION ACT 1996

CHAPTER 55

CAUSES RELATING TO INTELLECTUAL PROPERTY

CHAPTER 56

JUDGMENTS OF THE HOUSE OF LORDS

CHAPTER 57

ADMISSION OF ADVOCATES

CHAPTER 58

APPLICATIONS FOR JUDICIAL REVIEW

CHAPTER 59

APPLICATIONS FOR LETTERS

CHAPTER 60

APPLICATIONS FOR SUSPENSION, SUSPENSION AND INTERDICT, AND SUSPENSION AND LIBERATION

CHAPTER 61

JUDICIAL FACTORS

PART I

General Provisions

PART III

REGISTRATION OF AWARDS UNDER THE ARBITRATION (INTERNATIONAL INVESTMENTS DISPUTES) ACT 1966

PART IV

EUROPEAN COMMUNITY JUDGMENTS

PART V

RECOGNITION AND ENFORCEMENT OF JUDGMENTS UNDER THE CIVIL JURISDICTION AND JUDGMENTS ACT 1982 OR UNDER COUNCIL REGULATION (E.C.) NO. 44/2001 OF 22ND DECEMBER 2001

PART VI

REGISTRATION UNDER THE MERCHANT SHIPPING (LINER CONFERENCES) ACT 1982

PART III

ADOPTION

PART IV

CONVENTION ADOPTION ORDERS

CHAPTER 68

APPLICATIONS UNDER THE SOLICITORS (SCOTLAND) ACT 1980

CHAPTER 69

ELECTION PETITIONS

CHAPTER 70

APPLICATIONS UNDER THE CHILD ABDUCTION AND CUSTODY ACT 1985

PART I

GENERAL PROVISIONS

PART II

INTERNATIONAL CHILD ABDUCTION (THE HAGUE CONVENTION)

PART III

RECOGNITION AND ENFORCEMENT OF CUSTODY DECISIONS (THE EUROPEAN CONVENTION)

PART IV

APPLICATIONS UNDER THE HAGUE CONVENTION WHERE THE COUNCIL REGULATION APPLIES

CHAPTER 71

REGISTRATION AND ENFORCEMENT OF PART I ORDERS UNDER THE FAMILY LAW ACT 1986

CHAPTER 72

BANKRUPTCY (SCOTLAND) ACT 1985

CHAPTER 73

RECTIFICATION OF DOCUMENTS

CHAPTER 74

COMPANIES

PART I

GENERAL PROVISIONS

PART II

COMPANY VOLUNTARY ARRANGEMENTS

PART II

APPLICATIONS UNDER THE UNCERTIFIED SECURITIES REGULATIONS *1995*

CHAPTER 76

CAUSES IN RELATION TO CONFISCATION OF PROCEEDS OF CRIME

PART I

CAUSES UNDER THE PROCEEDS OF CRIME (SCOTLAND) ACT *1995*

PART II

APPLICATIONS UNDER THE PREVENTION OF TERRORISM (TEMPORARY PROVISIONS) ACT *1989* OR THE ORDER OF *1995*

PART III

APPLICATIONS UNDER THE PROCEEDS OF CRIME ACT 2002, THE OVERSEAS FORFEITURE ORDER OF 2005 AND THE POCA ORDER OF 2005

CIVIL RECOVERY PROCEEDINGS

CHAPTER 82

THE HUMAN RIGHTS ACT 1998

CHAPTER 83

APPLICATIONS FOR THE PURPOSES OF INVESTIGATIONS ORDERED PURSUANT TO ARTICLE 14 OF REGULATION 17 OF THE COUNCIL OF THE EUROPEAN COMMUNITIES

Revoked by S.S.I. 2005 No. 193.

CHAPTER 84

APPPLICATIONS UNDER THE TERRORISM ACT 2000

CHAPTER 85

APPLICATIONS UNDER THE PROTECTION FROM ABUSE (SCOTLAND) ACT 2001

CHAPTER 86

APPLICATIONS UNDER VARIOUS PROVISIONS OF THE COMPETITION ACT 1998

Preliminary

CHAPTER 1

[1] CITATION, APPLICATION, ETC.

Citation
1.1. These Rules may be cited as the Rules of the Court of Session 1994.

————

[1] Chapter heading amended by SI 1999 No. 1386 (effective 19th May 1999).

1.1.1   *General note*. The current rules of the Court of Session are to be found in Sched. 2 to the A.S. (R.C.S. 1994) 1994 [S.I. 1994 No. 1443]. They are a consequence of the reports of the Rules Review Group set up by the Lord President of the Court of Session in 1984 to examine the rules, Acts of Sederunt, statutes and practice notes, and, in light of, *inter alia*, experience of their use, (i) to recommend what changes in the layout of the rules were necessary and what changes in the rules were desirable, with a view to the simplification of procedure and to the promotion of the speedier and more economical despatch of court business; and (ii) to make proposals for an appropriate A.S. for consideration by the Rules Council and the court. The layout, order and numbering of the R.C.S. 1994 do not follow recommendations of the Rules Review Group. Not all the new provisions are recommendations of the Group. The Rules were made on 31st May, and came into force on 5th September 1994.

    The general statutory power of the Court of Session to make rules regulating its procedure is to be found in ss.5 and 6 of the C.S.A. 1988 (formerly ss.16 and 17 of the Administration of Justice (Scotland) Act 1933). It includes a power to make rules to carry out the provisions of any other Act conferring powers or imposing duties on the court or relating to proceedings in the court. An Act may include specific rule-making powers for the purposes of that Act in addition to this general power. The original statutory power was in the College of Justice Act 1540. Apart from its statutory powers, the court has an inherent right to regulate its business and procedure. The court has power, under s.5 (*m*) of the C.S.A. 1988, to modify, amend or repeal the provisions in any enactment relating to its procedure. There is often a power in particular statutes to make rules in respect of provisions contained in them.

1.1.2   *Acts of Sederunt and practice notes*. The court regulates its procedure by Acts of Sederunt. By s.10 of the Law Reform (Miscellaneous Provisions) (Scotland) Act 1966, an A.S. made under a statute passed after the commencement of the Statutory Instruments Act 1946 is to be by statutory instrument; and the provisions of the 1946 Act apply to such Acts of Sederunt. In practice, all Acts of Sederunt are made by statutory instrument. Practice notes are administrative directions indicating, where necessary, the way in which, for administrative purposes only, a particular rule in the R.C.S. or an administrative requirement may be complied with. They should not be used for any other purpose, such as to amend or suspend a rule of the R.C.S.

1.1.3   *Rules Council*. The Rules Council, set up under s.18 of the A.J.A. 1933 (now s.8 of the C.S.A. 1988), meets from time to time to consider draft rules (formerly prepared by the Counsel to the Lord President (who are also the clerks to the Rules Council)) or to frame them. Acts of Sederunt in the form of statutory instruments are signed by the Lord President (or, in his absence, the Lord Justice-Clerk) in the presence of a quorum of the judges. The procedure for statutory instruments is followed for bringing the Acts of Sederunt into force. Interested persons may submit suggestions for reform of the R.C.S. to the Lord President's Private Office to be considered. The Lord President's Court of Session Procedure Committee occasionally suggested reforms but fell into abeyance when the Rules Review Group was set up: see note 1.1.1. The Group was disbanded after it completed its review of the rules in 1992.

Application
1.2. These Rules apply to any cause whether initiated before or after the coming into force of these Rules.

1.2.1   *General note*. There are no transitional or savings provisions in the rules. In relation to savings, note the effect of ss.16 and 17, by virtue of s.23, of the Interpretation Act 1978 with regard to the revocation of the R.C.S. 1965. There are savings in relation to fees of solicitors, witnesses' fees and shorthand writers' fees in para. 3(5) of the A.S. (R.C.S. 1994) 1994, above, for work done before that A.S. came into force.

Interpretation etc.

1.3.—(1) In these Rules, unless the context otherwise requires—

"the Act of 1988" means the Court of Session Act 1988;

"act" means an order of the court which is extractable, other than a decree;

"agent", except in rule 16.2(2)(*e*)(service furth of United Kingdom by party's authorised agent) and rule 16.14(1) (arrestment of cargo), means a solicitor or person having a right to conduct the litigation;

"the Auditor" means the Auditor of the Court of Session;

"cause" means any proceedings;

"clerk of court" means the clerk of session acting as such;

"clerk of session" means a depute clerk of session or an assistant clerk of session, as the case may be;

"counsel" means a practising member of the Faculty of Advocates;

"depute clerk of session" means a depute clerk of session and justiciary;

"Deputy Principal Clerk" means the Deputy Principal Clerk of Session;

"document" has the meaning assigned to it in section 9 of the Civil Evidence (Scotland) Act 1988;

"the Extractor" means the Extractor of the Court of Session or the Extractor of the acts and decrees of the Teind Court, as the case may be;

"Keeper of the Records" means the Keeper of the Records of Scotland;

"Keeper of the Registers" means the Keeper of the Registers of Scotland;

"other person having a right of audience" means a person having a right of audience before the court by virtue of Part II of the Law Reform (Miscellaneous Provisions) (Scotland) Act 1990 (legal services) in respect of the category and nature of the cause in question;

"party" means a person who has entered appearance in an action or lodged a writ in the process of a cause (other than a minuter seeking leave to be sisted to a cause); and "parties" shall be construed accordingly;

"period of notice" means—

(*a*) in relation to service, or intimation on a warrant for intimation before calling, of a summons, the period determined in accordance with rule 13.4 (period of notice in summonses); and

(*b*) in relation to service of any other writ, intimation of a writ other than intimation referred to in sub-paragraph (*a*), or the period for lodging answers to a writ, the period determined in accordance with rule 14.6 (period of notice for lodging answers);

"person having a right to conduct the litigation" means a person having a right to conduct litigation by virtue of Part II of the Law Reform (Miscellaneous Provisions) (Scotland) Act 1990 in respect of the category and nature of the cause in question;

"Principal Clerk" means the Principal Clerk of Session and Justiciary;

"principal writ" means the writ by which a cause is initiated before the court;

"proof" includes a proof before answer;

"rolls" means the lists of the business of the court issued from time to time by the Keeper of the Rolls;

"send" includes deliver; and "sent" shall be construed accordingly;

"step of process" means a document lodged in process other than a production;

"summons" includes the condescendence and pleas-in-law annexed to it;

"vacation judge" means a judge of the court sitting as such in vacation;

"writ" means summons, petition, note, application, appeal, minute, defences, answers, counterclaim, issue or counter-issue, as the case may be.

(2) For the purposes of these Rules—

(a) "affidavit" includes an affirmation and a statutory or other declaration; and

(b) an affidavit shall be sworn or affirmed before a notary public or any other competent authority.

(3) Where a power is conferred in these Rules on the Lord President to make directions, the power may be exercised in his absence by the Lord Justice-Clerk.

(4) Where a provision in these Rules imposes an obligation on a principal officer, the obligation may be performed in his absence by a clerk of session authorised by him or by another principal officer; and in this paragraph "principal officer" means the Principal Clerk, Deputy Principal Clerk, Deputy Principal Clerk (Administration), Keeper of the Rolls or Principal Extractor.

(5) Unless the context otherwise requires, where a provision in these Rules requires a party to intimate, give written intimation or send a document, to another party, it shall be sufficient compliance with that provision if intimation is given or the document is sent, as the case may be, to the agent acting in the cause for that party.

(6) Unless the context otherwise requires, anything done or required to be done by a party under a provision in these Rules may be done by the agent for that party acting on his behalf.

[1] (7) Where a provision in these Rules requires a document to be lodged in an office or department of the Office of Court within or not later than a specified period and the last day of that period is a day on which that office or department is closed, the period shall be extended to include the next day on which that office or department, as the case may be, is open or on such other day as may be specified in a notice published in the rolls.

(8) Unless the context otherwise requires, a reference to a specified Chapter, Part, rule or form is a reference to the Chapter, Part, rule, or the form in the appendix, so specified in these Rules; and a reference to a specified paragraph, sub-paragraph or head is a reference to that paragraph of the rule or form, that sub-paragraph of the paragraph or that head of the sub-paragraph, in which the reference occurs.

Deriv. R.C.S. 1965, r. 68G (r. 1.3(3)) and r. 168(3) (r. 1.3(2))

---

[1] R. 1.3(7) amended by S.I. 1996 No. 2587 (effective 1st November 1996)

General note. Under s. 11 of the Interpretation Act 1978, where a statute confers power to **1.3.1** make subordinate legislation, expressions used in that legislation have the same meaning as they bear in the Act. Hence, words and expressions in the C.S.A. 1988 (under which Act the R.C.S. 1994 are made) have the same meaning in the R.C.S. 1994 unless a contrary intention appears. Further, in the R.C.S. 1994, words and expressions listed in Sched. 1 to the 1978 Act are, unless the contrary intention appears, to be construed according to that Schedule: Interpretation Act 1978, s. 5. Not all words and expressions having special meaning in the R.C.S. 1994, however, are defined in the 1978 Act or the C.S.A. 1988; accordingly, unless the contrary intention appears, those of common application in the R.C.S. 1994 are defined here. Rules may specifically import the meaning of words used in a particular enactment, although not made under that enactment. Particular rules may be made under particular statutes (apart from under the general power in the C.S.A. 1988); and where this is the case, it is not necessary to import the meaning of a word used in that statute. It will not be always readily apparent, however, that a rule has been made under reference to a statute other than the C.S.A. 1988; therefore, the meaning of a word is specifically defined in such a rule by a further interpretation rule where appropriate. Rules made under powers in enactments other than the C.S.A. 1988 can be ascertained from Sched. 1 to the A.S. (R.C.S. 1994) 1994, above.

The words defined by s. 51 of the C.S.A. 1988 for the purposes of that Act and the R.C.S. 1994 (unless the context otherwise requires or the R.C.S. 1994 provide otherwise) are as follows: "action", "the court", "enactment", "the Inner House", "the Lord President", "prescribed" and "solicitor". Although "action" is defined as a cause initiated by summons, under the R.C.S. 1994 (*a*) a cause transmitted or remitted from the sheriff court proceeds as if it had been initiated by summons (r. 32.4(2)) and (*b*) a petition for suspension, suspension and interdict or suspension and liberation also proceeds as an action (r. 60.5(2)).

1.3.2   *"act"*. An act is an interlocutor that does not contain a decerniture (*i.e.* the word "decern(s)", which is inserted only where the interlocutor finally determines a part, or the whole, of a cause); and, therefore, is an interlocutory or procedural order.

1.3.2A   *"document"*. A document is defined by reference to the inclusive definition in s.9 of the Civil Evidence (Scotland) Act 1988.

1.3.3   *"period of notice"*. The period of notice in a summons is the period *before* the last day of which the summons may not be lodged for calling (see r. 13.13(1)), whereas the period of notice in a petition or other writ (for the definition of which (see r. 1.3(1)) is the period *within* which any answers must be lodged.

1.3.4   *"other person having a right of audience" and "person having a right to conduct the litigation"*. A solicitor, under and by virtue of s. 25A of the Solicitors (Scotland) Act 1980 (inserted by the Law Reform (Miscellaneous Provisions) (Scotland) Act 1990, s. 24), may obtain an extended right of audience to appear (as an advocate) before the court. He also has the right to conduct litigation and instruct counsel: see s. 25 of the 1980 Act. The rights of other persons, other than an advocate, to have a right of audience or to conduct litigation (*i.e.* act as a solicitor) depend on any scheme made in respect of them under s. 25 of the 1990 Act: none has been made. "Solicitor" is defined in s. 51 of the C.S.A. 1988.

1.3.5   *"rolls"*. The rolls for the court are: (1) The General Roll, consisting of the registers of causes of the (*a*) General Department (the Ordinary, Admiralty and Commercial, and Family (including Consistorial) Rolls) and (*b*) the Petition Department. (2) The Daily Rolls—the printed rolls issued each weekday during term showing the causes in the General Roll appearing for business on a particular day, consisting of (*a*) in the Inner House (i) Single Bills, (ii) By Order Roll, (iii) Summar Roll and (iv) Advisings; and (*b*) in the Outer House (i) Calling List, (ii) Motion Roll, (iii) Diet Roll, (iv) Commercial Roll, (v) Adjustment Roll (and Continued Adjustment Roll), (vi) By Order (Adjustment) Roll, (vii) By Order Roll, (viii) Procedure Roll, (ix) Jury Trials, Proofs, Proofs before Answer and Hearings, (x) For Judgment and (xi) Undefended Consistorial Causes (in fact undefended divorce actions). In the Daily Rolls there are also printed notices of Acts of Sederunt, practice notes and other matters of administration. Rolls issued in vacation contain details of (2)(*a*)(i) and (iv) and (*b*)(i), (iii)–(xi).

1.3.6   *Lodging documents in a department of the Office of Court*. For office hours of the Office of Court and holidays, see note 3.1.2.

1.3.7   *"affidavit"*. An affidavit required by a rule of court or by order of the court is lodged as a step of process. An affidavit not so required is lodged as a production.
On lodging an affidavit as a step of process, see r. 4.4. It may be lodged by post: P.N. No. 4 of 1994, paras. 1 and 8; and see note 4.4.10. On lodging an affidavit as a production, see r. 4.5. A production may be lodged by post: P.N. No. 4 of 1994, para. 1, and see note 4.5.5.
An affidavit should be in the form of a statement of evidence written in the first person. The affidavit should contain evidence in support of, and expanding on, the averments in the pleadings. It should be sworn or affirmed and signed by the deponent before any person who may competently take an oath. Such a person includes a notary, a justice of the peace, a sheriff

or any judge (or in England a commissioner for oaths (includes any barrister or solicitor)). The person taking the oath or affirmation should also sign the affidavit. Witnesses are unnecessary. A child under the age of 14 should not swear an affidavit.

Where there are contradictions between affidavits, and no other evidence to support a conclusion one way or another, no conclusion can be drawn by the court: *D v. D*, 2002 S.C. 33, 37D (Extra Div.).

Forms

1.4. Where there is a reference to the use of a form in these Rules, that form in the appendix to these Rules, or a form substantially to the same effect, shall be used with such variation as circumstances may require.

General note. A form should normally be followed, but, as each form does not cover every **1.4.1** eventuality, changes may have to be made or more than one version of a form produced: each form is a style.

A form has the same number as the rule to which it relates. Where there is more than one form referred to in a rule the forms are also marked sequentially by letters of the alphabet: *e.g.* "13.2–A" and so on.

Direction relating to Advocate General

[1] **1.5.** The Lord President may, by direction, specify such arrangements as he considers necessary for, or in connection with, the appearance in court of the Advocate General for Scotland.

---

[1] R.1.5 inserted by S.I. 1999 No. 1386 (effective 19th May 1999) and correctly numbered by S.S.I. 2000 No. 66 (effective 7th April 2000).

General note. This rule was inserted by A.S. (R.C.S.A. No. 5) (Miscellaneous) 1999 [S.I. 1999 **1.5.1** No. 1386] to enable the Lord President to make a direction (if indeed a direction were necessary) providing for where the Advocate General may sit in court. By Direction No. 4 of 1999 the Advocate General shall be entitled, in court, to sit at the table within the Bar immediately below the Bench at the left hand side of the Chair (where the presiding judge sits); *i.e.* on the right hand side if facing the bench.

By convention the Lord Advocate is entitled to sit on the right hand side of the Chair at the table (*i.e.* on left if facing the bench). The Solicitor General is entitled to sit on the left hand side of the Chair at the table (*i.e.* on the right if facing the bench).

CHAPTER 2

RELIEF FROM COMPLIANCE WITH RULES

Relief for failure to comply with rules

2.1.—(1) The court may relieve a party from the consequences of a failure to comply with a provision in these Rules shown to be due to mistake, oversight or such other excusable cause on such conditions, if any, as the court thinks fit.

(2) Where the court relieves a party from the consequences of a failure to comply with a provision in these Rules under paragraph (1), the court may pronounce such interlocutor as it thinks fit to enable the cause to proceed as if the failure to comply with the provision had not occurred.

Deriv. A.S. (Rules of Court, consolidation and amendment) 1965, para. (4) [S.I. 1965 No. 321]

General note. This rule provides the court with an overriding discretion to excuse a failure to **2.1.1** comply with a rule where justice demands in the circumstances. The provision is substantially the same as the words used in para. (4) in the R.C.S. 1948 (in A.S. (Rules of Court, consolidation and amendment) 1948 [S.I. 1948 No. 1691]) and R.C.S. 1965, para. (4) and similar to that in the proviso to R.C.S. 1934 (in A.S. approving and embodying the Rules of Court [S.R. & O. 1934 No. 772]), in which it was first introduced, with this important difference: the phrase "mistake, oversight or other cause, not being wilful non-observance of the same" is replaced by the phrase "mistake, oversight or other excusable cause" (on which see note 2.1.2).

The power has been narrowly construed: "That dispensing power has been scantily applied, and generally where it is thought the novelty of the new procedure, or legitimate doubts as to the changes introduced, partly justified an oversight. Generally it requires for application some overlook or reasonable mistake" (*Richardson v. Ministry of Pensions* 1945 S.C. 363, 370 *per* Lord Mackay (motion for new trial not enrolled timeously)—R.C.S. 1934). "That discretion is conferred upon the Court not with a view to enabling the Court, wherever it thinks fit, to disregard the express provisions of the Rules. That provision is inserted to deal with some highly special circumstances, which may arise in some unusual case, and this discretion should only very rarely be employed" (*Grieve v. Batchelor and Buckling* 1961 S.C. 12, 16 *per* L. P. Clyde (late lodging of appeal after expiry of reponing days)—R.C.S. 1948, disapproved in *Grier v. Wimpey Plant & Transport Ltd* 1994 S.C. 385 and not followed in *X v. Galloway R.C.* 1994 S.C. 498). The dispensing power may be less likely to be exercised where there is a peremptory rule or a rule containing its own provision for relief (*cf. Flynn v. Morris Young (Perth) Ltd* 1996 S.C. 255 (relief from r. 37.1(6))). It has been suggested, obiter, in *Robertson v. Robertson's Trs* 1991 S.L.T. 875 that the dispensing power does not apply to R.C.S. 1965, r. 89(f) (now R.C.S. 1994, r. 19.2(2)–(4)), but it is not clear why; and the decision may be doubted: *cf. Thomson v. Omal Ltd* 1994 S.L.T. 705, *per* Lord MacLean and note 19.2.2. Because r. 37.1(2) (late lodging of proposed issue on cause shown) contains its own provision for granting relief, the court will not exercise the dispensing power in r. 2.1 unless in extraordinary circumstances: *McGee v. Matthew Hall Ltd* 1996 S.L.T. 399.

But it has been more widely construed: ". . . one finds the meaning of the proviso by paying attention to the words 'not being wilful non-observance of' the Rules. I think that the dispensing power was meant to enable the Court to do justice" (*Dalgety's Trs v. Drummond* 1938 S.C. 709, 715 *per* L. P. Normand (late lodging of appeal)—R.C.S. 1934); see also *Carroll v. Glasgow Corporation* 1965 S.L.T. 95 (failure to lodge closed record timeously). In *Graham v. John Tullis & Son (Plastics) Ltd (No. 1)* 1992 S.L.T. 507, 509, L.P. Hope said that the power extends to the time within which anything required or authorised to be done shall or may be made or done: in other words it applies not only to obligations imposed by the rules but to permissive powers. In *McDonald v. Kwok* 1999 S.L.T. 593, 595J and 596C, Lord Macfadyen said that the recent trend of authorities has been towards the view that it is always competent to invoke the dispensing power and that the terms of r. 2.1 were wholly unqualified as to the nature of the failure to comply. *McDonald* was overruled in *Brogan v. O'Rourke Ltd*, 2005 S.L.T. 29 (Extra Div.) where it was held that rr. 13.13(6) and 43.3(2) were plain and the meaning of "the instance shall fall" was perfectly understood: where the summons has not called within the specified period the instance falls and it is incompetent to apply to the court under r. 2.1.

There was always an inherent power of the court (superseded by the rule) to depart from the rules where justice demanded: "I doubt greatly whether the Court . . . is precluded by any Act of Sederunt from doing what it thinks according to justice and equity in any individual case before it" (*Boyd, Gilmour & Co. v. Glasgow & South Western Railway Co.* (1888) 16 R. 104, 109 *per* Lord Young (failure to lodge and box prints timeously); see also *Hutcheson v. Galloway Engineering Co.* 1922 S.C. 497 (note of objections to Auditor's report not timeously lodged)). In light of the (earlier) inherent power, the power in this rule should not receive, perhaps, too strict or rigid a construction. The new phrase "mistake, oversight or other excusable cause" may have resolved most of the former difficulties of interpretation and application of the provision: see further, note 2.1.2.

Non-compliance with the Rules is not necessarily to be excused simply because no particular prejudice can be identified. The rules are designed to regulate the general conduct of business, not just to suit the convenience of the parties: *Smith v. Smith* (I.H.), 23rd June 1995, unreported.

The power applies only in relation to the Court of Session rules: *G.A.S. Construction Co. Ltd v. Schrader* 1992 S.L.T. 505; *Graham*, above.

Where a rule provides a specific relief from its requirements, the court should hesitate to apply the wider power of relief in r. 2.1: *McGee v. Matthew Hall Ltd* 1996 S.L.T. 399 *per* Lord Caplan. In *Robertson v. Robertson's Trs,* 1991 S.L.T. 875 (OH), Lord Weir held that the dispensing power (now r. 2.1) could not apply where there was a provision containing its own dispensing power (in that case what is now r. 19.2(2)). In *Thomson v. Omal Ltd,* 1994 S. L.T. 705 (OH) Lord MacLean did not agree that exercise of the general dispensing power in r. 2.1 was incompetent in relation to r. 19.2(2) but, since that latter provision contained its own dispensing power the general dispensing power, the general dispensing power could be exercise only in exceptional circumstances. In *Semple Cochrane plc v. Hughes,* 2001 S.L.T. 1121 (OH) Lord Carloway was reluctant to qualify r. 2.1 by reading into it words such as "exceptional or extraordinary circumstances".

The dispensing power in r. 2.1 will not be exercised to allow, without leave, a reclaiming motion which required leave to proceed as that would frustrate the object of the rule requiring leave: *Robertson v. Robertson's Exr* 1991 S.C. 21.

Occasionally an A.S. is passed giving the court a discretion to relieve a party from the consequences of a failure to comply with the provisions of a rule or other enactment as a result of some particular emergency: see, for example, A.S. (Extension of Prescribed Time) 1971 [S.I. 1971 No. 356] (postal strike); A.S. (Emergency Powers) 1972 [S.I. 1972 No. 221] (coalminers' strike; see also A.S. (Suspension of Business) 1979 [S.I. 1979 No. 226] (civil service strike).

"mistake, oversight or other excusable cause". The replacement by this phrase of the phrase **2.1.2**
"mistake, oversight or other cause, not being wilful non-observance of the same" is intended to
deal with the not uncommon situation, not explicitly authorised by the previous rules, of the
court granting authority, often in advance, for the deliberate non-observance of a rule because
the rule cannot be complied with. The amendment has wider implications than to legitimise
such a necessary practice.

In relation to the previous rule, it was held in *Anderson v. British Coal Corporation* 1992
S.L.T. 398 that the dispensing power was normally exercised where there had been an excusable
mistake and not where a deliberate decision had been taken.

Ignorance of a rule may be an excusable cause: *Sutherland v. Duncan* 1996 S.L.T. 428 (case
concerned the equivalent O.C.R 1993, r. 2.1).

General and administration

CHAPTER 3

OFFICES OF THE COURT

Office of Court
   3.1.—(1) The Office of Court shall comprise—
   (a) the General Department,
   (b) the Petition Department,
   (c) the Rolls Department,
   (d) the Extracts Department, and
   (e) the Teind Office;
but shall not include the office of the Accountant of Court or the Auditor.

   (2) Each department of the Office of Court shall be under the charge of an
officer who shall act under the direction of the Principal Clerk in
consultation with the Lord President.

       Deriv. A.J.A. 1933, s.24(2); R.C.S. 1965, r. 12(a) (part) and (b) (part)

General note. There is provision in s.24 of the Administration of Justice (Scotland) Act 1933 **3.1.1**
(as originally enacted) for the offices of the court and the business of the departments. This was
repeated and extended (the Rolls Department) in the R.C.S. 1965, r.12.

Office hours and holidays. The offices of the court are open during the following hours: **3.1.2**
Monday .... 10.30 a.m. to 1 p.m. and 2 p.m. to 4 p.m.
Tuesday to Friday 10 a.m. to 1 p.m. and 2 p.m. to 4 p.m.
The offices are not open on Saturdays, Sundays or on public or local holidays. The public and
local holidays during the calendar year are as follows:
New Year's Day (1st January), or the following Monday if on a Saturday or Sunday
(bank holiday),
2nd January, or the following Monday (or Tuesday) if on a Saturday (or Sunday) (bank
holiday),
Spring Weekend (third Monday in April) (local holiday).
Good Friday (bank holiday),
Easter Monday,
May Day Holiday (first Monday in May) (bank holiday),
Victoria Day (local holiday),
September Weekend (third Monday in September),
Christmas Eve (24th December)—half day,
Christmas Day (25th December), or the following Monday if on a Saturday or Sunday
(bank holiday),
Boxing Day (26th December), or the following Monday (or Tuesday) if on a Saturday (or
Sunday).
The arrangements for urgent business when the offices are closed are as follows. Telephone the
Court of Session (0131–225 2595). The telephone is manned at all times. On telephoning, leave a
contact number. The security staff will contact a clerk who will contact you and make the
necessary arrangements. At weekends in session there is a rota for stand-by judges. In vacation
the vacation judge is the stand-by judge.
Accountant of Court. First appointed by s.9 of the Judicial Factors Act 1849 to superintend **3.1.3**
the conduct of judicial factors, tutors and curators, the office was re-appointed, and the office of
Accountant in Bankruptcy was subsumed under it, by ss.1 and 5 of the Judicial Factors
(Scotland) Act 1889; but, by s.1 of the Bankruptcy (Scotland) Act 1985, the Accountant of
Court is the Accountant in Bankruptcy created under that Act. The Accountant of Court is not,
however, an officer of the court.
The duties of the Accountant of Court are:
(1) In judicial factories—(a) to superintend the conduct of all judicial factors, curators, tutors,
guardians and others appointed by the court or the sheriff court to hold, administer and protect
property belonging to persons or estates in Scotland and to audit their accounts: Judicial
Factors Acts 1849, 1880 and 1889; (b) to superintend factors appointed to administer damages
awarded to a child under 16 under r.43.16(a); (c) to prepare an annual report on all judicial
factories: 1849 Act, above, s.18.
(2) Formerly in sequestrations as Accountant in Bankruptcy—(a) to supervise interim and
permanent trustees and commissioners in their functions, to maintain the register of
insolvencies and to prepare an annual report of sequestrations, etc: Bankruptcy (Scotland)
Act 1985, s.1(1); (b) to audit accounts of trustees under voluntary trust deeds for creditors
where sought: 1985 Act, Sch.5, para.1; and (c) to receive deposit receipts in respect of unclaimed
dividends and unapplied balances: 1985 Act, s.57(1). These functions have been transferred to
the Accountant in Bankruptcy: 1985 Act, ss.1, 1A and 1C inserted by the Bankruptcy
(Scotland) Act 1993, s.1.
(3) In liquidations—to determine the time of the release of liquidators: Insolvency Act 1986,
ss.173 and 174 and Insolvency (Scotland) Rules 1986, r.4.25 [SI 1986/1915].
(4) In relation to caution—(a) to fix the caution to be found by judicial factors, curators and
guardians: r.61.9(3); (b) to receive all bonds of caution lodged in any process: r.33.12(1).
(5) In relation to consignation—(a) to receive all monies consigned under order of the court
or otherwise: Court of Session Consignations (Scotland) Act 1895, s.3; (b) to receive
consignation receipts or other deposits in respect of (i) unclaimed dividends and unapplied
balances in judicial factories under his own supervision (Judicial Factors (Scotland) Act 1849,
s.35) and in liquidations (Insolvency Act 1986, s.193), and (ii) sums representing consideration
for shares acquired under s.430 of the Companies Act 1985 (as substituted by the Financial
Services Act 1986, Sch.12) in respect of person who cannot be found after 12 years (s.430(13));
(c) miscellaneous sums held at his discretion; (d) to maintain in the Consignation Book a record
of consignations: 1895 Act, above, s.4; and (e) to lodge detailed annual returns with the Lord
President: 1895 Act, above, s.9.
(6) To make reports on remits from the court.

(7) To superintend trusts in relation to arrestment and distribution of trust funds on the order of the court on the application of a trustee: Trusts (Scotland) Act 1921, s.17.

(8) To supervise administrators appointed under the Prevention of Terrorism (Temporary Provisions) Act 1989 or the Proceeds of Crime (Scotland) Act 1995.

(9) To perform any other special duties imposed by statute: *e.g.* War Loan (Supplemental Provisions) Act 1915, s.9 (investment of funds under any trade union rules).

3.1.4   *The Auditor.* This is the Auditor of the Court of Session: r.1.3(1) (definition of "the Auditor"). See further, r.3.7 and note 3.7.1.

General Department

3.2.—(1) The General Department shall be under the charge of the Deputy Principal Clerk.

(2) There shall be lodged in the General Department all processes in—
   (a) causes originating in the court and initiated by summons or simplified divorce application;
   (b) appeals from inferior courts, remits from the sheriff court, appeals, including references, submissions and applications of the nature of appeals under statute, stated cases and special cases;
   (c) causes transmitted from the sheriff court on contingency; and
   (d) appeals to the Lands Valuation Appeal Court.

(3) All processes lodged in the General Department shall be classified as—
   (a) ordinary actions;
   (b) Admiralty and commercial actions;
   (c) family (including consistorial) actions; or
   (d) lands valuation causes.

Deriv. A.J.A. 1933, s.24(2) and (3) and C.S.A. 1988, s.6(i) (r.3.2(3)); R.C.S. 1965, rr.12(b) (part) (r.3.2(1)), 13(a) amended by SI 1982/1679 (r.3.2(2)) and 15 (r.3.2(3))

3.2.1   *General Note.* The General Department is divided into three sections. The sections are:
A–F
G–Mac
Mad–Z.

A cause is assigned to a particular section according to (a) in the case of an individual, the initial letter of the surname of the pursuer, and (b) in the case of a firm or company, usually the initial letter of the first word where a descriptive name is used or the initial letter of the surname where a proper name is used, of the pursuer.

3.2.2   *"causes originating in the court".* Causes originating in the court are commenced by summons except (a) those commenced by petition (see rr.14.2 and 14.3), (b) special cases (see Chap. 77), (c) certain applications and references treated as appeals under various statutes (see note 3.2.3(d)(iii) and (iv)), (d) applications for divorce under the simplified divorce procedure (see r.49.73), and (f) applications (by minute, note or motion) treated as part of the original process.

3.2.3   *R. 3.2(2)(b). (A) Appeals from inferior courts.* (1) *The sheriff court*: Sheriff Courts (Scotland) Act 1907, s.28 as substituted by the Sheriff Courts (Scotland) Act 1913, s.2 and as amended by the Sheriff Courts (Scotland) Act 1971, Sch.2; 1971 Act, s.38(b) as amended by the Law Reform (Miscellaneous Provisions) (Scotland) Act 1985, s.18(4) (summary causes other than small claims) and s.37(3) as amended by the Law Reform (Miscellaneous Provisions) (Scotland) Act 1980, s.16(c) (appeals *re* remits of ordinary cause to summary cause and *vice versa*). (2) *The Lyon Court*: *Cunninghame v. Cunyngham* (1849) 11 D. 1139; Erskine, I.iv.32.
   (B) Remits from sheriff court: 1971 Act, above, s.37(1)(b) as amended by the 1980 Act, above, s.16 (ordinary cause), s.37(2A) as amended by the 1980 Act, above, s.16(b) and the Divorce Jurisdiction, Court Fees and Legal Aid (Scotland) Act 1983, Sch.1, para.12 (actions for divorce or relating to custody or adoption); Presumption of Death (Scotland) Act 1977, s.1(6) (action of declarator), s.4 (variation of declarator).
   (C) Appeals, etc., under particular statutes.
   (1) *Appeals.* These include—Taxes Management Act 1970, ss.53, 100B(3) and 100C(4) (appeals *re* penalties from General or Special Commissioners); Inheritance Tax Act 1984, s.222 (against determination of Commissioners of Inland Revenue), and ss.249(3) and 251(2)

(appeals *re* penalties from Special Commissioners); Oil Taxation Act 1975, s.1 and Sched.2, para. 1 (from Commissioners *re* penalties); Stamp Duty Reserve Tax Regulations 1986 [S.I. 1986 No. 1711], reg.8 (against determination of Commissioners of Inland Revenue); Tribunal and Inquiries Act 1992, s.11 (from VAT Tribunals); Burial Grounds (Scotland) Act 1855, s.10; Sheep Stocks Valuation (Scotland) Act 1937, s.2(2) (from sheriff from arbiter); Pharmacy Act 1954, ss.10 and 24(2) (against directions); Therapeutic Substances Act 1956, ss.2(4) and 6 (from suspension of licence); Teaching Council (Scotland) Act 1965, s.12 as substituted by Standards in Scotland's Schools etc. Act 2000 (appeal against direction *re* registration); Fair Trading Act 1973, s.42 (*re* protection of consumers from Restrictive Practices Court); Consumer Credit Act 1974, s. 41A inserted by Consumer Credit Act 2006, s. 57 (on point of law from Consumer Credit Appeals Tribunal); Control of Pollution Act 1974, s.85 (from sheriff); Restrictive Practices Court Act 1976, s.10(2) (from RPC in proceedings under Pt III of the Fair Trading Act 1973 (*re* protection of consumer)); Licensing (Scotland) Act 1976, s.39(8) (from sheriff from licensing board); Patents Acts: 1949 Act, s.87(3) and 1977 Act, Sched.4 (*re* decision of comptroller under 1949 Act, s.55), 1977 Act, s.97 (from comptroller); Estate Agents Act 1979, s.7(4) (from Secretary of State from Director General of Fair Trading *re* estate agency work); Education (Scotland) Act 1980, s.112(8) as amended by the Education (Scotland) Act 1981, s.1 and Sched.2, para. 3 (from Council *re* issue of practising certificate), ss.16 (from Council *re* restoration to roll) and 54 (from discipline tribunal); Public Passenger Vehicles Act 1981, s.51 (from Secretary of State from Traffic Commissioners); Civic Government (Scotland) Act 1982, s.4 and Sched.1, para. 12 (from sheriff from licensing authority), s.54 and Sched.2, para. 24(12) (from sheriff *re* licence of sex shop), s.64(9) (from sheriff *re* holding of procession), s.88(4) (from sheriff *re* installation of pipes through neighbouring property), s.106(5) (from sheriff *re* notices and expenses under Pt VIII); Representation of the People Act 1983, ss.56 and 57 (from sheriff from registration officer *re* registration to three judges of the court); Medical Act 1983, s.40 as amended by the NHS Reform and Health Care Professionals Act 2002, s.30 (from General Council); Dentists Act 1984, s.29 as amended by the NHS Reform and Health Care Professionals Act 2002, s.31 (appeal from Professional Conduct and Health Committees); Mental Health (Scotland) Act 1984, s.66A(1) (appeal from sheriff); Transport Act 1985, s.117(2) and Sched.4, para. 14(1) (from Transport Tribunal); Legal Aid (Scotland) Act 1986, s.31(4) (*re* exclusion of lawyer from selection in legal aid cases); Building Societies Act 1986, s.49(1) and (2) (from tribunal from B.S. Commission); Banking Act 1987, s.31 (from Banking Appeal Tribunal); Copyright, Designs and Patents Act 1988, s.152(1) (from Copyright Tribunal) and s.251(2) (from Comptroller General *re* design rights); Opticians Act 1989, s.23 as amended by the NHS Reform and Health Care Professionals Act 2002, s.32 (from Disciplinary Committee); Human Fertilisation and Embryology Act 1990, s.21 (*re* determination of licence by HFEA); Environmental Protection Act 1990, s.73 (from sheriff *re* waste on land); Child Support Act 1991, s.25 (from the Child Support Commissioner); Agricultural Holdings (Scotland) Act 1991, s.61 and Sched.7 (from sheriff from arbiter); Social Security Administration Act 1992, ss.18(3) and 58 (from decisions or determinations by the Secretary of State) and 24 (from the SS Commissioner); Local Government Finance Act 1992, s.82(4) (from valuation appeal committee *re* council tax); Friendly Societies Act 1992, s.61 (from tribunal *re* decision of Commission); Tribunal and Inquiries Act 1992, s.11 and Sched.1 (from various tribunals); Pension Schemes Act 1993, s.151(4) (from Pensions Ombudsman) and s.173(3) (from Occupational Pensions Board); Osteopaths Act 1993, ss.24 and 25 (against interim suspension order), s.29 (from Registrar); and s.31 as amended by the NHS Reform and Health Care Professionals Act 2002, s.33 (from Professional Conduct Committee); Chiropractors Act 1994, s.31 as amended by the NHS Reform and Health Care Professionals Act 2002, s.34 (from Professional Conduct Committee or appeal tribunal); Trade Marks Act 1994, s.76(2) (from registrar); Drug Trafficking Act 1994, s.45 (from forfeiture order by sheriff); Pensions Act 1995, s.97(3) (from Occupational Pensions Regulatory Authority); Industrial Tribunals Act 1996, s.37(1) (from Employment Appeal Tribunal); Architects Act 1997, s.22 (appeals *re* registration); Nurses, Midwives and Health Visitors Act 1997, s.12 (*re* removal from register); Special Immigration Appeals Commission Act 1997, s.7 (from Special Immigration Appeals Commission); Social Security Act 1998, s.15 (appeal from Social Security Commissioner with leave); Data Protection Act 1998, s.49(6) (on point of law from Data Protection Tribunal); Competition Act 1998, s.49 (on point of law from appeal tribunal); Social Security Act 1998, s.15 (from Social Security Commissioner); Road Traffic (NHS Charges) Act 1999, s.9(2) (on point of law from appeal tribunal); Immigration and Financial Services and Markets Act 2000, s.137(1) (from Financial Services and Markets Tribunal); Terrorism Act 2000, s.6(1) (from Proscribed Organisations Commission); Postal Services Act 2000, s.36(2) (by person aggrieved); Freedom of Information (Scotland) Act 2002, s.56 (from Scottish Information Commissioner on point of law); Proceeds of Crime Act 2002, s.299 (from sheriff); Enterprise Act 2002, s.114 (from Competition Appeal Tribunal); Nationality, Immigration and Asylum Act 2002, s.103 (from Immigration Appeal Tribunal).

(2) *References*. These include—Defamation Act 1952, s.4(4) (*re* steps in fulfilment of offer of amends): see r. 54.1; Copyright, Designs and Patents Act 1988, s.251(1) (from Comptroller General) and s.252 (disputes *re* Crown use of designs): see r. 55.14; Social Security Administration Act 1992, ss.18(1) and 58 (from Secretary of State: by stated case by virtue of r. 41.34); Pension Schemes Act 1993, ss.150(7) (from Pensions Ombudsman: by stated case by virtue of r. 41.34) and 173(1) (from Occupational Pensions Board: by stated case by virtue of r. 41.34); Trade Marks Act 1994, s.76(3) (from appointed person); Pensions Act 1995, s.97(1) (from Occupational Pensions Regulatory Authority by stated case by virtue of r. 41.34). Certain references are by petition and are therefore assigned to the Petition Department: see note 3.3.1.

(3) *Applications (of the nature of appeals)*. These include—Public Order Act 1936, ss.2(3) and 8(2) (*re* property of an association); Acquisition of Land (Authorisation Procedure) (Scotland) Act 1947, s.1 and Sched. 1, para. 15 (*re* validity of compulsory purchase order); Housing (Scotland) Act 1966, ss.36, 38, 43 and Sched. 2, para. 2 (*re* clearance orders); Fair Trading Act 1973, s.85 (*re* default of requirement to give evidence or produce documents to Monopolies and Mergers Commission); Ancient Monuments and Archaeological Areas Act 1979, s.55(1) (*re* validity of designation orders); Wildlife and Countryside Act 1981, ss.29, 34 and Sched. 11, para. 7 (*re* validity of order *re* areas of scientific interest), s.36 and Sched. 12, para. 8 (*re* validity of order *re* marine nature reserves); Civil Aviation Act 1982, Sched. 7, para. 7 (*re* validity of orders); Telecommunications Act 1984, s.18 (*re* orders of Secretary of State); Roads (Scotland) Act 1984, Sched. 2, para. 2 (*re* validity of orders and schemes); Films Act 1985, Sched. 2, para. 9 (from decision of Secretary of State to refuse to certify or to revoke certification for purposes of s.72 of the Finance Act 1982); Gas Act 1986, s.30 (*re* orders of Secretary of State); Petroleum Act 1998, s.42 (from decisions of the Secretary of State); National Heritage (Scotland) Act 1991, Sched. 5, para. 10 (*re* validity of irrigation control order); Railways Act 1993, s.57 (*re* validity of order); Coal Industry Act 1994, s.33 (*re* validity of enforcement order); Town and Country Planning (Scotland) Act 1997, s.238 (*re* validity of structure or local plan), s.239 (*re* validity of other orders, etc.); Planning (Listed Buildings and Conservation Areas) (Scotland) Act 1997, s.58 (*re* validity of orders etc.); Planning (Hazardous Substances) (Scotland) Act 1997, s.20 (*re* validity of decisions) Petroleum Act 1998, s.42 (from decisions of the Secretary of State).

(D) Stated cases. These include—Stamp Act 1891, s.13 (from Commissioners of Inland Revenue *re* assessment of duty); Taxes Management Act 1970, s.56 (from General or Special Commissioners); Inheritance Tax Act 1984, s.225 (from Special Commissioners); Stamp Duty Reserve Tax Regulations 1986 [S.I. 1986 No. 1711], reg. 10 (from Special Commissioners); Tribunals and Inquiries Act 1992, s.11 and Sched. 1 and Tribunals and Inquiries (Value Added Tax Tribunals) Order 1972 [S.I. 1972 No. 1210] (from VAT Tribunals); Pensions Appeal Tribunal Act 1943, ss.6 and 13 (from PAT); Lands Tribunal Act 1949, s.3(3) (from LT); Agricultural Marketing Act 1958, s.12(2) (from disciplinary committee); Building (Scotland) Act 1959, s.16(3) (from sheriff); Industrial and Provident Societies Act 1965, s.60(9) (*re* disputes involving registered society); Social Work (Scotland) Act 1968, s.50 (from sheriff from children's hearing); Administration of Justice (Scotland) Act 1972, s.3 (from arbiter); Town and Country Planning (Scotland) Act 1972, s.234 (from Secretary of State in determining planning permission under s.51); Social Security Act 1973, s.86 (from Occupational Pensions Board: by stated case by virtue of r. 41.34); Local Government (Scotland) Act 1973, s.103(2) (on special report to Commission by Controller of Audit); Friendly Societies Act 1974, s.78 (*re* certain disputes); Restrictive Practices Court Act 1976, s.10 (from RPC); Iron and Steel Act 1982, s.26(5)(a) (from Iron and Steel Arbitration Tribunal); Representation of the People Act 1983, s.134(1) (from sheriffs principal who cannot agree *re* election of councillors) and s.146(4) (from election court on admissibility of evidence, etc.); New Roads and Street Works Act 1991, s.158(2) (from arbiter); Social Security Administration Act 1992, ss.18(1) and 58 (from Secretary of State: by stated case by virtue of r. 41.34); Friendly Societies Act 1992, s.80(4) (from arbiter); Tribunal and Inquiries Act 1992, s.11 and Sched. 1 (from various tribunals).

(E) Special cases. These include—Compensation (Defence) Act 1939, ss.7 and 18(2) (from Shipping Tribunal or General Tribunal); Crofters (Scotland) Act 1961, s.4(3) (from Land Court); Control of Pollution Act 1974, s.39(8); Representation of the People Act 1983, s.146(1) (from election court); C.S.A. 1988, s.27: see Chap. 77; Scottish Land Court Rules 1992, r. 88 [S.I. 1992 No. 2656].

3.2.4 *Transmission from sheriff court on contingency*. For the meaning of contingency, see note 32.2.3.

3.2.5 *Lands Valuation Appeal Court*. The appeals to the Lands Valuation Appeal Court are under the following statutory provisions: Lands Valuation (Scotland) Act 1854, s.24 (as amended by the Railways (Valuation for Rating) Act 1930, s.22(4)) (against valuations of assessors of public undertakings); Lands Valuation (Scotland) Act 1857, as amended by the Valuation of Lands (Scotland) Amendment Act 1867, s.8 and the Valuation of Lands (Scotland) Amendment Act 1879, s.7 (both as amended by the Rating and Valuation (Amendment) (Scotland) Act 1984, s.13) (appeals against entries in valuation roll) (applied to the Rating (Scotland) Act 1926, s.14); Rating and Valuation (Apportionment) Act 1928, s.9(9); Local Government (Scotland) Act 1966, s.22(3); Rating (Disabled Persons) Act 1978, s.4(8); Water (Scotland) Act 1980, s.45(2).

The judges of the Lands Valuation Appeal Court are Lords Gill, Nimmo Smith, Philip, Kingarth and Clarke: A.S. (Lands Valuation Appeal Court) 2002 [S.S.I. 2002 No. 340].

Classification of General Department processes. Causes initiated by summons are so classified **3.2.6** by virtue of the C.S.A. 1988, s.6(i), which provides for (a) an Ordinary Roll, (b) an Admiralty and Commercial Roll and (c) a Family (including Consistorial) Roll. The classification is determined as follows: (i) an Admiralty cause is one defined by r. 46.1; (ii) a commercial action is one defined by r. 47.1(2); (iii) a family action is one defined by r. 49.1(1) (a consistorial cause is an action between husband and wife involving status); (iv) an ordinary action is any other cause initiated by summons; and (v) a lands valuation cause is an appeal to the Lands Valuation Court: see note 3.2.5.

Petition Department

3.3.—(1) The Petition Department shall be under the charge of the Deputy Principal Clerk.

(2) There shall be lodged in the Petition Department all processes in causes which are initiated by petition.

Deriv. A.J.A. 1933, s.24(2); R.C.S. 1965, r. 12(b) (part) (r. 3.3(1)) and r. 13(b) (r. 3.3(2))

Petition Department processes. The processes belonging to the Petition Department are: **3.3.1**
(1) Those listed in rr. 14.2 and 14.3.
(2) Certain references under particular statutes. These are— Railway and Canal Commission (Abolition) Act 1949, s.1(1): by petition by virtue of r. 14.2(h); Mines (Working Facilities and Support) Act 1966, s.4(3) (grant of right *re* minerals and compensation): by petition by virtue of r. 14.2(h); Defamation Act 1952, s.4(4) (*re* steps in fulfilment of offer of amends where no action for defamation taken): r. 54.2.

Petition register. For the 17 categories of petitions, see note 4.1.5. Petitions are kept and **3.3.2** recorded alphabetically according to subject-matter but recorded in the Petition register chronologically. To trace a process when the subject-matter under which the process has been recorded is not known the chronological register will have to be searched if the year is known. Alternatively, if there has been a final interlocutor or a year and a day has passed with no interlocutor, a search may be made in the index of processes in the process records department but only where the record number is known and the process is not a judicial factory or liquidation in which there has been no final discharge (r. 9.1(3)). See also note 7.1.5.

Rolls Department

3.4.—(1) The Rolls Department shall be under the charge of the Keeper of the Rolls, who shall be assisted by a clerk of session known as the Assistant Keeper of the Rolls.

(2) The Keeper of the Rolls shall be responsible for keeping the rolls of the court in consultation with the Lord President, the Lord Justice-Clerk and the Principal Clerk.

Deriv. R.C.S. 1965, r. 14 (r. 3.4(2))

General note. The Rolls Department did not previously exist in name, though the Keeper, and **3.4.1** the Assistant Keeper, of the Rolls and the work of the department did.

"rolls". These are the lists of business of the court: r. 1.3(1) (definition of "rolls"). The rolls　**3.4.2**
are: (1) The General Roll, consisting of the registers of causes of the (*a*) General Department
(the Ordinary, Admiralty and Commercial, and Family (including Consistorial) Rolls) and
(*b*) the Petition Department. (2) The Daily Rolls—the printed rolls issued each weekday during term showing the causes in the General Roll appearing for business on a particular day,
consisting of (*a*) in the Inner House (i) Single Bills, (ii) By Order Roll, (iii) Summar Roll and
(iv) Advisings; and (*b*) in the Outer House (i) Calling List, (ii) Motion Roll, (iii) Diet Roll,
(iv) Commercial Roll, (v) Adjustment Roll and Continued Adjustment Roll, (vi) By Order
(Adjustment) Roll, (vii) By Order Roll, (viii) Procedure Roll, (ix) Jury Trials, Proofs, Proofs
before Answer and Hearings, (x) For Judgment and (xi) Undefended Consistorial Causes (in
fact undefended divorce actions). In the Daily Rolls there are also printed notices of Acts of
Sederunt, practice notes and other acts of administration. Rolls issued in vacation contain
details of (2)(*a*)(i) and (iv) and (*b*)(i), (iii)–(xi).

Extracts Department

3.5.—(1) The Extracts Department shall be under the charge of the Principal Extractor who shall be assisted by a clerk of session known as the
Extractor.

(2) The Principal Extractor shall be responsible for extracting the acts
and decrees of the court except those in teind causes.

(3) Subject to rule 3.6(3) (duties of clerk of teinds), the Extractor shall
be the Keeper of—

    (*a*) the Register of Acts and Decrees;

    (*b*) the Register of Edictal Citations and Executions of Diligence; and

    (*c*) the Register of Decrees in Consistorial Causes.

(4) As Keeper of the Register of Edictal Citations and Executions of
Diligence, the Extractor shall—

    (*a*) record on the copy of the schedule of diligence received by him the
date of its receipt at his office;

    (*b*) record the details of that schedule and its receipt in the register;

    (*c*) preserve that schedule and any citation for a period of three years
from the date of receipt of the schedule or citation, as the case may
be; and

    (*d*) make the register and schedules of diligence and citations executed
on him available for inspection at his office during its normal business hours.

Deriv. R.C.S. 1965, r. 12(*b*) (part) (r. 3.5(1)); Debtors (Scotland) Act 1838, s. 18 and A.S.
(Edictal Citations, Commissary Petitions and Petitions of Service) 1971 [S.I. 1971 No. 1165],
para. 1(2) and (3) (r. 3.5(4))

General note. The business of the extractors was given to one Principal Extractor by the　**3.5.1**
Court of Session (No. 2) Act 1838, s. 18. These officials are now appointed under the Public
Records (Scotland) Act 1937, s. 31(1). The duty of the Principal Extractor, with the assistance
of the Extractor, is to prepare and issue extracts of the acts and decrees of the court as
required. The Extractor of acts and decrees in teind causes is the clerk of teinds: see note
3.6.4(*d*).

Duties of Extractor. These are:　**3.5.2**

(1) To assist the Principal Extractor in extracting the acts and decrees of the court including
decrees of the inferior courts (the sheriff court, Lyon Court and Employment Appeal Tribunal) appealed to the Court of Session and not transmitted back after disposal of the appeal
(because no further procedure is necessary in the lower court). In fact, all applications for
extracts are made to the Extractor: see r. 7.1(3).

(2) To keep the Register of Acts and Decrees of the court: see Public Records (Scotland)
Act 1937, s. 31(1). This is transmitted annually to the Keeper of the Records: r. 9.1(1).

(3) To receive executions of diligence on persons resident furth of Scotland, whose residence is not known and cannot reasonably be ascertained or on whom diligence cannot otherwise be executed: see r. 16.12(4).

(4) To edit and keep the Register of Edictal Citations and Executions of Diligence: r.
3.5(4); and see (A) below and note 3.5.3.

(5) To edit and keep the register of decrees of divorce, nullity and dissolution of marriage as
Keeper of the Register of Decrees of Consistorial Causes. This register contains decrees dis-

solving marriage and all other decrees in consistorial causes which used to be recorded in the Minute Book (now no longer kept, having been discontinued in January 1993). The register may be inspected at the Extracts Department.

(6) To receive offers in relation to rights of pre-emption of superiors: Conveyancing Amendment (Scotland) Act 1938, s. 9(2).

(7) To receive any notices of a requirement to grant a feu right under the Long Leases (Scotland) Act 1954, s. 23(1)(c).

(8) To receive notices of calling up or default in relation to standard securities: Conveyancing and Feudal Reform (Scotland) Act 1970, ss. 19(6) and 21(2).

The Extractors are not responsible for the Teind Court Minute Book or for teind extracts, the clerk of teinds being so responsible: see rr. 3.5(2) and 3.6(3).

The Extractor used to have the following duties:

(A) To receive all edictal citations, services and intimations as Keeper of the Register of Edictal Citations: Reorganisation of Offices (Scotland) Act 1928, s. 8. As Keeper, the Extractor (a) received citations and orders for service against persons whose whereabouts were unknown under R.C.S. 1965, r. 75A (a procedure discontinued under R.C.S. 1994: see r. 16.5 (service by advertisement)); and (b) received citations, charges, publications and orders for service under para. 1 of the A.S. (Edictal Citations, Commissary Petitions and Petitions of Service) 1971 [S.I. 1971 No. 1165] (revoked by A.S. (R.C.S. 1994) 1994 [S.I. 1994 No. 1443], Sched. 5).

(B) To edit and keep the Minute Book as Keeper of the Minute Book: Reorganisation of Offices (Scotland) Act 1928, s. 8 and the Order as to Transfer of Powers and Duties of the Office of Keeper of Minute Book and Record of Edictal Citations [S.R. & O. 1929 No. 588]. The Minute Book contained the minutes of the judicial business of the court—Acts of Sederunt, Practice Notes, minutes of General, and Petition, Department business including entries of intimations, decrees, acts admitting solicitors and notaries. The Minute Book was compiled weekly and published for subscribers and transmitted annually to the Scottish Record Office. It was discontinued in January 1993 because it was not cost effective and little used.

3.5.3   *Register of Edictal Citations and Executions of Diligence.* Although edictal citation has been abolished for citation of persons furth of Scotland or whose address is not known (see r. 16.5), the register of edictal citations has to be maintained for three years: r. 3.5(4)(c) and (d). Furthermore, although edictal citation has been abolished, a means had to continue to be provided for execution of diligence on such persons. Edictal execution of diligence was retained being the simplest, practical and inexpensive means rather than resort to advertisement. For this purpose edictal execution by executing a document of diligence on the Extractor of the Court of Session is used and for which purpose the Extractor must keep a Register of Edictal Executions of Diligence; after three years from the coming into force of the R.C.S. 1994 there will be no need for a register of edictal citations. The otiose provisions of s. 18 of the Debtors (Scotland) Act 1838 (edictal execution of arrestment) and para. 1(2) and (3) of the A.S. (Edictal Citations, Commissary Petitions and Petitions of Service) 1971 [S.I. 1971 No. 1165], are replaced by r. 3.5(4) and new rules for execution of diligence in r. 16.12.

Teind Office

3.6.—(1) The Teind Office shall be under the charge of a clerk of session known as the clerk of teinds.

(2) There shall be lodged in the Teind Office all processes which are dealt with by the Teind Court or the Lord Ordinary in teind causes.

(3) The clerk of teinds shall—

   (a) keep and index the records and processes in the Teind Office; and
   (b) be the Keeper of the Teind Rolls and the Keeper of the Minute Book of the Teind Court.

Deriv. R.C.S. 1965, rr. 12(b) (part) and 13(c) (r. 3.6(2))

3.6.1   *Teind Court.* The Kirk and Teinds Act 1706 transferred the powers of various commissions appointed to deal with teinds to the Court of Session. The judges of the Inner House and a Lord Ordinary as Lord Ordinary in teind causes, acting in their capacity as Lords Commissioners for teinds, are the judges of the Teind Court. Any five are a quorum of the Court of Commissioners for Teinds: C.S.A. 1839, s. 8 as amended by C.S.A. 1868, s. 9. Though known as the Teind Court, the court is not a separate court from the Court of Session; and the jurisdiction of the Court of Session sitting as the Teind Court includes the original jurisdiction of the Court of Session: *Presbytery of Stirling v. Heritors of Larbert & Dunpace* (1900) 2 F. 562.

The court meets once a fortnight on a Friday during session (when there is business) at such time as is convenient; the Lord Ordinary in teind causes sits every Friday at 10.00 am (when there is business), the roll of business is made up the preceding Tuesday: Church of Scotland (Property and Endowments) Act 1925, s.41; A.S. Procedure under Church of Scotland (Property and Endowments) Act 1925, s.10, etc. [S.R. & O. 1925 No. 1062], and C.A.S. 1913, H,I,7 [S.R. & O. 1913 No. 638]. The Lord Ordinary in teind causes is currently Lord Bonomy.

Jurisdiction. The Teind Court has jurisdiction—(a) to modify, settle and appoint teinds and **3.6.2** determine all points concerning teinds: Teinds Act 1690; (b) in respect of the teind rolls: Church of Scotland (Property and Endowments) Act 1925, s.11 and Sched. 5, and A.S. Procedure relating to Preparation of Teind Rolls etc., [S.R. & O. 1925 No. 1063]; over valuation and surrender of teinds under the 1925 Act, above, s.16 and Sched. 6; (c) in relation to disjunction and erection of parishes: New Parishes (Scotland) Act 1844, ss.1–6 and 8–11 and United Parishes (Scotland) Act 1868, ss.2 and 3; (d) in appeals in relation to (i) churches, manses and glebes: Ecclesiastical Buildings and Glebes (Scotland) Act 1868, s.14 and (ii) value of victual stipends: 1925 Act, above, s.2; (e) over the feuing of glebes: Glebe Lands (Scotland) Act 1866; and (f) over the transfer of a glebe to a new parish: United Parishes (Scotland) Act 1876.

Procedure. (1) In relation to teind rolls, see Church of Scotland (Property and Endowments) **3.6.3** Act 1925, s.11 and Sched. 5, and A.S. Procedure relating to Preparation of Teind Rolls, etc. [S.R. & O. 1925 No. 1063]. (2) In relation to other teind causes, see C.A.S. 1913, H, I,III–VII [S.R. & O. 1913 No. 638].

Clerk of teinds. Originally appointed under the C.S.A. 1821, the clerk is now appointed under **3.6.4** the Administration of Justice (Scotland) Act 1933, s.24 and this rule. The duties of the clerk are—(a) to prepare the teind rolls: Church of Scotland (Property and Endowments) Act 1925, s.11 and Sched. 5; (b) to officiate as clerk to the Teind Court: r. 3.6(3); (c) to keep and index the records and processes in the Teind Office: r. 3.6(3); (d) to act as extractor of acts and decrees of the Teind Court: Court of Session (No. 2) Act 1838, s.27. He is Keeper of the Teind Rolls and Keeper of the Minute Book of the Teind Court: r. 3.6(3).

[1] **Registers kept by the court**
   3.6A. Any register kept by the court, whether or not under or by virtue of **3.6A.1** these Rules, may be kept either—
   (a) in documentary form; or
   (b) in electronic form (that is to say in a form accessible only be electronic means).

_____

[1] R.3.6A inserted by S.I. 1998 No. 2637 (effective 1st December 1998) and numbered correctly by S.I. 1999 No. 1386 (effective 19th May 1999).

General note. This new rule, inserted by A.S. (R.C.S.A. No. 2) (Miscellaneous) 1998 [S.I. 1998 **3.6A.2** No. 2637], will enable the court to put its registers on computer in due course.

The Auditor
   3.7. The Auditor shall be responsible for the taxation of accounts of expenses in any cause.

The Auditor. This is the Auditor of the Court of Session: r. 1.3(1) (definition of "the **3.7.1** Auditor"). First appointed by A.S. 6th February 1806, the Auditor was made a permanent official and member of the College of Justice, formerly holding his appointment *ad vitam aut culpam* by s.32 of the C.S.A. 1821. He is now appointed under s.25 of the Administration of Justice (Scotland) Act 1933 until the age of 65 unless extended (1933 Act, s.26).
   The duties of the Auditor are:
   (1) To tax accounts of expenses in civil causes remitted by the court: rr. 3.7 and 42.1(1)(b)(ii).
   (2) To tax accounts incurred to solicitors under (a) the Legal Aid (Scotland) (Fees in Civil Proceedings) Regulations 1989, reg. 9 [S.I. 1989 No. 1490], (b) Criminal Legal Aid (Scotland) (Fees) Regulations 1989, reg. 11 [S.I. 1989 No. 1491] and (c) Legal Aid in Contempt of Court Proceedings (Scotland) (Fees) Regulations 1992, reg. 9 [S.I. 1992 No. 1228], if required.
   (3) To tax accounts incurred to solicitors by (a) judicial factors (see Notes for Guidance of J.F.s by Accountant of Court, n. 14(a)); (b) permanent trustees on sequestrated estates of debtors (see Bankruptcy (Scotland) Act 1985, s.53(2)); and (c) by administrators and liquidators of companies (under the Insolvency (Scotland) Rules 1986, rr. 2.16(3) and 4.32 [S.I. 1986 No. 1915] and applying s.53(2) of the 1985 Act, above; on the interpretation of s.53(2A) of the 1985 Act, see *Rankin, Noter*, 2003 S.L.T. 107 (OH)).

(4) To tax accounts incurred in private legislation procedure: Private Legislation Procedure (Scotland) Act 1936, s.6(6).

(5) To tax the accounts of returning officers in Parliamentary elections, if required: Representation of the People Act 1949, s.20(7).

(6) To fix the remuneration of a receiver where remuneration has not been agreed or is disputed: Insolvency Act 1986, s.58(2).

(7) To tax non-legal aid fees of counsel where not agreed under the Scheme for Accounting for and Recovery of Counsel's Fees between the Faculty of Advocates and the Law Society 1987, para. 5(4).

(8) To adjudicate on a reasonable fee where counsel's fee is challenged under the Standard Terms for Direct Professional Access to Counsel, para. 3.7.

The Auditor may also tax:

(1) Extra-judicial accounts remitted to him with consent of the parties.

(2) Accounts incurred to solicitors where client requires: Table of Fees for Conveyancing and General Business approved by the Council of the Law Society of Scotland, January [annually], Chap. 2, para. 5.

CHAPTER 4

THE PROCESS

Form, size, etc., of documents forming the process

4.1.—(1) In an action or petition, the principal summons or petition, as the case may be, shall be on a printed form approved by the court, completed in writing, typescript or print and backed with a printed backing approved by the court.

(2) A writ, other than a principal summons or petition, bringing a cause before the court shall be in writing, typescript or print, on paper of a texture and size approved by the court and backed with cartridge paper or paper of similar durability.

(3) A step of process lodged in a cause shall be in writing, typescript or print, on paper of a texture and size approved by the court and, except in the case of a motion, backed with cartridge paper or paper of similar durability.

(4) A step of process other than a motion shall be securely fastened, folded and backed lengthwise and shall bear, on the first page and on the backing, a delimited square for the cause reference number assigned to the principal writ on being lodged.

Deriv. R.C.S. 1965, r. 19

4.1.1   *"printed form approved by the court".* The printed forms of summons, petition and respective backings approved by the court are those in the form supplied by HMSO, Oyez Scotland, Clydebank and other stationers in accordance with Forms 13.2–A and 14.4 respectively. Only the first page and the backing are printed; additional pages must be inserted of such paper as is approved by the court—*i.e.* A4 paper (see note 4.1.3).

Any firm of solicitors wishing to produce forms on a word processor should contact the Deputy Principal Clerk of Session. Agents may now reproduce a facsimile of the Royal Arms in Scotland in order to produce a principal summons or petition.

For an experimental period from 23rd September, 1997, the following provision will apply instead of r. 4.1 (See P.N. No. 2 of 1997):—

    (a) In an action or petition the principal writ or other writ bringing a cause before the court shall be in the appropriate or prescribed form; it and all steps of process, except motion sheets, shall be completed in writing, transcript or print on durable quality paper of A4 size and shall be backed and securely fastened with a two-piece filing clip.

    (b) Motion sheets shall be in A4 size and consist of a backing sheet and two-piece filing clip.

4.1.2   *"writ".* This means summons (including a condescendence and pleas-in-law annexed to it), petition, note, application, appeal, minute, defences, answers, counterclaim or issue: r. 1.3(1).

4.1.3   *"paper . . . approved by the court".* A4 paper is now the approved paper and not foolscap. A process will not be accepted except in A4 size paper. There is no specified quality.

"step of process". This is any document lodged in process, other than a production (r.1.3(1)), including those listed in r.4.4(1) and any inventory of productions.

"cause reference number". The first part of the reference is a letter determined by the nature of the cause: *i.e.*:

     O = Ordinary;
     C = Family, including Consistorial;
     A = Admiralty and Commercial; and
     P = Petitions.

(The letter "C" has been retained for family actions whether consistorial or not.) Next is a number determined by the chronological order in which a cause is lodged and the year in which it is lodged. In the case of actions there follows the year in which the cause is lodged.

In the case of petitions, before the year is the number of the category of the petition in the petition register. The categories are:

1 – Inner House *nobile officium*;	8 – Entails;
2 – Curatories and Factories;	9 – Outer House company petitions;
3 – Adoptions;	10 – Inner House company petitions;
4 – Custody of children;	11 – Petitions by trustees for directions and variation of trusts;
5 – Sequestrations;	12 – Other Outer House petitions (e.g. judicial review);
6 – Outer House trust petitions;	13 – Other Inner House petitions;
7 – Suspensions, and Interdict;	14 – Dissolution of marriage (now obsolete as such causes are by action);

15 – Admission of solicitors;
16 – Admission of notaries;
17 – Admission of Advocates.

Petitions are filed alphabetically, however, in one of the following categories according to subject-matter:
    (a) Curatories and Factories;
    (b) Inner House;
    (c) Company;
    (d) Outer House.

Signature of documents

4.2.—(1) Subject to paragraph (5), each page of a summons and the condescendence and pleas-in-law annexed to it shall be signed by an agent.

(2) Subject to paragraph (5), a letter passing the signet shall be signed by an agent.

(3) Subject to paragraphs (5) and (9), a petition, note, application or minute shall be signed by counsel or other person having a right of audience, except that—
    (a) a petition for the sequestration of the estates of the petitioner, or for recall of his sequestration, may be signed by the petitioner or an agent;
    (b) a petition for suspension, suspension and interdict or suspension and liberation may be signed by an agent;
    (c) a simplified divorce application under rule 49.73 shall be signed by the applicant;
[1] (cc) a petition in Form 61.2 shall be signed only by the Accountant of Court;
    (d) an application for registration under Chapter 62 (recognition, registration and enforcement of foreign judgments, etc.) may be signed by the petitioner or an agent;
  (dd) a petition by the Council of the Law Society of Scotland for a person's admission as (either or both)—
      (i) a solicitor;
      (ii) a notary public,
    may be signed by any officer of the Society who is authorised by the Council to do so; and
    (e) a minute for variation of custody may be signed by a party litigant.

(4) Subject to paragraph (9), defences, answers and other writs (other than appeals) not referred to in paragraphs (1), (2) and (3), shall be signed by counsel or other person having a right of audience, or, in the case of a party litigant, the party litigant.

(5) Where a party litigant is unable to obtain the signature of counsel or other person having a right of audience or an agent on a document as required by paragraph (1), (2) or (3), he may request the Deputy Principal Clerk to place the document before the Lord Ordinary for leave to proceed without such signature; and the decision of the Lord Ordinary shall be final and not subject to review.

(6) Where the Lord Ordinary grants leave to proceed under paragraph (5), the interlocutor granting leave shall be written and signed on the face of the document and the party litigant shall sign the document.

(7) Where an agent signs a document under this rule, he shall append to his signature his business address—
    (a) in the case of a summons, at the end of the first page and on the last page after the pleas-in-law; and
    (b) in the case of any other document, at the end of the last page.

(8) Where counsel or other person having a right of audience has signed a writ, he shall be regarded as the drawer of it and answerable for what it contains.

(9) The following documents shall not require any signature—
(a) a minute of amendment;
(b) answers to a minute of amendment;
(c) a minute of sist;
(d) a minute of transference;
(e) a minute of objection to a minute of transference;
(f) a note of objection.

Deriv. R.C.S. 1965, r. 28(1) amended by S.I. 1991 No. 2483 (r. 4.2(3), (4) and (8)), r. 28(2) inserted by S.I. 1991 No. 2483 (r. 4.2(9)), r. 73(a) amended by S.I. 1991 No. 2483 (r. 4.2(1) and (7)), r. 73(b) (r. 4.2(2)), r. 193 amended by S.I. 1986 No. 514 and 1991 No. 2483 (r. 4.2(3) and (4).

---

[1] R. 4.2(3)(cc) inserted by S.I. 1997 No. 1720 (effective 1st August 1997).
[2] Re R.4.2(3) (dd) inserted by S.I. 1997 No. 3059 (effective 23rd December 1997).

4.2.1   *Signature.* (1) A party litigant may *not* normally sign (a) a summons, (b) a letter passing the signet, or (c) a petition for suspension, suspension and interdict, suspension and liberation, or a petition under the Bankruptcy (Scotland) Act 1985 other than one for his own sequestration or recall of that sequestration: but see r. 4.2(5) for exception and note 4.2.8. He may sign any other writs. (2) An agent (*i.e.* a solicitor or a person having a right to conduct litigation: see r. 1.3(1)) may *not* sign (a) a simplified divorce application for the applicant or (b) a writ required to be signed by counsel under r. 4.2(3) and (4). (3) Counsel may *not* sign (a) a summons, (b) a letter passing the signet or (c) a simplified divorce application for the applicant. (4) Special kinds of petitions may be signed only by a particular officer: see r.4.2(3)(ce) and (dd).

A minute which concludes part or the whole of a cause may only be signed by counsel or other person having a right of audience (for the meaning of which see r. 1.3(1)); it cannot be signed on his behalf. Such a minute is a minute of abandonment, tender, acceptance or joint minute.

4.2.2   *"agent".* This means a solicitor or a person having a right to conduct the litigation: see r. 1.3(1) (definition of "agent") and note 1.3.3. "Solicitor" is defined in s.51 of the C.S.A. 1988.

4.2.3   *"letter passing the signet".* There are now two kinds of letters passing the signet to note (letters of loosing of arrestments are rare as recall or restriction is usually sufficient). These are:
(1) Letters of inhibition. Letters are required for (a) inhibition in security for a future or contingent debt (unless sought in a depending family action: for which, see now s.19 of the Family Law (Scotland) Act 1985 and r. 49.7) where there are special circumstances, *e.g.*, the debtor is *vergens ad inopiam* or *in meditatione fugae* or putting away his funds to avoid fulfilling his obligations (*Symington v. Symington* (1875) 3 R. 205); (b) on a document of debt except possibly where the document is registered for execution; (c) inhibition on the dependence of an action in the sheriff court; and (d) inhibition in execution of a decree of the sheriff court or a decree of the Court of Session where inhibition was not sought on the dependence. Inhibition on the dependence of an action in the Court of Session usually proceeds on a warrant in the summons: r. 13.6(c)(i).
(2) Letters of arrestment. Letters are required (for arrestment in security) for a future or contingent debt (unless sought in a depending family action: for which, see now s.19 of the Family Law (Scotland) Act 1985 and r. 49.7) where there are special circumstances (see (1) above). Letters will be required on a document of debt not registered for execution. Letters of arrestment on the dependence of an action (in security) are rare because a warrant may be inserted in the summons (r. 13.6(c)(ii)) or applied for by motion (r. 13.8) or on a counterclaim (r. 25.2(1)) or third party notice (r. 26.3(1)). Letters in execution are rare as the warrant in the extract decree can be relied on: r. 7.10 and note 7.10.2.
Letters of inhibition or arrestment with warrant are obtained by application under r. 59.1. There may then be execution of the letters under r. 16.12. Letters of inhibition with warrant, once obtained, may be registered in the Register of Inhibitions and Adjudications under ss.155 and 156 of the Titles to Land Consolidation (Scotland) Act 1868.

4.2.4   *"counsel".* This means a practising member of the Faculty of Advocates: r. 1.3(1) (definition of "counsel").

4.2.5   *"other person having a right of audience".* See r. 1.3(1) (definition) and note 1.3.4.

4.2.6   *"party litigant".* In the Court of Session only a natural person in his own cause may be a party litigant. A company, firm, other artificial entity or non-natural person may not be a party litigant: see *Gordon v. Nakeski-Cumming* 1924 S.C. 939, 941–942 *per* L.P. Clyde; *Equity and Law Life Assurance Society v. Tritonia Ltd* 1943 S.C.(H.L.) 88.

"*writ*". This means summons (including a condescendence and pleas-in-law annexed to it), **4.2.7** petition, note, application, appeal, minute, defences, answers, counterclaim or issue: r. 1.3(1) (definition of "writ").

Leave for party litigant to proceed without signature. A party litigant may normally not sign **4.2.8** certain documents such as a summons, letter passing the signet and other writs: see r. 4.2(1), (2) and (3) and note 4.2.1. It was acknowledged in *Rennie v. Murray* (1850) 13 D. 36 that if counsel would not sign a petition the petitioner might apply to the court; but no procedure was mentioned or ever laid down. R. 4.2(5) introduces a procedure allowing a party litigant to seek leave of the court to proceed although he has not been able to obtain the necessary signature. A process is not required at this stage: see r. 4.3. Once leave has been obtained the interlocutor will be written on the face of the document and the party litigant must then sign it and, if he wishes to proceed, present the document in the appropriate department for registration and, where appropriate, signeting together with any necessary process. The document will be checked, against a copy of the original placed before the Lord Ordinary for leave to proceed, before it is registered.

The rule does not indicate what test the court would apply in considering whether to grant leave. The court may well wish to be satisfied that (a) there is a *prima facie* case, (b) the signature of counsel or agent has been unsuccessfully sought (for which the court may require documentary evidence) and (c) the litigant has not been declared a vexatious litigant under the Vexatious Actions (Scotland) Act 1898.

Where the party litigant is a vexatious litigant he must also seek leave to proceed with the proceedings by virtue of s.1 of the 1898 Act. An application for such leave is made by presenting the proposed writ to the Deputy Principal Clerk who puts it before the Lord Ordinary in chambers. A process is not required at this stage: see r. 4.3. A decision by the Lord Ordinary to refuse leave is final: 1898 Act, above, s.1A (inserted by the Law Reform (Miscellaneous Provisions) (Scotland) Act 1980, s.19). This application for leave may be dealt with at the same time as an application for leave to proceed without a signature of counsel or agent. On vexatious litigants, see further note 14.3.12.

"final and not subject to review". The decision of the Lord Ordinary may not be reclaimed **4.2.9** against.

Documents not requiring signature. The documents listed in r. 4.2(9) which formerly required **4.2.10** to be signed are accompanied by a motion. As certain motions and any document accompanying it may be faxed (see r. 23.2), the original document will not be lodged where the motion is faxed; and for this reason these documents need not be signed.

For minutes of amendment and answers to a minute of amendment, see r. 24.2. For minutes of sist, see r. 31.1. For minutes of transference, see r. 31.2. For minutes of objection to minutes of transference, see r. 31.2(2)(b). A note of objection may be lodged in relation to a report of the Auditor (r. 42.4) or to a state of funds or scheme of division prepared by a judicial factor in a factory on the estate of a deceased person (r. 61.26(1)).

Lodging of processes

4.3. A process shall be lodged in every cause commenced by summons or petition when—

(a) in the case of a summons, the summons is presented for signeting; and

(b) in the case of a petition, the petition is presented to the Petition Department;

[1] except that the foregoing provisions of this rule shall not apply where the petition is in Form 61.2.

Deriv. P.N. No. 3 of 1976, para. 3(i)

---

[1] R.4.3 amended by S.I. 1997 No. 1720 (effective 1st August 1997).

General note. A process is required for causes commenced by summons or petition. A **4.3.1** summons is presented when lodged for signeting and registration (r. 13.5(3)); a petition, when presented for lodging in the Petition Department. A process is also required in other causes such as appeals.

The agent for the pursuer or petitioner should write his reference on the backing of the principal writ in order to improve communications between him and court staff: see Notice, 11th December 1987 (pp. 2001 *et seq.*).

A process or step of process may be lodged by post: P.N. No. 4 of 1994, paras 1 and 8.

For an experimental period from 23rd September, 1997, the following provision will apply instead of r. 4.3 (see P.N. No. 2 of 1997):—

(a) A process shall be lodged in every cause commenced by summons or petition when—

    (i) in the case of a summons, the summons is presented for signeting; and

    (ii) in the case of a petition, the petition is presented to the Petition Department.

(b)

    (i) Subject to (b)(ii) below, a black process box shall be lodged by the agent for the pursuer or petitioner

      — along with the Open Record prescribed by rule of court 22.1 in a cause commenced by summons or

      — within 3 days of answers having been intimated in a cause commenced by petition.

    (ii) A red process box shall be lodged by the agent for the pursuer

      — within 3 days of defences having been intimated in a Commercial Action or

—   along with the Open Record prescribed by rule of court 22.1 in any cause relating to Intellectual Property.
(c) A process box shall conform to the following specification:
(i)   of durable plastic with secure fastener;
(ii) depth 245 mm × width 60 mm × height 330 mm;
(iii) with space for names of parties and a finger hole on its spine.

Steps of process
4.4.—(1) A process shall include the following steps of process—
(a) an inventory of process;
(b) the principal writ;
(c) an interlocutor sheet;
(d) a motion sheet; and
(e) a minute of proceedings.
(2) A step of process referred to in paragraph (1), other than the principal writ, shall contain at least two pages.
(3) A step of process shall be assigned a number of process which shall be marked on the backing with the cause reference number of the principal writ and recorded in the inventory of process.

Deriv. R.C.S. 1965, r. 20 (r. 4.4(1) and (2));
r. 78(d) amended by S.I. 1990 No. 705, and r. 194 (r. 4.4(3))

4.4.1   *General note.* When a process is lodged (that is, when a summons is presented for signeting or a petition is presented) it must include the steps specified in this rule. A duplicate inventory of process and a certified copy summons are no longer required: it was rarely completed and the latter is no longer acceptable as a substitute for a principal writ which has been lost; although it was relied on by the clerks of court if the principal had been borrowed. Additional pages may be added to the steps mentioned in r. 4.4(1) as required.
A step of process may be lodged by post: P.N. No. 4 of 1994, paras 1 and 8; and see note 4.4.10.

For an experimental period from 23rd September 1997, the following provision will apply instead of r.4.4 (see P.N. No. 2 of 1997):—
(a) The process shall include the following steps enumerated thus:
(1) the principal writ;
(2) certified copy principal writ;
(3) the interlocutor sheets;
(4) a motion sheet;
(5) a minute of proceedings;
(6) (*number reserved for pursuer's productions*)
(7) (*number reserved for defender's productions*)
an inventory of process.
(b) A step of process referred to in paragraph 2(a) above other than the principal writ, certified copy writ and motion sheet shall contain at least 2 pages.
(c) A step of process shall be assigned a number corresponding to (a) above where appropriate or another number consecutive thereto and said number shall be marked on the backing along with the cause reference number and recorded in the inventory of process.

4.4.2   *"step of process".* This is any document lodged in process, other than a production (r. 1.3(1)), including those listed in r. 4.4(1) and any inventory of productions.

4.4.3   *"inventory of process".* In this inventory there is listed every step of process lodged (together with its number of process in the margin). Details of productions lodged with an inventory of productions are not given, merely their number (*e.g.* "9 Inventory of productions and 6 writs"). The first five entries in the inventory of process (Nos 1–5 of Process), and any other step in the process when it is first lodged, are entered by the pursuer (the first four in a petition by the petitioner); thereafter all entries are made by the clerks of session. In this inventory there are written the receipts for any paper borrowed and the marking of any paper returned: r. 4.12.

4.4.4   *"principal writ".* This means the writ by which a cause is initiated before the court: r. 1.3(1) (definition of "principal writ").

"interlocutor sheet". In the interlocutor sheet the clerk of court writes the orders of the court, **4.4.5**
and each of these is then signed: see rr. 4.15 and 4.16 on interlocutors.

"motion sheet". To the motion sheet there is appended any application to the court for any **4.4.6**
order not made at the Bar: see r. 23.2.

"minute of proceedings". In the minute of proceedings the clerk of court keeps a record of **4.4.7**
hearings, proofs, etc., in the cause, including the time taken, the counsel who addressed the
court, the witnesses led and whether the judge made avizandum. Other information may be
inserted at the request of the court or parties, *e.g.* the terms of an undertaking given.

"number of process". The inventory of process has no number. The principal writ is number 1 **4.4.8**
of process and (during the experimental period mentioned in note 4.4.1) the certified copy
principal writ is number 2, the interlocutor sheet is number 3, the motion sheet is number 4 and
the minute of proceedings is number 5. Subsequent steps of process lodged are numbered
consecutively.

While an inventory of productions is numbered consecutively with other steps of process, the
productions in it are numbered from "1" prefixed by the number of the inventory (*e.g.* 5/1):
P.N. No. 4 of 1994, para. 8(1).

"cause reference number". See r. 4.1(4) and note 4.1.5. **4.4.9**

Steps of process lodged by post. A step of process may be lodged by post: P.N. No. 4 of 1994, **4.4.10**
para. 1. Where a step of process is lodged by post the party lodging it must contact the
appropriate section of the General Department or the Petition Department to ascertain the
correct number of process and mark the step of process accordingly before posting it: P.N. No.
4 of 1994, para. 8(3).

Fees. A court fee for lodging a step of process may be payable. For fee, see Court of Session **4.4.11**
etc. Fees Order 1997 [S.I. 1997 No. 688, as amended, pp.C1201 *et seq.*]. Certain persons are now
exempt from fees: see the 1997 Fees Order, art.5 substituted by S.S.I. 2002 No. 270. A fee
exemption certificate must be in existence in process: see P.N. No.1 of 2002.

Where the party enrolling a motion is represented, the fee may be debited under the credit
scheme introduced on 1st April by P.N. No.4 of 1976 to the account (if one is kept or permitted)
of the party's agent by the court cashier, and an account will be rendered weekly by the court
cashier's office to the agent for all court fees due that week for immediate settlement. Party
litigants, and agents not operating the scheme, must pay (by cash, cheque or postal order) at the
time of lodging at the counter of the appropriate department.

Productions

4.5.—(1) On each occasion a production is lodged in process—
(a) an inventory of productions shall be lodged in process; and
(b) a copy of the inventory of productions shall be sent to every other
party.
(2) A production shall be—
(a) marked with a number of process with the cause reference number
assigned to the principal writ; and
(b) if consisting of more than one sheet, securely fastened together.

Deriv. R.C.S. 1965, r. 25

"lodged in process". A production may be lodged by hand, or by post (P.N. No. 4 of 1994, **4.5.1**
paras. 1 and 8). For lodging a production by post, see note 4.5.5. For faxing productions in
support of motions, see r. 23.2 and note 23.2.9.

"inventory of productions". The inventory has its own number of process and productions **4.5.2**
lodged with it are numbered within it from "1" prefixed by the number of the inventory (*e.g.* 9/
1): P.N. No. 4 of 1994, para. 8. The numbers of the productions must also be marked in the
inventory in the margin beside the description of the production. Only a copy of the inventory is
required to be delivered to any other party (who may borrow up the productions to peruse or
copy: see r. 4.12).

For an experimental period from 23rd September, 1997, the following provision will apply
instead of r.4.5 (See P.N. No 2 of 1997):—
(a) On each occasion a production is lodged in process:
(i) an inventory of productions shall be lodged in process; and

      (ii) a copy of the inventory of productions shall be sent to every other party.
    (b) A production shall be:
      (i) marked with a number of process with the cause reference number assigned to the principal writ; and
      (ii) if consisting of more than one sheet, securely fastened together.
    (c) Productions should be numbered as follows:
      (i) where there is only one pursuer, all pursuer's productions will be assigned number 6 of process and will be numbered consecutively thereafter e.g. 6/l–6/x;
      (ii) where there is only one defender, all defender's productions will be assigned number 7 and will be numbered consecutively thereafter e.g. 7/l–7/x;
      (iii) where there are further pursuers/defenders another number of process will be assigned to each and productions should be enumerated as at (i) and (ii) above.

    In a defended action the back of the backing of the inventory must be docquetted with the word "Intimated" as evidence of intimation to the other parties required under r. 4.6.

4.5.3   *"sent"*. This includes delivered: see r. 1.3(1) (definition of "send").

4.5.4   *"cause reference number"*. See r. 4.1(4) and note 4.1.5.

4.5.5   *Productions lodged by post*. A production may be lodged by post: P.N. No. 4 of 1994, para. 1. Where a production is lodged by post the party lodging it must contact the appropriate section of the General Department or the Petition Department to ascertain the correct number of process and mark the inventory of productions and the productions accordingly before posting them: P.N. No. 4 of 1994, para. 8(3).

Intimation of steps of process

    4.6.—(1) A party lodging a step of process shall—
    (a) give written intimation of the lodgment of it to every other party; and
    (b) subject to any other provision in these Rules, send a copy of the step of process lodged to every such party.
    (2) A clerk of session shall not mark a step of process as received until a certificate of intimation has been endorsed on it.

Deriv. R.C.S. 1965, r. 21 (r. 4.6), r. 83(d) (r. 4.6(1)(b))

4.6.1   *General note*. Formerly it was not necessary to deliver a copy of the step of process to every other party as well as intimating the lodgment, though it has been the practice to do so. The practice is now the rule.

4.6.2   *"step of process"*. This is any document lodged in process, other than a production (r. 1.3(1)), including those listed in r. 4.4(1) and any inventory of productions.

4.6.3   *"written intimation"*. For method see r. 16.9.

4.6.4   *"subject to any other provision"*. Not less than four copies of an open record (r. 22.1(1)(a)) and six copies of a closed record (r. 22.3(2)(a)) must be delivered to each other party; and four copies of an open record after a third party notice (r. 26.7(1)(b)).

4.6.5   *"send"*. This includes deliver: r. 1.3(1) (definition of "send").

4.6.6   *"certificate of intimation"*. The back of the step of process is marked (docquetted) "Intimated" followed by the date of intimation.

Lodging of documents in Inner House causes

    4.7.—(1) A party, on lodging in a cause in the Inner House—
    (a) a petition or note,
    (b) an appeal, application for leave to appeal, stated case, special case, case, reference or submission,
    (c) answers,
[1]   (d) a reclaiming print required under rule 38.6(2) (reclaiming prints for reclaiming motions),
    (e) a print of the whole pleadings and other documents required under r. 39.1(4) (print of pleadings, etc., for motion for new jury trial),

(f) an appeal print required under rule 40.7(2)(a)(ii) (appeal print in appeal from inferior court), or

(g) an appendix required under rule 38.19 (lodging of appendices in reclaiming motions), 39.5 (lodging of appendix in application for new trial) or 40.17 (lodging of appendices in appeals from inferior court),

shall lodge in process six copies of the document; and, unless otherwise agreed, send six copies of it to every other party.

(2) Where a party intends to refer to a document, other than one mentioned in paragraph (1), at a hearing before a Division of the Inner House, he shall lodge four copies of it in process by 12 noon on the second sederunt day before the hearing.

Deriv. R.C.S. 1965, r. 26(b)

---

[1] R. 4.7(1)(d) amended by S.I. 1996 No. 1756 (minor correction).

Copies of documents for Inner House. As well as the principal, six copies of a document listed **4.7.1** in this rule must be lodged. One copy is for the Scottish Council of Law Reporting (*Session Cases*), one for W. Green & Son Ltd (*Scots Law Times*), three are for the court (it is rare now for four judges to sit in a Division) and one is the process copy.

"refer to a document". Only four copies of documents to be referred to other than those **4.7.2** mentioned in rule 4.7(1) must be lodged: but note the terms of rule 4.8 on documents which do not conform to a standard.

Copies of documents for use of court

4.8.—(1) A clerk of session shall refuse to accept a copy of a document for the use of the court which does not conform to a standard approved by the court in size, spacing, lettering, legibility, quality of paper or otherwise.

(2) A party tendering a document which is refused by a clerk of session shall have the right to appeal in writing to the Deputy Principal Clerk.

(3) Where the Deputy Principal Clerk refuses an appeal under paragraph (2), he may extend the time for lodging the document.

(4) A decision of the Deputy Principal Clerk under this rule shall be final and not subject to review.

Deriv. R.C.S. 1965, r. 26(a)

General note. The right of appeal against the refusal of a copy has rarely been exercised. This **4.8.1** may be because the clerks have not been rigorous in refusing illegible copies rather than because copies have been perfect.

"final and not subject to review". The decision cannot be appealed, reduced or otherwise **4.8.2** reviewed by the court.

Documents ordered or allowed to be lodged

4.9.—(1) Where the court pronounces an interlocutor ordering or allowing a document to be lodged in process, it shall specify a time within which the document shall be lodged.

(2) The time for lodging a document referred to in paragraph (1) may be prorogated by the court on an application by motion enrolled before the time for lodging has expired.

(3) A document lodged in process, in terms of an interlocutor ordering or allowing it to be lodged, shall have marked on it—

(a) the date of the interlocutor ordering or allowing it to be lodged;

(b) the date of any interlocutor prorogating the time originally allowed; and

(c) the time allowed for lodging it.

Deriv. R.C.S. 1965, r. 27

Prorogation. The opportunity for prorogating the time to lodge a document only arises where **4.9.1** an interlocutor has been pronounced specifying a time within which that document must be lodged. It does not normally apply, therefore, to the lodging of defences, where the time for the lodging of which depends on r. 18.1(2) and not on an interlocutor.

The former rule stated that cause must be shown for an extension of time. The requirement to show cause has been omitted from the rule as it did not accord with current practice. It does not follow, however, that the court may not require cause to be shown in a particular case, as prorogation is in the discretion of the court.

Application to lodge a document late must be made by motion to the court under r. 2.1(1) (relief for failure to comply with rules).

4.9.2   *"motion"*. For motions, see Chap. 23.

[NEXT TEXT PAGE IS C 51]

Date of interlocutor. It is no longer necessary to set out the interlocutor prescribing the time **4.9.3** for lodging the document: only the date of the interlocutor(s) and the time for lodging are required.

Receipt of documents

4.10.—(1) Subject to paragraph (2), a clerk of session shall mark the date of receipt on every document lodged in process other than a production.

(2) A clerk of session shall not accept, or mark as received, a document after the day on which it is due to be lodged.

Deriv. R.C.S. 1965, r. 29

General note. The time for lodging a document may be prorogated: see r. 4.9(2). Appli- **4.10.1** cation to lodge a document late must be made by motion to the court under r. 2.1(1) (relief for failure to comply with rules).

Documents not to be borrowed

4.11.—(1) Subject to paragraph (2), a writ shall remain in the Office of Court and shall not be borrowed from process, but may be inspected by any person having an interest.

(2) Paragraph (1) shall not apply to—
(a) a party borrowing his principal writ in order to do diligence for which a warrant mentioned in rule 13.6(c) has been obtained;
(b) a party borrowing his principal writ for the purpose of service or intimation; or
(c) a party borrowing his writ for the purpose of writing on it and authenticating an amendment which has been made.

(3) The following steps of process shall not be borrowed from process—
(a) the inventory of process;
(b) the interlocutor sheet;
(c) the motion sheet;
(d) the minute of proceedings;
(e) any inventory of productions;
(f) the principal copy of a report ordered by the court and lodged in process;
(g) the principal or any copy of a bond of caution or a consignation receipt lodged in process; and
(h) the principal copy of any other document by which an order of the court to find caution or give security is satisfied and lodged in process until the order is recalled.

Deriv. R.C.S. 1965, r. 31(a) (r. 4.11(1) and (2))

General note. While all writs lodged may be inspected, r. 4.11(2) provides for only three **4.11.1** situations in which they may be borrowed: (a) to do diligence on the dependence of an action (r. 13.6(c)) or a counterclaim (r. 25.2), the summons or counterclaim, as the case may be, being required by (i) the messenger-at-arms before executing a diligence and (ii) the Keeper of the Register of Inhibitions and Adjudications before registration of an inhibition (see r. 13.9(2)); (b) to have a principal writ served or intimated by a messenger-at-arms (r. 16.3); and (c) to write on the writ, *e.g.* a restriction of a conclusion (r. 7.3), a minute of election of expenses (r. 42.16, Table of Fees, Chap. III, Pt. I, para. 1) or an amendment (r. 7.3) before extract; and to authenticate any amendment (*e.g.* initialling by counsel). A certified copy interlocutor, and not the original writ, is required where diligence is to be done on a warrant applied for after signeting of a summons (r. 13.8(1) and (3)), on a minute of amendment (r. 13.8(2) and (3)), after allowance of a counterclaim on that counterclaim (r. 25.2(1) and (5)), or on a third party notice (r. 26.3(1) and (3)). A defender or respondent may not (now) borrow the principal writ on entering the process; there was never any need to do so: borrowing the summons prevented the pursuer from obtaining a decree in absence when defences were not lodged timeously.

Documents other than writs may be borrowed except the steps of process in r. 4.11(3). Documents no longer require to be borrowed for transmission to the Auditor for taxation as the process is transmitted by the clerks of session.

No document or step of process may be borrowed after final extract: r. 4.13.

Release 35: 6 February 1995

4.11.2   *"writ"*. This means summons (including a condescendence and pleas-in-law annexed to it), petition, note, application, appeal, minute, defences, answers, counterclaim or issue: r. 1.3(1) (definition of "writ").

4.11.3   *"any person having an interest"*. A party to the cause has an interest. Whether other persons have a sufficient interest is in the discretion of the Principal Clerk. The phrase might include a person who could be called in the cause. It is unlikely it would include a person, merely seeking information for the purposes of another cause, for whom there are procedures for recovery of documents in Chap. 35.

4.11.4   *"principal writ"*. This means the writ by which a cause is initiated before the court: r. 1.3(1) (definition of "principal writ").

4.11.5   *Documents not to be borrowed*. The principal copy of a report ordered by the court must remain in process; copies may be borrowed or made available. Bonds of caution and consignation receipts may not be borrowed but the principal of each is transmitted to the Accountant of Court and may be uplifted on discharge: see r. 33.12.

4.11.6   *"step of process"*. This is any document lodged in process, other than a production (r. 1.3(1)), including those listed in r. 4.4(1) and any inventory of productions.

Borrowing and returning documents

4.12.—(1) A party borrowing a document which may be borrowed shall give a receipt for it, dated and signed, on the inventory of process.

(2) Subject to paragraph (3), before a clerk of session accepts a document for return to process, he shall—

    (*a*) compare it with the inventory of process and receipt in the presence of the person returning it, delete the receipt and initial and date the deletion; or

    (*b*) in the case of a partial return, mark on the inventory of process the document so returned and initial and date the entry.

(3) Where the document being returned is bulky so that it cannot be examined conveniently at the time—

    (*a*) a clerk of session shall not accept the document without a separate slip accompanying it, dated and signed by the party returning it, specifying the number of process so returned; and

    (*b*) the clerk of session receiving it shall examine it before the close of the following business day and give written intimation to the party returning it of any inaccuracy in the slip accompanying it.

(4) Where written intimation is not given under paragraph (3)(*b*), the accuracy of the slip shall be presumed and the party returning the document shall be exonered as if the receipt had been deleted under paragraph (2)(*a*) or marked under paragraph (2)(*b*), as the case may be.

(5) A party returning more than one document shall ensure that the documents returned are arranged in consecutive order according to the inventory of process; and a clerk of session may refuse to accept documents which are not so arranged.

(6) The court may, on the motion of a party, ordain any other party who has borrowed a document to return that document within such period as the court thinks fit.

Deriv. R.C.S. 1965, r. 32(a) (r. 4.12(1) to (4)) and 32(b) (r. 4.12(5))

4.12.1   *"written intimation"*. For methods, see r. 16.9.

Finally extracted processes not to be borrowed

4.13. No step of process may be borrowed after a final extract has been issued.

4.13.1   *General note*. The reason for this rule is that the court is *functus* after final extract and the process must remain with the Extractor for subsequent transmission to the Keeper of the Records under r. 9.1. It may be retransmitted to the Office of Court from the Keeper: r. 9.2(1).

4.13.2   *"step of process"*. This is any document lodged in process, other than a production (r. 1.3(1)), including those listed in r. 4.4(1) and any inventory of productions.

Final extract. This is a final extract of an interlocutor which concludes the cause, leaving **4.13.3** nothing to be done, and after which the court is *functus* (*Taylor v. Jarvis* (1860) 22 D. 1031, 1034 *per* L.J.-C. Inglis) except for the possible rectification of errors (see note 7.9.2). See also notes 4.15.2(2) and 7.1.2(2).

Lost documents
4.14.—(1) Where—
 (*a*) a principal writ,
 (*b*) other pleadings, or
 (*c*) an interlocutor sheet,
is lost or destroyed, a copy of it may be substituted which is proved in the cause to the satisfaction of the court and authenticated in such manner as the court thinks fit.
 (2) A copy of a document substituted under paragraph (1) shall be equivalent to the original for the purposes of the cause and the process of which it forms a part, including the use of diligence.

Deriv. R.C.S. 1965, r. 23

General note. Application to substitute a copy for a lost document is made to the court by **4.14.1** motion. The court is usually satisfied on the explanation made at the Bar. Authentication is normally a signed certification on each page that the substituted document is a true copy. A copy of any citation, notice or intimation sent with any writ lost and which was served or intimated should also be produced.
 This rule and R.C.S. 1965, r. 23 are derived from s. 15 of the C.S.A. 1868 which was repealed by the C.S.A. 1988 as superseded by the rule.

Outer House interlocutors
4.15.—(1) This rule applies to interlocutors pronounced in the Outer House.
 (2) Subject to paragraph (3), an interlocutor pronounced by the Lord Ordinary may be written by the clerk of court and shall be signed by the Lord Ordinary.
 (3) Subject to any direction he may be given by the Lord Ordinary, a depute clerk of session may sign an interlocutor, other than a final interlocutor, in respect of a motion which is not starred; and that interlocutor shall be treated for all purposes as if it had been signed by the Lord Ordinary.
 (4) An interlocutor may be signed during session or in vacation.
 (5) An extract of an interlocutor which is not signed in accordance with the provisions of this rule shall be void and of no effect.
 (6) An interlocutor may, on cause shown, be corrected or altered at any time before extract by—
 (*a*) the Lord Ordinary who signed it or on whose behalf it was signed; or
 (*b*) in the event of the death, disability or absence of the Lord Ordinary, any other judge of the court.

Deriv. R.C.S. 1965, r. 30(1) substituted by S.I. 1984 No. 472 (r. 4.15(2) and (5)), r. 30(2) substituted by S.I. 1984 No. 472 and amended by S.I. 1986 No. 1937 (r. 4.15(6)), r. 30(3) substituted by S.I. 1984 No. 472 (r. 4.15(4)), and r. 93A inserted by S.I. 1978 No. 799 and amended by S.I. 1984 No. 472 (r. 4.15(3))

General note. Interlocutors are minutes (see *Clark & Macdonald v. Bain* (1895) 23 R. 102, **4.15.1** 104) of the official expressions of all orders of the court; where an extract is issued, the extract becomes the official expression. Originally, "interlocutor" meant an incidental order; the interlocutor determining a cause being called a decree: Stair, IV.46.2. Nowadays, and in the R.C.S. 1994, "interlocutor" is used for all orders of the court. A finding of the court not made in the form of an order is not an interlocutor: *Ranken v. Ranken* 1971 S.L.T. (Notes) 55 (entry in interlocutor sheet of findings sought on construction of an agreement not an interlocutor).

Classification of interlocutors. A distinction has to be made between interlocutory orders **4.15.2** (interlocutory decrees or incidental orders), interim decrees and final decrees. The distinction between interlocutory orders and final decrees is of importance (*a*) because, as a general rule, no motion can be made to the court after final decree (the principal exceptions being (i) to correct an error and (ii) to refer the cause to an opponent's oath) and (*b*) to ascertain whether leave is required to reclaim or to appeal to the House of Lords. It should be noted that all interlocutors are "final" in the Outer House: C.S.A. 1988, s. 18.

(1) An interlocutory order (interlocutory decree or incidental order) is one pronounced before the final decision disposing of the merits and expenses of the cause and is usually procedural. Many of these may be reclaimed against only with leave of the court: see r. 38.3(5); but there are a number of exceptions: see r. 38.3(4). In relation to appeal against interlocutory judgments to the House of Lords, see s. 40 of the C.S.A. 1988.

(2) A final decree or interlocutor is one, taken by itself or along with previous interlocutors, by which the whole subject-matter of the cause is disposed of: formerly C.S.A. 1868, s. 53. It has been authoritatively decided that the whole subject-matter of the cause is disposed of when both the merits and the question of expenses have been determined, though expenses may not have been taxed or decerned for: *Baird v. Barton* (1882) 9 R. 970 (subject-matter of cause includes expenses); *Burns v. Waddell & Co.* (1897) 24 R. 325 (interlocutor which did not deal with expenses not an interlocutor disposing of whole subject-matter of the cause and could not be reclaimed against without leave); *Caledonian Railway Co. v. Corporation of Glasgow* (1900) 2 F. 871 (as also reserved expenses). Subject to the correction of errors (see note 4.15.5) the decree is not capable of alteration (*U.C.B. Bank plc v. Dundas & Wilson, C.S.* 1990 S.L.T. 90) and further motions in relation to expenses cannot be entertained (*Henderson v. Peeblesshire C.C.* 1972 S.L.T. (Notes) 35; *Wilson v. Pilgrim Systems plc* 1993 S.L.T. 1252). Since 1983, in a cause in which the person liable for the expenses is not legally aided there are usually two interlocutors at the conclusion of a cause (or wherever expenses are dealt with): one disposing of the merits and the other decerning for expenses as taxed, the latter being strictly the last or final decree. An interlocutor awarding expenses against a non-legally aided party has a decerniture pronounced at the time the finding of expenses is made. Where a party liable in expenses is legally aided there is no decerniture when the finding is made: a finding of liability in expenses is made with a remit to the Auditor to tax and report. A decerniture is only made thereafter, after consideration of any objections or applications for modification. The reason for the difference in the case of a legally aided party is that it is not competent to modify expenses after decerniture: *Gilbert's Tr. v. Gilbert* 1988 S.L.T. 680 (modification incompetent after decerniture for expenses). The court is, as a general rule, bound to determine expenses when giving judgment on the merits; though it may do so later if, for instance, expenses are reserved (in which case the interlocutor is not final). An interlocutor, or the rules, may reserve to the parties the right to make further applications to the court (*e.g.* in cases of custody or aliment of children), in which case such an interlocutor cannot be a final decree and any extract is only an interim extract: *Sanderson v. Sanderson* 1921 S.C. 686, 692 *per* L.P. Clyde.

Final decrees are classified as follows: (*a*) decrees in absence: *i.e.* those pronounced against a defender who has not entered appearance or lodged defences (see r. 19.1); and (*b*) decrees *in foro contentioso* ("in a defended action"), *i.e.* decrees pronounced after defences have been lodged, including a decree by default (Court Act 1672, art. 19; and see further r. 20.1). Decrees in absence are not, and decrees *in foro* (except a decree of dismissal) are, *res judicata*. Note that a decree in absence may become a decree *in foro*: r. 19.1(7)). Final decrees may also be classified as (i) of dismissal (where the cause as laid is put out of court but is not *res judicata*), (ii) of absolvitor (a decree *in foro* in favour of the defender on the merits which is *res judicata*), (iii) of condemnator (a decree *in foro* against a defender which is *res judicata*) and (iv) a mixed decree of more than one of (i)–(iii) and a decree of refusal of a petition (for interdict): *Luxmoore v. The Red Deer Commission* 1979 S.L.T. (Notes) 53 (equivalent to decree of absolvitor). On *res judicata*, see note 18.1.4(B)(5).

(3) An interim decree is one which (*a*) makes some interim provision until the merits of the cause are determined (*e.g.* interim aliment or interim interdict) or (*b*) decides part of the merits (*e.g.* for payment of an admitted part of a debt): *Crawfurd v. Ballantine's Trs.* (1833) 12 S. 113.

4.15.3 *Signature.* An interlocutor is merely a minute of the judgment pronounced intended for use in preparing an extract. No authentication is necessary other than the judge's signature (or that of the clerk, where permitted): *Clark & Macdonald v. Bain* (1895) 23 R. 102, 104; though a correction ought to be initialled. Where an essential interlocutor is not signed, any extract is void: *Smith v. McAuley & Co.* (1846) 9 D. 190. The date of a decree is the date when it was signed: *Cruickshank v. Williams* (1848) 11 D. 601, 614 (date of signature different from date of interlocutor).

Whenever an interlocutor is pronounced it may be signed during session, or in vacation: r. 4.15(4).

4.15.4 *Signing of unstarred motions.* The signing of interlocutors in unstarred motions by depute clerks of session was introduced by A.S. (R.C.A. No. 5) (Depute Clerks of Session) 1978 [S.I. 1978 No. 799] (as amended by A.S. (R.C.A. No. 2) (Miscellaneous) 1984 [S.I. 1984 No. 472]) to facilitate the expedition of business. For motions which are unstarred, see notes 23.2.15 and 23.2.17. In fact interlocutors on unstarred motions granting interim aliment or the approval (and authentication) of issues and counter-issues are signed by the Lord Ordinary. In practice any interlocutor seen by the Lord Ordinary before signing will be signed by him.

Correction of interlocutors before extract. This does not include clarifying an ambiguity in a **4.15.5**
previous interlocutor: *Davidson & Syme W.S. v. Booth* 1971 S.L.T.(Notes) 11. It has been observed by Lord Penrose in *Laing v. Scottish Arts Council* 2000 S.L.T. 338, 341F (OH) that the former statement here, citing *Campbell v. Campbell* 1934 S.L.T. 45 as authority for the proposition that the power to correct did not apply to a motion for expenses not timeously made, is wrong and that *Campbell* is not authority for that proposition. Formerly at common law an interlocutor could be modified only if application was made *de recenti*: *Kennedy v. Clyde Shipping Co. Ltd* 1908 S.C. 895 (motion made some six weeks after interlocutor refused), *Bruce v. Bruce* 1945 S.C. 353; and not even then when the interlocutor has been acted upon if there would be prejudice. It would appear that now delay is just one of the factors to be taken into account, along with prejudice, in determining whether to allow correction: *Martinez v. Grampian Health Board*, 1995 S.C. 428; though the new rule merely repeats the old and the court appears to have overlooked the rule that a re-enactment does not change the law. In *Laing*, above, Lord Penrose distinguished between the word "corrected" in r.4.15(6), which implied that the interlocutor contained or reflected an error, and the word "altered" in r.4.15(6) which carries no such implication and that an interlocutor could be "altered" at least *de recenti* where there was a mistake. In that case the mistake was that the defender's counsel forgot to move for expenses from the date of the tender when the pursuer unexpectedly accepted the tender during a proof and moved for expenses to the date of the tender. It is not clear that "altered" is intended to be so different from "corrected". The latter clearly deals with a clerical error; but "altered" is intended to deal with an error of expression that would require more than correcting a word. Lord Penrose appeared to open up again the argument whether the rule replaces the common law or whether the rule and the common law exist side by side. But Lord Penrose was overruled by an Extra Division: *Laing v. Scottish Arts Council*, 2001 S.C. 493.

The general rule is that a Lord Ordinary cannot alter the substance of a prior interlocutor. Clerical errors may be corrected: *Hope v. Hamilton* (1851) 13 D. 1268 (wrong date of trust disposition). The rule is not limited to clerical errors (see dicta of L.P. Dunedin in *Kennedy*, above) and applies to errors of expression; however, although errors or mistakes in figures or expression may be corrected, a judgment cannot be altered in substance after it has been pronounced: *Cuthill v. Burns* (1862) 24 D. 849, 859 *per* L.J.-C. Inglis; *Campbell v. James Walker Insulation Ltd* 1988 S.L.T. 263; *Walker v. Walker (No. 2)* 1990 S.L.T. 248 *Laing v. Scottish Arts Council*, 2001 S.C. 493 (Extra Div.). In *Laing*, at p.498H para. 14, the Inner House confirmed that the intention of the rules is to give power to bring an interlocutor into line with the court's original intention: "[T]he limited changes which are envisaged in this context are changes which, like correction, will not involve any departures from what the court was trying to do when it issued the interlocutor." In *Burke v. Harvey* 1916 2 S.L.T. 315 a correction was made where there had been an oversight in seeking expenses for the pursuer's agent as agent disburser (to which he would have been entitled); but in *Bailey, Petrs* 1969 S.L.T.(Notes) 70, a motion to recall an interlocutor pronounced in ignorance of the existence of an interested party was refused as not being a mere mistake of fact (*cf. Rottenburgh v. Duncan* (1896) 24 R. 35 (interlocutor pronounced on undertaking in ignorance of circumstances making its fulfilment impossible)). In *Finlayson v. Turnbull*, (No. 2) 1997 S.L.T. 619 Lord Milligan altered an interlocutor on the ground of procedural error to delete an award of interest made in the mistaken belief that there had been no challenge to it. In *Carnegie v. Lord Advocate (No. 2)* 1999 S.L.T. 521 it was held that an interlocutor could be altered which failed to repel a plea on a point expressly dealt with in the judgment. In *Ewos Ltd v. Mainland*, 2005 S.L.T. 1227 (OH) two interlocutors were altered to reflect the intention that expenses were to be taxed on an agent and client basis and two were not.

A joint application or motion of consent is not enough, if not relating to a correction of a mistake, clerical error or omission which was not in any event put forward *de recenti*: see *Hutchison* 1965 S.C. 240.

The decision in *McIlwham v. Secretary of State for Scotland* 1989 S.L.T. 167 that apart from this rule the court has power at common law to review its own interlocutor *de recenti* must be wrongly decided: the common law is replaced by the rule. In *Hamilton Academical Football Club Ltd v. Flayest Ltd*, 29th November 1996, unreported (1997 G.W.D. 2–45), the defender had wished to go to procedure roll but the interlocutor (which stated that it was represented when it was not) allowed a proof which the pursuer said could not now be varied, altered or revoked by the Lord Ordinary. The Lord Ordinary, while accepting that no rule in the R.C.S. 1994 allowed him to revoke the interlocutor, was concerned that the court's general power to do justice between the parties did not enable him to rectify a genuine mistake, and appears to have exercised such a power to appoint the case to procedure roll. The Lord Ordinary's decision is clearly wrong in principle because he has no power either to alter the substance of his own interlocutor or to recall or revoke it except where the rules permit. The view expressed here, that the cases of *McIlwham* and *Hamilton Academical* have been wrongly decided, has been endorsed by Lord Eassie in *Black v. Somerfield Stores Ltd*, 1998 S.L.T. 1315.

Exceptionally a Lord Ordinary may (in effect) recall his own interlocutor, although an interlocutor of the Lord Ordinary is final in the Outer House (C.S.A. 1988, s.18): (1) Where a particular mode of inquiry has been allowed, the court is not precluded from reconsidering and altering the mode of inquiry following a minute of amendment (and answers) by which the pleadings are altered (this is not a true recall): *Bendex v. James Donaldson & Sons Ltd* 1990 S.C. 259. (2) Where the R.C.S. 1994 or other enactment permits: *e.g.* recall of a decree in absence (r. 19.2).

The rule states that a correction may be made *before* extract. It does not necessarily follow, however, that a correction may *not* be made *after* extract: see note 7.9.2.

4.15.6   *Units of measurement*. The Units of Measurement Directive (Council Directive 80/181 of 20th December 1979) was adopted by the E.C. in 1989 [Official Journal, 7th December 1989, L357/28]. From 1st January 1995 member states must use the metric system of measurement and, subject to certain transitional arrangements and exceptions, must cease to use imperial measurements for economic, public health, public safety and administrative purposes. Where a unit of measurement is used in pleadings it should be expressed as a metric unit, and court orders must be so expressed.

Exceptions are as follows: The nautical mile and knot are to be used for sea and air traffic and the foot is to be used for aircraft heights. Until 31st December 1999, fathom may be used for marine navigation; therm for gas supply; pint and fluid ounce for beer, cider, waters, lemonade and fruit juices on returnable containers; and ounce and pound for good sold loose from bulk. In perpetuity, acre may be used for land registration; troy ounce for transactions in precious metals; mile, yard, foot and inch for road traffic signs, distances and speed measurements; pint for draught beer, cider and milk in returnable containers.

4.15.7   *Issuing of judgments*. Unless otherwise ordered, judgments are issued without the necessity of the attendance of counsel or solicitor. A clerk of session will give agents notice of the date an opinion is to be issued (usually two days in advance). A copy of the opinion may be collected on or after the date of issue from the Opinions desk during office hours on payment of the prescribed fee. See Notice (*sic*) 4th September 1997.

Agents may obtain a copy in advance of the date of issue. Neither the opinion nor any of its contents may be revealed by agents or examined by any other person including a party in advance of the date of issue. See P.N. No. 4 of 1991.

Where the opinion does not deal with expenses, a party seeking expenses will have to enrol a motion. Unless opposed, or starred by the court, a motion for expenses will be dealt with in chambers: See Notice (*sic*) 4th September 1997.

Opinions or judgments of the court, from September 1998, are available on the Internet at The Scottish Courts Web Site at www.scotcourts.gov.uk. The site is updated at 2 p.m. every day on which opinions are issued.

4.15.8   *Schedule of Damages*. Under P.N. No. 3 of 1997 parties seeking decree in an action of reparation for personal injuries (except where that decree is sought of consent, *e.g.* because of a joint minute) must lodge in process a schedule of damages for the purposes of s.15(2) of the Social Security (Recovery of Benefits) Acts 1997 stating the amount of any compensation in respect of the relevant period under the heads of compensation in column 1 of Sched. 2 to the 1997 Act. It is apparent that the interlocutor subsequently pronounced will not itself specify the amounts under each head but will refer to a (or the) appended schedule which does. Clerks of Session have been issuing blank schedules in the following form:—

Schedule to interlocutor of even date (*amend as necessary*)
1. Solatium—
     To date:
     Future:
2. Loss of Earnings—
     To end of relevant period (date):
     Subsequent to end of relevant period:
3. Compensation for
     (1) cost of care
         to end of relevant period (date):
         subsequent to end of relevant
             period (date):
     (2) loss of mobility
         to end of relevant period (date):

subsequent to end of relevant
period (date):
4. Section 8 services:
5. Section 9 services:
6. Medical expenses:
7. Loss of pension rights, etc.:
TOTAL:
Less ()% due to contributory negligence:
Sum decerned for:

Inner House interlocutors

4.16—(1) This rule applies to interlocutors pronounced in the Inner House.

(2) Subject to paragraph (3), an interlocutor of the Inner House may be written by the clerk of court and shall be adjusted and signed by—
   (a) the judge who presided in the Division of the Inner House when the matter to be dealt with in the interlocutor was determined, or
   (b) in the event of the death, disability or absence of that judge, the next senior judge who sat in that Division when the matter to be dealt with in the interlocutor was determined, as soon as reasonably practicable and after such consultation as may be necessary with the other members of the Division who sat.

(3) An interlocutor of the Inner House in respect of a motion which is not starred shall be adjusted and signed by the judge presiding at the time when the motion was brought before the Division of the Inner House.

(4) An interlocutor may be signed during session or in vacation.

(5) The judge signing an interlocutor of the Inner House shall append the letters "I.P.D." to his signature as conclusive evidence that the requirements of the preceding paragraphs of this rule have been complied with.

(6) An extract of an interlocutor which is not signed in accordance with the provisions of this rule shall be void and of no effect.

(7) An interlocutor may, on cause shown, be corrected or altered at any time before extract by—
   (a) the judge who signed it; or
   (b) in the event of the death, disability or absence of that judge, the next senior judge of the same Division of the Inner House.

Deriv. R.C.S. 1965, r. 30(1) substituted by S.I. 1984 No. 472 (r. 4.16(6)), r. 30(2) substituted by S.I. 1984 No. 472 (r. 4.16(7)), r. 30(3) inserted by S.I. 1986 No. 1937 (r. 4.16(4)), and r. 295 (r. 4.16(2), (3) and (5))

General note. See notes to r. 4.15.   **4.16.1**

"I.P.D.". These initials mean *in praesentia dominorum*, and originally meant that the **4.16.2** interlocutor had been read and signed before a quorum of the judges as once required by the Interlocutors Act 1693.

Correction or alteration on cause shown. In assessing whether a party has shown cause the **4.16.3** court will take into account any undue delay in seeking the alteration and any prejudice which the alteration may cause to the other party: *Martinez v. Grampian Health Board* 1995 S.C. 428. Prejudice to the other party includes prejudice in presenting an appeal against the interlocutor in question: *Martinez*, above.

Issuing of judgments. Unless otherwise ordered, judgments are issued without the necessity of **4.16.4** the attendance of counsel or solicitor. A clerk of session will give agents notice of the date an opinion is to be issued (usually two days in advance). A copy of the opinion may be collected on or after the date of issue from the Opinions desk during office hours on payment of the prescribed fee. See Notice (*sic*) 4th September 1997.

Agents may obtain a copy in advance of the date of issue. Neither the opinion nor any of its contents may be revealed by agents or examined by any other person including a party in advance of the date of issue. See P.N. No. 4 of 1991.

Where the Opinion does not deal with expenses, a party seeking expenses will have to enrol a motion. Unless opposed, or starred by the court, a motion for expenses will be dealt with in chambers: See Notice (*sic*) 4th September 1997.

Opinions or judgments of the court, from September 1998, are available on the Internet at The Scottish Courts Web Site at www.scotcourts.gov.uk. The site is updated at 2 p.m. every day on which opinions are issued.

CHAPTER 5

CAVEATS

Orders against which caveats may be lodged
[1] **5.1.** Without prejudice to rule 5.1A., a person may only lodge a caveat against—

(a) an interim interdict sought in an action before he has lodged defences;

(b) an interim order sought in an action before the expiry of the period within which he could enter appearance;

(c) an interim order (other than an order under section 1 of the Administration of Justice (Scotland) Act 1972 (orders for inspection of documents and other property, etc.)) sought in a petition before he has lodged answers;

(d) an order for intimation, service and advertisement of a petition to wind up, or to appoint an administrator to, a company in which he has an interest; and

(e) an order for intimation, service and advertisement of a petition for his sequestration.

Deriv. R.C.S. 1965, r. 68H inserted by S.I. 1990 No. 2118 and r. 218A(1) inserted by S.I. 1986 No. 2298 (r. 5.1(d))

---

[1] R. 5.1 amended by S.S.I. 2001 No. 92, r.3 (effective 1st April 2001).

5.1.1   *General note.* A caveat is a document lodged in the Petition Department (r. 5.2(1)) by a person to ensure that certain orders may not be made against him without his receiving intimation of the application for the order and having an opportunity to be heard before the order may be made (r. 23.9 (motions where caveat lodged)).

A caveat may be general (affecting any order in r. 5.1) or particular (*i.e.* certain specified orders in r. 5.1).

The orders against which caveats could be lodged were never clear before A.S. (R.C.S. No. 5) (Miscellaneous) 1990 [S.I. 1990 No. 2118] (inserting R.C.S. 1965, r. 68H). This rule sets out the orders against which caveats may be lodged, and no caveat may be lodged against any other order.

5.1.2   *Multiple caveats.* These are single caveats lodged on behalf of a multiplicity of parties. The onus is on the caveator to justify such a caveat, for, as a general rule, such a caveat is not readily acceptable. It is justification that the parties named are liable to be sued together or in the alternative in the same cause: *e.g.* a company in receivership and its receiver; a partnership and the partners; the common owners of the same property. The Secretary of State for Scotland may lodge a caveat in his own behalf in respect of the departments he represents in the Scottish Office. It will not be permitted for a caveator to lodge a caveat in respect of all his clients.

5.1.3   "*interim order*". This would include interim interdict, custody or aliment, an interim judicial factor, an interim administrator or liquidator of a company, or interim suspension, interim liberation, or interim possession under s.47(2) of the C.S.A. 1988.

It is not permissible to lodge a caveat against an arrestment or inhibition on the dependence as they are not truly interim orders although granted "on the dependence" and because the pursuer is entitled, in general, as of right to preserve assets of the defender to satisfy any decree. It would defeat the purpose of not giving the defender prior warning so that he cannot dispose of his assets (see s.17 of the Debtors (Scotland) Act 1838 and s.18 of the C.S.A. 1868 which introduced execution of these diligences before service of the summons): see *Mackinlay*, 20th December 1988, unreported, *per* Lord Cullen (inhibition). It is possible to obtain interdict against the use of diligence on the dependence where it would be instantly verifiable as wrongful—*i.e.* without warrant, irregularly or with malice and want of probable cause (*Beattie & Son v. Pratt* (1880) 7 R. 1171) or the defender has consigned the principal sum (*Duff v. Wood* (1858) 20 D. 1231). An application for letters of arrestment or inhibition is not included in r. 5.1 as something against which a caveat may be lodged. A caveat may not be lodged against an application for arrestment or inhibition under s.27 of the C.J.J.A. 1982 (on which, see, e.g. *Stancroft Securities Ltd v. McDowall* 1990 S.C. 274).

A caveat may not be lodged against an order in an application for judicial review (as formerly under authority of *Kelly v. Monklands District Council* 1986 S.L.T. 165, 166F–G *per* Lord Ross (*obiter*)) except one which is truly interim: an order for production of documents in a first order is not an interim order.

A caveat against an order under s.1 of the Administration of Justice (Scotland) Act 1972 is also not competent under r. 5.1(c); but if another interim order under r. 5.1 is sought as well, a caveat will give notice of the 1972 Act application. On applications under s.1 of the 1972 Act, see r. 35.2 and note 35.2.6 and Chap. 64.

Interim orders relate mostly to the merits of the cause in which they are sought: *Kelly*, above, *per* Lord Ross at p. 167. An order is interim because of its character not merely because it is expressly granted "*ad interim*". "Interim" means for the time being or in the meantime.

Further restriction as to caveats
[1] **5.1A** A caveat shall not be lodged against an interim order sought in a petition under rule 83.2.

---

[1] R.5.1A inserted by SS.I. 2001 No. 92, r. 3 (effective 1st April 2001) and amended by SS.I. 2001 No. 305, r. 16 (effective September 18, 2001).

General note. This rule prohibits a caveat against a petition by authorised officials of the E.U. **5.1A.1** seeking assistance in an investigation by them into a breach of Art. 81(1) or 82 of the EC Treaty (bringing to light an agreement, decision or concerted practice prohibited by those articles).

The rules for petitions mentioned above are in Chap. 83 (erroneously numbered Chap.82 in the first S.S.I; hence the subsequent amendment).

Form, lodging and renewal of caveats
5.2.—(1) A caveat shall be in Form 5.2 and shall be lodged in the Petition Department.

(2) A caveat shall remain in force for a period of one year from the date on which it was lodged and may be renewed on its expiry for a further period of a year and yearly thereafter.

Deriv. R.C.S. 1965, r. 68I inserted by S.I. 1990 No. 2118

General note. A caveat is not a step of process in a process. It is given an index number and **5.2.1** year number, placed in a folder and entered in an alphabetical card index register in the Petition Department. A copy of the caveat is transmitted to the Signet Officer who retains a similar index register for use in the General Department. The register is consulted by the clerks before any order under r. 5.1 is applied for *ex parte*.

"one year after". The date of lodging is not counted in calculating the period. **5.2.2**

Motions where caveat lodged. When a motion is enrolled in a cause *ex parte* for an order **5.2.3** against which a caveat may be lodged the clerk of session in the General or Petition Department, as the case may be, checks the register of caveats to see if a caveat has been lodged. If a caveat has been lodged he informs the Keeper of the Rolls who arranges a hearing of the motion (day or night) at a time when both parties can attend: see r. 23.9. Where the motion is enrolled by a pursuer before the calling of the summons or by a petitioner before the granting of the first order, r. 23.8 will apply.

If the duty clerk of session has to be contacted after 5pm, ring the Court of Session (0131–225 2595), leave your name and telephone number, and the duty security guard will contact the duty clerk who will contact you.

Fee. There is a fee for lodging a caveat: see Court of Session etc. Fees Order 1997, Table of **5.2.4** Fees, Pt I, C, item 5 [S.I. 1997 No. 688, as amended, pp. C1201 *et seq.*].

Where the party enrolling a motion is represented, the fee may be debited under the credit scheme introduced on 1st April by P.N. No.4 of 1976 to the account (if one is kept or permitted) of the party's agent by the court cashier, and an account will be rendered weekly by the court cashier's office to the agents for all court fees due that week for immediate settlement. Party litigants, and agents not operating the scheme, must pay (by cash, cheque or postal order) at the time of lodging at the counter of the appropriate department.

CHAPTER 6

THE ROLLS

Printing and publishing of rolls
6.1. The rolls shall be printed and published, and delivered to subscribers, under directions made from time to time by the Lord President.

Deriv. R.C.S. 1965, r. 18

6.1.1 *"rolls"*. These are the lists of business of the court: r. 1.3(1) (definition of "rolls"). The rolls are: (1) The General Roll, consisting of the registers of causes of the (a) General Department (the Ordinary, Admiralty and Commercial, and Family (including Consistorial) Rolls) and (b) the Petition Department; (2) The Daily Rolls—the printed rolls issued each weekday during term showing the causes in the General Roll appearing for business on a particular day, consisting of (a) in the Inner House (i) Single Bills, (ii) By Order Roll, (iii) Summar Roll and (iv) Advisings; and (b) in the Outer House (i) Calling List, (ii) Motion Roll, (iii) Diet Roll, (iv) Commercial Roll, (v) Adjustment Roll and Continued Adjustment Roll, (vi) By Order (Adjustment) Roll, (vii) By Order Roll, (viii) Procedure Roll, (ix) Jury Trials, Proofs, Proofs before Answer and Hearings, (x) For Judgment and (xi) Undefended Consistorial Causes (in fact undefended divorce actions). In the Daily Rolls there are also printed notices of Acts of Sederunt, practice notes and other acts of administration. Rolls issued in vacation contain details of (2)(a)(i) and (iv) and (b)(i), (iii)–(xi).

The importance of the By Order Roll in the Inner and Outer Houses is that the court itself may order a cause put out on that Roll and require parties to appear before it. A court fee is now payable for a By Order Roll hearing under the Court of Session etc. Fees Order 1997, Table of Fees, Pt I, B, item 19 or 20, or C, item 18 or 19 for every 30 minutes [S.I. 1997 No. 688 as amended, pp. C1201 *et seq.*]. Certain persons are exempt from payment of fees: see 1997 Fees Order, art.5; substituted by SS.I. 2002 No. 270. A fee exemption certificate must be lodged in process: see P.N. No. 1 of 2002.

Fixing and allocation of diets in Outer House
6.2.—(1) This rule applies to the fixing and allocation of diets in the Outer House.
(2) The court shall not proceed to fix a diet where—
  (a) a proof is allowed;
  (b) issues are approved; or
  (c) a cause is appointed to the Procedure Roll.
(3) Subject to paragraph (4), a cause appointed to the Procedure Roll may be put out for hearing by the Keeper of the Rolls in the course of any week where, unless the parties otherwise agree, the diet has been published in the rolls on Thursday of the preceding week.
(4) Where a hearing on the Procedure Roll is anticipated to be of some length or complexity, the parties may arrange a fixed diet with the Keeper of the Rolls.
¹ (5) When a party enrols for a proof to be allowed or issues to be approved in a cause depending before the Outer House he shall include in the enrolled motion his estimate of the likely duration of the proof or jury trial and request that the diet be allocated accordingly.
¹ (6) If any other party considers that the estimate so included is too low, he shall record upon the enrolled motion his own estimate.
¹ (7) On such papers (whether or not the closed record) as are transmitted to the Keeper of the Rolls for the purpose of his allocating the diet, the clerk of court shall note the estimate provided in pursuance of paragraph (5) unless a higher estimate is recorded under paragraph (6), in which case the note shall only be of the higher (or as the case may be the highest) estimate so recorded; and the Keeper of the Rolls shall allocate the diet of proof or

jury trial accordingly and give written intimation of it to each party.

(8) [*Revoked by S.I. 1998 No. 870*]

(9) [*Revoked by S.I. 1998 No. 870*]

(10) [*Revoked by S.I. 1998 No. 870*]

(11) [*Revoked by S.I. 1998 No. 870*]

(12) [*Revoked by S.I. 1998 No. 870*]

(13) An application for the allocation of a special diet may be made to the Keeper of the Rolls—

   (a) on cause shown;

   (b) of consent of all parties; and

   (c) before a diet has been allocated under a preceding paragraph of this rule.

(14) Where an application under paragraph (13) is refused, the parties may bring the application before the Lord President; and the Lord President, or a judge nominated by him, shall determine the application in chambers.

(15) Parties shall attend on the Keeper of the Rolls for the purpose of fixing a diet for—

   (a) a proof or jury trial in a cause of exceptional length or complexity;

   (b) an undefended proof;

   (c) a continued proof;

   (d) a continued hearing; or

   (e) a hearing on evidence.

Deriv. R.C.S. 1965, r. 17 (r. 6.2(2)), r. 94(a) (r. 6.2(3)); P.N. 5th May 1972 (r. 6.2(4)), P.N. 29th May 1975 (r. 6.2(13) and (14)), P.N. No. 2 of 1987, para. 5 (r. 6.27 (part))

------

[1] Paras (5) to (7) of r. 6.2 substituted, and paras (8) to (12) revoked, by S.I. 1998 No. 890 (effective 21st April 1998).

General note. The former Form 6.2 procedure, introduced in 1987 by S.I. 1987 No. 1206 and **6.2.1** amended by S.I 1990 No. 2118, has been abolished and a new procedure provided for by A.S. (R.C.S.A.) (Miscellaneous) 1998 [S.I. 1998 No. 890]. The new procedure is for a party seeking a proof or jury trial to specify in the motion for proof or issues his estimate of the likely duration of the proof or jury trial: r. 6.2(5). Any other party who considers that that estimate is too low must mark on the motion his estimate (r. 6.2(6)) and the Keeper of the Rolls will allocate a diet on the highest estimate (r. 6.2(7)). In theory the new procedure dispenses with the need for a form because the information will be in the motion.

In practice the new procedure may be thought to have a number of drawbacks. (1) There is no sanction for failing to comply: one assumes that a motion without an estimate will be refused (to be accepted by the clerk of session) as incompetent. (2) Any higher estimate must be marked on the motion, not a notice of opposition, and accordingly cannot be done by fax but requires attendance at the General or Petition Department (as the case may be). (3) There is no provision for notification to the Keeper of revised estimates. (4) There is no provision for supplementary information of use to the Keeper, as in Form 6.2, such as the total number of witnesses, expert witnesses or witnesses from abroad (such information was, apparently, rarely given or used) or that a witness was disabled or that video equipment was to be used (regarded as necessary information). (5) The new provisions omit the former reference to the "fixing" of diets; accordingly, on a strict application of the canons of statutory interpretation, the fixing of diets has been abolished. Apparently, however, the Keeper of the Rolls will take note of revised estimates he receives; information about witnesses, etc., may be intimated by letter or telephone; and the fixing of diets continues. It is unfortunate that the new provisions do not even reflect the practice which they are intended to authorise and provide for, a situation which the R.C.S. 1994 had been intended by the Rules Review Group to overcome and avoid.

The purpose of the rule remains the same as before, namely, to ensure that, under our system of fixing or allocating diets, court time is not wasted by hearings going off for one reason or another or a hearing is adjourned to another date because it has taken longer than the time allocated.

Before making the weekly allocation of cases to the judges sitting in the Outer House for that week, the Keeper of the Rolls consults the senior Outer House judge. No later than 12 noon on the Friday of the week preceding the diet of their case, parties may inform the Keeper of any factors they consider may have a bearing on setting the priorities of their case: P.N. No.1 of

2001. The reason for this is that few cases are allocated to a particular judge and there are insufficient judges to hear the cases set down for hearing.

6.2.2　*Fixing and allocation of diets*. The former provision in r. 6.2(5) referred to diets being "fixed or allocated". The amendments and new provisions inserted by A.S. (R.C.S.A.) (Miscellaneous) 1998 [S.I. 1998 No. 890] omit the reference to the fixing of diets. Accordingly, applying strictly the canons of statutory interpretation, the fixing of diets has been abolished. Apparently, however, this is not so in practice and was not intended: the practice of fixing continues. It would be better if the rule reflected the practice.

A diet is "allocated" where the Keeper of the Rolls arranges a diet without consultation with parties: he normally does so in the case of (a) causes appointed to the Procedure Roll and (b) causes in which proof has, or issues have, been allowed. A diet is "fixed" where (a) the allocated diet is inconvenient and application is made to the Keeper to arrange an alternative diet (which will be done only on cause shown) or (b) the diet is arranged before or instead of allocation because (i) parties' estimated length varies substantially, (ii) the parties apply to the Keeper under r. 6.2(4) because a procedure roll hearing is anticipated to be of some length or complexity, (iii) the parties apply under r. 6.2(13) for a special diet, or (iv) the parties are required to attend the Keeper of the Rolls to fix diets in those causes to which r. 6.2(15) applies.

In relation to causes appointed to the Procedure Roll, the Keeper will publish in the rolls a Procedure Roll warning list two weeks before the Thursday's roll on which diets are allocated for hearing the following week. Such hearings will be put out for one day unless, in response to the warning list, the Keeper is requested to fix more than one day under r. 6.2(4) ("some length" in r. 6.2(4) means, in practice, more than one day). Where a party seeks to discharge a diet fixed by the Keeper under r. 6.2(4), a motion for discharge must now be enrolled: P.N. No. 7 of 2004.

In actions of damages for personal injuries or death of a person from personal injuries, proof diets are fixed by the Keeper on the lodging of defences: r. 43.6(1)(a). In existing actions the Keeper is reviewing diets for after 31st October 2003 and parties may apply for early or accelerated diets: P.N. No.3 of 2003.

6.2.3　*"The court shall not proceed to fix a diet"*. The interlocutor allowing a proof or issues for jury trial or appointing a cause to the Procedure Roll will provide for such a hearing "on the. . .day of. . .", but the Keeper of the Rolls will be responsible for fixing and inserting the actual date of the hearing: see note 6.2.2.

6.2.4　*"estimate of the likely duration"*. The party seeking proof or jury trial must specify in his motion for proof or issues his estimate of the likely duration of the proof or jury trial and request allocation of a diet: r. 6.2(5). One assumes that if he fails to comply, the motion will not be accepted by the clerk of session in the General or Petition Department (as the case may be) because it is incompetent.

Any other party who considers that that estimate is too low must mark *on the motion* his estimate: r. 6.2(6). He does not do so by or on a notice of opposition in Form 23.4. Accordingly this cannot be done by fax and attendance at the General or Petition Department will be required. It is understood, however, that, contrary to the *express* terms of the provision, account will be taken of a fax indicating a higher estimate from another party.

The Keeper of the Rolls allocates a diet (see n. 6.2.2) on the basis of the highest estimate: r. 6.2(7). There is no provision for informing the Keeper of the Rolls of a revised estimate. It is understood, however, that the Keeper will take account of a revised estimate intimated to him. Also, contrary to the apparently express terms of r. 6.2(7) the Keeper may still fix a diet in consultation with the parties instead of allocating it in accordance with the highest estimate: see note 6.2.2.

6.2.5　*Arranging diets for proofs or jury trials*. The Keeper relies primarily on the information provided in the motion as required by r. 6.2(5). He compares the information provided by each party. Where there is an estimate that the length of a proof or jury trial will not be more than four days, the Keeper will normally allocate a diet of the length sought. Where there is an estimate of more than four days or there is a substantial variation in the estimates given by each party, the Keeper will communicate with parties with a view to ascertaining a better estimate and fixing a diet. R.6.2(15) lists those hearings or proofs for which parties must attend on the Keeper to fix diets on the list printed on a Thursday for allocation of diets.

6.2.6　*"enrols"*. This means enrols a motion. This style is not used elsewhere in the R.C.S. 1994 (except in Chap. 23), and to be consistent with the other rules the phrase "applies by motion" should have been used.

On motions, see Chap. 23.

6.2.7　*"written intimation"*. For methods, see r. 16.9.

6.2.8　*Special diets*. Parties may apply to the Keeper of the Rolls for a special diet under r. 6.2(13) for a procedure roll hearing, proof, jury trial or other hearing; this will only be done (a) on cause shown, (b) with consent of parties and (c) before allocation of a diet by the Keeper (in the case of proofs or jury trials): r. 6.2(1). "Cause shown" should include complexity of the case, urgency or importance.

A decision on an application for a special diet which has been referred by the Keeper to the Lord President under r. 6.2(14) may not be reclaimed against: C.S.A. 1988, s.28.

"exceptional length". This means, in practice, a cause requiring over eight court days.   **6.2.9**

Fee. The court fee for fixing a proof or jury trial in an action is payable on the diet being **6.2.10** fixed. For fee, see Court of Session etc. Fees Order 1997, Table of Fees, Pt I, B, item 15 [S.I. 1997 No. 688, as amended, pp. C1201 *et seq.*]. Certain persons are exempt from payment of fees: see 1997 Fees Order, art.5 substituted by SS.I. 2002 No. 270. A fee exemption certificate must be lodged in process: see P.N. No.1 of 2002.

Where a party is legally represented, the fee may be debited under a credit scheme introduced on 1st April 1976 by P.N. No. 4 of 1976 to the account (if one is kept or permitted) of the agent by the court cashier, and an account will be rendered weekly by the court cashier's office to the agent for all court fees due that week for immediate settlement. Party litigants, and agents not operating the scheme, must pay (by cash, cheque or postal order) on each occasion a fee is due at the time of lodging at the counter at the appropriate department.

Allocation of diets in Inner House

[1] **6.3.**—(1) This rule applies to the allocation of diets in the Inner House.

(2) When a party enrols for a cause depending before the Inner House to be appointed to the Summar Roll for hearing he shall include in the enrolled motion his estimate of the likely duration of the hearing and request that the diet be allocated accordingly.

(3) If any other party considers that the estimate so included is too low, he shall record upon the enrolled motion his own estimate.

(4) On such papers (whether or not the reclaiming print) as are transmitted to the Keeper of the Rolls for the purpose of his allocating the diet, the clerk of court shall note the estimate provided in pursuance of paragraph (2) unless a higher estimate is recorded under paragraph (3), in which case the note shall only be of the higher (or as the case may be of the highest) estimate so recorded; and the Keeper of the Rolls shall allocate the diet for the hearing accordingly and give written intimation of it to each party.

(5) Not less than five weeks before the hearing of the cause on the Summar Roll, the Keeper of the Rolls shall put the cause out on the By Order Roll before a Division of the Inner House.

(6) At a hearing on the By Order Roll under paragraph (5), the parties shall—

  (a) advise the court whether or not the hearing on the Summar Roll is to proceed; and

  (b) where it is to do so, provide the court with a re-assessment of its likely duration.

Deriv. R.C.S. 1965, r. 294C (7) and (8) inserted by S.I. 1987 No. 1206 (rr. 6.3(2) to (7), (9) and (10)); P.N. No. 2 of 1987, para. 5 (r. 6.3(4))

[1] R. 6.3 substituted by S.I. 1998 No. 890 (effective 21st April 1998).

General note. The former Form 6.3 procedure, introduced in 1987 by S.I. 1987 No. 1206 and **6.3.1** amended by S.I 1990/2118, has been abolished and a new procedure provided for by A.S. (R.C.S.A.) (Miscellaneous) 1998 [S.I. 1998 No. 890]. The new procedure is for a party seeking a hearing on the Summar Roll to specify in the motion for the hearing his estimate of the likely duration of the hearing: r. 6.3(2). Any other party who considers that that estimate is too low must mark on the motion his estimate (r. 6.3(3)) and the Keeper of the Rolls will allocate a diet on the highest estimate (r. 6.3(4)). In theory the new procedure dispenses with the need for a form because the information will be in the motion.

In practice the new procedure may be thought to have a number of drawbacks. (1) There is no sanction for failing to comply: one assumes that a motion without an estimate will be refused (to be accepted by the clerk of session) as incompetent. (2) Any higher estimate must be marked on the motion, not a notice of opposition, and accordingly cannot be done by fax but requires attendance at the General or Petition Department (as the case may be). (3) There is no provision for notification to the Keeper of the Rolls of revised estimates. (4) There is no provision for supplementary information of use to the Keeper, as in Form 6.3. (5) The new provisions omit the former reference to the "fixing" of diets; accordingly, on a strict application of the canons of statutory interpretation, the fixing of diets has been abolished. Apparently, however, the Keeper of the Rolls will take note of revised estimates he receives; supplementary information may be intimated by letter or telephone; and the fixing of diets continues. It is unfortunate that the new provisions do not even reflect the practice which they are intended to authorise and provide for, a situation which the R.C.S. 1994 had been intended by the Rules Review Group to overcome and avoid.

The purpose of the rule remains the same as before, namely, to ensure that, under our system of fixing or allocating diets, court time is not wasted by hearings going off for one reason or another or a hearing is adjourned to another date because it has taken longer than the time allocated.

The procedure applies only where a hearing is sought on the Summar Roll. It does not apply if the reclaimer or appellant seeks early disposal on the Single Bills under r. 38.13 (for reclaiming motions) or 40.11 (for appeals from inferior courts).

The stage at which consideration should be given to the grounds on which the reclaiming motion or appeal is to be argued, so that the court can be told whether the hearing is to proceed and the dates set down registered, is at the time of the By Order hearing under r. 6.3(5): *Noble Organisation Ltd v. Kilmarnock and Loudoun District Council* 1993 S.L.T. 759, 761I. A sufficient opportunity must be given for the case to be reviewed before the By Order roll hearing for counsel to confirm that the grounds of appeal are adequate: *Eurocopy Rentals Ltd v. Tayside Health Board* 1996 S.L.T. 1322, 1324J.

6.3.2   *"enrols"*. This means enrols a motion. This style is not used elsewhere in the R.C.S. 1994 (except in Chap. 23), and to be consistent with the other rules the phrase "applies by motion" should have been used.

On motions, see Chap. 23.

6.3.3   *"depending"*. A cause is depending from the time it is commenced (*i.e.* from the time an action is served or a first order in a petition is made) until final decree, whereas a cause is in dependence until final extract. For the meaning of commenced, see note 13.4.4 (action) or 14.6.1 (petition). For the meaning of final decree, see note 4.15.2(2). For the meaning of final extract, see note 7.1.2(2).

6.3.4   *"Summar Roll"*. There was formerly a Summar Roll and a Short Roll in the Inner House. The former was for causes dealt with summarily (speedily) and the latter was for causes heard in ordinary course. The latter roll no longer exists and all causes for hearing are appointed to the Summar Roll if not dealt with in the Single Bills or on the By Order Roll.

6.3.5   *Fixing and allocation of diets.* The former provision in r. 6.3(1) referred to the "fixing and allocation" of diets. The amendments and new provisions inserted by A.S. (R.C.S.A.) (Miscellaneous) 1998 [S.I. 1998 No. 890] omit the reference to the fixing of diets. Accordingly, applying strictly the canons of statutory interpretation, the fixing of diets has been abolished. Apparently, however, this is not so in practice and was not intended: the practice of fixing continues. It would be better if the rule reflected the practice.

A diet is allocated where the Keeper of the Rolls arranges a diet without consultation with parties. A diet is fixed where (a) the allocated diet is inconvenient and application is made to the Keeper to arrange an alternative diet (which will be done only on cause shown) or (b) the diet is arranged before or instead of allocation because the parties' estimated length varies substantially.

6.3.6   *"estimate of the likely duration"*. The party seeking a hearing on the Summar Roll specifies in his motion for the hearing his estimate of the likely duration of the hearing: r. 6.3(2). One assumes that if he fails to comply the motion will not be accepted by the clerk of session in the General or Petition Department (as the case may be) because it is incompetent.

Any other party who considers that that estimate is too low must mark *on the motion* his estimate: r. 6.3(3). He does not do so by or on a notice of opposition in Form 23.4. Accordingly this cannot be done by fax and attendance at the General or Petition Department will be required. It is understood, however, that, contrary to the express terms of the provision, account will be taken of a fax indicating a higher estimate from another party.

The Keeper of the Rolls allocates a diet (see n. 6.3.5) on the basis of the highest estimate: r. 6.3(5). There is no provision for informing the Keeper of a revised estimate. It is understood, however, that the Keeper will take account of a revised estimate intimated to him. Also, contrary to the apparently express terms of r. 6.3(5) the Keeper may still fix a diet in consultation with the parties instead of allocating it in accordance with the highest estimate: see note 6.3.5.

6.3.7   *Arranging diets.* The Keeper relies primarily on the information provided in the motion as required by r.6.3(2). He compares the information provided by each party. Where there is an estimate that the length of a hearing will not be more than four days, the Keeper will normally allocate a diet of the length sought. Where there is an estimate of more than four days or there is a substantial variation in the estimates given by each party, the Keeper will communicate with parties with a view to ascertaining a better estimate and fixing a diet. In certain cases, even though a diet may have been allocated, a cause may be the subject of a short notice diet or peremptory short notice diet: see notes 6.3.8 and 6.3.9.

Short notice diets. Parties may agree with the Keeper that, notwithstanding the allocation of a   **6.3.8**
diet, notice may be given of an early diet. Agents indicate by letter what notice they would require for an early diet. When a diet is cancelled agents are either contacted about the possibility of an early diet according to the notice required or a notice appears periodically in the rolls of the short notice diets available. An offer of a short notice diet by the Keeper is not to be treated as a fixed diet until written intimation has been made by the Keeper: P.N. No. 2 of 1992. Certain sheriff court and statutory appeals may be subject to peremptory short notice diets: see note 6.3.9.

Peremptory short notice diets. In relation to certain sheriff court and statutory appeals the   **6.3.9**
Keeper may issue peremptory diets where the estimated length of the hearing is not more than two days. This provision applies generally to cases requiring some urgency. A minimum of two days notice of a diet will be given. A notice of causes to which this provision applies will be published periodically in the rolls. The fact that a later diet has been allocated does not preclude the issue of a short notice diet. See P.N. No. 6 of 1992.

"written intimation". For methods, see r.16.9.   **6.3.10**

R.6.3(5). The cause is put out by order not less than five weeks before the date arranged for   **6.3.11**
the hearing so that the court can discover (a) whether the hearing is to proceed and (b) the current estimated length of the hearing. On the basis of this information the court may be able to rearrange other business. There is little prospect of other business being arranged where a hearing goes off within two weeks of the diet.

It is at the stage of the by order hearing that consideration should be given to the grounds on which an appeal or reclaiming motion is to be argued. A sufficient opportunity must be given for the case to be reviewed prior to its appearance on the by order roll to enable counsel to confirm that the grounds of appeal are adequate and to provide a reasonably accurate forecast of the time which will be required: *Eurocopy Rentals Ltd v. Tayside Health Board* 1996 S.C. 410, 413–414 *per* L. P. Hope.

No court fee will be payable for this hearing on the By Order Roll.

Putting out causes for proof, jury trial or hearing
6.4—(1) The Keeper of the Rolls shall prepare and publish in the rolls from time to time lists of all causes in which diets have been fixed or allocated—
    (a) in the Summar Roll, or
    (b) for proof, jury trial or other hearing,
and put out such causes before such Division of the Inner House or Lord Ordinary, as the case may be, as may be convenient.

(2) Without prejudice to rule 6.2(3) (causes appointed to procedure roll put out for hearings), a cause published in the rolls for hearing on any roll or at any diet shall be published not later than the second day before the day on which the cause is to be heard.

Deriv. R.C.S. 1965, r.16

General note. Shortly after a proof, jury trial or other hearing has been allowed the Keeper   **6.4.1**
puts out a list in the daily rolls on a Thursday of the cases in which diets are to be fixed or allocated. The lists of fixed or allocated diets appear on a Thursday in the daily rolls within a few weeks thereafter.

CHAPTER 7

EXTRACTS AND OFFICIAL CERTIFIED COPY INTERLOCUTORS

Applications for extracts
7.1.—(1) Subject to the provisions of this Chapter mentioned in

paragraph (2), an application may be made for an extract of an act or a decree after the expiry of seven days after the date of the act or decree, as the case may be.

(2) The provisions referred to in paragraph (1) are—
> paragraph (4) of this rule,
> rule 7.2 (extracts of decrees in certain family actions),
> rule 7.3 (amendments to principal writ),
> rule 7.4 (return of steps of process and borrowing productions).

(3) An application under paragraph (1) shall be made by note to the Extractor in Form 7.1 lodged in the appropriate department of the Office of Court.

(4) The court may authorise immediate extract or supersede extract for such period as it thinks fit.

Deriv. P.N. 9th July 1980, reg.1 (r.7.1(1) and (3)) and reg.3 (r.7.1(2))

7.1.1   *General note.* An extract is a written instrument proceedings in the name of the Lords of Council and Session, signed by the Principal Extractor or the Extractor of the Court of Session in the case of Court of Session decrees or the Extractor of the acts and decrees of the Teind Court in the case of teind causes, containing a brief narrative of the cause and the procedure in it ending with the decision of the court (the interlocutor of which extract is sought) and, where appropriate, a warrant for execution. It is not a document of debt, but a certificate of the Extractor that such a decree exists in the records of the court: *Inglis v. McIntyre* (1862) 24 D. 541. It is the authority for doing diligence on a decree.

An extract is the proper evidence of the decree of the court and, if *ex facie* valid, proves itself: Stair, IV.xlii.10. It may be challenged, for example, on the ground that it does not conform to the decree or that it has been issued before time: *McKellar v. Dallas's Ltd* 1928 S.C. 503.

This rule does not apply to extracts of decrees of divorce or declarator of nullity of marriage: r.7.1(2); for these, see r.7.2.

7.1.2   *Classification of extracts.* Extracts may be classified as (1) interim extracts or (2) final extracts.

(1) An interim extract is of an act or decree during the dependence of a cause which does not dispose of the whole of the cause: *Crawfurd v. Ballantyne's Trs.* (1833) 12 S. 113. Such an act or decree is extractable *ad interim* unless the court otherwise directs: C.S.A. 1988, s.47(3) (formerly C.S.A. 1850, s.28). In general, if something remains to be done in the cause after extract, the extract is an interim extract: *Smith v. Smith* 1927 S.L.T. 462, 463 *per* Lord Moncreiff; *Brunt v. Brunt* 1958 S.L.T. (Notes) 41. An extract of a decree disposing only of the merits is an interim extract and does not preclude a subsequent decree and extract for expenses: *Crichton Brothers v. Crichton* (1901) 4 F. 271. Nowadays the decrees on the merits and for expenses are invariably in separate interlocutors: in this way extract of the former is not held up pending taxation and, if necessary, a decree for a principal sum can be enforced before waiting for taxation of expenses.

(2) A final extract is an extract of an interlocutor which concludes the cause, leaving nothing to be done and there being no other extractable interlocutor still outstanding. Since 1983, in a cause in which the person liable for the expenses is not legally aided there are usually two interlocutors at the conclusion of a cause (or wherever expenses are dealt with); one disposing of the merits and the other decerning for expenses as taxed (and when taxed, the amount of expenses authorised by the Auditor is inserted by the Extractor in the extract), the latter being the last or final interlocutor. An interlocutor awarding expenses against a non-legally aided party has a decerniture pronounced at the time the finding of expenses is made. Where a party liable in expenses is legally aided there is no decerniture when the finding is made: a finding of liability in expenses is made with a remit to the Auditor to tax and report. A decerniture is only made thereafter, after consideration of any objections or application for modification. The reason for the difference in the case of a legally aided party is that it is not competent to modify expenses after decerniture: *Gilbert's Tr. v. Gilbert* 1988 S.L.T. 680. The interlocutor awarding expenses as taxed (or as varied) is extractable. A final extract is not necessarily, but usually will be, an extract of a final decree; a final decree is one, taken by itself or along with previous interlocutors, by which the whole subject-matter of the cause is disposed of (including expenses: *Baird v. Barton* (1882) 9 R. 970): see note 4.15.2(2). The court is *functus* after a final extract (*Taylor v. Jarvis* (1860) 22 D. 1031, 1034 *per* L.J.-C. Inglis) except for the possible rectification of errors (see note 7.9.2). Parties cannot be deprived of their rights by the erroneous issue of a final, instead of an interim, extract: *Brunt*, above. If an interlocutor, or the rules, reserves to the parties the right to make a further application to the court (*e.g.* in cases of custody or aliment of children), it cannot be a final decree and the extract is only an interim extract: *Sanderson v. Sanderson* 1921 S.C. 686, 692 *per* L.P. Clyde.

Act or decree. An act is an interlocutor which does not contain a decerniture (*i.e.* the inclusion **7.1.3**
of the word "decern(s)" which is inserted only where the interlocutor finally determines a part
or the whole of a cause) and, therefore, is an interlocutory or procedural, and not a
determinative, order. A decree is a determinative order, an interlocutor which disposes of a part
or the whole of the cause and, therefore, includes the word "decern(s)". The word "decern(s)"
does not just give authority for extract; it gives effect to all that has gone before it: *Greig v.
Lamb's Trs.* (1830) 8 S. 908.

"expiry of seven days". Under s. 23 of the C.S.A. 1868 and then R.C.S. 1965, r. 89(*aa*) **7.1.4**
(inserted by A.S. (R.C.A. No. 2) (Miscellaneous) 1984 (S.I. 1984 No. 472)), a decree in absence
could be extracted only after 10 days whereas other interlocutors (other than divorce and nullity
decrees—which are not treated as decrees in absence) were extractable after seven days. Now
that a defender or respondent has at least 21 days notice of the calling of a summons (r. 13.4(1))
or of a petition (r. 14.6(1)), seven days before extract is thought to be sufficient in all cases
except divorce and nullity decrees. The date of the act or decree is not counted in calculating the
period.

As an act or decree may be extracted before the expiry of the reclaiming days where leave is
not required (21 or 14 days: see r. 38.3(2)–(4)), a party seeking to reclaim should notify his
opponent of his intention as soon as possible: for, while the successful party cannot be
prevented from obtaining an extract, execution and enforcement cannot be pursued without
leave of the court except in the case of orders for custody, access or aliment (r. 38.8(5)).

Application for extract. The persons entitled to apply for an extract are: (*a*) the party in whose **7.1.5**
favour the act or decree is made; (*b*) his solicitor holding a decree for expenses (to obtain
payment of his account and outlays); (*c*) his assignee, on production of the assignation and
evidence of intimation; and (*d*) his executor, on production of the confirmation.

The following paragraphs apply to applications for extracts of Court of Session decrees: for
extracts of decrees in teind causes, application at any time is made to the Extractor of the acts
and decrees of the Teind Court.

(1) Application for extract within five years of last interlocutor or, if none, date of calling of
summons or presentation of petition (because after that a process is transmitted to the Keeper
of the Records: see r. 9.1(2)). Where the process has gone to the process records department, it
must first be ordered up to the General or Petition Department, as the case may be, on a
transmission slip (which must show (i) year of last interlocutor, (ii) full names of parties, (iii)
name of person making application and (iv) date of application). The clerks of session are
responsible for the transmission of the process. A process goes to the process records
department after the final interlocutor or after a year and a day in which no interlocutor has
been pronounced (except in judicial factories and liquidations: r. 9.1(3)): an index is maintained
of processes alphabetically, each process having a record number. In fact, the first year of all
processes in the process records department are kept in the General or Petition Department, as
the case may be, and not in the process record department itself.

(*a*) Application is made by note in Form 7.1 (see note 7.1.5A) to the Extractor: r. 7.1(3). Rule
15.2 (applications by note) does not apply: r. 15.2(4). A note may contain more than one
interlocutor sought to be extracted. Only one principal extract will be issued. Where more than
one extract is required, the additional extracts will be extracts from the Register of Acts and
Decrees.

The process, together with the note to the Extractor, has to be transmitted by the party
applying for the extract from the General or Petition Department by way of the transmission
book to the Extracts Department. The book is receipted by the Extractor's staff and returned by
the party to the appropriate department.

When an extract is ready for issue, written intimation is sent to the party who applied
together with a note of the fee payable in cash: for fees, see Court of Session etc. Fees Order
1997, Table of Fees, Pt. I, G, item 1 [S.I. 1997 No. 688 as amended, pp. C1201 *et seq.*].

Where the extract is a final extract, the process is retained in the Extracts Department;
otherwise, the process is returned to the appropriate department by the Extracts Department by
way of the decreets (now decree) book kept by the Extractor. The book is receipted and
returned.

(*b*) If the interlocutor sought to be extracted has been extracted previously and the record
copy has not yet been transmitted to the Keeper of the Records (which is done within six

months after the end of the calendar year (see r. 9.1(1)), application for an extract is made to the Extractor for an extract from the Register of Acts and Decrees on payment of the appropriate fee (see Table of Fees, above, Pt. I, G, item 6). It is helpful to quote the extract number on the principal extract or from the decreets (decree) book or the Register of Extracted Processes kept by the Extractor.

(c) If the interlocutor sought to be extracted has been extracted previously and the record copy has been transmitted to the Keeper of the Records, application for an extract is made by letter or in person to the Keeper of the Records, Scottish Record Office, General Register House: see Public Records (Scotland) Act 1937, s. 9. The Register of Acts and Decrees containing the record copies of extracts (except extracts in cases of divorce, nullity or dissolution of marriage unless a full extract has been ordered under r. 7.1) for each calendar year is sent to the Keeper within six months of the end of each year: r. 9.1(1). It is helpful to quote the reference number in the Extract Book (which is the number allocated to it in the decreets book). This number and a process can also be traced through the Register of Extracted Processes kept by the Keeper of the Records (alphabetically by year and giving the extract number), a copy of which is also kept by the Extractor for the years up to 1982 (the Extractor keeps his own register from 1985 through which finally extracted processes may be traced). The Keeper will issue an extract prepared from the record copy in the Register on payment of the appropriate fee: for fees, see A.S. (Fees in the Scottish Record Office) 1990, Sched., Pt. III [S.I. 1990 No. 44].

(2) Application for extract after five years from last interlocutor or, if none, date of calling of summons or presentation of petition (because after that a process is transmitted to the Keeper of the Records: see r. 9.1(2)).

(a) Where extract is sought of an interlocutor not previously extracted in a process not finally extracted (*i.e.* for a first or principal extract), application must be made by the party seeking extract either in the General or Petition Department on a slip provided for that purpose or to the Keeper of the Records for the retransmission of the process to that department from the Keeper of the Records (see r. 9.2(1) and notes); there is a fee for transmission from the Keeper: see A.S. (Fees in the Scottish Record Office) 1990, above, Sched., Pt. IV, para. 1. Note that petitions for the appointment of judicial factors and winding up of companies are not transmitted to the Keeper until final discharge: r. 9.1(3). It is helpful to quote the reference number in the Register of Unextracted Processes kept by the Keeper when seeking retransmission (the Extractor has a copy of this register back to 1959 available for tracing processes). The process together with a note to the Extractor in Form 7.1 is then transmitted from the General or Petition Department to the Extracts Department by way of the transmission book by the party seeking extract and the book is receipted by the Extractor's staff and returned by the party to the appropriate department. When the extract is ready for issue, written intimation is sent to the party who applied together with a note of the fee payable in cash; for fees, see Court of Session etc. Fees Order 1997, Table of Fees, Pt. I, G, item 1 [S.I. 1997 No. 688, as amended, pp. C1201 *et seq.*]. The process is then returned to the Keeper of the Records by the Extractor.

(b) Where there has been a previous extract, application is made to the Keeper of the Records as in (1)(c) above.

7.1.5A   *Form 7.1.* A new Form 7.1 was provided for by A.S. (R.C.S.A. No. 3) (Miscellaneous) 1996 [S.I. 1996 No. 1756]. It is no longer necessary to set out the interlocutor(s) to be extracted. Part A is completed by the applicant; Part B by the Extracts Department.

Copies of the form are available from the Extracts Department.

7.1.6   *"immediate . . . or supersede extract"*. The court may order that any interim or final extract (see note 7.1.2) is extractable immediately, notwithstanding r. 7.1(1) which provides that seven days must elapse after decree before extract. Immediate extract will be granted only on cause shown where the justice of the case requires: see, *e.g. Gavin v. P. Henderson & Co.* 1910 S.C. 357. The provision under s. 28 of the Exchequer Court (Scotland) Act 1856 for the immediate extract of decrees in exchequer causes was repealed by the C.S.A. 1988 for lack of use.

Extract may be superseded until a certain event or for a specified period of time: see, *e.g. Fry v. North Eastern Railway Co.* (1882) 10 R. 290; this is often done in divorce cases in relation to the payment of a capital sum. The issue of an extract does not of itself preclude review by the Inner House: r. 38.9. Accordingly there is no need to supersede extract where, *e.g.* the court grants decree by default under r. 20.1: but see *Munro & Miller (Pakistan) Ltd v. Wyvern Structures Ltd* 1996 S.L.T. 135 where it was thought superseding extract might have some value; though this was commented on adversely by the First Division at 1997 S.C.1, 3C.

Extracts of decrees in certain family actions
    7.2.—(1) Subject to paragraph (2), a decree—
    (a) of divorce,

(b) of declarator of nullity of marriage, or

(c) in an action to which rule 49.28 (evidence in certain undefended family actions) applies,

shall be extracted automatically after the expiry of 21 days after the date of the decree unless a reclaiming motion has been enrolled.

(2) A decree of divorce in a simplified divorce application shall be extracted immediately.

(3) An extract under paragraph (1) or (2) shall be issued by the Extractor to the pursuer and a copy of it sent by the Extractor by first class post to the defender where his address is known.

(4) Additional extracts under this rule may be obtained from the Extracts Department.

Deriv. R.C.S. 1965, r. 168(11) substituted by S.I. 1978 No. 106 (r. 7.2(1)), r. 170K inserted by S.I. 1982 No. 1679 (r. 7.2(2)); P.N. 9th July 1980, regs. 6 to 8 (r. 7.2(3) and (4))

General note. An extract under this rule shows the ground of decree, findings as to custody, **7.2.1** access, reservation date, interdict, orders under the Matrimonial Homes (Family Protection) (Scotland) Act 1981, any order for financial provision under s. 8 of the Family Law (Scotland) Act 1985 (but not findings for capital sums unless also decerned for in the divorce interlocutor— this is to avoid the possibility of wrongful diligence should the decerniture be superseded but the extract contain warrant for diligence in respect of some other order) and any order for expenses. Extracts since 21st March 1985 should include all the necessary information of the decree and findings (and are to that extent full or complete) but are not "full" extracts as they are not obtained under rule 7.1 Between 23rd September 1975 and 21st March 1985 an extract showed only the divorce or nullity decree and findings as to custody, access, aliment and periodical allowance. Prior to 23rd September 1975 only a certificate of divorce was issued automatically.

(1) Accordingly, if a full extract is sought of a decree not previously extracted (prior to 23rd September 1975) or not fully extracted (between 23rd September 1975 and 21st March 1985, or possibly after 21st March 1985), application for a full extract may be made by the party seeking extract either to the appropriate section of the General Department or to the Keeper of the Records for retransmission of the process to that section from the Keeper of the Records (see r. 9.2(1) and note 9.2.1); there is a fee for retransmission from the Keeper: see A.S. (Fees in the Scottish Record Office) 1990, Sched., Pt. IV, para. 1 [S.I. 1990 No. 44]. It is helpful to quote the reference number in the Register of Unextracted Processes kept by the Keeper when seeking retransmission (the Extractor has a copy of this register back to 1959). The process together with a note to the Extractor in Form 7.1 where a full extract is required is then transmitted from the General Department by the party seeking extract to the Extracts Department by way of the transmission book (which is receipted by the Extractor's staff and returned to the General Department). When the extract is ready for issue, written intimation is sent to the party who applied together with a note of the fee payable in cash: for fees, see Court of Session etc. Fees Order 1984, Table of Fees, Pt. I, G, item 1 [S.I. 1984 No. 256, Table as amended, pp. C1202 *et seq.*]. The process is then returned to the Keeper of the Records by the Extractor.

Alternatively, in a decree prior to 23rd September 1975, application can be made for an extract from the Register of Decrees in Consistorial Causes kept by the Extractor; but it will not be a full extract. A note to the Extractor is not required, but the process must be obtained and transmitted direct to the Extractor as above. For fees, see Court of Session etc. Fees Order 1984, Table of Fees, Pt. I, G.

(2) If an extract is sought of such a decree which has been fully extracted, application is made to the Keeper of the Records in writing or in person to the Keeper of the Records, General Register House: see Public Records (Scotland) Act 1937, s. 9. The Register of Acts and Decrees containing the record copies of extracts for each calendar year is sent to the Keeper within six months of the end of each year: r. 9.1(1). It is helpful to quote the reference number in the extract (which is the number allocated in the Decreets Book). This number and the process can also be traced through the Register of Extracted Processes kept by the Keeper of the Records (alphabetically by year, giving the extract number) a copy of which is kept by the Extractor for the years up to 1982. The Keeper will issue an extract prepared from the record copy in the Register on payment of the appropriate fee: for fees, see A.S. (Fees in the Scottish Record Office) 1990, Sched., Pt. III [S.I. 1990 No. 44].

The clerks of court are responsible for the transmission of the process to the Extracts Department after decree for automatic and immediate extracts under this rule.

The pursuer has paid for an extract from the Register of Decrees in Consistorial Causes with the signeting dues: see Court of Session etc. Fees Order 1997, Table of Fees, Pt. I, B, items 3 and

4 [S.I. 1997 No. 688, as amended, pp. C1201 *et seq*.]. The defender is issued a copy free of charge.

7.2.2 *"expiry of 21 days"*. 21 days must elapse after decree of divorce or declarator of nullity of marriage because, as extract is automatic, the period of the reclaiming days must expire (21 days): see r. 38.3(2). The date of the decree is not counted in calculating the period.

7.2.3 *Extract of divorce in simplified divorce application.* Simplified divorce applications are undefended actions on the ground of two years separation with consent, or five years separation, where there are no children and no financial provision sought: see r. 49.72. An extract is issued immediately (*i.e.* after 4 p.m. on the date of decree).

7.2.4 *"Additional extracts"*. (1) Decrees prior to 23rd September 1975. (a) Where a full extract has been obtained previously and is sought, proceed as in note 7.1.5(1)(c). (b) Otherwise, application is made by letter to the Extractor for an extract from the Register of Decrees in Consistorial Causes.

(2) Decrees after 23rd September 1975. (a) Where a full extract has been obtained previously and is sought, proceed as in note 7.1.5(1)(c) (in fact all extracts after 21st March 1985 should be "full" or complete extracts). (b) Otherwise, application is made by letter to the Extractor for an extract from the Register of Decrees in Consistorial Causes.

(3) Decrees after 1st May 1984. (*a*) Where a full extract has been obtained previously and is sought, proceed as in note 7.1.5(1)(*c*) (in fact all extracts after 21st March 1985 should be "full" or complete extracts). (*b*) Otherwise, application is made (i) by letter to the Extractor for an extract from the Register of Decrees in Consistorial Causes or (ii) in divorce cases to the Keeper of the Records for an extract from the Central Divorce Registry kept by him of all decrees of divorce granted in Scotland (which is a copy of the extract decree issued under r. 7.2).

For fees, see Court of Session etc. Fees Order 1984, Table of Fees, Pt. I, G, item 5(*a*) [S.I. 1984 No. 256, Table as amended, pp. C1202 *et seq*.].

Amendments to principal writ

7.3. An amendment which has been allowed to the instance or a conclusion of a summons, or to a petition, shall be written on the principal writ before the process is transmitted to the Extracts Department for an extract.

Deriv. P.N. 9th July 1980, reg. 1

7.3.1 *General note.* This rule is required because (*a*) an error in an extract cannot be altered (see r. 4.15(6) and note 4.15.5) and (*b*) the Extractor proceeds primarily on the basis of the information in the principal writ and interlocutor to be extracted. Although the Extractor checks all the interlocutors and pleadings for amendments, he may overlook an amendment not actually made on the principal writ, and would be reluctant to proceed without the amendment having been made because the extract cannot be altered: the responsibility must be that of the party.

In relation to a petition, it is any amendment which must be written on the principal writ before transmission to the Extracts Department.

[NEXT TEXT PAGE IS C 67]

Amendment may be allowed at any time up to final judgment: r. 24.1(1). "Final judgment" is not the same as final decree (see note 4.15.2(2)) and must mean the last or final decree or judgment after any appeal to the House of Lords or expiry of the days of appeal without an appeal: see note 24.1.3(7). Appeal to the House of Lords must be made within three months of the interlocutor appealed against: House of Lords Directions, Direction 8.1.

Return of steps of process and borrowing productions

7.4. Before an application is made under rule 7.1 for a final extract—
(a) any step of process which has been borrowed shall be returned; and
(b) each party shall borrow the productions lodged by him.

Deriv. P.N. 9th July 1980, reg. 2

General note. A process sent for final extract is not returned to the General or Petition   **7.4.1**
Department, but is kept by the Extractor for five years and then transmitted to the Keeper of the Records under r. 9.1(2) and cannot be retransmitted. Accordingly, all steps of process must be returned to process and all productions borrowed from process. Where productions are not borrowed in an action of divorce or declarator of nullity of marriage (where extract is automatic or immediate: see r. 7.2), they are returned by post by the Office of Court to the party who lodged them.

"final extract". See note 7.1.2(2).   **7.4.2**

Decrees for payment in foreign currency

7.5.—(1) Where an application is made under rule 7.1 for an extract of a decree for payment in a foreign currency, the applicant shall lodge with the note to the Extractor a certified statement of the rate of exchange prevailing at—
(a) the date of the decree sought to be extracted,
(b) the date on which the note to the Extractor is lodged, or
(c) a date within three days before the date on which the note to the Extractor is lodged,
and the sterling equivalent of the principal sum, interest and expenses decerned for.

(2) The certified statement required under paragraph (1) shall be by an official in the Bank of England or an institution authorised under the Banking Act 1987.

Deriv. P.N. 9th July 1980, reg. 5A

General note. In *Commerzbank AS v. Large* 1977 S.C. 375, it was decided that a creditor   **7.5.1**
entitled to payment of a debt due in a foreign currency could conclude for and obtain decree in a foreign currency. The form of conclusion is usually "for payment of (*state sum in foreign currency*) with interest at the rate of…per cent a year or the sterling equivalent thereof at the date of payment or the date of extract whichever is the earlier". For the purposes of enforcement in Scotland it is necessary to provide for conversion into sterling at a particular date. For practical purposes the latest date is the date on which a note to the Extractor is lodged. The applicant must choose either the date of decree, the date the extract is applied for or (in the case of difficulty at a weekend) a date within three days before extract is applied for. This rule achieves fairness to both parties while giving the applicant some flexibility in converting at a favourable or not disadvantageous rate. As Lord President Emslie observed in *Commerzbank*, above at p. 383 "the search must be for the latest practical date for conversion in order to reduce to a minimum the risk that the foreign creditor who has to enforce his decree will suffer by reason of an adverse fluctuation of the value of sterling as against the currency of account."

A foreign pursuer in an action of delict may obtain decree in a foreign currency if that was the one in which he suffered his loss: *Fullemann v. McInnes's Exrs.* 1993 S.L.T. 259.

"certified statement". This must be a certificate signed by a bank official (of a bank which is an   **7.5.2**
institution authorised under the Banking Act 1987 or the Bank of England) stating the exchange rate and the sterling equivalent of the principal and of the interest and any expenses on a stated day. The certificate should be in the following form:
"I, (*state name and position of certifier*), hereby certify that the rate current in London for the purchase of (*state foreign currency*) at the close of business on the (*state date in*

prose) was (*state rate*) to the Pound Sterling. At this rate, the principal sum of (*state sum*) amounts to (*state sterling equivalent*), interest of (*state sum*) amounts to (*state sterling equivalent*) and expenses of (*state sum*) amounts to (*state sterling equivalent*).

> Signed for and on behalf of
> (*name of bank*)
> (Signature)

Dated this   day of   .".

The bank does not have to be an Edinburgh, or a Scottish, bank; but it may be more convenient if it is an Edinburgh bank. The Scottish banks are authorised institutions under the Banking Act 1987.

The certificate should accompany the note to the Extractor.

The Extractor will insert a docquet at the end of the extract as follows: "In terms of a certificate dated at [Edinburgh] the (*date*), the Sterling equivalent of the principal sum is £......, the interest on that sum is £......, and the expenses is £......, at the rate of exchange prevailing at that date.".

Decrees of adjudication

7.6. Where an application is made under rule 7.1 for an extract of a decree of adjudication for debt, the applicant shall lodge with the note to the Extractor a statement of the accumulated sum in Form 7.6.

Deriv. P.N. 9th July 1980, reg. 5

7.6.1   *General note.* There are two forms of adjudication in execution to be noted here: (a) adjudication on a *debitum fundi* against heritable property for a debt is available to a creditor of a heritable security, feuduty or ground annual in order to accumulate the debt with its interest into capital bearing interest: Bell's *Comm.*, i.753, and see further Graham Stewart on *Diligence*, pp. 592 *et seq.*; and (b) adjudication against heritable, or moveable (where other diligence not competent), property in satisfaction of a debt constituted by decree (or a document of debt).

Where it has been necessary first to take a decree of constitution of the debt, the expenses of that action may be added to the claim in the action of adjudication. As adjudication is a diligence, the action of adjudication should not include a claim for expenses of process; and such expenses do not form part of the accumulated sum in the action and are not adjudged for. The court may award expenses where the debtor opposes the action unnecessarily; but these expenses are taken and extracted in a separate decree: see Graham Stewart, p. 589.

7.6.2   *"statement of the accumulated sum".* This brings into one (total) amount the various items of debt—*i.e.* principal, interest to the date of decree, any liquid penalty (the purpose of which is to cover expenses) or expenses in the action of constitution (including dues of extract). Payments to account must be deducted. Different debts should be accumulated separately; there should be separate conclusions in the action and separate statements of accumulated sum. The accumulated sum bears interest from the date of decree at the rate concluded for.

Interest

7.7. Where interest is included in, or payable under, a decree, it shall be at the rate of 8 per cent a year unless otherwise stated.

Deriv. R.C.S. 1965, r. 66

7.7.1   *General note.* Until 1970 the rate of interest on any decree or extract was 5 per cent. Since then the rate has changed as follows:

In an action commenced on or after 6th January 1970: 7%
    A.S. (R.C.A. No. 5) 1969 [S.I. 1969 No. 1819]
In an action commenced on or after 7th January 1975: 11%
    A.S. (R.C.A. No. 7) 1974 [S.I. 1974 No. 2090]
On a decree or extract on or after 6th April 1983:   12%
    A.S. (R.C.A. No. 2) 1983 [S.I. 1983 No. 398]
On a decree or extract on or after 16th August 1985:   15%
    A.S. (R.C.A. No. 5) 1985 [S.I. 1985 No. 1178]
On a decree on or after 1st April 1993:   8%
    A.S. (R.C.S.A.) 1993 [S.I. 1993 No. 770]

Until 5th April 1983 any increase in the rate of interest applied only in an action *commenced* on or after the date of the increase. From 6th April 1983 any increase in the rate of interest applies to any decree pronounced, or in any extract issued, on or after the date of the increase, whenever the cause was commenced; there was no satisfactory reason for linking an alteration in the rate to the date that caused commenced rather than the date of the decree. From 1st April 1993, with interest rates coming down and to avoid any confusion arising where the interest rate changes between decree and extract, it is stated that the only relevant date is the date of decree: the parties should be in no better or worse position than that at the date of decree caused by the date on which extract was obtained; and the Extractor, in a case where the decree specified the rate, would not change the rate in the extract even though the rate had changed since the decree.

It is now sought to maintain a rate of interest which is about 1 per cent above the minimum lending rate of the clearing banks. This is the principle applied by the Lord Chancellor, with the concurrence of the Treasury, for interest on judgment debts (in England and Wales) under the Judgments Act 1838, s.17. The same rate as is applied to judgment debts is fixed for awards by certain tribunals in the U.K. sitting in Scotland: *e.g.* Employment Appeal Tribunal and industrial tribunals, fixed by the Secretary of State for Employment with approval of the Treasury (Industrial Tribunals Act 1996, ss.14 and 36(3)).

The phrase "per cent a year" is now more appropriate than "*per centum per annum*".

"*unless otherwise stated*". The interlocutor allowing decree will usually state the rate of **7.7.2** interest. It will not always be the case that the rate current in the rule and concluded for when the summons was signeted is the rate of the rule at the date of decree. A summons may be amended at any time before final judgment to conclude for the current rate (sometimes referred to (erroneously) as the legal rate). But, particularly when interest rates are or may be increasing, to avoid frequent amendment or amendment in an undefended cause (which would have to be re-served if a higher rate is sought than that originally claimed), it would seem appropriate to frame a conclusion for interest in the following or similar terms where the current rate is sought: "For interest from (*state date from which interest sought*) until payment" or "For interest at the rate in rule 7.7 of the Rules of Court of Session 1994 applicable at the date of decree from (*state date from which interest sought*) until payment". Strictly, it is not necessary to mention, or refer to, the rate in the conclusion because the rule applies the current rate where interest is included or payable; and it is not necessary to conclude for interest at all from the date of decree, for interest is due *ex lege* on the principal sum and expenses from the date of decree: *Dalmahoy and Wood v. Magistrates of Brechin* (1859) 21 D. 210. But it is the practice to have a conclusion for interest, and good practice to refer to the rate or the rule, as it is then clear to a defender what has full liability is alleged to be.

Where interest is concluded for from the date of decree, or where the conclusion is silent, and the cause has been reclaimed, the date of decree means the date of the interlocutor of the appellant court and not the date of the original degree. Interest from the date of the original decree will be considered only where there has been unjustifiable delay by the party liable: *McCormack v. National Coal Board* 1957 S.C. 277; *cf.* Maclaren on *Court of Session Practice*, p. 298. The House of Lords has a discretion whether to award interest on appeal to it, and if it does not award interest the Court of Session cannot do so in applying the judgment: *Roger v. J. P. Cochrane & Co.* 1910 S.C. 1.

The effect of s.1(1A) of the Interest of Damages (Scotland) Act 1958 (inserted by the Interest of Damages (Scotland) Act 1971, s.1) is mandatory, so that interest on damages for personal injuries must be included in a decree unless there are special reasons for not doing so. Therefore, the sum sued for must be deemed to cover all heads of damage and interest under that section. Accordingly, it is unnecessary to conclude for this element of interest specifically; a conclusion for £X (sufficient to cover this element of interest as well as damages) "with interest at Y per cent a year [or the rate in rule 7.7 of the Rules of the Court of Session 1994 applicable at the date of decree] from the date of decree until payment" is adequate and proper: *Orr v. Metcalfe* 1973 S.C. 57.

It is permissible to conclude for interest at a variable rate where this has been contracted for—*e.g.* "at X per cent a year above bank rate": *Bank of Scotland v. Forsyth* 1969 S.L.T.(Sh.Ct) 15; *cf. Royal Bank of Scotland plc v. Geddes* 1983 S.L.T.(Sh.Ct) 32.

The full rate or less or more. Where interest is sought from the date of decree, normally the **7.7.3** rate allowed will be the rate sought in the summons or the rate current in the rule. Where the rate in the rule is sought from a date earlier than the date of decree, interest will not necessarily be allowed at that rate because there may be fluctuations over the period for which interest is sought (in which case an average rate may be applied) or the sum awarded is for a cumulative loss (in which case half the rate applicable to that period may be applied).

In actions of reparation for personal injuries or death, the position appears to be as follows: (1) *Pre-decree loss of earnings and loss of support*. Since the Interest on Damages (Scotland) Act 1958, s.1 (as amended by the Interest on Damages (Scotland) Act 1971, s.1), the practice has been to award interest at half the current rate (or half the average rate where the rate has changed over the period in question) from the date the loss began (date of accident) to the date the loss ceased or, if it did not, to the date of decree: see, *e.g. Smith v. Middleton,* 1972 SC 30; *McCuaig v. Redpath Dorman Long Ltd,* 1972 S.L.T.(Notes) 42; *Ward v. Tarmac Civil Engineering Ltd,* 1972 S.L.T.(Notes) 52; *Wilson v. Chief Constable, Lothian and Borders Police* 1989 S.L.T. 97 (an adjusted average of two rates). (2) *Pre-decree solatium or loss of society.* In the early years of the 1971 Act amendment to the 1958 Act, interest on past solatium was because of the change in rates between the dates of accident and degree) an average rate: see *Smith*; *McCuaig*; *Ward*, above. Since then, though the rate remained at 11 per cent for eight years, the practice has been—(a) normally to adopt a similar rule to (1) above and award half the current rate; (b) where most solatium was before the proof, to award a higher rate than half; and (c) where all solatium was post solatium, to award the full rate. In *Starkey v. National Coal Board,* 1987 S.L.T. 103, Lord Morison held that there was no logical justification for the practice of calculating interest without regard to changes in the rate during the relevant period; instead of awarding half the current rate he adjusted the rate to take account of an increase in the rate during the latter part of the relevant period: see also *Wilson*, above. The award and payment of interim damages may affect the award of interest: see *Redman v. McRae,* 1991 S.L.T. 785; *Jarvie v. Sharp,* 1992 S.L.T. 350. (3) *Future loss.* No pre-decree interest can be awarded: *Macrae v. Reed & Mallik Ltd,* 1961 S.C. 68; *McCuaig,* above. (4) *Interest on the total award* (including pre-decree interest) is at the current rate in the rule. (5) *A selective and discriminating approach must be made* in relation to interest claimed under the 1958 Act: *Macrae*; *Smith*, above. The court may refuse to award interest if there are special reasons: 1958 Act, s.1(1A). The reasons must be special to the case—*e.g.* undue delay or abuse of process; and see further, note 7.7.8.

The Social Security (Recovery of Benefits) Act 1997 repeals s.103 of the Social Security (Administration) Act 1992 which provided that in assessing interest the award of damages is reduced by a sum equal to the amount of relevant benefits received. Section 81(5) of the 1992 Act has been re-enacted in s.17 of the 1997 Act which provides that in assessing damages the amount of any listed benefits paid is to be disregarded. The question arises whether, now, in assessing interest the whole of the listed benefits received should be deducted and interest applied only to the balance or that no deduction should be made and interest applied to the gross award. There is a divergence of judicial opinion. In *George v. George C. Peebles & Son,* 1998 S.L.T. 685, Lord Nimmo Smith held that, since the primary purpose of an award of interest is to compensate a pursuer for being deprived of the use of money which he would have received but for the accident, it was inappropriate to leave out of account the fact that he had received benefits in place of earnings he would have received. The inference was that Parliament intended that the discretion conferred by s.1(A) of the Interest on Damages (Scotland) Act 1958 should continue to be exercised; and interest was awarded in that case on the difference between the loss of earnings and income support received. In *Spence v. Wilson,* 1998 S.C. 433, Lord Eassie came to the opposite opinion. He held that s.103 and its statutory predecessor innovated on the preceding common law and that the repeal of s.103 and omission of a re-enactment implied a legislative intention that the receipt of benefits was to be disregarded in the assessment of interest just as in the assessment of damages (notwithstanding, it must be supposed, that there is an express provision for the latter). The issue has now been determined by the Inner House in a report from the Lord Ordinary in *Wisely v. John Fulton (Plumbers) Ltd,* 1998 S.C. 910 and confirmed by the House of Lords (2000 S.C.(H.L.) 95). It was held that, by virtue of s.17 of the 1997 Act, the court disregards any benefits received by the pursuer when working out interest and, therefore, calculates interest on the whole amount of the damages for past loss of earnings. The case of *George,* above, was wrongly decided because it is inconsistent with the scheme of the 1997 Act.

Interest may be sought at a rate which is more or less than that current in the rule. Little difficulty will be encountered in seeking a lower rate. Allowance of a rate which is higher will depend on the circumstances. A rate contracted for will be allowed (see, *e.g. Bank of Scotland v Davies,* 1982 S.L.T. 20) subject to the application of the Consumer Credit Act 1974, ss.134–140 to credit bargains, as to which, see *A. Ketley v. Scott* [1981] I.C.R. 241; otherwise, the court always has a discretion and will have regard to the circumstances of the case (*Ross v. Ross* (1896) 23 R. 802 (legitim)) and the court may refuse interest where it would normally be payable (*Waddell's Trs v. Crawford,* 1926 S.C. 654 (legacy)). Interest on a foreign debt may be allowed at the rate of the *lex loci contractus.* In *Presslie v Cochrane McGregor Ltd (No.2),* 1999 S.L.T. 1242, the question was left open whether the pursuer could charge interest on outlays at the bank rate on the overdraft he had to take out to fund them.

The Late Payment of Commercial Debts (Interest) Act 1998 (Commencement No. 1) Order 1998 [S.I. 1998 No. 2479], which came into force on 1st November 1998, brought into force the Late Payment of Commercial Debts (Interest) Act 1998 in relation to commercial contracts for the supply of goods or services where the supplier is a small business and the purchaser is a large business or a U.K. public authority. The Late Payment of Commercial Debts Act 1998

(Transitional Provisions) Regulations 1998 [S.I. 1998 No. 2481] provide that in any proceedings it shall be presumed, unless the contrary is proved, that the business of the purchaser is a large business. The Late Payment of Commercial Debts (Interest) Act 1998 (Commencement No. 2) Order 1999 [S.I. 1999 No. 1816] applies the Act to contracts between a small business supplier (as defined in art. 2(2) of the Order and not as in the first commencement order (S.I. 1998 No. 2479)) and a United Kingdom public authority (defined as the Scottish Parliamentary Corporate Body, the Scottish Administration, the Auditor General for Scotland, the National Assembly, and the Auditor General, for Wales). The Late Payments of Commercial Debts (Interest) Act 1998 (Commencement No. 4) Order 2001 (S.I. 2000 No. 2740) applies the 1998 Act to commercial contracts for the supply of goods or services where the supplier and the purchaser are both small businesses. The Late Payment of Commercial Debts (Rate of Interest) Order 1998 [S.I. 1998 No. 2480] sets the statutory interest which may be claimed at 8 per cent above the official dealing rate of the Bank of England. The official dealing rate, also called the U.K. clearing banks base lending rate, is announced from time to time by the Bank's Monetary Policy Committee and is published daily in the *Financial Times* (under London Money Rates), *The Scotsman* and elsewhere. The Late Payment of Commercial Debts (Interest) Act 1998 (Commencement No.6) (Scotland) Order 2002 [S.S.I. 2002 No.337] brought the remainder of the 1998 Act into force from 7th August 2002 for all remaining commercial contracts for the supply of goods and services.

Date from which interest may be sought.   Interest may be sought as follows: (1) From the **7.7.4** date of decree, as money wrongfully withheld: *Dalmahoy and Wood v. Magistrates of Brechin* (1859) 21 D. 210; *Macrae v. Reed & Mallik Ltd*, 1961 S.C. 68. (2) From the date of citation. This is where—(a) the debt is not liquid; (b) interest was not stipulated for; or (c) the principal sum was not due to be paid by agreement or custom of trade at a particular time: *Blair's Trs v. Payne* (1884) 12 R. 104. It is a rule of law that interest from the date of citation runs on claims for debt in these circumstances and cannot be modified by the exercise of any judicial discretion: *Dean Warrick Ltd v. Borthwick*, 1983 S.L.T. 533. The general rule that interest runs on contractual debts from judicial demand (*i.e.* citation) was confirmed in *Elliott v. Combustion Engineering Ltd*, 1997 S.C. 127, 131F (Extra Div.). In *Gaelic Assignments Ltd v. Sharp*, 2001 S.L.T. 914 (OH) the question arose as to whether a judicial demand had to be made by bringing a petitory action (or at least not earlier that the introduction of a petitory conclusion into an action). Lord Hamilton held that petitory form was not a prerequisite to a judicial demand and that bringing an action for declarator that a debt was due constituted a judicial demand. (3) From a date earlier than citation. For example, (a) where interest runs *ex lege* by statute—*e.g.* on bills of exchange and promissory notes from the date of presentation or maturity. Bills of Exchange Act 1882, s.57 or under the Late Payment Commercial Debts (Interest) Act 1998 (see further at the end of this note); (b) where interest is due by contract from a stipulated date; (c) where damages are claimed, interest is awarded from a date on or after the date when the right of action arose: Interest on Damages (Scotland) Act 1958, s.1(1) (substituted by the Interest on Damages (Scotland) Act 1971, s.1) (whereas at common law, it was only from the date damages were quantified and decree pronounced).

Interest may be restricted to a period shorter than that for which it might otherwise have been due because of unreasonable delay in proceedings with the action: *Nacap Ltd v. Moffat Plant Ltd*, 1986 S.L.T. 326 (limited to five years); *M. & I. Instrument Engineers Ltd v. Varsada*, 1991 S.L.T. 106 (from date of citation only).

Interest cannot be sought after final decree either at common law or under the 1958 Act: *Handren v. Scottish Construction Co. Ltd*, 1967 S.L.T.(Notes) 21.

The general rule is that interest is due by virtue of a contract express or implied or by virtue of the principal sum of money having been wrongfully withheld and not paid when it ought to have been paid *Carmichael v. Caledonian Railway Co.* (1870) 8 M.(H.L.) 119, 131 *per* Lord Westbury. Where, as in an arbitration, the Interest on Damages (Scotland) Act 1958 does not apply, a sum of damages is wrongfully withheld and unpaid only once it is liquidated to a specific figure: *Farrans (Construction) Ltd v. Dunfermline D.C.*, 1988 S.L.T. 466. Where a pursuer raises an action in England for payment of a liquid debt which he abandons and re-raises an action for the same debt in Scotland, the debt may be deemed to have been wrongfully withheld from the date of the raising of the English action: *Trans Barwil Agencies (U.K.) Ltd v. John S. Braid & Co. Ltd* (No. 2), 1990 S.L.T. 182. For a peculiar case where interest was awarded on a liquid debt in a building contract from before the date of citation, see *Robertson Construction Co. (Denny) Ltd v. Taylor*, 1990 S.L.T. 698. The general rule still applies following the 1958 Act; and, in relation to damages, interest may reasonably be held to run from the date when damages may reasonably be regarded as quantifiable or capable of ascertainment: *Boots the Chemist Ltd v. G.A. Estates Ltd*, 1992 S.C. 485. For a discussion of the circumstances and occasions where interest is due, see Erskine, III.iii.76 *et seq.*; Bell, *Comm.*, i,691 *et seq.* For interest on salvage awards, see *The "Ben Gairn"* 1979 S.C. 98; *cf. The "Rilland"* [1979] 1 Lloyd's Rep. 455; *Fairbairn v. Vennootschap G. Ver Vreis Zn*, 1987 S.L.T. 498.

It is an implied term, in a contract for the supply of goods or services (defined in s.2(2)) where the purchaser and supplier are each acting in the course of a business other than an excepted contract (see s.2(5)), that any qualifying debt carries simple statutory interest: Late Payment of Commercial Debts (Interest) Act 1998, s.1(1). A "qualifying debt" is one created by virtue of an obligation under a contract to pay the whole or part of the contract price unless (when created) the whole debt is prevented by s.3 from carrying statutory interest: 1998 Act, s.3. In certain circumstances contract terms to oust or vary the right to statutory interest are permitted by Pt II of the Act. Interest runs from the last day of 30 days beginning with the day of performance or the day on which the purchaser has notice of the amount of the debt (the relevant day), whichever is the later, unless another date has been agreed or the debt relates to an obligation to make an advance payment: 1998 Act, s.4. Statutory interest starts to run on the day after the relevant day at the rate prevailing in s.6 at the end of the relevant day: 1998 Act, s.4(2). The rate of statutory interest is fixed by the Secretary of State by statutory instrument: 1998 Act, s.6 (see end note 7.7.3). There may be remission of interest in the interests of justice: 1998 Act, s.5 (a provision providing a rich soil for litigation).

7.7.5   *Interest on judicial expenses.* As a general rule an award of expenses bears interest from the date of the interlocutor decerning for the taxed expenses (*Dalmahoy and Wood v. Magistrates of Brechin* (1859) 21 D. 210; *McCormack v. N.C.B.*, 1957 S.C. 277) or on an interim decree when extracted and charged upon (*Wallace v. Henderson* (1876) 4 R. 264).

That decerniture is usually in the final decree or interlocutor. A "final decree" is one, taken by itself or along with previous interlocutors, by which the whole subject–matter of the cause is disposed of including expenses (see note 4.15.2(2)). Where the person liable in expenses is not legally aided there is (since 1983) a decerniture for expenses in an interlocutor separate from that dealing with the merits decerning for expenses as taxed (the sum to be determined by the Auditor); whereas if the person liable is an assisted person there is no decerniture at that stage (merely a finding of expenses). The fact that the amount of expenses has not been determined should make no difference, and interest on expenses should be payable from a date no later than the date of the interlocutor finding a party liable in expenses (whether or not decerned for or the amount determined). Where the interlocutor is reclaimed, the relevant date is the date of the interlocutor affirming the original decree: *Roger v. J. & P. Cochrane & Co.*, 1910 S.C. 1.

In exceptional circumstances, interest might be given from a date before final decree: *e.g.* *McDowall v. McDowall* (1821) 1 S. 200; *Whitehead & Morton v. Cullen* (1861) 24 D. 86; *Phillips v. Upper Clyde Shipbuilders*, 1990 S.L.T. 887 (interest on outlays refused); and see *Presslie v. Cochrane McGregor Group Ltd (No. 3)*, 15th October 1998, unreported (1998 G.W.D. 35–1810).

Interim execution of expenses pending appeal to the House of Lords has not been allowed to include interest: *Dunlop v. Spier* (1825) 4 S. 179, though this may now be doubted. The House of Lords may award interest (simple or compound) in its discretion, but the expenses do not carry interest unless it has so ordered: C.S.A. 1988, s.42.

7.7.6   *Interest on interest and compound interest.* It is competent to sue for a principal sum and for a fixed sum of interest due on it with interest on both from the date of citation because both the principal and the interest are the subject-matter of the action (the interest also being money wrongly withheld: *Napier v. Gordon* (1831) 5 W. & S. 745. This is often done. In *Jolly v. McNeill* (1829) 7 S. 666 it was stated that such accumulation of interest on interest was not to be allowed in ordinary contract debts where interest was not due but might be allowed in certain cases. Such accumulation has been allowed: *Napier*, above (defender in mora for refusing to pay arrears of interest); *Maclean v. Campbell* (1856) 18 D. 609; *cf. Clyde Navigation Trs v. Kelvin Shipping Co.*, 1927 S.C. 622 (thought to be compound interest being claimed); and for a recent discussion where interest on interest allowed, see *Nash Dredging (U.K.) Ltd v. Kestrel Marine Ltd*, 1986 S.L.T. 67; and see Bell's *Comm.*, i,695.

But compound interest proper, as a general rule, is not allowed: *Maclean v. Campbell* (1856) 18 D. 609 (interest from citation on principal and interest calculated to date of citation allowed but no compound interest after that date); and in *Douglas v. Douglas's Trs* (1867) 5 M. 827, 836, L.J.-C. Patton said: "A claim for compound interest, with annual rests, is a demand which can only be maintained, either in the case of a fixed usage in commercial dealings, or where there has been an abuse in a party trusted with funds and violating his trust". Exceptions to the general rule are—(a) express agreement; (b) as a penalty for breach of trust or where a person fails in an obligation to invest and accumulate: *Cranston & Hay v. Scott* (1826) 5 S. 62 (judicial factor *loco tutoris*); (c) where there is a fixed commercial usage (*e.g.* bank loans: *Reddie v. Williamson* (1863) 1 M. 229, 237) but not on interest not yet applied (*Bank of Scotland v. Davies*, 1982 S.L.T. 20); (d) where advances are made by a factor on a trust estate, but not on solicitor's cash advances unless agreed or where as usually made: *Graham's Exrs v. Fletcher's Exrs* (1870) 9 M. 298.

7.7.7   *Interest in tenders.* Where a tender is lodged in an action for damages the tender is deemed to to be in full satisfaction of any claim to interest unless otherwise stated: Interest on Damages

(Scotland) Act 1958, s.1(1B) (inserted by the Interest on Damages (Scotland) Act 1971, s.1). Thus, if the total of principal and interest awarded exceeds the tender, the pursuer has beaten the tender: *The "Devotion II"* 1979 S.C. 80. In considering whether the tender is beaten the court may take into account such part of the interest it awarded as it thinks appropriate: 1958 Act, s.1(1B). Hence, if the tender were lodged some time before the proof so that the interest which accrued between the date of tender and the date of the award took the award over the tender, the pursuer might not be held to have beaten the tender: *cf. Quinn v. Bowie (No. 2)*, 1987 S.L.T. 576. A defender may expressly exclude interest from a tender—*e.g.* where he intends to argue that there are special reasons for refusing interest under s.1(1A) of the 1958 Act.

Where the 1958 Act does not apply, the rule is that interest must be expressly referred to in the tender if it is to be a tender including interest: *Riddell v. Lanarkshire & Ayrshire Railway Co.* (1904) 6 F. 432; *The "Devotion II"*, above.

See further, note 36.11.8.

Restriction of interest. As interest is in the discretion of the court, it may be restricted or **7.7.8** modified. This may be done, for example, where there has been unreasonable delay in pursuing a claim: *Nacap Ltd v. Moffat Plant Ltd*, 1986 S.L.T. 326 (limited to five years); *M. & I. Instrument Engineers Ltd v. Varsada*, 1991 S.L.T. 106 (from date of citation only).

Even inordinate delay in prosecuting an action should not result, however, in a pursuer being deprived of interest on items of property damage which were capable of being ascertained in respect of which expenditure had been incurred (*Boots the Chemist Ltd v. G.A. Estates Ltd*, 1992 S.C. 485—because the defenders have had use of money for a longer period than they should have had—*per* L.J.-C. Ross at p. 497) or on past loss of support and services (*Bhatia v. Tribax Ltd*, 1994 S.L.T. 1201).

Fees for extracts to be included in extracts

7.8.—(1) Where the court pronounces an interlocutor awarding a sum of expenses, the interlocutor shall be deemed to include, in addition to such sum, the fees for any extract required to enforce the award.

(2) In an extract of an interlocutor containing an award of expenses, the Extractor shall include the amount of the fee for the extract.

Deriv. R.C.S. 1965, r. 63A inserted by S.I. 1986 No. 1937

General note. The source of this rule in so far as it relates to modified expenses is s.33 of the **7.8.1** C.S.A. 1821 (repealed by A.S. (R.C.A. No. 8) (Miscellaneous) 1986 [S.I. 1986 No. 1937]).

Since 1983, when the court grants decree for expenses against a non-legally aided party, it pronounces one interlocutor finding a party entitled to expenses and another decerning against the party liable in expenses as taxed by the Auditor, although the amount has not then been determined (and when taxed, the amount of expenses authorised is inserted by the Extractor in the extract). In the case of a legally aided party being found liable in expenses the first interlocutor remits to the Auditor for taxation and there is no decerniture at that stage. The interlocutor decerning for expenses is only pronounced after the Auditor's report and after consideration of any objections or application for modification. The reason for the difference in the case of a legally aided party is that it is not competent to modify expenses after decerniture: *Gilbert's Tr. v. Gilbert*, 1988 S.L.T. 680. The fees for an extract of a decree for expenses are included automatically by the Extractor when preparing the extract.

For fees for extracts, see Court of Session etc. Fees Order 1984, Table of Fees, Pt I, G [S.I. 1984 No. 256, Table as amended, pp. **C** 1202 *et seq.*]. The credit scheme introduced by P.N. No. 4 of 1976 for debiting accounts of agents does not apply to extracts and the Extracts Department.

Form of extracts

7.9.—(1) Subject to paragraphs (2) and (3), the extract of an act or a decree shall be in such form as the Extractor thinks fit.

(2) An extract shall be—
   (a) partly or wholly written,
   (b) typewritten,
   (c) printed,
   (d) lithographed, or
   (e) photographed,
and subscribed on the last page by the Extractor and have each page impressed with the stamp of the Extractor.

(3) An alteration in an extract shall be authenticated by the initials of the Extractor.

(4) In this rule, a reference to the Extractor includes the Principal Extractor.

Deriv. R.C.S. 1965, r. 63(2) and (3) substituted by S.I. 1986 No. 1937

7.9.1   *General note.* Until A.S. (R.C.A. No. 8) (Miscellaneous) 1986 [S.I. 1986 No. 1937], the form of an extract was governed by the Court of Session (Extracts) Act 1916 (repealed by that A.S.). R. 7.9 is substantially the same.

Extracts are usually typewritten. Where there is more than one page, the pages are numbered and the total is stated in the extract. The place and date of the extract are stated at the end. The date of the act or decree extracted is stated at the beginning of the extract; where there are two decrees extracted together as one (*e.g.* a decree for a principal sum and another for the expenses as taxed or a decree and an interlocutor of the Inner House adhering to the interlocutor of the court below), the dates of both are stated. There will no longer be a recital of the claim and procedure in the cause. The extract will be in such form as will reflect the decree of the court and enable its execution.

Extracts are issued in the name of the Lords of Council and Session as a judgment of the whole court, even where the interlocutor is that of a Lord Ordinary.

In preparing an extract, the Extractor may refer to the opinion(s) of the court in construing the interlocutor to be extracted: *McKellar v. Dallas's Ltd*, 1928 S.C. 503.

Extracts are backed, but an extract will no longer be stitched unless specifically requested.

7.9.2   *Rectification of errors.* Rules 4.15(6) and 4.16(7) apply to the correction of errors before extract: and see note 4.15.5 on correction before extract. It does not necessarily follow that an interlocutor may not be corrected or altered after extract. An action of reduction may have to be brought. It may be possible to obtain an order by petition to rectify an error in an extract (though not where the error originates from the interlocutor): see, *e.g. Brown, Petr* (1840) 2 D. 1467; *Mitchell's Trs, Petrs*, 1930 S.C. 180. But corrections have been made after extract. The grounds for doing so must be no better than for correction before extract: see note 4.15.5. Where there is an error in the summons which is repeated in the extract, an order may be obtained by (petition) or motion to rectify the error: *Miller v. Lindsay* (1850) 12 D. 964; *Small's Trs, Petrs* (1856) 18 D. 1210; *Provan's Trs v. Provan*, 1987 S.L.T. 405. The application should be by petition where the record copy of the extract has reached the Keeper of the Records or the extract has been otherwise registered or recorded; otherwise it may be by motion.

An extract *ex facie* regular is a probative writ. It may be reduced (with difficulty), and any charge suspended, on the ground, for example, of not being in conformity with the decree: *McKellar v. Dallas's Ltd*, 1928 S.C. 503.

7.9.3   *Units of measurement.* The Units of Measurement Directive (Council Directive 80/181 of 20th December 1979) was adopted by the E.C. in 1989 [Official Journal, 7th December 1989. L357/28]. From 1st January 1995 member states must use the metric system of measurement and, subject to certain transitional arrangements and exceptions, must cease to use imperial measurements for economic, public health, public safety and administrative purposes. Where a unit of measurement is used in pleadings it should be expressed as a metric unit, and court orders must be so expressed.

Exceptions are as follows: The nautical mile and knot are to be used for sea and air traffic and the foot is to be used for aircraft heights. Until 31st December 1999, fathom may be used for marine navigation; therm for gas supply; pint and fluid ounce for beer, cider, waters, lemonade and fruit juices on returnable containers; and ounce and pound for goods sold loose from bulk. In perpetuity, acre may be used for land registration; troy ounce for transactions in precious metals; mile, yard, foot and inch for road traffic signs, distances and speed measurements; pint for draught beer, cider and milk in returnable containers.

Warrants for execution

7.10. An extract of a decree on which execution may proceed shall include a warrant for all lawful execution in the following terms: "and the Lords grant warrant for all lawful execution on this decree".

Deriv. R.C.S. 1965, r. 64

7.10.1   *General note.* By virtue of the warrant under this rule, an extract is its own warrant for all lawful execution (for which see note 7.10.2).

Decrees for the payment of money may be enforced by a charge and diligence following on this warrant. Exchequer decrees are enforced in the same manner, the forms of exchequer diligence under the Exchequer Court (Scotland) Act 1856 having been abolished by the Debtors (Scotland) Act 1987.

A charge for enforcing a decree *ad factum praestandum* (to perform a specific act) is no longer competent: 1987 Act, s. 100(2). If it is sought to enforce such a decree by imprisonment, application must be made to the court by minute for a warrant of imprisonment under s. 1(2) of the Law Reform (Miscellaneous Provisions) (Scotland) Act 1940. The court has power to substitute payment of damages in lieu of imprisonment or to make such other order as appears to be just and equitable.

"all lawful execution". (1) In the case of a decree for payment of money, the extract is warrant **7.10.2** for charging the debtor to pay, within 14 days if the debtor is in the UK (28 days if he is not or his whereabouts are unknown: Debtors (Scotland) Act 1987, s. 90(3)), the sums mentioned in the extract and any interest accrued; and, in the event of failure to pay, the execution of an earnings arrestment, the attachment of articles belonging to the debtor (including opening lockfast places in order to execute poinding), arrestment other than an earnings arrestment and, in the case of a maintenance order, a current maintenance arrestment: 1987 Act, s. 87(2). An "earnings arrestment" means a diligence under Part III of the 1987 Act (to enforce payment of a debt including maintenance) against the earnings of the debtor in the hands of his employer. A "current maintenance arrestment" means a diligence to enforce payment of maintenance as it falls due under Part III of the 1987 Act. The rules for attachment and auction sales are laid down in Parts 2 and 3 of the Debt Arrangement and Attachment (Scotland) Act 2002, and for arrestments in Part III of the 1987 Act.

(2) An extract of a decree in an action of poinding of the ground is warrant for a poinding of the ground: 1987 Act, s. 87(5).

With two exceptions, an extract is necessary to do diligence. The exceptions are (a) an official certified copy interlocutor for interim aliment (s. 7.11(2)) and (b) an interlocutor granting warrant for recovery of expenses in a matter before the Solicitors Disciplinary Tribunal (see note 68.2.1A).

There is no civil imprisonment for debt (Debtors (Scotland) Act 1880), even for Crown taxes (1987 Act, s. 74(2)), except on application by minute to the sheriff in the case of alimentary debts (Civil Imprisonment (Scotland) Act 1882, s. 4—which does not include failure to pay periodical allowance: *White v. White*, 1984 S.L.T. (Sh.Ct.) 30), or for rates (Local Government (Scotland) Act 1947, s. 247(5)), the community charge (Abolition of Domestic Rates Etc. (Scotland) Act 1987, Sched. 2, para. 7) or the council tax (Local Government Finance Act 1992, Sched. 8, para. 2): see *Hardie v. Hardie*, 1984 S.L.T. (Sh.Ct.) 49. There must be wilful refusal to pay (which is presumed until the contrary is proved by the debtor); mere want of means is not enough (unless the debtor can prove he has not been able to earn the means of paying the debt since the decree): 1882 Act, s. 4.

Adjudication to attach heritable property, though a diligence, requires the raising of an action of adjudication to obtain a decree for it. Inhibition in execution, though so called, is still a preventive diligence.

Official certified copy interlocutors

7.11.—(1) An application may be made to the appropriate department of the Office of Court for an official certified copy of an interlocutor in respect of—

   (a) the appointment of a judicial factor;

   (b) the approval of a scheme of arrangement in a petition for variation of a trust under section 1(1) of the Trusts (Scotland) Act 1961;

   (c) the approval of a cy près scheme or a scheme for the variation or reorganisation of a public trust; or

   (d) a decree for interim aliment.

(2) The Principal Clerk, the Deputy Principal Clerk, or a clerk of session authorised by either of them, may append to an official certified copy of an interlocutor granting decree for interim aliment a warrant for all lawful execution in the following terms: "and the Lords grant warrant for all lawful execution on this decree for interim aliment".

Deriv. R.C.S. 1965, r. 170D(6) inserted by S.I. 1976 No. 1994 (r. 7.11(2))

General note. A certified copy interlocutor (a "CCI") may be obtained for any interlocutor **7.11.1** (the certification being applied by the clerk of session to the copy prepared by the party), but in four instances an official copy may be obtained from the court—(a) the appointment of a judicial factor, (b) approval of a trust variation scheme, (c) a *cy près* scheme or a scheme of variation or reorganisation of a public trust under s.9 of the Law Reform (Miscellaneous Provisions) (Scotland) Act 1990 and (d) a decree for interim aliment (pending determination of the cause). These are permitted because it is quicker than an extract. An official CCI is required to enable the judicial factor to intromit with the estate of his ward; and to enforce a decree for interim aliment on a warrant for execution. The official CCI is on headed paper and backed. To the CCI of the appointment of a judicial factor there is a sheet containing the schedule of the estate of the ward; and more than one CCI may be obtained.

On judicial factors, see Chap. 61. On variation of trusts, see Chap. 63, Pt. I. On *cy près* schemes and variation and reorganisation of public trusts, see Chap. 63, Pt. III. On interim aliment, see Chap. 49.

7.11.2   *"all lawful execution"*. The warrant in a decree for interim aliment enables the creditor to charge the debtor to pay, within 14 days if the debtor is in the UK (28 days if he is not or his whereabouts are unknown: Debtors (Scotland) Act 1987, s. 90(3)), the sums mentioned in the extract and any interest accrued; and, in the event of failure to pay, to execute an earnings arrestment, to attach articles belonging to the debtor (including opening lockfast places in order to execute poinding), arrestment other than an earnings arrestment and, as a maintenance order, a current maintenance arrestment: 1987 Act, s. 87(2). An "earnings arrestment" means a diligence under Part III of the 1987 Act (to enforce payment of a debt including maintenance) against the earnings of the debtor in the hands of his employer. A "current maintenance arrestment" means a diligence to enforce payment of maintenance as it falls due under Part III of the 1987 Act. The rules for attachment and auction are laid down in Parts 2 and 3 of the Debt Arrangement and Attachment (Scotland) Act 2002, and for arrestments in Part III of the 1987 Act.

Because the official CCI contains the words "all lawful execution", an extract is not necessary in order to do diligence.

Civil imprisonment for failure to pay may be sought on application by minute to the sheriff: Civil Imprisonment (Scotland) Act 1882, s. 4. There must be wilful refusal to pay (which is presumed until the contrary is proved by the debtor); mere want of means is not enough (unless the debtor can prove he has not been able to earn the means of paying the debt since the decree); 1882 Act, s.4.

7.11.3   *Fees.* See Court of Session etc. Fees Order 1997, Table of Fees, Pt IV, J, items 2 and 3 [SI 1997/688, as amended, pp.C1201 *et seq.*]. Certain persons are exempt from payment of fees: see 1997 Fees Order, art.5 substituted by S.S.I. 2002 No. 270. A fee exemption certificate must be lodged in process: see P.N. No.1 of 2002.

Where a party is legally represented, the fee may be debited under a credit scheme introduced on 1st April 1976 by P.N. No. 4 of 1976 to the account (if one is kept or permitted) of the agent by the court cashier, and an account will be rendered weekly by the court cashier's office to the agent for all court fees due that week for immediate settlement. Party litigants, and agents not operating the scheme, must pay (by cash, cheque or postal order) on each occasion a fee is due at the time of lodging at the counter at the appropriate department.

CHAPTER 8

TAXES ON MONEY UNDER CONTROL OF THE COURT

[1] *Certificates by officer of Revenue and Customs*
  [1] **8.1.**—(1) Subject to paragraph (2), no—
  (a) decree or other interlocutor for payment to a person of any money consigned in the name of the Accountant of Court under the Court of Session Consignations (Scotland) Act 1895,
  (b) decree or other interlocutor for payment of consigned money, or for transfer or conveyance to a person of any heritable or moveable property, in a cause which seeks the distribution of the estate of a deceased person, or
  (c) decree of exoneration and discharge of a judicial factor appointed by the court to administer and distribute an estate, unless appropriate steps have been taken for the continued administration of a lapsed trust, intestate estate, partnership estate or other estate, heritable or moveable,
shall be pronounced until there has been lodged with the clerk of court a certificate by an authorised officer of the Revenue and Customs stating that

all taxes or duties payable to the Commissioners for Her Majesty's Revenue and Customs have been paid or satisfied.

(2) In relation to paragraph (1)(*b*), in an action of multiplepoinding it shall not be necessary for the issue of such a certificate that all of the taxes or duties payable on the estate of a deceased claimant have been paid or satisfied.

Deriv. R.C.S. 1965, r. 36

---

[1] Heading and r. 8.1 amended by S.S.I. 2005 No. 268 (effective 7th June, 2005).

Money consigned with Accountant of Court. Under the Court of Session Consignations **8.1.1** (Scotland) Act 1895, s. 3, the Accountant of Court is custodian of all sums lodged by order of the court. Consignation may be ordered—(*a*) in lieu of caution for expenses: *Morrison v. Morrison's Exrx.* 1912 S.C. 892; (*b*) in lieu of sisting a mandatory: *Bell v. Strathearn & Blair* 1953 S.L.T. (Notes) 23; (*c*) in lieu of caution in suspensions, suspension and interdict, and suspension and liberation: r. 60.3. For consignation, see note 33.4.3.

Certificate of Revenue and Customs. A certificate is required notwithstanding, in the case of **8.1.2** consignation, that income tax on interest in the hands of a deposit-taker (including an institution authorised under the Banking Act 1987) is deducted at source before payment: Income and Corporation Taxes Act 1988, s. 479. This deduction at source provision does not apply, however, where the beneficial owner of the deposit is not ordinarily resident in the UK.

CHAPTER 9

COURT RECORDS

Transmission of records

9.1.—(1) The Register of Acts and Decrees for each year shall be transmitted by the Extractor to the Keeper of the Records for permanent custody within six months after the end of that year.

(2) Subject to paragraph (3), a process, other than a teind process, shall be transmitted to the Keeper of the Records after the expiry of five years after—

(*a*) the date of the last interlocutor pronounced in the cause; or

(*b*) where no interlocutor has been pronounced, the date of the calling of the summons or the presentation of the petition, as the case may be.

(3) No process of a petition for—

(*a*) appointment of a judicial factor, or

(*b*) the winding up of a company,

shall be transmitted under this rule unless the factor or liquidator, as the case may be, has been granted a final discharge by the court.

Deriv. R.C.S. 1965, r. 32A inserted by S.I. 1976 No. 745 and amended by S.I. 1982 No. 1825

General note. This rule is made under s. 1(1) of the Public Records (Scotland) Act 1937: see **9.1.1** A.S. (R.C.S. 1994) 1994, Sched.1 [S.I. 1994 No. 1443].

The following records are transmitted to the Keeper of the Records (General Register House): (1) *The Books of Sederunt.* These are records of the administrative work of the court including Acts of Sederunt, acts appointing judges to particular functions and admission of advocates. At intervals (about 10 years) a collection is transmitted to the Keeper. (2) *Register of Acts and Decrees.* In this register are kept the record copies of every extract issued in the calendar year (and in which extracts are traced by reference to the extract number (number/ year)). The register for each year is transmitted to the Keeper. (3) *Processes.* All processes (except petitions for appointment of judicial factors or for the winding up of a company where there has been no final discharge) are transmitted to the Keeper after five years in terms of r. 9.1(2) and (3). (4) *Sequestrations.* The Accountant of Court transmits to the Keeper each year records of sequestrations which he considers should be preserved. (5) *Minute Book.* This was discontinued in January 1993. It recorded the minutes of the daily judicial business of the court including Acts of Sederunt, practice notes and decrees (including brief particulars of the causes). At the end of the judicial year the Minute Book was transmitted to the Keeper.

The Keeper of the Records maintains a Register of Unextracted Processes (an alphabetical index with the Court of Session basement Records Department number) and a Register of Extracted Processes (an alphabetical index by year with the extract number) for tracing processes.

9.1.2 *"within six months after", "after the expiry of five years after".* The date from which the period is calculated is not counted.

9.1.3 *R.9.1(3).* A petition for the appointment of a judicial factor or the winding up of a company in which there has been no final discharge is not transmitted. A judicial factor may be required to look after the estate of his ward for many years before he (or anyone else) petitions for his discharge; and applications may be made to the court in this process, including petitions for special powers or for discharge (which do not have processes of their own). It may take some years to complete a winding up, and during the course of it applications may be made to the court (by motion or note) in the winding-up process.

Retransmission of processes to Office of Court

9.2.—[1] (1) Where a person having an interest in a process in the custody of the Keeper of the Records (other than a finally extracted process), requires that process to be transmitted back to the Office of Court—

    (a) it shall be transmitted back on payment of such fee as may be due to the Keeper of the Records; and

    (b) an entry shall be made in a book to be kept by the Keeper of the Records recording the retransmission, which shall be signed by the clerk of session who receives the process.

(2) No document in a process, may be borrowed by any person while the process remains in the custody of the Keeper of the Records except under the provisions of paragraph (1).

(3) A process transmitted back to the Office of Court under paragraph (1) shall be returned by the Office of Court to the Keeper of the Records as soon as possible after it has ceased to be required.

Deriv. R.C.S. 1965, r. 34

---

[1] Rule 9.2(1) amended by S.I. 1994 No. 2901 (clerical error).

9.2.1 *General note.* This rule is made under s. 1(2) of the Public Records (Scotland) Act 1937: see A.S. (R.C.S. 1994) 1994, Sched. 1 [S.I. 1994 No. 1443].

Only a process in which there has not been a final extract may be transmitted back to the Office of Court under this rule. A finally extracted process may not be transmitted back to the Office of Court, though it may be inspected in the Scottish Record Office on payment of such fee as may be due (see note 9.2.3). The reason for this is to prevent further business being carried out in a process which has finished. This is consonant with r. 4.13 which provides that no part of a finally extracted process may be borrowed after final extract. If a finally extracted process or an unextracted process in the custody of the Keeper of the Records is required in court for the purposes of another litigation, it may be obtained by motion under r. 35.10(1). Where the process transmitted back has not been finally extracted, a borrowable document (for documents not borrowable, see r. 4.11) may be borrowed: r. 9.2(2).

Application under r. 9.2(1) may be made in the General, or Petition, Department, as the case may be, on a slip provided for that purpose, or to the Keeper of the Records, for transmission back from the Keeper. It is helpful to quote the reference number in the Index of Processes (which is maintained by the Keeper and available for inspection in the Scottish Record Office, General Register House) or to refer to the copy kept by the Extractor up to 1982. The process is transmitted back by the Keeper's transmission book which is receipted by a clerk of session and returned to the Keeper: r. 9.2(1)(b).

The clerks of session are responsible for returning the process to the Keeper as soon as possible after it has ceased to be required by a transmission book which is receipted by the Keeper's staff and returned: r. 9.2(3).

Where an interlocutor has been extracted and the record copy has been transmitted to the Keeper of the Records, application for an extract is made to the Keeper: see 1937 Act, s. 9; and note 7.1.5(1)(c). Where an application is made for an extract later than five years after the last interlocutor or, if none, the date of calling of the summons or presentation of the petition, it is made (a) where the interlocutor has not previously been extracted in a process not finally extracted, to the General or Petition Department or to the Keeper of the Records (see note 7.1.5(2)(a)); or (b) where there has been a previous extract, to the Keeper (see note 7.1.5(2)(b)).

"person having an interest". Whether a person has an interest is in the discretion of the **9.2.2** Keeper. Parties, solicitors, factors and researchers may have an interest.

There are special rules in relation to adoption processes (see r.67.32(2)).

Fees. There is a fee for inspection of a process (unless for historical or literary purposes) in the **9.2.3** Scottish Record Office, and a fee for transmission back from the Keeper to the Office of Court: A.S. (Fees in the Scottish Record Office) 1990, Sched., Pts. I and IV [SI 1990/44].

Where application for transmission back is made direct to the Keeper, the fee must be paid to him then. Where application is made in the Office of Court, on receipt of the application from the Office of Court the Keeper sends a bill to the party who applied.

"step of process". This is any document lodged in process, other than a production (r.1.3(1)), **9.2.4** including those listed in r.4.4(1) and any inventory of productions.

CHAPTER 10

SITTINGS OF THE COURT

Session and terms of court

10.1.—(1) The court shall be in session throughout the year except during such periods as the Lord President shall specify by direction as periods when the court shall be in vacation.

[1] (2) There shall be three terms during session when the court shall sit to conduct the ordinary business of the court, namely—

(*a*) a winter term,

(*b*) a spring term, and

[1] (*c*) a summer term,

the dates of which shall be such as the Lord President shall direct.

(3) The Lord President may, if at any time he considers the business of the court so requires, direct that a term of the court shall be extended for such period as may be necessary.

Deriv. R.C.S. 1965, r.68B inserted by S.I. 1987 No. 2160 (r.10.1(2) and (3))

---

[1] R.10.1(2) amended by S.S.I. 2004 No.52 (effective 1st March, 2004).

General note. The forerunner of this Chapter was introduced by A.S. (R.C.A. No. 5) **10.1.1** (Miscellaneous) 1987 [SI 1987/2160] replacing and repealing ss. 6, 7, 8 and 11 of the C.S.A. 1868, s. 4(2), (3) (part) and (5) of the Administration of Justice (Scotland) Act 1933, s. 2 of the Administration of Justice (Scotland) Act 1948, and s. 3 (part) of the Exchequer Court (Scotland) Act 1856 (see r.10.6).

In recognition, however, of the fact that the business of the court continues in vacation (except the hearing of proofs, jury trials and procedure roll hearings) and to avoid public misconception of the meaning of vacation, this rule provides for the court to be in session for most of the year (except in practice for one vacation at Christmas and New Year: see current direction at pp. **C** 1501 *et seq.*). In session outwith terms the Lord Ordinary's powers to deal with the business of the court may be more extensive than those of the vacation judge (for which see r.11.1) and are laid down and may be extended by the Lord President by direction: r.10.4; for the current direction, see pp. **C** 1501 *et seq*.

The legal year begins in September with the Winter term.

"terms". The terms of the court are what were formerly called the sessions of the court. The legal **10.1.2** year begins in September with the Winter term. For the current direction, see pp. **C** 1501 *et seq*.

Sederunt days

10.2.—[1] (1) A day on which the court sits during session under rule 10.3(1) or 10.4 shall be a sederunt day.

(2) The Lord President may, by direction, provide that such days in vacation as he may specify in the direction shall be sederunt days.

Deriv. R.C.S. 1965, r.68C inserted by SI 1987/2160

---

[1] R. 10.2(1) amended by S.I. 1994 No.2901 (effective 5th December, 1994).

General note. See note 10.1.1 for statutory history. For the first time, under R.C.S. 1965, **10.2.1** r.68C, a sederunt day was defined. The sederunt days during session are Tuesdays, Wednesdays, Thursdays and Fridays (see r.10.3(1)). The directions which provide for the annual session and terms of the court (r.10.1) also provide for the sederunt days in vacation under r.10.2(2): these are invariably every Wednesday and Thursday: for the current direction, see pp. **C** 1501 *et seq*. Historically, the business of the court could only be conducted on sederunt days.

On vacations, see r.10.5 and note 11.1.2.

Sittings during term

10.3.—(1) Subject to the following paragraphs of this rule, the court shall sit on Tuesday, Wednesday, Thursday and Friday of each week during a term at such times as the Lord President may direct.

(2) The court shall not sit during a term—

(*a*) subject to paragraph (3), on such public holidays, or

(*b*) on such other days in exceptional circumstances,

as the Lord President may direct.

(3) A Division of the Inner House or the Lord Ordinary may sit—

(*a*) on a Monday where it is considered necessary to hear and determine a cause; or

(*b*) on a Saturday, Sunday or public holiday to hear and determine a matter of urgency.

Deriv. R.C.S. 1965, r.68D inserted by SI 1987/2160

10.3.1   *General note*. See note 10.1.1 for statutory history. For the current direction, see pp. **C** 1501 *et seq*. The court does not normally sit on the following public holidays:

New Years Day (1st January), or the following Monday if on a Saturday or Sunday (bank holiday)

2nd January, or the following Monday (or Tuesday) if on a Saturday (or Sunday) (bank holiday)

Spring Weekend (third Monday in April) (local holiday)

Good Friday (bank holiday)

Easter Monday

May Day Holiday (first Monday in May) (bank holiday)

Victoria Day (local holiday)

September Weekend (third Monday in September)

Christmas Eve (24th December)—half day

Christmas Day (25th December), or the following Monday if on a Saturday or Sunday (bank holiday)

Boxing Day (26th December), or the following Monday (or Tuesday) if on a Saturday (or Sunday).

10.3.2   *"term"*. The terms of the court are what were formerly called the sessions of the court. The legal year begins in September with the Winter term. For the current direction, see pp. **C** 1501 *et seq*.

10.3.3   *"considered necessary" and "a matter of urgency"*. It is for the court to decide what is necessary or is a matter of urgency.

Sittings during session outwith terms

10.4.—(1) A Division of the Inner House or the Lord Ordinary may sit on any day when the court is in session after a term has ended to conclude a hearing which has commenced during a term.

(2) A Division of the Inner House may sit at any time when the court is in session outwith a term to hear and determine urgent Inner House business.

(3) At any time during session outwith a term, the Lord Ordinary shall—

(*a*) have the powers of the vacation judge in rule 11.1; and

(*b*) have such other powers to hear and determine a cause in the Outer House as the Lord President may from time to time direct.

10.4.1   *General note*. This is a new rule providing for the business of the Lord Ordinary in session but outwith a term.

10.4.2   *Sittings of Inner House outwith terms*. The Inner House may sit during session after a term has ended (*a*) to conclude a hearing commenced during term or (*b*) to hear and determine urgent Inner House business. The meaning of "urgent" has not been defined and is a matter for the court to decide. This provision is consistent with Inner House business during vacation: see r.10.5(3) and (4).

Powers of Lord Ordinary *outwith terms.* The Lord Ordinary may sit during session after a **10.4.3**
term has ended (a) to conclude a hearing commenced during term, (b) to deal with business
which in vacation the vacation judge would deal with and (c) to deal with such other business as
the Lord President may direct: r. 10.4(1) and (3). The Lord President has made no such direction
as yet, but it is not expected that the Lord Ordinary would hear proofs, jury trials and procedure
roll hearings as in term. The business under (b) and (c) is arranged in the same way as that of the
vacation court, see note 10.5.3.

The question of expenses not dealt with by the Inner House after a reclaiming motion is a
substantial issue beyond the powers that a Lord Ordinary sitting in session outwith a term has in
relation to interlocutory business of the Inner House: *Alliance & Leicester Building Society v.
Lindsays W.S.*, 25th July 1997 (G.W.D. 36–1862).

On the powers of the vacation judge in r. 11.1, see notes to that rule.

Sittings during vacation

10.5.—(1) During vacation, one or more of the judges of the court, other
than the Lord President and the Lord Justice-Clerk, shall act from time to
time as a vacation judge sitting in court or in chambers.

(2) The vacation judge shall deal with the business of the vacation judge
under rule 11.1(1) on such days and at such times as may be necessary or
convenient, subject to any direction of the Lord President.

(3) A Division of the Inner House or the Lord Ordinary may sit during
vacation, whether or not on a sederunt day, to conclude a hearing
commenced when the court was in session.

(4) A Division of the Inner House may sit during vacation, whether or not
on a sederunt day, to hear and determine urgent Inner House business which
cannot competently be heard and determined by the vacation judge.

Deriv. R.C.S. 1965, r. 68E inserted by S.I. 1987 No. 2160

General note. See note 10.1.1 for statutory history. Section 4(2) of the Administration of **10.5.1**
Justice (Scotland) Act 1933 provided for the hearing during vacation of causes "pending"
before the court; the current provision makes it clear that (a) the court may always sit in
vacation to conclude a hearing once begun in session and (b) a Division may sit to hear urgent
Inner House business which cannot be dealt with by the vacation judge even though it was not
pending during session.

"vacation". There is presently only one vacation in the legal year, the Christmas or Winter **10.5.2**
vacation (two weeks at Christmas and New Year). The actual dates depend on the dates of the
end of the Winter term (usually the Friday of the week before the week in which Christmas Day
falls) and the beginning of the Spring term (usually the first Tuesday after New Year's Day). See
r. 10.1(1) and the current direction at pp. 1501 *et seq.*

Sittings of vacation court. The vacation court normally sits at 10.30am, or as soon as possible **10.5.3**
thereafter, on Tuesdays to Fridays (except in public or local holidays or on a Tuesday where
Monday is a public or local holiday). During the Winter (Christmas) vacation there may be only
two vacation court days. Business is normally conducted in open court but may be conducted in
chambers or in private. The days on which the vacation court sits are published in the rolls about
four weeks before the end of the preceding term. The vacation court sits on such days and at
such times as may be convenient or necessary subject to any direction of the Lord President:
r. 10.5(2).

Lord Ordinary in Exchequer Causes

10.6. The Lord Ordinary in Exchequer Causes may hear and determine an
Exchequer cause when the court is in session or in vacation.

Deriv. R.C.S. 1965, r. 68F inserted by S.I. 1987 No. 2160

General note. See note 10.1.1 for statutory history. For Exchequer causes, see Chap. 48. **10.6.1**
The Lord Ordinary in Exchequer Causes is appointed by the Lord President under s.3 of the
C.S.A. 1988 (amended by the Law Reform (Miscellaneous Provisions) (Scotland) Act 1990,
Sched. 4, para. 4(3)). The Lord Ordinary in Exchequer Causes is currently Lord Cameron of
Lochbroom. In the absence or inability of the Lord Ordinary in Exchequer Causes, the business
of that judge may be dealt with by another Lord Ordinary: C.S.A. 1988, s.3 (as amended).

10.6.2   *"vacation".* There is presently only one vacation in the legal year, the Christmas or Winter vacation (two weeks at Christmas and New Year). The actual dates depend on the dates of the end of the Winter term (usually the Friday of the week before the week in which Christmas Day falls) and the beginning of the Spring term (usually the first Tuesday after New Year's Day). See r. 10.1(1) and the current direction at pp. 1501 *et seq.*

Hearing of commercial actions

10.7. A commercial judge nominated under rule 47.2 (proceedings before commercial judge) may hear and determine a commercial action as defined by rule 47.1(2) when the court is in session or in vacation.

R. 10.7 inserted by S.I. 1994 No. 2310 (effective 20th September 1994).

10.7.1   *General note.* This rule enables the commercial judge to hear commercial actions in all 52 weeks of the year. During about two weeks in April, the month of August and the Christmas and New Year vacation, only interlocutory or incidental business will normally be done: proofs and debates will not, as a general rule, be heard.

10.7.2   *"vacation".* There is presently only one vacation in the legal year, the Christmas or Winter vacation (two weeks at Christmas and New Year). The actual dates depend on the dates of the end of the Winter term (usually the Friday of the week before the week in which Christmas Day falls) and the beginning of the Spring term (usually the first Tuesday after New Year's Day). See r. 10.1(1) and the current direction.

CHAPTER 11

VACATION JUDGE

Powers of vacation judge

11.1.—(1) Subject to any other provision in these Rules and paragraph (2) of this rule, the vacation judge may, during vacation, hear and determine—

    (a) a motion which might be determined during session by the Lord Ordinary;

    (b) an application which might be determined during session by the Lord Ordinary in chambers; and

    (c) a motion which does not affect the merits, in a cause in dependence in the Inner House.

(1A) Subject to paragraph (2) of this rule, the vacation judge may, during vacation, in a case where early disposal of a reclaiming motion or appeal is sought by virtue of rule 38.7A or 40.7A make any order or refusal, or give any direction, under rule 38/14(6) or 40.12(6) which might be made or given during session by the nominated judge.

(2) The vacation judge shall not be bound to hear or determine any matter if, in his opinion, it would be more appropriate for the matter to be dealt with in the session of the court after the vacation.

Deriv. R.C.S. 1965, r. 1 amended by S.I. 1987 No. 1206
R. 11.1(1A) inserted by S.I. 1997 No. 2692 (effective 1st December 1997).

11.1.1   *General note.* The foundation of R.C.S. 1965, r. 1 was s.4(3) of the Administration of Justice (Scotland) Act 1933, the relevant part of which was repealed by A.S. (R.C.A. No. 5) (Miscellaneous) 1987 [S.I. 1987 No. 2160].

Any solicitor has a right of audience before the vacation judge: see C.S.A. 1988, s.48 (substituted by the Law Reform (Miscellaneous Provisions) (Scotland) Act 1990, Sched. 8, para. 38) and s.51.

11.1.2   *"vacation".* There is presently only one vacation in the legal year, the Christmas or Winter vacation (two weeks at Christmas and New Year). The actual dates depend on the dates of the end of the Winter term (usually the Friday of the week before the week in which Christmas Day falls) and the beginning of the Spring term (usually the first Tuesday after New Year's Day). See r. 10.1(1) and the current direction at pp. 1502 *et seq.*

"application". This includes a motion or other application, such as an application for letters **11.1.3**
of arrestment or inhibition under r. 59.1, for a simplified divorce under r. 49.73 or an
application by petition.

"in dependence". A cause is depending from the time it is commenced (*i.e.* from the time an **11.1.4**
action is served or a first order in a petition is made) until final decree, whereas a cause is in
dependence until final extract. For the meaning of commenced, see note 13.4.4 (action) or 14.6.1
(petition). For the meaning of final decree, see note 4.15.2(2). For the meaning of final extract,
see note 7.1.2(2).

"does not affect the merits". Interlocutory business of the Inner House may be dealt with in **11.1.5**
vacation, but not anything which will affect the merits of the cause.

In *Shell U.K. Exploration and Production Ltd v. Innes*, 1995 S.L.T. 807, it was held that the
question whether the respondents were in breach of interdict (on a minute and answers) was a
question which arose in the same cause as that in which the interim interdicts were pronounced
and it was not possible to regard the breach of interdict as a matter which did not affect the
merits of the cause, and the vacation judge or Lord Ordinary outwith a term could not deal with
the breach of interdict.

The vacation judge cannot deal, *e.g.*, with breach of interim interdict where a decision not to
recall the interim interdict has been reclaimed, because the minute and answers about breach of
interdict are part of the same process as that in which the interdict was pronounced, and it is not
possible to regard the breach of interdict as an interlocutory matter not affecting the merits:
Shell U.K. Exploration and Production Ltd v. Innes, 1995 S.L.T. 807.

The question of expenses not dealt with by the Inner House following are claiming motion is
a substantial issue outwith the powers that a vacation judge has in relation to interlocutory
business of the Inner House: *Alliance & Leicester Building Society v. Lindsays W.S.*, 25th July
1997 (1997 G.W.D. 36–1862).

"In a case where early disposal . . . is sought". Early disposal of a reclaiming motion may be **11.1.5A**
sought under r.38.13 or 40.11 respectively. Rules 38.7A and 40.7A state that in certain cases the
reclaimer or appellant must enrol for early disposal.

Rule 11.1(1A) empowers the vacation judge (and a Lord Ordinary sitting in session outwith a
term by virtue of r.10.4(3)(a), to deal with questions of competency under r.38.14(6) or 40.12(6).

"more appropriate". A vacation judge is not bound to deal with every matter brought before **11.1.6**
him; but vacation business is not limited to urgent matters as is sometimes thought: there is a
discretion where it would be more appropriate for the matter to be dealt with in the next term.
The vagueness of the rule is unfortunate as it cannot be certain that any particular motion will
necessarily be heard. The word "appropriate" may be less equivocal than the former word
"conveniently"; it carries no sense of personal convenience.

Vacation business under statute. Certain statutes make express reference to matters being dealt **11.1.7**
with by a vacation judge:
- (a) Companies Clauses Consolidation (Scotland) Act 1845, ss.3 and 134 (application for
  appointment of an umpire in an arbitration), incorporated in the Insolvency Act 1986,
  s.111(4);
- (b) Land Clauses Consolidation (Scotland) Act 1845, ss.3 and 27 (application for
  appointment of an oversman in an arbitration), incorporated in, *e.g.* Acquisition of
  Land (Authorisation Procedure) (Scotland) Act 1947, Sched. 2, Town and Country
  Planning (Scotland) Act 1997, s.188(2), Land Compensation (Scotland) Act 1973, s.63,
  Roads (Scotland) Act 1984, s.110(5);
- (c) Judicial Factors Act 1849, ss.1, 7 and 34 (application by judicial factor for special
  powers or petition for discharge of judicial factor, tutor or curator);

(*d*) Titles to Land Consolidation (Scotland) Act 1868, s. 158 (application for recall or restriction of inhibition on the dependence);

(*e*) Representation of the People Act 1983, s. 134(2) (discharge or variation of penalty by election court for local election);

(*f*) Companies Act 1985, s. 425(5) (order on summary application for compromise or arrangement);

(*g*) Insolvency Act 1986, ss. 111(4) (see (*a*) above) and 120(2) (jurisdiction to wind up companies).

Vacation business under the rules. Certain rules (other than r. 11.1(1)) make express refer- **11.1.8** ence to matters being dealt with in vacation:

(*a*) r. 10.5(3) and (4) (sittings of Inner House or Lord Ordinary to conclude a hearing commenced in term, or of Inner House to hear urgent business);

(*b*) r. 10.6 (Exchequer causes);

(*c*) r. 14.5(1)(*b*) (first order in petitions);

(*d*) r. 38.5(2) (leave to reclaim against certain interlocutors);

(*e*) r. 41.21(1) (orders for service and answers in statutory appeals);

(*f*) r. 43.20 (Optional Procedure in certain actions of damages heard by vacation judge (subject to r. 11.1));

(*g*) r. 47.2 (commercial actions heard by vacation judge (subject to r. 11.1));

(*h*) r. 55.2 (causes relating to intellectual property heard by vacation judge (subject to r. 11.1));

(*i*) r. 58.5 (applications for judicial review heard in vacation (subject to r. 11.1));

(*j*) r. 77.3(4) (summary trial).

Orders of vacation judge which are final. Certain orders of a vacation judge are by statute **11.1.9** expressly final and not subject to review:

(*a*) an order giving a judicial factor special powers or discharging or removing a judicial factor: Judicial Factors Act 1849, ss. 1, 7 (final and not subject to appeal) and 34 (final and conclusive);

(*b*) an order in relation to a sanction of compromise or scheme of arrangement: Companies Act 1985, s. 425(5) (not subject to review, reduction, suspension or stay of execution);

(*c*) orders under the following sections of the Insolvency Act 1986 (by virtue of s. 162(2) of that Act—(not subject to review, reduction, suspension or stay of execution)):

   (i) s. 153 (as to time for proving debts and claims);

   (ii) s. 195 (as to meetings for ascertaining wishes of creditors and contributories);

   (iii) s. 198 (as to examination of witnesses in regard to property or affairs of company).

Arrangement of business. All motions requiring appearance in session will require appear- **11.1.10** ance in vacation—*i.e.* starred motions; for such motions, see notes 23.2.14, 23.2.16 and 23.2.17(2). Unopposed motions are dealt with first, then opposed motions, all in alphabetical order. Motions of length or complexity (*e.g.* an application for judicial review) will usually be heard separately by another vacation judge if pressure of business requires it.

Sittings of the vacation court. For the power, see r. 10.5(2). A vacation court sits at **11.1.11** 10.30am, or as soon as possible thereafter, on Tuesdays to Fridays (except on public or local holidays or on a Tuesday where Monday is a public or local holiday). During the Winter or Christmas vacation there may be only two vacation court days. Business is usually conducted in open court but may be conducted in chambers or in private. The days on which the court sits in vacation are published in the rolls about four weeks before the end of the preceding term. The vacation court sits on such days and at such times as may be convenient or necessary subject to any direction of the Lord President: r. 10.5(2).

More than one judge may sit as a vacation judge if pressure of business requires it.

Exchequer causes. An Exchequer cause may be dealt with in vacation by the Lord Ordinary **11.1.12** in Exchequer Causes: r. 10.6. In his absence or inability an Exchequer cause may be dealt with by the vacation judge: C.S.A. 1988, s. 3 and r. 11.1(1)(*a*). Where this occurs any interlocutor begins with the words "The Vacation Judge in room and stead of the Lord Ordinary in Exchequer Causes".

Rights of audience. Counsel or other person having a right of audience before the Court of **11.1.13** Session may appear before the vacation judge. On the meaning of "counsel" and "other person having a right of audience", see definitions in r. 1.3(1). A solicitor also has a right of audience before the vacation judge: C.S.A. 1988, s. 48(2)(*a*) substituted by the Law Reform (Miscellaneous Provisions) (Scotland) Act 1990, Sched. 8, para. 38.

CHAPTER 12

ASSESSORS

Summoning of assessors

12.1.—(1) Subject to the following provisions of this Chapter, the court may, at its own instance or on the motion of a party, summon to its assistance a qualified person to sit with the court to act as an assessor at a proof or hearing in any cause.

(2) Where the court considers summoning an assessor at its own instance, it shall hear the parties on the matter before making a decision.

(3) Where an interlocutor is pronounced summoning an assessor, the court shall remit to the Deputy Principal Clerk to arrange for the attendance of the assessor selected.

Deriv. Nautical Assessors (Scotland) Act 1894, s. 2; R.C.S. 1965, r. 37 amended by S.I. 1978 No. 955, r. 38 (r. 12.1(1)), r. 40 (r. 12.1(2)) and r. 41 (r. 12.1(3))

12.1.1   *General note.* Under R.C.S. 1965, rr. 37 and 38, the court (*a*) could summon an assessor in any maritime or patent cause at its own instance, (*b*) had to summon an assessor in any maritime or patent cause on the application of any party and (*c*) could summon an assessor on the joint motion of parties in any other cause. The rule has been simplified and now is that the court may summon an assessor in any cause at its own instance or on the motion of a party. The Nautical Assessors (Scotland) Act 1894 is repealed in its application to the Court of Session.

The summoning of an assessor is appropriate where there are technical matters to be decided requiring special knowledge. In maritime matters, the functions of an assessor include advising on seamanship, the interpretation and application of the Regulations for Preventing Collisions at Sea, and whether the course of action taken was one which would have been taken by a skilful seaman: *McLean v. Johnstone* (1906) 8 F. 836, 838. The trustworthiness of the evidence is a matter for the judge: *Cambo Shipping Co. Ltd v. Dampskibssellskadet Carl* 1920 S.C. 26. See also generally *Owners of SS Australia v. Owners of Cargo of SS Nautilus* [1927] A.C. 145. The assessor does not determine the issues of fact: he provides expert advice on which the court may rely in determining the issues. The court is not bound to follow the advice; but it cannot follow the advice of the assessor on which there was no evidence: *Cambo Shipping Co. Ltd*, above.

12.1.2   *"motion of a party".* For motions, see Chap. 23.

12.1.3   *"proof or hearing".* "Hearing" includes a reclaiming motion or appeal in the Inner House or a hearing on evidence. Jury trial is excluded as it is not an appropriate mode of inquiry where an assessor is appointed, because questions appropriate for the assessor are unsuitable for a jury: *McLean v. Johnstone* (1906) 8 F. 836; *Leadbetter v. Dublin & Glasgow Steam Packet Co.* 1907 S.C. 538; *Kerr v. The Screw Collier Co. Ltd* (1907) 15 S.L.T. 444; *Rodger v. Glen-Coats* 1913 1 S.L.T. 434; *Williamson v. Richard Irvin & Sons Ltd* 1960 S.L.T. (Notes) 34.

12.1.4   *Arrangements for attendance of assessor.* The remit to the Deputy Principal Clerk to make the necessary arrangements is contained in the interlocutor. Where the parties select an assessor under r. 12.5(1), the pursuer should inform the Deputy Principal Clerk by letter of his name and address. Where the court selects an assessor (failing agreement by the parties) under r. 12.5(1), the clerk of court will inform the Deputy Principal Clerk.

Consignation of money for fees of assessors

12.2. An interlocutor summoning an assessor in a cause other than a cause under the Patents Act 1977 shall only be pronounced subject to the condition that there shall be consigned into court such sum as the court thinks fit to meet the fees and expenses of the assessor by—

(*a*) the party enrolling the motion; or
(*b*) where an assessor is summoned by the court at its own instance, the pursuer or petitioner, as the case may be, unless the court otherwise directs.

Deriv. R.C.S. 1965, r. 44(*c*)

Patents Act 1977. The remuneration of an assessor in a cause under the Patents Act 1977 is **12.2.1** governed by s. 98(2) of that Act which provides that the remuneration is to be determined by the Lord President with the consent of the Minister of the Civil Service to be defrayed out of monies provided by Parliament (and not by a party).

Consignation. The purpose of consignation is to ensure that the assessor is paid. It is not **12.2.2** clear, however, how the court can assess with accuracy what the sum to be consigned should be as the total fees and expenses will not be known in advance. A better provision might have been to make the agent for a party liable in the first instance to the assessor for his fees. The remuneration of an assessor (except in a patent action) is treated as expenses in the cause unless the court otherwise directs: r. 12.9. Once the remuneration and expenses of the assessor have been paid, the consigned money may be recovered.

For procedure for consignation, see r. 33.4 and note 33.4.3 and r. 33.12.

Motions to summon assessors

12.3. A party seeking to summon an assessor shall—
(*a*) enrol a motion for that purpose not less than 28 days before the diet of the proof or hearing at which the presence of an assessor is sought; and
(*b*) give written intimation of the motion to every other party not less than seven days before it is enrolled.

Deriv. R.C.S. 1965, r. 39(*a*)

General note. The purpose of this rule is to ensure that applications do not come so late as to **12.3.1** make arrangements for summoning the assessor difficult.

"motion". For motions, see Chap. 23. **12.3.2**

"not less than 28 days before" and *"not less than seven days before"*. The date from which the **12.3.3** period is calculated is not counted.

"proof or hearing". See note 12.1.3. **12.3.4**

Copies of pleadings for use of assessors

12.4.—(1) Where an assessor is summoned by the court at its own instance, the pursuer or petitioner, as the case may be, shall lodge in process such copy of the closed record or other pleadings in the cause as the court directs for the use of the assessor.

(2) Where a motion under rule 12.3 (motions to summon assessors) has been granted, the party who enrolled the motion shall lodge in process a copy of the closed record or other pleadings in the cause for the use of the assessor.

Deriv. R.C.S. 1965, r. 39(*c*)

Selection of assessors

12.5.—(1) Subject to paragraph (2), an assessor shall be selected by agreement between the parties, failing which, by the court on the motion of a party.

(2) A nautical assessor shall be selected from the list of persons—
(*a*) approved by the Lord President;
(*b*) kept by the Principal Clerk; and
(*c*) published as the Lord President shall direct.

(3) The list of nautical assessors published under paragraph (2) shall be in force for a period of three years; but a person on that list may be approved in any subsequent list.

Deriv. Nautical Assessors (Scotland) Act 1894, s. 4; R.C.S. 1965, r. 38 (r. 12.5(1)) and r. 46(*a*) (r. 12.5(2))

12.5.1   *General note.* Where the parties cannot agree on the person to be appointed, one party will have to enrol a motion to have the court appoint an assessor. The motion should include the names of one or more persons from whom the appointment may be made.

12.5.2   *"motion".* For motions, see Chap. 23.

12.5.3   *"list of nautical assessors".* [*Omitted by the Act of Sederunt (Rules of the Court of Session Amendment) (Miscellaneous) 2007 (S.S.I. 2007 No. 7), para. 2(2) (effective 26th February 2007).*]

Number of assessors

12.6.—(1) For a proof or hearing in the Outer House, only one assessor shall be summoned.

(2) In the case of—

(a) a proof or hearing ordered by a Division of the Inner House to be taken by one of the judges of the Inner House, or

(b) a hearing in the Inner House,

the number of assessors to be summoned shall be such number as the court thinks fit.

Deriv. R.C.S. 1965, r. 43

12.6.1   *General note.* Application of paragraph (2) of this rule is even more rare than the appointment of an assessor in the Outer House. A proof or hearing in the Inner House is also rare.

Skilled witnesses where assessors summoned

12.7.—(1) In a cause arising out of a collision at sea where the court is assisted by a nautical assessor at a proof, no party may lead a skilled witness on nautical matters.

(2) In a cause other than one to which paragraph (1) applies, where the court is assisted by an assessor at a proof, a party may not lead evidence from more than one skilled witness on any matter within the special qualifications of the assessor.

(3) Where a question arises at a proof in relation to the application of paragraph (2), the decision of the Lord Ordinary shall be final and not subject to review.

(4) In a cause to which paragraph (2) applies, the court may, on the motion of a party—

(a) enrolled not less than 14 days before the diet of proof, and

(b) of which written intimation has been given to every other party not less than seven days before the motion is enrolled,

on cause shown, allow evidence to be led from a greater number of skilled witnesses.

Deriv. R.C.S. 1965, r. 146 (r. 12.7(1)) and r. 42 (r. 12.7(2) to (4))

12.7.1   *General note.* The limitation on the number of skilled witnesses, other than one arising out of a collision at sea, is subject to the right to seek leave to allow additional skilled witnesses (r. 12.7(4)).

12.7.2   *"nautical matters".* In a cause arising out of a collision at sea where a nautical assessor is appointed, there can be no skilled witness on nautical matters: r. 12.7(1). "Nautical matters" must mean the matters on which a nautical assessor may advise: see *McLean v. Johnstone* (1906) 8 F. 836, 838; and see notes 12.1.1 and 12.7.3.

12.7.3   *"any matter within the . . . qualifications of the assessor".* A nautical assessor's special qualifications are as a seaman. In *The Nerano v. The Dromedary* (1895) 22 R. 237, it was held that deductions about the speed of a vessel were a matter of engineering and not of nautical skill and experience.

12.7.4   *"final and not subject to review".* The decision of the Lord Ordinary cannot be reclaimed against.

"not less than 14 days before" and "not less than 7 days before". The date from which the **12.7.5**
period is calculated is not counted.

"written intimation". For methods, see r. 16.9.   **12.7.6**

"motion". For motions, see Chap. 23.   **12.7.7**

Note of questions submitted to assessors

12.8. The judge who presides at a proof or hearing to which an assessor is summoned shall make a note of each question submitted to the assessor and of the answer; and the note shall be lodged in process.

Deriv. Nautical Assessors (Scotland) Act 1894, s.3; R.C.S. 1965, r. 45

General note. The importance of compliance with this rule was stressed by L.P. Clyde in *SS*   **12.8.1**
"Rowan" v. "West Camak" 1923 S.C. 316, 342, because it is necessary for the appeal court (and parties considering reclaiming) to know precisely what advice was given. An example of questions put to an assessor can be found in *Hoek van Holland Maatschappij v. Clyde Shipping Co. Ltd* (1902) 5 F. 227, 231.

Remuneration of assessors

12.9. The remuneration to be paid to an assessor, other than in a cause under the Patents Act 1977, shall, unless the court otherwise directs, be treated as expenses in the cause.

Deriv. Nautical Assessors (Scotland) Act 1894, s.5; R.C.S. 1965, r. 44(b)

General note. The remuneration of an assessor in a cause under the Patents Act 1977 is   **12.9.1**
governed by s.98(2) of that Act which provides that the remuneration is to be determined by the Lord President with the consent of the Minister of the Civil Service to be defrayed out of monies provided by Parliament (and not by a party). The remuneration of any other assessor will have to be agreed between the assessor and the party (or parties) seeking to appoint him. A sum which the court thinks fit to meet the fees and expenses of the assessor has to be consigned into court: r. 12.2. R.C.S. 1965, r. 46(b) which provided for an assessor to be paid £6.30 per day has not been re-enacted.

Initiation and progress of proceedings

CHAPTER 13

SUMMONSES, NOTICE, WARRANTS AND CALLING

Initiation of causes by summons

13.1. Subject to any other provision in these Rules, all causes originating in the court shall be commenced in the Outer House by summons.

Deriv. R.C.S. 1965, r. 69 (part)

"Subject to any other provision". The other provisions are: (a) petitions (rr. 14.2 and 14.3); (b)   **13.1.1**
a counterclaim (r. 25.1); (c) a third party notice (r. 26.1); (d) special cases under s.27 of the C.S.A. 1988 (r. 77.2); (e) applications and references treated as appeals or stated cases—see note 3.2.3; (f) applications made as part of an existing process—*i.e.* by minute, note or motion; (g) applications for letters of inhibition or arrestment: r. 59.1.

"summons". A summons is a writ running in the name of the Sovereign whereas a petition,   **13.1.2**
minute, note or other application is simply addressed to the court. A summons is the appropriate form for seeking to establish a right or remedy against a person; a petition is an *ex parte* application seeking the authority of the court for something to be done which otherwise the petitioner would not be able to do or cause to be done: see Maclaren on *Court of Session Practice*, p. 825. "The object of the summons is to enforce a pursuer's legal right against a defender who resists it, or to protect a legal right which the defender is infringing; the object of a petition, on the other hand, is to obtain from the administrative jurisdiction of the court power to do something or to require something to be done, which it is just and proper should be done, but which the petitioner has no legal right to do or to require, apart from judicial authority":

Report of the Royal Commission on the Court of Session 1927 (Cmd. 2801), pp. 49–50. A summons involves a more formal procedure than a petition.

The signeting of a summons confers authority, without more, to execute forms of diligence on the dependence and intimations stated in the warrant (see r. 13.6); in any other case the authority has to be applied for (see r. 13.8).

Form of summonses

13.2.—(1) Subject to any other provision in these Rules, a summons shall be in Form 13.2–A.

(2) A conclusion in a summons shall be stated in accordance with the appropriate style, if any, in Form 13.2–B.

(3) Subject to rule 46.6(3) (no condescendence or pleas-in-law in ship collision actions), there shall be annexed to a summons—

(a) a statement, in the form of numbered articles of the condescendence, of the averments of fact which form the grounds of the claim; and

(b) appropriate pleas-in-law.

(4) A condescendence shall include averments stating—

(a) in an action to which the Civil Jurisdiction and Judgments Act 1982 applies, the domicile of the defender (to be determined in accordance with the provisions of that Act) so far as known to the pursuer;

(b) the ground of jurisdiction of the court, unless jurisdiction would arise only if the defender prorogated the jurisdiction of the court without contesting jurisdiction;

(c) unless the court has exclusive jurisdiction, whether or not there is an agreement prorogating the jurisdiction of a court in another country; and

(d) whether or not there are proceedings involving the same cause of action in subsistence between the parties in a country to which the convention in Schedule 1 or 3C to the Civil Jurisdiction and Judgments Act 1982 applies and the date any such proceedings commenced.

(5) A summons may include warrants for diligence and intimation in so far as permitted under these Rules.

[1] (6) A summons may include a draft interlocutor in Form 43.1A (actions based on clinical negligence: authority to raise as ordinary action).

Deriv. R.C.S. 1965, r. 70(1)(a), (b) and (2) amended by S.I. 1984 No. 472 (r. 13.2(1) to (3) and (5)) and r. 70(1)(c) inserted by S.I.1986 No. 1941 and amended by S.I. 1987 No. 1206 (r. 13.2(4))

---

[1] Rule 13.2(6) inserted by S.S.I. 2007 No. 282 (effective 2nd May 2007).

13.2.1   *General note.* Before 1850 a summons was in four parts—the Address, Instance, Conclusions and the Will. S. 1 of the C.S.A. 1850 introduced the addition of a condescendence and pleas-in-law annexed to the summons. A summons is now commonly referred to as including these additional parts, as also in these Rules: see r. 1.3(1) (interpretation of "summons"). The form of a summons now is (1) Instance, (2) Address and Charge, (3) Warrants, (4) Conclusions, (5) Condescendence and (6) Pleas-in-law. The official heading before the instance since at least 1934 as set out in Form 13.2–A, is "In the Court of Session"; but this form has, unfortunately been ignored, and for some reason the subject heading for the Court of Session in the Statutory Instruments Index has been inappropriately used.

Form 13.2–A (in the form approved by the court: r. 4.1(1)) is to be used for every action commenced by summons except where otherwise provided. Variants are provided for in r. 43.19 (optional procedure in certain actions of damages), r. 46.2(2) (Admiralty actions) and r. 47.3 (election of procedure in commercial actions).

The form approved by the court is an official printed form of the first page and backing: see note 4.1.1.

For the use of Form 43.1A to transfer a personal injury action involving clinical negligence actions from the Chap. 43 procedure to ordinary procedure, see r.43.1A.

13.2.2   *Instance.* The instance is dealt with in this note under four headings.

(A) Names, designation and addresses of parties. The better practice is to state full names, but this is not essential. The test is that there must be such specification as identifies the parties intended: *Joel v. Gill* (1859) 22 D. 6, 12 *per* L.J.-C. Inglis; *Anderson v. Stoddart* 1923 S.C. 755; *Kay v. Morrison's Reps.* 1984 S.L.T. 175 ("the representatives of John Morrison" not sufficient). The defender should be a named individual or legal persona: *McLaren v. Procurator Fiscal for the Lothian and Borders* 1992 S.L.T. 844; *cf.* (D)(15) below. A person suing or being sued in a special character, such as a trustee, must have that character set forth: *Bell v. Trotter's Trs.* (1841) 3 D. 380; *Hunter v. L.M.S. Railway Co.* 1938 S.L.T. 598, 599 *per* Lord Jamieson. The practice of stating the occupation (other than a professional one) of parties has generally died out and is not essential.

The current address must be given. Where there has been a recent change of address there is a convenient practice to state the former address also; but a last known address alone where the current address is not known will not be sufficient for service (note repeal of s.3 of the Citation Amendment (Scotland) Act 1882 by the A.S. (R.C.S. 1994) 1994, Sched. 4) and the rules for service where the address is not known must be followed (see r. 16.5). An accommodation address is generally not sufficient, but disclosure of the actual address may be dispensed with by the court in certain circumstances (*e.g.* persistent harassment), the reason for non-disclosure being set out in the condescendence: *Doughton v. Doughton* 1958 S.L.T. (Notes) 34. In a family action, a party may be ordered to disclose an address where it has been withheld to enable access arrangements to work or to disclose a telephone number where the court cannot judge whether the fear of harassment was well-founded; *McLean v. McDonald*, 20th June, 1997, unreported (1997 G.W.D. 25–1236) (order on party's agent to disclose number overturned. Where a party is in prison it is desirable that he should not be designed "at present a prisoner in": P.N. 23rd July 1952; the home address should be stated.

Where a summons is posted to a person in HM Forces Northern Ireland to his private billet the envelope should be addressed as if he were a private citizen and should not disclose his rank and number; where the address of the barracks is known the summons should be sent there: P.N. 17th December 1974. Where the address of the defender is unknown this must be stated: r. 13.3(b); and see note 13.3.2.

A substantial error in the instance will invalidate the cause: *Brown v. Rodger* (1884) 12 R. 340; *Overseas League v. Taylor* 1951 S.C. 105, 107 *per* L.J.-C. Thomson; but not if not material (*Anderson v. Stoddart*, above) or if permitted by amendment under r. 24.1(2)(b)(i) (to correct or supplement designation of party).

(B) Capacity. As a general rule any adult person, sovereign power, corporate body, partnership, trade union or friendly society may, as such, invoke the jurisdiction of the court.

(B)(1) *Aliens.* (a) An alien outside British territory cannot sue the state for a wrong in the national interest (act of state). (b) A friendly alien may not sue the state in respect of wrongs in the national interest: *Poll v. Lord Advocate* (1897) 1 F. 823, 827 *per* Lord Kyllachy. But this dictum is of doubtful authority. The exception here is probably limited to (a) above: *Johnstone v. Pedler* [1921] 2 A.C. 262. (c) An enemy alien—*i.e.* a person of whatever nationality whose residence or place of business is in a foreign country with which the UK is at war (from the date of declaration) or occupied by such country—cannot sue: *Arnauld v. Boick* (1704) Mor. 10159; *Blomert v. Earl of Roxburgh* (1664) Mor. 16091; *Van Uden v. Burrell* 1916 S.C. 391; *Schulze* 1917 S.C. 113. An assignee is in no better position than the enemy alien: *Arnauld*, above; *Johnston Wright v. Goldsmid* 15 Feb. 1809 F.C. Where the pursuer is an enemy alien, the action is sisted until the end of the war: *Craig Line Steamship Co. Ltd v. North British Storage & Transit Co.* 1915 S.C. 113. An enemy alien may defend an action, including bringing a counterclaim arising out of the same cause: *Burgess v. Guild* 12 Jan. 1813 F.C.; but he cannot defend where his real character is that of pursuer: *Weber's Trs. v. Reimer* 1947 S.L.T. 295. A national of an enemy country resident or having a place of business here and complying with residence requirements may sue: *Schulze, Gow & Co. v. Bank of Scotland* 1914 2 S.L.T. 455; *Weiss v. Weiss* 1940 S.L.T. 447.

(B)(2) *Foreign states, diplomats, etc.* Jurisdiction over states is governed by the State Immunity Act 1978 which enabled the UK to ratify the Brussels Convention on Immunity of State-owned Vessels 1926 and Protocol (Cmnd. 7800 (1980)) and the European Convention on State Immunity 1972 (Cmnd. 7742 (1979)). A state (see s.14) is generally immune from the jurisdiction of the court: 1978 Act, s.1, but there are exceptions relating to submission (s.2), commercial transactions (s.3), contracts of employment (s.4), reparation for death, personal injury or damage to property (s.5), immoveable property in the UK (s.6), patents, trade marks, designs or plant breeder's rights (s.7), membership of corporate or unincorporated bodies or partnerships (s.8), disputes which the state has agreed to submit to arbitration (s.9), actions *in rem* or *in personam* against a ship of the state or against a cargo of that state in admiralty causes (s.10) and liability for VAT, customs and excise duty, agricultural levies or rates of commercial premises (s.11). There are exceptions to the exceptions: see ss.3, 4, 8, 9 and 10(6). Heads of state, their families and servants are assimilated (s.20) to that of diplomatic missions under the Diplomatic Privileges Act 1964 which divides diplomats into three categories (agents with immunity except for actions relating to immoveables, succession and activities outside their official functions; administration and technical staff with the same immunity but which does not extend to acts outside their duties; service staff with immunity for acts in the course of their duties). Consular staff of foreign and Commonwealth states and the Republic of Ireland are governed by the Consular Relations Act 1968. International organisations may be granted similar immunities under the International Organisations Act 1968 and 1981 by Order in Council under s.1 or 4 of the 1968 Act. In *Forth Tugs Ltd v. Wilmington Trust Co.* 1987 S.L.T. 153 the court held that the adjudicative jurisdiction of the court which arose in a petitory action by reason of the possession in Scotland of heritable property was not ousted by s.13(2)(b) (as applied by s.13(6)(b)) of the 1978 Act which applied only to enforcement jurisdiction. On enforcement, under s.13(2) of the 1978 Act the property of a State is not subject to diligence for enforcing a judgment unless the property is in use for commercial purposes: 1978 Act, s.13(4). A joint stock company in which a State has a contributing interest does not make the company or the property the property of the State: *Coreck Maritime GmbH v. Sevrybokholodflot* 1994 S.L.T. 893.

(B)(3) *Adults.* A person of 18 years or more (Age of Majority (Scotland) Act 1969, s.1) with ability to manage his own affairs has capacity to sue or be sued.

(B)(4) *Children.* The general rule is that a child (*i.e.* a person under the age of 16 years) has no legal capacity to bring or defend civil proceedings on or after 25th September 1991; the former law will apply to transactions entered into before that date: Age of Legal Capacity (Scotland) Act 1991, ss.1 and 9(e); "transaction" is defined in s.9. The right of a person under the age of 21 years to apply to the court to set aside a transaction entered into while he was over 16 but under 18 and which is a prejudicial transaction does not apply to the bringing or defending of legal proceedings: 1991 Act, s.3(3). A child under 16 does have legal capacity to enter into transactions commonly entered into by persons of his age and circumstances on terms which are reasonable or to consent to medical treatment; a person under 16 has legal capacity to instruct a solicitor in connection with a civil matter and to sue, or defend, if he has a general understanding of what it means to do so, and a child of 12, or over, is presumed to have that understanding; a child of 12 or over has testamentary capacity or capacity to consent to adoption: 1991 Act, s.2. Where a child has a guardian, proceedings may be taken in his or her name. A mother is guardian of her child (as is the father if married to the mother at the time of conception or subsequently), or a person appointed by the court or a person appointed by a parent to be guardian after his death: Law Reform (Parent and Child) (Scotland) Act 1986, ss.1, 3, 4, and 8 (definition of "parental rights"). The existing law in relation to a child who has no guardian, or whose guardian is unable because of a conflict of interest or otherwise or refuses to bring or defend civil proceedings, is retained: 1991 Act, s.1(3)(f). (a) Where a child has no guardian he may sue alone: *Hill v. City of Glasgow Bank* (1879) 7 R. 68, 74–75 *per* L.P. Inglis (a minor); *Ward v. Walker* 1920 S.C. 80. Once the action is in court he may seek appointment of a curator *ad litem*: *Young* (1828) 7 S.220. A defender is entitled to object to the action proceeding until the guardian is added or until the appointment of a curator *ad litem*: *Sinclair v. Stark* (1828) 6 S.336, 338. If the guardian refuses to act (*McConochie v. Binnie* (1847) 9 D. 791; *Kirk v. Scottish Gas Board* 1968 S.C. 328), has an adverse interest (*Bogie v. Bogie* (1840) 3 D. 309) or is incapacitated (*Rankine* (1821) 1 S.118), the action may be brought in the name of the child and the court may appoint a curator *ad litem*. Appointment of a curator *ad litem* is discretionary: *Kirk*, above; and may be made by the court at its own instance: *Drummond's Trs. v. Peel's Trs.* 1929 S.C. 481, 518 *per* Lord Murray. If there is no concurrence and no curator *ad litem* and the defender makes no objection, the defender is barred from contending that a decree against him is void: *Sinclair*, above. (b) Where a child defender has a guardian, the guardian (if known) should be called as defender as well as the child (*King's Trs. v. McLay* (1901) 8 S.L.T. 413) and the conclusions be against both: Stair, I.6.20. If the identity of the guardian is not known, or it is known the child has no guardian or it is not known whether he has a guardian, the action must be brought against the child and "his guardians if he any has"; if not, and it was known that the child had a guardian though his identity was not known, any decree will be null: *Earl of Craven v. Lord Elibank's Trs.* (1854) 16 D. 811. If the guardian cannot or should not act or does not appear, or the child has no guardian, the court will appoint a curator *ad litem*. If the guardian appears, the child is bound by any decree: *Earl of Craven*, above. If the guardian is called but does not appear and a curator *ad litem* was appointed, a decree will be valid (*Agnew v. Earl of Stair* (1822) 1 Shaw's App. 333); if no curator *ad litem* was appointed, the decree will be a valid decree in absence: *Sinclair*, above; *Drummond's Trs.*, above, *per* Lord Hunter at p. 505.

(B)(5) *Incapaces.* A person of unsound mind and incapable of managing his own affairs or of giving instructions for their management has no *persona standi in judicio*: *Reid v. Reid* (1839) 1 D. 400; *Moodie v. Dempster,* 1931 S.C. 553. In family actions special rules apply: see r. 49.17. **I.** The new law:—From 1st April 2002 it is not competent to appoint a curator *bonis*, tutor-dative or tutor-at-law to a person who is aged 16 or over: Adults with Incapacity (Scotland) Act 2000. Existing curators, tutor-dative or tutor-at-law become guardians under the 2000 Act: 2000 Act,

Sched.4, para. 1. Under Pt 2 (continuing attorneys and welfare powers of attorney) and Pt 6 (intervention and guardianship orders), there are already in force, there are continuing attorneys, welfare attorneys, withdrawers, holders of intervention orders and guardians. The scheme of the Act is that incapable adults need measures only to the extent of their incapacity. So, *e.g.* if they can manage their own affairs but need support in their personal welfare they may require one of these persons with powers only in respect of personal welfare either short term or long term. Unlike curators, a guardian may be appointed over property, financial affairs or personal welfare or all such matters. A guardian has power to act as the legal representative in relation to any matters within the scope of the guardianship: 2000 Act, s.64(3). A guardianship order lasts for such period, including an infinitive period, as the sheriff determines unless renewed. Intervention and guardianship orders are made on application to a sheriff. Accordingly, if an incapable adult is incapable of initiating or defending a particular cause, a guardian (or interventioner) may be appointed for that purpose. "Incapable" under the 2000 Act means incapable of acting, making discussions, communicating decisions or retaining the memory of decisions by reason of mental disorder or inability to communicate because of physical disability: 2000 Act, s.1(6) . **II.** The old law:—(a) Where an *incapax* has a guardian the action should be brought in the name of the guardian, *i.e.* a tutor-at-law (under the Curators Act 1585), a tutor-dative (under the common law; Stair I.6.25), or a *curator bonis* (see note 61.1.2); the action should be brought in the name of the tutor, failing whom the *curator bonis*: *Young v. Rose* (1839) 1 D.1242. If the tutor is unwilling to raise the action, a *curator bonis* may be appointed to do so (see note 61.1.2). Where an *incapax* has neither a tutor nor a *curator bonis*, the proper course is to petition for the appointment of a tutor-at-law, failing whom a tutor-dative, failing whom a *curator bonis* who may bring the action. It remains competent to petition for the appointment of the nearest male agnate as tutor-at-law under the Curators Act 1585: *Britton v. Britton's Curator Bonis* 1996 S.C. 178; and see note 14.2.11. A petition for the appointment of a *curator bonis* is made under Chap. 61. It is not competent to bring the action in the name of the *incapax* and thereafter seek appointment of a *curator ad litem*: *Moodie*, above. (b) Where an *incapax* defender has a tutor (at law or dative) or a *curator bonis*, the action is brought against both the incapax and his tutor, failing whom his *curator bonis*. Where, despite the appointment of a tutor (at law or dative) a *curator bonis* continues to have authority to manage the estate of the *incapax* (as in *Dick v. Douglas* 1924 S.C. 787), the action should be raised against both tutor and *curator bonis*. If an *incapax* defender has neither tutor (at law or dative) nor *curator bonis*, a *curator bonis* (and perhaps a *curator ad litem*) should be appointed before the action comes into court. If neither the *incapax* nor a relative is willing to petition for the appointment, the pursuer, having an interest in the estate of the *incapax* may do so: see note 61.1.2(1). (c) Where a person becomes *incapax* during the dependence of an action a *curator bonis* should be appointed by petition: *Anderson's Trs v. Skinner* (1871) 8 S.L.R. 325; or possibly a curator *ad litem*: *Moodie*, above.

   (C) Title and interest. A pursuer must have title and interest to sue. The pursuer must have title at the date of bringing the action; if not, the lack of it cannot subsequently be made good by assignation (*Symington v. Campbell* (1894) 21 R. 434) or by retrocession (*Bentley v. Macfarlane* 1964 S.C. 76), though a qualified title may be cleared or a title completed (*Bentley*, above). Title may be contingent: *Rae v. Meek* (1888) 15 R. 1033; affd (1889) 16 R.(H.L.) 31, 33. Title must be pled: *Bentley*, above; *Microwave Systems (Scotland) Ltd v. Electro-Physiological Instruments Ltd* 1971 S.C. 140; and must continue until judgment: *Donaghy v. Rollo* 1964 S.C. 278.
   There must be interest as well as title, though to some extent they run into each other: *Summerlee Iron Co. Ltd v. Lindsay* 1907 S.C. 1161, 1165 *per* L.P. Dunedin. Provided there is title the interest need not be large or pecuniary: *Strang v. Steuart* (1864) 2 M. 1015, 1029 *per* L.J.-C. Inglis, *obiter*, but see *Smith v. Shields* (1830) 8 S. 553 (pursuer could recover nothing); *School Boards of Dunlop & Stewarton v. Patrons of Cunninghame Graham Endowment Fund* 1910 S.C. 945 (interest too remote). A person may have an interest but no title to enforce it: *Adams v. Johnson* 1920 2 S.L.T. 328.
   Title to sue involves some legal relation which gives the pursuer some right which the defender either infringes or denies: *D. & J. Nicol v. Dundee Harbour Trs* 1915 S.C.(H.L.) 7, 12 *per* Lord Dunedin; *Simpson v. Edinburgh Corporation* 1960 S.C. 313. Interest means some benefit from asserting the right. In establishing interest, it is no longer necessary to show that the question at issue involves pecuniary rights or status as was stated by Lord Ardwell in *Swanson v. Manson* 1907 S.C. 426, at p. 429. There must be a real issue, the existence of a sufficient interest being essentially a matter depending on the circumstances of the case: *Lennox v. Scottish Branch of the British Show Jumping Association* 1996 S.L.T. 353 applying *Scottish Old People's Welfare Council, Ptrs* 1987 S.L.T. 179 (see also *Watson v. Independent Broadcasting Authority* 1979 S.C. 351; *Gunstone v. Scottish Women's Amateur Athletic Association* 1987 S.L.T. 611). In *Shariff v. Hamid* 2000 S.L.T. 294 (OH), Lord Nimmo Smith held that a person who regularly worshipped at and contributed financially to an Islamic Studies Centre had title and interest to sue in a petition for removal of trustees of the centre which was in public trust.

Every person called as a defender has title to defend, though the defence may not prevail as being irrelevant or because the defender has no interest. A person who has title and interest may be sisted as a defender. All interested persons should be called as defenders and a defender may plead that all parties have not been called (see note 18.1.4(A)(1)); but there is an equitable discretion in the court not to enforce this where it would defeat the action: *Gibson v. Smith* (1849) 11 D. 1024.

A defender objecting to the title or interest of the pursuer (see note 18.1.4(A)(7)) or to the fact that all parties are not called (see note 18.1.4(A)(1)) must state a preliminary plea to that effect: *Lade v. Largs Baking Co.* (1863) 2 M. 17.

(D) Title of particular persons.

(D)(1) *Administrator of company.* See corporate bodies, (D)(6) below.

(D)(1A) *Advocate General.* See Lord Advocate, (D)(12) below.

(D)(2) *Agent and principal.* An agent acting ostensibly as principal may sue or be sued in his own name; the principal may disclose himself and sue, or be sued if discovered, in which case the pursuer must elect which to sue as liability is alternative and not joint and several: Bell's *Comm.*, i,540; *Bennett v. Inveresk Paper Co.* (1891) 18 R. 975. It is suggested by Gloag that an undisclosed principal can sue only if the contract is assignable: Gloag on *Contract*, pp. 128–129; and see *Salton v. Clydesdale Bank* (1898) 1 F. 110. In the case of an agent acting as agent for an undisclosed principal there is little authority (Gloag, p. 138); but see *Ferrier v. Dods* (1865) 3 M. 561. A disclosed principal and not his agent, as a general rule, must sue or be sued in his own name: Bell's *Comm.*, i,540; *McIvor v. Roy* 1970 S.L.T.(Sh.Ct) 58; but the general rule does not apply if the agent has an interest in the transaction (*MacKenzie v. Cormack* 1950 S.C. 183), where obligations are undertaken by the agent (*Johnston v. Little* 1960 S.L.T. 129), where the principal is an unincorporated body which cannot be sued as a club (*Thomson v. Victoria Eighty Club* (1905) 43 S.L.R. 628) or where the agent acts for a company not yet formed (*Tinnevelly Sugar Refining Co. Ltd v. Mirrlees, Watson & Yaryan Co. Ltd* (1894) 21 R. 1009). There is a presumption of fact that an agent acting for a disclosed foreign principal intends to be bound and may sue and be sued in his own name: *Millar v. Mitchell* (1860) 22 D. 833.

(D)(3) *Assignee.* An assignee may sue in his own name or that of his cedent or sist himself as pursuer in his cedent's action: *Fraser v. Duguid* (1838) 16 S. 1130. It is permissible for persons to assign their right to sue to a person who sues as their assignee. He should sue as "assignee of (*name of cedent*)".

(D)(4) *Bankrupt.* The permanent trustee may sue or be sued or sist himself to a current action in relation to the debtor's estate vested in him (with consent of commissioners, creditors or the court where there are commissioners): Bankruptcy Act 1985, s.39(2)(b); but not in actions in respect of the debtor's status or personal affairs unless his estate is affected: *Corbidge v. Somerville* 1913 S.C. 858. He cannot initiate a claim for solatium, which is personal to the debtor (*Muir's Tr. v. Braidwood* 1958 S.C. 169); but once litiscontestation has taken place, the personal quality of the claim is shed so that it is capable of being acquired by the trustee (*Watson v. Thompson* 1991 S.C. 447). The bankrupt until discharged and reinvested with his estate (*Flett v. Mustard* 1936 S.C. 269) has no title to pursue actions which his trustee may and does pursue (*Dickson v. United Dominion Trusts Ltd* 1988 S.L.T. 19). The bankrupt may sue or be sued in respect of certain dealings with his sequestrated estate, *e.g.* where his trustee has abandoned to the bankrupt the property to which the dealing relates or he has authorised the dealing or is personally barred and the third party was unaware of the sequestration (1985 Act, s.32(9)); or he has abandoned the right to pursue the claim (*Dickson*, above); the right must be averred: *Grindall v. John Mitchell (Grangemouth) Ltd* 1984 S.L.T. 335. The trustee may sue or be sued in his own name as "trustee in sequestration of (*name of bankrupt*)".

(D)(5) *Beneficiary.* Where there is a trustee, or an executor, a beneficiary cannot sue the estate's debtor: *Hinton & Co. v. Connell's Trs* (1883) 10 R. 1110; *Morrison v. Morrison's Exrx* 1912 S.C. 892; though a special legatee may sue if he makes the executor a defender: *Young v. Ramage* (1838) 16 S. 572, 578 *per* Lord Corehouse. The beneficiary may compel the trustee to give the use of his name on security for expenses or to grant an assignation of his claim: *Morrison*, above. He has title to sue one or more of his trustees for breach of trust; if there are other beneficiaries, intimation should be made to the others as a decision might be *res judicata* against them: *Allen v. McCombie's Trs* 1909 S.C. 710.

(D)(6) *Corporate bodies.* (a) Corporations are constituted by Royal Charter, letters patent or by or under Act of Parliament (*e.g.* the Companies Acts). As a general rule an incorporated body alone and not its members has title to sue or be sued in respect of matters affecting them as a body. The majority of members has title to sue in respect of an act done irregularly without their approval (and not illegally or *ultra vires*) and the action is brought in the name of one against the corporation; if the act is *ultra vires*, illegal or a fraud on the minority, a member of the minority may sue: *North West Transportation Co. v. Beatty* (1887) 12 App.Cas. 589; and where a member complains that the affairs of a company are being conducted in a manner unfairly prejudicial to the interests of some of its members, he may apply to the court for certain orders including an order to authorise civil proceedings: Companies Act 1985, s.461. A company cannot sue for damages on a contract entered into on its behalf before it came into existence: *Tinnevelly Sugar Refining Co. Ltd v. Mirrlees, Watson & Yaryan Co. Ltd* (1894) 21 R. 1009. The means of incorporation should be stated in the instance. A registered company is a body corporate: 1985 Act, s.13(3). Industrial and provident societies are bodies corporate: Industrial and Provident Societies Act 1965, s.3. Building societies are incorporated under the Building Societies Act 1986. The Universities of St Andrews, Glasgow, Aberdeen and Edinburgh may sue and be sued as such: Universities (Scotland) Act 1858, s.25. The University courts of each university are corporate bodies: Universities (Scotland) Act 1889, s.5(3). The Scottish Parliament is a corporate body, Scotland Act 1998, s.21, the Scottish Parliamentary Corporate Body. A company in receivership which sues may be required to find caution for expenses as the receiver is not personally liable: Companies Act 1985, s.726(2). (b) Administrators and receivers. An administrator of a company appointed under s.8 or 13 of the Insolvency Act 1986 acts as agent of the company (s.14(5)) and may sue or be sued in the name of the company (Sched. 1, para. 5). Proceedings cannot be commenced or continued against a company without the consent of the administrator or the court: 1986 Act, s.11(3)(d); and on the meaning of "proceedings", note *Air Ecosse Ltd v. Civil Aviation Authority* 1987 S.L.T. 751, *Re Barrow Borough Transport Ltd* [1990] Ch. 227 and *Carr v. British International Helicopters Ltd* [1993] B.C.C. 855, and see further note 74.10.1. A receiver appointed under s.51 or s.54 of the 1986 Act para. 5). Proceedings cannot be commenced or continued against a company without the consent of the administrator or the court: 1986 Act, s.11(3)(d); and on the meaning of "proceedings", note *Air Ecosse Ltd v. Civil Aviation Authority* 1987 S.L.T. 751, *Re Barrow Borough Transport Ltd* [1990] Ch. 227 and *Carr v. British International Helicopters Ltd* [1993] B.C.C. 855, and see further note 74.10.1. A receiver appointed under s.51 or s.54 of the 1986 Act acts as agent of the company (s.57(1)) and may sue or be sued in the name of the company (Sched. 2, para. 5). An administrator or receiver has the right to take proceedings to take possession of and get in the property of the company (Scheds 1 and 2, para. 1) and this has been interpreted as giving either officer title to sue in his own name for possessory purposes; but where he seeks recovery of a debt due to the company in respect of a contract entered into before the receivership he must sue in the company's name: *Taylor v. Scottish and Universal Newspapers Ltd* 1981 S.C. 408; *Myles J. Callaghan Ltd v. City of Glasgow D.C.* 1988 S.L.T. 227. (c) Liquidators. The liquidator of a company sues or is sued in the name of the company: 1986 Act, s.165(3) and Sched. 4, Pt II. Proceedings against a company in liquidation may not be proceeded with or commenced without leave of the court (1986 Act, s.130(2)) but leave is not required for a counterclaim for set off against the sum due (*G. & A. (Hotels) Ltd v. T.H.B. Marketing Services Ltd* 1983 S.L.T. 497).

(D)(7) *Crown.* See Lord Advocate and Advocate General for Scotland, and Secretary of State for Scotland, (D)(12) and (15) below.

(D)(8) *Executors.* Executors hold the estate of the deceased *pro indiviso* and must concur in suing together in an action relating to the estate, though if any refuse or are called as defenders their consent is dispensed with: Stair, III.viii.59. The powers of an executor, nominate or dative, are the same as those of a trustee: Trusts (Scotland) Act 1921, s.2; Succession (Scotland) Act 1964, s.20. Where executors refuse to sue, beneficiaries may sue in name of the executors, giving indemnity for expenses: *Morrison v. Morrison's Exrx* 1912 S.C. 892. An executor has title before confirmation so long as he confirms before extract: *Fyffe v. Fergusson* (1842) 4 D. 1482; *Mackay v. Mackay* 1914 S.C. 200. As a general rule a cause of action which A has against B is not extinguished by the death of either A or B and the right survives in the executors; but there are exceptions: (a) In uncompleted contracts involving *delectus personae*: *Hoey v. McEwan & Auld* (1867) 5 M. 814. (b) A right to damages under s.1 of the Damages (Scotland) Act 1976 (as amended by s.1 of the Damages (Scotland) Act 1993) which is vested in a relative of the deceased transmits to the executor of the relative in respect of the period to the relative's death: 1976 Act, s.1A as amended by the 1993 Act, s.2. (c) A right to damages in respect of personal injuries including solatium sustained by the deceased and vested in him before his death transmits to his executor, other than patrimonial loss or solatium after the date of death: 1976 Act, s.2(1)–(3) as amended by the 1993 Act, s.3. (d) A right to sue in respect of defamation or other verbal injury or other injury to reputation if the action to enforce that right had been brought by the deceased and concluded before his death: 1976 Act, ss.2(4) and 2A(2) as amended by the 1993 Act, ss.3 and 4. Executors sue or are sued as "(*name and address*) the executor(s) [–nominate *or as the case may be*] of (*name of deceased*)".

(D)(9) *Insured person.* A person indemnified under an insurance policy against damage may sue or be sued. On the principle of subrogation, on payment under the policy to the insured, the insurer may sue in the name of the insured; if the insured, after payment, recovers from the third party he must account to the insurer: *Castellain v. Preston* (1883) 11 Q.B.D. 380; see also *Napier v. Hunter* [1993] 2 W.L.R. 42.

(D)(9A) *Guardian.* A guardian appointed to a person aged 16 or over under the Adults with

Incapacity (Scotland) Act 2000 normally has the power to act as the legal representative in relation to any matter within the scope of the power conferred by the guardianship order: 2000 Act, s.64(3). A guardian appointed under the 2000 Act may have conferred on him the power to pursue or defend an action of declarator of nullity of marriage or divorce or separation: 2000 Act, s.64(1)(c). A guardian to a child under 16 may be appointed to be the legal representative of the child: Children (Scotland) Act 1995, s.11(2)(b). A person given power under an intervention order under s. 53(1) of the 2000 Act, to make decisions and give instructions in respect of an action, does not require to be sisted as a party to the action, the order being sufficient authority: *Riley v. James Beaton & Co (Plumbers) Ltd*, 2004 S.L.T. 1083 (OH).

(D)(10) *Landlord and tenant.* Each has title to sue in respect of a nuisance by a third party and may sue in the same action if both are affected: *Jolly v. Brown* (1828) 6 S. 872.

(D)(11) *Liquidator.* See corporate bodies, (D)(6) above.

(D)(12) *Lord Advocate and Advocate General for Scotland.* Civil proceedings brought by or against any part of the Scottish Administration on or after 1st July 1999 are brought by or against the Lord Advocate; in any other case (including any U.K. Government department), the proceedings are brought by or against the Advocate General: Crown Suits (Scotland) Act 1857, ss.1–4A as amended by Sched. 8, para. 2 of the Scotland Act 1998. The "Scottish Administration" is defined by s.126(6)–(8) of the Scotland Act 1998 as meaning the office-holders (Scottish Executive, junior ministers and non-ministerial offices (*e.g.* Registrar General of Births, Deaths and Marriages for Scotland, Keeper of the Registers of Scotland, Keeper of the Records for Scotland) and staff). The Lord Advocate will retain most of his statutory and other functions he currently has of representing the public interest in litigation (because they are not reserved matters for the U.K. Government). But some functions are transferred to the Advocate General: see Transfer of Functions (Lord Advocate and Advocate General for Scotland) Order 1999 (S.I. 1999 No. 679). During the transitional period of 20th May (the date on which the Scottish Law Officers cease to be members of the U.K. Government: Scotland Act 1998 (Commencement) Order 1998, Art. 2(2) and Sched. 4 (S.I. 1998 No. 3216)) to 1st July 1999, unnecessarily complicated provisions apply. Devolved matters remain the responsibility of the U.K. Government; however, *new* civil proceedings brought by or against the U.K. Government during this period should be brought by or against the Advocate General and not the Lord Advocate. During this transitional period any interest of the Lord Advocate in *pending* civil proceedings by or against the Lord Advocate will (unless it relates to crime or deaths) transfer to the Advocate General: Scotland Act 1998 (General Transfer, Transitional and Savings Provisions) Order 1999, Art. 6 (S.I. 1999 No. 901); but, by virtue of Art. 8 of that Order it may not be necessary to amend the pleadings. From 1st July 1999 any interest of the Advocate General in civil proceedings will transfer to the Lord Advocate if they would have been taken by or against the Scottish Administration if they had been commenced on that date: S.I. 1999 No. 901, Art. 7. The Advocate General is, therefore, after 1st July 1999 the person to sue and be sued on behalf of the Crown and government departments in relation to matters for which he has authority to act: (a) Exchequer causes—*i.e.* all revenues and duties of customs and excise and all other revenues, duties, debts and profits of the Crown and fines, forfeitures and penalties arising to the Crown, except where otherwise provided in an enactment (*e.g.* the Inland Revenue Commissioners who sue and are sued as such in relation to matters under s.13 of the Stamp Act 1891 or s.56 of the Taxes Management Act 1970): C.S.A. 1988, s.22; (b) causes by or against the Crown or a public department other than the Scottish Administration (generally the U.K. or English departments including the Treasury and the Admiralty (*Lord Advocate v. Argyllshire C.C.* 1950 S.C. 304)): Crown Suits (Scotland) Act 1857, ss.1–4A (the sections are permissive and not exclusive); see also (D)(15) below and *Cameron v. Lord Advocate* 1952 S.C. 165, 169 *per* Lord Mackay. S.17 of the Crown Proceedings Act 1947 (which provides for government departments in England to sue and be sued in their own names) does not apply to Scotland: 1947 Act, s.42. It is not competent to challenge the title of the Lord Advocate or the Advocate General on the ground that he has produced no authority: 1857 Act, s.3. The Lord Advocate is styled "[The Rt Hon.] (*name*), The Lord Advocate, [as representing (*name of government department*)], Lord Advocate's Chambers, Crown Office, 25 Chambers Street, Edinburgh EH1 1LA". (The Lord Advocate is no longer styled "Her Majesty's Advocate" in the Crown Suits Act 1857, no doubt because a distinction has to be made between him and the Advocate General.) The Advocate General is styled "[The Rt Hon. (*if that is the case*)] (*name*), The Advocate General for Scotland [as representing (*name of Government department*)], Office of the Solicitor to the Advocate General for Scotland, Victoria Quay, Edinburgh, EH6 6QQ". It would appear that, in Exchequer causes (unless otherwise provided) by virtue of s.22 of the C.S.A. 1988 and in causes in relation to the interest of the Crown or a public department by virtue of s.1 of the 1857 Act (see *Lord Advocate v. Black* 1995 S.L.T. 540), the Law Officers may in fact sue or be sued as "The Lord Advocate" or "The Advocate General for Scotland", as the case may be, and need not be named.

(D)(13) *Partnership.* A firm (an association of persons carrying on business in common with a view to profit: Partnership Act 1890, ss.1, 4 and 45) has a legal persona distinct from its partners. A firm with a social name (the names of its partners past or present) may sue or be sued in the firm name alone: *Forsyth v. John Hare & Co.* (1834) 13 S. 42; *cf. Brims & Mackay v. Pattullo* 1907 S.C. 1106 (new firm cannot sue for debts of old firm unless suing under arrangement for debts of old firm when that capacity must be set forth in the instance). An individual partner may sue in the firm name for firm debts: *Kinnes v. Adam & Sons* (1882) 9 R. 698, 699 *per* Lord McLaren. A firm with a descriptive name may sue or be sued in the firm name together with three of its partners (or all if less than three): *Antermony Coal Co. v. Walter Wingate & Co.* (1866) 4 M. 1017. There is now no Business Names Register, but a duty to disclose the names of persons using business names was introduced by the Companies Act 1981, s.29 (now the Business Names Act 1985, s.4). A person in breach of these provisions may have a claim of his dismissed if a defender was unable to pursue his claim against that person: 1985 Act, s.5. Where surviving partners sue for a debt due to the firm it is good practice to name the dissolved firm in the instance. A limited liability partnership (LLP or llp) is a body corporate (see (D)(6), above), a legal personality separate from its members: Limited Liability Partnership Act 2000.

(D)(14) *Receiver.* See corporate bodies, (D)(6) above.

(D)(14A) *Scottish Administration.* Proceedings by or against the Scottish Administration are brought by or against the Lord Advocate (subject to transitional provisions): see (D)(12) above.

(D)(14B) *Scottish Parliament.* Proceedings by or against the Parliament are instituted by or against the Scottish Parliamentary Corporate Body: Scotland Act 1998, s.40(1). Proceedings by or against the Presiding Officer or a member of the staff of the Parliament are instituted by or against the corporate body on his behalf: 1998 Act, s.40(2). A member of the public does not have title to interdict a member of the Parliament to secure that the member complies with the rule about members' interests. In art.6 of the Scotland Act 1998 (transitory and Transitional Provisions) (Members' Interests) Order 1999 [S.I. 1999 No.1350]: *Whaley v. Lord Watson of Invergowrie* 2000 S.C. 340.

(D)(15) *Secretary of State for Scotland.* It is customary for him to sue and be sued (as an officer of state) for the Scottish Office and the departments for which he is responsible. The departments within the Scottish Office, which are not separate legal entities (Reorganisation of Offices (Scotland) Act 1939) are the Scottish Office Agriculture and Fisheries Department, the Scottish Office Education Department, the Scottish Office Environment Department, the Scottish Office Home and Health Department and the Scottish Office Industry Department. He sues or is sued as "The Secretary of State for Scotland"; it is not necessary to name him: 1939 Act, s.1(8).

(D)(16) *Several defenders.* A pursuer may not, as a general rule, sue more than one defender in one action with separate conclusions based on separate and independent debts: Maclaren on *Court of Session Practice,* p. 388; *Liquidators of the Western Bank of Scotland v. Douglas* (1860) 22 D. 447; *Treadwell's Drifters Inc. v. RCL Ltd* 1996 S.L.T. 1048. An exception arises where there is sufficient connection between individual defenders having regard to the subject-matter of the case and the circumstances before the court: *Yoker Housing Association Ltd v. McGurn Logan Duncan & Opfer,* 1998 S.L.T. 1334. Joint or conjunct obligants must be called together and each is liable *pro rata* for his share ("A and B jointly"): *Coats v. Union Bank* 1929 S.C.(H.L.) 114. Joint or conjunct and several obligants must be sued together if the obligation is not in writing or a decree: *Neilson v. Wilson* (1890) 17 R. 608; and each is liable for the whole debt ("A and B jointly and severally"). Where the obligation is in writing or a decree, one may be sued as each is liable in *solidum.* There is a general presumption in favour of liability *pro rata:* Stair, I.xvii.20; but there are many exceptions: parties to a bill or promissory note, partners (Partnership Act 1890, s.9), parties to an obligation *ad factum praestandum: Rankine v. Logie Den Land Co.* (1902) 4 F. 1074. Joint proprietors must all be called together. Proprietors in common should be called together. Joint delinquents may be sued together jointly and severally or severally, or any one of them may be sued as each is liable for the whole damage arising from the combined wrong; and where they are both liable the pursuer gets a joint and several decree he can enforce against any, or if one only is held liable, a decree against that one: *Ellerman Lines Ltd v. Clyde Navigation Trs* 1909 S.C. 690. If defenders are responsible for different acts for which they may be sued in one action, they may not be sued jointly and severally but separately for the wrong by each: *Barr v. Neilsons* (1868) 6 M. 651.

(D)(17) *Several pursuers.* The rule is that parties cannot conjoin in the same action unless there is some connection between the parties in the matters pursued for or they have been aggrieved by the same act: *H.M. Feuers of Orkney v. Steuart,* (1741) Mor. 11986; *Paxton v. Brown,* 1908 S.C. 406, 412–413, (1907) 15 S.L.T. 662, 666 *per* Dunedin, L.P; *Boulting v. Elias,* 1990 S.C. 135, 1990 S.L.T. 597 (First Div.). Although in Paxton, the L.P. said that the connection did not mean the same thing as joint interest in its legal sense, in *Boulting* the court held that the connection must be one in respect of the legal basis on which the claims in the action are made. Joint proprietors (one estate vested in them *pro indiviso*), proprietors of common property or parties having a joint title to enforce a debt or other obligation, as a general rule, must join in one action: *Lawson v. Leith & Newcastle Steam Packet Co.* (1850) 13 D. 175; *Johnston v. Crauford* (1855) 17 D. 1023; *Lade v. Largs Baking Co. Ltd* (1863) 2 M. 17, 21 *per* Lord Deas. But one of them may sue to protect the property from trespass or encroachment (*Warrand v. Watson* (1905) 8 F. 253) or where it would cause injustice not to allow him to do so (*Lawson,* above at 178 *per* L.J.-C. Hope (part-owner of ship entitled to sue for his share of damage)). Unconnected pursuers may sue together for protection of a common right or interest against different defenders (*Cowan & Sons v. Duke of Buccleuch* (1874) 4 R.(HL) 14); but not for the same wrong to different parties in respect of different interests (*Arthur v. Aird* 1907 S.C. 1170; *Smith-Shand's Trs v. Forbes* 1921 S.C. 820; *Concrete Products (Kirkcaldy) Ltd v. Anderson and Menzies* 1996 S.L.T. 587. Where several pursuers sue together the ground of action must be identical and there must be no material prejudice to the defender: *Buchan v. Thomson* 1976 S.L.T. 42, 44 *per* Lord Fraser. Several pursuers having a claim arising out of one injury and the same wrong may sue together; and for claims arising out of the death of a relative, must do so: *Darling v. Gray* (1892) 19 R.(HL) 31, 32 *per* Lord Watson; and see also rules for intimation to connected persons in actions of damages in respect of the death of a relative in Chap. 43, Pt I.

(D)(18) *Trustees.* A majority (other than those having an adverse interest) or all trustees, unless the truster specified a quorum, may sue: *Blisset's Trs v. Hope's Trs* (1854) 16 D. 482. Normally one trustee has no title to sue: *Neilson v. Mossend Iron Co.* (1884) 12 R. 499, 525; *Neilson v. Neilson's Trs* (1885) 12 R. 670, 673; unless to challenge the other trustees or to protect the estate. When suing trustees, all should be called as defenders; though it is competent to sue one trustee for breach of trust of all of them: *Allen v. McCombie's Trs* 1909 S.C. 710. Trustees must sue or be sued as "(*names and addresses*), the trustees of (*name of truster*)": *Bell v. Trotter's Trs* (1841) 3 D. 380.

(D)(19) *Unincorporated bodies.* A trade union or an unincorporated employers' association may sue or be sued in its own name: Trade Union and Labour Relations (Consolidation) Act 1992, ss.10(1)(b) and 127(2)(b). Other unincorporated bodies must sue in their own name with the addition of the names of members authorised to sue, the test being that they should be persons "responsible for the proper prosecution of the action and for giving obedience to the decrees that may be given under it": *Renton Football Club v. McDowall* (1891) 18 R. 670, 674 *per* Lord McLaren; it is sufficient when suing such a body to call the body with its office-bearers or a sufficient number of members to defend its interests: *Somerville v. Rowbotham* (1862) 24 D. 1187, 1189 *per* Lord Neaves. In relation to churches the position is somewhat complicated: on non-established churches, see Lyall, *Of Presbyters and Kings: Church and State in the Law of Scotland* (1980), Chap. 6.

"conclusions". Styles are to be found in Form 13.2–B. A summons may contain any number **13.2.3** of different conclusions. Decree for more than has been concluded for cannot be granted without amendment except in optional procedure reparation cases (see Form 43.18) or in actions of count, reckoning and payment where the words "or such other sum as may be found due" have been added (*Spottiswoode v. Hopkirk* (1853) 16 D. 59).

A single conclusion for payment of a lump sum may include within it a number of heads of specific non-random amounts arising from different events and on different grounds, provided that these are detailed in the condescendence and supported by adequate pleas in law: *Lord Advocate v. Duncan Logan (Construction) Ltd., 1964 S.L.T. 64; Western SMT Co. Ltd. v. Magistrates of Greenock,* 1957 S.L.T. (Notes) 22. It is competent to have alternative conclusions: *e.g.* for implement with damages in the alternative, or for payment failing which declarator of breach of contract and damages; where one conclusion is not satisfied decree may be sought for the alternative conclusion and the first cannot be enforced further: *Bosco Design Services Ltd v. Plastic Sealant Services Ltd* 1979 S.L.T. (Notes) 33. Alternative conclusions may be mutually incompatible: see *Norwich Union Life Insurance Society v. Tanap Investments V.K. Ltd (in liquidation) (No. 1)* 1998 S.L.T. 623, 628C *per* Lord Penrose (conclusions for declarator that sums were due under a minute of agreement and also for rectification of the agreement to reflect that this was the contractual intention). An ancillary conclusion (which fails if the main conclusion fails) is also competent: *Harvey v. Smith* (1904) 6 F. 511, 523.

Expenses as an incident of process may be awarded without being concluded for: *J. Heggie & Co. v. Stark & Selkrig* (1826) 4 S. 510; but it is usual to conclude for expenses, and wise to do so to give notice and if the case is undefended. Interest runs *ex lege* from the date of decree, but it is advisable to conclude for it and this must be done if claimed from a date earlier than decree or for a rate other than that in r. 7.7 (rate of interest on decrees): on interest, see notes 7.7.1–7.7.8. A conclusion for expenses only in the event of appearing and opposing or appearing and occasioning expense is competent, but mere appearance in such a case does not infer liability for expenses: *Henderson v. Innes* 1922 S.L.T. 550.

It is not competent for a defender to enrol a motion for decree in favour of the pursuer in terms of the conclusions of the summons: *Auld & Macdonald v. George Wimpey & Co.* 1977 S.L.T.(Notes) 23.

The absence of any conclusions in a summons is not a fundamental nullity where it is plain to the defender from the pleadings what the nature of the claim against him is, and amendment to add conclusions has been allowed under rr. 2.1 and 24.1.2(a): *Wilson v. Lothian R.C.* 1995 S.L.T. 991.

13.2.4 *"condescendence"*. Formerly each article of condescendence was very short. An unfortunate modern practice has developed of making articles long and cumbersome. Articles should be as short and concise as possible: different facts or events should be stated in separate articles, and a matter known or likely to be disputed should be in a separate article rather than amongst uncontroversial material; this forces a defender clearly to admit or deny and explain facts without hiding behind a general denial. Our whole system of pleading and disposal of cases upon preliminary pleas must depend upon each party stating with candour what are the material facts upon which he relies and admitting the facts stated by his opponent which he knows to be true: *Ellon Castle Estates Co. Ltd v. Macdonald* 1975 S.L.T.(Notes) 66 *per* Lord Stewart.

"It is not the function of pleadings to justify an inquiry which may result in evidence being led which might establish the pleader's case: on the contrary the pleadings must set forth clearly and specifically the facts upon which the pleader aims to succeed in his pleas, so that the other party may have notice of the case against him and the facts upon which it is founded: *Morrison v. Rendall* 1986 S.C. 69, 78 *per* Lord Robertson.

The condescendence must state the facts which, if true, entitle the pursuer to the decree concluded for. Averments are sufficient for relevancy if according to their primary meaning they are sufficient to support the conclusions: *Hope v. Hope's Trs* (1898) 1 F.(H.L.) 1, 3 *per* Lord Watson. The parties and their capacities must be identified. Title to sue must be set forth: *Bentley v. Macfarlane* 1964 S.C. 76, 83 *per* Lord Guthrie; *Microwave Systems (Scotland) Ltd v. Electro-Physiological Instruments Ltd* 1971 S.C. 140, 143 *per* Lord Thomson. The domicile of the defender, the ground of jurisdiction, whether there is an agreement prorogating another jurisdiction and whether there are proceedings elsewhere must be stated: r. 13.2(4). An account of the circumstances must be given. The legal grounds of the action must be set forth, each in separate articles (*Keenan v. Glasgow Corporation* 1923 S.C. 611, 621 *per* Lord Ormidale) and any statutory provision founded on specified (although this is not always essential: *NV Devos Gebroeder v. Sunderland Sportswear Ltd* 1987 S.L.T. 331). An averment which is essential must be stated: *Brown v. Redpath & Co. Ltd* 1963 S.L.T. 219, 222 *per* L.J.-C. Thomson and 224 *per* Lord Mackay (essential to prove reasonable practice). As evidence is relevant if logically connected with the matters in dispute (*Inland Revenue Commissioners v. Stenhouse's Trs* 1993 S.L.T. 248, 251E–F *per* Lord Coulsfield), "collateral" issues may to that extent be averred: *Strathmore Group Ltd v. Crédit Lyonnais* 1994 S.L.T. 1023.

"Believed and averred" is not sufficient except in relation to inferences drawn from facts already stated, or non-essential facts, within the defender's knowledge but not the pursuer's: *McCrone v. Macbeth, Currie & Co.* 1968 S.L.T.(Notes) 24 (facts within pursuer's knowledge); *McCrindle v. Sandelands* 1980 S.L.T.(Notes) 12 (non-essential averment); and see *Brown*, above, at 222 *per* L.J.-C. Thomson, *Strathmore Group Ltd*, above, at 1032K *per* Lord Osborne, *Littlejohn v. Wood & Davidson Ltd*, 1996 G.W.D. 3–168, unreported. Lord Osborne in *Strathmore*, described it as a formula which ought to be used where the pleader is averring, as a matter of inference, a fact which was sought to be inferred from other averments of primary fact: see also *Burnett v. Menzies Dougal WS*, 2006 S.C. 93 (Extra Div).

Alternative and even inconsistent averments of fact may be made: *e.g.* they may be alternative where the precise way in which an accident occurred is not known: *Finnie v. Logie* (1859) 21 D. 825, 829 *per* L. P. McNeill; *Clarke v. Edinburgh & District Tramways Co. Ltd* 1914 S.C. 775, 781 *per* L. P. Strathclyde; see also *M v. M* 1967 S.L.T. 157 (nullity on ground of impotence of pursuer or defender); *Safdar v. Devlin* 1995 S.L.T. 530. The relevancy of alternative averments is tested by reference to the weakest alternative, and if the weakest is irrelevant in law the whole action is irrelevant because the weakest alternative is the only one which the pursuer absolutely offers to prove: *Hope*, above. In *Haig & Ringrose Ltd v. Barrhead Buildings Ltd* 1981 S.L.T. 157, Lord Stott explained the "weakest alternative" test as meaning that if liability arises only on proof of A and the pursuer avers that the fact is A or B, the pleadings are irrelevant; but if both are relevant though one is irrelevant because of lack of specification the court is entitled to sever the irrelevant alternative. The rule that a party perils his case on the weaker alternative applies only where the alternative is weaker in law: *Stewart's Exrs v. Stewart* 1993 S.C. 427, 457A *per* L.P. Hope. If not alternative, averments must not be self-contradictory: Maclaren on *Court of Session Practice*, p. 31. Facts should not be averred for which there is no evidence: *Bousted v. Gardner* (1879) 7 R. 139, 145 *per* L.J.-C. Moncreiff.

In a case of fault, there must be specific averments of fault: *Thomson & Co. v. Pattison, Elder & Co.* (1895) 22 R. 432.

Where fraud is alleged, averments of fraud must be specific: *Shedden v. Patrick* (1852) 14 D. 721, 727 *per* Lord Fullerton. Averments of fraud in a commercial action must meet the same standard: *Kaur v. Singh*, 1998 S.C. 233. For what must be averred in a case of fraud, see *Royal Bank of Scotland plc v. Holmes* 1999 S.L.T. 563, 569K–L, *per* Lord Macfadyen.

The special mention of one thing may operate to exclude things differing from it (*expressio unius est exclusio alterius*): *Buglass v. British Railways Board*, 18th June 1997 (1997 G.W.D. 26–1303) (reference to working at a particular place would exclude evidence about any other place).

Evidence should not be pled (*i.e.* the manner in which the facts averred will be proved): *Tulloch v. Davidson* (1858) 20 D. 1045, 1056 *per* Lord Cowan. So, *e.g.* the contents of an affidavit should not be incorporated into the pleadings, the proper course being to plead the facts on which proof would be led: *Tough v. SPS (Holdings) Ltd*, 8th December 1998 (O.H.), unreported. Similarly, law should not be pled except (a) as a matter of practice, the duties owed in a reparation action; (b) a private Act of Parliament before 1850 (Interpretation Act 1978, s.3); and (c) foreign law if different from Scots law, otherwise it will be presumed to be the same as Scots law (*Emerald Stainless Steel Ltd v. South Side Distribution Ltd* 1982 S.C. 61) unless judicial knowledge must be taken of it (Macphail on *Evidence*, paras 2–04 to 2–07). The presumption that foreign law complies with Scots law is not displaced by a European Community (or Union) regulation which has no effect on the procedural rules applicable to the ascertainment of the proper law: *Kraus v. Sullivan*, 1998 S.L.T. 963 (averments of German law required). But foreign law does not have to be pled and proved where the purpose is not to determine an issue according to the foreign law but to assist in construing a remedy derived from that foreign law: *Roy v. MR Pearlman Ltd* 1999 S.C. 459, 469 *per* Lord Hamilton. In that case it was held proper to look at French law without averment or proof because, in the context of an E.U. directive which provided a remedy drawn from French law, assistance towards a harmonised approach might be obtained by having regard to the experience of the French courts in applying the remedy.

The condescendence must give fair notice of the pursuer's case: *Hope*, above; *Eadie Cairns v. Programmed Maintenance Painting Ltd* 1987 S.L.T. 777. Thus, *e.g.* an averment, that certain matters were stated to "several friends" who were not named, did not give adequate notice and was not admitted to probation: *Boulting v. Elias* 1990 S.C. 135. Also, in pleading vicarious liability, the person who is said to have been negligent should be named or identified; or, if not known, that fact and other circumstances from which the defender would be able to establish by inference that the negligent act had been committed by an employee of the defender should be averred: *Davaney v. Yarrow Shipbuilders Ltd*, 4th December 1998 (O.H.), unreported.

One cannot make a new case at proof for which there is no record: *Morrison's Associated Companies Ltd v. James Rome & Sons Ltd* 1964 S.C. 160, 182 *per* L.P. Clyde (when a duty in general terms is averred followed by a particularisation of the way in which it is alleged that the duty was breached, proof is restricted to the breach of which notice has been given and evidence directed to some other way is excluded); *Carroll v. Scott's Shipbuilding and Engineering Co. Ltd* 1969 S.L.T.(Notes) 46. In *Gibson v. British Rail Maintenance Ltd* 1995 S.L.T. 953 it was held that the breach of duty proved, although taking a different form from that which appeared in the averments, was within the case pled on record. A pursuer is entitled to rely, however, on the defender's averments of fact even if he does not succeed on his own facts so long as it does not involve more than a variation or modification of his own case on the ground pled by him: *O'Hanlon v. John G. Stein & Co.* 1965 S.C.(H.L.) 23. A variation, modification or development of what is averred in one's pleadings is permissible, but not something which is new, separate and distinct: *Burns v. Dixon's Iron Works Ltd* 1961 S.C. 102, 107 *per* L.J.-C. Thomson. The ultimate test is one of fairness: *Maclean v. Forestry Commission* 1970 S.L.T. 265, 272 *per* Lord Wheatley.

As no reference can be made to productions on procedure roll without agreement of parties, if reliance is to be placed for relevancy or specification in pleadings on documents they must be "adopted and held as repeated herein *brevitatis causa*": see *Gordon v. Davidson* (1864) 2 M. 758, 769 *per* L.J.-C. Inglis; *Eadie Cairns*, above *per* Lord Avonside at p. 780E and Lord Jauncey at p. 2783F. The wholesale incorporation of lengthy documents, only parts of which are relevant, is generally unsatisfactory, however, and may well be held not to give the specification required: *Royal Bank of Scotland plc v. Holmes* 1999 S.L.T. 563. In *Prophit v. BBC* 1997 S.L.T. 745, Temporary Judge T. G. Coutts refused to listen to a tape recording of a programme because the issues at procedure roll had to be tested solely on the averments and the tape had not been incorporated into the pleadings. The implication is that if it had been so incorporated, the court would have listened to it.

In general, what a party avers he undertakes the evidential burden of proving. In a reparation case founding on the statutory duty of an employer to provide a safe place of work so far as reasonably practicable, it is for the employer to aver and prove non-practicability: *Nimmo v. Alexander Cowan & Sons* 1967 S.C.(H.L.) 79. A pursuer may plead a particular method of reasonable practicability or no particular method; in the former case this does not discharge the onus on the defender and still entitles the pursuer to cross-examine on other methods: *Gibson v. B.C.C. Co. Ltd* 1963 S.C.(H.L.) 15. So also when the onus of showing that due diligence was exercised transfers to the defender on a case of fault against him: *Gunn v. John McAdam & Son Ltd* 1949 S.C. 31, 40 *per* L.P. Cooper.

In relation to damages, consideration should be given, in a complex case, to whether details of the heads of claim could be set out in a schedule attached to the summons: see, *e.g.*, Scott schedules in building contract cases in England.

13.2.5   *"pleas-in-law"*. These were first required by ss.9 and 11 of the C.S.A. 1825. A plea-in-law ought to be a distinct legal proposition, applicable to the facts of the case: *J. & R. Young & Co. v. Graham* (1860) 23 D. 36 *per* L.J.-C. Inglis. "In the circumstances condescended upon, the pursuer is entitled to decree in terms of the conclusions with expenses" and "The defender being due and resting owing to the pursuer in the sum sued for, decree therefor should be pronounced as concluded for" are not legal propositions.

13.2.6   *"domicile of the defender"*. This is required to be stated in actions to which the C.J.J.A. 1982 applies; it does not apply to causes excluded by Sched. 1, Art. 1 (substituted by the Civil Jurisdiction and Judgments Act 1982 (Amendment) Orders 1990 [S.I. 1990 No. 2591] and 2000 [S.I. 2000 No. 1824]) (the 1968 (or Brussels) Convention which applies between Denmark and the Member States of the European Community), Art.1 of the "Brussels I" Regulation in E.C. Council Regulation No.44/2001 which applies between the Member States of the E.U. except Denmark, Sched. 3C, Art. 1 (the Lugano (or "Parallel") Convention, inserted by s.1(3) of the C.J.J.A. 1991, which applies between the E.C. countries and the Member States of the European Free Trade Association which have ratified it and any other State which accedes to it, and very closely modelled on the 1968 Convention), Sched.4, substituted by the Civil Jurisdiction and Judgments Order 2001 [S.I. 2001 No.3929] based on the Brussels I Regulation (inter-U.K. jurisdiction) or Sched. 9 (proceedings excluded from Sched. 8 (jurisdiction of Scottish courts)). The importance of this provision is that the court must know in such actions which Schedule to apply; *e.g.* if the defender is domiciled in a country outside the U.K. to which Sched. 1 or 3C applies or in another part of the U.K., the court must sist the cause if it is not shown that the defender has been able to receive the summons (or that all steps have not been taken to this end) in sufficient time to arrange his defence: C.J.J.A. 1982, Scheds 1, and Sched.4, r.15(2); and Brussels I Regulation, Art.26(2), 3C, Art. 20(2). Furthermore the defender is made aware of what the court is being told about the jurisdiction alleged.

(1) Under the 1968 Convention and the Lugano Convention, whether a person is domiciled in the Contracting State whose courts are seized of a matter is determined in the case of individuals (natural persons) by applying its internal law (1982 Act, Scheds 1 and 3C, Art. 52(1)) and of other persons by applying its rules of private international law (1982 Act, Scheds 1 and 3C, Art. 53). Under the Brussels I Regulation the domicile of individuals (natural persons) is determined by the internal law, in order to determine whether a party is domiciled in a Member State whose courts are seized of a matter (Art.59(1)); and in the case of other persons, the domicile is the place where it has its statutory seat, central administration or principal place of business (Art.60(1)), but in the case of a trust domicile is determined by the court applying its private international law (Art.60(3)).

(2) If a party who is a natural person is not domiciled in a contracting state to which the 1968 Convention or the Lugano Convention applies or a Member State to which the Brussels I Regulation applies whose courts are not seized of the matter, then, in order to determine whether that person is domiciled in another contracting or Member State, the court applies the law of that state: C.J.J.A. 1982, Scheds 1 and 3C, Art.52(2); Brussels I Regulation, Art.59(2). A person cannot be sued in Scotland under either convention or the Brussels I Regulation by virtue of rules which confer jurisdiction on the basis of the presence of property or arrestment of moveables in Scotland (C.J.J.A. 1982, Scheds 1 and 3C, Art. 3; Brussels I Regulation, Art.3(2)).

(3) Subject to (1) and (2) above, the domicile of an individual (natural person) for the purposes of the 1968 Convention, the Lugano Convention or under UK jurisdiction or the general jurisdiction of the Scottish courts (C.J.J.A. 1982, Scheds 1, 3C, 4 and 8) or, for the purposes of the Brussels I Regulation, is determined by para.9 of Sched.1 to the Civil Jurisdiction and Judgments Order 2001 [S.I. 2001 No.3929], is determined by s.41 of the C.J.J.A. 1982 according to where he resides: *i.e.* (a) he is resident there and (b) the nature and circumstances of his residence indicate that he has a substantial connection with that place ((b) is presumed if he has been resident there for the last three months).

(4) The domicile of a company or other legal person is, in general, its seat. Under the C.J.J.A. 1982, a corporation or association has its seat (in the UK or elsewhere) in the place where it was incorporated or formed and has its registered office or other official address, or where its central management and control is exercised: C.J.J.A. 1982, s.42 (in the case of a trust in the UK, domicile is determined by s.45). For the purposes of the Brussels I Regulation, a company or

other legal person or association is domiciled at the place where it has its statutory seat, central administration or principal place of business: Brussels I Regulation, Art. 60 (in the UK and Ireland, "statutory seat" is the registered office or, if none, the place of incorporation or, if none, the place under the law of which formation took place). Under the C.J.J.A. 1982, in relation to proceedings concerning the validity of the constitution, nullity or dissolution of companies, other legal persons or associations or their decisions (C.J.J.A. 1982, Scheds 1 and 3C, Art. 16(2), Sched. 4, rr. 4 and 11(b) and Sched. 8, rr. 2(16) and 5(1)(b); Brussels I Regulation, Art. 22(2)), a corporation or association has its seat in a country to which the 1968 or Lugano Convention applies, or in the U.K., under whose laws it was incorporated or formed or where its central management and control is exercised, and has its seat in Scotland if it has its registered office or other official address there or where its central management and control is exercised: C.J.J.A. 1982, s.43; Civil Jurisdiction and Judgments Order 2001 [S.I. 2001 No.3929], Sched.1, para. 10.

(5) The domicile of the Crown is dealt with in s.46 of the C.J.J.A. 1982. Note that, whatever the domicile of the defender, there may be exclusive jurisdiction of a court under the 1968 or Lugano Convention (Scheds 1 and 3C, Art. 16), under Sched. 4, r. 11 (inter-U.K. jurisdiction), Sched. 8, r. 5 (Scottish jurisdictional rules or the Brussels I Regulation, Art. 22).

"ground of jurisdiction". The general jurisdiction of the court over persons who may be sued **13.2.7** there is contained in Sched. 8 to the C.J.J.A 1982: C.J.J.A. 1982, s.20 (Sched.8 was substituted by the Civil Jurisdiction and Judgments Order 2001 [S.I. 2001 No.3929]). Sched. 8 does not apply to (a) proceedings subject to the jurisdictional rules in the 1968 (or Brussels) Convention on jurisdiction and enforcement in civil and commercial matters between Denmark and the Member States of the European Community, or the similar Lugano (or "Parallel") Convention between the E.C. Member States and Member States of the European Free Trade Association which ratify it (and any other State which accedes to it), in Scheds 1 and 3C respectively to the 1982 Act (C.J.J.A. 1982, s.20(1)); (b) proceedings subject to the jurisdictional rules in the EC Council Regulation No.44/2001 on jurisdiction and enforcement of judgments in civil and commercial matters (known as the "Brussels I Regulation") between Member States of the EU except Denmark; (c) proceedings subject to the jurisdictional rules in Sched. 4 to the C.J.J.A. 1982 which determines the allocation of jurisdiction between the different courts of the U.K. (C.J.J.A. 1982, s.20(1)); (d) proceedings in respect of which any other enactment confers jurisdiction (C.J.J.A. 1982, s.21(1)(a)) and (e) proceedings listed in Sched. 9 as proceedings excluded from Sched. 8 (C.J.J.A. 1982, s.21(1)(b)). See notes 13.2.8 to 13.2.14 on the various grounds of jurisdiction.

Rule 13.2(4)(a) assumes the defender will only prorogate jurisdiction when he lodges answers and does not contest jurisdiction. But he might have prorogated jurisdiction in advance in which case the ground of jurisdiction can (and must) be averred.

Jurisdiction under the C.J.J.A. 1982, Sched. 8. Before 1st March 2002, Sched.8 was based on **13.2.8** the 1968 European (or Brussels) Convention. From that date, Sched.8, substituted by the Civil Jurisdiction and Judgments Order 2001 [S.I. 2001 No.3929], is based on the EC Council Regulation No.44/2001 (known as the "Brussels I Regulation"). Sched.4 to the C.J.J.A. 1982 is also substituted by the same S.I. and is now based on the Brussels I Regulation. In determining the meaning and extent of Sched.8 derived to any extent from Title II (Jurisdiction) of the 1968 Convention, (a) regard must be had to the relevant principles laid down by the European Court in connection with the jurisdictional rules in the 1968 Convention (though not necessarily followed as in a case under the 1968 Convention) and (b) the Jenard and Schlosser reports on that convention must be given such weight as is appropriate: C.J.J.A. 1982, s.20(5).

The following paragraphs deal with the rules of jurisdiction under Sched.8 to the C.J.J.A. 1982 as amended by S.I. 2001 No.3929 with references to Scheds 1 (the 1968 Convention), 3C (the Lugano Convention) and 4 (inter-UK) and to the Brussels I Regulation on which Scheds 4 and 8 are now based. Discussion of jurisdiction under the Brussels I Regulation can be found in note 13.2.12A.

(A) Domicile. The general and principal ground of jurisdiction is that a person shall be sued in the place of his domicile (C.J.J.A. 1982 (amended by S.I. 2001 No. 3929) Sched. 8, r. 1; see also Scheds 1 and 3C, Art. 2, Brussels I Regulation, Art. 2), that is a defender must be domiciled in Scotland. This rule is subject to the rules of special jurisdiction, jurisdiction over consumer contracts, exclusive jurisdiction, prorogation of jurisdiction, submission to jurisdiction and the proceedings excluded under Sched. 9. Domicile is defined in ss.41, 42, 43, 45 and 46 of the C.J.J.A. 1982 and is to be ascertained at the time when the cause is commenced, that is the time of citation: Erskine, III.iv.3; *Alston v. Macdougall* (1887) 15 R. 78; *Smith v. Stewart & Co.* 1960 S.C. 329, 334 *per* L.P. Clyde. (But this statement *may* have to be reconsidered: see *Canada Trust Co v. Stolzenberg (No.2)* 2000 All E.R. 481, 502C *per* Lord Hope of Craighead.)

(B) Rule 2 (special jurisdiction) provides that a person may also be sued in the Court of Session on 17 different grounds subject to rules concerning consumer contracts, exclusive jurisdiction, prorogation of jurisdiction, submission to jurisdiction and the proceedings excluded by Sched. 9. On the meaning of "special", see *Bank of Scotland v. Seitz* 1990 S.L.T. 584, 587H *per* L.P. Hope. A clear *prima facie* relevant case for the jurisdiction of the court must be averred: *Eddie v. ALPA slv*, 2000 S.L.T. 1062.

Rule 2(a) (no fixed residence: where personally cited). This was a common law jurisdiction and earlier case law will be relevant; it was available in respect of itinerant defenders who had no fixed place of residence anywhere: Erskine, I.ii.16.

Rule 2(b) (contract: place of performance of the obligation; see also C.J.J.A. 1982, Scheds 1, Art. 5(1)3C and Sched.4, r. 3(a), Brussels I Regulation, Art. 5(1)(a)). This rule is concerned with contractual obligations for which a particular place of performance is provided expressly or by implication: *Bank of Scotland v. I.M.R.O. Ltd* 1989 S.L.T. 432. Where not express the implication is that debts must be paid at the creditor's residence: *Bank of Scotland v. Seitz* 1990 S.L.T. 584. The court decides the place of performance in accordance with its own conflict of law rules: *Tessili v. Dunlop* [1976] E.C.R. 1473; *Custom Made Commercial v. Stawa Metallbau GmbH* [1994] E.C.R. I–2913. The assumption in art.5(1) of the 1968 Convention is that the obligation has to be performed in one place: *Bank of Scotland v. Seitz*, above. The sole place of performance has to arise as a matter of obligation and of choice by the debtor as to where he would pay: *Montague Evans v. Young*, 2000 S.L.T. 1083 (OH). In Sched. 1 whether an obligation is contractual under the 1968 Convention is a matter of community law: *Peters v. Zuid Nederlandse Aannemers Vereniging* [1983] E.C.R. 987; *Arcado v. Haviland* [1988] E.C.R. 1539. The existence of the contract is a matter relating to a contract: *Effer v. Kantner* [1982] E.C.R. 825. The words "relating to contract" do not apply to a non-contractual claim such as the *condictio indebiti*: *Strathaird Farmers Ltd v. Chataway & Co.* 1993 S.L.T. (Sh.Ct.) 36. In employment contracts, the obligation is the obligation which characterises the contract: *Ivenel v. Schwab* [1982] E.C.R. 1891. In other contracts, the obligation is the basis of the proceedings: *De Bloos v. Bouyer* [1976] E.C.R. 1497 followed in *Shenavai v. Kreischer* [1987] 3 C.M.L.R. 782 and supported by Lord Maxwell in *Bank of Scotland v. I.M.R.O. Ltd* 1989 S.L.T. 432, 446; see also *Engdiv Ltd v. G. Percy Trentham Ltd* 1990 S.C. 53. In *Kleinwort Benson Ltd v. Glasgow City Council (sic)* [1999] 1 A.C. 153, [1997] 4 All E.R. 641 (HL) it was held that a claim fell within art. 5(1) of Sched.4 (now r. 3(a)) if it was based on a particular contractual obligation, the place of performance of which was within the jurisdiction of the court; it did not under a supposed contract whereby the claim was for restitution based on unjust enrichment and not contract. The fact that the place at which a bill of lading fell to be delivered was within the jurisdiction did not mean that the location of the place of delivery was also within the jurisdiction: *Eddie v. Alpa srl*, 2000 S.L.T. 1062 (OH). Where there is a choice between the laws of different countries in a contractual obligation, the parties may choose the law by which the contract is to be governed failing which the law will be that of the country with which the contract has the closest connection (assumed to be that of the habitual residence of the person to effect performance): see the Contracts (Applicable Law) Act 1990, Sched.1, Art. 4 (this presumption in Art. 4(2) has material weight: *Caledonia Subsea Ltd v. Microperi Srl.*, 2001 S.C. 716, aff'd. 2003 S.C. 71 (First Div.)). It has been held in England, by a majority of the House of Lords in *Agnew v. Lansförsäkringsbolagens AB* [2000] All ER. 737, that an obligation to disclose in pre-contract negotiations can constitute "the obligation in question" for the purposes of art.5(1) of the Lugano Convention. The approach to a jurisdiction issue involving art. 4 of the Rome Convention in Sched. 1 to the 1990 Act and art. 5(1) of the 1968 Brussels Convention in the C.J.J.A. 1982 was dealt with by Lord Hamilton in *William Grant & Sons International Ltd v. Marie Brizard Espana SA* 1998 S.C. 536. First, determine by Scottish choice of law rules what system of law is applicable to the legal relation in question (*i.e.* which system under art. 4(3) of the Rome Convention); and secondly, apply the substantive rules of the legal system so ascertained to determine the place of performance of the contractual obligation under art. 5(1) of the 1968 Convention: see, *e.g. Ferguson Shipbuilders Ltd v. Voith Hydro GmbH & Co. KG* 2000 S.L.T. 229. Where a party relies on the special and derogative provisions of art. 5(1) of Sched.1, he has to set out a sufficient exposition of the contractual terms to show that there is a stateable basis for maintaining that the place of performance is within the jurisdiction of the court: *Eddie v. Alpa srl*, 2000 S.L.T. 1062 (OH); see also *Montague Evans v. Young*, 2000 S.L.T. 1083 (OH); and *Atlantic Telecom Gmbh, Noter*, 2004 S.L.T. 1031 (OH).

Rule 2(c) (delict and quasi-delict: place where harmful event occurred or may occur; see also C.J.J.A. 1982, Scheds 1 and 3C, Art. 5(3) and Sched.4, r. 3(c), Brussels I Regulation, Art. 5(3)). The words "or may occur" do not appear in Scheds 1 or 3C of the C.J.J.A. 1982 but are derived from Art. 5(3) of the Brussels I Regulation, Art. 5(3) in which they do appear. Matters relating to "delict and quasi-delict" in Art. 5(3) of the 1968 Convention in Sched.1 mean all actions which seek to establish the liability of the defender which are not related to contract: *Kalfelis v. Schröder, Münchmeyer, Hengst & Co.* [1988] E.C.R. 5565. An action based on a statutory right of recovery following an unsatisfied judgment in a delictual action is not a matter relating to delict or quasi-delict: *Davenport v. Corinthian Motor Policies at Lloyds* 1991 S.C. 372. Article

5(3) does not apply to a claim based on unjust enrichment, since such a claim does not generally presuppose either a harmful event or a threatened wrong: *Kleinwort Benson Ltd v. Glasgow City Council (sic)* [1997] 4 All E.R. 641; and *Compagnie Commercial Andre SA v. Artibell Shipping Co Ltd* 1999 S.L.T. 1051. Under the former Law Reform (Jurisdiction in Delict) Act 1971 it was held that the court had jurisdiction if there were a material element of delict in Scotland: *Russell v. F.W. Woolworth & Co. Ltd* 1982 S.L.T. 428. Under this ground the defender may be sued where the damage occurred or where the harmful event occurred which gave rise to the damage: *Beir v. Mines de Potasse d'Alsace* [1976] E.C.R. 1735. The place "where the harmful event occurred" means the place where the event giving rise to the damage directly produced its harmful effects on the person who is the immediate victim of the event: *Dumez France and Tracoba v. Hessiche Landesbank (Helaba)* [1990] E.C.R. I–49. The Conventions and the Brussels I Regulation do not specify what constitutes a "harmful event" and, accordingly, that is a matter to be determined by the national court applying the substantive law: *Shevill v. Presse Alliance SA* [1996] A.C. 959. The extension of jurisdiction to include harmful events that "may occur" is intended to cover interim remedies for threatened wrongs. In relation to delicts on the internet, a person setting up a website potentially commits a delict in any country where it can be seen; but whether he does so in any particular country depends on the *de minimis* principle, so that if the impact in a given country is insignificant, no delict is committed there: *Bonnier Media Ltd v Smith*, 2003 S.C. 36.

Rule 2(d) (damages or restitution based on criminal act: court seized of criminal proceedings to extent it can entertain civil proceedings); see also C.J.J.A. 1982, Scheds. 1 and 3C, Art.5(4) and Sched.4, r.3(d), Brussels I Regulation, Art.5(4)). A Scottish criminal court does not deal with civil proceedings.

Rule 2(e) (maintenance: where creditor domiciled or habitually resident or if ancillary to proceedings concerning status; see also C.J.J.A. 1982, Scheds. 1 and 3C, Art.5(2) and Sched.4, r.3(b), Brussels I Regulation, Art.5(2)). Rule 2(e) of Sched.8 does not include the provision in the other conventions or Regulation that jurisdiction over maintenance, if ancillary to an action about status, is excluded if based on the nationality of one of the parties.). An action of affiliation and aliment is not ancillary to proceedings concerning status (Sched. 8, r.2(d) and Sched. 9, r. 1). Proceedings concerning status include divorce, separation, declarator of marriage, nullity and custody. Maintenance includes aliment, periodical allowance and lump sum payments: see *De Cavel v. De Cavel (No. 2)* [1980] E.C.R. 731.

Rule 2(f) (disputes from operations of a branch, agency or other establishment: where branch, agency or establishment is situated; see also C.J.J.A. 1982, Scheds 1 and 3C, Art.5(5) and Sched.4, r.3(e), Brussels I Regulation, Art.5(5). "Operations" means actions relating to rights and contractual or non-contractual obligations concerning the management of the establishment, actions relating to undertakings which have been entered into there and actions concerning non-contractual obligations arising from activities in which the establishment has engaged at the place in which it is established: *Somafer v. Saar-Ferngas* [1978] E.C.R. 2183. A parent company may be acting as a branch etc. of one of the subsidiaries: *SHR Schotte GmbH v. Parfums Rothschild SARL* [1987] E.C.R. 4905. "Situated" is not the same as domicile. "Establishment" implies a place of business which has the appearance of permanence. The expression "dispute arising out of operations of a branch" in Art. 5(5) of Sched. 1 does not mean that undertakings giving rise to a dispute entered into by a branch in the name of a parent body have to be performed in the contracting state in which the branch is established: *Lloyd's Register of Shipping v. Société Compenon Bernard* [1995] E.C.R. I–961.

Rule 2(g) (in capacity as settler, trustee or beneficiary of an (express) trust domiciled in Scotland; see also C.J.J.A. 1982, Scheds. 1 and 3C, Art. 5(6) and Sched. 4, r. 3(f), Brussels I Regulation, Art.5(6)). A trust is domiciled in a part of the UK only if the system of law of that part is the system with which the trust has the most real connection: C.J.J.A. 1982, s.45 (for the purposes of Scheds 1, 3C, 4 and 8); and Civil Jurisdiction and Judgments Order 2001, Sched.1, para.12(3) [S.I. 2001 No.3929] (for the purposes of the Brussels I Regulation).

Rule 2(h) (where defender not domiciled in the U.K. or another 1968 or Lugano Convention country, or a Brussels I Regulation country (*i.e.* Member State of the EU except Denmark), and moveable property is arrested, or immoveable property is situated, in Scotland: *cf.* C.J.J.A. 1982, Scheds 1 and 3C, Art. 3(2); Brussels I Regulations, Art.2(2)). These were common law grounds of jurisdiction. At common law arrestment to found jurisdiction was available only in an action with conclusions to enforce pecuniary claims (*Union Electric Co. v. Holman & Co.* 1913 S.C. 954) and not to actions affecting status (*Morley v. Jackson* (1888) 16 R. 78), a bare declarator (*Williams v. Royal College of Veterinary Surgeons* (1897) 5 S.L.T. 208) or sequestration (*Crail, Petrs* (1863) 1 M. 509) and probably not in actions for a decree *ad factum praestandum* alone (*cf. Powell v. Mackenzie & Co.* (1900) 8 S.L.T. 182 and *Union Electric Co.*, above, *per* L.P. Dunedin at p. 958). The property arrested must be in the hands of a third party, be arrestable in execution (*Leggat Bros v. Gray* 1908 S.C. 67; *Stenhouse London Ltd v. Allright* 1972 S.C. 209) and have some commercial value (*Shaw v. Dow and Dobie* (1867) 7 M.

449, 455 *per* L.P. Inglis; *Trowsdale's Tr. v. Forcett Railway Co.* (1870) 9 M. 88). The subjects arrested must belong to the common debtor in the capacity in which he is being sued. Arrestment originally unauthorised may be ratified: *Alexander Ward & Co. Ltd v. Samyang Navigation Co. Ltd* 1975 S.C.(H.L.) 26. It is available to the pursuer's representatives but not against the defender's representatives as it is personal to the defender and does not transfer against his successor: *Cameron v. Chapman* (1838) 16 S. 907. It establishes jurisdiction only in the action in which it is used: *Cameron*, above. The pursuer must arrest on the dependence also if he wishes to secure the subjects arrested, as the effect of the arrestment is complete once the summons is served and creates no nexus over the subjects arrested: *Leggat Bros.*, above; *Fraser-Johnston Engineering Co. v. Jeffs* 1920 S.C. 222. At common law the ownership or tenancy of heritable property in Scotland founded jurisdiction in causes relating to that heritage (proprietary or possessory claims) or in petitory actions (personal claims). The basis of jurisdiction was effectiveness, though the value was immaterial: *McArthur v. McArthur* (1842) 4 D. 354, 362 *per* Lord Fullerton. The defender must have a beneficial interest (*Caledonian Fish-Selling and Marine Stores Co. Ltd v. Allard Hewson & Co.* 1970 S.C. 168; *cf. Embassy Picture House (Troon) Ltd v. Cammo Developments Ltd* 1971 S.C. 25; *Llewellyn v. Hebbert* 1983 S.C. 112 (existence of missives established only a personal right but no beneficial interest)), though he need not be infeft (*Fraser v. Fraser & Hibbert* (1870) 8 M. 400); a personal right under an unrecorded disposition is sufficient (*Embassy Picture House (Troon) Ltd*, above), as is a right under a lease (*Weinschel* 1916 2 S.L.T. 91, 205), a contingent right of reversion (*Smith v. Stuart* (1894) 22 R. 130) or a right of a trust beneficiary to a conveyance (*Caledonian*

[NEXT TEXT PAGE IS C 99]

Fish-Selling and Marine Stores Co. Ltd, above). The heritage must be held by the defender in the same capacity in which he is sued: *Mackenzie v. Drummond's Exrs.* (1868) 6 M. 932.

Rule 2(i) (proprietary and possessory causes relating to moveables in Scotland where defender not domiciled in another 1968 or Lugano Convention country or a Brussels I Regulation country: in the place where the property is situated; see also Sched. 4, r.3(h)(ii)). These are causes in respect of the property itself. At common law jurisdiction applies not to moveables merely found in Scotland but to moveables fixed in a legal or practical sense within Scotland: *e.g.* moveables of a foreigner held in virtue of a landlord's hypothec in sequestration for rent (*Duncan v. Lodijensky* (1904) 6 F. 408); and also enforcement of rights *in rem* against ships and multiplepoindings (*Bell v. Stewart* (1852) 14 D. 837).

Rule 2(j) (interdict: in the place where wrong likely to be committed). This was a common law jurisdiction: *Toni Tyres Ltd v. Palmer Tyre Co.* (1905) 7 F. 477. The Maxwell Committee (Report on Jurisdiction and Enforcement 1980, pp.246–247) recommended this rule because it was not clear that Art.5(3) of Sched.1 (the 1968 Convention) (and r.2(3) of Sched.8 in its original form) to the C.J.J.A. 1982, which deals with jurisdiction for delicts, included prospective wrongs. New Art.5(3) of the Brussels I Regulation, and new r.2(c) of Sched.8 of the C.J.J.A. 1982, refer expressly to delicts that "may occur".

Rule 2(k) (debts over immoveable property in Scotland where defender not domiciled in another 1968 or Lugano Convention country or a Brussels I Regulation country: in the place where the property is situated; see also Sched. 4, r.3(h)(i)). This was thought to be a useful jurisdiction by the Maxwell Committee (Report on Jurisdiction and Enforcement 1980, pp. 248–249). This ground is not fully covered by Sched. 8, r.2(h)(ii) or r.5(1)(a).

Rule 2(l) (decision of an organ of a company, other legal person or association in the place where it has its seat in Scotland; see also C.J.J.A. 1982, Sched. 4, r.4). Rule 2(l) (formerly r.2(12)) was modelled on Art.16(2) of the 1968 Convention which is an exclusive jurisdiction concerning constitution, whereas r.2(l) is a special but non-exclusive jurisdiction relating to decisions. In constitutional matters there is an exclusive jurisdiction in Sched. 8, r. 4(1)(b); winding up is excluded by Sched. 9, para. 5.

Rule 2(m) (arbitration in Scotland or where procedure governed by Scots law: in the Court of Session). The 1968 and Lugano Conventions and the Brussels I regulation do not apply to arbitration. The rule enables the court to appoint an arbiter or deal with a stated case.

Rule 2(n) (registration or validity of patents, trade marks, designs: in the Court of Session). Art.16(4) of the 1968 Convention and Art.22(4) of the Brussels I Regulation give an exclusive jurisdiction to the State of application or registration. There is no exclusive jurisdiction in Scotland in r.5(1) of Sched.8 because the registers are in London, but r.2(n) gives a special non-exclusive jurisdiction.

Rule 2(o) (several defenders, third parties and counterclaims; see also C.J.J.A. 1982 Scheds 1 and 3C, Art. 6 and Sched. 4, r.5, and Brussels I Legislation, Art.6). In relation to several defenders, there must be, when the proceedings are instituted, a connection between the claims by the pursuer against the several defenders of such a kind that it is expedient to determine the claims together in order to avoid the risk of irreconcilable judgments resulting from separate actions: r.2(o)(i) which is derived from *Kalfelis v. Schröder, Münchmeyer, Hengst & Co.* [1988] E.C.R. 5565. In *Compagnie Commercial Andre SA v. Artibell Shipping Co. Ltd* 1999 S.L.T. 1051 (OH). Lord Macfadyen held that in most cases the presence or absence of the risk of irreconcilable judgments will be obvious from the nature of the claims against the domiciled and non-domiciled defenders; but if not, a pursuer may have to make averments to demonstrate the risk.

The rule in relation to counterclaims is narrower than reconvention at common law (which applied not only to claims arising out of the same transaction but also where the claims arose *ex diversis causis* provided they were claims which could fairly be set against one another: *Thompson v. Whitehead* (1862) 24 D. 331; *Clydedock Engineering Ltd v. Cliveden Compania Naviera SA* 1987 S.L.T. 762). On counterclaims, see note 25.1.6.

On third parties, see note 26.1.2.

(C) Jurisdiction in consumer contracts (C.J.J.A. 1982, Sched. 8, r. 3; see also C.J.J.A. 1982, Scheds 1 and 3C, Arts 13, 14 and 15, and Sched. 4, r.7, and Brussels I Regulation, Art.15). This rule is subject to the rules of exclusive jurisdiction, prorogation of jurisdiction, submission to jurisdiction and the proceedings excluded by Sched. 9. A consumer may sue (a) in the place where the other party is domiciled, (b) where he himself is domiciled or (c) in the courts having jurisdiction under r.2(f) or (i) of Sched.8. The reference to instalment credit in Sched. 8, r. 3(1) means a transaction in which the price is paid by a series of payments or which is limited to a financing contract in Sched. 1, Art. 13 (Brussels I Regulation, Art.15(1)(a)): *Bertrand v. Ott* [1978] E.C.R. 1431.

Sched.8, r.3 (and Sched.4, r.7) now follows Art.15(1)(c) of the Brussels I Regulation, and the court has jurisdiction in relation to contracts concluded by a consumer with a person pursuing commercial activities in Scotland or, by any means, "directs such activities" to Scotland. This phrase is intended to cover contracts concluded through a website accessible in the consumer's domicile. The exclusion of transport contracts does not apply to such contracts which for an inclusive price provide for travel and accommodation (they are now treated as consumer contracts).

The jurisdiction of courts in a cause where the defender is not domiciled in a contracting state is governed not by the Brussels or Lugano Convention but by the law of the contracting state of the court in which the cause is brought. The only exception in consumer contracts is in Art. 13(2) (Brussels I Regulation, Art.15(2)) which applies where a consumer enters into a contract with a party not domiciled in a contracting state but which has a branch, agency or other establishment there and the dispute arises out of its operations: *Brenner and Noller v. Dean Witter Reynolds Inc.* [1994] E.C.R. I–4275.

(CA) Jurisdiction in contracts of employment (C.J.J.A. 1982, Sched.8, r.4; see also Sched.4, r.10 and Brussels I Regulation, Arts 18–21). This rule is subject to r.2(f) in Sched. 8 (operations of a branch etc). These rules replace those in former r.5(1). They may be departed from by agreement entered into after the dispute has arisen or which allows the employee to sue in another court. An employer may be sued (a) where he is domiciled, (b) where the employee habitually carries or carried out his work or (c) if the employee did not do so in one place, where the business employing him is situated. An employer may sue only in the courts where the employee is domiciled.

(D) Exclusive jurisdiction of courts of country in which property is situated (C.J.J.A. 1982, Sched. 8, r. 5; see also C.J.J.A. 1982, Scheds 1, Art. 16 and Sched.4, r.11, and Brussels I Regulation, Art.22). Rule 5(1) of Sched.8 does not include reference to jurisdiction over six-month tenancies found in the other documents. In *Sanders v. Van der Putte* [1977] E.C.R. 2383, the European Court opined that the exclusive jurisdiction of Art. 16 of the 1968 Convention related to disputes as to the existence, interpretation, the giving up of, or of compensation for damage under, a lease but held that it did not cover a dispute arising out of an agreement to take over the running of a florist's shop as the principal aim of the agreement was of a different nature, namely, the operation of a business; it also determined that the denial by the defender of the existence of the agreement was immaterial to the issue; see also *Barratt International Resorts Ltd v. Martin* 1994 S.L.T. 434. Art. 16(1) applies to actions which seek to determine the extent, content, ownership or possession of immoveable property or the existence of other rights *in rem* in it and does not cover a personal claim by a creditor seeking to have a donation of immoveable property rendered ineffective: *Reichert & Others v. Dresdner Bank* [1990] E.C.R. I–27.

The exclusive jurisdiction in Art. 16(1) of the 1968 Convention includes lettings (between two natural persons one of whom owns the property): *Rösler v. Rottwinkel* [1985] E.C.R. 99. It does not include a holiday let arranged between a natural person and a travel agent in a country other than where the property is situated: *Hacker v. Euro-Relais GmbH* [1992] E.C.R. I–1111 where the European Court held that Art. 16(1) did not apply to a contract concluded in a Contracting State whereby a travel business with its seat in that State undertakes to procure for a client domiciled in the same State the use for several weeks of holiday accommodation not owned by it in another Contracting State and to book the travel arrangements.

It is not sufficient that a right *in rem* in immoveable property is involved or that the action has a link with immoveable property; the action must be founded on a right *in rem* and not on a right *in personam* (except in relation to tenancies): *Webb v. Webb* [1994] E.C.R. I–1717 (proceedings for declaration that French property held as trustee for plaintiff and to execute documents to vest the property not an action in respect of such a right); *Lieber v. Göbel* [1994] E.C.R. I–2535 (claim for compensation for use of a flat after a settlement of an action transferring ownership was declared void was not a right *in rem*).

Art. 16(1) of Sched. 1 (the 1968 Convention) was amended by the 1989 Accession Convention (Spain and Portugal) by providing that, in the case of proceedings which have as their object tenancies of immoveable property for temporary private use for a maximum of six months, the courts of the Contracting State in which the defender is domiciled also have jurisdiction if the landlord and tenant are natural persons domiciled in the same Contracting State. (In the Lugano Convention in Sched. 3C only the tenant has to be a natural person and neither party must be domiciled in the Contracting State in which the property is situated. In the Brussels I Regulation, Art.22(1) proviso, and the C.J.J.A. 1982, Sched.4, r.1(a)(ii) and Sched.8, r.5(3), only the tenant need be a natural person but both landlord and tenant must be domiciled in the same Member State/part of the UK/Scotland.)

(E) Prorogation of jurisdiction (C.J.J.A. 1982, Sched. 8, r. 6; see also C.J.J.A. 1982, Scheds 1 and 3C, Art. 17 and Sched.4, r.12, and Brussels I Regulation, Art.23). Such an agreement must be evidenced in writing or in a form which accords with a practice. A communication by electronic means which provides a durable record is now a "writing". The court had previously adopted a restrictive approach to prorogation agreements in that they must be clear and express (*Scotmotors (Plant Hire) Ltd v. Dundee Petrosea Ltd* 1980 S.C. 351; *Morrison v. Panic Link Ltd* 1993 S.C. 631) as has the European Court (*Estasis Salotti v. RüWA* [1976] E.C.R. 1831; *cf.*

England where inference is sufficient in matters relating to contract: RSC 1965, Ord. 11, r. 1(1)(d)(iii)). But in *McGowan v. Summit at Lloyds,* 2002 S.L.T. 1259 (Ex Div), a case under old Sched.4, it was held that *Scotmotors,* even if still authoritative, did not lay down any general rule of law that a contractual clause will only be construed as conferring exclusive jurisdiction on a foreign court if it does so expressly. The only general principal is that the same canons of construction are to be applied to jurisdiction clauses as any other material contractual provision: it is a matter of construing the words used in accordance with their natural meaning and in the light of the surrounding circumstances in which the contract was made. A choice of law does not imply a choice of court: *Blasquez v. Levy & Sons* (1893) 1 S.L.T. 14. A prorogated jurisdiction under r. 12(1) of Sched. 4 and r. 6(1) of Sched. 8 (which omit the word "exclusive") of the C.J.J.A. 1982 is not an exclusive jurisdiction. A clause that "all disputes . . . shall be governed in London" does not prorogate the jurisdiction of the English courts: *Compagnie Commercial Andre SA v. Artibell Shipping Co. Ltd* 1999 S.L.T. 1051. In *McGowan,* above, it was held that the English courts did not have exclusive jurisdiction under a contractual clause that provided that "This Document shall be governed by the laws of England whose courts shall have jurisdiction . . . " The European Court has held that where an insurance contract between an insurer and a policy-holder for the benefit of a third party contains a prorogation clause, the third party can rely on it even though he has not signed it: *Gerling v. Amministrazione del Tesoro dello Stato* [1983] E.C.R. 2503; as can a third party acquiring a bill of lading issued by a carrier to a shipper containing such a clause: *Partenreederei ms Tilly Russ and Ernest Russ v. NV Haven & Vervoerbedrijf Nova* [1984] E.C.R. 2417. Art. 17 of the 1968 Convention applies to an oral agreement confirmed in writing: *Berghoefer v. ASA* [1985] E.C.R. 2699. A clause in the statutes or articles of a company limited by shares conferring jurisdiction on a court to settle disputes between the company and its shareholders is an agreement prorogating jurisdiction (binding any shareholder): *Powell Duffryn plc v. Petereit* [1991] E.C.R. I–1745. See also note 13.2.14.

Art. 17 of the 1968 Convention prevails over Art. 21 (*lis pendens*: see note 13.2.11): *Bank of Scotland v. S.A. Banque Nationale de Paris,* 1996 S.L.T. 103.

It is not clear whether the prorogated jurisdiction of another or foreign court means that the proceedings before this court should be dismissed or sisted. For a discussion, see *Compagnie Commercial Andre SA,* above. It should depend on the circumstances. In *Belgian International Insurance Group SA v. McNicoll,* 4th June 1999 (OH), unreported, it was indicated, *obiter*, that in that case, if, as a result of the prorogation clause, some questions had to be decided in the first instance by a Belgian court, that would not warrant dismissal, but a sist.

(F) Submission to jurisdiction (C.J.J.A. 1982, Sched. 8, r. 7; see also C.J.J.A. 1982, Scheds. 1 and 3C, Art. 18 and Sched. 4, r. 13, and Brussels I Regulation, Art. 24). A defender who enters appearance and lodges defences contesting jurisdiction and the merits is not taken to have submitted to jurisdiction on the merits: R.C.S. 1994, r. 18.2(1)(a) following *Elefanten Schuh v. Jacqmain* [1981] E.C.R. 1671 and *Rohr v. Ossberger* [1981] E.C.R. 2431. The English text of Art. 24(1) of the Brussels I Regulation accords with this interpretation of Art. 18 of the 1968 Convention (by omitting the word "solely" from the phrase "solely to contest jurisdiction" which appears in the English but not the French text of the latter convention).

(G) Verification of jurisdiction and admissibility (C.J.J.A. 1982, Sched. 8, rr. 8 and 9; see also C.J.J.A. 1982, Scheds. 1 and 3C, Arts 19 and 20 and Sched. 4, rr. 14 and 15, and Brussels I Regulation, Arts 25 and 26). The court must itself examine the question of jurisdiction for, (a) if another court has exclusive jurisdiction or (b) where the defender has not entered appearance, is not domiciled in Scotland and there is no ground of jurisdiction compatible with the C.J.J.A. 1982, the court must declare at its own instance that it has no jurisdiction. The reason for this is that in relation to the 1968 Convention in proceedings for recognition and enforcement of judgments there shall be no examination of the jurisdiction of the original court, and this principle is extended under Scheds 4 and 8.

Proceedings excluded from Sched.8.   **13.2.9**
(A) Where jurisdiction is conferred by any other enactment: C.J.J.A. 1982, s. 21(1)(a); *e.g.* Continental Shelf Act 1964, s. 3 superseded by the Oil and Gas (Enterprise) Act 1982, ss. 22 and 23 and consolidated in ss. 10 and 11 of the Petroleum Act 1998 (see *Johnston v. Heerema Offshore Contractors Ltd* 1987 S.L.T. 407); Domicile and Matrimonial Proceedings Act 1973; Council Regulation (EC) No. 2201/2003 of 27th November 2003 (new Brussels II, replacing No. 1347/2000 of 29th May 2000 (Brussels II)); Debtors (Scotland) Act 1987; and see statutes bringing the conventions into effect listed in note 13.2.12.
(B) Proceedings listed in Sched. 9: C.J.J.A. 1982, s. 21(1)(b).

Forum non conveniens. This is a basis for excluding jurisdiction. Ss. 22 and 49 of the C.J.J.A.   **13.2.10**
1982 save the application of this doctrine in relation to the jurisdiction of the court under Sched. 8, but it has no application to causes to which the 1968 Convention, Lugano Convention or Brussels I Regulation applies where the defender is domiciled in another Convention country

Convention, (or Member State in the case of Brussels I) or where Art. 16 of Sched. 1 or 3C, or Sched. 4, r. 5 to the C.J.J.A. 1982, or Art. 22 of the Brussels I Regulation, applies (exclusive jurisdiction). Under these provisions the doctrine of *lis pendens* applies. The doctrine of *forum non conveniens* applies "whenever it can be shown that the case cannot, consistently with fairness and justice, be tried in this country": *Sim v. Robinow* (1892) 19 R. 665, 666 *per* Lord Low; see also *Clements v. Macauley* (1866) 4 M. 583, 592 *per* L.J.-C. Inglis. Where the jurisdiction of the court is competently founded, the court has no discretion whether to exercise it or not: *Clements*, above; *Sim*, above, *per* Lord Kinnear at p. 668. Something more than mere practical inconvenience is required to sustain a plea of *forum non conveniens*. The proper translation of *"conveniens"* is "appropriate"; the actual convenience of the parties is not to be considered but that which is the appropriate forum for securing the ends of justice, and the decision must be taken in the light of the whole surrounding circumstances: *Société du Gaz de Paris v. Société Anonyme de Navigation "Les Armateurs Francais"* 1926 S.C.(HL) 13, 18 *per* Lord Dunedin. The general principles were recently set out by Lord Jauncey in *Crédit Chimique v. James Scott Engineering Group Ltd* 1979 S.C. 406. The initial onus is on the defender to raise and justify the plea: *De Mulder v. Jadranska Linijska (Jadrolinija)* 1989 S.L.T. 269. The mere fact that evidence of foreign law is required is not enough. It is not enough to show that the defence will have a better chance of succeeding elsewhere, as one must look to the interests of the pursuer as well as those of the defender "and the thing to be shown is not that there will be a disadvantage in that sense, but that there will be unfair disadvantage, so that justice is unlikely to be done": *Longworth v. Hope* (1865) 3 M. 1049, 1057 *per* Lord Deas. Once the defender has satisfied the initial onus it is for the pursuer to establish that to litigate abroad would deprive him of an advantage of such importance that it would cause injustice to deprive him of it: *De Mulder*, above. The plea will usually be inappropriate in causes relating to immoveables as the court of the *lex situs* will be the only court competent to grant decree *in rem*: *Foster v. Foster's Trs* 1923 S.C. 212.

13.2.11   *Lis alibi pendens*. This is a basis for excluding jurisdiction. The common law plea of *lis alibi pendens* does not apply where the prior action is in a foreign court: *Martin v. Stopford-Blair's Exrs* (1879) 7 R. 329, 331 *per* L.P. Inglis. Where the 1968 (Brussels) or Lugano Convention, or Brussels I Regulation, applies, the provisions of those conventions for *lis pendens* and related actions apply: C.J.J.A. 1982, Scheds 1 and 3C, Arts 21, 22 and 23, and Brussels I Regulation, Arts 27–30; and see notes 13.2.12 and 13.2.15. Where the prior action is in a foreign country to which those conventions do not apply or another part of the U.K., the plea of *forum non conveniens* must be relied on to exclude jurisdiction: see note 13.2.10. The plea is available unless jurisdiction is prorogated by the defender: *Longmuir v. Longmuir* (1850) 12 D. 926. If the plea is upheld the court dismisses the second action. When the plea is considered, which must be supported by relevant averments (*Flannigan v. British Dyewood Co.* 1971 S.C. 110, 111 and 114 *per* Lord Fraser), there must be (a) a prior action in dependence—after service of the summons and before the action is finally disposed of (including expenses) (*Aitken v. Dick* (1863) 1 M. 1038), and even if the action is asleep (*Denovan v. Cairns* (1845) 7 D. 378)—(b) in another or the same court in Scotland (*Martin*, above) of competent jurisdiction, (c) between the same parties in the same legal capacities or interest (*Longmuir*, above; *Alston v. Alston's Trs* 1912 2 S.L.T. 22), (d) in which the same question is raised (*Wilson v. Dunlop, Bremner & Co. Ltd* 1921 1 S.L.T. 35). Where the prior action is in the same court the plea is *lis pendens*. See also notes 13.2.15 and 18.1.4(A)(5).

13.2.12   *Jurisdiction under the 1968 and Lugano Conventions (C.J.J.A. 1982, Scheds 1 and 3C)*. The 1968 Brussels (or European) Convention in Sched.1 to the C.J.J.A. 1982 was substituted by the Civil Jurisdiction and Judgments Act 1982 (Amendment) Order 1990 [S.I. 1990 No. 2591]. The Lugano (or Parallel) Convention in Sched. 3C to the C.J.J.A. 1982 was inserted by s. 1(3) of the C.J.J.A. 1991. The conventions apply to "civil and commercial matters", a phrase which appears to limit jurisdiction to matters of private as opposed to public law. They supersede the conventions listed in Art. 55. They do not cover a public authority acting in the exercise of its statutory powers as distinct from it acting in the exercise of private law obligations: *LTU v. Eurocontrol* [1976] E.C.R. 154; *Netherlands State v. Rüffer* [1980] E.C.R. 3807. They do not extend to revenue, customs or administrative matters, the status or legal capacity of natural persons, rights in property arising out of a matrimonial relationship, wills, succession, bankruptcy, winding up, judicial arrangements, compositions and analogous proceedings, social security or arbitration (including proceedings concerning the appointment of an arbiter or the existence or validity of an arbitration agreement: *Marc Rich and Co. v. Società Italiana Impianti* [1991] E.C.R. I-3855): Scheds 1 and 3C, Art. 1. They do not apply to prevent a court assuming jurisdiction under the provisions of another convention even where the defender is domiciled in another Contracting State which is not a party to the other convention: Scheds 1 and 3C, Art. 57. Such other conventions will be those implemented by the U.K. under any statutory provision or rules of law: C.J.J.A. 1982, s. 9(1). These include:

the Warsaw Convention on international carriage by air, 1929, Protocol (1975): see Carriage by Air Act 1961, Sched. 1, Art. 28(1),

    the Guadalajara Convention on international carriage by air by a person other than a
        contracting carrier, 1961: see Carriage by Air (Supplementary Provisions) Act 1962,
        Sched., Art. VIII,

    the Brussels Convention on matters of collision, 1952, arts 1, 2 and 3: see Administration
        of Justice Act 1956, Pts I and V, s.45,

    the Brussels Convention relating to arrest of sea-going ships, 1952; see Administration of
        Justice Act 1956, Pts I and V,

    the Vienna Convention on Civil Liability for Nuclear Damage, 1963, Art. 11

    the Geneva Convention on carriage of goods by road, 1956: see Carriage of Goods by
        Road Act 1965, Sched., Art. 31(1),

    the Paris Convention on third party liability in the field of nuclear energy, 1960 (with
        Protocol (1964), Supplement (1960), Annex (1963), Protocol to Supplement (1964)),
        s. 13 and Art. 14: see Nuclear Installations Acts 1965 and 1969,

    the Brussels Conventions on liability for oil pollution damage, 1969 and 1984 (now 1992):
        see Merchant Shipping Act 1995, s.166,

    the Geneva Convention on international carriage of passengers and luggage by road,
        1973: see Carriage of Passengers by Road Act 1974, Sched., Art. 21(1),

    the Athens Convention on carriage of passengers and luggage by sea, 1974: see Merchant
        Shipping Act 1995, Sched. 6, Art. 17,

    the Berne Convention on international carriage by rail, 1980, App. A, Arts 52 and 60,
        App. B, Arts 56 and 63: see International Transport Conventions Act 1983,

    the UN Convention on the Law of the Sea 1982, Art. 28 (Cmnd 8941): see Merchant
        Shipping Act 1995, s. 129,

    the Brussels Conventions for international oil pollution damage fund, 1971 and 1984
        (now 1992): see Merchant Shipping Act 1995, s.177,

    the Seoul Convention establishing the multilateral investment guarantee agency, 1985: see
        Multilateral Investment Guarantee Agency Act 1988, Sched., Art. 44.

    the International Convention on Liability and Compensation for Damage in Connection
        with the Carriage of Hazardous and Noxious Substances by Sea 1996: see Merchant
        Shipping and Maritime Security Act 1997, Sched. 3, arts 38 and 39 inserted in the
        Merchant Shipping Act 1995 as Sched. 5A.

    Art. 57 precludes the application of the Brussels or Lugano Convention only in relation to
questions governed by the specialised convention. Thus, if the specialised convention has rules
for jurisdiction but no provision as to *lis pendens* or related actions, Arts 21 and 22 of the
Brussels or Lugano Convention (as the case may be) will apply: *Owners of Cargo lately laden on
Board Tatry v. Owners of Maceij Rataj* [1994] E.C.R. 5439.

    The pre-eminent rule of jurisdiction is that a person shall be sued in the courts of the
Contracting State in which he is domiciled (as defined by ss.41–46 of, and Scheds 1 and 3C, Arts
52 and 53 to, the C.J.J.A. 1982: see note 13.2.6 above). A person domiciled in one Contracting
State may be sued in another Contracting State only by virtue of the rules set out in ss.2 (special
jurisdiction: Arts 5, 6 and 6A), 3 (insurance: Arts 7–12A), 4 (consumer contracts: Arts 13–15), 5
(exclusive jurisdiction: Art. 16) and 6 (prorogation of, and submission to, jurisdiction: Arts 17 and
18) of the conventions: C.J.J.A. 1982, Scheds 1 and 3C, Art. 3. Where a defender is not domiciled
in a Contracting State jurisdiction shall, subject to Scheds 1 and 3C, Art. 16 (exclusive
jurisdiction), be determined by the laws of the country in which he is sued (in Scotland this is
determined by Sched. 8 to the 1982 Act). The court may decline jurisdiction under Arts 21–23 (*lis
pendens* and related actions). In relation to *lis pendens*, where proceedings involving the same
cause of action and the same parties are brought, any court other than the court first seized shall
sist its proceedings until jurisdiction of the court first seized is established. The court first seized is
the one before which the requirements for proceedings to become definitely pending are first
fulfilled: *Zelger v. Salinitri (No. 2)* [1984] E.C.R. 2397; in Scotland this is once service had been
executed and the action was therefore commenced: Erskine, III.iv.3; *Alston v. Macdougall* (1887)
15 R. 78; *Smith v. Stewart & Co.* 1960 S.C. 329, 334 *per* L.P. Clyde. As well as the same cause of
action and same parties, there must also be the same subject-matter: *Gubisch Maschinenfabrik v.
Palumbo* [1987] E.C.R. 4861; *Bank of Scotland v. S.A. Banque Nationale de Paris*, 1996 S.L.T. 103.

    See also discussion in note 13.2.8 of various grounds of jurisdiction in Sched. 8 to the C.J.J.A.
1982.

    The Lugano Convention does not prejudice the application by the E.C. Member States of the
1968 Convention; however, the Lugano Convention will apply (a) in matters of jurisdiction
where the defender is domiciled in a Contracting State which is not a member of the E.C. or
where Art. 16 (exclusive jurisdiction) or 17 (prorogation of jurisdiction) of the Lugano
Convention confers jurisdiction on the courts of such a State, or (b) in relation to *lis pendens* or
related actions as provided for in Arts 21 and 22 of the Lugano Convention, when proceedings
are instituted in a Lugano Contracting State which is not a member of the E.C. and in a Lugano
Contracting State which is.

The 1968 Brussels Convention has been superseded by the Council Regulation (EC) No. 44/2001 for participating Member States to the Regulation: i.e. all the Member States of the E.U. except Denmark. Accordingly the 1968 Convention applies only to *Denmark*, and will have to be used in relation to that country. For the Council Regulation, and participating Member States of the E.U., see note 13.2.12A.

The Lugano Convention has been superseded by the Council Regulation (EC) No. 44/2001 for participating States to the Convention. The Lugano Convention applies now only to the following countries:

> Denmark
> Iceland
> Norway.

The Council Regulation will apply to the Member States of the E.U. except Denmark.

13.2.12A   *Jurisdiction under the Brussels I Regulation (Council Regulation (EC) No.44/2001).* Jurisdiction in civil and commercial matters between the Member States of the EU, except Denmark, are governed by this Regulation. It is substantially similar to the 1968 Convention, but there are significant differences (some based on 1968 Convention case law), some of which have been noted in note 13.2.8 above. These differences are—

(1) In Art. 5(1), the place of performance of a contract is now defined, unless otherwise agreed, as (i) where under the contract the goods were or should have been delivered and (ii) in the case of services, where under the contract the services were or should have been provided.

(2) In Art. 5(3), in delict, a defender may now also be sued in the courts for the place where the harmful event may occur.

(3) In Art. 6(1), where there is more than one defender, jurisdiction where any of them is domiciled applies only where the claims are so closely connected that it is expedient to hear and determine them together to avoid risk of irreconcilable judgments. This follows the decision in *Kalfelis v. Schröder, Münchmeyer, Hengst & Co.,* [1988] E.C.R. 5565.

(4) In Arts 8–14, there are modifications to jurisdiction in insurance contracts.

(5) In Art. 15(1)(c), in consumer contracts, there is provision for jurisdiction where a person who pursues commercial or professional activities in a Member State or, by any means, directs such activities to that Member State. This is to cover e-commerce.

(6) Transport contracts providing for travel and accommodation are not now excluded from being consumer contracts (Art. 15(1)).

(7) In Arts 18–21 there are now rules for individual contracts of employment.

(8) In Art. 22(2), exclusive jurisdiction in relation to decisions of organs of companies, other legal persons or associations of persons is now limited to the validity of those decisions.

(9) In relation to exclusive jurisdiction over six-month tenancies, only the tenant need be a natural person although both landlord and tenant must still be domiciled in the same Member State.

(10) In Art. 23(1) (prorogation), there is an express statement that parties are allowed to give non-exclusive jurisdiction to the courts of a particular Member State.

(11) In relation to related actions (*lis pendens*), Art. 30 provides an autonomous rule that the court is seized of proceedings (a) at the time the document instituting the proceedings is lodged with the court (*i.e.* in Scotland, when the summons is presented for signeting (R.C.S. 1994, rr. 4.3, 4.4 and 13.5) or the petition is presented for a first order (R.C.S. 1994, rr. 4.3, 4.4 and 14.5) provided that the pursuer has not subsequently failed to take the steps he was required to take to effect service; or (b) if it has to be served before being lodged in court, when it is received by the authority responsible for service provided that the pursuer has not subsequently failed to take the steps required to have the document lodged in court. (In *Zelger v. Salinitri (No.2)* [1984] E.C.R. 2397 it had been held under the 1968 Convention that it was for the courts of each State to determine when a court was seized of an action.) In Scotland, the common law rule is that an action commences when it is served: see notes 13.2.5, 13.2.8(A) and 13.4.4.

The Member States of the EU to which the Brussels I Regulation applies are—

Austria	Latvia
Belgium	Lithuania
Cyprus	Luxembourg
Czech Republic	Malta
Estonia	Netherlands
Finland	Poland
France	Portugal
Germany	Slovakia
Greece	Slovenia
Hungary	Spain
Ireland	Sweden
Italy	United Kingdom

Allocation of jurisdiction between U.K. courts (C.J.J.A. 1982, ss.16 and 17 and Sched. 4).   **13.2.13**
These provisions determine which U.K. court has jurisdiction where the subject-matter is within the scope of the Brussels I Regulation and the defender is domiciled in the U.K. or the proceedings are of a kind mentioned in the Brussels I Regulation, Art. 22 (exclusive jurisdiction). Sched. 4 is subject to the 1968 Convention, Lugano Convention and the Brussels I Regulation. In interpreting Sched. 4, (a) regard must be had to relevant principles laid down by the European Court in connection with the jurisdictional rules in the 1968 Convention or Chap.II of the Brussels I Regulation and (b) the Jenard and Schlosser reports on the 1968 convention must be given such weight as is appropriate in the circumstances: C.J.J.A. 1982, s.16(3). Sched. 4 does not apply (a) to proceedings listed in Sched. 5 or (b) to proceedings in Scotland under any enactment which confers jurisdiction on a Scottish court in respect of a specific subject-matter on specific grounds: C.J.J.A. 1982, s.17(1). Sched.4 to the C.J.J.A. 1982 has been substituted by the Civil Jurisdiction and Judgments Order 2001 [S.I. 2001 No.3929]. Sched.4 is now a modified version of Chap. II of the Brussels I Regulation. There are the following differences—

(1) Only Art. 5(1)(a) of the Regulation appears in para. 3(a) of Sched.4 (place of performance of contract and not also place of obligation). The reason for this, apparently, is that it was thought that the additional ground would cause uncertainty initially. Certainty was considered to be more important within the UK.

(2) The special rules for insurance contracts in Arts 8–15 of the Regulation are not included.

(3) Paragraph 4 of Sched.4 deals with proceedings which have as their object a decision of an organ or a company, etc., and not merely the validity of such decisions as in Art. 22(4) of the Regulation.

(4) As before, the exception of contracts of transport from the rules for consumer contracts extends to insurance contracts in para. 7(2) of Sched.4. The application of the rules for consumer contracts to contracts for an exclusive price which provide for a combination of travel and accommodation, which appear in Art. 15(3) of the Regulation, appear in para. 7(2) of Sched.4.

(5) As before, the detailed provisions for the form that an agreement to prorogate jurisdiction, which appear in Art. 23(1) of the Regulation, do not appear in para. 12(1) of Sched.4. The law of the courts, the jurisdiction of which is prorogued, applies. In Scotland, that law is in para. 6(2) of new Sched.8: that provision repeats the text of Art. 23(1) of the regulation. The express statement in Art. 23(1) of the Regulation about agreeing non-exclusive jurisdiction does not appear in para. 12(1) of Sched.4. The absence of this statement would not seem to preclude agreeing a non-exclusive jurisdiction.

(6) The provisions of Arts 27–30 of the Regulation (Arts 21–23 of the 1968 Convention) relating to *lis pendens* and related actions are omitted; the principles of *forum non conveniens* must be applied (see note 13.2.10).

In relation to Sched. 4, Art. 6 (now 5(a) of the Brussels I Regulation) (where the defender is one of a number of defenders) it has been held in England (following the test in *Kalfelis v. Schröder, Münchmeyer, Hengst & Co.* [1988] E.C.R. 5565) that a number of separate unconsolidated actions (one of which involved a Scottish local authority) not heard together would not lead to irreconcilable decisions because the final arbiters would be the House of Lords whose decision would be binding in England and Scotland: *Barclays Bank plc v. Glasgow City Council* [1994] Q.B. 404.

"agreement prorogating the jurisdiction of a court" (R. 13.2(4)(c)). Under the 1968 or   **13.2.14**
Lugano Convention, the Brussels I Regulation or Scottish rules of jurisdiction (Sched.8), an agreement must be evidenced in writing or in a form which accords with a practice and gives the court exclusive jurisdiction unless it purports to exclude an exclusive jurisdiction or it does not satisfy the requirements of departure by agreement from the jurisdictional rules in consumer contracts (in which case it is invalid): C.J.J.A. 1982, Scheds 1 and 3C, Art. 17 and Sched. 8, r. 6, Brussels I Regulation, Art. 23, Art. 23(2) of the Regulation adds "writing" by electronic means. Under Scheds 1 and 3C, Art. 17, if the agreement was concluded for the benefit of one party, that party may, notwithstanding, bring proceedings in another court having jurisdiction under the 1968 or Lugano Convention. That provision is not repeated in Art. 23 of the Brussels I Regulation. In relation to trust instruments, agreements or provisions conferring jurisdiction have no legal force if contrary to the provisions on agreements in insurance contracts, consumer contracts, contracts of employment or which purport to exclude exclusive jurisdiction: Brussels I Regulation, Art. 23(5). See also note 13.2.8(E).

In connection with the allocation of jurisdiction within the U.K., parties may agree to prorogate the jurisdiction of a court. There is no rule that the agreement must be in writing, the only requirement being that the agreement would be treated as effective under the law of the court whose jurisdiction is prorogated (Sched. 8 does not apply where Sched. 4 applies); there are no rules of formal validity of such an agreement in Scots law. The court had previously adopted a restrictive approach to prorogation agreements in that they must be clear and express

(*Scotmotors (Plant Hire) Ltd v. Dundee Petrosea Ltd* 1980 S.C. 351 *Morrison v. Panic Link Ltd* 1993 S.C. 631) as has the European Court (*Estasis Salotti v. RüWA* [1976] E.C.R. 1831; *cf.* England where inference is sufficient in matters relating to contract: RSC 1965, Ord. 11, r. 1(1)(d)(iii)). But in *McGowan v. Summit at Lloyds,* 2002 S.L.T. 1259 (Extra Div), a case under Sched.4, it was held that *Scotmotors,* even if still authoritative, did not lay down any general rule of law that a contractual clause will only be construed as conferring exclusive jurisdiction on a foreign courts if it does so expressly. The only general principal is that the same canons of construction are to be applied to jurisdiction clauses as any other material contractual provision: it is a matter of construing the words used in accordance with their natural meaning and in the light of the surrounding circumstances in which the contract was made. A choice of law does not imply a choice of court: *Blasquez v. Levy & Sons* (1893) 1 S.L.T. 14. A prorogated jurisdiction under art. 17 of Sched. 4 (which omits the word "exclusive") is not an exclusive jurisdiction. A clause in the statutes or articles of a company limited by shares conferring jurisdiction on a court of a Contracting State to settle disputes between the company and its shareholders is an agreement prorogating jurisdiction (binding any shareholder): *Powell Duffryn plc v. Petereit* [1991] E.C.R. I–1745. A clause that "all disputes . . . shall be governed in London" does not prorogate the jurisdiction of the English courts: *Compagnie Commercial Andre SA v. Artibell Shipping Co. Ltd* 1999 S.L.T. 1051. In *McGowan,* above, it was held that the English courts did not have exclusive jurisdiction under a contractual clause that provided that "This Document shall be governed by the laws of England whose courts shall have jurisdiction . . . "

It is not clear whether the prorogated jurisdiction of another or foreign court means that the proceedings before this court should be dismissed or sisted. For a discussion, see *Compagnie Commercial Andre SA,* above.

Art. 17 of the 1968 or Lugano Convention prevails over Art. 21 of those conventions (*lis pendens*: see note 13.2.11): *Bank of Scotland v. S.A. Banque Nationale de Paris* 1996 S.L.T. 103.

Rule 13.2(4)(b) assumes the defender will only prorogate jurisdiction when he lodges answers and does not contest jurisdiction. But he might have prorogated jurisdiction in advance in which case the ground of jurisdiction can (and must) be averred.

13.2.15   *"proceedings involving the same cause of action".* Where proceedings involving the same cause of action between the same parties are brought in the courts of different Contracting States to the 1968 Convention in Sched. 1, or the Lugano Convention in Sched. 3C, to the C.J.J.A. 1982, or the Brussels I Regulation, any court other than the court first seized of the proceedings shall at its own instance sist the proceedings until the jurisdiction of the court first seized is established: C.J.J.A. 1982, Scheds 1 and 3C, Art. 21(1); Brussels I Regulation, Art. 27 [S.I. 2001 No. 3929].

This provision applies irrespective of the domicile of the parties, and the court other than the court first seized cannot examine the jurisdiction of the court first seized: *Overseas Union Insurance Ltd v. New Hampshire Insurance Co.* [1991] E.C.R. I–3317. As the court has to consider jurisdiction (and particularly if decree in absence is sought), the court must know (*ex facie* of the summons) whether it has jurisdiction.

Proceedings will have been brought in a court if the proceedings have commenced according to the procedural rules of that court: *Zelger v. Salinitri (No. 2)* [1984] E.C.R. 2397. In Scotland this is the date of execution of citation of the defender (Erskine, III.iv.3; *Alston v. Macdougall* (1887) 15 R. 78; *Smith v. Stewart & Co.* 1960 S.C. 329, 334 *per* L.P. Clyde; though in relation to the plea of *forum non conveniens* it has been affirmed that priority of process in terms of litiscontestation (when defences are lodged) is the normal test (*Argyllshire Weavers Ltd v. A. Macauley (Tweeds) Ltd* 1962 S.C. 388, 400 *per* L.P. Clyde). Under the Brussels I Regulation, Art. 30 provides an autonomous rule for when a court is seized of proceedings (see note 13.2.12A(11) above).

The nature and factual basis of the claim must be the same. As well as the same cause of action and same parties, there must also be the same subject-matter: *Gubisch Maschinenfabrik v. Palumbo* [1987] E.C.R. 4861; *Bank of Scotland v. S.A. Banque Nationale de Paris* 1996 S.L.T. 103. Actions do not cease to have the same cause of action and same object just because one was brought *in personam* and the other *in rem*: *Owners of Cargo lately laden on board Tatry v. Owners of Maceij Rataj,* E.C.J., 6th December, 1994. Article 21 applies even where there is a partial overlap in the bases of the actions in order to avoid irreconcilable judgments on similar facts in two contracting states: *William Grant & Sons Ltd v. Marie-Brizard & Roger International SA,* 16th May 1996, unreported (1996 G.W.D. 23–1347).

When jurisdiction of the first court is established the second court must decline jurisdiction (to the extent to which the parties to the action before it are also parties to the first action: *Owners of Cargo lately laden on Board Tatry,* above): C.J.J.A. 1982, Scheds 1 and 3C (1968 and Lugano Conventions), Art. 21(2); Brussels I Regulation, Art. 27(2). Where the concurrent proceedings do not involve the same parties or cause of action they may yet be related actions: in the case of related actions the second court may sist the action before it (Scheds 1 and 3C,

Art. 22(1); Brussels I Regulation, Art. 28(1)) or, on the application of a party, decline jurisdiction if the actions can be consolidated and there is jurisdiction over both actions in the first court (Art. 22(2); Brussels I Regulation, Art. 28(2)). "Related actions" means actions so closely connected that it is expedient to hear and determine them together to avoid the risk of irreconcilable judgments (Art. 22(3); Brussels I Regulation, Art. 28(3)). Where more than one court has exclusive jurisdiction any court other than the court first seized shall decline jurisdiction: Scheds 1 and 3C, Art. 23; Brussels I Regulation, Art. 29. In *Sarrio SA v. Kuwait Investment Authority* [1997] 4 All E.R. 929, the House of Lords held in an English appeal that the application of art. 22 was not limited to the primary issues necessary to establish a cause of action, but that the court should apply the simple wide test in art. 22 which was designed to cover a range of circumstances from cases where matters before the courts were virtually identical to those where the connection was close enough to make it expedient for them to be heard together to avoid the risk in question. For the application of the 1968 or Lugano Convention in Scheds 1 and 3C to the C.J.J.A. 1982, see note 13.2.12; and for the application of the Brussels I Regulation, see note 13.2.12A.

Arts 21–23 of Scheds 1 and 3C are not repeated in Scheds 4 and 8. The principles of *forum non conveniens* will apply: see note 13.2.10.

"warrants for diligence and intimation". See r. 13.6A and notes.   **13.2.16**

Signing of summons. A summons must be signed on every page by an agent (for definition of **13.2.17** whom, see r. 1.3(1)): r. 4.2(1). There is a special procedure for a party litigant who cannot obtain the signature of an agent: see r. 4.2(5) and (6) and note 4.2.8.

Units of measurement. The Units of Measurement Directive (Council Directive 80/181 of 20th **13.2.18** December 1979) was adopted by the E.C. in 1989 [Official Journal, 7th December 1989, L357/28]. From 1st January 1995 member states must use the metric system of measurement and, subject to certain transitional arrangements and exceptions, must cease to use imperial measurements for economic, public health, public safety and administrative purposes. Where a unit of measurement is used in pleadings it should be expressed as a metric unit, and court orders must be so expressed.

Exceptions are as follows: The nautical mile and knot are to be used for sea and air traffic and the foot is to be used for aircraft heights. Until 31st December 1999, fathom may be used for marine navigation; therm for gas supply; pint and fluid ounce for beer, cider, waters, lemonade and fruit juices on returnable containers; and ounce and pound for goods sold loose from bulk. In perpetuity, acre may be used for land registration; troy ounce for transactions in precious metals; mile, yard, foot and inch for road traffic signs, distances and speed measurements; pint for draught beer, cider and milk in returnable containers.

Declinature of jurisdiction. A judge may have to decline to hear a case. The grounds of **13.2.19** objection are (1) pecuniary interest of the judge in the cause and (2) personal interest including enmity, partiality, bribery or corruption. The objection may be taken by the judge or a party. Parties may agree to waive a declinature. It is not essential that the waiver be recorded in a joint minute or other document.

(1) Pecuniary Interest. No man may be a judge in his own cause: *Wildridge v. Anderson* (1892) 2 Adam 399, 410–411 *per* Lord Moncrieff. In general, a pecuniary interest, however small, will disqualify. The rule does not apply where the judge is a partner in a life or fire insurance company, or the holder as trustee of shares in an incorporated company, which is a party to the litigation: Court of Session Act 1868, s.103.

(2) Personal Interest. Where the interest is personal and not pecuniary, the interest must be substantial or calculated to cause bias in the mind of the judge: *Wildridge*, above; *Gorman v. Wright*, 1916 S.C. (J.) 44, 47 *per* L.J.-C. Scott Dickson. The test for declinature of jurisdiction by a judge on the ground of partiality is whether the fair-minded and informed observer, having considered the facts, would conclude that the tribunal was biased: *Gillies v. Secretary of State for Work and Pensions*, 2006 S.C. (H.L.) 71, 73, para. [3]. In that case Lord Hope of Craighead adopted the test he had formulated in the English case of *Porter v. Magill*, [2002] 2 A.C. 357, 494, para. 103 resolving a problem in England where the test was "real danger" (rather than "real likelihood" involving the objective test of the reasonable person) which placed England out of step with ECtHR, the rest of the Commonwealth and Scotland (where the test was whether there is a legitimate apprehension of a lack of impartiality, judged objectively: *Unity Trust Bank plc v. Frost (No. 2)*, 2001 S.C.L.R. 350 (Extra Div.)).

Address of defender
13.3. In a summons, the pursuer shall—
- (a) set out in the instance the known residence, registered office, other official address or place of business of the defender where he is to be served; or

(b) where that residence, office, address or place, as the case may be, is not known and cannot reasonably be ascertained, set out in the instance that the whereabouts of the defender are not known and aver in the condescendence what steps have been taken to ascertain his present whereabouts.

Deriv. R.C.S. 1965, r. 71

13.3.1   *General note.* R.C.S. 1965, r. 71 applied only where the defender was not designed as having an address in Scotland although in practice the substance of the rule applied in any case. The address can be amended: see r. 24.1(2)(b)(i). For the domicile of defenders, see note 13.2.6; and for jurisdiction, see notes 13.2.7 to 13.2.15.

13.3.2   *"not known".* The word "known" refers not to the pursuer's knowledge but to that of persons generally who had business or social dealings with the defender (*Young v. Harper* 1970 S.C. 174, 177 *per* Lord Fraser); accordingly the pursuer must take some steps to ascertain an address, and this is required for a motion in respect of service where the address of the defender is not known: r. 16.5(1)(c). Where the address is not known service by advertisement will be required unless dispensed with: r. 16.5.

Period of notice in summonses

13.4.—(1) Subject to any other provision in these Rules, the period of notice in a summons shall be—

(a) in the case of service within Europe, 21 days from whichever is the later of the date of execution of service or the giving of intimation before calling on a warrant for intimation;

(b) in the case of service furth of Europe under rule 16.2(2)(d) or (e) (service by an *huissier*, etc., or personally), 21 days from whichever is the later of the date of execution of service or the giving of intimation before calling on a warrant for intimation;

(c) in the case of service furth of Europe other than under sub-paragraph (b), 42 days from whichever is the later of the date of execution of service or the giving of intimation before calling on a warrant for intimation; and

(d) in the case of service by advertisement under rule 16.5 (service where address of person not known), other than in an action to which rule 49.12 (notice of family actions by advertisement) applies, six months from the date of publication of the advertisement.

(2) An application may be made by motion to shorten or extend the period of notice in a summons.

(3) Where a motion under paragraph (2) is made after signeting of the summons but before service—

(a) the summons shall be produced to the court; and

(b) the decision of the Lord Ordinary on the motion shall be final and not subject to review.

Deriv. R.C.S. 1965, r. 72(1) (r. 13.4(1)(a) to (c)), r. 72(3) (r. 13.4(3))
and r. 75(7) (r. 13.4(1)(d)), all substituted by S.I. 1986 No. 1941

13.4.1   *General note.* The phrase "period of notice" has replaced the word "*induciae*", but its effect is the same: the summons may not be called until after expiry of the period. The period of 21 days was introduced by A.S. (R.C.A. No. 9) (Jurisdiction and Enforcement) 1986 [S.I. 1986 No. 1941]. The former period of 14 days was the shortest in Europe; it was increased to 21 days following Art. 20 of the 1968 Convention in Sched. 1 (and of the Lugano Convention in Sched. 3C) to the C.J.J.A. 1982 and Art. 15 of the Hague Convention of 15th November 1965 on the Service Abroad of Judicial and Extrajudicial Documents in Civil or Commercial Matters (Cmnd. 3986 (1969)) which deal with the sisting of proceedings where it is not shown that the defender has been able to receive the document in sufficient time to arrange for his defence, and Art. 27(2) of the 1968 or Lugano Convention which entitles a court of a Contracting State to refuse to recognise a judgment in default of appearance for enforcement if the defender was not served with the summons in sufficient time to enable him to arrange for his defence: C.J.J.A. 1982, Scheds 1 and 3C, Art. 27(2).

[NEXT TEXT PAGE IS C 103]

"Subject to any other provision in these Rules". The period of notice where (a) notice is by **13.4.2** advertisement in a family action, is 21 days and not six months (r. 49.12) and (b) service is by advertisement in an action of declarator of death, is 21 days unless the court otherwise orders (r. 50.2(2)).

"whichever is the later". The period of notice expires on the last day of the period of notice, **13.4.3** which is calculated from (but excluding) the date on which the last execution of service or giving of intimation was made; the summons may be called on that last day (r. 13.13(1)). Usually service and intimation on a warrant for intimation are made at the same time; but they may not be, or service or intimation may have to be attempted again if at first unsuccessful.

"execution of service". The date of execution of service (citation) marks the commencement of **13.4.4** the action: Erskine, III.iv.3; *Alston v. Macdougall* (1887) 15 R. 78; *Smith v. Stewart & Co.* 1960 S.C. 329, 334 *per* L.P. Clyde. The period of notice will begin to run from midnight of that day; except where service is by post when time begins to run from midnight of the day after the date of posting (r. 16.4(6)). All days of the week are included in the period of notice, including Sundays and other public holidays.

For methods of service, see Chap. 16, Pt I.

"intimation before calling". A summons may not be called until the last day of the period of **13.4.5** notice: r. 13.13(1). A summons is called by appearing in the rolls in the calling list of causes called, *i.e.* brought into court.

Intimation on a warrant in a summons is provided for in r. 13.6(d): and see also note 13.6.6. Intimation on a warrant for intimation is given in the same manner as service: see r. 16.8.

"Europe". This word has not been defined; but probably means as far east as (the Ural **13.4.6** mountains in Russia and) the Black Sea but not Asian Russia or the Asian Republics of the former U.S.S.R., south to the Mediterranean islands but not Africa, and north to Norway, Iceland and Finland. It includes the whole of the British Isles. The word obviously includes all Member States of the European Union (though not their dependencies). Note also "Europe" for the purposes of the Royal Mail: leaflets, available in Post Offices, on mailing abroad, list the countries treated as in Europe by the Royal Mail.

Application to shorten or extend the period of notice. Such an application after signeting and **13.4.7** before service will be made before calling and the procedure for such is in r. 23.8. A motion which is made (*i.e.* heard) before service will have been enrolled before service.

Dispensing with period of notice. Where the defender's agent accepts service he may dispense **13.4.8** with the period of notice: see r. 16.10.

"final and not subject to review". The decision of the Lord Ordinary may not be reclaimed **13.4.9** against.

Signeting

13.5.—(1) A summons shall pass the signet.

(2) No summons shall bear any date but the date of signeting, which date shall be treated as the date of the summons.

(3) A summons shall be signeted and registered by a clerk of session acting under authority from the Principal Clerk (by virtue of a commission granted to him by the Keeper of the Signet).

(4) Subject to paragraph (5), a summons shall be presented to the General Department during its normal office hours for signeting and registration.

(5) In an emergency, a summons may be signeted and registered outwith the normal office hours.

Deriv. R.C.S. 1965, r. 74 (preamble (part)) (r. 13.5(1) and (2));
P.N. No. 3 of 1976 (r. 13.5(2) to (5))

General note. A summons must have the signet or seal of the sovereign bearing the Royal **13.5.1** Coat of Arms embossed upon it to authorise execution (service of the summons). The Keeper of the Signet, the Lord Clerk Register, granted a commission on 3rd May 1976 to the Principal Clerk of Session to signet summonses and diligence letters which was formerly done by members of the Society of Writers to the Signet. Summonses are signeted by an assistant clerk of session acting with authority from the Principal Clerk as provided in the commission. Although signeting is carried out by clerks of session, it is not a function of the court and remains a function of the Keeper of the Signet; it is not therefore a judicial act: see *Wall's Trs v. Drynan* (1888) 15 R. 359, 362 *per* L.P. Inglis.

13.5.2 *"signeting and registration"*. A summons may be lodged in person for signeting (r. 4.3) in the appropriate section in the General Department (see note 3.2.1) where the process is registered in the appropriate roll (see r. 3.2(3)), given a cause reference number (see r. 4.1(4) and note 4.1.5), signeted (if in order) and the principal summons will be available for collection the following day (by 10.30am if lodged before 4pm the preceding day). A summons may be lodged by post by a Court of Session account holder or if accompanied by a cheque for the fee (see note 13.5.5: P.N. No. 4 of 1994, paras 2 and 4) and if there are any defects which cannot be dealt with by telephone the summons will be returned by post by the Signeting Officer.

A summons must be executed (served) within a year and a day after being signeted or the instance will fall and a fresh action would have to be brought: r. 13.7(2).

On signeting, the summons will be returned to the pursuer for the purpose of service and diligence.

13.5.3 *"normal office hours"*. For office hours and holidays, see note 3.1.2.

13.5.4 *"emergency"*. An emergency would be the need for an interim interdict, suspension or imminent expiry of prescription or limitation period. To contact one of the clerks to obtain a signet and, if necessary, a judge after 5pm, ring the Court of Session (0131–225 2595), leave your name and telephone number and the duty security guard will contact a clerk who will contact you.

13.5.5 *Fee*. The court fee for signeting and all work up to the closed record (or determination of mode of inquiry) is payable at this stage. If signeting is outwith normal hours there is an extra fee. For fee, see Court of Session etc. Fees Order 1997, Table of Fees, Pt I, A, and B, item 1, [SI 1997/688, as amended, pp. C1201 *et seq*.]. Certain persons are exempt from payment of fees: see 1997 Fees Order, art.5 substituted by S.S.I. 2002 No.270. A fee exemption certificate must be lodged in process: see P.N. No.1 of 2002.

Where the pursuer is legally represented, the fee may be debited under a credit scheme introduced on 1st April 1976 by P.N. No. 4 of 1976 to the account (if one is kept or permitted) of the pursuer's agent by the court cashier, and an account will be rendered weekly by the court cashier's office to the agent for all court fees due that week for immediate settlement. Party litigants, and agents not operating the scheme, must pay (by cash, cheque or postal order) on each occasion a fee is due at the time of lodging at the counter at the General Department.

Authority for service and intimation on signeting

[1] **13.6.** When signeted, a summons shall be authority for—

   (a) service on the defender designed in the instance; and

   (b) intimation of the summons on any person on whom intimation is required in these Rules where a warrant for that purpose has been inserted in the summons.

Deriv. R.C.S. 1965, r. 74 (preamble (part))

---

[1] R. 13.6 substituted by S.S.I. 2003 No. 537 (effective 10th November 2003).

13.6.1 *General note*. Rule 13.6 as originally in R.C.S. 1994, has been divided into two by A.S. (R.C.S. A. No.6) (Diligence on the Dependence) 2003 [S.S.I. 2003 No. 537] and the automatic right to diligence on the dependence, or to found jurisdiction, has been abolished. The reason is that, following *Karl Construction Ltd v. Palisade Properties plc*, 2002 S.C. 270 (OH) and *Advocate General v. Taylor*, 2003 S.L.T. 1340 (Extra Div), concerning inhibition on the dependence, such diligence must now be applied for and considered by the court. Rule 13.6A provides the new procedure for application for such diligence. See note 13.6A.1A for a discussion of these cases.

13.6.2 *"signeted"*. For signeting, see r. 13.5.

13.6.3 *"service"*. For service, see Chap. 16.

13.6.4 *"intimation"*. For procedure for intimation see r. 16.8. For forms, see the particular rules. Intimation of a summons is required for example:

   (a) in actions relating to heritable property on persons having an interest as holders of heritable securities over it: r. 13.12;

   (b) in actions for damages for death of a relative, on connected persons: r. 43.3;

   (c) in an action under s.1 of the Merchant Shipping (Oil Pollution) Act 1971 (now s.153 of the Merchant Shipping Act 1995), to the International Oil Pollution Compensation Fund: r. 46.9;

   (d) in family actions:

      (i) where defender's address is unknown, on children and next of kin: see r. 49.8(1)(a);

  (ii) on person with whom defender is alleged to have committed adultery: r. 49.8(1)(b);

  (iii) where defender is suffering from a mental disorder, on children and next of kin and Mental Welfare Commission: r. 49.8(1)(c);

  (iv) where a party has more than one spouse, on any additional spouse: r. 49.8(1)(d);

  (v) where court may make an order about parental rights, on third parties concerned: r. 49.8(1)(e), (f) and (g);

  (vi) where court may make an order which affects a child, to that child, if not a party to the action: r. 49.8(1)(h);

  (vii) where order sought for transfer of property under s.8(1)(*aa*) of the Family Law (Scotland) Act 1985, on consenters and creditors in respect of a security over the property: r. 49.8(1)(i);

  (viii) where order sought under s.18 the Family Law (Scotland) Act 1985 relating to avoidance transactions, on third parties in whose favour a transaction is made: r. 49.8(1)(j);

  (ix) where order sought under the Matrimonial Homes (Family Protection) (Scotland) Act 1981, on interested persons: r. 49.8(1)(k);

  (x) where pursuer alleges a relevant (improper) association between defender and another, on that other person: r. 49.9;

(e) in an action of declarator of death, to the missing person's spouse and children, any other person having an interest and the Lord Advocate: r. 50.2(4).

Authority for diligence etc. before calling

[1] **13.6A.**—(1) Before the calling of a summons, the pursuer may apply by motion for authority for—

  (a) arrestment to found jurisdiction; or

  (b) diligence by—

    (i) inhibition on the dependence of the action;

    (ii) arrestment on the dependence of the action where there is a conclusion for the payment of money;

    (iii) arrestment *in rem*; or

    (iv) dismantling a ship,

    where a warrant in the appropriate form in Form 13.2-A has been inserted in the summons.

(2) Where a Lord Ordinary pronounces an interlocutor granting a motion under paragraph (1)—

  (a) he shall record his interlocutor by signing the warrant in the summons; and

  (b) the signed warrant shall be sufficient authority for execution of the arrestment to found jurisdiction or, as the case may be, the diligence.

----

[1] R.13.6A added by S.S.I. 2003 No. 537 (effective 10th November, 2003).

General note. Rule 13.6 as originally in R.C.S. 1994, has been divided into two by A.S. **13.6A.1A** (R.C.S. A. No.6) (Diligence on the Dependence) 2003 [S.S.I. 2003 No. 537] and the automatic right to diligence on the dependence, or to found jurisdiction, has been abolished. The reason is that, following *Karl Construction Ltd v. Palisade Properties plc*, 2002 S.C. 270 (OH) and *Advocate General for Scotland v. Taylor*, 2003 S.L.T. 1340 (Extra Div), concerning inhibition on the dependence, such diligence must now be applied for and considered by the court. Rule 13.6A provides the new procedure for application for such diligence.

The previous rule dealt with warrants for diligence before signeting. New r. 13.6A deals with authority for diligence before calling, which is by an unintimated motion. After calling (see r. 13.8A), authority will be sought, as before, by motion.

The appropriate warrant must be inserted in the summons. In *Anglo-Dutch Petroleum International Inc. v. Ramco Energy Plc*, 2006 S.L.T. 334 (OH), the warrant was for "warrant for inhibition and warrant on the dependence" on the basis of which arrestments were made. The defender obtained recall of the arrestments as the omission of the word "arrestment" was held to be critical.

In *Karl Construction Ltd v. Palisade Properties plc*, 2002 S.C. 270 (OH), on a motion for recall of an inhibition, Lord Drummond Young held that four requirements must be satisfied if a right of protective attachment of immoveable property during litigation is to conform to Art. 1 of the First Protocol to the ECHR. These are: (1) The pursuer must establish a *prima facie* case on the merits of the action. (2) The pursuer must establish that there is a specific need for an interim remedy; this will generally involve demonstrating either that there is a significant risk of the defender's insolvency or that the defender is taking steps to conceal or dissipate his assets or that there is a significant risk that the defender will remove his assets from the jurisdiction. (3) A hearing must take place before a judge at which the previous two matters are discussed. (4) If protective attachment is used without an objective justification, and in particular if the pursuer is unsuccessful in the action, the defender should be entitled to damages for any loss that he has suffered in consequence of the attachment. He held that the present law on inhibition on the dependence failed to meet these requirements and that the automatic right to inhibition conferred by Scots law (with very limited right to compensation) did not strike a fair balance between the interests of the pursuer in having assets available to satisfy his claim and the right of the defender recognised by Art. 1 of the 1st Protocol to dispose of his property as he wants; the requirement of proportionality was not satisfied.

In *Advocate General v. Taylor*, above, the Extra Division on a report to the Inner House on a motion for a warrant for inhibition following *Karl Construction*, held at para. [34] that for a warrant for inhibition (and it would also apply to arrestment) the applicant need only establish a prima facie case on the merits of the action; the necessity for diligence need not be demonstrated, although it may no doubt assist. The court also held that r. 13.6 was not compatible with ECHR. To bring the rule within art. 1 of the First Protocol, the grant of a warrant for any diligence on the dependence required a judicial act, and that it had to be judicially considered before being granted. The court did not consider that a hearing was required in every case as suggested in *Karl Construction*, above. The court recommended that the rules be changed.

In *Amalgamated Roofing and Building Co v. Wilkie*, 2004 S.L.T. 509 (OH), it was held that *Karl Construction*, above, applied prospectively and did not make invalid diligence obtained before that case.

13.6A.1   *"arrestment to found jurisdiction"*. Subject to exceptions in Admiralty causes, arrestment to found jurisdiction is available where the defender is not domiciled in the UK or a country to which the 1968 or Lugano Convention in Sched.1 or 3C to the C.J.J.A. 1982 applies: C.J.J.A. 1982, Scheds 1 and 3C, Art. 3(2), Sched.4, Art. 3 and Sched.8, r. 2(8). In relation to Admiralty actions (defined in r. 46.1), however, see notes 16.13.1, 16.13.3 and 16.14.1 to 16.14.4. There must be a pecuniary claim: *Leggat Bros v. Gray* 1908 S.C. 67; *Union Electric Co. v. Holman & Co.* 1913 S.C. 954. The schedule of arrestment executed must state that it is to found jurisdiction: *Sutherlands of Peterhead (Road Hauliers) Ltd v. Allard Hewson & Co.* 1972 S.L.T. (Notes) 83. The arrestment is personal to the defender, does not transfer against his successors and establishes jurisdiction only for the action in which it is used: *Cameron v. Chapman* (1838) 16 S. 907. The arrestment must be executed before service of the summons: *Wall's Trs v. Dryman* (1988) 15 R. 359; *cf.* arrestment or inhibition on the dependence. It creates no nexus over the property arrested: *Craig v. Burnsgaard Kjosternd & Co.* (1896) 23 R. 500, 503 *per* Lord McLaren. If the pursuer wishes to secure the subjects arrested for enforcement of any decree he must also arrest on the dependence: *Leggat Bros.*, above; *Fraser-Johnston Engineering Co. v. Jeffs* 1920 S.C. 222. See further note 13.2.8(B), Ground (8) on jurisdiction. See also Graham Stewart on *Diligence*, pp. 246 *et seq.* For subjects arrestable, see notes 13.6.3(5), and 13.6.4 (arrestment of ships).

A schedule of arrestment must be served on the arrestee in Form 16.15–A (for ships, it is Form 16.15–AA). For methods of execution of the schedule of arrestment, see r. 16.12.

13.6A.2   *"inhibition on the dependence"*. This is a preventive diligence in security restraining a debtor from burdening, alienating or otherwise affecting his heritable property to the prejudice of the inhibitor: Erskine, II.xi.2. See generally, Graham Stewart on *Diligence*, pp. 530 *et seq.* As a general rule prior to the incorporation of the ECHR into Scots law, a pursuer was entitled to insert a warrant for inhibition as of right in respect of a debt due. An inhibition on the dependence could be recalled in whole or in part with or without conditions (see r. 13.10); and the pursuer would be liable in damages only for its wrongful use where executed on a defective warrant, in an irregular manner or its use was unjustifiable, or with malice and without probable cause: see *Wolthekker v. Northern Agricultural Co.* (1862) 1 M. 211, 212 *per* L.J.-C. Inglis: *Grant v. Magistrates of Airdrie* 1939 S.C. 738, 758–759 *per* L.P. Normand.

Pursuers in certain foreign actions which have been commenced, but not concluded may present a petition to the Court of Session for a warrant to inhibit on the dependence of the foreign action: see C.J.J.A. 1982, s.27. They are not, however, entitled to the warrant to inhibit as of right: *Stancroft Securities v. McDowall*, 1990 S.C. 274, 277 *per* L.J.-C. Ross. The pursuer in the foreign action must comply with s.27 and demonstrate a colourable care in the foreign actions: *Clipper Shipping Co. Ltd v. San Vincente Partners*, 1989 S.L.T. 204, 207D, *per* Lord Coulsfield and *Stancroft Securities Ltd*, above. An affidavit of the foreign lawyer conducting the action may be sufficient: see *e.g. Clipper Shipping Co. Ltd*, above.

(1) The summons need not contain pecuniary conclusions: it is necessary only that there is a conclusion which can be secured by inhibition, *e.g.* implement of an obligation in respect of

heritage: *Barstow v. Menzies* (1840) 2 D. 611; *Seaforth's Trs v. Macauley* (1844) 7 D. 180. It cannot be used in an action only for divorce (*Burns v. Burns* (1879) 7 R. 355), declarator or reduction (*Stafford v. McLaurin* (1875) 3 R. 148) or where the only conclusion which can be secured is one for expenses (*Weir v. Otto* (1870) 8 M. 1070). The preventive diligence in security in an action of reduction or adjudication is the registration of a notice of litigiosity in the Register of Inhibitions and Adjudications: Titles to Land Consolidated (Scotland) Act 1868, s.159. Warrant for inhibition in an action of aliment or in respect of a claim for financial provision in an action of divorce or declarator of nullity of marriage can only be obtained by motion on cause shown: Family Law (Scotland) Act 1985, s.19(1) and r. 49.7.

(2) A schedule of inhibition must be served on the defender in Form 16.15–F. It may be executed at the same time as service of the summons or at any time thereafter (r. 13.8(1)) until the action is disposed of by a final decree. For methods of execution, see r. 16.12. It may not be used if the action has fallen asleep (*i.e.* where the action has been in court with no interlocutor having been pronounced for a year and a day: r. 13.7(2)). The inhibition must be registered in the Register of Inhibitions and Adjudications and takes effect from the date of such registration; except that where a notice of inhibition is registered before (or after) execution of the inhibition and the inhibition is registered not later than 21 days after the notice, the inhibition takes effect from the date of registration of the notice: Titles to Land Consolidation (Scotland) Act 1868, s.155. The register is in Meadowbank House (open 10am to 4pm Monday to Friday).

(3) Payment of future or contingent debt. As in arrestment; see note 13.6.3(3).

(4) Property which can be inhibited is heritable property (corporeal or incorporeal) which may be affected by adjudication (Bell's *Comm.*, ii,135) but not heritable bonds where there has been no infeftment (Graham Stewart on *Diligence*, pp. 548–549).

(5) Effect of inhibition. When executed and registered it prevents the debtor voluntarily alienating or affecting his heritable property (whether he is infeft or not) to the prejudice of the inhibiter and renders any such deed voidable. It effectively prevents any sale or creation of a heritable security. It secures a ranking in preference to that of ordinary creditors who have taken no steps to secure their debts and to that of creditors who have post-dated preferences: *Bank of Scotland v. Lord Advocate* 1977 S.L.T. 24. If decree in the action is not subsequently obtained by the pursuer the inhibition is of no effect: *Gordon v. Duncan* (1827) 5 S. 602. It has no effect on prior debts. It affects property belonging to the defender at the time of registration except property acquired after registration of the inhibition destined to him under an indefeasible title, which is then inhibited, but otherwise does not affect property acquired after registration: 1868 Act, s.157; *cf. Leeds Permanent Building Society v. Aitken Malone & Mackay* 1968 S.L.T. 338. It secures principal and interest and any expenses decerned for (*Weir v. Otto* (1870) 8 M. 1070) but not the expenses of the inhibition. An inhibition within 60 days before sequestration or winding up of the defender does not create a preference: Bankruptcy (Scotland) Act 1985, s.37(2), Insolvency Act 1986, s.185 (companies); otherwise the inhibiter has a preference over debts contracted subsequently: *Baird & Brown v. Stirrat's Tr.* (1872) 10 M. 414. Inhibition is personal to the inhibiter and unless followed by a separate action of adjudication gives no real right or title.

(6) An inhibition will fall if the summons is not called within a year and a day of the expiry of the period of notice: *Thorburn v. Cox* (1830) 8 S. 945; r. 13.7(2). An inhibition relating to land, a lease or a heritable security prescribes within five years from the date of registration: Conveyancing (Scotland) Act 1924, s.44(3)(a).

(7) An inhibition will be invalid if there is not strict accuracy (*e.g.* an error or misdescription in relation to the inhibiter or the person inhibited): *Walker v. Hunter* (1853) 16 D. 226; and see, *e.g. Allied Irish Bank plc v. G.P.T. Sales and Services Ltd* 1995 S.L.T. 163; *Modern Housing Ltd v. Love* 1998 S.L.T. 1188 (misdescription of registered office address as that of a place of business, held trivial). Where there is a disparity between the name used in the Register of Inhibitions and the Register of Sasines the test is whether the disparity is capable of misleading a third party inspecting or instructing a search: *Atlas Appointments Ltd v. Tinsley* 1994 S.C. 582; for the sequel after proof, see *Atlas Appointments Ltd v. Tinsley* 1997 S.C. 200.

"arrestment on the dependence". This is a preventive diligence restraining a debtor (arrestee)   **13.6A.3** from making payment of a debt or satisfying an obligation to the defender (common debtor). As a general rule, prior to the incorporation of the ECHR into Scots law a pursuer was entitled to insert a warrant for arrestment as a right in respect of a debt due. An arrestment on the dependence could be recalled or restricted with or without conditions (see r. 13.10); and the pursuer would be liable in damages only for its wrongful use where executed on a defective warrant, in an irregular manner, or with malice or without probable cause: see *Wolthekker v. Northern Agricultural Co.* (1862) 1 M. 211, 212 *per* L.J.-C. Inglis; *Grant v. Magistrates of Airdrie* 1939 S.C. 738, 758–759 *per* L.P. Normand.

In *Karl Construction Ltd v. Palisade Properties plc,* 2002 S.C. 270 (OH), on a motion for recall of an inhibition, Lord Drummond Young held that four requirements must be satisfied if a right of protective attachment of immoveable property during litigation is to conform to Art. 1 of the

First Protocol to the ECHR. These are: (1) The pursuer must establish a *prima facie* case on the merits of the action. (2) The pursuer must establish that there is a specific need for an interim remedy; this will generally involve demonstrating either that there is a significant risk of the defender's insolvency or that the defender is taking steps to conceal or dissipate his assets or that there is a significant risk that the defender will remove his assets from the jurisdiction. (3) A hearing must be take place before a judge at which the previous two matters are discussed. (4) If protective attachment is used without an objective justification, and in particular if the pursuer is unsuccessful in the action, the defender should be entitled to damages for any loss that he has suffered in consequence of the attachment. He held that the present law on inhibition on the dependence failed to meet these requirements and that the automatic right to inhibition conferred by Scots law (with very limited right to compensation) did not strike a fair balance between the interests of the pursuer in having assets available to satisfy his claim and the right of the defender recognised by Art. 1 of the 1st Protocol to dispose of his property as he wants; the requirement of proportionality was not satisfied. There is no distinction in principle between inhibition and arrestment on the dependence on this ground, and there is no reason why the reasoning in that case should not also apply to arrestment on the dependence. Accordingly, a pursuer will have to enrol a motion at the time of lodging the summons for signeting and persuade the court to grant inhibition on the dependence. The motion will not need to be intimated to any prospective defender: see r. 23.3(1).

Pursuers in certain foreign actions which have been commenced, but not concluded, may present a petition to the Court of Session for a warrant to arrest on the dependence of the foreign action: see C.J.J.A. 1982, s.27. They are not, however, entitled to the warrant to arrest as of right: *Stancroft Securities Ltd v. McDowall* 1990 S.C. 274, 277 *per* L.J.-C. Ross. The pursuer in the foreign action must comply with s.27 and demonstrate a colourable care in the foreign action: *Clipper Shipping Co. Ltd v. San Vincente Partner*, 1989 S.L.T. 204, 207D *per* Lord Coulsfield and *Stancroft Securities Ltd*, above. An affidavit of the foreign lawyer conducting the action may be sufficient: see *e.g. Clipper Shipping Co. Ltd*, above.

Use of diligence on the dependence against foreign state agencies is uncommon as they could normally be expected to meet any decree, and the use of such diligence in those circumstances would be oppressive. But a distinction is to be drawn in the case of bodies merely controlled or supported by foreign governments such as state-owned companies: *Tor Corporate AS v. China National Star Petroleum Corporation*, 27th July 2000 (OH), unreported.

(1) The summons must contain pecuniary conclusions, even if alternative or subsidiary: *Burns v. Burns* (1879) 7 R. 355, 356 *per* L.P. Inglis. Arrestment cannot be used in an action only for divorce (*Burns*, above), declarator or reduction (*Stafford v. McLaurin* (1875) 3 R. 148) or where the only conclusion which can be secured is one for expenses (*Weir v. Otto* (1870) 8 M. 1070). Warrant for arrestment in an action of aliment or in respect of a claim for financial provision in an action of divorce or declarator of nullity of marriage can only be obtained by motion on cause shown: Family Law (Scotland) Act 1985, s.19(1) and r. 49.7. In an action involving commercial activities the pursuer must provide at least basic specification of factual grounds and, where that was the case, it was proper to proceed on the basis that responsible counsel had evidence which warranted the basic averments: *Interconnection Systems Ltd v. Holland* 1994 S.L.T. 777, 781A–C *per* Lord Penrose; *cf. Beton v. Beton* 1961 S.L.T.(Notes) 19, and see comments of Lord Cameron in a different context in *Moore v. Greater Glasgow Health Board* 1978 S.C. 123, 130.

(2) A schedule of arrestment must be served on the arrestee in Form 16.15–B (or 16.15–BB in the case of a ship). For methods of execution, see r. 16.12. It may be executed at any time after signeting, before service of the summons and is effective provided the summons is served within 20 days of the diet of compearance or, if that date is in vacation, the next calling date: Debtors (Scotland) Act 1838, s.17. There is no equivalent to the diet of compearance in modern practice; it has been argued that its equivalent is the first day on which the summons can call at the expiry of the period of notice, but this was rejected in *Brash v. Brash* 1966 S.L.T. 157, 158 *per* Lord Kissen. Accordingly it is sufficient if the summons is served within 20 days after service of the arrestment. Arrestment may be executed after calling at any time until the action is disposed of by a final decree. It may not be used if the action has fallen asleep (*i.e.* where the action has been in court for a year and a day with no interlocutor having been pronounced). An arrestment will fall if the summons is not called within a year and a day of the expiry of the period of notice: *Thorburn v. Cox* (1830) 8 S. 945. It must not be executed before an arrestment to found jurisdiction, because the defender will not be subject to the jurisdiction until the latter has been effected: *Dramgate Ltd v. Tyne Dock Engineering Ltd*, 2000 S.C. 43 (Ex Div).

(3) Payment of future or contingent debt (*i.e.* liquid debt payable at a certain future date or on the occurrence of an uncertain future event: *Mitchell v. Scott* (1881) 8 R. 875, 879 *per* L.P. Inglis). Arrestment is competent in respect of a debt due (*i.e.* due for payment immediately *ex hypothesi* of the pursuer's case). If the debt is a future debt, although arrestable by a creditor of the common debtor, arrestment is not competent in security of another debt in an action to enforce the claim: *Costain Building & Civil Engineering Ltd v. Scottish Rugby Union plc* 1993 S.C. 650, overruling, on

this point *Taylor Woodrow Construction (Scotland) Ltd v. Sears Investment Trust Ltd* 1991 S.C. 140; *cf. Rippin Group Ltd v. ITP Interpipe SA* 1995 S.C. 302. Arrestment will only be granted at common law on a claim for a future debt where there are special circumstances averred, *e.g.* that the defender is *vergens ad inopiam* or *in meditatione fugae* or considering putting away his funds with the intention of not implementing any decree or not fulfilling his obligations: *Symington v. Symington* (1875) 3 R. 205; *Gillanders v. Gillanders* 1966 S.C. 54; *Wilson v. Wilson* 1981 S.L.T. 101. In an action of aliment or a claim for financial provision in an action of divorce or declarator of nullity of marriage, which is for a future or contingent debt, the position now is that warrant to arrest or inhibit may only be granted by the court (by motion: r. 49.7) on cause shown subject to any limit as to property or value (property only in inhibition), and is not limited to the common law grounds: Family Law (Scotland) Act 1985, s.19(1).

(4) Arrestment must be made in the hands of a person other than the pursuer or defender who is indebted, holds goods belonging, or is liable to account, directly not indirectly, to the defender: Graham Stewart on *Diligence*, pp. 105 *et seq.*; *McDonald v. Mize* 1989 S.L.T. 482. Exceptions to the rule that the arrestment must be in another's hands are (a) arrestment of ships or cargo (see note 13.6.4; but not aircraft: *Emerald Airways Ltd v. Nordic Oil Services Ltd*, 1996 S.L.T. 403, (b) arrestment by a pursuer in his own hands where he holds in a different character to that in which he is pursuer: *Landcatch Ltd v. Sea Catch plc* 1993 S.L.T. 451. The arrestee must be subject to the jurisdiction of the court: *Brash v. Brash* 1966 S.C. 56. The statement in Graham Stewart on *Diligence*, p. 37, that, where arrestment is directed against an arrestee in a fiduciary capacity, this must be stated in the schedule (*Graham v. Macfarlane & Co.* (1869) 7 M. 640) was disapproved in *Huber v. Banks* 1986 S.L.T. 58. The arrestment is valid if there is, at the time it is laid, a present obligation on the arrestee to account to the defender: *Commercial Bank of Scotland Ltd v. Eagle Star Insurance Co. Ltd* 1950 S.L.T. (Notes) 30. Where the arrestee is an agent, such as a solicitor, and not a trustee he is under no obligation to account until he has received the funds; no debt exists, therefore, until then and any arrestment in his hands before then is ineffective: *Royal Bank of Scotland plc v. Law* 1996 S.L.T. 83. Where the cheque is lodged with a bank, no obligation to account arises until the bank (the collecting bank) has presented the cheque for payment to the paying bank and the cheque is honoured, and there is no arrestable obligation until then: *McLaughlin v. Allied Irish Bank*, 2001 S.C. 485.

(5) Subjects arrestable, as a general rule, are all personal debts due to the defender or his moveable property: Stair, III.i.25; Erskine, III.vi.4; Graham Stewart on *Diligence*, pp. 44 *et seq.* Cargo on board ship may be arrested: see *Svenska Petroleum A.B. v. H.O.R. Ltd* 1982 S.L.T. 343; *West Cumberland Farmers Ltd v. Director of Agriculture of Sri Lanka* 1988 S.L.T. 296; and if the cargo cannot be discharged, the ship cannot be moved. Certain property is not arrestable: (a) wages or salary (including fees, bonuses and commissions) and pensions (including annuities for past services, any periodical payments in compensation for loss of employment and any disability pension): Law Reform (Miscellaneous Provisions) (Scotland) Act 1966, s.1; (b) property specially appropriated; (c) alimentary provision; (d) bills and negotiable instruments (though the debt may be); (e) joint property for debt of one of the joint owners. See generally, Graham Stewart on *Diligence*, pp. 78 *et seq.*; Wilson on the *Scottish Law of Debt*, 2nd ed., pp. 192–195. A book debt ceases to be arrestable where a receiver is appointed over the common debtor before the arrestment because the floating charge has effect as an assignation in security of the right to receive the debt in favour of the holder of the floating charge: *Forth & Clyde Construction Co. Ltd v. Trinity Timber & Plywood Co. Ltd* 1984 S.L.T. 94.

(6) Effect of arrestment. When executed it arrests all the readiest moveable goods and gear, debts, sums of money and other moveable effects belonging or due to the defender wherever and in whosoever's hands to remain under arrestment until sufficient caution be found that the same may be forthcoming to the pursuer: see Debtors (Scotland) Act 1838, s.16. It prohibits the arrestee from parting with the subjects to the prejudice of the pursuer: see Graham Stewart on *Diligence*, pp. 125 *et seq.* The arrestment covers the principal debt, interest on it, the expenses of the action but not expenses of the arrestment as they are not an expense of process (which should be sought in the action of furthcoming): *Symington v. Symington* (1874) 1 R. 1006. Arrestments are preferred according to their date of service, those on the same day rank *pari passu*. Arrestments within 60 days before or four months after apparent insolvency rank *pari passu* with the insolvency as if all used on the same day: Bankruptcy (Scotland) Act 1985, Sched. 7, para. 24. Arrestments within 60 days of sequestration or winding up are ineffectual to secure a preference in competition with other creditors: 1985 Act, s.37(4); Insolvency Act 1986, s.185 (companies). The effect of arrestment continues after final decree (even after decree of absolvitor if pursuer reclaims): *Countess of Haddington v. Richardson* (1822) 1 S.362) during the three-year prescriptive period (Debtors (Scotland) Act 1838, s.22 as amended by the Statute Law Revision Act 1893 and the Debtors (Scotland) Act 1987, Sched. 6, para. 3); and the arrestment remains in effect while a time to pay direction is in force: Debtors (Scotland) Act 1987, s.2(2). The pursuer does not have a complete right unless it is followed by decree in an action of furthcoming: *Lucas's Trs. v. Campbell* (1894) 21 R. 1096, 1103 *per* Lord Kinnear; but

in relation to an earnings arrestment, a current maintenance arrestment or a conjoined arrestment order within the meaning of Part III of the 1987 Act an action of furthcoming is not competent and such a diligence is subject to the provisions of that Part.

(7) An arrestment will fall if the summons is not called within a year and a day of the expiry of the period of notice: *Thorburn v. Cox* (1830) 8 S.945. It will prescribe after three years, originally from the date of execution under the Prescription Act 1669 (erroneously repealed) but generally treated as from the date of decree, or, in the case of future or contingent debts, from the date when the debt becomes due; and, in any case, excluding any period during which a time to pay direction, time to pay order or a s.6(3) interim order is in force: Debtors (Scotland) Act 1838, s.22 as amended by the Statute Law Revision Act 1893 and the Debtors (Scotland) Act 1987, Sched. 6, para. 3.

13.6A.4   *Arrestment of ships, cargo and arrestment in rem.* Arrestment of a ship or vessel is a real diligence: the ship is arrested and is fixed in the place in which it is arrested (*Carlberg v. Borjesson* (1877) 5 R. 188, 195 *per* Lord Shand), there is not an arrestment in the hands of an arrestee (*Barclay Curle & Co. Ltd v. Sir James Laing & Sons Ltd* 1908 S.C. 82, 89 *per* Lord McLaren). The exception in relation to ships does not extend to aircraft: *Emerald Airways Ltd v. Nordic Oil Services Ltd* 1996 S.L.T. 403. The diligence is completed not by an action of furthcoming but by an action of sale.

(1) There may be arrestment of a ship (a) on a warrant to found jurisdiction (see notes 13.6.1 and 16.13.1(1)) or (b) on the dependence of an Admiralty action *in personam* involving a claim in s.47(2) of the Administration of Justice Act 1956 (and note s.47(3)(a)) on a warrant to arrest on the dependence. Only one ship (the ship concerned or a sister ship) per action may be arrested on the dependence under s.47(1) of the 1956 Act: *Interatlantic (Namibia) (Pty) Ltd v. Okeasnki Ribolov Ltd* 1996 S.L.T. 819; reported as *The "Afala"* in [1995] 2 Lloyd's Rep. 286. There may also be an arrestment of a ship on the dependence of a foreign action on a petition to the Court of Session for such a warrant: see C.J.J.A. 1982, s.27.

The petitioner is not, however, entitled to the warrant to arrest as of right: *Stancroft Securities Ltd v. McDowall*, 1990 S.C. pp. 274, 277 *per* L.J.-C. Ross. The pursuer in the foreign action must comply with s.27 and demonstrate a colourable care in the foreign action: *Clipper Shipping Co. Ltd v. San Vincente Partners* 1989 S.L.T. 204, 207D *per* Lord Coulsfield and *Stancroft Securities Ltd*, above. An affidavit of the foreign lawyer conducting the action may be sufficient: see *e.g. Clipper Shipping Co. Ltd*, above.

It is good practice to mention the name of the ship in the warrant though not essential. A schedule of arrestment on the dependence in Form 16.15–B is attached to the mainmast (or if none, another prominent part) and the Royal initials chalked above it: see r. 16.13(1) and (2). A schedule of arrestment to found jurisdiction is in Form 16.15–AA.

(2) There may be an arrestment *in rem* (a) of a ship or cargo in an Admiralty action *in rem* (an action to enforce a maritime lien over a ship, cargo or freight for money due, but in respect of the ship, only where the claim is one in s.47(2) of the 1956 Act); or (b) of a ship in an Admiralty action *in personam* involving a claim in s.47(2)(p) to (s) of the 1956 Act in respect of a non-pecuniary claim (whether or not there is a lien) by virtue of s.47(3)(b) of that Act. In an Admiralty action *in rem* to arrest the *res* (ship or cargo) there must be an arrestment *in rem*, arrestment on the dependence is not sufficient: r. 46.2(1)(a); and see *Clan Line Steamers Ltd v. Earl of Douglas Steamship Co. Ltd* 1913 S.C. 967, 973 *per* L.P. Dunedin, *Mill v. Fildes* 1982 S.L.T. 147. In an action *in rem* an arrestment *in rem* founds jurisdiction. An arrestment *in rem* must be executed before service: *Mill*, above, at p. 150. The expenses of an arrestment *in rem* are recoverable as part of the expenses of the action: *Hatton v. A/S Durban Hansen* 1919 S.C. 154. A warrant for arrestment *in rem* must specify the particular *res*. A schedule of arrestment in Form 16.15–C (to enforce lien) or Form 16.15–D (to enforce non-pecuniary claim) is attached to the mainmast (or if none, a prominent part): rr. 16.13(1) and 16.15((1)(c) and (d). An arrestment *in rem* of cargo is competent on board ship or anywhere on dry land: r. 16.13(1) or 16.14. Arrestment in Form 16.15–C where the cargo is on board is made by fixing to the mainmast, etc., or, where the cargo is landed, is made in the hands of the custodian (or harbour master where in the harbour): rr. 16.13(1), 16.14 and 16.15(1)(c). There is some doubt whether cargo may be arrested at sea: *cf. Carron Co. v. Currie & Co.* (1896) 33 S.L.R. 578 and Graham Stewart on *Diligence*, p. 108.

(3) There may be arrestment of a cargo on board ship (a) on a warrant to found jurisdiction or (b) on the dependence of an Admiralty action *in personam* or an ordinary action. There is some doubt whether cargo may be arrested at sea: *cf. Carron Co. v. Currie & Co.* (1896) 33 S.L.R. 578 and Graham Stewart on *Diligence*, p. 108.

(4) A ship may be arrested in the harbour or at anchor in the roadstead, but not when she is on passage (set sail): *Carlberg v. Borjesson* (1877) 5 R. 188 and (H.L.) 215. Where the vessel has set sail and is in territorial waters it may be possible to seek a warrant (by motion) to take possession: Graham Stewart, p. 42; but this has been doubted: *The "Grey Dolphin"* 1982 S.C. 5, 7 *per* Lord Wylie. Alternatively caution or consignation may be sought: *Meron v. Umland* (1896) 3 S.L.T. 286. Once arrested the ship must remain where it is: *Carlberg* above, at p. 195 *per* Lord

Shand. If any interested person seeks to remove the vessel to a safer place or for any other reason a special warrant must be obtained by motion under r. 13.11: see *Turner v. Galway* (1882) 19 S.L.R. 892.

See further, arrestment of ships and cargo in rr. 16.13 and 16.14, and Admiralty actions in Chap. 46.

"dismantling a ship". Where an arrestment of a ship might be disregarded an additional **13.6A.5** warrant to dismantle may be inserted. The warrant authorises the taking of the sails, rudders,

anchors or a necessary part of the machinery. Dismantling is usually effected by a marine engineer under the superintendence of the messenger-at-arms executing the warrant.

"calling". For calling, see r. 13.13. Calling may not occur earlier than the day on which the **13.6A.6** period of notice of the summons expires: r. 13.13(1).

"motion". For motions, see Chap. 23.   **13.6A.7**
The motion need not be intimated to any prospective defender: see r. 23.3(1).
Rule 23.8 (motions by pursuer before calling or petitioner before first order) will apply. Rule 13.6A(1) is silent as to whether a hearing before the Lord Ordinary is required. Following the *dicta* in *Advocate General v. Taylor*, 2003 S.L.T. 1340 (Extra Div) at para. [33], a hearing will not normally be required unless the Lord Ordinary requires it. A hearing will not be required if the summons or the motion or other information before the Lord Ordinary contains averments which *prima facie* justify the diligence sought and are proportionate to the claim (see *Advocate General v. Taylor* at para. [34]).

"warrant". If the Lord Ordinary grants warrant for diligence, the blank warrant on the **13.6A.8** summons (see Form 13.2-A as amended) is completed and signed by the Lord Ordinary.

Service and intimation of summonses
13.7.—(1) Where a summons is to be executed, a copy of the summons which has passed the signet shall be—
  (a) served on the defender with a citation in Form 13.7 attached to it; and
  (b) intimated to any person named in a warrant for intimation.
(2) Where service of a summons is not executed within a year and a day after the date of signeting, the instance shall fall.

Deriv. A.S. 8th July 1831, para.III (r. 13.7(2))

General note. Citation is the proper term for the step which brings an action into existence by **13.7.1** giving the defender notice of it—*i.e.* by service of a copy of the summons on him. The word "service" has replaced "citation" in common usage and is used in these Rules.
The date of execution of service (citation) marks the commencement of the action: Erskine, III.iv.3; *Alston v. Macdougall* (1887) 15 R. 78; *Smith v. Stewart & Co.* 1960 S.C. 329, 334 *per* L.P. Clyde. The period of notice before which the summons may not be lodged for calling will begin to run from midnight of that day; except where service is by post when time begins to run from midnight of the day after the date of posting (r. 16.4(6)). For service and intimation, see Chap. 16, Pt. I. Service may be by advertisement: r. 16.5.
It may be necessary to serve other notices with the summons and citation on the defender, *e.g.*, the notice and form in relation to time to pay directions where there is a conclusion for a sum of money less than £10,000: see r. 44.2 and note 44.1.1.
The form of citation served must be signed by the person executing it: Citation Act 1592. See *Blackfriars (Scotland) Ltd v. Laurie*, 14th July 1999 (OH), unreported (citation not signed; r. 2.1 not available to cure failure to comply with Act; decree *de plano* granted). In *Colley v. Celtic Pacific Ship Management (Overseas) Ltd*, 6th October 2000, unreported (2000 G.W.D. 33–1260) the summons was served without any citation. Lord Macfadyen distinguished *Blackfriars*, above, holding that, while anomalously, service of an unsigned citation remained dependent on the 1592 Act, service of a summons was made under r. 13.7 and failure to serve a citation could be cured under r. 2.1 (in that case relief was granted as the failure was due to a genuine oversight). Relief was granted under r. 2.1 in *Greenwoods Ltd v. Ans Homes Ltd*, 2007 S.L.T. 149 (OH) where service by a process server in England was not witnessed.

"served". For methods of service, see Chap. 16, Pt. I.   **13.7.2**

"intimated". For methods, see r. 16.8.   **13.7.3**

"executed within a year and a day". The summons must be served by the end of the last day a **13.7.4** year and one day later. The reason for the additional day is historical, to ensure that a whole year has elapsed. Thereafter, a fresh action must be brought.
The laws of prescription and limitation may, however, have the effect of restricting the period for execution (service). Not only must a summons be executed within a year and a day, it must also be served within a year and a day, of the date of signiting: r. 13.13(6). See the discussion on the meaning of the instance falling in note 13.13.9.

Authority for intimation after signeting
[1] **13.8.** Where a warrant for intimation referred to in rule 13.6(b) is not

obtained when the summons is signeted, the pursuer may apply by motion for authority for intimation of the summons on any person on whom intimation is required in these Rules.

Deriv. R.C.S. 1965, r. 74(d) (r. 13.8A(1))

---

[1] R.13.8 substituted by S.S.I. 2003 No. 537 (effective 10th November, 2003).

13.8.1   *General note.* The previous r. 13.8 dealt with warrants for diligence after signeting. New r. 13.8 deals with intimation after signeting, a subject not previously tackled in the Rules. The R.C.S. 1994 and R.C.S. 1965 were silent about the subject. The rule conforms the practice that intimation to persons not mentioned in the warrant for intimation at the time of signeting is applied for by motion.
     Authority for diligence after calling is now dealt with in r. 13.8A.

13.8.2   *"intimation".* For procedure for intimation, see r. 16.8. For forms, see the particular rules. See also note 13.6.4 for the rules in which intimation of a summons is required.

13.8.3   *"motion".* For motions, see Chap. 23.

Authority for diligence etc. after calling
[1] **13.8A.**—(1) After the calling of a summons, a pursuer may apply by motion for authority for—
     (a) arrestment to found jurisdiction; or
     (b) diligence by—
          (i) inhibition on the dependence of the action;
          (ii) arrestment on the dependence of the action where there is a conclusion for the payment of money;
          (iii) arrestment in rem; or
          (iv) dismantling a ship.
     (2) A certified copy of an interlocutor granting a motion under paragraph (1) shall be sufficient authority for execution of the arrestment to found jurisdiction or, as the case may be, the diligence.

R.13.8A inserted by S.S.I. 2003 No. 537 (effective 10th November, 2003).

13.8A.1   *General note.* New r. 13.8A deals with authority for diligence after calling. As before, authority is sought by motion.
     The previous r. 13.8(2) dealt with diligence sought by motion on the lodging of a minute of amendment. This will still be the case, although not specially mentioned in new r. 13.8A.
     On intimation of motions, see note 13.8A.3 below.

13.8A.2   *"calling".* For calling, see r. 13.13. Calling may not occur earlier than the day on which the period of notice of the summons expires: r. 13.13(1).

13.8A.3   *"motion".* For motions, see Chap. 23. Where the defender has not entered appearance, intimation is not required: r. 23.3(1). Following the *dicta* in *Advocate General v. Taylor*, 2003 S.L.T. 1340 (Extra Div) at para. [33], it is likely that a hearing will not normally be required unless the Lord Ordinary requires it. A hearing will not, presumably, be required if the summons or the motion contains averments which *prima facie* justify the diligence sought and are proportionate to the claim (see *Advocate General v. Taylor* at para. [34]).

13.8A.4   *"arrestment to found jurisdiction".* See note 13.6A.1.

13.8A.5   *"inhibition".* See note 13.6A.2.

13.8A.6   *"arrestment on the dependence".* See note 13.6A.3.

13.8A.7   *"arrestment in rem".* See note 13.6A.4.

13.8A.8   *"dismantling a ship".* See note 13.6A.5.

13.8A.9   *"certified copy interlocutor".* A CCI is a copy of the interlocutor prepared by the party seeking the CCI, stamped and signed by a clerk of session in the General Department.

Effect of authority for inhibition on the dependence

[1] **13.9.**—(1) Where a pursuer has been granted authority for inhibition on the dependence of an action, the signed warrant or, as the case may be, a certified copy of the interlocutor granting the motion under rule 13.8A—

(a) shall have the same effect as letters of inhibition;

(b) may be executed at the same time as the summons is served or at any time thereafter; and

(c) may be registered with a certificate of execution in the Register of Inhibitions and Adjudications.

(2) A notice of a certified copy of an interlocutor granting authority for inhibition under rule 13.8A may be registered under section 155 of the Titles to Land Consolidation (Scotland) Act 1868(a); and such registration shall have the same effect as registration of a notice under that section.

Deriv. R.C.S. 1965, r. 70(2)(a) inserted by S.I. 1984 No.472 (r. 13.9(1)); and r. 74(e) amended by S.I. 1984 No.472 and r. 74(f) (r. 13.9(1) and (2)).

R.13.9 substituted by S.S.I. 2003 No. 537 (effective 10th November, 2003).

General note. Although new r. 13.9 replaces the old rule, the substance of it is the same. **13.9.1**

"same effect as letters of inhibition". For effect of inhibition, see note 13.6.2(5). Letters of **13.9.2** inhibition are used (a) in security on a document of debt where the term of payment is future (at a certain future date) or contingent (at an uncertain future date), (b) on the dependence of a sheriff court action, (c) in execution of Court of Session or sheriff court decrees, (d) in execution of writs registered in the Books of Council and Session or sheriff court books and (e) in execution on a document of debt though there is no decree.

Registration in Register of Inhibitions. To be effectual the inhibition and execution of service **13.9.3** of it on the defender must be registered in the Register of Inhibitions and Adjudications (sometimes known as the "personal" or "diligence" register). The principal signeted summons must be taken to the office of the register in Meadowbank House (open 10am to 4pm Monday to Friday) to be recorded.

An inhibition takes effect from the date of registration: Titles to Land Consolidation (Scotland) Act 1868, s.155. A notice of a summons with a warrant for inhibition may be registered before execution and, if the summons with the execution of service is registered within 21 days after the date of the recording of the notice, the inhibition takes effect from the date of recording of the notice: 1868 Act, s.155. By virtue of r. 13.9(3) the same applies to notice of the certified copy of the interlocutor granting warrant for inhibition (r. 13.9(3) does not refer to a summons because that is provided for in s.155 of the 1868 Act). The Keeper of the Records must enter on each title in the Land Register any subsisting entry in the Register of Inhibitions and Adjudications adverse to the interest: Land Registration (Scotland) Act 1979, s.6(1). A title registered under this Act is subject, generally, only to such rights as are entered in the title sheet (s.3) and an inhibition will not take effect until it is so entered. Practical difficulties arising out of these provisions are discussed in Halliday on *Conveyancing Law and Practice*, Vol. II, (2nd ed.), para. 38–35 and Gretton on *Law of Inhibition and Adjudication* (2nd ed.), pp.39–43.

Recall etc. of arrestment or inhibition

13.10.—(1) An application by any person having an interest—

(a) to loose, restrict or recall an arrestment; or

(b) to recall, in whole or in part, an inhibition,

shall be made by motion.

Deriv. Debtors (Scotland) Act 1838, s.20; R.C.S. 1965, r. 74(g) amended by S.I. 1990 No.705 and 1991 No.2483 (r. 13(10)(1) and (2)) and r. 74(h) amended by S.I. 1990 No.705 (r. 13.10(3)).

R.13.10 substituted by S.S.I. 2003 No. 537 (effective 10th November, 2003).

General note. New r. 13.10(1) was substituted by A.S. (R.C.S.A.No.5) (Diligence on the **13.10.1** Dependence) 2003 [S.S.I. 2003 No. 537]. The substance of r. 13.10(1) is the same, namely, that loosing, restricting or recalling is by motion. It is not competent to lodge a caveat against inhibition or arrestment, although interdict may be obtained (see note 5.1.3). The procedure under this rule may be used by a defender or other interested person at any time after signeting when the diligence has been executed.

The rule does not apply to arrestment to found jurisdiction or dismantling of a ship, for which provision is not necessary. In relation to arrestment to found jurisdiction, see *Greig & Brunsgaard, Kjosterud & Co.* (1896) 23 R. 500.

Where the motion is made before calling by an interested person other than the defender and before the defender has entered appearance, the motion does not have to be intimated to the defender (r. 23.3). There is no requirement for intimation to the pursuer; but the Deputy Clerk of Session will inform the pursuer and the Keeper will arrange a hearing for both parties to attend, usually the next day: r. 23.9. To obtain a judge after 5pm, ring the Court of Session (031–225 2595), leave your name and telephone number and the duty security guard will contact a clerk who will contact you.

13.10.2   *"any person having an interest"*. This includes the defender, an arrestee, owner of arrested property or other person affected by the diligence. Earlier difficulties about who could apply for recall are overcome by this provision. Thus an owner claiming the arrested property as his and not due to the debtor can apply for recall.

13.10.3   *Loosing of arrestment*. This means a permission to the defender (or other person) to obtain, or for the release of, the arrested property but which does not extinguish the arrestment of the legal nexus created until the property is uplifted by the defender. If a later arrestment is laid by another creditor before the property is uplifted, the loosing is ineffectual when the pursuer is notified of the later arrestment. In relation to ships, loosing means a permission to move the ship and does not recall the arrestment but postpones the arrestment until after the move: *Svenska Petroleum A.B. v. H.O.R. Ltd* 1982 S.L.T. 343; and see r. 13.11. Loosing is distinguished from restriction, and from recall which extinguishes the arrestment.

13.10.4   *Restriction or recall*. The grounds for restriction or recall include the following.

(1) *Where the arrestment or inhibition is nimious or oppressive*: Examples are: **(a)** Where the conclusions are extravagant or the sum arrested far exceeds the claim: *Shanks v. Thomson* (1838) 16 S. 1353 (arrestment); *Mylne v. Blackwood* (1832) 10 S. 430 (inhibition); *McInally v. Kildonal Homes Ltd* 1979 S.L.T. (Notes) 89. **(b)** Where the pursuer already has sufficient security: *Magistrates of Dundee v. Taylor and Grant* (1863) 1 M. 701 (arrestment); *Cullen v. Buchanan* (1862) 24 D. 1280 (inhibition). **(c)** Where there are more than sufficient funds to meet the claim and there are no prospects of it being defeated by other creditors: *Magistrates of Dundee*, above; *West Cumberland Farmers Ltd v. Director of Agriculture of Sri Lanka* 1988 S.L.T. 296 (arrestment); although this may be a ground for rejecting a plea of nimiety or oppression: *Mendok BV v. Cumberland Maritime Corporation* 1989 S.L.T. 192, 193 *per* Lord McDonald. The critical question to consider when determining the issue of insolvency in the context of recall of inhibition is whether a significant risk of insolvency exists at the time when the claim, if sustained by the court, falls to be paid; accordingly the future has to be considered and a balance sheet is not conclusive: *Barry D Trentham Ltd v. Lawfield Investments Ltd,* 2002 S.C. 401, 406, para.[13] (OH). **(d)** Where there is excessive delay in pursuing the action, where the defender has consigned the sum, where the purpose is not to protect legitimate interests but to embarrass the defender: *Levy v. Gardiner* 1964 S.L.T. (Notes) 68; *Conoco Speciality Products (Inc.) v. Merpro Montassa Ltd (No. 2)* 1991 S.L.T. 513; *Hydraload Research Ltd v. Bone Connell & Baxters Ltd* 1996 S.L.T. 219. **(e)** Where there is no colourable case or no intelligible and discernible cause of action, though the averments are not examined with the scrutiny of a procedure roll debate: *West Cumberland Farmers Ltd v. Ellon Hinengo Ltd* 1988 S.L.T. 294 *per* Lord Weir; *Clipper Shipping Co. Ltd v. San Vincente Partners* 1989 S.L.T. 204 (affidavit of foreign lawyer accepted); *Stratmail Ltd v. D. & A. Todd (Building Contractors) Ltd* 1990 S.L.T. 493 (unanswerable plea of *lis alibi pendens*); *Hydraload*, above. Indeed, the court is not confined to the pursuer's averments but may look at the material but may look at the material before it: *Stiell Facilities Ltd v. Sir Robert McAlpine Ltd,* 2001 S.L.T. 1229 (OH). **(f)** Where the diligence had only a nuisance value: *Taymech Ltd v. Rush & Tompkins Ltd* 1990 S.L.T. 681. **(g)** Where arrestment unduly interferes with ordinary trading activities without legitimate advantage: *Matheson v. Matheson* 1995 S.L.T. 765. **(h)** Use of diligence on the dependence against foreign state agencies is uncommon as they could normally be expected to meet any decree, and the use of such diligence in those circumstances would be oppressive. But a distinction is to be drawn in the case of bodies merely or supported by foreign governments such as state-owned companies: *Tor Corporate AS v. China National Star Petroleum Corporation,* 27th July 2000 (OH), unreported.

(2) *Where the debt is future or contingent and there are no averments of special circumstances—* e.g. that the debtor is *vergens ad inopiam* or *in meditatione fugae—*the diligence is in fact incompetent: see note 13.6.3(3).

(3) *Where there is a defect or irregularity in execution*: e.g. *Richards & Wallington (Earthmoving) Ltd v. Whatlings Ltd* 1982 S.L.T. 66 (action and arrestment in wrong name, the company having changed its name before the action; arrestment recalled). In *Dramgate Ltd v. Tyne Dock Engineering Ltd*, 2000 S.C. 43 (Ex Div.), an arrestment on the dependence was held wrongful because it had been executed before the arrestment to found jurisdiction (before which there was no jurisdiction). The arrestment on the dependence in that case being defective, it was not necessary to aver malice and want of probable cause.

(4) *Where the property arrested is not arrestable*: *Forth & Clyde Construction Co. Ltd v. Trinity Timber & Plywood Co. Ltd* 1984 S.L.T. 94; though this is usually determined in the action of furthcoming.

(5) *Where the property arrested is not that of the defender*: *Barclay Curle & Co. Ltd v. Sir James Laing & Sons Ltd* 1908 S.C. 82; *Blade Securities Ltd, Petrs.* 1989 S.L.T. 246; *Sunrise Trading Co. Ltd v. Mobil Sales and Supply Corporation*, 27th October 1995, unreported, 1996 G.W.D. 2–111 (separate companies allegedly a single economic unit).

(6) *Where caution or consignation is offered in lieu*, as diligence is simply to provide a security: see note 13.10.5.

(7) *Where the pursuer has not made out a prima facie case on the merits of the action.* In *Advocate General v. Taylor*, 2004 S.C. 339, 2003 S.L.T. 1340, para. [34], it was held by an Extra Division that for a warrant for inhibition (and it would also apply to arrestment) the applicant need only establish a prima facie case on the merits of the action; the necessity for diligence need not be demonstrated, although it may no doubt assist. In that event, a ground for recall must now be that the pursuer has not made out a prima facie case on the merits. The prima facie test is a substantial hurdle for the pursuer to surmount: *Gillespie v. Toondale Ltd*, 2006 S.C. 304, 308, para. [13] (Extra Div. approving Lord Drummond Young in *Barry D Trentham Ltd v. Lawfield Investments Ltd*, 2002 S.C. 401, 2002 S.L.T. 1094, at para. [6] on the meaning of "prima facie", i.e. a good arguable case).

If there is a disputed question of right to the subjects arrested it will not be decided in the application for recall unless instantly verifiable without a proof, or caution is offered for the recall: *Vincent v. Chalmers & Co.'s Tr.* (1877) 5 R. 43; *William Batey (Exports) Ltd v. Kent* 1987 S.L.T. 557.

Recall of arrestments may be of all arrestments used and to be used (general recall), or specified arrestments or those used (special recall); the warrant for arrestment being rarely recalled. In the recall of inhibitions, the warrant itself is recalled because the warrant authorises one diligence. Interim recall of diligence is not competent. When an inhibition has been recalled a certified copy interlocutor should be obtained (prepared by the applicant for certification by a clerk of session in the appropriate section of the General Department) and recorded in the Register of Inhibitions and Adjudications. If there is a partial recall, the interlocutor should contain an adequate description of the subjects excluded. This is to enable the Keeper of the Registers to make the appropriate entry in the Register of Inhibitions and Adjudications and, if appropriate, the Land Register. It is preferable for the interlocutor to specify the subjects excluded rather than those included for it is only in respect of the former that the defender has satisfied the court that the inhibition should be recalled. The recall ought not to be recorded until after the reclaiming days have expired (14 days: see r. 38.3(4)(*h*)).

Certain statutes confer particular powers for recall, loosing or restriction of arrestments and inhibitions. These include: Administration of Justice Act 1956, s. 47(5), proviso (arrestment of ship *in rem* for non-pecuniary claim); Merchant Shipping (Liability of Shipowners and Others) Act 1958, s. 6 (arrestment for claim for which limit is set by the Merchant Shipping Act 1894, s. 503); Merchant Shipping Act 1995, s. 159 (arrestment on dependence or *in rem* where defender can limit his liability); Debtors (Scotland) Act 1987, ss. 2(3) and 3(1) (arrestments in relation to time to pay directions); Criminal Justice Act 1988, s. 92(4) (arrestment or inhibition of property affected by restraint orders relating to the proceeds of crime); Prevention of Terrorism (Temporary Provisions) Act 1989, Sched.4, paras. 16 and 16A (inhibition or arrestment of property affected by restraint orders relating to property liable to forfeiture); Proceeds of Crime (Scotland) Act 1995, ss. 32(1) and 33(1) (inhibition or arrestment of property affected by restraint orders or interdict relating to the proceeds of crime).

Caution, other security or consignation. This may not be required where the diligence was **13.10.5** nimious or oppressive: e.g. where there is no colourable case; where its use is merely to embarrass the defender (*Levy v. Gardiner* 1964 S.L.T. (Notes) 68); where the debt is future or contingent and there are no special circumstances averred; where there was irregularity in execution; where the property arrested was not arrestable or was not the property of the defender (and this is instantly verifiable). Where the conclusions are extravagant or the sum arrested is excessive or the claim is for a random sum, caution will be fixed having regard to the nature of the action, the extent of the subjects affected by the diligence and the circumstances of the defender. Where the defender has ample funds he may be required to find caution or consignation as a condition of recall (*cf. West Cumberland Farmers Ltd v. Director of*

Agriculture of Sri Lanka 1988 S.L.T. 296). Failure to offer caution may be regarded as grounds for doubting an ability to meet the claim.

Caution in lieu of arrestment may be for the arrested property or its value, but usually for the whole debt including expenses; where caution is for the whole debt a general recall should be obtained, and where a general recall is sought caution must be for the whole debt including expenses. Where recall is made on caution for the whole debt the interlocutor recalls only the arrestments used and not future arrestments (special recall), future arrestments are not ineffectual or incompetent. Caution in lieu of inhibition is usually for the whole debt including expenses.

In deciding whether a guarantee offered is an adequate alternative security to replace that held by an arrestment, the relevant comparison is between the security afforded by the proposed guarantee on the one hand and that afforded by the arrestment (and not a guarantee by an independent financial institution) on the other: *Global Marine Drilling Co. v. Triton Holdings Ltd (No.2)*, 26th January 2000, (2000 G.W.D. 5-210) (OH). There is no rule that recall should normally be on the provision of a guarantee by such an institution: *Global Marine Drilling Co*, above.   Another form of security other than caution may be allowed: r. 33.4(2). Consignation may be ordered in lieu of caution: see *Fisher v. Weir* 1964 S.L.T. (Notes) 99.

13.10.6   *Expenses*. This depends on the circumstances of the arrestment or inhibition not the merits of the action: *Clark v. Loos* (1855) 17 D. 306. Where arrestment or inhibition was improperly used (nimiously, oppressively, incompetently or irregularly), the pursuer pays the judicial expenses incurred in the recall. Where properly used but loosed, restricted or recalled on caution, the defender may be required to pay the expenses. Expenses may be reserved where diligence is properly used and recalled on caution or consignation (*Dobbie v. Duncanson* (1872) 10 M. 810, 816 *per* L.P. Inglis). The expenses of an unsuccessful application for recall are borne by the applicant. See also Graham Stewart on *Diligence*, pp. 212 and 573; Gretton on the *Law of Inhibition and Adjudication*, pp. 39–41.

13.10.7   *"motion"*. For motions, see Chap. 23.

13.10.8   *Reclaiming*. An interlocutor loosing, recalling or restricting an arrestment or recalling, in whole or in part, an inhibition or refusing such, may be reclaimed without leave within 14 days: r. 38.3(4)(*h*).

Movement of arrested property

13.11.—[1](1) Any person having an interest may apply by motion for a warrant authorising the movement of a vessel or cargo which is the subject of an arrestment mentioned in rule 13.6A.

(2) Where the court grants a warrant sought under paragraph (1), it may make such further order as it thinks fit to give effect to that warrant.

(3) A warrant granted on a motion under paragraph (1) shall be without prejudice to the validity and subsistence of the arrestment.

Deriv. R.C.S. 1965, r. 74(*g*) and (*h*), and r. 140(*d*) and (*dd*), amended by S.I. 1990 No. 705

---

[1] R.13.11(1) amended by S.S.I. 2004 No. 537 (effective 10th November, 2003).

13.11.1   *General note*. Rule 13.11(1) was amended by A.S. (R.C.S.A.No.5) (Diligence on the Dependence) 2003 [S.S.I. 2003 No. 537] to include a reference to new r. 13.6A.

This rule was introduced to overcome difficulties associated with someone having an interest in a ship or cargo seeking to move a ship or cargo. A vessel might be obstructing or causing loss to an innocent third party.

This is really a species of loosing of an arrestment, but is dealt with separately for the reasons above and because in the case of arrestment of a ship there is no arrestee. If a cargo is arrested but cannot be unloaded the ship is effectively immobilised. See *Svenska Petroleum A.B. v. H.O.R. Ltd* 1982 S.L.T. 343; *West Cumberland Farmers Ltd v. Director of Agriculture of Sri Lanka* 1988 S.L.T. 296. Authority may be obtained to bring an arrested vessel into a safe harbour: *Turner v. Galway* (1882) 19 S.L.R. 892; *The "Grey Dolphin"* 1982 S.C. 5.

Where the motion is made by an interested person before the defender has entered appearance, the motion does not have to be intimated to the defender: see r. 23.3. There is no provision for intimation to the pursuer, but the Deputy Principal Clerk will inform the pursuer of the motion (whether made by the defender or an interested person) and the Keeper of the Rolls will arrange a hearing at short notice for both parties to attend, usually the next day; but it could be the same day or night: see r. 23.10. To obtain a judge after 5pm, ring the Court of Session (0131–225 2595), leave your name and telephone number and the duty security guard will contact a clerk who will contact you.

Reclaiming. An interlocutor granting authority to move an arrested vessel or cargo may be **13.11.3** reclaimed against without leave within 14 days: r. 38.3(4)(i).

Intimation of actions relating to heritable property

13.12.—(1) In an action relating to heritable property, it shall not be necessary to call a person as a defender by reason only of any interest he may have as the holder of a heritable security over the heritable property; but intimation of the summons shall be given to that person by a notice of intimation in Form 13.12 attached to a copy of the summons.

(2) A warrant for intimation under paragraph (1) shall be inserted in the summons by the pursuer in the following terms: "Warrant to intimate to (*name and address*) as a person who is believed to be a heritable creditor of the defender.".

(3) A person on whom intimation has been made under this rule may apply by motion for leave to be sisted as a party and to lodge defences.

Deriv. R.C.S. 1965, r. 76 amended by S.I. 1991 No. 2483

General note. The proper defender in an action is the person who has the real title and interest **13.12.1** to prevent the pursuer from obtaining decree. A person having a security over heritable property may have an interest in the action, but he is not the real owner of the property, hence the rule for intimation only.

The rule applies even in a family action where an order is sought in respect of heritable property.

A heritable creditor to whom intimation has been made under this rule may seek by motion to enter the process: r. 13.12(3). Defences (not a minute) should be lodged when the motion is enrolled. On defences, see Chap. 18.

"intimation". For procedure, see r. 16.8. Where the warrant is not inserted in the summons **13.12.2** before signeting it may be applied for by motion: r. 13.8.

Calling

13.13.—(1) A summons shall not be called earlier than the day on which the period of notice expires.

(2) A summons shall be lodged for calling not later than 12.30 p.m. on the second day before that on which it is to be called.

(3) A summons may be called—

(a) during session, on a sederunt day; or

(b) in vacation, on a calling day of which notice has been given in the rolls.

(4) A summons lodged for calling shall be accompanied by a typewritten slip containing the instance, subject to the following provisions—

(a) where there is more than one pursuer or defender, the slip shall contain only the name and designation of the first pursuer or defender, as the case may be, followed by the words "and Another [*or* Others, *as the case may be*]"; and

(b) in naming and designing a pursuer or defender which is a body of persons (such as a trust or partnership), whether individual members are also parties or not, it shall be sufficient to use the collective name of that body.

(5) The calling of a summons shall be published in the rolls on the date on which the summons calls.

(6) Where a summons has not called within a year and a day after the expiry of the period of notice, the instance shall fall.

Deriv. A.S. 8th July 1831, para. III, (r. 13.13(6)); R.C.S. 1965, r. 78(a) to (c) and (e) (r. 13.13(1) to (5)); P.N. No. 3 of 1976, para. 3(vi) (r. 13.13(1) and (2))

General note. The calling of a summons brings the action into court. This must be done within **13.13.1** a year and a day of the expiry of the period of notice (r. 13.13(1) and (6)) by publication in the calling list in the rolls (r. 13.13(5)).

For the summons to call the pursuer must return the summons to the process (which was lodged for signeting and registration (see rr. 4.3 and 13.5(3)) in the appropriate section of the General Department (see note 3.2.1) either in person or by post (P.N. No.4 of 1994, paras 1 and 4). Where the summons is lodged for calling by post the pursuer will be informed by letter if it is accepted for calling; where there are any defects which cannot be dealt with by telephone, the summons will be returned by post: P.N. No. 4 of 1994, para. 4(3).

13.13.2   *"not earlier than the day on which the period of notice expires"*. The summons may call on the last day of the period of notice. The period of notice runs (a) where service is by post, from midnight of the day after the day of posting: r. 16.3(6); and (b) in any other case, from midnight of the day on which service is executed.

13.13.3   *"period of notice"*. See r. 13.4.

13.13.4   *Session and vacation.* On sessions of the court, see rr. 10.1, 10.3 and 10.4. On vacations, see rr. 10.1 and 10.5.

13.13.5   *"sederunt day"*. This is a day on which the court sits: see r. 10.2.

13.13.6   *Calling days.* A summons may be called on a sederunt day: in session, Tuesday to Friday (see rr. 10.2(1) and 10.3(1)); or, in vacation, a day of which notice is given in the rolls about four weeks before the end of the preceding term, being a sederunt day specified by direction by the Lord President under r. 10.2(2) (usually every Thursday). For the office hours of the General Department and holidays, see note 3.1.2.

13.13.7   *Calling slip.* The typewritten slip referred to in r. 13.13(4) is a calling slip. It provides the information required for publication in the calling list (on the noticeboard at the top of the main corridor of Parliament House after the reception area at door 11). The list is published every sederunt day and contains the names and addresses of the parties in the summons including any capacity in which they sue or are sued (it is usually a repetition of the instance).

13.13.8   *"called within a year and a day"*. The period of notice expires at midnight on the last day of that period and time runs from then. The summons must call at the latest by the end of the last day a year and a day later. The reason for the additional day is historical, to ensure that a whole year elapsed. Thereafter a fresh action must be brought. Where the last day falls on a Saturday, Sunday or a public holiday on which the Office of Court is closed, the next available day is allowed: r. 1.3(7). For office hours and holidays, see note 3.1.2.

13.13.9   *"the instance shall fall"*. This rule repeats the rule in para.III of the A.S. of 8th July 1831 that if a summons is not called within a year and a day of the expiry of the period of notice the instance falls. The instance falling means, or meant, that the summons thereafter is at an end and has no existence: *Cumming v. Munro* (1833) 12 S. 61, 63 *per* Lord Cringletie; *McKidd v. Manson* (1882) 9 R. 790, 791 *per* L.P. Inglis. The consequence of the decision of Lord Macfadyen in *McDonald v. Kwok* 1999 S.L.T. 593 is that it can no longer be said or relied upon that an action has ceased to exist in that situation. In that case it was held that r. 2.1 (relief for failure to comply with rules) was a power that it was always competent to invoke and the terms of which were wholly unqualified. A motion, therefore, to invoke the power in r. 2.1 to enable a summons to call is, despite the terms of r. 13.13(6) according to Lord Macfadyen, competent. This decision is, to say the least, unfortunate as it negates the spirit and intention of r. 13.13(6); a defender will have hanging over him indefinitely (subject to prescription) an action which is capable of resuscitation. The remedy which Lord Macfadyen says the defender has, namely, protestation under r. 13.14, is not so much a remedy for the defender as a reminder to the pursuer. *McDonald*, above, was followed in *Kilna v. De La Salle*, 2005 S.C.L.R. 154 but overruled in *Brogan v. O'Rourke Ltd*, 2005 S.L.T. 29 (Extra Div.) where it was held that rr. 13.13(6) and 43.3(2) were plain and the meaning of "the instance shall fall" was perfectly understood: where the summons has not called within the specified period the instance falls and it is incompetent to apply to the court under r. 2.1.

13.13.10   *Documents founded on or adopted.* Any document founded on or adopted as incorporated in the summons must be lodged as a production when the summons is lodged for calling: see r. 27.1(1)(a). For lodging of productions, see r. 4.5. For the meaning of documents founded on or adopted, see note 27.1.2.

Protestation for not calling summons

13.14.—(1) Where the pursuer does not lodge the summons for calling within seven days after the date on which the period of notice expires, the defender, on production of the service copy summons, may apply by motion for an order ordaining the pursuer to lodge the summons for calling within seven days, or such other period as the court thinks fit, after the date of the order.

(2) Where the court pronounces an interlocutor under paragraph (1), the defender shall serve a certified copy of that interlocutor on the pursuer.

(3) Where the pursuer fails to lodge the summons within the period ordered by the court under paragraph (1), the defender may apply by motion—

(a) for declarator that the instance has fallen;

(b) for recall of any diligence mentioned in rule 13.6(c) which has been executed; and

(c) for payment to the defender of his expenses of process under this rule.

(4) An interlocutor granting a motion under paragraph (3) shall be final and not subject to review.

Deriv. R.C.S. 1965, r. 80(a)

General note. Protestation is the means by which a defender compels the pursuer who has not **13.14.1** lodged the summons for calling to proceed with his action or have the court bring the process to an end. The principle of protestation in R.C.S. 1965, r. 80 is retained, but the procedure is new.

"motion". For motions, see Chap. 23.   **13.14.2**

"within seven days". The date of expiry of the period of notice or of the order is not counted   **13.14.3**
in calculating the period; and the seventh day is included in the period. When the last day falls
on a public holiday, Saturday or Sunday or on which the Office of Court is closed, the next
available day is allowed: r. 1.3(7). For office hours and holidays, see note 3.1.2.

"diligence mentioned in rule 13.6(c)". The diligences are arrestment and inhibition on the   **13.14.4**
dependence, arrestment *in rem* and dismantling of a ship. Recall is not restricted to diligence
executed on a warrant inserted in a summons under r. 13.6.

certified copy interlocutor. For fee, see Court of Session etc. Fees Order 1984, Table of Fees,   **13.14.5**
Pt. IV, J, item 2 [SI 1984/256, Table as amended, pp. **C** 1202 *et seq.*].

"served". For service, see Chap. 16, Pt. I. A certificate of service must be lodged: r. 16.1(3).   **13.14.6**

Expenses. The expenses will usually be the judicial expenses of process. Expenses are in the   **13.14.7**
discretion of the court and, where awarded, are on a party and party basis unless otherwise
ordered: *Fletcher's Trs. v. Fletcher* (1888) 15 R. 862. Expenses may be modified (r. 42.5);
modification being the exact ascertainment of the precise sum that is to be paid: *Kintore v. Pirie*
(1904) 12 S.L.T. 385, 386 *per* Lord Kinnear.

Finality of protestation. A pursuer cannot now be reponed against a protestation. He receives   **13.14.8**
intimation of the order of the court (r. 13.14(2)) and can oppose the subsequent motion under r.
13.14(3) (the decision on which is final (r. 13.14(4)). Protestation does not prevent the pursuer
raising the action again because the plea of *res judicata* does not arise.

CHAPTER 14

PETITIONS

Application of this Chapter
14.1. Subject to any other provision in these Rules, this Chapter applies to
a petition presented to the court.

General note. This Chapter provides the general rules for applications by petition. But there   **14.1.1**
are a number of Chapters in the Rules providing special provisions for particular applications
by petition. The rules in this Chapter do not apply where they are excluded expressly or by
implication in a Chapter providing particular rules.

Distinction between petition and summons. A petition is an *ex parte* application addressed to   **14.1.2**
the Lords of Council and Session and seeks their aid for some purpose or other, by exercising
some statutory jurisdiction or the *nobile officium* in a variety of matters: *Tomkins v. Cohen* 1951
S.C. 22, 23 *per* Lord Keith. A petition involves a less formal procedure than a summons. "The
object of the summons is to enforce a pursuer's legal right against a defender who resists it, or to
protect a legal right which the defender is infringing; the object of a petition, on the other hand,
is to obtain from the administrative jurisdiction of the court power to do something or to
require something to be done, which is just and proper should be done, but which the
petitioner has no legal right to do or to require, apart from judicial authority": Report of the
Royal Commission on the Court of Session 1927 (Cmd. 2801), pp. 49–50. See also
Encyclopaedia of the Laws of Scotland (Dunedin edition), Vol.11, sv. "Petition", para. 696.

Applications by petition in the Outer House
14.2. Subject to any other provision in these Rules, the following
applications to the court shall be made by petition presented in the Outer
House:—
    (*a*) an application for the appointment of a judicial factor, a factor *loco
       absentis*, a factor pending litigation or a curator *bonis*;
    (*b*) an application for the appointment of a judicial factor on the estate
       of a partnership or joint adventure;
    (*c*) an application to the *nobile officium* of the court which relates to—
       (i) the administration of a trust;
       (ii) the office of trustee; or
       (iii) a public trust;
    (*d*) a petition and complaint for breach of interdict;
    (*e*) an application to the supervisory jurisdiction of the court;

(*f*) an application for suspension, suspension and interdict, and suspension and liberation;

(*g*) an application to recall an arrestment or inhibition other than in a cause depending before the court;

(*h*) a petition or other application under these Rules or any other enactment or rule of law; and

[1] (*i*) an application to the court in exercise of its *parens patriae* jurisdiction.

Deriv. R.C.S. 1965, r. 69, and r. 189(*a*) (preamble) (amended by SI 1970/134), (i), (ii), (iii) (substituted by SI 1987/1206), (iv) (amended by SI 1987/1206) and (xxxvii) (inserted by SI 1990/705), (r. 14.2(*a*)–(*h*))

---

[1] R. 14.2(*i*) inserted by SI 1996/1756 (effective 5th August 1996)

14.2.1   *General note.* Most petitions are dealt with at first instance in the Outer House. R. 14.2(*h*) is intended to catch applications to the court under primary or subordinate legislation, or the common law, whether or not specified to be by petition under the particular enactment or these Rules, except where specified to be an action or an application by minute (see, *e.g.* certain applications in family actions in Chap. 49), note (see, *e.g.* certain applications relating to companies in Chap. 74) or motion (see r. 23.11 (statutory applications by motion in causes depending before the court unless otherwise provided)). This rule is subject, therefore, to other provisions in the Rules and in particular to r. 14.3 which provides for Inner House petitions.

The list in r. 14.2(*a*)–(*g*) consists mostly of the common law petitions. All statutory applications by petition are Outer House petitions unless listed in r. 14.3 as Inner House petitions: r. 14.2(h).

14.2.2   *"presented in the Outer House".* A petition is presented by being lodged for the first order (granting warrant for all or any of service, intimation and advertisement): see r. 14.5. All petitions when presented to the court are lodged in the Petition Department: r. 3.3. The petition is given a cause reference number when presented: r. 4.1(4) and note 4.1.5.

14.2.3   *Judicial factors.* See Chap. 61.

14.2.4   *Factor on estate of partnership or joint adventure.* As the court has a common law power to sequestrate the estate of a partnership, a judicial factor may be appointed to protect the firm's assets until the firm is dissolved (*McCulloch v. McCulloch* 1953 S.C. 189) or where there is a dispute between the partners which may materially prejudice the affairs of the partnership (*Carabine v. Carabine* 1949 S.C. 521). (Sequestration is a judicial order divesting the person sequestrated of his estate by a judicial conveyance in favour of the trustee in the sequestration.) Where such an appointment is sought a crave for sequestration should be included: *Booth v. Mackinnon* (1908) 15 S.L.T. 848. When all the partners are dead the court will appoint a factor: *Dickie v. Mitchell* (1874) 1 R. 1030, 1033 *per* L.P. Inglis. Where there are surviving partners but they are by fault or incapacity unfitted to carry on the partnership or to wind it up, the court will appoint a judicial factor: *Dickie,* above. There must be some compelling cause to wind up a partnership or joint adventure such as fraud, abuse of power or unreasonable delay: Bell's *Comm.,* ii,527 (McLaren's note 3); *Collins v. Young* (1853) 1 Macq. 385. A petition to dissolve a partnership under s.35 of the Partnership Act 1890 is an Outer House petition: r. 14.2(h).

Jurisdiction. The court may have jurisdiction under Sched.8 to the C.J.J.A. 1982 (jurisdiction of Scottish courts), r. 1 (domicile), r. 2(9) (moveable property) or r. 4(1) (exclusive jurisdiction); see also the 1968 and Lugano Conventions, Scheds. 1 and 3C, Arts. 2 and 16, and Sched.4 (inter-UK jurisdiction), Arts. 1, 5A and 16, in the C.J.J.A. 1982.

14.2.5   *Administration of trust or office of trustee.*

(1) *Jurisdiction.* The court has jurisdiction over Scottish trusts. For what constitutes a Scottish trust, see *Clarke's Trs., Petrs.* 1966 S.L.T. 249, 251 *per* L.P. Clyde. A trust may also be a trust of another legal system. Jurisdiction over a trust for certain proceedings is determined by the C.J.J.A. 1982. Under Sched.8 (jurisdiction of Scottish courts) jurisdiction depends on where the trust is domiciled, but whether another court has exclusive jurisdiction in relation to particular proceedings has to be considered: see C.J.J.A. 1982, Sched.8, r. 4; see also jurisdiction under the 1968 and Lugano Conventions in C.J.J.A. 1982, Scheds. 1 and 3C. For the purposes of Scheds. 1, 3C and 8 to the C.J.J.A. 1982 a trust is domiciled in Scotland if it has its closest and most real connection there: C.J.J.A. 1982, s.45 (as amended by the C.J.J.A. 1991, Sched.2, para. 20). Not every aspect of a trust will be determined by the domicile of the trust,

but the appointment and removal of a trustee will be where the C.J.J.A. 1982 applies. Sch.8 to that Act does not determine jurisdiction where no decree is sought against a person: Sch.9, para.13. Accordingly, where the C.J.J.A. 1982 does not apply the common law is still relevant. At common law jurisdiction is determined by the principle that every person beneficially interested ought to seek his remedy in that court in which it is most for the benefit of the trust and all concerned that the litigation should be carried on: *Orr Ewing's Trs v. Orr Ewing* (1885) 13 R.(H.L.) 1, 31 *per* Lord Watson. Arts 6 and 7 of the Sched. to the Recognition of Trusts Act 1987 determines the choice of law governing a trust.

The court will assist the administration of an English trust in an ancillary role: *Evans-Freke's Trs, Petrs* 1945 S.C. 382.

(2) *Administration of trust.* See Wilson & Duncan on *Trusts, Trustees and Executors*, pp. 298–317. This does not include a petition for directions under Chap. 63, Part II, which is an Inner House petition (see r.14.3(e)).

(3) *Office of trustee.* This relates to the appointment and removal of trustees. The court has a common law power and a statutory power (ss.22 and 23 of the Trusts (Scotland) Act 1921). A person interested in the trust estate may petition. Where the ground is mental incapacity, two medical certificates (one from each of two medical practitioners following examination of the *incapax* dated within 30 days of the examination and one month of the presentation of the petition; the certificates do not have to be on soul and conscience: P.N. of 6th June 1968) are required as in the case of appointment of a curator *bonis* in similar circumstances: *Lees, Petr* (1893) 1 S.L.T. 42. If an appointment of a new trustee is of a person not resident in Scotland (see Wilson & Duncan on *Trusts, Trustees and Executors*, pp. 277–278) a bond of prorogation should be lodged: for a style, see McBryde & Dowie on *Petition Procedure*, 2nd ed., p. 164. Applications to the court under the 1921 Act are to the Lord Ordinary in the Outer House: 1921 Act, s.26. See Wilson & Duncan, pp. 270–280 and 293–297.

Breach of interdict. Breach of interim interdict in a depending cause is dealt with by minute in **14.2.6** that process: C.S.A. 1988, s.47(1). In any other case it is by petition and complaint. A cause is depending until final decree, whereas a cause is in dependence until final extract. For the meaning of final decree, see note 4.15.2(2). For the meaning of final extract, see note 7.1.2(2).

The petition (or minute) must have the concurrence of the Lord Advocate as public prosecutor because of its quasi-criminal character: *Gribben v. Gribben* 1976 S.L.T. 266. His concurrence is written on the principal petition (or minute). It is not necessary to intimate to the Lord Advocate all adjustment or amendments to the pleadings if these are averments which are part of the same course of conduct averred: *Byrne v. Ross* 1992 S.C. 498. Proceedings for breach of interdict are civil proceedings to which s.1(1) of the Civil Evidence (Scotland) Act 1988 (rule requiring corroboration abolished) applies: *Byrne*, above.

Care must be taken to name and design the respondent correctly as a material error will invalidate the petition: *Overseas League v. Taylor* 1951 S.C. 105; *cf. Anderson v. Stoddart* 1923 S.C. 755 (immaterial error). As breach of interdict constitutes a contempt of court which might lead to punishment, it is necessary in the interests of fairness that the alleged contempt is clearly and distinctly averred, and the proceedings for contempt should be confined to the averments: *Byrne*, above.

Jurisdiction. If the court has jurisdiction to grant the interdict it will have jurisdiction to deal with a breach unless jurisdiction has been lost. The court has jurisdiction under Sch.8 of the C.J.J.A. 1982 (jurisdiction of Scottish courts), r.1 (domicile) and r.2(j) (interdict where wrong to be committed). See also jurisdiction under Sch.1 (1968 Convention), Sch.3C (Lugano Convention) and Sch.4 (inter-U.K. jurisdiction), Art.5(3) (jurisdiction in delict) and Art.24 (protective measures), and s.24(2) (protective measures where jurisdiction doubtful) and s.27 (protective measures), and under the Brussels I Regulation, Arts.5(3) and 31.

Supervisory jurisdiction of the court. This phrase is nowhere defined but describes a **14.2.7** superintending authority over inferior jurisdictions to keep inferior jurisdictions and administrative bodies right: see *McCreadie v. Thomson* 1907 S.C. 1176, 1183 *per* L.J.-C. Macdonald; *Moss's Empires v. Assessor for Glasgow* 1917 S.C.(H.L.) 1, 11 *per* Lord Shaw of Dunfermline. This jurisdiction is now exercised on an application for judicial review by petition: see Chap. 58. It includes an application for an order for specific performance of a statutory duty under s.45(b) of the C.S.A. 1988.

Suspension, suspension and interdict, suspension and liberation. See Chap. 60. **14.2.8**

Recall of arrestment or inhibition. Where the arrestment or inhibition has been executed in a **14.2.9** depending action an application for recall may be made by motion: r.13.10. Recall of arrestment or inhibition obtained by petition under s.28 of the Proceeds of Crime (Scotland) Act 1995 or para.13 of Sch.4 to the Prevention of Terrorism (Temporary Provisions) Act 1989, must be made by note: rr.76.4(1)(c) (1987 Act) and 76.22(4)(c) (1989 Act). A cause is depending until final decree, whereas a cause is in dependence until final extract. For the meaning of final decree, see note 4.15.2(2). For the meaning of final extract, see note 7.1.2(2).

On recall of arrestment and inhibition, see note 13.10.4.

14.2.10   *Petitions or applications under these Rules or any other enactment.* Rule 14.2(h) is intended to catch applications to the court under primary or subordinate legislation, or the common law, whether or not specified to be by petition under the particular enactment or these Rules, except where (specified to be) an action or an application by minute (see, *e.g.* certain applications in family actions in Chap. 49), note (see, *e.g.* certain applications relating to companies in Chap. 74) or motion (see r.23.11 (statutory applications by motion in causes depending before the court unless otherwise provided)).

It is not always clear whether a statutory application should be by petition or summons, even from the apparent distinction between a petition and a summons mentioned in note 4.1.1.

Statutory applications include: Public Order Act 1936, ss.2(3) and 8(2) (*re* property of an association); Fair Trading Act 1973, s.85 (*re* default of requirement to give evidence or produce documents to Monopolies and Mergers Commission); Building Society Act 1986, s.36A* inserted by the Building Societies Act 1997 (prohibition orders); Access to Health Records Act 1990 (*re* failure to comply with requirements of the Act—see r.79.2); Law Reform (Miscellaneous Provisions) (Scotland) Act 1990, ss.17(6), 18(7) and 20(11) (*re* review of decisions of Conveyancing and Executry Services Board—see r.80.2) and s.21 (in relation to Board's intervention powers—see r.80.2); Proceeds of Crime (Scotland) Act 1995, s.17(1) compensation to person who held realisable property); Olympics Association Right (Infringement Proceedings) Regulations 1995, reg.3 (order for delivery up of infringing goods, materials or articles) and reg.5 (order as to disposal—see r.55.17); United Nations (International Tribunal) (Former Yugoslavia) Order 1995, reg.20 (enforcement of orders for preservation or restoration of property) and reg.21 (decision as to the ownership of property); Adults with Incapacity (Scotland) Act 2000, s.50(6) (application to determine whether treatment should be given).

Section 36A of the Building Societies Act 1986 provides for the Building Societies Commission to "certify" a contravention of a prohibition order (prohibiting an activity) to the Court of Session which the court may inquire into and deal with as if it were contempt of court. Parliament has made no attempt to explain how certification is done in the context of this court's civil procedure. It is submitted that the Commission would have to present a petition under Chap. 14 by virtue of r.14.2(h).

Applications under s.49 of the Insurance Companies Act 1982 and ss.136 and 425 of the Companies Act 1985 were Inner House petitions. By A.S. (R.C.S.A.) (Miscellaneous) 1998 [SI 1998/890] they are Outer House petitions if presented on or after 21st April 1998. On applications under the 1982 Act, see further note 14.2.12; and on the applications under the 1985 Act, see note 14.2.13. Although there is no provision for nominating a judge to deal with such petitions, Lord Eassie has been nominated to deal with them.

14.2.11   "*application to the court in exercise of its* parens patriae *jurisdiction*". Such applications in the Outer House were provided for by A.S. (R.C.S.A. No. 3) (Miscellaneous) 1996 [SI 1996/1756].

The continuing existence of the *parens patriae* jurisdiction of the court, to grant authority for taking steps in the best interests of those incapable of giving their authority or consent for that purpose, was confirmed in *Law Hospital N.H.S. Trust v. Lord Advocate*, 1996 S.C. 301; for a review of the history of this jurisdiction, see the opinion of Lord Cullen. In exercise of this jurisdiction the court has appointed tutors-dative and recently has given them particular powers to consent to medical treatment. It is now confirmed that the jurisdiction extends to the court to authorise the discontinuation of medical treatment, at least in relation to a person in a persistent vegetative state.

(1) *Tutors-dative and guardians.* In 1856, the duties previously performed by or incumbent upon the Court of Exchequer with regard to the nomination, appointment and control of tutors-dative were transferred to the Court of Session (as successor to the Court of Exchequer in exercise of the right of the Crown as *pater patriae*, Erskine, I.vii.8), involving a special procedure of summary petition to the Inner House: Exchequer Court (Scotland) Act 1856, s.19. That provision was repealed by the C.S.A. 1988, Sch.2 because it was thought the procedure was not used in practice and was superseded by the power of the court to appoint a factor *loco tutoris* by petition to the Outer House (see r.14.2(a)). Such a factor, however, has no authority over the person of his ward (unlike a tutor-dative). The appointment of tutors-dative to pupil children was effectively rendered obsolete by the Age of Legal Capacity (Scotland) Act 1991: see note 61.1.2(4). The appointment of tutors-dative to adults who are mentally *incapax* is noted in two articles in the *Scots Law Times* (referring to a number of recent unreported cases): see "Revival of Tutors-Dative" 1987 S.L.T.(News) 69, and "Tutors to Adults Development" 1992 S.L.T.(News) 325. With the repeal of s.19 of the 1856 Act, such an appointment was thought to be incompetent because Parliament repealed that section in the belief that it was a substantive

provision which had fallen into desuetude. Ironically, by the time the recommendation of the Scottish Law Commission had been enacted (indeed before its report) the appointment of tutors-dative to mentally incapacitated adults had, as disclosed by the above articles, revived. Fortunately in *Law Hospital N.H.S. Trust*, above, it was authoritatively expressed that s.19 of the 1856 Act was only a procedural provision and the power of the Court of Exchequer to make such appointments in exercise of its *parens patriae* jurisdiction remains and was transferred to the Court of Session by the unrepealed s.1 of that Act.

On such appointments, see the cases cited in the articles in the *Scots Law Times* mentioned above. For a recent example of a tutor-dative appointed with power to consent to medical treatment on his ward's behalf, see *L v. L's curator ad litem*, 1997 S.L.T. 167 and *Britton v. Britton's Curator Bonis* 1996 S.C. 178. For the distinction between a tutor-at-law and a tutor-dative, see Stair I.vi.25.

The position of a tutor dative is gratuitous: *AB v. CD* (1890) 18 R. 90, 97. A tutor dative will be appointed only where it is necessary for decisions to be taken about a person's personal welfare: *Chapman, Petrs* 1993 S.L.T. 955. A tutor dative may be appointed in respect of the ward's person and a curator *bonis* appointed in respect of the ward's estate: *Dickie v. Douglas* 1924 S.L.T. 578. Although in the majority of cases in which the appointment of a tutor dative is sought the only powers applied for will be concerned with the personal welfare of the ward, a tutor dative may be given powers with respect to the ward's estate such as power to make certain decisions or claims which may affect the amount of the ward's estate or the way in which it is administered. Where powers are sought only in relation to the ward's welfare, and not in relation to or such as to affect the administration of the ward's estate, there is no need for the petition to be intimated to the Accountant of Court. Where powers are sought which relate to any part of the ward's estate or to the making of any claim or the taking of any decision which will or may affect the amount of the ward's estate or the manner in which or purposes for which any part of it is administered or expended, intimation to the Accountant of Court will be required. In such a case the court will have to consider whether the tutor dative should be required to find caution. All petitions for the appointment of a tutor dative require to be served on the Mental Welfare Commission: P.N. No. 11 of 1994.

As from 1st April 2002 it is not competent to appoint a tutor-dative to a person aged 16 or over: Adults with Incapacity (Scotland) Act 2000, s.80. A guardian will have to be appointed under s.57 of the 2000 Act. A person who has been appointed a tutor-dative to an adult becomes a guardian under the 2000 Act with the powers he had as a tutor-dative: 2000 Act, Sch.4, para.1(4). The guardian would have the power to apply to the court to withdraw medical treatment as his legal representative.

(2) *Petitions to withdraw medical treatment.* In *Law Hospital N.H.S. Trust*, above, it was held that the court would authorise the withdrawal of treatment where a person is in a persistent vegetative state. The procedure to be followed in such an application was set out in the opinion of L.P. Hope and is as follows:

(a) All such application should be made by petition presented to the Outer House in the same way as if they were applications to which rule 14.2 apply: see now r. 14.2(i).

(b) The application may be presented by the area health authority or N.H.S. trust in whose care the patient is for the time being, or by any relative of the patient within the meaning of Sched. 1 of the Damages (Scotland) Act 1976.

(c) The application should be for the court to authorise the treatment or the withdrawal of treatment from the patient as the case may be.

(d) The proposed treatment or withdrawal of treatment should be specified in a statement of facts and in the prayer setting out the order which is being sought.

(e) The petition should be served on the Lord Advocate for the public interest, and it should also be served on the relevant area health authority or N.H.S. trust and on the relatives of the patient unless these parties are already petitioners.

(f) There should be lodged with the petition as productions at least two medical reports on the patient's condition, describing the treatment which it is proposed to carry out or to discontinue and, if treatment is to be discontinued, the steps which will be taken to allow the patient to die peacefully and with dignity.

(g) In view of the advice given in the B.M.A. Guidelines on Treatment Decisions for Patients in Persistent Vegetative State (July 1993) that life-prolonging treatment should continue until the patient has been insentient for at least twelve months, the statement of facts should include a narrative as to when the persistent vegetative state was first diagnosed and for how long life-prolonging treatment has been continued since that date.

(h) If the view of the patient about the giving of treatment or the discontinuing of treatment have previously been expressed in writing or otherwise, the statement of facts should include averments about the views which the patient has expressed.

(i) The court should be asked, in the prayer of the petition, to appoint a curator *ad litem* to the patient so that the application may be considered separately on behalf of the patient and the curator's views made known to the court after such inquiry as the curator may consider appropriate in the circumstances.

(j) Intimation on the walls of the court will be dispensed with and any proof or other hearing will be conducted in chambers, unless the public interest otherwise requires: see now r. 14.7(3).

14.2.12   *Applications under s.49 of the Insurance Companies Act 1982.* Formerly there had been doubt whether a petition under this provision was appropriately an Inner or Outer House petition. That doubt was settled in the R.C.S. 1994 as originally enacted which made it an Inner House petition. By A.S. (R.C.S.A.) (Miscellaneous) 1998 [S.I. 1998 No. 890] such a petition is now presented to the Outer House.

Section 49 of the 1982 Act provides for the court sanctioning a scheme transferring long term business from one insurance company to another and is useful where the transferor is in difficulty (thus avoiding liquidation).

The petition must be (i) accompanied by a report by an actuary (s.49(2)), (ii) served on the Secretary of State (Trade and Industry) (s.49(3)(c)) and (iii) open for inspection at the company's offices (s.49(3)(d)). A notice must be inserted in the London, Edinburgh and Belfast Gazettes and two national newspapers: s.49(3)(a). A statement will have to be sent to every policyholder unless the court otherwise directs (s.49(3)(b)); and the court may so direct if there has already been a statement or something similar or a meeting to consider the proposal. The minimum period of notice of the petition is 21 days: effect of s.49(3)(c) and (d).

Jurisdiction. The court has jurisdiction if either the transferor or transferee company has its registered office in Scotland or if both have: s.49(8). This is consistent with the C.J.J.A. 1982.

14.2.13   *Applications under ss.136 and 425 of the Companies Act 1985.* Jurisdiction. The court of the country which has jurisdiction to wind up the company—*i.e.* the court of the country in which the company is registered—has jurisdiction: Companies Act 1985, s.744 and Insolvency Act 1986, s.120. Jurisdiction under the C.J.J.A. 1982 is excluded: C.J.J.A. 1982, Scheds 1 and 3C, Art. 1, Sched. 5, para. 1 and Sched. 9, para. 4.

(1) *Reduction of capital*: Companies Act 1985, s.136. Whether a company can apply for confirmation of a special resolution to reduce capital is determined by s.135(1) of the 1985 Act; there must be a power in the Articles. A special resolution requires not less than 21 days' notice, which does not mean, unless the Articles say so (see Companies (Tables A to F) Regulations 1985 [S.I. 1985 No. 805], Table A, reg. 38), 21 clear days: *Neil McLeod & Sons Ltd, Petrs* 1967 S.C. 16 (*i.e.* the day the notice is served is not, but the last day is, included in the calculation). Any provisions for a quorum at a meeting must be complied with (*Neil McLeod & Sons Ltd*, above) and the procedure laid down for it followed and minuted: *Citizens Theatre Ltd, Petrs* 1946 S.C. 14; *Fraserburgh Commercial Co. Ltd, Petrs* 1946 S.C. 444. The special resolution must be registered with the Registrar of Companies within 15 days: 1985 Act, s.380(1).

There should be produced with the petition (a) a draft minute of reduction for approval by the court (1985 Act, s.138(1)) which, with the order of the court, is registered (s.138(4)); (b) a copy of the Memorandum and Articles; (c) a certified copy of the notice calling the meeting to consider the special resolution; (d) a certified copy of the minute of that meeting; (e) the receipt of the Registrar of Companies of the registering of the resolution; and (f) a certified copy of the latest annual report and accounts.

The first order under r. 14.5 will include a requirement to advertise in the *Edinburgh Gazette* and appropriate newspapers (for which there should be craves in the prayer). Normally there will be no one on whom to serve the petition. After expiry of the period of notice a motion should be enrolled to remit to a reporter and if necessary to dispense *in hoc statu* with the requirements of s.136(3)–(5) of the 1985 Act (objections by and lists of creditors, etc.). Any objections will be postponed until after the report of the reporter. It is the invariable practice to remit to a reporter (usually one of two solicitors nominated by the Lord President): *Scottish Stamping and Engineering Co. Ltd, Petrs* 1928 S.C. 484; *J. Hay & Sons Ltd, Petrs* 1928 S.C. 622. The petitioner is responsible for lodging four copies of the report in process for the hearing to approve the report: r. 4.7(2) (lodging of documents in Inner House). If there are no objections by creditors the petitioner may enrol for approval of the report and if necessary for a direction that s.136(3)–(5) of the 1985 Act does not apply and to grant the prayer of the petition. It there are objections a hearing will be placed on the Summary Roll. The court can dispense with a list of creditors entitled to object in certain circumstances: 1985 Act, s.136(6). In considering whether to dispense with the list the question is whether the interests of creditors are prejudiced: *Anderson, Brown & Co. Ltd, Petrs* 1965 S.C. 81. If a list is required, motions are required to fix a date for the list to be made up and lodged and for the list to be advertised in the *Gazette* and appropriate newspapers with a date by which creditors not listed can claim to be put on the list or be excluded.

In confirming the reduction the court has to consider the interests of creditors, shareholders and the public: (1985 Act, s.137(1); *Westburn Sugar Refineries Ltd, Petrs* 1951 S.C.(H.L.) 57) and whether the reduction is fair and equitable between different classes of shareholders (*Wilsons and Clyde Coal Co. Ltd v. Scottish Insurance Corporation Ltd* 1949 S.C.(H.L.) 90).

Where the petition is combined with a scheme of arrangement the procedure is modified: *Wilson Brothers and D.G. Howat & Co. Ltd, Petrs* 1939 S.L.T. 68.

(2) *Compromise or scheme of arrangement*: Companies Act 1985, s.425. This provision provides for a compromise or arrangement between a company and its creditors or members. "Compromise" means settlement of a claim where there is a dispute: Stair, I.xvii.2: but it may be more broadly interpreted: see *City of Glasgow Bank v. Geddes' Trs* (1880) 7 R. 731. In England there must be some dispute about rights: *Sneath v. Valley Gold Ltd* [1893] 1 Ch. 477. In relation to arrangement, there must be an element of give and take: *Re N.F.U. Development Trust Ltd* [1972] 1 W.L.R. 1548; *Re Savoy Hotel Ltd* [1981] Ch. 351. The section is interpreted broadly: *Singer Manufacturing Co. v. Robinow* 1971 S.C. 11, 13–14 *per* L.P. Clyde.

The petition should include a crave for class meetings of classes of shareholders whose interests are affected by the scheme but not a general meeting of all members of the company as the company has power to do that: *Cayzer Irvine & Co. Ltd, Petrs* 1963 S.L.T. 94. Notice of the scheme is given by advertisements in newspapers. After the meetings, a motion may be enrolled for sanction of the scheme. Before doing so the court will have to be satisfied that (a) the statutory provisions have been complied with, (b) those who attended the class meetings were fairly representative of the class, (c) the arrangement is such that a man of business would reasonably approve, (d) the majority has been acting bona fide and (e) the minority has not been overridden by the majority: *Edinburgh American Land Mortgage Co. Ltd v. Lang's Trs* (1909) S.C. 488; *Shandon Hydropathic Co. Ltd, Petrs* 1911 S.C. 1153, 1155 *per* L.P. Dunedin; *Re Anglo-Continental Supply Co., Ltd* [1922] 2 Ch. 723, 736 *per* Astbury J.

Applications by petition in the Inner House

14.3. Any of the following applications shall be made by petition presented in the Inner House:—

(a) a petition and complaint other than for breach of interdict;

(b) an application under any enactment relating to solicitors or notaries public;

(c) an application which is, by virtue of these Rules or any other enactment, to be by petition and is incidental to a cause depending before the Inner House;

(d) an application to the *nobile officium* of the court other than an application mentioned in rule 14.2(c) (applications relating to the administration of a trust, the office of trustee or a public trust);

(e) a petition by trustees for directions under Part II of Chapter 63;

(f) an application under section 1 of the Evidence (Proceedings in Other Jurisdictions) Act 1975 (assistance in obtaining evidence for civil proceedings in another jurisdiction);

(g) an application under section 1 of the Trusts (Scotland) Act 1961 (variation or revocation of trusts);

(h) [*Revoked by S.I. 1998 No. 890*];

(i) [*Revoked by S.I. 1998 No. 890*];

(j) an application under section 17(6), 18(7), 20(7), 20(11)(b), 21(5), 21(7) or 21(10) of, or under paragraph 20 of Schedule 1 to, the Law Reform (Miscellaneous Provisions) (Scotland) Act 1990 (orders in relation to conveyancing or executory practitioners); and

(k) an application required to be made to the Inner House under any enactment.

Deriv. RCS 1965, r. 190 (preamble) (amended by S.I. 1970 No. 134), (i) (amended by S.I. 1980 No. 1144), (iv) (amended by S.I. 1992 No. 1422), (vi) (amended by S.I. 1976 No. 283 and 1987 No. 1206), (vii) (amended by S.I. 1976 No. 283 and 1977 No. 1621), (viii)–(x) substituted by S.I. 1987 No. 1206, and (xi) (inserted by S.I. 1992 No. 1422), (r. 14.3(a) to (j))

General note. The number of petitions reserved to the Inner House has in recent years been reduced.   **14.3.1**

"presented in the Inner House". A petition is presented by being lodged for the first order (granting warrant for all or any of service, intimation and advertisement): see r. 14.5. All   **14.3.2**

petitions when presented to the court are lodged in the Petition Department: r. 3.3. The petition is given a cause reference number when presented: r. 4.1(4) and note 4.1.5.

14.3.3   *Petition and complaint other than for breach of interdict.* Such a petition is rare. The jurisdiction covers malversation, misconduct and gross neglect of inferior judges (other than sheriffs) and officers of court, the purpose of the petition being removal from office or the imposition of a penalty. Much may now be done by judicial review of the decision made by the inferior judge or officer of court. Otherwise these cases may be covered by statutory employment law rules.

     The procedure is similar to a petition and complaint for breach of interdict: see note 14.2.6. Being of a quasi-criminal character, the petition requires the concurrence of the Lord Advocate.

14.3.4   *Solicitors and notaries.* See Chap. 68.

14.3.5   *Nobile officium other than administration of trusts and trustees.* The *nobile officium* is an extraordinary equitable jurisdiction of the court to exercise jurisdiction in circumstances which would not be justified except by the necessity of intervening in the interests of justice; and although the court tends to limit the exercise of its jurisdiction to cases in which the power has already been exercised, it is neither possible nor desirable to define all the circumstances in which resort may be had to it: *Royal Bank of Scotland plc v. Gillies* 1987 S.L.T. 54, 55I per L.J.-C. Ross. It does not exist to deal with matters of disputed right; its chief object is to provide a means of rectifying obvious errors or omissions, principally of an administrative character, which cannot be dealt with in any other way: *London and Clydeside Estates Ltd v. Aberdeen D.C.* 1980 S.C.(H.L.) 1, 45 per Lord Keith of Kinkel. "The jurisdiction associated with the *nobile officium* in this court gives us a right to come to the assistance of the petitioners where no other remedy is available": *Glasgow Magdalene Institution, Petrs* 1964 S.C. 227, 229 per L.P. Clyde. It is reserved for cases of necessity or very strong expediency where the ordinary procedure would provide no remedy: *Gibson's Trs* 1933 S.C. 190, 205 per L.J.-C. Alness. It may be used to meet a *casus improvisus* in a statute: *Skinner, Petr* 1976 S.L.T. 60; *Sloan, Petr* 1991 S.C. 281. It cannot be used to extend or derogate from the scope of a statute (*Smart v. Registrar General for Scotland* 1951 S.C. 81, 85 per L.J.-C. Thomson); to supplement a statutory procedure which would in effect be an amendment of the statute (*Maitland, Petr* 1961 S.C. 291, 293 per L.P. Clyde); or to conflict with or defeat a statutory intention express or implied (*R., Petr* 1993 S.L.T. 910, 912 per L.P. Hope; a re-hearing of a referral under s.42 of the Social Work (Scotland) Act 1968 where the circumstances were unforeseen was not expressly or impliedly excluded by statute (*L., Petr (No. 1)* 1993 S.L.T. 1310 and *L., Petr (No. 2)* 1993 S.L.T. 1342). It cannot be invoked where the law already provides a remedy: *Central Motor Engineering Co. v. Gibbs* 1917 S.C. 490, 493 per Lord Skerrington. See also Stair, IV.iii.1 and Erskine, I.iii.22.

     Jurisdiction. Nothing in Sched. 8 to the C.J.J.A. 1982 affects the jurisdiction of the court in exercise of its *nobile officium*: C.J.J.A. 1982, s.22(3).

14.3.6   *Petitions by trustees for directions.* See Chap. 63, Pt II.

14.3.7   *Applications under s.1 of the Evidence (Proceedings in Other Jurisdictions) Act 1975.* See Chap. 66.

14.3.8   *Applications under s.1 of the Trusts (Scotland) Act 1961.* See Chap. 63, Pt I.

14.3.9   *Applications under s.49 of the Insurance Companies Act 1982.* Formerly there had been doubt whether a petition under this provision was appropriately an Inner or Outer House petition. That doubt was settled by this rule, by which paragraph (h) made it an Inner House petition. But A.S. (R.C.S.A.) (Miscellaneous) 1998 [S.I. 1998 No. 890] transferred such applications to the Outer House. This does not apply to a petition presented before 21st April 1998. See further, note 14.2.12.

14.3.10   *Applications under ss.136 and 425 of the Companies Act 1985.* By A.S. (R.C.S.A.) (Miscellaneous) 1998 [S.I. 1998 No. 890] these applications have been transferred to the Outer House. This does not apply to a petition presented before 21st April 1998. See further, note 14.2.13.

14.3.11   *Conveyancing and executry practitioners.* For applications in relation to conveyancing and executry practitioners under the Law Reform (Miscellaneous Provisions) (Scotland) Act 1990, see Chap. 81.

14.3.12   *Applications to Inner House under any other enactment.* R. 14.3(k) is a new provision and refers to any statute or statutory instrument. Another enactment may provide expressly for a petition to be presented to the Inner House.

     For example, an application to prevent vexatious legal proceedings must be made to the Inner House: Vexatious Actions (Scotland) Act 1898. The application is made by the Lord Advocate who has to satisfy the court that the respondent has habitually and persistently instituted vexatious legal proceedings without any reasonable ground for instituting them whether in the Court of Session or any inferior court. The Act was introduced to deal with such vexatious litigations which can obviously be oppressive and unfair to defenders: *Lord Advocate v. Rizza* 1962 S.L.T.(Notes) 8. An order under the Act is not compatible with Art. 6 of the ECHR: *Lord Advocate v. Bell,* 23rd March 2001 (IH), unreported. Whether a person is vexatious does not depend simply on the number of actions he has raised, it includes the manner in which he has conducted himself in the legal process, the taking of a succession of hopeless appeals and abuse of process: *Lord Advocate v. Cooney* 1984 S.L.T. 434. Where an order has been granted, leave must be obtained from the Lord Ordinary to pursue any cause in the Court of Session or an inferior court. The application is made by presenting the proposed writ to the Deputy Principal Clerk who puts it before the Lord Ordinary in chambers. The decision of the Lord Ordinary is sent by letter to the applicant. A decision of the Lord Ordinary to refuse leave is final: Vexatious Actions (Scotland) Act 1898, s.1A (inserted by the Law Reform (Miscellaneous Provisions) (Scotland) Act 1980, s.19). A process is not required: see r. 4.3 (lodging of processes). It may be necessary to combine such an application with an application for leave to proceed in a petition without counsel or other person having a right of audience, or an agent, having signed the petition: see note 4.2.8.

Form of petitions

14.4.—(1) A petition shall be in Form 14.4.

(2) A petition shall include—

   (*a*) a statement of facts in numbered paragraphs setting out the facts and circumstances on which the petition is founded; and

   (*b*) a prayer setting out the orders sought.

(3) In a petition presented under an enactment, the statement of facts shall expressly refer to the relevant provision under the authority of which the petition is presented.

(4) Where a petition is one to which the Civil Jurisdiction and Judgments Act 1982 applies, the statement of facts shall include averments stating—

   (*a*) the ground of jurisdiction of the court, unless jurisdiction would arise only if the respondent prorogated the jurisdiction of the court without contesting jurisdiction;

   (*b*) unless the court has exclusive jurisdiction, whether or not there is an agreement prorogating the jurisdiction of a court in another country; and

   (*c*) whether or not there are proceedings involving the same cause of action in subsistence between the parties in a country to which the convention in Schedule 1 or 3C to that Act applies and the date any such proceedings commenced.

(5) The prayer of a petition shall crave warrant for such intimation, service and advertisement as may be necessary having regard to the nature of the petition, or as the petitioner may seek; and the name, address and capacity of each person on whom service of the petition is sought shall be set out in a schedule annexed to, and referred to in, the prayer of the petition.

(6) Where it is sought in a petition—

   (*a*) to dispense with intimation, service or advertisement, or

   (*b*) to shorten or extend the period of notice,

the appropriate order shall be craved in the prayer, and the grounds on which the order is sought shall be set out in the statement of facts.

Deriv. R.C.S. 1965, r. 191 amended by S.I. 1987 No. 1206

General note. A petition consists of (1) the Address, (2) a statement of facts, (3) the prayer, **14.4.1** (4) a schedule for service and, where necessary, (5) an appendix containing any scheme or document requiring approval by the court. An Inner House petition should be marked "Inner House" on the backing.

   A petition must, unless otherwise provided, be on the official printed form in Form 14.4 approved by the court: r. 4.1(1); and see notes 4.1.1 and 4.1.3.

The Address. Petitions are addressed "Unto the Right Honourable the Lords of Council and **14.4.2** Session". The name, designation and address of the petitioner must be correctly stated: *Maccallum, Petrs.* (1883) 11 R. 60. The better practice is to state full names, but this is not essential. The capacity in which the petitioner presents the petition must be stated: this often identifies the subject-matter of the petition, *e.g.* as where the petitioner is a trustee; this is particularly important because petitions are kept in the Petition Department alphabetically within the categories under which petitions are filed (see note 4.1.5) according to the subject-matter (though recorded chronologically in the Petition Register)—*e.g.* the name of the trust, truster, incapax or company. The practice of stating the occupation of the petitioner (other than a professional one) has generally died out and is not essential. The current address must be given. Where there has been a recent change of address there is a convenient practice to state the former address also; but a last known address alone where the current address is not known will not be sufficient for service (note repeal of s. 3 of the Citation Amendment (Scotland) Act 1882 by the A.S. (R.C.S. 1994) 1994, Sched. 4) and the rules for service where the address is not known must be followed (see r. 16.5).

   It is not usual to name a respondent in the Address, as he is specified in the schedule for service, except (but it is not essential) in petitions where an order is sought against or in relation to a particular person, *e.g.* suspension and interdict and breach of interdict.

   There should then follow a brief description of the general nature of the petition, *e.g.* "for appointment of a judicial factor".

Statement of facts. This is the narrative, preceded by the words "Humbly sheweth", in **14.4.3** numbered paragraphs (each properly beginning with "That") setting out the facts, circumstances and grounds on which the petition is based. The first paragraph usually should identify the petitioner and the capacity in which he petitions. Where there has been a previous petition in relation to the same subject-matter reference should be made to it. One paragraph should refer to the persons to be served with the petition and the schedule for service. A paragraph should state the ground of jurisdiction where the C.J.J.A. 1982 applies: r. 14.4(4); and see further note 14.4.4. A paragraph (usually the last) specifies whether the petition is presented at common law or under statute (in which case the statutory provision must be stated: r. 14.4(3)). Paragraphs should be as short and concise as possible: different facts or events should be stated in separate paragraphs.

14.4.4   *Jurisdiction.* Formerly the ground of jurisdiction always had to be specified; now it is only required where the C.J.J.A. 1982 applies. Sched. 8 to the C.J.J.A. 1982 contains the general grounds of jurisdiction of the court: C.J.J.A. 1982, s. 20. Sched. 8 does not apply to (*a*) proceedings subject to the jurisdictional rules in the 1968 (or Brussels) Convention on jurisdiction and enforcement in civil and commercial matters between the Member States of the European Community, or the similar Lugano (or "Parallel") Convention between the EC Member States and Member States of the European Free Trade Association which ratify it (and any other State which accedes to it), in Scheds. 1 and 3C respectively to the 1982 Act (C.J.J.A. 1982, s. 20(1)), (*b*) proceedings subject to the jurisdictional rules in Sched. 4 to the C.J.J.A. 1982 which determines the allocation of jurisdiction between the different courts of the UK (C.J.J.A. 1982 s. 20(1)), (*c*) proceedings in respect of which any other enactment confers jurisdiction (C.J.J.A. s. 21(1)(*a*)) and (*d*) proceedings listed in Sched. 9 as proceedings excluded from Sched. 8 (C.J.J.A. 1982, s. 21(1)(*b*)). Sched. 9 excludes, *e.g.* proceedings regulating the custody of children, in respect of sequestration in bankruptcy, the winding up of a company, judicial arrangements or compositions with creditors, proceedings not in substance proceedings in which a decree against any person is sought, and proceedings in pursuance of a convention which in relation to particular matters govern jurisdiction other than the 1968 Convention. The C.J.J.A. 1982 will apply, therefore, where jurisdiction depends on Scheds. 1, 3C, 4 or 8. On jurisdiction, see further notes 13.2.6 (domicile) and 13.2.7 to 13.2.12 (grounds of jurisdiction).
     R. 14.4(4)(*a*) assumes the respondent will only prorogate jurisdiction when he lodges answers and does not contest jurisdiction. But he might prorogate jurisdiction in advance, in which case the ground of jurisdiction can (and must) be averred.

14.4.5   *"agreement prorogating jurisdiction of a court".* See note 13.2.14 on this subject in relation to actions.

14.4.6   *"proceedings involving the same cause of action".* See note 13.2.15 on this subject in relation to actions. The word "action" is not a term of art in the Conventions and will apply also to proceedings by petition. As the court has to examine jurisdiction itself (and particularly if it is sought to have the prayer granted without any respondent lodging answers), the court must know (*ex facie* of the petition) whether it has jurisdiction.

14.4.7   *Pleas-in-law.* It is not necessary to insert pleas-in-law in a petition unless answers are lodged by a respondent opposing the grant of the prayer. A practice has grown up of including pleas-in-law in a petition, when it is drawn, in petitions for suspension and interdict and the like, no doubt because it is expected that the respondent will appear to oppose the petition.

14.4.8   *The prayer.* The prayer of the petition consists of a series of craves setting out all the orders to be sought in the order in which they are sought.
     The first order is for intimation, service and advertisement: see r. 14.4(5). (1) Intimation. In a petition this usually means intimation on the walls of the court: see r. 14.7(1) and note 14.7.1. (2) Service on all persons having an interest (and specified in the schedule for service: r. 14.4(5)) has to be made and may include service by advertisement where a person's address is not known (see r. 14.7(2)). On service, see Chap. 16, Pt. I. (3) Advertisement. Certain petitions require public notice in one or more of the London, Edinburgh and Belfast *Gazettes* and national or local newspapers. Where it is sought to dispense with intimation, service or advertisement or to shorten or extend the period of notice this must be craved and the grounds stated in the statement of facts: r. 14.4(5). The prayer craves interested persons (whether the petition was served on them or not) to lodge answers, if so advised, within the period of notice: r. 14.6(1).
     There will be a crave for the orders sought for which the petition has been presented whether or not answers have been lodged and after any inquiry or remit to a reporter the court may order. The prayer concludes with a crave "to do further or otherwise in the premises as to your Lordships shall seem proper" which permits the court to make orders not sought in the prayer: see, *e.g. Davidson v. Bogle & Co.* (1837) 15 S. 421. There are limits as to what the court can do where notice of such an order has not been given. There then follow before the signature of the person signing the petition the words "According to justice, etc." which is a short form of a longer historical text.

The schedule. The schedule specifies the persons to be served with the petition. It should also **14.4.9** include anyone to whom the petition is to be intimated. The names and addresses must be accurate as a substantial error will invalidate the cause: *Overseas League v. Taylor* 1951 S.C. 105, 107 *per* L.J.-C. Thomson.

Signing of petition. The petition must be signed. On who should sign, see r. 4.2 and notes. It **14.4.10** was stated in *Marshall & Others, Petrs.* 1938 S.N. 18 that an appendix containing any facts which would normally form part of the petition and any scheme should also be signed; but this rule has not been followed for many years.

"intimation". See note 14.7.1(1).   **14.4.11**

"service". For methods, see Chap. 16, Pt I.   **14.4.12**

"advertisement". See note 14.7.1(2).   **14.4.13**

Units of measurement. The Units of Measurement Directive (Council Directive 80/181 of 20th **14.4.14** December 1979) was adopted by the E.C. in 1989 [Official Journal, 7th December 1989, L357/ 28]. From 1st January 1995 member states must use the metric system of measurement and, subject to certain transitional arrangements and exceptions, must cease to use imperial measurements for economic, public health, public safety and administrative purposes. Where a unit of measurement is used in pleadings it should be expressed as a metric unit, and court orders must be so expressed.

Exceptions are as follows: The nautical mile and knot are to be used for sea and air traffic and the foot is to be used for aircraft heights. Until 31st December 1999, fathom may be used for marine navigation; therm for gas supply; pint and fluid ounce for beer, cider, waters, lemonade and fruit juices on returnable containers; and ounce and pound for goods sold loose from bulk. In perpetuity, acre may be used for land registration; troy ounce for transactions in precious metals; mile, yard, foot and inch for road traffic signs, distances and speed measurements; pint for draught beer, cider and milk in returnable containers.

First order in petitions

14.5.—[1] (1) Subject to paragraph (2), on a petition being lodged, the court shall, without a motion being enrolled for that purpose, pronounce an interlocutor for such intimation, service and advertisement as may be necessary.

(2) Where a petitioner seeks—
  (a) to dispense with intimation, service or advertisement on any person, or
  (b) any interim order,
he shall apply by motion for such order as appears appropriate.

(3) On disposing of a motion under paragraph (2), the court shall make such order as it thinks fit.

Deriv. R.C.S. 1965, r. 195(a) (part)

[1] R. 14.5(1) substituted by S.I. 1996 No. 2168 (effective 23rd September 1996)

General note. The first order (often called the first deliverance) is for intimation, service and **14.5.1** any advertisement or interim order.

Formerly, during term a petition appeared in the rolls (motion roll or single bills) for a first order. The A.S. (R.C.S.A. No. 4) (Miscellaneous) 1996 [S.I. 1996 No. 2168] abolished this requirement following a recommendation of the Cullen *Review of Outer House Business* in December 1995. Now, whether a petition is lodged in or out of a term, it will not appear in the rolls for a first order.

In certain petitions there is no first order, other provisions apply and this rule is disapplied. These are: petitions for judicial review (r. 58.2), applications for recognition and enforcement of foreign judgments (r. 62.2), applications under the Evidence (Proceedings in Other Jurisdictions) Act 1975 (r. 66.2), adoption petitions (r. 67.2), causes under the Proceeds of Crime (Scotland) Act 1995 (r. 76.2), causes under the Prevention of Terrorism (Temporary Provisions) Act 1989 and the Enforcement of External Orders Order of 1995 under the Act (r. 76.20), summary trials (r. 77.2) and applications for parental orders under the Human Fertilisation and Embryology Act 1990 (r. 81.2).

"on a petition being lodged". A petition is lodged in the Petition Department: r. 3.3(2). A **14.5.2** process must be lodged with it: rr. 4.3 and 4.4. In Inner House petitions six copies of the petition

must be lodged in addition to the principal: r. 4.7(1) and note 14.7.1. In Outer House petitions, although there is no rule to this effect, one copy of the petition must be handed to the clerk of session at the department's public counter for the Advocates' Library (see P.N. No. 2 of 1988).

On being lodged the petition is assigned a cause reference number: see r. 4.1(4) and note 4.1.5.

A petition may be lodged in person in the Petition Department, or by post by a Court of Session account holder (see note 14.5.11) or if accompanied by a cheque (P.N. No. 4 of 1994, paras 1 and 2). Where lodged by post it should be accompanied by the motion in Form 23.2 for the first order: P.N. No. 4 of 1994, para. 6(1). Where an interlocutor for intimation and service is pronounced, a copy of it will be sent by post to the petitioner: P.N. No. 4 of 1994, para. 6(2).

A fee is payable on lodging a petition: see note 14.5.11.

14.5.3 *Documents founded on or adopted.* Any document founded on or adopted as incorporated in the petition must be lodged as a production when the petition is lodged: see r. 27.1(1)(a). For lodging of productions, see r. 4.5. For the meaning of documents founded on or adopted, see note 27.1.2.

14.5.4 *"without a motion being enrolled".* The first order is automatic and no motion or appearance is required unless an application under r. 14.5(2) (to dispense with service, etc., or for an interim order) or 14.6(2) (to shorten or extend the period of notice) is made.

14.5.5 *"dispense with intimation, service or advertisement".* Where dispensation is sought a motion must be enrolled, and if sought at the time of the first order that order will not be granted without enrolment under r. 14.5(1). On intimation, see note 14.7.1.

14.5.6 *"interim order".* Interim orders relate mostly to the merits of the cause in which they are sought: *Kelly v. Monklands D.C.* 1986 S.L.T. 165, 167 *per* Lord Ross. An order is interim because of its character not merely because it is expressly granted "*ad interim*". "Interim" means for the time being or in the meantime. Interim orders would include interim interdict, an interim judicial factor, an interim administrator or liquidator of a company, interim suspension, interim liberation, or interim possession under s.47(2) of the C.S.A. 1988. For urgent applications for interim orders when the petition is lodged, see r. 23.8.

14.5.7 *"motion".* For motions, see Chap. 23. The procedure for urgent motions before the first order under r. 14.5 is in r. 23.8.

14.5.8 *Fee.* The court fee for lodging a petition is payable on lodging. An additional fee is payable when the petition is presented outwith normal hours. For fee, see Court of Session etc. Fees Order 1997, Table of Fees, Pt I, C, item 1 and 2 [S.I. 1997 No. 688, as amended, pp. **C** 1201 *et seq.*]. Certain persons are exempt from payment of fees: see 1997 Fees Order, art.5, substituted by S.S.I. 2002 No. 270. A fee exemption certificate must be lodged in process: see P.N. No.1 of 2002.

Where the petitioner is legally represented, the fee may be debited under a credit scheme introduced on 1st April 1976 by P.N. No. 4 of 1976 to the account (if one is kept or permitted) of the agent by the court cashier, and an account will be rendered weekly by the court cashier's office to the agent for all court fees due that week for immediate settlement. Party litigants, and agents not operating the scheme, must pay (by cash, cheque or postal order) on each occasion a fee is due at the time of lodging at the counter at the Petition Department.

Period of notice for lodging answers

14.6.—(1) Subject to any other provision in these Rules, the period of notice for lodging answers to a petition shall be—

    (a) in the case of service, intimation or advertisement within Europe, 21 days from whichever is the later of the date of execution of service, the giving of intimation or the publication of the advertisement;

    (b) in the case of service or intimation furth of Europe under rule 16.2(2)(d) or (e) (service by an *huissier* etc. or personally), 21 days from whichever is the later of the date of execution of service or the giving of intimation;

    (c) in the case of service or intimation furth of Europe other than under sub-paragraph (b), or advertisement furth of Europe, 42 days from whichever is the later of the date of execution of service, the giving of intimation or the publication of the advertisement;

(d) in the case of service by advertisement under rule 16.5 (service where address of person is not known), six months from the date of publication of the advertisement.

(2) An application may be made by motion to shorten or extend the period of notice.

(3) Where a motion under paragraph (2) is made in a petition at the time that an order for intimation, service or advertisement is made under rule 14.5 (first order in petitions), the decision of the court on the motion shall be final and not subject to review.

Deriv. R.C.S. 1965, r. 75(7) (r. 14.4(1)(d)), r. 192(1) (r. 14.6(1)(a) to (c)), and r. 192(3) (r. 14.6(2)), all substituted by S.I. 1986 No. 1941

General note. The phrase "period of notice" has replaced the word "*induciae*", but its effect is **14.6.1** the same: the prayer of the petition may not be granted until after expiry of the period. The period of 21 days was introduced by A.S. (R.C.A. No. 9) (Jurisdiction and Enforcement) 1986 [S.I. 1986 No. 1941]. The former period of 14 days was the shortest in Europe; it was increased to 21 days following the application of Art. 20 of the 1968 Convention in Sched. 1 (and of the Lugano Convention in Sched. 3C) to the C.J.J.A. 1982 and Art. 15 of the Hague Convention of 15th November 1965 on the Service Abroad of Judicial and Extrajudicial Documents in Civil or Commercial Matters (Cmnd. 3986 (1969)) which deal with the sisting of proceedings where it is not shown that the respondent has been able to receive the document in sufficient time to arrange for his defence (oppose the petition), and Art. 27(2) of the 1968 or Lugano Convention which entitles a court of a Contracting State to refuse to recognise a judgment in default of appearance for enforcement if the respondent was not served with the petition in sufficient time to enable him to arrange for his defence (oppose the petition): C.J.J.A. 1982, Scheds. 1 and 3C, Art. 27(2).

This rule applies generally to all periods of notice other than the period of notice in a summons (before the expiry of which the summons cannot be called) by virtue of r. 1.3(1) (definition of "period of notice").

A petition is commenced when the first order is made under r. 14.5. *Cf.* the date on which an application is made to the court, for the purpose of determining whether it falls within the two year period under s. 7 of the Company Directors Disqualification Act 1986, which is the date on which the petition is lodged: *Secretary of State for Trade and Industry v. Normand* 1994 S.L.T. 1249.

"*Subject to any other provision in these Rules*". Other provision is expressly made for the **14.6.2** following petitions:—
   r. 57.2 (disapplication of petition rules in petitions for admission of Advocates);
   r. 62.2 (disapplication of r. 14.6 in petitions to register foreign judgments, etc.);
   r. 66.2 (disapplication of r. 14.6 in applications under the Evidence (Proceedings in Other Jurisdictions) Act 1975);
   r. 67.2 (disapplication of r. 14.6(1)(d) in adoption petitions);
   r. 69.4(1)(a) (period of notice in election petitions);
   rr. 70.4(1) and 70.8(1) (period of notice of four days to lodge answers to petition under the Child Abduction and Custody Act 1985);
   rr. 76.2 and 76.20 (disapplication of r. 14.6(1) to petitions relating to confiscation of proceeds of crime).
The period of notice where notice is given by advertisement in an action (other than in the summons: see definition of "period of notice" in r. 1.3(1)) is not six months (a) in a family action (r. 49.12) or (b) in an action of declarator of death (r. 50.2(2)).

"*whichever is the later*". The period of notice expires on the last day of the period of notice **14.6.3** which is calculated from (but excluding) the date on which the last execution of service, giving of intimation or advertisement was made. Usually service and intimation are made at the same time; but they may not be, or service or intimation may have to be attempted again if at first unsuccessful. Intimation to named persons is rare in petitions, service being the general rule.

"*execution of service*". The period of notice will begin to run from midnight of the day on **14.6.4** which service is executed; except where service is by post when time begins to run from midnight of the day after the date of posting (r. 16.4(6)). All days of the week are included in the period of notice, including Sundays and other public holidays. For methods of service, see Chap. 16, Pt. I.

A petition is commenced when the first order is made under r. 14.5 and not later when service is executed.

14.6.5   *"intimation"*. Intimation to named persons is rare in a petition, service being the general rule. A petition in a judicial factory has to be intimated to the Accountant of Court: r. 61.5(1). Intimation on the walls of the court has to be made: r. 14.7; and see note 14.7.1. On intimation by advertisement, see note 14.6.6.

14.6.6   *"advertisement"*. Certain petitions require public notice in one or more national or local newspapers either as a matter of practice or by the statute under which the petition is presented.

14.6.7   *"Europe"*. This word has not been defined; but probably means as far east as (the Ural mountains in Russia and?) the Black Sea but not Asian Russia or the Asian Republics of the former U.S.S.R., south to the Mediterranean islands but not Africa, and north to Norway, Iceland and Finland. It includes the whole of the British Isles. Note also "Europe" for the purposes of the Royal Mail.

14.6.8   *Application to shorten or extend the period of notice.* Such an application is made by motion and accordingly the first order will not be granted automatically without enrolment: for motions, see Chap. 23. The decision of the court on such an application is final (r. 14.6(3)) as is an application before service in an action (r. 13.4(3)).

14.6.9   *Dispensing with period of notice.* Where the respondent's agent accepts service he may dispense with the period of notice: see r. 16.10 and note 16.10.1.

14.6.10   *Prorogation of time for lodging answers.* The period within which answers have to be lodged may be prorogated: r. 4.9(2). The former rule (R.C.S. 1965, r. 27(a)) stated that cause must be shown for an extension of time. The requirement to show cause has been omitted from the rule as it did not accord with current practice. It does not follow, however, that the court may not require cause to be shown in a particular case, as prorogation is in the discretion of the court.

Application to lodge a document late must be made by motion to the court under r. 2.1(1) (relief for failure to comply with rules).

Intimation and service of petitions

14.7.—(1) A petition shall be intimated—

   (a) on the walls of the court; and

   (b) in such other manner as the court thinks fit.

(2) A copy of the petition shall be served on every person, specified in the petition or by the court as a person on whom the petition is to be served, with a citation in Form 14.7 attached to it.

[1] (3) A petition to the court in exercise of its *parens patriae* jurisdiction shall not be intimated on the walls of the court.

Deriv. R.C.S. 1965, r. 195(a) (past) (r. 14.7(1)), and
r. 195(c) amended by S.I. 1986 No. 1941 (r. 14.7(2))

---

[1] R. 14.7(3) inserted by S.I. 1996 No. 1756 (effective 5th August 1996).

14.7.1   *Intimation.* In a petition intimation usually refers only to intimation on the walls of the court as intimation to named persons is rare (service on named persons being the general rule). Intimation in the Minute Book was discontinued in January 1993 when the Minute Book was discontinued: on the Minute Book, see note 9.1.1. A petition in a judicial factory has to be intimated to the Accountant of Court: r. 61.5(1).

(1) Intimation on the walls of the court. A typed slip containing the details of the petition or a copy of the first page is handed to the clerk of session in the Petition Department or sent by post or fax: P.N. No. 7 of 1994. The details required are (a) the nature of the application (i.e. "petition" or "note"), (b) the name and address of the petitioner, (c) the general purposes of the petition and (d) the name of the petitioner's solicitor. The Petition Department is responsible for placing the slip, on the day the first order under r. 14.5 is pronounced, on a hook at the top of the main corridor of Parliament House nearest the reception area at door 11.

This form of intimation may be dispensed with by order of the court: *Low, Petr.* 1920 S.C. 351 (fear of mother disappearing with child). In certain petitions, intimation is expressly excluded or dispensed with: see—

r. 57.2 (disapplication of petition rules in petitions for admission of Advocates);
r. 62.2 (disapplication of r. 14.7 in petitions to register foreign judgments etc.);
r. 66.2 (disapplication of r. 14.7 in applications under the Evidence (Proceedings in Other Jurisdictions) Act 1975);
r. 67.2 (disapplication of r. 14.7 in adoption petitions);
rr. 76.2 and 76.20 (disapplication of r. 14.7 to petitions relating to confiscation of proceeds of crime).

(2) Intimation in such other manner as the court thinks fit (r. 14.7(1)(*b*)). This includes advertisement and notices in the *Gazettes*. Certain petitions require advertisement in one or more of the London, Edinburgh and Belfast *Gazettes* and national or local newspapers either as a matter of practice or by the statute under which the petition is presented.

Service. A petition is normally brought to the attention of all interested persons by service: for **14.7.2** methods of service, see Chap. 16, Pt. I. Intimation in the sense in which it is used in actions is uncommon. Intimation of a petition (or note) relating to a judicial factory has to be made, however, to the Accountant of Court: r. 61.5(1).

Lodging execution copy of petition. On expiry of the period of notice the petitioner must **14.7.3** lodge in process an execution copy of the petition (r. 16.1(4)) with a copy of the first order attached to it and the certificate of service attached to that: r. 16.1(3). A copy of any notice or advertisement ordered to be made must be lodged as a production and referred to in the certificate of service. A walling certificate is no longer required: P.N. No. 7 of 1994, para. 4.

"*petition to the court in exercise of its* parens patriae *jurisdiction*". See note 14.2.11.   **14.7.4**

[THE NEXT PAGE IS C 127]

Procedure where answers lodged

14.8. Where answers to a petition have been lodged, the petitioner shall, within 28 days after the expiry of the period of notice, apply by motion for such further procedure as he seeks, and the court shall make such order for further procedure as it thinks fit.

General note. Where a petition is opposed it may proceed in the same way as an action, being appointed to the Adjustment Roll, the subsequent closing of the record and appointment to the Procedure Roll or to proof. In the case of suspensions this is expressly provided: r. 60.5.   **14.8.1**

The Lord Ordinary has statutory powers under s. 25 of the C.S.A. 1988 (1) to determine a petition himself, (2) to make such investigation and require such assistance from professional person or persons of science or of skill as he thinks fit or (3) to grant commission to take the deposition of havers and the evidence of witnesses as provided by s. 10 of the 1988 Act (evidence on commission in actions). Evidence on commission in an Inner House petition may similarly be taken: C.S.A. 1988, s. 38. Under the R.C.S. 1994 all of Chap. 35 (recovery of evidence) is available. Particular rules or practice may provide for a particular form of inquiry such as by remit to a reporter.

Strictly, a person becomes a respondent only by lodging answers.

"answers". For the form and lodging of answers, see r. 18.3 and notes.   **14.8.2**

"within 28 days". The date from which the period is calculated is not counted. Where the last day falls on a Saturday or Sunday, or a public holiday on which the Office of Court is closed, the next available day is allowed: r. 1.3(7). For office hours and public holidays, see note 3.1.2.   **14.8.3**

Lodging of execution copy of petition. Before proceeding with a motion under this rule the execution copy of the petition certified as a true copy must be lodged with the certificates of service and any Post Office receipts for, or certificates of, posting attached, and a copy of the interlocutor ordering service, and there should be lodged as productions copies of the *Gazettes* and newspapers containing any advertisement ordered to be published: r. 16.1(3) and (4). A walling certificate is not required: P.N. No. 7 of 1994, para. 4. The position of the advertisement should be clearly marked on the front of the document lodged and at the place of the advertisement; alternatively, on analogy with r. 16.5(6)(*b*), a certificate of publication by the publisher stating the date of publication and the text of the advertisement may be accepted.   **14.8.4**

"motion". For motions, see Chap. 23.   **14.8.5**

Hearings and proofs. A hearing in a petition may be a proof (or proof before answer) or simply a hearing.   **14.8.6**

At a hearing the court may consider reports, affidavits and other documentary evidence and be addressed by the parties, but parole evidence is not led. A hearing is not a proof. The interlocutor appointing a petition to a hearing will not grant authority to cite witnesses; whereas an interlocutor appointing the cause to a proof would do so. It is, therefore, important to be clear whether a hearing or a proof is sought; and the depute clerk of session should inquire if this information is not volunteered so that any necessary warrant to cite may be included (where proof is sought).

In the Inner House where a proof is ordered the proof is taken by a judge of the Inner House and any ruling by him on the admissibility of evidence may be reviewed by the Inner House in the discussion of his report on the evidence: C.S.A. 1988, s. 37.

Unopposed petitions

14.9.—(1) Subject to paragraph (2), where the period of notice has expired without answers being lodged, the court shall, on the motion of the petitioner, after such further procedure and inquiry into the grounds of the petition, if any, as it thinks fit, dispose of the petition.

(2) Where—

(*a*) the prayer of the petition seeks an order directed against a person,

(*b*) service of the petition has been made on that person furth of the United Kingdom under rule 16.2, and

(*c*) such order has been granted without that person having lodged answers,

a certified copy of the interlocutor granting the order shall be served forthwith by the petitioner on that person.

(3) The court may, on the motion of a person to whom paragraph (2) applies, recall the interlocutor and allow answers to be lodged if—

(a) that person—
  (i) without any fault on his part, did not have knowledge of the petition in sufficient time to lodge answers;
  (ii) has disclosed a *prima facie* answer to the petition on the merits; and
  (iii) has enrolled the motion for recall within a reasonable time after he had knowledge of the petition; and
(b) the motion is enrolled before the expiry of one year from the date of the interlocutor sought to be recalled.

(4) The recall of an interlocutor under paragraph (3) shall be without prejudice to the validity of anything already done or transacted, of any contract made or obligation incurred, or of any appointment made or power granted, in or by virtue of that interlocutor.

(5) The provisions of this rule are without prejudice to the power of the court to make any interim appointment or order at any stage of the cause.

Deriv. R.C.S. 1965, r. 197 (preamble) (r. 14.9(1)), r. 197(a) (r. 14.9(2)), r. 197(b) (r. 14.9(3)), r. 197(c) (r. 14.9(4)), all substituted by S.I. 1986 No. 1941, and r. 197(d) (r. 14.9(5))

14.9.1 *Lodging of execution copy of petition.* Before proceeding with a motion under this rule the execution copy of the petition certified as a true copy must be lodged with the certificates of service and any Post Office receipts for, or certificates of, posting attached, and a copy of the interlocutor ordering service, and there should be lodged as productions copies of the *Gazettes* and newspapers containing any advertisement ordered to be published: r. 16.1(3) and (4). The position of the advertisement should be clearly marked on the front of the document lodged and at the place of the advertisement; alternatively, on analogy with r. 16.5(6)(b), a certificate of publication by the publisher stating the date of publication and the text of the advertisement may be accepted.

14.9.2 *"motion".* For motions, see Chap. 23.

14.9.3 *Court must be satisfied about service.* This is established by the appropriate certificates of service and copies of any notices or advertisements: see note 14.9.1.
  In relation to an unopposed petition in which an order is sought against a person there is this significance to this requirement. Under Art. 20(2) of Scheds. 1, 3C and 4, to the C.J.J.A. 1982 the court must sist the cause so long as it has not been shown that that person has been able to receive the petition in sufficient time to enable him to defend or that all necessary steps have been taken to effect service: "all necessary steps" means that all necessary approaches have been made to the competent authorities of the country in which that person is domiciled to reach him in sufficient time (Jenard report on 1968 Convention, p. 40). Art. 20 does not apply where his whereabouts are unknown.
  Under Art. 15 of the Hague Convention on Service Abroad of Judicial and Extrajudicial Documents in Civil or Commercial Matters, 1965 (Cmnd. 3986 (1969)), which may be used in a country to which the 1968 Convention applies (Art. 20(3) of Scheds. 1 and 3C to the C.J.J.A. 1982), the court must be satisfied that service was executed by a method prescribed by the internal law of the country concerned or delivered by a method provided for under the convention in sufficient time to enable the respondent to defend. Decree may be granted, however, even if no certificate of service or delivery has been received where the petition was transmitted by a method under the convention, six months have elapsed since the date of transmission and no certificate has been received even though every reasonable effort has been made to obtain it: the UK has made the necessary declaration to bring this provision into effect. Art. 15 does not apply where the whereabouts of the respondent are unknown: Art. 1(2). For the countries to which the Hague Convention applies, see note 16.2.3.
  In relation to any other civil procedure convention with a foreign country, regard will require to be had to its terms, if any, about the court's satisfaction about service. Where there is no convention, the court will be satisfied by any form of service under r. 16.2; it may not enquire whether, or require a certificate that, the form of service used is permitted by the laws of the country concerned, leaving it to the petitioner to take care to use a method which will enable him to enforce the decree there.

14.9.4 *Court must be satisfied it has jurisdiction.* Averments about jurisdiction are required in a petition to which the C.J.J.A. 1982 applies: r. 14.4(4)(a); the requirement is limited to such petitions because not many petitions will be subject to that Act. Under Art. 20(1) of Scheds. 1, 3C and 4, and r. 8 of Sched. 8, to the C.J.J.A. 1982 the court must be satisfied that it has jurisdiction in causes to which that Act applies where the defender has not entered appearance (the respondent does not lodge answers) or it must declare at its own instance that it has no jurisdiction. Notice also that under the C.J.J.A. 1982 where it appears to the court that a court in another country has exclusive jurisdiction it must at its own instance decline jurisdiction: Art. 19 of Scheds. 1, 3C and 4, and r. 7 of Sched. 8, to the C.J.J.A. 1982. The former requirement (R.C.S. 1965, r. 197(*e*)), to state the ground of jurisdiction in the motion for the prayer of the petition to be granted, is no longer required as it is considered unnecessary because the ground (except prorogation unless agreed in advance) is stated in the petition in those petitions to which the C.J.J.A. 1982 applies (see r. 14.4(4)).

Inquiry in unopposed petitions. Some unopposed petitions may require a hearing (*e.g.* **14.9.5** adoption petitions (Chap. 67)) or some other form of inquiry such as a remit to a reporter (*e.g.* in applications for schemes in relation to public trusts (Chap. 63, Pt. III) or confirmation of reduction of capital of a company (see note 14.3.10)) or a proof.

Service of interlocutor granting order. R. 14.9(2) requires service of an order directed against a **14.9.6** person furth of the UK and is equivalent to the rule for decrees in absence in r. 19.1(6). The purpose of this rule stems from Art. 47(1) of Sched. 1 to the C.J.J.A. 1982 which requires a judgment to have been served on the defender before an order for enforcement can be obtained in cases to which that Schedule applies. The provision is extended in this rule to all orders against persons furth of the UK.

"answers". For form and lodging of answers, see r. 18.3 and notes.   **14.9.7**

Recall of interlocutor granting order. R. 14.9(3) enables a person furth of the UK, served with **14.9.8** an order required by r. 14.9(2), to seek to recall it and is equivalent to the rule for recall of decrees in absence in r. 19.2. The basis for the procedure for recall under r. 14.9(3) is Art. 16 of the Hague Convention on Service Abroad of Judicial and Extrajudicial Documents in Civil or Commercial Matters, 1965 (Cmnd. 3986 (1969)) which is applied in this rule to any country furth of the UK whether or not one to which the convention applies. The UK made a declaration in relation to Scotland under Art. 16 limiting the period within which application may be made for recall to one year and this is enshrined in r. 14.9(3)(*b*). Although such a person has a year within which to seek recall, the decree may be extracted by the petitioner under r. 7.1.

Recall does not affect the validity of things done or transacted, or appointments made, in or by virtue of the decree: r. 14.9(4) and (5).

CHAPTER 15

APPLICATIONS BY MINUTE OR NOTE

Applications by minute
   15.1.—(1) Subject to paragraph (6) and to any other provision in these Rules, this rule applies to any application to the court by minute in a cause.
   (2) A minute shall—
   (*a*) include a crave, a statement of facts and appropriate pleas-in-law; and
   (*b*) be lodged in the process of the cause to which it relates.
   (3) On lodging a minute, the minuter shall enrol a motion, as appropriate—
   (*a*) for a warrant for service of the minute on a person who has not entered the process of the cause;
   (*b*) where the cause is not a depending cause, for service of the minute on parties to that cause;
   (*c*) for intimation of the minute to any person;
   (*d*) to dispense with service on, or intimation to, a person; and
   (*e*) for an order for any answers to the minute to be lodged in process within the period of notice.
   (4) A notice in Form 15.1 shall be attached to the minute to be served or intimated under paragraph (3).
   (5) After the expiry of the period of notice, the court shall, on the motion of any party, after such further procedure, if any, as it thinks fit, determine the application.
   (6) This rule shall not apply to—
   (*a*) a minute of abandonment;
   (*b*) a minute of amendment;

(*c*) a minute of sist;
(*d*) a minute of transference; or
(*e*) a minute of objection to a minute of transference.

15.1.1 *General note.* This is a new rule intended to provide a general provision for applications by minute. Particular rules may exclude or augment the provisions of this rule.

An application in an action, which may not be made by motion, is made by minute or where the court orders that a minute regarding the subject-matter of an application be lodged within a prescribed period (*e.g.* variation of aliment or access: *e.g.* rr. 49.42(4) and 49.43(4)).

15.1.2 *Form of minute.* The crave, statement of facts and pleas-in-law should follow the principles applicable to the conclusions, condescendence and pleas-in-law in an action. On conclusions, see note 13.2.3. On the condescendence, see note 13.2.4. On pleas-in-law, see notes 13.2.5 and 18.1.4. The instance should be the same as in the summons. On use of metric units of measurement, see note 13.2.18.

15.1.3 *"service".* For methods, see Chap. 16, Pt. 1.

15.1.4 *"intimation".* For methods, see rr. 16.7 and 16.8. Particular rules may require a warrant for intimation.

15.1.5 *"period of notice".* This period is determined in accordance with rule 14.6 (period of notice for lodging answers) by virtue of r. 1.3(1) (definitions of "period of notice" and "writ").

15.1.6 *"answers".* For form and lodging of answers, see r. 18.3 and notes.

15.1.7 *Fee.* The court fee for lodging a minute is payable on lodging by a person, other than an originating party, on first appearing, or for variation of an order in a family action. For fee, see Court of Session etc. Fees Order 1997, Table of Fees, Pt. I, B, item 2, 6 or 8 [S.I. 1997 No. 688, as amended, pp. C1201 *et seq.*]. Certain persons are exempt from payment of fees: see 1997 Fees Order, art.5, substituted by S.S.I. 2002 No. 270. A fee exemption certificate must be lodged in process: see P.N. No.1 of 2002.

Where the minuter is legally represented, the fee may be debited under a credit scheme introduced on 1st April 1976 by P.N. No. 4 of 1976 to the account (if one is kept or permitted) of the agent by the court cashier, and an account will be rendered weekly by the court cashier's office to the agent for all court fees due that week for immediate settlement. Party litigants, and agents not operating the scheme, must pay (by cash, cheque or postal order) on each occasion a fee is due at the time of lodging at the counter at the General Department.

15.1.8 *Minutes to which this rule does not apply.* The minutes listed in r. 15.1(6) have their own forms and procedures and r. 15.1 does not therefore apply. On minutes of abandonment, see Chap. 29. On minutes of amendment, see Chap. 24. On minutes of sist, see r. 31.1. On minutes of transference and minutes of objection to such a minute, see r. 31.2.

15.1.9 *Party minuters.* There are no rules as to the form of a minute to be lodged by a person seeking to be sisted as a party (a party minuter) other than a minute of sist by a person representing a deceased or incapacitated party (see r. 13.1). A variety of styles are encountered, namely, a simple minute of sist with no pleadings, a minute of sist with pleadings attached, or simply answers, each accompanied by a motion to be sisted. The appropriate form of writ will often depend on the circumstances. In some instances the form of intimation will specify the writ to be lodged. As a general rule, however, unless otherwise provided in the R.C.S. 1994, a minute should seek to be sisted stating the ground on which the person wishes to become a party. The minute should be accompanied by the appropriate writ containing the pleadings.

Applications by note

15.2.—(1) Subject to paragraph (4) and to any other provision in these Rules, this rule applies to any application to the court by note in a cause.

(2) A note shall—

(*a*) include a statement of facts and a prayer; and

(*b*) be lodged in the process of the cause to which it relates.

(3) The following provisions of Chapter 14 (petitions) shall, with the necessary modifications and the modification mentioned below, apply to a note under this rule as they apply to a petition:—

rule 14.5 (first order in petitions),

rule 14.6 (period of notice for lodging answers),

rule 14.7 (intimation and service of petitions) with the substitution in paragraph (2) of that rule of the words "a notice in Form 15.2" for

the words "a citation in Form 14.7",
rule 14.8 (procedure where answers lodged),
rule 14.9 (unopposed petitions).
(4) This rule shall not apply to—
  (*a*) a note to the Extractor; or
  (*b*) a note of objection.

General note. This is a new rule intended to provide a general provision for applications by **15.2.1**
note. Particular rules may exclude or augment the provisions of this rule.
  An application in a petition, which may not be made by motion, is made by note.
  For procedure, see the rules and corresponding annotations in Chap. 14 referred to in r.
15.2(3).

Form of note. The Address, statement of facts and prayer should follow the principles **15.2.2**
applicable to a petition. On the Address, see note 14.4.2. On the statement of facts, see note
14.4.3. On the prayer, see note 14.4.8. On use of metric units of measurement, see note 14.4.14.

Answers. For form and lodging of answers to a note, see r. 18.3 and notes. **15.2.3**

Fee. The court fee for lodging a note is payable on lodging by a person, other than an **15.2.4**
originating party, on first appearing. For fee, see Court of Session etc. Fees Order 1997, Table
of Fees, Pt. I, C, item 4 [S.I. 1997 No. 688, as amended, pp. **C** 1201 *et seq.*]. Certain persons are
exempt from payment of fees: see 1997 Fees Order, art. 5 substituted by S.S.I. 2002 No. 270. A
fee exemption certificate must be lodged in process: see P.N. No.1 of 2002.
  Where the noter is legally represented, the fee may be debited under a credit scheme
introduced on 1st April 1976 by P.N. No. 4 of 1976 to the account (if one is kept or permitted)
of the agent by the court cashier, and an account will be rendered weekly by the court cashier's
office to the agent for all court fees due that week for immediate settlement. Party litigants, and
agents not operating the scheme, must pay (by cash, cheque or postal order) on each occasion a
fee is due at the time of lodging at the counter at the Petition Department.

Notes to which this rule does not apply. The notes listed in r. 15.2(4) have their own forms and **15.2.5**
procedure and r. 15.2 does not therefore apply. On notes to the Extractor, see r. 7.1(3). On notes
of objections, see r. 42.4 (note of objection to Auditor's report) and r. 61.26 (note of objection
to state of funds or scheme of division in judicial factory on estate of deceased person).

CHAPTER 16

SERVICE, INTIMATION AND DILIGENCE

PART I

SERVICE AND INTIMATION

Methods and manner of service
  16.1.—(1) Subject to any other provision in these Rules or any other
enactment, service of a document required under these Rules on a person
shall be executed—
  (*a*) in the case of an individual—
    (i) personally, by tendering the document and any citation or
notice, as the case may be, to that individual;
    (ii) by leaving the document and any citation or notice, as the case
may be, in the hands of a person, or failing which, depositing it,
in a dwelling place where the person executing service, after due
enquiry, has reasonable grounds for believing that that
individual resides but is not available;
    (iii) by leaving the document and any citation or notice, as the case
may be, in the hands of a person at, or depositing it in, a place of

business where the person executing service, after due enquiry, has reasonable grounds for believing that that individual carries on business; or

  (iv) by posting the document and any citation or notice, as the case may be, to the known dwelling place of that individual;

 (b) in the case of any other person—

  (i) by leaving the document and any citation or notice, as the case may be, in the hands of an individual at, or depositing it in, the registered office, other official address or a place of business, of that other person, in such a way that it is likely to come to the attention of that other person; or

  (ii) by posting the document and any citation or notice, as the case may be, to the registered office, other official address or a place of business, of that other person.

(2) Service of a principal writ on a person whose known residence is the same as that of the party on whose behalf service is to be executed shall be executed personally.

(3) Subject to paragraph (4), where service has been executed, the party on whose behalf service has been executed shall attach to the document served and lodge in process—

 (a) a certificate of service as required by these Rules;

 (b) a copy of any notice or advertisement ordered to be published; and

 (c) a copy of any interlocutor ordering service of that document.

(4) In relation to a petition or note, where service has been executed by a petitioner or noter, he shall attach the documents required by paragraph (3)(a) and (b) to a copy of the petition or note, as the case may be, marked "Execution Copy" and certified a true copy.

Deriv. R.C.S. 1965, r. 74A(1) inserted by S.I. 1984 No. 472 and amended by S.I. 1985 No. 1600, 1986 No. 1941 and 1990 No. 705 (r. 16.1(1)), r. 74A(3) inserted by S.I. 1984 No. 472 and r. 77 (r. 16.1(3)), and r. 195(d) (r. 16.1(4))

16.1.1   *General note.* This rule, subject to any other provision in the R.C.S. 1994 or any other enactment, applies to the service of any document (including a summons, petition or note). The rule is subject, *e.g.* to the rules for service furth of the UK (r. 16.2) or where the address of the person to be served is not known (r. 16.5). The rules for execution of diligence are in Part II of this Chapter which apply certain of the rules for service in Part I to the execution of diligence: see r. 16.12.

Service of a summons marks the commencement of the action: Erskine, III.vi.3; *Alston v. Macdougall* (1887) 15 R. 78; *Smith v. Stewart & Co.* 1960 S.C. 329, 334 *per* L.P. Clyde. The cause is then in dependence: *Aitken v. Dick* (1863) 1 M. 1038, 1041 *per* Lords Deas and Ardmillan. A petition or note is commenced and is in dependence when the first order is granted. Service on a defender in an action (or a respondent in a petition) is often called citation. Although a cause is not in dependence until served, certain applications may be made to the court: *e.g.* motions before calling or first order (r. 23.8), motions where caveat lodged (r. 23.9) or motions by defender or other party before calling (r. 23.10).

16.1.2   *Service on an individual (a natural person).* There are six methods of service on natural persons provided in r. 16.1. These are of general application, subject to any other provision in the R.C.S. 1994 or any other enactment in particular the rules for service furth of the UK and the qualifications in rr. 16.3, 16.4 and 16.5.

(1) *Personal service*: r. 16.1(1)(a)(i). This may only be executed on a natural person and not a corporate or unincorporated body or firm: *cf.* r. 16.1(1)(b). It may only be executed in Scotland by a messenger-at-arms (or elsewhere in the UK by his equivalent: a process server) who must explain the purpose of the service to the person served: r. 16.3(1) and (6). The execution of service must be witnessed and the certificate of service signed by the witness: r. 16.3(2). The essential part of personal service is the tendering (giving or offering) of the citation or other document: Stair, IV.xxxviii.15. Hence personal service may be regarded as executed even if the document is refused (Stair, IV.xxxviii.15) or obstructed (*Busby v. Clark* (1904) 7 F. 162): if this occurs the fact should be stated in the certificate of service. The citation or other document should be delivered if possible and, if it is not possible to serve personally, another method should be attempted. Service must be personal where service is of a principal writ (defined in

r. 1.3(1)) on a person living at the same address as the party on whose behalf service is executed: r. 16.1(2). Personal service may not be executed on a Sunday: Bell's *Comm.*, ii,460; *Oliphant v. Douglas* (1633) Mor. 15002; *McNiven v. Glasgow Corporation* 1920 S.C. 584.

(2) *Leaving in the hands of a person in the dwelling place* where the person on whom service is to be executed resides: r. 16.1(1)(*a*)(ii). The person executing service (in Scotland, a messenger-at-arms: r. 16.3(1); or, elsewhere in the UK, his equivalent: r. 16.3(6)) must have reasonable grounds for believing that the person on whom service is to be executed normally resides there: r. 16.1(1)(*a*)(ii). A person's dwelling place is his usual place of residence: *Corstorphine v. Kasten* (1898) 1 F. 287. The name and designation of the person in whose hands the documents are left must be stated in the certificate of service: r. 16.3(5). The documents to be served must be placed in a sealed envelope: r. 16.3(3). The execution of service must be witnessed and the certificate of service signed by the witness: r. 16.3(2). It should be noticed that simply *leaving* the documents *at* the person's residence is not enough. This method of service may not be executed on a Sunday: Bell's *Comm.*, ii,460; *Oliphant v. Douglas* (1633) Mor. 15002; *McNiven v. Glasgow Corporation* 1920 S.C. 584.

(3) *Depositing in the dwelling place* where the person on whom service is to be executed resides: r.16.1(1)(a)(ii). The person executing service (in Scotland, a messenger-at-arms: r.16.3(1); or, elsewhere in the UK, his equivalent: r.16.3(6)) must have reasonable grounds for believing that the person on whom service is to be executed normally resides there: r.16.1(1)(a)(ii). A person's dwelling place is his usual place of residence: *Corstorphine v. Kasten* (1898) 1 F. 287. The execution of service must be witnessed and the certificate of service signed by the witness: r.16.3(2). It should be noticed that depositing *at* (*i.e.* simply leaving, fixing to the outside of the dwelling or in the lockhole) is not sufficient; the documents must be placed inside the dwelling (*e.g.* through the letterbox or under the door): *Docherty v. Docherty* 1981 S.L.T. (Notes) 24. This method of service may not be executed on a Sunday: Bell's *Comm.*, ii,460; *Oliphant v. Douglas* (1633) Mor. 15002; *McNiven v. Glasgow Corporation* 1920 S.C. 584.

(4) *Leaving in the hands of a person at a place of business* where the person on whom service is to be executed carries on business: r.16.1(1)(a)(iii). Service by leaving in the hands of a person at the workplace of the person on whom service is to be executed is permissible, but the documents must be placed in a sealed envelope: r.16.3(3). The name and designation of the person in whose hands the documents are left must be stated in the certificate of service: r.16.3(5). The person executing service (in Scotland, a messenger-at-arms: r.16.3(1); or, elsewhere in the UK, his equivalent: r.16.3(6)) must have reasonable grounds for believing that the person on whom service is to be executed normally carries on business there: r.16.1(1)(a)(iii). The execution of service must be witnessed and the certificate of service signed by the witness: r.16.3(2). This method of service may not be executed on a Sunday: Bell's *Comm.*, ii,460; *Oliphant v. Douglas* (1633) Mor. 15002; *McNiven v. Glasgow Corporation* 1920 S.C. 584.

(5) *Depositing in a place of business* where the person on whom service is to be executed carries on business: r.16.1(1)(a)(iii). The person executing service (in Scotland, a messenger-at-arms: r.16.3(1); or, elsewhere in the UK, his equivalent: r.16.3(6)) must have reasonable grounds for believing that the person on whom service is to be executed normally carries on business there: r.16.1(1)(a)(iii). The execution of service must be witnessed and the certificate of service signed by the witness: r.16.3(2). It should be noticed that depositing *at* (*i.e.* simply leaving, fixing to the outside of the workplace or in the lockhole) is not sufficient; the documents must be placed inside (*e.g.* through the letterbox or under the door): see *Docherty v. Docherty* 1981 S.L.T. (Notes) 24. This method of service may not be executed on a Sunday: Bell's *Comm.*, ii,460; *Oliphant v. Douglas* (1633) Mor. 15002; *McNiven v. Glasgow Corporation* 1920 S.C. 584.

(6) *By post*: r.16.1(1)(a)(iv). The detailed rules for service by post are in r.16.4.

Service on persons other than individuals (non-natural persons). There are three methods of **16.1.3** service on legal persons, subject to any other provision in the R.C.S. 1994 or any other enactment and in particular the rules for service furth of the UK and the qualifications in rr.16.3, 16.4 and 16.5.

(1) *Leaving in the hands of an individual* at the registered office or place of business, etc., of the person on whom service is to be executed: r.16.1(1)(b)(i). Service by leaving in the hands of a person at the registered office or place of business of the person on whom service is to be executed is permissible, but the documents must be placed in a sealed envelope: r.16.3(3). The name and designation of the person in whose hands the documents are left must be stated in the certificate of service: r.16.3(5). The person executing service (in Scotland, a messenger-at-arms: r.16.3(1); or, elsewhere in the UK, his equivalent: r.16.3(6)) must have reasonable grounds for believing that the person on whom service is to be executed normally carries on business there: r.16.1(1)(a)(iii). The execution of service must be witnessed and the certificate of service signed by the witness: r.16.3(2). This method of service may not be executed on a Sunday: Bell's *Comm.*, ii,460; *Oliphant v. Douglas* (1633) Mor. 15002; *McNiven v. Glasgow Corporation* 1920 S.C. 584.

(2) *Depositing in the registered office or place of business, etc.*, of the person on whom service is to be executed: r.16.1(1)(b)(i). The person executing service in Scotland must be a messenger-at-arms: r.16.3(1); or, elsewhere in the UK, his equivalent: r.16.3(6). The execution of service must be witnessed and the certificate of service signed by the witness: r.16.3(2). It should be noticed that depositing *at*, *e.g.* by leaving the documents to be served under a stone on a vacant piece of ground or tied to the railings where a building once was, does not constitute a valid service. The documents must be placed *in* a building; if there is no building service cannot be executed. This method of service may not be executed on a Sunday: Bell's *Comm.*, ii,460; *Oliphant v. Douglas* (1633) Mor. 15002; *McNiven v. Glasgow Corporation* 1920 S.C. 584.

Section 725(1) of the Companies Act 1985 provides for service of a document on a company by leaving it at, or sending by post to, the company's registered office; and s.695 of the 1985 Act provides for service of process or any notices on an overseas company which has established a place of business in Great Britain. But r.16.1(1)(b) of the R.C.S. 1994 is more particular. and must be followed with respect to service of documents under the R.C.S. 1994.

(3) *By post*: r.16.1(1)(b)(ii). The detailed rules for service by post are in r.16.4.
On service on companies, see para.(2), above.

16.1.3A   *Service on members of the armed forces in maintenance proceedings.* Where service in connection with maintenance proceedings is to be effected on a member of the armed forces, service may be made by post to the person's commanding officer. The service is of no effect if the commanding officer certifies that the defender is absent without leave or has deserted. It is also without effect if it was served in the U.K. and the defender would be required to appear in court but the commanding officer certifies that the defender is under orders for active service out of the U.K.: see Naval Forces (Enforcement of Maintenance Liabilities) Act 1947, Army Act 1955, section 153; and Air Force Act 1955, section 153).

16.1.4   *"citation or notice"*. A citation in Form 13.7 must be attached to a summons when served on a defender: r.13.7(1)(a). In the case of a petition a citation in Form 14.7 is attached to the petition served on any person: r.14.7(2). In the case of a minute served or intimated on a person there must be attached a notice in Form 15.1; and in the case of a note, a notice in Form 15.2. Other notices may be required to be served under particular rules.

16.1.5   *Evidence of service.* The evidence required by the court for service is (a) a certificate of service by the person executing it, (b) a copy of any notice (*e.g.* the London, Edinburgh or Belfast *Gazette*) or advertisement ordered to be served, and (c) a copy of any interlocutor ordering service: r.16.1(3). Where a form of notice is also required to be served on a person, a copy of that notice must also be lodged. The reason for the documents required in addition to the certificate of service is so that the clerk of session can check that what was served was in, referred to or complied with, the same terms of any original interlocutor ordering service, or is a form of notice in compliance with the R.C.S. 1994. In actions these documents are attached to the principal writ: r.16.1(3). The citation and certificate of service are stitched into the principal summons for lodging for calling. Where any service is executed after calling of a summons or lodging of an execution copy of a petition or note, any citation and certificate of service are lodged as a separate step of process (on which, see r.4.4). For petitions and notes, see note 16.1.6.

16.1.6   *"Execution copy" of petition or note.* In petitions and notes the documents required as evidence of service (see note 16.1.5) are attached (stitched in) to an execution copy of the principal writ: r.16.1(4). A walling certificate is no longer required: P.N. No. 7 of 1994, para.4.

Service furth of United Kingdom

16.2.—(1) Subject to any other enactment, this rule applies to service of a document on a person on whom service is to be executed in a country furth of the United Kingdom.

(2) Service under this rule may be executed by any of the following methods of service, if, and in a manner, permitted under a convention providing for service in that country or by the laws of that country:—

(a) by post to the known residence, registered office or place of business, as the case may be, of the person on whom service is to be executed;

(b) through the central, or other appropriate, authority of that country, at the request of the Secretary of State for Foreign and Commonwealth Affairs;

(c) through a British consular office in that country, at the request of the Secretary of State for Foreign and Commonwealth Affairs;

(d) by an *huissier*, other judicial officer or competent official of that country, at the request of a messenger-at-arms, a party or his agent; or

(e) personally by the party executing service or his authorised agent tendering the document and the citation (if any) to the person on whom service is to be executed.

(3) Where service is to be executed through a central, or other appropriate, authority, or through a British consular officer, at the request of the Secretary of State for Foreign and Commonwealth Affairs, the party executing service shall—

(a) send a copy of the document, with a request for service by the

method indicated in the request, to the Secretary of State for Foreign
and Commonwealth Affairs; and
  (b) lodge in process a certificate signed by the authority which executed
      service stating that it has been, and the manner in which it was,
      served.
  (4) Where service is to be executed by an *huissier*, other judicial officer or
competent official at the request of a messenger-at-arms—

(a) the messenger-at-arms shall send a copy of the document with a request for service by the method indicated in the request to the official in the country in which service is to be executed; and

(b) the party on whose behalf service has been executed shall lodge in process a certificate of the official who executed service stating that it has been, and the manner in which it was, served.

(5) Where service has been executed personally by the party executing service or his authorised agent—

(a) the execution of service shall be witnessed by one witness who shall sign the certificate of service (which shall state his name, occupation and address); and

(b) the person who executed service shall complete a certificate of service in Form 16.2.

(6) Where service is executed by a method mentioned in paragraph (2)(a) or (e), the party executing service shall lodge in process a certificate by a person qualified in the law of the country, or a duly accredited representative of the country, in which service was executed stating that the method of service used is permitted by the law of that country.

Deriv. R.C.S. 1965, r. 74B(1) (r. 16.2(2)), r. 74B(4) (r. 16.2(3)), r. 74B(5) (r. 16.2(4)) and r. 74B(6) (r. 16.2(5)), all inserted by S.I. 1986 No. 1941

General note. This rule provides for all the methods of service available under the Hague **16.2.1** Convention on the Service Abroad of Judicial and Extrajudicial Documents in Civil or Commercial Matters dated 15th November 1965 (Cmnd 3986 (1969)), and personal service, and applies to any country furth of the U.K. It is necessary, however, to check that, in any foreign country in which service is to be executed, the method to be used is permitted in that country and is one listed in r. 16.2(1) unless the method is one specifically permitted under a particular enactment (see note 16.2.2). This is particularly important in relation to postal or personal service under r. 16.2(2)(a) or (e) as there may be no intervening authority or official in the country concerned who would execute service by a permitted method; and in these two cases a certificate from a qualified person stating that the method is permitted must be lodged in process: r. 16.2(6).

Consideration has to be given as to whether the person on whom service is to be executed is in (a) a Hague Convention country, (b) a Brussels or Lugano Convention country (to which Sched.1 or 3C of the C.J.J.A. 1982 applies), (c) an EU Member State other than Denmark, (d) a country with which the U.K. has a bilateral civil procedure convention, or (e) a country with which the U.K. has no convention.

For service in Member States of the EU other than Denmark, see now r. 16.2A (service of judicial and extra judicial documents in civil or commercial matters under Council Regulation (EC) No. 1348/2000).

Guidance on service may be obtained from: Private International Law Branch, Civil Justice and International Division, Justice Department, Scottish Executive, St Andrew House, Regent Road, Edinburgh EH1 3DG, Tel. +44 (0)131-244 4826, Fax. +44 (0)131-244 4848; and the Foreign and Commonwealth Office, Treaty and Nationality Department, 1 Palace Street, London SW1E 5HE, tel. 0171–238 4575 or 4577.

"Subject to any other enactment". A statute may provide for a method of service other than **16.2.2** one listed in r. 16.2. For example, under s.12 of the State Immunity Act 1978 any writ or document to be served for instituting proceedings other than a counterclaim or an action *in rem* against a State is served by transmitting it through the Foreign and Commonwealth Office to the Minister of Foreign Affairs of the State concerned, and service is deemed effected when the document is received at that Ministry; time for entering appearance begins to run from two months after that date. On proceedings in respect of which the court has jurisdiction over a foreign State, see note 13.2.2(B)(2).

For service in Member States of the EU other than Denmark, see now r. 16.2A (service of judicial and extra judicial documents in civil or commercial matters under Council Regulation (EC) No. 1348/2000).

Service in Hague Convention countries. The Hague Convention countries under the Hague **16.2.3** Convention on the Service Abroad of Judicial and Extrajudicial Documents in Civil or Commercial Matters dated 15th November 1965 (Cmnd. 3986 (1969)) are:

Antigua and Barbuda	Italy
Bahamas	Japan
Barbados	Latvia
Belerus	Luxembourg
Belgium	Malawi
Botswana	Netherlands (and Aruba)
Canada	Norway
China	Pakistan
Cyprus	Poland
Czech Republic*	Portugal
Denmark	Seychelles
Egypt	Slovac Republic*
Estonia	Spain
Finland	Sweden
France	Switzerland
Germany	Turkey
Greece	UK (and dependent territories)
Hong Kong†	USA (and dependent territories)
Ireland	Venezuela
Israel	

*Czechoslovakia is now divided into the Czech and Slovak Republics.
†The correct designation of Hong Kong is now "Special Administrative Region of the People's Republic of China".
Of the Member States of the European Communities, only Ireland is not a Hague Convention country.
The Hague Convention has been extended to the following U.K. dependencies:—

Anguilla	Montserrat
Bermuda	Pitcairn
Caymen Islands	Saint Helena and
Falkland Islands	dependencies
Gibraltar	South Georgia and the
Guernsey	South Sandwich Islands
Hong Kong	Turks and Caicos Islands
Isle of Man	Virgin Islands
Jersey	

The USA dependencies are: Guam, Puerto Rico and the Virgin Islands.
On the Hague Convention countries and the methods of service acceptable in each country, see the Practical Handbook on the Operation of the Hague Convention on Service Abroad published for the Permanent Bureau of the Hague Convention on Private International Law by Maklu Uitgevers; and see also Bowman & Harris on *Multilateral Treaties*.
The Hague Convention only applies where the address of the person on whom service is to be executed is known: Art. 1. The central authorities of the requested State will help to find an address. Where the address of the person on whom service is to be executed is not known r. 16.5 will have to be resorted to for service by advertisement and decree in absence may be obtained after six months: rr. 13.4(1)(d) or 14.6(1)(d). The Hague Convention does not state what is a civil or commercial matter or whether the law of the requesting or the requested country applies. The Special Commission of April 1989 indicated that "civil or commercial matter" should be interpreted in an autonomous manner without reference exclusively to the law of the requesting or requested State or both. On the meaning of "civil and commercial matter" in the Brussels Convention in Sched.1 to the C.J.J.A. 1982, see note 13.2.12; on the meaning in the Hague Convention on the Taking of Evidence Abroad in Civil or Commercial Matters, 1970 (Cmnd. 6727 (1977)) and s.9(1) of the Evidence (Proceedings in Other Jurisdictions) Act 1975, see note 66.1.2.
Where the method of service is by transmission through the central authority (see r. 16.2(2)(b)), the forwarding (central) authority in the U.K. is the Secretary of State for Foreign and Commonwealth Affairs. The model form of request and certificate of service in the convention should be used and sent with the documents for service (all in duplicate: Art. 3(2)) to The Foreign and Commonwealth Office, Treaty and Nationality Department, 1 Palace Street, London SW1E 5HE. A translation may be required: r. 16.6.
The model form of request and certificate is as follows:—

REQUEST

FOR SERVICE ABROAD OF JUDICIAL OR EXTRAJUDICIAL DOCUMENTS

Convention on the service abroad of judicial and extrajudicial documents in civil or commercial matters, signed at The Hague, 15 November 1965.

Identity and address of the applicant	Address of receiving authority

The undersigned applicant has the honour to transmit—in duplicate—the documents listed below and, in conformity with article 5 of the above-mentioned Convention, requests prompt service of one copy thereof on the addressee, *i.e.*,

(identity and address) _____

_____

(a) in accordance with the provisions of sub-paragraph (a) of the first paragraph of article 5 of the Convention*.
(b) in accordance with the following particular method (sub-paragraph (b) of the first paragraph of article 5)*:

_____

_____

_____

(c) by delivery to the addressee, if he accepts it voluntarily (second paragraph of article 5)*.

The authority is requested to return or to have returned to the applicant a copy of the documents—and of the annexes*—with a certificate as provided on the reverse side.

List of Documents

_____
_____
_____
_____
_____
_____
_____   Done at
_____   Date
_____   Signature and/or stamp

*Delete if inappropriate

Reverse of the request

CERTIFICATE

The undersigned authority has the honour to certify, in conformity with article 6 of the Convention,

1) that the document has been served*

—the (date) _____

—at (place, street, number) _____

_____

—in one of the following methods authorised by article 5—

   (a) in accordance with the provisions of sub-paragraph (a) of the first paragraph of article 5 of the Convention*.

   (b) in accordance with the following particular method*: _____

   _____

   (c) by delivery to the addressee, who accepted it voluntarily*.

The documents referred to in the request have been delivered to:

—(identity and description of person) _____

_____

—relationship to the addressee (family, business or other): _____

_____

2) that the document has not been served, by reason of the following facts*:

_____

_____

_____

In conformity with the second paragraph of article 12 of the Convention, the applicant is requested to pay or reimburse the expenses detailed in the attached statement*.

Annexes

Documents returned: _____

_____

_____

In appropriate cases, documents establishing the service:	Done at
	Date
	Signature and/or stamp

_____

_____

_____

Delete if inappropriate

SUMMARY OF THE DOCUMENT TO BE SERVED

Convention on the service abroad of judicial and extrajudicial documents in civil or commercial matters, signed at The Hague, 15 November 1965.

(article 5, fourth paragraph)

Name and address of the requesting authority: _____

_____

_____

Particulars of the parties*: _____

_____

_____

JUDICIAL DOCUMENT**

Nature and purpose of the document: _____

_____

_____

Nature and purpose of the proceedings and, where appropriate, the amount in dispute:

_____

_____

Date and place for entering appearance**: _____

_____

Court which has given judgment**: _____

_____

Date of judgment**: _____

Time limits stated in the document**: _____

EXTRAJUDICIAL DOCUMENT**

Nature and purpose of the document: _____

_____

_____

Time limits stated in the document**: _____

_____

_____

If appropriate, identity and address of the person interested in the transmission of the document.
**Delete if inappropriate*

Service in Brussels or Lugano Convention countries. Art. IV of the Annexed Protocol to the **16.2.4**
1968 Brussels Convention in Sched.1, and Art. IV of the Protocol No. 1 to the Lugano
Convention in Sched.3C, to the C.J.J.A. 1982 provide for transmission of documents in
accordance with the conventions between the Member States (including the Hague Convention)
and by public officials in one State directly to public officials in another State. This latter
method is intended to provide for transmission by messengers-at-arms and their equivalents
such as *huissiers* and is covered by r. 16.2(2)(d): see P. Jenard at pp. 40–41.

The 1968 Brussels Convention has been superseded by the Council Regulation (EC) No. 44/
2001 for participating Member States to the Regulation: i.e. all the Member States of the E.U.
except Denmark. Accordingly, the 1968 Convention applies only to *Denmark*, and will have to
be used in relation to that country. For the Council Regulation, and participating Member
States of the E.U., see note 16.2A.1.

The Lugano Convention has been superseded by the Council Regulation (EC) No. 44/2001
for participating States to the Regulation. The Lugano Convention applies now only to the
following countries:

Denmark
Iceland
Norway.

The Council Regulation will apply to the Member States of the E.U. except Denmark.

For countries to which the conventions apply and the methods of service, further information
can be obtained from Private International Law Branch, Civil Justice and International
Division, Justice Department, Scottish Executive, St Andrew House, Regent Road, Edinburgh
EH1 3DG, Tel. +44 (0)131-244 4826, Fax. +44 (0)131-244 4848; and the Foreign and
Commonwealth Office, Treaty and Nationality Department, 1 Palace Street, London SW1E
5HE, tel. 0171–238 4575 or 4577; and see also Bowman & Harris on *Multilateral Treaties.*

Service in bilateral convention countries. In relation to countries with which the U.K. has **16.2.5**
bilateral civil procedure conventions and the methods of service, information can be obtained
from the Foreign and Commonwealth Office, Treaty and Nationality Department, 1 Palace
Street, London SW1E 5HE, tel. 0171–238 4575 or 4577. Countries with which the U.K. has
bilateral conventions are listed in the Practical Handbook on the Operation of the Hague
Convention on Service Abroad published for the Permanent Bureau of the Hague Convention
on Private International Law by Maklu Uitgevers.

The U.K. has bilateral conventions with the following countries which have been extended to
Scotland:

Austria	Israel
Czechoslovakia	Italy
Denmark	Norway
Finland	Portugal
France	Romania
Germany	Spain
Greece	Sweden
Hungary	Turkey
Iraq	Yugoslavia

Service by post: r. 16.2(2)(a). R. 16.4 (service by post) will apply, but service must be by **16.2.6**
registered post as the recorded delivery service is not available outside Great Britain, Northern
Ireland, the Channel Islands and the Isle of Man: it is not available in the Republic of Ireland.
Not every country permits service by post, including some Hague Convention countries.
Information can be obtained from the sources mentioned in note 16.2.1.

A certificate is required that the method of service is permitted in the country where service is
executed in addition to the certificate of service: r. 16.2(6). Where English is not an official
language a translation of the documents to be served will be required: r. 16.4(3). Such
certificates may be obtained from the accredited representatives (embassies and consulates) of
the countries concerned. Certificates from embassies and consulates can be cheaper and quicker
to obtain than those obtained from lawyers abroad.

Service through a central authority at request of the Foreign Office: r. 16.2(2)(b). The Hague **16.2.7**
Convention model form of request and certificate of service in the convention should be used
and sent with the documents for service (all in duplicate: Art. 3(2)), with a letter requesting
service, a summary of the documents to be served and any necessary translation certified as
correct (r. 16.6) and the appropriate Foreign Office fee, to The Foreign and Commonwealth
Office, Treaty and Nationality Department, 1 Palace Street, London SW1E 5HE. The certificate
of service (in the model form) will be signed by the authority executing service.

16.2.8   *Service through a British consular office: r. 16.2(2)(c).* The documents for service, any necessary translation certified as correct (r. 16.6) and a letter requesting service are sent to The Foreign and Commonwealth Office, Treaty and Nationality Department, 1 Palace Street, London SW1E 5HE. The certificate of service is signed by the authority executing service: r. 16.2(3). This method should only be used as a method of last resort.

16.2.9   *Service by an huissier etc.: r. 16.2(2)(d).* This method may be used at the request of a messenger-at-arms, a party or his agent as mentioned in the Hague Convention. The word "agent" means solicitor or a person having a right to conduct the litigation: r. 1.3(1). On messengers-at-arms, see note 16.3.1.

This method is surer than postal service and quicker and more reliable than transmission through the central authorities. The expression "competent official" would probably include an unofficial process server, who is permitted to serve documents in some countries. The certificate of service is signed by the official executing service: r. 16.2(4).

16.2.10   *Personal service by party or authorised agent: r. 16.2(2)(e).* Personal service by a party or his authorised agent is not mentioned in the Hague Convention but appears in the rule because such service is permitted in some countries, the authorised agent usually being a solicitor (or his equivalent) or a notary. In this provision "authorised agent" does not mean only a solicitor, or a person having a right to conduct the litigation, in Scotland: r. 1.3(1) (definition of "agent").

This form of service must be witnessed and the person serving completes a certificate of service in Form 16.2: r. 16.2(5). There must also be lodged a certificate that the method of service is permitted in the country in which service is executed: r. 16.2(6).

16.2.11   *"citation or notice".* A citation in Form 13.7 must be attached to a summons when served on a defender: r. 13.7(1)(a). In the case of a petition a citation in Form 14.7 is attached to the petition served on any person: r. 14.7(2). In the case of a minute served or intimated on a person there must be attached a notice in Form 15.1; and in the case of a note, a notice in Form 15.2. Other notices may be required to be served under particular rules.

Service under the Council Regulation

[1] **16.2A.**—(1) In this rule—

"competent receiving agency" and "Member State" have the same meaning as in the Council Regulation; and

"Council Regulation" means Council Regulation (E.C.) No. 1348/2000 on the service in the Member States of judicial and extrajudicial documents in civil or commercial matters.

---

[1] R. 16.2A inserted by S.S.I. 2004 No. 52 (effective 1st March, 2004).

16.2A.1   *General note.* Council Regulation (EC) No. 1348/2000 may be used for service in EU Member States except Denmark for judicial and extra-judicial documents in civil and commercial matters.

The Member States of the EU, other than Denmark, are—

Austria	Latvia (from 1st May 2004)
Belgium	Lithuania (from 1st May 2004)
Cyprus (from 1st May 2004)	Luxembourg
Czech Republic (from 1st May 2004)	Malta (from 1st May 2004)
Estonia (from 1st May 2004)	Netherlands
Finland	Poland (from 1st May 2004)
France	Portugal
Germany	Slovakia (from 1st May 2004)
Greece	Slovenia (from 1st May 2004)
Hungary (from 1st May 2004)	Spain
Ireland	Sweden
Italy	United Kingdom

The points to note for service under this Regulation are—

(1) The Regulation does not apply where the address of the person to be served is not known (art.1(2)).

(2) Service is made via the transmitting agency of one Member State and the receiving agency of the Member State in which the document is to be served (art.2). The central bodies and transmitting agencies for Scotland and other EU countries can be found at *http://ec.europa.eu/justice_home/judicialatlascivil/html/ds_docs_en.htm*. The central

body for Scotland is: Private International Law Branch, Civil and International Division, Justice Department, St Andrew's House, Regent Road, Edinburgh, EH1 3DG, Tel: +44 (0)131 244 4826, Fax: +44 (0)131 244 4848. The transmitting agencies in Scotland are Messengers-at-Arms and accredited solicitors.

(3) The document to be transmitted may not have to be translated if served via the transmitting and receiving agencies; but a document not translated into an official language of the receiving Member State may be refused to be accepted by the recipient (see arts. 5 and 8).

(4) Service will be by a method of the receiving Member State unless a particular form is requested which is also valid in that State (art.7).

(5) A request form in the Annex to the Regulation in an official language of the receiving Member State must accompany the document (art.4(3)). For form, see below.)

(6) A certificate of service in the form in the Annex to the regulation will be returned (art.10(1)).

(7) Service is free except costs occasioned by use of a judicial officer or other competent person or by use of a particular method requested (art.11).

(8) Service is also permitted, unless a Member State has made a derogation—
- by consular or diplomatic channels,
- directly by post,
- through a judicial officer (see r. 16.2(2)(d)).

The form of request for service in the Annex to the Regulation is as follows—

ANNEX

REQUEST FOR SERVICE OF DOCUMENTS

(Article 4(3) of Council Regulation (EC) No 1348/2000 on the service in the Member States of judicial and extrajudicial documents in civil or commercial matters ([1]))

Reference No: ....

1. TRANSMITTING AGENCY
   1.1. Identity:
   1.2. Address:
      1.2.1. Street and number/PO box:
      1.2.2. Place and code:
      1.2.3. Country:
   1.3. Tel:
   1.4. Fax (*):
   1.5. E-mail (*)

2. RECEIVING AGENCY
   2.1. Identity:
   2.2. Address:
      2.2.1. Street and number/PO box:
      2.2.2. Place and code:
      2.2.3. Country:
   2.3. Tel:
   2.4. Fax (*):
   2.5. E-mail (*):

_____

([1]) OJ L 160, 30.6.2000, p.37.
(*) This item is optional.

3. APPLICANT
   3.1. Identity:
   3.2. Address:
      3.2.1. Street and number/PO box:
      3.2.2. Place and code:
      3.2.3. Country:
   3.3. Tel (*):
   3.4. Fax (*):

3.5. E-mail (*):

4. ADDRESSEE
4.1. Identity:
4.2. Address:
    4.2.1. Street and number/PO box:
    4.2.2. Place and code:
    4.2.3. Country:
4.3. Tel (*):
4.4. Fax (*):
4.5. E-mail (*):
4.6. Identification number/social security number/organisation number/or equivalent (*):

5. METHOD OF SERVICE
5.1. In accordance with the law of the Member State addressed
5.2. By the following particular method:
    5.2.1. If this method is incompatible with the law of the Member State addressed, the document(s) should be served in accordance with the law:
        5.2.1.1. yes
        5.2.1.2. no

(*) This item is optional.

6. DOCUMENT TO BE SERVED
(a) 6.1. Nature of the document
        6.1.1. judicial
            6.1.1.1. writ of summons
            6.1.1.2. judgment
            6.1.1.3. appeal
            6.1.1.4. other
        6.1.2. extrajudicial
(b) 6.2. Date or time limit stated in the document (*):
(c) 6.3. Language of document:
        6.3.1. original DE, EN, DK, EL, FI, FR, GR, IT, NL, PT, SV, others:
        6.3.2. translation (*) DE, EN, DK, ES, FI, FR, EL, IT, NL, PT, SV, others:
    6.4. Number of enclosures:

7. A COPY OF DOCUMENT TO BE RETURNED WITH THE CERTIFICATE OF SERVICE (Article 4(5) of the Regulation)
7.1. Yes (in this case send two copies of the document to be served)
7.2. No

---

1. You are required by Article 7(2) of the Regulation to effect all steps required for service of the document as soon as possible. In any event, if it is not possible for you to effect service within one month of receipt, you must inform this agency by means of the certificate provided for in point 13.

2. If you cannot fulfil this request for service on the basis of the information or documents transmitted, you are required by Article 6(2) of the Regulation to contact this agency by the swiftest possible means in order to secure the missing information or document.

Done at:

Date:

Signature and/or stamp:

(*) This item is optional.

"service is to be executed in a Member State other than the United Kingdom". Notwithstanding **16.2A.2** these words in r.16.2A(2), the Regulation method does *not* apply to Denmark: r.16.2 will have to be used for service in Denmark.

"served by a competent receiving authority...rule16.6(1) (translation of documents) shall not **16.2A.3** *apply"*. One should not be confused into thinking that the document need never be translated. The form in the Annex to the Regulation accompanying the document must be in an official language of the receiving Member State if the Regulation method is used: art.4(3). The person to be served may, however refuse to accept the document if the document itself is not in an official language of the receiving Member State: art.8.

Translation required by r.16.6 will be necessary where service is by any of the other methods.

"certificate of service mentioned in Article 10". When service has been completed a certificate **16.2A.4** of service in the form provided in the Annex to the Regulation is sent to the transmitting agency in Scotland.

Service by messenger-at-arms

16.3.—(1) Service by a method mentioned in rule 16.1(1)(a)(i), (ii) or (iii), or (b)(i), shall be executed by a messenger-at-arms who shall—
- (a) explain the purpose of service to any person on whom he executes service;
- (b) complete a citation or notice, as the case may be, and a certificate of service in Form 16.3; and
- (c) send the certificate of service to the pursuer.

(2) Such service shall be witnessed by one witness who shall sign the certificate of service (which shall state his name, occupation and address).

(3) Where service is executed by a method mentioned in rule 16.1(1)(a)(ii) or (iii), or (b)(i), and the document served is left in the hands of a person other than the person on whom service is to be executed, that document and the citation or notice of intimation, as the case may be, shall be placed in an envelope (bearing the notice specified in rule 16.4(2)) and sealed by the messenger-at-arms.

(4) Subject to paragraph (4A), a messenger-at-arms shall, when he executes service of a document, have in his possession—
- (a) in the case of service of a copy of a principal writ, the principal writ or a copy of it certified as correct by the agent for the party whose writ it is, and
- (b) where an interlocutor has been pronounced allowing service of the document, a certified copy of that interlocutor,

which he shall show, if required, to the person on whom he executes service.

[1](4A) Where the firm which employs the messenger-at-arms has in its possession—
- (a) the principal writ or a certified copy of it, it shall be competent for the messenger-at-arms to execute service of the document without having that writ or certified copy in his possession, in which case he shall, if required to do so by the person on whom service is executed and within a reasonable time of being so required, show the principal writ or certified copy to the person;
- (b) a certified copy of the interlocutor, it shall be competent for the messenger-at-arms to execute service of the document if he has in his possession a facsimile copy of the certified copy interlocutor which he shall show, if required, to the person on whom he executes service.

(5) The certificate of service required under paragraph (1) shall include the full name and designation of any person in whose hands any document and the citation or notice, as the case may be, were left.

(6) In the application of this rule to service in a part of the United Kingdom furth of Scotland, reference to a messenger-at-arms shall be construed as a reference to a person entitled to serve Supreme Court writs in that part.

Deriv. R.C.S. 1965, r.74(*i*) (r.16.3(4)) and r.74A(4) substituted by SI 1984/472 and amended by SI 1990/705 and 1991/1157 (r.16.3(1), (2), (3), and (5))

———

[1] R.16.3(4A) inserted by SSI 2001/305, para.2(2) (effective 18th September 2001).

16.3.1   *General note.* Messengers-at-arms are members of the ancient corps of Her Majesty's officers-of-arms (heralds, pursuivants, macers and messengers-at-arms): see *Stair Memorial Encyclopedia of the Laws of Scotland*, Vol. 14, paras. 1501 *et seq.* A messenger-at-arms is appointed by the Lord Lyon King of Arms, but his qualifications, training, examination, discipline and, to some extent, functions, are governed by the Debtors (Scotland) Act 1987 and the A.S. (Messengers-at-Arms and Sheriff Officers Rules) 1991 [SI 1991/1397]. Appointment is made on the recommendation of the Court of Session: 1987 Act, s.77(1) and the Messengers-at-Arms and Sheriff Officers Rules, r.7. He must have a bond of caution of not less than £50,000, and a policy of professional indemnity insurance of not less than £100,000, in respect of each claim: 1991 Rules, r.9.

A messenger-at-arms executes all warrants of the Court of Session, the High Court of Justiciary (along with others empowered to do so: Criminal Procedure (Scotland) Act 1995, s.307(1)) and the Court of the Lord Lyon. In relation to the Court of Session his functions include (a) collecting any debt constituted by decree or summary warrant; (b) executing diligence; (c) executing a citation or serving any document in a legal process; and (d) unless otherwise provided, serving notices to be served under any enactment: 1991 Rules, rr.14(1) and 15(1). He may refuse to act if a reasonable fee is not tendered or it is not reasonably practicable for him to act: 1991 Rules, r.14(4). Solicitors are personally liable in the first instance for the fees of a messenger-at-arms instructed by them: Maclaren on *Court of Session Practice*, p. 1115 (and see *Stirling Park & Co. v. Digby Brown & Co.* 1995 S.C.L.R. 375 (sheriff officers)). A messenger-at-arms can do nothing without a legal warrant to do it and he must act in strict conformity with it. If he fails to do so he and his cautioner may be liable in reparation. For wrongful diligence the messenger-at-arms, the cautioner and the agent may be liable to the debtor: Graham Stewart on *Diligence*, p. 799.

In a sheriff court district where there is no resident messenger-at-arms, a sheriff officer authorised to practise in that district has the powers of a messenger-at-arms in regard to service of a summons, writ, citation or other proceeding, or the execution of or diligence on, any decree, warrant or order: Execution of Diligence (Scotland) Act 1926, s.1.

"one witness". S.32 of the Debtors (Scotland) Act 1838 and s.1 of the Citations (Scotland) Act **16.3.2** 1846 provide that more than one witness is not required; hence one witness is required to the execution of service by a messenger-at-arms. He does not sign any citation, but he does sign the certificate of service: r.16.3(2).

Documents to be served in sealed envelope. The documents served must be sealed in an **16.3.3** envelope where they are left (a) in the hands of a person other than the person on whom service is to be executed, (b) in the case of an individual by leaving it with a person at his dwelling or at his place of business, or (c) in the case of a person other than an individual, in the hands of a person at the registered or other office: r.16.1(1)(a)(ii), (iii) or (b)(i) respectively. The certificate of service must state that person's name and designation: r.16.3(5). The envelope must have on the face of it the notice which must appear on the envelope when service is by post (the notice which indicates what the contents are and what is to be done if they cannot be delivered to the person on whom service is to be executed: see r.16.4(2)): r.16.3(3).

"principal writ or a copy of it certified". The messenger-at-arms must have the principal writ **16.3.4** (defined in r.1.3(1)) or a copy of it in his possession (r.16.3(4)) or in the possession of his firm (r.16.3(4A). The reference to "the firm which employs him" in r.16.3(4A) is a reference to the firm of messenger-at-arms and not a reference to the agent (solicitor) instructing him or his firm.

Although the rule permits him or his firm to have a copy certified by the agent, a messenger-at-arms or his firm would not normally proceed without the principal writ because it has the Court of Session stamp on it.

Service elsewhere in U.K. A messenger-at-arms does not have jurisdiction outside Scotland. **16.3.5** There is no direct equivalent officer in England and Wales or Northern Ireland. In those jurisdictions the plaintiff or his agent may effect service, and this is usually done by an inquiry agent or a county court bailiff. Process servers are only appointed in England and Wales for the purposes of civil procedure conventions with foreign countries: R.S.C. 1965, Ord. 69, r.4.

"Supreme Court". Under Sch.1 to the Interpretation Act 1978, this means the Court of **16.3.6** Appeal, High Court and Crown Court in England and Wales or the Supreme Court of Judicature in Northern Ireland.

Service by post

16.4.—[1](1) This rule applies to service of a document by post but is subject to rule 61.2(3) and (4) (order as respects intimation of petition for appointments of judicial factor).

(2) Service by post shall be executed by—

(a) a messenger-at-arms, or

(b) an agent,

posting a copy of the document to be served with any citation or notice, as the case may be, by registered post or the first class recorded delivery service addressed to the person on whom service is to be executed and having on the face of the envelope a notice in the following terms: "This envelope contains a citation to, or intimation from, the Court of Session. If delivery of the letter cannot be made it must be returned immediately to the Deputy Principal Clerk of Session, Court of Session, 2 Parliament Square, Edinburgh EH1 1RQ.".

(3) Where English is not an official language of the country in which service is to be executed, a translation in an official language of that country of the notice required under paragraph (2) shall appear on the face of the envelope.

(4) The person executing service of a document shall complete—

(a) a citation or notice, as the case may be; and

(b) a certificate of service in Form 16.4.

(5) A Post Office receipt of posting by registered post or a certificate of posting by the first class recorded delivery service, as the case may be, issued and stamped by the Post Office shall be attached to the certificate of service.

(6) The date of execution of service shall be deemed to be the day after the date of posting.

(7) Subject to rule 16.11 (no objection to regularity of service or intimation), the execution of service by post shall be valid unless the person on whom service was sought to have been made proves that the envelope and its contents were not tendered or left at his address.

Deriv. R.C.S. 1965, r.68A inserted by S.I. 1968 No. 1150, r.74A(5) inserted by S.I. 1984 No. 472 and amended by S.I. 1991 No. 2483, and r.74B(3)(a) (part) inserted by S.I. 1986 No. 1941 and amended by S.I. 1991 No. 2483 (r.16.4(2)); r.72(2) and r.192(2), both substituted by S.I. 1986 No. 1941 (r.16.4(6)); r.74(a) (part) (r.16.4(4)); r.74A(6) (r.16.4(2)), r.74A(7) (r.16.4(4)) and r.74A(8) (r.16.4(7)), all inserted by S.I. 1984 No. 472; and r.74B(3)(b) (r.16.4(4)), and r.74B(7)(b) (r.16.4(3)), both inserted by S.I. 1986 No. 1941

---

[1] R. 16.4(1) amended by S.I. 1997 No. 1720 (effective 1st August 1997).

16.4.1 *General note.* Service by post must be to the known dwelling place of the person on whom service is to be executed, *i.e.* his usual place of residence: *Corstorphine v. Kasten* (1898) 1 F. 287. It is not enough to post the documents to the last known address of the person on whom service is to be executed if it is known he no longer lives there.

This rule replaces much of the Citation Amendment (Scotland) Act 1882 and ss.3, 4(1)–(4), 5 and 6 of, and Scheds 1 and 2 to, the 1882 Act are repealed by Sch.3 to the A.S. (R.C.S. 1994) 1994 [SI 1994/1443].

16.4.2 *"messenger-at-arms".* See note 16.3.1.

16.4.3 *"agent".* This means a solicitor or a person having a right to conduct the litigation: see r.1.3(1) (definition of "agent") and note 1.3.4. "Solicitor" is defined in the C.S.A. 1988, s.51.

16.4.4 *"citation or notice".* A citation in Form 13.7 must be attached to a summons when served on a defender: r.13.7(1)(a). In the case of a petition a citation in Form 14.7 is attached to the petition served on any person: r.14.7(2). In the case of a minute served or intimated on a person there must be attached a notice in Form 15.1; and in the case of a note, a notice in Form 15.2. Other notices may be required to be served under particular rules.

16.4.5 *"registered post".* Service by registered post was introduced by the Citation Amendment (Scotland) Act 1882. Such service could be made throughout the British Isles and in many foreign countries (*cf.* the recorded delivery service: see note 16.4.6). The Post Office receipt of posting must be attached to the certificate of service in Form 16.4: r.16.4(5).

Where the letter is returned to the Deputy Principal Clerk with the reason for failure to deliver marked on it, he intimates to the party on whose behalf service was attempted in order that re-service may be attempted or an order sought from the court: Citation Amendment (Scotland) Act 1882, s.4(5). If the court is satisfied that, in the case of a party, a letter was tendered at his proper address, it may hold the tender equal to a good citation: 1882 Act, s.4(5).

Registered post is a service no longer provided by the Post Office. It has been replaced by the Special Delivery service. The latter service is not provided for in r.16.4; and, accordingly, the only form of postal service available under R.C.S. 1994 is first class recorded delivery.

16.4.6 *"first class recorded delivery".* The use of the recorded delivery service as an alternative to registered post was introduced by the Recorded Delivery Service Act 1962 but is only available in the United Kingdom, the Channel Islands and the Isle of Man but not the Republic of Ireland. Service by this means must be by the first class recorded delivery service. The Post Office certificate of posting must be attached to the certificate of service in Form 16.4: r.16.4(5). Rule 16.4 does not mention the international recorded delivery service provided by the Royal Mail; accordingly this service may not be used for service abroad.

Where the letter is returned to the Deputy Principal Clerk with the reason for failure to deliver marked on it, he intimates to the party on whose behalf service was attempted in order that re-service may be attempted or an order sought from the court: Citation Amendment (Scotland) Act 1882, s.4(5). If the court is satisfied that, in the case of a party, a letter was tendered at his proper address, it may hold the tender equal to a good citation: 1882 Act, s.4(5).

Service on member of HM Forces in Northern Ireland. A document served on a person in HM **16.4.7** Forces in Northern Ireland at a private address should be addressed as if that person were a private citizen and should not state on the envelope his rank and number. Where the address of that person's barracks is known the document should preferably be sent there. See P.N. 17th December 1974.

Date of execution of service. The date of execution of service by post is the day *after* the date **16.4.8** of posting: r.16.4(6). This abrogates the provisions for the date of execution in s.4(1) of the Citation Amendment (Scotland) Act 1882; and is consistent with s.7 of the Interpretation Act 1978 as applied by s.23 of that Act. Any period of notice begins to run from the end of the day after the day of posting.

Service on a Sunday. Service by post cannot be executed on a Sunday. **16.4.9**

Validity of service. Service by post is deemed to be effected by properly addressing, pre-paying **16.4.10** and posting a letter containing the document to be served: Interpretation Act 1978, s.7 as applied by s.23. An execution of service by post is valid unless it is proved that the letter and its contents were not tendered or left at the address of the person on whom service is to be executed: r.16.4(7) replacing s.3 (part) of the Citation Amendment (Scotland) Act 1882. The "address" of the person on whom service is to be executed is the usual place of residence, registered office, etc., or place of business. Proof that the letter was not delivered to the address does not invalidate the service if the documents are nonetheless received: *Steuart v. Ree* (1885) 12 R. 563. If the person on whom service is to be executed appears in the process he cannot object to the irregularity of service: r.16.11. The question of validity can only be raised, therefore, in other proceedings, *e.g.* suspension or reduction.

Proof that a letter has been posted raises a presumption that it was duly addressed and delivered; and this presumption is still applicable notwithstanding the modern postal service: *Netherfield Visual Productions v. Caledonian Land Properties Ltd*, 21st March 1996 (1996 G.W.D. 19–1107). The presentation can be rebutted by positive evidence tending to show that the letter was not delivered to the addressee or that it was delivered to someone else: *Mackenzie v. Dott* (1861) 23 D. 1310.

A pursuer who accepts delivery of a letter to a defender enclosing documents served and does not see that the defender gets them cannot claim that the service was good: *Morrison v. Vallance's Exrs* 1907 S.C. 999.

Where a postal citation is returned marked "refused", the court is entitled to regard the refusal as having been deliberate and the citation properly served: *Arthur v. SMT Sales & Service Co Ltd* 1999 S.C. 109.

Service where address of person is not known

16.5.—(1) Where the residence of the person to be served with a document is not known and cannot reasonably be ascertained or service on that person cannot be executed under rule 16.1 (methods and manner of service) or 16.2 (service furth of United Kingdom), the party who wishes to execute service may apply by motion—
  (a) for an order for service by the publication of an advertisement in a specified newspaper circulating in the area of the last known residence of that person or elsewhere; or
  (b) on special cause shown, for an order to dispense with service; and
  (c) stating the last known residence of that person and what steps have been taken to ascertain his present whereabouts.

(2) On enrolling such a motion, a copy of the document to be served shall be lodged with the Deputy Principal Clerk who shall retain it for a period of three years and from whom it may be uplifted by the person for whom it is intended.

(3) Where an interlocutor has been pronounced ordering publication of an advertisement under this rule—
  (a) the advertisement shall be in Form 16.5; and
  (b) publication of the advertisement shall have effect as if service of the document had been executed on the date of publication.

(4) Where an interlocutor has been pronounced dispensing with service under this rule—

(a) service of the document shall be deemed to have been executed on the date of the interlocutor; and

(b) the period of notice shall be dispensed with.

(5) A motion under paragraph (1) made before calling shall be heard in chambers.

(6) Where publication of an advertisement has been made under this rule, there shall be lodged in process—

(a) a copy of the newspaper containing the advertisement; or

(b) a certificate of publication by the publisher stating the date of publication and the text of the advertisement.

Deriv. R.C.S. 1965, r.75(1) substituted by S.I. 1986 No. 1941 and amended by S.I. 1987 No. 1206 (r.16.5(1)); r.75(2) substituted by S.I. 1986 No. 1941 (r.16.5(1)); r.75(3) substituted by S.I. 1986 No. 1941 and amended by S.I. 1991 No. 2483 (r.16.5(5)); r.75(4) (r.16.5(3)), and r.75(5) (r.16.5(6)), both substituted by S.I. 1986 No. 1941

16.5.1   *General note.* Edictal citation has now been abolished and the only means of service where a person's whereabouts are unknown (as distinct from execution of diligence: *cf.* r.16.12(4)) is by advertisement under r.16.5. Steps, however, must have been taken to ascertain the address of the person on whom service is to be executed, and what those steps were and an explanation of why service cannot be executed must be stated in the motion; r.16.5(1); in a summons (or minute) all this must be stated in the condescendence (or statement of facts); r.13.3. In *Young v. Harper* 1970 S.C. 174, 177 Lord Fraser held that "known" (in relation to art. 1 of the A.S. 14th December 1805) did not mean known only to the pursuer but known generally to persons having business or social dealings with the defender; accordingly, some steps must be taken to find an address or else a belief that an address is not known must be based on some evidence that none is known. Service may be dispensed with on cause shown.

In the case of service by advertisement, the date of the advertisement is that date of execution of service: r.16.5(3)(b). That day is excluded in calculating the period of notice.

16.5.2   *"motion".* For motions, see Chap. 23.

16.5.3   *Motion before calling.* See r.23.8.

16.5.4   *Lodging of advertisement or certificate of publication.* The newspaper containing the advertisement or the publisher's certificate of publication required under r.16.5(6) is lodged as a production: see r.4.5.

Translations of documents served or advertised abroad

16.6.—[1](1) Subject to rule 16.2A (service under the Council Regulation) where English is not an official language of the country in which a document is to be served, the document shall be accompanied by a translation in an official language of that country.

(2) An advertisement authorised under rule 16.5 (service where address of person is not known) to be published in a newspaper in a country in which English is not an official language of that country shall be in an official language of that country.

(3) With any certificate of service, or advertisement under rule 16.5, in a language other than English there shall be lodged a translation in English.

(4) A translation under this rule shall be certified as correct by the translator; and the certificate shall include his full name, address and qualifications.

Deriv. R.C.S. 1965, r.74B(4)(b) and (6)(b) (r.16.6(3)), r.74B(7)(a) (r.16.6(1) and r.74B(8) (r.16.6(4)), all inserted by S.I. 1986 No. 1941; also amended by S.S.I. 2004 No. 52 (effective 1st March, 2004)

---

[1] R.16.6(1) amended by S.S.I. 2004 No. 52 (effective 1st March 2004).

16.6.1   *Dispensing with translation.* Where, for instance, the person on whom service is to be executed, in a country in which English is not an official language, is a British citizen who can be expected to speak English, the court might be persuaded to dispense with the requirement under r.2.1 to serve a translation of the documents to be served.

"Subject to rule 16.2A". Rule 16.2A provides for service of documents in Member States of **16.6.1A** the EU except Denmark under Council Regulation (EC) No. 1348/2000). A translation may not be required *only* where service is via the transmitting agency in Scotland (see note.16.2A.1) and the receiving agency in the Member State in which service is to be effected. It should be noted, however, that the person to be served may refused to accept a document served by this method if it is not translated into an official language of his Member State. Translations will be required where other methods of service are used.

Qualification of translator. There is no particular qualification or standard of qualification **16.6.2** required of a translator.

Obtaining and cost of translations. The responsibility for obtaining and paying for a **16.6.3** translation falls on the party serving the document.

In relation to simplified divorce applications under Pt XI of Chap. 49, service is made or arranged by the Deputy Principal Clerk of Session. Nonetheless, that service is made on behalf of the applicant who will be required to obtain and pay for any translation required for service abroad.

Intimation of documents

16.7—(1) Subject to rule 16.8 (intimation on a warrant to intimate), rule 16.9 (written intimation) and any other provision in these Rules, where intimation of a document is to be given under these Rules to any person, the intimation shall be given—

   (a) personally, by tendering the document and the notice of intimation (if any) to that person; or

   (b) by registered post or the first class recorded delivery service—

      (i) in the case of an individual, addressed to the known, or last known, dwelling place or a place of business of that individual; or

(ii) in the case of any other person, addressed to the registered office, other official address or a place of business of that person.

(2) Where intimation has been given in accordance with paragraph (1), the party on whose behalf intimation has been given shall attach to the principal writ or lodge in process, as the case may be—

(a) a certificate of intimation in Form 16.7;

(b) a copy of any notice of intimation which was intimated; and

(c) a copy of any interlocutor ordering the intimation.

General note. This rule and rr.16.8 and 16.9 are intended to introduce formality and **16.7.1** distinction between the methods of intimation, heretofore impliedly permitted under the R.C.S. 1965, by rationalizing "intimation" into three categories. Intimation may be (*a*) formal intimation of a cause or document for the purposes of information (r.16.7), (*b*) intimation on a warrant to intimate to a person informing him of the existence of a cause in which he may have an interest so that he can enter the process if he wishes (r.16.8), and (*c*) intimation usually restricted to informing a party of steps taken in a process (r.16.9).

Intimation of documents. R.16.7 provides for the category of intimation whereby a cause or **16.7.2** document is intimated to a person for the purposes primarily of information and not to enable him to enter the process or of a step taken in the process.

A certificate of intimation in Form 16.7 is stitched into the principal summons for lodging for calling or the execution copy of the petition or note for lodging after expiry of the period of notice. A separate certificate of intimation is lodged as a step of process when intimation is given after calling of the summons or the lodging of the execution copy of the petition or note. A copy of any notice of intimation required to be intimated must be attached to the certificate as well as any interlocutor ordering intimation (r.16.7(2)): the reason for this is so that the clerk of session can check that the notice of intimation intimated is in accord with that provided for in R.C.S. 1994 and that the interlocutor intimated was in the same terms as the interlocutor in the interlocutor sheet.

There are two methods of such intimation:—

(1) *Personal: r.16.7(1)(a).* This is the same as personal service; the rules of personal service apply: see note 16.1.2(1).

(2) *Registered post or the first class recorded delivery service.* In the case of an individual this may be to his known or last known dwelling place (*i.e.* his usual place of residence: *Corstorphine v. Kasten* (1898) 1 F. 287) or his place of business. It will be noticed that in this case intimation to a last known address is permitted (*cf.* service: see note 16.4.1). In the case of a person other than an individual intimation may be made to the registered office, other official address or place of business as in the case of service.

Intimation on a warrant to intimate

16.8.—[1](1) Where intimation of a document is to be given to a person for whom a warrant to intimate has been obtained, the intimation shall be made in the same manner as service of a document; and the following rules shall, with the necessary modifications, apply to that intimation as they apply to service of a document:—

rule 16.1 (methods and manner of service),

rule 16.2 (service furth of United Kingdom),

rule 16.2A (service under the Council Regulation),

rule 16.3 (service by messenger-at-arms),

rule 16.4 (service by post),

rule 16.5 (service where address of person is not known),

rule 16.6 (translations of documents served or advertised abroad).

(2) Where intimation has been given in accordance with paragraph (1), the party on whose behalf intimation has been given shall attach a copy of any notice of intimation to the certificate of intimation.

---

[1] R.16.8(1) amended by S.S.I. 2004 No. 52 (effective 1st March, 2004).

Intimation on a warrant. R.16.8 provides for the category of intimation on a warrant to **16.8.1** intimate to a person to bring to his attention a cause in which he may have an interest so that he can enter the process if he wishes. Intimation in this case is made in the same way as service, and the rules for service apply as modified.

The certificate of intimation which must be lodged will be the certificate of service required according to the method of intimation used. The certificate of intimation in Form 16.7 is stitched into the principal summons for lodging for calling or the execution copy of the petition or note for lodging after expiry of the period of notice. A separate certificate of intimation is lodged as a step of process when intimation is given after calling of the summons or the lodging of the execution copy of the petition or note. A copy of any notice of intimation required to be intimated must be attached to the certificate (r.16.8(2)) as well as any interlocutor ordering intimation (r.16.1(3) by virtue of r.16.8(2)): the reason for this is so that the clerk of session can check that the notice of intimation intimated is in accord with that provided for in R.C.S. 1994 and that the interlocutor intimated was in the same terms as the interlocutor in the interlocutor sheet.

[1] R.16.8.(1) amended by S.S.I. 2004 No. 52 (effective 1st March, 2004).

Written intimation

16.9. Where a provision in these Rules requires written intimation to be given to a person, that intimation may be made by first class post or other means of delivery to that person.

16.9.1 *Written intimation.* R. 16.9 provides for the category of intimation usually restricted to informing a party of a step taken in a cause, *e.g.* the lodging of a step of process (r.4.6(1)(*a*)), the enrolling of a motion (r.23.3(1)) or opposition to a motion (r.23.4(4)), or intimation by the Deputy Principal Clerk or a clerk of session of something done or a document sent to the court in a process.

Acceptance of service or intimation and dispensing with period of notice

16.10.—(1) An agent may accept service or intimation of a document on behalf of the person on whom service is to be executed or to whom intimation is to be given and may dispense with any period of notice.

(2) A person on whom service of a document is executed or to whom intimation of a document is given may dispense with any period of notice as respects him in relation to that document.

(3) Where a period of notice is dispensed with under paragraph (1) or (2), it shall be deemed to expire on the day on which the party on whose behalf service is executed or intimation is given receives written intimation that the period of notice has been dispensed with.

Deriv. R.C.S. 1965, r.74(*b*) amended by S.I. 1991 No. 2843

16.10.1 *General note.* An agent may accept service or intimation and dispense with a period of notice on his client's behalf: r.16.10(1). A person served may himself dispense with a period of notice to which he is entitled: r.16.10(2).

Acceptance of service or intimation is made by the agent for the party on whose behalf service or intimation is accepted endorsing a holograph docquet on the principal or a copy of the document served or intimated in the following terms:

"(*Place and date*). I, (*name of agent*), on behalf of and authorised by (*name of person on whom service is to be executed or to whom intimation to be given*) acknowledge to have received a service copy of the summons [*or as the case may be*]. I accept service [*or* intimation] on his [*or* her *or* its] behalf.

(*Signed*)".

If the period of notice is dispensed with the words "and dispense with the period of notice" are added after the word "service".

Where the person served with a document or who has a document intimated to him dispenses with a period of notice himself he should endorse a holograph docquet on the principal or a copy of the document served or intimated in the following terms:

"(*Place and date*). I, (*name of person served or to whom document intimated*), dispense with the period of notice in the summons [*or as the case may be*].

(*Signed*)".

On the meaning of "agent", see r.1.3(1) (definition of "agent"). On the meaning of "period of notice", see r.1.3(1) (definition of "period of notice") and rr.13.4 and 14.6.

16.10.2 *Written intimation of acceptance or dispensation.* The written intimation will usually consist of the return of the document docquetted with the holograph acceptance of service, intimation or dispensation with a period of notice, as the case may be. For methods of written intimation, see r.16.9.

No objection to regularity of service or intimation

16.11.—(1) A person who enters the process of a cause shall not be entitled to state any objection to the regularity of the execution of service or intimation of a document on him; and his appearance shall be deemed to remedy any defect in such service or intimation.

(2) Nothing in paragraph (1) shall preclude a person from pleading that the court has no jurisdiction.

Deriv. R.C.S. 1965, r. 82

Irregularity in service or intimation. The object of citation (or service or intimation) is to **16.11.1** bring to the knowledge of the defender (or other person) the proceedings against him in order for him to take steps to protect his interests. The phrase "no party appearing to object to regularity" in s. 21 of the C.S.A. 1868 (replaced by R.C.S. 1965, r. 82 and repealed by Sched. 2 to the C.S.A. 1988) shows that if the object (of citation, service or intimation) is attained by the defender appearing, it is immaterial whether or not there were irregularities: *Corstorphine v. Kasten* (1898) 1 F. 287, 296 *per* Lord Adam. Irregularities may consist in citation, service or intimation in accordance with a wrong or inappropriate rule or not in accordance with any rule, and in either case the objection is to regularity: *Corstorphine*, above *per* Lord McLaren at p. 297; see also *Struthers v. Magistrates of Kirkintilloch* 1951 S.L.T. (Notes) 77.

It is *pars judicis* to notice that service or intimation has been irregular.

A person seeking to challenge an irregular service or intimation should seek suspension or reduction of the execution of service or intimation. An irregular service on or intimation to a person may be challenged in the process in which the irregularity occurs by a person sisted in place of the person concerned: *Morrison v. Vallance's Exrs.* 1907 S.C. 999.

Plea of no jurisdiction. A person who enters the process of a cause to challenge jurisdiction **16.11.2** is not barred from challenging an irregularity of service on which the jurisdiction is based and his appearance does not remedy a defect in the service or intimation: *Dallas & Co. v. McArdle* 1949 S.C. 481 (no personal service to constitute jurisdiction). The fact that there has been an irregularity does not preclude such a person from entering the process simply to challenge the jurisdiction of the court: the C.J.J.A. 1982, Scheds. 1, 3C and 4, art. 18 and Sched. 8, r. 6(2) provide that a court does not have jurisdiction over the substance or merits of a cause where appearance is entered solely to contest jurisdiction, and this principle has been extended to all persons.

PART II

DILIGENCE

[1] *Execution of diligence*

16.12.—(1) This rule applies to—

(a) the execution of any diligence on a warrant, act or decree of the court other than—

 (i) an arrestment to which rule 16.13 (arrestment of ships and arrestment *in rem* of cargo on board ship) applies; or

 (ii) an arrestment to which rule 16.14(1) (arrestment *in rem* of cargo landed or transhipped) applies; and

(b) diligence in execution of a writ registered for execution in the Books of Council and Session.

(2) Subject to the following paragraphs of this rule, the execution of any diligence by virtue of these Rules on a person shall be executed by a messenger-at-arms in the same manner as service of a document is permitted under rule 16.1(1)(a)(i), (ii) or (iii) or (b)(i) (methods and manner of service); and, where appropriate, the following provisions of Part I (service and intimation) shall, with the necessary modifications, apply to the execution of diligence as they apply to service of a document:—

 rule 16.3(1) to (4) (service by messenger-at-arms),

 rule 16.4(2)(a), (3), (6) and (7) (service by post).

(3) In the application under this rule, by virtue of paragraph (2), of—

(a) sub-paragraph (b) of paragraph (1) of rule 16.3 (completion of citation or notice and certificate of service), for the reference to Form 16.3 in that sub-paragraph, there shall be substituted a reference to the appropriate form of certificate of execution in rule 16.15 (forms for diligence); and

(b) sub-paragraph (b) of paragraph (4) of rule 16.4 (completion of citation or notice and certificate of service), for the reference to Form 16.4 in that sub-paragraph, there shall be substituted a reference to the appropriate form of certificate of execution in rule 16.15.

(4) The execution of such diligence on—
  (a) an individual who is resident furth of Scotland,
  (b) a person who has no registered office, other official address or a place of business in Scotland,
  (c) a person whose residence is not known and cannot reasonably be ascertained, or
  (d) a person on whom service cannot be executed in a manner permitted under paragraph (2),

shall be executed edictally by a messenger-at-arms leaving or depositing the appropriate schedule mentioned in rule 16.15 at the office of the Extractor.

(5) Where the execution of diligence is made edictally under paragraph (4), a copy of the schedule left at the office of the Extractor shall be sent by a messenger-at-arms by registered post or the first class recorded delivery service to the place furth of Scotland where the person on whom diligence is executed edictally resides, has his registered office, official address or place of business, as the case may be, or such last known place.

(6) A messenger-at-arms executing diligence shall have in his possession—
  (a) in the case of diligence on a warrant in a principal writ, the principal writ or a copy of it certified as correct by the agent for the party whose writ it is,
  (b) in the case of diligence on a warrant in an interlocutor, a certified copy of that interlocutor, or
  (c) in the case of diligence on an extract of an act or a decree, or a document registered in the Books of Council and Session, the extract,

which he shall show, if required, to any person on whom he executes diligence.

(7) The party on whose behalf diligence has been executed in a cause depending before the court shall attach the certificate of execution to the document containing the warrant for diligence.

Deriv. R.C.S. 1965, r. 67 (r.16.12(2) (part)

---

[1] Heading amended by S.I. 1994 No. 2901 (clerical error).

16.12.1   *General note.* The rules which govern the execution of diligence have not been entirely clear. Pt. II of Chap. 16 is an attempt to provide a comprehensive code for the execution of diligence (a) following an order or warrant of the court or (b) on a writ registered for execution in the Books of Council and Session.

In general the rules for service of documents apply to the execution of diligence. In relation to execution on a person furth of Scotland or whose whereabouts are unknown or on whom execution cannot be made, however, execution by advertisement was seen to be impractical and productive of delay, and execution by post impractical and uncertain. Accordingly, edictal execution, abolished for service of documents, has been retained (or re-introduced) for execution of diligence in these circumstances.

Special rules apply in relation to arrestment of ships and cargo: see rr. 16.13 and 16.14 respectively.

16.12.2   *"writ registered for execution in the Books of Council and Session".* The Books of Council and Session were the court books of the Lords of Council and Session. There are three registers in the Books of Council and Session—the Register of Deeds and Probative Writs, the Register of Protests and the Register of Judgments. Registration for execution gives the holder a decree of registration which is in effect a decree of the Court of Session (Bell's *Comm.*, i,4; *Taylor, Petr.* 1931 S.L.T. 260, 261 *per* Lord Pitman) and on the warrant inserted by the Keeper of the Registers or his deputy on an extract of a registered document diligence may be executed against the debtor's moveable property under s. 3 of the Writs Execution (Scotland) Act 1877 as substituted by s. 87(4) of the Debtors (Scotland) Act 1987. Diligence against heritable property may be executed by inhibition on the grant of letters of inhibition (see Chap. 59) or by action of adjudication founding on the decree of registration.

Registration for execution of deeds and probative writs in the Books of Council and Session may be made of probative writs which contain a clause of consent to registration for execution (other than a regulated consumer credit agreement: Consumer Credit Act 1974, s.93A inserted by the Debtors (Scotland) Act 1987, Sched. 6, para. 16) where the granter of the obligation resides in Scotland or is otherwise subject to the jurisdiction of the court. A bond or obligation in favour of the Crown may be registered as if it contained a clause of registration: Exchequer Court (Scotland) Act 1856, s.38. The procedure (protesting) for enforcing bills of exchange and promissory notes, but not cheques, is contained in the Bills of Exchange Act 1882. Judgments of certain foreign courts, awards of arbiters and others under various statutory provisions may be registered in the Register of Judgments: see Chap. 62.

Execution by person acquiring right to the extract decree. Where a person acquires a right as **16.12.3** creditor, by assignation or confirmation as executor or otherwise, to a decree, or a document registered in the Books of Council and Session, he must apply to the Deputy Principal Clerk by letter enclosing the extract decree or document, the document establishing his right and, in the case of assignation, evidence of its intimation, for a warrant authorising execution at the instance of that creditor: Debtors (Scotland) Act 1987, s.88(2). If the warrant is granted the words "*Fiat ut petitur (Date and signature)*" are written on the extract which is then warrant for diligence at the hands of the new creditor.

"messenger-at-arms". See note 16.3.1.   **16.12.4**

Methods of execution of diligence. Subject to the special provisions for arrestment of ships and **16.12.5** cargo (for which, see rr. 16.13 and 16.14), the methods of execution of diligence (a) on a warrant, act or decree of the court or (b) in execution of a writ registered for execution in the Books of Council and Session are as follows:

(1) Execution on an individual (a natural person)—
  (a) personally: see note 16.1.2(1);
  (b) by leaving the execution in the hands of a person at the dwelling place of the person on whom execution is to be made: see note 16.1.2(2);
  (c) by depositing the execution at the dwelling place of the person on whom execution is to be made: see note 16.1.2(3);
  (d) by leaving the execution in the hands of a person at the place of business of the person on whom execution is to be made: see note 16.1.2(4);
  (e) by depositing the execution at the place of business of the person on whom execution is to be made: see note 16.1.2(5);
  (f) edictal execution where person on whom execution to be made is furth of Scotland or whose whereabouts are unknown or on whom execution cannot be made: see note 16.12.6.

(2) Execution on any other person (*i.e.* a non-natural person such as a corporate or unincorporated body or firm)—
  (a) by leaving the execution in the hands of a person at the registered office, other official address or place of business of the person on whom execution is to be made: see note 16.1.3(1);
  (b) by depositing the execution at the place of business of the person on whom execution is to be made: see note 16.1.3(2);
  (c) edictal execution where person on whom execution to be made is furth of Scotland or whose whereabouts are unknown or on whom execution cannot be made: see note 16.12.6.

The certificate of execution by the messenger-at-arms will be in the appropriate Form in r. 16.15 and not Form 16.3: r. 16.12(3). R. 16.3(1) to (4) in relation to messengers-at-arms applies. The application of provisions in r. 16.4 (service by post) only arises in edictal execution: see note 16.12.5.

Subject to r. 16.13(1) (arrestment of ships and arrestment of cargo *in rem*) and r. 16.14(2) (arrestment of cargo on board ship), diligence may not be executed on a Sunday: Stair, III.i.37; Bell's *Comm.*, ii,460; *Oliphant v. Douglas* (1633) Mor. 15002.

Edictal execution of diligence. This procedure has been retained for execution of diligence on **16.12.6** (a) an individual resident furth of Scotland, (b) a person having no registered office, etc., in Scotland or (c) a person on whom the diligence cannot be executed because, *e.g.* his address is unknown: r. 16.12(4). Execution is by a messenger-at-arms who leaves the appropriate schedule at the Office of the Extractor (as Keeper of the Register of Edictal Citations and Executions of Diligence), Parliament House, Edinburgh and sends a copy by registered letter or the first class recorded delivery service to the residence or place of business, on the last known place, of the debtor: r. 16.12(4) and (5). The recorded delivery service may be used in Great Britain, Northern Ireland, the Channel Islands and the Isle of Man but not the Republic of Ireland. R. 16.4(2)(a) (notice on envelope), (3) (translation), (6) (date of execution) and (7) (validity of execution) apply: r. 16.12(2).

16.12.7   *Execution of arrestment to found jurisdiction.* A schedule of arrestment in Form 16.15–A (or 16.15–AA in the case of arrestment of a ship to found jurisdiction) is served on the arrestee by a messenger-at-arms and a certificate of execution in Form 16.15–H (or 16.15–HH) completed: r. 16.15(1)(a). The certificate is attached to the summons: r. 16.12(7).

Arrestment to found jurisdiction may be obtained by a warrant in a summons (r. 13.6(b)). On arrestment to found jurisdiction generally, see note 13.6.1. On arrestment of ships to found jurisdiction, see note 16.13.1(1).

16.12.8   *Execution of arrestment on the dependence.* A schedule of arrestment in Form 16.15–B (or 16.15–BB in the case of a ship) is served on the arrestee by a messenger-at-arms and a certificate of execution in Form 16.15–H (or 16.15–J in the case of a ship) completed: r. 16.15(1)(b). The certificate is attached to the summons or other document: r. 16.12(7).

Arrestment on the dependence is a preventive diligence restraining a debtor (arrestee) from making payment of a debt or satisfying an obligation to the defender (common debtor). As a general rule, a pursuer is entitled to insert a warrant for arrestment as a right in respect of a debt due. It may be recalled or restricted with or without conditions (see r. 13.10); and the pursuer will be liable in damages only for its wrongful use where executed on a defective warrant, in an irregular manner, or with malice or without probable cause: see *Wolthekker v. Northern Agricultural Co.* (1862) 1 M. 211, 212 *per* L.J.-C. Inglis; *Grant v. Magistrates of Airdrie* 1939 S.C. 738, 758–9 *per* L.P. Normand. Arrestment on the dependence may be obtained by warrant in a summons (r. 13.6(c)(ii)), by motion after signeting in an action (r. 13.8(1)), by warrant in a counterclaim or motion thereafter (r. 25.2(2)), by motion on a third party notice (r. 26.3(2)) or by motion in a petition under s.27 of the C.J.J.A. 1982 on the dependence of foreign proceedings (on which, see, *e.g. Stancraft Securities Ltd v. McDowall* 1990 S.C. 274).

In relation to a summons, arrestment may be executed at any time after signeting and before service of the summons, and is effective provided the summons is served within 20 days of the diet of compearance or, if that date is in vacation, the next calling date: Debtors (Scotland) Act 1838, s.17. There is no equivalent to the diet of compearance in modern practice; it has been argued that its equivalent is the first day on which the summons can call at the expiry of the period of notice, but this was rejected in *Brash v. Brash* 1966 S.L.T. 157, 158 *per* Lord Kissen; accordingly it is sufficient if the summons is served within 20 days after service of the arrestment. Arrestment may be executed after calling at any time until the action is disposed of by a final decree. It may not be used if the action has fallen asleep (*i.e.* where the action has been in court for a year and a day with no interlocutor having been pronounced). An arrestment will fall if the summons is not called within a year and a day of the expiry of the period of notice: *Thorburn v. Cox* (1830) 8 S. 945. Arrestment is enforced, except in the case of an earnings arrestment, a current maintenance arrestment or a conjoined arrestment order within the meaning of Part III of the Debtors (Scotland) Act 1987 (which are subject to the provisions of that Part), by an action of furthcoming (*Lucas's Trs. v Campbell* (1894) 21 R. 1096, 1103 *per* Lord Kinnear) in which both the common debtor and the arrestee are called as defenders. The arrestee must be subject to the jurisdiction of the court and the debt must have been constituted by a decree.

On arrestment on the dependence generally, see further note 13.6.3.

16.12.9   *Execution of arrestment of ships.* See r. 16.13.

16.12.10   *Execution of arrestment of cargo.* See rr. 16.13 and 16.14.

16.12.11   *Execution of arrestment in execution.* A schedule of arrestment in Form 16.15–E is served by a messenger-at-arms on the arrestee and a certificate of execution in Form 16.15–H completed: r. 16.15(1)(f). In relation to an earnings arrestment, Form 30, or, in relation to a current maintenance arrestment Form 34, and a certificate of execution in Form 60, in the A.S. (Proceedings in the Sheriff Court under the Debtors (Scotland) Act 1987) 1988 [S.I. 1988 No. 2013] must be used.

Arrestment in execution follows a decree for payment in a decree of the court or a decree of registration in the Books of Council and Session (on which, see note 16.12.2). The warrant for arrestment is implied in the words "all lawful execution on this decree (or "hereon")" inserted in the extract decree by the Extractor under r. 7.10 (or the Keeper of the Registers in a decree of registration for execution in the Books of Council and Session) by virtue of s.87(2) of the Debtors (Scotland) Act 1987 (decrees of the court) and s.3 of the Writs Execution (Scotland) Act 1877 substituted by s.87(4) of the 1987 Act (decrees of registration). Arrestment of the debtor's earnings in the hands of his employer must be by an earnings arrestment, a current maintenance arrestment to enforce current maintenance or a conjoined arrestment order to enforce payment of debts due to different creditors from the same earnings: see Part III of the 1987 Act.

Arrestment is enforced, except in the case of an earnings arrestment, a current maintenance arrestment or a conjoined arrestment order within the meaning of Part III of the 1987 Act (which are subject to the provisions of that Part), by an action of furthcoming (*Lucas's*

Trs. v. Campbell (1894) 21 R. 1096, 1103 *per* Lord Kinnear) in which both the common debtor and the arrestee are called as defenders. The arrestee must be subject to the jurisdiction of the court and the debt must have been constituted by a decree.

On arrestment generally, see note 13.6.3.

Execution of inhibition. A schedule of inhibition in Form 16.15–F is served on the defender or **16.12.12** other person inhibited by a messenger-at-arms and a certificate of execution in Form 16.15–H is completed: r. 16.15(1)(h). Where inhibition is on the dependence of a cause the certificate is attached to the summons or other document containing the warrant for the diligence: r. 16.12(7).

Inhibition may be used to prevent heritable property being burdened or disposed of by the debtor (1) on the dependence of an action, (2) on a document of debt or (3) in execution of a decree. It is generally only competent in relation to debts due (*Dove v. Henderson* (1865) 3 M. 339) but in all three cases inhibition in security may be obtained in respect of future or contingent debts where there are special circumstances (for which see note 13.6.3(3)). Inhibition may only be obtained from the Court of Session. It may proceed on a warrant for inhibition on the dependence of an action in the Court of Session (r. 13.6(c)(i)), by motion after signeting in an action (r. 13.8(1)), by warrant in a counterclaim or motion thereafter (r. 25.2(2)), by motion on a third party notice (r. 26.3(2)) or by motion in a petition under s.27 of the C.J.J.A. 1982 on the dependence of foreign proceedings (on which, see, *e.g. Stancroft Securities Ltd v. McDowall* 1990 S.C. 274). In other instances (*i.e.* on the dependence of a sheriff court action, in execution of a Court of Session or sheriff court decree, in execution of writs and foreign judgments registered for execution in the Books of Council and Session (on which, see note 16.12.2), on a document of debt or in security of future or contingent debts other than on the dependence of a Court of Session process) inhibition is obtained by letters of inhibition: see Chap. 59.

(1) *Inhibition on the dependence.* See note 13.6.2.

(2) *Inhibition on a document of debt.* A document of debt is a probative writ in which the debtor binds himself to pay. A negotiable instrument such as a bill of exchange or a promissory note is a document of debt for this purpose: Stair, IV.xlii.6. Consent to registration in the Books of Council and Session is not required; but where such a document contains a clause of registration for execution, a warrant to inhibit may be obtained on the decree of registration rather than the document of debt.

(3) *Inhibition in execution.* Inhibition may be obtained on a decree of the Court of Session or the sheriff court or on a decree of registration of a writ or judgment registered for execution in the Books of Council and Session.

Execution of charge for payment. A charge for payment in Form 16.15–G is served on the **16.12.13** debtor and a certificate of execution in Form 16.15–K is completed: r. 16.15(1)(i).

The warrant in a decree of the court or a decree of registration of a writ or judgment registered for execution in the Books of Council and Session (on which, see note 16.12.2) authorises the charging of the debtor to pay a money debt within a specified period and, where the debtor fails to pay, an earnings arrestment and attachment: Debtors (Scotland) Act 1987, s.87(2)(a) (decrees of the court) and s.3 of the Writs Execution (Scotland) Act 1877 substituted by s.87(4) of the 1987 Act (decrees of registration), both Acts amended by para. 17 of Sched.3 to the Debt Arrangement and Attachment (Scotland) Act 2002. The period for payment is 14 days if the person on whom the charge is executed is in the U.K. and 28 days if he is furth of the U.K.: 1987 Act, s.90(3). A charge to enforce an obligation *ad factum praestandum* is no longer competent: 1987 Act, s.100(2).

An earnings arrestment (within the meaning of Part III of the 1987 Act) or a attachment is not competent unless a charge for payment has been served on the debtor and must be executed within two years after the date of service of the charge, a right which may be reconstituted by serving a further charge: 1987 Act, s.90 as amended by the 2002 Act, Sched.3, para. 17(10). Earnings arrestments are governed by Part III of the 1987 Act. Attachment is governed by Pt.2 of the 2002 Act. In relation to an earnings arrestment, Form 30, and a certificate of execution in Form 60, in the A.S. (Proceedings in the Sheriff Court under the Debtors (Scotland) Act 1987) 1988 [SI 1988/2013] must be used. In the case of attachment, a schedule in Form 3 and a report of attachment in Form 8 in Appendix 1 of Sched. 1 to the Act of Sederunt (Debt Arrangement and Attachment (Scotland) Act 2002) 2002 [S.S.I. 2002 No. 560] must be used.

Suspension of execution. Execution of diligence may be prevented or suspended by suspension **16.12.14** of the charge and diligence or by suspension of the diligence, by suspension and interdict (where real diligence has begun), or by suspension and liberation (where the debtor has been imprisoned). See further, Chap. 60.

Expenses of execution. The expenses of executing diligence by an earnings arrestment schedule **16.12.15** or a conjoined arrestment order (within the meaning of Part III of the Debtors (Scotland) Act 1987), are recoverable from the debtor by the diligence under s.93(1) of the 1987 Act. The expenses of executing a schedule of arrestment and an action of furthcoming or sale are recoverable from the debtor out of the arrested property, and the court shall grant decree in the action of furthcoming for any balance not so recovered: 1987 Act, s.93(2). The expenses incurred in executing a current maintenance arrestment (within the meaning of Part III of the 1987 Act) are recoverable by diligence other than a current maintenance arrestment: 1987 Act, s.93(6).

16.12.16   *Liability for wrongful diligence.* For wrongful diligence the messenger-at-arms, the cautioner and the agent may be liable to the debtor: Graham Stewart on *Diligence*, p. 799. The party executing diligence will be liable in damages for its wrongful use where executed on a defective warrant, in an irregular manner, or with malice or without probable cause: see *Wolthekker v. Northern Agricultural Co.* (1862) 1 M. 211, 212 *per* L.J.-C. Inglis; *Grant v. Magistrates of Airdrie* 1939 S.C. 738, 758–759 *per* L.P. Normand. Where the charge is irregularly or unwarrantably executed, an averment of "wrongful" diligence is sufficient: *Dramgate Ltd v. Tyne Dock Engineering Ltd*, 2000 S.C. 43.

Arrestment of ships and arrestment in rem *of cargo on board ship*

16.13.—(1) An arrestment of a ship *in rem* or on the dependence, or an arrestment *in rem* of cargo on board ship, may be executed on any day by a messenger-at-arms who shall affix the schedule of arrestment—

   (a) to the mainmast of the ship;
   (b) to the single mast of the ship; or
   (c) where there is no mast, to some prominent part of the ship.

(2) In the execution of an arrestment of a ship on the dependence, the messenger-at-arms shall, in addition to complying with paragraph (1), mark the initials "ER" above the place where the schedule of arrestment is fixed.

(3) On executing an arrestment under paragraph (1), the messenger-at-arms shall deliver a copy of the schedule of arrestment and a copy of the certificate of execution of it to the master of the ship, or other person on board in charge of the ship or cargo, as the case may be, as representing the owners of, or parties interested in, the ship or cargo, as the case may be.

(4) Where the schedule of arrestment and the copy of the certificate of execution of it cannot be delivered as required under paragraph (3)—

   (a) the certificate of execution shall state that fact; and
   (b) either—
      (i) the arrestment shall be executed by serving it on the harbour master of the port where the ship lies; or
      (ii) where there is no harbour master, or the ship is not in a harbour, the pursuer shall enrol a motion for such further order as to intimation and advertisement, if any, as may be necessary.

(5) A copy of the schedule of arrestment and a copy of the certificate of execution of it shall be delivered by the messenger-at-arms to the harbour master, if any, of any port where the ship lies.

(6) In this rule, "ship" has the meaning assigned in section 48(f) of the Administration of Justice Act 1956.

Deriv. R.C.S. 1965, r. 140(a) (r. 16.13(1) (part), (3) and (4))

16.13.1   *Arrestment of ships.* A ship is any description of vessel used in navigation not propelled by oars: r. 16.13(6) importing the definition in the Administration of Justice Act 1956, s.48(f). The phrase "used in navigation" means used in navigating the seas: *Oakes v. Monkland Iron Co.* (1884) 11 R. 579, 584 *per* L.J.-C. Moncreiff.

There are restrictions in, for example, the Brussels Convention relating to arrest of sea-going ships, 1952: see the 1956 Act; and the UN Convention on the Law of the Sea 1982, Art. 28 (Cmnd 8941): see Merchant Shipping Act 1995, s. 129.

(1) *Arrestment of ship to found jurisdiction.* Subject to two exceptions arrestment may not be executed where the defender is domiciled in the U.K. or a Contracting State to the 1968 Brussels or the Lugano Convention: C.J.J.A. 1982, Scheds 1 and 3C, Art. 3(2), Sched.4, Art. 3 and Sched.8, r. 2(8). The exceptions are: (a) In an action of reparation arising out of the collision or manoeuvring of ships, or non-compliance with ship collision regulations under s.45 of the Administration of Justice Act 1956 the restrictions of the C.J.J.A. 1982 do not apply to defenders domiciled outside the U.K.: C.J.J.A. 1982, Scheds 1 and 3C, Art. 54 and Sched.9, para. 6. (b) In an Admiralty cause where the defender is domiciled in the U.K. or elsewhere except another Contracting State to the 1968 or Lugano Convention: C.J.J.A. 1982, Sched.5,

para. 7 and Sched.9, para. 6. An Admiralty action is defined in R.C.S. 1994, r. 46.1. Arrestment of a ship to found jurisdiction is subject to the ordinary rules of arrestment of any property to found jurisdiction, and must be made in the hands of a third party: see note 13.6.1.

For a strange argument, doubted by Lord Prosser, that there can be no arrestment to found jurisdiction in Admiralty cases since the C.J.J.A. 1982, see *Ladgroup Ltd v. Euroeast Lines S.A.* 1997 S.L.T. 916.

A schedule of arrestment in Form 16.15–AA is served on the defender and a certificate of execution in Form 16.15–HH is completed: r. 16.15(1)(a). The certificate is attached to the summons or other document containing the warrant for the diligence: r. 16.12(7).

 [NEXT TEXT PAGE IS C 151]

(2) *Arrestment of ships in rem.* An arrestment *in rem* may be executed in (a) an Admiralty action *in rem* to enforce a maritime lien or (b) an Admiralty action *in personam* to enforce a non-pecuniary claim relating to the ship under s.47(2)(p)–(s) of the Administration of Justice Act 1956 by virtue of s.47(3) of that Act. An Admiralty action is defined in r. 46.1. Arrestment of a ship is a real diligence directed against the vessel itself: *Carlberg v. Borjesson* (1877) 5 R. 188, 195 *per* Lord Shand. There is no arrestee: *Barclay, Curle & Co. Ltd v. Sir James Laing & Sons Ltd* 1908 S.C. 82, 89 *per* Lord McLaren. The ship may be arrested while in the possession of the defender. Arrestment of the ship does not arrest the cargo or freight. Arrestment *in rem* founds jurisdiction. The ship is fixed in the place where she is at the time of the execution of the arrestment until a declarator of lien is obtained and a process of sale completed: *Carlberg,* above. The arrestment cannot be executed when the ship is on passage: *Carlberg,* above; 1956 Act, s.47(6). The expenses of arrestment are recoverable as expenses of process because they are essential to the obtaining of the decree *in rem*: *Hatton v. A/S Durban Hansen* 1919 S.C. 154.

(a) Arrestment *in rem* to enforce maritime lien. A maritime lien is a form of hypothec or security without possession over a ship, her apparel or cargo enforceable by an Admiralty action *in rem* in which the *res* is attached by the arrestment, declarator of the lien is granted and the *res* sold. Such a lien arises (i) at common law in respect of damage done by a ship, bonds of bottomry or *respondentia,* seamen's wages, salvage and (ii) by creation by statute—master's wages and disbursements (1995 Act, s.41), compensation to owners or occupiers of land for damage occasioned by shipwreck (Merchant Shipping Act 1995, s.234(5)), fees and expenses of receiver of wrecks (1995 Act, s.249(3)), remuneration for services of coastguard (1995 Act, s.250(3)(c)). Under s.47(1) of the 1956 Act arrestment *in rem* is only competent if the action involves a claim in s.47(2), and the statutory liens except master's wages and disbursements and rights to life and property salvage are probably excluded. A schedule in Form 16.15–C is used and a certificate of execution in Form 16.15–I is completed: r. 16.15(1)(c). The schedule is attached by a messenger-at-arms to the mainmast or other prominent part and a copy delivered to the master of the ship or person in charge whom failing the harbour master whom failing a motion for further procedure must be enrolled: r. 16.13(1), (3) and (4). This may be done on any day, including Sunday: r. 16.13(1). The certificate is attached to the summons or other document containing the warrant for the diligence: r. 16.12(7).

(b) Arrestment *in rem* in an Admiralty action *in personam* to enforce non-pecuniary claims under s.47(2)(p)–(s) of the 1956 Act by virtue of s.47(3) of that Act. These provisions relate to a dispute as to ownership or possession of or a share in a ship, between co-owners of a ship about ownership, possession, employment or earnings of that ship, the mortgage or hypothecation of or share in a ship, or the forfeiture or condemnation of a ship or goods or the restoration of the ship or goods. Arrestment may be used whether or not the ship belongs to the defender: Arrest of Ships—4, Scotland, p. 87, by I. G. Inglis (Lloyds of London, 1987). There is no declarator of lien and no sale and the arrestment simply secures implement of the decree. A schedule in Form 16.15–D is used and a certificate of execution in Form 16.15–I is completed: r. 16.15(1)(d). The schedule is attached by a messenger-at-arms to the mainmast or other prominent part and a copy delivered to the master of the ship or person in charge whom failing the harbour master whom failing a motion for further procedure must be enrolled: r. 16.13(1), (3) and (4). This may be done on any day, including Sunday: r. 16.13(1). The certificate is attached to the summons or other document containing the warrant for the diligence: r. 16.12(7).

(3) *Arrestment of ship on the dependence.* A ship may be arrested on the dependence of an Admiralty action *in personam* (a) to enforce or secure a claim in s.47(2) of the 1956 Act by virtue of s.47(1) of that Act where the ship is the ship with which the action is concerned (and is partly owned by the defender: see *e.g. William Batey & Co. (Exports) Ltd v. Kent* 1985 S.L.T. 490, affd. 1987 S.L.T. 557) or all the shares are owned by the defender or (b) to enforce a claim in s.47(2)(p)–(s) by virtue of s.47(3)(a) of the 1956 Act if the conclusion is a pecuniary conclusion and the ship is the ship to which the conclusion relates. An Admiralty action is defined in r. 46.1. It used not to be clear whether s.47(1) limits the common law right to arrest a sister ship: see *e.g. Sheaf Steamship Co. Ltd v. Compania Transmediterranea* 1930 S.C. 660; *cf.* Brussels Convention relating to the Arrest of Seagoing Ships, May 10, 1952, art. 3(3), *The "Banco"* [1971] P. 137 (English law) and comments in *Gatoil International Inc. v. Arkwright-Boston Manufacturers Mutual Insurance Co.* 1985 S.C.(H.L.) 1, 15 *per* Lord Keith of Kinkel. It has now been held in the Outer House that only one ship (the ship concerned or a sister ship) per action may be arrested on the dependence under s.47(1) of the Administration of Justice Act 1956: *Interatlantic (Namibia) (Pty) Ltd v. Okeasnki Ribolov Ltd* 1996 S.L.T. 819; reported as *The "Afala"* [1995] 2 Lloyd's Rep. 286. The action is directed against the defenders and not the ship. The expenses of the arrestment are not recoverable at common law as expenses of process because the arrestment is not essential to obtaining the decree *in personam*: *Black v. Jehangeer Framjee & Co.* (1887) 14 R. 678. *Quaere* whether they are recoverable as a debt due in a separate action or under s.93(2) of the Debtors (Scotland) Act 1987.

A schedule in Form 16.15–BB is used and a certificate of execution in Form 16.15–J is completed: r. 16.15(1)(e). The schedule is attached by a messenger-at-arms to the mainmast or other prominent part, the letters "ER" chalked above and a copy of the schedule delivered to the master of the ship or person in charge whom failing the harbour master whom failing a motion for further procedure must be enrolled: r. 16.13(1)–(4). This may be done on any day, including Sunday: r. 16.13(1). The certificate is attached to the summons or other document containing the warrant for the diligence: r. 16.12(7).

16.13.2   *Warrant to dismantle.* An arrestment on the dependence or *in rem* of a ship fixes her in the place where she is found. To make sure the ship is not moved a warrant to dismantle may be sought (in the summons (r. 13.6(c)(iv)) or subsequently by motion (r. 13.8)). Dismantling should be done by a suitably qualified person (such as a marine engineer) under the supervision of the messenger-at-arms. Dismantling may be unnecessary if the ship does not have customs clearance to sail.

16.13.3   *Arrestment in rem of cargo on board ship.* This arrestment may be executed in an Admiralty action (defined in r. 46.1) *in rem* to enforce a maritime lien (on which, see note 16.13.1(2)(a)). It temporarily detains the ship until the cargo is discharged. Where the cargo cannot be discharged the court may even loose the arrestment to enable this to be done out of the jurisdiction: *Svenska Petroleum A.B. v. H.O.R. Ltd* 1982 S.L.T. 343. It is not clear if the arrestment immobilises the ship where it is until the cargo is discharged or merely prevents the ship-master from sailing with the cargo out of the jurisdiction. It is probable that s.47(1) of the Administration of Justice Act 1956 does not apply to such an arrestment: see *e.g. Svenska Petroleum A.B. v. H.O.R. Ltd* 1982 S.L.T. 343, 1983 S.L.T. 493 and 1986 S.L.T. 513; *West Cumberland Farmers Ltd v. Ellon Hinengo Ltd* 1988 S.C. 294.

A schedule in Form 16.15–C is used and a certificate of execution in Form 16.15–I is completed: r. 16.15(1)(c). The schedule is attached by a messenger-at-arms to the mainmast or other prominent part and a copy delivered to the master of the ship or person in charge whom failing the harbour master whom failing a motion for further procedure must be enrolled: r. 16.13(1), (3) and (4). This may be done on any day, including Sunday: r. 16.13(1). The certificate is attached to the summons or other document containing the warrant for the diligence: r. 16.12(7).

16.13.4   *Movement of arrested ship or cargo.* Any person having an interest may apply by motion to move an arrested vessel or cargo. This may be to move a ship to a safe harbour (*Turner v. Galway* (1882) 19 S.L.R. 892; *The "Grey Dolphin"* 1982 S.C. 5) or to move her from a place where she is obstructing or causing loss to a third party. If a cargo is arrested but cannot be unloaded the ship is effectively immobilised: see *Svenska Petroleum A.B. v. H.O.R. Ltd* 1982 S.L.T. 343; *West Cumberland Farmers Ltd v. Director of Agriculture of Sri Lanka* 1988 S.L.T. 296. See also note 13.11.1.

16.13.5   *Arrestment on a Sunday.* R. 16.13(1) permits arrestment of a ship *in rem* or on the dependence, or an arrestment *in rem* of cargo on board ship, to be executed on any day. The common law prohibition of executing diligence on a Sunday gave rise to difficulty when the turn-round time of ships is often short and tankers and bulk-ore carriers are frequently discharged at weekends. The common law in relation to arrestment on the dependence in an Admiralty action was altered by *Nederlandse Scheepshypotheekbank v. Cam Standby* 1994 S.C.L.R. 956.

Arrestment of cargo

16.14.—(1) Where cargo has been, or is in the course of being, landed or transhipped, whether or not it has been delivered to its owner or his agent, any arrestment *in rem* of the cargo shall be executed by a messenger-at-arms who shall serve the schedule of arrestment—

    (a) on the custodian for the time being of such cargo; or

    (b) where the cargo has been landed on the quay or into a shed of any port or harbour authority, to the harbour master.

(2) An arrestment, other than an arrestment to which paragraph (1) applies, of cargo on board ship may be executed on any day by a messenger-at-arms who shall serve the schedule of arrestment on the owner of the cargo or other proper arrestee.

Deriv. R.C.S. 1965, r. 140(b)

16.14.1   *Arrestment of cargo to found jurisdiction.* Subject to an exception, arrestment may not be executed where the defender is domiciled in the U.K. or a Contracting State to the 1968 Brussels or the Lugano Convention: C.J.J.A. 1982, Scheds 1 and 3C, Art. 3(2), Sched. 4, Art. 3 and Sched. 8, r. 2(8). The exception is in an Admiralty cause where the defender is domiciled in the U.K. or elsewhere except another Contracting State to the 1968 or Lugano Convention: C.J.J.A. 1982, Sch.5, para.7 and Sch.9, para.6. An Admiralty action is defined in R.C.S. 1994, r.46.1. Arrestment of a cargo to found jurisdiction is subject to the ordinary rules of arrestment of any property to found jurisdiction, and must be made in the hands of a third party: see note 13.6.1.

A schedule of arrestment in Form 16.15–A is served by a messenger-at-arms on the defender or other person inhibited and a certificate of execution in Form 16.15–H is completed: r.16.15(1)(a). The certificate is attached to the summons or other document containing the warrant for the diligence: r.16.12(7).

Arrestment in rem of cargo landed or transhipped. This arrestment may be executed in an **16.14.2** Admiralty action (defined in r.46.1) to enforce a maritime lien (on which, see note 16.13.1(2)(a)).

A schedule in Form 16.15–C is served by a messenger-at-arms and a certificate of execution in Form 16.15–I is completed: r.16.15(1)(c). The certificate is attached to the summons or other document containing the warrant for the diligence: r.16.12(7). There is no provision for this arrestment to be executed on a Sunday and the common law applies: r.16.14(2); Stair, III.i.37; Bell's *Comm.*, ii,460; *Oliphant v. Douglas* (1633) Mor. 15002. Whether or not the cargo has been delivered to the owner, the messenger-at-arms serves the schedule on the custodian of the cargo or, where on the quay or harbour shed, on the harbour master. Where the cargo has been landed on the quay or in a harbour shed the option of serving on the custodian is still available: this is useful where, *e.g.* there is no harbour master.

Arrestment on the dependence of cargo landed or transhipped. Where the cargo has been or is in **16.14.3** the course of being landed or transhipped it no longer has the character of cargo on board ship and there is no reason for treating it as liable to an Admiralty arrestment; the arrestment must be in the hands of a third party: see note 13.6.3. Where cargo is in the possession of the cargo owner on land the ordinary rules of arrestment also apply: see note 13.6.3.

A schedule in Form 16.15–B is served on the arrestee by a messenger-at-arms and a certificate of execution in Form 16.15–H is completed: r.16.15(1)(b). The certificate is attached to the summons or other document containing the warrant for the diligence: r.16.12(7). There is no provision for this arrestment to be executed on a Sunday and the common law applies: r.16.14(2); Stair, III.i.37; Bell's *Comm.*, ii,460; *Oliphant v. Douglas* (1633) Mor. 15002; but *cf. Nederlandse Scheepshypotheekbank NV v. Cam Standby Ltd* 1994 S.C.L.R. 956.

Arrestment on the dependence of cargo on board ship. This arrestment may be used in an **16.14.4** ordinary action or in an Admiralty action *in personam.* An Admiralty action is defined in r.46.1. There must be an arrestee, *e.g.* a third party or the ship-master (even if he is the employee of the cargo owner) or the cargo owner himself: r.16.14(2).

A schedule in Form 16.15–B is served on the arrestee by a messenger-at-arms and a certificate of execution in Form 16.15–J is completed: r.16.15(1)(e). The arrestment may be executed on any day, including Sunday: r.16.14(2). The certificate is attached to the summons or other document containing the warrant for the diligence: r.16.12(7).

Movement of arrested ship or cargo. Any person having an interest may apply by motion to **16.14.5** move arrested cargo. If a cargo is arrested but cannot be unloaded the ship is effectively immobilised: see *Svenska Petroleum A.B. v. H.O.R. Ltd* 1982 S.L.T. 343; *West Cumberland Farmers Ltd v. Director of Agriculture of Sri Lanka* 1988 S.L.T. 296. See also note 13.11.1.

Arrestment of cargo on a Sunday. The common law prohibition of executing diligence on a **16.14.6** Sunday gave rise to difficulty when the turn-round time of ships is often short and tankers and bulk-ore carriers are frequently discharged at weekends. Arrestment of cargo on a Sunday is permitted: (a) *in rem* of cargo on board ship: r.16.13(1); (b) on the dependence of an Admiralty action *in personam*, or of an ordinary action, of cargo on board ship: r.16.14(2).

Forms for diligence

16.15.—(1) In the execution of diligence, the following forms shall be used—

[1](a) in the case of—

    (i) an arrestment to found jurisdiction (other than the arrestment of a ship), a schedule in Form 16.15–A and a certificate of execution in Form 16.15–H;

    (ii) an arrestment of a ship to found jurisdiction, a schedule in Form 16.15–AA and a certificate of execution in Form 16.15–HH;

  (b) subject to sub-paragraph (e), in the case of an arrestment on the dependence, a schedule in Form 16.15–B and a certificate of execution in Form 16.15–H;

[1] (c) in the case of an arrestment *in rem* of a ship, cargo or other maritime

res to enforce a maritime hypothec or lien, a schedule in Form 16.15–C and a certificate of execution in Form 16.15–I;

(d) in the case of an arrestment *in rem* of a ship to enforce a non-pecuniary claim, a schedule in Form 16.15–D and a certificate of execution in Form 16.15–I;

[1] (e) in the case of an arrestment on the dependence of—
   (i) a cargo on board a ship, a schedule in Form 16.15–B;
   (ii) a ship, a schedule in Form 16.15–BB, and a certificate of execution in Form 16.15–J;

(f) subject to paragraph (g), in the case of an arrestment in execution, a schedule in Form 16.15–E and a certificate of execution in Form 16.15–H;

(g) in the case of an earnings arrestment, or a current maintenance arrestment, within the meaning of Part III of the Debtors (Scotland) Act 1987, a schedule in Form 30 (in respect of an earnings arrestment), or Form 34 (in respect of a current maintenance arrestment), and a certificate of execution in Form 60, in the Schedule to the Act of Sederunt (Proceedings in the Sheriff Court under the Debtors (Scotland) Act 1987) 1988;

(h) in the case of an inhibition, a schedule in Form 16.15–F and a certificate of execution in Form 16.15–H;

(i) in the case of the execution of a charge for payment of money, a charge in Form 16.15–G and a certificate of execution in Form 16.15–K; and

[2] (j) in the case of an attachment, a schedule in form 3, and a report of attachment in form 8, in Appendix 1 of Schedule 1 to the Act of Sederunt (Debt Arrangement and Attachment (Scotland) Act 2002) 2002.

(2) Where two or more of the arrestments mentioned in paragraph (1)(a), (b), (c) and (d) are to be executed, they may be combined in one schedule of arrestment.

Deriv. R.C.S. 1965, r.74(c), and r.140(c) (r.16.15(2))

---

[1] R.16.15(1)(a), (c) and (e) substituted by SI 1998/2637 (effective December 1, 1998).
[2] R.16.15(1)(j) substituted by SSI 2002/560, art.4, Sch.3, para.5 (effective December 30, 2002).

16.15.1   *Forms for diligence.* In respect of the following forms in r.16.15, see the notes mentioned to which the forms relate:

Form 16.15–A—see notes 16.12.7, 16.13.1(1) and 16.14.1;
Form 16.15–AA—see notes 16.12.7 and 16.13.1(1);
Form 16.15–B—see notes 16.12.8, 16.13.1(3) and 16.14.3;
Form 16.15–BB—see notes 16.12.8 and 16.13.1(3);
Form 16.15–C—see notes 16.13.1(2)(a), 16.13.3 and 16.14.2;
Form 16.15–D—see note 16.13.1(2)(b);
Form 16.15–E—see note 16.12.11;
Form 16.15–F—see note 16.12.12;
Form 16.15–G—see note 16.12.13;
Form 16.15–H—see notes 16.12.7, 16.12.8, 16.12.11, 16.12.12, 16.13.1(1), 16.14.1 and 16.14.3;
Form 16.15–HH—see notes 16.12.7 and 16.13.1(1);
Form 16.15–I—see notes 16.13.1(2), 16.13.3 and 16.14.2;
Form 16.15–J—see notes 16.13.1(3) and 16.14.4;
Form 16.15–K—see note 16.12.13.

In respect of earnings arrestments and current maintenance arrestments within the meaning of Pt III of the Debtors (Scotland) Act 1987 the forms in the Schedule to the Act of Sederunt (Proceedings in the Sheriff Court under the Debtors (Scotland) Act 1987) 1988, and, in the case of attachment, the form in Appendix 1 of Sch.1 to the Act of Sederunt (Debt Arrangement and Attachment (Scotland) Act 2002) 2002 [SSI 2002/560], are to be used. Proceedings following the execution of such diligence are in the sheriff court.

CHAPTER 17

APPEARANCE IN ACTIONS

Entering appearance

17.1.—(1) Appearance in an action shall be entered within three days after the date on which the summons has called by the defender requesting a clerk of session in the appropriate section of the General Department to mark on the summons—

   (a) the names of the counsel, or other person having a right of audience, and the agent acting for him; or

   (b) that he appears for himself.

(2) On entering appearance, the defender shall give written intimation to the pursuer that appearance has been entered.

(3) On entering appearance, the defender shall have the right to borrow any production which has been lodged in process.

Deriv. R.C.S. 1965, r. 81(1) substituted by SI 1991/2483 (r. 17.1(1)), r. 81(1B) inserted by SI 1991/2483 (r. 17.1(2)) and r. 86 (r. 17.1(3))

General note. Appearance is no longer entered on the calling list but by a clerk of session on **17.1.1** the principal summons (heretofore an informal practice). The effect of entering appearance is (a) the defender cannot challenge a defective execution of service on himself (*Corstorphine v. Kasten* (1898) 1 F. 287) and (b) the defender may borrow any productions from process (r. 17.1(3)). If the defender does not enter appearance or having done so has not lodged defences, the pursuer may obtain a decree in absence which may become a decree *in foro*: r. 19.1(1) and (7).

   Entering appearance may be done in person at the public counter of the appropriate section of the General Department, or by post or fax (P.N. No. 4 of 1994, para. 5, or by e-mail (P.N. No. 2 of 2001). Where this is done by post, fax or e-mail details of the cause reference number, the parties, date of calling and the information required for the purposes of r. 17.1(1) must be given by 4 p.m. on the last day for entering appearance: P.N. No. 4 of 1994, para. 5(2); P.N. No. 2 of 2001, para. 2.

   "within three days". The day on which the summons calls is not counted in calculating the **17.1.2** period; but the third day is included in the period. Where the last day falls on a Saturday or Sunday or a public holiday on which the Office of Court is closed, appearance may be entered on the next available day: r. 1.3(7). For office hours and holidays, see note 3.1.2. For calling of summons, see r. 13.13.

   "counsel, or other person having a right of audience". See r. 1.3(1) (definitions of "counsel" and **17.1.3** "other person having a right of audience") and note 1.3.4.

   "agent". This means a solicitor or a person having a right to conduct the litigation: see r. **17.1.4** 1.3(1) (definition of "agent") and note 1.3.4. "Solicitor" is defined in the C.S.A. 1988, s.51.

   "written intimation". For methods, see r. 16.9. **17.1.5**

   Borrowing productions. The defender no longer has the right to borrow the principal **17.1.6** summons: there is no need for him to do so; and the only effect or purpose of the former right was to prevent the pursuer obtaining a decree in absence. For borrowing and returning productions, see r. 4.12.

Appearance not to imply acceptance of jurisdiction

17.2. The entering of appearance shall not imply acceptance of the jurisdiction of the court.

Deriv. R.C.S. 1965, r. 81(2) inserted by SI 1986/1941

General note. This rule was introduced by A.S. (R.C.A. No. 9) (Jurisdiction and **17.2.1** Enforcement) 1986 [SI 1986/1941] because the C.J.J.A. 1982, Scheds 1, 3C and 4, Art. 18 and Sched.8, r. 6(2) provide that a court does not have jurisdiction over the substance or merits of a cause where appearance is entered solely to contest jurisdiction.

   Defences may be lodged contesting jurisdiction only or contesting jurisdiction and defending on the merits: see r. 18.2(1). But, where the defender first admits jurisdiction and subsequently seeks to take a plea of jurisdiction, he may be taken as having consented to the jurisdiction of the court: *Clarke v. Fennoscandia Ltd (No.2)*, 10th March 2000, (2000 G.W.D. 11-377) (OH).

CHAPTER 18

DEFENCES AND ANSWERS

Form and lodging of defences

18.1.—(1) Defences to an action shall consist of—
  (a) numbered answers corresponding to the articles of the condescendence annexed to the summons; and
  (b) appropriate pleas-in-law.
(2) Subject to rule 46.6 (ship collisions and preliminary acts), defences to an action shall be lodged in process within 7 days after the date on which the summons has called, or, if the seventh day is in vacation, on the next day on which a summons may be called.

Deriv. R.C.S. 1965, r. 83(a) (r. 18.1(2)) and (b) (r. 18.1(1))

18.1.1   *General note.* Where defences are to be lodged, the principal must be taken to the clerk of session in the Signet Office in the General Department to be initialled by him before being presented at the section in the department in which the process of the action is lodged (see note 3.2.1 for departmental sections). Defences may be sent by post by a Court of Session account holder or if accompanied by a cheque for the court fee for lodging: P.N. No. 4 of 1994, paras 1, 2 and 8.

    Litiscontestation takes place when defences are lodged and any decree thereafter is a decree *in foro contentioso*: *Gow v. Henry* (1899) 2 F. 48, 52 *per* Lord Young; *Argyllshire Weavers Ltd v. A. Macauley (Tweeds) Ltd* 1962 S.C. 388, 394 *per* Lord Hunter.

18.1.2   *Form of defences.* "Our whole system of pleading and disposal of cases upon preliminary pleas must depend upon each party stating with candour what are the material facts upon which he relies and admitting the facts stated by his opponent which he knows to be true": *Ellon Castle Estates Co. Ltd v. Macdonald* 1975 S.L.T.(Notes) 66 *per* Lord Stewart.

    In family actions, defences may contain conclusions: r. 49.31(2)(b)(i). On answers to condescendence, see note 18.1.3; on pleas-in-law, see note 18.1.4.

    On the requirement for the use of metric units of measurement in pleadings, see note 13.2.18.

18.1.3   *Answers to condescendence.* There should be a concise, accurate and frank response to the articles of the condescendence. Every fact should be answered. In each answer to each article, these rules should be followed: First, admit specifically all those averments which are admitted ("Admitted that *(set out the averment)*"); one should not admit a variation of the averment. An averment may be admitted subject to an explanation ("Admitted that . . . under explanation that . . .") where it is convenient to include it and this can be done shortly; otherwise there should be no admission and the explanation dealt with after the general denial. An admission must be read with any qualification or explanation unless disproved (*Picken v. Arundale & Co.* (1872) 10 M. 987) or irrelevant (*Robertson & Co. v. Bird & Co.* (1897) 24 R. 1076). Where all averments are admitted, "Admitted." will do. Admissions exclude the need for evidence and are conclusive in that cause against the party making them (Erskine IV.ii.33) except in consistorial actions (*Macfarlane v. Macfarlane* 1956 S.C. 472); and if deleted from the record may yet be the subject of cross-examination (*Lennox v. National Coal Board* 1955 S.C. 438).

    Second (exceptionally), where facts are outwith the defender's knowledge but are believed to be true, these averments should be dealt with by "Believed to be true that *(set out averment)*": an averment that something is believed to be true is equivalent to an admission: *Scottish North Eastern Railway Co. v. Napier* (1859) 21 D. 700, 703 *per* L.J.-C. Inglis (the Acts of Sederunt containing this principle are no longer in force, but the principle remains). The party met by such a reply is entitled to take it that the point believed to be true is not disputed and is not one on which evidence is required: *Binnie v. Rederij Theodoro BV* 1993 S.C. 71, 86G *per* L.P. Hope.

    Thirdly, where averments are outwith the defender's knowledge and are not admitted, these should be dealt with by "Not known and not admitted that *(set out averment)*". Where all averments are not known and not admitted, "Not known and not admitted." will do.

    Fourthly, all other averments, being those which are denied, should be answered with a general denial, "Quoad ultra, denied.": this is because every averment of fact within the defender's knowledge which is not denied is deemed to be admitted: *Pegler v. Northern Agricultural Implements and Foundry Co. Ltd* (1877) 4 R. 435, 438 *per* L.P. Inglis; and knowledge means his state of knowledge (*Central Motor Engineering Co. v. Galbraith* 1918 S.C. 755, 756 *per* L.P. Strathclyde) on any matter which he does not have to make enquiries about to discover the truth (*O'Connor v. W. G. Auld & Co. (Engineering) Ltd* 1970 S.L.T.(Notes) 16).

The averment "Not admitted" or "No admission is made" is similarly treated: *Ellis v. Fraser* (1840) 3 D. 264, 271 *per* L.P. Hope; *Clark v. Clark* 1967 S.C. 296, 305 *per* Lord Milligan. An averment that the defender performed all statutory duties incumbent upon him may be treated as an admission of the applicability of the statute averred by the pursuer: *McNaught v. British Railways Board* 1979 S.L.T.(Notes) 99; but such an averment will not bar the defender from subsequently taking a plea to the relevancy if the statute does not apply: *Lamont v. Monklands D.C.* 1992 S.L.T. 428; and see the discussion in *Ballantyne v. John Young & Co. (Kelvinhaugh) Ltd* 1996 S.L.T. 358. An averment that a document is "referred to for its terms" is not an admission: *Pringle v. Bremner & Stirling* (1867) 5 M. (H.L.) 55; *Ballantyne*, above (statutory duty). Where all averments are denied, "Denied." will do. A defender's unqualified denial on record of a pursuer's detailed averments on matters within the defender's knowledge could indicate a lack of candour which entitled the court to proceed on the basis that the pursuer's averments were well founded and grant decree *de plano*: *EFT Finance Ltd v. Hawkins* 1994 S.C. 34. The form "it is specifically denied that . . .", sometimes seen in sheriff court pleadings, is an example of bad pleading and does not conform to the rules just set out.

There then follows the defender's explanation or version of the facts. The explanation and any additional facts averred should be such as is necessary to give fair notice of the line of the

defence or to provide the foundation for the substantive defence and the pleas-in-law without pleading evidence (*i.e.* the manner in which the facts averred will be proved): *Neilson v. Househill Coal and Iron Co.* (1842) 4 D. 1187, 1193 *per* L.J.-C. Hope "The beauty of the Scotch system is, that, without disclosing what is properly called evidence, you must at least state the line of the defence, and the main facts and points in the enquiry on which you rest, so that the other party shall be fully able previously to investigate the case, and be prepared for it." Law should not be pled except (a) as a matter of practice, in a reparation action the duties owed by the defender to the pursuer are pled; (b) a private Act of Parliament before 1850 (Interpretation Act 1978, s.3); and (c) foreign law if different from Scots law, otherwise it will be presumed to be the same as Scots law (*Emerald Stainless Steel Ltd v. South Side Distribution Ltd* 1982 S.C. 61), unless judicial knowledge must be taken of it (for which see Macphail on *Sheriff Court Practice*, paras 2–04 to 2–07).

The defender cannot normally raise issues not pled on record (*Smith v. Green* (1854) 16 D. 429) but a defence emerging in cross-examination and unforeseen may be put forward (*Bile Bean Manufacturing Co. v. Davidson* (1906) 8 F. 1181). All grounds of defence and pleas must be stated at the same time, except that of no jurisdiction (see r. 18.2). A defender may plead alternative defences: *Smart v. Bargh* 1949 S.C. 57, 61 *per* L.P. Cooper.

Skeletal defences—*i.e.* bare denials—are rarely proper or satisfactory: it is rare for a straight denial to be the whole of a defence, no alternative version of events can be put forward in evidence or cross-examination and they may result in the pursuer obtaining summary decree (see Chap. 21) or decree *de plano* at procedure roll (*Ellon Castle Estates Co. Ltd v. Macdonald* 1975 S.L.T.(Notes) 66; *Foxley v. Dunn* 1978 S.L.T.(Notes) 35; *cf. McManus v. Spiers Dick and Smith Ltd* 1989 S.L.T. 806 (circumstances where skeletal defences entitled defender to put pursuer to his proof).

Pleas-in-law. These are distinct legal propositions applicable to the facts of the case: *J. & R.* **18.1.4** *Young & Co. v. Graham* (1860) 23 D. 36 *per* L.J.-C. Inglis. Pleas may be divided into (1) preliminary pleas and (2) pleas on the merits (peremptory pleas). Pleas-in-law must be supported by averments.

(A) Preliminary pleas. These are decided before the merits are decided and if sustained lead to disposal of the action without inquiry into the merits. They result in dismissal (or sist) but do not make the cause *res judicata*, and the pursuer may raise a fresh action: *Menzies v. Menzies* (1893) 20 R.(H.L.) 108, 110 *per* Lord Watson. Where such a plea is so bound up with the merits, a proof before answer may be allowed instead of disposing of the action at procedure roll. It is good practice to disclose in the plea the ground on which the plea is taken, particularly in the case of general pleas of relevancy and specification: the practice heretofore of regarding proper notice of fact or the line of evidence as essential but not notice of the point of law is defective; the practice is tempered by the possibility of being required to lodge and intimate a note of argument (see rr. 22.4 (general provision), 43.24(8) (optional procedure in certain actions of damages), 47.12(1)(d) (commercial actions) and 55.3(4)(b) (causes relating to intellectual property)). The most common pleas are as follows:

(A)(1) "*All parties not called.*" This short form is normally used. The plea is that all persons whose absence from the cause will prejudice the defender in his defence or after the defence has been repelled (Maclaren on *Court of Session Practice*, p. 381; see *e.g. Arthur v. The SMT Sales & Service Co. Ltd*, 1999 S.C. 525) or whose presence is necessary to have the question at issue effectively disposed of (*Wilson v. Independent Broadcasting Authority* 1979 S.C. 351, 356 *per* Lord Ross) have not been called as defenders: *e.g.* where the party not called is a joint owner (*North British Railway Co. v. North Eastern Railway Co.* (1896) 24 R.(H.L.) 19); where a joint and several obligation has to be constituted by decree (*Neilson v. Wilson* (1890) 17 R. 608). Prejudice to the defender may not exist where third party procedure is available: *Lang v. Ure* 1994 S.L.T. 1235. It is *pars judicis* to notice that all parties are not called: *Connell v. Ferguson* (1857) 19 D. 482, 486 *per* Lord Deas.

(A)(2) *Competent and omitted*: "The present action being based on averments that (*briefly detail*) and having been omitted from that action, the present action is incompetent and the action should be dismissed [or the defender should be assoilzied]." The plea now seems to be regarded as a preliminary or dilatory plea: see, *e.g. Murray v. Seath* 1939 S.L.T. 348; *Cantors Properties (Scotland) Ltd v. Swears & Wells Ltd* 1978 S.C. 310. The plea should specify the grounds of objection and be supported by relevant averments. Where a defender has put forward a defence which is unsuccessful he cannot in a subsequent process challenge the prior judgment on grounds which it was competent to plead in the prior process but which he omitted to do: Maclaren on *Court of Session Practice*, p. 401; *Macdonald v. Macdonald* (1842) 1 Bell's App. 819, 829 *per* Lord Campbell; *Cantors Properties (Scotland) Ltd*, above; *Dickie v. Goldie* 1995 S.L.T. 780 (failure to plead compensation in prior action not a bar). It does not apply to a pursuer in a prior cause who can raise further actions based on different grounds: *Macdonald*, above. The considerations for this plea are similar to those in the plea of *res judicata*: *Rorie v. Rorie* 1967 S.L.T. 75, 78 *per* Lord Milligan. For *res judicata*, see (B)(5) below.

(A)(3) *Forum non conveniens*: "The court being *forum non conveniens*, the action should be dismissed [*or* sisted]." Ss.22 and 49 of the C.J.J.A. 1982 save the application of this doctrine in relation to the jurisdiction of the court under Sched. 8, but it has no application to causes to which either the 1968 or Lugano Convention applies where the defender is domiciled in another Convention country or where Sched. 1 or 4, Art. 16 applies (exclusive jurisdiction). Under these conventions the doctrine of *lis pendens* applies. The doctrine of *forum non conveniens* applies "whenever it can be shown that the case cannot, consistently with fairness and justice, be tried in this country": *Sim v. Robinow* (1892) 19 R. 665, 666 *per* Lord Low; see also *Clements v. Macauley* (1866) 4 M. 583, 592 *per* L.J.-C. Inglis. Where the jurisdiction of the court is competently founded, the court has no discretion whether to exercise it or not: *Clements*, above; *Sim*, above, *per* Lord Kinnear at p. 668. Something more than mere practical inconvenience is required to sustain a plea of *forum non conveniens*. The proper translation of "*conveniens*" is "appropriate"; the actual convenience of the parties is not to be considered but that which is the appropriate forum for securing the ends of justice, and the decision must be taken in the light of the whole surrounding circumstances: *Société du Gaz de Paris v. Société Anonyme de Navigation "Les Armateurs Français"* 1926 S.C.(H.L.) 13, 18 *per* Lord Dunedin. The general principles were recently set out by Lord Jauncey in *Crédit Chimique v. James Scott Engineering Group Ltd* 1979 S.C. 406. The initial onus is on the defender to raise and justify the plea: *De Mulder v. Jadranska Linijska (Jadrolinija)* 1989 S.L.T. 269. The mere fact that evidence of foreign law is required is not enough. It is not enough to show that the defence will have a better chance of succeeding elsewhere, as one must look to the interests of the pursuer as well as those of the defender "and the thing to be shown is not that there will be a disadvantage in that sense, but that there will be unfair disadvantage, so that justice is unlikely to be done": *Longworth v. Hope* (1865) 3 M. 1049, 1057 *per* Lord Deas. Once the defender has satisfied the initial onus it is for the pursuer to establish that to litigate abroad would deprive him of an advantage of such importance that it would cause injustice to deprive him of it (*De Mulder*, above) or that substantial justice could not be done in the other court (*Sokha v. Secretary of State for the Home Department* 1992 S.L.T. 1049, 1054 *per* Lord Prosser). In *Sokha*, above, at p. 1054A, it was observed by Lord Prosser that where the choice of jurisdiction was between competing jurisdictions within the U.K. a strong preference might be given to the forum chosen by the pursuer. The plea will usually be inappropriate in causes relating to immoveables as the courts of the *lex situs* will be the only courts competent to grant decree *in rem*: *Foster v. Foster's Trs* 1923 S.C. 212.

(A)(4) *Incompetency*: "The action, being incompetent [because (*state reason*)], should be dismissed." The ground on which objection is taken should be specified: *Coxall v. Stewart* 1976 S.L.T. 275. This plea is an objection to the form of the summons or condescendence and is distinguished from relevancy: Maclaren on *Court of Session Practice*, p. 387. Competency and relevancy run into each other: *Coutts v. Coutts* (1866) 4 M. 802, 803 *per* L.P. McNeill. A party acting inconsistently with his plea may be held to have waived it: *North British Railway Co. v. Carter* (1870) 8 M. 998. It is *pars judicis* to notice questions of competency, and an action may be dismissed without such a plea being stated: *Hamilton v. Murray* (1830) 9 S. 143.

(A)(5) "*Lis [alibi] pendens*." This short form is usually used. If the prior cause is in another court the plea is *lis alibi pendens*. If the prior cause is in the same court the plea is *lis pendens*: *Levy v. Gardiner* 1965 S.L.T.(Notes) 86. The common law plea of *lis alibi pendens* does not apply where the prior action is in a foreign court: *Martin v. Stopford-Blair's Exrs* (1879) 7 R. 329, 331 *per* L.P. Inglis. Where the 1968 (Brussels) or Lugano Convention applies, the provisions of those conventions for *lis pendens* and related actions apply: C.J.J.A. 1982, Scheds 1 and 3C, Arts 21–23; and see note 13.2.11. Where the prior action is in a foreign country to which those conventions do not apply or another part of the U.K., the plea of *forum non conveniens* must be relied on to exclude jurisdiction: see para. (A)(3) above. In consistorial causes the plea of *lis alibi pendens* is not usually taken, the position being governed by para. 9 of Sched. 3 to the Domicile and Matrimonial Proceedings Act 1973 so that where proceedings are continuing in another court relating to the marriage or its validity the court may, after considering the balance of fairness, convenience and all other relevant factors, grant a sist of the Scottish cause pending the outcome of those proceedings: see, *e.g. Mitchell v. Mitchell* 1992 S.C. 372.

(a) The common law plea. There must be supporting averments: *Flannigan v. British Dyewood Co.* 1971 S.C. 110, 111 and 114 *per* Lord Fraser. There must be, when the plea is considered (*Flannigan*, above), (a) a prior action in dependence—after service of the summons and before the action is finally disposed of (including expenses) (*Aitken v. Dick* (1863) 1 M. 1038), and even if the action is asleep (*Denovan v. Cairns* (1845) 7 D. 378)—(b) in another court in Scotland (*Martin*, above) of competent jurisdiction, (c) between the same parties in the same legal capacities or interest (*Longmuir v. Longmuir* (1850) 12 D. 926; *Alston v. Alston's Trs* 1912 2 S.L.T. 22), (d) in which the same question is raised (*Wilson v. Dunlop, Bremner & Co. Ltd* 1921 1 S.L.T. 35). The plea is avoided by abandonment (*Laidlaw v. Smith* (1834) 12 S. 538; *McAuley v. Cowel* (1873) 1 R. 307) or disclaimer (*Alston*, above) of the prior cause. The plea is not available if the defender prorogates the jurisdiction (*Longmuir*, above).

(b) Where proceedings involving the same cause of action between the same parties are brought in the courts of different Contracting States to the 1968 Convention in Sched. 1, or the Lugano Convention in Sched. 3C, to the C.J.J.A. 1982, any court other than the court first seized of the proceedings shall at its own instance sist the proceedings until the jurisdiction of the court first seized is established: C.J.J.A. 1982, Scheds 1 and 3C, Art. 21(1). As the court has to examine jurisdiction itself (and particularly if decree in absence is sought), the court must know (*ex facie* of the summons) whether it has jurisdiction. Proceedings will have been brought in a court if the proceedings have commenced according to the procedural rules of that court (*Zelger v. Salinitri (No. 2)* [1984] E.C.R. 2397). In Scotland this is the date of execution of citation of the defender (Erskine, III.iv.3; *Alston v. Macdougall* (1887) 15 R. 78; *Smith v. Stewart & Co.* 1960 S.C. 329, 334 *per* L.P. Clyde; though in relation to the plea of *forum non conveniens* it has been affirmed that priority of process in terms of litiscontestation (when defences are lodged) is the normal test (*Argyllshire Weavers Ltd v. A. Macauley (Tweeds) Ltd* 1962 S.C. 388, 400 *per* L.P. Clyde)). The nature and factual basis of the claim must be the same. As well as the same cause of action and same parties, there must also be the same subject-matter: *Gubisch Maschinenfabrik v. Palumbo* [1987] E.C.R. 4861. Where the foreign proceedings are only for protective measures and do not concern the substantive issues, there may not be a cause of action which has arisen between the parties: *Bank of Scotland v. S.A. Banque Nationale de Paris* 1996 S.L.T. 103. Where jurisdiction of the first court is contested the second court may sist the cause before it rather than decline jurisdiction: C.J.J.A. 1982, Scheds 1 and 3C, Art. 21(2). Where the concurrent proceedings do not involve the same parties or cause of action they may yet be related actions: in the case of related actions the second court may sist the action before it (Scheds 1 and 3C, Art. 22(1)) or on the application of a party decline jurisdiction if the actions can be consolidated and there is jurisdiction over both actions in the first court (Scheds 1 and 3C, Art. 22(2)); "related actions" means actions so closely connected that it is expedient to hear and determine them together to avoid the risk of irreconcilable judgments (Scheds 1 and 3C, Art. 22(3)). Where more than one court has exclusive jurisdiction any court other than the court first seized shall decline jurisdiction: Scheds 1 and 3C, Art. 23. Art. 17 (prorogation) prevails over Arts 21 and 22: *Bank of Scotland*, above. For the application of the 1968 or Lugano Convention in Scheds 1 and 3C to the C.J.J.A. 1982, see note 13.2.12.

(A)(6) *No jurisdiction*: "The court having no jurisdiction [because (*state reason*)], the action should be dismissed." The short form "No jurisdiction" has been criticised: *Love v. Love* 1907 S.C. 728, 729 *per* Lord Dundas; *cf. Carter v. Allison* 1966 S.C. 257. For jurisdiction, see notes 13.2.7 to 13.2.14. The plea should be taken at the first opportunity; if not, and the defender first admits jurisdiction but subsequently seeks to take the plea, he may be taken as having consented to the jurisdiction of the court: *Clarke v. Fennoscandia Ltd (No.2)*, 10th March 2000, (2000 G.W.D. 11-377) (OH).

(A)(7) *No title to sue*: "The pursuer having no title to sue [*or* no interest] to sue [because (*state reason*)], the action should be dismissed." The ground of objection must be specifically averred: *North British Railway Co. v. Brown, Gordon & Co.* (1857) 19 D. 840. A plea of no title permits the defender to contend that title fails through lack of any interest: *Agnew v. Laughlan* 1948 S.C. 656, 661 *per* Lord Macintosh. This plea is not appropriate where the pursuer's title is the *de quo* of the action: *Luss Estates Co. v. B.P. Oil Grangemouth Refinery Ltd* 1981 S.L.T. 97. The plea is judged as at the time the summons was served: *Swanson v. Manson* 1907 S.C. 426, 430 *per* L.P. Dunedin. See also, note 13.2.2(c) (title and interest).

(A)(8) *Reference to arbitration*: "The parties having agreed to arbitration upon the subject-matter of the action, the action should be sisted pending such arbitration." This is the correct form of the plea: *Inverclyde (Mearns) Housing Society Ltd v. Lawrence Construction Co. Ltd* 1989 S.L.T. 815, 821F *per* Lord McCluskey. It must be established that a valid contract exists (*Ransohoff & Wissler v. Burrell* (1897) 25 R. 284) and that there is a dispute (*Mackay & Son v. Leven Police Commissioners* (1893) 20 R. 1093, 1102 *per* Lord Adam; *Allied Airways (Gander Dower) Ltd v. Secretary of State for Air* 1950 S.C. 249) to which the arbitration clause applies (*Crawford Brothers v. Commissioners of Northern Lighthouses* 1925 S.C.(H.L.) 22). The action is sisted rather than dismissed so that recourse can be made to the court where the arbitration breaks down, other questions arise or to enforce an arbitral award: *Hamlyn & Co. v. Talisker Distillery* (1894) 21 R.(H.L.) 21, 27 *per* Lord Watson.

The plea should be taken early in the proceedings and before the record is closed: *Halliburton Manufacturing and Services Ltd v. Bingham Blades & Partners* 1984 S.L.T. 388. Failure to observe the proper practice could constitute a very strong indication that the right had been waived and, in any event, delay in taking the plea could render that party liable for expenses abortively incurred: *Presslie v. Cochrane McGregor Group Ltd* 1996 S.L.T. 988.

(A)(9) *Relevancy and specification*: "The pursuer's averments [in respect of (*refer to averment attacked*)] being irrelevant *et separatim* lacking in specification, the action should be dismissed [*or* should not be remitted to probation]." The ground on which the relevancy or specification of the pleadings is attacked ought to be specified; although a general plea is common, and the specific plea directed to exclusion of averments from probation. Where the pursuer does not offer to amend and the plea would otherwise be successful, the action will be dismissed. Where the plea is directed to the exclusion of certain averments, the action is not dismissed and the plea seeks exclusion of those averments from probation.

(a) A plea to the relevancy is that even on the assumption that the pursuer's averments are true in fact, he cannot succeed in law in obtaining the decree he has concluded for. The onus is on the defender: *Jamieson v. Jamieson* 1952 S.C.(H.L.) 44, 50 *per* Lord Normand. The proper approach is to consider whether, on a fair reading and assuming them to be true, the pursuer's case is bound to fail: *Wislon v. Norwich Union Fire Insurance Society Ltd*, 6 June 1999, unreported. In deciding relevancy, the pursuer's averments are considered; but, where the pursuer admits an averment of the defender, that too will be considered: *Pringle v. Bremner and Stirling* (1867) 5 M.(H.L.) 55, 58 *per* Lord Chelmsford L.C. A reparation action for personal injuries will rarely be dismissed on relevancy: *Miller v. South of Scotland Electricity Board* 1958 S.C.(H.L.) 20, 33 *per* Lord Keith of Avonholm; *cf. Davie v. Edinburgh Corporation* 1977 S.L.T.(Notes) 5 and *Robb v. Dundee D.C.* 1980 S.L.T.(Notes) 91; *Kemp v. Secretary of State for Scotland* 1997 S.L.T. 1174. The ultimate test of relevancy is whether the material in question has a reasonably direct bearing on the subject under investigation; it being a matter of degree in each case (in which expediency has a part to play): *Strathmore Group Ltd v. Credit Lyonnais* 1994 S.L.T. 1023, 1031H *per* Lord Osborne. Where a case is of doubtful relevancy a proof before answer will be allowed. See further on relevancy, note 13.2.4.

(b) A plea relating to specification is usually combined with the relevancy plea. It is to the effect that the pursuer has not given fair notice of the case the defender has to meet; the matter must be looked at broadly to ascertain whether fair notice has been given: *McMenemy v. James Dougal & Sons Ltd* 1960 S.L.T.(Notes) 84 *per* Lord Guest. The ultimate test is one of fairness: *Maclean v. Forestry Commission* 1970 S.L.T. 265, 272 *per* Lord Wheatley. In the field of criminal law it has been held that lack of fair notice can only be a justifiable complaint if it results in material prejudice: *Lockhart v. National Coal Board* 1981 S.L.T. 161, 170. The plea is available where the fact not averred is in the defender's knowledge: *Macdonald v. Glasgow Western Hospital's Board of Management* 1954 S.C. 453, 465 *per* L.P. Cooper. In modern practice calls are sometimes made in pleadings on a pursuer for further specification: this will alert him to a defective case (*Gordon v. Davidson* (1864) 2 M. 758, 768 *per* L.J.-C. Inglis) which he may improve and prevent the defender from obtaining dismissal; but if the plea is properly drafted the pursuer may be alerted anyway. A call to make an averment which the pursuer does not need to do to make his case relevant is of no effect: *Bonnor v. Balfour Kilpatrick Ltd* 1974 S.C. 223, 227 *per* Lord Kincraig, and 228 *per* L.P. Emslie. A party is not bound to answer a call (*Gordon*, above); and a call is not an averment of fact and does not amount to a denial of the pursuer's averments (*Bonnor*, above).

(A)(10) *Time-bar (limitation of action)*: "The action, not having been commenced timeously in terms of [section [17] of the Prescription and Limitation (Scotland) Act 1973], should be dismissed." An action is commenced on the date the citation is served on the defender: *Miller v. National Coal Board* 1960 S.C. 376. The period of limitation runs to midnight on the same day at the end of the limitation period: *Cavers Parish Council v. Smailholm Parish Council* 1909 S.C. 195; Bell's Prin., para. 46 (note). The limitation periods for actions of personal injuries or death in the 1973 Act are subject to the discretion of the court, under s.19A of the Prescription and Limitation (Scotland) Act 1973 (inserted by s.23 of the Law Reform (Miscellaneous Provisions) (Scotland) Act 1980 and amended by the Prescription and Limitation (Scotland) Act 1984, Sched. 1, para. 8), where it is equitable to do so, to allow the pursuer to bring the action outwith the limitation period. The court has an unfettered discretion to be exercised on all the relevant circumstances: *Donald v. Rutherford* 1984 S.L.T. 70; *Forsyth v. A. F. Stoddard & Co. Ltd* 1985 S.L.T. 51. On relevant factors, see *Carson v. Howard Doris Ltd* 1981 S.C. 278; *Donald*, above; *Forsyth*, above; *Anderson v. City of Glasgow D.C.* 1987 S.L.T. 279; and see summary in *McLaren v. Harland and Wolff Ltd* 1991 S.L.T. 85, 87 *per* Lord Milligan. It is relevant that the pursuer has a right of action against his legal advisors for their negligence in failing to raise the action timeously: *Donald, Forsyth*, above. An action of reparation for failing to raise an action of reparation for personal injuries is not an action of reparation for personal injuries: *McGahie v. Union of Shop Distributive & Allied Workers* 1966 S.L.T. 74. A preliminary proof may be required to determine the question of time-bar or the discretion to override it: *Donald*, above.

(A)(11) *Personal bar*. "The pursuer being personally barred from (*state reason*), the action should be dismissed [*or where the plea relates only to some of the averments in a specified article of condescendence*, the averments in article (*specify*) of condescendence should not be remitted to probation]." This includes acquiescence, holding out, personal bar by representation or notice, and waiver. On acquiescence, see definition in *Cairncross v. Lorimer* (1860) 3 Macq. 827, 829 *per* Lord Campbell L.C. On personal bar by representation, see definition in *Gatty v. Maclaine* 1921 S.C.(H.L.) 1, 7 *per* Lord Birkenhead L.C. On waiver, see *e.g. Armia Ltd v. Daejan Developments Ltd* 1979 S.C.(H.L.) 56. This plea is usually so tied up with the merits that a proof before answer is allowed and is not disposed of at procedure roll or a preliminary proof.

(A)(12) *Mora*. This plea is usually regarded as a peremptory plea: see (B)(3) below. Where the plea is directed to seeking proof instead of jury trial it is a preliminary plea: *Hunter v. John Brown & Co.* 1961 S.C. 231.

(B) Pleas to the merits (peremptory pleas). These pleas are dependent on the facts and circumstances of each case. They should not simply be a negative form of the pursuer's pleas. Such a plea where successful results in absolvitor for the defender if it affects the whole cause: *Forrest v. Dunlop* (1875) 3 R. 15; *cf. Matuszczyk v. National Coal Board* 1955 S.C. 418. Such pleas include:

(B)(1) *General pleas*. Where the facts are in dispute—*e.g.* "The pursuer's averments, so far as material, being unfounded in fact, the defender should be assoilzied."; "In any event the sum sued for being excessive, decree should not be pronounced as concluded for."

(B)(2) *Compensation or set-off*: "The defender, being entitled to retain (*specify*) due to the pursuer and to set that sum off against sums due by the defender, should be assoilzied [*or* the pursuer is not entitled to decree as concluded for]." Under the Compensation Act 1592 compensation may be pleaded where one debt is to be set off against another debt of the same nature (see *Mycroft, Petr.* 1983 S.L.T. 342), the debts must be due at the same time (*Paul & Thain v. Royal Bank of Scotland* (1869) 7 M. 361; but not where one party is insolvent when there may be a balancing of accounts), both debts must be liquid (*Hamilton v. Wright* (1839) 2 D. 86; *Scottish North Eastern Railway Co. v. Napier* (1859) 21 D. 700 (a claim for damages is illiquid)) and there must be *concursus debiti et crediti* (Bell's *Comm.*, ii, 124; *Stuart v. Stuart* (1869) 7 M. 366; *Matthews v. Auld & Guild* (1874) 1 R. 1224 (not where debt due by third party to disclosed principal and debt due by agent to third party); *cf. Macgregor's Tr. v. Cox* (1883) 10 R. 1028, *National Bank of Scotland v. Dickie's Tr.* (1895) 22 R. 740). The plea must be pled before decree: 1592 Act. As a general rule the plea is excluded after decree (when separate proceedings must be raised: *Cuninghame v. Wilson*, Jan. 17, 1809, FC); but the general rule does not apply to a decree for expenses (*Fowler v. Brown* 1916 S.C. 597). On set-off in balancing accounts in bankruptcy, see McBryde on *Contract*, paras 22–75 to 22–88. On compensation and set-off in relation to the Crown, see Crown Proceedings Act 1947, s.35 as applied by s.50; and see note 25.1.7.

(B)(3) *Mora*: "The pursuer being barred by mora, taciturnity and acquiescence from insisting in this action, the defender should be assoilzied." There must be supporting averments of prejudice or acquiescence because delay short of prescription is not a defence unless the defender is prejudiced or the pursuer has acquiesced: *Halley v. Watt* 1956 S.C. 370, 374 *per* L.P. Clyde. The plea may be pleaded as a preliminary plea as a ground for proof instead of jury trial: *Hunter v. John Brown & Co.* 1961 S.C. 231.

(B)(4) *Prescription*. Pleas based on the negative prescriptions are peremptory pleas: *Munro v. Tod* (1829) 7 S. 648; *Alcock v. Easson* (1842) 5 D. 356. It is *pars judicis* to take a plea of prescription (but not of limitation).

(B)(5) "*Res judicata*." This short form is used. A more detailed form may be used: see *e.g. Anderson v. Wilson* 1978 S.C. 147, 148. The plea is that the substantial merits of the cause have already been decided by a court of competent jurisdiction in an action about the same subject-matter on the same grounds between the same parties or parties having the same interest: *Esso Petroleum Co. Ltd v. Law* 1956 S.C. 33, 38 *per* Lord Carmont. There must have been a proper judicial determination of the merits—*i.e.* a decree *in foro*: see, *e.g. Margrie Holdings Ltd v. City of Edinburgh D.C.* 1994 S.C. 1 (where case settled extrajudicially (in the Inner House) there is nothing decided). A decree in absence (*Esso Petroleum*, above; including one pronounced after an undefended consistorial proof: *Paterson v. Paterson* 1958 S.C. 141), unless it has become *in foro* under r. 19.1(7), or a decree of dismissal on the ground of irrelevancy without inquiry into the merits (*Gillespie v. Russel* (1859) 3 Macq. 757; *Menzies v. Menzies* (1893) 20 R.(H.L.) 108, 111 *per* Lord Watson), will not found the plea.

A decree of dismissal (without inquiry into the merits, fact or law, as on relevancy) means that the pursuer is entitled to bring a fresh action on the same grounds: see *Menzies*, above. It has been said that the word "dismiss" is used when it is open to a party to bring another action and "assoilzie" where it is not: *Stewart v. Greenock Harbour Trs* (1868) 6 M. 954, 958 *per* Lord Deas. See also *Waydale Ltd v. DHL Holdings (UK) Ltd.* 2000 S.C. 172 (Extra Div.) overruling Lord Hamilton at 1999 S.L.T. 631, 637C (who held that where dismissal on relevancy followed inquiry, another action on the same grounds could be excluded) and doubting *Johnston v. Standard Property Investment Co. Ltd* 1909 1 S.L.T 23. A decree after a compromise or settlement (*Young v. Young's Trs* 1957 S.C. 318) or a decree of consent (*Glasgow and South-Western Railway Co. v. Boyd & Forrest* 1918 S.C.(H.L.) 14, 26 *per* Lord Dunedin; *Hynds v. Hynds* 1966 S.C. 201, 202 *per* Lord Cameron) can found the plea. Scots law does not recognise the doctrine of issue estoppel known to English law: *Clink v. Speyside Distillery Co. Ltd* 1995 S.L.T. 1344.

The court must be a court of competent jurisdiction, which includes the sheriff court: *Murray v. Seath* 1939 S.L.T. 348; *Hynds,* above; as also a foreign court. The subject-matter of the actions must be identical: *Leith Dock Commissioners v. Miles* (1866) 4 M.(H.L.) 14, 19 *per* Lord Chelmsford; and see, *e.g. Dollar Land (Cumbernauld) Ltd v. CIN Properties Ltd* 1996 S.C. 331. The parties must be the same or have the same interest: *Ryan v. McBurnie* 1940 S.C. 173; an *actio popularis* decided against one member of the public is *res judicata* against all: *Potter v. Hamilton* (1870) 8 M. 1064; a decree *in rem* is *res judicata* against any other person litigating about the same matter: *Administrator of Austrian Property v. Von Lorang* 1926 S.C. 598, 620 *per* Lord Sands, approved 1927 S.C.(H.L.) 80, 88 *per* Viscount Haldane and p. 91 *per* Viscount Dunedin. The grounds of action in fact and law (the *media concludendi*) must be the same: see *Edinburgh & District Water Trs v. Clippens Oil Co.* (1899) 1 F. 859, 907 *per* L.P. Robertson; a new *medium concludendi* elides the plea (*Edinburgh & District Water Trs,* above; *Short's Tr. v. Chung (No. 2)* 1998 S.L.T. 200; aff'd, 1999 S.C. 471 (Extra Div.)) unless irrelevant (*Earl of Perth v. Lady Willoughby de Eresby's Trs* (1877) 5 R.(H.L.) 26) or met by the plea of competent and omitted. Whether there was identity of *media concludendi* depends on the pleadings and decision of the previous action and not antecedent rights or equities: *Edinburgh & District Water Trs,* above. A plea of *res noviter veniens ad notitiam* elides it: *Phosphate Sewage Co. v. Molleson* (1879) 6 R.(H.L.) 113, 117 *per* Lord Cairns L.C.; on *res noviter,* see *McCarroll v. McKinstery* 1924 S.C. 396, rev. in 1926 S.C.(H.L.) 1; *Maltman v. Tarmac Civil Engineering Ltd* 1967 S.C. 177; and see further note 39.1.1(5).

18.1.5 *Signing of defences.* Only counsel, other person having a right of audience or a party litigant may sign defences: r. 4.2(4). Where counsel or other person having a right of audience sign defences they are regarded as the drawer of them and answerable for what they contain: r. 4.2(8). For the definition of "counsel" and "other person having a right of audience", see r. 1.3(1) and note 1.3.4.

18.1.6 *"Subject to rule 46.6".* Where the preliminary act procedure is followed in an action arising out of the collision of ships, the defender does not have to lodge defences until after the envelopes containing the preliminary acts have been opened: r. 46.6(10).

18.1.7 *"within 7 days".* The period of 14 days has been reduced to seven days because the defender has a minimum notice of the action of 21 days (the period of notice), giving him at least four weeks in which to prepare defences. The date of calling is not counted in calculating the period; but the seventh day is included in the period. When the last day falls on a Saturday or Sunday or a public holiday on which the Office of Court is closed, the defences may be lodged on the next available day: r. 1.3(7). For office hours and holidays, see note 3.1.2. Note the power of the court to relieve a party from failure to comply with a rule, under which power defences may be received late: r. 2.1(1). There is no provision for prorogating the time for lodging defences: see r. 4.9.

Defences may be lodged on any day, Monday to Friday, and not just on a sederunt day.

18.1.8 *Day on which a summons has or may be called.* In session a summons may be called on a sederunt day (r. 13.13(3)(a)); the sederunt days are Tuesdays to Fridays (r. 10.2(1) and 10.3(1)). In vacation a summons may call on a calling day (r. 13.13(3)(b)), which will be one of the sederunt days in vacation of which notice has been given in the rolls at the beginning of the vacation that it is a calling day.

18.1.9 *Documents founded on or adopted.* Any document founded on or adopted as incorporated in the defences must be lodged as a production when the defences are lodged: r. 27.1(1)(b). For lodging of productions, see r. 4.5.

18.1.10 *Intimation to other parties.* On lodging defences, the defender must give written intimation, and send a copy of the defences, to every other party: r. 4.6(1). There must be a docquet on the back of the backing with the word "Intimated" as evidence of intimation required by r. 4.6. For methods of written intimation, see r. 16.9.

18.1.11 *Fee.* The court fee for lodging defences is payable at this stage. For fee, see Court of Session etc. Fees Order 1997, Table of Fees, Pt I, B, item 2 or 6 (consistorial) [S.I. 1997 No. 688, as amended, pp. **C** 1201 *et seq.*]. Certain persons are exempt from payment of fees: see 1997 Fees Order, art.5, substituted by S.S.I. 2002 No. 270. A fee exemption certificate must be lodged in process: see P.N. No.1 of 2002.

Where the defender is legally represented, the fee may be debited under the credit scheme introduced on 1st April 1976 by P.N. No. 4 of 1976 to the account (if one is kept or permitted) of the defender's agent by the court cashier, and an account will be rendered weekly by the court cashier's office to agents for all court fees due that week for immediate settlement. Party litigants, and agents not operating the scheme, must pay (by cash, cheque or postal order) at the time of lodging at the counter at the General Department.

Contesting jurisdiction

18.2.—(1) Where a defender seeks to contest the jurisdiction of the court, he may—

(a) lodge defences relating both to jurisdiction and the substantive issues of the action without submitting to the jurisdiction of the court; or

(b) lodge defences relating only to the question of jurisdiction in the first instance.

(2) Where a defender lodges defences under paragraph (1)(b) and is unsuccessful in contesting jurisdiction, the court shall allow the defender to amend his defences to defend on the substantive issues of the action within such period as the court thinks fit.

Deriv. RCS 1965, r. 83(e) inserted by SI 1986/1941

General note. Under Art. 18 of Scheds 1 (the 1968 Convention), 3C (Lugano Convention), r. **18.2.1** 13(2) of Sched.4 (allocation of jurisdiction in U.K.), and r. 7(2) of Sched.8 (jurisdiction of Scottish courts), to the C.J.J.A. 1982, and Art. 24 of the Brussels I Regulation (Council Regulation (EC) No. 44/2001) a defender does not submit to the jurisdiction of the court by contesting jurisdiction alone or at the same time as defending on the merits: see *Elefanten Schuh v. Jacqmain* [1981] E.C.R. 1671; *Rohr v. Ossberger* [1981] E.C.R. 2431. But, where the defender first admits jurisdiction and subsequently seeks to take a plea of jurisdiction, he may be taken as having consented to the jurisdiction of the court: *Clarke v. Fennoscandia Ltd (No.2)*, 10th March 2000, (2000 G.W.D. 11-377) (OH).

This rule extends to all actions, whether governed by the C.J.J.A. 1982 or not.

Where a defender does enter appearance without contesting jurisdiction he will be held to have submitted to the jurisdiction unless another court has exclusive jurisdiction (under the C.J.J.A. 1982).

A defender contesting jurisdiction may not obtain an order for inspection under s.1(1) of the Administration of Justice (Scotland) Act 1972 or other order relating to the substantive issues before the plea of no jurisdiction has been repelled (unless, of course, the court has been given the power to do so): *MT Group v. James Howden & Co. Ltd* 1993 S.L.T. 409.

Under s.27 of the C.J.J.A. 1982 the court has power to grant warrant for arrestment or inhibition where proceedings have been commenced, or interim interdict where proceedings are to be commenced, in another Brussels or Lugano Contracting State, a Brussels I Regulation State, or in England and Wales or Northern Ireland. Under s.28 of the 1982 Act, where proceedings have been or are likely to be brought in another Brussels or Lugano Contracting State, a Brussels I Regulation State, or in England and Wales or Northern Ireland in respect of a matter which is within the scope of Art. 1 of the the Brussels Regulation, the court may make an order under s.1 of the 1972 Act. S.24 of the 1982 Act provides that any power of a court in Scotland to grant protective measures pending the decision of any hearing applies to a case where the subject of the proceedings includes a question as to the jurisdiction of the court to entertain them. The court's power to grant the warrants or orders above-mentioned is extended by the Civil Jurisdiction and Judgments Act 1982 (Provisional and Protective Measures) (Scotland) Order 1997 [SI 1997/2780] as follows:— (a) anything mentioned in s.27 or 28 of the C.J.J.A. 1982 in relation to proceedings commenced otherwise than in a Brussels or Lugano Contracting State or proceedings whose subject-matter is not within the scope of the 1968 Brussels Convention; and (b) the granting of interim interdict under s.27(1)(c), or an order under s.1 of the 1972 Act by virtue of s.28, of the C.J.J.A. 1982 in relation to proceedings which are to be commenced otherwise than in a Brussels or Lugano Contracting State.

Answers

18.3.—(1) This rule applies to answers lodged to a petition, counterclaim, minute or note.

(2) Answers shall consist of—

(a) numbered answers corresponding to the paragraphs of the statement of facts in the writ to which they apply; and

(b) appropriate pleas-in-law.

(3) Answers may be lodged at any time within the period of notice specified in the interlocutor calling for answers.

Deriv. R.C.S. 1965, r. 196(*a*) (r. 18.3(3)) and r. 196(*b*) (r. 18.3(2))

General note. Notes 18.1.2 to 18.1.5 are in general relevant to this rule.   **18.3.1**

A person should disclose his private address in his answers and not an accommodation address: *Stein v. Stein* 1936 S.C. 268.

A person entering the process of a petition or note who is not at issue with the petitioner or noter does not, as a matter of practice, lodge answers but a minute (unless he seeks for himself an order of the court): r. 15.1 (applications by minute) does not apply because the minute in this case is not an application to the court.

Answers may be lodged by post by a Court of Session account holder or if accompanied by a cheque for the court fee for lodging: P.N. No. 4 of 1994, paras. 1, 2 and 8.

Form of answers. Notes 18.1.2 to 18.1.5 on defences are relevant to answers. Any interlocutor **18.3.2** allowing the answers to be lodged must be written or typed above the instance of the answers. On the requirement for the use of metric units of measurement in pleadings, see note 14.4.14.

"period of notice". This period is determined in accordance with rule 14.6 (period of notice for **18.3.3** answers) by virtue of r. 1.3(1) (definitions of "period of notice" and "writ").

Prorogation of time. The time for lodging answers may be prorogated: r. 4.9(2). The former **18.3.4** rule (R.C.S. 1965, r. 27(a)) stated that cause must be shown for an extension of time. The requirement to show cause has been omitted from the rule as it did not accord with current practice. It does not follow, however, that the court may not require cause to be shown in a particular case, as prorogation is in the discretion of the court.
 Application to lodge a document late must be made by motion to the court under r. 2.1(1) (relief for failure to comply with rules).

Documents founded on or adopted. Any document founded on or adopted as incorporated in **18.3.5** the answers must be lodged as a production when the defences are lodged: r. 27.1(1)(b). For lodging of productions, see r. 4.5.

Intimation to other parties. On lodging answers, the respondent or as the case may be, must **18.3.6** give written intimation, and send a copy of the answers, to every other party: r. 4.6(1). There must be a docquet on the back of the backing with the word "Intimated" as evidence of intimation required by r. 4.6. For methods of written intimation, see r. 16.9.

Fee. The court fee for lodging answers on first entering the cause is payable on lodging. For **18.3.7** fee, see Court of Session etc. Fees Order 1997, Table of Fees, Pt. I, B, item 2 or C, item 4 [S.I. 1997 No. 688, as amended, pp. C 1201 *et seq.*]. Certain persons are exempt from payment of fees: see 1997 Fees Order, art.5, substituted by S.S.I. 2002 No.270. A fee exemption certificate must be lodged in process: see P.N. No.1 of 2002.
 Where the party is legally represented, the fee may be debited under a credit scheme introduced on 1st April 1976 by P.N. No. 4 of 1976 to the account (if one is kept or permitted) of the agent by the court cashier, and an account will be rendered weekly by the court cashier's office to the agent for all court fees due that week for immediate settlement. Party litigants, and agents not operating the scheme, must pay (by cash, cheque or postal order) on each occasion a fee is due at the time of lodging at the counter at the appropriate department.
 No fee is payable for answers lodged other than answers by a person, who is not an originating party, on first entering the cause.

CHAPTER 19

DECREES IN ABSENCE

Decrees in absence
 19.1.—(1) This rule applies to any action other than an action in which the court may not grant decree without evidence.
 (2) Where a defender—
  (a) fails to enter appearance in accordance with rule 17.1(1), or
  (b) having entered appearance, fails to lodge defences in accordance with rule 18.1(2),
the pursuer may apply by motion for decree in absence against him.
 (3) A motion enrolled under paragraph (2) shall specify—
  (a) the decree sought; and
  (b) where appropriate, whether expenses are sought—
   (i) as taxed by the Auditor; or
   (ii) as elected by the pursuer under Part I of Chapter III of the Table of Fees in rule 42.16.
 (4) Where a motion has been enrolled under paragraph (2), the court shall grant decree in absence in terms of all or any of the conclusions of the summons—
  (a) subject to such restrictions, if any, as may be set out in a minute appended to the summons and signed by the pursuer;
  (b) if satisfied that it has jurisdiction;
  (c) if satisfied that the rules of service have been complied with; and
  (d) where the summons was served on the defender furth of Scotland, if satisfied about service on the defender—

(i) in a case to which the Civil Jurisdiction and Judgments Act 1982 applies, as required by Article 20(2) or (3) of the convention in Schedule 1 or 3C, or Article 20(2) of Schedule 4, to that Act, as the case may be;

(ii) in a case in which service has been executed on the defender under the Hague Convention on the Service Abroad of Judicial and Extrajudicial Documents in Civil or Commercial Matters dated 15th November 1965, as required by Article 15 of that convention; or

(iii) in a case in which service has been executed on the defender under a convention between the United Kingdom and the country in which service was executed, as required by the provisions of that convention.

(5) In an undefended action in which a defender is designed as resident or carrying on business furth of the United Kingdom and has no known solicitor in Scotland, the court shall, in the interlocutor granting decree in absence against him, supersede extract of that decree for such period beyond seven days as it thinks fit to allow for the number of days required in the ordinary course of post for the transmission of a letter from Edinburgh to the residence, registered office, other official address or place of business, as the case may be, of that defender and the transmission of an answer from there to Edinburgh.

(6) Where a copy of the summons has been served on the defender furth of the United Kingdom under rule 16.2 and decree in absence is pronounced against him as a result of his failure to enter appearance, a certified copy of the interlocutor granting decree shall be served on him forthwith by the pursuer.

(7) Where a decree in absence on which a charge may be made has been granted after personal service of a summons on the defender or after the defender has entered appearance, and—

(a) the decree has not been recalled,

(b) the decree has been extracted,

(c) a charge on the decree has not been brought under review by suspension, and

(d) 60 days have elapsed since the expiry of the charge,

that decree shall have effect as a decree *in foro contentioso*.

Deriv. R.C.S. 1965, r. 89(a)(part) amended by S.I. 1984 No. 472 (r. 19.1(1) and (2)), r. 89(aa) inserted by S.I. 1984 No. 472 (r. 19.1(4)), r. 89(b) and (c) substituted by S.I. 1986 No. 1941 (r. 19.1(5) and (6)), and r. 89(i) inserted by S.I. 1984 No. 472 and amended by S.I. 1986 No. 1941 (r. 19.1(7))

19.1.1   *General note.* A decree in absence is not a decree *in foro contentioso* (which is *res judicata* between the parties unless a decree of dismissal: *Forrest v. Dunlop* (1875) 3 R. 15) until the conditions in rule 19.1(7) are met (see note 19.1.14). It must be distinguished from a decree by default which at common law is a decree obtained after defences have been lodged (*i.e.* litiscontestation has taken place) where a party has failed to comply with a statutory provision, a rule of court or an order of the court and irrespective of the merits of the action: *cf.* r. 20.1. A decree in absence does not imply an admission by the defender of the pursuer's claim: *Mackintosh v. Smith and Lowe* (1864) 2 M. 1261 *per* L.P. McNeill, (1865) 3 M.(H.L.) 6.

It is pointed out in Macfadyen *et al* in Court of Session Practice, p. K/5 para. 11, that a motion for recall may be allowed late where there has been a straightforward mistake in failing to enter appearance or lodge defences (*cf.* note 19.2.2). Because of this, a prudent agent for a pursuer will refrain from seeking decree in absence if aware that a defender intends to resist the claim and will intimate his intention to seek decree in absence. In *Wallace v. Keltbray Plant Ltd*, 2006 S.L.T. 428 (OH) Lady Paton did not grant decree in absence for £5 million in an action of reparation under the new Chap. 43 procedure (the summons, therefore, containing no detailed averments of how the first defender would be liable); intimation was ordered on the first defender.

Causes in which court cannot grant decree without evidence. Decree in absence may not be **19.1.2**
obtained where the court cannot grant decree in an action without evidence. These actions are:
an action of proving the tenor (see r. 52.3), an action of divorce, separation, declarator of marriage, nullity of marriage, legitimacy, legitimation, illegitimacy, parentage or non-parentage
(Civil Evidence (Scotland) Act 1988, s. 8), an action of declarator of freedom and putting to
silence, an action of reduction of divorce (*Acutt v. Acutt* 1935 S.C. 525), an action of declarator
of death and dissolution of marriage (Presumption of Death (Scotland) Act 1977, s. 2(1)).

Where there are several defenders and only some enter appearance and lodge defences,
decree in absence against the other defenders may be refused *in hoc statu* if it would be inequitable to grant it and prejudicial to other defenders: *Morrison v. Somerville* (1860) 22 D. 1082;
Symington, Son & Co. Ltd v. Larne Shipping Co. Ltd 1921 2 S.L.T. 32.

Decrees in absence against the Crown. A decree in absence against the Crown is not oper- **19.1.3**
ative without leave of the court after notice (intimation) to the Crown: Crown Proceedings
Act 1947, s. 35(2)(*a*) as applied by s. 50; leave is applied for by motion (for which, see Chap.
23).

"fails to enter appearance". A defender must enter appearance within three days after the **19.1.4**
date on which the summons has called: r. 17.1(1).

"fails to lodge defences". A defender must lodge defences, generally, within seven days **19.1.5**
after the date on which the summons has called: 18.1(2).

Time to pay directions. Although not entering appearance a defender may have applied for **19.1.6**
a time to pay direction under s. 1(1) of the Debtors (Scotland) Act 1987 in an action against an
individual including a conclusion for the payment of any principal sum of money not exceeding £10,000. If the pursuer does not object to the application by the defender he must state
this in the motion for decree in absence. If he does object he must intimate the motion to the
defender and state the grounds of objection in Form 44.3; the motion will require the attendance of counsel or other person having a right of audience whether or not the defender
appears. See generally, r. 44.3.

"pursuer may apply by motion for decree". A pursuer must now enrol a motion which will **19.1.7**
appear in the Motion Roll (unstarred where appearance is not required; starred where an
explanation, and therefore appearance, is required). The undefended causes roll (created by
A.S. 14th October 1868 following provision for undefended causes on the Motion Roll in s. 22
of the C.S.A. 1868 which was repealed by the C.S.A. 1988, Sched. 2 and superseded by
R.C.S. 1965, r. 89(*a*)) has been abolished as that part of R.C.S. 1965, r. 89(*a*) has not been re-enacted. An undefended cause slip is no longer required. For motions, see Chap. 23. Note
what is required in a motion where the defender has applied for a time to pay direction: see
note 19.1.6 and r. 44.3.

Expenses. The practice applicable to defended causes is now applied to undefended actions **19.1.8**
whereby, when expenses are sought as taxed, two interlocutors will be pronounced, namely,
one for the principal conclusion and the other a decerniture for the expenses. Where the election is made for the inclusive fee in Pt. I of Chapter III of the Table of Fees in r. 42.16, the
sum elected to be charged is included in the interlocutor granting decree. The election is made
by a minute of election attached to the summons; r. 15.1 (applications by minute) does not
apply. A blank form of minute of election may be obtained from the Office of Court. The
inclusive fee for which the pursuer may elect is the fee current at the date of signeting and not
the fee current at the date of decree. Under r. 19.1(3)(*b*)(ii) the pursuer must indicate
whether expenses are sought as taxed or whether an election is to be made to charge the
inclusive fee.

Minute of restriction. R. 19.1(4)(*a*) is originally derived from s. 23 of the C.S.A. 1868 **19.1.9**
(repealed by A.S. (R.C.A. No. 8) (Miscellaneous) 1986 [S.I. 1986 No. 1937] and re-enacted
in R.C.S. 1965, r. 89(*aa*) by A.S. (R.C.A. No. 2) (Miscellaneous) 1984 [S.I. 1984 No. 472]).
Notwithstanding that the pursuer must enrol for the particular decree sought under
r. 19.1(3)(*a*), including any restriction of the conclusions, he must also append a minute of
restriction to the summons signed by the pursuer or his agent indicating the extent to which
any conclusions are restricted (*e.g.* by taking a decree for less than the sum sued for). The
purpose of this provision is so that the Extractor can see on the face of the summons to what
the conclusions have been restricted. The minute is appended by writing it immediately
after the conclusions of the summons or on a paper apart attached; r. 15.1 (applications by
minute) does not apply.

Where a solicitor sues for his professional fees, those fees will be taxed before he can obtain
a decree (see r. 42.7(1)(*b*)); a minute of restriction may be required for the taxed amount.

Court must be satisfied it has jurisdiction. Under Art. 20(1) of Scheds. 1, 3C and Sched. 4, **19.1.10**
and r. 8 of Sched. 8, to the C.J.J.A. 1982 the court must be satisfied that it has jurisdiction in

actions to which that Act applies where the defender does not enter appearance or it must declare at its own instance that it has no jurisdiction. As a general rule the court will be concerned in any action to confirm it has jurisdiction. Whether the court has jurisdiction is discoverable from the averments about jurisdiction (except prorogation unless agreed in advance) in the summons required by r. 13.2(4)(b). Notice also that under the C.J.J.A. 1982 where it appears to the court that a court in another country has exclusive jurisdiction, it must at its own instance decline jurisdiction: Art. 19 of Scheds. 1, 3C and Sched. 4, and r. 7 of Sched. 8, to the C.J.J.A. 1982. The former requirement (in R.C.S. 1965, r. 89(ac)) to state the ground of jurisdiction in the motion for decree is no longer required as it is considered unnecessary because the ground (except prorogation unless agreed in advance) is stated in the summons.

19.1.11   *Court must be satisfied about service.* This is established by the appropriate certificates of service, intimation and copies of any newspaper advertisements: see Chap. 16, Pt. I, on service.

Under Art. 20(2) of Scheds. 1, 3C and 4 to the C.J.J.A. 1982 the court must sist the cause so long as it has not been shown that the defender has been able to receive the summons in sufficient time to enable him to defend or that all necessary steps have been taken to effect service: "all necessary steps" means that all necessary approaches have been made to the competent authorities of the country in which the defender is domiciled to reach him in sufficient time (Jenard report on 1968 Convention, p. 40). Art. 20 does not apply where the defender's whereabouts are unknown.

Under Art. 15 of the Hague Convention on Service Abroad (Cmnd. 3986 (1969)) (which may also be used in a country to which the 1968 or Lugano Convention applies: Art. 20(3) of Scheds. 1 and 3C to the C.J.J.A. 1982) the court must be satisfied that service was executed by a method prescribed by the internal law of the country concerned or delivered by a method provided for under the convention in sufficient time to enable the defender to defend. Decree may be granted, however, even if no certificate of service or delivery has been received where the summons was transmitted by a method under the convention, six months have elapsed since the date of transmission and no certificate has been received even though every reasonable effort has been made to obtain it: the UK has made the necessary declaration to bring this provision into effect. Art. 15 does not apply where the whereabouts of the defender are unknown: Art. 1(2). For the countries to which the Hague Convention applies, see note 16.2.3.

In relation to any other civil procedure convention with a foreign country, regard will require to be had to its terms, if any, about the court's satisfaction about service. Where there is no convention, the court will be satisfied by any form of service under r. 16.2; it may not enquire whether, or require a certificate that, the form of service used is permitted by the laws of the country concerned, leaving it to the pursuer to take care to use a method which will enable him to enforce the decree there.

Service under any convention must also be a form of service permitted under r. 16.2 unless otherwise provided in an enactment: r. 16.2(1).

19.1.12   *Superseding extract.* The reason for superseding extract where the defender is designed as furth of the UK under r. 19.1(5) is to give the defender time after he has received notice of the decree under r. 19.1(6) to apply to recall the decree under r. 19.2(6) before the pursuer can extract the decree.

19.1.13   *Service of decree on defender furth of UK.* The purpose of this rule stems from Art. 47(1) of Sched. 1 to the C.J.J.A. 1982 which requires a judgment to have been served on the defender before an order for enforcement can be obtained in cases to which that Schedule applies. The provision is extended to all decrees in absence against defenders furth of the UK.

19.1.14   *Decree in absence as decree in foro.* R. 19.1(7) is derived from s. 24 of the C.S.A. 1868 (repealed by A.S. (R.C.A. No. 8) (Miscellaneous) 1986 [S.I. 1986 No. 1937] and re-enacted in R.C.S. 1965, r. 89(i) by A.S. (R.C.A. No. 2) (Miscellaneous) 1984 [S.I. 1984 No. 472]). A decree is not *res judicata* between the parties unless *in foro contentioso* (*i.e.* one pronounced after defences have been lodged): *Forrest v. Dunlop* (1875) 3 R. 15.

A decree in absence in an action of removing under s. 9 of the Land Tenure Reform (Scotland) Act 1974 is not challengeable in a question with onerous third parties in good faith when an extract has been recorded in the Register of Sasines: 1974 Act, s. 9(7). A decree in absence after personal service of the defender cannot be challenged after his death: *Blair v. Common Agent in Sale of Kinloch* (1789) Mor. 12196.

19.1.15   *Decree in absence where charge may be made.* A charge may only be made on a decree for payment of money: Debtors (Scotland) Act 1987, s. 100(2) (a charge on a decree *ad factum praestandum* is no longer competent).

"*60 days have elapsed*". The last day of the period of charge is not counted in calculating the period. **19.1.16**

"*decree in foro contentioso*". This is a decree pronounced in a cause after defences have been lodged. See note 19.1.4. **19.1.17**

Recall of decrees in absence

19.2.—(1) A decree in absence may not be reclaimed against.

(2) A defender may, not later than—

(a) 7 days after the date of a decree in absence against him, or

(b) the last day of the period for which extract of the decree has been superseded,

apply by motion for recall of the decree and to allow defences to be received.

(3) Where a defender enrols a motion under paragraph (2), he shall—

(a) at the same time lodge defences in process;

(b) have paid the sum of £25 to the pursuer; and

(c) lodge the receipt for that sum in process.

(4) On compliance by the defender with paragraphs (2) and (3), the court shall recall the decree against him and allow the defences to be received; and the action shall proceed as if the defences had been lodged timeously.

(5) Where a summons has been served on a defender furth of the United Kingdom under rule 16.2 and decree in absence has been pronounced against him as a result of his failure to enter appearance, the court may, on the motion of that defender, recall the decree and allow defences to be received if—

(a) without fault on his part, he did not have knowledge of the summons in sufficient time to defend;

(b) he has disclosed a *prima facie* defence to the action on the merits; and

(c) the motion is enrolled within a reasonable time after he had knowledge of the decree or in any event before the expiry of one year from the date of the decree;

and, where that decree is recalled, the action shall proceed as if the defences had been lodged timeously.

(6) On enrolling a motion under paragraph (5), the defender shall lodge defences in process.

(7) The recall of a decree under this rule shall be without prejudice to the validity of anything already done or transacted, of any contract made or obligation incurred, or of any appointment made or power granted, in or by virtue of that decree.

Deriv. R.C.S. 1965, r. 89(ab) inserted by S.I. 1984 No. 472 (r. 19.2(1)), r. 89(d) substituted by S.I. 1986 No. 1941 (r. 19.2(5)), r. 89(e) and (f) (r. 19.2(2), (3) and (4)), and r. 89(j) amended by S.I. 1986 No. 1941 (r. 19.2(7))

General note. R. 19.2(1)–(4) is derived in part from s. 23 of the C.S.A. 1868 (repealed by A.S. (R.C.A. No. 8) (Miscellaneous) 1986 [S.I. 1986 No. 1937]). **19.2.1**

Recall under r. 19.2(4) on payment of the fee in r. 19.2(3)(b) to the pursuer is granted as a matter of course.

A defender furth of the UK has an additional opportunity to seek to recall the decree under r. 19.2(5). The basis for the procedure under r. 19.2(5) where a summons has been served on a defender furth of the UK is Art. 16 of the Hague Convention on Service Abroad of Judicial and Extrajudicial Documents in Civil or Commercial Matters, 1965 (Cmnd. 3986 (1969)) which is applied in r. 19.2(5) to any country furth of the UK whether or not one to which the convention applies. The UK made a declaration in relation to Scotland under Art. 16 limiting the period within which application may be made for recall to one year and this is enshrined in r. 19.2(5)(c). Although such a defender has a year within which to seek recall, the decree may be extracted (under r. 7.1) by the pursuer in accordance with r. 19.1(5) and may become a decree *in foro* under r. 19.1(7). There is an identical provision to art. 16 in art. 19(4) of the Council Regulation (EC) No.1348/2000 on Service in the Member States of Judicial and Extra Judicial Documents in Civil and Commercial Matters.

In *Bank of Scotland v. Kunkel-Griffin*, 2nd November 2004, unreported, it was argued that the lack of reference in r. 19.2(5) to the provision in the Hague Convention and the Service Regulation to "knowledge of the judgment in sufficient time to appeal" meant that the rule was deficient and deprived the defender of a second bite at the cherry. Lord Emslie considered, *obiter*, that r.19.2(2)–(4) might be regarded as a legitimate equivalent of the appeal envisaged and perhaps broader and more readily available. Of course, the argument overlooks the fact that r. 19.2 is concerned with recalling decrees in absence (granted for failing to lodge a notice of intention to defend or defences) from which there is no appeal. If one can rely on lack of knowledge of the summons one does not need to rely on lack of knowledge of the judgment. The provision for lack of knowledge of the judgment in order to appeal is not a provision for a second bite at the cherry, but a provision for a different situation with which this rule is not concerned.

Recall does not affect the validity of things done or transacted, or appointments made, in or by virtue of the decree: r. 19.2(7).

An interlocutor on a motion to recall a decree in absence out of time, being in respect of an incidental matter of procedure, requires leave under r. 38.3(5): *Robertson v. Robertson's Exr.* 1991 S.C. 21.

It may be possible to reduce a decree in absence in an action of reduction. In such an action it is not necessary to aver exceptional circumstances (*contra* a decree *in foro*), but the whole circumstances must be looked at: *Sinclair v. Brown* (1837) 15 S. 770, 772; *Robertson's Exr v. Robertson* 1995 S.C. 23; *Nunn v. Nunn* 1997 S.L.T. 182.

19.2.2   *"not later than"*. The period has been reduced from 10 to seven days in which to seek recall. The date of the decree or the last day of the period of supersession of extract is not counted in calculating the period. Where the last day falls on a Saturday or Sunday or a public holiday on which the Office of Court is closed, the next available day is allowed: r. 1.3(7). For office hours and public holidays, see note 3.1.2.

In *Robertson v. Robertson's Trs.* 1991 S.L.T. 875 Lord Weir decided that the period within which a defender could seek to recall a decree in absence was peremptory and the general dispensing power in A.S. (Rules of Court, consolidation and amendment) 1965, para. 4 [S.I. 1965 No. 321], now r. 2.1, did not apply to R.C.S. 1965, r. 89(f) (now R.C.S. 1994, r. 19.2(2)). The decision may be doubted as the discretionary dispensing power in r. 2.1 is apparently applicable to every rule and there is no reason in principle why it should not apply to r. 19.2(2) in a proper case bearing in mind the defender has recourse to reduction or suspension. Lord Weir went on to say that if the dispensing power applied the case was not a proper one for exercising the power. Cf. *Graham v. John Tullis & Son (Plastics) Ltd (No. 1)* 1992 S.L.T. 507, 509J per L.P. Hope (the power extends to the time within which anything required or authorised to be done shall or may be made or done). In *Thomson v. Omal Ltd*, 1994 S.L.T. 705, Lord MacLean, not following *Robertson;* above, on competency indicated that it could not be said that the dispensing power could never be exercised in relation to R.C.S. 1965, r. 89(f), but because that provision contained its own dispensing power the general dispensing power would only be exercised in very exceptional circumstances. In *Semple Cochrane plc v. Hughes*, 2001 S.L.T. 1121 (OH) Lord Carloway followed *Thomson*, above, but did not agree with Lord MacLean that the general dispensing power in r. 2.1 was qualified by the words "in exceptional circumstances" where there was an express dispensing power.

In *Strain v. Byers*, 2005 S.C.L.R. 157, Lord McCluskey held (with hesitation on an unopposed motion) that the fact that the decree had been extracted, was no absolute bar to the application of r. 19.2 coupled with the discretionary power in r. 2.1.

19.2.3   *"motion"*. For motions, see Chap. 23.

19.2.4   *"paid the sum of £25"*. This sum is a modest penalty to include the cost of the pursuer's agent writing to his client to inform him of the motion, booking the interlocutor and the like. These items would not normally be recoverable on a party and party taxation.

19.2.5   *Lodging receipt for payment of £25*. It may not always be possible to lodge the receipt timeously: the pursuer or his agent may be remote from Edinburgh or it might not be possible to obtain a receipt if, *e.g.* the pursuer's agent has withdrawn from acting. In such circumstances the defender should include in his motion under r. 19.2(2) a motion under r. 2.1 to relieve him from the failure to comply with the requirement.

CHAPTER 20

DECREES BY DEFAULT

Decrees where party in default

20.1.–(1) Without prejudice to the power of the court to grant decree by default in other circumstances, where a party fails to attend before the Lord Ordinary on the calling of a cause—

    (a) on the By Order Roll,

(b) on the Procedure Roll,
(c) for a proof, or
(d) for jury trial,
that party shall be in default.

(2) Where a pursuer is in default under paragraph (1)(a), (c) or (d), the court may grant decree by default against him with expenses.

(3) Where a pursuer is in default under paragraph (1)(b), the court may grant decree of dismissal with expenses.

(4) Where a defender is in default under paragraph (1), the court may grant decree by default against him with expenses.

(5) Where a third party is in default under paragraph (1), the court may grant decree by default against him with expenses or make such finding or order as it thinks fit.

Deriv. R.C.S. 1965, r. 94(d) amended by S.I. 1991 No. 2483 (r. 20.1(1)(b), (3) and (4)).

General note. There are now stipulated, in this rule, four circumstances in which decree by **20.1.1** default may be granted; but this does not exclude the granting of such decree in other circumstances, a decree by default being one pronounced after defences have been lodged (*i.e.* litiscontestation has taken place) for failure to comply with a statute, rule of court or other enactment, or an order of the court: Maclaren on *Court of Session Practice*, p. 1094; Mackay's

Manual of Practice, p. 310; and see *e.g. Mackenzie v. Scott* (1861) 23 D. 1201 and *Forrest v. Dunlop* (1879) 3 R. 15. For this reason the words "without prejudice to the power of the court to grant decree by default in other circumstances" appear in r. 20.1(1). The power of the court to grant decree of dismissal for failure to lodge rather than decree by default (properly so-called) should be noted: r. 22.1(3) (open record) and r. 22.3(3) (closed record). Rule 20.1 applies to any cause, not merely actions; it appears in that group of Chapters applying to all causes and expressly applies to "a cause". See further, note 20.1.5.

A decree by default at common law is a decree *in foro contentioso* (*i.e.* one pronounced after defences have been lodged): Courts Act 1672, art. 19; *Forrest*, above. Under this rule, however, where a pursuer is in default under paragraph (1)(a) decree of absolvitor (a decree by default) may be granted even where defences have not been lodged, and where a pursuer is in default under paragraph (1)(b) decree of dismissal (not a decree *in foro*) may be granted. A decree *in foro* (unless a decree of dismissal) is *res judicata* between the parties: *Forrest*, above; and see note 18.1.4(B)(5) on *res judicata*.

The court has a discretion to grant decree of default under r. 20.1 where an agent has intimated that he has withdrawn from acting and the party is in default by failing to appear: *Munro & Miller (Pakistan) Ltd v. Wyvern Structures Ltd* 1996 S.L.T. 135, affirmed 1997 S.C. 1.

A decree by default is distinguished from a decree in absence, the principal distinction being that the latter is not at first a decree *in foro*: see r. 19.1(7) and notes 19.1.1 and 19.1.14.

Decree is obtained by motion. For motions, see Chap. 23.

Where the court grants decree by default under r. 20.1, there is no need to supersede extract if the court wishes to give the party in default time to reclaim because, under r. 38.9, the fact that an extract has been issued does not of itself preclude review: see *Munro & Miller (Pakistan) Ltd*, above, where the superseding of extract was commented on adversely by the First Division.

Where pursuer in default. Where the pursuer is in default, the appropriate decree is one of **20.1.2** absolvitor and is *res judicata* between the parties; unless the default is failure to appear at procedure roll when decree of dismissal is granted (r. 20.1(3)) which is not *res judicata* and does not preclude the pursuer from raising a fresh action (*Stewart v. Greenock Harbour Trs* (1868) 6 M. 954).

A decree of dismissal (without inquiry into the merits, fact or law, as on relevancy) means that the pursuer is entitled to bring a fresh action on the same grounds: see *Menzies*, above. It has been said that the word "dismiss" is used when it is open to a party to bring another action and "assoilzie" where it is not: *Stewart*, above, at p. 958 *per* Lord Deas. See also *Waydale Ltd v. DHL Holdings (UK) Ltd*, 2000 S.C. 172 (Extra Div.) overruling Lord Hamilton at 1999 S.L.T. 631, 637C (who held that where dismissal on relevancy followed inquiry, another action on the same grounds could be excluded) and doubting *Johnston v. Standard Property Investment Co. Ltd* 1909 1 S.L.T. 23.

In an undefended consistorial action where decree is refused after evidence the appropriate decree is one of dismissal (*Paterson v. Paterson* 1958 S.C. 141); and it may be that, in an undefended consistorial action where a pursuer is in default under this rule, the appropriate decree should always be dismissal and not absolvitor.

Where a pursuer fails to appear at a jury trial the defender has the option of seeking decree by default under this rule or obtaining a verdict in his favour without leading evidence under r. 37.5(b).

Where defender in default. Where a defender is in default, the appropriate decree is usually as **20.1.3** concluded for (a decree of condemnator).

Decree by default where agent withdraws. Where a party's agent has intimated that he has **20.1.3A** withdrawn from acting and that party fails to attend a proof, the court has a discretion whether to grant decree by default under r. 20.1 or to ordain that party under r. 30.2 to intimate whether he intends to proceed: *Munro & Miller (Pakistan) Ltd v. Wyvern Structures Ltd* 1996 S.L.T. 135, affirmed 1997 S.C. 1. Where an agent withdraws on the morning of the proof, an order under r. 30.2 would be more appropriate.

Reclaiming. A decree by default may be reclaimed against without leave within 21 days: **20.1.4** r. 38.3(2). The decree may be recalled on such conditions as to expenses or otherwise as the court thinks fit: r. 38.11(2). Where the decree was granted because of a failure to lodge a step of process or other document, the document must be lodged on or before the motion is enrolled for recall: r. 38.11(1). The usual condition being payment of expenses: see *Bedfordshire Loan Co. v. Russell* 1909 2 S.L.T. 481. Where the decree has not been reclaimed within that period, an action of reduction must be brought. The remedy of reduction is not available as of right, and while the court has power to award substantial justice, it will require a strong statement of facts to support an application: *Forrest v. Dunlop* (1875) 3 R. 15. (In relation to decrees by default pronounced in the sheriff court, the court has emphasised that the remedy is not available as of right, but is only available in exceptional circumstances as a means of avoiding injustice: *Adair v. Colville & Sons*, 1926 S.C. (H.C.) 51, 56 *per* Viscount Dunedin; *Kirkwood v. City of Glasgow Council*, 1988 S.L.T. 430, 431 per Lord Weir (OH); *Shaw v. Performing Right Society Ltd*, 9th July 2002, unreported (OH).) A decree by default in the Inner House may be set aside by consent (*Tough v. Smith* (1832) 10 S. 619), by appeal to the House of Lords or by an action of reduction.

20.1.5   *Petitions, notes and minutes.* The language of paras (2)–(5) of this rule is appropriate to actions. But a party to a petition or note may still be in default under r. 20.1(1). Confirmation of this is hardly necessary, having regard to the position of the rule and the reference to "a cause", but is to be found in *Thomson v. Rush*, 26th May 2000, (2000 G.W.D. 24-9030 (OH). In such a case an equivalent decree appropriate to the circumstances will be pronounced: *i.e.* a decree of refusal with expenses against a petitioner or noter in default under r. 20.1(1)(a), (c) or (d) or a decree of dismissal with expenses where the default is under r. 20.1(1)(b); where the respondent is in default the prayer of the petition or note will usually be granted. A decree of refusal of a petition is equivalent to a decree of absolvitor: *Luxmoore v. The Red Deer Commission* 1979 S.L.T.(Notes) 53.

In the case of a minute the decree will be the same as that for an action.

Chapter 21

Summary Decrees

Application of this Chapter
   21.1. This Chapter applies to any action other than—
   (a) a family action within the meaning of rule 49.1(1);
   (b) an action of multiplepoinding;
   (c) an action of proving the tenor; or
   (d) an action under the Presumption of Death (Scotland) Act 1977.

Deriv. RCS 1965, r. 89B(1) inserted by S.I. 1984 No. 499 and amended by S.I. 1990 No. 705

21.1.1   *General note.* Certain actions are excluded from those in which summary decree may be obtained. These are: (1) Those actions for which summary decree is not appropriate (certain family actions and actions of multiplepoinding: r. 21.1(a), (b) and (c)). (2) Actions in which decree cannot be granted without evidence: actions of divorce, separation or declarator of marriage, nullity of marriage, legitimacy, legitimation, illegitimacy, parentage or non-parentage (Civil Evidence (Scotland) Act 1988, s. 8; and r. 21.1(a) (which is wider than the Act because of (1) above)), an action of proving the tenor (r. 52.3) and an action under the Presumption of Death (Scotland) Act 1977 (1977 Act, s. 2(1)). Although an action of damages for personal injuries or the death of a person is not excluded, it will be uncommon for summary decree to be obtained in such an action: see *e.g. McManus v. Speirs Dick and Smith Ltd* 1989 S.L.T. 806; *Ross v. British Coal Corporation* 1990 S.L.T. 854; *cf. Campbell v. Golding* 1992 S.L.T. 889 (decree granted where defender, convicted of offence relating to accident, failed to aver that the accident had occurred without fault on his part); *Frew v. Field Packaging Scotland Ltd* 1994 S.L.T. 1193; *Struthers v. British Alcan Rolled Products Ltd* 1995 S.L.T. 142.

21.1.2   *"action".* Summary decree is only obtainable in an action. An action is a cause initiated by summons: C.S.A. 1988, s. 51.

Applications for summary decree
   21.2.—(1) Subject to paragraphs (2) to (5) of this rule, a pursuer may, at any time after a defender has lodged defences while the action is depending before the court, apply by motion for summary decree against that defender on the ground that there is no defence to the action, or a part of it, disclosed in the defences.
   (2) In applying for summary decree, the pursuer may move the court—
   (a) to grant decree in terms of all or any of the conclusions of the summons;
   (b) to pronounce an interlocutor sustaining or repelling a plea-in-law; or
   (c) to dispose of the whole or a part of the subject-matter of the action.
   (3) The pursuer shall—
   (a) intimate a motion under paragraph (1) by registered post or the first

class recorded delivery service to every other party not less than 14 days before the motion is enrolled; and
(b) on enrolling the motion, lodge in process—
  (i) a copy of each letter of intimation; and
  (ii) the Post Office receipt or certificate of posting in respect of each letter of intimation.
(4) On a motion under paragraph (1), the court may—
(a) if satisfied that there is no defence to the action disclosed or to any part of it to which the motion relates, grant the motion for summary decree in whole or in part, as the case may be; or
(b) ordain any party, or a partner, director, officer or office-bearer of, any party—
  (i) to produce any relevant document or article;
  (ii) to lodge an affidavit in support of any assertion of fact made in the pleadings or at the bar.
(5) Notwithstanding the refusal of all or a part of a motion for summary decree, a subsequent motion may be made where there has been a change of circumstances.

Deriv. RCS 1965, r. 89B(2) to (6) inserted by S.I. 1984 No. 499 (r. 21.2(1) to (5))

General note. Summary decree was first suggested by the principal annotator (N. Morrison **21.2.1** Q.C.) to the Rules Council in 1979 as a means of preventing defenders delaying meeting unanswerable claims. These rules were introduced by A.S. (R.C.A. No. 3) (Summary Decree and Other Amend-ments) 1984 [S.I. 1984 No. 499] after consultation with the Faculty of Advocates, the Law Society and the Joint Committee of Legal Societies of Midlothian; considerable use was made of draft rules prepared by a committee of the Faculty of Advocates. Formerly it was difficult to prevent a defender with no obvious defence delaying decree against him by putting the pursuer to his proof: the record could be closed early on the Adjustment Roll; or the pursuer could seek decree *de plano* at procedure roll where skeletal defences were irrelevant (*Ellon Castle Estates Ltd v. Macdonald* 1975 S.L.T. (Notes) 66; *Foxley v. Dunn* 1978 S.L.T. (Notes) 35), but these means were inadequate.

In *McAlinden v. Bearsden and Milngavie D.C.*, 26th March 1985, unreported, Lord McDonald said that the procedure for summary decree is intended to deal with the situation where there is no valid stateable defence but procedural technicalities are used to delay settlement of the claim; but that it is not intended to provide opportunity on the Motion Roll for legal debate appropriate to the Procedure Roll. See also *Frimokar (UK) Ltd v. Mobile Technical Plant (International) Ltd* 1990 S.L.T. 180, 181L *per* Lord Caplan; *Brunswick Bowling and Billiards Corporation v. Bedrock Bowl Ltd* 1991 S.L.T. 187, 189F *per* Lord Allanbridge.

The distinction between the tests for summary decree and in a procedure roll debate was explained by Lord Johnston in *First Fidelity Bank, N.A. v. Hudson*, 1995 G.W.D. 28–1499, unreported. In the latter, the court is required to focus on relevancy; in the former, although relevancy arguments are permissible, the court is only required to be satisfied that there is an issue to try at all.

Summary decree does not apply to attempting to enforce an out of court settlement which is not a decree following a joint minute: *Gallacher v. Morrison & MacDonald (Paisley) Ltd.*, May 30, 2003, 2003 G.W.D. 23–670 (OH), *aff'd* on appeal, at 33–924 unreported.

Chap. 21 is permissive rather than mandatory and where issues of fact are to be investigated at proof the court should be slow to deny probation to some other aspects of fact and breach of duty in relation to the same conduct: *Frew v. Field Packaging Scotland Ltd* 1994 S.L.T. 1193 (summary decree in fact granted in relation to the statutory case).

There is divergence of opinion in the Outer House, about whether the court has an inherent power to dismiss an action for want of insistence or prosecution where there has been excessive delay by a pursuer in proceeding with the action. There is no express power, as there is for

class recorded delivery service to every other party not less than 14 days before the motion is enrolled; and
(b) on enrolling the motion, lodge in process—
   (i) a copy of each letter of intimation; and
   (ii) the Post Office receipt or certificate of posting in respect of each letter of intimation.
(4) On a motion under paragraph (1), the court may—
(a) if satisfied that there is no defence to the action disclosed or to any part of it to which the motion relates, grant the motion for summary decree in whole or in part, as the case may be; or
(b) ordain any party, or a partner, director, officer or office-bearer of, any party—
   (i) to produce any relevant document or article;
   (ii) to lodge an affidavit in support of any assertion of fact made in the pleadings or at the bar.
(5) Notwithstanding the refusal of all or a part of a motion for summary decree, a subsequent motion may be made where there has been a change of circumstances.

Deriv. RCS 1965, r. 89B(2) to (6) inserted by S.I. 1984 No. 499 (r. 21.2(1) to (5))

General note. Summary decree was first suggested by the principal annotator (N. Morrison **21.2.1** Q.C.) to the Rules Council in 1979 as a means of preventing defenders delaying meeting unanswerable claims. These rules were introduced by A.S. (R.C.A. No. 3) (Summary Decree and Other Amend-ments) 1984 [S.I. 1984 No. 499] after consultation with the Faculty of Advocates, the Law Society and the Joint Committee of Legal Societies of Midlothian; considerable use was made of draft rules prepared by a committee of the Faculty of Advocates. Formerly it was difficult to prevent a defender with no obvious defence delaying decree against him by putting the pursuer to his proof: the record could be closed early on the Adjustment Roll; or the pursuer could seek decree *de plano* at procedure roll where skeletal defences were irrelevant (*Ellon Castle Estates Ltd v. Macdonald* 1975 S.L.T. (Notes) 66; *Foxley v. Dunn* 1978 S.L.T. (Notes) 35), but these means were inadequate. The background and application of summary decree is summarised by Lord Rodger of Earlsferry in *Henderson v. 3052775 Nova Scotia Ltd*, 2006 S.C. (H.L.) 85: See note 21.2.6 below.

In *McAlinden v. Bearsden and Milngavie D.C.*, 26th March 1985, unreported, Lord McDonald said that the procedure for summary decree is intended to deal with the situation where there is no valid stateable defence but procedural technicalities are used to delay settlement of the claim; but that it is not intended to provide opportunity on the Motion Roll for legal debate appropriate to the Procedure Roll. See also *Frimokar (UK) Ltd v. Mobile Technical Plant (International) Ltd* 1990 S.L.T. 180, 181L *per* Lord Caplan; *Brunswick Bowling and Billiards Corporation v. Bedrock Bowl Ltd* 1991 S.L.T. 187, 189F *per* Lord Allanbridge.

The distinction between the tests for summary decree and in a procedure roll debate was explained by Lord Johnston in *First Fidelity Bank, N.A. v. Hudson*, 1995 G.W.D. 28–1499, unreported. In the latter, the court is required to focus on relevancy; in the former, although relevancy arguments are permissible, the court is only required to be satisfied that there is an issue to try at all.

Summary decree does not apply to attempting to enforce an out of court settlement which is not a decree following a joint minute: *Gallacher v. Morrison & MacDonald (Paisley) Ltd.*, May 30, 2003, 2003 G.W.D. 23–670 (OH), *aff'd* on appeal, at 33–924 unreported.

Chap. 21 is permissive rather than mandatory and where issues of fact are to be investigated at proof the court should be slow to deny probation to some other aspects of fact and breach of duty in relation to the same conduct: *Frew v. Field Packaging Scotland Ltd* 1994 S.L.T. 1193 (summary decree in fact granted in relation to the statutory case).

There is divergence of opinion in the Outer House, about whether the court has an inherent power to dismiss an action for want of insistence or prosecution where there has been excessive delay by a pursuer in proceeding with the action. There is no express power, as there is for summary decree sought by a pursuer against a defender who has no defence (although the principal annotator considered proposing it when summary decree was introduced). In *McKie v. MacRae*, 2006 S.L.T. (OH), Lord Glennie held that the court has an inherent power to bring a case to an end where delay has caused prejudice to a defender, or put in jeopardy the possibility of a fair trial. He disagreed with Lady Smith in *Tonner v. Reiach & Hall*, 2005 S.L.T. 936, who held that there was no such power.

"summary decree". This means any of the interlocutors sought in r. 21.2(2): *cf.* observation in **21.2.2**

Brunswick Bowling and Billiards Corporation v. Bedrock Bowl Ltd 1991 S.L.T. 187 at 189F *per* Lord Allanbridge, although he may have overlooked the terms of R.C.S. 1965, r. 89B(3).

21.2.3   *"at any time after a defender has lodged defences"*. Where the defender does not enter appearance or fails to lodge defences, the pursuer can obtain decree in absence: r. 19.1. Although summary decree is usually sought soon after defences have been lodged, it may be sought at any time up to final decree (see note 21.2.5). In, *e.g. Struthers v. British Alcan Rolled Products Ltd* 1995 S.L.T. 142, summary decree was sought and granted after proof before answer was allowed.

21.2.4   *"apply by motion"*. For motions, see Chap. 23.

21.2.5   *"depending"*. A cause is depending from the time it is commenced (*i.e.* from the time an action is served) until final decree, whereas a cause is in dependence until final extract. For the meaning of commenced in an action, see note 13.4.4. For the meaning of final decree, see note 4.15.2(2). For the meaning of final extract, see note 7.1.2(2).

21.2.6   *No defence disclosed.* The approach to be adopted is summarised by Lord Rodger of Earlsferry in *Henderson v. 3052775 Nova Scotia Ltd,* 2006 S.C. (H.L.) 85, 90, para. [19]: The judge is entitled to proceed not merely on what is said in the defences, but on the basis of any facts which can be clarified, from documents, articles and affidavits, without trespassing on the role of the proof judge in resolving factual disputes after hearing the evidence; the judge can grant summary decree if he is satisfied, first, that there is no issue raised by the defender which can be properly resolved only at proof and, secondly, that, on the facts which have been clarified in this way, the defender has no defence to all, or any part, of the action; in other words, before he grants summary decree, the judge has to be satisfied that, even if the defender succeeds in proving the substance of his defence as it has been clarified, his case must fail; so, if the judge can say no more than that the defender is unlikely to succeed at proof, summary decree will not be appropriate: it is only appropriate where the judge can properly be satisfied on the available material that the defender is bound to fail and so there is nothing of relevance to be decided in a proof.

The court is entitled to look beyond the defences to see if there is a defence. It is proper to take account of a minute of amendment: *Robinson v. Thomson* 1987 S.L.T. 120 *per* Lord Cullen, *obiter*. The court is concerned not only to test the relevancy of the defence but to see if there is a genuine defence, and the defender must be able to satisfy the court at the time of the motion that a proper defence was likely to be available: *Frimokar (UK) Ltd v. Mobile Technical Plant (International) Ltd* 1990 S.L.T. 180, 181L *per* Lord Caplan.

The court must be satisfied there is no defence disclosed. It has been held in the Outer House that "satisfied" means the same as in a motion for interim payment of damages under r. 43.9(3)—*i.e.* more than probability but less than complete certainty is required to succeed: *Watson-Towers Ltd v. McPhail* 1986 S.L.T. 617; *Robinson v. Thomson,* 6th May 1986, unreported on this point. But in *Keppie v. The Marshall Food Group Ltd* 1997 S.L.T. 305, Lord Hamilton doubted that the test was the same as for interim damages. He did so on the ground that on a motion for summary decree the court was concerned with whether a defence was disclosed and not with forecasting the outcome of a proof; the consequence of a successful motion was to exclude the relation issue from inquiry. In *P. & M. Sinclair v. The Bamber Gray Partnership* 1987 S.C. 203, 206, Lord Prosser referred to the "near certainty" required to justify summary decree. That case was applied in *Wyman-Gordon Ltd v. Proclad International Ltd,* 2006 S.L.T. 390 (OH). Summary decree is not limited to those cases where there is no defence stated at all or the stated defence is plainly irrelevant; the court is not barred from pronouncing decree simply because the defender makes unspecific assertions which, if established, would provide a defence where the defender does not offer to prove it: *Rankin v. Reid* 1987 S.L.T. 352. In *Pope v. James McHugh Contracts Ltd,* 2006 S.L.T. 386 (OH), summary decree was granted, with hesitation, where there was no defence on the merits but contributory negligence, apportionment and quantum was raised, with proof restricted to those issues.

Where there is more than one defence to the action, summary decree cannot be obtained against a defence to part of the action if there remains a defence to the whole of the action: *Brunswick Bowling and Billiards Corporation v. Bedrock Bowl Ltd* 1991 S.L.T. 187.

Summary decree is not a substitute for full procedure roll discussion: *P. & M. Sinclair,* above, *per* Lord Prosser at p. 207. But questions of law or fact may be dealt with in a motion for summary decree; and the court should not refuse, however, to deal with the matter on the Motion Roll merely because it involves a question of law: see *e.g. Royal Bank of Scotland plc v. Dinwoodie* 1987 S.L.T. 82. In relation to a question of law, the test is whether it admits of a clear and obvious answer in favour of the pursuer: *Mackays Stores Ltd v. City Wall (Holdings) Ltd* 1989 S.L.T. 835, 836E *per* Lord McCluskey.

If the defences raise questions of fact it may be difficult to be satisfied that there is no defence: *Patterson & O'Grady v. Alu-Lite Windows Ltd,* 10th September 1985, unreported. A defender may not be entitled, however, to put a pursuer to proof on a question of fact where it is apparent it is part of a tactic to delay progress of the action: *Spink & Son Ltd v. McColl* 1992 S.L.T. 470, 473D *per* Temp. Judge Horsburgh, Q.C.

It is permissible for the court to have regard to documents or other material not referred to in the pleadings, not agreed, or not ordered to be produced under r. 21.2(4)(b): *Spink & Son Ltd*, above. Hence, summary decree procedure is more far reaching than a procedure roll hearing where relevancy is tested only by reference to pleadings and incorporated documents: *Spink & Son Ltd*, above, *per* Temp. Judge Horsburgh, Q.C. at p. 472K.

In *Henderson v. 3052775 Nova Scotia Ltd*, 2006 S.L.T. 489, 492 (HL), para. [19] it was held by the House of Lords that a judge considering summary decree is entitled to proceed, not merely on what is said in the defences, but on the basis of any facts which can be clarified from documents, articles and affidavits, without trespassing on the role of the proof judge; and he can grant summary decree if satisfied that (1) there is no issue raised by the defender which can be properly resolved only at proof and (2) on the facts which have been clarified, the defender has no defence at all to all, or part, of the action: in other words, before he grants summary decree he has to be satisfied that, even if the defender succeeds in proving the substance of his defence as clarified, his case *must* fail.

"document or article". By virtue of r. 1.3(1) "document" has an extended meaning as defined in **21.2.7** s.9 of the Civil Evidence (Scotland) Act 1988. The word "article" should cover any other material.

Order to produce a document or lodge an affidavit. A document can be ordered to be produced **21.2.8** only if it is known to be in existence and can be identified by the party seeking summary decree: *M. & I. Instruments v. Varsada*, 9th May 1985, unreported.

Affidavits enable the court to go behind the bald assertions in the pleadings to see whether there is anything to support the pleadings: *Rankin v. Reid* 1987 S.L.T. 352, 354C *per* Lord McCluskey. R.21.2(4)(b)(ii) clearly envisages that the court may proceed on the basis of affidavit evidence even in the face of a denial: *Ingram Coal Co. v. Nugent* 1991 S.L.T. 603.

"subsequent motion on a change of circumstances". There may be more than one subsequent **21.2.9** motion. A change of circumstances must involve an alteration in the pleadings or the coming to light of a document (or information) not previously available to the pursuer. On analogy with variation of periodical allowance in a divorce action, there is no "change of circumstances" where the original decision was based on a failure to put all the information then available to the court: *Stewart v. Stewart* 1987 S.L.T. 246.

Reclaiming. An interlocutor pronounced under this rule may be reclaimed against with leave **21.2.10** of the Lord Ordinary or vacation judge within 14 days after the date of the interlocutor on such conditions, if any, as he thinks fit: r. 38.4(1).

Leave to reclaim must be sought whether the summary decree is a final or interlocutory decision. The suggestion by Lord Coulsfield in *Maus Freres S.A. v. Hoon*, 24th November 1995, 1996 G.W.D. 10.594, that leave to reclaim is not required where the summary decree is a final interlocutor, would defeat the purpose of the rule intended by the rule's clear and unambiguous terms. Paragraph (2) of r. 38.3 which provides for reclaiming a final interlocutor without leave, is, by virtue of para.(1) of that rule, subject to r. 38.4(1) (leave to reclaim summary decree). It is submitted that Lord Coulsfield's opinion is wrong on this point. It is understood that subsequently the Inner House directed that leave was required.

Application of summary decree to counterclaims etc.

21.3.—(1) Where a defender has lodged a counterclaim—

   (a) he may apply by motion for summary decree against the pursuer on that counterclaim on the ground that there is no defence to the counterclaim, or a part of it, disclosed in the answers to it; and

   (b) paragraphs (2) to (5) of rule 21.2 shall, with the necessary modifications, apply to a motion by a defender under this paragraph as they apply to a motion by a pursuer under paragraph (1) of that rule.

(2) Where a defender or third party has made a claim against another defender or third party who has lodged defences or answers, as the case may be—

   (a) he may apply by motion for summary decree against that other defender or third party on the ground that there is no defence to his claim, or a part of it, disclosed in the defences or answers, as the case may be; and

   (b) paragraphs (2) to (5) of rule 21.2 shall, with the necessary modifications, apply to a motion by a defender or third party under this paragraph as they apply to a motion by a pursuer under paragraph (1) of that rule.

Deriv. R.C.S. 1965, r. 89B(7) (r. 21.3(1)) inserted by SI 1984/499

21.3.1   *General note.* The application of the procedure for summary decree has been extended to third party pleadings as well as to counterclaims.

CHAPTER 22

MAKING UP AND CLOSING RECORDS

Making up open record
[1,2] **22.1.**—(1) Subject to any other provision in these rules—
  (a) where defences have been lodged, the pursuer in an action shall, within 14 days after the date on which the time for lodging defences expired or on which the defences were lodged (whichever date was the earlier); or
  (b) where in a cause a party is ordered by the court to make up an open record he shall within such period as is specified by the court,
lodge two copies of the open record in process; and on being given, in accordance with rule 22.2(1), a date for the commencement of the adjustment period and a date on which it shall close, he shall forthwith send a copy of the open record (endorsed in pursuance of that rule) to every other party.
  (2) Where the pursuer, petitioner, noter or minuter, as the case may be, fails to comply with the requirements of paragraph (1), the defender or other party may apply by motion for decree of dismissal.

[NEXT TEXT PAGE IS C 173]

(3) An open record shall consist of the pleadings of the parties and the interlocutors pronounced in the cause.

Deriv. R.C.S. 1965, r. 90(1) (r. 22.1(1)), and r. 90(2) (r. 22.1(3)), both amended by S.I. 1980 No. 1144

---

[1] Rule 22.1 substituted by S.I. 1998 No. 890 (effective 21st April 1998).
[2] Rule 22.1 amended by S.S.I. 2007 No. 7, para. 2(2) (effective 26th February 2007).

General note. The only difference in substance between the new rule (substituted by A.S. **22.1.1** (R.C.S.A.) (Miscellaneous) 1998 [S.I. 1998 No. 890]) and the former rule is the requirement on the pursuer (or other party ordered to make up an open record) to send the copies of the record to the other parties, not within the time for lodging the two court copies in process, but "forthwith" after being given the date for the commencement of the adjustment period by the clerk of session under r. 22.2(1).

The open record is an important part of the system of pleading: it is on this document that adjustments are made. In the open record in an action, the summons is set out in full, but, after each article of condescendence there is set out the relative answer in the defences of each defender in turn; after the pursuer's pleas there are set out the pleas of the defender(s). At the end there are set out the interlocutors pronounced before the open record was made up. On the front sheet of the record, below the cause reference number and the names of the parties, there are set out the names of the parties' solicitors (including any correspondents); and between that and a repetition of the instance a space is left for any interlocutor ordering the open record (there will be none for an open record made up under this rule).

The date of signeting of the summons should be included at the end of the Address in the summons in the open record print: this is all too often omitted.

An open record may be ordered under r. 14.8 in an opposed petition (or note); it may also be ordered (though rarely) in a minute and answers: the principles about form and practice of open records in actions apply in such cases. An open record may also be ordered where a closed record is opened up. The interlocutor ordering the open record in these instances will specify the period within which the open record must be sent to other parties and lodged in process. On the lodging of answers by a third party after a third party notice has been served an open record has to be lodged by the defender introducing the third party: r. 26.7(1)(a).

"Subject to any other provision". The other provisions are: (a) r. 43.23 (no record in optional **22.1.2** procedure); (b) r. 46.6(12) (open record in ship collision cases); (c) r. 47.4 (no open record in commercial action); (d) r. 49.33(1) (no record in family actions); (e) r. 51.4(3) (open record where objections to action of multiplepoinding); and (f) r. 51.7(1) (open record where defences lodged to condescendence of the fund *in medio* in action of multiplepoinding).

"where defences have been lodged". An open record is only made up in an action where **22.1.3** defences have been lodged. Where there is only one defender the record must be lodged within 14 days after the date defences were lodged or the date on which the time for lodging defences has expired. Where there is more than one defender and at least one of them has lodged defences the record must be lodged within 14 days after the date on which the time for lodging defences has expired. Where defences are allowed to be lodged late (under r. 2.1) no motion is required when lodging an open record incorporating late defences unless the record is also late. Where defences have been allowed to be lodged late and there is already an open record, a further open record incorporating the defences must be lodged by the pursuer (subject to any order of the court in relation to expenses occasioned by the late defences).

"within fourteen days". The date from which the period is calculated is not counted. Where **22.1.4** the last day falls on a Saturday or Sunday or a public holiday on which the Office of Court is closed, the next available day is allowed: r. 1.3(7). For office hours and public holidays, see note 3.1.2. Note the power of the court to relieve a party from failure to comply with a rule: r. 2.1.

"send". This includes deliver: r. 1.3(1) (definition of "send"). **22.1.5**

"two copies of the open record". One copy of the record is the process copy, the other is for the **22.1.6** Keeper of the Rolls and is used to regulate the progress of the cause on the Adjustment Roll. The latter copy is passed to the Keeper at the close of business on a Friday.

It is advisable to take a third copy which can have the dates of the adjustment period stamped on it (see r. 22.2(1) and also note 22.1.11), which will be the same date as that stamped on the court copies.

Party ordered to make up open record. A party may be ordered to make up an open record in **22.1.7** an opposed petition or note under r. 14.8, in a minute and answers or where the closed record is opened up. The period within which the record is to be sent and lodged under r. 22.1(2) may be prorogated: r. 4.9(2).

22.1.8   *"motion"*. For motions, see Chap. 23.

22.1.9   *"decree of dismissal"*. The penalty for failure of a pursuer to lodge or send the copies of the open record is dismissal of the action. This is not a decree by default (properly so-called). A decree of dismissal in an action is not *res judicata* between the parties and the pursuer may bring a fresh action: *Stewart v. Greenock Harbour Trs* (1868) 6 M. 954. The position is the same for a petitioner, noter or minuter.

Where the party who fails to lodge the open record is not the pursuer (or petitioner, noter or minuter) decree of dismissal is not the appropriate decree, the appropriate decree being decree *de plano* in an action or a decree granting the prayer of a petition or note, as the case may be.

Dismissal is not common for late lodging and recourse may be had to the dispensing power in r.2.1. If there is no satisfactory or reasonable explanation for the failure to lodge timeously, the dispensing power may not be exercised and dismissal may be granted: see, *e.g, Maund v. Julia Arredamenti SpA*, 9th October 2001 (OH), 2001 G.W.D. 38–1417.

22.1.10   *"or other party"*. This would be the respondent in a petition or note.

22.1.11   *"on being given . . . a date for the commencement of the adjustment period . . . forthwith send"*. The pursuer (or other party ordered to make up an open record) must now send the four or more copies of the record to the other parties, not within the time for lodging the two court copies in process, but "forthwith" after being given the date for the commencement of the adjustment period by the clerk of session under r. 22.2(1).

The word "forthwith" was banished from the R.C.S. 1994 as originally enacted because it lacked enforceable precision. Unfortunately it appears to be making a comeback.

Adjustment
[1] **22.2.**—(1) On an open record being lodged in process the Assistant Clerk of Session shall endorse it, and the interlocutor sheet, with a stamp so as to show the date of lodging, a date on which the adjustment period shall commence (which shall be a date determined by the Deputy Principal Clerk of Session, being ordinarily the first Wednesday which occurs at least three days after the date of lodging but which may be such later date as the Deputy Principal Clerk of Session considers appropriate) and a date on which that period shall end and the record shall close (which shall be the date eight weeks after that on which the adjustment period commences); but this paragraph is without prejudice to paragraph (3).

(2) During the adjustment period parties may adjust their respective pleadings and shall intimate any such adjustments to one another.

(3) At any time during the adjustment period the court may, on the motion of any party, pronounce an interlocutor—
    (a) closing the record; or
    (b) extending the period of adjustment to such date as the court thinks fit, on which date the record shall close.

[2] (4) On enrolling a motion under paragraph (3), a party shall make available for use of the court a copy of the open record (endorsed in pursuance of paragraph (1)) showing the adjustments, if any, as at the date of enrolment.

(5) An endorsement in pursuance of paragraph (1) may be corrected or altered by the Deputy Principal Clerk of Session at any time before the date for the time being shown in the endorsement as the date on which the record shall close.

(6) An endorsement which cannot be corrected or altered under paragraph (5) may, on cause shown, be corrected by the Lord Ordinary at any time.

Deriv. R.C.S. 1965, r. 90(3) (r. 22.2(2)), r. 90A(2)(a) and (3) (r. 22.2(3) and (4)) and r. 90A(3) (r. 22.2(3) and (4)), all inserted by S.I. 1980 No. 1144

---

[1] R. 22.2 substituted by S.I. 1998 No. 890 (effective 21st April 1998).
[2] R. 22.2(4) amended by S.S.I. 1999 No. 109 (effective 29th October 1999).

General note. The Adjustment Roll has been abolished by A.S. (R.C.S.A.) (Miscellaneous)   **22.2.1**
1998 [S.I. 1998 No. 890]. That said, lists of causes at adjustment are being printed in the Rolls
under the heading "Adjustment Roll"! (Thus already do we find practice and the rules parting
company—one of the problems the R.C.S.1994 were designed to overcome.) The erroneously
titled Continued Adjustment Roll is, as a consequence, also abolished: there never was any
provision for such a roll, cases being properly continued on the Adjustment Roll.

The new provision in r. 22.2(1) is that the assistant clerk of session (no other clerk of session
has authority apparently) will stamp the two court copies of the open record, and the
interlocutor sheet, with the date of (a) lodging, (b) commencement of the adjustment period and
(c) the end of the adjustment period. The pattern for the commencement of adjustment will be
like this:—

Records lodged	Adjustment commenced	Notice in Rolls
Monday 16th	Wednesday 25th	Friday 27th
Tuesday 17th	Wednesday 25th	Friday 27th
Wednesday 18th	Wednesday 25th	Friday 27th
Thursday 19th	Wednesday 25th	Friday 27th
Friday 20th	Wednesday 25th	Friday 27th

This new provision does not apply where an open record has been lodged before 21st April
1998.

During the adjustment period when parties may adjust their respective pleadings as of right.

A defended action will always have a period of adjustment (when the open record is lodged)
unless sought to be dispensed with. Any other defended cause will only have an adjustment
period if an open record is ordered by the court to be made up.

A list of causes at adjustment is published in the rolls on the Wednesday on which the
interlocutors appointing those causes to that roll are pronounced with a note of the date to
which each case has been continued and the names of parties' agents: P.N. 27th March 1987.

"eight weeks". The eight-week period at adjustment includes any period in vacation. The   **22.2.2**
inclusion of vacation days in calculating the period was introduced by A.S. (R.C.A. No. 5)
(Miscellaneous) 1987 [S.I. 1987 No. 2160]. The adjustment period is, however, suspended during
any time the cause is sisted. Once the sist is recalled time starts to run again including any period
of adjustment before the sist. R.C.S. 1965, r. 90(7) which so provided in relation to a sist is not
re-enacted, not because the provision no longer applies but because the obvious does not need
to be stated.

Adjustment of pleadings. The pleadings which may be adjusted in an action are the   **22.2.3**
condescendence and pleas-in-law annexed to the summons, the answers and pleas-in-law in the
defences, the statement of facts and pleas-in-law in a counterclaim and the answers and pleas-in-
law to it and answers and pleas-in-law to a third party notice. In a petition, note or minute, the
statement of facts and any pleas-in-law, and any answers and pleas, may be adjusted if a period
of adjustment is allowed. The instance in a cause and the conclusions in a summons (or defences
in a family action) may not be adjusted; these may only be amended: Maclaren on *Court of
Session Practice*, p. 450. On amendment, see r. 24.1.

Adjustments are made by counsel or other person having a right of audience. The
adjustments are written on, or typed on papers apart attached to, a copy of the open record.
Each party prepares an intimation print incorporating the adjustments which is intimated to the
other parties. Different colours should be used for adjustments made at different times and e
date on which those adjustments were made should be marked on the back of the backing of the
open record.

The court has no control over what averments are made by adjustment except in relation to
scandalous and irrelevant averments: *C v. W* 1950 S.L.T. (Notes) 8 (an exception which may
now be doubted). A party may radically alter his pleadings during the adjustment period and
may include a case not previously pled and even a case which is pled outwith a statutory time-
limit. Thus a new case may be added outwith the triennium in s.17 of the Prescription and
Limitation (Scotland) Act 1973 at adjustment: *Sellars v. IMI Yorkshire Imperial Ltd* 1986 S.L.T.
629. On the rules in relation to amendment, see note 24.1.2.

"motion". For motions, see Chap. 23.   **22.2.4**

Closing record at any time. Formerly a record could not be closed before the end of four   **22.2.5**
weeks of the adjustment period. There was no obvious reason for such a restriction which was
removed when the RCS 1994 were enacted.

22.2.6   *Extended adjustment.* Under r. 22.2(3)(b) the adjustment period may be extended. The motion for continuation must be enrolled before the expiry of the previous period of adjustment.

Closing record

22.3.—[1] (1) The pursuer shall, within four weeks after the date on which the record is closed—

[3] (a) send a copy of the closed record to the defender and to every other party; and

(b) lodge three copies of the closed record in process,

and if there is failure to do so the defender or any other party may apply by motion for decree of dismissal.

[1] (2) A closed record shall consist of the pleadings of the parties and the interlocutors pronounced in the action or cause (endorsed in pursuance of rule 22.2(1)).

(3) [*Revoked by S.I. 1998 No. 890.*]

(4) [*Revoked by S.I. 1998 No. 890.*]

[2] (5) The pursuer shall, on lodging the copies of the closed record as required by paragraph (1)(b), enrol a motion craving the court—

(a) where parties have agreed on further procedure, of consent—

    (i) to appoint the cause to the Procedure Roll for consideration of all the preliminary pleas of parties or such of the pleas as may be specified;

    (ii) to allow to parties a preliminary proof on specified matters or in respect of specified pleas;

    (iii) to allow to parties a proof before answer of their respective averments under reservation of such preliminary pleas as may be specified;

    (iv) to allow a proof;

    (v) to allow issues for jury trial; or

    (vi) to make some other specified order; or

(b) where parties have been unable to agree on further procedure, to appoint the cause to the By Order (Adjustment) Roll.

(6) In a cause which is one of more than one cause arising out of the same cause of action, the court may, on or after pronouncing an interlocutor ordering further procedure under paragraph (5)—

(a) on the motion of a party to that cause, and

(b) after hearing parties to all those causes,

appoint that cause or any other of those causes to be the leading cause and to sist the other causes pending the determination of the leading cause.

(7) In this rule, "pursuer" includes petitioner, noter or minuter, as the case may be.

Deriv. R.C.S. 1965, r. 91(1) and (2) (r. 22.3(1) and (2)), r. 91(3) (r. 22.3(5)), r. 91(5) (r. 22.3(3)), and r. 91(6) (r. 22.3(6)), all substituted by S.I. 1982 No. 1825

---

[1] R. 22.3(1) and (2) substituted for r. 22.3(1) to (4) by S.I. 1998 No. 890 (effective 21st April 1998).

[2] R. 22.3(5) amended by S.I. 1998 No. 890 (effective 21st April 1998).

[3] Rule 22.3(1)(a) amended by S.S.I. 2007 No. 7, para. 2(4) (effective 26th February 2007).

22.3.1   *General note.* With the abolition of the Adjustment Roll and the automatic closing of the record by virtue of new r. 22.2(1) substituted by A.S. (R.C.S.A.) (Miscellaneous) 1998 [S.I. 1998 No. 890], there is no need for an interlocutor closing the record as previously provided in r. 22.3(1). The A.S. accordingly removes that provision and paras (2) to (4) of r. 22.3 are now paras (1) to (2).

The period for lodging a closed record has been reduced from five to four weeks.

On the closing of the record parties must discuss the future procedure in the cause with particular regard to the resolution of points at issue without recourse to a hearing on the Procedure Roll: P.N. No. 3 of 1991, para. 1(a). Whether this has been done may be taken into account by the court in dealing with expenses: P.N. No. 3 of 1991, para. 2.

"within four weeks". The date from which the period is calculated is not counted. Where the **22.3.2** last day falls on a Saturday or Sunday or a public holiday on which the Office of Court is closed, the next available day is allowed: r. 1.3(7). For office hours and public holidays, see note 3.1.2.

"send". This includes deliver: r. 1.3(1) (definition of "send").   **22.3.3**

"three copies of the closed record". One copy is the process copy, one is for the clerk of court **22.3.4** and the third is for the Keeper of the Rolls (used by him in preparing the lists of causes for fixing diets).

Failure to send or lodge closed record. The penalty for failure by a pursuer (or petitioner, noter **22.3.5** or minuter) to lodge or send the copies of the closed record is dismissal of the cause. This is not a decree by default (properly so-called) as the pursuer may, in the case of dismissal, raise fresh proceedings: *Stewart v. Greenock Harbour Trs* (1868) 6 M. 954; *Forrest v. Dunlop* (1875) 3 R. 15. A party may seek to lodge a closed record late under r. 2.1: *Carroll v. Glasgow Corporation* 1965 S.L.T. 95. For a recent case in which an action was dismissed, and late lodging under r.2.1 refused, see *Clements v. Macleod*, 28th April 2000, (2000 GWD 17-676) (OH).

Where the party who fails to lodge the closed record is not the pursuer (or petitioner, noter or minuter), decree of dismissal is not the appropriate decree, the appropriate decree being decree *de plano* in an action or a decree granting the prayer of a petition or note, as the case may be.

"Procedure Roll". The Procedure Roll is where preliminary pleas (*e.g.* objections to the **22.3.6** instance, objections to jurisdiction, and pleas against the action itself such as competency, relevancy and specification of pleadings) are debated and disposed of, including whether inquiry is to be by proof or jury trial or whether there should be a preliminary proof if these matters are not agreed by the parties. Irrelevant averments should be excluded at procedure roll: *Inglis v. National Bank of Scotland Ltd* 1909 S.C. 1038.

A cause will be appointed to the Procedure Roll where parties are agreed to send it there or, where parties are not so agreed, may be sent there when the case is heard (because of the lack of agreement) at the By Order (Adjustment) Roll: r. 22.3(5). The interlocutor appointing a cause to the Procedure Roll should state on whose motion the cause has been so appointed and in relation to which plea(s)-in-law. A party who has not moved for the cause to be sent to procedure roll is not precluded from debating a plea of his at a hearing on that roll: *McIntosh v. Cockburn & Co. Ltd* 1953 S.C. 88.

On the closing of the record parties must discuss the future procedure in the cause with particular regard to the resolution of points at issue without recourse to a hearing on the Procedure Roll: P.N. No. 3 of 1991, para. 1(a). Whether this has been done may be taken into account by the court in dealing with expenses: P.N. No. 3 of 1991, para. 2.

An action of damages for personal injuries will rarely be dismissed on procedure roll on the ground of irrelevancy: *Miller v. South of Scotland Electricity Board* 1958 S.C.(H.L.) 20, 33 *per* Lord Keith of Avonholm. It is not normally appropriate (except on a point of law only), where the welfare of children is involved, to dispose of an application for an order relating to parental rights solely on the pleadings, some kind of inquiry into the facts being necessary: *O v. O* 1995 S.C. 569.

"preliminary pleas". A preliminary plea is one which, if sustained, leads to the disposal of the **22.3.7** whole or part of the cause without inquiry into the merits of that part of the cause: see further note 18.1.4(A).

"preliminary proof". Since proof is defined as including a proof before answer (see r. 1.3(1)), a **22.3.8** preliminary proof before answer may be allowed.

A preliminary proof is not usually allowed in respect of the merits of a cause but is confined to where an issue is raised in the pleadings which could bar the action from proceeding. Such cases fall into three categories: (a) cases in which there is a plea of no jurisdiction (see *McLeod v. Tancred, Arrol & Co.* (1890) 17 R. 514; *Dallas & Co. v. McArdle* 1949 S.C. 481), (b) cases of bar either in connection with the discharge of a claim or in connection with a statutory bar in the way of an action, and (c) cases which raise questions of title: *Burroughs Machines Ltd v. George Davie, Crawford & Partners* 1976 S.L.T.(Notes) 35 *per* Lord Grieve. A preliminary proof will not be allowed on an issue which is so bound up with the merits that they cannot be separated: *McCafferty v. McCabe* (1898) 25 R. 872; *cf. A.B. v. C.D.* 1937 S.C. 408. A preliminary proof may be required to determine the question of time-bar or the discretion to override it under s.19A of the Prescription and Limitation (Scotland) Act 1973: *Donald v. Rutherford* 1984 S.L.T. 70.

Proof before answer and proof. Probation may be by (a) proof *prout de jure* (without **22.3.9** restriction as to method: see (1) below), (b) proof by writ or oath only (*e.g.* in loan, payment of money exceeding £100 Scots, obligations of relief, gratuitous obligations and innominate

contracts of unusual character)—abolished for causes commenced on or after 1st August 1995 by s.11 of the Requirements of Writing (Scotland) Act 1995, (c) proof *habili modo* (this means proof by the manner competent to each part of the case—see (2A) below), (d) proof before answer (see (2) below) or (e) jury trial (see note 28.1.8 and Chap. 37).

(1) *Proof.* It is sometimes thought that the allowance of proof excludes consideration of questions of relevancy after the proof, but the matter is not free from doubt: *cf.* Mackay's *Practice of the Court of Session*, ii, 18 (although questions of law may be argued after proof, the party against whom facts are proved can no longer maintain no proof should have been allowed and facts disregarded) and *Duke of Hamilton's Trs v. Woodside Coal Co.* (1897) 24 R. 294, 296 *per* Lord McLaren (an interlocutor allowing parties proof of their averments leaves all questions of relevancy open to further consideration). In that case Lord McLaren said the words "before answer" were unnecessary for reserving questions of law and relevancy although the proper time for raising questions of law is when the Lord Ordinary is moved to allow a proof. Where a proof has been allowed evidence may be led which might have been excluded on the ground of irrelevance or lack of specification if such a plea had been taken: *Barr v. Bain* (1896) 23 R. 1090. Objection cannot be taken to proving an averment admitted to probation: *Scott v. Cormack Heating Engineers Ltd* 1942 S.C. 159, 162 *per* L.P. Normand.

(2) *Proof before answer.* Proof before answer may be allowed where there is a plea to the relevancy of averments, questions of law and relevancy being reserved until the evidence has been led: *Robertson v. Murphy* (1867) 6 M. 114; *Fleming v. Eadie & Son* (1897) 25 R. 3, 5–6 *per* Lord Young; *Moore v. Stephen & Sons* 1954 S.C. 331, 336 *per* Lord Patrick. Proof before answer strictly means proof before answer as to relevancy, but not competency: *Fleming*, above; *Macvean v. Maclean* (1873) 11 M. 506 *per* Lord Neaves; *cf.* L.J.-C. Moncreiff at p. 509 who thought it might be as to either. A proof before answer reserving a plea to competency may be allowed where evidence on the merits may be relevant to the question of competency (*Shaw v. Renton & Fisher Ltd* 1977 S.L.T.(Notes) 60) or even, in exceptional circumstances, jurisdiction (*McLeod v. Tancred, Arrol & Co.* (1890) 17 R. 514) although it would be more usual to allow a preliminary proof on issues of competency or jurisdiction (see note 28.1.5). A proof before answer may be allowed where it cannot be said in advance whether the facts averred are sufficient to support the legal conclusions or the law cannot be stated until the facts are determined: *Moore*, above, at p. 335 *per* L.J.-C. Thomson and p. 336 *per* Lord Patrick.

The allowance of a proof before answer does not authorise the admission of incompetent evidence: *Robertson*, above; and, *e.g.* confidentiality is not waived even if a proof before answer was of consent: *Duke of Argyll v. Duchess of Argyll* 1962 S.C.(H.L.) 88, 93–94 *per* Lord Reid and 97–98 *per* Lord Guest.

In an action of damages for personal injuries involving only two parties it should seldom be necessary to allow a proof (before answer) with all pleas standing including time-bar. The court, however, must determine whether averments relating to s.19A of the 1973 Act are relevant and, if so, if there is sufficient agreement on the material facts, adjudicate on the issue on the basis of submissions, or if there is insufficient agreement allow a preliminary proof: *Clark v. McLean*, 1994 S.C. 410.

(2A) *Proof habili modo.* As mentioned at the beginning of this note, a proof *habili modo* means that proof is allowed by the manner competent to each part of the case, *e.g.*, where parts of the cause may be proved *prout de jure* (according to law) and other parts are restricted. The judge rules on the admissibility of evidence with respect to a restricted part at the proof: *Clark's Exrx v. Brown* 1935 S.C. 110. Objection should be taken to the competency of a particular form of evidence at the time it is adduced: *Royal Bank of Scotland plc v. Malcolm*, (No. 2) 1999 S.C.L.R. 854. The judge may rule on it then or, more commonly, reserve consideration of it until the conclusion of the proof: *Gill v. Gill* 1907 S.C. 532; *Jackson v. Ogilvie's Exr* 1935 S.C. 154.

(3) *Interlocutors.* The interlocutor allowing probation will specify the nature of probation allowed.

(a) In relation to proof (at large) the possibilities are: (i) "allows to parties a proof of their respective averments on record" where each party makes averments, enabling each to lead evidence in support of his own case; (ii) "allows the pursuer a proof of his own averments and to the defender a conjunct probation" where the defender only denies the pursuer's averments, the conjunct probation permitting him to contradict the pursuer's case; and (iii) "allows the defender a proof of his averments and to the pursuer a conjunct probation" where the defender admits the pursuer's claim but makes counter-averments.

(b) In relation to a proof before answer the interlocutor is "allows to parties a proof before answer of their respective averments on record; appoints said proof to proceed on the day of 19 at 10 o'clock forenoon and grants diligence for citing witnesses and havers".

(c) In relation to jury trial the interlocutor is "approves of the proposed issue [and counter-issue] No(s). [and] of process and allows them as now authenticated to be the issue [and counter-issue] for the trial of the cause; appoints the said issue [and counter-issue] to be tried by jury on   the   day of   19 at 10 o'clock forenoon; authorises and appoints a jury to be summoned for that purpose in common form; grants warrant for citing witnesses and havers".

(d) In relation to proof by writ or oath the interlocutor is "allows the cause to proceed by writ or oath of the defender; appoints said proof to proceed on   the   day of   19 at 10 o'clock forenoon and grants diligence for citing the defender".

(e) In relation to proof *habili modo* the interlocutor is "allows to parties a proof *habili modo* of their averments on record; appoints said proof to proceed on   the   day of   19 at 10 o'clock forenoon and grants diligence for citing witnesses and havers".

(f) In relation to a preliminary proof the interlocutor is "allows a preliminary proof restricted solely to (*nature of proof or averments to go to proof*); appoints said proof to proceed on   the   day of   19 at 10 o'clock forenoon and grants diligence for citing witnesses and havers".

22.3.10   *"issues for jury trial".* Issues (and counter-issues) are the concise statements of the questions of fact to be answered by the jury: Bell's *Dictionary*. On the procedure for lodging issues, see r. 37.1.

22.3.11   *Proof or jury trial.* Certain causes, the "enumerated causes", must be sent to jury trial unless the parties otherwise agree or special cause is shown: C.S.A. 1988, s.9(b). The statutory provision is not modified by r. 28.1: *Graham v. Paterson & Son Ltd* 1938 S.C. 119. It has been held that, where the pursuer claims provisional damages under s.12 of the Administration of Justice (Scotland) Act 1982, Parliament has by implication deprived the pursuer of jury trial: *Potter v. McCulloch* 1987 S.L.T. 308, 311L *per* Lord Weir, although he also found special cause existed. It might be unwise, however, to rely on exclusion by implication: see note 28.1.8(B) (Special cause) and *McFadyen v. Crudens Ltd* 1972 S.L.T.(Notes) 62 *per* L.P. Emslie; *cf. Winchester v. Ramsay* 1966 S.C. 41 (effect of third party notice).

The court may allow jury trial in a cause other than an enumerated cause: *e.g. Fletcher v. Lord Advocate* 1923 S.C. 27; *Blount v. Watt* 1953 S.L.T.(Notes) 39. In this case the court has an unfettered discretion, although it may require a special reason (cause) to send a case which is not an enumerated cause to jury trial. According to present-day practice proof before a judge is the normal and convenient method of inquiry in actions which are not appropriated by statute to trial by jury: *Blount*, above, *per* Lord Guthrie at p. 40. The enumerated causes are: (a) an action of damages for personal injuries; (b) an action for libel or defamation; (c) an action founded on delinquency or quasi-delinquency where the conclusion is for damages only and expenses; and (d) an action of reduction on the ground of incapacity, essential error, or force and fear: C.S.A. 1988, s.11. The longer list in s.28 of the C.S.A. 1825 was replaced by this shorter list in the C.S.A. 1988 because none of the others had been sent to jury trial in living memory. S.49 of the C.S.A. 1850 had allowed proof on commission as an alternative in the enumerated causes except cases of libel, nuisance or damages; s.4 of the Evidence (Scotland) Act 1866 introduced the alternative of proof to jury trial where parties consented or special cause was shown (both these provisions are repealed by the C.S.A. 1988, Sched. 2).

A proof may, after amendment, be recalled and the cause sent for jury trial (*Higgins v. Burton* 1968 S.L.T.(Notes) 14); and, after amendment, allowance of issues recalled and a proof allowed (*Nicol v. McIntosh* 1987 S.L.T. 104 (*obiter*)).

For a more detailed discussion of the question of proof or jury trial, see note 28.1.8.

22.3.12   *By Order (Adjustment) Roll.* This roll generally involves a purely formal hearing where parties are not agreed as to the next step in procedure. The roll is of little value because where parties are not agreed about the next step at the hearing on this roll the cause will be sent to procedure roll. A party may not consent to the further procedure under r. 22.3(5)(a) if he seeks to have the other party lodge a note of argument for a procedure roll discussion (see r. 22.4) and that party does not agree. Should parties agree further procedure after a cause has been appointed to the By Order (Adjustment) Roll, a motion may be enrolled by any party of consent craving the court to make an order under r. 22.3(5)(a)(i)–(iv).

Where a By Order (Adjustment) Roll hearing occurs because a party has not intimated his wishes earlier and the other party would have agreed to the procedure proposed, thus obviating the need for the hearing, the court may award the expenses of that hearing to that other party.

22.3.13   *"leading cause".* It is possible to appoint one of a number of causes arising out of the same cause of action to be the leading cause and sist the others: r. 22.3(6). This procedure is infrequently used (similarly, conjunction); it is possible, administratively, to arrange for proofs of causes to be heard together. It is not essential to make the evidence in the leading cause the evidence in the other causes. The words "same cause of action" in r. 22.3(6) probably mean that the nature and factual basis of the causes must be the same.

In *Anderson v. The Braer Corporation* 1996 S.L.T. 779, Lord Gill decided that as r. 22.3(6) applies after the record has closed, he was precluded from exercising any discretion to sist a case and appoint a leading case before the record had closed. If he was wrong, he concluded that it was inappropriate to sist a number of actions and appoint leading actions, because (a) the time to decide the matter was when the issues of fact and law had been defined in the pleadings (*i.e.* when the record has closed), (b) it must be clear that the actions must arise out of the same cause of action, (c) there must be a clear and concise question of fact or law, and (d) the decisions in the leading action should resolve issues to reduce the time, effort and expense incurred overall, especially where there was no agreement that the decisions would be regarded as decisions of questions in other cases.

Reclaiming. An interlocutor allowing or refusing proof or proof before answer, jury trial, **22.3.14** limiting the mode of proof or adjusting issues, may be reclaimed against without leave within 14 days of the interlocutor being pronounced: r. 38.3(4).

Although an interlocutor of the Lord Ordinary is final in the Outer House (C.S.A. 1988, s. 18), a subsequent amendment of pleadings may have the result that a prior interlocutor as to the mode of inquiry can be regarded as superseded and the Lord Ordinary can consider the mode of inquiry of new without the prior interlocutor having to be reclaimed: *Bendex v. James Donaldson & Sons Ltd* 1990 S.C. 259; *Gillon v. Gillon* (No. 2) 1994 S.C. 162, 165F *per* L.P. Hope.

Fee. A court fee is payable on lodging a closed record or when the mode of inquiry is **22.3.15** determined. For fee, see Court of Session etc. Fees Order 1997, Table of Fees, Pt I, B, item 14 or C, item 11 [S.I. 1997 No. 688, as amended, pp. C1201 *et seq.*]. A court fee is also payable for fixing a proof: Court of Session etc. Fees Order 1997, Table of Fees, Pt I, B, item 15 or C, item 12. Certain persons are exempt from payment of fees: see 1997 Fees Order, art.5, substituted by S.S.I. 2002 No. 270. A fee exemption certificate must be lodged in process: see P.N. No.1 of 2002.

Where the party is legally represented, the fee may be debited under a credit scheme introduced on 1st April 1976 by P.N. No. 4 of 1976 to the account (if one is kept or permitted) of the agent by the court cashier, and an account will be rendered weekly by the court cashier's office to the agent for all court fees due that week for immediate settlement. Party litigants, and agents not operating the scheme, must pay (by cash, cheque or postal order) on each occasion a fee is due at the time of lodging at the counter at the appropriate department.

Notes of argument

[1] **22.4.**—(1) Where a cause has been appointed to the Procedure Roll, a party seeking to have a preliminary plea sustained shall—

(a) lodge in process a concise note of argument consisting of numbered paragraphs stating the grounds on which he proposes to submit that the preliminary plea should be sustained,

(b) lodge a copy of the note with the Keeper of the Rolls, and

(c) send a copy of the note to every other party.

(2) The note shall be lodged and sent in accordance with paragraph (1) within 28 days after the date of the interlocutor appointing the cause to the Procedure Roll unless the court, at its own instance or on the motion of a party, orders that the note be lodged and sent within a different period.

---

[1] R.22.4 substituted by S.S.I. 2004 No. 331 (effective 6th August 2004).

General note. This is a new provision giving the court a discretionary power at its own **22.4.1** instance or on the motion of a party to order a note of argument in any cause appointed to the Procedure Roll whether or not it has been on the Adjustment Roll or whether or not a record is required. An infelicitously drafted P.N. No. 4 of 1997 sought to provide a mandatory requirement for notes of argument. Furthermore, it did not indicate whether it superseded the requirement in para. 1(b) of P.N. No. 3 of 1991 to inform an opponent of the nature of the proposal argument at the earliest opportunity. The confusion and inconsistency between the rule and the P.N.s has recently been made by Lord Osborne, without reference or acknowledgement to the comments in this note up to Release 79 (January 2005) in *Fairbarn v. Vayro,* 2001 S.L.T. 1167.

This new rule sorts out the problem. It is now mandatory to lodge a note of argument in process, send a copy to the Keeper and to every other party after the interlocutor appointing the cause to the Procedure Roll. The only discretion is that the court may change the period of 28 days in which to do this: r. 22.4(2).

Special provision for notes of argument is made in the following causes: (a) commercial actions (r. 47.12(1)(d)); and (b) causes relating to intellectual property (r. 55.3(4)(b)).

A copy of the note of argument must also be sent to the Keeper of the Rolls: P.N. No. 6 of 1997.

"Procedure Roll". A cause is appointed to the Procedure Roll under r. 22.3(5) (where a record **22.4.2** is closed) or r. 14.8 (procedure where answers lodged in a petition), r. 15.1(5) (further procedure in minutes) or r. 15.2(3) (application of r. 14.8 to applications by note). A cause is so appointed where there are preliminary pleas (see note 22.3.6) to be argued. For Procedure Roll, see Chap. 28.

"note of argument". The note of argument does not require to be signed. R.15.2 (applications **22.4.3** by note) does not apply because a note of argument is not an application to the court.

A note of argument should set out the basis of the argument including any relevant authority but need not do so in detail.

The court may order different periods for lodging the note in process and sending a copy of it to the other parties concerned (not every party will necessarily be concerned with the plea).

A note of argument lodged in process must be backed and comply with r. 4.1(3) and (4). It need not be signed. It may be lodged by post: P.N. No. 4 of 1994, paras. 1 and 8.

"preliminary plea". See note 22.3.6.   **22.4.4**

"sent". This includes deliver: r. 1.3(1) (definition of "send").   **22.4.5**

"within 28 days after". The date from which the period is calculated is not counted.   **22.4.6**

"lodge in process". On lodging steps of process, see rr. 4.4–4.6.   **22.4.7**

CHAPTER 23

MOTIONS

Interpretation of this Chapter
23.1. In this Chapter, unless the context otherwise requires, "party" includes any person entitled under these Rules to enrol a motion or to whom intimation of a motion is required to be made by these Rules or the court.

General note. Persons entitled to enrol motions are generally only parties to the cause, but **23.1.1** there are exceptions: *e.g.* any person having an interest may apply by motion to the court for the loosing, restriction or recall of an arrestment or the recall of an inhibition (r. 13.10(1)) or to move arrested property (r. 13.11(1)) or a person seeking leave to be sisted as a party.

Enrolment of motions
23.2.—(1) A motion by a party may be—
 (a) made orally at the bar with leave of the court during any hearing of a cause; or
 (b) enrolled in the process of the cause to which it relates in accordance with paragraph (2).
(2) A motion may be enrolled—
 (a) by lodging it in Form 23.2, with any document which requires to be lodged with or which accompanies the motion, at the appropriate department of the Office of Court during its normal office hours;
 (b) subject to paragraph (3), by posting it in Form 23.2, with any document which requires to be lodged with or which accompanies the motion, to the appropriate department of the Office of Court; or
 (c) subject to paragraph (4), by sending it by facsimile transmission in Form 23.2, with any document which requires to be lodged with or which accompanies the motion, to the appropriate department of the Office of Court.
(3) A motion may not be enrolled under paragraph (2)(b) where a fee is payable with that motion unless—
 (a) the motion is enrolled by an agent who has a Court of Session account; or
 (b) is accompanied by a cheque from the agent for the fee.
(4) A motion may not be enrolled under paragraph (2)(c) where—
 (a) a document which requires to be lodged with, or which accompanies, the motion—
  (i) is a step of process which requires to be or is signed;

      (ii) is an open or closed record, reclaiming print, appeal print or appendix;
      (iii) consists of more than four pages (including the backing sheet); or
      (iv) does not fall within a class of documents prescribed by the Lord President by direction as a document which may be sent by facsimile transmission in support of a motion of a category, and on such conditions, prescribed by that direction;
    (*b*) a fee is payable with that motion unless the motion is enrolled by an agent who has a Court of Session account; or
    (*c*) it falls within a category of motions prescribed by the Lord President by direction as unsuitable for enrolment by facsimile transmission.

(5) On receipt of a motion lodged, sent by post or transmitted by facsimile under paragraph (2), a clerk of session shall attach the motion to the motion sheet.

(6) A motion sent by post or facsimile transmission under paragraph (2) shall be treated as enrolled when it is received in the appropriate department of the Office of Court.

(7) Where appearance for the party who enrolled the motion is required for a motion, the entry in the rolls in respect of that motion shall be starred.

Deriv. R.C.S. 1965, r. 93(*a*) (r. 23.2(1)), r. 93(*b*) and (*c*) (part), r. 198 amended by S.I. 1978 No. 799 and P.N. No. 8 of 1991, para. 10(3) (r. 23.2(2)), r. 93(*d*) (part) (r. 23.2(7)), P.N. No. 8 of 1991, para. 2 (r. 23.2(3)), and P.N. No. 8 of 1991, para. 10(2) and (5) (r. 23.2(4))

23.2.1   *General note.* A motion is the means by which the court is asked to grant some application in the cause (whether incidental or substantive) or to allow a document to be lodged.

23.2.2   *"made orally at the bar".* Motions must usually be made in writing in Form 23.2 and require to be intimated where there is an opposing party (see r. 23.3). A motion made at the bar can therefore really only be made with leave of the court. Since in a defended cause intimation is required, the court is unlikely to grant leave if the opponent does not consent, although the court does have a power to dispense with intimation (see r. 23.3(3)(*c*) which it may exercise if there is no prejudice). An opposing party concerned in the motion may object on the ground of prejudice because the motion has not been intimated. Certain motions require a lengthy period of intimation (see, *e.g.* a motion one year after the last interlocutor (r. 23.3(4)) and variation of certain orders in family actions (*e.g.* rr. 49.40(2), 49.41(2), 49.42(2), 49.43(2) and (5))) and such a motion will rarely be heard in the absence of such intimation without consent of the opposing party concerned.

23.2.3   *Enrolling a motion.* There are three methods of enrolling a motion: (*a*) lodging Form 23.2 (the motion form) at the appropriate public counter of the General or Petition Department; (*b*) sending Form 23.2 by post if, where a fee is payable with the motion, the party's agent has a Court of Session account (see P.N. No. 4 of 1976) or accompanied by a cheque for the fee (r. 23.2(3)); or (*c*) sending Form 23.2 by fax if it is not a motion to which r. 23.2(4) applies. The fax no. for the General Department is 031–225 5496; the fax no. for the Petition Department is 031–225 7233.

    For the categories of cause lodged in the General Department, see r. 3.2 and notes. The causes lodged in the Petition Department are all petitions and notes in petition processes and certain references under statute (see note 3.3.1).

23.2.4   *Form 23.2.* All motions must be written or typed on a form in Form 23.2 whether lodged in person at the public counter of the appropriate Department, posted or faxed. The form is in three parts. In the case of a motion in a cause lodged in the General Department, all three parts must be completed where the motion is enrolled by post or fax; only Parts II and III (the latter being a motion slip) need be completed where enrolment is by lodging in person. In the case of a cause lodged in the Petition Department, Parts I and II must be completed where the motion is enrolled by post or fax; only Part II need be completed where enrolment is by lodging in person (a motion slip (Part III) is not required because, given the variety of petitions and the need for accuracy in the rolls of court, the clerks in the Petition Department have, historically, always written the motion slips and transmitted them to the Keeper of the Rolls for publication in the rolls).

For the categories of cause lodged in the General Department, see r. 3.2 and notes. The causes lodged in the Petition Department are all petitions and notes in petition processes and certain references under statute (see note 3.3.1).

Under P.N. 10th December 1986, para. 3 certain motions require reasons or explanations to be given and this information must be included in Form 23.2; a document may also be required. The document may be a writ or a production lodged with an inventory.

A motion which is expected to be starred and to require more than 10 minutes' duration on the motion roll must have the estimated duration marked on the form: P.N. No. 4 of 1996.

"agent". This means a solicitor or a person having a right to conduct the litigation: see r. 1.3(1) **23.2.5** (definition of "agent") and note 1.3.4. "Solicitor" is defined in the C.S.A. 1988, s.51.

"Court of Session account". Fees may be debited under a credit scheme introduced on 1st **23.2.6** April 1976 by P.N. No. 4 of 1976 to the account (if one is kept or permitted) of the agent by the court cashier, and an account will be rendered weekly by the court cashier's office to the agent for all court fees due that week for immediate settlement. Party litigants are not allowed to use this scheme.

Documents lodged with motions. Such a document may be a writ, other step of process (a **23.2.7** document not a production: r. 1.3(1)) or a production. Note the extended meaning of document in r. 1.3(1). A document may be lodged in person or by post (P.N. No. 4 of 1994, paras 1 and 8).

To facilitate enrolling motions by fax certain documents no longer require to be signed: see r. 4.2(9). Certain documents may not be transmitted by fax; these are: steps of process which must be signed, an open or closed record, a reclaiming or appeal print or appendix, a document of more than four pages or a document which does not fall within a class prescribed by the Lord President by direction as a document which may be faxed (for which, see note 23.2.9): r. 23.2(4).

Certain motions may require a document to be lodged. In relation to unopposed motions an indication of what documents are required for particular motions is given in P.N. 10th December 1986. Certain documents in support of certain motions may be transmitted by fax: see Direction No. 3 of 1994 and note 23.2.9. In either case the document must be lodged as a production: see r. 4.5.

"step of process which requires to be or is signed". A step of process is any document lodged in **23.2.8** process, other than a production (r. 1.3(1)), including those listed in r. 4.4(1) and any inventory of productions. A step of process which requires to be or is signed would include, *e.g.* defences, answers (other than answers to a minute of amendment), a report by a reporter or a legal aid certificate. Note the documents which no longer require to be signed: r. 4.2(9), and see note 23.2.7.

Documents of a class prescribed as documents which may be faxed. The Lord President has **23.2.9** made a direction under r. 23.2(4)(iv) prescribing certain productions lodged solely in support of a particular motion as documents which may be sent by fax with a faxed motion: see Direction No. 3 of 1994 (Productions which may be sent by facsimile transmission) (formerly P.N. No. 8 of 1993, para. 10(5) and Appendix C): see Section Two, 2. If the production is more than four pages long it may not be faxed by virtue of r. 23.2(4)(a)(iii). Where a production is sent by fax the principal will subsequently have to be lodged before the motion is heard (a) where the motion is opposed or (b) at the request of the court: Direction No. 3 of 1994, para. 3.

Motions unsuitable for fax. The Lord President has not yet made a direction defining a **23.2.10** category of motions unsuitable for fax transmission.

"motion sheet". This is one of the steps of process (No. 3 of Process): r. 4.4. Motions lodged are **23.2.11** attached to the motion sheet by an india tag or other suitable fixing.

"appearance". Appearance may be by a party litigant, counsel or other person having a right **23.2.12** of audience. A solicitor also has a right of audience before the vacation judge: C.S.A. 1988, s. 48(2)(a).

For the meaning of party litigant, see note 4.2.6. For definitions of "counsel" and "other person having a right of audience", see r. 1.3(1).

"rolls". The rolls are the lists of the business of the court issued by the Keeper of the Rolls. **23.2.13**

"starred". A motion is starred (*i.e.* an asterisk is placed at the beginning of the entry in the **23.2.14** rolls for the Motion Roll or Single Bills) (a) where the appearance of a party litigant, counsel or other person having a right of audience is required (i) because the motion is not an unopposed motion to which P.N. 10th December 1986 applies or (ii) by the court (r. 23.2(7)); or (b) the motion is opposed (r. 23.4(6)). For starred unopposed motions requiring appearance, see notes 23.2.16 (Outer House) and 23.2.17(2) (Inner House). It should be noted that P.N. 10th December 1986 does not apply to motions in causes in the Inner House, although the spirit of it in relation to consultation with practitioners before motions are dropped is followed. On motions in the Inner House, see note 23.2.17.

23.2.15   *Unstarred unopposed motions in the Outer House.* These are unopposed motions which do not require the appearance of a party litigant, counsel or other person having a right of audience. The categories of unopposed motions in the Outer House are defined by P.N. 10th December 1986 as (1) those which according to present practice are unstarred, (2) those of a procedural nature which hitherto have required the appearance of counsel, and (3) those which hitherto required appearance of counsel and judicial consideration. Motions in categories (1) and (2) are dealt with by a depute clerk of session and the interlocutor is signed by him (r. 4.15(3)) or if the interlocutor is seen by the judge is signed by the judge. A motion in category (3) is dealt with, and the interlocutor signed by, the judge.

     (1) *Unopposed motions unstarred according to current practice.* These are:

        A sist of process, and recall of sist,

        Amendment (by motion or minute),

        Proof before answer,

        Commission and diligence for recovery of documents,

        Recovery of evidence under the Bankers' Books Evidence Act 1879,

        Third party notice procedure,

        Order for defences,

        Intimation of withdrawal of agent,

        Minute of sist applications,

        Minute of transference applications,

        Approval of issues,

        Allowance of issues.

     (2) *Unopposed unstarred motions of a procedural nature.* These are those listed in Appendix I to P.N. 10th December 1986. Written reasons and explanations (examples of which are given in column 2 of the appendix) must accompany the motion.

     (3) *Unopposed unstarred motions which require judicial consideration.* These are those listed in Appendix II in P.N. 10th December 1986. Written reasons and explanations and any documents required (examples of which are given in column 2 of the appendix) must accompany the motion.

     The lists above are not in fact exhaustive; the clerks of session should be consulted to determine which category a motion not listed falls into and what information and documentation is required.

     For starred unopposed motions which hitherto required appearance, see note 23.2.16.

23.2.16   *Starred unopposed motions in the Outer House.* These motions require the appearance of a party litigant, counsel or other person having a right of audience. They fall into two categories:

     (1) *A motion for which the court requires appearance for some reason requiring explanation or justification.*

     (2) *Motions which hitherto have required appearance.* These are:

        Interim interdict (before and after calling),

        Perpetual interdict,

        Interim orders under the Matrimonial Homes (Family Protection) (Scotland) Act 1981,

        Intimation and service in judicial review petitions where interim orders are sought.

23.2.17   *Motions in the Inner House.* The P.N. 10th December 1986 does not apply to the Inner House. The vacation judge has power to dispose of motions, of a procedural nature and which do not dispose of the merits, enrolled in causes pending before the Inner House (r. 11.1(1)(c)); and the interlocutors are signed by the vacation judge and not the clerk. The following practice applies during term.

     (1) *Unopposed unstarred motions in the Inner House.* These are scrutinised by the clerk to the Division and, if he is satisfied that the relevant procedural rules have been complied with, he prepares an interlocutor for signature by the chairman of the Division. All interlocutors are signed by the chairman and never the clerk. Such motions are:

        Order for grounds of appeal,

        Appointment of cause to Summar Roll,

        Sist of cause (reason stated in motion),

        Recall of sist,

        Ordaining party to intimate insistence of reclaiming motion or appeal where agent has withdrawn from acting,

        Refusing reclaiming motion or appeal following above,

        Motion by reclaimer/appellant to refuse reclaiming motion/appeal,

        Amendment (except amendment of pleadings: P.N. 26th March 1981),

        Expenses after judgment (unless starred by the court): see Notice 4th September 1997.

     (2) *Unopposed starred motions in the Inner House.* These fall into two categories:

     (a) A motion for which the court requires appearance for some reason requiring explanation or justification and could relate to any of the motions listed in note 23.2.15.

(b) Motions which hitherto have required appearance. These are:
> Late lodging of a document,
> Ordaining a party to find caution,
> Prorogation of time to find caution,
> Adjustment of a writ,
> Amendment of grounds of appeal previously lodged,
> Relief from compliance with rule (r. 2.1),
> Refusing opponent's reclaiming motion or appeal (except where consented to),
> Late motion for review,
> Prorogation of time to lodge document,
> Discharge of diet on Summar Roll,
> Interim interdict,
> Interim payment or execution,
> Sist of a mandatory,
> Lost step of process,
> Second sist for legal aid,
> Modification of liability for expenses of legally aided person,
> Expenses (except where consented to or unopposed: see Notice 4th September 1997 following a judgment unless starred by the court).

The lists above are not in fact exhaustive; the clerk of one of the Divisions should be consulted to determine which category a motion not listed falls into and what information and documentation is required.

Duration of motions. Where the hearing of a motion is likely to last more than 20 minutes, the **23.2.18** Keeper's office must be informed so that the Keeper can re-arrange other business, if necessary: Notice, 7th March 1990.

Fee. The court fee for a motion will be payable. For fee, see Court of Session etc. Fees Order **23.2.19** 1997, Table of Fees, Pt 1, B and C [S.I. 1997 No. 688, as amended, pp. C1201 *et seq.*]. A party making a first appearance in a cause by enrolling a motion is liable to a fee under the 1997 Fees Order, Table of Fees, Pt 1, B, item 2 or C item 5. Certain persons are exempt from paying fees: see 1997 Order, art.5, substituted by S.S.I. 2002 No.270. A fee exempt certificate must be in existence in process and a fee exemption slip must be lodged certifying that there has been no change in circumstances since the certificate: see P.N. No.1 of 2002. Certain motions are exempt from fees: see Fees Order, art. 5A, inserted by S.S.I. 1999 No.755.

Where the party enrolling the motion is represented, the fee may be debited under the credit scheme introduced on 1st April by P.N. No.4 of 1976 to the account (if one is kept or permitted) of the party's agent by the court cashier, and an account will be rendered weekly by the court cashier's office to the agents for all court fees due that week for immediate settlement. Party litigants, and agents not operating the scheme, must pay (by cash, cheque or postal order) at the time of lodging at the counter of the appropriate department.

Intimation of motions

23.3.—(1) Subject to paragraph (2) and any other provision in these Rules, the party enrolling a motion in a cause where—
> (a) appearance has been entered by a defender under rule 17.1(1),
> (b) defences, a minute or answers have been lodged by a party, or
> (c) provision for intimation of a motion to a party is made in these Rules,

shall give written intimation of his intention to make such enrolment, and of the terms of the motion, to every such party.

(2) The requirement under paragraph (1) to give written intimation of a motion to a party shall not apply where that party—
> (a) having entered appearance, fails to lodge defences within the period for lodging those defences;
> (b) has not lodged answers within the period of notice for lodging those answers; or
> (c) has withdrawn or is deemed to have withdrawn his defences, minute, note or answers, as the case may be.

(3) Such intimation shall be made so as to reach the other party not later than 12.30 p.m. on the day before enrolment, except where—
> (a) the other party concerned in the motion consents to a shorter period of intimation;

(b) the period of intimation is otherwise provided in these Rules; or

(c) the court shortens or extends the period of intimation or dispenses with intimation.

(4) Where a motion is enrolled after the lapse of one year from the date of the last interlocutor in the cause, written intimation shall be given to every other party not less than 14 days before the date of enrolment.

(5) Where written intimation of a motion has been given, the party enrolling the motion shall state that this has been done on the motion in Form 23.2.

Deriv. R.C.S. 1965, r. 93(c) amended by S.I. 1980 No. 1144 (r. 23.3(1) and (3)), r. 93(b) (part) (r. 23.3(5)) and r. 105 (r. 23.3(4))

23.3.1 *General note.* Intimation of a motion is not required by a pursuer of a motion made before calling of a summons or by a petitioner or noter before the interlocutor containing the first order is pronounced (for which see r. 23.8) unless expressly required by a rule. Provision is made in certain rules for intimation of a motion to a person who is not a party, *e.g.*:

    r. 35.3, to haver, and Lord Advocate,

    r. 35.8(3), to person claiming confidentiality where confidential envelope to be opened in recovery of evidence,

    r. 49.39, to local authority of motion relating to child under care or supervision of that local authority,

    r. 49.62, to local authority where court considering committing care or supervision of child to local authority.

Where intimation is required and has not been made the motion will be dropped by the court and will have to be re-enrolled after having been re-intimated as required under the relevant rule.

23.3.2 *"written intimation".* For methods, see r. 16.9.

23.3.3 *Period of intimation.* Where intimation is required, r. 23.3(3) provides that it must be made by 12.30 p.m. the day before enrolment unless (a) the other party consents, (b) the period is otherwise provided for or (c) the court shortens, extends or dispenses with the period.

For an experimental period from 25th November 1996, a motion should be intimated (subject to the exceptions in r. 23.3(3)) so that intimation reaches the other party not later than 12.30 p.m. two days before enrolment: P.N. No. 6 of 1996. The purpose of this is to enable a person opposing a motion to include in his notice of opposition a brief statement of the extent and bases of his opposition as required by that P.N.

Longer periods of intimation are required in the rules for some motions: see, *e.g.* a motion one year after the last interlocutor (r. 23.3(4)) and variation of certain orders in family actions (*e.g.* rr. 49.40(2), 49.41(2), 49.42(2), 49.43(2) and (5)). The court might shorten a period of intimation in, *e.g.* a motion to move arrested property (r. 13.11).

23.3.4 *Statement that written intimation given.* The date of intimation must now be inserted in Form 23.2. Where intimation is made to persons other than parties, this should be stated on Form 23.2.

23.3.5 *Wakening a cause.* R.C.S. 1965, r. 105 (now R.C.S. 1994, r. 23.3(4)) superseded the former procedure for wakening a cause which had fallen asleep because no interlocutor had been pronounced within a year of the last interlocutor (for which see Maclaren on *Court of Session Practice*, p. 462). Where the address of another party is unknown application to dispense with intimation will have to be made under r. 23.3(3)(c). Where a party seeks to enrol a motion to interpone authority to a joint minute or to obtain decree in terms of a minute of tender and minute of acceptance (where these have been recently lodged), the court will look favourably on a motion to dispense with the requirement to give 14 days' intimation under r. 23.3(4).

Opposition to motions

23.4.—(1) Where a party seeks to oppose a motion under rule 23.2, he shall—

(a) not later than the day and time as the Lord President shall prescribe by direction for the lodging of notices of opposition to motions, lodge a notice of opposition in Form 23.4 at the appropriate department of the Office of Court during its normal office hours;

(b) post a notice of opposition in Form 23.4 to the appropriate department of the Office of Court; or

(c) send by facsimile transmission a notice of opposition in Form 23.4 to the appropriate department of the Office of Court.

(2) Opposition to a motion sent by post or facsimile transmission under paragraph (1)(b) or (c) shall be treated as lodged when the notice of opposition is received in the appropriate department of the Office of Court.

(3) On receipt of a notice of opposition lodged, sent by post or facsimile transmission under paragraph (1), a clerk of session shall attach the notice to the motion sheet.

(4) A party who opposes a motion shall give written intimation of his opposition to every other party so as to reach such other party not later than 12.30 p.m. on the day on which the opposition is lodged or treated as lodged.

(5) Where written intimation of opposition to a motion has been given, the party who has given such intimation shall state that this has been done on the notice of opposition in Form 23.4.

(6) Where a motion is opposed, the entry in the rolls in respect of that motion shall be starred.

Deriv. R.C.S. 1965, r. 93(e) (part) (r. 23.4(1), (5) and (6)), and r. 93(e) (part) amended by S.I. 1980 No. 1144 (r. 23.4(4))

General note. If a motion is not timeously opposed and the motion is unstarred as not **23.4.1** requiring appearance, the opportunity to oppose it may be lost. If an approach to the clerk of court is made before the Motion Roll is heard (and the interlocutor is signed), it may be possible to postpone the motion to the next (convenient) day, particularly if the opposition was eventually intimated (although out of time). If the motion is starred the opponent can ask leave of the court to be heard when the motion is heard on the Motion Roll; and this will usually be granted if there is no prejudice to the party who enrolled the motion. In either case the question of whether the opponent should pay expenses of the motion may arise.

Day and time for opposition to motions prescribed by direction. The current direction is **23.4.2** Direction No. 4 of 1994 (Motions): see Directions, pp. C1501 *et seq.* The general rule is that a motion enrolled before 4pm on one weekday will be heard on the second sederunt day thereafter; and notice of opposition to a motion must be lodged by 12.30pm the weekday before the motion is due to be heard in court: Direction No. 4 of 1994, para. 2. Direction No. 4 of 1994 does not apply to insolvency and certain Companies Act 1985 proceedings: see Direction No. 3 of 2005.

Form 23.4. Opposition to a motion must be in this form. The form is in three parts. In the case **23.4.3** of a motion in a cause lodged in the General Department, all three parts must be completed where the motion is enrolled by post or fax; only Parts II and III (the latter being an opposition slip) need be completed where enrolment is by lodging in person. In the case of a cause lodged in the Petition Department, Parts I and II must be completed where the motion is enrolled by post or fax; only Part II need be completed where enrolment is by lodging in person (an opposition slip (Part III) is not required because, given the variety of petitions and the need for accuracy in the rolls of court, the clerks in the Petition Department have, historically, completed opposition slips and transmitted them to the Keeper of the Rolls for publication in the rolls). When a motion is opposed the opponent's agent's name is added (after a dash after the enroller's agent's name) to the entry in the Motion Roll and, if the entry was previously unstarred, an asterisk added at the beginning of the entry indicating that appearance is required at the hearing on the Motion Roll.

For the categories of cause lodged in the General Department, see r. 3.2 and notes. The causes lodged in the Petition Department are all petitions and notes in petition processes and certain references under statute (see note 3.3.1).

The expected duration of the hearing of the motion on the motion roll must be marked on the form: P.N. No. 4 of 1996.

For an experimental period from 25th November 1996, the notice of opposition in the form must include a brief statement of the extent and bases of opposition: P.N. No. 6 of 1996.

"written intimation". For methods, see r. 16.9.   **23.4.4**

Statement that written intimation given. The date of intimation must now be inserted in Form **23.4.5** 23.4.

"rolls". The rolls are the lists of the business of the court issued by the Keeper of the Rolls. **23.4.6**

"starred". An asterisk is placed at the beginning of the entry in the rolls for the Motion Roll **23.4.7** or Single Bills.

23.4.8   *Fee.* There is currently no court fee for a party opposing a motion, except for opposition to a motion for variation of an order in a consistorial cause (for which see Court of Session etc. Fees Order 1997, Table of Fees, Pt. I, B, item 9 [S.I. 1997 No. 688, as amended, pp. C1201 *et seq.*]). A fee is payable for opposing a motion by a person other than an originating party making his first appearance in the process (for which see Court of Session etc. Fees Order 1997, Table of Fees, Pt. I, B, item 2 or 6, or C, item 5). A person making a first appearance in a process by enrolling a motion is liable to pay a court fee under the Court of Session etc. Fees Order 1984, Table of Fees, Pt. I, B, item 2 or C, item 5. Certain persons are exempt from payment of fees: see 1997 Fees Order, art.5, substituted by S.S.I. 2002 No. 270. A fee exemption certificate must be lodged in process: see P.N. No.1 of 2002.

Where a party is legally represented, the fee may be debited under the credit scheme introduced on 1st April 1976 by P.N. No. 4 of 1976 to the account (if one is kept or permitted) of the defender's agent by the court cashier, and an account will be rendered weekly by the court cashier's office to agents for all court fees due that week for immediate settlement. Party litigants, and agents not operating the scheme, must pay (by cash, cheque or postal order) at the time of lodging at the counter at the appropriate department.

Consent to motions

23.5. Where a party seeks to consent to a motion, he may—

    (a) endorse the motion with his consent;

    (b) post a notice of consent in Form 23.5 to the appropriate department of the Office of Court; or

    (c) send by facsimile transmission a notice of consent in Form 23.5 to the appropriate department of the Office of Court.

23.5.1   *General note.* This is a new rule required to facilitate consent to motions by post or fax.

Hearing of motions

23.6.—(1) Subject to the rules mentioned in paragraph (2), the day of publication on the walls of the court and of the hearing of a motion enrolled on any day shall be determined in accordance with such provisions as the Lord President shall prescribe by direction.

(2) The rules referred to in paragraph (1) are:

    rule 23.7 (motions in session outwith a term or in vacation),

rule 23.8 (motions by pursuer before calling or petitioner before first order),

rule 23.9 (motions where caveat lodged),

rule 23.10 (motions by defender or other person before calling).

(3) A motion enrolled in a cause in the Outer House shall be heard by the Lord Ordinary.

(4) A motion enrolled in a cause in the Inner House shall be heard in the Single Bills by a Division of the Inner House.

Deriv. R.C.S. 1965, r. 93(d) (part) (r. 23.6(1))

23.6.1   *General note.* Paragraphs (3) and (4) of r. 23.6 are new provisions. A motion heard by the Lord Ordinary is not always heard in the Motion Roll: *i.e.* motions before calling in actions and motions before first order in petitions, and certain motions on the Diet Roll in actions under the optional procedure for actions of damages.

23.6.2   *Day of publication and hearing of motions prescribed by direction.* The current direction is Direction No. 5 of 1994: see Directions, pp. C1501 *et seq.* The general rule is that a motion enrolled before 4pm on one weekday will be heard on the second sederunt day thereafter: Direction No. 5 of 1994, para. 2. That Direction does not apply to insolvency and certain Companies Act 1985 proceedings: see Direction No. 3 of 2005.

The direction does not apply to rr. 23.8, 23.9 and 23.10: see those rules and Direction No. 3 of 1994, para. 2.

In commercial actions to which Chap. 47 applies, the direction applies subject to Direction No. 2 of 1995 which provides that opposed and other starred motions will be put out for hearing on such a date and at such a time as is convenient to the court and, where possible, the parties. The clerk of court will fix the date and time and intimate it to the parties. Urgent motions will be dealt with on a priority basis.

"publication on the walls of the court". Motions in the Single Bills and the Motion Roll are **23.6.3** published in the rolls and on the noticeboard outside the First Division courtroom (Court 1) under the courtroom and Division or Lord Ordinary before whom they are to be dealt with (if unstarred) or heard (if starred).

Motions in court or in chambers. Motions are usually heard in open court. A motion may be **23.6.4** heard in chambers in certain instances particularly where a cause has not yet called. Motions for interim interdict are sometimes heard in chambers for convenience, though the press and public are not excluded. Motions to shorten a period of notice before calling of an action or first order in petition (for which an agent has a right of audience: r. 23.14(1)) are always dealt with in chambers in term; in vacation they have been dealt with in the vacation court. Motions in proceedings under the Adoption (Scotland) Act 1978, the Solicitors (Scotland) Act 1980 and the Human Fertilisation and Embryology Act 1990 are always dealt with in chambers.

Urgent motions outwith court or office hours. The arrangements for urgent business when the **23.6.4A** offices are closed are as follows. Telephone the Court of Session (0131–225 2595). The telephone is manned at all times. On telephoning, leave a contact number. The security staff will contact a clerk who will contact you and make the necessary arrangements. At weekends in session there is a rota for stand-by judges. In vacation the vacation judge is the stand-by judge.

Hearing of motions. P.N. No. 4 of 1996 provides:— **23.6.5**
(1) Starred motions requiring no more than 10 minutes. A Lord Ordinary naming substantive business (*e.g.* a proof) may be allocated no more than three such motions. Allowance will be made for such other number of starred motions or other interlocutory business as can be accommodated up to 10.30am.
(2) Other starred motions and those likely to take more than 10 minutes. These will be assigned to a Lord Ordinary assigned to the motion roll for that day. Such motions will be published in the rolls in groups allocated to a specific half-hour period between 10am and 1pm; those remaining will be published for disposal not before 2pm. Motions will be heard in the order printed in the rolls which the court otherwise allows.
The former provision was that where the hearing of a motion is likely to last more than 20 minutes, the Keeper's office must be informed so that the Keeper can re-arrange other business, if necessary: Notice, 7th March 1990. This notice has not, for some reason, been revoked, although it is obviously superseded by P.N. No. 4 of 1996.

Fee. The court fee for a hearing of a motion on the Motion Roll or Single Bills is payable by **23.6.6** each party for every 30 minutes or part thereof after the first 30 minutes. For fee, see Court of Session etc. Fees Order 1997, Table of Fees, Pt 1, B, item 21 or 22 [S.I. 1997 No. 688, as amended, pp. C1201 *et seq.*]. A motion heard out of hours (*i.e.* after 4.30pm and before 8.30am unless parties were ready to proceed before 4.30pm) is subject to a higher fee: Table of Fees, Pt. I, B, item 24 or C, item 23. Certain persons are exempt from payment of fees: see 1997 Fees Order, art.5 substituted by S.S.I. 2002 No. 270. A fee exemption certificate must be lodged in process: see P.N. No. 1 of 2002.
Where a party is legally represented, the fee may be debited under a credit scheme introduced on 1st April 1976 by P.N. No. 4 of 1976 to the account (if one is kept or permitted) of the agent by the court cashier, and an account will be rendered weekly by the court cashier's office to the agent for all court fees due that week for immediate settlement. An agent not on the credit scheme will have an account opened for the purpose of lodging the fee: P.N. No. 2 of 1995.
A party litigant must pay (by cash, cheque or postal order) to the clerk at the end of the hearing or, if the hearing lasts more than a day, at the end of each day: P.N. No. 2 of 1995.

Motions in session outwith a term or in vacation

23.7.—(1) A motion which is to be heard by the Lord Ordinary in session outwith a term, or in vacation by the vacation judge, shall not appear in the rolls.

(2) A party enrolling such a motion shall be informed at the time of enrolment whether or not any appearance is required.

(3) Any such motion which is opposed in accordance with rule 23.4 shall require appearance for the party whose motion it is.

(4) On the afternoon of the day preceding each sitting of the Lord Ordinary in session outwith a term or of the vacation judge there shall be published on the walls of the court a list of unopposed motions for which appearance is required followed by a list of opposed motions, each in alphabetic order.

(5) Motions before the Lord Ordinary in session outwith a term or the vacation judge shall be called for hearing in the order in which they appear in the list published under paragraph (4).

Deriv. P.N. 31st March 1970

General note. Motions before the Lord Ordinary in session outwith a term will be subject to **23.7.1** the same procedure as motions in vacation.

The vacation court normally sits at 10.30am, or as soon as possible thereafter, on Tuesdays to Fridays (except on public or local holidays or on a Tuesday where Monday is a public or local holiday). During the Winter (Christmas) vacation there may be only two vacation court days. Business is normally conducted in open court but may be conducted in chambers or in private. The days on which the vacation court sits are published in the rolls about four weeks before the end of the preceding term. The vacation court sits on such days and at such times as may be convenient or necessary subject to any direction of the Lord President: r. 10.5(2).

More than one judge may sit as a vacation judge if pressure of business requires it.

"rolls". The rolls are the lists of the business of the court issued by the Keeper of the Rolls. **23.7.2** Motions in session outwith a term or in vacation are not published in the rolls, but they are displayed on the walls of the court: r. 23.7(4).

"appearance". Appearance in vacation may be by a party litigant, counsel or other person **23.7.3** having a right of audience. A solicitor also has a right of audience before the vacation judge: C.S.A. 1988, s. 48(2)(*a*) (substituted by the Law Reform (Miscellaneous Provisions) (Scotland) Act 1990, Sched. 8, para. 38).

For the meaning of party litigant, see note 4.2.6. For definitions of "counsel" and "other person having a right of audience", see r. 1.3(1).

Motions by pursuer before calling or petitioner before first order

23.8.—(1) A motion enrolled by a pursuer in an action before the calling of the summons or by a petitioner before an order under rule 14.5(1)(*a*) (order for intimation, service and advertisement in petitions) has been made—

(*a*) shall, subject to any other provision in these Rules, be brought as soon as reasonably practicable by the Keeper of the Rolls, or a clerk of session instructed by him, before the Lord Ordinary sitting in court or in chambers; and

(*b*) shall not require to be published in the rolls.

(2) On enrolling such a motion, the pursuer or petitioner, as the case may be, shall be informed whether or not appearance is required.

General note. A motion made under this rule is made before the calling of a summons (and **23.8.1** before the defender is able to enter appearance) or before a respondent has been served with a petition. Accordingly, neither the defender nor the respondent has a right to appear and, if the pursuer or petitioner is seeking protective measures such as arrestment, inhibition or interdict, should not have prior warning of the motion unless (where competent) he has lodged a caveat: see r. 5.1.

"subject to any other provision in these Rules". R. 23.8(1)(*a*) is subject to r. 23.9 under **23.8.2** which the caveator has the right to appear.

"sitting in court or in chambers". Motions are usually heard in open court. A motion may be **23.8.3** heard in chambers in certain instances particularly where a cause has not yet called. Motions for interim interdict are sometimes heard in chambers for convenience, though the

press and public are not excluded. Motions to shorten a period of notice before calling of an action or first order in petition (for which an agent has a right of audience: r. 23.14(1)) are always dealt with in chambers in term; in vacation they have been dealt with in the vacation court. Motions in proceedings under the Adoption (Scotland) Act 1978, the Solicitors (Scotland) Act 1980 and the Human Fertilisation and Embryology Act 1990 are always dealt with in chambers.

23.8.4 *"rolls"*. The rolls are the lists of the business of the court issued by the Keeper of the Rolls.

23.8.5 *"appearance"*. Appearance may be by a party litigant, counsel or other person having a right of audience. A solicitor also has a right of audience in such a motion: r. 23.14.

For the meaning of party litigant, see note 4.2.6. For definitions of "counsel" and "other person having a right of audience", see r. 1.3(1).

Motions where caveat lodged

23.9. Where a motion in respect of which a caveat has been lodged is enrolled, the Keeper of the Rolls shall—

(a) fix a hearing of the motion before the Lord Ordinary sitting in court or in chambers as soon as reasonably practicable; and

(b) inform the parties concerned of the date and time of the hearing.

Deriv. R.C.S. 1965, r. 79(1) (part) and (2), and r. 236(b) amended by S.I. 1984 No. 499

23.9.1 *General note.* When a motion is enrolled in a cause *ex parte* for an order against which a caveat may be lodged the clerk of session in the General or Petition Department, as the case may be, checks the register of caveats to see if a caveat has been lodged. If a caveat has been lodged he informs the Keeper of the Rolls who arranges a hearing of the motion (day or night) at a time when both parties can attend. Where the motion is enrolled by a pursuer before the calling of the summons or by a petitioner before the granting of the first order, r. 23.8 will apply.

If the duty clerk of session has to be contacted after 5pm, ring the Court of Session (031–225 2595), leave your name and telephone number, and the duty security guard will contact a clerk who will contact you.

For the orders against which a caveat may be lodged, see r. 5.1. For the form and lodging of caveats, see r. 5.2.

23.9.2 *"caveat"*. A caveat is a document lodged in the Petition Department (r. 5.2(1)) by a person to ensure that certain orders may not be made against him without his receiving intimation of the application for the order and having an opportunity to be heard before the order may be made.

23.9.3 *"sitting in court or in chambers"*. Motions are usually heard in open court. A motion may be heard in chambers in certain instances particularly where a cause has not yet called. Motions for interim interdict are sometimes heard in chambers for convenience, though the press and public are not excluded. Motions to shorten a period of notice before calling of an action or first order in petition (for which an agent has a right of audience: r. 23.14(1)) are always dealt with in chambers in term; in vacation they have been dealt with in the vacation court. Motions in proceedings under the Adoption (Scotland) Act 1978, the Solicitors (Scotland) Act 1980 and the Human Fertilisation and Embryology Act 1990 are always dealt with in chambers.

Motions by defender or other person before calling

23.10.—[1] (1) A motion, enrolled in an action before the calling of the summons by a person other than the pursuer shall be intimated forthwith by the Deputy Principal Clerk to the pursuer.

(2) The Keeper of the Rolls shall—

(a) fix a hearing of such a motion before the Lord Ordinary sitting in court or in chambers as soon as reasonably practicable; and

(b) inform the parties concerned of the date and time of the hearing.

---

[1] R. 23.10(1) amended by S.I. 1994 No. 2901 (clerical error).

23.10.1 *General note.* This is a new rule. This rule might apply, *e.g.* where a defender or a person having an interest applies for recall etc. of arrestment or inhibition under r. 13.10 or for warrant to move arrested property under r. 13.11.

"sitting in court or in chambers". Motions are usually heard in open court. A motion may be **23.10.2** heard in chambers in certain instances particularly where a cause has not yet called. Motions for interim interdict are sometimes heard in chambers for convenience, though the press and public are not excluded. Motions to shorten a period of notice before calling of an action (for which an agent has a right of audience: r. 23.14(1)) are always dealt with in chambers in term; in vacation they have been dealt with in the vacation court. Motions in proceedings under the Adoption (Scotland) Act 1978, the Solicitors (Scotland) Act 1980 and the Human Fertilisation and Embryology Act 1990 are always dealt with in chambers.

Statutory applications by motion
23.11. Unless otherwise provided in these Rules or any other enactment, an application to the court under any other enactment in a cause depending before the court shall be made by motion.

General note. This is a new rule. Unless the Rules or any other enactment provide that an **23.11.1** application to the court under an enactment (statute or statutory instrument) is to be by other means in a depending cause, it may be by motion.

A recent example would be an application under s.4(2) of the Requirements of Writing (Scotland) Act 1995 (endorsation or decree that document dated or signed at place on date on, or place at, which it bears so to be). The court might, if the motion were opposed and if the question raised were not straightforward, order the issue to be dealt with by minute and answers.

"depending". A cause is depending from the time it is commenced (*i.e.* from the time an action **23.11.2** is served or a first order in a petition is made) until final decree, whereas a cause is in dependence until final extract. For the meaning of commenced, see note 13.4.4 (action) or 14.6.1 (petition). For the meaning of final decree, see note 4.15.2(2). For the meaning of final extract, see note 7.1.2(2).

Expenses of motions
23.12. Where a motion is called for hearing in the Motion Roll or Single Bills and is dropped, the Auditor shall, in taxing any expenses found due to the party on whose behalf the motion was enrolled, disallow the expenses occasioned by the motion unless he is satisfied that the motion was properly enrolled and properly dropped.

Deriv. R.C.S. 1965, r. 93(f)

Expenses of motions. Often no motion is made for expenses of a motion and the court makes **23.12.1** no finding. In an opposed motion, a motion for expenses may well be made by the successful party. It had been thought that there should be a rule that, if expenses are not otherwise dealt with at the time of the motion, expenses are in the cause (*i.e.* whoever is ultimately successful in the cause and subsequently obtains a general order for the expenses of the cause gets the expenses of such a motion: *Glasgow and South-Western Railway Co. v. Magistrates of Ayr* 1911 S.C. 298) unless the court otherwise orders.

The problem with such a rule is that a motion might have to be opposed in order simply to ensure that expenses of a motion which the mover of the motion ought to pay (*e.g.* the allowance of a minute of amendment) are not "in the cause". The proposal has not been followed. The Auditor has no discretion where the court makes a finding of expenses in the cause: see note 42.5.2. But he does have a discretion where there is a general finding of expenses (usually at the end of a cause) to disallow a party so entitled to expenses on a matter on which he was in fact unsuccessful or he incurred expenses through his own fault: see r. 42.5(2). This discretion sufficiently covers the situation where no particular finding for expenses in respect of a motion has been made.

"properly enrolled and properly dropped". A motion which it was right to enrol but dropped **23.12.2** because its purpose was satisfied without the court having to adjudicate on the matter is one which the Auditor will allow the expenses for.

Conditions attached to granting of motions
23.13. Where the court grants a motion in whole or in part, it may do so subject to such conditions, if any, as to expenses or otherwise as it thinks fit.

General note. This is a new rule which states what the court may always do. **23.13.1**

Conditions as to expenses or otherwise. Apart from being found liable in expenses on losing a **23.13.2** motion, a party might be ordered to pay expenses as a condition of being allowed to proceed with a cause. This may arise where there has been a failure or delay such that, although it is in the interests of justice that the case proceeds, it is just and equitable that the opponent should be paid before the cause proceeds: see *Colbron v. United Glass Ltd* 1965 S.L.T. 366; *McGregor v. Rooney*, 5th February 1971, Outer House, unreported; *Masinimport v. Scottish Mechanical Light Industries Ltd*, 15th May 1973, unreported. Other conditions might be caution or consignation. On caution, see note 33.1.2. On consignation, see note 33.4.3.

Appearance by solicitor for certain motions

23.14.—(1) A solicitor shall have a right of audience before the court in respect of a motion which is heard in chambers under any of the following rules—

> rule 23.8 (motions by pursuer before calling or petitioner before first order),
>
> rule 23.9 (motions where caveat lodged),
>
> rule 23.10 (motions by defender or other person before calling).

(2) A solicitor shall have a right of audience before the Lord Ordinary sitting during session outwith a term in respect of any motion.

23.14.1   *General note.* This rule is made under s.48(2)(b) of the C.S.A. 1988 and in relation to r. 23.14(1) confirms the current practice. R. 23.14(2) provides for the right of audience of a solicitor before the Lord Ordinary in session outwith a term (a provision introduced by r. 10.4). The right of a solicitor to appear before the vacation judge is provided by s.48(2)(a) of the C.S.A. 1988 (substituted by the Law Reform (Miscellaneous Provisions) (Scotland) Act 1990, Sched. 8, para. 38).

CHAPTER 24

AMENDMENT OF PLEADINGS

Powers of court

24.1.—(1) In any cause the court may, at any time before final judgment, allow an amendment mentioned in paragraph (2).

(2) Paragraph (1) applies to the following amendments—

(a) an amendment of a principal writ which may be necessary for the purpose of determining the real question in controversy between the parties, notwithstanding that in consequence of such amendment—

   (i) the sum sued for in a summons is increased or restricted; or

   (ii) a different remedy from that originally concluded for or craved is sought;

(b) an amendment which may be necessary—

   (i) to correct or supplement the designation of a party to the cause;

   (ii) to enable a party who has sued or has been sued in his own right to sue or be sued in a representative capacity;

   (iii) to enable a party who has sued or has been sued in a representative capacity to sue or be sued in his own right or in a different representative capacity;

   (iv) to add the name of an additional pursuer, a petitioner or person whose concurrence is necessary;

   (v) where the cause has been commenced or presented in the name of the wrong person, or it is doubtful whether it has been commenced or presented in the name of the right person, to allow any other person to be sisted in substitution for, or in addition to, the original person; or

   (vi) to direct conclusions against a third party brought into an action under Chapter 26 (third party procedure);

(c) an amendment of a condescendence, defences, answers, pleas-in-law or other pleadings which may be necessary for determining the real question in controversy between the parties; and

(d) where it appears that all parties having an interest have not been called or that the cause has been directed against the wrong person, an amendment inserting in the instance of the principal writ an additional or substitute party and directing existing or additional conclusions or craves, averments and pleas-in-law against that party.

Deriv. R.C.S. 1965, r. 92(1) and (3) amended by SI 1967/1789

General note. The statutory origins of this Chapter are ss.20 and 29 of the C.S.A. 1868   **24.1.1** (repealed by the C.S.A. 1988, Sched.2). Alteration of the instance of a cause or the conclusions of a summons must always be by amendment under this rule. Alteration of any other pleadings (including the prayer of a petition) may be (a) during any adjustment period allowed by the court, by adjustment without permission of the court; and (b) at any other time, by amendment under this rule.

A wide reading should be given to the terms of the rule: *Rackstraw v. Douglas* 1919 S.C. 354, 357 *per* L.J.-C. Scott Dickson.

Amendment is in the discretion of the court, and in exercising it the court will consider delay in seeking the amendment, any prejudice to another party, the stage at which the amendment is sought to be made and any conditions which might be imposed for allowing the amendment. In deciding whether to allow an amendment the court seeks to do justice to all the parties: see *Dryburgh v. National Coal Board* 1962 S.C. 485, 492 *per* Lord Guthrie. It is not just to dismiss an action because of a formal pleading defect which can be put right without prejudice to the other party: *G.U.S. Property Management Ltd v. Littlewoods Mail Order Stores Ltd* 1982 S.C.(H.L.) 157, 178 *per* Lord Keith of Kinkel. The court will not amend a party's pleadings at its own instance: *Lord Advocate v. Johnston* 1983 S.L.T. 290.

Amendment is a question of discretion and not competency: *Thomson v. Glasgow Corporation* 1962 S.C.(H.L.) 36; and see note 24.1.2. Accordingly, the competency of the original cause is simply one of the factors to be taken into account in exercising the discretion: *Shanks v. Central R.C.* 1988 S.L.T. 212.

The general rule is that an interlocutor of a Lord Ordinary is final (s. 18 of the 1988 Act), and a Lord Ordinary cannot alter the substance of an interlocutor refusing a minute of amendment by subsequently allowing a minute of amendment in the same terms on a material change of circumstances. Such a motion was refused as incompetent in *Bremner v. Martin t/a George Martin Engineering*, 2006 S.L.T. 169 (OH).

Amendment after expiry of time-limit. "The court will not, in general, allow a pursuer by   **24.1.2** amendment to substitute the right defender for the wrong defender, or to cure a radical incompetence in his action, or to change the basis of his case if he only seeks to make such amendments after the expiry of a time limit which would have prevented him at that stage from raising fresh proceedings": *Pompa's Trs. v. Magistrates of Edinburgh* 1942 S.C. 119, 125 *per* L.J.-C. Cooper. This is a question of discretion not of competency: *O'Hara's Exx. v. Western Heritable Investment Co. Ltd* 1965 S.C. 97, 104 *per* L.J.-C. Grant; *Hynd v. West Fife Co-operative Ltd* 1980 S.L.T. 41, 42; *Sellars v. IMI Yorkshire Imperial Ltd* 1986 S.L.T. 629.

In respect of the discretionary power to allow an action of reparation for, or in respect of death from, personal injuries to be raised outwith the triennium under s.19A of the Prescription and Limitation (Scotland) Act 1973 (inserted by the Law Reform (Miscellaneous Provisions) (Scotland) Act 1980, s.23 and amended by the Prescription and Limitation (Scotland) Act 1984, Sched.1, para. 8), the question of amendment ought to be simply one of discretion in such cases. The notion that the question may have been one of competency might have been because of the unfortunate, if not erroneous, use of the word "competency" in R.C.S. 1965, r. 92 and its predecessors and the historical test of competency of amendment by reference to the competency of raising a supplementary summons: see *Mackie v. Glasgow Corporation* 1924 S.L.T. 510.

Changing the method of formulating the case is not changing the basis or substance of it: *McPhail v. Lanarkshire C.C.* 1951 S.C. 301. The introduction of a new ground will not be excluded where the case remains about the same accident and danger: *Hynd*, above, at p. 43.

The time for considering whether such an amendment should be allowed is at a hearing of the motion to allow the pleadings to be amended in terms of the minute of amendment: *Greenhorn v. J. Smart & Co. (Contractors) Ltd* 1979 S.C. 427, 432. It may be possible to consider it at the motion to allow the minute of amendment to be received: *Sellars*, above, at p. 638A *per* Lord Dunpark. It is too late to challenge an amendment on the basis of time-bar or prescription once the amendment has been allowed (and the record amended), unless the interlocutor is timeously reclaimed: *Jones v. Lanarkshire Health Board* 1991 S.C. 285.

The *punctum temporis* when the case commenced for considering a new case introduced by amendment is the date when the minute of amendment is lodged and the motion to allow it to be received is intimated and enroled: *Boyle v. Glasgow Corporation* 1975 S.C. 238; but not the date of the interlocutor allowing the amendment: see *Boyle v. Glasgow Corporation* 1973 S.L.T.(Notes) 42 *per* Lord Dunpark; *Morrison v. Scotstoun Marine Ltd* 1979 S.L.T.(Notes) 76 *per* Lord Ross.

Where a time-bar plea has been included in the answers to a minute but the exclusion of the amendment has been rejected, the plea should not be printed in the amended closed record: *Gibson v. Droopy & Browns Ltd* 1989 S.L.T. 172.

So long as an action to enforce an obligation is in court a "relevant claim" is being made and the prescriptive period under s.6 of the Prescription and Limitation (Scotland) Act 1973 recommences when the action is dismissed or abandoned. Hence, where a claim in a counterclaim was deleted a relevant claim was being made until the claim was deleted, the new prescriptive period ran from the time the claim was deleted and an amendment to re-introduce the claim after five years after the original counterclaim but within one year after its deletion was made within the new prescriptive period and the claim had not prescribed; in other words, an amendment deleting a ground of claim in a pending action will trigger the running of a fresh prescriptive period for that ground of claim and allow that ground to be re-introduced by a further amendment: *G. A. Estates Ltd v. Caviapen Trs. Ltd (No. 2)* 1993 S.L.T. 1045, 1049 *per* Lord Coulsfield; *G. A. Estates Ltd v. Caviapen Trs. Ltd* 1993 S.L.T. 1051, 1059 *per* Lord McCluskey, 1061 *per* Lord Weir, 1065 *per* Lord Penrose. Where an alternative case added by amendment is based on the same obligation or is fundamentally the same as the primary case timeously pled, a party will not be prevented from pursuing it because it was added after expiry of the quinquennial prescription under s.6 of the 1973 Act: *Devos Gebroeder, N.V. v. Sunderland Sportswear Ltd* 1990 S.L.T. 473; *Safdar v. Devlin* 1995 S.L.T. 530. It should be averred that the onus of proof of the negative presumptions falls on the party alleging the affirmative: *Strathclyde R.C. v. W.A. Fairhurst and Partners* 1997 S.L.T. 658.

The words "induced to refrain" in s.6(4) of the 1973 Act include not only a conscious act of self-restraint but also doing nothing to enforce the obligation because it is being concealed: *BP Exploration Operating Co Ltd v. Chevron Shipping Co.,* 2002 S.C. (H.L.) 19.

24.1.3 *"before final judgment".* (1) Amendment at or before procedure roll will generally be allowed unless there is prejudice or delay. At procedure roll the party amending, if he does not lodge a minute of amendment at the time, ought (and should be required) to indicate what the amendment will be, for he should not have the opportunity to amend if amendment could not cure a defect or assist his case. Any such indication may be sought to be noted by the clerk of court in the Minute of Proceedings.

(2) Amendment may be allowed when issues have, or a proof has, been allowed; *McKenna v. British Transport Commission* 1960 S.L.T.(Notes) 30; *cf. McFarquhar v. British Railways Board* 1976 S.L.T.(Notes) 102 and *Muldoon v. Carntyne Steel Castings Co. Ltd* 1965 S.L.T.(Notes) 63.

(3) Amendment near to the date of the proof (or trial) may be refused as too late if it would involve the discharge of the diet or the investigation by an opponent of a new case: *Dryburgh v. National Coal Board* 1962 S.C. 485; *cf. Doig v. Randsgrove Ltd* 1980 S.L.T.(Notes) 16 (new matter could not have been reasonably ascertained earlier); *Jones v. McDermott (Scotland)* 1986 S.L.T. 551 (new case on same facts); *cf. Cork v. Greater Glasgow Health Board* 1997 S.L.T. 404 (proof discharged when amendment allowed but motion to amend record made six months later; motion refused because defender prejudiced and second proof diet would have to be discharged), but overruled on reclaiming motion reported at 1997 S.L.T. 740.

(4) Amendment may be allowed during the proof or trial, and ought to be made as soon as the difficulty arises: *Lawrence v. Arrol* 1958 S.C. 348, 352 *per* L.P. Cooper (proof); *Rafferty v. Weir Housing Corporation Ltd* 1966 S.L.T.(Notes) 23 (jury trial); *Cameron v. Lanarkshire Health Board* 1997 S.L.T. 1040 (jury trial). The overriding consideration is fairness and the interests of justice: *Chapman v. James Dickie & Co. (Drop Forging) Ltd* 1985 S.L.T. 380 (amendment refused); *cf. Campbell v. Cordale Investment Ltd* 1985 S.L.T. 305 (amendment allowed). An adverse circumstance to allowing an amendment is where the facts were or should have been known to the party beforehand: *Thomson v. Glasgow Corporation* 1962 S.C.(H.L.) 36, 57 *per* Lord Macintosh. In such a case the diet may have to be discharged or witnesses recalled: see *Campbell,* above.

Where distinct grounds of action emerge during a proof which are not raised in the pleadings, the new grounds cannot be made the basis of decision unless the appropriate amendment is made: *Black v. John Williams & Co. (Wishaw) Ltd* 1924 S.C.(H.L.) 22; *"Vitruvia" SS Co. Ltd v. Ropner Shipping Co. Ltd* 1924 S.C.(H.L.) 31; both explained in *Gunn v. John McAdam & Son Ltd* 1949 S.C. 31, 39 *per* L.P. Cooper. The modern rule would appear to be that where no objection is taken to evidence led introducing a new ground of action for which there is no record, amendment may not be required: *McGlone v. British Railways Board Ltd* 1966 S.C.(H.L.) 1.

Amendment is not necessary if what is proved in evidence is merely a "variation, modification or development" of what is pled; but it is necessary if what is pled is "new, separate and distinct": *Burns v. Dixon's Iron Works Ltd* 1961 S.C. 102, 107 *per* L.J.-C. Thomson; see also

Cleisham v. British Transport Commission 1964 S.C.(H.L.) 8; *O'Hanlon v. John G. Stein & Co. Ltd* 1965 S.C.(H.L.) 23, 42 *per* Lord Guest; *Hamilton v. John Brown & Co. (Clydebank) Ltd* 1969 S.L.T.(Notes) 19; *McIntosh v. Walker Steam Trawl Fishing Co. Ltd* 1971 S.L.T.(Notes) 75; *McCusker v. Saveheat Cavity Wall Insulation* 1987 S.L.T. 24. See also *McCluskey v. Wallace* 1998 S.C. 711 (submission of joint fault, where sole fault averred and defender pled "caused or at least materially contributed to by the fault on the part of the said child" and had a plea of contributory negligence, allowed; use of the word "*esto*" was unnecessary).

(5) Amendment may be allowed before judgment itself. It may be refused on the grounds of prejudice and injustice: *Oswald v. Fairs* 1911 S.C. 257 (completely new defence raised in hearing on evidence); *McLean v. Victoria Spinning Co. Ltd* 1971 S.L.T.(Notes) 10 (lack of notice in hearing on evidence of evidence of earnings lower than they would have been before accident).

(6) Amendment may be allowed on, during or after reclaiming or an appeal. This is common after debate but uncommon after evidence has been led. In the former case, if allowed the Inner House may refuse to hear argument until the judge at first instance has reconsidered the amended pleadings and the case will be remitted for that purpose: *Wallace v. Scottish Special Housing Association* 1981 S.L.T.(Notes) 60; and see r. 38.21. In the latter case, amendment to raise fresh issues of fact may not be allowed because it could unjustly prejudice

the other party who might have conducted his case differently: *Thomson v. Glasgow Corporation* 1962 S.C.(H.L.) 36; *McGuffie v. Forth Valley Health Board* 1991 S.L.T. 231; *cf. Johnston v. Johnston* (1903) 5 F. 659 (allowed to aver facts not known at time of proof (*res noviter*)); *Moyes v. Burntisland Shipping Co.* 1952 S.C. 429 (allowed in exceptional circumstances to clarify existing controversy not a new one). For an example of amendment in the House of Lords, see *CIN Properties Ltd v. Dollar Land (Cumbernauld) Ltd* 1992 S.C.(H.L.) 104 (amendment to cover point not argued below allowed; no reasons given).

(7) "Final judgment" means a decree which can no longer be appealed: *i.e.* the reclaiming days have expired without a reclaiming motion having been enrolled or, a reclaiming motion having been determined, the period within which appeal to the House of Lords has expired (three months: H.L. Directions, Direction 8.1) without an appeal or where an appeal has been made and finally determined there.

"*necessary for . . . determining the real question in controversy*". Where the amendment is to **24.1.4** the conclusions, condescendence, or pleas-in-law, it must be necessary for the purpose of determining the real question in controversy between the parties: see, *e.g. Moyes v. Burntisland Shipbuilding Co.* 1952 S.C. 429 (allowed exceptionally after jury trial to clarify existing controversy). The amendment may include the introduction or elaboration of a new basis of action even if it is made after expiry of a limitation period: *O'Hara's Exx. v. Western Heritable Investment Co. Ltd* 1965 S.C. 97. Nothing in the dictum of L.J.-C. Cooper in *Pompa's Trs. v. Magistrates of Edinburgh* 1942 S.C. 119, 125 was intended to restrict the scope of what is now r. 24.1. The dictum had been interpreted erroneously, to suggest that the introduction of a new basis of action against an existing defender was incompetent: *Dryburgh v. National Coal Board* 1962 S.C. 485 and *O'Hara's Exx.* above. It is now clear that the court has complete discretion to consider an amendment to change the basis of a pursuer's case against an existing defender notwithstanding that it is made after the expiry of any limitation period: *Hynd v. West Fife Co-operative Ltd* 1980 S.L.T. 41, 42 and *Sellars v. I.M.I. Yorkshire Imperial Ltd* 1986 S.L.T. 629.

Even if the proposed amendment is necessary to determine the real question in controversy, the court must consider whether it is in the interests of justice to allow it: *Thomson v. Glasgow Corporation* 1962 S.C.(H.L.) 36, 51 per L.J.-C. Thomson. The court has a complete discretion in exercising the power of amendment: *Browns Trs. v. Hay* (1897) 24 R. 1108, *per* Lord McLaren. The timing of the proposed amendment and the prejudice caused to the other parties are significant factors. See also *Evans v. Northern Coasters Ltd* 1995 G.W.D. 9–515 (I.H.).

The absence of any conclusions in a summons is not a fundamental nullity where it is plain to the defender from the pleadings what the nature of the claim against him is, and amendment to add conclusions has been allowed under rr. 2.1 and 24.1(2)(a): *Wilson v. Lothian R.C.* 1995 S.L.T. 991.

"*the sum sued for in a summons is increased*". This is unaffected by any statutory time-limit for **24.1.5** bringing an action: *Mackie v. Glasgow Corporation* 1924 S.L.T. 510. Amendment may be made even after the defender has consented to decree against him: *Cowie v. Carron Co. Ltd* 1945 S.C. 280.

"*a different remedy from that originally concluded for or craved*". See, *e.g. Summerlee Iron Co.* **24.1.6** *Ltd v. Caledonian Railway Co.* 1911 S.C. 458; *Campbell v. Henderson* 1949 S.C. 172. But a petition for interdict may not be amended to become a petition for judicial review: *Sleigh v. Edinburgh D.C.* 1988 S.L.T. 253.

"*add the name of an additional pursuer*". Such an amendment may be made even where the **24.1.7** title to sue of the existing pursuer is or becomes defective: *Donaghy v. Rollo* 1964 S.C. 278. Such an amendment is subject to any statutory time-limit: see *McLean v. British Railways Board* 1966 S.L.T. 39.

A minute of sist is not required: *Stewart v. Highlands and Islands Development Board* 1991 S.L.T. 787, 790C–F per Lord MacLean.

"*cause . . . commenced . . . in the name of the wrong person*". See, *e.g. Morrison v. Morrison's* **24.1.8** *Exx.* 1912 S.C. 892. This may be done even if the original pursuer's title is defective: *A.C. Stewart & Partners v. Coleman* 1989 S.L.T. 430. See *Link Housing Association Ltd v. PBL Construction Ltd,* [2007] CSIH 4, 10th January 2007, unreported (First Div.) (whether amendment correcting designation or substituting party after expiry of triennium).

"*doubtful . . . commenced . . . in the name of the right person*". See, *e.g. Anderson v.* **24.1.9** *Balnagowan Estates Co.* 1939 S.C. 168.

"*cause . . . directed against the wrong person*". An amendment to rectify this is subject to any **24.1.10** statutory time-limit for bringing an action. "The court will not, in general, allow a pursuer by amendment to substitute the right defender for the wrong defender, or to cure a radical incompetence in his action, or to change the basis of his case if he only seeks to make such amendments after the expiry of a time limit which would have prevented him at that stage from raising fresh proceedings": *Pompa's Trs. v. Magistrates of Edinburgh* 1942 S.C. 119, 125 *per* L.J.-C. Cooper. It should be noted that an amendment to insert or substitute a new defender may constitute the "bringing of an action" under s.17 or 18 of the Prescription and Limitation (Scotland) Act 1973: *Miller v. National Coal Board* 1960 S.C. 376.

The *punctum temporis* for determining when an action commenced against a party added by amendment is the date when the amended pleadings are served on that party: *Miller*, above, where the pursuer sought to amend to introduce a new defender after the expiry of the limitation period the proposed amendment was held to be incompetent; *cf. Pompa's Trs.*, above.

Applications to amend

24.2.—(1) Subject to paragraph (2), a party seeking to amend shall lodge a minute of amendment in process setting out his proposed amendment and, at the same time, enrol a motion—

  (a) to allow the minute of amendment to be received; and

  (b) to allow—

    (i) amendment in terms of the minute of amendment and, where appropriate, to grant an order under rule 24.3(1) or (2) (service of amended pleadings); or

    (ii) in any other case, where the minute of amendment may require to be answered, any other party to lodge answers within a specified period or such period as the court thinks fit.

(2) Where the amendment proposed is of a minor and formal nature, the party seeking to amend may enrol a motion to allow amendment in the terms set out in the motion.

(3) Where the court has pronounced an interlocutor allowing a minute of amendment to be received and answered, then—

[1] (a) where answers have been lodged, unless the court otherwise orders parties may adjust the minute of amendment and answers within four weeks after the date on which answers were lodged or, where more than one set of answers have been lodged, the latest date on which answers were lodged;

  (b) the party who has lodged the minute of amendment shall—

    (i) where answers have been lodged, within 14 days after the expiry of the period for adjustment of the minute of amendment and answers or any continuation of it, or

    (ii) where no answers have been lodged, within 14 days after the expiry of the period for lodging answers or any prorogation of it, enrol a motion to amend the writ or other pleadings in terms of the minute of amendment and answers (if any) or for other further procedure, as the case may be.

(4) Where a party fails to enrol a motion under paragraph (3)(b), the court shall appoint the cause to be put out on the By Order Roll and, having heard parties on that roll, may—

  (a) if moved to do so, allow the amendment;

  (b) make such order as to further procedure as it thinks fit; and

  (c) in any event, make such order in respect of expenses as it thinks fit.

[2] (5) Where a party to a cause before the Inner House enrols a motion to amend a record in terms of a minute of amendment and answers (if any), he shall at the same time enrol for an order for further procedure, and if it is reasonably practicable to do so, the party shall specify the nature of such further procedure.

Deriv. P.N. 26th March 1981 (r. 24.2(5)) and P.N. 27th March 1986 (r. 24.2(3) and (4))

---

[1] R. 24.2(3)(a) amended by S.I. 1994 No. 2901 (effective 5th December 1994).
[2] R.24.2(5) amended by S.I. 1999 No.1386 (effective 19th May 1999).

General Note. On lodging a minute of amendment, written intimation must be given of its **24.2.1** lodging, and a copy sent, to every other party: r. 4.6(1); on methods of written intimation, see r. 16.9.

Form of minute of amendment. A minute of amendment is headed with the instance of the **24.2.2** cause. There follows a preamble:

"[X] for the pursuer [*or as the case may be*] craved and hereby craves leave of the court to amend the summons [*or as the case may be*] as follows:—".

The amendments to the pleadings are then listed in numbered paragraphs. The minute ends with the words "IN RESPECT WHEREOF". The minute no longer needs to be signed: r. 4.2(9)(a). R. 15.1 (applications by minute) does not apply to a minute of amendment: r. 15.1(6)(b).

No fee is payable on a party lodging a minute of amendment.

"period of notice". This period is determined in accordance with rule 14.6 (period of notice for **24.2.3** answers) by virtue of r. 1.3(1) (definitions of "period of notice" and "writ").

Form and lodging of answers. Where answers are lodged in response to a minute of **24.2.4** amendment, there must be inserted, above the instance of the answers, the date of the interlocutor allowing answers to be lodged and the time for lodging them: r. 4.9(3) (it is no longer necessary to insert the interlocutor). After the instance there follows a preamble:

"[Y] for the defender [*or as the case may be*] craved and hereby craves leave of the court to answer the Minute of Amendment for the pursuer [*or as the case may be*] No. (*insert number*) as follows:—".

The answers are then listed in numbered paragraphs. The answers end with the words "IN RESPECT WHEREOF". The answers no longer need to be signed: r. 4.2(9)(b).

On lodging answers, written intimation must be given of their lodging, and a copy sent, to every other party: r. 4.6(1); on methods of written intimation, see r. 16.9.

No fee is payable on a party lodging answers to a minute of amendment.

"within 4 weeks after". The date from which the period is calculated is not counted. **24.2.5**

"within 14 days". The date from which the period is calculated is not counted. Where the last **24.2.6** day falls on a Saturday or Sunday or a public holiday on which the Office of Court is closed, the next available day is allowed: r. 1.3(7). For office hours and public holidays, see note 3.1.2.

Amendments in Inner House. When pleadings are amended in the Inner House, it may refuse **24.2.7** to hear argument until the judge at first instance has considered the amended pleadings: *Wallace v. Scottish Special Housing Association* 1981 S.L.T. (Notes) 60; and see r. 38.21. In that case the Second Division awarded expenses of the reclaiming motion against the party amending because that party could have enrolled a motion to allow the reclaiming motion and remit to the Lord Ordinary for reconsideration. After this case P.N. 26th March 1981 (the foundation for r. 24.2.(5)) was issued requiring a motion to amend and for an order for further procedure (which may well be for a remit to the court below).

Note the statutory power of the court to allow amendment of a record in an appeal under s.28 of the Sheriff Courts (Scotland) Act 1907: C.S.A. 1988, s.32(1).

By Order Roll hearing. No court fee is payable for a hearing on this By Order Roll. **24.2.8**

Service of amended pleadings

24.3.—(1) In an undefended action where no appearance has been entered or in an unopposed petition or note, unless the amendment is formal in character, the court shall—

(a) order that a copy of the principal writ as amended be served on a specified person; and

(b) allow that person to lodge defences or answers, as the case may be, within such period as the court thinks fit.

(2) Where an amendment under rule 24.1(2)(d) (all parties not, or wrong person, called) has been made—

(a) the court shall order that a copy of the pleadings as so amended be served by the party who made the amendment on that additional or substitute party with a notice in Form 24.3 specifying the date by which defences or answers, as the case may be, must be lodged; and

(b) the party who made the amendment shall lodge in process—

(i) a copy of the pleadings as amended;

(ii) a copy of the notice mentioned in sub-paragraph (a);

(iii) a copy of the interlocutor ordering service; and

(iv) a certificate of service.

(3) When paragraph (2) has been complied with, the cause as so amended shall proceed in every respect as if that party had originally been made a party to the cause.

Deriv. R.C.S. 1965, r. 92(3) (r. 24.3(1))

"undefended action where no appearance has been entered". Where appearance has been **24.3.1** entered, only written intimation and not service is required: see r. 4.6.

"served". For methods of service, see Chap. 16, Part I. **24.3.2**

"answers". See note 24.2.4. **24.3.3**

"such period as the court thinks fit". It is usual to use the period of notice for service of a **24.3.4** summons or petition (21 days within Europe and 42 days furth of Europe: see rr. 13.4 and 14.6), but this may be shortened or extended, and any answers must be lodged *within* that period.

"lodge in process a copy of the pleadings" etc. The documents required to be lodged under **24.3.5** r. 24.3(2)(b) are made up as an execution copy of the pleadings (writ) and lodged as a step of process (on which, see r. 4.4).

Form 24.3. A copy of this form has to be lodged in process with the amended writ because the **24.3.6** court must be satisfied that service has been properly executed and that all that was required to be served was served.

Expenses and conditions of amendment

24.4. The court shall find the party making an amendment liable in the expenses occasioned by the amendment unless it is shown that it is just and equitable that the expenses occasioned by the amendment should be otherwise dealt with, and may attach such other conditions as it think fit.

Deriv. R.C.S. 1965, r. 92(2)

General note. The general rule is that the party making an amendment pays the expenses **24.4.1** occasioned by it (and these include the expenses of his opponent preparing answers: *Campbell v. Henderson* 1949 S.C. 172, 183). An amendment which so alters a case that what has gone before is rendered abortive will result in the party making the amendment being found liable to expenses at least from the date of the amendment: *Stevens v. Motherwell Entertainments Ltd* 1914 S.C. 957 (expenses since closed record); *Black v. John Williams & Co. (Wishaw) Ltd* 1924 S.C.(H.L.) 22, 27 (whole expenses of process to date). If amendment should have made earlier, expenses may be awarded from an earlier date than that of the amendment.

Where amendment is proposed at procedure roll, the party seeking to amend will, as a general rule, have to pay the expenses of the abortive hearing; and payment of those expenses may be made a condition precedent of that amendment: *Colbron v. United Glass Ltd* 1965 S.L.T. 366.

Payment of expenses may be made a condition precedent of further procedure: *Moyes v. Burntisland Shipbuilding Co.* 1952 S.C. 429; *Colbron*, above; cf. *The Edinburgh Modern Quarry Co. Ltd v. Eagle Star Insurance Co. Ltd* 1965 S.L.T.(Notes) 91. Cases cited in McLaren on *Expenses*, pp. 6–7, are no longer followed: *Smellie v. Smellie* 1953 S.L.T.(Notes) 53, 54 *per* L.P. Cooper. A time limit for payment may be laid down: *Stevens*, above.

Conditions are not limited to expenses: see *e.g. Duthie Bros. & Co. v. Duthie* (1892) 19 R. 905 (pursuer to be entitled to sist further pursuers); *Morrison v Marshall Henderson & Whyte SSC,* 28 May 2003 (OH), unreported (condition that evidence of a particular witness be taken on commission).

The conditions cannot be objected to after amendment has been made: *Duthie*, above.

Effect of amendment on diligence

24.5. Where an amendment has been allowed, the amendment shall—
- (a) not validate diligence used on the dependence of a cause so as to prejudice the rights of creditors, of the party against whom the diligence has been executed, who are interested in defeating such diligence; and
- (b) preclude any objection to such diligence stated by a party or any person by virtue of a title acquired or in right of a debt contracted by him subsequent to the execution of such diligence.

Deriv. R.C.S. 1965, r. 92(4)

24.5.1 *General note.* An amendment will not make good diligence used on the dependence before amendment so as to give the pursuer a preference over other creditors: *Fischer & Co. v. Andersen* (1896) 23 R. 395. In such a case, the pursuer will have to obtain a fresh warrant for diligence on the dependence.

CHAPTER 25

COUNTERCLAIMS

Counterclaims

25.1.—(1) In any action other than a family action within the meaning of rule 49.1(1) or an action of multiplepoinding, a defender may lodge a counterclaim against a pursuer—
- (a) where the counterclaim might have been made in a separate action in which it would not have been necessary to call as a defender any person other than the pursuer; and
- (b) in respect of any matter—
  - (i) forming part, or arising out of the grounds, of the action by the pursuer;
  - (ii) the decision of which is necessary for the determination of the question in controversy between the parties; or
  - (iii) which, if the pursuer had been a person not otherwise subject to the jurisdiction of the court, might have been the subject-matter of an action against that pursuer in which jurisdiction would have arisen by reconvention.

(2) A counterclaim may be lodged in process—
- (a) at any time before the record is closed; or
- (b) at any later stage, with leave of the court and subject to such conditions, if any, as to expenses or otherwise as the court thinks fit.

(3) A counterclaim shall be headed "Counterclaim for the defender" and shall contain—
- (a) conclusions, stated in accordance with the appropriate short style, if any, in Form 13.2–B which, if the counterclaim had been made in a separate action, would have been appropriate in the summons in that separate action;
- (b) a statement of facts in numbered paragraphs setting out the facts on

which the counterclaim is founded, incorporating by reference, if necessary, any matter contained in the defences; and

(c) appropriate pleas-in-law.

Deriv. R.C.S. 1965, r.84(a) (part) and (j) (r.25.1(1) and (2)), r.84(a) (part) (r.25.1(1)) and r. 84(b) (r.25.1(3))

General note. The present power to make rules for counterclaims is in s.6(v) of the C.S.A. 1988. **25.1.1** Not every claim may form the basis of a counterclaim: three conditions must be satisfied—(a) the counterclaim could have formed a separate action, (b) it would not have been necessary in that separate action to call another person as defender other than the pursuer and (c) the subject-matter of the counterclaim must (i) form part of the pursuer's action, or (ii) arise out of the grounds of it, or (iii) be a matter the decision of which is necessary for the determination of the question in controversy between the parties or (iv) if the pursuer had not otherwise been subject to the jurisdiction of the court, have arisen by reconvention. The rule is not limited to claims of compensation, set-off or other pecuniary claims: *e.g.* interdict (*McLean v. Marwhirn Developments Ltd* 1976 S.L.T.(Notes) 47), or a decree *ad factum praestandum* (*Borthwick v. Dean Warwick Ltd* 1985 S.L.T. 269 (delivery), *MacKenzie v. MacLeod's Exr.* 1988 S.L.T. 207 (delivery)).

The rationale for counterclaim procedure is expediency; that does not justify a third party minuter entering the process to maintain a claim against the pursuer, even as assignee of the defender's claim: *Tods Murray, W.S. v. Arakin Ltd* 2000 S.L.T. 758 (OH aff'd 2001 S.C. 840, 2001 S.L.T. 1193 (Extra Div.)). In that case Lord Macfadyen in the Outer House observed (p.760F (para.10)) that the position would be different if the minuter assumed the defender's liability to the pursuer and the pursuer consented to the substitution of the minuter for the defender.

Causes in which counterclaims excluded. There are special rules in family actions for making **25.1.2** claims against the pursuer in defences: see r.49.31. A counterclaim is inappropriate in an action of multiplepoinding, the nature of the process being one by which it is decided which persons who have lodged claims are entitled to a fund held by another: see Chap. 51.

Jurisdiction. Jurisdiction over the person sued in a counterclaim is now governed by the **25.1.3** C.J.J.A. 1982. Subject to the rules for consumer contracts, exclusive jurisdiction and prorogation, a person may be sued in the courts for the place in which he is domiciled or, in a counterclaim, in the court where the original claim is pending under the statutory rule for reconvention in the C.J.J.A. 1982. Where the person to be sued is domiciled furth of Scotland, jurisdiction will only be by reconvention and r.25.1(1)(b)(iii) will apply. For jurisdiction generally, see notes 13.2.7 to 13.2.14; and for reconvention, see note 25.1.6.

"forming part, or arising out of the grounds, of the action". Where a contract is one and **25.1.4** indivisible a counterclaim may be made in respect of one item in answer to a claim on the whole contract; but if there is a series of transactions forming separate contracts, a counterclaim in respect of one can only be pleaded in relation to that contract: *J.W. Chafer (Scotland) Ltd v. Hope* 1963 S.L.T.(Notes) 11.

"necessary for the determination of the question in controversy". The question in controversy is **25.1.5** ascertained from the whole pleadings and is wider than simply the pursuer's action: *Fulton Clyde Ltd v. J.F. McCallum & Co. Ltd* 1960 S.L.T. 253 (counterclaim for damages for breach of contract in action for payment of price); see also *Borthwick v. Dean Warwick Ltd* 1983 S.L.T. 269 (ancillary contracts).

Reconvention. A person not otherwise subject to the jurisdiction of the court may render **25.1.6** himself liable to its jurisdiction by litigating in it. This jurisdiction of reconvention is based solely on equity, the fundamental principle being that a party is not entitled to take the benefit of the jurisdiction of our courts, and at the same time refuse that jurisdiction in relative matters: *Thompson v. Whitehead* (1862) 24 D. 331, *per* L.J.-C. Inglis. At common law reconvention arises not only where the two claims arise *in eodem negotio* (arising out of the same matter), but also where they arise *ex diversis causis*, provided they are claims which can fairly be set against one another, without violating some other rule of pleading or principle of equity: *Thompson,* above, *per* L.J.-C. Inglis at p. 345; *MacKenzie v. MacLeod's Exr.* 1988 S.L.T. 207.

The common law now only applies to those matters (where applicable) in Sch.9 of the C.J.J.A. 1982 which are excluded from the application of Sch.8 to that Act. The rule now is, in all matters other than those in Sch.9, that, subject to the rules of jurisdiction over consumer contracts, exclusive jurisdiction and prorogation of jurisdiction in the 1982 Act, a person may be sued, on a counterclaim arising from the same contract or facts on which the original claim was based, in the court in which the original claim is pending (and not only in the courts for the place in which he is domiciled): C.J.J.A. 1982, Sch.8, r.2(15)(c). Where the person to be sued on the counterclaim is domiciled in a Contracting State to which the 1968 (Brussels) Convention, or the Lugano Convention, applies or is domiciled in another part of the UK, the same statutory rule applies: C.J.J.A. 1982, Sch.1 (1968 Convention), Art.6(3); Sch.3C (Lugano Convention), Art.6(3); Sch.4 (Inter-UK jurisdiction), Art.6(3). Note *Spitzley v. Sommer Exploitation* [1985] E.C.R. 787 where no objection to jurisdiction was entered in relation to a counterclaim on a contract not based on the same contract and in respect of which another court had exclusive jurisdiction by virtue of an agreement; it was held by the European Court that the court hearing the counterclaim had jurisdiction by virtue of Art.18 of the 1968 Convention (entering appearance without contesting jurisdiction).

25.1.7   *Counterclaims and the Crown.* A person is not allowed to avail himself of any set-off (see *Laing v. Lord Advocate* 1973 S.L.T.(Notes) 81) or counterclaim in proceedings by the Crown (a) for recovery of taxes, duties or penalties or (b) arising out of a right or claim to repayment of taxes, duties or penalties: Crown Proceedings Act 1947, s.35(2)(b) as applied by s.'50. A person is not entitled, without leave of the court, to avail himself of any set-off or counterclaim in any proceedings by the Crown if the subject-matter does not relate to the government department on whose behalf the proceedings are brought: 1947 Act, s.35(2)(c) as applied by s.50. Similarly, the Crown may not, without leave of the court, set-off or counterclaim if the subject-matter does not relate to the government department concerned: 1947 Act, s.35(2)(d) as applied by s.50.

     In considering whether leave to the Crown should be granted, where leave may be sought, the court will balance the common law right against the statutory duty to seek leave (*Smith v. Lord Advocate* 1980 SC 227, 237 *per* Lord Avonside) and take into account the similarity between the nature of the claims (*Laing*, above, at p. 82 *per* Lord Keith).

25.1.8   *Form and lodging of counterclaim.* A counterclaim must be in a separate writ and not alternatively, as formerly, in the defences (whether as drafted or by adjustment or amendment). If a counterclaim satisfies the conditions of r.25.1(1), the court, in general, has no discretion to refuse it if it is lodged before the record is closed. Exceptions to the general rule are—(a) counterclaims by or against the Crown (see note 25.1.7) or (b) where leave is required under the Insolvency Act 1986, s.130 (but leave is not required where set-off is for a lesser sum than that in the action: *G. & A. (Hotels) Ltd v. T.H.B. Marketing Services Ltd* 1983 S.L.T. 497).

     But the court has a discretion if the counterclaim is sought to be lodged after the record has closed: it may be refused as coming too late. It is not clear what factors the court would take into account in granting or refusing leave. The considerations may be similar to those in deciding whether to allow amendment, including delay, prejudice and the stage at which it is sought to lodge the counterclaim: see note 24.1.1. If it is sought to amend the defences in light of the counterclaim, then the circumstances in which amendment is allowed after the record has closed will apply: see r.24.1 and notes 24.1.1–24.1.3.

     On the form of pleadings and pleas-in-law, see notes 13.2.3–13.2.5.

     Where a counterclaim is lodged the record (open or closed) will contain it and any answers in addition to, but separate from, the summons and defences.

     On lodging a counterclaim the defender must give written intimation of its lodging, and send a copy of it, to every other party: r.4.6(1). On methods of written intimation, see r.16.9.

25.1.9   *Fee.* There is no court fee for lodging a counterclaim.

Authority for diligence etc. on counterclaims

   [1] **25.2.**—(1) A defender who lodges a counterclaim may apply by motion for authority for diligence by—

     (a) inhibition on the dependence of the action;

     (b) arrestment on the dependence of the action where there is a conclusion for the payment of money;

     (c) arrestment *in rem*; or

     (d) dismantling a ship.

     (2) A certified copy of an interlocutor granting a motion under paragraph (1) shall be sufficient authority for execution of the diligence.

     (3) A certified copy of an interlocutor granting authority for inhibition under this rule may be registered with a certificate of execution in the Register of Inhibitions and Adjudications.

     (4) A notice of a certified copy of an interlocutor granting authority for inhibition under this rule may be registered under section 155 of the Titles to Land Consolidation (Scotland) Act 1868; and such registration shall have the same effect as registration of a notice under that section.

Deriv. R.C.S. 1965, r.84(c)

---

[1] R.25.2 substituted by S.S.I. 2003 No. 537 (effective 10th November, 2003).

General note. On diligence, see notes 13.6A.1–13.6A.5; on the effect of authority for **25.2.1** inhibition on the dependence, see notes 13.9.2 and 13.9.3.

"motion". For motions, see Chap.23.   **25.2.2**

Answers to counterclaims

25.3.—(1) Answers to a counterclaim may be lodged by a pursuer—
- (a) where the counterclaim is lodged before the record is closed, within 14 days after the date on which the counterclaim is lodged; or
- (b) in any other case, within the period appointed by the interlocutor allowing the counterclaim to be received.

(2) Where answers to a counterclaim have been lodged, the court may, on the motion of the pursuer or defender, allow such period for adjustment as it thinks fit.

Deriv. R.C.S. 1965, r. 84(k)

Form and lodging of answers. For form of answers, see r. 18.3.   **25.3.1**
No court fee is payable on the lodging of answers by a party to a counterclaim.

"within 14 days". The date from which the period is calculated is not counted. Where the last **25.3.2** day falls on a Saturday or Sunday or a public holiday on which the Office of Court is closed, the next available day is allowed: r. 1.3(7). For office hours and public holidays, see note 3.1.2.

Effect of abandonment of action

25.4.—(1) The right of a pursuer to abandon his action under rule 29.1 shall not be affected by a counterclaim; and any expenses for which the pursuer is found liable as a condition, or in consequence, of such abandonment shall not include the expenses of the counterclaim.

(2) Notwithstanding abandonment by the pursuer, a defender may insist in his counterclaim; and the proceedings in the counterclaim shall continue in dependence as if the counterclaim were a separate action.

Deriv. R.C.S. 1965, r. 84(d) (r. 25.4(1)) and r. 84(f) (r. 25.4(2))

General note. On abandonment by pursuer, see r. 29.1; on abandonment by defender of **25.4.1** counterclaim, see r. 29.2.

Proof or jury trial of counterclaims

25.5.—(1) Where a proof or jury trial is allowed between parties to an action, the court may allow any counterclaim to proceed to proof or jury trial, as the case may be, before, at the same time as or after, the action as it thinks fit.

(2) Where evidence is led in a counterclaim separately from the evidence in the action, the evidence in one cause shall, so far as competent and relevant, be evidence in the other cause.

Deriv. R.C.S. 1965, r. 84(g)

General note. The court may, under r. 25.5(1), allow a counterclaim to proceed before, at the **25.5.1** same time as or after the action. The court may, of course, dismiss the action (see *e.g. Feld British Agencies Ltd v. James Pringle Ltd* 1961 S.L.T. 123), grant decree for a sum admittedly due (see *e.g. Fulton Clyde Ltd v. J. F. McCallum & Co. Ltd* 1960 S.L.T. 253) or for which there is no relevant defence stated and allow the counterclaim to proceed. Where the pursuer obtains decree it would not be usual, though not incompetent, to supersede extract.

Interlocutors in respect of counterclaims

25.6. A decree or other interlocutor which could have been pronounced in a separate action brought to enforce the conclusions stated in a counterclaim may be pronounced in respect of the counterclaim.

Deriv. R.C.S. 1965, r. 84(h)

[1] CHAPTER 25A

DEVOLUTION ISSUES

Interpretation of this Chapter
  25A.1 In this Chapter—
  "Advocate General" means the Advocate General for Scotland;
  "devolution issue" means a devolution issue within the meaning of—
      (a) Schedule 6 to the Scotland Act 1998;
      (b) Schedule 10 to the Northern Ireland Act 1998; or
      (c) Schedule 8 to the Government of Wales Act 1998,
    and any reference to Schedule 6, Schedule 10 or Schedule 8 is a
    reference to that Schedule to, respectively, the Scotland Act 1998,
    the Northern Ireland Act 1998 and the Government of Wales Act
    1998;
  "the Judicial Committee" means the Judicial Committee of the Privy
    Council;
  "relevant authority" means the Advocate General and—
      (a) in the case of a devolution issue within the meaning of
          Schedule 6, the Lord Advocate;
      (b) in the case of a devolution issue within the meaning of
          Schedule 10, the Attorney General for Northern Ireland, and
          the First Minister and deputy First Minister acting jointly;
      (c) in the case of a devolution issue within the meaning of
          Schedule 8, the National Assembly for Wales.

---

[1] Chap. 25A and r. 25A.1 invoked by S.I. 1999 No. 1345 (effective 6th May 1999).

25A.1.1   *General note.* Chap. 25A was inserted by A.S. (Devolution Issues Rules) 1999 [SI 1999/1345]. It makes provision for the manner and time in which a "devolution issue" (see note 25A.1.2) may be raised and dealt with.

25A.1.2   *"devolution issue"*. An Act of the Scottish Parliament is not law in so far as any provision is outside the legislative competence of the Parliament: Scotland Act 1998, s.29(1). It would appear that what is intended, although not clearly expressed, is that only the provision outwith legislative competence is affected and not the whole Act. Such an intention is clearly expressed in s.6(1) of the Northern Ireland Act 1998; and there were attempts to amend the Scottish provision to make it clearer. A provision of an Act is outside legislative competence if (a) it would form part of the law of a country or territory other than Scotland or confer or remove functions exercisable otherwise than in or as regards Scotland; (b) it relates to reserved matters (see s.30 and Sched.5 to the Scotland Act 1998); (c) it is in breach of the restrictions in Sched.4 (enactments protected from modification); (d) it is incompatible with any of the Convention rights in the Human Rights Act 1998 or European Community law; or (e) it would remove the Lord Advocate from his position as head of the systems of criminal prosecution and investigation of deaths in Scotland: Scotland Act 1998, s.29(2).
  The courts may be called upon to decide whether a provision in an Act is within or without the legislative competence of the Parliament. Sched.6 of the Scotland Act 1998 provides the mechanism for devolution issues raised in proceedings in Scotland, England and Wales and Northern Ireland. Similar provision is made for devolution issues with respect to Northern Ireland in Sched.10 to the Northern Ireland Act 1998, and to Wales in Sched.8 to the Government of Wales Act 1998 which may be raised in proceedings, in *e.g.* Scotland, including intimation of those proceedings to the other countries' law officers.

A "devolution issue" is defined in Sched. 6 to the Scotland Act 1998 as (a) a question whether an Act of the Scottish Parliament or any provision of it is within the legislative competence of the Parliament; (b) a question whether any function (purportedly or proposed to be exercised) is a function of the Scottish Ministers, the First Minister or the Lord Advocate; (c) a question whether the purported or proposed exercise of a function by a member of the Scottish Executive is or would be within devolved competence; (d) a question whether the purported or proposed exercise by a member of the Scottish Executive is or would be incompatible with any of the Convention rights or with Community law; (e) a question whether a failure to act by a member of the Scottish Executive is incompatible with any of the Convention rights or with Community law; (f) any other question about whether a function is exercisable within devolved competence in or as regards Scotland an any other question arising by virtue of the Scotland Act 1998 about reserved matters. Similar definitions are contained in the Northern Ireland Act 1998 and the Government of Wales Act 1998.

Under s.102 of the Scotland Act 1998 (and s.81 of the Northern Ireland Act and s.110 of the Government of Wales Act), where the court decides that an Act or a provision of an Act is not within the legislative competence of the Parliament or a member of the Scottish Executive does not have power to make, confirm or approve a provision of subordinate legislation, the court may remove or limit any retrospective effect or suspend the effect of the decision of the court.

Proceedings where devolution issue raised in principal writ
[1] **25A.2.** Where any summons, petition or other principal writ contains an averment or conclusion which raises a devolution issue, the principal writ shall be served on the relevant authority, unless he has initiated the proceedings.

----

[1] R.25A.2 inserted by S.I. 1999 No. 1345 (effective 6th May 1999).

"individual issue". See note 25A.1.2.   **25A.2.1**

"principal writ". This means the writ by which a cause is initiated before the court: r. 1.3(1).   **25A.2.2**

"served". For rules of service, see Chap. 16.   **25A.2.3**

Time for raising devolution issue
[1] **25A.3.**—(1) It shall not competent for a party to any proceedings to raise a devolution issue otherwise than in the pleadings before any evidence is led, unless the court, on cause shown, otherwise determines.

(2) Where the court determines that a devolution issue may be raised as mentioned in paragraph (1) it shall make such orders as to the procedure to be followed as appear to it to be appropriate and, in particular, it shall make such orders—

 (a) as are necessary to ensure that intimation of the devolution issue is given in writing to the relevant authority for the purposes of paragraph 5 of Schedule 6 or as the case may be paragraph 23 of Schedule 10 or paragraph 14(1) of Schedule 8; and

 (b) as to the time in which any step is to be taken by any party in the proceedings.

[1] R. 25A.3 inserted by S.I. 1999 No. 1345 (effective 6th May 1999).

General note. The general rule is that a devolution issue must be raised in pleadings and   **25A.3.1**
before any evidence is led: s.25A. 3(i). Cause will have to be shown to raise such an issue which is not in the pleadings or after evidence has begun.

No procedure is laid down for dealing with a devolution issue. A practice may develop in due course. What is apparent is that a devolution issue may not have to await a hearing on the Procedure Roll. As soon as the issue is raised in, *e.g.* the summons, a party may apply by motion or presumably the court may at its own instance (see the terms of r. 25A.3(2) although probably only after hearing parties on whether to do so), for the court to order the procedure to be followed.

The court has power to refer the issue to a higher court, *i.e.* the Outer House to the Inner House or the Inner House to the Judicial Committee of the Privy Council: Scotland Act 1998, Sched. 6, paras 7, 8 and 10.

"devolution issue". See note 25A.1.2.   **25A.3.2**

"relevant authority". See definition in r. 25A.1.   **25A.3.3**

Specification of devolution issue

[1] **25A.4.**—(1) Any party raising a devolution issue shall specify—

(a) where he initiates the action, in the principal writ;

(b) where a counterclaim is lodged, in the counterclaim;

(c) in any other case, in the defences or answers,

the facts and circumstances and contentions of law on the basis of which it is alleged that the devolution issue arises in sufficient detail to enable the court to determine, for the purposes of paragraph 2 of Schedule 6 or, as the case may be, of Schedule 10 or Schedule 8, whether a devolution issue arises in the proceedings.

(2) Where a party wishes to raise a devolution issue after the lodging of any writ mentioned in paragraph (1), he shall do so either by adjustment or amendment so as to specify in his pleadings the matters mentioned in that paragraph.

---

[1] R. 25A.4 inserted by S.I. 1999 No. 1345 (effective 6th May 1999).

25A.4.1 *"devolution issue"*. See note 25A.1.2.

25A.4.2 *"principal writ"*. This means the writ by which a cause is initiated before the court: r. 1.3(1).

25A.4.3 "paragraph 2 of Schedule 6", Paragraph 2 of Sched. 6 to the Scotland Act (and para. 2 of Sched. 10 to the Northern Ireland Act 1998 and Sched. 8 to the Government of Wales Act 1998) provides that a devolution issue shall not be taken to arise merely because of any contention of a party which appears to the court to be frivolous or vexatious.

Intimation of devolution issue

[1] **25A.5**—(1) Intimation of a devolution issue in pursuance of paragraph 5 of Schedule 6 or, as the case may be, paragraph 23 of Schedule 10 or paragraph 14(1) of Schedule 8 shall be given to the relevant authority (unless he is a party to the proceedings or has been served with the principal writ in pursuance of rule 25A.2) in accordance with this rule.

(2) Where the devolution issue is raised in the principal writ, service of the principal writ on the relevant authority shall be treated as such intimation.

(3) In any other case, the party raising the devolution issue shall, as soon as practicable, enrol a motion craving a warrant to intimate the devolution issue to the relevant authority and on hearing the motion, where it appears to the court that a devolution issue arises, the court shall order such intimation in Form 25A.5.

(4) The intimation of a devolution issue shall specify 14 days, or such other period as the court on cause shown may specify, as the period within which a relevant authority may give notice to the Deputy Principal Clerk of his intention to take part as a party in the proceedings as mentioned in paragraph 6 of Schedule 6 or, as the case may be, paragraph 24 of Schedule 10 or paragraph 14(2) of Schedule 8.

---

[1] R. 25.5 inserted by S.I. 1999 No. 1345 (effective 6th May 1999).

25A.5.1 *"devolution issue"*. See note 25A.1.2.

25A.5.2 *Intimation.* Subject to r. 16.8, for methods of intimation, see r. 16.7. Rule 16.8 deals with intimation on a warrant to intimate, such as under r. 25A.5(3).

Intimation has to be given, unless a party, to the Advocate General and the Lord Advocate under para. 5 of Sched. 6 to the Scotland Act 1998. Where a devolution issue under the Northern Ireland Act 1998 or the Government of Wales Act 1998 arises in civil proceedings in Scotland there are provisions for intimation in para. 23 of Sched. 10 and para. 14(1) of Sched. 8, respectively, to those Acts.

25A.5.3 *"relevant authority"*. See definition in r. 25A.1.

25A.5.4 *"motion"*. For motions, see Chap. 23.

Response to intimation
 [1] **25A.6**—(1) Where a relevant authority gives notice as mentioned in rule 25A.5(4), he shall, not later than 7 days after the date of such notice lodge a minute of his written submissions in respect of the devolution issue together with conclusions and pleas in law as appropriate.

 [2](1A) Where a relevant authority does not take part as a party in the proceedings at first instance the court may allow him to take part as a party in any subsequent appeal, reclaiming motion or reference to a higher court.

 (2) The minute lodged in accordance with paragraph (1) shall be intimated to all other parties in the proceedings.

---

 [1] R. 25A.6 inserted by S.I. 1999 No. 1345 (effective 6th May 1999).
 [2] R.25A.6(1A) inserted by S.S.I. 2000 No. 66, para. 2(3) (effective 7th April 2000).

"*not later than 7 days after*". The day of the date of the notice is not counted, the period of **25A.6.1** time commencing at the beginning of the following day and ending at the close of office hours of Office of Court on the seventh day after that date.

"*relevant authority*". See definition in r. 25A.1   **25A.6.2**

Reference of devolution issue to Inner House
 [1] **25A.7.** Where a devolution issue arises in any proceedings before the Lord Ordinary, any reference of the devolution issue to the Inner House as mentioned in paragraph 7 of Schedule 6 or, as the case may be, paragraph 25 of Schedule 10 or paragraph 15 of Schedule 8 shall by means of a report in accordance with Chapter 34 of these Rules.

---

 [1] R. 25A.7 inserted by S.I. 1999 No. 1345 (effective 6th May 1999).

General note. There is a statutory power for a Lord Ordinary to refer a devolution issue to the **25A.7.1** Inner House. The procedure is that for reporting to the Inner House in Chap. 34.

"*devolution issue*". See note 25A.1.2.   **25A.7.2**

Reference of devolution issue to Judicial Committee
 [1] **25A.8.**—(1) Where the court—
  (a) decides in accordance with paragraph 10 of Schedule 6 or, as the case may be, paragraph 28 of Schedule 10 or paragraph 18 of Schedule 8; or
  (b) is required as mentioned in paragraph 33 of Schedule 6 or, as the case may be, paragraph 33 of Schedule 10 or paragraph 30(1) of Schedule 8,
to refer a devolution issue to the Judicial Committee, it shall pronounce an interlocutor giving directions to the parties about the manner and time in which the reference is to be drafted and adjusted.

 (2) When the reference has been drafted at the sight of the court, the court shall make and sign the reference.

 (3) The reference shall include such matter as may be required by rule 2.9 of the Judicial Committee (Devolution Issues) Rules 1999, and shall have annexed to it the interlocutor making the reference.

 (4) Service of the reference in pursuance of rule 2.8 of the Judicial Committee (Devolution Issues) Rules 1999 may be effected by the Deputy Principal Clerk by first class recorded delivery post.

---

 [1] R. 25A.8 inserted by S.I. 1999 No. 1345 (effective 6th May 1999).

General note. Only a court of three or more judges of the Court of Session (*i.e.* the Inner **25A.8.1** House), and not the Lord Ordinary, may refer a devolution issue to the Judicial Committee of the Privy Council. There is also provision for appeals to the Judicial Committee: see r. 25A.11.

25A.8.2   *The reference*. The reference must set out (a) the questions referred; (b) the addresses of the parties; (c) the name and address of the person who applied for or required the reference; (d) a concise statement of the background to the matter including the facts of the case (including any findings in fact) and the main issues in the case and the contentions of the parties; (e) the relevant law including the relevant provisions of the Scotland Act 1998, and (f) the reasons why an answer to the question is considered necessary for the purpose of disposing of the proceedings: Judicial Committee (Devolution Issues) Rules Order 1999, r. 2.9(1) (S.I. 1999 No. 665).

     All judgments already given in the proceedings, including copies of any interlocutors and any notes attached to such interlocutors, must be annexed to the reference: r. 2.9(2) of the above Rules.

25A.8.3   "*Service of the reference*". Rule 2.8 of the Judicial Committee (Devolution Issues) Rules 1999 (S.I. 1999 No. 665) provides that the court lodging the reference must serve copies of it on the parties and law officer who is not already a party and who has a potential interest in the proceedings. Rule 2.8(3)(a) specifies that where the reference or appeal is from a court in Scotland the Law Officers having a potential interest will be the Lord Advocate and the Advocate General.

25A.8.4   "*devolution issue*". See note 25A.1.2.

Sist of cause on reference to Judicial Committee

[1] **25A.9.**—(1) Subject to paragraph (2), on a reference being made to the Judicial Committee as mentioned in rule 25A.8, the cause shall, unless the court when making the reference otherwise orders, be sisted until the Judicial Committee has determined the devolution issue.

     (2) The court may recall a sist made under paragraph (1) for the purpose of making any interim order which a due regard to the interests of the parties may require.

------

[1] R. 25A.9 inserted by S.I. 1999 No. 1345 (effective 6th May 1999).

Transmission of reference

[1] **25A.10.**—(1) The reference shall be transmitted by the Deputy Principal Clerk to the Registrar of the Judicial Committee.

     (2) Unless the court otherwise directs, the reference shall not be sent to the Registrar of the Judicial Committee where a reclaiming motion or an appeal against the making of the reference is pending.

     (3) For the purpose of paragraph (2), a reclaiming motion or an appeal shall be treated as pending—

     (a) until the expiry of the time for marking that reclaiming motion or appeal; or

     (b) where a reclaiming motion or an appeal has been made, until it has been determined.

------

[1] R. 25A.10 inserted by S.I. 1999 No. 1345 (effective 6 May 1999).

Appeals to the Judicial Committee

[1] **25A.11.**—(1) Where an appeal to the Judicial Committee is made—

     (a) under paragraph 12 of Schedule 6 or, as the case may be, paragraph 30 of Schedule 10 or paragraph 20 of Schedule 8; or

     (b) with leave or special leave, under paragraph 13(b) of Schedule 6 or, as the case may be, paragraph 31(b) of Schedule 10 or paragraph 21(b) of Schedule 8,

the court from whose determination the appeal is made may make such orders as it thinks fit, having regard to the interests of the parties to the cause, for the purpose of regulating the proceedings pending the determination of the appeal by the Judicial Committee, including orders relating to interim possession, execution and expenses already incurred.

(2) Where the determination of an appeal by the Judicial Committee does not dispose of the whole cause, the court against whose determination the appeal was made shall order such further procedure as is necessary to enable it to dispose of the whole cause.

————

[1] R. 25A.11 inserted by S.I. 1999 No. 1345 (effective 6th May 1999).

General note. There is a right of appeal to the Judicial Committee of the Privy Council from **25A.11.1** the Inner House against a determination by it of a devolution issue with leave of the Inner House or, failing which, with special leave of the Judicial Committee of the Privy Council: 1998 Act, Sch.6, para.13.

The word "determination" in para.13 of Sch.6 to the 1998 Act implies the making of a decision on the merits of a devolution issue and, where no such decision has been made, an application for leave to appeal is incompetent: *C v. Miller,* 2003 S.L.T. 1402 (Extra Div.).

Orders mitigating the effect of certain decisions

[1] **25A.12.**—(1) In any proceedings where the court is considering making an order under—

(a) section 102 of the Scotland Act 1998;

(b) section 81 of the Northern Ireland Act 1998; or

(c) section 110 of the Government of Wales Act 1998,

(power of the court to vary or suspend the effect of certain decisions), the court shall order intimation of the fact to be made by the Deputy Principal Clerk to every person to whom intimation is required to be given by that section.

(2) Intimation as mentioned in paragraph (1) shall—

(a) be made forthwith in Form 25A.12 by first class recorded delivery post; and

(b) specify 7 days, or such other period as the court thinks fit, as the period within which a person may give notice of his intention to take part in the proceedings.

----

[1] R. 25A.12 inserted by S.I. 1999 No. 1345 (effective 6th May 1999).

General note. Under s.102 of the Scotland Act 1998 (and s.81 of the Northern Ireland Act and **25A.12.1** s.110 of the Government of Wales Act), where the court decides that an Act or a provision of an Act is not within the legislative competence of the Scottish Parliament or a member of the Scottish Executive does not have power to make, confirm or approve a provision of subordinate legislation, the court may remove or limit any retrospective effect or suspend the effect of the decision of the court.

Where the court is considering whether to make such an order it must intimate that to the appropriate law officers mentioned in s.102 of the Scotland Act 1998 (or the equivalent provisions of the other Acts mentioned above, as the case may be).

CHAPTER 26

THIRD PARTY PROCEDURE

Applications for third party notice

26.1.—(1) Where, in an action, a defender claims that—

(a) he has in respect of the subject-matter of the action a right of contribution, relief or indemnity against any person who is not a party to the action, or

(b) a person whom the pursuer is not bound to call as a defender should be made a party to the action along with the defender in respect that such person is—

(i) solely liable, or jointly or jointly and severally liable with the defender, to the pursuer in respect of the subject-matter of the action, or

(ii) liable to the defender in respect of a claim arising from or in connection with the liability, if any, of the defender to the pursuer,

he may apply by motion for an order for service of a third party notice on that other person in Form 26.1–A for the purpose of convening that other person as a third party to the action.

(2) Where—

    (a) a pursuer against whom a counterclaim has been made, or

    (b) a third party convened in the action,

seeks, in relation to the claim against him, to make against a person who is not a party, a claim mentioned in paragraph (1) as a claim which could be made by a defender against a third party, he shall apply by motion for an order for service of a third party notice in Form 26.1–B (notice by pursuer) or Form 26.1–C (notice by third party), as the case may be, in the same manner as a defender under that paragraph; and rules 26.2 to 26.7 shall, with the necessary modifications, apply to such a claim as they apply in relation to such a claim by a defender.

Deriv. R.C.S. 1965, r.85(1) (preamble (part)) amended by SI 1980/1144 (r.26.1(1)) and r.85(1)(g) and (2) amended by SI 1980/1144 (r.26.1(2))

26.1.1   *General note.* First introduced in R.C.S. 1934, Ch. II, r.20(d) [S.R. & O. 1934 No. 967], third party procedure was abolished by A.S. 25th May 1937 [S.R. & O. 1937 No. 180] (about which, see 1937 S.L.T. (News) 98) and re-introduced by A.S. (R.C.A.) 1963 [SI 1963/380], and re-enacted in R.C.S. 1965, r.85, after the introduction of contribution between joint wrongdoers by s.3 of the Law Reform (Miscellaneous Provisions) (Scotland) Act 1940.

    The purpose of the rule is to enable questions arising out of one matter, including claims by a defender against a third party for contribution, relief or indemnity and liability between a defender and a third party, to be disposed of in one action, saving time and expenses: *Winchester v. Ramsay* 1966 S.C. 41, 46 *per* Lord Kissen; *Beedie v. Norrie* 1966 S.C. 207, 210 *per* L.P. Clyde; *Buchan v. Thomson* 1976 S.L.T. 42; *Nimmo's Exrs v. White's Exr.* 1976 S.L.T. 70, 71 *per* Lord Grieve. It enables a third party to be heard on any matter in which he has a relevant interest in relation to the case between the pursuer and defender: *Barton v. William Low & Co. Ltd* 1968 S.L.T. (Notes) 27, 28 *per* Lord Stott.

The rule is procedural and is not concerned with substantive right: *Findlay v. National Coal Board* 1965 S.L.T. 328, 330 *per* Lord Kissen; *Aitken v. Norrie* 1966 S.C. 168, 174 *per* L.P. Clyde.

It is an advantage to the defender to convene a third party where he has a right of contribution, relief or indemnity, or for apportionment of liability, against the third party because it saves intimating progress of the action and raising a separate action of relief (*Dorman, Long & Co. v. Harrower* (1899) 1 F. 1109, 1115 *per* Lord Kinnear). Where liability is either solely that of the defender or a third party, the defender may prefer not to convene the third party, thus avoiding paying expenses to the third party if he himself is found wholly liable.

The rule applies to a pursuer against whom a counterclaim is made or to a third party seeking to bring in a second third party (see, *e.g. Nicol Homeworld Contracts Ltd v. Charles Gray Builders Ltd* 1986 S.L.T. 317).

The court has a discretion whether to grant an order for service of a third party notice. In considering the question it will have regard to what would be in the interests of doing justice between the parties: *Rodgers v. James Crow & Sons Ltd* 1971 S.C. 155. That a party may lose his right to jury trial or other mode of inquiry is not a relevant factor: *Rodgers*, above. An order may be refused if there has been inordinate delay in seeking the order and the prejudice in refusing is outweighed by the prejudice to the other party in postponing the determination of the action: *Tait v. Leslie & Saddler Ltd* 1971 S.L.T.(Notes) 79; *Halbert v. British Airports Authority plc* 1996 S.L.T. 97.

Jurisdiction. The rule is, in all matters other than those in Sched. 9 to the C.J.J.A. 1982, that, **26.1.2** subject to the rules of jurisdiction over consumer contracts, exclusive jurisdiction and prorogation of jurisdiction in the 1982 Act, a person may be sued, as a third party in an action on a warranty or guarantee or in any other third party proceedings, in the court seized of the original proceedings (and not only in the courts for the place in which he is domiciled) unless solely for the purpose of removing him from the jurisdiction of a competent court: C.J.J.A. 1982, Sched. 8, r. 2(15)(b). Where the person to be sued as a third party is domiciled in a Contracting State to which the 1968 (Brussels) Convention, or the Lugano Convention, applies or is domiciled in another part of the UK, the same statutory rule applies: C.J.J.A. 1982, Sched. 1 (1968 Convention), Art. 6(2); Sched. 3C (Lugano Convention), Art. 6(2); Sched. 4 (Inter-UK jurisdiction), Art. 6(2). Jurisdiction may be invoked whatever the ground of jurisdiction in the original proceedings unless the jurisdiction of another court has been prorogated by agreement. Note *Hagen v. Zeehaghe* [1990] E.C.R. I–1845 where it was held that Art. 6 merely determines jurisdiction and is not concerned with the procedural rules for determining what third party claims the national court will admit to be heard under its own procedural rules provided the effectiveness of the convention is not impaired.

"subject-matter of the action". This means no more than the claim by the pursuer: *Buchan v.* **26.1.3** *Thomson* 1976 S.L.T. 42, 45 *per* Lord Fraser.

"right of contribution, relief or indemnity". This is the first ground on which a defender may **26.1.4** bring in a third party. Such a right gives rise to a separate claim by the defender against the third party only, ancillary to the action between the pursuer and defender but incorporated with it in the same process. A third party may be convened by a defender after the expiry of a time-limit for the raising of the main action: see, *e.g. Findlay v. National Coal Board* 1965 S.L.T. 328. Where there are two or more pursuers, one may be convened as a third party: *Buchan v. Thomson* 1976 S.L.T. 42.

The defender must have title and interest at the time of service of the third party notice: *Cobham v. Minter* 1986 S.L.T. 336. He may have an interest although he does not have an enforceable right to recover until he has paid the pursuer: *Findlay v. National Coal Board* 1965 S.L.T. 328, 330 *per* Lord Kissen; *Beedie v. Norrie* 1966 S.C. 207, 210 *per* L.P. Clyde (cases on whether a third party could be convened with respect to a claim under s.3(2) of the Law Reform (Miscellaneous Provisions) (Scotland) Act 1940).

(1) *Right of contribution.* Technically this exists only where the defender and third party are co-obligants to the same principal: *Lanarkshire Speedway and Sports Stadium Ltd v. Gray* 1970 S.L.T.(Notes) 54. But, following *Anderson v. Anderson* 1981 S.L.T. 271, "contribution" should no longer be regarded as a term of art and third party procedure is not limited to its technical meaning: and see (2) below. Under s.3(1) of the Law Reform (Miscellaneous Provisions) (Scotland) Act 1940 persons found jointly and severally liable in damages or expenses for wrongful or negligent acts or omissions are liable *inter se* to contribute to those damages or expenses in such proportions as the court may deem just; but this does not affect the right of the pursuer to obtain decree against one or any of them, leaving it to him or them to recover from the others.

(2) *Right of relief.* The better view now is that "relief" here is not a term of art and is not limited to claims which would constitute an action of relief proper; and third party procedure may be used even where the defender seeks relief only in respect of part of the pursuer's claim, not just where the liability of the third party is commensurate or co-extensive with his:

Nimmo's Exrs. v. White's Exr. 1976 S.L.T. 70; *Anderson v. Anderson* 1981 S.L.T. 271; *Nicol Homeworld Contracts Ltd v. Charles Gray Builders Ltd* 1986 S.L.T. 317. The view that the term is limited to its technical meaning (see *Lanarkshire Speedway and Sports Stadium Ltd v. Gray* 1970 S.L.T.(Notes) 54) must now be regarded as no longer the law. An action of relief proper arises generally where the pursuer and defender were under a common obligation which ought first to have been performed by the defender (*Caledonian Railway Co. v. Colt* (1860) 3 Macq. 833) and the damages claimed must be to a certain extent commensurate and must be founded on the same kind of liability (*Caledonian Railway Co.*, above; *Ovington v. McVicar* (1864) 2 M. 1066, 1073 *per* L.J.-C. Inglis; *Buchanan & Carswell v. Eugene Ltd* 1936 S.C. 160, 182 *per* Lord Murray). A defender sued in contract cannot claim a right of relief based on negligence under s.3(2) of the Law Reform (Miscellaneous Provisions) (Scotland) Act 1940 because that provision is concerned with joint wrongdoers: *National Coal Board v. Knight Bros.* 1972 S.L.T.(Notes) 24. Also, if sued for negligence, a defender cannot claim a right of relief on the ground that the third party was in breach of a duty to him because liability to make a contribution under s.3(2) of the 1940 Act arises out of a duty by the third party to the pursuer: *R. & W. Watson Ltd v. David Traill & Sons Ltd* 1972 S.L.T.(Notes) 38. Abandonment by a pursuer of an action so far as directed against a defender does not affect a claim under s.3(2) of the 1940 Act between defenders (or between a defender and a third party): *Singer v. Gray Tool Co. (Europe) Ltd* 1984 S.L.T. 149. The extinction of the obligation to contribute under s.3(2) of the 1940 Act which has subsisted for two years after the date on which the right to recover the contribution became enforceable without a relevant claim or acknowledgement should be noted: Prescription and Limitation (Scotland) Act 1973, s.8A inserted by the Prescription and Limitation (Scotland) Act 1984, s.1.

(3) *Right of indemnity.* An indemnity arises where, by law or agreement, one person is liable for the liability of another. It should not be regarded as a term of art and in third party procedure is not limited to any technical meaning: and see (2) above.

26.1.5   *Third party solely, jointly or jointly and severally liable.* This is the second ground on which the defender can bring in a third party. Under this head the defender claims the third party is (to some extent) liable to the pursuer: *Buchan v. Thomson* 1976 S.L.T. 42, 45 *per* Lord Fraser. The pursuer can only recover from the third party if he amends to include a claim against him: *Findlay v. National Coal Board* 1965 S.L.T. 328, 329 *per* Lord Kissen. If the pursuer does not make a claim against the third party or call him as a defender he cannot succeed against him: *Aitken v. Norrie* 1966 S.C. 168. The pursuer does not have to make the third party a defender (*Jack v. Glasgow Corporation* 1965 S.L.T. 227) though he may do so (*Thomson v. Greig* 1967 S.L.T.(Notes) 113). If a defender claims the third party is solely liable and the pursuer does not make a case against the third party, the latter can obtain dismissal of the defender's case against him: *Connor v. Andrew Main & Sons* 1967 S.L.T.(Notes) 71 (no claim of indemnity or joint liability). If the pursuer does not amend where joint or joint and several liability is averred and established, the court grants decree to the pursuer against the defender, finds the defender entitled to a right of relief against the third party for his proportion of the liability to the pursuer and decerns against the third party for payment to the defender for that proportion. If the defender does not pay the pursuer, the latter may sue the third party (subject to prescription and limitation).

A pursuer may not amend to add a claim against a third party after expiry of a limitation or prescriptive period (*Aitken v. Norrie* 1966 S.C. 168) unless he can invoke s.19A of the Prescription and Limitation (Scotland) Act 1973 (inserted by the Law Reform (Miscellaneous Provisions) (Scotland) Act 1980, s.23 and amended by the Prescription and Limitation (Scotland) Act 1984, Sched. 1, para. 8) (discretion to dispense with limitation period) or the time-limit runs from a date other than the date on which the injuries or death occurred. It is sufficient if the conclusions are amended before expiry of the limitation or prescriptive period: *Cross v. Noble* 1975 S.L.T.(Notes) 33. It is sufficient if the minute of amendment is allowed to be received and intimated before expiry of its limitation or prescriptive period and it is not required that the record be amended in terms of the minute of amendment: *Boyle v. Glasgow Corporation* 1975 S.C. 238, 251 *per* L.J.-C. Wheatley.

Joint liability means liability pro rata, each liable for his proportionate share. Joint and several liability means liability *in solidum*, each liable for the whole amount.

26.1.6   *Arising from or in connection with the liability of the defender.* This is the third ground on which the defender can bring in a third party. This head was proposed by the Rules Review Group. It is wide enough to include the other two grounds in r. 26.1 (see notes 26.1.4 and 26.1.5) and anything left out by them and overcomes any doubt about the meaning of the phrase "right of contribution, relief or indemnity".

26.1.7   *"motion".* For motions, see Chap. 23.

Jury trial. The presence of a third party may result in the pursuer losing his right to jury trial, **26.1.8** because the discretion in this rule supersedes the pursuer's statutory right (C.S.A. 1988, s.11) to jury trial: *Winchester v. Ramsay* 1966 S.C. 41, 45 *per* Lord Kissen. In deciding whether to grant an order for service of a third party notice it is not relevant to consider whether a party may lose his right to jury trial: *Rodgers v. James Crow & Sons Ltd* 1971 S.C. 155.

Averments where order for service of third party notice sought

26.2.—(1) Where a defender intends to apply by motion for an order for service of a third party notice before the closing of the record, he shall, before enrolling the motion, set out in his defences, by adjustment to those defences, or in a separate statement of facts annexed to those defences—

(a) averments setting out the grounds on which he maintains that the proposed third party is liable to him by contribution, relief or indemnity or should be made a party to the action; and

(b) appropriate pleas-in-law.

(2) Where a defender applies by motion for an order for service of a third party notice after the closing of the record, he shall, on enrolling the motion, lodge a minute of amendment containing—

(a) averments setting out the grounds on which he maintains that the proposed third party is liable to him by contribution, relief or indemnity or should be made a party to the action, and

(b) appropriate pleas-in-law,

unless those grounds and pleas-in-law have been set out in the defences in the closed record.

Deriv. R.C.S. 1965, r.85(1) (preamble (part)) amended by S.I. 1980 No. 1144

General note. If application for a third party notice is made before the record has been closed, **26.2.1** an adjusted print of the open record (or other pleadings) should be lodged showing the averments which would justify the third party notice.

Authority for diligence etc. on third party notices

[1] **26.3.**—(1) A defender who applies for an order for service of a third party notice may apply by motion for authority for—

(a) arrestment to found jurisdiction; or

(b) diligence by—

(i) inhibition on the dependence of the action;

(ii) arrestment on the dependence of the action where there is a conclusion for the payment of money;

(iii) arrestment *in rem*; or

(iv) dismantling a ship.

(2) A certified copy of an interlocutor granting a motion under paragraph (1) shall be sufficient authority for execution of the arrestment to found jurisdiction or, as the case may be, the diligence.

(3) A certified copy of an interlocutor granting authority for inhibition under this rule may be registered with a certificate of execution in the Register of Inhibitions and Adjudications.

(4) A notice of a certified copy of an interlocutor granting authority for inhibition under this rule may be registered under section 155 of the Titles to Land Consolidation (Scotland) Act 1868; and such registration shall have the same effect as registration of a notice under that section.

Deriv. R.C.S. 1965, r.85(1)(b)

---

[1] R.26.3 substituted by S.S.I. 2004 No. 537 (effective 10th November, 2003).

General Note. For diligence, see notes 13.6A.1–13.6A.5; on the effect of authority for **26.3.1** inhibition on the dependence, see notes 13.9.2 and 13.9.3.

"motion". For motions, see Chap.23. **26.3.2**

Service on third party

26.4.—(1) A third party notice shall be served on the third party within such period as the court shall specify in the interlocutor allowing service of that notice.

(2) Where service of a third party notice has not been made within the period specified by virtue of paragraph (1), the order for service of it shall cease to have effect; and no service of the notice may be made unless a further order for service of it has been applied for and granted.

(3) There shall be served with a third party notice—

    (*a*) a copy of the pleadings (including any adjustments and amendments);

    (*b*) a copy of the interlocutor allowing service of the notice; and

[1] (*c*) where the pleadings have not been amended in accordance with the minute of amendment, a copy of that minute.

(4) The defender who served the third party notice shall lodge in process—

    (*a*) a copy of the third party notice; and

    (*b*) a copy of the interlocutor allowing service of it; and

    (*c*) a certificate of service.

Deriv. R.C.S. 1965, r.85(1)(a)

---

[1] R.26.4(3) amended by S.S.I. 2001 No. 305, para.3 (effective 18th September 2001).

26.4.1   *Service within the period specified.* The court will usually specify the period of notice for service of a summons (21 days within Europe and 42 days furth of Europe: see r.13.4), but this may be shortened or extended, and the notice must be served *within* that period. For methods of service, see Chap. 16, Pt. I.

26.4.2   *"copy of the interlocutor ordering service".* A copy of this interlocutor will have been served with the third party notice. A copy must be lodged in process with a certificate of service and a copy of the third party notice, as an execution copy, so that the clerk of session can check the copy of the interlocutor served against the interlocutor itself. The execution copy is lodged as a step of process: see r.4.4.

Answers to third party notice

26.5.—(1) An order for service of a third party notice shall specify 28 days, or such other period as the court on cause shown may specify, as the period within which the third party may lodge answers.

(2) Answers for a third party shall include—

    (*a*) answers to the averments of the defender against him in the form of numbered paragraphs corresponding to the numbered articles of the condescendence annexed to the summons and incorporating, if the third party so wishes, answers to the averments of the pursuer; or

    (*b*) where a separate statement of facts has been lodged by the defender under rule 26.2(1), answers to the statement of facts in the form of numbered paragraphs corresponding to the numbered paragraphs of the statement of facts; and

    (*c*) appropriate pleas-in-law.

Deriv. R.C.S. 1965, r.85(1) (preamble (part)) amended by S.I. 1980 No. 1144

26.5.1   *Form and lodging of answers.* These are dealt with in r.26.5(2).

26.5.2   *Fee.* The court fee for lodging answers is payable on lodging by a person who is entering the process for the first time. For fee, see Court of Session etc. Fees Order 1984, Table of Fees, Pt. I, B, item 6 [SI 1984/256, Table as amended, pp. C1202 *et seq.*]. The fee may be debited under a credit scheme introduced on 1st April 1976 by P.N. No. 4 of 1976 to the account (if one is kept or permitted) of the agent by the court cashier, and an account will be rendered weekly by the court cashier's office to the agent for all court fees due that week for immediate settlement. Party litigants and agents not operating the scheme must pay cash on each occasion a fee is due at the time of lodging at the counter at the General Department.

Consequences of failure to lodge answers

26.6.—(1) Where a third party fails to lodge answers, the defender may apply by motion for such finding, order or decree against the third party as may be appropriate to give effect to the claim in the third party notice.

[1] (1A) Where a minute of amendment under rule 26.2(2) has been lodged, the defendants may not apply by motion under paragraph (1) unless, at or before the date on which he makes the application, he applies by motion to amend the pleadings in terms of the minute of amendment.

(2) Where such a finding, order or decree is pronounced by the court, rule 19.2 (recall of decrees in absence) shall, with the necessary modifications, apply to that finding, order or decree as it applies to recall of a decree in absence by a defender.

---

[1] R.26.6(1) revoked and r. 26.6(1A) inserted by S.S.I. 2004 No. 52 (effective 1st March, 2004).

"motion". For motions, see Chap.23.   **26.6.1**

"paragraph (1)". This presumably means para.(1) of this rule (r. 26.6).   **26.6.2**

Procedure following answers

26.7.—(1) Within 14 days after the date on which answers are lodged by the third party, the defender who has served the third party notice shall—

(a) make up an open record incorporating the pleadings of all parties;
(b) deliver four copies of that record to every other party; and
(c) lodge two copies of that record in process.

(2) When an open record is lodged in process under paragraph (1), the action shall be put out on the Adjustment Roll and the court shall pronounce an interlocutor continuing the action on that roll for six weeks.

(3) Where a proof or jury trial is necessary between parties to the action, the court may allow the action so far as directed against the third party to proceed to proof or jury trial, as the case may be, before, at the same time as or after, the action between the pursuer and the defender as the court thinks fit.

(4) Where a third party challenges the case pled by the pursuer, he may appear at the proof or jury trial of the pursuer's case and lead evidence as if he were a defender; and such evidence, so far as competent and relevant, shall be evidence for or against the pursuer or for or against the defender, as the case may be, and shall be available to all the parties in the action.

(5) Subject to the preceding provisions of this Chapter and unless the context otherwise requires, the other provisions of these Rules in relation to actions shall, with the necessary modifications, apply as between the defender and a third party or the pursuer and a third party, as the case may be, as they apply to the action between the pursuer and defender.

Deriv. R.C.S. 1965, r. 85(1)(c) (part) amended by S.I. 1976 No. 2197 and 1980 No. 1144 (r. 26.7(1)) and r. 85(1)(e) (r. 26.7(3) and (4))

"within 14 days". The date from which the period is calculated is not counted. Where the last **26.7.1** day falls on a Saturday or Sunday or a public holiday on which the Office of Court is closed, the next available day is allowed: r. 1.3(7). For office hours and public holidays, see note 3.1.2.

"open record". See r. 22.1(4). **26.7.2**

Adjustment. For the Adjustment Roll, see r. 22.2. **26.7.3**

Proof of claim against third party. It may sometimes be appropriate to sist the action between **26.7.4** the pursuer and defender until the determination of the dispute between the defender and third party: *Cookney v. Laverty* 1967 S.L.T. (Notes) 89.
In *Vetco Gray UK Ltd v. Slessor*, 2006 S.C. 398 (Second Div.), it was held that r. 26.7(3), though slightly differently worded than the former R.C.S. 1965, r. 85(e), did not exclude the two stages being conducted by different modes of inquiry (and pursuer not deprived of right to jury trial because of proof before answer on indemnity issue).

Third party challenging pursuer's case. As the third party is entitled to be heard on any matter **26.7.5** in which he has a relevant interest (*Barton v. William Low & Co. Ltd* 1968 S.L.T. (Notes) 27, 28 *per* Lord Stott), he may challenge the claim of the pursuer against the defender; he may adopt the pursuer's case against the defender and blame the defender (see, *e.g. Algeo v. Melville Dundas & Whitson Ltd* 1973 S.L.T. (Notes) 90).

Application of other rules. R. 26.7(5) is necessary to ensure the application, where appropriate, **26.7.6** of rules which apply to a pursuer or defender to a third party.

CHAPTER 27

DOCUMENTS FOUNDED ON OR ADOPTED IN PLEADINGS

Lodging of documents founded on or adopted

27.1.—(1) Any document founded on by a party, or adopted as incorporated, in his pleadings shall, so far as in his possession or within his control, be lodged in process as a production by him—

(a) when founded on or adopted in a summons, at the time of lodging the summons for calling;

(b) when founded on or adopted in a petition, note, application, minute, defences, counterclaim or answers, at the time of lodging that writ; and

(c) when founded on or adopted in an adjustment to any pleadings, at the time when such adjustment is intimated to any other party.

(2) Paragraph (1) shall be without prejudice to any power of the court to order the production of any document or to grant a commission and diligence for recovery of it.

Deriv. R.C.S. 1965, r. 134E inserted by S.I. 1990 No. 705

27.1.1   *General note.* This provision originated from s.3 of the C.S.A. 1825 which was formally repealed by the C.S.A. 1988, Sched. 2. R.C.S. 1965, r. 134E, which was inserted by A.S. (R.C.S.A. No. 1) (Miscellaneous) 1990 [S.I. 1990 No. 705], replaced R.C.S. 1965, r. 78(d) (part) which applied to summonses only.

27.1.2   *Documents founded on or adopted.* Documents founded on are those which are not merely evidence but on which the action is based, though only if in the party's possession or control: *Western Bank of Scotland v. Baird* (1863) 2 M. 127. For the consequences of failure to lodge a document, see r. 27.2.

Documents adopted as incorporated in the pleadings (*brevitatis causa*) may not necessarily be documents founded on; but by virtue of this rule, even where they are not founded on, documents which are adopted in the pleadings must now be lodged with the pleadings if in the party's possession or control. As no reference can be made to productions on procedure roll without agreement of parties, if reliance is to be placed for relevancy or specification in pleadings on documents they must be "adopted and held as repeated herein *brevitatis causa*": see *Gordon v. Davidson* (1864) 2 M. 758, 769 *per* L.J.-C. Inglis; *Eadie Cairns v. Programmed Maintenance Painting Ltd* 1987 S.L.T. 777, *per* Lord Avonside at p. 780E and Lord Jauncey at p. 783F.

In *Prophit v. BBC* 1997 S.L.T. 745, Temporary Judge T. G. Coutts refused to listen to a tape recording of a programme because the issues at procedure roll had to be rested solely on the averments and the tape had not been incorporated into the pleadings. The implication is that if it had been so incorporated, the court would have listened to it.

The other party is entitled to see such documents; for any other document a commission and diligence has to be obtained unless there is agreement to disclose it: *Reavis v. Clan Line Steamers Ltd* 1926 SC 215.

In family actions marriage and birth certificates which are referred to in the pleadings must be lodged with the pleadings: see r. 49.10.

The rule does not apply to statutes, Royal proclamations, Orders in Council or other statutory instruments or European Community legislation. Judicial notice is taken of an Act of Parliament passed after 1850 (s.3 of, and Sched. 2, para. 2 to, the Interpretation Act 1978), a statutory instrument as defined by the Statutory Instruments Act 1946 (Walkers on *Evidence*, para. 198(c); *Macmillan v. McConnell* 1917 J.C. 43, 47 *per* L.J.-C. Scott Dickson) and European Community legislation (ss.2 and 3 of the C.J.J.A. 1982). They do not have to be produced and proved. In fact, Acts of Parliament before 1850, including pre-1707 Acts do not have to be proved: *Macmillan*, above. Should a question arise about the terms of a statute, its terms are established by a copy printed by the Queen's Printer or under authority of HMSO: Dickson on *Evidence*, para. 1105. In the case of a Scots' statute, the Record edition should be produced: Walkers on *Evidence*, para. 194(a). In case of doubt, the terms of a statutory instrument are established by an HMSO copy (Documentary Evidence Acts of 1868 and 1882) and of its date of issue by a list issued by HMSO under s.3(1) of the Statutory Instruments Act 1946. Law reports do not have to be produced and proved.

By virtue of r. 1.3(1) (definition of "document"), "document" has an extended meaning as defined in s.9 of the Civil Evidence (Scotland) Act 1988.

27.1.3   *"lodged in process".* The documents are lodged as productions with an inventory of productions in accordance with r. 4.5.

27.1.4   *Power of court to order production or recovery.* The court has a statutory power to order production or recovery under s.1(1) of the Administration of Justice (Scotland) Act 1972. For commission and diligence for recovery of documents, see Chap. 35.

Consequences of failure to lodge documents founded on or adopted

27.2. Where a party fails to lodge a document in accordance with rule 27.1(1), he may be found liable in the expenses of any order for the production or recovery of it obtained by any other party.

General note. Failure to lodge documents founded on or adopted as incorporated may result **27.2.1** in expenses being awarded against that party for any order for production or recovery.

CHAPTER 28

PROCEDURE ROLL

Hearings on procedure roll

28.1.—(1) When a cause calls on the Procedure Roll and no counsel, other person having a right of audience or party attends, the Lord Ordinary may pronounce an interlocutor dismissing or refusing the cause, as the case may be, and finding no expenses due to or by any party.

(2) An interlocutor pronounced under paragraph (1) may, if reclaimed, be recalled on such conditions, if any, as to expenses or otherwise as the court thinks fit.

(3) The court, after hearing parties on the Procedure Roll, may dispose of all or any of the preliminary pleas and may—

    (a) allow parties a preliminary proof on specified matters or in respect of specified pleas;

    (b) allow parties a proof before answer of their respective averments under reservation of such preliminary pleas as may be specified;

    (c) allow a proof;

    (d) allow issues for jury trial; or

    (e) may make such other order as it thinks fit.

(4) Where a cause has been appointed to the Procedure Roll, parties may, of consent, apply by motion to withdraw the cause from that roll and for any order which might have been pronounced at the hearing of the cause on that roll.

Deriv. R.C.S. 1965, r. 94(c) amended by S.I. 1991 No. 2483 (r. 28.1(1) and (2)) and r. 94(e) (r. 28.1(4))

General note. The Procedure Roll is where preliminary pleas (*e.g.* objections to the instance, **28.1.1** objections to jurisdiction, and pleas against the action itself such as competency, relevancy and specification of pleadings) are debated and disposed of, including whether inquiry is to be by proof or jury trial or whether there should be a preliminary proof if these matters are not agreed by the parties. Irrelevant averments should be excluded at procedure roll: *Inglis v. National Bank of Scotland Ltd* 1909 S.C. 1038.

A cause will be appointed to the Procedure Roll where parties are agreed to send it there or, where parties are not so agreed, may be sent there when the case is heard (because of the lack of agreement) at the By Order (Adjustment) Roll: r. 22.3(5). The interlocutor appointing a cause to the Procedure Roll should state on whose motion the cause has been so appointed and in relation to which plea(s)-in-law.

On the closing of the record parties must discuss the future procedure in the cause with particular regard to the resolution of points at issue without recourse to a hearing on the Procedure Roll: P.N. No. 2 of 2004, para. 2. Whether that has been done may be taken into account by the court on the question of expenses: P.N. No. 2 of 2004, para. 3.

A cause may be finally disposed of on procedure roll where the parties have renounced probation.

A party who has not moved for the cause to be sent to procedure roll is not precluded from debating a plea of his at a hearing on that roll: *McIntosh v. Cockburn & Co. Ltd* 1953 S.C. 88.

Although a particular mode of inquiry has already been allowed, the court is not precluded from reconsidering and altering the mode of inquiry on a minute of amendment altering the pleadings: *Bendex v. James Donaldson & Sons Ltd* 1990 S.C. 259. For an example of the court refusing to allow alteration of the mode of proof after amendment, see *Johnston v. Clark* 1998 S.L.T. 139.

Fixing and allocation of hearings on procedure roll. The Keeper of the Rolls puts out causes **28.1.2** which are estimated to last one or two days on procedure roll in the rolls the Thursday of the week preceding the date on which the cause is to be heard, unless parties agree otherwise or they wish to arrange a fixed diet where the cause is of some length or complexity: see r. 6.2(3) and (4). The Keeper will publish in the rolls a Procedure Roll warning list two weeks before the Thursday's roll on which diets are allocated for hearing the following week. Such hearings will be put out for one day unless, in response to the warning list, the Keeper is requested to fix more than one day under r. 6.2(4) ("some length" in r. 6.2(4) means, in practice, more than one day). On fixing and allocation of diets in the Outer House, see generally r. 6.2 and note 6.2.2.

28.1.2A *Unallocated procedure roll hearings.* A debate may not have been allocated to a particular Lord Ordinary on the first day of the diet. A representative of the agents for each party in such a case must attend the Keeper's office between 10 am and 10.20 am. The Keeper must be informed about the existence of any discussions with a view to settlement. Agents may be required to attend later at intervals during the day. See generally, Notice [*i.e.* P.N.], 13th June 1996.

28.1.3 *Non-appearance at procedure roll.* R.28.1(1) deals with the situation where no party appears or is represented. Such a decree may be recalled with or without conditions: r. 28.1(2).

The calling of a cause on procedure roll is peremptory and if any party does not appear any other party who does appear is entitled to a decree of dismissal or default, as the case may be; and such a decree may also be recalled in the same way: see Chap. 21 (decrees by default).

28.1.4 *Preliminary pleas.* A preliminary plea is one which, if sustained, leads to the disposal of the whole or part of the cause without inquiry into the merits of that part of the cause. If such a plea is sustained it results in dismissal (or sist) but does not make the cause *res judicata*, and the pursuer may raise a fresh action: *Menzies v. Menzies* (1893) 20 R.(H.L.) 108, 110 *per* Lord Watson; and see further note 18.1.4(A). Where a preliminary plea is to be argued at procedure roll the court expects the party whose plea is to be argued to inform his opponent of the nature of his proposed argument at the earliest opportunity: P.N. No. 3 of 1991. The court may, at its own instance or on the motion of a party, order a party to lodge a note of argument on a preliminary plea: r. 22.4 (general rule), r. 43.24(8) (on Diet Roll in actions for damages for personal injuries or death under optional procedure), r. 47.5(6) (on Commercial Roll in commercial causes) and r. 55.3(4)(b) (pre-proof hearing in causes relating to intellectual property).

As no reference can be made to productions on procedure roll without agreement of parties, if reliance is to be placed for relevancy or specification in pleadings on documents they must be "adopted and held as repeated herein *brevitatis causa*": see *Gordon v. Davidson* (1864) 2 M. 758, 769 *per* L.J.-C. Inglis; *Eadie Cairns v. Programmed Maintenance Painting Ltd* 1987 S.L.T. 777, *per* Lord Avonside at p. 780E and Lord Jauncey at p. 783F.

As to particular preliminary pleas, see note 18.1.4(A).

28.1.5 *Preliminary proof.* Since proof is defined as including a proof before answer (see r. 1.3(1)), a preliminary proof before answer may be allowed.

A preliminary proof is not usually allowed in respect of the merits of a case but is confined to where an issue is raised in the pleadings which could bar the action from proceeding. Such cases fall into three categories: (a) cases in which there is a plea of no jurisdiction (see *McLeod v. Tancred, Arrol & Co.* (1890) 17 R. 514; *Dallas & Co. v. McArdle* 1949 S.C. 481), (b) cases of bar either in connection with the discharge of a claim or in connection with a statutory bar in the way of an action, and (c) cases which raise questions of title: *Burroughs Machines Ltd v. George Davie, Crawford & Partners* 1976 S.L.T.(Notes) 35 *per* Lord Grieve. A preliminary proof will not be allowed on an issue which is so bound up with the merits that they cannot be separated: *McCafferty v. McCabe* (1898) 25 R. 872; *cf. A.B. v. C.D.* 1937 S.C. 408. A preliminary proof may be required to determine the question of time-bar or the discretion to override it under s. 19A of the Prescription and Limitation (Scotland) Act 1973: *Donald v. Rutherford* 1984 S.L.T. 70.

It is doubtful whether it would ever be proper to hold a preliminary proof as to the motive of a pursuer in bringing an action: *Mullan v. Anderson (No. 2)* 1997 S.L.T. 93, 97D–F per Temp. Judge Coutts, Q.C.

28.1.6 *Proof before answer and proof.* Probation may be by (a) proof *prout de jure* (without restriction as to method: see (1) below), (b) proof by writ or oath only (*e.g.* in loan, payment of money exceeding £100 Scots, obligations of relief, gratuitous obligations and innominate contracts of unusual character)—abolished for causes commenced on or after August 1, 1995 by s.11 of the Requirements of Writing (Scotland) Act 1995, (c) proof *habili modo* (where parts of a cause may be proved *prout de jure* and other parts may be restricted, the decision being made at the proof), (d) proof before answer (see (2) below) or (e) jury trial (see note 28.1.8 and Chap. 37).

(1) *Proof.* It is sometimes thought that the allowance of proof excludes consideration of questions of relevancy after the proof, but the matter is not free from doubt: *cf.* Mackay's *Practice of the Court of Session*, ii, 18 (although questions of law may be argued after proof, the party against whom facts are proved can no longer maintain no proof should have been allowed and facts disregarded) and *Duke of Hamilton's Trs. v. Woodside Coal Co.* (1897) 24 R. 294, 296

per Lord McLaren (an interlocutor allowing parties proof of their averments leaves all questions of relevancy open to further consideration). In that case Lord McLaren said the words "before answer" were unnecessary for reserving questions of law and relevancy although the proper time for raising questions of law is when the Lord Ordinary is moved to allow a proof. Where a proof has been allowed evidence may be led which might have been excluded on the ground of irrelevance or lack of specification if such a plea had been taken: *Barr v. Bain* (1896) 23 R. 1090. Objection cannot be taken to proving an averment admitted to probation: *Scott v. Cormack Heating Engineers Ltd* 1942 S.C. 159, 162 *per* L.P. Normand.

(2) *Proof before answer.* Proof before answer may be allowed where there is a plea to the relevancy of averments, questions of law and relevancy being reserved until the evidence has been led: *Robertson v. Murphy* (1867) 6 M. 114; *Fleming v. Eadie & Son* (1897) 25 R. 3, 5–6 *per* Lord Young; *Moore v. Stephen & Sons* 1954 S.C. 331, 336 *per* Lord Patrick. Proof before answer strictly means proof before answer as to relevancy, but not competency: *Fleming*, above; *Macvean v. Maclean* (1873) 11 M. 506 *per* Lord Neaves; *cf.* L.J.-C. Moncreiff at p. 509 who thought it might be as to either. A proof before answer reserving a plea to competency may be allowed where evidence on the merits may be relevant to the question of competency (*Shaw v. Renton & Fisher Ltd* 1977 S.L.T.(Notes) 60) or even, in exceptional circumstances, jurisdiction (*McLeod v. Tancred, Arrol & Co.* (1890) 17 R. 514) although it would be more usual to allow a preliminary proof on issues of competency or jurisdiction (see note 28.1.5). A proof before answer may be allowed where it cannot be said in advance whether the facts averred are sufficient to support the legal conclusions or the law cannot be stated until the facts are determined: *Moore*, above, at p. 335 *per* L.J.-C. Thomson and p. 336 *per* Lord Patrick.

The allowance of a proof before answer does not authorise the admission of incompetent evidence: *Robertson*, above; and, *e.g.* confidentiality is not waived even if a proof before answer was of consent: *Duke of Argyll v. Duchess of Argyll* 1962 S.C.(HL) 88, 93–94 *per* Lord Reid and 97–98 *per* Lord Guest.

The Lord Ordinary who hears the proof is not bound by the views on legal questions of the judge who allowed the proof before answer: *Forbes v. Forbes Trs.* 1957 S.C. 325, 337–338 *per* Lord Guthrie.

(3) *Interlocutors.* The interlocutor allowing probation will specify the nature of probation allowed.

(a) In relation to proof (at large) the possibilities are: (i) "allows (both) parties a proof of their respective averments" where each party makes averments, enabling each to lead evidence in support of his own case; (ii) "allows the pursuer a proof of his own averments and to the defender a conjunct probation" where the defender only denies the pursuer's averments, the conjunct probation permitting him to contradict the pursuer's case; and (iii) "allows the defender a proof of his averments and to the pursuer a conjunct probation" where the defender admits the pursuer's claim but makes counter-averments.

(b) In relation to a proof before answer the interlocutor is "allows to parties a proof before answer of their respective averments on record; appoints said proof to proceed on the day of 19   at 10 o'clock forenoon and grants diligence for citing witnesses and havers".

(c) In relation to jury trial the interlocutor is "approves of the proposed issue [and counter-issue] No(s).   [and   ] of process and allows them as now authenticated to be the issue [and counter-issue] for the trial of the cause; appoints the said issue [and counter-issue] to be tried by jury on the day of 19   at 10 o'clock forenoon; authorises and appoints a jury to be summoned for that purpose in common form; grants warrant for citing witnesses and havers".

(d) In relation to proof by writ or oath the interlocutor is "allows the cause to proceed by writ or oath of the defender; appoints said proof to proceed on the day of 19   at 10 o'clock forenoon and grants diligence for citing the defender".

(e) In relation to proof *habili modo* the interlocutor is "allows to parties a proof *habili modo* of their averments on record; appoints said proof to proceed on the day of 19   at 10 o'clock forenoon and grants diligence for citing witnesses and havers".

(f) In relation a preliminary proof the interlocutor is "allows a preliminary proof restricted solely to (*nature of proof or averments to go to proof*); appoints said proof to proceed on the   day of 19   at 10 o'clock forenoon and grants diligence for citing witnesses and havers".

Issues. Issues (and counter-issues) are the concise statements of the questions of fact to be answered by the jury: Bell's *Dictionary.* On the procedure for lodging issues, see r. 37.1. **28.1.7**

Proof or jury trial. Certain causes, the "enumerated causes" (see (A) below), must be sent to jury trial unless the parties otherwise agree or special cause is shown (see (B) below): C.S.A. 1988, s.9(b). The statutory provision is not modified by r. 28.1: *Graham v. Paterson & Son Ltd* 1938 S.C. 119. It has been held that, where the pursuer claims provisional damages under s.12 of the Administration of Justice (Scotland) Act 1982, Parliament has by implication deprived the pursuer of jury trial: *Potter v. McCulloch* 1987 S.L.T. 308, 311L *per* Lord Weir, although he also found special cause existed. It might be unwise, however, to rely on exclusion by implication: see (B) below (Special cause) and *McFadyen v. Crudens Ltd* 1972 S.L.T.(Notes) 62 *per* L.P. Emslie; *cf. Winchester v. Ramsay* 1966 S.C. 41 (effect of third party notice). **28.1.8**

The court may allow jury trial in a cause other than an enumerated cause: *e.g. Fletcher v. Lord Advocate* 1923 S.C. 27; *Blount v. Watt* 1953 S.L.T.(Notes) 39. In this case the court has an unfettered discretion, although it may require a special reason (cause) to send a case which is not an enumerated cause to jury trial. According to present day practice proof before a judge is the normal and convenient method of inquiry in actions which are not appropriated by statute to trial by jury: *Blount,* above, *per* Lord Guthrie at p. 40.

In choosing proof or jury trial (whether in an enumerated cause or not) the question is essentially one of discretion, the object being to select as between the alternative methods of inquiry which type of tribunal would best secure justice between the parties: *Graham v. Associated Electrical Industries Ltd* 1968 S.L.T. 81, 82 *per* L.P. Clyde; *Blount,* above.

A proof may, after amendment, be recalled and the cause sent for jury trial (*Higgins v. Burton* 1968 S.L.T.(Notes) 14); and, after amendment, allowance of issues recalled and a proof allowed (*Nicol v. McIntosh* 1987 S.L.T. 104 (*obiter*)).

(A) The enumerated causes. These are: (1) an action of damages for personal injuries; (2) an action for libel or defamation; (3) an action founded on delinquency or quasi-delinquency where the conclusion is for damages only and expenses; and (4) an action of reduction on the ground of incapacity, essential error, or force and fear: C.S.A. 1988, s.11. The longer list in s.28 of the C.S.A. 1825 was replaced by this shorter list in the C.S.A. 1988 because none of the others had been sent to jury trial in living memory. S.49 of the C.S.A. 1850 had allowed proof on commission as an alternative in the enumerated causes except cases of libel, nuisance or damages; s.4 of the Evidence (Scotland) Act 1866 introduced the alternative of proof to jury trial where parties consented or on special cause shown (both these provisions are repealed by the C.S.A. 1988, Sched. 2).

(1) *Action of damages for personal injuries.* This phrase in s.11(a) of the C.S.A. 1988, which is a consolidating measure, was not intended to and did not change the law, from that under s.28

of the C.S.A. 1825, to exclude claims for loss of society as a result of the death of a relative: *Morris v. Drysdale* 1992 S.L.T. 186. In *McFarlane v. Thain*, 2006 S.C. 360; 2006 S.L.T. 107 (Second Div.), the Motor Insurers' Bureau was a party minuter seeking a ruling on the applicability of their liability, where it was alleged that the pursuer knew, or ought to have know, that the vehicle he was in was uninsured. The opinion was expressed at para. [21] of the judgment that the case was a hybrid case going beyond the issue of personal injuries and was, therefore, not an enumerated cause.

(2) *An action for libel or defamation.* This means an action for written or oral defamation, the former being sometimes known as libel and the latter as slander. Defamation means a communication to the injured party or another of a false statement or idea which is an imputation injurious to the character or credit of the injured party: *Brownlie v. Thomson* (1859) 21 D. 480, 485 *per* L.J.-C. Inglis; *A.B. v. C.D.* (1904) 7 F. 22. Malice only requires to be proved where qualified privilege is claimed: *Langlands v. Leng* 1916 S.C.(H.L.) 102, 109 *per* Lord Shaw of Dunfermline. Other types of verbal injury are *convicium*, slander of title, property, or goods or business, and malicious falsehood, which require proof of malice: these are not included in the meaning of defamation.

(3) *Action founded on delinquency and quasi-delinquency.* Delinquency means fault or violation of duty and these terms are, therefore, synonymous with delict and quasi-delict.

(4) *Action of reduction on ground of incapacity, essential error, or force or fear.* (a) Incapacity may arise through nonage (a child under 16: Age of Legal Capacity (Scotland) Act 1991, s.1(1)(a)) or insanity or other mental incapacity (including drunkenness: Stair, I.x.13; Erskine, III.i.16; Taylor v. Provan (1864) 2 M. 1226). (b) Essential error: see *Stewart v. Kennedy* (1890) 17 R.(H.L.) 25; *Menzies v. Menzies* (1893) 20 R.(H.L.) 108, 142 *per* Lord Watson; *Woods v. Tulloch* (1893) 20 R.(H.L.) 477 *per* Lord Watson; *Westville Shipping Co. v. Abram Steamship Co.* 1922 S.C. 571. (c) Force and fear. A contract induced by threats or violence sufficient to overcome the fortitude of a reasonable man is void: Stair, I.ix.8; Erskine, III.i.16; but a bill of exchange is voidable (Bills of Exchange Act 1882, ss.29(2), 30(2) and 38).

(B) Special cause. The cause must be special to the particular case and not a general cause: *Taylor v. Dumbarton Tramways Co. Ltd* 1918 S.C.(H.L.) 96, 108 *per* Lord Shaw of Dunfermline; *Walker v. The Pitlochry Motor Co.* 1930 S.C. 565, 575 *per* L.P. Clyde. It is not a "special clause" that the right to a fair trial under Art. 6 of the European Convention on Human Rights might be infringed by jury trial as that cause would apply to almost every case: *Gunn v. Newman*, 2001 S.C. 525. What constitutes special cause is within the discretion of the Lord Ordinary, and the Inner House will be slow to interfere with that discretion: *Vallery v. McAlpine & Sons* (1905) 7 F. 640; *Walker*, above; *Graham v. Paterson & Son Ltd* 1938 S.C. 119, 136 *per* Lord Wark; *McLellan v. Western S.M.T. Co. Ltd* 1950 S.C. 112, 116 *per* Lord Russell. The Inner House will interfere, however, where the Lord Ordinary has proceeded on a consideration which is general and not special to the particular case or he has not had material before him upon which to exercise a discretion.

In *Sandison v. Graham Begg Ltd*, 2001 S.C. 821 (OH), it was decided, *obiter,* that it was not necessary for detailed reasons to be given by a jury before a party dissatisfied with its decision on quantum could exercise the statutory right to apply for a new trial and there was, therefore, no risk of infringing Art. 6 of the ECHR.

A plea appropriate to the special cause should be stated (*Rigley v. Remington Rand Ltd* 1964 S.L.T.(Notes) 100) supported by specific averments (*McFaull v. Compania Navigacion Sota y Anzar* 1937 S.L.T. 118, 123 *per* Lord Russell).

Since special cause must be special to the particular case, one case is of little guidance when considering another: *Walters v. National Coal Board* 1961 S.L.T.(Notes) 82. The cases appear to disclose that only a case which is straightforward in relation to the legal and factual issues should be sent for jury trial. Special cause has been found on the following grounds, among others:

(a) Difficult and complex questions of fact: *Robertson v. T. & H. Smith Ltd* 1962 S.C. 628; and see *Miller v. Lanarkshire Health Board* 1993 S.L.T. 453 (medical issue); *McKechnie's C.B. v. Gribben* 1996 S.L.T. 136 (post-traumatic stress, cost of administration and special needs); *Johnston v. Clark* 1997 S.L.T. 923 (interpretation of patrimonial losses); *McInnes v. Kirkforthar Brick Co. Ltd* 1998 S.L.T. 568 (medical issues; loss of employability); *McKenna v. Sharp* 1998 S.C. 297, *sub. nom. McKenna v. Chief Constable Strathclyde Police* 1998 S.L.T. 1161 (issues allowed as jury able to discriminate between medical opinions).

(b) A question of law in relation to which it would be difficult to give the jury an effective direction: *Caldwell v. Wright* 1970 S.C. 24, 28 *per* Lord Avonside; *Potter v. McCulloch* 1987 S.L.T. 308, 312C *per* Lord Weir; and see also *Cassidy v. Argyll and Clyde Health Board* 1997 S.L.T. 934 (difficult and delicate questions of law could arise about foreseeability); *Ireland v. Dunfermline D.C.* 1998 S.L.T. 321. But, that a legal question may arise is not generally a sufficient ground (*Gardner v. Hastie* 1928 S.L.T. 497, 499 *per* Lord Fleming; *cf. Sneddon v. Baxter* 1967 S.L.T.(Notes) 67) and a difficult question of statutory construction is not a sufficient ground for withholding jury trial (*McIntosh v. Commissioners of Lochgelly* (1897) 25 R. 32; *cf. Potter*, above, in conjunction with another factor). In *McFarlane v. Thain*, 2006 S.C. 360; 2006 S.L.T. 107 (Second Div.), it was held that the phrase "ought to have known" (that the pursuer knew that the driver was uninsured) in relation to the Motor Insurers' Bureau Agreement would give rise to difficulties in charging a jury.

(c) Questions of mixed fact and law in respect of which it would be difficult to give the jury an effective direction: *Bygate v. Edinburgh Corporation* 1967 S.L.T.(Notes) 65; *Morris v. Drysdale* 1992 S.L.T. 186; *Pietryea v. Strathclyde R.C.* 1998 S.L.T. 184 (fact). *Cf Robertson v. Smith*, 2000 S.L.T. 1013 (Extra Div.) (an argument, that the decision in *Wells v. Wells* [1999] 1 A.C. 345 meant that future loss of earnings had to be quantified with greater precision and that greater precision is averment or that difficult questions of fact and law would arise, was not sustained in that case); *Morris v. Fife Council,* 2003 S.L.T. 926 (OH); *aff'd* 2004 S.L.T. 1139 (Extra Div.) (risk of prejudice to defenders *re* evidence of consequences of sexual abuse that direction could not remove). See also *Potts v. McNulty*, 2000 S.L.T. 1269 (insufficient specification about claim relating to pension).

(d) Where there are averments of doubtful relevancy: *Robertson*, above; *Walters*, above; *Englert v. Stakis p.l.c.*, 5th July 1996, unreported; *Gibson v. McAndrew Wormald & Co Ltd* 1998 S.L.T. 562; *Currie v. Strathclyde Regional Council Fire Brigade*, 1999 S.L.T. 62.

(e) Where the law applicable to the facts cannot be stated with precision until the facts are determined, as jury trial proceeds on the basis that questions of relevancy have been disposed of: *Moore v. Alexander Stephen & Sons Ltd* 1954 S.C. 331, 334 *per* L.J.-C. Thomson; and see *Miller*, above. See also *Higgins v. DHL International (UK) Ltd,* 2003 S.L.T. 1301 (pleadings under new Chap. 43 insufficient).

(f) Where there are several grounds of action: *Mackenzie v. John Smith & Sons* 1955 S.L.T.(Notes) 25.

(g) Where a third party is brought in, particularly where this could otherwise involve two different modes of inquiry: *Winchester v. Ramsay* 1966 S.C. 41; *Rodgers v. James Crow & Sons Ltd* 1971 S.C. 155. *Cf. Vetco Gray UK Ltd v. Slessor*, 2006 S.C. 398 (Second Div), and note 26.7.4.

(h) Where it might be impossible for the court to identify, for the purposes of the Interest on Damages (Scotland) Act 1958 (as amended by the Act of 1971), the elements of the lump sum awarded by the jury: *Cooper v. Pat Munro (Alness) Ltd* 1972 S.L.T.(Notes) 21; *cf. McMahon v. J. & P. Coats (United Kingdom) Ltd* 1972 S.L.T.(Notes) 16, *McFadyen v. Crudens Ltd* 1972 S.L.T.(Notes) 62. Most of the difficulties may be overcome by the practice of a form of issue in which the claim is broken down into various heads of claim: *McDonald v. Glasgow Corporation* 1973 S.C. 52.

(i) Where prejudice is caused by delay in raising or proceeding with an action (*mora*): *Hunter v. John Brown & Co. Ltd* 1961 S.C. 231, 236 *per* L.P. Clyde and Lord Guthrie. The delay must be inordinate, that is, beyond what normally occurs: *Conetta v. Central S.M.T. Co. Ltd* 1966 S.L.T. 302, 305 *per* Lord Migdale. The delay may be due to some factor outside the party's control: *Conetta*, above. The party relying on delay must be prejudiced, *e.g.* in preparation or presentation of the case because of the dimming of the recollection of witnesses: *Hunter*, above; *cf. Davidson v. Chief Constable, Fife Police* 1995 S.L.T. 545.

(j) Where there are difficulties for the jury in the proper assessment of damages. For example, where, in a claim for services under s.9 of the Administration of Justice Act 1982, the averments are not clear, precise and defined to an obvious basis rendering it difficult to instruct a jury as to the approach to valuing the services: *Stark v. Ford* 1995 S.L.T. 69, aff'd on appeal in *Stark v. Ford (No. 2)* 1996 S.L.T. 1329; *Johnston v. Clark* 1997 S.L.T. 923; *Marshall v. PLM Helicopter Ltd* 1997 S.L.T. 1039 (on "services", see *Ingham v. John G. Russell (Transport) Ltd* 1991 S.C. 201 and *O'Brien's C.B. v. British Steel plc* 1991 S.C. 315). See also *Potts v. McNulty*, 2000 S.L.T. 1269 (different multipliers to various injuries); *Forrest v. Gourlay*, 2003 S.L.T. 783 (pursuer left open a range of issues which created uncertainty and would necessitate the formulation of many directions about a multiplicity of possible situations relating to disability).

"may make such other order". This is a catch-all provision. It would, *e.g.* permit the court to allow an amendment (see note 28.1.10).   **28.1.9**

Amendment at procedure roll. Where a cause has been sent to procedure roll, an offer to amend cannot usually be resisted unless it can be said that no amendment could cure the defect. It is not just to dismiss an action because of a formal pleading defect which can be put right without prejudice to the other party: *G.U.S. Property Management Ltd v. Littlewoods Mail Order Stores Ltd* 1982 S.C.(H.L.) 157, 178 *per* Lord Keith of Kinkel. Nowadays the party seeking to amend at the hearing on procedure roll will usually, and ought to, be required to indicate what the proposed amendment will be if a minute of amendment is not already lodged; any such indication may be sought by any other party to be noted (by the clerk of court) in the minute of proceedings. Any other party who appears at the hearing will be entitled to the   **28.1.10** expenses of a discharge of the procedure roll hearing occasioned by leave to amend being granted.

Although it is for the party seeking to amend to move the court for leave to do so, it is not incompetent for the Lord Ordinary to put the cause out By Order **after a hearing** on the Procedure Roll expressly or impliedly reserving the right of a party to apply for leave to amend: *Kennedy v. Norwich Union Fire Insurance Society Ltd* 1993 S.C. 578; see also *Craig v. Jarvis (Scotland) Ltd*, 30th May, 1997 unreported.

On the grounds on which amendment may be allowed, see r. 24.1 and notes 24.1.1–24.1.10.

Although a particular mode of inquiry has already been allowed, the court is not precluded from reconsidering and altering the mode of inquiry on a minute of amendment altering the pleadings: *Bendex v. James Donaldson & Sons Ltd* 1990 S.C. 259. For an example of the court refusing to allow alteration of the mode of proof after amendment, see *Johnston v. Clark* 1998 S.L.T. 139.

Where amendment is proposed at procedure roll, the party seeking to amend will, as a general rule, have to pay the expenses of the abortive hearing, and payment of these expenses may be made a condition precedent of that amendment: *Colbron v. United Glass Ltd* 1965 S.L.T. 366.

28.1.11   *"motion".* For motions, see Chap. 23.

28.1.12   *Reclaiming.* A decision on the Procedure Roll which disposes of a cause (*i.e.* the subject-matter), whether or not expenses are dealt with, may be reclaimed against without leave within 21 days of the interlocutor: r. 38.3(2) and (5). An interlocutor allowing or refusing proof, proof before answer, jury trial, limiting the mode of proof, or adjusting issues may be reclaimed against without leave within 14 days: r. 38.3(4).

28.1.13   *Judgment: authorities not cited by counsel etc.* If, at avizandum, the Lord Ordinary discovers an authority not cited by parties which he is inclined to rely on, a new argument occurs to him or a question arises about the appropriate interlocutor, the case should be put out by order to allow parties to make further submissions: *Lees v. North East Fife D.C.* 1987 S.C. 265, 273 *per* L.J.-C. Ross; *Brebner v. British Coal Corporation*, 1988 S.C. 333, 340 *per* L.J.-C. Ross; *Kennedy v. Norwich Union Fire Insurance Society* 1994 S.L.T. 617. If the only outstanding issue is the form of the interlocutor, the Lord Ordinary may give judgment expressing his conclusions but should allow parties an opportunity to address him on that point: *Libertas-Kommerz v. Johnson* 1977 S.C. 191. See generally, *Osborne v. British Coal Property* 1996 S.L.T. 736.

28.1.14   *Fee.* The court fee for a hearing on the Procedure Roll is payable by each party for every 30 minutes or part thereof. For fee, see Court of Session etc. Fees Order 1997, Table of Fees, Pt I, B, item 16 or C, item 16 [S.I. 1997 No. 688, as amended, pp. C 1201 *et seq.*]. Certain persons are exempt from payment of fees: see 1997 Fees Order, art.5, substituted by S.S.I. 2002 No. 270. A fee exemption certificate must be lodged in process: see P.N. No. 1 of 2002.

Where a party is legally represented, the fee may be debited under a credit scheme introduced on 1st April 1976 by P.N. No. 4 of 1976 to the account (if one is kept or permitted) of the agent by the court cashier, and an account will be rendered weekly by the court cashier's office to the agent for all court fees due that week for immediate settlement. An agent not on the credit scheme will have an account opened for the purpose of lodging the fee: P.N. No. 2 of 1995. A debit slip and a copy of the court hearing time sheet will be delivered to the agent's box or sent by DX or post.

A party litigant must pay (by cash, cheque or postal order) to the clerk of court at the end of the hearing or, if the hearing lasts more than a day, at the end of each day: P.N. No. 2 of 1995. A receipt will be issued. The assistant clerk of session will acknowledge receipt of the sum received from the clerk of court on the Minute of Proceedings.

28.1.15   *Documents not pled.* As no reference can be made to productions on procedure roll without agreement of parties, if reliance is to be placed for relevancy or specification in pleadings on documents they must be "adopted and held as repeated herein *brevitatis causa*": see *Gordon v. Davidson* (1864) 2 M. 758, 769 *per* L.J.-C. Inglis; *Eadie Cairns*, above *per* Lord Avonside at p.780E and Lord Jauncey at p.783F. The wholesale incorporation of lengthy documents, only parts of which are relevant, is generally unsatisfactory, however, and may well be held not to give the specification required: *Royal Bank of Scotland plc v. Holmes*, 1999 S.L.T. 563. In *Prophit v. BBC*, 1997 S.L.T. 745, Temporary Judge T. G. Coutts refused to listen to a tape recording of a programme because the issues at procedure roll had to be tested solely on the averments and the tape had not been incorporated into the pleadings. The implication is that if it had been so incorporated, the court would have listened to it.

28.1.16   *Citation of authorities.* The general rule is that when a case has been reported in Session Cases or the (English) Law Reports, it should be cited from that source: *McGowan v. Summit at Lloyds*, 2002 S.L.T. 1258, 1273 at para.[57] (Ex Div.). See also now, P.N. No. 5 of 2004. The citation of cases from reproduction of electronic formats is permitted by that P.N.

[1] CHAPTER 28A

NOTICES TO ADMIT AND NOTICES OF NON-ADMISSION

Notices to admit and notices of non-admission
[1] **28A.1.**—(1) At any time after the record has closed, a party may intimate to any other party a notice or notices calling on him to admit for the purposes of that cause only—
  (a) such facts relating to an issue averred in the pleadings as may be specified in the notice;
  (b) that a particular document lodged in process and specified in the notice is—
   (i) an original and properly authenticated document; or
   (ii) a true copy of an original and properly authenticated document.
(2) Where a party on whom a notice is intimated under paragraph (1)—
  (a) does not admit a fact specified in the notice, or
  (b) does not admit, or seeks to challenge, the authenticity of a document specified in the notice,
he shall, within 21 days after the date of intimation of the notice under paragraph (1), intimate a notice of non-admission to the party intimating the notice to him under paragraph (1) stating that he does not admit the fact or document specified.
(3) The party intimating a notice under paragraph (1) or (2) shall lodge a copy of it in process.
(4) The court may, at any time, allow a party to amend or withdraw an admission made by him on such conditions, if any, as it thinks fit.
(5) A party may, at any time, withdraw in whole or in part a notice of non-admission by intimating a notice or withdrawal.

---

[1] Chap. 28A and r. 28A.1 inserted by S.I. 1996 No. 2168 (effective 23rd September 1996).

General note. Chapter 28A was inserted by A.S. (R.C.S.A. No. 4) (Miscellaneous) 1996 [S.I. **28A.1.1** 1996 No. 2168]. It was formerly r. 36.6 which permitted a notice to admit to be served at any time after a proof had been allowed. The Cullen *Review of Outer House Business* of December 1995 recommended that a notice to admit should be permitted at any time after the lodging of defences. This recommendation did not find favour and the Rules Council recommended that such notices be permitted after the record has closed. This recommendation is now in the rule: see r. 28A.1(1). If and when records are abolished following the Cullen review, a further change will be required. Because the rule now is to permit such notices *before* a proof has been allowed, r. 36.6 has been taken out of Chap. 36 (proofs) and has had to be given a Chapter of its own.
  The opportunity has been taken to divide r. 36.6 into two rules in Chap. 28A, r. 28A.1 providing for the procedure for notices and r. 28A.2 dealing with the consequences of failure to intimate a notice of non-admission.

Chap. 28A (formerly r. 36.6) was originally suggested by the principal annotator to the Jauncey Working Party on Patent Litigation which recommended its adoption in the intellectual property rules, and this was done in R.C.S. 1965, r. 253 as amended by A.S. (R.C.S.A. No. 7) (Patent Rules) 1991 [S.I. 1991 No. 1621] (now R.C.S. 1994, r. 55.4).

It might be thought that Chap. 28A is not necessary when the system of Scottish pleadings should result in it being clear by the time proof has been allowed what is in issue and what has to be proved. Not all relevant documentary material, however, previously in dispute will be in dispute by the time the proof approaches, and the authenticity of such material, or an averment, may be the subject of a general denial which would otherwise necessitate proof. It may, of course, be possible to obtain agreement by consent. The purpose of the rule is to provide an additional means to assist in reducing documentary material and averments having to be proved which in the end of the day do or did not require proof and the time taken in proving them. It is also considered that this might be a more effective way of obtaining admissions than calls in the pleadings.

The relationship of Chap. 28A to rr. 36.7 and 36.8 should be noticed. The possibility of a minute of admission by one or more parties is not affected by Chap. 28A. A deemed admission may arise, however, under r. 28A.2(1) if a notice of non-admission is intimated in response to a notice to admit. Under s.2(1)(b) of the Civil Evidence (Scotland) Act 1988 any document (including an affidavit) may be received in evidence without being spoken to by a witness as evidence not merely that it was made but as to the truth of its contents, and r. 36.8 provides the mechanism for obtaining the permission of the court to produce such evidence without being spoken to. In respect of the authenticity of a document it may also be possible to use the procedure in Chap. 28A.

Form of notices. A notice of admission and a notice of non-admission do not require to be **28A.1.2** formal signed documents in the style of a Minute ("X for the pursuer called and hereby calls on the defender to admit:—"). It is preferred that the notice is headed (after the cross-heading "In the Court of Session") "Notice to Admit [*or* of non-admission]" with the instance of the cause.

"intimate". For methods, see r. 16.7.   **28A.1.3**

"within 21 days". The date from which the period is calculated is not counted. Where the last **28A.1.4** day falls on a Saturday or Sunday or a public holiday on which the Office of Court is closed, the next available day is allowed: r. 1.3(7). For office hours and public holidays, see note 3.1.2.

"lodge a copy of it in process". The copy is lodged as a step of process and not as a **28A.1.5** production: r. 1.3(1) (definition of "step of process"). On steps of process, see r. 4.4.

Consequences of failure to intimate notice of non-admission
[1] **28A.2.**—(1) A party who fails to intimate a notice of non-admission under paragraph (2) of rule 28A.1 shall be deemed to have admitted the fact or document specified in the notice intimated to him under paragraph (1) of that rule; and such fact or document may be used in evidence at a proof if otherwise admissible in evidence, unless the court, on special cause shown, otherwise directs.

(2) [Revoked by S.I. 1997 No. 1050.]

(3) A deemed admission under paragraph (1) of this rule shall not be used against the party by whom it was deemed to be made other than in the cause for the purpose for which it was deemed to be made or in favour of any person other than the party by whom the notice was given under rule 28A.1(1).

---

[1] R. 28A.2 inserted by S.I. 1996 No. 2168 (effective 23rd September 1996).

General note. This rule was formerly part of r. 36.6. For the history of the rule, see note **28A.2.1** 28A.1.1.

The rule as originally enacted was not entirely satisfactory: if a fact is deemed to be admitted by virtue of r. 28A.2(1), proof is unlikely to be required and the provision for the expenses of proving it under r. 28A.2(2), is unnecessary. The latter provision has been revoked by A.C. (R.C.S.A. No. 4) (Miscellaneous) 1997 [S.I. 1997 No. 1050]. Accordingly, now failure to lodge a notice of non-admission of a fact or document results in it being deemed to be admitted. The party serving the notice to admit does not have to prove the fact or document, and there is no need for the rule to deal with expenses.

It might have been better if the rule provided, where there is a failure to lodge a notice of non-admission, (a) in relation to facts, for the expenses of proving facts set out in the notice (no deemed admission), and (b) in relation to documents, for a deemed admission of their authentication.

28A.2.2 *"intimate"*. For methods, see r. 16.7.

28A.2.3 *"within 21 days"*. The date from which this period is calculated is not counted. Where the last day falls on a Saturday or Sunday or a public holiday on which the Office of Court is closed, the next available day is allowed: r. 1.3(7). For office hours and public holidays, see note 3.1.2.

CHAPTER 29

ABANDONMENT

Abandonment of actions

29.1.—(1) A pursuer may abandon an action by lodging a minute of abandonment in process and—

    (a) consenting to decree of absolvitor; or

    (b) seeking decree of dismissal.

(2) The court shall not grant decree of dismissal under paragraph (1)(b) unless—

    [1](a) full judicial expenses have been paid to the defender, and to any third party against whom the pursuer has directed any conclusions, within 28 days after the date of intimation of the report of the Auditor on the taxation of the account of expenses of that party; and

    (b) where abandonment is made in a proof or jury trial, the minute of abandonment is lodged before avizandum is made in the proof or the charge to the jury by the presiding judge has begun in the jury trial, as the case may be.

(3) If the pursuer fails to pay the expenses referred to in sub-paragraph (a) of paragraph (2) to the party to whom they are due within the period specified in that sub-paragraph, that party shall be entitled to decree of absolvitor with expenses.

Deriv. R.C.S. 1965, r. 91A inserted by S.I. 1984 No. 472 (r. 29.1(b), (2) and (3)).

---

[1] R.29.1(2)(a) amended by S.S.I. 2001 No.305 (effective 18th September 2001).

29.1.1 *General note.* R.C.S. 1965, r. 91A (now R.C.S. 1994, r. 29.1(1)(b) and (2)) was inserted by A.S. (R.C.A. No. 2) (Miscellaneous) 1984 [S.I. 1984 No. 472], r. 29.1(1)(b) and (2) replacing s.10 of the C.S.A. 1825 (repealed by A.S. (R.C.A. No. 8) (Miscellaneous) 1986 [S.I. 1986 No. 1937]) which was extended by s.39 of the C.S.A. 1868 (repealed by A.S. (R.C.S. 1994) 1994, Sched. 5 [S.I. 1994 No. 1443]. Abandonment at common law meant the pursuer was prepared to release the defender for all time without reservation, the defender could obtain decree of absolvitor and the court had discretion only in relation to expenses; whereas abandonment under statute (s.10 of the C.S.A. 1825 as extended by s.39 of the C.S.A. 1868 and substituted by R.C.S. 1965, r. 91A) was under reservation (of his right to raise a fresh action) involving payment of expenses with a view to obtaining dismissal: see *Esso Petroleum Co. Ltd v. Hall Russell & Co. Ltd* 1988 S.L.T. 33, 39E–I *per* L.P. Emslie. At common law the court had no discretion to prevent a party abandoning, he having an unfettered right to abandon subject to the conditions which the court could lawfully impose (*i.e.* expenses): *Lee v. Pollock's Trs* (1906) 8 F. 857, 860 *per* L.P. Dunedin; *Castlegreen Storage & Distributors Ltd v. Schreiber* 1982 S.L.T. 269, 271 *per* Lord Murray; *Esso Petroleum*, above, *per* L.P. Emslie.

Up to release 63 this annotation contained the statement "R.29.1(1)(a) replaced the common law and r.29.1(1)(b) and (2) replaces R.C.S. 1965, r.91A and the former statutory rules." Rule 91A(1) was intended by the draftsman (W. Galbraith Q.C.) to replace the common law rule of abandonment under reservation. In *Beattie v The Royal Bank of Scotland plc*, 2003 S.L.T 564 (OH), Lord Reed held that the common law right to abandonment under reservation had not been abolished by r.29.1 or by the former r.91A. The distinction between abandonment under r.29.2(1)(b) (dismissed on payment of expenses required by r.29.1(2)) and common law abandonment under reservation is that under common law abandonment it is in the discretion of the court what, if any, expenses are to be paid as a condition of obtaining the decree of dismissal. In fact payment of expenses was the "normal" condition: *Singer v. Gray Tool Co. (Europe) Ltd*, 1984 S.L.T. 149, 150 *per* Emslie, L.P. In *Beattie*, resort to the common law rule was made because expenses had been agreed and not taxed as stipulated in r. 29.1(2). In *VP Packaging Ltd v. The ADF Partnership*, 2002 S.L.T. 1224 (OH) it had been held in a similar situation that as expenses had been agreed and not taxed as required by r. 29.1(2)(a) there could be no abandonment under r. 29.1(1)(b) and the pursuer must be presumed to have waived any right to ask for dismissed under that rule. In *Beattie*, Lord Reed held that if he was wrong about the continuing existence of the common law right, it would have been competent to exercise, and he would have exercised, the dispensing power under r. 2.1. He did not follow *VP Packaging* in which Lord Wheatley held that r. 2.1 could not apply where the failure to comply with r. 29.1(2)(a) was deliberate.

Abandonment may be made at any time after calling and before final decree; but the decree on abandonment and the conditions for abandonment differ depending on the time at which abandonment is sought. Abandonment may be against one or more or all other parties; it does not have to be abandonment against all parties. The pursuer cannot obtain abandonment in respect of part of the action in which the defender has obtained a (final) decree although the whole action has not been disposed of: formerly A.S. 11th July 1828, s.115.

Abandonment by a pursuer under r. 29.1 is of right, and is not in the discretion of the court: *Frost v. Unity Trust Bank plc* 1997 S.L.T. 1358. It should be obvious that the word "may" in the opening words of r. 29.1(1) is not conferring a discretion on the court but an option for the pursuers which he may or may not choose to take ("shall" could not be substituted because the pursuer cannot be obliged to abandon his action).

(1) *Abandonment with consent to decree of absolvitor* may be obtained at any time after calling and before final decree without conditions imposed by the court (*cf.* common law when the court had a discretion as to dismissal or absolvitor). A decree of absolvitor is a decree *in foro* in favour of a defender on the merits which is *res judicata*: *Forrest v. Dunlop* (1875) 3 R. 15; on *res judicata*, see note 18.1.4(B)(5). When the defender moves for decree of absolvitor he may seek an order for expenses, and he would be entitled to expenses of the cause unless otherwise agreed or determined. The court has a discretion in relation to expenses: see *Esso Petroleum Co. Ltd v. Hall Russell & Co. Ltd* 1988 S.L.T. 33, 39F *per* L.P. Emslie.

(2) *Abandonment with a decree of dismissal.* Since a decree of dismissal (which is not *res judicata*) enables a pursuer to raise a fresh action (*Menzies v. Menzies* (1893) 20 R.(H.L.) 108, 110 *per* Lord Watson), it is subject to the two conditions in r. 29.1(2). The restriction of abandonment before avizandum or the charge to the jury derives from s.39 of the C.S.A. 1868. The minute of abandonment for decree of dismissal must be accompanied by a motion for decree of dismissal and for finding the party abandoning liable in expenses as taxed. On payment of expenses, see note 29.1.4. Dismissal, carrying with it the right to bring a new action, is a remedy that has to be acquired by taking certain steps in terms of the rules. If dismissal is not available then the only appropriate course is absolvitor: *VP Packaging Ltd v. The ADF Partnership*, 29th January 2002, unreported, 2002 G.W.D. 5–144 (OH).

A decree of dismissal (without inquiry into the merits, fact or law, as on relevancy) means that the pursuer is entitled to bring a fresh action on the same grounds: see *Menzies*, above. It has been said that the word "dismiss" is used when it is open to a party to bring another action and "assoilzie" where it is not: *Stewart v. Greenock Harbour Trs* (1868) 6 M. 954, 958 *per* Lord Deas. See also *Waydale Ltd v. DHL Holdings (UK) Ltd*, 2000 S.C. 172 (Extra Div.) overruling Lord Hamilton at 1999 S.L.T. 631, 637C (who held that where dismissal on relevancy followed inquiry, another action on the same grounds could be excluded) and doubting *Johnston v. Standard Property Investment Co. Ltd* 1909 1 S.L.T. 23.

A solicitor should obtain a special mandate to abandon: *Urquhart v. Grigor* (1857) 19 D. 853, 855 *per* L.J.-C. Hope. Counsel may abandon without instructions but usually does not do so: *Batchelor v. Pattison and Mackery* (1876) 3 R. 914, 918 *per* L.J.-C. Inglis.

A party might abandon at the Bar in the course of a cause without lodging a minute.

The question arises as to the meaning of "full judicial expenses" in r. 29.1(2)(a): see note 29.1.4.

Minute of abandonment. Rule 15.1 (form of applications by minute, etc.) does not apply: **29.1.2** r. 15.1(6). The minute has to be signed, and accordingly a pursuer's motion for decree of dismissal and the minute of abandonment cannot be faxed to the court: see r. 23.2(4).

The minute should not include any conditions or qualifications: *Adamson, Howie & Co. v. Guild* (1868) 6 M.347, 358 *per* L.P. Inglis; *Stewart v. Stewart* (1906) 8 F. 769. The minute may only be signed by the counsel or other person having a right of audience responsible for the cause; it cannot be signed on his behalf.

The text of the minute under r. 29.1(1)(a) should be along the following lines:

"[X] for the pursuer stated and hereby states to the court that the pursuer abandons this cause [in so far as it relates to the [first] defender] under rule 29.1(1)(a) of the Rules of the Court of Session 1994 and consents to decree of absolvitor [in favour of the [first] defender]."

The text of the minute under r. 29.1(1)(b) should be along the following lines:

"[X] for the pursuer stated and hereby states to the court that the pursuer abandons this cause under rule 29.1(1)(b) of the Rules of the Court of Session 1994 and seeks decree of dismissal."

29.1.3 *Intimation of minute of abandonment.* Written intimation of the lodging of the minute must be given to every other party and a copy of it sent to every such party: r. 4.6(1). For methods of written intimation, see r. 16.9. The back of the minute must be marked "Intimated".

29.1.4 *Payment of expenses to obtain decree of dismissal.* The minute of abandonment for decree of dismissal must be accompanied by a motion to find the party abandoning liable in expenses as taxed and to appoint the defender to lodge an account of expenses within a specified period (usually four months as this is the period specified in r. 42.1(2)) and to remit that account for taxation. The pursuer must specify a period otherwise the defender could delay lodging an account indefinitely and prevent the pursuer obtaining decree of dismissal. If the defender fails to lodge an account the pursuer will no doubt have to resort to the dispensing power in r. 2.1 to dispense with the requirement to pay the expenses and obtain decree of dismissal. The court pronounces an interlocutor in those terms remitting the defender's account of expenses to the Auditor to tax and report but with no decerniture for the expenses as taxed. The object of remitting for taxation is to get a fixed sum which the pursuer has to pay: *Lee v. Pollock's Trs* (1906) 8 F. 857. When the Auditor reports a note of objection may be taken to the report in the usual way. There is, however, no award or decerniture for the expenses as taxed, but the pursuer has 28 days under r. 29.1(2)(a) to pay the expenses. If he pays he should obtain a receipt which he lodges in process and is entitled to decree of dismissal. A pursuer who agrees to settle expenses without reference to the Auditor must be presumed to have abandoned any right to ask for dismissal in terms of r. 29.1: *VP Packaging Ltd v. The ADF Partnership,* 29th January 2002, unreported, 2002 G.W.D. 5–144 (OH).

The expenses recoverable by the defender are the expenses which he could have recovered from the pursuer under a decree of absolvitor with expenses had the action not been abandoned (*i.e.* he is not entitled to recover expenses for procedure in which he was unsuccessful and earlier expenses awarded against him may not be recovered): *Nobel's Explosives Co. Ltd v. British Dominions General Insurance Co. Ltd* 1919 S.C. 455; *Lord Hamilton v. Glasgow Dairy Co.* 1933 S.C. 18. The pursuer is not liable for the expenses of a counterclaim as a condition or consequence of abandonment: r. 24.5.

What does "full judicial expenses" mean? Generally expenses will be awarded on a party and party basis, but may be awarded on a solicitor and client basis in appropriate circumstances: *P v. P* 1940 S.C. 389, 391 *per* L.J.-C. Aitchison; followed in *Lord Advocate v. ASAU JV*, 24th March 2006, 2006 G.W.D. 21-454 (OH), [2006] CSOH 50.

It has been held that r. 29.1(2)(a) does not apply to a pursuer who agrees expenses and does not submit an account for taxation: *VP Packaging Ltd v. The ADF Partnership*, 2002 S.L.T. 1224 (OH). In that case it was held that the pursuer must be presumed to have abandoned any right to ask for dismissal in terms of r. 29.1 and that the dispensing power in r. 2.1 could not apply because the agreement on expenses was deliberate. But in *Beattie v. The Royal Bank of Scotland plc*, 2002 S.L.T. 564 (OH), Lord Reed held that the dispensing power in r. 2.1 could be applied as the failure to comply with the taxation provision was an excusable cause. He observed that an agreement on expenses might be regarded as equivalent to the intimation of the auditor's report on taxation required by r. 29.1(2)(a).

Where the pursuer is legally aided there is no power for the court to modify the expenses the pursuer is liable to pay either instead of remitting to the Auditor (*Johnston v. Johnston* 1985 S.L.T. 510, 512 *per* Lord Cowie) or on a motion to modify under s.18(2) of the Legal Aid (Scotland) Act 1986 (*Collum v. Glasgow Corporation* 1964 S.L.T. 199 not following *Thompson v. Fairfield Shipbuilding and Engineering Co.* 1954 S.C. 354) because there is no "award" of expenses made by the court.

If the pursuer fails to pay the expenses the defender or other party to whom they are due is entitled to absolvitor: r. 29.1(3). This accords with *Ross v. Mackenzie* (1889) 16 R. 871 and *Donnelly v. Morrison* (1895) 2 S.L.T. 582. There is no discretion in the court to grant decree of dismissal: *Cobb v. Baker Oil Tools (U.K.) Ltd* 1984 S.C. 60.

29.1.5 *Abandonment of family action.* Where a pursuer abandons a family action (as defined by r. 49.1(1)), the defender may continue with any conclusions for custody, aliment or access in his defences: r. 49.32.

29.1.6 *Effect of abandonment on counterclaim.* The right of a pursuer to abandon is not affected by the presence of a counterclaim, the pursuer is not liable for any expenses of the counterclaim as a condition or consequence of abandonment and the counterclaim continues as if a separate action: r. 25.4.

Withdrawal of minute. A minute of abandonment may be withdrawn before final decree: *Lee* **29.1.7**
v. Pollock's Trs (1906) 8 F. 857. The minute must be withdrawn by motion. The defender may
move for absolvitor which will be granted unless the pursuer shows his proceedings have been
bona fide, in which case the pursuer may proceed subject to any conditions the court imposes:
Lee, above, *per* L.P. Dunedin at p. 861. The pursuer will usually have to pay the expenses
connected with the aborted abandonment: *Todd & Higginbotham v. Corporation of Glasgow*
(1879) 16 S.L.R. 718; *Dalgleish v. Mitchell* (1886) 23 S.L.R. 552.

Application of abandonment of actions to counterclaims

29.2. Rule 29.1 shall, with the necessary modifications, apply to the
abandonment by a defender of his counterclaim as it applies to the
abandonment of an action.

Deriv. RCS 1965, r. 84(e)

General note. This rule applies r. 29.1 to counterclaims. The principles are the same.   **29.2.1**

Abandonment of petitions, minutes and notes

29.3.—(1) A petition, minute or note may be abandoned by the petitioner,
minuter or noter, as the case may be—
  (a) enrolling a motion for abandonment of the cause; and
  (b) intimating the motion to every person who lodged answers.
  (2) The court may grant a motion under paragraph (1) subject to such
conditions as to expenses or otherwise, if any, as it thinks fit.

General note. This new rule provides for abandonment of petitions, minutes and notes. **29.3.1**
Intimation only has to be made to those who have entered the process: r. 23.3.
  Where a petition for sequestration or liquidation is dismissed, there is an order for
advertisement of the interlocutor dismissing the petition.

CHAPTER 30

WITHDRAWAL OF AGENTS

Intimation of withdrawal of agent to court

30.1.—(1) Where an agent withdraws from acting on behalf of a party, he
shall intimate his withdrawal by letter to the Deputy Principal Clerk and to
every other party.
  (2) The Deputy Principal Clerk shall cause such letter to be lodged in
process.

General note. This Chapter contains new rules which reflect the current practice on **30.1.1**
withdrawal of solicitors from acting.
  When intimating his withdrawal the agent must disclose to every other party his former
client's current address if known to him and different from that stated in the pleadings so that
the procedure under r. 30.2 can be carried out: *Sime, Sullivan & Dickson's Tr. v. Adam* 1908 S.C.
32.
  Leave of the court to withdraw is not required: *Scott v. Christie* (1856) 19 D. 178.
  Notwithstanding that an agent has withdrawn, the court has a discretion, where a party is in
default under r. 20.1 for failure to appear, to grant decree of default: *Munro & Miller
(Pakistan) Ltd v. Wyvern Structures Ltd* 1996 S.L.T. 135, affirmed 1997 S.C. 1.

"agent". This means a solicitor or a person having a right to conduct the litigation: see **30.1.2**
r. 1.3(1) (definition of "agent") and note 1.3.4. "Solicitor" is defined in the C.S.A. 1988, s.51.

"intimate". For methods, see r. 16.7.   **30.1.3**

"lodged in process". The letter becomes a step in process.   **30.1.4**

Intimation to party whose agent has withdrawn

30.2.—[1] (1) The court shall, on the motion of any other party, pronounce
an interlocutor ordaining the party whose agent has withdrawn from acting
to intimate to the Deputy Principal Clerk within 14 days (or such other
period as the court, on cause shown, thinks fit) after service of the notice as

required by paragraph (2) whether or not he intends to proceed, under certification that if he fails to intimate whether or not he intends to proceed, the court may grant such decree or make such order or finding as it thinks fit.

[1] (2) The party who enrolled a motion under paragraph (1) shall forthwith serve a notice in Form 30.2 to the party whose agent has withdrawn from acting.

[1] R. 30.2(1) and (2) amended by S.I. 1996 No. 2168 (effective 23rd September 1996)

30.2.1 *General note.* On receiving intimation of withdrawal under r. 30.1(1) any other party may enrol a motion for an order under r. 30.2 ordaining the party whose agent has withdrawn to intimate whether he intends to proceed. The motion is unstarred unless a period of notice other than 14 days is sought. The notice in Form 30.2 must be served. The A.S. (R.C.S.A. No. 4) (Miscellaneous) 1996 [S.I. 1996 No. 2168] abolished the requirement to serve the interlocutor as well as the notice in order to save duplication: all that is necessary is in the notice.

For a case in which this was not done and the defender sought and was granted decree of absolvitor at a proof at which the pursuer did not appear following withdrawal of its agents from acting, see *Munro & Miller (Pakistan) Ltd v. Wyvern Structures Ltd* 1996 S.L.T. 135.

Where the whereabouts of the party on whom the notice is to be served becomes unknown, it may be necessary to serve the notice by advertisement: see r. 16.5.

30.2.2 *"motion".* For motions, see Chap. 23.

30.2.3 *"within 14 days".* The date from which the period is calculated is not counted. Where the last day falls on a Saturday or Sunday or a public holiday on which the Office of Court is closed, the next available day is allowed: r. 1.3(7). For office hours and public holidays, see note 3.1.2.

30.2.4 *"serve".* For methods, see Chap. 16, Pt I.

30.2.5 *Intimation of intention by party whose agent has withdrawn.* Form 30.2 explains that the party whose agent has withdrawn must write to the Deputy Principal Clerk indicating whether he intends to proceed. If he does intend to proceed he will be informed what the next step is which is required to be done in the cause. The letter will be placed in process by the Deputy Principal Clerk. A form on which to do this is sent with Form 30.2. The language of Form 30.2 is clear and peremptory, and a cogent reason for its being disregarded would be required: *Connelly v. Lanarkshire Health Board* 1999 S.C. 364.

If the party whose agent has withdrawn intimates that he does not intend to proceed, the Deputy Principal Clerk causes the letter to be lodged in process. The other party must check the process after the period for intimation has expired. If there is no letter intimating an intention to proceed he may enrol a motion for such decree or other order as is appropriate in the circumstances.

30.2.6 *"decree, order or finding".* The decree or other order will depend on the circumstances, including which party's agent has withdrawn. The decree could be *de plano*, absolvitor or dismissal or the grant or refusal of the prayer of a petition.

30.2.7 *Decree by default where agent withdraws.* Where a party's agent has withdrawn from acting and that party fails to attend a proof, the court has a discretion whether to grant decree by default under r. 20.1 or to ordain that party under r. 30.2 to intimate whether he intends to proceed: *Munro & Miller (Pakistan) Ltd v. Wyvern Structures Ltd* 1996 S.L.T. 135, affirmed 1997 S.C. 1.

Consequences of failure to intimate intention to proceed

[1] **30.3.** Where a party on whom a notice has been served under rule 30.2(2) fails to intimate to the Deputy Principal Clerk within the period specified in the notice that he intends to proceed, the court shall, on the motion of any other party where a certificate of service of the notice has been lodged in process, grant such decree, order or finding as it thinks fit.

[1] R. 30.3 amended by S.I. 1997 No. 1050 (effective 6th April 1997).

30.3.1 *"certificate of service".* The certificate of service signed by the person executing service (with the requisite proof of delivery where service is by post), a copy of the notice and the interlocutor served must be lodged as a step of process (not a production): r. 16.1(3). On lodging steps of process, see r. 4.1(3) and (4).

"decree, order or finding". The decree or other order will depend on the circumstances **30.3.2** including which party's agent has withdrawn. The decree could be *de plano*, absolvitor or dismissal, or the grant or refusal of the prayer of a petition and an order or finding for expenses.

A decree of dismissal after defences have been lodged, granted when the defender failed to intimate his intention to proceed after withdrawal of his agents, is a decree *in foro* but not *res judicata*: *Mason v. A. & R. Robertson & Black* 1993 S.L.T. 773.

Reclaiming. Where a decree passes against a party under r. 30.3, the decree may be reclaimed **30.3.3** against, without leave, within 21 days after the date on which the decree was pronounced (r. 38.3(2)). Failing that, an action of reduction would have to be brought. For a recent case, see *Dundee Football Club Ltd v. Souter*, 6th December 1996, unreported (action unsuccessful).

CHAPTER 31

MINUTES OF SIST AND TRANSFERENCE

Minutes of sist
31.1.—(1) Where a party dies or comes under legal incapacity while a cause is in dependence, any person claiming to represent that party or his estate may apply to the court by minute to be sisted as a party to the cause.
(2) Intimation of such an application shall be made to each party.

Deriv. R.C.S. 1965, r. 106 (part)

General note. This rule deals with only two situations in which a sist of a person as a party **31.1.1** may arise (on which see notes 31.1.2 and 31.1.3); there are others.

(1) *General rule as to sist of person as party*. Any person having sufficient title and interest may apply to be sisted as a party to an action: see *e.g. Muir v. Corporation of Glasgow* 1917 2 S.L.T. 106. On title and interest, see note 13.2.2(C). It is *par judicis* to allow a person to appear whom the court considers may have an interest: *Lord Blantyre v. Lord Advocate* (1876) 13 S.L.R. 213, 214 *per* Lord Deas; to this end the court may order intimation to enable that person to be sisted if so advised: *Orr Ewing's Trs v. Orr Ewing* (1884) 12 R. 343. As a general rule, in petitions and notes there is no need to be sisted as a party because any person may lodge answers as the first order under r. 14.5 states. The procedure for sisting a person to a cause is the same as the procedure in r. 31.1.

(2) *Sist of person as pursuer or petitioner*. This may arise on the motion of any party or the person lodging a minute of sist seeking to be sisted. Note, however, the provisions of r. 24.1(1)(b)(iv) (adding name of additional pursuer by amendment), r. 24.1(1)(d) (additional or substitute party by amendment) and r. 24.2 (applications to amend). A connected person (as defined by r. 43.1(2)) may apply by minute to be sisted to an action of damages arising out of the death of a person from personal injuries under r. 43.6. An executor may sist himself to an action of damages for personal injuries in respect of any rights transmitted to him: Damages (Scotland) Act 1976, s.2A inserted by the Damages (Scotland) Act 1993, s.4.

(3) *Sist of person as defender*. This may arise on the person's own motion or the motion of a party lodging a minute of sist seeking to be sisted as a defender. If he can show title and interest he may be sisted and allowed to lodge defences: see *e.g. Macfie v. Scottish Rights of Way and Recreation Society (Ltd)* (1884) 11 R. 1094. Note, however, the provisions of r. 24.1(2)(d) (additional or substitute party) and r. 24.2 (applications to amend) to bring in a person by amendment.

(4) *Transmission of interest*. The interest in the subject-matter of a cause may pass to another party other than by death or incapacity. A transferee is entitled to take the place of the party who is divested of the interest which is in the subject-matter of the action: *Waddell v. Hope* (1843) 6 D. 160; *Fearn v. Cowper* (1899) 7 S.L.T. 68 (assignee); *Mavor v. Governors of Aberdeen Educational Trust* (1902) 10 S.L.T. 156 (disponee).

Sist of representative on death of party. On death of a party during the dependence of a cause **31.1.2** all procedure is suspended (including extract) and any further proceedings are null and void unless that party's representatives sist themselves or the action is transferred against them (see r. 31.2): Maclaren on *Court of Session Practice*, p. 466; *Davidson v. Robertson* (1827) 5 S. 751; *Thompson v. Crawfurd* 1979 S.L.T.(Notes) 91. The cause must be one which transmits against representatives (*Gibson v. Barbour's Reps.* (1846) 8 D. 427) although the representatives may be sisted reserving all questions as to their right to insist in the cause to be subsequently determined (*Martin's Exx. v. McGhee* 1914 S.C. 628).

Representatives may be sisted at any stage while the cause is in dependence, *i.e.* until final extract (see note 31.1.4): *Marquis of Douglas v. Earl of Dalhousie*, 15th November 1811, F.C.; *Gibson's Trs. v. Gibson* (1869) 7 M. 1061; *Cumming v. Stewart* 1928 S.C. 709.

R. 31.1 is procedural and does not affect the substantive rules of law in relation to time bar: see *Marshall v. Black* 1981 S.L.T. 228; and see further on time bar note 24.1.2.

31.1.3   *Sist of representative on incapacity of party*. Incapacity includes sequestration.

(1) *Sequestration*. A bankrupt until discharged and reinvested with his estate (*Flett v. Mustard* 1936 S.C. 269) has no title to pursue actions which his trustee may and does pursue (*Dickson v. United Dominion Trusts Ltd* 1988 S.L.T. 19). Where a person is sequestrated the permanent trustee may, with the consent of any commissioners, be sisted to continue to pursue or defend a cause if he considers it would be beneficial to the estate: Bankruptcy (Scotland) Act 1985, s.39(2)(b). A bankrupt may bring and continue proceedings relating to his status or personal affairs or where he may do so by virtue of s.32(9) of the Bankruptcy (Scotland) Act 1985: see further note 13.2.2(D)(4).

A liquidator of a company being wound up may be sisted to continue to pursue or defend a cause: Insolvency Act 1986, s.165(3) (in voluntary winding up without sanction of court), or s.167(1)(b) (in winding up by the court with court's sanction), and Sched. 4, para. 4. Note also the power of an administrator or receiver to bring or defend legal proceedings as agent of the company: Insolvency Act 1986, ss.14 and 55.

(2) *Incapacity*. A person of unsound mind and incapable of managing his own affairs or of giving instruction for their management has no *persona standi in judicio* (*Reid v. Reid* (1839) 1 D. 400; *Moodie v. Dempster* 1931 S.C. 553) and if a person becomes incapable during the dependence of a cause no further steps can be taken in his name and any subsequent interlocutors are null and void. Accordingly, under the old law in respect of a person aged 16 or over, a curator *bonis* would be appointed, although there may be cases where appointment of a curator *ad litem* was sufficient: *Moodie*, above. The curator *bonis* may apply to sist himself to the cause. In family actions the procedure is to appoint a curator *ad litem*: r. 49.17. A curator *bonis* is appointed to a person by presenting a petition for appointment of a curator *bonis*.

As from 1st April 2002 a curator *bonis* may no longer be appointed to a person aged 16 or over and a guardian must be appointed instead: Adults with Incapacity (Scotland) Act 2000, ss.57, 64 and 80. Where a curator *bonis* has been appointed he will become a guardian under the 2000 Act with power to manage the property and financial affairs of the adult: 2000 Act, Sch. 4, para. 1(1). He would have the power to act as the adult's legal representative. "Incapable" under the 2000 Act means incapable of asking, making decisions, communicating decisions or retaining memory of decisions by reason of mental disorder or of inability to communicate because of physical disability: 2000 Act, s. 1(6).

A person given power under an intervention order under s. 53(1) of the 2000 Act, to make decisions and give instructions in respect of an action, does not require to be sisted as a party to the action, the order being sufficient authority: *Riley v. James Beaton & Co (Plumbers) Ltd*, 2004 S.L.T. 1083 (OH).

31.1.4   *"in dependence"*. A cause is depending from the time it is commenced (*i.e.* from the time an action is served or a first order in a petition is made) until final decree, whereas a cause is in dependence until final extract. For the meaning of commenced, see note 13.4.4 (action) or 14.6.1 (petition). For the meaning of final decree, see note 4.15.2(2). For the meaning of final extract, see note 7.1.2(2).

31.1.5   *"minute"*. R. 15.1 (applications by minute) does not apply to a minute of sist: r. 15.1(6)(c). The minute of sist must narrate the death and the representative's title and crave to be sisted in room and place of the deceased or incapacitated person. The minute does not require to be signed: r. 4.2(9)(c). Any documents proving title have to be lodged (*e.g.* an extract confirmation). A motion will have to accompany the minute seeking to have it sustained.

31.1.6   *"intimation"*. For methods, see r. 16.7. Written intimation of the motion to allow the person to be sisted must be given: for methods, see r. 16.9.

31.1.7   *Expenses*. A person who sists himself or is sisted as a party may not impose conditions about his liability for expenses: *Ellis v. Ellis* (1870) 8 M. 805. A person who sists himself or is sisted as an additional party but has no title to appear may be liable in expenses from the date of the minute of sist: *Hope v. Landward District Committee of Parish Council of Inveresk* (1906) 8 F. 896. A person who sists himself in place of another may be liable for all expenses: *Torbet v. Borthwick* (1849) 11 D. 694; *Ellis*, above.

31.1.8   *Fee*. There is currently no fee for lodging a minute of sist.

Minutes of transference

31.2.—(1) Where a party dies or comes under legal incapacity while a cause is depending before the court and the provisions of rule 31.1 (minutes of sist) are not invoked, any other party may apply to the court by minute to have the cause transferred in favour of or against, as the case may be, any person who represents that party or his estate.

[NEXT TEXT PAGE IS C 217]

[1] (1A) Where—

(a) a question of liability is the subject of proceedings before the court; and

(b) the effect of any statutory transfer while the cause is depending before the court is to transfer the liability if proved to a person other than an existing party to the cause,

any party to the proceedings may apply to the court by minute to have the cause transferred in favour of or against, as the case may be, the person to whom the liability has been transferred.

(2) Where a minute of transference has been lodged in process, the court shall pronounce an interlocutor—

(a) granting warrant for service of a copy of the minute of transference, a copy of the pleadings (including any adjustments and amendments) and a copy of that interlocutor on such person; and

(b) allowing such person to lodge a minute of objection to the minute of transference within such period as the court thinks fit.

Deriv. R.C.S. 1965, r. 106 (part)

---

[1] R.31.2(1A) inserted by S.S.I. 2001 No. 305, para. 5 (effective 18th September 2001).

Transference on death or legal incapacity. Where a party dies or comes under legal incapacity **31.2.1** and his representatives do not sist themselves under r. 31.1, another party may apply under r. 31.2 to have them sisted (on the minute of transference, see note 32.2.4). The representatives must be subject to the jurisdiction of the court, *e.g.* domicile: *Mackenzie v. Drummond's Exrs.* (1868) 6 M. 932.

In the case of transference sought by a party instead of a representative seeking to be sisted, the cause must be one which is depending (see note 31.2.2) before the court: *Forbes v. Clinton* (1872) 10 M. 449.

The rule is silent on what happens if there is no appearance in response to a minute of transference. If the representatives do not appear the other party may (a) in the case of death, take decree of constitution against a deceased defender's estate (a decree *cognitionis causa tantum*) or decree of absolvitor against a deceased pursuer; or (b) in the case of incapacity, a decree which has effect as a decree in absence. In the case of transference sought against a person to whom an interest has been alienated or otherwise transferred (a) if the transferee would be the pursuer but fails to sist himself, the action may be dismissed; or (b) if the transferee would be the defender but he fails to sist himself, the pursuer may amend and call the transferee as an additional defender: r. 24.1(b)(v) or (d).

Statutory transference. Rule 31.2(1A), inserted by A.S. (R.C.S.A. No.4) (Miscellaneous) 2001 **31.2.1A** [S.S.I. 2001 No.305], applies the transference rules to, and provides for joining the new owner of an undertaking to, an action where statute has transferred the relevant liability of an undertaking to the new owner.

The word "undertaking" has not been defined. It commonly refers to water, electricity, telephone, gas and other services.

"depending". A cause is depending from the time it is commenced (*i.e.* from the time an action is **31.2.2** served or a first order in a petition is made) until final decree, whereas a cause is in dependence until final extract. For the meaning of commenced, see note 13.4.4 (action) or 14.6.1 (petition). For the meaning of final decree, see note 4.15.2(2). For the meaning of final extract, see note 7.1.2(2).

"service". For methods, see Chap. 16, Pt. I.   **31.2.3**

"minute of transference". R. 15.1 (applications by minute) does not apply to a minute of **31.2.4** transference: r. 15.1(6)(d). The minute must narrate the death and the representative's name and title and crave warrant to serve a copy of the pleadings on him, for him to lodge a minute of objection if so advised and to transfer the cause against the representative. The minute does not require to be signed: r. 4.2(9)(d). A motion will have to accompany the minute seeking to have it sustained.

"minute of objection". R. 15.1 (applications by minute) does not apply to a minute of **31.2.5** objection: r. 15.1(6)(e). The minute will be a form similar to a note of objection. The minute does not require to be signed: r. 4.2(9)(e).

Fee. There is currently no fee for lodging a minute of transference or a minute of objection to **31.2.6** a minute of transference.

Death of party: further provisions

[1] **31.3.**—(1) Subject to rule 43.20 (Rights of Relatives to Damages (Mesothelioma) (Scotland) Act 2007), as soon as reasonably practicable after the death of a party, any agent who immediately prior to the death was instructed in a cause by that party shall notify the court of the death.

(2) The notification under paragraph (1) shall be by letter to the Deputy Principal Clerk and shall be accompanied by a certified copy of the death certificate relative to the deceased party.

(3) The letter shall include an estimate of the length of time required for confirmation to the deceased party's estate by an executor.

(4) On receipt of the letter, the Deputy Principal Clerk shall place it in the process and shall place the cause before a Lord Ordinary in chambers.

(5) The Lord Ordinary may, if satisfied that the party has died and after considering the estimate provided under paragraph (3), pronounce a sist in the cause for a specified period of not less than three months.

(6) A party may apply by motion for—
 (a) recall of a sist pronounced under paragraph (5); or
 (b) variation of the specified period referred to in paragraph (5).

(7) A motion under paragraph (6)(b) shall be granted only on cause shown.

(8) On pronouncing a sist under paragraph (5); recalling a sist under paragraph (6)(a); or, varying a specified period under paragraph (6)(b), the Lord Ordinary may make such order as regards further procedure as he thinks fit including, in the case of a personal injuries action, such variation of the timetable issued under rule 43.6 as he thinks fit.

(9) Any personal injuries action in which a sist has been pronounced under paragraph (5) and the period of sist has expired may be put out by order by the Keeper of the Rolls.

(10) In this rule, "personal injuries action" has the same meaning as in rule 43.1(2).

---

[1] Rule 31.3 inserted by S.S.I. 2007 No. 282 (effective 2nd May 2007).

CHAPTER 32

TRANSMISSION AND REMIT OF CAUSES

Remits to sheriff court

32.1.—(1) An application by a party under section 14 of the Law Reform (Miscellaneous Provisions) (Scotland) Act 1985 (remit from court to sheriff) shall be made by motion.

(2) Where an action is remitted to a sheriff under section 14 of the Law Reform (Miscellaneous Provisions) (Scotland) Act 1985, the Deputy Principal Clerk shall, within four days after the interlocutor remitting the cause has been pronounced, transmit the process to the sheriff clerk of the sheriff court specified in the interlocutor.

(3) When transmitting a process under paragraph (2), the Deputy Principal Clerk shall—
 (a) give written intimation of the transmission to the parties; and
 (b) certify on the interlocutor sheet that such written intimation has been given.

(4) Failure by the Deputy Principal Clerk to comply with paragraph (3) shall not affect the validity of a remit made under paragraph (1).

Deriv. R.C.S. 1965, r. 104B inserted by S.I. 1986 No. 1955 and amended by S.I. 1987 No. 1206

32.1.1   *General note.* S. 14 of the Law Reform (Miscellaneous Provisions) (Scotland) Act 1985 allows the court at its own instance or on the motion of a party to remit a particular action before it to a sheriff before whom it could competently have been brought where in the opinion of the court the nature of the action makes it appropriate to do so. This provision was introduced as a corollary of the powers to transfer a cause from the sheriff to the court. The then Lord Advocate indicated a remit might be appropriate where other related proceedings are pending before the sheriff and where for reasons of efficiency and convenience of the parties it is desirable that all proceedings be dealt with by the sheriff: H.L. Debates, Vol. 467, col. 194 *per* Lord Mackay of Clashfern. But the fact that there is an action in the sheriff court is not determinative: *Rae v. Rae* 1991 S.L.T. 45.

The provision is there to meet the needs of particular cases and not to effect a general redistribution of work between the courts: *McIntosh v. British Railways Board (No. 1)* 1990 S.L.T. 637, 639 *per* L.P. Hope. Actions inappropriate to the sheriff court are not to be sent there: *McIntosh*, above. The fact that an action is small in value or simple is not, except in extreme cases (*i.e.* where the pursuer could not recover more than the privative limit of the sheriff court (currently £1,500)), enough to justify a remit: *McIntosh*, above, *per* L.P. Hope at p. 640A. Where there is concurrent jurisdiction the pursuer is not to be deprived of his choice of court on grounds which would apply generally to every case: *McIntosh*, above, *per* L.P. Hope at p. 640D. The court is entitled to have regard to practical and procedural advantages in adopting one forum rather than another: *McIntosh*, above, *per* L.P. Hope at p. 640L overruling *Hamilton v. British Coal Corporation* 1990 S.L.T. 287 and *Westcott v. James Dickie & Co. Ltd* 1991 S.L.T. 200. S. 14 of the 1985 Act is not to be used as a means for the defender to avoid being exposed to an award trivial in relation to expense unless the pursuer could not recover more than the privative amount: *McIntosh*, above, *per* L.P. Hope at p. 641D. A remit has been made on the grounds of expense of defending a divorce action in the Court of Session: *Gribb v. Gribb* 1993 S.L.T. 178. A remit was refused on the grounds of procedural advantage to the pursuer because of his union's policy of pursuing all actions of reparation in the Court of Session and the availability of optional procedure: *McIntosh*, above. For recent examples of remits, see *McKay v. Lloyds TSB Mortgages Ltd*, 2004 G.W.D. 37-757, 2nd November 2004 (OH); and *Drimsynie Estate Ltd v. Ramsay*, 2006 S.L.T. 528 (OH) (action of declarator and removing).

The power in s.14 of the 1985 Act does not affect the power of the court to modify an award of expenses to one of the sheriff court scales where appropriate: *McIntosh*, above, *per* L.P. Hope at 641B; see *e.g. Smith v. British Railways Engineering Ltd* 1985 S.L.T. 463.

Note also remit to the sheriff court of a winding up petition under s.120(3)(a)(i) of the Insolvency Act 1986.

Transmission to sheriff court. Where the action could be transmitted to more than one sheriff **32.1.2** court the action will be transmitted to the court of the pursuer's choice leaving it to the sheriff to determine under the sheriff court rules whether the action should be remitted to another sheriff court: *McIntosh v. British Railways Board (No. 1)* 1990 S.L.T. 637, 641F–G *per* L.P. Hope.

"written intimation". For methods, see r. 16.9. **32.1.3**

Transmissions on contingency

32.2.—(1) An application under section 33 of the Act of 1988 (transmission from sheriff on ground of contingency) shall be made—

  (a) by motion at the instance of a party to the cause depending before the court; or

  (b) by minute at the instance of any other person having an interest (including a party to the cause depending before the sheriff).

  (2) A copy of the pleadings and the interlocutors in the cause depending before the sheriff, certified by the sheriff clerk, shall be lodged with any motion enrolled or any minute lodged under paragraph (1).

  (3) A decision made on an application under paragraph (1) may not be reclaimed; but where an application has been refused, a subsequent application may be made where there has been a change of circumstances.

Deriv. R.C.S. 1965, r. 104A inserted by S.I. 1984 No. 472

General note. R.C.S. 1965, r. 104A, inserted by A.S. (R.C.A. No. 2) (Miscellaneous) 1984 [S.I. **32.2.1** 1984 No. 472], derived from ss.74 and 75 of the C.S.A. 1868 (s.74 being repealed by Sched. 2 to the C.S.A. 1988 and s.75 being repealed by A.S. (R.C.A. No. 8) (Miscellaneous) 1986 [S.I. 1986 No. 1937]). s.74 of the C.S.A. 1868 and R.C.S. 1965, r. 104A were in part replaced by s.33 of the C.S.A. 1988.

32.2.2   *Transmission on contingency.* S.33 of the C.S.A. 1988 allows the Court of Session, on an application to it, to order a sheriff court cause to be transferred to the Court of Session if it is of opinion that there is contingency between the sheriff court cause and a cause depending before the Court of Session. The expression "sheriff court cause" means a cause depending before the sheriff principal or the sheriff: C.S.A. 1988, s.33(2). A cause is depending from the time it is commenced (*i.e.* from the time it is served) until final decree. For the meaning of commenced, see note 13.4.4 or 14.6.4. For the meaning of final decree, see note 4.15.2(2). On contingency, see note 32.2.3.

32.2.3   *Contingency.* Causes may be transmitted *ob contingentiam* where a contingency exists in a cause in the Court of Session and a cause in the sheriff court. No satisfactory definition of contingency has been made. It is not very easy to define the legal term "contingency": *Liquidators of Western Bank v. Douglas* (1860) 22 D. 447, 472 *per* L.P. Inglis. In *Duke of Athole v. Robertson* (1869) 8 M. 304, 305, L.J.-C. Moncreiff said "I do not think there is a contingency unless a decision in one of the actions would decide the other in whole or in part".

A contingency may be said to exist (a) where the same parties dispute the same subject-matter; (b) where one action arises directly out of the other; (c) where the result of one action may affect the consequences of the other; (d) where the parties are different but the subject-matter is or may be the same and the decision in one will decide the dispute in both actions; and (e) where the parties are different but it is expedient to have the dispute decided once and for all in one action: see *Reid's Trs. v. Reid* (1873) 45 Sc. Jur. 191, *sub nom. Reid v. Reid's Trs.* (1893) 10 S.L.R. 168; *McFadyen v. United Alkali Co. Ltd* (1897) 4 S.L.T. 321; *Wilson v. Junor* (1907) 15 S.L.T. 182; Maclaren on *Court of Session Practice*, pp. 490 *et seq.*

Although the sheriff court action is transmitted the actions are not necessarily conjoined. Conjunction is in the discretion of the court and will only be appropriate if "the same issue will try both causes" but not if they are complicated or there are such shades of distinction that confusion and embarrassment may be produced: *Duke of Buccleuch v. Cowan* (1866) 4 M. 475, 480 *per* L.J.-C. Inglis (affd. (1876) 4 R.(H.L.) 14). The parties seeking conjunction must be connected with one another in the matters pursued for or have been aggrieved by the same act: *Boulting v. Elias* 1990 S.C. 135. There will be no conjunction if a party is prejudiced: *Gatt v. The Angus Shipping Co. Ltd* (1907) 14 S.L.T. 749. Conjunction is rarely resorted to except where different pursuers raise separate actions of damages arising out of the same circumstances: see, *e.g. Gatt*, above; *Simpson v. Imperial Chemical Industries Ltd* 1983 S.L.T. 601. An alternative arrangement is to appoint one cause to be the leading cause and to sist the others: r. 22.3(6). Another alternative is to appoint simultaneous proof (or hearing) diets.

A conjoined action may be disjoined: see, *e.g. Turner v. Tunnock's Trs.* (1864) 2 M. 509, 514.

32.2.4   *"motion".* The sheriff court process number must be stated in the motion to be incorporated in the interlocutor. For motions, see Chap. 23.

32.2.5   *"minute".* R. 15.1 (applications by minute) applies to a minute under this rule.

32.2.6   *"subsequent application".* There may be more than one subsequent application on a change of circumstances. On analogy with variation of periodical allowance in a divorce action, there is no "change of circumstances" where the original decision was based on a failure to put all the information then available to the court: *Stewart v. Stewart* 1987 S.L.T. 246.

Intimation of receipt of process transmitted from sheriff court

32.3. On receipt of a process transmitted by a sheriff clerk by virtue of an order made under any enactment to remit a cause to the court, the Deputy Principal Clerk shall—

(a) write the date of receipt on the interlocutor sheet of the sheriff court process; and

(b) give written intimation of that date to each party.

Deriv. R.C.S. 1965, r. 274 substituted by S.I. 1980 No. 1801

32.3.1   *"order made under any enactment".* The enactments under which a cause may be remitted from the sheriff court to the Court of Session include:

(1) *S.44 of the Crown Proceedings Act 1947.* Proceedings against the Crown must be remitted from the sheriff to the Court of Session if a certificate of the Lord Advocate is produced stating that the proceedings may involve an important question of law, or may be decisive of other cases, or are for other reasons more fit for trial (*sic*) in the Court of Session.

(2) *S.8(3) of the Law Reform (Miscellaneous Provisions) (Scotland) Act 1966.* An appeal to the sheriff to vary or recall a decree of the Court of Session for aliment, periodical allowance, or an order under s.9 of the Conjugal Rights (Scotland) (Amendment) Act 1861, Pt II of the

Matrimonial Proceedings (Children) Act 1958 or Pt II of the Guardianship Act 1973 shall be remitted to the Court of Session on the request of any other party.

(3) *S.37(1)(b) of the Sheriff Courts (Scotland) Act 1971* (as amended by s.16 of the Law Reform (Miscellaneous Provisions) (Scotland) Act 1980). A cause in the sheriff court may be remitted by the sheriff principal or the sheriff on condition that (a) the value of the cause exceeds the privative limit of sheriff court jurisdiction (currently £1,500: Sheriff Courts (Scotland) Act 1907, s.7 and S.I. 1988 No. 1993), (b) application is made by a party and (c) the importance or difficulty of the cause makes it appropriate. An action should not be remitted on a ground which would justify a remit in every case of its kind but on grounds particular to the cause: *Dunbar v. Dunbar* 1912 S.C. 19, 21 *per* Lord Kinnear. In *Mullan v. Anderson* 1993 S.L.T. 835 a bench of five judges decided (overruling *Data Controls (Middlesbrough) Ltd v. British Railways Board* 1991 S.C. 105) that importance or difficulty were not the only factors to be taken into account. The majority held that there was a single stage determination which included consideration of the characteristics of the *fora* and the question of importance to the parties when deciding whether the importance or difficulty of the cause made it appropriate to remit; and observations in *Shaw v. Lanarkshire Health Board* 1988 S.C.L.R. 13 were disapproved.

(4) *S.1(6) or 4(4) of the Presumption of Death (Scotland) Act 1977*. An action of declarator of death or an application for variation or recall of a decree in such an action in the sheriff court may be remitted by the sheriff at his own instance or on the motion of a party or on the order of the Court of Session on the motion of a party where the sheriff or the Court of Session, as the case may be, considers such remit desirable because of the importance or complexity of the matters at issue.

(5) *S. 63(3) of the Bankruptcy (Scotland) Act 1985*. This provides for an application to cure defects of procedure in a sequestration to be remitted to the Court of Session by the sheriff at his own instance or on the motion of a person having an interest or by the Court of Session on an application by any such person.

(6) *S. 120(3)(a)(ii) of the Insolvency Act 1986*. This provides for the Court of Session to require a petition in the sheriff court to wind up a company to be remitted to the Court of Session.

(7) *S. 33 of the C.S.A. 1988*. This is transmission from the sheriff on the ground of contingency between a sheriff court cause and a cause depending in the Court of Session: see r. 32.2 and notes.

"written intimation". For methods, see r. 16.9.   **32.3.2**

Lodging of process and motion for further procedure

32.4.—(1) Within 14 days after the date of receipt of a process referred to in rule 32.3 (intimation of receipt of process transmitted from sheriff court)—

  (*a*) the party on whose motion the remit was made, or
  (*b*) in a cause remitted by the sheriff at his own instance, the pursuer or first pursuer,

shall make up and lodge in the General Department a process incorporating the sheriff court process.

(2) On lodging a process under paragraph (1), the party lodging it shall apply by motion for an order for such further procedure as he desires; and the cause shall proceed as if it had been an action in the court initiated by a summons.

(3) A motion under paragraph (2) shall be disposed of by the Lord Ordinary.

Deriv. R.C.S. 1965, r. 275(2) substituted by S.I. 1982 No. 1825 (r. 32.4(1))

General note. This and the following rules in this Chapter provide the procedure for the transmission or remit of a cause from the sheriff court under any enactment. Formerly such a cause was dealt with initially in the Inner House, but this is no longer the case and such a cause is dealt with in the Outer House: r. 32.4(3).   **32.4.1**

"within 14 days". The date from which the period is calculated is not counted. Where the last day falls on a Saturday or Sunday or a public holiday on which the Office of Court is closed, the next available day is allowed: r. 1.3(7). For office hours and public holidays, see note 3.1.2.   **32.4.2**

"lodge a process". See rr. 4.3 and 4.4.   **32.4.3**

32.4.4   *"motion"*. For motions, see Chap. 23.

32.4.5   *Sist of process*. It will be necessary to seek a sist of process to prevent time-limits running. If legal aid has been granted in the sheriff court, an application will have to be made to the Scottish Legal Aid Board to extend the certificate to the Court of Session: a sist may be required for this to be done.

Reponing against failure to comply with rule 32.4(1) or (2)
32.5.—(1) Where—
  (*a*) the party on whose motion the remit was made, or
  (*b*) in a cause remitted by the sheriff at his own instance, the pursuer or first pursuer,
fails to comply with the requirements of rule 32.4(1) or (2) (lodging of process and motion for further procedure), he may, within seven days after the expiry of the period specified in rule 32.4(1), apply by motion to be reponed.

(2) The party enrolling a motion under paragraph (1), where the failure is a failure to lodge a process under rule 32.4(1), shall on enrolling the motion, lodge such a process and shall apply by motion for an order for such further procedure as he desires.

(3) A motion under paragraph (1) shall be granted only on cause shown and on such conditions, if any, as to expenses or otherwise as the court thinks fit.

Deriv. R.C.S. 1965, r. 275(5)(*a*) and (*b*)(i) substituted by S.I. 1982 No. 1825

32.5.1   *"within seven days"*. The date from which the period is calculated is not counted. Where the last day falls on a Saturday or Sunday or a public holiday on which the Office of Court is closed, the next available day is allowed: r. 1.3(7). For office hours and public holidays, see note 3.1.2.

32.5.2   *"motion"*. For motions, see Chap. 23.

32.5.3   *"lodge a process"*. See rr. 4.3 and 4.4.

Insistence in remit by another party
32.6. Where—
  (*a*) the party on whose motion the remit was made, or
  (*b*) in a cause remitted by the sheriff at his own instance, the pursuer or first pursuer,
has failed to comply with the requirements of paragraph (1) or (2) of rule 32.4 (lodging of process and motion for further procedure), any other party to the cause may, within seven days after the expiry of the period specified in rule 32.4(1) comply with the requirements of those paragraphs himself and insist in the remit.

Deriv. R.C.S. 1965, r. 275(5)(*b*)(ii) substituted by S.I. 1982 No. 1825

32.6.1   *"within seven days"*. The date from which the period is calculated is not counted. Where the last day falls on a Saturday or Sunday or a public holiday on which the Office of Court is closed, the next available day is allowed: r. 1.3(7). For office hours and public holidays, see note 3.1.2.

Re-transmission to sheriff clerk
32.7. Where, on the expiry of 21 days after the date of receipt of the process referred to in rule 32.3 (intimation of receipt of process transmitted from sheriff court), no motion has been enrolled under rule 32.5(1) (reponing against failure to comply with rule 32.4(1) or (2)) and no motion has been enrolled under rule 32.6 (insistence in remit by another party), the remit shall be deemed to be abandoned and the Deputy Principal Clerk shall—
  (*a*) write on the interlocutor sheet the words "Re-transmitted in respect that the remit has been abandoned.";

(b) add his signature and the date; and

(c) transmit the process to the sheriff clerk.

Deriv. R.C.S. 1965, r. 275(6) substituted by S.I. 1982 No. 1825

"expiry of 21 days". The date from which the period is calculated is not counted.　　**32.7.1**

---

[1] CHAPTER 32A

TRANSFER OF CAUSES TO AND FROM THE COMPETITION APPEAL TRIBUNAL

Transfers to the Competition Appeal Tribunal

[1] **32A.1.**—(1) An application to transfer a cause to the Competition Appeal Tribunal shall be made by motion.

(2) Where a cause is transferred to the Competition Appeal Tribunal, the Deputy Principal Clerk of Session shall, within four days after the interlocutor transferring the cause has been pronounced, transmit the process to the party on whose motion the transfer was made together with a certified copy of the interlocutor granting the motion under paragraph (1).

(3) When transmitting a process under paragraph (2), the Deputy Principal Clerk shall—

(a) give written intimation of the transmission to—

(i) the other parties;

(ii) the Registrar of the Competition Appeal Tribunal; and

(b) certify on the interlocutor sheet that such written intimation has been given.

(4) A failure by the Deputy Principal Clerk to comply with paragraph (3) shall not affect the validity of any transfer of a cause.

---

[1] Chap.32A and r. 32A.1 inserted by S.S.I. 2004 No. 52 (effective 1st March, 2004).

General note. The Competition Appeal Tribunal (CAT), as it now is, was created by the **32A.1.1** Enterprise Act 2002. The new tribunal takes over the functions of the Competition Commission Appeal tribunal under the Competition Act 1998. The power to transfer to CAT from the court is provided in s. 16 of the 2002 Act. The court may transfer to CAT so much of any proceedings before it as relate to a claim to which s. 47A of the 1998 Act applies. Section 47A, inserted by s. 18 of the 2002 Act, deals with monetary claims before CAT being claims for damages, or other claims for a sum of money, which a person who has suffered loss or damage as a result of an infringement of a relevant prohibition under the 1998 Act or Art. 81 or 82 of the EC Treaty or art. 65 or 66 of the ECSC Treaty may make in civil proceedings. It is not clear what the test would be for a transfer. It is thought that CAT would be better placed as a specialist tribunal to resolve such issues.

The Lord Chancellor has power by regulation to transfer from the court to CAT so much of any proceedings that relate to an infringement issue: 2002 Act, s. 16(1).

"motion". For motions, see Chap.23.　　**32A.1.2**

"written intimation". For method, see r. 16.9.　　**32A.1.3**

Receipt of transfers from the Competition Appeal Tribunal

32A.2. On receipt of documentation in respect of a claim which has been directed to be transferred to the court by the Competition Appeal Tribunal, the Deputy Principal Clerk of Session shall—

(a) mark the first page of the documentation or, as the case may be, the interlocutor sheet, with the date of receipt; and

(b) give written intimation of that date to each party.

---

[1] R.32A.2 inserted by S.S.I. 2004 No. 52 (effective 1st March, 2004).

32A.2.1   *General note.* The Competition Appeal Tribunal, may transfer proceedings under s. 47A of the Competition Act 1998 before it to the Court of Session. On s. 47A of the 1998 Act, see note 32A.1.1.

32A.2.2   *"written intimation".* For method, see r. 16.9.

Motion for further procedure and lodging of process in transfers from the Competition Appeal Tribunal
    32A.3.—(1) Within 14 days after the date of receipt of documentation referred to in rule 32A.2 (receipt of transfers from the Competition Appeal Tribunal)—
    (a) the party at whose request the transfer was directed, or
    (b) in proceedings in which the transfer was directed by the Tribunal at its own initiative, the party who initiated the proceedings,
shall apply by motion for an order for such further procedure as he desires; and the cause shall proceed as if it had been an action in the court initiated by summons.
    (2) On applying by motion under paragraph (1) the party shall make up and lodge a process incorporating the documentation referred to in rule 32A.2 (receipt of transfers from the Competition Appeal Tribunal) unless the documentation includes a process previously transferred to the Competition Appeal Tribunal under rule 32A.1 (transfers to the Competition Appeal Tribunal).
    (3) A motion under paragraph (1) shall be disposed of by the Lord Ordinary.

---

[1] R.32A.3 inserted by S.S.I. 2004 No. 52 (effective 1st March, 2004).

32A.3.1   *"Within 14 days".* The date from which the period is calculated is not counted. Where the last day falls on a Saturday or Sunday or a public holiday on which the Office of Court is closed, the next available day is allowed: r. 1.3(7). For office hours and public holidays, see note 3.1.2.

32A.3.2   *"motion".* For motions, see Chap.23.

32A.3.3   *"process".* For rules about a process, see Chap.4.

Reponing against a failure to comply with rule 32A.3(1) or (2)
    32A.4.—(1) Where
    (a) the party at whose request the transfer was directed; or
    (b) in proceedings in which the transfer was directed by the Tribunal at its own initiative, the party who initiated the proceedings, fails to comply with the requirements of rule 32A.3(1) or (2) (motion for further procedure and lodging of process), he may, within seven days after the expiry of the period specified in rule 32A.3(1), apply by motion to be reponed.
    (2) The party enrolling a motion under paragraph (1), where the failure is a failure to lodge a process under rule 32A.3, shall on enrolling the motion, lodge such a process and shall apply by motion for an order for such further procedure as he desires.
    (3) A motion under paragraph (1) shall be granted only on cause shown and on such conditions, if any, as to expenses or otherwise as the court thinks fit.

---

[1] R.32A.4 inserted by S.S.I. 2004 No. 52 (effective 1st March, 2004).

32A.4.1   *"within seven days".* The date from which the period is calculated is not counted. Where the last day falls on a Saturday or Sunday or a public holiday on which the Office of Court is closed, the next available day is allowed: r. 1.3(7). For office hours and public holidays, see note 3.1.2.

"motion". For motions, see Chap.23.

Insistence in transfer by another party

32A.5. Where—

(a) the party at whose request the transfer was directed; or

(b) in proceedings in which the transfer was directed by the Tribunal at its own initiative, the party who initiated the proceedings, has failed to comply with the requirements of paragraph (1) or (2) of rule 32A.3 (motion for further procedure and lodging of process), any other party to the proceedings may, within seven days after the expiry of the period specified in rule 32A.3(1), comply with the requirements of those paragraphs himself and insist in the transfer.

---

[1] R.32A.5 inserted by S.S.I. 2004 No. 52 (effective 1st March, 2004).

"within seven days". The date from which the period is calculated is not counted. Where the last day falls on a Saturday or Sunday or a public holiday on which the Office of Court is closed, the next available day is allowed: r. 1.3(7). For office hours and public holidays, see note 3.1.2.   32A.5.1

Re-transmission to Registrar of the Competition Appeal Tribunal

32A.6. Where, on the expiry of 21 days after the receipt of the documentation referred to in rule 32A.2 (intimation of the date of receipt of documentation), no motion has been enrolled under rule 32A.4 (reponing against failure to comply with rule 32A.3(1) or (2)) and no motion has been enrolled under rule 32A.5 (insistence on transfer by another party), the transfer shall be deemed to be abandoned and the Deputy Principal Clerk shall—

(a) write on the first page of the documentation or, as the case may be, the interlocutor sheet the words "Re-transmitted in respect that transfer has been abandoned.";

(b) add his signature and the date; and

(c) transmit the documentation to the Registrar of the Competition Appeal Tribunal.

---

[1] R.32A.6 inserted by S.S.I. 2004 No. 52 (effective 1st March, 2004).

"on the expiry of 21 days after". The first day is excluded.   32A.6.1

"motion". For motions, see Chap.23.   32A.6.2

CHAPTER 33

CAUTION AND SECURITY

Application of this Chapter

33.1. Subject to any other provisions in these Rules, this Chapter applies to—

(a) any cause in which the court has power to order a person to find caution or give other security; and

(b) security for expenses ordered to be given under section 136 of the Representation of the People Act 1983 in an election petition.

Caution or other security. "Caution" (or "cautionary") is the Scots legal term for the obligation by which a person becomes surety for another: Bell's *Dictionary*, p. 151. The English word "surety" includes the concept of caution but has a wider meaning and would include a personal surety by a person in addition to the original obligation. A bond of caution is a particular form of written surety whereby one person obligates himself for another that he will pay a certain sum or perform a certain act: Bell's *Dictionary*, p. 128. Formerly the rules   33.1.1

permitted only surety by caution, but the new rules permit other forms of security so that surety may be given by guarantee (a difference in form rather than substance) or consignation (see note 33.4.3).

Caution or guarantee does not require the advance of money, but consignation would require the lodging of money (although consigned money would earn interest).

33.1.2   *Circumstances in which caution required.* Caution may be required in the following circumstances.

(A) For expenses as a condition precedent to proceed with or defend a cause.

(1) *Common law.* This is entirely within the discretion of the court: *Will v. Sneddon, Campbell & Munro* 1931 S.L.T. 125; *Stevenson v. Midlothian District Council* 1983 S.C.(H.L.) 50. It should only be ordered where the interests of justice require it and may be required of a pursuer or defender: *Thom v. Andrew* (1888) 15 R. 780, 782 *per* Lord Young. The Lord Ordinary's discretion will only be overturned on appeal if his discretion was so unreasonable that no other judge could have pronounced it: *Stevenson*, above *per* L.P. Emslie at p. 52. It is usually only ordered in the situations mentioned below.

Poverty alone is not a ground for ordering caution: *Walker v. Kelty's Tr.* (1839) 1 D. 1066, 1070 *per* L.P. Hope. A person with a statable case should not be excluded from the court unless in exceptional circumstances: *Stevenson*, above, *per* Lord Fraser of Tullybelton at p. 58. If he does not have a statable case he may be required to find caution, even if he is not in a financial position to provide a sum, as it would be unfair to oblige his opponent to carry on defending the action: *Rush v. Fife R.C.* 1985 S.L.T. 451.

In *McTear's Exrx v. Imperial Tobacco Ltd* 1997 S.L.T. 530, the Extra Div. considered that although impecuniosity alone was not sufficient, a wide variety of factors could be taken into account, the overriding principle being that the defender was entitled to be protected against the necessity of incurring heavy expenses where the nature of the litigation or the conduct of the pursuer was such that the interests of justice required such protection; but this was subject to what was said in *Stevenson*, above, that it would be wrong that a litigant with a statable case should be in effect excluded from the court by an order for caution unless in exceptional circumstances. In that case the court said it had to consider whether the factors advanced by the defenders were so cogent and compelling that they overcame the general principle that an impecunious litigant is entitled to advance a statable case. The court held that the Lord Ordinary's decision to refuse to order caution should be upheld.

In *Monarch Energy Ltd v. Powergen Retail Ltd*, 2006 S.L.T. 743 (OH), a case under s. 726(2) of the Companies Act 1985 (see (A)(2) below), it was held that the right of access to a court under Art. 6 of the ECHR, was not absolute and the requirement that a litigant should provide security for expenses had been held to be a permissible limitation, provided it pursued a legitimate aim and that there was a reasonable relationship of proportionality between the means employed and the legitimate aim sought to be achieved.

There is no rule that a person on legal aid may not be ordered to find caution: *Stevenson*, above.

A motion for caution to be found may be made at any time: *Mackinnon, Noter*, 5th March 1999, unreported.

There is no general rule that the court should be reluctant to adopt a step-by-step approach to caution, ordering caution up to a particular stage such as Procedure Roll: *Merrick Homes Ltd v. Duff* 1995 S.L.T. 932.

A defender would not normally be required to find caution because he is exercising his right to defend; *cf. Robertson v. McCaw* 1911 S.C. 650. The common law test is even more difficult to satisfy in the case of a defender than in the case of a pursuer because a defender is in the action only because he has been brought into it by the pursuer and is seeking to defend himself: *Balfour Beatty Ltd v. Brinmoor Ltd* 1997 S.L.T. 888, 891F, *per* Lord Abernethy. The court is always slow to ordain a defender to find caution for payment of any expenses that may ultimately be awarded against him, but the court is entitled in the exercise of its discretion to ordain any party, including a defender, to find caution if the circumstances are special: *Matheson v. Marsh* 1996 S.C. 25.

Caution is ordered, at common law, only in the case of bankruptcy or other exceptional circumstances:

(a) Bankruptcy of pursuer. The general rule is that where the pursuer is, or *pendente lite* becomes, bankrupt he must find caution; and leave to proceed without caution is only granted in exceptional circumstances: *Clarke v. Muller* (1884) 11 R. 418, 419 *per* L.P. Inglis. For an example of such circumstances, see *Neil v. South East Lancashire Insurance Co.* 1930 S.C. 629 where pursuer made bankrupt by defender *re* expenses of reclaiming and *McCue v. Scottish Daily Record & Sunday Mail Ltd* 1999 S.C. 332. Actual sequestration is not necessary: see generally *Maxwell v. Maxwell* (1847) 9 D. 797, 802–803 *per* Lord Jeffrey; *Clarke*, above. An admission of insolvency may be sufficient: *Maxwell*, above; *cf. Hegard v. Hegard* 1981 S.L.T.

(Notes) 45 (no evidence of practical insolvency). One reason for the rule is that the bankrupt is usually seeking to recover what belongs to his estate: *Stevenson v. Midlothian D.C.* 1983 S.C.(H.L.) 50, 58 *per* Lord Fraser of Tullybelton. A discharged bankrupt may sue without caution for sums not recovered by his trustee: *Cooper v. Frame & Co.* (1893) 20 R. 920. A person nominally the pursuer but in substance the defender (as in suspension) is not ordinarily required to find caution: *Stephen v. Skinner* (1800) 22 D. 1122. Where a pursuer becomes bankrupt *pendente lite*, caution may well be ordered for past as well as future expenses: *Torbet v. Borthwick* (1849) 11 D. 694; *Mackersy v. Muir* (1850) 12 D. 1057; *cf. Maxwell*, above; *Ramedy v. Stenhouse and Grant* (1847) 10 D. 234.

(b) Bankruptcy of defender. As a general rule, caution is not ordered of a bankrupt defender as he is entitled to defend himself (*Lawrie v. Pearson* (1888) 16 R. 62; *Johnstone v. Henderson* (1906) 8 F. 689) unless he is in substance the pursuer: *Ferguson Lamont & Co.'s Trs v. Lamont* (1889) 17 R. 282—*e.g.* where the only dispute is a counterclaim: *Robb v. Dickson* (1901) 9 S.L.T. 224; see also Goudy on *Bankruptcy*, pp. 365–367 and Maclaren on *Court of Session Practice*, pp. 239 *et seq*.

(c) Other circumstances. These include: (i) Where the pursuer did not disclose her address: *Murdoch v. Young* (1909) 2 S.L.T. 450. (ii) Where a ship's master broke an arrestment on the dependence: *Meron v. Umland* (1896) 3 S.L.T. 286. (iii) Where the pursuer is a mere catspaw: *Porteous v. Pearl Life Assurance Co. Ltd* (1901) 8 S.L.T. 430, 431 *per* Lord Stormonth Darling; or where the pursuer is not the true *dominus litis*. (iv) Where there are exceptional circumstances: *Rush v. Fife R.C.* 1985 S.L.T. 451 (impecunious pursuer pursuing irrelevant action); *Kennedy v. Hamilton Brothers Oil and Gas Ltd* 1986 S.L.T. 110 (pursuer of admittedly no substance who had failed to satisfy two decrees).

In deciding whether to order a party to find caution, regard may be had to the nature of the claim or defence as disclosed in the pleadings, and also to whether that party is on legal aid.

It is not essential that there are averments in the pleadings or in a separate minute in support of a motion to ordain a party to find caution so long as there has been proper notice: *Hegard*, above; *cf. Nakeski-Cumming v. Gordon's J.F.* 1923 S.C. 770. An order for caution, being an incidental order, may be modified or superseded on a change of circumstances: *Whyte v. City of Perth Co-operative Society* 1932 S.C. 482. Consignation may be allowed in lieu of caution: *Morrison v. Morrison's Exx* 1912 S.C. 892; and see note 33.4.3.

(2) *S.726 of the Companies Act 1985.* A limited company pursuer to which the Companies Act applies may be required to find caution if it appears by credible testimony that there is reason to believe that the company will be unable to pay the defender's expenses: see *e.g. Dean Warwick Ltd v. Borthwick* 1981 S.L.T.(Notes) 18; *Merrick Homes Ltd v. Duff* 1996 S.L.T. 932. The common law power is unaffected: see below.

In *Monarch Energy Ltd v. Powergen Retail Ltd*, 2006 S.L.T. 743 (OH), it was held that the right of access to a court under Art. 6 of the ECHR was not absolute and the requirement that a litigant should provide security for expenses had been held to be a permissible limitation, provided it pursued a legitimate aim and that there was a reasonable relationship of proportionality between the means employed and the legitimate aim sought to be achieved.

If a liquidator sues in his own name rather than in the name of the company he should not be ordered to find caution as he has accepted responsibility for the expenses (unless it appears that he would be unable to pay): *Arch Joinery Contracts Ltd v. Arcade Building Services Ltd* 1992 S.L.T. 755. While a liquidator enjoys a special position as an officer of the court and subject to its supervision, creditors and contributories granted leave to raise an action in the name of an insolvent company are not and caution is required: *Caledonian Produce (Holdings) Ltd v. Price Waterhouse* 1993 S.C. 181.

A company which opposes a reclaiming motion or appeal as successful pursuer is not a pursuer for the purposes of s. 726(2) of the 1985 Act (*Star Fire and Burglary Insurance Co. Ltd v. Davidson & Sons* (1902) 4 F. 997); similarly, a company appearing as unsuccessful defender (*Sinclair v. Glasgow and London Contract Corporation Ltd* (1904) 6 F. 818). In *Assuranceforeningen Skuld v. International Oil Pollution Compensation Fund (No.3)*, 2000 S.L.T. 1352 (OH) Lord Gill, distinguishing *Star Fire*, above, held that *Assuranceforeningen*, formerly a pursuer in an action against the Braer Corporation and had become a claimant in the limitation fund action seeking compensation arising out of the Braer oil tanker disaster, could be ordered to find caution for expenses as it was a "pursuer" in "other legal proceedings" within s. 726(2) of the 1985 Act. Lord Gill held that one looked at the realities of the situation.

"Credible testimony" may be in the pleadings, documents, affidavits or asserted at the bar where not disputed or satisfactorily explained (*New Mining and Exploring Syndicate Ltd v. Chalmers & Hunter* 1909 S.C. 1390; *Dean Warwick Ltd v. Borthwick* 1981 S.L.T.(Notes) 18); but probably not merely an assertion at the bar on its own (*Edinburgh Modern Quarry Co. Ltd v. Eagle Star Insurance Co. Ltd* 1965 S.L.T.(Notes) 91): *Edinburgh Entertainments Ltd v. Stevenson* 1925 S.C. 848; *Dean Warwick Ltd*, above; *UK Leasing Ltd v. Bremners plc* 1990 S.L.T. 684. It may include the company's balance sheets or other documents lodged with the Registrar of

Companies: *Dean Warwick Ltd*, above. Even if satisfied by that testimony the court still has a discretion whether to order caution: *Brownrigg Coal Co. Ltd v. Sneddon* 1911 S.C. 1064, *per* Lord Salvesen at p. 1068 and *per* Lord Mackenzie at p. 1069.

The power to ordain a party to find caution at common law is independent of the statutory power under s. 726(2). While the legislation makes clear that it is not possible to ordain a limited company defender to find caution for expenses in terms of s. 726(2), there is nothing there which prevents the court from ordaining such a company to find caution for expenses at common law: *Kaiser Bautechnik GmbH v. G.A. Group Ltd* 1993 S.L.T. 826; *Balfour Beatty Ltd v. Brinmoor Ltd*, 1997 S.L.T. 888, 891A *per* Lord Abernethy.

A motion for caution is competent where the company is a defender and has counterclaimed against the pursuer: *Atlas Hydraulic Loads Ltd v. Seaton Ltd*, 22nd April, 1997 unreported (1997 G.W.D. 15–683).

There is no general rule that the court should be reluctant to adopt a step-by-step approach to caution, ordering caution up to a particular stage such as Procedure Roll: *Merrick Homes Ltd v. Duff* 1996 S.L.T. 932.

In considering the question of additional caution, it is not relevant to consider whether the litigation was a simple one in which the approach to expenses would be straightforward (which was relevant only to whether caution should be ordered at all): *Merrick Homes Ltd*, above.

Where the company is ordered to find caution, the court should sist the cause while caution is found rather than set a time limit for doing so: *Pioneer Seafoods Ltd v. The Braer Corporation*, 21st May 1999 (OH), unreported (1999 G.W.D. 20–956). Lod Gill indicated in that case that if caution was not found in a reasonable time, the defender could move the court to recall the sist and grant decree in absolvitor.

(B) As a condition for recall of arrestment or inhibition. Caution may be offered or required as a condition of recall of an arrestment or inhibition on the dependence. Caution is expressly referred to in r. 13.10(2). Recall of arrestment will be made on caution being found on the basis that the arrested fund, subject or value of it, or the whole debt including principal, interest and expenses to the extent of the arrested fund will be made forthcoming. Recall may be made where less than full caution is offered depending on the circumstances. If the arrested property exceeds the debt, caution should be required only to the extent of the debt. Where the sum sued for is a random sum (as in an action of damages) caution will be fixed having regard to the nature of the claim, the likely award, the amount arrested and the financial circumstances of the common debtor: see Graham Stewart on *Diligence*, pp. 202–204; see also *Henderson v. George Outram and Co. Ltd* 1993 S.L.T. 824.

Caution may be not only for the principal sum and interest but also for expenses: *McPhedron and Currie v. McCallum* (1888) 16 R. 45.

Caution will not be required where arrestment is nimious or oppressive, wrongful or where the subjects are not arrestable: see Bell's *Principles*, s. 2280 and note 13.10.5.

The principle in relation to recall of arrestment on caution is the same in relation to recall of inhibition: see, *e.g. Fisher v. Weir* 1964 S.L.T.(Notes) 99. In deciding whether a guarantee offered is an adequate alternative security to replace that held by an arrestment, the relevant comparison is between the security afforded by the proposed guarantee on the one hand and that afforded by the arrestment (and not a guarantee by an independent financial institution) on the other: *Global Marine Drilling Co. v. Triton Holdings Ltd (No.2)*, 26th January 2000, (2000 G.W.D. 5–210) (OH). There is no rule that recall should normally be on the provision of a guarantee by such an institution: *Global Marine Drilling Co*, above.

Consignation may be ordered instead of caution (*Fisher*, above) or the debtor may be given the option (*McPhedron and Currie*, above). See further, note 13.10.5.

(C) In lieu of sisting a mandatory. Caution for expenses cannot be required of foreigners seeking redress, or in the enforcement of certain foreign judgments, under certain international and European conventions. Such conventions which are adopted as part of the law of the U.K. include:

> the Brussels and Lugano Conventions on jurisdiction and enforcement of judgments in civil and commercial matters, 1968, in the C.J.J.A 1982, Scheds 1 and 3C, Art. 45 (no security, bond or deposit however described shall be required of a party in one Contracting State seeking to enforce a judgment in another Contracting State on the ground that he is a foreign national or that he is not domiciled or resident in that State);
>
> the Geneva Convention on contract for international carriage of goods by road, 1965, in the Carriage of Goods by Road Act 1956, Sch., Art. 31(5);
>
> the Geneva Convention on carriage of passengers and luggage by road, 1956, in the Carriage of Passengers by Road Act 1974, Sch., Art. 21(5);
>
> the Berne International Convention on Carriage by Rail, 1980, Art. 18(4): see International Transport Conventions Act, 1983, s.1.

A pursuer resident abroad is usually required to sist a mandatory, rather than provide security by caution or consignation (see (1) below). Where a convention provides that a foreign party shall not be required to find caution for expenses ("security for costs"), the question arises whether he can be required to sist a mandatory. In *General Trading Corporation v. James Mills (Montrose) Ltd* 1982 S.L.T. (Sh. Ct.) 30 it was decided in a case under the Geneva Convention on Carriage of goods by road that sisting a mandatory was not excluded. The Maxwell Report on Jurisdiction and Enforcement (HMSO 1980), pp. 143–144, appears to consider the requirement would not be imposed in enforcement proceedings under the 1968 Convention in Sched. 1 to the C.J.J.A. 1982 (and see *Mund & Fester v. Hatrex International Transport* [1994] E.C.R. I–467 (a right to seizure of assets simply on the ground that judgment is to be enforced abroad in another Member State is contrary to the prohibition of discrimination in art. 6 of the EC Treaty)); and it was waived in proceedings for enforcement of judgments under the Judgments Extension Act 1868 and has been waived under the Foreign Judgments (Reciprocal Enforcement) Act 1933. Requiring a mandatory may be because providing security for payment of expenses is not the sole purpose of sisting a mandatory; it also ensures that there is someone within the jurisdiction responsible for the proper conduct of the cause (see *Lawson's Trs. v. British Linen Co.* (1874) 1 R. 1065, 1066 *per* L.P. Inglis). In any event, the sisting of a mandatory is in the discretion of the court (*Fellowes' Exr. v. Fellowes' Trs.* 1988 S.L.T. 730), and the provisions of a convention against security for costs must be a relevant and important consideration. The point was not raised in *Kaiser Bautechnik GmbH v. G A Group Ltd* 1993 S.L.T. 826.

(1) *Circumstances in which mandatory sisted.* Subject to what is stated in the next paragraph, a pursuer or defender resident furth of Scotland (including a domiciled Scotsman) may be required to sist a mandatory to have someone in the jurisdiction responsible for the conduct of the cause: *Renfrew and Brown v. Magistrates of Glasgow* (1861) 23 D. 1003, 1005 *per* L.J.-C. Inglis. The matter is entirely in the discretion of the court: *Lawson's Trs.*, above. Factors to be considered in exercising the discretion are as follows: (i) impecuniosity is not in itself a sufficient ground: *Dessau v. Daish* (1897) 24 R. 976; (ii) the enforceability of a decree for expenses abroad: *Kaiser Bautechnik GmbH*, above; (iii) the applicability of a convention containing a protection against requiring security for costs; (iv) the ownership of heritable property in Scotland which is not the subject-matter of the cause and of sufficient value: *Smith v. Norval* (1828) 6 S. 852, *Caledonian and Dumbartonshire Railway Co. v. Turner* (1849) 12 D. 406, *Lawson's Trs.*, above; (v) where there has been established a *prima facie* case: *McLean v. McGarvey* (1908) 16 S.L.T. 174; *N.V. Ondix International v. James Landay Ltd* 1963 S.C. 270; (vi) where pursuer is suing on a protested bill of exchange: *N.V. Ondix International*, above; (vii) where he is a claimant in a multiplepoinding: *Stow's Trs. v. Salvester* (1900) 8 S.L.T. 253.

A party who is a national of and resident in another member state of the EU which is a party to the 1968 Brussels Convention on Jurisdiction and Enforcement of Judgments (see C.J.J.A. 1982, Sched. 1) should not be required to sist a mandatory: *Dieter Rossmeier v. Mounthooly Transport* 2000 S.L.T. 208 (First Div.). The reasons are that it is discrimination contrary to art.12 of the EC Treaty to require such a sist for such a national, and the convention makes relevant orders enforceable in other states which are parties to the convention. (The 1968 Convention now applies between the Member States of the EU and Denmark; between the other Member States of the EU, the relevant "convention" is the Council Regulation (EC) No. 44/2001 (the "Brussels I Regulation").) A party resident in another part of the U.K. should not be required to sist a mandatory: *Lawson's Trs*, above. The reason is that since the Judgments Extension Act 1868, relevant judgments of the court may be enforced throughout the U.K.

An assisted person resident outside Scotland may be ordered to sist a mandatory: *Herzberg v. Herzberg* 1952 S.L.T. (Sh. Ct.) 65; *cf. Harley v. Kinnear Moodie & Co. Ltd* 1964 S.L.T. 64 (order refused, it being observed that s. 2(6)(e) of the Legal Aid (Scotland) Act 1967 (now s. 18(2) of the Legal Aid (Scotland) Act 1986) only applied to expenses against an assisted person not his mandatory).

A court has a larger discretion in requiring a defender to sist a mandatory than a pursuer and will do so less usually: *Simla Bank v. Home* (1878) 8 M. 781; *N.V. Ondix International*, above. A refusal to sist a mandatory is always *in hoc statu* and a further motion may be made on a change of circumstances: *Aitkenhead v. Bunton & Co.* (1892) 19 R. 803, 804 *per* L.P. Robertson.

(2) *Procedure for sisting a mandatory.* The court may order a party to sist a mandatory within a specified time. Time may be prorogated: *Murray v. Murray* (1845) 7 D. 1000. The order may be recalled on a change of circumstances: *N.V. Ondix International*, above. A minute of sist must be lodged in process by the named mandatory, thereafter an interlocutor is pronounced sisting the mandatory as a party to the cause. The mandate itself is not required (*Elder v. Young & Co.* (1854) 16 D. 1003) unless demanded by the other party (*Gunn & Co. v. Couper* (1871) 10 M. 116). The court will normally accept as mandatory any person who is solvent (*Railton v. Mathews* (1844) 7 D. 105) other than another party to the cause (*Scott & Steven's Tr. v. Smith* (1851) 13 D. 854). Whether a solicitor may be mandatory for his client depends on the extent of

his authority: *Knight v. Freeto* (1863) 2 M. 386. If a pursuer fails to obtemper an order to sist a mandatory, the defender is assoilzied: *Masinimport v. Scottish Mechanical Light Industries* 1972 S.L.T. (Notes) 76; if a defender fails, the pursuer is entitled to decree. Either may be reponed on lodging a minute of sist: *Thomson v. Woodthorpe* (1863) 1 M. 635.

(3) *Liability of mandatory*. A mandatory will be liable for all expenses of the cause including those incurred before his appointment: *Robertson & Co. v. Exley, Dinsdale & Co.* (1833) 11 S. 320. He has general authority to take all usual steps (*Renfrew and Brown v. Magistrates of Glasgow* (1861) 23 D. 1003, 1005 *per* L.J.-C. Inglis) though he requires special authority to settle an action (*Thoms v. Bain* (1888) 15 R. 613). He is not liable to implement any decree, he is merely the security that it will be binding on his principal: *Thoms*, above.

(4) *Withdrawal of mandatory*. A mandatory may withdraw on lodging a minute of resignation (*Martin v. Underwood* (1827) 5 S. 783) though he remains liable for expenses prior to his withdrawal (*Chapman v. Balfour* (1875) 2 R. 291). He may be removed if he becomes insolvent: *Harker v. Dickson* (1856) 18 D. 793.

(5) *Death of mandatory*. On death the mandatory's estate is liable for expenses prior to his death: *Barclay & Ewart's Reps. v. Barclay* (1850) 12 D. 1253.

(D) In suspension, suspension and interdict, and suspension and liberation. See r. 60.3.

(E) In judicial factories, by a judicial factor on his appointment. See Judicial Factors Acts 1849, s.2, and 1889, s.6; and see r. 61.9(1).

(F) By administrators appointed under para. 1(8) of Sched. 1 to the Proceeds of Crime (Scotland) Act 1995. See r. 75.11.

33.1.3   *"any cause in which the court has power"*. The court is given express power in certain rules to order caution, *e.g.* r. 13.10(2) (recall etc. of arrestment or inhibition), r. 35.2(4) (recovery of documents etc.).

The court also has power to grant motions subject to such conditions, if any, as to expenses or otherwise as it thinks fit (r. 23.13); and this could include caution or other security.

The court has power under certain statutes to order caution: *e.g.* Judicial Factors Act 1849, s.2; Bills of Exchange Act 1882, s.100; Sale of Goods Act 1979, s.11(5); Proceeds of Crime (Scotland) Act 1995, Sched. 1, para. 1(8).

33.1.4   *Security for expenses under the Representation of the People Act 1983*. The methods of caution or security under s.136 of the Representation of the People Act 1983 are governed by r. 69.4.

Form of applications

33.2.—(1) An application for an order for caution or other security, or for variation or recall of such an order, shall be made by motion.

(2) The grounds on which such an application is made shall be set out in the motion.

33.2.1   *"motion"*. The grounds of the motion must be set out in the motion: r. 33.2(2). For motions, see Chap. 23.

Orders to find caution or other security

33.3. Subject to section 726(2) of the Companies Act 1985 (order on company to find caution), an order to find caution or give other security shall specify the period within which such caution is to be found or such security given.

33.3.1   *Period within which caution to be found*. The former rule in R.C.S. 1965, r. 200(c) in relation to judicial factors stipulated one month as the period in which caution had to be found. There is not now a fixed period, but the period fixed must be specified. The period fixed may be prorogated: r. 4.9(2).

The court must fix a reasonable time within which to find caution; failure to find caution within that time (unless prorogated) will result in decree in favour of the other party except in judicial factories (see note 61.9.3). This rule applies also to s.726 of the Companies Act 1985: *Augustinus Ltd v. Anglia Building Society* 1990 S.L.T. 298.

33.3.2   *Companies Act 1985, s.726(2)*. Where a limited company to which the Companies Act applies is pursuer in an action or other legal proceedings, the court may, if it appears by credible testimony that there is reason to believe the company will be unable to pay the defender's expenses if successful in his defence, order the company to find caution and sist the proceedings until caution is found: Companies Act 1985, s.726(2). The common law power is unaffected. See further, note 33.1.2(A)(2).

Methods of finding caution or giving security

33.4.—(1) A person ordered—

(a) to find caution, shall do so by obtaining a bond of caution; or

(b) to consign a sum of money into court, shall do so by consignation under the Court of Session Consignations (Scotland) Act 1895 in the name of the Accountant of Court.

(2) The court may approve a method of security other than one mentioned in paragraph (1), including a combination of two or more methods of security.

(3) Subject to paragraph (4), any document by which an order to find caution or give other security is satisfied shall be lodged in process.

(4) Where the court approves a security in the form of a deposit of a sum of money in the joint names of the agents of parties, a copy of the deposit receipt, and not the principal, shall be lodged in process.

(5) A bond of caution or consignation receipt lodged in process shall be accompanied by a copy of it.

Bonds of caution. Where caution is by bond of caution, the bond may be (a) by an insurance **33.4.1** company authorised to conduct such business (see r. 33.5) or (b) by any person, in which case it is more likely that the sufficiency of the caution will have to be established: r. 33.7(2). In (a), there is usually a formal bond; otherwise a letter from the cautioner indicating that he will satisfy the obligation in the amount of the caution will suffice. All bonds must comply with the requirements of r. 33.6. A consignation receipt for the full amount of the caution is acceptable in place of a bond (see note 33.4.3).

Except in relation to judicial factors, a bond (or letter) must be lodged as a step of process and marked with a number of process (r. 4.4(3)) and intimated to other parties (r. 4.6). In the case of a bond other than a bond by an insurance company, it is docquetted by the Deputy Principal Clerk (or on his behalf) confirming that the bond of caution or other document is in proper form (he is no longer concerned with sufficiency, which is a matter for the parties: see r. 33.7). The bond is transmitted by the party required to lodge it to the Accountant of Court by the transmission book for safekeeping; the book is receipted and returned to the appropriate department of the Office of Court. When the bond is allowed to be uplifted, it is transmitted by the Accountant of Court's transmission book to the appropriate department of the Office of Court; the book is receipted and returned. Transmission is undertaken by the party concerned. The Accountant of Court is custodian of all bonds of caution: Judicial Factors Act 1849, s. 35. In relation to judicial factories, see r. 61.9.

Security other than bonds of caution. This might be a guarantee rather than a formal bond, a **33.4.2** consignation receipt (see note 33.4.3) or a deposit receipt in joint names of parties' agents.

Consignation. This may be ordered or allowed by the court: (a) in lieu of caution for **33.4.3** expenses: *Morrison v. Morrison's Exx.* 1912 S.C. 892; (b) in lieu of sisting a mandatory: *Bell v. Strathearn & Blair* 1953 S.L.T. (Notes) 23; (c) in lieu of diligence in security; or (d) in lieu of caution in suspensions, suspension and interdict, and suspension and liberation: r. 60.2(2). Consignation is less common than caution because a party will be out of his money until the dispute is settled, although interest will be earned. Furthermore, the procedure is more complicated than for bonds of caution because, before an interlocutor allowing the consigned money to be uplifted may be granted, a certificate from the Inland Revenue under r. 8.1(1)(a) must be produced.

Under the Court of Session Consignations (Scotland) Act 1895, ss. 2 and 3, the Accountant of Court is custodian of all sums lodged by order of the court or under any Act of Parliament ("consignations").

By a Notice [*i.e.* P.N. No. 1 of 1996] the former procedure for consignation receipts has been abolished. Such receipts were subject to criticism because of the low rate of interest and their use, as a consequence, was rare. The low rate of interest was justified by the banks on the ground that consignation receipts were expensive to administer. The new form, a special deposit account, allows a higher rate of interest. Consignation receipts had an advantage over ordinary deposit receipts in that partial upliftment was possible. Partial upliftment will be possible from a special deposit account.

The new procedure is that where consignation is ordered, the consigned funds should be lodged in a special deposit account opened at any branch of the Royal Bank of Scotland (though the amounts will be held at the Edinburgh North Bridge Branch, 31 North Bridge, EH1 1SF, of that bank). An opening statement of account should then be sent to the Accountant of Court. The Accountant will then write to inform the Deputy Principal Clerk of Session of the consignation (this will replace the copy consignation receipt formerly lodged in process). Existing consignations will be transferred to the new account by the Accountant of Court.

Applications to uplift consigned sums will be made by motion under reference to the special deposit accounts. When a certified copy interlocutor authorising upliftment is shown to the Accountant of Court, he will draw on the account and make payment as directed by the court.

An interlocutor permitting the uplifting of the whole or a part of the sum consigned should clearly state to whom the Accountant should pay any sum ("pay to A" does not include A's solicitor) and whether interest is to be included. Such an interlocutor will not be signed by the court until a tax clearance certificate from the Inland Revenue as required under r. 8.1(1)(a) has been produced, notwithstanding that income tax on interest in the hands of a deposit taker (including an authorised institution or a municipal bank within the meaning of the Banking Act 1987) is deducted at source before payment: Income and Corporation Taxes Act 1988, s. 479. This deduction at source provision does not apply, however, where the beneficial owner of the deposit is not ordinarily resident in the UK.

Copy bonds of caution or consignation receipts. A copy of a bond of caution or a consignation **33.4.4** receipt has to be lodged because the principal may not be borrowed out of process: r. 4.11(3)(g).

Cautioners and guarantors
[1] **33.5.** A bond of caution or other security shall be given only by a person

authorised to carry on a regulated activity under section 31 of the Financial Services and Markets Act 2000.

---

[1] Rule 33.5 amended by S.S.I. 2004 No. 331 (effective 6th August 2004).

33.5.1   *General note.* This is a new rule, replacing R.C.S. 1965, r. 200(e)(iv) which provided for a list of guarantee companies for the purposes of obtaining caution in judicial factories (the list was used more widely in fact). That rule arose out of s. 27 of the Judicial Factors Act 1849 which provided for the court to authorise bonds or policies of certain companies carrying on guarantee business in Scotland in relation to caution to be found by factors. This led to a list of "approved" guarantee companies imposing a burden on the Accountant of Court to investigate to satisfy himself that a company could be approved by the Lord President for the list. There is no requirement in s. 27 of the 1849 Act for the court to approve a list of companies. Regard must now be had to Arts. 59 and 60 of the EEC Treaty which allow a company from another Member State to supply services here.

The solution was to abandon the list of approved guarantee companies and to provide for companies authorised to carry on business in class 15 in Sched. 2 to the Insurance Companies Act 1982. That Act is now replaced by reference to those authorised under s. 31 of the Financial Services and Markets Act 2000.

Form of bonds of caution and other securities

[1] **33.6.**—(1) A bond of caution shall oblige the cautioner, his heirs and executors to make payment of the sums for which he has become cautioner to the party to whom he is bound, as validly and in the same manner as the party and his heirs and successors, for whom he is cautioner, are obliged.

(2) [*Revoked by S.S.I. 2004 No.514.*]

Deriv. R.C.S. 1965, r. 238(a)

33.6.1   *General note.* Rule 33.6(2) required a bond by an insurance company to state whether the insurance company was authorised under the Insurance Companies Act 1982. That Act was repealed by the Financial Services and Markets Act 2000.

Sufficiency of caution or security and objections

33.7.—(1) The Deputy Principal Clerk shall satisfy himself that any bond of caution or other document, lodged in process under rule 33.4(3), is in proper form.

(2) A party who is dissatisfied with the sufficiency or form of the caution or other security offered in obedience to an order of the court may apply by motion for an order under rule 33.10 (failure to find caution or give security).

33.7.1   *General note.* The practice has been for the Deputy Principal Clerk to satisfy himself as to the sufficiency of caution found, a matter which is really not his concern. It is for the party who is dissatisfied with the caution found by another party to raise the matter with the court and if necessary seek decree by default: r. 33.10. The Deputy Principal Clerk is concerned only with the form of the document of caution or security.

33.7.2   *"motion".* For motions, see Chap. 23.

Juratory caution

33.8.—(1) Where a pursuer in an action with a conclusion for suspension is ordered to find caution or give other security, he may offer to do so by juratory caution.

(2) Such an offer shall be made—

(a) at the time the order for caution or other security is made; or

(b) by enrolling a motion within the period allowed for finding caution or giving other security, as the case may be, or any prorogation of it, for the appointment of a commissioner.

(3) Where such an offer is made, the court shall—

(a) appoint a commissioner to take the deposition of the pursuer at a time and place to be fixed by the commissioner;

(b) ordain the pursuer to give notice of at least seven days of the time and place so fixed by the commissioner to every other party to the action; and

(c) where the offer has been made by motion under paragraph (2)(b), prorogate the time for finding caution or giving other security, as the case may be, by such period as it thinks fit.

(4) At the time and place fixed by the commissioner in accordance with paragraph (3)(a), the pursuer shall be examined as to the nature and extent of his whole estate wheresoever situated and the other parties to the action shall be entitled to cross-examine him.

(5) After his examination, the pursuer shall send to the Deputy Principal Clerk—

(a) a bond of caution;

(b) a full inventory of his whole estate;

(c) a declaration attached to the inventory, stating that he will not dilapidate or dispose of any of his property or uplift any of the debts due to him, without the authority of the court (under pain of imprisonment or being otherwise punished as being guilty of fraud) or the consent of the party entitled to the benefit of the caution until the interlocutor disposing of the subject-matter of the action has become final and, where he has been found liable to pay any sum, including expenses, 12 weeks (and any further period that the court, on the motion of any party, may grant) have passed since the interlocutor became final;

(d) the vouchers of any debts due to the pursuer;

(e) the title deeds of any heritable property belonging to the pursuer, so far as in his possession or under his control; and

(f) where required by the party entitled to the benefit of the caution—

(i) a standard security in favour of such party over any heritable property belonging to the pursuer, and

(ii) an assignation of all debts or other rights due to the pursuer, prepared at the expense of the pursuer.

(6) Subject to rule 33.12(1) (bond of caution or consignation receipt transmitted to Accountant of Court), the Deputy Principal Clerk shall retain any documents lodged under paragraph (5) of this rule until further order of the court.

Deriv. R.C.S. 1965, r. 240

General note. Juratory caution is rare. It only arises in a suspension where offered, which is **33.8.1** infrequent, and involves the appointment of a commissioner in a process with intimations of bankruptcy procedure.

"suspension". Suspension is the means of preventing execution of diligence, to stop **33.8.2** infringement of a right or to bring a decree under review: see Chap. 60.

"caution or other security". See note 33.1.1. **33.8.3**

"motion". For motions, see Chap. 23. **33.8.4**

Insolvency or death of cautioner or guarantor
33.9. Where caution has been found by bond of caution or security has been given by guarantee and the cautioner or guarantor, as the case may be—

(a) becomes apparently insolvent within the meaning assigned by section 7 of the Bankruptcy (Scotland) Act 1985 (constitution of apparent insolvency),

(b) calls a meeting of his creditors to consider the state of his affairs,

(c) dies unrepresented, or

(d) is a company and—

    (i) an administration or winding up order has been made, or a resolution for a voluntary winding up has been passed, with respect to it,

    (ii) a receiver of all or any part of its undertaking has been appointed, or

    (iii) a voluntary arrangement (within the meaning assigned by section 1(1) of the Insolvency Act 1986) has been approved under Part I of that Act,

the party entitled to benefit from the caution or guarantee may apply by motion for a new security or further security to be given.

Deriv. R.C.S. 1965, r. 238(f)

33.9.1   *General note.* The party whose cautioner becomes bankrupt or insolvent, etc., or dies should apply for new caution. If he does not the other party may object to further procedure without this being done: *A.B. v. C.D.* (1836) 15 S. 158.

33.9.2   *"apparent insolvency".* S. 7 of the Bankruptcy (Scotland) Act 1985 lists the events which give rise to the constitution of apparent insolvency.

33.9.3   *Administration or winding up orders or appointment of receiver.* An administration order is made under Part II of the Insolvency Act 1986, a receiver is appointed under Part III of that Act and a winding up order made under Part IV of that Act. An insurance company (a body of persons, whether incorporated or not, carrying on insurance business) whether established within or outside the UK, carrying on business in the UK may be wound up under the 1986 Act: Insurance Companies Act 1982, ss. 15, 53, 54 and 96(1).

33.9.4   *"voluntary arrangement".* The directors of a company (in respect of which an administration order is not in force) may propose under Part I of the Insolvency Act 1986 to the company and its creditors a composition in satisfaction of its debts or a scheme of arrangement of its affairs: 1986 Act, s. 1(1). The word "composition" means an arrangement whereby the creditors will not be paid in full or will have their debts postponed.

33.9.5   *"motion".* For motions, see Chap. 23.

Failure to find caution or give security

33.10. Where a party fails to find caution or give other security (such a party being in this rule referred to as "the party in default"), any other party may apply by motion—

    (*a*) where the party in default is a pursuer, for decree of absolvitor; or

    (*b*) where the party in default is a defender or a third party, for decree by default or for such other finding or order as the court thinks fit.

33.10.1   *General note.* This rule enshrines the current practice.

33.10.2   *"motion".* For motions, see Chap. 23.

33.10.3   *"decree of absolvitor".* This is the decree when the court decides finally in the (defender's) favour; it is a decree *in foro* and is one which is *res judicata* between the parties: see note 20.1.1; and on *res judicata*, see note 18.1.4(B)(5).

33.10.4   *"decree by default".* A decree by default is a decree *in foro* and is one which is *res judicata* between the parties: see note 20.1.1; and on *res judicata*, see note 18.1.4(B)(5).

33.10.5   *Reclaiming.* A decree by default may be reclaimed against without leave within 21 days: r. 38.3(2). The decree may be recalled on such conditions as to expenses or otherwise as the court thinks fit: r. 38.11(2). The document of caution or security must be lodged on or before the reclaiming motion is enrolled: r. 38.11(1).

Interlocutors authorising uplifting of consignation receipts

33.11. An interlocutor authorising a party to uplift a consignation receipt from the Accountant of Court shall state the name of the person entitled to any interest which has accrued on the sum consigned.

33.11.1   *General note.* This is a new rule which reflects existing practice.

33.11.2   *"consignation receipt".* See note 33.4.3.

Accountant of Court

33.12.—(1) A bond of caution or a consignation receipt lodged in any process shall be transmitted by the party lodging it, after the Deputy Principal Clerk has complied with rule 33.7(1), to the Accountant of Court.

(2) A bond of caution may be uplifted from the Accountant of Court on exhibition to him of the interlocutor granting discharge.

(3) A consignation receipt may be uplifted from the Accountant of Court on exhibition to him of a certified copy of the interlocutor authorising it.

(4) The form of the book to be kept by the Accountant of Court under section 4 of the Court of Session Consignations (Scotland) Act 1895 (consignations to be entered in books kept by Accountant of Court) shall be in Form 33.12.

Deriv. R.C.S. 1965, r. 13(d) (r. 33.12(1)); P.N. 14th May 1970 (r. 33.12(2))

Accountant of Court. See note 3.1.3.   33.12.1

Transmission to Accountant of Court. The clerk of session at the appropriate public counter 33.12.2 of the Petition or General Department will enter particulars of the process in a transmission book. The party who lodged the document of caution or other security will take the document and the transmission book to the Accountant of Court's office. On a receipt being entered in the book by the Accountant's staff the book is taken back to the Petition or General Department.

Uplifting of bond of caution or consignation receipt. On bonds of caution, see note 33.4.1; on 33.12.3 consignation receipts, see note 33.4.3.

CHAPTER 34

REPORTS TO INNER HOUSE

Report by Lord Ordinary to Inner House

34.1.—(1) The Lord Ordinary may, at any stage of a cause on intimation to the parties, report the cause or any incidental matter which arises in the course of it, to the Inner House for a ruling.

(2) The Lord Ordinary shall give effect to the ruling of a Division of the Inner House on a report to the Inner House unless the Division decides the cause or incidental matter itself or remits to the Lord Ordinary with directions to proceed in a particular way.

Deriv. R.C.S. 1965, r. 91B(1) inserted by S.I. 1984 No. 472 and amended by S.I. 1986 No. 1937, and r. 198A(1) inserted by S.I. 1986 No. 1937

General note. This Chapter is derived from s.19 of the C.S.A. 1825 (incidental matter) and s.14 34.1.1 of the C.S.A. 1850 (whole cause), both replaced by R.C.S. 1965, r. 91B (and R.C.S. 1965, r. 198A) and repealed by A.S. (R.C.A. No. 8) (Miscellaneous) 1986 [S.I.1986 No. 1937].

"report the cause". Report of a whole cause (see *e.g. Borland v. Borland* 1947 S.C. 432) to the 34.1.2 Inner House has fallen into desuetude.

"incidental matter". Any incidental matter in the course of a cause may be reported to the 34.1.3 Inner House. Such a matter would include a point on which there is a difference of practice in the Outer House (*e.g. Johnson v. Caledonian Railway Co.* (1892) 20 R. 222) or a matter of practice about which there is doubt (*e.g. Gould v. Gould* 1966 S.C. 88).

Where the Inner House has made an order, such as for a particular mode of inquiry, which subsequently appears to be inappropriate, the proper course is for the Lord Ordinary to report the matter back to the Inner House: *Kerr v. John Brown & Co.* 1965 S.C. 144.

It is incompetent for a Lord Ordinary to remit a cause to the Inner House *simpliciter*, it must be done in an appropriate case by a report under this Chapter: *Alliance & Leicester Building Society v. Lindsays W.S.*, 25th July (1997 G.W.D. 36–1862).

Fixing hearings for reports

34.2.—(1) Where the Lord Ordinary reports a cause, or any incidental matter in a cause, under rule 34.1(1) to the Inner House, each party shall, within seven days after the date on which the report of the Lord Ordinary is issued, inform the Keeper of the Rolls of the estimate of counsel or other person having a right of audience of the duration of the hearing before the Inner House.

(2) If a party fails to comply with paragraph (1), the Keeper of the Rolls may put the cause out on the By Order Roll before a Division of the Inner House.

(3) Where, at any time after an estimate has been given to the Keeper of the Rolls under paragraph (1), a party's estimate of the likely length of the hearing alters materially, that party shall inform the Keeper of the Rolls of the new estimated length.

(4) On the basis of the information provided to him under this rule, the Keeper of the Rolls shall—

(a) put the cause out for hearing before a Division of the Inner House in the Single Bills or on the Summar Roll as he thinks fit; and

(b) give written intimation of the date of the hearing to each party.

34.2.1   *General note.* This rule sets out expressly the procedure to be followed when a report is made.

34.2.2   *"counsel or other person having a right of audience".* See r. 1.3(1) (definitions of "counsel" and "other person having a right of audience").

34.2.3   *"written intimation".* For methods, see r. 16.9.

34.2.4   *Copies of documents for use of the court.* There must be lodged four copies of any document a party wishes to refer to at the hearing in the Inner House on the second sederunt day before the hearing: r. 4.7(2). This should be the responsibility of the party on whose motion the court decided to report.

34.2.5   *By Order Roll hearing.* No court fee is payable for a hearing on this By Order Roll.

Disposal of reports

34.3.—(1) On considering the report of the Lord Ordinary and hearing parties, the Inner House may—

(a) dispose of the cause or matter reported to it; or

(b) remit to the Lord Ordinary with such directions as it thinks fit.

(2) The decision of the Inner House on a report to it under rule 34.1(1) shall be final.

(3) The Inner House may determine any question of expenses in respect of the matter reported to it or may reserve any such question.

(4) An interlocutor pronounced by the Lord Ordinary in obedience to directions given under paragraph (1) shall be deemed to be an interlocutor of the Inner House.

Deriv. R.C.S. 1965, r. 91B(2), inserted by S.I. 1984 No. 472 and amended by S.I. 1986 No. 1937 (r. 34.3(1) to (3)), and r. 198A(2) and (3) inserted by S.I. 1986 No. 1937.

34.3.1   *Disposal by Inner House or Lord Ordinary.* Disposal by either the Inner House or remit to the Outer House may be adopted. Formerly, where the whole cause was reported the cause became an Inner House cause: *Gould v. Gould* 1966 S.C. 88.

An interlocutor of the Lord Ordinary following a report includes the words "having advised with the Lords of the First [*or* Second] Division".

The Lord Ordinary should not sit with the Division considering the report: *F v. F* 1945 S.C. 202, 212 *per* Lord Moncrieff.

[1] CHAPTER 34A

PURSUERS' OFFERS

Application and interpretation of this Chapter
[1] **34A.1.** *[Revoked by S.I. 1996 No. 2769.]*

---

[1] Chap. 34A and r. 34A.1 inserted by S.I. 1996 No. 2168 (effective 23rd September 1996).

General note. Chapter 34A was inserted by A.S. (R.C.S.A. No. 4) (Miscellaneous) 1996 [S.I. **34A.1.1**
1996 No. 2168] following a recommendation of the Cullen *Review of Outer House Business* in
December 1995. The Chapter was revoked with effect from 14th November 1996 by A.S.
(R.C.S.A. No. 6) 1996 [S.I. 1996 No. 2769]. The revocation does not affect offers made before it
came into effect.

The idea of pursuers' offers was first proposed by Lord President Hope after he discovered its
existence in Canada in 1991. Research was carried out by the Lord President's Private Office
and a consultation exercise carried out on proposals for its introduction. Not all those consulted
were in favour, but the majority were; and the Rules Council was persuaded reluctantly to
accept it. It was agreed that Chap. 34A would be in operation as an experiment for two years
after which it would be reviewed. Pursuers' offers were brought to the attention of the Woolf
Committee examining English procedure by the Lord President's office; the idea was taken up
and adopted in Lord Woolf's interim and final reports (without acknowledgement).

Rules for such offers exist in Canada (British Columbia, New Brunswick, Nova Scotia,
Ontario and Saskatchewan) and Australia (New South Wales, Queensland, South Australia and
Victoria).

Chap. 34A was introduced as part of the armoury of procedures to increase early settlements.
The policy behind the rules (applying to both pursuers and defenders) in the other jurisdictions
mentioned was to encourage settlement and replaced the English-based rules for payment into
court (where our procedure for tenders appears not to have existed). Anecdotal evidence
suggests the procedure works successfully in these jurisdictions, but no statistics were available
to show how significant the contribution of offers to settle to early settlements has been. In
South Australia an offer to settle must be made at the end of a pre-trial conference.

The success or failure of pursuers' offers will depend on the appropriate form of sanction
being imposed on a defender who, having refused to accept an offer, does not succeed at proof
in achieving a lower award or in winning the case. It would be unfortunate if the procedure
failed because an inappropriate sanction were chosen; and the penalty in r. 34A.6(2)(b) is not
the most appropriate.

Few other jurisdictions have elected for a rule for up to a 100 per cent uplift in expenses. A notable
exception is British Columbia where the double costs rule applies only to tariff items covering
preparation for trial, trial and proceedings after trial other than appeal, exclusive of disbursements
and expenses. It may be that Chap. 34A has been revoked because of the unsatisfactory nature of r.
34A.6 which provides for a 100 per cent uplift in the whole expenses (except any additional fee). The
100 per cent uplift should be a general rule "unless the court otherwise orders" rather than a fixed
100 per cent or any figure between 0 and 100 per cent. Consideration should be given to limiting
expenses to those incurred after the offer is lodged, as with tenders.

In *Taylor v. Marshalls Food Group Ltd (No. 2)* 1998 S.C. 841 (First Div.), it was held that the
provision in r.34A.6, for the pursuer to be entitled on beating his own offer to a sum equal to
the taxed expenses, was *ultra vires.* But all is not lost. Pursuers' offers may have experienced a
form of reprieve in *Cameron v. Kvaerner Govan Ltd* 1999 S.L.T. 638. In that case the pursuer
was held to be entitled to an additional fee under r.42.14(2)(g) (settling or limiting matters)
where the pursuer offered to settle for a fixed sum, thus encouraging the issues to be focused,
and the defender subsequently tendered that sum. Lord Bonomy said any step which might
clarify the position of a party or limit the areas in dispute should be encouraged. At present it
cannot be said that a pursuer's offer can be equiperated with a tender and any law and
procedure applicable to tenders: *Tenbey v. Stolt Comex Seaway Ltd*, 2001 S.C. 638.

Offers to settle
[1] **34A.2.** *[Revoked by S.I. 1996 No. 2769.]*

---

[1] R. 34A.2 inserted by S.I. 1996 No. 2168 (effective 23rd September 1996).

34A.2.1 *General note.* For the history of this rule, see note 34A.1.1.

Protection of offers from disclosure
[1] **34A.3.** *[Revoked by S.I. 1996 No. 2769.]*

---

[1] R. 34A.3. inserted by S.I. 1996 No. 2168 (effective 23rd September 1996).

34A.3.1 *General note.* For the history of this rule, see note 34A.1.1.

Withdrawal or capers of offers
[1] **34A.4.** *[Revoked by S.I. 1996 No. 2769.]*

[1] R. 34A.4 inserted by S.I. 1996 No. 2168 (effective 23rd September 1996).

34A.4.1 *General note.* For the history of this rule, see note 34A.1.1.

Acceptance of offers
[1] **34A.5.** *[Revoked by S.I. 1996 No. 2769.]*

---

[1] R. 34A.5 inserted by S.I. 1996 No. 2168 (effective 23rd September 1996).

34A.5.1 *General note.* For the history of this rule, see note 34A.1.1.

Consequences of failure to accept an offer to settle
[1] **34A.6.** *[Revoked by S.I. 1996 No. 2769.]*

---

[1] R. 34A.6 inserted by S.I. 1996 No. 2168 (effective 23rd September 1996).

34A.6.1 *General note.* For the history of this rule, see note 34A.1.1.
    In *Taylor v. Marshalls Food Group Ltd (No. 2)* 1998 S.C. 841 (First Div.), it was held that the provision in r.34A.6, for the pursuer to be entitled on beating his own offer to a sum equal to the taxed expenses, was *ultra vires*.

CHAPTER 35

RECOVERY OF EVIDENCE

Application and interpretation of this Chapter
    35.1.—(1) This Chapter applies to the recovery of any evidence in a cause depending before the court.
    (2) In this Chapter, "the Act of 1972" means the Administration of Justice (Scotland) Act 1972.

35.1.1 *General note.* This Chapter applies to the recovery of evidence in a depending cause (on the meaning of which, see note 35.1.2). If the cause is not depending, *e.g.* the summons has not been served, recovery may not be sought. An application, *e.g.* under s.1(1) of the Administration of Justice (Scotland) Act 1972 for preservation, custody or detention of documents before a cause has been commenced would have to be by petition under Chap. 64.

35.1.2 *"depending".* A cause is depending from the time it is commenced (*i.e.* from the time an action is served or a first order in a petition is made) until final decree, whereas a cause is in dependence until final extract. For the meaning of commenced, see note 13.4.4 (action) or 14.6.1 (petition). For the meaning of final decree, see note 4.15.2(2). For the meaning of final extract, see note 7.1.2(2).

Applications for commission and diligence for recovery of documents or for orders under section 1 of the Act of 1972
    35.2.—(1) An application by a party for—
    (a) a commission and diligence for the recovery of a document, or
    (b) an order under section 1 of the Act of 1972,
shall be made by motion.

(2) At the time of enrolling a motion under paragraph (1), a specification of—
- (a) the document or other property sought to be inspected, photographed, preserved, taken into custody, detained, produced, recovered, sampled or experimented on or with, as the case may be, or
- (b) the matter in respect of which information is sought as to the identity of a person who might be a witness or a defender,

shall be lodged in process.

(3) A copy of the specification lodged under paragraph (2) and the motion made under paragraph (1) shall be intimated by the applicant to—
- (a) every other party;
- (b) in respect of an application for an order under section 1(1) of the Act of 1972, any third party haver; and
- [1] (c) where necessary—
  - (i) the Advocate General for Scotland (in a case where the document or other property sought is in the possession of either a public authority exercising functions in relation to reserved matters within the meaning of Schedule 5 to the Scotland Act 1998, or a cross-border public authority within the meaning of section 88(5) of that Act); or
  - (ii) the Lord Advocate (in any other case),
  and if there is any doubt, both.

(4) Where the Lord Ordinary grants a motion made under paragraph (1), in whole or in part, in an action before calling of the summons, he may order the applicant to find such caution or give such other security as he thinks fit.

(5) The decision of the Lord Ordinary on a motion under paragraph (1) in an action before calling of the summons shall be final and not subject to review.

[2] (6) The Advocate General for Scotland or the Lord Advocate or both, as appropriate, may appear at the hearing of any motion under paragraph (1).

Deriv. R.C.S. 1965, r. 95(a)(part) amended by SI 1992/88 (r. 35.2(5) and (6)), r. 95(b) (r. 35.2(1)(a), (2) and (3), r. 95A(a)(part) inserted by SI 1972/2021 and amended by SI 1992/88 (r. 35.2(5) and (6)); r. 95A(b) inserted by SI 1972/2021 (r. 35.2(1) to (4); r. 95A(d)(i) substituted by SI 1987/1206 (r. 35.2(1)(b))

[1] R.35.2(3)(c) substituted by SSI 2001 No. 305, para. 6 (effective 18th September 2001).
[2] Rule 35.2(6) substituted by S.S.I. 2007 No. 7, para. 2(5) (effective 26th February 2007).

General note. This rule is the principal provision for obtaining an order to recover documents **35.2.1** or for an order under s. 1 of the Administration of Justice (Scotland) Act 1972 in a depending cause (on which, see note 35.1.2). Where there is no depending cause the application is by petition under Chap. 64.

A commission and diligence to recover documents refers strictly to the common law rules for recovery of documents (on which, see note 35.2.5). The power of the court to take the depositions of havers on commission is preserved by s. 10(a) (and in relation to the Inner House, s. 38) of the C.S.A. 1988. Under s. 1 of the Act of 1972 orders may be sought (for a commission and diligence) for the inspection, photographing, preservation, custody and detention of documents and other property and for their production and recovery, the taking of samples or the carrying out of experiments or for disclosure of information about the identity of a potential witness or defender. A motion for a commission and diligence must be accompanied by a specification of the documents or property sought: r. 35.2(2); and see note 35.2.10.

In relation to actions of damages for personal injuries or the death of a relative where the optional procedure has been adopted there is a procedure for automatic mandatory disclosure of documents: r. 43.25.

A commission and diligence may not be obtained to recover from the keeper of any public record original registers or deeds in his custody or processes kept by the Keeper of the Records of Scotland or an inferior court; the procedures in rr. 35.9 or 35.10 respectively must be used.

A party who has obtained possession of documents or other items under a commission and diligence at common law or under s. 1 of the 1972 Act is subject to an implied obligation or undertaking to the court not to use them or allow them to be used for any purpose other than the conduct of the actual or proposed proceedings for which there were recovered: *Iomega Corporation v. Myrica (U.K.) Ltd* 1998 S.C. 636 (I.H.).

35.2.2   *"commission and diligence"*. In granting a motion for recovery of documents the court, where appropriate, (a) appoints a commissioner with a warrant under which the commissioner may enter premises and search for the documents or property, (b) authorises a named person to photograph, inspect, take samples of, or carry out an experiment on the property, (c) grants warrant to cite a party or third party haver to appear before a commissioner to produce the document or other property or answer questions about where it is or with whom it is or has been, or (d) authorises one or more of the above either at the same time or one at a time: for execution of commissions, see r. 35.4. Where it is not possible for a commissioner to blank out commercially confidential material in excerpting from documents the court has authorised counsel, solicitors and an independent expert to inspect the documents provided they signed an undertaking about non-disclosure: *Iomega Corporation v. Myrica (U.K.) Ltd (No.1)* 1999 S.L.T. 793.

Before a commission is executed there is an optional procedure for serving the order for recovery of a document (but not other property) on the haver to obtain voluntary production: r. 35.3.

Documents or other property recovered are not productions in the cause. They only become so if subsequently lodged as productions by a party.

The Lord Ordinary cannot sist a commission and diligence after it has been granted: *Exal Sampling Services Ltd v. Massie* 1993 S.L.T. 1220.

The court has power to impose conditions for the use of information recovered by commission and diligence, although it is not normal practice for the court to do so: *McInally v. John Wyeth & Brother Ltd* 1992 S.L.T. 344; *Union Carbide Corporation v. B.P. Chemicals Ltd* 1995 S.C. 398, 404G *per* L. Hope.

35.2.3   *"document"*. This word has been defined in the R.C.S. 1994 by reference to the inclusive definition in s. 9 of the Civil Evidence (Scotland) Act 1988: r. 1.3(1).

35.2.4   *"other property"*. This phrase is not defined in the R.C.S. 1994. In s. 1(1) of the Act of 1972 the phrase is defined as "including, where appropriate, land". "Property" in the Act of 1972 means corporeal property; but the court has a common law power to order inspection and video recording of things such as a process or activity: *Christie v. Arthur Bell & Sons Ltd* 1989 S.L.T. 253; and see cases there cited.

35.2.5   *Recovery of documents (common law)*. The purpose of a commission and diligence is to put the court in possession of documents about the issues of fact which have to be determined: *Paterson v. Paterson* 1919 1 S.L.T. 12. Hence a fishing diligence by a party to discover material for a case not pled will not be allowed: *County Council of Fife v. Thoms* (1898) 25 R. 1097; *Earl of Morton v. Fleming* 1921 1 S.L.T. 205. A fishing diligence is one for which there is no basis in the averments or one which involves too wide a search among all the papers of the haver: *Civil Service Building Society v. MacDougall* 1988 S.C. 58, 62 *per* L.J.-C. Ross. Real evidence is not recoverable by this means: *Mactaggart v. MacKillop* 1938 S.L.T. 559; *cf.* s. 1 of the Act of 1972.

The suggested rule for the recovery of documents in Walker and Walker on *The Law of Evidence in Scotland* (p. 321) is: "Subject to confidentiality and relevancy, a document is recoverable if it is a deed granted by or in favour of a party or his predecessor in title, or a communication sent to, or by or on behalf of, a party, or a written record kept by or on behalf of a party."; and "A document is not recoverable if it has not been communicated to or by one of the parties and if it can be used only to provide material for the examination-in-chief or in cross-examination of a witness who is not a party". No judge can be called on to produce his notebook in order for it to be ascertained what the reasons for his decision were: *Behrent v. MacKillop,* 2003 S.L.T. 1049 (OH).

The document must be relevant to the facts averred but it does not have to be admissible in evidence: *Admiralty v. Aberdeen Steam Trawling and Fishing Co. Ltd* 1909 S.C. 335, 340 *per* L.P. Dunedin (*de recenti* report by ship master to owner); *Black v. Bairds & Dalmellington* 1939 S.C. 472 (post-mortem medical report); *Johnston v. South of Scotland Electricity Board* 1968 S.L.T. (Notes) 7 (*de recenti* statements to third party). A commission and diligence may not be refused because averments remitted to probation are irrelevant or of doubtful relevance: *Duke of Hamilton's Trs. v. Woodside Coal Co.* (1897) 24 R. 294.

Documents prepared for the purposes or in anticipation of the litigation are as a general rule not recoverable: *Anderson v. St Andrew's Ambulance Association* 1942 S.C. 555; *Young v. National Coal Board* 1957 S.C. 99; and see note 35.2.7 on confidentiality.

At common law a commission and diligence was not normally granted before the closed record, and was granted after the open record (but before proof was allowed) only to enable a party to make more specific averments already pled or to answer averments or calls for further specification but not to gather material for evidence in preparation for proof: *Boyle v. Glasgow Royal Infirmary and Associated Hospitals* 1969 S.C. 72, 77 *per* L.P. Clyde. That power has been extended, by the effect of s.1(2) of the Act of 1972, to any time from the time the cause has commenced (*i.e.* the action has been served or the first order in a petition has been granted): *Moore v. Greater Glasgow Health Board* 1978 S.C. 123, 131 *per* Lord Cameron. On the granting of a commission and diligence after the record has closed but where the cause has been appointed to the Procedure Roll, see *Graham Builders Merchants Ltd v. The Royal Bank of Scotland plc* 1992 S.C.L.R. 402; *Bank of East Asia Ltd v. Shepherd and Wedderburn, W.S.* 1994 S.C.L.R. 526. The grounds on which the commission will be granted at any time before the record has closed are the same as in *Boyle*, above: *Moore*, above: it must be shown that the documents are necessary for the purpose of enabling a party to make more pointed or more specific what is already averred or to enable him to make adequate and specific replies to his opponent's averments; in short "what he must show is that the documents sought to be recovered are required to serve the purposes of the pleadings as those pleadings stand at the time the diligence is sought": *Moore*, above, *per* Lord Cameron at p. 131. S.1(2) has not inverted the onus on the party seeking to establish that the commission and diligence should be granted: *Civil Service Building Society v. MacDougall* 1988 S.C. 58; and see note 35.2.6.

In the Cullen *Review of Outer House Business* in December 1995, it was recommended that there should be no difference between the test for recovery applied before the closing of the record and the test applied after the record has closed, subject to a proviso that the court may refuse to allow recovery where it is related to amendments in respect of which there is an unresolved dispute as to whether probation should be allowed. This is similar to the position adopted by Lord Grieve in *McGown v. Erskine* 1987 S.L.T.(Notes) 4 but not followed by the Inner House in *Moore*, above and *Civil Service Building Society*, above. No rule has been promulgated to alter the common law in the hope that the judicial climate will change.

There is a divergence of opinion about the time when recovery of documents may be allowed on the strength of averments in a minute of amendment. Some clerks and judges take the view that a commission and diligence may be granted when the minute of amendment is allowed to be received, while others take the view that the commission and diligence may only be granted when the record (or other pleadings) are amended in terms of the minute of amendment. The latter view may be based on the principle that until the record is amended the averments in the minute do not form part of the pleadings. In theory the averments might be adjusted out, the minute not insisted in or the amendment of the record not allowed (*e.g.* it is at the motion to amend the record that normally the issue of amendment after expiry of a limitation or prescriptive period is determined: *Greenhorn v. J. Smart & Co. (Contractors) Ltd* 1979 S.C. 427, 432). No such purist view is taken about a commission and diligence sought on the basis of adjustments prior to a record closing. It may be that a distinction is to be made between, on the one hand, a commission and diligence to enable a party to make more specific certain averments or to answer calls and, on the other hand, a commission and diligence to prepare for the proof. This distinction has been made with respect to recovery of documents sought before the record has closed (or proof allowed), the former being allowed and the latter not: see *Boyle v. Glasgow Royal Infirmary and Associated Hospitals* 1969 S.C. 72 and note 35.2.4 above.

There must be a specification of the documents sought which is intimated to every other party and, where necessary, the Lord Advocate or Advocate General (see note 35.2.14): r. 35.2(2) and (3).

Orders under s.1 of the Administration of Justice (Scotland) Act 1972. Under s.1(1) of the Act **35.2.6** of 1972 orders may be sought (for a commission and diligence) for the inspection, photographing, preservation, custody and detention of documents and other property and for their production and recovery, the taking of samples or the carrying out of experiments (even if this involves destruction). The court may also order any person (not just a party) to disclose any

information he has about the identity of any person who appears to the court to be a person who might be a witness in any existing civil proceedings: Act of 1972, s.1(1A) inserted by the Law Reform (Miscellaneous Provisions) (Scotland) Act 1985, s.19 (for information about possible witnesses or defenders in proceedings which are likely to be brought, see Chap. 64): for a recent unsuccessful attempt under s.1(1A) of the Act of 1972, see *Pearson v. Educational Institute of Scotland* 1997 S.C. 245. These provisions do not affect the law and practice about privilege or witnesses and havers, confidentiality or public interest, and s.47 of the Crown Proceedings Act 1947 (recovery of documents in possession of the Crown) applies: Act of 1972, s.1(4). The privilege against self-incrimination cannot be claimed in respect of certain proceedings under s.1(1) of the Act of 1972 for infringement relating to intellectual property: see note 35.2.7(6).

Section 1(1A) of the Act of 1972 cannot be used simply to get an order for the disclosure of the identity of witnesses in an action early unless there are circumstances which in justice required that the ordinary rule in P.N. No. 8 of 1994 (exchange of list of witnesses 28 days before proof) should yield in favour of early disclosure: *Boyce v. Cape Contracts Ltd*, 1998 S.L.T. 889; *Moffat v. News Group Newspapers Ltd* (O.H.) 19th June 1999, unreported (1999 G.W.D. 24–1126).

An order may be sought at any time after the cause has commenced (*i.e.* the action has been served or the first order in a petition has been granted) unless there is special reason why the application should not be granted: Act of 1972, s.1(2)(a). This provision was designed to overrule the common law practice (see note 35.2.5) that a commission and diligence was rarely granted before the record was closed. In *Baxter v. Lothian Health Board* 1976 S.L.T.(Notes) 37 Lord Dunpark said that s.1(2)(a) of the Act of 1972 meant that the common law test applied so that a person seeking an order before the closed record had to show cause why recovery should be allowed although even if a prima facie case was made out there may yet be a special reason for refusing it. In *McGown v. Erskine* 1987 S.L.T.(Notes) 4 Lord Grieve held that if it was in the interests of justice to grant the motion it should be granted unless there were special reasons for refusing it. The decision of the Inner House in *Moore v. Greater Glasgow Health Board* 1978 S.C. 123 (in which *Baxter*, and *McGown*, above were cited but not referred to in the judgments) indicates that the former view prevails, and this was confirmed in *Civil Service Building Society v. MacDougall* 1988 S.C. 58: on *Moore*, see note 35.2.5.

In the Cullen *Review of Outer House Business* in December 1995, it was recommended that there should be no difference between the test for recovery applied before the closing of the record and the test applied after the record has closed, subject to a proviso that the court may refuse to allow recovery where it is related to amendments in respect of which there is an unresolved dispute as to whether probation should be allowed. This is similar to the position adopted by Lord Grieve in *McGown v. Erskine*, above, but not followed by the Inner House in *Moore*, above and *Civil Service Building Society*, above. No rule has been promulgated to alter the common law in the hope that the judicial climate will change.

There must be a specification of the documents or property sought which must be intimated to any third party haver as well as the other parties and, where necessary, the Lord Advocate (see note 35.2.14): r. 35.2(2) and (3).

The optional procedure for serving the order for recovery of documents to obtain voluntary production does not apply: r. 35.3(1).

A defender contesting jurisdiction may not obtain an order for inspection under s.1 of the Act of 1972 before the plea of no jurisdiction has been repelled: *M. T. Group v. James Howden & Co. Ltd* 1993 S.L.T. 409.

Medical examination and blood tests. Medical examinations are usually arranged by **35.2.6A** agreement between parties in actions of damages for personal injuries. The court may order a pursuer to be medically examined in such an action: *Junner v. North British Railway Co.* (1877) 4 R. 686.

Such an examination might extend to a psychological examination as distinct from a physical one (*McLaren v. Remploy Ltd* 1996 S.L.T. 382 *per* Lord Macfadyen as a preliminary view) but may not extend to examination by a person without any medical or professional qualification (*Mearns v. Smedvig Ltd* 1999 S.C. 243). The court may have to consider whether an examination may be made a condition of pursuing a claim where there is a refusal to undergo it; the test is whether the refusal prevents the just determination of the cause: *Mearns*, above, at p. 249E *per* Lord Eassie. In *McMurray v. Safeway Stores plc*, 2000 S.L.T. 1033, Lady Paton held that the defender had to demonstrate the appropriate validation of the system of tests by a physiotherapist in a physical evaluation company; and since tests would be painful and it was questionable whether confidentiality would be maintained, the pursuer's opposition to the test was reasonable.

An order may not be made in respect of a witness, and evidence sought to be adduced which cannot be tested by the other party without obtaining a medical examination to which there is no consent will be excluded: *Davidson v. Davidson* (1860) 22 D. 749. A party cannot, at common law, be ordered to undertake an examination because if he refused he could, in theory, be imprisoned for contempt: *Whitehall v. Whitehall* 1958 S.C. 252, 258 *per* L.J.-C. Thomson. In practice, therefore, only an adverse inference may be drawn (*Docherty v. McGlynn* 1983 S.C. 202, 214, *per* Lord Cameron).

An adult may consent to a blood test; but he cannot be compelled to provide a blood sample: *Torrie v. Turner* 1990 S.L.T. 718. Under s.6 of the Law Reform (Parent and Child) (Scotland) Act 1986 (as amended by s.70(3) of the Law Reform (Miscellaneous Provisions) (Scotland) Act 1990) consent to a blood test or to the taking of other body fluids or tissue of a child under 16 for evidence relating to the determination of parentage in civil proceedings may be given, but cannot be compelled to be given, by his guardian or the person having custody or care and control of the child or, where the child cannot give consent, by the court. By s.70 of the 1990 Act a party to any civil proceedings may be requested to give a sample of blood, other body fluid or tissue for analysis or to consent to the taking of such a sample from a child in relation to whom he has power to give consent, and where that party refuses or fails to do so an adverse inference may be drawn.

A curator *ad litem* cannot consent to the taking of blood samples from his ward: *Docherty*, above. This rule is unaffected by s.70 of the 1990 Act: *Cameron v. Carr's curator ad litem* 1998 S.L.T.(Sh.Ct) 22.

35.2.7   *Confidentiality or privilege.* Certain communications are recognised to be confidential and privileged.

(1) *Solicitor and client.* The general rule is that communications between solicitor and client for professional purposes are confidential and cannot be recovered. There are exceptions where fraud or other illegality is alleged against a party in relation to a transaction in which the solicitor was concerned (*Micosta S.A. v. Shetland Islands Council* 1983 S.L.T. 483), where the very existence of the solicitor and client relationship is in issue or where the communication is the subject-matter of the cause for which it is sought to be recovered (*Kid v. Bunyan* (1842) 5 D. 193) or where solicitor and client are involved in a transaction to derive benefit for a client from his knowledge of fraud by another (*Conoco (U.K.) Ltd v. The Commercial Law Practice*, 1997 S.L.T. 372). The client may waive the privilege for a series of communications but not for an isolated document in a series: *Wylie v. Wylie* 1967 S.L.T.(Notes) 9. There is no rule that there is no confidentiality in the identity of a client or that by waiving confidentiality in relation to the contents of a letter the client has waived it in relation to his identity: *Conoco (U.K.) Ltd*, above. Under s.1 of the Evidence (Scotland) Act 1852, where a party adduces his agent (solicitor) as a witness on any matter which he could not otherwise competently be led, that party cannot object on the ground of confidentiality to any question on a matter pertinent to the issue.

(2) *Solicitor and solicitor.* Communications between solicitors with a view to achieving settlement of litigation are confidential and not recoverable: *Fyfe v. Miller* (1835) 13 S. 809. Stating that a communication is "without prejudice", however, will not make it privileged (*Burns v. Burns* 1964 S.L.T.(Sh.Ct.) 21); and a statement of fact is not protected from use as an admission because the words "without prejudice" have been used: *Watson-Towers Ltd v. McPhail* 1986 S.L.T. 617; *Daks Simpson Group plc v. Kuiper*, 1994 S.L.T. 689.

(3) *Communications post litem motam.* Documents prepared for the purposes or in anticipation of the litigation are confidential and as a general rule are not recoverable: *Anderson v. St Andrew's Ambulance Association* 1942 S.C. 555; *Young v. National Coal Board* 1957 S.C. 99. The question of whether a report is one prepared *post litem motem* requires the court to make a judgment as to whether or not the document has been prepared in anticipation of litigation or in response to a development in litigation already raised; and it is not appropriate to take a broad brush approach to the issue based on the interests of justice or fairness: *Hepburn v. Scottish Power Plc.* 1997 S.L.T. 859.

Accordingly, reports of accidents are generally excluded. The reason is that after an accident each party must be able to investigate free from the risk of having to reveal his information to the other side: *Johnstone v. National Coal Board* 1968 S.C. 128.

(a) An exception to this general rule is that a report by an employee, present at the time of the accident, to his employer is not confidential (it is a *de recenti* statement or a spontaneous report on a matter of fact) and may be recovered by the opponent: *Young*, above. Photographs fall into the same category as reports: *More v. Brown & Root Wimpey Highland Fabricators Ltd* 1983 S.L.T. 669 (in which the general rule and its only exception were reaffirmed). An employer's accident book is not recoverable unless an entry in it comes within the exception: *Dobbie v. Forth Ports Authority* 1974 S.C. 40. A medical report instructed for the purposes of the litigation is not recoverable: *Teece v. Ayrshire & Arran Health Board* 1990 S.L.T. 512. Reports of a receiver or liquidator on the conduct of directors prepared under s.7(3) of the Company Directors Disqualification Act 1986 are not recoverable: *Secretary of State for Trade and Industry v. Houston* 1995 S.L.T. 196.

Reports prepared to ascertain and present facts (scientifically and objectively) rather than with an aim to litigation are, on the other hand, recoverable: *Waddington v. Buchan Poultry Products Ltd* 1961 S.L.T. 428; *Marks & Spencer Ltd v. British Gas Corporation* 1983 S.L.T. 196.

(b) The only other exception is where an examination undertaken in anticipation or in development of a party's case destroys or materially alters the subject-matter with the result that the person in possession of the report of the examination is in a position of knowledge about the cause and circumstances of the incident which the other party is unable to acquire: *Black v. Bairds & Dalmellington* 1939 S.C. 472. A report may contain observations of the fact as well as expressions of opinion; and there may be circumstances in which an opinion as to the cause of an accident may be difficult to disentangle from observations of fact; in such a case a commissioner should be appointed to take exception from the report: *Hepburn v. Scottish Power plc.* 1997 S.L.T. 859, 864H.

Confidentiality does not cease on completion of the case for which the report was prepared: *Hunter v. Douglas Reyburn & Co. Ltd* 1993 S.L.T. 637; and see *Ward v. Marine Harvest Ltd* 1997 S.L.T. 469.

(4) *Public policy (public interest immunity).* The only situation in which a document or other property may be withheld on the ground of public policy or public interest is where the interest is a national one put forward by the Crown: *Higgins v. Burton* 1968 S.L.T.(Notes) 52. The view that the law of Scotland does not recognise the concept of public interest immunity beyond that of Crown privilege, and does not divide confidentiality into public interest immunity and private confidentiality, was confirmed in *Parks v. Tayside R.C.* 1989 S.L.T. 345, 348A–348F *per* Lord Sutherland. See note 35.2.8 on Crown privilege or immunity.

(5) *Spouses.* Communications between spouses are confidential and one is not a competent or compellable witness against the other (Evidence (Scotland) Act 1853, s. 3) except where the cause is concerned with their conduct towards each other, *e.g.* in a divorce (*MacKay v. MacKay* 1946 S.C. 78). The privilege subsists after death or divorce: Dickson on *Evidence*, para. 1660.

(6) *Self-incrimination of haver.* As a general rule a document or other property which would render the haver liable to prosecution because it is self-incriminating is privileged. There is an exception. The privilege against self-incrimination cannot be claimed in respect of proceedings under s. 1(1) of the Act of 1972 for infringement, to obtain disclosure of information about infringement, or to prevent any apprehended infringement, of intellectual property rights or passing off: Law Reform (Miscellaneous Provisions) (Scotland) Act 1985, s. 15.

(7) *Clergy, doctors and journalists.* It is sometimes said that communications to such persons are confidential. This is true in a popular but not a legal sense. Confidentiality does not appear to attach to communications to clergy. It does not attach to communications to doctors or journalists. The ordinary rule excluding recovery in relation to a medical report made in connection with the litigation would, however, apply to a doctor.

(8) *Communications made as a matter of duty.* "A communication honestly made upon any subject in which a person has an interest, social or moral, or in reference to which he has a duty, is privileged if made to a person having a corresponding interest or duty.": *James v. Baird* 1916 S.C. 510, 517 *per* L.P. Strathclyde. For a recent example of this type of privilege, see *Pearson v. Educational Institute of Scotland,* 1997 S.C. 245.

Waiver of confidentiality will not necessarily result from documents being referred to in open court by the party entitled to the privilege; it depends on the purpose and whether there was publication of the contents: *Barclay v. Morris,* 1998 S.C. 74. See also *Duke of Argyll v. Duchess of Argyll,* 1962 S.C.(H.L.) 88 (admission on record of specific entries in diaries not waiver of whole contents); and *Cunningham v. The Scotsman Publications Ltd,* 1987 S.C. 107.

Where confidentiality is claimed the documents or property, where practicable, are sealed in an enclosed packet and a motion has to be enrolled to have the packet opened up or such recovery allowed: r. 35.8.

Crown privilege or immunity. Commission and diligence may be granted for recovery, etc., of   **35.2.8** documents or property in the possession of the Crown, whether or not a party, subject to two provisos, (i) a document or property may be withheld on the ground that its disclosure would be injurious to the public interest and (ii) the existence of a document or property shall not be disclosed if in the opinion of a Minister of the Crown it would be injurious to the public interest to disclose the existence of it: Crown Proceedings Act 1947, s. 47; Act of 1972, s. 1(4). The first proviso relates to a particular document and the second to a class. The court has, however, an inherent power to overrule an objection by the Crown which is preserved by s. 47 of the 1947 Act. The test to be applied is whether the public interest in the administration of justice not being frustrated outweighs the objection: *Glasgow Corporation v. Central Land Board* 1956 S.C.(H.L.) 1 confirming the law of Scotland recognised in *Sheridan v. Peel* 1907 S.C. 577, 580 *per* L.P. Dunedin; *Henderson v. McGowan* 1916 S.C. 821, 826 *per* L.P. Strathclyde. It is based on the ground that the fair administration of justice between subject and subject and between the subject and the Crown is a public interest of a high order, and that its protection is in the care of the courts: *Glasgow Corporation,* above, *per* Viscount Normand at pp. 12–13. Where objection is taken to a class of documents the court can take into account not only the interests of the applicant but also the interests of the public as a whole: *Friel, Petr.* 1981 S.C. 1.

The court is bound to accept the assertion of the Crown that there is an aspect of public policy to protect: *Admiralty v. Aberdeen Steam Trawling and Fishing Co. Ltd* 1909 S.C. 335; *Friel*, above; *AB v. Glasgow and West of Scotland Blood Transfusion Service* 1993 S.L.T. 36.

The court may inspect the document to decide whether it, or parts of it which are relevant, should be produced: *Science Research Council v. Nassé* [1980] A.C. 1028; *Air Canada v. Secretary of State for Trade (No. 2)* [1983] 2 A.C. 394.

In order to persuade the court even to inspect the documents the party seeking recovery ought at least to satisfy the court that they are very likely to contain material which would give substantial support to his contention on an issue which arises in the case, and that without them he might be deprived of the means of proper presentation of his case: *Air Canada*, above, *per* Lord Fraser of Tullybelton at p. 435; followed in *Somerville v. The Scottish Ministers*, 2007 S.L.T. 96 (First Div).

Immunity does not apply to documents or property which do not come into the possession of a servant or agent of the Crown in the ordinary course of his official duties: *Whitehall v. Whitehall* 1957 S.C. 30. Immunity only arises where the public interest is a national one: *Higgins v. Burton* 1968 S.L.T. (Notes) 52; *Parks v. Tayside R.C.* 1989 S.L.T. 345, 348A–F *per* Lord Sutherland.

"motion". For motions, see Chap. 23.   **35.2.9**

"specification". A specification consisting of numbered paragraphs or "calls" of the **35.2.10**
documents, property or information sought to be recovered (or as the case may be) must be
lodged with the motion to grant the order. Calls should be framed with reference to the issues of
fact on which the documents etc. are supposed to have a bearing (*Paterson v. Paterson* 1919 1
S.L.T. 12) and the averments in the pleadings. The names of persons thought to be in possession
of documents, property or information do not require to be stated in the specification.
   Where it is sought to recover information from a document which may contain matters not
relevant to the pleadings, the words "in order that excerpts may be taken therefrom at the sight
of the commissioner of all entries showing or tending to show (*the information relevant to the
matters averred*)" are used. It is customary to insert a final call in these terms: "Failing
principals, drafts, copies or duplicates of the above or any of them".
   Deletions may be required or the specification otherwise adjusted when the motion is heard.
The interlocutor should record what calls or parts of calls were allowed or refused where the
whole of the specification is not granted.
   A specification for the recovery of documents at common law is intimated to every other
party and, where necessary, the Lord Advocate or Advocate General (see note 35.2.14); a
specification for an order under s. 1 of the Act of 1972 is also intimated to any third party haver:
r. 35.2(3).
   The specification is lodged in process as a step of process: see r. 4.4 and r. 1.3(1) (definition of
"step of process"). It may be sent by post or fax with the motion: P.N. No. 4 of 1994, paras. 1,
8(2) and 9.

   "haver". A haver is a person who has (is believed to have or has had) the document or other **35.2.11**
property sought. He may be a party or anyone else ("a third party haver").

   Caution on application before calling. This is rarely required. On caution generally, see Chap. 33. **35.2.12**

   "final and not subject to review". The decision of the Lord Ordinary may not be reclaimed **35.2.13**
against.

   Intimation to and appearance of Lord Advocate or Advocate General. This must be done where **35.2.14**
recovery is sought of a document belonging to or in possession of the Crown: *Sheridan v. Peel*
1907 S.C. 577, 580 *per* L.P. Dunedin; *Henderson v. McGowan* 1916 S.C. 821, 825 *per* L.P.
Strathclyde; *Whitehall v. Whitehall* 1957 S.C. 30, 42 *per* Lord Sorn. This used to apply also to
records of an NHS hospital: *Glacken v. National Coal Board* 1951 S.C. 82; but the practice of
intimating to the Lord Advocate, deriving from a P.N. in 1950, is now considered no longer
necessary in relation to the recovery of medical records: P.N. No. 2 of 2006. Care should be
taken about whether a document relates to a "reserved matter", in which case intimation is to
the Advocate General; or a "developed matter", in which case intimation is to the Lord
Advocate. The provision for intimation to both in case of doubt avoids a difficulty when
intimation has been on the wrong law officer. When intimation has been made the back of the
specification should be marked (docquetted) with the words "Intimated to Lord Advocate [*or
Advocate General as the case may be*]".
   The Lord Advocate may appear or be represented at any motion under this rule: r. 35.2(6).
No mention is made of appearance by the Advocate General; but if he has an interest, he would
hardly be denied a hearing.

   Caveats. A caveat may not be lodged against an order under s. 1 of the Act of 1972: r. 5.1(c). **35.2.15**

   Bankers' books. A commission and diligence may be sought to recover bank books although **35.2.16**
it is often possible to agree excerpts with the bank and the opponent. Certain statutory
provisions should be noted.
   A copy of any document purporting to be authenticated by a person responsible for making
the copy shall, unless the court otherwise directs, be deemed a true copy and treated as if it were
the document itself, and ss. 3–5 of the Bankers' Books Evidence Act 1879 do not apply: Civil
Evidence (Scotland) Act 1988, s. 6. A document may be taken to form part of the record of a
business or undertaking if certified as such by a docquet signed by a officer of the business, and
a statement contained in the certified document may be received in evidence without being
spoken to by a witness: 1988 Act, s. 5. The evidence of an officer of a business that a statement
is not contained in the records of the business is admissible as evidence of that fact, whether or
not the records have been produced, and such evidence may be given by affidavit: 1988 Act, s. 6.
On receiving affidavits in evidence, see r. 36.8.
   Where a bank is not a party it cannot be compelled to produce books the contents of which
can be proved under the 1879 Act or the 1988 Act: 1879 Act, s. 6 as amended by the 1988 Act,
s. 7(4).
   S.7 of 1879 Act contains provisions for the court to order, in any legal proceedings, the
inspection and taking of copies of entries in banker's books, the order being served three clear

days before it is to be obtempered unless the court otherwise directs. The grounds on which, and the time at which, an order may be made are probably the same as for recovery of documents at common law or under s. 1 of the Act of 1972. "Bank" means an institution authorised under the Banking Act 1987 or a municipal bank, a building society, National Savings Bank or the Post Office: 1987 Act, s. 9.

35.2.17   *Reclaiming.* A motion for an order under r. 35.2 may be reclaimed against with leave within 14 days after the date of the interlocutor: r. 38.3(5).

Optional procedure before executing commission and diligence
[1] **35.3.**—(1) Subject to rule 35.3A (optional procedure where there is a party litigant or confidentiality is claimed), this rule applies where a party has obtained a commission and diligence for the recovery of a document on an application made under rule 35.2(1)(a).

(2) Such a party may, at any time before executing the commission and diligence against a haver, serve on the haver an order in Form 35.3–A (in this rule referred to as "the order").

(3) The order and a copy of the specification referred to in rule 35.2(2), as approved by the court, shall be served on the haver or his known agent and shall be complied with by the haver in the manner and within the period specified in the order.

(4) Not later than the day after the day on which the order, and any document recovered, is received from a haver by the party who obtained the order, that party—
  (a) shall give written intimation of that fact in Form 35.3–B to the Deputy Principal Clerk and every other party; and
  (b) shall—
    (i) if the document has been sent by post, send a written receipt for the document in Form 35.3–C to the haver; or
    (ii) if the document has been delivered by hand, give a written receipt in Form 35.3–C to the person delivering the document.

(5) Where the party who has recovered any such document does not lodge in it process within 14 days of receipt of it, he shall—
  (a) forthwith give written intimation to every other party that that party may borrow, inspect or copy the document within 14 days after the date of that intimation; and
  (b) in so doing, identify the document.

(6) Where any party, who has obtained any such document under paragraph (5), wishes to lodge the document in process, he shall—
  (a) lodge the document within 14 days after receipt of it; and
  (b) at the same time, send a written receipt for the document in Form 35.3–D to the party who obtained the order.

(7) Where—
  (a) no party wishes to lodge or borrow any such document under paragraph (5), the document shall be returned to the haver by the party who obtained the order within 14 days after the expiry of the period specified in sub-paragraph (a) of that paragraph; or
  (b) any such document has been uplifted by another party under paragraph (5) and that party does not wish to lodge it in process, the document shall be returned to the haver by that party within 21 days after the date of receipt of it by him.

(8) Any such document lodged in process shall be returned to the haver by the party lodging it within 14 days after the expiry of any period allowed for appeal or reclaiming or, where an appeal or reclaiming motion has been marked, from the disposal of any such appeal or reclaiming motion.

(9) If any party fails to return any such document as provided for in paragraph (7) or (8), the haver shall be entitled to apply by motion (whether or not the cause is in dependence) for an order that the document he returned to him and for the expenses occasioned by that motion.

(10) The party holding any such document (being the party who last issued a receipt for it) shall be responsible for its safekeeping during the period that the document is in his custody or control.

(11) If the party who served the order is not satisfied that—

(a) full compliance has been made with the order, or

(b) adequate reasons for non-compliance have been given,

he may execute the commission and diligence under rule 35.4.

(12) Where an extract from a book of any description (whether the extract is certified or not) is produced under the order, the court may, on the motion of the party who served the order, direct that that party shall be allowed to inspect the book and take copies of any entries falling within the specification.

(13) Where any question of confidentiality arises in relation to a book directed to be inspected under paragraph (12), the inspection shall be made, and any copies shall be taken, at the sight of the commissioner appointed in the interlocutor granting the commission and diligence.

(14) The court may, on cause shown, order the production of any book (not being a banker's book or book of public record) containing entries falling under a specification, notwithstanding the production of a certified extract from that book.

Deriv. R.C.S. 1965, r. 96(a) to (f)

---

[1] R. 35.3 substituted by S.I. 1996 No. 2168 (effective 23rd September 1996).

Optional procedure before executing commission and diligence. The Cullen *Review of Business* **35.3.1** *of the Outer House of the Court of Session* in December 1995 recommended that a procedure should be devised for documents recovered under a commission and diligence to be sent by the haver directly to the party who obtained the order rather than to the Deputy Principal Clerk of Session, and made available to all parties as soon as possible. A working group was set up to devise such a procedure, now enacted in substance by the A.S. (R.C.S.A. No. 4) (Miscellaneous) 1996 [S.I. 1996 No. 2168]. The group foresaw difficulties in the case of documents recovered where there was a party litigant in the process or in respect of which confidentiality was claimed: a separate procedure for such situations is provided in r. 35.3A.

This procedure is available for recovery of documents at common law except where one of the parties is a party litigant or confidentiality is claimed: r. 35.3(1). The order in Form 35.3 and the specification as approved by the court is served on the haver or his known agent (on which, see definition in r. 1.3(1)). The form specifies seven days as the period within which the order must be obtempered. The haver must complete the certificate in the order stating what documents are produced, that he has no such documents, that such documents are in existence but not in his possession or that he knows of the existence of no such documents. If confidentiality is claimed the documents should be put in a sealed packet: r. 35.8.

The documents and the order duly certified are sent by the haver to the party who obtained the order, who informs the Deputy Principal Clerk and every other party of their receipt. The party who recovered the documents must lodge them in process within 14 days or give written intimation to every other party that he may borrow, inspect or copy them within 14 days.

"commission and diligence". See note 35.2.2.   **35.3.2**

"document". See note 35.2.3.   **35.3.3**

"serve". For methods, see Chap. 16, Pt. I.   **35.3.4**

"haver". See note 35.2.11.   **35.3.5**

"written intimation". For methods, see r. 16.9.   **35.3.6**

"extract from a book of any description". The provision in r. 35.3(9) is required because there **35.3.7** will be no commissioner who can inspect the books and make the necessary excerpts at this stage. A difficulty arises, however, in granting such a motion as a party obtaining the order may have access to material he ought not to see, and accordingly r. 35.3(10) provides for the commissioner appointed in the original interlocutor granting the commission and diligence to deal with this.

"confidentiality". On the meaning of confidentiality, see note 35.2.7. Where confidentiality is **35.3.8**

claimed, r.35.8 applies, the document must be put in a sealed packet and a motion must be enrolled by the party seeking to open it which is intimated to the haver concerned.

35.3.9   *Production of original books notwithstanding production of extract.* Ss. 5 and 6 of the Civil Evidence (Scotland) Act 1988 provide for production as evidence of copies of business records and other documents. The court retains a power under the optional procedure (because the originals will not normally have been inspected by the party seeking recovery or by a commissioner) to order production of the original documents. There are exceptions in relation to bankers' books and public records.

In relation to bankers' books the exception was no doubt made because the Bankers' Books Evidence Act 1879 was introduced in the interests of bankers to prevent interference with their business and to facilitate the giving in evidence of information from their books. Ss. 3–5 of the 1879 Act have been superseded by rules of evidence of general application in ss. 5 and 6 of the 1988 Act. See further, note 35.2.16.

In relation to public records, see r. 35.9.

35.3.10   *Lodge in process.* On lodging documents recovered in process, see r. 4.5 (productions).

Optional procedure where there is a party litigant or confidentiality is claimed

[1] **35.3A.**—(1) This rule shall apply where—

(a) any of the parties to the action is a party litigant; or

(b) confidentiality is claimed for any document in the possession of a haver.

(2) Rule 35.3 (optional procedure before executing commission and diligence) shall not apply where paragraph (1) of this rule applies.

(3) The party who has obtained a commission and diligence for the recovery of a document on an application made under rule 35.2(1)(a) may, at any time before executing it against a haver, serve on the haver an order in Form 35.3A–A (in this rule referred to as "the order").

(4) The order and a copy of the specification referred to in rule 35.2(2), as approved by the court, shall be served on the haver or his known agent and shall be complied with by the haver in the manner and within the period specified in the order.

(5) Not later than the day after the date on which the order, and any document recovered, is received from a haver by the Deputy Principal Clerk, he shall give written intimation of that fact to each party.

(6) No party, other than the party who served the order, may uplift any such document until after the expiry of 7 days after the date of intimation under paragraph (5).

(7) Where the party who served the order fails to uplift any such document within 7 days after the date of intimation under paragraph (5), the Deputy Principal Clerk shall give written intimation of that failure to every other party.

(8) Where no party has uplifted any such document within 14 days after the date of intimation under paragraph (7), the Deputy Principal Clerk shall return it to the haver who delivered it to him.

(9) Where a party who has uplifted any such document does not wish to lodge it, he shall return it to the Deputy Principal Clerk who shall—

(a) give written intimation of the return of the document to every other party; and

(b) if no other party uplifts the document within 14 days after the date of intimation, return it to the haver.

(10) Any such document lodged in process shall be returned to the haver by the party lodging it within 14 days after the expiry of any period allowed for appeal or reclaiming or, where an appeal or reclaiming motion has been marked, from the disposal of any such appeal or reclaiming motion.

(11) If any party fails to return any such document as provided for in paragraph (9) or (10), the haver shall be entitled to apply by motion (whether or not the cause is in dependence) for an order that the document be returned to him and for the expenses occasioned by that motion.

(12) The party holdings any such document (being the party who last

issued a receipt for it) shall be responsible for its safekeeping during the
period that the document is in his custody or control.

(13) If the party who served the order is not satisfied than—

(a) full compliance has been made with the order, or

(b) adequate reasons for non-compliance have been given,

he may execute the commission and diligence under rule 35.4.

(14) Where an extract from a book of any description (whether the extract
is certified or not) is produced under the order, the court may, on the motion
of the party who served the order, direct that that party shall be allowed to
inspect the book and take copies of any entries falling within the
specification.

(15) Where any question of confidentiality arises in relation to a book
directed to be inspected under paragraph (14), the inspection shall be made,
and any copies shall be taken, at the sight of the commissioner appointed in
the interlocutor granting the commission and diligence.

(16) The court may, on cause shown, order the production of any book
(not being a banker's book or book of public record) containing entries
falling under a specification, notwithstanding the production of a certified
extract from that book.

---

[1] R. 35.3A inserted by S.I. 1996 No. 2168 (effective 23rd September 1996).

General note. This rule was inserted by A.S. (R.C.S.A. No. 4) (Miscellaneous) 1996 [S.I. 1996   **35.3A.1**
No. 2168] following recommendations of the Cullen *Review of Business of the Outer House of
the Court of Session* in December 1995 and a working group, in relation to a new procedure for
documents recovered under the optional procedure under r. 35.3 to be sent directly to the party
obtaining the order rather than to the Deputy Principal Clerk. That new procedure in r. 35.3
does not apply where one of the parties is a party litigant or where confidentiality is claimed.
The procedure for these exceptions is that of the former r. 35.3—*i.e.* the haver sends the
documents to the Deputy Principal Clerk.

"*confidentiality*". On the meaning of confidentiality, see note 35.2.7. Where confidentiality is   **35.3A.2**
claimed, r.35.8 applies, the document must be put in a sealed packet and a motion must be
enrolled by the party seeking to open it which is intimated to the haver concerned.

"*document*". See note 35.2.3.   **35.3A.3**

"*commission and diligence*". See note 35.2.2.   **35.3A.4**

"*serve*". For methods, see Chap. 16, Pt. I.   **35.3A.5**

"*haver*". See note 35.2.11.   **35.3A.6**

"*written intimation*". For methods, see r. 16.9.   **35.3A.7**

"*lodged in process*". See r. 4.5.   **35.3A.8**

"*extract from a book of any description*". See note 35.3.7.   **35.3A.9**

Production of original books notwithstanding production of extract. See note 35.3.9.   **35.3A.10**

Execution of commission and diligence for recovery of documents

35.4.—(1) The party who seeks to execute a commission and diligence for
recovery of a document obtained on an application under rule 35.2(1)(a)
shall—

(a) provide the commissioner with a copy of the specification, a copy of
the pleadings (including any adjustments and amendments) and a
certified copy of the interlocutor of his appointment;

(b) fix a diet for the execution of the commission in consultation with
every other party;

(c) instruct the clerk and any shorthand writer; and

(d) be responsible, in the first instance, for the fees of the commissioner,
his clerk and any shorthand writer.

(2) The interlocutor granting such a commission and diligence shall be
sufficient authority for citing a haver to appear before the commissioner.

(3) A haver shall be cited to appear at a commission for the recovery of documents by service on him of a citation in Form 35.4–A—
(a) by registered post or the first class recorded delivery service; or
(b) personally, by messenger-at-arms.
(4) A certificate of citation of a haver—
(a) under paragraph (3)(a) shall be in Form 35.4–B; and
(b) under paragraph (3)(b) shall be in Form 35.4–C.
(5) There shall be served on the haver with the citation a copy of the specification and, where necessary for a proper understanding of the specification, a copy of the pleadings (including any adjustments and amendments).
(6) The agent for a party, or a party litigant, as the case may be, shall be personally liable, in the first instance, for the fees and expenses of a haver cited to appear at a commission for that party.
(7) The parties and the haver shall be entitled to be represented by counsel or other person having a right of audience, or an agent, at the execution of the commission.
(8) At the commission, the commissioner shall—
(a) administer the oath *de fideli administratione* to the clerk and shorthand writer appointed for the commission; and
(b) administer to the haver the oath in Form 35.4–D, or, where the haver elects to affirm, the affirmation in Form 35.4–E.
(9) The report of the execution of the commission and diligence, any document recovered and an inventory of that document, shall be sent by the commissioner to the Deputy Principal Clerk.
(10) Not later than the day after the date on which such a report, any document recovered and an inventory of that document are received by the Deputy Principal Clerk, he shall give written intimation to the parties that he has received them.
(11) No party, other than the party who served the order, may uplift such a document until after the expiry of 7 days after the date of intimation under paragraph (10).
¹ (12) Where the party who served the order fails to uplift such a document within 7 days after the date of intimation under paragraph (10), the Deputy Principal Clerk shall give written intimation of that failure to every other party.
(13) Where no party has uplifted such a document within 14 days after the date of intimation under paragraph (12), the Deputy Principal Clerk shall return it to the haver.
(14) Where a party who has uplifted such a document does not wish to lodge it, he shall return it to the Deputy Principal Clerk who shall—
(a) give written intimation of the return of the document to every other party; and
(b) if no other party uplifts the document within 14 days of the date of intimation, return it to the haver.

Deriv. R.C.S. 1965, r. 97

---

¹ R. 35.4(12) amended by S.I. 1994 No. 2901 (minor correction).

35.4.1 *"commission and diligence"*. See note 35.2.2.

35.4.2 *"document"*. See note 35.2.3.

35.4.3 *"commissioner"*. The commissioner is appointed and named in the interlocutor granting the commission and diligence. If the original appointee has to be replaced before the commission this change may be done by the clerk of court after consultation with the judge.
The commissioner is usually a member of the Bar.

35.4.4 *"certified copy of the interlocutor"*. The copy is prepared by the party and is stamped, dated, certified a true copy and signed by the clerk of session at the public counter of the appropriate department.

"instruct the clerk and shorthand writer". The clerk and shorthand writer are usually the same **35.4.5** person.

Responsibility for fees of commissioner, clerk and shorthand writer. The party obtaining the **35.4.6** commission and diligence is responsible in the first instance for the fees of the commissioner, clerk and shorthand writer and must pay them: r. 35.4(1)(d). On expenses, see note 35.4.17.

"haver". See note 35.2.11.   **35.4.7**

Service of citation on haver. Service of the citation, specification and any pleadings is by **35.4.8** registered or first class recorded delivery post (see r. 16.4) or personally by messenger-at-arms (see r. 16.3). A citation furth of Scotland cannot be enforced. Resort can be made to letters of request: see r. 35.15. On failure of a haver to attend a commission, see note 35.4.13.

Responsibility for fees and expenses of haver. The agent for the party, or the party litigant, **35.4.9** obtaining the commission and diligence is responsible in the first instance for the fees and expenses of the haver: r. 35.4(6). The haver is entitled to an attendance fee at the commission and a fee for searching for the documents, subject to taxation, but not for copying when the call is merely to produce: *Forsyth v. Pringle Taylor & Lamond Lawson* (1906) 14 S.L.T. 658; *Mackinnon v. Guildford* (1894) 2 S.L.T. 309.

"counsel or other person having a right of audience, or agent". See r. 1.3(1) (definitions of **35.4.10** "counsel", "other person having a right of audience" and "agent") and note 1.3.4. It is suggested by Maclaren that the expense of counsel is not usually allowed at a commission for examination of a haver unless there are questions of nicety: Maclaren on *Expenses*, p. 449.

The commission. The purpose of the commission is to achieve the handing over of docu- **35.4.11** ments or to ascertain where they are or what has happened to them: see *Sommervell v. Sommervell* (1900) 8 S.L.T. 84. The commission is under the charge of the commissioner. The commissioner puts the clerk and shorthand writer on oath to "faithfully discharge the duties of clerk and shorthand writer at this commission" and administers the oath or affirmation to the haver: r. 35.4(8). The party seeking recovery asks questions first after any introduction by the commissioner.

The haver may be asked: (1) If he has the document. (2) If he has had the document in his possession at any time. (3) If he no longer has the document, (*a*) if he knows or suspects where it is and (*b*) who has or may have it. (4) If the document has or has not ever existed. (5) If the document has been destroyed. (6) If the document has been destroyed, (*a*) when and where it was destroyed and (*b*) by whom. The haver may not be asked about the merits of the cause or about the terms of a document. See generally, Maclaren on *Court of Session Practice*, p. 1079. The haver need not answer any question which may incriminate him except in respect of proceedings under s. 1(1) of the Act of 1972 for infringement, to obtain disclosure of information about infringement, or to prevent any apprehended infringement, of intellectual property rights or passing off: Law Reform (Miscellaneous Provisions) (Scotland) Act 1985, s. 15.

Whoever represents the haver and any other party at the commission may then ask questions to achieve a full and fair disclosure: *Dunlop's Trs. v. Lord Belhaven* (1852) 14 D. 825.

Objections to questions should as a general rule be dealt with by the commissioner. Where objection relates to confidentiality the proper course is to repel the objection and allow the document to be recovered subject to competency and relevancy; the document is sealed up by the commissioner and parties can argue the point before the court on a motion to open up the sealed packet. Other matters of difficulty the commissioner may prefer to leave to the court to decide, in which case he repels the objection under reservation of competency and relevancy; and the document is sealed up to await the decision of the court on a motion to open up the packet.

Where a document is produced which should be, but is not, subject to a restriction in the call for excerpting at the sight of the commissioner, it may be agreed at the commission that this in fact be done. A document subject to excerpting in a call may be agreed to be handed over in its entirety without excerpting. Where there is a call for excerpting the haver is obliged only to produce the document and not to excerpt the material himself: *Forsyth v. Pringle Taylor & Lamond Lawson* (1906) 14 S.L.T. 658. Excerpting is done by the commissioner and his clerk.

The commissioner may seek or may be given authority by the court to have the assistance of a qualified person in looking at documents and excerpting entries and to give him advice in determining what documents fall within a call: *Argyllshire Weavers Ltd v. A. Macauley (Tweeds) Ltd* 1962 S.L.T. (Notes) 96; *Santa Fe International Corporation v. Napier Shipping S.A.* 1985 S.L.T. 430.

Where a haver refuses to produce a document the commissioner has no power to order production, the commission has to be adjourned and the commissioner will usually report to the court. On the motion of the party whose commission it is, the court may, after hearing parties and the haver (see *e.g. Montgomerie v. A. B.* (1845) 7 D. 553; *Train & McIntyre Ltd v. Forbes* 1925 S.L.T. 286), order production. A failure to produce thereafter renders the haver liable to penalty for contempt of court (letters of second diligence are inappropriate: *National Exchange Co. v. Drew and Dick* (1858) 20 D. 837). An alternative is for the haver to be cited to appear at the proof to produce the document.

At the end of the diet of commission the commission may be closed or, if all the documents sought are not recovered, it may be adjourned. If there is no adjournment, although not all the documents are recovered, and the commission is closed, a further commission and diligence has to be sought from the court.

For failure of haver to appear at a commission, see note 35.4.13.

35.4.12 *Commissions furth of Scotland.* Commissions may be taken outside Scotland on an interlocutor granting a commission and diligence where the foreign country does not object and the haver is willing. Where either is not the case an application will have to be made by minute for a letter of request: see r. 35.15. But note the provisions in the Hague Convention on the Taking of Evidence Abroad in Civil or Commercial Matters, 18th March 1970 (Cmnd. 6727 (1977)) for the taking of evidence by diplomatic or consular officials, or by a commissioner, and the powers of compulsion they may be able to seek: see further note 35.15.2.

35.4.13 *Failure of haver to appear at commission.* If a haver in Scotland fails to appear at a commission in Scotland the modern practice is to adjourn the commission (the commissioner will report) and for the party whose commission it is to enrol a motion for warrant to messengers-at-arms to apprehend the haver and bring him to the adjourned diet. The historical practice of obtaining letters of second diligence (in effect having the same result) is no longer followed.

Where the commission in the UK is furth of Scotland, resort may be had to letters of request under the Evidence (Proceedings in Other Jurisdictions) Act 1975: see note 35.15.3. Where the commission is furth of the UK, resort may be had to the Hague Convention on the Taking of Evidence in Civil or Commercial Matters, 18th March 1970 (Cmnd. 6727 (1977)) under which powers of compulsion may be exercised under letters of request by the convention country or may be applied for by diplomatic or consular officials or a commissioner in certain convention countries: see note 35.15.2.

35.4.14 *Report of commission.* The report (or interim report) of a commission (adjourned or closed) includes a transcript of the deposition of the haver, the documents recovered and those sealed up, and an inventory of those documents: for form of report, see Maclaren on *Court of Session Practice*, p. 1081. The report is signed by the commissioner and sent (or delivered: r. 1.3(1) (definition of "send") to the Deputy Principal Clerk: r. 35.4(8).

35.4.15 *Uplifting documents recovered.* The Deputy Principal Clerk intimates to parties that he has received the report and any documents recovered; and during the first seven days after such intimation only the party whose commission it was may uplift the documents, failing which the Deputy Principal Clerk intimates that failure to every other party who have seven days after that to uplift them: r. 35.4(10) and (11). If the documents are not uplifted 14 days after that the documents are returned to the haver: r. 35.4(12).

35.4.16 *"written intimation".* For methods, see r. 16.9.

35.4.17 *Expenses.* Expenses are in the cause (*i.e.* expenses follow success) if the documents recovered are lodged as productions, unless some other order has been made: *Mackie & Stark v. Cruickshank* (1896) 4 S.L.T. 84. It is suggested by Maclaren that the expense of counsel is not usually allowed at a commission for examination of a haver unless there are questions of nicety: Maclaren on *Expenses*, p. 449.

Execution of orders for production or recovery of documents or other property under section 1(1) of the Act of 1972

35.5.—(1) An order under section 1(1) of the Act of 1972 for the production or recovery of a document or other property shall grant a commission and diligence for the production or recovery of that document or other property.

(2) Rule 35.3 (optional procedure before executing commission and diligence) and rule 35.4 (execution of commission and diligence for recovery of documents) shall apply to an order to which paragraph (1) applies as they apply to a commission and diligence for the recovery of a document.

35.5.1 *General note.* See rr. 35.3 and 35.4 and notes.

Execution of orders for inspection etc. of documents or other property under section 1(1) of the Act of 1972

35.6.—(1) An order under section 1(1) of the Act of 1972 for the inspection or photographing of a document or other property, the taking of samples or the carrying out of any experiment thereon or therewith, shall authorise and appoint a specified person to photograph, inspect, take samples of, or carry out any experiment with or on, any such document or other property, as the case may be, subject to such conditions, if any, as the court thinks fit.

(2) A certified copy of the interlocutor granting such an order shall be sufficient authority for the person specified to execute the order.

(3) When such an order is executed, the party who obtained the order shall serve on the haver a certified copy of the interlocutor granting it, a copy of the specification and, where necessary for a proper understanding of the specification, a copy of the pleadings (including any adjustments and amendments).

General note. The person carrying out the inspection etc. must be named in the interlocutor **35.6.1** and a certified copy of the interlocutor, the specification and any necessary pleadings served on the haver.

Execution of orders for preservation etc. of documents or other property under section 1(1) of the Act of 1972

35.7.—(1) An order under section 1(1) of the Act of 1972 for the preservation, custody and detention of a document or other property shall grant a commission and diligence for the detention and custody of that document or other property.

(2) The party who has obtained an order under paragraph (1) shall—
  (a) provide the commissioner with a copy of the specification, a copy of the pleadings (including any adjustments and amendments) and a certified copy of the interlocutor of his appointment;
  (b) be responsible for the fees of the commissioner and his clerk; and
  (c) serve a copy of the order on the haver.

(3) The report of the execution of the commission and diligence, any document or other property taken by the commissioner and an inventory of such property, shall be sent by the commissioner to the Deputy Principal Clerk for the further order of the court.

General note. The commissioner appointed will be named in the interlocutor granting the **35.7.1** commission and diligence. The interlocutor granting the order must be served on the haver: r. 35.7(2)(c).

Responsibility for fees of commissioner and clerk. See r. 35.4.6.   **35.7.2**

"further order of the court". Where a document or other property has been recovered at **35.7.3** common law or under s.1 of the Act of 1982 and it is subsequently sought to use it for the purposes of foreign proceedings, it is not necessary to present a petition under s.1 of the Evidence (Proceedings in Other Jurisdictions) Act 1975 or s.1 of the Act of 1972 as extended by s.28 of the C.J.J.A. 1982 or by S.I. 1997 No. 2780. The application for such permission, which is in the court's power to grant, may be made in the process in which the evidence was recovered. The better practice is to proceed by minute rather than by motion. See *Iomega Corporation v. Myrica (U.K.) Ltd* 1998 S.C. 636 (First Div.).

Confidentiality

35.8.—(1) Where confidentiality is claimed for any document or other property sought to be recovered under any of the following rules, such document or other property shall, where practicable, be enclosed in a sealed packet:
  rule 35.3 (optional procedure before executing commission and diligence),
  rule 35.4 (execution of commission and diligence for recovery of documents),
  rule 35.5 (execution of orders for production or recovery of documents or other property under section 1(1) of the Act of 1972),
  rule 35.7 (execution of orders for preservation etc. of documents or other property under section 1(1) of the Act of 1972).

(2) A motion to have such a sealed packet opened up or such recovery allowed may be made by—
(a) the party who obtained the commission and diligence; or
(b) any other party after the date of intimation by the Deputy Principal Clerk under rule 35.3(5) or 35.4(12) (intimation of failure to uplift documents).

(3) In addition to complying with rule 23.3 (intimation of motions), the party enrolling such a motion shall intimate the terms of the motion to the person claiming confidentiality by registered post or the first class recorded delivery service.

(4) The person claiming confidentiality may oppose a motion made under paragraph (2).

Deriv. R.C.S. 1965, r. 98

35.8.1   *"confidentiality"*. On the meaning of confidentiality, see note 35.2.7.

35.8.2   *"motion"*. For motions, see Chap. 23. The person claiming confidentiality must have the motion to open up the packet or allow the recovery intimated to him so that he may appear and oppose it: r. 35.8(4).

35.8.3   *Opening the sealed packet*. The haver, or commissioner, seals up the documents and delivers or sends them to the DPCS who informs the parties (r.35.3A(5)). By virtue of r.35.3A(7), the party seeking the document has seven days (any other party has 14 days) to enrol a motion to open the sealed packet. The motion, made under r.35.8(2), must be intimated to the haver so that he may oppose it if he wishes under r.35.8(4).

Warrants for production of original documents from public records

35.9.—(1) Where a party seeks to obtain from the keeper of any public record production of the original of any register or deed in his custody for the purposes of a cause, he shall apply to the court by motion.

(2) Written intimation of a motion under paragraph (1) shall be given to the keeper of the public record concerned at least two days before the motion is enrolled.

(3) Where it appears to the court that it is necessary for the ends of justice that a motion under this rule should be granted, authority shall be given to such keeper, on production of a certified copy of the interlocutor granting the motion, to produce or exhibit, as the case may be, the original register or deed to the court.

(4) The expense of the production or exhibition of such an original register or deed shall be met, in the first instance, by the party who applied by motion under paragraph (1).

Deriv. R.C.S. 1965, r. 103(a) to (c)

35.9.1   *General note*. The original of any register or deed in the custody of the keeper of a public record may not be recovered by commission and diligence. Extracts are usually sufficient: see Registration Act 1617, Titles to Land Consolidation (Scotland) Act 1868, s.142 and Conveyancing and Feudal Reform (Scotland) Act 1970, s.45 (extracts of Register of Sasines); Writs Execution (Scotland) Act 1877, s.5 (extracts of the Books of Council and Session). If an original is required the keeper of the record will be ordered to bring it to court and one of his officials will do so, but it will remain in his custody.

35.9.2   *"public record"*. This term is not statutorily defined. It obviously extends to the public records kept by the Keeper of the Records of Scotland, the registers kept by the Keeper of the Registers of Scotland, the records of the Court of the Lord Lyon King of Arms, the registers of births, marriages and deaths kept by the Registrar General for Scotland, and deeds registered in sheriff court books and other sheriff court records (other than processes: for which see r. 35.10) before transfer to the Keeper of the Records (not sooner than 25 years: Public Records (Scotland) Act 1937, s.2(1)). On the sheriff court records transferred to the Keeper of the Records, see the Preservation of Sheriff Court Records Regulations 1969, Sched. 2 [S.I. 1969 No. 1756].

This rule does not apply to processes in the custody of the Keeper of the Records (Court of Session processes after five years (r. 9.1(2)) and sheriff court processes after 25 years (see paragraph above)) or processes of inferior courts not in the custody of the Keeper of the Records. Recovery of such processes for use in another cause is governed by r. 35.10. A process of the Court of Session in the custody of the Keeper of the Records which is not a finally extracted process may be transmitted back to the court under r. 9.2 to be looked at or for something to be done in it; and r. 35.9 does not apply.

An order for production of a public record for evidence in foreign proceedings may be made under s. 1 of the Evidence (Proceedings in Other Jurisdictions) Act 1975 (formerly R.C.S. 1965, r. 103(d)).

"motion". For motions, see Chap. 23. The Keeper of the Records must have two days' written **35.9.3** intimation (see r. 16.9) of the motion.

Expenses. Fees may be due for inspection, searches, extracts, copyings and attendance at **35.9.4** court: see *e.g.* Sheriff Court Fees Order 1985 [S.I. 1985 No. 827], Act of Sederunt (Fees in the Scottish Record Office) 1990 [S.I. 1990 No. 44], Fees in the Registers of Scotland Order 1991 [S.I. 1991 No. 2093].

Warrants for transmission of processes

35.10.—(1) A party who seeks to lodge in process any process in the custody of the Keeper of the Records, or any process depending or which depended in any inferior court in Scotland, may apply by motion to the court for a warrant to authorise and direct the Keeper of the Records or the clerk of the inferior court, as the case may be, on production of a certified copy of the interlocutor granting the motion, to transmit that process to the Deputy Principal Clerk.

(2) A party who enrols a motion under paragraph (1) shall give written intimation of the motion to the Keeper of the Records or the clerk of the inferior court, as the case may be, at least two days before the motion is enrolled.

(3) The Deputy Principal Clerk shall grant a receipt for any process transmitted to him under an order made under paragraph (1) and lodge it in the process of the cause.

(4) No process transmitted under paragraph (1) may be borrowed.

(5) After a process transmitted under paragraph (1) ceases to be required, the Deputy Principal Clerk shall return it to the Keeper of the Records or the clerk of the inferior court, as the case may be.

Deriv. R.C.S. 1965, r. 104

General note. This rule is concerned with processes in one cause in the custody of the Keeper **35.10.1** of the Records or an inferior court which are required as evidence in another; a commission and diligence is not competent. The rule applies to processes in the custody of the Keeper of the Records (Court of Session processes after five years (r. 9.1(2)) and sheriff court processes after 25 years (not sooner than 25 years: Public Records (Scotland) Act 1937, s.2(1))) or processes of inferior courts not in the custody of the Keeper of the Records. On the sheriff court records transferred to the Keeper of the Records, see the Preservation of Sheriff Court Records Regulations 1969, Sched. 2 [S.I. 1969 No. 1756].

A process of the Court of Session in the custody of the Keeper of the Records which is not a finally extracted process may be transmitted back to the court under r. 9.2 to be looked at or for something to be done in it; and r. 35.10 does not apply.

"process". This means the documents constituting the cause.   **35.10.2**

"Keeper of the Records". The Keeper of the Records of Scotland is appointed under the **35.10.3** Public Registers and Records (Scotland) Act 1948. Under ss.1 and 2 of the Public Records (Scotland) Act 1937 processes of the Court of Session and the sheriff court are transferred to the custody of the Keeper after a certain passage of time (on which, see note 35.10.1).

"inferior court". This includes the Lyon Court, the sheriff court and the district court.   **35.10.4**

"motion". For motions, see Chap. 23.   **35.10.5**

"written intimation". For methods, see r. 16.9.   **35.10.6**

Commissions for examination of witnesses

35.11.—(1) This rule applies to a commission—

(a) to take the evidence of a witness on a ground mentioned in section 10(b) of the Act of 1988;

(b) in respect of the evidence of a witness which is in danger of being lost, to take the evidence to lie *in retentis*; or

(c) on special cause shown, to take the evidence of a witness on a ground other than one mentioned in sub-paragraph (a) or (b).

(2) An application by a party for a commission to examine a witness shall be made by motion; and that party shall specify in the motion the name and address of at least one proposed commissioner for approval and appointment by the court.

(2A) A motion under paragraph (2) may include an application for authority to record the proceedings before the commissioner by video recorder.

(3) Where a motion under paragraph (2) is made in an action before calling of the summons—

(a) the applicant shall give written intimation of the motion to every other person named in the instance; and

(b) the decision of the Lord Ordinary shall be final and not subject to review.

(4) The interlocutor granting such a commission shall be sufficient authority for citing the witness to appear before the commissioner.

(5) A witness shall be cited to give evidence at a commission by service on him of a citation in Form 35.11–A—

(a) by registered post or the first class recorded delivery service; or
(b) personally, by a messenger-at-arms.

(6) The certificate of citation of a witness—

(a) under paragraph (5)(a) shall be in Form 35.11–B; and
(b) under paragraph (5)(b) shall be in Form 35.11–C.

(7) The agent for a party, or a party litigant, as the case may be, shall be personally liable, in the first instance, for the fees and expenses of a witness cited to appear at a commission for that party.

(8) At the commission, the commissioner shall—

(a) administer the oath *de fideli administratione* to the clerk and any shorthand writer appointed for the commission; and
(b) administer to the witness the oath in Form 35.4–D, or, where the witness elects to affirm, the affirmation in Form 35.4–E.

(9) In a cause involving the collision of ships, such an application shall be granted on condition, where necessary, that the applicant shall, at least 24 hours before the evidence is taken, lodge in process a preliminary act which the commissioner shall be entitled to open before the witness is examined.

(10) Where a commission is granted for the examination of a witness, the court may, on the motion of any party and on cause shown, dispense with interrogatories.

Deriv. R.C.S. 1965, rr. 100 and 101

---

[1] Rule 35.11(2A) inserted by S.S.I. 2007 No. 282, para. 2 (effective 2nd May 2007).

35.11.1   *General note.* Until the middle of the last century proof was usually on commission, a practice virtually abolished by s.2 of the Evidence (Scotland) Act 1866. The evidence of witnesses must now usually be heard by the court at a proof or jury trial. There are three exceptions to the modern rule—evidence on commission permitted under s.10 of the C.S.A. 1988, evidence in danger of being lost to lie *in retentis* and evidence on any other ground on special cause shown. The exception in relation to evidence to lie *in retentis* is part of the existing practice of the court preserved by s.10 of the C.S.A. 1988. S.10 of the C.S.A. 1988 re-enacted the first two exceptions which were in s.2 of the 1866 Act. S.10 of the C.S.A. 1988 did not (apparently inadvertently) re-enact a proviso in s.2 of the 1866 Act which preserved the right of the court to grant a commission to take the evidence of a witness according to the existing law and practice on special cause shown or of consent of parties. Although only the proviso in relation to evidence in danger of being lost has been preserved it could not have been intended by Parliament in a consolidating statute to deprive the court of a power to grant a commission in other circumstances in which it has even today been used to do, such as where a witness (other than perhaps a crucial witness) is going abroad. The Scottish Law Commission recommendations to the Bill (now the C.S.A. 1988) did not mention repeal of the proviso. The court's power to grant a commission in circumstances other than those referred to in s.10 of the C.S.A. 1988 is preserved in this rule by virtue of the general rule-making power in s.5 of that Act.

35.11.2   *S.10 of the C.S.A. 1988.* S.10 of the C.S.A. 1988 applies to actions in the Outer House and is applied to petitions by s.25(3), and to the Inner House by s.38, of the C.S.A. 1988. There are two statutory grounds.

(1) *Witness resident beyond the jurisdiction of the court.* A commission may be granted and executed where the foreign country does not object and the witness is willing. Where either is not the case an application will have to be made by minute for a letter of request: see r. 35.15. But note the provisions in the Hague Convention on the Taking of Evidence Abroad in Civil or Commercial Matters, 18th March 1970 (Cmnd. 6727 (1977)) for the taking of evidence by diplomatic or consular officials, or by a commissioner, and the powers of compulsion they may be able to seek: see further note 35.12.2.

A motion for such a commission may be refused if the evidence of the witness is of primary importance for the proper determination of the issue between the parties or if the party against whom the witness is to be adduced would be prejudiced by having the evidence taken on commission: *Grant v. Countess of Seafield* 1926 S.C. 274.

(2) *Witness unable to attend court by reason of age, infirmity or sickness.*

(a) Age. The practice is to treat a person who is 70 years old or more as a person whose evidence may be taken on commission: *Wilson v. Young* (1896) 4 S.L.T. 73. A birth certificate should be produced.

(b) Infirmity. This means a permanent disability which prevents the witness coming to court. A medical certificate is required.

(c) Sickness. This is not limited to such illness as would give rise to a risk that the evidence of the witness may be lost (as that is covered by the common law exception) but includes someone whose illness is such that he cannot come to court. A medical certificate is required. If the witness is an important one the proper course might be to discharge the diet of proof or jury trial; and see *Grant*, above.

Evidence to lie in retentis. The only ground for taking the evidence of a witness to be retained **35.11.3** until the proper time for using it is where evidence is in danger of being lost because a witness is aged or infirm. The matter is in the discretion of the Lord Ordinary. Even the pursuer's evidence may in appropriate circumstances be taken on commission: *Anderson v. Morrison* (1905) 7 F. 561.

(1) *Aged.* The practice is to treat a person who is 70 years old or more as aged even if hale and hearty: *Wilson v. Young* (1896) 4 S.L.T. 73. A birth certificate should be produced.

(2) *Infirmity.* This means any illness or disability which gives rise to a risk or danger of the evidence of that witness being lost. A medical certificate is required.

Evidence on commission on special cause shown. The court has for long enough been used to **35.11.4** granting commissions to take the evidence of witnesses on grounds other than those mentioned in notes 35.11.2 and 35.11.3. Grounds have included a witness about to go abroad of necessity, *e.g.* pre-arranged holidays, attending a professional conference, a person in HM Forces called for duty or a merchant seaman called to his ship: see *dicta* in *Grant v. Countess of Seafield* 1926 S.C. 274 and *Tonner*, below. A commission may be allowed in the case of *penuria testium* (lack of witnesses): *Maltman's Factor v. Cook* (1867) 5 M. 1076. The court may not grant such a commission where the witness is important or an opponent would be prejudiced (in which case the diet of proof or jury trial would have to be discharged): *Grant v. Countess of Seafield* 1926 S.L.T. 213. A balance has to be struck between the importance of the witness's evidence and the loss or inconvenience which would result if the commission were not granted, and the fact that the motion is unopposed or consented to is a point to be taken into account: *Tonner v. FT Everard & Sons Ltd* 1994 S.C. 593, 599B *per* L.P. Hope (witness due to go on holiday and another to sit examination during proof).

"motion". For motions, see Chap. 23.   **35.11.5**

"commissioner". Where the commission is on interrogatories the commissioner may be a **35.11.6** member of the Bar or, where the witness is remote from Edinburgh, a sheriff or solicitor. Where the commission is an open commission (*i.e.* interrogatories have been dispensed with) the commissioner will usually be a member of the Bar. Where the commission is furth of the U.K. the commissioner will usually be a member of the Bar, or a lawyer of the country concerned or even a British consular officer (who has power to administer oaths and take affidavits: Commissioners for Oaths Act 1889, s.6). The practice is to specify that "X" whom failing "Y" be nominated and appointed. A Lord Ordinary may be appointed to be the commissioner.

Motion before calling of a summons. See r. 23.8.   **35.11.7**

"written intimation". For methods, see r. 16.9.   **35.11.8**

Citation of witness. Citation is by registered or first class recorded delivery post (see r. 16.4) or **35.11.9** personally by messenger-at-arms (see r. 16.3).

Citation of a witness furth of the U.K. and Ireland cannot be enforced. In the case of citation elsewhere in the U.K. and Ireland, and on failure of a witness to appear at a commission, see note 35.11.12.

On competence and compellability of witnesses, see note 36.2.8.

Responsibility for fees and expenses of witness. The agent for the party, or the party litigant, **35.11.10** obtaining the commission is responsible in the first instance for the fees and expenses of the haver: r. 35.11(7). For witnesses' fees, see Chap. II of the Table of Fees in r. 42.16.

The commission. The form of the commission depends on whether the commission is with or **35.11.11** without interrogatories: see notes 35.12.5 and 35.13.5.

Failure of witness to appear at commission. If a witness in Scotland fails to appear at a **35.11.12** commission in Scotland the modern practice is to adjourn the commission (the commissioner will report) and for the party whose commission it is to enrol a motion for warrant to messengers-at-arms to apprehend the witness and bring him to the adjourned diet. The historical practice of obtaining letters of second diligence (in effect having the same result) is not usually followed.

Attendance at a commission in Scotland of a witness who resides in the U.K. furth of Scotland or in Ireland, may be enforced under the Attendance of Witnesses Act 1854 as extended by s.4 of the Evidence (Proceedings in Other Jurisdictions) Act 1975. The 1854 Act applies to Northern Ireland by virtue of the General Adaptation of Enactments (Northern Ireland) Order 1921 [S.R. & O. 1921 No. 1804] and to the Republic of Ireland by virtue of the Irish Free State (Consequential Adaptation of Enactments) Order 1923 [S.R. & O. 1923 No. 405] (preserved by the Ireland Act 1949). Under ss.1, 2 and 3 of the 1854 Act the court may order a warrant of citation in special form containing a notice that it is issued by special order of the court, and on proof of service and default of appearance the court may transmit a certificate to the Supreme Court in which jurisdiction the witness resides for that court to punish the witness (but he cannot otherwise be forced to go). The witness must have had tendered to him his attendance money: 1854 Act, s.4. An alternative is to apply for letters of request: see r. 35.15.

Where the commission is furth of the U.K., resort may be had to the Hague Convention on the Taking of Evidence in Civil or Commercial Matters, 18th March 1970 (Cmnd. 6727 (1977)) under which powers of compulsion may be exercised under letters of request by the convention country or may be applied for by diplomatic or consular officials or a commissioner in certain convention countries: see note 35.15.2.

35.11.13   *Collision of ships and preliminary acts.* A preliminary act is a document setting out certain specified details where an Admiralty action of damages arising out of the collision of ships has been brought: see r. 46.6. A preliminary act may be dispensed with under r. 46.7. It may be required for the purpose of taking evidence on commission and if so must be lodged before the commission where it has not already been lodged.

35.11.14   *"dispense with interrogatories".* A commission is on interrogatories unless these are dispensed with: r. 35.11(10). On interrogatories, see note 35.12.1. Interrogatories are not a satisfactory means of obtaining evidence except for straightforward evidence or to save expense where a witness is abroad.

Interrogatories may be dispensed with, *e.g.* where the witness is in the U.K. (this ground was expressly mentioned in R.C.S. 1965, r. 100(c) but is not excluded because it is not now mentioned) or where credibility and reliability of the witness is in issue (*Nicolson v. McLachlan and Brown* 1985 S.L.T. 132 (for which interrogatories are a wholly inadequate expedient)).

The matter is in the discretion of the Lord Ordinary: *Dexter & Carpenter v. Waugh & Robertson* 1925 S.C. 28, 32 *per* Lord Skerrington. *Venter v. Scottish Legal Aid Board* 1993 S.L.T. 147, 153F *per* L.P. Hope.

Where the party seeking a commission without interrogatories (or any other course of action of an unusual nature or involving unusually large expenditure) is legally aided, that party should seek the prior approval of the Legal Aid Board before that course of action is proposed to the court: *Venter v. Scottish Legal Aid Board* 1993 S.L.T. 147, 154D *per* L.P. Hope at p. 154D.

35.11.15   *Expenses.* Expenses are in the cause (*i.e.* expenses follow success) if the evidence taken on commission is used at the proof or jury trial. If the witness is subsequently examined at the proof the expenses of the commission may not be allowed unless the expense was incurred on reasonable necessity, a question which is for the Auditor to decide: *Webster & Others v. Simpson's Motors & Others* 1967 S.L.T. 287. The expenses may not be allowed where a proof was not subsequently allowed (*Gilchrist v. National Cash Register Co.* 1929 S.C. 272, 274 *per* Lord Sands) or where the evidence is not used at the proof or jury trial.

Commissions on interrogatories

35.12.—(1) Where interrogatories have not been dispensed with, the party who obtained the commission to examine a witness under rule 35.11 shall lodge draft interrogatories to be adjusted at the sight of the clerk of court.

(2) Any other party may lodge cross-interrogatories to be adjusted at the sight of the clerk of court.

(3) The interrogatories and any cross-interrogatories, when adjusted, shall be extended and returned to the clerk of court for approval.

(4) The party who has obtained the commission shall—

(a) provide the commissioner with a copy of the pleadings (including any adjustments and amendments), the approved interrogatories and any cross-interrogatories and a certified copy of the interlocutor of his appointment;

(b) instruct the clerk; and

(c) be responsible, in the first instance, for the fee of the commissioner and his clerk.

(5) The commissioner shall, in consultation with the parties, fix a diet for the execution of the commission to examine the witness.

(6) The executed interrogatories, any document produced by the witness and an inventory of that document, shall be sent by the commissioner to the Deputy Principal Clerk.

(7) Not later than the day after the date on which the executed interrogatories, any document and an inventory of that document, are received by the Deputy Principal Clerk, he shall give written intimation to each party that he has received them.

(8) The party who obtained the commission to examine the witness shall lodge in process—

(a) the report of the commission; and

(b) the executed interrogatories and any cross-interrogatories.

General note. Interrogatories are written numbered questions. They are intimated in draft form to the other parties and lodged in process. Any other party may intimate and lodge draft cross-interrogatories. These may be adjusted at the sight of the clerk of court: see note 35.12.2. Cross-interrogatories cannot be postponed until answers to the interrogatories are lodged: *Charteris v. Charteris* 1967 S.C. 33. **35.12.1**

"adjusted at the sight of the clerk of court". This means that the questions are checked by the clerk to see that they are relevant and relate to matters on record. If he has a doubt he consults a judge. Once adjusted the clerk adds the following docquet to the interrogatories:
    "Edinburgh, (*date*). These interrogatories consisting of this and the preceding   pages adjusted at my sight.
                                        (*Signed*), Depute Clerk of Session". **35.12.2**

"commissioner". See note 35.11.6. **35.12.3**

Responsibility for fees of commissioner and clerk. The party obtaining the commission and diligence is responsible in the first instance for the fees of the commissioner and his clerk and must pay them: r. 35.4(1)(d). On expenses, see note 35.11.15. **35.12.4**

The commission. The commissioner puts the clerk on oath to "faithfully discharge the duties of clerk at this commission" and administers the oath or affirmation to the witness: r. 35.11(8). He reads the questions to the witness writing down the answers to each, numbering them in accord with the numbers of the questions. He may put further questions to the witness to add to or explain an answer. **35.12.5**
    The commissioner and the witness sign each page of the answers: *Elrick v. Elrick* 1967 S.L.T. (Notes) 68.
    Any report, the executed interrogatories and cross-interrogatories and any document produced are sent or delivered to the Deputy Principal Clerk.

Commissions furth of Scotland. Commissions may be taken outside Scotland on an interlocutor granting a commission where the foreign country does not object and the witness is willing. Where either is not the case an application will have to be made by minute for a letter of request: see r. 35.15. But note the provisions in the Hague Convention on the Taking of Evidence Abroad in Civil or Commercial Matters, 18th March 1970 (Cmnd. 6727 (1977)) for the taking of evidence by diplomatic or consular officials, or by a commissioner, and the powers of compulsion they may be able to seek: see further note 35.15.2. **35.12.6**

"written intimation". For methods, see r. 16.9. **35.12.7**

Commissions without interrogatories

35.13.—(1) Where interrogatories have been dispensed with, the party who has obtained a commission to examine a witness under rule 35.11 shall—

(a) provide the commissioner with a copy of the pleadings (including any adjustments and amendments) and a certified copy of the interlocutor of his appointment;

(b) fix a diet for the execution of the commission in consultation with the commissioner and every other party;

(c) instruct the clerk and any shorthand writer; and

(d) be responsible, in the first instance, for the fees of the commissioner, his clerk and any shorthand writer.

(2) All parties shall be entitled to be present and represented by counsel or other person having a right of audience, or agent, at the execution of the commission.

(3) The report of the execution of the commission, any document produced by the witness and an inventory of that document, shall be sent by the commissioner to the Deputy Principal Clerk.

(4) Not later than the day after the date on which such a report, any document and an inventory of that document are received by the Deputy Principal Clerk, he shall give written intimation to each party that he has received them.

(5) The party who obtained the commission to examine the witness shall lodge the report in process.

35.13.1   *General note.* A commission without interrogatories is called an open commission. It is conducted according to the normal rules of evidence and procedure.

35.13.2   *"commissioner".* See note 35.11.6.

35.13.3   *Responsibility for fees of commissioner and clerk.* See note 35.12.4.

35.13.4   *"counsel or other person having a right of audience, or an agent".* See r. 1.3(1) (definitions of "counsel", "other person having a right of audience" and "agent") and note 1.3.4.

35.13.5   *The commission.* The commissioner puts the clerk and shorthand writer on oath to "faithfully discharge the duties of clerk and shorthand writer at this commission" and administers the oath or affirmation to the witness: r. 35.11(8). The commission is conducted according to the normal rules of evidence with examination-in-chief, cross-examination and re-examination at which the parties may all be present or represented. The commissioner will have to rule on objections but, in cases of difficulty or on request of a party, he may allow evidence subject to competency and relevancy (on which the court will decide at the proof or jury trial).
On competence and compellability of witnesses, see note 36.2.8.

35.13.6   *Report of commission.* The report (or interim report) of a commission (adjourned or closed) includes a transcript of the deposition of the witness, any documents produced and an inventory of those documents: for form of report, see Maclaren on *Court of Session Practice*, p. 1052. The report is signed by the commissioner and sent (or delivered: r. 1.3(1) (definition of "send")) to the Deputy Principal Clerk: r. 35.13(3).

Evidence taken on commission

35.14.—(1) Subject to the following paragraphs of this rule and to all questions of relevancy and admissibility, evidence taken on commission under rule 35.12 or 35.13 may be used as evidence at any proof or jury trial of the cause.

(2) Any party may object to the use of such evidence at a proof or jury trial; and the objection shall be determined by the court.

(3) Such evidence shall not be used at a proof or jury trial if the witness becomes available to attend the diet of proof or jury trial, as the case may be.

(4) A party may use such evidence in accordance with the preceding paragraphs of this rule notwithstanding that it was obtained at the instance of another party.

Deriv. A.S. 16th February 1841, s. 17

35.14.1   *General note.* The deposition should be made expressly part of the proof. Any party may use the evidence: r. 35.14(4).

Evidence on commission in one action has been allowed in a subsequent action on the same circumstances where the witness had since died: *Hogg v. Frew and Another* 1951 S.L.T. 397. *Quaere* whether this would be allowed under the terms of r. 35.14(1).

If the deponent gives evidence at the proof or jury trial the evidence on commission may not be used: r. 35.14(3). It may not be used, apparently, to contradict his evidence because it is superseded by the oral evidence, although the witness may be asked if he has given different evidence on a previous occasion: *Forrests v. Low's Trs.* 1907 S.C. 1240 (although in that case what was sought to be done was to contradict the evidence at the proof by referring, at a reclaiming motion, to the evidence on commission).

Letters of request

35.15.—(1) This rule applies to an application for a letter of request to a court or tribunal outside Scotland to obtain evidence of the kind specified in paragraph (2), being evidence obtainable within the jurisdiction of that court or tribunal, for the purposes of a cause depending before the Court of Session.

(2) An application to which paragraph (1) applies may be made in relation to a request—

(*a*) for the examination of a witness,

(*b*) for the inspection, photographing, preservation, custody, detention, production or recovery of, or the taking of samples of, or the carrying out of any experiment on or with, a document or other property, as the case may be,

(*c*) for the medical examination of any person,

(*d*) for the taking and testing of samples of blood from any person, or

(*e*) for any other order for obtaining evidence,

for which an order could be obtained in the Court of Session.

(3) Such an application shall be made by minute in Form 35.15–A with a proposed letter of request in Form 35.15–B.

(4) It shall be a condition of granting a letter of request that the agent for the applicant, or a party litigant, as the case may be, shall be personally liable, in the first instance, for the whole expenses which may become due and payable in respect of the letter of request to the court or tribunal obtaining the evidence and to any witness or haver who may be examined for the purpose; and he shall consign into court such sum in respect of such expenses as the court thinks fit.

(5) Unless the court or tribunal to which a letter of request is addressed is a court or tribunal in a country or territory—

(*a*) where English is an official language, or

(*b*) in relation to which the Deputy Principal Clerk certifies that no translation is required,

then the applicant shall, before the issue of the letter of request, lodge in process a translation of that letter and any interrogatories and cross-interrogatories into the official language of that court or tribunal.

(6) The letter of request when issued, any interrogatories and cross-interrogatories adjusted as required by rule 35.12 and the translations (if any), shall be forwarded by the Deputy Principal Clerk to such person and in such manner as the Lord President may direct.

Deriv. R.C.S. 1965, r. 102 substituted by S.I. 1976 No. 283

General note. This rule applies to the obtaining of evidence for a depending cause in the Court of **35.15.1** Session from a witness or haver furth of Scotland; where proceedings are contemplated, letters of request may be sought by petition. There is an international convention (the Hague Convention; on which, see note 35.15.2) which many countries have ratified and to which resort may be had to assist in obtaining such evidence (see note 35.15.2) and, within the UK, resort may be had to the Evidence (Proceedings in Other Jurisdictions) Act 1975 (see note 35.15.3). Letters of request should be used not only in the UK or a Hague Convention country but in any foreign country (whether a Hague Convention country or not) as many such countries will in fact assist. For requests to a court in a Member State of the European Union other than Denmark, see. r. 35.16.

Further information and guidance may be obtained from: Justice Department, Division II, Branch 1, Hayweight House, 23 Lauriston Street, Edinburgh EH3 9DQ, tel. 0131–229 9200; and The Foreign and Commonwealth Office, Nationality and Treaty Department, Clive House, Petty France, London SW1H 9HD, tel. 071–270 4086 or 4087.

The Hague Convention. The Hague Convention on the Taking of Evidence Abroad in Civil or **35.15.2** Commercial Matters, 18th March 1970 (Cmnd.6727 (1977)), provides for letters of request to convention countries seeking the assistance of the judicial authorities of the foreign country to take the evidence of a witness or haver in proceedings which are pending (or contemplated). The Contracting State may use methods of compulsion to assist in obtaining the evidence.

Under the convention two other methods are available. (1) A UK diplomatic officer or consular agent in the country in which he exercises his functions may take the evidence of a UK national in respect of proceedings in the UK and, with the consent of the convention country, a national of that country: Arts. 15 and 16. (2) A commissioner (appointed by the court) may take evidence in the territory of another Contracting State with its consent: Art. 17. The diplomatic officer, consular agent or commissioner may apply to the competent authority of the convention country for assistance to obtain evidence by compulsion if a declaration has been made to that effect: Art. 18. Only Czechoslovakia, Italy and the USA have made such a declaration.

The Hague Convention countries are:

Argentina	Mexico
Barbados	Monaco
Cyprus	Netherlands
Czechoslovakia*	Norway
Denmark	Portugal
Finland	Singapore
France	Spain
Germany	Sweden
Israel	UK (with extensions)
Luxembourg	USA (with extensions)

*Czechoslovakia is now divided into the Czech and Slovak Republics.

The UK extensions are to: the Sovereign Base areas of Akrotiri and Dhekelia, the Cayman Islands, Falkland Islands and dependencies, Gibraltar, Hong Kong and the Isle of Man.

The USA extensions are to: Guam, Puerto Rico and the Virgin Islands.

On the Hague Convention countries, see the *Practical Handbook on the Operation of the Hague Convention on the Taking of Evidence Abroad* published for the Permanent Bureau of the Hague Convention on Private International Law published by Maarten Kluwers, Antwerp; and Bowman & Harris on *Multilateral Treaties* published by Butterworths.

The Hague Convention does not state what is a civil or commercial matter. It has been held in England in a case under the Evidence (Proceedings in Other Jurisdictions) Act 1975 that the words "civil or commercial matter" have a wide meaning and include all proceedings other than criminal proceedings (a meaning broader than the same words in the C.J.J.A. 1982): *Re State of Norway's Application (Nos. 1 and 2)* [1990] 1 A.C. 723, 806F *per* Lord Goff of Chieveley. It was also held in that case that whether proceedings are civil is a matter of law and practice of the requesting court: *per* Lord Goff of Chieveley at p. 805B.

A requested court can only grant orders it can ordinarily grant. The witness or haver may be legally represented: Art. 20.

A convention country may declare that it will not execute letters of request issued for the purpose of obtaining pre-trial discovery of documents as known in Common Law countries (the UK has made such a declaration).

35.15.3   *Evidence (Proceedings in Other Jurisdictions) Act 1975.* This Act enabled the UK to ratify the Hague Convention on the Taking of Evidence Abroad in Civil or Commercial Matters, 1970 (Cmnd. 6727 (1977)) in 1976. An application may be made to the Court of Session for letters of request to the High Court in England and Wales or Northern Ireland for an order to obtain evidence there provided that the steps taken to obtain it are steps which could be required there: 1975 Act, ss. 1 and 2.

An order may not be made by the requested court which would require a person (*a*) to state what documents relevant to the proceedings to which the application relates are or have been in his possession, custody or power, or (*b*) to produce any documents other than particular documents specified in the order as being documents appearing to the court making the order (the requested court) to be, or to be likely to be, in his possession, custody or power. In England the words "particular documents specified in the order" is given a strict construction. A compendious description of a number of documents is permitted provided that the exact document in each case is clearly indicated, and recovery will be ordered only of documents which the court is satisfied do or did exist: see *Re Westinghouse Uranium Contract* [1978] A.C. 547, 609 and 635; *Re Asbestos Insurance* [1985] 1 W.L.R. 331, 337 and 338 *per* Lord Fraser of Tullybelton.

35.15.4   *"depending".* A cause is depending from the time it is commenced (*i.e.* from the time an action is served or a first order in a petition is made) until final decree, whereas a cause is in dependence until final extract. For the meaning of commenced, see note 13.4.4 (action) or 14.6.1 (petition). For the meaning of final decree, see note 4.15.2(2). For the meaning of final extract, see note 7.1.2(2).

35.15.5   *Orders which may be obtained.* Two conditions must be met: the order must be one which can be obtained (*a*) within the jurisdiction of the requested court and (*b*) from the Court of Session in the cause for which the letters of request are sought.

For the circumstances in which an order may be obtained in the Court of Session:

(1) *Examination of witnesses.* See notes 35.11.2–35.11.4. On compellability of witnesses, see 36.2.8.

(2) *Recovery of documents.* See note 35.2.5.

(3) *Inspecting, photographing, etc., of documents or other property.* See note 35.2.6.

(4) *Medical examinations and blood tests.* See note 35.2.6A

"application". The application is by minute in Form 35.15–A and r. 15.1 applies except as to   **35.15.6**
the form. The form of letters of request (Form 35.15–B) is the style in the Hague Convention on
the Taking of Evidence Abroad in Civil or Commercial Matters (Cmnd. 6727 (1977)).

The letters of request will be forwarded by the Deputy Principal Clerk to the foreign court (r.
35.15(6)), but not before consignation as required by r. 35.15(4) for the expenses of executing
them (for which the agent for the applicant or the party litigant is, in the first instance, liable: r.
35.15(4)). A translation may be required.

Fee. A court fee for a letter of request is payable. For fee, see Court of Session etc. Fees   **35.15.7**
Order 1997, Table of Fees, Pt I, B, item 11 [S.I. 1997 No. 688, as amended, pp. C 1201 *et seq.*].
Certain persons are exempt from payment of fees: see 1997 Fees Order, art.5 substituted by
S.S.I. 2002 No. 270. A fee exemption certificate must be lodge in process: see P.N. No. 1 of
2002.

Where the applicant is legally represented, the fee may be debited under a credit scheme
introduced on 1st April 1976 by P.N. No. 4 of 1976 to the account (if one is kept or permitted)
of the agent by the court cashier, and an account will be rendered weekly by the court cashier's
office to the agent for all court fees due that week for immediate settlement. Party litigants, and
agents not operating the scheme, must pay (by cash, cheque or postal order) on each occasion a
fee is due at the time of lodging at the counter at the appropriate department.

Applications for requests that evidence be taken under the Council Regulation

35.16.—(1) In this rule—

"the Council Regulation" means the Council Regulation (EC) No.
1206/2001 of 28 May 2001 on co-operation between the courts of
the Member States in the taking of evidence in civil or commercial
matters;

"Member State" has the same meaning as in Article 1(3) of the Council
Regulation;

"request" means a request to which Article 1(1)(a) of the Council
Regulation applies; and

"requested court" has the same meaning as in Article 2(1) of the
Council Regulation.

(2) This rule applies to an application under the Council Regulation for a
request to a requested court in a Member State other than the United
Kingdom for the purposes of a cause depending before the Court of Session.

(3) An application to which paragraph (2) applies shall be made by
minute in Form 35.16-A with a proposed request in form A (request for the
taking of evidence) or form I (request for direct taking of evidence) set out in
the Annex to the Council Regulation.

(4) It shall be a condition of granting an application for a request that the
agent for the applicant, or a party litigant, as the case may be, shall be
personally liable, in the first instance, for any reimbursement required by the
requested court in respect of any fees paid to experts and interpreters and
the costs occasioned by the use of any requested special procedure in
executing the request for evidence, or the use of requested communications
technology at the performance of the taking of evidence; and that he shall
consign into court any such sum as is required by the requested court as
deposit or advance towards the costs of executing the request.

(5) Unless the requested court is in a country or territory—

(a) where English is an official language, or

(b) in relation to which the Deputy Principal Clerk certifies that no
translation is required,

then the applicant shall, before the issue of the request, lodge in process a
translation of the request and any interrogatories and cross-interrogatories
into the official language of that country or territory.

(6) Where an application under this rule has been granted, the request
shall be forwarded by the Deputy Principal Clerk to—

(a) the requested court; or

(b) the central body or competent authority designated by the other
Member State to be responsible for taking decisions on requests to
take evidence directly.

(7) The Deputy Principal Clerk shall, as soon as reasonably practicable after receipt of any communication from the requested court, send written intimation of that communication to the parties.

(8) If a request is made to take the evidence of a witness directly in another Member State, the Deputy Principal Clerk shall intimate to the witness who is to give evidence, a notice in Form 35.16–B and the witness shall return Form 35.16–C to the Deputy Principal Clerk, within 14 days after the date of intimation of the notice.

---

[1] Inserted by S.S.I. 2004 No.514 (effective 30th November 2004).

35.16.1 *General note.* Rule 35.16 was inserted by A.S. (R.C.S. A. No. 6) (Miscellaneous) 2004 [S.S.I. 2004 No. 514].

Under Council Regulation (EC) No. 1206/2001 of 28th May 2001 on co-operation between Member States of the EU in the taking of evidence in civil or commercial matters, evidence may be taken in another Member State for proceedings in Scotland. The Council Regulation does not apply to Denmark. The Hague Convention of 18th March 1970 (see note 35.15.2) applies only to 11 Member States of the EU.

35.16.2 *"Member State".* This means Member State of the EU other than Denmark: Council Regulation, art.1(3).

35.16.3 *The Council Regulation.* There are a number of points to notice.

(1) There is no definition of civil or commercial matter. On the interpretation of this phrase under the Hague Convention, see note 35.15.2.

(2) The request may be made only for use in judicial proceedings commenced or contemplated: art.1(2).

(3) There may be direct transmission between courts.

(4) Member States draw up lists of courts competent to take evidence.

(5) The central body for Scotland for information to courts, and forwarding a request in exceptional circumstances is:- Private International Law Branch, Civil and International Division, Justice Department, St Andrew's House, Regent Road, Edinburgh EH1 3DG; tel. +44 (0)131-244 4826; fax. +44 (0)131-244 4848.

(6) The request is made in Form A (where evidence is to be taken by the requested court) or Form I (where evidence to be taken by the requesting court) in the Annex to the Regulation, with a translation in the language of the requested court:

    (a) in a request in Form A—
- it must be executed within 90 days in accordance with the law of the requested State or in accordance with a special procedure of the requesting State, unless incompatible with the law of the requested State: art. 10;
- if provided for by the law of the *requesting* State, the parties and their representatives may be present at the taking of evidence (art. 11) as also may representatives of the requested court (art. 12);
- a person may refuse to give evidence under the law of the requesting or requested court and on grounds in art. 14;

    (b) a request in Form I—
- is made via the central body or competent authority;
- only if it can be done voluntarily without the need for coercive measures;
- the requested State may assign a court to take part to ensure compliance with art. 17.

35.16.4 *"consign".* For consignation, see r. 33.4 and note 33.4.3.

35.16.5 *"lodge in process".* The translation lodged under r. 35.16(5) will be lodged as a step of process (and must therefore be intimated to other parties): rr. 4.4 and 4.6.

35.16.6 *"written intimation".* For methods, see r. 16.9.

35.16.7 *"intimate".* It may have been intended that intimation by the DPCS under r. 35.16(8) would be written intimation under r. 16.9; however, the methods under r. 16.7 have been stipulated.

35.16.8 *Fee.* A court fee for a request is payable. For fee, see Court of Session etc. Fees Order 1997, Table of Fees, Pt I, B, item 11 [S.I. 1997 No. 688 as amended, pp. C1201 *et seq.*]. Certain persons are exempt from payment of fees: see 1997 Fees Order, art.5 substituted by S.S.I. 2002 No. 270. A fee exemption certificate must be lodged in process: see P.N. No. 1 of 2002.

Where the pursuer is legally represented, the fee may be debited under a credit scheme introduced on 1st April 1976 by P.N. No. 4 of 1976 to the account (if one is kept or permitted) of the pursuer's agent by the court cashier, and an account will be rendered weekly by the court cashier's office to the agent for all court fees due that week for immediate settlement. Party litigants and agents not operating the scheme must pay (by cash, cheque or postal order) on each occasion a fee is due at the time of lodging at the counter at the General Department.

CHAPTER 36

PROOFS

Hearing parts of proof separately

36.1.—(1) In any cause the court may—
  (a) at its own instance, or
  (b) on the motion of any party,
order that proof on liability or any other specified issue be heard separately from proof on any other issue and determine the order in which the proofs shall be heard.

(2) The court shall pronounce such interlocutor as it thinks fit at the conclusion of the first proof of any cause ordered to be heard in separate parts under paragraph (1).

Deriv. R.C.S. 1965, r. 108

General note. The restriction in R.C.S. 1965, r. 108 limiting separation of parts of a proof to **36.1.1** an action with pecuniary conclusions and to the merits and quantum has been omitted. It is now possible to separate any issue from any other issues and hear them separately, although in practice the circumstances in which such separation is appropriate may be limited. Obvious examples are (a) separation of proof on liability and quantum and (b) preliminary proofs (on which, see note 22.3.8).

The court will not, however, use its procedures to order issues to be heard separately to assist a party to avoid the consequences of current legislation: *Dyer v. Balfour Beattie Construction (Northern) Ltd*, 10th January 1997 (1997 G.W.D. 5–178) (motion to postpone proof on quantum until changes in rules on deduction of benefits on damages awards refused).

The appropriate stage at which to apply for an order under r. 36.1 is when an order for proof is first made: *BP Exploration Operating Co. Ltd v. Chevron Shipping Co. Ltd (No.2)*, 13th November 2002, 2002 G.W.D. 37–1217 (OH).

Citation of witnesses

36.2.—(1) A witness shall be cited for a proof by service on him of a citation in Form 36.2–A—
  (a) by registered post or the first class recorded delivery service, by the agent for the party on whose behalf he is cited; or
  (b) personally, by a messenger-at-arms.

(2) A certified copy of the interlocutor allowing a proof shall be sufficient warrant to a messenger-at-arms to cite a witness on behalf of a party.

(3) A certificate of citation of a witness—
  (a) under paragraph (1)(a) shall be in Form 36.2–B; and
  (b) under paragraph (1)(b) shall be in Form 36.2–C.

(4) The agent for a party, or a party litigant, as the case may be, shall be personally liable, in the first instance, for the fees and expenses of a witness cited by him to appear at a proof.

(5) Where a party to a cause is a party litigant, he shall—
  (a) not later than 12 weeks before the diet of proof, apply to the court by motion to fix caution for the expenses of witnesses in answering a citation in such sum as the court considers reasonable having regard to the number of witnesses he proposes to cite and the period for which they may be required to attend court; and
  (b) before instructing a messenger-at-arms to cite a witness, find the caution which has been fixed.

(6) A party litigant who does not intend to cite all the witnesses referred to in his application under paragraph (5)(a) may apply by motion for variation of the amount of caution.

Deriv. R.C.S. 1965, r. 106A inserted by S.I. 1984 No. 472 (r. 36.2(2)) and r. 106B inserted by S.I. 1986 No. 1955 (r. 36.2(5))

36.2.1   *General note.* A witness is a person who gives evidence at a proof or jury trial for any purpose and includes a haver cited to produce a document at a proof or jury trial.

The interlocutor allowing a proof or jury trial contains the warrant to cite witnesses and havers.

For exchange of lists of witnesses, see note 36.2.9.

36.2.2   *"citation".* Service of the citation is by registered or first class recorded delivery post (see r. 16.4) or personally by messenger-at-arms (see r. 16.3). On witnesses in custody, see note 36.2.3.

Citation of a witness furth of the U.K. and Ireland cannot be enforced. In the case of citation elsewhere in the U.K. and Ireland, and on failure of a witness to attend, see note 36.2.7.

Travelling expenses should be tendered with the citation and other arrangements made for outlays and attendance. A witness is entitled to demand his travelling expenses before answering the citation.

36.2.3   *Witnesses in custody.* A written application should be made to the Governor of the institution in Scotland or to the Home Office, Cleland House, Page Street, London SW1P 4LN, where the prisoner is elsewhere in the U.K. The letter should give details of the case and the reason why the evidence of the witness is required because it is for the Minister responsible to be satisfied that the attendance of the prisoner is desirable in the interests of justice: Criminal Justice Act 1961, s. 29(1).

36.2.4   *Responsibility for fees and expenses of witness.* The agent for the party or the party litigant who cites the witness is responsible in the first instance for the fees and expenses of the witness: r. 36.2(4). For witnesses' fees, see Ch.II of the Table of Fees in r. 42.16.

36.2.5   *Witnesses of party litigant.* R.C.S. 1994, r. 36.2(5) was introduced in R.C.S. 1965, r. 106B by A.S. (R.C.A. No. 10) (Miscellaneous) 1986 [S.I. 1986 No. 1955] to deal with party litigants citing numerous witnesses from the Sovereign down. The rule does not empower the court directly to limit the number of witnesses, but simply to order the party litigant to find caution to ensure that the witness's expenses are covered.

The first step is for the party litigant to ask the court at least 12 weeks before the proof to fix the amount of caution he should find in respect of all the witnesses having regard to the number of witnesses he proposes to cite and the period for which they may each be required to attend court. Thereafter before any witness is cited the party litigant must find that caution.

A party litigant may only cite witnesses by messenger-at-arms, he is not entitled to cite witnesses by post: r. 16.4(2).

On finding caution, see Chap. 33.

36.2.6   *"motion".* For motions, see Chap. 23.

Failure of witness to attend court. If a witness in Scotland fails to appear at a proof or jury   **36.2.7** trial the modern practice is for the party whose witness he is to enrol a motion for warrant to messengers-at-arms to apprehend the witness and bring him to the proof. The historical practice of obtaining letters of second diligence (in effect having the same result) is not usually followed, although it may be where it is known in advance that the witness will not attend. Before granting the warrant the court must be satisfied that citation has been executed; a certificate of execution must be produced.

Attendance at a proof or jury trial in the Court of Session of a witness who resides in the U.K. furth of Scotland or in Ireland, may be enforced under the Attendance of Witnesses Act 1854 as extended by s.4 of the Evidence (Proceedings in Other Jurisdictions) Act 1975. The 1854 Act applies to Northern Ireland by virtue of the General Adaptation of Enactments (Northern Ireland) Order 1921 [S.R. & O. 1921 No. 1804] and to the Republic of Ireland by virtue of the Irish Free State (Consequential Adaptation of Enactments) Order 1923 [S.R. & O. 1923 No. 405] (preserved by the Ireland Act 1949). Under ss.1, 2 and 3 of the 1854 Act the court may order a warrant of citation in special form containing a notice that it is issued by special order of the court, and on proof of service and default of appearance the court may transmit a certificate to the Supreme Court in which jurisdiction the witness resides for that court to punish the witness (but he cannot otherwise be forced to go). The witness must have had tendered to him his attendance money: 1854 Act, s.4. On the application of the 1854 Act, see "Witnesses from England in the Court of Session" by DIK MacLeod, W.S. in the Civil Practice Bulletin, 1996, Issue 12, p. 9. An alternative is to apply for letters of request to take his evidence in that country: see r. 35.15; and this would also apply to a witness furth of the U.K. and Ireland who cannot be compelled to attend.

The historical practice for an application under the 1854 Act needs to be brought up to date. An application should now be made by minute in an action (see r. 15.1 and note 15.1.1) or note in a petition (see r. 15.2 and note 15.2.1) in the following form. Theoretically, the application could be made by motion, but it is convenient (though not essential) to make it by minute (or note) so that the warrant of the citation issued by the court and the clerk's certificate attached the minute can be served as one document. The crave and plea in a minute (or prayer in a note) may be simply expressed. The statement of facts may be expressed thus in one paragraph:

"The Honourable Lord (*name*) has appointed a proof to take place in this cause on (*day*) the (*date*) of (*month*) (*year*). I, (*solicitor's name, designation and address*) have reason to believe that the following necessary witness for the [*pursuer or defender*] resident in England, namely, (*full name and address*) will not attend at the proof unless commanded by your Lordships in a warrant of citation in the special form referred to in section 1 of the Attendance of Witnesses Act 1854."

The warrant and certificate, which may be added at the end of the minute (leaving blanks for the court to complete) or which the court should issue, should be in the following form:

"EDINBURGH (*date to be inserted*), The Lords of Council and Session by the Honourable Lord (*name to be inserted*) one of the judges of the Court of Session, having considered the foregoing minute, hereby grant warrant for citation in this the special form used in the Court, commanding the above named witness (*full name of witness*) to attend the proof on (*day*) the (*date*) of (*month*) (*year*) and subsequent days wherever (s)he may be within the United Kingdom, to answer at the instance of the pursuer, [AB] (*or* the defender [CD]); and grant authority to all officers of the law to cite the said witness accordingly, in terms of the Attendance of Witnesses Act 1854.

(*signed by the judge*)

I hereby certify that this warrant of citation in the special form used in the Court of Session is issued on the special orders of the Court of Session by the Honourable Lord (*name to be inserted*), one of the judges of that Court.

2 Parliament Square
Edinburgh
(*date*)

(*signed*)
[Depute] Clerk of Session"

A citation and execution of which should be prepared by the party calling the witness in accordance with the motion forms in Forms 36.2–A and 36.2–C, modified for use under the 1854 Act, for the foreign process server to use.

Competence and compellability of witnesses.   **36.2.8**

(1) *Heads of State.* They are probably competent but not compellable: see Macphail on *Evidence*, para. 3.04.

(2) *Diplomatic missions etc.* See the Diplomatic Privileges Act 1964, Consular Relations Act

1968, Diplomatic and Other Privileges Act 1971 and International Organisations Act 1981.

(3) *Judges.* Supreme court judges are not competent witnesses about judicial proceedings which took place before them: *Muckarsie v. Wilson* (1834) Bell's Notes to Hume, 99; *H.M. Advocate. v. Monaghan* (1844) 2 Broun 131.

(4) *Bankers.* Where a bank is not a party it cannot be compelled to produce books the contents of which can be proved under the Bankers' Books Evidence Act 1879 or the Civil Evidence (Scotland) Act 1988: 1879 Act, s.6 as amended by the 1988 Act, s.7(4).

(5) *Spouses.* Under s.3 of the Evidence (Scotland) Act 1853 a spouse is a competent witness, but nothing in the section renders a spouse a competent or compellable witness against the other spouse of any matter communicated by one to the other during the marriage. A spouse is not compellable to give evidence about whether marital intercourse took place at any time: Law Reform (Miscellaneous Provisions) Act 1949, s.7. In consistorial causes (or any family action perhaps) the court should have all available and relevant evidence before it and should not be deprived of it by *e.g.* a defender (not called as a witness by the pursuer) not calling any evidence (including his own): *Bird v. Bird* 1931 S.C. 731, 734 *per* L.J.-C. Alness; *White v. White* 1947 S.L.T. (Notes) 51 *per* L.P. Cooper.

(6) *Parties.* A party is competent and compellable: Evidence (Scotland) Act 1853, s.3; Evidence Further Amendment (Scotland) Act 1874, s.1.

(7) *Advocates and solicitors.* An advocate is a competent witness, even if he is conducting the case. A party's solicitor's evidence is admissible even if he is conducting the case: Evidence (Scotland) Act 1852, s.1 as amended by the 1853 Act, s.1; 1853 Act, s.2. Under s.1. of the Evidence (Scotland) Act 1852, where a party adduces his agent (solicitor) as a witness on any matter which he could not otherwise competently be led, that party cannot object on the ground of confidentiality to any question on a matter pertinent to the issue.

(8) *Persons not cited as witnesses.* A person is not excluded from giving evidence because he was not cited: 1852 Act, s. 1.

(9) *Person in breach of court order.* Such a person may not be compellable as a witness on proof of the breach.

36.2.9   *Exchange of lists of witnesses.* Under P.N. No. 8 of 1994, not later than 28 days before the diet fixed for a proof (or jury trial) each party must give written intimation to every other party of a list of his witnesses and lodge a copy in process. Leave is required to call a witness not on the list. This P.N. does not apply to optional procedure cases under Chap. 43, Pt V or to commercial actions under Chap. 47 for which express similar provision is made.

Lodging productions

36.3.—(1) Where a proof has been allowed, all productions which are intended to be used at the proof shall be lodged in process not later than 28 days before the diet of proof.

(2) A production which is not lodged in accordance with paragraph (1) shall not be used or put in evidence at a proof unless—

(a) by consent of parties; or

(b) with the leave of the court on cause shown and on such conditions, if any, as to expenses or otherwise as the court thinks fit.

Deriv. R.C.S. 1965, r. 107(part) amended by S.I. 1972 No. 2022

36.3.1   *General note.* Documents founded on or incorporated in the pleadings must be lodged as productions when the pleadings in which they are referred to are lodged: r. 27.1. Other productions must be lodged 28 days before the proof (r. 36.3(1)), otherwise (with one exception noted in note 36.3.2) they may not be referred to without consent of parties or leave of the court (r. 36.3(2)): On lodging productions, see r. 4.5. Consent of other parties is either orally at the Bar or by marking the back of the inventory of productions of the late production "Of consent *(date and name of solicitor)*". Productions borrowed out must be returned by 12.30pm the day before the proof: r. 36.5.

36.3.2   *Documents used to test credibility.* A document used to test the credibility of a witness may be produced during the proof without having been previously lodged: *Paterson & Sons (Camp Coffee) v. Kit Coffee Co. Ltd* (1908) 16 S.L.T. 180. The reason is said to be because it will not be known in advance whether the witness will be adduced by the other party; and for this reason it had been thought that a document used to test the credibility of a *party* should be lodged before the proof in accordance with r. 36.3. In *Robertson v. Anderson,* 15th May 2001, unreported (OH), Lord Carloway held that there was no distinction between a party and any other witness and that a document not lodged as a production could be put to a party in cross-examination to test credibility.

A statement made by a witness otherwise than in the course of the proof is admissible as evidence in so far as it tends to reflect favourably or unfavourably on the witness's credibility: Civil Evidence (Scotland) Act 1988, s.3. There are exceptions: statements collateral to the issue (*A v. B* (1895) 22 R. 402, 404 *per* L.P. Robertson), precognitions (see *Kerr v. H.M. Advocate* 1958 J.C. 14, 19 *per* L.J.-C. Thomson) and reports in accident books unless they were written by the witness (*Dobbie v. Forth Ports Authority* 1974 S.C. 40, 44 *per* L.J.-C. Wheatley).

Copy productions

36.4.—[1] (1) A copy of every documentary production, marked with the appropriate number of process of the principal production, shall be lodged for the use of the court at a proof not later than 48 hours before the diet of proof.

(2) Each copy production consisting of more than one sheet shall be securely fastened together by the party lodging it.

---

[1] R. 36.4(1) amended by S.I. 1996 No. 2168 (effective 23rd September 1996).

General note. The provisions of r. 4.8 should be noted. A clerk of session may refuse to accept **36.4.1** a copy for use of the court if, *e.g.* it is not legible.

This rule applies, obviously, only to documentary productions.

Returning borrowed documents before proof

36.5. All steps of process and productions which have been borrowed shall be returned to process before 12.30 p.m. on the day preceding the diet of proof.

Deriv. R.C.S. 1965, r. 107(part)

General note. On borrowing productions, see r. 4.12. **36.5.1**

Notices to admit and notices of non-admission

36.6. [*Revoked by S.I. 1996 No. 2168.*]

General note. For notices to admit and notices of non-admission, see now Chap. 28A. That Chapter was inserted by the A.S. (R.C.S.A. No. 4) (Miscellaneous) 1996 [S.I. 1996 No. 2168] following a recommendation of the Cullen *Review of Outer House Business* in December 1995 that such notices should be permitted before a proof was allowed. Rule 36.6 applied only where proof had been allowed. The new provisions which apply after the record has closed is not appropriate to this chapter on proofs.

Admissions by parties

36.7.—[1] (1) Where a party admits—
  (a) any matter of fact whether averred in the pleadings or not;
  (b) the authenticity of any document; or
  (c) the sufficiency of a copy or extract of such a document as equivalent to the original,
which has not been admitted in the pleadings or in respect of which a notice under rule 28A.1(1) has not been intimated, a minute of admission signed by counsel or other person having a right of audience for the party making such admission, shall be lodged in process.

(2) An admission made in a minute of admission may be used in evidence at a proof if otherwise admissible in evidence.

(3) In taxing any account of expenses, the Auditor shall disallow the expenses of any evidence led on matters covered by a minute of admission, unless special cause is shown to him.

Deriv. R.C.S. 1965, r. 109

---

1 R. 36.7(1) amended by S.I. 1997 No. 1050 (minor correction).

36.7.1   *General note.* A minute of admission may be by one party or, more commonly, by more than one party (a joint minute).

A (joint) minute of admission(s) is conclusive for the purposes of the action in which it is made. A joint minute of admission is a contract by which the parties accept as true the facts stated in it: *Carswell & Son v. Finlay* (1887) 24 S.L.R. 643, 645 *per* L.P. Inglis. A joint minute may agree facts, that a document bears to be what it is, that the facts in it are true or that it is the evidence of its author.

Parties should agree what can be agreed because, where evidence is led of a skilled witness on a matter not in issue which could have been incorporated in a joint minute, the court may refuse to note the witness in the Minute of Proceedings as a skilled witness in attendance at court and direct that his fee is not chargeable against the opponent: *Ayton v. National Coal Board* 1965 S.L.T. (Notes) 24.

R. 15.1 does not apply to a minute of admission because it is not an application to the court.

36.7.2   *"counsel or other person having a right of audience".* See definitions of "counsel" and "other person having a right of audience" in r. 1.3(1).

36.7.3   *"lodged in process".* The minute of admission is lodged as a step of process and not as a production: r. 1.3(1) (definition of "step of process"). On steps of process, see r. 4.4.

36.7.4   *Expenses.* Expenses in relation to proof of matters in a minute of admission are disallowed unless special cause is shown to the Auditor: r. 36.7(3). It is not clear what the special cause might be. It might include evidence led before the minute of admission was signed.

See also note 36.7.1 on disallowance by the court of expenses of a skilled witness whose evidence is not in issue.

Lodging of certain written statements

[1] **36.8.** A party who wishes to have any written statement (including an affidavit) or report, admissible under section 2(1)(b) of the Civil Evidence (Scotland) Act 1988, received in evidence shall lodge the statement or report in process and shall intimate such lodging to the other party or parties.

------

[1] R.36.8 substituted by S.S.I. 2001 No. 305, para. 7(1) (effective 18th September 2001).

36.8.1   *General note.* Following the passing of the Civil Evidence (Scotland) Act 1988 which abolished the (secondary) hearsay rule (s.2 of the 1988 Act), a somewhat cumbersome mechanism was provided for obtaining the permission of the court to allow any document (including an affidavit) to be received in evidence without being spoken to by a witness as evidence not merely that it was made but as to the truth of its contents: see R.C.S. 1994, r. 36.8 which in its original form was derived from R.C.S. 1965, r. 108A which was inserted by A.S. (R.C.S.A. No. 1) (Witness Statements) 1989 [S.I. 1989 No. 435]. Such evidence was made admissible under s.2(1)(b) of the 1988 Act.

In *Ebrahem v. Ebrahem* 1989 S.L.T. 808, 809J–K, Lord Caplan indicated, *obiter*, that r. 36.8 was not suitable where the witness was speaking to critical matters in dispute and was not intended to supplant the taking of evidence by commission where that alternative was available. It would, however, be possible for the court to allow an affidavit as evidence in chief without depriving another party of having the witness called to cross-examine him. It would curtail the usefulness of r. 36.8 if affidavits could not be admitted merely because the evidence could be taken on commission. It has since been held that there is nothing in s.2 of the 1988 Act or r. 36.8 (formerly R.C.S. 1965, r. 108A) which is restrictive or which suggests that the evidence must be undisputed: *Smith v. Alexander Baird Ltd* 1993 S.C.L.R. 563, 564D *per* Lord Cameron of Lochbroom. In *McVinnie v. McVinnie* 1995 S.L.T.(Sh.Ct.) 81, Sheriff Macphail, Q.C., went further and stated that a statement admissible in evidence under s.2(1)(b) of the 1988 Act by affidavit by virtue of r. 36.8 cannot be excluded because part of the statement is disputed or because the other party claims he would be prejudiced. There is no prejudice in a party not being able to cross-examine because the court would take account of the fact that the evidence had not been subjected to cross-examination: *Smith*, above, at p. 565B; *McVinnie*, above, at p. 85F.

In *Glaser v. Glaser* 1997 S.L.T. 456, Lord Macfadyen approved *McVinnie*, above, and held that the court has no discretion to refuse an application to admit an affidavit using the procedure under r. 36.8. (It has been observed here until Release 61 that if the court is to have no discretion, there is little point in an elaborate procedure involving an application to the court, and the affidavit may as well simply be lodged and intimated to the other side.)

Rule 36.8 has been changed following *Glaser*, above. Now the statement or report is simply lodged in process, and intimated, for what it is worth: A.S. (R.C.A. No.4) (Miscellaneous) 2001 [S.S.I. 2001 No.305]. Some questions remain unanswered, such as how is the other party to react when he has no idea what credence the court may give to the statement.

S.2(1)(b) of the 1988 Act provides that a statement made by a person otherwise than in the course of proof shall be admissible as evidence of any matter contained in the statement of which direct oral evidence by that person would be admissible. The test in s.2(1)(b) is one of admissibility and not one of competency: *T v. T*, 2001 S.C. 337 overruling *F v. Kennedy*, 1992 S.C. 28 and cases following it. A copy of a document (a statement of the signatories) is not admissible as evidence of the contents of the principal because it is not a statement made by a person otherwise than in the course of proof, as only the principal would be such a statement; and direct oral evidence of the signatories would not otherwise be admissible because, under the best evidence rule, their oral evidence would be inadmissible: *Japan Leasing (Europe) plc v. Weir's Trs (No. 2)* 1998 S.C. 543.

Affidavits. As to the form of a statement lodged as an affidavit, see note 1.3.7.   **36.8.2**

Where there are contradictions between affidavits, and no other evidence to support a conclusion one way or another, no conclusion can be drawn by the court: *D v. D*, 2002 S.C. 33, 37D (Extra Div.).

Provisions to which this rule does not apply. Express provision is made in certain rules for   **36.8.3** certain evidence to be adduced without resort having to be made to this rule. These are: (a) evidence in certain undefended family actions (r. 49.28) and (b) affidavits in causes under the Adoption (Scotland) Act 1978 (r. 67.6(2)), (c) affidavits in causes under the Matrimonial Homes (Family Protection) (Scotland) Act 1981 (r. 49.71) and (d) affidavits in causes under the Human Fertilisation and Embryology Act 1990 (r. 81.6(2)).

"motion". For motions, see Chap. 23.   **36.8.4**

Lodge in process as a production. On lodging productions, see r. 4.5.   **36.8.5**

Attendance, and lists, of witnesses

36.9.—(1) It shall be the duty of each party to ensure that his witnesses, if any, are—

(a) in attendance in the vicinity of the courtroom; and

(b) available when called to give evidence.

(2) Each party shall, before his case begins, give to the macer of the court a numbered list of any witnesses of his in the order in which it is proposed to call them.

(3) No witness at a proof shall, except with leave of the court—

(a) be present in the courtroom during the proceedings prior to the giving of his evidence; or

(b) leave the courtroom after giving evidence.

(4) No party, other than the party citing a witness, shall have access to that witness while he is in attendance at court.

Deriv. RCS 1965, r. 111(a) to (d)

General note. Witnesses should be advised not to discuss evidence they are giving (if during an **36.9.1** adjournment) or have given during the course of a proof. Counsel and agents may not discuss with a witness during an adjournment the evidence he is giving.

Witnesses not to be in court before giving evidence. The general rule is stated in r. 36.9(3); it **36.9.2** does not apply to a party who may be present in court. Under s.3 of the Evidence (Scotland) Act 1840 the court may admit the evidence of a witness who was in court before he gave evidence if his presence was not due to culpable negligence or intent and the witness was not unduly instructed or influenced by what he heard; it does not apply to a party.

Even though parties consent to a witness being in court before he gives evidence, the leave of the court must also be obtained: r. 36.9(3).

Leave is often sought and granted to allow a skilled witness to hear the evidence of an opponent's witness(es), but not usually an opponent's skilled witness, or to assist counsel during the course of the proof.

Witness leaving court after giving evidence. The purpose of the provision in r. 36.9(3) that a **36.9.3** witness may not leave the court after giving evidence without leave of the court is that in granting leave the witness is released from his citation.

Unallocated proofs. A proof may not have been allocated to a particular Lord Ordinary on **36.9.4** the first day of the diet. A representative of the agents for each party in such a case must attend the Keeper's Office between 10am and 10.20am. The Keeper must be informed about the existence of any discussions with a view to settlement. Agents may be required to attend later at intervals during the day. See generally, Notice [*i.e.* P.N.], 13th June 1996.

Administration of oath or affirmation to witnesses

36.10. The Lord Ordinary shall administer the oath to a witness in Form 36.10–A or, where the witness elects to affirm, the affirmation in Form 36.10–B.

Deriv. RCS 1965, r. 122A(2) inserted by S.I. 1984 No. 472

General note. The oath is usually taken by the witness raising his right hand and repeating the **36.10.1** oath after the judge who also stands with right hand raised. It is permissible to take the oath in another form appropriate to one's religious belief; but where it is not practicable without inconvenience or delay to administer an oath in the manner appropriate to his religious belief the witness shall affirm: Oaths Act 1978, s.5(2). A person who objects to being sworn may affirm: 1978 Act, s.5(1). The fact that a person without religious belief takes an oath does not affect the validity of the oath: 1978 Act, s.4(2).

The affirmation is administered in the same way as an oath but without the judge or the witness raising his right hand.

Children and other vulnerable witnesses. The oath is not usually administered to a child under **36.10.2** the age of 12; he is admonished to tell the truth. A child between 12 and 14 is sworn or admonished at the judge's discretion; and a child over 14 is usually sworn. The competency test of ascertaining whether a child under 14 knew the difference between the truth and lies, in order to be allowed to give evidence, has been abolished by s. 24 of the Vulnerable Witnesses (Scotland) Act 2004 and came into force on 1st April 2005. That section provides (1) that the evidence of *any* witness is not inadmissible solely because the witness does not understand (a) the nature of the duty to give truthful evidence or (b) the difference between truth and lies; and (2) that the court must not, before that witness gives evidence, take any steps intended to establish whether the witness understands those matters.

Recording of evidence

36.11.—(1) Subject to any other provision in these Rules, evidence at a proof shall be recorded by—

(a) a shorthand writer to whom the oath *de fideli administratione officii* has been administered on his appointment as a shorthand writer in the Court of Session; or

(b) tape recording or other mechanical means approved by the Lord President.

(2) The record of the evidence at a proof shall include—

(a) any objection taken to a question or to the line of evidence;

(b) any submission made in relation to such an objection; and

(c) the ruling of the court in relation to the objection and submission.

(3) A transcript of the record of the evidence shall be made only on the direction of the court; and the cost shall, in the first instance, be borne—

(a) in an undefended cause, by the agent for the pursuer; and

(b) in a defended cause, by the agents for the parties in equal proportions.

(4) The transcript of the record of the evidence provided for the use of the court shall be certified as a faithful record of the evidence by—

(a) the shorthand writer or shorthand writers, if more than one, who recorded the evidence; or

(b) where the evidence was recorded by tape recording or other mechanical means, the person who transcribed the record.

(5) The court may make such alterations to the transcript of the record of the evidence as appear to it to be necessary after hearing the parties; and, where such alterations are made, the Lord Ordinary shall authenticate the alterations.

(6) Where a transcript of the record of the evidence has been made for the use of the court, copies of it may be obtained by any party from the shorthand writer on payment of his fee.

(7) Except with leave of the court, the transcript of the record of the evidence may be borrowed from process only for the purpose of enabling a party to consider whether to reclaim against the interlocutor of the court on the proof.

(8) Where a transcript of the record of the evidence is required for the purpose of a reclaiming motion but has not been directed to be transcribed under paragraph (3), the reclaimer—

(a) may request such a transcript from the shorthand writer, or as the case may be, the cost of the transcript being borne by the agent for the reclaimer in the first instance; and

(b) shall lodge the transcript in process;

and copies of it may be obtained by any party from the shorthand writer, or as the case may be, on payment of his fee.

Deriv. RCS 1965, r. 110 (r. 36.11(2)), r. 113(a) (r. 36.11(1), (4) and (5)), r. 113(b) (r. 36.11(3) and (8)), r. 113(c) (r. 36.11(7)), and r. 113(d) (r. 36.11(6)); P.N. 2nd March 1972 (r. 36.11(2))

36.11.1   *General note.* R. 36.11 includes a reference to recording evidence by tape recording or other mechanical means as well as to recording by a shorthand writer. With effect from 1st April 1997, proofs are recorded by mechanical means: Notice (*sic*), 6th March 1997.

36.11.2   *The proof.* For the distinction between proof, proof before answer and proof *habili modo*, see note 22.3.9.

A few points are mentioned here about proofs in general.

(1) Proofs heard in public. A proof is conducted in open court: see C.S.A. 1693. There are statutory exceptions: see, *e.g.* Adoption (Scotland) Act 1978, s. 57.

(2) Judge's rôle. The judge's rôle is to see that the litigation is carried out fairly between the parties: *Thomson v. Glasgow Corporation* 1962 S.C.(H.L.) 36, 52 *per* L.J.-C. Thomson. He should not interrupt so as to frustrate the development of a line of examination-in-chief or cross-examination. He may question witnesses with caution (*Thomson*, above, *per* L.J.-C. Thomson at p. 52), usually after cross-examination to clear up an obscurity or ambiguity. If he elicits new matter, parties should be given an opportunity to question the witness again on that matter.

(3) Duties of advocates and agents. On the duties of advocates and agents, see *Batchelor v. Pattison and Mackersy* (1876) 3 R. 914, 918 *per* L.P. Inglis. Lord Hope of Craighead translated what Lord Inglis, L.P., said into modern practice in *Arthur JS Hall v. Simons*, [2002] 1 A.C. 615, 725-726.

(4) Leading at proof. The party on whom the initial onus of proof lies leads at a proof, and, unless the contrary is stated in an interlocutor before proof, that party is the pursuer. The defender may be ordained to lead where so much of the pursuer's case is admitted that the onus is transferred to him. Where each party has to rebut a presumption, who leads depends on a comparison of the strengths of the presumptions. The question of who leads is not merely dependent on where the initial onus lies but sometimes on consideration of convenience: *Macfarlane v. Macfarlane* 1947 S.L.T.(Notes) 34 *per* L.P. Cooper.

(5) Objections. Objections to evidence must be made when the evidence is sought to be given, otherwise it may become part of the evidence on which reliance may be made. Evidence objected to may, however, be allowed subject to competency and relevancy, to be argued about at the end in submissions.

(6) Presence of witnesses in court. Parties may be present in court during the examination of witnesses. The common law rule, that a witness other than a skilled witness may be excluded if he has been in court during the evidence of previous witnesses, is modified by s. 3 of the Evidence (Scotland) Act 1840. This provides that if objection is taken that a witness has been present without the permission of the court or the consent of the party objecting, the court may admit the witness if his presence was not through culpable negligence or criminal intent and he has not been unduly instructed or influenced by what took place while he was in court or that injustice will not be done by his examination.

Skilled witnesses may remain in court during the evidence of witnesses (of fact) other than the evidence of other skilled witnesses, unless of consent.

(7) Examination-in-chief. It is the invariable practice in Scotland to ask a witness his age; this is because it may indicate the witness's capacity, maturity and understanding, and ought not to be omitted: *Meiklejohn v. Stevenson* (1870) 8 M. 890.

Leading questions (questions which suggest the answer) must not be asked which relate to the facts in issue. They may be asked about purely formal matters, matters not in dispute, matters established by other evidence or with the consent of the other party. The answer to a leading question may be regarded as of little weight: *Bishop v. Bryce* 1910 S.C. 426, 435 *per* L.P. Dunedin; *McKenzie v. McKenzie* 1943 S.C. 108, 109 *per* L.J.-C. Cooper. Leading questions are permitted of an hostile witness, and leave of the court is not required for this purpose: *Lowe v. Bristol Omnibus Co.* 1934 S.C. 1; *Avery v. Cantilever Shoe Co. Ltd* 1942 S.C. 469.

Published academic material may be put to an expert witness in evidence in chief without being produced beforehand as a production: *Roberts v. British Railways Board* 1998 S.C.L.R. 577.

(8) Cross-examination. The order for cross-examination of a pursuer's witnesses where there is more than one defender is 1D, 2D, 3D; for cross-examination of a second defender's witnesses, it is 3D, 1D, P.

The purpose of cross-examination is to weaken or destroy the witness's version of facts and to elicit evidence favourable to the cross-examiner. Cross-examination is not limited to the evidence-in-chief.

Leading questions are permitted, though sometimes evidence not so elicited has more weight.

Nowadays, failure to cross-examine on a point does not preclude a party leading evidence to contradict that point, but such evidence will be subject to comment (*Dawson v. Dawson* 1956 S.L.T.(Notes) 58), may be given little weight, may result in the opponent being allowed to lead evidence in replication (*Wilson v. Thomas Usher & Son Ltd* 1934 S.C. 332, 338 *per* L.J.-C. Aitcheson), or may result in the witness being recalled for further cross-examination (expenses may be awarded: *Bishop*, above *per* L.P. Dunedin at p. 431). The modern practice was confirmed in *Bryce v. British Railways Board* 1996 S.L.T. 1378 in which the 2nd Div held that a Lord Ordinary was entitled to have regard to evidence from a medical witness for the defender which had not been put in cross-examination to the pursuer's witness, which had not be objected to by the pursuer and on which the pursuer had not cross-examined the witness. In *Dollar Air Services Ltd v. Highland Council*, 11th July 1997, unreported (1997 G.W.D. 28–1435),

Proofs (Chap. 36)

Lord Marnoch, because there had been a failure to put an opposing version of an important telephone call in cross-examination of the pursuer's witness, was disinclined to make any adverse findings about that witness's credibility. In *Roberts v. John Johnston & Son*, 26th June 1998, unreported on this point, Lord Osborne, while acknowledging that a failure to put to the pursuer the defender's case of contributory negligence might not be fatal, refused to infer any failure because no challenge to the pursuer's case was made in cross-examination and no evidence in support of the defender's case was led. See also *Currie v. Clamp's Exr*, 27th February 2001, unreported (2001 G.W.D. 16–625). Where no evidence is led contradicting the pursuer's version of events, the court is entitled to draw the most favourable inferences of which the evidence is reasonably capable: *O'Donnell v. Murdoch Mackenzie & Co. Ltd* 1967 S.C. (H.L.) 63, 71 *per* Lord Upjohn.

If intending to treat a witness's evidence as incredible or unreliable, the witness must be questioned about that evidence to give him the opportunity to respond to the challenge, and the evidence which contradicts him must be put to him: *Avery*, above. Similarly, where the evidence of the witness about the issues is to be contradicted, the contradictory evidence should be put to the witness: *McKenzie*, above. Where the character or honesty of the witness is questioned, there must be a basis for it in fact.

Where credibility of a witness is in issue, the witness is open to challenge in cross-examination on the truth of any statement made by him during his evidence even if it is collateral to the crucial facts (*King v. King* (1841) 4 D. 124) and even if there is no record for the questions: *Clinton v. News Group Newspapers Ltd* 1999 S.C. 367 *per* Lord Nimmo Smith. In *Clinton*, the pursuer stated in cross-examination that he had not had sexual relations with any woman. The defender's counsel was permitted to put to the pursuer that he had had sexual relations with another woman (not the 2nd pursuer) even though there was no record for it (nor would there have been for it was not crucial to the defender's case). Opinion was reserved as to whether the defender would be allowed to lead evidence to support the line (in fact it was lead without objection). It would surely have to follow, from the fact that the witness could be questioned as to certain facts, that evidence in support of the line would have to be allowed.

A document used to test the credibility of a witness may be produced during the proof without having been previously lodged: *Paterson & Sons (Camp Coffee) v. Kit Coffee Co. Ltd* (1908) 16 S.L.T. 180. The reason is said to be because it will not be known in advance whether the witness will be adduced by the other party; and for this reason it had been thought that a document used to test the credibility of a *party* should be lodged before the proof in accordance with r. 36.3. In *Robertson v. Anderson*, 15th May 2001, unreported (OH), Lord Carloway held that there was no distinction between a party and any other witness, and that a document not lodged as a production could be put to a party in cross-examination to test credibility.

A statement made by a witness otherwise than in the course of the proof is admissible as evidence in so far as it tends to reflect favourably or unfavourably on the witness's credibility: Civil Evidence (Scotland) Act 1988, s. 3. There are exceptions: statements collateral to the issue (*A v. B* (1895) 22 R. 402, 404, *per* L.P. Robertson), precognitions (see *Kerr v. H.M. Advocate* 1958 J.C. 14, 19, *per* L.J.-C. Thomson) and reports in accident books unless they were written by the witness (*Dobbie v. Forth Ports Authority* 1974 S.C. 40, 44, *per* L.J.-C. Wheatley). Evidence of a different statement made on a previous occasion is not admissible unless a foundation has been laid in cross-examination: *Hoey v. Hoey* (1884) 11 R. 578.

(9) Re-examination. This is restricted to matters (though it may include new facts) arising out of or relating to the points raised in cross-examination. Where re-examination is permitted on a new matter, further cross-examination will be allowed on it. Leading questions are no more allowed in re-examination than in examination-in-chief.

(10) Recall of, and additional, witnesses. A witness who has given evidence may be recalled at the judge's instance or on the motion of a party: Evidence (Scotland) Act 1852, s. 4. The power may be exercised, *e.g.* where the pursuer would be prejudiced by the defender's case not being properly put in cross-examination: *Wilson v. Thomas Usher & Son* 1934 S.C. 332, 338–339 *per* L.J.-C. Aitchison. The court might recall a witness to clear up an ambiguity: Dickson on *Evidence*, para. 1769. Under s. 4 of the Civil Evidence (Scotland) Act 1988 and for the purposes of s. 2 (admissibility of hearsay) or s. 3 (statement as evidence as to credibility), at any time before closing submissions a person may be recalled as a witness (whether or not he was present in court after first giving evidence) or a person may be called as an additional witness (whether or not he was present in court during the proof). This would enable a party to call the maker of a statement to give evidence. In *Davies v. McGuire* 1995 S.L.T. 755 Lord Gill held that evidence of statements made by eyewitnesses to a police officer could not be allowed (in cross in this case) in advance of the evidence of the eyewitnesses, this not being warranted by s. 2 or 3 of the 1988 Act; but the police officer could be recalled under s. 4 of that Act after the eyewitnesses had given evidence.

(11) Views. A view may be made of a place or object in relation to any matter arising at the proof at the instance of the judge or a party. The purpose of a view is to enable the judge to understand the evidence not to criticise or contradict it: *Hattie v. Leitch* (1889) 16 R. 1128. The judge, the clerk of court and representatives of the parties should be present.

(12) Hearing on evidence. The hearing on evidence is usually heard as soon as the proof is finished, but may be postponed through lack of time or in order to obtain the notes of evidence. The party who leads at the proof speaks first (pursuer) and the other party (defender) or parties may each reply. It is in the discretion of the court to grant the pursuer a right of reply (P.N. 14th May 1970), and this is exercised where, *e.g.* a defender referred to authorities not mentioned by the pursuer.

The Lord Ordinary may request, or a party may proffer without a request, a written skeletal (or full) submission for the hearing on evidence.

The citation of cases from reproduction of electronic formats is permitted by P.N. No. 5 of 2004. A case reported in Session Cases must be cited from that source: P.N. No. 5 of 2004; the general rule is that when a case has been reported in Session Cases or the (English) Law Reports, it should be cited from that source: *McGowan v. Summit at Lloyds*, 2002 S.L.T. 1258, 1273 at para.[57] (Extra Div.).

(13) Judgment. In giving his opinion, the Lord Ordinary has a duty to record all the arguments and submissions made to him and his views upon them: *Morrow v. Enterprise Sheet Metal Works (Aberdeen) Ltd* 1986 S.C. 96, 101; *Hogan v. Highland R.C.* 1995 S.C. 1, 2C, *per* L.J.-C. Ross. Where a decision on a fact is based on credibility, the Lord Ordinary should leave no doubt as to the grounds of decision: *Duncan v. Watson* 1940 S.C. 221, 225, *per* L.P. Normand.

If, at avizandum, the Lord Ordinary discovers an authority not cited by parties which he is inclined to rely on, or a new argument occurs to him or a question arises about the appropriate interlocutor, the case should be put out by order to allow parties to make further submissions: *Lees v. North East Fife D.C.* 1987 S.C. 265; *Kennedy v. Norwich Union Fire Insurance Society* 1994 S.L.T. 617. If the only outstanding issue is the form of the interlocutor, the Lord Ordinary may give judgment expressing his conclusions but should allow parties an opportunity to address him on that point: *Libertas-Kommerz v. Johnson* 1977 S.C. 191. See generally, *Osborne v. British Coal Property* 1996 S.L.T. 736.

The form of opinions and neutral citation of cases is dealt with in P.N. No. 5 of 2004.

(14) The best evidence rule. The rule is that only the best obtainable evidence is admissible: Dickson on *Evidence*, p. 195. Thus, hearsay evidence (and in particular secondary hearsay) was, with exceptions, excluded until s. 2(1) of the Civil Evidence (Scotland) Act 1988. The expression "best evidence rule" has tended to be used with reference to documentary or real evidence, the word "hearsay" to oral statements.

A procedure for admitting evidence under s. 2(1) of the 1988 Act is laid down in RCS 1994, r. 36.8 (on which see note 36.8.1). It is now up to the court to assess all the evidence which is led (including admissible hearsay) and to determine its weight: *L. v. L.* 1998 S.L.T. 672, 676H *per* L.P. Rodger.

(A) *(Secondary) hearsay evidence*. There were exceptions to the general common law rule excluding hearsay. The statutory rule now is that (a) evidence is not excluded solely on the ground that it is heresay and (b) a statement made by a person otherwise than in the course of the proof is admissible of any matter in it of which direct oral evidence by that person would be admissible, and (c) a fact may be proved by hearsay evidence (secondary hearsay): 1988 Act, s. 2(1). Nothing in s. 2(1) affects the rule about the admissibility of a statement as evidence that it was made (primary hearsay as distinct from secondary hearsay which goes to the truth of the statement).

A statement is admissible as evidence as to credibility whether favourable or unfavourable: 1988 Act, s. 3. But it is still the law that the hearsay evidence of what the maker of the statement said on a previous occasion may be led only after the maker of the statement has given evidence: *Davies v. McGuire* 1995 S.L.R. 755 (such evidence could not be led in advance, but the witness could be recalled after the maker of the statement had given evidence). Section 2 of the 1988 Act overrides the best evidence rule so that the fact that the maker of the statement has given oral evidence does not prevent hearsay evidence being given of what he said on another occasion: *F. v. Kennedy (No. 2)* 1993 S.L.T. 1284 (I.H.) (evidence of social workers about what children said when interviewed).

Section 2(1)(b) of the 1988 Act allows hearsay evidence of a statement to be admissible if it relates to a matter on which direct oral evidence by the maker of the statement would be admissible. It does not involve a competency test but a test of admissibility of evidence, namely, that hearsay evidence is admissible unless direct oral of the matter would be inadmissible: *T v. T*, 2001 S.C. 337 overruling *F v. Kennedy*, 1992 S.C. 28 and cases following it (*e.g. L v. L*, 1996 S.L.T. 767).

While a statement in a precognition is inadmissible, what was said by a person to a precognoscer is admissible: *Anderson v. Jas. B. Fraser & Co. Ltd* 1992 S.L.T. 1129. Similarly in *Ellison v. Inspirations East Ltd*, 2002 S.L.T. 291 (OH) evidence from a solicitor who had taken notes of a statement by a coach driver was admitted. But, where there is no precise record of what was asked and answered, evidence of the precognoscer might be of little weight: see *Cavanagh v. BP Chemicals Ltd* 1995 S.L.T. 1287.

The admissibility of hearsay evidence does not breach the right to a fair hearing under ECHR art.6(1): *Irvine v. Arco Atholl Ltd*, 2002 S.L.T 931 (OH) (infringement argued because the third party had not cited for health reasons the maker of the statement relied on by defender).

(B) *Best evidence rule (documents or real evidence)*. This rule exists to prevent prejudice to one party and unfair advantage to the other party to a dispute where better evidence than that before the court exists. It does not apply to exclude evidence of a party which is no longer capable of being examined usefully; but where that is the case, that party's case will be examined with greater care and a heavier burden of proof will be imposed: *Stirling Aquatic Technology Ltd v. Farmocean AB (No. 2)* 1996 S.L.T. 456 (fish nets).

In relation to documents, the best evidence rule requires that the contents of a document have to be proved by the document itself and not by a copy or parole evidence: *S & U Newspapers Ltd v. Gherson's Trs* 1987 S.C. 27; *Inverkip D.C. v. Carswell* 1987 S.C.L.R. 145. The rule in s. 2(1) of the 1988 Act applies to (statements in) documents other than precognitions: 1988 Act, s. 9. But a copy of a document is inadmissible unless authenticated by the maker of it under s. 6 of the 1988 Act or it is agreed by the parties. The reason for exclusion of a copy is that a copy cannot be evidence of the principal admissible under s. 2(1)(b) of the 1988 Act because it is not "a statement made by a person otherwise than in the course of the proof", a "statement" could only apply to the principal document: *Japan Leasing (Europe) plc v. Weir's (No. 2)* 1998 S.C. 543 (I.H.) (copy of hire purchase contract). In that case the court went on to say that direct oral evidence of the signatories about the contents of the document would not be admissible, apart from s. 2 of the 1988 Act, because of the best evidence rule (which states that the principal document is the best evidence). The trouble with the case of *Japan Leasing* is that it appears, on the one hand, to treat the document as the "statement" of the signatories while, on the other hand, the court excludes evidence of the signatories about what is in the document because the best evidence is not their statement but the principal document itself. Does this mean that s. 2 of the 1988 Act has abolished the best evidence rule in relation to oral statements but has not abolished the rule in relation to documents?

(15) Corroboration. Section 1(1) of the Civil Evidence (Scotland) Act 1988 abolishes the requirement for corroboration. There is now no rule that requires the court to scrutinise with special care the evidence of a witness simply because he made prior statements to persons not led in evidence: *L. v. L.* 1998 S.L.T. 672. *Per* Lord Coulsfield in that case, it was doubted that there was now any validity in the previous rule (see *McLaren v. Caldwell's Paper Mill Co. Ltd*, 1973 S.L.T. 158) that failure to lead other (corroborative) evidence which was available should lead a judge to regard such evidence with special care and attention. This case was distinguished by Lord Marnoch in *Rae v. The Chief Constable, Strathclyde Police* 1998 Rep.L.R. 63 where he said that, in relation to the weight to be attached to a single witness's evidence, the court may be disinclined to give maximum weight to uncorroborated testimony where a crucial witness is not led to substantiate a party's position.

(16) Expenses. An extra-judicial offer, whenever made, that has not been accepted may be taken into account in considering an award of expenses: *Pearce & Co. v. Owners of SS Hans Maersk* 1935 S.C. 703 (during action by pursuer); *O'Donnell v. A.M. & G. Robertson* 1965 S.L.T. 155 (before action brought). The old practice (see *Gunn v. Hunter* (1886) 13 R. 573, 574 *per* LP Inglis) that, if an offer was made before litiscontestation (when defences lodged) which was repeated on record and the pursuer was awarded less, expenses were awarded to the defender; but if the offer was not repeated on record, there were no expenses due to or by, is long since dead. It is rare to find offers on record as pleadings are not regarded as the place for providing the basis for arguments about expenses: *O'Donnell, above*.

(17) Citation of authorities. The general rule is that when a case has been reported in Session Cases or the (English) Law Reports, it should be cited from that source: *McGowan v. Summit at Lloyds*, 2002 S.L.T. 1258, 1273 at para.[57] (Ex Div.). See also now, P.N. No. 5 of 2004. The citation of cases from reproduction of electronic formats is permitted by that P.N.

(18) Fee for proof. See note 36.11.6.

36.11.3   *Reports of proofs*. The Judicial Proceedings (Regulation of Reports) Act 1926 regulates the publishing of indecent material. S.46 of the Children and Young Persons (Scotland) Act 1937 empowers the court to direct that the identity of a child should not be disclosed. Under s. 4(2) of the Contempt of Court Act 1981 an order may be made to postpone a report of proceedings to avoid substantial risk of prejudice to the administration of justice. Under s. 11 of the 1981 Act, where the court allows a name or other matter to be withheld from the public, it may prohibit publication of that name or matter in connection with the proceedings.

36.11.4   *Transcripts of evidence*. These are ordered by the court either at the request of the court to assist in writing the judgment or at the request of a party (r. 36.11(3)), or requested by a party from the shorthand writers for the purposes of a reclaiming motion (r. 36.11(8)).

Transcripts, if ordered, are not usually available for some weeks after the proof; but daily transcripts may be ordered and obtained by arrangement with the shorthand writers at extra cost.

Although r. 36.11(7) provides for borrowing the record of the evidence to enable a party to consider whether to reclaim, a transcript of the evidence is rarely available before the expiry of the reclaiming days unless there are daily transcripts.

The court shorthand writers are William Hodge (Shorthand Writers) Ltd, 20 York Place, Edinburgh EH1 3EP (tel. 0131–556 5660).

Shorthand writer's fee. For shorthand writer's fees, see r. 42.16, Table of Fees, Chap. IV.   **36.11.5**

Fee. The court fee for a proof is payable by each party for every 30 minutes or part thereof.   **36.11.6**
For fee, see Court of Session etc. Fees Order 1997, Table of Fees, Pt I, B, item 16 or C, item 16 [S.I. 1997 No. 688, as amended, pp. **C** 1201 *et seq.*]. Certain persons are exempt from payment of fees: see 1997 Fees Order, art.5 substituted by S.S.I. 2002 No. 270. A fee exemption certificate must be lodge in process: see P.N. No. 1 of 2002.

Where a party is legally represented, the fee may be debited under a credit scheme introduced on 1st April 1976 by P.N. No. 4 of 1976 to the account (if one is kept or permitted) of the agent by the court cashier, and an account will be rendered weekly by the court cashier's office to the agent for all court fees due that week for immediate settlement. An agent not on the credit scheme will have an account opened for the purpose of lodging the fee: P.N. No. 2 of 1995. A debit slip and a copy of the court hearing time sheet will be delivered to the agent's box or sent by DX or post.

A party litigant must pay (by cash, cheque or postal order) to the clerk of court at the end of the hearing or, if the proof lasts more than a day, at the end of each day: P.N. No. 2 of 1995. A receipt will be issued. The assistant clerk of session will acknowledge receipt of the sum received from the clerk of court on the Minute of Proceedings.

Extra-judicial settlements. Where a case is settled there are three possible ways of bringing the   **36.11.7**
cause to an end:— (a) the court is asked to grant the agreed decree at the proof and the proof is discharged, (b) a joint minute is lodged setting out the terms of settlement and a motion is enrolled for the court to interpone authority to the joint minute and for decree in terms of it (or such parts of it as the court may grant) and for discharge of the proof, or (c) a motion (usually at the bar) to discharge the proof because the cause has settled and a joint minute is subsequently lodged.

(1) *Joint minutes.* The joint minute sets out the terms of settlement. It is lodged in process (or tendered at the bar) with a motion to interpone authority to it, for decree in terms of it (or such parts of it as the court may grant decree for) and to discharge any proof diet fixed. The settlement is binding on the parties even though the court has not interponed authority to it: *McAthey v. Patriotic Investment Co Ltd*, 1910 S.C. 584. Once lodged the minute cannot be withdrawn unless the court could not grant decree in terms of it at all: *McAthey*, above (where agreement with liquidator to settle dispute on payment to pursuer thus giving a creditor a preference); or possibly in other exceptional circumstances: *Paterson v. Magistrates of St Andrews* (1880) 7 R. 712. In *Paterson* it appears there was a doubt whether the town council really had properly authorised the settlement and there is hint in Lord Ormidale's opinion that the minute could be withdrawn as not moved for and because authority had not been interponed to it by the court (Lord Young's dissenting view in *Gow v. Henry* (1899) 2 F. 48). The case of *Paterson* is not mentioned in *McAthey*. The court will grant decree in terms of the joint minute insofar as its terms are within the perimeters of the conclusions: *McAthey*, above. It is not necessary to postpone decree where the action is settled with respect to one defender in order to preserve another defender's rights of relief under s. 3 of the Law Reform (Miscellaneous Provisions) (Scotland) Act 1940: *Singer v. Gray Tool Co (Europe) Ltd*, 1984 S.L.T. 149 (First Div.). The form of a joint minute is:

"[X] for the pursuer and
[Y] for the defender stated and hereby state to the court that the parties are agreed that . . ."

(2) *Disputes about settlements.* In *Dixon v. Van de Weterfing*, 17th March 2000 (OH), unreported (2000 G.W.D. 12-409), parties thought that the case was settled on the morning of the proof but the defender refused to pay because he thought he had been induced to agree by misrepresentation by the pursuer. The pursuer enrolled for decree. Lord Bonomy considered that, where the court was being asked to give effect to an agreement the terms of which were not clearly stated and acknowledged and was arguably reducible, the issue must be plainly and quickly identified in writing. He ordered the pursuer to lodge in seven days a minute setting out the facts relating to the settlement, the remedy sought and pleas and the defender to lodge answers in seven days thereafter. It might be possible to determine the matter at a subsequent hearing. If not, further procedure (amendment, debate and proof) would be necessary. There is nothing new about this procedure (see *Lawrence v. Knight*, 1972 S.C. 26 (OH)) but it is useful to be reminded of it. The procedure is at the discretion of the court. There may be circumstances,

however, where the better course is for the party alleging settlement to bring an action of declarator (or specific implement): *North British Railway Co. v. Bernards Ltd*, (1900) 7 S.L.T. 329 (OH).

(3) *Expenses*. Expenses "as taxed" means the expenses of process, but does not include expenses incurred before the cause was brought: *Clyde Nail Co Ltd v. A. G. Moore & Co Ltd*,1949 S.L.T. (Notes) 43. Expenses include expenses appropriate to the case, which may include an additional fee under r. 42.14 whether or not expressly included in the terms of settlement (but not if excluded): *Marks and Spencer Ltd v. British Gas Corporation*, 1984 S.C. 86 (Second Div.); *UCB Bank plc v. Dundas & Wilson C.S.*, 1990 S.C. 377 (First Div.). Where a party wishes to reserve the right to seek modification of a liability for expenses as a legally assisted person, this should be stated in the settlement otherwise the right will be held to have been surrendered: *Boughen v. Scott*, 1983 S.L.T. (Sh. Ct.) 94; *Roy, Nicholson, Becker & Day v. Clarke*, 1984 S.L.T. (Sh. Ct.) 16.

36.11.8   *Judicial settlements—Tenders*. A tender is a judicial offer because it is a formal written offer by a defender (or third party) to a pursuer (or a pursuer to a defender in a counterclaim) in the process of the cause. A tender may be made in the pleadings or, more commonly, in a separate minute of tender lodged in process. A tender may be lodged at any time from the bringing of the proceedings until final judgment. The money is not lodged in court.

A tender may be withdrawn by a minute of withdrawal of tender at any time before the tender is accepted. A tender may lapse, e.g. because of subsequent events: see *Macrae v. Edinburgh Street Tramway Co*, (1885) 13 R, 365 (tender sought to be accepted after referee's lower award); *Bright v. Weatherspoon*, 1940 S.C. 280 (tender accepted after reclaiming judgment of Lord Ordinary). A tender is not brought to the attention of the judge until the question of expenses is dealt with: *Avery v. Cantilever Shoe Co*, 1942 S.C. 469, 470 *per* L.P. Normand.

(1) *Form of tender*. The form of a tender is:

"[Y] for the defender stated and hereby states to the court that, without admitting liability and under reservation of his [*or* its] whole rights and pleas, the defender tendered and hereby tenders to the pursuer the sum of (*state in words and figures*) sterling together with the taxed expenses of process to the date hereof in full of the conclusions of the summons."

A tender should be in clear and unambiguous terms. It has been said that it should be unqualified and unconditional: *Bisset v. Anderson* (1847) 10 D. 233, 234 (*obiter*) and *Gunn v. Marquis of Breadalbane* (1849) 11 D. 1040, 1050-1052 (*obiter*). But in *Ferguson v. Maclennan Salmon Co Ltd*, 1990 S.C. 45, 51, Lord McCluskey held that a tender did not have to be unqualified. The principle was that if one party made a judicial offer in clear and unambiguous terms which was open to the other party to accept, thereby ending the litigation, and the other party did not accept it, then if, after further litigation, the court made an award which benefits the non-accepting party to no greater extent than he would have benefited by accepting the offer, then, in the absence of other considerations, it is he and not the offerer who should pay for the unnecessary litigation subsequent to its date.

(2) *Expenses*. The tender must contain an unconditional offer to pay the expenses to the date of the tender: *Little v. Burns* (1881) 9 R. 118. An exception may be where the pursuer unreasonably failed to intimate the claim before raising the action and the tender is lodged with defences: *Lees v. Gordon* 1929 S.L.T. 400 (OH). Phrases such as "such expenses as the court may award" and "such expenses as the court considers proper" should not be used: see *McKenzie v. H.D. Fraser & Sons*, 1990 S.C. 311, 321 *per* L.P. Hope (the dispute was whether the usual form of tender, or another, should be used when a defender wished to argue that expenses should be awarded on a sheriff court scale; the court adhered to the usual form of tender). The phrase "expenses of process" means that the court has a discretion as to the level or amount of expenses: *McKenzie*, above; see also *Gillespie v. Fitxpatrick*, 2003 S.L.T. 999 (motion for expenses on sheriff court ordinary scale granted). The expenses of process will include any additional fee awarded. See also *Martin v. Had-Fab Ltd*, 2005 S.C.L.R. 129 (defenders unsuccessfully argued that "expenses to date" entitled the court to award expenses to the date of an earlier tender). See also *Brackencroft Ltd v. Slivers Marine Ltd*, 2006 S.L.T. 85.

The pursuer has a reasonable time to consider the tender: *Wood v. Miller* 1960 S.C. 86, 98 *per* LJ-C Thomson. For a case where it was held that it was reasonable to accept a tender, made on the first day, on the third day of a proof, see *Pagan v. The Miller Group Ltd*, 2002 S.C. 150 (OH). Accordingly, where the pursuer accepts the tender, expenses "to the date of tender" includes that reasonable time thereafter. Determination of this true date of the tender is very much the province of the auditor: *Smeaton v. Dundee Corporation*, 1941 S.C. 600. But where the court has all the facts, the court may determine the date: see, e.g. *Morton v. O'Donnell*, 1979 S.L.T. (Notes) 26. The pursuer's expenses will include the expenses of considering the tender: *Jack v. Black*, 1911 S.C. 691, 700 *per* L.P. Dunedin. For expenses where the tender is not accepted, see (5) below.

(3) *Interest*. Interest may be excluded or restricted. Unless otherwise stated, in an action of damages, a tender is in full satisfaction of any claim for interest: Interest on Damages (Scotland)

Act 1958, s. 1(1B). In considering whether an award is equal to or greater than the sum tendered, therefore, the court will have to take account of such part as it considers appropriate of any interest awarded under the Act. See, *e.g. Manson v. Skinner*, 2002 S.L.T. 448 in (5) below. In *Tait v. Campbell*, 2004 S.L.T. 187, it was held that the pursuer was entitled to interest at the full rate until payment (but liable for expenses from the date of the second tender) notwithstanding an unsuccessful motion for a new trial as it was only in exceptional circumstances that a pursuer should suffer a lower award as a result of the passage of time arising from the exercise of a right to such a new trial.

In any other case whether interest is included will depend on construction of the terms of the tender. The words "in full satisfaction and settlement of the claim" may not include interest: see *Carmichael v. Caledonian Railway Co*, (1868) 6 M. 671, 681, *Riddell v. Lanarkshire and Ayrshire Railway Co*, (1904) 6 F. 432 and *The "Devotion II"*, 1979 S.C. 80, 91 *per* Lord Wylie.

(4) *Acceptance of tender*. The form of acceptance is:

[X] for the pursuer stated and hereby states to the court that the pursuer accepted and hereby accepts the tender contained in the minute of tender, No. of Process, in full of the conclusion(s) of the summons."

A motion for decree in terms of the minutes of tender and acceptance has also to be made. The pursuer has a reasonable time to consider the tender: *Wood v. Miller* 1960 S.C. 86, 98 *per* LJ-C Thomson.

(5) *Expenses where tender not accepted*. The general principles are these. (A) Where the pursuer beats the tender by being awarded more than the tender, he is entitled to the whole expenses of process: *Heriot v. Thomson*, (1833) 12 S. 145. (B) Where the pursuer fails to beat the tender by being awarded less or no more than the tender, the pursuer gets expenses to the date of the tender (not the date he should have accepted the tender) and the defender gets expenses from that date. Circumstances may justify another determination. Thus, although an award of damages may exceed the tender, where that excess is due to interest accrued since the date of the tender, the court may in effect treat the tender as not being beaten and award expenses to the defender from the date of the tender. Such a course of action would arise where the refusal of the tender unnecessarily prolonged the proceedings to no purpose and the excess of the award over the tender was due to the interest accrued since the date of tender: *Manson v. Skinner*, 2002 S.L.T. 448.

(6) *Plurality of parties*. Where there is more than one pursuer, each having separate conclusions, there must be a tender to each pursuer: *Flanagan v. Dempster, Moore & Co*, 1928 S.C. 308 (First Div.).

A defender sued jointly and severally may alone tender to a pursuer. If for the full sum and the pursuer accepts and is paid, the pursuer may not continue his action against the other defenders. Where the averments of the defender making the tender make it prudent for the pursuer to call a second defender, the tender of expenses includes a right of the pursuer to relief from the tendering defender for any expenses awarded against the pursuer in favour of the second defender: *Clegg v. McKirdy & MacMillan*, 1932 S.C. 442, 446 (Second Div.); *cf Mitchell v. Redpath Engineering Ltd*, 1990 S.L.T. 259.

(7) *Tender by one defender to pursuer and other defenders*. One of jointly and severally sued defenders may tender to the pursuer and to the other defenders that they contribute in certain proportions: see, e.g. *Houston v. British Road Services Ltd*, 1967 S.L.T. 329.

(8) *Williamson tenders*. One of jointly and severally sued defenders may offer to the other defenders that he will admit liability to the pursuer if the other defenders will contribute with that defender in certain proportions: *Williamson v. McPherson*, 1951 S.C. 438. If agreed a joint tender is then made to the pursuer.

The form of a Williamson tender is:

[Y] for the first (-named) defender stated and hereby states to the court that, without prejudice to and under reservation of his whole rights and pleas, the first defender offered and hereby offers to the second defender to admit liability to make reparation to the pursuer jointly and severally with the second defender on the basis that the defenders shall be liable *inter se* to contribute to any damages and expenses awarded to the pursuer in the proportion of ..."

Finality of decision on sufficiency of stamp

36.12. The decision of the Lord Ordinary that a document adduced in evidence is sufficiently stamped, or does not require to be stamped, shall be final and not subject to review.

Deriv. RCS 1965, r. 264(f)

General note. Judicial notice must be taken of the omission or insufficiency of the stamp on a **36.12.1** document subject to stamp duty: Stamp Act 1891, s. 14(1).

Under s. 14(4) of the 1891 Act an instrument in Sched. 1 to that Act executed in the U.K., or relating wherever executed to any property, or to any matter or thing or to be done, in the U.K., shall not be given in evidence or be available for any purpose whatsoever unless it be stamped in accordance with the law in force at the time it was first executed.

The duty due and a penalty may be paid at the proof to the clerk of court: 1891 Act, s. 14(1).

Death, disability, retiral, etc., of Lord Ordinary

36.13.—(1) Where the Lord Ordinary, before whom proof has been taken, in whole or in part, dies, retires or otherwise becomes unable to give judgment or to hear further proof, as the case may be, any party to the cause may apply by motion to the Inner House for directions—

(a) that the cause shall be continued before, and shall be disposed of by, another Lord Ordinary;

(b) that the notes of evidence already taken, as certified by the shorthand writer, shall be evidence in the cause; and

(c) that the notes of the Lord Ordinary taken at the proof shall be made available to the Lord Ordinary before whom the cause is to be continued.

(2) On making directions under paragraph (1), the Inner House may make such other order as it thinks fit.

(3) On enrolling a motion under paragraph (1), the party enrolling it shall—

(a) lodge in process four copies of the closed record (incorporating all interlocutors pronounced in the cause and amendments to the record allowed since the closing of the record); and

(b) send one copy of that record to every other party.

[NEXT TEXT PAGE IS C 263]

(4) It shall not be necessary for any documents to be lodged in support of such a motion unless the court otherwise directs.

(5) The vacation judge may not hear or determine a motion under paragraph (1).

Deriv. R.C.S. 1965, r. 112 amended by S.I. 1976 No. 137

"motion". For motions, see Chap. 23. **36.13.1**

"lodge in process". The closed records are lodged in process as a step of process: r. 1.3(1) **36.13.2** (definition of "step of process"). On steps of process, see r. 4.4.

CHAPTER 37

JURY TRIALS

Applications for jury trial

37.1.—(1) Within 14 days after the date of an interlocutor allowing issues in an action, the pursuer shall lodge in process the proposed issue for jury trial and a copy of it for the use of the court.

(2) Where a pursuer fails to lodge a proposed issue for jury trial under paragraph (1), he shall, unless—

(*a*) the court, on cause shown, otherwise orders, or

(*b*) a proposed issue is lodged by another party under paragraph (3),

be held to have departed from his right to jury trial; and any other party may apply by motion for a proof.

(3) Where a pursuer fails to lodge a proposed issue under paragraph (1), any other party may, within seven days after the expiry of the period specified in that paragraph, lodge in process a proposed issue for jury trial and a copy of it.

(4) Where a proposed issue has been lodged under paragraph (1) or (3), any other party may, within seven days after the date on which the proposed issue has been lodged, lodge in process a proposed counter-issue and a copy of it.

(5) A proposed counter-issue lodged by a party under paragraph (4) may include any question of fact which is made the subject of a specific averment on record or is relevant to his pleas-in-law notwithstanding that it does not in terms meet the proposed issue.

(6) The party lodging a proposed issue under paragraph (1) or (3) shall, on the day after the date on which the period for lodging a proposed counter-issue under paragraph (4) expires, apply by motion for approval of the proposed issue.

(7) Any party who has lodged a proposed counter-issue under paragraph (4) shall, within seven days after the enrolment of a motion for approval of a proposed issue under paragraph (6), apply by motion for approval of his proposed counter-issue.

(8) Where a proposed counter-issue has been lodged, the motion for approval of a proposed issue shall be heard at the same time as the motion for approval of the proposed counter-issue.

(9) The Lord Ordinary, on granting a motion for approval of a proposed issue or proposed counter-issue, shall authenticate with his signature the proposed issue or proposed counter-issue as lodged or as adjusted.

(10) Where an issue or counter-issue has been approved by the court, the party whose issue or counter-issue it is shall lodge 18 copies of the approved issue or counter-issue for the use of the court; and such copies need not contain the authentication of the Lord Ordinary.

Deriv. R.C.S. 1965, r. 114(1) to (5) (r. 37.1(1) to (5)), r. 114(6) (r. 37.1(6) and (7)) and r. 114(7) (r. 37.1(9)), all substituted by S.I. 1982 No. 1825; P.N. 28th February 1955 (r. 37.1(10))

37.1.1   *General note.* Civil jury trial was introduced in Scotland with the Jury Court by the Jury Trials (Scotland) Act 1815, after a lengthy debate, begun perhaps by Lord Swinton in a pamphlet in 1789, as a means of dealing with the dire state into which the forms of Scottish pleading and litigation had fallen by the end of the 18th century. Furthermore the House of Lords saw in it a means of improving Scottish litigation and discouraging appeals, they being also more familiar with the English (jury) trial system. The Jury Court was abolished and the power to try causes by jury transferred to the Court of Session by the C.S.A. 1830.

Civil jury trial does not infringe art.6(1) of the ECHR (right to fair trial): *Heasman v J M Taylor & Partners*, 2002 S.C. 326; 2002 S.L.T. 451 (Ex Div). The grounds of challenge in that case were that no meaningful guidance was given to juries on levels of solatium and the jury gave no reasons for its decision. The case was reported to the Inner House. The challenge was unsuccessful and the Extra Division held that the procedures followed were adequate to give the assurance that the jury was directed to the proper questions and the appellate procedure ensured that a party did not suffer the consequences of an unfair trial.

37.1.2   *Causes for jury trial.* Certain causes, the "enumerated causes", must be sent to jury trial unless the parties otherwise agree or special cause is shown: C.S.A. 1988, s. 9(b). The court may allow jury trial in a cause other than an enumerated cause: *e.g. Fletcher v. Lord Advocate* 1923 S.C. 27; *Blount v. Watt* 1953 S.L.T. (Notes) 39. In this case the court has a discretion, although it may require a special reason (cause) to send a case which is not an enumerated cause to jury trial.

The enumerated causes are: (1) an action of damages for personal injuries; (2) an action for libel or defamation; (3) an action founded on delinquency or quasi-delinquency where the conclusion is for damages only and expenses; and (4) an action of reduction on the ground of incapacity, essential error, or force and fear: C.S.A. 1988, s. 11. The longer list in s. 28 of the C.S.A. 1825 was replaced by this shorter list in the C.S.A. 1988 because none of the others had been sent to jury trial in living memory. S. 49 of the C.S.A. 1850 had allowed proof on commission as an alternative in the enumerated causes except cases of libel, nuisance or damages; s. 4 of the Evidence (Scotland) Act 1866 introduced the alternative of proof to jury trial where parties consented or on special cause shown (both these provisions are repealed by the C.S.A. 1988, Sched. 2).

(1) *Action of damages for personal injuries.* This phrase in s. 11(a) of the C.S.A. 1988, which is a consolidating measure, was not intended to and did not change the law, from that under s. 28 of the C.S.A. 1825, to exclude claims for loss of society as a result of the death of a relative: *Morris v. Drysdale* 1992 S.L.T. 186.

(2) *Action for libel or defamation.* This means an action for written or oral defamation, the former being sometimes known as libel and the latter as slander. Defamation means a communication to the injured party or another of a false statement or idea which is an imputation injurious to the character or credit of the injured party: *Brownlie v. Thomson* (1859) 21 D. 480, 485 *per* L.J.-C. Inglis; *A.B. v. C.D.* (1904) 7 F. 22. Malice only requires to be proved where qualified privilege is claimed: *Langlands v. Leng* 1916 S.C.(H.L.) 102, 109 *per* Lord Shaw of Dunfermline. Other types of verbal injury are *convicium*, slander of title, property, or goods or business, and malicious falsehood, which require proof of malice: these are not included in the meaning of defamation.

(3) *Action founded on delinquency and quasi-delinquency.* Delinquency means fault or violation of duty and these terms are, therefore, synonymous with delict and quasi-delict.

(4) *Action of reduction on ground of incapacity, essential error, or force or fear.* (a) Incapacity may arise through nonage (a child under 16: Age of Legal Capacity (Scotland) Act 1991, s. 1(1)(a)) or insanity or other mental incapacity (including drunkenness: Stair, I.x.13; Erskine, III.i.16; *Taylor v. Provan* (1864) 2 M. 1226). (b) Essential error: see *Stewart v. Kennedy* (1890) 17 R.(H.L.) 25; *Menzies v. Menzies* (1893) 20 R.(H.L.) 108, 142 *per* Lord Watson; *Woods v. Tulloch* (1893) 20 R.(H.L.) 477 *per* Lord Watson; *Westville Shipping Co. v. Abram Steamship Co.* 1922 S.C. 571. (c) Force and fear. A contract induced by threats or violence sufficient to overcome the fortitude of a reasonable man is void: Stair, I.ix.8; Erskine, III.i.16; but a bill of exchange is voidable (Bills of Exchange Act 1882, ss. 29(2), 30(2) and 38).

See note 28.1.8(B) for a discussion of special cause for disallowing jury trial.

37.1.3   *"within 14 days", "within seven days".* The date from which the period is calculated is not counted. Where the last day falls on a Saturday or Sunday or a public holiday on which the Office of Court is closed, the next available day is allowed: r. 1.3(7). For office hours and public holidays, see note 3.1.2.

37.1.4   *"interlocutor allowing issues".* This will be the interlocutor pronounced (a) after the record has closed either of consent under r. 22.3(5)(*a*)(v) or at the By Order (Adjustment) Roll appointed under r. 22.3(5)(*b*), or (*b*) after a hearing on the Procedure Roll under Chap. 28.

"proposed issue". R.C.S. 1965, r. 115 which provided for jury trial without issues has not been **37.1.5** re-enacted because it is thought to have fallen into desuetude, although jury trial without issues was ordered in *Ryan v. Orr* 1965 S.L.T. 12.

Issues are concise statements of questions of fact to be decided by the jury: Bell's *Dictionary*, p. 586. They are a device to simplify the jury's task: *Lawrie v. Glasgow Corporation* 1952 S.C. 361, 366 *per* L.J.-C. Thomson. They must be in conformity with the averments on record: *Lawrie*, above. The issues put before the jury should be as uncomplicated as is compatible with a fair representation of the rival pleas: *Taylor v. National Coal Board* 1953 S.C. 349, 354 *per* L.J.-C. Thomson. It is a long established practice that a jury has to answer the question of a defender's liability, and an issue should include a question as to the defender's liability: *Black v. North British Railway*, 1908 S.C. 444: *Mitchell v. Laing*, 1998 S.C. 342, 353A-C *per* Rodger, L.P. In a case where liability has been admitted, the answer to the question is a formality; but the jury must still give an affirmative answer by direction of the judge, the answer must be recorded by the clerk of court on the issue as being the verdict of the jury (r.37.9): *Benson v. Scottish Lion Engineering Ltd*, 2002 S.C. 228.

Issues may be general or particular. A general issue is an issue specific as to time and place but general as to other facts and where there are no separate grounds on which the case rests, and is the usual form in actions for damages for personal injuries: Maclaren on *Court of Session Practice*, p. 565; *e.g.* "Whether on or about (*date*) at (*place*) the pursuer was injured through the fault of the defenders to his loss, injury and damage?". A particular issue is one which includes a particular averment which the pursuer must prove in order to succeed: *e.g.* that the pursuer was in the employment of the defenders or that there was a negligent exercise of a statutory duty.

Several pursuers injured by the same conduct of the defender have separate conclusions and separate issues except in the case of pursuers suing for death of a relative. A pursuer suing several defenders for the same delict may have one issue against all and, if in the alternative, with the addition of the words "or one or other and which of them"; although separate issues may be necessary to distinguish different damages claimed against each: *Smith v. Taylor* (1882) 10 R. 291, 299 *per* L.P. Inglis. On styles for issues, see *Christie's Tutor v. Kirkwood* 1991 S.L.T. 805 (issue where contributory negligence and damages claimed against both defenders or one of them); *Hayden v. Glasgow Corporation* 1948 S.C. 143 (issue and counter-issue in personal injury action with contributory negligence); *McLean v. The Admiralty* 1960 S.C. 199 (issue in personal injury action where no contributory negligence); *Stewart v. Blythswood Shipbuilding Co. Ltd* 1951 S.L.T.(Notes) 47 (issue where existence of accident in dispute); *Cairnie v. Secretary of State for Scotland* 1966 S.L.T.(Notes) 57 (issue where there is a third party).

At the end of the issue there will be a schedule of the damages claimed. In an action of damages for personal injuries, there are separate entries in the schedule for solatium past and future, and for loss of earnings past and future: *MacDonald v. Glasgow Corporation* 1973 S.C. 52, 55 (where the style is set out). In an action of damages for the death of a relative, there are separate entries for loss of society (or its recent replacement) past and present: *McAllister v. Abram* 1981 S.L.T. 85. Where there is more than one pursuer there are separate entries for heads of claim for each pursuer. Where more than one wrong is alleged there may be more than one schedule corresponding to the separate conclusions; there will not be more than one schedule simply because there is a common law case and a statutory case alleged in an action for personal injuries. Loss of employability may be divided into past and future loss: *Hill v. Watson* 1998 S.C. 81.

Where the pursuer received benefits to which the Social Security (Recovery of Benefits) Act 1997 applies, the issue for the pursuer will have to be framed in such a way that the jury can specify the damages it is awarding under each, if any, of the heads of compensation in column 1 of Sched. 2 to the 1997 Act. The reason is that the court, on pronouncing decree for payment of the damages, must specify the amount of compensation payment in the case of each head of compensation: 1997 Act, s.15(2). Under the 1997 Act, the person (the compensator) compensating the victim of an accident, injury or disease is liable to pay in full to the Secretary of State for Social Security the amount of the recoverable social security benefits (for which see column 2 of Sched. 2 to the 1997 Act) paid to the victim. The compensator is entitled to deduct, from certain specified heads of compensation he is to pay to the victim, the amount of the recoverable benefits (see 1997 Act, s.8). These heads, specified in column 1 of Sched. 2 to the 1997 Act, are the compensation for earnings lost, the compensation for cost of care, and the compensation for loss of mobility, during the relevant period. The compensator will then pay the sum deducted to the Secretary of State (to the CRU). The "relevant period" is the five years immediately following the date of the accident or injury or, in the case of disease, the date on which the victim first claimed a listed benefit: see 1997 Act, s.3(2) and (3). If at any time before the end of that period a compensation payment is made in final discharge of any claim, the relevant period ends on that date: 1997 Act, s.3(4)(a). The £2,500 small payments threshold has been abolished. A difficulty arises where the final decree is pronounced within the five-year relevant period: is the court required to specify the damages for a period ending on the date of payment (not then determinable) after final decree, the final discharge occurring and the relevant period ending, under s.3(4)(a) of the 1997 Act, on the date of payment; or is the date of decree to be deemed to be the date of payment? The solution has been provided by the Inner House in *Mitchell v. Laing*, 1998 S.C. 342. The court held that the intention of the legislation was that the amount of recoverable benefits to be deducted from the heads of compensation was the amount payable over the whole five-year period. Accordingly, the court in pronouncing decree would specify the damages due for the specified heads of compensation for the full five years; and the issue must, therefore, be framed in such a way that the jury can specify the damages due for earnings lost, cost of care or loss of mobility for the five years following the date of the accident or injury, or, in the case of disease, the date on which a listed benefit was first claimed.

The relevant part of the issue approved in *Mitchell*, above, was in the following terms:

Damages claimed	£75,000
Past solatium	£
Future solatium	£
Past wage loss	£
Past services by stepmother	£
(cost of care component:— £)	£
(loss of mobility component:— £)	£
Past cost of tradesmen	£
Past cost of physiotherapy	£
Past cost of medical care	£
Future cost of medical care	£
(amount to 26.7.98— £)	£
Cost of cancellation of Africa trip	£
Total damages	£

A schedule of reference for lengthy documents founded on, as in a defamation action, may be attached to an issue.

If no proposed issue is lodged and no other party lodges a proposed issue, the pursuer is deemed to have departed from his right to jury trial: r. 37.1(2). The court may, on cause shown, allow a proposed issue to be received late under r. 37.1(2)(a): see, *e.g. McGee v. Matthew Hall Ltd*, 1996 S.L.T. 399 (narrow case of agents' inadvertence). Because r. 37.1(2) contains its own provision for granting relief, the court will not exercise the dispensing power in r. 2.1 unless in extraordinary circumstances: *McGee*, above, *obiter per* Lord Caplan.

On counter-issues, see note 37.1.8.

37.1.6   *"lodge in process"*. The issue is lodged in process as a step of process: r. 1.3(1) (definition of "step of process"). On steps of process, see r. 4.4.

37.1.7   *"motion"*. For motions, see Chap. 23.

37.1.8   *"counter-issue"*. Counter-issues are concise statements of questions of fact to be decided by the jury: Bell's *Dictionary*, p. 586. They must be in conformity with the averments on record: *Lawrie v. Glasgow Corporation* 1952 S.C. 361, 366 *per* L.J.-C. Thomson. The issues put before the jury should be as uncomplicated as is compatible with a fair representation of the rival pleas: *Taylor v. National Coal Board* 1953 S.C. 349, 354 *per* L.J.-C. Thomson.

The circumstances in which a counter-issue may or may not be appropriate were considered by Lord Patrick in *Taylor v. National Coal Board* 1953 S.C. 349, 363–368. He made the following points:

(a) A counter-issue is not necessary where the defence is a direct negative of the pursuer's issue.

(b) A counter-issue is not allowed if it is not a counter to the pursuer's issue, because if a counter-issue is answered in the defender's favour he should get the verdict.

(c) If in a case of slander the defender wishes to prove *veritas* as a complete defence he must lodge a counter-issue but not if he merely wishes to prove circumstances in order to reduce the damages.

(d) A counter-issue should not be allowed unless the fact on which the defender founds is one which, if proved, is a complete defence.

(e) The words "notwithstanding that it does not in terms meet the proposed issue" in r. 37.1(5) (in the same terms as those introduced in R.C.S. 1934, Chap. II, r. 34(c)) mean that facts which the defender will have to establish to support the counter-issue which are different from the facts the pursuer will have to establish to support the issue may be contained in a counter-issue.

(f) A counter-issue of contributory negligence is viewed as, if not necessary, at least expedient for the due administration of justice: see also *Lawrie*, above; and see *Hayden v. Glasgow Corporation* 1948 S.C. 143, 146 *per* L.P. Cooper and *Christie's Tutor v. Kirkwood* 1991 S.L.T. 805 *per* Lord McCluskey for styles. The words "they have proved that" should not be added: *Gallagher v. National Coal Board* 1962 S.L.T. 160.

(g) If the pursuer's issue is to prove a breach of statutory duty and the defender has to prove that if there was such a breach it was not reasonably practicable to prevent it, the defender must have a counter-issue.

(h) A counter-issue is appropriate where it is expedient for the due administration of justice and is in the Lord Ordinary's discretion.

If, in a defamation action where the defender pleads *veritas*, the counter-issue simply mirrors the issues, it may be appropriate for the defender to lead at the proof.

On styles for counter-issues, see *Hayden*, above (counter-issue in personal injury action with contributory negligence); *Gallagher*, above (counter-issue where defender alleging impracticability of preventing breach of statutory duty); *Christie's Tutor*, above (apportionment between defenders under s.3 of the Law Reform (Miscellaneous Provisions) (Scotland) Act 1940).

Approval of issues. On lodging the proposed issue the pursuer must enrol a motion for **37.1.9** approval of issues the day after the expiry of the period for lodging a counter-issue (seven days after proposed issue): r. 37.1(4) and (6). The court may relieve a party under r. 2.1 of his failure to move for approval of issues timeously: *Flynn v. Morris Young (Perth) Ltd* 1996 S.C. 255. The Lord Ordinary must authenticate any proposed issue and counter-issue by signing them; and an interlocutor approving issues is dealt with by the Lord Ordinary and not a clerk of session under r. 4.15. The docquet of authentication does not have to be reproduced on the copies for use of the court: P.N. 21st January 1955.

In approving issues the court can insist in modification of them (*Hayden v. Glasgow Corporation* 1948 S.C. 143, 145 *per* L.P. Cooper); and did so in *MacDonald v. Glasgow Corporation* 1973 S.C. 52 to specify separately the several heads of claim. Although a proposed issue is deficient because it lacks the essential question about liability, it does not follow that it is not a proposed issue as it may require to be, and may be, adjusted to meet the court's approval: *Benson v. Scottish Lion Engineering Ltd (No.2)*, 2002 S.C. 228 (2nd Div.).

Reclaiming. An interlocutor adjusting issues may be reclaimed against without leave within 14 **37.1.10** days of the interlocutor: r. 38.3(4)(d). The issue (or counter-issue) must be lodged and a copy sent to every other party: r. 38.12.

Fees. A court fee for a jury trial is payable by each party for every 30 minutes or part thereof. **37.1.11** For fee, see Court of Session etc. Fees Order 1997, Table of Fees, Pt I, B, item 18 [S.I.1997 No.688, as amended, pp.C1201 *et seq.*]. Certain persons are exempt from payment of fees: see 1997 Fees Order, art.5, substituted by S.S.I. 2002 No.270. A fee exemption certificate must be lodged in process: see P.N. No.1 of 2002.

Where a party is legally represented, the fee may be debited under a credit scheme introduced on 1st April 1976 by P.N. No. 4 of 1976 to the account (if one is kept or permitted) of the agent by the court cashier, and an account will be rendered weekly by the court cashier's office to the agent for all court fees due that week for immediate settlement. Agents on the credit scheme will be billed in the usual way. An agent not on the credit scheme will have an account opened for the purpose of lodging the fee: P.N. No. 2 of 1995. A debit slip and a copy of the court hearing time sheet will be delivered to the agent's box or sent by DX or post. A party litigant must pay (by cash, cheque or postal order) to the clerk of court at the end of the hearing or, if the hearing lasts more than a day, at the end of each day: P.N. No. 2 of 1995. A receipt will be issued. The assistant clerk of session will acknowledge receipt of the sum received from the clerk of court on the Minute of Proceedings.

Citation of jurors

37.2.—[1] (1) Not less than 28 days before the diet for jury trial, the pursuer shall attend at the General Department and request the issue of a jury precept.

[1] (2) Where the pursuer has failed to request the issue of a jury precept

under paragraph (1), any other party may request a jury precept not less than 21 days before the diet for jury trial.

(3) A jury precept shall be in Form 37.2–A.

(4) Where a jury precept is issued, it shall be transmitted by a clerk of session to the sheriff principal of the sheriffdom of Lothian and Borders who shall cause a list of jurors to be prepared of an equal number of men and women in accordance with the precept.

(5) A citation of a person to attend as a juror shall be in Form 37.2–B and shall be executed by the sheriff clerk at Edinburgh (or a depute authorised by him) by post by the first class recorded delivery service.

(6) Where no party requests the issue of a jury precept under paragraph (1) or (2), each party shall be held to have departed from the application for a jury trial and inquiry into the facts of the cause shall be taken by proof.

Deriv. RCS 1965, r. 117A(1) (r. 37.2(1)), r. 117A(2) (r. 37.2(4)), both substituted by S.I. 1990 No. 2118; r. 119(b) (r. 37.2(5))

----

[1] R.37.2 (1) and (2) amended by S.I. 1999 No. 1386 (effective 19th May 1999).

"jury precept". The jurors for a jury trial must be summoned by virtue of an authority or **37.2.1**
precept signed by the Lord Ordinary or a clerk of court and issued to the sheriff principal:
C.S.A. 1988, s.12. Under r. 37.2(4) the precept is transmitted to the sheriff principal of the
Sheriffdom of the Lothian and Borders, and jurors are selected from the list kept by the sheriff
clerk of that sheriffdom of persons living in the sheriff court districts of Edinburgh, Linlithgow
and Haddington (see form of precept in Form 37.2–A).

If there is no precept the jury cannot be summoned. The pursuer's agent would have to bear
the expenses of the discharge of any diet fixed: see *Center v. Duncan* 1965 S.L.T. 168.

There is a fee due for the precept: see note 37.2.3.

Jurors. The sheriff clerk must cite 36 jurors of an equal number of men and women in terms **37.2.2**
of the precept in Form 37.2–A.

The general qualifications for jury service are set out in s.1 of the Law Reform (Miscellaneous
Provisions) (Scotland) Act 1980, *i.e.* every person who is a registered parliamentary or local
government elector not less than 18 nor more than 65 years old ordinarily resident in the U.K.,
the Channel Islands or the Isle of Man for any period of at least five years since the age of 13
and not among those listed in Pt I or II of Sched. 1. On ineligibility, disqualification and excusal
from jury service, see notes to r. 37.3.

Fee. The court fee for citation of a jury is payable on receipt of instructions for precept. For **37.2.3**
fee, see Court of Session etc. Fees Order 1997, Table of Fees, Pt I, B, item 12 [S.I. 1997 No. 688,
as amended, pp.C1201 *et seq.*]. Certain persons are exempt from payment of fees: see 1997 Fees
Order, art.5, substituted by S.S.I. 2002 No.270. A fee exemption certificate must be lodged in
process: see P.N. No.1 of 2002.

Where a party is legally represented, the fee may be debited under a credit scheme introduced
on 1st April 1976 by P.N. No. 4 of 1976 to the account (if one is kept or permitted) of the agent
by the court cashier, and an account will be rendered weekly by the court cashier's office to the
agent for all court fees due that week for immediate settlement. Party litigants and agents not
operating the scheme must pay (by cash, cheque or postal order) at the time at the counter at the
General Department.

Ineligibility for, and excusal from, jury service

37.3.—(1) A person summoned to serve on a jury may, as soon as possible
after receipt of his citation, apply in writing to the Deputy Principal Clerk to be
released from his citation; and the Deputy Principal Clerk may, if he is satisfied
that there are good and sufficient grounds for excusal, grant the application.

(2) The Lord Ordinary to preside at the jury trial may, at any time before
the jury is empanelled, excuse any person summoned to attend as a juror
from attendance if he is satisfied that there are good and sufficient grounds
for doing so.

Deriv. RCS 1965, r. 119(a) and (c)

General note. A person may be ineligible or disqualified for, or excused as of right from, jury **37.3.1**
service under statute; or excused on application in writing to the Deputy Principal Clerk before
the trial diet or by the judge at the trial. A notice is sent to persons about to be put on the
register of jurors on the exemptions.

A person cited who fails to attend is liable to a fine: Law Reform (Miscellaneous Provisions)
(Scotland) Act 1980, s.2.

Jurors are entitled to travelling and subsistence for attending court, whether selected for the
jury or not, and for serving on the jury: Juries Act 1949, s.24 as amended by the 1980 Act,
Sched. 2, para. 3; and see Jurors Allowances (Scotland) Regulations 1977 [S.I. 1977 No. 445].

Ineligibility, disqualification and excusal under statute. S.1 of and Sched. 1 to the Law Reform **37.3.2**
(Miscellaneous Provisions) (Scotland) Act 1980 reforms and restates the law on qualification
and ineligibility for, and excusal from, jury service previously in some 10 statutes. Pt I of Sched.
1 to the 1980 Act lists those ineligible for jury service and Pt II lists those who are disqualified
from jury service. Pt III of Sched. 1 lists those who shall be excused as of right on attending
court in answer to a citation or on writing to the clerk who issued the citation (in fact the
Deputy Principal Clerk): 1980 Act, s.1(2) and (3).

Excusal from jury service by Deputy Principal Clerk. Under r. 37.3(1) the Deputy Principal **37.3.3**
Clerk may excuse a person from jury service before the trial diet if there are good and sufficient
grounds. This is discretionary. The matter is dealt with initially by a clerk of session in the
Signet Office. Such grounds might include illness or disability, work or holiday commitments,
depending on the circumstances.

37.3.4   *Excusal from jury service by Lord Ordinary.* Under r. 37.3(2) the Lord Ordinary to preside at the trial may excuse a person from jury service if there are good and sufficient grounds. This is discretionary. Such grounds might include illness or disability, work or holiday commitments, depending on the circumstances.

Application of certain rules relating to proofs

[1] **37.4.** The following provisions of these Rules shall apply in relation to an action in which issues have been approved for jury trial as they apply to a cause in which a proof has been allowed:—

> rule 36.2 (citation of witnesses),
> rule 36.3 (lodging productions),
> rule 36.4 (copy productions),
> rule 36.5 (returning borrowed documents before proof),
> rule 36.7 (admissions by parties),
> rule 36.8 (conditions for receiving certain written statements in evidence),
> rule 36.9 (attendance, and lists, of witnesses),
> rule 36.10 (administration of oath or affirmation to witnesses).

Deriv. RCS 1965, r. 121, r. 122, r. 122A(2) (inserted by S.I. 1984 No. 472),
and r. 123, (r. 37.4 (part))

---

[1] R. 37.4 amended by S.I. 1998 No. 890 (effective 21st April 1998).

37.4.1   *General note.* This rule simply imports rules relating to proofs which are of equal application to jury trial.

     The A.S. (R.C.S.A.) (Miscellaneous) 1998 [S.I. 1998 No. 890] removes the references to r. 36.6 (notices to admit and notices of non-admission), for which provision is now in Chapter 28A, and r. 36.11 (recording of evidence) for which provision is now made in r. 37.5A.

37.4.2   *The trial.*

     (1) *Selection of the jury.* A jury of 12 persons is selected by ballot: C.S.A. 1988, s.13(1). The selection of any juror may be challenged for an assigned reason: C.S.A. 1988, s.13(3). Such a reason might be enmity against a party or interest in the cause. Each party may also challenge four jurors without assigning any reason: C.S.A. 1988, s.13(3); "each party" meaning each set of pursuers and defenders: *Dobbie v. Johnston and Russell* (1861) 23 D. 1139. It is no longer possible for a jury to be chosen of all men or all women, proviso (b) to s.1 of the Sex Disqualification (Removal) Act 1919 having been repealed by the Statute Law (Repeals) Act 1989, Sched. 1. Jurors are sworn in: r. 37.6.

     (2) *Illness of jurors.* If the presiding judge is satisfied that a juror is through illness unable to continue, or ought for any other reason to be discharged, he may discharge the juror so long as the jury does not fall below 10 jurors: C.S.A. 1988, s.15.

     (3) *Opening speeches.* The main purpose is to inform the jury of the nature and character of the case and to bring to its notice the issue to be tried, and the speech must be fairly related to the record and the issue: *Robertson v. Federation of Icelandic Co-operative Societies* 1948 S.C. 565, 569 *per* L.J.-C. Thomson. It need not be co-extensive with the pleadings, the test is one of fairness: *Greig v. Sir William Arrol & Co. Ltd* 1965 S.L.T. 242, 244 *per* Lord Wheatley. It offends against standards of advocacy simply to read the record: *Greig*, above. The jury does not have the record. The facts should be briefly outlined and reference should be made to all the grounds of fault averred and alleged. The jury should be told how it is sought that the question in the issue is to be answered. Objection can be made to evidence not covered by the opening speech: *Robertson*, above; and evidence not covered should be objected to as there may be circumstances in which an omission to refer to part of a case might be interpreted as a departure from it. If a party departs deliberately from part of his case he should say so at the close of his opening speech: *Greig*, above, *per* Lord Walker at p. 245. A party may ask for clarification at the end of a vague opening speech (and clarification of any matter should be sought whenever it arises in the course of the trial so that it is recorded in the notes): see *Jamieson v. W. Brown & Sons (Hamilton) Ltd* 1938 S.C. 456, 456 *per* L.J.-C. Aitchison. The jury should not be referred to authorities. If reliance is to be placed on particular authorities which it is thought necessary to bring to the judge's attention at an early stage, the authorities should be mentioned to the judge at the end of the opening speech. While a precise figure for damages may not be mentioned (because assessment of damages is for the jury), the jury may be told that the sum sued for, stated in the schedule of damages attached to the issue, is a ceiling or maximum figure.

     The first opening speech is by the party on whom the initial burden of proof rests (usually the pursuer): the speech is normally delivered by the junior counsel.

After the pursuer has led his evidence, if no motion is made to withdraw the case from the jury (see (7) below), an opening speech may be made for the defender (normally by junior counsel) before he leads any evidence. Again the purpose of this speech is to explain his case. Reference is made to the pursuer's case only where it is necessary to explain his own case. There should be no reasoned attack on the pursuer's case: Maclaren on *Court of Session Practice*, p. 607. Where there is a counter-issue it is undesirable not to make an opening speech: *Dellett v. Winter* 1969 S.L.T. (Notes) 27, 28 *per* Lord Hunter.

(4) *Objections*. Notwithstanding any objection taken in the course of the trial to the opinion or direction of the judge, the trial proceeds until the jury returns a verdict (C.S.A. 1988, s.16) or until the case is withdrawn from the jury.

(5) *Views*. Any party may apply to a Lord Ordinary to view any heritable or moveable property: C.S.A. 1988, s.14.

(6) *Motion to withdraw case from jury*. Such a motion may be made, *e.g.* if the facts in evidence are different from the averments on record on the faith of which the issue was obtained (*Tully v. North British Railway Co.* (1907) 46 S.L.R. 715, 718 *per* L.P. Dunedin) or if the pursuer failed to adduce legal evidence of averments on record (*McCafferty v. Lanarkshire Tramways Co.* 1910 S.C. 797).

(7) *Amendment*. This is very difficult during a jury trial: *Rafferty v. Weir Housing Corporation Ltd* 1966 S.L.T. (Notes) 23 *per* Lord Hunter. On amendment, see r. 24.1.

(8) *Closing speeches*. First the party who led (usually the pursuer) and then the defender may address the jury on the evidence. The jury should not be told what counsel thinks the general damages should be (*e.g.* it should not be suggested that solatium is worth "£10,000 to £15,000"), although it may be suggested that the claim is worth several thousands of pounds. It is permissible to state what the wage loss is and to suggest what multiplier might be applied. If reliance is to be placed on particular authorities not previously referred to, the authorities should be mentioned to the judge.

(9) *Judge's charge to jury*. It is the jury's function to decide the facts. The judge will direct them on the standard of proof, on whom the burden lies and the principles of law to be applied. He may explain what facts have to be established and inform them what parts of the case have to be ignored as not supported by the evidence. The jury's function is to decide not only what evidence is credible but also what weight is to be attached to the evidence. The judge will explain the issues and counter-issues. The judge may add supplementary questions to the issues: see r. 37.8. He will tell them that the verdict may be by a simple majority (C.S.A. 1988, s.17). He may not mention precise figures for damages but should inform them that the figure in the issue is a maximum which has no bearing on what would be a proper award. On exceptions to the charge, see r. 37.7.

(10) *Fee for jury trial*. For court fees payable for jury trial, see note 37.1.10.

Failure of party to appear at jury trial

37.5. Where a party does not appear at the diet for jury trial, then—

   (a) if the party appearing is the pursuer or the party on whom the burden of proof lies, he shall be entitled to lead evidence, and go to the jury for a verdict;

   (b) if the party appearing is the defender or the party on whom the burden of proof does not lie, he shall be entitled to obtain a verdict in his favour without leading evidence.

Deriv. R.C.S. 1965, r. 127

Recording of proceedings at jury trial

[1] **37.5A.**—(1) Subject to any other provision in these Rules, proceedings at a jury trial shall be recorded by—

   (a) a shorthand writer to whom the oath *de fideli administratione officii* has been administered on his appointment as a shorthand writer in the Court of Session; or

   (b) tape recording or other mechanical means approved by the Lord President.

(2) In paragraph (1), "the proceedings" means the whole proceedings including, without prejudice to that generality—

   (a) discussions—

      (i) with respect to any challenge of a juror; and

      (ii) on any question arising in the course of the trial;

   (b) the decision of the Lord Ordinary on any matter referred to in sub-paragraph (a);
   (c) the evidence led at the trial;
   (d) the Lord Ordinary's charge to the jury;
   (e) the speeches of counsel or agents;
   (f) the verdict of the jury; and
   (g) any request for a direction to be given under rule 37.7, any hearing in relation to such a request and any direction so given.

   (3) A transcript of the record of proceedings shall be made only on the direction of the court; and the cost shall, in the first instance, be borne by the agents for the parties in equal proportions.

   (4) Any transcript so made shall be certified as a faithful record of proceedings—
   (a) where the recording was under sub-paragraph (a) of paragraph (1), by whoever recorded the proceedings; and
   (b) where it was under sub-paragraph (b) of that paragraph, by whoever transcribed the record.

   (5) The Lord Ordinary may make such alterations to the transcript as appear to him to be necessary after hearing the parties; and, where such alterations are made, he shall authenticate the alterations.

   (6) Where a transcript has been so made for the use of the court, copies of it may be obtained by any party from the transcriber on payment of his fee.

   (7) Except with leave of the court, the transcript may be borrowed from process only for the purpose of enabling a party to consider whether to reclaim against the interlocutor of the court applying the verdict of the jury or whether to apply for a new trial.

   (8) Where a transcript is required for a purpose mentioned in paragraph (7) but has not been directed to be transcribed under paragraph (3), a party—
   (a) may request such a transcript from the shorthand writer, or as the case may be, from a person who might have transcribed the recording had there been such a direction, the cost of the requested transcript being borne by the agent for the requester in the first instance; and
   (b) shall lodge the transcript in process;

and copies of it may be obtained by any party from the transcriber on payment of his fee.

---

[1] R. 37.5A inserted by S.I. 1998 No. 890 (effective 21st April 1998).

37.5A.1   *General note.* This rule was inserted by A.S.(R.C.S.A.) (Miscellaneous) 1998 [S.I. 1998 No. 890]. The purpose, and reason for a provision different from r. 36.11 (recording of evidence in proofs), is that (as in criminal jury trials) the whole of the proceedings in a civil jury trial will now be recorded.

   Rule 37.5A(1) includes a reference to recording by tape recording or other mechanical means as well as to recording by a shorthand writer. With effect from 1st April 1997, jury trials are recorded by mechanical means: Notice (*sic*), 6th March 1997.

37.5A.2   *Reports of jury trials.* The Judicial Proceedings (Regulation of Reports) Act 1926 regulates the publishing of indecent material. S.46 of the Children and Young Persons (Scotland) Act 1937 empowers the court to direct that the identity of a child should not be disclosed. Under s.4(2) of the Contempt of Court Act 1981 an order may be made to postpone a report of proceedings to avoid substantial risk of prejudice to the administration of justice. Under s.11 of the 1981 Act, where the court allows a name or other matter to be withheld from the public, it may prohibit publication of that name or matter in connection with the proceedings.

37.5A.3   *Transcripts of evidence.* These are ordered by the court either at the request of the court to assist in writing the judgment or at the request of a party (r. 36.11(3)), or requested by a party from the shorthand writers for the purposes of a reclaiming motion (r. 36.11(8)). Arrangements for transcription of tape recorded evidence must be made by a party personally with a contractor of his choice who will obtain the tapes from the court: Notice (*sic*), 6th March 1997.

Transcripts, if ordered, are not usually available for some weeks after the jury trial; but daily transcripts may be ordered and obtained by arrangement with the shorthand writers at extra cost.

Although r. 36.11(7) provides for borrowing the record of the evidence to enable a party to consider whether to reclaim, a transcript of the evidence is rarely available before the expiry of the reclaiming days unless there are daily transcripts.

The court shorthand writers are William Hodge (Shorthand Writers) Ltd, 20 York Place Edinburgh EH1 3EP (tel. 0131–556 5660).

Shorthand writer's fee. For shorthand writer's fees, see r. 42.16, Table of Fees, Chap. IV.   **37.5A.4**

Fee. The court fee for a jury trial is payable by each party for every 30 minutes or part thereof.   **37.5A.5**
For fee, see Court of Session etc. Fees Order 1984, Table of Fees, Pt I, B, item 17 [S.I. 1984 No. 256, Table as amended, pp. **C** 1202 *et seq.*]. The fee may be debited under a credit scheme introduced on 1st April 1976 by P.N. No. 4 of 1976 to the account (if one is kept or permitted) of the agent by the court cashier, and an account will be rendered weekly by the court cashier's office to the agent for all court fees due that week for immediate settlement. An agent not on the credit scheme will have an account opened for the purpose of lodging the fee: P.N. No. 2 of 1995. A debit slip and a copy of the court hearing time sheet will be delivered to the agent's box or sent by DX or post.

A party litigant must pay cash to the clerk of court at the end of the hearing or, if the proof lasts more than a day, at the end of each day: P.N. No. 2 of 1995. A receipt will be issued. The assistant clerk of session will acknowledge receipt of the sum received from the clerk of court on the Minute of Proceedings.

Administration of oath or affirmation to jurors

37.6.—(1) Subject to paragraph (2), the clerk of court shall administer the oath collectively to the jury in Form 37.6–A.

(2) Where a juror elects to affirm, the clerk shall administer the affirmation to that juror in Form 37.6–B.

Deriv. R.C.S. 1965, r. 122A(1) inserted by S.I. 1984 No. 472

Exceptions to judge's charge

37.7.—(1) Where a party seeks to take exception to a direction on a point of law given by the Lord Ordinary in his charge to the jury or to request the Lord Ordinary to give a direction differing from or supplementary to the directions in the charge, he shall, immediately on the conclusion of the charge, so intimate to the Lord Ordinary, who shall hear counsel for the parties in the absence of the jury.

(2) The party dissatisfied with the charge to the jury shall formulate in writing the exception taken by him or the direction sought by him; and the exception or direction, as the case may be, and the judge's decision on it, shall be recorded in a note of exception under the direction of the Lord Ordinary and shall be certified by him.

(3) After the note of exception has been certified by the Lord Ordinary, he may give such further or other directions to the jury in open court as he thinks fit before the jury considers its verdict.

Deriv. R.C.S. 1965, r. 124

Note of exception(s). A note of exception(s) is a contemporaneous record of what has taken   **37.7.1**
place drawn up by counsel and signed by the judge who gave the direction to which exception is taken and/or the direction sought. It must be made at the conclusion of the charge: r. 37.7(1). It is useful to have a blank prepared in advance in case of need. It is a summary and informal procedure because exceptions are made on the spur of the moment in the heat of battle, and it is out of keeping to demand a precise meticulous exposition of the point at issue: *Robertson v. Federation of Icelandic Co-operative Societies* 1948 S.C. 565, 572 *per* L.J.-C. Thomson. In some cases it may be enough to object to what the judge said for the purpose of having him withdraw what he said and otiose to invite him to state the opposite, or to invite him to make a direction in certain terms and otiose to table an exception that he was silent, or it may be enough where the terms of the direction sought clearly imply the terms of the direction objected to: *Robertson*, above. The note should be short and explicit. For a style of a note of exception, see *McArthur v. Weir Housing Corporation Ltd* 1970 S.C. 135, 137.

Release 49: August 1998

Any direction sought must be a direction in law: *McDougall v. Girdwood* (1867) 5 M. 937, 941 *per* Lord Curriehill.

Whatever happens to the exception taken the trial proceeds to a verdict: C.S.A. 1988, s.16.

Withdrawal of a case from the jury is not a charge to the jury and the jury does not return a verdict; and a note of exceptions is not taken against a withdrawal of the case from the jury.

On applications for new trial on the ground of misdirection, the note of exceptions must be lodged: r. 39.1.

Further questions for jury

37.8. The Lord Ordinary may, after the evidence has been led, submit to the jury in writing along with the issue and any counter-issue such further questions as he thinks fit.

Deriv. R.C.S. 1965, r. 116(b)

37.8.1   *General note.* R.C.S. 1965, r. 128 provided for special verdicts whereby the jury could be asked to answer specific questions, to which the judge applied the law, and did not give a verdict for either party. That rule has not been re-enacted. The view has been taken that they are obsolete. The judge, however, may ask the jury additional questions under r. 37.8.

Verdicts

37.9. After a verdict has been returned by a jury, the verdict shall be written on the issue and dated and signed by the clerk of court.

Deriv. R.C.S. 1965, r. 125(a)

37.9.1   *General note.* The verdict can be by a simple majority: C.S.A. 1988, s.17(2). The verdict is not operative until applied on an application under r. 37.10.

The jury may be discharged if it has been enclosed for three hours and is unable to agree: C.S.A. 1988, s.17(2).

The jury is asked to return a verdict on the issues and not to give a verdict for a party. If the verdict on the issue is in the negative the jury is not asked to give a verdict on the counter-issue.

Withdrawal of a case from the jury is not a charge to the jury and the jury does not return a verdict.

On applications for a new trial, see r. 39.1. On applications to the Inner House on a point of law to enter a jury verdict, see r. 39.6.

Application of verdicts

37.10. Any party may, after the expiry of seven days after the date on which the verdict was written on the issue and signed, apply by motion to apply the verdict, grant decree in accordance with it and make any award in relation to expenses.

Deriv. R.C.S. 1965, r. 125(b)

37.10.1   *General note.* The verdict is a finding in fact and is not operative until applied on an application under r. 37.10 to apply the verdict, for judgment (including interest) and expenses. The motion is dealt with by the presiding judge. He applies the legal result of the verdict and cannot amend it: *Morgan v. Morris* (1858) 20 D.(H.L.) 18. The judge can only look at the verdict and the issues in construing the verdict: *Morgan*, above. A verdict negative of the pursuer's case but not affirmative of the defender's results in the defender being assoilzied: *Melrose v. Hastie* (1854) 17 D.(H.L.) 4. An ambiguous verdict will result in a new trial: *Morgan*, above.

On applications to the Inner House on a point of law to enter a jury verdict, see r. 39.6.

CHAPTER 38

RECLAIMING

Interpretation of this Chapter

38.1. In this Chapter, "reclaiming days" means the days within which an interlocutor may be reclaimed against.

Reclaiming

38.2. Subject to any other provision in these Rules or any other enactment, any party to a cause who is dissatisfied with an interlocutor pronounced by—
 (a) the Lord Ordinary,
 (b) the Lord Ordinary in Exchequer Causes, or
 (c) the vacation judge,
and who seeks to submit that interlocutor to review by the Inner House shall do so by reclaiming in accordance with the provisions of this Chapter.

Deriv. R.C.S. 1965, r. 153C inserted by S.I. 1984 No. 472 and r. 261(a)(part)

"reclaiming". Reclaiming is a power of review of an interlocutor pronounced by a Lord **38.2.1** Ordinary exercised by the Inner House. Other powers of review of the court are suspension (see Chap. 60), reduction (see Chap. 53) and appeals from inferior courts (see Chap. 40) and under various statutes (see Chap. 41). Reclaiming is a re-hearing by three or more senior judges from a decision of a single judge derived from the days when the court was a unitary court: *Clippens Oil Co. Ltd v. Edinburgh and District Water Trs.* (1906) 8 F. 731, 750 *per* L.P. Dunedin. A re-hearing does not mean that the evidence is heard afresh but that the cause may be reconsidered on the evidence which was led before the Lord Ordinary as well as on a point of law.
 The statutory power for reclaiming is s.28 of the C.S.A. 1988.
 An interlocutor reclaimed against need not be implemented except if it is an award of custody, access or aliment, in which case it must be implemented unless the court otherwise orders (r. 38.8(5)). Oddly, an interlocutor (except in relation to certain family actions: see r. 7.2) may be extracted before the days within which the interlocutor may be reclaimed against have expired (*i.e.* seven days: r. 7.1(1)), and, theoretically, enforced before the end of that period. The fact, however, that an interlocutor has been extracted within the reclaiming days does not of itself prevent the interlocutor being reclaimed against: r. 38.9.
 It had been thought that it is incompetent for a party to reclaim against an interlocutor pronounced on his own motion: *Watson v. Russell* (1894) 21 R. 433; *McGuinness v. Bremner plc* 1988 S.L.T. 340; *Jongejan v. Jongejan* 1993 S.L.T. 595. But in *McCue v. Scottish Daily Record* 1998 S.C. 811, a court of five judges indicated that, where a party sought to reclaim against an interlocutor pronounced on his own motion in order to submit to review a prior interlocutor (as in *McGuinness v. Bremner plc* 1988 S.L.T. 340), this was not a question of competency but that the court would not normally countenance it. Accordingly, there may be circumstances in which the court would permit it.
 Where an interlocutor has been pronounced "of consent", both parties may be barred from challenging it: *Anderson v. British Coal Corporation* 1992 S.L.T. 398, 400I *per* L.J.-C. Ross (*obiter*); *Jongejan*, above. But, where the Lord Ordinary has indicated that he is minded to grant an order which has been opposed and requests parties to discuss its terms, the party who opposed the order is not precluded from reclaiming against the granting of the order merely because he complied with the request to discuss it and even proposed terms to be included in it: *Osborne v. British Broadcasting Corporation* 2000 S.L.T. 150 (Extra Div.). Mere acquiescence in the terms of an interlocutor does not debar a party from reclaiming on a point of law: *Vetco Gray UK Ltd v. Slessor*, 2006 S.C. 398 (Second Div.).

"Subject to any other provision". Certain interlocutors, by virtue of a rule to that effect, may **38.2.2** not be reclaimed against. A statute or other enactment may state that a particular decision may not be reclaimed.
 The following provisions in these Rules provide that certain interlocutors of a Lord Ordinary may not be reclaimed:
 r. 4.2(5) (decision to allow party litigant to proceed with action or petition without signature),
 r. 12.7(3) (decision in relation to leading evidence from one skilled witness where evidence is within the qualifications of the assessor),
 r. 13.4(3)(b) (decision to shorten or extend period of notice in a summons before service),
 r. 14.6(3) (decision to shorten or extend period of notice in a petition at time of first order),
 r. 19.2(1) (decree in absence),
 r. 35.2(5) (decision on application for recovery of evidence made before calling of summons),
 r. 36.12 (decision on sufficiency of stamp duty on a document),
 r. 38.5(6) (decision to grant or refuse leave to reclaim),
 r. 49.79 (decree in a simplified divorce application),

r. 59.1(5) (decision on application for letters of arrestment or inhibition in which a claim under s.19 of the Family Law (Scotland) Act 1985 is made).

Some interlocutors may only be reclaimed against with leave of the Lord Ordinary: see rr. 38.3(5) and 38.4.

Reclaiming days

38.3.—(1) This rule applies subject to any other provision in these Rules or any other enactment.

(2) An interlocutor disposing, either by itself or taken along with a previous interlocutor, of—

  (a) the whole subject-matter of the cause, or

[1] (b) the whole merits of the cause whether or not the question of expenses is reserved or not disposed of,

may be reclaimed against, without leave, within 21 days after the date on which the interlocutor was pronounced.

[2] (2A) Where an interlocutor which reserves or does not dispose of the question of expenses is the subject of a reclaiming motion under paragraph (2)(b), any party to the cause who seeks an order for expenses before the disposal of the reclaiming motion shall apply by motion to the Lord Ordinary for such an order within 14 days of the date of enrolment of that reclaiming motion.

(3) An interlocutor disposing of the merits of an action and making an award of provisional damages under section 12(2)(a) of the Administration of Justice Act 1982 may be reclaimed against, without leave, within 21 days after the date on which the interlocutor was pronounced.

(4) An interlocutor—

  (a) disposing of part of the merits of a cause,

  (b) allowing or refusing proof, proof before answer or jury trial (but, in the case of refusal, without disposing of the whole merits of the cause),

  (c) limiting the mode of proof,

  (d) adjusting issues for jury trial,

  (e) granting, refusing, recalling, or refusing to recall, interim interdict or interim liberation,

  (f) in relation to an exclusion order under section 4 of the Matrimonial Homes (Family Protection) (Scotland) Act 1981,

  (g) granting, refusing or recalling a sist of execution or procedure,

  (h) loosing, restricting or recalling an arrestment or recalling in whole or in part an inhibition used on the dependence of an action or refusing to loose, restrict or recall such arrestment or inhibition,

  (i) granting authority to move an arrested vessel or cargo,

  (j) deciding (other than in a summary trial) that a reference to the European Court should be made,

may be reclaimed against, without leave, within 14 days after the date on which the interlocutor was pronounced.

(5) An interlocutor (other than a decree in absence or an interlocutor mentioned in paragraph (2), (3) or (4) of this rule) may be reclaimed against, with leave, within 14 days after the date on which the interlocutor was pronounced.

Deriv. R.C.S. 1965, r. 264(a)(part) substituted by S.I. 1990 No. 705 (r. 38.3(2)), r. 134D inserted by S.I. 1984 No. 919 (r. 38.3(3)), r. 264(b) amended by S.I. 1977 No. 1621, 1980 No. 1144 and 1985 No. 1600 (r. 38.3(4)), and r. 264(c)(part) (r. 38.3(5))

---

[1] R. 38.3(2)(b) amended by S.I. 1994 No. 2901 (clerical error).
[2] R.38.3(2A) inserted by S.S.I. 2000 No. 66, para. 2(4) (effective 7th April 2000).

38.3.1 *General note.* There are three general time-limits in the R.C.S. 1994 for reclaiming: (1)

reclaiming, without leave within 21 days, of interlocutors which dispose of the whole cause or the whole merits (r. 38.3(2) and (3)); (2) reclaiming, without leave within 14 days, of certain interlocutors which do not dispose of the whole cause (r. 38.3(4)); and (3) reclaiming, with leave within a specified period, of any other interlocutor (rr. 38.3(5) and 38.4).

The provision in r. 38.7 for allowing a reclaiming motion to proceed out of time should be noted.

The date from which the reclaiming days are calculated is the date of the issue of the interlocutor containing the decision in question. See also note 38.3.6.

Where an *ex tempore* judgment is given, that date will normally be the same as the day of the *ex tempore* judgment; it will not be the date of issue of any subsequent written opinion: P.N. No. 2 of 1990. Similarly, where a decision is given with reasons to be given later, the relevant date will normally be the date on which the decision was given as that will be the date of the interlocutor.

There is an exception in relation to undefended divorce actions dealt with wholly by affidavit procedure. The relevant date is the date on which the public notice of the decree appears in the rolls and not the date on which the interlocutor is signed: *Smith v. Smith* 1989 S.L.T. 668.

"subject to any other provision". In particular, r. 38.4 provides for reclaiming against certain **38.3.2** interlocutors only with leave obtained within a certain time. Statutes or other enactments may provide for different time-limits. Where leave is required, days during which a motion for leave to reclaim is continued until the Lord Ordinary who pronounced the decision concerned is available are not counted in calculating the reclaiming days: r. 38.5(4).

"subject-matter of the cause". This means that the whole merits of the cause (whether or not **38.3.3** evidence was led) and expenses have been decided, although expenses may not have been taxed, modified or decerned for: *Baird v. Barton* (1882) 9 R. 970. Such an interlocutor may be reclaimed against without leave within 21 days of being pronounced: r. 38.3(2)(a).

Whole merits of the cause whether or not expenses disposed of. This provision was introduced **38.3.4** by A.S. (R.C.S.A. No. 1) (Miscellaneous) 1990 [S.I. 1990 No. 705] following *McGuinness v. Bremner plc* 1988 S.L.T. 340. In that case it was argued that a difficulty was created by a Lord Ordinary pronouncing a decree on the merits before dealing with expenses, as leave was required to reclaim the former interlocutor and could only be reclaimed without leave when the interlocutor for expenses was pronounced thereby disposing of the whole subject-matter of the cause. Under r. 38.3(2)(b) an interlocutor disposing of the merits either by itself or along with a previous interlocutor may be reclaimed against without leave within 21 days of the interlocutor being pronounced whether or not expenses have been dealt with.

Where an interlocutor which reserves expenses or does not dispose of expenses is reclaimed, a party who seeks those expenses before disposal of the reclaiming motion must apply by motion to the Lord Ordinary within 14 days of the marking of the reclaiming motion: r.38.3(4A).

"without leave". The permission of the Lord Ordinary or vacation judge who made the **38.3.5** decision is not required.

"within 21 days". The date from which the period is calculated is not counted. Where the last **38.3.6** day falls on a Saturday or Sunday or a public holiday on which the Office of Court is closed, the next available day is allowed: r. 1.3(7). For office hours and public holidays, see note 3.1.2.

The 21 days are, therefore, counted from the day after the date of the interlocutor reclaimed against. Where the interlocutor to be reclaimed disposes of the merits, the start of the period is not postponed because questions of expenses are not dealt with: *Dingley v. Chief Constable, Strathclyde Police*, 6th December 1996 (IH), unreported (1996 G.W.D. 39–2250); and see Notice, 6th February 1997.

"award of provisional damages". See r. 43.12.   **38.3.7**

"adjusting issues for jury trial". See note 37.1.9.   **38.3.8**

"sist of execution or procedure". This applies not only to sist of execution and diligence but **38.3.9** also sist of process which is a stoppage of procedure, and "procedure" does not relate only to the former: *Thornton v. North Star Fishing Co. Ltd* 1983 S.L.T. 530.

"loosing, restricting or recalling an arrestment or recalling an inhibition". See notes 13.10.3 and **38.3.10** 13.10.4.

"authority to move an arrested vessel or cargo". See note 13.11.1.   **38.3.11**

"reference to the European Court". See Chap. 65.   **38.3.12**

"without leave, within 14 days". The date from which the period is calculated is not counted. **38.3.13**

Where the last day falls on a Saturday or Sunday or a public holiday on which the Office of Court is closed, the next available day is allowed: r. 1.3(7). For office hours and public holidays, see note 3.1.2.

38.3.14 *"with leave, within 14 days"*. The permission of the Lord Ordinary or vacation judge who made the decision must be sought before the interlocutor may be reclaimed against: r. 38.3(5). If the Lord Ordinary is not available another Lord Ordinary or the vacation judge may decide whether to grant leave: r. 38.5(2). In the event that such a judge continues a motion for leave until the Lord Ordinary who made the decision sought to be reclaimed is available, the days during which the motion is continued are not counted in calculating the reclaiming days: r. 38.5(4). The decision to grant or refuse leave to reclaim is final and not subject to review: r. 38.5(6).

R. 38.3(5) which provides for reclaiming against interlocutors other than those in r. 38.3(2), (3) or (4), or decrees in absence, is subject to r. 38.4 which provides for leave in certain cases.

The reclaiming motion must be enrolled (see r. 38.6) within 14 days; accordingly care must be taken to obtain leave within such period as to leave time to mark the reclaiming motion. The date from which the period is calculated is not counted. Where a motion for leave is continued until the Lord Ordinary who made the decision is available, the days during which the motion is continued are not counted in calculating the period of the reclaiming days: r. 38.5(4).

[NEXT TEXT PAGE IS C 275]

Where, *e.g.* it is sought to reclaim against a decision involving the exercise of a discretion it is essential to ask the Lord Ordinary for an opinion at the earliest opportunity; this may be when leave is sought: *Hodge v. British Coal Corporation* 1992 S.L.T. 484, 486K *per* L.P. Hope.

Interlocutors in respect of all incidental matters of procedure except interlocutors mentioned in r. 38.3(4) require leave to reclaim: *Robertson v. Robertson's Exr.* 1991 S.C. 21. The dispensing power in r. 2.1 will not be exercised to allow, without leave, a reclaiming motion which required leave to proceed as that would frustrate the object of the rule requiring leave: *Robertson*, above.

"decree in absence". A decree in absence may not be reclaimed against, but may be recalled by **38.3.15** the Lord Ordinary: r. 19.2.

An interlocutor on a motion to recall a decree in absence out of time, being in respect of an incidental matter of procedure, requires leave under r. 38.3(5): *Robertson v. Robertson's Exr.* 1991 S.C. 21.

Leave to reclaim etc. in certain cases

38.4.—(1) An interlocutor granting or refusing a motion for summary decree may be reclaimed against only with the leave of the Lord Ordinary within 14 days after the date on which the interlocutor was pronounced.

(2) In the application of section 103(3) of the Debtors (Scotland) Act 1987 (appeals on questions of law arising from making, variation or recall of time to pay directions)—

(a) leave to appeal shall be sought within 14 days after the date of the decision of the Lord Ordinary appealed against; and

(b) an appeal shall be made by motion to the Inner House within 14 days after the date on which leave was granted.

(3) An interlocutor pronounced under rule 43.24 (diet roll in optional procedure cases) which does not, either by itself or taken along with a previous interlocutor, dispose of the whole merits of the action whether or not the question of expenses is reserved or not disposed of, may be reclaimed against, only with the leave of the Lord Ordinary, within 14 days after the date on which the interlocutor was pronounced.

(4) An interlocutor, other than an interlocutor determining the application, pronounced under Chapter 58 (applications for judicial review) may be reclaimed against only with the leave of the Lord Ordinary within 14 days after the date on which the interlocutor was pronounced.

(5) The decision of the Lord Ordinary on a note of objection to the report of the Auditor under rule 42.4 may be reclaimed against only with the leave of the Lord Ordinary within 7 days after the date on which the decision was made.

(6) An interlocutor granting or refusing a motion under rule 47.10(1) (appointing action to be a commercial action) may be reclaimed against only with the leave of the commercial judge within 14 days after the date on which the interlocutor was pronounced.

[1] (7) An interlocutor pronounced on the Commercial Roll, other than an interlocutor which such disposal as is mentioned in rule 38.3(2), may be reclaimed against only with the leave of the commercial judge within 14 days after the date on which the interlocutor was pronounced.

Deriv. R.C.S. 1965, r. 89B(8) inserted by S.I. 1984 No. 499 (r. 38.4(1)), r. 88G(3) inserted by S.I. 1988 No. 2060 (r. 38.4(2)), r. 188P inserted by S.I. 1985 No. 227 (r. 38.4(3)), r. 260B(21) inserted by S.I. 1985 No. 500 (r. 38.4(4)), r. 349(7) substituted by S.I. 1983 No. 836 (r. 38.4(4))

R. 38.4(6) and (7) inserted by S.I. 1994 No. 2310 (effective 20th September 1994).

[1] R. 38.4(7) amended by S.I. 1998 No. 890 (effective 21st April 1998).

General note. This rule contains special provisions for reclaiming certain interlocutors with **38.4.1** leave.

38.4.2 *"summary decree"*. See Chap. 21. The purpose of this provision is to prevent further delay by a defender who has no defence to an action reclaiming against a summary decree.

Leave to reclaim must be sought whether the summary decree is a final or interlocutory decision. The suggestion by Lord Coulsfield in *Maus Feres S.A. v. Hoon*, 24th November 1995, 1996 G.W.D. 10.594, that leave to reclaim is not required where the summary decree is a final interlocutor, would defeat the purpose of the rule intended by the rule's clear and unambiguous terms. Paragraph (2) of r. 38.3 which provides for reclaiming a final interlocutor without leave, is, by virtue of para. (1) of that rule, subject to r. 38.4(1) (leave to reclaim summary decree). It is submitted that Lord Coulsfield's opinion is wrong on this point. It is understand that subsequently the Inner House directed that leave was required.

38.4.3 *"section 103(3) of the Debtors (Scotland) Act 1987"*. An appeal may be made on a question of law with leave from the Lord Ordinary against a decision by him on an application for a time to pay direction, or variation or recall of a time to pay direction, or recall or restriction of an arrestment in respect of the debt for which decree containing a time to pay direction has been granted: 1987 Act, s.103(3). Not only must leave be sought within 14 days but the reclaiming motion must be enrolled (see r. 38.6) within 14 days thereafter: r. 38.4(2).

38.4.4 *Interlocutor on the Diet Roll.* To assist with the speedy determination of actions of damages for personal injuries or death of a relative which are pursued under the optional procedure in Part V of Chap. 43, an interlocutor pronounced on the Diet Roll which does not dispose of the whole merits may only be reclaimed against with leave within 14 days of the interlocutor: r. 38.4(3).

38.4.5 *"judicial review"*. To assist with the speedy determination of applications for judicial review, an interlocutor other than one disposing of the application may only be reclaimed against with leave within 14 days of the interlocutor: r. 38.4(4).

38.4.6 *"note of objection to the report of the Auditor"*. While it is competent to reclaim against the decision of the Lord Ordinary with leave within seven days (r. 38.4(5)) on a matter of expenses, such motions are not encouraged unless a point of principle is involved: *Aird v. School Board of Tarbert* 1907 S.C. 22, 24 per Lord McLaren; *Ramm v. Lothian and Borders Fire Board* 1994 S.C. 226.

On the report of the Auditor on a taxation of an account of expenses on a judicial account (or, by virtue of r. 42.7(9), on a solicitor's own account), see r. 42.3.

38.4.7 *"with the leave"*. The permission of the Lord Ordinary who made the decision must be sought before the interlocutor may be reclaimed against. If the Lord Ordinary is not available another Lord Ordinary or the vacation judge may decide whether to grant leave: r. 38.5(2). In the event that such a judge continues a motion for leave until the Lord Ordinary who made the decision sought to be reclaimed is available, the days during which the motion is continued are not counted in calculating the reclaiming days: r. 38.5(4). The decision to grant or refuse leave to reclaim is final and not subject to review: r. 38.5(6).

Where, *e.g.* it is sought to reclaim against a decision involving the exercise of a discretion it is essential to ask the Lord Ordinary for an opinion at the earliest opportunity; and this may be when leave is sought: *Hodge v. British Coal Corporation* 1992 S.L.T. 484, 486K per L.P. Hope.

The dispensing power in r. 2.1 will not be exercised to allow, without leave, a reclaiming motion which required leave to proceed as that would frustrate the object of the rule requiring leave: *Robertson v. Robertson's Exr.* 1991 S.C. 21.

It is not a breach of art.6(1) of the ECHR for the judge at first instance, who determined the substantive issue, to be the judge who also decides whether leave to appeal should be granted: *Umair v Umair*, 2002 S.C.153 (Ex Div).

38.4.8 *"within 14 days", "within 7 days"*. The reclaiming motion must be enrolled (see r. 38.6) within the period specified; accordingly care must be taken to obtain leave within such period as to leave time to mark the reclaiming motion. Where a motion for leave is continued until the Lord Ordinary who made the decision is available, the days during which the motion is continued are not counted in calculating the period of the reclaiming days: r. 38.5(4).

The date from which the period is calculated is not counted.

38.4.9 *Leave to reclaim decisions of the commercial judge.* The commercial judge is appointed under r. 47.2. He hears a motion to transfer an ordinary action to be a commercial action on the Commercial Roll: r. 47.10(2); a decision to grant or refuse the motion may only be reclaimed against with his leave within 14 days of the interlocutor: r. 38.4(6). To assist with the principle of speedy determination of actions on the Commercial Roll (for which, see r. 47.8), an interlocutor, other than an interlocutor disposing of the whole subject-matter of the cause or the whole merits but not necessarily the expenses, pronounced in a commercial action may only be reclaimed against with leave of the commercial judge within 14 days of that interlocutor: r. 38.4(7).

On the meaning of "final interlocutor", see note 4.15.2(2).

Applications for leave to reclaim

38.5.—(1) An application for leave to reclaim against an interlocutor shall be made by motion.

(2) A motion under paragraph (1) shall be brought—
  (a) before the Lord Ordinary who pronounced the interlocutor;
  (b) where that Lord Ordinary is, for whatever reason, unavailable, before another Lord Ordinary; or
  (c) before the vacation judge.

(3) Where a motion under paragraph (1) is brought before a judge under paragraph (2)(b) or (c), that judge shall—
  (a) continue the motion until the Lord Ordinary who pronounced the interlocutor is available; or
  (b) where the matter is of such urgency that a continuation would not be appropriate, grant or refuse leave, as the case may be.

(4) Any period during which a motion under paragraph (1) is continued by virtue of an order under paragraph (3)(a) shall not be taken into account in calculating the reclaiming days under rule 38.3(5) (reclaiming days with leave) or rule 38.4 (leave to reclaim etc. in certain cases).

(5) In granting leave to reclaim, the Lord Ordinary may impose such conditions, if any, as he thinks fit.

(6) The decision of the Lord Ordinary or the vacation judge to grant or refuse leave to reclaim shall be final and not subject to review.

(7) Leave to reclaim against an interlocutor shall not excuse obedience to or implement of the interlocutor unless by order of the Lord Ordinary, the Inner House or the vacation judge.

Deriv. R.C.S. 1965, r. 264(c)(part) (r. 38.5(2), (6) and (7))

"motion". For motions, see Chap. 23.　　**38.5.1**

"conditions". Conditions may be imposed in respect, *e.g.* of expenses, caution or consignation.　　**38.5.2**

"final and not subject to review". The decision of the Lord Ordinary may not be reclaimed against.　　**38.5.3**
While r. 38.5(6) excludes from review the decision to grant or refuse leave to appeal against an interlocutor, the interlocutor in respect of which leave was sought may be submitted to review as a prior interlocutor under r. 38.1(1) unless it is expressly or by implication a final interlocutor: *McCue v. Scottish Daily Record* 1998 S.C. 811 (court of five judges). On what is expressly or by implication a final interlocutor, see note 38.81(1).

Leave to reclaim does not excuse obedience. The granting of leave to reclaim does not excuse obedience to or implement of an interlocutor unless the court otherwise orders: r. 38.5(7). Once the reclaiming motion is enrolled (see r. 38.6) the interlocutor need not be implemented unless it is an award of custody, access or aliment in respect of which the court has not excused obedience: see r. 38.8(5).　　**38.5.4**

Human rights. It is not a breach of art.6(1) of the ECHR for the judge at first instance, who determined the substantive issue, to be the judge who also decides whether leave to appeal should be granted: *Umair v. Umair*, 2002 S.C. 153 (Ex Div).　　**38.5.5**

Time-limit. There is no time-limit for leave to reclaim under this rule (there may be time-limits under other provisions—e.g. r. 38.4(1)). If leave to reclaim is sought outwith the reclaiming days from a Lord Ordinary from his decision, it is not incompetent to seek *leave* to reclaim (unless that is outwith a time-limit); it is for the Inner House to decide in due course under r. 38.7 whether to allow a reclaiming motion, enrolled out of time, to proceed out of time: *Bank of Scotland v. Kunkel-Griffin*, [2005] CSIH 18, 15th February 2005, unreported (First Div.).　　**38.5.6**

Method of reclaiming

38.6.—(1) A party who seeks to reclaim against an interlocutor shall mark a reclaiming motion by enrolling a motion for review in Form 38.6 before the expiry of the reclaiming days.

(2) On enrolling a motion for review under paragraph (1), the reclaimer shall lodge a reclaiming print which complies with rule 38.18.

Deriv. R.C.S. 1965, r. 262(a) and (b) (r. 38.6(1))

38.6.1 *General note*. When enrolling a reclaiming motion in a cause in which no opinion has yet been issued by the Lord Ordinary, his clerk should be informed that the motion has been enrolled and that an opinion is required: P.N. No. 7 of 1991, para. 1. Where a point likely to be at issue in the reclaiming motion is one which the Lord Ordinary has not dealt with in his opinion, this should be indicated in the motion sheet and his clerk informed that an opinion is required on the point: P.N. No. 7 of 1991, para. 2.

Where no opinion is available and a reclaiming motion has been enrolled, the clerk of one of the Divisions will write to the Lord Ordinary drawing his attention to the fact that no opinion has yet been lodged, that a reclaiming motion has been marked and that grounds of appeal have to be lodged by a certain date. If the opinion is not to be available by that date, the Lord Ordinary should inform his clerk who will advise the reclaimer who, in turn, may enrol for prorogation of the time to lodge grounds of appeal.

38.6.2 *"motion"*. For motions, see Chap. 23.

38.6.3 *"lodge a reclaiming print"*. The print is lodged as a step of process: r. 1.3(1) (definition of "step of process"). On lodging the principal reclaiming print when enrolling the motion for review under r. 38.6(2), six copies must be lodged for use of the court and six copies sent to every other party: r. 4.7(1).

On what must be contained in a reclaiming print, see r. 38.18.

38.6.4 *Fee*. A court fee is payable on enrolling a reclaiming motion. For fee, see Court of Session etc. Fees Order 1997, Table of Fees, Pt I, B, item 13, or C, item 10 [S.I. 1997 No. 688, as amended, pp. C 1201 *et seq*.]. Certain persons are exempt from payment of fees: see 1997 Fees Order, art.5, substituted by S.S.I. 2002 No.270. A fee exemption certificate must be lodged in process: see P.N. No.1 of 2002.

Where the reclaimer is legally represented, the fee may be debited under a credit scheme introduced on 1st April 1976 by P.N. No. 4 of 1976 to the account (if one is kept or permitted) of the agent by the court cashier, and an account will be rendered weekly by the court cashier's office to the agent for all court fees due that week for immediate settlement. Party litigants, and agents not operating the scheme, must pay (by cash, cheque or postal order) on each occasion a fee is due at the time of lodging at the counter at the appropriate department.

Leave to reclaim out of time

38.7.—(1) In a case of mistake or inadvertence, the Inner House may, on an application to it, allow a motion for review to be received outwith the reclaiming days and to proceed out of time on such conditions as to expenses or otherwise as the court thinks fit.

(2) An application under paragraph (1) shall be made by motion included in the motion for review made under rule 38.6(1).

Deriv. R.C.S. 1965, r. 264(d)

38.7.1 *General note*. The reclaiming print will have to be lodged when enrolling the motion for review under this rule: r. 38.6. On lodging the principal reclaiming print under r. 38.6(2), six copies must be lodged for use of the court and six copies sent to every other party: r. 4.7(1).

The dispensing power in r. 38.7 will not be exercised so as to have the effect of avoiding the necessity for leave to appeal if this would otherwise be required: see *Robertson v. Robertson's Exr* 1991 S.C. 21.

38.7.2 *"mistake or inadvertence"*. Similar considerations to those arising in the application of the dispensing power in r. 2.1 occur in applying this rule.

38.7.3 *"motion"*. For motions, see Chap. 23.

[1] *Required application for early disposal of certain reclaiming motions*

38.7A. Where a party reclaims against an interlocutor mentioned in paragraph (4) or (5) of rule 38.3, he shall, under rule 38.13(1)(a), seek early disposal of the reclaiming motion.

[1] R. 38.7A inserted by S.I. 1997 No. 2692 (effective 1st December 1997).

General note. The reasons for positioning this rule here are not all clear since the rule is **38.7A.1** unconnected with the rules surrounding it and is separated from the rule with which it is connected (r. 38.13).

The rule is inserted by A.S. (R.C.S.A. No. 8) (Early Disposal of Reclaiming Motions and Appeals) 1997 [S.I. 1997 No. 2692].

Required applications for early disposal. With respect to reclaiming motions marked on or **38.7A.2** after 1st December 1997, the reclaimer must enrol for early disposal under r. 38.13(1) where he is reclaiming against an interlocutor to which r. 38.3(4) or (5) applies.

Paragraph (4) of r. 38.3 lists those interlocutors which may be reclaimed against without cause within 14 days after the date on which the interlocutor was pronounced. Paragraph (5) of r. 38.3 provides for these interlocutors which may be reclaimed against only with leave within 14 days. In substance, these interlocutors are those not disposing of the cause.

If an appendix is required, it may be necessary to apply to the court by motion to order that paras (1) to (4) shall not apply or shall be modified: r. 38.19(5).

Effect of reclaiming

38.8.—[1](1) Subject to paragraph (2), a reclaiming motion shall have the effect of submitting to the review of the Inner House all previous interlocutors of the Lord Ordinary or any interlocutor of the Lord Ordinary in a motion under rule 38.3(2A), not only at the instance of the party reclaiming, but also at the instance of any other party who appeared in the cause, and without the necessity of any counter-reclaiming motion.

(2) Where an interlocutor, either by itself or taken along with a previous interlocutor, has disposed of the whole merits of the cause, a reclaiming motion against a subsequent interlocutor dealing with expenses shall have the effect of submitting to review only that interlocutor and any other interlocutor in so far as it deals with expenses.

(3) After a reclaiming motion has been enrolled, the reclaimer shall not be at liberty to withdraw it without the consent of the other parties who have appeared in the cause; and if he does not insist on the reclaiming motion, any other party may do so in the same way as if the motion had been enrolled at his instance.

(4) An unopposed motion by a party to refuse a reclaiming motion shall be treated as if all parties consented to it.

(5) Where an interlocutor contains an award of custody, access or aliment, the marking of a reclaiming motion shall not excuse obedience to or implement of the award of custody, access or aliment, as the case may be, unless by order of the court.

Deriv. R.C.S. 1965, r. 262(c) (r. 38.8(1) and (3)), r. 264(a)(part) substituted by S.I. 1990 No. 705 (r. 38.8(5))

[1]R.38.8(1) as amended by S.S.I. 2000 No. 66, para. 2(5) (effective 7th April 2000).

General note. As well as submitting to review the interlocutor reclaimed against, all previous **38.8.1** interlocutors are submitted to review at the instance of either party (r. 38.8(1)) subject to two exceptions.

(1) A prior interlocutor which is expressly or by implication a final interlocutor is not submitted to review. A prior interlocutor expressly final is one not reclaimed against within the time prescribed under the R.C.S. 1994 or another enactment: *Copeland v. Lord Wimborne* 1912 S.C. 355; *Cumptsie v. Waterston* 1933 S.C. 1. A prior interlocutor which is final by implication is one which has been acted on as the basis of subsequent proceedings: *Macaskill v. Nicol* 1943 S.C. 17, 20 *per* L.J.-C. Cooper; see also *Spencer v. Macmillan* 1957 S.L.T.(Notes) 32, *Campbell v. James Walker Insulation Ltd* 1988 S.L.T. 263, *Gillon v. Gillon* 1994 S.C. 162. It had been thought that a prior interlocutor was also expressly final where leave to reclaim is required and has been refused in respect of it: *Marsh v. Baxendale* 1994 S.C. 157. But in *McCue v. Scottish Daily Record* 1998 S.C. 811 a court of five judges held that this was not so. A distinction has to be drawn between, on the one hand, a rule which excludes subsequent review of an interlocutor

if not reclaimed against within a specified time (*e.g.* final if not reclaimed against within X days: *Copeland*, above; *Cumptsie*, above) and, on the other hand, one which merely delimits the period within which an interlocutor may be reclaimed. The former is excluded from review by r. 38.1(1) but the latter is not (unless excluded by actings). Thus, while r. 38.5(6) excludes from review the interlocutor granting or refusing leave to appeal against an interlocutor, the interlocutor in respect of which leave was sought may be submitted to review as a prior interlocutor under r. 38.1(1). The decisions in *Marsh*, above, and *Mowbray v. D.C. Thomson Ltd* 1996 S.C. 197 (appeal without the necessary leave from the sheriff court held expressly final and incapable of review as a prior interlocutor under s. 29 of the Sheriff Courts (Scotland) Act 1907) are overruled.

In *McCue*, above, the court went on to say that actings after an interlocutor which may exclude review of that interlocutor was not a matter of competency but because the court considers that it should not exercise the power of review in respect of it.

Also in *McCue*, above, it was stated that, where a party sought to reclaim against an interlocutor pronounced on his own motion in order to submit to review a prior interlocutor (as in *McGuinness v. Bremner plc* 1988 S.L.T. 340), this was not a question of competency but that the court would not normally countenance it. Accordingly, there may be circumstances in which the court would permit it.

It should be noted that an interlocutor pronounced by the Lord Ordinary is final in the Outer House subject to the provisions for review (C.S.A. 1988, s. 18); an exception being an interlocutor as to the mode of proof which is superseded as a result of subsequent amendments (*Bendex v. James Donaldson & Sons Ltd* 1990 S.C. 259).

(2) Where an interlocutor, either by itself or taken with another has disposed of the merits, a reclaiming motion against a subsequent interlocutor dealing with expenses only submits for review the interlocutor dealing with expenses and any other interlocutor in so far as it deals with expenses: r. 38.8(2). To reclaim against the previous interlocutors on the merits the interlocutor dealing with the merits must be reclaimed timeously.

38.8.2 *Effect of reclaiming on interlocutor reclaimed against.* When an interlocutor is reclaimed, the effect of that appeal, from the time the reclaiming motion is marked, is to sist all execution on the decree until the reclaiming motion has been determined: *Macleay v. Macdonald* 1928 S.C. 776, 782, *per* Lord Anderson. The exception is that awards of custody, access or aliment are not affected by the marking of a reclaiming motion and must be complied with unless the court otherwise orders: r. 38.8(5). The court will be the court which made the order, or the vacation judge, where the application is made before (or at the time) the reclaiming motion is marked; once the reclaiming motion has been marked, the application must be made to the Inner House.

Execution before the marking of the appeal will not be affected unless and until the interlocutor is successfully reclaimed against or some interim order is sought from the court such as will suspend or sist the execution.

The marking of a reclaiming motion precludes extract of the interlocutors subject to review: see *Fowler v. Fowler (No. 2)* 1981 S.L.T.(Notes) 78.

38.8.3 *Interlocutory matters while reclaiming motion pending.* As a general rule, when an interlocutor has been reclaimed, nothing can be done in the Outer House in the cause pending in the Inner House. There are two unreported cases which support this statement. In *Shell UK Exploration and Production Ltd v. Innes*, 31st August 1995 (First Div.), unreported, it was held that a cause cannot be in both Houses of the Court at the same time. The crucial date for deciding when the case is in the Inner House is the date of marking of the reclaiming motion (under r. 38.6): *Bonnier Media Ltd v. Smith*, 23rd August 2002, unreported (First Div.). In both cases, after a reclaiming motion had been marked against refusal to recall of interdict a minute for breach of interdict was enrolled. In fact it may be possible for the Lord Ordinary to deal with certain interlocutory matters notwithstanding the cause is in the Inner House; but he would not be able to do so where the interlocutory matter would affect, (a) the effect of an interlocutor previous to that which has been reclaimed (because under r. 38.8(1) all previous interlocutors are submitted for review), or (b) the finality of the interlocutor reclaimed against (because s. 18 of the C.S.A. 1988 provides that every interlocutor is final in the Outer House—*i.e.* the Lord Ordinary cannot reconsider his own decisions except where recall is permitted by law or rule). An example might be a motion for commission and diligence to recover documents or for evidence. A specific exception is now in r. 38.3(2A) which allows a Lord Ordinary to deal with a question of Outer House expenses of a case reclaimed to the Inner House. The creation of this exception lends support to the truth of the statement in the first sentence.

Effect of extracted interlocutor

38.9. Review by the Inner House of an interlocutor shall not be prevented by reason only that extract has been issued before the expiry of the reclaiming days.

Reclaiming against decree by default (r. 38.11)   **C 280/1**

Deriv. R.C.S. 1965, r. 63B inserted by S.I. 1986 No. 1937

"extract". On extracts, see Chap. 7.   **38.9.1**

Land Tenure Reform (Scotland) Act 1974. R. 38.9 is subject to s. 9(7) of the Land Tenure **38.9.2**
Reform (Scotland) Act 1974 which provides that a decree in an action of removing for breach of
condition of a long lease is, in a question with third parties who have acted onerously and in
good faith, to be final when the extract is recorded in the Register of Sasines.

Superseding extract. Where, *e.g.*, the court grants decree by default under r. 20.1, there is no **38.9.3**
need to supersede extract if the court wishes to give the party in default time to reclaim because,
under r. 38.9, the fact that an extract has been issued does not of itself preclude review: *cf.*
Munro & Miller (Pakistan) Ltd v. Wynern Structures Ltd 1996 S.L.T. 135 where the court
superseded extract, though this was commented on adversely by the First Division at 1997 S.C.
1, 3C.
    See also note 7.1.6.

Appeals treated as reclaiming motions
38.10. In respect of the following appeals, the rules in this Chapter shall
apply to those appeals as they apply to reclaiming:—
   (a) an appeal from a decision of the Lord Ordinary under section 6 of,
       and Article 37 or 41 of the convention in Schedule 1 or 3C to, the
       Civil Jurisdiction and Judgments Act 1982 (appeals in relation to
       decisions on enforcement); and
   (b) an appeal from a decision of the Lord Ordinary under section 103(3)
       of the Debtors (Scotland) Act 1987 (appeals on questions of law).

General note. This is a new rule to take account of the references in the enactments specified in **38.10.1**
the rule to "appeal".

C.J.J.A. 1982, Sched. 1 or 3C, Art. 37 or 41. A decision authorising enforcement of a **38.10.2**
judgment given in another Contracting State to the 1968 (Brussels) Convention or the Lugano
Convention may be appealed against to the Inner House on a point of law by the party against
whom enforcement was sought: C.J.J.A. 1982, s. 6 and Sched. 1 or 3C, Arts 36 and 37. A
decision refusing enforcement of such a judgment may be appealed against to the Inner House
on a point of law by the applicant for enforcement: C.J.J.A. 1982, s. 6 and Sched. 1 or 3C, Arts
40 and 41. These provisions are extended to authentic instruments and court settlements:
C.J.J.A. 1982, Sched. 1 or 3C, Art. 50.
    Art. 37 of the 1968 Brussels Convention in Sched. 1 to the C.J.J.A. 1982, limiting appeals
against decisions authorising enforcement of foreign judgments, has to be construed strictly and
a court seized of an appeal does not have power to impose or re-impose a sist: *Société
D'Informatique Service Réalisation Organisation (SISRO) v. Ampersand Software BV, The
Times,* 25th September 1995.

"section 103(3) of the Debtors (Scotland) Act 1987". An appeal may be made on a question **38.10.3**
of law with leave from the Lord Ordinary against a decision by him on an application for a time
to pay direction, or variation or recall of a time to pay direction, or recall or restriction of an
arrestment in respect of the debt for which decree containing a time to pay direction has been
granted: 1987 Act, s. 103(3). Not only must leave be sought within 14 days but the reclaiming
motion must be enrolled (see r. 38.6) within 14 days thereafter: r. 38.4(2).

Reclaiming against decree by default
38.11.—(1) Where decree by default has been granted against a party in
respect of his failure to lodge a step of process or other document, a motion
for review by that party of the interlocutor granting such decree shall be
refused unless the document is lodged on or before the date on which the
motion is enrolled.
    [1] (2) A decree by default may, if reclaimed against, be recalled on such
conditions, if any, as to expenses or otherwise as the court thinks fit.

Deriv. R.C.S. 1965, r. 264(e)

---

[1] R. 38.11(2) amended by S.I. 1994 No. 2901 (minor correction).

38.11.1 *"decree by default".* See Chap. 20.

38.11.2 *Recall of decree by default.* Whether a decree by default should be recalled under r. 38.11(2) is a matter for the discretion of the court, in the exercise of which the guiding principle is what would do justice between the parties in the particular circumstances of the case: *Hyslop v. Flaherty*, 1933 S.C. 588. Even where carelessness on the part of the defender has delayed the course of the procedure of the action, the court still may be prepared to consider whether the decree should be recalled, provided that the case as pleaded discloses a substantial defence: *McKelvie v. Scottish Steel Scaffolding Co. Ltd*, 1938 S.C.278.

Reclaiming against interlocutor adjusting issues

38.12. A party who reclaims against an interlocutor adjusting issues for jury trial shall, on enrolling the motion for review—

(a) lodge in process the issue or counter-issue proposed by him showing the amendment to the issues, as adjusted, sought to be made; and

(b) send a copy of the issue or counter-issue, as the case may be, to every other party.

Deriv. R.C.S. 1965, r. 117

38.12.1 *General note.* Six copies of the issue will have to be lodged as well as six copies of the print of the pleadings: r. 4.7(1). They are lodged as steps of process: r. 1.3(1) (definition of "step of process").

On issues, see notes 37.1.5, 37.1.8 and 37.1.9.

Early disposal of reclaiming motion

[1] **38.13.**—(1) A party who seeks early disposal of a reclaiming motion (in the case of the reclaimer, whether or not by virtue of rule 38.7A) shall—

(a) where he is the reclaimer, include in his motion under rule 38.6(1) (method of reclaiming) either the words "and for early disposal on the Summar Roll" or the words "and for early disposal in the Single Bills"; or

(b) where he is the respondent—

(i) within the period allowed for opposing the motion, endorse on the motion of the reclaimer made under rule 38.6(1), or send by post or facsimile transmission a notice of opposition in Form 23.4 including the words "The respondent (*name*) seeks early disposal."; or

(ii) add, to his opposition under rule 38.14(1) (objections to competency of reclaiming motion), the words "and for early disposal".

(2) The entry in the rolls in respect of the motion for early disposal shall be starred; and the parties shall, at the hearing of that motion, provide the Inner House with an assessment of the likely duration of the hearing to determine the reclaiming motion.

(3) At the hearing of the motion for early disposal, the Inner House may—

(a) appoint the cause to the Summar Roll for hearing; or

(b) direct that the cause be heard in the Single Bills,

and may make such order as to the lodging of grounds of appeal as it thinks fit.

(4) At any hearing of the reclaiming motion in the Single Bills, the Inner House may determine the motion or make such other order as it thinks fit.

---

[1] R. 38.13(1) amended, and paras (2) to (4) substituted, by S.I. 1997 No. 2692 (effective 1st December 1997).

38.13.1 *General note.* The original rule was proposed by the Rules Review Group to provide a formal means for seeking early disposal of urgent reclaiming motions.

Rule 38.13 has been amended by A.S. (R.C.S.A. No. 8) (Early Disposal of Reclaiming

Motions and Appeals) 1997 [S.I. 1997 No. 2692] for reclaiming motions marked on or after 1st December 1997. Reclaiming motions marked before that date are governed by P.N. No. 1 of 1995.

The reclaimer, on enrolling for early disposal, must specify whether he seeks early disposal on the Single Bills or on the Summar Roll: r. 38.13(1). It does not follow that because early disposal is sought in the Single Bills that the court will not determine that the reclaiming motion should be disposed of on the Summar Roll: see r. 38.13(3)(a). On Single Bills (and reclaiming motions appropriate for it), see note 38.17.4; on the Summar Roll, see note 38.17.3.

Grounds of appeal do not have to be lodged for the motion seeking early disposal. At the hearing of the motion, the court will decide when and if grounds of appeal should be lodged: r. 38.13(3).

Under r. 38.7A, early disposal must be sought in reclaiming motions against certain interlocutors.

A motion for early disposal will be starred requiring appearance of counsel or other person having a right of audience; and the court will wish to know parties' estimate of the duration of the hearing: r. 38.13(2).

"motion". For motions, see Chap. 23.   **38.13.2**

Lodging grounds of appeal. The grounds of appeal are lodged as a step of process (r. 1.3(1)   **38.13.3** (definition of "step of process")), intimated, and a copy sent, to every other party (r. 4.6).

Objections to competency of reclaiming motion

38.14.—(1) After a reclaiming motion has been marked by a reclaimer, any other party may oppose the motion on the ground that the reclaiming motion is incompetent.

(2) Where a reclaiming motion has been opposed under paragraph (1), the cause shall be put out for hearing in the Single Bills before a Division of the Inner House.

(3) At the hearing in the Single Bills arranged under paragraph (2), the Inner House may—

(a) dispose of the objection to competency and, where it repels the objection, order grounds of appeal to be lodged;

(b) appoint the cause to the Summar Roll for a hearing on the objection;

(c) reserve the objection until grounds of appeal have been lodged and order such grounds to be lodged;

(d) reserve the objection for hearing with the merits and order grounds of appeal to be lodged.

(4) Where the Deputy Principal Clerk considers that a reclaiming motion may be incompetent, whether or not any other party has opposed the reclaiming motion under paragraph (1), he may, before the cause is brought before the Inner House, refer it to a single judge in accordance with paragraph (5).

(5) Any referral by the Deputy Principal Clerk under paragraph (4) shall be made to a judge nominated for that purpose by the Lord President.

(6) Where a referral is made under paragraph (4), the judge may—

(a) order any party to make representations to him in respect of the competency of the reclaiming motion;

(b) refuse the reclaiming motion on the ground that it is incompetent;

(c) direct that the reclaiming motion is to proceed as if the referral had not been made;

(d) make such order as to expenses or otherwise as he thinks fit.

(7) Any decision of a judge in respect of a reclaiming motion referred to him under paragraph (4) shall be final and not subject to review.

Deriv. R.C.S. 1965, r. 263(b) (r. 38.14(1) to (3))

"oppose the motion". See r. 23.4.   **38.14.1**

"incompetency". A reclaiming motion may be opposed on being enrolled (on which, see r.   **38.14.2** 38.6) on the ground that it is incompetent. Opposition to the motion will be made on Form 23.4.

A reclaiming motion may be incompetent, *e.g.* because the reclaiming days have expired before the reclaiming motion was enrolled, because leave was not sought or because the interlocutor may not be reclaimed against. It had been thought that it is incompetent to reclaim against an interlocutor because it was pronounced on the motion of the party seeking to reclaim (*Watson v. Russell* (1894) 21 R. 433; *McGuinness v. Bremner plc* 1988 S.L.T. 340). But in *McCue v. Scottish Daily Record*, 5th June 1998, unreported (1998 G.W.D. 23–1153), a court of five judges indicated that, where a party sought to reclaim against an interlocutor pronounced on his own motion in order to submit to review a prior interlocutor (as in *McGuinness v. Bremner plc* 1988 S.L.T. 340), this was not a question of competency but that the court would not normally countenance it. Accordingly, there may be circumstances in which the court would permit it.

The court may take the objection itself and will not entertain an incompetent appeal even if objection is waived by the respondent: *Governors of Strichen Endowments v. Diverall* (1891) 19 R. 79.

Although a respondent has not marked a reclaiming motion as incompetent, it is still open to him to raise the matter of competency at the reclaiming motion: see *A.B. and C.D., Petrs* 1992 S.L.T. 1064.

38.14.3   *Referral of reclaiming motion to single judge.* This is a new provision introduced to prevent the time of the Inner House being wasted on a reclaiming motion (particulary by party litigants) which is incompetent.

The decision of the judge is final and not subject to review: r. 38.14(7).

Procedure where no objection to competency

38.15.—(1) Subject to paragraph (2), where a reclaiming motion is not opposed on the ground of competency, the Inner House shall, without hearing parties, order grounds of appeal to be lodged.

(2) This rule shall not apply where an application is made under rule 38.13(1) (early disposal of reclaiming motion).

Deriv. R.C.S. 1965, r. 263(a)

38.15.1   *"grounds of appeal".* See r. 38.16.

Grounds of appeal in reclaiming motions

38.16.—(1) An order for grounds of appeal shall require—

(a) the reclaimer, and

(b) any respondent seeking to bring an interlocutor under review or to challenge the grounds on which the Lord Ordinary has pronounced the interlocutor under review,

to lodge grounds of appeal in process within 28 days after the date of the interlocutor making the order.

(2) Grounds of appeal shall consist of brief specific numbered propositions stating the grounds on which it is proposed to submit that the reclaiming motion should be allowed or as the case may be.

(3) On lodging grounds of appeal, the party lodging them shall—

(a) lodge three copies of them in process; and

(b) send a copy of them to every other party.

(4) A party who has lodged grounds of appeal may at any time apply for leave to amend his grounds of appeal on cause shown.

[1] (5) Where a reclaimer fails to lodge grounds of appeal in accordance with paragraph (2) within the period prescribed under paragraph (1), the Inner House may, at its own instance or on the motion of a respondent, refuse the reclaiming motion with or without hearing parties as the court thinks fit.

Deriv. R.C.S. 1965, r. 294B(2) inserted by S.I. 1987 No. 1206 and amended by S.I. 1991 No. 1157 (r. 38.16(1)), r. 294B(3) inserted by S.I. 1987 No. 1206 (r. 38.16(2)), r. 294B(5)(a) inserted by S.I. 1987 No. 1206 (r. 38.16(3)), r. 294B(6) inserted by S.I. 1987 No. 1206 (r. 38.16(4)), r. 294B(4) inserted by S.I. 1987 No. 1206 (r. 38.16(5))

---

[1] R. 38.16(5) amended by S.I. 1994 No. 2901 (effective 5th December 1994).

General note. On lodging grounds of appeal a motion should be enroled for a hearing of the **38.16.1** reclaiming motion (r. 38.17(1)), unless early disposal was sought under r. 38.13 in which case the hearing will have been ordered at the motion for early disposal.

"grounds of appeal". These are brief specific numbered propositions (see r. 38.16(2)) for which **38.16.2** the reclaimer contends which, if correct, should result in the reclaiming motion being granted. The authorities on which the propositions are based should be mentioned. It is not necessary to detail all the propositions or to list every authority which will be referred to at the hearing of the reclaiming motion. Where grounds of appeal do not comply with the requirement of r. 38.16(2) the reclaiming motion may be refused: r. 38.16(5); and see note 38.16.6.

The purpose of grounds of appeal is to give notice to the parties and to the court of the grounds on which the reclaiming motion is to be argued: *Eurocopy Rentals Ltd v. Tayside Health Board* 1996 S.C. 410, 413G *per* L.P. Hope. The purpose of grounds of appeal is to give notice to the parties and to the court of the grounds on which the appeal is to be argued: *Eurocopy Rentals Ltd v. Tayside Health Board*, 1996 S.C. 410, 413 *per* L.P. Hope.

A statement that the Lord Ordinary "erred in fact and law" is insufficient as a ground of appeal to afford a proper notice of what is to be contended: *Clark v. Chief Constable, Lothian and Borders Police* 19th February 1993, unreported on this point, 1993 G.W.D. 11–759; see also *McAdam v. Shell U.K. Ltd* 1991 S.C. 360, 364 *per* L.P. Hope and *City of Glasgow D.C. v. Secretary of State for Scotland (No. 1)* 1993 S.L.T. 198, 204E–G *per* Lord Caplan.

Grounds of appeal do not have to be signed.

Grounds of appeal are lodged as a step of process: see note 38.16.3.

Cross-grounds of appeal may be lodged within the 28 day period notwithstanding the cause has been appointed to the Summar Roll.

It should be noted that the Lord Ordinary has a duty to record in his opinion all the arguments and submissions made to him and his views upon them: *Morrow v. Enterprise Sheet Metal Works (Aberdeen) Ltd* 1986 S.C. 96, 101; *Hogan v. Highland R.C.* 1995 S.C. 1. 2C *per* L.J.-C. Ross.

"lodge grounds of appeal". Grounds of appeal are lodged as a step of process (r. 1.3(1) **38.16.3** (definition of "step of process")). On lodging the principal, three copies must be lodged: r. 38.16(3)(a). They may be lodged in person at the public counter of the appropriate department or sent by post (P.N. No. 4 of 1994, paras. 1 and 8).

Written intimation of the lodging of grounds of appeal must be given, as well as one copy sent, to every other party: rr. 4.6(1) and 38.16(3).

"within 28 days". The period, which will be specified in an interlocutor, may be prorogated: r. **38.16.4** 4.9(2). This may be necessary, *e.g.* because the Lord Ordinary's opinion is not yet available: see, *e.g. McAdam v. Shell U.K. Ltd* 1991 S.C. 360, 363 *per* L.P. Hope.

The date from which the period is calculated is not counted. Where the last day falls on a Saturday or Sunday or a public holiday on which the Office of Court is closed, the next available day is allowed: r. 1.3(7). For office hours and public holidays, see note 3.1.2.

"leave to amend grounds of appeal". This may be done to include additional grounds or to **38.16.5** alter grounds already stated. It is done by motion or a minute of amendment (and a motion). Appearance will be required for such a motion. Cause must be shown for leave to be granted: r. 38.16(4).

On amending grounds of appeal at the hearing of the reclaiming motion, see *McInnes v. Lawrence* 1996 S.C.L.R. 169, where leave was refused on a motion at the start of an appeal because no special cause had been shown and proper notice had not been given so as to get a proper allocation of court time. See also *Eurocopy Rentals Ltd v. Tayside Health Board* 1996 S.C. 410 (motion to amend to add new grounds refused). The time for a reclaimer considering whether the grounds of appeal are adequate is before the By Order hearing under r. 6.3(9): *Noble Organisation Ltd v. Kilmarnock and Loudoun D.C.* 1993 S.L.T. 759, 761I; *Eurocopy*, above, at p. 1324J.

"fails to lodge grounds of appeal in accordance with paragraph (2)". A respondent may apply **38.16.6** by motion to have a reclaiming motion refused (a) because there are no grounds of appeal lodged or (b) because the grounds lodged do not comply with the requirement of paragraph (2) (*i.e.* they are not brief specific numbered propositions stating the grounds on which it is

proposed to submit that the reclaiming motion should be allowed or they do not disclose such a ground). The court may at its own instance refuse a reclaiming motion on the same grounds.

For an example of an appeal being refused because the grounds of appeal were inadequate under the equivalent r. 40.14(5), see *Ferguson v. Whitbread and Co. plc* 1996 S.L.T. 659.

38.16.7   *Circumstances in which Inner House will interfere with decision of the Lord Ordinary.*

(1) *Facts.* Review of facts will depend on examination and assessment of the evidence and rules of evidence, and credibility, reliability, weight and sufficiency. In relation to credibility, the Inner House will be reluctant to reverse findings of credibility for the reason that it is denied the advantage of the judge at first instance who saw and heard the witnesses. The court must be persuaded, and come to the clear conclusion, that the judge who had that advantage was plainly wrong: *Clarke v. Edinburgh and District Tramways Co.* 1919 S.C.(H.L.) 35, 37, *per* Lord Shaw of Dunfermline. Where an appellate court is disposed to come to a different conclusion, it should not do so unless it is satisfied that any advantage enjoyed by the judge at first instance could not be sufficient to explain or justify his conclusion; where the reasons given by that judge are not satisfactory or it unmistakenly so appears from the evidence, the appellate court may be satisfied he has not taken proper advantage of seeing and hearing the witnesses and the matter will be at large for the appellate court: *Thomas v. Thomas* 1947 S.C.(H.L) 45, 54, *per* Lord Thankerton. Where a decision on fact is based on credibility, the judge at first instance should leave no doubt as to the grounds of his decision: *Duncan v. Watson* 1940 S.C. 221, 225, *per* L.P. Normand. The appellate court will more readily treat the matter as at large where clear and satisfactory reasons are not given: *Morrison v. J. Kelly & Sons Ltd* 1970 S.C. 65. In *Hamilton v. Allied Domecq plc*, 2006 S.C. 221, 242, para. [84], Lord Hamilton said that the constraints on an appeal court, in relation to matters of fact, did not absolve the appeal court from reconsidering the evidence and determining whether critical findings of fact were justified.

(2) *Discretion.* A discretion will not be lightly interfered with. It is not enough that the appellate court would have exercised the discretion differently. The tests have been variously described, depending to some extent on the area of law concerned. The tests may be stated as follows: (a) has there been a failure to exercise the discretion at all (*Orr Pollock & Co. (Printers) Ltd v. Mulholland* 1983 S.L.T. 558), (b) has the judge misdirected himself in law (*Forsyth v. A. F. Stoddard & Co. Ltd* 1985 S.L.T. 51), (c) has the judge misunderstood, misused or failed to balance the evidence (*Skiponian Ltd v. Barratt Developments (Scotland) Ltd* 1983 S.L.T. 313, 314), (d) has the judge taken into account an irrelevant factor (*Thomson v. Glasgow Corporation* 1962 S.C.(H.L.) 36, 66, *per* Lord Reid), (e) has the judge failed to take into account a relevant factor (*Thomson, above*), (f) is the decision unreasonable (*Thomson, above*), (g) is the decision unjudicial (*Thomson, above*). See also *Brittan v. Central R.C.* 1986 S.L.T. 407.

38.16.8   *Argument not presented to Lord Ordinary.* There is no general rule, unlike in the House of Lords, that the Inner House will not entertain an argument not advanced before the Lord Ordinary; although it may be unfortunate that the argument was not so advanced (*Varney (Scotland) Ltd v. Lanark Town Council* 1974 S.C. 245, 249, *per* L.J.-C. Wheatley.) It is always open to the court to consider competency which strikes at the root of the proceedings: *Wolfson v. Glasgow District Licensing Board* 1980 S.C. 136, 128, *per* L.J.-C. Wheatley.

There are exceptions. A fresh argument which cannot be advanced without amendment to the pleadings will generally not be heard because the court will usually wish the judge at first instance to consider the amended pleadings (if allowed: on which see note 38.21.1) and have the benefit of his opinion: see *e.g. Wallace v. Scottish Special Housing Association* 1981 S.L.T. (Notes) 60 and r. 38.21. A new argument cannot be advanced other than on evidence led unless the court has allowed that further evidence or is willing to consider a change of circumstances since the hearing before the Lord Ordinary.

Orders for hearing

38.17.—(1) Subject to rule 38.13 (early disposal of reclaiming motion), on lodging grounds of appeal—

    (a) the reclaimer who has lodged grounds of appeal, or

    (b) where the reclaimer no longer insists in his reclaiming motion, a respondent who has lodged grounds of appeal,

shall apply by motion to the Inner House for an order for hearing.

    (2) On a motion under paragraph (1), the Inner House may—

    (a) appoint the cause to the Summar Roll for hearing; or

    (b) direct that the cause be heard in the Single Bills.

    (3) In a cause in which an objection to competency has been reserved under rule 38.14(3)(c), the motion under paragraph (1) of this rule shall require the attendance of counsel or other person having a right of audience, and, at the hearing of that motion in the Single Bills, the Inner House may—

  (a) dispose of the objection, and, where it repels the objection, either dispose of the merits in the Single Bills or appoint the cause to the Summar Roll for hearing;

  (b) appoint the cause to the Summar Roll for hearing on the objection; or

  (c) reserve the objection for hearing with the merits and appoint the cause to the Summar Roll for hearing.

Deriv. R.C.S. 1965, r. 294B(5)(b) inserted by S.I. 1987 No. 1206 (r. 38.17(1))

"Subject to rule 38.13". Where early disposal has been sought the grounds of appeal will have **38.17.1** been lodged and an order for an early or other hearing already made.

"motion". For motions, see Chap. 23. Appearance is not required unless an objection to **38.17.2** competency (see r. 38.14) has been reserved (r. 38.17(3)) or a motion under r. 2.1 is made to relieve a party from the consequences of a failure to comply with a rule.

Summar Roll. As a general rule, reclaiming motions are appointed to and heard on the **38.17.3** Summar Roll. Originally the Summar Roll was the roll for dealing with causes summarily and the Short Roll was for more complicated causes; the latter, however, has fallen into desuetude. Once appointed to the Summar Roll a diet is fixed by the Keeper of the Rolls in accordance with r. 6.3 after parties have sent him Form 6.3 duly completed.

Single Bills. The Single Bills is the motion roll of the Inner House. **38.17.4**
  As a general rule reclaiming motions are not heard in the Single Bills. Reclaiming motions dealt with on the Single Bills might include an urgent reclaiming motion, an appeal clearly incompetent, a reclaiming motion in respect of recall of arrestment or inhibition or interlocutory decisions where, *e.g.* an imminent proof might be saved. Determination of a reclaiming motion in the Single Bills may be appropriate for a short, sharp point.

Hearings before Inner House. A reclaiming motion will be heard by a Division of the Inner **38.17.5** House. A Division consists of four judges, but three are a quorum: C.S.A. 1988, s. 2(2) and (4). Because of pressure of criminal business in the High Court of Justiciary and other civil business it is unusual nowadays for a Division to sit with more than three judges. The Lord President may direct three judges to sit as an Extra Division: C.S.A. 1988, s. 2(3).
  Where a Division before whom a cause is pending (a) considers the cause to be one of difficulty or importance or (b) the Division is equally divided in opinion, it may appoint the cause to be reheard by such larger court as is necessary for the proper disposal of the cause: C.S.A. 1988, s. 36. A larger court would in the first instance be a court of five judges; a rehearing of a cause on a point which had been decided by a court of five judges would be heard by a court of seven judges and so on. It is not always necessary for the cause to be heard by the Division before it is reheard by a larger court, particularly where all parties are agreed. A larger court will be required where consideration has to be given as to whether to overturn a previous decision of a Division. Hearings before a larger court may be appropriate on questions of practice or procedure. Where the question at issue is construction of a U.K. statute the preferable course is for appeal to the House of Lords: see *Drummond v. I.R.C.* 1951 S.C. 482.
  The general rule is that when a case has been reported in Session Cases or the (English) Law Reports, it should be cited from that source: *McGowan v. Summit at Lloyds*, 2002 S.L.T. 1258, 1273 at para.[57]. See also now, P.N. No. 5 of 2004. The citation of cases from reproduction of electronic formats is permitted by that P.N.

Fee. The court fee for the hearing of a reclaiming motion on the Summar Roll is payable by **38.17.6** each party for every 30 minutes or part thereof. For fee, see Court of Session etc. Fees Order 1997, Table of Fees, Pt I, B, item 14 or C, item 16 [S.I. 1997 No. 688, as amended, pp. C 1201 *et seq.*]. The fee for a reclaiming motion in the Single Bills will be under Pt I, B, item 22 or C, item 21. Certain persons are exempt from payment of fees: see 1997 Fees Order, art.5, substituted by S.S.I. 2002 No. 270. A fee exemption certificate must be lodged in process: see P.N. No.1 of 2002.
  Where a party is legally represented, the fee may be debited under a credit scheme introduced on 1st April 1976 by P.N. No. 4 of 1976 to the account (if one is kept or permitted) of the agent by the court cashier, and an account will be rendered weekly by the court cashier's office to the agent for all court fees due that week for immediate settlement. An agent not on the credit scheme will have an account opened for the purpose of lodging the fee: P.N. No. 2 of 1995. A debit slip and a copy of the court hearing time sheet will be delivered to the agent's box or sent by DX or post.
  A party litigant must pay cash to the clerk of court at the end of the hearing or, if the hearing lasts more than a day, at the end of each day: P.N. No. 2 of 1995. A receipt will be issued. The

assistant clerk of session will acknowledge receipt of the sum received from the clerk of court on the Minute of Proceedings.

Reclaiming prints

38.18. A reclaiming print shall be in the form of a record and shall contain—

    (a) the whole pleadings and interlocutors in the cause;

    (b) where the reclaiming motion is directed at the refusal of the Lord Ordinary to allow the pleadings to be amended in terms of a minute of amendment and answers, the text of such minute and answers; and

    (c) where available, the opinion of the Lord Ordinary.

Deriv. P.N. No. 2 of 1989, para. 2(1)

38.18.1   *General note.* If the Lord Ordinary's opinion is not available when the reclaiming print is lodged, it will have to be included in an appendix: r. 38.19(1)(a).

Lodging of appendices in reclaiming motions

38.19.—(1) Where, in a reclaiming motion—

    (a) the opinion of the Lord Ordinary has not been included in the reclaiming print, or

    (b) it is sought to submit notes of evidence or documents for consideration by the court,

the reclaimer shall lodge an appendix incorporating such documents within three months after the cause has been appointed to the Summar Roll.

(2) Where the reclaimer considers that an appendix is not necessary, the reclaimer shall, by the date specified in paragraph (1)—

    (a) give written intimation of that fact to the Deputy Principal Clerk; and

    (b) send a copy of that intimation to the respondent.

(3) Where a respondent in a reclaiming motion seeks to submit notes of evidence or documents for consideration by the court which the reclaimer has given written intimation to the respondent he does not intend to include in his appendix, the respondent shall incorporate such notes or documents in an appendix which he shall lodge within one month after the date on which intimation under paragraph (2) or this paragraph, as the case may be, was given.

(4) Where a reclaimer fails to lodge an appendix in accordance with paragraph (1), a respondent may apply by motion to the Inner House to have the reclaiming motion refused.

[1] (5) In a case where early disposal is sought by virtue of rule 38.7A, the Inner House may, on the application by motion of the reclaimer, determine that paragraphs (1) to (4) shall not apply or shall apply subject to such modifications as it considers appropriate.

Deriv. R.C.S. 1965, r. 294A(a)(part) inserted by S.I. 1972 No. 2022, and P.N. No. 2 of 1989, para. 2(2)

---

[1] R.38.19(5) inserted by S.I. 1997 No. 2692 (effective 1st December 1997).

38.19.1   *General note.* The reclaimer must lodge any appendix within three months after the cause has been appointed to the Summar Roll. If he does not intend to lodge an appendix the reclaimer must give written intimation of that to the respondent: r. 38.19(2) and (3). Where the appellant does not intend to include in his appendix documents which the respondent wishes to be lodged, the clear implication of r. 38.19(3) is that he must given written intimation of that fact to the respondent to enable the latter to lodge an appendix. Parties should discuss and try to agree the documents to be lodged in one appendix.

If the respondent wishes to lodge an appendix he has one month from the date of such intimation to do so: r. 38.19(3).

If a reclaimer fails to lodge an appendix timeously the respondent may apply by motion to have the reclaiming motion refused: r. 38.19(4). The reclaiming motion is not, as previously under R.C.S. 1965, r. 294A(b), deemed to be abandoned.

Where a motion for early disposal has been granted under r. 38.13, the interlocutor may have to make special provision for the lodging of an appendix.

Under r. 38.7A early disposal must be sought of reclaiming motion against certain interlocutors. It may be necessary to ask the court not to apply or to modify the application of r. 38.19(1) to (4): r. 38.19(5).

"within three months", "within one month". The date from which the period is calculated is **38.19.2** not counted. Where the last day falls on a Saturday or Sunday or a public holiday on which the Office of Court is closed, the next available day is allowed: r. 1.3(7). For office hours and public holidays, see note 3.1.2.

"written intimation". For methods, see r. 16.9.　**38.19.3**

"motion". For motions, see Chap. 23.　**38.19.4**

Notes of evidence not extended when agreed

38.20. Where, in a reclaiming motion, the parties are agreed that on any particular issue the interlocutor reclaimed against is not to be submitted to review, it shall not be necessary to reproduce the notes of evidence or documents relating to that issue.

Deriv. R.C.S. 1965, r. 262(d)

Amendment of pleadings in reclaiming motions

38.21.—(1) Where, after a reclaiming motion has been marked, any party applies by motion to have the pleadings amended in terms of a minute of amendment and answers, he shall apply for a direction as to further procedure.

(2) Where it appears to the Inner House that the proposed amendment makes a material change to the pleadings, it may recall the interlocutor of the Lord Ordinary reclaimed against and remit the cause back to the Lord Ordinary for a further hearing.

Deriv. P.N. 26th March 1981

General note. Amendment may be allowed on, during or after reclaiming. This may occur **38.21.1** after debate but is uncommon after evidence has been led. In the former case, if allowed, the Inner House may refuse to hear argument until the judge at first instance has reconsidered the amended pleadings and the case will be remitted for that purpose: *Wallace v. Scottish Special Housing Association* 1981 S.L.T. (Notes) 60. In the latter case, amendment to raise fresh issues of fact may not be allowed because it could unjustly prejudice the other party who might have conducted his case differently: *Thomson v. Glasgow Corporation* 1962 S.C.(H.L.) 36; *McGuffie v. Forth Valley Health Board* 1991 S.L.T. 231; *cf. Moyes v. Burntisland Shipping Co.* 1952 S.C. 429 (allowed in exceptional circumstances to clarify existing controversy not a new one).

The purpose of r. 38.21 is to give the Inner House the opportunity to consider, before the reclaiming motion is heard, whether the amendment involves a material change as requires consideration by the Lord Ordinary.

"motion". For motions, see Chap. 23. A motion enrolled under r. 38.21 will require **38.21.2** appearance on behalf of the party enrolling the motion.

CHAPTER 39

APPLICATIONS FOR NEW TRIAL OR TO ENTER JURY VERDICTS

Applications for new trial

39.1.—(1) An application under section 29(1) of the Act of 1988 (application for new trial) shall be made by motion within 7 days after the date on which the verdict of the jury was written on the issue and signed.

(2) A motion under paragraph (1) shall specify the grounds on which the application is made.

(3) An application under section 29(1)(a), (b) or (c) of the Act of 1988

may not be made unless—
- (a) in the case of an application under section 29(1)(a) (misdirection of judge), the procedure in rule 37.7 (exceptions to judge's charge) has been complied with;
- (b) in the case of an application under section 29(1)(b) (undue admission or rejection of evidence), objection was taken to the admission or rejection of the evidence at the trial and recorded in the notes of evidence under direction of the judge presiding at the trial;
- [1] (c) in the case of an application under section 29(1)(c) (verdict contrary to evidence) it sets out in brief specific numbered propositions the reasons the verdict is said to be contrary to the evidence.

(4) On enrolling a motion for a new trial under paragraph (1), the party enrolling it shall lodge—
- (a) a print of the whole pleadings and interlocutors in the cause incorporating the issues and counter-issues;
- (b) the verdict of the jury; and
- (c) any exception and the determination on it of the judge presiding at the trial.

(5) Rule 38.8 (effect of reclaiming) shall, with the necessary modifications, apply to an application for a new trial under section 29 of the Act of 1988 as it applies to a reclaiming motion.

Deriv. R.C.S. 1965, r. 126(a) (r. 39.1(1) to (3))

---

[1] Rule 39.1 amended by S.S.I. 2004 No.331 (effective 6th August 2004).

39.1.1 *Grounds of application for new trial.* The grounds are set out in s. 29(1) of the C.S.A. 1988. They are: (a) misdirection by the judge; (b) undue admission or rejection of evidence; (c) that the verdict is contrary to the evidence; (d) excess or inadequacy of damages; (e) *res noviter veniens ad notitiam*; or on such other ground as is essential to the justice of the cause. These are dealt with in turn below.

A motion for a new trial on any of the statutory grounds in (a) to (e) is subject to the statutory proviso that it will only be granted if it is essential to the justice of the case: *Tate v. Fischer* 1998 S.L.T. 1419.

(1) *Misdirection by the presiding judge.* It is not necessary to show that the jury was misled, it is sufficient to show that the misdirection was calculated to mislead: *Cleland v. Weir* (1847) 6 Bell's App. 70, 76 *per* Lord Cottenham, L.C. There must have been a note of exception(s) drawn up: r. 39.1(3)(a); and see r. 37.7. The fact that the court has only the note of exception and not the shorthand writer's record of the judge's charge has been criticised, and it has been suggested that the whole of the charge should be available to the appeal court: see *Douglas v. Cunningham* 1963 S.C. 564, 570 *per* Lord Guthrie and *McArthur v. Weir Housing Corporation Ltd* 1970 S.C. 135, 138–139 *per* Lord Wheatley.

(2) *Undue admission or rejection of evidence.* Objection must have been taken at the time in the trial: r. 39.1(3)(b). (a) A new trial will not be allowed if the exclusion of the evidence admitted would not have led to a different verdict: C.S.A. 1988, s. 30(1). The onus of showing that the evidence adduced, but which should have been excluded, was immaterial rests on the party who adduced it: *Livingstone v. Strachan, Crerer & Jones* 1923 S.C. 794. Evidence admitted which is objectionable on the ground of surprise is a ground for allowing a new trial, but the surprise must be of such a character which the party taken by surprise could not reasonably

have been expected to anticipate: *Christie's Curator ad litem v. Kirkwood* 1996 S.L.T. 1299, 1300I. (b) Where the presiding judge rejected parole evidence it must be shown that the evidence was wrongly rejected and that its admission might have led to a different result; if it can be demonstrated that, whatever that evidence, no reasonable jury would have returned a verdict for the aggrieved party there will be no new trial: *Greig v. Sir William Arrol & Co. Ltd* 1965 S.L.T. 242. If the evidence rejected is documentary evidence, a new trial may be refused if its admission would not have affected the result: C.S.A. 1988, s.30(2).

(3) *Verdict contrary to the evidence.* It is not the court's function to review the jury's verdict. The test is whether the jury came to a conclusion to which reasonable people of ordinary intelligence could have come on the whole evidence: *Keenan v. Scottish Co-operative Society Ltd* 1914 S.C. 959, 961 *per* Lord Johnston, approved in *Potec v. Edinburgh Corporation* 1964 S.C.(H.L.) 1, 7 *per* Lord Guest, in *Macarthur v. Chief Constable, Strathclyde Police* 1989 S.L.T. 517 and *Currie v. Kilmarnock and Loudoun D.C.* 1996 S.L.T. 481. A verdict will not be lightly set aside: *Robertson v. John White & Son* 1963 S.C.(H.L.) 22, 29 *per* Lord Guest. The verdict must be either one for which there was no evidence to support it or one flagrantly opposed to the evidence: *Magistrates of Elgin v. Robertson* (1862) 24 D. 301, 305 *per* Lord Wood. The verdict must be one, on the evidence, to which no jury properly directed could reasonably have come (*Robertson*, above, *per* Lord Guest at p. 29) or it must be a verdict which cannot from any point of view be reconciled with the evidence (*Kinnell v. Peebles* (1890) 17 R. 416, 424 *per* Lord McLaren). It is not enough that the court might have reached a different conclusion and disagrees with the jury's findings: *Keenan*, above. For a recent example of a verdict set aside on this ground, see *Ross v. Fife Healthcare NHS Trust*, 2000 S.C.L.R. 620 (First Div.).

(4) *Excess or inadequacy of damages.* The test laid down in *Landell v. Landell* (1841) 3 D. 819, 825 to establish that damages were excessive is: "It is evidently not enough, in order to bring the damages within the description of excessive, that they are more, and even a great deal more, than the amount at which the injury sustained might have been estimated, in the opinion of the individual members of the Court to whom the application is made . . . It is clear that, in order to warrant the application of the term 'excessive', the damages must be held to exceed, not what the Court might think enough, but even that latitude which, in a question of amount so very vague, any set of reasonable men could be permitted to indulge. The excess must be such as to raise on the part of the Court the moral conviction that the jury, whether from wrong intention or incapacity or some mistake, have committed gross injustice, and have given higher damages than any jury of ordinary men, fairly and without gross mistake exercising their functions, could have awarded." That this is the correct approach was confirmed by the House of Lords in *Girvan v. Inverness Farmers Dairy*, 1998 S.C. 1. A right to a fair trial under Art. 6 of the European Convention on Human Rights is not infringed by the court applying the test in *Landell*, above: *McLeod v. British Railways Board*, 2001 S.C. 534, 536–537 (First Div.).

The modern statement of the proper approach is in *Girvan*, above. To be "excessive" the damages awarded have to exceed the latitude which any reasonable jury could be permitted to indulge and have to raise a conviction in the court that a gross injustice had been committed (p. 31 C–D). A fairly broad approach has to be taken to the question whether the jury has committed a gross injustice or reached a palpably wrong result. The matter can be considered in two stages. First, the court can make a judicial assessment of the value of the claim, taking into account judicial and jury awards and secondly it can compare that with the award of the jury (p. 16G–17C). In comparing the awards, the 100 per cent working rule (derived from *Young v. Glasgow Tramway and Omnibus Co. (Ltd)* (1882) 10 R. 242, 245 *per* L.P. Inglis) can be considered in relation to solatium only; the rule has no application to other elements of an award which are capable of reasonable precision (patrimonial loss, multipliers): a relatively small departure from a judicial assessment maybe excessive in relation to patrimonial loss. The working rule is not, however, a formula; it is no more than a rule of thumb or a check which the court may use as a guide (p. 17G). It is legitimate to take into account assessments made by previous juries in the same case (p. 18A—C, H).

(5) "*res noviter veniens ad notitiam*" (information newly discovered). The allowance of *res noviter* is more or less in the nature of an indulgence: *Miller v. Mac Fisheries Ltd* 1922 S.C. 157, 160 *per* L.P. Clyde. There may be new evidence or new fact: *Miller*, above, *per* L.P. Clyde at p. 162. New evidence must not be merely additional evidence of a fact originally averred and spoken to: *Miller*, above, *per* L.P. Clyde at p. 160. The new material must have been unknown and not available at the time of the trial to the party moving for a new trial through no fault of his: *Bannerman v. Scott* (1846) 9 D. 163, 165 *per* L.P. Boyle; *Miller*, above, *per* L.P. Clyde at p. 162; *Maltman v. Tarmac Civil Engineering Ltd* 1967 S.C. 177, 181 *per* L.P. Clyde. It must be material to the justice of the cause: *Miller*, above, *per* L.P. Clyde at p. 160. The court does not have to be convinced that the evidence certainly or probably would lead to a different verdict: *Bannerman*, above, *per* L.P. Boyle at p. 166; *Maltman*, above, *per* L.P. Clyde at p. 182. If *res nova* is of a fact, it may require amendment of the pleadings, unless it is extraneous to the pleadings, in which case a minute should be lodged recording it; if it is new evidence which does

not affect the pleadings, a minute should be lodged setting out what it is and how it is to be proved: *Miller*, above, *per* L.P. Clyde at p. 161. Answers may be lodged to a minute of amendment or minute.

(6) "*such other ground essential to the justice of the cause*". S.29(1) of the C.S.A. 1988 ends with a general catch-all provision. It depends on the circumstances what would be included in this ground. It may include evidence not presaged on record, taking the other party by surprise (*Smith v. The Anchor Line Ltd* 1961 S.L.T.(Notes) 54) or unfair conduct of the case (*Reekie v. McKinven* 1921 S.C. 733, 734–735 *per* L.P. Clyde). It may also include wrongful withdrawal of the case from the jury: see *Gibson v. Nimmo & Co.* (1895) 22 R. 491.

Where there are two or more defenders a verdict cannot stand against one and be set aside against any others, the whole verdict has to go: *Simpson v. Glasgow Corporation* 1916 S.C. 345.

39.1.2   "*within 7 days*". The date from which the period is calculated is not counted. Where the last day falls on a Saturday or Sunday or a public holiday on which the Office of Court is closed, the next available day is allowed: r. 1.3(7). For office hours and public holidays, see note 3.1.2. Note the provision for applications out of time: r. 39.2.

39.1.3   "*motion*". For motions, see Chap. 23.

39.1.4   *Lodging copies of documents.* Six copies of an appeal print of the record, the issues and the note of exceptions, and of any appendix, must be lodged when the motion for a new trial is enrolled (and four copies of any other document the day before the hearing): r. 4.7.

39.1.5   *Expenses.* If a new trial is granted expenses are generally dealt with at the time the new trial is ordered: *McInnes v. British Transport Commission* 1961 S.C. 156; *cf. Watson v. British Transport Commission* 1961 S.C. 152, 155 *per* L.J.-C. Thomson.

39.1.6   *Fee.* The court fee for a hearing on the Summar Roll is payable by each party for every 30 minutes or part thereof. For fee, see Court of Session etc. Fees Order 1997, Table of Fees, Pt I, B, item 17 [S.I. 1997 No. 688, as amended, pp. C 1201 *et seq.*]. Certain persons are exempt from payment of fees: see 1997 Fees Order, art.5, substituted by S.S.I. 2002 No.270. A fee exemption certificate must be lodged in process: see P.N. No.1 of 2002.

Where a party is legally represented, the fee may be debited under a credit scheme introduced on 1st April 1976 by P.N. No. 4 of 1976 to the account (if one is kept or permitted) of the agent by the court cashier, and an account will be rendered weekly by the court cashier's office to the agent for all court fees due that week for immediate settlement. An agent not on the credit scheme will have an account opened for the purpose of lodging the fee: P.N. No. 2 of 1995. A debit slip and a copy of the court hearing time sheet will be delivered to the agent's box or sent by DX or post.

A party litigant must pay (by cash, cheque or postal order) to the clerk of court at the end of the hearing or, if the hearing lasts more than a day, at the end of each day: P.N. No. 2 of 1995. A receipt will be issued. The assistant clerk of session will acknowledge receipt of the sum received from the clerk of court on the Minute of Proceedings.

Applications out of time

39.2.—(1) Where an application for a new trial under section 29(1) of the Act of 1988 is made outwith the period specified in rule 39.1(1) the motion made in accordance with that rule shall include an application to allow the motion to be received and for leave to proceed out of time.

(2) Where the court grants an application under paragraph (1), it shall—
(a) where the motion has been opposed as incompetent, make such order as may be made under rule 39.3(2); or
(b) where no such opposition has been marked, appoint the cause to the Summar Roll for hearing or dispose of the motion in the Single Bills.

39.2.1   *General note.* An application out of time for a new trial may only be made provided the verdict has not been applied or a motion to apply it has not been enrolled.

39.2.2   "*motion*". For motions, see Chap. 23.

39.2.3   "*leave to proceed out of time*". The considerations for leave to proceed out of time may well include mistake or inadvertence and those arising in the application of the dispensing power in r. 2.1.

Objections to competency of application

39.3.—(1) Where an application for a new trial under section 29(1) of the

Act of 1988 is made by a party, any other party may oppose the motion on the ground that it is incompetent.

(2) At the hearing in the Single Bills of the motion referred to in paragraph (1), the court may—

(a) dispose of the objection to competency; and, where it repels the objection, appoint the cause to the Summar Roll for hearing or determine the motion in the Single Bills;

(b) appoint the cause to the Summar Roll for a hearing on the objection; or

(c) reserve the objection for hearing with the merits and appoint the cause to the Summar Roll for hearing.

"motion". For motions, see Chap. 23.   **39.3.1**

"incompetency". An application for a new trial may be opposed on being enrolled on the   **39.3.2**
ground that it is incompetent. Opposition to the motion will be made on Form 23.4.

The application may be incompetent, *e.g.* because the period within which the application may be made has expired.

The court may take the objection itself and will not entertain an incompetent appeal even if objection is waived by the respondent: *Governors of Strichen Endowments v. Diverall* (1891) 19 R. 79.

Procedure where no objections to competency

39.4. Where an application for a new trial under section 29(1) of the Act of 1988 is—

(a) made timeously, and

(b) not opposed on the ground of competency,

the court shall, without hearing parties, appoint the cause to the Summar Roll or direct that it be put out in the Single Bills for hearing.

Summar Roll. As a general rule, applications for a new trial are appointed to and heard on the   **39.4.1**
Summar Roll. Originally the Summar Roll was the roll for dealing with causes summarily and the Short Roll was for more complicated causes; the latter, however, has fallen into desuetude. Once appointed to the Summar Roll a diet is fixed by the Keeper of the Rolls in accordance with r. 6.3 after parties have sent him Form 6.3 duly completed.

Single Bills. The Single Bills is the motion roll of the Inner House. As a general rule,   **39.4.2**
applications for a new trial are not heard in the Single Bills.

Speeches application for new trial. At the hearing the convention is that there is only one   **39.4.3**
speech for each party.

Lodging of appendix

39.5. Rule 38.19 (lodging of appendices in reclaiming motions) shall, with the necessary modifications, apply to an application for a new trial under section 29(1) of the Act of 1988 as it applies to a reclaiming motion.

Appendix. This would include the notes of evidence (so far as relevant) and other documents   **39.5.1**
to be considered by the court. The appendix has to be lodged within three months after the cause has been appointed for hearing on the Summar Roll: r. 38.19(1). Where the party moving for a new trial does not intend to lodge an appendix, he must inform the other party in case he does: see r. 38.19(2) and (3). Six copies of the appendix must be lodged: r. 4.7(1)(f).

Applications to enter jury verdict

39.6.—(1) An application under section 31(1) of the Act of 1988 (verdict returned subject to opinion of Inner House on point reserved) shall be made by motion.

(2) On enrolling a motion under paragraph (1), the party enrolling it shall lodge in process four copies of the closed record incorporating—

(a) all interlocutors pronounced in the cause and any amendments to the record allowed;

(b) the issues and counter-issues;

(c) any exception taken during the trial and the determination on it of the judge presiding at the trial; and

(d) the verdict of the jury;
and send one copy of it to every other party.

(3) Unless the court otherwise directs, it shall not be necessary for the purposes of such a motion to print the notes of evidence, but the notes of the judge presiding at the trial may be produced at any time if required.

(4) In a case of complexity or difficulty, the Inner House may appoint an application referred to in paragraph (1) to the Summar Roll for hearing.

Deriv. R.C.S. 1965, r. 125(c) inserted by S.I. 1984 No. 472 (r. 39.6(3))

39.6.1   *General note.* Where the presiding judge has directed the jury on a question of law (subject to the opinion of the court on the direction), a party against whom the verdict was given may apply to the Inner House to enter the verdict for him on the ground that (a) the direction was erroneous and that he was truly entitled to the verdict in whole or in part, or (b) it is necessary to set aside the verdict and order a new trial: C.S.A. 1988, s. 31(1).

39.6.2   *"motion".* For motions, see Chap. 23.

39.6.3   *Fee.* The court fee for a hearing on the Summar Roll is payable by each party for every 30 minutes or part thereof. For fee, see Court of Session etc. Fees Order 1997, Table of Fees, Pt. I, B, item 17 [S.I. 1997 No. 688, as amended, pp. C 1201 *et seq.*]. Certain persons are exempt from payment of fees: see 1997 Fees Order, art.5, substituted by S.S.I. 2002 No.270. A fee exemption certificate must be lodged in process: see P.N. No.1 of 2002.

Where a party is legally represented, the fee may be debited under a credit scheme introduced on 1st April 1976 by P.N. No. 4 of 1976 to the account (if one is kept or permitted) of the agent by the court cashier, and an account will be rendered weekly by the court cashier's office to the agent for all court fees due that week for immediate settlement. An agent not on the credit scheme will have an account opened for the purpose of lodging the fee: P.N. No. 2 of 1995. A debit slip and a copy of the court hearing time sheet will be delivered to the agent's box or sent by DX or post.

A party litigant must pay (by cash, cheque or postal order) to the clerk of court at the end of the hearing or, if the hearing lasts more than a day, at the end of each day: P.N. No. 2 of 1995. A receipt will be issued. The assistant clerk of session will acknowledge receipt of the sum received from the clerk of court on the Minute of Proceedings.

CHAPTER 40

APPEALS FROM INFERIOR COURTS

Application and interpretation of this Chapter

40.1.—(1) This Chapter applies to an appeal to the court from any decision pronounced by an inferior court which may be appealed to the court.

(2) In this Chapter—
(a) "appeal process" means—
    (i) the process of the inferior court; or
    (ii) where the cause is recorded in an official book of an inferior court, a copy of the record in that book certified by the clerk of the inferior court;
(b) "decision" includes interlocutor, judgment or other determination;
[1] (c) "inferior court" means—
    (i) the Lyon Court;
    [2] (ii) the sheriff with respect to judgments or interlocutors to which section 28 of the Sheriff Courts (Scotland) Act 1907, or s. 38(b) of the Sheriff Courts (Scotland) Act 1971, applies.

Deriv. R.C.S. 1965, r. 267.

---

[1] R. 40.1(2)(c) amended by S.I. 1996 No. 1756 (effective 5th August 1996).
[2] R. 40.1(2)(c)(ii) amended by S.I. 1996 No. 2587 (effective 1st November 1996).

"inferior court". This term is now defined. The sheriff court is an inferior court as is the Lyon   **40.1.1**
Court (*Cunninghame v. Cunyngham* (1849) 11 D. 1139; Erskine, I.iv.32).

The A.S. (R.C.S.A. No.3) (Miscellaneous) 1996 [SI 1996/1756] removed the Employment
Appeal Tribunal from the definition or inferior court. Thus appeals from the EAT will no
longer be dealt with under Chap.40 but under Chap.41 Part II (appeals in Form 41.19).

The Employment Appeal Tribunal found it difficult administratively to deal with appeals to
the Court of Session under this Chapter.

"the sheriff". This Chapter applies to appeals under s.28 of the Sheriff Courts (Scotland) Act   **40.1.2**
1907, or s.38(b) of the Sheriff Courts (Scotland) Act 1971. It does not apply to appeals under
other enactments, to which Chap.41 applies.

Applications for leave to appeal from inferior court

40.2.—(1) Where leave to appeal is required, an application for such leave
shall be made in the first instance to the inferior court unless the enactment
allowing the appeal requires the application to be made to the court.

(2) Where—
  (a) the inferior court has refused leave to appeal and such refusal is not
    final, or
  (b) leave to appeal is required from the court and not the inferior court,
any application to the court for leave to appeal shall be made in Form 40.2
to the Inner House.

(3) An application to the court under paragraph (2) for leave to appeal
shall be lodged in the General Department—
  (a) within the period prescribed by the enactment by virtue of which it is
    made; or
  (b) where no such period is prescribed, within 14 days after the date
    specified in paragraph (4).

(4) The date referred to in paragraph (3)(b) is—
  (a) the date on which the decision of the inferior court refusing leave to
    appeal was intimated to the appellant; or
  (b) where the application for leave to appeal is required to be made to
    the court and not the inferior court—
    (i) the date on which the decision of the inferior court complained
      of was issued; or
    (ii) where the inferior court issued reasons for its decision later than
      the decision, the date of issue of the reasons.

(5) An application to the court for leave to appeal shall include a
statement setting out the proposed grounds of appeal and the grounds on
which leave to appeal is sought.

(6) There shall be lodged with an application to the court under
paragraph (3)—
  (a) a process in accordance with rule 4.4 (steps of process);
  (b) where applicable—
    (i) evidence that leave to appeal has been refused by the inferior
      court;
    (ii) a copy of the grounds of appeal intimated to the inferior court;
      and
    (iii) any note by the inferior court setting out the reasons for its
      refusal;
  (c) a copy of the decision of the inferior court complained of and any
    reasons for that decision; and
  (d) where the inferior court itself exercised an appellate function, a copy
    of the decision of the tribunal from which that appeal was taken and
    any reasons given for that decision.

Deriv. P.N. 6th November 1986 (r.40.2(5) and (6))

General note. Some enactments require either the inferior court or the Court of Session to grant   **40.2.1**
leave to appeal. Where leave may be sought from either court, r.40.2(1) requires leave to be
sought in the first instance from the inferior court. Where leave must be sought from the inferior

court, application to the Court of Session for leave to appeal where the sheriff has refused leave is incompetent because the sheriff's decision is final: *Frost v. Bulman* 1995 S.C.L.R. 579.

The sole function of r.40.2 is to lay down a procedure for applying for leave to appeal; the right to appeal to the court has to be found in the enactment providing for the inferior court's decision to be appealed against: *Bulman v. Frost* 1995 G.W.D. 17–971 (sheriff's decision to refuse leave under s.103(1) of the Debtors (Scotland) Act 1987 is final).

It is not a breach of art.6(1) of the ECHR for the judge at first instance, who determined the substantive issue, to be the judge who also decides whether leave to appeal should be granted: *Umair v Umair*, 2002 S.C. 153 (Ex Div.).

(1) *Sheriff court*. Under subs. (1)(d) of s.28 of the Sheriff Courts (Scotland) Act 1907, leave to appeal is required from the sheriff or sheriff principal against an interlocutor not specified in that subsection. Under s.38(b) of the Sheriff Courts (Scotland) Act 1971, an appeal in a summary cause (other than a small claim, in respect of which there is no appeal) lies on a point of law where the sheriff principal certifies the cause as suitable for such appeal. And see further, note 40.4.2.

If leave to appeal is required from the sheriff court but not sought before the appeal is marked, the appeal will (usually) fail because once an appeal has been marked the procedure for the appeal is then regulated by the Court of Session under Chap. 40 and it is no longer competent for the sheriff court to deal with the cause: *McArthur v. McArthur's Tr.* 1997 S.L.T. 926 (Extra Div.); and see *Sheltered Housing Management Ltd v. Aitken* 1998 S.C. 150 (Extra Div.). So leave to appeal cannot be granted by the sheriff court after the appeal has been marked. But the Court of Session cannot supply the want of leave unless an application has been made to and refused by the sheriff court. A way out of this vicious circle has been found. In *DTL Gas Supplies Ltd v. Protan SRL*, 1999 S.L.T. 397 (First Div.) the Inner House (where the sheriff principal said leave was not necessary but the I.H. said it was) remitted back to the sheriff under s.32(2) of the C.S.A. 1988 to consider whether to exercise the dispensing power and a late application for leave. The court held that s.32(2) of the C.S.A. 1988 does not apply only to appeals properly taken under s.28 of the 1907 Act but may also apply to an appeal marked late or for which the required leave had not been granted. *DTL Gas*, above, was distinguished in *Walker v. Tidewater Cyprus Ltd*, December 5, 2003, 2003 G.W.D. 40-1070 (First Div.) where it was held that an appellant was not entitled as a matter of course to a remit (there was a plain failure to apply for leave).

The absence of a decerniture is not decisive against the finality of an interlocutor for the purpose of determining whether leave to appeal is required. Leave to appeal is not required for an appeal from a sheriff's decision under s.49(6) of the Bankruptcy (Scotland) Act 1985 to admit the claim of a creditor in sequestration proceedings: *Japan Leasing (Europe) plc v. Weir's Tr.* 1998 S.L.T. 224.

(2) *Employment Appeal Tribunal*. Under s.136(4) of the Employment Protection (Consolidation) Act 1978 an appeal lies to the Court of Session on a question of law with leave of the tribunal or the court. In considering whether to grant leave, the court has to consider whether the applicant has shown a *probabilis causa* in his grounds of appeal in relation to a genuine point of law: *Campbell v. Dunoon & Cowal Housing Association Ltd* 1992 S.L.T. 1136, 1137F *per* Lord Murray.

40.2.2   *"sheriff"*. The "sheriff" includes the sheriff principal: Interpretation Act 1978, Sch.1.

40.2.3   *Fee*. There is no fee for lodging an application for leave to appeal. There will be a fee for the hearing of the motion to grant the application under r.40.3: see note 40.3.2.

Determination of applications for leave to appeal from inferior court

40.3.—(1) On lodging an application for leave to appeal under rule 40.2, the applicant shall apply by motion to the Inner House for an order for intimation and service.

(2) On expiry of the period within which answers may be lodged, the applicant may apply by motion to the Inner House for the application to be granted.

40.3.1   *"motion"*. For motions, see Chap. 23.

40.3.2   *Fee*. A court fee for the hearing of the application will be payable. Notwithstanding the terms of the Court of Session etc. Fees Order 1984, Table of Fees [SI 1984/256, Table as amended, pp. C 1202 *et seq*.], the fee for the application, which is heard in the Single Bills, will be the same as for a motion on the Motion Roll, namely, a fee payable by each party for every 30 minutes after the first 30 minutes under Pt I, B, item 17.

The fee may be debited under a credit scheme introduced on 1st April 1976 by P.N. No. 4 of 1976 to the account (if one is kept or permitted) of the agent by the court cashier, and an account will be rendered weekly by the court cashier's office to the agent for all court fees due that week for immediate settlement. An agent not on the credit scheme will have an account opened for the purpose of lodging the fee: P.N. No. 2 of 1995. A debit slip and a copy of the court hearing time sheet will be delivered to the agent's box or sent by DX or post.

A party litigant must pay cash to the clerk of court at the end of the hearing or, if the hearing lasts more than a day, at the end of each day: P.N. No. 2 of 1995. A receipt will be issued. The assistant clerk of session will acknowledge receipt of the sum received from the clerk of court on the Minute of Proceedings.

Time and method of appeal

40.4.—(1) An appeal from an inferior court shall be made—

(a) within the period prescribed by the enactment by virtue of which the appeal is made; or

(b) where no such period is prescribed, within 21 days after—

   (i) the date on which the decision appealed against was given;

   (ii) where the inferior court issued written reasons for its decision later than the decision, the date on which the written reasons were issued; or

   (iii) where leave to appeal was granted by the inferior court or application for leave to appeal was made to the court under rule 40.2(2), the date on which leave was granted by the inferior court or the court, as the case may be.

[1] (2) A party seeking to appeal from an inferior court shall mark an appeal by writing a note of appeal in Form 40.4—

(a) on the interlocutor sheet, minute of court or other written record containing the decision appealed against; or

(b) where such a decision is not available or the proceedings of the inferior court are recorded in an official book, on a separate sheet lodged with the clerk of the inferior court.

(3) A note of appeal shall—

(a) be signed by the appellant or his agent;

(b) bear the date on which it is signed; and

(c) where the appellant is represented, specify the name and address of the agent who will be acting for him in the appeal.

Deriv. R.C.S. 1965, r. 268(1) substituted by SI 1990/2118 and amended by SI 1991/2483

---

[1] R. 40.4(2) amended by SI 1996/2587 (effective 1st November 1996).

General note. The appeal is marked in the inferior court process. In the sheriff court, O.C.R. **40.4.1** 1993, r. 31.3(1) and (2) and Summary Cause Rules 1976, r. 84(3) and (4) mirror R.C.S. 1994, r. 40.4.

Once an appeal has been marked, the procedure governing the appeal is regulated by Chap. 40 of R.C.S. 1994; *McArthur's Tr. v. McArthur*, 1997 S.C.L.R. 252, 1997 S.L.T. 926.

Appeals from sheriff court. **40.4.2**

(1) *Sheriff Courts (Scotland) Act 1907.* An appeal lies to the Court of Session (a) without leave against a judgment of the sheriff principal or the sheriff which is a final judgment or an interlocutor granting interim decree for payment of money (other than a decree for expenses). sisting an action or refusing a reponing note; or (b) against any other interlocutor with leave of the sheriff principal or sheriff: Sheriff Courts (Scotland) Act 1907, s. 28(1). There are two exceptions: A cause not exceeding £1,500 in value exclusive of interest and expenses competent in the sheriff court shall be brought there and shall not be subject to review by the Court of Session: 1907 Act, s. 7. Nothing in s. 28(1) or s. 27 affects any right or exclusion of appeal provided by any Act of Parliament: 1907 Act, s. 28(2); and see s. 7 of the 1907 Act above and (3) below (restriction of appeal in summary cause).

(a) Final judgment. This means an interlocutor which, by itself, or taken along with previous interlocutors, disposes of the subject-matter of the cause, notwithstanding that judgment may not have been pronounced on every question raised, and that the expenses found due may not have been modified, taxed or decerned for: 1907 Act, s. 3(h). If liability for expenses has not been decided the appellant will have to obtain such a decree in order to present an appeal: see *Russell v. Allan* (1877) 5 R. 22.

A prior interlocutor which is expressly or by implication a final interlocutor cannot be submitted to appeal. A prior interlocutor expressly final is one not appealed within the time prescribed: *Copeland v. Lord Wimborne* 1912 S.C. 355; *Cumptsie v. Waterston* 1933 S.C. 1. A prior interlocutor which is final by implication is one which has been acted on as the basis of subsequent proceedings: *Macaskill v. Nicol* 1943 S.C. 17, 20 *per* L.J.-C. Cooper; see also *Spencer v. Macmillan* 1957 S.L.T.(Notes) 32, *Campbell v. James Walker Insulation Ltd* 1988 S.L.T. 263. It had been thought that a prior interlocutor was also expressly final where leave to appeal is required and has been refused in respect of it: *Marsh v. Baxendale* 1994 S.C. 157. But in *McCue v. Scottish Daily Record* 1998 S.C. 811 a court of five judges held that this was not so. A distinction has to be drawn between, on the one hand, a rule which excludes subsequent review of an interlocutor if not reclaimed against (or appealed) within a specified time (*e.g.* final if not reclaimed against within X days: *Copeland*, above; *Cumptsie*, above) and, on the other hand, one which merely delimits the period within which an interlocutor may be reclaimed (or appealed). The former is excluded from review by s. 29 of the 1907 Act but the latter is not (unless excluded by actings). Thus, where an interlocutor granting or refusing leave to appeal against an interlocutor excludes from review the interlocutor appealed against, the interlocutor in respect of which leave was sought may be submitted to review as a prior interlocutor under s. 29 of the 1907 Act. The decisions in *Marsh*, above, and *Mowbray v. D.C. Thomson Ltd* 1996 S.C. 197 (appeal without the necessary leave from the sheriff court held expressly final and incapable of review as a prior interlocutor under s. 29) are overruled.

In *McCue*, above, the court went on to say that actings after an interlocutor which may exclude review of that interlocutor was not a matter of competency but because the court considers that it should not exercise the power of review in respect of it.

Also in *McCue*, above, it was stated that, where a party sought to reclaim against an interlocutor pronounced on his own motion in order to submit to review a prior interlocutor (as in *McGuinness v. Bremner plc* 1988 S.L.T. 340), this was not a question of competency but that the court would not normally countenance it. Accordingly, there may be circumstances in which the court would permit it.

A distinction falls to be drawn, in bankruptcy cases at least, between those cases where an application is made to the sheriff for some kind of order or determination which he makes in the first instance and those cases where the sheriff acts as an appeal court from a decision taken in the first instance by someone else: *per* L.P. Rodger in *Japan Leasing (Europe) plc. v. Weir's Tr.* 1997 S.C.L.R. 519 1998 S.L.T. 224 (First Div.). Leave is required in respect of the first category of cases, of which *Ingle's Tr. v. Ingle* 1996 S.L.T. 26 and *Gupta's Tr. v. Gupta* 1996 S.C. 82 are examples. Appeals in the second category, not requiring leave, include decisions taken under ss. 26(4), 26(A)(5), 27(4), 28(7)(b), 53(6)(b), 57(4) and 58(A)(5) of the Bankruptcy (Scotland) Act 1985: *Japan Leasing*, above.

(b) Interim decree for payment of money. Payment of money means payment to the other party and does not include an interim order for consignation (*Maxton v. Bone* (1886) 13 R. 912), although it does include an order to release such money to a party (*Sinclair v. Baikie* (1884) 11 R. 413).

(c) Sisting an action. The court looks at the practical effect of the interlocutor not the form of words to determine whether the action has been sisted: *Watson v. Stewart* (1872) 10 M. 494.

(d) Refusal of reponing note. Since the decision in a reponing note is discretionary, the court will only overrule the decision if there was an error of law, if an irrelevant factor was taken into account, if a relevant factor was not taken into account or if the decision was unreasonable or unjudicial: *Guardian Royal Exchange Group v. Moffat* 1986 S.L.T. 262, 266 *per* L.J.-C. Wheatley.

(2) *Remit of ordinary cause.* An appeal lies to the Court of Session from a decision to remit an ordinary cause to the Court of Session: Sheriff Courts (Scotland) Act 1971, s. 37(3).

(3) *Appeal in summary cause.* A summary cause other than a small claim (which cannot be appealed) may be appealed to the Court of Session on a point of law from the final judgment of the sheriff principal if he certifies the cause as suitable for such appeal: 1971 Act, s. 38(b).

40.4.3   *Effect of appeal.* The effect of marking an appeal is to sist all execution on the decree appealed against until the appeal is determined: *Macleay v. Macdonald* 1928 S.C. 776, 782 *per* Lord Anderson. An appeal precludes extract: *Fowler v. Fowler (No. 2)* 1981 S.L.T.(Notes) 78.

Execution before the marking of the appeal will not be affected unless and until the interlocutor is successfully reclaimed against or some interim order is sought from the court such as will suspend or sist the execution.

Once an appeal has been marked, the procedure governing the appeal is regulated by r. 40.6 and the other provisions of Chap. 40: *McArthur v. McArthur's Tr.* 1997 S.L.T. 926. The lower court is no longer competent to deal with matters relating to the appeal, such as the granting of leave to appeal or relief from a party's failure to mark the appeal, or to seek leave to do so, in time. The actual marking of the appeal is the act which constitutes the appeal. Accordingly, when that has been done the lower court's jurisdiction is removed, except in so far as otherwise provided (on which see note 40.6.2 on interim orders and O.C.R. 1993, r. 31.6 on interim possession etc.). This would appear to have two consequences. First, if the appeal has been marked after the prescribed time-limit for making it (see r. 40.4), the appellant will have to apply to the Court of Session under r. 40.5 to be allowed to proceed out of time, rather than moving the lower court to exercise a power to relieve him of his failure to mark timeously (*e.g.* O.C.R. 1993, r. 2.1). Secondly, if leave to bring the appeal is required but not sought before it is marked, it would seem the appeal must fail, unless the enactment under which it is brought actually requires leave to be sought from the Court of Session. With the exception of that situation, r. 40.2 provides that the Court of Session can only supply the want of leave where an application for it has been made to and refused by the inferior court in the first instance. As the lower court could not consider an application after the appeal is marked, the incompetency of the appeal could not be cured and it should be refused under r. 40.12. See *McArthur*, above.

A way out of this vicious circle has been found for appropriate cases. In *DTL Gas Supplies Ltd v. Protan SRL*, 19th August 1998, unreported, the Inner House (where the sheriff principal said leave was not necessary but the I.H. said it was) remitted back to the sheriff under s.32(2) of the C.S.A. 1988 to consider whether to exercise the dispensing power and a late application for leave. The court held that s.32(2) of the C.S.A. 1988 applies not only to appeals properly taken under s.28 of the Sheriff Courts (Scotland) Act 1907 but may also apply to an appeal marked late or for which the required leave had not been granted.

Leave to appeal out of time

40.5.—(1) An application to allow an appeal to be received outwith the time prescribed for marking an appeal and to proceed out of time shall be included in the note of appeal.

(2) Within 14 days after the date of receipt by the Deputy Principal Clerk of the appeal process from the clerk of the inferior court under rule 40.6(1), the appellant shall apply by motion to allow the appeal to be received outwith the time prescribed for marking an appeal and for leave to proceed out of time.

(3) The decision of the Inner House on a motion under paragraph (2) shall be final and not subject to review.

(4) Where a motion under paragraph (2) is refused, the Deputy Principal Clerk shall—

  (a) give written intimation to the clerk of the inferior court that leave to appeal out of time has been refused; and

  (b) transmit the appeal process and note of appeal to him.

Deriv. R.C.S. 1965, r. 268(2) substituted by S.I. 1990 No. 2118

General note. No test is laid down for allowing an appeal out of time. The equivalent rule for **40.5.1** allowing a reclaiming motion to be marked out of time provides that it can only be done in the case of mistake or inadvertence: see r. 38.7.

In the case of an appeal under statute which specifies a time-limit for lodging an appeal, the court may grant leave to appeal out of time, unless it is apparent that the rule is imperative, where the failure to comply was caused by excusable mistake or some cause over which the appellant had no control and there is no substantial prejudice to the respondent: see *National Commercial Bank of Scotland v. Assessor for Fife* 1963 S.C. 197.

Transmission of appeal process

40.6.—(1) Within four days after an appeal has been marked, the clerk of the inferior court shall—

  (a) give written intimation of the appeal to every other party and certify on the interlocutor sheet, other record or separate note of appeal, as the case may be, that he has done so; and

  (b) transmit—

    (i) the appeal process, and

    (ii) any separate note of appeal,

    to the Deputy Principal Clerk.

(2) On receipt of an appeal process sent to him under paragraph (1), the Deputy Principal Clerk shall—

  (a) mark the date of receipt on the interlocutor sheet, other record or separate note of appeal, as the case may be; and

(b) give written intimation of that date to the appellant.

(3) Where the clerk of the inferior court or the Deputy Principal Clerk fails to comply with a provision of this rule, the appeal shall not be invalidated; but the court may give such remedy for any disadvantage or inconvenience occasioned thereby as it thinks fit.

Deriv. R.C.S. 1965, r. 268(3) and (4) amended by S.I. 1990 No. 2118

40.6.1 *General note.* In the sheriff court, O.C.R. 1993, r. 31.3(3) to (5) mirrors this rule.
Within 14 days of lodging the appeal process of the inferior court, the name and address of the appellant's agent must be given (r. 40.7(1)) and within 28 days a Court of Session process must be lodged (r. 40.7(2)).

40.6.2 *Interim orders.* Pending the making up of a Court of Session process, interim orders of possession, aliment and adjustment of rights should be sought in and regulated by the inferior court: *Cunningham v. Cunningham* 1965 S.C. 78; *cf. Macleay v. Macdonald* 1928 S.C. 776 (interim liberation sought from and granted by Court of Session).
Once an appeal is marked it passes to the Court of Session, and the sheriff has no power to pronounce an interlocutor granting leave: *McArthur v. McArthur's Tr.* 1997 S.L.T. 926 (Ex Div.).
The Deputy Principal Clerk has no power to do anything other than comply with r. 40.6(2). He does not have the right to return the process (*e.g.* to have leave to appeal sorted out because the sheriff has no power to grant it after the appeal has been marked). But, as Lord Prosser remarks at p. 932L, that does not mean to say there might not be other situations in which it may be proper for the DPCS to return a process for some administrative matter to be sorted out before marking the process as received. See *McArthur*, above (in that case what the DPCS should have done was bring the matter before a judge under r. 40.12(4) and (5)). In *Sheltered Housing Management Ltd v. Aitken* 1998 S.C. 150 (Ex Div.) the DPCS did so refer the matter (because the appeal was out of time and leave had not been granted). Representations were sought from the parties, but the defender indicated he was not insisting on his appeal "at this stage". The process was returned; the defender subsequently sought and was granted leave to appeal out of time by the sheriff principal and an appeal was again marked to the Court of Session. It was held that the Lord Ordinary should have refused the appeal when it was placed before him. In any event, in returning the process to the sheriff court after the defender indicated he was not insisting in his appeal, the interlocutor of the sheriff principal incompetently appealed against ceased to be reviewable and became final. Following *McArthur*, above, it was not competent for the sheriff principal to grant leave out of time after the appeal had been marked.

40.6.3 *"within four days".* The date from which the period is calculated is not counted. Where the last day falls on a Saturday or Sunday or a public holiday on which the Office of Court is closed, the next available day is allowed: r. 1.3(7). For office hours and public holidays, see note 3.1.2.

40.6.4 *"written intimation".* For methods, see r. 16.9.

Procedure following transmission of appeal process

40.7.—(1) Within 14 days after the date of receipt by the Deputy Principal Clerk of the appeal process, each party seeking to appear in the appeal shall—
(a) give written intimation to the Deputy Principal Clerk of, or
(b) state by note written on the interlocutor sheet, minute of court, or other record containing the decision appealed against or on the separate note of appeal, as the case may be,
his name and address and that of his agent (if any).

(2) Subject to rule 40.9(2) (appeals deemed abandoned), within 28 days after the date of receipt by the Deputy Principal Clerk of the appeal process, or the date of the interlocutor granting a motion made under rule 40.5(2) (leave to appeal out of time), whichever is the later, the appellant shall—
(a) lodge—
(i) a process, including each part of the appeal process, in accordance with rule 4.4 (steps of process); and
(ii) an appeal print; and
(b) send a copy of the appeal print in accordance with rule 4.6(1) (intimation of steps of process).

(3) Subject to rule 40.11 (early disposal of appeal), on lodging in process

the documents required under paragraph (2), the appellant shall apply by motion to the Inner House for an order for grounds of appeal to be lodged.

Deriv. R.C.S. 1965, r. 269(a) amended by S.I. 1974 No. 845 and 1991 No. 2483, and P.N. 13th November 1969, para. 2 (r. 40.7(1)), r. 269(b)(part) amended by S.I. 1974 No. 845 (r. 40.7(2)) and r. 269(c) (r. 40.7(3))

"within 14 days". The date from which the period is calculated is not counted. Where the last **40.7.1**
day falls on a Saturday or Sunday or a public holiday on which the Office of Court is closed, the
next available day is allowed: r. 1.3(7). For office hours and public holidays, see note 3.1.2.

"written intimation". For methods, see r. 16.9.   **40.7.2**

"within 28 days". Failure to lodge the process or appeal print timeously will result in the **40.7.3**
appeal being deemed to be abandoned unless the appellant is reponed: rr. 40.9(1) and 40.10. In
an appropriate case the dispensing power in r. 2.1 may be applied: *X v. Dumfries and Galloway
R.C.* 1994 S.C. 498

The date from which the period is calculated is not counted. Where the last day falls on a
Saturday or Sunday or a public holiday on which the Office of Court is closed, the next
available day is allowed: r. 1.3(7). For office hours and public holidays, see note 3.1.2.

"appeal print". See r. 40.16. Six copies are required as well as the principal: r. 4.7(1). The **40.7.4**
appeal print is lodged as a step of process (r. 1.3(1) (definition of "step of process")). On lodging
steps of process, see r. 4.4.

"send". This includes deliver: r. 1.3(1) (definition of "send").   **40.7.5**

"in accordance with rule 4.6(1)". This provision requires a copy of a step of process lodged to **40.7.6**
be sent to every other party.

"motion". For motions, see Chap. 23.   **40.7.7**

"grounds of appeal". See r. 40.14.   **40.7.8**

Fee. The court fee for lodging the appeal is payable on lodging the appeal process. For fee, see **40.7.9**
Court of Session etc. Fees Order 1997, Table of Fees, Pt I, B, item 2 [S.I. 1997 No. 688, as
amended, pp. C 1201 *et seq.*]. Certain persons are exempt from payment of fees: see 1997 Fees
Order, art.5, substituted by S.S.I. 2002 No. 270. A fee exemption certificate must be lodged in
process: see P.N. No.1 of 2002.

Where the appellant is legally represented, the fee may be debited under a credit scheme
introduced on 1st April 1976 by P.N. No. 4 of 1976 to the account (if one is kept or permitted)
of the agent by the court cashier, and an account will be rendered weekly by the court cashier's
office to the agent for all court fees due that week for immediate settlement. Party litigants, and
agents not operating the scheme, must pay (by cash, cheque or postal order) on each occasion a
fee is due at the time of lodging at the counter at the General Department.

Required application for early disposal of appeal against interlocutor other than final judgment

[1] **40.7A.** On lodging an appeal print under rule 40.7(2)(a)(ii) in respect of
an appeal marked against—
   (a) an interlocutor of an inferior court in a case where the interlocutor is
       not a final judgment; or
[2] (b) an interlocutor of an inferior court containing an order made under
       the Adoption Act 1978 or under section 11(1) of the Children
       (Scotland) Act 1995,
the appellant shall make application under rule 40.11(1)(a) for early disposal
of the appeal.

---

[1] Rule 40.7A inserted by S.I. 1997 No. 2692 (effective 1st December 1997).
[2] Rule 40.7A (b) inserted by S.S.I. 2001 No. 305 (effective 18th September 2001) and amended
by S.S.I. 2004 No. 331 (effective 6th August 2004).

General note. The reasons for positioning this rule here are not at all clear since the rule is **40.7A.1**
unconnected with the rules surrounding it and is separated from the rule with which it is
connected (r. 40.11).

The rule is inserted by A.S.C. (R.C.S.A. No. 8) (Early Disposal of Reclaiming Motions and
Appeals) 1997 [S.I. 1997 No. 2692].

Required applications for early disposal. With respect to appeals marked on or after 1st **40.7A.2**
December 1997, the reclaimer must enrol for early disposal under r. 4.11(1)(a) where he is
appealing against an interlocutor which is not a final interlocutor.

If an appendix is required, it may be necessary to apply to the court by motion to order that
paras (1) to (4) shall not apply or shall be modified: r. 40.17(5).

Sist of process of appeal

40.8.—(1) Within 14 days after the date of receipt by the Deputy Principal Clerk of the appeal process, the appellant may apply by motion to the Inner House for a sist of process.

(2) On enrolling a motion under rule 40.5(2) (leave to appeal out of time) or under paragraph (1) of this rule, the appellant shall lodge a motion sheet and an interlocutor sheet, if not already lodged.

(3) Where the court grants a motion under paragraph (1), the period of 28 days mentioned in rule 40.7(2) shall not run during any period in which the appeal is sisted.

Deriv. R.C.S. 1965, r. 269(b)(part) amended by S.I. 1974 No. 845

40.8.1   *General note.* Where the appeal is sisted the period for lodging the process and appeal print is suspended. Once the sist is recalled the period begins to run again, including any days before the sist was granted: this interpretation was confirmed in *X v. Dumfries and Galloway R.C.* 1994 S.C. 498.

40.8.2   *"motion".* For motions, see Chap. 23.

40.8.3   *"period of 28 days mentioned in r. 40.7(2)".* This is the period within which the appeal print must be lodged.

Appeals deemed abandoned

40.9.—(1) If an appellant fails—
    (a) to apply by motion in accordance with rule 40.5(2) (leave to appeal out of time), or
[1] (b) to comply with the requirements of rule 40.7(2) (lodging process etc.) which, in a case where rule 40.7A is applicable, shall mean the requirements of rule 40.7(2) as read with rules 40.7A and 40.11(1)(a),
he shall be deemed to have abandoned his appeal on the expiry of the period for marking an appeal or for complying with the requirements of rule 40.7(2), as the case may be.

(2) Where an appeal has been deemed to be abandoned by reason of paragraph (1)(b), a respondent may, within seven days after the date on which the appeal is deemed to be abandoned, comply with the requirements of rule 40.7(2) (lodging process etc.) and thereafter insist in the appeal as if it had been marked by him; and the following provisions of this Chapter applying to an appellant shall, with the necessary modifications, apply to an appeal by a respondent under this paragraph.

(3) Where a respondent insists in an appeal under paragraph (2), the appellant shall be entitled to insist in the appeal notwithstanding that his appeal has been deemed to be abandoned.

(4) If, on the expiry of seven days after the date on which an appeal is deemed to be abandoned by virtue of paragraph (1)—
    (a) the appellant has not been reponed under rule 40.10, and
    (b) the respondent does not insist in the appeal under paragraph (2) of this rule,
the decision appealed against shall be treated in all respects as if no appeal had been marked, and the Deputy Principal Clerk shall transmit the appeal process to the clerk of the inferior court in accordance with paragraph (5) of this rule.

(5) Where an appeal process falls to be transmitted to the inferior court under paragraph (4), the Deputy Principal Clerk shall—
    (a) write on the interlocutor sheet, minute of court or other record containing the decision appealed against or on the separate note of appeal, as the case may be, a certificate in Form 40.9;
    (b) send the appeal process to the clerk of the inferior court; and
    (c) give written intimation to each party to the appeal of the date on which the appeal process was transmitted.

(6) Where an appeal—

(a) is deemed to be abandoned under paragraph (1) and has been transmitted to an inferior court under paragraph (5), the respondent in the appeal may apply by motion to that court for an award of the expenses of the abandoned appeal; and

(b) the inferior court shall on such motion grant decree for payment to that respondent of those expenses as taxed by the Auditor of the Court of Session.

Deriv. R.C.S. 1965, r. 269(b)(part) amended by S.I. 1974 No. 845 (r. 40.9(1)) and r. 272 amended by S.I. 1985 No. 1600 (r. 40.9(2) to (6))

---

[1] R. 40.9(1)(b) amended by S.I. 1997 No. 2692 (effective 1st December 1997).

General note. If there is no motion under r. 40.10 to be reponed against a deemed **40.9.1** abandonment, the interlocutor appealed against becomes final: *Watt Brothers & Co. v. Foyn and Ors* (1879) 7 R. 126. Notwithstanding that the interlocutor appealed against has become final, an appellant may, provided that at the time of the motion the process has not been transmitted to the clerk of the inferior court, make a motion under r. 2.1 (power of relief) for relief from any failure mentioned in r. 40.9(1): *Grieve v. Batchelor and Buckling* 1961 S.C. 12; and *X v. Dumfries and Galloway R.C.* 1994 S.C. 498.

Circumstances in which it might be possible to reduce a deemed abandonment should be noted: see *Bain v. Hugh L.S. McConnell Ltd* 1991 S.L.T. 691.

The respondent may insist in an appeal deemed abandoned. If so, the appellant may insist in his appeal although previously deemed abandoned: r. 40.9(2) and (3).

Expenses of abandoned appeal. The motion is made to the inferior court but any award of **40.9.2** expenses is subject to taxation by the Auditor of the Court of Session: r. 40.9(6). The clerk of the inferior court must incorporate in the interlocutor for expenses a remit to the Auditor of the Court of Session.

Reponing against deemed abandonment

40.10.—(1) An appellant may, within seven days after the date on which the appeal has been deemed to be abandoned under rule 40.9(1), apply by motion to be reponed.

(2) The court may grant a motion under paragraph (1) on such conditions as to expenses or otherwise as it thinks fit.

(3) On enrolling a motion under paragraph (1), the appellant shall lodge a process (or such necessary steps of process as have not already been lodged) and an appeal print.

Deriv. R.C.S. 1965, r. 271 (r. 40.10(1) and (2))

General note. If there is no motion to be reponed the interlocutor appealed against becomes **40.10.1** final.

Circumstances in which it might be possible to reduce a deemed abandonment should be noted: see *Bain v. Hugh L.S. McConnell Ltd* 1991 S.L.T. 691.

"motion". For motions, see Chap. 23. Appearance is required for a motion under r. 40.10.   **40.10.2**

"lodge a process . . .". Part of the process may have been lodged under r. 40.8(2) if a sist has **40.10.3** been sought. The necessary steps of process at this stage are Nos. 1 to 4: see r. 4.4(1) and note 4.4.8.

On the meaning of appeal print, see r. 40.16. Six copies are required as well as the principal: r. 4.7(1). The appeal print is lodged as a step of process (r. 1.3(1) (definition of "step of process")). On lodging steps of process, see r. 4.4.

Grounds for reponing. No test is laid down in the rule. Mistake and inadvertence are obvious **40.10.4** factors to be considered.

Early disposal of appeal

[1] **40.11.**—(1) A party who seeks early disposal of an appeal (in the case of the appellant, whether or not by virtue of rule 40.7A) shall—

(a) where he is the appellant, instead of enrolling for an order for grounds of appeal under rule 40.7(3), apply by motion to the Inner

House for early disposal of the appeal, specifying in the motion whether he seeks disposal on the Summar Roll or in the Single Bills; or

(b) where he is the respondent—
   (i) within the period allowed for opposing the motion, endorse, on the motion of the appellant made under rule 40.7(3), the words "The respondent (*name*) seeks early disposal.";
   (ii) who is insisting in an appeal deemed abandoned by virtue of rule 40.9(1), instead of enrolling for an order for grounds of appeal under rule 40.7(3) (by virtue of rule 40.9(2)), apply by motion to the Inner House for early disposal of the appeal; or
   (iii) add, to his opposition under rule 40.12(1) (objections to competency of appeals), the words "and for early disposal".

(2) The entry in the rolls in respect of the motion for early disposal shall be starred; and the parties shall, at the hearing of that motion, provide the Inner House with an assessment of the likely duration of the hearing to determine the appeal.

(3) At the hearing of the motion for early disposal, the Inner House may—
  (a) appoint the cause to the Summar Roll for hearing; or
  (b) direct that the cause be heard in the Single Bills,
and may make such order as to the lodging of grounds of appeal as it thinks fit.

(4) At any hearing of the appeal in the Single Bills, the Inner House may determine the appeal or make such order as it thinks fit.

----

[1] R. 40.11(1) amended, and paras (2) to (4) substituted, by S.I. 1997 No. 2692 (effective 1st December 1997).

40.11.1   *General note.* The original rule was proposed by the Rules Review Group to provide a formal means for seeking early disposal of urgent appeals. Such a motion is made instead of a motion for an order for hearing under r. 40.7(3).

Rule 40.11 has been amended by A.S. (R.C.S.A. No. 8) (Early Disposal of Reclaiming Motions and Appeals) 1997 [S.I. 1997 No. 2692] for appeals marked on or after 1st December 1997. Reclaiming motions marked before that date are governed by P.N. No. 1 of 1995.

The appellant, on enrolling for early disposal, must specify whether he seeks early disposal in the Single Bills or on the Summar Roll: r. 40.11(1).

It does not follow that because early disposal is sought in the Single Bills that the court will not determine that the appeal should be disposed of on the Summar Roll: see r. 40.11(3)(a).

On Single Bills (and appeals appropriate for it), see note 40.15.3; on the Summar Roll, see note 40.15.2.

Grounds of appeal do not have to be lodged for the motion seeking early disposal. At the hearing of the motion, the court will decide when and if grounds of appeal should be lodged: r. 40.11(3).

Under r. 40.7A, early disposal must be sought in appeals against interlocutors which are not final.

A motion for early disposal will be starred requiring appearance of counsel or other person having a right of audience; the court will wish to know parties' estimate of the duration of the hearing: r. 40.11(2).

Note also Short Notice Diets in P.N. No. 6 of 1992 under which the Keeper of the Rolls may issue peremptory diets where the hearing has been assessed as being not more than two days. A notice is published in the rolls of causes which may be subject to this procedure. At least two days' notice of a short notice diet will be given. The assessment of duration will normally be made on the basis of the estimate given in Form 6.3 where the appeal has been appointed to the Summar Roll. An appeal will not normally be considered for a short notice diet unless any appendix required has been lodged.

40.11.2   *"written intimation".* For methods, see r. 16.9.

Objections to competency of appeals

40.12.—(1) Where a motion for grounds of appeal under rule 40.7(3) has been enrolled by an appellant, any other party may oppose the motion on the ground that the appeal is incompetent.

(2) Where a motion has been opposed under paragraph (1), the cause shall be put out for hearing in the Single Bills before a Division of the Inner House.

(3) At the hearing in the Single Bills arranged under paragraph (2), the court may—

(a) dispose of the objection to competency and, where it repels the objection, order grounds of appeal to be lodged;

(b) appoint the cause to the Summar Roll for a hearing on the objection;

(c) reserve the objection until grounds of appeal have been lodged and order such grounds to be lodged;

(d) reserve the objection for hearing with the merits and order grounds of appeal to be lodged.

[1] (4) Where the Deputy Principal Clerk considers that an appeal may be incompetent, he may, at any time before the cause is brought before the Inner House, refer it to a single judge in accordance with paragraph (5).

(5) Any referral by the Deputy Principal Clerk under paragraph (4) shall be made to a judge nominated for that purpose by the Lord President.

(6) Where a referral is made under paragraph (4), the judge may—

(a) order any party to make representations to him in respect of the competency of the appeal;

(b) refuse the appeal on the ground that it is incompetent;

(c) direct that the appeal is to proceed as if the referral had not been made;

(d) make such order as to expenses or otherwise as he thinks fit.

(7) Any decision of a judge in respect of an appeal referred to him under paragraph (4) shall be final and not subject to review.

Deriv. R.C.S. 1965, r. 270 (r. 40.12(1) to (3))

---

[1] R. 40.12(4) amended by S.I. 1996 No. 1756 (effective 5th August 1996).

"oppose the motion". See r. 23.4.   **40.12.1**

"incompetency". An appeal may be incompetent, *e.g.* because the days for appeal have **40.12.2** expired before the appeal was enrolled, because leave was not sought or because the interlocutor may not be appealed. It had been thought that it is incompetent to reclaim against an interlocutor because it was pronounced on the motion of the party seeking to appeal (see *Watson v. Russell* (1894) 21 R. 433; *McGuinness v. Bremner plc* 1988 S.L.T. 340). But in *McCue v. Scottish Daily Record* 1998 S.C. 811, a court of five judges indicated that, where a party sought to reclaim against an interlocutor pronounced on his own motion in order to submit to review a prior interlocutor (as in *McGuinness v. Bremner plc* 1988 S.L.T. 340), this was not a question of competency but that the court would normally countenance it. Accordingly, there may be circumstances in which the court would permit it.

When leave to appeal is required, it is not competent to seek leave out of time subsequent to having marked an (incompetent) appeal without leave: *McArthur v. McArthur's Tr.* 1997 S.L.T. 926, 1997 S.C.L.R. 252 (Extra Div.).

The court may take the objection itself and will not entertain an incompetent appeal even if objection is waived by the respondent: *Governors of Strichen Endowments v. Diverall* (1891) 19 R. 79.

Although a respondent has not marked an appeal as incompetent, it is still open to him to raise the matter of competency at the appeal: *A.B. and C.D. Ptrs* 1992 S.L.T. 1064.

Referral of appeal to single judge. This is a new provision introduced to prevent the time of the **40.12.3** Inner House being wasted on an appeal (particularly by party litigants) which is incompetent because, *e.g.* it seeks to review a final interlocutor.

In *Sheltered Housing Management Ltd v. Aitken* 1998 S.C. 150 (Extra Div.) the Deputy Principal Clerk, no doubt smarting after the decision in *McArthur v. McArthur's Tr.* 1997 S.L.T.

926; 1997 S.C.L.R. 252 (Extra Div.), referred an appeal because the appeal was out of time and leave had not been granted instead of returning the process to the sheriff court as had been done in *McArthur*, above. Representations were sought from the parties, but the defender indicated he was not insisting on his appeal "at this stage". The process was returned; the defender subsequently sought and was granted leave to appeal out of time by the sheriff principal and an appeal was again marked to the Court of Session. It was held that the Lord Ordinary should have refused the appeal when it was placed before him. In any event, in returning the process to the sheriff court after the defender indicated he was not insisting in his appeal, the interlocutor of the sheriff principal incompetently appealed against ceased to be reviewable and became final. Following *McArthur*, above, it was not competent for the sheriff principal to grant leave out of time after the appeal had been marked.

The single judge may allow the appeal to proceed under r. 40.12(6)(c) where the position about competency is uncertain: see, *e.g. M and K, Appellants*, 23rd May 2002, 2002 G.W.D. 18–585 (OH) *per* Lord Hamilton.

The decision of the judge is final and not subject to review: r. 38.14(7).

The judge nominated to deal with a referral was, when the rule was introduced, always an Inner House judge. There are now a number of nominated judges.

A.S. (R.C.S.A. No. 3) (Miscellaneous) 1996 [S.I. 1996 No. 1756] amended r. 40.12(4) to enable the Deputy Principal Clerk of Session to refer an appeal, which it is considered may be incompetent, as soon as it is marked rather than for the Deputy Principal Clerk of Session to wait until a motion for grounds of appeal has been enrolled.

Procedure where no objection to competency of appeal

40.13.—(1) Subject to paragraph (2), where an appeal is not opposed on the ground of competency, the Inner House shall, without hearing parties, order grounds of appeal to be lodged.

(2) This rule shall not apply where an application is made under rule 40.11(1) (early disposal of appeal).

Deriv. R.C.S. 1965, r. 294B(1) inserted by S.I. 1987 No. 1206 (r. 40.13(1))

"grounds of appeal". See r. 40.14.   **40.13.1**

Grounds of appeal

40.14.—(1) An order for grounds of appeal shall require—
  (a) the appellant, and
  (b) any respondent seeking to appeal against any interlocutor or challenge the grounds on which the inferior court has made its decision,
to lodge grounds of appeal within 28 days after the date of the interlocutor making the order.

(2) Grounds of appeal shall consist of brief specific numbered propositions stating the grounds on which it is proposed to submit that the appeal should be allowed or as the case may be.

(3) On lodging grounds of appeal, the party lodging them shall send a copy of them to every other party to the appeal.

(4) A party who has lodged grounds of appeal may at any time apply for leave to amend his grounds of appeal on cause shown.

[1] (5) Where an appellant fails to lodge grounds of appeal in accordance with paragraph (2) within the period prescribed under paragraph (1), the Inner House may, at its own instance or on the motion of a respondent, refuse the appeal with or without hearing parties as the court thinks fit.

Deriv. R.C.S. 1965, r. 294B(2) to (6) inserted by S.I. 1987 No. 1206 and amended by S.I. 1991 No. 1157

---

[1] R.40.14(5) amended by S.I. 1994 No. 2901 (effective 5th December 1994).

40.14.1   *General note.* Paragraph (5) of r. 40.14 was amended by A.S. (R.C.S.A. No.3) (Miscellaneous) 1994 [S.I. 1994 No. 2901]. The words "with or without hearing parties as the court thinks fit" were added.

On failing to lodge grounds, see further note 40.14.5.

40.14.2   *"grounds of appeal"*. These are brief specific numbered propositions (see r. 38.16(2)) for which the appellant contends, which, if correct, should result in the appeal being granted. The authorities on which the propositions are based should be mentioned. It is not necessary to detail all the propositions or to list every authority which will be referred to at the hearing of the appeal. Where grounds of appeal do not comply with the requirement of r. 40.14(2) the appeal may be refused: r. 40.14(5); and see note 40.14.5. The purpose of grounds of appeal is to give notice to the parties and to the court, of the grounds on which the appeal is be argued: *Eurocopy Rentals Ltd v. Tayside Health Board* 1996 S.C. 410, 413 *per* L.P. Hope.

A statement that the Lord Ordinary "erred in fact and law" is an insufficient ground of appeal to afford a proper notice of what is to be contended: *Clark v. Chief Constable, Lothian and Borders Police* 19th February 1993, unreported on this point (1993 G.W.D. 11–759); see also *McAdam v. Shell U.K. Ltd* 1991 S.C. 360, 364 *per* L.P. Hope; and *City of Glasgow D.C. v. Secretary of State for Scotland (No. 1)* 1993 S.L.T. 198, 204E–F *per* Lord Caplan in relation to the similarly worded r. 41.19(2)(e), that: "The purpose of the rule is obviously to ensure that the respondent will receive fair advance notice of any points to be taken on appeal."

Grounds of appeal do not have to be signed.

Grounds of appeal are lodged as a step of process; written intimation of the lodging of them must be given, as well as one copy sent, to every other party: rr. 4.6(1) and 40.14(3). They may be lodged in person at the public counter of the appropriate department or sent by post (P.N. No. 4 of 1994, paras 1 and 8).

Only the principal copy of the grounds of appeal must be lodged unless early disposal has been applied for (in which case three copies will have had to be lodged: r. 40.11(3)). Where the grounds of appeal are to be referred to at any hearing (on the Single Bills or the Summar Roll or otherwise) and copies have not previously been lodged for the motion for early disposal, four copies must be lodged by 12 noon on the second sederunt day before the hearing: r. 4.7(2).

40.14.3   *"within 28 days"*. The period, which will be specified in an interlocutor, may be prorogated: r. 4.9(2). This may be necessary, *e.g.* because the Lord Ordinary's opinion is not yet available: see, *e.g. McAdam v. Shell U.K. Ltd* 1991 S.C. 360, 363 *per* L.P. Hope.

The date from which the period is calculated is not counted. Where the last day falls on a Saturday or Sunday or a public holiday on which the Office of Court is closed, the next available day is allowed: r. 1.3(7). For office hours and public holidays, see note 3.1.2.

40.14.4   *"leave to amend grounds of appeal"*. This may be done to include additional grounds or to alter grounds already stated. It is done by motion or a minute of amendment (and a motion). Appearance will be required for such a motion. Cause must be shown for leave to be granted: r. 40.14(4).

On amending grounds of appeal at the hearing of the appeal, see *McInnes v. Lawrence* 1996 S.C.L.R. 169, where leave was refused on a motion made at the start of the appeal because no special cause had been shown and proper notice had not been given so as to get a proper allocation of court time; see also *Eurocopy Rentals Ltd v. Tayside Health Board* 1996 S.L.T. 1322 (motions to amend to add new grounds refused). The time for an appellant considering whether the grounds of appeal are adequate is before the By Order hearing under r. 6.3(9): *Noble Organisation Ltd v. Kilmarnock and Loudoun D.C.* 1993 S.L.T. 759, 761I, *Eurocopy*, above, at p. 1324.

40.14.5   *"fails to lodge grounds of appeal in accordance with paragraph (2)"*. A respondent may apply by motion to have an appeal refused (a) because there are no grounds of appeal lodged or (b) because the grounds lodged do not comply with the requirement of paragraph (2) (*i.e.* they are not brief specific numbered propositions stating the grounds on which it is proposed to submit that the appeal should be allowed or they do not disclose such a ground). The court may at its own instance refuse an appeal on the same grounds.

For an example of an appeal being refused because the grounds of appeal were inadequate, see *Ferguson v. Whitbread and Co. plc* 1996 S.L.T. 659 (the courts below had "erred"); and *S v. S*, 4 July 2002, 2002 G.W.D. 24–758 (Ex Div.).

40.14.6   *Circumstances in which appellate court will interfere with decision of the court below.*

(1) *Facts.* Review of facts will depend on examination and assessment of the evidence and rules of evidence, and credibility, reliability, weight and sufficiency. In relation to credibility, the appellate court will be reluctant to reverse findings of credibility for the reason that it is denied the advantage of the judge at first instance who saw and heard the witnesses. The court must be persuaded, and come to the clear conclusion, that the judge who had that advantage was plainly wrong: *Clarke v. Edinburgh and District Tramways Co.* 1919 S.C.(H.L.) 35, 37, *per* Lord Shaw

of Dunfermline. Where an appellate court is disposed to come to a different conclusion, it should not do so unless it is satisfied that any advantage enjoyed by the judge at first instance could not be sufficient to explain or justify his conclusion; where the reasons given by that judge are not satisfactory or it unmistakenly so appears from the evidence, the appellate court may be satisfied he has not taken proper advantage of seeing and hearing the witnesses and the matter will be at large for the appellate court: *Thomas v. Thomas* 1947 S.C.(H.L.) 45, 54, *per* Lord Thankerton. Where a decision on fact is based on credibility, the judge at first instance should leave no doubt as to the grounds of his decision: *Duncan v. Watson* 1940 S.C. 221, 225, *per* L.P. Normand. The appellate court will more readily treat the matter as at large where clear and satisfactory reasons are not given: *Morrison v. J. Kelly & Sons Ltd* 1970 S.C. 65.

Where the Court of Session is reviewing concurrent findings as to credibility by the judge at first instance and an intermediate court of appeal (*i.e.* the sheriff principal), the following rules apply: (a) Concurrent findings-in-fact, depending on an assessment of credibility, ought only to be reviewed when it can be clearly demonstrated that the findings were erroneous. It is not enough that the court would have taken a different view of the facts: a concurrent finding can only be reversed where it could be demonstrated either that some cardinal fact had been overlooked, or that some altogether erroneous view had been taken of the bearing of the evidence on the case. (b) The court will reverse concurrent findings-of-fact where these do not depend upon as assessment of credibility. (c) A reluctance to reverse a concurrent finding-in-fact will not be shown where the finding is not a finding of a specific fact but is really an inference from facts specifically found. See *Brodie v. British Railways Board* 1972 S.L.T.(Notes) 37.

(2) *Discretion.* A discretion will not be lightly interfered with. It is not enough that the appellate court would have exercised the discretion differently. The tests have been variously described, depending to some extent on the area of law concerned. The tests may be stated as follows: (*a*) has there been a failure to exercise the discretion at all (*Orr Pollock & Co. (Printers) Ltd v. Mulholland* 1983 S.L.T. 558), (*b*) has the judge misdirected himself in law (*Forsyth v. A. F. Stoddard & Co. Ltd* 1985 S.L.T. 51), (*c*) has the judge misunderstood, misused or failed to balance the evidence (*Skiponian Ltd v. Barratt Developments (Scotland) Ltd* 1983 S.L.T. 313, 314), (*d*) has the judge taken into account an irrelevant factor (*Thomson v. Glasgow Corporation* 1962 S.C.(H.L.) 36, 66, *per* Lord Reid), (*e*) has the judge failed to take into account a relevant factor (*Thomson, above*), (*f*) is the decision unreasonable (*Thomson, above*), (*g*) is the decision unjudicial (*Thomson, above*). See also *Brittan v. Central R.C.* 1986 S.L.T. 407.

Argument not presented to court below. There is no general rule, unlike in the House of Lords, **40.14.7** that the appellate court will not entertain an argument not advanced before the court below; although it may be unfortunate that the argument was not so advanced (*Varney (Scotland) Ltd v. Lanark Town Council* 1974 S.C. 245, 249, *per* L.J.-C. Wheatley.) It is always open to the court

to consider competency which strikes at the root of the proceedings: *Wolfson v. Glasgow District Licensing Board* 1980 S.C. 136, 128, *per* L.J.-C. Wheatley.

There are exceptions. A fresh argument which cannot be advanced without amendment to the pleadings will generally not be heard because the court will usually wish the judge at first instance to consider the amended pleadings (if allowed: on which see note 38.21.1) and have the benefit of his opinion: see *e.g. Wallace v. Scottish Special Housing Association* 1981 S.L.T. (Notes) 60 and r. 38.21. A new argument cannot be advanced other than an evidence led unless the court has allowed that further evidence or is willing to consider a change of circumstances since the hearing in the court below.

Orders for hearing of appeal

40.15.—(1) Within seven days after the expiry of the period prescribed for lodging grounds of appeal—

(*a*) the appellant who has lodged grounds of appeal, or

(*b*) where the appellant no longer insists in his appeal, a respondent who has lodged grounds of appeal,

shall apply by motion to the Inner House for an order for hearing.

(2) On a motion under paragraph (1), the court may—

(*a*) appoint the cause to the Summar Roll for hearing; or

(*b*) direct that the cause be heard in the Single Bills.

(3) In a cause in which an objection to competency has been reserved under rule 40.12(3)(*c*), the motion under paragraph (1) of this rule shall require the attendance of counsel or other person having a right of audience, and, at the hearing of that motion in the Single Bills, the court may—

(*a*) dispose of the objection and, where it repels the objection, either dispose of the merits on the Single Bills or appoint the cause to the Summar Roll for hearing;

(*b*) appoint the cause to the Summar Roll for hearing on the objection; or

(*c*) reserve the objection for hearing with the merits and appoint the cause to the Summar Roll for hearing.

"motion". For motions, see Chap. 23. Appearance is not required unless an objection to competency (see r. 40.12) has been reserved: r. 40.15(3). **40.15.1**

Summar Roll. As a general rule, appeals are appointed to and heard on the Summar Roll. **40.15.2** Originally the Summar Roll was the roll for dealing with causes summarily and the Short Roll was for more complicated causes; the latter, however, has fallen into desuetude. Once appointed to the Summar Roll a diet is fixed by the Keeper of the Rolls in accordance with r. 6.3 after parties have sent him Form 6.3 duly completed.

Single Bills. The Single Bills is the motion roll of the Inner House. As a general rule appeals **40.15.3** are not heard in the Single Bills. Appeals dealt with on the Single Bills might include an urgent appeal, an appeal clearly incompetent or an appeal in respect of recall of arrestment or inhibition or interlocutory decisions where, *e.g.* an imminent proof might be saved.

Hearings before Inner House. An appeal will be heard by a Division of the Inner House. A **40.15.4** Division consists of four judges, but three are a quorum: C.S.A. 1988, s. 2(2) and (4). Because of pressure of criminal business in the High Court of Justiciary and other civil business it is unusual nowadays for a Division to sit with more than three judges. The Lord President may direct three judges to sit as an Extra Division: C.S.A. 1988, s. 2(3).

Where a Division before whom a cause is pending (*a*) considers the cause to be one of difficulty or importance or (*b*) the Division is equally divided in opinion, it may appoint the cause to be reheard by such larger court as is necessary for the proper disposal of the cause: C.S.A. 1988, s. 36. A larger court would in the first instance be a court of five judges; a rehearing of a cause on a point which had been decided by a court of five judges would be heard by a court of seven judges and so on. It is not always necessary for the cause to be heard by the Division before it is reheard by a larger court, particularly where all parties are agreed. A larger court will be required where consideration has to be given as to whether to overturn a previous decision of a Division. Hearings before a larger court may be appropriate on questions of practice or procedure. Where the question at issue is construction of a UK statute the preferable course is for appeal to the House of Lords: see *Drummond v. I.R.C.* 1951 S.C. 482.

The general rule is that when a case has been reported in Session Cases or the (English) Law Reports, it should be cited from that source: *McGowan v. Summit at Lloyds*, 2002 S.L.T. 1258, 1273 at para.[57] (Ex Div.). See also now P.N. No. 5 of 2004 (in respect of Session Cases).

40.15.5   *Fee.* The court fee for the hearing of an appeal on the Summar Roll is payable by each party for every 30 minutes or part thereof. For fee, see Court of Session etc. Fees Order 1997, Table of Fees, Pt I, B, item 17 or C, item 17 [S.I. 1997 No. appeal heard in the Single Bills will under Pt I, B, item 22, or C, item 21. Certain persons are exempt from payment of fees: see 1997 Fees Order, art.5, substituted by S.S.I. 2002 No. 270. A fee exemption certificate must be lodged in process: see P.N. No. 1 of 2002.

Where a party is legally represented, the fee may be debited under a credit scheme introduced on 1st April 1976 by P.N. No. 4 of 1976 to the account (if one is kept or permitted) of the agent by the court cashier, and an account will be rendered weekly by the court cashier's office to the agent for all court fees due that week for immediate settlement. An agent not on the credit scheme will have an account opened for the purpose of lodging the fee: P.N. No. 2 of 1995. A debit slip and a copy of the court hearing time sheet will be delivered to the agent's box or sent by DX or post.

A party litigant must pay (by cash, cheque or postal order) to the clerk of court at the end of the hearing or, if the hearing lasts more than a day, at the end of each day: P.N. No. 2 of 1995. A receipt will be issued. The assistant clerk of session will acknowledge receipt of the sum received from the clerk of court on the Minute of Proceedings.

40.15.6   *Remit to sheriff court, or proof or additional proof.* The powers of the court in s. 32 of the C.S.A. 1988 (to remit to the sheriff court or order proof or additional proof) should be noted. The court may order proof or additional proof: see *e.g. Pirie v. Leask* 1964 S.C. 103 (*res noviter*). The power is exercised only under exceptional circumstances: *Coul v. Ayrshire C.C.* 1909 S.C. 422; *Mitchell v. Sellar* 1915 S.C. 360, 361 *per* L.P. Strathclyde. The court may remit to the sheriff principal or sheriff: *e.g.* for a report on the accuracy of an interlocutor (*Whyte v. Whyte* (1895) 23 R. 320). That the power to remit was one to be exercised only in circumstances which justify this as an exceptional course of action was mentioned in *Japan Leasing (Europe) plc v. Weir's Tr (No. 2)* 1998 S.C. 543. In *DTL Gas Supplies Ltd v. Protan Srl*, 1999 S.L.T. 397 (First Div.), a remit was made under s. 32(2) of the 1988 Act for the sheriff to consider whether to exercise the dispensing power in a late application for leave to appeal. A remit was not made for this purpose in *Walker v. Tidewater Cyprus Ltd*, December 5, 2003, 2003 G.W.D. 40-1070 (First Div.) where it was held that an appellant was not entitled as a matter of course to a remit (there was a plain failure to apply for leave).

Although the court has to consider the interests of justice in considering a motion for additional proof, it will be slow to reopen a proof which has been concluded when both parties were legally represented at the proof and where judgment has been issued determining all matters ventilated at the proof: *Ralston v. Secretary of State for Scotland* 1991 S.C. 336 (*dicta* of L.P. Dunedin in *Coul*, above, at p. 424 applied that the court will not make an order on light grounds particularly where a party has by his own negligence failed to bring forward available evidence or where a party seeks leave to introduce new evidence to strengthen a weak point).

Appeal prints

40.16. An appeal print shall be in the form of a record and shall contain—

(a) the whole pleadings and interlocutors in the cause;

(b) where the appeal is directed at the refusal of the inferior court to allow the pleadings to be amended, the text of the proposed amendment; and

(c) where available, the judgment of the inferior court (including in an appeal in a summary cause under the Summary Cause Rules of the Sheriff Court, the stated case of the sheriff).

Deriv. P.N. No. 2 of 1989, para. 2(1)

40.16.1   *General note.* If the judgment of the inferior court is not available when the appeal print is lodged, it will have to be included in an appendix: r. 40.17(1)(*a*).

Lodging of appendices in appeals

40.17.—[1] (1) Where, in an appeal—

(a) the judgment of the inferior court has not been included in the appeal, or

(b) it is sought to submit notes of evidence or other documents for consideration by the court,

the appellant shall lodge an appendix incorporating such documents within three months after the cause has been appointed to the Summar Roll.

(2) Where the appellant considers that an appendix is not necessary, the appellant shall, by the date specified in paragraph (1)—

(a) give written intimation of that fact to the Deputy Principal Clerk; and

(b) send a copy of that intimation to the respondent.

(3) Where a respondent in an appeal seeks to submit notes of evidence or other documents for consideration by the court which the appellant has given written intimation to the respondent he does not intend to include in his appendix, the respondent shall incorporate such notes or documents in an appendix which he shall lodge within one month after the date on which intimation under paragraph (2) or this paragraph, as the case may be, was given.

(4) Where an appellant fails to lodge an appendix in accordance with paragraph (1), a respondent may apply by motion to the Inner House to have the appeal refused.

[2] (5) In a case where early disposal is sought by virtue of rule 40.7A, the Inner House may, on the application by motion of the appellant, determine that paragraphs (1) to (4) shall not apply or shall apply subject to such modifications as it considers appropriate.

Deriv. R.C.S. 1965, r.294A(a)(part) inserted by SI 1972/2022, and P.N. No. 2 of 1989, para.2(2) (r.40.17(1))

---

[1] R.40.17(1) amended by S.I. 1994 No. 2901 (minor correction).
[2] R.40.17(5) inserted by S.I. 1997 No. 2692 (effective 1st December 1997).

General note. The appellant must lodge any appendix within three months after the cause has **40.17.1** been appointed to the Summar Roll. If he does not intend to lodge an appendix, the appellant must give written intimation of that to the respondent: r.40.17(2) and (3). Where the appellant does not intend to include in his appendix documents which the respondent wishes to be lodged, the clear implication of r.40.17(3) is that he must given written intimation of that fact to the respondent to enable the latter to lodge an appendix. Parties should discuss and try to agree the documents to be lodged in one appendix.

If the respondent wishes to lodge an appendix he has one month from the date of such intimation to do so: r.40.17(3).

If an appellant fails to lodge an appendix timeously the respondent may apply by motion to have the appeal refused: r.40.17(4). The appeal is not, as previously under R.C.S. 1965, r.294A(b), deemed to be abandoned.

Where a motion for early disposal has been granted under r.40.11, the interlocutor may have to make special provision for the lodging of appendices.

Under r.40.7A early disposal must be sought of an appeal against an interlocutor which is not final. It may be necessary to ask the court not to apply or to modify the application of r.40.17(1) to (4): r.40.17(5).

"within three months", "within one month". The date from which the period is calculated is **40.17.2** not counted. Where the last day falls on a Saturday or Sunday or a public holiday on which the Office of Court is closed, the next available day is allowed: r.1.3(7). For office hours and public holidays, see note 3.1.2.

"written intimation". For methods, see r.16.9.   **40.17.3**

"motion". For motions, see Chap. 23.   **40.17.4**

Notes of evidence not extended when agreed in appeals

40.18. Where, in an appeal, the parties are agreed that on any particular issue the decision appealed against is not to be submitted to review, it shall not be necessary to reproduce the notes of evidence or documents relating to that issue.

Deriv. R.C.S. 1965, r.262(d)

Amendment of pleadings in appeals

40.19.—(1) Where, after an appeal has been marked, a party applies by motion to have the pleadings amended in terms of a minute of amendment and answers, he shall apply for a direction as to further procedure.

(2) Where it appears to the Inner House that the proposed amendment makes a material change to the pleadings, it may set aside the decision, or

recall the interlocutor, as the case may be, of the inferior court appealed against and remit the cause back to the inferior court for a further hearing.

Deriv. P.N. 26th March 1981

40.19.1   *General note.* Amendment may be allowed on, during or after an appeal. This may occur after debate but is uncommon after evidence has been led. In the former case, if allowed the Inner House may refuse to hear argument until the judge at first instance has reconsidered the amended pleadings and the appeal will be remitted for that purpose: *Wallace v. Scottish Special Housing Association* 1981 S.L.T.(Notes) 60. In the latter case, amendment to raise fresh issues of fact may not be allowed because it could unjustly prejudice the other party who might have conducted his case differently: *Thomson v. Glasgow Corporation* 1962 S.C.(H.L.) 36; *McGuffie v. Forth Valley Health Board* 1991 S.L.T. 231; *cf. Moyes v. Burntisland Shipping Co.* 1952 S.C. 429 (allowed in exceptional circumstances to clarify existing controversy not a new one).

    The purpose of r.40.19 is to give the Inner House the opportunity to consider, before the appeal is heard, whether the amendment involves a material change as requires consideration by the Lord Ordinary.

40.19.2   *"motion".* For motions, see Chap. 23. A motion enrolled to amend pleadings will require appearance on behalf of the party enrolling the motion.

Referral to family mediation in appeals from sheriff court

[1] **40.20.** In an appeal from the sheriff court in which an order in relation to parental responsibilities or parental rights under section 11 of the Children (Scotland) Act 1995 is in issue, the court may, where it considers it appropriate to do so, refer that issue to a mediator accredited to a specified family mediation organisation.

———

[1] R.40.20 inserted by S.I. 1996 No. 2587 (effective 1st November 1996).

40.20.1   *General note.* This rule was inserted to enable the court to refer a case on appeal from the sheriff court to mediation if it so wished. Rule 40.20 is in the same terms as r.49.23 which applies to family actions in the Court of Session and O.C.R. 1993, r.33.22 which applies to such motions in the sheriff court.

    On referral to mediation, see note 49.23.1.

Use of Gaelic

[1] **40.21.**—(1) This rule applies where an inferior court has authorised the use of Gaelic by a party.

    (2) If—

      (a) the party wishes to address the Inner House in the appeal; or

      (b) where proof has been ordered by the Inner House, the party wishes to give oral evidence or to address the judge to whom the Inner House has remitted the cause, in Gaelic,

he may apply by motion for authority to do so.

    (3) Where the court has granted authority under paragraph (2), an interpreter shall be provided by the court.

———

[1] R.40.21 inserted by S.S.I. 2004 No. 305 and substituted by S.S.I. 2004 No. 52 (effective 1st March, 2004).

40.21.1   *General note.* The former mysterious and badly drafted rule, inserted by A.S. (R.C.S.A. No.4) (Miscellaneous) 2001 [S.S.I. 2001 No. 305], has been replaced by this rule. The former rule applied only to an appeal against an interlocutor which granted an application by a party litigant to address the court or give evidence in Gaelic. The new rule applies to any appeal in which the inferior court authorized the use of Gaelic by a party.

    The Act of Court (No.1 of 2001) of the Sheriffdom of Grampian, Highlands and Islands permits the use of Gaelic in Portree, Lochmaddy and Stornoway sheriff courts.

40.21.2   *"inferior court".* This is defined in r.40.1(2)(c) as the Lyon Court or the sheriff. This Chapter applies only to decisions of an inferior court. The use of the expression "inferior court" in r.40.21(1) is, therefore, superfluous.

"*motion*". For motions, see Chap.23.   **40.21.3**

CHAPTER 41

APPEALS UNDER STATUTE

PART I

GENERAL PROVISIONS

Application and interpretation of this Chapter
    41.1.—(1) This Chapter applies to an appeal to the court from a decision of a tribunal other than a decision in the Outer House or a court to which Chapter 40 (appeals from inferior courts) applies.
    [1] (2) In this Chapter, unless the context otherwise requires—
        "appeal" includes stated case, case, special case (other than a special case under section 27 of the Act of 1988), reference or submission, or an application under an enactment by virtue of which a person may question the validity of a decision;
        "case" means stated case, special case (other than a special case under section 27 of the Court of Session Act 1988), reference or submission;
        "decision" includes assessment, determination, order or scheme;
        "party" means the person appearing before the tribunal against the decision of which appeal is taken;
        "tribunal" means court, Secretary of State, Minister, Department, statutory tribunal, referee, authority or arbiter, as the case may be, against whose decision the appeal is taken.

Deriv. RCS 1965, r. 276 amended by S.I. 1972 No. 2021, and r. 290(a)(part) amended by S.I. 1973 No. 540 and 1986 No. 1955

---

[1] Rule 41.1(2) was amended by S.I. 1996 No. 1756 (effective 5th August 1996).

General note. Most statutory appeals are directed to be to the Court of Session and, following **41.1.1** a long tradition, are dealt with in the Inner House. An enactment may, however, provide that an appeal is to be heard by the Lord Ordinary or a single judge in which case r. 41.43 (appeals to Lord Ordinary) will apply.
    Appeal processes are lodged in the General Department: r. 3.2(2)(b).

Stated case and appeals in Form 41.19. This Chapter provides two forms of appeal, stated case **41.1.2** and appeals made in Form 41.19.
    (1) Stated case procedure applies to a stated case, case, special case (other than one under s. 27 of the C.S.A. 1988: for which see Chap. 78), reference and submission. It requires the tribunal to state findings-in-fact on which its decision was based, rehearse the evidence relevant to those findings and give its reasons, these often not all being given in full at the time of the decision. The procedure is cumbersome but appropriate in such cases.

(2) Appeal under the Form 41.19 procedure is a simpler procedure involving reproducing in or appending to the appeal in Form 41.19 the decision appealed against. It is the appropriate procedure where a reasoned decision has been given by the tribunal or findings-in-fact are not required.

Applications for leave to appeal

[1] **41.2.**—(1) Where leave to appeal is required, an application for such leave shall be made, in the first instance, to the tribunal which made the decision sought to be appealed against unless—

(a) the enactment allowing the appeal requires the application to be made to the court; or

(b) there are special circumstances which make it impracticable or impossible to apply to the tribunal.

(2) Where—

(a) the tribunal has refused leave to appeal and such refusal is not final, or

(b) leave to appeal is required from the court and not the tribunal,

any application to the court for leave to appeal shall be made in Form 40.2 to the Inner House.

(3) An application to the court under paragraph (2) for leave to appeal shall be lodged in the General Department—

(a) within the period prescribed by the enactment by virtue of which it is made; or

(b) where no such period is prescribed, within the period mentioned in paragraph (1)(b) of rule 41.20 (lodging of appeal in court).

(4) An application to the court for leave to appeal shall include a statement setting out the proposed grounds of appeal and the grounds on which leave to appeal is sought.

(5) There shall be lodged with an application to the court under paragraph (3)—

(a) a process in accordance with rule 4.4 (steps of process);

(b) where applicable—

(i) evidence that leave to appeal has been refused by the tribunal;

(ii) a copy of the grounds of appeal submitted to the tribunal; and

(iii) any note by the tribunal setting out the reasons for its refusal;

(c) a copy of the document issued by the tribunal setting out the decision complained of and any reasons for that decision; and

(d) where the tribunal itself exercised an appellate function, a copy of the decision of the tribunal from which that appeal was taken and any reasons given for that decision.

Deriv. P.N. 6th November 1986 (41.2(4) and (5))

---

[1] R.41.2 amended by SI 1996/1756 (effective 5th August 1996).

General note. An enactment may require either the tribunal or the Court of Session to grant **41.2.1** leave to appeal. Where leave may be sought from either the tribunal or the court, r. 41.2(1) requires leave to be sought in the first instance from the tribunal.

Time for seeking leave. Following the amendment in A.S. (R.C.S.A. No. 3) (Miscellaneous) **41.2.2** 1996 [SI 1996/1756], the rule now is that where leave to appeal is sought from the court it must be sought within the period specified in the enactment under which it is made or, where there is no such period, within the period for lodging the appeal in the RCS 1994, *i.e.*, within 42 days after the date specified in rule 41.20(1)(b) (lodging of appeal in court): r. 41.2(3)(b).

It may be that when leave is sought from the court the time for lodging an appeal may be close to expiry (because of, *e.g.* the time taken in seeking leave from the tribunal) and the time for lodging the appeal may expire before or by the time leave is granted. To deal with this problem created by having to seek leave from the court within the same period as the time for lodging the appeal, r. 41.20(3) provides that (so long as leave is sought timeously) the period for lodging the appeal after leave is granted is extended by 7 days.

A further problem is that an appellant may be presented with a difficulty in obtaining leave from the tribunal, imperilling his ability to seek leave from the court within the 42 day period for lodging the appeal. For example, the tribunal may not have decided to refuse leave or even not been able to consider it, but the time limit for seeking leave of the court and lodge the appeal is about to expire. To meet this difficulty, r. 41.2(1)(b) provides for seeking leave of the court without first seeking leave of the tribunal where it is impracticable or impossible to do so.

Rules 41.2 and 41.20(2) do not deal with a situation where leave must be sought from a tribunal first and is refused, there being a right to apply after the refusal to the court for leave. That is, where the 42 day period, from the (substantive) decision sought to be appealed against, required by rr. 41.2 and 41.20(1)(b), has expired before leave is refused or an appeal to the court can thereafter be made. In *Hakim v. Secretary of State for the Home Department,* 2001 S.C. 789 it was held by an Extra Div, unattracted to requiring an appellant to seek judicial review or to use the dispensing power in r. 2.1, that the 42 day period runs from the date of refusal of leave. What is odd about this case is that the appellant still had eight days remaining, of the 42 day period after the date of intimation of refusal of leave, in which to lodge an application to the court for leave. No explanation was given or sought for his not doing so.

The former provisions in r. 41.2 created an unsatisfactory position, in certain circumstances giving an appellant 42 days to seek leave from the tribunal, 14 days to seek leave from the court and a further 42 days to lodge the appeal.

41.2.3   *Leave to appeal out of time.* In the case of an appeal under statute which specifies a time-limit for lodging an appeal, the court may grant leave to appeal out of time, unless it is apparent that the rule is imperative, where the failure to comply was caused by excusable mistake or some cause over which the appellant had no control and there is no substantial prejudice to the respondent: see *National Commercial Bank of Scotland v. Assessor for Fife,* 1963 S.C. 197.

41.2.3A   *Human rights.* It is not a breach of art.6(1) of the ECHR for the judge at first instance, who determined the substantive issue, to be the judge who also decides whether leave to appeal should be granted: *Umair v. Umair,* 2002 S.C.153 (Ex Div.).

41.2.4   *Fee.* There is no fee for lodging an application for leave to appeal.

Determination of applications for leave to appeal

41.3.—(1) On lodging an application for leave to appeal under rule 41.2, the applicant shall apply by motion to the Inner House for an order for intimation and service.

[1] (1A) An order for intimation and service under paragraph (1) shall include a requirement to intimate the application to the clerk of the tribunal.

(2) On expiry of the period within which answers may be lodged, the applicant may apply by motion to the Inner House for the application to be granted.

(3) Where an application for leave to appeal has been granted—

(a) the Deputy Principal Clerk shall send a certified copy of the interlocutor granting the application to the tribunal; and

(b) in an appeal by stated case within 14 days after the date on which the certified copy of the interlocutor was sent to it, the tribunal shall state a case in accordance with rule 41.9 (preparation and issue of case).

[1] (4) Where an application for leave to appeal has been refused, the Deputy Principal Clerk shall send to the tribunal a copy of the interlocutor refusing the application.

---

[1] Rule 41.3(1A) inserted by S.S.I. 2006 No. 83 (effective 17th March 2006).

41.3.1   *"motion".* For motions, see Chap. 23. A motion in the Inner House is heard in the Single Bills: r. 23.6(4).

41.3.2   *"intimation and service".* For methods, see Chap. 16, Pt I.

41.3.3   *"period within which answers may be lodged".* The court will usually fix a period of 21 days.

41.3.3A   *"send".* This includes deliver: r. 1.3(1) (definition of "send").

41.3.4   *Fee.* A court fee for the hearing of the application will be payable by each party for every 30 minutes after the first 30 minutes or part thereof. For fee, see Court of Session etc. Fees Order 1997, Table of Fees, Pt I, item 22 [S.I. 1997 No. 688, as amended, pp.C1201 *et seq.*]. Certain persons are exempt from payment of fees: see 1997 Fees Order, art.5, substituted by S.S.I. 2002 No 270. A fee exemption certificate must be lodged in process: see P.N. No. 1 of 2002.

Where a party is legally represented, the fee may be debited under a credit scheme introduced on 1st April 1976 by P.N. No. 4 of 1976 to the account (if one is kept or permitted) of the agent by the court cashier, and an account will be rendered weekly by the court cashier's office to the agent for all court fees due that week for immediate settlement. An agent not on the credit scheme will have an account opened for the purpose of lodging the fee: P.N. No. 2 of 1995. A debit slip and a copy of the court hearing time sheet will be delivered to the agent's box or sent by DX or post.

A party litigant must pay cash to the clerk of court at the end of the hearing or, if the hearing lasts more than a day, at the end of each day: P.N. No. 2 of 1995. A receipt will be issued. The assistant clerk of session will acknowledge receipt of the sum received from the clerk of court on the Minute of Proceedings.

Competency of appeals

[1] **41.3A.**—(1) Where the Deputy Principal Clerk considers that an appeal may be incompetent, he may, at any time before the cause is brought before the Inner House, refer it to a single judge in accordance with paragraph (2).

(2) Any referral by the Deputy Principal Clerk under paragraph (1) shall be made to a judge nominated for that purpose by the Lord President.

(3) Where a referral is made under paragraph (1), the judge may—
- (a) order any party to make representations to him in respect of the competency of the appeal;
- (b) refuse the appeal on the ground it is incompetent;
- (c) direct that the appeal is to proceed as if the referral had not been made;
- (d) make such order as to expenses or otherwise as he thinks fit.

(4) Any decision of a judge in respect of an appeal referred to him under paragraph (1) shall be final and not subject to review.

---

[1] Rule 41.3A inserted by S.S.I. 2004 No.331 (effective 6th August 2004).

General note. This rule replicates the provisions in r. 38.14 (objections to competency of **41.3A.1** reclaiming motions) and r. 40.12 (objections to competency of appeals from inferior courts) in respect of other appeals. The DPCS refers an (allegedly) incompetent appeal to a single judge. It is introduced to prevent the time of the Inner House being wasted by incompetent appeals (particularly by party litigants).

"*incompetent*". An appeal may be incompetent because, *e.g.*, the appeal days have expired **41.3A.2** before the appeal was made or because the decision may not be appealed.

"*final and not subject to review*". The decision of the single judge may not be reclaimed against. **41.3A.3**

Intimation of final interlocutor

[1]**41.3B.** The Deputy Principal Clerk shall send to the tribunal a copy of the final interlocutor in an appeal.

---

[1] Rule 41.3B inserted by S.S.I. 2006 No. 83 (effective 17th March 2006).

"*send*". This includes deliver: r. 1.3(1) (definition of "send"). **41.3B.1**

PART II

APPEALS BY STATED CASE ETC.

Application and interpretation of this Part

41.4. [1] Subject to the provisions of the enactment providing for appeal and to Parts III to XIII, this Part shall regulate the procedure in—
- (a) an appeal by stated case, special case, case, reference or submission against the decision of a tribunal;
- (b) a case stated by an arbiter;
- (c) all statutory proceedings for obtaining the opinion of the court on a

question before the issue of a decision by a tribunal or by appeal against such a decision; and

(d) a case required to be stated by a tribunal referred to in subsection (1), as modified by subsection (7), of section 11 of the Tribunals and Inquiries Act 1992.

Deriv. R.C.S. 1965, r. 276 amended by S.I. 1972 No. 2021

---

[1] Rule 41.4 amended by S.S.I. 2004 No. 52 (effective from 1st March, 2004) and by S.S.I. 2004 No. 331 (effective August 6, 2004).

41.4.1   *General note.* Stated case procedure applies to a stated case, case, special case (other than one under s. 27 of the C.S.A. 1988: for which see Chap. 78), reference and submission. It involves the tribunal in stating findings-in-fact on which its decision was based, rehearsing the evidence relevant to those findings and giving its reasons, these often not all being given in full at the time of the decision. The procedure is cumbersome but appropriate in such cases.

Appeals to which this Part applies include the following:

(1) *Stated cases.* These include—Stamp Act 1891, s. 13 (from Commissioners of Inland Revenue *re* assessment of duty); Taxes Management Act 1970, s. 56 (from General or Special Commissioners); Inheritance Tax Act 1984, s. 225 (from Special Commissioners); Stamp Duty Reserve Tax Regulations 1986 [S.I. 1986 No. 1711], reg.10 (from Special Commissioners); Tribunals and Inquiries Act 1992, s. 11 and Sched. 1 and Tribunals and Inquiries (Value Added Tax Tribunals) Order 1972 [S.I. 1972 No. 1210] (from VAT and Duties Tribunals); Pensions Appeal Tribunal Act 1943, ss. 6 and 13 (from PAT); Lands Tribunal Act 1949, s. 3(3) (from LT); Agricultural Marketing Act 1958, s. 12(2) (from disciplinary committee); Building (Scotland) Act 1959, s. 16(3) (from sheriff); Industrial and Provident Societies Act 1965, s. 60(9) (*re* disputes involving registered society); Social Work (Scotland) Act 1968, s. 50 (from sheriff from children's hearing); Administration of Justice (Scotland) Act 1972, s. 3 (from arbiter); Town and Country Planning (Scotland) Act 1972, s. 234 (from Secretary of State in determining planning permission under s. 51); Social Security Act 1973, s. 86 (from Occupational Pensions Board: by stated case by virtue of r. 41.34); Local Government (Scotland) Act 1973, s. 103(2) (on special report to Commission by Controller of Audit); Friendly Societies Act 1974, s. 78 (*re* certain disputes); Restrictive Practices Court Act 1976, s. 10 (from RPC); Iron and Steel Act 1982, s. 26(5)(a) (from Iron and Steel Arbitration Tribunal); Representation of the People Act 1983, s. 134(1) (from sheriffs principal who cannot agree *re* election of councillors) and s. 146(4) (from election court on admissibility of evidence etc.); New Roads and Street Works Act 1991, s. 158(2) (from arbiter); Social Security Administration Act 1992, ss. 18(1) and 58 (from Secretary of State: by stated case by virtue of r. 41.34); Friendly Societies Act 1992, s. 80(4) (from arbiter); Tribunal and Inquiries Act 1992, s. 11 and Sched. 1 (from various tribunals).

(2) *Special cases.* These include—Compensation (Defence) Act 1939, ss. 7 and 18(2) (from Shipping Tribunal or General Tribunal); Crofters (Scotland) Act 1961, s. 4(3) (from Land Court); Scottish Land Court Rules 1992, r. 88 [S.I. 1992 No. 2656]; Representation of the People Act 1983, s. 146(1) (from election court).

(3) *References.* These include—Defamation Act 1952, s. 4(4) (*re* steps in fulfilment of offer of amends): see r. 54.1; Social Security Administration Act 1992, ss. 18(1) and 58 (from Secretary of State: by stated case by virtue of r. 41.34); Pension Schemes Act 1993, s. 150(7) (from Pensions Ombudsman: by stated case by virtue of r. 41.34) and s. 173(1) (from Occupational Pensions Board: by stated case by virtue of r. 41.34). Certain references are by petition and not by appeal (and are assigned to the Petition Department). These are—Railway and Canal Commission (Abolition) Act 1949, s. 1(1): by petition by virtue of r. 14.2(h); Mines (Working Facilities and Support) Act 1966, s. 4(3) (grant of right *re* minerals and compensation): by petition by virtue of r. 14.2(h); Defamation Act 1952, s. 4(4) (*re* steps in fulfilment of offer of amends where no action for defamation taken): r. 54.2.

41.4.2   *Case by tribunal under section 11(1)of the Tribunals and Inquiries Act 1992.* S.11(1) as modified by s. 11(7) of the 1992 Act provides that any party to proceedings before certain specified tribunals in Sched. 1 to the Act who is dissatisfied in point of law with a decision of the tribunal may appeal to, or require the tribunal to state a case for the opinion of, the Court of Session.

Applications for case

41.5.—(1) An application for a case for the opinion of the court on any question shall be made by minute setting out the question on which the case is applied for.

(2) A minute under paragraph (1) shall be sent to the clerk of the tribunal—

   (a) where the application must be made before the issue of the decision of the tribunal, at any time before the issue of the decision; or

¹ (b) where the application may be made—

      (i) after the issue of the decision of the tribunal, or

      (ii) in a cause in which a statement of the reasons for the decision was given later than the issue of the decision, after the issue of that statement,

    within the period mentioned in paragraph (3).

² (3) The period referred to in paragraph (2)(b) is—

   (a) the period prescribed by the enactment under which the appeal is made; or

   (b) where no such period is prescribed, within 14 days after the issue of the decision or statement of reasons, as the case may be.

Deriv. R.C.S. 1965, r. 277(a) amended by S.I. 1982 No. 1825 (r. 41.5(1) and (2))

---

¹ Rule 41.5(2)(b) amended by S.I. 1996 No. 1756 (effective 5th August 1996).
² Rule 41.5(3) inserted by S.I. 1996 No. 1756 (effective 5th August 1996).

"minute". R.15.1 (applications by minute) does not apply as the minute is not an application to the Court of Session.   **41.5.1**

"sent". This includes deliver: r. 1.3(1) (definition of "send").   **41.5.2**

"within 14 days". The date from which the period is calculated is not counted.   **41.5.3**

Period for lodging appeal. This rule was amended by A.S. (R.C.S.A. No. 3) (Miscellaneous) 1996 [S.I. 1996 No. 1756] to allow for enactments which provide a time-limit for appeals by stated case: this brings r. 41.5 into line with r. 41.20 in this respect. Where the enactment under which the appeal is made does not prescribe a time-limit, r. 41.5 prescribes 14 days after the issue of the decision or reasons.   **41.5.4**

It should be noted that in appeals to which this part applies (stated cases), the period for appealing under r. 41.5(2)(b) is 14 days and not 42 days as in the case of appeals to which Pt III applies (see r. 41.20(1)(b)). Such a mistake was made in *City of Edinburgh Council v. Rapley*, 2000 S.C. 78.

Additional questions by other parties

41.6.—(1) On receipt of an application under rule 41.5 (applications for case), the clerk of the tribunal shall send a copy of the minute to every other party.

(2) Within 14 days after the date on which the clerk of the tribunal complied with paragraph (1), any other party may lodge with the clerk a minute setting out any additional question he proposes for the case; and on so doing he shall send a copy of it to every other party.

Deriv. R.C.S. 1965, r. 277(b)

"send". This includes deliver: r. 1.3(1) (definition of "send").   **41.6.1**

"within 14 days". The date from which the period is calculated is not counted.   **41.6.2**

"minute". R.15.1 (applications by minute) does not apply as the minute is not an application to the Court of Session.   **41.6.3**

Consideration of application by tribunal

41.7.—(1) Within 21 days after the expiry of the period allowed for lodging a minute under rule 41.6(2) (additional questions by other parties), the tribunal shall—

    (a) decide to state a case on the basis of the questions set out in the application for a case under rule 41.5(1) and any minute under rule 41.6(2);

    (b) where it is of the opinion that the proposed question—
        (i) does not arise,
        (ii) does not require to be decided for the purposes of the appeal, or
        (iii) is frivolous,
        refuse to state a case on that question; or

    (c) where the application under rule 41.5(1) is made before the facts have been ascertained and the tribunal is of the opinion that it is necessary or expedient that the facts should be ascertained before the application is disposed of, defer further consideration of the application until the facts have been ascertained by it.

(2) Where the tribunal has deferred a decision under paragraph (1)(c), it shall, within 14 days after it has ascertained the facts, decide whether to state or refuse to state a case.

(3) Where the tribunal makes a decision under paragraph (1) or (2), the clerk of the tribunal shall intimate that decision to each party.

(4) Where the tribunal has refused to state a case on any question, there shall be sent to the applicant with the intimation under paragraph (3)—

    (a) a certificate specifying—
        (i) the date of the decision of the tribunal; and
        (ii) the reasons for refusal; and

    (b) where the refusal has been made after the facts have been ascertained, a note of the proposed findings-in-fact on which the tribunal proposes to base its decision; or

    (c) where the refusal has been made before the facts have been ascertained, a note of, or sufficient reference to, the averments of the parties in the appeal on which the refusal is based.

Deriv. R.C.S. 1965, r. 277(c) and (d)

41.7.1   *"within 14 days"*. The date from which the period is calculated is not counted.

41.7.2   *"intimate"*. For methods, see r. 16.7.

41.7.3   *"sent"*. This includes deliver: r. 1.3(1) (definition of "send").

41.7.4   *"Where the tribunal refuses to state a case"*. In an arbitration the arbiter has a discretion on an application to state a case to postpone further consideration of the application until the facts have been ascertained, and it is inappropriate for the court to require him to do so under s. 3 of the Administration of Justice Act 1972: *Edmond Nuttall Ltd v. Amec Projects Ltd* 1992 S.C. 133. But the arbiter's decision might be judicially reviewed: *Shanks & McEwan (Contractors) Ltd v. Mifflin Construction Ltd* 1993 S.L.T. 1124.

Procedure for ordaining tribunal to state a case

41.8.—(1) Where the tribunal has refused to state case on any question, the party whose application has been refused may, within 14 days after the date on which intimation of such refusal was made under rule 41.7(3), lodge in the General Department—

    (a) an application by note to the Inner House for an order to require the other party to show cause why a case should not be stated;

    (b) the certificate and any note issued under rule 41.7(4); and

    (c) a process in accordance with rule 4.4 (steps of process).

(2) A note under paragraph (1)(*a*) shall—
  (*a*) state briefly the grounds on which the application is made; and
  (*b*) specify the order and any incidental order sought.
(3) An application under paragraph (1) shall be put out in the Single Bills before the Inner House on the first available day after the date on which the note under paragraph (1)(*a*) was lodged for an order for service of the note on—
  (*a*) the tribunal; and
  (*b*) every other party.
(4) After the period for lodging answers has expired, the Inner House shall, on a motion by the noter, without hearing parties—
  (*a*) appoint the note to the Summar Roll for hearing; or
  (*b*) direct that the note be heard in the Single Bills.
(5) The noter shall intimate the decision of the Inner House on the note to the tribunal.

Deriv. R.C.S. 1965, r. 278

"refused to state a case". A tribunal refuses to state a case where it agrees to state a case on **41.8.1** certain questions but refuses to do so in respect of others: *John G. McGregor (Contractors) Ltd v. Grampian R.C.* 1989 S.L.T. 299.

"within 14 days". The date from which the period is calculated is not counted. Where the **41.8.2** last day falls on a Saturday or Sunday or a public holiday on which the Office of Court is closed, the next available day is allowed: r. 1.3(7). For office hours and public holidays, see note 3.1.2.

"note". R. 15.2 (applications by note) applies. The grounds for the application must be **41.8.3** briefly stated and must specify any incidental order sought (as well as an order requiring any other party to the proceedings before the tribunal to show cause why a case should not be stated): r. 41.8(1) and (2).

"order for service". The note and the interlocutor must be served on the tribunal as well as **41.8.4** every other party to the proceedings before the tribunal: r. 41.8(3). Where the tribunal has a clerk, the order may be served on him, otherwise it should be served on the chairman of the tribunal.
For service, see Chap. 16, Pt. I.

Summar Roll. As a general rule, appeals are appointed to and heard on the Summar Roll. **41.8.5** The court must be satisfied that service has been executed. An execution copy of the appeal must be lodged before the motion is enrolled for a hearing. Originally the Summar Roll was the roll for dealing with causes summarily and the Short Roll was for more complicated causes; the latter, however, has fallen into desuetude. Once appointed to the Summar Roll a diet is fixed by the Keeper of the Rolls in accordance with r. 6.3 after parties have sent him Form 6.3 duly completed.

Single Bills. The Single Bills is the motion roll of the Inner House. As a general rule, **41.8.6** appeals are not heard in the Single Bills. Appeals dealt with on the Single Bills might include an urgent appeal or an appeal clearly incompetent.

"intimate". For methods, see r. 16.7.   **41.8.7**

Preparation and issue of the case
41.9.—(1) Where the tribunal has decided, or is ordered under rule 41.8, to state a case, the tribunal shall, within 14 days after the date of intimation of its decision to the parties, cause the case to be prepared in Form 41.9 and copies of it to be submitted in draft to each party.
(2) The case shall—
  (*a*) specify the relevant provision of the enactment under which it is prepared;
  (*b*) state in numbered paragraphs the facts and circumstances out of which the case arises, as agreed or found, or as the case may be, the decision of the tribunal and the reasons for the decision; and
  (*c*) set out the question for answer by the court.

(3) Within 21 days after the date on which the draft case is submitted under paragraph (1), each party shall—

(a) return a copy of it to the clerk of the tribunal with a note of any amendments which he seeks to have made; and

(b) intimate such amendments to every other party.

(4) Within 28 days after the expiry of the period for return of the case under paragraph (3), the tribunal—

(a) shall adjust and settle the case; and

(b) may, when so doing, add such further or additional findings-in-fact and such additional questions as it thinks necessary for the disposal of the subject-matter of the case.

(5) Where the tribunal does not accept any amendment sought by a party, it shall append to the case a note of—

(a) the terms of the amendment proposed by the party and any statement by that party in support of the proposal; and

(b) its reasons for rejecting the proposed amendment.

(6) When the case has been settled by the tribunal, the case shall be authenticated by the clerk of the tribunal who shall send it to the party, or first party, who applied for it.

Deriv. R.C.S. 1965, r. 279 (r. 41.9(1)(part) and (2))

41.9.1   *"within 14 days", "within 21 days", "within 28 days"*. The date from which the period is calculated is not counted.

41.9.2   *"send"*. This includes deliver: r. 1.3(1) (definition of "send").

Intimation of intention to proceed

41.10.—(1) The party to whom the case has been sent under rule 41.9(6) or paragraph (3) of this rule shall, within 14 days after the date of receipt of it—

(a) intimate to every other party a notice stating whether or not he intends to proceed with the case; and

(b) send a copy of the case to every other party.

(2) Where the party to whom the case has been sent under rule 41.9(6) does not intend to proceed with it, he shall, on intimating that fact to every other party under paragraph (1), send the case back to the clerk of the tribunal.

(3) On receipt of the case sent back under paragraph (1), the clerk of the tribunal shall send it to any other party who had applied for a case.

Deriv. R.C.S. 1965, r. 277(h)(i) (r. 41.10(1)) and r. 277(j) (r. 41.10(2) and (3))

41.10.1   *"within 14 days"*. The date from which the period is calculated is not counted.

41.10.2   *"intimate"*. For methods, see r. 16.7.

41.10.3   *"send"*. This includes deliver: r. 1.3(1) (definition of "send").

Lodging of case in court

41.11.—(1) The party who applied for the case shall, within the period mentioned in paragraph (2)—

(a) lodge in the General Department—
  (i) the case; and
  (ii) a process in accordance with rule 4.4 (steps of process) including any productions to be referred to in the appeal;

(b) on giving written intimation to every other party of the lodging of the case, send four copies of the case to every other party; and

(c) endorse and sign a certificate on the case that the requirements of rule 4.6 (intimation of steps of process) have been complied with.

(2) The period referred to in paragraph (1) shall be—
(a) the period prescribed by the enactment under or by virtue of which the appeal is brought; or
(b) where no such period is prescribed, within 28 days after the date on which the case was received by him from the clerk of the tribunal by virtue of rule 41.9(6) or 41.10(3), as the case may be.

Deriv. R.C.S. 1965, r. 277(*h*)(ii)(part) and (*k*)(i)(part) amended by S.I. 1984 No. 499

General note. On lodging a case a motion must be enrolled for a hearing: r. 41.15(1).   **41.11.1**

"lodge in the General Department". Six copies of the case must be lodged with the principal: r.   **41.11.2** 4.7(1). Four copies of any productions must be lodged. Lodging may be done by post: P.N. No. 4 of 1994, paras. 1 and 8.

"within 28 days". The date from which the period is calculated is not counted. Where the last   **41.11.3** day falls on a Saturday or Sunday or a public holiday on which the Office of Court is closed, the next available day is allowed: r. 1.3(7). For office hours and public holidays, see note 3.1.2.

Fee. The court fee for lodging the appeal is payable on lodging the stated case. For fee, see   **41.11.4** Court of Session etc. Fees Order 1997, Table of Fees, Pt. I, B, item 1 [S.I. 1997 No. 688, as amended, pp. C1201 *et seq.*]. Certain persons are exempt from payment of fees: see 1997 Fees Order, art.5 substituted by S.S.I. 2002 No. 270. A fee exemption certificate must be lodged in process: see P.N. No. 1 of 2002.
Where the appellant is legally represented, the fee may be debited under a credit scheme introduced on 1st April 1976 by P.N. No. 4 of 1976 to the account (if one is kept or permitted) of the agent by the court cashier, and an account will be rendered weekly by the court cashier's office to the agent for all court fees due that week for immediate settlement. Party litigants, and agents not operating the scheme, must pay (by cash, cheque or postal order) on each occasion a fee is due at the time of lodging at the counter at the General Department.

Abandonment of appeal
41.12.—(1) If a party—
(a) fails to comply with a requirement of rule 41.11(1) (lodging of case in court), and
(b) does not apply to be reponed under rule 41.13 (reponing against deemed abandonment),
he shall be deemed to have abandoned his appeal.
(2) Where a party is deemed to have abandoned his appeal under paragraph (1) and another party has also applied for a case and has had no opportunity of proceeding with his appeal, the party deemed to have abandoned his appeal shall—
(a) intimate to that other party that his appeal is abandoned, and
(b) send the case to that other party;
and that other party shall be entitled to proceed in accordance with rule 41.11.
(3) In the application of rule 41.11 to a party entitled to proceed by virtue of paragraph (2) of this rule, for the words "on which the case" to "rule 41.9(6) or 41.10(3), as the case may be" in paragraph (2)(b) of that rule, there shall be substituted the words "of intimation of abandonment under rule 41.12(2)".

Deriv. R.C.S. 1965, r. 277(*k*)(part) (r. 41.12(1)) and r. 277(*k*)(ii) (r. 41.12(2))

General note. If there is no motion under r. 41.13 to be reponed against a deemed   **41.12.1** abandonment, the decision appealed against becomes final. The circumstances in which it might be possible to reduce a deemed abandonment should be noted: see *Bain v. Hugh L.S. McConnell Ltd,* 1991 S.L.T. 691.
Where another party wishes to take up the appeal which has been deemed to be abandoned, he has 28 days to do so from the date on which the party whose appeal is deemed to be abandoned has intimated that fact to him: r. 41.12(3).

"intimate". For methods, see r. 16.7.   **41.12.2**

41.12.3   *"send"*. This includes deliver: r. 1.3(1) (definition of "send").

Reponing against deemed abandonment
41.13. A party may apply by motion to the Inner House, within seven days after the expiry of the period specified in rule 41.11(2) (period for lodging of case in court), to be reponed against a failure to comply with a requirement of rule 41.11(1).

Deriv. R.C.S. 1965, r. 277(*k*)(i)(part)

41.13.1   *General note*. If there is no motion to be reponed the decision appealed against becomes final. The circumstances in which it might be possible to reduce a deemed abandonment should be noted: see *Bain v. Hugh L.S. McConnell Ltd,* 1991 S.L.T. 691.

On enrolling to be reponed the appellant must lodge the stated case and a process as required by r. 41.11(1) and the six copies of the stated case as required by r. 4.7(1).

41.13.2   *"motion"*. For motions, see Chap. 23.

41.13.3   *"within seven days"*. The date from which the period is calculated is not counted. Where the last day falls on a Saturday or Sunday or a public holiday on which the Office of Court is closed, the next available day is allowed: r. 1.3(7). For office hours and public holidays, see note 3.1.2.

41.13.4   *Grounds for reponing*. No test is laid down in the rule. Mistake and inadvertence are obvious factors to be considered.

Procedure on abandonment
41.14.—(1) On the abandonment of the appeal by all parties entitled to proceed, the case shall be sent to the Deputy Principal Clerk.

(2) On receiving a case sent to him under paragraph (1), the Deputy Principal Clerk shall—
    (*a*) endorse the case with a certificate in Form 41.14; and
    (*b*) transmit the case to the clerk of the tribunal.

(3) Where a case has been transmitted under paragraph (2), the tribunal shall, on a motion being made to it to that effect—
    (*a*) dispose of the cause; and
    (*b*) where one party only has applied for a stated case, find him liable for payment to the other party in the appeal of the expenses of the abandoned appeal as taxed by the Auditor of the Court of Session.

Deriv. R.C.S. 1965, r. 277(*k*)(iii)

41.14.1   *"sent"*. This includes deliver: r. 1.3(1) (definition of "send"). The party last in possession of the stated case will be the party responsible for sending the case to the Deputy Principal Clerk.

41.14.2   *Expenses of abandoned appeal*. The motion is made to the tribunal but any award of expenses is subject to taxation by the Auditor of the Court of Session: r. 41.14(3). The tribunal should make a finding in relation to expenses and "remit to the Auditor of the Court of Session to tax".

This provision does not apply to appeals under the Social Work (Scotland) Act 1968: r. 41.33(2).

Motions for hearing of appeals
41.15.—(1) On lodging a case under rule 41.11 (lodging of case in court), the party lodging it shall apply by motion to the Inner House for an order for a hearing.

(2) The Inner House shall, on a motion under paragraph (1), without hearing parties—
    (*a*) appoint the cause to the Summar Roll for hearing; or
    (*b*) direct that the cause be heard in the Single Bills.

Deriv. R.C.S. 1965, r. 280(*a*)

41.15.1   *"motion"*. For motions, see Chap. 23.

Summar Roll. As a general rule, appeals are appointed to and heard on the Summar Roll. **41.15.2**
Originally the Summar Roll was the roll for dealing with causes summarily and the Short Roll
was for more complicated causes; the latter, however, has fallen into desuetude. Once appointed
to the Summar Roll a diet is fixed by the Keeper of the Rolls in accordance with r. 6.3 after
parties have sent him Form 6.3 duly completed.

Single Bills. The Single Bills is the motion roll of the Inner House. As a general rule, appeals **41.15.3**
are not heard in the Single Bills. Appeals dealt with on the Single Bills might include an urgent
appeal or an appeal clearly incompetent.

Hearings before Inner House. An appeal will be heard by a Division of the Inner House. A **41.15.4**
Division consists of four judges, but three are a quorum: C.S.A. 1988, s. 2(2) and (4). Because of
pressure of criminal business in the High Court of Justiciary and other civil business it is
unusual nowadays for a Division to sit with more than three judges. The Lord President may
direct three judges to sit as an Extra Division: C.S.A. 1988, s. 2(3).
    Where a Division before whom a cause is pending (*a*) considers the cause to be one of
difficulty or importance or (*b*) the Division is equally divided in opinion, it may appoint the
cause to be reheard by such larger court as is necessary for the proper disposal of the cause:
C.S.A. 1988, s. 36. A larger court would in the first instance be a court of five judges; a rehearing
of a cause on a point which had been decided by a court of five judges would be heard by a court
of seven judges and so on. It is not always necessary for the cause to be heard by the Division
before it is reheard by a larger court, particularly where all parties are agreed. A larger court will
be required where consideration has to be given as to whether to overturn a previous decision of
a Division. Hearings before a larger court may be appropriate on questions of practice or
procedure. Where the question at issue is construction of a U.K. statute the preferable course is
for appeal to the House of Lords: see *Drummond v. I.R.C.* 1951 S.C. 482.
    The general rule is that when a case has been reported in Session Cases or the (English) Law
Reports, it should be cited from that source: *McGowan v. Summit at Lloyds*, 2002 S.L.T. 1258,
1273 at para.[57] (Ex Div.). See also now P.N. No. 5 of 2004 (in respect of Session Cases).

Fee. The court fee for the hearing of an appeal on the Summar Roll is payable by each party **41.15.5**
for every 30 minutes or part thereof. For fee, see Court of Session etc. Fees Order 1997, Table of
Fees, Pt I, B, item 17 [S.I. 1997 No. 688, as amended, pp. C1201 *et seq.*]. The fee for an appeal
heard in the Single Bills will under Pt I, B, item 22. Certain persons are exempt from payment of
fees: see 1997 Fees Order, art.5 substituted by S.S.I. 2002 No. 270. A fee exemption certificate
must be lodged in process: see P.N. No. 1 of 2002.
    Where a party is legally represented, the fee may be debited under a credit scheme introduced
on 1st April 1976 by P.N. No. 4 of 1976 to the account (if one is kept or permitted) of the agent by
the court cashier, and an account will be rendered weekly by the court cashier's office to the agent
for all court fees due that week for immediate settlement. An agent not on the credit scheme will
have an account opened for the purpose of lodging the fee: P.N. No. 2 of 1995. A debit slip and a
copy of the court hearing time sheet will be delivered to the agent's box or sent by DX or post.
    A party litigant must pay (by cash, cheque or postal order) to the clerk of court at the end of
the hearing or, if the hearing lasts more than a day, at the end of each day: P.N. No. 2 of 1995.
A receipt will be issued. The assistant clerk of session will acknowledge receipt of the sum
received from the clerk of court on the Minute of Proceedings.

Circumstances in which appellate court will interfere with decision of the court below. **41.15.6**
    (1) *Facts.* Review of facts will depend on examination and assessment of the evidence and
rules of evidence, and credibility, reliability, weight and a sufficiency. In relation to credibility,
the appellate court will be reluctant to reverse findings of credibility for the reason that it is
denied the advantage of the judge at first instance who saw and heard the witnesses. The court
must be persuaded, and come to the clear conclusion, that the judge who had that advantage
was plainly wrong: *Clarke v. Edinburgh and District Tramways Co.* 1919 S.C. (H.L.) 35, 37, *per*
Lord Shaw of Dunfermline. Where an appellate court is disposed to come to a different
conclusion, it should not do so unless it is satisfied that any advantage enjoyed by the judge at
first instance could not be sufficient to explain or justify his conclusion; where the reasons given
by that judge are not satisfactory or it unmistakenly so appears from the evidence, the appellate
court may be satisfied he has not taken proper advantage of seeing and hearing the witnesses
and the matter will be at large for the appellate court: *Thomas v. Thomas* S.C. (H.L.) 45, 54, *per*
Lord Thankerton. Where a decision on fact is based on credibility, the judge at first instance
should leave no doubt as to the grounds of his decision: *Duncan v. Watson* 1940 S.C. 221, 225,
per L.P. Normand. The appellate court will more readily treat the matter as at large where clear
and satisfactory reasons are not given: *Morrison v. J. Kelly & Sons Ltd* 1970 S.C. 65.
    The question of the Court of Session reviewing concurrent findings of credibility of the tribunal
at first instance as an intermediate court of appeal will arise infrequently in statutory appeals to
which Chap. 41 applies. In an appeal in which this issue does arise, see note 40.14.6(1).

(2) *Discretion.* A discretion will not be legally interfered with. It is not enough that the appellate court would have exercised the discretion differently. The tests have been variously described, depending to some extent on the area of law concerned. The tests may be stated as follows: (a) has there been a failure to exercise the discretion at all (*Orr Pollock & Co. (Printers) Ltd v. Mulholland* 1983 S.L.T. 558), (b) has the judge misdirected himself in law (*Forsyth v. A. F. Stoddard & Co. Ltd* 1985 S.L.T. 51), (c) has the judge misunderstood, misused or failed to balance the evidence (*Skiponian Ltd v. Barratt Developments (Scotland) Ltd* 1983 S.L.T. 313, 314), (d) has the judge taken into account an irrelevant factor (*Thomson v. Glasgow Corporation* 1962 S.C. (H.L.) 36, 66 *per* Lord Reid), (e) has the judge failed to take into account a relevant factor (*Thomson, above*), (f) is the decision unreasonable (*Thomson, above*), (g) is the decision unjudicial (*Thomson, above*). See also *Brittan v. Central R.C.* 1986 S.L.T. 407.

41.15.7   *Argument not presented to court below.* There is no general rule, unlike in the House of Lords, that the appellate court will not entertain an argument not advanced before the court below; although it may be unfortunate that the argument was not so advanced (*Varney (Scotland) Ltd v. Lanark Town Council* 1974 S.C. 245, 249, *per* L.J.-C. Wheatley.) It is always open to the court to consider competency which strikes at the root of the proceedings: *Wolfson v. Glasgow District Licensing Board* 1980 S.C. 136, 128, *per* L.J.-C. Wheatley.

There are exceptions. A fresh argument which cannot be advanced without amendment to the pleadings will generally not be heard because the court will usually wish the judge at first instance to consider the amended pleadings (if allowed: on which see note 38.21.1) and have the benefit of his opinion: see *e.g. Wallace v. Scottish Special Housing Association* 1981 S.L.T. (Notes) 60 and r. 38.21. A new argument cannot be advanced other than on evidence led unless the court has allowed that further evidence or is willing to consider a change of circumstances since the hearing in the court below.

Amendment or re-statement of case

41.16. The Inner House may, at any time before the final determination of the case—

    (a) allow the case to be amended with the consent of the parties; or

    (b) remit the case for re-statement, or further statement, in whole or in part by the tribunal.

Deriv. R.C.S. 1965, r. 280(b)(part)

Remit to reporter

41.17.—(1) Where, in order to determine the case, any inquiry into matters of fact may be made, the Inner House may remit to a reporter, the Lord Ordinary or one of its own number to take evidence and to report to the court.

(2) On completion of a report made under paragraph (1), the reporter shall send his report and three copies of it, and a copy of it for each party, to the Deputy Principal Clerk.

(3) On receipt of such a report, the Deputy Principal Clerk shall—

    (a) cause the report to be lodged in process; and

[1] (b) give written intimation to each party that this has been done and that he may uplift a copy of the report from process.

(4) After the lodging of such a report, any party may apply by motion for an order in respect of the report or for further procedure.

Deriv. R.C.S. 1965, r. 280(b)(part)

———————

[1] R.41.17(3)(b) amended by S.I. 1994 No. 2901 (clerical error).

41.17.1   *General note.* Where a remit is made the solicitors for the parties will be personally liable in the first instance for the reporter's fees and outlays unless the court otherwise orders and one party will be made liable: r. 42.15.

41.17.2   *"send".* This includes deliver: r. 1.3(1) (definition of "send").

41.17.3   *"written intimation".* For methods, see r. 16.9.

41.17.4   *"motion".* For motions, see Chap. 23.

PART III

APPEALS IN FORM 41.19

Application of this Part
41.18. Subject to the provisions of the enactment providing for appeal, this Part applies to an appeal against a decision of a tribunal other than an appeal to which Part II (appeals by stated case, etc.) applies.

Deriv. R.C.S. 1965, r. 290(a)(part) amended by S.I. 1973 No. 540

General note. Appeal under the Form 41.19 procedure is a simpler procedure than that of the **41.18.1** stated case involving reproducing in or appending to the appeal in Form 41.19 the decision appealed against. It is the appropriate procedure where a reasoned decision has been given by the tribunal or findings-in-fact are not required: *cf.* notes 41.1.2 and 41.4.1 on stated case procedure.

Appeals to which the Form 41.19 procedure applies. These include—Taxes Management Act **41.18.2** 1970, ss. 53, 100B(3) and 100C(4) (appeals *re* penalties from General or Special Commissioners); Inheritance Tax Act 1984, s. 222 (against determination of Commissioners of Inland Revenue), and ss. 249(3) and 251(2) (appeals *re* penalties from Special Commissioners); Oil Taxation Act 1975, s. 1 and Sched. 2, para. 1 (from Commissioners *re* penalties); Stamp Duty Reserve Tax Regulations 1986 [S.I. 1986 No. 1711], reg.8 (against determination of Commissioners of Inland Revenue); Tribunal and Inquiries Act 1992, s. 11 (from VAT Tribunals); Burial Grounds (Scotland) Act 1855, s. 10; Pharmacy Act 1954, ss. 10 and 24(2) (against directions); Therapeutic Substances Act 1956, ss. 2(4) and 6 (from suspension of licence); Teaching Council (Scotland) Act 1965, s. 12 as substituted by Standards in Scotland's Schools etc. Act 2000 (appeal against direction *re* registration); Fair Trading Act 1973, s. 42 (*re* protection of consumers from Restrictive Practices Court); Consumer Credit Act 1974, s. 41A inserted by Consumer Credit Act 2006, s. 57 (on point of law from Consumer Credit Appeals Tribunal); Control of Pollution Act 1974, s. 85 (from sheriff); Restrictive Practices Court Act 1976, s. 10(2) (from RPC in proceedings under Pt III of the Fair Trading Act 1973 (*re* protection of consumer); Patents Acts: 1949 Act, s. 87(3) and 1977 Act, Sched. 4 (*re* decision of comptroller under 1949 Act, s. 55), 1977 Act, s. 97 (from comptroller); Estate Agents Act 1979, s. 7(4) (from Secretary of State from Director General of Fair Trading *re* estate agency work); Education (Scotland) Act 1980, s. 112(8) as amended by the Education (Scotland) Act 1981, s. 1 and Sched. 2, para. 3 (from Council *re* issue of practising certificate), ss. 16 (from Council *re* restoration to roll) and 54 (from discipline tribunal); Public Passenger Vehicles Act 1981, s. 51 (from Secretary of State from Traffic Commissioners); Medical Act 1983, s. 40 as amended by the NHS Reform and Health Care Professionals Act 2002, s. 30 (from General Council); Dentists Act 1984, s. 29 as amended by the NHS Reform and Health Care Professionals Act 2002, s. 31 (appeal from Professional Conduct and Health Committees)); Mental Health (Scotland) Act 1984, s. 66A(1) (appeal from sheriff); Transport Act 1985, s. 117(2) and Sched. 4, para. 14(1) (from Transport Tribunal); Legal Aid (Scotland) Act 1986, s. 31(4) (*re* exclusion of lawyer from selection in legal aid cases); Building Societies Act 1986, s. 49(1) and (2) (from tribunal from B.S. Commission); Banking Act 1987, s. 31 (from Banking Appeal Tribunal); Copyright, Designs and Patents Act 1988, s. 152(1) (from Copyright Tribunal) and s. 251(2) (from Comptroller General *re* design rights); Opticians Act 1989, s. 23 as amended by the NHS Reform and Health Care Professionals Act 2002, s. 32 (from Disciplinary Committee); Human Fertilisation and Embryology Act 1990, s. 21 (*re* determination of licence by HFEA); Child Support Act 1991, s. 25 (from the Child Support Commissioner); Social Security Administration Act 1992, ss. 18(3) and 58 (from decisions or determinations by the Secretary of State) and 24 (from the SS Commissioner); Local Government Finance Act 1992, s. 82(4) (from valuation appeal committee *re* council tax); Friendly Societies Act 1992, s. 61 (from tribunal *re* decision of Commission); Tribunal and Inquiries Act 1992, s. 11 and Sched. 1 (from various tribunals); Railways Act 1993, s. 57 (*re* validity of order); Pension Schemes Act 1993, s. 151(4) (from Pensions Ombudsman) and s. 173(3) (from Occupational Pensions Board); Osteopaths Act 1993, ss. 24 and 25 (against interim suspension orders, s. 29 (from Registrar), and s. 31 as amended by the NHS Reform and Health Care Professionals Act 2002, s. 33 (from Professional Conduct Committee); Chiropractors Act 1994, s. 31 as amended by the NHS Reform and Health Care Professionals Act 2002, s. 34 (from Professional Conduct Committee or appeal tribunal); Trade Marks Act 1994, s. 76(2) (from registrar); Drug Trafficking Act 1994, s. 45 (from forfeiture order by sheriff); Pensions Act 1995; s. 97(3) (from Occupational Pensions Regulatory Authority); Industrial Tribunals Act 1996, s. 37(1) (from Employment Appeal Tribunal); Architects Act 1997, s. 22 (*re* registration); Nurses, Midwives and Health Visitors Act 1997, s. 12 (*re* removal from register); Special Immigration Appeals Commission Act 1997, s. 7

(from Special Immigration Appeals Commission); Social Security Act 1998, s. 15 (with leave from Social Security Commissioner); Data Protection Act 1998, s. 49(6) (on point of law from Data Protection Tribunal); Competition Act 1998, s. 49 (on point of law from appeal tribunal); Road Traffic (NHS Charges) Act 1999, s. 9(2) (on point of law from appeal tribunal); Financial Services and Marketing Act 2000, s. 137(1) (from Financial Services and Markets tribunal); Terrorism Act 2000, s. 6(1) (from Proscribed Organisations Commission); Postal Services Act 2000, s. 36(2) (by person aggrieved); Freedom of Information (Scotland) Act 2002, s. 56 (from Scottish Information Commissioner on point of law); Proceeds of Crime Act 2002, s. 299 (from sheriff); Enterprise Act 2002, s. 114 (from Competition Appeal Tribunal); Nationality, Immigration and Asylum Act 2002, s. 103 (from Immigration Appeal tribunal); Trade Union and Labour Relations (Consolidation) Act 1992, s. 212A(7) and R.C.S. 1994, 4. 41.58(1) (appeal from ACAS scheme).

The appeals in Form 41.19 procedure also applies to applications to challenge the validity of a decision which are of the nature of an appeal (by virtue of r. 41.1). These include—Acquisition of Land (Authorisation Procedure) (Scotland) Act 1947, s. 1 and Sched. 1, para. 15 (*re* validity of compulsory purchase order); Housing (Scotland) Act 1966, ss. 36, 38, 43 and Sched. 2, para. 2 (*re* clearance orders); Ancient Monuments and Archaeological Areas Act 1979, s. 55(1) (*re* validity of designation orders); Wildlife and Countryside Act 1981, ss. 29, 34 and Sched. 11, para. 7 (*re* validity of order *re* areas of scientific interest), s. 36 and Sched. 12, para. 8 (*re* validity or order *re* marine nature reserves); Civil Aviation Act 1982, Sched. 7, para. 7 (*re* validity of orders); Telecommunications Act 1984, s. 18 (*re* orders of Secretary of State); Roads (Scotland) Act 1984, Sched. 2, para. 2 (*re* validity of orders and schemes); Films Act 1985, Sched. 2, para. 9 (from decision of Secretary of State to refuse to certify or to revoke certification for purposes of s. 72 of the Finance Act 1982); Gas Act 1986, s. 30 (*re* orders of Secretary of State); National Heritage (Scotland) Act 1991, Sched. 5, para. 10 (*re* validity of irrigation control order); Railways Act 1993, s. 57 (*re* validity of order); Coal Industry Act 1994, s. 33 (*re* validity of enforcement order); Town and Country Planning (Scotland) Act 1997, s. 238 (*re* validity of structure or local plan), s. 239 (*re* validity of other orders, etc.); Planning (Listed Buildings and Conservation Areas) (Scotland) Act 1997, s. 58 (*re* validity of orders etc.); Planning (Hazardous Substances) (Scotland) Act 1997, s. 20 (*re* validity of decisions); Petroleum Act 1998, s. 42 (decisions from the Secretary of State); Social Security Act 1998, s. 15 (appeal from Social Security Commissioner); Immigration and Asylum Act 1999, Sched. 5, para. 33 (appeal from Immigration Appeal tribunal); Financial Services and Markets Act 2000, s. 137(1) (appeal from Financial Services and Markets tribunal); Terrorism Act 2000, s. 6(1) (appeal from Proscribed Organisations Commission); Postal Services Act 2000, s. 36(2) (appeal by person aggrieved).

Form of appeal

41.19.—(1) An appeal to which this Part applies shall be made in Form 41.19 presented to the Inner House.

(2) An appeal referred to in paragraph (1) shall—

    (a) specify the relevant provision of the enactment under the authority of which the appeal is brought;

    (b) specify the decision complained of, the date on which the decision was made and on which it was intimated to the appellant, and any other necessary particulars;

    (c) where the appeal is against only a part of such a decision, specify or distinguish that part;

    (d) set out the decision appealed against or refer to the decision (a copy of which shall be appended to the appeal);

    (e) state, in brief numbered propositions, the grounds of appeal; and

    (f) set out in a schedule the names and addresses of the respondents in the appeal and the name and address, so far as known to the appellant, of any other person who may have an interest in the appeal.

Deriv. R.C.S. 1965, r. 290(a)(part) and (d) (r. 41.19(1)(part)) and r. 290(a)(part), (b) and (c) (r. 41.19(2))

41.19.1   *General note.* It is not essential to repeat in the appeal the decision appealed against if a copy of it can more conveniently be appended to the appeal.

41.19.2   *"state, in brief numbered propositions, the grounds of appeal".* "The purpose of the rule is obviously to ensure that a respondent will receive fair advance notice of any points to be taken on appeal": *City of Glasgow District Council v. Secretary of State for Scotland (No. 1)* 1993 S.L.T. 198, 204E–G *per* Lord Caplan (bare averment that decision contrary to the principles of natural justice not enough); see also *Eurocopy Rentals Ltd v. Tayside Health Board* 1996 S.C. 410, 413G *per* L.P. Hope.

Lodging of appeal in court
[1] **41.20.**—(1) Subject to paragraphs (2) and (3), the appeal shall be lodged in the General Department—
   (a) within the period prescribed by the enactment under which it is brought; or
   (b) where no such period is prescribed, within 42 days after—
      (i) the date on which the decision appealed against was intimated to the appellant; or
      (ii) where the tribunal issued a statement of reasons for its decision later than the decision, the date of intimation of that statement of reasons to the appellant.
   (2) Where leave to appeal to the court has been granted by the tribunal under any of the following enactments, the appeal shall be lodged in the General Department within 42 days after the date on which the decision to grant leave was intimated to the appellant:—
   (a) section 25 of the Child Support Act 1991 (appeal from decision of a commissioner on a question of law with leave of the commissioner);
   (b) section 24 of the Social Security Administration Act 1992 (appeal from decision of a commissioner on a question of law with leave of the commissioner); and
[2] (c) section 103E of the Nationality, Immigration and Asylum Act 2002 (appeal from the Asylum and Immigration Tribunal).
   (3) Where an application for leave to appeal was made to the court within the period specified in paragraph (1)(b) but that period has expired before leave has been granted, the appeal may be lodged within 7 days after the date on which that leave was granted.
   (4) There shall be lodged with the appeal under paragraph (1)—
   (a) a process in accordance with rule 4.4 (steps of process), unless an application has already been made to the court for leave to appeal;
   (b) where appropriate, evidence that leave to appeal has been granted by the tribunal;
   (c) the documents mentioned in rule 41.2(6)(c) and (d) (copies of decisions of tribunal) unless already lodged; and
   (d) such other documents founded on by the appellant so far as in his possession or within his control.

Deriv. R.C.S. 1965, r. 290(*a*)(part) amended by S.I. 1984 No. 499 (r. 41.20(1)(part)), and r. 290(*i*) inserted by S.I. 1982 No. 1825 (r. 41.20(1)(*b*)(ii))

---

[1] Rule 41.20 amended by S.I. 1996 No. 1756 (effective 5th August 1996).
[2] Rule 41.20(2) (c) amended S.S.I. 2004 No. 331 (effective 6th August 2004) and S.S.I. 2005 No. 198 (effective 4th April 2005).

General note. Unless the statute under which the appeal is made otherwise provides, the **41.20.1** general rule now is that the appeal must be lodged within 42 days after the date of intimation of the decision or, if later, of intimation of reasons for the decision: r. 41.20(1)(b). Where leave to appeal is sought from the tribunal or, under r. 41.2, from the court, it must be sought (where r. 41.20(1)(b) applies) within the 42 day period for lodging the appeal. Where leave to appeal is sought from the court, the 42 day period may be extended by 7 days after the date on which leave was granted: r. 41.20(3). The former rule for the 42 day period for lodging an appeal to begin to run from the date of leave being granted was revoked by A.S. (R.C.S.A. No. 3) [S.I. 1996 No. 1756]. The reason for this was that the provision resulted in there being no period within which to seek leave from, *e.g.*, the Employment Appeal Tribunal.
   There are three exceptions to the general rule provided for in r. 41.20(2) as inserted by the amending S.I. 1996 No. 1756. The reason is that in relation to the tribunals in the enactments mentioned, provision is made for the period within which leave to appeal must be sought from the tribunal (on which, see notes 41.20.5 and 41.20.6).

Rules 41.2 and 41.20(2) do not deal with a situation where leave must be sought from a tribunal first and is refused, there being a right to apply after the refusal to the court for leave. That is, where the 42 day period, from the (substantive) decision sought to be appealed against, required by rr. 41.2 and 41.20(1)(b), has expired before leave is refused or an appeal to the court can thereafter be made. In *Hakim v. Secretary of State for the Home Department*, 2001 S.C. 789 it was held by an Ex Div, unattracted to requiring an appellant to seek judicial review or to use the dispensing power in r. 2.1, that the 42 day period runs from the date of refusal of leave. What is odd about this case is that the appellant still had eight days remaining, of the 42 day period after the date of intimation of refusal of leave, in which to lodge an application to the court for leave. No explanation was given or sought for his not doing so.

41.20.2   *"appeal shall be lodged in the General Department"*. Six copies of the appeal must be lodged with the principal (r. 4.7(1)) as well as a process (r. 41.20(4)).

41.20.3   *"within 42 days"*. The date from which the period is calculated is not counted. Where the last day falls on a Saturday or Sunday or a public holiday on which the Office of Court is closed, the next available day is allowed: r. 1.3(7). For office hours and public holidays, see note 3.1.2.

It should be noted that in appeals by stated case under Pt II the period for appealing under r. 41.5(2)(b) is 14 days (or 28 days for lodging it) and not 42 days as in the case of appeals to which this part applies (see r. 41.20(1)(b)). Such a mistake was made in *City of Edinburgh Council v. Rapley*, 2000 S.C. 78.

41.20.4   *Fee.* The court fee for lodging the appeal is payable on lodging the stated case. For fee, see Court of Session etc. Fees Order 1997, Table of Fees, Pt I, B, item 1 [S.I. 1997 No. 688, as amended, pp.C1201 *et seq.*]. Certain persons are exempt from payment of fees: see 1997 Fees Order, art.5 substituted by S.S.I. 2002 No. 270. A fee exemption certificate must be lodged in process: see P.N. No. 1 of 2002.

Where the appellant is legally represented, the fee may be debited under a credit scheme introduced on 1st April 1976 by P.N. No. 4 of 1976 to the account (if one is kept or permitted) of the agent by the court cashier, and an account will be rendered weekly by the court cashier's office to the agent for all court fees due that week for immediate settlement. Party litigants, and agents not operating the scheme, must pay (by cash, cheque or postal order) on each occasion a fee is due at the time of lodging at the counter at the General Department.

41.20.5   *Appeal from Child Support and Social Security Commissioners.* An appeal to the court on a question of law from a Child Support Commissioner is made under s. 25 of the Child Support Act 1991 with leave of the commissioner or, if he refuses, the court. Under reg.25 of the Child Support Commissioners (Procedure) Regulations 1992 [S.I. 1992 No. 2640], an appeal to the commissioner for leave to appeal to the court must be made within three months from the date on which the appellant was given written notice of the decision.

An appeal to the court on a question of law from a Social Security Commissioner is made under s. 24 of the Social Security Administration Act 1992 with leave of the commissioner or, if he refuses leave, the court. Under reg.31 of the Social Security Commissioners (Procedure) Regulations 1987 [S.I. 1987 No. 214], an application to the commissioner for leave to appeal to the court must be made within three months from the date on which the applicant was given written notice of the decision.

41.20.6   *Appeals from Asylum and Immigration Tribunal.* An appeal to the court on a point of law from the Asylum and Immigration Tribunal is made under s. 103E of the Nationality, Immigration and Asylum Act 2002 inserted by s. 26 of the Asylum and Immigration (Treatment of Claimants, etc.) Act 2004 with leave of the tribunal or, if it refuses leave, the court.

The test for leave to appeal (from the former Immigration Appeal Tribunal) is whether the appeal would have a real prospect of success: *Hoseini v. Secretary of State for the Home Department*, 2005 S.L.T. 550 (First Div.).

There are time-limits for permission from the tribunal to appeal to the court: Asylum and Immigration Tribunal (Procedure) Rules 2005, r. 34 [S.I. 2005 No. 230].

Orders for service and answers

41.21.—(1) The appeal shall, without a motion being enrolled—
- (a) during session, appear in the Single Bills on the first available day after being lodged for an order for—
  - (i) service of the appeal on the respondent and such other person as the court thinks fit; and
  - (ii) any person on whom the appeal has been served, to lodge answers, if so advised, within the period of notice; and
- (b) during vacation, be brought before the vacation judge for such an order.

(2) In the application of paragraph (1) to an appeal under section 9(5) of the Transport Act 1985 (appeal from decision of the Secretary of State), the order for service under that paragraph shall include a requirement to serve the appeal on—

(*a*) the Secretary of State; and

[1] (*b*) every person who had, or if aggrieved would have had, a right to appeal to the Secretary of State, whether or not he has exercised that right.

[2] (3) In the application of paragraph (1) to an appeal under section 25(1) of the Child Support Act 1991 (appeal from Child Support Commissioner) or section 24(1) of the Social Security Administration Act 1992 (appeal from Social Security Commissioner), the order for service under that paragraph shall include a requirement to serve the appeal on—

(*a*) the Secretary of State for Social Security and the Chief Child Support Officer or the Chief Adjudication Officer, as the case may be; and

(*b*) if it appears to the court that a person has been appointed by the Secretary of State to pursue a claim for benefit to which the appeal relates, that person.

(4) In the application of paragraph (1) to an appeal from a tribunal referred to in subsection (1), as modified by subsection (7), of section 11 of the Tribunals and Inquiries Act 1992, the order for service pronounced under that paragraph shall include a requirement to serve the appeal on every other party to the proceedings before the tribunal and on the clerk of the tribunal.

(5) In the application of paragraph (1) to an appeal to which subsection (6), as modified by subsection (7), of section 11 of the Tribunals and Inquiries Act 1992 (which relates to an appeal from a decision under section 41 of the Consumer Credit Act 1974) applies—

(*a*) the order for service under that paragraph shall include a requirement to serve the appeal on—

(i)   the Secretary of State; and
(ii) where the appeal is by a licensee under a group licence against compulsory variation, suspension or revocation of that licence, the original applicant, if any; and
(b)   the court may remit to the Secretary of State for him to provide the court with such further information as the court may require.

Deriv. R.C.S. 1965, r. 290(e) (r. 41.21(1)), r. 293(a) amended by S.I. 1972 No. 1835 (r. 41.21(2)), r. 293B(5) inserted by S.I. 1980 No. 1754 and amended by S.I. 1992 No. 2289 (r. 41.21(3)), r. 292(a) amended by S.I. 1972 No. 1835 (r. 41.21(4)) and r. 293A(a) amended by S.I. 1976 No. 847 (r. 41.21(5))

---

[1] R. 41.21(2)(b) amended by S.I. 1994 No. 2901 (minor correction).
[2] R. 41.21(3) amended by S.I. 1996 No. 1756 (effective 5th August 1996).

"service". For methods, see Chap. 16, Pt. I.   **41.21.1**

"vacation". See note 11.1.11.   **41.21.2**

"answers". R. 18.3 does not apply. Where appropriate, the principles of answers to a **41.21.3** condescendence apply: see r. 18.1.3. It is usual also to include pleas-in-law. The primary purpose of the answers is to respond to the contentions of the appellant.

Section 11(1) of the Tribunals and Inquiries Act 1992. S. 11(1) as modified by s. 11(7) of the **41.21.4** 1992 Act provides that any party to proceedings before certain specified tribunals in Sched. 1 to the Act who is dissatisfied in point of law with a decision of the tribunal may appeal to, or require the tribunal to state a case for the opinion of, the Court of Session.

"section 9(5) of the Transport Act 1985". This provides for an appeal on a point of law from **41.21.5** a decision of the Secretary of State in relation to traffic regulation conditions.

"section 25(1) of the Child Support Act 1991". This is the general provision for appeals on a **41.21.5A** question of law, from Child Support Commissioners, with leave of the Commissioner or, if he refuses, the court. The Child Support Commissioners are also the Social Security Commissioners.

"section 24(1) of the Social Security Administration Act 1992". This is the general provision **41.21.6** for appeals from Social Security Commissioners, with leave of the commissioners or the court, on a question of law.

Section 11(6) of the Tribunals and Inquiries Act 1992. Provision is made in s. 11(6) as **41.21.7** modified by s. 11(7) of the 1992 Act for appeal to the Court of Session on a point of law from a decision of the Secretary of State on an appeal under s. 41 of the Consumer Credit Act 1974 from a determination of the Director General of Fair Trading in relation to licensing of credit and hire businesses by a company registered in Scotland or by any other person whose principal or prospective principal place of business in the UK is in Scotland.

Motion for further procedure

41.22.—(1) Within 14 days after the expiry of the period allowed for lodging answers to an appeal, whether or not answers have been lodged, the appellant shall apply by motion to the Inner House for—
(a)   such order for further procedure as is sought; or
(b)   an order for a hearing.
(2) The Inner House shall, on a motion under paragraph (1)—
(a)   in relation to a motion under paragraph (1)(a), make such order as it thinks fit; or
(b)   in relation to a motion under paragraph (1)(b), without hearing parties—
(i)   appoint the cause to the Summar Roll for hearing; or
(ii) direct that the cause be heard in the Single Bills.

"within 14 days". The date from which the period is calculated is not counted. Where the last **41.22.1** day falls on a Saturday or Sunday or a public holiday on which the Office of Court is closed, the next available day is allowed: r. 1.3(7). For office hours and public holidays, see note 3.1.2.

41.22.2   *"motion"*. For motions, see Chap. 23.

41.22.3   *Summar Roll*. As a general rule, appeals are appointed to and heard on the Summar Roll. Originally the Summar Roll was the roll for dealing with causes summarily and the Short Roll was for more complicated causes; the latter, however, has fallen into desuetude. Once appointed to the Summar Roll a diet is fixed by the Keeper of the Rolls in accordance with r. 6.3 after parties have sent him Form 6.3 duly completed.

41.22.4   *Single Bills*. The Single Bills is the motion roll of the Inner House. As a general rule, appeals are not heard in the Single Bills. Appeals dealt with on the Single Bills might include an urgent appeal or an appeal clearly incompetent.

41.22.5   *Hearings before Inner House*. An appeal will be heard by a Division of the Inner House. A Division consists of four judges, but three are a quorum: C.S.A. 1988, s. 2(2) and (4). Because of pressure of criminal business in the High Court of Justiciary and other civil business it is unusual nowadays for a Division to sit with more than three judges. The Lord President may direct three judges to sit as an Extra Division: C.S.A. 1988, s. 2(3).

Where a Division before whom a cause is pending (*a*) considers the cause to be one of difficulty or importance or (*b*) the Division is equally divided in opinion, it may appoint the cause to be reheard by such larger court as is necessary for the proper disposal of the cause: C.S.A. 1988, s. 36. A larger court would in the first instance be a court of five judges; a rehearing of a cause on a point which had been decided by a court of five judges would be heard by a court of seven judges and so on. It is not always necessary for the cause to be heard by the Division before it is reheard by a larger court, particularly where all parties are agreed. A larger court will be required where consideration has to be given as to whether to overturn a previous decision of a Division. Hearings before a larger court may be appropriate on questions of practice or procedure. Where the question at issue is construction of a UK statute the preferable course is for appeal to the House of Lords: see *Drummond v. I.R.C.* 1951 S.C. 482.

41.22.6   *Fee*. The court fee for the hearing on an appeal on the Summar Roll is payable by each party for every 30 minutes or part thereof. For fee, see Court of Session etc. Fees Order 1997, Table of Fees, Pt. I, B, item 17 [S.I. 1997 No. 688, as amended, pp. C1201 *et seq.*]. The fee for an appeal heard in the Single Bills will under Pt. I, B, item 22. Certain persons are exempt from payment of fees: see 1997 Fees Order, art.5 substituted by S.S.I. 2002 No. 270. A fee exemption certificate must be lodged in process: see P.N. No. 1 of 2002.

Where a party is legally represented, the fee may be debited under a credit scheme introduced on 1st April 1976 by P.N. No. 4 of 1976 to the account (if one is kept or permitted) of the agent by the court cashier, and an account will be rendered weekly by the court cashier's office to the agent for all court fees due that week for immediate settlement. An agent not on the credit scheme will have an account opened for the purpose of lodging the fee: P.N. No. 2 of 1995. A debit slip and a copy of the court hearing time sheet will be delivered to the agent's box or sent by DX or post.

A party litigant must pay (by cash, cheque or postal order) to the clerk of court at the end of the hearing or, if the hearing lasts more than a day, at the end of each day: P.N. No. 2 of 1995. A receipt will be issued. The assistant clerk of session will acknowledge receipt of the sum received from the clerk of court on the Minute of Proceedings.

41.22.7   *Circumstances in which appellate court will interfere with decision of the court below.*

(1) *Facts*. Review of facts will depend on examination and assessment of the evidence and rules of evidence, and credibility, reliability, weight and sufficiency. Issues in relation to credibility will not arise often in appeals to which this Part of Chap. 41 applies; where it does, see note 41.15.6.

The question of the Court of Session reviewing concurrent findings of credibility of the tribunal at first instance as an intermediate court of appeal will arise infrequently in statutory appeals to which Chap. 41 applies. In an appeal in which the issue does arise, see note 40.14.6(1).

(2) *Discretion*. A discretion will not be legally interfered with. It is not enough that the appellate court would have exercised the discretion differently. The tests have been variously described, depending to some extent on the area of law concerned. The tests may be stated as follows: (*a*) has there been a failure to exercise the discretion at all (*Orr Pollock & Co. (Printers) Ltd v. Mulholland* 1983 S.L.T. 558), (*b*) has the judge misdirected himself in law (*Forsyth v. A.F. Stoddard & Co. Ltd* 1985 S.L.T. 51), (*c*) has the judge misunderstood, misused or failed to balance the evidence (*Skiponian Ltd v. Barratt Developments (Scotland) Ltd* 1983 S.L.T. 313, 314), (*d*) has the judge taken into account an irrelevant factor (*Thomson v. Glasgow Corporation* 1962 S.C. (H.L.) 36, 66 *per* Lord Reid), (*e*) has the judge failed to take into account a relevant factor (*Thomson, above*), (*f*) is the decision unreasonable (*Thomson, above*), (*g*) is the decision unjudicial (*Thomson, above*). See also *Brittan v. Central R.C.* 1986 S.L.T. 407.

Argument not presented to court below. There is no general rule, unlike in the House of Lords, **41.22.8** that the appellate court will not entertain an argument not advanced before the court below; although it may be unfortunate that the argument was not so advanced (*Varney (Scotland) Ltd v. Lanark Town Council* 1974 S.C. 245, 249 *per* L.J.-C. Wheatley.) It is always open to the court to consider competency which strikes at the root of the proceedings: *Wolfson v. Glasgow District Licensing Board* 1980 S.C. 136, 128 *per* L.J.-C. Wheatley.

There are exceptions. A fresh argument which cannot be advanced without amendment to the pleadings will generally not be heard because the court will usually wish the judge at first instance to consider the amended pleadings (if allowed: on which see note 38.21.1) and have the benefit of his opinion: see *e.g. Wallace v. Scottish Special Housing Association* 1981 S.L.T. (Notes) 60 and r. 38.21. A new argument cannot be advanced other than on evidence led unless the court has allowed that further evidence or is willing to consider a change of circumstances since the hearing in the court below.

PART IV

EXCHEQUER APPEALS

Revenue appeals by stated case
[1] **41.23.**—(1) This rule applies to an appeal to the court as the Court of Exchequer in Scotland under any of the following provisions:—

[2,4] (a) section 13(5) of the Stamp Act 1891 (appeal from Commissioners for Her Majesty's Revenue and Customs);

(b) section 705A of the Income and Corporation Taxes Act 1988 (case for opinion of court from tribunal); and

(c) regulation 20(1) of the General Commissioners (Jurisdiction and Procedure) Regulations 1994.

[3] (1A) In relation to appeals in respect of instruments executed before 1st October 1999, paragraph (1)(a) above has effect as if the reference to section 13(5) of the Stamp Act 1891 were a reference to section 13(1) of that Act as it has effect in relation to such instruments.

(2) Subject to paragraph (3), Part II (appeals by stated case etc.) shall apply to an appeal to which paragraph (1) applies.

(3) The following provisions of Part II shall not apply to an appeal to which this rule applies:—

rule 41.5 (applications for case),

rule 41.6 (additional questions by other parties),

rule 41.7 (consideration of application by tribunal),

rule 41.8 (procedure for ordaining tribunal to state a case),

rule 41.9 (preparation and issue of the case),

rule 41.10 (intimation of intention to proceed).

Deriv. R.C.S. 1965, r. 281(1)(part) substituted by S.I. 1976 No. 1849 and amended by S.I. 1984 No. 499

---

[1] Rule 41.23 substituted by S.I. 1994 No. 2901 (effective 5th December 1994).
[2] Rule 41.23(1)(a) as amended by S.S.I. 1999 No. 192 (effective 14th January 2000).
[3] Rule 41.23(1A) inserted by S.S.I. 1999 No. 192 (effective 14th January 2000).
[4] Rule 41.23 amended by S.S.I. 2005 No. 268 (effective 7th June, 2005).

General note. Stated case procedure applies in principle, but rr. 41.5–41.11 do not apply **41.23.1** because the enactments under which the appeals are made provide for the procedure to be followed.

Only the party who was unsuccessful in the appeal to or proceedings before the Commissioners is "dissatisfied" in point of law, and there should only be one stated case even if the other party raises a point of law: *Gordon v. Inland Revenue Commissioners* 1991 S.C. 149.

"section 13(5) of the Stamp Act 1891". A person dissatisfied with the assessment of the **41.23.2** Commissioners of Inland Revenue (now Commissioners for Her Majesty's Revenue and Customs) may, within 30 days of notice of the decision, appeal to the Court of Session and require the Commissioners to state a case: Stamp Act 1891, s. 13(1) substituted by Sched. 12 to the Finance Act 1999. Section 13B of the 1891 Act as amended contains the procedural

41.23.3   *"section 705A of the Income and Corporation Taxes Act 1988"*. This section was inserted by the General and Special Commissioners (Amendment of Enactments) Regulations 1994 [S.I. 1994 No. 1813]. It provides for an appeal to the Court of Session by stated case by a person dissatisfied with a decision as being erroneous in point of law of a tribunal to which an appeal has been made against a determination of the Special Commissioners in relation to a notice with respect to the cancellation of a tax advantage from certain transactions in securities. The procedure is laid down in the section. The application for a stated case must be made within 30 days of the decision of the tribunal and the case lodged (in the General Department under r. 41.11) within 30 days of receiving it.

41.23.4   *"regulation 20(1) of the General Commissioners (Jurisdiction and Procedure) Regulations 1994"*. Reg.20(1) of the 1994 Regulations [S.I. 1994 No. 1812] provides a general provision for appeal to the Court of Session by stated case from an appeal to or proceedings before the General Commissioners under the Taxes Acts by a person dissatisfied with a decision or determination as being erroneous in point of law. It would apply to an appeal (by stated case) under s. 100B(3) of the 1970 Act (see the "without prejudice" provision) against the imposition of a penalty, as opposed to the amount of the penalty (see r. 41.25(1)(b)) to which in fact the same procedure applies (see 4. 41.25(3)(a)). The procedure is laid down in regs 20–23 of the 1994 Regulations. The application for a stated case must be made within 30 days of the determination and the case lodged (in the General Department under r. 41.11) within 30 days of receiving it.

41.23.5   *"written intimation"*. For methods, see r. 16.9.

Revenue appeals from Special Commissioners

[1] **41.24.**—(1) This rule applies to an appeal to the court under any of the following provisions:—

    (a) section 56A of the Taxes Management Act 1970;
    (b) section 225 of the Inheritance Tax Act 1984; and
    (c) regulation 10(1) of the Stamp Duty Reserve Tax Regulations 1986.

    (2) Part III (appeals in Form 41.19) shall apply to an appeal to which paragraph (1) applies.

---

[1] Rule 41.24 substituted by S.I. 1994 No. 2901 (effective 5th December 1994).

41.24.1   *General note*. Because the Special Commissioners give reasoned decisions it is no longer considered appropriate to use the cumbersome method of stated case procedure for appeals from them. Regulations provide for this in respect of appeals from Special Commissioners under the enactments mentioned in r. 41.24(1) and such appeals are dealt with under Form 41.19 procedure: r. 41.24(2). No period within which the appeal must be made is laid down in any of the provisions listed in r. 41.24(1); accordingly the appeal must be made within 42 days after the relevant date mentioned in r. 41.20(1)(b).

    Only the party who was unsuccessful in the appeal to or proceedings before the Commissioners is "dissatisfied" in point of law, and there should only be one stated case even if the other party raises a point of law: *Gordon v. Inland Revenue Commissioners* 1991 S.C. 149.

41.24.2   *"section 56A of the Taxes Management Act 1970"*. This section was substituted by the General and Special Commissioners (Amendment of Enactments) Regulations 1994 [S.I. 1994 No. 1813]. It provides for an appeal to the Court of Session by a person dissatisfied in point of law with a decision of the Special Commissioners. The procedure in Pt III of Chap. 41 (appeals in Form 41.19) applies: r. 41.42(2). S.56A of the 1970 Act would apply to an appeal under s. 100B of the 1970 Act (see the "without prejudice" provision) against the imposition of a penalty, as opposed to the amount of the penalty (see r. 41.25(1)(b)) to which in fact the same Form 41.19 procedure applies (see r. 41.25(3)(b)).

41.24.3   *"section 225 of the Inheritance Tax Act 1984"*. This section was substituted by the General and Special Commissioners (Amendment of Enactments) Regulations 1994 [S.I. 1994 No. 1813]. It provides for an appeal to the Court of Session by a person dissatisfied in point of law with a decision of the Special Commissioners. The procedure in Pt III of Chap. 41 (appeals in Form 41.19) applies: r. 41.42(2).

41.24.4   *"regulation 10(1) of the Stamp Duty Reserve Tax Regulations 1986"*. This regulation was substituted by the General and Special Commissioners (Amendment of Enactments) Regulations 1994 [S.I. 1994 No. 1813]. It provides for an appeal to the Court of Session by a person dissatisfied in point of law with a determination of the Special Commissioners. The procedure in Pt III of Chap. 41 (appeals in Form 41.19) applies: r. 41.42(2).

Appeals relating to penalties
 [1] **41.25.**—(1) This rule applies to an appeal to the court as the Court of Exchequer in Scotland under any of the following provisions:—
 [2] (za) section 13A(7) of the Stamp Act 1891 (appeals from Special Commissioners in relation to penalties);
   (a) section 53(1) or 100C(4) of the Taxes Management Act 1970 (appeals from General or Special Commissioners in relation to penalties);
   (b) an appeal against the amount of a penalty under section 100B(3) of the Taxes Management Act 1970;
 [3] (c) section 249(3) or 251(2) of the Inheritance Tax Act 1984 (appeals from Special Commissioners in relation to penalties);
 [3] (d) paragraph 10(3) of Schedule 12 to the Value Added Tax Act 1994 (appeal from VAT tribunal in relation to penalty);
 [2,5] (e) paragraph 12(2) of Schedule 17 to the Finance Act 1999 (appeals from Special Commissioners in relation to penalties);
 [4,5] (f) paragraph 4(1) of Schedule 2 to the Tax Credits Act 2002 (appeals from General or Special Commissioners in relation to penalties); and
   (g) paragraph 6(1) of Schedule 14 to the Finance Act 2003 appeals from General or Special Commissioners in relation to penalties)
 [3] (2) Part III (appeals in Form 41.19) shall apply to an appeal to which paragraph (1)(za), (a), (c), (d), (e) or (f) applies.
 [5] (3) In relation to paragraph (1)(b), and (g)—
   (a) Part II (appeals by stated case etc.) shall apply to an appeal from the General Commissioners; and
   (b) Part III shall apply to an appeal from the Special Commissioners.
 [4] (4) Within 30 days after service on them of an appeal in Form 41.19, the General Commissioners, the Special Commissioners or the VAT tribunal, as the case may be, shall—
   (a) send six copies of a note of their findings and of the reasons for their decision to the Deputy Principal Clerk; and
   (b) send a copy of that note to every party to the appeal.

---

[1] Rule 41.25 substituted by S.I. 1994 No. 2901 (effective 5th December, 1994).
[2] Rule 41.25(1)(za) and (e) inserted by S.S.I. 1999 No. 192 (effective 14th January, 2000).
[3] Rule 41.25(c), (d) and (2) amended by S.S.I. 1999 No. 192 (effective 14th January, 2000).
[4] Rule 41.25(1)(f), (2) and (4) inserted by S.S.I. 2004 No. 52 (effective 1st March, 2004).
[5] Rule 41.25(1)(e) and (f) and (3) amended by S.S.I. 2005 No. 193 (effective 1st April, 2005).

General note. Appeal against penalties under s. 13A(7) of the Stamp Act 1891, s. 53(1) or **41.25.1**
100C(4) of the Taxes Management Act 1970, s. 249(3) or 251(2) of the Inheritance Tax Act 1984 or para. 10(3) of Sched. 12 to the Value Added Tax Act 1994 is in Form 41.19 and stated case procedure does not apply: r. 41.25(2).
  No period within which the appeal must be made is laid down in any of the provisions listed in r. 41.24(1); accordingly the appeal must be made within 42 days after the relevant date mentioned in r. 41.20(1)(b). The Special Commissioners or the VAT Tribunal, as the case may be, must provide a note of the findings and reasons within 30 days of service of the appeal on them: r. 41.25(4).

Appeals against amount of a penalty under s. 100B(3) of the Taxes Management Act 1970. **41.25.2**
The procedure differs depending whether the appeal is from the General or Special Commissioners. If the appeal is from the General Commissioners, the stated case procedure in Pt II of Chap. 41 applies; if from the Special Commissioners, the Form 41.19 procedure applies (with the addition of the provision in r. 41.25(4)): r. 41.25(3). If the appeal is against the imposition of a penalty by the General Commissioners, the appeal should be by stated case under reg.20(1) of the General Commissioners (Jurisdiction and Procedure) Regulations 1994 [S.I. 1994 No. 1812] and r. 41.23; if by the Special Commissioners, the appeal should be in Form 41.19 under s. 56A of the Taxes Management Act 1970 and r. 41.24.
  No period within which the appeal must be made is laid down in s. 100B(3) of the 1970 Act. Accordingly, if the appeal is from the General Commissioners, the appeal must be made within

14 days after the relevant date mentioned in r. 41.5(2)(b); if from the Special Commissioners, the appeal must be made within 42 days after the relevant date mentioned in r. 41.20(1)(b).

41.25.3   *"send".* This includes deliver: r. 1.3(1) (definition of "send").

Appeals relating to certain determinations of the Commissioners for Her Majesty's Revenue and Customs

[1] **41.26.**—(1) This rule applies to an appeal against a determination of the Commissioners for Her Majesty's Revenue and Customs specified in a notice to the appellant under section 221 of the Inheritance Tax Act 1984 or regulation 6 of the
Stamp Duty Reserve Tax Regulations 1986.

(2) Where the Inner House grants leave to appeal under rule 41.3(2) in an application to it under section 222(3) of the said Act or regulation 8(3) of the said Regulations, as the case may be, or it is agreed between the appellant and the Commissioners of Inland Revenue that the appeal is to be to the court, the appellant shall, within 30 days after the date on which leave to appeal is granted or, as the case may be, after the date on which the Board intimates its agreement to the appellant—

(a) lodge a statement of facts and grounds of appeal in Form 41.19, and a process unless a process has already been lodged under rule 41.2(6) (lodging process in applications for leave to appeal), in which case the statement of facts and grounds of appeal shall be lodged in that process; and

(b) on so doing, apply by motion for an order for service in accordance with rule 41.21 (orders for service and answers).

(3) The appellant shall—

(a) following the lodging of answers or on the expiry of any period of adjustment allowed, or

(b) where no answers have been lodged, on the expiry of the period allowed for lodging answers,

apply by motion to the Inner House for an order for a hearing.

[2] (4) A motion under paragraph (3) shall be intimated to the solicitor in Scotland to the Commissioners of Her Majesty's Revenue and Customs whether or not answers have been lodged by the Commissioners.

(5) Rule 41.22(2)(b) shall apply to a motion under paragraph (3) of this rule as it applies to a motion under paragraph (1)(b) of that rule.

(6) If an appellant fails to comply with any time-limit imposed by this rule, he shall be deemed to have abandoned his appeal.

(7) Where it appears to the Inner House in an appeal under this rule that any question as to the value of land in the United Kingdom requires to be determined, the court shall remit the cause—

(a) where the land is in Scotland, to the Lands Tribunal for Scotland,

(b) where the land is in England and Wales, to the Lands Tribunal,

(c) where the land is in Northern Ireland, to the Lands Tribunal for Northern Ireland,

to determine that question and remit back to the Inner House for further procedure.

Deriv. R.C.S. 1965, r. 283(1), (2), (5) and (11) to (13) substituted by S.I. 1976 No. 1849 and amended by S.I. 1990 No. 705.

---

[1] Rule 41.26 amended by S.S.I. 2005 No. 268 (effective 7th June, 2005).
[2] Rule 41.26(4) amended by S.I. 1994 No. 2901 (effective 5th December, 1994).

41.26.1   *General note.* The appeals in this rule are made in Form 41.19.

41.26.2   *"lodge a statement of facts and grounds of appeal".* In addition to lodging the principal, six copies have to be lodged (r. 4.7(1)).

"service". For methods, see Ch.16, Pt I.   **41.26.3**

"motion". For motions, see Ch.23.   **41.26.4**

PART V

APPEALS UNDER THE PENSIONS APPEAL TRIBUNALS ACT 1943

Form of appeal under the Act of 1943
41.27. An appeal from a Pensions Appeal Tribunal under section 6(2) of the Pensions Appeal Tribunals Act 1943 shall be by a case, stated by the chairman of the tribunal, to which Part II (appeals by stated case etc.) shall apply.

Deriv. R.C.S. 1965, r.286(1)

General note. R.41.27 relates to appeals from Pension Appeal Tribunals to which an appeal **41.27.1** may be made under ss.1–4 of the Pension Appeal Tribunals Act 1943 in respect of war pensions claims.
  Appeal is on a point of law with leave of the tribunal or the court.

[1] PART VI

APPEALS UNDER SECTION 51 OF THE CHILDREN (SCOTLAND) ACT 1995

Application of Part II to this Part
[1] **41.28.** Part II (appeals by stated case etc.) shall apply to an appeal to the court by stated case under section 51(11)(b) of the Act of 1995 subject to the following provisions of this Part.

---

[1] Pt. VI and r.41.28 substituted by S.I. 1998 No. 2637 (effective 1st December 1998).

General note. Section 50 of the Social Work (Scotland) Act 1968 provided for an appeal by **41.28.1** stated case on a point of law or an irregularity from a decision of the sheriff. Section 50 of the 1968 Act has been replaced by s.51(11) of the Children (Scotland) Act 1995 which makes provision for an appeal by stated case on a point of law, but with one variation. Under the new provision the appeal may be made to the sheriff principal or to the Court of Session. If an appeal is made to the sheriff principal, a further appeal may be made to the Court of Session with leave of the sheriff principal. Section 50 of the 1968 Act continues to apply to proceedings not concluded when that section was repealed (1st April 1997). The stated case should be confined to proper findings-in-fact and should not include extraneous comments or questions not asked for by a party: *Kennedy v A*. 1986 S.L.T. 358; *Sloan v B*. 1991 S.L.T. 530, 544I–545E *per* L.P. Hope; *Kennedy v R's Curator ad Litem* 1992 S.C. 300, 305 *per* L.P. Hope.

Interpretation of this Part
[1]**41.29.** In this Part—
  "the Act of 1995" means the Children (Scotland) Act 1995; and
  "the Principal Reporter" means the Principal Reporter appointed under section 127 of the Local Government etc. (Scotland) Act 1994 or any officer of the Scottish Children's Reporter Administration to whom there is delegated, under section 131(1) of that Act, any function of the Principal Reporter under the Act of 1995.

---

[1] Rule 41.29 substituted by S.I. 1998 No. 2637 (effective 1st December 1998).

Lodging of reports and statements with sheriff
[1] **41.30.** Where, on application being made under subsection (13) of section 51 of the Act of 1995 to state a case for the purposes of an appeal under subsection (11)(b) of that section—

  (a) it appears to the sheriff (or as the case may be to the sheriff principal) that any report or statement lodged under subsection (2), or report lodged under subsection (3), of that section in the appeal to him is relevant to any issue which is likely to arise in the stated case; and

  (b) the report or statement has been returned to the Principal Reporter, the sheriff (or sheriff principal) may require the Principal Reporter to lodge the report or statement with the sheriff clerk; but on the stated case being sent to the person who applied for it, the sheriff clerk shall return the report or statement to the Principal Reporter.

Deriv. R.C.S. 1965, r. 289A(2) and (4)(part) inserted by S.I. 1971 No. 203

————

[1] R. 41.30 substituted by S.I. 1998 No. 2637 (effective 1st December 1998).

Lodging etc. of reports and statements in court
[1] **41.31.**—(1) Within seven days after the date on which the case is lodged under rule 41.11(1), the Principal Reporter shall send to the Deputy Principal Clerk the principal and three copies of every report or statement which he was required, under rule 43.30, to lodge.

(2) Neither the principal nor any copy of any such report or statement shall be made available to any of the other parties unless the court otherwise orders.

(3) Subject to any such order, every such report or statement shall remain in the custody of the Deputy Principal Clerk until the appeal has been determined or abandoned; and then shall be returned by him to the Principal Reporter.

Deriv. R.C.S. 1965, r. 289A(6) and (8) inserted by S.I. 1971 No. 203

————

[1] R. 41.31 substituted by S.I. 1998 No. 2637 (effective 1st December 1998).

"within seven days". The date from which the period is calculated is not counted. Where the **41.31.1** last day falls on a Saturday or Sunday or a public holiday on which the Office of Court is closed, the next available day is allowed: r. 1.3(7). For office hours and public holidays, see note 3.1.2.

"send". This includes deliver: r. 1.3(1) (definition of "send").   **41.31.2**

Hearing in private
[1] **41.32.** The court may direct that all or any part of the appeal shall be heard in private.

Deriv. R.C.S. 1965, r. 289A(7) inserted by S.I. 1971 No. 203

————

[1] R. 41.32 substituted by S.I. 1998 No. 2637 (effective 1st December 1998).

General note. The rule substituted by A.S. (R.C.S.A. No. 2) (Miscellaneous) 1998 [S.I. 1998 **41.32.1** No. 2637] is in identical terms to the rule it replaced.

Expenses
[1] **41.33.**—(1) No expenses shall be awarded to or against any party in respect of the appeal.

(2) Rule 41.14(3)(b) (award of expenses in abandoned appeal) shall not apply to an appeal to which this Part applies.

Deriv. R.C.S. 1965, r. 289A(9) inserted by S.I. 1971 No. 203

————

[1] R. 41.32 substituted by S.I. 1998 No. 2637 (effective 1st December 1998).

General note. The rule substituted by A.S. (R.C.S.A. No. 2) (Miscellaneous) 1998 [S.I. 1998 No. 2637] is in identical terms to the rule it replaced.

Part VII

APPEALS UNDER THE REPRESENTATION OF THE PEOPLE ACT 1983

Application of this Part
41.34. This Part applies to an appeal under section 56, as applied by section 57, of the Representation of the People Act 1983 (registration appeals).

Deriv. R.C.S. 1965, r. 284(preamble) amended by S.I. 1980 No. 1144

41.34.1 *General note.* S.56, as applied by s.57, of the Representation of the People Act 1983 provides for appeal on a point of law from a decision of the sheriff from a decision of the registration officer in relation to local government elections. Appeal is to three judges of the Court of Session appointed by A.S. (1983 Act, s.57(2)) and known as the Registration Appeal Court: see r. 41.37.

Form of appeal under this Part
41.35. An appeal to which this Part applies shall be made by stated case to which Part II (appeals by stated case etc.) shall apply subject to the following provisions of this Part.

Deriv. R.C.S. 1965, r. 284(preamble) amended by S.I. 1980 No. 1144

Consolidated appeals
41.36.—(1) Where several persons have applied for a stated case and it appears to the sheriff that such applications, or any two or more of them, raise the same question of law, he may consolidate the appeals into one stated case and, where he does so, he shall—
(a) state in the case the reasons why he has consolidated the appeals; and
(b) name one of the appellants as the appellant.
(2) Where appeals have been consolidated under paragraph (1), the appellant named under paragraph (1)(b), on receiving the stated case from the sheriff clerk, shall send a copy of it to every other appellant on request.

Deriv. R.C.S. 1965, r. 284(a)

41.36.1 *"send".* This includes deliver: r. 1.3(1) (definition of "send").

Hearing before Registration Appeal Court
41.37.—(1) On the stated case being lodged in accordance with rule 41.11, the appeal shall be put out for hearing before the Registration Appeal Court on the earliest available day.
(2) Rule 41.15 (motions for hearing of appeals) shall not apply to an appeal to which this Part applies.

Deriv. R.C.S. 1965, r. 284(b)

41.37.1 *General note.* The Registration Appeal Court is constituted under s.57(2) of the Representation of the People Act 1983.
The judges of the court are currently Lords Abernethy, Nimmo Smith and Emslie; A.S. (Registration Appeal Court) (No. 2) 2005 [S.S.I. 2005 No. 382].

Decision of Registration Appeal Court
41.38.—(1) The Registration Appeal Court shall, in its decision, specify any alteration or correction to be made on the register in pursuance of such decision.

(2) The Deputy Principal Clerk shall send a copy of the decision of the Registration Appeal Court to the registration officer within four days after the date of the decision.

Deriv. R.C.S. 1965, r. 284(c)

"send". This includes deliver: r. 1.3(1) (definition of "send").   **41.38.1**

PART VIII

STATED CASES UNDER SECTION 11(3) OF THE TRIBUNALS AND INQUIRIES ACT 1992

Case stated by tribunal at its own instance
41.39.—(1) A tribunal referred to in subsection (1), as modified by subsection (7), of section 11 of the Tribunals and Inquiries Act 1992 may, at its own instance, state a case for the opinion of the court on any question arising in the course of proceedings before it.
(2) Part II (appeals by stated case etc.) shall apply to a case stated under paragraph (1) subject to the following provisions of this Part.

Deriv. R.C.S. 1965, r. 291(2)(preamble)

General note. S.11(1), as modified by s.11(7), of the Tribunals and Inquiries Act 1992 **41.39.1** provides that any party to proceedings before certain specified tribunals in Sched. 1 to the Act who is dissatisfied in point of law with a decision of the tribunal may appeal to, or require the tribunal to state a case for the opinion of, the Court of Session.

Modifications of Part II to appeals under this Part
41.40.—(1) The following rules shall apply to a case to which this Part applies subject to the following provisions of this rule:—
    rule 41.9 (preparation and issue of the case),
    rule 41.11 (lodging of case in court),
    rule 41.15 (motions for hearing of appeals).
(2) For paragraph (1) of rule 41.9 there shall be substituted the following paragraph:—
    "(1) Where the tribunal decides to state a case at its own instance, it shall intimate that decision to each party.".
(3) For paragraph (6) of rule 41.9 there shall be substituted the following paragraphs:—
    "(6) When the case has been settled by the tribunal, the case shall be authenticated by the clerk of the tribunal who shall—
    (a) send a copy of the case to each party; and
    (b) transmit to the Deputy Principal Clerk the case with a certificate endorsed on it and signed by him certifying that sub-paragraph (a) has been complied with.
    (7) The Deputy Principal Clerk shall endorse the case with the date on which he received it from the clerk of the tribunal and return it to the clerk.".
(4) For rule 41.11 there shall be substituted the following rule:—
    "**41.11.** Not earlier than seven days and not later than 14 days after the date on which the case was received by the Deputy Principal Clerk, the clerk of the tribunal shall—
    (a) lodge in the General Department—
      (i) the case; and
      (ii) a process in accordance with rule 4.4 (steps of process) including any productions to be referred to in the appeal;
    (b) on giving written intimation to every other party of the lodging of the case, send five copies of the case to every such party; and
    (c) endorse and sign a certificate on the case that the requirements of

rule 4.6 (intimation of steps of process) have been complied with.".

(5) Rule 41.15 shall apply to the clerk of the tribunal in a cause to which this Part applies as it applies to the party lodging a case under rule 41.11.

Deriv. R.C.S. 1965, r. 291(a), (b), (c) and (d) (amended by S.I. 1985 No. 1600)

41.40.1   *General note.* The modifications are necessary because the clerk of the tribunal is requested to send the case to the Deputy Principal Clerk before lodging it in the General Department within a period determined from the date it was received by the Deputy Principal Clerk.

41.40.2   *"intimate".* For methods, see r. 16.7.

41.40.3   *"send".* This includes deliver: r. 1.3(1) (definition of "send").

41.40.4   *"lodge in the General Department".* Six copies of the case must be lodged with the principal: r. 4.7(1). Four copies of any productions must be lodged. Lodging may be done by post: P.N. No. 4 of 1994, paras. 1 and 8.

Part IX

Appeals under Social Security Acts

Form of appeal under certain Social Security Acts
41.41. A reference or appeal under any of the following provisions shall be by stated case to which Part II (appeals by stated case etc.) shall apply:—
  [3] (a) an appeal under section 15(1) of the Social Security Act 1998;
      (b) [*Omitted by the Act of Sederunt (Rules of the Court of Session Amendment) (Miscellaneous) 2007 (S.S.I. 2007 No. 7), para. 6(b) (effective 26th February 2007).*]
  [1] (c) a reference by the Pensions Ombudsman under section 150(7) of the Pension Schemes Act 1993;
      (d) an appeal under section 151(4), or section 173(3), of the Pension Schemes Act 1993;
  [2] (e) a reference by the Occupational Pensions Regulatory Authority under section 97(1) of the Pensions Act 1995; and
      (f) an appeal under section 97(3) of the Pensions Act 1995.

Deriv. R.C.S. 1965, r. 288(1) substituted by S.I. 1992 No. 2289

---

[1] Rule 41.41(b) amended by S.I. 1997 No. 853 (effective 6th April 1997).
[2] Rule 41.41(e) and (f) inserted by S.I. 1997 No. 853 (effective 6th April 1997).
[3] Rule 41.41(a) substituted by S.S.I. 2007 No. 7, para. 6(a) (effective 26th February 2007).

41.41.1   *Section 15(1) of the Social Security Act 1998.* Section 15 of the 1998 Act provides for an appeal on a question of law arising out of certain adjudications of the Secretary of State.

41.41.2   *Regulations under section 58(8) of the Social Security Administration Act 1992.* S. 58(8) of the 1992 Act allows for regulations in connection with the Social Security Contributions and Benefits Act 1992 and to provide for references or appeals to the Court of Session on questions of law. This provision of the 1992 Act has been repealed by the Social Security Act 1998.

41.41.3   *Pension Schemes Act 1993.* S. 150(7) of the 1993 Act provides for a reference to the Court of Session of a question of law arising from a determination in connection with a complaint or dispute investigated by the Pensions Ombudsman. S. 151(4) of the 1993 Act provides for an appeal on a point of law to the Court of Session from a determination of the Pensions Ombudsman at the instance of certain persons.
Section 173(1) of the 1993 Act provided for references to the Court of Session by the Occupational Pensions Board of questions of law and s. 173(3) of that Act provided for appeal by a person aggrieved by a determination of the Board involving a question of law which has not been referred by the Board to the court.
Section 173 of the Pension Schemes Act 1993 has been repealed and replaced by s. 97 of the Pensions Act 1995. The Occupational Pensions Board has been replaced by the Occupational Pensions Regulatory Authority: 1995 Act, s. 1. The Authority may make a reference on a

question of law to the court under s. 97(1), and an aggrieved person may appeal against a determination of the Authority involving a question of law (which has not been referred by the Authority to the court) under s. 97(3), of the 1995 Act.

Modifications of Part II to appeals under this Part

41.42.—(1) The following rules shall apply to a cause to which this Part applies subject to the following provisions of this rule:—

rule 41.9 (preparation and issue of the case),

rule 41.11 (lodging of case in court),

rule 41.15 (motions for hearing of appeals).

(2) For paragraph (1) of rule 41.9 there shall be substituted the following paragraph:—

"(1) Where the tribunal decides to state a case at its own instance, it shall intimate that decision to each party.".

(3) For paragraph (6) of rule 41.9 there shall be substituted the following paragraphs:—

"(6) When the case has been settled by the tribunal, the case shall be authenticated by the clerk of the tribunal who shall—

(a) send a copy of the case to each party; and

(b) transmit to the Deputy Principal Clerk the case with a certificate endorsed on it and signed by him certifying that sub-paragraph (a) has been complied with.

(7) The Deputy Principal Clerk shall endorse the case with the date on which he received it from the clerk to the tribunal and return it to the clerk.".

(4) For rule 41.11 there shall be substituted the following rule:—

"**41.11.** Not earlier than seven days and not later than 14 days after the date on which the case was received by the Deputy Principal Clerk, the clerk of the tribunal shall—

(a) lodge in the General Department—

(i) the case; and

(ii) a process in accordance with rule 4.4 (steps of process) including any productions to be referred to in the appeal;

(b) on giving written intimation to every other party of the lodging of the case, send five copies of the case to every such party; and

(c) endorse and sign a certificate on the case that the requirements of rule 4.6 (intimation of steps of process) have been complied with.".

(5) Rule 41.15 shall apply to the clerk of the tribunal in a cause to which this Part applies as it applies to the party lodging a case under rule 41.11.

Deriv. R.C.S. 1965, r. 288(3) and (4) substituted by S.I. 1992 No. 2289

General note. The modifications are necessary because the clerk of the tribunal is required to **41.42.1** send the case to the Deputy Principal Clerk before lodging it in the General Department within a period determined from the date it was received by the Deputy Principal Clerk.

"intimate". For methods, see r. 16.7. **41.42.2**

"send". This includes deliver: r. 1.3(1) (definition of "send"). **41.42.3**

"lodge in the General Department". Six copies of the case must be lodged with the principal: r. **41.42.4** 4.7(1). Four copies of any productions must be lodged. Lodging may be done by post: P.N. No. 4 of 1994, paras 1 and 8.

Part X

Appeals to Lord Ordinary

Application of Parts II and III to this Part

41.43. Unless otherwise provided in these Rules, in an appeal to the court which is directed by these Rules or any other enactment to be made to a

single judge of the court, the Outer House or the Lord Ordinary, Part II (appeals by stated case etc.) or Part III (appeals in Form 41.19), as the case may be, shall apply to that appeal subject to the following modifications:—
  (a) for references to the Inner House there shall be substituted references to the Lord Ordinary;
  (b) for references to the Single Bills there shall be substituted references to the Motion Roll; and
  (c) for references to the Summar Roll there shall be substituted references to a hearing.

41.43.1   *General note.* This is a new rule. Although most appeals are dealt with by the Inner House, an enactment may specify that an appeal is to be dealt with by a single judge or the Lord Ordinary.
  Appeals to the court under, *e.g.* the Patents Acts 1949 and 1977, and the Trade Marks Act 1994, are heard by the patents judge: see rr. 55.14 and 55.19 respectively. Under s. 97 of the Patents Act 1977 an appeal from the Comptroller of Patents, Designs and Trade Marks is to the Outer House in the first instance.

Appeals to be heard in Outer House
  [1] **41.44.**—(1) Subject to paragraph (2), an appeal to the court to which this Chapter applies may be remitted by the Inner House to the Outer House to be heard by the Lord Ordinary in the first instance—
  (a) at its own instance after hearing parties, or
  (b) on the motion of a party,
on a motion being enrolled under rule 41.15 (motions for hearing appeals by stated case) or rule 41.22 (motion for further procedure in appeals in Form 41.19), as the case may be.
  (2) Paragraph (1) shall not apply to the following appeals:—
  (a) an appeal under an enactment which specifies that the appeal is to the Inner House;
  (b) an appeal to which Part IV of this Chapter applies (Exchequer appeals);
  (c) an appeal to which Part VI of this Chapter applies (appeals under section 50 of the Social Work (Scotland) Act 1968);
  (d) an appeal to which Part VII of this Chapter applies (appeals under the Representation of the People Act 1983);
  (e) an appeal from the Land Court;
  (f) an appeal from the Lands Tribunal for Scotland;
  (g) an appeal under section 10 of the Restrictive Practices Court Act 1976 (appeal from the Restrictive Practices Court);
  (h) an appeal under paragraph 14 of Schedule 4 to the Transport Act 1985 (appeal from the Transport Tribunal);
  (i) an appeal under section 25(1) of the Child Support Act 1991 (appeal from the Child Support Commissioner);
  (j) an appeal under section 24(1) of the Social Security Administration Act 1992 (appeal from the Social Security Commissioner);
  (k) an appeal under section 9 of the Asylum and Immigration Appeals Act 1993 (appeal from the Immigration Appeal Tribunal);
  (l) an appeal under section 37(1) of the Industrial Tribunals Act 1996.
  [2](m) an appeal under section 49 of the Competition Act 1998 (appeal from the Competition Commission).

---

  [1] R. 41.44 inserted by S.I. 1996 No. 2168 (effective 23rd September 1996).
  [2] R.41.44(2)(m) inserted by S.S.I. 2000 No. 144, para. 2 (effective 12th June 2000).

41.44.1   *General note.* Public concern has been expressed about the apparent delay in hearing some statutory appeals, such as planning appeals, in the Inner House. Some statutory appeals are more akin to judicial review proceedings. In U.K. statutes, where an appeal in England and Wales is to the High Court or the Court of Appeal, the Scottish provision provides simply for the Court of Session in either case. The historical convention is that all such statutory appeals are heard in the Inner House.

Rule 41.44, inserted by A.S. (R.C.S.A. No. 4) (Miscellaneous) [1996 No. 2168], provides for the Inner House to remit statutory appeals to which Chap. 41 applies, subject to certain exceptions, to the Outer House for a Lord Ordinary to determine in the first instance.

The exceptions are, in principle, appeals under an enactment which stipulates appeals which the Inner House wishes to retain (Exchequer and Social Work appeals); appeals from tribunals consisting of a (judicial) panel of two or more (*e.g.* the Lands Tribunal); and appeals under U.K. statutes which, in relation to England and Wales, specify the Court of Appeal as the appeal court.

Remit to Outer House. There is no indication in r. 41.44(1) as to the circumstances in which a **41.44.2** remit might be appropriate. Regard would be had to the principle which is behind the choice of some of the appeals listed in r. 41.44(2) as appeals which cannot be remitted. These principles are that the enactment under which the appeal is made specifies the Inner House; appeals which the Inner House wishes to retain (Exchequer and Social Work appeals); appeals from a tribunal consisting of a (judicial) panel of two or more; and appeals under U.K. statutes which, in relation to England and Wales, specify the Court of Appeal as the appeal court.

Other factors might include the fact that the appeal was a test case, or raised a point of public importance or a novel point of law on which there was no judicial authority. Another factor might be the urgency for a decision.

Reclaiming against decision of Lord Ordinary

[1] **41.45.** The decision of the Lord Ordinary on an appeal heard in the Outer House by virtue of rule 41.44 (appeals to be heard in Outer House) may be reclaimed against.

---

[1] Rule 41.45 inserted by S.I. 1996 No. 2168 (effective 23rd September 1996).

General note. This rule is a consequence of the insertion of r. 41.44 for the remit of certain **41.45.1** statutory appeals of the Outer House, and was inserted by the A.S. (R.C.S.A. No. 4) (Miscellaneous) 1996 [S.I. 1996 No. 2168].

Although delay in hearing appeals might be overcome by a power to remit to the Outer House, delay could be built back in by providing for a further appeal to the Inner House. Provision for a further appeal, however, is inevitable if, under a U.K. statute, a party to an appeal in England and Wales would have the opportunity to appeal from the High Court to the Court of Appeal.

[1] PART XI

NATIONALITY, IMMIGRATION AND ASYLUM ACT 2002

Interpretation of this Part

[1] **41.46.** In this Part—

"the Act of 2002" means the Nationality, Immigration and Asylum Act 2002;

"the Act of 2004" means the Asylum and Immigration (Treatment of Claimants, etc.) Act 2004;

"the Tribunal" means the Asylum and Immigration Tribunal;

"filter provision" means paragraph 30 of Schedule 2 to the Act of 2004.

---

[1] Part IX and Rule 41.46 substituted by S.S.I. 2005 No. 198 (effective 4th April 2005) and by S.S.I. 2007 No. 283 (effective 2nd May 2007).

General note. Part XI, inserted by A.S. (R.C.S.A. No. 3) (Applications under the Nationality, **41.46.1** Immigration and Asylum Act 2002) 2003 [S.S.I. 2003 No. 223], was substituted by A.S. (R.C.S.A. No. 6) (Asylum and Immigration (Treatment of Claimants, etc.) Act 2004) 2005 [S.S.I. 2005 No. 198].

The Act of 2004 replaced the provision for review in s. 102(2) of the Act of 2002 with an application under s. 103A of the Act of 2002 to the Court of Session, on the grounds of error of law, for an order requiring the Asylum and Immigration tribunal to reconsider its decision on an appeal under s. 82 or 83 of the Act of 2002. The AIT was created by s. 81 of the 2002 Act, as substituted by s. 26 of the 2004 Act.

Following reconsideration by the AIT, there is a right of appeal to the Court of Session under s. 103B of the Act of 2002 inserted by s. 26 of the Act of 2004. There is also a right of appeal from a decision of the AIT sitting as a panel under s. 103E of the Act of 2002. These appeals will be dealt with under Pt III of Chap. 49 (appeals in form 41.19)

There is also provision, in r. 41.53, in an application under s. 103A of the Act of 2002 for a reference to the Inner House instead of an order for reconsideration by the AIT.

There are transitional provisions in the A.S. for reviews under the former s. 102(2) of the 2002 Act.

Disapplication of certain rules to this Part

[1] **41.47.** The following rules shall not apply to a petition to which this Part applies—

    rule 14.4 (form of petition),
    rule 14.5 (first order in petitions),
    rule 14.6 (period of notice for lodging answers),
    rule 14.7 (intimation and service of petitions),
    rule 14.8 (procedure where answers lodged),
    rule 14.9 (unopposed petitions).

---

[1] Rule 41.47 substituted by S.S.I 2005 No. 198 (effective 4th April 2005) and by S.S.I. 2007 No. 283 (effective 2nd May 2007).

Applications for orders requiring reconsideration

[1] **41.48.**—(1) The following shall be made to the Outer House—

(a) an application under section 103A(1) of the Act of 2002 for an order requiring the Tribunal to reconsider a decision on an appeal;

(b) a notification under paragraph 30(5)(a) of Schedule 2 to the Act of 2004 that the applicant wishes the court to consider his application under section 103A(1) of the Act of 2002.

(2) The application or notification shall be by petition in Form 41.48.

(3) There shall be lodged with the petition—

(a) the asylum and immigration decision to which the application relates, and any document giving reasons for the decision;

(b) the grounds of appeal to the Tribunal;

(c) the Tribunal's decision;

(d) a copy of any case report upon which the applicant wishes to rely;

(e) any other documents material to the application which were before the Tribunal; and

(f) where applicable, a copy of any decision under paragraph 30(4) of Schedule 2 to the Act of 2004 (decision of a member of the Tribunal during the period the filter provision has effect).

(4) The petition shall set out—

(a) the grounds upon which it is contended that the Tribunal made an error of law;

(b) reasons in support of those grounds,

and may set out comments on the reasons given in any decision under paragraph 30(4) of Schedule 2 to the Act of 2004.

(5) Where the applicant—

(a) was the respondent to the appeal; and

(b) was required to serve the Tribunal's determination, or any decision of a member of the Tribunal during the period the filter provision has effect, on the appellant,

the petition shall contain a statement of the date on which, and the means by which, the determination or any such decision was served.

(6) An application to which paragraph 30(2) of Schedule 2 to the Act of 2004 applies may be signed by a solicitor.

---

[1] Rule 41.48 substituted by S.S.I. 2005 No. 198 (effective 4th April 2005) and by S.S.I. 2007 No. 283 (effective 2nd May 2007).

General note. The Act of 2004 replaced the provision for review in s. 102(2) of the Act of 2002 **41.48.1**
with an application under s. 103A of the Act of 2002 to the Court of Session, on the grounds of
error of law, for an order requiring the Asylum and Immigration tribunal to reconsider its
decision on an appeal under s. 82 or 83 of the Act of 2002.

The proper test for determining the adequacy of reasons given by an adjudicator is that set
out in *Wordie Property Co Ltd v. Secretary of State for Scotland,* 1984 S.L.T. 345: *Esen v.
Secretary of State for the Home Department,* 2006 S.C. 555 (Extra Div.).

The correct test in relation to art. 6 of ECHR in asylum cases is that it must be shown that a
person has suffered or risks suffering a flagrant denial of a fair trial: *Torabi v. Secretary of State
for the Home Department,* 2006 S.C. 567 (Extra Div.).

"petition". A petition is presented to the Outer House: r. 14.2(h). The petition must be in **41.48.2**
Form 86.3 in the official printed form (r. 4.1). The petition must be signed by counsel or other
person having a right of audience: r. 4.2; and see r. 1.3(1) (definition of "counsel" and "other
person having a right of audience") and note 1.3.4.

The petitioner must lodge the petition with the required steps of process (r. 4.4). A fee is
payable on lodging the petition: see note 14.5.10.

On petitions generally, see Chap. 14.

Productions. On productions and the lodging of them, see r. 4.5 and note 4.5.2.   **41.48.3**

Exclusion of days

[1] **41.49.**—(1) In applying section 103A(3)(a) or section 103A(3)(c) of the
Act of 2002 (time limits) any day which is not a business day shall be
disregarded.

(2) In this rule "business day" means any day other than a Saturday,
Sunday, or public holiday as directed by the Lord President of the Court of
Session.

---

[1] Rule 41.49 substituted by S.S.I. 2005 No. 198 (effective 4th April 2005) and by S.S.I. 2007 No. 283 (effective 2nd May 2007).

General note. There is a power in s. 103A(4) of the 2002 Act to exclude, from calculating the
time limits set out in s. 103A(3), certain days. This rule does that.

Extension of time limit for application

[1] **41.50.** An application under section 103A(4) of the Act of 2002 for
permission to make an application under section 103A(1) of that Act
(applications for orders requiring reconsideration) outside the period
specified in section 103A(3) of that Act (time limits) shall be made in the
petition and supported by an affidavit.

---

[1] Rule 41.50 substituted by S.S.I. 2005 No. 198 (effective 4th April 2005) and by S.S.I. 2007 No. 283 (effective 2nd May 2007).

General note. There is a power in s. 103A(4) of the 2002 Act to allow an application under s. **41.50.1**
103A to be made out of time.

"affidavit". On affidavits, see r. 1.3(2) and note 1.3.7.   **41.50.2**

Other written submissions

[1] **41.51.** Where a petition is for reconsideration of a decision of the
Tribunal to grant an appeal the court may order that written submissions
may be lodged by the other party within a time limit to be fixed by the court.

---

[1] Rule 41.51 substituted by S.S.I 2005 No. 198 (effective 4th April 2005) and by S.S.I. 2007 No. 283 (effective 2nd May 2007).

Service of petition etc.

[1] **41.52.**—(1) Where an order has been made under rule 41.51 (order for other written submissions) the petitioner shall serve on the other party copies of—

(a) the petition;

(b) the interlocutor made under rule 41.51; and

(c) each of the documents lodged in support of the petition, except for documents that come from or have already been served on the other party,

with a citation in Form 41.52 attached to the petition.

(2) The petitioner shall lodge in process a certificate of service as required by these Rules at least 7 days before the expiry of the time limit fixed by the court under rule 41.51.

[1] Rule 41.52 substituted by S.S.I. 2005 No. 198 (effective 4th April 2005) and by S.S.I. 2007 No. 283 (effective 2nd May 2007).

41.52.1   *"serve".* For methods, see Chap. 16, Pt I.

Reference to Inner House

[1] **41.52A.** A reference under section 103C(1) of the Act of 2002 shall be made by report to the Inner House under rule 34.1.

[1] Rule 41.52A substituted by S.S.I. 2005 No. 198 (effective 4th April 2005), re-numbered by S.S.I. 2005 No. 268 (effective 7th June 2005) and substituted by S.S.I. 2007 No. 283 (effective 2nd May 2007).

41.52A.1   *General note.* There is provision, in an application under s. 103A of the Act of 2002, for a reference to the Inner House instead of an order for reconsideration by the AIT: Act of 2002, s. 103C inserted by s. 26 of the 2004 Act.

41.52A.2   *"report to the Inner House".* For procedure, see Chap. 34.

Service of order

[1] **41.52B.**—(1) After consideration of a petition under rule 41.48 (applications for orders requiring reconsideration) the Deputy Principal Clerk of Session shall send copies of the order of the court to—

(a) the applicant and other party to the appeal, except where paragraph (2) applies; and

(b) the Tribunal.

(2) Where the application relates, in whole or in part, to a claim for asylum, the Deputy Principal Clerk of Session shall send a copy of the order of the court to the Secretary of State, who shall serve the order on the applicant and the other party.

(3) Where the Secretary of State has served an order in accordance with paragraph (2), he shall notify the court of the date and method of service.

(4) The Secretary of State shall provide the notification required by paragraph (3) within 28 days after the date on which the Deputy Principal Clerk of Session sends him a copy of the order of the court.

(5) If, 28 days after the date on which the Deputy Principal Clerk of Session sends a copy of the order of the court to the Secretary of State in accordance with paragraph (2), the Secretary of State has not provided the notification required by paragraph (3), the Deputy Principal Clerk may, on receipt of a request, serve the order on the applicant and the other party.

---

[1] Rule 41.52B substituted by S.S.I. 2005 No. 198 (effective 4th April 2005), re-numbered by S.S.I. 2005 No. 268 (effective 7th June 2005) and substituted by S.S.I. 2007 No. 283 (effective 2nd May 2007).

"*send*". This includes deliver: r. 1.3(1) (definition of "send").   **41.52B.1**

"*28 days after*". The date of sending is not included in the calculation.   **41.52B.2**

Continuing application or appeal otherwise treated as abandoned

[1] **41.52C.**—(1) This rule applies to—

(a) an application under section 103A(1) of the Act of 2002;

(b) an application under sections 103B or 103E of the Act of 2002 for leave to appeal;

(c) an appeal under sections 103B or 103E of the Act of 2002; or

(d) a reference under section 103C of the Act of 2002.

(2) Where an application or appeal mentioned in paragraph (1) would be treated as abandoned under section 104(4A) of the Act of 2002 but—

(a) meets the conditions set out in section 104(4B) or (4C) of the Act of 2002, and

(b) the applicant or appellant, as the case may be, wishes to pursue his application or appeal,

the applicant or appellant, as the case may be, must lodge a notice in Form 41.52C.

(3) A notice in Form 41.52C must be lodged—

(a) where section 104(4B) of the Act of 2002 applies, within 28 days of the date on which the applicant or appellant, as the case may be, received notice of the grant of leave to enter or remain in the United Kingdom for a period exceeding 12 months; or

(b) where section 104(4C) of the Act of 2002 applies, within 28 days of the date on which the applicant or appellant, as the case may be, received notice of the grant of leave to enter or remain in the United Kingdom.

(4) Where the applicant or appellant, as the case may be, does not comply with the time limit specified in paragraph (3) the application or appeal will be treated as abandoned in accordance with section 104(4) of the Act of 2002.

(5) The applicant or appellant, as the case may be, must serve a copy of the Form 41.52C on the respondent.

(6) Where the applicant or appellant, as the case may be, has lodged a notice under paragraph (2) the Deputy Principal Clerk of Session shall—

(a) notify the applicant or appellant, as the case may be, of the date on which the Form was received, and

(b) send a copy of the notification to the respondent.

---

[1] Rule 41.52C inserted by S.S.I. 2007 No. 283 (effective 2nd May 2007).

[1] PART XII

APPEALS UNDER THE PROCEEDS OF CRIME ACT 2002

Form of appeal under section 299 of the Proceeds of Crime Act 2002

[1] **41.53.**—(1) In this rule "the Act of 2002" means the Proceeds of Crime Act 2002.

(2) This rule applies to an appeal under section 299 of the Act of 2002.

(3) An appeal under paragraph (2) shall be to the Lord Ordinary.

[1] Pt XII and r. 41.53 inserted by S.S.I. 2003 No. 222 (effective 28th March, 2003) and amended by S.S.I. 2004 No. 331 (effective 6th August, 2004).

41.53.1 *General note.* An appeal under s. 299 of the Act of 2002 is an appeal against an order for forfeiture by the sheriff of cash (under s. 298), which is recoverable property or intended for use in unlawful conduct, detained (under s. 295) after being seized by a customs officer or constable (under s. 294).

The appeal must be made within 30 days beginning with the date of the forfeiture order, and is a rehearing: Act of 2002, s. 299.

41.53.2 *Form of appeal.* As an appeal from the decision of a sheriff, the appeal should probably be under Chap. 40 (appeals from inferior courts). The appeal will instead be one to which Pt III of Chap. 41 applies, and the appeal will be in Form 41.19. Pt X (appeals to Lord Ordinary) will also apply.

Reclaiming against decision of the Lord Ordinary
[1] **41.54.** The decision of the Lord Ordinary on an appeal under rule 41.53 shall be final and shall not be subject to review.

[1] R.41.54 inserted by S.S.I. 2003 No. 222 (effective 28th March, 2003) and as amended by S.S.I. 2004 No. 331 (effective 6th August, 2004).

41.54.1 *"final and shall not be subject to review".* The decision may not be reclaimed against.

[1] PART XIII

REFERENCES AND APPEALS UNDER AN ACAS ARBITRATION SCHEME

Definitions
[1] **41.55.** In this Part, "an ACAS Scheme" means an arbitration scheme set out in an order under section 212A(7) of the Trade Union and Labour Relations (Consolidation) Act 1992.

[1] Part XIII and r. 41.55 inserted by S.S.I. 2004 No. 331 (effective 6th August 2004).

41.55.1 *General note.* Section 212A of the Trade Union and Labour Relations (Consolidation) Act 1992 was inserted by s. 7 of the Employment Rights (Dispute Resolution) Act 1998. It provides that ACAS may prepare a scheme for arbitration in disputes involving proceedings in, or claims which could be proceedings before, an employment tribunal arising out of an (alleged) contravention of Pt X of the 1996 Act (unfair dismissal) or other enactment specified by the Secretary of State.

Such a scheme may provide, in an arbitration conducted in accordance with Scots law, for a reference on a preliminary point, or a right of appeal, to the Court of Session: 1992 Act, s. 212A(7).

References under an ACAS Scheme
[1] **41.56.**—(1) A reference on a preliminary point under an ACAS Scheme shall be made to the Outer House in Form 41.56 and shall—
  (a) state in numbered paragraphs the facts and circumstances out of which the reference arises; and
  (b) set out the question for answer by the court.
(2) On a reference under paragraph (1) being lodged, the court shall, without a motion being enrolled for that purpose, pronounce an interlocutor for—
  (a) service of the reference on such persons as appears necessary; and
  (b) any person on whom the reference has been served, to lodge answers, if so advised, within such period as is specified by the court.
(3) Within 14 days after the expiry of the period allowed for the lodging of answers, the person making the reference shall apply by motion for such

further procedure as he seeks, and the court shall make such order for further procedure as it thinks fit.

———

[1] Rule 41.56 inserted by S.S.I. 2004 No. 331 (effective 6th August 2004).

"reference". The only initiating processes in R.C.S. 1994 are summons and petition; there are   **41.56.1** no general rules for a reference. In other cases of references to the court, the usual course is to provide for the reference to be by petition, thus attracting the general (or such general) rules for petitions as may be necessary. Since there is no initiating process known as a reference, there are no rules which can be applied to it. Are petition rules or rules for actions to apply? Is the reference lodged in the Petition or General Department (one assumes the former)?

"service". See Chap. 16, Pt.1.   **41.56.2**

"answers". See r. 18.3 for guidance.   **41.56.3**

"Within 14 days". The date from which the period is calculated is not counted. Where the last   **41.56.4** day falls on a Saturday or Sunday or a public holiday on which the Office of Court is closed, the next available day is allowed: r. 1.3(7). For office hours and public holidays, see note 3.1.2.

"motion". For motions, see Chap. 23.

Reclaiming against decision of the Lord Ordinary
[1] **41.57.** The decision of a Lord Ordinary on a reference on a preliminary point under rule 41.56 may be reclaimed against.

———

[1] Rule 41.57 inserted by S.S.I. 2004 No. 331 (effective 6th August 2004).

"reclaimed". For reclaiming, see Chap. 38.

Appeals
[1] **41.58.**—(1) Subject to paragraph (2), Part III (appeals in Form 41.19) shall apply to appeals under an ACAS Scheme.

(2) An appeal under an ACAS Scheme shall be made within the time limits specified in that scheme.

———

[1] Rule 41.58 inserted by S.S.I. 2004 No. 331 (effective 6th August 2004).

CHAPTER 42

TAXATION OF ACCOUNTS AND FEES OF SOLICITORS

PART I

TAXATION OF ACCOUNTS

Remit to the Auditor
42.1.—(1) Where expenses are found due to a party in any cause, the court shall—
    (a) pronounce an interlocutor finding that party entitled to expenses and, subject to rule 42.6(1) (modification of expenses awarded against assisted persons), remitting to the Auditor for taxation; and

(b) without prejudice to rule 42.4 (objections to report of the Auditor), unless satisfied that there is special cause shown for not doing so, pronounce an interlocutor decerning against the party found liable in expenses as taxed by the Auditor.

(2) Any party found entitled to expenses shall—

[1] (a) lodge an account of expenses in process not later than 4 months after the final interlocutor in which a finding in respect of expenses is made;

[2] (aa) if he has failed to comply with sub-paragraph (a), lodge such account at any time with leave of the court but subject to such conditions (if any) as the court thinks fit to impose; and

(b) give written intimation of the lodging of the account, and send a copy of it, to the party found liable to pay those expenses.

(3) Rule 4.6(1) (intimation of steps of process) shall not apply to the lodging of an account of expenses.

Deriv. R.C.S. 1965, r. 348(1) and (2) substituted by S.I. 1983 No. 826

---

[1] R.42.1(2)(a) amended by S.I. 1995 No. 1396 (effective 22nd June 1995), S.I. 1996 No. 1756 (effective August 5, 1996) and S.S.I. 2001 No. 305 (effective September 18, 2001).

[2] R.42. 1(2)(aa) inserted by S.I. 1998 No. 890 (effective April 21, 1998).

General note. The principle upon which the court proceeds in awarding expenses is that the **42.1.1** cost of litigation should fall on him who has caused it, unless the circumstances justify otherwise: *Shepherd v. Elliot* (1896) 23 R. 695. Allowance of a late plea of arbitration clause does not fall within the exception to the general rule that expenses follow success: *Presslie v. Cochrane McGregor Group Ltd (No. 2)* 1997 S.C. 159. Disputed compensation cases under the Land Compensation (Scotland) Acts where an advance payment, but no tender, has been made, follow the general principle: *City of Aberdeen D.C. v. Emslie & Simpson Ltd* 1995 S.C. 264.

The general rule that expenses follow success applies even though the whole of the sum awarded is paid to the CRU (Compensation Recovery Unit) of the DSS under the Social Security (Recovery of Benefits) Act 1997: *Gray v. Lanarkshire Health Board* 1998 S.L.T. 1378.

There are three forms of taxation—(1) party and party, (2) agent and client, client paying, and (3) agent and client, third party paying. An interlocutor awarding expenses without qualification implies taxation on a party and party basis; if expenses are to be taxed on another basis, that must be specified: *Fletcher's Trs v. Fletcher,* (1888) 15 R. 862; *Magistrates of Aberchirder v. Banff District Committee,* (1906) 8 F. 571, 573 *per* Lord McLaren. (1) Expenses on a party and party basis means expenses reasonable for conducting the litigation in a proper manner. Expenses are taxed on the scale in r. 42.16, unless otherwise specifically ordered (e.g. on a sheriff court scale). (2) Expenses in a solicitor and client basis without further specification will be solicitor and client, client paying: see *Milligan v. Tinnes's Trs,* 1971 S.L.T. (Notes) 64. A client is liable for all expenses reasonably incurred by the agent for the protection of the client's interest, and those specifically authorised, even though not (otherwise) recoverable from the other party: Mackay's Practice, ii, 585; Maclaren on Expenses, p. 431. In exceptional circumstances the court may award expenses on an "agent and client" basis (*Plasticisers Ltd v. William R. Stewart & Sons (Hacklemakers) Ltd* 1973 S.L.T. 58, 63. It has been said that all the expenses incurred by the client are allowable except those unreasonably or extravagantly incurred, or unreasonable in amount, the benefit of any doubt being given to the receiving party. In no case are expenses which are not expenses of process allowable: *Milligan,* above. (3) Expenses on a solicitor and client, third party paying (i.e. the opposite side) is not so generous as in the case of client paying, but not as rigorous as on a party and party basis: Maclaren on Expenses, p. 509. The expenses are those that would be incurred by a prudent man of business: *Hood v. Gordon,* (1896) 23 R. 675, 676 *per* Lord Patrick. It is said to be the appropriate basis where statute authorises expenses as between agent and client (*Hood,* above) and in multiplepoindings where expenses are awarded on an agent and client basis out of the fund *in medio* (*Park v. Colvilles Ltd,* 1960 S.C. 143, 153).

The taxation of accounts, whether between party and party (Chap. 42, Pt II), or agent and client (r. 42.7), is left almost entirely to the Auditor. The court has shown reluctance, except in exceptional circumstances, to interfere with his discretion. It is not the function of the court in reviewing an exercise of discretion to substitute its own views of the material under consideration: *Wood v. Miller* 1960 S.C. 86, 97 *per* L.J.-C. Thomson.

The Auditor has no power to refuse or modify the expenses of proceedings ordered by the court (*Stott v. McWilliam* (1856) 18 D. 716, 719 *per* Lord Ivory), even when these proceedings have been held as incompetent (*Sleigh v. City of Edinburgh D.C.* 1988 S.L.T. 253); and unusually in a cause which was abandoned the petitioner was still awarded expenses (*Laing's Tr. v. Messenger* 1993 G.W.D. 12–898).

Expenses of a deemed abandoned appeal are dealt with by the inferior court but require to be remitted to the Auditor of the Court of Session for taxation: r. 40.9(6).

The Auditor's power in taxing an account includes not only taxing off and reducing items which appear to have been improperly charged but also to increase items that he considers as understated, not filled up, or altogether omitted: *Reeve v. Dykes* (1829) 7 S.632.

42.1.2   *"Where expenses are found due"*. The court has no power to award expenses against a person who was not a party to, or associated with, the litigation: *Meekison v. Uniroyal Engelbert Tyres Ltd* 1995 S.L.T.(Sh.Ct.) 63.

The court, when granting decree for expenses, must pronounce an interlocutor finding a party entitled to expenses and, unless satisfied that there is special cause for not doing so, it must further (a) decern against the party found liable as taxed and (b) remit the account of expenses to the Auditor to tax. It has been held that where an interlocutor refers to expenses as taxed there is no need for an express remit, that being implied in cases where it is not expressed: *Gilbert's Tr. v. Gilbert* 1988 S.L.T. 680. Special cause for postponement of an immediate for modification as the court is *functus*: *Stewart v. Stewart* 1989 S.L.T. 80. Since 1983, in a cause in which the person liable for the expenses is not legally aided there are usually two interlocutors at the conclusion of a cause (or wherever expenses are dealt with); one disposing of the merits and the other decerning for expenses as taxed (and when taxed, the amount of expenses authorised by the Auditor is inserted by the Extractor in the extract), the latter being the last or final interlocutor. An interlocutor awarding expenses against a non-legally-aided party has a decerniture pronounced at the time the finding of expenses is made. Where a party liable in expenses is legally aided there is no decerniture when the finding is made: a finding of liability in expenses is made with a remit to the Auditor to tax and report. A decerniture is only made thereafter after consideration of any objections or application for modification. The reason for the difference in the case of a legally aided party is that it is not competent to modify expenses after decerniture: *Gilbert's Tr.*, above.

A decerniture for expenses cannot be altered or recalled: *U.C.B. Bank plc v. Dundas & Wilson, C.S.* 1991 S.L.T. 90, 93L *per* L.P. Hope; and see, *e.g. Davis v. British Coal Corporation* 1993 S.L.T. 697 (further expenses sought not allowed after expenses decerned for).

Expenses may be awarded even if not concluded for: *Elliot & Stewart v. McDougall* 1956 S.L.T.(Notes) 36.

Expenses of an appeal include expenses of adjustment and preparation of stated case or appeal: *Macdonald v. Stornoway Trust* 1989 S.L.T. 87.

An award of "expenses of process as taxed" does not refer to the expenses of another process: *Rankin v. Upper Clyde Shipbuilders Ltd* (*in liquidation*) 1990 G.W.D. 3–139.

As reserved expenses will be carried automatically along with the expenses of the cause awarded by the final interlocutor; if it is desired that they be dealt with differently it is important that they be specifically dealt with as soon as possible after being reserved: *Bank of Scotland v. Morrison* 1911 S.C. 593.

A party may not be awarded expenses where he has no separate interest from another party which renders his appearance necessary: *Robertson v. City of Edinburgh District Licensing Board* 1994 S.C. 83.

Where a party succeeded in an appeal upon a different ground from that advanced in the lower court and which emerged only in the course of the appeal no award of expenses was made: *Speyside Electronics Ltd v. The Royal Bank of Scotland plc*, 2nd Div., 10th February 1995, 1995 G.W.D. 12–629.

Where the original action was incompetent and irrelevant and a minute of amendment constituted a new action based on a different ground and seeking a different result the successful pursuer was found liable in expenses: *Manson v. Manson*, O.H., 12th January 1996, 1996 G.W.D. 11–645.

The general rule as to expenses in tenders where there are two or more defenders is that, if a pursuer convenes two or more defenders and one or more is assoilzied, the pursuer and not the unsuccessful defender pays the expenses of the successful defender: *Mitchell v. Redpath Engineering Ltd* 1990 S.L.T. 259. That case lays down the principles to be applied. There is an exception where a defender causes or induces the pursuer to convene another party. Where by tender a defender had, in effect, accepted full liability although in the defences had made a bare denial of the pursuer's averments and adopted the averments of fault against the pursuer of other defenders which required the pursuer to maintain his action against the other defenders until the lodging of the tender following upon which the pursuer lodged a minute of abandonment in respect of the other defenders, the defender was found liable in the whole expenses of the cause: *Bremner v. Press Offshore Ltd*, 1994, S.C.L.R. 772.

It is not competent to award expenses against counsel personally: see *Reid v. Edinburgh Acoustics Ltd (No. 2)*, 1995 S.L.T. 982.

An award of expenses may be made, in exceptional circumstances, against a solicitor personally: *Blyth v. Watson* 1987 S.L.T. 616; *Stewart v. Stewart* 1984 S.L.T.(Sh.Ct) 58; *L., Petitioners (No. 6)*, 1st Div., 24th October 1995, 1995 G.W.D. 39–2025. (Failure to apply timeously for legal aid.) For example where he acted in excess of instructions or without due regard to his duty to the court or his responsibilities to the Legal Aid Fund. But not where the solicitor acted on the advice of counsel: *Reid*, above.

Reclaiming motions on expenses are discouraged by the court: *Ramm v. Lothian and Borders Fire Board*, 1994 S.C. 226.

"account of expenses". The account should be typed on A4 size account paper with columns **42.1.3** for figures to the left and right of the text of the items claimed; the left hand column is for the Auditor to enter figures taxed off or added. The dates of the items of work are entered in chronological order with the details of the work being succinctly stated, giving sufficient information to show the nature of the work carried out for which the charge is claimed. The outlays should be numbered to correspond with the numbers on the vouchers to be produced to support them. The account is stitched into a process backing sheet showing the names of parties (the instance) and the cause reference number. The interlocutor containing the finding to which the account relates must be reproduced on the first page of the account.

"lodge the account of expenses in process". The account of expenses is lodged as a step in **42.1.4** process; it must be backed and have the number of process and the cause reference number marked on it: see rr. 4.1(3) and 4.4(3). It may be lodged by post: P.N. No. 4 of 1994, paras 1 and 8.

A fee is payable on lodging the account: see note 42.1.9.

The four-month rule. The general rule is that an account of expenses must be lodged not later **42.1.5** than four months after a final interlocutor (on which see note 4.15.2(2)) in which a *finding* in respect of expenses was made (*i.e.* not just the one which awards a specified sum of expenses): r. 42.1(2)(a). A "month" means a calendar month. Hence, if the final interlocutor is dated 20th October the account must be lodged by the end of 20th February; if the final interlocutor is dated 30th October, the account must be lodged by the end of 28th February (or 29th in a leap year). The time-limit does not apply to an account of expenses prepared on a finding of expenses in a final interlocutor pronounced before September 5, 1994: Interpretation Act 1978, s. 16(1) as applied by s. 23(1); and the presumption against retrospectivity.

The provision was changed (by A.S. (R.C.S. A No. 2) (Fees of Solicitors) 1995 [S.I. 1995 No. 1396]) from "within a period of 4 months" to "not later than 4 months" to avoid a notion that an account for an incidental award of expenses may be lodged only within the four month period after the *final* interlocutor.

The reason for the four month rule is so that the paying party may know the amount of his liability within a reasonable period. In *King v. Global Marine (UK) Ltd*, 2003 S.C. 269 (Second Div.), it was argued for the pursuer, seeking leave to lodge an account late, that the change of wording in r. 42.1(2)(a) from "*a* final interlocutor" to "*the* final interlocutor" made by A.S. (R.C.S.A. No.3) (Miscellaneous) 1996 [S.I. 1996 No. 1756] meant the final interlocutor (the very last in the process) on the subject of expenses pronounced in the cause. It was submitted that otherwise a series of individual accounts of expenses during the course of the litigation would have to be lodged instead of at the end. It was held that "the final interlocutor" referred to was not necessarily the final interlocutor on the subject of expenses in the process, but, in this case the final interlocutor on expenses between this pursuer in the cause and the defender. Otherwise, the unreasonable result would be that where one party settled with an award of expenses and the process continued for resolution of the other claims, that party could delay lodging an account until the end of the case. The purpose of the rule is to ensure that when a decree for expenses was granted, the party liable should receive an account of them promptly; and the change of wording is of no significance.

An application for prorogation of the period by which an account may be lodged in terms of the rule must be made within the four month period otherwise application for late lodging will require to be made under r. 42.1(2)(aa). Some solicitors resented the four-month rule and sought its abolition or a less onerous timetable. They have been to some extent successful in that r. 42.1(2)(aa) has been inserted by A.S. (R.C.S.A.) (Miscellaneous) 1998 [S.I. 1998 No. 890]. This provision allows late lodging of an account with leave of the court subject to any conditions it may impose. The provision does not state that cause has to be shown to obtain leave. It is inconceivable, however, that some cause does not have to be shown: if leave is required it may be withheld, and, therefore, a reason (cause) must be given. Formerly resort had to be made to the dispensing power, for cause, under r. 2.1. What is the perceived difference between the new provision in r. 42.1(2)(aa) and "other excusable cause" in r. 2.1? This new provision bears all the hallmarks of an unsatisfactory compromise between two opposing camps. The new provision also states that leave to lodge the account late may be granted on such conditions (if any) as the court may impose. But what conditions can the court impose (the expenses of the motion will have to be paid in any event)? In relation to the meaning of "conditions" in r. 42.1(2)(aa), it was held in *Finlayson v. British Steel plc,* 2003 S.L.T. 903 (OH) that a condition of a financial penalty could not be imposed as the court had no power to impose penalties. In *Finlayson's Guardian v. Scottish Rig Repairers,* 2006 S.L.T. 329 (OH), leave to lodge an account late was refused.

Under the original provision in r. 42.1(2)(a) special cause had to be shown for an extension of the four months. Following the new provision for late lodging introduced in r. 42.1(2)(aa) (inserted by S.I. 1998 No. 890), it made little sense to require special cause for an extension of time under r. 42.1(2)(a). The provision for late lodging on special cause shown in r. 42.1(2)(a) has been removed by A.S. (R.C.S.A. No.4) (Miscellaneous) 2001 [S.S.I. 2001 No. 305].

The law, under the former strict four-month rule, on an application under r. 2.1, appears from the following cases. In *Fane v. Murray* 1996 S.C. 51 (I.H.), late lodging was refused by the Extra Division where the delay was due to absence of the solicitor and subsequent negotiations; the case indicates a strict compliance with r. 42.1(2)(a) is required. In *Stakeman v. Brien,* 6th September 1996, unreported (1996 G.W.D. 33–1980), it was held that it was not special cause that there was no prejudice or that there was a belief that the parties would endeavour to agree a sum for expenses. Although r. 2.1 does not require the very high test of "special cause shown" the court may be less willing to exercise its discretion when specific provision has been made for extension of the period: see *Smith v. Smith* (I.H.), 23rd June 1995, unreported; *McGee v. Matthew Hall Ltd* 1996 S.L.T. 399, 399K *per* Lord Caplan (a case on r. 37.1(2)(a)).

If the final substantive interlocutor of the Inner House is appealed to the House of Lords, the four-month period will not commence until that appeal has been determined.

Decerniture for expenses principally occurs in causes where the person found liable in expenses is in receipt of legal aid in which case he is entitled to apply to the court for modification: r. 42.5. If, however, the court has gone on to make a decerniture for expenses it is incompetent to apply.

A solicitor acting for an assisted person awarded expenses must (unless perhaps where both parties are legally aided and the unsuccessful party had his liability modified within the four month period) prepare (a) a party and party account of expenses and lodge it in court within the four month period and (b) the agent and client account for lodging within the Legal Aid Board. The cost of taxation may be included in the agent and client account or a supplementary account lodged with the Board.

The clerk of session in the appropriate department will check that the account is being lodged within the required period. If it is not, a motion will need to be enrolled seeking to prorogate the time for lodging under r. 42.1(2)(a), failing which enrolling a motion for leave to lodge the account late under r. 2.1.

The date from which the period is calculated is not counted. Where the last day falls on a Saturday or Sunday or a public holiday on which the Office of Court is closed, the next available day is allowed: r. 1.3(7). For office hours and public holidays, see note 3.1.2.

In *Canon (UK) Ltd v. Craig,* 2005 G.W.D. 10-156, 2nd February 2005 (OH), it was argued that, as the principal summons had not been served though signeted, there was no process in which the defender could lodge an account. It was held that the requirement under r. 42. 1(2)(a) was met by the existence of a process in the sense of a bundle of documents with a reference number.

42.1.6   *"final interlocutor in which a finding in respect of expenses is made".* A "final interlocutor" is one which, by itself or along with previous interlocutors, disposes of the whole subject-matter of the cause. An interlocutor final in the Outer House by virtue of s.18 of the C.S.A. 1988 is not a "final interlocutor" in this sense (which is the sense used in this rule). In *King v. Global Marine (UK) Ltd,* 2003 S.C. 269, 272, 2003 S.L.T. 1334, 1336, para. [14] the Second Division held that a "final interlocutor" in r. 42.1(2)(a) means the final interlocutor on expenses in the claim between the parties concerned (in that case the first pursuer and the first defender) and not the final interlocutor in the process. In *Scottish Enterprise v. Archibald Russell of Denny Ltd,* 22nd August 2003, unreported (Second Div.), it was held that an interlocutor by a sheriff principal allowing a proof before answer was not a final interlocutor. In *Canon (UK) Ltd v. Craig,* 2005 G.W.D. 10-156, 2nd February 2005 (OH), it was said that "final" is not a point in time but relates to the determinative or decisive quality of the interlocutor.

In a cause in which the person liable in expenses is not legally aided, wherever expenses are dealt with there are usually two interlocutors at the conclusion of the cause: one disposing of the merits and the other decerning for expenses as taxed (the latter being the final interlocutor). Where the party liable in expenses is legally aided a finding for expenses is made with a remit to the Auditor to tax and report, but there is no decerniture for expenses until after the Auditor has reported and after consideration of any objections or an application for modification. See further, note 4.15.2(2).

The expression "finding for expenses" was changed to "finding in respect of expenses" by A.S. (R.C.S.A. No. 3) (Miscellaneous) 1996 [S.I. 1996 No. 1756]. It was thought that the former expression excluded a finding of no expenses due to or by and would mean that a party could not lodge an account of expenses in respect of an earlier interlocutor making a finding for expenses if that interlocutor was more than four months before the final interlocutor.

"written intimation of the lodging of the account, and send a copy of it, to the party found liable". It is not necessary to intimate the account of expenses to a party not found liable to pay those expenses, hence the disapplication of r. 4.6(1): see rr. 4.1(2) and (3). **42.1.7**

Under P.N. No. 3 of 1993, para. 2.1, the copy of the account should be sent to the paying party at least 10 days before the account is lodged for taxation, and this will constitute compliance with r. 42.1(2)(b). The account should be accompanied by the information required in P.N. No. 3 of 1993, paras 2.2 and 2.3.

For methods of written intimation, see r. 16.9. "Send" includes deliver: r. 1.3(1) (definition of "send").

Transmission of the process to the Auditor. Formerly this was done by the party seeking to have the account taxed. Nowadays the process is transmitted (by court messenger) from the appropriate department with the department's transmission book to the office of the Auditor. The entry in the transmission book for the cause is receipted and returned to the department from which it came. **42.1.8**

Fee. The Auditor's fee for lodging an account of expenses is payable on receipt of the account in the Auditor's office. For fee, see Court of Session etc. Fees Order 1984, Table of Fees, Pt III, I, 1(a) [S.I. 1984 No. 256, Table as amended, pp. **C** 1202 *et seq.*]. The fee may be debited under a credit scheme introduced on 1st April 1976 by P.N. No. 4 of 1976 to the account (if one is kept or permitted) of the agent by the court cashier, and an account will be rendered weekly by the court cashier's office to the agent for all court fees due that week for immediate settlement. **42.1.9**

An agent not on the credit scheme or a party litigant will be billed by the Auditor's office for the fee. A diet of taxation will not be fixed until the fee is paid.

Expenses against party litigating in a representative capacity. The general rule is that a person who litigates in a representative capacity may still expose himself to personal liability in expenses but may be entitled to relief from the funds he holds in that capacity. In *Dyer v. Craiglaw Developments Ltd*, 29th October 1998, unreported (1998 G.W.D. 39–2015) Lord Hamilton gave guidance on the form of words to be used in the interlocutor awarding expenses to such a party:—(1) Where the award is to be against the party in his representative capacity and therefore limited to the funds he holds, the interlocutor should state that the award of expenses is against him with the expression "as" followed by his particular capacity (*Craig v. Hogg* (1896) 24 R. 6), *e.g.* "as liquidator". (2) Where the award is against him personally while preserving his right of relief against the funds he holds, the interlocutor should state that the award of expenses is against him without qualification, *e.g.* "pursuer" or as the case may be. (3) Where the award is against him personally but is intended to be unrestricted without a right of relief against the funds he holds, the interlocutor should state that the award of expenses is against him "personally" (*Kilmarnock Theatre Co. v. Buchanan* 1911 S.C. 607). **42.1.10**

Diet of taxation

42.2.—(1) On receipt of the process of the cause, the Auditor shall—
(a) fix a diet for taxation; and
(b) intimate the diet to—
   (i) the party found entitled to expenses; and
   (ii) the party found liable in expenses.

¹(1A) The party found liable in expenses shall, not later than 3 working days prior to the diet of taxation, intimate to the Auditor and to the party found entitled to expenses, specific points of objection, setting out each item objected to and stating concisely the nature and ground of objection in each case.

¹(1B) Subject to paragraph (1C), if the party found liable in expenses fails to intimate points of objection under paragraph (1A) within the time limit set out there, the Auditor shall not take account of them at the diet of taxation.

¹(1C) The Auditor may relieve a party from the consequences of a failure to comply with the requirement contained in paragraph (1B) because of mistake, oversight or other excusable cause on such conditions, if any, as the Auditor thinks fit.

(2) At the diet of taxation, the party found entitled to expenses shall

make available to the Auditor all vouchers, documents, drafts or copies of documents sought by the Auditor and relevant to the taxation.

Deriv. R.C.S. 1965, r. 348(3) and (4) substituted by S.I. 1983 No. 826

[1] R.42.2(1A)–42.2(1C) inserted by S.S.I. 2001 No. 305, para. 11 (effective 18th September 2001).

42.2.1 *"diet of taxation"*. A diet of taxation is a hearing conducted by the Auditor in his Office at which the receiving and paying parties attend personally, or at which they may be represented by their respective solicitors or such other persons as the Auditor may allow.

The Auditor appoints a day and time for the taxation. This is notified to the receiving and paying parties, who are required to attend the diet under certification that if the paying party does not appear to state any objections to the account the Auditor may proceed to tax the account forthwith.

A strict time-table for, and written specification of, the points of objection are now required: r.42.1(1A) and (1B). The Auditor has a similar discretion to that of the court in r.2.1 to relieve a party from the consequences of a failure to comply with these requirements (which is that the objections will not be considered: r.42.2(1B)) r.42.2(1C). These provisions replace para 4.1 and 4.2 of P.N. No. 3 of 1993.

At the diet the Auditor hears parties orally on the points of objections and he will usually give his decisions on these as they arise, but he may require to take time to consider them along with information given to him at the diet.

It is the duty of parties appearing at the diet to make full submissions to the Auditor to help him in reaching decisions: *Griffiths v. Kerr* 1992 S.L.T. 1024.

A tender of expenses prior to taxation does not entitle the paying party to the expenses of attendance at the diet of taxation even when the amount taxed is less than the amount tendered: *Gilmour's Tutor v. Renfrew C.C.* 1970 S.L.T.(Notes) 47.

Before the Auditor completes his taxation of the account he adds a charge in respect of fee fund dues: see note 42.2.5. The fee is added to the taxed account. The Auditor taxes off a sum proportionate to the amount taxed off from the account, so that the receiving party recovers only that proportion of the fee fund dues he has to pay which bears to the net amount of the account after taxation.

42.2.2 *"intimate"*. For methods, see r. 16.7.

42.2.3 *"all vouchers, documents, drafts or copies of documents"*. At the diet the Auditor is entitled to see all necessary documentation and to receive such information as he may require to enable him to complete the taxation of the account: on documentation, see also P.N. No. 3 of 1993, para. 5. The Auditor cannot allow an outlay which has not been adequately vouched: *Goldie v. Mohr*, 18th November 1992 (1993 G.W.D. 1–40). The paying party is entitled to see receipts and vouchers in respect of all outlays claimed: r. 42.16, Table of Fees, Chap. II, para. 8. All vouchers should be numbered separately and correspondingly numbered in the account: P.N. No. 3 of 1993, para. 6.

As far as charges for professional and skilled witnesses are concerned, the Auditor requires to see full details of the work done, the time taken to do it, and the hourly rate claimed for it. An interlocutor must have been pronounced certifying them as skilled witnesses: see r. 42.13(3). The court may, on cause shown, allow late certification: *Mains v. Uniroyal Englebert Tyres Ltd (No. 2)* 1995 S.C. 538. The Auditor has no such discretion: *Clark v. Laddaws Ltd* 1994 S.L.T. 792.

As far as an employed witness is concerned, the Auditor requires to see satisfactory evidence of lost wages or remuneration. This information will usually take the form of a certificate from the employer on his notepaper stating the actual (net) loss sustained by the witness.

In the case of a witness who is self-employed, the Auditor will have to be satisfied that the witness has sustained a loss; therefore, the vouching must show objective information as to the amount of the actual net loss.

Claims can be made only for those witnesses who have actually given evidence or whose names have been noted in the Minute of Proceedings as having been in attendance or as having been held as concurring with a witness who has given evidence.

If an item is challenged and the necessary information is not made available to the Auditor at the diet of taxation, the Auditor may disallow it entirely. If satisfactory vouching has not been exhibited before the diet of taxation to the paying party, in response to his request for it (see r. 42.16, Table of Fees, Chap. II, para. 8), the Auditor may modify or tax off completely the receiving party's fee for attendance at the taxation. If the paying party has not requested sight of a voucher in respect of any outlay, other than counsel's fees, charged in the account, then he will be deemed to have accepted that charge. As counsel's fees are charged on an agent and client basis (see "Scheme for Accounting for and Recovery of Counsel's Fees" entered into between the Faculty of Advocates and the Law Society of Scotland (1987), para. 5(5)), the Auditor alone has the right to see these vouchers but the paying party is entitled to have confirmed to him by the Auditor that counsel has done the work charged for in the account, and to dispute the amount charged as being excessive on a party and party basis: *Macnaughton v. Macnaughton* 1949 S.C. 42, 46 *per* L.P. Cooper.

"not later than 3 working days prior to the diet of taxation". The first question is what is meant **42.2.3A** by "working day": whose working day? This phrase in r. 42.2(1A) is not felicitously drafted (it should also be "before" not "prior to"). In *Coyle v. Auditor of the Court of Session*, 2006 S.L.T. 1045 (OH), the court proceeded, after discussion, on the basis that it meant the working day of the Auditor whose office closes at 4pm (objections being lodged at 4.46pm at the end of the fourth day). It was held in a judicial review that, though technically late (on the basis that there was no gap between the end of a working day and the beginning of the next, they were at most one minute late), the Auditor had acted unreasonably in exercising his discretion (presumably that in r. 42.2(1C)).

Objections to accounts. At least three working days before the diet the Auditor must receive a **42.2.4** note of all outstanding points of objection to items in the account and a copy of it must also be sent to the receiving party: P.N. No. 3 of 1993, para. 4.1. Where it is intended to refer to any authorities at the diet, prior notification of these should also be given both to the other party and the Auditor. The Auditor will not expect to be addressed on any points of objection not previously intimated both to him and the other party: P.N. No. 3 of 1993, para. 4.2.

At the diet the Auditor hears parties orally on the points of objection and he will usually give his decisions on these as they arise, but he may require to take time to consider them along with information given to him at the diet. It is the duty of parties appearing at the diet to make full submissions to the Auditor to help him in reaching decisions: *Griffiths v. Kerr* 1992 S.L.T. 1024.

The Auditor may, however, at his own instance, report or reserve points of objection for consideration by the court either during the taxation or in his report at the conclusion of it.

If the Auditor sustains an objection to any extent to an item in the account, he records his decision by marking in the left-hand margin of the account the amount disallowed or abated.

Fee. The fee for taxing the account is payable on issue of the Auditor's report. For fee, see **42.2.5** Court of Session etc. Fees Order 1984, Table of Fees, Pt III, I, item 1(b) [SI 1984/256, Table as amended, pp. **C** 1202 *et seq.*]. The fee is a fixed sum for accounts under £300, and £4 for every additional £100 of the gross amount of the account lodged for taxation.

The fee may be debited under a credit scheme introduced on 1st April 1976 by P.N. No. 4 of 1976 to the account (if one is kept or permitted) of the agent by the court cashier, and an account will be rendered weekly by the court cashier's office to the agent for all court fees due that week for immediate settlement. Party litigants and agents not operating the scheme must pay cash on each occasion a fee is due at the time of the issue of the Auditor's report at the office of the Auditor (from whence it will be remitted to the court cashier's office).

Report of taxation

42.3.—(1) The Auditor shall—
  (a) prepare a report of the taxation of the account of expenses, stating the amount of expenses as taxed;
  (b) transmit the process of the cause and the report to the appropriate Department of the Office of Court; and
  (c) on the day on which he transmits the process, intimate that fact and the date of his report to each party to whom he intimated the diet of taxation.

(2) The party found entitled to expenses shall, within seven days after the date of the report prepared under paragraph (1), exhibit the taxed account, or send a copy of it, to the party found liable to pay the expenses.

Deriv. RCS 1965, r. 349(1) substituted by SI 1983/826

"report of the taxation". The report of the taxation, which is prepared by the Auditor, **42.3.1** commences with a reference to each of the interlocutor(s) awarding expenses to the party covered by items contained in the taxed account, specifies the total in words and figures of the amount of the taxed account and names the party who has been found liable to pay the taxed expenses. The report which forms a step in the process is not borrowable.

"transmit the process of the cause and the report". This is done by a court messenger taking the **42.3.2**

process from the office of the Auditor with a transmission book to the department from which the process came. The entry in the transmission book for the cause is receipted and returned to the office of the Auditor. At the same time a notification slip is placed in the box allocated to each of the firms of solicitors acting for the respective parties concerned in the taxation. These boxes are located in the office of the General Department. Where a party does not have a box, notification is sent direct to the party.

42.3.3   *"intimate"*. For methods, see r. 16.7.

42.3.4   *"within seven days"*. The date from which the period is calculated is not counted.

42.3.5   *"send a copy of it, to the party found liable"*. As the Auditor's taxations appear on only the process copy of the account the receiving party is obliged to send the taxed account, or a full copy of it, to the paying party within seven days after the date of the Auditor's report: r. 42.3(2). This gives respective parties time to decide whether to accept the taxations or take a note of objection to the report within 14 days after the date of the report (see r. 42.4(1)). "Send" includes deliver: r. 1.3(1) (definition of "send").

42.3.6   *Motion for approval of report and decree in terms of it*. Where the party found liable for the expenses is not an assisted person, it is not usually necessary for the party entitled to the expenses to enrol a motion for approval of the report and for decree in terms of it because of the interlocutor containing the decerniture against the paying party for the expenses as taxed. In such a case all that is necessary is for the Extractor, when the application for an extract is made, to enter the taxed amount in the extract of the interlocutor decerning for expenses as taxed.

Where the party found liable for the expenses is legally aided, on receipt of the taxed account the receiving party may enrol a motion for approval of the report and for decree in terms of it after expiry of the days within which a party can lodge a note of objection or modification (14 days: see rr. 42.4(1) and 42.6(2)).

Objections to report of the Auditor

42.4.—(1) Any party to a cause who has appeared or been represented at the diet of taxation may state any objection to the report of the Auditor by lodging in process a note of objection within 14 days after the date of the report.

(2) A party lodging a note of objection shall—

[1] (a)   intimate a copy of the note to any other party who appeared or was represented at the diet of taxation and to the Auditor;

(b)   apply by motion for an order—

   (i)   allowing the note to be received; and

   (ii)   ordaining the Auditor to state by minute, within 14 days after intimation under sub-paragraph (c), the reasons for his decision in relation to the items to which objection is taken in the note; and

(c)   intimate forthwith to the Auditor a copy of the interlocutor pronounced on a motion under sub-paragraph (b).

(3) After the minute of the Auditor has been lodged in process, the party who lodged the note of objection shall, in consultation with any other party wishing to be heard, arrange with the Keeper of the Rolls for a diet of hearing before the appropriate court.

(4) At the hearing on the note of objection, the court may—

(a)   sustain or repel any objection in the note or remit the account of expenses to the Auditor for further consideration; and

(b)   find any party liable in the expenses of the procedure on the note.

(5) In the event of an objection being sustained, the court shall ordain the Auditor to amend his report to give effect to the decision of the court.

Deriv. RCS 1965, r. 349(2) substituted by SI 1992/1433 (r. 42.4(1)), r. 349(3) substituted by SI 1983/826 and amended by SI 1991/1157 (r. 42.4(2)), and r. 349(4) to (6) substituted by SI 1983/826 (r. 42.4(3) to (5))

---

[1] R. 42.4(2)(a) amended by SI 1996/1756 (effective 5th August 1996).

42.4.1   *General note.* Rule 42.4 is designed to deal with objections to specific items in the auditor's report. The rule does not envisage that there will be disputed questions of evidence or that there will be a challenge because of some fundamental irregularity: *Urquhart v. Ayrshire and Arran Health Board*, 2000 S.L.T. 829 (OH).

Before taking or replying to a note of objection(s) consideration should be given to whether or not any principle is involved, since the expenses of the note of objections which may be awarded against the unsuccessful party may equal or exceed the sum in dispute. If on reflection the party, whose objection was sustained by the Auditor, no longer wishes to insist in the objection that should be intimated to the Auditor as soon as possible to minimise expense.

Parties can at any time consent in a request to the Auditor to tax an account at an agreed sum with fee fund dues in addition.

The court can only interfere with the decision of the Auditor if he misdirected himself as to the considerations which regulate his discretion (irrelevant material taken into account, relevant material not taken into account, he misunderstood or misdirected himself as to the facts or law): *Wood v. Miller* 1960 S.C. 86, 98 *per* LJ-C Thomson. The procedure is limited in scope and the court cannot carry out a complete rehearing of matters debated before the Auditor and substitute its own assessment; and the court's practice was not to hear oral evidence about what happened during taxation: *Tods Murray, WS v. Arakin Ltd (No.2)*, 5 April 2002, 2002 G.W.D. 13–420 (OH).

"note of objection". R. 15.2 (applications by note) does not apply to a note of objection: r. **42.4.2**
15.2(4). The note must specify the grounds of objection and the appropriate alteration sought: *Crossan v. Caledonian Railway Co.* (1902) 5 F. 187, 190 *per* Lord Trayner; *Mowbray v. Kirkcaldy D.C.*, 10th December 1993 (Extra Div.), unreported, 1994 G.W.D. 3–153. The note need not be signed: r. 4.2(9)(f).

"lodge in process". The note of objection is lodged in person or by post (P.N. No. 4 of 1994, **42.4.3**
paras 1 and 8) in process as a step of process (see rr. 4.4 and 4.6).

"within 14 days". It may be possible to persuade the court to exercise its dispensing power **42.4.4**
under r. 2.1 to allow late lodging of a note of objection, but mere oversight to lodge the note within the required period may not of itself be a good reason to excuse more especially as it further delays payment of expenses. In any event, if an interlocutor has been pronounced approving the Auditor's report and decerning for expenses, no note of objection may be lodged.

The date from which the period is calculated is not counted. Where the last day falls on a Saturday or Sunday or a public holiday on which the Office of Court is closed, the next available day is allowed: r. 1.3(7). For office hours and public holidays, see note 3.1.2.

"intimate". For methods, see r. 16.7.   **42.4.5**

"motion". For motions, see Chap.23.   **42.4.6**

"minute". R. 15.1 does not apply as the minute is not an application to the court. The minute **42.4.7**
is headed with the instance of the cause. Unless the reasons are very short the Auditor gives his reasons in an appendix.

"intimate forthwith to the Auditor". On the meaning of "forthwith", see *Brown v. Magistrates* **42.4.8**
of Bonnyrigg and Lasswade 1936 S.C. 258, 265 *per* L.P. Normand (it must be construed according to the circumstances).

"arrange with the Keeper of the Rolls for a diet". Once the Auditor has lodged his minute it is **42.4.9**
the responsibility of the party who lodged the note of objections to consult immediately with any other party wishing to be heard and arrange with the Keeper of the Rolls for a diet of hearing before the appropriate court. The Keeper must be informed whether it is sought to have the diet assigned to a particular judge and, if so, the reason for it: P.N. No. 1 of 1994. As the procedure involves delay, it should be carried through with the utmost expedition since it prevents the receiving party from obtaining even the undisputed amount of expenses as taxed. Interest on expenses runs only from the date of the decree of the taxed amount: *Dalmahoy & Wood v. Magistrates of Brechin* (1859) 21 D. 210.

Although it may be necessary to have the note heard by a particular judge, it may not be necessary to delay the hearing so that counsel previously instructed can conduct it. It is always open to a party to enrol for a hearing on the note if he considers that the other party is unreasonably delaying it.

"hearing on the note of objection". As the Auditor is not present at the hearing on the note of **42.4.10**
objections, the party whose objection was sustained on taxation and objected to in the note should appear at the hearing in support of it, but the court will not automatically grant the note of objection if there is no contradictor. Although a note of objections has been lodged, it remains open to parties to resolve objections informally, and have the note refused or agree by joint minute with a request to the court that the Auditor give effect to the agreement reached. In the absence of any such agreement the court will hear parties on the note and the Auditor's

minute. It may sustain or repel any objection or remit the account to the Auditor for further consideration.

The procedure is limited in scope and the court cannot carry out a complete rehearing of matters debated before the Auditor and substitute its own assessment; and the court's practice was not to hear oral evidence about what happened during taxation: *Tods Murray, WS v. Arakin Ltd (No.2)*, 5th April 2002, 2002 G.W.D. 13–420 (OH). The possibility of factual disputes cannot be ruled out, but the correct procedure is for the hearing to proceed by way of legal submissions and if factual issues arose it would be necessary to address at that point how to resolve them: *Tods Murray, WS*, above. On the grounds on which the court can interfere, see last paragraph of note 42.4.1.

Once the court has ruled on the note the successful party must move for the expenses of the hearing immediately thereafter and before the interlocutor dealing with it is signed. Where the Auditor has himself reported or reserved a point for the consideration of the court, the court usually makes no award of expenses.

42.4.11   *Reclaiming.* The decision of the Lord Ordinary on a note of objection may be reclaimed against with leave of the Lord Ordinary within seven days after the date of the decision: r. 38.4(5). Subject to r. 38.5, leave must be sought, and the reclaiming motion if leave granted must be marked, within seven days.

While it is competent to reclaim against the decision of the Lord Ordinary on a matter of expenses, such motions are not encouraged unless a point of principle is involved: *Aird v. School Board of Tarbert* 1907 S.C. 22, 24 *per* Lord McLaren; *Ramm v. Lothian and Borders Fire Board* 1994 S.C. 226; see also *Gray v. Babcock Power Ltd* 1990 S.L.T. 693, 694K–L *per* L.P. Hope.

Modification or disallowance of expenses

42.5.—(1) In any cause where the court finds a party entitled to expenses, the court may direct that expenses shall be subject to such modification as the court thinks fit.

(2) Where it appears to the Auditor that a party found entitled to expenses—

(a) was unsuccessful, or

(b) incurred expenses through his own fault,

in respect of a matter which would otherwise be included in those expenses, the Auditor may disallow the expenses in respect of that matter in whole or in part.

Deriv. R.C.S. 1965, r. 347(c) (r. 42.5(1))

42.5.1   *"modification".* Where the court has awarded expenses subject to modification it is the duty of the Auditor to tax the account without regard to modification and then to give effect to the modification in the final sum taxed: *McIlroy & Sons v. Tharsis Sulphur and Copper Co.* (1879) 6 R. 1119; *Arthur v. Lindsay* (1895) 22 R. 904. Where a tender specified the amount of expenses to be paid it was not considered to be a judicial tender but nevertheless when the pursuer recovered less than the sum offered he was found liable to the defender in the expenses of the cause modified to one half: *Banks v. D.R.G. plc* 1988 S.L.T. 825.

The general rule is that a party put to the expense of vindicating his rights is entitled to recover the expense from the person by whom it was created: *Howitt v. Alexander & Sons Ltd* 1948 S.C. 124; *William Nimmo & Co. Ltd v. Russell Construction Co. Ltd (No. 2)* (2nd Div.) 1997 S.L.T. 122. It is not incompatible with art.6 of ECHR to award expenses to a successful party: *Ackerman v. Logan's Exrs (No.2)*, November 1, 2001, 2001 G.W.D. 35–1346 (Extra Div.).While it is permissible to take into account time spent on matters on which the party awarded expenses was unsuccessful, that did not necessarily lead to any diminution of expenses: *Howitt*, above. Where a party has misjudged the correct scope and character of his claim and where the other party advanced a number of points which failed to affect their case and thereby both parties contributed to the length and expense of the proof, no expenses were found due to or by either party: *Elf Caledonia Ltd v. London Bridge Engineering Ltd (No. 2)*, 10th December 1997 (1998 G.W.D. 2–86). In *Gray v. Lanarkshire Health Board* 1998 S.L.T. 1378 Lord Abernethy modified the account of expenses by 15 per cent as a substantial part of the pursuer's case was misconceived prolonging the proof by about a day.

A pursuer who brings his action in the Court of Session may, if he receives only a trivial award in relation to the expenses, suffer modification of his account: *McIntosh v. British Railways Board (No. 1)* 1990 S.L.T. 637. The wish to have a jury trial in order to test the adequacy of the level of damages awarded by the courts regarded as being too low is not in itself adequate justification for selecting the Court of Session: *Smillie v. Lanarkshire Health Board,*

8th May 1996, unreported (1996 G.W.D. 22–1288). The court may award expenses limited to one of the sheriff court scales (with or without sanction of counsel) where decree is for a small amount. While the amount of any settlement or award is relevant, the proper approach is to determine whether the initial choice of forum of the Court of Session was justified in the circumstances known to the pursuer's advisers when the action was brought having regard to the high level of expenses likely to be incurred by bringing the action there, judgment on the matter being assisted by consideration of events subsequent to that date including the result of the case: *Coyle v. William Fairey Installations Ltd* 1991 S.C. 16; see also *Kinnaird v. Walter Alexander (Falkirk) Ltd*, 28th June 1995 (unreported, 1995 G.W.D. 32–1648), where the court refused to modify expenses. The size of the award is not therefore the only test: see, *e.g. Campbell v. SCA Packaging Ltd (No. 2)* 1995 G.W.D. 23–1253; *Gordon v. Strathclyde Buses Ltd* 1995 S.L.T. 1019 (case settled at less than sheriff court summary cause maximum limit. Expenses modified to sheriff court ordinary cause scale on ground that award might have been just outside sheriff court privative jurisdiction of £1,500). The saga continues of the court, on the one hand, not wishing to be troubled with reparation actions of small value, and on the other hand of awarding expenses on the Court of Session scale rather than a sheriff court scale in such actions brought under Chap. 43 procedure, on the anecdotal submissions that the Court of Session procedure is cheaper and quicker than the sheriff court procedure: see *Galbraith v. First Glasgow (No. 1) Ltd*, 2006 S.L.T. 317 (OH), and cases there cited.

Where a defender achieved a measure of success in showing that the level of support was considerably less than the pursuer had claimed in her evidence which was exposed as unreliable in regard to matters within her knowledge and documents under her control, her award of expenses was restricted to three quarters: *Bhatia v. Tribax Ltd* 1994 S.L.T. 1201.

The fact that a pursuer has claimed custody in a concurrent petition for custody and an action of divorce will not necessarily result in a refusal or modification of expenses: *Shishodia v. Shishodia (No. 3)*, 13th June 1995, unreported (1995 G.W.D. 34–1742).

The court still has power to modify where a tender offers expenses of process to date: *Neilson v. Motion* 1992 S.L.T. 124; *McKenzie v. H.D. Fraser & Sons* 1990 S.L.T. 629.

There must be an award of expenses against a party before he can seek modification of them. So, when a minute of abandonment is lodged, as no "award" of expenses falls to be made against the pursuer before or as a condition precedent of dismissal, the court has no jurisdiction to modify expenses: *Mica Insulator Co. Ltd v. Bruce Peebles & Co. Ltd* 1907 S.C. 1293; see also *Frost v. Unity Trust Bank plc* 1997 S.L.T. 1358. If the taxed amount of the expenses is not paid within a reasonable time the receiving party is entitled to enrol for absolvitor: *Collum v. Glasgow Corporation* 1964 S.L.T. 199.

Where the court proposes to restrict the expenses of a cause to the sheriff court scale and is also prepared to sanction the employment of counsel, it should be asked to specify if that includes both senior and junior counsel or solely one of them. It is competent for senior counsel to appear without junior counsel: see Resolution of the Faculty of Advocates, 4th February 1977: see 1977 S.L.T.(News) 142.

For modification of expenses against legally aided persons, see r. 42.6.

The principle that expenses follow success is not applied with full rigour in divorce (or other family) actions: *Little v. Little* 1990 S.L.T. 785, 790C *per* L.P. Hope. For recent examples, see *Whittome v. Whittome (No. 2)* 1994 S.L.T. 130 (to wife defender); *Macdonald v. Macdonald* 1995 S.L.T. 72, 75F *per* Lord Caplan (60% to wife pursuer); *Adams v. Adams (No. 2)* 1997 S.L.T. 150 (husband defender awarded expenses of proof; otherwise, no expenses due to or by); *De Winton v. De Winton*, 29th November 1996, unreported (1996 G.W.D. 2–58) (no expenses due to or by).

Leave to lodge productions late may result in the party lodging them being held liable in the whole expenses of the cause to date: *Readman v. McGregor*, 15th January, 1997, unreported (1997 G.W.D. 8–302).

That a cause cannot proceed by reason of a judge's other judicial commitments does not justify any special disposal of associated expenses: *Independent Pension Trustee Ltd v. L A W Construction Co. Ltd (No. 2)*, 17th December, 1996, unreported (1997 G.W.D. 8–336).

Disallowance of expenses by Auditor in respect of a matter. R. 42.5(2) is a statement of the **42.5.2** current practice. Although the court may itself award expenses against a party who has been shown to have caused unnecessary expense through failure to observe correct procedure (*Franchetti v. Franchetti* 6th July 1993, unreported), the Auditor is empowered to tax off all expenses incurred by a party unnecessarily or due to that party's own fault or where in his opinion it appears that a party has been unsuccessful in any part of a cause: *Aitken v. Classen* 1928 S.C. 628; and see *Mica Insulator Co. Ltd v. Bruce Peebles & Co. Ltd* 1907 S.C. 1293, 1300 *per* L.P. Dunedin.

Where the court awarded full expenses to the pursuer in a cause where the major part of the proof was taken up with matters in which the pursuer failed, the court on a reclaiming motion allowed the defender one half of his expenses: *Alvis v. Harrison* 1989 S.C. 136; see also *William Nimmo & Co. Ltd v. Russell Construction Ltd (No. 2)* (2nd Div.) 1997 S.L.T. 122, a substantial part of pursuers' claim had been rejected and the defenders found liable in expenses, but excluding therefrom one half of the expenses incurred by the pursuer which were occasioned by the proof. See also *Whittome v. Whittome* above, where partial expenses were awarded to successful defender.

In *Elliot v. J. & C. Finney (No. 2)* 1989 S.L.T. 241, upheld in *Elliot v. J. & C. Finney* 1989 S.L.T. 605, an award of full expenses was made after a preliminary proof on a plea of time-bar in which the pursuer persuaded the court to exercise its discretion to allow the claim to proceed under section 19A of the Prescription and Limitation (Scotland) Act 1973, although the pursuer had amended just prior to the proof to bring in a point about the date of the start of the triennium on which point he failed and notwithstanding the time taken up by the evidence on the unsuccessful point. In such a case it would not be open to the Auditor to tax off expenses in respect of the unsuccessful work.

Where there is a general finding of expenses in favour of a party who was unsuccessful in an earlier part of the cause and in respect of which the court has made no finding of expenses, it may be difficult to persuade the Auditor that r. 42.5(2) applies merely because a plea was refused since that does not of itself signify lack of success in a particular branch or part of the case. It is therefore essential to bring fully to the attention of the court any special circumstances or conditions by reference to which the exercise of its discretion should be guided: *Howitt v. Alexander & Sons Ltd* 1948 S.C. 124. Similarly where the court finds expenses of any part of the cause to be expenses in the cause, the Auditor has no discretion in the matter even if it is submitted to him that the party was truly unsuccessful in that part of the cause. It is, therefore, essential to ensure that the court, when considering the question of expenses, is fully aware that by making an award of expenses "to be expenses in the cause", it is thereby removing the Auditor's discretion: *Turner v. Thomson* 1991 G.W.D. 19–1159.

Where a defender has incurred expense between the date of lodging a minute of tender and the date of the minute of acceptance of it and he wishes to recover these expenses, he must seek these prior to the decerniture for expenses following the interponing of authority by the court to the minutes of tender and acceptance; it is too late to seek these expenses thereafter, even before the Auditor: *Wilson v. Pilgrim Systems plc* 1993 S.L.T. 1252; for a contrary view, see article at 1994 S.L.T.(News) 159. In a case where the pursuer had beaten two tenders (one in the Outer House and one in the Inner House), and the Inner House reduced the award made in the Outer House—but which award still exceeded the higher sum tendered—the defender was nevertheless awarded expenses. It was held that the ordinary rule that expenses followed success applied and the defender was entitled to the expenses of the reclaiming motion irrespective of whether the award was reduced to any figure tendered; the pursuer could have made an extra-judicial offer which, while not conclusive, might have been relevant to the question whether any expenses had been incurred unnecessarily: *Morrison v. Barton* 1994 S.C. 100.

Where a pursuer was successful at procedure roll as a result of crucial late adjustments to

answers to a minute of amendment based on facts known to him before the action was raised, a finding of no expenses due to or by either party was made: *McSkimming v. The Royal Bank of Scotland plc*, 4th April 1996, unreported (1996 G.W.D. 31–1881).

Even though a party at a late stage in a cause successfully pleads an arbitration clause, that party will not be liable for the whole of the antecedent expenses caused by him, because the time for dealing with expenses is when the case is determined unless the case involves an exception of the rule that expenses follow success: *Presslie v. Cochrane McGregor Group Ltd* 1997 S.C. 159.

Where there has been divided success in a procedure roll debate expenses were made expenses in the cause: *Third v. North East Ice & Storage Co. Ltd (No. 2)*, 31st October 1996, unreported (1996 G.W.D. 37–2167).

Modification of expenses awarded against assisted persons

42.6.—(1) In a cause in which the court finds an assisted person liable in expenses, the court may, on the motion of any party to the cause, instead of remitting the account of expenses of the party in whose favour the finding is made to the Auditor for taxation, determine to what extent the liability of the assisted person for such expenses shall be modified under—

(a) section 2(6)(e) of the Legal Aid (Scotland) Act 1967; or

(b) section 18(2) of the Legal Aid (Scotland) Act 1986.

(2) Where a remit is made to the Auditor for taxation in a cause in which an assisted person is found liable in expenses, an application for modification under a statutory provision mentioned in paragraph (1) may be made by motion within 14 days after the date of the report of the Auditor made under rule 42.3 (report of taxation).

Deriv. R.C.S. 1965, r. 349(8) substituted by S.I. 1983 No. 826; P.N. January 16, 1970

42.6.1   *General note.* A legally assisted person may apply to the court to have modified (or assessed) his liability to pay the expenses of an unassisted person in whose favour the cause has been finally determined. The court may, without the necessity of having an account of expenses taxed, proceed to modify the expenses to a fixed sum or to nil. Section 18(2) of the Legal Aid (Scotland) Act 1986 (formerly s.2(6)(e) of the Legal Aid (Scotland) Act 1967) does not require that the account of expenses be taxed before a decision can be made on the question of modification and set-off, but there has to be sufficient financial information available to enable a proper decision to be made: *McInally v. Clackmannan D.C.* 1993 S.C. 314. The 1967 Act only has application to legal aid granted under that Act.

If the court does remit an account of expenses for taxation then the assisted person may, within 14 days of the date of the Auditor's report, ask the court to modify these expenses: r. 42.6(2).

The court must have regard to all the circumstances including the means of all the parties and their conduct in connection with the dispute in determining the amount; but the assisted person's house, wearing apparel, household furniture and the tools and implements of his trade or profession are not taken into account in assessing his means: 1986 Act, s.18(3). There must be an award of expenses by the court against the legally assisted person and he must be afforded a reasonable time to pay before the defender can enrol for absolvitor: *Collum v. Glasgow Corporation* 1964 S.L.T. 199. On "having regard to all the circumstances", see *Douglas v. Cunningham* 1966 S.L.T. (Notes) 7 (Motor Insurance Bureau behind legally assisted defender). On "the means of all the parties", see *Ballantyne v. Douglas* 1953 S.C. 258; *Todd v. Todd* 1966 S.L.T. 50; *Armstrong*, below. In considering means, the court is entitled to take any damages recovered into account: *MacKenzie v. Lothian and Borders Police* 1995 S.L.T. 1332. On "conduct in connection with the dispute", see *Burns v. James McHaffie & Sons Ltd* 1965 S.L.T. 238; *O'Donnell v. A.M. & G. Robertson* 1965 S.L.T. (Notes) 32; *Armstrong*, below; *Clelland v. Clelland* 1988 S.L.T. 674; *Cullen v. Cullen*, 22nd November 1996, unreported (1997 G.W.D. 2–59) (modification to £20,000 where conduct reprehensible).

The general principle governing modification is indicated in *Armstrong v. Armstrong* 1970 S.C. 161, 166 by the First Division: "The figure should not be so high as to render it for practical purposes impossible for the party, with the resources available to him, to meet the liability. It equally seems clear that it was not intended that the liability should as a matter of course be fixed at a nominal sum or even at nil." The matter is one of discretion. The award to the legally aided person may be taken into account: *McInally*, above. For a recent example see *Jack v. McIntyre's Exrs*, 1999 S.L.T. 85.

Failure to mark the steps of process with the words: "Assisted Person" following issue of a legal aid certificate as required by r. 3(1) of the A.S. (Civil Legal Aid Rules) 1987 [S.I. 1987 No.

492] may result in the court not only pronouncing a finding of liability for expenses against the assisted person but also a decerniture for these expenses as taxed. This point is important because, once expenses have been decerned for, it is incompetent thereafter to apply for modification of the taxed expenses under s.18(2) of the 1986 Act: *Gilbert's Tr. v. Gilbert* 1988 S.L.T. 680; *Stewart v. Stewart* 1989 S.L.T. 80. It is therefore essential that the assisted person's solicitor mark the process appropriately immediately the legal aid certificate is issued; the legal aid certificate must, however, be lodged in process first.

Where a pursuer who is an assisted person abandons his action the court has no jurisdiction to modify his liability for expenses either under the legal aid provisions or at common law because there is no "award" of expenses made by the court: *Collum*, above (not following *Thompson v. Fairfield Shipbuilding and Engineering Co.* 1954 S.C. 354); *Johnston v. Johnston* 1985 S.L.T. 510, 512 *per* Lord Cowie.

Where a legally-aided pursuer accepted a tender but was found liable to the defender in the latter's expenses post-tender he was able to have his liability reduced to nil: *Ross v. McDermott International Inc* 1987 G.W.D 36–1284.

Rules in relation to the making of awards of expenses against assisted persons are in r. 4 of the A.S. (Civil Legal Aid Rules) 1987 [S.I. 1987 No. 4921].

The defender, if an unassisted person, may be entitled to claim expenses against the Legal Aid Fund (*Walker v. Walker* 1987 S.L.T. 129); but only on conclusion of the whole case (*Moss v. Penman (No. 2)* 1994 S.L.T. 602), and only if a motion under s. 19(1) of the 1986 Act is made to the court awarding expenses: see *Fulton v. Bell*, 22nd November 1996, unreported (1997 G.W.D. 1–29). The limitation imposed by *Moss*, above, does not apply in the House of Lords: *Herd v. Clyde Helicopters Ltd*, 1997 S.L.T. 672.

Where a defender who is an assisted person enters into a joint minute agreeing to be found liable as an assisted person, he is entitled to seek modification of his liability: *Jeffrey v. Jeffrey* 1987 S.L.T 488.

An appeal for re-assessment of the amount of an award of expenses to which s.18(2) of the 1986 Act applies may be made on a relevant change of circumstances within one year after the date of the award: 1986 Act, s.20(4) and Civil Legal Aid (Scotland) Regulations 1987 [S.I. 1987 No. 331], reg. 38. It is thought that the application may be made by motion under this rule although the cause may no longer be depending (*cf*. r. 23.11); otherwise the application would have to be by petition by virtue of r. 14.2(h).

Article 26 of Sched. 1 to the Child Abduction and Custody Act 1985 (Hague Convention) does not apply to expenses not normally covered by legal aid: *Matznick v. Matznick* 1998 S.L.T. 636.

It is competent to reclaim against a decision on modification of expenses awarded against an assisted person: *Cullen v. Cullen* 2000 S.C. 396 (Ct of Five Judges) overruling in part *Todd v. Todd* 1966 S.L.T. 50. But as assessment is intended to be carried out by the Lord Ordinary, in the event of a successful reclaiming motion, the re-assessment of liability should be carried out by the Lord Ordinary subject to whatever directions the Inner House considers appropriate: *Cullen*, above.

"motion". For motions, see Chap. 23.   **42.6.2**

Taxation of solicitors' own accounts

42.7.—(1) Subject to section 61A(1) of the Solicitors (Scotland) Act 1980, the court may remit to the Auditor the account of a solicitor to his client—
  (a) where the account is for work done in relation to a cause in the Court of Session, on the motion of the solicitor or the client; or
  (b) in an action in which the solicitor or his representative sues the client for payment of the account.

(2) A motion under paragraph (1)(a) may be enrolled notwithstanding that final decree in the cause has been extracted.

(3) The account referred to in paragraph (1) shall—
  (a) be in such form as will enable the Auditor to establish the nature and extent of the work done to which the account relates;
  (b) detail the outlays incurred by the solicitor; and
  (c) be accompanied by such supporting material as is necessary to vouch the items in the account.

(4) The Auditor shall—
  (a) fix a diet of taxation not earlier than 14 days after the date on which he receives the account; and
  (b) intimate the diet to the solicitor.

(5) On receipt of intimation of the diet of taxation from the Auditor, the solicitor shall forthwith send to his client by registered post or the first class recorded delivery service—

(a) a copy of the account to be taxed;

(b) a copy of the interlocutor remitting the account; and

(c) a notice in Form 42.7 of the date, time and place of the diet of taxation.

(6) In taxing an account remitted to him under paragraph (1), the Auditor—

(a) shall allow a sum in respect of such work and outlays as have been reasonably incurred;

(b) shall allow, in respect of each item of work and outlay, such sum as may be fair and reasonable having regard to all the circumstances of the case;

(c) shall, in determining whether a sum charged in respect of an item of work is fair and reasonable, take into account any of the following factors:—

 (i) the complexity of the cause and the number, difficulty or novelty of the questions raised;

 (ii) the skill, labour, and specialised knowledge and responsibility required, of the solicitor;

 (iii) the time spent on the item of work and on the cause as a whole;

 (iv) the number and importance of any documents prepared or perused;

 (v) the place and circumstances (including the degree of expedition required) in which the work of the solicitor or any part of it has been done;

 (vi) the importance of the cause or the subject-matter of it to the client;

 (vii) the amount or value of money or property involved in the cause; and

 (viii) any informal agreement relating to fees;

(d) shall presume (unless the contrary is demonstrated to his satisfaction) that—

 (i) an item of work or outlay was reasonably incurred if it was incurred with the express or implied approval of the client;

 (ii) the fee charged in respect of an item of work or outlay was reasonable if the amount of the fee or the outlay was expressly or impliedly approved by the client; and

 (iii) an item of work or outlay was not reasonably incurred, or that the fee charged in respect of an item of work or outlay was not reasonable if the item of work, outlay or fee charged, was unusual in the circumstances of the case, unless the solicitor informed the client before carrying out the item of work or incurring the outlay that it might not be allowed (or that the fee charged might not be allowed in full) in a taxation in a cause between party and party; and

(e) may disallow any item of work or outlay which is not vouched to his satisfaction.

(7) The Auditor shall—

(a) prepare a report of the taxation of the account remitted to him under paragraph (1);

(b) transmit his report to the appropriate Department of the Office of Court; and

(c) send a copy of his report to the solicitor and the client.

Deriv. R.C.S. 1965, r. 350 substituted by S.I. 1992 No. 1433

42.7.1   *General note.* The court is not concerned with identifying the applicability of any of the heads in r. 42.7(6) in the taxation of a solicitor's business account with his client: *Bradnock v. Liston (No. 2)* 1994 S.L.T. 1195.

As to the Auditor's general power to recognise responsibility when taxing a solicitor's business account, see *Davidson & Syme, W.S. v. Booth* 1972 S.L.T. 122.

The solicitor's account must be lodged in process before the court will remit the account to the Auditor for taxation.

A certificate of audit is not a taxation—see Law Society of Scotland's Table of Fees for Conveyancing and General Business, Chapter 2.1(d)—and must not be represented to the client or a court as such: *Rollo Davidson & McFarlane v. Anderson*, 18th February, 1997, unreported (1997 G.W.D. 12–522).

"Subject to section 61A(1) of the Solicitors (Scotland) Act 1980". Where a solicitor and his **42.7.2** client have reached agreement in writing as to the solicitor's fees it is not competent for the court, in any litigation arising out of a dispute as to the amount due under the agreement, to remit the solicitor's account for taxation: 1980 Act, s.61A(1) inserted by the Law Reform (Miscellaneous Provisions) (Scotland) Act 1990, s.36(3).

"the account of a solicitor to his client". It is the client's own solicitor's account which may be **42.7.2A** lodged, and that account may include as an outlay any account incurred to other solicitors employed by the client's solicitor. The employed solicitor, who is not directly the client's solicitor, has a right to be reimbursed by the instructing (Scottish) solicitor unless the employing solicitor has expressly disclaimed liability: Solicitors (Scotland) Act 1980, s. 30.

"final decree". This is the decree disposing of the whole subject-matter of the cause including **42.7.3** expenses: see note 4.15.2(2).

"not earlier than seven days after". The date from which the period is calculated is not **42.7.4** counted.

"any informal agreement relating to fees". R.42.7(6)(c)(viii) is a new factor to be considered. It **42.7.5** may be that there was no written agreement about fees but that an hourly rate was quoted to which the client may have acquiesced.

Fee. The fee for taxing the account is payable on issue of the Auditor's report. For fee, see **42.7.6** Court of Session etc. Fees Order 1984, Table of Fees, Pt III, I, item 1(b) [S.I. 1984 No. 256, Table as amended, pp. C 1202 *et seq*.]. The fee is a fixed sum for accounts under £300, and £4 for every additional £100 of the gross amount of the account lodged for taxation.

Lodging dues and fee fund dues must be paid to the Auditor's office. The Auditor's office issues invoices or the collection of lodging dues and fee fund dues are paid on taxation of the account. Party litigants must pay cash when lodging dues or fee fund dues are incurred.

PART II

FEES OF SOLICITORS

Application and interpretation of this Part

42.8.—(1) This Part applies to fees of solicitors in a cause other than fees—

(a) provided for by regulations made by the Secretary of State under section 14A of the Legal Aid (Scotland) Act 1967; or

(b) for which the Secretary of State may make regulations under section 33 of the Legal Aid (Scotland) Act 1986.

(2) In this Part, "the Table of Fees" means the Table of Fees in rule 42.16.

Deriv. RCS 1965, r. 347(aa) inserted by S.I. 1984 No. 499 (r. 42.8(1))

General note. The regulations made under s. 14A of the Legal Aid (Scotland) Act 1967 are the **42.8.1** Legal Aid (Scotland) (Fees in Civil Proceedings) Regulations 1984 [S.I. 1984 No. 519]. The regulations made under s. 33 of the Legal Aid (Scotland) Act 1986 are the Civil Legal Aid (Scotland) (Fees) Regulations 1989 [S.I. 1989 No. 1490].

Form of account of expenses

42.9. An account of expenses presented to the Auditor in accordance with an order of the court shall set out in chronological order all items in respect of which fees are claimed and shall be taxed as if the whole work in the cause had been carried out by one solicitor.

Deriv. RCS 1965, r. 347(a)(part) inserted by S.I. 1974 No. 1686

General note. The remuneration of a foreign solicitor is treated as an outlay in the account of **42.9.1** expenses. The account of expenses of a non-Scottish solicitor in a Scottish litigation must be stated in such a form as to make it clear what items of work were done by the foreign solicitor and admissible in a party-and-party account. The Auditor has then to ascertain what charges for these admitted items are appropriate in accordance with the law and practice of the foreign jurisdiction: *Wimpey Construction (U.K.) Ltd v. Martin Black & Co. (Wire Ropes) Ltd*, 1988 S.C. 264, 1988 S.L.T. 637 (Ct. of 7 judges).

It is not competent to award an additional fee under r. 42.14 for the work of a foreign solicitor, because it is treated as an outlay and the amount of the foreign solicitor's fees are not determined by the table of fees in r. 42. 16, but by the law and practice of the foreign country; but it may be allowed as part of the outlay if permitted under the law and practice of the foreign court, which the Auditor must ascertain: *Scottish Lion Insurance Co Ltd v. National Grid Insurance Co (Isle of Man) Ltd, Petr.*, 2006 S.L.T. 686.

Basis of charging

42.10.—(1) Only such expenses as are reasonable for conducting the cause in a proper manner shall be allowed.

[1] (2) Where the work can properly be performed by a local solicitor, the

Auditor in taxing an account shall allow such expenses as would have been incurred if the work had been done by the nearest local solicitor, including reasonable fees for instructing and corresponding with him, unless the Auditor is satisfied that it was in the interests of the client that the solicitor in charge of the cause should attend personally.

(3) Subject to paragraph (4), a solicitor may charge an account either on the basis of Chapter I or on the basis of Chapter III of the Table of Fees, but he may not charge partly on one basis and partly on the other.

(4) Where the inclusive fees set out in Chapter III of the Table of Fees are not conveniently applicable or do not properly cover the work involved, an account may be charged on the basis of Chapter I of that Table.

(5) The Auditor may increase or reduce an inclusive fee in Chapter III of the Table of Fees in appropriate circumstances whether or not those circumstances fall under Part IX of that Chapter.

Deriv. RCS 1965, r. 347(a)(part) inserted by S.I. 1974 No. 1686 (r. 42.10(1)); r. 347, Table of Fees, Chap. I, note 5 (r. 42.10(2)); r. 347(e)(part) substituted by S.I. 1970 No. 1746 and amended by S.I. 1981 No. 497 (r. 42.10(3)); and r. 347(f) substituted by S.I. 1970 No. 1746 (r. 42.10(5))

---

[1] R. 42.10(2) amended by SI 1994/2901 (minor correction).

42.10.1   *"Only such expenses as are reasonable"*. The only relevant test in deciding what expenses should be allowed is that of reasonableness, the references in earlier editions of the RCS to "necessary" and "economy" no longer appearing: *Ahmed's Tr. v. Ahmed (No. 1)* 1993 S.L.T. 390; and see *City of Aberdeen Council v. Fairhurst*, 2000 S.C.L.R. 392 (OH)) per Lord Penrose. The Auditor should only disallow an item if it can truly be said that it was unreasonable to incur the expense in the sense that a competent solicitor acting reasonably would not have incurred it: *Malpas v. Fife Council* 1999 S.L.T. 499, 501E per Lord Bonomy. Under r. 42.10(1) the outlay must be in respect of work reasonably undertaken to conduct the cause, that is to say, to prepare and pursue the litigation to conclusion including rebuttal of the opponent's contentions; and in a party and party taxation, what is reasonable undertaken to conduct a cause cannot normally vary according to the economic circumstances or needs of the litigant: *McNair's Exrx v. Wrights Insulation Co Ltd,* 2003 S.L.T. 1311 (OH), 1315E, para.[9] per Lord Carloway (payment into Law Society Compensation Scheme to secure insurance against liability to pay defender's expenses in event of unsuccessful action not an expense "for conducting the cause").

In commercial actions, which depend on co-operation of parties, expenses may be awarded on an agent and client, client paying, basis where any irresponsibility is shown by a party in the conduct of the litigation: *North East Ice & Cold Storage Co. Ltd v. Third*, 4th June 1996, unreported (1996 G.W.D. 27–1616).

Trustees whose actions are *bona fide* to secure the best interests of the beneficiaries of a trust are entitled to be indemnified for ordinary expenses: *Independent Pension Trustee v. LAW Construction Co. Ltd*, 17th December, 1996 unreported (1997 G.W.D. 8–336).

The mere fact that a litigant was a party litigant is irrelevant to the auditor's determination of the reasonableness of charges by counsel for the opposing party: *Frost v. Unity Trust Bank plc,* 2000 S.L.T. 952 (OH) (objection to allowance to counsel of element of his fee to reflect fact that pursuer was a party litigant was sustained).

42.10.2   *Counsel's fees*. The concern is not what fees a particular counsel is justly entitled to receive from his client for his services but what fees can reasonably be made a charge against an unsuccessful opponent: *MacNaughton v. MacNaughton* 1949 S.C. 42, 46 per L.P. Cooper; and see *City of Aberdeen Council v. Fairhurst*, 20th July 1999, unreported (1999 G.W.D. 31–1493) per Lord Penrose.

As the Auditor is charged with determining what expenses are reasonable, he may disallow fees for senior counsel: *McDonald v. Salmond* 1999 S.C. 396, 400G per Lord Philip.

There is no rule that a fee for senior counsel revising a summons will be allowed only in the most exceptional case; it is always a question of circumstances: *J.M. Mitchell & Sons v. Lord Advocate* 1994 S.C.L.R. 522.

There is no "rule" that the fee for a junior counsel is two-thirds of senior counsel's fee: *McCance v. Newalls Insulation Ltd (No. 2)* 1996 S.L.T. 1133.

The use of English counsel other than as a skilled witness is not a reasonable party and party expense: *First Tokyo Index Trust Ltd v. Gould* 1994, O.H., 16th November 1994, unreported (1994 G.W.D. 40–2390).

The illness of counsel for a successful pursuer resulting in a lost day of proof is not "a vagary of litigation" for which the defender is required to pay: *Elliot v. Abela*, 10th May 1996, unreported (1996 G.W.D. 23–1338).

The employment of senior counsel may not always be allowed: *Signet Group plc v. C. & J. Clark Retail Properties Ltd*, 23rd June 1995, unreported, (1995 G.W.D. 27–1454). Likewise, the employment of junior counsel with senior counsel may be disallowed if senior counsel has not been asked if he is willing to appear without a junior: see "Guide to the Professional Conduct of Advocates"—June 1988, para. 4.8.3; Resolution of the Faculty of Advocates 4th February 1977—1977 S.L.T.(News) 142.

In *Gorrie's Exrx v. Ciba Geigy Ltd*, 26th June 1996, unreported (1996 G.W.D. 28-1685), it was held that there is no place for a disappointment fee for counsel in respect of a settled action removed from counsel's diary since such fees are the creature of special bargains. But in *City of Aberdeen Council v. Fairhurst*, 20th July 1999, unreported (1999 G.W.D. 31–1493), Lord Penrose disagreed with the decision in *Gorrie's Exrx*, above if it meant that a commitment fee could never be recovered. He held that the test in r. 42.10(1) was whether the expenses were reasonable for conducting the cause in a proper manner. In applying that test the auditor should bear in mind that the successful party should not be allowed to throw an unnecessary burden on the other party and bear in mind the public interest in maintaining control over the cost of litigation. But that the auditor also has to bring to bear his wide knowledge and experience of proper and responsible practice. A special bargain personal to selected counsel may be considered a reasonable approach in the circumstances of a particular case. Commitment fees could reasonably have been expected as an expense in this case. An account of expenses should still include any fee charged by counsel, by virtue of para. 5.12 of the *Guide to Professional Conduct of Advocates*, June 1988, where he has been instructed for a case which has subsequently settled or the diet has been discharged: P.N. No. 5 of 1996. At taxation the Auditor will consider whether the fee charged is appropriate, having regard to the factors mentioned in para. 5.12 of the Guide.

Posts and incidental expenses
42.11.—[Revoked by S.I. 1998 No. 2674.]

Deriv. R.C.S. 1965, r. 347(g) substituted by S.I. 1974 No. 1686 (r. 42.11(1) and (2))

General note. Postages and incidents could formerly be charged at 12 per cent of the total fees; **42.11.1** except where a solicitor elected to charge the inclusive fee in para. 1 of Chap. III of the Table of Fees. Rule 42.11 was revoked, with respect to work on or after 1st December 1998 by A.S. (R.C.S.A. No. 3) (Fees of Solicitors) 1998 [SI 1998/2674] as part of a policy to eliminate the disparity between the expenses recoverable from a paying party and the cost of the case to a successful party. No additions for posts and incidents, either the 12 per cent sum or those actually incurred, may now be made.

Value added tax
42.12.—(1) Where work done by a solicitor constitutes a supply of services in respect of which value added tax is chargeable by him, there may be added to the amount of fees an amount equal to the amount of value added tax chargeable.

(2) An account of expenses or a minute of election to charge the inclusive fee in paragraph 1 of Chapter III of the Table of Fees shall contain a statement as to whether or not the party entitled to the expenses is registered for the purposes of value added tax.

Deriv. R.C.S. 1965, r. 347(h) inserted by S.I. 1973 No. 360

Charges for witnesses
42.13.—(1) Charges for the attendance at a proof or jury trial of a witness—
⁴(a) present but not called to give evidence, or
(b) who is held as concurring with another witness who has been called, may be allowed if a party has, at any time before the diet of taxation, enrolled a motion for the name of that witness to be noted in the minute of proceedings in the cause.
¹(2) Subject to paragraph (3), where it was reasonable in any cause to employ a skilled person to make investigations or to report for any purpose, any charges for such investigations and report and for any attendance at any proof or jury trial shall be allowed in addition to the ordinary witness fee of

such person at such rate as the Auditor shall determine is fair and reasonable.

[2] (2A) Subject to paragraph (3)(a) in the case of a skilled witness and paragraph (3)(b) in the case of a professional witness, in any cause in which evidence has been given by affidavit, charges shall be allowed to the deponent in terms of paragraph (2) of this rule or of paragraph (2)(a)(iii) of Chapter II of the Table of Fees as the case may be.

[3] (3) The Auditor may make no determination under paragraph (2) or (2A) unless the court has, on granting a motion made for the purpose, before or at the time at which it awarded expenses or on a motion enrolled at any time thereafter but before the diet of taxation—

[6] (a) certified that the witness was a skilled witness;
[7] (aa) certified that it was reasonable to employ that person to make investigations or to report; and
   (b) recorded the name of that witness in the interlocutor pronounced by the court.

[5] (4) Where a motion under paragraph (3) is enrolled after the court has awarded expenses, the expenses of the motion shall be borne by the party enrolling it.

Deriv. R.C.S. 1965, r. 347, Table of Fees, Chap. II, para. 8 (r. 42.13(1)), and r. 347, Table of Fees, Chap. II, para. 9 (r. 42.13(2) and (3))

---

[1] Rule 42.13(2) substituted by S.S.I. 2006 No. 294 (effective 1st July 2006).
[2] Rule 42.13(2A) inserted by S.I. 1995 No. 1396 (effective 22nd June 1995).
[3] Rule 42.13(3) amended by S.I. 1996 No. 1756 (effective 5th August 1996) and S.S.I. 2006 No. 294 (effective 1st July 2006).
[4] Rule 42.13(1)(a) amended by S.S.I. 2001 No. 305, para. 12(1) (effective 18th September 2001).
[5] Rule 42.13(4) inserted by S.S.I. 2001 No. 305, para. 12(3) (effective 18th September 2001).
[6] Rule 42.13(3)(a) amended by S.S.I. 2006 No. 294 (effective 1st July 2006).
[7] Rule 42.13(3)(aa) inserted by S.S.I. 2006 No. 294 (effective 1st July 2006).

42.13.1   *General note.* The fees allowable for a skilled witness exclude all charges for assistance given to counsel in both the Outer and the Inner House. The allowance is only for the expert *qua* witness and may include the expenses of a consultation with counsel as to the line or material of intended evidence. The time and expenses incurred by an expert adviser in relation to the advisability of instituting or defending proceedings is not allowable: *Caledonian Railway Co. v. Greenock Corporation* 1922 S.C. 299, 313 *per* L.P. Clyde.

The cost of a service agency between a skilled witness and litigant is allowable: *Macken v. Boag-Warner Chemicals Ltd* 1989 G.W.D. 14–604.

42.13.2   *Certification of witness as skilled person.* Rule 42.13(2) has been radically amended by A.S. (R.C.S.A. No. 4) (Fees of Solicitors) 2006 [2006 No. 294].

The former r. 42.13(2) was that it had to be (a) "necessary" to employ a skilled person, (b) to make investigations, (c) in order to qualify him to give evidence, (d) in a prospective proof or jury trial. The court had to satisfied that the skilled person was necessary and that *special* investigations or preparations had been carried out (*William Nimmo & Co. Ltd v. Russell Construction Ltd (No. 2)*, 20th June 1995, 1995 G.W.D. 26-1408 (OH)); and to show necessity something special to the cause or party ought to be the norm (*Snelling v. Thomson Alarm and Communication System Ltd*, 12th June 2003, *unreported* (OH) *per* Temp Judge Coutts, QC). The person had to be employed by or for the party seeking certification, and the investigations had to have been in order to give evidence (as specified in the rule: *Delaney v. Finlay Park t/a Park Hutchison*, 27th September 2002, 2002 G.W.D. 30-1045 (OH). Certification could only be sought if the skilled person was or might be a witness, and at one time could not apply where no proof or jury trial had been allowed (*Parratt v. Ceiling Decor Ltd*, 1998 S.C. 179 (OH)); although in *Clements v. Edinburgh Corporation*, (1905) 7 F. 651 it was held that where settlement took place before a proof a party entitled to expenses could include reasonable remuneration for an expert including remuneration for investigations. A practice had grown up of seeking certification where proof or jury trial had been allowed but did not proceed: *Devenney v. Greater Glasgow Health Board*, 1989 S.L.T. 578. (It should be noted that at that time the rule referred to investigations "before a proof or jury trial".) By A.S. (R.C.S.A.) (Miscellaneous) 1998 [S.I. 1998 No. 890], r. 42.13(2) was amended to cover the situation of a "prospective" proof; but this phrase was criticised in this note as ambiguous and not clarifying the position as to whether a proof had to be allowed or not. Lord Eassie agreed with that criticism in *Earl v. Kvaerner Energy Ltd*, 2002 S.L.T. 1167, para. [4] and, in the light of *Clements*, above, did not understand the utility of extending the previous rule.

The new provision in r. 42.13(2) made by A.S. (R.C.S.A. No. 4) (Fees of Solicitors) 2006 [2006 No. 294] is the latest attempt to clarify and widen the provision. In part this must be in consequence of the criticisms previously in this note and in *Earl,* above. The provision in r. 42.13(2) now is that it only has to be (a) "reasonable" to employ a skilled person, (b) to make investigations or to report. Thus (i) "reasonable" is substituted for "necessary", (ii) reports are covered as well as investigations, (iii) it is no longer necessary that the investigations or reports have to be carried out in order to qualify the skilled person to give evidence, and (iv) a proof or jury trial does not have to have been allowed or even be in prospect. The provision is, therefore, much wider than the previous provision. The "reasonable" test must be wider (that is less stringent) than "necessary". It is not clear if the investigations still have to be special (see *William Nimmo & Co. Ltd,* above). The appropriate point at which to test the necessity of instructing an expert witness was at the time of his being instructed: *Allison v. Chief Constable, Strathclyde Police,* 2004 S.C. 453, 2004 S.L.T. 341 (First Div.) (where it was held to be unnecessary to employ an expert to value loss of employability). The appropriate point for determining whether it was reasonable to employ a skilled person must also be at the time of instructing him.

Under r. 42.13(3), however, no fees or charges may be allowed to skilled person until the court has made a certification. Certification by the court under that provision, however, is still only of a "witness". As was held by Lord Maclean in *Parratt,* above, before a proof has been allowed or issues approved a person cannot be said to be a "witness". If it was intended by the new r. 42.13(2) to include investigations before a proof has been allowed, the continued use of the word "witness" in r. 42.13(3) might be said to preclude it. It has to be said that the position remains confused.

It is essential that the court certifies all skilled witnesses and that it was reasonable to employ them to make investigations reports for whom additional remuneration is to be sought, even where the case is settled before the diet of proof or jury trial. The Auditor has no discretion to allow any remuneration for a skilled witness who has not been certified: *Clark v. Laddaws Ltd* 1994 S.L.T. 792. If it is considered that a party seeks to have too many witnesses certified that must be raised before the court. The Auditor's function is solely to assess the remuneration to be paid to a witness who has been certified: *Anderson v. Strathclyde Passenger Transport Executive* 1986 S.L.T. 619.

Certification is required whether the witness attended the proof or jury trial or not or gave evidence or not (the expenses of a skilled witness who prepared a report and was certified, but not called, were allowed in *Herd and Mackenzie (Buckie) Ltd v. Mackenzie* 1987 G.W.D. 37–1329; see also *Merrick Homes Ltd v. Duff (No. 2)* 1997 S.L.T. 53). It is also required even if the cause has been settled extra-judicially.

Formerly the motion for certification had to be made at the proof or before decerniture for expenses. Although decerniture for expenses had been made it was not too late to seek certification of a skilled witness, even in a cause in which he has given evidence, on the exercise of the dispensing power under r. 2.1, because certification would not imply any alteration or recall of the decerniture: *Mains v. Uniroyal Englebert Tyres Ltd (No. 2)* 1995 S.C. 538, 1st Div., overruling *Hodge v. British Coal Corporation* 1992 G.W.D. 15–890. The position now is that certification may be sought at any time before the diet of taxation: r. 42.13(1) and (3) as amended by A.S. (R.C.S.A. No.4) (Miscellaneous) 2001 [SSI 2001 No.305]. It also gets round the problem, where cases settle before a proof is allocated at the diet to a particular judge, of there not being a judge to deal with certification.

The certification of a skilled person or recording of the name of a professional person now applies also to such a person giving evidence by affidavit: see r. 42.13(2A) and note 42.13.2A. The skilled witness must have carried out "investigations" under r. 42.13(2): cf. *Ferguson v. Johnston,* (1886) 13 R.635 and *Earl v. Kvaerner Energy Ltd,* 2002 S.L.T. 1167.

Evidence given on affidavit. With the increasing occurrence of affidavit evidence by skilled or professional witnesses it has been thought appropriate to allow such witnesses a fee for investigations (or examining papers) before giving affidavit evidence as would be allowed if that witness gave oral evidence or attended at the proof or jury trial. This provision was inserted by A.S. (R.C.S. 1994 Amendment No. 2) (Fees of Solicitors) 1995 [S.I. 1995 No. 1396].   **42.13.2A**

"any attendance at a proof or jury trial". When a skilled witness was in attendance to speak to facts which had been agreed the expenses of his attendance were refused: *Ayton v. National Coal Board* 1965 S.L.T.(Notes) 24.   **42.13.3**

"motion". For motions, see Chap. 23.   **42.13.4**

Additional fee
42.14.—(1) An application for the allowance of an additional fee shall be made by motion to the court.

(2) The court may, on such an application to it—

(a) determine the application itself; or

(b) remit the application to the Auditor for him to determine whether an additional fee should be allowed.

(3) In determining whether to allow an additional fee under paragraph (2), the court or the Auditor, as the case may be, shall take into account any of the following factors:—

(a) the complexity of the cause and the number, difficulty or novelty of the questions raised;

[1] (b) the skill, time and labour, and specialised knowledge required, of the solicitor or the exceptional urgency of the steps taken by him;

(c) the number or importance of any documents prepared or perused;

(d) the place and circumstances of the cause or in which the work of the solicitor in preparation for, and conduct of, the cause has been carried out;

(e) the importance of the cause or the subject-matter of it to the client;

(f) the amount or value of money or property involved in the cause;

(g) the steps taken with a view to settling the cause, limiting the matters in dispute or limiting the scope of any hearing.

(4) In fixing an additional fee, the Auditor shall take into account any of the factors mentioned in paragraph (3).

Deriv. RCS 1965, r. 347(d) substituted by S.I. 1970 No. 1746 and amended by S.I. 1991 No. 272

---

[1] R. 42.14(3)(b) amended by S.S.I 1999 No. 109 (effective 29th October 1999).

42.14.1   *General note.* R. 42.14 includes a new provision allowing the court to remit to the Auditor the question of whether an additional fee should be allowed. Whether to remit the question to the Auditor is a matter for the court (even where the parties agree: *Young v. Blue Star Line Ltd,* 1998 S.L.T. 109); and (a) the court must be satisfied that the case is one in which an additional fee would be appropriate and (b) there must be something out of the ordinary in the facts and circumstances of the case which persuades the court not to make a determination itself: *Kennedy v. British Coal Corporation* 1997 S.L.T. 151 *per* Lord Cameron of Lochbroom (counsel had little involvement—case settled after exchange of correspondence and reports between agents). That there may be circumstances when the court feels unable on the information before it to determine the question itself, may not, therefore, be a sufficient reason; although this was a consideration in providing for remit to the Auditor.

A motion for an additional fee should be made at the same time as the motion for expenses; but a motion for an additional fee is not incompetent after the interlocutor decerning for expenses as taxed (but before taxation) because an allowance of an additional fee does not imply any alteration or recall of the decerniture in the decree for expenses: *U.C.B. Bank plc v. Dundas £ Wilson, C.S.* 1991 S.L.T. 90. A motion for an additional fee is, however, incompetent after the auditor has issued his report of taxation because then the matter of expenses has been finally determined (subject to the objection procedure under r.42.4): *Taylor v. Marshalls Food Group Ltd (No. 3),* 1999 S.L.T. 629.

It is competent to deal with a motion for an additional fee under reg. 5(4) of the Civil Legal Aid (Scotland) (Fees) Regulations 1989 [S.I. 1989 No. 1490] at the same time as a motion under the same provisions of r. 42.14: *McVey v. Secretary of State for Scotland,* 2nd August 1996, unreported (1996 G.W.D. 31–1880).

Where the question of whether an additional fee should be allowed is remitted to the Auditor, he will consider the question at the diet of taxation. On lodging the account of expenses, a note of the reasons for which an additional fee is sought must also be lodged: P.N. No. 3 of 1995.

Where an interim award of expenses has been made in respect of proceedings to date without mention of an additional fee and an account for that work has been taxed and paid, an award of an additional fee at the conclusion of the cause applies to the whole work in the cause: *Masterton v. Thomas Smith & Sons (Kirkoswald) Ltd,* 1998 S.L.T. 699. The auditor should determine the application for an additional fee and give his reasons in the course of the taxation of the account and can be challenged in a note of objection under r. 42.4: *Petrie v. North Milk Co-Operative Ltd,* [2005] CSOH 45, 24th March 2005, para. [19], unreported.

Where an account of expenses has been prepared on an inclusive fee basis, the court may remit the question of an additional fee to the Auditor to consider: *Young v. Blue Star Line Ltd* 1998 S.L.T. 109.

It is not competent to award an additional fee under r. 42.14 for the work of a foreign solicitor because it is treated as an outlay (see *Wimpy Construction (UK) Ltd v. Martin Black & Co (Wire Ropes) Ltd*, 1988 S.C. 264 and note 42.9.1) and the amount of the foreign solicitor's fees are not determined by the table of fees in r. 42. 16 but by the law and practice of the foreign country: but it may be allowed as part of the outlay if permitted under the law and practice of the foreign court, which the Auditor must ascertain: *Scottish Lion Insurance Co Ltd*, Ptnr., 2006 S.L.T. 606.

The factors to be taken into account. Only one factor need be recognised by the court as **42.14.2** sufficient to justify it allowing an additional fee: *Hill v. Lovett (No. 2)* 1992 G.W.D. 7–380.

The court should record in the interlocutor the factor(s) it considered appropriate: *Gray v. Babcock Power Ltd* 1990 S.L.T. 693. The Auditor must have regard to all the factors set out in the rule notwithstanding the fact that the court has specified only one or more: *Gray*, above. It was confirmed in *Petrie v. North Milk Co-Operative Ltd*, [2005] CSOH 45, 24th March 2005, para. [19], unreported, that the inclusion of the words ("any of" in "any of the following factors" in r. 42.14(3) (which were not in R.C.S. 1965, r. 347(d)) implied that the court and the auditor were not required to have regard to *all* the factors and could allow an additional fee taking into account only one or more of the factors.

In relation to the factor in r. 42.14(2)(c) (importance to the client), it is not sufficient merely that the cause was important to the client, but that in the particular circumstances the cause was of such importance as to justify an additional fee: *Zyszkiewicz v. University of Glasgow*, 7th July 1995, unreported (1995 G.W.D. 31–1614).

With regard to the factor in sub-para. (g) (formerly RCS 1965, r. 347(d)(8)—settling or limiting matters), see *Boal v. Newalls Insulation Co. Ltd* 1994 S.C.L.R. 534. An additional fee was granted under r. 42.14(2)(g) where a pursuer offered to settle for a fixed sum, thus encouraging the issues to be focused, and the defender subsequently tendered that sum: *Cameron v. Kvaerner Govan Ltd*, 1999 S.L.T. 638. This was so even though the provisions for pursuer's offers has been revoked (and the rule about expenses declared *ultra vires* in *Taylor v. Marshall's Food Group (No. 2)* 1998 S.C. 841). Lord Bonomy said that any step which might clarify the position of a party or limit the areas in dispute should be encouraged.

Where persistent denial of liability and refusal to agree any item of claim may justify an additional fee, see *William Nimmo & Co. Ltd v. Russell Construction Ltd (No. 2)* (O.H.), 20th June 1995, unreported (1995 G.W.D. 26–1408).

(A) **Cases where additional fee allowed:**

(i) *Dunfermline District Council v. James Parr & Partners*, 10th February 1989, unreported: Productions voluminous both in content and in physical extent; need to investigate a width of material and a number of separate but related topics.

(ii) *Montgomery v. Shell U.K. Ltd*, 11th May 1995, unreported (1995 G.W.D. 30–1579) (the process shows that the reclaiming motion was refused—no written opinions issued).

(iii) *Wood v. Hall Russell & Co. Ltd* 1989 G.W.D. 14–603 (no reason to refuse additional fee because solicitor was experienced);

(iv) Where a pursuer had made a genuine attempt at least to limit the issues in dispute and the defender had increased the pursuer's work by not responding and opened settlement negotiations only within a week of the proof, the pursuer was found entitled to an additional fee under head (8) of RCS 1965, r. 347(d) (now RCS 1994, r. 42.14(2)(g)): *Boal v. Newalls Insulation Co. Ltd* 1994 S.C.L.R. 534.

(v) Where a *prima facie* case under only sub-paragraph (g) had been made out it was considered appropriate to remit the matter to the Auditor for determination: *Campbell v. Talbot*, O.H., 8th September 1995, unreported (1995 G.W.D. 36–1831); but see *Independent Pension Trustee Ltd v. LAW Construction Co. Ltd*, 17th December, 1997, unreported (1997 G.W.D. 8–336) where the court itself awarded an additional fee only on factor (g).

(vi) *Shishodia v. Shishodia (No. 2)*, O.H., 13th June 1995, unreported (1995 G.W.D. 34–1742) (lengthy custody and access dispute which went to proof).

(B) **Cases where additional fee refused:**

(i) Where the solicitor's role is subordinate to counsel: *Keystone Properties Ltd v. Sun Alliance & London Insurance plc*, 7th June 1995, unreported (1994 G.W.D. 25–1511); *Whittome v. Whittome (No. 2)*, 1994 S.L.T. 130, 133.

(ii) *Gilgis v. Currie*, 1992 G.W.D. 23–1326.

(C) **Additional fee in respect of sheriff court expenses where expenses not already dealt with there:**

The court should be invited to remit to the sheriff to determine the question of the allowance of an additional fee in respect of the expenses in that court and, if allowed, the percentage increase. Thereafter the accounts of expenses in both courts will be remitted to the Auditor to tax: see *L Petrs. (No. 5)* (1st Div.), 7th April 1995, unreported (1995 G.W.D. 34–1747).

Fees of a reporter

42.15. Subject to any other provision in these Rules, any order of the court or agreement between a party and his solicitor, where any matter in a cause is remitted by the court, at its own instance or on the motion of a party, to a reporter or other person to report to the court—

(a) the solicitors for the parties shall be personally liable, in the first instance, to the reporter or other person for his fee and outlays unless the court otherwise orders; and

(b) where—

(i) the court makes the remit at its own instance, the party ordained by the court, or

(ii) the court makes the remit on the motion of a party, that party, shall be liable to the reporter or other person for his fee and outlays.

Deriv. RCS 1965, r. 347(b) substituted by S.I. 1970 No. 1746

Table of fees

[19] **42.16.**—(1) The Table of Fees shall regulate the fees of a solicitor charged in an account in any cause between party and party.

(2) In the Table of Fees, "sheet" means a page of 250 or more words or numbers.

(3) The Table of Fees is as follows.

[11,13] TABLE OF FEES

[1,5,6] CHAPTER I

TABLE OF DETAILED CHARGES

Paragraph

£

[13,18] **1. Framing documents**

(a) Framing precognitions and other papers (but not including affidavits), per sheet 16.10

(b) Framing formal documents such as inventories, title pages and accounts of expenses, etc., per sheet 6.70

(c) Framing affidavits, per sheet 23.70

(d) Framing accounts of expenses, per sheet 15.50

Notes.

1. *[Revoked by S.I. 1998 No. 2674.]*

[5] 2. Where a skilled witness prepares his own precognition or report, the solicitor shall be allowed half drawing fees for perusing it (whether or not in the course of doing so he revises or adjusts it).

[5] **2. Copying**

For the copying of papers by whatever means—

(a) where a copy is required to be lodged, or sent, in pursuance of any of rules 4.7, 22.1 and 22.3, such charge as the Auditor may from time to time determine (and he may make different provision for different classes of case); and

(b) in any other case, if the Auditor determines (either or both) that—

(i) the copying had to be done in circumstances which were in some way exceptional;

(ii) the papers which required to be copied were unusually numerous having regard to the nature of the cause, such charge, if any, as the Auditor considers reasonable (but a charge based on time expended by any person in copying shall not be allowed).

£

Notes
1. Where a determination is required under sub-paragraph (b), the purpose of copying, the number of copies made and the charge claimed shall be shown in the account.
2. Copying done other than in the place of business of the solicitor shall be shown as an outlay.

[13,18] **3. Revising**
Papers drawn by counsel, open and closed records, etc., for each five sheets or part of a sheet 6.70

[13,18] **4. Citation of parties, witnesses, havers and instructions to messenger-at-arms**
(a) Each party 16.10
(b) Each witness or havers 16.10
(c) Instructing messenger-at-arms including examining, execution and settling fee 16.10

[13,18] **5. Time charge**
(a) Preparation for proof, jury trial or any other hearing at court, per quarter hours 32.00
  or such other sum as in the opinion of the Auditor is justified.
(b) Attendance at meetings, proof, jury trial or any other hearing at court including waiting time, or consultation with counsel, per quarter hour 32.00
  or such other sum as in the opinion of the Auditor is justified.
(c) Perusal of documents, per quarter hour 32.00
  or such other sum as in the opinion of the Auditor is justified.
(d) Allowance for time of clerk, one-half of the above.
(e) Attendance at Office of Court—
  (i) for making up and lodging process 16.10
  (ii) for lodging all first steps of process 16.10
  (iii) for performance of formal work (other than work under head (ii)) 6.70

Notes.
1. Time necessarily occupied in travelling is to be regarded as if occupied on business. Reasonable travelling and maintenance expenses are to be allowed in addition.
2. In the event of a party in a proof or jury trial being represented by one counsel only, allowance may be made to the solicitor should the case warrant it, for the attendance of a clerk at one half the rate chargeable for the attendance of the solicitor.

[13,18] **6. Correspondence**
(a) Letters including instruction to counsel (whether sent by hand, post, telex or facsimile transmission), each page of 125 words 16.10
(b) Formal letters 3.70
(c) Telephone calls (except under sub-paragraph (d)) 6.70
(d) Telephone calls (lengthy), to be charged at attendance rate.

Note. In relation to sub-paragraph (d), whether a telephone call is "lengthy" will be determined by the Auditor.

^{1,7} CHAPTER II

WITNESSES' FEES

1. Skilled Persons

Where it was reasonable to employ a skilled person to make investigations or to report for any purpose, any charges for such investigations and report and for any attendance at any proof or jury trial shall be allowed at a rate which the Auditor of Court shall determine is fair and reasonable.

2. Witnesses

A person who is cited to give evidence and in consequence incurs financial loss shall be allowed reimbursement, being such reasonable sum as the Auditor may determine to have been reasonably and necessarily incurred by the witness, but not exceeding £400 per day.

3. Travelling Allowance

In respect of any witness there shall be allowed a travelling allowance, being such sum as the Auditor may determine to have been reasonably and necessarily incurred by the witness in travelling from and to the witness's residence or place of business and the Court.

4. Subsistence Allowance

In respect of any witness there shall be allowed a subsistence allowance, being such sum as the Auditor may determine to have been reasonably incurred by the witness for the extra cost of subsistence during the witness's absence from the witness's home or place of business for the purpose of giving evidence, and where the witness reasonably requires to stay overnight, for the reasonable cost of board and lodging.

5. Value Added Tax

Where any witness is a taxable person in terms of the Value Added Tax Act 1983, the amount of value added tax may be added by the witness to the witness's note of fee, and may be paid to the witness by the Solicitor.

6. Receipts and Vouchers

Receipts and detailed vouchers for all payments claimed in respect of a witness shall be produced to the party found liable in expenses, prior to the taxation of the Account of Expenses, and to the Auditor, if the Auditor requires.

7. Account of Fees of Witnesses

The fees charged for any witness shall be stated in the Account of Expenses in a lump sum and the details of the charges shall be entered in a separate schedule appended to the Account as follows:

Name & Designation	Where From	Days Charged	Rate per Day	Travelling Subsistence Allowance	Total	Taxed Off

---

¹ Revoked by S.S.I. 2002 No. 31 (effective 1st July 2002) and substituted by S.S.I. 2007 No. 7, para. 7 (effective 26th February 2007).

[5,6] CHAPTER III

PART I

UNDEFENDED CAUSES
(other than consistorial actions)

£

[18] **1. Inclusive fee**

In all undefended causes where no proof is led, the pursuer's solicitor may at his option elect to charge an inclusive fee to cover all work from taking instructions up to and including obtaining extract decree. The option shall be exercised by the solicitor for the pursuer endorsing a minute of election to the above effect on the principal summons or petition before decree is taken.

(a) All work up to and obtaining extract decree 288.05

[5] (b) Outlays to an amount not exceeding £365.45 (exclusive of value added tax) shall also be allowed.

[13,18] PART II

UNDEFENDED CONSISTORIAL ACTIONS
(other than by affidavit procedure in Part III of this Chapter)

£

1. All work (other than precognitions) up to and including the calling of the summons in court 404.40

Note. Precognitions to be charged as in paragraph 5 of Part v. of this Chapter of this Table.

2. Incidental procedure

Fixing diet, enrolling action, preparing for proof, citing witnesses, etc 231.35

3. Amendment

(a) Where summons amended, re-service is not ordered and motion is not starred 59.40

(b) Where summons amended, re-service is not ordered and motion is starred 85.70

(c) Where summons amended and re-service is ordered 106.55

4. Commission to take evidence on interrogatories

(a) All work up to and including lodging of completed interrogatories, but excluding attendance at execution of commission 104.05

(b) Attendance at execution of commission (if required), per quarter hour 32.00

(c) In addition a fee per sheet for completed interrogatories, including all copies, of 17.80

5. Commission to take evidence on open commission

(a) All work up to and including lodging of report of commission, but excluding attendance at execution of commission 96.15

(b) Attendance at execution of commission, per quarter hour 32.00

£

6. Other matters
Where applicable, charges under paragraphs 6, 7, 10, 14, 16 and 21 of Part v. of this Chapter of this Table.

7. Proof and completion fee
All work to and including sending extract decree, but excluding account of expenses 288.05

8. Accounts
Framing and lodging account and attending taxation 88.75

PART III

UNDEFENDED CONSISTORIAL ACTIONS

(affidavit procedure)

1.—(1) This paragraph applies to any undefended action of divorce or separation where—
   (a) the facts set out in section 1(2)(a) (adultery) or section 1(2)(b) (unreasonable behaviour) of the Divorce (Scotland) Act 1976 ("the 1976 Act") are relied on;
   (b) there are no conclusions relating to any ancillary matters; and
   (c) the pursuer seeks to prove those facts by means of affidavits.

(2) The solicitor for the pursuer may, in respect of the work specified in column 1 of Table A below, charge the inclusive fee specified in respect of that work in column 2 of that Table.

(3) Where the pursuer has been represented in respect of work specified in column 1 of Table A below by an Edinburgh solicitor and a solicitor outside Edinburgh, the Auditor may, where he is satisfied that it was appropriate for the pursuer to be so represented, allow the inclusive fee specified in column 3 instead of the inclusive fee specified in column 2 of that Table.

[13,18] TABLE A

Column 1 *Work done*	Column 2 *Inclusive fee* £	Column 3 *Discretionary inclusive fee Edinburgh solicitor and solicitor outside Edinburgh* £
1. All work to and including calling of the summons	635.45	725.70
2. All work from calling to and including swearing affidavits	451.85	548.55
3. All work from swearing affidavits to and including sending extract decree	138.65	203.60
4. All work to and including sending extract decree	1225.90	1478.30

2.—(1) This paragraph applies to any undefended action of divorce or separation where—
   (a) the facts set out in section 1(2)(c) (desertion), section 1(2)(d) (two

years' non-cohabitation and consent) or section 1(2)(e) (five years'
non-cohabitation) of the 1976 Act are relied on;
(b) there are no conclusions relating to any ancillary matters; and
(c) the pursuer seeks to prove those facts by affidavit.

(2) The solicitor for the pursuer may, in respect of the work specified in
column 1 of Table B below, charge the inclusive fee specified in respect of
that work in column 2 of that Table.

(3) Where the pursuer has been represented in respect of work specified in
column 1 of Table B below by an Edinburgh solicitor and a solicitor outside
Edinburgh, the Auditor may, where he is satisfied that it was appropriate for
the pursuer to be so represented, allow the inclusive fee specified in respect
of that work in column 3 instead of the inclusive fee specified in column 2 of
that Table.

TABLE B [13,18]

Column 1 *Work done*	Column 2 *Inclusive fee* £	Column 3 *Discretionary* *inclusive fee* *Edinburgh* *solicitor and* *solicitor outside* *Edinburgh* £
1. All work to and including calling of the summons	522.80	613.05
2. All work from calling to and including swearing affidavits	251.50	319.45
3. All work from swearing affidavits to and including sending extract decree	138.65	203.60
4. All work to and including sending extract decree	912.85	1135.80
Add session fee	of 7.5%	of 10%

3. If—
(a) the solicitor for the pursuer charges an inclusive fee under either
paragraph 1 or 2 of this Part, and
(b) the action to which the charge relates includes a conclusion relating
to an ancillary matter,
in addition to that fee he may charge in respect of the work specified in
column 1 of Table C below the inclusive fee specified in respect of that work
in column 2 of that Table.

TABLE C [13,18]

Column 1 *Work done*	Column 2 *Inclusive fee* £
1. All work to and including calling of the summons	118.70
2. All work from calling to and including swearing affidavits	133.20
3. All work under items 1 and 2	251.65

PART IV [13,18]

OUTER HOUSE PETITIONS

£

1. Unopposed petition
   (a) All work including precognitions and all copyings, up to and obtaining extract decree 599.40
   (b) Where the party has been represented by an Edinburgh solicitor and a solicitor outside Edinburgh, the Auditor may, where he is satisfied that it was necessary for the party to be so represented, allow a fee of 830.40
   (c) Outlays including duplicating charges to be allowed in addition.

2. Opposed petition
   (a) All work (other than precognitions) up to and including lodging petition, obtaining and executing warrant for service 441.85
   (b) Outlays including duplicating charges to be allowed in addition.
   [15] (c) Where applicable, charges under paragraphs 1A, 2, 3 and 5 to 21 of Part v. of this Chapter of this table.

3. Reports in opposed petitions
   (a) For each report by the Accountant of Court 67.30
   (b) For any other report, as under paragraph 6 of Part v. of this Chapter of this Table.

4. Obtaining bond of caution 68.60

PART V [13,18]

DEFENDED ACTIONS

£

[6] **1. Instruction**
   (a) All work (apart from precognitions) from commencement until lodgment of open record 613.00
   (b) Instructing re-service where necessary 66.10
   (c) If counterclaim lodged, additional fee for each party 128.95

[6] **1A. Work before action commences**
   All work which the Auditor is satisfied has reasonably been undertaken in contemplation of, or preparatory to, the commencement of proceedings 392.80
   or such other sum as in the opinion of the Auditor is justified.

[6] **2. Record**
   (a) All work in connection with adjustment and closing of record including subsequent work in connection with By Order Adjustment Roll 651.75
   (b) All work as above, so far as applicable, where cause settled or disposed of before record closed 403.20
   (c) If consultation held before record closed, additional fees may be allowed as follows—
       (i) arranging consultation 66.10
       (ii) attendance at consultation, per quarter hour 34.80

£

(d) Additional fee to sub-paragraph (a) or (b) (to include necessary amendments) to the pursuer and existing defender, to be allowed for each pursuer, defender or third party brought in before the record is closed, each of 193.40

(e) If an additional pursuer, defender or third party is brought in after the record is closed, an additional fee shall be allowed to the existing pursuer and the existing defender or defenders, each of 287.10

[15,16] 2A. Notes of Argument

(a) Instructing, perusing and lodging first Note of Arguments (either party) 127.85

(b) Perusing opponent's Note of Arguments 69.60

(c) Instructing, perusing and lodging any further Note of Arguments (either party) 69.60

3. Procedure Roll or hearing

(a) Preparing for hearing including all work incidental work and instruction of counsel 128.95

(b) Attendance fee, per quarter hour 34.80

(c) Advising and work incidental to it 96.45

4. Adjustment of issues and counter-issues

(a) All work in connection with and incidental to the lodging of an issue, and adjustment and approval of it 122.55

(b) If one counter-issue, additional fee to pursuer of 34.80

(c) Where more than one counter-issue, an additional fee to pursuer for each additional counter-issue 17.45

(d) All work in connection with lodging of counter-issue and adjustment and approval of it 122.55

(e) Fee to defender or third party for considering issue where no counter-issue lodged 34.80

(f) Fee to defender or third party for considering each additional counter-issue 17.45

5. Precognitions

Taking and drawing precognitions, per sheet 64.85

[5] *Notes.*

1. *[Revoked by S.I. 1998 No. 264.]*

2. Where a skilled witness prepares his own precognition or report, the solicitor shall be allowed, for perusing it (whether or not in the course of doing so he revises or adjusts it), half of the taking and drawing fee per sheet.

6. Reports obtained under order of court excluding Auditor's report

(a) All work incidental to it 138.90

(b) Additional fee for perusal of report, per quarter hour ..... 19.35 or such other sum as in the opinion of the Auditor is justified.

7. Specification of documents

(a) Instructing counsel, revising and lodging and all incidental procedure to obtain a diligence up to and including obtaining interlocutor 129.00

(b) Fee to opponent 62.65

(ba) Additional fee 121.75

(bb) Fee to opponent 62.65

£

(c) Attendance at execution of commission, per quarter hour, of   34.80
(d) If alternative procedure adopted, a fee per person on whom order served, of 51.60
[11] (e) Fee for perusal of documents recovered under a specification of documents (or by informal means) where not otherwise provided for in the Table of Fees, per quarter hour 34.80

8. Commission to take evidence on interrogatories
(a) Applying for commission to cover all work up to and including lodging report of commission with completed interrogatories and cross-interrogatories 240.30
(b) Fee to opponent if cross-interrogatories lodged 209.80
(c) Fee to opponent if no cross-interrogatories lodged 77.45
(d) In addition to above, fee per sheet to each party for completed interrogatories or cross-interrogatories, including all copies, of 19.35

9. Commission to take evidence on open commissions
(a) Applying for commission up to and including lodging report of commission, but excluding sub-paragraph (c) 287.10
(b) Fee to opponent 128.95
(c) Fee for attendance at execution of commission, per quarter hour, of 34.80

10. Miscellaneous motions and minutes where not otherwise covered by this Part
(a) Where attendance of counsel and/or solicitor not required   34.80
(b) Where attendance of counsel/or solicitor required, inclusive of instruction of counsel, not exceeding half hour 96.45
(c) Thereafter attendance fee, per additional quarter hour 34.85
(d) Instructing counsel for a minute (other than a minute ordered by the court), revising and lodging as a separate step in process including any necessary action 96.45
(e) Perusing a minute of admission or abandonment 34.80

11. Incidental procedure (not chargeable prior to approval of issue or allowance of proof)
Fixing diet, obtaining note on the line of evidence, etc., borrowing and returning process, lodging productions, considering opponent's productions and all other work prior to the consultation on the sufficiency of evidence 364.80

12. Amendment of record
(a) Amendment of conclusions only, fee to proposer 96.45
(b) Amendment of conclusions only, fee to opponent 34.80
(c) Amendment of pleadings after record closed, where no answers to the amendment are lodged, fee to prosper 141.80
(d) In same circumstances, fee to opponent 65.15
(e) Amendment of pleadings after record closed, where answers are lodged, fee for proposer and each party lodging answers   330.30
(f) Fee for adjustment of minute and answers, where applicable, to be allowed in addition to each party, of 183.75

13. Preparation for proof or jury trial (to include fixing consultation on the sufficiency of evidence, fee-funding precept, citing witnesses, all work checking and writing up process and preparing for proof or jury trial)

£

(a) If action settled before proof or jury trial, or lasts only one
day, to include, where applicable, instruction of counsel .. 886.90
(b) For each day or part of day after the first, including
instruction of counsel 79.00
(c) Preparing for adjourned diets and all work incidental to it as
in sub-paragraph (a), if adjourned for more than five days 161.65
(d) If consultation held before proof or jury trial, attendance at
it, per quarter hour 34.80

[6] 14. Copying
For the copying of papers by whatever means—
(a) where a copy is required to be lodged, or sent, in pursuance
of any of rules 4.7, 22.1 and 22.3, such charge as the Auditor
may from time to time determine (and he may make
different provisions for different classes of case); and
(b) in any other case, if the Auditor determines (either or both)
that—
    (i) the copying had to be done in circumstances which were
in some way exceptional;
    (ii) the papers which required to be copied were unusually
numerous having regard to the nature of the cause,
such charge, if any, as the Auditor considers reasonable (but
a charge based on time expended by any person in copying
shall not be allowed).

Notes.
1. Where a determination is required under sub-paragraph (b),
the purpose of copying, the number of copies made and the
charge claimed shall be shown in the account.
2. Copying done other than in the place of business of the
solicitor shall be shown as an outlay.

Note. When copied by photostatic or similar process, each page to
be charged as one sheet.

15. Settlement
(a) Settlement by tender
    (i) Lodging or considering first tender 193.40
    (ii) Lodging or considering each further tender 128.95
    (iii) If tender accepted, an additional fee to each accepting
party 128.95
(b) Extrajudicial settlement—advising on, negotiating and
agreeing extrajudicial settlement (not based on judicial
tender) to include preparation and lodging of joint minute 322.60
(c) The Auditor may allow a fee in respect of work undertaken
with a view to settlement (whether or not settlement is in fact
agreed), including offering settlement, of 548.40
(d) 34.80

16. Hearing limitation fee
To include all work undertaken with a view to limiting the
matters in dispute or limiting the scope of any hearing, and
including exchanging documents, precognitions and expert
reports, agreeing any fact, statement or document, and
preparing and lodging any joint minute 685.65

17. Proof or jury trial
Attendance fee, per quarter hour 34.80

£

18. Accounts
    (a) To include framing, adjusting and lodging account 208.80
[15,16](b) To include considering Notes of Objections, and generally
        preparing for taxation 208.80
[15,16](c) Attendance at taxation, per quarter hour 34.80

19. Ordering and obtaining extract 51.60

20. Final procedure
    (a) If case goes to proof or jury trial, or is settled within 14 days
        before the diet of proof or jury trial, to include all work to
        close of cause so far as not otherwise provided for 261.35
    (b) In any other case 79.00

[12,13,18] PART VA

DEFENDED PERSONAL INJURIES ACTIONS COMMENCED ON OR AFTER
1 APRIL 2003

Fee
£

1. Precognitions / Expert Reports / Factual Reports
    (a) Taking and drawing precognitions, per sheet 64.75
    (b) Perusal fee for consideration of Reports (whether or not in
        the course of doing so he revises or adjusts it), half thereof,
        per sheet 32.40

2. Pre-Litigation Fee
All work which the Auditor is satisfied has reasonably been
undertaken in contemplation of, or preparatory to the commencement of proceedings particularly to include communications
between parties in relation to areas of medical/quantum/discussion
re settlement or such other sum as in the opinion of the Auditor is
justified 392.00

3. Instruction
    (a) To cover all work (except as otherwise specially provided for
        in this Chapter) from commencement to the lodging of
        Defences 611.75
    (b) Specification of Documents per Form 43.2-B 85.95
  (ba) Fee to opponent for considering Specification of Documents 62.55
    (c) In the event of the Summons being drafted without the
        assistance of Counsel or a Solicitor-Advocate such further
        fee will be allowed as the Auditor considers appropriate .. 208.45
    (d) Instructing re-service where necessary 66.00
    (e) If counterclaim lodged, additional fee for each party to
        include Answers 208.45
    (f) Arranging commission to recover documents, citing havers,
        instructing Commission and shorthand writer and prepara-
        tion for commission 116.45
    (g) Attendance at execution of commission, per quarter hour of 34.80
    (h) If alternative procedure adopted, a fee per person on whom
        order served of 51.50
    (i) Fee for perusal of documents recovered under a specification
        of Documents (or by informal means) where not otherwise
        provided for in the Table of Fees, per quarter hour 34.80

4. Record
    (a) All work in connection with adjustment and closing of
        record 650.40

Fee
£

(b) All work as above, so far as applicable, where cause settled
    or disposed of before record closed 402.40
(c) If consultation held before record closed, additional fees
    may be allowed as follows—
    (i) arranging consultation 66.00
    (ii) attendance at consultation, per quarter hour 34.80
(d) Additional fee to sub-paragraph (a) or (b), (to include
    necessary Amendments) to the pursuer and existing defen-
    der, to be allowed for each pursuer, defender or third party
    brought in before the record is closed, each of 193.00
(e) If an additional pursuer, defender or third party is brought
    in after the record is closed, an additional fee shall be
    allowed to the existing pursuer and the existing defender or
    defenders, each of 286.60

4A. Notes of Arguments
(a) Instructing, perusing and lodging first Note of Arguments,
    where ordained by the Court (either party) 127.85
(b) Perusing opponent's Notes of Arguments 69.60
(c) Instructing, perusing and lodging any further Note of
    Arguments, where ordained by the Court (either party) 69.60

5. Valuation of claim
(a) Fee to cover Note on Quantum/Valuation of Claim 417.00
(b) Opponent's fee for inspection of Valuation of Claim 208.45
(c) Inspection of documents, per quarter hour 34.80

6. Adjustment of issues and counter-issues
(a) All work in connection with and incidental to the lodging of
    an issue, and adjustment and approval of it 122.30
(b) If one counter-issue, additional fee to pursuer of 34.80

**7. By Order Roll/Variation of timetable order/Adjustment on Final
Decree/Interim Payment of Damages**
(a) Fee to cover preparing and instruction of Counsel, to
    include attendance not exceeding half an hour 96.25
(b) Thereafter attendance fee, per additional quarter hour 34.80
(c) In the event of a separate Advising/Opinion and all work
    incidental thereto 96.25

8. Reports obtained under order of court excluding Auditor's Report
(a) All work incidental to it 138.50
(b) Additional fee for perusal of report, per quarter hour or such
    other sum as in the opinion of the Auditor is justified 19.35

9. Incidental Procedure
(not chargeable prior to approval of issue or allowance of proof)
Noting diet, obtaining note on the line of evidence, etc, borrowing
and returning process, and all other work prior to the consultation
on the sufficiency of evidence 363.95

**10. Specification of documents (if further Specification considered
necessary)**
(a) Instructing counsel, revising and lodging and all incidental
    procedure to obtain a diligence up to and including
    obtaining interlocutor 128.75
(b) Fee to opponent 62.55

Fee
£

(c) Arranging commission to recover documents, citing havers, instructing commissioner and shorthand writer and preparation for commission 116.45
(ca) Fee to opponent 62.65
(d) Attendance at execution of commission, per quarter hour, of 34.80
(e) If alternative procedure adopted, a fee per person on whom order served, of 51.50
(f) Fee for perusal of documents recovered under a specification of documents (or by informal means) where not otherwise provided for in the Table of Fees, per quarter hour 34.80

11. Commission to take evidence on interrogatories
(a) Applying for commission to cover all work up to and including lodging report of commission with completed interrogatories and cross-interrogatories 260.85
(b) Fee to opponent if cross-interrogatories lodged 209.35
(c) Fee to opponent if no cross-interrogatories lodged 78.00
(d) In addition to above, fee per sheet to each party for completed interrogatories or cross-interrogatories, including all copies, of 19.35

12. Commission to take evidence on open commission
(a) Applying for commission up to and including lodging report of commission, but excluding sub-paragraph (c) 286.60
(b) Fee to opponent 128.75
(c) Fee for attendance at execution of commission, per quarter hour, of 34.80

13. Miscellaneous motions and minutes where not otherwise covered by this Part
(a) Where attendance of counsel and/or solicitor not required 34.80
(b) Where attendance of counsel and/or solicitor required inclusive of instruction of counsel, not exceeding half hour 99.15
(c) Thereafter attendance fee, per quarter hour 34.80
(d) Instructing counsel for a minute/note on further procedure (if applicable), revising and lodging as a separate step in process including any necessary action 96.25
(e) Perusing a minute of admission or abandonment/note ordered by Court/notice of grounds 34.80

14. Amendment of record
(a) Amendment of conclusions only, fee to proposer 96.25
(b) Amendment of conclusions only, fee to opponent 34.80
(c) Amendment of pleadings after record closed, where no answers to the amendment are lodged, fee to proposer 141.60
(d) In same circumstances, fee to opponent 65.05
(e) Amendment of pleadings after record closed, where answers are lodged, fee for proposer and each party lodging answers 329.50
(f) Fee for adjustment of minute and answers, where applicable, to be allowed in addition to each party, of 183.40

15. Copying
For the copying of papers by whatever means—
(a) where a copy is required to be lodged—or sent, in pursuance of any Rules 4.7, 22.1 and 22.3, such charge as the Auditor may from time to time determine (and he may make different provision for different classes of case); and

Fee
£

(b) in any other case, if the Auditor determines (either or both) that—
   (i) the copying had to be done in circumstances which were in some way exceptional;
   (ii) the papers which required to be copied were unusually numerous having regard to the nature of the cause, such charge, if any, as the Auditor considers reasonable (but a charge based on time expended by any person in copying shall not be allowed).

Notes.
   1. Where a determination is required under sub-paragraph (b), the purpose of copying, the number of copies made and the charge claimed shall be shown in the account.
   2. Copying done other than in the place of business of the solicitor shall be shown as an outlay.

16. Preparation for proof or jury trial
(to include fixing consultation on the sufficiency of evidence, fee-funding precept, citing witnesses, all work checking and writing up process and preparing for proof or jury trial)
   (a) If action settled before proof or jury trial, or lasts only one day, to include where applicable, instruction of counsel ...   885.10
   (b) For each day or part of day after the first, including instruction of counsel 78.80
   (c) Preparing for adjourned diets and all work incidental to it as in sub-paragraph (a), if adjourned for more than five days   161.15
   (d) If consultation held before proof or jury trial, attendance at it, per quarter hour 34.80

17. Pre-trial meeting
   (a) Fee arranging pre-trial meeting (each occasion) 66.00
   (b) Fee preparing for pre-trial meeting 347.50
   (c) Fee attending pre-trial meeting, per quarter hour 34.80
   (d) Joint Minute of pre-trial meeting—
      (i) in respect of Section 1 only 107.35
      (ii) in respect of Sections 1 and 2 only 214.60
      (iii) in respect of Sections 1 and 3 only 249.75
      (iv) in respect of Sections 1, 2 and 3 only 321.95

18. Hearing limitation fee
For any work undertaken to limit matters in dispute not otherwise provided for—subject to details being provided 278.10

19. Settlement
   (a) Settlement by tender
      (i) Lodging or considering first tender 193.10
      (ii) Lodging or considering each further tender 128.75
      (iii) If tender accepted, an additional fee to each accepting party 128.75
   (b) Extrajudicial settlement—advising on, negotiating and agreeing extrajudicial settlement (not based on judicial tender or joint minute) to include preparation and lodging of joint minute 321.95
   (c) The Auditor may allow a fee in respect of work undertaken with a view to settlement (whether or not settlement is in fact agreed), including offering settlement, of 547.15

Fee
£

(d) If consultation held to consider tender, extrajudicial settlement (not based on judicial tender) or with a view to settlement (whether or not settlement is in fact agreed), attendance at it, per quarter hour 34.80

20. Proof or jury trial
Attendance fee, per quarter hour 34.80

21. Accounts
(a) Preparation of judicial account, to include production of vouchers and adjustment of expenses 278.10
(b) Perusal of points of objections, per quarter hour 23.15
(c) Attendance at taxation, per quarter hour 23.15

22. Ordering and obtaining extract 51.50

23. Final procedure
(a) If case goes to proof or jury trial, or is settled within 14 days before the diet of proof or jury trial, to include all work to close of cause so far as not otherwise provided for 260.85
(b) In any other case 78.55

PART VI [13,18]

INNER HOUSE BUSINESS

£

1. Reclaiming motions
(a) Fee for appellant for all work up to interlocutor sending cause to roll 193.40
(b) Fee for respondent 96.45
(c) Additional fee for each party for preparing or revising every 50 pages of Appendix 80.90

2. Appeals from inferior courts
(a) Fee for appellant 233.75
(b) Fee for respondent 115.85
(c) Additional fee for each party for preparing or revising every 50 pages of Appendix 79.00

3. Summar Roll
(a) Preparing for discussion and instructing counsel 193.45
(b) Attendance fee, per quarter hour 34.80

4. Other matters
Where applicable, charges under Part v. of this Chapter of this Table.

5. Special cases, Inner House petitions and appeals other than under paragraph 2 of this Part
According to circumstances of the case.

6. Obtaining bond of caution 79.00

PART VII

ADMIRALTY AND COMMERCIAL CAUSES, MERCANTILE SEQUESTRATIONS AND APPLICATIONS FOR SUMMARY TRIAL UNDER SECTION 26 OF THE ACT OF 1988 AND CAUSES REMITTED FROM THE SHERIFF COURT

Charges under this Part shall be based on this Table according to the circumstances.

PART VIII

SOLICITORS EXERCISING RIGHTS OF AUDIENCE UNDER SECTION 25 OF THE SOLICITORS (SCOTLAND) ACT 1980

1. The Auditor shall allow to a solicitor who exercises a right of audience by virtue of section 25A of the Solicitors (Scotland) Act 1980 such fee for each item of work done by the solicitor in the exercise of such right as he would allow to counsel for an equivalent item of work.

2. Where a solicitor exercises a right of audience by virtue of section 25A of the Solicitors (Scotland) Act 1980, and is assisted by another solicitor or a clerk, the Auditor may also allow attendance fees in accordance with Parts IV and V of this Chapter of this Table.

PART IX

GENERAL

The Auditor shall have power to apportion the foregoing fees in this Chapter between parties' solicitors in appropriate circumstances or to modify them in the case of a solicitor acting for more than one party in the same cause or in the case of the same solicitor acting in more than one cause arising out of the same circumstances or in the event of a cause being settled or disposed of at a stage when the work covered by an inclusive fee has not been completed.

[2,3,4,8,10,12,14,17,20] CHAPTER IV

TRANSCRIPTS OF EVIDENCE ETC.

	£
1. Attendance of shorthand writer	
Attendance by shorthand writer at proof, jury trial or commission, per hour, with a minimum fee of £140.04 per day	35.03
2. Notes of evidence: extension by shorthand writer or transcriber	
(a) Except where these are transcribed daily, per sheet	5.73
(b) Where these are transcribed daily, per sheet	7.02
(c) Where notes of evidence have been directed to be supplied for the use of the court, copies may be made available to parties, payable to the shorthand writer or transcriber by the solicitor for the parties obtaining the copies, per sheet	0.46

Notes.

1. Transcripts of evidence will be made only on directions from the court, and the cost of them in defended causes will, in the first instance, be payable by the solicitors for the parties in equal proportions. The daily transcripts of evidence shall be made only if all compearing parties consent. When an undefended cause is continued, or where for other

reasons the court considers it necessary that transcripts be made for the use of the court and so directs, the cost will be borne by the solicitor for the pursuer in the first instance. In any cause where transcripts have not been made but are required for a reclaiming motion, the solicitor for the reclaimer may request that they be made; and when they are thus available they will be lodged in court, the cost of transcription being payable in the first instance by the solicitor for the reclaimer.

2. In any cause where the court, on a motion enrolled for the purpose, certifies that there is reasonable ground for reclaiming and that the reclaimer is unable, for financial reasons, to meet the cost of the necessary transcription from which copies for the use of the Inner House are made, the cost of such transcription will be paid out of public funds.

Deriv. R.C.S. 1965, r. 347(a)(part) substituted by S.I. 1970 No. 1746 and amended by S.I. 1992 No. 1433; and Table of Fees amended by S.I. 1971 No. 1161, 1989 No. 445, 1993 No. 900 and 1357, 1994 Nos 1139 and 1140

[1] Chaps I and III (solicitors' fees) fees substituted by S.I. 1998 No. 2674 (effective 1st December 1998).
[2] Chap. IV (shorthand writers' fees) fees substituted by S.I. 1996 No. 754 (effective 1st May 1996).
[3] Chap. IV amended (and fees in para. 1 increased) by S.I. 1997 No. 1260 (effective 1st May 1997).
[4] Chap. IV amended by S.I. 1998 No. 993 (effective 1st May 1998).
[5] Chap. I, para. 1 notes and Chap. III, Pt V, para. 5 notes amended by S.I. 1995 No. 1376 (effective 22nd June 1995).
[6] Chap. I, para. 1 notes, para. 2 and Chap. III, Pt I, para. 1(b), Pt IV, para. 2(c) and Pt V. paras 1, 2, 5 notes and para. 14 amended by, and Chap. III Pt V, para. 1A inserted by S.I. 1998 No. 2674 (effective 1st December 1998).
[7] Chap. II revoked by S.S.I. 2002 No. 301 (effective 1st July 2002). See now the Act of Sederunt (Rules of the Court of Session Amendment) (Fees of Solicitors, Shorthand Writers and Witnesses) 2002 (S.S.I. 2002 No. 301), Sched. 2 for witnesses' fees (reproduced at page C 1208).
[8] Chap. IV amended by S.I. 1999 No. 615 (effective 1st May 1999).
[9] Chaps I and III amended by S.S.I. 1999 No. 166 (effective 1st January 2000).
[10] Chap. IV amended by S.S.I. 2000 No. 143, para. 2 (effective 1st June 2000).
[11] Table of Fees amended by S.S.I. 2000 No. 450 & Chap. III, Part, para. 7(e) inserted by S.S.I. 2000 No. 450 (effective 1st January 2001); and S.S.I. 2002 No. 301 (effective 1st July, 2002).
[12] As amended by S.S.I. 2001 No. 135, para. 2 (effective 1st May 2001) and by S.S.I. 2002 No. 301, and S.S.I. 2003 No. 194, (effective 1st July 2002 and 1st April 2003 respectively).
[13] As amended by S.S.I. 2005 No. 147, para. 2 (effective 25th April 2005).
[14] As amended by S.S.I. 2005 No. 148, para. 2 (effective 25th April 2005).
[15] Inserted by S.S.I. 2004 No. 151, para. 2 (effective 4th May 2004).
[16] Amended by S.S.I. 2005 No. 147, para. 2 (effective 25th April 2005).
[17] Amended by S.S.I. 2006 No. 87, para. 2 (effective 1st May 2006).
[18] As amended by S.S.I. 2006 No. 294, para. 2 (effective 1st July 2006).
[19] As amended by S.S.I. 2007 No. 86 (effective 1st April 2007).
[20] As amended by S.S.I. 2007 No. 234 (effective 1st May 2007).

42.16.1   *General note.* Since 20th July 1992 the Table of Fees regulates only the charges between party and party. Charges in accounts between a solicitor and his client are regulated by r. 42.7.

Party litigants' expenses are regulated by the Litigants in Person (Costs and Expenses) Act 1975 and para. 2 of the A.S. (Expenses of Party Litigants) 1976 [S.I. 1976 No. 1606]. See, *e.g. Bell v. McGlennan (No. 2)*, 1st Div., 10th June 1994, unreported (1994 G.W.D. 25–1512).

The A.S. (R.C.S.A. No. 3) (Fees of Solicitors) 1998 [S.I. 1998 No. 2674], which came into force on 1st December 1998, makes radical changes to the Table of Fees. There was growing disquiet at the disparity between expenses recoverable from a paying party and the cost of the case to the successful party. Recommendations were made to the Lord President to eliminate the differential between the rates chargeable under the Judicial Table and the General Table. It was also recognised that the Judicial Tables require modernisation. After consulting a wide group of interested parties this A.S. was promulgated. The principal changes are as follows. (1) Rule 42.11 (which provides for a sum to cover posts and incidents) is omitted and a separate charge for posts and incidental expenses is abolished. (2) Rule 42.16 is amended by omitting the first note to para. 1 of Chap. I (which allows copies of precognitions) and, in note 2 of that paragraph, the wording is changed to allow perusal of a skilled witness' precognition or report, "whether or not the solicitor in doing so revives or adjusts it". (3) The copying charges in Chap. I para. 2 are abolished except where a copy of documents is required to be sent or lodged in terms of rr. 4.7 (lodging of documents in Inner House), 22.1 open record) and 22.3 closed record). The auditor is given the discretion to fix the copying rates and he may also allow copying charges where the copying undertaken is "exceptional" or the documents copied "unusually numerous". (4) There are significant increases in the block fees Chap. III Pts I, II, III and IV. (5) In Pt V, a new fee for work before action commences is introduced. The Auditor may award a fee up to £250.00 for "all work which the Auditor is satisfied has reasonably been undertaken in contemplation of, or preparatory to, the commencement of proceedings". Para. 5 is amended in line with Chap. I para. 1, above. Para. 14 (copyings) is abolished and copies are allowed as set out in Chap. I para. 2, above. (6) The repeal of r. 42.11 abolishes the 12 per cent charge for posts and incidental expenses.

Precognitions: Table of Fees, Chap I, para. 1 notes. By A.S. (R.C.A. No. 3) (Fees of Solicitors) **42.16.1A** 1998 [S.I. 1998 No. 2674], no charge may be made, with respect to work on or after 1st December 1998, for copies of precognitions for use by the solicitor or counsel.

The A.S. extends note 2 so that a charge may be made for perusing a precognition or report a skilled witness whether or not the solicitor revises or adjusts it.

Copyings: Table of Fees, Chap I, para. 2. The A.S. (R.C.S.A. No. 3) (Fees of Solicitors) 1998 **42.16.1B** [S.I. 1998 No. 2674] abolishes copying charges in respect of work on or after 1st December 1998 with exceptions. The exceptions are: (1) Copies required under r. 4.7 (lodging of documents in the Inner House, r. 22.1 (open record) and r. 22.3 (closed record) which may be charged at such rate as the Auditor may determine. (2) In any other case, if the Auditor determines that the copying was required in exceptional circumstances and, or, that the papers to be copies were unusually numerous.

Travelling expenses: Table of Fees, Chap. II (Witnesses' Fees), para. 3. Where a party does **42.16.2** not formally agree or abandon a matter requiring proof the other party is entitled to claim the travelling expenses of a necessary witness: *Gow v. Gow* 1987 G.W.D. 24–887.

Chap. II (witnesses' fees) was revoked (in error) and replaced by A.S. (R.C.S.A) (Fees of Solicitors, Shorthand Writers and Witnesses) 2002 [S.S.I. 2002 No. 301] and reinstated by A.S. (R.C.S.A.) (Miscellaneous) 2007 [S.S.I. 2007 No. 7].

Maritime witness: Table of Fees, Chap. II (Witnesses' Fees). See *Ellerman Lines v. Dundee* **42.16.3** *Harbour Trs* 1922 S.C. 646.

Chap. II (witnesses' fees) was revoked (in error), replaced by A.S. (R.C.S.A) (Fees of Solicitors, Shorthand Writers and Witnesses) 2002 [S.S.I. 2002 No. 301] and reinstated by A.S. (R.C.S.A.) (Miscellaneous) 2007 [S.S.I. 2007 No. 7].

Receipts and vouchers: Table of Fees, Chap. II (Witnesses' Fees), para. 6. As the Auditor has **42.16.4** little discretion to allow payments to a witness in the absence of satisfactory vouching, the witness should be specifically requested to obtain and produce receipts in support of his claim: *Goldie v. Mohr* 1993 G.W.D. 1–40.

Chap. II (witnesses' fees) was revoked (in error), replaced by A.S. (R.C.S.A) (Fees of Solicitors, Shorthand Writers and Witnesses) 2002 [S.S.I. 2002 No. 301] and reinstated by A.S. (R.C.S.A.) (Miscellaneous) 2007 [S.S.I. 2007 No. 7].

Account of fees of witnesses: Table of Fees, Chap. II (Witnesses' Fees), para. 7. It is doubtful if **42.16.5** the court has power to increase witness fees since these are promulgated in the name of the whole court: *Mica Insulator Co. Ltd v. Bruce Peebles & Co. Ltd* 1907 S.C. 1293, 1301 *per* L.P. Dunedin.

It is for the Auditor to fix the level of remuneration payable to a skilled witness: *Wilkie v. Scottish Aviation Ltd* 1956 S.C. 198.

A skilled witness should not be told, "your usual fees will be met", when what is intended is that he will be paid only such fees as are allowed by the Auditor on a party-and-party taxation or as otherwise prescribed. If the witness is not prepared to undertake the work on such a basis another witness should be sought, otherwise the solicitor may be liable to the witness for his fee on an agent-and-client basis: *John R. Dick & Co. v. Drummond & Co., W.S.* 1988 G.W.D. 17–749.

A solicitor who cites a witness is personally responsible for the payment of that witness's charges and out-of-pocket expenses: r. 36.2(4). The witness is entitled to receive his travelling expenses and reasonable conduct money in sufficient time to enable him to make arrangements to appear at court on the date on which he is required to attend. In the event of the failure of a witness to appear at the diet to which he has been cited, then if further procedure is required, it will be necessary to exhibit to the court not only proof of timeous citation but also that reasonable conduct money has been paid in a readily negotiable form. Payment of a witness's other out-of-pocket expenses and fees should not be delayed until recovery has been made following on payment of a taxed account.

Chap. II (witnesses' fees) was revoked (in error), replaced by A.S. (R.C.S.A) (Fees of Solicitors, Shorthand Writers and Witnesses) 2002 [S.S.I. 2002 No. 301] and reinstated by A.S. (R.C.S.A.) (Miscellaneous) 2007 [S.S.I. 2007 No. 7].

42.16.6   *Inclusive fee: Table of Fees, Chap. III, Part I (Undefended Causes), para. 1.* A pro forma minute of election is available from the Office of Court which can be attached to the principal writ.

Where a solicitor elects to charge the inclusive fee in para. 1 of Chap. III of the Table of Fees in rule 42.16, only the posts and incidents actually incurred may be charged: r. 42.11.

An amount equal to the VAT may be added to the inclusive fee in para. 1(a): r. 42.12(1).

A "consistorial action" is not synonymous with "family action" although the rules for consistorial actions and all other family actions are now the same (see Chap. 49). A consistorial action is an action between husband and wife involving status.

42.16.7   *Procedure Roll or hearing: Table of Fees, Chap. III, Part v. (Defended Actions), para. 3.* As a "hearing" does not require the leading of evidence, charges for the attendance of witnesses will not be allowed unless the court otherwise orders.

42.16.7A   *Work before action commences: Table of Fees, Chap. IV, Pt V, para. 1A.* This provision, for a charge for work undertaken in contemplation of, or in preparation to, the commencement of proceeding, was introduced by A.S. (R.C.S.A no. 3) (Fees of Solicitors) 1998 [SI 1998/2674]. It applies to work done on or after 1st December 1998.

42.16.8   *Precognitions: Table of Fees, Chap. III, Part v. (Defended Actions), para. 5.* Where neither party was found entitled to the expenses of a first jury trial nevertheless the party successful after a second trial was found entitled to the precognitions taken for the first trial: *McKnight v. General Motor Carrying Co. Ltd* 1936 S.L.T. 289.

Charges for precognitions were revoked by A.S. (R.C.S. No. 2) (Fees of Solicitors) 1995 [S.I. 1995 No. 1396]. The original note in the R.C.S. 1965 applied to attendances and precognitions. In the R.C.S. 1994, charges for attendances are dealt with in r. 42.13. The implication of leaving precognitions in the note was that if a witness's name is not recorded in the minute of proceedings then charges for that witness's precognition would be disallowed. This implication was not intended and had never been the practice. The charge for any precognition is entirely in the discretion of the Auditor, the test being one of reasonableness in the circumstances.

By A.S. (R.C.A. No. 3) (Fees of Solicitors) 1998 [S.I. 1998 No. 2674], note 1 is revoked and no charge may be made, with respect to work on or after 1st December 1998, for copies of precognitions for use by the solicitor or counsel.

The A.S. extends note 2 so that a charge may be made for perusing a precognition or report a skilled witness whether or not the solicitor revises or adjusts it. In *Delaney v. Finlay Park t/a Park Hutchison,* September 27, 2002, 2002 G.W.D. 30 1045 (OH), para.[8], Temp. Judge. Coutts, Q.C., considered, *obiter,* that it was not a pre-requisite for the court to certify a witness as a skilled witness for the purposes of the auditor allowing a fee under note 2 to para. 5.

42.16.9   *Specification of documents: Table of Fees, Chap. III, Part v. (Defended Actions), para. 7.* It may not always be reasonable to instruct counsel to examine a haver unless there is a matter of nicety or special importance: *Fairley v. McGowan* (1836) 14 S. 470. The haver is entitled to payment of his reasonable charges before being called on to produce under a specification and for his trouble in searching out documents called, but not for copying extracts unless specially requested by the party citing him (who should therefore make that clear to the haver): *Forsyth v. Pringle Taylor & Lamond Lowson* (1906) 14 S.L.T. 658.

Parties should be represented locally at commissions to examine havers: *Tennant, Walker & Co. v. Hannay & Sons* (1874) 1 R. 440.

A.S. (R.C.S.A. No.8) (Fees of Solicitors) 2000 [S.S.I. 2000 No. 450] inserted a new provision (para. 7(e)) allowing an agent to charge for perusing documents recovered under a specification, or by informal means, where not otherwise provided for in the Table of Fees. A.S. (R.C.S.A.No.5) (Fees of Solicitors) 2001 [SSI 2001/441] inserted para. 7(ba) allowing a new fee for work done up to the commission.

42.16.9A   *Incidental procedure fee: Table of Fees, Chap. III, Part v. (Defended Actions), para. 11.* As to the importance of a note on the line of evidence, see (1948) 64 S.L.Rev. 53.

42.16.10   *Copyings: Table of Fees, Chap. III, Part v. (Defended Actions), para. 14.* Until 1st December, 1998 the position was thus. The court and the Auditor discouraged any unnecessary copyings: *McIntyre v. Munro* 1989 S.C.L.R. 766 (Notes). In *Main v. McAndrew Wormald Ltd* 1988 S.L.T. 141, 143, Lord McDonald noted that it is the skilled witness's own direct experience which is of prime importance and only when it is to be challenged may there be need for him to refer to published work. Parties should therefore ascertain, in advance of copying, to what extent any material requires to be copied. This also applies to the copying, as distinct from the lodging, of medical records. A skilled medical witness can be asked when preparing a report to indicate which parts of the medical records he will require to be copied in the event of there not being agreement on the matters contained in them: *McIntyre*, above. Failure to make any prior enquiry of other parties about copying of documents may result in copying charges being disallowed, in whole or part. See also, Hearing limitation fee, Table of Fees, Chap. III, Pt V, para. 16 and note 42.16.11.

The A.S. (R.C.S.A. No. 3) (Fees of Solicitors) 1998 [S.I. 1998 No. 2674] abolishes copying charges in respect of work on or after 1st December 1998 with exceptions. The exceptions are: (1) Copies required under r. 4.7 (lodging of documents in the Inner House, r. 22.1 (open record) and r. 22.3 (closed record) which may be charged at such rate as the Auditor may determine; (2) In any case, if the Auditor determines that the copying was required in exceptional circumstances and, or, that the papers to be copies were unusually numerous.

Settlement: Table of Fees, Chap.III, Part V, (Defender Actions), para. 15. For the avoidance of doubt, A.S. (R.C.S.A.No.5) (Fees of Solicitors) 2001 [S.S.I. 2001 No. 441] added sub-para. (d) to make it clear that a fee is chargeable for considering a tender or extra-judicial settlement at a consultation.   **42.16.10A**

Hearing limitation fee: Table of Fees, Chap. III, Part v. (Defended Actions), para. 16. The Auditor encourages and recognises the fullest use of this term and expects the successful party to demonstrate to him that every reasonable effort has been made to minimise expense by endeavouring to agree as much as possible with the other party: *Boal v. Newalls Insulation Co. Ltd* 1994 S.C.L.R. 534.   **42.16.11**

Ordering and obtaining extract: Table of Fees, Chap. III, Part v. (Defended Actions), para. 19. Although the work has not been done at the time of the taxation, the item must be included in the account for it cannot be recovered later if an extract is required of the taxed amount of expenses. In the event of payment being made before an extract has been ordered then the paying party may deduct this charge from the amount of the taxed account together with the appropriate proportion of the session fee, posts and incidents and value added tax: *Allan v. Allan's Trs* (1851) 13 D. 1270. The fee fund dues of an extract decree are added by the Extractor to the taxed amount of expenses.   **42.16.12**

Commercial actions: Table of Fees, Chap. III, Part VII. In commercial actions, the procedure may not take the form of traditional pleadings. The system depends on co-operation of parties to make proper use of the resources of the court and to disclose the basis on which the litigation proceeds. They require a thorough analysis of the issues before action is initiated, and a party's failure to focus the issues in dispute at an early stage may result in an award of expenses being made against that party on an agent and client basis for any wasted procedure: *North East Ice & Cold Storage Co. Ltd v. Third*, 4th June 1996, unreported (1996 G.W.D. 27–1616).   **42.16.13**

Shorthand writers; transcripts of evidence: Table of Fees, Chapter IV. From April 1, 1997, proceedings formerly recorded by a shorthand writer are recorded by mechanical means: Notice [*sic*], 6th March, 1997. Chapter IV of the Table of Fees has been amended by A.S. (R.C.S.A. No. 5) (Transcripts of Evidence and Attendance Fees for Shorthand Writers etc.) 1997 [S.I. 1997 No. 1260] to reflect this change. The notes to Chapter IV and to the Notice, 6th March 1997 are not clear, but presumably as shorthand writers will record evidence where (and only where) daily transcripts are consented to.   **42.16.14**

PART III

FEES IN SPECULATIVE CAUSES

Fees of solicitors in speculative causes

42.17.—(1) Where—
  (a) any work is undertaken by a solicitor in the conduct of a cause for a client,
  (b) the solicitor and client agree that the solicitor shall be entitled to a fee for the work only if the client is successful in the cause, and
  (c) the agreement is that the fee of the solicitor for all work in connection with the cause is to be based on an account prepared as between party and party,

the solicitor and client may agree that the fees element in that account shall be increased by a figure not exceeding 100 per cent.

(2) The client of the solicitor shall be deemed to be successful in the cause where—

(a) the cause has been concluded by a decree which, on the merits, is to any extent in his favour;

(b) the client has accepted a sum of money in settlement of the cause; or

(c) the client has entered into a settlement of any other kind by which his claim in the cause has been resolved to any extent in his favour.

(3) In paragraph (1), "the fees element" means all the fees in the account of expenses of the solicitor—

(a) for which any other party in the cause other than the client of the solicitor has been found liable as taxed or agreed between party and party;

(b) before the deduction of any award of expenses against the client; and

(c) excluding the sums payable to the solicitor in respect of—

(i) any fees payable for copying documents and the proportion of any session fee in the Table of Fees and posts and incidental expenses under rule 42.11;

(ii) any additional fee allowed under rule 42.14 to cover the responsibility undertaken by the solicitor in the conduct of the cause; and

(iii) any charges by the solicitor for his outlays.

Deriv. R.C.S. 1965, r. 350A inserted by S.I. 1992 No. 1898

General note. R.42.17 (formerly R.C.S. 1965, r. 350A) arises out of s. 61A(3) of the Solicitors **42.17.1** (Scotland) Act 1980 (inserted by s. 36(3) of the Law Reform (Miscellaneous Provisions) (Scotland) Act 1990), which provides for a solicitor and his client to agree, in relation to a litigation undertaken on a speculative basis, that in the event of success the solicitor's fee chargeable against his client may be increased by such a percentage as has been agreed. The uplift is based on the taxed or agreed expenses recovered from the paying party but excluding copyings and any additional fee allowed.

In relation to the fees of counsel a similar rule for an increase not exceeding 100 per cent is provided for in A.S. (Fees of Advocates in Speculative Actions) 1992 [S.I. 1992 No. 1897].

Special provisions in relation to particular proceedings

[1] CHAPTER 43

ACTIONS OF DAMAGES FOR, OR ARISING FROM, PERSONAL INJURIES

Application and interpretation of this chapter

[1,2] **43.1.**—(1) Subject to rule 43.1A (actions based on clinical negligence) this Chapter applies to a personal injuries action.

(2) In this Chapter—

"connected person" means a person, not being a party to the action, who has title to sue the defender in respect of the personal injuries from which a deceased died or in respect of his death;

"personal injuries" includes any disease or impairment, whether physical or mental;

"personal injuries action" means an action of damages for, or arising from, personal injuries or death of a person from personal injuries; and

"relative" has the meaning assigned to it in Schedule 1 to the Damages (Scotland) Act 1976.

[1] (3) The following rules shall not apply to an action to which this Chapter applies—

rule 4.9(2) (prorogation of time for lodging document),

rule 6.2 (fixing and allocation of diets in Outer House)
rule 13.2 (form of summonses),
rule 13.6A(1)(a) (arrestment to found jurisdiction),
rule 13.7 (service and intimation of summonses),
rule 13.13(6) (falling of instance),
rule 18.1(1)(b) (defences to include pleas-in-law),
rule 22.1 (making up open record),
rule 22.2 (adjustment),
rule 22.3 (closing record),
rule 36.3 (lodging productions).

Deriv. R.C.S. 1965, r. 75A(2) substituted by S.I. 1984 No. 920 and amended by S.I. 1986 No. 1941 (r. 43.1(2) (part))

---

[1] Chap. 43 and r. 43.1 substituted by S.S.I. 2002 No. 570 (effective 1st April 2003) and r. 43.1(3) substituted by S.S.I. 2004 No. 291 (effective 29th June 2004).
[2] Rule 43.1 amended by S.S.I. 2007 No. 282 (effective 2nd May 2007).

43.1.1   *General note.* In respect of actions commenced (on the meaning of which see notes 13.2.8(A) and 13.4.4) on or after 1st April 2003, new *obligatory* rules for all actions of reparation for personal injuries or death of a relative were introduced by A.S. (R.C.S.A. No. 2) (Personal Injuries Actions) 2002 [S.S.I. 2002 No. 570]. The former Chap. 43 still applies to actions commenced before 1st April 2003.

The old Chap. 43 had six parts, Part v. of which contained the Optional Procedure Rules introduced in 1985. The new Chap. 43 applies to all actions of damages for, or arising from, personal injuries or death of a person from personal injuries. These rules are obligatory, that is, they apply in all such actions unless a motion is made successfully under r. 43.5, after defences have been lodged, to have the action proceed as an ordinary action. There are no distinct or discreet parts in the new chapter, and the former Parts dealing with connected persons, interim damages and further damages have been tacked on to the end of the chapter and provisions for provisional damages are subsumed into r. 43.2(2).

The new Chap. 43 has been some seven years in gestation and is considerably watered down from the detailed proposals in 1995. The story begins with the publication of the Cullen *Review of Business of the Outer House of the Court of Session* in December 1995. That review contained radical proposals for reform with 63 recommendations. The then Lord President (Hope of Craighead) accepted the recommendations and resolved to bring the reforms into effect in stages. Some of the reforms were implemented in 1996, *e.g.* permitting notices to admit before proof is allowed (Chap. 28A) and averments about medical treatment and lodging of medical reports (rr. 43.29–43.31 in Pt VI of old Chap. 43). The more radical proposals, including abbreviated pleadings and case management in all actions, were postponed to a later stage. That never happened. In January 1997 some judges expressed concern about case management hearings in all defended actions as just another expensive layer of procedure. The new Lord President (by this time Rodger of Earlsferry) set up a working party on Court of Session procedure under Lord Coulsfield in October 1997. The remit was to consider whether a simplified procedure eliminating unnecessary delay and expense could be devised for routine cases.

The working party produced its report in 2000 (www.scotcourts.gov.uk/session/report/coulreport.htm). The working party ascertained that over a three-week period, of 97 cases, 71 were routine of which 57 were personal injury cases. In personal injury and death actions, it is the case that 98.2 per cent settle before proof; one-third of those being in the week before proof. Also, apparently, such cases take on average two years to reach a conclusion. That report recommended limited reforms in relation only to personal injury reparation actions and abandoned the Cullen proposal for case management by the court. Late settlement is a cause of inconvenience to the courts, the parties and other litigants. The working party wished to replicate the circumstances that brought about late settlement at an earlier stage, including the exchange of information about quantum which could lead to settlement. The proposals were for (1) an automatic timetable triggered by the lodging of defences; (2) policing or monitoring by the court (which seemed to be limited to reminding parties what the next automatic stage is); (3) discouraging sists, and in particular the granting of sists for legal aid except on cause shown; (4) action following a failure to comply with a procedural step (limited to requiring an explanation); (5) initially, minimal pleadings; (6) automatic recovery of documents; (7) both parties to lodge a valuation of the claim; (8) a pre-trial settlement meeting between the parties; and (9) judgments within eight weeks of the conclusion of the proof. Any notion that the judiciary should be pro-active in litigation has been abandoned in favour of a principle of minimum intervention (which explains the limited policing role). Case management consists of an automatic timetable. The optional procedure rules restricting the number of experts (*contra* England & Wales) and listing witnesses is allegedly not followed, having been seen to be too restrictive. Although initially a success, by this time the Optional Procedure Rules had, apparently, fallen into disfavour as having a relatively rigid structure together with the inconsistent approach by the judges including their approach to vague pleadings. It is imagined that judges will adopt a consistent approach in relation to the new rules, which they did not do with the Optional Procedure Rules, particularly with regard to simple pleadings. As the working party recognises, however, it is not a change of rules that will produce consistency.

The proposals in the *Report of the Working Party on Court of Session Procedure* (referred to in this chapter as "the 2000 Report") were rejected by the Rules Council which endorsed the view that more than skeletal pleadings were necessary. A representative group of the working party was asked by the Lord President (now Lord Cullen) to meet again. In July 2002 the Group presented a supplementary report to the Lord President (www.scotcourts.gov.uk/session/report/supplementary.htm). That report endorsed the working party's approach and reiterated the need for short pleadings that excluded stylistic standard phrases and ritual incantations (which one might think were the hallmark of short pleadings!). The group considered that "pleadings should be couched in such a way as to requiring individual answers to individual averments of fact", which "discouraged general denials". This *crie de coeur* has been made in note 13.2.4 since the Annotations were first published in 1994. The Group provided illustrations of appropriate pleadings. Finally, the rules were promulgated together with a practice note (P.N. No. 2 of 2003) and new fees for solicitors in A.S. (R.C.S.A.) (Fees of Solicitors) 2003 [S.S.I. 2003 No. 194].

A users' group is to be set up to monitor the effectiveness of the new rules.

"personal injuries action". Notwithstanding the title of the chapter, Chap. 43 applies to actions **43.1.2** in relation to death of a relative from personal injuries. The definition of "personal injuries action" includes actions of "damages for, or *arising from*, personal injuries or death of a person from personal injuries". Does this mean that an action of damages, against a solicitor arising out of his failure to raise an action of damages for personal injuries, is an action of damages *arising from* personal injuries? In *Mackenzie v. Digby Brown & Co.,* 1992 S.L.T. 891, it was held that the expression "an action of damages for personal injuries" in old r. 43.8 (about interim damages) did not include such an action. An action of that kind could, however, be said to *arise from* personal injuries, although remote and not directly. It is to be hoped that it is not a natural consequence of personal injuries that the subsequent and consequent action is not raised timeously. P.N. No. 2 of 2003 offers no guidance, indicating only that it is not intended that "actions of defamation or any *similar* actions" should be covered by Chap. 43. Insofar as it is relevant to an interpretation of the definition, the 2000 Report states in the sixth paragraph of Chap. 1 (introductory) that it devised a scheme to deal with routine reparation actions. In *Tudhope v. Finlay Park t/a Park Hutchison, Solicitors,* 2003 S.L.T. 1305 (OH), however, at the time of lodging the summons it was held, relying on *Mackenzie,* above, the Working Party Reports and P.N. No.2 of 2003, that an action for professional negligence in a personal injuries action was an action "arising from" personal injuries. But in this case at 2004 S.L.T. 783 (OH), on the defender's motion to have the case withdrawn from Chap. 43, it was held that the action was not one for personal injuries and the action was appointed to proceed as an ordinary action.

The definition of personal injuries includes "any disease or impairment whether physical or mental": r. 43.1(2). The definition in old Chap. 43 is that used in s. 10(1) of the Damages (Scotland) Act 1976 (dealing with death claims) and s. 13(1) of the Administration of Justice Act 1982 (which introduced provisional damages): *i.e.* "any disease or any impairment of a person's physical or mental condition". It is not clear that any difference of meaning was intended in the new definition; but it is also not clear why a slightly different definition, from that found in statutes in this area, is used.

An action for damages for harassment is not an action for personal injuries; a distinction has to be made between actions, which in a broad sense might be described as actions, of damages for personal injuries and those which fell within the narrow definition of "personal injuries" in r. 43.1(2): *G v. S,* 2006 S.L.T. 795 (OH).

Non-application of certain rules. For obvious reasons, certain general rules are inapplicable to **43.1.3** the new procedure; and these are listed in r. 43.1(3). It is not entirely clear, however, why arrestment to found jurisdiction is excluded from personal injuries actions in Chap. 43. Is a pursuer to be denied the right to subject a person to the jurisdiction of the court who would not otherwise be subject to it? Since one cannot apply to have the action proceed as an ordinary action until defences have been lodged (see r. 43.5), it may be too late by then.

Jurisdiction. For jurisdiction in delict, see note 13.2.8(A) and (B) Rule, Ground (3).   **43.1.4**

Actions based on clinical negligence

[1] **43.1A.**—(1) At the same time as a summons which includes a draft interlocutor in Form 43.1A is presented for signeting, a pursuer may apply by motion for authority to raise a personal injuries action which is based on alleged clinical negligence as an ordinary action.

(2) On the making of a motion under paragraph (1), the summons shall be placed before a Lord Ordinary in chambers and in the absence of the parties.

(3) On consideration of the summons in accordance with paragraph (2), the Lord Ordinary may—

(a) if he considers that there are exceptional reasons for not following the procedure in the other rules in this Chapter such as would justify the granting of a motion under rule 43.5(1) (application to have action withdrawn from personal injuries procedure), grant authority for the cause to proceed as an ordinary action by signing the draft interlocutor in the summons; or

(b) fix a hearing.

(4) The Keeper of the Rolls shall notify the parties of the date and time of any hearing under paragraph (3)(b).

(5) At a hearing under paragraph (3)(b), the Lord Ordinary may refuse the application or, if he considers that there are exceptional reasons for not following the procedure in this Chapter such as would justify the granting of a motion under rule 43.5(1) (application to have action withdrawn from personal injuries procedure), grant authority for the cause to proceed as an ordinary action by signing the draft interlocutor in the summons.

(6) The other rules of this Chapter shall not apply to a cause commenced by a summons in respect of which a Lord Ordinary has granted an application under paragraph (1).

(7) In this rule—

"clinical negligence" means a breach of a duty of care by a health care professional in connection with that person's diagnosis or the care or treatment of any person, by act or omission, whilst the health care professional was acting in his professional capacity; and

"health care professional" includes doctors, dentists, nurses, midwives, health visitors, pharmacy practitioners, registered ophthalmic practitioners, registered dispensing opticians, members of Professions Allied to Medicine, members of the Allied Health Professions, ambulance personnel, laboratory staff and relevant technicians.

---

[1] Rule 43.1A inserted by S.S.I. 2007 No. 282 (effective 2nd May 2007).

43.1A.1   *General note.* By including the draft interlocutor in Form 43.1A and enrolling a motion under r.43.1A(1), a personal injury action involving clinical negligence (defined in r.43.1A(7)) may be removed from the special Chap. 43 procedure, and be treated as an ordinary action if the motion is granted for "exceptional reasons".

43.1A.2   *"motion".* For motions, see Chap. 23.

Form of summons

[1] **43.2.**—(1) The summons shall be in Form 43.2-A and there shall be annexed to it a brief statement containing—

(a) averments in numbered paragraphs relating only to those facts necessary to establish the claim; and

(b) the names of every medical practitioner from whom, and every hospital or other institution in which, the pursuer or, in an action in respect of the death of a person, the deceased received treatment for the personal injuries.

(2) An application for an order under section 12(2)(a) of the Administration of Justice Act 1982 (provisional damages for personal injuries) shall

be made by including in the summons a conclusion for provisional damages; and, where such an application is made, averments as to the matters referred to in paragraphs (a) and (b) of section 12(1) of that Act shall be included in the statement made under paragraph (1)(a).

(3) In paragraph (2) above "provisional damages" means the damages referred to in section 12(4)(a) of the Administration of Justice Act 1982.

(4) A summons may include—

(a) warrants for intimation in so far as permitted under these Rules; and

(b) a specification of documents in Form 43.2-B.

(5) In relation to an action to which this Chapter applies, any references to the condescendence of a summons and to articles of the condescendence shall be construed as a reference to the statement required under paragraph (1) above and numbered paragraphs of that statement.

Deriv. R.C.S. 1965, r. 134B inserted by S.I. 1984 No. 919 (r. 43.2(2)).

---

[1] R.43.2 substituted by S.S.I. 2002 No. 570 (effective 1st April, 2003).

General note. On the introduction of the new Chap. 43 and this rule, see note 43.1.1. Rule 13.2 **43.2.1** (form of summons) does not apply.

Summons in Form 43.2-A. A summons no longer has a condescendence (with articles) **43.2.2** attached to it or pleas-in-law, but simply a statement of claim (not facts) with numbered paragraphs. It seems a pity to dispense with the word condescendence, as if a change of name will produce a change of practice P.N. No. 3 of 2004 confirms that pleas-in-law should not be inserted in pleadings.

The new brief form of statement of claim is remarkably similar to the old optional procedure Form 43.18, a style to which the judges, according to the 2000 Report, were inconsistent in demanding adherence. P.N. No. 2 of 2003 quotes from the 2000 Report and the Supplementary Report as to what is required: "the briefest description of the events on which the claim is based together with a brief indication of the ground for alleged kindly specific reference to any statutory provision". The detail of the financial aspects of the claim will be in the statement of value of claim (see r. 43.9). The supplementary report contains three illustrations of the new style of brief pleading. It is not entirely clear how brief pleadings can be "couched in such a way as to require individual answers to particular averments of fact", as stated in the supplementary report: that requires a large number of detailed paragraphs. The requirement in r. 43.2(1)(a) to aver facts "necessary to establish the claim" should be observed with care; failure to aver sufficient facts could result in the pursuer being denied issues for jury trial: see, eg, *Higgins v. DHL International (UK) Ltd*, 2003 S.L.T. 1301 (OH) (insufficient facts pled).

Under the old optional procedure rules, it was said that the requirement of fair notice in a broad rather than a narrow technical sense is one which should be reasonably met: *McFarnon v. British Coal Corporation*, 1988 S.L.T. 242 (OH), 243B *per* Lord Murray; and see *Rodgers v. British Steel plc*, 1990 S.L.T. 642 (OH) where an alternative case not pled could not be advanced.

Form 42.2-A contains no pleas-in-law. Chap. 43 makes no provision for defences; accordingly, r. 18.1 applies and defences in a Chap. 43 action should contain please-in-law, although they frequently do not. There is nothing in Chap. 43 about the defences having to be brief.

The following example of a statement of claim (with modifications to style of layout, grammar, syntax and punctuation) is taken from one of the illustrations in the Supplementary Report. The illustration uses letters of the alphabet; *e.g.* paras 1–11 below were 1A–1K. That system has not been followed here, although a hint of it as a possibility is to be found in para. 12.

STATEMENT OF CLAIM

1. On 3rd June 1998 the pursuer was a bus assembler employed by the defender.

2. On that date, the pursuer was working on the Olympian Line fitting an anti-roll bar to a bus which consisted of a rod 5cm (2 inches) in diameter and about 304cm (10 feet) in length and of a solid metal construction.

3. A rod was fitted across the width of the bus around 91cm (three feet) from ground height.

4. This was not the pursuer's normal job as the employee who did the job, Thomas Ferguson, was absent for a week.

5. The pursuer was carrying out the job in the way that he had seen Mr Ferguson doing it, and had not been otherwise trained or instructed in the job.

6. To fit the rod, the pursuer exerted force from a crouching position on one knee placing the end of the rod onto the front of the chassis where it was bolted.

7. The pursuer used a pinch bar held in his left hand to wedge the end of the rod in the proper place for connection to the chassis.

8. There was no mechanical device to guide the rod to where it was fitted.

9. The pursuer was locating the rod when the pinch bar jammed and suddenly released, and released the rod with the pinch bar hitting the pursuer on his right shin and the rod on his right knee.

10. There was no harness provided to support the rod while being located.

11. Following the accident the defender provided an alternative type of pinch bar and instructed operators as to the correct method of construction.

12. The defender was in breach of the following duties of care.
    (1) [or 12A] The defender failed to take reasonable care for the safety of the pursuer and exposed him to risk of injury by not devising a safe system of work.
    (2) [or 12B] The defender failed to take reasonable care to provide safe and adequate plant and equipment.

13. The defender was in breach of the following statutory duties.
    (1) Regulation 13 of the Workplace (Health, Safety and Welfare) Regulations 1992.
    (2) Regulation 5 of the Provisions and Use of Work Equipment Regulations 1992.
    (3) Regulation 20 of the Provisions and Use of Work Equipment Regulations 1992.

14. The pursuer suffered the following injuries—
    (i) damaged anterior cruciate ligament bucket handle tear of the cartilage of the right knee; and
    (ii) adjustment disorder with mixed anxiety and depressed mood.

15. The pursuer was treated by—
    (i) Dr McCreadie, Almswell Road, Kilwinning, Ayrshire (*insert for what?*); and
    (ii) Crosshouse Hospital, Kilmarnock (*insert for what?*)

16. The pursuer seeks damages under the following heads of claim.
    (1) Solatium (*insert amount if known?*).
    (2) Earnings lost till June 2000 (*insert amount if known?*).
    (3) Earnings loss from employment he would have obtained (*insert amount if known?*).
    (4) Future earnings loss or failing which, loss of employability on the open labour market (*insert amount if known?*).
    (5) Cost of travelling for medical treatment (*insert amount if known?*).
    (6) Prescription costs (*insert amount if known?*).
    (7) Services provided by the pursuer that he can no longer perform for his parents since the year 2000 (*insert amount if known?*).
    (8) Services that the pursuer is unable to carry out by way of home decoration, gardening and car maintenance (*insert amount if known?*).

The requirement under the old r. 43.30 in relation to averments about medical treatment is now contained in r. 43.2 (1)(b).

Whereas under the optional procedure rules it was possible for the sum awarded to be greater than the sum sued for (see first conclusion in old Form 43.18), this is not provided for in the new Chap.43. The requirement for a specific sum to be concluded for is related to jury trial.

For the rules in relation to "connected persons" to whom intimation of an action of damages for death of a person from personal injuries should be given, see rr. 43.14–43.19.

43.2.3   *Social Security (Recovery of Benefits) Act 1997.* For a discussion of this Act and its effect on payment of damages, see note 43.9.10.

43.2.4   *"provisional damages".*
    (1) General. In old Chap. 43, the rules for provisional and further damages were in Part III. The rules for further damages are now in r. 43.13. An application for provisional damages may be made only by the injured person: Administration of Justice Act 1982, s. 12(2).
    (2) Section 12 of the 1982 Act. This provision sets out the circumstances in which provisional damages may be claimed: (a) there must be a risk that, at some definite or indefinite time in the

future, the pursuer will, as a result of the act or omission which gave rise to the cause of action, develop some serious disease or suffer some serious deterioration of his physical or mental condition; and (b) that the defender was, at the time of the act or omission which gave rise to the cause of action, a public authority, public corporation or insured or otherwise indemnified in respect of the claim. Evidence of risk that the pursuer will, as a result of the act or omission which gave rise to the cause of action, develop some serious disease or suffer some serious deterioration in his condition, should be led and the court asked to make a finding that there is such a risk, but to assess and award damages on the assumption that the pursuer will not develop the disease or suffer the deterioration. In making the award the court may order that an application for further damages may only be made within a specified period: 1982 Act, s. 12(2).

(3) Interpretation; meaning of "serious" and "future deterioration". The word "serious" primarily qualifies the word disease or deterioration rather than the effects of the disease or deterioration, although in assessing seriousness account must be taken of effects on the pursuer's physical abilities: *White v. Inveresk Paper Co. Ltd,* 1988 S.L.T. 2 (OH), 5L *per* Lord Murray; *Robertson v. British Bakeries Ltd,* 1991 S.L.T. 434 (OH), 439G *per* Lord Osborne. It is not the case that a triggering incident causing future deterioration means that s. 12 of the 1982 Act does not apply. The question is whether the deterioration is the result of the act or omission which gave rise to the cause of action, and that could be the case notwithstanding that the deterioration is brought about by an interaction between the condition produced by the original act and a future triggering event: *Meek v. Burton's Gold Medal Biscuits Ltd,* 1989 S.L.T. 338 (OH).

(4) Social Security (Recovery of Benefits) Act 1997. For a discussion of this Act and its effect on payment of damages, see note 43.9.10.

"warrants for intimation". See generally, note 13.6.6. The obvious example in reparation **43.2.5** actions is intimation to connected persons: see further, in r. 43.15.

Diligence. Is a warrant for arrestment or inhibition on the dependence allowed to be included **43.2.6** in the summons? Rule 13.2 (form of summons), which refers to warrants for diligence in the summons, is excluded and Form 43.2-A contains no reference to a warrant for diligence. Rule 13.6 (warrants in summons) is, however, excluded only in so far as it relates to arrestment to found jurisdiction; thus a warrant for arrestment or inhibition would appear to be technically competent. On the other hand one must have regard to the decision in the Outer House in *Karl Construction Ltd v. Palisade Properties plc,* 2002 S.C. 270 in relation to inhibition and its effect on arrestment: see further, notes 13.6.2 and 13.6.3. The effect of that case is that diligence must be applied for and granted by a judge and that the warrant in the summons is insufficient authority. The decision of the Inner House on appeal has been awaited since the hearing in August 2002. Currently any warrant for diligence in a summons is referred to the Lord Ordinary.

"specification of documents". Rule 43.2(4) provides that the summons may "include" a **43.2.7** specification of documents. In r. 43.4(5) the specification is referred to as being annexed to the summons. It is not clear if it is really intended that the specification be part of the summons, for it would not be in accordance with normal practice to serve the summons on a haver other than a party. If the specification is part of the summons it is not a separate step of process and is not given a separate process number and will not incur a separate fee. Clearly the specification has to be served with the summons on the defender so that he has notice that the standard form of specification has been applied for and granted. It would have been better to provide for the pursuer, on lodging the summons, to apply by motion *ex parte* for a commission and diligence for recovery of documents on a specification containing the standard calls, which document would be supplied by the court in the order.

No distinction is made, as in Chap. 35, between recovery of documents by a represented party and a party litigant; indeed, Form 43.2-B assumes that the pursuer is legally represented. Following the Cullen *Review of Business of the Outer House of the Court of Session,* where the party is represented r. 35.3 provides the procedure for the haver to send the documents directly to the party's agent; but in the case of a party litigant r. 35.3A follows the old rule that documents have to be sent to the DPCS: see notes 35.3.1 and 35.3A.1. Form 43.2-B as substituted by S.S.I. 2004 No. 291 now provides for the documents to be sent to the pursuer's agent: the alternative in the old form for sending them to the Office of Court has been removed; but there is still no alternative procedure provided for where the pursuer is a party litigant as in r. 35.3A.

In any event, this is the automatic recovery of documents' procedure. Under the optional procedure (old r. 43.25), each party had to disclose documents in his possession to the other side, but documents in possession of a haver had to be sought by commission and diligence in the normal way. The new procedure is that the pursuer is entitled, on lodging the summons, to (an order for) recovery of documents in a standard specification in Form 43.2-B without prior intimation to the defender. The standard calls are for recovery of the relevant medical records, earnings and accident reports.

Unfortunately, the specification of documents is provided by the pursuer and not the court.

The clerk of session will have to check the document very carefully to see that it is word for word in identical terms to Form 43.2-B.

The pursuer is not precluded from seeking recovery of these documents at a later stage or any other documents or property at common law or under s. 1 of the Administration of Justice (Scotland) Act 1972: r. 43.4(5).

For execution of the order for recovery of documents, see r. 43.4.

Service and calling of summons

[1] **43.3.**—(1) Where a summons in an action to which this Chapter applies is to be executed, a copy of the summons which has passed the signet shall be—

  (a) served on the defender with a citation in Form 43.3 attached to it; and

  (b) intimated to any person named in a warrant for intimation.

(2) Where a summons has not called within three months and a day after the date of signeting, the instance shall fall.

(3) Where a summons cannot be served within the period of notice determined in accordance with rule 13.4 and called before the expiry of the period mentioned in paragraph (2), the court may—

  (i) on the application of the pursuer by motion; and

  (ii) on cause shown,

extend that period.

(4) An application under paragraph (3) shall be made before the expiry of the period mentioned in paragraph (2).

---

[1] R.43.3 substituted by S.S.I. 2002 No. 570 (effective 1st April 2003).

43.3.1   *General note.* On the introduction of the new Chap. 43 and this rule, see note 43.1.1. Rule 13.7 (service and intimation of summons) does not apply.

43.3.2   *"served".* For service, see Chap. 16. The citation on the defender is in Form 43.3 and not Form 13.7. The only difference is the second paragraph which states that the action is a claim for reparation.

43.3.3   *"intimated".* For methods, see r. 16.8.

43.3.4   *"called within three months and a day".* The period expires at the end of the last day, three months and a day after the day of signeting (that day will not be included in the calculation). The reason for the extra day is connected to the historically "year and a day" provisions now in rr. 13.7(2) and 13.13. The general rule that the instance falls if the summons is not executed within a year and a day after signeting (r. 13.7(2)) or if the summons is not called within a year and a day after the expiry of the period of notice (r. 13.13(6)) does not apply. Instead, under r. 43.3(2), the instance falls if the summons is not *called* within *three months* and a day after signeting. Although the defender has the right of protestation under r. 13.14 if the summons is not called within seven days after the expiry of the period of notice, this rule ensures that there is no delay. Rule 43.3(3) provides for the situation where the summons cannot be served within the period of notice and called within three months and a day of signeting. On cause shown, the three-month cut-off period may be prorogued. No other situation is provided for. Having regard to the decision in *MacDonald v. Kwok*, 1999 S.L.T. 593 (OH), on which see note 13.13.9, it was argued that relief from the rigours of the rule may be sought under r. 2.1. This was done in *Jackson v. McDougall*, 2004 S.L.T. 770 (OH) and *Roberts v. Chisholm*, 2004 S.L.T. 1171 following *MacDonald*, above. *McDonald*, however, was overruled in *Brogan v. O'Rourke Ltd*, 2005 S.L.T. 29 (Extra Div.) where it was held that rr. 13.13(6) and 43.3(2) were plain and the meaning of "the instance shall fall" was perfectly understood: where the summons has not called within the specified period the instance falls and it was incompetent to apply to the court under r. 2.1. Sense having prevailed in *Brogan*, it ought to follow that *Jackson* and *Roberts*, though not referred to in *Brogan*, are no longer good law.

For calling of the summons, see r. 13.13.

43.3.5   *Fee.* The court fee for signeting a summons is payable. For fee, see Court of Session etc. Fees Order 1997, Table of Fees, Pt I, A and B, item 1 [S.I. 1997 No. 688 as amended, pp.C1201 *et seq.*]. Certain persons are exempt from payment of fees: see 1997 Fees Order, art. 5 substituted by S.S.I. 2002 No. 270. A fee exemption certificate must be lodged in process: see P.N. No. 1 of 2002.

Where the pursuer is legally represented, the fee may be debited under a credit scheme introduced on 1st April 1976 by P.N. No. 4 of 1976 to the account (if one is kept or permitted) of the pursuer's agent by the court cashier, and an account will be rendered weekly by the court cashier's office to the agent for all court fees due that week for immediate settlement. Party litigants and agents not operating the scheme must pay (by cash, cheque or postal order) on each occasion a fee is due at the time of lodging at the counter at the General Department.

Inspection and recovery of documents

[1] **43.4.**—(1) This rule applies where the summons contains a specification of documents by virtue of rule 43.2(4)(b).

(2) Upon signet an order granting commission and diligence for the production and recovery of the documents mentioned in the specification shall be granted and the Deputy Principal Clerk of Session shall certify Form 43.2-B to that effect.

(3) An order under paragraph (2) shall be treated for all purposes as an interlocutor of the court granting commission and diligence signed by the Lord Ordinary.

(4) The pursuer may serve an order under paragraph (2) and the provisions of rule 35.2 shall thereafter apply, subject to any necessary modifications, as if the order were an order obtained on an application made under rule 35.2(1)(a).

(5) Nothing in this rule shall affect the right of a party to apply under rule 35.2 for a commission and diligence for recovery of documents or for an order under section 1 of the Administration of Justice (Scotland) Act 1972 in respect of any document or other property not mentioned in the specification annexed to the summons.

-----

[1] R.43.4 substituted by S.S.I. 2002 No. 570 (effective 1st April 2003).

General note. On the introduction of the new Chap. 43 and this rule, see note 43.1.1.   **43.4.1**

"an order granting commission and diligence". Rule 43.4(2) states that an order is granted and **43.4.2** that the DPCS certifies that it has been. The rule does not state who has granted the order. Rule 43.4(3) implies that it is not granted by a Lord Ordinary but is to be treated as if it had been. Either the DPCS, or some other clerk of session, has granted the order or r. 43.4(2) should have made it clear that an order is *deemed* to have been granted and is certified by the DPCS. It would have been better to provide for the pursuer, on lodging the summons, to apply by motion *ex parte* for a commission and diligence for recovery of documents on a specification containing the standard calls, which document would be supplied by the court.

For the meaning of commission and diligence, see note 35.2.2.

Form 43.2-B is a confused document. The description of the form is that it is an order, but the document itself does not state that it is an order of the court and there is no official place for the certificate of the DPCS (the certificate may be stamped on). The form itself is headed "Specification of Documents" (rather than "Order of the Court of Session", as in Form 35.3-A, or "Order for Recovery of Documents") which, in our procedure, is not the order for a commission and diligence but the document lodged that specifies the documents for which the commission and diligence is sought and accompanies the order.

Rule 43.4(4). This provision states that r. 35.2 applies to an order "made" under rule 43.4(2) **43.4.3** as if it were obtained on application under rule 35.2(1)(a). This makes no sense. Rule 35.2 applies to applications *before* they are granted not after: *i.e.* it states how the application is made (by motion) and to whom the application must be intimated before it is dealt with. That this was not intended may be confirmed by P.N. No 2 of 2003 which indicates that intimation is not made to the Lord Advocate (a requirement of r. 35.2(3)). This must be a drafting error and some other rule was intended: probably r. 35.3 or a combination of rr. 35.3 and 35.3A. It is not possible for only one of these rules to apply because Form 43.2-B begins by requiring the haver to produce the documents to the pursuer's agent but later states that he may produce the documents either to the pursuer's agent or by lodging them in the Office of Court. Rule 35.3 provides for the former and r. 35.3A provides for the latter. The distinction between these procedures was introduced following a recommendation in the Cullen *Review of Business of the Outer House of the Court of Session* (para. 5.12) to allow documents to be sent directly to the pursuer's agent. A working group devised such a scheme in 1996 but decided that, in the case of a party litigant, the haver should send documents to the DPCS: see note 35.3.1 and 35.3A .1. Form 43.2-B assumes that the pursuer is legally represented. Notes (3) and (4) in the form require the haver to send documents for which confidentiality is claimed in a sealed packet to the DPCS.

A pursuer, or any other party, is not precluded by the automatic procedure from applying for recovery of documents under Chap.35 in the normal way: r. 43.4(5).

43.4.4   *Intimation and service.* Rule 35.2 cannot apply, notwithstanding r. 43.3(3), because there is no motion and the order is granted automatically. Intimation is not, therefore, made to the Lord Advocate or the Advocate General. P.N. No. 2 of 2003 confirms this in relation to the Lord Advocate.

In relation to medical records, the order should be served on the Central Legal Office for the Scottish Health Service, Trinity Park House, South Trinity Road, Edinburgh: P.N. No. 2 of 2003 (for "sent" read "served").

Motions to dispense with timetable

[1] **43.5.**—(1) Any party to an action may, within 28 days of the lodging of defences, by motion apply to have the action withdrawn from the procedure in this Chapter and to be appointed to proceed as an ordinary action.

(2) No motion under paragraph (1) shall be granted unless the court is satisfied that there are exceptional reasons for not following the procedure in this Chapter.

(3) In determining whether there are exceptional reasons justifying the granting of a motion made under paragraph (1), the Lord Ordinary shall have regard to—

   (a) the likely need for detailed pleadings;
   (b) the length of time required for preparation of the action; and
   (c) any other relevant circumstances.

(4) Where the court appoints the cause to proceed as an ordinary action under paragraph (1)—

   (a) the pursuer shall, within seven days, lodge an open record in terms of rule 22.1; and
   (b) rules 43.11, 43.12 and 43.13 shall apply to the action.

----

[1] R.43.5 substituted by S.S.I. 2002 No. 570 (effective 1st April 2003).

43.5.1   *General note.* On the introduction of the new Chap. 43 and this rule, see note 43.1.1.

This rule provides a "get out" for any party, once defences have been lodged, by application to have the case proceed as an ordinary action. This may be achieved only if there are "exceptional reasons": see note 43.5.5.

43.5.2   *"within 28 days".* The date from which the period is calculated is not counted. Where the last day falls on a Saturday or Sunday, or a public holiday on which the Office of Court is open, the next available day is allowed: r. 1.3(7). For office hours and public holidays, see note 3.1.2.

43.5.3   *"lodging of defences".* On defences, see generally Chap.18. On lodging defences, see r. 18.1(2).

43.5.4   *"motion".* For motions, see generally Chap.23.

43.5.5   *"exceptional reasons".* An action to which Chap.43 applies may only proceed as an ordinary action if there are exceptional reasons for not allowing the procedure in Chap.43: r. 43.5(2). Guidance as to the meaning of this phrase is given in r. 43.5(3) and P.N. No. 2 of 2003. Rule 43.5(3) requires the Lord Ordinary to have regard, *inter alia*, to (a) the need for detailed pleadings, and (b) the length of time and required to prepare the case. The P.N. states that a transfer to the ordinary roll is likely to be granted only in cases of exceptional complexity. A motion should detail specifically all the items in para.(3) of r. 43.5: *Broadfoot's CB v. Forth Valley Acute Hospitals NHS Trust,* July 3, 2003, 2003 G.W.D. 26–729 (OH).

It should not be assumed that merely because an action involves professional negligence that it will automatically be appointed to proceed as an ordinary action: *Broadfoot's CB,* above.

Where a case is transferred to the ordinary roll, r. 43.5(4) provides that the rules relating to interim and further damages (rr. 43.11–43.13) continued to apply. Nothing, however, is said about rr. 43.17–43.19 relating to connected persons continuing to apply.

43.5.6   *"within seven days".* The date from which the period is calculated is not counted. Where the last day falls on a Saturday or Sunday, or a public holiday on which the Office of Court is open, the next available day is allowed: r. 1.3(7). For office hours and public holidays, see note 3.1.2.

Allocation of diets and timetables

[1] **43.6.**—(1) The Keeper of the Rolls shall, on the lodging of defences or, where there is more than one defender the first lodging of defences—

(a) allocate a diet for proof of the action;

(b) issue a timetable stating the date mentioned in sub-paragraph (a) and calculated by reference to periods specified from time to time by the Lord President, in accordance with which—

 (i) an application for a third party notice under rule 26.1 may be made;

 (ii) the pursuer may execute a commission for recovery of documents under rule 43.4;

 (iii) parties may adjust their pleadings;

 (iv) the pursuer shall lodge a statement of valuation of claim in process;

 (v) the pursuer shall lodge a record;

 (vi) the defender (and any third party to the action) shall lodge a statement of valuation of claim in process;

 (vii) the parties shall each lodge in process a list of witnesses together with any productions upon which they wish to rely; and

 (viii) the pursuer shall lodge in process the minute of the pre-trial meeting.

(2) A timetable issued under paragraph (1) shall be in Form 43.6 and shall be treated for all purposes as an interlocutor of the court signed by the Lord Ordinary; and so far as the timetable order is inconsistent with any provision in these rules which relates to a matter to which the timetable relates, the timetable shall prevail.

(3) Where a party fails to comply with any requirement of a timetable other than that referred to in paragraph (7), the Keeper of the Rolls may put the cause out to be heard on the By Order roll.

(4) The pursuer shall lodge two copies of the record, which shall consist of the pleadings of the parties, in process by the date specified in the timetable and shall at the same time send one copy to the defender and any other parties.

(5) The pursuer shall, on lodging the copies of the record as required by paragraph (4), enrol a motion craving the court—

(a) to allow to parties a preliminary proof on specified matters;

(b) to allow a proof;

(c) to allow issues for jury trial; or

(d) to make some other specified order.

(6) In the event that any party proposes to ask the court to make any order other than one of those specified in sub-paragraphs (b) or (c) of paragraph (5), that party shall, on enrolling or opposing (as the case may be) the pursuer's motion, specify the order to be sought and give full notice in the motion or notice of opposition, of the grounds thereof.

(7) Where a pursuer fails to lodge a record by the date specified in a timetable issued under paragraph (1), the Keeper of the Rolls may put the case out to be heard on the By Order roll.

(8) A production which is not lodged in accordance with paragraph (1)(b)(vii) shall not be used or put in evidence at a proof unless—

(a) by consent of parties; or

(b) with the leave of the court on cause shown and on such conditions, if any, as to expenses or otherwise as the court thinks fit.

(9) In a cause which is one of more than one cause arising out of the same cause of action, the court may—

(a) on the motion of a party to that cause; and

(b) after hearing parties to all those causes,

appoint that cause or any other of those causes to be the leading cause and to sist the other causes pending the determination of the leading cause.

(10) In this rule, "pursuer " includes additional pursuer, noter or minuter, as the case may be.

_____

[1] R. 43.6 substituted by S.S.I. 2002 No. 570 (effective 1st April 2003) and amended by the Act of Sederunt (Rules of the Court of Session Amendment No. 4) (Personal Injuries Actions etc.) 2007, para. 2 (effective 2nd May 2007).

43.6.1   *General note.* On the introduction of the new Chap. 43 and this rule, see note 43.1.1. Rules 4.9(2) (prorogation of time for lodging documents), 6.2 (fixing and allocation of diets in the Outer House), 22.1 (open records), 22.2 (time for adjustment on Adjustment Roll), 22.3 (closing of record) and 36.3 (lodging of productions) do not apply.

   This rule is crucial to the success of the scheme. A rigid timetable must be adhered to once defences have been lodged. Following the US Federal model, a date for the proof (or jury trial) is fixed when defences are lodged. The date for a proof will be about 12 months after the date on which defences are lodged. Thus parties know the date to which they have to work. The 2000 Report indicates that the working party considered that, instead of judicial case management, which it concluded would be an unnecessary and unjustified expense in most cases, there should be an automatic timetable with which parties would have to comply. Although adjustment of the timetable may be required, that should be done where possible without affecting the date allocated for proof or jury trial.

43.6.2   *"The Keeper of the Rolls shall, on the lodging of defences".* Rule 43.6(1) would appear to require that the timetable will be issued by the Keeper on the day that the defences, or the first defences, are lodged.

43.6.3   *"timetable".* The period of time for the doing or completion of various stages and the proof date will all be set out in the timetable issued to the parties by the Keeper in Form 43.6. The stages include application for third party notices, execution of commission and diligence, adjustment, lodging of statements of value of claim, lodging of record, list of witnesses and productions, and minute of pre-trial meeting.

   The Keeper will calculate these periods according to periods specified by the Lord President: r.43.6(1)(b). The rule makes no provision for publication by a P.N. The periods currently envisaged are set out in Table 1 to P.N. No. 2 of 2003.

   P.N. No. 2 of 2003 stipulates that the period set out in the timetable order will be strictly insisted on. If they are not adhered to, the cause may be put out on the By Order Roll. As to the sanctions available day by order hearing, see r.43.7(2) and note 43.7.2.

43.6.4   *"allocate a diet for proof".* Rule 43.6(1)(a) refers to allocating a diet for proof of the action, which must mean proof or jury trial. The timetable order in Form 43.6 on the other hand refers to the diet of *trial*: it should be a reference to proof or jury trial.

   Normally, four days are allocated. If four days is not appropriate, the Keeper should be contacted: P.N. No. 2 of 2003.

   In *Hamilton v. Seamark Systems Ltd*, 2004 S.C. 543 (OH), it was held that as "proof" included proof before answer (see r. 1.3), and as examination of questions of law after evidence was not excluded by the new Chap. 43 procedure, there could be a proof before answer where appropriate. Lady Paton, *obiter*, at para. [23], indicated that there might be little difference between proof and proof before answer, as parties may make submissions about the law after proof (see note 28.1.6).

43.6.5   *"commission for recovery of documents".* The reference in r.43.6(1)(b)(ii) to a commission should be to a commission and diligence. It refers only to the automatic or standard specification provided for in r.43.4, *i.e.* the one that may be included in (*sic*) the summons. If the pursuer has not already executed it, this must be done by the date specified in the timetable order.

43.6.6   *"statement of valuation of claim".* The pursuer first, and then by a later date, the defender must lodge a statement of the value of claim. On the statement of value of claim, see r.43.8.

43.6.7   *"list of witnesses together with any productions".* The 2000 Report indicates in Chap. 5 that the requirement in the old optional procedure rules for a list of witnesses had been found to be unduly restrictive. New r.43.6(1)(b)(vii), however, requires that parties must lodge a list of witnesses and any productions by the date stipulated in the timetable order. Unlike old r.43.26, there is no express provision prohibiting the calling of witnesses not on the list without leave. It may not, however, be implied that there is such a prohibition in relation to witnesses under the new provision because there is an express prohibition in relation to productions: see below in this note.

It should be noted that the action will be subject to P.N. No. 4 of 1994 which not only "requires" parties to exchange lists of witnesses 28 days before the proof or jury trial but states in para.2 that a party may call a witness not on his list subject to such conditions, if any, as the court may impose. This is, of course, only a P.N. and not a rule.

A production not lodged timeously under r.43.6(1)(b)(vii), on the other hand, may not be used or put in evidence unless with the consent of parties or with leave of the court on cause shown and on such conditions, if any, as the court may impose: r.43.6(7). This provision appears to prohibit the putting of documents not lodged to a witness to test credibility, on which see notes 36.3.2 and 36.11.2(8). But, since leave of the court can be obtained under r.43.6(7), it will presumably be granted for this purpose. In P.N. No. 1 of 2007 practitioners are reminded that parties are expected (in accordance with the principle of early disclosure) to lodge all expert reports within a reasonable time after receipt; failure to do so may have consequences in expenses.

On lodging such steps of process, see rr.4.4–4.6 and notes.

"pre-trial meeting". Parties must hold a joint pre-trial (*sic*) meeting and lodge a minute in **43.6.8** respect of it. On pre-trial meetings, see r.43.10.

"lodge...in process". On lodging steps of process, see rr.4.4–4.6.   **43.6.9**

Lodging of records. It should be noted that unlike a record in any other action (see r.22.3(2)), **43.6.10** the record in an action under Chap. 43 contains only the pleadings and not any of the interlocutors.

Two copies of the record are required as one is the process copy and the other is for the use of the Keeper of the Rolls. (In other actions, three copies are required, the third being required for the clerk of court.)

Where the record is not lodged by the date in the timetable order, the case will, not may, be put out by order for an explanation. On the by order hearing and sanctions for failure to comply with the timetable order, see r.43.7.

Motions for further procedure. On the lodging of the record the pursuer must enrol a motion **43.6.11** for a preliminary proof, a proof, issues for jury trial or some other specified order: r.43.6(6). The court expects that a proof will be sought: P.N. No. 2 of 2003. If a debate is sought, or any other specified order is sought, a motion will have to be accompanied by written notice of the grounds: r.43.6(7) and P.N. No. 2 of 2003 (P.N. No. 3 of 1991 may also be applicable). Such a motion will not be lightly granted, and normally questions of specification of pleadings will be dealt with at the motion.

"motion". For motions, see Chap. 23.   **43.6.12**

Appointing cause to be the leading cause. See note 22.3.13.   **43.6.13**

Hearings on the By Order roll

[1] **43.7.**—(1) Where the Keeper of the Rolls puts a case out to be heard on the By Order roll under paragraphs (3) or (7) of rule 43.6 or paragraph (3) of rule 43.10 he shall—

  (a) put the cause out to be heard not less than seven days after the date of the notice referred to in sub-paragraph (b) on the By Order roll; and

  (b) give notice to the parties to the action—

    (i) of the date of the hearing of the cause on the By Order roll; and

    (ii) requiring the party in default to lodge in process a written explanation as to why the timetable has not been complied with and to intimate a copy to all other parties, not less than two clear working days before the date of the hearing.

(2) At a hearing on the By Order roll under any of the provisions mentioned in the foregoing paragraph, the Lord Ordinary—

  (a) shall consider any explanation provided by the party in default;

  (b) may award expenses against that party; and

  (c) may make any other appropriate order, including decree of dismissal.

(3) Expenses awarded under paragraph (2)(b) shall not exceed the expenses of the process before the date of the hearing on the By Order roll.

---

[1] R. 43.7 substituted by S.S.I. 2002 No. 570 (effective 1st April 2003).

43.7.1   *General note.* On the introduction of the new Chap. 43 and this rule, see note 43.1.1.

The party in default must lodge in process a written explanation for the default: r.43.7(1)(b)(ii). The by order hearing will still take place even if the party in default has since complied: P.N. No. 2 of 2003.

43.7.2   *Sanctions.* From the 2000 Report, Chap. 10, it appears that it is hoped that a state of co-operation will become the new culture and that bludgeoning parties into compliance may be counter-productive. The working party recognised that the sanction of expenses could lose its bite if parties settled and dealt with expenses as part of the settlement (although they could not directly defeat an award). The working party considered that, generally, failure to comply with a step should result in the party having to explain the failure to the court. Hence the provision for the by order hearing. In two situations the working party considered severe sanctions should be imposed: (1) failure to lodge a document or comply with a date in the timetable order, by awarding expenses of process to date against the party in default; and (2) failure to lodge a statement of value of claim, by dismissing the action (if pursuer in default) or granting decree for the amount in the claim (if defender in default). The former is dealt with in r.43.7(2) and the latter in r.43.9(7).

The sanctions in r.43.7 are (a) expenses, which are not to exceed the expenses of process to date (r. 43.7(2)(b) and (3)), and (b) any other appropriate order, including dismissal (r. 43.7(2)(c)). Expenses could be party in party, agent and client, or modified expenses. Other appropriate orders may include: payment of expenses as a condition precedent to further procedure; and liability for an additional fee. Absolvitor is not specifically excluded but may be implied by the rule being inclusive of dismissal.

43.7.3   *"not less than seven days after".* The date of notice of the date of the by order hearing is not counted.

43.7.4   *"lodge in process".* The written explanation will be a step in process (r.1.3(1)). On lodging steps of process, see rr.4.4–4.6.

43.7.5   *"not less than two clear working days before".* The date of the hearing is not counted.

Applications for sist or for variation of timetable order

[1] **43.8.**—(1) The action may be sisted or the timetable issued under rule 43.6 may be varied by the court on an application by any party to the action by motion.

(2) An application under paragraph (1)—

(a) shall be placed before the Lord Ordinary; and

(b) shall be granted only on special cause shown.

(3) Any sist of an action shall be for a specific period.

(4) Where a timetable issued under rule 43.6 is varied under this rule, the Keeper of the Rolls shall issue a revised timetable in Form 43.6.

(5) A revised timetable issued under paragraph (4) shall have effect as if it were a timetable issued under rule 43.6 and any reference in this Chapter to any action being taken in accordance with the timetable shall be construed as a reference to its being taken in accordance with the timetable as varied under this rule.

---

[1] R. 43.8 substituted by S.S.I. 2002 No. 570 (effective 1st April 2003).

43.8.1   *General note.* On the introduction of the new Chap. 43 and this rule, see note 43.1.1.

43.8.2   *Sist.* Applications for sist, such as for legal aid, should be made before, or when, defences are lodged in order to avoid the need to vary the timetable order: P.N. No. 2 of 2003.

The 2000 Report, Chap. 4, suggests that sists should be discouraged and that all grants of sist should be for a fixed period. A sist for legal aid should be granted only on special cause shown. If legal aid has not already been applied for, an interlocutor granting a sist should be intimated to SLAB. Delay in applying for legal aid may result in a motion to sist being refused.

43.8.3   *Variation of timetable.* A motion to extend the timetable is unlikely to be granted, whereas one to accelerate the timetable (particularly where the pursuer's life expectancy is within the period of the timetable) is more likely to be favourably considered: P.N. No. 2 of 2003.

Any motion should contain full details of the grounds, including any relevant supporting medical evidence: P.N. No. 2 of 2003.

"motion". For motions, see Chap. 23.

Statements of valuation of claim

[1] **43.9.**—(1) Each party to an action shall make a statement of valuation of claim in Form 43.9.

(2) A statement of valuation of claim (which shall include a list of supporting documents) shall be lodged in process.

(3) Each party shall, on lodging a statement of valuation of claim—

(a) intimate the list of documents included in the statement of valuation of claim to every other party; and

(b) lodge each of those documents.

(4)–(5) [*Omitted by S.S.I. 2007 No. 282 (effective 2nd May 2007).*]

(6) Nothing in paragraph (3) shall affect—

(a) the law relating to, or the right of a party to object to the recovery of a document on the ground of, privilege or confidentiality; or

(b) the right of a party to apply under rule 35.2 for a commission and diligence for recovery of documents or an order under section 1 of the Administration of Justice (Scotland) Act 1972.

(7) Without prejudice to paragraph (2) of rule 43.7 (hearings on the By Order roll), where a party has failed to lodge a statement of valuation of claim in accordance with a timetable issued under paragraph (2) of rule 43.6 (allocation of diets and timetables) the court may at a hearing of the cause on the By Order roll under paragraph (3) of that rule—

(a) where the party in default is the pursuer, dismiss the action; or

(b) where the party in default is the defender, grant decree against the defender for an amount not exceeding the amount of the pursuer's valuation.

---

[1] Rule 43.9 substituted by S.S.I. 2002 No. 570 (effective 1st April 2003) and amended by S.S.I. 2007 No. 282 (effective 2nd May 2007).

General note. On the introduction of the new Chap. 43 and this rule, see note 43.1.1. **43.9.1**
The statement of value of claim is one of the cornerstones of the scheme. The 2000 Report states, in Chap. 7, that the object is to bring forward the point at which a party can see how each other party is approaching the valuation of the claim and what material supports it. There are draconian sanctions available to the court for failure to comply: see r.43.9(7) and note 43.9.9.

"statement of value of claim". The statement must be in Form 43.9. The form has no heading **43.9.2** or instance; but the statement should be headed up, have the court reference number and the instance in order to identify the case to which it refers. The form is a template or *pro forma* and may be adjusted to suit the particular case: *Logie v. Fife Council*, 16th August 2006, 2006 G.W.D. 26-585 (OH), [2006 CSOH] 127.
Each party must lodge a statement of valuation. According to the timetable order issued under r.43.6(1), the pursuer will do so first and the defender will do so some eight weeks later. It should be noted that under r.4.6 a copy of the statement should be sent to every other party.
In addition to lodging a statement of valuation, each party must (a) give written intimation to every other party of the list of documents that support the valuation, and (b) lodge that list in process: r.43.9(2) and (3).
P.N. No. 2 of 2003, although not a statement, or rule, of law, states (a) that the statement of valuation is not binding on a party, yet (b) can be founded on by any party.

"documents". The word "document" has been defined in R.C.S. 1994 by reference to the **43.9.3** inclusive definition in s.9 of the Civil Evidence (Scotland) Act 1988: see r.1.3(1). The documents in support of the valuation might include medical report, wage certificates, the report in respect of any special needs claim, and statements and vouching of any claim for services.

"lodged in process". The statements of valuation of claim will be lodged as steps of process **43.9.4** (r.1.3(1) (definition of "step of process"). On lodging a step of process, see rr.4.4–4.6).

"written intimation". For methods, see r.16.9. **43.9.5**

"within 14 days after". The date of receipt of the list is not counted. The difficulty with **43.9.6** calculating the date from the date of receipt, rather than the date of sending the list, is that the date of receipt is not a definitely known and instantly verifiable date.

43.9.7 *Inspection of documents.* Rule 43.9(4)–(6) has been taken from old r.43.25.
Parties should agree the time and place for inspection. If a party is being unreasonable, the other party could apply to the court for an order for which failure to obtemper would constitute contempt.

43.9.8 *"privilege or confidentiality".* For privilege and confidentiality, see note 35.2.7.

43.9.9 *Sanctions.* Rule 43.9(7) follows the proposal in the 2000 Report, Chap. 10, for failure to lodge a statement of claim in accordance with the timetable order.
Where a party fails to lodge a statement of claim in accordance with the timetable, the court may, at the by order hearing held under r.43.7, (a) dismiss the action, if the pursuer is in default, or (b) grant decree for an amount not exceeding the pursuer's valuation, if the defender is in default: r.43.9(7).
For the hearing on the By Order Roll, see r.43.7.

43.9.10 *Social Security (Recovery of Benefits) Act 1997.* Under the Social Security (Recovery of Benefits) Act 1997, the person (the compensator) compensating the victim of an accident, injury or disease is liable to pay in full to the Secretary of State for Social Security the amount of the recoverable social security benefits (for which see column 2 of Sched. 2 to the 1997 Act) paid to the victim in respect of payment of damages on or after 6th October 1997. The compensator is entitled to deduct, from certain specified heads of compensation he is to pay to the victim, the amount of the recoverable benefits (see 1997 Act, s.8). These heads, specified in column I of Sched. 2 to the 1997 Act, are the compensation for earnings lost, the compensation for cost of care, and the compensation for loss of mobility, during the relevant period. The compensator will then pay the sum deducted to the Secretary of State (to the CRU). The "relevant period" is the five years immediately following the date of the accident or injury or, in the case of disease, the date on which the victim first claimed a listed benefit: see 1997 Act, s.3(2) and (3). If at any time before the end of that period a compensation payment is made in final discharge of any claim, the relevant period ends on that date: 1997 Act, s.3(4)(a). The £2,500 small payments threshold has been abolished.
Where the pursuer received benefits to which the 1997 Act applies, the court, on pronouncing decree for payment of the damages, must specify the amount of compensation payment in the case of each head of compensation: 1997 Act, s.15(2). A difficulty arises where the final decree is pronounced within the five-year relevant period: is the court required to specify the damages for a period ending on the date of payment (not then determinable) after final decree, the final discharge occurring and the relevant period ending, under s.3(4)(a) of the 1997 Act, on the date of payment; or is the date of decree to be deemed to be the date of payment? The solution has been provided by the Inner House in *Mitchell v. Laing,* 1998 S.C. 342 (First Div). The court held that the intention of the legislation was that the amount of recoverable benefits to be deducted from the heads of compensation was the amount payable over the whole five-year period. Accordingly, the court in pronouncing decree would specify the damages due for the specified heads of compensation for the full five years.
Other points raised by the 1997 Act are:
(1) *Tenders.* There are five possibilities: (a) a tender in the usual form (*i.e.* stipulating a total or global sum); (b) a tender containing specification or a breakdown of the offer of damages for loss of earnings, and any cost of care and loss of mobility attributable to the relevant period; (c) a tender in the usual form accompanied by a back letter giving the breakdown; (d) a tender of an offer of damages stating that it is net of benefits; or (e) a tender of an offer of damages stating that it is net of benefits accompanied by a back letter giving the breakdown. All have their drawbacks. A pursuer will not wish to accept a tender in form (a) because he will not know whether the element from which the deductions are to be made may be the largest part of the offer. It may be that a tender in form (b) would satisfy all those having an interest. It has now been confirmed, in *Spence v. Wilson (No.2),* 1998 S.L.T. 959 (OH), that a tender in form (a) is invalid and, accordingly, a tender should be in form (b). For tenders generally, see 36.11.8.
(2) *Contributory negligence.* This will reduce the amount of damages to the pursuer but not the amount of recoverable benefits payable by the defender to the CRU.
(3) *Interest.* The 1997 Act repeals s.103 of the Social Security (Administration) Act 1992 which provided that in assessing interest the award of damages is reduced by a sum equal to the amount of relevant benefits received. Section 81(5) of the 1992 Act has been re-enacted in s.17 of the 1997 Act which provides that in assessing damages the amount of any listed benefits paid is to be disregarded. The question arises whether, now, in assessing interest the whole of the listed benefits received should be deducted and interest applied only to the balance or that no deduction should be made and interest applied to the gross award. There was a divergence of judicial opinion in the Outer House. In *George v. George C. Peebles & Son,* 1998 S.L.T. 685 (OH), Lord Nimmo Smith held that, since the primary purpose of an award of interest is to compensate a pursuer for being deprived of the use of money which he would have received but for the accident, it was inappropriate to leave out of account the fact that he had received benefits in place of earnings

he would have received. The inference was that Parliament intended that the discretion conferred by s.1(1A) of the Interest on Damages (Scotland) Act 1958 should continue to be exercised; and interest was awarded in that case on the difference between the loss of earnings and income support received. In *Spence v. Wilson*, 1998 S.C. 433 (OH), Lord Eassie came to the opposite opinion. He held that s.103 and its statutory predecessor innovated on the preceding common law and that the repeal of s.103 and omission of a re-enactment implied a legislative intention that the receipt of benefits was to be disregarded in the assessment of interest just as in the assessment of damages (notwithstanding, it must be supposed, that there is an express provision for the latter). The issue has now been determined by the Inner House in a report from the Lord Ordinary in *Wisely v. John Fulton (Plumbers) Ltd*, 1998 S.C. 910 and confirmed by the House of Lords (2000 S.L.T. 494). It was held that, by virtue of s.17 of the 1997 Act, the court disregards any benefits received by the pursuer when working out interest and, therefore, calculates interest on the whole amount of the damages for past loss of earnings. The case of *George*, above, was wrongly decided because it is inconsistent with the scheme of the 1997 Act.

The compensation for earnings lost during the relevant period in col. 1 of Sched. 2 to the 1997 Act, against which the compensator may set off his liability to repay the listed benefits, includes any sum of interest on damages for past loss of earnings: *Wisely*, above.

(4) *The interlocutor granting decree.* Under P.N. No. 3 of 1997, parties seeking decree in an action of reparation for personal injuries (except where that decree is sought of consent, *e.g.* because of a joint minute) must lodge in process a schedule of damages for the purposes of s.15(2) of the Social Security (Recovery of Benefits) Acts 1997 stating the amount of any compensation in respect of the relevant period under the heads of compensation in column 1 of Sched. 2 to the 1997 Act. It is apparent that the interlocutor subsequently pronounced will not itself specify the amounts under each head but will refer to a (or the) appended schedule which does. Clerks of session have been issuing blank schedules in the following form:

Schedule to interlocutor of even date *(amend as necessary)*
1.   Solatium—To date:
            Future:
2.   Loss of Earnings— To end of relevant period *(date)*:
            Subsequent to end of relevant period:
3.   Compensation for
            (1) cost of care:
                 to end of relevant period *(date)*:
                 subsequent to end of relevant period *(date)*:
            (2) loss of mobility
                 to end of relevant period date:
                 subsequent to end of relevant period *(date)*:
4.   Section 8 services:
5.   Section 9 services:
6.   Medical expenses:
7.   Loss of pension rights, etc.:
                                              TOTAL:
Less ( )% due to contributory negligence:
Sum decerned for:

(5) *Benefits disregarded.* Section 17 of the 1997 Act provides that, in respect of any accident, injury or disease, the amount of any listed benefits paid or likely to be paid is to be disregarded. That does not include benefits received prior to the accident: *McKenna v. Sharp*, 1998 S.C. 297 (OH), *sub. nom. McKenna v. Chief Constable Strathclyde Police*, 1998 S.L.T. 1161.

(6) *Heads of compensation from which relevant benefits may be deducted.* These heads, specified in column 1 of Sched. 2 to the 1997 Act, are the compensation for earnings lost, the compensation for cost of care, and the compensation for loss of mobility, during the relevant period. In *Mitchell v. Laing*, 1998 S.C. 342 (First Div.) it was held that "loss of mobility" means damages for patrimonial loss suffered as a result of loss of mobility due to the accident, injury or disease. In *McManus' Exrx v. Babcock Energy Ltd*, 1999 S.C. 569 (OH) it was held that an award for services rendered to an injured person under s. 8 of the Administration of Justice Act 1982 was not "compensation for cost of care" and, therefore, benefits such as attendance allowance could not be deducted under s. 8 of the 1997 Act.

(7) *Expenses.* The general rule that expenses follow success applies even though the whole of the sum awarded is paid to the CRU (Compensation Recovery Unit) of the DSS under the Social Security (Recovery of Benefits) Act 1997: *Gray v. Lanarkshire Health Board*, 1998 S.L.T. 1378 (OH).

Pre-trial meetings

[1] **43.10.**—(1) For the purposes of this rule, a pre-trial meeting is a meeting between the parties, which shall be held not later than four weeks before the date assigned for the proof or trial to discuss—

(a) settlement of the action; and

(b) to agree, so far as is possible, the matters which are not in dispute between them.

(2) A joint minute of a pre-trial meeting, made in Form 43.10, shall be lodged in process by the pursuer not less than three weeks before the date assigned for the proof or trial.

(3) Where a joint minute in Form 43.10 has not been lodged in accordance with paragraph (2) and by the date specified in the timetable order the Keeper of the Rolls shall put the case out to be heard on the By Order roll.

(4) During the pre-trial meeting, the representative of each party to the action shall have access to the party or another person who has authority to commit the party in the settlement of the action.

---

[1] R.43.10 substituted by S.S.I. 2002 No. 570 (effective 1st April 2003).

43.10.1   *General note.* On the introduction of the new Chap. 43 and this rule, see note 43.1.1.

Since most reparation actions go to proof (or prove before answer), it would have been better to call this a pre-proof hearing rather than to use the Anglo-American terminology of a pre-trial hearing. The word "proof" does not exclude jury trial as even in a trial there must be proof; whereas the word "trial" excludes the Scottish concept of a proof.

The Cullen *Review of the Business of the Outer House of the Court of Session* in 1995 recommended a pre-proof hearing before a judge. The 2000 Report proposed that the pre-proof hearing should simply be a meeting between the parties. It was considered, without reference to any empirical evidence, that the Cullen model added a stage that was expensive for parties and burdensome for parties and the court. That proposal is reflected in r. 43.10. Thus the court has gone against the trend in other common law jurisdictions such as the US and England and Wales. In the US, for example, the pre-trial hearing does not have to be chaired by a judge, but there is always a facilitator (*e.g.* a judge or another lawyer) to chair the meeting. It is not clear how the Court of Session model will work to achieve settlements where there is no person at the meeting to facilitate, mediate or direct the settlement discussion between parties already locked in combat. All that this model is doing, rather than increase the number of settlements, is to bring forward the door-of-court-settlement process to a date some three weeks before the proof.

43.10.2   *"pre-trial meeting".* Rule 43.10(1) states that the pre-trial, or more correctly pre-proof, meeting is between parties. The 2000 Report and P.N. No. 2 of 2003 make it clear that the meeting will be conducted by the legal advisers. In fact it is not necessary that the person with authority to settle the action for a party need be present, so long as he is contactable during the meeting: r. 43.10(4). It is envisaged that the meeting could be by video conferencing. It is expected that counsel will attend the meeting, because the joint minute of the meeting must be signed by counsel (or solicitor-advocate).

Parties are expected to discuss two things: (a) settlement, and (b) in any event, agree matters not in dispute: r. 43.10(1).

From the terms of the form of joint minute of the meeting in Form 43.10, it is clear that a number of questions *must* be answered on detailed aspects of the case. They must, therefore, be discussed at the pre-proof meeting.

Parties are expected to take such steps as are necessary to comply with the spirit as well as the letter of the rule.

43.10.3   *"not later than four weeks before".* The day from which the calculation is made is not counted.

43.10.4   *Joint minute.* The joint minute must be in Form 43.10. The timetable order will specify the date by which the joint minute of the pre-proof meeting must be lodged, failing which there will be a by order hearing (see note 43.10.7). That date cannot be less than three weeks before the proof date: r. 43.10(2). The joint minute must be signed by counsel or other person having a right of audience (solicitor-advocate).

Section 2 of the joint minute may assume that parties will have used the notices to admit and non-admission procedure in Chap. 28A, as the section has space for the calls made to admit certain facts and whether they were admitted or denied. It would be possible for calls to be made at the pre-proof meeting without using the Chap. 28A procedure.

It is the responsibility of the pursuer to lodge the joint minute in process: r. 43.10(2).

"lodged in process". The joint minute will be lodged as a step of process (r. 1.3(1) (definition of **43.10.5** "step of process"). On lodging a step of process, see rr. 4.4–4.6).

"not less than three weeks before". The day from which the calculation is made is not counted. **43.10.6** Where the last day falls on a Saturday or Sunday, or a public holiday on which the Office of Court is closed, the next available day is allowed: r. 1.3(7). For office hours and public holidays, see note 3.1.2.

By Order Roll. Where the joint minute is not lodged by the date in the timetable order, there **43.10.7** must be a by order hearing: r. 43.10(3). At that hearing the court will require an explanation and may award (a) expenses against a party, or (b) make any other order, including dismissal (if the pursuer is at fault). See further, r. 43.7.

Applications for interim payments of damages

[1] **43.11.**—(1) A pursuer may, at any time after defences have been lodged, apply by motion for an order for interim payment of damages to him by the defender or, where there are two or more of them, by any one or more of them.

(2) The pursuer shall give written intimation of a motion under paragraph (1) to every other party not less than 14 days before the date on which the motion is enrolled.

[3] (3) On a motion under paragraph (1), the court may ordain—
  (a) any defender who has admitted liability to the pursuer in the action; or
  (b) where the court is satisfied that, if the action proceeded to proof, the pursuer would succeed on the question of liability without any substantial finding of contributory negligence on his part, or on the part of any person in respect of whose injury or death the claim of the pursuer arises, and would obtain decree for damages, any defender who has not admitted liability to the pursuer in the action,
to make an interim payment to the pursuer of such amount as it thinks fit, not exceeding a reasonable proportion of the damages which, in the opinion of the court, are likely to be recovered by the pursuer.

(4) Any such payment may be ordered to be made in one lump sum or otherwise as the court thinks fit.

(5) No order shall be made against a defender under this rule unless it appears to the court that the defender is—
  (a) a person who is insured in respect of the claim of the pursuer;
[2] (aa) a person who is not insured but in respect of whose liability the Motor Insurers' Bureau will be liable to make payment;
  (b) a public authority; or
  (c) a person whose means and resources are such as to enable him to make the interim payment.

(6) Notwithstanding the grant or refusal of a motion for an interim payment, a subsequent motion may be made where there has been a change of circumstances.

(7) Subject to Part IV (management of money payable to children), any interim payment shall be made to the pursuer unless the court otherwise directs.

(8) This rule shall, with the necessary modifications, apply to a counterclaim for damages for personal injuries made by a defender.

(9) In this rule "defender" includes a third party against whom the pursuer has a conclusion for damages.

Deriv. R.C.S. 1965, r. 89A(1)(a) to (g) (r. 43.11(1)–(8)) inserted by S.I. 1974 No. 845; and R.C.S. 1994, old r. 43.8(2) (part) (r. 43.11(9)).

---

[1] Rule 43.11 substituted by S.S.I. 2002 No. 570 (effective 1st April, 2003).
[2] Rule 43.11(5)(aa) inserted by S.S.I. 2004 No.331 (effective 6th August 2004).
[3] Rule 43.11(3) inserted by S.S.I. 2006 No. 83 (effective 17th March 2006).

43.11.1   *General note.* Rule 43.11(1)–(8) is in the same terms as old r. 43.9, even including the reference to Part IV of old Chap. 43, which was revoked by the A.S. (R.C.S.A. No. 2) (Personal Injuries Actions) 2002 [S.S.I. 2002 No. 570], the rules in that Part having been revoked by SI 1996/2587!

    Temp. Judge Coutts, Q.C., has suggested, in *Hogg v. Carrigan's Exr*, 2001 S.C. 542, 554D (para.[9]), that r. 43.9 (now r. 43.11) should be radically rephrased. Rule 43.9(3)(a) did not, it was suggested, indicate whether it is liability to make reparation or an admission of fault that is meant. This invitation has not so far been taken up.

    An amendment has been made to r. 43.11(3) by A.S. (R.C.S.A.) (Miscellaneous) 2006 [S.S.I. 2006 No. 83], but not as suggested in that case. The amendment deals with a problem that the previous wording of r. 43.11(3)(b) referred to "that defender". Although r.43.11(3) has been set out slightly differently, the only change is to make "that defender" now "any defender": thus restoring the rule to its form in R.C.S. 1965, r. 89A(1); and see further note 43.11.7 for the reason for this.

43.11.2   *What documents may be considered?* It was held by Lord Allanbridge in *McCann v. Miller Insulation and Engineering Ltd,* 1986 S.L.T. 147 (OH), that, when considering the question of liability and contributory negligence, the court must look at the pleadings alone and not medical reports or other productions. But in *Stone v. Mountford*, 1995 S.L.T. 1279 (OH), Lord Johnston did not follow *McCann*, and held that the approach in that case did not amount to a general rule, that the discretion available to the court is wide enough to enable the court to review material before it other than the pleadings and to look at productions. It is, however, entitled, when looking at the pleadings, to consider notorious facts: *Reith v. Aberdeen Mineral Water Co., 1987* S.C.L.R. 689 (OH). The court may look at reports and other productions when considering quantification of the interim payment.

43.11.3   *"motion".* For motions, see Chap. 23.

43.11.4   *"written intimation".* For methods, see r. 16.9.

43.11.5   *"satisfied".* Satisfaction is less than complete certainty but it requires more than probability or even high probability: *Douglas's C.B. v. Douglas*, 1974 S.L.T. (Notes) 67 (OH) *per* Lord Maxwell. It means "almost certainly": *Nelson v. Duraplex Industries Ltd*, 1975 S.L.T. (Notes) 31 (OH), 33 *per* Lord Grieve. This approach was accepted by counsel in *Walker v. Infabco Diving Services Ltd*, 1983 S.L.T. 633 (Extra Div.), and confirmed in *Cowie v. Atlantic Drilling Co. Ltd*, 1995 S.C. 288 (First Div.), where it was held (p. 1154H–J *per* Hope, L.P.) that the pursuer has to show that it was practically certain that he would succeed on the question of liability or that he would almost certainly do so.

    On the question of liability, a relevant conviction may assist the court in being satisfied: *Reid v. Planet Welding Equipment Ltd*, 1980 S.L.T. (Notes) 7 (OH). It may be difficult to be satisfied where the defender denies material averments: *Reid v. J. Smart & Co. Ltd*, 1981 S.L.T. (Notes) 20 (OH); *McCann v. Miller Insulation and Engineering Ltd*, 1986 S.L.T. 147 (OH).

    Proximity of the motion for interim payment to the proof is a relevant factor, but only in exceptional circumstances would it justify making no award: *Kay v. G.P. Inveresk Corporation*, 1988 S.L.T. 711 (OH), 713E *per* Lord Dervaird.

43.11.6   *"without any substantial finding of contributory negligence".* The better view is that "substantial" means a considerable amount, and does not mean of substance in the sense of not being *de minimis*, because the fact that the pursuer was contributorily negligent to some extent does not mean he will get nothing when damages are ultimately assessed: *Reid v. Planet Welding Equipment Ltd*, 1980 S.L.T. (Notes) 7 (OH); *McNeill v. Roche Products Ltd*, 1988 S.L.T. 705 (OH); *cf Nelson v. Duraplex Industries Ltd*, 1975 S.L.T. (Notes) 31 (OH); *Noble v. Noble*, 1979 S.L.T. (Notes) 75 (OH) and *Herron v. Kennon*, 1986 S.L.T. 260 (OH). This view was upheld in *Cowie v. Atlantic Drilling Co. Ltd*, 1995 S.C. 288 (First Div.), 294D *per* Hope, L.P: "substantial" means something of real importance to the assessment of the extent of the defender's liability; and the court must be satisfied that the finding of contributory negligence will not be so large as to have a material effect on the assessment of damages the pursuer is likely to recover.

    In *Reid*, above, Lord Ross did not regard contributory negligence which would not exceed one-quarter or a third as substantial. In *Hogg v. Carrigan's Exr*, 2001 S.C. 542 (OH), 544F at para.[10], it was suggested that even contributory negligence of 50 per cent was not "substantial".

43.11.7   *"would obtain decree for damages against any defender".* Under R.C.S. 1965, r. 89A(l), where the court was satisfied the pursuer was likely to succeed against at least one of a number of defenders, it could make an award against any one or more of the defenders from whom an interim payment was sought: *Walker v. Infabco Diving Services Ltd*, 1983 S.L.T. 633 (Extra Div.). Under R.C.S. 1994, r. 43.11(3), before amendment in 2006, interim damages could only be obtained from the defender against whom the pursuer would be likely to succeed. This was because the phrase "the defender" in the former rule was replaced by *"that* defender" in the latter rule; hence, the rule in *Walker,* above, could not apply. An amendment has been made to r. 43.11(3) by A.S. (R.C.S.A.) (Miscellaneous) 2006 [S.S.I. 2006 No. 83]. The amendment deals with a problem that the previous wording of r. 43.11(3)(b) referred to "that defender". Although r. 43.11(3) has been set out slightly differently, the only change is to make "that defender" now "any defender": thus restoring the rule to its form in R.C.S. 1965, r. 89A(1). Accordingly, the decision in *Walker,* can be applied.

"such amount . . . not exceeding a reasonable proportion . . . likely to be recovered". **43.11.8** Quantification is a matter of discretion. The restraint of the words "not exceeding" provides a ceiling, and, as the limit is a proportion, a conservative and moderate approach is necessary: *Nisbet v. The Marley Roof Tile Co. Ltd,* 1988 S.L.T. 608 (OH). In *D's Parent and Guardian v. Argyll and Clyde Acute Hospitals NHS Trust,* 2003 S.L.T.511 (OH), Lord Carloway considered that 75% or more should not necessarily be seen as exceeding a "reasonable proportion", especially where a minimum figure of likely damages is accepted by the defender in a given case. In *Lennox v. Bishop,* 2005 G.W.D. 32-613, 1st July 2005 (OH), it was held that there was no justification for taking, as a starting point, the minimum award likely and then applying a conservative percentage around 30 to 40 per cent.

The stage which an action has reached is a relevant but not determinative consideration.

An award may be made notwithstanding: (a) that the intention is to spend the award to meet expenditure which is not a head of claim *(Thompson's C.B. v. Burnett* 1989 S.L.T. 264 (OH)); or (b) that the award may involve payment which exceeds the value of the claim for loss to date *(Nisbet,* above; *Thompson's C.B.,* above).

The pursuer does not have to show he is suffering actual hardship *(McNicol v. Buko Ltd,* 1986 S.L.T. 12 (OH), 14E *per* Lord McCluskey; *Curran v. H.A.T. Painters (Scotland) Ltd,* 1987 S.L.T. 98 (OH) *per* Lord Cullen; *McNeill v. Roche Products Ltd,* 1988 S.L.T. 705 (OH), 706H *per* Lord Coulsfield), although it may be a relevant factor *(McNicol,* above).

State benefits may have to be taken into account: *Curran,* above.

"lump sum or otherwise". An interim payment of damages may, where parties consent, be **43.11.9** ordered to be paid in the form of periodical payments: Damages Act 1996, s. 2.

"a person who is insured...a public authority...a person whose means and resources are such". **43.11.10** "[A] person whose means and resources" refers to a person who can meet the obligation to pay out of funds which are his or his to dispose of at will: *Ferguson v. McGrandles,* 1993 S.L.T. 822 (OH), 823 *per* Lord Penrose.

"subsequent motion". There may be more than one subsequent motion. **43.11.11**

Management of money payable to children. Where the interim payment is for the benefit of a **43.11.12** child the court will have to consider the management of that money: see Children (Scotland) Act 1995, s. 13; and note 49.88.2 for detailed discussion.

Social Security (Recovery of Benefits) Act 1997. Under the Social Security (Recovery of **43.11.13** Benefits) Act 1997, the person (the compensator) compensating the victim of an accident, injury or disease is liable to pay in full to the Secretary of State for Social Security the amount of the recoverable social security benefits (for which see column 2 of Sched. 2 to the 1997 Act) paid to the victim in respect of payment of damages on or after 6th October 1997. The compensator is entitled to deduct, from certain specified heads of compensation he is to pay to the victim, the amount of the recoverable benefits (see 1997 Act, s. 8). These heads, specified in column 1 of Sched. 2 to the 1997 Act, are the compensation for earnings lost, the compensation for cost of care, and the compensation for loss of mobility, during the relevant period. The compensator will then pay the sum deducted to the Secretary of State (to the CRU). The "relevant period" is the five years immediately following the date of the accident or injury or, in the case of disease, the date on which the victim first claimed a listed benefit): see 1997 Act, s. 3(2) and (3). If at any time before the end of that period a compensation payment is made in final discharge of any claim, the relevant period ends on that date: 1997 Act, s. 3(4)(a). The £2,500 small payments threshold has been abolished.

Where the pursuer received benefits to which the 1997 Act applies, the court, on pronouncing decree for payment of the interim damages, must specify the amount of compensation payment in the case of each head of compensation: 1997 Act, s. 15(2). A difficulty arises where the decree is pronounced *within* the five-year relevant period: is the court required to specify the damages for a period ending on the date of payment (not then determinable) after decree, the final discharge occurring and the relevant period ending, under s. 3(4)(a) of the 1997 Act, on the date of payment; or is the date of decree to be deemed to be the date of payment? The solution has

been provided by the Inner House in *Mitchell v. Laing*, 1998 S.C. 342. The court held that the intention of the legislation was that the amount of recoverable benefits to be deducted from the heads of compensation was the amount payable over the whole five-year period. Accordingly, the court in pronouncing decree would specify the damages due for the specified heads of compensation for the full five years. As at the date of interim damages, the benefits recoverable from the relevant heads of compensation are the listed benefits paid or likely to be paid during the period from the date of injury (or claim for benefit in the case of disease) to the date of payment of interim damages or the end of the five year period, whichever is earlier.

The court also held in that case that the words "loss of mobility" in column 1 of Sched. 2 to the 1997 Act mean damages for patrimonial loss suffered as a result of loss of mobility due to the accident, injury or disease.

Adjustment on final decree

[1] **43.12.** Where a defender has made an interim payment order under rule 43.11(3), the court may make such order, when final decree is pronounced, with respect to the interim payment as it thinks fit to give effect to the final liability of that defender to the pursuer; and in particular may order—

  (a) repayment by the pursuer of any sum by which the interim payment exceeds the amount which that defender is liable to pay the pursuer; or

  (b) payment by any other defender or a third party of any part of the interim payment which the defender who made it is entitled to recover from him by way of contribution or indemnity or in respect of any remedy or relief relating to, or connected with, the claim of the pursuer.

Deriv. R.C.S. 1965, r.89A(2) inserted by S.I. 1974 No. 845; and R.C.S. 1994, old r.43.10

---

[1] R. 43.12 substituted by S.S.I. 2002 No. 570 (effective 1st April 2003).

General note. Rule 43.12 is in the same terms as old r.43.10. **43.12.1**

"may make such order . . . . as it thinks fit". That the court may make such order as it thinks fit, **43.12.2** gives the court a wide general discretion; and the words "and in particular may order" is a clear indication that what follows are two examples of what the court may do, without prejudice to the generality.

In *Walker v. Infabco Diving Services Ltd*, 1983 S.L.T. 633 (Extra Div.), Lord Cowie observed that r.43.10(a) (now r.43.12(a)) allows the court to adjust the position whether liability to the pursuer is established or not; and r.43.10(b) (now r.43.12(b)) allows the court to adjust the position between defenders and envisages the position that one defender, against whom an order for interim payment has been made, may be assoilzied and may recover that amount from a defender against whom liability has been established.

Where a final award is made, care must be taken to ensure that interest is not applied to that portion which formed an interim award after the date on which that interim award was paid.

"final decree". This relates individually to the position of any particular defender and not **43.12.3** simply to the last of a number of defenders whose position is considered; so, where a pursuer, who was paid interim damages by two defenders, abandoned against one of them, it was competent for that defender to recover his share from the other defender: *Mitchell v. H.A.T. Contracting Services Ltd (No. 3)*,1993 S.L.T. 1199 (OH).

Interest on repayment. In *Walker v. Infabco Diving Services Ltd*, 1983 S.L.T. 633 (Extra Div.), **43.12.4** Lord Ross observed at p.641 that interest would be due on repayment of the interim damages; but Lord Stott at p.638, and Lord Cowie at p.642, took a contrary view as the rule made no mention of interest. The fact that the rule does not specifically mention interest is not conclusive; the rule gives the court a wide discretion to make such order as it thinks fit, which could include an order relating to interest.

Applications for further damages

[1] **43.13.**—(1) An application for further damages by a pursuer in respect of whom an order under section 12(2)(b) of the Administration of Justice Act 1982 has been made shall be made by minute and shall include—

(a) a conclusion in Form 43.13-A; and

(b) averments in the statement of facts supporting that conclusion.

(2) On lodging such a minute in process, the pursuer shall apply by motion for warrant to serve the minute on—

(a) every other party; and

(b) where such other party is insured or otherwise indemnified, his insurer or indemnifier, if known to the pursuer.

(3) A notice of intimation in Form 43.13-B shall be attached to the copy of the minute served on a warrant granted on a motion under paragraph (2).

(4) Any such party, insurer or indemnifier may lodge answers to such a minute in process within 28 days after the date of service on him.

Deriv. R.C.S. 1965, r.134C inserted by S.I. 1984 No. 919; and R.C.S. 1994 old r.43.13

---

[1] R. 43.13 substituted by S.S.I. 2002 No. 570 (effective 1st April 2003).

43.13.1 *General note.* Rule 43.13 is in the same terms as old r.43.13, save that the minute has no pleas-in-law: see r.43.13(1).

43.13.2 *'minute".* For applications by minute, see r.15.1.

43.13.3 *"lodging such a minute in process".* The minute is lodged as a step of process (r.1.3(1) (definition of "step of process")) in the process of the action to which it relates. On lodging a step of process, see rr.4.4–4.6.

43.13.4 *"serve".* For methods, see Chap. 16, Pt I.

43.13.5 *Evidence of service.* See note 16.1.5. On expiry of the period of notice after service, the certificate of service must be attached to the minute lodged under this rule.

43.13.6 *"answers".* See r.18.3.

43.13.7 *"within 28 days".* The date from which the period is calculated is not counted. Where the last day falls on a Saturday or Sunday, or a public holiday on which the Office of Court is closed, the next available day is allowed: r.1.3(7). For office hours and public holidays, see note 3.1.2.

Actions by connected persons

[1] **43.14.**—(1) In an action of damages in which, following the death of any person from personal injuries, damages are claimed—

(a) by the executor of the deceased, in respect of the injuries from which the deceased died; or

(b) by any relative of the deceased, in respect of the death of the deceased,

the pursuer shall make the averments specified in paragraph (2).

(2) The pursuer in an action to which paragraph (1) applies shall aver in the condescendence, as the case may be—

(a) that there are no connected persons;

(b) that there are connected persons, being persons specified in the warrant for intimation; or

(c) that there are connected persons in respect of whom intimation should be dispensed with on the ground that—

(i) the names or whereabouts of such persons are not known to, and cannot reasonably be ascertained by, the pursuer; or

(ii) such persons are unlikely to be awarded more than the sum of £200 each.

Deriv. R.C.S. 1965, r.75A(1) and (2) substituted by S.I. 1984 No. 920 and amended by S.I. 1986 No. 1941; and R.C.S. 1994, old r.43.1(1) and 43.2

---

[1] R. 43.14 substituted by S.S.I. 2002 No. 570 (effective 1st April 2003).

General note. Rule 43.14 is substantially in the same terms as old rr.43.1(1) and 43.2. **43.14.1**

Section 5 of the Damages (Scotland) Act 1976 first introduced detailed provisions for avoidance of multiplicity of actions in respect of the death of a relative requiring the pursuer to serve a notice on every person not a party who would have title to sue the defender as executor or relative of the deceased in an action based on the injuries or death. This proved cumbersome and expensive and s.5 was repealed by s.14(2) of the Administration of Justice Act 1982 following a report of the Scottish Law Commission (Scot. Law Com. No. 64), leaving it to the court to make appropriate provision in the rules. Such rules were made by A.S. (A.R.C. No. 5) (Intimation in Fatal Accident Cases) 1984 [S.I. 1984 No. 920].

The rules for intimation to connected persons are plainly intended to ensure that intimation is only required when it is sensible: *Henderson v. Occidental Petroleum (Caledonia) Ltd,* 1990 S.L.T. 315 (OH), 316G *per* Lord Prosser.

"personal injuries". The definition is now in r.43.1(2): see note 43.1.2. **43.14.2**

"relative". This means only those listed in Sched. 1 to the Damages (Scotland) Act 1976 as **43.14.3** amended by s.14(4) of the Administration of Justice Act 1982. A relative belonging to the deceased's immediate family (for which see the 1976 Act, s.l0(2) as amended by the 1982 Act, s.14(4)) may sue for (what was formerly called) loss of society and loss of support, and a remoter relative may sue for loss of support (actual or likely), where the deceased died in consequence of personal injuries as a result of an act or omission of another unless the liability to the deceased or his executor was excluded or discharged before his death: 1976 Act, s.1 as amended by the Damages (Scotland) Act 1993, s.1. Such a right transfers to the relative's executor (1976 Act, s.1A inserted by the 1993 Act, s.2) but not solatium or "loss of society" (1976 Act, s.3). The deceased's claim for damages for personal injuries (except patrimonial loss after death) transmits to his executor: 1976 Act, s.2 substituted by the 1993 Act, s.3.

Civil partners, or persons in a relationship which has the same characteristics as a civil partnership (same sex relationship), are now relatives: 1976 Act, Sched. 1 as amended by the Civil Partnership Act 2004, Sched. 28, para. 42. *Telfer v. Killock,* 2004 S.L.T. 1291 (OH) is thus overruled.

"connected person". The definition in r.43.1(2), as in old r.43.1(2), is "a person, not being a **43.14.4** party to the action, who has title to sue the defender in respect of the personal injuries from which a deceased died or in respect of his death". The connected persons to the deceased are thus (a) the executors, (b) the immediate family relatives (for which, see Damages (Scotland) Act 1976, s.10(2) as amended by the Administration of Justice Act 1982, s.14(4)), and (c) remoter relatives.

Intimation to connected persons. Intimation should be made to (a) the executors of the **43.14.5** deceased, (b) members of the deceased's immediate family, and (c) remoter relatives. A relative belonging to the deceased's immediate family will probably be known and should be named and receive intimation because he or she may sue for loss of society and loss of support (unless unlikely to receive more than £200); a remoter relative may sue only for loss of actual or likely support: see note 43.14.3.

In the case of relatives remoter than the immediate family (for which, see Damages (Scotland) Act 1976, s.10(2) as amended by the Administration of Justice Act 1982, s.14(4)), it has been held that it is not necessary to set out the names and whereabouts of such persons, even when these are known, and no need to take any steps to ascertain names or whereabouts which are unknown. In the absence of current or specific likelihood of support, the grounds for seeking dispensation, and the reasons for granting it, do not turn on identification of the relative or the number or relationship of such relatives. It is sufficient to aver that there are persons other than the pursuer(s) having title as relatives of the deceased, that no such person was receiving, or is likely in the future to receive, support from the deceased; and that in these circumstances it is believed and averred that none of those persons is likely to be awarded more than £200: *Henderson v. Occidental Petroleum (Caledonia) Ltd,* 1990 S.L.T. 315 (OH), 316K *per* Lord Prosser.

Warrants for intimation in actions by connected persons

[1] **43.15.**—(1) Where the pursuer makes averments under rule 43.14(2)(b) (existence of connected persons), he shall insert a warrant for intimation in the summons in the following terms:—

"Warrant to intimate to (*name and address*) as a person who is believed to have title to sue the defender in an action in respect of the personal injuries from which the late (*name and last place of residence*) died [or the death of the late (*name and last place of residence*)]".

(2) A notice of intimation in Form 43.15 shall be attached to the copy of the summons where intimation is given on a warrant under paragraph (1).

Deriv. R.C.S. r.75A(6) and (7) (part) substituted by S.I. 1984 No. 920 and amended by S.I. 1986 No. 1941; and R.C.S. 1994, old r.43.3

---

[1] R. 43.15 substituted by S.S.I. 2002 No. 570 (effective 1st April 2003).

43.15.1 *Intimation.* For methods, see r.16.8. For evidence of intimation, see note 16.8.1.

Applications to dispense with intimation in actions by connected persons
[1] **43.16.**—(1) Where the pursuer makes averments under rule 43.14(2)(c) (dispensing with intimation to connected persons), he shall apply by motion for an order to dispense with intimation.

(2) In determining a motion under paragraph (1), the court shall have regard to—

(a) the desirability of avoiding multiplicity of actions; and

(b) the expense, inconvenience or difficulty likely to be involved in taking steps to ascertain the name or whereabouts of the connected person.

(3) Where the court is not satisfied that intimation to a connected person should be dispensed with, it may—

(a) order intimation to a connected person whose name and whereabouts are known;

(b) order the pursuer to take such further steps as it may specify in the interlocutor to ascertain the name or whereabouts of any connected person; and

(c) order that such advertisement be made in such manner, in such place and at such times as it may specify in the interlocutor.

Deriv. R.C.S. 1965, r.75A(4) (r. 43.16(1)), and r.75A(5) (r. 43.16(2) and (3), both substituted by S.I. 1984 No. 920 and amended by S.I. 1986 No. 1941; and R.C.S. 1994, old r.43.4.

---

[1] R. 43.16 substituted by S.S.I. 2002 No. 570 (effective 1st April 2003).

43.16.1 *General note.* Rule 43.16 is in the same terms as old r.43.4.

43.16.2 *Dispensing with intimation.* Intimation should only be required on anyone beyond the immediate family (for which, see Damages (Scotland) Act 1976, s.10(2) as amended by the Administration of Justice Act 1982, s.14(4)) in those cases (presumably rare) in which the pursuer's agents have reason to believe that some particular relative has suffered an actual loss of support, or is for specific reasons to be regarded as someone who the deceased would have supported in the future: *Henderson v. Occidental Petroleum (Caledonia) Ltd,* 1990 S.L.T. 315 (OH), 316H *per* Lord Prosser. See further, notes 43.14.2 to 43.14.5.

Where a relative in respect of whom the court has dispensed with intimation becomes known, intimation may be required: r.43.17; and see note 43.17.2.

43.16.3 *"motion".* For motions, see Chap. 23.

Subsequent disclosure of connected persons
[1] **43.17.** Where the name or whereabouts of a person, in respect of whom the court has dispensed with intimation on a ground specified in rule 43.14(2)(c) (dispensing with intimation to connected persons), subsequently becomes known to the pursuer while the action is depending before the court, the pursuer shall apply by motion under rule 13.8(1) (warrants after signeting) for a warrant for intimation to such a person; and such intimation shall be made in accordance with rule 43.15(2).

Deriv. R.C.S. 1965, r.75A(7) (part) substituted by S.I. 1984 No. 920 and amended by S.I. 1986 No. 1941; and R.C.S. 1994, old r.43.5.

---

[1] R. 43.17 substituted by S.S.I. 2002 No. 570 (effective 1st April 2003).

General note. Rule 43.17 is in the same terms as old r.43.5. **43.17.1**

Is intimation mandatory? Having regard to what Lord Prosser said in *Henderson v. Occidental* **43.17.2** *Petroleum (Caledonia) Ltd*, 1990 S.L.T. 315 (OH), at 316H about the only persons on whom intimation ought to be required (see note 43.16.2), intimation on a relative may, notwithstanding the terms of r.43.17, be dispensed with.

"depending" A cause is depending from the time it is commenced *(i.e.* from the time an action **43.17.3** is served) until final decree, whereas a cause is in dependence until final extract. For the meaning of "commenced", see note 13.4.4. For the meaning of final decree, see note 4.15.2(2). For the meaning of final extract, see note 7.1.2(2).

"motion". For motions, see Chap. 23. **43.17.4**

Connected persons entering the process
[1] **43.18.**—(1) A connected person may apply to the court by minute in the process of the action craving leave to be sisted as an additional pursuer to the action.

(2) Any such minute shall be placed before the Lord Ordinary who may grant the minute and shall make such order as he considers appropriate, having regard to the provisions in this Chapter.

Deriv. R.C.S. 1965, r.75A(9) (part) substituted by S.I. 1984 No. 920 and amended by S.I. 1986 No. 1941; and R.C.S. 1994, old r.43.6(1)

---

[1] R. 43.18 substituted by S.S.I. 2002 No. 570 (effective 1st April 2003).

General note. A connected person should join the existing action otherwise he will not be **43.18.1** awarded expenses in any separate action raised by him: r.43.19.

"minute". Old r.43.6(2) required the minuter to crave leave to adopt the existing pleadings for **43.18.2** the pursuer or set out separate pleadings. That provision has not been repeated in the new rule. A fee will be payable for entering the process.

Procedure on minute. Old r.43.6(3) and (4) provided for intimation of the minute to other **43.18.3** parties before the minute was lodged. That provision has not been repeated.

Failure by connected person to enter process
[1] **43.19.**—(1) Where a connected person to whom intimation is made—
  (a) does not apply to be sisted as an additional pursuer to the action;
  (b) subsequently brings a separate action against the same defender in respect of the same personal injuries or death; and
  (c) would, apart from this rule, be awarded the expenses or part of the expenses of that action,
he shall not be awarded those expenses except on cause shown.

Deriv. R.C.S. 1965, r.75A(1) substituted by S.I. 1984 No. 920 and amended by S.I. 1986 No. 1941; and R.C.S. 1994, old r.43.7.

---

[1] R. 43.19 substituted by S.S.I. 2002 No. 570 (effective 1st April 2003).

General note. Rule 43.19(1) (there is in fact no r.43 19(2)) is in the same terms as old r.43.7. **43.19.1**
It behoves a connected person to join an existing action to avoid having to pay his or her own expenses for not doing so.

Mesothelioma actions: special provisions

[1] **43.20**—(1) This rule applies where liability to a relative of the pursuer may arise under section 1(2A) and (2B) of the Damages (Scotland) Act 1976 (liability where the personal injury in consequence of which the deceased died is mesothelioma).

(2) On settlement of the pursuer's claim, the pursuer may apply by motion for any or all of the following:–

   (a) a sist for a specified period;

   (b) discharge of the proof;

   (c) variation of the timetable issued under rule 43.6.

(3) Paragraphs (4) to (7) apply where a motion under paragraph (2) has been granted.

(4) As soon as reasonably practicable after the death of the pursuer, any agent who immediately prior to the death was instructed in a cause by the deceased pursuer shall notify the court of the death.

(5) The notification under paragraph (4) shall be by letter to the Deputy Principal Clerk and shall be accompanied by a certified copy of the death certificate relative to the deceased pursuer.

(6) A relative of the deceased may apply by motion for the recall of the sist and for an order for further procedure.

(7) On the expiration of the period of any sist pronounced on a motion under paragraph (2) the Keeper may put the case out to be heard on the By Order roll.

---

[1] Rule 43.20 inserted by the Act of Sederunt (Rules of the Court of Session Amendment No. 4) (Personal Injuries Actions etc.) 2007, para. 2 (effective 2nd May 2007).

[1] (OLD) CHAPTER 43   **Old**

ACTIONS OF DAMAGES

[1] Chap.43 was substituted by S.S.I. 2002 No. 570 (effective 1st April 2003). The following version of Chapter 43 applies to any action raised before 1st April 2003 (see S.S.I. 2002 No. 570, para.3), and is reproduced accordingly.

PART I

INTIMATION TO CONNECTED PERSONS IN CERTAIN ACTIONS OF DAMAGES

Application and interpretation of this Part

43.1.—(1) This Part applies to an action of damages in which, following the death of any person from personal injuries, damages are claimed—

   (a) by the executor of the deceased, in respect of the injuries from which the deceased died; or

   (b) by any relative of the deceased, in respect of the death of the deceased.

(2) In this Part—

   "connected person" means a person, not being a party to the action, who has title to sue the defender in respect of the personal injuries from which the deceased died or in respect of his death;

   "relative" has the meaning assigned to it in Schedule 1 to the Damages (Scotland) Act 1976.

Deriv. R.C.S. 1965, r. 75A(1) and (2) substituted by S.I. 1984 No. 920 and amended by S.I. 1986 No. 1941

43.1.1   *General note.* Section 5 of the Damages (Scotland) Act 1976 first introduced detailed provisions for avoidance of multiplicity of actions in respect of the death of a relative requiring the pursuer to serve a notice on every person not a party who would have title to sue the

Old

defender as executor or relative of the deceased in an action based on the injuries or death. This proved cumbersome and expensive and s.5 was repealed by s.14(2) of the Administration of Justice Act 1982 following a report of the Scottish Law Commission (Scot. Law Com. No. 64), leaving it to the court to make appropriate provision in the rules. Such rules were made by A.S. (A.R.C. No. 5) (Intimation in Fatal Accident Cases) 1984 [S.I. 1984 No. 920].

The rules for intimation to connected persons are plainly intended to ensure that intimation is only required when it is sensible: *Henderson v. Occidental Petroleum (Caledonia) Ltd* 1990 S.L.T. 315, 316G *per* Lord Prosser.

"personal injuries". These include any disease or any impairment of a person's physical or **43.1.2** mental condition: Damages (Scotland) Act 1976, s.10(1).

"relative". This means only those listed in Sched. 1 to the Damages (Scotland) Act 1976 as **43.1.3** amended by s.14(4) of the Administration of Justice Act 1982. A relative belonging to the deceased's immediate family (for which see Damages (Scotland) Act 1976, s.10(2) as amended by the Administration of Justice Act 1982, s.14(4)) may sue for (what was formerly called) loss of society and loss of support, and a remoter relative may sue for loss of support (actual or likely), where the deceased died in consequence of personal injuries as a result of an act or omission of another unless the liability to the deceased or his executor was excluded or discharged before his death: 1976 Act, s.1 as amended by the Damages (Scotland) Act 1993, s.1. Such a right transfers to the relative's executor (1976 Act, s.1A inserted by the 1993 Act, s.2) but not solatium or "loss of society" (1976 Act, s.3). The deceased's claim for damages for personal injuries (except patrimonial loss after death) transmits to his executor: 1976 Act, s.2 substituted by the 1993 Act, s.3.

Averments in actions to which this Part applies

43.2. In an action to which this Part applies, the pursuer shall aver in the condescendence, as the case may be—
  (a) that there are no connected persons;
  (b) that there are connected persons, being the persons specified in the warrant for intimation;
  (c) that there are connected persons in respect of whom intimation should be dispensed with on the ground that—

Old

(i) the names or whereabouts of such persons are not known to, and cannot reasonably be ascertained by, the pursuer; or

(ii) such persons are unlikely to be awarded more than the sum of £200 each.

Deriv. R.C.S. 1965, r. 75A(3) substituted by S.I. 1984 No. 920 and amended by S.I. 1986 No. 1941

General note. A relative belonging to the deceased's immediate family (for which see Damages **43.2.1** (Scotland) Act 1976, s.10(2) as amended by the Administration of Justice Act 1982, s.14(4)) should be named and receive intimation because he or she may sue for loss of society and loss of support whether receiving it or not.

In the case of relatives remoter than the immediate family, it is not necessary to set out the names and whereabouts of such persons, even when these are known, and no need to take any steps to ascertain names or whereabouts which are unknown. In the absence of current or specific likelihood of support the grounds for seeking dispensation, and the reasons for granting it, do not turn on identification of the relative or the number or relationship of such relatives. It is sufficient to aver that there are persons other than the pursuer(s) having title as relatives of the deceased, that no such person was receiving, or is likely in the future to receive, support from the deceased; and that in these circumstances it is believed and averred that none of these persons is likely to be awarded more than £200: *Henderson v. Occidental Petroleum (Caledonia) Ltd* 1990 S.L.T. 315, 316K *per* Lord Prosser.

Warrants for intimation

43.3.—(1) Where the pursuer makes averments under rule 43.2(*b*) (existence of connected persons), he shall insert a warrant for intimation in the summons in the following terms:– "Warrant to intimate to (*name and address*) as a person who is believed to have title to sue the defender in an action in respect of the personal injuries from which the late (*name and last place of residence*) died [*or* the death of the late (*name and last place of residence*)]".

(2) A notice of intimation in Form 43.3 shall be attached to the copy of the summons where intimation is given on a warrant under paragraph (1).

Deriv. R.C.S. 1965, r. 75A(6) and (7)(part) substituted by S.I. 1984 No. 920 and amended by S.I. 1986 No. 1941

Intimation. For methods, see r. 16.8. For evidence of intimation, see note 16.8.1.   **43.3.1**

Applications to dispense with intimation

43.4.—(1) Where the pursuer makes averments under rule 43.2(*c*) (dispensing with intimation to connected persons), he shall apply by motion for an order to dispense with intimation.

(2) In determining a motion under paragraph (1), the court shall have regard to—

(*a*) the desirability of avoiding multiplicity of actions; and

(*b*) the expense, inconvenience or difficulty likely to be involved in taking steps to ascertain the name or whereabouts of the connected person.

(3) Where the court is not satisfied that intimation to a connected person should be dispensed with, it may—

(*a*) order intimation to a connected person whose name and whereabouts are known;

(*b*) order the pursuer to take such further steps as it may specify in the interlocutor to ascertain the name or whereabouts of any connected person; and

(*c*) order that such advertisement be made in such manner, in such place and at such times as it may specify in the interlocutor.

Deriv. R.C.S. 1965, r. 75A(4) (r. 43.4(1)), and r. 75A(5) (r. 43.4(2) and (3)), both substituted by S.I. 1984 No. 920 and amended by S.I. 1986 No. 1941

43.4.1   *General note.* Intimation should only be required on anyone beyond the immediate family | **Old**
(for which see, Damages (Scotland) Act 1976, s.10(2) as amended by the Administration of
Justice Act 1982, s.14(4)) in those cases (presumably rare) in which the pursuer's agents have
reason to believe that some particular relative has suffered an actual loss of support, or is for
specific reasons to be regarded as someone whom the deceased would have supported in the
future: *Henderson v. Occidental Petroleum (Caledonia) Ltd* 1990 S.L.T. 315, 316H *per* Lord
Prosser.

     Where a relative in respect of whom the court has dispensed with intimation becomes known,
intimation may be required: r. 43.5.

43.4.2   *"motion".* For motions, see Chap. 23.

Subsequent disclosure of connected persons

43.5. Where the name or whereabouts of a person, in respect of whom the
court has dispensed with intimation on a ground specified in rule 43.2(*c*)
(dispensing with intimation to connected persons), subsequently becomes
known to the pursuer while the action is depending before the court, the
pursuer shall apply by motion under rule 13.8(1) (warrants after signeting)
for a warrant for intimation to such a person; and such intimation shall be
made in accordance with rule 43.3(2).

Deriv. R.C.S. 1965, r. 75A(7)(part) substituted by S.I. 1984 No. 920 and amended by S.I. 1986
No. 1941

43.5.1   *General note.* Having regard to what Lord Prosser said in *Henderson v. Occidental Petroleum
(Caledonia) Ltd* 1990 S.L.T. 315 at 316H about the only persons on whom intimation ought to
be required (see note 43.4.1), intimation on a relative may, notwithstanding the terms of r. 43.5,
be dispensed with.

43.5.2   *"depending".* A cause is depending from the time it is commenced (*i.e.* from the time an action
is served) until final decree, whereas a cause is in dependence until final extract. For the meaning
of commenced, see note 13.4.4. For the meaning of final decree, see note 4.15.2(2). For the
meaning of final extract, see note 7.1.2(2).

43.5.3   *"motion".* For motions, see Chap. 23.

Connected persons entering process

43.6.—(1) A connected person may apply to the court by minute in the
process of the action craving leave to be sisted as an additional pursuer to
the action.

     (2) Such a minute shall also—
       (*a*) crave leave of the court to adopt the existing grounds of action and
            to amend the conclusions, condescendence and pleas-in-law; or
       (*b*) set out separate conclusions, a statement of facts and appropriate
            pleas-in-law.

     (3) Before lodging such a minute in process, the minuter shall intimate to
every party a copy of the minute and the date on which it will be lodged.

     (4) Any party may lodge answers to such a minute in process within 14
days after the minute has been lodged.

Deriv. R.C.S. 1965, r. 75A(9) and (10) substituted by S.I. 1984 No. 920 and amended by S.I.
1986 No. 1941

43.6.1   *General note.* A connected person should join the existing action otherwise he will not be
awarded expenses in any separate action raised by him: r. 43.7.

     After the period for lodging answers to the minute has expired, a motion should be enrolled,
in respect of any minute, sisting any additional pursuer(s) as a party to the action and amending
the summons accordingly.

43.6.2   *"minute".* A fee will be payable on a connected person first entering the process.

43.6.3   *"intimate".* For methods, see r. 16.7.

"within 14 days". The date from which the period is calculated is not counted. Where the last **43.6.4**
day falls on a Saturday or Sunday or a public holiday on which the Office of Court is closed, the
next available day is allowed: r. 1.3(7). For office hours and public holidays, see note 3.1.2.

Failure to enter process
43.7. Where a connected person to whom intimation is made in
accordance with this Part—
   (a) does not apply to be sisted as an additional pursuer to the action,
   (b) subsequently brings a separate action against the same defender in
       respect of the same personal injuries or death, and
   (c) would, apart from this rule, be awarded the expenses or part of the
       expenses of that action,
he shall not be awarded those expenses except on cause shown.

Deriv. R.C.S. 1965, r. 75A(11) substituted by S.I. 1984 No. 920 and amended by S.I. 1986 No.
1941

PART II

INTERIM PAYMENTS OF DAMAGES

Application and interpretation of this Part
43.8.—(1) This Part applies to an action of damages for personal injuries
or the death of a person from personal injuries.
   (2) In this Part—
      "defender" includes a third party against whom the pursuer has a
         conclusion for damages;
      "personal injuries" includes any disease or impairment of a physical or
         mental condition.

Deriv. R.C.S. 1965, r. 89A(1)(h) inserted by S.I. 1974 No. 845 (r. 43.8(2)(part))

"action of damages for personal injuries". This does not include an action of damages against **43.8.1**
a solicitor arising out of his failure to raise an action of damages for personal injuries within the
triennium: *Mackenzie v. Digby Brown & Co.* 1992 S.L.T. 891.

Applications for interim payment of damages
43.9.—(1) In an action to which this Part applies, a pursuer may, at any
time after defences have been lodged, apply by motion for an order for
interim payment of damages to him by the defender or, where there are two
or more of them, by any one or more of them.
   (2) The pursuer shall give written intimation of a motion under paragraph
(1) to every other party not less than 14 days before the date on which the
motion is enrolled.
   (3) On a motion under paragraph (1), the court may, if satisfied that—
   (a) the defender has admitted liability to the pursuer in the action, or
   (b) if the action proceeded to proof, the pursuer would succeed in the
       action on the question of liability without any substantial finding of
       contributory negligence on his part, or on the part of any person in
       respect of whose injury or death the claim of the pursuer arises, and
       would obtain decree for damages against any defender,
ordain that defender to make an interim payment to the pursuer of such
amount as it thinks fit, not exceeding a reasonable proportion of the
damages which, in the opinion of the court, are likely to be recovered by the
pursuer.
   (4) Any such payment may be ordered to be made in one lump sum or
otherwise as the court thinks fit.
   (5) No order shall be made against a defender under this rule unless it
appears to the court that the defender is—
   (a) a person who is insured in respect of the claim of the pursuer;

    (b) a public authority; or

    (c) a person whose means and resources are such as to enable him to make the interim payment.

    (6) Notwithstanding the grant or refusal of a motion for an interim payment, a subsequent motion may be made where there has been a change of circumstances.

    (7) Subject to Part IV (management of money payable to children), any interim payment shall be made to the pursuer unless the court otherwise directs.

    (8) This rule shall, with the necessary modifications, apply to a counterclaim for damages for personal injuries made by a defender as it applies to an action in which the pursuer may apply for an order for interim payment of damages.

Deriv. R.C.S. 1965, r. 89A(1)(a) to (g) inserted by S.I. 1974 No. 845

43.9.1   *General note.* It was held by Lord Allanbridge in *McCann v. Miller Insulation and Engineering Ltd* 1986 S.L.T. 147 that when considering the question of liability and contributory negligence the court must look at the pleadings alone and not medical reports or other productions. But in *Stone v. Mountford* 1995 S.L.T. 1279 Lord Johnston did not follow *McCann*, and held that the approach in that case did not amount to a general rule, that the discretion available to the court is wide enough to enable the court to review material before it other than the pleadings and to look at productions. It is, however, entitled, when looking at the pleadings, to consider notorious facts: *Reith v. Aberdeen Mineral Water Co.* 1987 S.C.L.R. 689. The court may look at reports and other productions when considering quantification of the interim payment.

    An interim payment of damages may, where parties consent, be ordered to be paid in the form of periodical payments: Damages Act 1996, s.2.

    Temp. Judge Coutts, Q.C., has suggested, in *Hogg v. Carrigan's Exr*, 2001 S.C. 542, 554D (para. 9), that r.43.9 should be radically rephrased. Rule 43.9(3)(a) did not indicate whether it is liability to make reparation or an admission of fault that is meant. This invitation has not so far been taken up.

43.9.2   *"motion".* For motions, see Chap. 23.

43.9.3   *"written intimation".* For methods, see r. 16.9.

43.9.4   *"satisfied".* Satisfaction is less than complete certainty but it requires more than probability or even high probability: *Douglas's C.B. v. Douglas* 1974 S.L.T. (Notes) 67 *per* Lord Maxwell. It means "almost certainly": *Nelson v. Duraplex Industries Ltd* 1975 S.L.T. (Notes) 31, 33 *per* Lord Grieve. This approach was accepted by counsel in *Walker v. Infabco Diving Services Ltd* 1983 S.L.T. 633 and confirmed in *Cowie v. Atlantic Drilling Co. Ltd* 1995 S.C. 288, where it was held (p. 1154H–J *per* L.P. Hope) that the pursuer has to show that it was practically certain that he would succeed on the question of liability or that he would almost certainly do so.

    On the question of liability, a relevant conviction may assist the court in being satisfied: *Reid v. Planet Welding Equipment Ltd* 1980 S.L.T. (Notes) 7. It may be difficult to be satisfied where the defender denies material averments: *Reid v. J. Smart & Co. Ltd* 1981 S.L.T. (Notes) 20; *McCann v. Miller Insulation and Engineering Ltd* 1986 S.L.T. 147.

    Proximity of the motion for interim payment to the proof is a relevant factor, but only in exceptional circumstances would it justify making no award: *Kay v. G.P. Inveresk Corporation* 1988 S.L.T. 711, 713E *per* Lord Dervaird.

43.9.5   *"without any substantial finding of contributory negligence".* The better view is that "substantial" means a considerable amount, and does not mean of substance in the sense of not being *de minimis*, because the fact that the pursuer was contributorily negligent to some extent does not mean he will get nothing when damages are ultimately assessed: *Reid v. Planet Welding Equipment Ltd* 1980 S.L.T. (Notes) 7; *McNeill v. Roche Products Ltd* 1988 S.L.T. 705; *cf. Nelson v. Duraplex Industries Ltd* 1975 S.L.T. (Notes) 31; *Noble v. Noble* 1979 S.L.T. (Notes) 75 and *Herron v. Kennon* 1986 S.L.T. 260. This view was upheld in *Cowie v. Atlantic Drilling Co. Ltd* 1995 S.C. 288, 294D *per* L.P. Hope: "Substantial" means something of real importance to the assessment of the extent of the defender's liability; and the court must be satisfied that the finding of contributory negligence will not be so large as to have a material effect on the assessment of damages the pursuer is likely to recover.

    In *Reid*, above, Lord Ross did not regard contributory negligence which would not exceed one-quarter or a third as substantial. In *Hogg v. Carrigan's Exr*, 2001 S.L.T. 444, it was suggested that even contributory negligence of 50 per cent was not "substantial".

Old

"would obtain decree for damages against any defender". Under R.C.S. 1965, r. 89A(1), where **43.9.6** the court was satisfied the pursuer was likely to succeed against at least one of a number of defenders, it could make an award against any one or more of the defenders from whom an interim payment was sought: *Walker v. Infabco Diving Services Ltd* 1983 S.L.T. 633. But under R.C.S. 1994, r. 43.9(3), interim damages may only be obtained from the defender against whom the pursuer would be likely to succeed. This is because the phrase "the defender" in the former rule has been replaced by "*that* defender" in the latter rule; hence, the rule in *Walker*, above, cannot now apply.

"such amount . . . not exceeding a reasonable proportion . . . likely to be recovered". **43.9.7** Quantification is a matter of discretion. The restraint of the words "not exceeding" provides a ceiling, and, as the limit is a proportion, a conservative and moderate approach is necessary: *Nisbet v. The Marley Roof Tile Co. Ltd* 1988 S.L.T. 608. In *D's Parent and Guardian v Argyll and Clyde Acute Hospitals NHS Trust*, 2003 S.L.T. 511 (OH), Lord Carloway considered that 75 per cent or more should not necessarily be seen as exceeding a "reasonable proportion", especially where a minimum figure of likely damages is accepted by the defender in a given case.

The stage which an action has reached is a relevant but not determinative consideration.

An award may be made notwithstanding (*a*) that the intention is to spend the award to meet expenditure which is not a head of claim (*Thompson's C.B. v. Burnett* 1989 S.L.T. 264) or (*b*) that the award may involve payment which exceeds the value of the claim for loss to date (*Nisbet*, above; *Thompson's C.B.*, above).

The pursuer does not have to show he is suffering actual hardship (*McNicol v. Buko Ltd* 1986 S.L.T. 12, 14E *per* Lord McCluskey; *Curran v. H.A.T. Painters (Scotland) Ltd* 1987 S.L.T. 98, *per* Lord Cullen; *McNeill v. Roche Products Ltd* 1988 S.L.T. 705, 706H *per* Lord Coulsfield), although it may be a relevant factor (*McNicol*, above).

State benefits may have to be taken into account: *Curran*, above.

"a person who is insured . . . a public authority . . . a person whose means and resources are **43.9.8** *such"*. "A person whose means and resources" refers to a person who can meet the obligation to pay out of funds which are his or his to dispose of at will: *Ferguson v. McGrandles* 1993 S.L.T. 822, 823 *per* Lord Penrose.

"subsequent motion". There may be more than one subsequent motion. **43.9.9**

Management of money payable to children. Where the interim payment is for the benefit of a **43.9.10** child the court will have to consider the management of that money: see Children (Scotland) Act 1995, s.13; and note 49.88.2 for detailed discussion.

Social Security (Recovery of Benefits) Act 1997. Under the Social Security (Recovery of **43.9.11** Benefits) Act 1997, the person (the compensator) compensating the victim of an accident, injury or disease is liable to pay in full to the Secretary of State for Social Security the amount of the recoverable social security benefits (for which see column 2 of Sched. 2 to the 1997 Act) paid to the victim in respect of payment of damages on or after 6th October 1997. The compensator is entitled to deduct, from certain specified heads of compensation he is to pay to the victim, the amount of the recoverable benefits (see 1997 Act, s.8). These heads, specified in column 1 of Sched. 2 to the 1997 Act, are the compensation for earnings lost, the compensation for cost of care, and the compensation for loss of mobility, during the relevant period. The compensator will then pay the sum deducted to the Secretary of State (to the CRU). The "relevant period" is the five years immediately following the date of the accident or injury or, in the case of disease, the date on which the victim first claimed a listed benefit): see 1997 Act, s.3(2) and (3). If at any time before the end of that period a compensation payment is made in final discharge of any claim, the relevant period ends on that date: 1997 Act, s.3(4)(a). The £2,500 small payments threshold has been abolished.

Where the pursuer received benefits to which the 1997 Act applies, the court, on pronouncing decree for payment of the interim damages, must specify the amount of compensation payment in the case of each head of compensation: 1997 Act, s.15(2). A difficulty arises where the decree is pronounced *within* the five-year relevant period: is the court required to specify the damages for a period ending on the date of payment (not then determinable) after decree, the final discharge occurring and the relevant period ending, under s.3(4)(a) of the 1997 Act, on the date of payment; or is the date of decree to be deemed to be the date of payment? The solution has been provided by the Inner House in *Mitchell v. Laing*, 1998 S.C. 342. The court held that the intention of the legislation was that the amount of recoverable benefits to be deducted from the heads of compensation was the amount payable over the whole five-year period. Accordingly, the court in pronouncing decree would specify the damages due for the specified heads of compensation for the full five years. As at the date of interim damages, the benefits recoverable from the relevant heads of compensation are the listed benefits paid or likely to be paid during the period from the date of injury (or claim for benefit in the case of disease) to the date of payment of interim damages or the end of the five year period, whichever is earlier.

The court also held in that case that the words "loss of mobility" in column 1 of Sched. 2 to the 1997 Act mean damages for patrimonial loss suffered as a result of loss of mobility due to the accident, injury or disease.

Adjustment on final decree

43.10. Where a defender has made an interim payment ordered under rule 43.9(3), the court may make such order, when final decree is pronounced, with respect to the interim payment as it thinks fit to give effect to the final liability of that defender to the pursuer; and in particular may order—

   (a) repayment by the pursuer of any sum by which the interim payment exceeds the amount which that defender is liable to pay the pursuer; or

   (b) payment by any other defender or a third party of any part of the interim payment which the defender who made it is entitled to recover from him by way of contribution or indemnity or in respect of any remedy or relief relating to, or connected with, the claim of the pursuer.

Deriv. R.C.S. 1965, r. 89A(2) inserted by S.I. 1974 No. 845

43.10.1   *General note.* That the court can make such order as it thinks fit gives the court a wide general discretion; and the words "and in particular may order" is a clear indication that what follows are two examples of what the court may do, without prejudice to the generality.

In *Walker v. Infabco Diving Services Ltd* 1983 S.L.T. 633, Lord Cowie observed that r. 43.10(a) allows the court to adjust the position whether liability to the pursuer is established or not and r. 43.10(b) allows the court to adjust the position between defenders and envisages the position that one defender, against whom an order for interim payment has been made, may be assoilzied and may recover that amount from a defender against whom liability has been established.

Where a final award is made, care must be taken to ensure that interest is not applied to that portion which formed an interim award after the date on which that interim award was paid.

43.10.2   *"final decree".* This relates individually to the position of any particular defender and not simply to the last of a number of defenders whose position is considered; so, where a pursuer, who was paid interim damages by two defenders, abandoned against one of them, it was competent for that defender to recover his share from the other defender: *Mitchell v. H.A.T. Contracting Services Ltd (No. 3)* 1993 S.L.T. 1199.

43.10.3   *Interest on repayment.* In *Walker v. Infabco Diving Services Ltd* 1983 S.L.T. 633, Lord Ross observed at p. 641 that interest would be due on repayment of the interim damages; but Lord Stott at p. 638, and Lord Cowie at p. 642, took a contrary view as the rule made no mention of interest. The fact that the rule does not specifically mention interest is not conclusive; the rule gives the court a wide discretion to make such order as it thinks fit, which could include an order relating to interest.

PART III

PROVISIONAL DAMAGES FOR PERSONAL INJURIES

Application and interpretation of this Part

43.11.—(1) This Part applies to an action of damages for personal injuries.

   (2) In this Part—

      "the Act of 1982" means the Administration of Justice Act 1982;

      "further damages" means the damages referred to in section 12(4)(b) of the Act of 1982;

      "provisional damages" means the damages referred to in section 12(4)(a) of the Act of 1982.

Deriv. R.C.S. 1965, r. 134A inserted by S.I. 1984 No. 919

43.11.1   *"personal injuries".* These include any disease or any impairment of a person's physical or mental condition: Administration of Justice Act 1982, s.13(1).

Old

"further damages", "provisional damages". Provisional damages are damages assessed on the   **43.11.2**
assumption that the injured person will not develop some serious disease or suffer some serious
deterioration in his condition. Further damages are those the pursuer may be awarded if he does
develop the disease or suffer the deterioration.

Applications for provisional damages

43.12. Any application under section 12(2)(a) of the Act of 1982 for
provisional damages for personal injuries shall be made by including in the
summons—

   (a) a conclusion in Form 43.12;

   (b) averments in the condescendence supporting the conclusion, includ-
      ing averments—

      (i) that there is a risk that, at some definite or indefinite time in the
         future, the pursuer will, as a result of the act or omission which
         gave rise to the cause of action, develop some serious disease or
         suffer some serious deterioration of his physical or mental
         condition; and

      (ii) that the defender was, at the time of the act or omission which
         gave rise to the cause of action, a public authority, public
         corporation or insured or otherwise indemnified in respect of the
         claim; and

   (c) an appropriate plea-in-law.

Deriv. R.C.S. 1965, r.134B inserted by SI 1984/919

General note. R. 43.12(b) repeats s.12(1)(a) and (b) of the Act of 1982.   **43.12.1**
An application for provisional damages can be made only by the injured person: Act of 1982,
s.12(2).
Evidence of risk that the pursuer will, as a result of the act or omission which gave rise to the
cause of action, develop some serious disease or suffer some serious deterioration in his
condition, should be led and the court asked to make a finding that there is such a risk, but to
assess and award damages on the assumption that the pursuer will not develop the disease or
suffer the deterioration. In making the award the court may order that an application for
further damages may only be made within a specified period: Act of 1982, s.12(2).

"averments in the condescendence". On pleadings, see note 13.2.4.   **43.12.2**

"develop some serious disease or suffer some serious deterioration". The word "serious"   **43.12.3**
primarily qualifies the word disease or deterioration rather than the effects of the disease or
deterioration, although in assessing seriousness account must be taken of effects on the
pursuer's physical abilities: *White v. Inveresk Paper Co. Ltd* 1988 S.L.T. 2, 5L *per* Lord Murray;
Robertson v. British Bakeries Ltd 1991 S.L.T. 434, 439G *per* Lord Osborne.
It is not the case that a triggering incident causing future deterioration means that s.12 of the
Act of 1982 does not apply. The question is whether the deterioration is the result of the act or
omission which gave rise to the cause of action, and that could be the case notwithstanding that
the deterioration is brought about by an interaction between the condition produced by the
original act and a future triggering event: *Meek v. Burton's Gold Medal Biscuits Ltd* 1989 S.L.T.
338.

Social Security (Recovery of Benefits) Act 1997. For a discussion of this Act and the effect on   **43.12.4**
payment of damages, see note 43.18.4.

Applications for further damages

43.13.—(1) An application for further damages by a pursuer in respect of
whom an order under section 12(2)(b) of the Act of 1982 has been made
shall be made by minute and shall include—

   (a) a conclusion in Form 43.13–A;

   (b) averments in the statement of facts supporting that conclusion; and

   (c) appropriate pleas-in-law.

(2) On lodging such a minute in process, the pursuer shall apply by
motion for warrant to serve the minute on—

   (a) every other party; and

(b) where such other party is insured or otherwise indemnified, his | **Old**
insurer or indemnifier, if known to the pursuer.

(3) A notice of intimation in Form 43.13–B shall be attached to the copy of the minute served on a warrant granted on a motion under paragraph (2).

(4) Any such party, insurer or indemnifier may lodge answers to such a minute in process within 28 days after the date of service on him.

Deriv. R.C.S. 1965, r.134C inserted by SI 1984/919

43.13.1   *"minute".* For applications by minute, see r.15.1.

43.13.2   *"lodging such a minute in process".* The minute is lodged as a step of process (r.1.3(1) (definition of "step of process")) in the process of the action to which it relates. On lodging a step of process, see r.4.4. The note may be lodged by post: P.N. No. 4 of 1994, paras 1 and 8; and see note 4.4.10.

43.13.3   *"serve".* For methods, see Chap. 16, Pt I.

43.13.4   *Evidence of service.* See note 16.1.5. On expiry of the period of notice after service, the certificate of service shall be attached to the minute lodged under this rule.

43.13.5   *"answers".* See r.18.3.

43.13.6   *"within 28 days".* The date from which the period is calculated is not counted. Where the last day falls on a Saturday or Sunday or a public holiday on which the Office of Court is closed, the next available day is allowed: r.1.3(7). For office hours and public holidays, see note 3.1.2.

PART IV

MANAGEMENT OF MONEY PAYABLE TO CHILDREN

Interpretation of this Part
43.14. [Revoked by S.I. 1996 No. 2587 (effective 1st November 1996).]

43.14.1   *General note.* Part IV has been revoked by the A.S. (R.C.S.A. No. 5) (Family Actions and Miscellaneous) 1996 [SI 1996/2587] because s.13 of the Children (Scotland) Act 1995 contains the substantive provisions for the management of money payable to children in any court proceedings.

Section 13 of the 1995 Act implements the recommendations of the Scottish Law Commission *Report on Family Law*, para.4.6 [Scot. Law Com. No. 135]. Advice that rr.43.14 to 43.17 implemented these recommendations and that they were more flexible in rules than in primary legislation was not accepted.

The only rule which survives in the R.C.S. 1994 is a rule for administration now in r.49.88, which replaces r.43.17 (subsequent orders). Full notes on management of money payable to children are now to be found in notes 49.88.1–49.88.4.

Full notes on management of money payable to children are now to be found in notes 49.88.1–49.88.4.

Orders for payment and management of money
43.15. [Revoked by S.I. 1996 No. 2587 (effective 1st November 1996).]

43.15.1   *General note.* See note 43.14.1.

Methods of management
43.16. [Revoked by S.I. 1996 No. 2587 (effective 1st November 1996).]

Subsequent orders
43.17. [Revoked by S.I. 1996 No. 2587 (effective 1st November 1996).]

43.17.1   *General note.* See note 43.14.1.

PART V

OPTIONAL PROCEDURE IN CERTAIN ACTIONS OF DAMAGES

Application and election of optional procedure

43.18.—(1) This Part applies to an action of damages for personal injuries or the death of a person in consequence of personal injuries in which the pursuer has made an election under paragraph (2).

(2) The pursuer may elect to adopt the procedure in this Part by bringing an action in Form 43.18.

Deriv. R.C.S. 1965, r. 188E(1) inserted by S.I. 1985 No. 227 (r. 43.18(1)) and r. 188F(1) inserted by S.I. 1985 No. 227 (r. 43.18(2))

General note. In 1979 the Lord President's Committee on Procedure in the Court of Session **43.18.1** chaired by Lord Kincraig made recommendations to give the court more control over, and for the simplification of procedures and to speed up the progress of, personal injuries litigation. Actions subject to the new proposals would not be tried by jury. Action was not taken immediately because it was not thought that anything could be done while jury trial remained a right of both pursuers and defenders. The draftsman (N.M.P. Morrison) devised a means whereby the bringing of an action in a particular form (now Form 43.18) would constitute a waiver by the pursuer of his right to jury trial (see r. 43.19(a)) and if the defender did not apply for jury trial on lodging defences he would be deemed to have waived his right to jury trial (see r. 43.22). The new procedure which a pursuer could elect to use for actions of damages for personal injuries or death of a person (known as the Optional Procedure) was introduced by A.S. (R.C.A. No. 1) (Optional Procedure in Certain Actions of Reparation) 1985 [S.I. 1985 No. 227].

On the objects of the procedure, see *Giles v. Fleming Bros. Structural Engineers Ltd* 1987 S.L.T. 114, 115J *per* Lord Jauncey, *Dunbar v. British Coal Corporation* 1988 S.L.T. 437, 438H *per* Lord Weir and *Matheson v. Press Offshore Ltd* 1992 S.L.T. 288, 290G–K *per* Lord McCluskey. The procedure is ideally suited for actions of damages arising out of road traffic accidents and industrial accidents where the facts are within relatively small compass (*Giles*, above, *per* Lord Jauncey at p. 115K) but is not limited to such cases. For a discussion of the Optional Procedure, see 1991 S.L.T.(News) 17.

The success of the procedure may be measured by the fact that it is now possible to obtain a date for a proof within a relatively short time after the calling of the summons.

Jurisdiction. See notes 13.2.8 to 13.2.14.   **43.18.2**

"action in Form 43.18". The principal features of the summons in this form are (1) that the **43.18.3** words "Action of Reparation (Optional Procedure)" must be inserted; (2) that the sum awarded may be an amount greater than that sued for; and (3) that the articles of condescendence relating to the grounds of fault may be brief consonant with fair notice and, in relation to breaches of statutory duty, it may be enough to specify the statutory provision. The form is a style which may be varied according to the circumstances: r. 1.4; *White v. Inveresk Paper Co. Ltd* 1987 S.L.T. 586, 587 *per* Lord Cullen.

Cases appropriate for optional procedure do not require the careful and comprehensive pleading standards appropriate for an ordinary action: *Noble v. National Coal Board* 1989 S.L.T. 303, 304H *per* Lord Caplan. Nonetheless, the requirement of fair notice in a broad rather than a narrow technical sense is one which should be reasonably met: *McFarnon v. British Coal Corporation* 1988 S.L.T. 242, 243B *per* Lord Murray; and see *Rodgers v. British Steel plc* 1990 S.L.T. 642 where an alternative case not pled could not be advanced.

Social Security (Recovery of Benefits) Act 1997. Under the Social Security (Recovery of **43.18.4** Benefits) Act 1997, the person (the compensator) compensating the victim of an accident, injury or disease is liable to pay in full to the Secretary of State for Social Security the amount of the recoverable social security benefits (for which see column 2 of Sched. 2 to the 1997 Act) paid to the victim in respect of payment of damages on or after 6th October 1997. The compensator is entitled to deduct, from certain specified heads of compensation he is to pay to the victim, the amount of the recoverable benefits (see 1997 Act, s.8). These heads, specified in column 1 of Sched. 2 to the 1997 Act, are the compensation for earnings lost, the compensation for cost of care, and the compensation for loss of mobility, during the relevant period. The compensator will then pay the sum deducted to the Secretary of State (to the CRU). The "relevant period" is the five years immediately following the date accident or injury or, in the case of disease, the date on which the victim first claimed a listed benefit: see 1997 Act, s.3(2) and (3). If at any time before the end of that period a compensation payment is made in final discharge of any claim, the relevant period ends on that date: 1997 Act, s.3(4)(a). The £2,500 small payments threshold has been abolished.

Where the pursuer received benefits to which the 1997 Act applies, the court, on pronouncing decree for payment of the damages, must specify the amount of compensation payment in the case of each head of compensation: 1997 Act, s.15(2). A difficulty arises where the final decree is pronounced *within* the five-year relevant period: is the court required to specify the damages for a period ending on the date of payment (not then determinable) after final decree, the final discharge occurring and the relevant period ending, under s.3(4)(a) of the 1997 Act, on the date of payment; or is the date of decree to be deemed to be the date of payment? The solution has been provided by the Inner House in *Mitchell v. Laing*, 1998 S.C. 342. The court held that the intention of the legislation was that the amount of recoverable benefits to be deducted from the heads of compensation was the amount payable over the whole five-year period. Accordingly, the court in pronouncing decree would specify the damages due for the specified heads of compensation for the full five years.

Other points raised by the 1997 Act are:

(1) *Tenders.* There are five possibilities:- (a) a tender in the usual form (*i.e.* stipulating a total or global sum); (b) a tender containing specification or a breakdown of the offer of damages for loss of earnings, and any cost of care and loss of mobility attributable to the relevant period; (c) a tender in the usual form accompanied by a back letter giving the breakdown; (d) a tender of an offer of damages stating that it is net of benefits; or (e) a tender of an offer of damages stating that it is net of benefits accompanied by a back letter giving the breakdown. All have their drawbacks. A pursuer will not wish to accept a tender in form (a) because he will not know whether the element from which the deductions are to be made may be the largest part of the offer. It may be that a tender in form (b) would satisfy all those having an interest. It has now been confirmed, in *Spence v. Wilson (No. 2)* 1998 S.L.T. 959, that a tender in form (a) is invalid and, accordingly a tender should be in form (b). For tenders generally, see 36.11.8.

(2) *Contributory negligence.* This will reduce the amount of damages to the pursuer but not the amount of recoverable benefits payable by the defender to the CRU.

(3) *Interest.* The 1997 Act repeals s.103 of the Social Security (Administration) Act 1992 which provided that in assessing interest the award of damages is reduced by a sum equal to the amount of relevant benefits received. S.81(5) of the 1992 Act has been re-enacted in s.17 of the 1997 Act which provides that in assessing damages the amount of any listed benefits paid is to be disregarded. The question arises whether, now, in assessing interest the whole of the listed benefits received should be deducted and interest applied only to the balance or that no deduction should be made and interest applied to the gross award. There was a divergence of judicial opinion in the Outer House. In *George v. George C. Peebles & Son*, 1998 S.L.T. 685, Lord Nimmo Smith held that, since the primary purpose of an award of interest is to compensate a pursuer for being deprived of the use of money which he would have received but for the accident, it was inappropriate to leave out of account the fact that he had received benefits in place of earnings he would have received. The inference was that Parliament intended that the discretion conferred by s.1(A) of the Interest on Damages (Scotland) Act 1958 should continue to be exercised; and interest was awarded in that case on the difference between the loss of earnings and income support received. In *Spence v. Wilson* 1998 S.C. 433, Lord Eassie came to the opposite opinion. He held that s.103 and its statutory predecessor innovated on the preceding common law and that the repeal of s.103 and omission of a re-enactment implied a legislative intention that the receipt of benefits was to be disregarded in the assessment of interest just as in the assessment of damages (notwithstanding, it must be supposed, that there is an express provision for the latter). The issue has now been determined by the Inner House in a report from the Lord Ordinary in *Wisely v. John Fulton (Plumbers) Ltd* 1998 S.C. 910 and confirmed by the House of Lords (2000 S.L.T. 494). It was held that, by virtue of s.17 of the 1997 Act, the court disregards any benefits received by the pursuer when working out interest and, therefore, calculates interest on the whole amount of the damages for past loss of earnings. The case of *George*, above, was wrongly decided because it is inconsistent with the scheme of the 1997 Act.

The compensation for earnings lost during the relevant period in col. 1 of Sched. 2 to the 1997 Act, against which the compensator may set off his liability to repay the listed benefits, includes any sum of interest on damages for past loss of earnings: *Wisely*, above.

(4) *The interlocutor granting decree.* Under P.N. No. 3 of 1997 parties seeking decree in an action of reparation for personal injuries (except where that decree is sought of consent, *e.g.* because of a joint minute) must lodge in process a schedule of damages for the purposes of s.15(2) of the Social Security (Recovery of Benefits) Acts 1997 stating the amount of any compensation in respect of the relevant period under the heads of compensation in column 1 of Sched. 2 to the 1997 Act. It is apparent that the interlocutor subsequently pronounced will not itself specify the amounts under each head but will refer to a (or the) appended schedule which does. Clerks of session have been issuing blank schedules in the following form:—

Old

Schedule to interlocutor of even date (*amend as necessary*)
1. Solatium—
      To date:
      Future:
2. Loss of Earnings—
      To end of relevant period (date):
      Subsequent to end of relevant period:
3. Compensation for
      (1) cost of care:
            to end of relevant period (date):
            subsequent to end of relevant
                  period (date):
      (2) loss of mobility
            to end of relevant period date:
            subsequent to end of relevant
                  period (date):
4. Section 8 services:
5. Section 9 services:
6. Medical expenses:
7. Loss of pension rights, etc.:
                                                  TOTAL:
      Less ( )% due to contributory negligence:
      Sum decerned for:

(5) *Benefits disregarded.* Section 17 of the 1997 Act provides that, in respect of any accident, injury or disease, the amount of any listed benefits paid or likely to be paid is to be disregarded. That does not include benefits received prior to the accident: *McKenna v. Sharp* 1998 S.C. 297, *sub. nom. McKenna v. Chief Constable Strathclyde Police* 1998 S.L.T. 1161.

(6) *Heads of compensation from which relevant benefits may be deducted.* These heads, specified in column 1 of Sched.2 to the 1997 Act, are the compensation for earnings lost, the compensation for cost of care, and the compensation for loss of mobility, during the relevant period. In *Mitchell v. Laing* 1998 S.C. 342 it was held that "loss of mobility" means damages for patrimonial loss suffered as a result of loss of mobility due to the accident, injury or disease. In *McManus' Exrx v. Babcock Energy Ltd* 1999 S.C. 569 (OH) it was held that an award for services rendered to an injured person under s.8 of the Administration of Justice Act 1982 was not "compensation for cost of care" and, therefore, benefits such as attendance allowance could not be deducted under s.8 of the 1997 Act.

(7) *Expenses.* The general rule that expenses follow success applies even though the whole of the sum awarded is paid to the CRU (Compensation Recovery Unit) of the DSS under the Social Security (Recovery of Benefits) Act 1997: *Gray v. Lanarkshire Health Board* 1998 S.L.T. 1378.

Effect of election on right to jury trial
43.19. Service of a summons in Form 43.18—
   (a) shall constitute a waiver by the pursuer of his right to jury trial;
   (b) shall not, subject to rule 43.22(2) (waiver by defender of right to jury trial), affect any right of a defender to apply for jury trial.

Deriv. R.C.S. 1965, r. 188F(3) inserted by S.I. 1985 No. 227

General note. The pursuer waives his right to jury trial by serving a summons in Form 43.18. **43.19.1** This does not affect the defender's right to jury trial which will only be deemed to be waived if the defender does not serve a minute with his defences stating his intention to apply for jury trial: r. 43.22.

Period of notice. The period of notice for the lodging of the summons is now the same as for **43.19.2** an ordinary action and not 28 days as in R.C.S. 1965, r. 188G(1).

"Service". For methods, see Chap. 16, Pt. I. **43.19.3**

Proceedings before nominated judge
43.20. All hearings on the Diet Roll shall be brought before a judge of the court nominated for that purpose by the Lord President or, where a nominated judge is not available, before any other judge of the court (including the vacation judge).

43.20.1 *General note.* The provision for nominated judges is to obtain a consistency of approach and to attempt to bring a particular case before the same judge at different hearings on the Diet Roll.

43.20.2 *Nominated judge.* The nominated judges for the Optional Procedure are currently Lords MacLean, Osborne, Abernethy and Johnston and Lady Cosgrove.

43.20.3 *"vacation judge".* The powers of the vacation judge are limited by r. 11.1.

Defences in optional procedure action

43.21. Defences to the action shall be in the form of brief answers to the condescendence and appropriate pleas-in-law.

Deriv. R.C.S. 1965, r. 188H inserted by S.I. 1985 No. 227

43.21.1 *General note.* Defences must be lodged within seven days after the date on which the summons has called: r. 18.1(2). The period of notice for the lodging of the summons is now the same as for an ordinary action and not 28 days as in R.C.S. 1965, r. 188G(1).

No higher standard of averment is required in relation to contributing negligence than is required of a pursuer who need not aver specific duties of care: *Dalson v. Tayside Health Board* 1998 Rep. L.R. 40.

43.21.2 *"Defences".* See notes to r. 18.1 and r. 18.2.

Application by defender for jury trial

43.22.—(1) Where a defender intends to apply for jury trial in the action, he shall, at the same time as lodging defences, lodge a minute in process stating his intention to apply for jury trial.

(2) Where a defender does not lodge a minute under paragraph (1), he shall be taken to have waived his right to jury trial.

(3) Where a defender lodges a minute under paragraph (1)—

(a) the provisions of this Chapter and the waiver by the pursuer of his right to jury trial shall cease to have effect; and

(b) the action shall proceed as an ordinary action.

Deriv. R.C.S. 1965, r. 188I inserted by S.I. 1985 No. 227

43.22.1 *General note.* Where the defender intends to apply for jury trial the court will direct that the action proceeds as an ordinary action and that an open record be lodged within 14 days after the lodging of the defences and minute.

43.22.2 *"minute".* R. 15.1 does not apply because the minute is not an application to the court but a statement of intention. The minute should be in such a form as this:

"[X] for the defender stated and hereby states to the court that he intends to apply for jury trial in this action.

IN RESPECT WHEREOF   (*Signed*)".

Disapplication of requirement for open record

43.23. An open record shall not be made up in, and Chapter 22 (making up and closing records) shall not apply to, the action unless otherwise ordered by the court.

Deriv. R.C.S. 1965, r. 188J(5) inserted by S.I. 1985 No. 227

43.23.1 *General note.* A record is not necessary unless there have been considerable adjustments (for which there should not, in fact, be a need). The authority of the court must be obtained to make up and lodge a record on the summons and defences as adjusted: see r. 43.24(9). Where no such authority has been obtained the Auditor may not allow a charge in any judicial account for making up a record.

Diet Roll

43.24.—(1) Within 14 days after defences have been lodged, the action shall appear on the Diet Roll for a hearing on a specified date.

Old

(2) The appearance of the action on the Diet Roll for a hearing on a specified date shall not affect the right of any party to apply by motion at any time under these Rules.

(3) Where an action appears on the Diet Roll, a motion (other than a motion for a commission and diligence for the recovery of medical records heard before the first hearing on the Diet Roll) which requires the attendance of counsel, or a motion mentioned in paragraph (5), shall be heard on the Diet Roll.

(4) At any hearing on the Diet Roll, the court may, at its own instance or on the motion of a party, on special cause shown where it is satisfied that the difficulty or complexity of the action makes it unsuitable for procedure under this Chapter, order that the action shall proceed as an ordinary action and ordain the pursuer to make up an open record.

(5) At any hearing on the Diet Roll, the court may, on the motion of any party—

    (a) on special cause shown, allow a specified period of adjustment;

    (b) on special cause shown, allow an amendment of the instance or conclusions of the summons;

    (c) on special cause shown, ordain a party to give further specification of his case in his pleadings;

    (d) on cause shown, grant warrant for service of a third party notice: provided that—

        (i) no such warrant may be granted after the final appearance on the Diet Roll unless on special cause shown; and

        (ii) rule 43.21 (defences in optional procedure action) shall, with the necessary modifications, apply to answers by a third party as it applies to a defender;

    (e) remit to a man of skill.

(6) At any hearing on the Diet Roll where adjustment has not been allowed or the period for adjustment has expired, the court shall—

    (a) where necessary, continue the action on the Diet Roll;

    (b) on special cause shown, appoint the action to the Procedure Roll;

    (c) allow a proof or proof before answer, as appropriate—

        (i) on the question of liability and the question of quantum of damages;

        (ii) where liability is admitted, on the question of quantum of damages;

        (iii) where quantum of damages is admitted or agreed, on the question of liability; or

        (iv) where there is an issue between a defender and a third party, on that issue; or

    (d) make such other order, if any, as it considers necessary for the further progress of the action.

(7) Where the court allows a proof or proof before answer under paragraph (6)(c)(i) or (iv), it shall determine whether—

    (a) the questions of liability and quantum of damages should be heard together or separately; and

    (b) any issue between a defender and a third party should be heard with or separately from any question of liability or quantum of damages.

(8) Where the court makes an order under paragraph (6)(b), it may ordain a party—

    (a) to lodge in process a concise note of argument consisting of numbered paragraphs stating the grounds on which he proposes to submit that any preliminary plea should be sustained, and

    (b) to send a copy of it to every other party concerned,

within such period as the court thinks fit.

(9) When making an order under paragraph (6)(b) or (c), the court shall determine whether a record should be made up.

(10) Where the court orders a record to be made up under paragraph (8),

rule 22.3(2) and (3) (lodging etc. of closed records) shall apply to the action as it applies to an ordinary action.

Deriv. R.C.S. 1965, r. 188J(1) to (4) and (6) to (8) inserted by S.I. 1985 No. 227 and amended by S.I. 1990 No. 2118 and 1992 No. 88

43.24.1 *General note.* A special roll rather than the Motion Roll was devised for dealing with optional procedure cases. Originally it was thought the roll would be heard once a week, but this was abandoned because it would cause delays. Once a cause is on the Diet Roll, any motion (subject to one exception in r. 43.24(3): see note 43.24.4) is heard on that roll: r. 43.24(3). Once a case has left the Diet Roll it cannot go back there: *Anderson v. British Coal Corporation* 1992 S.L.T. 398 (2nd Div.). In practice, motions on the Diet Roll are heard at the same time as motions on the Motion Roll.

Because the concept of the procedure and the Diet Roll was new, R.C.S. 1965, r. 188J (now R.C.S. 1994, r. 43.24) contained detailed provisions about what was to be done in order to give guidance to the judges and the legal profession as to its purpose, involving greater and tighter judicial control and expeditious progress of causes. So, *e.g.* if a subsequent hearing after the first on the Diet Roll is required, the court will fix the date of the next hearing. The court is not limited to doing what is listed in r. 43.24 where it is not inconsistent with a particular provision of the rule and the policy of the optional procedure. The other rules of the R.C.S. 1994 of general application apply unless excluded: it has not been found necessary, therefore, in the structure of the R.C.S. 1994 to repeat R.C.S. 1965, r. 188E(2) (application of other rules)). Hence, *e.g.* summary decree may be obtained in an optional procedure cause (*MacNeil v. U.I.E. Shipbuilding (Scotland) Ltd* 1988 S.L.T. 167); and a conclusion for decree of declarator *cognitionis causa tantum* may be inserted (*Garland v. Fairnington* 1993 S.L.T. 711).

Unless there is urgency, instead of enrolling motions *ad hoc*, parties should consider enrolling for a number of orders they require, to be heard together at a hearing on the Diet Roll.

43.24.2 *"within 14 days"*. The date from which the period is calculated is not counted.

43.24.3 *"motion"*. For motions, see Chap. 23.

43.24.4 *"motion for a commission and diligence"*. Allowing a motion for a commission and diligence to recover medical records to be heard other than on the Diet Roll was introduced so that such a motion could be made before having to wait for the first hearing on the Diet Roll.

43.24.5 *"on special cause shown where it is satisfied that the difficulty or complexity of the action makes it unsuitable"*. Special cause must be special to the case in question: *Giles v. Fleming Bros. Structural Engineers Ltd* 1987 S.L.T. 114, 115J *per* Lord Jauncey. The procedure is ideally suited for actions of damages arising out of road traffic accidents and industrial accidents where the facts are within relatively small compass (*Giles*, above, *per* Lord Jauncey at p. 115K) but is not limited to such cases.

Difficulties of investigation can amount to difficulties of the case: *Glennie v. Gillies* 1987 S.L.T. 308. The inclusion of a conclusion for provisional damages does not necessarily make an action difficult or complex: *Duke v. Plessey plc* 1987 S.L.T. 638.

Industrial deafness cases have been withdrawn from the optional procedure: *Giles*, above; *Carr v. British Coal Corporation* 1990 S.L.T. 702. Asbestosis cases have been similarly treated: *Glennie*, above; *Paterson v. Henry Robb Ltd* 1989 S.C. 64.

The motion to have a case withdrawn from optional procedure must be made on the Diet Roll and cannot be made after proof has been allowed: *Roberts v. Lord Advocate* 1990 S.L.T. 317; *Anderson v. British Coal Corporation* 1992 S.L.T. 398 (2nd Div.).

43.24.6 *"Procedure Roll"*. Where the defender has accepted that a case should be under the optional procedure, only in exceptional circumstances, where a point of law is sharply raised, will a plea for dismissal based on a criticism of the relevancy and specification of the pleadings be likely to succeed: *Prest v. Seaforth Maritime Ltd* 1988 S.L.T. 745, 747C *per* Lord Weir; see also *Noble v. National Coal Board* 1989 S.L.T. 303, 304L *per* Lord Caplan; and *Easson v. Dundee Teaching Hospitals NHS Trust* 2000 S.L.T. 345, 348F-I *per* Lord Macfadyen. The proper way to deal with a (belief of) lack of specification in the pursuer's pleadings in an optional procedure case is for the defender to seek an order under r.43.24(5)(c).

43.24.7 *Fixing of hearings on the Procedure Roll or proofs.* For the fixing of hearings, see r. 6.2.

43.24.8 *"send"*. This includes deliver: r. 1.3(1) (definition of "send").

43.24.9 *Reclaiming.* An interlocutor on the Diet Roll which does not dispose of the whole merits of the action (whether or not expenses are dealt with) may be reclaimed against, only with leave of the Lord Ordinary, within 14 days after the date of the interlocutor.

Old

Fee. The court fee for a hearing on the Diet Roll is payable by each party for every 30 minutes   **43.24.10**
or part thereof. For fee, see Court of Session etc. Fees Order 1997, Table of Fees, Pt. I, A and B,
item 16 [S.I. 1997 No.688, Table as amended, pp. C1201 *et seq.*]. The fee may be debited under a
credit scheme introduced on 1st April 1976 by P.N. No. 4 of 1976 to the account (if one is kept
or permitted) of the agent by the court cashier, and an account will be rendered weekly by the
court cashier's office to the agent for all court fees due that week for immediate settlement. An
agent not on the credit scheme will have an account opened for the purpose of lodging the fee:
P.N. No. 2 of 1995. A debit slip and a copy of the court hearing time sheet will be delivered to
the agent's box or sent by DX or post.

A party litigant must pay (by cash, cheque or postal order) to the clerk of court at the end of
the hearing: P.N. No. 2 of 1995. A receipt will be issued. The assistant clerk of session will
acknowledge receipt of the sum received from the clerk of court on the Minute of Proceedings.

Inspection and recovery of documents in optional procedure
43.25.—(1) Without prejudice to rule 43.27 (exchange of reports of skilled
witnesses), within 14 days after an order has been pronounced under rule
43.24(6)(*c*) (allowance of proof), each party to the action shall—
  (*a*) give written intimation to every other party of a list of the documents
      which are, or to the best of his knowledge have been, in his
      possession or control relating to the matters at issue between them;
  (*b*) where such documents have been in his possession or control, state in
      that list the place where and the person with whom, to the best of his
      knowledge, those documents may be found; and
  (*c*) lodge a copy of that list in process.
(2) A party who has received a list of documents from another party
under paragraph (1) may inspect those documents which are in the
possession or control of the party intimating the list within 14 days after the
receipt of the list at a time and place which is reasonable to both parties.
(3) A party inspecting documents under paragraph (2) shall have the right
to obtain a copy or copies of any such document on payment of a copying
fee of not more than that prescribed in Chapter I of the Table of Fees in rule
42.16.
(4) Nothing in this rule shall affect—
  (*a*) the law relating to, or the right of a party to object to the inspection
      of a document on the ground of, privilege or confidentiality; or
  (*b*) the right of a party to apply under rule 35.2 for a commission and
      diligence for recovery of documents or an order under section 1 of
      the Administration of Justice (Scotland) Act 1972.

Deriv. R.C.S. 1965, r. 188K inserted by S.I. 1985 No. 227 and amended by S.I. 1992 No. 88

General note. R.C.S. 1965, r. 188K (now R.C.S. 1994, r. 43.25) was proposed by the   **43.25.1**
draftsman to assist with the policy of the optional procedure.

Parties should agree the time and place for inspection of documents. If a party is being
unreasonable the other party could apply to the court for an order, for which a failure to
obtemper would constitute a contempt.

For a discussion of the interpretation and application of this provision, see "Recovery of
Documents – New Rules?" 1994 S.L.T. (News) 43.

"within 14 days". The date from which the period is calculated is not counted. In relation to r.   **43.25.2**
43.25(1), where the last day falls on a Saturday or Sunday or a public holiday on which the
Office of Court is closed, the next available day is allowed: r. 1.3(7). For office hours and public
holidays, see note 3.1.2.

"written intimation". For methods, see r. 16.9.   **43.25.3**

"documents". The word "document" has been defined in the R.C.S. 1994 by reference to the   **43.25.4**
inclusive definition in s.9 of the Civil Evidence (Scotland) Act 1988: r. 1.3(1).

"lodge a copy of that list in process". The list of documents is lodged as a step of process   **43.25.5**
(r. 1.3(1) (definition of "step of process")). On lodging steps of process, see r. 4.4. The list may
be lodged by post: P.N. No. 4 of 1994, paras. 1 and 8; and see note 4.4.10.

"privilege or confidentiality". For privilege or confidentiality, see note 35.2.7.   **43.25.6**

Exchange of lists of witnesses in optional procedure　　　　　**Old**

43.26.—(1) Within 28 days after an order has been pronounced under rule 43.24(6)(*c*) (allowance of proof), each party to the action shall—

(*a*) give written intimation to every other party of a list containing the name, occupation (if known) and address of each person whom he intends to call as a witness; and

(*b*) lodge a copy of that list in process.

(2) A party who seeks to call as a witness a person not on his list intimated under paragraph (1) shall, if any other party objects to such a witness being called, seek leave of the court to call that person as a witness; and such leave may be granted on such conditions, if any, as the court thinks fit.

Deriv. R.C.S. 1965, r. 188L inserted by S.I. 1985 No. 227 and amended by S.I. 1992 No. 88

43.26.1　　*General note.* All witnesses must be included in the list. Each party must prepare a complete list including a witness he proposes to call who may also happen to be on another party's list. A skilled witness must be included in the list even though his report does not have to be disclosed until 28 days before the proof under r. 43.27: *Gray v. Shearer Shipping Services Ltd* 1991 S.L.T. 355, 357D *per* Lord Sutherland; *Matheson v. Press Offshore Ltd* 1992 S.L.T. 288 (2nd Div.).

If it is sought to add further witnesses before the proof, a supplementary list should be lodged with a motion.

A motion by a defender after the close of the pursuer's proof to lead witnesses not on his list (although on the pursuer's list) was refused in *McGunnigal v. D.B. Marshall (Newbridge) Ltd* 1993 S.L.T. 769.

43.26.2　　*"within 28 days".* The date from which the period is calculated is not counted. Where the last day falls on a Saturday or Sunday or a public holiday on which the Office of Court is closed, the next available day is allowed: r. 1.3(7). For office hours and public holidays, see note 3.1.2.

43.26.3　　*"written intimation".* For methods, see r. 16.9.

43.26.4　　*"lodge a copy of that list in process".* The list of witnesses is lodged as a step of process (r. 1.3(1) (definition of "step of process")). On lodging steps of process, see r. 4.4. The list may be lodged by post: P.N. No. 4 of 1994, paras 1 and 8; and see note 4.4.10.

Exchange of reports of skilled witnesses in optional procedure

43.27.—(1) Not less than 28 days before the diet of proof, a party shall—

(a) disclose to every other party in the form of a written report the substance of the evidence of any skilled person whom he intends to call as a witness; and

(b) lodge a copy of that report in process.

(2) Except on special cause shown, a party may only call as a skilled witness any person the substance of whose evidence has been disclosed in accordance with paragraph (1).

(3) Except on cause shown, the number of skilled witnesses for any party shall be limited to one medical expert and one expert of any other kind.

Deriv. R.C.S. 1965, r. 188M inserted by S.I. 1985 No. 227

43.27.1　　*General note.* R. 43.27 does not derogate from r. 43.26 and a skilled witness should be intimated in the list under r. 43.26 even though his report does not have to be disclosed until 28 days before the proof under r. 43.27: *Gray v. Shearer Shipping Services Ltd* 1991 S.L.T. 355, 357D *per* Lord Sutherland; *Matheson v. Press Offshore Ltd* 1992 S.L.T. 288 (2nd Div.).

The purpose of r. 43.27(2) is to exclude the calling of expert evidence where there is no real dispute as to its substance: *Matheson*, above.

The purpose of r.43.27(3) is to avoid the unnecessary duplication of expert evidence in any particular field: *Nelson v. Fife Council,* 20th December 2001 (OH), unreported (2001 G.W.D. 1–43).

43.27.2　　*"Not less than 28 days before".* The first and last days are included in the calculation.

43.27.3　　*"lodge a copy of that report in process".* The report is lodged as a step of process (r. 1.3(1)

Old

(definition of "step of process")). On lodging steps of process, see r. 4.4. The list may be lodged by post: P.N. No. 4 of 1994, paras 1 and 8; and see note 4.4.10.

Evidence generally in optional procedure
43.28. Where possible, the parties shall agree photographs, sketch plans and any statement or document not in dispute.

Deriv. R.C.S. 1965, r. 188N inserted by S.I. 1985 No. 227

General note. This rule is in form less a rule and more a statement of general principle. It **43.28.1** envisages that parties will come together in advance of the proof to agree as much of the evidence as possible, thereby focusing the matters still dividing them and minimising the amount of court time required for the hearing of evidence.

R.C.S. 1965, r. 188N(2) and (3) (evidence by affidavit etc.) has not been repeated because use can be made of r. 36.8 (conditions for receiving written statements in evidence).

[1] PART VI

PRODUCTIONS IN CERTAIN ACTIONS OF DAMAGES

Application of this Part
43.29. This Part applies to an action of damages for personal injuries or the death of a person in consequence of personal injuries.

———

[1] Pt. VI and r. 43.29 inserted by S.I. 1996 No. 2168 (effective 23rd September 1996).

General note. Part VI was inserted by the A.S. (R.C.S.A. No. 4) (Miscellaneous) 1996 [S.I. **43.29.1** 1996 No. 2168] following recommendations of the Cullen *Review of Business in the Outer House of the Court of Session* in December 1995. These related to averments of medical treatment and medical reports: they are dealt with in the following rules.

Averments of medical treatment
[1] **43.30.** The condescendence of the summons in an action to which this Part applies shall include averments naming—
(a) every medical practitioner from whom, and
(b) every hospital or other institution in which,
the pursuer or, in an action in respect of the death of a person, the deceased received treatment for the injuries sustained, or disease suffered, by him.

———

[1] R. 43.30 inserted by S.I. 1996 No. 2168 (effective 23rd September 1996).

General note. For the history of this rule, see note 43.29.1.   **43.30.1**

"condescendence". See note 13.2.4.   **43.30.2**

Lodging of medical reports
[1] **43.31.**—[2](1) At any time up to and including the calling of a summons in an action to which this Part applies, the pursuer shall lodge as productions all medical reports then available to him and in his possession or control on which he intends, or intends to reserve the right, to rely in the action.
(2) Where no medical report is lodged as required by paragraph (1), the defender may apply by motion for an order specifying a period within which such a report shall be lodged in process.

———

[1] R. 43.31 inserted by S.I. 1996 No. 2168 (effective 23rd September 1996).
[2] R.43.31(1) as amemded by S.S.I. 2000 No. 66, para.2(6) (effective 7th April 2000).

43.31.1   *General note.* For the history of this rule, see note 43.29.1.

In *Pollock v Thomson*, 21st January 2003, unreported (OH), Lord Wheatley, in a motion for interim damages, ignored the element relating to a medical condition because the medical records had not been lodged in accordance with r.43.31. There was no duty, he said, on the defender to obtain the records under r.43.31(2).

43.31.2   *"lodge as productions".* On lodging productions, see r. 4.5.

43.31.3   *"then available to him".* Not all reports in respect of his then medical condition may be available to the pursuer when the summons is lodged for signeting. Where, *e.g.*, the triennium is about to expire, it would be wrong to preclude the lodging of the summons because a medical report was not available. Where no medical report is lodged, the defender may enrol a motion under r. 43.31(2) for an order to lodge such a report.

Subsequent reports may require to be lodged by virtue of r. 36.3 (lodging productions), r. 43.25 (inspection and recovery of documents), or r. 43.27 (exchange of reports of skilled witnesses).

43.31.4   *Application by defender for order for reports.* Rule 43.31(2) was devised to meet the situation where the pursuers did not lodge reports when the summons was lodged for signeting.

43.31.5   *"motion".* For motions, see Chap. 23.

CHAPTER 43A

ACTIONS OF HARASSMENT

[1] *Application and interpretation of this Chapter*
43A.1.—(1) This Chapter applies to an action of harassment within the meaning of section 8(2) of the 1997 Act.
(2) In this Chapter—
    "the 1997 Act" means the Protection from Harassment Act 1997;
"non-harassment order" means an order granted under section 8(5)(b)(ii) of the 1997 Act.

_____

[1] Chap. 43A and r. 43A.1 inserted by S.I. 1997 No. 1527 (effective 16th June 1997).

General note. The Protection from Harassment Act 1997 was originally conceived because of **43A.1.1** the inadequacies of English criminal law to deal with harassment of women, which was given media attention in 1996. For Scotland, the Act creates a (statutory) delict of harassment. Our criminal law is already able to deal with harassment as a breach of the peace, although the 1997 Act provides for the obtaining of non-harassment orders against an offender.

The new delict of harassment occurs where there is an actual or apprehended breach of the duty not to pursue a course of conduct which amounts to harassment of another and is intended to amount to harassment or occurs in circumstances where it would appear to a reasonable person that it would amount to harassment: 1997 Act, s.8(1) and (2). "Conduct" includes speech and "harassment" includes alarm or distress. The court may award damages, grant interdict or interim interdict or a non-harassment order: 1997 Act, s.8(5). There are statutory defences of authorisation by enactment or rule of law, preventing or detecting crime, or reasonableness: 1997 Act, s.8(4).

Procedure for variation or revocation of non-harassment order
    43A.2. An application under section 8(7) of the 1997 Act after final decree in an action of harassment for the variation or revocation of a non-harassment order shall be made by minute in the process of the action to which the application relates.

_____

[1] R. 43A.2 inserted by S.I. 1997 No. 1527 (effective 16th June 1997).

General note. On the Protection from Harassment Act 1997, see note 43A.1.1.   **43A.2.1**

"section 8(7) of the 1997 Act". Where a non-harassment order has been made under **43A.2.2** s.8(5)(b)(ii) of the 1997 Act in an action of harassment to protect a person against further harassment, either the harasser or the harassed person may apply to the court which made the order to revoke or vary the order.

"minute". For applications by minute, see r. 15.1.   **43A.2.3**

CHAPTER 44

TIME TO PAY DIRECTIONS

Application and interpretation of this Chapter
    44.1.—(1) This Chapter applies to an action in which a person may apply under section 1(1) of the Debtors (Scotland) Act 1987 for a time to pay direction.
(2) In this Chapter—
    "the Act of 1987" means the Debtors (Scotland) Act 1987;
"time to pay direction" means a direction made under section 1(1) of the Act of 1987.

Deriv. R.C.S. 1965, r. 88A inserted by S.I. 1988 No. 2060 (r. 44.1(2))

44.1.1   *General note.* S. 1(1) of the Act of 1987 enables the court, on an application made to it by an individual debtor, to direct that any principal sum of money decerned for in a decree (and, subject to certain conditions, any interest and expenses for which that debtor is found liable) be paid by that debtor either by instalments or as a deferred lump sum.

An application for a time to pay direction must be made before the court grants decree. The right to apply may be exercised by any individual debtor who is a party to any cause and against whom a decree for payment of a sum of money is pronounced, *e.g.* a pursuer held liable in a counterclaim, or a third party minuter.

Time to pay directions are competent only in actions where the principal sum of money being decerned for is less than £10,000 (exclusive of interest, whenever accruing, and expenses), or such other amount as may be prescribed in regulations made by the Lord Advocate: Act of 1987, s.1(5)(a). It is not competent for the court to make a time to pay direction where the decree contains an award of a capital sum on divorce, on the granting of a declarator of nullity of marriage, in connection with a maintenance order or in actions for payment of various rates, taxes and duties: Act of 1987, s.1(5). Although not a time to pay direction, it is possible to achieve payment of a capital sum in a divorce action by instalments.

Notice about time to pay directions

44.2.—(1) In an action in which a defender may apply to the court for a time to pay direction, the pursuer shall serve on that defender a notice in Form 44.2–A and an application in Form 44.2–B at the same time as he serves a copy of the summons, or pleadings, as amended by a minute of amendment calling him as a defender.

(2) Before serving a notice and an application under paragraph (1), the pursuer shall insert in Form 44.2–A the date by which Form 44.2–B must be returned to the court by the defender (being the date on which the period of notice expires) and shall complete Part A of Form 44.2–B.

Deriv. R.C.S. 1965, r. 88B inserted by S.I. 1988 No. 2060

44.2.1   *General note.* Form 44.2–A is a notice informing the defender of his right under the Act of 1987 to apply for a time to pay direction which must be served with the application form for a time to pay direction in Form 44.2–B.

44.2.2   *"service".* For methods, see Chap. 16, Pt. I. The certificate of service required under r. 16.1(2) must state that Forms 44.2–A and 44.2–B have been served in a cause in which they are required.

44.2.3   *"period of notice".* This period is determined in accordance with rule 14.6 (period of notice for answers) by virtue of r. 1.3(1) (definitions of "period of notice" and "writ").

Applications for time to pay directions where appearance not entered

44.3.—(1) Where a defender—
(a) does not enter appearance in an action,
(b) intends to apply to the court for a time to pay direction, and
(c) where appropriate, seeks recall or restriction of an arrestment,
he shall complete and send the application in Form 44.2–B to the Deputy Principal Clerk before the date specified in Form 44.2–A.

(2) On receipt of an application for a time to pay direction, the Deputy Principal Clerk shall—
 (*a*) cause the application to be lodged in the process to which it relates; and
 (*b*) give written intimation to the pursuer that he has received the application.

(3) Where the pursuer does not object to the application by a defender for a time to pay direction or the recall or restriction of an arrestment, he may apply by motion for decree in absence stating that he does not object to the application.

(4) Where the pursuer objects to the application by a defender for a time to pay direction or the recall or restriction of an arrestment, he shall intimate—
 (*a*) the motion for decree in absence, and
 (*b*) the grounds of objection to the application by the defender,
in Form 44.3 to the defender not less than seven days before the date on which the motion is enrolled.

(5) On enrolling a motion for decree in absence, the pursuer shall lodge in process a copy of Form 44.3 intimated to the defender.

(6) The defender need not appear at the hearing of the motion for decree in absence and may send to the Deputy Principal Clerk written representations in response to the grounds of objection of the pursuer.

(7) A motion for decree in absence to which paragraph (4) applies shall require the appearance of counsel or other person having a right of audience.

Deriv. R.C.S. 1965, r. 88C inserted by S.I. 1988 No. 2060

General note. A defender may apply for a time to pay direction even though he admits the **44.3.1** debt and does not enter appearance. He may also apply for the recall or restriction of an arrestment which the court may consider when making the time to pay direction: Act of 1987, s. 2(3).

"enter appearance". A defender must enter appearance within three days after the calling of **44.3.2** the summons if he intends to defend: r. 17.1.

"recall or restriction of arrestment". The arrestment may be on the dependence of the action **44.3.3** or in security of the debt concerned: see Act of 1987, s. 2(2). On recall of arrestment, see note 13.10.4.

"written intimation". For methods, see r. 16.9.   **44.3.4**

"decree in absence". A decree in absence may be granted where a defender fails to enter **44.3.5** appearance, or having entered appearance, fails to lodge defences in a cause in which the court may grant decree without evidence: r. 19.1. On decrees in absence generally, see Chap. 19.

"intimate". For methods, see r. 16.7.   **44.3.6**

"counsel or other person having a right of audience". See definitions in r. 1.3(1).   **44.3.7**

Appeals. An "appeal" against a decision of the Lord Ordinary on an application for a time to **44.3.8** pay direction may be made on a question of law with leave of the Lord Ordinary: Act of 1987, s. 103(3). The application for leave must be made within 14 days of the decision and the reclaiming motion enrolled within the next 14 days: r. 38.4(2). Such an appeal is treated as a reclaiming motion: r. 38.10(*b*). The decision of the Lord Ordinary whether or not to grant leave is final: r. 38.5(6).

Applications for time to pay directions where appearance entered but defences not lodged

44.4.—(1) Where a defender—
 (*a*) after entering appearance does not lodge defences,
 (*b*) intends to apply to the court for a time to pay direction, and
 (*c*) where appropriate, seeks recall or restriction of an arrestment, then, notwithstanding the date specified in Form 44.2–A as the date by

which Form 44.2–B must be returned, he shall complete and send the application in Form 44.2–B to the court not later than the day on which defences would have had to be lodged in process.

(2) Paragraphs (2) to (7) of rule 44.3 (applications for time to pay directions where appearance not entered) shall apply to an application under this rule as they apply to an application under that rule.

Deriv. R.C.S. 1965, r. 88D inserted by S.I. 1988 No. 2060

44.4.1   *General note.* See r. 44.3 and notes.

44.4.2   *Lodging defences.* Defences must be lodged in process within seven days after the calling of the summons or, if the seventh day is in vacation, on the next day on which a summons may call: r. 18.1(2).

Applications for time to pay directions where defences lodged

44.5. An application for a time to pay direction by—

(a) a defender in an action in which defences have been lodged by that defender, or

(b) any other party,

shall be made by motion.

Deriv. R.C.S. 1965, r. 88E inserted by S.I. 1988 No. 2060

44.5.1   *General note.* Any party intending to apply for a time to pay direction in a cause after defences have been lodged should particularly note the provisions of the Act of 1987 in relation to expenses. In the Court of Session, expenses are not quantified when decree is granted. Where the party liable for expenses is not legally aided the court's practice since 1983 is usually to pronounce two interlocutors, one disposing of the merits and finding that party liable in expenses and the other decerning for expenses as taxed by the Auditor (the sum being entered in any extract by the Extractor after taxation). Where a party liable in expenses is legally aided there is no decerniture for expenses when the finding is made: a finding of liability is made with a remit to the Auditor to tax and report (on which, see Chap. 42). A decerniture is only made after the Auditor has reported and any objections or an application for modification have been determined. See further, note 4.15.2. The expenses decree in either case cannot be extracted until the expenses have been taxed, and that extract, when it becomes available will specify the amount of the expenses as taxed.

S. 1(3) of the Act of 1987 provides that where the court grants a decree which contains a finding as to liability for expenses, but does not at the same time make a time to pay direction, it shall not at any time thereafter for the court to make a time to pay direction in relation to those expenses. In order therefore to obtain a direction covering the expenses awarded against him, the debtor must apply expressly for it before the court makes a finding as to liability for expenses. The reasoning behind this rule is that the court should only be required to exercise its discretion to make a time to pay direction on one occasion only during a court action for payment of a principal sum: see Scottish Law Commission Report on Diligence and Debtor Protection (Scot. Law Com. No. 95) at para. 3.19.

44.5.2   *"any other party".* This would include a pursuer in a counterclaim or a third party.

44.5.3   *"motion".* The motion ought to be made at the same time as decerniture for payment is sought. For motions, see Chap. 23.

44.5.4   *Appeals.* An "appeal" against a decision of the Lord Ordinary on an application for a time to pay direction may be appealed on a question of law with leave of the Lord Ordinary: Act of 1987, s. 103(3). The application for leave must be made within 14 days of the decision and the reclaiming motion enrolled within the next 14 days: r. 38.4(2). Such an appeal is treated as a reclaiming motion: r. 38.10(b). The decision of the Lord Ordinary whether or not to grant leave is final: r. 38.5(6).

Applications for variation or recall of time to pay directions or arrestments

44.6.—(1) An application under section 3(1) of the Act of 1987 (variation or recall of time to pay direction or recall or restriction of arrestment) shall be made by motion.

(2) The applicant shall—

(*a*) in a motion under paragraph (1), state briefly the grounds on which the order is sought; and

(*b*) give written intimation of the motion to the debtor or creditor, as the case may be, not less than 14 days before the date on which the motion is enrolled.

(3) On enrolling a motion under paragraph (1), the applicant shall lodge in process—

(*a*) a copy of the letter of intimation;

(*b*) the Post Office receipt or certificate of posting of that letter; and

(*c*) any document he intends to rely on at the hearing of the motion.

Deriv. R.C.S. 1965, r. 88F inserted by S.I. 1988 No. 2060

General note. Either the debtor or the creditor may apply to the court to vary or recall a **44.6.1** time to pay direction. The court will only grant such application "if it is satisfied that it is reasonable to do so": Act of 1987, s. 3(1)(*a*).

Similarly, the debtor or creditor may apply to the court for recall or restriction of any arrestment in effect in respect of the debt concerned, and the court may order variation, recall or restriction of the arrestment, subject to the fulfilment by the debtor of such conditions as it thinks fit: Act of 1987, s. 3(1)(*b*) and (2). Where an arrestment on the dependence was in place before the granting of a decree containing a time to pay direction, the effect of the granting of the decree is to convert the arrestment on the dependence into an arrestment in execution. The consequence of the time to pay direction being attached, however, is that no action of furthcoming or sale is competent: Act of 1987, s. 2(1)(*b*)(i).

While a time to pay direction is in effect, the creditor is not entitled to seek to enforce payment of the debt by means of serving a charge or the diligences of arrestment and action of furthcoming or sale, poinding and sale, earnings arrestment or adjudication for debt: Act of 1987, s. 2(1). The creditor does however retain his entitlement to inhibit. The right of a creditor to call up a heritable security, exercise a lien or utilise any of those special diligences available to enforce a heritable debt or arrears of a ground annual is similarly not affected by the making of a time to pay direction.

The right of the creditor to exercise the ordinary diligences available to him in respect of an unpaid debt revives where the time to pay direction is recalled, or has lapsed as a consequence of default or death on the part of the debtor: Act of 1987, s. 2(5). On recall or where lapse has occurred, as described in ss. 4 and 14(2) of the Act of 1987, the creditor may proceed with diligence without returning to court for the recall of the time to pay direction.

"motion". For motions, see Chap. 23.   **44.6.2**

"written intimation". For methods, see r. 16.9.   **44.6.3**

"lodge in process". The copy letter of intimation, the certificate of posting and any **44.6.4** document which the applicant intends to rely on are lodged in process as productions: r. 4.5.

Appeals. An "appeal" against a decision of the Lord Ordinary on an application for vari- **44.6.5** ation or recall of a time to pay direction or arrestment may be made on a question of law with leave of the Lord Ordinary: Act of 1987, s. 103(3). The application for leave must be made within 14 days of the decision and the reclaiming motion enrolled within the next 14 days: r. 38.4(2). Such an appeal is treated as a reclaiming motion: r. 38.10(*b*). The decision of the Lord Ordinary whether or not to grant leave is final: r. 38.5(6).

Notice to debtor for payment of interest on decrees

44.7. Where a creditor seeks to recover interest (other than interest awarded as a specific sum) under a decree containing a time to pay direction, the notice to be served under section 1(7) of the Act of 1987 shall be served on the debtor by the creditor—

(*a*) in the case of a decree containing a time to pay direction for payment by instalments, not less than 14 days before the date on which the last instalment is due to be paid; and

(*b*) in the case of a decree which includes a time to pay direction for payment by deferred lump sum, not less than 14 days before the date on which the lump sum is due to be paid.

Deriv. R.C.S. 1965, r. 88H inserted by S.I. 1988 No. 2060

44.7.1   *General note.* This rule applies where a creditor seeks to recover interest which was not quantified and included in the decree or which has accrued subsequent to the decree being granted. The creditor must, in terms of s. 1(7) of the Act of 1987, and within the periods specified in r. 44.7(*a*) and (*b*), serve a notice on the debtor stating that he is claiming interest and specifying the amount claimed. Unless this is done timeously, the right to recover such interest is lost: Act of 1987, s. 1(6).

As a consequence of s. 1(6) and 1(7) of the Act of 1987, the normal rule that payments made by a debtor are ascribed to interest before capital must be reversed where interest is payable under a decree subject to a time to pay direction. Where the time to pay direction is for payment by instalments, payments to account are applied to the capital sum outstanding until it has been recovered in full. Only then are payments applied to any interest which is claimed. Where the time to pay direction is for payment by deferred lump sum, the principal sum and the interest become payable together at the end of such period as was specified by the court, following intimation by the creditor to the debtor of an extract of the decree containing the time to pay application.

44.7.2   *"served"*. For methods, see Chap. 16, Pt. I.

CHAPTER 45

ACTIONS OF DIVISION AND SALE

Remit to reporter to examine property
    45.1.—(1) In an action of division and sale of heritable property, the court shall, in accordance with paragraph (2), remit to a reporter to examine the property and to report to the court—
    (*a*) whether the property is capable of division in a manner equitable to the interests of the *pro indiviso* proprietors and, if so, how such division may be effected; and
    (*b*) in the event that the property is to be sold—
        (i) whether the property should be sold as a whole or in lots and, if in lots, what those lots should be;
        (ii) whether the property should be exposed for sale by public roup or private bargain;
        (iii) whether the sale should be subject to any upset or minimum price and, if so, the amount;
        (iv) the manner and extent to which the property should be advertised for sale; and
        (v) any other matter which the reporter considers pertinent to a sale of the property.
    (2) A remit under paragraph (1) shall be made—
    (*a*) where the action is undefended, on the motion of the pursuer at any time after the period for lodging defences has expired;
    (*b*) where the action is defended—
        (i) at the closing of the record, on the motion of any party to the action;
        (ii) on the court finding, after a hearing on the Procedure Roll or a proof, that the pursuer is entitled to bring and insist in the action of division and sale; or
        (iii) at such other time as the court thinks fit.
    (3) On completion of a report made under paragraph (1), the reporter shall send the report, with a copy for each party, to the Deputy Principal Clerk.
    (4) On receipt of such a report, the Deputy Principal Clerk shall—
    (*a*) cause the report to be lodged in process; and
    (*b*) give written intimation to each party that this has been done and that he may uplift a copy of the report from the process.

[Release 32: 6 May 1994]

(5) After the lodging of such a report, any party may apply by motion for further procedure or for approval of the report.

(6) At the hearing of a motion under paragraph (5), the court may—

(a) in the event of challenge to any part of the report, order a note of objection to the report and answers to the note to be lodged within such period as the court thinks fit; or

(b) in the absence of such challenge, order that the property be divided or sold, as the case may be, in accordance with the recommendations of the reporter, subject to such modification, if any, as the court thinks fit.

(7) Where, in accordance with paragraph (6)(a), the lodging of a note of objection and answers has been ordered, the cause shall be put out on the By Order Roll before the Lord Ordinary after the expiry of the period for lodging the note of objection and answers; and the court may make such order for further procedure as it thinks fit.

General note. The distinctive feature of common property, derived from the fact that each **45.1.1** co-owner has a separate and separable interest (in a legal, rather than a physical, sense), is the absolute right of every co-owner to terminate the community at will: *Banff Magistrates v. Ruthin Castle Ltd* 1944 S.C. 36, 68 *per* L.J.-C. Cooper. The *pro indiviso* proprietor is entitled to have the property divided, or if division is impracticable or would operate unfairly, to have it sold and the price divided: *Morrison v. Kirk* 1912 S.C. 44, 49 *per* Lord Salvesen. Accordingly, the right to insist on an action of division and sale at any time cannot be affected by considerations of the financial position, present or contingent, of any *pro indiviso* proprietor or other equitable consideration. The proper context for equitable considerations is the working out of the remedy (*i.e.* division or sale, and, if sale, by what method): *Upper Crathes Fishings Ltd v. Bailey's Executors* 1991 S.L.T. 747, 750L *per* L.P. Hope. Personal bar is not a relevant defence to an action of division and sale, though it might be relevant to determine how the property is to be divided up as a consequence of some agreement or acting of the parties: *Riddell v. Morisetti (No. 2),* 22 November 1996, unreported (1996 G.W.D. 40–2292). The absolute nature of this right is justified on grounds of public policy, and especially to ensure the advantageous management of such property: *Brock v. Hamilton* (1852) 19 D. 701, 703 *per* Lord Rutherford.

There are, however, circumstances in which the exercise of this right may be denied. For instance, it is always open to a person to deprive himself of his right to such an action by contract, or by the operation of personal bar: *Upper Crathes Fishings Ltd*, above, *per* L.P. Hope at p.749C–D. An action of division and sale may not lie in respect of a thing of common and indispensable use, such as a staircase or vestibule: Bell's *Prin.*, s. 1082. In relation to matrimonial homes owned in common by a husband and wife, s. 19 of the Matrimonial Homes (Family Protection) (Scotland) Act 1981 confers on the court a discretion to refuse to grant decree, postpone the granting of decree, or grant decree subject to conditions, in an action of division and sale brought by a spouse.

"heritable property". The absolute entitlement of each co-owner to terminate the community **45.1.2** by means of an action of division and sale applies to all common property, whether heritable or moveable, corporeal or incorporeal: see Bell's *Comm.*, i, 62 (references to ships) and *Robertson's Tr. v. Roberts* 1982 S.L.T. 22 (concerning a lease). This Chapter refers specifically to, and deals only with, heritable property.

"remit to a reporter". Whether the division of the property which is the subject of an action of **45.1.3** division and sale is reasonably practicable has in the past been determined by means of proof, *e.g. Bryden v. Gibson* (1837) 15 S. 486, but in general, the question is far better decided on a remit to a person of skill and experience: *Thom v. Macbeth* (1875) 3 R. 161, 165 *per* Lord Gifford. R. 45.1(1) provides that in an action of division and sale of heritable property, the court *shall* remit to a reporter, the implication of which is that proof is no longer a competent means of establishing whether heritable subjects are capable of equitable division.

Where there has been a remit to a reporter, that becomes the exclusive mode of proof of the issues comprised in the remit: *Williams v. Cleveland and Highland Holdings Ltd* 1993 S.L.T. 398 at 400K–L *per* Lord Penrose. The interlocutor ordering the remit both defines the issues for the reporter and prescribes the procedure to be followed by him: *Williams*, above, at 401B–C. Therefore, in approaching the question of a remit to a reporter in the context of division or sale, the parties have both an opportunity and an obligation to define the issues with clarity, since it is they who have to determine the scope of the reporter's power to bind them by his decision: *Williams*, above, at 401L. It has been pointed out that the observations of Lord Penrose in *Williams*, above, were made before the promulgation of the present r. 45.1. In *Riddell v. Morisetti (No. 2),* 22 November 1996, unreported (1996 G.W.D. 40–2292), the court declined to order the reporter to consider specified matters. Counsel in that case were asked to produce an agreed formula as to the matters to which the reporter ought to have regard, which failing the court desired further submissions.

It is open to the court to give the reporter instructions about further particular matters to which he should have regard in addition to those mentioned in r. 45.1: *Riddell v. Morisetti*, 19th January 1996, unreported.

The solicitors for the parties are personally liable for the fees and outlays of the reporter and the court will order which party is liable: r. 42.15.

45.1.4   *"capable of division in a manner equitable to the interests of the pro indiviso proprietors"*. Only if it is established that the subjects cannot be divided in a manner equitable to the interests of the *pro indiviso* proprietors is the remedy of sale under authority of the court and division of the price available to a pursuer. It may be physically possible to divide most subjects if all considerations of expense of division and of deterioration or possible destruction of the subjects are disregarded. These considerations, however, cannot be left out of view, and it is on them that, in most cases, the answer to the question whether the subjects should be divided will depend: *Thom v. Macbeth* (1875) 3 R. 161, 165 *per* Lord Gifford. Sale and subsequent division of the price will be resorted to where division is not reasonably practicable without sacrificing to an appreciable extent the interests of some or all of the parties: *Thom*, above, *per* L.J.-C. Moncrieff at p. 164. For instance, sale would be appropriate where division would sacrifice a considerable portion of the value of the property: *Thom*, above, *per* Lord Ormidale at p. 164. Factors such as the emotional attachment of parties to the subjects are not relevant considerations in assessing the feasibility of the physical division of land: *Williams v. Cleveland and Highland Holdings Ltd* 1993 S.L.T. 398 at 402H–I *per* Lord Penrose. A remit is necessary even in undefended actions to establish that sale is expedient and necessary: *Bryden v. Gibson* (1837) 15 S. 486, 487 *per* Lord Balgray.

45.1.5   *"sale by public roup or private bargain"*. The question of whether a sale under the authority of the court for the purpose of division should be by public roup or private bargain is essentially a practical one, in which the court is exercising an equitable jurisdiction. The aim must be to effect a sale which is fair to all parties, and the common goal of all parties is to achieve the best bargain which can be obtained in all the circumstances: *The Miller Group Ltd v. Tasker* 1993 S.L.T. 207, 208H–K *per* Lord Weir. Before the decision of the Inner House in *Campbells v. Murray* 1972 S.C. 310, a sale for the purpose of division was invariably effected by public roup. In *Campbells*, the court held that this practice was not in the nature of a rule of law, and that sale by private bargain, after an adequate test of the relevant market, was now more likely to lead to sale at the best price which could reasonably be obtained. Since then, private bargain has usually been the preferred method of conducting a sale under the authority of the court for the purpose of division, but there may be situations in which a sale by public roup is to be preferred: *The Miller Group Ltd*, above. In terms of the r. 45.1(1)(*b*)(ii), the reporter to whom the examination of the property is remitted may recommend which of the two methods is appropriate in the circumstances of the case.

It is not settled whether it is competent for the court, in the absence of agreement between the parties, to order that the subjects be disposed of by means other than public roup or sale by private bargain in the open market. In *Scrimgeour v. Scrimgeour* 1988 S.L.T. 590, Lord McCluskey was prepared, on the basis of civilian and institutional authority, in an undefended action, to grant warrant in terms of the pursuer's conclusion for the sale of the defender's one-half *pro indiviso* share in the former matrimonial home to the pursuer at the price fixed on an open market valuation by the reporter appointed by the court. A motion in similar terms, however, was refused in *Berry v. Berry (No. 2)* 1989 S.L.T. 292, Lord Cowie rejecting the proposition that he had a wide discretion to lay down how the subjects should be disposed of and commenting that even if he had such a discretion, he would not regard the method of sale proposed as being in the best interests of the parties, which would be properly served by obtaining the highest price for the property through sale by private treaty in the open market.

45.1.6   *"motion"*. For motions, see Chap. 23.

45.1.7   *"send"*. This includes deliver: r. 1.3(1) (definition of "send").

45.1.8   *Objections to the report.* The reporter's findings are final, subject only to a remit for reconsideration, by the same reporter, if available, on the basis of articulate objections made to the report provided and on restricted grounds. Whether a further remit will be made depends on the cogency of the objections, considered in the light of the original remit, and on those objections relating to the performance by the reporter of his duty under the remit, or to some issue or principle identifiable on the face of the report: *Williams v. Cleveland and Highland Holdings Ltd* 1993 S.L.T. 398, 401J–K *per* Lord Penrose. It is not legitimate for a party to include in a note of objections, contentions on the approach which the reporter might have adopted in carrying out the remit, where such contentions are in substance innovations on the procedure provided for in the remit, nor to use the procedure by way of objection to present arguments which might have been presented on the making of the original remit: *Williams*, above, *per* Lord Penrose at p. 401D–E.

45.1.9   *"note of objection"*. R. 15.2 does not apply to the note of objection (r. 15.2(4)(*b*)) and the note does not have to be signed (r. 4.2(9)(*f*)). The note is lodged as a step of process (r. 1.3(1) (definition of "step of process")). On lodging steps of process, see r. 4.4. The list may be lodged by post: P.N. No. 4 of 1994, paras. 1 and 8; and see note 4.4.10.

Division or sale of property

45.2.—(1) Where the court orders the division or sale of heritable property, it shall direct that the division or sale, as the case may be, shall be conducted under the oversight and direction of the Deputy Principal Clerk or any other fit person whom it may appoint for that purpose.

(2) The Deputy Principal Clerk or person appointed under paragraph (1), as the case may be, may report any matter of difficulty arising in the course of the division or sale to the court.

(3) At a hearing on a report made under paragraph (2), the court may give such directions as it thinks fit, including authority to the Deputy Principal Clerk to sign, on behalf of any proprietor, a disposition of his interest in the property.

(4) On the conclusion of a sale of property—

(a) the proceeds of the sale, under deduction of the expenses of the sale, shall be consigned into court; and

(b) the Deputy Principal Clerk or the person appointed under paragraph (1), as the case may be, shall lodge in process a report of the sale and a proposed scheme of division of the proceeds of sale.

(5) At the hearing of a motion for approval of a report of the sale of property lodged under paragraph (4) and a proposed scheme of division, the court may—

(a) approve the report and scheme of division, and direct that payment of the proceeds of sale be made in terms of the report;

(b) deal with any question as to the expenses of process or of sale; and

(c) make such other order as it thinks fit.

"authority to the Deputy Principal Clerk to sign . . . a disposition". This may be necessary **45.2.1** where a defender refuses to obtemper an order to sign and deliver a disposition of the subjects: *e.g. Whyte v. Whyte* 1913 2 S.L.T. 85.

A sale under r. 45.2 is not a sale by the parties; the person appointed to carry out the sale does not act as the agent of the proprietors but as a court authorised officer who enters into missives and procures a disposition: see *Kenneil v. Kenneil*, 2006 S.L.T. 449 (OH).

"consigned into court". For consignation into court, see r. 33.4(1)(b) and note 33.4.3.   **45.2.2**

"motion". For motions, see Chap. 23.   **45.2.3**

[1] CHAPTER 45A

ACTIONS OF REMOVING

Application of this Chapter

[1] **45A.1.**—(1) Subject to paragraph (2), this Chapter applies only to a conclusion for removing in an action of removing against a person or persons in possession of heritable property without right or title to possess the property.

(2) This Chapter shall not apply with respect to a person who has or had a title or other right to occupy the heritable property and who has been in continuous occupation since that title or right is alleged to have come to an end.

_____

[1] Chap. 45A and r. 45A.1 inserted by S.I. 1996 No. 2168 (effective 23rd September, 1996).

General note. Chapter 45A was inserted by A.S. (R.S.C.A. No. 4) (Miscellaneous) 1996 [S.I. **45A.1.1** 1996 No. 2168]. It implements recommendations 103 to 105 in Scot. Law Com. Report No. 118 on *Recovery of Possession of Heritable Property*.

The Scottish Law Commission felt that something was needed to be done about the problem of removing unidentified and unlawful occupants (*e.g.* trespassers or squatters) of land or buildings against whom it is difficult to bring proceedings because a writ cannot be served on them, and to do so speedily. Procedure exists in England and Wales: C.P.R. 1998, r. 55.6.

Before Chap. 45A was inserted, resort was made, where the identity of the occupiers was known, to a petition under s. 46 of the C.S.A. 1988 for reinstatement of a possessory right to heritable property. For use of s. 46 of the C.S.A. 1988 where the names of the occupiers are not known, see note 45A.1.3.

Chapter 45A provides (a) a means of service on occupiers whose names are not known, (b) a means for such persons to enter the process, and (c) for shortening or dispensing with periods of time under the RCS 1994.

45A.1.2   *Actions of removing*. The conventional wisdom is that an action of removing without any other substantive conclusion is not competent in the Court of Session, although there is no statute or rule of law excluding it: see Scot. Law Com. report no. 118 at para. 9.1. The competency of a simple action of removing in the Court of Session was questioned but not decided by Lord Penrose in *Marco's Leisure Ltd v. Occupiers of the subjects known as the Corn Exchange, New Market Road, Edinburgh*, 25th May 1999, unreported (and no judgment) and referred to in *Oliver & Son Ltd, Petrs*, 1999 S.L.T. 1039. In *Marco's Leisure Ltd*, the motion for interim orders was dropped and in *Oliver & Son Ltd* the answer was not necessary for the decision. The matter was resolved in *Beriston Ltd v. Dumbarton Motor Boat and Sailing Club*, 2007 S.L.T. 227 (OH). It was held that the Court of Session has no jurisdiction in "pure" actions of removing or actions that do not contain a conclusion as a preliminary step towards removing; it has concurrent jurisdiction with the sheriff court where declarator is sought as a preliminary step; and it has exclusive jurisdiction where reduction is sought as a preliminary to removing. Nothing in rule 45A.1 could change the substantive law as to what was competent in the Court of Session.

It is accepted that an action with a conclusion for removing is competent if associated with another conclusion such as interdict. In relation to the difficulties with interdict associated with this procedure, see note 45A.1.3.

45A.1.3   *"Chapter applies only to a conclusion for removing"*. It is not uncommon for a pursuer to seek to reinforce a decree of removing with an interdict. In relation to interdict, however, it is not competent to obtain an interdict against unnamed persons such as "any other person having notice of said interlocutor": *Lord Advocate v. The Scotsman Publications Ltd* 1989 S.C. (H.L.) 122, 135, 147, 155 and 161 (founding on *Pattison v. Fitzgerald* (1823) 2 S. 536), approved by the Inner House and not overruled by the House of Lords. It would be inappropriate to affect the law on this point by a side wind in altering procedure in relation to removing. Accordingly r. 45A.1(1) makes it clear that Chap. 45A, which provides for effective service on unnamed persons, applies *only* with respect to a conclusion for removing.

It was explained in *Oliver & Son Ltd, Petrs*, 1999 S.L.T. 1039, by the First Div. on a report to the Inner House by Lord Penrose, that the underlying reasoning in *The Scotsman Publications*, above, and *Pattison*, above, was that it is incompetent to pronounce an interdict on persons on whom the proceedings are not served or to move for its recall. In *Oliver*, the petitioners sought an order under s. 46 of the C.S.A. 1988 to be reinstated in their possessory right to heritable property which was occupied by persons whose names were unknown to them but who could be identified as the occupiers of the petitioners' land. A first order for service was sought on the unnamed persons; those who were served would be able to enter the process and resist the making of any substantive order. The First Div. held that the persons on whom service was to be made were sufficiently identified; were it otherwise the court would be powerless to act and would be handing to those who concealed their identity a weapon to wreak injustice. It was indicated for the petitioners that messengers-at-arms would hand copies of the petition to individuals they found occupying the land and record what they had done and might photograph those on the land and the steps taken to serve the petition. Accordingly it should be possible to bring an action for removing with conclusions for interdict and interim interdict against unnamed persons and to seek service of the action on those who can be found and identified with respect to the conclusions for interdict. But it would not be possible to seek interim interdict on those unnamed persons before service.

45A.1.4   *"without right or title to possess the property"*. The procedures in Chap. 45A are intended to be available only against persons who enter or remain in property without licence or consent such as trespassers or squatters. The purpose of r. 45A.1(2) is to exclude tenants or persons remaining after termination of a tenancy.

Service on unnamed occupiers
[1] **45A.2.**—(1) Where the name of a person in occupation of a heritable property is not known and cannot reasonably be ascertained, the pursuer shall call that person as a defender by naming him as an "occupier".

(2) Where the name of a person in occupation of the heritable property is not known and cannot reasonably be ascertained, the summons shall be

served (whether or not it is also served on a named person), unless the court otherwise directs, by a messenger-at-arms—

(a) affixing a copy of the summons and a citation in Form 45A.2 addressed to "the occupiers" to the main door or other conspicuous part of the premises, and if practicable, depositing a copy of each of those documents in the premises; or

(b) in the case of land only, inserting stakes in the ground at conspicuous parts of the occupied land to each of which is attached a sealed transparent envelope containing a copy of the summons and a citation in Form 45A.2 addressed to "the occupiers".

(3) Paragraphs (1), (2) and (4) of rule 16.3 (service by messenger-at-arms) shall apply to service of a summons under this rule as they apply to service by a method to which those paragraphs apply.

---

[1] R. 45A.2 inserted by S.I. 1996 No. 2168 (effective 23rd September 1996).

General note. For the history of the rule, see note 45A.1.1. This rule provides the means for   **45A.2.1**
service on occupiers whose names are not known or cannot reasonably be ascertained.

In *Marco's Leisure Ltd v. Occupiers of the subjects known as the Corn Exchange, New Market Road, Edinburgh,* 25th May 1999, unreported (and no judgment) and referred to in *Oliver & Son Ltd, Petrs* 1999 S.L.T. 1039, Lord Penrose questioned the *vires* of r. 45A.2, but did not decide the issue because the motion for interim orders was dropped. The court has power to regulate and prescribe the procedure and practice of the court under s.5(a) of the C.S.A. 1988. If the court may provide rules for service by virtue of that power, the court may make provision for service on unnamed persons.

"not known and cannot reasonably be ascertained". Steps must have been taken to ascertain   **45A.2.2**
the address of the person on whom service is to be executed, and what those steps were and an explanation of why service cannot be executed must be stated in the summons: r. 13.3. In *Young v. Harper* 1970 S.C. 174, 177 Lord Fraser held that "known" (in relation to art. 1 of the A.S. 14th December 1805) did not mean known only to the pursuer but known generally to persons having business or social dealings with the defender; accordingly, some steps must be taken to find an address or else a belief that an address is not known must be based on some evidence that none is known.

Methods of service. The two methods for service on unnamed persons are (1) in the case of   **45A.2.3**
buildings affecting and depositing in, or (2) in the case of land without buildings, inserting stakes in the ground with the summons and citation attached.

Service on named persons will be in accordance with normal rules of service, on which see Chap. 16, Pt I.

"in the case of land only". The provision in r. 45A.2(2)(b) for inserting stakes in the ground in   **45A.2.4**
the case of land only, is designed for (a) land occupied on which there are no buildings, or (b) where there is a building but the land and not the building is occupied.

Shortening or dispensing with periods of time

[1] **45A.3.** Where the action is directed against a person in occupation of the heritable property *vi clam aut precario*, the pursuer may apply by motion to shorten or dispense with the period of notice or other period of time in these Rules relating to the conduct of the action or the extracting of any decree.

---

[1] R. 45A.3 inserted by S.I. 1996 No. 2168 (effective 23rd September 1996).

General note. For the history of this rule, see note 45A.1.1.   **45A.3.1**

Where a person is in possession of property *vi clam aut precario* and without right or title to process or occupy that property, the court may shorten or dispense with (a) the period of notice, or (b) any other period of time specified in the RCS 1994 relating to the action: r. 45A.3.

The power of the court under r. 7.1(4) to authorise immediate extract or to supersede extract for such period as it thinks fit should be noted.

"vi clam aut precario". This phrase means by force, stealth or precarious possession.   **45A.3.2**

"motion". For motions, see Chap. 23.   **45A.3.3**

Application by occupiers to become defenders
     [1] **45A.4.** A person not named as a defender in the summons who is in occupation of the heritable property may, within the period of notice, apply by minute to be sisted as a defender to the action.

---

[1] R. 45A.4 inserted by S.I. 1996 No. 2168 (effective 23rd September 1996).

45A.4.1 *General note*. For the history of this rule, see note 45A.1.1.
      An unnamed occupier enters the process by applying by minute to be sisted as a defender: r. 45A.4. Once he identifies himself by doing so, he will become a named defender and be liable as any named defender to, *e.g.*, interdict.

45A.4.2 *"apply by minute to be sisted"*. On a minute of sist, see note 15.1.9.

45A.4.3 *Expenses*. The question arises about obtaining expenses against unnamed occupiers.

CHAPTER 46

ADMIRALTY ACTIONS

Interpretation of this Chapter
     46.1. In this Chapter—
          "Admiralty action" means an action having a conclusion appropriate
               for the enforcement of a claim to which section 47(2) of the
               Administration of Justice Act 1956 applies or in respect of a
               contract of *respondentia*;
          "ship" has the meaning assigned in section 48(f) of that Act.

Deriv. RCS 1965, r. 135

46.1.1 *"Admiralty action"*. The definition of "Admiralty action" follows a proposal of the Scottish Law Commission's Discussion Paper on Diligence on the Dependence and Admiralty Arrestments (Scot. Law Com. Discussion Paper No. 84) to define Admiralty actions by reference to the list of claims in s.47(2) of the Administration of Justice Act 1956 being the claims in respect of which arrestments may be laid. This brings Scots law into line with English law and the theory that Admiralty jurisdiction is over ships and that the appropriate remedy lies in proceedings against the ship (see "The Scottish Court of Admiralty: A Retrospect" (1922) 34 J.R. 38). An arrestment on the dependence or *in rem* is different from an ordinary arrestment and is a real diligence against the ship itself: *Carlberg v. Borjesson* (1877) 5 R. 188, 195 *per* Lord Shand. S.47 of the 1956 Act was enacted to enable the U.K. to ratify the Brussels International Convention relating to the Arrest of Sea-going Ships 1952 (Cmnd. 1128 (1960)). Contracts of *respondentia* have been added to the definition, only bottomry bonds being mentioned in s.47(2)(h) of the 1956 Act, although both are obsolete. Under the Merchant Shipping (Salvage and Pollution) Act 1994 (replaced by s.224 of the Merchant Shipping Act 1995), implementing the London International Convention on Salvage 1989 (Cm. 1526), s.47(2)(c) of the 1956 Act is amended to refer to the Salvage Convention 1989 and to contracts of salvage; accordingly, any claim not covered by the Convention will not properly be salvage to which s.47(2) of the 1956 Act applies and will not be an Admiralty action.
      S.47 of the 1956 Act does not define the jurisdiction of the Scottish courts.
      The purpose of Chap. 46 is to provide for the special rules of arrestment in relation to ships and their cargo and completion of these arrestments by sale, and for the special rules for ship collision cases, salvage and the International Oil Pollution Compensation Fund.
      Maritime or Admiralty actions not included in s.47(2) of the 1956 Act could proceed as commercial actions under Chap. 47. An Admiralty action mentioned in s.47(2) of the 1956 Act which relates to a dispute of a commercial nature may also proceed as a commercial action: see r. 47.1(1)(b).

46.1.2 *"ship"*. S.48(f) of the Administration of Justice Act 1956 defines "ship" as including any description of vessel used in navigation not propelled by oars. The meaning of "ship" or "vessel" is important in determining what subjects are arrestable by Admiralty arrestments. In a case under the Merchant Shipping Act 1854, "ship" was held to be a vessel which goes to sea, and "used in navigation" meant "used in navigating the seas": *Oakes v. Monkland Iron Co.* (1884) 11 R. 579, 583 and 584 *per* L.J.-C. Moncreiff. This definition is rather limiting.

"Ship" includes hovercraft: Hovercraft Act 1968, s.2(1).

Note also s.87(1) of the Civil Aviation Act 1982 and the Aircraft (Wreck and Salvage) Order 1938 [S.R. & O. 1938 No. 136] which apply Admiralty jurisdiction (and arrestments) to claims for salvage of aircraft.

Jurisdiction. S.47(2) of the Administration of Justice Act 1956 does not define the jurisdiction **46.1.3** of the Scottish courts; but to the extent that Admiralty jurisdiction is over ships and the appropriate remedy lies in proceedings against the ship (see note 46.1.1), that provision, by listing those claims in respect of which arrestment may be laid, provides a sort of indirect definition of jurisdiction. The limits of Admiralty jurisdiction are not entirely clear.

Under Art. 5(7) of Scheds 1 (Brussels 1968 Convention), 3C (Lugano Convention) and 4 (inter-U.K. jurisdiction) of the C.J.J.A. 1982, in relation to remuneration for salvage of cargo or freight, a person domiciled in one country may be sued in the courts of another country under the authority of which the cargo or freight was or could have been arrested. Sched. 8 (jurisdiction of Scottish courts) does not apply to Admiralty actions where jurisdiction is based on arrestment *in rem* or to found jurisdiction of a ship, cargo or freight: C.J.J.A. 1982, Sched. 9, para. 6.

In actions of reparation arising out of ship collisions, close manoeuvring or non-compliance with collision regulations (but not an action *in rem* to enforce a collision lien), the court has jurisdiction if (a) the defender has his habitual residence or place of business within the jurisdiction, (b) the cause of action arose within the jurisdiction and either within inland waters or the limits of a port, (c) an action arising out of the same incident(s) is proceeding or has been heard or determined in the court, (d) the defender has prorogated the jurisdiction of the court, or (e) a ship in which the defender owns shares has been arrested to found jurisdiction or on the dependence within the jurisdiction: 1956 Act, s.45.

In relation to salvage, under the Merchant Shipping (Salvage and Pollution) Act 1994 (replaced by s.224 of the Merchant Shipping Act 1995), implementing the London International Convention on Salvage 1989 (Cm. 1526), any claim not covered by the Convention will not properly be salvage to which s.47(2) of the 1956 Act applies and will not be an Admiralty action. This will not affect any possible "salvage" claims based on *negotiorum gestio*. Note also s.87(1) of the Civil Aviation Act 1982 and the Aircraft (Wreck and Salvage) Order 1938 [S.R. & O. 1938 No. 136] which apply Admiralty jurisdiction (and arrestments) to claims for salvage of aircraft.

Forms of action

46.2.—(1) An Admiralty action against the owners of, or parties interested in, a ship or cargo may be brought—

(a) *in rem*, where the conclusion of the summons is directed to recovery in respect of a maritime lien against the ship or cargo or the proceeds of it as sold under order of the court or where arrestment *in rem* may be made under section 47(3) of the Administration of Justice Act 1956;

(b) *in personam*, where the conclusion of the summons is directed to a decree in common form against the defender; or

(c) both *in rem* and *in personam*, where sub-paragraphs (a) and (b) apply.

(2) When bringing an Admiralty action, the pursuer shall insert the words "Admiralty Action *in rem*", "Admiralty Action *in personam*" or "Admiralty Action *in rem* and *in personam*", as the case may be, immediately below the words "IN THE COURT OF SESSION" where they occur above the instance, and on the backing, of the summons and any copy of it.

Deriv. R.C.S. 1965, r. 136

General note. On Admiralty actions *in rem*, see r. 46.3 and notes. On Admiralty actions *in*   **46.2.1** *personam*, see r. 46.4 and notes.

Actions in rem

46.3.—(1) In an Admiralty action *in rem*—
(a) where the owners of, or parties interested in, the ship or cargo against which the action is directed are known to the pursuer, they shall be called as defenders by name;
(b) where such owners or parties are unknown to the pursuer—
   (i) he may call them as defenders as "the owners of or parties interested in the ship (*name and identify by its port of registry*) [*or* cargo]"; and
   (ii) the master, if known, shall also be called as a defender representing the owners.

(2) In an Admiralty action *in rem*, the ship or cargo shall be arrested *in rem* and a warrant for such arrestment shall be inserted in the summons in the form in Form 13.2–A.

Deriv. R.C.S. 1965, r. 137(a) and (b)

Admiralty actions in rem. An Admiralty action *in rem* is directed against the ship or cargo   **46.3.1** itself, as the case may be, to enforce a maritime lien. The action has conclusions for declarator that the pursuer has a maritime lien over the ship or cargo for a specified sum and interest preferable to the rights of others and for warrant to sell the ship or cargo on the lien being declared and to apply the proceeds in satisfaction of the lien: see Form 13.2–B(9). The action can only proceed on an arrestment *in rem*: r. 46.3(2). The arrestment *in rem* is an integral part of the action and should be sought in the summons when signeted. It is now possible to convert an Admiralty action *in personam* into an action *in rem* after signeting: see r. 13.8; *cf. Mill v. Fildes* 1982 S.L.T. 147 under R.C.S. 1965. The arrestment attaches the whole ship or cargo, as the case may be, the whole being subject to sale. On arrestment *in rem*, see further notes 46.3.2 to 46.3.4.

A maritime lien is a form of hypothec or security without possession over a ship, her apparel or cargo enforceable by an Admiralty action *in rem* in which the *res* is attached by the arrestment, declarator of the lien is granted and the *res* sold. Such a lien arises (i) at common law in respect of damage done by a ship, bonds of bottomry or *respondentia*, seamen's wages, salvage and (ii) by creation of statute—master's wages and disbursements (Merchant Shipping Act 1995, s.41), compensation to owners or occupiers of land for damage occasioned by shipwreck (1995 Act, s.234(5)), fees and expenses of receiver of wrecks (1995 Act, s.249(3)), remuneration for services of coastguard (1995 Act, s.250(3)(c)). Under s.47(1) of the Administration of Justice Act 1956, arrestment *in rem* is only competent if the action involves a claim in s.47(2), and the statutory liens except master's wages and disbursements and rights to life and property salvage are probably excluded.

Arrestment of ships in rem. An arrestment *in rem* may be executed in (a) an Admiralty   **46.3.2** action *in rem* to enforce a maritime lien or (b) an Admiralty action *in personam* to enforce a non-pecuniary claim relating to the ship under s.47(2)(p)–(s) of the Administration of Justice Act 1956 by virtue of s.47(3) of that Act. An Admiralty action is defined in r. 46.1. Arrestment of a ship is a real diligence directed against the vessel itself: *Carlberg v. Borjesson* (1877) 5 R. 188, 195 *per* Lord Shand. There is no arrestee: *Barclay, Curle & Co. Ltd v. Sir James Laing & Sons Ltd* 1908 S.C. 82, 89 *per* Lord McLaren. The ship may be arrested while in the possession of the defender. Arrestment of the ship does not arrest the cargo or freight. Arrestment *in rem* founds jurisdiction. The ship is fixed in the place where she is at the time of the execution of the arrestment until a declarator of lien is obtained and a process of sale completed: *Carlberg*, above. The arrestment cannot be executed when the ship is on passage:

Carlberg, above; 1956 Act, s.47(6). The expenses of arrestment are recoverable as expenses of process because they are essential to the obtaining of the decree *in rem*: *Hatton v. A/S Durban Hansen* 1919 S.C. 154. Under s.47(1) of the 1956 Act arrestment *in rem* is only competent if the action involves a claim in s.47(2), and the statutory liens except master's wages and disbursements and rights to life and property salvage are probably excluded. On maritime liens, see note 46.3.1. Note also arrestment *in rem* in an Admiralty action *in personam* to enforce a non-pecuniary claim under s.47(2)(p)–(s) of the 1956 Act: see note 46.4.4.

A schedule in Form 16.15–C is used and a certificate of execution in Form 16.15–I is completed: r. 16.15(1)(c). The schedule is attached by a messenger-at-arms to the mainmast or other prominent part and a copy delivered to the master of the ship or person in charge whom failing the harbour master whom failing a motion for further procedure must be enrolled: r. 16.13(1), (3) and (4). This may be done on any day, including Sunday: r. 16.13(1). The certificate is attached to the summons or other document containing the warrant for the diligence: r. 16.12(7).

46.3.3 *Arrestment in rem of cargo on board ship.* This arrestment may be executed in an Admiralty action *in rem* to enforce a maritime lien (on which, see note 46.3.1). It temporarily detains the ship until the cargo is discharged. Where the cargo cannot be discharged the court may even loose the arrestment to enable this to be done out of the jurisdiction: *Svenska Petroleum A.B. v. H.O.R. Ltd* 1982 S.L.T. 343. It is not clear if the arrestment immobilises the ship where it is until the cargo is discharged or merely prevents the ship-master from sailing with the cargo out of the jurisdiction. It is probable that s.47(1) of the Administration of Justice Act 1956 does not apply to such an arrestment: see *e.g. Svenska Petroleum A.B. v. H.O.R. Ltd* 1982 S.L.T. 343, 1983 S.L.T. 493 and 1986 S.L.T. 513; *West Cumberland Farmers Ltd v. Ellon Hinengo Ltd* 1988 S.L.T. 294.

A schedule in Form 16.15–C is used and a certificate of execution in Form 16.15–I is completed: r. 16.15(1)(c). The schedule is attached by a messenger-at-arms to the mainmast or other prominent part and a copy delivered to the master of the ship or person in charge whom failing the harbour master whom failing a motion for further procedure must be enrolled: r. 16.13(1), (3) and (4). This may be done on any day, including Sunday: r. 16.13(1). The certificate is attached to the summons or other document containing the warrant for the diligence: r. 16.12(7).

46.3.4 *Arrestment in rem of cargo landed or transhipped.* This arrestment may be executed in an Admiralty action to enforce a maritime lien (on which, see note 46.3.1).

A schedule in Form 16.15–C is served by a messenger-at-arms and a certificate of execution in Form 16.15–I is completed: r. 16.15(1)(c). The certificate is attached to the summons or other document containing the warrant for the diligence: r. 16.12(7). There is no provision for this arrestment to be executed on a Sunday and the common law applies: r. 16.14(2); Stair, III.i.37; Bell's *Comm.*, ii, 460; *Oliphant v. Douglas* (1663) Mor. 15002 (*quaere* whether arrestment permitted following *Nederlandse Scheepshypotheekbank v. Cam Standby* 1994 S.C.L.R. 956). Whether or not the cargo has been delivered to the owner, the messenger-at-arms serves the schedule on the custodian of the cargo or, where on the quay or harbour shed, on the harbour master. Where the cargo has been landed on the quay or in a harbour shed the option of serving on the custodian is still available: this is useful where, *e.g.* there is no harbour master.

46.3.5 *Warrant to dismantle.* An arrestment *in rem* of a ship fixes her in the place where she is found. To make sure the ship is not moved a warrant to dismantle may be sought (in the summons (r. 13.6(c)(iv)) or subsequently by motion (r. 13.8)). Dismantling should be done by a suitably qualified person (such as a marine engineer) under the supervision of the messenger-at-arms. Dismantling may be unnecessary if the ship does not have customs clearance to sail.

46.3.6 *Movement of arrested ship or cargo.* Any person having an interest may apply by motion to move an arrested vessel or cargo. This may be to move a ship to a safe harbour (*Turner v. Galway* (1882) 19 S.L.R. 892; *J.W.A. Upham v. Torode* 1982 S.L.T. 229, *sub nom. The "Grey Dolphin"* 1982 S.C. 5) or to move her from a place where she is obstructing or causing loss to a third party. If a cargo is arrested but cannot be unloaded the ship is effectively immobilised: see *Svenska Petroleum A.B. v. H.O.R. Ltd* 1982 S.L.T. 343; *West Cumberland Farmers Ltd v. Director of Agriculture of Sri Lanka* 1988 S.L.T. 296. See also note 13.11.1.

46.3.7 *Arrestment on a Sunday.* R. 16.13(1) permits arrestment of a ship *in rem*, or an arrestment *in rem* of cargo on board ship, to be executed on any day. The common law prohibition of executing diligence on a Sunday gave rise to difficulty as the turn-round time of ships is often short and tankers and bulk-ore carriers are frequently discharged at weekends.

Actions in personam

46.4.—(1) In an Admiralty action *in personam* directed against the owners of a ship or cargo, such owners shall, if known to the pursuer, be called as defenders by name.

(2) In such an action, where—
  (a) the vessel is not a British ship, and
  (b) the names of the owners are not known to the pursuer,
the master of the ship may be called as the defender representing the owners.

(3) In an action to which paragraph (2) applies, any warrant to arrest to found jurisdiction shall be executed against the master of the ship in his representative capacity.

(4) In an action to which paragraph (2) applies, any decree shall be pronounced against the master in his representative capacity.

(5) A decree in an Admiralty action *in personam* may be pronounced against an owner of, or a party interested in, the ship or cargo only where that owner or party interested, as the case may be, has been called or added as a defender.

Deriv. R.C.S. 1965, r. 138 (r. 46.4(1) to (3)) and r. 142 (r. 46.4(4) and (5))

Admiralty actions in personam. An Admiralty action *in personam* is an Admiralty action other **46.4.1** than one *in rem* (on which, see note 46.3.1) listed in s.47(2) of the Administration of Justice Act 1956; but note arrestment *in rem* in an Admiralty action *in personam* to enforce a non-pecuniary claim under s.47(2)(p)–(s) of the 1956 Act: see note 46.4.4. An Admiralty action *in personam* may be a petitory action (an action for payment or performance) to enforce an obligation secured by a maritime lien but does not enforce the lien itself. The action is directed against a person and not the ship or cargo, although the master of the ship may be called as a defender if the ship is not British and the owners are not known: r. 46.4(1). Arrestment (on the dependence) is not essential. To found jurisdiction an arrestment to found jurisdiction must be executed. Arrestment attaches the share(s) of the ship owned by the defender, only the share(s) arrested being subject to sale. The whole ship is detained by the arrestment if the ship is the ship with which the action is concerned or all the shares in it are owned by the defender against whom the conclusion is directed: 1956 Act, s.47(1).

Arrestment of ship or cargo to found jurisdiction. Subject to two exceptions arrestment to **46.4.2** found jurisdiction may not be executed where the defender is domiciled in the U.K. or a Contracting State to the 1968 Brussels, or the Lugano, Convention: C.J.J.A. 1982, Scheds 1 and 3C, Art. 3(2), Sched. 4, Art. 3 and Sched. 8, r. 2(8). The exceptions are: (a) In an action of reparation arising out of the collision or manoeuvring of ships, or non-compliance with ship collision regulations under s.45 of the Administration of Justice Act 1956, the restrictions of the C.J.J.A. 1982 do not apply to defenders domiciled outside the U.K.: C.J.J.A. 1982, Scheds 1 and 3C, Art. 54 and Sched. 9, para. 6. (b) In an Admiralty action where the defender is domiciled in the U.K. or elsewhere except another Contracting State to the 1968 Brussels, or the Lugano, Convention: C.J.J.A. 1982, Sched. 5, para. 7 and Sched. 9, para. 6. (For an argument that the 1968 Brussels Convention and Sched. 8 to the C.J.J.A. 1982 have affected and do not permit our law of arrestment to found jurisdiction, see *Ladgroup Ltd v. Euroeast Lines SA* 1997 S.L.T. 916.) Arrestment of a ship or cargo to found jurisdiction is subject to the ordinary rules of arrestment of any property to found jurisdiction, and must be made in the hands of a third party: see note 13.6.1. There are also restrictions in the UN Convention on the Law of the Sea 1982, Art. 28 (Cmnd 8941): see Merchant Shipping Act 1995, s. 129.

A schedule of arrestment in Form 16.15–A is served on the defender and a certificate of execution in Form 16.15–H is completed: r. 16.15(1)(a). The certificate is attached to the summons or other document containing the warrant for the diligence: r. 16.12(7).

Arrestment of ships on the dependence. A ship may be arrested on the dependence of an **46.4.3** Admiralty action *in personam* (a) to enforce or secure a claim in s.47(2) of the Administration of Justice Act 1956 by virtue of s.47(1) of that Act where the ship is the ship with which the action is concerned (and is partly owned by the defender: see *e.g. William Batey & Co. (Exports) Ltd v. Kent* 1985 S.L.T. 490, *affd.* 1987 S.L.T. 557) or all the shares are owned by the defender or (b) to enforce a claim in s.47(2)(p)–(s) by virtue of s.47(3)(a) of the 1956 Act if the conclusion is a pecuniary conclusion and the ship is the ship to which the conclusion relates. An Admiralty action is defined in r. 46.1. It is not clear whether s.47(1) limits the common law right to arrest a sister ship: see *e.g. Sheaf Steamship Co. Ltd v. Compania Transmediterranea* 1930 S.C. 660; *cf. Brussels Convention relating to the Arrest of Seagoing Ships, 10th May 1952, art. 3(3), The "Banco"* [1971] P. 137 (English law) and comments in *Gatoil International Inc. v. Arkwright-Boston Manufacturers Mutual Insurance Co.* 1985 S.C.(H.L.) 1, 15 *per* Lord Keith of Kinkel. The action is directed against the defenders and not the ship. The expenses of the arrestment are not recoverable at common law as expenses of process because the arrestment is not essential to obtaining the decree *in personam: Black v. Jehangeer Framjee & Co.* (1887) 14 R. 678. *Quaere* whether they are recoverable as a debt due in a separate action or under s.93(2) of the Debtors (Scotland) Act 1987. There are also restrictions in the UN Convention on the Law of the Sea 1982, Art. 28 (Cmnd 8941): see Merchant Shipping Act 1995, s. 129.

A schedule in Form 16.15–B is used and a certificate of execution in Form 16.15–J is completed: r. 16.15(1)(e). The schedule is attached by a messenger-at-arms to the mainmast or other prominent part, the letters "ER" chalked above and a copy of the schedule delivered to the master of the ship or person in charge whom failing the harbour master whom failing a motion for further procedure must be enrolled: r. 16.13(1)–(4). This may be done on any day, including Sunday: r. 16.13(1). The certificate is attached to the summons or other document containing the warrant for the diligence: r. 16.12(7).

46.4.4   *Arrestment in rem in an Admiralty action in personam.* Such an arrestment may be executed to enforce a non-pecuniary claim under s.47(2)(p)–(s) of the Administration of Justice Act 1956 by virtue of s.47(3) of that Act. These provisions relate to a dispute as to ownership or possession of or a share in a ship, between co-owners of a ship about ownership, possession, employment or earnings of that ship, the mortgage or hypothecation of or share in a ship, or the forfeiture or condemnation of a ship or goods or the restoration of the ship or goods. Arrestment may be used whether or not the ship belongs to the defender: *Arrest of Ships*—4, Scotland, p. 87, by I. G. Inglis (Lloyds of London, 1987). There is no declarator of lien and no sale and the arrestment simply secures implement of the decree. There are also restrictions in the UN Convention on the Law of the Sea 1982, Art. 28 (Cmnd 8941): see Merchant Shipping Act 1995, s. 129.

A schedule in Form 16.15–D is used and a certificate of execution in Form 16.15–I is completed: r. 16.15(1)(d). The schedule is attached by a messenger-at-arms to the mainmast or other prominent part and a copy delivered to the master of the ship or person in charge whom failing the harbour master whom failing a motion for further procedure must be enrolled: r. 16.13(1), (3) and (4). This may be done on any day, including Sunday: r. 16.13(1). The certificate is attached to the summons or other document containing the warrant for the diligence: r. 16.12(7).

46.4.5   *Arrestment on the dependence of cargo landed or transhipped.* Where the cargo has been or is in the course of being landed or transhipped it no longer has the character of cargo on board ship and there is no reason for treating it as liable to an Admiralty arrestment; the arrestment must be in the hands of a third party: see note 13.6.3. Where cargo is in the possession of the cargo owner on land the ordinary rules of arrestment also apply: see note 13.6.3.

A schedule in Form 16.15–B is served on the arrestee by a messenger-at-arms and a certificate of execution in Form 16.15–H is completed: r. 16.15(1)(b). The certificate is attached to the summons or other document containing the warrant for the diligence: r. 16.12(7). There is no provision for this arrestment to be executed on a Sunday and the common law applies: r. 16.14(2); Stair, III.i.37; Bell's *Comm.*, ii, 460; *Oliphant v. Douglas* (1633) Mor. 15002; but *cf. Nederlandse Scheepshypotheekbank NV v. CAM Standby Ltd* 1994 S.C.L.R. 956.

46.4.6   *Arrestment on the dependence of cargo on board ship.* This arrestment may be used in an ordinary action or in an Admiralty action *in personam*. There must be an arrestee, *e.g.* a third party or the ship-master (even if he is the employee of the cargo owner) or the cargo owner himself: r. 16.14(2).

A schedule in Form 16.15–B is served on the arrestee by a messenger-at-arms and a certificate of execution in Form 16.15–J is completed: r. 16.15(1)(e). The arrestment may be executed on any day, including Sunday: r. 16.14(2). The certificate is attached to the summons or other document containing the warrant for the diligence: r. 16.12(7).

46.4.7   *Warrant to dismantle.* An arrestment on the dependence of a ship fixes her in the place where she is found. To make sure the ship is not moved a warrant to dismantle may be sought (in the summons (r. 13.6(c)(iv)) or subsequently by motion (r. 13.8)). Dismantling should be done by a suitably qualified person (such as a marine engineer) under the supervision of the messenger-at-arms. Dismantling may be unnecessary if the ship does not have customs clearance to sail.

46.4.8   *Movement of arrested ship or cargo.* Any person having an interest may apply by motion to move an arrested vessel or cargo. This may be to move a ship to a safe harbour (*Turner v. Galway* (1882) 19 S.L.R. 892; *J.W.A. Upham v. Torode* 1982 S.L.T. 229, *sub nom. The "Grey Dolphin"* 1982 S.C. 5) or to move her from a place where she is obstructing or causing loss to a third party. If a cargo is arrested but cannot be unloaded the ship is effectively immobilised: see *Svenska Petroleum A.B. v. H.O.R. Ltd* 1982 S.L.T. 343; *West Cumberland Farmers Ltd v. Director of Agriculture of Sri Lanka* 1988 S.L.T. 296. See also note 13.11.1.

46.4.9   *Arrestment on a Sunday.* The common law prohibition of executing diligence on a Sunday gave rise to difficulty when the turn-round time of ships is often short and tankers and bulk-ore carriers are frequently discharged at weekends. Arrestment on any day, including Sunday, is permitted on the dependence of an Admiralty action *in personam*, or of an ordinary action, of cargo on board ship: r. 16.14(2). The common law in relation to arrestment on the dependence in an Admiralty action was altered by *Nederlandse Scheepshypotheekbank v. Cam Standby* 1994 S.C.L.R. 956 in which Lord Allanbridge permitted arrestment on a Sunday.

Sale of ship or cargo
46.5.—(1) This rule shall not apply to the sale of a cargo arrested on the dependence of an Admiralty action *in personam*.

(2) Where, in an Admiralty action or an action of declarator and sale of a ship—

(a) the court makes a finding that the pursuer has a claim which falls to be satisfied out of an arrested ship or cargo, or

(b) a decree for a sum of money has been granted in an action in which a ship has been arrested on the dependence,

the pursuer may apply by motion for an order for the sale of that ship or a share in it, or the cargo, as the case may be, by public auction or private bargain.

(3) Before making such an order, the court shall remit to a reporter for the purpose of obtaining—

(a) an inventory of,

(b) a valuation and recommended upset price for, and

(c) any recommendation as to the appropriate advertisement for the sale of,

the ship, share or cargo.

(4) Where a remit is made under paragraph (3), the pursuer shall instruct the reporter within 14 days after the date of the interlocutor making the remit and be responsible, in the first instance, for payment of his fee.

(5) On completion of a report following a remit under paragraph (3), the reporter shall send the report and a copy for each party to the Deputy Principal Clerk.

(6) On receipt of such a report, the Deputy Principal Clerk shall—

(a) give written intimation to each party of receipt of the report;

(b) request the pursuer to show to him a discharge in respect of the fee for which he is responsible under paragraph (4); and

(c) after sight of such a discharge—

(i) lodge the report in process;

(ii) give written intimation to each party that this has been done and that he may uplift a copy of the report from process; and

(iii) cause the action to be put out on the By Order Roll before the Lord Ordinary.

(7) Where the court orders the sale of a ship, share or cargo, the conduct of the sale, including any advertisement of it, shall be under the direction of the Deputy Principal Clerk.

(8) Where such a sale is the sale of a ship or a share in it, the interlocutor ordering the sale shall include a declaration that the right to transfer the ship or share to the purchaser is vested in the Deputy Principal Clerk.

(9) Where, in such a sale, no offer to purchase the ship, share or cargo, as the case may be, has reached the upset price, the pursuer may apply by motion for authority to expose such ship, share or cargo for sale at a reduced upset price.

(10) The proceeds of such a sale shall be consigned into court, under deduction of all dues to the date the court adjudges the ship, share or cargo to belong to the purchaser under paragraph (11)(a), payable to Her Majesty's Customs and Excise or to the port or harbour authority within the jurisdiction of which the ship or cargo lies and in respect of which such port or harbour authority has statutory power to detain the ship or cargo.

(11) On consignation being made under paragraph (10), the court shall—

(a) adjudge the ship, share or cargo, as the case may be, declaring the same to belong to the purchaser, freed and disburdened of all bonds, mortgages, liens, rights of retention and other incumbrances affecting it and ordering such ship, share or cargo to be delivered to the purchaser on production of a certified copy of the interlocutor pronounced under this sub-paragraph; and

(b) order such intimation and advertisement, if any, for claims on the consigned fund as it thinks fit.

(12) The court shall, after such hearing or inquiry as it thinks fit—

(a) determine all questions of expenses;

(*b*) rank and prefer any claimants in order of preference; and
(*c*) make such other order, if any, as it thinks fit.

Deriv. R.C.S. 1965, r. 143

46.5.1   *Sale of ship or cargo.* Sale is the completion of the arrestment of a ship either *in rem* or on the dependence, or of cargo *in rem*. The sale is under r. 46.5 under the direction of the Deputy Principal Clerk. In the case of an arrestment on the dependence of an Admiralty action *in personam*, a separate action of declarator and sale is competent; but it is now specified in r. 46.5(2) (to clear up a doubt) that such a sale in a separate action is subject to r. 46.5. It is clear from the terms of r. 46.5(1) and (2) that r. 46.5 applies to arrestment on the dependence of an Admiralty action *in personam*; and see *Banque Indo Suez v. Maritime Co. Overseas Inc.* 1985 S.L.T. 517 where this seems to have been assumed.

Where the arrestment is of cargo on the dependence of an Admiralty action *in personam*, the appropriate process to complete the arrestment is an action of furthcoming, and r. 46.5 does not apply: r. 46.5(1).

Where the arrestment is of a ship or cargo in execution of a decree in an Admiralty action *in personam*, or an ordinary action for payment, the appropriate process for completion of the arrestment is an action of furthcoming.

Sale may be by public auction or private bargain: r. 46.5(2). Often the price obtained at auction is less than can be obtained by private bargain.

46.5.2   *"motion".* For motions, see Chap. 23.

46.5.3   *"within 14 days".* The date from which the period is calculated is not counted.

46.5.4   *Remit to a reporter.*

46.5.5   *"send".* This includes deliver: r. 1.3(1) (definition of "send").

46.5.6   *"written intimation".* For methods, see r. 16.9.

46.5.7   *"consigned into court".* On consignation, see r. 33.4(1)(*b*) and note 33.4.3.

46.5.8   *"freed and disburdened".* The reasoning for freeing the ship, share or cargo, as the case may be, from all claims on its sale is explained by Lord Fleming in *The "Sierra Nevada"* (1932) 42 Ll.L.Rep. 309, 310. That case was an action *in rem* but the reasoning is said to be equally applicable in an action *in personam*, and r. 46.5(11) applies to both.

Ship collisions and preliminary acts

46.6.—(1) Subject to rule 46.7 (applications to dispense with preliminary acts), this rule applies to an Admiralty action of damages arising out of a collision between ships at sea.

(2) An action to which this rule applies may be brought *in rem*, *in personam* or *in rem* and *in personam*.

(3) A summons in such an action shall not contain a condescendence or pleas-in-law.

(4) Where such an action is brought *in personam*, the conclusion of the summons shall contain sufficient detail to enable the defender to identify the date and place of, and the ships involved in, the collision.

(5) Within seven days after the summons has called, the pursuer shall lodge in process a sealed envelope containing—
(*a*) a preliminary act in Form 46.6; and
(*b*) a brief condescendence and appropriate pleas-in-law.

(6) Within 28 days after the preliminary act for the pursuer has been lodged under paragraph (5), the defender shall lodge in process a sealed envelope containing a preliminary act in Form 46.6.

(7) A party who lodges a preliminary act under paragraph (5) or (6) shall not send a copy of it to any other party.

(8) On the lodging of a preliminary act by the defender under paragraph (6), a clerk of session in the General Department shall—
(*a*) open both sealed envelopes;
(*b*) mark the contents of those envelopes with appropriate numbers of process; and

(c) give written intimation to each party that sub-paragraphs (a) and (b) have been complied with.

(9) On receipt of the written intimation under paragraph (8)(c), the pursuer and defender shall exchange copies of the contents of their respective envelopes.

(10) Within 7 days after the sealed envelopes have been opened up under paragraph (8), the defender may lodge defences to the action in process and any counterclaim on which he proposes to found.

(11) Within 7 days after a counterclaim has been lodged under paragraph (10), the pursuer may lodge answers to it in process.

(12) Within 14 days after defences have been lodged under paragraph (10) or answers have been lodged under paragraph (11), whichever is the earlier, the pursuer shall make up an open record with a copy of each of the preliminary acts appended to it; and Chapter 22 (making up and closing records) shall, subject to paragraph (13) of this rule, apply to the action as it applies to an ordinary action.

(13) No amendment, adjustment or alteration may be made to a preliminary act except by order of the court.

Deriv. R.C.S. 1965, r. 144

Preliminary acts. The procedure for preliminary acts is an English importation of 1934 **46.6.1** introduced there in 1855 by Dr Lushington (see *The "Inflexible"* (1856) Sw. 32, 34 n. (a)) to get a statement from the parties of the circumstances *recenti facto* and to prevent the defender from shaping his case to meet the pursuer's case: *The "Vortigern"* (1859) Sw. 518. "They are not merely pleading allegations. They are statements of fact made under such circumstances that they rank as formal admissions of fact binding the party making them perhaps as strongly as any admissions of fact can do. An admission of fact, as such, does not constitute an estoppel. It may be shown that it was made under mistake, and the Court may be satisfied that such was the case; but it is evidence against the party making it, its strength varying according to the conditions under which it is made. An admission under circumstances which necessitate that it must have been made after full consideration, has an evidential value far higher than a casual admission made without any opportunity of reflection or verification. The statements of fact in a preliminary act are statements which must be presumed to be made after the most careful examination and consideration. To my mind they carry such weight, from the nature of a preliminary act and from the circumstances under which it is made, that I should doubt whether otherwise than under the most special circumstances and with the special leave of the court, a party would be allowed to depart from the admissions in the preliminary act, at all events as far as evidence-in-chief is concerned": *The "Seacombe"* [1912] P. 21, 59 *per* Fletcher Moulton L.J; and see also *The "Channel Queen"* [1928] P. 157 and *The "Semiramis"* [1952] 2 Lloyd's Rep. 86; 93 *per* Willmer J.

In *Regent Shipping Co. (Aberdeen) v. George Robb & Sons* 1940 S.N. 50, *sub nom. The "Barbara Robb"* (1940) 67 Ll.L.Rep. 407, 411 *affd.* H.L. (1941) 70 Ll.L.Rep. 227, L.P. Normand said that the statements which a preliminary act contains "are as much binding on the party who makes them as averments in the condescendence of an ordinary action, and the adverse party is entitled to found on them as judicial admissions. Great care should be taken to fill in the preliminary act intelligibly as well as candidly; and a motion to amend it should rarely be granted, since its purpose is to obtain from the parties a statement of the facts *de recenti*, and to prevent one party from shaping his case to meet the facts alleged by the other". In *Morrison v. Scott (The "Scottish Maid")*, 15th June 1979, unreported, Lord Grieve said that statements "made in a preliminary act have effect as formal admissions of fact (Rule of Court 144(g)) and, in my opinion, that means that parties must be held bound by the statements in their respective preliminary acts and cannot seek to controvert them in evidence. Where the evidence led on behalf of a party is in conflict with a statement of fact in that party's preliminary act, the latter must be preferred . . . Preliminary acts are intended to be final documents capable of alteration only by order of the court." It is not thought that the absence of the express provisions, (a) for making additions with the leave of the court where the statements required by the preliminary act are not fully set out and (b) that the statements have effect as formal admissions, in R.C.S. 1965, r. 144(g) from R.C.S. 1994, r. 46.6(13) is intended to alter the law.

The requirement for preliminary acts applies even where a party is not the owner of a colliding ship. Where such is the case, however, application may be made to dispense with a preliminary act: see r. 46.7.

46.6.2   *Jurisdiction.* In actions of reparation arising out of ship collisions, close manoeuvring or non-compliance with collision regulations (but not an action *in rem* to enforce a collision lien), the court has jurisdiction if (*a*) the defender has his habitual residence or place of business within the jurisdiction, (*b*) the cause of action arose within the jurisdiction and either within inland waters or the limits of a port, (*c*) an action arising out of the same incident(s) is proceeding or has been heard or determined in the court, (*d*) the defender has prorogated the jurisdiction of the court, or (*e*) a ship in which the defender owns shares has been arrested to found jurisdiction or on the dependence within the jurisdiction: 1956 Act, s. 45.

46.6.2A   *"arising out of a collision between ships at sea".* On the meaning of "collision at sea", see *The "Star of the Isles"* (1938) 61 Ll.L.Rep. 168 (Outer House) and *Baird* v. *Aberdeen Coal & Shipping Co. Ltd* 1975 S.L.T. (Notes) 50.

46.6.3   *"within 7 days", "within 28 days".* The date from which the period is calculated is not counted. Where the last day falls on a Saturday or Sunday or a public holiday on which the Office of Court is closed, the next available day is allowed: r. 1.3(7). For office hours and public holidays, see note 3.1.2.

46.6.4   *"lodge in process".* A preliminary act is lodged as a step of process (r. 1.3(1) (definition of "step of process")). On lodging steps of process, see r. 4.4. The list may be lodged by post: P.N. No. 4 of 1994, paras. 1 and 8; and see note 4.4.10.

46.6.5   *"written intimation".* For methods, see r. 16.9.

Applications to dispense with preliminary acts

46.7.—(1) Within 7 days after the date on which the summons has called, any party may apply for an order to dispense with preliminary acts in an action to which rule 46.6 applies.

(2) An application under paragraph (1) shall be made by minute craving the court to dispense with preliminary acts and setting out the grounds on which the application is made.

(3) Before lodging such a minute in process, the party making the application shall intimate a copy of the minute, and the date on which it will be lodged, to every other party.

(4) Any other party may lodge in process answers to such a minute within 14 days after such a minute has been lodged.

(5) After the expiry of the period mentioned in paragraph (4), the court may, on the motion of any party, after such further procedure, if any, as it thinks fit, dispense with preliminary acts.

(6) Where the court dispenses with preliminary acts, the pursuer shall lodge a condescendence with appropriate pleas-in-law within such period as the court thinks fit; and the action shall thereafter proceed in the same way as an ordinary action.

(7) Where the court refuses to dispense with preliminary acts, it shall ordain a party or parties, as the case may be, to lodge preliminary acts under rule 46.6 within such period as it thinks fit.

(8) An interlocutor dispensing or refusing to dispense with preliminary acts shall be final and not subject to review.

Deriv. R.C.S. 1965, r. 145

46.7.1   *General note.* Where a party is not the owner of a colliding ship, such as the owner of a third vessel, the crew of a colliding ship or the cargo owner, that party may not be in a position to complete a preliminary act. On the exercise of the discretion to dispense with a preliminary act in England, which arises where there is no mutuality, see *The "El Oso"* (1925) 21 Ll.L.Rep. 340; *The "Carlston" and the "Balcombe"* [1926] P. 82; and see, more recently, *The "Beaverford"* [1960] 2 Lloyd's Rep. 216.

46.7.2   *"within 7 days", "within 14 days".* The date from which the period is calculated is not counted. Where the last day falls on a Saturday or Sunday or a public holiday on which the Office of Court is closed, the next available day is allowed: r. 1.3(7). For office hours and public holidays, see note 3.1.2.

46.7.3   *"minute".* For applications by minute, see r. 15.1.

46.7.4   *"intimate".* For methods, see r. 16.7.

Ship collision and salvage actions
    46.8.—(1) Without prejudice to rule 36.3(1) (lodging productions for proof), in an Admiralty action arising out of a collision between ships at sea or salvage, the parties shall—
    (*a*) within 4 days after the interlocutor allowing proof,
    (*b*) within 4 days before the taking of evidence on commission, or
    (*c*) on or before such other date as the court, on special cause shown, shall determine,
lodge in process the documents, if any, mentioned in paragraph (2).
    (2) The documents to be lodged under paragraph (1) are—
    (*a*) the log books, including scrap log books, of the ships concerned;
    (*b*) all *de recenti* written reports in connection with the collision or salvage, as the case may be, by the masters or mates of the vessels concerned to their respective owners; and
    (*c*) reports of any surveys of the ship in respect of which damage or salvage is claimed.

[THE NEXT PAGE IS C 385]

[THE NEXT PAGE IS 2356]

Deriv. RCS 1965, r. 147

General note. It is usual to have an assessor sitting with the court in a ship collision case. On **46.8.1** assessors, see Chap. 12.

"within 4 days after". The date from which the period is calculated is not counted. Where the **46.8.2** last day falls on a Saturday or Sunday or a public holiday on which the Office of Court is closed, the next available day is allowed: r. 1.3(7). For office hours and public holidays, see note 3.1.2.

"lodge in process". The documents are lodged as productions. On lodging productions, see r. **46.8.3** 4.5.

International Oil Pollution Compensation Fund

[1,2] **46.9.**—(1) In this rule—
"the Act of 1995" means the Merchant Shipping Act 1995;
"the Fund" means the International Fund established by the Fund
    Convention referred to in section 172(1)(b) of the Act of 1995;
"the Supplementary Fund" has the meaning given in section 172(1)(f)
    of the Act of 1995.

(2) In an action in respect of liability under section 153 of the Act of 1995, intimation of the action under section 177(2) of that Act to the Fund shall be given by the pursuer in accordance with paragraphs (3) and (4) of this rule.

(3) Where intimation is to be made under paragraph (2), the pursuer shall insert a warrant for intimation in the summons in the following terms:—"Warrant to intimate to the International Oil Pollution Compensation Fund (*address*) as a person having an interest in this action.".

(4) Intimation under paragraph (2) shall be given by a notice of intimation in Form 46.9 attached to a copy of the summons.

(5) Where the Fund or the Supplementary Fund is not a party to an action to which this rule applies, a defender may apply by motion for warrant to serve a third party notice on the Fund or the Supplementary Fund, as the case may be.

(6) Where, in an action under section 175 of the Act of 1995 (compensation from Fund for persons suffering pollution damage) or section 176A of that Act (liability of the Supplementary Fund), the court grants decree against the Fund or the Supplementary Fund, as the case may be, the clerk of court shall, within 14 days after the date of the decree, send a copy of it by first class post to the Fund or the Supplementary Fund, as the case may be.

(7) Any notice under section 176(3)(b) or section 176B(2)(b) of the Act of 1995 (notification of whether amount of claim to be reduced) by the Fund to the court shall be sent to the Deputy Principal Clerk.

(8) An application by virtue of section 176(3)(a) or section 176B(2)(a) of the Act of 1995 for leave to enforce a decree against the Fund or the Supplementary Fund, as the case may be shall be made by motion.

Deriv. RCS 1965, r. 147A inserted by S.I. 1979 No. 670

---

[1] R. 46.9 amended by S.I. 1996 No. 1756 (effective 5th August 1996).
[2] Rule 46.9 amended by S.S.I. 2007 No. 7, para. 8 (effective 26th February 2007).

General note. The Merchant Shipping (Oil Pollution) Act 1971 (now Pt VI, Chap. III of the **46.9.1** Merchant Shipping Act 1995) provides for civil liability for oil pollution caused by merchant ships. It implements the Brussels International Convention on Civil Liability for Oil Pollution Damage 1969 (Cmnd. 6183 (1975)) as amended by Protocol in 1984 (Cmnd. 9927 (1986)). By the Merchant Shipping (Salvage and Pollution) Act 1994, the U.K. implemented the amendment to this convention (the Liability Convention) by the Protocol of November 27, 1992 (now the Liability Convention of 1992 which provides for strict liability and limitation of liability for oil pollution damage caused by oil tankers): see now Pt VI, Chap. III of the 1995 Act which replaces the 1994 Act as well as the 1971 Act. Under the 1971 Act (now s.158 of the 1995 Act) the owner of a ship alleged to have incurred liability may apply to the court for limitation of that liability.

By the Act of 1974 (now Pt VI, Chap. IV of the Merchant Shipping Act 1995) the U.K. ratified the Brussels International Convention on Establishment of an International Fund for

Compensation for Oil Pollution Damage 1971 (Cmnd. 7383). By the Merchant Shipping (Salvage and Pollution) Act 1994, the U.K. implemented the amendment to the convention by the Protocol of November 27, 1992 (now the Fund Convention of 1992 which changes the entry into force requirements of the 1984 protocols): see now Pt VI, Chap. IV of the 1995 Act which replaces the 1994 Act as well as the 1974 Act. Under this convention (the Fund Convention) victims of oil pollution damage unable to obtain a complete remedy from the liable shipowner under the 1971 Act (now the 1995 Act) may make a claim against the Fund: see 1995 Act, s.175. Where a claim is subsequently amended outwith that period, the test is whether the modified version of the claim is presented on a fundamentally different basis: *Assuranceforeningen Skuld v. International Oil Pollution Compensation Fund (No.2)*, 2000 S.L.T. 1348.

Section 5(3) of the1971 Act is not intended to extinguish a claim made out of time but is merely a procedural provision regulating the making of the claim, and the court might allow further time after the appointed day has passed: *Assuranceforeningen Skuld v. International Oil Pollution Compensation Fund (No.1)*, 2000 S.L.T. 1333.

Liability under the 1971 Act and the 1974 Act does not extend to liability for economic loss of a secondary or relational kind: *Landcatch Ltd v. International Oil Pollution Compensation Fund*, 1999 S.L.T. 1208. "Damage" under the 1971 and 1974 Acts may include psychological conditions such as stress, anxiety and depression: *Black v. The Braer Corporation* 1999 S.L.T. 1401 (OH).

Section 9 of the 1971 Act (now s.162 of the 1995 Act) creates one prescriptive period of three years applicable to all claims after the claim arose: *Gray v. The Braer Corporation*, 1999 S.L.T. 141. The effect of s.9 of the 1971 Act is that a claim is extinguished on the third anniversary of its emergence: *Eunson v. The Braer Corporation* 1999 S.L.T. 1405 (OH).

The purpose of intimation to the Fund under r. 46.9 is that where the Fund is given notice of proceedings against an owner or guarantor in respect of liability under s.153 of the 1995 Act any judgment in the proceedings becomes binding on the Fund: Act of 1974, s.6(2) (now 1995 Act, s.177(2)).

The liability of the Fund may be limited under the Fund Convention. The court must notify the Fund of a judgment in proceedings under s.4 of the Act of 1974 (now s.175 of the 1995 Act) and no steps may be taken to enforce the judgment unless the court gives leave to enforce it: Act of 1974, s.4A(3)(a) inserted by the Merchant Shipping Act 1988, Sched. 4, para. 17(5) (now 1995 Act, s.176(3)(a)). Leave shall not be given until the Fund notifies the court that the amount of the claim is or is not to be reduced: Act of 1974, s.4A(3)(b) (now 1995 Act, s.176(3)(b)).

For parties to the Liability Convention, see the Merchant Shipping (Oil Pollution) (Parties to Convention) Order 1986 [S.I. 1986 No. 2225]. On parties to the Fund Convention, see the International Oil Pollution Compensation Fund (Parties to Convention) Order 1986 [S.I. 1986 No. 2223].

46.9.2   *"intimate"*. For methods, see r. 16.8.

46.9.3   *"motion"*. For motions, see Chap. 23.

46.9.4   *"third party notice"*. For third party procedure, see Chap. 26.

46.9.5   *"within 14 days"*. The date from which the period is calculated is not counted.

46.9.6   *"send"*. This includes deliver: r. 1.3(1) (definition of "send").

46.9.7   *Limitation actions under the Merchant Shipping (Oil Pollution) Act 1971.* A limitation action is one brought by the owner of a ship to limit his liability, for damage or costs incurred where oil is discharged or escapes from his ship, to an amount determined by the court under the Act. The court directs distribution of the amount among those making claims in the proceedings in proportion to their claims. By P.N. No. 1 of 1999, a procedure is provided in a limitation action under s.5 of the 1971 Act for advertisement for, the lodging of, objections to, and adjustment of any condescendence and claims, and for a by order hearing for further procedure. The P.N. also provides that, where a condescendence and claim is based on an existing (presumably "depending") action, all steps of process in that action become steps of process in the limitation action (how they are numbered is not explained).

One imagines, although it is not expressed, that the P.N. is intended to apply also to a limitation action brought under s.158 of the Merchant Shipping Act 1995 which repeals and re-enacts s.5 of the 1971 Act.

CHAPTER 47

COMMERCIAL ACTIONS

Application and interpretation of this Chapter

[1] **47.1.**—(1) This Chapter applies to a commercial action.

(2) In this Chapter—

"commercial action" means an action arising out of, or concerned with, any transaction or dispute of a commercial or business nature in which an election has been made under rule 47.3(1) or which has been transferred under rule 47.10;

"preliminary hearing" means a hearing under rule 47.11;

"procedural hearing" means a hearing under rule 47.12.

[1] R. 47.1 substituted by S.I. 1994 No. 2310 (effective 20th September 1994).

General note. This Chapter was substituted by A.S. (R.C.S. 1994 Amendment No. 1) **47.1.1** (Commercial Actions) 1994 [S.I. 1994 No. 2310] replacing Chap. 47 in RCS 1994 (A.S. (R.C.S. 1994) 1994 [S.I. 1994 No. 1443]) which repealed the rules in RCS 1965 as substituted by A.S. (R.C.S.A. No. 4) (Commercial Actions) 1988 [S.I. 1988 No. 1521] as amended by A.S. (R.C.S.A. No. 5) (Miscellaneous) 1990 [S.I. 1990 No. 2118]. It follows recommendations of the Working Party on Commercial Causes (see note 47.1.2). It was not possible to include those new rules in the RCS 1994 as originally drafted because of lack of time caused by the need for consultation on the draft rules for commercial actions.

The rules in this Chapter make available for the disposal of commercial actions a procedure swifter, more flexible and with less of an emphasis on written pleadings than ordinary procedure. The procedure on the Commercial Roll enables disputes of a business or commercial nature to be dealt with as quickly as possible under the close supervision of the court: *Stirling Aquatic Technology Ltd v. Farmocean AB* 1993 S.L.T. 713, 715L *per* L.P. Hope. Once a case has been put in the list of commercial actions the court has all the powers it requires to secure its speedy disposal: *Jones & Bailey Contractors Ltd v. George H. Campbell & Co. (Glasgow) Ltd* 1983 S.L.T. 461, 462 *per* L.P. Emslie. These points made in these cases under the former Rules apply equally to the new rules. The new procedures are the answer to the perception of the business community that the court's procedures caused delay and lacked expertise.

The introduction of special rules of procedure to govern the conduct of disputes of a business or commercial nature represents an attempt by the court not only to respond to the demands of the business and commercial community for a quick and relatively straight-forward means of resolving the sort of disputes which arise in the course of business, but also to compete more effectively with other forums available (*e.g.* the courts of other jurisdictions, arbitrations, ADR, etc.) for the resolution of these disputes.

In the light of experience the rules may be amended.

Working Party on commercial causes. The rules on commercial actions as previously **47.1.2** constituted, in 1978 by A.S. (R.C.A. No. 4) (Commercial Causes) 1978 [S.I. 1978 No. 690] and A.S. (R.C.S.A. No. 4) (Commercial Actions) 1988 [S.I. 1988 No. 1521] as amended by A.S. (R.C.S.A. No. 5 (Miscellaneous) 1990 [S.I. 1990 No. 2218], had only limited success. Only 55 cases called on the Commercial Roll in 1991. 1992 saw a slight increase (to 66) in the number

of causes brought under this procedure, but there were only 50 in 1993. This low level of use is thought most unlikely to reflect the true level of commercial disputes in Scotland: Report of the Working Party on Commercial Causes, November 1993, para. 3. Accordingly, the Lord President set up a Working Party, under the chairmanship of Lord Coulsfield (a nominated commercial judge) with terms of reference to "examine the existing practice in relation to the hearing of commercial litigation in the Court of Session . . . to consider any changes which may be desirable in order to improve the handling of such cases and to make this more expeditious and more convenient to litigants". After wide-ranging consultation with representatives of the commercial and legal communities, the Working Party reported in November 1993. It did not recommend radical departures from the existing scheme. It advocated that familiar procedures be adapted rather than new ones devised or imported. The recommendations, and the rules in this Chapter, are the answer to the perception of the business community that in commercial litigation the court's procedures were slow and lacking in expertise.

It will be necessary to read the rules in Chap. 47 in conjunction with P.N. No. 6 of 2004 (and subsequent P.N.s). In due course, a Guide for Practitioners will be published from time to time to keep readers up to date with the developing practice of the commercial judges. For an introductory overview of the operation of the rules for commercial actions, including a discussion of what "judicial proactivity" has meant in practice, based upon analysis of 180 actions brought under the new procedure, see: Ronald Clancy, Andrew Murray and Rachel Wardia: "The New Commercial Cause Rules" in 1997 S.L.T.(News) 45, 58.

Jurisdiction. For jurisdiction, see notes 13.2.8 to 13.2.15.   **47.1.3**

"commercial action". The definition of a commercial action is in the widest terms. It will **47.1.4** include those matters previously listed in R.C.S. 1994, r. 47.1(2) (see new P.N. No. 6 of 2004, para. 1), namely:

    (i)   the construction of a commercial or mercantile document,
    (ii) the sale or hire purchase of goods,
   (iii) the export or import of merchandise,
   (iv) the carriage of goods by land, air or sea (other than an Admiralty action within the meaning of rule 46.1),
    (v) insurance,
   (vi) banking,
  (vii) the provision of financial services,
 (viii) mercantile agency,
   (ix) mercantile usage or a custom of trade,
    (x) a building, engineering or construction contract, and
   (xi) a commercial lease.

It would also include an action which would otherwise be an Admiralty action *in personam* which does not require the special rules in r. 46 where the identity of the ship owners is not known (P.N. No. 6 of 2004, para. 1). Any other Admiralty action could not be brought as a commercial action by election under r. 47.3, but it might be transferred to the Commercial Roll in an appropriate case under r. 47.10.

It is unlikely that a consumer contract would ordinarily be treated as a commercial action. The new procedures are not intended to resolve disputes between a commercial organisation and a lay purchaser. Such an action would probably be withdrawn from the Commercial Roll under new rule 47.9 if a motion were made to that effect. An exception would be where it could be demonstrated, for example, that the case turned on an interpretation of a standard commercial document the construction of which was important not simply in the case in question.

The phrase "any transaction or dispute of a commercial or business nature" in r. 47.1(2) is intended to be of broad scope and is habile to include an action by a trustee in sequestration for declarator of vesting of acquirenda, where the issue was one of insolvency and not of succession: *Rankin's Trs v. H.C. Somerville & Russell*, 1999 S.C. 166.

It is not competent to bring as, or incorporate into, a commercial action an application which under the R.C.S. 1994 requires to be brought by petition. So, e.g., in *Ross v. Davy*, 1996 S.C.L.R. 369, a commercial action at the instance of a liquidator against a company director and founded on that director's alleged breach of fiduciary duty, the court refused as incompetent an attempt by the liquidator to seek to add by minute of amendment an order under s. 212 of the Insolvency Act 1986, where such an application must, by virtue of r. 74.2, be brought as a petition.

Proceedings before commercial judge

[1] **47.2.** All proceedings in the Outer House in a commercial action shall be brought before a judge of the court nominated by the Lord President as a commercial judge or, where a commercial judge is not available, any other judge of the court (including the vacation judge); and "commercial judge" shall be construed accordingly.

Deriv. R.C.S. 1965, r. 149 substituted by S.I. 1988 No. 1521

---

[1] R. 47.2 substituted by S.I. 1994 No. 2310 (effective 20th September 1994).

47.2.1   *General note.* In March 1994, L. P. Hope appointed Lord Penrose to be, in effect, a full-time commercial judge. The commercial judge has no duties as a trial judge in the High Court of Justiciary and commercial actions in the Court of Session have priority. He will be assisted by two other judges and arrangements will be made to ensure that at least one of these other two will always be available. There should always, therefore, be two commercial judges available at any time.

Under r. 10.7 the commercial judge can hear and determine a commercial action when the court is in session or in vacation. A commercial judge will be available all 52 weeks of the year. During about two weeks in April, the month of August and the Christmas and New Year vacation, only interlocutory or incidental business will normally be done: proofs and debates will not, as a general rule, be heard.

Steps will be taken to ensure that all appearances on the Commercial Roll of a particular action will be before the same commercial judge: P.N. No. 6 of 2004, para. 19(1).

47.2.2   *Nominated judges.* The current commercial judges are Lord Clarke, assisted by Lords Eassie, Reed and Drummond Young.

47.2.3   *"vacation judge".* The powers of the vacation judge are limited by r. 11.1.

Election of procedure for commercial actions

[1] **47.3.**—(1) The pursuer may elect to adopt the procedure in this Chapter by bringing an action in which there are inserted the words "Commercial Action" immediately below the words "IN THE COURT OF SESSION" where they occur above the instance, and on the backing, of the summons and any copy of it.

(2) A summons in a commercial action shall—

   (a) specify, in the form of conclusions, the orders sought;

   (b) identify the parties to the action and the transaction or dispute from which the action arises;

   (c) summarise the circumstances out of which the action arises; and

   (d) set out the grounds on which the action proceeds.

(3) There shall be appended to a summons in a commercial action a schedule listing the documents founded on or adopted as incorporated in the summons.

Deriv. R.C.S. 1965, r. 148(3) substituted by S.I. 1988 No. 1521 (r. 47.3(1))

---

[1] R.47.3 substituted by S.I. 1994 No. 2310 (effective 20th September 1994).

47.3.1   *General note.* Prior to reform in 1988, an action could proceed as a commercial cause only with the consent of the other parties. Where such consent was not forthcoming, a pursuer who wished to employ commercial cause procedure required to raise an ordinary action and then enrol a motion seeking that it be placed on the list of commercial causes. It was then for that party to persuade the court that his action was one appropriate to be dealt with under commercial cause procedure. The requirement of consent was perceived to be an obstacle in the way of the success of commercial cause procedure, and so in 1988 the rules were changed to permit a pursuer to elect, at the outset, to bring an action under the procedure in this Chapter; and this provision is repeated in R.C.S. 1994, r. 47.3(1). Defenders are, however, protected from the consequences of inappropriate adoption by a pursuer of this procedure r. 47.9(1), which provides for the withdrawal of a commercial action from this procedure by the court, on the motion of any party (but not now at its own instance, strangely), where it considers that the speedy and efficient determination of the action would not be served by the cause being dealt with as a commercial action. The onus then appears to have shifted on to the defender to explain why a dispute is inappropriate to be dealt with according to the procedure under the Chapter.

47.3.2   *"instance".* On the instance, see note 13.2.2.

47.3.3   *Form of summons.* Underlying the procedure in this Chapter is the principle that the normal requirements of pleadings in ordinary actions may be dispensed with. The nature of the dispute between the parties may determine the form of pleading adopted in a particular commercial action. R.47.3(2) is intended to indicate that a summons may be short and simple; the only formal requirements being set out in r. 47.3(2). The purpose is to identify the subject-matter of the dispute and the legal issues. Lengthy narrative is to be discouraged.

Summonses may still be drawn with the familiar three parts of conclusions, condescendence and pleas-in-law, however brief; although a summons without such formal parts as a condescendence and pleas-in-law will not be incompetent. Where only the construction of a document is sought, a pursuer may serve a summons consisting solely of conclusions specifying the document in dispute and the pursuer's preferred construction of it: P.N. No. 6 of 2004, para. 3(1).

It should be noted, however, that while in many commercial actions, detailed written pleadings may be inappropriate generally, or appropriate only in relation to particular issues, it by no means follows that the requirements of fair notice are dispensed with. On the contrary, it is a cardinal feature of commercial action business that parties make full and frank disclosure. Sometimes, such disclosure may be in a form other than formal pleadings, but when, for instance, an allegation of fraud is made, the basis for that allegation must be set forth to the same standard of relevancy and specification as is required for such an allegation in any other proceedings: *Kaur v. Singh* 1998 S.C. 233, 237C *per* Lord Hamilton. If not in formal pleadings, material adequate for the purposes of fair notice and enabling the court to determine whether or not inquiry was justified must be provided: *Johnston v. WH Brown Construction (Dundee) Ltd* 2000 S.L.T. 223.

Initial pleadings are expected to be in abbreviated form: the purpose of the pleadings is to give notice of the essential elements of the case to the court and other parties: P.N. No. 6 of 2004, para. 3(1). Before a commercial action is commenced, save exceptionally, matters in dispute should have been discussed and focused in pre-litigation communications: P.N. No. 6 of 2004, para. 11(1).

Schedule of documents. Documents founded on or adopted in the summons must be lodged as **47.3.4** productions when the summons is lodged for calling: r. 27.1(1)(*a*). Such documents must also be listed in a schedule to the summons. Rule 47.3(3) is intended to require a party to produce the "core" or essential documents to establish a contract or transaction: P.N. No. 6 of 2004, para. 3(2).

Commercial action registration form. A special registration form (Form CA1), copies of which **47.3.5** are obtainable from the General Department, must be completed and signed by the pursuer when the summons is lodged for signeting: P.N. No. 6 of 2004, para. 3(3). The form identifies the parties, the nature of the case, the legal advisers, etc. The form is in duplicate: one of the copies is retained in process and the other must be attached to the copy summons served on the defender.

Disapplication of certain rules
[1] **47.4.**—(1) The requirement in rule 4.1(4) for a step of process to be folded lengthwise shall not apply in a commercial action.

(2) An open record shall not be made up in, and Chapter 22 (making up and closing records) shall not apply to, a commercial action unless otherwise ordered by the court.

(3) The following rules shall not apply to a commercial action—
   rule 6.2 (fixing and allocation of diets in Outer House),
   rule 25.1(3) (form of counterclaim),
   rule 25.2(3) (application of warrants for diligence in counterclaims),
   rule 36.3 (lodging productions).

---

[1] R. 47.4 substituted by S.I. 1994 No. 2310 (effective 20th September 1994).

General note. The other rules of the R.C.S. 1994 apply to a commercial action to which Chap. **47.4.1** 47 applies except in so far as specifically excluded under r. 47.4 or excluded by implication because of a provision in Chap. 47. This statement is repeated in P.N. No. 6 of 2004, para. 4.

Flat processes. R. 47.4(1) is intended to permit flat (*i.e.* unfolded) A4 processes and the **47.4.2** lodging of steps of process in flat form rather than folded.

Procedure in commercial actions

[1] **47.5.** Subject to the provisions of this Chapter, the procedure in a commercial action shall be such as the commercial judge shall order or direct.

---

[1] R. 47.5 substituted by S.I. 1994 No. 2310 (effective 20th September 1994).

47.5.1   *General note.* This rule enables the commercial judge to direct the procedure to be followed where the specific rules in Chap. 47 are silent and in so far as not inconsistent with them. The commercial judge will take a pro-active approach: P.N. No. 6 of 2004, para. 5.

In spite of the wide scope afforded under r. 47.5 to the commercial judge relating to procedure in commercial actions, an application in a depending commercial action, which would otherwise be precluded by this Chapter from being brought as a commercial action, will not be entertained. In *Ross v. Davy*, 1996 S.C.L.R. 369, a commercial action at the instance of a liquidator against a director of the company and founded on that director's alleged breach of fiduciary duty, the liquidator attempted to seek by minute of amendment an order under s. 212 of the Insolvency Act 1986 (being a summary remedy). Any application under that section must be brought by petition and must be brought before the insolvency judge nominated under r. 74.2. The court refused the liquidator's minute of amendment, to the extent that it sought an order under s. 212 of the 1986 Act, as incompetent.

Defences

[1] **47.6.**—(1) Defences in a commercial action shall be in the form of answers to the summons with any additional statement of facts or legal grounds on which it is intended to rely.

(2) There shall be appended to the defences in a commercial action a schedule listing the documents founded on or adopted as incorporated in the defences.

---

[1] R. 47.6 substituted by S.I. 1994 No. 2310 (effective 20th September 1994).

47.6.1   *General note.* Defences will be in an abbreviated form similar to that of a summons: see note 47.3.3. Where the summons has a numbered condescendence, the answers should be in the form of equivalently numbered responses. It is not necessary that each allegation in the summons is admitted or denied provided that the extent of the dispute is reasonably well identified; compliance with the requirement for pre-litigation communications between law agents will enable essential elements of the defence to be presented in the defences in succinct form: P.N. No. 6 of 2004, paras. 6(1) and 11 (pre-litigation communications). One of the objectives of the commercial procedure is to make the extent of written pleadings subject to the control of the court: P.N. No. 6 of 2004, para. 6(1). On defences generally, see r. 18.1.

There is no power under r. 4.9(2) to prorogate the time for lodging defences. Application may be made under r. 2.1 for the lodging of defences late.

It should be noted that a counterclaim or third party notice cannot be proceeded with except with the leave of the court sought by motion: r. 47.7(1).

47.6.2   *Schedule of documents.* Documents founded on or adopted in the defences must be lodged as productions when the defences are lodged: r. 27.1(1)(*b*). Such documents must also be listed in a schedule to the defences.

47.6.3   *Commercial action registration form.* The defender must complete either the service copy of the registration form CA1 served with the summons (and lodge it in process with his defences) or complete the process copy of the form. The form requires details of the nature of the defences, the names of the legal advisers, etc.: P.N. No. 6 of 2004, para. 6(4).

Counterclaims and third party notices

[1] **47.7.**—(1) A party seeking to lodge a counterclaim or to serve a third party notice shall apply by motion to do so.

(2) The commercial judge shall, on a motion to lodge a counterclaim or to serve a third party notice, make such order and give such directions as he thinks fit with regard to—

   (a) the time within which a counterclaim may be lodged or a third party notice served and any answers lodged;

(b) where the motion is made before the preliminary hearing, a date for the preliminary hearing if it is to be a date other than the date referred to in rule 47.11(4); and

(c) any application for a warrant to use any form of diligence which would have been permitted under rule 13.6(*c*) (warrants for diligence in summons) had the warrant been sought in a summons in a separate action.

(3) Paragraphs (2) and (3) of rule 47.3 shall apply to the form of a counterclaim as they apply to the form of a summons.

---

[1] R. 47.7 substituted by S.I. 1994 No. 2310 (effective 20th September 1994).

General note. The rule in ordinary actions, that a defender does not require the authority of **47.7.1** the court to lodge a counterclaim with his defences, does not apply in the case of commercial actions: the authority of the commercial judge to proceed with a counterclaim must be sought by motion: r. 47.7(1). The reason for this is that the introduction of a counterclaim might make the action unsuitable for procedure under Chap. 47.

R. 47.7(1) follows r. 26.1(1) in requiring a motion for authority to serve a third party notice.

"motion". For motions, see Chap. 23. **47.7.2**

"counterclaim". The form of the substance of a counterclaim will be the same as that of a **47.7.3** summons: r. 47.7(3).

On counterclaims generally, see Chap. 25.

"third party notice". On third party procedure, see Chap. 26. **47.7.4**

Commercial Roll

[1] **47.8.**—(1) All proceedings in an action in which an election has been made under rule 47.3(1) or which has been transferred under rule 47.10 shall, in the Outer House, be heard and determined on the Commercial Roll on such dates and at such times as shall be fixed by the commercial judge.

(2) A commercial action shall call on the Commercial Roll for a preliminary hearing within 14 days after defences have been lodged.

(3) The appearance of a commercial action on the Commercial Roll for a hearing on a specified date shall not affect the right of any party to apply by motion at any time under these Rules.

---

[1] R. 47.8 substituted by S.I. 1994 No. 2310 (effective 20th September 1994).

The Commercial Roll. All proceedings in a commercial action are dealt with on the **47.8.1** Commercial Roll including motions: r. 47.8(1). The date and time of any hearing of an action on the Commercial Roll will be determined by the commercial judge: r. 47.8(1).

Motions. The ordinary rules for enrolment and intimation of motions in Chap. 23 apply. Rr. **47.8.2** 23.6 to 23.10 apply subject to the modification that the control of the date and time of the motions are in the hands of the commercial judge.

Except in cases of urgency, a motion enrolled before the date for a preliminary hearing will probably be heard at that hearing; a motion enrolled after the preliminary hearing may be heard on the Monday following enrolment on Monday to Thursday or, if a subsequent hearing on the Commercial Roll has been fixed for a date within a reasonable time, at that hearing.

In commercial actions to which Chap. 47 applies, the direction applies subject to Direction No. 2 of 1995 which provides that opposed and other starred motions will be put out for hearing on such a date and at such a time as is convenient to the court and, where possible, the parties. The clerk of court will fix the date and time and intimate it to the parties. Urgent motions will be dealt with on a priority basis.

Greater discretion may be exercised by the commercial judge in dealing with unopposed motions without requiring the appearance of counsel or other person having a right of audience than is the case in respect of unopposed motions on the Motion Roll (for which, see notes 23.2.15 and 23.2.16).

47.8.4   "*within 14 days*". The date from which the period is calculated is not counted. Where the last day falls on a Saturday or Sunday or a public holiday on which the Office of Court is closed, the next available day is allowed: r. 1.3(7). For office hours and public holidays, see note 3.1.2.

47.8.5   *Reclaiming.* To assist with the principle of speedy determination of actions on the Commercial Roll, an interlocutor, other than a final interlocutor, pronounced in a commercial action may only be reclaimed against with leave of the commercial judge within 14 days of that interlocutor: r. 38.4(7).

Withdrawal of action from Commercial Roll

[1] **47.9.**—(1) At any time before or at the preliminary hearing, the commercial judge shall—

    (*a*) on the motion of a party, withdraw a commercial action from the procedure in this Chapter and appoint it to proceed as an ordinary action where, having regard to—

        (i) the likely need for detailed pleadings to enable justice to be done between the parties,

        (ii) the length of time required for preparation of the action, or

        (iii) any other relevant circumstances,

    he is satisfied that the speedy and efficient determination of the action would not be served by the cause being dealt with as a commercial action; and

    (*b*) on the motion of a party with the consent of all other parties, withdraw a commercial action from the Commercial Roll and appoint it to proceed as an ordinary action.

[2] (1A) At any time before or at the preliminary hearing, the commercial judge may—

    (a) on the motion of a party; or

    (b) *ex proprio motu*, after hearing the parties to the action,

if he is satisfied that the action is not a commercial action, withdraw it from the procedure in this Chapter and appoint it to proceed as an ordinary action.

(2) If a motion to withdraw a commercial action from the Commercial Roll made before or renewed at a preliminary hearing is refused, no subsequent motion to withdraw the action from the Commercial Roll shall be considered except on special cause shown.

---

[1] R. 47.9 substituted by S.I. 1994 No. 2310 (effective 20th September 1994)
[2] R. 47.9(1A) as inserted by S.S.I. 2000 No. 66, para. 2(7) (effective 7th April 2000).

47.9.1   *General note.* This rule provides some protection for a defender against the potentially adverse consequences for him of the election by a pursuer to adopt the procedure under this Chapter in an action ill-suited to it. A party may, at any time before or at the preliminary hearing, enrol a motion to have that action withdrawn from the Commercial Roll and, if granted, the action reverts to being an ordinary action. Commercial procedure is not limited to straightforward or simple cases and does not exclude cases involving investigation or difficulty and complicated facts: P.N. No. 6 of 2004, para. 9.

Originally, in r. 47.6(1) the commercial judge could, at his own instance, withdraw an action from the Commercial Roll and make it an ordinary action. When Chap. 47 was re-written in September 1994 this provision was not re-enacted in r. 47.9 in order to encourage commercial actions. The rule has been changed again and r. 47.9(1A) now permits the commercial judge to withdraw an action from the Commercial Roll at his own instance.

Although the motion to withdraw must be made at or before the preliminary hearing, a subsequent motion (if the earlier motion is refused) may be made at any time; but it may be made only on special cause shown.

47.9.2   "*motion*". For motions, see Chap. 23.

47.9.3   "*speedy and efficient determination of the action*". The test for withdrawal of an action from the Commercial Roll is whether the commercial judge is satisfied that the "speedy and efficient determination of the action would not be served by the cause being dealt with as a commercial action": r. 47.9(1)(*a*). In applying that test certain factors (items (i)–(iii) in para.(1)(*a*)) must be considered.

Transfer of action to Commercial Roll

[1] **47.10.**—(1) In an action within the meaning of rule 47.1(2) (definition of commercial action) in which the pursuer has not made an election under rule 47.3(1), any party may apply by motion at any time to have the action appointed to be a commercial action on the Commercial Roll.

(2) A motion enrolled under paragraph (1) shall be heard by the commercial judge.

(3) Where an interlocutor is pronounced under paragraph (1) appointing an action to be a commercial action on the Commercial Roll, the action shall be put out by order for a preliminary hearing within 14 days—

(a) if defences have been lodged, after the date of that interlocutor; or

(b) if defences have not been lodged, after defences have been lodged.

---

[1] R. 47.10 substituted by S.I. 1994 No. 2310 (effective 20th September 1994).

General note. It is not open to the court at its own instance to appoint an ordinary action to proceed as a commercial action. **47.10.1**

"motion". The date and time of a motion to transfer an action will be fixed by the commercial judge: r. 47.10(2). **47.10.2**

For motions generally, see Chap. 23.

Reclaiming. The former rule (in r. 47.7(3)) provided that the decision whether or not to transfer was final. The rule now is that the decision may only be reclaimed against with the leave of the commercial judge within 14 days of the date of the interlocutor: r. 38.4(6). **47.10.3**

Preliminary hearing

[1] **47.11.**—(1) Unless a commercial action is withdrawn under rule 47.9 from the Commercial Roll then, at the preliminary hearing of a commercial action in which an election has been made under rule 47.3(1), the commercial judge—

(a) shall determine whether and to what extent and in what manner further specification of the claim and defences should be provided;

(b) may make an order in respect of any of the following matters:

(i) detailed written pleadings to be made by a party either generally or restricted to particular issues;

(ii) a statement of facts to be made by one or more parties either generally or restricted to particular issues;

(iii) the allowing of an amendment by a party to his pleadings;

(iv) disclosure of the identity of witnesses and the existence and nature of documents relating to the action or authority to recover documents either generally or specifically;

(v) documents constituting, evidencing or relating to the subject-matter of the action or any invoices, correspondence or similar documents relating to it to be lodged in process within a specified period;

(vi) each party to lodge in process, and send to every other party, a list of witnesses;

(vii) reports of skilled persons or witness statements to be lodged in process;

(viii) affidavits concerned with any of the issues in the action to be lodged in process; and

(ix) the action to proceed to a hearing without any further preliminary procedure either in relation to the whole or any particular aspect of the action;

(c) may fix the period within which any such order shall be complied with;

(d) may continue the preliminary hearing to a date to be appointed by him; and (*e*) may make such other order as he thinks fit for the speedy determination of the action.

(2) Where the commercial judge makes an order under paragraph 1(*b*)(i) or (ii) or (*c*), he may ordain the pursuer to—

(*a*) make up a record; and

(*b*) lodge that record in process within such period as the commercial judge thinks fit.

(3) At the conclusion of the preliminary hearing, the court shall, unless it has made an order under rule 47.11(*a*)(ix) (order to proceed without a further hearing), fix a date for a procedural hearing to determine further procedure.

(4) The date fixed under paragraph (3) for a procedural hearing shall not be extended except on special cause shown on a motion enrolled not less than 7 days before the date fixed for the procedural hearing.

---

[1] R. 47.11 substituted by S.I. 1994 No. 2310 (effective 20th September 1994).

47.11.1   *General note.* The preliminary hearing is one of the two critical hearings in the preparation of a commercial action for debate or proof; the other is the procedural hearing (for which, see r. 47.12). It is unlikely that at the preliminary hearing (which is held within 14 days after defences have been lodged: r. 47.8(2)) the action will be ready to go to debate or proof; if it is, the commercial judge may order that at once: r. 47.11(1)(*b*)(ix). More commonly, at this hearing there will be a discussion about what is required more clearly to identify and disclose the factual and legal issues to be decided and how long will be needed to do this. To this end further specification of pleadings, the disclosure of the identity of witnesses and documents, and the ordering of the production of documents, may be required: r. 47.11(1)(*b*). Time-limits will be set within which any matter required is to be done: for the consequences of failure to observe time-limits, see r. 47.16. It is likely that it will not be possible to settle all these matters at one hearing; the hearing may, therefore, be continued to another date to deal with remaining issues: r. 47.11(1)(*d*).

At the (final) preliminary hearing a date will be fixed for the next critical hearing, the procedural hearing: r. 47.11(3).

47.11.2   *Form of the preliminary hearing.* The hearing will normally be conducted on the basis that the pre-action communications provisions of para. 11 of the P.N. No. 6 of 2004 have been complied with: P.N. No. 6 of 2004, para. 12(1). A continuation of a hearing brought about by a failure to comply with para. 11 may result in an adverse finding of expenses on an agent and client basis; and motions for continuations to obtain information which should have been obtained may be refused: P.N. No. 6 of 2004, para. 12(3).

Parties should lodge before the hearing all correspondence and other documents which set out their material contentions of fact and law which show their compliance with para. 11: P.N. No. 6 of 2004, para. 12(2) (and this is supplemental to the requirement in rr. 47.3(3) and 47.6(2) for a schedule of documents).

Parties should be in a position to lodge a document (where possible, agreed) setting out concisely the issues requiring judicial determination: P.N. No. 6 of 2004, para. 12(4).

Time-limits will be expected to be achieved and extensions of time will only be granted in certain circumstances: P.N. No. 6 of 2004, para. 12(5).

It is anticipated that the hearing will be rather less formal than hearings on the motion or diet rolls. It is more likely that, at a hearing which is more in the nature of a round-table discussion, agreement can be reached on how cases proceed and what needs to be done than in the more adversarial context of a hearing in court.

The main purpose of the hearing, in achieving a speedy resolution of cases, is to reduce to a minimum the time spent in preparing cases for proof or debate, and the time spent in court on proof or debate, proving or arguing points which at the end of the day are not disputed or which turn out to be immaterial.

It is important that the counsel or other persons having rights of audience and the agents actually involved in the case are present at this hearing because the commercial judge will expect such persons to be fully informed about the case, see P.N. No. 6 of 2004, para. 19(1).

47.11.3   *"detailed written pleadings", "amendment", "record".* The detailed written pleadings necessary in an ordinary action are neither encouraged nor required, as a general rule, in a commercial action. It is unlikely, therefore, that there should be a need in most cases for further specification, amendment or a record (as a consequence of either of the former). Although in an ordinary action, if a defender raises an issue in his defences, the pursuer would require to plead an answer to it, such a rule will not normally apply in a commercial action so long as it is clear to the parties and the court at the preliminary hearing (or at the latest, the procedural hearing) what the issues are, what the position of the parties is to them and what each party is intending to establish.

Where pleadings or other documents are to be adjusted, a fresh copy of the writ must be prepared with new material shown in under-lining, side-lining, red-lining, a different type face or other means: P.N. No. 6 of 2004, para. 19(2).

Recovery and disclosure of documents. The procedures in Chap. 35 for recovery of evidence **47.11.4** are still available to parties. The former rule (in r. 47.8) is not explicitly re-enacted. In new r. 47.11(1)(*b*)(iv) and (v), for example, there are powers for parties to seek, and for the commercial judge to order at his own instance or on the motion of a party, disclosure of documents relating to the dispute. If these powers are exercised, resort to Chap. 35 may be unnecessary.

The word "document" has been defined in the R.C.S. 1994 by reference to the inclusive definition in s. 9 of the Civil Evidence (Scotland) Act 1988: r. 1.3(1).

Exchange of lists of witnesses. This may be ordered at this stage: r. 47.11(1)(*b*)(vi). There is a **47.11.5** requirement to lodge and exchange such lists before the procedural hearing where a proof is sought: r. 47.12(1)(*b*).

The list of witnesses is lodged as a step of process (r. 1.3(1) (definition of "step of process")). On lodging steps of process, see r. 4.4. The list may be lodged by post: P.N. No. 4 of 1994, paras. 1 and 8; and see note 4.4.10.

Reports of skilled persons and witness statements. These may be ordered to be lodged under r. **47.11.6** 47.11(1)(*b*)(vii).

A witness statement is not the same as a precognition and should be signed.

As these documents are ordered by the court to be lodged they will be lodged as steps of process (r. 1.3(1) (definition of "step of process")) and not as productions. On lodging steps of process, see r. 4.4. The reports may be lodged by post: P.N. No. 4 of 1994, paras. 1 and 8; and see note 4.4.10.

"affidavits". As these documents are ordered by the court to be lodged they will be lodged as **47.11.7** steps of process (r. 1.3(1) (definition of "step of process")) and not as productions. On lodging steps of process, see r. 4.4. The affidavits may be lodged by post: P.N. No. 4 of 1994, paras. 1 and 8; and see note 4.4.10.

"speedy determination". While the speedy determination of the question in dispute between **47.11.8** the parties may be the primary objective of the procedure under this Chapter, it may be stated as a general principle that this objective is not to be achieved at the expense of a thorough examination of the issues and the correctness and fairness of the court's eventual decision. Where it becomes apparent that speed in disposal cannot be reconciled with a thorough examination of the issues, this may indicate that it is inappropriate for the action to continue under the procedure in this Chapter.

Fee. The court fee for a preliminary hearing is payable by each party for every 30 minutes or **47.11.9** part thereof. For fee, see Court of Session etc. Fees Order 1984, Table of Fees, Pt I, B, item 16 [S.I. 1984 No. 256, Table as amended, pp. C1202 *et seq.*]. The fee may be debited under a credit scheme introduced on 1st April 1976 by P.N. No. 4 of 1976 to the account (if one is kept or permitted) of the agent by the court cashier, and an account will be rendered weekly by the court cashier's office to the agent for all court fees due that week for immediate settlement. An agent not on the credit scheme will have an account opened for the purpose of lodging the fee: P.N. No. 2 of 1995. A debit slip and a copy of the court hearing time sheet will be delivered to the agent's box or sent by DX or post.

A party litigant must pay cash to the clerk of court at the end of the hearing: P.N. No. 2 of 1995. A receipt will be issued. The assistant clerk of session will acknowledge receipt of the sum received from the clerk of court on the Minute of Proceedings.

Procedural hearing

[1] **47.12.**—(1) Not less than 3 days before the date fixed under rule 47.11(3) for the procedural hearing, each party shall—

    (*a*) lodge a written statement of his proposals for further procedure which shall, *inter alia*, state—

        (i) whether he seeks to have the commercial action appointed to debate or to have the action sent to proof on the whole or any part of it; and

(ii) what the issues are which he considers should be sent to debate or proof;

(b) lodge a list of the witnesses he proposes to cite or call to give evidence, identifying the matters to which each witness will speak;

(c) lodge the reports of any skilled persons before the procedural hearing;

(d) where it is sought to have the action appointed to debate, lodge a note of argument consisting of concise numbered paragraphs stating the legal propositions on which it is proposed to submit that any preliminary plea should be sustained or repelled with reference to the principal authorities and statutory provisions to be founded on; and

(e) send a copy of any such written statement, lists, reports or note of argument, as the case may be, to every other party.

(2) At the procedural hearing, the commercial judge—

(a) shall determine whether the commercial action should be appointed to debate or sent to proof on the whole or any part of the action;

(b) where the action is appointed to debate or sent to proof, may order that written arguments on any question of law should be submitted;

(c) where the action is sent to proof, may determine whether evidence at the proof should be by oral evidence, the production of documents or affidavits on any issue;

(d) may determine, in the light of any witness statements, affidavits or reports produced, that proof is unnecessary on any issue;

(e) may direct that there should be consultation between skilled persons with a view to reaching agreement about any points held in common;

(f) without prejudice to Chapter 12 (assessors), may appoint an expert to examine, on behalf of the court, any reports of skilled persons or other evidence submitted and to report to the court within such period as the commercial judge may specify;

(g) may direct that proof of the authenticity of a document or other formal matters may be dispensed with;

(h) if invited to do so by all parties, direct the action to be determined on the basis of written submissions, or such other material, without any oral hearing; and

(i) may continue the procedural hearing to a date to be appointed by him.

---

[1] R. 47.12 inserted by S.I. 1994 No. 2310 (effective 20th September 1994).

47.12.1   *General note.* The procedural hearing is the second critical hearing held before debate or proof unless the action has been appointed to debate or proof at the preliminary hearing under r. 47.11(1)(b)(ix). If the action has not been so appointed, the procedural hearing is the hearing at which the decision is taken whether the action is to be sent to debate or proof, what issues have to be decided and the form in which either debate or proof is to be undertaken.

Parties will be expected to discuss realistically the issues involved and the methods of disposing of them; parties' positions will have been ascertained and identified and all prospects for settlement fully discussed and exhausted: P.N. No. 6 of 2004, para. 13(1).

For the procedural hearing each party must, not less than three days before the hearing, (a) lodge a statement of his proposals for further procedure stating, among other things, whether he seeks debate or proof and on what issues, and (b) lodge a note of argument for the debate or certain productions for the proof, as the case may be: r. 47.12(1). These requirements are mandatory and are necessary to enable the commercial judge to make an informed decision about the orders he will make under r. 47.12(2).

There is unlikely to be more than one procedural hearing. But note the pre-proof by order hearing: see note 47.15.2.

47.12.2   *Form of procedural hearing.* It is anticipated that the hearing will be rather less formal than hearings on the motion or diet rolls. It is more likely that, at a hearing which is more in the nature of a round-table discussion, agreement can be reached on how cases proceed and what needs to be done than in the more adversarial context of a hearing in court.

The main purpose of the hearing, in achieving a speedy resolution of cases, is to reduce to a minimum the time spent in preparing cases for proof or debate, and the time spent in court on proof or debate, proving or arguing points which at the end of the day are not disputed or which turn out to be immaterial.

It is important that the counsel or other persons having rights of audience and the agents actually involved in the case are present at this hearing because the commercial judge will expect such persons to be fully informed about the case. See P.N. No. 6 of 2004, para. 19(1).

"not less than 3 days before". This is synonymous with clear days, and the day from which the   **47.12.3**
period is calculated is not included.

"written statement of his proposals for further procedure". Parties must have a clear idea about   **47.12.4**
what they want, what has to be established and what issues have to be determined.

The requirements of r. 47.12(1)(a) are mandatory and are necessary to enable the commercial judge to make an informed decision about the orders he will make under r. 47.12(2).

The statement should be lodged as a step of process (r. 1.3(1) (definition of "step of process")). On lodging steps of process, see r. 4.4. The written statement may be lodged by post: P.N. No. 4 of 1994, paras. 1 and 8; and see note 4.4.10. A copy of the written statement must be sent to the other parties: r. 47.12(1)(e).

"lodge a list of witnesses". The former provision was in r. 47.9(1). This must be done   **47.12.5**
notwithstanding that an order to lodge a list may previously have been made and obtempered under r. 47.11(1)(b)(vi) unless the list is the same as that previously ordered and lodged.

The list of witnesses is lodged as a step of process (r. 1.3(1) (definition of "step of process")). On lodging steps of process, see r. 4.4. The list may be lodged by post: P.N. No. 4 of 1994, paras. 1 and 8; and see note 4.4.10. A copy of the list must be sent to the other parties: r. 47.12(1)(e).

In *McGunnigal v. D. B. Marshall (Newbridge) Ltd* 1993 S.L.T. 769, under the optional (reparation) procedure, the defender was refused leave to lead witnesses because it had not lodged a list of witnesses.

"lodge the report of any skilled persons". This means the reports of skilled persons who may   **47.12.6**
give evidence.

This may already have been done following an order under r. 47.11(1)(b)(vii).

Any report is lodged as a production. On lodging productions, see r. 4.5. The report may be lodged by post: P.N. No. 4 of 1994, paras. 1 and 8; and see note 4.5.5. A copy of the report must be sent to the other parties: r. 47.12(1)(e).

"lodge a note of argument". This is required under r. 47.12(1) (d) where a party seeks to have a   **47.12.7**
case sent to debate. The note of argument should consist of numbered paragraphs setting out briefly the legal propositions to be advanced at debate by the party lodging it, supported by citations of the principal authorities for those propositions and any statutory provisions relied on.

A note of argument is lodged in process as a step of process (r. 1.3(1) (definition of "step of process")) and does not require to be signed. R.15.2 does not apply. On lodging a step of process, see r. 4.4. The note may be lodged by post: P.N. No. 4 of 1994, paras. 1 and 8; and see note 4.4.10. A copy of the note must be sent to the other parties: r. 47.12(1)(e).

"debate". See r. 47.13.   **47.12.8**

It is for the court to determine whether an action should be sent to debate or proof and, unlike in an ordinary action, a party with a preliminary plea may not insight on a debate: *Highland and Universal Properties Ltd v. Safeway Properties Ltd* 1996 S.C. 424.

"proof". Chap. 36 applies except that r. 47.14 (lodging productions) replaces r. 36.3. In the   **47.12.9**
application of r. 36.4 (lodging copies of productions for use of the court), the requirement of P.N. No. 12 of 1994, para. 14 is that parties should agree a single paginated working bundle of productions for the judge.

There is no present intention to depart from the principle of the adversarial nature of a proof.

It is for the court to determine whether an action should be sent to debate or proof and, unlike in an ordinary action, a party with a preliminary plea may not insight on a debate: *Highland and Universal Properties Ltd v. Safeway Properties Ltd* 1996 S.C. 424.

The normal form of interlocutor, allowing parties a proof [before answer] of their respective averments, may not always be appropriate in a commercial action. Because the condescendence and defences may be brief (see rr. 47.3(2) and 47.6(1)), the written statement lodged under r. 47.12(1)(a) may contain, in the statement of issues sought to be sent to proof, matters on which it is intended to lead evidence which are not spelt out in the pleadings. In such a case the interlocutor should allow a "proof [before answer] of their respective averments and of the issues set forth in the written statements lodged under rule 47.12(1) of the Rules of the Court of Session 1994". See *Highland and Universal Properties Ltd*, above, at pp. 425H–426D.

"written arguments". These may be ordered on questions of law at debate or proof, even   **47.12.10**
though a note of argument has been lodged under r. 47.12(1)(d): r. 47.12(2)(b). In *Deans v. Thus*

plc, 2005 S.C.L.R. 148. 149, Lord Clarke indicated that it was not for parties to ignore such an order on the basis that their earlier note (under r. 47.12(1)(d)) was sufficient, because the purpose of the order was to ensure that a party applied his mind to what exactly was the position he wished to adopt at debate.

A written argument is lodged in process as a step of process (r. 1.3(1) (definition of "step of process")) and does not require to be signed. On lodging a step of process, see r. 4.4. The written argument may be lodged by post: P.N. No. 4 of 1994, paras. 1 and 8; and see note 4.4.10.

47.12.11   *"affidavits"*. These may be ordered on any issue or in respect of any witness instead of oral evidence; r. 47.12(2)(c). It is conceivable that evidence-in-chief of a witness could be ordered in the first instance to be by affidavit, the position about cross-examination being reserved or preserved.

An affidavit is lodged in process as a step of process (r. 1.3(1) (definition of "step of process")). On lodging a step of process, see r. 4.4. The affidavit may be lodged by post: P.N. No. 4 of 1994, paras. 1 and 8; and see note 4.4.10.

47.12.12   *"consultation between skilled persons"*. Consultation between experts is sometimes "ordered" by reporters in planning inquiries, and can be useful in reducing if not eliminating an area of disagreement.

47.12.13   *"appoint an expert"*. It is a novel provision to empower the court to appoint its own expert to examine reports of skilled persons or other evidence (*e.g.* on a matter of trade or business practice).

47.12.14   *"remit to a person of skill"*. This provision enables the commercial judge, *e.g.* to remit questions of measurement in building and engineering contract cases once issues of principle or law have been determined by him.

The provision would also allow the judge to remit a question of a custom of trade or commercial usage to a person to report to the court. This provision replaces the former detailed rule in r. 47.11, the following paragraphs of which may still be relevant—

"(5) A remit under this paragraph shall be made to one or more persons engaged in the particular trade in question to report on the existence and scope of the custom or usage, on which matters the report shall be conclusive.

(6) Where a remit is made under paragraph (5), the party who pleads the custom or usage shall instruct the reporter within 14 days after the date of the remit and be responsible, in the first instance, for payment of his fee.

(7) On completion of a report following a remit under paragraph (5), the reporter shall send the report and a copy for each party to the Deputy Principal Clerk.

(8) On receipt of such a report, the Deputy Principal Clerk shall—

(*a*) give written intimation to each party of receipt of the report;

(*b*) request the party responsible for payment of the fee under paragraph (6) to show to him a discharge in respect of that fee; and

(*c*) after sight of such discharge—

(i) lodge the report in process; and

(ii) give written intimation to each party that this has been done and that he may uplift a copy of the report from process.".

47.12.15   *"written submissions"*. If invited to do so by the parties, the commercial judge may determine an action in a suitable case by written submissions or other material without any oral hearing of a debate or proof.

Written submissions are lodged in process as a step of process (r. 1.3(1) (definition of "step of process")). On lodging a step of process, see r. 4.4. The written submissions may be lodged by post: P.N. No. 4 of 1994, paras. 1 and 8; and see note 4.4.10.

47.12.16   *"document"*. The word "document" has been defined in the R.C.S. 1994 by reference to the inclusive definition in s. 9 of the Civil Evidence (Scotland) Act 1988: r. 1.3(1).

47.12.17   *Fee*. The court fee for a procedural hearing is payable by each party for every 30 minutes or part thereof. For fee, see Court of Session etc. Fees Order 1997, Table of Fees, Pt I, B, item 16 [S.I. 1997 No. 688, as amended, pp. C1201 *et seq.*]. Certain persons are exempt from payment of fees: see 1997 Fees Order, art.5 substituted by S.S.I. 2002 No. 270. A fee exemption certificate must be lodged in process: see P.N. No.1 of 2002.

Where a party is legally represented, the fee may be debited under a credit scheme introduced on 1st April 1976 by P.N. No. 4 of 1976 to the account (if one is kept or permitted) of the agent by the court cashier, and an account will be rendered weekly by the court cashier's office to the agent for all court fees due that week for immediate settlement. An agent not on the credit scheme will have an account opened for the purpose of lodging the fee: P.N. No. 2 of 1995. A debit slip and a copy of the court hearing time sheet will be delivered to the agent's box or sent by DX or post.

A party litigant must pay (by cash, cheque or postal order) to the clerk of court at the end of the hearing: P.N. No. 2 of 1995. A receipt will be issued. The assistant clerk of session will acknowledge receipt of the sum received from the clerk of court on the Minute of Proceedings.

Debates
[1] **47.13.** Chapter 28 (procedure roll) shall apply to a debate ordered in a commercial action under rule 47.12(2)(*a*) as it applies to a cause appointed to the Procedure Roll.

[1] R. 47.13 inserted by S.I. 1994 No. 2310 (effective 20th September 1994).

General note. A note of argument will have been lodged under r. 47.12(1)(*d*).   **47.13.1**

Lodging of productions for proof
[1] **47.14.**—(1) Any document not previously lodged required for any proof in a commercial action shall be lodged as a production not less than 7 days before the date fixed for the proof.

(2) No document may be lodged as a production after the date referred to in paragraph (1), even by agreement of all parties, unless the court is satisfied that any document sought to be lodged could not with reasonable diligence have been lodged in time.

[1] R. 47.14 inserted by S.I. 1994 No. 2310 (effective 20th September 1994).

General note. R. 47.14 replaces r. 36.3 on lodging productions for the proof.   **47.14.1**
In relation to productions not lodged timeously, the commercial judge will not allow late lodging unless satisfied that the document could not with reasonable diligence have been lodged in time: r. 47.14(2).
In the application of r. 36.4 (lodging copies of productions for use of the court), the requirement of P.N. No. 6 of 2004, para. 16 is that parties should agree a single paginated working bundle of productions for the judge.

"*document*". The word "document" has been defined in the R.C.S. 1994 by reference to the   **47.14.2**
inclusive definition in s. 9 of the Civil Evidence (Scotland) Act 1988: r. 1.3(1).

"*not less than 7 days before*". This is synonymous with clear days, and the day from which the   **47.14.3**
period is calculated is not included.

Hearings for further procedure
[1] **47.15.** At any time before final judgment, the commercial judge may, at his own instance or on the motion of any party, have a commercial action put out for hearing for further procedure; and the commercial judge may make such order as he thinks fit.

[1] R. 47.15 inserted by S.I. 1994 No. 2310 (effective 20th September 1994).

General note. Where a proof or proof before answer has been allowed, there will, e.g., be a   **47.15.1**
pre-proof hearing: P.N. No. 6 of 2004, para. 15.

Pre-proof By Order hearings. P.N. No. 6 of 2004, para. 15, provides that where a proof or   **47.15.2**
proof before answer is allowed there will be a pre-proof by order hearing to ascertain the parties' state of preparation and to review the estimated length of that hearing. Also there will be:— (1) Consideration of any joint minutes of admissions (to be lodged 2 days before the hearing). (2) A review of documents and productions to be relied on (to be lodged 2 days before the hearing). (3) The update position re expert reports and what consultation between experts to agree points has taken place. (4) Where there is to be a proof before answer, a statement of legal argument lodged and lists of authorities which may be relied on.

Failure to comply with rule or order of commercial judge

47.16. Any failure by a party to comply timeously with a provision in these Rules or any order made by the commercial judge in a commercial action shall entitle the judge, at his own instance—

    (*a*) to refuse to extend any period for compliance with a provision in these Rules or an order of the court,

    (*b*) to dismiss the action or counterclaim, as the case may be, in whole or in part,

    (*c*) to grant decree in respect of all or any of the conclusions of the summons or counterclaim, as the case may be, or

    (*d*) to make an award of expenses,

as he thinks fit.

---

[1] R. 47.16 inserted by S.I. 1994 No. 2310 (effective 20th September 1994).

47.16.1   *General note.* This rule provides the commercial judge with the sanctions open to him as the means of imposing discipline on parties in pursuit of the aim to achieve speedy determination of commercial actions.

    The sanctions most likely to be frequently used are refusal to extend time-limits and awards of expenses. Where, *e.g.* a party fails to lodge a document within the specified period, he may have to proceed without that document or be found liable in expenses occasioned by delay. In *McGunnigal v. D. B. Marshall (Newbridge) Ltd* 1993 S.L.T. 769, under the optional (reparation) procedure, the defender was refused leave to lead witnesses because it had not lodged a list of witnesses.

CHAPTER 48

EXCHEQUER CAUSES

Proceedings before Lord Ordinary in Exchequer Causes

48.1.—(1) Subject to Part IV of Chapter 41 (Exchequer appeals), all proceedings in an Exchequer cause shall be brought before the Lord Ordinary in Exchequer Causes.

    (2) An application for the suspension of a decree, charge, threatened charge or diligence in an Exchequer cause shall be made to the Lord Ordinary in Exchequer Causes.

    (3) Where another judge of the court acts in place of the Lord Ordinary in Exchequer Causes, any interlocutor pronounced by him shall state that he acted in the absence of the Lord Ordinary in Exchequer Causes.

Deriv. R.C.S. 1965, r. 153A(2) (r. 48.1(1)), and r. 153B (r. 48.1(2)), both inserted by S.I. 1984 No. 472

48.1.1   *General note.* Article XIX of the Treaty of Union between Scotland and England ratified by the Union with England Act 1706 and the Union with Scotland Act 1707 stipulated that there be a Court of Exchequer in Scotland after the Union for deciding questions concerning the revenues of customs and excises there. The Exchequer Court (Scotland) Act 1707 established a new Court of Exchequer in Scotland. It was to have the same power and authority within Scotland as the Court of Exchequer had in England. The procedures of the new court were also based on the English model. The Court of Exchequer in Scotland was, with the Courts of Session and Justiciary, one of the three Supreme Courts of Scotland and appeals were taken from it to the House of Lords: *e.g.* see *Brand v. Mackenzie* (1710) 1 Robert 8 (HL).

    The jurisdiction of the Court of Exchequer in Scotland was defined as encompassing all the revenues and duties and profits appertaining to the Crown, all forfeited lands and all the remedies and means for the recovering of the same; all forfeitures and penalties due and payable in Scotland by force or virtue of any law or statute touching on or relating to the custom and excise or by force or virtue of any penal or other laws or statutes whatsoever and also all fines, issues, forfeitures or penalties arising to the Crown, and all actions, securities, prosecutions and remedies concerning the same: 1707 Act, s. 7. In essence, the purpose of the Court of Exchequer in Scotland was to receive the King's custom and other things that belonged thereto and to make reckoning and give count thereof at the King's Chequer: Clerk and Scrope, *A Historical View of the Forms and Powers of the Court of Exchequer in Scotland* (1820), p. 98.

The whole power, authority and jurisdiction of the Court of Exchequer in Scotland was transferred to and vested in the Court of Session by the Exchequer Court (Scotland) Act 1856, s. 1. That jurisdiction has been augmented by subsequent taxation legislation to include various new taxes and duties.

Any tax may be sued for and recovered from the person charged therewith in the Court of Session sitting as the Court of Exchequer as a debt due to the Crown: Taxes Management Act 1970, s. 68. Today, the core of Exchequer causes consists in actions for the recovery of central government taxes due to the Board of Inland Revenue and the various customs, excise and other duties due to the Board of Customs and Excise: Scottish Law Commission *Report on Diligence and Debtors Protection* (Scot. Law Com. No. 95), para. 7.81. The Crown, as part of its prerogative power, may insist on any cause falling within this jurisdiction which has been raised in another court (the sheriff court) being remitted to the Court of Session as the Court of Exchequer: *Sharpe v. Miller* (1861) 23 D. 1015. On remits to the court, see rr. 32.3 *et seq.*

The court, as the Court of Exchequer in Scotland, has three further areas of jurisdiction:—

(1) It exercises an appellate function: see rr. 41.23 to 41.25.

(2) The Lord Ordinary in Exchequer Causes, in exercise of the ministerial jurisdiction of the Court of Exchequer, has various responsibilities in relation to Crown writs. (a) Where, in the course of an application for a Crown writ, a mistake in the terms of the last Crown writ or retour or decree of service comes to light, no rectification of such mistake shall be allowed, nor shall the draft Crown writ be held as finally revised or authenticated as such, until the same have been reported to and approved of by the Lord Ordinary in Exchequer Causes: Titles to Land Consolidation (Scotland) Act 1868, ss. 66 and 67. (b) Where a note of objections is lodged, by the person applying for it, to the revisals made to a draft Crown writ, the Lord Ordinary in Exchequer Causes hears the parties and adjudicates on the objection. Where it appears to him that the objections should to any extent receive effect, he shall cause such alterations and corrections as seem to him proper to be made, and shall authenticate them with his signature: 1868 Act, ss. 75 and 76. (c) Where a note of objection is lodged by an applicant who has sought but has been refused a Crown writ for want of sufficient production of titles, the Lord Ordinary in Exchequer Causes must hear the parties and sustain or repel such objection, or pronounce such judgment or deliverance on it as seems to him just: 1868 Act, s. 77.

(3) It exercises the jurisdiction, derived from the Sovereign as *pater patriae*, to grant authority for taking steps in the best interests of those who are incapable of giving their authority or consent for the purpose.

In 1856, the duties previously performed by or incumbent upon the Court of Exchequer with regard to the nomination, appointment and control of tutors-dative were transferred to the Court of Session (as successor to the Court of Exchequer in exercise of the right of the Crown as *pater patriae*: Erskine, I.vii.8), involving a special procedure of summary petition to the Inner House: Exchequer Court (Scotland) Act 1856, s. 19. That provision was repealed by the C.S.A. 1988, Sched. 2 because the procedure was not used in practice and was superseded by the power of the court to appoint a factor *loco tutoris* by petition to the Outer House (see r. 14.2(a)). Such a factor, however, has no authority over the person of his ward (unlike a tutor-dative). The appointment of tutors-dative to pupil children was effectively rendered obsolete by the Age of Legal Capacity (Scotland) Act 1991: see note 61.1.2(4). The appointment of tutors-datives to adults who are mentally *incapax* is noted in two articles in the *Scots Law Times* (referring to a number of recent unreported cases): see "Revival of Tutors-Dative" 1987 S.L.T.(News) 69, and "Tutors to Adults: Developments", 1992 S.L.T.(News) 325. With the repeal of s. 19 of the 1856 Act, such an appointment was thought (and was stated in this note) to be incompetent because Parliament repealed that section in the belief that it was a substantive provision which had fallen into desuetude. Ironically, by the time the recommendation of the Scottish Law Commission had been enacted (indeed before its report) the appointment of tutors-datives to mentally incapacitated adults had, as disclosed by the above articles, revived. In *Law Hospital N.H.S. Trust v. Lord Advocate* 1996 S.C. 301, it was authoritatively expressed that s. 19 of the 1856 Act was only a procedural provision and the power of the Court of Exchequer to make such appointments in exercise of its *parens patriae* jurisdiction remains and was transferred to the Court of Session by the unrepealed s. 1 of the Act. See further, note 14.2.11.

"Lord Ordinary in Exchequer Causes". A judge of the court who usually sits as a Lord   **48.1.2**
Ordinary is appointed by the Lord President to act as the Lord Ordinary in Exchequer Causes, and no other judge shall so act unless and until such judge is appointed in his place; in the event of the absence or inability of the Lord Ordinary in Exchequer Causes, for whatever reason, any of his duties may be performed by any other Lord Ordinary acting in his place: C.S.A. 1988, s. 3 (as amended by the Law Reform (Miscellaneous Provisions) (Scotland) Act 1990, Sched. 4, para. 4(3)) and r. 48.1(3).

The present Lord Ordinary in Exchequer Causes is Lord Hodge.

An Exchequer cause may be dealt with in vacation by the Lord Ordinary in Exchequer Causes: r. 10.6. In his absence or inability an Exchequer cause may be dealt with by another Lord Ordinary (C.S.A. 1988, s. 3) or, in vacation, by the vacation judge (C.S.A. 1988, s. 3 and r. 11.1(1)(a)). Where this occurs any interlocutor begins with the words "The Lord Ordinary [*or* Vacation Judge] in room and stead of the Lord Ordinary in Exchequer Causes". Where the Lord Ordinary in Exchequer Causes is the vacation judge, an interlocutor in an Exchequer cause begins with the words "The Lord Ordinary in Exchequer Causes".

Procedure in Exchequer causes

48.2. An Exchequer cause commenced by summons shall proceed as an ordinary action.

Deriv. R.C.S. 1965, r. 153A(1) inserted by S.I. 1984 No. 472

48.2.1   *General note.* The specialities of procedure based on the procedure of the English Court of Exchequer, to which Exchequer causes were originally subject, survived the transfer of the jurisdiction of the Court of Exchequer in Scotland to the Court of Session in 1856, but the consequence of a number of twentieth-century enactments is that an Exchequer cause now follows the same procedure as an ordinary action, subject to three exceptions: (1) Exchequer causes at all times take precedence and have preference over all other causes in the court: C.S.A. 1988, s. 21. (2) All Exchequer causes brought on behalf of the Crown, or by any person alleging any ground of action against the Crown, are respectively at the instance of or directed against the Lord Advocate, except where any enactment otherwise provides: C.S.A. 1988, s. 22. Examples of enactments which do otherwise provide include s. 13 of the Stamp Act 1891 and s. 56 of the Taxes Management Act 1970. (3) In all Exchequer causes the Lord Advocate, in pleading on behalf of the Crown, has the privilege of being heard last: C.S.A. 1988, s. 23.

Because the eighteenth-century English Exchequer Court would not have entertained an action against a person who was not served within the jurisdiction, it follows that the existence of a subsisting general jurisdiction over non-residents, without personal service, cannot be asserted simply on the basis that the 1707 Act empowered the Court of Exchequer in Scotland to adjudicate on revenue matters pertaining to Scotland: *Lord Advocate v. Tursi*, 1998 S.L.T. 1035 *per* Lord Penrose.

The special modes of diligence, under distinctive forms of warrant, for the enforcement of Crown debts, constituted by a decree of the Court of Session sitting as the Court of Exchequer, available formerly to the Crown, were abolished by the Debtors (Scotland) Act 1987, s. 74(5). Now an Exchequer decree will contain a warrant for execution of the ordinary diligences: 1987 Act, s. 87. The Inland Revenue and H.M. Customs and Excise must proceed by way of summary warrant in the sheriff court to take advantage of summary diligence: 1987 Act, s. 74(1) and (2), Scheds 4 and 5.

In relation to counterclaims and the Crown, see note 25.1.7.

48.2.2   *Appeals.* An interlocutor of the Lord Ordinary in Exchequer Causes may be reclaimed against to the Inner House in the ordinary way: see C.S.A. 1988, s. 28; and see Chap. 38. An appeal may be brought to the House of Lords against the judgment of the Inner House in an Exchequer cause as if it were a judgment of the Inner House on the whole merits of the case in an ordinary action: C.S.A. 1988, s. 24.

Precedence of extracts

48.3. The Extractor shall give priority to extracts in Exchequer causes over all other business.

Deriv. R.C.S. 1965, r. 153E inserted by S.I. 1984 No. 472

48.3.1   *General note.* On the Extracts Department, see r. 3.5. On the duties of the Extractor, see note 3.5.2. On extracts, see Chap. 7.

CHAPTER 49

FAMILY ACTIONS

PART I

GENERAL PROVISIONS

Interpretation of this Chapter
[1] **49.1.**—(1) In this Chapter, "family action" means—
(a) an action of divorce;
(b) an action of dissolution of a civil partnership;
(c) an action of separation of spouses or of civil partners;
(d) an action of declarator of nullity of marriage or civil partnership;
(e) an action of declarator of marriage;
(f) an action of declarator of legitimacy;
(g) an action of declarator of illegitimacy;
(h) an action of declarator of parentage;
(i) an action of declarator of non-parentage;
(j) an action of declarator of legitimation;
(k) an action or application for, or in respect of, an order under section 11 of the Children (Scotland) Act 1995 (court orders relating to parental responsibilities etc.) except a petition for the appointment of a judicial factor;
(l) an action of, or application for or in respect of, aliment;
(m) an action or application for financial provision after a divorce or annulment an in overseas country with the meaning of Part IV of the Matrimonial and Family Proceedings Act 1984;
(n) an action or application for financial provision after a dissolution or annulment of a civil partnership in an overseas country within the meaning of section 125 of and Schedule 11 to the Civil Partnership Act 2004;
(o) an action or application for an order under the Matrimonial Homes (Family Protection) (Scotland) Act 1981;
(p) an action or application for an order under Chapter 3 or 4 of Part 3 of the Civil Partnership Act 2004;
[2] (q) an application under section 28 or 29 of the Family Law (Scotland) Act 2006 (financial provision for former co-habitants).
(2) In this Chapter, unless the context otherwise requires—
"the Act of 1975" means the Children Act 1975;
"the Act of 1976" means the Divorce (Scotland) Act 1976;
"the Act of 1973" means the Domicile and Matrimonial Proceedings Act 1973;
"the Act of 1981" means the Matrimonial Homes (Family Protection) (Scotland) Act 1981;
"the Act of 1985" means the Family Law (Scotland) Act 1985;
"the Act of 1995" means the Children (Scotland) Act 1995;
"the Act of 2004" means the Gender Recognition Act 2004;
"the CP Act of 2004" means the Civil Partnership Act 2004;
"civil partnership" has the same meaning as in section 1(1) of the CP Act of 2004;
"contact order" has the same meaning as in section 11(2)(d) of the Act of 1995;
"corrected gender recognition certificate" means a certificate issued under section 6(4) of the Act of 2004;
"dissolution of a civil partnership" means a decree granted under section 117(2) of the CP Act of 2004;
"full gender recognition certificate" and "interim gender recognition certificate" have the same meanings as in section 25 of the Act of 2004;

"local authority" means a council constituted under section 2 of the
Local Government etc. (Scotland) Act 1994;

"mental disorder" has the same meaning as in section 328 of the Mental
Health (Care and Treatment) (Scotland) Act 2003;

"action for declarator of nullity of a civil partnership" means an action
for declarator that a civil partnership is void within the meaning of
section 123 of the CP Act of 2004;

"order for financial provision" means, except in Parts VII and VIIA of
this Chapter (financial provision after overseas divorce, dissolution
of a civil partnership, or annulment of marriage or civil partnership), an order mentioned in section 8(1) of the Act of 1985;

"parental responsibilities" has the same meaning as in section 1(3) of
the Act of 1995;

"parental rights" has the same meaning as in section 2(4) of the Act of
1995;

"residence order" has the same meaning as in section 11(2) of the Act of
1995;

"section 11 order" means an order under section 11 of the Act of 1995;

"action of separation of civil partners" means an action for decree
under section 120 of the CP Act of 2004.

(3) For the purposes of rule 49.2 (averments in certain family actions
about other proceedings) and rule 49.3 (averments where section 11 order
sought), and in relation to proceedings in another jurisdiction, Schedule 3 to
the Act of 1973 (sisting of consistorial actions in Scotland) and rule 49.18A
(applications for sist in actions involving civil partnerships), proceedings are
continuing at any time after they have commenced and before they are
finally disposed of.

Deriv. R.C.S. 1965, r. 154(1) and (2) substituted by S.I. 1976 No. 1994 and amended by S.I.
1986 No. 1231 (r. 49.1(1) and (2))

---

[1] Rule 49.1 substituted by S.S.I. 2005 No. 632 (effective 8th December 2005).
[2] Rule 49.1(q) inserted by S.S.I. 2006 No. 206 (effective 4th May 2006).

49.1.1 *General note.* Family causes (called "family actions" and defined in r. 49.1(1)), including all
applications for custody (see now "residence order"), are now initiated by summons; none is
commenced by petition. The difficulty in *Hogg v. Dick* 1987 S.L.T. 716 that an application for
custody could not be sought in an action of declarator of paternity should now be overcome: see
rr. 49.1(1), 49.58(1) and 49.59.

A consistorial action, included in the family actions to which Chap. 49 applies, is an action
between husband and wife involving status. An application for custody (see now a residence
order) is not a consistorial action: *Hogg*, above.

49.1.2 *"section 11 order".* This means an order under s. 11 of the Children (Scotland) Act 1995.
Under that section the court may make an order in relation to parental responsibilities (defined
in s. 1), parental rights (defined in s. 2), guardianship and administration of a child's property.
Without prejudice to that generality, the court may (a) make an order depriving a person of
parental responsibilities or parental rights in respect of a child under 18, (b) make an order
imposing such responsibilities or rights in respect of a child under 18, (c) make a residence order
in respect of a child under 16, (d) make a contact order in respect of a child under 16, (e) make a
specific issue order in relation to a matter arising out of or in connection with a matter in (a) to
(d), (f) grant interdict in relation to parental responsibilities, parental rights or the
administration of property of a child under 18, (g) appoint a judicial factor in respect of a
child under 18, or (h) appoint or remove a guardian of a child under 18.

49.1.3 *Civil Partnership Act 2004.* Chap. 49 has been amended to take account of this Act, which
provides for registered partnerships between people of the same sex.

Averments in certain family actions about other proceedings
49.2.—[2] (1) This rule applies to an action of divorce, separation,
declarator of marriage, declarator of nullity of marriage, dissolution of a

civil partnership, separation of civil partners or declarator of nullity of a civil partnership.

(2) In an action to which this rule applies, the pursuer shall state in the condescendence of the summons—

[2] (a) whether to his knowledge any proceedings are continuing in Scotland or in any other country in respect of the marriage or civil partnership to which the summons relates or are capable of affecting its validity or subsistence; and

(b) where such proceedings are continuing—

(i) the court, tribunal or authority before which the proceedings have been commenced;

(ii) the date of commencement;

(iii) the names of the parties;

(iv) the date, or expected date of any proof (or its equivalent), in the proceedings; and

[3] (v) such other facts as may be relevant to the question of whether or not the action in the Court of Session should be sisted under Schedule 3 to the Act of 1973, or rule 49.18A.

(3) Where—

(a) such proceedings are continuing;

(b) the action in the Court of Session is defended; and

(c) either—

(i) the summons does not contain the statement referred to in paragraph (2)(b), or

[1] (ii) the particulars mentioned in paragraph (2)(b) as set out in the summons are incomplete or incorrect,

any defences or minute, as the case may be, lodged by any person to the action shall include that statement and, where appropriate, the further or correct particulars mentioned in paragraph (2)(b).

Deriv. R.C.S. 1965, r. 157(3) substituted by S.I. 1976 No. 1994

---

[1] R. 49.2(3)(c)(ii) amended by S.I. 1994 No. 2901 (minor correction).
[2] Rule 49.2(1) & (2)(a) amended by S.S.I. 2005 No. 632 (effective 8th December 2005).
[3] Rule 49.2(2)(b)(v) substituted by S.S.I. 2005 No. 632 (effective 8th December 2005).

General note. The Domicile and Matrimonial Proceedings Act 1973 and the Council **49.2.1** Regulation (EC) No. 2201/2003 of 27th November 2003 (new Brussels II, replacing 1347/2000 of 29th May 2000) contain provisions for the jurisdiction of the court in actions of divorce, declarator of marriage, declarator of nullity of marriage and judicial separation. The 1973 Act has been amended by the European Communities (Matrimonial and Parental Responsibility Jurisdiction and Judgments) (Scotland) Regulations 2005 (S.S.I. 2005 No. 42) to take account of the Council Regulation (EC) No. 1347/2000 of 29th May 2000 (Brussels II). The Council Regulation has had direct effect in the U.K. since 1st March 2001 with respect to the jurisdiction and enforcement of judgments in matrimonial matters and matters of parental responsibility for children of both spouses. The Council Regulation makes provisions for common rules on jurisdiction in matrimonial proceedings to apply throughout the member states of the E.U. other than Denmark. Matrimonial matters are defined in Art. 2 of the Council Regulation as divorce, separation or marriage annulment. Parental responsibility is defined in art. 2(7) as meaning all rights and duties relating to the person or property of a child including custody and access; and art. 1(2) is referred to as including also guardianship, curatorship, etc., placement in foster care and child protection. It does not apply to paternity, adoption, maintenance, trusts or succession.

In general, jurisdiction is no longer determined by domicile but by habitual residence in the territory of a member state and, also in the case of U.K. and Ireland, the domicile of both spouses: Art. 3(1). The courts of that country have jurisdiction. There is an exception in the 1973 Act for an "excluded action" of divorce or separation and either of the parties is domiciled in Scotland on the date the action is begun: 1973 Act, s. 7(2A) as inserted by S.S.I. 2001 No. 36. Such an action is defined as an action in respect of which no court of a contracting state has jurisdiction and the defender is not a national of a contracting state (other than the U.K. or Ireland) or domiciled in Ireland: 1973 Act, s. 12 as amended by S.S.I. 2001 No. 36 (i.e. the member states of the EU except Denmark). There is a similar but not identical exception for excluded actions of declarator of nullity of marriage in s. 7(3A) of the 1973 Act: for a recent example, see *Singh v. Singh,* 2005 S.L.T. 749 (OH).

On the meaning of domicile, see *Bell v. Kennedy* (1868) 6 M. (H.L.) 69 and *Udny v. Udny* (1869) 7 M. (H.L.) 89. On a recent case on domicile of choice, see *Spence v. Spence* 1995 S.L.T. 335. On the meaning of habitual residence, see *Dickson v. Dickson* 1990 S.C.L.R. 692 (1st Div), *Rellis v. Hart* 1993 S.L.T. 738; *Scullion v. Scullion* 1990 S.C.L.R. 577, 581A *per* Sheriff Stoddart. An action is begun when it is served on the defender: Erskine, III. vi. 3; *Alston v. Macdougall* (1887) 15 R. 78; *Smith v. Stewart & Co.* 1960 S.C. 329, 334 *per* L.P. Clyde; *Miller v. National Coal Board* 1960 S.C. 376.

The 1973 Act gives the court having jurisdiction in divorce etc., jurisdiction over ancillary matters such as custody and access and other parental rights (but not in declarator of marriage), aliment and financial provision: 1973 Act, s. 10 (as modified by s. 13 of the Family Law Act 1986) and (in relation to parental rights) the C.S.A. 1988, s. 20(1).

Sched. 3 to the 1973 Act contains a duty to give certain information to the court about other related proceedings in any other court. It also contains provisions for the mandatory sist of proceedings before the court in certain circumstances and for a discretionary sist in others. On the exercise of the discretionary sist, see *Mitchell v. Mitchell* 1991 S.L.T. 410. An application for a sist is made by motion: r. 49.18. Under Art. 19(1) of the Council Regulation, the court in a member state that is second seized of proceedings must sist those proceedings until the court in the member state first seized of the proceedings has determined the question of jurisdiction.

Part 3 of Chap. 5 of the Civil Partnership Act 2004 contains provisions for jurisdiction in relation to proceedings under that Act.

49.2.2   *"condescendence".* See generally, note 13.2.4.

[1] *Averments where section 11 order sought*

49.3.—[1] (1) A party to a family action, who makes an application in that action for a section 11 order in respect of a child, shall include in his pleadings—

[2] (a)   where that action is an action of divorce, separation, declarator of nullity of marriage, dissolution of a civil partnership, separation of civil partners or declarator of nullity of a civil partnership averments giving particulars of any other proceedings known to him, whether in Scotland or elsewhere and whether concluded or not, which relate to the child in respect of whom the section 11 order is sought;

(b)   in any other family action—

(i)   the averments mentioned in sub-paragraph (a); and

[2] (ii)   averments giving particulars of any proceedings known to him which are continuing, whether in Scotland or elsewhere, and which relate to the marriage or civil partnership of the parents or either of the parents of that child.

[1] (2) Where such other proceedings are continuing or have taken place and the averments of the applicant for such a section 11 order—

(a)   do not contain particulars of the other proceedings, or

(b)   contain particulars which are incomplete or incorrect,

any defences or minute, as the case may be, lodged by any person to the family action shall include such particulars or such further or correct particulars as are known to him.

(3) In paragraph (1)(b)(ii), "child" includes a child of the family within the meaning assigned in section 42(4) of the Family Law Act 1986.

Deriv. R.C.S. 1965, r. 170B(11) (inserted by S.I. 1988 No. 615), r. 260EA (inserted by S.I. 1988 No. 615) and the Family Law Act 1986, (r. 49.3(1)).

---

[1] Heading and r. 49.3(1) and (2) amended by S.I. 1996 No. 2587 (effective 1st November 1996).
[2] Rule 49.3(1)(a) & (b)(ii) amended by S.S.I. 2005 No. 632 (effective 8th December 2005).

49.3.1   *General note.* The jurisdiction of the court to entertain an application for residence, custody, care or control of a child, or contact with or access to a child (all included in the meaning of a "Part I order" under the Act) in proceedings other than divorce, nullity of marriage or judicial separation is governed by ss. 9 (habitual residence), 10 (presence of child), 12 (emergency) and

15(2) (original order granted by court) of the Family Law Act 1986 as amended first by the European Communities (Matrimonial Jurisdiction and Judgments) (Scotland) Regulations 2001 [S.S.I. 2001 No. 36] and second by the European Communities (Matrimonial and Parental Responsibility and Judgments) (Scotland) Regulations 2005 [S.S.I. 2005 No. 42]. The pre-eminent ground in such proceedings is habitual residence, on the meaning of which see *Dickson v. Dickson* 1990 S.C.L.R. 692 (1st Div); *Rellis v. Hart* 1993 S.L.T. 738; *Scullion v. Scullion* 1990 S.C.L.R. 577, 581A *per* Sheriff Stoddart. The jurisdiction of the court in relation to custody in actions of divorce, nullity and judicial separation is governed by the Domicile and Matrimonial Proceedings Act 1973 (as modified by s. 13 of the 1986 Act) and amended by European Communities (Matrimonial Jurisdiction and Judgments) (Scotland) Regulations 2001 (S.S.I. 2001 No. 36) and the Council Regulation (EC) No. 1347/2000 of 27th November 2003 (new Brussels II, replaces the Regulation No. 1347/2000).

The Family Law Act 1986 contains provisions for avoiding conflict of jurisdiction within the U.K. in relation to Part I orders. The court in matrimonial proceedings may decline jurisdiction if it would be more appropriate for the matter to be dealt with in another court having jurisdiction: 1986 Act, s. 13(6).

Under s. 14(2) of the 1986 Act, where, at any stage of the proceedings for a Part I order, it appears to the court (a) that proceedings with respect to matters to which the application relates are continuing outside Scotland or in another court in Scotland or (b) that it would be more appropriate for those matters to be determined in proceedings outside Scotland or in another court in Scotland and such proceedings are likely to be taken there, the court may sist the proceedings. It has been held by Lord McCluskey, in *Hill v. Hill* 1991 S.L.T. 189 and by Lord MacLean in *B v. B* 1998 S.L.T. 1245 that the principle of *forum non conveniens* (whether it would be more appropriate for another court to determine the matter) applies both to para.(a) and (b) of s. 14(2) of the 1986 Act.

"*section 11 order*". See note 49.1.2.   **49.3.2**

Averments where identity or address of person not known
49.4. In a family action, where the identity or address of any person referred to in rule 49.8 as a person in respect of whom a warrant for intimation requires to be applied for is not known and cannot reasonably be ascertained, the party required to apply for the warrant shall include in his pleadings an averment of that fact and averments setting out what steps have been taken to ascertain the identity or address, as the case may be, of that person.

Deriv. R.C.S. 1965, r. 157(1) substituted by S.I. 1976 No. 1994

"*not known*". The word "known" refers not to the pursuer's knowledge but to that of persons **49.4.1** generally who had business or social dealings with the defender (*Young v. Harper* 1970 S.C. 174, 177 *per* Lord Fraser); accordingly the pursuer must take some steps to ascertain an address, and this is required for a motion in respect of service where the address of the defender is not known: r. 16.5(1)(c). Where the address is not known service by advertisement will be required unless dispensed with: r. 16.5. That rule applies by virtue of r. 16.8(1) which applies rules for service to persons for whom a warrant to intimate has been obtained.

Averments about maintenance orders
49.5. In a family action in which an order for aliment or periodical allowance is sought, or is sought to be varied or recalled, by any party, the pleadings of that party shall contain an averment stating whether and, if so, when and by whom a maintenance order (within the meaning of section 106 of the Debtors (Scotland) Act 1987) has been granted in favour of or against that party or any other person in respect of whom the order is sought.

General note. S.106 of the Debtors (Scotland) Act 1987 contains a convenient list of **49.5.1** maintenance orders.

Averments where aliment sought for a child
49.6.—(1) In this rule—
"the Act of 1991" means the Child Support Act 1991;
"child" has the meaning assigned in section 55 of the Act of 1991;
"conclusion relating to aliment" means—

(a) for the purposes of paragraph (2), a conclusion for decree of aliment in relation to a child or for recall or variation of such a decree; and

(b) for the purposes of paragraph (3), a conclusion for decree of aliment in relation to a child or for recall or variation of such a decree or for the variation or termination of an agreement on aliment in relation to a child;

"maintenance assessment" has the meaning assigned in section 54 of the Act of 1991.

(2) A family action containing a conclusion relating to aliment to which section 8(6), (7), (8) or (10) of the Act of 1991 (top up maintenance orders) applies shall—

(a) include averments stating, where appropriate—

   (i) that a maintenance assessment under section 11 of that Act is in force;

   (ii) the date of the maintenance assessment;

   (iii) the amount and frequency of periodical payments of child support maintenance fixed by the maintenance assessment; and

   (iv) the grounds on which the sheriff retains jurisdiction under section 8(6), (7), (8) or (10) of that Act; and

(b) unless the court on cause shown otherwise directs, be accompanied by any document issued by the Secretary of State to the party intimating the making of the maintenance assessment referred to in sub-paragraph (a).

(3) A family action containing a conclusion relating to aliment to which section 8(6), (7), (8) or (10) of the Act of 1991 does not apply, shall include averments stating—

(a) that the habitual residence of the absent parent, person with care or qualifying child, within the meaning of section 3 of that Act, is furth of the United Kingdom;

(b) that the child is not a child within the meaning of section 55 of that Act; or

(c) the grounds on which the court retains jurisdiction.

(4) In an action for declarator of non-parentage or illegitimacy—

(a) the summons shall include an article of condescendence stating whether the pursuer previously has been alleged to be the parent in an application for a maintenance assessment under section 4, 6 or 7 of the Act of 1991 (applications for maintenance assessment); and

(b) where an allegation of paternity has been made against the pursuer, the Secretary of State shall be named as a defender in the action.

(5) A family action involving parties in respect of whom a decision has been made in any application, review or appeal under the Act of 1991 relating to any child of those parties, shall—

(a) include averments stating that such a decision has been made and giving details of that decision; and

(b) unless the court on cause shown otherwise directs, be accompanied by any document issued by the Secretary of State to the parties intimating that decision.

49.6.1   *General note.* Where the Child Support Agency has jurisdiction the court may nonetheless have jurisdiction to make a maintenance order including a maintenance order to top up child support maintenance and orders to meet expenses of education and training, to meet expenses attributable to a disability or where the order is to be made against a person with care of the child: Child Support Act 1991, s. 8. An order may be made where the Child Support Agency does not have jurisdiction, *i.e.* where the child, parent with care or absent parent is not habitually resident in the UK or the child is not a qualifying child within the meaning of s. 3 of the Act of 1991. When a statutory instrument is made to that effect, the court will retain jurisdiction to make a maintenance order where a written agreement provides for an absent parent to make periodic payments to or for the child and that agreement is not enforceable and the maintenance order made by the court is in all material respects in the same terms as that agreement. The court retains jurisdiction during the transitional period (from 5th March 1993 for an indefinite period: Child Support Act 1995, s. 18), where a maintenance provision already exists to deal with applications for variation of such provision whether under order of the court or a maintenance agreement until a child maintenance assessment is made, or to deal with a conclusion for aliment in a pending action: Child Support Act 1991 (Commencement No. 3 and Transitional Provisions) Amendment Order 1992 [S.I. 1992 No. 2644].

A maintenance agreement for less than could be awarded under a maintenance assessment will be insecure because an application to the Child Support Agency for a maintenance assessment cannot be prevented: 1991 Act, s. 9.

Warrants for arrestment or inhibition on dependence

49.7.—(1) A warrant for inhibition or arrestment on the dependence in a family action or in respect of a claim to which section 19 of the Act of 1985 (action for aliment or claim for order for financial provision) applies shall be applied for by motion.

(2) A certified copy of the interlocutor granting warrant for diligence applied for under paragraph (1) shall be sufficient authority for execution of the diligence.

(3) A certified copy of the interlocutor containing a warrant for inhibition granted under this rule and an execution of service of it may be registered in the Register of Inhibitions and Adjudications.

(4) A notice of the certified copy of the interlocutor containing a warrant for inhibition granted under this rule may be registered under section 155 of the Titles to Land Consolidation (Scotland) Act 1868 (inhibitions to take effect from date of registration of notice); and such registration shall have the same effect as registration of a notice under that section.

Deriv. R.C.S. 1965, r. 155A(1) inserted by S.I. 1991 No. 1157

General note. In an action of aliment or a claim for financial provision in an action of divorce   **49.7.1**
or declarator of nullity of marriage, which is for a future or contingent debt, warrant to arrest or inhibit may only be granted by the court (by motion: r. 49.7) on cause shown subject to any limit as to property or value (property only in inhibition), and is not limited to the common law grounds: Family Law (Scotland) Act 1985, s. 19(1). Arrestment can only be granted at common law on a claim for a future debt where there are special circumstances averred, *e.g.* that the defender is *vergens ad inopiam* or *in meditatione fugae* or considering putting away his funds with the intention of not implementing any decree or not fulfilling his obligations: *Symington v. Symington* (1875) 3 R. 205; *Gillanders v. Gillanders* 1966 S.C. 54; *Wilson v. Wilson* 1981 S.L.T. 101.

See further, notes 13.6.2 (inhibition) and 13.6.3 (arrestment).

Execution of warrants for arrestment or inhibition. See Chap. 16, Pt. II.   **49.7.2**

Warrants for intimation in family actions

49.8.—[2] (1) Subject to paragraphs (5) and (8), in the summons in a family action, the pursuer shall insert a warrant for intimation—
[3] (a) in an action where the address of the defender is not known to the pursuer and cannot reasonably be ascertained, to—
    (i) every child of the marriage between the parties, or child who has been accepted by both partners of a civil partnership as a child of the family, who has reached the age of 16 years, and
    (ii) one of the next-of-kin of the defender who has reached that age, unless the address of such a person is not known to the pursuer and cannot reasonably be ascertained, in the following terms:— "Warrant to intimate to (name and address) as a child of the marriage [or to (name and address) as a child who has been accepted by both partners of a civil partnership as a child of the family] [or to (name and address) the (relationship to defender), as one of the next-of-kin of the defender]."
  (b) in an action where the pursuer alleges that the defender has committed adultery with another person, to that person, unless—
    (i) that person is not named in the summons and, if the adultery is

relied on for the purposes of section 1(2)(a) of the Act of 1976 (irretrievable breakdown of marriage by reason of adultery), the summons contains an averment that his or her identity is not known to the pursuer and cannot reasonably be ascertained, or

  (ii) the pursuer alleges that the defender has been guilty of rape upon or incest with, that named person,

in the following terms:— "Warrant to intimate to (*name and address*) as a person with whom the defender is alleged to have committed adultery.";

³ (c) in an action where the defender is a person who is suffering from a mental disorder, to—

  (i) those persons mentioned in sub-paragraph (a)(i) and (ii), unless the address of such person is not known to the pursuer and cannot reasonable be ascertained;

  (ii) any person holding the office of curator bonis to the defender, if one has been appointed; and

  (iii) any person holding the office of guardian, or continuing or welfare attorney to the defender under or by virtue of the Adults with Incapacity (Scotland) Act 2000, if one has been appointed,

in the following terms:— "Warrant to intimate to (name and address) as a child of the marriage [or to (name and address) as a child who has been accepted by both partners of a civil partnership as a child of the family], (name and address) the (relationship to the defender) as one of the next-of-kin of the defender and (name and address) guardian [or continuing [or welfare] attorney] to the defender."

  (ii) the curator *bonis* to the defender, if one has been appointed,

in the following terms:— "Warrant to intimate to (*name and address*) as a child of the marriage, (*name and address*) the (*relationship to defender*) as one of the next-of-kin of the defender and (*name and address*), curator *bonis* to the defender.";

  (d) in an action relating to a marriage which was entered into under a law which permits polygamy where—

  (i) one of the decrees specified in section 2(2) of the Matrimonial Proceedings (Polygamous Marriages) Act 1972 is sought; and

  (ii) either party to the marriage in question has any spouse additional to the other party,

to any such additional spouse in the following terms:— "Warrant to intimate to (*name and address*) as an additional spouse of the pursuer [*or* defender].";

³ (e) in an action of divorce, separation, declarator of nullity of marriage, dissolution of a civil partnership, separation of civil partners or declarator of nullity of a civil partnership where the court may make a section 11 order in respect of a child—

  (i) who is in the care of a local authority, to that local authority in the following terms:— "Warrant to intimate to the chief executive of (name and address of local authority) as the local authority having care of (name and address of child).";

  (ii) who, being a child of one party to the marriage who has been accepted as a child of the family by the other party to the marriage or is a child of one partner in a civil partnership who has been accepted by both partners as a child of the family, and who is liable to be maintained by a third party, to that third party in the following terms:— "Warrant to intimate to (name and address) as a person liable to maintain (name and address of child)."; or

  (iii) in relation to whom a third party in fact exercises care or control, to that third party in the following terms:— "Warrant to intimate to (name and address) as a person who in fact exercises care or control of (name and address of child)."

[2] (f) in an action where the pursuer concludes for a section 11 order, to any parent or guardian of the child who is not a party to the action in the following terms:— "Warrant to intimate to (*name and address*) as a parent [*or guardian*].";

[2] (g) in an action where the pursuer concludes for a residence order in respect of a child and he is—

(i) not a parent of that child, and

(ii) resident in Scotland when the summons is presented for signeting,

to the local authority within which area the pursuer resides in the following terms:— "Warrant to intimate to the chief executive of (*name and address of local authority*) as the local authority within which area the pursuer, not being a parent of (*name and address of child*), resides.";

(h) in an action which includes a conclusion for a section 11 order, to the child to whom the section 11 order would relate, if not a party to the action, in the following terms:—"Warrant to intimate to (*name and address*) as a child who may be affected by the action.";

(i) in an action where the pursuer makes an application for an order under section 8(1)(aa) of the Act of 1985 (transfer of property) and—

(i) the consent of a third party to such a transfer is necessary by virtue of an obligation, enactment or rule of law, or

(ii) the property is subject to a security,

to the third party or creditor, as the case may be, in the following terms:— "Warrant to intimate to (*name and address*) as a person the consent of whom is required in respect of the transfer sought [*or as a person who is believed to be a creditor of (name of party*) in respect of the property sought to be transferred] in the (*number*) conclusion of this summons.";

(j) in an action where the pursuer makes an application for an order under section 18 of the Act of 1985 (which relates to avoidance transactions), to—

(i) any third party in whose favour the transfer of, or transaction involving, the property is to be or was made, and

(ii) any other person having an interest in the transfer of, or transaction involving, the property,

in the following terms:— "Warrant to intimate to (*name and address*) as the person in whose favour the transfer of [*or transaction involving*] property referred to in the condescendence attached to this summons was made [*or is to be made*] [*or is a person having an interest in the transfer of [or transaction involving*] property referred to in the condescendence attached to this summons].";

[3] (k) in an action where the pursuer makes an application for an order under the Act of 1981—

(i) where he is a non-entitled partner and the entitled partner has a spouse, or civil partner, to that spouse or civil partner, or

(ii) where the application is under section 2(1)(e), 2(4)(a), 3(1), 3(2), 4, 7, 13, or 18 of that Act, and the entitled spouse or entitled partner is a tenant or occupies the matrimonial home by permission of a third party, to the landlord or the third party, as the case may be,

in the following terms:— "Warrant to intimate to (name and address) as a person with an interest in the order sought in the (number) conclusion of this summons."

(l) in an action where the pursuer makes an application for an order under—

(i) section 8(1)(ba) of the Act of 1985 (orders under s. 12A of the Act of 1985 for pension lump sum), or

(ii) section 8(1)(baa) of that Act (pension sharing orders), to the person responsible for the pension arrangement, in the following terms—"Warrant to intimate to (*name and address*) as the person responsible for the pension arrangement in respect of which an order is sought in the (*number*) conclusion of this summons.";

[4] (m) in an action where the pursuer makes an application for an order under Chapter 3 of Part 3 of the CP Act of 2004 where the application is under section 102(1)(e), 102(4)(a), 103(1), 103(2), 104, 107 or 112 of that Act and the entitled civil partner is a tenant or occupies the family home by permission of a third party, to the landlord or the third party, as the case may be, in the following terms:— "Warrant to intimate to (*name and address*) as a person with an interest in the order sought in the (*number*) conclusion of this summons;"

[5] (n) in an action where the pursuer makes an application for an order under section 29(2) of the Act of 2006 (application by survivor for provision on intestacy) to any person having an interest in the deceased's net intestate estate, in the following terms:— "Warrant to intimate to (name and address) as a person having an interest in the deceased's net intestate estate referred to in the condescendence attached to this summons."

(2) Expressions used in—

    (i) paragraph (1)(k) which are also used in the Act of 1981;

    (ii) paragraph (1)(m) which are also used in the CP Act of 2004; and

    (iii) paragraph (1)(n) which are also used in section 29 of the Act of 2006,

have the meanings given in those Acts, or that section, as the case may be.

[2] (3) A notice of intimation shall be attached to the copy of the summons where intimation is given on a warrant—

(a) under paragraph (1)(a) (address of defender not known), in Form 49.8–A;

(b) under paragraph (1)(b) (allegation of adultery), in Form 49.8–B;

(c) under paragraph (1)(c) (mental disorder of defender), in Form 49.8–C;

(d) under paragraph (1)(d) (polygamous marriage), in Form 49.8–D;

(e) under paragraph (1)(e)(i) or (ii) (where section 11 order may be made in respect of a child in care of local authority or accepted as a child of the marriage), in Form 49.8–E;

(f) under paragraph (1)(e)(iii) (where section 11 order may be made in respect of a child in relation to whom a third party in fact exercises care or control), in Form 49.8–F;

(g) under paragraph (1)(f) (section 11 order sought by guardian), in Form 49.8–G;

(h) under paragraph (1)(g) (residence order sought by non-parent resident in Scotland), in Form 49.8–H;

(i) [Revoked by SI 1996/2587 (effective 1st November 1996).]

(j) under paragraph (1)(i) (transfer of property), in Form 49.8–J;

(k) under paragraph (1)(j) (avoidance transactions), in Form 49.8–K;

(l) under paragraph (1)(k) (orders sought under the Act of 1981), in Form 49.8–L;

(m) under—

    (i) paragraph (1)(l)(i) (orders for pension lump sums) in Form 49.8–M; and

    (ii) paragraph (1)(l)(ii) (person sharing orders), in Form 49.8MA;

[4] (n) under paragraph (l)(m) (order sought under Chapter 3 of Part 3 of the CP Act of 2004), in Form 49.8–O; and

[5] (o) under paragraph (1)(n)(order under section 29 of the Act of 2006), in Form 49.8–P

(4) In a family action, where the pursuer—

[2] (a) concludes for a residence order in respect of a child;

(b) is not a parent of the child; and

(c) is not resident in Scotland when the summons is presented for signeting,

he shall, on presenting the summons for signeting, apply by motion for an order for intimation in Form 49.8–H to such local authority as the court thinks fit.

[1] (5) Where the address of a person mentioned in paragraph (1)(b), (d), (e), (f), (g), (i), (j), (k), (l) or (m) is not known and cannot reasonably be ascertained, the pursuer shall, immediately after the calling of the summons, apply by motion to dispense with intimation; and the court may grant that motion or make such other order as it thinks fit.

(6) Where the identity or address of a person to whom intimation of a family action is required becomes known during the course of the action, the party who would have been required to insert a warrant for intimation to that person shall apply by motion for a warrant for intimation to that person or to dispense with such intimation.

[2] (7) In relation to paragraph (1)(h) (action which affects a child), a copy of the summons shall not be intimated to the child but a notice of intimation shall be intimated to him in Form 49.8–N.

[2] (8) Where a pursuer considers that a warrant for intimation to a child under paragraph (1)(h) is inappropriate, he shall—

(a) apply by motion to dispense with intimation to that child; and

(b) include in the condescence of the summons averments setting out the reasons why such intimation is appropriate,

and the court may dispense with such intimation or make such other order as it thinks fit.

Deriv. R.C.S. 1965, r. 155(3)(a) and (4) substituted by S.I. 1976 No. 1994 (r. 49.8(1)(a)); r. 155(1) and (2) substituted by S.I. 1976 No. 1994 (r. 49.8(1)(b)); r. 155(3)(b) and (4) substituted by S.I. 1976 No. 1994 (r. 49.8(1)(c)); r. 155(5) substituted by S.I. 1976 No. 1994 (r. 49.8(1)(d)); r. 155(6) substituted by S.I. 1976 No. 1994, and r. 170B(6)(a) inserted by S.I. 1976 No. 1994 and amended by S.I. 1986 No. 1955 and 1990/705, (r. 49.8(1)(e)); Children Act 1975, s. 48 amended by Law Reform (Parent and Child) (Scotland) Act 1986, Sched. 2 (r. 49.8(1)(f)); Children Act 1975, s. 49(1)(a) amended by Law Reform (Parent and Child) (Scotland) Act 1986, Sched. 1, para. 14 (r. 49.8(1)(g)); r. 170D(9) inserted by S.I. 1986 No. 1231 (r. 49.8(1)(i)); r. 155(7) inserted by S.I. 1982 No. 1825, and r. 170D(4)(c) substituted by S.I. 1977 No. 1621 and amended by S.I. 1986 No. 1231 (r. 49.8(1)(j)); r. 188D(7) and (10) inserted by S.I. 1982 No. 1381 (r. 49.8(1)(k)); Children Act 1975, s. 49(1)(b) amended by Law Reform (Parent and Child) (Scotland) Act 1986, Sched. 1, para. 14 (r. 49.8(4))

---

[1] R. 49.8(5) amended by S.I. 1996 No. 1756 (effective 5th August 1996) and (1)(l) substituted by S.S.I. 2000 No. 412 (effective 1st December 2000).

[2] R. 49.8(1), (3), (4) and (7) amended, and r. 49.8(8) inserted, by S.I. 1996 No. 2587 (effective 1st November 1996).

[3] Rule 49.8(1)(a), (c), (e) & (k) substituted by S.S.I. 2005 No. 632 (effective 8th December 2005).

[4] Rule 49.8(1)(m)& (3)(n) inserted by S.S.I. 2005 No. 632 (effective 8th December 2005) and substituted by S.S.I. 2006 No. 206 (effective 4th May 2006).

[5] Rule 49.8(1)(n) and r.49.8(3)(o) inserted by, and r.49.8(2) and r.49.8(3)(m) substituted by, S.S.I. 2006 No. 206 (effective 4th May 2006).

"warrants for intimation". For methods of intimation, see r. 16.8. **49.8.1**

"child who may be affected by the action". R. 49.8(1)(h) provides for a warrant to intimate to a **49.8.2** child a family action which may affect him. Under art. 12 of the UN Convention on the Rights of the Child (Cm. 1976 (1992)), ratified by the UK on 16th December 1991, a child who is capable of forming his own views has the right to express those views freely in all matters affecting him and his views must be given due weight in accordance with his age and maturity. For this purpose the child must be given the opportunity to be heard in any judicial and administrative proceedings affecting him, either directly or through a representative or appropriate body, in a manner consistent with the procedural rules of national law. This principle is now enshrined in s. 11(7) of the Children (Scotland) Act 1995.

The child need not become a party, and may express his views by writing a letter or be given an opportunity to express his views orally to the judge in private: a form (Form 49.8–N) is sent to the child. A child should be able to instruct a solicitor: Age of Legal Capacity (Scotland) Act 1991, s. 2(1)(a).

The court cannot always know in advance whether a child is capable of forming his own views and a minimum age cannot be laid down. On the other hand a child cannot know he has the right to be heard unless he is informed of that right. There appears to be no alternative but to provide for intimation in every case while providing in r. 49.8(8) for the court to dispense with intimation in certain circumstances (*e.g.* the child is a baby). There is a statutory presumption that a child of 12 or more is of sufficient age and maturity to form a view: Act of 1995, s. 11(10).

In *S v. S*, 2002 S.C. 246 (Ex Div.), *sub nom. Shields v. Shields*, 2002 S.L.T. 579, paras [10] and [11], it was observed (1) that in affording a child the opportunity to make known his views the only test is practicality; (2) how the child should be given that opportunity depends on the circumstances including the child's age, and could be (a) by intimation in Form [49.8–N] (b) by seeing the child in chambers, (c) by the views of the child being made known to the court by a person known to the child or a child psychologist; (3) if it was practicable to give the child an opportunity to express his views, the only safe course was to employ whatever method was practicable; (4) the formal process of intimation in Form [49.8-N] should not be the principal mode of complying with s. 11(7)(b) of the Children (Scotland) Act 1995 and other methods must be preferable, particularly where younger children are involved or there is risk of upsetting the child; and (5) the duty on the court to comply with s. 11(7)(b) continues until the order is made and dispensing with formal intimation does not relieve the court from complying with that continuing duty.

R. 49.8(7) provides that the summons is not intimated to the child but that a notice in Form 49.8–N is sent to him.

49.8.3 *"motion"*. For motions, see Chap. 23.

49.8.4 *"section 11 order"*. See note 49.1.2.

Intimation where relevant association

49.9.—(1) In a family action where the pursuer alleges an association as defined in paragraph (4) between the defender and another named person, the pursuer shall, when the summons is presented for signeting, apply by motion for an order for intimation to that person or to dispense with such intimation.

(2) In determining a motion under paragraph (1), the court may—

(a) make such order for intimation as it thinks fit; or

(b) dispense with intimation; and

(c) where it dispenses with intimation, order that the name of that person be deleted from the condescendence of the summons.

(3) Where intimation is ordered under paragraph (2), a notice of intimation in Form 49.9 shall be attached to the copy of the summons to be intimated.

[1] (4) In paragraph (1), "relevant association" means sodomy, incest or any homosexual relationship, and where the family action is in relation to a civil partnership shall include any heterosexual relationship.

Deriv. R.C.S. 1965, r. 162 substituted by S.I. 1976 No. 1994

[1] Rule 49.9 substituted by S.S.I. 2005 No. 632 (effective 8th December 2005).

49.9.1 *"motion"*. For motions, see Chap. 23.

49.9.2 *"intimation"*. For methods, see r. 16.8.

[1] *Productions in action of divorce or where section 11 order may be made*

[1] **49.10.**—(1) There shall be lodged as a production with the principal writ when first lodged in process—

(a) in an action of divorce—

(i) an extract or certified copy of the relevant entry in the register of marriages; and

(ii) where an action relies on section 1(1)(b) of the Act of 1976 (grounds of divorce: interim gender recognition certificate), the interim gender recognition certificate or a certified copy of it;

(b) in an action of dissolution of a civil partnership—
    (i) an extract or certified copy of the relevant entry in the civil partnership register; and
    (ii) where the action relies on section 117(2)(b) of the CP Act of 2004 (grounds for dissolution of civil partnership: interim gender recognition certificate), the interim gender recognition certificate or a certified copy of it; and
(c) in a family action in which the court may make a section 11 order, an extract or certified copy of the relevant entry in the register of births.

(2) In the application of sub-paragraph (a) of paragraph (1) to an action of divorce, or sub-paragraph (b) of paragraph (1) in an action of dissolution of a civil partnership, where the address of the defender is not known, the documents to be lodged under those sub-paragraphs, as the case may be, shall be obtained and dated within three months before the date on which it is lodged.

Lodging productions. See r. 4.5.   **49.10.1**

---

[1] Rule 49.10 substituted by S.S.I. 2005 No. 632 (effective 8th December 2005).

Execution of service on, or intimation to, local authority
  49.11.—[1] (1) Where a local authority referred to in rule 49.8(1)(g) (residence order sought by non-parent resident in Scotland) or rule 49.8(4) (residence order sought by non-parent not resident in Scotland) is called as a defender in a summons at the time of signeting, service of the summons on that local authority shall be executed within seven days after the date of signeting.

(2) Where in a family action—
  (a) to which rule 49.8(1)(g) applies, or
  (b) in which a motion under rule 49.8(4) is required,
the local authority referred to in that provision is called as a defender in the summons at the time of signeting, a notice in Form 49.8–H shall be attached to the copy of the summons served on that local authority unless the court otherwise orders.

(3) In any family action, the court may, if it thinks fit, order intimation to a local authority, and such intimation shall be in Form 49.8–H.

[1] (4) Where, by virtue of paragraph (3) of this rule or rule 49.8(1)(g), 49.8(4) or 49.15(3), intimation of an application for a section 11 order is to be made to a local authority, intimation to that local authority shall be given within seven days after the date of signeting or order for intimation, as the case may be; and a notice in Form 49.8–H shall be attached to the copy of the summons intimated to that local authority.

Deriv. Children Act 1975, s. 49 amended by Law Reform (Parent and Child) (Scotland) Act 1986, Sched. 1, para. 14

General note. Under s. 49 of the Children Act 1975 where the pursuer was not the parent of **49.11.1** the child, an order for custody could be made unless, where he resided in Scotland, he had given notice within seven days of making the application to the local authority of the area in which he resided or, in any other case (*i.e.* he did not reside in Scotland), he gave notice within such period and to such local authority as the court directed. On receipt of the notice the local authority had to investigate and report to the court on the circumstances of the child and on the proposed arrangements for his care and upbringing.

Section 49 of the 1975 Act was repealed, but *not* replaced, by the Children (Scotland) Act 1995. A local authority is no longer required to provide such a report; but it is understood that local authorities are prepared to continue to do so. Rule 49.11 remains, therefore, but in an amended form; and the court is only able to *request* such a report.

"within seven days". The date from which the period is calculated is not counted.   **49.11.2**

49.11.3 *"residence order"*. This replaces, but is not the whole of, what was formerly custody. It means an order regulating arrangements as to with whom or with whom during what periods a child under 16 is to live: Children (Scotland) Act 1995, s. 11(2)(c).

49.11.4 *"section 11 order"*. See note 49.1.2.

Notice of actions by advertisement

49.12. Where notice of a family action is given by advertisement under rule 16.5 (service where address of person is not known), the period of notice shall be 21 days from the date of publication of the advertisement unless the court otherwise orders.

Deriv. R.C.S. 1965, r. 159(2) substituted by S.I. 1986 No. 1941 and amended by S.I. 1987 No. 1206

49.12.1 *General note.* The normal period of notice by advertisement is six months, which is inappropriate in family actions.

Service in cases of mental disorder of defender

49.13.—(1) In a family action where the defender suffers or appears to suffer from mental disorder and is resident in a hospital or other similar institution, service of the summons shall be executed in accordance with rule 16.4 (service by post) addressed to the medical officer in charge of that hospital or institution; and there shall be included with the copy of the summons—

[1] (a) any notice required by rule 49.14(1) (notices in certain actions of divorce or separation) or by rule 49.14A(1) (notices in certain actions of dissolution of civil partnership or separation of civil partners);

   (b) request in Form 49.13–A requesting the medical officer to—

      [2] (i) deliver and explain the summons, citation and any notice or form of notice of consent required under rule 49.14(1) or rule 49.14A(1); or

      (ii) certify that such delivery or explanation would be dangerous to the health or mental condition of the defender; and

      (iii) complete the certificate in Form 49.13–B; and

   (c) a stamped envelope addressed for return of that certificate to the pursuer or his agent, if he has one.

(2) The medical officer referred to in paragraph (1) shall send the certificate in Form 49.13–B duly completed to the pursuer or his agent, as the case may be.

(3) The certificate mentioned in paragraph (2) shall be attached to the summons when it is lodged for calling.

(4) Where such a certificate bears that the summons has not been delivered to the defender, the court may, at any time while the action is depending—

   (a) order such further medical inquiry, and

   (b) make such order for further service or intimation,

as it thinks fit.

Deriv. R.C.S. 1965, r. 159(5) and (6) substituted by S.I. 1976 No. 1994

---

[1] Rule 49.13(1)(a) substituted by S.S.I. 2005 No. 632 (effective 8th December 2005).
[2] Rule 49.13(1)(b)(i) amended by S.S.I. 2005 No. 632 (effective 8th December 2005).

49.13.1 *"send"*. This includes deliver: r. 1.3(1) (definition of "send").

49.13.2 *"depending"*. A cause is depending from the time it is commenced (*i.e.* from the time an action is served) until final decree, whereas a cause is in dependence until final extract. For the meaning of commenced, see note 13.4.4. For the meaning of final decree, see note 4.15.2(2). For the meaning of final extract, see note 7.1.2(2).

"mental disorder". This is defined in r. 49.1(2) as "mental illness or mental handicap however caused or manifested". In the R.C.S. 1965, r. 15.4(3) "mental deficiency" appeared in place of mental handicap. The definition in the R.C.S. 1994 is now the same as that in s. 1 of the Mental Health (Scotland) Act 1984.

Notices in certain actions of divorce or separation

49.14.—(1) In the following actions of divorce or separation, there shall be attached to the copy of the summons served on the defender—

² (a) in an action relying on section 1(2)(d) of the Act of 1976 (no cohabitation for one year with consent of defender to decree)—

  (i) which is an action of divorce, a notice in Form 49.14–A and a form of notice of consent in Form 49.14–B;

  (ii) which is an action of separation, a notice in Form 49.14–C and a form of notice of consent in Form 49.14–D;

² (b) in an action relying on section 1(2)(e) of the Act of 1976 (no cohabitation for two years)—

  (i) which is an action of divorce, a notice in form 49.14–E;

  (ii) which is an action of separation, a notice in Form 49.14–F.

¹ (c) in an action relying on section 1(1)(b) of the Act of 1976 (grounds for divorce: interim gender recognition certificate), a notice in Form 49.14–G.

(2) The certificate of service of a summons in an action mentioned in paragraph (1) shall state which notice or form mentioned in paragraph (1) has been included with the summons.

Deriv. R.C.S. 1965, r. 161 substituted by S.I. 1976 No. 1994

———

¹ Rule 49.14(1)(c) inserted by S.S.I. 2005 No. 193 (effective 1st April, 2005).
² Rule 49.14(1)(a) and (b) amended by S.S.I. 2006 No. 206 (effective 4ᵗʰ May 2006).

49.14.1
General note. Where amendment is made changing the ground of divorce, the appropriate notice will have to be sent. In certain circumstances this may be dispensed with: see *Duncan v. Duncan* 1986 S.L.T. 17.

Notices in certain actions of dissolution of civil partnership or separation of civil partners

¹ **49.14A.**—(1) In the following actions of dissolution of civil partnership or separation of civil partners, there shall be attached to the copy of the summons served on the defender—

² (a) in an action relying on section 117(3)(c) of the CP Act of 2004 (no cohabitation for one year with consent of defender to decree)—

  (i) which is an action of dissolution of a civil partnership, a notice in Form 49.14A–A and a form of notice of consent in Form 49.14A–B;

  (ii) which is an action of separation of civil partners, a notice in Form 49.14A–C and a form of notice of consent in Form 49.14A–D;

² (b) in an action relying on section 117(3)(d) of the CP Act of 2004 (no cohabitation for two years)—

  (i) which is an action of dissolution of a civil partnership, a notice in Form 49.14A–E;

  (ii) which is an action of separation of civil partners, a notice in Form 49.14A–F;

  (c) in an action relying on section 117(2)(b) of the CP Act of 2004 (grounds of dissolution: interim gender recognition certificate), a notice in Form 49.14A–G.

(2) The certificate of service of a summons in an action mentioned in paragraph (1) shall state which notice or form mentioned in paragraph (1) has been included with the summons.

[1] Rule 49.14A inserted by S.S.I. 2005 No. 632 (effective 8th December 2005).
[2] Rule 49.14(1)(a) and (b) amended by S.S.I. 2006 No. 206 (effective 4th May 2006).

Orders for intimation by the court

[1] **49.15.**—(1) In any family action, the court may, at any time—

   (a) subject to paragraph (2), order intimation to be made to such person as it things fit;

   (b) postpone intimation, where it considers that such postponement is appropriate and in that case, the court shall make such order in respect of postponement of intimation as it thinks fit; or

   (c) dispense with intimation, where it considers that such dispensation is appropriate.

[2] (2) Where the court is considering whether to make a section 11 order by virtue of section 12 of the Act of 1995 (restrictions on decrees for divorce, separation, annulment, dissolution of civil partnership, separation of civil partners, or annulment of civil partnership affecting children), it shall, subject to paragraph (1)(c) and without prejudice to paragraph (1)(b) of this rule, order intimation to the child to whom the section 11 order would relate unless—

   (a) intimation has been given to the child under rule 49.8(7); or

   (b) the court considers that the child is not of sufficient age or maturity to express his views.

(3) Where a party makes an application or averment in a family action which, had it been made in a summons when presented for signeting, would have required a warrant for intimation under rule 49.8, that party shall apply by motion for a warrant for intimation or to dispense with such intimation; and rule 49.8 shall, with the necessary modifications, apply to a warrant under this paragraph as it applies to a warrant under that rule.

Deriv. R.C.S. 1965, r. 164 substituted by S.I. 1976 No. 1994 (r. 49.15(1))

[1] Rule 49.15 amended by S.I. 1996 No. 2587 (effective 1st November 1996).
[2] Rule 49.15(2) amended by S.S.I. 2005 No. 632 (effective 8th December 2005).

49.15.1   *"motion"*. For motions, see Chap. 23.

49.15.2   *"intimation"*. For methods, see r. 16.8.

49.15.3   *"section 11 order"*. See note 49.1.2.

49.15.4   *Lord Advocate.* Under s. 19(1) of the C.S.A. 1988 the court shall, where it considers it necessary for the proper disposal of an action of declarator of nullity of marriage or for divorce, direct intimation to the Lord Advocate so that he can determine whether to enter appearance. He might do so, *e.g.* where there was allegedly *lenocinium* (connivance at adultery).

No expenses can be claimed from or by the Lord Advocate in an action in which he has entered appearance.

Interested persons entering process

49.16.—(1) A person on whom intimation has been made of a family action or an application in a family action, may apply by minute for leave to be sisted as a party and to lodge defences, answers or a minute, as the case may be—

   (a) where the intimation was made on a warrant in a summons, within 7 days after the summons is lodged for calling; and

   (b) in any other case, within the period of notice.

(2) Where the court grants a motion under paragraph (1), it shall make such order for further procedure as it thinks fit.

Appointment of curators ad litem to defenders (r. 49.17) **C** 410/9

Deriv. R.C.S. 1965, r. 165 substituted by S.I. 1976 No. 1994

"minute". See r. 15.1. A fee will be payable on lodging a minute under this rule: see note 15.1.7. **49.16.1**

"within 7 days". The date from which the period is calculated is not counted. Where the last **49.16.2** day falls on a Saturday or Sunday or a public holiday on which the Office of Court is closed, the next available day is allowed: r. 1.3(7). For office hours and public holidays, see note 3.1.2.

Lord Advocate. Under s. 19(1) of the C.S.A. 1988 the Lord Advocate may enter appearance as **49.16.3** a party in any action of declarator of nullity of marriage or for divorce and lead such evidence and maintain such pleas as he thinks fit. This will no doubt be even rarer than it ever was when adultery was regarded as the crime it once was.

No expenses can be claimed from or by the Lord Advocate in an action in which he has entered appearance.

Appointment of curators ad litem to defenders

49.17.—[1] (1) This rule applies to an action of divorce, separation, dissolution of a civil partnership, or separation of civil partners, where it appears to the court that the defender is suffering from a mental disorder.

(2) In an action to which this rule applies, the court shall, after the expiry of the period for lodging defences—

(a) appoint a curator *ad litem* to the defender; and

[1,2] (b) where the facts set out in section 1(2)(d) of the Act of 1976 or section 117(3)(c) of the CP Act of 2004 (no cohabitation for one year with consent of defender to decree) are relied on—

(i) make an order for intimation of the ground of the action to the Mental Welfare Commission for Scotland; and

(ii) include in such an order a requirement that the Commission sends to the Deputy Principal Clerk a report indicating whether in its opinion the defender is capable of deciding whether or not to give consent to the granting of decree.

(3) Within 7 days after the appointment of a curator *ad litem* under paragraph (2)(a), the pursuer shall send to him a copy of the summons and any defences lodged (including any adjustments and amendments).

(4) On receipt of a report required under paragraph (2)(b)(ii), the Deputy Principal Clerk shall—

(a) cause the report to be lodged in process; and

(b) give written intimation that this has been done to—

(i) the pursuer;

(ii) the agent for the defender, if known; and

(iii) the curator *ad litem*.

(5) The curator *ad litem* shall lodge in process one of the writs mentioned in paragraph (6)—

(a) within 14 days after the report required under paragraph (2)(b)(ii) has been lodged in process; or

(b) where no such report is required, within 21 days after the date of his appointment under paragraph (2)(a).

(6) The writs referred to in paragraph (5) are—

(a) defences to the action;

(b) a minute adopting defences already lodged in process; and

(c) a minute stating that the curator *ad litem* does not intend to lodge defences.

(7) Notwithstanding that he has lodged a minute stating that he does not intend to lodge defences, a curator *ad litem* may appear at any stage of the action to protect the interests of the defender.

(8) If, at any time, it appears to the curator *ad litem* that the defender is not suffering from mental disorder, he may report that fact to the court and seek his own discharge.

(9) The pursuer shall be responsible, in the first instance, for payment of the fees and outlays of the curator *ad litem* incurred during the period from his appointment until—

(a) he lodges a minute stating that he does not intend to lodge defences;
(b) he decides to instruct the lodging of defences or a minute adopting defences already lodged; or
(c) being satisfied after investigation that the defender is not suffering from mental disorder, he is discharged.

Deriv. R.C.S. 1965, r. 167(1) substituted by S.I. 1976 No. 1994 (r. 49.17(1) to (7)); P.N. 10th February 1983 (r. 49.17(9))

---

[1] Rule 49.17(1) & (2)(b) inserted by S.S.I. 2005 No. 632 (effective 8th December 2005).
[2] Rule 49.14(1)(a) and (b) amended by S.S.I. 2006 No. 206 (effective 4th May 2006).

49.17.1   *General note.* R. 49.17 is made under s. 11 of the Divorce (Scotland) Act 1976.

49.17.2   *"mental disorder".* This is defined in r. 49.1(2) as mental illness or mental handicap however caused or manifested. This is the definition in s. 1 of the Mental Health (Scotland) Act 1984.
It will not be every mental disorder which will justify the appointment of a curator *ad litem*. Although it is not stated in the rule, the implication is, and the court would not normally make the appointment unless, the defender is incapable of managing his affairs or of giving instructions for their management. The practice is for the pursuer to produce medical certificates from two doctors (although with the abolition of the rule for corroboration by s. 1(1) of the Civil Evidence (Scotland) Act 1988, one should be sufficient).
On the duties of a curator *ad litem*, see *Finlay v. Finlay* 1962 S.L.T. (Sh.Ct.) 43.

49.17.2A   *Guardians.* Under s. 64(1)(c) of the Adults with Incapacity (Scotland) Act 2000, a guardian may be appointed to a person aged 16 or over, who is suffering from a mental disorder, with power to pursue or defend an action of nullity of marriage or divorce or separation.

49.17.3   *"Within 7 days", "within 14 days".* The date from which the period is calculated is not counted. In relation to r. 49.17(5), where the last day falls on a Saturday or Sunday or a public holiday on which the Office of Court is closed, the next available day is allowed: r. 1.3(7). For office hours and public holidays, see note 3.1.2.

49.17.4   *"send".* This includes deliver: r. 1.3(1) (definition of "send").

49.17.5   *"seek his own discharge".* The curator should seek his discharge by minute: *Walls v. Walls* 1953 S.L.T. 269.

Applications for sist
49.18. An application for a sist, or the recall of a sist, under Schedule 3 to the Domicile and Matrimonial Proceedings Act 1973 shall be made by motion.

Deriv. R.C.S. 1965, r. 167(2) substituted by S.I. 1976 No. 1994

49.18.1   *General note.* Sched. 3 to the Domicile and Matrimonial Proceedings Act 1973 contains provisions for the mandatory sist of proceedings before the court in certain circumstances and for a discretionary sist in others. On the exercise of the discretionary sist, see *Mitchell v. Mitchell* 1991 S.L.T. 410.

49.18.2   *"motion".* For motions, see Chap. 23.

Applications for sist in actions involving civil partnerships
[1] **49.18A.**—(1) Schedule 3 to the Act of 1973 (sisting of consistorial actions in Scotland) shall apply to actions for dissolution of civil partnerships, separation of civil partners or declarator of nullity of civil partnerships subject to the following modifications—
(a) for "consistorial action", wherever it appears, there shall be substituted "action concerning a civil partnership";
(b) for "divorce", wherever it appears there shall be substituted "dissolution of a civil partnership";
(c) for "separation", wherever it appears, there shall be substituted "separation of civil partners";
(d) for "declarator of nullity of marriage", wherever it appears, there shall be substituted "declarator of nullity of a civil partnership";

(e) for "marriage", wherever it appears, there shall be substituted "civil partnership";

(f) for "spouse", wherever it appears, there shall be substituted "civil partner";

(g) in paragraph 2 "declarator of marriage" shall be omitted;

(h) in paragraph 8(b) for "marriage was contracted" there shall be substituted "civil partnership was registered";

(i) in paragraphs 4(a), 7, and 9(4) "or in a sheriff court" shall be omitted;

(j) in paragraph 8 "or in the Sheriff Court" shall be omitted;

(k) in paragraph 9(1) "or in a sheriff court" shall be omitted.

(2) An application for a sist or a recall of a sist under Schedule 3 to the Act of 1973 as it applies under paragraph (1) shall be made by motion.

---

[1] Rule 49.18A inserted by S.S.I. 2005 No. 632 (effective 8th December 2005).

General note. Sched. 3 to the Domicile and Matrimonial Proceedings Act 1973 contains **49.18A.1** provisions for mandatory sist of proceedings before the court in certain circumstances and for a discretionary sist in others. On the exercise of the discretionary sist, see *Mitchell v. Mitchell*, 1991 S.L.T. 410.

"motion". For motions, see Chap. 23. **49.18A.2**

[1] *Notices of consent to divorce, separation, dissolution of civil partnership or separation of civil partners*
  49.19.—[1,3] (1) Where, in an action of divorce, or separation in which the facts in section 1(2)(d) of the Act of 1976, or dissolution of a civil partnership or separation of civil partners in which the facts in section 117(3)(d) of the CP Act of 2004, (no cohabitation for one year with consent of defender to decree) are relied on, the defender wishes to consent to the grant of decree—

(a) of divorce or separation he shall do so by giving notice in writing in Form 49.14–B (divorce) or Form 49.14–D (separation), as the case may be; or

(b) of dissolution of a civil partnership or separation of civil partners, he shall do so by giving notice in writing in Form 49.14A–B (dissolution) or Form 49.14A–D (separation of civil partners), as the case may be;

to the Deputy Principal Clerk.

(2) The evidence of one witness shall be sufficient for the purpose of establishing that the signature on a notice of consent under paragraph (1) is that of the defender.

[1] (3) In an action of divorce, separation, dissolution of a civil partnership, or separation of civil partners where the summons includes for the purposes of section 1(2)(d) of the Act of 1976, or section 117(3)(d) of the CP Act of 2004, as the case may be, an averment that the defender consents to the grant of decree, the defender may give notice by letter to the Deputy Principal Clerk stating that he has not so consented or that he withdraws any consent which he has already given.

(4) On receipt of a letter under paragraph (3), the Deputy Principal Clerk shall—

(a) cause the letter to be lodged in process; and

(b) give written intimation of the terms of the letter to the pursuer.

[2] (5) On receipt of an intimation under paragraph (4)(b), the pursuer may, within 14 days after the date of the intimation, if none of the other facts mentioned in section 1(2) of the Act of 1976 or section 117(3) of the CP Act of 2004, as the case may be, is averred in the summons, apply by motion for the action to be sisted.

(6) If no such motion is enrolled, the pursuer shall be deemed to have abandoned the action and the action shall be dismissed.

(7) If a motion under paragraph (5) is granted and the sist is not recalled or renewed within a period of six months from the date of the interlocutor granting the sist, the pursuer shall be deemed to have abandoned the action and the action shall be dismissed.

Deriv. R.C.S. 1965, r. 166 substituted by S.I. 1976 No. 1994

---

[1] Heading and Rule 49.19(1) & (3) substituted by S.S.I. 2005 No. 632 (effective 8th December 2005).

[2] Rule 49.19(5) amended by S.S.I. 2005 No. 632 (effective 8th December 2005).

[3] Rule 49.14(1)(a) and (b) amended by S.S.I. 2006 No. 206 (effective 4th May 2006).

49.19.1   *"sent"*. This includes deliver: r. 1.3(1) (definition of "send").

49.19.2   *"within 14 days"*. The date from which the period is calculated is not counted. Where the last day falls on a Saturday or Sunday or a public holiday on which the Office of Court is closed, the next available day is allowed: r. 1.3(7). For office hours and public holidays, see note 3.1.2.

49.19.3   *"motion"*. For motions, see Chap. 23.

Procedure in respect of children
[1] **49.20.**—(1) In a family action in relation to any matter affecting a child, where that child has—
    (a) returned Form 49.8–N, or
    (b) otherwise indicated to the court a wish to express views on a matter affecting him,
the court shall not grant any order unless an opportunity has been given for the views of that child to be obtained or heard.

(2) Where a child has indicated his wish to express his views, the court shall order such steps to be taken as it considers appropriate to ascertain the views of that child.

(3) The court shall not grant an order in a family action, in relation to any matter affecting a child who has indicated his wish to express his views, unless due weight has been given by the court to the views expressed by that child, having regard to his age and maturity.

---

[1] R. 49.20 Substituted by S.I. 1996 No. 2587 (effective 1st November 1996).

49.20.1   *General note.* Under art. 12 of the UN Convention on the Rights of the Child (Cm. 1976 (1992)), ratified by the UK on 16th December 1991, a child who is capable of forming his own views has the right to express those views freely in all matters affecting him and his views must be given due weight in accordance with his age and maturity. For this purpose the child must be given the opportunity to be heard in any judicial and administrative proceedings affecting him, either directly or through a representative or appropriate body, in a manner consistent with the procedural rules of national law. This principle is now enshrined in s. 11(7) of the Children (Scotland) Act 1995.

The child need not become a party, and may express his views by writing a letter or be given an opportunity to express his views orally to the judge in private: a form (Form 49.8–N) is sent to the child. The formal process of intimation in Form 49.8-N should not be the principal mode of complying with s. 11(7)(b) of the Children (Scotland) Act 1995: *S v. S*, 2002 S.C. 246 (Ex Div.) *sub nom. Shields v. Shields*, 2002 S.L.T.579 and see further, note 49.20.2. A child should be able to instruct a solicitor: Age of Legal Capacity (Scotland) Act 1991, s. 2(1)(a).

The court cannot always know in advance whether a child is capable of forming his own views and a minimum age cannot be laid down. On the other hand a child cannot know he has the right to be heard unless he is informed of that right. There appears to be no alternative but to provide for intimation in every case while providing in r. 49.8(8) for the court to dispense with intimation in certain circumstances (*e.g.* the child is a baby). There is a statutory presumption that a child of 12 or more is of sufficient age and maturity to form a view: Act of 1995, s. 11(10). See further, note 49.20.2.

R. 49.8(7) provides that the summons is not intimated to the child, but that a notice in Form 49.8–N is sent to him.

"*such steps to be taken as it considers appropriate*". It is not clear what steps will be **49.20.2**
appropriate to ascertain the views of a child. One view is that a curator *ad litem* must be
appointed in every case.

In *S v. S*, 2002 S.C. 246 (Ex Div.), *sub nom. Shields v. Shields*, 2002 S.L.T. 579, paras [10]
and [11], it was observed (1) that in affording a child the opportunity to make known his views
the only test is practicality; (2) how the child should be given that opportunity depends on the
circumstances including the child's age, and could be (a) by intimation in Form [49.8-N] (b) by
seeing the child in chambers, (c) by the views of the child being made known to the court by a
person known to the child or a child psychologist; (3) if it was practicable to give the child an
opportunity to express his views, the only safe course was to employ whatever method was
practicable; (4) the formal process of intimation in Form [49.8-N] should not be the principal
mode of complying with s. 11(7)(b) of the Children (Scotland) Act 1995 and other methods
must be preferable, particularly where younger children are involved or there is risk of upsetting
the child; and (5) the duty on the court to comply with s. 11(7)(b) continues until the order is
made and dispensing with formal intimation does not relieve the court from complying with
that continuing duty.

Reports by local authorities under section 49(2) of the Act of 1975
49.21. [Revoked by SI 1996/2587 (effective 1st November 1996).]

General note. Reports by local authorities were required where the applicant for custody of a **49.21.1**
child was not a parent of the child under s. 49 of the Children Act 1975. Section 49 of the 1975
Act has been repealed, but not replaced, by the Children (Scotland) Act 1995. A report may still
be requested: see r. 49.11 and note 49.11.1.

Appointment of local authority or reporter to report on a child
49.22.—(1) This rule applies where, at any stage of a family action, the
court appoints—
[1] (a) a local authority, whether under section 11(1) of the Matrimonial
   Proceedings (Children) Act 1958 or otherwise, or
 (b) another person (referred to in this rule as a "reporter"), whether
   under a provision mentioned in sub-paragraph (a) or otherwise,
to investigate and report to the court on the circumstances of a child and on
proposed arrangements for the care and upbringing of the child.

(2) On making an appointment referred to in paragraph (1), the court
shall direct that the party who sought the appointment or, where the court
makes the appointment at its own instance, the pursuer or minuter, as the
case may be, shall—
 (a) instruct the local authority or reporter; and
 (b) be responsible, in the first instance, for the fees and outlays of the
   local authority or reporter appointed.

(3) Where a local authority or reporter is appointed—
 (a) the party who sought the appointment, or
 (b) where the court makes the appointment at its own instance, the
   pursuer or minuter, as the case may be,
shall, within seven days after the date of the appointment, intimate the name
and address of the local authority or reporter to any local authority to which
intimation of the family action has been made.

(4) The local authority or reporter, as the case may be, shall, on
completion of a report referred to in paragraph (1), send the report, and a
copy of it for each party, to the Deputy Principal Clerk.

(5) On receipt of such a report, the Deputy Principal Clerk shall—

(a) cause the report to be lodged in process; and
(b) give written intimation to each party that this has been done and that he may uplift a copy of the report from process.

[1] (6) Where a local authority or reporter has been appointed to investigate and report in respect of a child, an application for a section 11 order in respect of that child shall not be determined until the report of the local authority or the reporter, as the case may be, has been lodged in process.

Deriv. R.C.S. 1965, r. 170B(14)(c), (d), (f) and (g) inserted by S.I. 1990 No. 705, and r. 260D(4), (5), (7) and (8) inserted by S.I. 1986 No. 515, (r. 49.22(1), (4) and (5)); P.N. November 13, 1969, para. 3 (r. 49.22(2)(b))

---

[1] R. 49.22(1)(a) and (6) amended by S.I. 1996 No. 2587 (effective 1st November 1996).

General note. S. 11(1) of the Matrimonial Proceedings (Children) Act 1958 gives the court a **49.22.1** power in proceedings between husband and wife to order a report from a local authority, without prejudice to its power to order a report from any other person, on the circumstances of the child and the proposed arrangements for his care and upbringing. The reporter may be required to appear and be examined and cross-examined on oath: 1958 Act, s. 11(4). The reporter should not be cited as a witness unless so required: P.N. 6th June 1968.

The court's powers under the above statutory provision is without prejudice to its power, recognised in r. 49.22(1)(b), to appoint any person to investigate and report.

The court is free to accept statements of fact in the report along with any other relevant facts proved in the action: *Macintyre v. Macintyre* 1962 S.L.T. (Notes) 70.

"section 11 order". See note 49.1.2. **49.22.2**

"send". This includes deliver: r. 1.3(1) (definition of "send"). **49.22.3**

Referral to family mediation

[1,2] **49.23.** In any family action in which an order in relation to parental responsibilities or parental rights is in issue, the court may, at any stage of the action where it considers it appropriate to do so, refer that issue to a mediator accredited to a specified family mediation organisation.

Deriv. R.C.S. 1965, r. 170B(15), and r. 260D(10), both inserted by S.I. 1990 No. 705

---

[1] R. 49.23 and heading amended by S.I. 1996 No. 1756 (effective 5th August 1996).
[2] R. 49.23 amended by S.I. 1996 No. 2587 (effective 1st November 1996).

General note. Mediation is concerned with helping parties resolve difficulties arising out of the **49.23.1** breakdown of a marriage, particularly in relation to residence and contact (custody and access) of children. There are mediation services available throughout Scotland. For further information, contact Family Mediation Scotland, 127 Rose Street South Lane, Edinburgh EH2 4BB (tel. 0131–220 1610). The Law Society of Scotland also accredits mediators, most of whom join C.A.L.M. (Comprehensive Accredited Lawyer Mediators) who mediate on financial matters as well. For further information, contact Law Society of Scotland, Law Society's Hall, 26 Drumsheagh Gardens, Edinburgh EH3 7YR (0131–226 7411).

Under s. 1 of the Civil Evidence (Family Mediation) (Scotland) Act 1995, information as to what occurred during family mediation (whether or not on a referral by the court) conducted by an accredited mediator of an approved organisation is not admissible in evidence in civil proceedings. S. 1 of the 1995 Act does not apply to civil proceedings in which evidence has been given or heard (in whole or in part) at any time prior to 19th February 1996: Civil Evidence (Family Mediation) (Scotland) Act 1995 (Commencement and Transitional Provision) Order 1996. S.2 of the 1995 Act contains exceptions to the inadmissibility rule.

Family Mediation Scotland and C.A.L.M. are approved organisations.

Approval of an organisation concerned with mediation is given by the Lord President; and applications by organisations for approval should be made to the Legal Assistant to the Lord President, Lord President's Private Office, Parliament House, Edinburgh EH1 1RQ.

The requirement of consent of parties to mediation was removed by A.S. (R.C.S.A. No. 3) (Miscellaneous) 1996 [S.I. 1996 No. 1756]. This brings r. 49.23 into line with the sheriff court rule (O.C.R. 1993, r. 33.22).

There are no legal requirements for consideration to be given to reconciliation between husband and wife. If the court considers there are prospects for reconciliation it may continue an action for such attempts to be made: Divorce (Scotland) Act 1976, s. 2(1). P.N. 11th March 1977 invites legal practitioners to encourage parties to seek advice and guidance from a marriage counsellor in those cases in which parties might be thought to benefit from it.

Applications for orders to disclose whereabouts of children

49.24.—(1) An application for an order under section 33(1) of the Family Law Act 1986 (which relates to the disclosure of the whereabouts of a child) shall be made by motion.

(2) Where the court makes an order under section 33(1) of the Family Law Act 1986, it may ordain the person against whom the order has been made to appear before it or to lodge an affidavit.

Deriv. R.C.S. 1965, r. 170B(12), and r. 260EB, both inserted by S.I. 1988 No. 615

49.24.1   *General note.* The court may order a person to disclose information about the whereabouts of a child: Family Law Act 1986, s. 33(1). Such a person may not refuse to answer on the ground of incrimination, and any answer may not be used in evidence for an offence other than perjury: 1986 Act, s. 33(2). The court has a common law power to order a person to make such a disclosure, to take evidence from such a person and to grant warrant to messengers-at-arms to search for children: *Abusaif v. Abusaif* 1984 S.L.T. 90, 91 *per* L.P. Emslie.

49.24.2   *"motion".* For motions, see Chap. 23.

Applications in relation to removal of children

49.25.—[1] (1) An application for leave under section 51(1) of the Act of 1975 (authority to remove a child from the care and possession of the applicant for a residence order) or for an order under section 35(3) of the Family Law Act 1986 (application for interdict or interim interdict prohibiting removal of child from jurisdiction)—
  (a) by a party, shall be made by motion;
  (b) by a person other than a party, shall be made by minute in the process of that action.

(2) An application under section 35(3) of the Family Law Act 1986 need not be served or intimated.

(3) An application under section 23(2) of the Child Abduction and Custody Act 1985 (declarator that removal of child from United Kingdom was unlawful) shall be made—
  (a) in an action depending before the court—
    (i) by a party, in the summons, defences or minute, as the case may be, or by motion; or
    (ii) by any other person, by minute; or
  (b) after final decree, by minute in the process of the action to which the application relates.

Deriv. R.C.S. 1965, r. 170B(13), and r. 260EC, both inserted by S.I. 1988 No. 615 (r. 49.25(1)(part)); r. 170C(2), and r. 260E(2) and (3), both inserted by S.I. 1986 No. 515 (r. 49.25(1)(part))

---

[1] R. 49.25(1) amended by S.I. 1996 No. 2587 (effective 1st November 1996).

49.25.1   *Section 51(1) of the Act of 1975.* Leave is required to remove a child from the care of the applicant for a residence order because it is an offence to remove the child without the authority of the court or an enactment: Children Act 1975, s. 51(1).

49.25.1A   *"residence order".* This replaces, but is not the whole of, what was formerly custody. It means an order regulating arrangements as to with whom or with whom during what periods a child under 16 is to live: Children (Scotland) Act 1995, s. 11(2)(c).

49.25.2   *Section 35(3) of the Family Law Act 1986.* The court may interdict a person from removing a child, in respect of whom it has jurisdiction to make an order, from not only Scotland but from anywhere in the UK: Family Law Act 1986, s. 35(3). The court has jurisdiction other than in matrimonial proceedings to make an order as provided in ss. 9 (habitual residence), 10 (presence of child), 12 (emergency) and 15(2) (original order granted by court) of the 1986 Act. The court's jurisdiction in matrimonial proceedings (divorce, nullity or separation) is unaffected; and the court dealing with matrimonial proceedings has primacy in dealing with residence, custody, care or control of or contact with a child: 1986 Act, s. 11.

Interim interdict will be refused if there is no evidence that the child is likely to be removed furth of the UK: *Woodcock v. Woodcock* 1990 S.L.T. 848.

"*minute*". See r. 15.1.   **49.25.3**

"*motion*". For motions, see Chap. 23.   **49.25.4**

[1] *Intimation to local authority before supervised contact order*
49.26.—[1] (1) Where the court, at its own instance or on the motion of a party, is considering making a contact order or an interim contact order subject to supervision by the social work department of a local authority, it shall ordain the party moving for such an order to intimate to the chief executive of that local authority (unless a party to the action and represented at the hearing at which the issue arises)—
  (a) the terms of any relevant motion;
  (b) the intention of the court to order that the contact order be supervised by the social work department of that local authority; and
  (c) that the local authority shall, within such period as the court has determined—
    (i) notify the Keeper of the Rolls whether it intends to make representations to the court through counsel or other person having a right of audience or in writing; and
    [2] (ii) where it intends to make representations in writing, do so within that period.
(2) After receiving notice or written representations, as the case may be, under paragraph (1)(c), the Keeper of the Rolls shall put the action out on the By Order Roll before the Lord Ordinary on such a date as may be convenient, for the court to determine, after considering any representations of a local authority under paragraph (1), whether to order such supervision.

Deriv. P.N. No. 1 of 1988

---

[1] R. 49.26(1) and heading amended by S.I. 1996 No. 2587 (effective 1st November 1996).
[2] Rule 49.14(1)(a) and (b) amended by S.S.I. 2006 No. 206 (effective 4th May 2006).

"*intimate*". For methods, see r. 16.7.   **49.26.1**

"*contact order*". A contact order is an order regulating the arrangements for maintaining **49.26.2** personal relations and direct contact between a child under 16 and a person with whom he is not, or will not be, living: Children (Scotland) Act 1995, s. 11(2)(d).

Joint minutes
[1] **49.27.** Where any parties have reached agreement in relation to—
  (a) a section 11 order,
  (b) aliment for a child, or
  (c) an order for financial provision,
a joint minute may be entered into expressing that agreement; and, subject to rule 49.20(3) (no order before views of child expressed), the court may grant decree in respect of those parts of the joint minute in relation to which it could otherwise make an order, whether or not such a decree would include a matter for which there was no conclusion or crave.

Deriv. R.C.S. 1965, r. 170B(5) inserted by S.I. 1976 No. 1994

---

[1] R. 49.27 amended by S.I. 1996 No. 2587 (effective 1st November 1996).

49.27.1　*General note.* A joint minute may record an agreement with provisions other than those mentioned in r. 47.27 and the court may interpone authority to such an agreement. But the court cannot grant decree in respect of anything in the joint minute *except* in relation to a matter listed in r. 47.27.

There are four points to note about the form of the joint minute. (1) The effect of the court interponing authority is to show that the agreement was made in the presence of the court and the court did not object to it: *Gow v. Henry* (1899) 2 F. 48, 53 *per* Lord Young *obiter*. The authority of the court is not required, however, to bind the parties to the agreement signed by or on their behalf, and there is no *locus poenitentiae* until such authority is interponed: *Gow*, above; *McAthey v. Patriotic Investment Society Ltd* 1910 1 S.L.T. 121; *Lothian v. Lothian* 1965 S.L.T. 368; *Jongejan v. Jongejan* 1993 S.L.T. 595. The fact that the joint minute is stated to be conditional "in the event of decree of divorce being pronounced" does not enable one party to resile from it: *Lothian*, above. (2) Where a joint minute requests the court to "interpone authority hereto and to grant decree in terms thereof [*or in terms of specified paragraphs*]", the subsequent decree and not the agreement regulates those provisions of the agreement in respect of which decree has been granted. (3) Where a joint minute records an agreement and requests the court to "interpone authority hereto and to make no order for aliment [*or financial provision*] [*or to assoilzie the defender from the ... conclusion of the summons* (*or as the case may be*)]", if the court grants decree accordingly, the agreement in the joint minute will regulate the position of the parties. (4) The joint minute must clearly state what the parties are requesting the court to do, *i.e.* to interpone authority to it, to grant decree in terms of all or some (and if so which) of its paragraphs; or, in granting decree in terms of some of it, to assoilzie any party from a particular conclusion or crave.

Even an agreement in a joint minute will be subject to the power of the court under s. 16 of the Act of 1985 to vary or set aside a term relating to periodical allowance where the agreement expressly provides for the court to do it or a term where the agreement was not fair and reasonable at the time it was made. An agreement relating to periodical allowance may also be set aside or varied which is affected by sequestration or a voluntary trust deed of one of the parties or where a maintenance assessment has been made under the Child Support Act 1991.

It should also be noted that a joint minute which is a maintenance agreement (*i.e.* an agreement for making or securing periodical payment of aliment to or for the benefit of a child) for less than could be awarded under a maintenance assessment will be insecure because an application to the Child Support Agency for a maintenance assessment cannot be prevented: Child Support Act 1991, s. 9. The court's power to award aliment for a child is dealt with in ss. 3 and 8 of the 1991 Act.

49.27.2　*Fee.* A court fee is payable on lodging a joint minute by a party other than an originating party who makes his first appearance by signing a joint minute. For fee, see Court of Session etc. Fees Order 1997, Table of Fees, Pt. I, B, item 6 [S.I. 1997 No. 688, as amended, pp. C1201 *et seq.*]. Certain persons are exempt from payment of fees: see 1997 Fees Order, art. 5 substituted by S.S.I. 2002 No. 270. A fee exemption certificate must be lodged in process: see P.N. No.1 of 2002.

Where the new party is legally represented, the fee may be debited under a credit scheme introduced on 1st April 1976 by P.N. No. 4 of 1976 to the account (if one is kept or permitted) of the agent by the court cashier, and an account will be rendered weekly by the court cashier's office to the agent for all court fees due that week for immediate settlement. Party litigants, and agents not operating the scheme, must pay (by cash, cheque or postal order) on each occasion a fee is due at the time of lodging at the counter at the General Department.

Expenses of curator ad litem appointed to a child

[1] **49.27A.** Where in any family action a curator *ad litem* is appointed to a child, the pursuer shall be responsible, in the first instance, for payment of the fees and outlays of the curator *ad litem* incurred during the period from his appointment until the occurrence of any of the following events—

　(a)　the lodging of a minute by the curator stating that he does not intend to lodge defences;

　(b)　the curator instructing the lodging of defences or a minute adopting defences which are already lodged; or

　(c)　the discharge, before the occurrence of the events mentioned in sub-paragraphs (a) and (b), of the curator.

---

[1] Rule 49.27A inserted by S.S.I. 1999 No. 109 (effective 29th October 1999).

General note. The problem that this new rule addresses is the funding of work of a curator *ad*   **49.27A.1**
litem appointed before legal aid is granted directly to a child.
   The rule was inserted by A.S. (R.C.S.A. No. 7) (Miscellaneous) 1999 [S.S.I. 1999 No. 109].
The pursuer is analogous to that for appointment of a curator *ad litem* to a defender in a divorce
act under r. 49.17.

Curators ad litem. A curator *ad litem* is a person appointed by the court to act for a child, or a   **49.27A.2**
person under some disability, to protect the child's interests in the action. The common law
power of the court to appoint a curator *ad litem* to a child under the age of 16 is preserved by
the Age of Legal Capacity (Scotland) Act 1991, s. 1(3)(f)(ii). Normally the child's parent or
guardian will act as the child's legal representative, but in a family action there may be a conflict
of interest between the child and that representative. The circumstances in which a curator may
be appointed include:- where there is no parent or guardian; where the action is by the legal
representative against the child or the child against the legal representative; where the child
brings an action and the legal representative will not act; where there is a conflict of interest
between the child and the legal representative; where there is not necessarily a conflict of interest
but the child's interests nonetheless require protection.
   A curator *ad litem* takes the oath *de fideli administratione*. The responsibilities of the curator
do not extend beyond the subject of the action. They do not extend to the estate of the child.
The appointment may be recalled by the court and in any event terminates with the action. The
curator must exercise independent judgment. He may conduct or compromise the action and is
the *dominus litis* (*M'Cuaig v. M'Cuaig* 1909 S.C. 355, 357 *per* L.P. Dunedin): *Dewar v. Dewar's
Trs* (1906) 14 S.L.T. 238, 239 *per* Lord Dundas. In relation to remuneration and outlays, where
the pursuer is not the child to whom the curator is appointed, the pursuer is, by r. 49.27A,
responsible in the first instance for these expenses. Where the pursuer is the child to whom the
curator is appointed, the curator (if the court has not made another party responsible) may
apply to the court to direct that funds are made available from any appropriate source or he
should apply for legal aid: see *L, Petr. (No. 4)* 1997 S.L.T. 44. In that case the curator was not
covered by legal aid for part of his work and, because the court considered that no other party
should bear the cost, the court ordered payment out of public funds. The curator is not
personally responsible for expenses if not successful in the action.

Corrected gender recognition certificates

[1] **49.27B.**—(1) An application after final decree for a corrected gender
recognition certificate under section 6 of the Act of 2004 shall be made by
minute in the process of the action in which the full gender recognition
certificate was issued.
   (2) Where the court issues a corrected gender recognition certificate, the
Deputy Principal Clerk shall send a certified copy of the certificate to the
Secretary of State.

---

[1] Rule 49.27B inserted by S.S.I. 2005 No. 193 (effective 1st April, 2005).

"corrected gender recognition certificate". Under the Gender Recognition Act 2004 a person   **49.27B.1**
may apply for a gender recognition certificate on the basis of living in the other gender or
having changed gender. Where the certificate was issued by the court (which would occur in
divorce proceedings) and there is an error in the certificate, an application may be made to the
court for a corrected certificate under s. 6.

"minute". For applications by minute, see r. 15.1.   **49.27B.2**

"send". This includes deliver: r. 1.3(1) (definition of "send").   **49.27B.3**

Applications for postponement of decree under section 3A of the Act of 1976

[1] **49.27C.** An application under section 3A(1) (application for postponement of decree where impediment to religious marriage exists) or section
3A(4) (application for recall of postponement) of the Act of 1976 shall be
made by minute in the process of the action to which the application relates.

---

[1] Rule 49.27(C) inserted by S.S.I. 2006 No. 206 (effective 4th May 2006) and amended by S.S.I.
2007 No. 7, para. 9 (effective 26th February 2007).

"minute". For applications by minute, see r. 15.1.   **49.27C.1**

PART II

UNDEFENDED FAMILY ACTIONS

Evidence in certain undefended family actions
  49.28.—(1) This rule—
  (a) subject to sub-paragraph (b), applies to all family actions in which no
      defences have been lodged, other than a family action—
      ² (i) for a section 11 order;
      (ii) for financial provision after an overseas divorce or annulment
           within the meaning of Part IV of the Matrimonial and Family
           Proceedings Act 1984; or
      (iii) for an order under the Act of 1981;
      ³ (iv) for financial provision after overseas proceedings to dissolve or
           annul a civil partnership within the meaning of Schedule 11 to
           the CP Act of 2004; or
      ³ (v) for an order under Chapter 3 or 4 of Part 3 of the CP Act of
           2004;
  (b) applies to a family action in which a curator *ad litem* has been
      appointed under rule 49.17(2)(a) where the curator *ad litem* to the
      defender has lodged a minute intimating that he does not intend to
      lodge defences;
  (c) applies to any family action which proceeds at any stage as
      undefended where the court so directs;
  (d) applies to the merits of a family action which is undefended on the
      merits where the court so directs, notwithstanding that the action is
      defended on an ancillary matter.
  (2) Unless the court otherwise directs, evidence shall be given by affidavit.
  (3) Unless the court otherwise directs, evidence relating to the welfare of a
child shall be given by affidavit, at least one affidavit being sworn by a
person other than a parent or party to the action.
  (4) Evidence in the form of a written statement bearing to be the
professional opinion of a duly qualified medical practitioner, which has been
signed by him and lodged in process, shall be admissible in place of parole
evidence by him.
  ¹ (5) Rule 36.8 (lodging of certain written statements) shall not apply in an
undefended family action to which this rule applies.

Deriv. R.C.S. 1965, r. 168(1), (2), (5) and (6) substituted by S.I. 1978 No. 106 and amended by
S.I. 1980 No. 1144 (r. 49.28(1) to (4))

_____

  ¹ Rule 49.28(5) amended by S.S.I. 2001 No. 305, para. 7(2) (effective 18th September 2001).
  ² Rule 49.28(1)(a)(i) amended by S.I. 1996 No. 2587 (effective 1st November 1996).
  ³ Rule 49.28(1)(a)(iv) & (v) inserted by S.S.I. 2005 No. 632 (effective 8th December 2005).

49.28.1   *General note.* In certain family actions, even if undefended, decree cannot be granted without
the grounds of action being established by evidence; these are actions for divorce, separation,
declarator of marriage, nullity of marriage, legitimacy, legitimation, illegitimacy, parentage or
non-parentage: Civil Evidence (Scotland) Act 1988, s. 8(1) and (2). The grounds of action are
not limited to the conclusion concerning status (*e.g.* divorce) but include a conclusion for
financial provision. Except where parties are agreed, there must be evidence before the court
which must be considered by the judge before an award for financial provision can be made:
Gould v. Gould, 1966 S.C. 88; *Ali v. Ali,* 2001 S.C. 618.
  In undefended family actions specified in r. 49.28(1), the evidence may be by affidavit
evidence alone. Although the requirement for corroboration has been abolished by s. 1(1) of the
1988 Act, in an action of divorce, separation, declarator of marriage or nullity of marriage
evidence must consist of or include evidence other than that of a party to the marriage: 1988
Act, s. 8(3).

[NEXT TEXT PAGE IS C 415]

If the court is not satisfied on the evidence, it may continue the case to enable the pursuer to adduce additional evidence: *Paterson v. Paterson* 1958 S.C. 141, 146 *per* L.P. Clyde.

"section 11 order". See note 49.1.2.   **49.28.2**

"affidavits". On the form and requirements of an affidavit, see Notes by the Dean of the **49.28.3** Faculty of Advocates and the President of the Law Society in regard to Affidavit Evidence in Undefended Divorce Actions, 11th April 1978 (see Section Two, 3).
Note also the definition of an affidavit in r. 1.3(2).

"any family action which proceeds at any stage as undefended where the court so directs". The **49.28.4** court so directs in undefended divorce actions even where custody, access or aliment is sought.

Fee. A court fee is payable for initial lodging of affidavits in a family action where proof by **49.28.5** affidavit evidence has been allowed on the Procedure Roll. For fee, see Court of Session etc. Fees Order 1997, Table of Fees, Pt. I, B, item 7 [S.I. 1997 No. 688, as amended, pp. **C** 1201 *et seq.*]. Certain persons are exempt from payment of fees: see 1997 Fees Order, art. 5 substituted by S.S.I. 2002 No. 270. A fee exemption certificate must be lodged in process: see P.N. No.1 of 2002.
Where the pursuer is legally represented, the fee may be debited under a credit scheme introduced on 1st April 1976 by P.N. No. 4 of 1976 to the account (if one is kept or permitted) of the agent by the court cashier, and an account will be rendered weekly by the court cashier's office to the agent for all court fees due that week for immediate settlement. An agent not on the credit scheme or a party litigant must pay (by cash, cheque or postal order) at the public counter of the General Department.

Procedure for decree in actions under rule 49.28

49.29.—(1) In an action to which rule 49.28 (evidence in certain undefended family actions) applies, if counsel or other person having a right of audience, on consideration of the available affidavits and supporting documents, is satisfied that a motion for decree may properly be made, he may, at any time after the expiry of the period for lodging defences, move the court by minute in Form 49.29–A to grant decree in terms of the conclusions of the summons or in such restricted terms as may be appropriate.

(2) On lodging such a minute in process, the pursuer shall—

(a) lodge in process the documents specified in the schedule to the minute; and

(b) send to the Deputy Principal Clerk, Form 49.29–B duly completed.

(3) The court may, at any time after the minute and other documents referred to in paragraph (2) have been lodged, without requiring the appearance of counsel or other person having a right of audience—

(a) grant decree in terms of the motion for decree contained in the minute; or

(b) put the action out on the By Order Roll before the Lord Ordinary for such further procedure, if any, including proof by parole evidence, as the court thinks fit.

(4) Notice shall be given in the rolls of all decrees granted under paragraph (3)(a).

Deriv. R.C.S. 1965, r. 168(7) to (11) substituted by S.I. 1978 No. 106

Date of decree. The date of the decree will be the date on which notice of the decree appears in **49.29.1** the rolls under r. 49.29(4) and not the date on which the interlocutor was signed: *Smith v. Smith* 1989 S.L.T. 668.

[1] No suspension in undefended actions of divorce or civil partnerships

49.30. A defender may not bring any proceedings for the suspension of any decree of divorce or dissolution of a civil partnership pronounced in an undefended action.

Deriv. R.C.S. 1965, r. 170A inserted by S.I. 1976 No. 1994

¹ Heading and r. 49.30 amended by S.S.I. 2005 No. 632 (effective 8th December 2005).

49.30.1   *General note.* As suspension of decree of divorce in an undefended action is not competent, such a decree can be reduced only in an action of reduction or *ope exceptiones* in another action. The Court of Session has jurisdiction to reduce any decree granted by a Scottish court whether or not jurisdiction exists independently in the action of reduction: Law Reform (Miscellaneous Provisions) (Scotland) Act 1980, s. 20. On reduction generally, see Chap. 53.

A defender may not reclaim a decree in an undefended family action if he has not entered appearance: rr. 38.2, 38.3 and 1.3(1) (definition of "party"). It should be noted that R.C.S. 1965, r. 169(1)(c) (power of court to allow defender not present at proof in an undefended consistorial action to reclaim) has not been re-enacted.

PART III

DEFENDED FAMILY ACTIONS

Defences in family actions
    49.31.—(1) This rule applies where the defender in a family action seeks—
    (a) to oppose any conclusion in the summons;
    (b) to make a claim for—
        (i) aliment;
        (ii) an order for financial provision within the meaning of section 8(3) of the Act of 1985; or
    ¹ (iii) a section 11 order; or
    (c) an order—
        (i) under section 16(1)(b) or (3) of the Act of 1985 (setting aside or varying agreement as to financial provision);
        (ii) under section 18 of the Act of 1985 (which relates to avoidance transactions); or
        (iii) under the Act of 1981; or
    ² (iv) under Chapter 3 or 4 of Part 3 of the CP Act of 2004
    (d) to challenge the jurisdiction of the court.
    (2) In an action to which this rule applies, the defender shall—
    (a) lodge defences to the action in process; and
    (b) make any claim or seek any order, as the case may be, referred to in paragraph (1) in those defences by setting out in those defences—
        (i) conclusions;
        (ii) averments in the answers to the condescendence in support of those conclusions; and
        (iii) appropriate pleas-in-law.

Deriv. R.C.S. 1965, r. 170B(3) and (4) inserted by S.I. 1976 No. 1994; r. 170D(2) inserted by S.I. 1976 No. 1994 and amended by S.I. 1986 No. 1231, 1990 No. 705 and 1991 No. 1157; r. 170D(4)(a) substituted by S.I. 1977 No. 1621 and amended by S.I. 1986 No. 1231; r. 170D(5) substituted by S.I. 1986 No. 1231; and r. 170D(7)(b) inserted by S.I. 1986 No. 1231

―――――

¹ R. 49.31(1)(b)(iii) amended by S.I. 1996 No. 2587 (effective 1st November 1996).
² Rule 49.31(1)(c)(iv) inserted by S.S.I. 2005 No. 632 (effective 8th December 2005).

49.31.1   *General note.* It is not competent for a pursuer to have a conclusion craving an order on behalf of the defender: *T. v. T.* 1987 S.L.T. (Sh.Ct.) 74 (custody); *Young v. Young* 1991 G.W.D. 13–798 (financial provision). The defender must seek his own remedies.

A defender may not counterclaim in a family action (r. 25.1(1)), and in order to avoid him having to bring a cross-action, he may exceptionally conclude for certain remedies (see r. 49.31(1)) in his defences: r. 49.31(2)(b)(i).

49.31.2   "*section 11 order*". See note 49.1.2.

49.31.3   "*defences*". See rr. 18.1 and 18.2.

Abandonment by pursuer
49.32. Notwithstanding abandonment by a pursuer, the court may allow a defender to pursue an order or claim sought in his defences; and the proceedings in relation to that order or claim shall continue in dependence as if a separate cause.

"abandonment". On abandonment of actions, see Chap. 29.   **49.32.1**

"in dependence". A cause is depending until final decree, whereas a cause is in dependence   **49.32.2**
until final extract. For the meaning of final decree, see note 4.15.2(2). For the meaning of final
extract, see note 7.1.2(2).

Adjustment and further procedure
49.33.—(1) Chapter 22 (making up and closing records) shall not apply to a family action.

(2) The court shall, 14 days after the date on which defences were lodged, or a minute by a person on whom intimation has been made under rule 49.8, 49.9 or 49.15 was lodged, pronounce an interlocutor allowing the parties a proof of their respective averments.

(3) Notwithstanding the pronouncement of an interlocutor under paragraph (2), the parties may adjust their respective pleadings until 28 days before the diet of proof; and any such adjustments shall be written on the summons, defences or minute, as the case may be.

(4) Not earlier than 28 days after the allowance of proof, the court may, on cause shown, withdraw the allowance of proof and appoint the action to the Procedure Roll.

(5) The pursuer shall, within seven days after the end of the adjustment period under paragraph (3) or the appointment of the action to the Procedure Roll, as the case may be—
   (a) subject to rule 49.68 (procedure for minutes in causes under the Act of 1981) or rule 49.71E (procedure for minutes in causes under Chapters 3 and 4 of Part 3 of the CP Act of 2004) as the case may be, make up a copy of the adjusted pleadings in the form of a record;
   (b) send not less than three copies of the record to every other party; and
   (c) not later than 48 hours before the diet of proof or hearing on the Procedure Roll, as the case may be, lodge two copies of the record in process.

Deriv. R.C.S. 1965, r. 168A inserted by S.I. 1980 No. 1144 and amended by S.I. 1982 No. 1381
(r. 49.33(5)(part))

———————

[1] Rule 49.33(5)(a) amended by S.S.I. 2005 No. 632 (effective 8th December 2005).

General note. R. 49.33 sets out a new procedure for defended family actions. 14 days after   **49.33.1**
defences have been lodged an interlocutor is automatically pronounced allowing parties a proof,
but parties are entitled to adjust their pleadings until 28 days before the diet of proof. An action
may, however, be sent to procedure roll: r. 49.33(4).

Procedure Roll. A hearing on the Procedure Roll is rare in a family action. It is not normally   **49.33.2**
appropriate (except on a point of law only), where the welfare of children is involved, to dispose
of an application for an order relating to parental rights solely on the pleadings, some kind of
inquiry into the facts being necessary: *O. v. O.* 1994 S.C. 569.
   On the Procedure Roll, see Chap. 28.

Late appearance by defenders
49.34.—(1) In a family action, the court may, at any time while the action is depending, make an order with such conditions, if any, as it thinks fit, allowing a defender—
   (a) to lodge defences to the action; and
   (b) to appear and be heard at a diet of proof although he has not lodged

defences, but he shall not, in that event, be allowed to lead evidence without the pursuer's consent.

(2) Where the court makes an order under paragraph (1)(a), the pursuer may recall a witness already examined or lead other evidence whether or not he closed his proof before that order was made.

Deriv. R.C.S. 1965, r. 169 substituted by S.I. 1976 No. 1994

49.34.1   *General note.* The court has a discretion to refuse to allow a defender to lodge defences or appear: see, *e.g. Watt v. Watt* 1978 S.L.T. (Notes) 55; *cf. Stirton v. Stirton* 1969 S.L.T. (Notes) 48.

While r. 49.34(1)(b) gives the court a discretion to allow a defender to appear at the proof, where the proof has in fact been heard it would probably not allow the defender a further diet of proof without him lodging defences.

The provision in R.C.S. 1965, r. 169(1)(c), by virtue of which the court could allow a defender who had not appeared at the proof to reclaim, has not been re-enacted in r. 49.34. Accordingly, only reduction is competent if the defender did not enter appearance (rr. 38.2 and 1.3(1) (definition of "party")); if the action was defended but the defender failed to appear at the proof, he would still have a right to reclaim under r. 38.3.

49.34.2   *"defences".* See rr. 18.1 and 18.2.

49.34.3   *"depending".* A cause is depending until final decree, whereas a cause is in dependence until final extract. For the meaning of final decree, see note 4.15.2(2). For the meaning of final extract, see note 7.1.2(2).

PART IV

APPLICATIONS AND ORDERS RELATING TO CHILDREN IN CERTAIN ACTIONS

[1] *Application of this Part*
    [1] **49.35.** This Part applies to actions of divorce, separation, declarator of nullity of marriage, dissolution of a civil partnership, separation of civil partners and declarator of nullity of a civil partnership.

Deriv. R.C.S. 1965, r. 170B(1)(b) inserted by S.I. 1976 No. 1994 (r. 49.35(1))

---

[1] Heading and r. 49.35 substituted by S.S.I. 2005 No. 632 (effective 8th December 2005).

49.35.1   *General note.* Applications in relation to parental rights in family actions other than an action of divorce, separation or declarator of nullity of marriage are dealt with in Pt. IX (rr. 49.58 to 49.63).

49.35.2   *Jurisdiction.* The court having jurisdiction in an action of divorce, separation or declarator of nullity of marriage has jurisdiction in relation to parental rights (as defined by s. 8 of the Law Reform (Parent and Child) (Scotland) Act 1986 (and see note 49.36.4)): Domicile and Matrimonial Proceedings Act 1973, s. 10 (as modified by s. 13 of the Family Law Act and reg. 2(4) of the European Communities (Matrimonial Jurisdiction and Judgments) (Scotland) Regulations 2000 (S.S.I. 2000 No. 36)), and secondly by the European Communities (Matrimonial and Parental Responsibility and Judgments) (Scotland) Regulations 2005 [S.S.I. 2005 No. 42] the C.S.A. 1988, s. 20(1) (which re-enacts s. 9 of the Conjugal Rights (Scotland) Amendment Act 1861, as substituted by para. 2 of Sched. 1 to the Law Reform (Parent and Child) (Scotland) Act 1986, referred to in s. 10 of, and Sched. 2 to, the 1973 Act), and the Council Regulation (E.C.) No. 2201/2003 of 27th November 2003 (new Brussels II) which replaced the Council Regulation (EC) No. 1347/2000 of 29th May 2000 (Brussels II) which applies between member states of the E.U.

Applications in actions to which this Part applies
    49.36.—(1) An application for an order mentioned in paragraph (2) shall be made—
    (a) by a conclusion in the summons or defences, as the case may be, in an action to which this Part applies; or
    (b) where the application is made by a person other than the pursuer or defender, by minute in that action.

(2) The orders referred to in paragraph (1) are—
[1] (a) an order for a section 11 order; and
(b) an order for aliment for a child.

"*summons*". On form of summons, see r. 13.2.   **49.36.1**

"*defences*". On form of defences, see r. 18.1.   **49.36.2**

"*minute*". On applications by minute, see r. 15.1.   **49.36.3**

"*section 11 order*". See note 49.1.2.   **49.36.4**
Any person claiming an interest may apply for an order relating to parental rights: Children (Scotland) Act 1995, s. 11(3)(a). On the meaning of "interest" under s. 3(1) of the Law Reform (Parent and Child) (Scotland) Act 1986, see *D. v. Grampian R.C.* 1995 S.C.(H.L.) 1. In any proceedings for a section 11 order the court shall regard the welfare of the child as the paramount consideration and shall not make any order unless it would be better for the child that an order be made than that none be made and having regard to views expressed by the child: Act of 1995, s. 11(7).

A mother always has parental responsibilities and parental rights in relation to her child; a father has them only if he is married to the child's mother or was married to her at the time of or after the child's conception: Act of 1995, s. 3. The right to parental responsibilities is subject to what is in the interests of the child: Act of 1995, s. 1(1).

The advantage to a very young child of being with its mother is a consideration which has to be taken into account in deciding where its best interests lie but which will yield to competing advantages which more effectively promote the welfare of the child: *Brixey v. Lynas* 1997 S.C. (H.L.) 1.

In relation to contact orders, where a person has parental rights, it is not required to aver in detail the basis on which contact is sought: *O. v. O.* 1995 S.L.T. 238. It should be noted that a parent does not have an absolute right of contact with his or her child, he or she is only entitled to contact if the court is satisfied that it is in the best interests of the child: *Porchetta v. Porchetta* 1986 S.L.T. 105; and see now the Act of 1995, s. 11(7). In *Sanderson v. McManus* 1996 S.L.T. 751 the majority in the Extra Division held that (1) s. 3(2) of the Law Reform (Parent and Child) (Scotland) Act 1986 (see now s. 11(7) of the Act of 1995) sets out the only test; (2) the child's father if not married to its mother does not have parental rights; (3) there is no "right" in a parent to access; and (4) although the parent-child relationship may have intrinsic value, and the status quo should be preserved (*Brixey v. Lynas*, 1994 S.C. 606), these are not propositions of law capable of being determinative but are simply factors which may or may not be significant. Lord McCluskey, dissenting, took the view that the "traditional approach" that the link between a child and his natural parent would be conducive to the child's welfare or should be preserved unless there were strong reasons to the contrary (*Blance v. Blance* 1978 S.L.T. 74; *Brannigan v. Brannigan* 1979 S.L.T. (Notes) 73) was not altered by s. 3(2) of the 1986 Act or *Porchetta*, above. The majority opinion in *Sanderson*, above was upheld in the House of Lords in 1997 S.L.T. 629. In *White v. White*, 2001 S.C. 689, it was held that the court requires where regard to the welfare of the child as its paramount consideration and will generally consider that it is conducive to the welfare of children if the absent parents maintain personal relations and direct contact on a regular basis (see also Lord Hope of Craighead in *Sanderson*). There is, however, no legal onus on the person seeking a contact order, the court simply considers all the relevant material and decides what is conducive to the child's welfare: *White*, above, *per* L.P. Rodger at p.698H.

The parent having a residence order does not fulfil his or her obligations where a contact order is awarded by leaving it to the child to decide whether to go or not; that parent must encourage and persuade, although not physically coerce, the child to accept contact by the other parent: see *Blance*, above, *per* Lord Stewart at p. 75.

In an action of divorce, separation or nullity of marriage, the court must consider whether to make a section 11 order or a reference to the Principal Reporter; and where it is of the opinion that such action may be required, or that it is not in a position to take such action without further consideration, or that it is not desirable in the interests of the child to grant decree until it is in a position to do so, it shall postpone its decision to grant decree: Act of 1995, s. 12(1).

It is not appropriate to dispose of an appeal for parental rights solely on the pleadings: *O.*, above.

"*aliment*". See ss. 1 to 7 of the Family Law (Scotland) Act 1985.   **49.36.5**

Intimation before committal to care or supervision
49.37. [Revoked by S.I. 1996 No. 2587 (effective 1st November 1996).]

Care or supervision orders
49.38. [Revoked by S.I. 1996 No. 2587 (effective 1st November 1996).]

Intimation of certain applications to local authorities or other persons
49.39. [Revoked by S.I. 1996 No. 2587 (effective 1st November 1996).]

Applications in depending actions by motion
[1,2] **49.40.**—(1) An application by a party in an action depending before the court to which this Part applies for, or for variation of, an order for—
 (a) interim aliment for a child under the age of 18, or
 (b) an interim residence order or an interim contact order,
shall be made by motion.
[3] (2) Written intimation of a motion under paragraph (1) shall be given to every other party not less than 7 days before the date on which the motion is enrolled.

---

[1] R. 49.40 substituted by S.I. 1996 No. 2587 (effective 1st November 1996).
[2] R. 49.40 amended by S.I. 1997 No. 1050 (effective 6th April 1997: insertion of "(1)").
[3] R. 49.40(2) inserted by S.I. 1997 No. 1050 (effective 6th April 1997).

49.40.1 *"depending".* A cause is depending from the time it is commenced (*i.e.* from the time an action is served) until final decree, whereas a cause is in dependence until final extract. For the meaning of commenced, see note 13.4.4. For the meaning of final decree, see note 4.15.2(2). For the meaning of final extract, see note 7.1.2(2).

49.40.2 *"residence and contact orders".* A residence order replaces, but is not the whole of, what was formerly custody. It means an order regulating arrangements as to with whom or with whom during what periods a child under 16 is to live: Children (Scotland) Act 1995, s. 11(2)(c).
 A contact order replaces access. It is an order regulating the arrangements for maintaining personal relations and direct contact between a child under 16 and a person with whom he is not, or will not be, living: Act of 1995, s. 11(2)(d).

49.40.3 *"motion".* For motions, see Chap. 23.

[1] *Applications after decree relating to a section 11 order*
49.41.—[1] (1) An application after final decree for, or for the variation or recall of, a section 11 order other than a contact order shall be made by minute in the process of the action to which the application relates.
[2] (2) Where a minute has been lodged under paragraph (1), any party—
 (a) may apply by motion for any interim order which may be made pending the determination of the application; and

(b) shall intimate any such motion to every other party not less than 7 days before the date on which the motion is enrolled.

---

[1] R. 49.41(1) and heading amended by S.I. 1996 No. 2587 (effective 1st November 1996).
[2] R. 49.41(2) amended by S.I. 1996 No. 2587 (clerical error).

General note. In relation to parental rights, a party (*i.e.* person in the process: r. 1.3(1)) may **49.41.1** apply under this rule, as also may any person claiming interest: Children (Scotland) Act 1995, s.11(3)(a). On the meaning of "interest" under s.3(1) of the Law Reform (Parent and Child) (Scotland) Act 1986, see *D. v. Grampian R.C.* 1995 S.C.(H.L.) 1. The court's power is derived from s. 9(2) of the 1986 Act and s. 20(1) of the C.S.A. 1988.

"section 11 order other than a contact order". A section 11 order is an order under s. 11 of the **49.41.2** Children (Scotland) Act 1995. Under that section the court may make an order in relation to parental responsibilities (defined in s. 1), parental rights (defined in s. 2), guardianship and administration of a child's property. Without prejudice to that generality, the court may (a) make an order depriving a person of parental responsibilities or parental rights in respect of a child under 18, (b) make an order imposing such responsibilities or rights, (c) make a residence order in respect of a child under 16, (d) make a contact order in respect of a child under 16, (e) make a specific issue order in relation to the matter arising out of or in connection with a matter in (a) to (d), (f) grant interdict in relation to parental responsibilities, parental rights or the administration of property of a child under 18, (g) appoint a judicial factor in respect of a child under 18, or (h) appoint or remove a guardian of a child under 18.

"minute". On applications by minute, see r. 15.1. Apart from the provision for a fee due by a **49.41.3** person first entering the process, a court fee will be payable by a party on lodging a minute for variation of an order in a family action: see note 15.1.7.

"motion". For motions, see Chap. 23.   **49.41.4**

"intimate". For methods, see r. 16.7.   **49.41.5**

"party". See definition in r. 1.3(1).   **49.41.6**

[1] *Applications after decree relating to a contact order*
49.42.—[1] (1) An application after final decree for, or for the variation or recall of a contact order shall be made by motion in the process of the action to which the application relates.
(2) A motion under paragraph (1) shall—
(a) include a brief statement of the reasons for the order sought, and
(b) be intimated by registered post or the first class recorded delivery service to—
  (i) any person concerned or a solicitor known to be acting on behalf of that person, and
  (ii) where appropriate, the local authority concerned,
  not less than 14 days before the date on which the motion is enrolled.
(3) On enrolling a motion under paragraph (1), the applicant shall lodge in process—
(a) a copy of the letter of intimation; and
(b) the Post Office receipt or certificate of posting of that letter.
(4) At the hearing of a motion under paragraph (1), the court may order that the application be made by minute; and, in such a case, shall make an order for the lodging of answers to the minute in process within such period as it thinks fit.
(5) Where the court makes an order under paragraph (4), any party may apply by motion for an interim order pending the determination of the application.

Deriv. R.C.S. 1965, r. 170B(10) inserted by S.I. 1977 No. 1621 (r. 49.42(1) to (4))

---

[1] R. 49.42(1) amended by S.I. 1996 No. 2587 (effective 1st November 1996).

49.42.1　*General note.* In relation to parental rights, a party (*i.e.* a person in the process: r. 1.3(1)), may apply under this rule, as also may any person claiming interest: Children (Scotland) Act 1995, s. 11(3)(a). On the meaning of "interest" under s. 3(1) of the Law Reform (Parent and Child) (Scotland) Act 1986, see *D. v. Grampian R.C.* 1995 S.C.(H.L.) 1. The court's power is derived from s. 9(2) of the 1986 Act and s. 20(1) of the C.S.A. 1988.

49.42.2　*"contact order".* A contact order replaces access. It is an order regulating the arrangements for maintaining personal relations and direct contact between a child under 16 and a person with whom he is not, or will not be, living: Children (Scotland) Act 1995, s. 11(2)(d).

　　The test for variation of a contact order is the same as in seeking a contact order and is that laid down in *Sanderson v. McManus* 1997 S.C. (H.L.) 55: *Thomson v. Thomson*, 14th June 2000, unreported, 2000 G.W.D. 23–874 (First Div.).

49.42.3　*"motion".* For motions, see Chap. 23.

49.42.4　*"not less than 14 days before".* The first and last days are included in calculating the period so that there are 14 clear days.

49.42.5　*"lodge in process".* The copy letter of intimation of the motion and certificate of posting are lodged in process as productions. On lodging productions, see r. 4.5. Productions may be lodged by post: P.N. No. 4 of 1994, paras. 1 and 8; and see note 4.5.5.

49.42.6　*"minute".* On applications by minute, see r. 15.1. Apart from the provision for a fee due by a person first entering the process, a court fee will be payable by a party on lodging a minute for variation of an order in a consistorial cause: see note 15.1.7.

49.42.7　*"answers".* See r. 18.3.

49.42.8　*"party".* See definition in r. 1.3(1).

Applications after decree relating to aliment

49.43.—(1) An application after final decree for, or for the variation or recall of, an order for aliment for a child shall be made by motion in the process of the action to which the application relates.

(2) A motion under paragraph (1) shall—

(a) include a brief statement of the reasons for the order sought; and

(b) be intimated by registered post or the first class recorded delivery service to any person concerned or a solicitor known to be acting on behalf of that person, not less than 14 days before the date on which the motion is enrolled.

(3) On enrolling a motion under paragraph (1), the applicant shall lodge in process—

(a) a copy of the letter of intimation;

(b) the Post Office receipt or certificate of posting of that letter; and

(c) written evidence of the earnings or other income of the applicant or, if not employed, written evidence of that fact.

(4) At the hearing of a motion under paragraph (1), the court may order that the application be made by minute; and, in such a case, shall make an order for the lodging of answers to the minute in process within such period as the court thinks fit.

(5) Where the court makes an order under paragraph (4), any party—

(a) may apply by motion for an interim order pending the determination of the application; and

(b) shall give written intimation of any such motion to every other party not less than seven days before the date on which the motion is enrolled.

Deriv. R.C.S. 1965, r. 170B(10) inserted by S.I. 1977 No. 1621

49.43.1　*"final decree".* This is the decree disposing of the whole subject-matter of the cause including expenses: see note 4.15.2(2).

49.43.2　*"aliment".* See ss. 1 to 7 of the Family Law (Scotland) Act 1985.

　　Before an award of aliment can be varied or recalled by virtue of s. 5 of the 1985 Act the court has to be satisfied that there has been a material change of circumstances; and it is not a material change that the original award has been made on the basis of incomplete or inaccurate information: *Walker v. Walker* 1994 S.C. 482 applying *Stewart v. Stewart* 1987 S.L.T. 246.

An obligation of aliment is owed by a husband to his wife, a wife to her husband, a father or mother to his or her child and a person to a child (other than a child who has been boarded out to him by a local or public authority or voluntary organisation) who has been accepted by him as a child of the family: Family Law (Scotland) Act 1985, s. 1(1).

The obligation subsists until the child is 18 or, if the child is undergoing education at an educational establishment or training for a profession, trade or vocation, until the age of 25; and while under 18, aliment must be claimed on the child's behalf and not by the child: Act of 1985, s. 1. Both parents owe an obligation to aliment their child: Act of 1985, s. 1(1)(c); and see, *e.g. Howarth v. Howarth* 1990 S.L.T. 289. The obligation is to provide such support as is reasonable in the circumstances, having regard to the needs and resources of the parties, their earning capacities and all the circumstances of the case (subject to s. 4(3)): Act of 1985, ss. 1(2) and 4(1). The award may be backdated: Act of 1985, s. 3(1).

The court may order a party to provide details of his or her resources or those relating to a child: Act of 1985, s. 20.

The court has a very wide discretion in awarding interim aliment (which is provided for in s. 6(2) of the Act of 1985). Interim aliment is for the relief of need. An award may be reclaimed only with leave of the Lord Ordinary (r. 38.3(5)) unless the interlocutor contains an order not requiring leave. Interim aliment is determined on the basis of gross earnings not net earnings after tax: *MacInnes v. MacInnes* 1993 S.L.T. 1108.

As a general rule aliment is paid out of post-tax income, the payer receives no allowance for it and the recipient is not taxed on it: Income and Corporation Taxes Act 1988, s. 347A (inserted by s. 36(1) of the Finance Act 1988). An exception is provided for qualifying maintenance payments (*i.e.* a periodic payment under a court order by a party to the marriage to a child of the family) whereby a payer receives an allowance against his income by deducting such payments from his total income equal to the married couple's allowance: 1988 Act, s. 347B. It is not now, therefore, necessary or effective to make the payment payable to a parent as guardian of the child (see formerly *Huggins v. Huggins* 1981 S.L.T. 179). The small maintenance payment regime has also gone. For a discussion of the pre-, and post-, 1988 law, see Alan Barr "*A Vintage Year for Aliment*" 1989 S.L.T.(News) 57.

Variation or recall of a decree for aliment may only be made on a material change of circumstances: Act of 1985, s. 5(1). That incomplete or incorrect information was before the court on the previous occasion is not a change of circumstances: *Walker v. Walker* 1994 S.C. 482, 486F–H *obiter per* 2nd Div. The making of a maintenance assessment by the C.S.A. is a material change: Act of 1985, s. 5(1A). Interim aliment may be varied or recalled: Act of 1985, s. 6(4). The court has power to order repayment of aliment where a variation or recall of an award of aliment is made and backdated (Act of 1985, s. 5(4)) but has no such power where the award is of interim aliment (*McColl v. McColl* 1993 S.C. 276).

"*motion*". For motions, see Chap. 23. Apart from the provision for a fee due by a person first entering the process, a court fee will be payable by a party on lodging a minute for variation of an order in a consistorial cause: see note 23.2.18. **49.43.3**

"*lodge in process*". The copy letter of intimation of the motion and certificate of posting are lodged in process as productions. On lodging productions, see r. 4.5. Productions may be lodged by post: P.N. No. 4 of 1994, paras 1 and 8; and see note 4.5.5. **49.43.4**

"*minute*". On applications by minute, see r. 15.1. Apart from the provision for a fee due by a person first entering the process, a court fee will be payable by a party on lodging a minute for variation of an order in a family action: see note 15.1.7. **49.43.5**

"*answers*". See r. 18.3. **49.43.6**

"*party*". See definition in r. 1.3(1). **49.43.7**

Applications after decree by persons over 18 years for aliment

49.44.—(1) A person—

(a) to whom an obligation of aliment is owed under section 1 of the Act of 1985,

(b) in whose favour an order for aliment while under the age of 18 years was made in an action to which this Part applies, and

(c) who seeks, after attaining that age, an order for aliment against a person in that action against whom the order for aliment in his favour was made,

shall apply by minute in the process of that action.

(2) An application for interim aliment pending the determination of an application under paragraph (1) shall be made by motion.

(3) Where a decree has been pronounced in an application under paragraph (1) or (2), any application for variation or recall of any such decree shall be made by motion; and rule 49.43 (applications after decree relating to aliment) shall apply to a motion under this paragraph as it applies to a motion under that rule.

49.44.1   *General note.* The obligation to aliment a child exists after the child is 18 years old until the age of 25 if the child is undergoing instruction at an educational establishment or training for a profession, trade or vocation: Act of 1985, s. 1(5).

See further, note 49.43.2.

49.44.2   *"minute".* For applications by minute, see r. 15.1.

49.44.3   *"motion".* For motions, see Chap. 23.

PART V

ORDERS RELATING TO FINANCIAL PROVISION ETC.

Application and interpretation of this Part
49.45.—[1] This Part applies to an action of divorce, declarator of nullity of marriage, dissolution of a civil partnership, or declarator of nullity of a civil partnership.

(2) In this Part, "incidental order" has the meaning assigned in section 14(2) of the Act of 1985.

Deriv. R.C.S. 1965, r. 170D(11) inserted by S.I. 1986 No. 1231 (r. 49.45(1))

---

[1] Rule 49.45(1) substituted by S.S.I. 2005 No. 632 (effective 8th December 2005).

49.45.1   *General note.* For aliment in family actions other than an action of divorce or declarator of nullity of marriage, see Pt. VIII (rr. 49.54 to 49.57).

Applications in actions to which this Part applies
49.46.—(1) An application for an order mentioned in paragraph (2) shall be made—
(a) by a conclusion in the summons or defences, as the case may be, in an action to which this Part applies; or
(b) where the application is made by a person other than the pursuer or defender, by minute in that action.
(2) The orders referred to in paragraph (1) are—
(a) an order for financial provision within the meaning of section 8(3) of the Act of 1985;
(b) an order under section 16(1)(b) or (3) of the Act of 1985 (setting aside or varying agreement as to financial provision);
(c) an order under section 18 of the Act of 1985 (which relates to avoidance transactions); and
(d) an order under section 13 of the Act of 1981 (transfer or vesting of tenancy of a matrimonial home).
[1](e) an order under section 112 of the CP Act of 2004.

Deriv. R.C.S. 1965, r. 170D(1) and (2)(part) inserted by S.I. 1976 No. 1994 and amended by S.I. 1986 No. 1231; r. 170D(4)(a) substituted by S.I. 1977 No. 1621; r. 188D(4)(part) and (5)(part) inserted by S.I. 1982 No. 1381

---

[1] Rule 49.46(1)(e) inserted by S.S.I. 2005 No. 632 (effective 8th December 2005).

General note. It is permissible to add a conclusion "For such other order as the court may **49.46.1** consider appropriate." The reason for this is that it is not always possible to have a conclusion to meet every circumstance which may arise, particularly in relation to incidental orders relating to capital payments.

In the R.C.S. 1965, r. 156(2) expressly provided for such a conclusion but in Chap. 49 of the R.C.S. 1994 there is no convenient peg on which to have such a rule. It is not thought that a rule is a prerequisite.

General note. It is permissible to add a conclusion "For such other order as the court may **49.46.1** consider appropriate." The reason for this is that it is not always possible to have a conclusion to meet every circumstance which may arise, particularly in relation to incidental orders relating to capital payments.

In the R.C.S. 1965, r. 156(2) expressly provided for such a conclusion but in Chap. 49 of the R.C.S. 1994 there is no convenient peg on which to have such a rule. It is not thought that a rule is a prerequisite.

"summons". On form of summons, see r. 13.2.   **49.46.2**

"defences". On form of defences, see r. 18.1.   **49.46.3**

"minute". On applications by minute, see r. 15.1.   **49.46.4**

"order for financial provision within the meaning of section 8(3) of the Act of 1985". The orders **49.46.5** for financial provision defined in s. 8(3) of the Act of 1985 are those listed in s. 8(1), namely, capital sum (including a pension lump sum), transfer of property, periodical allowance, a pension sharing order, and an incidental order (defined in s. 14(2)). An order must be justified by the principles set out in s. 9 *and* reasonable having regard to the resources of the parties: Act of 1985, s. 8(2)(a) and (b). Both conditions must be satisfied: *Latter v. Latter* 1990 S.L.T. 805, 807F *per* Lord Marnoch; *Wallis v. Wallis* 1993 S.C.(H.L.) 49, 56C *per* Lord Jauncey of Tullichettle. There are restrictions in ss. 12 and 15.

The court of first instance is entitled to take a broad and practical approach as a matter of discretion: *Little v. Little* 1990 S.L.T. 785, 786K, 787D *per* L.P. Hope; *Peacock v. Peacock* 1993 S.C. 88, 92C *per* L.J.-C. Ross; *Jacques v. Jacques* 1995 S.C. 327. The discretion of the Lord Ordinary will only be interfered with by the Inner House if it can be shown that he misdirected himself in law, failed to take into account a relevant and material factor (or took into account an irrelevant factor) or reached a result which is manifestly inequitable or plainly wrong: *Gray v. Gray* 1968 S.C. 185, 193 *per* Lord Guthrie; *Little*, above, *per* L.P. Hope at p. 786K.

One of the principles in s. 9 is that the net value (as at the relevant date: s. 10(2)) of matrimonial property (defined in s. 10(4); and see *Mitchell v. Mitchell* 1994 S.C. 601) should be shared fairly (*i.e.* equally or in such other proportions as are justified by special circumstances: s. 10(1)). The relevant date is the earlier of the date on which the parties ceased to cohabit or the date of service of the summons: Act of 1985, s. 10(3). There is nothing in s. 10 of the Act of 1985 which requires an unequal division whenever special circumstances are found to exist; the court must determine, first, whether an event in s. 10(6) amounted to special circumstances and, secondly, if so, whether it justifies an unequal division: *Jacques v. Jacques* 1997 S.C.(H.L.) 20. By virtue of s. 16 of the Family Law (Scotland) Act 2006, in relation to orders for the transfer of property (s. 8(1)(aa) of the 1985 Act), the valuation date is not now the relevant date but the "appropriate valuation date" (i.e. the date the parties agree, failing which the date of the order or, in exceptional cases, such other date as the court may determine).

The net value of any property for the purposes of s. 10(2) of the Act of 1985 is the price a hypothetical willing purchaser would pay and a hypothetical willing seller receive for that property on a hypothetical sale at the (relevant) date in question; it is not constituted by that price less any costs, such as capital gains tax, that the seller would incur: *Sweeney v. Sweeney*, 2004 S.C. 372, S.L.T. 125 (Extra Div.)

In assessing the net value of matrimonial property at the relevant date after deduction of debts under s. 10(2) of the 1985 Act, the incidence of any capital gains tax or other contingent tax liability hypothetically incurred at the relevant date should not be deducted from the valuation of realizable assets: *Sweeney v. Sweeney,* 2004 S.C. 372 (Extra Div.). In *Sweeney v. Sweeney (No. 2),* 2006 S.C. 82, 90 paras. [20] and [21], it was held by the Extra Division that, although a contingent tax liability should not be brought into account by reducing the net value of the matrimonial home, it could be brought into account in determining the proportions in which matrimonial property would be shared fairly and in determining what was reasonable having regard to the parties' resources.

Nothing in the Act of 1985 justifies a division of the increase in the net value which has taken place at the time of the proof: *Wallis*, above. A change in the value of matrimonial property between the relevant date and the proof does not amount to special circumstances for the purposes of s. 10(1): *Wallis*, above, *per* Lord Keith of Kinkel at p. 55D (*obiter*); *Welsh v. Welsh* 1994 S.L.T. 828.

On the meaning and effect of s. 8(2) of the Act of 1985 (order reasonable having regard to parties' resources), see *Wallis*, above; *Welsh*, above, *per* Lord Osborne at p. 835L.

On payment of a capital sum out of a pension, at a present or future date, see *Bannon v. Bannon* 1993 S.L.T. 999; *McEwan v. McEwan* (Extra Div.), 29th August 1995, unreported, 1995 G.W.D. 31–1610.

S.12A of the Act of 1985 (inserted by s. 167(3) of the Pensions Act 1995) provides for orders for payment of pension lump sums. Under that section the court may order the trustees or managers of the pension scheme (to whom intimation must be made under r. 49.8(1)(l)) to pay a whole or part of the lump sum, when it becomes due, to the other party of the marriage. If the trustees or managers of the pension scheme do not enter the process, any order of the court would require to be intimated to them by order of the court.

A pension sharing order may be made, as from 1st December 2000, by virtue of s. 8(1)(baa) of the Act of 1985 inserted by s. 20(1) of the Welfare and Pensions Reform Act 1999. The order is one which provides that one party's shareable rights under a pension arrangement or shareable state scheme rights are made subject to pension sharing for the benefit of the other party to a specified percentage value or amount transferred to the other party: Act of 1985, s. 27(1) definition inserted by s. 20(3) of the 1999 Act. The mechanics are dealt with in Chaps.I and II of Pt.IV of the 1999 Act. The idea is to give the other spouse a pension that continues during the life of the recipient.

A widow's (or spouse's) prospective pension rights do not form part of the matrimonial property for the purpose of division: *Dible v. Dible* 1997 S.C. 134.

"Resources" under s. 27(1) of the Act of 1985 include prospective earnings: *Cunniff v. Cunniff* 1999 S.C. 537 (Extra Div.).

Pleadings should specify which of the principles in s. 9(1) of the Act of 1985 are being relied on: *Toye v. Toye* 1991 G.W.D. 32–1922. The pleas-in-law should not merely state that the party is "entitled", but that the orders sought are "justified by the principles in s. 9 and are reasonable having regard to the resources of the parties".

In the case of an order for transfer of property, the interlocutor must contain a sufficiently detailed description of the subject to be transferred to enable the necessary conveyance to be made and to distinguish the property from other property: *Walker v. Walker* 1991 S.L.T. 157.

The principles for the award of periodical allowance are set out in s. 13 of the Act of 1985. An award may be varied or recalled on a material change of circumstances: Act of 1985, s. 13(4). That incomplete or incorrect information was before the court on the previous occasion is not a change of circumstances: *Stewart v. Stewart* 1987 S.L.T. 246.

The loss of a right to aliment on divorce, even though aliment was not enforced after the separation, would itself be a hardship brought about by the divorce rather than by the separation and an award of periodical allowance was competent under s. 9(1)(e) of the Act of 1985: *Hangan v. Hangan* 1996 S.L.T. 321.

An incidental order under s. 14(2) of the Act of 1985 must be an order in connection with a financial provision; it does not include, *e.g.* a provision for security for educational expenses because an order for such would be alimentary: *Macdonald v. Macdonald* 1995 S.L.T. 72, 74D *per* Lord Caplan. An application for an incidental order must be ancillary to a claim for financial provision: *Demarco v. Demarco* 1990 S.C.L.R. 635, 638D *obiter per* Lord Cameron of Lochbroom; *MacClue v. MacClue* 1994 S.C.L.R. 933, 934F *per* Sheriff Principal Cox, Q.C., relying on *Reynolds v. Reynolds* 1991 S.C.L.R. 175, 176 *per* Sheriff Simpson. There does not, however, have to be an *order* to which an order under s. 14(2) is incidental; but the order under s. 14(2) must be aimed at financial provision, justified by the principles in s. 9 and be reasonable having regard to the resources of the parties: *Reynolds*, above.

The court may order a party to provide details of his or her resources: Act of 1985, s. 20.

49.46.6 *"an order under section 16(1)(b)"*. The court has power, (a) at any time after granting divorce, to set aside or vary an agreement relating to periodical allowance which expressly provided for it or (b) on granting divorce or within a specified period after that, to set aside or vary an agreement if the agreement was not fair and reasonable at the time it was entered into. In (a), the agreement must expressly state that the power is exercisable *by the court*: *Ellerby v. Ellerby* 1991 G.W.D. 15–936. In relation to (b), it is not possible to contract out of the right to apply to set aside or vary an agreement as to financial provision: Act of 1985, s. 16(4). In considering the issue of fairness and reasonableness, which has to be looked at in relation to the agreement as a whole, one has to look at all the circumstances; and the quality of legal advice available to a party might be a relevant factor: *Gillon v. Gillon (No. 1)* 1994 S.L.T. 978. The principles to be applied are summarised in *Gillon v. Gillon (No. 3)* 1995 S.L.T. 678.

49.46.7 *"an order under section 18"*. An application to set aside or vary a transaction or transfer involving property effected by the other party not more than five years before the claim for financial provision must be made not later than one year from the date that the claim was disposed of: Act of 1985, s. 18(1). The court must be satisfied that the transaction or transfer had the effect of or is likely to have the effect of defeating in whole or in part the claim for aliment or claim for, or for variation or recall of a decree for, financial provision: Act of 1985, s. 18(2). On the similar wording of the previous law in s. 6 of the Divorce (Scotland) Act 1976, see *Leslie v. Leslie* 1987 S.L.T. 232.

An order does not prejudice a third party (a) who has in good faith acquired the property or any rights in relation to it for value or (b) who derives title to it or rights from any person who has done so: Act of 1985, s. 18(3).

A third party who might be affected by such an order must be given an opportunity to be heard: *Harris v. Harris* 1988 S.L.T. 101.

Applications in depending actions relating to incidental orders

49.47.—(1) In an action depending before the court to which this Part applies—

(a) the pursuer or defender, notwithstanding rule 49.31(2) (application by defender for order for financial provision) and rule 49.46(1)(a) (application for order for financial provision in summons or defences), may apply by motion for an incidental order; and

(b) the court shall not be bound to determine such a motion if it considers that the application should properly be by a conclusion in the summons or defences, as the case may be.

(2) In an action depending before the court to which this Part applies, an application under section 14(4) of the Act of 1985 for the variation or recall of an incidental order shall be made by motion.

"depending". A cause is depending from the time it is commenced (*i.e.* from the time an action **49.47.1** is served) until final decree, whereas a cause is in dependence until final extract. For the meaning of commenced, see note 13.4.4. For the meaning of final decree, see note 4.15.2(2). For the meaning of final extract, see note 7.1.2(2).

"motion". For motions, see Chap. 23.   **49.47.2**

"incidental order". This is an order under s.14(2) of the Act of 1985. On incidental orders, see **49.47.3** note 49.46.5.

"section 14(4) of the Act of 1985". On incidental orders, see note 49.46.5.   **49.47.4**

Applications relating to interim aliment

49.48.—(1) An application for, or for the variation or recall of, an order for interim aliment for the pursuer or defender shall be made by motion.

(2) Written intimation of a motion under paragraph (1) shall be given not less than 7 days before the date on which the motion is enrolled.

Deriv. P.N. 13th November 1969, para. 1 (r. 49.48(2))

General note. The court has a very wide discretion in awarding interim aliment (which is **49.48.1** provided for in s.6(2) of the Family Law (Scotland) Act 1985). Interim aliment is for the relief of need.

An award of interim aliment may be varied or recalled: Act of 1985, s.6(4). A requirement of the common law is that there must be a material change of circumstances. An award may be varied or recalled on a material change of circumstances: Act of 1985, s.13(4). That incomplete or incorrect information was before the court on the previous occasion is not a change of circumstances: *Stewart v. Stewart* 1987 S.L.T. 246; *Walker v. Walker* 1994 S.C. 482, 486F–H *obiter per* 2nd Div.

An award of interim aliment may be reclaimed only with the leave of the Lord Ordinary (r. 38.3(5)) unless the interlocutor contains an order not requiring leave.

"motion". For motions, see Chap. 23.   **49.48.2**

"written intimation". For methods, see r. 16.9.   **49.48.3**

"not less than 7 days before". The first and last days are included in calculating the period so **49.48.4** that there are seven clear days.

Applications relating to orders for financial provision

49.49.—(1) An application—

(a) after final decree under any of the following provisions of the Act of 1985—

(i) section 8(1) for periodical allowance,

(ii) section 12(1)(b) (payment of capital sum or transfer of property),

(iii) section 12(4) (variation of date or method of payment of capital sum or date of transfer of property), or

      (iv) section 13(4) (variation, recall, backdating or conversion of
          periodical allowance), or
  (b) after the grant or refusal of an application under—
      (i) section 8(1) or 14(3) for an incidental order, or
      (ii) section 14(4) (variation or recall of incidental order),
shall be made by motion in the process of the action to which the
application relates.
  ¹ (2) Rule 49.43 (applications after decree relating to aliment) shall apply
to a motion under paragraph (1) of this rule as it applies to a motion under
that rule.
  ² (3) The application under—
  (a) paragraph (5) of section 12A of the Act of 1985 (recall or variation of
      order in respect of a pension lump sum), or
  (b) paragraph (7) of that section (variation of order in respect of pension
      lump sum to substitute person responsible for the pension arrange-
      ment),
shall be made by minute in the process of the action to which the application
relates.

Deriv. R.C.S. 1965, r. 170D(1) and (2)(part) inserted by S.I. 1976 No. 1994 and amended by S.I. 1986 No. 1231, r. 170D(7)(a) and (8) inserted by S.I. 1986 No. 1231 (r. 49.49(1) and (2))

---

[1] R. 49.49(2) amended by S.I. 1996 No. 1756 (effective 5th August 1996).
[2] R. 49.49(3) inserted by S.I. 1996 No. 1756 (effective 5th August 1996) and (3)(b) amended by S.S.I. 2000 No. 412 (effective 1st December 2000).

General note. On financial provision, see note 49.46.5. **49.49.1**

"final decree". This is the decree disposing of the whole subject-matter of the cause including **49.49.2**
expenses: see note 4.15.2(2).

"motion". For motions, see Chap. 23. Apart from the provision for a fee due by a person first **49.49.3**
entering the process, a court fee will be payable by a party on lodging a minute for variation of
an order in a family action: see note 23.2.18.

Section 12A of the Act of 1985. S. 12A of the Act of 1985 (inserted by s. 167(3) of the **49.49.4**
Pensions Act 1995) provides for orders for payment of pension lump sums. Where such an order
is made any person having an interest (*e.g.* the pension scheme trustees or managers) may apply
to the court for recall or variation of an order where the liability of the liable party has been
discharged in whole or in part other than by a payment by the trustees or managers under a
court order: s. 12A(5). It also enables application to the court for substitution of the pension
managers or trustees in circumstances where there has been a transfer or partial transfer of the
pension rights to a new pension scheme: s. 12A(7). In both cases, intimation will be required to
the recipient.
The application by minute will have to be served on other interested parties. If the trustees or
managers do not become parties, any order will have to be intimated to them by order of the
court.

"minute". On applications by minute, see r. 15.1. **49.49.5**

Variation of periodical allowance. For variation there must be a material change of **49.49.6**
circumstances: Act of 1985, s.13(4). The starting point is to assume that the original order was
correct and to consider whether the change of circumstances justifies a variation: *Macpherson v.*
Macpherson, 1989 S.L.T. 231, 235A-B *per* LJ-C Ross. To discover that the information before
the court when the original order was made is not a material change of circumstances: *Stewart v.*
Stewart, 1987 S.L.T. 246 (OH).
There is no statutory power for the court to vary post-decree agreements. In such an
agreement it is important to be clear whether the decree is superseded by the agreement,
otherwise the decree could be varied. That this could occur arose in *McDonnell v. McDonnell,*
2001 S.C. 877 (Extra Div.), an unsatisfactory decision in many ways as, though it was held that
the decree could be varied, the agreement was unaffected by the variation. One method adopted
in post-decree agreements, to invoke the power for variation s.7(2) of the Act of 1985 over
agreements on aliment, is to treat the variation of periodical allowance as (a variation of)
aliment for a child (if there is one).

Applications after decree relating to agreements or avoidance transactions
49.50. An application for an order—
   (a) under section 16(1)(a) or (3) of the Act of 1985 (setting aside or
       varying agreement as to financial provision), or
   (b) under section 18 of the Act of 1985 (which relates to avoidance
       transactions),
made after final decree shall be made by minute in the process of the action
to which the application relates.

Deriv. R.C.S. 1965, r. 170D(7)(c) inserted by S.I. 1986 No. 1231

General note. It is not possible to contract out of the right to apply for an order to set aside or **49.50.1**
vary an agreement as to financial provision: Family Law (Scotland) Act 1985, s. 16(4).
For applications in family actions other than an action of divorce or declarator of nullity of
marriage, see r. 49.51.
On setting aside or variation of agreements (s. 16 of the Act of 1985), see note 49.46.6. On
avoidance transactions, see note 49.46.7.

"final decree". This is the decree disposing of the whole subject-matter of the cause including **49.50.2**
expenses: see note 4.15.2(2).

"minute". For applications by minute, see r. 15.1. **49.50.3**

Release 64: March 2002

PART VI

APPLICATIONS RELATING TO AVOIDANCE TRANSACTIONS

Form of applications relating to avoidance transactions
49.51.—(1) An application for an order under section 18 of the Act of 1985 (which relates to avoidance transactions) by a party to a family action shall be made by including in the summons, defences or minute, as the case may be, appropriate conclusions, averments and pleas-in-law.

(2) An application for an order under section 18 of the Act of 1985 after final decree in a family action, shall be made by minute in the process of the action to which the application relates.

Deriv. R.C.S. 1965, r. 170D(4)(a) substituted by S.I. 1977 No. 1621 and amended by S.I. 1986 No. 1231 (r. 49.51(1)); r. 170D(7)(c) inserted by S.I. 1986 No. 1231 (r. 49.51(2))

49.51.1   *General note.* An application, to set aside or vary a transaction or transfer involving property effected by the other party not more than five years before the claim for financial provision, must be made not later than one year from the date that the claim was disposed of: Act of 1985, s. 18(1). The court must be satisfied that the transaction or transfer had the effect of or is likely to have the effect of defeating in whole or in part the claim for aliment or claim for, or for variation or recall of a decree for, financial provision: Act of 1985, s. 18(2). On the similar wording of the previous law in s. 6 of the Divorce (Scotland) Act 1976, see *Leslie v. Leslie* 1987 S.L.T. 232.

An order does not prejudice a third party (a) who has in good faith acquired the property or any rights in relation to it for value or (b) who derives title to it or rights from any person who has done so: Act of 1985, s. 18(3).

A third party, who may be affected by an order under s. 18 of the Family Law (Scotland) Act 1985 to set aside or vary a transaction involving property, has a right to be heard: *Harris v. Harris* 1988 S.L.T. 101.

For applications in actions of divorce or declarator of nullity of marriage, see r. 49.50.

49.51.2   *"summons".* On form of summons, see r. 13.2.

49.51.3   *"defences".* On form of defences, see r. 18.1.

49.51.4   *"minute".* On applications by minute, see r. 15.1.

49.51.5   *"final decree".* This is the decree disposing of the whole subject-matter of the cause including expenses: see note 4.15.2(2).

PART VII

FINANCIAL PROVISION AFTER OVERSEAS DIVORCE OR ANNULMENT

Interpretation of this Part
49.52. In this Part—
  "the Act of 1984" means the Matrimonial and Family Proceedings Act 1984;
  "order for financial provision" has the meaning assigned in section 30(1) of the Act of 1984;
  "overseas country" has the meaning assigned in section 30(1) of the Act of 1984.

Applications for financial provision after overseas divorce or annulment
49.53.—(1) An application under section 28 of the Act of 1984 for an order for financial provision after a divorce or annulment in an overseas country shall be made by summons.

(2) An application for an order in an action to which paragraph (1) applies—
  (a) made before or after final decree under—
    (i) section 13 of the Act of 1981 (transfer of tenancy of matrimonial home),

   (ii) section 29(4) of the Act of 1984 for interim periodical allowance, or

   (iii) section 14(4) of the Act of 1985 (variation or recall of an incidental order), or

  (b) made after final decree under—

   (i) section 12(4) of the Act of 1985 (variation of date or method of payment of capital sum or date of transfer of property),

   (ii) section 13(4) of the Act of 1985 (variation, recall, backdating or conversion of periodical allowance), or

   (iii) section 14(4) of the Act of 1985 (variation or recall of incidental order),

shall be made by motion.

[1] (3) Rule 49.43 (applications after decree relating to aliment) shall apply to a motion under paragraph (2) of this rule as it applies to a motion under that rule.

[2] (4) An application under—

  (a) paragraph (5) of section 12A of the Act of 1985 (recall or variation of order in respect of a pension lump sum), or

  (b) paragraph (7) of that section (variation of order in respect of pension lump sum to substitute person responsible for the pension arrangement),

shall be made by minute in the process of the motion to which the application relates.

Deriv. R.C.S. 1965, r. 170M inserted by S.I. 1986 No. 1231

---

[1] R. 49.53(3) amended by S.I. 1996 No. 1756 (effective 5th August 1996).
[2] R. 49.53(4) inserted by S.I. 1996 No. 1756 (effective 5th August 1996 and (4)(b) amended by S.S.I. 2000 No. 412 (effective 1st December 2000).

General note. The Family Law Act 1986 contains provisions for the recognition in Scotland of **49.53.1** divorces obtained elsewhere in the British Islands and furth of the British Islands. A divorce, annulment or separation by a court of civil jurisdiction (subject to two exceptions) within the British Islands (*i.e.* the UK, Channel Islands and Isle of Man: Interpretation Act 1978, Sched. 1) is recognised throughout the UK. An overseas divorce (*i.e.* one obtained outside the British Islands) by a court or by other means is recognised if it satisfies certain conditions.

  Certain ancillary orders of an overseas divorce may be enforceable here, *e.g.* under the Foreign Judgments (Reciprocal Enforcement) Act 1933, the Maintenance Orders (Reciprocal Enforcement) Act 1972, the C.J.J.A. 1982 or the Council Regulation (E.C.) No. 2201/2003 of 27th November 2003 (new Brussels II) which replaced the Council Regulation (EC) No. 1347/2000 of 29th May 2000 (Brussels II) which applies between member states of the E.U. The Court of Session may, however, be able to make an order for financial provision following an overseas divorce under Pt. IV of the Matrimonial and Family Proceedings Act 1984. There are jurisdictional requirements including that the applicant is domiciled or habitually resident in Scotland and that the other party to the marriage is or must have been domiciled here when they last lived together or owns or is the tenant of property in Scotland which had been the matrimonial home: Act of 1984, s. 28(2).

  The orders which the court may make are any one or more of the orders in s. 8(1) of the Act of 1985 (capital sum, transfer of property, periodical allowance or incidental order) or an order under s. 13 of the Act of 1981 (transfer of tenancy of matrimonial home): Act of 1984, s. 30(1). For a recent example, see *Tahir v. Tahir (No. 2)* 1995 S.L.T. 451.

"summons". On form of summons, see r. 13.2.   **49.53.2**

"final decree". This is the decree disposing of the whole subject-matter of the cause including **49.53.3** expenses: see note 4.15.2(2).

"motion". For motions, see Chap. 23.   **49.53.4**

[1] PART VIIA

FINANCIAL PROVISION AFTER OVERSEAS DISSOLUTION OR ANNULMENT OF A CIVIL PARTNERSHIP

Interpretation of this Part
[1] **49.53A.** In this Part—
"order for financial provision" has the meaning given in paragraph 4 of Part 4 of Schedule 11 to the CP Act of 2004;
"overseas proceedings" means proceedings in a country or territory outside the British Islands.

---

[1] Part VIIA and r. 49.53A inserted by S.S.I. 2005 No. 632 (effective 8th December 2005).

Applications for financial provision after overseas dissolution or annulment of civil partnership
[1] **49.53B.**—(1) An application under paragraph 2 of Schedule 11 to the CP Act of 2004 for an order for financial provision after a dissolution or annulment of a civil partnership in overseas proceedings shall be made by summons

(2) An application for an order in an action to which paragraph (1) applies—
(a) made before or after final decree under—
(i) section 112 of the CP Act of 2004 (transfer of tenancy of family home);
(ii) paragraph 3(4) of Schedule 11 to the CP Act of 2004 (interim periodical allowance);
(iii) section 14(4) of the Act of 1985 (variation or recall of an incidental order); or
(b) made after final decree under—
(i) section 12(4) of the Act of 1985 (variation of date or method of payment of capital sum of date of transfer of property);
(ii) section 13(4) of the Act of 1985 (variation, recall, backdating or conversion of periodical allowance); or
(iii) section 14(4) of the Act of 1985 (variation or recall of incidental orders);
shall be made by motion.
(3) Rule 49.43 (applications after decree relating to aliment) shall apply to a motion under paragraph (2) of this rule as it applies to a motion under that rule.
(4) An application under—
(a) paragraph (5) of section 12A of the Act of 1985 (recall or variation of order in respect of a pension lump sum); or
(b) paragraph (7) of that section (variation of order in respect of pension lump sum to substitute person responsible for the pension arrangement);
shall be made by minute in the process of the motion to which the application relates.

---

[1] Rule 49.53B inserted by S.S.I. 2005 No. 632 (effective 8th December 2005).

49.53B.1   *General note.* Chap. 3 of Pt. 5 of the Civil Partnership Act 2004 contains provisions for the recognition of overseas civil partnerships.

49.53B.2   *"summons".* On the form of a summons, see r. 13.2.

49.53B.3   *"motion".* For motions, see Chap. 23.

PART VIII

ACTIONS OF ALIMENT

Interpretation of this Part
49.54. In this Part, "action of aliment" means a claim for aliment under section 2(1) of the Act of 1985.

General note. The court may entertain a claim for aliment (1) in an action for aliment or (2) in **49.54.1** proceedings (a) for divorce, separation, declarator of marriage or declarator of nullity of marriage, (b) relating to orders for financial provision, (c) concerning rights and obligations relating to children, (d) concerning parentage or legitimacy and (e) of any other kind where the court considers it appropriate: Family Law (Scotland) Act 1985, s. 2(1) and (2).

A claim for interim aliment may be sought in an action of aliment: Family Law (Scotland) Act 1985, s. 6(1).

Jurisdiction. The jurisdiction of the court will depend on the jurisdiction to entertain the **49.54.2** proceedings in which the claim for aliment is made.

Jurisdiction in an action for aliment alone depends on the C.J.J.A. 1982, Sched. 8, r. 1 (defender's domicile in Scotland), r. 2(1) (personal citation), r. 2(2) obligation in contract to be performed in Scotland), r. 2(5) (domicile or habitual residence of pursuer in an action relating to maintenance), r. 2(8) (where defender not domiciled in UK has moveable property which has been arrested, or has immoveable property, here). Where a person is domiciled in a Brussels or Lugano Convention country or elsewhere in the UK, jurisdiction is on the grounds of domicile of defender, contract or domicile or habitual residence of pursuer in an action relating to maintenance: C.J.J.A. 1982, Scheds. 1, 3C and 4, Arts. 2 and 5(1) and (2). See further, notes 13.2.8 to 13.2.15.

Jurisdiction with respect to aliment (including variation and recall) in an action of divorce, separation, declarator of marriage or declarator of nullity of marriage will arise if the court has jurisdiction to determine that action: Domicile and Matrimonial Proceedings Act 1973, s. 10 and Sched. 2, para. 2A; C.J.J.A. 1982, Scheds. 1, 3C and 4, Art. 5(2) if ancillary to proceedings concerning status in the court which according to its own law has jurisdiction to entertain those proceedings; the Council Regulation (E.C.) No. 2201/2003 of 27th November 2003 (new Brussels II) which replaced and the Council Regulation (EC) No. 1347/2000 of 29th May 2000 (Brussels II) which applies between member states of the E.U.: see note 49.2.1. But the court will not have jurisdiction to entertain the ancillary application if the court is exercising a jurisdiction by virtue of Art. 2 of the Council Regulation and the making or variation of the order in consequence of the application would contravene Art. 7 (exclusive jurisdiction of member state of habitual residence, etc., of the defender): 1973 Act, s. 10(1B) inserted by the European Communities (Matrimonial Jurisdiction and Judgments) (Scotland) Regulations 2001 (S.S.I. 2001 No. 36) and amended by the European Communities (Matrimonial and Parental Responsibility and Judgments) (Scotland) Regulations 2005 [S.S.I. 2005 No. 42]. The court's jurisdiction to entertain those proceedings is dealt with in s. 7 of the 1973 Act: see note 49.2.1.

Undefended actions of aliment
49.55.—(1) Where a motion for decree in absence is enrolled in an action of aliment, the pursuer shall, on enrolling the motion, lodge all documentary evidence of the means of the parties available to him in support of the amount of aliment sought.

(2) Where the court requires any appearance for the pursuer, the cause shall be put out for hearing on the Motion Roll.

Deriv. R.C.S. 1965, r. 170N inserted by S.I. 1986 No. 1231

"motion". For motions, see Chap. 23. Wage certificates etc. may be sent by fax: Direction No. **49.55.1** 3 of 1994.

"decree in absence". See Chap. 19. **49.55.2**

Applications relating to aliment
49.56.—(1) An application for, or for the variation of, an order for interim aliment in an action of aliment depending before the court shall be made by motion.

(2) Written intimation of a motion under paragraph (1) shall be given not less than seven days before the date on which the motion is enrolled.

(3) An application after final decree for the variation or recall of an order for aliment in an action of aliment shall be made by motion; and rule 49.43 (applications after decree relating to aliment) shall apply to a motion under this paragraph as it applies to a motion under that rule.

(4) A person—

    (a) to whom an obligation of aliment is owed under section 1 of the Act of 1985,

    (b) in whose favour an order for aliment while made under the age of 18 years was made in an action of aliment, or

    (c) who seeks, after attaining that age, an order for aliment against the person in that action against whom the order for aliment in his favour was made,

shall apply by minute in the process of that action.

(5) An application for interim aliment pending the determination of an application under paragraph (4) shall be made by motion.

(6) Where a decree has been pronounced in an application under paragraph (3) or (4), any application for variation or recall of any such decree shall be made by motion; and rule 49.43 (applications after decree relating to aliment) shall apply to a motion under this paragraph as it applies to a motion under that rule.

Deriv. R.C.S. 1965, r. 170P inserted by S.I. 1986 No. 1231

49.56.1   *General note.* An obligation of aliment is owed by a husband to his wife, a wife to her husband, a father or mother to his or her child and a person to a child (other than a child who has been boarded out to him by a local or public authority or voluntary organisation) who has been accepted by him as a child of the family: Family Law (Scotland) Act 1985, s. 1(1).

The obligation subsists until the child is 18 or, if the child is undergoing education at an educational establishment or training for a profession, trade or vocation, until the age of 25; and while under 18, aliment must be claimed on the child's behalf and not by the child: Act of 1985, s. 1. Both parents owe an obligation to aliment their child: Act of 1985, s. 1(1)(c); and see, *e.g. Howarth v. Howarth* 1990 S.L.T. 289. The obligation is to provide such support as is reasonable in the circumstances, having regard to the needs and resources of the parties, their earning capacities and all the circumstances of the case (subject to s. 4(3)): Act of 1985, s. 1(2) and 4(1). The award may be backdated: Act of 1985, s. 3(1).

The court may order a party to provide details of his or her resources or those relating to a child: Act of 1985, s. 20.

The court has a very wide discretion in awarding interim aliment (which is provided for in s. 6(2) of the Act of 1985). Interim aliment is for the relief of need. An award may be reclaimed only with leave of the Lord Ordinary (r. 38.3(5)) unless the interlocutor contains an order not requiring leave. Interim aliment is determined on the basis of gross earnings, not net earnings after tax: *MacInnes v. MacInnes* 1993 S.L.T. 1108.

As a general rule aliment is paid out of post-tax income, the payer receives no allowance for it and the recipient is not taxed on it: Income and Corporation Taxes Act 1988, s. 347A (inserted by s. 36(1) of the Finance Act 1988). An exception is provided for qualifying maintenance payments (*i.e.* a periodic payment under a court order by a party to the marriage to a child of the family) whereby a payer receives an allowance against his income by deducting such payments from his total income equal to the married couple's allowance: 1988 Act, s. 347B. It is not now, therefore, necessary or effective to make the payment payable to a parent as guardian of the child (see formerly *Huggins v. Huggins* 1981 S.L.T. 179). The small maintenance payment regime has also gone. For discussion of the pre-, and post-, 1988 law, see Alan Barr *"A Vintage Year for Aliment"* 1989 S.L.T.(News) 57.

The court's power to deal with aliment is now restricted. Where the Child Support Agency has jurisdiction, the court may nonetheless have jurisdiction to make a maintenance order including a maintenance order to top up child support maintenance and orders to meet expenses of education and training, to meet expenses attributable to a disability or where the order is to be made against a person with care of the child: Child Support Act 1991, s. 8. An order may be made where the Child Support Agency does not have jurisdiction, *i.e.* where the child, parent with care or absent parent is not habitually resident in the U.K. or the child is not a qualifying child within the meaning of s. 3 of the 1991 Act. The court retains jurisdiction (even though a child support officer has jurisdiction) to make a maintenance order where a written agreement (whether or not enforceable) provides for an absent parent to make periodic payments to or for the child and the maintenance order made by the court is in all material respects in the same terms as that agreement: Child Support (Written Agreements) (Scotland) Order 1997 [S.I. 1997 No. 2943]. The court retains jurisdiction during the transitional period (5th March 1993 to 6th April 1997), where a maintenance provision already exists, to deal with applications for variation of such provision whether under order of the court or a maintenance agreement until a child maintenance assessment is made, or to deal with a conclusion for aliment in a pending action: Child Support Act 1991 (Commencement No. 3 and Transitional Provisions) Amendment Order 1992 [S.I. 1992 No. 2644].

A maintenance agreement for less than could be awarded under a maintenance assessment will be insecure because an application to the Child Support Agency for a maintenance assessment cannot be prevented: 1991 Act, s. 9.

"motion". For motions, see Chap. 23. **49.56.2**

"minute". For applications by minute, see r. 15.1. **49.56.3**

Variation or recall of aliment. Before an award of aliment can be varied or recalled by virtue **49.56.4** of s. 5 of the Family Law (Scotland) Act 1985 the court has to be satisfied that there has been a material change of circumstances; and it is not a material change that the original award has been made on the basis of incomplete or inaccurate information: *Walker v. Walker* 1994 S.C. 482, 486H *obiter per* 2nd Div. applying *Stewart v. Stewart* 1987 S.L.T. 246. The making of a maintenance assessment by the C.S.A. is a material change: Act of 1985, s. 5(1A).

Interim aliment may be varied or recalled: Act of 1985, s. 6(4).

The court has power to order repayment of aliment where a variation or recall of an award of aliment is made and backdated (Act of 1985, s. 5(4)) but has no such power where the award is of interim aliment: *McColl v. McColl* 1993 S.C. 276.

Applications relating to agreements on aliment

49.57. An application under section 7(2) of the Act of 1985 (variation or termination of agreement on aliment) shall be made by summons or in defences in a family action, as the case may be.

Deriv. R.C.S. 1965, r. 170R inserted by SI 1096/1231

General note. A provision in an agreement which purports to exclude future liability for **49.57.1** aliment or to restrict any right to bring an action for aliment has no effect unless it was fair and reasonable in all the circumstances at the time the agreement was made: Act of 1985, s. 7(1). If the agreement will terminate on the granting of divorce, an application for variation of the agreement in a divorce action is misconceived (*Mackenzie v. Mackenzie* 1987 S.C.L.R. 671) unless, perhaps, interim aliment is sought.

An application under s. 7(2) of the Act of 1985 may be made only in respect of an obligation created by s. 1(1) of that Act and cannot be invoked where a couple are merely cohabiting or have been divorced: *Drummond v. Drummond* 1995 S.C. 321. Variation or termination of an agreement on aliment may be made on a material change of circumstances: Act of 1985, s. 7(2). The making of a maintenance assessment in respect of a child is a material change of circumstances: Act of 1985, s. 7(2A).

The court has no power to backdate a variation: *Ellerby v. Ellerby* 1991 G.W.D. 15–936.

The power to vary an agreement relating to aliment of a child is restricted: Child Support Act 1991, s. 9(5).

Jurisdiction. The court has jurisdiction to entertain an application under s. 7(2) of the Act of **49.57.2** 1985 if it would have jurisdiction to entertain an action for aliment between the parties to the agreement: Act of 1985, s. 7(5).

On jurisdiction in an action for aliment, see note 49.54.2.

PART IX

[1] APPLICATIONS FOR ORDERS UNDER SECTION 11 OF THE CHILDREN (SCOTLAND) ACT 1995

Application of this Part

[2] **49.58.** This Part applies to an application for a section 11 order in a family action other than in an action of divorce, separation, declarator of nullity of marriage, dissolution of a civil partnership, separation of civil partners, or declarator of nullity of a civil partnership.

C 434   *Family Actions (Chap. 49)*

Deriv. R.C.S. 1965, r. 260C(1) inserted by S.I. 1986 No. 515

---

[1] Cross-heading to Pt. IX substituted by S.I. 1996 No. 2587 (effective 1st November 1996).
[2] Rule 49.58 substituted by S.S.I. 2005 No. 632 (effective 8th December 2005).

49.58.1   *General note.* For applications for section 11 orders in actions of divorce, separation or declarator of nullity of marriage, see Pt. IV (rr. 49.35 to 49.42).

49.58.2   *Jurisdiction.* The jurisdiction of the court in a family action other than an action of divorce, separation or declarator of marriage is determined, in relation to residence, custody, care or control of a child, contact with or access to (but not guardianship of a child), by ss. 9 (habitual residence), 10 (presence of child), 12 (emergency) and 15(2) (original order granted by court) of the Family Law Act 1986 except where the Council Regulation (E.C.) No. 2201/2003 of 27th November 2003 (new Brussels II) which replaced the Council Regulation (EC) No. 1347/2000 of 29th May 2000 (Brussels II) applies (it applies between member states of the E.U.). The pre-eminent ground in such proceedings is habitual residence, on the meaning of which see *Dickson v. Dickson* 1990 S.C.L.R. 692 (1st Div.); *Rellis v. Hart* 1993 S.L.T. 738; *Scullion v. Scullion* 1990 S.C.L.R. 577, 581A *per* Sheriff Stoddart.

     An order under s. 11(1) of the 1985 Act may not be made by the court where (a) the court is exercising a jurisdiction in proceedings by virtue of Art. 3 of the Council Regulation and (b) the making of such an order would contravene Art. 6 of the Council Regulation (exclusive jurisdiction of member state of habitual residence, etc., of the defender): 1995 Act, s. 11(1A). The Council Regulation applies to matrimonial matters and matters of parental responsibility for the children of both spouses. Under Art. 6, a spouse, who is (a) habitually resident in the territory of a member state of the E.U. or is a national of a member state or (b) in the case of U.K. or Ireland has his domicile in that state, may be sued in another member state only in accordance with Arts 3–5 of the Council Regulation.

49.58.3   *"section 11 order"*. See note 49.1.2.

---

[1] *Form of applications relating to section 11 orders*
     [1] **49.59.** Subject to any other provision in this Chapter, an application for a section 11 order shall be made—
     (a) by a section 11 order;
     (b) by a conclusion in the summons or defences, as the case may be, in any other family action to which this Part applies; or
     (c) where the application is made by a person other than a party to an action mentioned in paragraph (a) or (b), by minute in that action.

---

[1] R. 49.59 and heading amended by S.I. 1996 No. 2587 (effective 1st November 1996).

49.59.1   *"section 11 order"*. See note 49.1.2.

     Any person claiming an interest may apply for an order relating to parental rights: Children (Scotland) Act 1995, s. 11(3)(a). On the meaning of "interest" under s. 3(1) of the Law Reform (Parent and Child) (Scotland) Act 1986, see *D. v. Grampian R.C.* 1995 S.C.(H.L.) 1. In any proceedings for a section 11 order the court shall regard the welfare of the child as the paramount consideration and shall not make any order unless it would be better for the child that an order be made than that none be made and having regard to the views expressed by the child: Act of 1995, s. 11(7).

     A mother always has parental responsibilities and parental rights in relation to her child; a father has them only if he is married to the child's mother or was married to her at the time of or after the child's conception: Act of 1995, s. 3(1). The right to parental responsibilities is subject to what is in the best interests of the child: Act of 1995, s. 1(1).

     The advantage to a very young child of being with its mother is a consideration which has to be taken into account in deciding where its best interests lie but which will yield to competing advantages which more effectively promote the welfare of the child: *Brixey v. Lynas* 1997 S.C.(H.L.) 1.

     In relation to a contact order, where a person has parental rights, it is not required to aver in detail the basis on which contact is sought: *O. v. O.* 1995 S.L.T. 238. It should be noted that a parent does not have an absolute right to contact with his or her child. He or she is only entitled to contact if the court is satisfied that it is in the best interests of the child: *Porchetta v. Porchetta* 1986 S.L.T. 105; and see now the Act of 1995, s. 11(7). In *Sanderson v. McManus* 1996 S.L.T. 751, the majority in the Extra Division held that (1) s. 3(2) of the Law Reform (Parent and

Child) (Scotland) Act 1996 (see now s. 11(7) of the Act of 1995) sets out the only test; (2) the child's father if not married to its mother does not have parental rights; (3) there is no "right" in a parent to access; and (4) although the parent-child relationship may have intrinsic value, and the status quo should be preserved (*Brixey v. Lynas*, 1994 S.C. 606), these are not propositions of law capable of being determinative but are simply factors which may or may not be significant. Lord McCluskey, dissenting, took the view that the "traditional approach" that the link between a child and his natural parent would be conducive to the child's welfare or should be preserved unless there were strong reasons to the contrary (*Blance v. Blance* 1978 S.L.T. 74; *Brannigan v. Brannigan* 1979 S.L.T.(Notes) 73) was not altered by s. 3(2) of the 1986 Act or *Porchetta*, above.) The majority opinion in *Sanderson*, above was upheld in the House of Lords in 1997 S.L.T. 629. Lord Hope of Craighead stated at p. 634E that the party who seeks the order (for contact or residence) must show on a balance of probabilities, that the welfare of the child requires that the order be made in the child's best interests. In *White v. White*, 2001 S.C. 689 it was held that the court required to have regard to the welfare of the child as its paramount consideration and will generally consider that it is conducive to the welfare of children if the absent parents maintain personal relations and direct contact on a regular basis (see also Lord Hope of Craighead in *Sanderson*, above). There is, however, no legal onus on the person seeking a contact order, the court simply considers all the relevant material and decides what is conducive to the child's welfare: *White*, above, *per* L.P. Rodger at p. 698H.

The parent having a residence order does not fulfil his or her obligations where a contact order is awarded by leaving it to the child to decide whether to go or not; that parent must encourage and persuade, although not physically coerce, the child to accept contact by the other parent (*Blance*, above, *per* Lord Stewart at p. 75).

In an action of divorce, separation or nullity of marriage the court must consider whether to make a section 11 order or a reference to the Principal Reporter; and where it is of the opinion that such action may be required, or that it is not in a position to take such action without further consideration, or that it is not desirable in the interests of the child to grant decree until it is in a position to do so, it shall postpone its decision to grant decree: Act of 1995, s. 12(1).

It is not appropriate to dispose of an appeal for parental rights solely on the pleadings: *O.*, above.

"summons". On form of summons, see r. 13.2.   **49.59.2**

"defences". On form of defences, see r. 18.1.   **49.59.3**

"minute". On applications by minute, see r. 15.1.   **49.59.4**

Defenders in actions for a section 11 order

[1] **49.60.** In an action for a section 11 order, the pursuer shall call as a defender—

(a) the parents or other parent of the child in respect of whom the order is sought;

(b) any guardian of the child;

(c) any person who has treated the child as a child of his family;

(d) any person who in fact exercises care or control in respect of the child; and

(e) in any case where there is no person falling within paragraphs (a) to (d), the Lord Advocate.

---

[1] R. 49.60 amended by S.I. 1996 No. 2587 (effective 1st November 1996).

General note. Rule 49.60(e), which provided for calling the Lord Advocate as a defender   **49.60.1**
where there was no one in the other paragraphs to call, was revoked by A.S. (R.C.S.A.) (Miscellaneous) 1998 [S.I. 1998 No. 890]. Paragraph (e) had been inserted at the suggestion of the Rules Review Group in case there was no one else to call as a defender. Such a situation was rather remote. It had been thought such an event might arise, *e.g.* where a sole surviving parent required a formal order for immigration purposes. The court might subsequently require intimation to the local authority in whose area the child resides.

"section 11 order". See note 49.1.2.   **49.60.2**

Applications relating to interim orders in depending actions

49.61.—[1] (1) An application, in an action depending before the court to which this Part applies, for, or for the variation or recall of, an interim residence order or an interim contact order shall be made by motion.

(2) Written intimation of a motion under paragraph (1) shall be given not less than 7 days before the date on which the motion is enrolled.

Deriv. P.N. 13th November 1969, para. 1 (r. 49.61(2))

---

[1] R. 49.61(1) amended by S.I. 1996 No. 2587 (effective 1st November 1996).

49.61.1   *"depending"*. A cause is depending until final decree, whereas a cause is in dependence until final extract. For the meaning of final decree, see note 4.15.2(2). For the meaning of final extract, see note 7.1.2(2).

49.61.2   *Residence and contact orders*. A residence order replaces, but is not the whole of, what was formerly custody. It means an order regulating arrangements as to with whom or with whom during what periods a child under 16 is to live: Children (Scotland) Act 1995, s. 11(2)(c).

A contact order replaces access. It is an order regulating the arrangements for maintaining personal relations and direct contact between a child under 16 and a person with whom he is not, or will not be, living: Act of 1995, s. 11(2)(d).

49.61.3   *"motion"*. For motions, see Chap. 23.

49.61.4   *"written intimation"*. For methods, see r. 16.9.

49.61.5   *"not less than 7 days before"*. The first and last days are included in calculating the period so that there are seven clear days.

Care and supervision by local authorities
49.62. [*Revoked by S.I. 1996 No. 2587 (effective 1st November 1996).*]

Applications after decree
49.63.—[1] (1) An application after final decree for the variation or recall of a section 11 order other than a contact order shall be made by minute in the process of the action to which it relates.

(2) Where a minute has been lodged under paragraph (1), any party—
  (a) may apply by motion for an interim order pending the determination of the application; and
  (b) shall intimate such a motion to every other party not less than seven days before the date on which the motion is enrolled.

[1] (3) An application after final decree for, or for the variation or recall of, a contact order shall be made by motion; and rule 49.43 (applications after decree relating to aliment) shall apply to a motion under this paragraph as it applies to a motion under that rule.

Deriv. R.C.S. 1965, r. 260E(1)(b) inserted by S.I. 1986 No. 515

49.63.1   [1] R. 49.63(1) and (3) amended by S.I. 1996 No. 2587 (effective 1st November 1996).

"section 11 order". See note 49.1.2.

49.63.2   *"minute"*. For applications by minute, see r. 15.1.

49.63.3   *"motion"*. For motions, see Chap. 23.

PART X

CAUSES UNDER THE MATRIMONIAL HOMES (FAMILY PROTECTION) (SCOTLAND) ACT 1981

Interpretation of this Part
49.64. Unless the context otherwise requires, words and expressions used in this Part which are also used in the Act of 1981 have the same meaning as in that Act.

Deriv. R.C.S. 1965, r. 188D(1)(c) inserted by S.I. 1982 No. 1281

Form of applications under the Act of 1981

49.65. Subject to any other provision in this Chapter, an application for an order under the Act of 1981 shall be made—

(a) by an action for such an order;

(b) by a conclusion in the summons or in defences, as the case may be, in any other family action; or

(c) where the application is made by a person other than a party to an action mentioned in paragraph (a) or (b), by minute in that action.

Deriv. R.C.S. 1965, r. 188D(2), (4)(b) and (5) inserted by S.I. 1982 No. 1381

"summons". On form of summons, see r. 13.2.   **49.65.1**

"defences". On form of defences, see r. 18.1.   **49.65.2**

"minute". On applications by minute, see r. 15.1.   **49.65.3**

Jurisdiction. The jurisdiction of the court depends on the proceedings in which the application   **49.65.4**
under the Act of 1981 is brought. The court may make an order under the Act of 1981 as an ancillary order by virtue of s. 14(2) of the Family Law (Scotland) Act 1985 in an action of divorce or declarator of nullity of marriage. The jurisdiction of the court to entertain either of those proceedings is found in s. 7 of the Domicile and Matrimonial Proceedings Act 1973 and the Council Regulation (E.C.) No. 2201/2003 of 27th November 2003 (new Brussels II) which replaced the Council Regulation (EC) No. 1347/2000 of 29th May 2000 (Brussels II) which applies between member states of the E.U.: see note 49.2.1. But the court will not have jurisdiction to entertain the ancillary application if the court is exercising a jurisdiction by virtue of Art. 3 of the Council Regulation and the making or variation of the order in consequence of the application would contravene Art. 6 (exclusive jurisdiction of member state of habitual residence, etc., of the defender): 1973 Act, s. 10(1B) inserted by the European Communities (Matrimonial Jurisdiction and Judgments) (Scotland) Regulations 2001 (S.S.I. 2001 No. 36) and amended by the European Communities (Matrimonial and Parental Responsibility and Judgments) (Scotland) Regulations 2005 [S.S.I. 2005 No. 42].

Jurisdiction in an action for an order under the Act of 1981 only, will be determined by the C.J.J.A. 1982. The Scottish courts have, amongst other grounds, exclusive jurisdiction in proceedings which have as their object, rights *in rem* in or tenancies of immoveable property: Scheds 1, 3C and 4, Art. 16(1) and Sched. 8, r. 4(1)(a).

Defenders in causes under the Act of 1981

49.66. The applicant for an order under the Act of 1981 shall call as a defender—

(a) where he is seeking an order as a spouse, the other spouse;

(b) where he is a third party making an application under section 7(1) (dispensing with consent of non-entitled spouse to a dealing), or section 8(1) (payment from non-entitled spouse in respect of loan), of the Act of 1981, both spouses;

(c) where the application is made under section 18 of the Act of 1981 (occupancy rights of cohabiting couples), or is one to which that section applies, the other partner; and

¹ (d) where the application is made under section 18A of the Act of 1981 (application for domestic interdict), the other partner.

Deriv. R.C.S. 1965, r. 188D(7)(a) and (b) inserted by S.I. 1982 No. 1381

---

¹ Rule 49.66(d) inserted by S.S.I. 2006 No. 206 (effective 4ᵗʰ May 2006).

"non-entitled spouse". The "entitled spouse" is the spouse entitled, or permitted by a third   **49.66.1**
party, to occupy a matrimonial home (defined in s. 22 of the Act of 1981) and the other spouse who is not so entitled or permitted is the "non-entitled spouse"; and the non-entitled spouse has a right to enter into and occupy or to continue to occupy the matrimonial home with any child of the family: 1981 Act, s. 1(1).

"occupancy rights of cohabiting couples". If a man and a woman are living together as man   **49.66.2**
and wife, or two persons of the same sex living together as civil partners, in a house which one

of them (the "entitled partner") is entitled, or permitted by a third party, to occupy and the other (the "non-entitled partner") is not so entitled or permitted, the court may grant occupancy rights to the non-entitled partner for a period not exceeding six months (or extend such period for a further period not exceeding six months): Act of 1981, s. 18(1).

Applications by motion under the Act of 1981

49.67.—(1) An application under any of the following provisions of the Act of 1981 shall be made by motion—

(a) section 3(4) (interim order for regulation of rights of occupancy etc.);

(b) section 4(6) (interim order suspending occupancy rights);

(c) section 5 (variation and recall of orders regulating occupancy rights and of exclusion order);

(d) [*Rule 49.67(1)(d) omitted by S.S.I. 2006 No. 206 (effective 4th May 2006)*]

(e) [*Rule 49.67(1)(e) omitted by S.S.I. 2006 No. 206 (effective 4th May 2006)*]

(f) the proviso to section 18(1) (extension of period of occupancy rights).

(2) Written intimation of a motion under paragraph (1) shall be given not less than 7 days before the date on which the motion is enrolled—

(a) to the other spouse or partner, as the case may be;

(b) where the motion is under paragraph (1)(a), (b), (c) or (f) and the entitled spouse or partner is a tenant or occupies the matrimonial home by the permission of a third party, to the landlord or third party, as the case may be; and

(c) to any other person to whom intimation of the application was or is to be made by virtue of rule 49.8(1)(k) (warrant for intimation to certain persons in actions for orders under the Act of 1981) or 49.15 (orders for intimation by the court).

Deriv. R.C.S. 1965, r. 188D(3) (r. 49.67(1)), and r. 188D(7) and (9) (r. 49.67(2)), both inserted by S.I. 1982 No. 1381

49.67.1　　*"motion"*. For motions, see Chap. 23.

49.67.2　　*Section 3(4) of the Act of 1981.* An entitled or non-entitled spouse (see s. 1(1)) may apply for an order declaring, enforcing, restricting, regulating or protecting occupancy rights in the matrimonial home (see s. 22): Act of 1981, s. 3(1). On such an application the court may make such interim order as is necessary or expedient in relation to the residence of either spouse in the home, their personal effects or the furniture and plenishings: Act of 1981, s. 3(4).

49.67.3　　*Section 4(6) of the Act of 1981.* A spouse (or partner of a cohabiting couple), whether entitled, non-entitled (see s. 1(1) or where both spouses are entitled, or permitted by a third party, to occupy a matrimonial home (see s. 22), may, whether in occupation or not, apply for an exclusion order suspending the occupancy rights of the other spouse in the home: Act of 1981, s. 4(1). Pending the making of an exclusion order the court may make an interim order suspending the occupancy rights of the non-applicant spouse including summary ejection and interdict: Act of 1981, s. 4(6).

The test for the grant of an interim order is the same as that for an exclusion order (for which see s. 4(2)): *Brown v. Brown* 1985 S.L.T. 376.

An interim order may only be made if the non-applicant spouse has been given an opportunity to be heard: Act of 1981, s. 4(6) proviso.

Affidavits, permitted under r. 49.71, may be required so that relevant evidence is before the court. The Lord Ordinary may interview the parties (*Bell v. Bell* 1983 S.L.T. 224; *Smith v. Smith* 1983 S.L.T. 275) or refer to a custody report (*Ward v. Ward* 1983 S.L.T. 472).

As an interim order is in the discretion of the Lord Ordinary, a decision may be successfully reclaimed against only if he erred in law or his decision was unwarranted (*i.e.* so unreasonable no other judge would have reached it): *Brown*, above; *McCafferty v. McCafferty* 1986 S.L.T. 650.

49.67.4　　*Section 5 of the Act of 1981.* An order regulating occupancy rights (see s. 3) in the matrimonial home, or an exclusion order (see s. 4), may be varied or recalled under s. 5 of the Act of 1981. Such an order will, in any event, cease to have effect on the termination of the marriage, on the entitled spouse ceasing to be entitled or, where both are entitled or permitted, on both ceasing so to be: Act of 1981, s. 5(1).

Section 15 of the Act of 1981. A power of arrest must be attached to (*a*) a matrimonial **49.67.5** interdict which is ancillary to an exclusion order or an interim exclusion order (on which see s. 4 of the Act of 1981 and note 49.67.3), or (*b*) any other matrimonial interdict where the non-applicant spouse (or partner of a cohabiting couple) has had the opportunity of being heard by the court unless in all the circumstances such a power is unnecessary: Act of 1981, s. 15(1). A "matrimonial interdict" means an interdict or interim interdict which restrains or prohibits the conduct of one spouse against the other spouse or a child of the family or prohibits a spouse from entering or remaining in or in the vicinity of the matrimonial home: Act of 1981, s. 14(2). On the form of words for a non-molestation interdict, see *Murdoch v. Murdoch* 1973 S.L.T. (Notes) 13 in which the court said it would have to be satisfied that the pursuer, unless interdict is granted, is likely to be exposed, without adequate protection, to conduct by the defender which will put her at risk or in fear, alarm or distress.

A copy of (*a*) the application for interdict, (*b*) the interlocutor granting interdict and the power of arrest attached and (*c*) a certificate of service of the interdict must be intimated, after service of it, to the chief constable of the police area in which the matrimonial home is situated and, if the applicant spouse resides in another area, to the chief constable of that police area: Act of 1981, s. 15(4). For certificates of execution of such intimation, see r. 49.70.

A power of arrest under s. 15 of the Act of 1981 may not be imposed if the non-applicant spouse (or partner of a cohabiting couple) would be subject to a power of arrest under that Act and the Protection from Abuse (Scotland) Act 2001: Act of 1981, s. 15(1A) inserted by s. 6 of the 2001 Act.

For applications for a power of arrest in interdicts for protection from abuse, see Chap. 85.

"written intimation". For methods, see r. 16.9.   **49.67.6**

"not less than 7 days before". The first and last days are included in calculating the period so **49.67.7** that there are seven clear days.

Procedure for minutes

49.68. Where an application is made by minute under rule 49.65(*c*) (form of application under the Act of 1981 by a person other than a party) and answers to that minute are lodged, the minute and answers shall not be included with the other pleadings in the action in any record, but shall be made up separately in the form of a record; and rule 49.33(5)(*b*) and (*c*) (lodging etc. of records) shall apply to that record as it applies to a record under that rule.

Deriv. R.C.S. 1965, r. 188D(6) inserted by S.I. 1982 No. 1381

Sist of actions to enforce occupancy rights

49.69. Unless the court otherwise directs, the sist of an action by virtue of section 7(4) of the Act of 1981 (where action raised by non-entitled spouse to enforce occupancy rights) shall apply only to such part of the action as relates to the enforcement of occupancy rights by a non-entitled spouse.

Deriv. R.C.S. 1965, r. 188D(11) inserted by S.I. 1982 No. 1381

General note. As a general rule the exercise of occupancy rights by a non-entitled spouse is **49.69.1** protected against any dealing (*e.g.* sale or lease) of the entitled spouse relating to the matrimonial home without consent of the non-entitled spouse: Matrimonial Homes (Family Protection) (Scotland) Act 1981, s. 6. The court can dispense with that consent on an application to it under s. 7 of the Act of 1981. Where such an application has been made and the non-entitled spouse has brought an action to enforce occupancy rights, that action or that part of it which relates to the claim for occupancy rights can be sisted pending the proceedings in the application: Act of 1981, s. 7(4).

Certificates of execution of delivery of documents to chief constable

49.70.—(1)–(2) [*Rule 49.70 omitted by S.S.I. 2006 No. 206 (effective 4ᵗʰ May 2006)*]

Evidence in causes under the Act of 1981

49.71.—(1) For the purposes of proof in any application for an order under the Act of 1981, evidence by affidavit shall be admissible in place of parole evidence.

(2) Rule 36.8 (conditions for receiving certain written statements in evidence) shall not apply in a cause to which paragraph (1) of this rule applies.

Deriv. R.C.S. 1965, r. 188D(15) inserted by S.I. 1982 No. 1381

49.71.1   *General note.* The reference in R.C.S. 1965, r. 188D(15) to evidence by affidavit not being insufficient by reason only that it is not supported by parole evidence has been omitted as unnecessary; see also s. 1 of the Civil Evidence (Scotland) Act 1988.

49.71.2   *"affidavit".* Note meaning in r. 1.3(1).

[1] PART XA

CAUSES UNDER CHAPTERS 3 AND 4 OF PART 3 OF THE CIVIL PARTNERSHIP ACT 2004

Interpretation of this Part
  [1] **49.71A.**—(1) In this Part, unless the context otherwise requires, words and expressions used in this Part which are also used in Chapters 3 and 4 of Part 3 of the CP Act of 2004 have the meaning given in those Chapters.

---

[1] Part XA and r. 49.71A inserted by S.S.I. 2005 No. 632 (effective 8th December 2005).

49.71A.1   *General note.* Pt. XA contains rules similar to those in Pt. X for proceedings under the Matrimonial Homes (Family Protection) (Scotland) Act 1981.

Forms of applications under Chapters 3 and 4 of Part 3 of the Act of 2004
  [1] **49.71B.** Subject to any other provision in this Chapter, an application for an order under Chapter 3 or 4 of Part 3 of the CP Act of 2004 shall be made—
  (a) by an action for such an order;
  (b) by a conclusion in the summons or in defences, as the case may be, in any other family action; or
  (c) where the application is made by a person other than a party to an action mentioned in paragraph (a) or (b), by minute in that action.

---

[1] Rule 49.71B inserted by S.S.I. 2005 No. 632 (effective 8th December 2005).

49.71B.1   *"summons".* On form of summons, see r. 13.2.

49.71B.2   *"defences".* On form of defences, see r. 18.1.

49.71B.3   *"minute".* On applications by minute, see r. 15.1.

Defenders in causes under Chapters 3 and 4 of Part 3 of the CP Act of 2004
  [1] **49.71C.** The applicant for an order under Chapter 3 or 4 of Part 3 of the CP Act of 2004 shall call as a defender—
  (a) where he is seeking an order as a civil partner, the other civil partner; and
  (b) where he is a third party making an application under section 107(1) (dispensing with the consent of non-entitled partner to a dealing), or section 108(1) (payment from non-entitled partner in respect of loan) of the CP Act of 2004, both partners.

---

[1] Rule 49.71C inserted by S.S.I. 2005 No. 632 (effective 8th December 2005).

Applications by motion under Chapters 3 and 4 of the CP Act of 2004
  [1] **49.71D.**—(1)–(2) [*Rule 49.71D omitted by S.S.I. 2006 No. 206 (effective 4th May 2006)*]

Procedure for minutes
[1] **49.71E.** Where an application is made by minute under rule 49.71B(c) (form of application under Chapter 3 or 4 of Part 3 of the CP Act of 2004) by a person other than a party and answers to that minute are lodged, the minute and answers shall not be included with the other pleadings in the action in any record, but shall be made up separately in the form of a record; and rule 49.33(5)(b) and (c) (lodging etc. of records) shall apply to that record as it applies to a record under that rule.

_____

[1] Rule 49.71E inserted by S.S.I. 2005 No. 632 (effective 8th December 2005).

Sist of actions to enforce occupancy rights
[1] **49.71F.** Unless the court otherwise directs, the sist of an action by virtue of section 107(4) of the CP Act 2004 (where the action raised by non-entitled partner to enforce occupancy rights) shall apply only to such part of the action as relates to the enforcement of occupancy rights by a non-entitled partner.

_____

[1] Rule 49.71F inserted by S.S.I. 2005 No. 632 (effective 8th December 2005).

Certificates of execution of delivery to the chief constable
[1] **49.71G.**—(1)–(2) [*Rule 49.71G omitted by S.S.I. 2006 No. 206 (effective 4th May 2006)*]

Evidence in causes under Chapter 3 or 4 of Part 3 of the Act of 2004
[1] **49.71H.**—(1) For the purposes of proof in any application for an order under Chapter 3 or 4 of the CP Act of 2004, evidence by affidavit shall be admissible in place of parole evidence.

(2) Rule 36.8 (conditions for receiving certain written statements in evidence) shall not apply in a cause to which paragraph (1) of this rule applies.

_____

[1] Rule 49.71H inserted by S.S.I. 2005 No. 632 (effective 8th December 2005)

"affidavit". Note the meaning of affidavit in r. 1.3(1); and see note 1.3.7 on affidavits.   **49.71H.1**

Part XI

Simplified Divorce Applications

Application and interpretation of, and directions under, this Part
49.72.—(1) This Part applies to an application for divorce by a party to a marriage made in the manner prescribed in rule 49.73 (form of applications for simplified divorce) if, but only if—
[1,2] (a) that party relies on the facts set out in section 1(2)(d) (no cohabitation for one year with consent of defender to decree), section 1(2)(e) (no cohabitation for two years) or section (1)(1)(b) (issue of interim gender recognition certificate), of the Act of 1976;
(b) in an application under section 1(2)(d) of the Act of 1976, the other party consents to decree of divorce being granted;
(c) no other proceedings are pending in any court which could have the effect of bringing the marriage to an end;
(d) there are no children of the marriage under the age of 16 years;
(e) neither party to the marriage applies for an order for financial provision on divorce;
(f) neither party to the marriage suffers from mental disorder; and

[3] (g) neither party to the marriage applies for postponement of decree under section 3A of the Act of 1976 (postponement of decree where impediment to religious marriage exists).

(2) If an application ceases to be one to which this Part applies at any time before final decree, it shall be deemed to be abandoned and shall be dismissed.

(3) In this Part, "simplified divorce application" means an application mentioned in paragraph (1).

(4) The Principal Clerk shall give directions in relation to the administrative procedures to be followed on the lodging of a simplified divorce application for—

(a) the registration and service of such an application,

(b) having it brought before the court for consideration,

(c) in the event of decree of divorce being granted, for notification to the parties, and

(d) connected purposes,

and such directions shall have effect subject to the provisions of this Part.

Deriv. R.C.S. 1965, r. 170E inserted by S.I. 1982 No. 1679 (r. 49.72(1) to (3)); and r. 170H(1) inserted by S.I. 1982 No. 1679 (r. 49.72(4))

---

[1] Rule 49.72(1)(a) amended by S.S.I. 2005 No. 632 (effective 8th December 2005).
[2] Rule 49.72(1)(a) amended by S.S.I. 2006 No. 206 (effective 4th May 2006).
[3] Rule 49.72(1)(g) inserted by S.S.I. 2006 No. 206 (effective 4th May 2006) and substituted by S.S.I. 2007 No. 7, para. 10 (effective 26th February 2007).

49.72.1 *General note.* Simplified (or "do-it-yourself") divorce procedure was introduced by A.S. (R.C.A. No. 6) (Simplified Divorce Procedure) 1982 [S.I. 1982 No. 1679].

49.72.2 *"final decree".* This is the decree disposing of the whole subject-matter of the cause including expenses: see note 4.15.2(2).

49.72.3 *Directions by the Principal Clerk.* There are none.

Form of applications for simplified divorce

49.73.—[2] (1) A simplified divorce application in which the facts set out in section 1(2)(d) of the Act of 1976 (no cohabitation for one year with consent of defender to decree) are relied on shall be made in Form 49.73–A and shall only be of effect if—

(a) it is signed by the applicant; and

(b) the form of consent in Part 2 of Form 49.73–A is signed by the party to the marriage giving consent.

[2] (2) A simplified divorce application in which the facts set out in section 1(2)(e) of the Act of 1976 (no cohabitation for two years) are relied on shall be made in Form 49.73–B and shall only be of effect if it is signed by the applicant.

[1] (3) A simplified divorce application in which the facts set out in section 1(1)(b) of the Act of 1976 (grounds of divorce: interim gender recognition certificate) are relied on shall be made in Form 49.73–C and shall only be of effect if signed by the applicant.

Deriv. R.C.S. 1965, r. 170F inserted by S.I. 1982 No. 1679

---

[1] Rule 49.73(3) inserted by S.S.I. 2005 No. 632 (effective 8th December 2005).
[2] Rule 49.73(1) and (2) amended by S.S.I. 2006 No. 206 (effective 4th May 2006).

Lodging and registration of simplified divorce applications

49.74.—(1) The applicant shall send a simplified divorce application to the Deputy Principal Clerk with—

[1] (a) an extract or certified copy of the marriage certificate;

[1] (b) the appropriate fee; and

[1] (c) an application under section 1(1)(b) of the Act of 1976, the interim gender recognition certificate or a certified copy.

(2) Subject to the following rules of this Part, a simplified divorce application shall, on being registered in accordance with any directions made under rule 49.72(4), be treated as a summons in an action of divorce which has commenced.

Deriv. R.C.S. 1965, r. 170G inserted by S.I. 1982 No. 1679 (r. 49.74(1)); and r. 170H(2) inserted by S.I. 1982 No. 1679 (r. 49.74(2)).

---

[1] Rule 49.74(1)(a) & (b) amended and r. 49.74(1)(c) inserted by S.S.I. 2005 No. 632 (effective 8th December 2005).

Fee. A fee is payable by the applicant. For fee, see Court of Session etc. Fees Order 1997, **49.74.1** Table of Fees, Pt. I, B, item 4 [S.I. 1997 No. 688, as amended, pp.C1201 *et seq.*]. Certain persons are exempt from payment of fees; see 1997 Fees Order, art. 5 substituted by S.S.I. 2002 No. 270.

Warrants for service or intimation of simplified divorce applications

49.75.—(1) On registration of a simplified divorce application where the address of the other party to the marriage is known, a clerk of session shall grant warrant for service of the application.

[1,2] (2) On registration of an application in which the facts set out in section 1(2)(*e*) of the Act of 1976 (no cohabitation for two years) or section 1(1)(b) of the Act of 1976 (grounds of divorce: interim gender recognition certificate) are relied on where the address of the other party to the marriage is not known to the applicant and cannot reasonably be ascertained—

  (*a*) the Deputy Principal Clerk shall grant warrant for intimation of the application to—
    (i) every child of the marriage, and
    (ii) one of the next of kin of the other party who has reached the age of 16 years,
    unless the address of such person is not known and cannot reasonably be ascertained; and
  (*b*) the application shall thereafter be placed before the Lord Ordinary for such order under rule 16.5 (service where address of person is not known) as he thinks fit.

(3) A warrant granted under paragraph (1) or (2)(*a*) shall be sufficient authority for such service and intimation.

Deriv. R.C.S. 1965, r. 170I(1) inserted by S.I. 1982 No. 1679 (r. 49.75(1)), and r. 170I(3) inserted by S.I. 1982 No. 1679 and amended by S.I. 1987 No. 1206 (r. 49.75(2)).

---

[1] Rule 49.75(2) amended by S.S.I. 2005 No. 632 (effective 8th December 2005).
[2] Rule 49.75(2) amended by S.S.I. 2006 No. 206 (effective 4th May 2006).

Execution of service or intimation of simplified divorce applications

49.76.—(1) Subject to the following paragraphs, service or intimation of a simplified divorce application on a warrant granted under rule 49.75 on any person whose address is known to the applicant shall be made—

  (*a*) by the Deputy Principal Clerk by post in accordance with rule 16.4 (service by post); or
  (*b*) by a messenger-at-arms.

(2) In the application of Part I of Chapter 16 (service and intimation) to service or intimation under this rule, the following provisions of that Part of that Chapter shall not apply:—

    rule 16.1(3) (which relates to a party lodging a certificate of service in process), rule 16.3(1)(*b*) (form of citation and certificate of service by messenger-at-arms),

rule 16.4(2)(*b*) (service by post by agent),

rule 16.4(4) (form of citation in service by post).

[1,2] (3) In the case of service of a simplified divorce application on the other party to the marriage under paragraph (1), the person executing service shall complete a citation in Form 49.76–A (no cohabitation for one year with consent to divorce) Form 49.76–B (no cohabitation for two years) or Form 49.76–BA (interim gender recognition certificate), as the case may be.

(4) In the case of intimation of a simplified divorce application on a person under paragraph (1), the person giving intimation shall complete a notice of intimation in Form 49.76–C.

(5) A certificate of service or intimation in Form 49.76–D (certificate by Deputy Principal Clerk) or Form 49.76–E (certificate by messenger-at-arms), as the case may be, shall be—

(*a*) completed by the person executing service or giving intimation;

(*b*) in the case of a certificate completed by a messenger-at-arms, sent to the Deputy Principal Clerk; and

(*c*) attached to the application by the Deputy Principal Clerk.

---

[1] Rule 49.76(3) amended by S.S.I. 2005 No. 632 (effective 8th December 2005).
[2] Rule 49.76(3) amended by S.S.I. 2006 No. 206 (effective 4th May 2006).

Opposition to simplified divorce applications

49.77.—(1) Any person on whom service or intimation of a simplified divorce application has been made may give notice by letter sent to the Deputy Principal Clerk within the period of notice that he challenges the jurisdiction of the court or opposes the grant of decree of divorce and giving the reasons for his opposition to the application.

(2) Where opposition to a simplified divorce application is made under paragraph (1), the court shall dismiss the application unless it is satisfied that the reasons given for the opposition are frivolous.

(3) The Deputy Principal Clerk shall give written intimation of the decision under paragraph (2) to the applicant and the respondent.

(4) The sending of a letter under paragraph (1) shall not imply acceptance of the jurisdiction of the court.

Deriv. R.C.S. 1965, r. 170J inserted by S.I. 1982 No. 1679

49.77.1   *"frivolous"*. Reasons which do not amount in law to a defence are frivolous.

Evidence in simplified divorce applications

49.78.—(1) Parole evidence shall not be given in a simplified divorce application.

(2) Rule 36.8 (conditions for receiving certain written statements in evidence) shall not apply in a simplified divorce application.

No reclaiming in simplified divorce applications

49.79. A decree pronounced in a simplified divorce application may not be reclaimed against.

49.79.1   *General note.* To set aside a decree pronounced in a simplified divorce action, an action of reduction would have to be brought. On actions of reduction, see Chap. 53.

Applications after decree in simplified divorce applications

49.80.—(1) Any application to the court after decree of divorce has been granted in a simplified divorce application which could have been made if it had been an action of divorce shall be made by minute.

(2) On lodging a minute under paragraph (1), the minuter shall lodge a process.

Deriv. R.C.S. 1965, r. 170L inserted by S.I. 1982 No. 1679

"minute". For applications by minute, see r. 15.1.   **49.80.1**

[1] PART XIA

SIMPLIFIED APPLICATIONS FOR DISSOLUTION OF CIVIL PARTNERSHIPS

Application and interpretation of, and directions under, this Part
[1] **49.80A.**—(1) In this Part—
     [2] "child of the family" has the meaning given in section 12(4)(b) of the Act of 1995;
     "simplified dissolution application" means an application mentioned in paragraph (2).
(2) This Part applies to an application for dissolution of a civil partnership by a party to a civil partnership made in the manner prescribed in rule 49.80B (form of application for simplified dissolution of a civil partnership) if, but only if—
[2] (a) that party relies on the facts set out in section 117(3)(c) (no cohabitation for one year with consent of defender to decree), section 117(3)(d) (no cohabitation for two years), or section 117(2)(b) (issue of a gender recognition certificate) of the CP Act of 2004,
  (b) in an application under section 117(3)(c) of the CP Act of 2004, the other party consents to a decree of dissolution being granted;
  (c) no other proceedings are pending in any court which could have the effect of bringing the civil partnership to an end;
  (d) there are no children of the family under the age of 16 years;
  (e) neither party to the civil partnership applies for an order for financial provision on dissolution of the civil partnership; and
  (f) neither party to the civil partnership suffers from a mental disorder.
(3) If an application ceases to be one to which this Part applies at any time before final decree, it shall be deemed to be abandoned and shall be dismissed.
(4) The Principal Clerk shall give directions in relation to the administrative procedures to be followed on the lodging of a simplified dissolution application for—
  (a) the registration and service of such an application;
  (b) having it brought before the court for consideration;
  (c) in the event of decree of dissolution of the civil partnership being granted, for notification to the parties; and
  (d) connected purposes;
and such directions shall have effect subject to the provisions of this Part.

---

[1] Part XIA and r. 49.80A inserted by S.S.I. 2005 No. 632 (effective 8th December 2005).
[2] Rule 49.80A(1) and (2)(a) amended by S.S.I. 2006 No. 206 (effective 4th May 2006).

General note. Pt. XIA contains provisions similar to simplified divorce applications under Pt. XI.   **49.80A.1**

"final decree". This is the decree disposing of the whole subject-matter of the cause including   **49.80A.2**
expenses: see note 4.15.2(2).

Directions by the Principal Clerk. There are none.   **49.80A.3**

Form of application for simplified dissolution of a civil partnership
[1] **49.80B.**—[2] (1) A simplified dissolution application in which the facts set out in section 117(3)(c) of the CP Act of 2004 (no cohabitation for one year with consent of defender to decree) are relied on shall be made in Form 49.80B–A and shall only be of effect if—

(a) it is signed by the applicant; and
(b) the form of consent in Part 2 of Form 49.80B–A is signed by the party to the civil partnership giving consent.

[2] (2) A simplified dissolution application in which the facts set out in section 117(3)(d) of the CP Act of 2004 (no cohabitation for two years) are relied on shall be made in Form 49.80B–B and shall only be of effect if signed by the applicant.

(3) A simplified dissolution application in which the facts set out in section 117(2)(b) of the CP Act of 2004 (issue of interim gender recognition certificate) are relied on shall be made in Form 49.80B–C and shall only be of effect if signed by the applicant.

---

[1] Rule 49.80B inserted by S.S.I. 2005 No. 632 (effective 8th December 2005).
[2] Rule 49.80B(1) and (2) amended by S.S.I. 2006 No. 206 (effective 4th May 2006).

Lodging and registration of simplified dissolution applications
[1] **49.80C.**—(1) The applicant shall send a simplified dissolution application to the Deputy Principal Clerk with—
(a) an extract or certified copy of the certificate of civil partnership;
(b) the appropriate fee; and
(c) in an application under section 117(2)(b) of the CP Act of 2004, the interim gender recognition certificate or a certified copy.

(2) Subject to the following rules of this Part, a simplified dissolution application shall, on being registered in accordance with any directions made under rule 49.80A(4), be treated as a summons in an action of dissolution of a civil partnership which has commenced.

---

[1] Rule 49.80C inserted by S.S.I. 2005 No. 632 (effective 8th December 2005).

49.80C.1   *Fee.* A fee is payable by the applicant. For fee, see Court of Session, etc. Fees Order 1997, Table of Fees, Pt. I, B, [S.I. 1997 No. 688, as amended, pp C1201 *et seq.*] Certain persons are exempt from payment of fees: see 1997 Fees Order, art. 5 substituted by S.S.I. 2002 No. 270.

Warrants for service or intimation of simplified dissolution applications
[1] **49.80D.**—(1) On registration of a simplified dissolution application where the address of the other party to the civil partnership is known, a clerk of session shall grant warrant for service of the application.

[2] (2) On registration of an application in which the facts set out in section 117(3)(d) (no cohabitation for two years) or section 117(2)(b) (issue of interim gender recognition certificate) of the Act of 2004 are relied on where the address of the other party to the civil partnership is not known to the applicant and cannot reasonably be ascertained—
(a) the Deputy Principal Clerk shall grant warrant for intimation of the application to–
(i) every child of the family, and
(ii) one of the next-of-kin of the other party who has reached the age of 16 years,
unless the address of such person is not known an cannot reasonably be ascertained; and
(b) the application shall thereafter be placed before the Lord Ordinary for such order under rule 16.5 (service where address of person is not known) as he thinks fit.

(3) A warrant granted under paragraph (1) or (2)(a) shall be sufficient authority for such service and intimation.

---

[1] Rule 49.80D inserted by S.S.I. 2005 No. 632 (effective 8th December 2005).
[2] Rule 49.80D(2) amended by S.S.I. 2006 No. 206 (effective 4th May 2006).

Execution of service or intimation of simplified dissolution application

[1] **49.80E.**—(1) Subject to the following paragraphs, service or intimation of a simplified dissolution application on a warrant granted under rule 49.80D on any person whose address is known to the applicant shall be made—

(a) by the Deputy Principal Clerk by post in accordance with rule 16.4 (service by post); or

(b) by a messenger-at-arms.

(2) In the application of Part I of Chapter 16 (service and intimations) to service and intimation under this rule, the following provisions of that Part of that Chapter shall not apply:—

rule 16.1(3) (which relates to party lodging a certificate of service in process),

rule 16.3(1)(b) (form of citation and certificate of service by messenger-at-arms),

rule 16.4(2)(b) (service by post by agent),

rule 16.4(4) (form of citation in service by post).

[2] (3) In the case of service of a simplified dissolution application on the other party to the civil partnership under paragraph (1), the person executing service shall complete a citation in Form 49.80E–A (no cohabitation for one year with consent to divorce), Form 49.80E–B (no cohabitation for two years), or Form 49.80E–C (interim gender recognition certificate) as the case may be.

(4) In the case of intimation of a simplified dissolution application on a person under paragraph (1) the person giving intimation shall complete a notice of intimation in Form 49.80E–D.

(5) A certificate of service or intimation in Form 49.80E–E (certificate by Deputy Principal Clerk) or Form 49.80E–F (certificate by messenger-at-arms), as the case may be, shall be–

(a) completed by the person executing service or giving intimation;

(b) in the case of a certificate completed by a messenger-at-arms, sent to the Deputy Principal Clerk; and

(c) attached to the application by the Deputy Principal Clerk.

---

[1] Rule 49.80E inserted by S.S.I. 2005 No. 632 (effective 8th December 2005).
[2] Rule 49.80E(3) amended by S.S.I. 2006 No. 206 (effective 4th May 2006).

Opposition to simplified dissolution application

[1] **49.80F.**—(1) Any person on whom service or intimation of a simplified dissolution application has been made may give notice by letter sent to the Deputy Principal Clerk within the period of notice that he challenges the jurisdiction of the court or opposes the grant of the decree of dissolution and giving the reasons for his opposition to the application.

(2) Where opposition to a simplified dissolution application is made under paragraph (1), the court shall dismiss the application unless it is satisfied that the reasons given for the opposition are frivolous.

(3) The Deputy Principal Clerk shall give written intimation of the decision under paragraph (2) to the applicant and the respondent.

(4) The sending of a letter under paragraph (1) shall not imply acceptance of jurisdiction of the court.

---

[1] Rule 49.80F inserted by S.S.I. 2005 No. 632 (effective 8th December 2005).

"frivolous". Reasons which do not amount in law to a defence are frivolous.   **49.80F.1**

Evidence in simplified dissolution applications
[1] **49.80G.**—(1) Parole evidence shall not be given in a simplified dissolution application.

(2) Rule 36.8 (conditions for receiving certain written statements in evidence) shall not apply in a simplified dissolution application.

---

[1] Rule 49.80G inserted by S.S.I. 2005 No. 632 (effective 8th December 2005).

No reclaiming in simplified dissolution applications
[1] **49.80H.** A decree pronounced in a simplified dissolution application may not be reclaimed against.

---

[1] Rule 49.80H inserted by S.S.I. 2005 No. 632 (effective 8th December 2005).

49.80H.1   *General note.* To set aside a decree pronounced in a simplified dissolution application, an action of reduction would have to be brought. On actions of reduction, see Chap. 53.

Applications after decree in simplified dissolution applications
[1] **49.80I.**—(1) Any application to the court after decree of dissolution has been granted in a simplifed dissolution application which could not have been made if it had been an action of dissolution of a civil partnership shall be made by minute.

(2) On lodging a minute under paragraph (1), the minuter shall lodge a process.

---

[1] Rule 49.80I inserted by S.S.I. 2005 No. 632 (effective 8th December 2005).

49.80I.1   *"minute".* For applications by minute, see r. 15.1.

PART XII

CHILD SUPPORT ACT 1991

Interpretation of this Part
[1] **49.81.** In this Part—
    "the Act of 1991" means the Child Support Act 1991;
    "child" has the meaning assigned in section 55 of the Act of 1991;
    "maintenance assessment" has the meaning assigned in section 54 of
        the Act of 1991.

---

[1] R. 49.81 amended by SI 1996/1756 (minor correction).

49.81.1   *General note.* On averments required in a family action where aliment is sought for a child, see r. 49.6. For jurisdiction of the court in relation to aliment which may be affected by the Child Support Act 1991, see note 49.6.1.

Restriction of expenses
49.82. Where the Secretary of State is called as a defender in an action for declarator of non-parentage or illegitimacy, and the Secretary of State does not defend the action, no expenses shall be awarded against the Secretary of State.

49.82.1   *General note.* The Secretary of State may be made a defender to an action of declarator of non-parentage or illegitimacy: Child Support Act, s. 28; and r. 49.6(4)(b) provides that where an allegation of paternity is made against the pursuer the Secretary of State must be called as a defender. Such an action is brought under s. 7 of the Law Reform (Parent and Child) (Scotland)

Act 1986. The Secretary of State is likely only to defend where the mother of the child does not defend and where there are strong grounds; accordingly expenses may not be recovered from him if he does not defend.

Effect of maintenance assessments

49.83. The Deputy Principal Clerk shall, on receiving notification that a maintenance assessment has been made, cancelled or has ceased to have effect so as to affect an order of a kind prescribed for the purposes of section 10 of the Act of 1991, endorse on the interlocutor sheet relating to that order a certificate in Form 49.83–A or 49.83–B, as the case may be.

General note. A court order for aliment may cease to have effect when a maintenance **49.83.1** assessment is made which supersedes it. Form 49.83–A applies where a maintenance assessment has been made, and Form 49.83–B applies where it is cancelled or ceases to have effect. Extracts may also be affected: see r. 49.84.

Effect of maintenance assessments on extracts relating to aliment

49.84.—(1) Where an order relating to aliment is affected by a maintenance assessment, any extract of that order issued by the Extractor shall be endorsed with a certificate in Form 49.84–A.

(2) Where an order relating to aliment has ceased to have effect on the making of a maintenance assessment, and that maintenance assessment is later cancelled or ceases to have effect, any extract of that order issued by the Extractor shall be endorsed also with a certificate in Form 49.84–B.

General note. A court order for aliment may cease to have effect when a maintenance **49.84.1** assessment is made which supersedes it. Where an extract of the order which is affected by a maintenance assessment is issued the certificate in Form 49.84–A will be endorsed on it. A certificate in Form 49.84–B will be endorsed on the extract when the maintenance assessment is cancelled or ceases to have effect. These certificates can only be endorsed on the extract if the extract happens to be sought after one of the foregoing events has occurred.

[1] PART XIII

REFERRALS TO PRINCIPAL REPORTER

Application and interpretation of this Part

[1] **49.85.**—(1) This Part applies where the court, in a family action, refers a matter to the Principal Reporter under section 54 of the Act of 1995 (reference to the Principal Reporter by court).

(2) In this Part, "Principal Reporter" has the meaning assigned in section 93(1) of the Act of 1995.

_____

[1] Pt. XIII and r. 49.85 inserted by S.I. 1996 No. 2587 (effective 1st November 1996).

Intimation to Principal Reporter

[1] **49.86.** Where a matter is referred by the court to the Principal Reporter under section 54 of the Act of 1995, the clerk of court shall give written intimation of the interlocutor making the reference to the Principal Reporter; and that intimation shall specify which of the conditions in section 52(2)(a) to (h), (j), (k) or (l) of that Act it appears to the court have been satisfied.

_____

[1] R. 49.86 inserted by S.I. 1996 No. 2587 (effective 1st November 1996).

"section 54 of the Act of 1995". In an action of divorce, judicial separation, or for declarator **49.86.1** of marriage, nullity of marriage, percentage or non-percentage, or proceedings relating to parental responsibilities or parental rights, the court may refer a child (see s. 93(2)(b)) to the Principal Reporter if any of the conditions in s. 52(2)(a) to (h), (j), (k) or (l) are satisfied:

Children (Scotland) Act 1995, s. 54. Those conditions relate to the circumstances in which compulsory measures of supervision may be required.

49.86.2   *"written intimation"*. For methods, see r. 16.9.

Intimation of decision by Principal Reporter

[1] **49.87.**—(1) Where a matter has been referred by the court to the Principal Reporter under section 54 of the Act of 1995 and the Principal Reporter, having made such investigation as he thinks appropriate and having reached the view that compulsory measures of supervision are necessary, arranges a children's hearing under section 69 of that Act (continuation or disposal of referral by children's hearing), the Principal Reporter shall give written intimation to the court which referred the matter to him of—

   (a) the decision to arrange such children's hearing;

   (b) where there is no appeal made against the decision of that children's hearing once the period for appeal has expired, the outcome of the children's hearing; and

   (c) where such an appeal has been made, that an appeal has been made and, once determined, the outcome of that appeal.

(2) Where a matter has been referred by the court to the Principal Reporter under section 54 of the Act of 1995 and the Principal Reporter, having made such investigation as he thinks appropriate and having considered whether compulsory measures of supervision are necessary, decides not to arrange a children's hearing under section 69 of that Act, the Principal Reporter shall give written intimation of that decision to the court which referred the matter to him.

---

[1] R. 49.87 inserted by S.I. 1996 No. 2587 (effective 1st November 1996).

49.87.1   *"section 54 of the Act of 1995"*. See note 49.86.1.

49.87.2   *"written intimation"*. For methods, see r. 16.9.

[1] PART XIV

MANAGEMENT OF MONEY PAYABLE TO CHILDREN

[2] *Application under section 11(1)(d) of the Act of 1995 following order under section 13 of that Act*

[1] **49.88.** Where the court has made an order under section 13 of the Act of 1995 (awards of damages to children), an application by a person for an order by virtue of section 11(1)(d) of that Act (administration of child's property) may be made by minute in the process of the cause in which the order under section 13 of that Act was made.

---

[1] Pt. XIV and r. 49.88 inserted by S.I. 1996 No. 2587 (effective 1st November 1996).
[2] Heading to r. 49.88 inserted by S.I. 1997 No. 1050.

49.88.1   *General note.* Part IV of Chap. 43 has been revoked by the A.S. (R.C.S.A. No. 5) (Family Actions and Miscellaneous) 1996 [S.I. 1996 No. 2587] because s. 13 of the Children (Scotland) Act 1995 contains the substantive provisions for the management of money payable to children in any court proceedings.

    S.13 of the 1995 Act implements the recommendations of the Scottish Law Commission *Report on Family Law*, para. 4.6 [Scot. Law Com. No. 135]. Advice that rr. 43.14 to 43.17 implemented these recommendations and were more flexible in rules than in primary legislation was not accepted.

    The only rule which survives in the R.C.S. 1994 is a rule for administration now in r. 49.88 which replaces r. 43.17 (subsequent orders).

49.88.2   *"section 13 of the Act of 1995"*. The side-note to s. 13 of the Children (Scotland) Act 1995 states that the section deals with awards of damages payable to children. In fact its terms are very wide and extend to where any "sum of money becomes payable to, or for the benefit of, a child under the age of sixteen years". It applies in any court proceedings. An extra-judicial settlement after an action or other proceedings have been brought would arise in court proceedings and would be covered by s. 13.

The court may make such order relating to the payment and management of that sum as it thinks fit: 1995 Act, s. 13(1).

Without prejudice to that generality, the court may—

(a) appoint a judicial factor to invest, apply or otherwise deal with the money for the benefit of the child;

(b) order the money to be paid to the sheriff clerk or the Accountant of Court, or to a parent or guardian of the child, to be invested, applied or otherwise dealt with under directions of the court for the benefit of the child; or

(c) order the money to be paid directly to the child.

A receipt by such a person is a sufficient discharge of the obligation to make payment.

Some guidance on the appropriateness of the alternative orders is needed. No criterion is laid down in the Act. In *IC v. Argyll and Clyde Health Board*, 21st November 2002, unreported (OH), reference is made to a report by the Accountant of Court in which comments are made on some of the merits and the demerits of appointing a factor or the Accountant of Court. In that case Lord Carloway observed that, especially where there is no criticism or suspicion about the ability of parents to look after their child's funds, there is no obligation on a defender to raise s. 13 of the 1995 Act with the court.

(1) **Judicial factor**. Where the sum is very large the appointment of a judicial factor may be appropriate, but not otherwise because the costs of appointment and administration are substantial: there have to be paid annually the caution premium, the factor's commission and the statutory fees payable to the Accountant of Court including the audit fee (in the case of damages, the award could attempt to take account of these). The audit fee includes a fee currently of 17.5 per cent of the factor's commission: see Court of Session etc. Fees Order 1984, Table of Fees, Pt. II, item 3 [SI 1984/256, Table as amended, pp. **C** 1202 *et seq.*]. The running cost depends on the amount of capital, the level of activity and the demands on the time of the factor. It might be thought that a judicial factory was not appropriate for sums less than £50,000. A judicial factor is subject to the Judicial Factors Act 1849, the Judicial Factors (Scotland) Act 1889, the Trusts (Scotland) Acts 1921 and 1961 and the Trustee Investments Act 1961. He is subject to the supervision of the Accountant of Court. He must find caution.

On judicial factors, see further Chap. 61.

(2) **Sheriff clerk**. In this case the expense of a judicial factor or the Accountant of Court is avoided. There is no charge for administration by the sheriff clerk. Money paid to the sheriff clerk passes out of the control of the court to that of the sheriff court unless an order is subsequently sought under r. 49.88 to make a change. The Ordinary Cause Rules 1993 in Sched. 1 to the Sheriff Courts (Scotland) Act 1907 were substituted for the previous rules by A.S. (Sheriff Court Ordinary Cause Rules) 1993 [SI 1993/1956]. Management of money paid to the sheriff clerk is dealt with in O.C.R. 1993, r. 36.17 (in Pt. IV of Chap. 36). Money has to be invested in accordance with the Trustee Investments Act 1961: O.C.R. 1993, r. 36.17(4).

(3) **Accountant of Court**. The Accountant might be appropriately appointed in cases where the sum is less than £50,000 (see note 43.16.2) but more than £5,000 or where the amount of administration is likely to be less than that which would justify a factor. £50,000, however should not be regarded as an upper limit. A lower limit of £5,000 is intended to cover those cases where the money is not so substantial as to justify being invested but should rather be placed in a bank account as the transactions in relation to it are likely to be few. As there is no statutory provision for the Accountant to be paid, the interlocutor appointing him should find him entitled to the expenses and outlays incurred. The costs of administration would be less than that of a judicial factory: that would be no caution premium, no inventory or audit fees (see note 43.16.2) and the overall cost saving could be 25 per cent or more compared to the costs of a judicial factory.

(4) **Guardian**. A guardian normally includes the child's parents as one of their parental rights, any person on application to the court may be appointed a guardian and a parent may appoint any person to be the child's guardian: Law Reform (Parent and Child) (Scotland) Act 1986, ss. 2–4 and 8 as amended by the Age of Legal Capacity (Scotland) Act 1991, Sched. 1.

A guardian is a trustee subject to the Trusts (Scotland) Acts 1921 and 1961 and the Trustee Investments Act 1961. It might be thought that sums of up to £20,000 could be administered by a guardian (or £5,000 where there was concern about the ability of the guardian to handle the money): see Report on Family Law, Scot. Law Com. No. 135, para. 4.17.

The court might require a guardian to take the advice of a (named) person, such as a solicitor.

In *IC v. Argyll and Clyde Health Board*, above, Lord Carloway observed that it may be prudent in the case of even reliable and trustworthy parents, who are appointed to be paid and to manage the award, to attach some form of reporting requirement at least where the sum is very large and on which the child may be largely dependent in later life. In that case, on the recommendation of the Accountant of Court, Lord Carloway attached the following conditions to the payment of the funds to the parents: (i) confirmation to the Accountant of investment of funds in accordance with disclosed advice; (ii) lodging with the Accountant a voucher of the level of initial investment; (iii) the funds to be held in the parents' joint names for the child; (iv) withdrawals in excess of 2.5 per cent of capital to require the Accountant's approval; (v) all revenue spent to be for the benefit of the child; and (vi) an annual report to the Accountant of the   level   of   funds   and   expenditure.

(5) **Payment direct to child**. Payment of only small sums may be appropriate, having regard particularly to the restrictions on transactions under the Age of Legal Capacity (Scotland) Act 1991.

A decree for payment will arise on an award of damages, interim damages or provisional damages. A payment arising on decree of absolvitor would occur where there is an extra-judicial settlement: see, *e.g. Scott v. Occidental Petroleum (Caledonia) Ltd* 1990 S.C.L.R. 278.

Damages awarded for future necessary services under s. 3 of the Administration of Justice Act 1982 (substit.uted by the Law Reform (Miscellaneous Provisions) (Scotland) Act 1990, s. 69(1)) would appear to be for the child's benefit and subject to s. 13 of the Act of 1995.

49.88.3   *Curator* ad litem. Where a curator *ad litem* has been appointed to the child, he should prepare a report detailing the arrangements for the payment and management of the money: *Riddoch v. Occidental Petroleum (Caledonia) Ltd* 1991 S.L.T. 721, 722L *per* Lord McCluskey.

49.88.4   *"minute"*. For applications by minute, see r. 15.1.

[1] PART XV

MANAGEMENT OF CHILD'S PROPERTY BY VIRTUE OF SECTION 9(5)(A) OR 11(2)(G) OF THE ACT OF 1995

Directions
[1] **49.89.** In making an appointment under section 9(5)(a) or 11(2)(g) of the Act of 1995, or when it receives a report under the said section 11(2)(g), the court may give such directions as it thinks fit regarding the management of the property concerned, and it may from time to time, on the application of a judicial factor so appointed, of the Accountant of Court or of any other person having an interest, give further such directions.

---

[1] Pt. XV and r. 49.89 inserted by S.I. 1997 No. 1720 (effective 1st August, 1997); heading inserted by S.S.I. 2004 No. 52 (effective 1st March, 2004).

49.89.2   *Section 9(5)(a) of the Children (Scotland) Act 1995*. Subject to section 13 of the Act of 1995 (court awards of money to children), where property is owned by or due to a child, is held by a person other than a parent or guardian, would otherwise require to be transferred to a parent with parental responsibilities, or to a guardian, for administration for the child (unless appointed a trustee under a trust deed to administer the property for the child) and (1) the person holding the property is a trustee or executor, then (a) if the value of the property exceeds £20,000, he shall, (b) if the value of the property is not less than £5,000 and does not exceed £20,000, he may, or (2) the person holding the property is not a trustee or executor, he may, apply to the Accountant of Court for directions: Act of 1995, s. 9(1), (2) and (3). When such an application is made to the Accountant of Court, he may, among other things, apply to the Court for the appointment of a judicial factor: Act of 1995, s. 9(5)(a).

49.89.3   *Section 11(2)(g) of the Children (Scotland) Act 1995*. Section 11(1) of the Act of 1995 empowers the court to make an order in any proceedings for the administration of a child's property (subject to the jurisdictional rules in s. 14(1) and (2)). The court may appoint a judicial factor or remit the matter to the Accountant of Court to report on suitable arrangements: Act of 1995, s. 11(2)(g).

49.89.4   *"application"*. Strictly, by virtue of r. 14.2(h), an application under r. 49.89 is by petition to the Outer House. This is clearly not intended (possibly because the current draftsman may not be familiar with the structure of the Rules). There is no reason why such an application may not be by motion or minute, where there is a depending process in which it could be made.

¹ PART XVA

APPLICATION BY SURVIVOR FOR PROVISION ON INTESTACY

¹ **49.90.**—(1) The applicant for an order under section 29(2) of the Act of 2006 (application by survivor for provision on intestacy) shall call the deceased's executor as a defender.

(2) An application under section 29(9) of the Act of 2006 for variation of the date or method of payment of the capital sum shall be made by minute in the process of the action to which the application relates.

(3) Words and expressions used in this Part shall have the same meaning as in section 29 of the Act of 2006.

---

² Part XVA and r. 49.90 inserted by S.S.I. 2006 No. 206 (effective 4ᵗʰ May 2006).

General note. Where two people are living together as man and wife, or as civil partners, and one dies intestate, the survivor may apply for payment of a capital sum out of the deceased's net intestate estate, or for the transfer of property: Act of 2006, s. 29.   **49.90.1**

"minute". For applications by minute, see rule 15.1.   **49.90.2**

CHAPTER 50

CAUSES UNDER THE PRESUMPTION OF DEATH (SCOTLAND) ACT 1977

Interpretation of this Chapter
  50.1. In this Chapter—
    "the Act of 1977" means the Presumption of Death (Scotland) Act 1977;
    "action of declarator" means an action under section 1(1) of the Act of 1977;
    "missing person" has the meaning assigned in section 1(1) of the Act of 1977.

Deriv. RCS 1965, r. 188B(1) inserted by S.I. 1978 No. 161

General note. A question as to whether a person has died may be dealt with (a) in an action of **50.1.1** declarator of death under the Act of 1977; or (b) incidentally to some other process (*Bruce v. Smith* (1871) 10 M. 130 (action of multiplepoinding); *Secretary of State for Scotland v. Sutherland* 1944 S.C. 79 (application for state pension)).
  A natural person is presumed to live for 80 to 100 years: Stair, IV.xlv.17; Bankton, II.vi.31. Anyone who requires to prove that a person has died has to overcome this presumption on a balance of probabilities: Act of 1977, s. 2(1) and (3).

"missing person". This is a person who is thought to have died or has not been known to be **50.1.2** alive for a period of at least seven years: Act of 1977, s. 1(1).

Jurisdiction. The court has jurisdiction where (a) the pursuer is the spouse of the missing **50.1.3** person and is domiciled in Scotland at the date of raising the action or was habitually resident in Scotland throughout the period of one year ending in that date, or (b) in any other case the missing person was domiciled in Scotland on the date on which he was last known to be alive or had been habitually resident there throughout the period of one year ending with that date: Act of 1977, s. 1(3).

The pursuer. The pursuer may be any person having an interest: Act of 1977, s. 1(1); *e.g.* **50.1.4** spouse, beneficiary in succession, factor *loco absentis*, etc. The Lord Advocate may be a pursuer: Act of 1977, ss. 1(1) and 17.

Parties to, and service and intimation of, actions of declarator
  50.2.—(1) The missing person shall be called as the defender in an action of declarator and service on that person shall be by advertisement in such newspaper or other publication as the court thinks fit of such of the facts

relating to the missing person and set out in the summons as the court may specify.

[1] (2) The period of notice where service is executed in accordance with paragraph (1) rule shall be 21 days from the date of publication of the advertisement unless the court otherwise orders.

(3) [Revoked by SI 1999/1386 (effective 19th May 1999).]

(4) Subject to paragraph (6), in the summons in an action of declarator, the pursuer shall insert a warrant for intimation to—

(a) the missing person's—

[2] (i) spouse or civil partner, and

(ii) children or, if he has no children, nearest relative known to the pursuer,

(b) any person, including any insurance company, who so far as known to the pursuer, has any interest in the action, and

(c) the Lord Advocate,

in the following terms:— "Warrant for intimation to (*name and address*) as [husband *or* wife, child *or* nearest relative] [a person having an interest in the presumed death] of (*name and last known address of the missing person*) and to the Lord Advocate.".

(5) A notice of intimation in Form 50.2–B shall be attached to the copy of the summons where intimation is given on a warrant under paragraph (4).

(6) The court may, on the motion of the pursuer, dispense with intimation on a person mentioned in paragraph (4)(a) or (b).

(7) Notwithstanding the reference in subsection (5) of section 1 of the Act of 1977 (person interested in seeking determination or appointment not sought by pursuer) to lodging a minute, an application under that subsection shall be made by lodging defences containing a conclusion for the determination or appointment sought, averments in the answers to the condescendence in support of that conclusion and an appropriate plea-in-law.

(8) On lodging defences under paragraph (7), the defender shall, as well as complying with rule 4.6 (intimation of steps of process)—

(a) send a copy of the defences by registered post or the first class recorded delivery service to each person to whom intimation of the action has been made under paragraph (4); and

(b) lodge in process the Post Office receipt or certificate of posting of those defences.

Deriv. RCS 1965, r. 188B(3) and (4)(part) (r. 50.2(4)), r. 188B(4)(part) and (5) (r. 50.2(5)), and r. 188B(6) (r. 50.2(6)), all inserted by S.I. 1978 No. 161

---

[1] Rule 50.2(1) and (2) amended by S.I. 1999 No. 1386 (effective 19th May 1999).

[2] Rule 50.2(4)(a)(i) amended by S.S.I. 2005 No. 632 (effective 8th December 2005).

50.2.1   *Service by advertisement.* As by definition the current address of the missing person will not be known service of the summons has to be executed by advertisement: r. 50.2(1).

Advertisement is no longer in Form 16.5 because the references in r. 50.2 to Form 16.5 (service by advertisement) were revoked by A.S. (R.C.S.A. No. 5) (Miscellaneous) 1999 [S.I. 1999 No. 1386]. The reason is simply that the rule now provides that the advertisement must contain such facts relating to the missing person set out in the summons as the court may specify. Nonetheless the form or style of the advertisement should, apart from this and the 21 day period of notice, comply with that in Form 16.5. The motion for service by advertisement should set out the averred facts about the missing person that the pursuer considers might be included in the advertisement, or the motion should be accompanied by a draft advertisement containing such averred facts, for approval by the court.

The new procedure for the first service by advertisement rolls into one the former two-stage process whereby, if no defences were lodged after the first advertisement, a second advertisement containing facts relating to the missing person was required (r. 50.3(1)). Rule 50.3(1) is accordingly revoked.

"period of notice". The period of notice in an action of declarator of death is 21 days from the **50.2.2** date of publication of the advertisement: r. 50.2(2). This contrasts with the general provision of six months: r. 13.4(1)(d). An application to shorten or extend the period of notice may be made by motion: r. 13.4(2).

Intimation. The warrant should be inserted in the summons after the address and charge, and **50.2.3** before the conclusions: r. 13.2 and Form 32.2.A. For methods of service, see r. 16.8.

Defences. See rr. 18.1 and 18.2. **50.2.4**

Lodge in process the certificate of posting. The certificate of posting and a copy of the notice of **50.2.5** intimation in Form 50.2–B must be lodged as productions. On lodging productions, see r. 4.5.

Further advertisement and procedure
50.3.—(1) [Revoked by SI 1999/1386 (effective 19th May 1999).]
(2) At any time before the determination of the action, the court may, at its own instance or on the motion of a party, make such order for further advertisement as it thinks fit.

General note. Rule 50.3(1) (derived from RCS 1965, r. 188B (7) inserted by S.I. 1978 No. 161) **50.3.1** provided for advertisement containing facts relating to the missing person where no defences were lodged within the period of notice. The new procedure for the first service by advertisement rolls into one the former two-stage process whereby, if no defences were lodged after the first advertisement, a second advertisement containing facts relating to the missing person was required (r. 50.3(1)). Rule 50.3(1) is accordingly revoked. But, because the effect of a decree is that the missing person is deemed to be dead for all civil law purposes (Act of 1977, s. 3(1)), an additional safeguard remains in r. 50.3(2) for further advertisement if required.

"motion". For motions, see Chap. 23. **50.3.2**

Applications for proof
50.4. In an action of declarator where no defences have been lodged, the pursuer shall, after such further advertisement as may be ordered under rule 50.3, apply by motion for an order for a proof.

"motion". For motions, see Chap. 23. **50.4.1**

Proof. See generally, Chap. 36. **50.4.2**
Any person (including the Secretary of State for Social Services) who possesses information relating to the survival or death of the missing person and who is aware that an action of declarator has been raised or an application for a variation order made, must disclose that information by letter to the Principal Clerk: Act of 1977, s. 9(1). The usual rules on inadmissibility on grounds of privilege or confidentiality apply: Act of 1977, s. 9(2). A statement purporting to be an instrument made or issued by or on behalf of any Minister of the Crown containing facts relating to an action of declarator or application for a variation order is sufficient evidence of the facts stated therein: Act of 1977 s. 9(3). The reporting of the action by the press is not restricted by the Judicial Proceedings (Regulation of Reports) Act 1926 (which prohibits the printing or publishing in relation to any judicial proceedings, any indecent matter the publication of which would be calculated to injure public morals): Act of 1977, s. 14; the missing person is decreed to be dead for all civil law purposes..

Effect of decree. The decree takes effect on the expiry of the time for reclaiming with no **50.4.3** reclaiming motion having been marked or on the withdrawal or refusal of a reclaiming motion; the missing person is deemed to be dead for all civil law purposes: Act of 1977, s. 3(1). The time for reclaiming is 21 days after the date on which the interlocutor granting decree was pronounced: r. 38.3(2).
The missing person is automatically deprived of any rights from the expiry of the reclaiming days after the granting of decree: Act of 1977, s. 3(1). Even if the missing person re-appears and obtains a recall or variation of the decree under s. 4 of the Act of 1977, he is not *per se* entitled to recover his former property: Act of 1977, s. 5(1).

Intimation to Registrar General. Where the court has granted decree of declarator of death or **50.4.4** pronounced a variation order and the reclaiming days have expired with no reclaiming motion having been marked or the reclaiming motion has been refused, the clerk of court must notify the prescribed particulars in connection with such decree or order to the Registrar General for Births, Marriages and Deaths for Scotland: Act of 1977, s. 12(1). The prescribed particulars in so far as known are (a) the date of decree or variation order; (b) the full name, last known usual residence and last known occupation of the deceased; (c) the date of birth or age of the deceased; (d) the time and date of death as determined by the court; (e) the marital status of the deceased at the date of death and if married the name and address of the surviving spouse; (f) the full name and address of the pursuer in the action or applicant in the application and his or her relationship (if any) to the deceased; and (g) the name and address of the agent for said pursuer or applicant: Registration of Presumed Deaths (Prescription of Particulars) (Scotland) Regulations 1978 [S.I. 1978 No. 160], Reg. 3. There is a form of Notice of import of decree or order for variation or recall of declarator of death which the clerk completes.

Applications for variation or recall of decrees
  50.5.—(1) An application under section 4(1) of the Act of 1977 (variation or recall of decree) shall be made by minute in the process of the action to which the application relates.
  (2) On the lodging of such a minute, the minuter shall apply by motion for an order—
  (*a*) for service on the missing person, where his whereabouts have become known;
  (*b*) for intimation to those persons mentioned in rule 50.2(4) or to dispense with intimation to a person mentioned in rule 50.2(4)(*a*) or (*b*); and
  (*c*) for any answers to the minute to be lodged in process within such period as the court thinks fit.
  (3) An application under section 4(3) of the Act of 1977 (person interested seeking determination or appointment not sought by applicant for variation order) shall be made by lodging answers containing a crave for the determination or appointment sought.
  [1] (4) A person lodging answers containing a crave under paragraph (3) shall, as well as sending a copy of the answers to the minuter—
  (*a*) send a copy of the answers by registered post or the first class recorded delivery service to each person on whom service or intimation of the minute was ordered; and
  (*b*) lodge in process the Post Office receipt or certificate of posting of those answers.

Deriv. R.C.S. 1965, r. 188B(2), (3), (5) and (6) inserted by S.I. 1978 No. 161 (r. 50.5(1) and (2))

———

[1] R. 50.5(4) amended by S.I. 1994 No. 2901 (minor correction).

General note. A variation order is an order varying or recalling a decree in an action of declarator of death: Act of 1977, s. 4(1). The variation order may vary or recall the decree in any matter which could have been dealt with in the original decree except in relation to any property acquired as a result of the original decree: Act of 1977, ss. 4(2) and 1(1). A variation order may not revive a marriage: Act of 1977, s. 4(5).   **50.5.1**
  If following an application made no later than five years after the date of the original decree the court pronounces a variation order, the court may make such further order in relation to any property rights acquired as a result of the original decree as it considers fair and reasonable in all the circumstances: Act of 1977, s. 5(2) and (4). Such further order may not affect the entitlement to any income accruing between the date of the decree and the variation order: Act of 1977, s. 5(2). The further order may be craved in the minute for the variation order.
  Any person having an interest may apply: Act of 1977, s. 4(1). This includes the Lord Advocate for the public interest: Act of 1977, s. 17.

Jurisdiction. The court has jurisdiction where: **50.5.2**
  (1) it granted the decree of declarator of death which is sought to be varied or recalled: Act of 1977, s. 4(1); or
  (2) the sheriff or the court itself remits an application under s. 4(1) of the Act of 1977 to the court due to the importance or complexity of the matters at issue: Act of 1977, s. 4(4); and see rr. 50.5 and 32.3.

"minute". See r. 15.1. The minute may include a crave for a further order in relation to   **50.5.3**
property under s. 5(2) of the Act of 1977.

"motion". For motions, see Chap. 23.   **50.5.4**

"service". For methods, see Chap. 16.   **50.5.5**

"intimation". For methods, see r. 16.8.   **50.5.6**

"answers". See r. 18.3.   **50.5.7**

Proof. See note 50.4.2.   **50.5.8**

Intimation to Registrar General. See note 50.4.4.   **50.5.9**

Applications for remit from sheriff court

50.6.—(1) An application by a person for a direction under section 1(6) or 4(4) of the Act of 1977 (remit of action or application to the court) shall be made by petition.

(2) An action of declarator or an application which is remitted to the court under section 1(6) or 4(4) of the Act of 1977 shall proceed in the Outer House as if it were an action brought or an application made, as the case may be, in that court.

Deriv. R.C.S. 1965, r. 188B(8) and (9) inserted by S.I. 1978 No. 161

50.6.1   *General note.* An application to the court for a remit of an application or action from the sheriff to the court may be made by any party to the application or action: Act of 1977, ss. 1(6) and 4(4).

50.6.2   *"petition".* For petitions generally, see Chap. 14.
An application to the court for a remit of an application or action from the sheriff to the court may be made by any party to the application or action: Act of 1977, ss. 1(6) and 4(4).

50.6.3   *Further procedure.* Where the petition is granted, for further procedure see rr. 32.3 *et seq.*

Appointment of judicial factors

50.7.—(1) Rule 61.6 (documents relating to judicial factories for Accountant of Court) shall apply to an application for the appointment of a judicial factor under section 2(2)(c) or section 4(2) of the Act of 1977 as it applies to a petition for the appointment of a judicial factor.

(2) Where, in an action of declarator or an application under section 4(1) of the Act of 1977 (variation or recall of decree), a judicial factor on the estate of the missing person is appointed, the process shall forthwith be transmitted to, and retained by, the Petition Department; and the judicial factory shall proceed as if the judicial factor had been appointed in a petition for that purpose.

(3) In the application of rule 50.5 (applications for variation or recall of decrees) to an application under section 4(1) of the Act of 1977 in a cause transmitted to the Petition Department under paragraph (2), for references to a minute there shall be substituted references to a note.

50.7.1   *General note.* On judicial factories generally, see Chap. 61.

CHAPTER 51

ACTIONS OF MULTIPLEPOINDING

Application of this Chapter
51.1. This Chapter applies to an action of multiplepoinding.

51.1.1   *General Note.* The purpose of an action of multiplepoinding is to enable a person, pursued by different pursuers upon distinct rights, to cite all persons in a single process, so that he may be liable only in once and single payment and performance and free from subsequent claims: Stair, IV.xvi.3. It is an action by which property, whether heritable or moveable, claimed by different parties is brought into court either by the holder of the property or by one of the claimants, in order that the true ownership of, or respective rights to, the property can be determined. Accordingly, "a process of multiplepoinding implies all powers necessary for determining the rights of the parties . . . the effect being such as to authorise the court to discuss incidentally all such points arising in the course of it, as are necessary for extricating the rights of the parties": More's Notes to Stair, ccclxxviii–ccclxxix. It has been described as a "congeries of actions" in which, as a general rule, "all deeds and decrees founded on by one claimant may be set aside by other claimants *ope exceptionis* without the necessity of a substantive action of reduction": *Jarvie's Trs. v. Bannatyne* 1927 S.C. 34, 36 *per* Lord Fleming. Sometimes thought cumbersome and slow, a multiplepoinding has been (unfairly) described as a process in which, if there is anything left in the fund *in medio* at the conclusion of the action, some step of procedure has been omitted. Examples of issues which have been tried in an action of multiplepoinding include: reduction *ope exceptionis* of a decree in absence (*Jarvie's Trs.*, above); looking beyond the terms of a decree and to examine its *media concludendi* (*Thomson & Co. v. Friese-Greene's Tr.* 1944 S.C. 336); the existence or validity of a marriage (*Dean's J.F. v. Deans* 1912 S.C. 441); legitimacy (*Brook's Exx. v. James* 1970 S.C. 147, affd. 1971 S.C.(H.L.) 77); presumption of death (*Tait's Factor v. Meikle* (1890) 17 R. 1182: the court may sist the cause to enable a separate process for the declarator of death to be presented (*Clark's Exr. v. Clark* 1953 S.L.T. (Notes) 58), as was done in *Shepherd's Trs. v. Brown* (1902) 9 S.L.T. 487); the effect of the passing of an Act of Parliament on a bequest (*McClement's Trs. v. Lord Advocate* 1949 S.L.T. (Notes) 59) or whether the fund *in medio* (or part of it) fell to be regarded as heritable or moveable in a question of succession (*Cowan's Trs. v. Cowan* (1887) 14 R. 670). It is competent, though unusual, to set up a claim by one claimant in a multiplepoinding by reference to the oath of a competing claimant: *Farquhar v. Farquhar* (1886) 13 R. 596.

An action of multiplepoinding may involve a succession of separate actions to determine (1) objections to the raising of the action (usually by taking a plea to the competency), (2) the extent and identity of the fund *in medio* and (3) the claims of the respective claimants in a competition on that fund. Each of these distinct stages, if necessary (because an objection has been made), proceeds as an ordinary action, complete with a condescendence, defences and open record.

Jurisdiction. R. 2(9) of Sched. 8 to the C.J.J.A. 1982, relating to "proceedings . . . to assert, **51.1.2** declare or determine proprietary or possessory rights . . . in or over moveable property . . . in the courts for the place where the property is situated", is sufficiently broad to encompass an action of multiplepoinding. If the fund *in medio* is comprised of or includes immoveable property situated in Scotland, r. 4(1)(a) of Sched. 8 to the C.J.J.A. 1982 will also confer jurisdiction on the court, even if the defender's domicile is outwith the UK: C.J.J.A. 1982, Sched. 8, r. 2(8)(d). Further, it will be sufficient to establish jurisdiction in a multiplepoinding if at least one of the defenders is domiciled in Scotland: C.J.J.A. 1982, Sched. 8, r. 2(15)(a).

The existence of the fund *in medio* in Scotland is sufficient to found jurisdiction and supersedes the necessity of arrestment to found jurisdiction: *Miller v. Ure* (1838) 16 S. 1204.

Parties to actions of multiplepoinding

51.2.—(1) An action of multiplepoinding may be brought by any person holding, or having an interest in, or claim on, the fund *in medio*, in his own name.

(2) The pursuer shall call as defenders to such an action—

(*a*) all persons so far as known to him as having an interest in the fund *in medio*; and

(*b*) where he is not the holder of the fund, the holder of that fund.

Deriv. R.C.S. 1965, r. 175 substituted by S.I. 1986 No. 1941

"action of multiplepoinding". See note 51.1.1. **51.2.1**

"any person holding . . . the fund". The holder of the property in dispute (the "fund *in* **51.2.2** *medio*") is always known as the pursuer. If the holder of the fund raises the action, he is known as the "pursuer and real raiser". If someone other than the holder of the fund raises the action (the "real raiser"), the holder is known as the "pursuer and nominal raiser".

"in his own name". The person who raises an action of multiplepoinding, regardless of **51.2.3** whether or not he is the holder of the property in dispute (the "fund *in medio*"), is known as the "real raiser". The real raiser, if he holds the fund *in medio*, is also the pursuer. If he is not the pursuer (*i.e.* the holder of the fund) he is known as the "defender and real raiser". The real raiser should always conclude for distribution of the fund *in medio* among the claimants found entitled thereto: see the style in Form 13.2–B. If the real raiser is also the holder, he may also conclude for his exoneration and discharge. If the action is raised by someone other than the holder of the fund, the holder may, at a later stage, apply for his exoneration and discharge: see, *e.g.* r. 51.10 (consignation of fund into court after approval of the condescendence of the fund *in medio*) and r. 51.15 (consignation and exoneration at the conclusion of the multiplepoinding). Other conclusions in an action brought by the holder of the fund *in medio* may include: that he should be found liable only in once and single payment (or consignation) of the fund for the behoof of the persons who may have right thereto; that all claimants and others pretending right to the fund ought to produce their respective grounds of debt or other interest in the fund, and dispute their preference; and for his expenses out of the fund (on which see note 51.1.3): see Mackay's *Manual of Court of Session Practice*, ii.117–118.

A judicial factor may not competently obtain his exoneration and discharge in the course of a multiplepoinding, although he may competently raise such an action if competing claims are made on the estate under his charge: *Campbell v. Grant* (1890) 8 M. 988. Others holding funds in a fiduciary capacity, such as trustees and executors, may seek their exoneration and discharge in the course of an action of multiplepoinding only in limited circumstances: see note 51.4.1(4).

51.2.4   *"having an interest in, or claim on"*. As the purpose of a multiplepoinding is to free the holder from a multitude of claims in respect of the fund *in medio*, all persons who have made or are believed entitled to make a claim should be called as defenders. Persons not called may be allowed to lodge a claim at a later stage than they would otherwise would be: *Morgan v. Morris* (1856) 18 D. 797; affd. *sub. nom. Young v. Morris* (1858) 20 D.(H.L.) 12. This is the justification for the provisions for advertisement inviting objections to the action (r. 51.5) and claims on the fund (r. 51.8). The holder of the fund may also make a claim on the fund. When the holder of the fund is the real raiser, he does so in the condescendence of the fund. If the holder is not the real raiser, he states his claim in his objections to the action itself (stated in his defences, in terms of r. 51.4(1)) or in a separate condescendence of the fund (r. 51.3(2)(*a*)).

51.2.5   *"pursuer"*. For an action raised by a person falling within the terms of r. 51.2(2)(*b*), the reference to the pursuer in the beginning of r. 51.2(2) should be read as a reference to the pursuer as nominal raiser. Otherwise, the person holding the fund and raising the action is known as the "pursuer and real raiser".

51.2.6   *"defenders"*. In an action of multiplepoinding, the holder of the fund is always the pursuer. All persons having an interest in the fund should be called as defenders, of which there must be at least two. On the requirement of double distress generally, see note 51.4.1(4).

51.2.7   *"fund in medio"*. The property in dispute, whatever form it takes, is known as the "fund *in medio*". The fund *in medio* may be comprised of heritable property (*e.g. Edinburgh Merchant Maiden's Hospital v. Greig's Exrs.* (1902) 12 S.L.T. 317; *Boyd's Trs. v. Boyd* (1906) 13 S.L.T. 878; the statement in Bell's *Comm.*, ii,276 and Mackay's *Practice of the Court of Session*, ii, p. 113 to the contrary are incorrect), moveable property (including determination of right to title deeds: *Baillie v. Baillie* (1830) 8 S. 318) or a combination of heritable and moveable (*Logan v. Byres* (1895) 2 S.L.T. 455). In the course of a multiplepoinding the court may have to decide whether the fund *in medio* falls to be regarded as heritable or moveable, *e.g.* in determining rights of succession to the property comprising that fund: *Cowan v. Cowan* (1887) 14 R. 670. Rights *in spe* cannot alone form the fund *in medio* (*Provan v. Provan* (1840) 23 D. 298), although an unascertained amount may (*Highland Railway Co. v. British Linen Co.* (1901) 38 S.L.R. 584). The fund *in medio* should only include what is the subject-matter of the dispute and no other property: *McNab v. Waddell* (1894) 21 R. 827; *MacGillvray's Trs. v. Dallas* (1905) 7 F. 733. The court may dismiss such an action as incompetent (*McNab*, above) or allow the holder to amend the condescendence of the fund (*MacGillvray's Trs.*, above). Where the holder loses title to property in the fund *in medio* (*i.e.* by reduction of that title in a separate action) before the action of multiplepoinding is concluded, that property to which the holder no longer has valid title should be excluded from the condescendence of the fund: *Dunn's Trs. v. Barstow* (1870) 9 M. 281.

51.2.8   *Effect of raising action.* Bell noted in his *Commentaries* (ii,276), that because of its effect on diligence, an action of multiplepoinding was also known as "suspension of double poinding". He further stated that the effect of raising the action was to render the fund litigious, *i.e.* to prevent the holder from granting any voluntary conveyance of the fund while the action of multiplepoinding was in dependence: Bell's, *Comm.*, ii,278. It has been stated that the raising of an action of multiplepoinding does not sist all diligence against the fund, but any creditor who appears as a claimant could not proceed with diligence: Graham Stewart on *Diligence*, pp. 136–137. The point is not free from doubt. In *Ferguson v. Bothwell* (1882) 9 R. 786, a poinding creditor proceeded with diligence notwithstanding being cited as a defender in the multiplepoinding raised by his debtor. In that case the court observed that the proper course for the debtor would have been to raise his own action of suspension of the diligence.

Condescendence of fund in medio

51.3.—(1) Where the pursuer is the holder of the fund *in medio*, he shall include a detailed statement of the fund in the condescendence annexed to the summons.

(2) Where the pursuer is not the holder of the fund *in medio*, the holder shall, unless he has lodged defences in accordance with rule 51.4 (objections to actions of multiplepoinding), lodge in process a condescendence of the fund *in medio*, stating—

(*a*) any claim or lien which he may profess to have on that fund, and
(*b*) all persons so far as known to him as having an interest in the fund,
within seven days after the date on which the summons has called.

Deriv. R.C.S. 1965, r. 176 substituted by S.I. 1986 No. 1941

"where the pursuer is the holder of the fund". The pursuer is the real raiser.   **51.3.1**

"where the pursuer is not the holder . . . ". The real raiser is not the "pursuer", in the sense   **51.3.2** of being the holder of the fund. In such an action the holder of the fund is designed as the "pursuer and nominal raiser" and the real raiser is himself one of the defenders and is designed as "defender and real raiser".

"detailed statement of the fund". It should be sufficient to identify the property comprising   **51.3.3** the fund: see, *e.g.* the style in Green's *Encyclopaedia of Styles*, vol. 7, p. 105 (No. 74).

"condescendence of the fund in medio". The purpose of the condescendence of the fund,   **51.3.4** annexed to the summons by the pursuer and real raiser (under r. 51.3(1)) or lodged in process where the holder is not the real raiser (under r. 51.3(2)), is to enable the court to establish the extent, if any, of the fund *in medio*. This is an essential prior step to determining the rights of the respective claimants thereto. There must be a condescendence: *Carmichael v. Todd* (1853) 15 D. 473 (real raiser criticised by the court for, *inter alia*, failing to have a condescendence of the fund).

"lodged defences". The holder of the fund may object to the action of multiplepoinding and   **51.3.5** does so by lodging defences in accordance with r. 51.4(1).

"claim or lien". The holder may have a claim upon, or a lien over, the fund *in medio* (or   **51.3.6** that part of the fund in his possession). A holder's failure to assert a claim at this stage, *i.e.* in objections to the action itself, may not bar the claim, if the claim is stateable by way of retention or compensation, when objections to the condescendence of the fund are determined: *Ramsay's J.F. v. British Linen Bank* 1912 S.C. 206, 208. Trustees holding a fund for administration are obliged to lodge a claim, as trustees, for the whole fund for the purpose of administration: *Hall's Trs. v. McDonald* (1892) 19 R. 567, 577 *per* Lord Kinnear.

"summons". See Chap. 13.   **51.3.7**

"has called". On calling of a summons, see r. 13.13.   **51.3.8**

Objections to actions of multiplepoinding

51.4.—(1) Any objection to an action of multiplepoinding on any ground shall be made by lodging defences.

(2) Where the holder of a fund *in medio* lodges defences under paragraph (1), he shall, notwithstanding his objection to the action, disclose all persons so far as known to him and reasonably ascertainable who have an interest in that fund.

(3) On defences being lodged under paragraph (1), the pursuer shall comply with rule 22.1 (making up open records); and the action shall proceed for the purpose of determining the objection stated in the defences as an ordinary action.

(4) Where the holder of the fund *in medio* has lodged defences, the court shall, on determining those defences without dismissing the action, ordain the holder of the fund to lodge a condescendence of the fund *in medio* stating any claim or lien which he may profess to have on that fund, within such period as it thinks fit.

Deriv. R.C.S. 1965, r. 176(b)(part) amended by S.I. 1986 No. 1941 (r. 51.4(1)(part), (2) and (4)), r. 177(a) amended by S.I. 1986 No. 1941 (r. 51.4(1)(part)), and r. 177(b) (r. 51.4(3))

"objection . . . on any ground". An objection to an action of multiplepoinding must be   **51.4.1** dealt with before all other questions: *Connell v. Ferguson* (1861) 23 D. 683, 686 *per* Lord Neaves; *Clark v. Campbell* (1873) 1 R. 281 (*e.g.* before determining whether a foreign-domiciled real raiser was required to sist a mandatory).
The following objections have been taken:
(1) *No jurisdiction.* The situation of any part of the fund *in medio* in Scotland is sufficient to confer jurisdiction on the court: see note 51.1.2. Accordingly, the court has jurisdiction over a

foreign-domiciled defender in an action of multiplepoinding, but that does not otherwise make that person subject to the jurisdiction of the court in another action brought by a third party: *Bell v. Stewart* (1852) 14 D. 837.

(2) *Forum non conveniens.* See, *e.g. Okell v. Foden* (1884) 11 R. 906.

(3) *No fund in medio.* It is a valid objection to the competency of an action of multiplepoinding that there is no fund: see, *e.g. Provan v. Provan* (1840) 23 D. 298 (where the Lord Ordinary raised the question of competency on this ground at his own instance); but see *Crombie v. Crombie's Trs.* (1830) 8 S. 745, which is to the contrary effect. This defence is peculiar to the pursuer and nominal raiser: MacLaren on *Court of Session Practice*, p. 660. An objection that the real raiser is not entitled to the fund is not an objection to the competency of the action, but one which affects the merits: *Greenshield's Trs. v. Greenshield* 1915 2 S.L.T. 189.

(4) *No double distress.* In its original form, multiplepoinding (or "double poinding" in Stair's usage (Stair, IV.xvi.1) required double distress in the technical sense of double diligence. In his proposed style, Stair referred to multiple arrestments or poindings, from which the name of this action is presumably derived: Stair, IV.xvi.7. The nineteenth century saw some modification of this prerequisite for double diligence, as long as there was a double claim on the fund: "it is still however necessary to the validity of the action that there should be a true case of double claim to one fund or property on separate and hostile grounds, not a mere ostensible case got up in order to try a question of debt or obligation between two individuals, the proper mode of trying which is a direct action": *Russel v. Johnston* (1859) 21 D. 886, 887 *per* Lord Kinloch, quoted with approval by Lord Johnston in *Glen's Trs. v. Miller* 1911 S.C. 1178, 1185. If a direct action is available to the claimant, an action of multiplepoinding will be incompetent. So, *e.g.* an action of multiplepoinding has been held incompetent to determine a dispute between debtor and creditor (*Clark v. Campbell* (1873) 1 R. 281), between cedent and assignee (*Russel*, above), between trustees and beneficiaries (*Robb's Trs. v. Robb* (1880) 7 R. 1049), to determine whether the real raiser was entitled to *legitim* (*Scott's J.F. v. Richardson* (1905) 13 S.L.T. 537) and where it was used in lieu of an action of count and reckoning (*Carmichael v. Todd* (1853) 15 D. 473, 476 *per* Lord Cuninghame; *Park v. Mackersy* (1843) 5 D. 482; *cf. National Providential Institute v. Mcleod* 1915 2 S.L.T. 329 (in which an originally competent action of multiplepoinding became, because of the withdrawal of other claims, a direct action of count and reckoning)). A distinction, however, falls to be drawn between an action raised by a claimant and one raised by the holder of the fund: *Russel*, above. In the latter case, greater latitude is allowed. The holder of the fund "is entitled to be relieved by means of an action of multiplepoinding . . . and accordingly it is sufficient justification of the institution of the action, and is the criteria of its competency, that the claims intimated make it impossible for the depositary to pay to one of the parties without running the risk of an action at the instance of the other.": *Winchester v. Blakey* (1890) 17 R. 1046, 1050 *per* Lord MacLaren. The rationale is that a holder "can never raise a direct action, and is not bound to remain a depositary till the day of his death": *Winchester*, above. Accordingly, it is sufficient if there are competing claims which the holder of the fund is unable to meet: *Winchester*, above. So, *e.g.* actions of multiplepoinding which would otherwise have been dismissed as incompetent, because only raising an issue between two claimants triable by direct action, were nonetheless allowed when raised by the holders: *Royal Bank of Scotland v. Price* (1893) 20 R. 290; *Commercial Bank of Scotland v. Muir* (1897) 25 R. 219.

Resort to an action of multiplepoinding should not be made by trustees, executors and those who hold monies on behalf of others simply as a means to determine disputes in relation to those monies where there is no genuine double distress. So, *e.g.* an action of multiplepoinding raised by trustees was refused where the only dispute was between a beneficiary and a creditor on the estate (*Glen's Trs. v. Miller* 1911 S.C. 1178; *cf. Ogilvie's Trs. v. Chevalier* (1874) 1 R. 693 (in which a multiplepoinding by testamentary trustees was only reluctantly allowed where the only dispute was between the sole beneficiary and her creditor)) or where a solicitor was called upon to pay over the estate to the confirmed executor and another party claimed right to those funds (*Adam Cochran & Co. v. Conn* 1989 S.L.T. (Sh. Ct.) 27). An attempt to use an action of multiplepoinding in this way may be an abuse of process: *Ogilvie's Trs.*, above. Nor should executors or trustees resort to a multiplepoinding in order to obtain exoneration and discharge where there is no difficulty obtaining this extrajudicially: *Mackenzie's Trs. v. Gray* (1895) 2 S.L.T. 422. It has been held competent, however, for those holding monies in a fiduciary capacity, such as trustees and executors, to raise an action of multiplepoinding to obtain their exoneration and discharge if those in whose power it is to grant this refuse to do so (*Fraser's Exr. v. Wallace's Trs.* (1893) 20 R. 374, 379 *per* Lord MacLaren; *Mackenzie's Trs. v. Sutherland* (1894) 22 R. 233, 237 *per* Lord Kinnear), are otherwise unable to grant sufficient exoneration (*Davidson v. Ewen* (1895) 3 S.L.T. 162) or because of doubts as to the construction of testamentary bequests it is unclear who is entitled to the fund and able to give valid discharge (*McClement's Trs. v. Lord Advocate* 1949 S.L.T. (Notes) 59).

A judicial factor may not competently obtain his exoneration and discharge in the course of an action of multiplepoinding. A judicial factor is appointed by the court in the exercise of its *nobile officium* and his ultimate discharge is likewise granted in exercise of those powers: *Campbell v. Grant* (1869) 7 M. 227, 233 *per* Lord Deas, (1870) 8 M. 988.

(5) *All parties not called.* See, *e.g. Connell v. Ferguson* (1861) 23 D. 683.

(6) *Irregular statement of facts.* For an unusual case in which objection was taken to the statement of facts by the defender and real raiser, see *Carmichael v. Todd* (1853) 15 D. 473, in which the single beneficiary under a trust deed raised an action of multiplepoinding in the name of the judicial factor appointed to manage the estate after the death of all the testamentary trustees. The real raiser proceeded to make detailed allegations of misconduct against the judicial factor. The court dismissed the multiplepoinding as both incompetent, there being no double distress, and irregular, in that the statement of facts contained averments which the nominal raiser, in whose name the action had been raised, was bound to deny.

"*an ordinary action*". The action proceeds as an ordinary action for the purpose of deter-   **51.4.2** mining the objections to the raising of the action of multiplepoinding stated in the defences. An open record is made up. This is only one of several records within an action of multiplepoinding, the others concerning the ascertainment of the fund *in medio*, if objections are taken to the condescendence of the fund (as opposed to the action itself) and, thirdly, the competition (if any) of the claimants on the fund.

"*holder . . . lodges defences*". These may be preliminary (*e.g.* because there is no double   **51.4.3** distress or no fund) or substantive.

"*lodge a condescendence of the fund*". If the holder is the real raiser, he will have annexed a   **51.4.4** condescendence of the fund to the summons. Where, however, he is only the nominal raiser, he should lodge a condescendence of the fund in terms of r. 51.3(2). Alternatively, the holder may, under this rule (r. 51.4(4)), be ordained to lodge a condescendence, once the objections to the action have been determined by the court. On the condescendence of the fund, see note 51.3.4.

"*for the purpose of determining the objection*". This only determines objections to the   **51.4.5** action. The court may, by separate causes each with its own record, have to determine objections to the condescendence of the fund *in medio* and, finally, to determine the respective rights of the claimants to that fund.

Advertisement for objections to condescendence and claims

51.5.—(1) The pursuer may—

    (*a*) after the expiry of the period for lodging defences without defences having been lodged, or

    (*b*) where defences have been lodged, after those defences have been repelled and, where an order is made under rule 51.4(4), the condescendence of the fund has been lodged,

apply by motion for the orders mentioned in paragraph (2).

(2) The orders referred to in paragraph (1) are—

    (*a*) the ordaining of any objection to the condescendence of the fund *in medio* and claims on the fund to be lodged within such period as the court thinks fit; and

    (*b*) advertisement of the call for any objection and claims in such newspapers or other publications and for such number of insertions as the court thinks fit.

(3) An advertisement ordered under paragraph (1) shall be in Form 51.5.

Deriv. R.C.S. 1965, r. 182(*a*) (r. 51.5(1) and (2)(*a*))

"*expiry of the period for lodging defences*". This will be seven days after the date on which   **51.5.1** the summons has called or, if the seventh day falls in vacation, the next day on which a summons may be called: r. 18.1(2).

"*motion*". For motions, see Chap. 23.   **51.5.2**

"*advertisement*". The purpose of intimating the raising of an action of multiplepoinding is   **51.5.3** to ensure that all persons entitled to make a claim have an opportunity to do so. It has been stated to be "an essential prerequisite to any judgment in [a] competition": *Connell v. Ferguson* (1861) 23 D. 683, 687 *per* Lord Neaves. Failure to make an order for claims would render a decree of preference "ineffectual or unsafe as an exoneration of the nominal raisers, if no such interlocutor allowing claims should ever have been pronounced": *Connell*, above. The court may at its own instance order advertisement or other intimation: see r. 51.9, and *Connell*, above. The newspaper containing the advertisement or the publisher's certificate of publication required under r. 51.9(*a*) is lodged as a production: see r. 4.5.

Form of objection to condescendence and claims

51.6.—(1) An objection to a condescendence of the fund *in medio* shall be made by lodging defences.

(2) A claim on the fund *in medio* shall be made in the form of a condescendence, claim and appropriate pleas-in-law.

(3) On lodging a condescendence and claim, a claimant shall lodge his ground of debt and all other documents supporting his claim.

(4) Where a person intends to—

(*a*) object to the condescendence on the fund *in medio*, and

(*b*) make a claim on the fund,

he shall lodge defences and a separate condescendence and claim.

Deriv. R.C.S. 1965, r. 180

51.6.1 *"An objection to a condescendence of the fund"*. The condescendence of the fund *in medio* will have been lodged by the holder under r. 51.3(1) or (2) or under r. 51.4(4). If objections are stated to the condescendence of the fund *in medio*, the adjudication of those objections forms a separate cause within the multiplepoinding. A separate record is made up. The objections must be stated in defences (see r. 51.6(1)) as a separate statement of facts on which the objections are based, pleas-in-law are annexed to the condescendence and are signed by counsel or other person having a right of audience (see definition in r. 1.3(1)). The most common objection is that there is some property or monies which should be excluded from the condescendence of the fund: see, *e.g. Walker's Tr. v. Walker* (1878) 5 R. 678; *Donaldson's Trs. v. Beattie* 1914 1 S.L.T. 170. Objections, however, that clearly undisputed property has been included in the condescendence of the fund *in medio* appear to be treated as raising questions as to the competency of the action (*e.g. McNab v. Waddell* (1894) 21 R. 827), rather than stated at this stage. Objection to the condescendence of the fund should not be combined with objections (if any) to the competency of the action itself. The court will have dealt with objections to the latter under r. 51.4. In *Walker's Trs.*, above, the court allowed objections to the condescendence of the fund *in medio* to be made, notwithstanding that it had already pronounced an interlocutor finding the holder and real raiser liable only in once and single payment.

51.6.2 *"condescendence"*. A claimant's condescendence should give the factual basis on which his claim is founded. A condescendence by a claimant (under r. 51.1(2)) should not be confused with the holder's condescendence of the fund *in medio* (although the holder should state his own claim (if any) in the condescendence of the fund). A claimant's condescendence is in the same form as the condescendence in other actions (on which, see note 13.2.4), but must conclude with a separate short claim (on which, see note 51.6.3).

51.6.3 *"claim"*. The claim is a short sentence in which the claimant claims to be ranked and preferred to the whole (or a specified portion) of the fund *in medio*. If a condescendence does not contain a claim, the claimant cannot be preferred to the fund *in medio*: *Connell v. Ferguson* (1861) 23 D. 683, 686 *per* Lord Neaves. A holder's claim may include a right of retention or compensation. Notice of such a claim should be given as early as possible in the process: *Ramsay's J.F. v. British Linen Bank* 1912 S.C. 206, 208.

In some circumstances, by what is known as a "riding claim", a person may claim to be ranked on the fund *in medio* by virtue of his debtor's claim in the multiplepoinding. However, the debtor's claim, through which the creditor is asserting a riding claim, must be a direct one and not, *e.g.* through the debtor's debtor: *Gill's Trs. v. Patrick* (1889) 16 R. 403. A riding claim must be constituted (*Royal Bank of Scotland v. Stevenson* (1849) 12 D. 250) and liquid (*Home's Trs. v. Ralston's Trs.* (1834) 12 S. 727; *Wilson v. Young* (1851) 13 D. 1366). The riding claim must be lodged before decree for payment is pronounced in favour of the original claimant (*i.e.* the debtor): *Anglo-Foreign Banking Co.* (1879) 16 S.L.R. 731. A riding claim has been described as a *surrogatum* of arrestment or assignation to prevent the fund being taken out of court: *Royal Bank of Scotland*, above, *per* Lord Jeffrey at p. 252. It would appear competent, though no reported decision has been found, for more than one riding claim to be ranked on a principal claim, compelling a separate competition in respect of those several riding claims on the principal claimant's share of the fund: Thomson & Middleton, *Manual of Court of Session Practice*, p. 124. The court has refused a riding claim where, after consideration of the *media concludendi* of the decree on which the riding claim was based, it was regarded as an attempt to obtain a preference: *Thomson & Co. v. Friese-Greene's Tr.* 1944 S.C. 336.

"pleas-in-law". The plea is that the claimant is entitled to be ranked and preferred to the fund **51.6.4** *in medio* in terms of his claim. On pleas-in-law generally, see note 18.1.4.

"ground of debt and all other documents". Any document of debt founded on or adopted in **51.6.5** the defences must be lodged as a production when the defences are lodged: r. 27.1(1)(b). For lodging productions, see r. 4.5.

"defences and a separate condescendence and claim". That is, an objection to the **51.6.6** condescendence of the fund, separate from objections to the action itself. On claims, see note 51.6.3.

Procedure following call for objections

51.7.—(1) Where defences are lodged under rule 51.6 (form of objection to condescendence and claims), an open record shall be made up on the condescendence and such objection, and the pursuer shall comply with rule 22.1 (making up open records); and the cause shall proceed for the purposes of determining the objection as an ordinary action.

(2) No order shall be pronounced in relation to any claims on the fund *in medio* until any defences under rule 51.6 have been disposed of and the condescendence of the fund *in medio* approved.

(3) Where the court disposes of defences, or where no defences have been lodged under rule 51.6, the court shall—

(a) approve the condescendence of the fund *in medio*, subject to such alteration as it may make in disposing of any objection;

(b) find the pursuer, or where he is not the holder of the fund, the holder, liable only in once and single payment;

(c) make such further order, if any, for claims as it thinks fit.

Deriv. R.C.S. 1965, r. 182(c) (r. 51.7(1)) and r. 179(part) amended by S.I. 1986 No. 1941 (r. 51.7(3))

"objection to condescendence". See note 51.6.1. **51.7.1**

"as an ordinary action". This is the second of several separate causes in the course of a **51.7.2** multiplepoinding. The purpose is to adjudicate on the objections (if any) to the fund, in order to ascertain its extent.

"approve the condescendence of the fund in medio". This is a final interlocutor, which may be **51.7.3** reclaimed without leave: *School Board of Harris v. Davidson* (1881) 9 R. 375; *Walker's Tr. v. Walker* (1878) 5 R. 678.

"once and single payment". The purpose of finding the holder liable "only in once and single **51.7.4** payment", once the objections (if any) are determined and the fund is approved, is to enable the holder to make payment (usually by consigning the fund into court) and effectively drop out of the action (unless the holder also wishes to assert a claim to the fund): see, *e.g.* r. 51.10. The court does not always require consignation: *British Linen Co. v. Breadalbane's Trs.* (1836) 15 S. 356.

Advertisement of dependence of actions

51.8. The court may, at its own instance or on the motion of a party, at any time order—

(a) such advertisement of the dependence of the action as it thinks fit; and

(b) intimation of the dependence of the action to any person not called as a defender.

Deriv. R.C.S. 1965, r. 178(part) amended by S.I. 1986 No. 1941

"advertisement". See note 51.5.3. **51.8.1**

"dependence of the action". A cause is depending from the time it is commenced (*i.e.* from the **51.8.2** time an action is served) until final decree, whereas a cause is in dependence until final extract. For the meaning of commenced, see note 13.4.4. For the meaning of final decree, see note 4.15.2(2). For the meaning of final extract, see note 7.1.2(2).

Evidence of advertisement and intimation
  51.9. Where the court orders advertisement or intimation under this Chapter, the party required to make such advertisement or intimation shall lodge in process, as the case may be—
    (a) a copy of the newspaper or other publication containing the advertisement or a certificate of publication by the publisher stating the date of publication and the text of the advertisement; or
    (b) the certificate of intimation.

Deriv. R.C.S. 1965, r. 178(part) amended by S.I. 1986 No. 1941

51.9.1   *"advertisement"*. See note 51.5.3.

51.9.2   *"intimation"*. For methods, see rr. 16.7 and 16.8.

Consignation of fund and discharge of holder
  51.10.—(1) On approval of the condescendence of the fund *in medio*, the holder of the fund may apply by motion for—
    (a) a finding that he is entitled to his expenses out of the fund; and
    (b) authority to consign the fund into court, after deduction of his expenses as taxed by the Auditor.
  (2) Where consignation is made by virtue of an authority under paragraph (1)(b), the holder of the fund may apply by motion for his exoneration and discharge.

51.10.1   *"approval of the condescendence of the fund in medio"*. The court's approval of the fund is essential, as the interlocutor determines the amount for which the holder is liable to account. An interlocutor approving of the fund becomes final if not reclaimed against before the expiry of the period for so doing.

51.10.2   *"motion"*. For motions, see Chap. 23.

51.10.3   *"expenses out of the fund"*. If the holder of the fund is not the real raiser (*i.e.* he is the nominal raiser), he will be entitled to the expenses of the condescendence of the fund out of that fund. If the holder is the real raiser and the action was justified, he will generally be entitled to expenses *primo loco* out of the fund. If trustees raise an action of multiplepointing which is subsequently found to be unjustified, they may be found personally liable in expenses: *Mackenzie's Trs. v. Sutherland* (1894) 22 R. 233; *Paterson's Trs. v. Paterson* (1897) 7 S.L.T. 134; *cf. Gill's Trs. v. Miller* 1911 S.C. 1178.

51.10.4   *"consignation"*. The amount consigned is the balance in the hands of the holder after deduction of the holder's taxed expenses (if any). The form of the fund, or a part of it, may make consignation difficult. In one case, where part of the fund was a bond and disposition in security, the court ordered the holder to execute and lodge in process an assignation of the bond in favour of the successful claimant: *Currie's Trs. v. Bothwell* 1954 S.L.T.(Sh.Ct.) 87. On consignation generally, see note 33.4.3. The court may require an agent of the holder to consign the fund, reserving all claims by the agent: *Long v. Downie* (1872) 9 S.L.R. 308.

51.10.5   *"exoneration and discharge"*. The effect is to take the holder out of the action and to free him from all future claims by any person: see, *e.g. Farquhar v. Farquhar* (1896) 13 R. 596. Exoneration and discharge is not normally granted until consignation of the fund *in medio* has been effected to the satisfaction of the court.

Claims not timeously lodged
  51.11.—(1) A claimant who fails to lodge his claim within the period specified in the order under rule 51.5(2)(a) (order for any objections and for claims) may apply by motion to have his claim received.
  (2) The court may allow such a claim to be received on such conditions as to expenses, if any, as it thinks fit.

Deriv. R.C.S. 1965, r. 181

51.11.1   *"fails to lodge his claim within the period specified"*. It has been observed that "the process of multiplepointing admits ... of a very great latitude in the lodging of claims, both by those who have been called as defenders and by those who have not. Claims are constantly received long after the prescribed time for lodging them has expired": *Landale v. Wilson* (1900) 2 F. 1047, 1048–1049 *per* Lord Stormonth-Darling. It is a matter for the court's discretion whether to allow a late claim: *Young v. Morris* (1858) 20 D.(H.L.) 12. Once a decree of ranking and preference has been pronounced the fund is no longer *in medio* and the late claimant cannot demand of right to lodge a claim: *Young*, above. *A fortiori*, the court will not entertain a late claim where the decree of ranking and preference has been substantially implemented and the fund paid away: *Stodart v. Bell* (1860) 22 D. 1092. Generally, a late claim will be allowed, unless an interlocutor pronounced on a ranking and preference of the claimant's respective claims has become final: *Landale*, above; *Ramsay's J.F. v. British Linen Bank* 1911 S.C. 832. If the interlocutor is final, the Lord Ordinary is *functus* (*Ramsay's J.F.*, above; *Terrell v. Kerr* (1900) 2 F. 1055) and it is beyond the competence of the Lord Ordinary to review that interlocutor (*Duncan's Factor v. Duncan* (1874) 1 R. 964, 965 *per* Lord Gifford). Nor is it within the power of a Lord Ordinary to allow a late claim, where the Inner House had pronounced decree of ranking and preference and thereafter remitted the cause to the Lord Ordinary to carry its judgment into effect: *Landale*, above. In the absence of a decree of preference being final, the Inner House may recall *in hoc statu* the interlocutor of the Lord Ordinary and, subject to payment of expenses, allow a late claim to be lodged. Leave to lodge a late claim has been allowed in relation to a person who was called as a defender but who had never appeared (*Binnie's Trs. v. Henry's Trs.* (1883) 10 R. 1075), a person who had entered appearance but had never lodged a claim (*Jaffe v. Carruthers* (1860) 22 D. 936), a person who had lodged, and then before the closing of the record withdrew, an earlier claim (*Binnie's Trs.*, above) and a fresh claim by an unsuccessful claimant after judgment on a new ground (*Dymond v. Scott* (1877) 5 R. 196). The court may be more disposed to allow a late claim by a person who was never called in the multiplepoinding: compare the court's treatment of the first and second groups of late claimants in *Morgan v. Morris* (1856) 18 D. 797. The Inner House has permitted, at the bar in a reclaiming motion, amendment of a claim by the holder of the fund: *Hall's Trs. v. McDonald* (1892) 19 R. 567. In an unusual case a claim was rejected as too late, coming as it did after the expiry of the reclaiming days for the decree of ranking and preference (*Ramsay's J.F.*, above), but was subsequently allowed to be stated by way of plea of compensation or retention in the objections to the condescendence of the fund: *Ramsay's J.F v. British Linen Bank* 1912 S.C. 206. Greater latitude, however, is allowed in respect of the late lodging of a riding claim (on which see note 51.6.3) because such a claim would not disturb the existing decree of ranking and preference, but simply substitute the creditor with a riding claim in place of the successful claimant: see, *e.g. Scottish Life Assurance Co. Ltd v. John Donald Ltd* (1902) 9 S.L.T. 348; *Ramsay's J.F. v. British Linen Bank* 1911 S.C. 832, 834 *per* Lord Mackenzie, 1912 S.C. 206, 210 *per* Lord Salvesen. It is too late to lodge a riding claim once a decree for payment in favour of the claimant has been made: *Anglo-Foreign Banking Co.* (1879) 16 S.L.R. 731.

"*motion*". For motions, see Chap. 23.   **51.11.2**

"*such conditions as to expenses … as it thinks fit*". The court may order payment of a   **51.11.3** proportion of the successful claimant's expenses, usually in the same proportion as the late claimant is likely to benefit from the successful claimant's efforts: *e.g.* one-half (*Morgan v. Morris* (1856) 18 D. 797), one-quarter (*Cowan's Trs. v. Cowan* (1887) 14 R. 670), one-third (*National Bank of Scotland v. City Commercial Restaurant* (1901) 9 S.L.T. 211). If the person seeking leave to lodge a late claim fails to meet the condition (*i.e.* payment of expenses), his application for leave will be refused: *Morgan v. Morris*, above, 818–819; affd. *sub nom. Young v. Morris* (1858) 20 D.(H.L.) 12.

Procedure following approval of fund in medio

51.12.—(1) After the condescendence of the fund *in medio* has been approved, and it appears that there is no competition, the court may, on the motion of any claimant, rank and prefer the parties who have lodged claims.

(2) After the condescendence of the fund *in medio* has been approved and where there is competition—

(a) any party may apply by motion for an order to print a record in the competition and, on such an order being made, an open record shall be made up on the condescendences and claims and the pursuer shall comply with rule 22.1 (making up open records); and the action shall proceed for the purpose of determining the competition as an ordinary action; and

(b) during the period of adjustment, a claimant may adjust his condescendence to state any objection to any other claim.

(3) When pronouncing any decree of ranking on the fund *in medio*, the court may determine any question of expenses; and, where it finds any party entitled to expenses out of the fund *in medio*, notwithstanding rule 42.1(1)(b) (decerniture for expenses as taxed) it shall not at the same time decern for payment of those expenses.

Deriv. R.C.S. 1965, r. 183(part) (r. 51.12(1)) and r. 185 (r. 51.12(2))

51.12.1   *"condescendence of the fund in medio … has been approved"*. See note 51.7.4.

51.12.2   *"competition"*. A competition arises where the claims exceed the value of the fund or are competing in respect of a particular part of the fund. If there is no competition, the Lord Ordinary gives effect to the claimants' respective claims by a decree of ranking and preference (on which, see note 51.12.3). Thereafter, a decree of payment is pronounced: see, *e.g. Morgan v. Morris* (1856) 18 D. 797. If there is a competition, this forms a separate cause within the multiplepoinding. Again, a decree of ranking and preference will follow, once the claimants' respective claims have been allowed or repelled.

51.12.3   *"rank and prefer the parties who have lodged claims"*. If there is no competition, the parties may agree in a joint minute to a ranking of their respective claims, though this is not necessary. The court may refuse a joint minute purporting to agree a scheme of division which is not in accordance with the claimants' respective entitlements in terms of the decree of ranking and preference: *Tennent's J.F. v. Tennent* 1956 S.L.T.(Notes) 39. A decree of ranking and preference may be granted without proof: *Union Bank v. Gracie* (1887) 25 S.L.R. 61. The court may refuse to pronounce a decree of ranking and preference, notwithstanding that there is no competition, if it appears *ex facie* of a claimant's claim that he has no right to that part of the fund to which he lays claim: *Clark's Exr. v. Clark* 1953 S.L.T. (Notes) 58. The court has refused to pronounce a decree of ranking and preference, except for "aught yet seen" (on which, see note 51.13.2), where the existence of claimants was not known and had not been excluded (*i.e.* by a separate declarator of presumption of death): *Kerr's Trs.* (1894) 2 S.L.T. 10. A decree of ranking and preference in favour of one party, by its nature, excludes every other party: *Duncan's Factor v. Duncan* (1874) 1 R. 964, 968 *per* L.P. Inglis. Once final, a decree of ranking and preference can only be brought under review by a person called as a defender in the multiplepoinding in which the decree was pronounced, by an action of reduction: *Stodart v. Bell* (1860) 22 D. 1092, 1093 *per* Lord Cowan.

51.12.4   *"motion"*. For motions, see Chap. 23.

51.12.5   *"as an ordinary action"*. This is another of several potential separate causes in the course of a multiplepoinding. The purpose is to adjudicate on the claimants' respective claims, which are either repelled or allowed, to the fund itself.

51.12.6   *"to state any objections to any other claim"*. It is competent for a claimant to challenge the ground of any other claimant's claim, including a decree which may be irregular (*Fischer & Co. v. Anderson* (1896) 23 R. 395) or otherwise incompetent (*Dickson & Walker v. Mitchell & Co.* 1910 S.C. 139).

Decrees for payment
51.13.—(1) No decree for payment out of the fund *in medio*, whether consigned into court or not, following an order for ranking (whether for aught yet seen or otherwise) shall be made until—
[1] (a) all accounts of expenses found payable out of the fund *in medio* have been taxed and the report of the Auditor on those accounts has been approved; and
(b) the certificate referred to in rule 8.1(1)(b) (Inland Revenue certificate of taxes or duties paid) has been lodged.
(2) Where the fund *in medio* has been consigned into court, any decree for payment out of the fund shall include—
(a) warrant to the bank, on production of a certified copy of the interlocutor granting decree, to pay to each party the sums for which he has been ranked; and

(*b*) warrant to the Accountant of Court, on production of a certified copy of the interlocutor granting decree, to endorse and deliver the consignation receipt to the bank in order that the payments may be made.

Deriv. R.C.S. 1965, r. 183(part)

---

[1] R. 51.13(1)(*a*) amended by S.I. 1994 No. 2901 (minor correction).

"decree for payment". An interlocutor ranking and preferring the successful claimants in terms of their claims may include, or be followed by, an order for payment or transfer of the fund *in medio* to the claimants preferred. The interlocutor ranking and preferring the claimants determines the merits, while the decree for payment (or warrant for payment from consigned funds) is the mechanism for giving effect to the order for ranking and preference. Once decerniture for payment has been made, the holder is secure against any further claims at the instance of persons called in that action: Erskine, IV.iii.23; Mackay's *Manual of Court of Session Practice*, ii.118.   **51.13.1**

"for aught yet seen". A decree of ranking and preference "for aught yet seen" may be granted notwithstanding the possibility that other claimants may subsequently emerge with a preferable title to the fund *in medio*: *Clark's Exr. v. Clark* 1953 S.L.T. (Notes) 58. The wording "for aught yet seen" imports a qualification of that decree of ranking and preference. A decree for aught yet seen has been held conclusive against persons cited, and who neither appeared in the original action of multiplepoinding nor reclaimed against the decree of preference: Mackay's *Manual of Court of Session Practice*, ii.110. Compare the position of persons not called (but who should have been): *Johnston v. Elder* (1832) 10 S. 195.   **51.13.2**

"Inland Revenue certificate". The purpose of this rule is to provide a safeguard for the Inland Revenue by preventing any payment out of the fund *in medio* until the court has been satisfied that all government duties have been paid. If unauthorised payments have been made out of the fund, the court may not grant the holder of the fund exoneration and discharge: *Simpson's Trs. v. Fox* 1954 S.L.T. (Notes) 12. In *Simpson's Trs.*, in which *per incuriam* payment had been made to beneficiaries (in whose favour an order of ranking and preference had been made), the court granted exoneration and discharge after the certificates had been lodged. See Chap. 8 generally for taxes on funds in the control of the court.   **51.13.3**

"consigned into court". On consignation into court, see notes 51.10.4 and 33.4.3.   **51.13.4**

"certified copy of the interlocutor". A copy of the interlocutor is typed by the agent and presented to the clerk of session at the appropriate section of the General Department or at the Petition Department. The clerk checks it, certifies it as a true copy and stamps it with the court stamp.   **51.13.5**

Reclaiming by claimant against ranking for aught yet seen

51.14.—(1) A claimant who has failed to lodge his claim on the fund *in medio* before a ranking for aught yet seen, may reclaim against the interlocutor making such ranking at any time while the action is depending.

(2) The Division of the Inner House before which a motion for review of an interlocutor is brought under paragraph (1) may recall that interlocutor and remit the cause to the Lord Ordinary to receive the claim on such conditions as to expenses, if any, as it thinks fit.

Deriv. R.C.S. 1965, r. 184

"for aught yet seen". See note 51.13.2.   **51.14.1**

"depending". A cause is depending from the time it is commenced (*i.e.* from the time an action is served) until final decree, whereas a cause is in dependence until final extract. For the meaning of commenced, see note 13.4.4. For the meaning of final decree, see note 4.15.2(2). For the meaning of final extract, see note 7.1.2(2).   **51.14.2**

"such conditions as to expenses. . .as it thinks fit". In an unusual case, no condition as to expenses was imposed where the person seeking leave to lodge a late claim after decree of preference had been pronounced ought (as an arresting creditor) to have been called as a defender in the action: *Johnston v. Elder* (1832) 10 S. 195.   **51.14.3**

Exoneration of holder where no consignation

51.15. Where the holder of the fund *in medio* has not been exonerated and discharged, he may—

(a) following a decree for payment,

(b) on production of the receipts of the persons entitled to payment under that decree, and

(c) on consignation of any balance of the fund remaining,

apply by motion for his exoneration and discharge.

51.15.1   *"decree for payment"*. See note 51.13.1.

51.15.2   *"motion"*. For motions, see Chap. 23.

CHAPTER 52

ACTIONS OF PROVING THE TENOR

Parties to action of proving the tenor

52.1. In an action of proving the tenor, the pursuer shall call as a defender—

(a) any person having an interest in the document to be proved; or

(b) where only the pursuer has such an interest, the Lord Advocate as representing the public interest.

Deriv. R.C.S. 1965, r. 186

52.1.1   *General note.* An action to prove the tenor is an action to obtain an order containing the tenor (*i.e.* terms or content) of any part of a lost or destroyed document. The order has the same effect as the original document would have had. The action is declaratory in effect but it is not a species of action of declarator: *Dunbar & Co. v. Scottish County Investment Co. Ltd* 1920 S.C. 210, 213 *per* L.J.-C. Scott Dickson. The document the tenor of which is sought to be proved must have been lost or destroyed erroneously. Generally, a document (*e.g.* a testamentary writing) which has been destroyed legitimately for the purpose of revocation may not be the subject of an action to prove the tenor (see *e.g. Bonthrone v. Ireland* (1883) 10 R. 779). Occasionally the court may grant the order containing the tenor of the document but under reservation of any question of its validity at the date of granting: *Falconer v. Stephen* (1849) 11 D. 1338.

52.1.2   *Necessity for the action.* The action is necessary where a person requires the principal of the lost or destroyed document to establish a title to sue (*Shaw v. Shaw's Trs.* (1876) 3 R. 813) or where the document is the subject-matter of an action (*Dow v. Dow* (1848) 10 D. 1465 (action of nullity of testamentary writing)).

   The action is unnecessary where the lost or destroyed document is merely a part of the evidence in a cause: *Young v. Thomson* 1909 S.C. 529; *Maxwell v. Reid* (1863) 1 M. 932. It is equally unnecessary where it is founded on by a defender or a respondent as part of a defence: *Drummond v. Thomson's Trs.* (1834) 7 W. & S. 564, 572 *per* Lord Brougham. Where a party to a cause has destroyed the document on which the other party (usually pursuer or petitioner) founds, he cannot plead that the other party must raise an action to prove the tenor of that document: *Seton v. Paterson* (1766) 5 Brown's Supp. 924; *Ross v. Fisher* (1833) 11 S. 467.

   The person who requires the document may also overcome the need for an action to prove its tenor by agreeing its terms in a joint minute of agreement for the purposes of a proposed litigation with the other likely party. Following the widespread use of photocopying machines this may be a possible solution. Where, however, there is no other party (*e.g.* in a petition for appointment as an executor-dative) an action of proving the tenor may still be required to establish title to sue on the basis of the lost document.

52.1.3   *Jurisdiction.* The applicability of the C.J.J.A. 1982 depends to some extent on the subject-matter of the document sought to be proved. Thus:

   (1) *In a jurisdictional issue between states party to the 1968 or Lugano Convention*, these conventions do not apply to matters relating to status or legal capacity of natural persons, wills and succession, bankruptcy, etc., social security and arbitration (C.J.J.A. 1982, Scheds. 1 and 3C, Art. 1).

   (2) *In a jurisdictional issue between U.K. legal systems.* Sched. 4 to the C.J.J.A. 1982 would appear to apply.

   (3) *In a jurisdictional issue between Scotland and any other legal system not mentioned in (1) and (2) above* because an action of proving the tenor involves an exercise of the *nobile officium* (see below), Sched. 8 to the C.J.J.A. 1982 does not apply: C.J.J.A. 1982, s. 22(3). The common law, therefore, does apply.

Jurisdiction at common law rests with the *nobile officium* of the court: *Dunbar & Co. v. Scottish County Investment Co.* 1920 S.C. 210, 217 *per* Lord Salvesen. Until the A.S. 20th March 1907, after the action had been raised in the Outer House, the Lord Ordinary made avizandum in the cause to the Inner House where the proof was heard and the interlocutor on the merits pronounced. Since 1907 the exercise of the *nobile officium* has been delegated to the Outer House. An action of proving the tenor is not a species of action of declarator and accordingly the sheriff does not have jurisdiction: *Dunbar & Co.*, above.

The pursuer. Any person with a *prima facie* interest in the lost or destroyed document may be **52.1.4** a pursuer: *Winchester v. Smith* (1863) 1 M. 685, 692 *per* Lord Deas. This may include a signatory of the document, an assignee of the signatory, a representative of a deceased signatory or a grantee of a unilaterally signed recorded document (*Brown v. Orr* (1872) 10 M. 397).

The defender. Every person having an interest should be called as a defender: r. 52.1(a). **52.1.5** Where the pursuer alone has an interest he should call the Lord Advocate as representing the public interest: r. 52.1(b).

Lodging of supporting evidence
52.2. On lodging the summons for signeting, supporting documentary evidence of the tenor of the document to be proved in an action of proving the tenor, so far as in the possession or control of the pursuer, shall be lodged in process.

Deriv. RCS 1965, r. 187

Summons. For form of summons, see r. 13.2. In the conclusions, apart from the statutory **52.2.1** requirements of r. 13.2(2) and Form 13.2–B(6), there should be a conclusion for expenses against the defender "in the event of a defender appearing to oppose the action".

In the condescendence the pursuer should aver:

(1) *The terms of the document.* These should be narrated in the conclusions. It may be sufficient only to incorporate the terms in the condescendence by reference to the conclusion.

(2) *Existence of adminicles.* These are any writs which tend to establish the contents of the document sought to be proved. They may include drafts (*McLeod v. Leslie* (1865) 3 M. 840) or informal copies (*e.g.* photocopies) or correspondence (Erskine, IV.i.55). Where the document lost or destroyed is one where copies, drafts or other written evidence of the contents may reasonably be expected to exist, the pursuer must produce and aver such an adminicle: Erskine, IV.i.55; *Winton & Co. v. Thomson & Co.* (1862) 24 D. 1094. An example of such a document is a formal document prepared by a law agent: *Graham v. McFarlane* (1847) 10 D. 45 (deed of entail). Where the document is not one where an adminicle would reasonably be expected (*e.g.* where a law agent was not involved) then an adminicle need not be averred: *Winton & Co.*, above; *Lithgow v. Murray* (1680) Mor. 15799; *A. v. B.* (1749) Mor. 15823. Adminicles, in so far as in the possession or control of the pursuer, should be lodged in process at the signeting of the summons: rr. 52.2 and 27.1;

(3) *The casus amissionis.* This is the circumstance of the loss or destruction of the document. There are two types of *casus amissionis* for which different levels of specification are required—

(a) Special *casus amissionis.* Where the document to be proved is one which may be destroyed for the purpose of revocation or termination (*e.g.* a personal bond, bill of exchange, or a writing with testamentary effect), the pursuer must aver the particular circumstances of loss or destruction: Erskine, IV.i.54; *Winchester v. Smith* (1863) 1 M. 685, 689 *per* L.P. McNeill, Lords Curriehill and Ardmillan (mutual will); *Smith v. Ferguson* (1882) 9 R. 866, 879 *per* Lord Shand (ante-nuptial marriage contract). Averments that a testator ordered a testamentary writing to be destroyed (*Bonthrone v. Ireland* (1883) 10 R. 779), that a testator destroyed it while of unsound mind (*Laing v. Bruce* (1838) 1 D. 59) or that the testator's mental health was deteriorating (*Lander v. Briggs*, 1999 S.C. 453), have been held to be sufficient for a proof: *cf. Smith v. Ferguson* (1882) 9 R. 866 (*casus amissionis* insufficiently averred).

(b) General *casus amissionis.* Where the document lost or destroyed was intended to remain constantly with the grantee or is one which requires a contrary document to be extinguished, the pursuer need only aver bare loss or destruction *casu fortuito* (an accident): Erskine, IV.i.54; *Winton & Co. v. Thomson & Co.* (1862) 24 D. 1094 (composition agreement).

Where any *casus amissionis* is that the document has been lost the pursuer must aver the steps taken in search of the document: *Walker v. Brock* (1852) 14 D. 362; *McKean* (1857) 19 D. 448.

The summons should be signed by an agent or a party litigant with leave of the court: r. 4.2.

52.2.2   *Lodging of documentary evidence.* See r. 4.5.

Proof in undefended actions

52.3. Where no appearance has been entered or no defences have been lodged in an action of proving the tenor, the pursuer shall apply by motion for an order for proof.

Deriv. RCS 1965, r. 188

52.3.1   *Proof.* For proofs generally, see Chap. 36.

Proof in an action of proving the tenor must cover (1) the tenor of the document; and (2) the *casus amissionis*: *Bonthrone v. Ireland* (1883) 10 R. 779, 786 *per* Lord Craighill.

(1) The terms of the document may be proved by the adminicles alone if they are in a formal writing (or if part of the records of a business or undertaking are docquetted by an officer of that business or undertaking: Civil Evidence (Scotland) Act 1988, s.5): *Graham v. McFarlane* (1847) 10 D. 45, 49 *per* Lord Jeffrey. Usually a combination of the adminicles and oral evidence is sufficient. Where oral evidence alone is relied on it must be specific about the terms of the document and not merely about the general effect of the document: *Rannie v. Ogg* (1891) 18 R. 903, 910 *per* Lord Kinnear.

(2) The *casus amissionis* may be proved by any competent and admissible evidence. It is usually necessary to prove that the *casus amissionis* did not affect the validity of the document: *Bonthrone*, above. Exceptionally, however, the court may hold the tenor of the document proved under reservation of the question of its validity: *Falconer v. Stephen* (1849) 11 D. 1338.

52.3.2   *"motion".* For motions, see Chap. 23.

Chapter 53

Actions of Reduction

Conclusions for suspension etc.

53.1. In an action where real or personal diligence may proceed on a document sought to be reduced in the action, the pursuer may include in the summons, in relation to that diligence, such conclusions for suspension, interdict, and liberation as circumstances may require.

53.1.1   *"real or personal diligence".* Diligence is the procedure by which a creditor attaches the property of his debtor, with the object of forcing his debtor either to appear in court to answer an action at the instance of the creditor (*e.g.* an arrestment to found jurisdiction), to find security for implement of the judgment which may be pronounced against him in such an action (*e.g.* arrestment on the dependence, inhibition) or to implement a judgment already obtained against the debtor: Graham Stewart on *Diligence*, p. 1. Real diligences are the means of enforcing rights which a creditor already possesses, and include real poinding (also known as poinding of the ground), sequestration for rent, maills and duties and real adjudication. Personal diligences are the methods for obtaining rights which the creditor does not yet possess and include arrestment, inhibition, poinding and adjudication.

53.1.2   *"suspension, interdict, and liberation".* On these remedies, see Chap. 60.

Intimation to clerk of inferior court or tribunal

53.2.—(1) In an action in which reduction of a decree, order, decision or warrant of whatever nature of an inferior court or tribunal is concluded for, intimation of the action shall be made to the clerk of that court or tribunal.

(2) In an action to which paragraph (1) applies, the pursuer shall insert a warrant for intimation in the summons in the following terms:— "Warrant to the (*designation of the clerk of the relevant court or tribunal*) being the court [*or* tribunal] in which the decree [*or as the case may be*] was granted [*or* made] which is sought to be reduced in this action.".

(3) A notice of intimation in Form 53.2 shall be attached to the copy of the summons where intimation is given on a warrant under paragraph (2).

(4) An interlocutor granting reduction in an action to which paragraph (1) applies shall include a direction to the clerk of court to send a copy of the interlocutor to the clerk of the inferior court or tribunal to whom intimation of the action was made.

(5) Where such an interlocutor is reclaimed against or appealed to the House of Lords, the reclaimer or appellant, as the case may be, shall give written intimation of that fact to the clerk of the inferior court or tribunal forthwith after the reclaiming motion has been marked or the petition of appeal to the House of Lords has been lodged, as the case may be.

(6) The interlocutor disposing of such a reclaiming motion or giving effect to the judgment of the House of Lords shall include a direction to the clerk of court to send a copy of that interlocutor to the clerk of the inferior court or tribunal to whom intimation of the action was made.

General note. The Court of Session has exclusive, inherent power to reduce its own decrees as **53.2.1** well as the decrees of inferior courts: *Doherty v. Norwich Union Fire Insurance Society Ltd* 1975 S.L.T. 41, 43 *per* Lord Robertson. In these circumstances reduction is a mode of review, and decree, if granted, is given in exercise of the court's supervisory jurisdiction.

The relationship between applications to the court for reduction and judicial review should be noted. Judicial review has not superseded actions of reduction. The reference to the "supervisory jurisdiction of the court" in r. 58.1(1) (applications for judicial review) must be construed as excluding procedures for which specific provision is made elsewhere in the RCS 1994 and is confined to the type of jurisdiction described in *West v. Secretary of State for Scotland* 1992 S.C. 385: *Bell v. Fiddes*, 1996 S.L.T. 51, 52H, *per* Lord Marnoch (disapproving the statement made in this note before release 38 that reduction as a mode of review in exercise of the supervisory jurisdiction was superseded by Chap. 58). In that case it was held that judicial review for reduction of a decree in absence in the sheriff court and interim interdict against enforcement was incompetent and reduction should be sought in an action of reduction.

On reduction of sheriff court decrees, note *Bain v. L. S. McConnell* 1991 S.L.T. 691; *Johnstone & Clark (Engineers) v. Lockhart* 1995 S.L.T. 440.

The courts commonly observe that reduction is an equitable remedy and, where other means for review of a decree are available and either utilised or the person seeking reduction has failed to utilise such means, then reduction may not be granted. In relation to an attempt to reduce an award of sequestration, see *Arthur v. S.M.T. Sales and Service Co. Ltd* 1999 S.C. 109 (First Div.). In that case, the court held that a delay of 12 years on the part of the pursuer in seeking reduction of his sequestration was fatal.

On the test applicable and the averments required for reduction of a decree in absence, see *Robertson's Exr v. Robertson* 1995 S.C. 23 and the subsequent application of that case in *Nunn v. Nunn* 1997 S.L.T. 182: there is no precise test, but the *whole* circumstances of the case have to be looked at. While the party seeking to reduce a decree in absence is not required to aver "exceptional circumstances" justifying the order sought, as is required in an action for reduction of a decree *in foro*, the party seeking reduction must aver that in the whole circumstances of the case the decree in absence was not justified in fact and in law. One important factor to which the court will have regard is a candid explanation of how the decree in absence came to be granted without any opposition: *Nunn*, above, at 184D–E. For important observations on the sufficiency of averments of interest to sue, see *Lennox v. Scottish Branch of the British Show Jumping Association* 1997 S.L.T. 353 and *Cameron v. Lightheart* 1995 S.C. 341.

It should be noted that the availability of reduction is not restricted to writings but is available to reduce illegal acts: *Lennox*, above.

Jurisdiction. An action of reduction is within the court's privative jurisdiction and may be **53.2.2** brought as a principal action, with or without other conclusions, or stated by way of exception (see r. 53.8) without the necessity of raising a separate action.

The Court of Session has jurisdiction to reduce any decree granted by a Scottish court whether or not jurisdiction exists independently in the action of reduction: Law Reform (Miscellaneous Provisions) (Scotland) Act 1980, s.20.

"intimation". For methods, see r. 16.8. For evidence of intimation, see note 16.8.1.   **53.2.3**

"send". This includes deliver: r. 1.3(1) (definition of "send").   **53.2.4**

"written intimation". For methods, see r. 16.9.   **53.2.5**

Objection by defenders to production

53.3.—(1) Where a defender objects to satisfying a conclusion for production of a document sought to be reduced in an action, he shall state in his defences—

    (a) his grounds of objection; and

    (b) any defence on the merits of the action.

(2) Where a defender objects to satisfying such a conclusion, he shall not be required to satisfy production at the time of lodging his defences.

(3) Where the court repels or reserves an objection to satisfying a conclusion for production, it shall, in the interlocutor repelling or reserving such objection, ordain the defender to satisfy production within such period as it thinks fit.

(4) Where—

    (a) the defender obtempers an order made under paragraph (3), he shall, on lodging in process any such document as is in his possession or within his control, apply by motion to hold production either satisfied or satisfied in respect of the document lodged, as the case may be; or

    (b) the defender fails to obtemper an order made under paragraph (3), the pursuer may apply by motion for decree by default.

Deriv. RCS 1965, r. 171 (r. 53.3(1)) and r. 173(part) (r. 53.3(4))

53.3.1   *"production"* The pursuer should conclude for production of the deeds or other writings to be reduced, unless they are in his own possession. A defender may only be called upon to produce documents which are in his possession or within his control, *e.g.* documents held on his behalf by an agent: *Elder v. Smith* (1829) 7 S. 656. The court will usually order production under reservation of the defenders' pleas to the relevancy and competency of the pursuer's action, including a plea of all parties not called (*Officers of State v. Magistrates of Brechin* (1827) 5 S. 672): see, *e.g. Cochran v. Dunlop* (1872) 9 S.L.R. 597; *Fraser v. Macleay* (1882) 9 R. 1036; *cf. Earl of Perth v. Lady Willoughby de Eresby's Trs.* (1869) 7 M. 642. Prescriptive possession is no defence to a conclusion for production in an action for reduction of a heritable title: *Earl of Perth*, above. A defender should not lodge documents or writings which truly belong to third parties: see, *e.g. Mackintosh v. Arkley* (1868) 6 M.(HL) 141, 143 *per* L.J.-C. Inglis.

    The proper evidence to be produced in reduction of a decree, those decrees being *in publica custodia*, is an extract: *Miller & Son v. Oliver & Boyd* (1901) 9 S.L.T. 287, 287 *per* Lord Pearson. In *Miller* the arbiter refused to allow the decree arbitral to be lodged until his fees had been paid. The pursuers declined to pay those fees and the court held that the onus of production of a decree arbitral under reduction was on the defenders. It is not competent to bring a decree under review by reduction until it has been extracted (*Scouler v. M'Laughlan* (1864) 2 M. 955, 959 *per* Lord Mackenzie), although reduction of an unextracted decree may be permitted in special circumstances (*Scouler*, above, *per* L.P. McNeill at p. 962). Where an extract of the decree sought to be reduced is available or can be obtained, it is lodged by the pursuer when the summons is signeted.

    If the deed under reduction has been registered in the Books of Council and Session, it is sufficient to satisfy production for the defender to lodge a note of the date of its being so registered: Mackay's *Practice of the Court of Session*, p. 160.

    If the defender fails to satisfy production the pursuer may move for decree *contra non producta* (*Miller & Son*, above; *Elder v. Smith* (1829) 7 S. 656), the effect of which is that the deed challenged is held to be void. The interlocutor pronounced in such a case would include the words "hold production satisfied and that for non-production".

53.3.2   *"defences"*. For defences, see Chap. 18.

53.3.3   *"document"*. This is wide enough to encompass reduction of decrees, whether *in foro* or otherwise, in exercise of the court's supervisory jurisdiction, or of any other deed or writing in exercise of the court's ordinary jurisdiction. It is not competent, however, to reduce a decree of adoption: *J. and J. v. C's Tutor* 1948 S.C. 642, 643 *per* L.P. Cooper. See also the definition of "document" in r. 1.3(1).

53.3.4   *"objection"*. The court appears reluctant to uphold a defender's objection to production, the duty to do so generally being on the defender, even where it is within the power of either party to obtain the document to be reduced. See, *e.g. Miller & Son v. Oliver & Boyd* (1901) 9 S.L.T. 287.

In *Fraser v. Macleay* (1882) 9 R. 1036 the court repelled the defender's objection to producing a second document, where the objection was that the pursuers would only have title to reduce the second document if they successfully reduced the first of which production was sought.

"lodge in process". For lodging productions, see r. 4.5. **53.3.5**

"motion". For motions, see Chap. 23. **53.3.6**

"decree by default". For decrees by default, see Chap. 20. **53.3.7**

Preventive diligence. In an action of reduction, the preventive diligence in security is the registration of a notice of litigiosity in the Register of Inhibitions and Adjudications: Titles to Land Consolidation (Scotland) Act 1868, s. 159. Inhibition on the dependence cannot be used in an action of reduction or declarator: *Stafford v. McLaurin* (1875) 3 R. 148. **53.3.8**

Production by defenders where no objection

53.4.—(1) Where a defender does not state an objection against satisfying a conclusion for production of a document sought to be reduced, he shall—

(a) on lodging his defences, lodge in process any such document as is in his possession or within his control; and

(b) apply by motion to hold production either satisfied or satisfied in respect of the document lodged.

(2) Where a defender—

(a) does not state an objection against satisfying a conclusion for production, and

(b) fails to comply with paragraph (1)(a),

the pursuer may apply by motion for decree by default.

Deriv. RCS 1965, r. 172 (r. 53.4(1)) and r. 173 (part) (r. 53.4(2)).

"objection". See note 53.3.4. **53.4.1**

"conclusion for production". See note 53.3.1. **53.4.2**

"defences". For defences, see Chap. 18. **53.4.3**

"motion". For motions, see Chap. 23. **53.4.4**

"decree by default". For decrees by default, see Chap. 20. **53.4.5**

Pursuers to satisfy production

53.5.—(1) Where a document, in respect of which reduction is concluded for, is in the possession or the control of the pursuer, he shall lodge it in process on lodging the summons for calling.

(2) The court may, at any stage of an action, ordain the pursuer to satisfy a conclusion for production of a document sought to be reduced.

(3) The pursuer shall, on lodging a document under paragraph (1) or (2), apply by motion to hold production satisfied.

(4) Where a pursuer fails to obtemper an order made under paragraph (2), the defender may apply by motion for dismissal of the action.

"lodge in process". For lodging productions, see r. 4.5. **53.5.1**

Calling of summons. For calling of the summons, see r. 13.13. **53.5.2**

"motion". For motions, see Chap. 23. **53.5.3**

"production". See note 53.3.1. **53.5.4**

Joint minutes for reduction

53.6. In an action in which a conclusion for production has not been satisfied and parties enter into a joint minute in terms of which decree of reduction is to be pronounced—

(a) the document to be reduced shall be lodged in process with the joint minute; and

(b) the terms of the joint minute shall be such as to enable the court, when interponing authority to it, to hold production satisfied.

"production". See note 53.3.1. **53.6.1**

Production satisfied by copies

53.7. The court may, with the consent of the parties, hold production satisfied by a copy of the document sought to be reduced.

Deriv. R.C.S. 1965, r. 173(part)

General note. See, *e.g. Law v. Law's Trs.* (1903) 11 S.L.T. 155 (production of copy disposition **53.7.1** allowed where original under reduction had already been delivered by defender to his disponee).

"production". See note 53.3.1. **53.7.2**

Challenge of deeds or writings ope exceptionis

53.8. Where, in an action, a deed or other writing is founded on by a party, any objection to it may be stated by way of exception, unless the court considers that the objection would be more conveniently disposed of in a separate action of reduction.

Deriv. R.C.S. 1965, r. 174

General note. The pursuer must have fair notice of any plea of reduction *ope exceptionis* (by **53.8.1** force of exception): *Oswald v. Fairs* 1911 S.C. 257. A decree may be reduced *ope exceptionis*: *Thomson's Trs. v. Muir* (1867) 6 M. 145. For an example of the court's refusal to allow the plea, see *Duke of Argyll v. Muir* 1910 S.C. 96.

A defender may challenge the validity of the decision of an adjudicator (a creature created by the Housing Grants, Construction and Regeneration Act 1996) *ope exceptiones* in his defences and is not obliged to petition for judicial review as he is not in effect making an application to the court for the exercise of its supervisory jurisdiction by doing so: *Vaughan Engineering Ltd v. Hinkins & Frewin Ltd,* 2003 S.L.T. 428 (OH). An argument in that case, that the defender could not seek reduction in a separate *action* but would have to proceed by petition for judicial review and therefore could not plead by way of exception under r. 53.8, was rejected.

CHAPTER 54

APPLICATIONS UNDER THE DEFAMATION ACT 1996

Form of application to court where proceedings have been taken
   [1] **54.1.**—(1) An application to the court under section 3 of the Defamation Act 1996 (which relates to offers to make amends) where proceedings for defamation have been taken shall be by minute lodged in the process of those proceedings.
   (2) A minute lodged under paragraph (1) shall set out—
      (a) the questions to be determined by the court; and
      (b) the contentions of the minuter,
and shall have appended to it a copy of the offer to make amends.

Deriv. R.C.S. 1965, r. 188A(a)(part) inserted by S.I. 1966 No.868

---

[1] R. 54.1 substituted by S.S.I. 2001 No. 93 (effective 1st April 2001).

54.1.1   *General note.* Sections 2 to 4 of the Defamation Act 1996 provide for the defence of an offer to make amends before a defence is served in any proceedings or before a summons has even been served or lodged. These provisions replace the statutory defence of *unintentional* defamation in s. 4 of the Defamation Act 1952 which was little used.
   The offer must include an offer to make a suitable correction and apology. It must also include an offer to pay such compensation (if any) as may be agreed by the parties (s. 2(4)(c) of the 1996 Act) or determined by the court (s. 3(5) of the 1996 Act).
   The 1996 Act and the rules do not lay down any time-limit for the pursuer to respond to the offer. It is not clear if the defender should be able to impose a limit. One would expect a defender to make an offer open for acceptance within a specified period and s. 4(1) of the 1996 Act clearly envisages that an offer may be withdrawn. In *Moore v. The Scottish Daily Record and Sunday Mail Ltd,* 2007 S.L.T. 217 (OH) it was held that in order to rely on the s. 4(2) defence a defender is obliged to maintain an offer of amends duly made and *which has not been withdrawn.* The offer may, therefore, be accepted at any time; and the defender (or the court) cannot impose a time limit for its acceptance. The length of time in accepting it may be met in expenses.
   Where an offer to make amends is not withdrawn it may be relied on as a defence; but where it is, the defender may not rely on any other defence: 1996 Act, s. 4(2) and (4). The offer may be relied on in mitigation of damages whether or not it was relied on as a defence: 1996 Act, s. 4(5).

Form of application to court where proceedings have not been taken
   [1] **54.2** An application to the court under the said section 3 where proceedings for defamation have not been taken shall be by petition presented in the Outer House.

Deriv. R.C.S. 1965, r. 188A(a)(part) and (b) inserted by S.I. 1966 No.868

---

[1] R. 54.2 substituted by S.S.I. 2001 No. 93 (effective 1st April 2001).

54.2.1   *General note.* See generally, note 54.1.1 on offer of amends.
   Where an offer of amends is accepted any question about the steps to be taken in fulfilment of the offer are, in default of agreement, to be referred to the court whose decision is final. Where no action has been commenced the reference is made to the court by petition: r. 54.2.
   An application may be made to the court by petition, where there is no action, by the aggrieved person to seek an order for expenses reasonably incurred or to be incurred in consequence of the publication.

54.2.2   *"petition".* A petition is presented in the Outer House: r. 54.2. The petition must be in Form 14.4 in the official printed form: rr. 4.1 and 14.4. The petition must be signed by counsel or other person having a right of audience: r. 4.2; and see r. 1.3(1) (definition of "counsel" and "other person having a right of audience") and note 1.3.4.
   The petitioner must lodge the petition with the required steps of process (r. 4.4). A fee is payable on lodging the petition: see note 14.5.10.
   On petitions generally, see Chap. 14.

CHAPTER 55

CAUSES RELATING TO INTELLECTUAL PROPERTY

Application and interpretation of this Chapter
    [1] **55.1.**—(1) This Chapter applies to any cause—
    (a) under the Patents Act 1949;
    (b) under the Registered Designs Act 1949;
    (c) under the Defence Contracts Act 1958;
    (d) under the Patents Act 1977;
    (e) under the Copyright, Designs and Patents Act 1988;
    (f) under the Trade Marks Act 1994;
    (g) under the Olympics Association Right (Infringement Proceedings) Regulations 1995; or
    (h) for the determination of a question relating to a patent under the inherent jurisdiction of the court.
    (2) In this Chapter—
        "the Act of 1949" means the Patents Act 1949;
        "the Act of 1977" means the Patents Act 1977;
        "the Comptroller" means the Comptroller-General of Patents, Designs and Trade Marks;
        "the Copyright Act of 1988" means the Copyright, Designs and Patents Act 1988;
        "existing patent" means a patent mentioned in section 127(2)(a) or (c) of the Act of 1977;
        "the Journal" means the journal published in accordance with rules made under section 123(6) of the Act of 1977;
        "patent" means an existing patent or a patent under the Act of 1977;
        "patentee" has the meaning assigned to it in section 101(1) of the Act of 1949.

Deriv. RCS 1965, r. 250 substituted by S.I. 1991 No. 1621

-----

[1] R. 55.1(1) amended by S.I. 1996 No. 1756 (effective 5th August 1996).

General note. The Registered Designs Act 1949 as amended is set out in Sched. 4 to the Act of **55.1.1** 1988.
    The Patents Act 1949 continues to apply to patents before the Act of 1977. The Act of 1977 was passed following the Banks Report on the British Patent System (Cmnd. 4407 (1970)). It was intended to permit ratification of the Patents Co-operation Treaty 1970 (Cmnd. 7340), the European Patent Convention 1973 (Cmnd. 8510 (1982)) and the Community Patent Convention 1975 (Cmnd. 6553).

Jurisdiction. Under the 1968 Brussels and the Lugano Conventions, in proceedings **55.1.2** concerning the registration or validity of patents, trade marks, designs, or other similar rights required to be deposited or registered, the courts of the Contracting State, in which the deposit or registration has been applied for, has taken place or is under the terms of an international convention deemed to have taken place, have exclusive jurisdiction: C.J.J.A. 1982, Scheds 1 and 3C, Art. 16(4).
    There is no similar rule in Sched. 4 (inter-U.K. jurisdiction) or Sched. 8 (jurisdiction of Scottish courts) of the C.J.J.A. 1982. The ordinary non-exclusive rules of jurisdiction will apply: see notes 13.2.8 to 13.2.15.

Proceedings before patents judge
    [1] **55.2.** All proceedings in the Outer House in a cause to which this Chapter applies shall be brought before a judge of the court nominated by the Lord President as the intellectual property judge or, where the intellectual property judge is not available, any other judge of the court (including the vacation judge).

Deriv. RCS 1965, r. 251 substituted by S.I. 1991 No. 1621

[1] R. 55.2 amended by S.I. 1999 No. 1785 (effective 12th July 1999).

55.2.1   *"intellectual property judge"*. In order to ensure that intellectual property causes will be heard by a judge with knowledge of and expertise in what is a specialised area of the law, intellectual property causes are, where possible, brought before the judge nominated by the Lord President as the patents judge.

The intellectual property judges are currently Lord Emslie and Glennie.

55.2.2   *"vacation judge"*. The powers of the vacation judge are limited by r. 11.1.

Requirement for marking

[1] **55.2A.** In a cause to which this Chapter applies, initiated—

(a) by summons, the pursuer shall, before presenting the summons to the General Department for signeting;

(b) by petition, the petitioner shall, before lodging the petition in the Petition Department,

mark it distinctly in red, both on the first page and on the backing, with the words "Intellectual Property Cause"; and thereafter every step of process in the cause shall be so marked by the person lodging it.

[1] R. 55.2A inserted by S.I. 1999 No. 1785 (effective 12th July 1999).

Procedural hearings

[1] **55.3.**—(1) In a cause to which this Chapter applies, not later than five weeks after—

(a) if it is a cause initiated by summons, the closing of the record; or

(b) if it is a cause initiated by petition, the expiry of any period of adjustment allowed,

the pursuer or petitioner shall enrol a motion, which shall be put out unstarred, for a date to be fixed for a hearing in accordance with this rule (a "procedural hearing"); and after consultation with the intellectual property judge the Keeper of the Rolls shall fix a date accordingly and shall notify it to the parties.

(2) Unless the parties have otherwise agreed, notification under paragraph (1) shall be given at least 14 days before the date so fixed.

(2A) Not later than 7 days after notification under paragraph (1) the parties may, having conferred with one another, jointly attend the Keeper of the Rolls that he may fix a different date, more convenient to them, for the procedural hearing.

(2B) To any motion enrolled by him under paragraph (1) the pursuer or petitioner shall append a note—

(a) identifying the points which he intends to raise, other than on a preliminary plea, at the procedural hearing; and

(b) giving his estimate of the likely duration of that hearing.

(3) Not less than seven days before the date notified under paragraph (1), each party shall lodge in process and send to every other party, a notice of any issue sought to be raised on a preliminary plea against any other party.

(4) At a procedural hearing, the court shall consider—

(a) whether to direct that any issue of law or fact (including validity, infringement, an application for amendment of a patent under section 75 of the Act of 1977, damages or other remedies sought) should be determined separately from any other issue;

(b) whether the cause should be appointed to the Procedure Roll for consideration of any preliminary plea, and may order—

      (i) a party, whose plea is to be considered, to lodge in process a concise note of argument consisting of numbered paragraphs stating the grounds on which he proposes to submit that the preliminary plea should be sustained, and to send a copy of it to every other party concerned within such period as the court thinks fit;

     (ii) any other party to lodge in process a note of argument in reply and to send a copy of it to every other party, within a specified period thereafter; and

(c) whether—

      (i) to remit to the Patent Office for a report and what the terms of the remit should be;

     (ii) to order a party to make available to any other party a copy of any documents;

   (iii) to appoint an assessor or assessors;

   (iv) a meeting of experts should be held for the purpose of producing a joint report on the general state of the art;

    (v) to order each party to make available to every other party a copy of any precognitions, or reports, of skilled witnesses on any matter which is not the subject of a joint report under head (iv) and the time by which they were to be made available;

   (vi) to order the advisers of the parties to meet for the purpose of agreeing and preparing a single paginated inventory of productions and, if necessary, to fix a date by which this is to be done;

 (vii) to make an order regulating the making of any experiment, inspection, test or report;

(viii) to fix a date by which a notice under rule 55.4 (notices to admit and notices of non-admission) shall be served; and

   (ix) to fix the time within which, notwithstanding rule 36.3 (lodging productions for proofs), any production shall be lodged or within which any other step may be taken.

(5) At a procedural hearing, the court may—

(a) continue the hearing to another date;

(b) without prejudice to paragraph (6), order a further pre-proof hearing on a specified date or a date to be afterwards fixed; or

(c) give such further directions as to the conduct of the cause as it thinks fit.

(6) The court may order a further procedural hearing at any time of its own motion or on the motion of any party.

(7) Where a party intends to seek a particular order at a procedural hearing, he shall give written intimation, to the court and to every other party not less than seven days before the hearing, of the order sought and the reason for seeking it.

Deriv. RCS 1965, r. 252 substituted by S.I. 1991 No. 1621

---

[1] Heading and r. 55.3(1) and (e) substituted, and (3) to (7) amended by S.I. 1999 No. 1785 (effective 12th July 1999).

General note. R. 55.3 was originally introduced by A.S. (R.C.S.A. No. 7) (Patent Rules) 1991 **55.3.1** [S.I. 1991 No. 1621] following a recommendation of the Working Party on the White Paper on Intellectual Property and Innovation (Patent Litigation) chaired by Lord Jauncey. The concept of a pre-proof hearing was recommended in the Banks Report on the British Patent System 1970 (Cmnd. 4407). The Working Party considered the pre-proof hearing to be of very considerable importance. The idea is that the judge takes a firm grip of the case at a very early stage, to focus the main issues, reduce the amount of evidence required and indicate the areas in which he requires assistance on technical matters. The Working Party envisaged that the pre-proof hearing might involve more than one stage. It was thought that the success of the procedure would depend on the same judge hearing the proof as the pre-proof hearing.

The Cullen Report on the Business of the Outer House (1995) accepted a suggestion that r. 55.3 should be extended to all causes to which this Chapter applies. This reform was introduced by the A.S. (R.C.S.A. No. 3) (Miscellaneous) 1996 [S.I. 1996 No. 1756]. Formerly, r. 55.3 applied only to causes under the Patent Act of 1949 or 1977.

The pre-proof hearing is now called the "procedural hearing": A.S.(R.C.S.A. No.6) 1999 [S.I. 1999 No. 1785]. The main purpose of the A.S. is to provide, in new paras (1) and (2) in r. 55.3, greater flexibility in fixing a date for the procedural hearing.

55.3.2 *"not later than five weeks after"; "not later than seven days after"*. The first day is not counted in the calculation.

55.3.3 *"at least 14 days before" "not less than seven days before"*. There must be at least 14, or seven, clear days.

55.3.4 *"unstarred"*. A motion which requires appearance for a party is starred: r. 23.2(7). An unstarred motion does not require an appearance.

55.3.5 *"concise note of argument"*. A concise note of argument and a note of argument in reply may be ordered where a cause is sent to the Procedure Roll. Each should consist of numbered paragraphs setting out briefly the legal propositions to be advanced at debate by the party lodging it, supported by citations of the principal authorities for those propositions and any statutory provisions relied on.

A note of argument is lodged in process as a step of process (r. 1.3(1) (definition of "step of process")) and does not require to be signed. R. 15.2 does not apply. On lodging a step of process, see r. 4.4. The note may be lodged by post: P.N. No. 4 of 1994, paras 1 and 8; and see note 4.4.10.

55.3.6 *Patent Office report.* This would be a technical report dealing with, *e.g.* obviousness. Views on its usefulness vary.

55.3.7 *Joint report of experts.* It can be advantageous in reducing the length of a proof to obtain, if possible, a joint or agreed report by expert witnesses on the general scientific principles applicable to the case.

55.3.8 *Exchange of expert reports etc.* The view held by some that exchange of reports lengthens cross-examination is not encountered in practice in England.

55.3.9 *Paginated inventory of productions.* To reduce the duplication of documentary material by both sides, agents may be required to get together to agree one set of paginated productions.

55.3.10 *"give such further directions as to the conduct of the cause"*. At the pre-proof hearing, the court may wish to consider, for example, whether a reading guide should be prepared by the parties in consultation with each other. The guide should indicate the documents the judge should read before the proof and in what order and an up-to-date list of the principal issues to be resolved. Another consideration might be (although this may be too early a stage to contemplate it) to consider the requirement of written skeletal submissions for the hearing of evidence at the end of the proof.

55.3.11 *"written intimation"*. For methods, see r. 16.9.

Notices to admit and notices of non-admission
    55.4.—[1](1) In a cause under the Act of 1949 or the Act of 1977, at any time after defences or answers have been lodged but not later than such date as has been fixed by the court at a procedural hearing, a party may intimate to any other party to the cause a notice or notices calling on him to admit for the purposes of that cause only—
    (a) such facts relating to an issue averred in the pleadings as may be specified in the notice;
    (b) that a particular document lodged in process and specified in the notice is—
        (i) an original and properly authenticated document;
        (ii) a true copy of an original and properly authenticated document; or
        (iii) correct in the particular respects specified in the notice.
    (2) Where a party on whom a notice has been served under paragraph (1)—
        (a) does not admit any of the facts specified in the notice, or
        (b) does not admit, or seeks to challenge, the authenticity or correctness of any document specified in the notice,

he shall, within 28 days after the date of intimation of the notice under paragraph (1), intimate a notice of non-admission to the party intimating the notice to him under paragraph (1) stating that he does not admit the fact or document specified.

(3) A party who fails to serve a notice of non-admission under paragraph (2) shall be deemed to have admitted the matters specified in the notice intimated to him under paragraph (1); and such matters may be used in evidence at a proof if otherwise admissible in evidence unless the court, on special cause shown, otherwise directs.

(4) A party who fails to intimate a notice of non-admission under paragraph (2) within 28 days after the notice to admit intimated to him under paragraph (1) shall be liable to the party intimating the notice to admit for the expenses of proving the matters specified in that notice unless the court otherwise directs.

(5) The party intimating a notice under paragraph (1) or (2) shall lodge a copy of it in process.

(6) A deemed admission under paragraph (3) shall not be used against the party by whom it was deemed to be made other than in the cause for the purpose of which it was deemed to be made or in favour of any person other than the party by whom the notice was given under paragraph (1).

(7) The court may, at any time, allow a party to amend or withdraw an admission made by him on such conditions, if any, as it thinks fit.

Deriv. RCS 1965, r. 253 substituted by S.I. 1991 No. 1621

---

[1] R. 55.4(1) amended by S.I. 1999 No. 1785 (effective 12th June 1999)

General note. The Jauncey Working Party on Patent Litigation recommended adoption of **55.4.1** this rule, and this was done in RCS 1965, r. 253 as amended by A.S. (R.C.S.A. No. 7) (Patent Rules) 1991 [S.I. 1991 No. 1621] (now RCS 1994, r. 55.4).

It might be thought that r. 55.4 is not necessary when the system of Scottish pleadings should result in it being clear by the time proof has been allowed what is in issue and what has to be proved. Not all relevant documentary material, however, previously in dispute will be in dispute by the time the proof approaches, and the authenticity of such material, or an averment, may be the subject of a general denial which would otherwise necessitate proof. It may, of course, be possible to obtain agreement by consent. The purpose of the rule is to provide an additional means to assist in reducing documentary material and averments having to be proved which at the end of the day do or did not require proof and the time taken in proving them. It is also considered that this might be a more effective way of obtaining admissions than calls in the pleadings. It also provides a penalty by imposing the burden of expenses on the party who has caused unnecessary proof.

The relationship of this rule to rr. 36.7 and 36.8 should be noticed. The possibility of a minute of admission by one or more parties is not affected by r. 55.4. A deemed admission may arise, however, under r. 55.4(3) if a notice of non-admission is not intimated in response to a notice to admit. Under s.2(1)(b) of the Civil Evidence (Scotland) Act 1988 any document (including an affidavit) may be received in evidence without being spoken to by a witness as evidence not merely that it was made but as to the truth of its contents, and r. 36.8 provides the mechanism for obtaining the permission of the court to produce such evidence without being spoken to. In respect of the authenticity of a document it may also be possible to use the procedure in r. 55.4.

"intimated". For methods, see r. 16.7.   **55.4.2**

"within 28 days". The date from which the period is calculated is not counted.   **55.4.3**

"lodge a copy of it in process". The copy is lodged as a step of process and not as a production: **55.4.4** r. 1.3(1) (definition of "step of process"). On steps of process, see r. 4.4.

Applications for leave to amend specifications

55.5.—(1) A patentee or the proprietor of a patent intending to apply to the court under section 30 of the Act of 1949 or section 75 of the Act of 1977 (which provide for leave to amend specification) shall give notice of his intention to the Comptroller and at the same time deliver to him a form of advertisement—

(a) identifying the proceedings depending before the court in which it is intended to apply for such leave;

(b) giving particulars of the amendment sought;

(c) stating the address of the applicant for service within the United Kingdom; and

(d) stating that any person intending to oppose the amendment who is not a party to the proceedings must, within 28 days after the appearance of the advertisement, give written notice of that intention to the applicant and to the Deputy Principal Clerk.

(2) On receipt of a form of advertisement under paragraph (1), the Comptroller shall cause the advertisement to be inserted once in the Journal.

(3) A person who gives notice of intention to oppose the amendment in accordance with the advertisement shall be entitled to be heard on the application subject to any order of the court as to expenses.

(4) Within 35 days after the appearance of the advertisement, the applicant shall make his application under section 30 of the Act of 1949 or section 75 of the Act of 1977, as the case may be, by motion intimated, with a copy of the specification certified by the Comptroller and showing in coloured ink the amendment sought, to—

(a) the Comptroller;

(b) every other party; and

(c) any person who has intimated his intention to oppose the amendment.

(5) On enrolling a motion under paragraph (4), the applicant shall lodge in process—

(a) a copy of the Journal containing the advertisement referred to in paragraph (2); or

(b) a certificate of publication by the publisher stating the date of publication and the text of the advertisement.

(6) At the hearing of a motion under paragraph (4)—

(a) where there is no opposition to the amendment sought, the court may—

(i) grant the application; or

(ii) make such order for further procedure as it thinks fit; or

(b) where there is opposition to the amendment sought, the court shall ordain the applicant to lodge a minute setting out the grounds of his application within such period as the court thinks fit, and allow any party or person opposing the amendment to lodge answers to the minute in process within a specified period.

(7) Within seven days after the expiry of the time for lodging answers under paragraph (6)(b), the applicant shall apply by motion for an order for further procedure.

(8) On a motion under paragraph (7), the court may—

(a) grant the application;

(b) determine whether the motion shall be heard at the same time as the hearing of the cause depending before the court relating to the patent in question or at a different time;

(c) determine the manner in which evidence shall be given and, if the evidence is to be given by affidavit, the period within which affidavits must be lodged; or

(d) make such other order for further procedure as it thinks fit.

(9) Where the court allows the specification to be amended, the applicant shall forthwith—

(a) lodge with the Comptroller a certified copy of the interlocutor; and
(b) if so required by the court or the Comptroller, leave at the Patent Office a new specification and drawings as amended, prepared in compliance with the Act of 1949 or the Act of 1977, as the case may be, and any rules made under either of those Acts.

(10) On receiving the certified copy interlocutor under paragraph (9), the Comptroller shall cause it to be inserted at least once in the Journal.

Deriv. R.C.S. 1965, r. 254 substituted by S.I. 1991 No. 1621

55.5.1   *General note.* Where the validity of a patent is put in issue the court may allow the proprietor of the patent to amend the specification. The Comptroller has a similar power.

55.5.2   *"within 35 days", "within seven days".* The date from which the period is calculated is not counted. Where the last day falls on a Saturday or Sunday or a public holiday on which the Office of Court is closed, the next available day is allowed: r. 1.3(7). For office hours and public holidays, see note 3.1.2.

55.5.3   *"motion".* For motions, see Chap. 23.

Applications for revocation of patents

55.6.—(1) Subject to paragraph (2), an application under section 72 of the Act of 1977 (revocation of a patent) shall be made by petition.

(2) Where an action is depending before the court between the same parties in relation to the patent in question, such an application may be made by counterclaim in that action; and Chapter 25 (counterclaims) shall apply to any such counterclaim.

Deriv. R.C.S. 1965, r. 255 substituted by S.I. 1991 No. 1621

55.6.1   *General note.* S.72 of the Act of 1977 specifies the grounds on which a patent may be revoked by the court. The Comptroller has a similar power.
Note also r. 55.8 on challenges to the validity of a patent in proceedings for revocation.
In England, U.K. and European patents are given a "purposive" construction as set out in *Catnic Components v. Hill & Smith* [1982] R.P.C. 237 (H.L.).

55.6.2   *"petition".* A petition is presented in the Outer House: r. 14.2(h). The petition must be in Form 14.4 in the official printed form: rr. 4.1 and 14.4. The petition must be signed by counsel or other person having a right of audience: r. 4.2; and see r. 1.3(1) (definition of "counsel" and "other person having a right of audience") and note 1.3.4.
The petitioner must lodge the petition with the required steps of process (r. 4.4). A fee is payable on lodging the petition: see note 14.5.10.
On petitions generally, see Chap. 14.

55.6.3   *"depending".* A cause is depending from the time it is commenced (*i.e.* from the time an action is served) until final decree, whereas a cause is in dependence until final extract. For the meaning of commenced, see note 13.4.4. For the meaning of final decree, see note 4.15.2(2). For the meaning of final extract, see note 7.1.2(2).

Proceedings for infringement

55.7.—(1) In any cause in which it is alleged that a patent has been infringed, the person alleging infringement must aver in the petition or summons, as the case may be, particulars of the infringement relied on, showing which of the claims in the specification of the patent are alleged to have been infringed and giving at least one instance of each type of infringement alleged.

(2) Where, as a defence to such an allegation, it is averred that—
(a) at the time of the infringement there was in force a contract or licence relating to the patent made by or with the consent of the person alleging the infringement, and
(b) containing a condition or term void by virtue of section 44 of the Act of 1977,

the person stating that defence must aver particulars of the date of, and the parties to, each such contract or licence and particulars of each such condition or term.

Deriv. R.C.S. 1965, r. 256 substituted by S.I. 1991 No. 1621

General note. Under s. 61 of the Act of 1977 proceedings for infringement of a patent may be **55.7.1**
brought in the Court of Session or referred to the Comptroller by agreement. The court may
grant (*a*) interdict, (*b*) delivery or destruction, (*c*) damages, (*d*) an account of profits or (*e*)
declarator of validity and infringement. The Comptroller may only grant an order in (*c*) or (*e*).

A conclusion for infringement should refer to the claims in the specification: *Ygnis S.A. v.
McFarlane Bros. (Heat) Ltd* 1969 S.L.T. (Notes) 77.

A patentee's claim has to explain his monopoly in terms which a man, reasonably competent
in the art, could understand so as to enable him to work out for himself precisely what the
forbidden area was for the purposes of deciding both what activities would constitute
infringement and whether the patent itself was invalidated by prior art. *Smoothysigns v. Metro
Products (Accessories and Leisure) Ltd*, *The Times*, 4th August 1995.

Objections to validity of patent
55.8.—(1) A person who—
  (*a*) brings an action under section 32 of the Act of 1949 or presents a
        petition under section 72 of the Act of 1977 for revocation of a patent,
        or
  (*b*) being a party to an action relating to a patent—
        (i) challenges the validity of the patent, or
        (ii) applies by counterclaim in the action for revocation of the
             patent,
shall aver the grounds on which the validity of the patent is challenged.

(2) Where the grounds in respect of which averments are required under
paragraph (1) include—
  (*a*) want of novelty, or
  (*b*) want of any inventive step,
the averments shall include the matters mentioned in paragraph (3).

(3) The matters referred to in paragraph (2) are—
  (*a*) the manner, time and place of every prior publication or use relied on;
        and
  (*b*) where prior use is alleged—
        (i) specification of the name of every person alleged to have made
            such use;
        (ii) an averment as to whether such use is alleged to have continued
             until the priority date of the claim in question or of the invention,
             as the case may be, and, if not, the earliest and latest date on
             which such use is alleged to have taken place;
        (iii) a description accompanied, if necessary, by drawings sufficient to
              identify such use; and
        (iv) if such use relates to machinery or apparatus, an averment as to
             whether the machinery or apparatus is in existence and where it
             can be inspected.

(4) Where, in the case of an existing patent—
  (*a*) one of the grounds on which the validity of the patent is challenged is
        that the invention, so far as claimed in any claim of the complete
        specification, is not useful, and
  (*b*) it is intended, in connection with that ground, to rely on the fact that
        an example of the invention which is the subject of any such claim
        cannot be made to work, either at all or as described in the
        specification,
the averments shall specify that fact and identify each such claim and shall
include particulars of each such example, specifying the respects in which it
is alleged that it does not work or does not work as described.

Deriv. R.C.S. 1965, r. 257 substituted by S.I. 1991 No. 1621

General note. A patent may only be granted if it is new, involves an inventive step, is capable **55.8.1**
of industrial application and is not excluded by subsection (2) or (3): Act of 1977, s. 1(1).

"novelty". The applicant for a patent must not have disclosed details of his invention by, **55.8.2**
e.g. publishing an article or demonstrating it other than at an international exhibition: Act of
1977, s. 2; *cf. Quantel Ltd v. Spaceworld Microsystems Ltd* [1990] R.P.C. 83. An invention is
not new if it does not form part of the state of the art: Act of 1977, s. 2(1). State of the art

includes all material available to the public (Act of 1977, s. 2(2)) or matter contained in a prior application (Act of 1977, s. 2(3)). The test is whether a person of ordinary knowledge of the subject would be able to replicate the invention from study of its alleged progenitor: *Hill v. Evans* (1862) 31 L.J.Ch. 457.

55.8.3   *"inventive step"*. An invention shall be taken to involve an inventive step if it is not obvious to a person skilled in the art, having regard to any matter which forms part of the state of the art which is matter available to the public: Act of 1977, s. 3.

The criteria for deciding whether or not the claimed invention involves an inventive step is wholly objective and requires a qualitative not a quantitative test: *Mölnycke A.B. v. Proctor & Gamble (No. 5)* [1994] R.P.C. 49.

Determination of question or application where Comptroller declines to deal with it

55.9. Where the Comptroller—

(*a*) declines to deal with a question under the following sections of the Act of 1977:—

(i) section 8 (entitlement to patents etc.),

(ii) section 12 (entitlement to foreign and convention patents),

(iii) section 37 (right to patent after grant), or

(iv) section 61(3) (infringement of patent),

(*b*) declines to deal with an application under section 40 of that Act (compensation of employees for certain inventions), or

(*c*) issues a certificate under section 72(7) of that Act (revocation of patent should be determined by the court),

any person entitled to do so may, within 28 days after the decision of the Comptroller, apply by petition to have the question or application, as the case may be, determined by the court.

Deriv. R.C.S. 1965, r. 257A substituted by S.I. 1991 No. 1621

55.9.1   *"petition"*. A petition is presented in the Outer House: r. 14.2(*h*). The petition must be in Form 14.4 in the official printed form: rr. 4.1 and 14.4. The petition must be signed by counsel or other person having a right of audience: r. 4.2; and see r. 1.3(1) (definition of "counsel" and "other person having a right of audience") and note 1.3.4.

The petitioner must lodge the petition with the required steps of process (r. 4.4). A fee is payable on lodging the petition: see note 14.5.10.

On petitions generally, see Chap. 14.

Applications by employees for compensation under section 40 of the Act of 1977

55.10.—(1) An application under section 40(1) or (2) of the Act of 1977 (compensation of employees for certain inventions) shall be made by summons commenced within the period which begins when the relevant patent is granted and which expires one year after it has ceased to have effect.

(2) Where a patent has ceased to have effect by reason of a failure to pay any renewal fee within the period prescribed for the payment of that fee and an application is made to the Comptroller under section 28 of the Act of 1977 (restoration of lapsed patent), the period within which the application by summons is to be made shall—

(*a*) if restoration is ordered, continue as if the patent has remained continuously in effect; or

(*b*) if restoration is refused, be treated as if expiring one year after the patent ceased to have effect or six months after the refusal, whichever is the later.

Deriv. R.C.S. 1965, r. 257B substituted by S.I. 1991 No. 1621

55.10.1   *General note.* An employee may be compensated for an invention he made belonging to his employer which is of outstanding benefit to the employer, and compensation is determined under s. 41: Act of 1977, s. 40. Whether the invention belongs to the employer is determined by s. 39 of the Act of 1977.

55.10.2   *"summons"*. See Chap. 13.

Proceedings for determination of certain disputes

55.11. A reference or application under any of the following provisions shall be made by petition:—

(a) a reference under—
   (i) section 48 of the Act of 1949 or section 58 of the Act of 1977 (which provide for disputes as to Crown use);
   (ii) paragraph 3 of Schedule 1 to the Registered Designs Act 1949 (disputes as to Crown use);
   (iii) section 4 of the Defence Contracts Act 1958 (payments for use and determination of disputes);
   (iv) section 251(1) (design right matters), or section 252(1) (disputes as to Crown use), of the Act of 1988; and
(b) an application under section 45(3) of the Act of 1977 (variation of certain contracts).

Deriv. RCS 1965, r. 257C substituted by S.I. 1991 No. 1621

"petition". A petition is presented in the Outer House: r. 14.2(h). The petition must be in **55.11.1** Form 14.4 in the official printed form: rr. 4.1 and 14.4. The petition must be signed by counsel or other person having a right of audience: r. 4.2; and see r. 1.3(1) (definition of "counsel" and "other person having a right of audience") and note 1.3.4.

The petitioner must lodge the petition with the required steps of process (r. 4.4). A fee is payable on lodging the petition: see note 14.5.10.

On petitions generally, see Chap. 14.

Applications for rectification of Register of Designs or Patents

55.12.—(1) Subject to paragraph (2), an application under section 20(1) of the Registered Designs Act 1949 (rectification of Register of Designs) or section 34(1) of the Act of 1977 (rectification of Register of Patents) shall be made by petition.

(2) Where an action for infringement of a patent is depending before the court, an application mentioned in paragraph (1) may be made by a counterclaim in that action; and Chapter 25 (counterclaims) shall apply to any such counterclaim.

(3) In an application under section 34(1) of the Act of 1977, the applicant shall intimate the application to the Comptroller, who may lodge answers in process and be heard on the application.

Deriv. RCS 1965, r. 257D substituted by S.I. 1991 No. 1621

"petition". A petition is presented in the Outer House: r.14.2(h). The petition must be in **55.12.1** Form 14.4 in the official printed form: rr. 4.1 and 14.4. The petition must be signed by counsel or other person having a right of audience: r. 4.2; and see r. 1.3(1) (definition of "counsel" and "other person having a right of audience") and note 1.3.4.

The petitioner must lodge the petition with the required steps of process (r. 4.4). A fee is payable on lodging the petition: see note 14.5.10.

On petitions generally, see Chap. 14.

"intimate". For methods, see r. 16.7.   **55.12.2**

"answers". See r. 18.3.   **55.12.3**

Counterclaim for rectification of Register of Designs

55.13.—(1) Where, in any cause, an infringement of the copyright in a registered design is alleged, the party against whom the allegation is made may—

(a) put in issue the validity of the registration of that design;
(b) counterclaim for an order that the Register of Designs be rectified by cancelling or varying the registration; or
(c) put in issue such validity and make such a counterclaim.

(2) A party to any such cause who counterclaims for an order that the Register of Designs be rectified shall intimate to the Comptroller a copy of

the counterclaim; and the Comptroller may, or (if ordered to do so by the court) shall, lodge answers in process and be heard in any such cause.

(3) Chapter 25 (counterclaims) shall apply to any such counterclaim.

Deriv. RCS 1965, r. 257E substituted by S.I. 1991 No. 1621

55.13.1   *General note.* For infringement of copyright of a registered design, see Pt I of the Act of 1988.

55.13.2   *"intimate".* For methods, see r. 16.7.

Appeals and references from Comptroller

55.14.—[1,2] (1) Subject to the following paragraphs of this rule, an appeal under the Act of 1949, the Act of 1977 or the Copyright Act of 1988 from a decision of, or a reference under the Copyright Act of 1988 from, the Comptroller shall be heard in the Outer House by the intellectual property judge.

[1] (2) In the application of Part III of Chapter 41 (appeals in Form 49.19) by virtue of rule 41.43 (appeals to Lord Ordinary) to an appeal or a reference made in paragraph (1) of this rule—

(a) for references to the Inner House there shall be substituted references to the intellectual property judge; and

(b) the following paragraphs of this rule shall apply.

[1] (3) Subject to paragraph (4), an appeal or a reference shall be lodged in the General Department—

(a) in the case of a decision on a matter of procedure, within 14 days after the date of the decision appealed against; and

(b) in any other case, within six weeks after the date of the decision appealed against or the decision referring the proceedings to the court, as the case may be.

(4) Except with the leave of the court, no appeal under this rule shall be entertained unless it has been lodged within the period specified in paragraph (3) or within such further period as the Comptroller may allow on an application made to him before the expiry of that period.

(5) Any determination by the Comptroller that a decision is on a matter of procedure shall be treated as being itself a decision on a matter of procedure.

(6) In the application of paragraph (1) of rule 41.21 (orders for service and answers), the order under that paragraph shall include a requirement to—

(a) intimate the appeal to the Comptroller; and

(b) serve the appeal on every other party to the proceedings before the Comptroller.

(7) On receiving intimation of the appeal, the Comptroller shall forthwith transmit to the Deputy Principal Clerk all the papers relating to the matter which is the subject of the appeal.

(8) A respondent who, not having appealed from the decision of the Comptroller, wishes to contend at the hearing of the appeal that the decision or the grounds of the decision should be varied shall—

(a) specify the grounds of that contention in his answers; and

(b) intimate those answers to the Comptroller and to every other party to the proceedings before the Comptroller.

(9) Intimation of the date of the hearing of the appeal shall be made to the Comptroller by the appellant not less than seven days before that date, unless the court otherwise directs.

(10) An appeal under this rule shall be a re-hearing and the evidence led on appeal shall be the same as that led before the Comptroller; and, except with the leave of the court, no further evidence shall be led.

Deriv. RCS 1965, r. 257F substituted by S.I. 1991 No. 1621

---

[1] R. 55.14 (1) to (3) amended by S.I. 1994 No. 2901 (effective 5th December 1994).
[2] R. 55.14(1) and (2)(a) amended by S.I. 1999 No. 1785 (effective 12th July 1999).

General note. R. 41.43 provides for appeals to the Outer House or a single judge under any **55.14.1**
enactment. S. 97 of the Act of 1977 provides for appeal from the Comptroller to the Outer
House.

"within 14 days". The date from which the period is calculated is not counted. Where the last **55.14.2**
day falls on a Saturday or Sunday or a public holiday on which the Office of Court is closed, the
next available day is allowed: r. 1.3(7). For office hours and public holidays, see note 3.1.2.

"intimate"; "Intimation". For methods, see r. 16.7.   **55.14.3**

Intimation to Comptroller of reclaiming motion
55.15. The marking of a reclaiming motion from a decision of the patents
judge on an appeal from a decision of the Comptroller shall be intimated by
the reclaimer to the Comptroller as well as to the other parties to the appeal.

Deriv. RCS 1965, r. 257G substituted by S.I. 1991 No. 1621

"intimated". For methods, see r. 16.7.   **55.15.1**

Communication of information to European Patent Office
55.16.—(1) The court may authorise the communication to the European
Patent Office or the competent authority of any country which is a party to
the European Patent Convention of any such information in the records of
the court as the court thinks fit.
(2) An application for such information shall be made by letter addressed
to the Deputy Principal Clerk.
(3) Before complying with an application for the disclosure of information
under paragraph (1), any person appearing to be affected by the application
shall be given the opportunity of making representations to the patents
judge in chambers on the question whether the information should be
disclosed; and the decision of the patents judge shall be final and not subject
to review.
(4) In this rule, "the European Patent Convention" has the meaning
assigned in section 130(1) and (6) of the Act of 1977.

Deriv. RCS 1965, r. 257H substituted by S.I. 1991 No. 1621

General note. The European Patents Convention 1973 (Cmnd. 8510 (1982)) established the **55.16.1**
concept of a single European patent which may be issued by the European Patent Office valid in
all or specified Contracting States.

"final and not subject to review". The decision of the Lord Ordinary may not be reclaimed **55.16.2**
against.

[2] *Intimation and service of certain statutory applications for orders for
disposal of infringing matter*
[1,2] **55.17.** An application under section 114, 204 or 231 of the Copyright Act
of 1988 (which provide for orders for disposal in respect of infringement of
copyright, rights in performances and design rights), section 19 of the Trade
Marks Act 1994 (order as to disposal of infringing goods, material or
articles) or regulation 5 of the Olympics Association Right (Infringement
Proceedings) Regulations 1995 (order as to disposal of infringing goods,
materials or articles etc.), shall be made—
(a) in a cause depending before the court, by motion; or
(b) where there is no depending cause, by petition; and

the applicant shall intimate the motion to, or serve the petition on, as the case may be, all persons, so far as known to the applicant or reasonably ascertainable, having an interest in the copy, article, recording or other thing which is the subject of the application, including any person in whose favour an order could be made in respect of the copy, article, recording or other thing under any of the said sections of the Copyright Act of 1988, section 19 of the said Act of 1994 or regulation 5 of the said Regulations.

Deriv. RCS 1965, r. 257I substituted by S.I. 1991 No. 1621

---

[1] R. 55.17 amended by S.I. 1994 No. 2901 (effective 5th December 1994).
[2] R. 55.17 and heading amended by S.I. 1996 No. 1756 (effective 5th August 1996).

55.17.1   *"depending"*. A cause is depending from the time it is commenced (*i.e.* from the time an action is served or a first order in a petition is made) until final decree, whereas a cause is in dependence until final extract. For the meaning of commenced, see note 13.4.4 (action) or 14.6.1 (petition). For the meaning of final decree, see note 4.15.2(2). For the meaning of final extract, see note 7.1.2(2).

55.17.2   *"motion"*. For motions, see Chap. 23.

55.17.3   *"petition"*. A petition is presented in the Outer House: r. 14.2(h). The petition must be in Form 14.4 in the official printed form: rr. 4.1 and 14.4. The petition must be signed by counsel or other person having a right of audience: r. 4.2; and see r. 1.3(1) (definition of "counsel" and "other person having a right of audience") and note 1.3.4.
    The petitioner must lodge the petition with the required steps of process (r. 4.4). A fee is payable on lodging the petition: see note 14.5.10.
    On petitions generally, see Chap. 14.

55.17.4   *"intimate"*. For methods, see r. 16.7.

55.17.5   *"service"*. For methods, see Chap. 16, Pt I.

55.17.6   *Olympics Association Right (Infringement Proceedings) Regulations 1995 [S.I. 1995 No. 3325]*. The Olympics Association right consists of rights and remedies conferred by the Olympic Symbol etc. (Protection) Act 1995 similar to a registered trade mark. Under the 1995 Regulations the proprietor of the right (the British Olympics Association) may apply to the court for an order for delivery up of infringing goods, materials or articles. Where any such items have been delivered up an application may be made under reg. 5 for disposal.

Applications for leave to proceed
55.18.—(1) Where leave of the court is required under the Copyright Act of 1988 before an action may proceed, the pursuer shall apply by motion for leave to proceed before the summons is signeted.
    (2) A motion under paragraph (1) shall be heard in chambers.
    (3) Where such leave is granted, a copy of the interlocutor allowing leave shall be attached to the copy of the summons served on the defender.

Deriv. RCS 1965, r. 257J substituted by S.I. 1991 No. 1621

55.18.1   *"motion"*. For motions, see Chap. 23.

Appeals and references under the Trade Marks Act 1994
[1] **55.19.**—(1) Subject to the following paragraphs of this rule, an appeal or reference under section 76 of the Trade Marks Act 1994 (appeal from registrar or reference from appointed person) shall be heard in the Outer House by the patents judge.
    (2) In the application of Part III of Chapter 41 (appeals in Form 41.19) by virtue of rule 41.43 (appeals to Lord Ordinary) to an appeal or reference under paragraph (1) of this rule—
    (a) for references to the Inner House there shall be substituted references to the patents judge; and
    (b) the following paragraphs of this rule shall apply.

(3) Subject to paragraph (4), an appeal or reference shall be lodged in the General Department—
  (a) in the case of a decision on a matter of procedure, within 14 days after the date of the decision appealed against; and
  (b) in any other case, within 6 weeks after the date of the decision appealed against or the decision referring the proceedings to the court, as the case may be.

(4) Except with the leave of the court, no appeal or reference under this rule shall be entertained unless it has been lodged within the period specified in paragraph (3) or within such further period as the Comptroller may allow on an application made to him before the expiry of that period.

(5) Any determination by the Comptroller that a decision is on a matter of procedure shall be treated as being itself a decision on a matter of procedure.

(6) In the application of paragraph (1) of rule 41.21 (orders for service and answers), the order under that paragraph shall include a requirement to—
  (a) intimate the appeal to the Comptroller; and
  (b) serve the appeal on every other party to the proceedings before the Comptroller.

(7) On receiving intimation of the appeal, the Comptroller shall forthwith transmit to the Deputy Principal Clerk all the papers relating to the matter which is the subject of the appeal.

(8) A respondent who, not having appealed from the decision of the Comptroller, wishes to contend at the hearing of the appeal that the decision or the grounds of the decision should be varied shall—
  (a) specify the grounds of that contention in his answers;
  (b) intimate those answers to the Comptroller and to every other party to the proceedings before the Comptroller.

(9) Intimation of the date of the hearing of the appeal shall be made to the Comptroller by the appellant not less than 7 days before that date, unless the court otherwise directs.

(10) An appeal under this rule shall be a re-hearing and the evidence led on appeal shall be the same as that led before the Comptroller; and, except with the leave of the court, no further evidence shall be led.

---

[1] R. 55.19 inserted by S.I. 1994 No. 2901 (effective 5th December 1994).

General note. R. 41.43 provides for appeals to the Outer House or a single judge under any enactment. **55.19.1**

"within 14 days". The date from which the period is calculated is not counted. Where the last **55.19.2** day falls on a Saturday or Sunday or a public holiday on which the Office of Court is closed, the next available day is allowed: r. 1.3(7). For office hours and public holidays, see note 3.1.2.

"intimate"; Intimation". For methods, see r. 16.7. **55.19.3**

CHAPTER 56

JUDGMENTS OF THE HOUSE OF LORDS

Applications to apply judgments of the House of Lords
56.1.—(1) An application to apply a judgment of the House of Lords in a cause shall be made by motion in the Single Bills.

(2) On enrolling a motion under paragraph (1), the party enrolling it shall lodge four copies of the House of Lords judgment in process.

General note. Where the House of Lords affirms the decision of the Court of Session and **56.1.1** there is nothing else to be done in the cause (*i.e.* the subject-matter of the cause is disposed of), the Court of Session decree can be extracted and it is not necessary to apply to the court to apply the House of Lords judgment: *Peters v. Magistrates of Greenock* (1893) 20 R. 924.
  A judgment of the House of Lords may have to be put into a form to allow extract of a decree

to carry the judgment into effect, *e.g.* where the decision of the Court of Session is reversed. A motion to apply the judgment will be required. In such a case, where the Court of Session is simply giving effect to the judgment of the House of Lords, it is acting in a ministerial or administrative capacity and cannot add to or alter the judgment of the House of Lords: *Maclachlan's Trs v. Yuill's Trs* 1939 S.C. 500; *Grant v. Sun Shipping Co. Ltd* 1949 S.C. 19.

Where the judgment of the House of Lords does not exhaust the whole cause (because, *e.g.* it was an interlocutory judgment), an appropriate interlocutor of the Court of Session will have to be pronounced for further procedure. A motion to apply the judgment will be required.

A petition to apply a judgment of the House of Lords is no longer required.

56.1.2   *"motion"*. For motions, see Chap. 23.

56.1.3   *Appeals to the House of Lords*. Section 40 of the C.S.A. 1988, subject to the provisions of any other Act restricting or excluding appeal, governs appeals to the House of Lords. Appeal can only be from the Inner House, it not being possible to appeal to the House of Lords from the decision of the Lord Ordinary. The procedure is regulated by the House of Lords Directions as to Procedure and Standing Orders regulating judicial business. On time-limits for appeal, see House of Lords Directions, Direction 7 (reprinted in Division **B**).

Appeal is from a judgment of the court: see C.S.A. 1988, s.40(1) and Appellate Jurisdiction Act 1876, s.3. There is no appeal from an opinion of the court expressed in a stated case from an arbiter under s.3 of the Administration of Justice (Scotland) Act 1972 or a special case for the opinion of the court (rather than judgment) under s.27 of the C.S.A. 1988: *John G. McGregor (Contractors) Ltd v. Grampian R.C.* 1991 S.C.(H.L.) 1; *cf.* Tribunals and Inquiries Act 1992, s.11(6)(d), which provides for appeal to the House of Lords in stated cases to which s.11 of that Act applies. On appeals from the sheriff court, see note 56.1.4.

(1) *Appeal without leave*. A judgment on the whole merits of the cause, or an interlocutory judgment where there is a difference of opinion among the judges or it sustains a dilatory defence and dismisses the action, may be appealed against without leave. An interlocutor allowing or refusing a new jury trial is appealable without leave. See C.S.A. 1988, s.40(1)(a).

(2) *Appeal with leave*. An interlocutory judgment other than one mentioned above may be appealed against with leave of the Inner House: C.S.A. 1988, s.40(1)(b). A particular statute may provide for a final interlocutor to be appealable only with leave. Leave might not be granted unless there is a novel point of law, a point of law on which there is a conflict of judicial authority or a point of law of public importance: see also *Costain Building and Civil Engineering Ltd v. Scottish Rugby Union plc* 1993 S.C. 650, 663H *per* L.P. Hope. Leave may be refused where the question raised is one purely of Scottish procedure and practice (*McIntosh v. British Railways Board* 1990 S.C. 339) or against an interim order (*Ferguson v. Maclennan Salmon Co. Ltd* 1990 S.L.T. 658). The House of Lords has reiterated the point that it is not appropriate to refer matters of the procedure and practice of the Court of Session for decision by the House of Lords: *Girvan v. Inverness Farmers Dairy* 1998 S.C. 1, 21C–G *per* Lord Hope of Craighead. As a general rule, at the interlocutor stage it is not the court's function to resolve difficult questions of law which call for detailed and mature reflection; and the fact that a matter of public importance was raised was not a relevant consideration in determining whether to grant leave: *Houston v. BBC* 1995 S.C. 433 (First Div. refused leave against interim interdict). Leave will not usually be granted to enable a party to advance an argument not previously put forward: *Strathclyde R.C. v. Gallagher* 1995 S.C. 241.

In *Ross v. Ross* 1927 S.C.(H.L.) 4, 6, Viscount Dunedin stated that the right of appeal (without leave) remains where the judgment, though interlocutory, is final in substance; the test of finality in substance is to see whether the case would have been equally decided in substance whether the interlocutor had been pronounced as it was or to the opposite effect.

The House of Lords will not usually hear a new argument not made in the courts below: *British Oxygen Co. Ltd v. South West Scotland Electricity Board* 1956 S.C.(H.L.) 112, 119–120 *per* Lord Normand. It may do so where justice requires, *e.g.*, where the point would have to be decided in a later case or there is no other means of having the point decided: *British Oxygen Co. Ltd*, above; *Stonehaven Magistrates v. Kincardinshire C.C.* 1940 S.C.(H.L.) 56; *CIN Properties Ltd v. Dollar Land (Cumbernauld) Ltd* 1992 S.C.(H.L.) 104.

Where the House of Lords is reviewing concurrent findings as to credibility by the judge at first instance and the appellate court, the following rules apply: (a) concurrent findings-in-fact, depending on the assessment of credibility, ought only to be reviewed when it can be clearly demonstrated that the findings were erroneous. It is not enough that the court would have taken a different view of the facts: a concurrent finding can only be reversed where it could be demonstrated either that some cardinal fact had been overlooked, or that some altogether erroneous view had been taken of the hearing of the evidence on the case. (b) The court will reverse concurrent findings-of-fact where these do not depend upon an assessment of credibility. (c) A reluctance to reverse a concurrent finding-in-fact will not be shown where the finding is not a finding of specific fact but is really an inference from facts specifically found. See *Brodie v. British Railways Board* 1972 S.L.T.(Notes) 37.

Appeals to House of Lords from sheriff court. Under s. 32(5) of the C.S.A. 1988, an appeal to **56.1.4** the House of Lords from the Inner House in an appeal from the sheriff court under s. 28 of the Sheriff Courts (Scotland) Act 1907 is appealable only on matters of law. The House of Lords cannot embark on an examination of the evidence in the sheriff court but is restricted to genuine questions of law: *Laing v. Scottish Grain Distillers* 1992 S.C.(H.L.) 64, 69 *per* Lord Jauncey of Tullichettle and cases there cited; see also *Martinez v. Grampian Health Board* 1996 S.C.(H.L.) 1, 50–F *per* Lord Jauncey of Tullichettle.

Interim possession, execution and expenses. Under s.41(1) of the C.S.A. 1988, the Inner House **56.1.5** may regulate all matters relating to interim possession, execution and expenses pending appeal to the House of Lords. "Interim possession" has been held to include orders relating to custody of a child: *Brixey v. Lynas (No. 2)* 1996 S.L.T. 651.

<h1 style="text-align:center">CHAPTER 57</h1>

ADMISSION OF ADVOCATES

Form of petition for admission as advocate
57.1. A petition by a person for admission to the public office of advocate shall be in such form as the Lord President shall, in consultation with the Dean of the Faculty of Advocates, determine.

General note. The petition for admission as an Advocate is in a special form and the ordinary **57.1.1** rules for petitions do not apply. The petition form is obtainable from the Faculty of Advocates on applying to become an intrant of the Faculty of Advocates, and the petition is presented on the intrant's behalf by the Faculty.

An Advocate is not called to the Bar, he or she is admitted to the Faculty of Advocates and passes advocate after making, before a Lord Ordinary in a ceremony in open court, a declaration of allegiance to the Sovereign (or where allegiance is not owed, because, *e.g.* the person concerned is a foreign national not permitted to owe allegiance to a sovereign of another country, a declaration to faithfully discharge the office of advocate). The Advocate signs a parchment recording the declaration, the Lord Ordinary signs an interlocutor in the petition for an act of admission by the Lords of Council and Session, which is duly recorded in the Books of Sederunt.

Disapplication of rules in relation to petitions
57.2. The following provisions of these Rules shall not apply to a petition by a person for admission to the public office of advocate:—
    rule 4.1 (form, size, etc., of documents forming the process),
    rule 4.3 (lodging of processes), and
    Chapter 14 (petitions).

Admission as advocate
57.3.—(1) On presentation of the petition, the court shall pronounce an interlocutor remitting to the Dean and Faculty of Advocates to take trial of the qualifications of the petitioner for the public office of advocate and to report to the court.

(2) The Faculty of Advocates shall, subject to the approval of the court, make such rules and regulations with respect to the terms and conditions of admission to the Faculty of Advocates as it may from time to time think fit.

Deriv. R.C.S. 1965, r. 351 substituted by S.I. 1968 No. 1016 (r. 57.3(2))

General note. On presentation of the petition, the Lord President signs an interlocutor in the **57.3.1** petition remitting to the Faculty of Advocates. The qualifications, entry and training requirements are regulated by the Faculty of Advocates and are set out in Regulations as to Intrants approved by the court. Further information can be obtained from The Clerk of Faculty, Faculty of Advocates, Advocates' Library, Parliament House, Edinburgh EH1 1RF.

CHAPTER 58

APPLICATIONS FOR JUDICIAL REVIEW

Application and interpretation of this Chapter
58.1.—(1) This Chapter applies to an application to the supervisory jurisdiction of the court.
(2) In this Chapter—
"the first hearing" means a hearing under rule 58.9;
"the second hearing" means a hearing under rule 58.10.

58.1.1   *General note.* The special procedure in this Chapter is derived from R.C.S. 1965, r. 260B inserted by A.S. (R.C.A. No. 2) (Judicial Review) 1985 [S.I. 1985 No. 500]. This A.S. was made following a recommendation of the Dunpark Working Party on Procedure for Judicial Review of Administrative Action. The Working Party itself was set up by L.P. Emslie following remarks made by Lord Fraser of Tullybelton in *Brown v. Hamilton D.C.* 1983 S.C.(H.L.) 1, 49. Lord Fraser of Tullybelton contrasted the cumbersome ordinary action procedure then used in Scotland for judicial review, with the speedy and cheap prerogative order procedure used in England since 1973. The remarks of Lord Fraser of Tullybelton about speed and cost are reflected in the judicial review procedure. Accordingly the rules should be interpreted and applied with these elements in mind.

58.1.2   *The supervisory jurisdiction of the court.* This Chapter provides procedure for all applications to the supervisory jurisdiction of the Court of Session for the judicial review of certain types of conduct of certain natural and non-natural persons and the pronouncement of an order relating to the status of such conduct. The scope of this Chapter is limited by the extent of the court's supervisory jurisdiction. The rules in this Chapter do not change the substantive law regarding the extent of the court's supervisory jurisdiction or the extent of its jurisdiction: *West v. Secretary of State for Scotland* 1992 S.C. 385, 404 per L.P. Hope.
The "supervisory jurisdiction of the court" excludes procedures for which specific provision is made elsewhere in the R.C.S. 1994 (*e.g.* reduction in Chap. 53 or suspension in Chap. 60) where the jurisdiction which is the subject of review is not of a kind as defined in *West*, above: *Bell v. Fiddes* 1996 S.L.T. 51, 52H per Lord Marnoch; *Saunders, Ptnr*, 1999 S.C. 564 (OH) (petition dismissed because reduction of sheriff court decrees was dealt with under r.53.2).
A petition may be refused because of inordinate delay in seeking judicial review, on the ground of *mora*, taciturnity and acquiescence: *Atherton v. Strathclyde R.C.* 1995 S.L.T. 557.

58.1.3   *Jurisdiction.* See note 58.3.5.

Disapplication of certain rules to this Chapter
58.2. The following rules shall not apply to a petition to which this Chapter applies:
rule 14.4 (form of petitions),
rule 14.5 (first order in petitions),
rule 14.9 (unopposed petitions).

58.2.1   *General note.* Special rules apply to petitions for judicial review and, accordingly, rr. 14.1, 14.5 and 14.9 do not apply.

Applications for judicial review
58.3.—(1) Subject to paragraph (2), an application to the supervisory jurisdiction of the court, including an application under section 45(b) of the Act of 1988 (specific performance of statutory duty), shall be made by petition for judicial review.
(2) An application may not be made under paragraph (1) if that application is made, or could be made, by appeal or review under or by virtue of any enactment.

Deriv. R.C.S. 1965, r. 260B(1), (2) and (3) inserted by S.I. 1985 No. 500

58.3.1   *General note.* An application to the supervisory jurisdiction of the court may only be made by a petition for judicial review. It follows that any cause which is based on the exercise of the supervisory jurisdiction (in the sense of jurisdiction as described in *West v. Secretary of State for*

Scotland 1992 S.C. 385) which before 1985 could be brought by action or petition must now be brought by petition for judicial review: r. 58.3(1).

An application may not be made for judicial review where the remedy may be sought by appeal or review or under any enactment: r. 58.3(2). It does not apply, *e.g.* to applications under para. 15 of Sched. 1 to the Acquisition of Land (Authorisation Procedure) (Scotland) Act 1947 (validity of compulsory purchase order), s.232 (validity of structure plans) and s.233 (validity of other orders, decisions and directions) of the Town and Country Planning (Scotland) Act 1972 or para. 2 of Sched. 2 to the Roads (Scotland) Act 1984 (validity of orders). See further note 58.3.3.

"petition". The petition is presented in the Outer House: r. 14.2(e). The petition must be in **58.3.2** Form 58.6: r. 58.6(1). The petition must be in the official printed form: r. 4.1. The petition must be signed by counsel or other person having a right of audience: r. 4.2; and see r. 1.3(1) (definition of "counsel" and "other person having a right of audience") and note 1.3.4.

The petitioner must lodge the petition with the required steps of process (r. 4.4). A fee is payable on lodging the petition: see note 14.5.10.

On petitions generally, see Chap. 14.

Competency and relevancy of the petition. The extent of the supervisory jurisdiction is limited **58.3.3** by—(1) the type of person whose conduct may be reviewed; (2) the type of conduct which may be reviewed; and (3) the availability of any other statutory remedy to the petitioner. These matters affect the competency of a petition. In addition the petitioner must show title and interest to sue: this affects the relevancy of a petition. The principles by reference to which the competency of applications for judicial review is to be determined are set out in *West v. Secretary of State for Scotland* 1992 S.C. 385, 412–413 *per* L.P. Hope.

(A) Persons whose conduct may be reviewed. These are persons to whom a "jurisdiction" has been delegated or entrusted by statute, agreement, or other instrument: *West*, above *per* L.P. Hope at p. 412. In *West*, above, L.P. Hope at p. 413 said, "Contractual rights and obligations, such as those between employer and employee, are not as such amenable to judicial review. The cases in which the exercise of the supervisory jurisdiction is appropriate involve a tripartite relationship, between the person or body to whom the jurisdiction, power or authority has been delegated or entrusted, the person or body by whom it has been delegated or entrusted and the person or persons in respect of or for whose benefit that jurisdiction, power or authority is to be exercised.". The need for a tripartite relationship to exist has been doubted as inflexible: *Naik v. University of Stirling* 1994 S.L.T. 449, 451L–A *per* Lord Maclean; and see comments of Lord Prosser in *Joobeen v. University of Stirling* 1995 S.L.T. 120, 122F–K. A tripartite relationship is not formed when one of two parties to a relationship delegates a decision to an employee or agent: *Fraser v. Professional Golfers Association* 1999 S.C.L.R. 1032 (OH). In *Crocket v. Tantallon Golf Club*, 2005 S.L.T. (OH), para. [40], Lord Reed indicated that the concept of a tripartite relationship should not be applied inflexibly. In that case, in holding that the petition was competent, it was held that there was no distinction between a decision taken by the council of a club and a decision taken by a general meeting of members; the essence of the supervisory jurisdiction was described in para. [37].

A person to whom a jurisdiction has been delegated may be a natural or non-natural person. For a recent example of a debate about who was the "decision maker" to be called as respondent, see *Thomson v. Chief Constable of Grampian Police*, 2001 S.C. 443.

There are a number of persons who have been recognised to have a jurisdiction and whose conduct in the exercise of that jurisdiction has been judicially reviewed.

(1) *Inferior civil courts and tribunals*. It has been stated in numerous cases that the decisions of inferior civil courts and tribunals are reviewable (but note r. 58.3(2)). These have included—

(a) Church courts and office bearers: see, *e.g. Earl of Kinnoul v. Presbytery of Auchterarder* (1838) 16 S. 661 (aff'd (1839) Mac. & Rob. 220); *McMillan v. Free Church* (1861) 23 D. 1314; *Peake v. Association of English Episcopalians* (1884) 22 S.L.R. 3; *Moffat v. Kirk Session of Canonbie* 1936 S.C. 209; *Macdonald v. Burns* 1940 S.C. 376. The court has no jurisdiction, however, with respect to the exclusive jurisdiction of the courts of the Church of Scotland to legislate and adjudicate in relation to "all matters of doctrine, worship, government and discipline in the Church" including the determination of all questions covering the membership and office in the Church, the constitution and membership of its courts, the mode of election of its office bearers, and the definition of the boundaries of the spheres of labour of its ministers and other office bearers: *Logan v. Presbytery of Dumbarton* 1995 S.L.T. 1229; *Ballantyne v. Presbytery of Wigtown* 1936 S.C. 625.

(b) Lyon Court: see *Macrae's Trs. v. Lord Lyon* 1927 S.L.T. 285.

(c) Sheriff court in civil matters: see, *e.g. Murchie v. Fairbairn* (1863) 1 M. 800; *Maclachlan v. Rutherford* (1854) 16 D. 937; *Mackenzie v. Munro* (1894) 22 R. 45; *Mathewson v. Yeaman* (1900) 2 F. 873; *Adair v. Colville & Sons* 1926 S.C.(H.L.) 51; *Lothian R.C. v. Lord Advocate* 1993 S.C.L.R. 565 (fatal accident inquiry); *cf. Riverford Finance v. Kelly* 1991 S.L.T. 300, and *Bain v. Hugh L.S. McConnell Ltd* 1991 S.L.T. 691. In *Gupta's Tr. v. Gupta,* 1996 S.C. 82, Lord Morrison at p. 84F said it was questionable whether *ultra vires* actings of a sheriff in making an order he had no power or right to pronounce, could be challenged only by judicial review. Where the R.C.S. 1994 provide specific procedures (*e.g.* reduction in Chap. 53 or suspension in Chap. 60) and the jurisdiction which is the subject of review is not of a kind as defined in *West,* above, a petition for judicial review is not competent: *Bell v. Fiddes* 1996 S.L.T. 51, 52H *per* Lord Marnoch. In *Ingle v. Ingle's Tr* 1997 S.L.T. 160, the point was not argued but parties appeared to accept that such a petition was competent. In *Saunders v. Royal Insurance plc,* 1999 S.C. 564, 2000 S.L.T. 597 Lord MacLean held that since rule 53.2 provided for reduction of a sheriff court decree, a petition for judicial review was incompetent and it was irrelevant that the case also fell within the principles of *West,* above. In *Glasgow City Council, Ptrs,* 2004 S.L.T. 61, Lord Menzies disapproved of *Saunders,* did not follow it, distinguished *Bell,* and held judicial review was competent of a sheriff's refusal of a summary application against a decision of an education authority's appeal committee. In relation to "administrative" decisions of this kind by a sheriff from which there is no appeal, Lord Menzies' approach would seem correct. If the decision is in a criminal matter the High Court of Justiciary may exercise its supervisory jurisdiction: *Reynolds v. Christie* 1988 S.L.T. 68. The exercise by the Secretary of State of a power to refer a criminal case to the High Court of Justiciary under s.263 of the Criminal Procedure (Scotland) Act 1995 is reviewable by the Court of Session: *McDonald v. Secretary of State for Scotland* 1996 S.L.T. 16.

(d) *Justice of the peace in civil matters:* see *Stakis plc v. Boyd* 1989 S.C.L.R. 290.

(e) *District licensing boards.* A decision of a licensing board which is not appealable under the Licensing (Scotland) Act 1976 is reviewable: see, *e.g. Main v. City of Glasgow District Licensing Board* 1987 S.L.T. 305; *Tait v. City of Glasgow District Licensing Board* 1987 S.L.T. 340; *Argyll Arms (McManus) Ltd v. Lorn, Mid-Argyll etc., Licensing Board* 1988 S.L.T. 290; *J. & J. (Inns) Ltd v. Angus District Licensing Board* 1992 S.L.T. 931; *Brechin Golf and Squash Club v. Angus District Licensing Board* 1993 S.L.T. 547.

(f) *Valuation Appeal Committee:* see, *e.g. I.C.I. plc v. Central Region Valuation Appeal Committee* 1988 S.L.T. 106.

(g) *Reporter to the Secretary of State for Scotland.* This is a reporter who determines an appeal to the Secretary of State under, *e.g.* the Town and Country Planning (Scotland) Act 1997: see, *e.g. City of Aberdeen D.C. v. Hickman* 1993 S.C.L.R. 488.

(2) *Arbiters.* It is clear that their conduct in exercise of their jurisdiction is reviewable. This may be notwithstanding the power of an arbiter under s.3 of the Administration of Justice (Scotland) Act 1972 to state a case on a question of law to the Court of Session: see, *e.g. Macpherson v. Ross* (1831) 9 s.797; *Walsh v. Pollockshaws Magistrates* (1905) 7 F. 1009, 1018; *Kyle and Carrick D.C. v. A.K. Kerr and Sons* 1992 S.L.T. 629; *Shanks & McEwan (Contractors) Ltd v. Mifflin Construction Ltd* 1993 S.L.T. 1124. An arbiter's acceptance of appointment may also be reviewable: *Haden Young Ltd v. William McCrindle & Son Ltd* 1994 S.L.T. 221.

(3) *Local authorities.* A local authority has a general jurisdiction to do anything to facilitate or be conducive or incidental to the carrying out of its functions: Local Government (Scotland) Act 1973, s.69(1). In addition to this a local authority exercises other particular functions as education authority, valuation authority, council tax authority, planning authority, public authority, fire authority, etc. The core of a local authority's jurisdiction is conferred by the Local Government (Scotland) Act 1973. Additional jurisdiction is conferred by individual statutes applicable to specific areas (*e.g.* Social Work etc. (Scotland) Act 1968). Local authorities, like government ministers, exercise, *inter alia,* an executive function and a legislative function. Both of these functions may involve the exercise of a jurisdiction which has to be exercised *intra vires* and is reviewable: see, *e.g. Nicol v. Magistrates of Aberdeen* (1870) 9 M. 306; *Caledonian Railway Co. v. Glasgow Corporation* (1905) 7 F. 1020; *Moss' Empires v. Assessor for Glasgow* 1917 S.C.(H.L.) 1; *Walker v. Strathclyde R.C.* 1986 S.C. 1; *Tarmac Econowaste Ltd v. Assessor for Lothian Region* 1991 S.L.T. 77.

(3A) *Scottish Parliament.* The Scottish Parliament is the creature of statute and derives its' powers from statute and, unless otherwise excluded, the courts are the final authority in the interpretation of the governing legislation of the Parliament: *Whaley v. Lord Watson of Invergowrie* 2000 S.C. 340 (First Div.) The court may grant a declarator but may not grant interdict, reduction, specific implement or any like order: Scotland Act 1998, s.40(3). It may not grant an order against a member of the Parliament if its effect would be to give relief against the Parliament prohibited by s.40(3): 1998 Act, s.40(4).

(4) *The Crown and ministers.* A minister may act on behalf of the Crown using the prerogative power or a power delegated by statute.

(a) Prerogative power. This is the remaining part of the sovereign's power which has not been delegated to Parliament by statute, and which is exercised by ministers at their discretion. The type of power which is a prerogative power and its rationale for so being has been explained as follows: "Prerogative powers such as those relating to the making of treaties, the defence of the realm, the prerogative of mercy, the grant of honours, the dissolution of Parliament, and the appointment of ministers, as well as others, are not, I think susceptible to judicial review because their nature and subject-matter is such as not to be amenable to the judicial powers. The courts are not the place wherein to determine whether a treaty should be concluded, or the armed forces disposed in a particular manner and Parliament dissolved on one date or another.": *Council of Civil Service Unions v. Minister for the Civil Service* [1985] A.C. 374, 418B *per* Lord Roskill. A new prerogative power cannot now be created (*B.B.C. v. Johns* [1965] Ch. 32) but an existing power may be modified by statute (*Attorney-General v. De Keyser's Royal Hotel* [1920] A.C. 508; *Burmah Oil Ltd v. Lord Advocate* 1964 S.C.(H.L.) 117). The predominant view is that a decision based solely on a prerogative power is not reviewable in England: *Chandler v. Director of Public Prosecutions* [1964] A.C. 763; *Blackburn v. Attorney General* [1971] 1 W.L.R. 1037. It is thought that this is also the Scottish position: see, *e.g. McCormick v. Lord Advocate* 1953 S.C. 396; *Gibson v. Lord Advocate* 1975 S.C. 136, 143 *per* Lord Keith.

(b) Delegated (statutory) power. This is power given to a minister by statute. A decision using such a power is reviewable; see, *e.g. re* delegated legislation, *Air 2000 v. Secretary of State for Scotland (No. 2)* 1990 S.L.T. 335, *Singh v. Secretary of State for the Home Department* 1990 S.L.T. 300; and *re* delegated executive decision, *Lakin v. Secretary of State for Scotland* 1988 S.L.T. 780, *London and Clydeside Estates Ltd v. Secretary of State for Scotland* 1987 S.L.T. 459, *Ryrie (Blingery) Wick v. Secretary of State for Scotland* 1988 S.L.T. 806, *Johnston v. Secretary of State for Scotland* 1992 S.L.T. 387 and *Mensah v. Secretary of State for the Home Department* 1992 S.L.T. 177.

(5) *Trustees of public trusts*. The trustees must have a "jurisdiction" delegated to them either by statute or by private instrument: *West v. Secretary of State for Scotland* 1992 S.C. 385, 412–413 *per* L.P. Hope. It is suggested that for the trustees to have such a jurisdiction, the trust must have a public purpose: see, *e.g. Magistrates of Perth v. Trustees of the Road from Queensferry to Perth* (1756) Kilkerron's Notes, Brown's Suppl., Vol. 5, 318; *D. & J. Nicol v. Dundee Harbour Trs.* 1915 S.C.(H.L.) 7.

(6) *Other statutory and non-statutory bodies*. The body must be an administrative body to which a "jurisdiction" has been delegated: *West*, above, *per* L.P. Hope at pp. 412–413. It is suggested that such a body to which an administrative jurisdiction has been delegated by statute or private instrument must have some public or quasi-judicial function. Thus corporate bodies with purely private functions, *e.g.* banks, manufacturing companies, retailing companies, etc., would not be covered. On the other hand corporate bodies with public functions, *e.g.* regulatory organisations (commonly referred to as "quangos" (quasi-autonomous non-governmental organisations)) would be covered. Each body must be considered on its own facts. The following have been held to exercise a jurisdiction which is reviewable—

(a) Financial services regulatory organisation: *Bank of Scotland v. Investment Management Regulatory Organisations Ltd* 1989 S.C. 107.

(b) Scottish Legal Aid Board: see, *e.g. K. v. Scottish Legal Aid Board* 1989 S.L.T. 617; *Venter v. Scottish Legal Aid Board* 1993 S.L.T. 147.

(c) Criminal Injuries Compensation Board: *Gray v. Criminal Injuries Compensation Board* 1993 S.L.T. 28.

(d) Public broadcasting authorities: see, *e.g. Wilson v. Independent Broadcasting Authority* 1979 S.C. 351; and *Wilson v. Independent Broadcasting Authority (No. 2)* 1988 S.L.T. 276.

(e) Agricultural Marketing Boards: see, *e.g. Barrs v. British Wool Marketing Board* 1957 S.C. 72.

(f) Forestry Commissioners: *Kincardine and Deeside D.C. v. Forestry Commissioners* 1992 S.L.T. 1180.

(g) Harbour and airport authorities: see, *e.g. Air Ecosse Ltd v. Civil Aviation Authority* 1987 S.L.T. 751; *Peterhead Towage Services Ltd v. Peterhead Bay Authority* 1992 S.L.T. 594.

(h) Monopoly public industries: *British Oxygen Company Ltd v. South of Scotland Electricity Board* 1956 S.C.(H.L.) 112.

(i) Housing Benefit Review Boards: *Macleod v. Banff and Buchan Housing Benefit Review Board* 1988 S.L.T. 753.

(j) The Keeper of the Registers of Scotland: *Short's Tr. v. The Keeper of the Registers* 1994 S.C. 122, aff'd 1996 S.C.(H.L.) 14; *Millar & Bryce Ltd v. Keeper of the Registers of Scotland* 1997 S.L.T. 1000.

(k) The Scottish Football Association: *St Johnstone Football Club v. Scottish Football Association Ltd* 1965 S.L.T. 171.

(l) Universities: *Naik v. University of Stirling* 1994 S.L.T. 449; *Carlton v. Glasgow Caledonian University* 1994 S.L.T. 549.

(m) Rail authorities: *Highland R.C. v. British Railway Board* 1996 S.L.T. 274.

(n) Chief Constable: *Looney v. Chief Constable Strathclyde Police* 1997 S.C.L.R. 367; *Thomson v. Chief Constable of Grampian Police*, 2001 S.C. 443 (police pension regulations).

(o) Political parties: *Brown v. Executive Committee of Edinburgh Labour Party* 1995 S.L.T. 985.

(p) Housing associations: *Boyle v. Castlemilk East Housing Co-operative Ltd* 1998 S.L.T. 56.

(q) Adjudicators (creatures in construction contracts by virtue of the Housing Grants, Construction and Regeneration Act 1996): They are equiperated with arbiters. See *Ballast Plc v. The Burrell Company (Construction Management) Ltd*, 2001 S.L.T. 1039 (OH), *Homer Burgess Ltd v. Chirex (Annan) Ltd*, 2000 S.L.T. 277 (OH) and *SL Timber Systems Ltd v. Carillion Construction Ltd*, 2002 S.L.T. 997 (OH).

There is some doubt whether the decision of a club which is owned by its members involves the exercise of a jurisdiction for the purposes of judicial review: see *Graham v. Ladeside of Kilbirnie Bowling Club* 1990 S.C. 865.

(B) The type of conduct which may be reviewed. The conduct must involve the exercise of a jurisdiction: *West v. Secretary of State for Scotland* 1992 S.C. 385, 412 *per* L.P. Hope. Where the decision is simply to enter into a contract which could be entered into by private persons, the decision is not reviewable: *West*, above. On a "decision" which was not reviewable, see *Maguire v. Secretary of State for Scotland*, 9th March 1994 (1994 G.W.D. 17–1044). Suspension from duties of a chief executive could not be judicially reviewed because the true nature of the dispute was contractual: *Blair v. Lochaber D.C.* 1995 S.L.T. 407. In *WM Fotheringham & Son v. The British Limousin Cattle Society Ltd*, 6th August 2002, unreported (OH), it was held that the true nature of the dispute was an action of reparation for breach of s. 18 of the Competition Act 1998 by abuse of a dominant position and not a challenge of the validity of bye-laws which caused the loss.

The jurisdiction of the court is not, however, limited to something identifiable as a "decision"; it includes, for example, acts, omissions and statements denying the alleged rights are subject to review, the wider basis of the jurisdiction being recognised by the terms of r. 58.6(4): *Elmsford Ltd v. City of Glasgow Council (No.2)*, 2001 S.C. 267 (declaration of rights of access over strip of land where local authority by its acts, omissions and statements over a period of time denying alleged rights).

(C) The availability of any other statutory remedy. The supervisory jurisdiction is residuary to the court's appellate jurisdiction. The petitioner must have had no other statutory remedy available to him or have exhausted any such remedy: see also r. 58.3(2). Often there exist special statutory appeal procedures from a person's exercise of a jurisdiction. If these exist, then, subject to exceptional circumstances, the aggrieved person may not apply to the supervisory jurisdiction for judicial review: see, *e.g. Crawford v. Lennox* (1852) 14 D. 1029; *Maclachlan v. Rutherford* (1854) 16 D. 937; *Philp v. Reid* 1927 S.C. 224; *British Railways Board v. Glasgow Corporation* 1976 S.C. 224; *Simpson v. Inland Revenue Commissioners* 1992 S.L.T. 1069; *Sangha v. Secretary of State for Home Department* 1997 S.L.T. 545 (faulty advice by agent or lay adviser not exceptional circumstances). Exceptional circumstances may include where the decision-maker breached his statutory duty to inform the aggrieved person of the right of appeal under statute: *Moss' Empires v. Assessor for Glasgow* 1917 S.C.(H.L.) 1. See also discussion of s. 45(b) of the C.S.A. 1988 in note 58.3.4.

Where a remedy is available under another specific procedure in the Rules, a petition for judicial review may be refused as incompetent: see note 58.1.2.

(D) Title and interest to sue. The petitioner must have title and interest to sue, otherwise the petition will be irrelevant. There is no comprehensive definition of what amounts to title and interest in relation to the exercise of a jurisdiction which is complained of. It has been said that the petitioner "must be a party (using the word in its widest sense) to some legal relationship which gives him some right which the person against whom he raised the action either infringes or denies": *D. & J. Nicol v. Dundee Harbour Trs* 1915 S.C.(H.L.) 7, 12 *per* Lord Dunedin; see also, *e.g. Simpson v. Edinburgh Corporation* 1960 S.C. 313. A commercial interest *per se* does not give title or interest to sue: *Bondway Properties Ltd v. City of Edinburgh Council* 1999 S.L.T. 127.

A council tax payer has a clear title and interest to see local authority accounts as a "person interested" under s. 101(1) of the Local Government (Scotland) Act 1973, and his motive for doing so is irrelevant: *Stirrat v. City of Edinburgh Council* 1999 S.L.T. 274.

The petitioner must have title and interest at or about the time of the presentation of the petition and not at some point in the future: *Shaw v. Strathclyde R.C.* 1988 S.L.T. 313; see also *Air 2000 v. Secretary of State for Scotland (No. 2)* 1990 S.L.T. 335. The petitioner may become personally barred from proceeding by judicial review: see (F) below.

(E) Grounds of review under supervisory jurisdiction. Where the petition is competent the court will, in exercise of its supervisory jurisdiction, review the decision to see whether it is defective thereby entitling the petitioner to the remedy which he seeks. There is no substantial difference between English law and Scots law on the grounds of defectiveness: *West v. Secretary of State for Scotland* 1992 S.C. 385, 413 *per* L.P. Hope. Accordingly English cases may be referred to.

There are a number of grounds of defectiveness, for which see *Council of Civil Service Unions v. The Minister for the Civil Service* [1985] A.C. 374 *per* Lord Diplock and 414F *et seq. per* Lord Roskill.

(F) Mora, taciturnity and acquiescence. A petitioner may become personally barred from pursuing a judicial review because, *e.g.* of delay or silence indicating acquiescence: *Hanlon v. Traffic Commissioner* 1988 S.L.T. 802 (petition 10 months after decision); *Ingle v. Ingle's Tr.* 1997 S.L.T. 160 (acquiescence in decision of sheriff over four years earlier); and see *McIntosh v. Aberdeenshire Council* 1999 S.L.T. 93 (*obiter*); *Devine v. McPherson,* 2002 S.L.T. 213 (delay of seven months for judicial review of planning decision inferred acquiescence in its validity).

Section 45 of the C.S.A. 1988. The court may order the specific performance of any statutory **58.3.4** duty, under such conditions and penalties in the event of the order not being implemented as seems proper: C.S.A. 1988, s. 45(b). Only this provision is specifically included in r. 58.3(1), the implication being that s. 45(a) of the C.S.A. 1988 (restoration of possession of property of which one has been violently or fraudulently deprived) is not included because it was thought not to be appropriate for judicial review. The remedies in s. 45 of the C.S.A. 1988 are not available against the Crown: Crown Proceedings Act 1947, s. 21(1) (declarator available instead); see, *e.g. Davidson v. Scottish Ministers,* 2002 S.C. 205 (Extra Div.).

The precise terms of the order sought under s. 45(b) of the C.S.A. 1988 must be stated: *Carlton Hotel Co. v. Lord Advocate* 1921 S.C. 237. The remedy under this provision used not to be precluded because an alternative remedy was available: *T. Docherty Ltd v. Burgh of Monifieth* 1971 S.L.T. 13. It would appear, because such a remedy must be sought by judicial review and no remedy of appeal or review be available (r. 58.3), that the availability of this remedy is restricted.

Jurisdiction. The scope of the supervisory jurisdiction of the court covers a wide range of decisions **58.3.5** made by a wide variety of decision-makers. Accordingly it is impossible to give an exhaustive list of the various cases of jurisdiction. Rather the following is intended to give an indication of the factors to be considered in deciding whether a particular basis of jurisdiction applies.

(1) *Review of decision of a tribunal.* "Tribunal" may include inferior civil court for this purpose. The C.J.J.A. 1982 does not apply: C.J.J.A. 1982, ss. 17 and 21, Sched. 5, para. 4 and Sched. 9, para. 12. The common law applies under which the court's supervisory jurisdiction extends to the conduct of all inferior courts or tribunals situated within Scotland: see Maclaren on *Court of Session Practice,* pp. 118 and 119.

(2) *Review of decision of any other person.* Where an issue of jurisdiction exists between Scotland and another part of the U.K. it is determined by the C.J.J.A. 1982, s. 16 and Sched. 4. Where an issue of jurisdiction arises between Scotland and any other country outwith the U.K. (including a country which is party to the 1968 Brussels Convention or the Lugano Convention) it is determined by the C.J.J.A. 1982, s. 20 and Sched. 8. The bases of jurisdiction under these Schedules are largely the same and it is convenient to deal with them together—

(a) Domicile of the respondent (C.J.J.A. 1982, Sched. 4, Art. 2 and Sched. 8, r. 1). This is determined according to whether the respondent is an individual (C.J.J.A. 1982, s. 41), a body corporate or an unincorporated body of persons (C.J.J.A. 1982, s. 45), or the Crown (C.J.J.A. 1982, s. 46).

(b) The place where the threatened wrong is likely to occur (C.J.J.A. 1982, Sched. 4, Art. 5(3) and Sched. 8, r. 2(10));

(c) The seat of the legal person or association of natural or legal persons whose decision is the object of the litigation (Sched. 4, Art. 5A and Sched. 8 r. 2(12); see *Bank of Scotland v. Investment Management Regulatory Organisation Ltd* 1989 S.C. 107).

(d) In arbitration proceedings conducted in Scotland, the Court of Session (Sched. 8, r. 2(13)).

Where a case may be tried more suitably for the interests of all and of justice elsewhere, the court may decline jurisdiction on the ground of *forum non conveniens: Sokha v. Secretary of State for the Home Department* 1992 S.L.T. 1049.

Powers of court in judicial review

58.4. The court, in exercising its supervisory jurisdiction on a petition for judicial review, may—

    (a) grant or refuse any part of the petition, with or without conditions;

    (b) make such order in relation to the decision in question as it thinks fit, whether or not such order was sought in the petition, being an order that could be made if sought in any action or petition, including an order for reduction, declarator, suspension, interdict, implement, restitution, payment (whether of damages or otherwise) and any interim order;

(c) subject to the provisions of this Chapter, make such order in relation to procedure as it thinks fit.

Deriv. R.C.S. 1965, r. 260B(4) inserted by S.I. 1985 No. 500

58.4.1 *Powers of the court*. The court, if it holds that the decision is defective or that there is an apprehended wrong, may grant such order in relation to the decision as it thinks fit: r. 58.4(b). This rule re-states the common law position. Once a petition has been presented the court has, except where the cause is directed against the Crown, complete discretion in dealing with the decision on review. It may pronounce an order at its own instance.

The orders include—

(1) Reduction. The court may reduce the decision and remit for the decision-maker to reconsider: *McCormick v. Subscription Services Ltd* 1994 G.W.D. 40–2336.

(2) Declarator.

(3) Interdict (including interim interdict). This remedy is not available in a cause against the Crown, though a declaratory order may be available instead: Crown Proceedings Act 1947, s. 21. In the House of Lords, in *Davidson v. The Scottish Ministers*, 2006 S.L.T. 110, it was held that the reference to "civil proceedings" in s. 21 is to be read as not including proceedings for judicial review in respect of the Crown. The bar to certain remedies in s. 21 does not apply, therefore, in judicial review of acts or omissions of the Crown (and *McDonald v. Secretary of State for Scotland*, 1994 S.C. 234 (Second Div.) correctly decided for the wrong reasons). Where a petitioner seeks judicial review of the Crown's conduct as *ultra vires* of E.C. law, he may be able to obtain interdict against the Crown: *R. v. Secretary of State for Transport, ex parte Factortame Ltd* [1990] 2 A.C. 85 and *R. v. Secretary of State for Transport, ex parte Factortame Ltd (No. 2)* [1991] E.C.R. I–3905; see also Chap. 60.

(4) Suspension. Particular contractual decisions are not open to challenge by judicial review, and suspension of such decisions will not be granted: *Millar & Bryce Ltd v. Keeper of the Registers of Scotland* 1997 S.L.T. 1000. Interim suspension is not so distinct from interdict or specific performance as to escape the prohibition in s. 21(1)(a) of the 1947 Act: *Ralston v. The Scottish Ministers*, 2004 S.L.T. 1263 (OH). On suspension generally, see Chap. 60.

(5) Specific implement or specific performance of a statutory duty. Specific implement is a common law remedy. Specific performance of a statutory duty is available under s. 45(b) of the C.S.A. 1988 (formerly C.S.A. 1868, s. 91). Neither of these remedies is available against the Crown, although a declarator may be available instead: Crown Proceedings Act 1947, s. 21(1). See also note 58.3.4.

(6) Delivery or restoration of possession of violently or fraudulently deprived real or personal property. Delivery is a common law remedy. Restoration of possession of violently or fraudulently deprived real or personal property is available under s. 45(a) of the C.S.A. 1988 (formerly C.S.A. 1868, s. 91). Neither of these remedies is available against the Crown, although a declarator may be available instead: Crown Proceedings Act 1947, s. 21(1). The remedy under s. 45(a) of the C.S.A. 1988 is not specifically included in r. 58.3(1) and by implication may be excluded from being sought by means of judicial review: see also note 58.3.4.

(7) Damages. See, *e.g. Mallon v. Monklands D.C.* 1986 S.L.T. 347. If a petitioner wishes to claim damages, it is desirable that he should claim for and quantify these at the presentation for the petition: see *Shetland Line (1984) Ltd v. Secretary of State for Scotland* 1996 S.L.T. 653, 658 I *per* Lord Johnston.

(8) Protective order for expenses. On the competency of and circumstances for a protective order for expenses, see *McArthur v. Lord Advocate*, 2006 S.L.T. 170 (OH).

58.4.2 *"the decision in question"*. This phrase is used in r. 58.4(b). The supervising jurisdiction of the court is not, however, limited to decisions and the wider jurisdiction is recognised by the words used in r. 58.6(4): *Elmsford Ltd v. City of Glasgow Council (No.2)*, 2001 S.C. 267; and see note 58.3.3(B) above.

58.4.3 *Protective orders for expenses*. In *McArthur v. Lord Advocate*, 2006 S.L.T. 170, 2006 S.C.L.R. 654 (OH), the petitioners sought a protective order before the first hearing of no expenses to be found against the petitioners. It was held that it was competent to make such an order, although it was not granted in the circumstances of the case. Lord Glennie laid down the procedure to be followed when such a motion was made: full details of the petitioner's case to be given to the respondent in the petition or a note under r. 15.2, including intimation of the order sought and financial position of the petitioner, the public interest and other discretionary factors referred to in *R (Corner House Research) v. Secretary of State for Trade and Industry*, [2005] 1 W.L.R. 2600; and the order should be sought only after the respondent has had an opportunity to answer the petition or note and, if the respondent opposed it he had to set out his own position in respect of the same matters.

Nominated judge

58.5. A petition for judicial review shall be heard by a judge nominated by the Lord President for the purposes of this Chapter or, where such a judge is not available, any other judge of the court (including the vacation judge).

Deriv. R.C.S. 1965, r. 260B(6) inserted by SI 1985/500

General note. The aim of this rule is to have a petition for judicial review decided by a judge   **58.5.1** who is experienced in judicial review and administrative law matters.

Nominated judges. The judges currently nominated to hear petitions for judicial review are   **58.5.2** Lords Milligan, Cameron of Lochbroom, Marnoch, MacLean, Osborne and Abernethy.

"vacation judge". The powers of the vacation judge are limited by r. 11.1.   **58.5.3**

Form of petition

58.6.—(1) A petition for judicial review shall be in Form 58.6.

(2) The petitioner shall lodge with the petition all relevant documents in his possession and within his control.

(3) Where the petitioner founds in the petition on a document not in his possession or within his control, he shall append to the petition a schedule specifying the document and the person who possesses or has control over the document.

(4) Where the decision, act or omission in question and the basis on which it is complained of is not apparent from the documents lodged with the petition, an affidavit shall be lodged stating the terms of the decision, act or omission and the basis on which it is complained of.

Deriv. R.C.S. 1965, r. 260B(5) inserted by SI 1985/500 and amended by SI 1990/705 (r. 58.6(1));
r. 260B(8) to (10) inserted by SI 1985/500 (r. 58.6(2) to (4))

Form of petition. The petition must be in Form 58.6: r. 58.6(1). The petition must be signed by   **58.6.1** counsel or other person having a right of audience: r. 4.2(3); and see r. 1.3(1) (definition of "counsel" and "other person having a right of audience") and note 1.3.4.

Where the petition is in respect of a decision of an adjudicator appointed under s. 12 of the Immigration Act 1971, the Home Secretary should be called as respondent and the adjudicator should receive intimation as a person having an interest: P.N. No. 1 of 1992.

"all relevant documents in his possession". The general rule is that where any party founds on,   **58.6.2** or incorporates, a document in his pleadings he must, so far as the document is in his possession or within his control, lodge it in process with those pleadings: r. 27.1(1). R. 58.6(2) extends the general rule by requiring all relevant documents to be lodged whether or not the petitioner founds on or incorporates them in his pleadings.

The proper evidence to be produced in reduction of a decree, those decrees being *in publica custodia*, is an extract: *Miller & Son v. Oliver & Boyd* (1901) 9 S.L.T. 287, 287 *per* Lord Pearson. In *Miller* the arbiter refused to allow the decree arbitral to be lodged until his fees had been paid. The pursuers declined to pay those fees and the court held that the onus of production of a decree arbitral under reduction was on the defenders. It is not competent to bring a decree under review by reduction until it has been extracted (*Scouler v. McLaughlan* (1864) 2 M. 955, 959 *per* Lord Mackenzie), although reduction of an unextracted decree may be permitted in special circumstances (*Scouler*, above, *per* L.P. McNeill at p. 962). Where an extract of the decree sought to be reduced is available or can be obtained, it is lodged by the pursuer when the summons is signeted.

Schedule of documents. The purpose of the schedule of documents is to let the judge know the   **58.6.3** identity and location of any document which the petitioner founds on but is outwith his possession or control. The document may be located (a) in the hands of any party named as respondent in the petition or (b) in the hands of any other person.

Where the document is in the hands of the respondent, the petitioner may (a) at any time before or after the presentation of the petition apply for an order under s. 1 of the Administration of Justice (Scotland) Act 1972 (see Chaps. 35 and 64); or (b) at the first hearing make a motion for the production of the document under r. 58.9(2)(b)(vii) (see, *e.g. Kelly, Petr.* 1985 S.C. 333). When the document is in the hands of a person who has not appeared in the petition the petitioner may only apply for an order under the Administration of Justice (Scotland) Act 1972.

58.6.4   *Affidavits.* Affidavits are extensively used in judicial review procedure in place of oral evidence. Once again the reasoning behind this is to provide speed and flexibility. The deponent of the affidavit does not need to be the petitioner. The deponent should be a person who has direct knowledge of the conduct sought to be reviewed.

The affidavit should be in the form of a statement of evidence written in the first person. The affidavit should contain evidence in support of, and expanding, the averments in the petition. It should be sworn and signed by the deponent before any person who may competently take an oath. Such a person may include a notary public (including one who has ceased to be a solicitor), a justice of the peace, a sheriff, or any judge. The person taking the oath should also sign the affidavit. Witnesses to an affidavit are unnecessary. And see definition of affidavit in r. 1.3(1).

First order

58.7. On being lodged, the petition shall, without appearing in the Motion Roll, be presented forthwith to the Lord Ordinary in court or in chambers for—
    (a) an order specifying—
        (i) such intimation, service and advertisement as may be necessary;
        (ii) any documents to be served with the petition;
        (iii) a date for the first hearing, being a date not earlier than seven days after the expiry of the period specified for intimation and service; or
    (b) any interim order;
and, having heard counsel or other person having a right of audience, the Lord Ordinary may grant such an order.

Deriv. RCS 1965, r. 260B(1) inserted by SI 1985/500

58.7.1   *General note.* On lodging the petition, it is scrutinised and registered by a clerk of session in the Petition Department. A motion is enrolled by the petitioner for a first order and any interim orders. The clerk will ascertain if any caveat (on which, see Chap. 5) has been lodged on behalf of a respondent. The existence or otherwise of a caveat will be docquetted on the backing of the petition by the clerk. If there is a caveat, a copy of it will be placed with the process. The process is taken by a clerk of session from the Petition Department to the Keeper of the Rolls. If a caveat has been lodged in respect of an order which the petitioner seeks in the first order, intimation of the petition and of the hearing for the first order will be given to the respondent or his agent by a clerk in the office of the Keeper of the Rolls. A record of the intimation will be marked in the Motion Sheet. The Keeper will arrange for the motion for the first order to be heard by a nominated judge. The process is then taken to the nominated judge's clerk. At the arranged time the cause will be called. On the first order being pronounced, the period of notice is noted by the clerk of court in the Minute of Proceedings.

The appearance of counsel or other person having a right of audience is required for a first order.

A petition can be disposed of at a motion for a first order: *Sokha v. Secretary of State for the Home Department* 1992 S.L.T. 1049; *Butt v. Secretary of State for the Home Department*, 15th March 1995, unreported (1999 G.W.D. 16–905). In *Butt*, Lord Gill suggested that it would be appropriate to determine a petition at a motion for a first order where (1) the respondent is represented, (2) all necessary documents are to hand, (3) the respondent wishes to dispose of the petition then and is in a position to present a fully prepared case, and (4) there is no dispute of a factual nature such as to prevent the court from making a properly informed decision at that stage.

58.7.2   *Intimation, advertisement and service.* For rules, see Chap. 16. This will proceed on a warrant in the first order.

58.7.3   *Service of documents.* The Lord Ordinary may order that specific documents be served with the petition: r. 58.7(a)(ii). The aim of this rule is to speed up the procedure. Any potential respondent will know what documents the petitioner has lodged without having to examine the process.

58.7.4   *Date of first hearing.* The petitioner should apply to the Keeper of the Rolls for a date for the first hearing, and this may be done before the motion for the first order. The Keeper has complete discretion in allocating a diet, although certain factors may be taken into account (*e.g.* the availability of counsel). The first hearing must be on a date at least seven days after the expiry of the period of notice.

A full copy of the petition will be required by the Keeper's Office when applying for a date for a hearing: Notice (*i.e.* P.N.), 4th July 1996.

"interim order". This includes interim interdict, interim suspension, interim liberation, and **58.7.5** any interim order which the court may make and relates to the merits of the petition. In this context it does not include an order for the production of documents: *Kelly, Petr.* 1985 S.C. 333; *cf.* r. 58.9(2)(b)(vii). A caveat may be lodged against any interim order sought in a petition for judicial review: r. 5.1(c).

"counsel or other person having a right of audience". For definition see r. 1.3(1) and note 1.3.4. **58.7.6**

Reclaiming. An interlocutor pronounced under Chap. 58 which does not determine the **58.7.7** application may be reclaimed against only with the leave of the Lord Ordinary within 14 days after the date on which the interlocutor was pronounced: r. 38.4(4).

Compearing parties

58.8.—(1) A person to whom intimation of the first hearing has been made and who intends to appear—
    (a) shall intimate his intention to do so to—
        (i) the agent for the petitioner, and
        (ii) the Keeper of the Rolls,
        not less than 48 hours before the date of the hearing; and
    (b) may lodge answers and any relevant documents.
[1] (2) Any person not specified in the first order made under rule 58.7 as a person on whom service requires to be made, and who is directly affected by any issue raised, may apply by motion for leave to enter the process; and if the motion is granted, the provisions of this Chapter shall apply to that person as they apply to a person specified in the first order.

    Deriv. RCS 1965, r. 260B(13) and (14) inserted by S.I. 1985 No. 500
[1] R. 58.8 amended by S.S.I. 2000 No. 317 (effective 2nd October, 2000).

"intimate". For methods, see r. 16.7. **58.8.1**

"lodge answers and any relevant documents". Any person who has received intimation of the **58.8.2** petition may oppose the petition. The interlocutor appointing the first hearing does not include a call for answers, although a respondent appearing at the first hearing may seek leave to lodge them. It is not a prerequisite to appearance by a respondent at the first hearing that he tenders answers; but it is appropriate to do so, and to intimate them to the petitioner and other respondents in advance (and this is often done), to give notice of the argument against the order sought in the petition: see now comments in *Blair v. Lochaber D.C.* 1995 S.L.T. 407, 408D *per* Lord Clyde. Answers are called for by the court if it orders a second hearing: r. 58.9(2)(b)(iv). For form of answers, see r. 18.3.
    "Relevant documents" include any documents founded on or incorporated in the answers and any other documents in the respondent's control which are relevant to the determination of the petition. If a respondent wishes to keep certain documents confidential on grounds of privilege, the documents should be placed in a sealed packet: see also notes 35.2.7 and 35.2.8.

Appearance of person on whom petition not served. A person who has not been served with a **58.8.3** copy of the petition under the first order but who has nevertheless become aware of the petition, may make a motion for leave to enter the process: r. 58.8(2). The motion to enter the process should state the title and interest of the person. It should be made as soon as possible so that that person can lodge answers.

"motion". For motions, see Chap. 23. **58.8.4**

Applications for public interest intervention

[1] **58.8A.**—(1) A person to whom rule 58.8(2) does not apply may make an application to the court for leave to intervene—
    (a) in a petition for judicial review;
    (b) in an appeal in connection with such a petition.
    (2) An application for leave to intervene shall be by way of a minute of intervention in Form 58.8A, and the applicant shall—
    (a) send a copy of it to all the parties; and
    (b) lodge it in process, certifying that sub-paragraph (a) above has been complied with.
    (3) A minute of intervention shall set out briefly—

(a) the name and description of the applicant;
(b) any issue in the proceedings which the applicant wishes to address and the applicant's reasons for believing that any such issue raises a matter of public interest; and
(c) the propositions to be advanced by the applicant and the applicant's reasons for believing that they are relevant to the cause and that they will assist the court.

(4) The court may—
(a) refuse leave without a hearing;
(b) grant leave without a hearing unless a hearing is requested under paragraph (5) below; or
(c) fuse or grant leave after such a hearing.

(5) A hearing, at which the applicant and the parties may address the court on the matters referred to in paragraph (6)(c) below, may be held if, within 14 days of the minute of intervention being lodged, any of the parties lodges a request for a hearing.

(6) The court may grant leave only if it is satisfied that—
(a) the cause raise, and an issue in the cause which the applicant wishes to address raises, a matter of public interest;
(b) the propositions to be advanced by the applicant are relevant to the cause and are likely to assist the court; and
(c) the intervention will not unduly delay or otherwise prejudice the rights of the parties, including their potential liability for expenses.

(7) In granting leave, the court may impose such terms and conditions as it considers desirable in the interests of justice, including making provision in respect of any additional expenses incurred by the parties as a result of the intervention.

(8) Where leave is granted—
(a) an intervention shall be by way of a written submission which (including any appendices) does not exceed 5000 words; and
(b) the applicant shall lodge the submission and send a copy of it to all the parties by such time as the court may direct.

(9) The court may in exceptional circumstances—
(a) allow a longer written submission to be made;
(b) direct that an oral submission is to be made.

(10) The Clerk of court shall give written intimation of a grant or refusal of leave to the applicant and all the parties.

(11) Any diet in pursuance of paragraph (5) or (9)(b) above shall be fixed by the Keeper of the Rolls and who shall give written intimation of the dict to the applicant and all the parties.

(12) Nothing in this rule shall affect the power of the court to make such other direction as it considers appropriate in the interests of justice.

(13) Any decision of the court in under this rule shall be final cause and not subject to review.

----

[1] R. 58.8A inserted by S.S.I. 2000 No. 317 (effective 2nd October, 2000) and amended by S.S.I. 2004 No. 52 (effective 1st March, 2004).

58.8A.1   *General note.* This rule, inserted by A.S. (R.C.S.A. No.5) (Public Interest Intervention in Judicial Review) 2000 [SSI 2000 No.317], allows, with leave of the court, a person or organisation to make submissions in a judicial review involving other parties on the ground that the cause raises an issue of public interest.

58.8A.2   *"send".* This includes deliver: see r. 1.3(1).

58.8A.3   *"public interest".* The cause must raise a matter of public interest that the applicant wishes to address. What "public interest" means is not defined. It is submitted that the phrase is used as a term of art rather than as a legal term.

Leave of the court. An applicant is allowed to intervene (r. 58.8A(6)) only where—   **58.8A.4**
- the cause raises an issue of public interest,
- the applicant wishes to address that issue,
- the applicant's propositions are relevant to the cause and likely to assist the court, and
- the intervention will not unduly delay or prejudice parties' rights.

There is nothing in the rule about the applicant being an appropriate person or body to raise the issue or make submissions.

"intervention". The form of intervention is normally to be by written submissions; but, in **58.8A.5** exceptional circumstances, may be by oral submissions: r. 58.8A(8) and (9).

"written intimation". For methods, see r. 16.9.   **58.8A.6**

"final and not subject to review". The decision may not be reclaimed against.   **58.8A.7**

First hearing

58.9.—(1) At the first hearing, the Lord Ordinary shall—
- (a) satisfy himself that the petitioner has duly complied with the first order made under rule 58.7; and
- (b) hear the parties.

(2) After hearing the parties, the Lord Ordinary may—
- (a) determine the petition; or
- (b) make such order for further procedure as he thinks fit, and in particular may—
  - (i) adjourn or continue the first hearing to another date;
  - (ii) order service on a person not specified in the first order made under rule 58.7;
  - (iii) make any interim order;
  - (iv) order answers to be lodged within such period as he shall specify;
  - (v) order further specification in the petition or answers in relation to such matters as he shall specify;
  - (vi) order any fact founded on by a party at the hearing to be supported by evidence on affidavit to be lodged within such period as he shall specify;
  - (vii) order any party who appears to lodge such documents relating to the petition within such period as the Lord Ordinary shall specify;
  - (viii) appoint a reporter to report to him on such matters of fact as the Lord Ordinary shall specify; or
  - (ix) order a second hearing on such issues as he shall specify.

Deriv. RCS 1965, r. 260B(15) and (16) inserted by S.I. 1985 No. 500

General note. The purpose of the first hearing is to enable the Lord Ordinary to ascertain the **58.9.1** respective positions of the parties, to determine any outstanding issues which may be disposed of at the first hearing, and to make any order appropriate to secure the disposal at any subsequent hearing of any issue not disposed of at the first hearing. If it is sought to print a record the authority of the court must be obtained and will normally be granted only where adjustment has been allowed. The Lord Ordinary will dispose of any plea to the competency. The list of orders in r. 58.9(2)(b) is not exhaustive. Before the hearing, the parties should agree on the subject-matter to be covered so that the judge can be informed at the outset. The Lord Ordinary may determine the petition either on competency or on the merits at the first hearing. Most petitions are determined at the first hearing.

Reclaiming. An interlocutor pronounced under Chap. 58 which does not determine the **58.9.2** application may be reclaimed only with leave of the Lord Ordinary within 14 days after the date on which the interlocutor was pronounced: r. 38.4(4).

Fee. The court fee for the first hearing is payable by each party for every 30 minutes or part **58.9.3** thereof. For fee, see Court of Session etc. Fees Order 1997, Table of Fees, Pt. I, C, item 19 [S.I. 1997 No. 688, as amended, pp. C 1201 *et seq.*]. Certain persons are exempt from payment of fees: see 1997 Fees Order, art. 5 substituted by S.S.I. 2002 No. 270. A fee exemption certificate must be lodged in process: see P.N. No.1 of 2002.

Where a party is legally represented, the fee may be debited under a credit scheme introduced on 1st April 1976 by P.N. No. 4 of 1976 to the account (if one is kept or permitted) of the agent by the court cashier, and an account will be rendered weekly by the court cashier's office to the agent for all court fees due that week for immediate settlement. An agent not on the credit scheme will have an account opened for the purpose of lodging the fee: P.N. No. 2 of 1995. A debit slip and a copy of the court hearing time sheet will be delivered to the agent's box or sent by DX or post.

A party litigant must pay (by cash, cheque or postal order) to the clerk of court at the end of the hearing or, if the hearing lasts more than a day, at the end of each day: P.N. No. 2 of 1995.

A receipt will be issued. The assistant clerk of session will acknowledge receipt of the sum received from the clerk of court on the Minute of Proceedings.

Second hearing

58.10.—(1) Where the Lord Ordinary orders a second hearing under rule 58.9(2)(b)(ix), the Keeper of the Rolls shall, in consultation with the Lord Ordinary and the parties, fix a date for the second hearing as soon as reasonably practicable.

(2) Subject to the terms of any order for further procedure made under rule 58.9(2)(b), the parties shall, not less than seven days before the date of the second hearing, lodge all documents and affidavits to be founded on by them at the second hearing with copies for use by the court.

(3) At any time before the date of the second hearing, the Lord Ordinary may cause the petition to be put out for hearing on the By Order Roll for the purpose of obtaining such information from the parties as he considers necessary for the proper disposal of the petition at the hearing.

(4) At a hearing on the By Order Roll under paragraph (3), the Lord Ordinary may make such order as he thinks fit, having regard to all the circumstances, including an order appointing a commissioner to recover a document or take the evidence of a witness.

(5) At the second hearing, the Lord Ordinary may—

(a) adjourn the hearing;
(b) continue the hearing for such further procedure as he thinks fit; or
(c) determine the petition.

Deriv. R.C.S. 1965, r. 260B(17) to (20) inserted by S.I. 1985 No. 500

General note. If the Lord Ordinary has ordered a second hearing he will have specified the **58.10.1** issues to be dealt with at that hearing.

By Order Roll. The purpose of the By Order Roll hearing is to enable the Lord Ordinary to **58.10.2** keep a tight control of procedure to avoid delay. If a party discovers that he will have a problem in preparing adequately for the second hearing he should inform the Petition Department as soon as possible. The clerk of court will raise the matter with the Lord Ordinary who will decide whether and for what purpose there should be a hearing on the By Order Roll.

"obtaining such information as he considers necessary". The court may order the petition to be **58.10.3** put out on the By Order Roll on the request of any party or at its own instance. The By Order Roll hearing may enable the Lord Ordinary to obtain any information which he considers necessary to help him to determine any remaining issues.

No court fee is payable for the By Order Roll hearing under r. 58.10(3).

Fee. The court fee for a second hearing is payable by each party for every 30 minutes or part **58.10.4** thereof. For fee, see Court of Session etc. Fees Order 1984, Table of Fees, Pt. I, C, item 17 (or as appropriate) [S.I. 1984 No. 256, Table as amended, pp. C 1202 *et seq.*]. The fee may be debited under a credit scheme introduced on 1st April 1976 by P.N. No. 4 of 1976 to the account (if one is kept or permitted) of the agent by the court cashier, and an account will be rendered weekly by the court cashier's office to the agent for all court fees due that week for immediate settlement. An agent not on the credit scheme will have an account opened for the purpose of lodging the fee: P.N. No. 2 of 1995. A debit slip and a copy of the court hearing time sheet will be delivered to the agent's box or sent by DX or post.

A party litigant must pay cash to the clerk of court at the end of the hearing or, if the hearing lasts more than a day, at the end of each day: P.N. No. 2 of 1995. A receipt will be issued. The assistant clerk of session will acknowledge receipt of the sum received from the clerk of court on the Minute of Proceedings.

CHAPTER 59

APPLICATIONS FOR LETTERS

Applications for letters of arrestment or inhibition

59.1.—(1) An application for letters of arrestment or inhibition may be made, as the case may be, in—

(a) Form 59.1–A (arrestment);

[1] (b) Form 59.1–B (inhibition where decree granted, foreign judgment registered for execution or other document having the same force and effect as an extract of a decree of the Court of Session);

[3] (c) Form 59.1–C (inhibition on deed registered for execution);

[3] (d) Form 59.1–D (inhibition on dependence of action in sheriff court);

[3] (e) Form 59.1–E (inhibition in respect of future or contingent debt); or

[5] (f) Form 59.1–F (inhibition on contract for transfer of heritable property).

[2] (2) An application under paragraph (1) shall be presented to the Deputy Principal Clerk together with any relevant supporting documents.

[4,6] (3) Except where the application is in Form 59.1–D or 59.1–E, if the Deputy Principal Clerk is satisfied that the applicant for such letters is entitled to a warrant for arrestment or inhibition—

(a) he shall sign and date the warrant in such an application; and

(b) the application shall be signeted;

and such signeted application and warrant shall constitute letters of arrestment or inhibition, as the case may be.

[5,6] (4) Where the application is in any of Forms 59.1–A to 59.1–C or is in Form 59.1–D or 59.1–F, if the Deputy Principal Clerk refuses to sign and date such warrant, the application shall, on request, be placed before the Lord Ordinary; and the decision of the Lord Ordinary shall be final and not subject to review.

[3,6] (4A) Where the application is in Form 59.1–D or 59.1–E, it shall be placed before the Lord Ordinary together with any such documents as are mentioned in paragraph (2); and if the Lord Ordinary is satisfied as is mentioned in paragraph (3)—

(a) he shall sign and date the warrant in the application; and

(b) the application shall be signeted,

and such signeted application and warrant shall constitute letters of inhibition.

[3,6] (4B) The decision of the Lord Ordinary as respects an application in Form 59.1–D or 59.1–E shall be final and not subject to review.

(5) An application for letters of arrestment or inhibition on the dependence of an action to which a claim under section 19 of the Family Law (Scotland) Act 1985 applies shall be placed before the Lord Ordinary; and the decision of the Lord Ordinary shall be final and not subject to review.

Deriv. R.C.S. 1965, r. 68J(1) (r. 59.1(2)), r. 68J(2) (r. 59.1(4)), and r. 68J(3) (r. 59.1(5)), all inserted by S.I. 1991 No. 2483

---

[1] R. 59.1(1)(b) amended by S.S.I. 2004 No.331 (effective 6th August 2004).

[2] R. 59.1(2) amended by S.I. 1997 No. 1050 (effective 6th April, 1997).

[3] R. 59.1(1)(e) and (4A) and (4B) inserted by S.I. 1998 No. 890 (effective 21st April, 1998).

[4] R. 59.1(3) and (4) amended by S.I. 1998 No. 890 (effective 21st April, 1998).

[5] R. 59.1(1)(f) inserted, and r. 59.1(4) amended, by S.S.I. 1999 No. 109 (effective 29th October, 1999).

[6] R. 59.1(3), (4), (4A) and (4B) amended by S.S.I. 2004 No. 537 (effective 10th November, 2003).

59.1.1 *General note.* Modern forms of applications for letters of arrestment or inhibition are now provided. The form of inhibition in Sched. QQ to the Titles to Land Consolidation (Scotland) Act 1868 has been repealed and replaced by the forms in r. 59.1(1).

There is one document constituting the application and letters, the documents being the letters of arrestment or inhibition, as the case may be, on the warrant being granted and the application signeted.

On arrestment on the dependence, see note 13.6.2. On arrestment in execution, see note 16.12.11. On execution of letters of arrestment, see r. 16.12 and note 16.12.11.

59.1.3 *Letters of inhibition.* These are required for inhibition (a) on the dependence of a sheriff court action, (b) in execution of a Court of Session or sheriff court decree, (c) in execution of writs and foreign judgments registered for execution in the Books of Council and Session, (d) in execution on a document of debt, and (e) in security of future or contingent debts other than on the dependence of a Court of Session process.

Inhibition is a preventive diligence in security restraining a debtor from burdening, alienating or otherwise affecting his heritable property to the prejudice of the inhibitor: Erskine, II.xi.2. See generally, Graham Stewart on *Diligence*, pp. 530 *et seq.* As a general rule, a pursuer is entitled to insert a warrant for inhibition as of right in respect of a debt due. It may be recalled in whole or in part with or without conditions; and the pursuer will be liable in damages only for its wrongful use where executed on a defective warrant, in an irregular manner, or with malice or without probable cause: see *Wolthekker v. Northern Agricultural Co.* (1862) 1 M. 211, 212 *per* L.J.-C. Inglis: *Grant v. Magistrates of Airdrie* 1939 S.C. 738, 758–9 *per* L.P. Normand.

(1) The initial writ in a sheriff court action need not contain pecuniary conclusions: it is necessary only that there is a conclusion which can be secured by inhibition, *e.g.* implement of an obligation in respect of heritage: *Barstow v. Menzies* (1840) 2 D. 611; *Seaforth's Trs v. Macauley* (1844) 7 D. 180. It cannot be used in an action only for divorce (*Burns v. Burns* (1879) 7 R. 355), declarator or reduction (*Stafford v. McLaurin* (1875) 3 R. 148) or where the only conclusion which can be secured is one for expenses (*Weir v. Otto* (1870) 8 M. 1070). Warrant for inhibition in an action of aliment or in respect of a claim for financial provision in an action of divorce or declarator of nullity of marriage can only be obtained by motion on cause shown: Family Law (Scotland) Act 1985, s.19(1).

(2) A schedule of inhibition must be served on the defender or debtor in Form 16.15–F. The inhibition must be registered in the Register of Inhibitions and Adjudications and takes effect from the date of such registration; except that where a notice of inhibition is registered before (or after) execution of the inhibition and the inhibition is registered not later than 21 days after the notice, the inhibition takes effect from the date of registration of the notice: Titles to Land Consolidation (Scotland) Act 1868, s.155. The register is in Meadowbank House, 153 London Road, Edinburgh EH8 7AU, tel. 0131–659 6111, fax 0131–459 1221, DX ED 300 (open 10am to 4pm Monday to Friday).

(3) Inhibition is competent on a claim for payment of future or contingent debt (*i.e.* liquid debt payable at a certain future date or on the occurrence of an uncertain future event: *Mitchell v. Scott* (1881) 8 R. 875, 879 *per* L.P. Inglis). Arrestment is competent in respect of a debt due (*i.e.*, due for payment immediately *ex hypothesi* of the pursuer's case). If the debt is a future debt, although arrestable by a creditor of the common debtor, arrestment is not competent in security of another debt in an action to enforce the claim: *Costain Building & Civil Engineering Ltd v. Scottish Rugby Union plc* 1993 S.C. 650 overruling, on this point, *Taylor Woodrow Construction (Scotland) Ltd v. Sears Investment Trust Ltd* 1991 S.C. 140. Inhibition will only be granted at common law on a claim for a future debt where there are special circumstances averred, *e.g.* that the defender is *vergens ad inopiam* or *in meditatione fugae* or considering putting away his funds with the intention of not implementing any decree or not fulfilling his obligations: *Symington v. Symington* (1875) 3 R. 205; *Gillanders v. Gillanders* 1966 S.C. 54; *Wilson v. Wilson* 1981 S.L.T. 101. In an action of aliment or a claim for financial provision in an action of divorce or declarator of nullity of marriage, which are future or contingent debts, the position now is that warrant to inhibit may be granted on cause shown subject to any limit as to property or value (property only in inhibition), and is not limited to the common law grounds: Family Law (Scotland) Act 1985, s.19(1).

(4) Property which can be inhibited is heritable property (corporeal or incorporeal) which may be affected by adjudication (Bell's *Comm.*, ii,135) but not heritable bonds where there has been no infeftment (Graham Stewart on *Diligence*, pp. 548–549).

(5) Inhibition on a document of debt. A document of debt is a probative writ in which the debtor binds himself to pay. A negotiable instrument such as a bill of exchange or a promissory note is a document of debt for this purpose: Stair, IV.xlii.6. Consent to registration in the Books of Council and Session is not required; but where such a document contains a clause of registration for execution, a warrant to inhibit may be obtained on the decree of registration rather than the document of debt.

(6) Inhibition in execution. Inhibition may be obtained on a decree of the Court of Session or the sheriff court or on a decree of registration of a writ or judgment registered for execution in the Books of Council and Session.

(7) Effect of inhibition. When executed and registered it prevents the debtor voluntarily alienating or affecting his heritable property (whether he is infeft or not) to the prejudice of the inhibiter and renders any such deed voidable. It effectively prevents any sale or creation of a heritable security. It secures a ranking in preference to that of ordinary creditors who have taken no steps to secure their debts and creditors who have post-dated preferences: *Bank of Scotland v. Lord Advocate* 1977 S.L.T. 24. If decree in the action is not subsequently obtained by the pursuer the inhibition is of no effect: *Gordon v. Duncan* (1827) 5 S. 602. It has no effect on prior debts. It affects property belonging to the defender or debtor at the time of registration except property acquired after registration of the inhibition destined to him under an

indefeasible title, which is then inhibited, but otherwise does not affect property acquired after registration: 1868 Act, s.157; *cf. Leeds Permanent Building Society v. Aitken Malone & Mackay* 1968 S.L.T. 338. It secures principal and interest and any expenses decerned for (*Weir v. Otto* (1870) 8 M. 1070) but not the expenses of the inhibition. An inhibition within 60 days before sequestration or winding up of the defender or debtor does not create a preference: Bankruptcy (Scotland) Act 1985, s.37(2), Insolvency Act 1986, s.185 (companies); otherwise the inhibiter has a preference over debts contracted subsequently: *Baird & Brown v. Stirrat's Tr.* (1872) 10 M. 414. Inhibition is personal to the inhibitor and unless followed by a separate action of adjudication gives no real right or title.

(8) An inhibition relating to land, a lease or a heritable security prescribes within five years from the date of registration: Conveyancing (Scotland) Act 1924, s.44(3)(a).

On execution of inhibition, see r. 16.12 and note 16.12.12.

(9) An inhibition may be invalid if there is not strict accuracy (*e.g.* as an error or misdescription in relation to the inhibitor or the person inhibited): *Walker v. Hunter* (1853) 16 D. 226; and see, *e.g. Allied Irish Bank plc v. GPT Sales and Services Ltd* 1995 S.L.T. 163. Where there is a disparity between the name used in the Register of Inhibitions and the Register of Sasines the test is whether the disparity is capable of misleading a third party inspecting or instructing a search: *Atlas Appointments Ltd v. Tinsley* 1997 S.C. 200.

59.1.4 *"final and not subject to review"*. The decision of the Lord Ordinary may not be reclaimed against.

59.1.5 *Fee*. The court fee for an application for letters is payable for the fiat. For fee, see Court of Session etc. Fees Order 1997, Table of Fees, Pt I, C, item 7 [S.I. 1997 No. 688, as amended, pp. C1201 *et seq.*]. Certain persons are exempt from payment of fees: see 1997 Fees Order, art.5 substituted by S.S.I. 2002 No. 270. A fee exemption certificate must be lodged in process: see P.N. No.1 of 2002.

Where the applicant is legally represented, the fee may be debited under a credit scheme introduced on 1st April 1976 by P.N. No. 4 of 1976 to the account (if one is kept or permitted) of the agent by the court cashier, and an account will be rendered weekly by the court cashier's office to the agent for all court fees due that week for immediate settlement. Party litigants, and agents not operating the scheme, must pay (by cash, cheque or postal order) on each occasion a fee is due at the time of lodging at the counter at the General Department.

CHAPTER 60

APPLICATIONS FOR SUSPENSION, SUSPENSION AND INTERDICT, AND SUSPENSION AND LIBERATION

Application of this Chapter

60.1. Subject to rule 53.1 (conclusions for suspension etc., in action of reduction), this Chapter applies to an application for suspension, suspension and interdict, or suspension and liberation.

60.1.1 *General note*. This Chapter provides special rules for applications for (1) suspension; (2) suspension and interdict; and (3) suspension and liberation. Strictly, a petition for interdict alone (historically a heresy but now not uncommon) is not subject to the special rules in this Chapter; although in practice it probably would be.

(1) *Suspension*. The remedy of suspension is an ancient one. Originally a process of suspension was directed solely against any person who had obtained a decree or had obtained letters for charging or letters of caption (for civil imprisonment) or had carried out a poinding *simpliciter*, poinding of the ground or an adjudication: Stair, IV.lii.8. By the eighteenth century the scope of the remedy had expanded and Erskine described it thus: "Anywhere there is no decree there may be a suspension, though not in the strict acceptance of that word, for suspension is a process authorized by law for putting a stop not only to the execution of iniquitous decrees but to all encroachments either on property or possessions and in general to every unlawful proceeding": Erskine, IV.iii.20.

The purpose of suspension is thus to stop unlawful conduct (including execution of a decree) either temporarily or permanently. A suspension, however, has only retrospective effect. In this it is akin to arrestment. Suspension is also akin to reduction but differs in that (a) a decree of suspension cannot itself be suspended, and (b) a person seeking suspension may obtain an interim order: see Stair IV.lii.3 and 4. Often a suspension may be sought as a temporary measure preceding an action of reduction: *e.g. McCarroll v. McKinstery* 1923 S.C. 94 (suspension of charge leading to reduction of the execution of charge and underlying decree).

Suspension is thus used (1) to sist diligence and proceedings and (2) to review a decree in absence or a decree of an inferior court. Suspension of a charge following a decree merely suspends diligence whereas suspension as a mode of review challenges the decree: Mackay's Practice, 610-611; *Macdonald v. Denoon,* 1928 S.L.T. 439. In *Ali v. Ali,* 2001 S.C. 618, 622 (paras 8–11), an Extra Div. expressed the view, without deciding the issue, that in modern times the usual practice for seeking review of a decree, having obtained sist of diligence by suspension, is to bring an action of reduction. (Suspension may, of course, be sought in an action of reduction: r. 53.1.) It has also been held that reduction is the appropriate remedy where it is sought to set aside a decree on the ground of fraud or on a ground extrinsic to the case: *Smith v. Kirkwood* (1897) 24 R. 872. (There was some doubt expressed in *Smith* as to the competency of suspension of a final decree of an inferior court after the C.S.A. 1868 regarding review.) It should be noted that s. 35 of the C.S.A. 1988 recognises the suspension of sheriff court decrees. Suspension of a decree is limited. It is excluded where (a) review by appeal is competent (Mackay's Practice, ii, pp.482-3); (b) the party seeking suspension has been unsuccessful on appeal on the merits or by default (*Lamb v. Thompson* (1901) 4 F. 88, 92 *per* Lord Moncreiff; (c) the decree has been implemented (Mackay's Practice, ii, p.483); (d) the decree is one of absolvitor *in foro* (*McGregor v. Lord Strathallan,* (1862) 24 D. 1006); (e) the decree is for a sum within the privative jurisdiction of the sheriff court (*Brown & Critchley Ltd v. Decorative Art Journals Ltd,* 1922 S.C. 192); (f) the decree is that of the Court of Session: *McCarroll v. McKinstery,* 1923 S.C. 94. Suspension of a decree in absence before extract is in effect superseded by reponing in the sheriff court. As to reduction, see note 53.2.1.

The test of relevancy for suspension permanently of a sheriff court decree is the same as would be applicable in an action of reduction of that decree: *Ali,* above. On that test, see note 53.2.1.

Until 1933 suspension was obtainable by a note of suspension presented to the Lord Ordinary on the Bills sitting in the Bill Chamber. Since 1933, when the Bill Chamber was abolished, suspension may be obtained either by petition (*simpliciter*) or petition for judicial review (see Chap. 58). In many older cases suspension is used as a remedy to review the decisions of inferior courts or tribunals: see, *e.g. Manson v. Smith* (1871) 9 M. 492; *McCarroll,* above; and see note 60.6.1. It is also available as a remedy to review a decree in absence of the Court of Session: C.S.A. 1988, s. 34. An interim order of suspension may be obtained: see r. 14.5 and note 14.5.8. Suspension, including interim suspension, may be obtained through a conclusion ancillary to other conclusions in an action: *Gilmont Transport Services Ltd v. Renfrew District Council* 1982 S.L.T. 290.

Where the court has granted a decree of suspension, including interim suspension, it may not be appropriate for the court to ordain the respondent *ad factum praestandum* (to perform a certain act) under s. 46 of the C.S.A. 1988: *Maersk Co. Ltd v. National Union of Seamen* 1988 S.L.T. 828, 831 *per* Lord Cullen.

(2) *Suspension and interdict.* Suspension merely affects past and not future conduct. Accordingly, where a person wishes also to prohibit future conduct he must include a crave for interdict in the prayer of the petition. Where interdict, alone or with suspension, is sought, procedure is usually by way of petition. It is nevertheless competent to conclude solely for interdict in an action: *Dunn v. Hamilton* (1837) 15 S. 853, (1838) 3 S. & M. 356 (HL); and *Exchange Telegraph Co. v. White* 1961 S.L.T. 104. Where interdict is sought with other remedies, such as damages or declarator, procedure is usually by way of action.

Interdict prohibits reasonably apprehended future breaches of duty by the respondent or defender to the petitioner or pursuer: *Inverurie Magistrates v. Sorrie* 1956 S.C. 175. Interdict is a preventive remedy prohibiting action which is threatened or continuing and looks to the future not the past; its purpose is not to compel a defender (or respondent) to restore parties to the position they were in previously, although that might be its indirect effect, but to preserve the status quo: *Church Commissioners for England v. Abbey National plc* 1994 S.C. 651 approving *Grosvenor Developments (Scotland) plc v. Argyll Stores Ltd* 1987 S.L.T. 738; and see *Retail Parks Investments v. Royal Bank of Scotland plc* 1996 S.L.T. 1156. Hence, "positive" interdicts so-called are not granted; in *Hampden Park Ltd v. Dow,* 13th July 2001 (OH), ureported, Lord Drummond Young set out a three stage approach to determining whether an interdict was truly a negative order. Under s. 46 (reinstating petitioner in possessory right or granting specific relief) and s. 47(2) (interim possession) of the C.S.A. 1988 enable the court to make interim orders to restore a party to the position he was in prior to the wrongful act (*Church Commissioners for England,* above (and see the cases cited at p. 965)) and an order may be made under s. 46 of the C.S.A. 1988 for reinstatement before a final hearing to dispose of the petition (*Maersk Co. Ltd v. National Union of Seamen* 1988 S.L.T. 828, 831G *per* Lord Cullen; *Five Oaks Properties Ltd v. Granite House Ltd* 1994 S.C.L.R. 740). (On the other hand, a party to a contract is generally entitled to specific implement (the decree for which passes the test of precision, specification, definition and notice) of a contractual obligation subject to the residual discretion of the court to refuse it in exceptional circumstances where cogent reasons exist as where to grant it would be inconvenient and unjust or it would cause exceptional hardship. For the most recent statement of the law, see *Highland and Universal Ltd v. Safeway Properties Ltd* 2000 S.C. 297 (First Div.)). The court always retains an equitable discretion to refuse a permanent decree of interdict: *Wm. Grant & Sons. Ltd v. Glen Catrine Bonded Warehouse Ltd.*, 2001 S.L.T. 1419, 1437 *per* Rodger, L.P.

An interim order of interdict may be obtained: see note 60.3.2.

The remedy of interdict is not available in civil proceedings against the Crown, though a declaratory order may be available instead: Crown Proceedings Act 1947, s. 21; and see *McDonald v. Secretary of State for Scotland* 1994 S.C. 234 on "civil proceedings against the Crown". But note that in *Davidson v. The Scottish Ministers*, 2006 S.C. (H.L.) 41; 2006 S.L.T. 110, the House of Lords held that the bar in s. 21 did not apply to judicial review as that was not "civil proceedings". In *Beggs v. The Scottish Ministers*, 2005 S.L.T. 305 (First Div.), it was held that s. 21 did not make it incompetent to find the respondents in contempt of court by reason of a breach of an undertaking to the court. In *Beggs*, it was also decided that the proceedings against the respondents were not against the Crown. The question whether the Scottish Ministers were the Crown was reserved in *Davidson*. Interdict may, however, be available where it is reasonably apprehended that the Crown will be in breach of E.C. law: see *R. v. Secretary of State for Transport, ex parte Factortame Ltd* [1990] 2 A.C. 85 and *R. v. Secretary of State for Transport, ex parte Factortame Ltd (No. 2)* [1991] 1 A.C. 603.

The remedy of interdict is not available against the Scottish Parliament, but the court may, instead, make a declarator: Scotland Act 1998, s. 40(3).

An interdict may apply to future conduct outwith Scotland: *Barratt International Resorts Ltd v. Martin* 1994 S.L.T. 434, 437L *per* Lord Sutherland. For enforcement of such an interdict under the C.J.J.A. 1982, see rr. 62.40 and 62.42.

On the factors to be considered in determining whether to grant interdict in contractual cases (*e.g.* of landlord and tenant), see *Church Commissioners for England v. Nationwide Anglia Building Society* 1994 S.L.T. 897, 899A–D *per* Lord Clyde.

Where a court is considering whether to grant (interim) interdict which might affect freedom of expression under ECHR, the court has to be satisfied not only that there is a prima facie case and that the balance of convenience favours granting the order but also that on a final determination the petitioner would be likely to succeed: Human Rights Act 1998, s. 12; *Dickson Minto WS v. Bonnier Media Ltd*, 2002 S.L.T. 776.

On interdict to prohibit pursuing action abroad, see *Shell U.K. Exploration and Production Ltd v. Innes* 1995 S.L.T. 807. In *FMC Corporation v. Russell* 1999 S.L.T. 99, Lord Bonomy reviewed the authorities when considering the issues to be determined in deciding whether there is a prima facie case for interim interdict for pursuing an action abroad. There must be a prima facie case that Scotland is the natural forum and that pursuing the proceedings in the foreign court is vexatious or oppressive.

In a petition for interim interdict under s. 27 of the C.J.J.A. 1982 the court may, in the exercise of comity, grant an order similar to the foreign order even though it would not have been able to do so in Scottish proceedings provided that there was a prima facie case according to the jurisprudence of the originating jurisdiction: *G. v. Caledonian Newspapers Ltd* 1995 S.L.T. 559.

Interdict may not be granted to circumvent those provisions of the C.J.J.A. 1982 which exclude the court from interfering with a judgment made elsewhere which is to be registered in Scotland: *Clarke v. Fennoscandia Ltd* 1998 S.C. 464; and see *Clark v. Fennoscandia Ltd (No. 3)*, 2005 S.L.T. 511 (Second Div.).

The court will only interfere in the proceedings of a voluntary association in extraordinary circumstances: *Brown v. Executive Committee of the Edinburgh District Labour Party* 1995 S.L.T. 985 (court interfered where there was an apprehension of denial of natural justice).

(3) *Suspension and liberation.* Where a person who is imprisoned, following the granting of a warrant to apprehend after a breach of a civil decree, wishes to be released before the expiry of his period of imprisonment, his remedy is to apply to the court for (a) suspension of any unlawful step of procedure which led to imprisonment and liberation from his place of imprisonment; or (b) liberation *simpliciter* where he has been imprisoned after refusal to comply with a decree *ad factum praestandum* and while in prison he has either complied with the decree or no longer wilfully refuses to comply (Law Reform (Miscellaneous Provisions) (Scotland) Act 1940, s. 1(1)(ii)).

Suspension and liberation may also be sought be a person who has been detained by an immigration officer pending either a decision on leave to enter the U.K. or following directions for removal from the U.K.: see *Sokha v. Secretary of State for the Home Department* 1992 S.L.T. 1049.

Where a person seeks a suspension and liberation, the application will usually seek to review the exercise of a jurisdiction of a court or public official. Accordingly the application will usually require to be made in a petition for judicial review: see *West v. Secretary of State for Scotland* 1992 S.L.T. 636, 645J *per* L.P. Hope; and r. 58.4. An order for interim liberation may be obtained: C.S.A. 1988, s. 47(1). For grounds for civil imprisonment, see note 60.3.4. For grounds for suspension and liberation, see Maclaren on *Bill Chamber Practice*, p. 76.

Forms of applications

60.2.—(1) An application to which this Chapter applies shall be made by petition.

(2) It shall not be necessary in any such petition to make an offer of caution or consignation.

Deriv. R.C.S. 1965, r. 234 (part)

"petition". A petition is presented in the Outer House: r. 14.2(f). The petition must be in **60.2.1** Form 14.4 in the approved printed form: rr. 4.1 and 14.4. The petition must be signed by counsel or other person having a right of audience, or an agent: r. 4.2(3); and see r. 1.3(1) (definition of "counsel", "other person having a right of audience" and "agent") and note 1.3.4.

The petitioner must lodge the petition with the required steps of process (r. 4.4) and any documents founded on or adopted (r. 27.1(1)). A fee is payable on lodging the petition: see note 14.5.10.

On petitions generally, see Chap. 14.

Caution. Caution from the petitioner is no longer ordered as a general rule in suspension and **60.2.2** interdict unless there is a question of the petitioner's solvency or if the respondent might have a substantial damages claim in the event of the interim interdict proving wrongous: *Wright v. Thomson* 1974 S.L.T.(Notes) 15 *per* Lord Maxwell. For procedure for finding caution, see Chap. 33.

First order

60.3. Where the interlocutor ordering intimation, service or advertisement contains an interim suspension of execution, interim interdict or interim liberation, subject to the finding of caution or the giving of other security or any other conditions, the petition shall not be intimated, served or advertised until such condition has been met.

Deriv. R.C.S. 1965, r. 236(d) (part)

Intimation, service or advertisement. See r. 14.7; and for methods of service and intimation, see **60.3.1** Chap. 16, Pt I.

Interim interdict. Where a petition or summons contains a crave or conclusion for interdict or **60.3.2** liberation the court may, on the motion of any party, grant interim interdict or interim liberation: C.S.A. 1988, s.47(1). The motion may be made at any time after the presentation of the petition or signeting of the summons: *National Cash Register Co. Ltd v. Kinnear* 1948 S.L.T.(Notes) 83. No special crave or conclusion for the interim order is required, although this is usually inserted: *National Cash Register Co. Ltd,* above. When the court considers a motion for interim interdict it first considers whether the petitioner or pursuer has made out a *prima facie* case, and if he has, it then considers whether the balance of convenience favours the petitioner or pursuer: *W.A.C. Ltd v. Whillock* 1989 S.C. 397, 410 *per* L.J.-C. Ross.

A motion for interim interdict is often made and dealt with in the absence of the person against whom the order is sought. Exceptions are:

(a) Where that person has lodged a caveat (see Chap. 5).

(b) Where that person has already entered the process.

(c) Section 221(1) of the Trade Union and Labour Relations (Consolidation) Act 1992. This provides that where an application for interdict is made *ex parte* and the respondent (or defender) claims or would be likely to claim that he acted in furtherance of a trade dispute, the court will not grant interdict unless satisfied that all reasonable steps have been taken to secure that notice of the application and an opportunity of being heard has been given to the respondent.

(1) *Prima facie case.* The petitioner or pursuer must show that his case as averred and amplified by submissions, taken on the basis of all available information, gives him a reasonable prospect of success: *W.A.C. Ltd,* above. The court is not at this stage concerned to arrive at definite conclusions on the legal issues: *W.A.C. Ltd,* above, Where a motion for recall of interim interdict would determine the cause and balance of convenience is not an issue, the motion should be dealt with on the Procedure Roll: *Zebmoon Ltd v. Akinbrook Investment Developments Ltd* 1988 S.L.T. 146, 174C *per* Lord Clyde. The correct test where no injury or delict has yet been committed is to consider whether the interdictor is in reasonable apprehension that a serious delict or injury will be, or is likely to be, committed against him by

the defender or respondent: *Allseas UK Ltd v. Greenpeace Ltd,* 2001 S.C. 844 (OH).

(2) *Balance of convenience.* The petitioner or pursuer must show that the inconvenience to him in not obtaining the interim interdict outweighs the inconvenience to the respondent or defender in obtaining interim interdict. The following is a list of factors (in no particular order of importance) which have been considered:

(a) Irreparable nature of apprehended wrong: *Baird v. Monkland Iron and Steel Co.* (1862) 24 D. 1418, 1425 *per* L.J.-C. Inglis (flooding of petitioner's coal mines); *Pease v. Pease* 1967 S.C. 112 (marriage); *McGuinness v. Renfrewshire Upper District Committee* 1907 S.C. 1117 (discharge of sewage); *British Coal Corporation v. South of Scotland Electricity Board* 1988 S.L.T. 446 (catastrophic effect on pursuer's market); *Secretary of State for Scotland v. Highland Council* 1998 S.L.T. 222 (demolition of listed building); *Allied Domeq Spirits and Wine Ltd v. Murray McDavid Ltd* 1999 S.L.T. 157 (low likelihood of damage to pursuer's businesses).

(b) Offering of caution, other security or undertaking by the respondent or defender: *Forth Yacht Marina Ltd v. Forth Road Bridge Joint Board* 1984 S.L.T. 177 (undertaking to reduce nuisance); *Highland Distilleries Co. plc v. Speymalt Whisky Distributors Ltd* 1985 S.L.T. 85 (undertaking to keep accounts); *Knox v. Paterson* (1861) 23 D. 1263 (offer of caution); *Bernard v. Bernard* (1893) 1 S.L.T. 29 (undertaking to keep accounts); *Waste Systems International Inc. v. Eurocare Environmental Services Ltd* 1999 S.L.T. 198 (undertaking to keep accounts).

(c) Degree of likelihood of ultimate success: *Toynar Ltd v. Whitbread & Co. plc* 1988 S.L.T. 433, 434C–D *per* Second Div.

(d) Financial effect of interim interdict on respondent or defender: *Orkney Seafoods Ltd, Petrs* 1991 S.L.T. 891 (minor change of name for newly established company); *Dash Ltd v. Philip King Tailoring Ltd* 1989 S.L.T. 39 (minor effect from change of name of new business); *Steiner v. Breslin* 1979 S.L.T.(Notes) 34 (major financial hardship); *Salon Services (Hairdressing Supplies) Ltd v. Direct Salon Services Ltd* 1988 S.L.T. 414 (whole savings threatened); *Waste System International Inc,* above (cessation of whole business).

(e) Ease of quantification of putative damages: *Conoco Speciality Products (Inc.) v. Merpro Montassa Ltd (No. 1)* 1991 S.L.T. 222 (damages for loss of monopoly patent right market); *Dash Ltd v. Philip King Tailoring Ltd* 1989 S.L.T. 39 (damages for passing off); *C R Smith Glaziers (Dunfermline) Ltd v. Greenan* 1993 S.L.T. 1221, 1224G *per* L.J.-C. Ross (damages for breach of employee's restrictive covenant).

(f) Adequacy of putative damages: *William E. Selkin Ltd v. Proven Products Ltd* 1992 S.L.T. 983 (damages for infringement of patent).

(g) Safety implications: *Shell U.K. Ltd v. McGillivray* 1991 S.L.T. 667, 672I–L *per* Lord Cameron of Lochbroom; *Waste Systems International Inc,* above (disposal of hazardous medical waste).

(h) Public interest: *Scottish Milk Marketing Board v. Paris* 1935 S.C. 287 (preservation of statutory public monopoly); *Forth Yacht Marina Ltd,* above (maintenance of public bridge); *Johnston v. Dumfriesshire Road Trustees* (1867) 5 M. 1127 (construction of public bridge); *Waste Systems International Inc,* above (operation of hazardous medical waste-disposal factories).

(i) Undue delay in making motion: *William Grant & Sons Ltd v. William Cadenhead Ltd* 1985 S.L.T. 291.

(3) *Undertaking or caution by respondent or defender.* An undertaking may be recorded in the interlocutor or in the minute of proceedings. Breach of an undertaking does not *per se* entitle the aggrieved party to obtain an order for the party in breach to appear at the bar of the court: *Stirling Shipping Co. Ltd v. National Union of Seamen* 1988 S.L.T. 832, 834K–L *per* Lord Cullen. The breach may, however, be contempt of court: *Graham v. Robert Younger Ltd* 1955 J.C. 28; and see *Cordiner, Petr* 1973 S.L.T. 125. For procedure for finding caution, see Chap. 33.

(4) *Wrongous interdict.* Interim interdict is obtained *periculo petentis* (at the risk of the person seeking it): *Fife v. Orr* (1895) 23 R. 8. Where a party obtains interim interdict which is then to any extent recalled as unjustified, that party may be sued by the person interdicted for wrongous interdict and be found liable in damages: *Fife,* above; *Clippens Oil Co. Ltd v. Edinburgh and District Water Trustees* (1906) 8 F. 731.

(5) *Duration of interdict.* Interim interdict lasts from the time it is granted until it is recalled or made perpetual. An order of interim interdict may be superseded: *Phonographic Performance Ltd v. McKenzie* 1982 S.L.T. 272. Interim interdict may be recalled on a reclaiming motion, on a motion to the Lord Ordinary for recall, or on the determination of the crave or conclusion for interdict. The interim interdict may be recalled in part: *Steiner v. Breslin* 1979 S.L.T.(Notes) 34. In any event, subject to reclaiming, the interim interdict will cease on final determination by the Lord Ordinary when it is either made perpetual or recalled. If there is an appeal from the final determination the interim interdict ceases on determination of the appeal: *Clippens Oil Co. Ltd,* above *per* L.P. Dunedin at pp. 749–751.

(6) *Operation of interdict.* Although an interim interdict is valid from when it is granted, it only becomes operative when the respondent or defender becomes sufficiently aware of its

contents: *Clark v. Stirling* (1839) 1 D. 955. This would apply even in the absence of service, although service is usually made. Knowledge of the interdict by the respondent's agent may raise a presumption of knowledge by the respondent: *Henderson v. Maclellan* (1874) 1 R. 920, 923 *per* L.P. Inglis. Awareness by the respondent of the terms of an interim interdict does not *per se* make him aware of the terms of a perpetual interdict even if in identical terms: *Stewart v. Stallard* 1995 S.C.L.R. 167. Interdict cannot affect unnamed persons (*e.g.* "any other person having notice of the interlocutor"): *Lord Advocate v. The Scotsman Publications Ltd* 1989 S.C.(H.L.) 122; and *Pattison v. Fitzgerald* (1823) 2 S. 536. It was explained in *Oliver & Son Ltd Ptrs.* 1999 S.L.T. 1039, by the First Div. on a report to the Inner House by Lord Penrose, that the underlying reasoning in *The Scotsman Publications*, above, and *Pattison*, above, was that it is incompetent to pronounce an interdict on persons on whom the proceedings are not served or to move for its recall. In *Oliver*, the petitioners sought an order under s.46 of the C.S.A. 1988 to be reinstated in their possessory right to heritable property which was occupied by persons whose names were unknown to them but who could be identified as the occupiers of the petitioners' land. A first order for service was sought on the unnamed persons those who were served would be able to enter the process and resist the making of any substantive order. The First Div. held that the persons on whom service was to be made were sufficiently identified were it otherwise the court would be powerless to act and would be handing to those who concealed their identity a weapon to wreak injustice. It was indicated for the petitioners that messengers-at-arms would hand copies of the petition to individuals they found occupying the land and record what they had done and might photograph those on the land and the steps taken to serve the petition. Accordingly it should he possible to bring an action for removing with conclusions for interdict and interim interdict against unnamed persons and to seek service of the action on those who can be found and identified with respect to the conclusions for interdict. But it would not be possible to seek interim interdict on those unnamed persons before service. Where interim interdict is granted on condition that the pursuer finds caution it becomes operative only on the finding of caution: *Wilson v. Gilchrist* (1900) 2 F. 391; and see Chap. 33. Where the interim interdict is the first order in a petition process, the court will also automatically pronounce an order for intimation and service of the petition: r. 14.5(1). Service by registered letter tendered at the respondent's or defender's address but refused may amount to a good citation: Citation Amendment (Scotland) Act 1882, s.4(5); *Matheson v. Fraser* 1911 2 S.L.T. 493.

Breach of interdict. Breach of interim interdict in a depending cause (whether action or **60.3.3** petition) is dealt with by minute in that process: C.S.A. 1988, s.47(1). Breach of perpetual interdict is dealt with by petition and complaint. A cause is depending until final decree, whereas a cause is in dependence until final extract. For the meaning of final decree, see note 4.15.2(2). For the meaning of final extract, see note 7.1.2(2).

The petition (or minute) must have the concurrence of the Lord Advocate as public prosecutor because of its quasi-criminal character: *Gribben v. Gribben* 1976 S.L.T. 266. In the case of a matrimonial interdict against molestation, the docquet is a means of informing the court that no criminal proceedings are being pursued against the alleged offender, avoiding double jeopardy. The Lord Advocate's concurrence is written on the principal petition (or minute), usually by one of his deputes. The concurrence is obtained by sending the principal of the writ to the Lord Advocate at the Lord Advocate's Chambers, Crown Office, 25 Chambers Street, Edinburgh, EH1 1LA. It is not necessary to intimate to the Lord Advocate all adjustment or amendments to the pleadings if these are averments which are part of the same course of conduct averred: *Byrne v. Ross* 1992 S.C. 498. Proceedings for breach of interdict are civil proceedings to which s.1(1) of the Civil Evidence (Scotland) Act 1988 (rule requiring corroboration abolished) applies: *Byrne*, above.

Care must be taken to name and design the respondent correctly as a material error will invalidate the petition: *Overseas League v. Taylor* 1951 S.C. 105; *cf. Anderson v. Stoddart* 1923 S.C. 755 (immaterial error). As breach of interdict constitutes a contempt of court which might lead to punishment, it is necessary in the interests of fairness that the alleged contempt is clearly and distinctly averred, and the proceedings for contempt should be confined to the averments: *Byrne*, above.

(1) *Jurisdiction.* If the court has jurisdiction to grant the interdict it will have jurisdiction to deal with a breach unless jurisdiction has been lost. The court has jurisdiction under Sch.8 to the C.J.J.A. 1982 (jurisdiction of Scottish courts), r.1 (domicile) and r.2(10) (interdict where wrong to be committed). See also jurisdiction under Sch.1 (1968 Convention), Sch.3C (Lugano Convention) and Sch.4 (inter-U.K. jurisdiction), Art.5(3) (jurisdiction in delict) and Art.24 (protective measures), and s.24(2) (protective measures where jurisdiction doubtful) and s.27 (protective measures), and the Brussels I Regulation (Council Regulation (EC) No.44/2001).

(2) *Procedure by minute.* On the form of the minute, see r.15.1. The minute docqueted with the Lord Advocate's concurrence is lodged and a motion enrolled for the minute to be received and to ordain the party in breach (the respondent, defender or as the case may be) to appear at the bar and to explain the alleged breach. The motion will be intimated in the usual way (see r.23.3) to that party's agent or, if he has not entered the process, to that party himself by letter. At the motion, if the respondent denies the breach, an interlocutor will be pronounced ordaining him to lodge answers within a specified time; thereafter the procedure will be that for a minute and answers. If the breach is admitted, he will be dealt with there and then if he is personally present; if not, but he is represented or there is no appearance, an interlocutor will be pronounced ordaining him to appear on a particular date (usually a week later). A certified copy of that interlocutor must be served on the respondent, personally in the case of a natural person: on personal service, see note 16.1.2(1). At the second hearing the clerk may request the presence of police officers if this is thought to be necessary. If found to be in breach the respondent may be admonished, fined or imprisoned (on which, see note 60.3.4). Where the respondent is not a natural person, it may appear by one of its office-bearers to explain the breach or be represented by counsel or other person having a right of audience. If the respondent does not appear, and he is a natural person, an interlocutor will be pronounced granting warrant to messengers-at-arms and other officers of the law to apprehend him, granting warrant to Governors of H.M. Prisons to receive and detain him pending his appearance in court, and execution of the interlocutor to proceed on a certified copy of the interlocutor. The messenger-at-arms will inform the petitioner's agent once the respondent has been apprehended.

(3) *Procedure by petition and complaint.* This is an Outer House petition: r.14.2(*d*). The concurrence of the Lord Advocate must be docqueted on the principal petition before it is presented. The petition proceeds in the usual way for a petition with a first order being obtained for intimation and service. If no answers are lodged, the petitioner can enrol a motion to ordain the respondent to appear at the bar and to explain the alleged breach of interdict. The procedure thereafter is the same as that of a minute for breach of interim interdict. If answers are lodged the procedure will be similar to that for a minute and answers.

Civil imprisonment. This is available in three circumstances.   **60.3.4**
(1) Contempt of court in a civil cause.
(2) As a remedy for breach of interdict: see note 14.2.6.
(3) As a diligence for the enforcement of—
(*a*) Failure to pay a fine for contempt of court in a civil proceeding: Debtors (Scotland) Act 1880, s.4 as amended by the Debtors (Scotland) Act 1987, Sch.6, para.8;
(*b*) Failure to comply with an order under s.45 of the C.S.A. 1988: 1880 Act, s.4 as amended by the 1987 Act, Sch.6, para.8;
(*c*) Failure to pay any sum decerned for aliment: 1880 Act, s.4; and
(*d*) Failure to comply with a decree *ad factum praestandum* (for the performance of a certain act): 1880 Act, s.4 and the Law Reform (Miscellaneous Provisions) (Scotland) Act 1940, s.1. A decree of registration obtained following default on an obligation *ad factum praestandum* in a document registered in the Books of Council and Session or in the sheriff court books is not *per se* enforceable by imprisonment: 1987 Act, s.100(1). It is unclear whether an order under s.45 of the C.S.A. 1988 is a decree *ad factum praestandum* for the purposes of the Law Reform (Miscellaneous Provisions) (Scotland) Act 1940, s.1(1)(ii).

"finding of caution or granting of other security". See Chap. 33 for procedure.   **60.3.5**

Further petition following refusal by default

60.4. Where a petition for suspension, suspension and interdict, or suspension and liberation has been refused—
  (a) for failure by the petitioner to—

     (i) find caution or give other security, or to consign money into court, or

     (ii) comply with any other condition imposed by the court under rule 60.3 (first order), or

  (b) on any other ground other than on the merits,

the petitioner may, having paid any expenses in which he was found liable, present another petition for suspension, suspension and interdict, or suspension and liberation, as the case may be.

Deriv. R.C.S. 1965, r.243

Appointing petition to Adjustment Roll

60.5.—(1) Any party may, within seven days after any answers have been lodged, apply by motion for an order appointing the petition and answers to the Adjustment Roll.

(2) Where the court grants a motion under paragraph (1), the petitioner shall, within 14 days after the interlocutor granting the motion—

  (a) send at least four copies of the petition and answers in the form of an open record to the respondent; and

  (b) lodge two copies of the record in process;

and thereafter the cause shall proceed as an action.

Deriv. R.C.S. 1965, r.247

60.5.1   *General note.* Traditionally, a party who seeks interdict alone presents a petition although an action concluding solely for interdict has been held to be competent: *Dunn v. Hamilton* (1837) 15 S. 853, (1838) 3 S. & M. 356 (H.L.); *Exchange Telegraph Co. v. White* 1961 S.L.T. 104. Where other remedies connected with interdict such as reduction are also sought, an action should be raised. In any event, a petition presented under this Chapter which is opposed proceeds as an action.

60.5.2   *"within seven days", "within 14 days".* The date from which the period is calculated is not counted. Where the last day falls on a Saturday or Sunday or a public holiday on which the Office of Court is closed, the next available day is allowed: r.1.3(7). For office hours and public holidays, see note 3.1.2.

60.5.3   *"motion".* For motions, see Chap. 23.

60.5.4   *"open record".* This consists of the pleadings of the parties and the interlocutors so far pronounced: r.22.1(4); and see note 22.1.1. Where the petitioner fails to comply with r.60.5(2) the respondent may apply by motion to have the petition refused: see note 22.1.9.

60.5.5   *"send".* This includes deliver: r.1.3(1) (definition of "send").

60.5.6   *"lodge two copies of the open record in process".* The open records are lodged as steps of process (r.1.3(1) (definition of "step of process")). On lodging steps of process, see r.4.4. The list may be lodged by post: P.N. No. 4 of 1994, paras. 1 and 8; and see note 4.4.10.

    One copy of the record is the process copy, the other is for the Keeper of the Rolls and is used to regulate the progress of the cause on the Adjustment Roll.

Suspension of decree of inferior court or tribunal

60.6.—(1) This rule applies to a petition for the suspension of a decree, order, decision or warrant of whatever nature of an inferior court or tribunal.

(2) The petition shall be served on the clerk of the inferior court or tribunal to which the petition relates.

(3) The Lord Ordinary may pronounce an interlocutor ordering production to the court of any part of the proceedings in the inferior court or tribunal within such period as he thinks fit.

(4) On an interlocutor being pronounced under paragraph (1), the petitioner shall exhibit to the clerk of the inferior court or tribunal a certified copy of the interlocutor; and that clerk shall transmit the documents ordered to be produced to the Deputy Principal Clerk.

(5) Where the petitioner fails to comply with the requirement on him under paragraph (4), the petition shall be refused.

(6) An interlocutor granting suspension shall include a direction to the clerk of court to send a copy of the interlocutor by post to the clerk of the inferior court or tribunal on whom service was executed under paragraph (2).

(7) Where an interlocutor granting suspension is reclaimed against, the reclaimer shall give written intimation of that fact to the clerk of the inferior court or tribunal as soon as possible after the reclaiming motion has been marked.

(8) The interlocutor disposing of such a reclaiming motion shall include a direction to the clerk of court to send a copy of that interlocutor to the clerk of the inferior court or tribunal on whom service was executed under paragraph (2).

Deriv. R.C.S. 1965, r. 242(a)

General note. It had been thought that it was unclear whether it was competent to present an **60.6.1** ordinary petition for suspension of a decree, order or decision of an inferior court or tribunal following the introduction of applications for judicial review as the means of the court exercising its supervisory jurisdiction. It has now been held that the reference to the "supervisory jurisdiction of the court" in r. 58.1(1) (applications for judicial review) must be construed as excluding procedures for which specific provision is made elsewhere in the R.C.S. 1994 and as confined to the type of jurisdiction described in *West v. Secretary of State for Scotland* 1992 S.C. 385: *Bell v. Fiddes* 1996 S.L.T. 51, 52H *per* Lord Marnoch. In that case it was held that judicial review for reduction of a decree in absence in the sheriff court and interim interdict against enforcement was incompetent and reduction should be sought in an action of reduction.

It is not competent to suspend an unextracted decree: *Turner v. Gray* (1824) 3 S.235. It is not competent to suspend a decree of absolvitor or a decree for expenses arising to any extent from it: *McGregor v. Lord Strathallan* (1862) 24 D. 1006, 1009 *per* L.J.-C. Inglis. The court may not suspend a sheriff court decree where its value (exclusive of interest) brings it within the sheriff's privative jurisdiction (currently £1,500: Sheriff Courts (Scotland) Act 1907, s.7 as amended by the Sheriff Courts (Scotland) Act 1971 (Privative Jurisdiction and Summary Cause) Order 1988 [S.I. 1988 No. 1993]): *Brown and Critchley Ltd v. The Decorative Art Journals Co. Ltd* 1922 S.C. 192; such a suspension must be brought before the sheriff (Sheriff Courts (Scotland) Act 1907, s.5(5) and A.S. (Summary Suspension) 1993 [S.I. 1993 No. 3128]).

"served". For methods, see Chap. 16, Pt I.   **60.6.2**

Interlocutor ordering production. This may be pronounced on the motion of any party or by **60.6.3** the court at its own instance.

Reclaiming. See Chap. 38.   **60.6.4**

"written intimation". For methods, see r. 16.9.   **60.6.5**

Interlocutor refusing suspension after proof

60.7. Where the Lord Ordinary, after a proof, refuses a petition for suspension of a decree or decision of an inferior court or tribunal, he shall specify in his interlocutor the relevant facts of the case which he finds to be established and the points of law which he has applied to such facts.

Deriv. R.C.S. 1965, r. 242(b)

CHAPTER 61

JUDICIAL FACTORS

PART I

GENERAL PROVISIONS

Application and interpretation of this Chapter

61.1.—(1) This Chapter applies to an application for the appointment of a judicial factor, and to a judicial factor appointed by the court.

(2) In this Chapter, unless the context otherwise requires—
"the Act of 1849" means the Judicial Factors Act 1849;
[1] "the Act of 1995" means the Children (Scotland) Act 1995;
"judicial factor" includes a curator *bonis*, a factor *loco absentis*, a factor on trust or other estates, and a guardian.

Deriv. R.C.S. 1965, r. 199 (r. 61.1(2))

---

[1] Definition inserted by S.I. 1997 No. 1720 (effective 1st August 1997).

61.1.1 *General note.* This Chapter provides rules for the appointment and subsequent conduct of judicial factors appointed by the court. It applies, subject to any other specific provisions in the R.C.S. 1994, to all judicial factors of whatever type. Until the mid-nineteenth century there was a division between (a) judicial factors appointed to manage the estates of natural persons under a legal incapacity (*e.g.* curators *bonis* (to a minor or an *incapax*), factors *loco tutoris*, factors *loco absentis*); and (b) judicial factors appointed to ingather and distribute the estates of legally capable persons, natural and non-natural, due to insolvency or other financial or administrative difficulties. This was reflected in the application of different Acts of Sederunt to these different types of factor. Both types of factor could only be appointed by application to the *nobile officium* of the Inner House. By the C.S.A 1857 this jurisdiction was delegated to the Outer House where, but for minor exceptions, it remains. Following the Judicial Factors (Scotland) Act 1880, the sheriff court was given power to appoint some types of factor and, after s.14 of the Law Reform (Miscellaneous Provisions) Act 1980, the sheriff court has concurrent jurisdiction. The fact that the application is still technically to the *nobile officium* is reflected in judicial dicta to the effect that the remedy is only available in absolute deadlock (*e.g.* between parties, shareholders, co-owners) and no other legal remedy is available.

The first statute to cover judicial factors was the Judicial Factors Act 1849 (the "Act of 1849"; originally referred to as the Pupils Protection (Scotland) Act 1849 which indicates its original purpose to supervise, *inter alia*, factors managing the estates of pupils and minors). S.1 of the Act of 1849 defined judicial factor as "factor *loco absentis*, and *curator bonis*". This definition and the scope of the Act of 1849 was extended to all types of judicial factor by s.6 of the Judicial Factors (Scotland) Act 1889. With effect from 1st April 2002, the words "and *curator bonis*" in s.1 of the 1849 Act were repealed and no longer form part of that definition: Adults with Incapacity (Scotland) Act 2000, Sched. 6.

The rules in this Chapter have been made under the powers in s.5 of the C.S.A. 1988, s.40 of the Act of 1849 and s.21 of the 1889 Act (see A.S. (R.C.S. 1994) 1994, Sched. 1 [S.I. 1994 No. 1443]). Accordingly, following the Interpretation Act 1978, s.11, unless the context otherwise requires, words and expressions used in this Chapter which are also used in the C.S.A. 1988, the Act of 1849 or the 1889 Act have the same meaning as in those Acts, as the case may be.

61.1.2 *Judicial factor.* There is no precise definition of a judicial factor. This is a result of the historical origin of judicial factors, who may be appointed by, *inter alia*, the exercise of the *nobile officium* of the court in a number of different situations for a number of different purposes. Irons on *Judicial Factors* (1908) described a judicial factor as "an officer appointed by the Court, to whose care, custody and management under its supervision, are committed estates and interests which are without capable administration, or are the subject of litigation, in order that such estates or interests may . . . be preserved for [the beneficiaries'] behoof and of all having interest therein".

It has also been said that "there is no limit to the circumstances under which the Court . . . may appoint a judicial factor provided that the appointment is necessary to protect against loss or injustice which cannot in the circumstances be prevented by allowing the ordinary legal remedies to take their course": *Leslie's Judicial Factor* 1925 S.C. 464, 469 *per* L.P. Clyde. For an example of a case where an appointment was not competent, see *Institute of Chartered Accountants in Scotland v. Kay*, 2001 S.L.T. 1449 (appointment over estate of unfit CA recalled as petitioners had no interest in his estate).

Nevertheless there are a number of generally recognised types of judicial factor according to the reasons for appointment. These may be listed as follows:

(1) *Curator* bonis. The power to appoint a *curator bonis* was abolished by the Adults with Incapacity (Scotland) Act 2000 from 1st April 2002. Latterly there was only one type of curator *bonis*, namely a curator *bonis* to an *incapax*. The appointment was made where a disabled person was incapable of managing his affairs and no-one wished to be appointed tutor-at-law (under the Curators Act 1585: see note 14.2.11) or tutor-dative (under the common law: see note 14.2.11). This included inability to supervise properly an attorney: *Fraser v. Paterson* 1987 S.L.T. 562. Physical disability may (*e.g. Blaikie* (1827) 5 S. 268) or may not (*e.g. Kirkpatrick* (1853) 15 D. 734) render a disabled person *incapax*. The petitioner could be any person having an interest in the estate of the *incapax*, including the *incapax* himself (*e.g. Mark* (1845) 7 D. 882; *A.B.*, Petr. (1908) 16 S.L.T. 557). In particular a local authority (regional or islands council) or the Mental Welfare Commission could, in certain circumstances, present a petition: Mental Heath (Scotland) Act 1984, ss. 92 and 93. The appointment of a curator *bonis* supersedes the functions of any attorney previously appointed by the *incapax*: *Dick* (1901) 9 S.L.T. 177; *Fraser*, above.

The appointment of a tutor-at-law or tutor-dative, except in so far as it provides otherwise, supersedes the appointment of a curator bonis and brings it to an end: *Young v. Rose* (1839) 1D 1242; and *Dick v. Douglas* 1924 S.C. 787. For a conflict between a person wishing to be appointed a tutor-at-law and a curator *bonis*, see *Britton v. Britton's Curator Bonis* 1996 S.C. 178.

General Guidance Notes for Curator *Bonis* have been issued by the Office of the Accountant of Court following the 2000 Act.

As from 1st April 2002 a curator *bonis* may not be appointed to a person with incapacity aged 16 or over, but can be if the person is under 16: Adults with Incapacity (Scotland) Act 2000, s. 80. Where a person already has a curator *bonis*, the curator becomes a guardian under the 2000 Act with power over the property and financial affairs of the adult: 2000 Act, Sched. 4, para. 1(1). Where the person is under 16, the curator becomes the guardian upon the child's 16th birthday: 2000 Act, Sched. 4, para. 1(2). [The effect of repeals, by Sched. 6 to the 2000 Act, to the Judicial Factors Acts is that even curators to children are not subject to the Judicial Factors Acts.] Applications for appointment of guardianship orders are to the sheriff. A tutor-dative or tutor-at-law may also not be appointed to person aged 16 or over: 2000 Act, s. 80.

Guardians are subject to the controls in the 2000 Act.

The Hague Convention on the International Protection of Adults of 13th January 2000, was ratified by Scotland on 4th November 2003.

(2) *Factor* loco absentis. The appointment is made where a person has left Scotland leaving nobody to manage his affairs here. Following improvements in transport and communication a court will be more reluctant to make the appointment than it once was. An appointment will be inappropriate when there is evidence that the absent person has died or no evidence that he has been alive for the previous seven years. In that situation an action of declarator of death should be raised; and on decree being pronounced an application may be made to appoint an executor. The petitioner may be any person having an interest in the estate of the absent person, including a relative (*e.g. Dobson* (1903) 11 S.L.T. 44) or a creditor (*Lunan v. Macdonald* 1927 S.L.T. 661).

(3) *Factor on trust estate*. The appointment may be made in a number of situations where no other remedy is available. Generally these occur when there is nobody to manage the trust estate (*e.g.* no surviving trustee, death of *sine qua non* trustee, or lack of quorum). If the difficulty lies with the trust purposes the remedy is a petition for their variation (see Chap. 63, Pt. I). A factor is appropriate if there is a problem with the trustee as such. Other examples include, trustees' indefinite absence from Scotland (*Nisbet* (1835) 13 S. 384; *Dean* (1852) 15 D. 17), conflict of interest between trustee *qua* trustee and *qua* individual or between trustees to two antagonistic trusts (*Thomson v. Dalrymple* (1865) 3 M. 336; *Henderson v. Henderson* (1893) 20 R. 536), deadlock in management, trustees' malversation of office, etc.; see also Irons on *Judicial Factors*, pp. 12 and 13 and Walker on *Judicial Factors* (1974), pp. 28 *et seq.*

(4) *Guardian to a child*. Any person who after 1st November 1996 becomes a guardian to a child or acquires parental rights or responsibilities for that child, is no longer subject to the legislation covering judicial factors: Children (Scotland) Act 1995, s. 105(5) and Sched. 5.

A person who before 25th September 1991 was appointed factor *loco tutoris* (to a pupil child) or curator *bonis* (to a minor child), or from 25th September 1991 was appointed by a court, or a deceased parent, guardian to a child, appears to remain subject to the legislation covering judicial factors: Act of 1849, s. 1 saved by Interpretation Act 1978, s. 16(1)(c). The change of the factor's title to "guardian" was made by ss. 1(4) and 5(1) of the Age of Legal Capacity

(Scotland) Act 1991. For a guardian subject to the judicial factor legislation there are certain exemptions (*e.g.* no requirement for caution: Act of 1849, s. 25(2)).

Where a guardian has been appointed the guardianship continues until the child attains the age of 16 years: 1991 Act, s. 1(1)(b).

A judicial factor to a child (known as a factor on damages) may be appointed for the purpose of receipt and management of a sum of money to which the child became entitled as a result of an action for damages: see Chap. 43, Pt. IV.

(5) *Factor on estate of deceased person without executor.* See r. 61.16 and note 61.16.1 for appointment under s. 11A of 1889 Act. An appointment may also be made at common law: see Irons on *Judicial Factors*, pp. 143 *et seq.*

(6) *Factor on partnership estate.* The appointment may be made (a) before the dissolution of the partnership or (b) as part of or following the dissolution of the partnership.

(a) Appointment before dissolution of the partnership. The court may appoint a judicial factor where the surviving partners are unfit through health or from breach of duty to carry on the partnership: *Dickie v. Mitchell* (1874) 1 R. 1030, 1033 *per* L.P. Inglis. Generally, however, this will be in exceptional circumstances where dissolution or common law sequestration of the partnership is not appropriate: *Dickie*, above.

(b) Appointment as part of or following dissolution of the partnership. For circumstances constituting dissolution, see the Partnership Act 1890, ss. 32–35. Following dissolution the surviving former partner or partners are expected to gather in the assets of the partnership, pay off its liabilities, and distribute the surplus to each other according to their entitlement: 1890 Act, s. 39; *Gow v. Schultze* (1877) 4 R. 928. Where a former partner fails to carry out his duties under s. 39 of the 1890 Act, thereby prejudicing the assets of the partnership, any other former partner may present a petition for the appointment of a judicial factor and for sequestration of the partnership estate: 1890 Act, s. 39; *Dickie*, above; *Allan v. Gronmeyer* (1891) 18 R. 784; *Carabine v. Carabine* 1949 S.C. 521. The effect of the sequestration order is to transfer control of the partnership assets from the possessor to the judicial factor. Often an interim judicial factor is appointed: see, *e.g. McCulloch v. McCulloch* 1953 S.C. 189.

(7) *Factor on company estate.* The appointment may be made, at common law, following illegal or dishonest conduct by the directors (*Fraser, Petr.* 1971 S.L.T. 146) or following voting deadlock between shareholders (*McGuiness v. Black* 1990 S.C. 21, 24 *per* Lord McCluskey). The aim of the appointment is to preserve the assets of the company. The common law power overlaps with the statutory provisions allowing remedies to a minority shareholder in the event of prejudice under the Companies Act 1985, s. 459. The petitioner may be a shareholder or anybody with a sufficient interest.

Often the circumstances require appointment of an interim judicial factor: *Fraser*, above; *McGuiness*, above. Special powers (*e.g.* the same as those of a receiver) may be sought in the petition: *McGuiness*, above. Averments must be made in the petition stating the reasons why an interim appointment should be made.

The appointment may be made under various private Acts for more limited purposes of clearing secured creditors' debts: see, *e.g. Greenock Harbour Trs. v. Judicial Factor of Greenock Harbour Trust* 1910 S.C.(H.L.) 32.

The appointment may be made under s. 41 of the Solicitors (Scotland) Act 1980 to an incorporated solicitors' practice where the practice has failed to comply with the Solicitors (Scotland) Accounts Rules: see (8) below. The same rules as for an individual solicitor apply.

(8) *Factor on solicitor's estate.* The appointment may be made where the Council of the Law Society of Scotland is satisfied (a) that the solicitor has breached the accounts rules; and (b) in connection with his practice, (i) his liabilities exceed his assets, (ii) it is not reasonably practicable to ascertain definitely from his books, accounts and other documents whether his liabilities exceed his assets or (iii) there is reasonable ground for apprehending that a claim on the guarantee fund may arise: Solicitors (Scotland) Act 1980, s. 41.

The purpose of the appointment is to ensure the proper application of the funds in the solicitor's estate with a view to settling the solicitor's liabilities: *Council of the Law Society of Scotland v. McKinnie (No. 2)* 1995 S.C. 94, 111C *per* Lord Penrose and 115G–116B *per* L.P. Hope.

The petitioner is the Council of the Law Society: 1980 Act, s. 41. The petition must be to the Inner House: r. 14.3(b). Before any order is pronounced in the petition the solicitor must have the opportunity to be heard: 1980 Act, s. 41.

Special rules apply to the conduct of the judicial factor in addition to his normal duties: 1980 Act, s. 42; and see *Ross v. Gordon's Judicial Factor* 1973 S.L.T. (Notes) 91 and *Scottish Council of the Pontifical Society of St Peter Apostle for Native Clergy v. McGregor's Judicial Factor* 1974 S.C. 106. Any estate administered by the judicial factor does not vest in a trustee in sequestration who is appointed subsequently to the judicial factor: *Council of the Law Society of Scotland v. McKinnie* 1993 S.L.T. 238.

(9) *Factor on common property*. The appointment may be made where the common owners of property owned by them *pro indiviso* disagree over any act of management or dealing in relation to the property which they do not wish to sell: *Mackintosh* (1849) 11 D. 1029; *Bailey v. Scott* (1860) 22 D. 1105. The court will only appoint a judicial factor where there is deadlock and no other way out, *e.g.* agreement on (non-judicial) factor: *Allan* (1898) 6 S.L.T. 152.

(10) *Factor on money payable to a child in an action of damages*. The appointment of such a factor (known as a factor on damages) may be made by the court in any action in which a sum of money becomes payable by virtue of a decree or an extra-judicial settlement to or for the benefit of the child in an action of damages: rr. 43.15(1) and 43.16(a). The order may be pronounced by the court at its own instance: r. 43.3(a); and see note 43.16.2.

(11) *Factor pending litigation*. The appointment is made to secure the management of heritable or moveable property which is in dispute. Often the appointment is only an interim one. It may be made where the party not in possession contests the peaceful right to possess of the party in possession: see, *e.g. Russell* (1847) 9 D. 989. Where the party in possession has a strong *prima facie* right to possess, it will not usually be appropriate to appoint a judicial factor

pending the outcome of an action concerning the property: *Campbell v. Campbell* (1864) 2 M.(H.L.) 41, 45 *per* Lord Westbury L.C. Where nobody is in possession (*e.g.* on death of owner occupier), the court will appoint a factor where each claimant presents a stateable case for his claim leading to a competition: *Pringle Pattison's Curator Bonis* (1898) 5 S.L.T. 400.

Jurisdiction. This lies with the *nobile officium* of the Court of Session exercised, with two **61.1.3** exceptions, by the Outer House: r. 14.2(a). An application for a factor to a solicitor's estate or to the estate of an incorporated practice of solicitors is to the Inner House: r. 14.3(b). An application for a guardian to a child is by action: Age of Legal Capacity (Scotland) Act 1991, s.5(2).

Factor's fees and outlay. The fees and outlays of a judicial factor are a prior claim over all **61.1.4** other competing claims on the factory estate: *Council the Law Society of Scotland v. McKinnie* 1995 S.C. 94.

Application for appointment of judicial factor

[1] **61.2.**—(1) An application for the appointment of a judicial factor shall be made by petition.

(2) An application under section 9(5)(a) of the Act of 1995 (application by Accountant of Court for appointment of judicial factor to administer certain property of a child) shall be made by petition in Form 61.2; and Chapter 14 shall not apply as respects any such petition.

(3) A petition in Form 61.2 shall, after being lodged in the Petition Department and recorded in the Petitions Register but without appearing in the Motion Roll, be presented to the Lord Ordinary in court or in chambers; and he may—

(a) forthwith make the appointment sought; or

(b) make an order—

    (i) for such intimation, service and advertisement of the petition as he considers appropriate; and

    (ii) for a hearing, on such date as he may specify, as respects the petition.

(4) Without prejudice to the generality of paragraph (3)(b)(i), any order under that paragraph as to intimation may specify that rule 16.4 shall not apply and that the Accountant of Court shall make intimation by post in such manner as the Lord Ordinary thinks fit.

---

[1] R.61.2 substituted by S.I. 1997 No. 1720 (effective 1st August 1997).

"petition". The petition may be presented by anyone with an interest in the estate. This may **61.2.1** include the *incapax* himself where he is aware that he may soon be unable to manage his affairs: *A.B., Petr.* (1908) 16 S.L.T. 557.

The petition is, subject to exceptions (see note 61.1.3), presented in the Outer House: r. 14.2(a). For form of petitions see r. 14.4. The petition must be signed by counsel or other person having a right of audience: r. 4.2(3); and see r. 1.3(1) (definition of "counsel" and "other person having a right of audience") and note 1.3.4. A fee is payable on lodging the petition and process: see note 14.5.10.

For petitions generally, see Chap. 14. For applications under s.9(5)(a) of the Act of 1995, see note 61.2.4.

Eligibility to be judicial factor. In general any natural person of full legal capacity is eligible. A **61.2.2** non-natural person is ineligible: *Brogan, Petr.* 1986 S.L.T. 420. A bankrupt (*Miller* (1849) 12 D. 941), or a person having an ineligible adverse interest (*Leslie* (1908) 12 S.L.T. 359), is incligible.

Only one factor may be appointed to each estate: *Sloan, Petr.* (1844) 7 D. 227.

Interim judicial factor. An interim judicial factor may be appointed in a situation of urgency **61.2.3** where the intimation of the petition and the lodging of answers would cause prejudicial delay: see *McGuiness v. Black* 1990 S.C. 21; Irons on *Judicial Factors*, Chap. XIV. An interim judicial factor must be specifically craved for in the prayer of the petition: *McGuiness*, above. The special reasons of urgency should be averred where the appointment of an interim factor is sought immediately: *Cuthbertson v. Gibson* (1887) 14 R. 736.

A motion for the appointment of an interim judicial factor may be enrolled at any time after the presentation of the petition. If the motion is enrolled before the first order it may be heard *ex parte* (*i.e.* without intimation) unless any person with an interest had lodged a caveat: rr. 23.8 and 23.9. The interlocutor appointing an interim judicial factor should contain, *inter alia*, an express direction to the factor to report to the Accountant of Court so long as his appointment is interim (normally at intervals of not less than one month): *McCulloch v. McCulloch* 1953 S.C. 189, 192 *per* L.P. Cooper (in which such an appointment was described as an extremely rare remedy).

The person to whose estate a factor is sought to be appointed ought to be given the opportunity of being heard on the motion for appointment of an interim judicial factor unless there is reason to suppose that such intimation is likely to place the estate in jeopardy: *Institute of Chartered Accountants in Scotland v. Kay* 2001 S.L.T. 1449, 1451L *per* Lord Carloway.

The court may restrict the power of the interim judicial factor, *e.g.* by prohibiting the sale of certain assets in the estate of a dissolved partnership: *Hunter v. Hunter*, 1999 S.C. 1, 3C *per* Lord Osborne.

An interim judicial factor must still find caution in the usual way and is restricted in what he can do until he does so: see notes 61.9.1 *et seq.*

61.2.4 *Applications under section 9(5)(a) of the Children (Scotland) Act 1995.* Subject to s.13 of the Act of 1995 (court awards of money to children), where property is owned by or due to a child, is held by a person other than a parent or guardian, would otherwise require to be transferred to a parent with parental responsibilities, or to a guardian, for administration for the child (unless appointed a trustee under a trust deed to administer the property for the child) and (1) the person holding the property is a trustee or executor, then (a) if the value of the property exceeds £20,000, he shall, (b) if the value is not less than £5,000 and does not exceed £20,000, he may, or (2) the person holding the property is not a trustee or executor, he may, apply to the Accountant of Court for directions: Act of 1995, s.9(1), (2) and (3). Where such an application is made to the Accountant of Court, he may, among other things, apply to the court for the appointment of a judicial factor: Act of 1995, s.9(5)(a).

An application under s.9(5)(a) of the Act of 1995 may be signed only by the Accountant of Court (r. 4.2(3)(cc)) and must be in Form 61.2 (r. 61.2(2)). A process is not required: r. 4.3. The rules of service by post in r. 16.4 do not apply: r. 61.2(4).

Crave to dispense with service on incapax

61.3. Where, in a petition for the appointment of a curator *bonis* to an *incapax*, dispensation of service on the *incapax* is craved on the ground that such service would be injurious to the health of the *incapax*, two medical certificates to that effect shall be lodged in process.

61.3.1 *General note.* If it is sought to dispense with service on an *incapax*, this should be craved in the prayer of the petition and supported by averments: r. 14.4(6).

A motion to grant the dispensation of service must be enrolled and sought at the time of the first order: r. 14.5(2).

It should be noted that injury to health is not the only ground for dispensing with personal service. Personal service on an *incapax* in a remote part of Scotland may be deferred with due regard to cost in relation to the moveable estate of the *incapax*: *Robertson, Petr.* 1978 S.L.T. (Notes) 39.

61.3.2 *"two medical certificates".* The examination of the *incapax* must be done separately by each of the two medical examiners. Notwithstanding s.1 of the Civil Evidence (Scotland) Act 1988 (rule requiring corroboration abolished), a certificate from each of two doctors is required primarily because two medical recommendations are required for the admission and detention of a patient under the Mental Health (Scotland) Act 1984.

Formerly the certificates had to be adopted as holograph, if not holograph and signed. Since the coming into force of the Requirements of Writing (Scotland) Act 1995 on 1st August 1995, which abolished the privilege of documents adopted as holograph, the practice of the court is as follows. A certificate will be accepted which is signed by the certifying doctor provided it is on headed notepaper with details of the doctor's professional practice and address; it need not be witnessed. Such a certificate frequently bears to be on soul and conscience, although this is not necessary following P.N. 6th June 1968 (soul and conscience medical certificates).

The certificates, which normally contain the words "having seen and examined (*name of incapax*)", must not pre-date the presentation of the petition by more than 30 days.

61.3.3 *"lodged in process".* The medical certificates are lodged as productions. On lodging productions, see r. 4.5.

Incidental applications

61.4. Unless otherwise provided in this Chapter, an incidental application to the court in a petition for the appointment of a judicial factor shall be made by note.

"Unless otherwise provided in this Chapter". See, *e.g.* applications by letter to the Accountant **61.4.1**
of Court for authority to encroach on capital (r. 61.13) and applications for consent to do an act
outwith the purpose of the factory (r. 61.14).

"note". For applications by note, see r. 15.2.   **61.4.2**

Intimation and service

61.5.—[1] (1) The order for intimation and service under rule 14.5 (first order in petitions) in a petition or note relating to a judicial factory shall include a requirement for intimation to the Accountant of Court (except where the petition is in Form 61.2) by first class recorded delivery post of the petition or note, as the case may be, and any production lodged with the petition or note.

(2) The Lord Ordinary may order publication of an advertisement of the petition in Form 61.5–A in the case of a petition for the appointment of a judicial factor or in Form 61.5–B in the case of a petition for the discharge of a judicial factor.

(3) Where publication of an advertisement has been made under paragraph (2), there shall be lodged in process—

(a) a copy of the newspaper or other publication containing the advertisement; or

(b) a certificate of publication by the publisher stating the date of publication and the text of the advertisement.

[2] (4) After a petition for the appointment of a judicial factor is lodged in the Petition Department, the Clerk of Session in that department may (wether or not any order is made, or is competent, under rule 14.5(1)(a)) provide any interested party with details of the petition.

----

[1] R.61.5(1) amended by S.I. 1997 No. 1720 (effective 1st August 1997).
[2] R.61.5(4) inserted by S.I. 1997 No. 1720 (effective 1st August 1997).

"intimation and service". For intimation and service generally, see r. 14.7 and Chap. 16, Pt I. **61.5.1**

"advertisement". The advertisement may be in one or more or both of a national or local **61.5.2**
newspaper of the area where persons likely to be interested in the estate may be situated.

"lodged in process". The copy of the newspaper or other publication containing the **61.5.3**
advertisement (or the certificate required under r. 61.5(3)(b)) is lodged as a production. On
lodging productions, see r. 4.5.

Documents for Accountant of Court

61.6.—(1) A person who lodges any document in a cause relating to a judicial factory (other than a petition for appointment of a judicial factor) shall send a copy of that document to the Accountant of Court.

(2) The clerk of session in the Petition Department shall transmit to the Accountant of Court any part of a process in a cause relating to a judicial factory as the Accountant of Court may request unless such part of the process is, at the time of request, required by the court.

Deriv. R.C.S. 1965, r. 200(a) (r. 61.6(1)) and r. 200(b) (r. 61.6(2))

"send". This includes deliver: r. 1.3(1) (definition of "send").   **61.6.1**

Accountant of Court. The Accountant of Court is appointed under s.1 of the Judicial Factors **61.6.2**
(Scotland) Act 1889. He has, *inter alia,* the duty to superintend the conduct of all judicial factors
whether appointed in the Court of Session or sheriff court: Act of 1849, s.10; 1889 Act, s.6. He
has numerous duties under the various Acts and subordinate legislation on judicial factors. He

may report any misconduct or breach of duty by a factor to the Lord Ordinary for disposal: Act of 1849, s.20. His address is 2 Parliament Square, Edinburgh EH1 1RQ; tel. 0131–554 2422; fax 0131–554 3632; DX ED311.

Accountant of Court to send information on prior application

61.7. The Accountant of Court, on receiving intimation of a petition for the appointment of a judicial factor, shall report any information he may possess which he considers may be of use to the court in disposing of the petition.

61.7.1   *General note.* The Accountant of Court may for example have comments on the eligibility or suitability of the proposed judicial factor.

Transmission of process to Accountant of Court to find caution

61.8. The clerk of session in the Petition Department shall, on the appointment of the judicial factor being made by the court, transmit the process of the petition to the Accountant of Court for the fixing and finding of caution.

Deriv. R.C.S. 1965, r. 200(*e*)(preamble)

Finding caution

61.9.—(1) The appointment of a person as a judicial factor shall be subject to his finding caution; and the interlocutor appointing a judicial factor shall ordain him to find caution.

(2) The court may, on cause shown, on a motion made before the expiry of the period for finding caution specified by virtue of rule 33.3 (orders to find caution or other security), allow further time for finding caution.

(3) The Accountant of Court shall, on receiving the process in a petition for the appointment of a judicial factor transmitted to him under rule 61.8, fix the caution to be found by the judicial factor.

(4) Where the Accountant of Court considers that any caution fixed by the court under section 27 of the Act of 1849 (amount of caution limited by court), should be increased—

(*a*) the Accountant of Court may increase the amount unless the judicial factor requires him to report to the court;

(*b*) where the judicial factor requires him to report to the court, the Accountant of Court shall do so; and

(*c*) on the report mentioned in sub-paragraph (*b*) being received, the cause shall be put out on the By Order Roll before the Lord Ordinary to determine the amount of caution.

(5) A bond of caution or other security offered by a judicial factor shall be delivered to the Accountant of Court; and rule 33.4(3) (lodging of bond of caution in process) and rule 33.7(1) (Deputy Principal Clerk to satisfy himself that bond of caution or other security is in proper form) shall not apply.

(6) Except in relation to paragraph (7), where caution has been found to the satisfaction of the Accountant of Court, he shall endorse and sign, on the interlocutor sheet of the process appointing the judicial factor, a certificate stating that caution has been found, the amount of caution and the date of the certificate.

(7) During the subsistence of a judicial factory, the Accountant of Court may, at any time—

(*a*) require the judicial factor to increase the amount of, or find new or additional, caution; or

(*b*) authorise the judicial factor to reduce the amount of existing caution.

Deriv. R.C.S. 1965, r. 200(*c*)(part) (r. 61.9(2)), r. 200(*d*) (r. 61.9(5)), r. 200(*e*)(i)(part) (r. 61.9(3)), r. 200(*e*)(ii)(part) (r. 61.9(4)), and r. 200(*e*)(i)(part) (r. 61.9(6)); and r. 200(*e*)(iii) amended by S.I. 1985 No. 1600 (r. 61.9(7))

General note. The present practice is for the court, in the interlocutor appointing a judicial **61.9.1** factor, to state that the factor may not obtain the official certified copy of the interlocutor appointing him until he has found caution; it does not usually order him to find caution. He must, however, find caution for his intromissions with and management of the estate: Act of 1849, s. 2.

A judicial factor may not, except in exceptional circumstances, enter on the duties of his office until after caution has been found and received as sufficient: Act of 1849, s. 2; *Donaldson v. Kennedy* (1833) 11 S. 740; see also note 61.11.1.

Caution. For the meaning of caution, see note 33.1.1. Usually caution will be in the form of a **61.9.2** bond of caution (r. 33.4(1)(*a*)), or it may be any other method of security approved by the court (r. 33.4(2)). Where caution is by bond of caution the bond may be by (*a*) an insurance company authorised to conduct such business (see r. 33.5); or (*b*) any other person, in which case the court must satisfy itself as to the sufficiency of the caution. The form of all bonds must comply with r. 37.6. A bond must be sent to the Accountant of Court (together with a copy): r. 61.9(5).

The Accountant then satisfies himself as to the caution offered. On being satisfied the Accountant will sign and endorse on the interlocutor sheet of the process a certificate that caution has been found and the amount: r. 61.9(6). The Accountant of Court will then transmit the process back to the Petition Department to enable an official certified copy of the interlocutor of appointment to be issued to the factor. The Accountant of Court will, however, retain the principal bond of caution as custodian: Act of 1849, s. 35.

Caution should be sought without delay, and agreement should be reached between the petitioner and the nominated factor before the petition is presented as to whose is the responsibility for arranging caution: P.N. No. 2 of 1994.

61.9.3   *Period for finding caution.* The former rule in R.C.S. 1965 r. 200(*c*) which stipulated a period of one month has not been re-enacted. There is not now a fixed period, but a period must be specified in the interlocutor appointing the factor: Act of 1849, s. 2. The period may be extended if a motion is made before its expiry: r. 61.9(2). Failure to find caution within the period specified will result in the appointment falling: Act of 1849, s. 2. In this case a motion must be enrolled for re-appointment. Such a motion requires appearance, and will be granted only on cause shown. Caution should, however, be sought without delay: P.N. No. 2 of 1994.

61.9.4   *"motion".* For motions, see Chap. 23.

61.9.5   *Amount of caution.* S. 27 of the Act of 1849 enables the court to limit the amount of caution to a specified sum less than the value of the estate. Where the Accountant of Court wishes to increase the amount of caution (which he has power to do), the judicial factor may insist on the matter being decided by the court: r. 61.9(4). The former requirement in R.C.S. 1965, r. 200(*e*)(ii) that, where the question of the increase is referred to the court, the amount fixed by the court must not be less than two-thirds of the value of the moveable and other realisable estate has not been re-enacted; although the fraction still provides a useful rule of thumb.

61.9.6   *Death or insolvency of cautioner.* The factor must intimate in writing the death or insolvency of the cautioner to the Accountant of Court: Act of 1849, s. 11. The Accountant of Court will then give notice in writing to the factor requiring new caution to be found: Act of 1849, s. 11. A new cautioner may be liable for the loss resulting from misconduct by the factor before the granting of new caution: *Grant* (1828) 6 S. 982; *Wallace's Factor v. McKissock* (1898) 28 R. 642.

61.9.7   *Bond of caution for curator* bonis. In addition to the usual requirements (see note 61.9.2), a bond of caution for a curator *bonis* to a person suffering from mental disorder within the meaning of the Mental Health (Scotland) Act 1984 must contain a consent to the registration of the bond for execution in the Books of Council and Session: Act of 1849, s. 26. Before it is sent to the Accountant of Court it must be sent to the Keeper of the Registers for registration for execution: Act of 1849, s. 26. See also Irons on *Judicial Factors*, pp. 469 and 470.

Issue of official certified copy interlocutor

61.10. An official certified copy of the interlocutor appointing a judicial factor shall not be issued by a clerk of session without a certificate having been endorsed on the interlocutor sheet in accordance with rule 61.9(6).

Deriv. R.C.S. 1965, r. 200(*e*)(i)(part) amended by S.I. 1967 No. 487

61.10.1   *Official certified copy interlocutor.* This is issued by the Petition Department on application being made to it: r. 7.11; see also note 7.11.1.

Judicial factor's title to act

61.11. A judicial factor shall not be entitled to act until he has received the official certified copy of the interlocutor appointing him.

61.11.1   *Capacity to act.* In general a judicial factor is not entitled to act until he has received the official certified copy interlocutor ("CCI") appointing him: Act of 1849, s. 2; and r. 61.11.

He may, however, act immediately on appointment to preserve the estate in a situation of urgent necessity: *Calver v. Howard Baker & Co.* (1894) 22 R. 1 (raising of court action). He cannot, however, actively intromit with estate property until he has the CCI: *Donaldson v. Kennedy* (1833) 11 S. 740.

Title of judicial factor. The effect of the issue of the official CCI of appointment is to assign to **61.11.2** the factor all funds, property and effects situated or invested in any part of the British dominions, including Scotland, belonging to the estate: Judicial Factors (Scotland) Act 1889, s.13; and see *Council of the Law Society of Scotland v. McKinnie* 1995 S.C.L.R. 53, 71F *per* Lord Penrose.

Stamp duty. As the official CCI is a "conveyance" it is liable to the fixed duty of 50p payable **61.11.3** by the judicial factor: Stamp Act 1891, s.1 and Sched. The Inland Revenue allows timeous stamping within 30 days of issue after which time penalty duty must be paid.

Remission or modification of penal interest

61.12. The Accountant of Court may, if satisfied that the circumstances justify it, remit or modify any interest incurred by a judicial factor under section 5(1) of the Act of 1849 (interest incurred for failure by factor to lodge money in bank etc.).

Deriv. R.C.S. 1965, r. 200(g)

Section 5(1) of the Act of 1849. S.5(1) of the Act of 1849 provides, *inter alia*, that where a **61.12.1** judicial factor has left more than £500 of money in his hands for over 10 days he shall be charged penalty interest at the rate of 20 per cent a year on the excess over £500 held for every day over 10 days. It also provides that unless the factor has kept such money from innocent causes, he shall be dismissed by the Accountant of Court and have no claim for commission.

Applications to encroach on capital

61.13.—(1) Where the income from the estate of a ward is insufficient for the maintenance of the ward, the judicial factor may apply to the Accountant of Court for his consent to encroach on the capital of the estate for the purpose of maintaining the ward.

(2) An application under paragraph (1) shall be made by letter and shall be supported by such information as the Accountant of Court may require.

[1] (3) On receipt of such an application, the Accountant of Court—

(a) may, if the proposed encroachment does not exceed 5% of the capital value of the estate as that the date when application is first made under paragraph (1), consent to the application subject to such conditions as he thinks fit to impose; and

(b) if he is unable, or declines, to consent under sub-paragraph (a), shall—

   (i) ordain the judicial factor to intimate, in accordance with paragraphs (5) and (6), the making of the application; or

   (ii) ordain him to apply by note to the Lord Ordinary for special powers.

(4) A person to whom intimation is given in accordance with paragraphs (5) and (6) may object to the application by—

(a) lodging an objection in writing with the Accountant of Court; and

(b) sending a copy of his objection to the judicial factor within 28 days after the date on which intimation was given to him.

[2] (5) The persons to whom intimation under paragraph (3)(b)(i) is to be given are—

(a) any cautioner of the judicial factor;

(b) any petitioner for the appointment of the judicial factor (other than a petitioner using Form 61.2);

(c) the ward, unless the circumstances of the ward are such as would warrant dispensing with service on him of a petition for the appointment of a judicial factor on his estate;

(d) the persons on whom the petition for appointment of the judicial factor was served and whose whereabouts are known to the judicial factor; and

(e) all other persons who have an interest in the estate and whose identity and whereabouts are known to the judicial factor.

[2] (6) The intimation under paragraph (3)(b)(i) shall include—
(a) a copy of the letter of application; and
(b) a notice setting out—
(i) the right of the person receiving the notice to object to the application in the manner provided in paragraph (4); and
(ii) that, in the absence of any such objection, the Accountant of Court may consent to the application.
[2] (7) The judicial factor shall, on giving intimation under paragraph (3)(b)(i), send to the Accountant of Court a certificate of intimation in Form 16.7 with a copy of the notice sent attached to it; and rule 16.7(2) (attaching certificate of intimation to principal writ or lodging it in process) shall not apply.
(8) Where no objections have been lodged under paragraph (4), the Accountant of Court may, on the expiry of the period for lodging objections—
(a) consent to the application subject to such conditions as he thinks fit; or
(b) require the judicial factor to apply to the court for special powers.
(9) Where any objection has been lodged under paragraph (4), the judicial factor shall, on expiry of the period for lodging objections, apply to the court for special powers.

Deriv. R.C.S. 1965, r. 200B inserted by S.I. 1990 No. 705

---

[1] R.61.13(3) substituted by S.I. 1997 No. 1720 (effective 1st August 1997).
[2] R.61.13(5), (6) and (7) amended by S.I. 1997 No. 1720 (effective 1st August 1997).

61.13.1 *General note.* This rule will apply largely to curators *bonis* and guardians to a child. Other factors will not have a ward. The purpose of this rule is to provide an expedited procedure which avoids the need to obtain special powers. The predecessor to R.C.S. 1994, r. 61.13 was R.C.S. 1965, r. 200B which was introduced to provide a formal procedure (in relation to what was done in practice) for application to the Accountant of Court by a curator for authority to encroach on the capital of his ward's estate in certain circumstances instead of the curator having to petition the court for special powers. That a rule should be provided was suggested by the Second Division in *Broadfoot's Curator Bonis* 1989 S.C. 90, 101. In that case it was held (1) that a curator did not have power to encroach on the capital of the ward's estate at his own hand, (2) that the Accountant of Court could authorise encroachment where (a) the estate was sufficient to meet his ward's requirements during the ward's life or (b) in the case of small estates, exhaustion of the estate would result in greater income from state funds, and (3) that in all other circumstances the curator had to apply to the court for special powers.

61.13.2 *Applications for special powers.* If the judicial factor is nevertheless required by the Accountant of Court to obtain special powers he must apply for these by note: see r. 61.15.

61.13.3 *Intimation by judicial factor.* For methods, see r. 16.7.

61.13.4 *"sending", "send".* This includes deliver: r. 1.3(1) (definition of "send").

61.13.5 *Cautioner.* A judicial factor who is a guardian of a person under 16 years of age may not have a cautioner as he is not bound to find caution: Act of 1849, s.25(2) inserted by the Law Reform (Parent and Child) (Scotland) Act 1986, Sched. 1, para. 1.

61.13.6 *"date on which intimation given".* Where intimation is by post the date of intimation is the day after the date of posting: r. 16.4(9). Where intimation is by any other method the date of intimation is the date of execution.

Applications under section 2(3) of the Trusts (Scotland) Act 1961

61.14.—(1) An application under section 2(3) of the Trusts (Scotland) Act 1961 to the Accountant of Court for his consent to the doing of an act to which that section applies shall be made by letter and shall be supported by such information as the Accountant of Court may require.
(2) Any person to whom intimation requires to be given in accordance with paragraph (3) may object to the application by lodging any objection with the Accountant of Court, and sending a copy of it to the judicial factor, within 28 days after the date on which the intimation was given.

(3) On the date on which he makes the application referred to in paragraph (1), the judicial factor shall intimate the application to—
 (a) any cautioner of the judicial factor;
 [1] (b) any person who petitioned for the judicial factor to be appointed (except where the petition was in Form 61.2);
 (c) the ward, unless the circumstances of the ward are such that would warrant dispensing with service on him of a petition for the appointment of a judicial factor on his estate;
 (d) the persons upon whom the application for appointment of the judicial factor was served and whose whereabouts are known to the judicial factor; and
 (e) all other persons who have an interest in the estate and whose identity and whereabouts are known to the judicial factor.
(4) The intimation to be given under paragraph (3) shall include—
 (a) a copy of the letter of application, and
 (b) a notice setting out—
  (i) the right of the person receiving the notice to object to the application in the manner provided in paragraph (2); and
  (ii) that, in the absence of any such objection, the Accountant of Court may consent to the application.
(5) The judicial factor shall, on giving intimation under paragraph (3), send to the Accountant of Court a certificate of intimation in Form 16.7 with a copy of the notice required under paragraph (4) attached to it; and rule 16.7(2) (attaching certificate of intimation to principal writ or lodging it in process) shall not apply.

Deriv. R.C.S. 1965, r. 200A inserted by S.I. 1980 No. 1803

---

[1] R.61.14(3)(b) substituted by S.I. 1997 No. 1720 (effective 1st August 1997).

General note. Where a judicial factor thinks it expedient to do an act described in paras (a) to (ee) of s.4 of the Trusts (Scotland) Act 1921 but feels that the act may be at variance with the terms of his appointment or the purposes of the judicial factory, he may apply to the Accountant of Court for the consent of the Accountant of Court to the doing of the Act: Trusts (Scotland) Act 1961, s.2(3). This rule does not cover consenting to encroachment on capital which is to be expended on the maintenance of a ward: *Broadfoot's Curator Bonis* 1989 S.C. 90, 100 *per* L.J.-C. Ross; for power to encroach on the capital of the estate of a ward application must be made to the Accountant of Court in an appropriate case (see r. 61.13) or for special powers under r. 61.15. **61.14.1**

Intimation by judicial factor. For methods, see r. 16.7. **61.14.2**

"sending", "send". This includes deliver: r. 1.3(1) (definition of "send"). **61.14.3**

"date on which intimation given". Where intimation is by post the date of intimation is the day after the date of posting: r. 16.4(9). Where intimation is by any other method the date of intimation is the date of execution. **61.14.4**

Cautioner. A judicial factor who is a guardian of a person under 16 years of age may not have a cautioner as he is not bound to find caution: Act of 1849, s.25(2) inserted by the Law Reform (Parent and Child) (Scotland) Act 1986, Sched. 1, para. 1. **61.14.5**

Applications for special powers or authority under section 5 of the Trusts (Scotland) Act 1921

61.15.—(1) This rule applies to an application by a judicial factor—
 (a) for special powers at common law or under section 7 of the Act of 1849; or
 (b) under section 5 of the Trusts (Scotland) Act 1921 (application for authority to do an act at variance with terms or purposes of the judicial factory).

(2) An application may be made—
(a) in the petition for the appointment of the judicial factor; or
(b) by note in the process of that petition.

(3) Before making an application, the judicial factor shall apply to the Accountant of Court for an opinion by lodging with him a report explaining why the special powers or authority are necessary and concluding with a statement of the precise powers he seeks.

(4) The Accountant of Court shall, after making any necessary inquiry, send his written opinion to the judicial factor.

(5) The judicial factor shall lodge in process his report to, and the opinion of, the Accountant of Court.

(6) The judicial factor shall send to the Accountant of Court a copy of the interlocutor disposing of the application within two days after the date of the interlocutor.

(7) An application by a judicial factor for special powers under this rule shall not be made before he has received an official certified copy of the interlocutor appointing him.

(8) An application by a judicial factor in respect of special powers sought in the petition for his appointment shall be made by him by motion.

61.15.1   *General note.* A judicial factor is appointed to take charge of an estate for a specific purpose. The purpose will differ depending on the nature of the estate and any ward. In most factories the main purpose will be to conserve the value of the estate. In some factories, *e.g.* on a bankruptcy estate or estate of a solicitor, distribution of all or part of the estate will be a purpose.

At common law a judicial factor has power to do anything reasonable to fulfil the purpose of the factory (usually to conserve the estate): see Irons on *Judicial Factors*, pp. 49 *et seq.*; Walker on *Judicial Factors*, Chap. XIII.

In addition a judicial factor has the powers, so far as exercisable by a factor, listed in s.4(1) of the Trusts (Scotland) Act 1921, provided they are not at variance with the terms or purposes of the factory. Where a factor wishes to exercise a power under s.4(1) of the 1921 Act he should also obtain the prior consent of the Accountant of Court to ensure that the subsequent transaction has the benefit of s.2(1) of the Trusts (Scotland) Act 1961 (making the transaction unchallengeable on the ground of *ultra vires*). A factor also has the power and duties of a trustee under the 1961 Act and the Trustee Investments Act 1961: see Trusts (Scotland) Act 1961, s.6, and Trustee Investments Act 1961, s.17(5).

A judicial factor has no powers other than these. In particular he does not have any additional power in a trust deed of a trust estate to which he is appointed: *Carmichael's Judicial Factor* 1971 S.L.T. 336. If a judicial factor wishes further powers, known as "special powers" then he must apply to the court for them: see note 61.15.2.

A *curator bonis* is in the same category as an agent appointed by a *capax* to manage his affairs, rather than that of a trustee under a deed; his powers are not, therefore, less than that of his ward's, and his duty is to manage the estate for the benefit of the ward: *D's Curator Bonis*, 1998 S.L.T. 2, 3L *per* Lord Nimmo Smith. This dictum must be read as subject to the rules regarding encroachment on capital of the ward: see note 61.13.1.

61.15.2   *Special powers.* There is no fixed list of acts for which a factor requires special powers. Where a factor is in any doubt whether a proposed act is within the terms and purposes of the judicial factory he should seek a special power to do it: *Marquess of Lothian's Curator Bonis* 1927 S.C. 579. An act which may not require special power in one factory may require special power in another factory due to the difference in the estates: contrast *Marquess of Lothian's Curator Bonis*, above, with *Barclay* 1962 S.C. 594 (power to sell heritage). Acts which have required special powers have included granting heritable security (*Maconochie, Noter* (1857) 19 D. 366), compromising a litigation (*Tennent's Judicial Factor v. Tennent* 1954 S.C. 215), retention of shares in a private limited company in face of the duties under the Trustee Investments Act 1961 (*Fraser v. Paterson* (*No. 2*) 1988 S.L.T. 124) and donating heritable property for the purpose of inheritance tax planning (*D's Curator Bonis, Noter* 1998 S.L.T. 2).

Special powers may be granted retrospectively: *Blair's Curator Bonis, Petr* 1921 1 S.L.T. 248; *Hamilton's Tutors* 1924 S.C. 364.

Special power to encroach on the capital of the estate of a ward where the estate is insufficient for the ward's maintenance may be sought from the Accountant of Court under r. 61.13.

For guidance on the granting of special powers to a curator *bonis* to make gifts of substantial parts of the ward's estate for inheritance tax planning, see *D's Curator Bonis, Noter* 1998 S.L.T. 2.

In *Bell's C.B., Noter* 1998 S.C. 365 it was held competent for a *curator bonis* to be given power to enter into a structured settlement of his ward's reparation action for personal injuries, involving the purchase of an annuity. Guidance must be provided to show that the proposed insurance arrangements are satisfactory. A guardian appointed under the Adults with Incapacity (Scotland) Act 2000 could be given that express power by the sheriff under s. 64(1) of that Act.

Jurisdiction. The court has jurisdiction to grant special powers: **61.15.3**
(a) under the *nobile officium* of the Inner House: *Tennent's Judicial Factor v. Tennent* 1954 S.C. 215;
(b) formerly under s. 7 of the Act of 1849; and
(c) in respect of some acts under s. 5 of the Trusts (Scotland) Act 1921.
Where a statutory application would encompass a common law application, the statutory application should be followed: *Tennent's Judicial Factor*, above, *per* L.P. Cooper at p. 225.
With effect from 1st April 2002, the definition of the term "judicial factor" appearing in s. 1 of the 1849 Act ceased to extend curators *bonis*: Adults with Incapacity (Scotland) Act 2000, Sched. 6. The reference in s. 7 of the 1849 Act to "factor" thus excludes "curator *bonis*". On 1st April 2002, any person holding office as curator *bonis* to an adult became guardian of that adult with power to manage the property or financial affairs of that adult: 2000 Act, Sched. 4, para. 1(1).
For a recent example of the exercise of the power under s. 5 of the 1921 Act, see *Inverclyde Council v. Dunlop,* 2005 S.L.T. 967 (Second Div.).

"petition". See note 61.2.1. If special powers are sought immediately the specific power sought   **61.15.4** must be craved in the prayer and supported by averments. The power sought must be for a specific act and not general in nature: *Carmichael's Judicial Factor* 1971 S.L.T. 336.

"note". For applications by note, see r. 15.2.   **61.15.5**

"send". This includes deliver: r. 1.3(1) (definition of "send").   **61.15.6**

"lodge in process his report". The report of the judicial factor to the Accountant of Court for   **61.15.7** special powers and the Accountant's opinion on it must be lodged in process as steps of process (r. 1.3(1) (definition of "step of process")). On lodging steps of process, see r. 4.4. They may be lodged by post: P.N. No. 4 of 1994, paras 1 and 8; and see note 4.4.10.

"motion". For motions, see Chap. 23.   **61.15.8**

PART II

APPLICATIONS UNDER SECTION 11A OF THE JUDICIAL FACTORS (SCOTLAND) ACT 1889

Application of this Part

61.16. This Part applies to a petition under section 11A of the Judicial Factors (Scotland) Act 1889 (appointment of a judicial factor on estate of person deceased).

Deriv. R.C.S. 1965, r. 201(preamble) substituted by S.I. 1986 No. 514

General note. A judicial factor appointed to the estate of a deceased person is akin to a trustee **61.16.1** in a sequestration or an executor creditor. The appointment is made where it appears that the deceased died intestate and nobody wishes to be executor-dative or a named executor refuses to be confirmed: Judicial Factors (Scotland) Act 1889, s. 11A(1) inserted by the Bankruptcy (Scotland) Act 1985, Sched. 7, para. 4. The appointment may also be made where an executor has to resign due to conflict of interest: see *Murray's Judicial Factor v. Thomas Murray & Sons (Ice Merchants) Ltd* 1992 S.C. 435. The petitioner may be a creditor or anyone with an interest in the estate of the deceased (*e.g.* a beneficiary or his representative).

Once appointed the duty of the judicial factor is to ingather the estate and then to distribute it to those entitled according to the proper order of ranking and succession.

Form of applications under section 11A of the Judicial Factors (Scotland) Act 1889

61.17. A petition to which this Part applies shall include averments stating—

(*a*) the name, last known address and date of death of the deceased person;

(*b*) the reasons for the appointment being necessary;

(*c*) the interest of the petitioner, including—

  (i) if a creditor, the nature and amount of the debt, how constituted, vouched or established, or

  (ii) if a person having an interest in the succession to the estate, the nature of that interest;

(*d*) details of the estate of the deceased person so far as known to the petitioner including heritable and moveable property, any stock in trade, interests in any business or partnership, debts owed to or by the deceased and any other relevant facts;

(*e*) the names and addresses of all persons known to the petitioner as having an interest in the estate either as creditors or in the succession to the estate, and the nature of the interest in each case; and

(*f*) the name, designation and address of the person nominated to be the judicial factor.

Deriv. R.C.S. 1965, r. 201(*a*) amended by S.I. 1986 No. 514

"petition". The application is by petition: Judicial Factors (Scotland) Act 1889, s. 11A(1). The **61.17.1** petition is presented in the Outer House: r. 14.2(*h*). The petition must be in Form 14.4 in the official printed form: rr. 4.1 and 14.4. The petition must be signed by counsel or other person having a right of audience: r. 4.2; and see r. 1.3(1) (definition of "counsel" and "other person having a right of audience") and note 1.3.4.

The petitioner must lodge the petition with the required steps of process (r. 4.4) and any documents founded on or adopted (r. 27.1(1)). A fee is payable on lodging the petition: see note 14.5.10.

On petitions generally, see Chap. 14.

Intimation and service of section 11A petition

61.18. The order for intimation and service under rule 14.5 (first order in petitions) in a petition under this Part shall include a requirement for—

(*a*) a notice of the petition in the Edinburgh Gazette in Form 61.18; and
(*b*) service of the petition on such persons named in the petition as personal representatives of the deceased who are not parties to the petition.

Deriv. R.C.S. 1965, r. 201(*b*)(part)

61.18.1   *"intimation and service".* See r. 14.7; and see Chap. 16, Pt. I.

61.18.2   *Advertisement in the Edinburgh Gazette.* The Edinburgh Gazette is published weekly by HMSO. Notices for advertisement should be sent to: HMSO Scotland, 71 Lothian Road, Edinburgh EH3 9AZ; tel: 031–228 4964; fax: 031–229 2734.

Interim appointment
61.19. The court may make an interim appointment of a judicial factor in a petition to which this Part applies when the petition is presented or at any time thereafter.

Deriv. R.C.S. 1965, r. 201(*c*)(part)

61.19.1   *Interim judicial factor.* An interim judicial factor may be appointed in a situation of urgency where the intimation of the petition and lodging of answers would cause prejudicial delay to the estate. The special reasons of urgency should be averred in the petition if the interim factor is sought immediately: *Cuthbertson v. Gibson* (1887) 14 R. 776; see also note 61.2.3.

Notice calling for claims
61.20.—(1) In order to ascertain the claims on the estate, the judicial factor shall, within 14 days after he has received the official certified copy of the interlocutor appointing him, place a notice in the Edinburgh Gazette, and in such other newspaper as he thinks fit, in Form 61.20.
(2) The judicial factor shall lodge in process—
(*a*) a copy of each newspaper containing the notice under paragraph (1); or
(*b*) a certificate of publication by the publisher of each such newspaper stating the date of publication and text of the notice.
(3) The period within which a creditor shall intimate a claim on the estate to the judicial factor shall be four months from the date of publication of the notice under paragraph (1).

Deriv. R.C.S. 1965, r. 201(*d*) amended by S.I. 1967 No. 487

61.20.1   *Notice in the Edinburgh Gazette.* The Edinburgh Gazette is published weekly by HMSO. Notices for advertisement should be sent to: HMSO Scotland, 71 Lothian Road, Edinburgh EH3 9AZ; tel: 031–228 4964; fax: 031–229 2734.

61.20.2   *"lodge in process".* The copy of the newspaper or publisher's certificate is lodged in process as a production. On lodging productions, see r. 4.5.

Claims
61.21.—(1) The judicial factor shall examine the claims of creditors in order to ascertain whether the debts are properly due from the estate of the deceased, and may—
(*a*) call for further evidence in support of the claims;
(*b*) if he thinks fit, require a creditor to constitute such claim by decree in a competent court in an action in which the judicial factor shall be called as a defender.
(2) For the purpose of ranking and payment of creditors, the date of the appointment of the judicial factor shall be deemed to be equivalent to the date of sequestration.

Deriv. R.C.S. 1965, r. 201(*e*)

"date of appointment of judicial factor". This will be the date of the interlocutor appointing **61.21.1** the judicial factor rather than the date of the official certified copy interlocutor.

"date of sequestration". For the meaning of this, see s. 12(4) of the Bankruptcy (Scotland) **61.21.2** Act 1985 substituted by s. 4(5) of the Bankruptcy (Scotland) Act 1993. The date is significant because it determines whether diligence on a debt has given it a preferred ranking. For the purposes of ranking and payment of creditors, a judicial factor acts as a trustee in sequestration.

Section 51 of the Bankruptcy (Scotland) Act 1985. An order of priority for the unsecured **61.21.3** debts of the creditors is provided in s. 51 of the Bankruptcy (Scotland) Act 1985. Unsecured debts rank after secured debts.

Custody and inspection of inventory of estate, etc.

61.22. There shall remain in the possession of the Accountant of Court and be open to inspection, within his office, by any creditor or person in the succession of the deceased—

(*a*) the inventory of estate, when adjusted and approved by the Accountant of Court and signed by him and the judicial factor;

(*b*) any report of the state of debts; and

(*c*) all subsequent accounts submitted by the judicial factor to the Accountant of Court.

Deriv. R.C.S. 1965, r. 201(*f*)(part) amended by S.I. 1967 No. 487

Inventory of estate. The judicial factor must lodge an inventory of the estate to which he has **61.22.1** been appointed with the Accountant of Court within six months of the lodging of his bond of caution: Act of 1849, s. 3.

Copies of documents. The Accountant of Court may issue signed copies of any document **61.22.2** lodged with him which shall have the same effect as originals: Act of 1849, s. 36.

Fees for inspection and copies. There is a fee for examining the inventory of the estate and a **61.22.3** fee for copying (and any searching). For fees, see Court of Session etc. Fees Order 1984, Table of Fees, Pt. II, H, item 2 and Pt. IV, J, items 3 and 4 [S.I. 1984 No. 256, Table as amended, pp. C1202 *et seq.*].

Administration, deathbed and funeral expenses

61.23.—(1) Out of the first funds realised by him, the judicial factor shall reserve sufficient funds to defray the estimated costs of his administration including the legal expenses of the judicial factory.

(2) On the expiry of the period for lodging claims, the judicial factor shall be entitled to pay out of such funds, with the prior approval of the Accountant of Court, those debts listed in paragraphs (*a*) to (*e*) of section 51(1) of the Bankruptcy (Scotland) Act 1985 (order of priority in distribution).

Deriv. R.C.S. 1965, r. 201(*n*)

Reserve fund for administration expenses. On the initial disposal of the assets of the estate, **61.23.1** the factor must set aside part of the funds thereby realised to form a reserve fund to meet the estimated costs of administration of the factor: r. 61.23(1).

"expiry of the period for lodging claims". This occurs on a date four months after the last **61.23.2** publication of the notice calling for claims in the Edinburgh Gazette and/or another newspaper: r. 61.20(3).

"such funds". These are the reserve fund created by the judicial factor under r. 61.23(1). **61.23.3**

"debts listed in paragraphs (a) to (e) of section 51(1) of the Bankruptcy (Scotland) Act **61.23.4** *1985"*. These include outlays and remuneration of an interim factor (1985 Act, s. 51(1)(*a*)), outlays and remuneration of the permanent factor (1985 Act, s. 51(1)(*b*)), reasonable deathbed and funeral expenses (1985 Act, s. 51(1)(*c*)), reasonable expenses of the petitioner for the factor (1985 Act, s. 51(1)(*d*)) and preferred debts (excluding any interest accrued thereon to the date of appointment) (1985 Act, s. 51(1)(*e*)).

Preferred debts include (*a*) debts to Inland Revenue and Customs and Excise; (*b*) Class 1, 2 or 4 National Insurance contributions; pension contributions under Schedule 3 to the Social Security Pensions Act 1975; and (*c*) debts to employees, including employees' remuneration not exceeding £800: Bankruptcy (Scotland) Act 1985, s. 51(2) and Sched. 3.

Procedure where there are creditors
61.24.—(1) Where claims are lodged, the judicial factor shall—
(*a*) where funds remain available for division after payment of the claims referred to in rule 61.23(2), prepare a state of funds and scheme of division amongst the creditors; or
(*b*) where no such funds remain after payment of those claims, prepare a state of funds only.
(2) The judicial factor shall—
(*a*) lodge with the Accountant of Court—
 (i) the state of funds and any scheme of division,
 (ii) all relevant writings and documents; and
(*b*) provide the Accountant of Court with such explanations as he may require.
(3) The Accountant of Court shall prepare a written report on the state of funds and any scheme of division containing such observations as he thinks fit for consideration by the court.
(4) The Accountant of Court shall issue the report under paragraph (3) to the judicial factor.

Deriv. R.C.S. 1965, r. 201(g)(part)

61.24.1 *General note.* Rr. 61.24 to 61.28 apply where creditors have lodged claims within the four month period of notice. R. 61.29 applies where no creditor has lodged a claim.

Notice to creditors
61.25.—(1) As soon as the report of the Accountant of Court under rule 61.24(3) has been issued, the judicial factor shall—
(*a*) lodge in process that report, the state of funds and any scheme of division;
(*b*) send to each person who has lodged with him a claim on the estate of the deceased a notice by first class post, or, if that person is furth of Europe, by air mail, stating—
 (i) that the state of funds and scheme of division or state of funds only, as the case may be, and a report have been lodged in court; and
 (ii) the amount for which the creditor has been ranked and whether his claim is to be paid in full or by a dividend and the amount of it; or
 (iii) that his claim has been rejected; or
 (iv) that no funds are available for division;
(*c*) place a notice in Form 61.25 in the Edinburgh Gazette; and
(*d*) if—
 (i) any person, other than a person who has lodged a claim with him, is stated in the application or in the books, deed of settlement, or other papers of the deceased, to be a creditor of the estate or has an interest in the estate, or
 (ii) he has reason to believe that any other person is either a creditor of the estate or has an interest in the estate,
 give notice to such person, by first class post or, if that person is furth of Europe, by air mail, that no dividend is allotted to him in the scheme of division.
(2) Any creditor or person having an interest in the succession to the deceased's estate shall be entitled to examine—
(*a*) the state of funds and any scheme of division lodged in process; and
(*b*) the claims and supporting vouchers or evidence lodged with the judicial factor.

Deriv. R.C.S. 1965, r. 201(*h*) (r. 61.25(1)) and r. 201(*j*)(part) (r. 61.25(2))

"lodge in process". The report, etc., is lodged in process as a step of process (r. 1.3(1) (defi- **61.25.1**
nition of "step of process")). On lodging steps of process, see r. 4.4. They may be lodged by
post: P.N. No. 4 of 1994, paras. 1 and 8; and see note 4.4.10.

"send". This includes deliver: r. 1.3(1) (definition of "send"). **61.25.2**

"each person who has lodged with him a claim". This includes creditors and beneficiaries **61.25.3**
with rights of succession.

Edinburgh Gazette. The Edinburgh Gazette is published weekly by HMSO. Notices for **61.25.4**
advertisement should be sent to: HMSO Scotland, 71 Lothian Road, Edinburgh EH3 9AZ;
tel: 031–228 4964; fax: 031–229 2734.

Approval of state of funds or scheme of division
61.26.—(1) Any creditor or person having an interest in the succession
to the estate of the deceased who is dissatisfied with the state of funds or
any scheme of division may lodge in process a note of objection within 28
days after the date of the notice given under rule 61.25(1)(*b*) and, until the
expiry of that period, the court shall not approve the state of funds and any
scheme of division.
(2) Where a note of objection under paragraph (1) is lodged, the court
shall dispose of the note after hearing any objector and the judicial factor
and making such investigations as it thinks fit.
(3) If any objection is sustained to any extent, the necessary alterations
shall be made to the state of funds and any scheme of division, and shall be
approved by the court.
(4) Where no note of objection is lodged, the court shall approve the
state of funds and any scheme of division.

Deriv. R.C.S. 1965, r. 201(*f*)(part) (r. 61.26(1)) and r. 201(*k*) (r. 61.26(2) and (3))

"lodge in process". The note of objection is lodged in process as a step of process (r. 1.3(1) **61.26.1**
(definition of "step of process")). On lodging steps of process, see r. 4.4. The note may be
lodged by post: P.N. No. 4 of 1994, paras. 1 and 8; and see note 4.4.10.

"note of objection". The note does not have to be signed: r. 4.2(9)(*f*). R. 15.2 (applications **61.26.2**
by note) does not apply: r. 15.2(4)(*b*).

Payment following approval of scheme of division
61.27. After the court has approved a scheme of division, the judicial
factor shall pay, deliver or convey to the parties the sums or other property
to which they are entitled under the scheme.

Deriv. R.C.S. 1965, r. 201(*l*)

Partial division on first scheme of division
61.28.—(1) Where, in the opinion of the judicial factor, a partial division
of funds among the creditors who have claimed may be made with safety in
the interests of all concerned, the judicial factor may, with the approval of
the Accountant of Court, prepare a state of funds and first scheme of division as soon as possible after the period for lodging claims has expired.
(2) The following provisions of this Part shall apply to a state of funds
and first scheme of division prepared under paragraph (1) of this rule as
they apply to a state of funds and scheme of division prepared under rule
61.24(1)(*a*):—
   rule 61.24(2) (lodging of state of funds etc. with Accountant of Court),
   rule 61.24(3) (report by Accountant of Court on state of funds),
   rule 61.25 (notice to creditors),
   rule 61.26 (approval of state of funds or scheme of division), subject to
        paragraph (3) of this rule.
(3) Subject to paragraph (4), the court may, not earlier than six months

after the death of the deceased, approve the first scheme of division and, where it so approves, the judicial factor shall pay, deliver or convey to the parties the sums or other property to which they are entitled under the first scheme.

(4) Out of the funds there shall be retained and deposited in an institution authorised under the Banking Act 1987 or other appropriate institution a sufficient sum to meet—

(a) the amount of the claims of creditors whose debts have not at that time been admitted by the judicial factor, or whose debts are future or contingent; and

(b) the full amount of such debts as are claimed as preferable but the priority of which is not admitted by the judicial factor.

Deriv. R.C.S. 1965, r. 201(m)

61.28.1   *"after the period for lodging claims has expired"*. This occurs on a date four months after the last publication of the notice calling for claims in the Edinburgh Gazette or another newspapers: r. 61.20(3).

61.28.2   *"institution authorised under the Banking Act 1987"*. This is a body corporate or partnership formed under the law of any part of the E.C. or a savings bank which has been authorised by the Bank of England to accept a deposit in the course of carrying on a deposit-taking business for the purposes of the Banking Act 1987: Banking Act 1987, ss. 9, 104 and 106.

61.28.3   *"other appropriate institution"*. This includes, *e.g.* the National Savings Bank, or a building society incorporated (or deemed to be incorporated) under the Building Societies Act 1986; *cf.* Act of 1849, s. 5(1).

Procedure where no creditors

61.29. Where, on the expiry of the period for lodging claims, no creditor has lodged a claim, the judicial factor shall not lodge a state of funds but shall prepare a report with regard to the disposal of the surplus estate in accordance with rule 61.30.

Deriv. R.C.S. 1965, r. 201(g)(part)

Disposal of surplus estate

61.30.—(1) Where, after payment of the creditors, there is a surplus, the judicial factor shall lodge with the Accountant of Court a statement of—

(a) the amount of the surplus;

(b) the parties claiming that surplus and their respective grounds of claim; and

(c) those parties who, in the opinion of the judicial factor, are entitled to the surplus and the reasons for his opinion.

(2) The Accountant of Court shall prepare a written opinion on the statement of the judicial factor lodged under paragraph (1) and issue that opinion to the judicial factor.

(3) On receipt of the opinion of the Accountant of Court under paragraph (2), the judicial factor shall—

(a) lodge in process that opinion and the statement prepared under paragraph (1); and

(b) give notice to each party claiming an interest or apparently entitled to any part of the estate, by first class post or, if that person is furth of Europe, by air mail, that—

(i) the statement of the judicial factor and the opinion of the Accountant of Court have been lodged in process; and

(ii) should any such party wish to lodge any objection to the statement, he shall lodge a note of objection with the Deputy Principal Clerk within 28 days after the date of the posting of the notice by the judicial factor.

(4) On expiry of the period for lodging objections under paragraph (3)(b)(ii), the court, on considering the statement, opinion, and any note of objection and, after such procedure as it thinks fit, shall—
  (a) determine which parties are entitled to the surplus estate and direct the judicial factor to make payment accordingly; or
  (b) if the court considers that it is desirable that the judicial factor should continue to administer the surplus estate, direct the judicial factor to do so.

Deriv. R.C.S. 1965, r. 201(o)

"lodge in process". The opinion of the Accountant of Court and the statement prepared **61.30.1**
under r. 61.30(1) by the judicial factor are lodged in process as steps of process (r. 1.3(1)
(definition of "step of process")). On lodging steps of process, see r. 4.4. They may be lodged by
post: P.N. No. 4 of 1994, paras. 1 and 8; and see note 4.4.10.

"note of objection". The note does not have to be signed: r. 4.2(9)(f). R. 15.2 (applications by **61.30.2**
note) does not apply: r. 15.2(4)(b).

"within 28 days". The date from which the period is calculated is not counted. Where the last **61.30.3**
day falls on a Saturday or Sunday or a public holiday on which the Office of Court is closed, the
next available day is allowed: r. 1.3(7). For office hours and public holidays, see note 3.1.2.

<h2 style="text-align:center">PART III</h2>

<h3 style="text-align:center">DISCHARGE OF JUDICIAL FACTORS</h3>

Applications for discharge to Accountant of Court

61.31.—(1) This rule applies to a judicial factor appointed as a—
  (a) curator *bonis*;
  (b) guardian;
  (c) factor *loco absentis*; or
  (d) commissary factor.

(2) Where a judicial factory is terminated by reason of the recovery, death or coming of age of the ward, or by reason of the exhaustion of the estate, the judicial factor, or where he has died, his representative, may apply to the Accountant of Court for a certificate of discharge.

(3) The judicial factor shall intimate a notice in Form 61.31 of an application under paragraph (2) to—
  (a) the cautioner; and
  (b) any person having an interest in the estate of the ward.

(4) Any person to whom intimation has been given under paragraph (3) may make written representations relating to the application to the Accountant of Court within 21 days after the date of such intimation.

(5) On the expiry of the period specified in paragraph (4), the Accountant of Court shall, after considering the application and representations made, send to—
  (a) the factor,
  (b) the Deputy Principal Clerk, and
  (c) any person who has made representations,
a copy of his decision to issue or refuse to issue a certificate of discharge and a note of his reasons for making that decision.

(6) The Accountant of Court—
  (a) shall not sign a certificate of discharge until the time for lodging an appeal under rule 61.32 has expired; and
  (b) shall, on issuing a certificate of discharge, give written intimation of the issue of the certificate to the Deputy Principal Clerk.

(7) The issue of a certificate of discharge shall be sufficient authority for the judicial factor to uplift his bond of caution.

Deriv. R.C.S. 1965, r. 201Z (r. 61.31(1)), r. 201AA (r. 61.31(2)), r. 201BB(1) (r. 61.31(3)),
r. 201CC (r. 61.31(4)), r. 201DD (r. 61.31(5)) and r. 201EE (r. 61.31(6) and (7)), all inserted
by S.I. 1991 No. 1915

61.31.1   *General note.* Generally a judicial factor must, at the termination of his office, present a
petition to the court for his discharge: Act of 1849, s.34. The purpose of this rule is to avoid the
necessity for certain types of judicial factor to present separate petitions to the court for
discharge. The power to make this rule is in s.34A of the Act of 1849, which permits the court to
make provision for the discharge of factors in cases where the judicial factory is terminated by
reason of the recovery, death or coming of age of the ward, or by reason of the exhaustion of the
estate (on which see note 61.31.2A). This rule applies only to judicial factors appointed as
curators *bonis*, guardians, factors *loco absentis*, or commissary factors: r. 61.31(1).

Where an application for discharge is made under this rule it will be unnecessary for the factor
to petition for recall of his appointment.

61.31.2   *Form of application.* The application is by letter. The letter should be addressed to: The
Accountant of Court, Parliament House, Parliament Square, Edinburgh EH1 1RF; tel.
0131–554 2422; fax 0131–554 3632; DX ED311.

61.31.2A   *"by reason of exhaustion of the estate".* The power to provide for an application to the
Accountant of Court for a discharge is, and this phrase appears, in s.34A of the 1849 Act. In
some cases the estate will be constructively exhausted: *e.g.* where the expenses of the factory
exceed the interest on the capital, where the capital is rapidly disappearing in nursing home fees,
or where the cost of the factory or the petition for discharge will use up what little is left of the
estate. It is thought that in cases where a factory is exhausted in the sense that its assets will not
cover its future liabilities, then administrative discharge is available. The Notes for the
Guidance of Curators prepared by the Accountant of Court (see *P.H. Book*, Vol. 5, **M** 301)
refer to situations where the "estate is substantially exhausted" (p. 11) on the death of a curator.
It is thought that administrative discharge may be sought in similar cases of constructive
exhaustion, even where the curator has not died.

61.31.3   *"intimate".* For methods, see r. 16.7.

61.31.4   *"within 21 days".* The date from which the period is calculated is not counted.

61.31.5   *"send".* This includes deliver: r. 1.3(1) (definition of "send").

61.31.6   *Grounds of termination of factory.* In relation to termination of a factory by means of
recovery of the ward, the question has arisen as to the sufficiency of evidence. Either the
common law rule of corroboration does not apply to the Accountant of Court (who acts in an
administrative capacity) or, if an application under r. 61.31 is a civil proceeding, the rule has
been abolished by s.1 of the Civil Evidence (Scotland) Act 1988. It is understood that the
Accountant of Court may be satisfied on the evidence from one source.

Appeals against decisions under rule 61.31

61.32.—(1) The judicial factor, or any person who has made representations under rule 61.31(4), may, within 14 days after intimation of a decision
to him under rule 61.31(5), appeal to the Lord Ordinary against the
determination of the Accountant of Court.

(2) An appeal under paragraph (1) shall be—
(a) made by letter to the Deputy Principal Clerk containing a statement
of the grounds of appeal; and
(b) intimated to the Accountant of Court.

(3) On receipt of an appeal under paragraph (1), the Deputy Principal
Clerk shall place the appeal before the Lord Ordinary in chambers for
determination.

(4) On disposing of such an appeal, the Lord Ordinary may—
(a) direct the Accountant of Court to sign the certificate of discharge;
(b) ordain the judicial factor to lodge a petition for his discharge; or
(c) make such other order as he thinks fit.

(5) The decision of the Lord Ordinary on an appeal to him under
paragraph (1) shall be final and not subject to review.

Deriv. R.C.S. 1965, r. 201FF inserted by S.I. 1991 No. 1915

61.32.1   *"within 14 days".* The date from which the period is calculated is not counted. Where the last
day falls on a Saturday or Sunday or a public holiday on which the Office of Court is closed, the
next available day is allowed: r. 1.3(7). For office hours and public holidays, see note 3.1.2.

"letter to the Deputy Principal Clerk". The address and telephone number, etc., of the Deputy **61.32.2**
Principal Clerk are: The Deputy Principal Clerk of Session, Court of Session, 2 Parliament
Square, Edinburgh EH1 1RQ; tel. 0131–225 2595; fax 0131–225 8213; DX ED306.

"final and not subject to review". The decision of the Lord Ordinary may not be reclaimed **61.32.3**
against.

Applications for discharge to court

61.33.—(1) Where a judicial factor, other than one to whom rule 61.31
(applications for discharge to Accountant of Court) applies, seeks his
discharge, he, or where he has died, his representative, shall apply to the
court by petition for his discharge.

(2) The order for intimation and service under rule 14.5 (first order in
petitions) in a petition for discharge of a judicial factor appointed under
section 11A of the Judicial Factors (Scotland) Act 1889 shall include a
requirement for—

(a) a notice of the petition in the Edinburgh Gazette in Form 61.33; and

[THE NEXT PAGE IS C 507]

Note under TEXT editing here. The address and telephone number are:—The Deputy Principal Clerk of Session, Court of Session, 2 Parliament Square, Edinburgh EH1 1RQ (tel 0131-225 2595; fax 0131-225 6313; DX ED36).

proof and are not for review. The decision of the Lord Ordinary may not be reclaimed against.

Application for discharge to court

61.13.—(1) Where a patient liable, other than one to whom rule 61.3 applies, applications for discharge to a tribunal, or of court, applies, seeks his discharge to one, or where he has filed, his representative, shall apply to the court by petition for his discharge.

(2) The order for intimation and service under rule 14.5 (first order in petitions), in a petition for discharge of a patient liable, proceeded under section 114A of the Judicial Factors (Scotland) Act 1889, shall intimate to representation:—

(a) a notice of the petition in the Edinburgh Gazette in Form 61.35; and

[THE NEXT PAGE IS 9097]

(b) service on the cautioner and on the personal representatives of the deceased person in respect of whom the appointment was made.

(3) The court shall remit a petition under paragraph (1) to the Accountant of Court to report to the court on the petition.

Deriv. R.C.S. 1965, r. 201(*p*)

General note. A judicial factor, other than a curator *bonis*, guardian, factor *loco absentis* or **61.33.1** commissary factor, requires to apply to the court for his discharge: Act of 1849, s. 34.

The most frequent reasons for a petition for discharge are death of the person in respect of whose estate the appointment was made, all monies having been disbursed, and death or retiral of the factor. In the latter case it is common practice to crave in the petition for the appointment of a new factor. The new factor will normally be appointed at the time when the remit is made under r. 61.33(3) to the Accountant of Court to report on the intromissions of the deceased or retiring factor. In some cases it may be appropriate to seek an appointment of an interim factor pending the full appointment: see note 61.2.3.

"petition". A petition is presented in the Outer House: r. 14.2(*h*). The petition must be in **61.33.2** Form 14.4 in the official printed form: rr. 4.1 and 14.4. The petition must be signed by counsel or other person having a right of audience: r. 4.2; and see r. 1.3(1) (definition of "counsel" and "other person having a right of audience") and note 1.3.4.

The petitioner must lodge the petition with the required steps of process (r. 4.4) and any documents founded on or adopted (r. 27.1(1)). A fee is payable on lodging the petition: see note 14.5.10.

On petitions generally, see Chap. 14.

Edinburgh Gazette. The *Edinburgh Gazette* is published weekly by HMSO. Notices for **61.33.3** advertisement should be sent to: HMSO Scotland, 71 Lothian Road, Edinburgh EH3 9AZ; tel. 0131–228 4964; fax 0131–229 2734.

"service". For methods, see Chap. 16, Pt. I.   **61.33.4**

Remit to Accountant of Court. After intimation and service of the petition an execution copy **61.33.5** of the petition must be lodged in process: see r. 16.1(4) and note 16.1.6. A motion should then be enrolled for the remit to the Accountant of Court "to inquire into and report to the court on the factor's [*or* curator's] intromissions with the factory [*or* curatory] estate with a view to discharge". On the motion being granted the process is transmitted by the Petition Department to the Accountant of Court.

On completion of the Accountant's report, it is lodged in process and the process returned to the Petition Department by the Accountant of Court's office. The petitioner may then enrol a motion in respect of the report (if favourable) to grant the prayer of the petition for discharge. The interlocutor pronounced "exoners and discharges the factor [*or* curator] and grants authority for delivery of his bond of caution".

Other proceedings in relation to statutory applications

CHAPTER 62

RECOGNITION, REGISTRATION AND ENFORCEMENT OF FOREIGN JUDGMENTS, ETC.

PART I

GENERAL PROVISIONS

Disapplication of certain rules to this Chapter
[1] **62.1.** Subject to Part XIII the following rules shall not apply to a petition or application under this Chapter:

    14.5 (first order in petitions),

    14.6 (period of notice for lodging answers),

    14.7 (intimation and service of petitions),

    14.9 (unopposed petitions).

[1] Rule 62.1 amended by S.S.I. 2006 No. 199 (effective 6th April 2006).

62.1.1   *General note.* The recognition and enforcement of judgments or awards from outwith Scotland should ideally be a speedy and inexpensive process. The merits of the judgment or award will already have been decided. Essentially the involvement of the Scottish court should be to check that it has jurisdiction under the relevant statutory provisions under which the application for enforcement is made. The jurisdiction provisions of the C.J.J.A. 1982 do not apply to an application for the recognition and enforcement of a judgment from a non-contracting state: *Owens Bank Ltd v. Bracco* [1994] 2 W.L.R. 759. For the meaning of "contracting state", see note 62.36.3.

The rules in Chap. 62 provide for enforcement to be by petition dealt with *ex parte* with any submission which may be required being dealt with in chambers. The procedures for service of the cause on the judgment debtor vary in detail but the general approach is for the debtor to receive notice only after the court has determined the application. After receiving notice of the cause and any determination, a debtor who wishes to object to enforcement must either comply with a specified statutory procedure or present a petition for suspension and interdict.

Certificate of currency conversion

62.2.—(1) Where the sum payable under a judgment, award, recommendation or determination to be registered in accordance with a provision of this Chapter is expressed in a currency other than sterling, the petitioner or applicant, as the case may be, before applying to the Keeper of the Registers for registration of such a document, shall lodge in the Petition Department—

(*a*) a certified statement of the rate of exchange prevailing at—

(i) the date of the judgment, award, recommendation or determination,

(ii) the date on which the certified statement is lodged, or

(iii) a date within three days before the date on which the certified statement is lodged,

and of the sterling equivalent, at that rate, of the principal sum, interest and expenses contained in the judgment, award, recommendation or determination, as the case may be; and

(*b*) a certificate of currency conversion in Form 62.2.

(2) The certified statement required under paragraph (1) shall be by an official in the Bank of England or an institution authorised under the Banking Act 1987.

(3) On receipt of the documents specified in paragraph (1), the clerk of session shall, if satisfied with the terms of those documents, sign and date the certificate of currency conversion.

Deriv. P.N. No. 7 of 1988

62.2.1   *General note.* R. 62.2 is a new rule which applies to the recognition and enforcement of any non-Scottish judgment or award which is expressed in a currency other than sterling. It replaces the fragmented and unclear position under the R.C.S. 1965.

62.2.2   *"certified statement of the rate of exchange".* The petitioner or applicant should obtain from an official in the Bank of England or an institution authorised under the Banking Act 1987 (see note 62.2.3) a certified statement of the rate of exchange prevailing at the date of conversion from the foreign currency into sterling: r. 62.2(1)(*a*). The petitioner should obtain the statement before applying to the Keeper of the Registers for registration of the judgment: r. 62.2(1).

62.2.3   *"institution authorised under the Banking Act 1987".* This is any corporate body, whenever incorporated, any UK partnership or Scottish savings bank established under the Savings Bank (Scotland) Act 1819 which has been authorised by the Bank of England to carry on a deposit-taking business: Banking Act 1987, s. 106. In practice this will include most UK banks, but not building societies.

62.2.4   *Date of conversion.* When the petitioner or applicant requests a bank for a certified statement of the rate of exchange he may request for the rate to be at any one of three dates of conversion, namely (1) the date of the judgment or award; (2) the date the statement is issued provided that later that day he lodges the statement and certificate of currency conversion with the Petition Department; or (3) any date within three days before the date when he lodges those items with the Petition Department.

It follows that where the petitioner or applicant does not wish to have the date of the judgment or award as the date of conversion, he must within three days of the date of conversion in the statement lodge with the Petition Department the certified statement together with the certificate of currency conversion. If the petitioner or applicant fails to meet this deadline, he must obtain a fresh certified statement of the rate of exchange.

Certificate of currency conversion. This should be in Form 62.2 and lodged completed but **62.2.5** unsigned by the petitioner or applicant together with the certified statement of the rate of exchange with the Petition Department within any applicable time limit: r. 62.2(1).

Where the documents lodged are in order the clerk of session in the Petition Department will sign and date the certificate of currency conversion and return it to the petitioner or applicant: r. 62.2(3).

On receipt of the signed certificate of conversion the petitioner or applicant will be entitled to apply to the Keeper of the Registers for registration of the judgment or award.

Translation of document lodged

62.3. Where a judgment, award, or other document lodged with a petition or application to which this Chapter applies is in a language other than English, there shall be produced with the petition a translation into English certified as correct by the translator; and the certificate shall include his full name, address and qualification.

Deriv. R.C.S. 1965, r. 249E(2)(*a*)(v) inserted by S.I. 1986 No. 1941

General note. A translation of any judgment or award not in English should be lodged with **62.3.1** the petition: r. 62.3. The translation should bear the certificate required by r. 62.3.

PART II

REGISTRATION AND ENFORCEMENT UNDER THE ADMINISTRATION OF JUSTICE ACT 1920 AND THE FOREIGN JUDGMENTS (RECIPROCAL ENFORCEMENT) ACT 1933

Application and interpretation of this Part

62.4.—(1) This Part applies to an application to the court under the Administration of Justice Act 1920 or the Foreign Judgments (Reciprocal Enforcement) Act 1933.

(2) In this Part—

"the Act of 1920" means the Administration of Justice Act 1920;

"the Act of 1933" means the Foreign Judgments (Reciprocal Enforcement) Act 1933.

General note. Until Pt. II of the Act of 1920 only judgments from other UK jurisdictions could **62.4.1** be enforced in Scotland by registration. Registration was under the Judgments Extension Act 1868 or (in the sheriff court) the Inferior Courts Judgments Extension Act 1882. Where a person wished to enforce any non-UK judgment in Scotland he required to raise a common law action for a decree conform. The common law action is still required to enforce a judgment where none of the provisions of Chap. 62 apply. In practice, the common law action still covers judgments from most countries. For a discussion of the common law action, see Anton on *Private International Law*, 2nd ed., pp. 220 *et seq.* and Graham Stewart on *Diligence*, pp. 430 *et seq.* Where there is a statutory procedure for recognition and enforcement of judgments, the use of the common law action is prohibited or discouraged through the exclusion of recovery of expenses of enforcement: see the Act of 1920, s. 9(5); the Act of 1933, s. 6; and the C.J.J.A. 1982, s. 18(8).

Part II of the Act of 1920 followed the Sumner *Report on the Conduct of Legal Proceedings between Parties in this Country and Parties Abroad and the Enforcement of Judgments and Awards* 1919 (Cmd. 251). The aim of the report was to examine the feasibility of giving the judgment of a supreme court in any part of the British Empire equal validity in any other part, merely on compliance with formalities along the lines of the intra-UK Act of 1868. Accordingly decisions under the Act of 1868 may to some extent be used in considering the provisions of the Act of 1920.

The Act of 1933 was passed to provide a parallel requirement for countries outwith the British Empire with which the UK concluded bilateral conventions on recognition and enforcement of certain judgments of certain courts. At the same time the Act of 1920 was restricted to those territories already covered by it (see note 62.5.3) and the Act of 1933 was put forward as the UK model for any future bilateral conventions for reciprocal recognition and enforcement of judgments.

62.4.2   *Definitions in the Act of 1920.* Part II of this Chapter is made under s. 11 of the Act of 1920 in relation to proceedings under that Act: A.S. (R.C.S. 1994) 1994, Sched. 1 [S.I. 1994 No. 1443]. Accordingly a word or expression used in Pt. II which is also used in the Act of 1920 has the meaning given in that Act unless the contrary intention appears: Interpretation Act 1978, s. 11. The following are definitions used in both Pt. II of the Act of 1920 and Pt. II of this Chapter:

(1) *"judgment"*. This is any judgment or order given or made by a court in civil proceedings whereby a sum of money is made payable: Act of 1920, s. 12(1). It includes an award in proceedings or an arbitration if, in the place where the award was made, it became enforceable in the same way as a judgment of a court: Act of 1920, s. 12(1). A judgment reducing or annulling an assignation is not *per se* a judgment whereby a sum of money is made payable: *Platt v. Platt* 1958 S.C. 95. A decree for a sum of money obtained by the registration of a probative writ for execution is a judgment for this purpose: *Taylor, Petr.* 1931 S.L.T. 260. A judgment has to be a decision of some description: *Ivory, Petr.*, 2006 S.L.T. 758 (OH).

(2) *"judgment creditor"*. This is the person who obtained the judgment or award and includes the successors and assignees of that person: Act of 1920, s. 12(1).

(3) *"judgment debtor"*. This is the person against whom the judgment or award was given and includes any person against whom the judgment or award is enforceable in the place where it was given: Act of 1920, s. 12(1).

(4) *"original court"*. This is the court (or arbiter) which gave the judgment or award: Act of 1920, s. 12(1).

62.4.3   *Definitions in the Act of 1933.* Part II of this Chapter is made under s. 12(*b*) of the Act of 1933 in relation to proceedings under that Act: A.S. (R.C.S. 1994) 1994, Sched. 1 [S.I. 1994 No. 1443]. Accordingly a word or expression used in Pt. II which is also used in the Act of 1933 has the meaning given in that Act unless the contrary intention appears: Interpretation Act 1978, s. 11. The following are definitions used in both the Act of 1933 and Pt. II of this Chapter:

(1) *"appeal"*. This includes any proceeding by way of discharging or setting aside a judgment or an application for a new trial or a stay of execution: Act of 1933, s. 11(1).

(2) *"court"*. This includes a tribunal, but not in relation to the enforcement of an arbitral award in the country of origin: Act of 1933, s. 11(1).

(3) *"judgment"*. This is a judgment or order given or made by a court in any civil proceedings, or a judgment or order given or made by a court in any criminal proceedings, for the payment of a sum of money in respect of compensation or damages to an injured party: Act of 1933, s. 11(1). Subject to ss. 1(5) and 6 of the Act of 1933 an award in an arbitration is treated as a judgment if, in the place where the award was made, it became enforceable in the same way as a judgment of a court: Act of 1933, s. 10A inserted by the C.J.J.A. 1982, Sched. 10, para. 4. A judgment reducing or annulling an assignation is not *per* se a judgment whereby a sum of money is made payable: *Platt v. Platt* 1958 S.C. 95. A judgment includes a decree for a sum of money obtained by the registration of a probative writ for execution: *Taylor, Petr.* 1931 S.L.T. 260. A judgment has to be a decision of some description: *Ivory, Petr.*, 2006 S.L.T. 758 (OH).

(4) *"judgment creditor"*, *"judgment debtor"* and *"original court"*. These have the same meaning as in the Act of 1920: see note 62.4.2.

Applications for registration under the Act of 1920 or 1933

62.5.—(1) An application under section 9 of the Act of 1920 (enforcement in United Kingdom of judgments obtained in superior courts in other British Dominions etc.) shall be made by petition.

(2) An application under section 2 of the Act of 1933 (application for registration of a foreign judgment) shall be made by petition.

Deriv. R.C.S. 1965, r. 248(*a*)(part) (r. 62.5(1)) and r. 249.1 (r. 62.5(2))

62.5.1   *Jurisdiction under the Act of 1920.* The court has jurisdiction for an application under s. 9 of the Act of 1920 where—

(*a*) the application is made within 12 months after the date of the judgment to be enforced, or such longer period as the court may allow;

(*b*) the application is in respect of a "judgment" as defined in s. 12(1) of the Act of 1920 (see note 62.4.2) from a superior court (Act of 1920, s. 3(1));

(*c*) Part II of the Act of 1920 applies to the judgment (see note 62.5.3); and

(*d*) jurisdiction is not otherwise excluded: Act of 1920, s. 9(1); and see note 62.5.4.

Time-limit under s.9 of the Act of 1920. The court has a discretion to allow an application to be **62.5.2**
made after the expiry of the 12-month period after the date of the judgment to be enforced: Act
of 1920, s.9(1).

Applicability of Pt II of the Act of 1920. Part II of the Act of 1920 applies to a judgment of a **62.5.3**
superior court in (1) any part of H.M. Dominions outside the United Kingdom, or (2) any
territory under H.M. protection or for which a government of any Dominion exercises a
mandate, to which Pt II of the Act has been applied by Order in Council: Act of 1920, ss.9(1), 13
and 14.

Part II of the Act of 1920 may not now be extended to any territory to which it did not apply
on 10th November 1933: Act of 1933, s.7(1) and the Reciprocal Enforcement of Judgments
(General Application to His Majesty's Dominions, etc.) Order 1933 [S.R. & O. 1933 No. 1073].
In addition Pt II of the Act of 1920 may be disapplied from any territory to which it previously
applied by the extension of the Act of 1933 to that territory by Order in Council: Act of 1933,
s.7(2). Where this happens transitional provisions apply: Administration of Justice Act 1956,
s.51.

The countries and territories to which Pt II of the Act of 1920 applies are listed in the
Reciprocal Enforcement of Judgments (Administration of Justice Act 1920, Part II) (Consoli-
dation) Order 1984 [S.I. 1984 No. 129] as amended by the Reciprocal Enforcement of
Judgments (Administration of Justice Act 1920, Part II) (Amendment) Order 1985 [S.I. 1985
No. 1994], the Reciprocal Enforcement of Judgments (Australia) Order 1994 [S.I. 1994 No.
1901] and the Reciprocal Enforcement of Judgments (Administration of Justice Act 1920, Pt II)
(Amendment) Order 1997 [S.I. 1997 No. 2601]. They are:

Anguilla	Malta
Antigua and Barbuda	Mauritius
Bahamas	Montserrat
Barbados	New Zealand
Belize	Nigeria
Bermuda	Territory of Norfolk Island
Botswana	Papua New Guinea
British Indian Ocean Territory	St Christopher and Nevis
British Virgin Islands	St Helena
Cayman Islands	St Lucia
Christmas Island	St Vincent and the Grenadines
Cocos (Keeling) Islands	Seychelles
Republic of Cyprus	Sierra Leone
Dominica	Singapore
Falkland Islands	Soloman Islands
Fiji	Sovereign Base Area of Akrotíri and
The Gambia	Dhekelia in Cyprus
Ghana	Sri Lanka
Grenada	Swaziland
Guyana	Tanzania
Jamaica	Trinidad and Tobago
Kenya	Turks and Caicos Islands
Kiribati	Tuvalu
Lesotho	Uganda
Malawi	Zambia
Malaysia	Zimbabwe

Exclusion of jurisdiction under the Act of 1920. S.9(2) of the Act of 1920 excludes the **62.5.4**
jurisdiction of the court where—
   (a) the original court acted without jurisdiction;
   (b) the judgment debtor did not carry on business or was not resident within the jurisdiction
of the original court and did not voluntarily appear or otherwise submit to that court's
jurisdiction;
   (c) the judgment debtor was ordinarily resident or carried on business within or agreed to
submit to the jurisdiction of the original court but was not served in the process of the original
court and did not appear;
   (d) the judgment was obtained by fraud: see *Owens Bank Ltd v. Bracco* [1992] 2 A.C. 444, 480
et seq. per Lord Bridge of Harwich;
   (e) the judgment debtor satisfies the court that either an appeal is pending or that he is
entitled and intends to appeal against the judgment: or

(f) the judgment was in respect of a course of action which for reasons of public policy or for some other reason could not have been entertained by the court (*e.g.* the judgment included penalty damages).

62.5.5   *Jurisdiction under the Act of 1933.* The court has jurisdiction under s.2 of the Act of 1933 where—
    (a) the application is made within six years of—
        (i) the date of the judgment; or
        (ii) where the judgment has been appealed against, the date of the last judgment given in the appeal;
    (b) the application is in respect of a "judgment" as defined in s.11(1) as extended by s.10A of the Act of 1933 (see note 62.4.3);
    (c) the Act of 1933 applies to the judgment (see note 62.5.7); and
    (d) jurisdiction is not otherwise excluded (see note 62.5.8).

62.5.6   *Time-limit under s.2 of the Act of 1933.* The six-year time-limit for the presentation of a petition is imposed under s.2 of the Act of 1933. Accordingly there is no scope for the use of the dispensing power under r. 2.1.

62.5.7   *Applicability of the Act of 1933.* The Act of 1933 has been applied to judgments in two ways, (1) by reference to the court of the territory where the judgment was given and (2) by reference to the subject-matter of the judgment.

(1) *Territorial applicability.* The Act of 1933 applies to judgments or any class of judgments given by a recognised court of a foreign country or any part of H.M. Dominions (including mandated territories) to which the Act has been extended by Order in Council: Act of 1933, ss.1(1) and 7(2) and (3).

The Act of 1933 has been extended to the recognised courts (specified in the relevant Order in Council) of the following countries:

Country (S.R. & O. or S.I.)

Australia (1994 No. 1901)
Austria (1962 No. 1339)
Belgium (1936) No. 1169)
Canada:
    Federal Court (1987 N. 468)
    British Columbia (1987 No. 468)
    Manitoba (1987 No. 468)
    New Brunswick (1987 No. 468)
    Nova Scotia (1987 No. 468)
    Ontario (1987 No. 468)
    Yukon Territory (1987 No. 2211)
    Prince Edward Island (1988 No. 1304)
    Saskatchewan (1988 No. 1853)
    Northwest Territories (1989 No. 987)
    Newfoundland (1991 No. 1724)

France (metropolitan) (1936 No. 609)
Germany (including former G.D.R.) (1961 No. 1199)
Guernsey (1973 No. 610)
India (states and territories listed) (1958 No. 425)
Isle of Man (1973 No. 611)
Israel (1971 No. 1039)
Italy (1973 No. 1894)
Jersey (1973 No. 612)
Netherlands (1969 No. 1063)
    Netherlands Antilles (1977 No. 2149)
Norway (1962 No. 636)
Pakistan (1958 No. 141)
Suriname (1981 No. 735)
Tonga (1980 No. 1523)

Where any Order in Council made before 1st January 1987 specifies a court of a country to be a "superior court", then it is to be treated as a recognised court for the purposes of s.1 of the Act of 1933: Act of 1933, s.1(5).

The above extensions of the Act cover only a judgment of a recognised court which is—
    (a) given at first instance;
    (b) either final or conclusive between the judgment debtor and the judgment creditor or requires the former to make an interim payment to the latter (notwithstanding that it may still be subject to appeal);
    (c) requires payment of a sum of money, not being a sum payable in respect of taxes, or other charges of a like nature or in respect of a fine or other penalty: see *S.A. Consortium General Textiles v. Sun and Sand Ltd* [1978] Q.B. 279;
    (d) given after the Order in Council which made the court which gave it (a "recognised court") had come into force;
    (e) not regarded as a judgment of the recognised court just for the purposes of enforcement and which was given or made in another country; or
    (f) not given by the recognised court in proceedings founded on a judgment of a court in another country and having as their object enforcement of that judgment: Act of 1933, s.1(2), (2A) and (3).

(2) *Applicability related to subject-matter.* The Act of 1933 (subject to variation) applies to judgments of a certain subject-matter to which it has been applied by the following Acts:

Carriage of Goods by Road Act 1965, ss.4 and 11(2) in respect of any judgment given by a court or tribunal of a party to the 1950 Geneva Convention on the Contract for the International Carriage of Goods by Road ("the C.M.R. Convention") in proceedings arising out of carriage under the Convention;

Nuclear Installations Act 1965, s.17(4) in respect of any judgment of any foreign country which is certified by the Secretary of State to be a judgment which is enforceable under the 1960 Paris Convention on Third Party Liability in the Field of Nuclear Energy (as amended) (Cmnd. 2514) in a country bound by that Convention;

Carriage of Passengers by Road Act 1974, s.5: not yet in force;

Civil Aviation (Eurocontrol) Act 1983, s.1 in respect of any determination made by a relevant authority in a state designated by Order in Council as a party to the 1981 Multilateral Agreement relating to Route Charges, to enforce a sum due to Eurocontrol in respect of air navigation charges;

International Transport Conventions Act 1983, s.6 in respect of a judgment pronounced by the court of a state designated by Order in Council as a member state of the 1980 Berne Convention Concerning International Carriage by Rail to enforce a claim pronounced under the Convention;

Merchant Shipping Act 1995, s.166(4) in respect of any judgment given by a court in a country in respect of which the Brussels International Convention on Civil Liability for Oil Pollution Damage 1992 (formerly 1969 and 1984 (Cmnd. 6183)) is in force, to enforce a claim for the discharge or escape of persistent oil from a ship (the Convention is in force in many major shipping countries including the UK, Bahamas, Panama, Liberia: see Merchant Shipping (Oil Pollution) (Parties to Convention) Order 1986 [S.I. 1986 No. 2225]);

Merchant Shipping Act 1995, s.177(4) and (5) in respect of any judgment given by a court in a country in respect of which the Brussels International Convention on the Establishment of an International Fund for Cooperation for Oil Pollution Damage 1992 (formerly 1971) is in force, to enforce a claim for liability for pollution damage.

Exclusion of jurisdiction under the Act of 1933. The jurisdiction of the court is excluded under **62.5.8** the Act of 1933 where—

(a) the judgment has at the time of the application been wholly satisfied (Act of 1933, s.2(1)(a));

(b) the judgment could not be enforced by execution at the date of the application in the country of the original court: Act of 1933, s.2(1)(b), and see *S.A. Consortium General Textiles v. Sun and Sand Ltd* [1978] Q.B. 279, 300 *per* Goff L.J.); or

(c) the Act of 1933 has been superseded by the 1968 Brussels or 1988 Lugano Convention (C.J.J.A. 1982, s.9(1) and Scheds. 1 and 3C, Art. 1).

"petition". A petition is presented in the Outer House: r. 14.2(h). The petition must be in **62.5.9** Form 14.4 in the approved printed form: rr. 4.1 and 14.4. The petition may be signed by the petitioner, counsel or other person having a right of audience, or an agent: r. 4.2(3)(d); and see r. 1.3(1) (definition of "counsel", "other person having a right of audience" and "agent") and note 1.3.4.

The petitioner must lodge the petition with the required steps of process (r. 4.4) and any documents founded on or adopted (r. 27.1(1)). A fee is payable on lodging the petition: see note 14.5.10.

On petitions generally, see Chap. 14.

Supporting documents

62.6.—(1) There shall be produced with the petition for registration referred to in rule 62.5 an affidavit—

(a) referring to the judgment or a certified copy of the judgment issued by the original court and authenticated by its seal; and

(b) stating—

    (i) the full name, title, trade or business and the usual or last known place of residence or business of the judgment creditor and the judgment debtor respectively;

    (ii) that the petitioner is entitled to have the judgment registered under the Act of 1920 or the Act of 1933, as the case may be;

    (iii) where the judgment is in respect of several matters, only some of which may be registered, those in respect of which the petitioner seeks registration;

(iv) the amount of the interest, if any, which under the law of the country of the original court has become due under the judgment up to the date of the affidavit;

(v) the amount of the judgment which is unsatisfied;

(vi) that at the date of presentation of the petition the judgment may be enforced by execution in the country of the original court;

(vii) that if the judgment were registered, the registration would not be, or be liable to be, set aside under section 4 of the Act of 1933; and

(viii) that the judgment is not a judgment to which section 5 of the Protection of Trading Interests Act 1980 (restriction on enforcement of certain overseas judgments) applies.

(2) There shall be produced with a petition referred to in rule 62.5 such other evidence with respect to the matters referred to in sub-paragraphs (b)(iv) and (b)(vi) of paragraph (1) as may be required having regard to the provisions of an order in Council made under section 1 of the Act of 1933 (power to extend the Act of 1933 to the country of the original court).

Deriv. R.C.S. 1965, r. 248(a)(part), and r. 249.2 amended by S.I. 1980 No. 891

62.6.1   *Productions.* The petitioner must produce with the petition (a) a certified copy of the judgment issued by the original court and authenticated by its seal (r. 27.1); (b) if necessary, a translation of any document lodged (r. 62.3); (c) an affidavit (r. 62.6(1)); and (d) if necessary, documents certifying the amount of interest which has become due under the judgment to the date of the affidavit and that at the date of the presentation of the petition the judgment may be enforced by execution in the country of the original court (r. 62.6(2)).

62.6.2   *Affidavit.* The affidavit should be in the form of a statement of evidence written in the first person. The affidavit should contain the evidence of the deponent in support of the averments in the petition. In particular the affidavit should deal with the matters listed in r. 62.6(1).

An affidavit should be sworn and signed by the deponent before any person who may competently take an oath, whether in Scotland or in any other country. In Scotland such a person may include a notary public, justice of the peace, sheriff, or any judge. The person taking the oath should also sign the affidavit. Where the affidavit is not in English a duly certified translation should also be lodged.

See also the definition of affidavit in r. 1.3(1).

62.6.3   *Setting aside of registration.* For circumstances where a judgment registered under the Act of 1933 may be set aside, see note 62.10.1.

62.6.4   *Protection of Trading Interests Act 1980, s.5.* This prohibits the recovery of any sum under the Act of 1920 or 1933 or at common law, in a judgment for multiple damages: Protection of Trading Interests Act 1980, s.5(1) and (2). A judgment for multiple damages is defined as a judgment for an amount arrived at by doubling, trebling, or otherwise multiplying a sum assessed as compensation for the loss or damage sustained by the person in whose favour the judgment is given: 1980 Act, s.5(3). Even the compensatory part of such a judgment may not be recovered. The Secretary of State also has powers under s.5(4) of the 1980 Act to extend the prohibitions to any judgment based on any rule of law appearing to him to be designed to restrain, distort, restrict or promote business competition: 1980 Act, s.5(2)(a) and (4). To date this power has not been exercised.

Warrant for registration under the Act of 1920 or 1933

62.7.—(1) The court shall, on being satisfied that the petition complies with the requirements of the Act of 1920 or the Act of 1933, as the case may be, pronounce an interlocutor granting warrant for the registration of the judgment.

(2) The interlocutor under paragraph (1) shall specify a date by which the judgment debtor may apply to the court to set aside the registration; and in fixing such date, regard shall be had to the place of residence of the judgment debtor.

(3) In fixing the date under paragraph (2), the court shall have regard, in the case of a judgment debtor furth of Scotland, to the periods for superseding extract of a decree in absence in rule 19.1(5).

Deriv. R.C.S. 1965, r. 248(b) amended by S.I. 1980 No. 891 and r. 249.5(1) (r. 62.7(1)); and r. 248(c) and r. 249.5(2) and (3) (r. 62.7(2) and(3))

General note. In Scotland a foreign judgment is enforced under statute by the court granting a **62.7.1** warrant for the judgment to be registered in the register of judgments of the Books of Council and Session (or sheriff court books in the case of certain maintenance judgments) for execution. On registration, the foreign judgment becomes a Scottish decree of registration and may be enforced by any diligence or sequestration or liquidation. Registration for execution gives the holder a decree of registration which is in effect a decree of the Court of Session (Bell's *Comm.*, i,4; *Taylor, Petr.* 1931 S.L.T. 260, 261 *per* Lord Pitman), and, on the warrant inserted by the Keeper of the Registers or his deputy on an extract of a registered document, diligence may be executed against the debtor's moveable property under s.3 of the Writs Execution (Scotland) Act 1877 as substituted by s.87(4) of the Debtors (Scotland) Act 1987. Diligence against heritable property may be executed by inhibition on the grant of letters of inhibition (see Chap. 59) or by action of adjudication founding on the decree of registration.

Period for setting aside registration under the Act of 1933. Under s.4 of the Act of 1933 the **62.7.2** judgment debtor may apply to the court for the setting aside of any registration which has taken place. The judgment creditor may not proceed to any step of execution until the expiry of the period for an application under s.4 of the Act of 1933 or if an application has been made within that period until the determination of the application.

Accordingly, the interlocutor granting warrant for registration must specify the date when the period for such an application expires: r. 62.7(1). In determining the period and date the court must have regard to the residence of the judgment debtor and, if he resides furth of Scotland, have regard to the periods for superseding extract of a decree of absence: r. 62.7(1) and (2). These are the number of days required in the ordinary course of post for the transmission of a letter from Edinburgh to the residence, registered office, other official address or place of business, as the case may be, of that defender and the transmission of an answer from there to Edinburgh being more than seven days: r. 19.1(5).

Expenses of petition and registration procedure. The reasonable costs of and incidental to the **62.7.3** registration procedure (including the obtaining of a certified copy judgment and the petition proceedings) are recoverable as if they were sums contained in the judgment being enforced: Act of 1920, s.9(3)(c); Act of 1933, s.2(6). The interlocutor granting the warrant for registration should provide for the awarding of expenses in relation to the petition procedure.

Registration of judgments under the Act of 1920 or 1933

62.8.—(1) Where the court pronounces an interlocutor under rule 62.7(1) granting warrant for registration, the Deputy Principal Clerk shall enter details of the judgment in a register of judgments under the Act of 1920 or the Act of 1933, as the case may be, kept in the Petition Department.

(2) On presentation by the petitioner to the Keeper of the Registers of—
   (a) a certified copy of the interlocutor under rule 62.7(1) granting warrant for registration,
   (b) the judgment or a certified copy of the judgment and any translation of it, and
¹ (c) any certificate of currency conversion under rule 62.2(1)(b),
they shall be registered in the register of judgments of the Books of Council and Session.

(3) An extract of a registered judgment with a warrant for execution shall not be issued by the Keeper of the Registers until the certificate mentioned in rule 62.10(3) is produced to him.

Deriv. R.C.S. 1965, r. 249.6 (r. 62.8(1)); and r. 248(d), and r. 249.7, both amended by S.I. 1986 No. 1941 (r. 62.8(2) and (3))

---

¹ R. 62.8(2)(c) amended by S.I. 1996 No. 2168 (minor correction).

"Keeper of the Registers". This is the Keeper of the Registers of Scotland: r. 1.3(1). The **62.8.1** Register of Judgments is at Meadowbank House, 153 London Road, Edinburgh EH8 7AU; tel. 0131–659 6111; fax 0131–459 1221; DX ED300.

"certified copy of the interlocutor". A copy of the interlocutor is typed by the agent and **62.8.2** presented to the clerk of session in the Petition Department. The clerk checks it, certifies it as a true copy and stamps it with the court stamp.
   A fee is payable.

62.8.3   *"certified copy of the judgment".* The copy of the judgment should be authenticated with the seal of the original court.

62.8.4   *"translation".* See r. 62.3.

62.8.5   *"certificate of currency conversion".* This should be obtained from the clerk of session in the Petition Department duly signed by him: r. 62.2(3); and see notes 62.2.4 and 62.2.5.

62.8.6   *Registration fee.* A fee will be payable to the Keeper of the Registers for registration and any extract: see the Fees in the Registers of Scotland Order 1991 [S.I. 1991 No. 2093].

62.8.7   *Certificate of confirmation of registration.* Where the court either receives no application by the judgment debtor to set aside the registration within the period stated in the interlocutor or refuses such an application, the Deputy Principal Clerk may, at the request of the petitioner, issue a certificate certifying this: r. 62.10(3). The petitioner has to produce this certificate to the Keeper of the Registers before he can obtain an extract of the registered judgment and proceed to execution: r. 62.8(3).

Service on judgment debtor

62.9. On registration of a judgment under rule 62.8(2), the petitioner shall serve a notice of the registration on the judgment debtor in Form 62.9.

Deriv. R.C.S. 1965, r. 248(e) amended by S.I. 1986 No. 1941 and r. 249.8

62.9.1   *General note.* The purpose of service on the judgment debtor is to enable him to apply under s.9(4)(b) of the Act of 1920 or s.4 of the Act of 1933 to set aside the registration or, in the case of registration under the Act of 1920, to present a petition for suspension and interdict.

62.9.2   *"serve".* For methods, see Chap. 16, Pt. I.

62.9.3   *"judgment debtor".* See note 62.4.2.

Application to set aside registration under the Act of 1920 or 1933

62.10.—(1) An application by a judgment debtor to set aside the registration of a judgment shall be made by note and supported by affidavit and any documentary evidence.

(2) In relation to such an application, the court may order such inquiry as it thinks fit.

(3) Where no such application is made by the date specified in the interlocutor pronounced under rule 62.7(2) or where the application has been made and refused, the Deputy Principal Clerk shall, at the request of the petitioner, issue a certificate to that effect.

(4) Subject to paragraph (5), where such an application is granted, a certificate to that effect issued by the Deputy Principal Clerk shall be sufficient warrant to the Keeper of the Registers to cancel the registration and return the judgment to the petitioner.

(5) Where the court makes an order under section 5(3) of the Act of 1933 (judgment ordered to be registered for balance payable), it shall pronounce an interlocutor—

(a) recalling the warrant for registration granted under rule 62.7; and
(b) granting warrant for registration of the judgment in respect of the balance remaining payable at the date of the original petition for registration.

Deriv. R.C.S. 1965, r. 249.9 (r. 62.10(1) and (2)), r. 248(f)(part) and r. 249.11 (r. 62.10(3))
and r. 248(g) (r. 62.10(4))

62.10.1   *General note.* Following registration under Pt. II of the Act of 1920, the court may set aside the registration of a judgment on such terms as it thinks fit: Act of 1920, s.9(4)(b).
Following registration under the Act of 1933, the court—
(a) shall set aside the registration if it is satisfied—

(i) that the judgment is not a "judgment" under the Act and so was registered in contravention of the Act;

(ii) that the courts of the country of the original court had no jurisdiction in the circumstances of the case (see note 62.10.2);

(iii) that the judgment debtor, being the defender in the proceedings in the original court, did not (notwithstanding that process may have been duly served on him in accordance with the law of the country of the original court) receive notice of those proceedings in sufficient time to enable him to defend the proceedings and did not appear;

(iv) that the judgment was obtained by fraud: see *Owens Bank Ltd v. Bracco* [1992] 2 A.C. 444, 480 *et seq. per* Lord Bridge of Harwich;

(v) that the enforcement of the judgment would be contrary to public policy in this country; or

(vi) that the rights under the judgment were not vested in the person by whom the application for registration was made (Act of 1933, s. 4(1)(*a*)); or

(*b*) may set aside the registration if it is satisfied that the matter in dispute in the proceedings in the original court had, previously to those proceedings, been the subject of a final and conclusive judgment of a court having jurisdiction in the matter (Act of 1933, s. 4(1)(*b*)); or

(*c*) may, if the applicant satisfies it that either an appeal is pending or that he is entitled and intends to appeal, set aside the registration or adjourn the application to set aside until the expiry of a period which appears to the court to be reasonably sufficient for the applicant to have the appeal disposed on such terms as it thinks just (Act of 1933, s. 5(1); and see *S.A. Consortium General Textiles v. Sun and Sand Ltd* [1978] Q.B. 279, 306 *per* Goff, L.J.).

Jurisdiction of the courts of the country of the original court. Where the courts have had no jurisdiction the registration of the judgment may be set aside: Act of 1933, s. 4(1)(*a*)(ii). These courts are deemed to have jurisdiction if paragraphs (*a*) to (*c*) in s. 4(2) of the Act of 1933 apply. In relation to paragraph (*a*), see *Société Co-opérative Sidmetal v. Titan International Ltd* [1966] 1 Q.B. 828 (*re* submission to the jurisdiction) and *S.A. Consortium General Textiles v. Sun and Sand Ltd* [1978] Q.B. 279 (*re* prorogation agreement under s. 4(1)(*a*)(iii)). **62.10.2**

Application for enforcement abroad under the Act of 1920 or 1933

62.11.—(1) An application under section 10 of the Act of 1920 or the Act of 1933, as the case may be, for a certified copy of a judgment pronounced by the court shall be made by letter to the Deputy Principal Clerk.

(2) On receipt of such an application, the Deputy Principal Clerk shall issue under the seal of the court a copy of the judgment certified by him in Form 62.11.

(3) Where such an application is made under section 10 of the Act of 1933, the Deputy Principal Clerk shall issue with the certified copy of the judgment a further certificate under the seal of the court signed by him containing the details, and having appended the documents, mentioned in paragraph (4).

(4) A certificate under paragraph (3) shall—

(*a*) state—

(i) the manner in which the principal writ or counterclaim was served on the judgment debtor;

(ii) whether or not the judgment debtor entered appearance or lodged answers in the process of the cause;

(iii) any objection made to the jurisdiction;

(iv) that the time limit for appeal has expired and that no appeal has been taken, or that an appeal was taken but was refused; and

(v) such other particulars as may be required by the foreign court which may enable execution of the judgment; and

(*b*) number, identify and have appended to it a copy of—

(i) the principal writ or counterclaim showing the manner in which such writ was served on the judgment debtor;

(ii) the pleadings, if any, in the cause resulting in the judgment; and

(iii) a copy of the opinion, if any, of the judge or judges who issued the judgment.

(5) Where necessary, the applicant shall provide the copies of the documents mentioned in paragraph (4).

Deriv. R.C.S. 1965, r. 248(*h*) and r. 249.13

62.11.1   *General note*. Recognition and enforcement of judgments is almost invariably done on a reciprocal basis. Accordingly this rule provides for the obtaining of a certified copy of a judgment together with an additional certificate of particulars for the purpose of enforcement abroad under either the Act of 1920 or the Act of 1933.

62.11.2   *"judgment"*. For definition, see notes 62.4.2 (Act of 1920) and 62.4.3 (Act of 1933). The Act of 1920 allows only judgments obtained in the Court of Session to be enforced abroad: Act of 1920, s. 10(1)(*a*). This includes a decree obtained by the registration of a document of debt in the Books of Council and Session: *Taylor, Petr.* 1931 S.L.T. 260.

The Act of 1933 allows any judgment given by a court or tribunal in the UK under which a sum of money is payable, not being a sum payable in respect of taxes or other charges of a like nature or in respect of a fine or other penalty, to be enforced abroad: Act of 1933, s. 10(2). Presumably this will include sums awarded in sheriff court decrees, or industrial tribunal decisions, and compensation orders under s. 58(1) of the Criminal Justice (Scotland) Act 1980, amongst others. R. 62.11, however, applies only to judgments pronounced by the Court of Session: r. 62.11.

62.11.3   *"letter to the Deputy Principal Clerk"*. The address and telephone number, etc., of the Deputy Principal Clerk are: The Deputy Principal Clerk of Session, Court of Session, 2 Parliament Square, Edinburgh EH1 1RQ; tel. 031–225 2595; fax 031–225 8213; DX ED306.

PART III

REGISTRATION OF AWARDS UNDER THE ARBITRATION (INTERNATIONAL INVESTMENT DISPUTES) ACT 1966

Application and interpretation of this Part
62.12.—(1) This Part applies to the registration of awards under the Arbitration (International Investment Disputes) Act 1966.

(2) In this Part—
"the Act of 1966" means the Arbitration (International Investment Disputes) Act 1966;
"award" has the meaning assigned to it in section 1(7) of the Act of 1966;
"the Convention" means the Convention mentioned in section 1(1) of the Act of 1966.

Deriv. R.C.S. 1965, r. 249A.1 inserted by S.I. 1971 No. 1809 (r. 62.12(2))

62.12.1   *General note*. Part III of this Chapter provides rules for the recognition and enforcement in Scotland of awards made by the International Centre for Settlement of Investment Disputes. The International Centre acts under the 1965 Washington Convention on the Settlement of Investment Disputes Between States and Nationals of Other States. The Arbitration (International Investment Disputes) Act 1966 was passed, *inter alia*, to allow for recognition and enforcement in the UK of awards made by the International Centre.

Part III of this Chapter has been made under s. 7 of the Act of 1966: A.S. (R.C.S. 1994) 1994, Sched. 1 [S.I. 1994 No. 1443]. Accordingly a word or expression used in Pt. III which is also used in the Act of 1966 has the meaning given in that Act unless the contrary intention appears: Interpretation Act 1978, s. 11.

62.12.2   *"award"*. This includes any decision interpreting, revising, or annulling an award being a decision under the Convention and any decision as to costs which under the Convention is to form part of the award: Act of 1966, s. 1(7)(*a*).

62.12.3   *"the Convention"*. This is the Convention on the Settlement of Investment Disputes Between States and Nationals of Other States opened for signature in Washington on 18th March 1965, set out in the Schedule to the Act of 1966.

Applications for registration under the Act of 1966
62.13.—(1) An application for recognition or enforcement of an award under Article 54 of the Convention shall be made by petition.

(2) There shall be produced with such a petition an affidavit–
(a) exhibiting a copy of the award certified under the Convention; and
(b) stating—
    (i) the full name, title, trade or business and the usual or the last known place of residence or, where appropriate, of the business of the petitioner and of the party against whom the award was made;
    (ii) that the petitioner is entitled to have the award registered under the Act of 1966;
    (iii) the amount of the award which is unsatisfied;
    (iv) whether the enforcement of the award has been sisted (provisionally or otherwise) under the Convention and whether any, and if so what, application has been made under the Convention which, if granted, might result in a sist of enforcement of the award.

Deriv. R.C.S. 1965, r. 249A.2 and 3 inserted by S.I. 1971 No. 1809

"petition". A petition is presented in the Outer House: r. 14.2(h). The petition must be in **62.13.1** Form 14.4 in the official printed form: rr. 4.1 and 14.4. The petition may be signed by the petitioner, counsel or other person having a right of audience, or an agent: r. 4.2(3)(d); and see r. 1.3(1) (definition of "counsel", "other person having a right of audience" and "agent") and note 1.3.4.

The petitioner must lodge the petition with the required steps of process (r. 4.4) and any documents founded on or adopted (r. 27.1(1)). A fee is payable on lodging the petition: see note 14.5.10.

On petitions generally, see Chap. 14.

Productions. The petitioner must produce with the petition (a) a copy of the award under the **62.13.2** Convention certified by the Secretary-General of the International Centre (Act of 1966, Sched., Art. 54(2); and r. 17.1); (b) an affidavit (r. 62.13(2)); and (c) if necessary, a translation of any document lodged (r. 62.3).

Affidavit. The affidavit should be in the form of a statement of evidence written in the first **62.13.3** person. The affidavit should contain the evidence of the deponent in support of the averments in the petition. In particular the affidavit should deal with the matters listed in r. 62.6(1).

An affidavit should be sworn and signed by the deponent before any person who may competently take an oath, whether in Scotland or in any other country. In Scotland such a person may include a notary public, justice of the peace, sheriff, or any judge. The person taking the oath should also sign the affidavit. Where the affidavit is not in English a duly certified translation should also be lodged.

See also the definition of affidavit in r. 1.3(1).

Warrant for registration under the Act of 1966

62.14. The court shall, subject to rule 62.17 (sist of enforcement), on being satisfied that the petition complies with the requirements of the Act of 1966, pronounce an interlocutor granting warrant for the registration of the award.

Deriv. R.C.S. 1965, r. 249A.5 inserted by S.I. 1971 No. 1809

Registration under the Act of 1966

62.15.—(1) Where the court pronounces an interlocutor under rule 62.14 granting warrant for registration, the Deputy Principal Clerk shall enter details of the interlocutor and the award in a register of awards under the Act of 1966.

(2) On presentation by the petitioner to the Keeper of the Registers of—
(a) a certified copy of the interlocutor under rule 62.14,
(b) a certified copy of the award and any translation of it; and
¹ (c) any certificate of currency conversion under rule 62.2(1)(b),
they shall be registered in the register of judgments of the Books of Council and Session.

Release 42: 14 November 1996

(3) An extract of the registered award with warrant for execution shall not be issued by the Keeper of the Registers until a certificate of service under rule 62.16 is produced to him.

Deriv. R.C.S. 1965, r. 249A.6 (r. 62.15(1)), and r. 249A.7(3)(part) (r. 62.15(3)), both inserted by S.I. 1971 No. 1809

---

[1] R. 62.15(2)(c) amended by S.I. 1996 No. 2168 (minor correction).

62.15.1 *"Keeper of the Registers".* This is the Keeper of the Registers of Scotland: r. 1.3(1). The Register of Judgments is at Meadowbank House, 153 London Road, Edinburgh EH8 7AU; tel. 031–659 6111; fax 031–459 1221; DX ED300.

62.15.2 *"certified copy of the interlocutor".* A copy of the interlocutor is typed by the agent and presented to the clerk of session in the Petition Department. The clerk checks it, certifies it as a true copy and stamps it with the court stamp.
A fee is payable.

62.15.3 *"certified copy of the award".* The copy of the award should be certified by the Secretary-General of the International Centre for Settlement of Investment Disputes: Act of 1966, Sched., Art. 54(2).

62.15.4 *"translation".* See r. 62.3.

62.15.5 *"certificate of currency conversion".* In obtaining this, notwithstanding the provisions of r. 62.2(1), the date of conversion in the certified statement should be the date of the award: Act of 1966, s. 1(3).
The certificate should be obtained from the clerk of session and should be signed by him: r. 62.2(3); and see notes 62.2.4 and 62.2.5.

62.15.6 *Registration fee.* A fee will be payable to the Keeper of the Registers for registration and any extract: see the Fees in the Registers of Scotland Order 1991 [S.I. 1991 No. 2093].

Service on party against whom award made
62.16. On registration under rule 62.15, the petitioner shall forthwith serve a notice of the registration on the party against whom the award was made in Form 62.16.

Deriv. R.C.S. 1965, r. 249A.7(1) and (2) inserted by S.I. 1971 No. 1809

62.16.1 *"serve".* For methods of service, see Chap. 16, Pt. I.

Sist of enforcement under the Act of 1966
62.17.—(1) Where it appears to the court that—
(a) the enforcement of the award has been sisted (whether provisionally or otherwise) under the Convention, or
(b) any application has been made under the Convention which, if granted, might result in a sist of the enforcement of the award,
the court shall, or in the case referred to in sub-paragraph (b) may, sist the petition for such time as it thinks fit.
(2) Where the court has granted a warrant for registration under rule 62.14, the party against whom the award was made may apply to the court for suspension or interdict of execution of the award.
(3) An application under paragraph (2) shall—
(a) be made on ground (a) or (b) of paragraph (1);
(b) notwithstanding rule 60.2 (form of applications for suspension), be made by note in the process of the petition under rule 62.13; and
(c) be accompanied by an affidavit stating the relevant facts.

Deriv. R.C.S. 1965, r. 249A.8 and 9 inserted by S.I. 1971 No. 1809

62.17.1 *"suspension or interdict".* See Chap. 60.

62.17.2 *"note".* For applications by note, see r. 15.2.

PART IV

EUROPEAN COMMUNITY JUDGMENTS

Interpretation of this Part
   62.18.—(1) In this Part—
     "Community judgment" means any decision, judgment or order which
       is enforceable under or in accordance with—
  [2] (a) Article 244 or 256 of the E.E.C. Treaty,
     (b) Article 18, 159 or 164 of the Euratom Treaty,
     (c) Article 44 or 92 of the E.C.S.C. Treaty, or
  [1] (d) Article 82 of Regulation 40/94 of December 20, 1993 (regula tion
       of the Council of the European Union: on the community trade
       mark).
     "Euratom inspection order" means an order made by or in the exercise
       of the functions of the President of the European Court or by the
       Commission of the European Communities under Article 81 of the
       Euratom Treaty;
     "European Court" means the Court of Justice of the European
       Communities;
     "order for enforcement" means an order by or under the authority of
       the Secretary of State that the Community judgment to which it is
       appended is to be registered for enforcement in the United
       Kingdom.
   (2) In paragraph (1), the expressions "E.E.C. Treaty", "Euratom Treaty"
and "E.C.S.C. Treaty" have the meanings assigned respectively in Schedule
1 to the European Communities Act 1972.

Deriv. R.C.S. 1965, r. 296F inserted by S.I. 1972 No. 1982

---

  [1] R. 62.1.8(1)(d) inserted by S.I. 1998 No. 2637 (effective 1st December 1998).
  [2] R. 62.18(1)(a) amended by S.I. 1999 No.1281 (effective 1st May 1999).

  General note. Part IV of this Chapter provides rules for the enforcement of (a) decisions of the   **62.18.1**
Council and Commission of the E.C. which impose pecuniary obligations on persons other than
States or (b) orders made by the President of the European Court or the Commission under Art.
81 of the Euratom Treaty.
  The term "European Economic Community" in the E.E.C. Treaty was replaced by the term
"European Community" by Art. G(1) of Title II of the Treaty on European Union (Maas
tricht): see European Communities Act 1972, s.1(2)(k) as amended by the European Commu
nities (Amendment) Act 1993, s.1(1).
  The reference to Art. 82 of Regulation 40/94 may be found in the Official Journal (of the
E.U.) 1994, 11/1.

Register of European Community judgments
   62.19. A register shall be kept by the Deputy Principal Clerk for the
purpose of registering—
     (a) any Community judgment to which the Secretary of State has at
       tached an order for enforcement;
     (b) any Euratom inspection order; or
     (c) any order of the European Court that enforcement of a registered
       Community judgment shall be suspended.

Deriv. R.C.S. 1965, r. 296G inserted by S.I. 1972 No. 1982

Applications for registration of European Community judgments
   62.20.—(1) An application for registration of a Community judgment or
Euratom inspection order shall be made by petition.
   (2) Where the application is for registration of a Community judgment
under which a sum of money is payable, the petition shall set out—
     (a) the name, trade or business and the usual or last known place of
       residence or business of the judgment debtor, so far as known to the
       petitioner; and

(b) the amount of the judgment which remains unsatisfied.

(3) There shall be produced with a petition referred to in paragraph (1) the Community judgment and the order for its enforcement or the Euratom inspection order, as the case may be, or a copy of it.

Deriv. R.C.S. 1965, r. 296H(i)(part) (r. 62.20(1)), r. 296H(iii)(a) and (b) (r. 62.20(2)), and r.296H(ii)(part) (r. 62.20(3)), all inserted by S.I. 1972 No. 1982

62.20.1   *"petition"*. A petition is presented in the Outer House: r. 14.2(h). The petition must be in Form 14.4 in the official printed form: rr. 4.1 and 14.4. The petition may be signed by the petitioner, counsel or other person having a right of audience, or an agent: r. 4.2; and see r.1.3(1) (definition of "counsel", "other person having a right of audience" and "agent") and note 1.3.4.

The petitioner must lodge the petition with the required steps of process (r. 4.4) and any documents founded on or adopted (r. 27.1(1)). A fee is payable on lodging the petition: see note 14.5.10.

On petitions generally, see Chap. 14.

Warrant for registration of European Community judgments

62.21.—(1) On an application being made under rule 62.20, the court shall direct that any Euratom inspection order or any Community judgment which has appended to it an order for enforcement shall be entered in the register kept under rule 62.19 and—

(a) in respect of a Community judgment, subject to paragraph (2), pronounce an interlocutor granting warrant for registration of the judgment in the Books of Council and Session; or

(b) in respect of a Euratom inspection order, pronounce such inter locutor as is necessary for the purpose of ensuring that effect is given to that order.

(2) Where it appears that a Community judgment under which a sum of money is payable has been partly satisfied at the date of the application under rule 62.20, warrant for registration in the Books of Council and Session shall be granted only in respect of the balance remaining payable at that date.

Deriv. R.C.S. 1965, r. 296H(i)(part) (r. 62.21(1)) inserted by S.I. 1972 No. 1982

Registration of European Community judgments

62.22.—(1) On presentation by the petitioner to the Keeper of the Registers of—

(a) a certified copy of an interlocutor pronounced under rule 62.21(1)(a),

(b) the Community judgment or a certified copy of it and any translation of it, and

[1] (c) any certificate of currency conversion under rule 62.2(1)(b), ik t3they shall immediately be registered in the register of judgments of the Books of Council and Session.

(2) On registration under paragraph (1), the Keeper of the Registers shall issue an extract of the registered Community judgment with a warrant for execution.

———

[1] R. 62.22(1)(c) amended by S.I. 1996 No. 2168 (minor correction).

62.22.1   *"Keeper of the Registers"*. This is the Keeper of the Registers of Scotland: r. 1.3(1). The Register of Judgments is at Meadowbank House, 153 London Road, Edinburgh EH8 7AU; tel. 0131–659 6111; fax 0131–459 1221; DX ED300.

62.22.2   *"certified copy of the interlocutor"*. A copy of the interlocutor is typed by the agent and presented to the clerk of session in the Petition Department. The clerk checks it, certifies it as a true copy and stamps it with the court stamp.

A fee is payable.

62.22.3   *"translation"*. See r. 62.3.

62.22.4   *"certificate of currency conversion"*. The certificate should be obtained from the clerk of session in the Petition Department and should be signed by him: r. 62.2(3); and see notes 62.2.4 and 62.2.5.

62.22.5   *Registration fee*. A fee will be payable to the Keeper of the Registers for registration and any extract: see the Fees in the Registers of Scotland Order 1991 [S.I. 1991 No. 2093].

Service on judgment debtor of European Community judgment

62.23. On an interlocutor being pronounced under rule 62.21(1)(a), the petitioner shall forthwith serve a copy of it on the person against whom the Community judgment was given or the Euratom inspection order was made, as the case may be.

Deriv. R.C.S. 1965, r.296H(iv)(part) inserted by S.I. 1972 No. 1982

"serve". For methods of service, see Chap. 16, Pt I.   **62.23.1**

Variation or cancellation of registration

62.24.—(1) An application for the variation or cancellation of any registration shall be made by note in the process of the petition under rule 62.20(1).

(2) Where the court grants an application under paragraph (1), it may direct that the entry in the register kept under rule 62.19, and, in the case of variation of a Community judgment, the entry in the Books of Council and Session, shall be varied as sought by the noter.

Deriv. R.C.S. 1965, r.296J inserted by S.I. 1972 No. 1982

"note". For applications by note, see r.15.2.   **62.24.1**

Suspension of enforcement of Community judgments

62.25.—(1) An order of the European Court that enforcement of a registered Community judgment be suspended—
  (a) shall—
    (i) on production of the order to the Court of Session, and
    (ii) on application made by note,
    be registered forthwith, and
  (b) shall be of the same effect as if the order had been an order made by the Court of Session on the date of its registration suspending the execution of the judgment for the same period and on the same conditions as are stated in the order of the European Court.

(2) No steps to enforce the judgment mentioned in paragraph (1) shall be taken while such an order of the European Court remains in force.

Deriv. R.C.S. 1965, r.296K inserted by S.I. 1972 No. 1982

General note. Enforcement of a community judgment enforceable under Art.192 of the E.C. **62.25.1**
Treaty may be suspended only by a judgment of the European Court: E.C. Treaty, Art.192. R. 62.25 provides for (a) the procedure to enforce a European Court order suspending a community judgment; and (b) the effect of a European Court order suspending a community judgment.

[1] PART V

RECOGNITION AND ENFORCEMENT OF JUDGMENTS UNDER THE CIVIL
JURISDICTION AND JUDGMENTS ACT 1982 OR UNDER COUNCIL REGULATION
(E.C.) NO. 44/2001 OF 22ND DECEMBER 2001

Application and interpretation of this Part

[1] **62.26.**—(1) This Part applies to the recognition and enforcement of a judgment under the Civil Jurisdiction and Judgments Act 1982 or under the Council Regulation.

(2) Unless the context otherwise requires, in this Part—
  "the Act of 1982" means the Civil Jurisdiction and Judgments Act 1982;
  "Contracting State" has the meaning assigned in section 1(3) of the Act of 1982;

"judgment" includes an authentic instrument or court settlement.

"the Council Regulation" means Council Regulation (E.C.) No. 44/2001 of 22nd December 2000 on jurisdiction and the recognition and enforcement of judgments in civil and commercial matters;

"Member State" has the same meaning as Member State in the Council Regulation.

Deriv. R.C.S. 1965, r. 249D(1)(part) (r. 62.26(2)) inserted by S.I. 1986 No. 1941

---

[1] Part V and r.62.26 substituted by S.S.I. 2004 No. 52 (effective 1st March 2004).

62.26.1   *General note.* Many foreign judgments are now enforced in Scotland under the C.J.J.A. 1982. The C.J.J.A. 1982 did two things in the field of recognition and enforcement, namely (1) replaced the Judgments Extension Act 1868 or (in the sheriff court) the Inferior Courts Judgments Extension Act 1882 in relation to reciprocal recognition and enforcement of judgments between different U.K. jurisdictions; and (2) provided a new regime for the reciprocal recognition and enforcement of judgments between the U.K. and other member States of the E.C. The latter regime uses the 1968 Brussels Convention as amended by the 1971 Protocol and the 1978, 1982, and 1989 Accession Conventions with regard to the other member States of the E.C. (see note 62.26.2). The C.J.J.A. 1982 was amended on each occasion a new state acceded to the 1968 Convention to include a reference to the new state. Following the 1989 Accession Convention to admit Spain and Portugal some additional textual changes were made to the 1968 Convention. These were brought into force in the U.K. by the Civil Jurisdiction and Judgments Act 1982 (Amendment) Order 1990 [S.I. 1990 No. 2591] on 1st December 1991.

The major amendment to the C.J.J.A. 1982 was made by the C.J.J.A. 1991 which came into force on 1st May 1992. This introduced a requirement for reciprocal recognition and enforcement parallel to the 1968 Brussels Convention built on the almost identically worded 1988 Lugano Convention between the U.K. and the member States of the European Free Trade Association (EFTA). As states leave EFTA and join the E.C. they will have to accede to the 1968 Brussels Convention: C.J.J.A. 1982, Sched. 1, Art. 63. To fill their absence the 1988 Lugano Convention envisages the accession to it of non-EFTA States, perhaps from Eastern Europe: C.J.J.A. 1982, Sched. 3C, Art. 62(1)(b) (see note 62.26.3).

In addition the C.J.J.A. 1982 provided that Her Majesty could by Order in Council, apply the terms of the 1968 Brussels Convention for the regulation of jurisdiction and the recognition and enforcement of judgments between the U.K., the Isle of Man, any Channel Island, and any U.K. colony. C.J.J.A. 1982, s.39. Her Majesty has used this power to regulate the jurisdiction and enforcement of judgments between the U.K. and Gibraltar (apply articles 1–54, 57 and 65 of the Convention): Civil Jurisdiction and Judgments Act 1980 (Gibraltar) Order 1997 (S.I. 1997 No. 2602).

Pt V and r.62.26 were replaced by A.S. (R.C.S.A. (Miscellaneous) 2004 [S.S.I. 2004 No. 52]. The purpose of the A.S. was to include in Pt. V of Chap.62 references to the Council Regulation (EC) No. 44/2001 on jurisdiction and the recognition and enforcement of judgments in civil and commercial matters between Member States of the EU except Denmark (the Brussels I Regulation). Under this new regime a judgment is enforceable immediately on completion of the formalities in art. 53; refusal of recognition is further restricted.

62.26.2   *Commencement date of Convention.* Under Art. 54 of the 1968 and Lugano Conventions, in order to maintain reciprocity, it is provided that the conventions apply to a judgment the proceedings for which were instituted, or an authentic instrument which was drawn up or registered, after the relevant convention came into force in both the state of origin and the state of destination of the judgment. An exception to this is when the judgment was given after the Convention had come into force on proceedings started before the date of operation but was founded in jurisdictional rules which accorded either with the relevant convention or were contained in a separate convention between the two states: C.J.J.A. 1982, Scheds 1 and 3C, Art. 54.

Accordingly it is important to know the date when the relevant convention came first into force in *both* the U.K. *and* the other contracting state. These are as follows:

(1) *1968 Brussels Convention*:
   (a) with regard to Belgium, France, Germany, Italy, Luxembourg, Netherlands, and Denmark, 1st January 1987;
   (b) with regard to the Republic of Ireland, 1st June 1988;
   (c) with regard to Greece, 1st October 1989;
   (d) with regard to Spain, 1st December 1991;
   (e) with regard to Portugal, 1st July 1992.
   (f) with regard to Gibraltar, 1st February 1998.

(2) *1988 Lugano Convention*:
- (a) with regard to Switzerland, 1st May 1992;
- (b) with regard to Sweden, 1st January 1993;
- (c) with regard to Norway, 1st May 1993;
- (d) with regard to Finland, 1st July 1993;
- (e) with regard to Iceland, 1st December 1995;
- (f) with regard to Austria, 1st September 1996.

Further information on the dates when the convention came into force in other states may be obtained from the Treaty Records Section, Foreign and Commonwealth Office, Room CL 505, Clive House, Petty France, London SW1H 9HD; tel. 0171–270 4079.

Definitions in the Act of 1982. Part V of this Chapter has been made under s.48 of the C.J.J.A. **62.26.3** 1982 (rr. 62.28 and 62.40 are made under s.12 of the C.J.J.A. 1982). Accordingly a word or expression used in Pt V which is also used in the C.J.J.A. 1982 has the meaning given in that Act unless the contrary intention appears: Interpretation Act 1978, s.11. The following are important definitions used in Pt V:

(1) "*Contracting State*". By themselves these words mean—
(a) in the application of the provisions in relation to the Brussels Convention, a Brussels Contracting State; and
(b) in the application of the provisions in relation to the Lugano Convention, a Lugano Contracting State.
A Brussels Contracting State is either one of the original parties to the 1968 Convention or a party acceding to that convention under the relevant Accession Convention when the Accession Convention has come into force in both it and the U.K. (see note 62.26.2). A Lugano Contracting State is one of the original parties to the 1988 Convention in relation to which that convention has taken effect in both it and the U.K. (see note 62.26.2).

(2) "*judgment*". The C.J.J.A. 1982 gives three separate definitions, namely—
(a) for general purposes, any judgment or order (by whatever name called) given or made by a court in civil proceedings: C.J.J.A. 1982, s.50;
(b) for the purpose of recognition and enforcement of judgments from another part of the UK it includes—
- (i) any judgment or order (by whatever name called) given or made by a court of law in the UK;
- (ii) any judgment or order not covered by (a) which has been entered in England and Wales or Northern Ireland in the High Court or County Court;

    (iii) any document registered for execution in the Books of Council and Session or in the sheriff court books;

    (iv) any award or order made by a tribunal in any part of the UK which is enforceable there without a court order;

    (v) any arbitration award which is enforceable in the part of the UK in which it was made in the same way as a court judgment: C.J.J.A. 1982, s.18(2); and

(c) for the purpose of enforcement of judgments from another Contracting State it means any judgment given by a court or tribunal of a Contracting Member State whatever the judgment may be called, including a decree, order, decision, or writ of execution as well as the determination of costs or expenses by an officer of the court: C.J.J.A. 1982, Scheds. 1 and 3C, Art. 25; Council Regulation, Art. 32.

In (2) above the meaning must be read subject to the restrictions on the subject-matter of judgments contained in s.18 of the C.J.J.A. 1982. In (3) above the meaning must be read subject to the restrictions on subject-matter contained in Art. 1 of the 1968 and Lugano Convention in Scheds. 1 and 3C to the C.J.J.A. 1982 and Art. 1 of the Council Regulation..

(3) *"authentic instrument"*. This is a document which has been formally drawn up and registered as an authentic instrument in the Contracting Member State and is enforceable in accordance with the procedures for judgments in another Contracting Member State: C.J.J.A. 1982, Scheds. 1 and 3C, Art. 50; Council Regulation, Art. 57. In the Scottish context this would include a document registered for execution in the Books of Council and Session or sheriff court books.

(4) *"court settlement"*. This is a settlement which has been approved by a court in the course of proceedings and is enforceable in the state in which it was concluded: C.J.J.A. 1982, Scheds. 1 and 3C, Art. 51; Council Regulation, Art. 58.

Disapplication of certain rules to this Part

[1] **62.27.** The following provisions shall not apply to an application under this Part in addition to those rules mentioned in rule 62.1:—

    rule 4.1(1) (printed form for petition),

    rule 14.4 (form of petitions).

-----

[1] R.62.27 substituted by S.S.I. 2004 No. 52 (effective 1st March, 2004).

General note. The official printed form of petition does not have to be used where a petition is **62.27.1** required under this Part of Chap. 62. Special forms of petition are provided in Forms 62.28 and 62.38 for petitions under the rules to which they relate.

The new rule is in identical terms to the old rule.

Enforcement of judgments, authentic instruments or court settlements from another Contracting State or Member State

[1] **62.28.**—(1) An application under—

(a) section 4 of, and Article 31 (enforcement of judgment from another Contracting State) or Article 50 (enforcement of authentic instrument or court settlement from another Contracting State) of the Convention in Schedule 1 or 3C to, the Act of 1982; or

(b) Article 38 (enforcement of judgment from Member State), Article 57 (enforcement of authentic instrument from another Member State) or Article 58 (enforcement of court settlement from another Member State) of the Council Regulation,

shall be made by petition in Form 62.28.

(2) Subject to paragraph (3), there shall be produced with the petition—

(a) an authentic copy of the judgment to be registered;

(b) a document which establishes that, according to the law of the country in which the judgment has been given, the judgment is enforceable and has been served;

(c) where judgment has been given in absence (that is to say, in default of appearance), the original or a certified copy of the document which establishes that the party against whom judgment was given in

absence was served with the document initiating the proceedings or
with an equivalent document;
  (d) where applicable, a document showing that the applicant is in receipt
of legal aid in the country in which the judgment was given;
  (e) an affidavit stating—
    (i) whether the judgment provides for the payment of a sum of money;
    (ii) whether interest is recoverable on the judgment under the law of
the country in which judgment was given and, if so, the rate of
interest, the date from which interest is due and the date on
which interest ceases to accrue;
    (iii) an address within the jurisdiction of the court for service on or
intimation to the petitioner;
    (iv) the usual or last known place of residence or business of the
person against whom the judgment was given;
    (v) the grounds on which the petitioner is entitled to enforce the
judgment; and
    (vi) the part of the judgment which is unsatisfied.
  (3) Paragraph (2)(b) and (d) shall not apply to a petition under Article 38
(enforcement of judgment from another Member State), Article 57
(enforcement of authentic instrument from another Member State) or
Article 58 (enforcement of settlement from another Member State) of the
Council Regulation but there shall be produced with such a petition a
certificate under Article 54 (standard form of certificate of judgment),
Article 57 (standard form of certificate of authentic instrument) or Article 58
(standard form of certificate of court settlement) of the Council Regulation.
  (4) Where the petitioner does not produce a document required under
paragraph (2)(a) to (d) or (3), the court may—
  (a) fix a period within which that document is to be lodged;
  (b) accept an equivalent document; or
  (c) dispense with the requirement to produce the document.

Deriv. R.C.S. 1965, r.249E(1)(a) (r.62.28(1)), and r.249E(2) and (3) (r.62.28(2) and (3)), both
inserted by S.I. 1986 No. 1941.

---

[1] R.62.28 substituted by S.S.I. 2004 No. 52 (effective 1st March, 2004).

62.28.1 *Jurisdiction.* The court has jurisdiction for an application under Art. 31 of the 1968 Brussels
or 1988 Lugano Convention in Sched. 1 or 3C to the C.J.J.A. 1982 and Council Regulation,
Arts 38, 57 and 58 where—
  (a) the application is in respect of a judgment, authentic instrument or court settlement;
  (b) the relevant convention was in force in both the state of origin and the state addressed at
the time the proceedings leading to the judgment were instituted or the authentic instrument
was drawn up or registered, or the judgment was given after the relevant convention came into
force in both states in proceedings instituted before the coming into force which were based on
jurisdictional rules which accorded with the relevant convention or with a bilateral Convention
between the state of origin and the state addressed (C.J.J.A. 1982, Scheds. 1 and 3C, Art. 54;
and Council Regulation, Art. 66, and see note 62.26.2);
  (c) the subject-matter of the judgment, authentic instrument, or court settlement is covered by
the relevant convention (see C.J.J.A. 1982, Scheds. 1 and 3C, Art. 1 and Council Regulation,
Art. 1); and
  (d) jurisdiction is not otherwise excluded (see note 62.28.2).

62.28.2 *Exclusion of jurisdiction.* The jurisdiction of the court will be excluded where it cannot
recognise the judgment because:—
  (a) Recognition would be contrary to public policy in the UK (C.J.J.A. 1982, Scheds. 1 and
3C, Arts. 27(1) and 34). Art. 27(1), which will only be applied in exceptional circumstances
when no other ground under Art. 27 was available (*Hoffman v. Kreig* [1988] E.C.R. 645), is
concerned with substantive matters and not the procedural requirements for the application for
recognition: *Artic Fish Sales Co. Ltd v. Adam (No. 2)* 1996 S.L.T. 970, 973I. For a recent
example, where the public policy exception was argued unsuccessfully on the ground that there
had been a breach of art.6(1) of ECHR in French proceedings (which it was held there had not

been), see *SA Marie Brizzard et Roger International v William Grant & Sons Ltd (No.2)*, 2002 S.L.T. 1365 (OH). Under art.34(1) of the Council Regulation the public policy ground is restricted to cases *manifestly* contrary to public policy.

(b) Where given in default of appearance, the defender had not been served with the document instituting the proceedings or with an equivalent document in sufficient time to enable him to arrange for his defence (C.J.J.A. 1982, Scheds. 1 and 3C, Arts. 27(2) and 34): see, *e.g. Artic Fish Sales Co. Ltd (No. 2)*, above and *Selco Ltd v. Mercier* 1996 S.L.T. 1247. Under art.34(2) of the Council Regulation the exclusion of recognition will not apply where the defender failed to commence proceedings to challenge the judgment in default when it was possible for him to do so.

(c) It is irreconcilable with a judgment between the same parties given in the UK (C.J.J.A. 1982, Scheds. 1 and 3C, Arts. 27(3) and 34) and Council Regulation, Art. 34(3). A court settlement (which is essentially contractual) is not a judgment for the purposes of Art. 27(3): *Solo Kleinmotoren v. Boch* [1994] E.C.R. I–2237. In Scotland, where the court grants decree in terms of part or all of a joint minute settling an action, that decree *is* a judgment.

(d) The adjudicating court has answered a preliminary question concerning an excluded matter in Art. 1(1) (relating to the subject-matter scope of the convention) in a way inconsistent with Scots international private law (C.J.J.A. 1982, Scheds. 1 and 3C, Arts. 27(4) and 34). This ground does not appear in the Council Regulation.

(e) It is irreconcilable with a prior non-contracting Member state judgment which involves the same cause of action, is between the same parties, and which is entitled to be recognised in the UK (C.J.J.A. 1982, Scheds. 1 and 3C, Arts. 27(5) and 34). This ground under Art. 34(4) of the Council Regulation is the same.

(f) It conflicts with the particular jurisdictional provisions in Arts. 7 to 16 of the relevant convention (C.J.J.A. 1982, Scheds. 1 and 3C, Arts. 28 and 34) or arts. 8–17, 22 and 72 of the Council Regulation (art.35(1)).

(g) It is against a person who was not domiciled in the state of origin of the judgment and an Order in Council has designated a provision in a treaty (permitted by Art. 59) between the UK and a non-contracting state to allow the UK not to recognise judgments given in a Contracting State against a defender domiciled or habitually resident in the non-contracting state in question (C.J.J.A. 1982, s.9(2) and Scheds. 1 and 3C, Arts. 28, 34 and 59; and see the Reciprocal Enforcement of Judgments (Canada) Order 1987 [S.I. 1987 No. 468] as amended by the Reciprocal Enforcement of Judgments (Canada) (Amendment) Order 1987 [S.I. 1987 No. 2211]).

"petition". A petition is presented in the Outer House: r. 14.2(h). The petition must be in Form 62.28 but does not have to be in the official printed form (see r. 62.27). The petition may be signed by the petitioner, counsel or other person having a right of audience, or an agent: r. 4.2(3)(d); and see r. 1.3(1) (definition of "counsel", "other person having a right of audience", and "agent") and note 1.3.4. **62.28.3**

The petitioner must lodge the petition with the required steps of process (r. 4.4) and any documents founded on or adopted (r. 27.1(1)). A fee is payable on lodging the petition: see note 14.5.10.

On petitions generally, see Chap. 14.

Under R.C.S. 1965, r. 249E(1)(a) a simple form of application was provided for instead of a formal petition in the official printed form, the purpose being to enable an application to be made from anywhere in the E.C. In practice, as a process is required, it is unlikely that an application would be made directly from abroad; the official printed form is, however, not required in case an application is made from abroad, but it may be used.

Productions. Under the Brussels and Lugano Conventions: The petitioner must produce with the petition (a) an authentic copy of the judgment, authentic instrument or court settlement which meets the conditions of C.J.J.A. 1982, s.11 (C.J.J.A. 1982, s.11 and Scheds 1 and 3C, Art. 46(1); and r. 62.28(2)(a)); (b) a document which establishes that according to the law of the country of origin the judgment is enforceable and has been served (C.J.J.A. 1982, Scheds 1 and 3C, Art. 47(1) and r. 62.28(2)(b)); (c) where judgment has been given in absence, the original or a certified copy of the document which establishes that the defender in the judgment was served with the document initiating proceedings against him or an equivalent document (C.J.J.A. 1982, Scheds 1 and 3C, Art. 46(2); and r. 68.28(2)(c) and see *Artic Fish Sales Co. Ltd v. Adam (No. 2)* 1996 S.L.T. 970); (d) where applicable, a document showing that the applicant is in receipt of legal aid in the country of origin (C.J.J.A. 1982, Scheds 1 and 3C, Art. 47(2); and r. 62.28(2)(d)); (e) an affidavit (r. 62.28(2)(e)); and (f) a translation of any document lodged (r. 62.3). **62.28.4**

Under the Council Regulation: The petitioner needs to produce only the documents referred to in r.62.28(2)(a), (c) and (e): r.62.28(3). But, in addition, there must be a certificate required by art. 54 (the form in Annex V for a judgment), art. 57 (the form in Annex VI for an authentic instrument) or art. 58 (the form on Annex V for a court settlement). The Council Regulation in

fact requires only two documents, namely, the copy of the judgment, authentic instrument or
court settlement and the appropriate certificate. It is not at all clear why r.62.28 requires a
document establishing service if judgment was obtained in default when this is provide for in the
form in Annex V; or an affidavit under r.62.28(2)(e). Furthermore, r.62.28(3) dopes not provide,
as does art. 55 of the Council Regulation, for the court receiving the application to accept a
document equivalent to the certificate in Annex V or VI.

Where the petitioner fails in the first place to lodge a necessary document, he may do so
subsequently (a photocopy may be accepted), even during an appeal against the grant of a
warrant of registration: r. 68.28(3); and *Artic Fish Sales Co. Ltd (No. 2)*, above. In such an
appeal under r. 62.34, the court may recall the original interlocutor if *ex facie* there is a
fundamental flaw in the documents produced: *Artic Fish Sales Co. Ltd v. Adam (No. 1)* 1996
S.L.T. 968, 969L.

An interlocutor dispensing with a document showing that a foreign judgment had been
properly served and allowing registration has been recalled: *Selco Ltd v. Mercier*, 1996 S.L.T.
1247.

62.28.5   *Conditions for authentication of judgment etc.* These are that the copy judgment (a) bears the
seal of the court which gave it, or (b) is certified by any person in his capacity as a judge or
officer of that court to be a true copy of a judgment given by that court: C.J.J.A. 1982, s.11.

62.28.5A   *"served with the document initiating the proceedings".* Art. 27(2) of Scheds 1 and 3C of the
C.J.J.A. 1982 and Art. 34(2) of the Council Regulation provide that where judgment is given in
default of appearance, the judgment shall not be recognised if the defender was not duly served
with the document which instituted the proceedings or in sufficient time to enable him to
arrange for his defence. In *Selco Ltd v. Mercier* 1996 S.L.T. 1247 (where registration was
recalled because the writ had not been served at the defender's domicile as required by the
Belgian Civil Code), Lord Coulsfield opined that if there had been proper service, one month
between service and the date of judgment would not have been unreasonable.

62.28.6   *Legal aid.* Where a petitioner has benefited from complete or partial legal aid or exemption
from costs or expenses in the state of origin, he is entitled to the most favourable legal aid or the
most extensive exemption from costs and expenses provided for under Scots law: C.J.J.A. 1982,
Scheds 1 and 3C, Art. 44; Council Regulation, Art. 50.

62.28.7   *Affidavit.* The affidavit should be in the form of a statement of evidence written in the first
person by the deponent. It should contain the evidence of the deponent in support of the
averments in the petition. In particular the affidavit should deal with the matters listed in
r. 62.28(2)(e).

An affidavit should be sworn and signed by the deponent before any person who may
competently take an oath, whether in Scotland or in any other country. In Scotland such a
person may include a notary public, justice of the peace, sheriff or any judge. The person taking
the oath should also sign the affidavit. Where the affidavit is not in English a duly certified
translation should also be lodged.

See also the definition of affidavit in r. 1.3(1).

62.28.8   *Interest on the judgment.* Where the judgment provides for the payment of money and the law
of the country where it was given provides for interest to be paid on the judgment from a
specified date, the rate of interest and the date from which it is due shall be registered with the
judgment. Once registered any interest will be in accordance with the registered particulars:
C.J.J.A. 1982, s.7.

Protective measures and interim interdict

[1] **62.29.**—(1) On lodging a petition, the petitioner may, at any time until
the expiry of the period for lodging an appeal referred to in rule 62.34 or its
disposal, apply by motion for a warrant for the execution of protective
measures.

(2) On lodging such a petition, the petitioner may, at any time until the
expiry of the period for lodging an appeal mentioned in rule 62.34 or its
disposal, apply by motion for an interim interdict.

---

[1] R.62.29 substituted by S.S.I. 2004 No. 52 (effective 1st March, 2004).

62.29.1   *"protective measures".* These are nowhere defined in the 1968 Brussels Convention or the
1988 Lugano Convention or the Council Regulation but are taken to refer to steps taken by the
petitioning creditor to prevent the debtor from disposing of assets against which he may wish to
enforce the judgment and which are available under the law of the country in which the
protective measure is sought. Section 27 of the C.J.J.A. 1982 provides for the protective

measures (arrestment, inhibition and interim interdict) which may be applied for to protect a foreign judgment, instrument or settlement in the absence of substantive proceedings in Scotland.

A litigant may apply to the court for protective measures (1) during the dependence of any action in another contracting state to which the relevant convention applies (C.J.J.A. 1982, s.27 (on which see *Stancroft Securities Ltd v. McDowall* 1990 S.C. 274) and Scheds 1 and 3C, Art. 24 or Council Regulation, Art.31); or (2) after a judgment has been given in such an action and the litigant has applied under Art. 31 of the relevant convention for enforcement of the judgment (r. 62.29).

The power of the court to grant warrant for arrestment, inhibition or interim interdict under r. 27 of the C.J.J.A. 1982 is extended by the Civil Jurisdiction and Judgments Act 1982 (Provisional and Protective Measures) (Scotland) Order 1997 [S.I. 1997 No. 2780] to proceeding commenced otherwise than in a Brussels or Lugano Contrasting State or to proceeding whose subject-matter is not within the scope of the 1968 Brussels Convention.

Where a petitioner has obtained an interlocutor granting warrant for the registration of the judgment, he will be entitled to proceed to execute protective measures as of right: C.J.J.A. 1982, Scheds 1 and 3C, Art. 39 and Council Regulation, Art. 47(2); r. 62.30(1)(b); *Capelloni and Aquilini v. Pelkmans* [1985] E.C.R. 3147, 3160.

In particular, protective measures will include arrestment on the dependence, inhibition on the dependence, interim interdict, arrestment of a ship on the dependence (*Clipper Shipping Co. Ltd v. San Vincente Partners* 1989 S.L.T. 204) and possibly arrestment *in rem* or arrestment of cargo on board ship: see C.J.J.A. 1982, s.27 and notes 13.6.2 *et seq.* For an English example, see *Republic of Haiti v. Duvalier* [1990] 1 Q.B. 202.

Interim interdict. Until the court grants warrant for, *inter alia*, the registration of a   **62.29.2** prohibitory judgment, the usual rules for obtaining interim interdict apply: see note 60.3.2. Once the court has granted a warrant for the registration of such a judgment (see r. 62.30), standing the decision in *Capelloni and Aquilini v. Pelkmans* [1985] E.C.R. 3147, it is suggested that the petitioner may proceed directly to execute the interdict by serving the interlocutor on the person affected.

"motion". For motions, see Chap. 23.   **62.29.3**

Warrant for registration under the Act of 1982 or the Council Regulation
[1] **62.30.**—(1) The court shall, on being satisfied that the petition complies with the requirements of the Act of 1982 or, as the case may be, the Council Regulation, pronounce an interlocutor—
  (a) granting warrant for the registration of the judgment;
  (b) granting warrant for the execution of protective measures; and
  (c) where necessary, granting decree in accordance with Scots law.
(2) The interlocutor pronounced under paragraph (1) shall specify—
  (a) the period within which an appeal mentioned in rule 62.34 against the interlocutor may be made; and
  (b) that the petitioner—
    (i) may register the judgment under rule 62.32; and
    (ii) may not proceed to execution until the expiry of the period for lodging such an appeal or its disposal.

Deriv. R.C.S. 1965, r.249G(1) and (2) inserted by S.I. 1986 No. 1941

---

[1] R.62.30 substituted by S.S.I. 2004 No. 52 (effective 1st March, 2004).

Determination of the petition. The petition must be determined *ex parte* without delay (1968 Brussels Convention or Lugano Convention C.J.J.A. 1982, Scheds 1 and 3C, Art. 34 or immediately (Council Regulation, Art. 41). Usually this will be done in chambers.

"complies with the requirements of the Act of 1982 or the Council Regulation". See notes   **62.30.2** 62.28.1 and 68.28.2.

Warrant for registration. The warrant will be for registration in the register of judgments of   **62.30.3** the Books of Council and Session for execution. On registration the foreign judgment becomes a Scottish decree of registration and may be enforced by any Scottish diligence or sequestration or liquidation: C.J.J.A. 1982, s.4(3) (1968 Brussels and Lugano Conventions); Civil Jurisdiction and Judgments Order 2001 (S.I. 2001 No. 3929), Sched. 1, para.2(2) (Council Regulation). Registration for execution gives the holder a decree of registration which is in effect a decree of the Court of Session (Bell's *Comm.*, i,4; *Taylor, Petr.* 1931 S.L.T. 260, 261 *per* Lord Pitman); and, on the warrant inserted by the Keeper of the Registers or his deputy on an extract of a registered document, diligence may be executed against the debtor's moveable property under s.3 of the Writs Execution (Scotland) Act 1877 as substituted by s.87(4) of the Debtors (Scotland) Act 1987. Diligence against heritable property may be executed by inhibition on the grant of letters of inhibition (see Chap. 59) or by action of adjudication founding on the decree of registration.

62.30.4   *Decree in accordance with Scots law*. This would be pronounced where the form of the foreign judgment is not suitable for a Scottish decree of registration (*e.g.* in a foreign decree of interdict or where *ad factum praestandum*).

62.30.5   *Expenses of petition and registration procedure*. The reasonable costs or expenses of the registration (and presumably petition) procedure are recoverable as if they were contained in the judgment being enforced: C.J.J.A. 1982, s. 4(2) (1968 Brussels and Lugano Conventions); Civil Jurisdiction and Judgments Order 2001 [S.I. 2001 No. 3929], Sched. 1, para.2(1) (Council Regulation). The interlocutor granting the warrant or decree accordingly should provide for the awarding of expenses in relation to the petition procedure.

62.30.6   *Period for marking appeal*. Where the appeal is by the judgment debtor it is (a) one month from the date of service under r. 62.33, or (b) two months from the date of service under r. 62.33 where he is domiciled in another Contracting State to the 1968 Brussels or Lugano Conventions (C.J.J.A. 1982, Scheds. 1 and 3C, Art. 36; and r. 62.34(1)) or Member State under the Council Regulation (Council Regulation, Art. 43(5); and r. 62.34(1)). The appropriate period should be specified in the interlocutor granting the warrant or decree: r. 60.30(2)(a).

Where the appeal is by the petitioner, see note 62.34.2.

62.30.7   *Execution pending marking or disposal of appeal*. An interlocutor granting warrant for registration or decree will specify, *inter alia*, that the petitioner may not proceed to execution until the expiry of the period for lodging such an appeal or its disposal: r. 60.30(2)(b). Execution presumably begins with the execution of diligence or the presentation of a petition for sequestration or liquidation. It is unclear whether service of a charge for payment is a step in execution, rather than a preliminary step. In relation to interdict and obligations *ad factum praestandum* execution begins presumably with the service of the interlocutor: on interim interdict, see note 60.3.2.

In any event during the appeal period the petitioner is automatically entitled to execute protective measures (but no other enforcement) if he has not already done so: C.J.J.A. 1982, Scheds. 1 and 3C, Art. 39 (1968 Brussels and Lugano Conventions); Council Regulation, Art. 47 (EU Member States except Denmark); and see note 62.29.1.

Intimation to petitioner
[1] **62.31.** Where the court pronounces an interlocutor under rule 62.30(1) granting warrant for registration, the Deputy Principal Clerk shall intimate such interlocutor to the petitioner by sending to his address for service in Scotland a certified copy of the interlocutor by registered post or the first class recorded delivery service.

Deriv. R.C.S. 1965, r. 249H inserted by S.I. 1986 No. 1941

---

[1] R.62.31 substituted by S.S.I. 2004 No. 52 (effective 1st March, 2004).

62.31.1   *General note*. The substituted r.62.31 is in the same terms as its predecessor.

Registration under the Act of 1982 or the Council Regulation
62.32.—(1) Where the court pronounces an interlocutor under rule 62.30(1) granting warrant for registration, the Deputy Principal Clerk shall enter the judgment in a register of judgments, authentic instruments and court settlements under the Act of 1982 and the Council Regulation kept in the Petition Department.

(2) On presentation by the petitioner to the Keeper of the Registers of—
  (a) a certified copy of the interlocutor under rule 62.30(1) granting warrant for registration;
  (b) an authentic copy of the judgment and any translation of it; and
  (c) any certificate of currency conversion under rule 62.2(1)(b),
they shall be registered in the register of judgments of the Books of Council and Session.

(3) On registration under paragraph (2), the Keeper of the Registers shall issue an extract of the registered judgment with a warrant for execution.

Deriv. R.C.S. 1965, r. 249K inserted by S.I. 1986 No. 1941

---

[1] R.62.34 inserted by S.S.I. 2004 No. 52 (effective 1st March 2004).

"Keeper of the Registers". This is the Keeper of the Registers of Scotland: r. 1.3(1). The **62.32.1** Register of Judgments is at Meadowbank House, 153 London Road, Edinburgh EH8 7AU; tel. 0131–659 6111; fax 0131–459 1221; DX ED300.

"certified copy of the interlocutor". A copy of the interlocutor is typed by the agent and **62.32.2** presented to the clerk of session in the Petition Department. The clerk checks it, certifies it as a true copy and stamps it with the court stamp.
A fee is payable.

"authentic copy of the judgment". See note 62.28.5. **62.32.3**

"translation". See r. 62.3. **62.32.4**

"certificate of currency conversion". The certificate should be obtained from the clerk of **62.32.5** session in the Petition Department and should be signed by him: r. 62.2(3) and see note 62.2.5.

Registration fee. A fee will be payable to the Keeper of the Registers for registration and any **62.32.6** extract: see the Fees in the Registers of Scotland Order 1991 [S.I. 1991 No. 2093].

Service of warrant for registration under the Act of 1982 or the Council Regulation

[1]**62.33.** The petitioner shall serve a copy of the interlocutor granting warrant for registration of a judgment and a notice in Form 62.33 on the person liable under the judgment.

Deriv. R.C.S. 1965, r.249J(1) inserted by S.I. 1996 No. 1941.

---

[1] R.62.33 substituted by S.S.I. 2004 No. 52 (effective 1st March 2004).

General note. The substituted r.62.33 is in the same terms as its predecessor. **62.33.1**

"serve". For methods of service, see Chap. 16, Pt. I. **62.33.2**

Appeals under the Act of 1982 or the Council Regulation

[1] **62.34.**—(1) An appeal under Article 37 of the convention in Schedule 1 or 3C to the Act of 1982 (appeal against granting of warrant for registration) or an appeal under Article 43 (appeals by either party) of the Council Regulation against the granting of a warrant for registration shall be made by motion—
  (a) to the Lord Ordinary; and
  (b) within one month of service under rule 62.33 (service of warrant for registration under the Act of 1982 or the Council Regulation) or within two months of such service where service was executed on a person domiciled in another Contracting State or, as the case may be, Member State.
(2) An appeal under Article 40 of the convention in Schedule 1 or 3C to the Act of 1982 (appeal against refusal to grant warrant for registration) or an appeal under Article 43 (appeals by either party) of the Council Regulation against a refusal to grant warrant for registration shall be made by motion—
  (a) to the Lord Ordinary; and
  (b) within one month of the interlocutor pronounced under rule 62.30(1) (warrant for registration under the Act of 1982 or the Council Regulation).
(3) Where the respondent in any such appeal is domiciled furth of the United Kingdom—
  (a) in relation to an appeal under paragraph (1), intimation of the motion shall be made to the address for service of the respondent in Scotland; and
  (b) in relation to an appeal under paragraph (2), intimation of the motion shall be made in accordance with rule 16.2 (service furth of

United Kingdom) or rule 16.5 (service where address of person is not known, as the case may be).

(4) Where an appeal under paragraph (1) is successful, the court shall, on the motion of the appellant, pronounce an interlocutor recalling any protective measure or interim interdict.

Deriv. R.C.S. 1965, r.249K inserted by S.I. 1986 No. 1941.

[1] R.62.34 substituted by S.S.I. 2004 No. 52 (effective 1st March 2004).

62.34.1   *General note.* Under Art. 37 or 40 of the 1968 Brussels or 1988 Lugano Convention, or Art. 43 of the Council Regulation, there is a two-stage appeal process. The first stage is (with the exception of maintenance judgments) in the Outer House. The second stage is a right of appeal to the Inner House: C.J.J.A. 1982, s.6(1)(b) and Sched. 1, Art. 37(2) in relation to the 1968 Brussels and Lugano Conventions, and art. 44 and Annex IV and para. 4(1)(b) of the Jurisdiction and Judgments Order 2001 [S.I. 2001 No. 3929] in relation to the Council Regulation. Rules 62.34 and 62.35 provide the procedural framework. Art. 37 of the 1968 Brussels Convention in Sched. 1 of the C.J.J.A. 1982, limiting appeals against decisions authorising endorsement of foreign judgments, has to be construed strictly and a court seized of an appeal does not have power to impose or re-impose a sist: *Société D'Informatique Service Réalisation Organisation (SISRO) v. Ampersand Software BV*, [1996] Q.B. 127 (ECJ). Art. 44 of the Council Regulation would no doubt be similarly interpreted.

Under R.C.S. 1965, r. 249K appeals had to be in the appeal form in Form 42 because the application for registration was not a petition and there were no formal requirements for a process (although in practice one was lodged). Now that applications for registration are made by petition, the appeal to the Lord Ordinary can readily be made by motion in the petition process.

62.34.2   *Time-limits.* Where the prospective appellant is the judgment debtor the time-limits are imposed under Art. 36 of the 1968 Brussels and Lugano Conventions and art. 43(5) of the Council Regulation: see note 62.30.6. No extension of time may be granted on account of distance: C.J.J.A. 1982, Scheds 1 and 3C, Art. 36 (Brussels and Lugano Conventions); Council Regulation, art.43(5). Accordingly there is no scope for the use of the dispensing power in r. 2.1 to relieve a party from a failure to comply with a time-limit.

Where the prospective appellant is the petitioning creditor, the time-limit is one month from the date of the interlocutor refusing warrant or decree: r. 62.34(2)(a); this is not imposed under either convention or the Council Regulation.

Art. 37(2) of the 1968 Brussels and Lugano Conventions which provides for the second appeal on a point of law (to the Inner House), is restrictively interpreted and the words "judgment given on the appeal" cannot be extended to enable an appeal to be lodged against a judgment other than that given on the first appeal: *Brennero v. Wendel* [1984] E.C.R. 3971; *Van Dalfsen v. Van Loon and Berendsen* [1991] E.C.R. I–4743. A decision to sist enforcement under Art. 38, by the court on the first appeal under Art. 37(1), may not be contested on the second appeal under Art. 37(2) as it does not constitute a judgment given on the appeal under Art. 37(1); and this is so whether or not the sist is granted in the same interlocutor as the judgment on the appeal under Art. 37(1).

In deciding whether to grant a sist of enforcement proceedings under Art. 38 of the Brussels and Lugano Conventions, the court may take into account only such submissions as the appellant was unable to make before the court of the state in which the original judgment was given: *Van Dalfsen*, above.

62.34.3   *"motion".* For motions, see Chap. 23. Note the special rules on intimation in r. 62.34(3).

62.34.4   *"domiciled".* This is determined under ss.41 to 45 of the C.J.J.A. 1982 in relation to the 1968 Brussels and Lugano Conventions, and in paras. 9 to 12 of Sched. 1 to the Civil Jurisdiction and Judgments Order 2001 in relation to the Council Regulation. See also note 13.2.6.

62.34.5   *The appeal.* In *Artic Fish Sales Co. Ltd v. Adam (No. 1)* 1996 S.L.T. 968, 969L Lord Cameron of Lochbroom considered, without deciding the point, that, if there was a fundamental flaw in the documentation produced under r. 62.28(2), the court could recall the original interlocutor or require the proper document to be produced (or otherwise) as provided in r. 62.28(3).

In *Artic Fish Sales*, above, Lord Cameron of Lochbroom held that where the appellant wished to place evidence before the court which contradicted the petitioner's case, the court could not proceed on *ex parte* statements but would require evidence (whether by affidavit or otherwise). In that case, the appellant was disputing having had notice of the foreign proceedings in respect of which enforcement of a decree was being sought.

In an appeal under Art. 37 of the 1968 Brussels Convention, the court is not limited to the grounds of challenge in Arts 27 and 28, and an appeal may be on the ground that the proper formalities were not observed in presenting the appeal: *Artic Fish Sales Co. Ltd (No. 1)*, above.

Reclaiming under the Act of 1982 or the Council Regulation

[1] **62.35.**—(1) Any party dissatisfied with the interlocutor of the Lord Ordinary in any appeal mentioned in rule 62.34 (appeals under the Act of 1982 or the Council Regulation) may reclaim on a point of law against that interlocutor.

(2) Where a reclaiming motion under paragraph (1) against the registration of a judgment is successful, the court shall, on the motion of the appellant, pronounce an interlocutor recalling any protective measure or interim interdict.

Deriv. R.C.S. 1965, r.249 inserted by S.I. 1986 No. 1941

———

[1] R.62.35 substituted by S.S.I. 2004 No. 52 (effective 1st March 2004).

Reclaiming. See, in general, Chap. 38. The interlocutor pronounced by the Lord Ordinary **62.35.1** under r. 62.34 disposes of the subject-matter of the cause and may be reclaimed against, without leave, within 21 days after its date: r. 38.3(2). This is now judicially confirmed by *Selco Ltd v. Mercier (*No. 2), 1997 S.L.T. 687.

"point of law". These words are used in Arts 37 and 41 of the 1968 Brussels or 1988 Lugano **62.35.2** Convention. Accordingly it is appropriate to have regard to the tools of interpretation listed in s.3 of the C.J.J.A. 1982 if any doubt arises whether a matter is a "point of law".

Recognition of judgments from another Contracting State or Member State

[1]**62.36.**—(1) For the purposes of Article 26 of the convention in Schedule 1 or 3C to the Act of 1982 of the Council Regulation an interlocutor pronounced under rule 62.30(1) (warrant for registration under the Act of 1982 and Article 33 or the Council Regulation) shall imply recognition of the judgment so dealt with.

(2) In an application under Article 26(2) of the convention in Schedule 1 or 3C to the Act of 1982 (application for recognition of a judgment) or Article 33(2) of the Council Regulation (application for recognition of judgment), rules 62.26 to 62.35 shall apply to such an application as they apply to an application under Article 31 of that convention, subject to the following provisions—

(a) it shall not be necessary to produce any documents required by rule 62.28(2)(b) and (d); and
(b) rule 62.32 shall not apply.

Deriv. R.C.S. 1965 r.249M inserted by S.I. 1986 No. 1941

———

[1] R.62.36 substituted by S.S.I. 2004 No. 52 (effective 1st March 2004).

Jurisdiction. The court has jurisdiction where the petitioner has raised the recognition of the **62.36.1** judgment sought to be recognised as the principal issue in a dispute: C.J.J.A. 1982, Scheds 1 and 3C, Art. 26 (in relation to the 1968 Brussels and Lugano Conventions) and art. 33 of the Council Regulation). Where proceedings before the court depend on the determination of an incidental question of recognition the court has jurisdiction: C.J.J.A. 1982, Sched. 1 and 3C, Art. 26.

Enforcement of judgments from another part of the United Kingdom in Scotland (money provisions)

[1] **62.37.**—(1) An application under paragraph 5 of Schedule 6 to the Act of 1982 (application for registration in the Court of Session of a certificate in relation to a money provision in a judgment from another part of the United Kingdom) shall be made by presenting to the Keeper of the Registers—

(a) a certificate under paragraph 4(1) of Schedule 6 to the Act of 1982; and
(b) any certificate of currency conversion under rule 62.2(1)(b).

(2) On presentation of the certificate mentioned in paragraph (1)(a), the Keeper of the Registers shall—

    (a) register the certificate in the register of judgments of the Books of Council and Session; and

    (b) issue an extract of the certificate with a warrant for execution.

(3) An application under—

    (a) paragraph 9 of Schedule 6 to the Act of 1982 (application to sist proceedings for enforcement of a certificate registered under paragraph (2) of this rule); or

    (b) paragraph 10 of Schedule 6 to the Act of 1982 (application for reduction of registration),

shall be made by petition.

Deriv. R.C.S. 1965, r. 249P(2), (3) and (4) inserted by S.I. 1986 No. 1941.

---

[1] R.62.37 substituted by S.S.I. 2004 No. 52 (effective 1st March 2004).

62.37.1A   *General note.* The substituted r.62.37 is in the same terms as its predecessor (as amended by S.I. 1996 No. 2168).

62.37.1   *Jurisdiction.* The Keeper of the Registers of Scotland, as "the proper officer" of the court under para. 5 of Sched. 6 to the C.J.J.A. 1982, has jurisdiction to register a certificate under that paragraph where (a) it is presented within six months of the date of its issue, and (b) it is in respect of a "judgment": see note 62.26.3; and C.J.J.A. 1982, s.18(2).

    A person who has obtained an English judgment cannot be interdicted from enforcing it under Sched. 6, para. 5 of the C.J.J.A. 1982 on the ground that the judgment was defective in its merits: *Clarke v. Fennscandia Ltd* 1998 S.C. 464.

62.37.2   *"Keeper of the Registers".* This is the Keeper of the Registers of Scotland: r. 1.3(1). The Register of Judgments is at Meadowbank House, 153 London Road, Edinburgh EH8 7AU; tel. 0131–659 6111; fax 0131–459 1221; DX ED300.

62.37.3   *Certificate of money provision in judgment to be registered.* The applicant should obtain this from the "proper officer" of the English, Welsh, or Northern Irish court where the judgment was given or entered or in whose books it was registered: C.J.J.A. 1982, Sched. 6, para. 2. In this context "judgment" has a limited meaning: see note 62.26.3; and C.J.J.A. 1982, s. 18(2).

62.37.4   *"certificate of currency conversion".* This should, if necessary, be obtained from the clerk of session in the Petition Department duly signed by him: r. 62.2(3) and see notes 62.2.4 and 62.2.5.

62.37.5   *Registration fee.* A fee will be payable to the Keeper of the Registers for registration and any extract: see the Fees in the Registers of Scotland Order 1991 [S.I. 1991 No. 2093].

62.37.6   *Costs and expenses of registration procedure.* The reasonable costs or expenses of and incidental to the obtaining of the certificate of the money provision in a judgment and its registration shall be recoverable as if they were costs and expenses contained in the original judgment: C.J.J.A. 1982, Sched. 6, para. 7.

62.37.7   *Interest.* See C.J.J.A. 1982, Sched. 6, para. 8.

Enforcement of judgments from another part of the United Kingdom in Scotland (non-money provisions)

[1] **62.38.**—(1) An application under paragraph 5 of Schedule 7 to the Act of 1982 (application for registration in the Court of Session of a non-money provision in a judgment from another part of the United Kingdom) shall be made by petition in Form 62.38.

(2) There shall be produced with the petition under paragraph (1)—

    (a) a certified copy of the judgment of the original court; and

    (b) a certificate under paragraph 4(1)(b) of Schedule 7 to the Act of 1982.

(3) The petition under paragraph (1) shall be heard by the Lord Ordinary in chambers and shall not require any appearance for the applicant unless the court so requires.

(4) The court shall, on being satisfied that the petition complies with the requirements of section 18 of, and Schedule 7 to, the Act of 1982, pronounce an interlocutor—

(a) granting warrant for the registration of the judgment; and

(b) where necessary, granting decree in accordance with Scots law.

(5) Where the court pronounces an interlocutor under paragraph (4), rule 62.32 shall apply to the registration of a judgment under this rule as it applies to the registration of a judgment under that rule.

(6) An application under—

(a) paragraph 8 of Schedule 7 to the Act of 1982 (application to sist proceedings for enforcement of a judgment registered under paragraph (5) of this rule); or

(b) paragraph 9 of Schedule 7 to the Act of 1982 (application to reduce the registration under paragraph (5) of this rule),

shall be made by petition.

Deriv. R.C.S. 1965, r.249Q(4) to (9) inserted by S.I. 1986 No. 1941.

———

[1] R.62.38 substituted by S.S.I. 2004 No. 52 (effective 1st March 2004).

General note. The substituted r.62.38 is in the same terms as its predecessor.   **62.38.1**

A decree of registration is not generally a suitable method to enforce a judgment which is not for the payment of money. Accordingly r. 62.38 requires an application to the court by petition.

Petition under C.J.J.A. 1982, Sched. 7, para. 5. A petition is presented in the Outer House: r. **62.38.2**
14.2(h). The petition must be in Form 62.38 but does not have to be in the official printed form
(see r. 62.27). The petition may be signed by the petitioner, counsel or other person having a
right of audience, or an agent: r. 4.2; and see r. 1.3(1) (definition of "counsel", "other person
having a right of audience", and "agent") and note 1.3.4.

The petitioner must lodge the petition with the required steps of process (r. 4.4) and any
documents founded on or adopted (r. 27.1(1)). A fee is payable on lodging the petition: see note
14.5.10.

On petitions generally, see Chap. 14.

Productions. The petitioner must produce with the petition (1) a certified copy of the **62.38.3**
judgment obtained from the "proper officer" of the original court (C.J.J.A. 1982, Sched. 7,
para. 5(3)(a); and r. 62.38(a)); and (2) a certificate under para. 4(1)(b) of Sched. 7 to the C.J.J.A.
1982.

"certificate under paragraph 4(1)(b)". This certifies that the period for making an appeal **62.38.4**
against the judgment has expired with no appeal having been made or that any appeal has been
finally disposed of: C.J.J.A. 1982, Sched. 7, para. 3.

Warrant for registration. The warrant will be for registration in the register of judgments of **62.38.5**
the Books of Council and Session for execution. On registration the foreign judgment becomes
a Scottish decree of registration and may be enforced by any Scottish diligence or sequestration
or liquidation: C.J.J.A. 1982, s. 4(3). Registration for execution gives the holder a decree of
registration which is in effect a decree of the Court of Session (Bell's *Comm.*, i,4; *Taylor, Petr.*
1931 S.L.T. 260, 261 *per* Lord Pitman); and, on the warrant inserted by the Keeper of the
Registers or his deputy on an extract of a registered document, diligence may be executed
against the debtor's moveable property under s. 3 of the Writs Execution (Scotland) Act 1877 as
substituted by s. 87(4) of the Debtors (Scotland) Act 1987. Diligence against heritable property
may be executed by inhibition on the grant of letters of inhibition (see Chap. 59) or by action of
adjudication founding on the decree of registration.

Decree in accordance with Scots law. This would be pronounced where the form of the foreign **62.38.6**
judgment is not suitable for a Scottish decree of registration (*e.g.* in a foreign decree of interdict
or where *ad factum praestandum*).

Costs and expenses of registration procedure. The reasonable costs or expenses of and **62.38.7**
incidental to the obtaining of the certified copy judgment, the certificate under para. 4(1)(b) of
Sched. 7 to the C.J.J.A. 1982 and the petition and any registration procedure are recoverable as
if they were costs and expenses incidental to registration of a money provision in a judgment:
C.J.J.A. 1982, Sched. 7, para. 7(1).

Any costs and expenses recovered shall bear interest from the "date of registration" of the
judgment as in accordance with Scots law: C.J.J.A. 1982, Sched. 7, para. 7(2).

Petition under C.J.J.A. 1982, Sched. 7, para. 8 or 9. A petition is presented in the Outer **62.38.8**
House: r. 14.2(h). The petition need not be in the official printed form: r. 62.27. The petition
may be signed by the petitioner, counsel or other person having a right of audience, or an agent:
r. 4.2; and see r. 1.3(1) (definition of "counsel", "other person having a right of audience" and
"agent") and note 1.3.4.

The petitioner must lodge the petition with the required steps of process (r. 4.4) and any
documents founded on or adopted (r. 27.1(1)). A fee is payable on lodging the petition: see note
14.5.10.

On petitions generally, see Chap. 14.

Cancellation of registration under the Act of 1982 or the Council Regulation
[1]**62.39.** Where—
   (a) an interlocutor under rule 62.30(1) (warrant for registration under
      the Act of 1982 or the Council Regulation) is recalled and
      registration under rule 62.32 (registration under the Act of 1982 or
      the Council Regulation) is ordered to be cancelled after an appeal
      under Article 37 of the convention in Schedule 1 or 3C to the Act of
      1982 or an appeal under Article 43 of the Council Regulation; or
   (b) registration under rule 62.37(2) (registration of judgments from
      another part of the United Kingdom in Scotland (money provisions))
      or rule 62.38(5) (registration of judgments from another part of the
      United Kingdom in Scotland (non-money provisions)) is reduced,
a certificate to that effect by the Deputy Principal Clerk shall be sufficient

warrant to the Keeper of the Registers to cancel the registration and return the judgment, certificate or other documents to the person who applied for registration.

Deriv. R.C.S. 1965, r.249R inserted by S.I. 1986 No. 1941.

---

[1] R.62.39 substituted by S.S.I. 2004 No. 52 (effective 1st March 2004).

Enforcement in another Contracting State of Court of Session judgments etc.
  [1] **62.40.**—(1) Where a person seeks to apply under section 12 of the Act of 1982 for recognition or enforcement in another Contracting State of a judgment given by the court or a court settlement in the court, he shall apply by letter to the Deputy Principal Clerk for—
    (a) a certificate in Form 62.40–A;
    (b) a certified copy of the judgment; and
    (c) if required, a certified copy of the opinion of the court.
  (2) Where a person seeks to apply under Chapter III of the Council Regulation for recognition or enforcement in another Member State of a judgment given by the court, he shall apply by letter to the Deputy Principal Clerk for—
    (a) a certificate under Article 54 of the Judgments Regulation;
    (b) a certified copy of the judgment; and
    (c) if required, a certified copy of the opinion of the court.
  (3) The Deputy Principal Clerk shall not issue a certificate under paragraph (1)(a) or 2(a) unless there is produced to him an execution of service of the judgment on the person on whom it is sought to be enforced.
  (4) Where a person seeks to apply under Article 50 of the convention in Schedule 1 or 3C to the Act of 1982 for enforcement of an authentic instrument or court settlement registered for execution in the Books of Council and Session, he shall apply by letter to the Keeper of the Registers for—
    (a) a certificate in Form 62.40-B or; and
    (b) an extract of the authentic instrument or court settlement.
  (5) Where a person seeks to apply under Article 57 or 58 of the Council Regulation for enforcement in another Member State of an authentic instrument or court settlement registered for execution in the Books of Council and Session, he shall apply by letter to the Keeper of the Registers for—
    (a) a certificate under Article 57 or 58 of the Council Regulation; and
    (b) an extract of the authentic instrument or court settlement.
  (6) The Keeper of the Registers shall not issue a certificate under paragraph (4) or (5) unless there is produced to him an affidavit verifying that enforcement has not been suspended and that the time available for enforcement has not expired.

Deriv. R.C.S. 1965, r.249N inserted by S.I. 1986 No. 1941.

---

[1] R.62.40 substituted by S.S.I. 2004 No. 52 (effective 1st March 2004).

62.40.1   *"letter to the Deputy Principal Clerk"*. The address and telephone number, etc., of the Deputy Principal Clerk are: The Deputy Principal Clerk of Session, Court of Session, 2 Parliament Square, Edinburgh EH1 1RQ; tel. 031–225 2595; fax 031–225 8213; DX ED306.

62.40.2   *"letter to the Keeper of the Registers"*. The address of the Keeper of the Registers is: Meadowbank House, 153 London Road, Edinburgh EH8 7AU; tel. 0131–659 6111; fax 0131–459 1221; DX ED300.

62.40.3   *Affidavit*. The affidavit should be in the form of a statement of evidence written in the first person. The affidavit should contain the evidence of the deponent in support of the application. In particular the affidavit should deal with the matters mentioned in r. 62.40(4).
  An affidavit should be sworn and signed by the deponent before any person who may competently take an oath, whether in Scotland or in any other country. In Scotland such a

person may include a notary public, justice of the peace, sheriff, or any judge. The person taking the oath should also sign the affidavit. Where the affidavit is not in English a duly certified translation should also be lodged.

See also, definition of affidavit in r. 1.3(1).

Enforcement in another part of the United Kingdom of Court of Session judgments or documents registered for execution (money provisions)

[1] **62.41.**—(1) Where a person seeks to apply under Schedule 6 to the Act of 1982 for enforcement in another part of the United Kingdom of a money provision in a judgment given by the court, he shall apply by letter to the Deputy Principal Clerk for a certificate in Form 62.41 A.

(2) The Deputy Principal Clerk shall not issue a certificate under paragraph (1) unless there is produced to him an affidavit stating—

  (a) the sum or aggregate of sums including interest and expenses payable and unsatisfied;

  (b) that the time for making an appeal against such judgment has expired or such appeal has been finally determined;

  (c) that enforcement of the judgment has not been suspended and the time available for its enforcement has not expired; and

  (d) the address of the party entitled to enforce, and the usual or last known address of the party liable to execution on, the judgment.

(3) Where a person seeks to apply under Schedule 6 to the Act of 1982 for enforcement in another part of the United Kingdom of a document registered for execution in the Books of Council and Session, he shall apply by letter to the Keeper of the Registers for—

  (a) a certificate in Form 62.41–B; and

  (b) an extract of the document.

(4) The Keeper of the Registers shall not issue a certificate under paragraph (3) unless there is produced to him an affidavit which includes the statements required under paragraph (2)(a), (c) and (d).

Deriv. R.C.S. 1965, r.249P(1) and (2) inserted by S.I. 1986 No. 1941.

---

[1] R.62.41 substituted by S.S.I. 2004 No. 52 (effective 1st March 2004).

General note: The substituted r. 62.41 is in the same terms as its predecessor (as amended by **62.41.1A** S.I. 1996 No. 1756).

"letter to the Deputy Principal Clerk". The address and telephone number, etc., of the Deputy **62.41.1** Principal Clerk are: The Deputy Principal Clerk of Session, Court of Session, 2 Parliament Square, Edinburgh EH1 1RQ; tel. 0131–225 2595; fax 0131–225 8213; DX ED306.

Affidavit. The affidavit should be in the form of a statement of evidence written in the first **62.41.2** person. The affidavit should contain the evidence of the deponent in support of the application. In particular the affidavit should deal with the matters listed in r. 62.41(2).

An affidavit should be sworn and signed by the deponent before any person who may competently take an oath, whether in Scotland or in any other country. In Scotland such a person may include a notary public, justice of the peace, sheriff, or any judge. The person taking the oath should also sign the affidavit. Where the affidavit is not in English a duly certified translation should also be lodged.

See also, definition of affidavit in r. 1.3(1).

"letter to the Keeper of the Registers". The address of the Keeper of the Registers is: **62.41.3** Meadowbank House, 153 London Road, Edinburgh EH8 7AU; tel. 0131–659 6111; fax 0131–459 1221; DX ED300.

Enforcement in another part of the United Kingdom of Court of Session judgments or documents registered for execution (non-money provisions)

[1] **62.42.**—(1) Where a person seeks to apply under Schedule 7 to the Act of 1982 for enforcement in another part of the United Kingdom of a non-money provision in a judgment of the court, he shall apply by letter to the Deputy Principal Clerk for—

(*a*) a certificate in Form 62.42–A; and

(*b*) a certified copy of such judgment.

(2) The Deputy Principal Clerk shall not issue a certificate under paragraph (1) unless there is produced to him an affidavit stating—

(*a*) that the time for making an appeal against such judgment has expired or such appeal has been finally determined; and

(*b*) the address of the party entitled to enforce, and the usual or last known address of the party liable to execution on, the judgment or registered document.

(3) Where the Deputy Principal Clerk issues a certificate in Form 62.42–A, he shall attach it to the certified copy judgment.

(4) Where a person seeks to apply under Schedule 7 to the Act of 1982 for enforcement in another part of the United Kingdom of a non-money provision in a document registered for execution in the Books of Council and Session, he shall apply by letter to the Keeper of the Registers for—

(*a*) a certificate in Form 62.42–B; and

(*b*) an extract of the document.

(5) The Keeper of the Registers shall not issue a certificate under paragraph (4) unless there is produced to him an affidavit referred to in paragraph (2).

(6) Where the Keeper of the Registers issues a certificate in Form 62.42–B, he shall attach it to the extract of the document.

Deriv. R.C.S. 1965, r.249O(1) to (3) inserted by S.I. 1986 No. 1941

———

[1] R.62.42 substituted by S.S.I. 2004 No. 52 (effective 1st March 2004).

62.42.1A   *General note.* The substituted r.62.42 is in the same terms as its predecessor.

62.42.1   *"letter to the Deputy Principal Clerk".* The address and telephone number, etc., of the Deputy Principal Clerk are: The Deputy Principal Clerk of Session, Court of Session, 2 Parliament Square, Edinburgh EH1 1RQ; tel. 0131–225 2595; fax 0131–225 8213; DX ED306.

62.42.2   *Affidavit.* The affidavit should be in the form of a statement of evidence written in the first person. The affidavit should contain the evidence of the deponent in support of the application. In particular the affidavit should deal with the matters listed in r. 62.42(2).

An affidavit should be sworn and signed by the deponent before any person who may competently take an oath, whether in Scotland or in any other country. In Scotland such a person may include a notary public, justice of the peace, sheriff, or any judge. The person taking the oath should also sign the affidavit. Where the affidavit is not in English a duly certified translation should also be lodged.

See also definition of affidavit in r. 1.3(1).

62.42.3   *"letter to the Keeper of the Registers".* The address of the Keeper of the Registers is: Meadowbank House, 153 London Road, Edinburgh EH8 7AU; tel. 0131–659 6111; fax 0131–459 1221; DX ED300.

PART VI

REGISTRATION UNDER THE MERCHANT SHIPPING (LINER CONFERENCES) ACT 1982

Application and interpretation of this Part

62.43.—(1) This Part applies to an application under section 9 of the Merchant Shipping (Liner Conferences) Act 1982 (recognition and enforcement of recommendations, etc., of conciliators).

(2) In this Part, "the Liner Conferences Act" means the Merchant Shipping (Liner Conferences) Act 1982.

62.43.1   *General note.* The Merchant Shipping (Liner Conferences) Act 1982 was passed to give certain parts of the 1979 Geneva Convention on a Code of Conduct for Liner Conferences the force of law in the UK. The Liner Conference Code provides machinery for the settlement of disputes relating to the application or operation of its provisions between shipping lines, shippers' organisations or representatives, and liner conferences. That machinery involves the use of conciliation by which conciliators make recommendations which bind the parties to the dispute. Part VI of this Chapter is thus concerned principally with the enforcement of the recommendations of the conciliators in Scotland. It also enables the enforcement of ancillary determination of costs of conciliation and awards of costs for vexatious and frivolous proceedings.

Definitions in the Liner Conferences Act. The rules in Pt. VI of this Chapter are made under s.   **62.43.2** 9(5) of the Liner Conferences Act. Accordingly a word or expression used in Pt. VI which is also used in the Liner Conferences Act has the meaning given in that Act unless the contrary intention appears: Interpretation Act 1978, s. 11.

The word "conference" (including "liner conference") means a group of two or more vessel-operating carriers which provides unilateral liner services for the carriage of cargo on a particular route or routes within specified geographical limits and which has an agreement or arrangement whatever its nature within the framework of which they operate under uniform or common freight rates and any other agreed condition with respect to the provisions of liner services: Liner Conferences Act, s. 14(1) and Sched., Chap. 1.

Applications for registration under the Liner Conferences Act

62.44.—(1) An application under—
- (*a*) section 9(1)(*b*) of the Liner Conferences Act (application for registration for enforcement of a recommendation, determination or award), or
- (*b*) section 9(3) of that Act (application for registration for enforcement of a determination of costs),

shall be made by petition.

(2) A petition under section 9(1)(*b*) of the Liner Conferences Act shall include averments in relation to—
- (*a*) the reasons for the petition; and
- (*b*) where appropriate, the limited extent to which the recommendation is enforceable under section 9(2) of that Act.

(3) There shall be produced with the petition—
(a) a certified copy of the recommendation, the reasons for the recommendation and the record of settlement;
(b) a copy of the acceptance of the recommendation by the parties on whom it is binding.

(4) There shall be produced with a petition under section 9(3) of the Liner Conferences Act a certified copy of the determination of costs.

Deriv. RCS 1965, r. 249B(1) to (4) inserted by S.I. 1986 No. 799

Jurisdiction under the Liner Conferences Act. The court has jurisdiction for an application **62.44.1** under s.9(1)(b) of the Liner Conferences Act where—
(a) the application is in respect of a recommendation of conciliators which has become binding as between two or more parties under Art. 37 of the Code in the Schedule to the Act; and
(b) the recommendation is unaffected by any matter in Art. 39, para. 2(a) to (d) of the Code (disability, fraud, coercion, public policy or composition or procedure of the conciliators).

The court may have jurisdiction in respect of some parts of the recommendation but not others provided the court is satisfied the parts may be severed: Liner Conferences Act, s.9(2) and Sched., Art. 39(3).

"petition". A petition is presented in the Outer House: r. 14.2(h). The petition must be in **62.44.2** Form 14.4 in the official printed form: rr. 4.1 and 14.4. The petition may be signed by the petitioner, counsel or other person having a right of audience, or an agent: r. 4.2; and see r. 1.3(1) (definition of "counsel", "other person having a right of audience" and "agent") and note 1.3.4.

The petitioner must lodge the petition with the required steps of process (r. 4.4) and any documents founded on or adopted (r. 27.1(1)). A fee is payable on lodging the petition: see note 14.5.10.

On petitions generally, see Chap. 14.

Certified copy of recommendation and reasons. There should be included the reasons of the **62.44.3** conciliators: Liner Conferences Act, Sched., Art. 36. Ideally, there should be included the matters listed in r. 11 of the Model Rules annexed to the Schedule to the Liner Conferences Act. A certified copy recommendation, determination or award, if necessary, should be obtained from the Registrar based at the U.N. Office in Geneva: Liner Conferences Act, Sched., Art. 46(2)(d).

"record of settlement". This document is drawn up and signed by the conciliators when their **62.44.4** recommendation has been accepted by the parties. On signature of the record of settlement the recommendation becomes binding, and thus enforceable: Liner Conferences Act, Sched., Art. 37(4).

Warrant for registration under the Liner Conferences Act

62.45. The court, on being satisfied that the recommendation, determination or award may be registered, shall pronounce an interlocutor granting warrant for registration of the recommendation, determination or award, as the case may be.

Deriv. RCS 1965, r. 249C(1) inserted by S.I. 1986 No. 799

General note. In Scotland a foreign judgment is enforced under statute by the court granting a **62.45.1** warrant for the judgment to be registered in the register of judgments of the Books of Council and Session for execution. On registration, the foreign judgment becomes a Scottish decree of registration and may be enforced by any diligence or sequestration or liquidation. Registration for execution gives the holder a decree of registration which is in effect a decree of the Court of Session (Bell's *Comm.*, i,4; *Taylor, Petr.* 1931 S.L.T. 260, 261 *per* Lord Pitman); and, on the warrant inserted by the Keeper of the Registers or his deputy on an extract of a registered document, diligence may be executed against the debtor's moveable property under s.3 of the Writs Execution (Scotland) Act 1877 as substituted by s.87(4) of the Debtors (Scotland) Act 1987. Diligence against heritable property may be executed by inhibition on the grant of letters of inhibition (see Chap. 59) or by action of adjudication founding on the decree of registration.

62.45.2 *Expenses of petitions and registration procedure.* The reasonable costs of and incidental to the registration procedure are recoverable as if they were sums recoverable under the recommendation, determination or award, except that they carry interest, as they would if they were an amount of costs or expenses made by the court on the date of registration: Liner Conferences Act, s.9(7).

Registration under the Liner Conferences Act

62.46.—(1) Where the court pronounces an interlocutor under rule 62.45 granting warrant for registration—
  (a) the Deputy Principal Clerk shall enter the warrant in the register of recommendations, determinations and awards to be registered under section 9 of the Liner Conferences Act; and
  (b) the petitioner shall serve a copy of the interlocutor containing such warrant on the party against whom the recommendation, determination or award may be enforced.
(2) On presentation by the petitioner to the Keeper of the Registers of—
  (a) a certified copy of the interlocutor under rule 62.45 granting warrant for registration,
  (b) a certified copy of the recommendation, determination or award to be registered and any translation of it, and
  [1] (c) where necessary, a certificate of currency conversion under rule 62.2(1)(b),
they shall be registered in the register of judgments of the Books of Council and Session.
(3) On registration under paragraph (2), the Keeper of the Registers shall issue an extract of the registered recommendation, determination or award, as the case may be, with a warrant for execution.

Deriv. RCS 1965, r. 249C(2) and (3) inserted by S.I. 1986 No. 799

---

[1] R. 62.46(2)(c) amended by S.I. 1996 No. 2168 (minor correction).

62.46.1 *"serve".* For methods of service, see Chap. 16, Pt I.

62.46.2 *"certified copy of the interlocutor".* A copy of the interlocutor is typed by the agent and presented to the clerk of session in the Petition Department. The clerk checks it, certifies it as a true copy and stamps it with the court stamp.
   A fee is payable.

62.46.3 *"Keeper of the Registers".* This is the Keeper of the Registers of Scotland: r. 1.3(1). The Register of Judgments is at Meadowbank House, 153 London Road, Edinburgh EH8 7AU; tel. 0131–659 6111; fax 0131–459 1221; DX ED300.

62.46.4 *Certified copy of the recommendation etc.* See note 62.44.3.

62.46.5 *"translation".* See r. 62.3.

62.46.6 *"certificate of currency conversion".* The certificate should be obtained from the clerk of session in the Petition Department and should be signed by him: r. 62.2(3) and see note 62.2.5.

62.46.7 *Registration fee.* A fee will be payable to the Keeper of the Registers for registration and any extract: see the Fees in the Registers of Scotland Order 1991 [S.I. 1991 No. 2093].

PART VII

[2] **RECIPROCAL ENFORCEMENT OF ORDERS IN RELATION TO CONFISCATION OF PROCEEDS OF CRIME AND TO FORFEITURE OF PROPERTY USED IN CRIME**

Interpretation of this Part
  [1] **62.47.** In this Part—
     "the Act of 1989" means the Prevention of Terrorism (Temporary Provisions) Act 1989;

"the Act of 1995" means the Proceeds of Crime (Scotland) Act 1995;

"the Act of 2000" means the Terrorism Act 2000;

"money order" means an order for the payment of money;

"non-money order" means an order which is not a money-order;

"the Order of 1995" means the Prevention of Terrorism (Temporary Provisions) Act 1989 (Enforcement of External Orders) Order 1995;

"the Order of 1999" means the Criminal Justice (International Co-operation) Act 1990 (Enforcement of Overseas Forfeiture Orders) (Scotland) Order 1999;

"the Overseas Forfeiture Order of 2005" means the Criminal Justice (International Co-operation) Act 1990 (Enforcement of Overseas Forfeiture Orders) (Scotland) Order 2005;

"the POCA Order of 2005" means the Proceeds of Crime Act 2002 (External Requests and Orders) Order 2005;

"relevant enactment" means the Act of 1989, the Act of 1995, the Order of 1995, the Order of 1999, the Overseas Forfeiture Order of 2005 or the POCA Order of 2005, as the case may be.

Deriv. RCS 1965, r. 249S(1) inserted by S.I. 1987 No. 12 and amended by S.I. 1990 No. 705 and 1991 No. 1183

---

[1] Rule 62.47 amended by S.I. 1996 No. 1756 (effective 5th August 1996) and S.I. 1999 No. 1220 (effective 1st May 1999) and S.I. 1996 No. 2168 (effective 23rd September 1996) and S.I. 2001 No.494 (effective 22nd December 2001) and by S.S.I. 2005 No. 663 (effective 31st December 2005).

[2] Heading to Pt. II amended by S.I. 1999 No. 1220 (effective 1st May 1999).

General note. Part VII of this Chapter is made under s. 36(1) of the Act of 1995, and originally **62.47.1** para. 19 of Sched. 4 to the Prevention of Terrorism (Temporary Provisions) Act 1989 (now replaced by para. 27 of Sched. 4 to the Terrorism Act 2000). Accordingly, a word or expression used in Pt. VII which is also used in those Acts has the meaning respectively given in those Acts unless the contrary intention appears: Interpretation Act 1978, s. 11.

[1] *Applications for registration under the relevant enactment*

62.48.—(1) An application to which this rule applies shall be made by petition.

[1,2] (2) This rule applies to an application under any of the following provisions:—

(a) paragraph 19(2) of Schedule 4 to the Act of 1989 (application for registration of an England and Wales order, Northern Ireland order or Islands order);

(b) section 36(1) of the Act of 1995 (application for registration of an order to which section 35 of the Act of 1995 applies);

(c) section 41(1) of the Act of 1995 (application for registration of external confiscation order);

(d) article 15(1) of the Order of 1995 (application for registration of external forfeiture order in relation to terrorism);

(e) article 16(1) of the Order of 1995 (application for registration of external restraint order);.

[3] (f) article 5(1) of the Order of 1999 (application for registration of external forfeiture order other than in relation to terrorism).

[3] (g) paragraph 27(3) of Schedule 4 to the Act of 2000 (application for registration of an England and Wales order, Northern Ireland order or Islands order);

[5] (h) article 13(1) of the Overseas Forfeiture Order of 2005 (applications to give effect to external forfeiture orders);

[5] (i) article 66(1) of the POCA Order of 2005 (applications to give effect to external orders).

(3) There shall be produced with a petition under paragraph (1) a certified copy of the order which is sought to be registered.

Deriv. RCS 1965, r. 249T(1) substituted by S.I. 1991 No. 1157, r. 249T(1A) inserted by S.I. 1991 No. 1157 and amended by S.I. 1991 No. 1183, and r. 249T(2) inserted by S.I. 1987 No. 12

---

[1] Rule 62.48(2) and heading amended by S.I. 1996 No. 1756 (effective 5th August 1996).
[2] Rule 62.48(2) amended by S.I. 1996 No. 2168 (effective 23rd September 1996).
[3] Rule 62.48(2)(d) amended and (2)(f) inserted, by S.I. 1999 No. 1220 (effective 1st May 1999).
[4] Rule 62.48(2)(g) inserted by S.S.I. 2001 No. 494 (effective 22nd December 2001).
[5] Rule 62.48(2)(h) & (i) inserted by S.S.I. 2005 No. 663 (effective 31st December 2005).

62.48.1   *General note.* Part VII of this Chapter provides rules for the enforcement in Scotland under the Acts of 1988, 1989, 1995, 2000 (replacing the 1989 Act), and the Orders of 1995 and 1999 listed in r. 62.47 of various orders made in England and Wales or Northern Ireland under the Drug Trafficking Act 1994, Pt. VI of the Act of 1988, the Act of 1989 (now replaced by the Act of 2000), and external orders under the Order of 1995 and overseas forfeiture orders under the Order of 1999. The orders are listed in each section which gives the court jurisdiction to deal with an application.

[1] *Warrant for registration under the relevant enactment*
[1] **62.49.** The court shall, on being satisfied that the application complies with the requirements of the relevant enactment, as the case may be—
 (a) pronounce an interlocutor granting warrant for execution of a non-money order; or
 (b) pronounce an interlocutor granting warrant for the registration of a money order.

Deriv. RCS 1965, r. 249U(1) inserted by S.I. 1987 No. 12 and amended by S.I. 1990 No. 705 and 1991 No. 1183

---

[1] R. 62.49 and heading amended by S.I. 1996 No. 1756 (effective 5th August 1996).

[1] *Registration under the relevant enactment*
 62.50.—[1] (1) Where the court pronounces an interlocutor under rule 62.49, the Deputy Principal Clerk shall enter the order in the register for the registration of orders under the relevant enactment.
 (2) On presentation by the petitioner to the Keeper of the Registers of—
 (a) a certified copy of the interlocutor pronounced under rule 62.49(b), and
 (b) a certified copy of the order to be registered,
they shall be registered in the register of judgments of the Books of Council and Session.
 (3) On registration under paragraph (2), the Keeper of the Registers shall issue an extract of the registered order with a warrant for execution.

Deriv. RCS 1965, r. 249U(2) inserted by S.I. 1987 No. 12 and amended by S.I. 1990 No. 705 and 1991 No. 1183, and r. 249U(3) inserted by S.I. 1987 No. 12

---

[1] R. 62.50(1) and heading amended by S.I. 1996 No. 1756 (effective 5th August 1996).

62.50.1   *"Keeper of the Registers".* This is the Keeper of the Registers of Scotland: r. 1.3(1). The Register of Judgments is at Meadowbank House, 153 London Road, Edinburgh EH8 7AU; tel. 0131–659 6111; fax 0131–459 1221; DX ED300.

62.50.2   *"certified copy of the interlocutor".* A copy of the interlocutor is typed by the agent and presented to the clerk of session in the Petition Department. The clerk checks it, certifies it as a true copy and stamps it with the court stamp.
    A fee is payable.

Registration fee. A fee will be payable to the Keeper of the Registers for registration and any **62.50.3** extract: see the Fees in the Registers of Scotland Order 1991 [S.I. 1991 No. 2093].

[1] *Service of warrant for registration under the relevant enactment*
   62.51. The petitioner shall serve a copy of the interlocutor, pronounced under rule 62.49 granting warrant for registration, and a notice in Form 62.51 on the person against whom the order may be enforced.

Deriv. RCS 1965, r. 249V inserted by S.I. 1987 No. 12 and amended by S.I. 1991 No. 1183

[1] Heading of r. 62.51 amended by S.I. 1996 No. 1756 (effective 5th August 1996).

"serve". For methods of service, see Chap. 16, Pt. I.   **62.51.1**

Further provisions as respects warrant for registration
   62.51A. Where an interlocutor granting warrant for the registration of an external confiscation order is pronounced and the order falls to be remitted for enforcement to the Sheriff of Lothian and Borders at Edinburgh, the Deputy Principal Clerk shall send a certified copy of the interlocutor, within four days after it is pronounced, to the sheriff clerk at Edinburgh.

[1] R. 62.51A inserted by S.I. 1999 No. 1220 (effective 1st May 1999).

"external confiscation order". An external confiscation order is an order, made by a court in a **62.51A.1** county designated by an Order in Council, for recovering payments or other reward or property or other economic advantage received, in connection with certain offences or drug trafficking, or the value of such payments, property, reward or economic advantage: Proceeds of Crime (Scotland) Act 1995, s. 40(2). Registration is by virtue of s. 41(1) of the Act of 1995.

[1] *Suspension of enforcement under the Act of 1995*
   62.52.—[1] (1) Where an order under section 36(1) of the Act of 1995 has been registered under rule 62.50, the court may, on the application of the person against whom the order may be enforced, if satisfied that an application has been made to the court which made the order to have it set aside or quashed—
   (a) suspend enforcement of the order; and
   (b) sist any proceedings for enforcement of the order.
   (2) Notwithstanding rule 60.2 (form of applications for suspension), an application under paragraph (1) shall be made by note in the process in the petition under rule 62.48(1).

Deriv. R.C.S. 1965, r. 249W inserted by S.I. 1987 No. 12 and amended by S.I. 1990 No. 705

[1] R. 62.52(1) and heading amended by S.I. 1996 No. 1756 (effective 5th August 1996) and S.I. 1996 No. 2168 (effective 23rd September 1996).

"note". For applications by note, see r. 15.2.   **62.52.1**

[1,2] *Modification and cancellation of registration under the Act of 1989 or 1995 or 2000*
   62.53.—[1,2] (1) An application to modify or cancel the registration of an order under the Act of 1989 or 1995 or 2000 registered under rule 62.50 shall be made—
   (a) by the petitioner, by motion; or
   (b) by any other interested party, by note.
   (2) There shall be produced with the application under paragraph (1) a certified copy of any order which modifies or revokes the registered order or which causes the order to cease to have effect.

[1] (3) The court shall, on being satisfied—

(a) that the registered order has been modified, revoked or has ceased to have effect, or

(b) that the registration of an external confiscation order should be cancelled in terms of section 41(3) of the Act of 1995,

pronounce an interlocutor so modifying or cancelling the registration, as the case may be, and grant warrant for the registration of a certified copy of the interlocutor in the register of judgments of the Books of Council and Session.

(4) Where the court pronounces an interlocutor under paragraph (3), the Deputy Principal Clerk shall modify or cancel the registration in the register kept under rule 62.50(1) in accordance with that interlocutor.

Deriv. R.C.S. 1965, r. 249X inserted by S.I. 1987 No. 12 and amended by S.I. 1991 No. 1157

---

[1] R. 62.53(1) and (3) and heading amended by S.I. 1996 No. 1756 (effective 5th August 1996).
[2] R. 62.53(1) and heading amended by S.I. 1996 No. 2168 (effective 23rd September 1996) and S.S.I. 2001 No. 494 (effective 22nd December 2001).

62.53.1   *"motion"*. For motions, see Chap. 23.

62.53.2   *"note"*. For applications by note, see r. 15.2.

Incidental applications

[1] **62.54.**—(1) Any of the following applications shall be made in the prayer of the petition under rule 62.48(1) to which it relates or, if the prayer of that petition has been granted, by motion in the process of that petition:—

 (a) an application under section 32(1) of the Act of 1995 for a warrant for inhibition;

 (b) an application under section 33(1) of the Act of 1995 (warrant for arrestment);

 (c) an application under paragraph 16(1) (warrant for inhibition), or paragraph 16A(1) (warrant for arrestment), of Schedule 4 to the Act of 1989 as applied by paragraph 19(5) of that Schedule or by article 18 of the Order of 1995, as the case may be.

(2) Either of the following applications shall be made in the prayer of the petition under rule 62.48(1) to which it relates or, if the prayer of the petition has been granted, by note in the process of that petition:—

 (a) an application under sub-paragraph (4) of paragraph 19 of Schedule 4 to the Act of 1989 for an order in implementation of an England and Wales, Northern Ireland or Islands forfeiture order registered in the Court of Session under that paragraph;

 (b) an application under article 17 of the Order of 1995 for an order in implementation of an external forfeiture order registered in the Court of Session under article 15(1) of that Order.

(3) Where the court makes an order by virtue of paragraph 19(4) of Schedule 4 to the Act of 1989 or article 17 of the Order of 1995 appointing an administrator, rules 76.24 to 76.26 (which relate to the duties of an administrator) shall apply to an administrator appointed by virtue of that paragraph or article as they apply to an order in implementation of a forfeiture order.

Deriv. R.C.S. 1965, r. 249Y inserted by S.I. 1987 No. 12 and amended by S.I. 1990 No. 705 and 1991 No. 1183

---

[1] R. 62.54 substituted by S.I. 1996 No. 2168 (effective 23rd September 1996).

"motion". For motions, see Chap. 23. **62.54.1**

Inhibition and arrestment. On inhibition on the dependence, see note 13.6.2. On arrestment on **62.54.2** the dependence, see note 13.6.3.

Applications to recall lease or restrict an arrestment or inhibition under the following enactments are by motion by virtue of r. 23.11:—

(a) with respect to inhibition—s. 32(1)(a) and (5) of the Act of 1995; para. 16(2)(a) and (6)(a) of Sched. 4 to the Act of 1989 as applied by para. 19(5) of Sched. 4 (in relation to restraint orders elsewhere in UK registered in the Court of Session) or as applied by art. 18 of the Order of 1995 (in relation to external restraint orders of a designated country registered in the Court of Session);

(b) with respect to arrestment—s. 33(2) and (4) of the Act of 1995; para. 16A(2) and (4) of Sched. 4 to the Act of 1989 as applied by para. 19(5) of Sched. 4 (in relation to relevant orders elsewhere in UK registered in the Court of Session) or as applied by art. 18 of the Order of 1995 (in relation to external restraint orders of a designated country registered in the Court of Session).

"note". For applications by note, see r. 15.2. **62.54.3**

Cancellation of registration or variation of property under the Overseas Forfeiture Order of 2005 or the POCA Order of 2005

[1] **62.54A.**—(1) An application under article 16(3) of the Overseas Forfeiture Order of 2005 (application for cancellation of registration or variation of property) or article 69(3) of the POCA Order of 2005 (application for cancellation of registration or variation of property) shall be made—

 (a) by the Lord Advocate, by motion; or

(b) by any other interested party, by note.

(2) There shall be produced with an application under paragraph (1), a certified copy of any order which modifies or revokes the registered order or which causes the registered order to cease to have effect.

(3) The court shall, on pronouncing an interlocutor granting an application under paragraph (1), grant warrant for the registration of a certified copy of the interlocutor in the register of judgments of the Books of Council and Session.

(4) Where the court pronounces an interlocutor granting an application under paragraph (1), the Deputy Principal Clerk shall cancel or, as the case may be, vary the registration in the register kept under rule 62.50(1) in accordance with that interlocutor.

---

[1] Rule 62.54A inserted by S.S.I. 2005 No. 663 (effective 31st December 2005).

Registration under the POCA Order in Council of 2005: further provision

[1] **62.54B.**—(1) Rule 62.2 (certificate of currency conversion) shall not apply to an application under article 66(1) of the POCA Order of 2005 (application to give effect to external orders).

(2) An application under article 72(4) (payment within a specified period) or article 72(6) (extension of specified period) of the POCA Order of 2005 shall be made by motion in the process relating to the granting of the application under article 66(1) of the POCA Order of 2005.

(3) The Deputy Principal Clerk shall send to the sheriff clerk appointed under article 69(1)(c) of the POCA Order of 2005 a certified copy of the interlocutor granting warrant for registration under rule 62.49 and of any subsequent interlocutor granting an application under–

(a) rule 62.54A(1) (application for cancellation of registration or variation of property);

(b) paragraph (3) of this rule (payment within specified period and extension of specified period);

(c) rule 76.28(1)(i) (enforcement administrators); or

(d) rule 76.28(3)(i) (recall and variation of order appointing administrator),

in respect of the registered order.

---

[1] Rule 62.54B inserted by S.S.I. 2005 No. 663 (effective 31st December 2005).

PART VIII

REGISTRATION OF AWARDS UNDER THE MULTILATERAL INVESTMENT GUARANTEE AGENCY ACT 1988

Registration of awards under the Multilateral Investment Guarantee Agency Act 1988

62.55. Part III shall, with the necessary modifications, apply to an award under Article 4 of Annex II to the convention referred to in section 1(1) of the Multilateral Investment Guarantee Agency Act 1988 as it applies to an award under the convention mentioned in section 1(1) of the Arbitration (International Investment Disputes) Act 1966.

Deriv. R.C.S. 1965, r. 249AA inserted by S.I. 1990 No. 705

62.55.1 *General note.* Part VIII of this Chapter is made under s. 7(e) of the Multilateral Investment Guarantee Agency Act 1988.

Under the Convention establishing the Multilateral Investment Guarantee Agency (Cm. 150 (1987)), disputes between the Agency and a member under Art. 57 may be settled by arbitration under Annex II to the convention. An award may be registered on application to the court under s. 4, as applied by s. 7, of the 1988 Act.

The convention is intended to promote private sector investment in developing countries by providing insurance for investors against certain kinds of non-commercial risks.

PART IX

RECOGNITION AND ENFORCEMENT OF ARBITRAL AWARDS UNDER THE MODEL LAW ON INTERNATIONAL COMMERCIAL ARBITRATION

Application and interpretation of this Part

62.56.—(1) This Part applies to an application under article 35 of the Model Law in Schedule 7 to the Law Reform (Miscellaneous Provisions) (Scotland) Act 1990 (applications for enforcement of arbitral award).

(2) In this Part—

"the Act of 1990" means the Law Reform (Miscellaneous Provisions) (Scotland) Act 1990;

"arbitral award" means an award to which the Model Law, as applied by section 86 of the Act of 1990, applies;

"the Model Law" means the Model Law on International Commercial Arbitration as set out in Schedule 7 to the Act of 1990.

General note. Part IX of this Chapter provides rules for the enforcement in Scotland of an **62.56.1** award made whether in Scotland or abroad under the UNCITRAL Model Law on International Commercial Arbitration adopted by the U.N. Commission on International Trade Law on 21st June 1985. The Model Law was given the force of law in Scotland by s. 66 of the Act of 1990. It applies automatically, unless excluded, to any international commercial arbitration as defined in Art. 1 of the Model Law commencing on or after 1st January 1991, and may be extended by agreement to any other arbitration.

Applications for registration under the Act of 1990

62.57.—(1) An application for enforcement of an arbitral award under article 35 of the Model Law shall be made by petition.

(2) There shall be produced with such a petition—

(a) the authenticated original arbitral award or a certified copy of it;

(b) the original arbitration agreement referred to in article 7 of the Model Law or a certified copy of it;

(c) an affidavit stating—

(i) the full name, title, trade or business and the usual or last known place of residence or, where appropriate, of the business of the petitioner and the party against whom the arbitral award was made;

(ii) the amount of the arbitral award which is unsatisfied;

(iii) that the arbitral award has become binding on the parties and has not been set aside or suspended by a court of the country in which, or under the law of which, the award was made; and

(iv) whether any application has been made under the Model Law which, if granted, might result in the setting aside of the award.

Deriv. R.C.S. 1965, r. 249AB inserted by S.I. 1991 No. 2213

Jurisdiction under the Model Law. The court has jurisdiction under art. 35 of the Model Law **62.57.1** where—

(a) the application is made in respect of an award made in an international commercial arbitration conducted under the Model Law;

(b) the Model Law applies to the award (see note 62.57.2); and

(c) the jurisdiction is not otherwise excluded (see note 62.57.3).

[THE NEXT PAGE IS C 543]

Applicability of the Model Law. The Model Law will not apply for enforcement (even where it **62.57.2** was used to conduct the arbitration) where—

(a) the award was made in a state party to the 1958 New York Convention (Act of 1990, Sched. 7, Art. 1(1) and the Arbitration Act 1975); or

(b) the award was made in a state party to the 1927 Geneva Convention on the Execution of Foreign Arbitral Awards (Act of 1990, Sched. 7, Art. 1(1) and Arbitration Act 1950, Pt. II).

Subject to the above, the Model law enforcement provisions apply to all awards, whether domestic or foreign, made under the Model Law.

Exclusion of jurisdiction. Art. 36(1)(b) excludes the jurisdiction of the court where it finds **62.57.3** that—

(a) the subject-matter of the dispute is not capable of settlement by arbitration under Scots law; or

(b) recognition or enforcement of the award would be contrary to public policy.

"petition". A petition is presented in the Outer House: r. 14.2(h). The petition must be in **62.57.4** Form 14.4 in the official printed form: rr. 4.1 and 14.4. The petition may be signed by the petitioner, counsel or other person having a right of audience, or an agent: r. 4.2; and see r. 1.3(1) (definition of "counsel", "other person having a right of audience" and "agent") and note 1.3.4.

The petitioner must lodge the petition with the required steps of process (r. 4.4) and any documents founded on or adopted (r. 27.1(1)). A fee is payable on lodging the petition: see note 14.5.10.

On petitions generally, see Chap. 14.

Productions. The petitioner must produce with the petition (1) the items listed in r. 68.57(2), **62.57.5** those listed in sub-paras. (a) and (b) of r. 68.57(2) being also required by the Model Law; and (2) if necessary, a translation of any document lodged (r. 62.3).

Affidavit. The affidavit should be in the form of a statement of evidence written in the first **62.57.6** person. The affidavit should contain the evidence of the deponent in support of the averments in the petition. In particular the affidavit should deal with the matters listed in r. 62.57(2)(c).

An affidavit should be sworn and signed by the deponent before any person who may competently take an oath, whether in Scotland or in any other country. In Scotland such a person may include a notary public, justice of the peace, sheriff, or any judge. The person taking the oath should also sign the affidavit. Where the affidavit is not in English a duly certified translation should also be lodged.

See also definition of affidavit in r. 1.3(1).

Registration under the Act of 1990

62.58.—(1) The court, on being satisfied that the arbitral award may be registered, shall grant warrant for registration.

(2) Where the court pronounces an interlocutor under paragraph (1), the Deputy Principal Clerk shall enter the arbitral award in a register of arbitral awards under article 35 of the Model Law.

(3) On presentation by the petitioner to the Keeper of the Registers of—

(a) a certified copy of the interlocutor of the warrant for registration,

(b) a certified copy of the arbitral award to be registered, and any translation of it, and

[1] (c) any certificate of currency conversion under rule 62.2(1)(b), they shall be registered in the register of judgments of the Books of Council and Session.

(4) An extract of a registered arbitral award with warrant for execution shall not be issued by the Keeper of the Registers until a certificate of service under rule 62.59 (service on party against whom arbitral award made) is produced to him.

Deriv. R.C.S. 1965, r. 249AC inserted by S.I. 1991 No. 2213

---

[1] R. 62.58(3)(c) amended by S.I. 1996 No. 2168 (minor correction).

"Keeper of the Registers". This is the Keeper of the Registers of Scotland: r. 1.3(1). The **62.58.1** Register of Judgments is at Meadowbank House, 153 London Road, Edinburgh EH8 7AU; tel. 0131–659 6111; fax 0131–459 1221; DX ED300.

62.58.2   *"certified copy of the interlocutor"*. A copy of the interlocutor is typed by the agent and presented to the clerk of session in the Petition Department. The clerk checks it, certifies it as a true copy and stamps it with the court stamp.

A fee is payable.

62.58.3   *"certified copy of the award"*. It is not clear how the award should be certified; but presumably this may be done by the arbiter or his clerk.

62.58.4   *"translation"*. See r. 62.3.

62.58.5   *"certificate of currency conversion"*. The certificate should be obtained from the clerk of session in the Petition Department and should be signed by him: r. 62.2(3) and see note 62.2.5.

62.58.6   *Registration fee*. A fee will be payable to the Keeper of the Registers for registration and any extract: see the Fees in the Registers of Scotland Order 1991 [S.I. 1991 No. 2093].

Service on party against whom arbitral award made

62.59. On registration under rule 62.58, the petitioner shall forthwith serve a notice of registration on the party against whom the arbitral award was made in Form 62.16.

62.59.1   *"serve"*. For methods of service, see Chap. 16, Pt. I.

Application for refusal of recognition or enforcement under the Act of 1990

62.60.—(1) An application under article 36(1)(a) of the Model Law (request by party against whom arbitral award made for refusal of recognition or enforcement) shall be made by note.

(2) A note referred to in paragraph (1)—

(a) may crave—

   (i) suspension or interdict of any past or future steps in the execution of the arbitral award, including registration or enforcement of the award; and

   (ii) recall of any interlocutor pronounced under rule 62.58(1) (registration under the Act of 1990); and

(b) shall be supported by affidavit and any documentary evidence.

(3) Where any interlocutor pronounced under rule 62.58(1) is recalled, a certificate to that effect issued by the Deputy Principal Clerk shall be sufficient warrant to the Keeper of the Registers to cancel the registration and return the documents registered to the petitioner on whose application the interlocutor under that rule was pronounced.

62.60.1   *General note*. For the grounds on which an application may be made for refusal of recognition or enforcement of an arbitral award under the Model Law, see Art. 36(1)(a) in Sched. 7 to the Act of 1990.

62.60.2   *"note"*. For applications by note, see r. 15.2.

62.60.3   *"affidavit"*. See note 62.57.6.

[1]PART X
RECOGNITION, REGISTRATION AND ENFORCEMENT OF MISCELLANEOUS DECISIONS

Application and interpretation of this Part

[1] **62.61**—(1) This Part applies to the recognition, registration or enforcement, as the case may be, of an award, decision, judgment or order under any of the following instruments:—

(a) Article 34.1 (enforcement of arbitral award) of the procedural rules on conciliation and arbitration of contracts financed by the European Development Fund;

(b) Article 20 of the United Nations (International Tribunal) (Former Yugoslavia) Order 1996 (enforcement of orders for the preservation or restitution of property).

[2] (c) Article 20 of the United Nations (International Tribunal) (Rwanda) Order 1996 (enforcement of orders for the preservation or restitution of property).

(2) In this Part—

"decision" includes award, judgment or order;

"relevant instrument" means an instrument mentioned in paragraph (1).

---

[1] Pt. X and r. 62.61 inserted by S.I. 1996 No. 2168 (effective 23rd September 1996).

[2] R.62.61(1)(c) inserted by S.S.I. 2001 No. 305, para. 14 (effective 18th September 2001).

General note. Part X was devised as a general provision for the growing number of obscure **62.61.1** decisions of bodies which may require registration and enforcement in Scotland. The rules in this Part (based on Pt III) are of general application and apply where appropriate to decisions listed in r. 62.61(1). The idea is that, to save adding new Parts to Chap. 62 where the general rules are sufficient, subsequent appropriate enactments or other instruments containing provisions for registration and enforcement of decisions can be inserted in r. 62.61(1). Had the principal annotator thought of this idea when drafting the original Chap. 62, he would have inserted Pts III and VIII at least into this miscellaneous Part.

Article 34.1 of EDF contracts. Under Art. 233 of the Lomé Convention of 15th December **62.61.2** 1989 (Cmnd. 1999 UKTS 47 (1992)) the European Development Fund may be used to finance projects and programmes in those African, Caribbean and Pacific (ACP) states which are parties to the Convention. Art. 307 provides for disputes between an ACP state and a contractor, supplier or provider of services during the performance of a trans-national contract financed by the Fund to be settled by arbitration in accordance with procedural rules adopted by decisions of the Council of Ministers. The procedural rules mentioned in r. 62.61(1)(a) are Annex V of Decision No. 3/90 of the ACP/EEC Council of Ministers of 29th March 1990 (O.J. L–382 of 31st December 1990).

Article 20 of the Former Yugoslavia Order, and the Rwanda Order. The United Nations **62.61.3** (International Tribunal) (Former Yugoslavia) Order 1996 (S.I. 1996 No. 716) enables the U.K. to co-operate with the International Tribunal for the Prosecution of Persons Responsible for Serious Violations of International Humanitarian Law Committed in the Territory of the Former Yugoslavia since 1991 established by the UN Security Council Resolution 827 (1993) in the investigation and prosecution of persons before the tribunal. Article 20 provides for registration and enforcement of orders for the preservation or restitution of property.

A similar provision is made in Art. 20 of the United Nations (International Tribunal) (Rwanda) Order 1996 (S.I. 1996 No. 1296) in respect of genocide in that country following the UN Security Council Resolution 955 (1994).

Applications under this Part

[1] **62.62.**—(1) An application for recognition, registration or enforcement, as the case may be, of a decision under a relevant instrument shall be made by petition.

(2) There shall be produced with such a petition an affidavit—

(a) exhibiting a copy of the decision certified under the relevant instrument; and

(b) stating—

   (i) the full name, title, trade or business and the usual or the last known place of residence or, where appropriate, of business of the petitioner and of the party against whom the decision was made;

   (ii) that the petitioner is entitled to have the decision recognised, registered or enforced, as the case may be, under the relevant instrument;

   (iii) the extent to which the decision is unsatisfied; and

   (iv) whether the enforcement of the decision has been sisted (provisionally or otherwise) under the relevant instrument and whether any, and if so what, application has been made under the relevant instrument which, if granted, might result in a sist of enforcement of the decision.

---

[1] R. 62.62 inserted by S.I. 1996 No. 2168 (effective 23rd September 1996).

62.62.1   *General note.* For the history of this rule, see note 62.62.1.

62.62.2   *"petition".* A petition is presented in the Outer House: r. 14.2(h). The petition must be in Form 14.4 in the official printed form: rr. 4.1 and 14.4. The petition may be signed by the petitioner, counsel or other person having a right of audience, or an agent: r. 4.2(3)(d); and see r. 13(1) (definition of "counsel", "other person having a right of audience" and "agent") and note 1.3.4.

On petitions generally, see Chap. 14.
The petitioner must lodge the petition with the required steps of process (r. 4.4) and any documents founded on or adopted (r. 27.1(1)). A fee is payable on lodging the petition: see note 14.5.10.

On petitions generally, see Chap. 14.

62.62.3   *Productions.* The petitioner must produce with the petition the relevant documents. On lodging productions, see r. 4.5.

62.62.4   *Affidavit.* The affidavit should be in the form of a statement of evidence written in the first person. The affidavit should contain the evidence of the deponent in support of the averments in the petition. In particular the affidavit should deal with the matters listed in r. 62.62(2).

An affidavit should be sworn and signed by the deponent before any person who may competently take an oath, whether in Scotland or in any other country. In Scotland such a person may include a notary public, justice of the peace, sheriff, or any judge. The person taking the oath should also sign the affidavit. Where the affidavit is not in English a duly certified translation should also be lodged.

See also the definition of affidavit in r. 1.3(1).

Recognition, or warrant for registration or for enforcement under this Part

[1] **62.63.** The court shall, on being satisfied that the petition complies with the requirements of the relevant instrument, pronounce an interlocutor recognising or granting warrant for the registration or enforcement of the decision, as the case may be.

[1] R. 62.63 inserted by S.I. 1996 No. 2168 (effective 23rd September 1996).

62.63.1   *General note.* For the history of this rule, see note 62.61.1.

Registration for enforcement under this Part

[1] **62.64.**—(1) Where the court pronounces an interlocutor under rule 62.63 granting warrant for registration or enforcement, as the case may be, the Deputy Principal Clerk shall enter details of the interlocutor and the decision in a register of decisions under this Part.

(2) On presentation by the petitioner to the Keeper of the Registers of—
   (a) a certified copy of the interlocutor under rule 62.63,
   (b) a certified copy of the decision and any translation of it, and
   (c) any certificate of currency conversion under rule 62.2(1)(b),
they shall be registered in the register of judgments of the Books of Council and Session.

(3) An extract of a registered decision with warrant for execution shall not be issued by the Keeper of the Registers until a certificate of service under rule 62.65 is produced to him.

[1] R. 62.64 inserted by S.I. 1996 No. 2168 (effective 23rd September 1996).

62.64.1   *General note.* For this history of this rule, see note 62.61.1.

62.64.2   *"Keeper of the Registers".* This is the Keeper of the Registers of Scotland: r. 1.3(1). The Register of Judgments is at Meadowbank House, 153 London Road, Edinburgh EH8 7AU; tel. 0131–659 6111; fax 0131–459 1221; DX ED300.

62.64.3   *"certified copy of the interlocutor".* A copy of the interlocutor is typed by the agent and presented to the clerk of session in the Petition Department. The clerk checks it, certifies it as a true copy and stamps it with the court stamp.

A fee is payable.

"*translation*". See r. 62.3.   **62.64.4**

"*certificate of currency conversion*". In obtaining this, notwithstanding the provisions of r.   **62.64.5**
62.2(1), the date of conversion in the certified statement may be regarded by the relevant
instrument to be the date of the decision.

The certificate should be obtained from the clerk of session and should be signed by him: r.
62.2(3); and see notes 62.2.4 and 62.2.5.

Registration fee. A fee will be payable to the Keeper of the Registers for registration and any   **62.64.6**
extract: see the Fees in the Registers of Scotland Order 1991 [S.I. 1995 No. 1945].

Service on party against whom award made
[1] **62.65.** On registration under rule 62.64, the petitioner shall forthwith
serve a notice of the registration on the party against whom the decision was
made in Form 62.65.

------

[1] R. 62.65 inserted by S.I. 1996 No. 2168 (effective 23rd September 1996).

General note. For the history of this rule, see note 62.61.1.   **62.65.1**

"*serve*". For methods of service, see Chap. 16, Pt. I.   **62.65.2**

Sist of enforcement under this Part
62.66.—(1) Where it appears to the court that—
  (a) the enforcement of the decision has been sisted (whether provision-
     ally or otherwise) under the relevant instrument, or
  (b) any application has been made under the relevant instrument which,
     if granted, might result in a sist of the enforcement of the award,
the court shall, or in the case referred to in sub-paragraph (b) may, sist the
petition for such period as it thinks fit.

(2) Where the court has granted a warrant for registration under rule
62.63, the party against whom the decision was made may apply to the court
for suspension or interdict of execution of the award.

(3) An application under paragraph (2) shall—
  (a) be made on ground (a) or (b) of paragraph (1);
  (b) notwithstanding rule 60.2 (form of applications for suspension), be
     made by note in the process of the petition under rule 62.62; and
  (c) be accompanied by an affidavit stating the relevant facts.

------

[1] R. 62.66 inserted by S.I. 1996 No. 2168 (effective 23rd September 1996).

General note. For the history of this rule, see note 62.61.1.   **62.66.1**
The relevant instrument may not provide for a sist, in which case this rule would not apply.

"*suspension or interdict*". See Chap. 60.   **62.66.2**

"*note*". For applications by note, see r. 15.2.   **62.66.3**

EDF contracts. There is no provision in the procedural rules on arbitration of contracts financed   **62.66.4**
by the European Development Fund (see r. 62.61(1)(a) and note 62.61.2) for sist of enforcement.

[1] **PART XI**

REGISTRATION AND ENFORCEMENT OF JUDGMENTS UNDER COUNCIL REGULATION (E.C.) No. 2201/2003 OF 27TH NOVEMBER 2003(C)

Application and interpretation of this Part
[1] **62.67.**—(1) This Part applies to the registration and enforcement of a
judgment under the Council Regulation.

(2) In this Part, unless the context otherwise requires—
    "the Council Regulation" means Council Regulation (E.C.) No. 2201/

2003 of 27th November 2003 on jurisdiction and the recognition and enforcement of judgments in matrimonial matters and matters of parental responsibility;

"judgment" includes an authentic instrument or enforceable agreement; and

"Member State" has the same meaning as in Article 2(3) of the Council Regulation.

———

[1] Part XI and r. 62.67 inserted by S.S.I. 2005 No. 135 (effective 2nd March 2005).

62.07.1   *General note.* The Council Regulation No. 2201/2003 (new Brussels II) replaces Council Regulation No 1347/2000 (for which there was no special provision in the RCS 1994). It deals with jurisdiction as well as recognition and enforcement of judgments in matrimonial matters and matters of parental responsibility.

The new Council Regulation has effect from 1st March 2005. Proceedings started under C.R. No. 1347/2000 may continue under that Regulation.

Matrimonial matters and matters of parental responsibility with which the new Council Regulation is concerned are defined in art. 1 as (a) divorce, legal separation, annulment; (b) attribution, exercise, delegation, restriction or termination of parental responsibility (which includes custody, access, guardianship, curatorship and similar institutions, designation and functions of a person or body over a child's person or property or representing or assisting a child, placement in a foster family or institution, and protection of a child's property). It does *not* cover establishing or contesting a parent-child relationship, adoption or freeing for or revocation of adoption, names, emancipation, maintenance, trusts or succession, or measures as a result of criminal offences by a child.

The term "child" is not defined in the Regulation.

The Regulation applies to Member States of the E.U. except Denmark.

Chapter III of the Regulation (arts. 21-52) deals with recognition and enforcement. A judgment in a Member State will be recognised without special procedure, but application may be made for a decision of a court in another Member State to be or not to be recognised: art. 21. A decision in relation to parental responsibility must be registered for enforcement in the UK, which is by petition: art. 28(2) and RCS 1994, r. 62.69.

Disapplication of certain rules to this Part
[1] **62.68.** The following rules shall not apply to an application under this Part:—

4.1(1) (printed form for petition),
14.4 (form of petitions),
14.5 (first order in petitions),
14.6 (period of notice for lodging answers),
14.7 (intimation and service of petitions),
14.9 (unopposed petitions).

———

[1] Rule 62.68 inserted by S.S.I. 2005 No. 135 (effective 2nd March 2005).

Enforcement of judgments from another Member State
[1] **62.69.**—(1) An application under Article 28 of the Council Regulation (enforceable judgments) shall be made by petition in Form 62.69.

(2) There shall be produced with the petition—

(a) an authentic copy of the judgment to be registered;
(b) a certificate under Article 39 of the Council Regulation (standard forms of certificate);
(c) where judgment has been given in absence (that is to say, in default of appearance)—
(i) the original or a certified copy of the document which establishes that the party against whom judgment was given in absence was served with the document initiating proceedings or with an equivalent; or

    (ii) a document indicating that the party against whom the judgment was given in absence has accepted the judgment unequivocally;
  (d) where applicable, a document showing that the applicant is in receipt of legal aid in the country in which the judgment was given;
  (e) an affidavit stating—
    (i) an address within the jurisdiction of the court for service on or intimation to the petitioner;
    (ii) the name and address of the petitioner and his interest in the judgment;
    (iii) the name and date of birth of each child in respect of whom the judgment was made, the present whereabouts or suspected whereabouts of that child and the name of any person with whom he is alleged to be;
    (iv) the name and address of any other person with an interest in the judgment;
    (v) whether the judgment is already registered and, if so, where it is registered;
    (vi) details of any order known to the petitioner which affects a child in respect of whom the judgment was made and fulfils the conditions necessary for its recognition in Scotland.

  (3) Where the petitioner does not produce a document required by paragraph (2)(b) to (e), the court may—
  (a) fix a period within which that document is to be lodged;
  (b) accept an equivalent document; or
  (c) dispense with the requirement to produce the document.

----

[1] Rule 62.69 inserted by S.S.I. 2005 No. 135 (effective 2nd March 2005).

General note. The only judgments to which art. 28 applies are those relating to parental **62.69.1** responsibility. In the UK, such judgments from another Member State must be registered for enforcement before they can be enforced: art. 28(2). Registration is by petition: r. 62.69.
  On the meaning of parental responsibility, see Art. 1 of the Regulation and note 62.67.1.
  An address of the applicant for service in Scotland must be given or a representative ad litem appointed: art. 30(2).

"petition". A petition is presented to the Outer House: r. 14.2(h). The petition must be in **62.69.2** Form 86.3 in the official printed form (r. 4.1). The petition must be signed by counsel or other person having a right of audience: r. 4.2; and see r. 1.3(1) (definition of "counsel" and "other person having a right of audience") and note 1.3.4.
  The petitioner must lodge the petition with the required steps of process (r. 4.4). A fee is payable on lodging the petition: see note 14.5.10.
  On petitions generally, see Chap. 14.

Productions. The documents referred to in r. 62.69(2)(a)-(c) are those required by art. 30(3). **62.69.3**
On productions and the lodging of them, see r. 4.5 and note 4.5.2.

"affidavit". The affidavit should be in the form of a statement of evidence written in the first **62.69.4** person. The affidavit should contain the evidence of the deponent in support of the averments in the petition. In particular, the affidavit should deal with the matters listed in r. 62.69(2)(e).
  An affidavit should be sworn and signed by the deponent before any person who may competently take an oath, whether in Scotland or any other country. In Scotland, such a person may include a notary public, justice of the peace, sheriff, or any judge. Where the affidavit is not in English, a duly certified translation should also be lodged.
  See also the definition of affidavit in r. 1.3(1).

Translations of judgments. A translation of a judgment not in English must be lodged with the **62.69.5** petition with a certificate by the translator: r. 62.3.

Warrant for registration under the Council Regulation
  [1] **62.70.**—(1) The court shall, on being satisfied that the petition complies with the requirements of the Council Regulation, pronounce an interlocutor—

(a) granting warrant for the registration of the judgment; and

(b) where necessary, granting decree in accordance with Scots law.

(2) The interlocutor pronounced under paragraph (1) shall specify—

(a) the period within which an appeal mentioned in rule 62.74 (appeals under the Council Regulation) against the interlocutor may be made; and

(b) that the petitioner—

(i) may register the judgment under rule 62.72 (registration under the Council Regulation); and

(ii) may not proceed to execution until the expiry of the period for lodging such appeal or its disposal.

---

[1] Rule 62.70 inserted by S.S.I. 2005 No. 135 (effective 2nd March 2005).

62.70.1   *Warrant for registration.* The warrant will be for registration in the register of judgments in the Petition Department and in the Books of Council and Session for execution: see r. 67.72.

62.70.2   *Decree in accordance with Scots Law.* This would be pronounced where the form of the foreign judgment is not suitable for a Scottish decree of registration.

62.70.3   *Period for marking appeal.* The period, for appeal by either party, is set out in r. 62.74(1).

Intimation to the petitioner

[1] **62.71.** Where the court pronounces an interlocutor under rule 62.70(1) the Deputy Principal Clerk shall intimate such interlocutor to the petitioner by sending to his address for service in Scotland a certified copy of the interlocutor by registered post or the first class recorded delivery service.

---

[1] Rule 62.71 inserted by S.S.I. 2005 No. 135 (effective 2nd March 2005).

Registration under the Council Regulation

[1] **62.72.**—(1) Where the court pronounces an interlocutor under rule 62.70(1) granting warrant for registration, the Deputy Principal Clerk shall enter the judgment in the register of judgments, authentic instruments and court settlements kept in the Petition Department.

(2) On presentation by the petitioner to the Keeper of the Registers of—

(a) a certified copy of the interlocutor under rule 62.70(1) granting warrant for registration,

(b) an authentic copy of the judgment and any translation of it, and

(c) any certificate of currency conversion under rule 62.2(1)(b) for any order concerning costs and expenses of proceedings under the Council Regulation;

they shall be registered in the register of judgments of the Books of Council and Session.

(3) On registration under paragraph (2), the Keeper of the Registers of Scotland shall issue an extract of the registered document with a warrant for execution.

---

[1] Rule 62.72 inserted by S.S.I. 2005 No. 135 (effective 2nd March 2005).

62.72.1   *Keeper of the Registers.* This is the Keeper of the Registers of Scotland: r. 1.3(1). The address of the Keeper of the Registers is Meadowbank House, 153 London Road, Edinburgh EH8 7AU; tel. 0131-659 6111; fax 0131-459 1221; DX ED300.

62.72.2   *"certified copy interlocutor".* A copy of the interlocutor is typed by the agent and presented to the clerk of session in the Petition Department. The clerk checks it, certifies it as a true copy and stamps it with the court stamp.

"translation". A translation of a judgment not in English will have been lodged with the **62.72.3** petition with a certificate by the translator: r. 62.3.

"certificate of currency conversion". The certificate should be obtained from the clerk of **62.72.4** session and should be signed by him: r. 62.2(3); and see notes 62.2.4 and 62.2.5.

Registration fee. A fee will be payable to the Keeper of the Registers for registration and any **62.72.5** extract: see the Fees in the Registers of Scotland Order 1995 [S.I. 1995 No. 1945].

"warrant for execution". Registration for execution gives the holder a decree of registration **62.72.6** which is in effect a decree of the Court of Session: Bell's Comm., I, 4; *Taylor, Petr.*, 1931 S.L.T. 260, 261 per Lord Pitman); and, on the warrant inserted by the Keeper of the Registers or his deputy on an extract of a registered document, diligence may be executed against the debtor's moveable property under s. 3 of the Writs Execution (Scotland) Act 1877 as substituted by s. 87(4) of the Debtors (Scotland) Act 1987. Diligence against heritable property may be executed by inhibition on the grant of letters of inhibition (see Chap. 59) or by action of adjudication founding on the decree of registration.

Service of warrant for registration under the Council Regulation

[1] **62.73.** The petitioner shall serve a copy of the interlocutor under rule 62.70(1) granting warrant for registration of a judgment and notice in Form 62.73 on the person against whom enforcement is sought.

---

[1] Rule 62.73 inserted by S.S.I. 2005 No. 135 (effective 2nd March 2005).

Service. For methods, see Chap. 16, Pt. I.   **62.72.6**

Appeals under the Council Regulation

[1] **62.74.**—(1) An appeal under Article 33 (appeals against the enforcement decision) of the Council Regulation shall be made by motion—
  (a) to the Lord Ordinary; and
  (b) where the appeal is against the granting of warrant for registration under rule 62.70(1) within one month of service under rule 62.73 (service of warrant for registration under the Council Regulation) or within two months of such service where service was executed on a person domiciled in another Member State.

(2) Where the respondent in any such appeal is domiciled furth of the United Kingdom—
  (a) in relation to an appeal against the granting of warrant for registration under rule 62.70(1), intimation of the motion shall be made to the address for service of the respondent in Scotland;
  (b) in relation to an appeal against a refusal to grant warrant for registration under rule 62.70(1), intimation of the motion shall be made in accordance with rule 16.2 (service furth of United Kingdom) or rule 16.5 (service where address of the person is not known), as the case may be.

---

[1] Rule 62.74 inserted by S.S.I. 2005 No. 135 (effective 2nd March 2005).

General note. Art. 33 of the Council Regulation No. 2201/2003 provides for an appeal against **62.74.1** a decision on the application for a declaration of enforceability under arts. 28 and 29.

The first appeal under the RCS 1994 is to the Lord Ordinary: r. 62.74(1)(a). There is a further appeal by reclaiming to the Inner House against the decision of the Lord Ordinary under r. 62.75.

An appeal against a declaration of enforceability must be lodged within one month (or two months if habitual residence is in another Member State) of service of the declaration of enforceability: art. 33(5). The declaration of enforceability referred to will be the interlocutor pronounced under r. 62.70.

Reclaiming under the Council Regulation

[1]**62.75.** Any party dissatisfied with the interlocutor of the Lord Ordinary in any appeal mentioned in rule 62.74 (appeals under the Council Regulation) may reclaim on a point of law against that interlocutor.

---

[1] Rule 62.75 inserted by S.S.I. 2005 No. 135 (effective 2nd March 2005).

62.75.1   *"reclaim".* For reclaiming, see Chap. 38.

The right of appeal under art. 33 of the Council Regulation No 2201/2003 is dealt with in r. 62.74. Reclaiming under r. 62.75 represents a further right of appeal. Do art. 33, and the time limits in art. 33(5), apply to reclaiming?

Recognition of judgments from another Member State

[1]**62.76.**—(1) For the purpose of Article 21 of the Council Regulation (recognition of a judgment), an interlocutor pronounced under rule 62.70(1) (warrant for registration under the Council Regulation) shall imply recognition of the judgment so dealt with.

(2) In an application under Article 21(3) of the Council Regulation for recognition of a judgment, rules 62.67 to 62.75 shall apply to such an application as they apply to an application under Article 28 of the Council Regulation (declarator of enforceability).

(3) In an application under Article 21(3) of the Council Regulation for non-recognition of a judgment, the rules under this part shall apply to such an application as they apply to an application under Article 28 of the Council Regulation (declarator of enforceability) subject to the following provisions—

(a) where the application relies on grounds under Article 22(b) or 23(c) of the Council Regulation (judgment given in default of appearance) for the judgment not to be recognised, it shall not be necessary to produce documents required by rule 62.69(2)(c) (document establishing service or acceptance of judgment); and

(b) rule 62.69(2)(b) (certificate under Article 39 of the Council Regulation);

(c) rule 62.70 (warrant for registration under the Council Regulation); and

(d) rule 62.72 (registration under the Council Regulation); shall not apply.

---

[1] Rule 62.76 inserted by S.S.I. 2005 No. 135 (effective 2nd March 2006).

62.76.1   *General note.* Under art. 21(1) of the Council Regulation No. 2201/2003, a judgement in a Member State is to be recognised without any special procedure being required. Notwithstanding that, an interested party may apply to a court for a decision that a judgment be, or not be, recognised: art. 21(3). For a judgment relating to parental responsibility to be enforced, however, it must be registered for enforcement, for which an application to the court is required: arts. 28 and 29 and R.C.S. 1994, r. 62.69.

Rule 62.76 states that a warrant for registration for enforcement under r. 62.70 (in respect of an application under r. 62.69) implies recognition for the purposes of art. 21. This no doubt refers to, and dispenses with the need for, an application for recognition under art. 21(3); although, of course, by virtue of art. 21(1) the judgment must automatically be recognised (while not automatically enforceable).

62.76.2   *Applications for recognition or non-recognition of a judgment.* Since a judgment to which the Council Regulation No. 2201/2003 given in another Member State must be recognised, one might wonder why it would be necessary to apply for recognition as distinct from non-recognition. One situation, perhaps, would be where it is necessary to "convert" the foreign judgment into an equivalent decree known to Scots law.

Cancellation of registration under the Council Regulation

[1] **62.77.** Where an interlocutor under rule 62.70(1) (warrant for registration under the Council Regulation) is recalled and registration under rule 62.72(2) (registration under the Council Regulation) is ordered to be cancelled after an appeal under Article 33 of the Council Regulation (appeal against decision on enforceability) a certificate to that effect by the Deputy Principal Clerk shall be sufficient warrant to the Keeper of the Registers to cancel the registration and return the judgment, certificate or other documents to the person who applied for registration.

---

[1] Rule 62.77 inserted by S.S.I. 2005 No. 135 (effective 2nd March 2005).

Enforcement in another Member State of Court of Session judgments etc.

[1] **62.78.**—(1) Where a person seeks to apply under the Council Regulation for recognition or enforcement in another Member State of a judgment given by the court, he shall apply by letter to the Deputy Principal Clerk for—
  (a) a certificate under Article 39 of the Council Regulation (certificates concerning judgments in matrimonial matters or on matters of parental responsibility);
  (b) a certified copy of the judgment; and
  (c) if required, a certified copy of the opinion of the court.

(2) The Deputy Principal Clerk shall not issue a certificate under paragraph (1)(a) above unless there is produced to him an execution of service of the judgment on the person against whom it is sought to be enforced.

(3) Where a judgment granting rights of access delivered by the Court of Session acquires a cross-border character after the judgment has been delivered and a party seeks to enforce the judgment in another Member State, he shall apply by letter to the Deputy Principal Clerk for—
  (a) a certificate under Article 41 of the Council Regulation (certificate concerning rights of access); and
  (b) a certified copy of the judgment.

---

[1] Rule 62.78 inserted by S.S.I. 2005 No. 135 (effective 2nd March 2005).

"letter to the Deputy Principal Clerk". The address and telephone number, etc., are: The 62.78.1
Deputy Principal Clerk of Session, Court of Session, 2 Parliament Square, Edinburgh EH1
1RQ; tel. +44 (0)131- 225 2595; fax +44 (0)131 225 8213; DX ED306.

"certificate under Article 39". This is a document which gives basic details of the case. 62.78.2

"cross-border character". The English version of art. 41(3) refers to the situation of rights of 62.78.3
access acquiring a cross-border character after judgment has been issued. A certificate under art.
41 will be issued at the request of a party. (If the case involves a "cross-border situation" at the
time of the judgment, the certificate will be issued automatically.)

"certificate under Article 41". This is a document which gives basic details of the case. 62.78.4

Rectification of certificates under Articles 41 and 42 of the Council Regulation

[1] **62.79.** Where a party seeks rectification of a certificate issued under Article 41 or 42 of the Council Regulation (certificate concerning rights of access or return of a child) he shall apply by letter to the Deputy Principal Clerk stating the details of the certificate that are to be rectified.

---

[1] Rule 62.79 inserted by S.S.I. 2005 No. 135 (effective 2nd March 2005).

General note. Rectification of certificates is provided for in art. 43 of the Council Regulation 62.79.1
2201/2003.

62.79.2   *"letter to the Deputy Principal Clerk"*. The address and telephone number, etc., are: The Deputy Principal Clerk of Session, Court of Session, 2 Parliament Square, Edinburgh EH1 1RQ; tel. +44 (0)131- 225 2595; fax +44 (0)131 225 8213; DX ED306.

Practical arrangements for the exercise of rights of access

[1] **62.80.**—(1) An application by a party having an enforceable judgment granting a right of access, that has been certified under Article 41 of the Council Regulation or registered for enforcement, seeking an order making practical arrangements for organising the exercise of rights of access under Article 48 of the Council Regulation, shall be made by petition.

(2) There shall be produced with the petition—

(a) an authentic copy of the judgment;

(b) any certificate under Article 41 of the Council Regulation;

(c) any extract of the registered judgment with a warrant for execution; and

(d) where applicable, a document showing that the applicant is in receipt of legal aid in the country where the judgment was given.

---

[1] Rule 62.80 inserted by S.S.I. 2005 No. 135 (effective 2nd March 2005).

62.80.1   *General note*. Art. 48 of the Council Regulation No. 2201/2003 provides for practical arrangements for organising rights of access to be made by the courts in the country for enforcement where they have not, or not sufficiently, been made in the original judgment.

62.80.2   *"petition"*. A petition is presented to the Outer House: r. 14.2(h). The petition must be in Form 86.3 in the official printed form (r. 4.1). The petition must be signed by counsel or other person having a right of audience: r. 4.2; and see r. 1.3(1) (definition of "counsel" and "other person having a right of audience") and note 1.3.4.

The petitioner must lodge the petition with the required steps of process (r. 4.4). A fee is payable on lodging the petition: see note 14.5.10.

On petitions generally, see Chap. 14

62.80.3   *Productions*. The documents referred to in r. 62.69(2)(a)-(c) are those required by art. 30(3). On productions and the lodging of them, see r. 4.5 and note 4.5.2.

[1] PART XII

EUROPEAN ENFORCEMENT ORDERS

Interpretation and application of this Part

[1] **62.81.**—(1) In this Part—

"the Regulation" means Regulation (EC) No. 805/2004 of the European Parliament and of the Council of 21 April 2004 creating a European Enforcement Order for uncontested claims;

"Council Regulation (EC) No. 44/2001" means Council Regulation (EC) No. 44/2001 of 22 December 2000 on jurisdiction and the recognition and enforcement of judgments in civil and commercial matters;

"authentic instrument" has the same meaning as in Article 4(3) of the Regulation;

"court settlement" means a settlement where the debtor has expressly agreed to a claim within the meaning of Article 4(2) of the Regulation by admission or by means of a settlement which has been approved by a court or concluded before a court in the course of proceedings; and

"judgment" has the same meaning as in Article 4(1) of the Regulation.

(3) This Part applies to judgments, court settlements and authentic instruments on uncontested claims certified as European Enforcement Orders under the Regulation.

(4) Subject to rule 62.84 (certification of authentic instrument), rule 62.87

(rectification or withdrawal of certificate), rule 62.88(1) (application for registration), and rule 62.88(3) (application for refusal, stay or limitation of enforcement), an application shall be made to the Deputy Principal Clerk by letter.

(5) Rule 62.1 shall not apply to a petition under rule 62.88(3) of this Part (application for refusal, stay or limitation of enforcement).

---

[1] Part XII and r. 62.81 inserted by S.S.I. 2005 No. 521 (effective 21st October, 2005).

General note. The EU Regulation (EC) No. 805/2004 of 21st April 2004 provides for orders in **62.81.1** uncontested claims made in one Member State to be enforced in another Member State. It does not apply, however, to Denmark.

It applies in civil and commercial matters except those relating to—
- revenue, customs, administrative matters or liability of the State in the exercise of State authority;
- status or legal capacity of natural persons, rights in property arising out of matrimonial relationship, wills and succession;
- bankruptcy, winding up of companies or other legal persons, judicial arrangements, compositions etc;
- social security;
- arbitration.

A claim is uncontested if—
- the debtor expressly agreed by admission or by a settlement approved by a court or concluded before a court in course of proceedings;
- the debtor has never objected to it, incompliance with relevant procedural requirements in the course of court proceedings;
- the debtor has not appeared or been represented at a court hearing regarding the claim after having initially objected to the claim in the course of the court proceedings, provided that it amounts to tacit admission of the claim or facts alleged by the creditor;
- the debtor has expressly agreed to it in an authentic instrument.

Certification of decree in absence or decree by default
[1] **62.82.**—(1) An application for certification under Article 6(1) (judgment on uncontested claim) or Article 8 (partial European Enforcement Order) of the Regulation shall be accompanied by an affidavit—
- (a) verifying that the judgment was of an uncontested claim within the meaning of Article 3(1)(b) or (c) of the Regulation and that the court proceedings met the requirements set out in Chapter III of the Regulation (minimum standards for uncontested claims procedures);
- (b) providing the information required by the form of certificate in Annex I to the Regulation (European Enforcement Order—judgment);
- (c) verifying that the judgment is enforceable in Scotland, and does not conflict with the rules of jurisdiction laid down in Articles 3 and 6 of Chapter II of Council Regulation (EC) No. 44/2001; and
- (d) stating that where the debtor was a consumer and the judgment related to a contract concluded by the debtor for a purpose outside his trade or profession the judgment was given in the Member State of the debtors domicile within the meaning of Article 59 of Council Regulation (EC) No. 44/2001.

(2) The Deputy Principal Clerk shall not issue a certificate under paragraph (1) unless there is produced to him an execution of service of the judgment on the person against whom it is sought to be enforced.

---

[1] Rule 62.82 inserted by S.S.I. 2005 No. 521 (effective 21st October, 2005).

"affidavit". On affidavits, see r. 1.3(2) and note 1.3.7.   **62.82.1**

Certification of court settlement
[1] **62.83.** An application for certification under Article 24 of the Regulation (court settlement) shall be accompanied by an affidavit—

(a) verifying that the debtor admitted the claim or entered into a settlement that was approved by the court or concluded before the court in the course of proceedings and is enforceable in Scotland;

(b) verifying that the settlement concerned a claim within the meaning of Article 4(2) of the Regulation (payment of money); and

(c) providing the information required by the form of certificate in Annex II to the Regulation (European Enforcement Order—court settlement).

_____

[1] Rule 62.83 inserted by S.S.I. 2005 No. 521 (effective 21st October, 2005).

62.83.1   *"affidavit".* On affidavits, see r. 1.3(2) and note 1.3.7.

Certification of authentic instrument
[1] **62.84.** An application for certification under Article 25(1) of the Regulation (authentic instrument) shall be by letter to the Keeper of the Registers and shall be accompanied by an affidavit—

(a) verifying that the authentic instrument concerns a claim within the meaning of Article 4(2) of the Regulation (payment of money);

(b) verifying that the authentic instrument is enforceable in Scotland; and

(c) providing the information required by the form of certificate in Annex III to the Regulation (European Enforcement Order—authentic instrument).

_____

[1] Rule 62.84 inserted by S.S.I. 2005 No. 521 (effective 21st October, 2005).

62.84.1   *Keeper of the Registers.* This is the Keeper of the Registers of Scotland: r. 1.3(1). The address of the Keeper of the Registers is Meadowbank House, 153 London Road, Edinburgh EH8 7AU; tel. 0131-659 6111; fax 0131-459 1221; DX ED300.

62.84.2   *"affidavit".* On affidavits, see r. 1.3(2) and note 1.3.7.

Certificate of lack or limitation of enforceability
[1] **62.85.** An application for certification under Article 6(2) of the Regulation (lack or limitation of enforceability) shall be accompanied by an affidavit—

(a) stating the date on which the judgment, court settlement or authentic instrument was certified as a European Enforcement Order; and

(b) providing the information required by the form of certificate in Annex IV to the Regulation (certificate of lack or limitation of enforceability).

_____

[1] Rule 62.85 inserted by S.S.I. 2005 No. 521 (effective 21st October, 2005).

62.85.1   *"affidavit".* On affidavits, see r. 1.3(2) and note 1.3.7.

Replacement certificate
[1] **62.86.** An application under Article 6(3) of the Regulation (replacement certificate) shall be accompanied by an affidavit providing the information required by the form of certificate in Annex v. to the Regulation (European Enforcement Order—replacement certificate following a challenge).

_____

[1] Rule 62.86 inserted by S.S.I. 2005 No. 521 (effective 21st October, 2005).

"affidavit". On affidavits, see r. 1.3(2) and note 1.3.7.　　　　　　　　　**62.86.1**

Rectification or withdrawal of certificate
[1] **62.87.** An application under Article 10(1) of the Regulation (rectification or withdrawal of European Enforcement Order certificate) shall be made in the form set out in Annex VI to the Regulation and, subject to rule 62.1 (disapplication of certain rules in Chapter 14 to this Chapter), shall be treated as a petition.

---

[1] Rule 62.87 inserted by S.S.I. 2005 No. 521 (effective 21st October, 2005).

"petition". On petitions, see Chap. 14.　　　　　　　　　**62.87.1**

Registration for enforcement
[1] **62.88.**—(1) An application for registration for enforcement of a judgment, court settlement or authentic instrument certified as a European Enforcement Order shall be made by presenting to the Keeper of the Registers—
　　(a) a certificate under Article 20(2)(b) of the Regulation (European Enforcement Order certificate);
　　(b) a copy of the judgment, court settlement, or authentic instrument in accordance with Article 20(2)(a) of the Regulation (enforcement procedure);
　　(c) where the certificate under Article 20(2)(b) is in a language other than English, a translation of the certificate into English certified as correct by the translator and stating the full name, address and qualification of the translator; and
　　(d) any certificate of currency conversion under rule 62.2(1)(b).
　(2) On presentation of the documents mentioned in sub-paragraphs (a) to (d) of paragraph (1) the Keeper of the Registers shall—
　　(a) register the certificate in the register of judgments of the Books of Council and Session; and
　　(b) issue an extract of the certificate with a warrant for execution.
　(3) An application under—
　　(a) Article 21 of the Regulation (refusal of enforcement); or
　　(b) Article 23 of the Regulation (stay or limitation of enforcement), shall be made by petition.

---

[1] Rule 62.88 inserted by S.S.I. 2005 No. 521 (effective 21st October, 2005).

"Keeper of the Registers". See note 62.84.1.　　　　　　　　　**62.88.1**

"petition". A petition is presented to the Outer House: r. 14.2(h). The petition must be in **62.88.2** Form 86.3 in the official printed form (r. 4.1). The petition must be signed by counsel or other person having a right of audience: r. 4.2; and see r. 1.3(1) (definition of "counsel" and "other person having a right of audience") and note 1.3.4.

The petitioner must lodge the petition with the required steps of process (r. 4.4). A fee is payable on lodging the petition: see note 14.5.10.

On petitions generally, see Chap. 14.

Refusal, stay or limitation of enforcement
[1] **62.89.** An interlocutor certified by the Deputy Principal Clerk shall be sufficient warrant to the Keeper of the Registers—
　　(a) where enforcement is refused under rule 62.88(3)(a), to cancel the registration of the certificate of the European Enforcement Order and return the judgment, certificate or other documents to the person who sought registration; or

(b) where enforcement is stayed or limited under rule 62.88(3)(b), to—
    (i) register the interlocutor in the register of judgements of the Books of Council and Session; and
    (ii) issue an extract of the interlocutor.

---

[1] Rule 62.88 inserted by S.S.I. 2005 No. 521 (effective 21st October, 2005).

[1] PART XIII

UNCITRAL MODEL LAW ON CROSS-BORDER INSOLVENCY

Application and interpretation of this Part
[1] **62.90.**—(1) This Part applies to applications under the Model Law and applications under the Scottish Provisions.
(2) In this Part—
    "application for an interim remedy" means an application under article 19 of the ModelLaw for an interim remedy by a foreign representative;
    "former representative" means a foreign representative who has died or who for any other reason has ceased to be the foreign representative in the foreign proceeding in relation to the debtor;
    "main proceeding" means proceedings opened in accordance with Article 3(1) of the EC Insolvency Regulation and falling within the definition of insolvency proceedings in Article 2(a) of the EC Insolvency Regulation;
    "the Model Law" means the UNCITRAL Model Law on Cross-Border Insolvency as set out in Schedule 1 to the Cross-Border Insolvency Regulations 2006;
    "modification or termination order" means an order by the court pursuant to its powers under the Model Law modifying or terminating recognition of a foreign proceeding, the restraint, sist and suspension referred to in article 20(1) of the Model Law or any part of it or any remedy granted under article 19 or 21 of the Model Law;
    "recognition application" means an application by a foreign representative in accordance with article 15 of the Model Law for an order recognising the foreign proceeding in which he has been appointed;
    "recognition order" means an order by the court recognising a proceeding as a foreign main proceeding or a foreign non-main proceeding, as appropriate;
    "review application" means an application to the court for a modification or termination order;
    "the Scottish Provisions" are the provisions of Schedule 3 to the Cross-Border Insolvency Regulations 2006; and
words and phrases defined in the Model Law have the same meaning when used in this Part.
(3) References in this Part to a debtor who is of interest to the Financial Services Authority are references to a debtor who—
    (a) is, or has been, an authorised person within the meaning of section 31 of the Financial Services and Markets Act 2000 (authorised persons);
    (b) is, or has been, an appointed representative within the meaning of section 39 (exemption of appointed representatives) of that Act; or
    (c) is carrying on, or has carried on, a regulated activity in contravention of the general prohibition.
(4) In paragraph (3) "the general prohibition" has the meaning given by section 19 of the Financial Services and Markets Act 2000 and the reference to "regulated activity" shall be construed in accordance with—

(a) section 22 of that Act (classes of regulated activity and categories of investment);
(b) any relevant order under that section; and
(c) Schedule 2 to that Act (regulated activities).

––––––––

[1] Part XIII and r. 62.90 inserted by S.S.I. 2006 No. 199 (effective 6th April 2006).

General note. The UNCITRAL Model Law on Cross-Border Insolvency is set out in Sched. 1 **62.90.1**
to the Cross-Border Insolvency Regulations 2006 [S.I. 2006 No. 1030].

General
[1]**62.91.**—(1) Rule 62.1 (disapplication of certain rules to Chapter 62) shall not apply to an application to which this Part relates.
(2) Unless otherwise specified in this Part, an application under the Model Law or the Scottish Provisions shall be made by petition.
(3) For the purposes of the application of rule 14.5(1) (first order for intimation, service and advertisement) to a petition under this Part, where necessary, the petitioner shall seek an order for service of the petition on:—
(a) the foreign representative;
(b) the debtor;
(c) any British insolvency officeholder acting in relation to the debtor;
(d) any person appointed an administrative receiver of the debtor or as a receiver or manager of the property of the debtor in Scotland;
(e) any member State liquidator who has been appointed in main proceedings in relation to the debtor;
(f) any foreign representative who has been appointed in any other foreign proceeding regarding the debtor;
(g) if there is pending in Scotland a petition for the winding up or sequestration of the debtor, the petitioner in those proceedings;
(h) any person who is or may be entitled to appoint an administrator of the debtor under paragraph 14 of Schedule B1 to the Insolvency Act 1986 (appointment of administrator by holder of qualifying floating charge); and
(i) the Financial Services Authority if the debtor is a debtor who is of interest to that Authority.
(4) On the making of—
(a) a recognition order;
(b) an order granting an interim remedy under article 19 of the Model Law;
(c) an order granting a remedy under article 21 of the Model Law;
(d) an order confirming the status of a replacement foreign representative; or
(e) a modification or termination order,
the Deputy Principal Clerk shall send a certified copy of the interlocutor to the foreign representative.

––––––––

[1] Rule 62.91 inserted by S.S.I. 2006 No. 199 (effective 6th April 2006).

"petition". A petition is presented to the Outer House: r.14.2(h). The petition must be in **62.91.1**
Form 86.3 in the official printed form (r.4.1). The petition must be signed by counsel or other person having a right of audience: r.4.2; and see r.1.3(1) (definition of "counsel" and "other person having a right of audience") and note 1.3.4.
The petitioner must lodge the petition with the required steps of process (r.4.4). A fee is payable on lodging the petition: see note 14.5.10.
On petitions generally, see Chap.14.

"send". This includes deliver: r. 1.3(1) (definition of "send"). **62.91.2**

Recognition application

¹**62.92.**—(1) A petition containing a recognition application shall include averments as to—

(a) the name of the applicant and his address for service in Scotland;

(b) the name of the debtor in respect of which the foreign proceeding is taking place;

(c) the name or names in which the debtor carries on business in the country where the foreign proceeding is taking place and in this country, if other than the name given under sub-paragraph (b);

(d) the principal or last known place of business of the debtor in Great Britain (if any) and, in the case of an individual, his last known place of residence in Great Britain, (if any);

(e) any registered number allocated to the debtor under the Companies Act 1985;

(f) the foreign proceeding in respect of which recognition is applied for, including the country in which it is taking place and the nature of the proceeding;

(g) whether the foreign proceeding is a proceeding within the meaning of article 2(i) of the Model Law;

(h) whether the applicant is a foreign representative within the meaning of article 2(j) of the Model Law;

(i) the address of the debtor's centre of main interests and, if different, the address of its registered office or habitual residence as appropriate;

(j) if the debtor does not have its centre of main interests in the country where the foreign proceeding is taking place, whether the debtor has an establishment within the meaning of article 2(e) of the Model Law in that country, and if so, its address.

(2) There shall be lodged with the petition—

(a) an affidavit sworn by the foreign representative as to the matters averred under paragraph (1);

(b) the evidence and statement required under article 15(2) and (3) respectively of the Model Law;

(c) any other evidence which in the opinion of the applicant will assist the court in deciding whether the proceeding in respect of which the application is made is a foreign proceeding within the meaning of article 2(i) of the Model Law and whether the applicant is a foreign representative within the meaning of article 2(j) of the Model Law; and

(d) evidence that the debtor has its centre of main interests or an establishment, as the case may be, within the country where the foreign proceeding is taking place.

(3) The affidavit to be lodged under paragraph (2)(a) shall state whether, in the opinion of the applicant, the EC Insolvency Regulation applies to any of the proceedings identified in accordance with article 15(3) of the Model Law and, if so, whether those proceedings are main proceedings, secondary proceedings or territorial proceedings.

(4) Any subsequent information required to be given to the court by the foreign representative under article 18 of the Model Law shall be given by amendment of the petition.

---

¹ Rule 62.92 inserted by S.S.I. 2006 No. 199 (effective 6th April 2006).

62.92.1   *"lodged"*. See rr. 4.4 and 4.5.

62.92.2   *"affidavit"*. See r. 1.3(2) and note 1.3.7.

Application for interim remedy

[1]**62.93.**—(1) An application for an interim remedy shall be made by note in process.

(2) There shall be lodged with the note an affidavit sworn by the foreign representative stating—

(a) the grounds on which it is proposed that the interim remedy applied for should be granted;

(b) the details of any proceeding under British insolvency law taking place in relation to the debtor;

(c) whether to the foreign representative's knowledge, an administrative receiver or receiver or manager of the debtor's property is acting in relation to the debtor;

(d) an estimate of the assets of the debtor in Scotland in respect of which the remedy is applied for;

(e) all other matters that would in the opinion of the foreign representative assist the court in deciding whether or not to grant the remedy applied for, including whether, to the best of the knowledge and belief of the foreign representative, the interests of the debtor's creditors (including any secured creditors or parties to hire-purchase agreements) and any other interested parties, including if appropriate the debtor, are adequately protected; and

(f) whether to the best of the foreign representative's knowledge and belief, the grant of any of the remedy applied for would interfere with the administration of the foreign main proceeding.

---

[1] Rule 62.93 inserted by S.S.I. 2006 No. 199 (effective 6th April 2006).

"note". See r. 15.2.   **62.93.1**

"affidavit". See r. 1.3(2) and note 1.3.7.   **62.93.2**

Application for remedy

[1]**62.94.**—(1) An application under article 21 of the Model Law for a remedy shall be made by note in process.

(2) There shall be lodged with the note an affidavit sworn by the foreign representative stating—

(a) the grounds on which it is proposed that the remedy applied for should be granted;

(b) an estimate of the value of the assets of the debtor in Scotland in respect of which the remedy is requested;

(c) in the case of an application by a foreign representative who is or believes that he is a representative of a foreign non-main proceeding, the reasons why the applicant believes that the remedy relates to assets that, under the law of Great Britain, should be administered in the foreign non-main proceeding or concerns information required in that proceeding; and

(d) all other matters that would in the opinion of the foreign representative assist the court in deciding whether or not it is appropriate to grant the remedy requested, including whether, to the best of the knowledge and belief of the foreign representative, the interests of the debtor's creditors (including any secured creditors or parties to hire-purchase agreements) and any other interested parties, including if appropriate the debtor, are adequately protected.

---

[1] Rule 62.94 inserted by S.S.I. 2006 No. 199 (effective 6th April 2006).

"note". See r. 15.2.   **62.94.1**

62.94.2   *"lodged"*. See rr. 4.4 and 4.5.

62.94.3   *"affidavit"*. See r. 1.3(2) and note 1.3.7.

Application for confirmation of status of replacement foreign representative
[1] **62.95.**—(1) An application under paragraph 2(3) of the Scottish Provisions for an order confirming the status of a replacement foreign representative shall be made by note in process.

(2) The note shall include averments as to—

(a) the name of the replacement foreign representative and his address for service within Scotland;

(b) the circumstances in which the former foreign representative ceased to be foreign representative in the foreign proceeding in relation to the debtor (including the date on which he ceased to be the foreign representative);

(c) his own appointment as replacement foreign representative in the foreign proceeding (including the date of that appointment).

(3) There shall be lodged with the note—

(a) an affidavit sworn by the foreign representative as to the matters averred under paragraph (2);

(b) a certificate from the foreign court affirming—

(i) the cessation of the appointment of the former foreign representative as foreign representative, and

(ii) the appointment of the applicant as the foreign representative in the foreign proceeding, or

(c) in the absence of such a certificate, any other evidence acceptable to the court of the matters referred to in sub-paragraph (a).

---

[1] Rule 62.95 inserted by S.S.I. 2006 No. 199 (effective 6th April 2006).

62.95.1   *"note"*. See r. 15.2.

62.95.2   *"lodged"*. See rr. 4.4 and 4.5.

62.95.3   *"affidavit"*. See r. 1.3(2) and note 1.3.7.

Review application
[1] **62.96.**—(1) A review application shall be made by note in process.

(2) There shall be lodged with the note an affidavit sworn by the applicant as to—

(a) the grounds on which it is proposed that the remedy applied for should be granted; and

(b) all other matters that would in the opinion of the applicant assist the court in deciding whether or not it is appropriate to grant the remedy requested, including whether, to the best of the knowledge and belief of the applicant, the interests of the debtor's creditors (including any secured creditors or parties to hire-purchase agreements) and any other interested parties, including if appropriate the debtor, are adequately protected.

---

[1] Rule 62.96 inserted by S.S.I. 2006 No. 199 (effective 6th April 2006).

62.96.1   *"note"*. See r. 15.2.

62.96.2   *"lodged"*. See rr. 4.4 and 4.5.

62.96.3   *"affidavit"*. See r. 1.3(2) and note 1.3.7.

CHAPTER 63

APPLICATIONS RELATING TO TRUSTS

PART I

VARIATION OR REVOCATION OF TRUSTS

Interpretation of this Part
63.1. In this Part, "the Act of 1961" means the Trusts (Scotland) Act 1961.

Form of petitions under section 1(4) of the Act of 1961
63.2. In a petition under section 1(4) of the Act of 1961 (petition to vary or revoke purposes of an alimentary trust), it shall not be necessary to aver the amount or details of the income of an alimentary beneficiary from all sources.

Deriv. R.C.S. 1965, r. 260(d)

Petition under s. 1(4) of the Act of 1961. A petition under s. 1(4) of the Act of 1961 is for the **63.2.1** authorisation by the court of an arrangement varying or revoking a trust purpose entitling a beneficiary to an alimentary liferent or alimentary income from the trust estate: Act of 1961, s. 1(4).

The petition may be presented by a beneficiary or trustee under the trust: Act of 1961, s. 1(4). "Beneficiary" for the purposes of s. 1 of the Act of 1961 includes any person having, directly or indirectly, an interest, whether vested or contingent, under the trust: Act of 1961, s. 1(6). This may include the beneficiary under a trust set up by the beneficiary of another trust the purposes or powers of which are sought to be varied: *Countess of Lauderdale, Petr.* 1962 S.C. 302. It does not include a remote contingent beneficiary whose interest is negligible: *Phillips and Others, Petrs* 1964 S.C. 141; *Morris, Petr.* 1985 S.L.T. 252.

For cases on the meaning of "alimentary" for the purposes of s. 1(4) of the Act of 1961: see *Strange and Another, Petrs* 1966 S.L.T. 59; *Pearson and Others, Petrs* 1968 S.L.T. 46; *Sutherland and Others, Petrs* 1968 S.L.T. 252. For necessity of the petition, see note 63.3.5.

Form of petition. See in general note 63.3.6. In a petition under s.1(4) of the Act of 1961 it is   **63.2.2** unnecessary to aver the amount or details of the income of an alimentary beneficiary: r. 63.2. It is sufficient for the income to be vouched by the documents lodged in the petition process: *Robertson and Others, Petrs.* 1962 S.C. 196, 203 *per* L.P. Clyde. An actuarial report on the apportionment of the trust fund between an alimentary liferenter and a prospective fiar should be produced: *Gibson's Trustee, Petr.* 1962 S.C. 204.

Service on certain persons

63.3. In a petition under section 1 of the Act of 1961 (petition for variation or revocation of trust purposes or extension of trustees' powers), the order under rule 14.5 (first order in petitions)—

(a) shall include a requirement for the petition to be served—
  (i) where the trust deed is registered in a register kept by the Keeper of the Registers or the Keeper of the Records, on the relevant Keeper; or
  (ii) where the trust deed is registered in a sheriff court book, on the sheriff clerk who keeps the relevant sheriff court book; and
(b) may include a requirement for the petition to be served on a truster or settlor or any other person who has contributed or is liable to contribute to the trust estate which may be affected by the petition.

Deriv. R.C.S. 1965, r. 260(c) and (e)

General note. At common law the purposes of a private trust could only be changed where all   **63.3.1** of the beneficiaries and potential beneficiaries were identified, fully *capax*, and in complete agreement with the proposed changes. If this happened they could direct the trustee to administer the property accordingly. This very rigid system caused difficulties with the implementation of long standing trust purposes which were affected by frequent changes in taxation law and levels, and inflation.

Following the Variation of Trusts Act 1958, which allowed variation of trust purposes in England and Wales, the Law Reform Committee in Scotland in its Ninth Report (Cmnd. 1102 (1960)) recommended the introduction of similar legislation in Scotland. In particular the report recommended the creation of a right for the trustees or any one or more of the beneficiaries to present a petition to the Outer House of the court, for approval on behalf of any unidentified, incapable, or unborn beneficiaries of an arrangement varying the purposes of the trust. The committee also recommended that the powers of the trustees could be varied in the same way. The result of the committee's recommendations was s.1(1) of the Act of 1961.

The committee also recommended changes which led to s.1(4) of the Act of 1961: see note 63.2.1.

Jurisdiction. The grounds of jurisdiction for a petition under s.1(1) or s.1(4) of the Act of 1961   **63.3.2** are largely similar.

(1) *Petition under s.1(1) of the Act of 1961.* In view of the nature of the petition it does not appear to involve any person "being sued" or to be in substance a proceeding in which a decree against any person is sought. Accordingly the C.J.J.A. 1982 would appear not to apply: C.J.J.A. 1982, Scheds 1 and 3C, Art. 3 and 4; Sched. 4, Arts 2 and 3; ss.20(1), 21(1)(b) and Sched. 9, para. 13. In addition a petition may be outwith the subject-matter scope of the C.J.J.A. 1982: C.J.J.A. 1982, Scheds 1 and 3C, Art. 1; ss.17(1) and 21(1)(a).

As the C.J.J.A. 1982 does not apply, the common law applies. At common law, the court has jurisdiction over all types of applications relating to Scottish trusts: *Clarke's Trs., Petrs.* 1966 S.L.T. 249, 251 *per* L.P. Clyde.

The test to decide whether a trust is Scottish is not wholly clear. It is clear that if (1) a trust was constituted in Scotland in a Scottish form, and (2) the trustees were at the time of its constitution domiciled (in the common law sense) in Scotland, the trust is Scottish: *Brockie and Another, Petrs.* (1875) 2 R. 923; *Ashburton v. Escombe* (1892) 20 R. 187, 196 *per* Lord Kinnear; and *Clarke's Trs.*, above. It is unclear what the position would be if only one of these requirements was fulfilled. If a trust deed declares that the trustees are to have the powers and immunities of trustees under Scots law, or some of the initial trustees are domiciled in Scotland, or the trust purposes are to be fulfilled in Scotland, these features will point towards the trust being a Scottish trust: see *Orr Ewing's Trs. v. Orr Ewing* (1885) 13 R.(H.L.) 1, 23 *per* Lord Watson; *Betts Brown Trust Fund Trs., Petrs.* 1968 S.C. 170.

With regard to non-Scottish trusts, at common law the court has jurisdiction (a) in an action against trustees provided they are resident, or administer trust property, in Scotland (see *Orr*

Ewing's Trs., above, *per* Lord Watson at p. 26); and (b) in any other application where the court is satisfied that the remedy sought is in conformity with the law of the trust (*Allan's Trs., Petrs.* (1897) 24 R. 238, 718; *Lipton's Trs., Petrs.* 1943 S.C. 521, 527 *per* L.J.-C. Cooper; *Bateman, Petr.* 1972 S.L.T.(Notes) 78; *cf. Hall and Others, Petrs.* (1869) 7 M. 667, and *Brockie*, above). The jurisdiction in relation to (b) has been described as an auxiliary jurisdiction of the court; and a request for its exercise will, where practicable, be sympathetically considered: *Lipton's Trs.*, above, *per* L.J.-C. Cooper at p. 525. The court may nevertheless refuse jurisdiction on the ground of *forum non conveniens*: see *Orr Ewing's Trs.*, above, *per* Lord Watson at pp. 26 *et seq.*

It is suggested that the court has jurisdiction for a petition under s.1(1) of the Act of 1961 in respect of a non-Scottish trust where the remedy sought would be approved by the courts of the law of the trust.

(2) *Petition under s.1(4) of the Act of 1961.* The grounds of jurisdiction will be the same as for a petition under s.1(1) of the Act of 1961: see (1) above.

63.3.3 *Choice of law.* Where the court has jurisdiction and the petition relates to a trust created voluntarily and evidenced in writing the court must apply the governing law of the trust as determined under Arts 6 and 7 of the Schedule to the Recognition of Trusts Act 1987: Act of 1987, Sched., Art. 6.

Effectively this means that in the exceptional situations where a "Scottish trust" was governed by a foreign law, the court could only grant the remedies sought in s.1(1) and (4) of the Act of 1961 if the courts in the country of the governing law would have been able to grant similar remedies. In that situation the court might well decline jurisdiction on grounds of *forum non conveniens*: see similar cases discussed by Lord Watson in *Orr Ewing's Trs. v. Orr Ewing* (1885) 13 R.(H.L.) 1, 26 *et seq.*

63.3.4 *Petition under s.1(1) of the Act of 1961.* This is a petition for approval by the court on behalf of (a) any beneficiary who because of legal incapacity is incapable of assenting, (b) any person who may become one of the beneficiaries at a future date or event being a person of a specified description or member of a specified class provided that if he had become a beneficiary on the date of the presentation of the petition he would not have been capable of assenting, or (c) any person unborn, of an arrangement varying or revoking all or any of the trust purposes or enlarging the power of the trustees of managing and administering the trust estate: Act of 1961, s.1(1). The petition may be presented by a trustee or beneficiary. The jurisdiction of the court is, essentially, a curatorial function on behalf of beneficiaries unborn or not *sui juris* in granting consent (or not) on their behalf. The following issues have arisen:

(1) *"Beneficiary".* This includes any person having directly or indirectly an interest whether vested or contingent under the trust: Act of 1961, s.1(6). This may include the beneficiary under a trust set up by a beneficiary of another trust the purposes or powers of which are sought to be varied: *Countess of Lauderdale, Petr.* 1962 S.C. 302. It does not include a remote contingent beneficiary whose interest is negligible: *Phillips and Others, Petrs.* 1964 S.C. 141; *Morris, Petr.* 1985 S.L.T. 252.

(2) *Legal incapacity of beneficiary.* A person who is over the age of 16 years and under the age of 18 years is legally incapable of assenting for the purpose of s.1(1): Act of 1961, s.1(2).

(3) *Contingent beneficiary.* The category in s.1(1)(b) of the Act of 1961 refers to a contingent beneficiary who is more than one contingency away from being a direct beneficiary: see (in relation to an almost identical English provision) *Knocker v. Youle* [1986] 2 All E.R. 914, 917 *per* Warner J.

(4) *Trust purposes.* The arrangement may provide for the setting up of a new trust: *Aikman, Petr.* 1968 S.L.T. 137.

(5) *Trustees' powers.* The arrangement may propose the extension of the powers of the trustees beyond those permitted by the trust deed or the Trustee Investments Act 1961: *Henderson, Petr.* 1981 S.L.T.(Notes) 40. It may include a power to assume new trustees (provided they are suitable having regard to the nature of the trust): see *Ommanney, Petr.* 1966 S.L.T.(Notes) 13.

63.3.5 *Necessity for petition under s.1(4) of the Act of 1961.* Unless there is an alimentary beneficiary the petition may be dismissed as being unnecessary: see *Strange and Another, Petrs.* 1966 S.L.T. 59; *Pearson and Others, Petrs.* 1968 S.L.T. 46. Where the alimentary purpose is contingent and revocable (*e.g.* where it is in a marriage contract trust and the alimented spouse has not begun to benefit) the petition may be dismissed as being unnecessary: *Findlay's Petrs.* 1962 S.C. 210.

63.3.6 *Form of petition under s.1(1) or (4) of the Act of 1961.* The petition is presented in the Inner House: r. 14.3(g). The petition must be in Form 14.4 in the official printed form: rr. 4.1 and 14.4. The petition must be signed by counsel or other person having a right of audience: r. 4.2(3); and see r. 1.3(1) (definition of "counsel" and "other person having a right of audience") and note 1.3.4.

The petitioner must lodge the petition with the required steps of process (r. 4.4), and any documents founded on or adopted (r. 27.1(1)) including detailed and accurate documents as evidence in support of the petition: *Young's Trs., Petrs.* 1962 S.C. 293. A fee is payable on lodging the petition: see note 14.5.10.

On petitions generally, see Chap. 14.

The crave in the prayer should follow the express wording of the statute: *Robertson and Others, Petrs.* 1962 S.C. 196, 203 *per* L.P. Clyde. Any proposed arrangement should be set out in a scheme annexed to the petition, which may, if necessary, be thereafter registered in the Books of Council and Session or sheriff court books for preservation: *Colville, Petr.* 1962 S.C. 185, 195 *per* L.P. Clyde; *Gibson's Tr., Petr.* 1962 S.C. 204, 209 *per* L.P. Clyde. The proposed trust purposes or trustees' powers should be set out in full in the arrangement in an appendix to the petition and not merely incorporated by reference to another deed: *Nimmo and Another, Petrs.* 1972 S.L.T.(Notes) 68.

The petition must set forth the effect of the proposed arrangement on persons on whose behalf the court's approval is sought.

For specialities in relation to a petition under s.1(4) of the Act of 1961, see note 63.2.2.

Service. The petition on being lodged shall, without a motion being enrolled, appear in the **63.3.7** rolls for the day after lodging in the Single Bills for an order for service: r. 14.5(1). The petition should be served on any interested party. This will include any trustee or beneficiary who is not a petitioner but may exclude a remote contingent beneficiary: *Phillips and Others, Petrs.* 1964 S.C. 141; *Morris, Petr.* 1985 S.L.T. 252. Where there are a number of contingent beneficiaries at the date of the lodging of the petition, the petition should be served on those who would become vested if the direct beneficiary died on that date: *Buchan, Petr.* 1964 S.L.T. 51. Where an interested party is a child the petition should be served on his parent or guardian. For whether a father has parental rights, see note 67.24.6. Where the purpose sought to be varied is testamentary and revocable (*e.g.* where a testamentary trustee is still alive) service on a beneficiary under the purpose is unnecessary: *Evetts v. Galbraith's Trs.* 1970 S.C. 211.

Where the trust deed has been registered in a register (*e.g.* the Books of Council and Session or General Register of Sasines) kept by the Keeper of the Registers or Keeper of the Records, the petition should be served on the relevant keeper: r. 63.3(a)(i). The same applies to registering in the sheriff court books and the sheriff clerk who keeps those books: r. 63.3(a)(ii).

The petition may also be served on a trustee or any other person who has contributed to the trust estate which may be affected by the petition: r. 63.3(b).

For methods of service, see Chap. 16, Pt I.

"Keeper of the Registers". This is the Keeper of the Registers of Scotland: r. 1.3(1). The **63.3.8** address for service on the Keeper of the Registers is: Meadowbank House, 153 London Road, Edinburgh EH8 7AU.

"Keeper of the Records". This is the Keeper of the Records of Scotland: r. 1.3(1). The address **63.3.9** for service on the Keeper of the Records is: Scottish Record Office, HM General Register House, Edinburgh EH1 3YY.

Curator ad litem. Where there are several beneficiaries whose interests do not conflict, the **63.3.10** same curator *ad litem* may be appointed to represent all those beneficiaries. Where any person with an interest (including one on whose behalf approval is sought) is *incapax* for whatever cause or where a beneficiary is as yet unborn, the court will always in its first order appoint a curator *ad litem* to represent that person in the petition proceedings: *Tulloch's Trs., Petrs.* 1962 S.C. 245. The court's power to appoint a curator *ad litem* arises at common law by virtue of the undisputed power to regulate its own practice and procedure, the court performing the "duty it owes to all helpless persons brought to its cognisance" (*Drummond's Trs v. Peel's Trs* 1929 S.C. 484, *per* L.P. Clyde). In view of s.1(2) of the Act of 1961 (see note 63.3.4(2), the court would appoint a curator *ad litem* to a 16 to 18 year old person in a petition under s.1(1) of the Act of 1961: this position is preserved by s.1(3)(f) of the Age of Legal Capacity (Scotland) Act 1991. Despite the appointment, the petition will still be served on the person's parents, guardian or curator *bonis*.

Where a curator *ad litem* is sought to be appointed the motion for the first order will be starred, requiring appearance.

A curator *ad litem* is appointed, usually an advocate, from lists kept by the clerks to the two Divisions. It is not usually necessary for an advocate to take the oath *de fideli administratione* on each appointment. The petitioner's agent will inform the curator *ad litem* that he has been appointed and of the details of the process, and should provide the curator with a copy of the interlocutor appointing him. The curator *ad litem* will have to decide whether to oppose the petition by lodging answers or consent to the petition by lodging a minute of consent.

The curator's duties. The court does not adhere to strict rules of evidence; if essential facts are disputed, enquiry is by remit (or even a proof, but that is rare) and documents produced which are accepted or not disputed may be accepted by the court without proof: *Colville, Ptnr* 1962 S.C. 185, 192 *per* L.P. Clyde. A curator's task should not, therefore, be underestimated.

It is the duty of the curator to exercise an independent judgment, by advising the ward where he is capable of concurring, and by acting for him where he is not, according to the true interest of the ward: *MacKay's Manual of Practice*, p. 150.

In *Drummond's Trs*, above, L.P. Clyde at pp. 496–498 stated that the court committed to the curator the duty of getting in touch with his ward and making such enquiry as to his ward's position as the court could not itself make; he must not independently; his professional responsibility is a guarantee of the purity and independence with which his duty to the ward and the court is performed; as a judicial officer as well as guardian of the ward's interests, if he found himself in difficulty, he can always report to the court. In relation to the equivalent procedure in England, Brightman, J, in *In re Whittall* [1973] 1 W.L.R. 1027, said that the guardian had the duty, under proper legal advice, to apprise himself fully of the notice of the application, of the existing beneficial interest of the infant, and of the manner in which that interest is proposed to be affected, and to inform the solicitor whom he has retained of the course he considers in the light of legal advice should be taken.

One of the first matters the curator will have to consider is whether he should be separately represented and advised in order to perform his duties. Where there are no disputed facts, and provided there are separate counsel to represent the conflicting interests, it is competent for the same agent to instruct them all: *Robertson, Petrs* 1962 S.C. 196, 203 *per* L.P. Clyde. Where facts are or may be in dispute, the curator should instruct separate agents to act on his behalf: it might be better to err on the side of caution if in doubt and instruct separate agents. The curator will generally wish to take the advice of counsel before determining how he should proceed; and the trustees must find the funds out of the trust to enable him to take the opinion of counsel: *Smith v. Smith's Tr*. 1900 S.L.T. 226. There may be circumstances in which the curator requires other expert advice, *e.g.* to assess material evidence: see "Variation of Trust Purposes" by Michael Bruce (now Lord Marnoch) in 1967 S.L.T.(News) 193.

The court may approve a scheme which positively benefits the person on whose behalf approval is sought or where the variation puts the person in question in no worse position than before: *Colville, Ptnr*, above, per L.P. Clyde at p. 194. The test will be whether, on a balance of probabilities, the arrangement not be prejudicial in the circumstances most likely to occur: Elliot in *Wilson & Duncan on Trusts, Trustees and Executors* at para. 13–31. It may be possible to eliminate the risk of potential prejudice by insurance (see *e.g. Robertson, Petrs*, above) or by a retained fund (*cf. Lobnitz* 1966 S.L.T.(Notes) 81): for a useful discussion, see *Stair Memorial Encyclopedia*, Vol. 24, para. 80. The court may approve an arrangement where the interests of the beneficiaries are remote and defeasible.

Where the curator is not satisfied that what is proposed is not prejudicial to his ward, the usual practice is for the counsel instructed on his behalf to raise his concerns with counsel for the petitioners. If the matter is not resolved to the curator's satisfaction, or there is a dispute of fact which he considers should be brought to the court, the curator will instruct answers to be lodged to the petition. Where the curator is satisfied that there is no prejudice he will instruct a minute of consent. On the form of such a minute, see note 63.3.12.

The curator is entitled to remuneration and should render a note of his fee to the petitioners agents.

63.3.11 *Representation.* Where no facts in the petition are disputed the parties may be represented by the same agent provided that they are represented by different counsel: *Robertson and Others, Petrs*. 1962 S.C. 196.

63.3.12 *Minute of consent.* Where a person who has had the petition served on him does not wish to lodge answers opposing it, he should lodge a minute to that effect and appear at the hearing to ensure that he does not suffer prejudice from any amendment to the petition which may be made at the hearing: *Findlay's Petrs*. 1962 S.C. 210, 214 *per* L.P. Clyde. Where the court amends the arrangement the minute of consent will have to be altered to show consent to the amendment.

A minute of consent should be in the following form:

"X for the Minuter, — and hereby states to the court that the Minuter, having examined the terms of the Arrangement [as amended] in the appendix to the petition, and having been separately advised, considers that the Arrangement [as so amended] would not be prejudicial to the interests of his ward, and consents to approval [and authorisation (*if this petition has been presented also under section 1(4) of the Trusts (Scotland) Act 1961 concerning remuneration of an alimentary liferent*)] being granted to the Arrangement [as amended].

IN RESPECT WHEREOF
(*signed by counsel*)"

No fee is payable on lodging such a minute. R. 15.1 does not apply because the minute is not an application to the court.

Objection to the petition. The first order calls for answers. It has been known for minutes to be **63.3.13** lodged; but obedience to the interlocutor would require answers.

Summar Roll. After the expiry of the period of notice, the lodging of the execution copy of the **63.3.14** petition (containing all executions) and the lodging of minutes of consent, and any answers, the petitioner should enrol a motion to appoint the cause to the Summar Roll. For fixing and allocation of the diet on the Summar Roll, see r. 6.3 and notes.

Granting of the petition. Where the court grants the prayer of the petition the chairman of the **63.3.15** court will sign a docquet attached to the arrangement in the form—
"Edinburgh, *(date)*. The foregoing arrangement is signed and authenticated relative to the interlocutor of this date."
Where the arrangement requires to be registered in the Books of Council and Session or sheriff court books, the agent for the petitioner should (a) apply to the Petition Department for an official certified copy of the interlocutor granting the prayer (see r. 7.11); (b) make up and certify a copy of the docquetted arrangement; (c) send these two items to the Inland Revenue with a remittance for stamp duty; and on return (d) stitch the two items together and send them to the Keeper of the Registers at Meadowbank House, 153 London Road, Edinburgh EH8 7AU (DX ED300), or the sheriff clerk who keeps the relevant sheriff court books, for registration.
At the same time the clerk of session in the Petition Department will send a letter confirming the variation to the appropriate keeper.

Amendment of interlocutor or arrangement. An amendment of an interlocutor or an approved **63.3.16** arrangement, which is not related to a mistake, clerical error, or omission in it is incompetent: *Hutchison* 1965 S.C. 240; *Bailey and Another, Petrs.* 1969 S.L.T. (Notes) 70. This is particularly important where an arrangement requires an insurance policy to be obtained by a certain date and it is not obtained in time. In that situation a fresh petition must be sought: see *Hutchison*, above.

PART II

PETITIONS BY TRUSTEES FOR DIRECTIONS

Application of this Part
[1] **63.4.** This Part applies to an application for which provision is to be made by virtue of section 6(vi) of the Act of 1988 (provision to enable trustees under any trust deed to obtain direction of the court).

Deriv. R.C.S. 1965, r. 232

---

[1] Rule 63.4 amended by S.S.I. 2006 No. 83 (effective 17th March 2006).

General note. Part II of this Chapter has been made under s.6(vi) of the C.S.A. 1988 which **63.4.1** enables the court, with a view to securing that causes coming before it may be determined with as little delay as possible and to the simplification of procedure and reduction of expense, to provide by A.S. for enabling trustees under any trust deed to obtain the directions of the court on certain questions or the exercise of any of their powers or duties. This provision replaced the identically worded s.17(vi) of the Administration of Justice (Scotland) Act 1933.
The purpose of the provision was to enable the court to make rules for the summary disposal of urgent requests by trustees acting under a trust deed for disposal of the issues listed.
The procedure has been infrequently used since the 1930s following a number of cases which restricted its scope. A petition for directions is competent where (1) the question raised is (a) one mentioned in s.6(vi) of the C.S.A. 1988 and (b) requires immediate decision by the trustees; (2) at the hearing all parties are represented who would have had to be represented if the question had been submitted in a competent special case; and (3) the pleadings must afford a satisfactory basis for answering the question put: *Peel's Trs. v. Drummond* 1936 S.C. 787, 794 *per* L.P. Normand. A petition for directions cannot be resorted to at will in preference to a special case. The procedure, being a summary procedure, ought to be resorted to where justified by some emergency or where a more formal procedure is inefficacious or incompetent: *Henderson's Trs. v. Henderson* 1938 S.C. 461, 464 *per* L.P. Normand. Complex questions of law or where the facts are disputed may be better dealt with in a special case or other procedure (*e.g.* action or multiplepoinding): *Andrew's Trs. v. Maddeford* 1935 S.C. 857, 864–865 *per* L.P. Normand; *Henderson's Trs.*, above.

63.4.2 *"any trust deed".* Although s.6(vi) of the C.S.A. 1988, as did s.17(vi) of the Administration of Justice (Scotland) Act 1933, gives the court power to make rules for applications for directions by trustees under any "trust deed", that term is not defined. R.C.S. 1965, r. 232 defined "trust deed" by reference to the definition in s.2 of the Trusts (Scotland) Act 1921 without power to do so, and no attempt is made to define it, without a power to do so, in this Part of this Chapter of the R.C.S. 1994. It is not clear whether Parliament intended the remedy to apply to all trustees, and it is not available to trustees in a trust arising merely by operation of law.

In *Chisholm, Ptnrs.,* 2006 S.L.T. 394 (First Div), it was held that "trustees" in s. 6(vi) of the 1988 Act, could be read as including executors nominate, and the deed by which they were nominated, together with the associated testamentary writing and confirmation, could be regarded as a "trust deed".

Form and service of application

63.5.—(1) An application to which rule 63.4 applies shall be made by petition.

[1] (2) Subject to rule 63.6A (executors of underwriting members of Lloyd's of London), the petition shall set out the question on which the direction of the court is sought and may include, in an appendix, any relevant documents.

(3) The court may, in any order made under rule 14.5 (first order in petitions) or in any subsequent order, include a requirement to serve the petition on creditors, beneficiaries or other persons interested in the subject-matter of the petition.

Deriv. R.C.S. 1965, r. 233(a) (r. 63.5(1) and (2)) and r. 233(b) (r. 63.5(3))

---

[1] Rule 63.5 (2) amended by S.S.I. 2006 No. 83 (effective 17th March 2006).

63.5.1 *"petition".* The petition may be presented by a trustee appointed under a trust deed: C.S.A. 1988, s.6(vi); and see note 63.4.2.

The petition is presented to the Inner House: r. 14.3(e). The petition must be in Form 14.4 in the official printed form: rr. 4.1 and 14.4. The petition must be signed by counsel or other person having a right of audience: r. 4.2(3); and see r. 1.3(1) (definition of "counsel" and "other person having a right of audience") and note 1.3.4.

The petitioner must lodge the petition with the required steps of process (r. 4.4) and any documents founded on or adopted (r. 27.1(1)). A fee is payable on lodging the petition: see note 14.5.10. On petitions generally, see Chap. 14.

The averments should set out, *inter alia,* (a) the facts of the matter which give rise to the questions on which directions are sought (*Henderson's Trs. v. Henderson* 1938 S.C. 461, 464 *per* L.P. Normand); (b) the immediacy or emergency which requires the question to be resolved by a petition for directions (*Andrew's Trs. v. Maddeford* 1935 S.C. 857, 864 *per* L.P. Normand; and *Henderson's Trs.,* above, *per* L.P. Normand at p. 464); and (c) that all persons with an interest in the trust agree with the facts as averred in the petition (*Andrew's Trs.,* above). The crave in the prayer should set out the question on which the direction of the court is sought: r. 63.5(2). The question should not be one where all persons interested are agreed on the answer: *Henderson's Trs.,* above; and see also *Grant's Trs. v. Hunter* 1938 S.C. 501.

63.5.2 *Jurisdiction.* See in general note 63.3.2. In *Clarke's Trs.* 1966 S.L.T. 249 trustees petitioned for directions on whether the court would have jurisdiction to present petitions under s.1 of the Act of 1961.

63.5.3 *"serve".* The petition will usually be served on persons interested in the subject-matter in the usual way: see r. 14.5. In some situations it may be dealt with *ex parte* or with a reduced period of notice. For methods of service, see Chap. 16, Pt. I.

Determination of petition

63.6.—[1] (1) Subject to rule 63.6A (executors of underwriting members of Lloyd's of London), the petition shall be disposed of at a hearing on the Summar Roll.

(2) At the hearing on the Summar Roll, the court may order inquiry by—
(a) proof,
(b) remit to a reporter, or
(c) affidavit,
as it thinks fit.

Executors of underwriting members of Lloyd's of London (r. 63.6A) **C** 551

Deriv. R.C.S. 1965, r. 233(c)

[1] Rule 63.6(1) amended by S.S.I. 2006 No. 83 (effective 17th March 2006).

Summar Roll. After the expiry of the period of notice (if any) the agent for the petitioner **63.6.1**
should enrol a motion to appoint the cause to the Summar Roll. For fixing and allocation of the
diet on the Summar Roll, see r. 6.3 and notes.

Where the direction sought is on a comparatively simple question of investment, distribution,
administration or a power or duty of trustees, only the petitioners need be represented.
Otherwise every person who would have an interest if the direction was sought in a special case
should be represented at the hearing on the Summar Roll: *Peel's Trs. v. Drummond* 1936 S.C.
786, 794 *per* L.P. Normand.

"proof". See Chap. 36. **63.6.2**

"remit to a reporter". The terms of the remit should be in the interlocutor ordering the remit: **63.6.3**
see *Williams v. Cleveland and Highland Holdings Ltd* 1993 S.L.T. 398, 401B–C *per* Lord
Penrose. Where there is a remit to a reporter the report becomes the exclusive mode of proof of
the issues compiled in the remit: see *Williams*, above, *per* Lord Penrose at p. 400L. It is not
appropriate to lodge answers to the report: *Scotstown Moor Children's Camp* 1948 S.C. 630.
Objections to the report may be made by lodging a note of objections.

The duties of the reporter are similar to those of a reporter appointed in a petition concerning
a public trust: see note 63.12.3.

The agents for the parties are personally liable for the fees and outlays of the reporter and the
petitioner's agent will usually be made responsible: r. 42.15.

"affidavit". The affidavit should be in the form of a statement of evidence written in the first **63.6.4**
person. The affidavit should contain the evidence of the deponent in support of the averments in
the petition.

An affidavit should be sworn and signed by the deponent before any person who may
competently take an oath, whether in Scotland or in any other country. In Scotland such a
person may include a notary public, justice of the peace, sheriff, or any judge. The person taking
the oath should also sign the affidavit. Where the affidavit is not in English a duly certified
translation should also be lodged.

See also the definition of affidavit in r. 1.3(1).

Executors of underwriting members of Lloyd's of London
   [1] **63.6A.**—(1) This rule applies to a petition under this Part for directions
as to the distribution of, or the administration of any trust relating to, the
estate of a deceased underwriting member of Lloyd's of London, where—
   (a) all liabilities of the estate in respect of syndicates of which the
       deceased was a member have been reinsured (whether directly or
       indirectly) or are otherwise the subject of indemnity; and
   (b) the only reason for the executor delaying distribution of the estate is
       the possibility of personal liability to creditors of Lloyd's of London.
   (2) The petition shall—
   (a) state that this rule applies; and
   (b) contain averments as to the matters mentioned in paragraph (1).
   (3) There shall be lodged with the petition all affidavits and other
documents available to the petitioner in respect of the matters mentioned in
paragraph (1).
   (4) If, on the expiry of the period of notice, no answers have been
lodged—
   (a) the petitioner shall apply by motion for a remit to a reporter
       approved by the court for that purpose; and
   (b) where a report has been lodged in process by the reporter, the
       petitioner may apply by motion for an order granting the prayer of
       the petition.
   (5) Where answers have been lodged—
   (a) the parties may adjust the petition and answers within 28 days after
       the date on which the answers were lodged ("the adjustment period")
       and shall intimate such adjustments to one another;

(b) within 14 days after the expiry of the adjustment period, the petitioner shall apply by motion for such further procedure as may be specified in the motion.

(6) Where the petitioner fails to comply with the requirements of paragraph (5), a respondent may apply by motion for decree of dismissal.

---

[1] Rule 63.6(A) amended by S.S.I. 2006 No. 83 (effective 17th March 2006).

63.6A.1   *General note.* Guidance on the application of this rule is to be found in P.N. No.1 of 2006. In *Chisholm, Ptnrs*, 2006 S.L.T. 394 (First Div.), the court identified the issues that would normally be sufficient in a remit to a reporter. These are repeated in P.N. No.1 of 2006.

63.6A.2   *"affidavit".* On affidavits, see notes 63.6.4 and 1.3.7.

PART III

PUBLIC TRUSTS

Application and interpretation of this Part
  63.7.—(1) This Part applies to—
  (a) an application to the *nobile officium* of the court for approval of a *cy près* scheme in relation to a public trust; or
  (b) an application to the court under—
    (i) Part VI of the Education (Scotland) Act 1980 (reorganisation of endowments); or
    (ii) Part I of the Law Reform (Miscellaneous Provisions) (Scotland) Act 1990 (charities and reorganisation of public trusts).
  (2) In this Part, "the Act of 1990" means the Law Reform (Miscellaneous Provisions) (Scotland) Act 1990.

Deriv. R.C.S. 1965, r. 233A inserted by S.I. 1992 No. 1533 (r. 63.7(2))

63.7.1   *Application for approval of a* cy près *scheme for a public trust.* This is an application to the *nobile officium* of the court for approval of a scheme varying the purposes of a public trust, which have failed because (a) no means have been provided to effect the public purpose, (b) the truster's directions cannot be carried out but there is a general charitable intention or (c) there is a bequest to a particular public object but that object has failed after the bequest has taken effect, to approximate to those purposes: see *Gibson's Trs.* 1933 S.C. 190.
  A public trust includes, but is not restricted to, charitable trusts, and the *cy près* jurisdiction applies to all public trusts: *Anderson's Trs. v. Scott* 1914 S.C. 942. A public trust is a trust for the benefit of the public; whereas a private trust is for the benefit of a third party. A public trust is valid even though it is not charitable. Only charitable trusts, however, attract the favourable income tax regime: *Commissioners for the Special Purposes of Income Tax v. Pemsel* [1891] A.C. 531; *Inland Revenue v. Glasgow Police Athletic Association* 1953 S.C. (H.L.) 13.

63.7.2   *Application under Pt. VI of the Education (Scotland) Act 1980.* There are six types of application, namely:—
  (1) For the giving of effect to a draft scheme for the future government and management of any university, theological or less than 20 years old educational endowment or of a Carnegie Trust: Education (Scotland) Act 1980, s. 105(4A) (as inserted by the Education (Scotland) Act 1981, Sched. 6, para. 4(g)) and s. 122(2); see, *e.g. University of Glasgow, Petrs.* 1991 S.L.T. 604.
  (2) By a governing body for the giving of effect to a draft scheme for the future government or management of an educational endowment which is at least 20 years old: 1980 Act, s. 105(4C) (as inserted by the 1981 Act, Sched. 6, para. 4(g)) and s. 122(1) and (2).
  (3) By a governing body for the giving of effect to a draft scheme for the future government or management of a non-educational endowment: 1980 Act, s. 108 as amended by the 1981 Act, Sched. 6, para. 7(a).
  (4) By the Lord Advocate for the giving of effect to a draft scheme for the future government or management of a non-educational endowment; 1980 Act, s. 108A renumbered and amended by the 1981 Act, Sched. 6, para. 7(b).
  (5) For amendment or substitution of a scheme made by an education authority for the future government or management of an educational endowment which is at least 20 years old: 1980 Act, s. 112(7) (as substituted by the 1981 Act, Sched. 6, para. 11(i)) and s. 122(1) and (2).

(6) By the Lord Advocate for summarily compelling governing bodies of certain educational endowments to give effect to a provisional order or scheme made under Part VI of the Act of 1980 or its predecessors: 1980 Act, s. 120(1) as amended by the 1981 Act, Sched. 6, para. 18.

Applications under Pt. I of the Act of 1990. These applications include: **63.7.3**
(1) An application by the Lord Advocate in relation to the management or misconduct in the administration of a charitable body: see Act of 1990, s. 7.

(2) An application by trustees of a public trust for approval of a scheme for the reorganisation of trust purposes: see Act of 1990, s. 9; see, *e.g. Mining Institute of Scotland Benevolent Fund Trs., Petrs.* 1994 S.L.T. 785.

Proceedings before nominated judge

63.8. Subject to rule 63.9 (referral to Inner House), all proceedings in an application to which this Part applies shall be brought before a judge of the court nominated for that purpose by the Lord President or, where the nominated judge is not available, any other judge of the court (including the vacation judge); and, in this Part, "Lord Ordinary" shall be construed accordingly.

Deriv. RCS 1965, r. 233C inserted by S.I. 1992 No. 1533

Nominated judge. The nominated judge is Lord Drummond Young.   **63.8.1**

Remit to Inner House

63.9. The Lord Ordinary, if he thinks fit, may at any time remit a petition to which this Part applies to the Inner House to be determined by a Division of the Inner House.

General note. This is a new rule to enable the Lord Ordinary to refer a petition to which this   **63.9.1** rule applies to the Inner House (which formerly dealt with such petitions).

Form of applications

63.10.—(1) Subject to the following paragraphs of this rule, an application to which this Part applies shall be made by petition.

(2) An application for an order in a petition to which this Part applies which is in dependence shall be made by motion.

(3) At the hearing of a motion under paragraph (2), the court may order that the application be made by note; and, in such a case, shall make an order for the lodging of answers to the note in process within such period as the court thinks fit.

[1] (4) Intimation to the court by the Scottish Ministers under section 1(6) or 5(13) of the Act of 1990 (interdict until intimation to court) shall be made by motion for recall of the interlocutor.

Deriv. RCS 1965, r. 233B(1) (r. 63.10(1)), r. 233B(2) (r. 63.10(2)), and r. 233H(1) (r. 63.10(4)), all inserted by S.I. 1992 No. 1533

---

[1] R. 63.10(4) amended by S.I. 1999 No. 1386 (effective 1st July 1999).

"petition". The petition is presented to the Outer House: r. 14.2(c)(iii) and (h). The petition   **63.10.1** must be in Form 14.4 in the official printed form: rr. 4.1 and 14.4. The petition must be signed by counsel or other person having a right of audience: r. 4.2(3); and see r. 1.3(1) (definition of "counsel" and "other person having a right of audience") and note 1.3.4.

The petitioner must lodge the petition with the required steps of process (r. 4.4) and any documents founded on or adopted (r. 27.1(1)). A fee is payable on lodging the petition: see note 14.5.10. On petitions generally, see Chap. 14.

The crave in the prayer should follow the express wording of the statutory provision founded on. Any proposed scheme should be set out in an appendix annexed to the petition. The proposed trust purposes or trustees' powers and duties should be set out in full in the scheme in the appendix.

In a petition under s. 9 of the Act of 1990 the application should be framed with particular reference to the conditions there set out and which have to be satisfied before the court can approve the scheme: *Mining Institute of Scotland Benevolent Fund Trs., Petrs.* 1994 S.L.T. 785.

63.10.2   *Jurisdiction.* The grounds of jurisdiction depend principally on the type of petition.

(1) *Petitions for the approval of a* cy près *scheme.* Jurisdiction is under the *nobile officium* but is otherwise akin to that in a petition under s. 1(1) of the Trusts (Scotland) Act 1961: see note 63.3.2(1). In addition, standing that the petition is to the *nobile officium*, Sched. 8 to the C.J.J.A. 1982 is disapplied: C.J.J.A. 1982, s. 22(3).

The petition is not a process for resolving preliminary matters such as whether the trust exists or whether there is uncertainty of gift or absence of charitable intention: *Church of Scotland Trust v. O'Donoghue* 1951 S.C. 85.

(2) *Petition under Pt. VI of the Education (Scotland) Act 1980.* Part VI of the Act of 1980 relates to "endowments". An "endowment" is any property heritable or moveable dedicated to charitable purposes: 1980 Act, s. 122(1). There is no specific reference to an endowment having to be a trust let alone a Scottish trust. Nevertheless in practice most endowments will be held in Scottish trusts.

Where the petition is directed against a person, jurisdiction will be based on the C.J.J.A. 1982 except where its subject-matter is outwith the scope of the C.J.J.A. 1982: see notes 13.2.8 to 13.2.14.

Where the petition is not directed against a person the position will be akin to that in a petition under s. 1(1) of the Trusts (Scotland) Act 1961 and the common law will apply: see note 63.3.2(1).

(3) *Petition under Pt. I of the Act of 1990.* With regard to a petition under s. 7 of the Act of 1990, in most instances the order sought will be directed against a person. Accordingly the C.J.J.A. 1982 will usually apply.

With regard to a petition under s. 9 of the Act of 1990, the position will be akin to that in a petition under s. 1(1) of the Trusts (Scotland) Act 1961 and the common law will apply: see note 63.2.2.

63.10.3   *"in dependence".* A cause is depending from the time it is commenced (*i.e.* from the time a first order in a petition is made) until final decree, whereas a cause is in dependence until final extract. For the meaning of commenced, see note 14.6.1. For the meaning of final decree, see note 4.15.2(2). For the meaning of final extract, see note 7.1.2(2).

63.10.4   *"motion".* For motions, see Chap. 23.

63.10.5   *"note".* For applications by note, see r. 15.2.

63.10.6   *"answers".* For form and procedure, see r. 18.3.

63.10.7   *"Scottish Ministers".* This expression means, collectively, the members of the Scottish Executive, *i.e.* the First Minister, the Ministers appointed by him under s. 47, the Lord Advocate and the Solicitor General for Scotland: Scotland Act 1998, s. 44(2). Sections 1(6) and 5(13) of the Act of 1990 refer to the Lord Advocate, but his functions in relation to charities under Pt. I of the Act of 1990 were transferred to the Secretary of State by the Transfer of Functions (Lord Advocate and Secretary of State) Order 1999 [S.I. 1999 No. 678] on 19th May 1999. The Lord Advocate now exercises only those functions he had immediately before he ceased to be a Minister of the Crown: Scotland Act 1998, s. 54. He ceased to be a Minister of the Crown and became a member of the Scottish Executive on 20th May 1999: The Scotland Act 1998 (Commencement) Order 1998 [S.I. 1998 No. 3178]. Accordingly the Lord Advocate does not exercise any functions in relation to charities under Pt I of the Act of 1990. Those functions were transferred from the Secretary of State to the Scottish Ministers by s.53(2)(c) of the Scotland Act 1998 which came into force on 1st July 1999 (The Scotland Act (Commencement) Order [S.I. 1998 No. 3178], art. 3). Oddly, Pt I of the Act of 1990 has not been amended.

Service on interested persons

63.11. A petition to which this Part applies shall be served on all persons who may have an interest in the subject-matter of the petition.

Deriv. RCS 1965, r. 233D inserted by S.I. 1992 No. 1533

63.11.1   *"served".* For methods of service, see Chap. 16, Pt I.

Procedure where no answers lodged

63.12.—(1) If, on the expiry of the period of notice, no answers have been lodged, the petitioner may apply by motion for an order granting the prayer of the petition.

(2) On a motion under paragraph (1), the Lord Ordinary may, before determining that motion—

[NEXT TEXT PAGE IS C 553]

(a) remit to a reporter to inquire into, and report on, the petition and any scheme appended to it;
(b) order the petitioner to lodge evidence by affidavit or documentary evidence;
(c) order a further hearing; or
(d) make such other order as he thinks fit.

Deriv. R.C.S. 1965, r. 233E inserted by S.I. 1992 No. 1533

"period of notice". This is the period within which answers may be lodged: see r. 1.3(1) **63.12.1** (definition of "period of notice") and r. 14.6.

"motion". For motions, see Chap. 23.   **63.12.2**

"remit to a reporter". This is the most common method used by the court in determining the **63.12.3** facts of a petition relating to a public trust. A motion will usually be made for such an appointment by the petitioner on the expiry of the period of notice and before applying for the prayer of the petition to be granted; in some circumstances (generally exceptional) a reporter may not be necessary. An advocate is usually appointed. The terms of the remit should be in the interlocutor ordering the remit: see *Williams v. Cleveland and Highland Holdings Ltd* 1993 S.L.T. 398, 401B–C *per* Lord Penrose. Where there is a remit to a reporter the report becomes the exclusive mode of proof of the issues compiled in the remit: see *Williams*, above, *per* Lord Penrose at p. 400L. It is not appropriate to lodge answers to the report: *Scotstown Moor Children's Camp* 1948 S.C. 630. Objections to the report may be made by lodging a note of objections. In most cases, points raised by the reporter can be dealt with at the bar on the motion to grant the prayer.

The duties of the reporter are invariably specified in the interlocutor of appointment as being to "inquire into and report on the facts and circumstances" of the petition. This means more than simply perusing and commenting on the petition and draft scheme. The reporter must ascertain whether the facts averred are correct and whether the scheme is justified (or too broad or too narrow) by the facts established; to do this he must carry out a full investigation himself. The reporter is not acting as counsel, advising the petitioner(s). The reporter will invariably find it essential to visit the petitioner(s) or a representative (such as the trust's chairman, treasurer, secretary) or all of them to establish the facts and discuss the scheme. Depending on the circumstances, the reporter may wish to speak to those involved in financial arrangements, to see accounts, records and other documents. In preparing the report, the reporter should comment on the scheme, recommending any drafting improvements, or changes to the scheme in the light of the investigations, including whether the scheme should be more restricted or widened (in the latter case the question whether further service or intimation is required will have to be considered). The process will have to be examined to ascertain whether intimation and service has been properly made, all persons whom the reporter has identified as having an interest have been appropriately notified, whether any advertisement has been made and the advertisements gave proper notice, whether any answers or other communication in response to the petition have been lodged and whether the period of notice has expired.

The agents for the parties are personally liable for the reporter's fees and outlays; and the petitioner's agent will usually be responsible: r. 42.15.

"affidavit". The affidavit should be in the form of a statement of evidence written in the first **63.12.4** person. The affidavit should contain the evidence of the deponent in support of the averments in the petition.

An affidavit should be sworn and signed by the deponent before any person who may competently take an oath, whether in Scotland or in any other country. In Scotland such a person may include a notary public, justice of the peace, sheriff, or any judge. The person taking the oath should also sign the affidavit. Where the affidavit is not in English a duly certified translation should also be lodged.

See also the definition of affidavit in r. 1.3(1).

Procedure where answers lodged
63.13.—(1) Where answers are lodged in a petition, the parties may adjust the petition and answers during the period of 28 days from the date on which answers are lodged or from the expiry of the period of notice, whichever is the later.

(2) Within 14 days after the expiry of the period allowed for adjustment under paragraph (1), the petitioner shall enrol a motion for an order for such further procedure as he shall specify.

(3) On a motion under paragraph (2), the Lord Ordinary shall make such order as he thinks fit for the further procedure of the petition; and, in particular—
  (a) may—
    (i) remit to a reporter to inquire into, and report on, the petition and any scheme appended to it;
    (ii) order a party to lodge evidence by affidavit or documentary evidence; and
  (b) then, or thereafter, shall appoint the cause to a hearing.
(4) At a hearing appointed under paragraph (3)(b), the Lord Ordinary shall—
  (a) determine the petition; or
  (b) make such order for further procedure as he thinks fit.
(5) If at any stage answers are withdrawn, the petition shall proceed as if answers had not been lodged.

Deriv. R.C.S. 1965, r. 233F inserted by S.I. 1992 No. 1533

63.13.1   *Adjustment of pleadings.* See note 22.2.3.

63.13.2   *"period of notice".* This is the period within which answers may be lodged: see r. 1.3(1) (definition of "period of notice") and r. 14.6.

63.13.3   *"motion".* For motions, see Chap. 23.
Where answers to the petition relate to a preliminary matter (*e.g.* whether a trust exists or whether there is uncertainty of gift or absence of charitable intention), the petitioner should enrol a motion to sist the cause pending resolution of the matter in another process: *Church of Scotland Trust v. O'Donoghue* 1951 S.C. 85.

63.13.4   *"remit to a reporter."* See note 63.12.4.

63.13.5   *"evidence by affidavit".* The affidavit should be in the form of a statement of evidence written in the first person. The affidavit should contain the evidence of the deponent in support of the averments in the petition.
An affidavit should be sworn and signed by the deponent before any person who may competently take an oath, whether in Scotland or in any other country. In Scotland such a person may include a notary public, justice of the peace, sheriff, or any judge. The person taking the oath should also sign the affidavit. Where the affidavit is not in English a duly certified translation should also be lodged.
See also the definition of affidavit in r. 1.3(1).

63.13.6   *"hearing".* The hearing is fixed once the report has been lodged: r. 63.13(3). Usually it will involve the making of submissions on the pleadings and productions without the leading of evidence.

Warrants for registration

63.14. An interlocutor approving a *cy près* scheme or a scheme for the variation or reorganisation of a public trust shall contain a warrant for the registration of an official certified copy of the interlocutor, and a copy of the scheme certified by the agent to the petitioner, in the Books of Council and Session or the books of a specified sheriff court.

Deriv. R.C.S. 1965, r. 233G inserted by S.I. 1992 No. 1533

63.14.1   *Granting of the petition.* Where the court grants the prayer of a petition for the approval of a *cy près* scheme or for the variation or reorganisation of a public trust under the Education (Scotland) Act 1980 or the Act of 1990, the Lord Ordinary will sign a docquet attached to the scheme in the form—
    "Edinburgh, (*date*). The foregoing arrangement is signed and authenticated relative to the interlocutor of this date."
The interlocutor will contain a warrant for the registration of an official certified copy of it with a copy of the scheme, certified by the agent to the petitioner in the Books of Council and Session or the books of a specified sheriff court: r. 63.14.

On the interlocutor granting the prayer of the petition being pronounced the agent for the petitioner should (a) apply to the Petition Department for an official certified copy of the interlocutor (see r.7.11); (b) make up and certify a copy of the docquetted scheme; and (c) stitch the two items together and send them to the Keeper of the Registers at Meadowbank House, 153 London Road, Edinburgh EH8 7AU (DX ED300) or the sheriff clerk who keeps the relevant sheriff court for registration.

At the same time the clerk of session in the Petition Department will send a letter confirming the variation to the appropriate keeper.

Advertisement of court orders

63.15. An order made under paragraph (a) or (g) of section 7(4) of the Act of 1990 (interim interdict or interdict of body holding itself out as a charity etc.) shall, unless the court otherwise directs, be advertised forthwith in one or more newspapers as the court shall direct for ensuring that it comes to the notice of persons dealing with a non-recognised body within the meaning of section 2(2) of that Act.

Deriv. R.C.S. 1965, r.233I inserted by S.I. 1992 No. 1533

[1] CHAPTER 64

APPLICATIONS UNDER SECTION 1 OF THE ADMINISTRATION OF JUSTICE (SCOTLAND) ACT 1972

Application of this Chapter

[1] **64.1.** This Chapter applies to an application for an order under section 1 of the Administration of Justice (Scotland) Act 1972 made where a cause is not depending before the court in which the application may be made.

---

[1] Chap. 64 and r.64.1 substituted by S.S.I. 2000 No. 319 (effective from 2nd October 2000).

General note. This Chapter was replaced by A.S. (R.C.S.A. No.4) (Applications under section **64.1.1** 1of the Administration of Justice (Scotland) Act 1972) 2000 (SSI 2000/3190). The new rules were introduced to make the procedure for applications under s.1 of 1972 Act (known as "dawn raids") comply with Art.8 of the European Convention of Human Rights. These rules introduce safeguards present in Anton Piller orders in England which were commented on by the European Court of Human Rights in *Chappell v. United Kingdom* (1998) 12 E.H.R.R. 1 as necessary safeguards. One safeguard was that an order would not be made unless the court was satisfied that (a) there was a very strong *prima facie* case, (b) the actual or potential damage to the petitioner was very serious and (c) there was clear evidence that the respondent had incriminating material in his possession and that there was a real possibility that he might destroy it if forewarned. The second safeguard relates to the manner of execution of the order which must ensure proportionality between the rights of the petitioner to recover property and the rights of the respondent to respect for his private life.

Rule 64.1 is in the same terms as the previous rule.

This Chapter applies to the recovery of documents and other property under s.1 of the Administration of Justice (Scotland) Act 1972 where there is no depending cause (on the meaning of which, see note 64.1.2). Where there is a depending cause the application may be made by motion in that cause under r.35.2.

The Act of 1972 is concerned with recovery and production of evidence for use in litigation in Scotland; recovery and production of evidence for use in foreign civil proceedings (following a letter of request) is regulated by Chap. 66. Where, however, documents or other items have been recovered by a commission and diligence at common law under s.1 of the Act of 1972, the court may, on an application to it in the process of the cause in which that recovery was made, permit those documents or other items to be used for those proceedings in Scotland or elsewhere. It is not necessary, where there is such a process, to bring fresh proceedings under s.1 of the Act of 1972 or the Evidence (Proceedings in Other Jurisdictions) Act 1975: *Iomega Corporation v. Myrica (UK) Ltd* 1998 S.C. 636 (I.H.) overruling *Dailey Petroleum Services Corporation v. Pioneer Oil Tools Ltd* 1994 S.L.T. 757.

In relation to the application of s.1 of the 1972 Act to proceedings by virtue of s.28 of the C.I.J.A. 1982, see note 64.1.7.

A party who has obtained possession of documents or other items under a commission and diligence at common law or under s.1 of the Act of 1972 is subject to an implied obligation or undertaking to the court not to use them or allow them to be used for any purpose other than the conduct of the actual or proposed proceedings for which they were recovered: *Iomega Corporation*, above.

64.1.2   "*depending*". A cause is depending from the time it is commenced (*i.e.* from the time an action is served or a first order in a petition is made) until final decree, whereas a cause is in dependence until final extract. For the meaning of commenced, see note 13.4.4 (actions) and note 14.6.1 (petitions). For the meaning of final decree, see note 4.15.2(2). For the meaning of final extract, see note 7.12.2(2).

64.1.3   *Orders under s.1 of the Administration of Justice (Scotland) Act 1972.* Under s.1(1) of the Act of 1972 orders may be sought (for commission and diligence) for the inspection, photographing, preservation, custody and detention of documents and other property (including land) which appear to be property as to which any question may relevantly arise in civil proceedings which are likely to be brought, and for their production and recovery, the taking of samples or the carrying out of experiments.

The court may also order any person (not just a party) to disclose any information he has about the identity of any person who appears to the court to be a person who might be a witness or defender in any civil proceedings which are likely to be brought: Act of 1972, s.1(1A) inserted by the Law Reform (Miscellaneous Provisions) (Scotland) Act 1985, s.19. for a recent unsuccessful attempt under s.1(1A) of the Act of 1972, see *Pearson v. Educational Institute of Scotland* 1997 S.C. 245 (Second Div.). In *Pearson*, it was confirmed that the test for an application under s.1(1A) of the 1972 Act is that (1) the proceedings are likely to be brought and (2) in relation to those proceedings the petitioner has a *prima facie*, intelligible and stateable case. In order to determine whether such a case exists, it is neither necessary nor appropriate to subject the pursuer's pleadings to a detailed examination: *Harwood v. Jackson*, 2003 S.L.T. 1026 (OH), 1029H, para. [8].

The order under s.1 of the Act of 1972 may only be made where civil proceedings are likely to be brought. It is not enough that proceedings are merely a possibility but would be rendered likely on the basis of the documents recovered: *Colquhoun, Petr* 1990 S.L.T. 43, 44L *per* Lord Prosser. There need not be full averments of fact which would make an action relevant: *Friel, Petr* 1981 S.C. 1. There must be adequate averments about the substance of and basis for the case proposed to be made before the order is granted: *Dominion Technology Ltd v. Gardner Cryogenics Ltd (No. 1)* 1983 S.L.T. 828, 832C *per* Lord Cullen. "Civil proceedings" has a general wide meaning, applying to proceedings of a civil character irrespective of the court or tribunal and includes arbitration: *Anderson v. Gibb* 1983 S.L.T. 726. "Property" means corporeal property; but the court has a common law power to order inspection and video recording of things such as a process or activity: *Christie v. Arthur Bell & Sons Ltd* 1989 S.L.T. 253; and see cases there cited.

These provisions do not affect the law and practice about privilege of witnesses and havers, confidentiality or public interest, and s.47 of the Crown Proceedings Act 1947 (recovery of documents in possession of the Crown) applies: Act of 1972, s.1(4). The privilege against self-incrimination cannot be claimed in respect of certain proceedings under s.1(1) of the Act of 1972 for infringement, to obtain disclosure of information about infringement relating to intellectual property: see note 64.1.4(6). On confidentiality, see note 61.1.4.

The same considerations for determining whether an order should be granted as in a depending cause and as set out in *Moore v. Greater Glasgow Health Board* 1978 S.C. 123 apply: *Thorne v. Strathclyde R.C.* 1984 S.L.T. 161. These are that it must be shown that the documents are necessary for the purpose of enabling a party to make more pointed or more specific what is already averred or to enable him to make adequate and specific replies to his opponent's averments, in short "what he must show is that the documents sought to be recovered are required to serve the purposes of the pleadings as those pleadings stand at the time the diligence is sought": see *Moore*, above, *per* Lord Cameron at p.131. there must be a *prima facie* case: *Smith, Petr* 1985 S.L.T. 461.

An order may be sought at any time after the cause has commenced (*i.e.* the action has been served or the first order in a petition or note has been granted) unless there is a special reason why the application should not be granted: Act of 11972, s.1(2)(a). This provision was designed to overrule the common law practice (see note 35.2.5) that a commission and a diligence was rarely granted before the record was closed. In *Baxter v. Lothian Health Board* 1976 S.L.T. (Notes) 37 Lord Dunpark said that s.1(2)(a) of the Act of 1972 meant that the common law test applied so that a person seeking an order before the closed record has to show cause why recovery should be allowed although even if a *prima facie* case was made out there may yet be a special reason for refusing it. The decision of the Inner House in *Moore v. Greater Glasgow Health Board* 1978 S.L.T. 123 (in which *Baxter* and *McGown*, above were cited but not referred to in judgments) indicates that the former view prevails, and this was confirmed in *Civil Service Building Society v. MacDougall* 1988 S.C. 58.

On seeking redelivery of documents and property, see note 64.13.1.

On *ex parte* applications, see note 64.5.2.

Caveats. A caveat may not be lodged in respect of an order under s.1 of the Act of 1972.   **64.1.4**

Section 28 of the C.J.J.A. 1982. When any proceedings have been brought, or are likely to be   **64.1.5**
brought, in another Brussels or Lugano Convention State, a Brussels I Regulation State, or in
England and Wales or Northern Ireland in respect of any matter within the scope of Art.1 of the
Brussels I Regulation, the Court of Session has the like power to make an order under s.1 of the
Administration of Justice (Scotland) Act 1972 as if the proceedings had been or were likely to be
brought, in that court: C.J.J.A. 1982 s.28. The court's power to grant an order under s.1 of the
1972 Act is extended by the Civil Jurisdiction and Judgements Act 1982 (Provisional and
Protective Measures) (Scotland) Order 1977 [S.I. 1997 No. 2780] as follows: (a) anything
mentioned in s.28 of the C.J.J.A. 1982 in relation to proceedings commenced otherwise than in a
Brussels or Lugano Contracting State or proceedings whose subject matter I not within the
scope of the 1968 Brussels Convention; and (b) the granting of an order under s.1 of the 1972
Act by virtue of s.28, of the C.J.J.A. 1982 in relation to proceedings which are to be commenced
otherwise than in a Brussels or Lugano Contracting State. In *Liffe Administration and
Management v. The Scottish Ministers*, 2004 S.L.T. 2 it was held that proceedings under a
Complaints Ombudsman Scheme under the Financial Services and Markets Act 2000 were
concerned with an administrative rather than a civil or commercial matter to which the 1968
Convention would apply and s.28 of the C.J.J.A. 1982 did not, therefore, apply and the petition
under s.1 of the 1972 Act was incompetent.
    Guidance has been given by the Inner House in *Union Carbide Corporation v. B.P. Chemicals
Ltd* 1995 S.C. 398 on how the power in s.28 should be exercised. (1) Section 28 of the 1972 Act is
partly based on Art.24 of the Conventions above and, as only an order under s.1 of the 1972 Act
for preservation and detention as opposed to production and recovery would be "provisional"
or "protective" in nature, s.28 of the C.J.J.A. 1982 goes beyond the requirements of the
Convention by allowing the court to make an order for production and recovery of information
for use in foreign litigation. (2) Although the remedies available are the remedies under the law
of Scotland whether available in the foreign jurisdiction or not, the question whether the Scots
or a similar remedy is available in the foreign jurisdiction is an important factor to which regard
must be had by the Scottish courts in determining whether to exercise the power to assist the
foreign proceedings. (3) Where a party to proceedings in another country claims that an order
should be made under s.28 of the C.J.J.A. 1982 to enable him to satisfy a rule of that country, it
is the rule and practice of that country that the court has to consider in order to decide what
order is a reasonably necessary. (4) The court must ask itself whether it will be consistent with
the ends of justice for the power in s.28 to be exercised and, if so, on what terms; and an order
should be refused if vexatious or oppressive. (5) There is a distinction between (a) cases where
the party against whom the s.28 order is sought is the same party as that against whom the
proceedings in the other jurisdiction have been brought, and (b) cases where the proceedings
have not yet been brought or the party is a stranger to those proceedings. In (a) the court must
be careful not to be drawn into a situation where it is where it is persuaded to grant a
discretionary remedy which the foreign court possessed of a similar power would not provide in
the same circumstances. (6) The court has power to attach conditions to the use of information
recovered by commission and diligence, although it is normal practice for the court to do so.
    Where a document or other property has been recovered by petition under s.1 of the Act of
1972 and recovery or production of it is sought for civil proceedings in any foreign country, a
separate petition need not be presented under the Evidence (Proceedings in Other Jurisdictions)
Act 1975: *Iomega Corporation v. Myrica (UK) Ltd*, 1998 S.C. 636 overruling *Dailey Petroleum
Services Corporation v. Pioneer Oil Tools Ltd* 1994 S.L.T. 757. The application may be made in
the petition under s.1 of the Act of 1972 because the documents or property are held until
further order of the court. The better procedure is to proceed by note rather than motion:
Iomega Corporation, above. See also Chap.66.
    In relation to the rest of the U.K. and Brussels or Lugano Convention Contracting States, or
Brussels I Regulation States, there is an overlap of the 1975 Act and s.28 of the C.J.J.A. 1982.

Form and content of application
    [1] **64.2.** (1) An application to which this Chapter applies shall be made by
petition.
    [2] (2) The statement of facts shall set out—
    (a) a list of documents and other property (in this Chapter and in Form
        64.6 referred to as the "listed items") which the petitioner wishes to
        be made the subject of the order;

   (b) the address of the premises within which the petitioner believes the listed items are to be found;

   (c) the facts which give rise to the petitioner's belief that were the order not to be granted the listed items or any of them would cease to be available for the purposes of the said section 1.

Deriv. RCS 1965, r.95A(c) (part) inserted by S.I. 1972 No. 2021 and r.95A(d)(ii) substituted by S.I. 1987 No. 1206.

---

[1] R.64.2 substituted by S.S.I. 2000 No. 319 (effective from 2nd October, 2000).
[2] R.64.2(2)(a) amended by S.S.I. 2004 No. 52 (effective 1st March, 2004).

64.2.1   *General note.* See note 64.1.1. The provision in this Chapter for applications where there is no depending cause by petition is an exercise of the power in s.1(3) of the Act of 1972.

64.2.2   *"petition".* A petition is presented in the Outer House: r.14.2 (h). The petition must be in Form 14.4 in the official printed form: rr.4.1 and 14.4. The petition must be signed by counsel or other person having a right of audience: r.4.2; and see r.1.3(1) (definitions of "counsel" and "other person having right of audience"), and note 1.3.4.

The petitioner must lodge the petition with the required steps of process (r.4.4). A fee is payable on lodging the petition: see note 14.5.10.

On petitions generally, see Chap. 14.

Accompanying documents

[1] **64.3.** The petitioner shall lodge with the application—

   (a) an affidavit supporting the averments in the petition;

   (b) an undertaking by the petitioner that he—

     (i) will comply with any order of the court as to payment of compensation if it is subsequently discovered that the order, or the implementation of the order, has caused loss to the respondent or, where the haver is not the respondent, to the haver; and

     (ii) will bring within a reasonable time of the execution of the order any proceedings which he decides to bring; and

     (iii) will not, without leave of the court, use any information, documents or other property obtained as a result of the order, except for the purpose of any proceedings which he decides to bring and to which the order relates.

---

[1] Rule 64.3 substituted by S.S.I. 2000 No. 319 (effective 2nd October, 2000).

64.3.1   *General note.* See note 64.1.1.

64.3.2   *"affidavit".* The affidavit should be in the form of a statement written in the first person. The affidavit should contain the evidence of the deponent in support of the averments in the petition.

An affidavit should be sworn and signed by the deponent before any person who may competently take an oath, whether in Scotland or in any other country. In Scotland such a person may include a notary public, justice of the peace, sheriff, or any judge. The person taking the oath should also sign the affidavit. Where the affidavit is not in English a duly certified translation should also be lodged.

See also the definition of affidavit in r.1.3(1).

Modification of undertakings

[1] **64.4.** The court may, on cause shown, modify, by addition, deletion or substitution, the undertaking mentioned in rule 64.3(b).

---

[1] R.64.5 substituted by S.S.I. 2000 No. 319 (effective 2nd October 2000).

General Note. See note 64.1.1.

Intimation and service of application

[1] **64.5.** (1) Before granting the application, the court may order such intimation and service of the petition to be given or executed, as the case may be, as it thinks fit.

(2) Any person receiving intimation or service of the petition by virtue of an order under paragraph (1) may appear and oppose the application.

---

[1] R.64.5 inserted by S.S.I. 2000 No. 319 (effective 2nd October, 2000).

General note. See note 64.1.1.   64.5.1
This rule is in the same terms as the former r.64.3.
Petitions are not usually intimated and served in the normal way before the order sought under s.1 of the Act of 1972 is granted because most applications are *ex parte* applications (on which, see note 64.2.3). The court may order service on the third party haver as in intimation of a motion under s.1 of the Act of 1972 (see r.35.2(3)) and on the Lord Advocate (see note 64.3.3).

Ex parte applications. The court may grant the application *ex parte* and the respondent can   64.5.2
only object to it after the event.
An application may be granted *ex parte* where (a) the documents are essential to the petitioner's case and (b) are at risk of destruction or concealment: *The British Phonographic Industry Ltd v. Cohen, Cohen, Kelly, Cohen & Cohen Ltd*, 1983 S.L.T. 137.
Where the order is sought *ex parte* a motion is enrolled for intimation, service and the order sought. If granted the court pronounces an interlocutor ordering intimation on the walls of the court, grants warrant for service, appoints a commissioner (usually a Q.C.), authorises recovery and orders the commissioner to transmit the documents, etc., with an inventory, to the Deputy Principal Clerk "to await the further orders of the court". Once recovered, a further order may be sought (if craved in the prayer) for inspection or the carrying out of experiments, etc., and thereafter returned to the Deputy Principal Clerk (a period of time sometimes being specified).

Service on Lord Advocate. This must be done where recovery is sought of a document   64.5.3
belonging to or in possession of the Crown: *Sheridan v. Peel* , 1907 S.C. 821, 825 *per* L.P. Strathclyde; *Whitehall v. Whitehall*, 1957 S.C. 30, 42 *per* Lord Sorn. This applies also to records of an NHS hospital: *Glacken v. National Coal Board*, 1951 S.C. 82.

Form of order

[1] **64.6.** An order made under this Chapter shall be in Form 64.6.

---

[1] Rule 64.6 inserted by S.S.I. 2000 No. 319 (effective 2nd October, 2000) and amended by S.S.I. 2004 No. 52 (effective 1st March, 2004).

General note. See note 64.1.1.   64.6.1

"Form". On forms, see note 1.4.1.   64.6.2

Caution and other security

[1] **64.7.** On granting, in whole or in part, the application the court may order the petitioner to find such caution or other security as it thinks fit.

[1] Deriv. RCS 1965, R.95A(C) (part) inserted by SI 1972/2021

---

[1] Chap. 64 and r.64.7 inserted by S.S.I. 2000 No. 319 (effective 2nd October 2000).

General note. See note 64.1.1.   64.7.1
This rule is in the same terms as the former r.64.4.
The ordering of caution or other security is rare. But, *e.g.* where the haver has a right of lien over them, the petitioner may only recover them by consignation in respect of the debt due: *Yau v. Ogilvie & Co.*, 1985 S.L.T. 91.

Execution of order

[1] **64.8.** The order of the court shall be served by the Commissioner in person and it shall be accompanied by the affidavit referred to in rule 64.3(a).

64.8.1   *General note.* See note 64.1.1.

64.8.2   *"served".* For personal service, see r.16.1. Rule 64.8 does not indicate on whom service is to be made or how. By reading the rule with r.64.9(a), it is clear that personal service under r.16.1(1)(a)(i) is intended.

64.8.3   *Commission and diligence.* If the prayer is granted an interlocutor will be pronounced granting a commission and diligence. The court, where appropriate and sought, (a) appoints a commissioner with a warrant under which the commissioner may enter premises and search for the documents or property, (b) authorises a named person to photograph, inspect, take samples of, or carry out an experiment on the property, (c) grants warrant to cite a haver to appear before a commissioner to produce the document or other property or answer questions about where it is or with whom it is or has been, or (d) authorises one or more of the above either at the same time or one at a time. Were it is not possible for a commissioner to blank out commercially confidential material in excerpting from documents, the court has authorised counsel, solicitors and an independent expert to inspect the documents provided they signed an undertaking about disclosure: *Iomega Corporation v. Myrica (UK) Ltd (No.1)*, 1999 S.L.T. 793.

The court has power to impose conditions for the use of information recovered by commission and diligence, although it is normal practice for the court to do so: *McInally v. John Wyeth & Brother Ltd*, 1992 S.L.T. 344; *Union Carbide Corporation v. B.P. Chemicals Ltd*, 1995 S.C. 398, 404G *per* L.P. Hope.

The interlocutor should indicate which of the powers in rr.35.5, 35.6 or 35.7 should apply. Note *ex parte* applications in note 64.5.2.

Care must be taken in identifying correctly in the interlocutor and by the commissioner the place to be searched. Where documents are recovered erroneously at a wrong place (and therefore unlawfully) the court cannot subsequently make them competently recovered: *Dominion Technology Ltd v. Gardner Cryogenics Ltd (No.2)*, 1993 S.L.T. 832.

Duties of commissioner

[1] **64.9.** The Commissioner appointed by the court shall, on executing the order—

[2] (a) give to the haver a copy of the notice in Form 64.9;

(b) explain to the haver—
  (i) the meaning and effect of the order;
  (ii) that he may be entitled to claim that some or all of the listed items are confidential or privileged;

(c) inform the haver of his right to seek legal advice;

(d) enter the premises and take all reasonable steps to fulfil the terms of the order;

(e) where the order has authorised the recovery of any of the listed items, prepare an inventory of all the listed items to be recovered before recovering them;

(f) send any recovered listed items to the Deputy Principal Clerk of Session to await the further order of the court.

64.9.1   *General note.* See note 64.1.1.

64.9.2   *"send".* This includes deliver: see r.1.3(1).

Confidentiality

[1] **64.10.** (1) Where confidentiality is claimed for any listed item, that listed item shall, where practicable, be enclosed in a sealed envelope.

(2) A motion to have such a sealed envelope opened may be made by the party who obtained the order and he shall intimate the terms of the motion, by registered post or first class delivery, to the person claiming confidentiality.

(3) A person claiming confidentiality may oppose a motion made under paragraph (2).

---

[1] R.64.10 inserted by S.S.I. 2000 No. 319 (effective 2nd October, 2000).

General note. See note 64.1.1.   **64.10.1**

"motion". For motions, see Chap. 23.   **64.10.2**

Confidentiality or privelege. Certain communications are recognised to be confidential and   **64.10.3** privileged.

(1) *Solicitor and client.* The general rule is that communications between solicitor and client for professional purposes are confidential and cannot be recovered. There are exceptions where fraud or other illegality is alleged against a party in relation to a transaction in which the solicitor was concerned (*Micosta S.A. v. Shetland I.C.*, 1983 S.L.T. 483), where the very existence of the solicitor and client relationship is in issue or where the communication is the subject-matter of the cause for which it is sought to be recovered (*Kid v. Bunyan* (1842) 5 D. 193). See further, under the fraud exception, *Conoco (U.K.) Ltd v. The Commercial Law Practice*, 1996 S.C.L.R. 446, 1997 S.L.T. 372, for an order against solicitors for disclosure of the identity of their client who was in possession of information relating to a fraud on the petitioners. The client may waive the privilege for a series of communications but not for an isolated document in a series: *Wylie v. Wylie*, 1967 S.L.T. (Notes) 9.

(2) *Solicitor and solicitor.* Communications between solicitors with a view to achieving settlement of litigation are confidential an d not recoverable: *Fyfe v. Miller* (1835) 13 S. 809. Stating that a communication is "without prejudice", however, will not make it privileged (*Burns v. Burns*, 1964 S.L.T. (Sh.Ct) 21); and a statement of fact is not protected from use as an admission because the words "without prejudice" have been used: *Watson-Towers Ltd v. McPhail*, 1986 S.L.T. 617; *Daks Simpson Group plc v. Kuiper*, 1994 S.L.T. 689.

(3) *Communications post litem motam.* Documents prepared for the purposes or in anticipation o the litigation are confidential and as a general rule are not recoverable: *Anderson v. St Andrew's Ambulance Association*, 1942 S.C. 99. Accordingly, reports of accidents are generally excluded. The reason is that after an accident each party must be able to investigate free from the risk of having to reveal his information to the other side: *Johnstone v. National Coal Board*, 1968 S.C. 128. The only exception to this general rule is that a report by an employee present at the time of the accident to his employer is not confidential (it is a *de recenti* statement) and may be recovered by the opponent: *Young*, above. Photographs fall into the same category as reports: *More v. Brown & Root Wimpey Highland Fabricators Ltd*, 1983 S.L.T. 669 (in which the general rule and its only exception was reaffirmed). An employer's accident book is not recoverable unless the entry in it comes within the exception: *Dobbie v. Forth Ports Authority*, 1974 S.C. 40. A medical report instructed for the purposes of the litigation is not recoverable: *Teece v. Ayrshire & Arran Health Board* 1990 S.L.T. 512. Confidentiality does not cease on completion if the case fir which the report was prepared: *Hunter v. Douglas Reyburn & Co. Ltd* 1993 S.L.T. 637.

(4) *Public policy (public interest immunity).* The only situation in which a document or other property may be withheld on the ground of public policy or public interest is where the interest is a national one put forward by the Crown: *Higgins v. Burton* 1986 S.L.T. (Notes) 52. The view that the law of Scotland does not recognise the concept of public interest immunity beyond that of Crown privilege, and does not divide confidentiality into public interest immunity and private confidentiality, was confirmed in *Parks v. Tayside R.C.* 1989 S.L.T. 345, 348a–348F *per* Lord Sutherland. See note 64.1.5 on Crown privilege or immunity.

(5) *Spouses.* Communications between spouses are confidential and one is not a competent or compellable witness against the other (Evidence (Scotland) Act 1853, s.3) except where the cause is concerned with their conduct towards each other, *e.g.* in a divorce (*MacKay v. MacKay* 1946 S.C. 78). The privilege subsists after death or divorce: Dickson on *Evidence*, para.1660.

(6) *Self-incrimination of haver.* As a general rule a document or other property which would render the haver liable to prosecution because it is self-incriminating is privileged. There is an exception. The privilege against self-incrimination cannot be claimed in respect of proceedings under s.1(1) of the Act of 1972 for infringement, to obtain disclosure of information about infringement or to prevent any apprehended infringement of intellectual property rights or passing off: Law Reform (Miscellaneous Provisions) (Scotland) Act 19875, s.15.

(7) *Clergy, doctors and journalists.* It is sometimes said that communications to such persons are confidential. This is true in a popular but not a legal sense. Confidentiality does not appear to attach much to communications to clergy. It does not attach to communications to doctors or journalists. The ordinary rule excluding recovery in relation to a medical report made in connection with the litigation would, however, apply to a doctor.

(8) *Communications as a matter of duty.* "A communication honestly made upon any subject in which a person has an interest, social or moral, or in reference to which he has a duty, is privileged if made to a person having a corresponding interest or duty": *James v. Baird* 1916 S.C. 510, 517 *per* L.P. Strathclyde. For a recent example of this type of privilege , see *Paterson v. Education Institution of Scotland*, 1997 S.C. 245.

Waiver of confidentiality will not necessarily result from documents being referred to in open court by the party entitled to the privilege; it depends on the purpose and whether there was publication of the contents: *Barclay v. Morris* 1998 S,C, 74. See also *Duke of Argyll v. Duchess of Argyll* 1962 S.C. (H.L.) 88 (admission on record of specific entries in diaries not waver of whole contents); and *Cunningham v. The Scotsman Publication Ltd* 1987 S.C. 107.

64.10.4   Crown *privilege or immunity.* Commission and diligence may be granted for recovery etc. of documents or property in possession of the Crown whether or not a party subject to two provisos, (i) a document or property may be withheld on the ground that its disclosure would be injurious to the public interest and (ii) the existence of a document or property shall not be disclosed if in the opinion of a Minister of the Crown it would be injurious to the public interest to disclose the existence of it; Crown Proceedings Act 1947, s.1(4). The first proviso relates to a particular document and the second to a class. The court has, however, an inherent power to overrule an objection by the Crown which is preserved by s.47 of the 1947 Act. The test to be applied is whether the public interest in the administration of justice not being frustrated outweighs the objection: *Glasgow Corporation v. Central Land Board* 1956 S.C. (H.L.) 1 confirming the law of Scotland recognised in *Sheridan v. Peel* 1907 S.C. 577, 580 *per* L.P. Dunedin; *Henderson v. McGowan* 1916 S.C. 821, 826 *per* L.P. Strathclyde. It is based on the ground that the fair administration of justice between subject and subject and between the subject and the Crown is a public interest of a high order, and that its protection is in the care of the courts: *Glasgow Corporation*, above, *per* Viscount Normand at pp. 12–13. Where objection is taken to a class of documents the court can take into account not only the interests of the applicant but also the interests of the public as a whole: *Friel, Petr* 1981 S.C. 1.

The court is bound to accept the assertion of the Crown that there is an aspect of public policy to protect: *Admiralty v. Aberdeen Steam Trawling and Fishing Co. Ltd*1909 S.C. 335; *Friel*, above; *A.B. v. Glasgow and West of Scotland Blood Transfusion Service* 1993 S.L.T. 36.

The court may inspect the document in deciding whether it should be reproduced or to decide whether parts of it which are relevant might be produced: *Science Research Council v. Nasse* [1980] A.C. 1028; *Air Canada v. Secretary of State for Trade (No. 2)* [1986] 2 A.C. 394.

In order to persuade the court even to inspect the documents the party seeking recovery ought at least to satisfy the court that they are very likely to contain material which would give substantial support to his contention on an issue which arises in the case and that without them he might be deprived of the means of proper presentation of his case: *Air Canada*, above, *per* Lord Fraser of Tullybelton at p.435.

Immunity does not apply to documents or property which do not come into the possession of a servant or agent of the Crown in the ordinary course of his official duties: *Whitehall v. Whitehall* 1957 S.C. 30. Immunity only arises where the public interest is a national one: *Higgins v. Burton* 1968 S.L.T. (Notes) 52; *Parks v. Tayside R.C.* 1989 S.L.T. 345, 345A *per* Lord Sutherland.

Restrictions on service

[1] **64.11.** (1) Except on cause shown, the order may be served on Monday to Friday only, between the hours of 9am and 5pm only.

(2) The order shall not be served at the same time as a search warrant granted in the course of a criminal investigation.

(3) The Commissioner may be accompanied only by—

(a) any person whom he considers necessary to assist him to execute the order;

(b) such representatives of the petitioner as are named in the order, and if it is likely that the premises will be occupied by an unaccompanied female and the Commissioner is not herself female, one of the people accompanying the Commissioner shall be female.

(4) If it appears to the Commissioner when he comes to serve the order that the premises are occupied by an unaccompanied female and the Commissioner is neither female nor accompanied by a female, the Commissioner shall not enter the premises.

[1] Rule 64.11 inserted by SSI 2000/319 (effective from 2nd October 2000).
General note. See note 64.1.1.   **64.11.1**

Right of haver to consult
[1] **64.12.** The haver may seek legal or other professional advice of his choice and where the purpose of seeking this advice is to help him to decide whether to ask the court to vary the order the Commissioner shall not commence to search for or to take any other steps to take possession of or preserve the listed items.

———

[1] Rule 64.12 inserted by SSI 2000/319 (effective from 2nd October 2000).

General note. See note 64.1.1.   **64.12.1**

Return of documents etc. to haver
[1] **64.13.** The Deputy Principal Clerk of Session shall return the recovered listed items to the haver if the petitioner has taken no further action within 8 weeks of the date on which they are sent to him under rule 64.9(f).

———

[1] Rule 64.13 inserted by SSI 2000/319 (effective from 2nd October 2000).

General note. See note 64.1.1.   **64.13.1**
This rule deals with a problem referred to in note 64.2.3 to the previous Chap. 64 (which last appeared in Release 53). In view In the view of the large number of recoveries kept by the Deputy Principal Clerk in respect of which no further action was taken, it was thought that the court might have to consider either (a) inserting in a interlocutor granting a commission and diligence a time-limit after the expiry of which the documents will be returned to the haver or (b) putting out petitions on the By Order Roll to ascertain whether the property may be returned. The haver could enter the process by lodging answers (or perhaps by motion) to recover his property, although in doing so he would be liable in the first instance to a court fee for entering the process. In *Olsen v. Forrest Estate Ltd,* 14th June 1994, unreported (1994 G.W.D. 24–1472), a motion by the havers to have documents returned was refused on the ground that the court would not be generally order return, except in exceptional circumstances, before the determination of the petition. This decision overlooked the point made above that a number of such petitions are not concluded but no further action is taken in the process after the recoveries are lodged with the Deputy Principal Clerk.
Where it can be summarily and conclusively shown that the basis on which an order for recovery of documents and property, under s. 1 of the Act of 1972 has been obtained, is false, the court can order redelivery: *Olsen,* above; *Iomega Corporation Petr*, 14th August 1994, unreported.

CHAPTER 65

REFERENCES TO THE EUROPEAN COURT OF JUSTICE

Interpretation of this Chapter
65.1.—(1) In this Chapter—
    "appeal" includes an application for leave to appeal;
    "the European Court" means the Court of Justice of the European Communities;
    "reference" means a reference to the European Court for—
        [1] (a) a preliminary ruling under Article 234 of the E.E.C. Treaty, Article 150 of the Euratom Treaty, or Article 41 of the E.C.S.C. Treaty;
        (b) a preliminary ruling on the interpretation of the Conventions, mentioned in Article 1 of Schedule 2 to the Civil Jurisdiction and Judgments Act 1982, under Article 3 of that Schedule; or
        (c) a preliminary ruling on the interpretation of the instruments, mentioned in Article 1 of Schedule 3 to the Contracts (Applicable Law) Act 1990, under Article 2 of that Schedule.

(2) The expressions "E.E.C. Treaty", "Euratom Treaty" and "E.C.S.C. Treaty" have the meanings assigned respectively in Schedule 1 to the European Communities Act 1972.

Deriv. RCS 1965, r. 296A inserted by SI 1972/1981

---

[1] R. 65.1 amended by SI 1999/1281 (effective 1st May 1999).

65.1.1   *General note.* The term "European Economic Community" in the E.E.C. Treaty was replaced by the term "European Community" by Art.G(1) of Title II of the Treaty on European Union (Maastricht): see European Communities Act 1972, s. 1(2)(k) as amended by the European Communities (Amendment) Act 1993, s. 1(1).

The E.C. Commission has expressed its willingness to respond to formal requests by national courts for advice and information about the application of Arts 85 and 86 (which relate to competition law) of the E.C. (formerly E.E.C.) Treaty: see Notice on co-operation between national courts and the Commission in applying Articles 85 and 86 of the E.E.C. Treaty, Official Journal [1993] c. 39/6. The court could write directly after hearing parties, or the court could request a party (or parties jointly) to write (no doubt in terms approved by the court) to the Commission for particular advice or information. The Commission could be invited to appear and make representations. No express provision is made, or required, in the RCS 1994 for this procedure.

Applications for reference

65.2. A reference may be made by the court at its own instance or on the motion of a party.

Deriv. RCS 1965, r. 296B inserted by S.I. 1972 No. 1981

---

[1] Rule 65.2 amended by S.I. 1999 No. 1281 (effective 1st May 1999).

General note. Where the decision of the court is one against which there is no judicial remedy under the national law (*i.e.* no right of appeal in the proceedings in question), the court is bound to bring before the European Court for a preliminary ruling a question of Community law arising in the proceedings pending before it: E.E.C. Treaty, Art. 234(3) (177(3) before the Treaty of Amsterdam). The duty to refer does not arise (a) in respect of an interlocutory decision against which there is no appeal if the question of Community law may be reviewed at a later stage of the case (*Hoffmann-La Roche v. Centrafarm Vertreibsgesellschaft* [1977] E.C.R. 957) or (b) where a previous decision of the European Court is directly in point or where the correct application of Community law is obvious to all national courts (*CILFIT Srl. v. Ministry of Health* [1982] E.C.R. 3415).

    65.2.1

A judge at first instance or the Inner House (at first instance, in a reclaiming motion or an appeal) has a discretion to request a preliminary ruling under Art. 177(2) (now Art. 234(2)) of the E.E.C. Treaty where a decision on a question of Community law is necessary to enable judgment to be given. The exercise of the discretion is itself subject to review.

The test in both cases is whether the decision on a question of Community law is necessary to decide the dispute: *CILFIT Srl.*, above. The court may decide the question itself if the point is free from doubt and obvious to all national courts: *CILFIT Srl.*, above.

A reference may be made at any time, though it is probably not appropriate before the closing of the record: *Prince v. Secretary of State for Scotland* 1985 S.C. 8.

The provisions for preliminary rulings under Art. 3 of Sched. 2 to the C.J.J.A. 1982 and Art. 2 of Sched. 3 to the Contracts (Applicable Law) Act 1990 are to similar effect. The 1990 Act implements the Rome Convention on the Law Applicable to Contractual Obligations 1980 made to achieve unification of rules of international private law in relation to contractual obligations within the E.C.

[1] The form for the reference is now provided for in r. 65.3.

"motion". For motions, see Chap. 23.   **65.2.2**

Preparation of case for reference

65.3.—(1) Where the court decides that a reference shall be made, it shall pronounce an interlocutor giving directions to the parties about the manner and time in which the reference is to be drafted and adjusted.

[1] (1A) Except in so far as the court may otherwise direct, a reference shall be prepared in accordance with Form 65.3.

[3] (1B) In preparing a reference, the parties shall have regard to guidance issued by the European Court of Justice.

[2] (2) When the reference has been drafted and any adjustments required by the court have been made, the court shall make and sign the reference.

(3) A certified copy of the interlocutor making the reference shall be annexed to the reference.

---

[1] Rule 65.3(1A) inserted by S.I. 1999 No. 1281 (effective 1st May 1999).
[2] R. 65.3(2) amended by S.I. 1999 No. 1281 (effective 1st May 1999).
[3] Rule 65.3(1B) inserted by S.I. 1999 No. 1281 and substituted by S.S.I. 2005 No. 521 (effective 21st October, 2005).

65.3.1   *"adjustment required by the court".* The reference is checked by the clerk of court in the first instance to see that it is in conformity with any requirement of the interlocutor allowing the reference and the ground on which the reference was allowed. If he has a doubt he consults the judge. Adjustments may be required by the court. Once adjusted the clerk may add the following docquet to the reference:

> "Edinburgh, *(date)*. This reference consisting of this and the preceding pages adjusted at my sight.

> *(Signed)*, Depute Clerk of Session".

65.3.2   *Guidance from the ECJ.* The European Court of Justice (of the European Communities) has issued guidance on the making of a reference. This should be consulted when preparing the reference in Form 65.3. The guidance was reproduced in an Annex to the Rules in the amendment to r. 65.3 in S.I. 1999 No.1281 which inserted para (1B), but, because the guidance is updated and may change from time to time, was sensibly removed in the amendment in 2005 substituting a new para (1B). The guidance referred to can be found in an information note published by the Court of Justice of the European Communities on its website at: *www.curia.eu.int/en/instit/txtdocfr/autrestxts/txt8.pdf.*

Sist of cause

65.4.—(1) Subject to paragraph (2), on a reference being made, the cause shall, unless the court when making such a reference otherwise orders, be sisted until the European Court has given a preliminary ruling on the question referred to it.

(2) The court may recall a sist made under paragraph (1) for the purpose of making an interim order which a due regard to the interests of the parties may require.

Deriv. RCS 1965, r. 296C inserted by S.I. 1972 No. 1981

Transmission of reference

65.5.—(1) Subject to paragraph (2), a copy of the reference, certified by the Deputy Principal Clerk, shall be transmitted by him to the Registrar of the European Court.

(2) Unless the court otherwise directs, a copy of the reference shall not be sent to the Registrar of the European Court where a reclaiming motion or appeal against the making of the reference is pending.

(3) For the purpose of paragraph (2), a reclaiming motion or an appeal shall be treated as pending—

    (a) until the expiry of the time for marking that reclaiming motion or appeal; or

    (b) where a reclaiming motion or an appeal has been made, until it has been determined.

Deriv. RCS 1965, r. 296D inserted by S.I. 1972 No. 1981

65.5.1   *General note.* When the reference is received by the Registrar of the European Court in Luxembourg it is translated into all the official languages of the court, the order of the Court of Session for the reference is served on the parties to the action, the Member States and Community institutions, all of whom may lodge written observations within two months of service. After expiry of the time to lodge observations the judge rapporteur prepares and presents a preliminary report; the Advocate-General writes an opinion. There follows a hearing at which parties can present oral argument.

For procedure generally before the European Court, see Rules of Procedure of the Court of Justice published by the court.

65.5.2   *Reclaiming or appeal.* The period within which a cause may be reclaimed or appealed is determined by the enactment under which the reclaiming motion or appeal is made. Subject to any other enactment, under the RCS 1994, the time for reclaiming is determined by rr. 38.3 and 38.4 and the time for appeal determined by r. 40.4 (appeals from inferior courts), rr. 41.5 and 41.11 (appeals by stated case etc.) or r. 41.20 (appeals in Form 41.19). "Appeal" includes appeal to the House of Lords, which must be made within three months of the date on which the order appealed from was made: House of Lords Directions, Direction 8.1.

CHAPTER 66

APPLICATIONS UNDER THE EVIDENCE (PROCEEDINGS IN OTHER
JURISDICTIONS) ACT 1975

Interpretation of this Chapter
66.1. In this Chapter—
"the Act of 1975" means the Evidence (Proceedings in Other
Jurisdictions) Act 1975;
"civil proceedings" has the meaning assigned in section 9(1) of the Act
of 1975;
"requesting court" has the meaning assigned in section 9(1) of the Act
of 1975.

General note. R.C.S. 1965, r. 102A, from which this Chapter is derived, was introduced **66.1.1**
following the enactment of the Evidence (Proceedings in Other Jurisdictions) Act 1975. Until
this Act the taking of evidence of a witness or haver resident in Scotland for the purpose of
proceedings in a foreign court or tribunal was regulated by the Evidence by Commission Acts
1859 and 1885 (for requests by a court in another of H.M. Dominions (including England and
Wales and Ireland)) and the Foreign Tribunals Evidence Act 1856 (for requests by a court in
any "foreign country"; and extended to criminal proceedings by s.24 of the Extradition Act
1870). The Act of 1975 repealed the 1856, 1859 and 1885 Acts and s.24 of the 1870 Act, and
replaced these with a new unified regime for civil and criminal proceedings. The Criminal
Justice (International Co-operation) Act 1990, however, replaced the Act of 1975 in respect of
criminal proceedings. The Act of 1975 also enabled the U.K. to ratify the Hague Convention on
the Taking of Evidence Abroad in Civil or Commercial Matters, 1970 (Cmnd. 6727 (1977)) in
1976. With effect from 1st April 2000 the authority functions under Art. 24 of the Convention
transferred from the Crown Agent for Scotland to the Scottish Executive Justice Dept, Civil
Justice and International Division, Hayweight House, 23 Lauriston Street, Edinburgh, EH3
9DQ. This followed the devolution settlement, which gave rise to responsibility passing to the
Scottish Ministers for whom the function is exercised by the Minister for Justice.
    The Act of 1975, however, is broader than the convention in that it allows letters of request
from any country and not just the parties to the convention; it also applies to courts within the
U.K. Under s.6 of the Act of 1975, the Act may be applied to international proceedings. By
Order in Council the Act of 1975 was extended to proceedings before the Court of Justice of the
European Communities: Evidence (European Court) Order 1976 [S.I. 1976 No. 428]. With
regard to U.K. dependencies the Act, as modified, applies to the Cayman Islands (S.I. 1978 No.
1890), the Falkland Islands and Dependencies (S.I. 1978 No. 1891), the Sovereign base areas of
Akrotiri and Dhekelia (S.I. 1978 No. 1920), the Isle of Man (S.I. 1979 No. 1711), Guernsey (S.I.
1980 No. 1956), Jersey (S.I. 1983 No. 1700), Anguilla (S.I. 1986 No. 218), and the Turks and
Caicos Islands (S.I. 1987 No. 1266).
    This Chapter is made under s.1(3) of the Administration of Justice (Scotland) Act 1972 as
well as under s.5 of the C.S.A. 1988.

"civil proceedings". This means, in relation to the requesting court, proceedings in any civil or **66.1.2**
commercial matter: Act of 1975, s.9(1). It has been held in England that the words "civil or
commercial matter" have a wide meaning and include all proceedings other than criminal
proceedings (a meaning broader than the same words in the C.J.J.A. 1982): *Re State of
Norway's Application (Nos 1 and 2)* [1990] 1 A.C. 723, 806F *per* Lord Goff of Chieveley. It was
also held in that case that whether proceedings are civil is a matter of law and practice of the
requesting court: *per* Lord Goff of Chieveley at p. 805B.

"requesting court". This means the court or tribunal making the request: Act of 1975, ss.1(a) **66.1.3**
and 9(1).

Disapplication of certain rules to this Chapter
66.2. The following rules shall not apply to an application to which this
Chapter applies:—
rule 14.5 (first order in petitions),
rule 14.6 (period of notice for lodging answers),
rule 14.7 (intimation and service of petitions),
rule 14.9 (unopposed petitions).

66.2.1   *Ex parte application.* An application under the Act is made *ex parte* without any requirement for intimation, service or answers. This is to enable the evidence to be obtained speedily. If a witness or haver against whom an order has been made and intimated under r. 66.4 objects to it, he must apply to the court by note to have it varied or recalled: r. 66.5. Accordingly the rules in Chap. 14 mentioned in this rule are disapplied.

Form of applications under the Act of 1975

66.3.—(1) An application under section 1 of the Act of 1975 (application for assistance in obtaining evidence for foreign civil proceedings) shall be made by petition.

(2) *[Revoked by S.I. 1998 No. 2637.]*

(3) Where the letter of request is in a language other than English, there shall be produced with the petition a translation into English certified as correct by the translator; and the certificate shall include his full name, address and qualifications.

Deriv. R.C.S. 1965, r. 102A(2) inserted by S.I. 1976 No. 283 and amended by S.I. 1982 No. 1825 (r. 66.3(1))

66.3.1   *Applications under s.1 of the Act of 1975.* All applications under the Act of 1975 are made under s.1 which relates only to evidence for civil proceedings, its application formerly by s.5 (now repealed) to criminal proceedings (furth of the U.K.) being replaced by the Criminal Justice (International Co-operation) Act 1990.

The application may be made by any court furth of Scotland including a court elsewhere in the U.K.

66.3.2   *"petition".* The petition is presented in the Inner House: r. 14.3(f). The vacation judge may not determine the petition though he may make an incidental order: r. 11.1(c). For the form of the petition see r. 14.4. The petition must be signed by counsel or other person having a right of audience: r. 4.2(3); and see r. 1.3(1) (definitions of "counsel" and "other person having a right of audience") and note 1.3.4.

Where the application relates to oral evidence, the petition should include averments—(a) referring to the request giving rise to the application; (b) that the requesting court requires oral evidence for use in a trial or proof of fact in civil proceedings before it (*Lord Advocate, Petr.* 1993 S.C. 638); and (c) to satisfy the court that if a similar situation arose in civil proceedings before it, the court could grant a commission for the examination of a witness (Act of 1975, s.2(3)). The prayer of the petition should contain a crave for the appointment of a commissioner.

Where the application relates to real or documentary evidence, the petition should include averments—(a) similar to (a) and (b) above; and (b) to satisfy the court that if a similar situation arose in civil proceedings before it, the court could order recovery, inspection, preservation, etc., of the material sought (Act of 1975, s.2(3)). The prayer of the petition should include craves corresponding to the order sought (see, *e.g.* note 64.2.3). It is suggested that one of the craves may, for convenience, refer to a schedule (akin to a specification of documents) listing the real or documentary evidence sought to be recovered.

66.3.3   *Evidence is to be obtained for civil proceedings.* The meaning of the word "evidence" in the Act of 1975 was discussed inconclusively in *In re Westinghouse Uranium Contract* [1978] A.C. 547. Lord Diplock, with whom Lord Keith of Kinkel agreed, considered (pp. 633–634) that evidence might be obtained by an applicant to ascertain whether there existed admissible evidence to support his case or to contradict his opponent's case if that was permitted by the system of the requesting court, the only limit to fishing discovery (diligence) being in s.2 of the Act of 1975 (see note 66.3.7). Viscount Dilhorne thought (p. 619) the Act was limited to direct evidence for use at the trial (proof); and see Lord Fraser of Tullybelton at pp. 641–645. In *Lord Advocate, Petr* 1993 S.C. 638, a letter of request for the dual purpose of trial testimony and deposition testimony was allowed to the extent of trial testimony and the sheriff principal was directed to allow a legal representative of the witness to attend to object to questions on the ground of competency or relevancy. The Inner House has approved Viscount Dilhorne's views in *In re Westinghouse Uranium Contract*, above: *Lord Advocate, Petr* 1998 S.C. 87, 94H *per* Extra Div.; and see *First American Corporation v. Sheikh Zayed Al-Nahyan* [1998] 4 All E.R. 437 (CA).

"requesting court". See note 66.1.3. **66.3.4**

Certificate about the proceedings. Formerly, r. 66.3(2) required a certificate that the **66.3.5** application was made by virtue of a request for evidence for the purpose of civil proceedings commenced or contemplated before the foreign court. This requirement was revoked by A.S. (R.C.S.A. No. 2) (Miscellaneous) 1998 [S.I. 1998 No. 2637] as an unnecessary formality which was in excess of the requirements of the 1970 Hague Convention (see note 66.1.1).

"civil proceedings". See note 66.1.2. **66.3.6**

Orders which may be obtained. S.2 of the Act of 1975 specifies the scope of an order under it. **66.3.7** The order must (a) give effect to the request in the application by providing for the obtaining of the evidence requested, and (b) require a person specified to take such steps as the court considers appropriate for the obtaining of the evidence requested. In giving effect to the request the court cannot make an order which it could not normally make in relation to domestic proceedings before it (Act of 1975, s.2(3); and see *Lord Advocate, Petr* 1993 S.C. 638 and *Lord Advocate, Petr* 1998 S.C. 87), or which would require a person to state what relevant documents are in his possession or to produce documents not specified in the order (Act of 1975 s.2(4)).

The restriction of the Act of 1975 in s.4 of the Protection of Trading Interests Act 1980 should be noted. Where the order provides for the obtaining of oral evidence, the order should narrate that the evidence is "for the purpose of trial testimony only": *Lord Advocate, Petr* 1993 S.C. 638, 641H.

The court can order a commission for the taking of evidence from a witness. It can also order recovery of documents from a haver at common law (see note 35.2.5) or under s.1 of the Administration of Justice (Scotland) Act 1972 (see note 35.2.6) or inspection, preservation, etc., under s.1 of the 1972 Act. An order for production of a public record for evidence in foreign proceedings may be made. In relation to medical examinations, see restriction in s.2 of the Age of Legal Capacity (Scotland) Act 1991. In relation to the taking of blood or other samples, see powers in s.6 of the Law Reform (Parent and Child) (Scotland) Act 1986 and s.70 of the Law Reform (Miscellaneous Provisions) (Scotland) Act 1990; and see note 35.15.5(4).

In relation to public records and entries in public registers, extracts should be sufficient. Writs in the Books of Council and Session may not be given out without the authority of the court: Writs Registration (Scotland) Act 1868; by the Writs Execution (Scotland) Act 1877, extracts are equivalent. The court is reluctant to allow original records out of the country: see *Kennedy* (1880) 7 R. 1129. Where the court does so, it may require the document to remain in the custody of an official of the public register: *Campbell's Trs* 1934 S.C. 8.

Commissioner. Where the application is made by the Lord Advocate on behalf of the **66.3.8** Secretary of State for Foreign and Commonwealth Affairs who has received a letter of request from a foreign government official, the commissioner should be the sheriff principal or sheriff of the sheriffdom in whose jurisdiction the witness or haver resides: *Lord Advocate, Petr* 1909 S.C. 199; and see, *e.g. Lord Advocate v. Sheriffs* 1978 S.C. 56 and *Lord Advocate, Petr* 1993 S.C. 638. Where the application is made by an agent of a party to foreign proceedings or a representative of a foreign country directly and not the Lord Advocate, the court will appoint any commissioner it thinks fit in the normal way for a commission but not a sheriff: *Baron de Bildt, Petr* (1905) 7 F. 899.

The commission. The commission ought to be conducted in the same way as a commission to **66.3.8A** take the evidence of a witness under Chap. 35 (see notes 35.12.5 (on interrogatories) and 35.13.5 (without interrogatories)). In *Lord Advocate, Petr* 1994 S.L.T. 852, the court considered it was taking an unusual step, which would not normally be ordered as a matter of course, by directing the sheriff principal to allow a legal representative of the witness (as distinct presumably from the lawyer for the party whose witness he would be) to attend to object to questions on the ground of competency or relevancy.

66.3.9   *Identity of witness or haver.* Where the applicant wishes to examine unknown representatives of a company or similar legal persona or partnership the names of which the applicant does not know, there is no need to identify the individuals by their names in the petition and the court will ordain the company to name them: *Lord Advocate, Petr* 1925 S.C. 568.

Intimation of order and citation

66.4.—(1) Where the court pronounces an interlocutor making an order under section 2(1) of the Act of 1975, the petitioner shall—
  (a) intimate a certified copy of that interlocutor to any witness or haver named in the interlocutor; and
  (b) cite such witness or haver to give evidence.
  (2) Rule 35.4(3) and (4) (citation of haver to commission) and rule 35.11(5) and (6) (citation of witness to commission) shall, with the necessary modifications, apply to the citation of a haver or witness, as the case may be, under this rule.

66.4.1   *Expenses of witness or haver.* A witness or haver who is cited following an order under s.1 of the Act of 1975 is entitled to payment of expenses for attendance: s.2(5) of the Act of 1975. The solicitor for the petitioner will be responsible for the expenses. Where the application is not made by the Lord Advocate caution may be required for these expenses.

66.4.2   *Intimation.* For methods, see r. 16.7.

66.4.3   *Certified copy interlocutor.* The applicant should prepare a copy for certification by the clerk of session.

66.4.4   *Citation of witness or haver.* This should be done at the same time as intimation.

Variation or recall of orders

66.5. A witness or haver who has received intimation and citation under rule 66.4 may apply to the court by motion to have the order under section 2(1) of the Act of 1975 varied or recalled.

Deriv. RCS 1965, r. 102A(5) inserted by S.I. 1990 No. 705

66.5.1   *"motion".* For motions, see Chap. 23. The special provisions where a witness or haver claims he is not compellable should be noted: see r. 66.6.
  For an example of variation of an order, see *Lord Advocate, Petr* 1993 S.C. 638.

Procedure where witness claims he is not compellable

66.6.—(1) Where a witness or haver who has received intimation and citation under rule 66.4—
  (a) claims that he is not a compellable witness or haver by virtue of section 3(1)(b) of the Act of 1975, and
  (b) is required to give evidence,
the court or any commissioner appointed by the court shall take the evidence and record it in a document separate from the record of any other evidence; and that document shall be kept by the Deputy Principal Clerk.
  (2) Where evidence is taken under paragraph (1) of this rule, the court or the commissioner, as the case may be, shall certify the grounds of the claim made under section 3(1)(b) of the Act of 1975.
  (3) On certification under paragraph (2), the Deputy Principal Clerk shall send the certificate to the requesting court with a request to it to determine the claim.
  (4) On receipt of the determination from the requesting court, the Deputy Principal Clerk shall—

(*a*) give written intimation of the determination to the witness or haver who made the claim; and

(*b*) in accordance with the determination, send the document in which the evidence is recorded to, as the case may be—

(i) the requesting court, or

(ii) where the claim is upheld, the witness or haver.

Deriv. R.C.S. 1965, r. 102A(3) inserted by S.I. 1976 No. 283

Compellability. A witness or haver may claim he is not compellable in relation to oral or **66.6.1** documentary evidence which he is ordered to give or produce (*a*) where he would be able to do so in Scottish civil proceedings (Act of 1975, s. 3(1)); (*b*) where he would be able to do so in the country of the requesting court (Act of 1975, s. 3(2)); or (*c*) where the evidence would be prejudicial to UK security, in respect of which a certificate by or on behalf of the Secretary of State is conclusive (Act of 1975, s. 3(3)). In respect of proceedings in the country of the requesting court the question of non-compellability should be supported by a statement in the request or conceded by the applicant for the order: Act of 1975, s. 3(2). Where the claim of non-compellability is not so supported the witness or haver may be required to give evidence (Act of 1975, s. 3(2)) in which case the procedure in this rule is followed.

Where a witness fails or refuses to attend, the modern practice is to enrol a motion for warrant to messengers-at-arms to apprehend the witness. The historical practice of obtaining letters of second diligence (in effect having the same result) is not usually followed, although it may be where it is known in advance that the witness will not attend. Before granting the warrant the court must be satisfied that citation has been executed; a certificate of execution must be produced.

On compellability of witnesses, see note 36.2.8.

At common law in England the court may refuse to give effect to letters of request where it would be prejudicial to the Sovereignty of the UK: *In re Westinghouse Uranium Contract* [1978] A.C. 547.

Where the evidence is taken by a commissioner he will have to send or deliver the record of the evidence to the Deputy Principal Clerk.

"requesting court". See note 66.1.3. **66.6.2**

"written intimation". For methods, see r. 16.9. **66.6.3**

Applications for evidence for proceedings under the European Patent Convention

66.7. Where the court makes an order under section 1 of the Act of 1975 as applied by section 92(1) of the Patents Act 1977, an officer of the European Patent Office may apply by motion—

(*a*) to examine any witness; or

(*b*) to request the court or commissioner, as the case may be, to put specified questions to any witness.

Deriv. R.C.S. 1965, r. 102A(4) inserted by S.I. 1978 No. 955

European Patent Office. The European Patent Office was established under Convention on **66.7.1** the Grant of European Patents (Cmnd. 8510 (1982)). By virtue of s. 92(1) of the Patents Act 1977, ss. 1 to 3 of the Act of 1975 apply to proceedings before a relevant convention court under the convention.

"motion". For motions, see Chap. 23. **66.7.2**

CHAPTER 67

APPLICATIONS UNDER THE ADOPTION (SCOTLAND) ACT 1978

PART I

GENERAL PROVISIONS

Application and interpretation of this Chapter

67.1.—(1) This Chapter applies to applications under the Adoption (Scotland) Act 1978.

(2) In this Chapter, unless the context otherwise requires—

"the Act of 1978" means the Adoption (Scotland) Act 1978;

[1] "the Act of 1995" means the Children (Scotland) Act 1995;

"freeing for adoption order" means an order made in accordance with section 18(1) of that Act;

[2] "the Act of 2002" means the Adoption and Children Act 2002;

"Her Majesty's Forces" means the Royal Navy, the regular armed forces as defined in section 225 of the Army Act 1955, the regular air force as defined in section 223 of the Air Force Act 1955 and the Queen Alexandra's Royal Naval Nursing Services;

[1] "parental responsibilities" has the meaning given by section 1(3) of the Act of 1995;

[1] "parental rights" has the meaning given by section 2(4) of that Act;

"section 49 order" means an order made in accordance with section 49(1) of the Act of 1978.

———

[1] R. 67.1 amended by S.I. 1997 No. 853 (effective 1st April 1997)
[2] Rule 67.1 amended by S.S.I. 2007 No. 7, para. 11 (effective 26th February 2007).

Deriv. R.C.S. 1965, r. 219(1) substituted by S.I. 1984 No. 997 (r. 67.1(2))

General note. The provisions of this Chapter are made under s.59(1) of the Adoption   **67.1.1** (Scotland) Act 1978 (as well as under s.5 of the C.S.A. 1988): see A.S. (R.C.S. 1994) 1994, Sched. 1 [S.I. 1994 No. 1443]. Accordingly, words and expressions used in this Chapter which are used in the Act of 1978 have the same meaning as in that Act unless the contrary intention appears: Interpretation Act 1978, s.11. Definitions in the Act of 1978 are in s.65(1) of that Act and include "adoption agency", "adoption order", "Convention adoption order", "local authority", "child", "parent", "guardian" and "approved adoption society".

Disapplication of certain rules to this Chapter

67.2. Unless otherwise provided in this Chapter, the following rules shall not apply to a petition or note to which this Chapter applies:—

rule 14.5 (first order in petitions),

rule 14.6(1)(d) (period of notice for lodging answers where service by advertisement),

rule 14.7 (intimation and service of petitions),

rule 14.8 (procedure where answers lodged),

rule 14.9 (unopposed petitions).

Deriv. R.C.S. 1965, rr. 220(2), 221(2), 222(2) and 226(2), all substituted by S.I. 1984 No. 997

General note. The primary consideration in an adoption order is the need to safeguard and   **67.2.1** promote the welfare of the child: Act of 1978, s.6. The rules therefore provide an expedited procedure to which certain ordinary petition rules (listed in this rule) do not apply. On the need to avoid delay in adoption petitions, see *Lothian R.C. v. A.* 1992 S.L.T. 858, 861F *per* L.P. Hope.

Confidentiality of documents in process

67.3. Unless the court otherwise directs, in any cause to which this Chapter applies—

(a) any document lodged in process, including a report by a local authority, an adoption agency, a reporting officer or a curator *ad litem*, shall be treated as confidential and open only to the court, the parties, the reporting officer and the curator *ad litem*; and

    (b) a reporting officer or curator *ad litem* shall treat any information obtained by him in relation to the cause as confidential, and shall not disclose any such information to any person unless it is necessary for the proper execution of his duties.

Deriv. R.C.S. 1965, r. 230(6) substituted by S.I. 1984 No. 997

67.3.1   *General note.* Confidentiality is necessary to ensure that a person is not reluctant to provide relevant information. All documents in process are confidential, not just the various reports. The court may order non-disclosure of a document to a person, even a party where appropriate.

67.3.2   *Inspection and borrowing of documents.* Writs (defined in r. 1.3(1)) and certain documents may not be borrowed from process, although a person interested (such as those mentioned in r. 67.3) may inspect them: r. 4.11. A party who is an individual may be given access (*i.e.* allowed to inspect) to a document: r. 67.3(2).

Selection of reporting officer or curator ad litem

[1] **67.4.** Where the court appoints a reporting officer or a curator *ad litem* and there is an established panel of persons from whom the appointment may be made, the reporting officer or curator *ad litem* shall be selected from that panel unless the court considers that it would be appropriate to appoint a person who is not on the panel.

Deriv. R.C.S. 1965, r. 230(8) substituted by S.I. 1984 No. 997

---

[1] R.67.4 substituted by S.I. 1997 No. 853 (effective 1st April 1997).

67.4.1   *General note.* The court is not obliged to appoint a curator *ad litem* or a reporting officer from the panel established under the Curators *ad Litem* and Reporting Officers (Panels) (Scotland) Regulations 1984 [S.I. 1984 No. 566], if it considers it appropriate to appoint someone not on the panel.

    S. 58(1) of the Act of 1978 specifies the general duties of the curator *ad litem* as being to safeguard the interests of the child in the proceedings, and of the reporting officer as being to witness agreements to adoption and to perform such other duties as may be prescribed by rules. On the appointment of a reporting officer, see r. 67.10(1) (freeing for adoption) and r. 67.23(1) (adoption etc.); on the duties of a reporting officer, see r. 67.11(1) (freeing for adoption) and r. 67.24(1) (adoption etc.). On the appointment of a curator *ad litem*, see r. 67.10(1) (freeing for adoption), r. 67.14(2)(b) (revocation of freeing for adoption) and r. 67.23(1) (adoption etc.); on the duties of a curator *ad litem*, see r. 67.11(2) (freeing for adoption), r. 67.14(5) (revocation of freeing for adoption), r. 67.24(2) (adoption etc.) and r. 67.36 (additional duties in applications for Convention adoption order).

    The court may appoint the same person to be both reporting officer and curator *ad litem*: Act of 1978, s.58(2).

67.4.2   *The Panel.* A local authority (a regional or islands council) is required to establish a panel for its own area after consultation with the sheriff principal for the area of suitably qualified and experienced persons under the Curators *ad Litem* and Reporting Officers (Panels) (Scotland) Regulations 1984 [S.I. 1984 No. 566]. Panels may include social workers, solicitors and advocates. There are restrictions on the appointment from a panel of a person employed by an adoption agency in certain circumstances: Act of 1978, s.58(2).

    The expenses of a reporting officer or curator *ad litem* appointed in a particular case from the panel are paid for by the local authority: 1984 Regulations, reg. 10 as substituted by the Curators *ad Litem* and Reporting Officers (Panels) (Scotland) Amendment Regulations 1985 [S.I. 1985 No. 1556]. Local authorities have laid down their own scales. Where additional fees or expenses are claimed these may be met by the local authority; but if not, the balance could be claimed from the petitioner on an order for expenses being obtained from the sheriff under r. 67.7.

    A person appointed to the panel takes the oath *de fideli administratione* on his appointment to the panel.

67.4.3   *Persons not on the panel.* The court may, where it considers it appropriate, appoint a person to be reporting officer or curator *ad litem* who is not on the panel of the local authority established under the Curators *ad Litem* and Reporting Officers (Panels) (Scotland) Regulations 1984 [S.I.

1984 No. 566]. Where this happens the local authority will not pay the fee of the person appointed, and the fee will usually be the responsibility of the petitioner. The court may make any order it thinks fit in relation to expenses including those of a reporting officer or curator *ad litem*: r. 67.7.

There are restrictions on the appointment of a person employed by an adoption agency in certain circumstances: Act of 1978, s.58(2).

A person not on the panel appointed to be a curator *ad litem* must take the oath *de fideli administratione* on his appointment.

¹ *Timetable for resolving question as to whether agreement to adoption order etc. should be dispensed with*
67.4A—(1) A timetable shall be drawn up forthwith under section 25A of the Act of 1978 by the court when any of the following occurs–
  (a) there is presented to it a petition with a crave for any agreement of the parent or guardian of a child to be dispensed with on a ground specified in section 16(2) of that Act;
  (b) it appears to the court, from the report of an adoption agency, local authority or reporting officer that the question of dispensing with such agreement on a ground so specified arises; or
  (c) such agreement (being agreement which, if not given, it would be competent to dispense with on a ground so specified) is given but is afterwards withdrawn.
  (2) To ensure, so far as is reasonably practicable, that the timetable is adhered to, the court shall give such directions as it considers appropriate.

---

¹ R.67.4A inserted by S.I. 1997 No. 853 (effective 1st April 1997).

General note. The insertion of r.67.4A by A.S. (R.C.S.A. No. 2) (Adoption Applications) **67.4A.1**
1997 [S.I. 1997 No. 853] does not apply to applications for adoption or freeing for adoption made before 1st April 1997.

Timetable. S. 25A of the Act of 1978 (inserted by para. 18 of Sch. 2 to the Children (Scotland) **67.4A.2**
Act 1995) requires the court, in proceedings in which the question arises as to whether there is agreement to adoption or freeing for adoption, to draw up a timetable specifying periods within which certain steps must be taken and to give directions to ensure the timetable is adhered to so as to determine the question without delay.

R.67.4A(2) repeats, in a different word order, s.25A(b) of the 1995 Act and ought not to have been enacted.

Form of agreements and consents
  67.5.—(1) An agreement by a parent or guardian—
¹ (a) for the purposes of section 16(1)(b) of the Act of 1978 (agreement to adoption), shall be in Form 67.5–A unless the applicant for the adoption order is such person as is mentioned in section 15(1)(aa) of that Act, in which case it shall be in Form 67.5–F;
  (b) for the purposes of section 16(1)(b), by virtue of section 49 of that Act (adoption of child abroad), shall be in Form 67.5–A; or
  (c) for the purposes of section 18(1)(a) of that Act (agreement to freeing for adoption), shall be in Form 67.5–B.
  (2) A consent—
  (a) by a child for the purposes of section 12(8) of the Act of 1978 (consent to adoption), shall be in Form 67.5–C;
  (b) by a parent or guardian for the purposes of section 18(2)(a) of that Act (consent to application for freeing for adoption), shall be in Form 67.5–D; or
  (c) by a child for the purposes of section 18(8) of that Act (consent to freeing for adoption), shall be in Form 67.5–E.

(3) An agreement or consent referred to in this rule which is executed furth of Scotland shall be witnessed—
  (a) where it is executed in England, Wales or Northern Ireland, by a justice of the peace or commissioner for oaths;
  (b) where it is executed furth of the United Kingdom—
    (i) in the case of a parent or guardian serving in Her Majesty's Forces, by an officer holding a commission in those forces; or
    (ii) by a British consular official or any person authorised, by the law of the country where the agreement or consent is executed, to administer an oath for any legal purpose.

Deriv. R.C.S. 1965, r. 220(4) (r. 67.5(2)(b)), r. 220(8)(a) (r. 67.5(1)(c)), r. 220(8)(b) (r. 67.5(2)(c)), r. 222(9)(a) (r. 67.5(1)(a) and (b)), r. 222(9)(b) (r. 67.5(2)(a)) and r. 230(1) (r. 67.5(3)), all substituted by S.I. 1984 No. 997

---

[1] R.67.5(1)(a) amended by S.I. 1997 No. 853 (effective 1st April 1997).

67.5.1   *General note.* Where the agreement or consent is executed in Scotland it should be witnessed by the reporting officer: rr. 67.11(1)(c) and 24.(1)(c). Where the agreement or consent is executed outside Scotland it should be witnessed in accordance with r. 67.5(3).
  By virtue of s.81 of the Solicitors Act 1974 every solicitor who holds a practising certificate in England and Wales has the power of a commissioner for oaths under the Commissioners for Oaths Acts 1889 and 1891. The power was extended to public notaries (members of the Incorporated Company of Scriviners) within their jurisdiction by s.65 of the Administration of Justice Act 1985. Under s.113 of the Courts and Legal Services Act 1990, the power was extended to authorised persons and general notaries in England and Wales. An "authorised person" is an authorised advocate or litigator other than a solicitor, or a member of a body prescribed by the Lord Chancellor. From 1st August 1995 legal executives who are fellows of the Institute of Legal Executives may act as commissioners for oaths in England and Wales. Every such solicitor, notary or authorised person has the right to use the title "Commissioner for Oaths" and should use that title (although a solicitor may accidentally omit to do so).
  An agreement or consent witnessed in accordance with the forms by virtue of r. 67.5 is sufficient evidence without further proof of signature of the person by whom it was executed: Act of 1978, s.55(1).

[1] *Consideration of views of child and of certain reports*
  67.5A In a cause to which this Chapter applies, the court shall not grant an adoption order or grant or revoke an order freeing a child for adoption–
  (a) where the child has indicated to the court, or his curator *ad litem* if one has been appointed under this Chapter, a wish to express views on a matter affecting the child unless–
    (i) an opportunity has been given for those views to be obtained or heard (the court ordering such steps to be taken in that regard as it considers appropriate); and
    (ii) due weight has been given by the court to such views as the child does express (account being taken of his age and maturity); and
  (b) where a report has been received in relation to the child by virtue of section 73(13) of the Act of 1995 (report of children's hearing where child subject to supervision requirement), unless the court has first considered the report.

---

[1] R.67.5A inserted by S.I. 1997 No. 853 (effective 1st April 1997).

67.5A.1   *General note.* The insertion of r.67.5A by A.S. (R.C.S.A. No. 2) (Adoption Applications) 1997 (S.I. 1997 No. 853] does not apply to applications for adoption or freeing for adoption, made before 1st April 1997.

Orders for evidence
67.6.—(1) In a cause to which this Chapter applies, the court may, before determining the cause, order—
  (a) production of further documents (including affidavits); or
  (b) parole evidence.
(2) A party may apply by motion for the evidence of a person to be received in evidence by affidavit; and the court may make such order as it thinks fit.

Deriv. R.C.S. 1965, r. 230(5) substituted by S.I. 1984 No. 997 (r. 67.6(1)), and r. 230D (part) inserted by S.I. 1978 No. 1373 (r. 67.6(2))

"affidavits". The affidavit should be in the form of a statement of evidence written in the first   **67.6.1**
person. The affidavit should contain evidence in support of, and expanding on, the averments in the petition. It should be sworn and signed by the deponent before any person who may competently take an oath. Such a person includes a notary public, a justice of the peace, a sheriff, or any judge. The person taking the oath should also sign the affidavit. Witnesses to the affidavit are unnecessary. And see definition of affidavit in r. 1.3(1).

[1] *Children who may require compulsory measures of supervision*
67.6A Where, under subsection (1) of section 54 of the Act of 1995 (question arising as to whether compulsory measures of supervision are necessary) a matter is referred to the Principal Reporter, the clerk of court shall given him written intimation of the court's decision, which shall include a certified copy of the interlocutor, and shall specify in the intimation which of the conditions referred to in that subsection it appears to the court has been satisfied.

---

[1] R.67.6A inserted by S.I. 1997 No. 853 (effective 1st April 1997).

General note. The insertion of r.67.6A by A.S. (R.C.S.A. No. 2) (Adoption Applications)   **67.6A.1**
1997 [S.I. 1997 No. 853] does not apply to applications for adoption or freeing for adoption made before 1st April 1997.

"written intimation". For methods, see r. 16.9.   **67.6A.2**

Expenses
67.7. In a cause to which this Chapter applies, the court may make such order as to expenses, including the expenses of a local authority or an adoption agency which prepared a report, a reporting officer, a curator *ad litem*, or any other person who attended a hearing, as it thinks fit.

Deriv. R.C.S. 1965, r. 230(7) substituted by S.I. 1984 No. 997

General note. In relation to the expenses of a reporting officer and curator *ad litem*, note that   **67.7.1**
the fees of such persons appointed from a panel established under the Curators *ad Litem* and Reporting Officers (Panels) (Scotland) Regulations 1984 [S.I. 1984 No. 566] are paid for by the local authority; but not if the person appointed is not on the panel, in which case the petitioner will normally be responsible for the fee.

PART II

FREEING FOR ADOPTION

Interpretation of this Part
67.8. In this Part, "petition" means the petition referred to in rule 67.9(1).

Applications for freeing for adoption order

67.9.—(1) An application under section 18(1) of the Act of 1978 (freeing child for adoption) shall be made by petition.

(2) The petition shall include averments in relation to, or refer to a report or other documents produced which deal with—

(a) whether the petition is presented with the consent of a parent or guardian;

(b) whether the petitioner is applying for dispensation with the agreement of a parent or guardian under section 18(2)(b) of the Act of 1978 (agreement to freeing for adoption) and the ground on which dispensation is sought;

(c) how the needs of the child came to the notice of the petitioner;

(d) any relevant family circumstances of the child;

(e) a description of the physical and mental health of the child (including any special needs) and his emotional, behaviourial and educational development;

(f) the discussion by the petitioner with the parents or guardians of the child and, if appropriate, with the child about their wishes and the alternatives to adoption;

(g) the knowledge of the petitioner of the position of other relatives or persons likely to be involved;

(h) the search by the petitioner for any parent or guardian who cannot be found;

(i) the likelihood of placement of the child for adoption and whether a petition for an adoption order is likely in the near future;

(j) the arrangements of the petitioner for the care of the child in the event of the granting of the prayer of the petition;

(k) whether the petitioner has given each parent or guardian who can be found an opportunity to make a declaration for the purposes of section 18(6) of the Act of 1978 (declaration of preference not to be involved in future questions concerning the adoption);

[1] (l) whether the petitioner has considered the position of any person claiming to be the child's father (being a person who is not married to the mother); and

[1] (m) whether the petitioner intends to give notice to a relevant parent under section 19(2) and (3) of that Act (progress reports).

(3) On presentation of the petition, there shall be lodged in process as a production—

(a) an extract or a certified copy of any entry in the register of births relating to the child; and

(b) any consent of a parent or guardian required by section 18(2)(a) of the Act of 1978 (consent to freeing for adoption).

Deriv. R.C.S. 1965, r. 220(1) (r. 67.9(1)), r. 220(3) (r. 67.9(2)) and r. 220(5) (r. 67.9(3)), all substituted by S.I. 1984 No. 997

---

[1] R.67.9.(2)(l) and (m) substituted by S.I. 1997 No. 853 (effective 1st April 1997).

67.9.1   *General note.* A petition to free a child for adoption may only be presented by an adoption agency: Act of 1978, s.18(1). An adoption agency is a local authority or an approved adoption society (Act of 1978, s.1(4)) and in certain cases includes an adoption agency under s.1 of the (English) Adoption Act 1976 (Act of 1978, s.65(1)). An approved adoption society means an adoption society approved by the Secretary of State (Act of 1978, s.65(1)) and in certain cases includes an adoption society under the (English) Adoption Act 1976.

Freeing for adoption is a procedure introduced following a recommendation of the Houghton Committee in its report on the Adoption of Children (Cmnd. 5107 (1972)) to provide a procedure for a parent to relinquish parental rights to overcome the problem of indecisiveness of a parent and insecurity for adopters when a parent can withdraw agreement to adoption at any time before the order is made. A parent can, however, withdraw agreement to a freeing for adoption order before it is made, and in certain circumstances may seek to have such an order revoked under s.20 of the Act of 1978 before an adoption order is made.

When freeing for adoption was introduced, many children tended to be placed for adoption at or shortly after birth. Times have changed. Also, the ECtHR has ruled that attempts should be made first to get natural parents to bring up their own children, and that adoption should be considered only if this fails: see, e.g., *Johansen v. Norway,* (1996) 23 EHRR 33. A result of this approach is that by the time adoption has to be pursued some bond exists between the natural parents and the child and there will be some form of contact between them while the child is in care. The natural parents want to continue that contact, but there is no provision in the Scottish freeing for adoption legislation to allow for contact in making a freeing order. In that event natural parents oppose freeing applications. For a discussion of the issues and appropriate course to be followed in this conflict between freeing and contact, see *City of Edinburgh Council v. S,* 2000 S.L.T. (Sh. Ct.) 147; *City of Edinburgh Council v. D,* 2001 S.L.T. (Sh. Ct.) 135. These concerns were taken up by the Inner House in *West Lothian Council v. McG,* 2002 S.C. 411.

It has been held that, while the effect of making a freeing order interfered with the rights of a natural parent to respect for family life under art. 8(1) of ECHR, it could be justified under art. 8(2) if it pursued the legitimate aim of welfare of the child: *Dundee City Council v. GK,* 2006 S.C. 326 (First Div) (a declaration of incompatibility was refused). Lord Hamilton, LP, comments at p. 336, under reference to the approach taken by Sheriff Horsburgh QC in *Midlothian Council v. W,* 2005 S.L.T. (Sh. Ct.) 146 (dismissing a freeing application without hearing evidence as an infringement of art. 8) that, in the absence of inquiry, it may be impossible to conclude that making a freeing order was such an infringement. The approach taken in *City of Edinburgh Council v. D,* above, was that evidence had to be heard.

In reaching any decision relating to the adoption of a child the court or adoption agency staff shall have regard to all the circumstances, first consideration being given to the need to safeguard and promote the welfare of the child throughout his chilood; and so far as practicable the child's wishes should be ascertained and due consideration given to them: Act of 1978, s.6.

The amendments to r.67.9(2)(l) and (m) by A.S. (R.C.S.A. No. 2) (Adoption Applications) 1997 [S.I. 1997 No. 853] do not apply to freeing for adoption petitions made before 1st April 1997.

It has been argued that freeing for adoption is an infringement of Art. 8 of ECHR where there is (or should be) contact by a parent with a child. In *Dundee City Council v. K,* 2006 S.L.T. 63. 69, para [28], Lord Hamilton, LP, said that in the absence of inquiry into the facts (or agreement of the facts) it may be impossible to conclude that freeing is an infringement of Art. 8.

Jurisdiction. The court has jurisdiction where the child is in Scotland or not in Great Britain **67.9.2** when the application for a freeing for adoption order is made: Act of 1978, s.56(1) to (3).

"petition". A petition for a freeing for adoption order is presented in the Outer House: **67.9.3** r. 14.2(h). The petition must be in Form 14.4 in the official printed form: rr. 4.1 and 14.4. The petition must be signed by counsel or other person having a right of audience: r. 4.2; and see r. 1.3(1) (definitions of "counsel" and "other person having a right of audience") and note 1.3.4.

The petitioner must lodge the petition with the required steps of process (r. 4.4) and the productions required by r. 67.9(3) and any others (including those founded on or adopted (r. 27.1)) with an inventory of productions (r. 4.5).

A fee is payable on lodging the petition: see note 14.5.10.

"parent". This means, irrespective of whether or not they are or have been married to each **67.9.4** other, (a) the mother of the child where she has parental rights or responsibilities in relation to him; (b) the father of the child where he has such responsibilities or rights; and (c) both of his parents where both have such responsibilities or rights: Act of 1978, s.65(1) inserted by Children (Scotland) Act 1995.

"guardian". This is defined in s.65(1) of the Act of 1978 and means a person appointed by **67.9.5** deed, a will or by the court to be a guardian: Act of 1978, s.65(1) as amended by the Law Reform (Parent and Child) (Scotland) Act 1986, the Age of Legal Capacity (Scotland) Act 1991 and the Children (Scotland) Act 1995.

Declaration not to be involved in future questions. The court has to be satisfied that each **67.9.6** parent or guardian who can be found has an opportunity of making a declaration that he prefers not to be involved in future questions concerning the adoption of the child: Act of 1978, s.18(6) as amended by the Health and Social Services and Social Security Adjudications Act 1983, Sched. 2, para. 40. See further r. 67.12. If such a declaration is made by a person, he will not receive progress reports about the adoption process and will not be able to apply for revocation of the freeing for adoption order: Act of 1978, ss.19 and 20.

Progress reports under s.19 of the Act of 1978. A parent or guardian who has not made a **67.9.7** declaration that he prefers not to be involved in future questions concerning the adoption must be informed of certain matters in the adoption process by the adoption agency: Act of 1978, s.19. This could be important if the child is not subsequently adopted and the parent wishes to be involved again with the child. Such a parent has the right after 12 months from the making of the freeing order to seek revocation of it in order to resume parental rights: Act of 1978, s.20.

67.9.8   *Applications for parental rights when petition for freeing for adoption pending.* An application for parental rights may have been made when a petition for a freeing order has been presented or *vice versa.* It is not incompetent for one court to consider a freeing order while another is considering parental rights, and the two concepts are different: *Borders R.C. v. M.* 1986 S.C. 63. A freeing order is not binding on a court considering custody: *F. v. F.* 1991 S.L.T. 357, 362L *per* L.P. Hope. It is desirable for questions about parental rights and adoption to be considered by the same judge and for questions about parental rights to be sisted pending a decision about adoption: *F. v. F.* 1991 S.L.T. 357, 363 *per* L.P. Hope. A similar solution should be adopted where applications for parental rights and a freeing order are made.

67.9.9   *Applications for parental rights after child freed for adoption.* Under s.11(1) and (3) of the Children (Scotland) Act 1995 any person claiming an interest in, or who has had, parental rights or responsibilities, may apply for an order relating to parental rights or responsibilities in the child. "Interest" in s.11(3)(a) may mean either some personal interest, or, in the context of title and interest to sue, an interest in the application itself and its outcome: *D. v. Grampian R.C.* 1995 S.C. (H.L.) 1.

Appointment of reporting officer and curator ad litem

67.10.—(1) On presentation of the petition, the court shall pronounce an interlocutor—

(a) appointing a reporting officer; and

(b) appointing a curator *ad litem* where it appears desirable in order to safeguard the interests of the child.

(2) Where a curator *ad litem* is appointed, the court may order—

(a) the petitioner,

(b) a local authority, or

(c) the reporting officer,

to make available to the curator *ad litem* any report or information in relation to the child and the natural father and mother of the child.

(3) A person may, before presenting the petition, apply by letter to the Deputy Principal Clerk for the appointment of a reporting officer.

(4) An application under paragraph (3) shall—

(a) set out the reasons for which the appointment is sought;

(b) not require to be intimated to any person;

(c) be accompanied by an interlocutor sheet; and

(d) be placed by the Deputy Principal Clerk before the Lord Ordinary for his decision.

(5) The Deputy Principal Clerk shall give written intimation to the applicant under paragraph (3) of the decision of the Lord Ordinary.

(6) The decision of the Lord Ordinary on an application under paragraph (3) shall be final and not subject to review.

(7) The letter and the interlocutor sheet in an application under paragraph (3) shall be kept in the Petition Department and subsequently placed in the process of the petition.

Deriv. R.C.S. 1965, r. 220(6) and (7) (r. 67.10(1) and (2)), r. 225 (r. 67.10(3) to (7)), all substituted by S.I. 1984 No. 997

67.10.1   *Reporting officer and curator* ad litem. Such persons may be appointed from a panel established under the Curators *ad Litem* and Reporting Officers (Panels) (Scotland) Regulations 1984 [S.I. 1984 No. 566]: see r. 67.4. Subject to certain restrictions in relation to a person employed by an adoption agency, the same person may be appointed to be reporting officer and curator *ad litem*: Act of 1978, s.58(2).

The general duties of a reporting officer are to witness agreements to adoption and to perform such other duties as may be prescribed by rules, and of the curator *ad litem* to safeguard the interests of the child: Act of 1978, s.58(1); and see r. 67.11.

A curator *ad litem* may be appointed where it is desirable to safeguard the interests of the child: r. 67.10(1)(b). It will be so desirable, *e.g.* where the adoption agency is applying for dispensation of the agreement of a parent or guardian or where it is sought to dispense with the consent of a child who is 12 or over: see Act of 1978, s.18(8).

"local authority". A local authority is a council constituted under s.2 of the Local **67.10.2** Government etc. (Scotland) Act 1994: Act of 1978, s.65(1).

Appointment of reporting officer or curator ad litem *before petition presented.* An adoption **67.10.3** agency may wish to have a reporting officer appointed before a petition is presented, for example, where a parent or guardian of the child to be freed for adoption whose agreement is required is going abroad.

"final and not subject to review". The decision of the Lord Ordinary may not be reclaimed **67.10.4** against.

Duties of reporting officer and curator ad litem
67.11.—(1) A reporting officer appointed under rule 67.10 shall—
   (a) inquire into the facts and circumstances averred in the petition;
   (b) ascertain the whereabouts of each parent or guardian and, if practicable, meet him;
   (c) witness any execution in Scotland of any agreement in Form 67.5–B by a parent or guardian under section 18(1)(a) of the Act of 1978 (agreement to freeing for adoption) and investigate whether the agreement is given freely, unconditionally and with full understanding of what is involved and, where the reporting officer has been appointed before the petition has been presented, any consent in Form 67.5–D by a parent or guardian under section 18(2)(a) of that Act (consent to freeing for adoption);
   (d) where a parent or guardian is furth of Scotland, confirm his views in writing, ensure that any agreement under section 18(1) of the Act of 1978 is witnessed in accordance with rule 67.5(3) and investigate whether the agreement is given freely, unconditionally and with full understanding of what is involved;
   (e) ensure that each parent or guardian who can be found and who has executed an agreement for the purposes of section 18(1)(a) of the Act of 1978 understands that he may renounce that agreement at any time before a freeing for adoption order is made;
   (f) witness any execution in Scotland of a consent of a child in Form 67.5–E under section 18(8) of the Act of 1978 (consent to freeing for adoption) and ensure that he understands the consequences of that consent;
   (g) where a child in respect of whom a consent under section 18(8) of the Act of 1978 is required is furth of Scotland, confirm his consent in writing and ensure that the consent is witnessed in accordance with rule 67.5(3);
   (h) consider whether the petitioner has made every reasonable effort to find every person whose agreement is required;
   (i) investigate whether there are any other persons with a relevant interest and whether they should be informed of the petition;
 [1] (j) ascertain whether the petitioner has considered the position of any person claiming to be the child's father (being a person who is not married to the mother);
 [2] (k) where such a person so claiming does not have parental responsibilities or parental rights in relation to the child, ascertain the likelihood of that person—
      (i) applying for an order under section 11(1) of the Act of 1995 (orders relating to parental responsibilities etc.);
      (ii) being refused such an order if he does so apply; or
      (iii) entering into an agreement with the mother under section 4(1) of that Act (natural father's acquisition of parental responsibilities etc. by agreement);

(l) discuss alternatives to adoption with each parent or guardian who can be found;

(m) explain the consequences of a freeing for adoption order to each parent or guardian who can be found;

(n) ensure that each parent or guardian who can be found understands he may be able to apply under section 20 of the Act of 1978 and rule 67.14 for revocation of a freeing for adoption order, and the procedure for making such an application;

(o) ensure that each parent or guardian who can be found has been given an opportunity to make a declaration under section 18(6) of the Act of 1978 that he prefers not to be involved in future questions concerning the adoption of the child;

(p) consider why the application is for a freeing for adoption order and not a full adoption order;

(q) consider whether the account by the petitioner of the likelihood of arranging adoption after a freeing for adoption order is correct;

(r) consider whether any payment or reward prohibited by section 51 of the Act of 1978 (prohibition on certain payments) has been received or agreed upon;

(s) ensure that each parent or guardian who can be found is aware of the date (if known) of the hearing to determine the application if he wishes to appear, and confirm that such person whose agreement is required and has not been dispensed with understands that he may withdraw his agreement at any time before the freeing for adoption order is made;

[1] (ss) ascertain whether the child is subject to a supervision requirement;

(t) draw to the attention of the court any matter which may be of assistance; and

(u) prepare a report in relation to the exercise of his duties within such period as the court may specify.

(2) A curator *ad litem* appointed under rule 67.10(1)(b) shall—

(a) safeguard generally the interests of the child;

(b) inquire, so far as he considers necessary, into the facts and circumstances averred in the petition;

[2](bb) ascertain from the child whether he wishes to express any views as respects the petition;

(bc) ascertain whether it would be better for the child that an order were made under section 18(1) of the Act of 1978 than that it were not made;

(c) confirm any consent by a child under section 18(8) of the Act of 1978 (consent to freeing for adoption);

(d) inquire into any matters not averred in the petition which appear to him to be relevant to the making of a freeing for adoption order;

(e) ascertain the current circumstances and care of the child;

(f) where the agreement or consent of a parent or guardian or the consent of a child is sought to be dispensed with, consider whether the ground of dispensation has been made out;

(g) consider whether, in his opinion, the child should be present at the hearing to determine the petition;

(h) perform such other duties as appear to him to be necessary or as the court may require;

[2](hh) in performing his duties under this paragraph, regard the need to safeguard and promote the welfare of the child throughout the child's life as the paramount consideration; and

(i) prepare a report in relation to the exercise of his duties within such period as the court may specify.

(3) The reporting officer shall, on completion of his report, send to the Deputy Principal Clerk—

(a) the report and a copy of it for each party;

(b) any agreement for the purposes of section 18(1)(a) of the Act of 1978 (agreement of parent or guardian to freeing for adoption);

(c) any declaration for the purposes of section 18(6) of the Act of 1978 (declaration of preference not to be involved in future questions concerning adoption); and

(d) any consent under section 18(8) of the Act of 1978 (consent of child to freeing for adoption).

(4) The curator *ad litem* shall, on completion of his report, send the report, and a copy of it for each party, to the Deputy Principal Clerk.

Deriv. R.C.S. 1965, r. 224(1) (r. 67.11(1)), r. 224(4) (r. 67.11(2)), r. 220(8) (r. 67.11(3)) and r. 220(9) (r. 67.11(4)), all substituted by S.I. 1984 No. 997

---

[1] R.67.11(1)(j) amended by S.I. 1997 No. 853 (effective 1st April 1997).
[2] R.67.11(1)(k) and (ss) and (2)(bb), (bc) and (hh) inserted by S.I. 1997 No. 853 (effective 1st April 1997).

General note. The essential difference between the duties of reporting officers and curators *ad litem* in freeing for adoption petitions and adoption petitions is that in the former the court is not concerned with the suitability of any prospective parents.   **67.11.1**

The general duties of a reporting officer are to witness agreements to adoption and to perform such other duties as may be prescribed by rules, and of the curator *ad litem* to safeguard the interests of the child: Act of 1978, s.58(1); and see r. 67.11.

The duties of the curator *ad litem* are to provide the court with evidence of the history of the child, his current parents and his situation. The curator *ad litem*'s function is to carry out an inquiry into all the enumerated matters on behalf of the court. It is not his function to express an opinion on matters of law: *T, Petr.*, 1997 S.L.T. 724, 731B–C *per* L.P. Hope (on r. 67.24(2)).

The amendments to r. 67.11(1) and (2) by A.S. (R.C.S.A. No. 2) (Adoption Applications) 1997 [S.I. 1997 No. 853] do not apply to freeing for adoption petitions made before 1st April 1997.

"parent". This means, irrespective of whether or not they are or have been married to each other, (a) the mother of the child where she has parental rights or responsibilities in relation to him; (b) the father of the child where he has such responsibilities or rights; and (c) both of his parents where both have such responsibilities or rights: Act of 1978, s.65(1) inserted by Children (Scotland) Act 1995.   **67.11.2**

"guardian". This is defined in s.65(1) of the Act of 1978 and means a person appointed by deed, a will or by the court to be a guardian: Act of 1978, s.65(1) as amended by the Law Reform (Parent and Child) (Scotland) Act 1986, the Age of Legal Capacity (Scotland) Act 1991 and the Children (Scotland) Act 1995.   **67.11.3**

"agreement by a parent or guardian". A freeing for adoption order can only be made where each parent or guardian agrees to the order unless his agreement is dispensed with on a ground mentioned in s.16(2) of the Act of 1978: Act of 1978, s.18(1).   **67.11.4**

"consent of a child". A freeing for adoption order cannot be made without the consent of a child who is 12 years old unless his consent is dispensed with on grounds of incapacity to give consent: Act of 1978, s.18(8) as amended by the Age of Legal Capacity (Scotland) Act 1991, s.2(3)(b).   **67.11.5**

Declaration not to be involved in future questions. The court has to be satisfied that each parent or guardian who can be found has an opportunity of making a declaration that he prefers not to be involved in future questions concerning the adoption of the child: Act of 1978, s.18(6) as amended by the Health and Social Services and Social Security Adjudications Act 1983, Sched. 2, para. 40. See further r. 67.12. If a declaration is made by a person, he will not receive progress reports about the adoption process and will not be able to apply for revocation of the freeing for adoption order: Act of 1978, ss.19 and 20.   **67.11.6**

"payment or reward prohibited by section 51 of the Act of 1978". It is unlawful to make or receive a payment or reward for the adoption of a child, any agreement or consent in that connection, the transfer of the care and possession of a child with a view to adoption of the child or the making of any arrangement for the child's adoption; and a person who does so is liable on summary conviction to a fine or imprisonment: Act of 1978, s.51.   **67.11.7**

"send". This includes deliver: r. 1.3(1) (definition of "send").   **67.11.8**

67.11.9   *Lodging of reports etc.* A report by the reporting officer and any agreements or declarations, and any report of a curator *ad litem*, are, on receipt of them by the Deputy Principal Clerk, lodged in process as a step in process: r. 67.13(1) and r. 1.3(1) (definition of "step of process").

Declaration of preference not to be involved

67.12.—[1] (1) A declaration under section 18(6) or 19(4) of the Act of 1978 (declaration of preference not to be involved in future questions concerning adoption) shall be in Form 67.12–A; and any withdrawal of either such declaration shall be in Form 67.12–B.

(2) A declaration referred to in paragraph (1) which is executed furth of Scotland shall be witnessed in accordance with rule 67.5(3).

(3) The making of a declaration referred to in paragraph (1) shall be recorded in an interlocutor pronounced by the court.

(4) For the purposes of section 19(4)(a) of the Act of 1978, the adoption agency shall—

(a) lodge the declaration, and

(b) apply to the court by motion,

in the process of the petition to which the declaration relates to have that declaration recorded.

[2] (5) Where a withdrawal such as is referred to in paragraph (1) is lodged, it shall be recorded in an interlocutor pronounced by the court and then intimated forthwith to the adoption agency by the clerk of court.

Deriv. R.C.S. 1965, r. 220(8)(c) (r. 67.12(1)), r. 220(14) (r. 67.12(3)) and r. 230(2) (r. 67.12(4)), all substituted by S.I. 1984 No. 997

---

[1] R.67.12(1) amended by S.I. 1997 No. 853 (effective 1st April 1997).
[2] R.67.12(5) inserted by S.I. 1997 No. 853 (effective 1st April 1997).

67.12.1   *Declaration not to be involved in future questions under s.18(6) of the Act of 1978.* The court has to be satisfied that each parent or guardian who can be found has an opportunity of making a declaration that he prefers not to be involved in future questions concerning the adoption of the child: Act of 1978, s.18(6) as amended by the Health and Social Services and Social Security Adjudications Act 1983, Sched. 2, para. 40. If a declaration is made by a person, he will not receive progress reports about the adoption process and will not be able to apply for revocation of the freeing for adoption order: Act of 1978, ss.19 and 20.

The reporting officer has a duty to ensure that each parent or guardian who can be found is given the opportunity to make such a declaration and that it is given freely, unconditionally and with full understanding: r. 67.11(1)(c) and (o). The declaration must be witnessed by the reporting officer if executed in Scotland (r. 67.11(1)(c)) or in accordance with r. 67.5(3) if executed furth of Scotland and recorded by the court (r. 67.12(3)).

67.12.2   *Declaration not to be involved in future questions under s.19(4) of the Act of 1978.* A former parent or guardian who was given an opportunity to make a declaration not to be involved in future questions concerning the adoption but did not do so before the freeing for adoption order, may do so subsequently; and if he does the adoption agency need not give him further progress reports: Act of 1978, s.19(4). The declaration must be in Form 67.12–A and must be recorded by the court on a motion by the adoption agency under r. 67.12(4).

Hearing of freeing for adoption petition

67.13.—(1) On receipt of the reports mentioned in rule 67.11(3) and (4), the Deputy Principal Clerk shall—

(a) cause the reports and any other documents to be lodged in process;

(b) give written intimation to each party of the lodging of those documents and make them available to each party; and

(c) within seven days thereafter, cause—

(i) the petition to be put out on the By Order Roll before the Lord Ordinary; and

(ii) written intimation of the date of the hearing on the By Order Roll to be given to each party.

(2) At the hearing on the By Order Roll, the court—

(a) shall pronounce an interlocutor appointing the petition to a hearing to determine the petition; and

(b) may, in such interlocutor—

    (i) order any person whose agreement or consent is required to be given or dispensed with to attend the hearing;

[1] (ii) order intimation of the date of the hearing to any person not mentioned in paragraph (3)(a), (aa), (b) or (c); and

    (iii) order the reporting officer or curator *ad litem*, as the case may be, to perform any additional duties to assist the court in determining the petition.

(3) The petitioner shall intimate the date of the hearing ordered under paragraph (2)(a) in Form 67.13 to—

(a) every person whose whereabouts are known to him and whose agreement or consent is required to be given or dispensed with;

[2](aa) where the child's mother is not married to his father, any person whose whereabouts are so known and who, being a person who claims to be the child's father, is neither the child's guardian nor a person with regard to whom an order in relation to parental responsibilities as respects the child has been made under section 11(1) of the Act of 1995;

(b) the reporting officer appointed under rule 67.10 (1)(a);

(c) any curator *ad litem* appointed under rule 67.10(1)(b); and

(d) any person on whom intimation was ordered under paragraph (2)(b)(ii) of this rule.

(4) At the hearing ordered under paragraph (2)(a)—

(a) the petitioner, the reporting officer and, where one has been appointed, the curator *ad litem* shall, if required by the court, appear and may be represented;

(b) any person required by the court to attend the hearing shall appear and may be represented; and

[1] (c) any other person to whom intimation was made under paragraph (3)(a), (aa) or (d) may appear or be represented.

Deriv. R.C.S. 1965, r. 220(10) to (13) substituted by S.I. 1984 No. 997

---

[1] R. 67.13(2)(b)(ii) and (4)(c) amended by S.I. 1997 No. 853 (effective 1st April 1997).
[2] R. 67.13(3)(aa) inserted by S.I. 1997 No. 853 (effective 1st April 1997).

"party". The petitioner is a party. A person objecting to a petition becomes a party **67.13.1** (respondent) on lodging answers: see r. 14.8 and note 14.8.1.

"written intimation". For methods, see r. 16.9.   **67.13.2**

By Order Roll hearing. The purpose of this hearing is to enable the court (a) to clarify the **67.13.3** issues to be resolved at the (full) hearing and (b) to determine the form of the (full) hearing. Parties should be clear before the By Order Roll hearing what has to be resolved and what form the (full) hearing should take. If oral evidence is required there must be an interlocutor allowing proof and the citing of witnesses.

The issues to be resolved may include the effect of the process on an application for parental rights (see note 67.9.8), the effect of any existing or proposed action of paternity or the reasonableness of the refusal of a parent or guardian to agree to the order.

The (full) hearing could take the form of a procedure roll discussion, a proof (or proof before answer) or the interview of a parent or guardian withholding consent followed by a hearing without oral evidence.

"intimation", "intimate". For methods, see r. 16.7.   **67.13.4**

Persons to whom intimation of hearing to be made. R. 67.13 provides for this and includes **67.13.5** intimation to any person. Such a person might include a father not married to the mother, where the court thinks it appropriate, in order to be satisfied about whether the father is not claiming or would be likely to obtain parental rights. Such a person has a locus to be heard as he can only be excluded from making submissions on the freeing application when the court is satisfied under s. 18(7) that it is likely that he will not be awarded parental rights: *City of Edinburgh Council v. G*, 2002 S.C. 440, 443 para.[9] (Ex Div.).

67.13.6 *Hearing to determine the petition.* The (full) hearing could take the form of a procedure roll discussion, a proof (or proof before answer) or possibly the interview of a parent or guardian withholding agreement followed by a hearing without oral evidence. If oral evidence is required there must have been an interlocutor pronounced allowing proof and the citing of witnesses.

Where the court is considering whether to dispense with the agreement of a parent or guardian, there are two stages involved, (a) whether one of the grounds in s. 16(2) of the Act of 1978 has been established and (b) if so, whether an order to dispense should be made; s. 6 of the Act of 1978 (welfare of the child) is strictly relevant only at the second stage, although the same considerations as in that section are matters to be taken into account in the first stage when the question is whether agreement is withheld unreasonably: *Lothian R.C. v. A*. 1992 S.L.T. 858.

67.13.7 *Privacy of hearings.* Any hearing in a petition for a freeing for adoption order is heard in private unless the court otherwise directs: Act of 1978, s. 57.

The court may otherwise direct, *e.g.* to enable a person to appear as *amicus curiae: Strathclyde R.C., Petrs* 1996 S.L.T. (Sh. Ct) 65.

67.13.8 *Representation.* A person appearing may be represented by counsel or other person having a right of audience (on the meaning of which, see definitions of "counsel" and "other person having a right of audience" in r. 1.3(1)).

Intimation of making of order freeing a child for adoption where he is subject to a supervision requirement

67.13A Where on making an order under section 18 of the Act of 1978 in relation to a child who is subject to a supervision requirement the court makes a determination under subsection (9) of that section (that is to say, a determination that the child shall forthwith cease to be subject to that requirement), the clerk of court shall intimate the determination to the Principal Reporter.

---

[1] R. 67.13A inserted by S.I. 1997 No. 853 (effective 1st April 1997).

67.13A.1 *General note.* The insertion of r. 67.13A by A.S. (R.C.S.A. No. 2) (Adoption Applications) 1997 [S.I. 1997 No. 853] does not apply to freeing for adoption petitions made before 1st April 1997.

67.13A.2 *"intimate".* This is clearly a drafting error for "give written intimation of". A clerk of court would normally give written intimation under r. 16.9 rather than be required to follow the procedure for intimation under r. 16.7.

Applications for revocation of freeing for adoption order

67.14.—[1] (1) An application under section 20(1) or (1A) of the Act of 1978 (application for revocation of freeing for adoption order) shall be made by note.

(2) On presentation of a note under paragraph (1), the court shall pronounce an interlocutor—

    (a) ordering service of the note on—

        [1] (i) the relevant parent if the application is under section 20(1A);

        (ii) any person who appeared or was represented at the hearing for the freeing for adoption order except a parent or guardian who has made a declaration under section 18(6) or 19(4) of the Act of 1978 (declaration of preference not to be involved in future questions concerning adoption); and

        [2] (iii) the adoption agency (or any substitute adoption agency) having the parental responsibilities and parental rights in relation to the child if the application is under section 20(1); and

    (b) where it appears desirable in order to safeguard the interests of the child, appointing a curator *ad litem*.

(3) A note under paragraph (1) shall not be intimated on the walls of the court or advertised.

(4) Where a curator *ad litem* is appointed under paragraph (2)(b), the court may order—

    (a) the adoption agency,

    (b) a local authority, or

    (c) the reporting officer appointed in the petition,

to make available to the curator *ad litem* any report or information in relation to the child and the natural father and mother of the child.

(5) A curator *ad litem* appointed under paragraph (2)(b) shall—

    (a) inquire into the facts and circumstances averred in the note;

[3]   (aa) ascertain from the child whether he wishes to express any views as respects the application;

    (b) ascertain whether 12 months have elapsed between the making of the freeing for adoption order and the date of presentation of the note;

[2]   (c) where the application is under—

      (i) subsection (1) of section 20 of the Act of 1978 and a previous application under that subsection was refused; or

      (ii) subsection (1A) of that section and a previous application under that subsection was refused,

    inquire whether there has been any change of circumstances, or there is any other reason for the current application, of which the court should be aware in determining the note;

    (d) inquire into any other matter which appears to him to be relevant for determination of the note;

    (e) consider whether, in his opinion, the child should be present at the hearing to determine the note;

    (f) perform such other duties as appear to him to be necessary or as the court may require; and

[3](ff) in performing his duties under this paragraph, regard the need to safeguard and promote the welfare of the child throughout the child's life as the paramount consideration;

    (g) prepare a report in relation to the exercise of his duties within such period as the court may specify.

(6) The curator *ad litem* shall, on completion of his report, send the report, and a copy of it for each party, to the Deputy Principal Clerk.

Deriv. R.C.S. 1965, r. 221(1) to (5) (r. 67.14(1) to (4) and (6)), and r. 224(5) (r. 67.14(5)), both substituted by S.I. 1984 No. 997

---

[1] R.67.14(2)(a)(i) amended by S.I. 1997 No. 853 (effective 1st April 1997).

[2] R.67.14(2)(a)(iii) and (5)(c) substituted by S.I. 1997 No. 853 (effective 1st April 1997).

[3] R.67.14(5)(aa) and (ff) inserted by S.I. 1997 No. 853 (effective 1st April 1997).

General note. A parent or guardian who was given the opportunity to make a declaration not **67.14.1** to be involved in future questions concerning the adoption before the freeing for adoption order but did not do so, may apply after 12 months after the making of a freeing for adoption order for an order to revoke it on the ground that he wishes to resume parental rights if no adoption order has been made and the child does not have his home with a person with whom he has been placed for adoption: Act of 1978, s.20(1). An adoption agency is given a similar right to seek revocation, but there is no time-limit on making the application: Act of 1978, s.20(1A) inserted by the Children (Scotland) Act 1995, Sch. 2, para. 13(b).

Where an application to revoke is refused on the grounds of the welfare of the child a subsequent application may only be made with leave of the court: Act of 1978, s.20(4) and (5). The court may grant leave if there has been a change of circumstances or for any other reason: Act of 1978, s.20(5).

The amendments to r. 67.14 by A.S. (R.C.S.A. No. 2) (Adoption Applications) 1997 [S.I. 1997 No. 853] do not apply to freeing for adoption petitions made before 1st April 1997.

Jurisdiction. The court which made the freeing for adoption order has exclusive jurisdiction: **67.14.2** Act of 1978, s.20(1).

"note". For form of note see r. 15.2 and notes. Where leave is required by virtue of s.20(4) **67.14.3**

and (5) of the Act of 1978, the note should contain a crave for leave with supporting averments in the statement of facts and an appropriate plea-in-law.

A fee is payable, by a person not already a party to the cause first entering the process, on lodging a note, see note 15.2.4.

67.14.4   *"service"*. For methods, see Chap. 16, Pt I.

67.14.5   *Curator* ad litem. A curator *ad litem* may be appointed from a panel established under the Curators *ad Litem* and Reporting Officers (Panels) (Scotland) Regulations 1984 [S.I. 1984 No. 566] or, where appropriate, may be a person not on the panel: see r. 67.4.

67.14.6   *"send"*. This includes deliver: r. 1.3(1) (definition of "send").

Hearing of application for revocation of freeing for adoption order

67.15.—(1) Where no curator *ad litem* has been appointed under rule 67.14(2)(b), the notes shall, within seven days after the expiry of the period of notice for lodging answers, apply by motion for a hearing to determine the note.

(2) Where a curator *ad litem* has been appointed under rule 67.14(2)(b)—
   (a) the Deputy Principal Clerk shall—
      (i) cause the report sent to him under rule 67.14(5) to be lodged in process; and
      (ii) give written intimation of the lodging of the report to the noter and any person on whom service was executed by virtue of rule 67.14(2)(a) and make that report available to them; and
   (b) within seven days after receipt of a copy of the intimation under sub-paragraph (a)(ii), the noter shall apply by motion for a hearing to determine the note.

(3) Where a noter has previously made an application under section 20(1) of the Act of 1978 (application for revocation of freeing for adoption order) which has been refused by any court, he shall, in his motion under paragraph (1) or (2), seek leave under section 20(5) of that Act to allow the note to proceed.

(4) On a date being fixed for a hearing to determine the note, the noter shall intimate the date of the hearing in Form 67.15 to any person to whom intimation was given by virtue of rule 67.14(2).

(5) At the hearing to determine the note, the noter and any person who received intimation under paragraph (4) shall appear and may be represented.

Deriv. R.C.S. 1965, r. 221(6) to (9) substituted by S.I. 1984 No. 997 (r. 67.15(2) to (5))

67.15.1   *"within seven days"*. The date from which the period is calculated is not counted. Where the last day falls on a Saturday or Sunday or a public holiday on which the Office of Court is closed, the next available day is allowed: r. 1.3(7). For office hours and public holidays, see note 3.1.2.

67.15.2   *"motion"*. For motions, see Chap. 23.

67.15.3   *"written intimation"*. For methods, see r. 16.9.

67.15.4   *"make available"*. Unless the court otherwise orders, parties may borrow the reports and other documents lodged in process.

67.15.5   *Leave under s.20(5) of the Act of 1978*. Leave is required by virtue of s.20(4) and (5) of the Act of 1978 where a previous application for revocation has been refused. The note should contain a crave for leave with supporting averments in the statement of facts and an appropriate plea-in-law.

67.15.6   *"intimate"*, *"intimation"*. For methods, see r. 16.7.

67.15.7   *Privacy of hearings*. Any hearing in a petition to revoke a freeing for adoption order is heard in private unless the court otherwise directs: Act of 1978, s.57.

67.15.8   *Representation*. A person appearing may be represented by counsel or other person having a right of audience (on the meaning of which, see definitions of "counsel" and "other person having a right of audience" in r. 1.3(1)).

Parental responsibilities and parental rights when order freeing a child for adoption is revoked

67.15A The court, on revoking an order freeing a child for adoption shall, by order under section 11(1) of the Act of 1995, specify on whom are to be imposed the parental responsibilities, and to whom are to be given the parental rights, in relation to the child; and the clerk of court shall give written intimation accordingly to any person so specified.

---

[1] R.67.15A inserted by S.I. 1997 No. 853 (effective 1st April 1997).

General note. Apart from the requirement by written intimation, r. 67.15A repeats in **67.15A.1** substance s.20(3) of the Act of 1978 as substituted by para. 13(d) of Sch. 2 to the Act of 1995, and ought not, therefore, to have been enacted.

The insertion of r. 67.15A by A.S. (R.C.S.A. No. 2) (Adoption Applications) 1997 [S.I. 1997 No. 853] does not apply to freeing for adoption petitions made before 1st April 1997.

"written intimation". For methods, see r. 16. 9.   **67.15A.2**

Applications to place child for adoption

67.16. An application under section 20(2) of the Act of 1978 (application by adoption agency for leave to place a child) shall be made by motion.

Deriv. R.C.S. 1965, r. 221(10) substituted by S.I. 1984 No. 997

General note. While an application to revoke a freeing for adoption order is pending, the **67.16.1** adoption agency having parental rights and duties may not place the child for adoption without leave of the court: Act of 1978, s.20(2). An application for revocation is presumably pending while it is depending. A cause is depending from the time it is commenced (*i.e.* from the time a first order in the note is made) until final decree, whereas a cause is in dependence until final extract. For the meaning of commenced, see note 14.6.1. For the meaning of final decree, see note 4.15.2(2). For the meaning of final extract, see note 7.1.2(2).

"motion". For motions, see Chap. 23.   **67.16.2**

[1] Applications for transfer of parental responsibilities and parental rights from one adoption agency to another

[1] 67.17. An application under section 21 of the Act of 1978 (variation of order under section 18 of that Act so as to substitute one adoption agency for another) shall be made by note.

Deriv. R.C.S. 1965, r. 226(1) substituted by S.I. 1984 No. 997

---

[1] R.67.17 substituted by S.I. 1997 No. 853 (effective 1st April 1997).

General note. A transfer of parental responsibilities and parental rights between adoption **67.17.1** agencies may be made on the joint application of the two agencies: Act of 1978, s.21. On the meaning of adoption agencies, see s.65(1) of the Act of 1978.

The amendment to r. 67, by A.S. (R.C.S.A. No. 2) (Adoption Applications) 1997 [S.I. 1997 No. 853] does not apply to freeing for adoption petitions made before 1st April 1997.

"note". For form of note see r. 15.2 and notes. A fee is payable, by a person not already a **67.17.2** party to the cause first entering the process, on lodging a note, see note 15.2.4.

Applications relating to return, removal or prohibition of removal of child

67.18. An application under section 29 of the Act of 1978 (order to return a child to, or not to remove a child from, the care of the applicant)—
[1](a) in relation to a breach of section 27(1) of the Act of 1978 (restrictions on removal of child where application for freeing for adoption order pending), an application under section 29 of that Act, or
[1](b) an application for leave under section 27(1) of that Act (leave to remove a child where application for freeing for adoption order pending),

shall be made by note.

Deriv. R.C.S. 1965, r. 227(1)(b) and (2)(b) substituted by S.I. 1984 No. 997

---

[1] R.67.18 amended by S.I. 1997 No 853 (effective 1st April 1997).

67.18.1   *General note.* The amendments to r. 67.18 by A.S. (R.C.S.A. No. 2) (Adoption Applications) 1997 [S.I. 1997/No. 853 do not apply to adoption petitions made before 1st April 1997. The amendments are to substitute references to s.27(1) for the references to s.27(2). Subsections (1) and (2) of s.27 have been substituted by para. 19(a) of Sch. 2 to the Act of 1995 (on which see note 67.18.2). Unfortunately, the amendments do not go far enough. The words in parenthesis in r. 67.18(a) and (b) are no longer an accurate description of s.27(1) of this Act of 1978 as substituted: s.27(1) is not limited to where a freeing for adoption order is pending. Furthermore, r. 67.18 ought to be further amended to make it clear that the application will be by note in a petition for a freeing for adoption petition only when the petition is pending.

67.18.2   *Restrictions on removal etc. of children.*Where a child has been placed by an adoption agency with a person with a view to being adopted and the consent of each parent or guardian has been obtained to that placement, no parent or guardian may remove the child against the will of the person with whom the child has his home except with leave of either the adoption agency or the court: Act of 1978, s.27(1). It is an offence for such a person to remove the child: Act of 1978, s.27(3).

An application by a person from whose care a child has been removed in breach of s.27(1) or who has reasonable grounds for suspecting another person is intending to remove the child may apply to the court for an order to return the child or not to remove the child, as the case may be: Act of 1978, s.29. Where a petition for a freeing for adoption order is pending, the application is made by note in that process.

67.18.3   *"note".* For form of note, see r. 15.2 and notes. A fee is payable, by a person not already a party to the cause first entering the process, on lodging a note, see note 15.2.4.

PART III

ADOPTION

Interpretation of this Part
   67.19. In this Part, unless the context otherwise requires, "the petition" means the petition referred to in rule 67.22(1).

Protection of identity of petitioner
   67.20.—(1) Where a person, who seeks to apply for an adoption order, wishes to prevent his identity being disclosed to any person whose agreement is required under section 16(1)(b) of the Act of 1978 (agreement of parent or guardian to adoption), he may, before presenting a petition, apply by letter to the Deputy Principal Clerk for a serial number to be assigned to him.
   (2) On receipt of such a letter, the Deputy Principal Clerk shall assign a serial number to the applicant and shall enter a note of it opposite the name of the applicant in a register of serial numbers.
   (3) Where a serial number has been assigned under paragraph (2)—
   (a) the record of the serial number and the person to whom it applies shall be treated as confidential and disclosed only to the court;
   (b) any agreement under section 16(1)(b) of the Act of 1978 shall not name or design the petitioner but shall refer to him by means of the serial number;
   (c) it shall be used to name or design the petitioner for all purposes connected with the petition.

Deriv. R.C.S. 1965, r. 222(3) substituted by S.I. 1984 No. 997

67.20.1   *General note.* An application for a serial number to prevent disclosure of the identity of the petitioner to a parent or guardian whose agreement is required under s.16(1)(b) of the Act of 1978 will only arise if the child has not been freed for adoption.

The letter should be addressed to the Deputy Principal Clerk of Session, Court of Session, 2 Parliament Square, Edinburgh EH1 1RQ.

Reports by local authority or adoption agency
   [4] **67.21.**—(1) A report by a local authority under section 22(2), or by an adoption agency under section 23, of the Act of 1978 shall include the following matters:—

(a) information about how the needs of the child came to the notice of the local authority or the adoption agency;
(b) the family circumstances of the child;
(c) where the child was placed for adoption by an adoption agency, a description of the physical and mental health of the child (including any special needs) and his emotional, behaviourial and educational development;
(d) where the child is not subject to a freeing for adoption order, an account of the discussion with the parents or guardians of the child about their wishes and the alternatives to adoption;
(e) where appropriate, an account of the discussion with the child about his wishes and, if the child is of or over the age of 12 years, his capability to decide to consent to the making of the adoption order;
(f) the position of other relatives or persons likely to be involved;
(g) an account of the search for a parent or guardian who cannot be found;
(h) information about the mutual suitability of the petitioner and the child for the relationship created by adoption and the ability of the petitioner to bring up the child including an assessment of the personality of the petitioner and, where appropriate, that of the child;
(i) particulars of all members of the household of the petitioner and their relationship to the petitioner;
(j) a description of the accommodation in the home of the petitioner;
(k) where a sole petitioner is married, why the other spouse has not joined in the petition;
(l) whether the petitioner understands the nature and effect of an adoption order and in particular that the order, if made, will make the petitioner responsible for the maintenance and upbringing of the child;
(m) whether the means and standing of the petitioner are such as to enable him to maintain and bring up the child suitably;
(n) what right or interest in property the child has;
[1] (o) whether any payment or reward prohibited by section 51 of the Act of 1978 (prohibition on certain payments), has been received or agreed upon;
(p) whether the life of the child has been insured and for what sum;
[2] (q) information about the religious persuasion, (if any), racial origin and cultural and linguistic background both of the child and of the petitioner;
(r) considerations arising from the difference in age between the petitioner and the child if this is more or less than the normal difference in age between parents and children;
[1] (s) whether adoption is likely to safeguard and promote the welfare of the child throughout its life;
[3] (ss) whether arrangements for the adoption of the child have been made in contravention of section 11 of the Act of 1978 or the child has been placed for adoption in contravention of that section;
(t) whether the child is subject to a supervision requirement and, if so, what steps have been taken to comply with subsections (4)(c), (5),

and (13) of section 73 (duration and review of supervision requirement) of the Act of 1995.

(u) where paragraph (1A) applies, the information mentioned in paragraph (1B); and

(v) any other information which may be of assistance to the court.

(1A) This paragraph applies where—

(a) the child was placed for adoption under section 19(1) (placement with parental consent: England and Wales) of the Act of 2002;

(b) the child was placed for adoption under a placement order made under section 21(1) (placement orders: England and Wales) of the Act of 2002; or

(c) each parent or guardian has consented under section 20(1) (advance consent to adoption: England and Wales) of the Act of 2002 to the making of a future adoption order.

(1B) Where paragraph (1A) applies, the report mentioned in paragraph (1) shall also include any available information about whether—

(a) any placement order has been revoked;

(b) any of the consents referred to in section 16(3D) (consents to placement: England and Wales) of the Act of 1978 have at any time been withdrawn;

(c) a parent or guardian of the child wishes to seek leave to oppose the petition; and

(d) there has been a change of circumstances since the consent of the parent or guardian was given or, as the case may be, the order under section 21(1) (placement orders: England and Wales) of the Act of 2002 was made.

(2) On completion of the report referred to in paragraph (1), the local authority or the adoption agency, as the case may be, shall send the report, and a copy of it for each party, to the Deputy Principal Clerk.

(3) On receipt of the report referred to in paragraph (2), the Deputy Principal Clerk shall—

(a) where the petition has been presented, cause the report to be lodged in process; and

(b) where the petition has not yet been presented, cause the report to be retained in the Petition Department for lodging in process when the petition is presented.

Deriv. R.C.S. 1965, r. 222(7) and (8) substituted by S.I. 1984 No. 997

---

[1] R.67.21(1) (o) and (s) amended by S.I. 1997 No. 853 (effective 1st April 1997).
[2] R.67.21(1)(q) substituted by S.I. 1997 No. 853 (effective 1st April 1997)
[3] R.67.21(1)(s) inserted by S.I. 1997 No. 853 (effective 1st April 1997).
[4] Rule 67.21 amended by S.S.I. 2007 No. 7, para. 12 (effective 26th February 2007).

67.21.1 *General note.* A person who wishes to adopt a child who has not been placed with him for adoption must, at least three months before the date of the adoption, give notice to the local authority in whose area he has his home of his intention to apply for the adoption order: Act of 1978, ss.22(1). It might be sensible to give notice before the petition is presented; the petition will, of course, be served on the local authority r. 67.23(1)(a)(ii). The reason for this requirement is that where the child has been placed for adoption the adoption agency will be in a position to report whereas if the child has not been so placed the agency might not yet have become involved. The local authority must investigate and submit a report to the court dealing with the matters in s.22(3) of the Act of 1978 (and r. 67.21(1)): Act of 1978, s.22(2).

Where the child has been placed for adoption the adoption agency (a local authority or approved adoption society: Act of 1978, s.1(4)) which placed the child will provide a report under s.23 of the Act of 1978 dealing with the matters mentioned in that section and r. 267.21(1). The adoption agency will receive notice of the petition when it is served under r. 267.23(1)(a)(i).

On style of reports, see McNeill on *Adoption of Children in Scotland*, 2nd ed., p. 203.

The amendments to r. 67.21(1) by A.S. (R.C.S.A. No. 2) (Adoption Applications) 1997 [S.I. 1997 No. 853] do not apply to adoption petitions made before 1st April 1997.

"search for parent or guardian who cannot be found" (r.67.21(1)(g)). Section 16(1) and (2)(a) **67.21.1A**
of the Act of 1978 provides that the agreement of a parent or guardian to an adoption may be
dispensed with on the ground that he cannot be found. This means that all reasonable steps
have to be taken to find him or her; and, if even only one reasonable step has been omitted, it
cannot be said that that person could not be found: *S v. M* 1999 S.C. 388 (Extra Div.).

"send". This includes deliver: r. 1.3(1) (definition of "send").   **67.21.2**

Lodging of reports. A report by the local authority or the adoption agency is, on receipt of it **67.21.3**
by the Deputy Principal Clerk, lodged in process as a step of process: r. 67.13(1) and r. 1.3(1)
(definition of "step of process").

Applications for adoption order

67.22.—(1) An application for an adoption order shall be made by
petition in Form 67.22.

(2) On presentation of the petition, there shall be lodged in process as
productions—

(a) an extract or a certified copy of any entry in the register of births
relating to the birth of the child;

(b) an extract or a certified copy of any entry in the register of births
relating to the birth of the petitioner;

(c) where the petition is by a married couple, an extract or a certified
copy of the entry in the register of marriages relating to their
marriage;

(d) where the child was not placed for adoption with the applicant by an
adoption agency, a medical report showing the physical and mental
health of the child (including any special needs) and his emotional,
behavioral and educational development;

(e) a medical certificate of the health of the petitioner except where the
petitioner is a parent of the child;

(f) where the child has been freed for adoption, a certified copy of the
interlocutor granting the freeing for adoption order in respect of that
child; and

[1] (g) where appropriate, the consent under section 19(1) (placing children
with parental consent: England and Wales) of the Act of 2002 of each
parent or guardian to the child being placed for adoption in the form
prescribed under section 52(7) of that Act;

[1] (h) where appropriate, the consent under section 20(1) (advance consent
to adoption: England and Wales) of the Act of 2002 of each parent or
guardian to the making of a future adoption order, in the form
prescribed under section 52(7) of that Act;

[1] (i) any notice given under section 20(4) (notice that information about
application for adoption order not required: England and Wales) of
the Act of 2002 by a parent or guardian of the child to an adoption
agency;

[1] (j) a certified copy of any placement order made under section 21(1)
(placement orders: England and Wales) of the Act of 2002.

[1] (3) If any of the documents required to be lodged in process under
paragraph (2)(g), (h), (i) or (j) is unavailable to be lodged by reason of its
being in the possession of an adoption agency, the court shall pronounce an
interlocutor requiring the agency to lodge the document within four weeks.

---

[1] Rule 67.22 (2)(g)–(j) and (3) inserted by S.S.I. 2007 No. 7, para. 13 (effective 26th February
2007).

Deriv. R.C.S. 1965, r. 222(1) (r. 67.22(1)), and r. 222(4) (r. 67.22(2)), both substituted by
S.I. 1984 No. 997

General note. An application for an adoption order is made under s.12 of the Act of 1978. **67.22.1**
Adoption extinguishes the parental rights and duties of a parent or guardian (not being one of

the adopters) in whom those rights were vested before the order: Act of 1978, s.12(3). The child must not have attained the age of 18 years: Act of 1978, s.65(1).

Where more than one child is sought to be adopted there should be a separate petition for each child. The two petitions can be heard together and the evidence in one can be ordered to be evidence in the other: see, *e.g. F. v. F.* 1991 S.L.T. 357.

An adopter (subject to an exception) must have attained the age of 21 years, and adoption may be sought by a married couple, or (in certain circumstances) by one person, domiciled in the UK, the Channel Islands or the Isle of Man: Act of 1978, ss.14 and 15. The exception is where the married couple or where one of them is the father or mother of the child and his or her spouse has attained the age of 18 and the other 21 years: Act of 1978, s.14(1B) inserted by the Children Act 1989, Sched. 10, para. 33.

Where a petitioner is a parent, step-parent or relative of the child, or the child was placed with the petitioner by an adoption agency, the child must be at least 19 weeks old and have had his home with (one of) the petitioner(s) during the preceding 13 weeks when the adoption order is made; in any other case the child must be at least 12 months old and have had his home with (one of) the petitioner(s) during the preceding 12 months: Act of 1978, s.13.

An adoption order may not be made in respect of a child of 12 years of age or more without his consent unless the court is satisfied he is incapable of giving his consent: Act of 1978, s.12(8) as substituted by the Age of Legal Capacity (Scotland) Act 1991, s.2(3)(a).

In reaching any decision relating to the adoption of a child the court or adoption agency staff shall have regard to all the circumstances, first consideration being given to the need to safeguard and promote the welfare of the child throughout his childhood; and so far as practicable the child's wishes should be ascertained and due consideration given to them: Act of 1978, s.6.

67.22.2 *Jurisdiction.* The court has jurisdiction where the child is in Scotland or not in Great Britain when the application for the adoption order is made: Act of 1978, s.56(2) and (3).

67.22.3 *"petition".* A petition for an adoption order is presented in the Outer House: r. 14.2(h). The petition must be in Form 67.22 in the official printed form: rr. 4.1 and 14.4. The petition must be signed by counsel or other person having a right of audience: r. 4.2; and see r. 1.3(1) (definitions of "counsel" and "other person having a right of audience") and note 1.3.4.

The petitioner must lodge the petition with the required steps of process (r. 4.4) and the productions required by r. 67.22(2) and any others (including those founded on or adopted (r. 27.1)) with an inventory of productions (r. 4.5). Other productions which should be lodged include any consent of the child under s.12(8), or agreement of a parent or guardian to the adoption under s.16(1)(b), of the Act of 1978.

A fee is payable on lodging the petition: see note 14.5.10.

Notice of petition and appointment of reporting officer and curator ad litem
  [1] **67.23.**—(1) On the presentation of the petition, the court shall pronounce an interlocutor—
  (a) requiring the petitioner to serve a notice in Form 67.23—
      (i) where the child has been placed for adoption, on the adoption agency which placed the child; and
      (ii) where the child has not been placed for adoption, on the local authority within whose area the petitioner has his home;
  (b) appointing a reporting officer; and
  (c) appointing a curator *ad litem* where it appears desirable in order to safeguard the interests of the child.
  (1A) The court shall not appoint a reporting officer where either or both of the following paragraphs applies:–
  (a) the child is free for adoption and is under the age of 12 years;
  (b) the petition is founded on one or other or both of section 16(1)(aa) (advance consent to adoption: England and Wales) and section 16(1)(ab) (placement of child: England and Wales) of the Act of 1978,
but, for the avoidance of doubt, a reporting officer shall be appointed in any case in which the petition is founded on section 16(1)(b) of the Act, whether or not it is also founded on section 16(1)(aa) or (ab) of the Act of 1978.
  (2) Where a curator *ad litem* is appointed under paragraph (1), the court may order—
  (a) the adoption agency,

(b) the local authority, or
(c) the reporting officer,
to make available to the curator *ad litem* any report or information in relation to the child and the natural father and mother of the child.

(3) A person may, before presenting the petition, apply by letter to the Deputy Principal Clerk for the appointment of a reporting officer.

(4) An application under paragraph (3) shall—
(a) set out the reasons for which the appointment is sought;
(b) not require to be intimated to any person;
(c) be accompanied by an interlocutor sheet; and
(d) be placed by the Deputy Principal Clerk before the Lord Ordinary for his decision.

(5) The Deputy Principal Clerk shall give written intimation to the applicant under paragraph (3) of the decision of the Lord Ordinary.

(6) The decision of the Lord Ordinary on an application under paragraph (3) shall be final and not subject to review.

(7) The letter and the interlocutor sheet in an application under paragraph (3) shall be kept in the Petition Department and subsequently placed in the process of the petition.

Deriv. R.C.S. 1965, r. 222(5) and (6) (r. 67.23(1) and (2)), and r. 225 (r. 67.23(3) to (7)), both substituted by S.I. 1984 No. 997

———

[1] Rule 67.23 amended by S.S.I. 2007 No. 7, para. 14 (effective 26th February 2007).

General note. The petition has to be served, where the child has been placed for adoption, on **67.23.1** the adoption agency which placed him or, where not placed, on the local authority in whose area the petitioner has his home: r. 67.23(1). The local authority or adoption agency has to investigate and report to the court: Act of 1978, ss.22(2) and 23; and see r. 67.21.

"serve". For methods of service, see Chap. 16, Pt I.   **67.23.2**

Appointment of reporting officer and curator ad litem. A reporting officer must be appointed.   **67.23.3** A curator *ad litem* may be appointed where it appears desirable (r. 67.23(1)(c)). The view of the Houghton Committee in its Report on the Adoption of Children (Cmnd. 5107 (1972)) was that a curator *ad litem* should be appointed only where a parent or guardian did not agree to the adoption, but this is too restrictive and r. 67.23(1)(c) gives the court a discretion. It would be desirable to appoint a curator *ad litem, e.g.* where the child has not been freed for adoption and a parent or guardian may be unwilling to agree to the adoption or where it is sought to dispense with the consent of a child who is 12 or over (see Act of 1978, s.12(8)). The court will usually appoint a person from a panel established by the local authority under the Curators *ad Litem* and Reporting Officers (Panels) (Scotland) Regulations 1984 [S.I. 1984 No. 566], but may appoint someone not on the panel where appropriate. Subject to certain restrictions in relation to persons employed by the adoption agency, the court may appoint the same person to be both reporting officer and curator *ad litem*: Act of 1978, s.58(2). See further, r. 67.4 and notes.

Appointment of a reporting officer may be sought before the petition is presented, for example, where a parent or guardian whose agreement is required is going abroad: r. 67.23(3)–(7).

The general duties of a reporting officer are to witness agreements to adoption and to perform such other duties as may be prescribed by rules: Act of 1978, s.58(1). The general duty of the curator *ad litem* is to safeguard the interests of the child: Act of 1978, s.58(1); and see r. 67.24.

"final and not subject to review". The decision of the Lord Ordinary may not be reclaimed **67.23.4** against.

Duties of reporting officer and curator ad litem

67.24.—(1) A reporting officer appointed under rule 67.23(1)(b) shall, where appropriate—
(a) inquire into the facts and circumstances averred in the petition and the report of the local authority or adoption agency;

(b) where the child is not free for adoption, ascertain the whereabouts of each parent or guardian and, if practicable, meet him;

¹ (c) witness any execution in Scotland of any agreement in Form 67.5–A or 67.5–F by a parent or guardian under section 16(1)(b) of the Act of 1978 (agreement to adoption), and investigate whether the agreement is given freely, unconditionally and with full understanding of what is involved;

(d) where a parent or guardian is furth of Scotland, confirm his views in writing, ensure that any agreement under section 16(1)(b) of the Act of 1978 is witnessed in accordance with rule 67.5(3) and investigate whether the agreement is given freely, unconditionally and with full understanding of what is involved;

(e) witness any consent of a child in Form 67.5–C under section 12(8) of the Act of 1978 (consent to adoption) and ensure that he understands the consequences of that consent;

¹ (f) ensure that each parent or guardian whose agreement is required understands that in agreeing to the adoption he is (except where the adoption order falls to be made by virtue of section 15(1)(aa) of the Act of 1978) giving up all future claims to the child and that all parental responsibilities and parental rights will (with that exception) be transferred to and will vest in the adopter;

(g) where the child is not free for adoption, consider whether the local authority or adoption agency has made every reasonable effort to find every person whose agreement is required;

(h) investigate whether there are any other persons with a relevant interest and whether they should be informed of the petition;

(i) ascertain from any parent or guardian who can be found whether alternatives to adoption have been discussed with him;

(j) ensure that each parent or guardian whose agreement is required or may be dispensed with is aware of the date (if known) of the hearing to determine the application if he wishes to appear, and confirm that such person whose agreement is required and has not been dispensed with understands that he may withdraw his agreement at any time before the adoption order is made;

² (jj) ascertain whether the child is subject to a supervision requirement;

(k) draw to the attention of the court any matter which may be of assistance; and

(l) prepare a report in relation to the exercise of his duties within such period as the court may specify.

(2) A curator *ad litem* appointed under rule 67.23(1)(c) shall—

(a) safeguard generally the interests of the child;

(b) inquire, so far as he considers necessary, into the facts and circumstances averred in the petition;

²(bb) ascertain from the child whether he wishes to express any views as respects the petition;

²(bc) ascertain whether it would be better for the child that an adoption order were made than that it were not made.

(c) ascertain particulars of the condition of, and accommodation in, the home of the petitioner;

(d) ascertain particulars of all members of the household of the petitioner and their relationship to the petitioner;

(e) where a sole petitioner is married, ascertain why the other spouse has not joined in the petition;

(f) ascertain whether the means and status of the petitioner are sufficient to enable him to maintain and bring up the child suitably;

(g) ascertain any rights or interests in property of the child;

(h) ascertain whether a payment or reward prohibited by section 51 of the Act of 1978 (prohibition on certain payments) has been received or agreed upon;

[1] (i) establish that the petitioner understands that the nature and effect of an adoption order is to transfer the parental responsibilities and parental rights in relation to the child to the petitioner and make him responsible for the maintenance and upbringing of the child;

(j) where applicable, ascertain when the mother of the child ceased to have the care and possession of the child and to whom care and possession were transferred;

[1] (k) ascertain whether the proposed adoption is likely to safeguard and promote the welfare of the child throughout his life;

(l) ascertain whether the life of the child has been insured and for what sum;

(m) ascertain whether it may be in the interests of the child that the court should pronounce an interlocutor making an order under section 25 of the Act of 1978 (interim orders), or make an adoption order subject to particular conditions including the making of special provision for the child, or whether an order such as is mentioned in section 11(2)(b) of the Act of 1995 (imposing parental responsibilities or giving parental rights) should be made;

(n) where the petitioner is not ordinarily resident in the United Kingdom, ascertain whether a report has been obtained on the house and living conditions of the petitioner from a reliable agency in the country of his ordinary residence;

(o) ascertain the reasons why the petitioner wishes to adopt the child;

[3] (p) ascertain the religious persuasion (if any), racial origin and cultural and linguistic background both of the child and of the petitioner;

(q) where the difference in age between the petitioner and the child is greater or less than the normal difference between parent and child, assess the implications of that difference in relation to the petition;

(r) consider any other matter, including the personality of the petitioner and where appropriate, that of the child which might affect the suitability of the petitioner to be a parent bringing up the child;

(s) [Revoked by S.I. 1997 No. 853.]

(t) [Revoked by S.I. 1997 No. 853.]

(u) where the agreement of a parent or guardian or the consent of a child is sought to be dispensed with, consider whether the ground of dispensation has been made out;

(v) consider whether, in his opinion, the child should be present at the hearing to determine the petition;

(w) perform such other duties as appear to him to be necessary or as the court may require;

[2](ww) in performing his duties under this paragraph, regard the need to safeguard and promote the welfare of the child throughout the child's life as the paramount consideration; and

(x) prepare a report in relation to the exercise of his duties within such period as the court may specify.

(3) The reporting officer shall, on completion of his report, send to the Deputy Principal Clerk—

(a) the report and a copy of it for each party;

(b) any agreement for the purposes of section 16(1)(b) of the Act of 1978 (agreement of parent or guardian to adoption); and

(c) any consent under section 12(8) of the Act of 1978 (consent of child to adoption).

(4) The curator *ad litem* shall, on completion of his report, send the report, and a copy of it for each party, to the Deputy Principal Clerk.

Deriv. R.C.S. 1965, r. 222(9) and (10) (r. 67.24(3) and (4)), r. 224(2) and (3) (r. 67.24(1)) and r. 224(6) (r. 67.24(2)), all substituted by S.I. 1984 No. 997

[1] R.67.24(1)(c) and (f), and (2)(i) and (k) amended by S.I. 1997 No. 853 (effective April 1, 1997).

[2] R.67.24(1)(jj) and (2)(bb), (bc) and (ww) inserted by S.I. 1997 No. 853 (effective April 1, 1997).

[3] R.67.24(2)(p) substituted by S.I. 1997 No. 853 (effective 1st April 1997) and amended by S.I. 1998 No. 890 (effective 21st April 1998).

67.24.1   *General note.* The essential difference between the duties of reporting officers and curators *ad litem* in freeing for adoption petitions and adoption petitions is that in the former the court is not concerned with the suitability of the prospective adopters. The duties of the reporting officer are largely administrative. The duties of the curator *ad litem* are to provide the court with evidence of the history of the child, his parents, the current situation and prospects of the adopters. The curator *ad litem*'s function is to carry out an inquiry into all the enumerated matters on behalf of the court. It is not his function to express an opinion on matters of law: *T, Petr.,* 1997 S.L.T. 724, 731C *per* L.P. Hope.

There is no need to appoint a reporting officer where the child is freed for adoption and under the age of 12 years. If appointed where the child is freed for adoption and is over 12, not all the duties in r. 67.24(1) will apply.

67.24.2   *"parent".* This means, irrespective of whether or not they are or have been married to each other, (a) the mother of the child where she has parental rights or responsibilities in relation to him; (b) the father of the child where he has such responsibilities or rights; and (c) both of his parents where both have such responsibilities or rights: Act of 1978, s.65(1) inserted by the Children (Scotland) Act 1995.

67.24.3   *"guardian".* This is defined in s.65(1) of the Act of 1978 and means a person appointed by deed, a will or by the court to be a guardian: Act of 1978, s.65(1) as amended by the Law Reform (Parent and Child) (Scotland) Act 1986, the Age of Legal Capacity (Scotland) Act 1991 and the Children (Scotland) Act 1995.

67.24.4   *"agreement by a parent or guardian".* Where a child has not been freed for adoption each parent or guardian must agree to the adoption unless his agreement is dispensed with on certain grounds: Act of 1978, s.16(1).

67.24.5   *"consent of a child".* An adoption order cannot be made without the consent of a child who has reached the age of 12 years unless the court is satisfied he is incapable of giving consent: Act of 1978, s.12(8) as amended by the Age of Legal Capacity (Scotland) Act 1991, s.2(3)(a).

67.24.6   *"parental responsibilities and parental rights".* These rights are defined in ss.1 and 2 respectively of the Children (Scotland) Act 1995.

A father may not have parental responsibilities or parental rights where he has never had them or has lost them. Where a child is born to parents who are not married at conception or subsequently, only the mother has parental rights at birth: Act of 1995, s.3(1)(b). The father may obtain such rights by marriage to the mother (Act of 1995, s.3(1)(b)), on an application to the court (Act of 1995, s.11) for which he may also require a declarator of parentage (a family action: r. 49.1(1)), by being appointed guardian by testamentary deed (Act of 1995, s.7) or by agreement (Act of 1995, s.4). Parental responsibilities and parental rights may be lost if taken away by the court on divorce or otherwise.

67.24.7   *Child to live with adopter before order made.* Where a petitioner is a parent, step-parent or relative of the child, or the child was placed with the petitioner by an adoption agency, the child must be at least 19 weeks old and have had his home with (one of) the petitioner(s) during the preceding 13 weeks when the adoption order is made; in any other case the child must be at least 12 months old and have had his home with (one of) the petitioner(s) during the preceding 12 months: Act of 1978, s.13.

67.24.8   *Section 24 of the Act of 1978.* The court shall not determine an application for adoption where a previous application for a British adoption order has been refused unless on the previous occasion the court directed that this provision should not apply or there is a change of circumstances or there is another proper reason: Act of 1978, s.24(1). The court shall not make an adoption order unless satisfied that the petitioners have not contravened s.51 of the Act of 1978 (see note 67.24.9): Act of 1978, s.24(2).

67.24.9   *"payment or reward prohibited by section 51 of the Act of 1978".* It is unlawful to make or receive a payment or reward for the adoption of a child, any agreement or consent in that connection, the transfer of the care and possession of a child with a view to adoption of the child or the making of any arrangement for the child's adoption; and a person who does so is liable on summary conviction to a fine or imprisonment: Act of 1978, s.51.

"*section 25 of the Act of 1978*". The court may postpone the determination of an adoption **67.24.10**
petition and give a petitioner custody for a probationary period of not more than two years: Act
of 1978, s.25. The curator *ad litem* must consider whether such an interim order is appropriate.

"*send*". This includes deliver; r. 1.3(1) (definition of "send").   **67.24.11**

Lodging of reports etc. A report by the reporting officer and any agreements, and any report **67.24.12**
of a curator *ad litem*, are, on receipt of them by the Deputy Principal Clerk, lodged in process as
a step in process: r. 67.25(1) and r. 1.3(1) (definition of "step of process").

Hearing of adoption petition
67.25.—(1) On receipt of the reports referred to in rules 67.21 and 67.24,
the Deputy Principal Clerk shall—
  (a) cause the reports and any other documents to be lodged in process;
  (b) give written intimation to each party of the lodging of those
      documents and make them available to each party; and
  (c) within seven days thereafter, cause—
      (i) the petition to be put on the By Order Roll before the Lord
          Ordinary; and
      (ii) written intimation of the date of the hearing on the By Order
           Roll to be given to each party.
(2) At the hearing on the By Order Roll, the court—
  (a) shall pronounce an interlocutor appointing the petition to a hearing
      to determine the petition; and
  (b) may, in such interlocutor—
      (i) order any person whose agreement or consent is required to be
          given or dispensed with to attend the hearing;
    ¹ (ii) order intimation of the date of the hearing to any person not
           mentioned in paragraph (3)(a) to (dc); and
      (iii) order the reporting officer or curator *ad litem* to perform
            additional duties to assist the court in determining the petition.
  (3) The petitioner shall intimate the date of the hearing ordered under
paragraph (2)(a) in Form 67.25 to—
  ³ (a) in a petition for an adoption order—
      (i) every person who can be found and whose agreement or consent
          to the making of such an order is required to be given or
          dispensed with; or
      (ii) where the petition is founded on either or both of section
           16(1)(aa) (advance consent to adoption: England and Wales) or
           section 16(1)(ab) (placement of child: England and Wales) of the
           Act of 1978 (but not also section 16(1)(b) (agreement to adoption
           order) of the Act of 1978), each parent or guardian of the child
           except a parent or guardian who has given notice under section
           20(4)(a) of the Act of 2002 that he does not wish to be informed
           of the application for an adoption order;
  (b) the reporting officer appointed under rule 67.23(1)(b);
  (c) any curator *ad litem* appointed under rule 67.23(1)(c);
  (d) the local authority or adoption agency referred to in rule 67.21;
  ²(da) any person keeping the child by virtue of a child protection order, of
        a supervision requirement or of a warrant granted by a children's
        hearing;
  ²(db) any person to whom the parental responsibilities and parental rights
        in relation to the child have been transferred by a parental
        responsibilities order or an order under section 11 of the Act of 1995;
  ²(dc) any person having parental responsibility (within the meaning of the
        Children Act 1989) for the child by virtue of section 5 of that Act or
        of a care order or residence order within the meaning of that Act; and
  (e) any person on whom intimation has been ordered under paragraph
      (2)(b)(ii).
  (4) At the hearing ordered under paragraph (2)(a)—
  (a) the petitioner, the adoption agency, the reporting officer and, where

one has been appointed, the curator *ad litem* shall, if required by the court, appear and may be represented;
   (b) any person required by the court to attend the hearing shall appear and may be represented;
   (c) any other person to whom intimation was made under paragraph (3)(a) or (e) may appear or be represented.

Deriv. R.C.S. 1965, r. 222(11) to (14) substituted by S.I. 1984 No. 997

---

[1] R.67.25(2)(b)(ii) amended by S.I. 1997 No. 853 (effective 1st April 1997).
[2] R.67.25(3) (da), (db), and (dc) inserted by S.I. 1997 No. 853 (effective 1st April 1997).
[3] Rule 67.21 inserted by S.S.I. 2007 No. 7, para. 15 (effective 26th February 2007).

67.25.1   *"party"*. The petitioner is a party. A person objecting to a petition becomes a party (respondent) on lodging answers: see r. 14.8 and note 14.8.1.

67.25.2   *"written intimation"*. For methods, see r. 16.9.

67.25.3   *"make available"*. Unless the court otherwise orders, parties may borrow the reports and other documents lodged in process.

67.25.4   *By Order Roll hearing*. The purpose of this hearing is to enable the court (a) to clarify the issues to be resolved at the (full) hearing and (b) to determine the form of the (full) hearing. Parties should be clear before the By Order Roll hearing what has to be resolved and what form the (full) hearing should take. If oral evidence is required there must be an interlocutor allowing proof and the citing of witnesses.
   The issues to be resolved may include the effect of any existing or proposed action of paternity or the reasonableness of the refusal of a parent or guardian to agree to the order.
   The (full) hearing could take the form of a procedure roll discussion, a proof (or proof before answer) or the interview of a parent or guardian withholding consent followed by a hearing without oral evidence. The interlocutor should state, *inter alia*, the form of the hearing.
   No court fee is payable for this By Order Roll hearing.

67.25.5   *"intimation"*, *"intimate"*. For methods, see r. 16.7.

67.25.6   *Hearing to determine the petition*. The (full) hearing could take the form of a procedure roll discussion, a proof (or proof before answer) or possibly the interview of a parent or guardian withholding agreement followed by a hearing without oral evidence. If oral evidence is required there must have been an interlocutor pronounced allowing proof and the citing of witnesses.
   Where the court is considering whether to dispense with the agreement of a parent or guardian, there are two stages involved, (a) whether one of the grounds in s. 16(2) of the Act of 1978 has been established and (b) if so, whether an order to dispense should be made; s. 6 of the Act of 1978 (welfare of the child) is strictly relevant only at the second stage, although the same considerations as in that section are matters to be taken into account in the first stage when the question is whether agreement is withheld unreasonably: see *Lothian R.C v. A.* 1992 S.L.T. 858 (freeing for adoption).

67.25.7   *Privacy of hearings*. Any hearing in an adoption petition is heard in private unless the court otherwise directs: Act of 1978, s. 57.
   The court may otherwise direct, *e.g.* to enable a person to appear as *amicus curiae: Strathclyde R.C. Petrs*, 1996 S.L.T. (Sh. Ct.) 65.

67.25.8   *Representation*. A person appearing may be represented by counsel or other person having a right of audience (on the meaning of which, see definitions of "counsel" and "other person having a right of audience" in r. 1.3(1)).

67.25.9   *Multiple adoptions*. Where the court is presented with two petitions for adoption—each should be heard separately and the court should issue separate interlocutors in each petition: *A.B. v. C.B.* 1985 S.L.T. 514, 561, *per* L.J.-C Wheatley. In practice, the petitions of siblings are by agreement often heard together and the evidence in one treated as evidence in the other petition.

67.25.10   *Fee*. The court fee for the full hearing is payable by each party for every 30 minutes or part thereof. For fee, see Court of Session etc. Fees Order 1984, Table of Fees, Pt. I, C, item 17 (or as appropriate) [S.I. 1984 No. 256, Table as amended, pp. C1202 *et seq.*]. The fee may be debited under a credit scheme introduced on 1st April 1976 by P.N. No. 4 of 1976 to the account (if one is kept or permitted) of the agent by the court cashier, and an account will be rendered weekly by the court cashier's office to the agent for all court fees due that week for immediate settlement. An agent not on the credit scheme will have an account opened for the purpose of lodging the fee: P.N. No. 2 of 1995. A debit slip and a copy of the court hearing time sheet will be delivered to the agent's box or sent by DX or post.

A party litigant must pay cash to the clerk of court at the end of the hearing or, if the hearing lasts more than a day, at the end of each day: P.N. No. 2 of 1995. A receipt will be issued. The assistant clerk of session will acknowledge receipt of the sum received from the clerk of court on the Minute of Proceedings.

No fee is payable for the By Order Roll hearing under r. 67.25(2).

Intimation of making of adoption order where child subject to supervision requirement

[1] **67.25A.** Where on making an adoption order in relation to a child who is subject to a supervision requirement the court makes a determination under section 12(9) of the Act of 1978 (that is to say, a determination that the child shall forthwith cease to be subject to that requirement), the clerk of court shall intimate the determination to the Principal Reporter.

---

[1] R. 67.25A inserted by S.I. 1997 No. 853 (effective April 1, 1997).

General note. The insertion of r. 67.25A by A.S. (R.C.S.A. No. 2) (Adoption Applications) **67.25A.1** 1997 [S.I. 1997 No. 853] does not apply to adoption petitions made before 1st April 1997.

"intimate", This is clearly a drafting error for "give written intimation of". A clerk of court **67.25A.2** would normally give written intimation under r. 16.9 rather than be required to follow the procedure for intimation under r. 16.7.

Supervision by or committal to care of local authority

67.26.—[Revoked by S.I. 1997 No. 853 (effective April 1, 1997)].

General note. The revocation of r. 67.26 by A.S. (R.C.S.A. No. 2) (Adoption Applications) **67.26.1** 1997 [S.I. 1997 No. 853] does not apply to applications for adoption made before 1st April 1997.

Applications under section 49(1) of the Act of 1978

67.27.—(1) An application under section 49(1) of the Act of 1978 (application to adopt a child abroad) shall be made by petition.

(2) The provisions of this Part shall, with the necessary modifications, apply to an application under section 49(1) of the Act of 1978 as they apply to an application for an adoption order.

(3) Evidence that the child in respect of whom the application is made may be adopted under the law of or in the country in which the petitioner is domiciled may be given by a signed statement by a person qualified in the law of that country.

Deriv. R.C.S. 1965, r. 223 substituted by S.I. 1984 No. 997 (r. 67.27(1) and (2))

General note. A person not domiciled in the UK may obtain an order (a "section 49 order": r. **67.27.1** 67.1(2)) granting him the parental rights and duties relating to a child whom he wishes to adopt under the law of the country in which he is domiciled: Act of 1978, s. 49. A Convention adoption order is made where a child habitually resident in one Contracting State is being adopted in another under the Hague Convention on Protection of Children and Co-operation in respect of Interventory Adoption see Pt. IV of this Chapter. The reporting officer only has to obtain a statement about whether there are obstacles to adoption in a country where the child is to be.

In the application of s. 13 of the Act of 1978 to a petition for a section 49 order, where a petitioner is a parent, step-parent or relative of the child, or the child was placed with the petitioner by an adoption agency, the child must be at least 32 weeks old and have had his home with (one of) the petitioner(s) during the preceding 26 weeks when the adoption order is made (in any other case the position is the same as in adoption, namely, that the child must be at least 12 months old and have had his home with (one of) the petitioner(s) during the preceding 12 months): Act of 1978, s. 49(2).

Ss. 12(1), 14(2), 15(2), 17–21 and 25 of the Act of 1978 do not apply: Act of 1978, s. 49(2).

67.27.2 *Jurisdiction*. The court has jurisdiction (a) where the child is in Scotland or not in Great Britain when the application for the section 49 order is made and (b) the petitioner is domiciled furth of England, Wales, Scotland and Northern Ireland: Act of 1978, ss. 49(1) and 56(2) and (3).

67.27.3 *"petition"*. A petition for a section 49 order is presented in the Outer House: r. 14.2(h). The petition must be in Form 67.22 in the official printed form: rr. 4.1 and 14.4. The petition must be signed by counsel or other person having a right of audience: r. 4.2; and see r. 1.3(1) (definitions of "counsel" and "other person having a right of audience") and note 1.3.4.

The petitioner must lodge the petition with the required steps of process (r. 4.4) and the productions required by r. 67.22(2) and any others (including those founded on or adopted (r. 27.1)) with an inventory of productions (r. 4.5). Other productions which should be lodged include a copy of any interlocutor freeing the child for adoption and any consent of the child under s. 12(8), or agreement of a parent or guardian to the adoption under s. 16(1)(b), of the Act of 1978.

A fee is payable on lodging the petition: see note 14.5.10.

67.27.4 *"signed statement"*. This should be an affidavit or an equivalent document permitted in the country concerned.

Applications for return, removal or prohibition of removal of child

67.28.—(1) An application under section 29 of the Act of 1978 (order to return a child to, or not to remove a child from, the care of the applicant) shall be made—

(a) in relation to a breach of section 27(1) or 28(1) of that Act (restrictions on removal of child where application for adoption order pending), by note in the process of the petition for an adoption order or a section 49 order to which it relates; or

(b) in relation to a breach of section 28(3) (restriction on removal where child was or is in care of the local authority) of that Act, by petition.

(2) An application for leave—

(a) under section 27(1) or 28 of the Act of 1978 (leave to remove a child) shall be made by note in the process of the petition for an adoption order or a section 49 order to which it relates;

(b) under section 30(2) of that Act (leave to adoption agency to give notice of intention to remove child) shall be made by note in the process of the petition for an adoption order or the application for a section 49 order to which it relates.

(3) Subject to paragraph (4), rule 67.2 (disapplication of certain rules to this Chapter) shall not apply to an application mentioned in paragraph (1) or (2) of this rule.

(4) An application mentioned in paragraph (1) or (2) shall not be intimated on the walls of the court or advertised.

Deriv. R.C.S. 1965, r. 227(1)(a) and (c) (r. 67.28(1)), r. 227(2)(a) and (c) (r. 67.28(2)) and r. 227(3) (r. 67.28(3) and (4)), all substituted by S.I. 1984 No. 997

67.28.1 *General note*. An application by a person, from whose care a child has been removed in breach of s.27(1) or 28 of the Act of 1978 or who has reasonable grounds for suspecting another person is intending to remove the child, may be made to the court for an order to return the child or to prohibit the removal of the child, as the case may be: Act of 1978, s.29.

67.28.2 *Section 27(1) of the Act of 1978*. Where a child has been placed by an adoption agency with a person with a view to being adopted and the consent of the parent or guardian has been obtained to that placement, the parent or guardian may not remove the child against the will of the person with whom the child has his home except with leave of either the adoption agency or the court: Act of 1978, s.27(1). It is an offence for such a person to remove the child: Act of 1978, s.27(3).

Section 28(1) of the Act of 1978. While a petition for an adoption order in respect of a child   **67.28.3**
made by a person with whom the child has had his home for five years is pending, no person is
entitled to remove the child from his care without leave of the court: Act of 1978, s.28(1).

Section 28(3) of the Act of 1978. There are restrictions imposed on a local authority removing   **67.28.4**
a child from a person who has had care of the child for five years other than in accordance with
s.30 or 31 or with leave of the court: Act of 1978, s.28(3).

Leave under s.27(1), 28, or 30(2) of the Act of 1978. Leave of the court is normally required   **67.28.5**
to remove a child from a prospective adopter's care. Where a child has been placed for adoption
the adoption agency cannot give notice of an intention not to allow the child to remain with the
person with whom the child has been placed without leave of the court: Act of 1978, s.30(2).

"note". For form of note, see r. 15.2 and notes. A fee is payable, by a person not already a   **67.28.6**
party to the cause first entering the process, on lodging a note: see note 15.2.4. The note does
not have to be intimated on the walls of court or advertised: r. 67.28(4).

"petition". A petition is presented in the Outer House: r. 14.2(h). The petition must be in   **67.28.7**
Form 14.4 in the official printed form: rr. 4.1 and 14.4. The petition must be signed by counsel
or other person having a right of audience: r. 4.2; and see r. 1.3(1) (definitions of "counsel" and
"other person having a right of audience") and note 1.3.4.
  The petitioner must lodge the petition with the required steps of process (r. 4.4) and the
productions required by r. 67.9(3) and any others (including those founded on or adopted
(r. 27.1)) with an inventory of productions (r. 4.5).
  A fee is payable on lodging the petition: see note 14.5.10.
  The ordinary petition rules apply to a petition under r. 67.28 except that it is not intimated on
the walls of court or advertised: r. 67.28(4).

Privacy of hearings. Any hearing in an application under s.29 of the Act of 1978 is heard in   **67.28.8**
private unless the court otherwise directs: Act of 1978, s.57.

Applications to amend or revoke a direction in, or revoke, an adoption order

67.29.—(1) An application—

(a) under paragraph 4(1) of Schedule 1 to the Act of 1978 (amendment, or revocation of a direction in, an adoption order), or

(b) under section 46 of that Act (revocation of an adoption order on legitimation),

shall be made by petition.

(2) Subject to paragraph (3), rule 67.2 (disapplication of certain rules to this Chapter) shall not apply to an application mentioned in paragraph (1) of this rule.

(3) An application mentioned in paragraph (1) shall not be intimated on the walls of the court or advertised.

Deriv. R.C.S. 1965, r. 228 substituted by S.I. 1984 No. 997

General note. An application by the adopter or adopted child to amend an adoption order in   **67.29.1**
respect of a new name given to the adopted child must be made within one year of the order:
Act of 1978, Sched. 1, para. 4(1)(a). The court may amend an adoption order by correcting any
errors in its particulars, or to revoke a direction for the marking of an entry in the register of
births or the Adopted Children Register, at any time: Act of 1978, Sched. 1, para. 4(1).
  An application by the natural married parents of a child, one of whom adopted the child
before marriage, or by the child to revoke an adoption order on legitimation, is made under s.46
of the Act of 1978.

Jurisdiction. The court has jurisdiction only if it made the adoption order sought to be   **67.29.2**
amended or revoked in relation to s.46(1) or Sched. 1, para. 4 of the Act of 1978; only the Court
of Session has jurisdiction in relation to an application under s.46(2) of the Act of 1978: Act of
1978, s.46 and Sched. 1, para. 4.

"petition". A petition is presented in the Outer House: r. 14.2(h). The petition must be in   **67.29.3**
Form 14.4 in the official printed form: rr. 4.1 and 14.4. The petition must be signed by counsel
or other person having a right of audience: r. 4.2; and see r. 1.3(1) (definitions of "counsel" and
"other person having a right of audience") and note 1.3.4.
  The petitioner must lodge the petition with the required steps of process (r. 4.4) and the
productions required by r. 67.9(3) and any others (including those founded on or adopted
(r. 27.1)) with an inventory of productions (r. 4.5).

A fee is payable on lodging the petition: see note 14.5.10.

The ordinary petition rules apply to a petition under r. 67.29 except that it is not intimated on the walls of court or advertised: r. 67.29(3).

Registration of certified copy interlocutor

67.30. On the court pronouncing an interlocutor making—

(a) an adoption order,

(b) an amendment to, or a revocation of a direction in, an adoption order,

(c) a revocation of an adoption order,

(d) a section 49 order, or

(e) a Convention adoption order,

the clerk of court shall forthwith send a certified copy of that interlocutor to the Registrar General for Scotland in a sealed envelope marked "confidential".

Deriv. R.C.S. 1965, r. 229 substituted by S.I. 1984 No. 997

67.30.1 *Registrar General for Scotland.* This is the Registrar General of Births, Marriages and Deaths for Scotland: Act of 1978, s.65(1). He maintains the Adopted Children Register in which the orders mentioned in r. 67.30 are registered: Act of 1978, ss.45 and 49(3).

The address is: New Register House, West Register Street, Edinburgh EH1 3YT; tel. 031-334 0380; fax 031-314 4400.

67.30.2 *"send".* This includes deliver: r. 1.3(1) (definition of "send").

Extract of order

67.31. An extract of an adoption order or a section 49 order shall not be issued except by order of the court on an application to it—

(a) where there is a petition for the adoption order or the section 49 order, as the case may be, depending before the court, by motion; or

(b) where there is no such petition depending before the court, by petition.

Deriv. R.C.S. 1965, r. 230(3) substituted by S.I. 1984 No. 997

67.31.1 *General note.* The primary evidence that an adoption order, or a section 49 order (see r. 67.27), has been made is the entry in the Adopted Children Register which is not open to inspection except by order of the court or a sheriff: Act of 1978, s.45(5). An extract of the court's interlocutor granting the order would not be so confidential and is not, therefore, normally available. R. 67.31 applies also to a Convention adoption order: r. 67.34.

67.31.2 *"depending".* A cause is depending from the time it is commenced (*i.e.* from the time the first order in the petition is made) until final decree, whereas a cause is in dependence until final extract. For the meaning of commenced, see note 14.6.1. For the meaning of final decree, see note 4.15.2(2). For the meaning of final extract, see note 7.1.2(2).

67.31.3 *"motion".* For motions, see Chap. 23.

67.31.4 *"petition".* A petition for an extract is presented in the Outer House: r. 14.2(h). The petition must be in Form 14.4 in the official printed form: rr. 4.1 and 14.4. The petition must be signed by counsel or other person having a right of audience: r. 4.2; and see r. 1.3(1) (definitions of "counsel" and "other person having a right of audience") and note 1.3.4.

The petitioner must lodge the petition with the required steps of process (r. 4.4) and the productions required by r. 67.9(3) and any others (including those founded on or adopted (r. 27.1)) with an inventory of productions (r. 4.5).

A fee is payable on lodging the petition: see note 14.5.10.

Procedure after intimation to Registrar General or issue of extract

67.32.—[1] (1) After a certified copy of an interlocutor mentioned in rule 67.30 has been sent to the Registrar General for Scotland, the clerk of court or the Extractor, as the case may be, shall—

(a) place the whole process in an envelope bearing only—

(i) the name of the petitioner;

(ii) the full name of the child to whom the process relates; and
(iii) the date of the order; and
(b) seal the envelope and mark it "confidential".
(2) No person shall open a process referred to in paragraph (1) or inspect its contents within 100 years after the date of the adoption order or the section 49 order, as the case may be, except—
[2] (a) the person adopted under the order after he has reached the age of 16 years;
(b) any other person or body entitled under section 45(5) of the Act of 1978 to access to the registers and books kept under section 45(4) of that Act, with the written authority of the adopted person;
(c) the Deputy Principal Clerk or Extractor, as the case may be, on the written application to him by an adoption agency with the written agreement of the adopted person for the purpose of ascertaining the name of the adoption agency responsible for the placement of that person for adoption;
(d) by order of the court on an application made by petition presented by another court or authority (whether within the United Kingdom or not) having the power to authorise an adoption for the purpose of obtaining information in connection with an application to it for adoption;
(e) by order of the court on an application made by petition presented by any person; and
(f) a person who is authorised in writing by the Secretary of State to obtain information from the process for the purpose of research designed to improve the working of adoption law and practice.

Deriv. R.C.S. 1965, r. 230(4) substituted by S.I. 1984 No. 997

---

[1] R. 67.32(1) amended by S.I. 1994 No. 2901 (minor correction).
[2] R. 67.32(2)(a) amended by S.I. 1997 No. 853 (effective 1st April, 1997).

General note. The purpose of r. 67.32 is to maintain confidentiality of the process and of an **67.32.1** adoption order or a section 49 order (for which, see r. 67.27) in respect of a child during his lifetime. R. 67.32 also applies to Convention adoption orders: r. 67.34.
After five years a process is transmitted from the Court of Session to the Keeper of the Records: r. 9.1.
The amendment to r. 67.32(2)(b) by A.S. (R.C.S.A. No. 2) (Adoption Applications) 1997 [SI 1997/853 does not apply to adoption petitions made before 1st April 1997.

Registrar General for Scotland. See note 67.30.1.   **67.32.2**

PART IV

CONVENTION ADOPTION ORDERS

Interpretation of this Part
[1] **67.33.**—(1) In this Part—
    "the petition" means the petition referred to in rule 67.35 or 67.41, as the case may be;
    "receiving State" has the same meaning as in the Convention; and
    "State of origin" has the same meaning as in Article 2 of the Convention.

Deriv. R.C.S. 1965, r. 230A inserted by S.I. 1978 No. 1373 and amended by S.I. 1984 No. 997.

---

[1] R. 67.33 substituted by S.S.I. 2004 No. 52 (effective 1st March, 2004).

General note. A Convention adoption order is made where a child habitually resident in one **67.33.1** Contracting State (State of origin) has been, or is being, or is to be moved to another

Contracting State (receiving State) either after adoption in the State of origin by spouses or a person habitually resident in the receiving State, or for the purposes of such adoption in the receiving State or State of origin: the Hague Convention on Protection of Children and Co-operation in respect of Intercountry Adoption, 29th May 1993, signed by the UK on 12th January 1994, art. 2. The Convention has been brought into effect in the UK by the Adoption (Intercountry Aspects) Act 1999.

This convention replaces the Hague Convention on the Jurisdiction, Applicable Law and Recognition of Decrees Relating to Adoptions, November 15, 1965 (Cmnd. 7342) which was ratified only by Austria, Switzerland and the UK.

Application of Part III to this Part

[1] **67.34.** Part III (adoption), except the following rules, shall apply to the petition—

   rule 67.19 (interpretation of Part III),
   rule 67.20 (protection of identity of petitioner),
   rule 67.27 (applications under section 49),
   rule 67.29 (applications to amend or revoke a direction in, or revoke, an adoption order).

Deriv. R.C.S. 1965, r. 230B inserted by S.I. 1978 No. 1373 and amended by S.I. 1984 No. 997.

---

[1] R. 64.34 substituted by SS.I. 2004 No. 52 (effective 1st March, 2004).

67.34.1   *General note.* An adoption order is made as a Convention adoption order if the application is for a Convention adoption order and a petitioner or the child is habitually resident in a Convention country, and the rules of Pt. III relating to adoption except those mentioned in r. 67.34 apply.

Applications for Convention adoption orders

[1] **67.35.**—(1) An application for a Convention adoption order shall be made by petition in Form 67.22.

(2) The petition shall include averments in relation to—
   (a) the age of the child;
   (b) the place and the country where the petitioner habitually resides;
   (c) the period of time for which the petitioner has resided there;
   (d) the place and the country where the child habitually resides;
   (e) the period of time for which the child has resided there; and
   (f) whether the child is, or has been, married.

(3) Where the United Kingdom is the receiving state, and the child is over the age of twelve years the petition shall also include averments in relation to—
   (a) whether the child is capable of giving consent, and
   (b) whether the child has consented,
to the making of the order.

(4) Where the United Kingdom is the State of origin, the petition shall also include averments as to whether the child is free for adoption by virtue of an order made under section 18 of the Act of 1978, section 18 of the Adoption Act 1976, or article 17(1) or 18(1) of the Adoption (Northern Ireland) Order 1987.

(5) The prayer of the petition shall include a crave that the court direct the Registrar General for Scotland to insert the words "Convention Order" in the entry to be made by him in the Adopted Children Register regarding the adoption.

Deriv. R.C.S. 1965, r. 230(1), (2) and (4) inserted by S.I. 1978 No. 1373

---

[1] R. 67.35 substituted by S.S.I. 2004 No. 52 (effective 1st March, 2004).

67.35.1   *General note.* See note 67.33.1.

Jurisdiction. If the child to be adopted is in Scotland when the petition is presented, the Court **67.35.2**
of Session and the sheriff court of the sheriffdom where the child is have jurisdiction to make a
Convention adoption order: Act of 1978, s. 56(2) and (4).

"petition". A petition for a Convention adoption order is presented in the Outer House: r. **67.35.3**
14.2(h). The petition must be in Form 67.22 in the official printed form: rr. 4.1 and 14.4. The
petition must be signed by counsel or other person having a right of audience: r. 4.2; and see r.
1.3(1) (definitions of "counsel" and "other person having a right of audience") and note 1.3.4.

The petitioner must lodge the petition with the required steps of process (r. 4.4) and the
productions required by r. 67.22(2) and any others (including those founded on or adopted (r.
27.1)) with an inventory of productions (r. 4.5). Other productions which should be lodged
include any consent of the child under s. 12(8), or agreement of a parent or guardian to the
adoption under s. 16(1)(b), of the Act of 1978.

A fee is payable on lodging the petition: see note 14.5.10.

"State of origin". This is defined in art. 2 of the Convention.   **67.35.4**

Registrar General for Scotland. See note 67.30.1.   **67.35.5**

Investigations by curator ad litem

[1] **67.36.**—(1) The curator ad litem appointed under rule 67.23(1)(b) by
virtue of rule 67.34 (application of Part III to this Part) shall also investigate
the averments referred to in rule 67.35(2) and shall include the results of his
investigations in his report.

(2) Where in the course of his investigations, the curator ad litem requires
a report from any authority outside Great Britain, he shall request the local
authority to request that other authority to provide that report.

Deriv. R.C.S. 1965, r. 230(3) inserted by S.I. 1978 No. 1373.

───────────

[1] R. 67.36 substituted by S.S.I. 2004 No. 52 (effective March 1, 2004).

General note. The substituted r. 67.36 is in the same terms as its predecessors.   **67.36.1**

Annulment etc. of overseas adoptions

[1] **67.37.**—(1) This rule applies to an application for an order under section
47 of the Act of 1978 (annulment etc. of overseas adoptions).

(2) An application mentioned in paragraph (1) shall be made by petition.

(3) An application under section 47(1) of the Act of 1978 shall not, except
with the leave of the court, be made later than two years after the date of the
adoption to which it relates.

(4) Where the adopted person is under the age of 18 years on the date of
the presentation of a petition under this rule, the court shall appoint a
curator ad litem with the duties mentioned in rule 67.24(2).

(5) On the court pronouncing an interlocutor making an order referred to
in paragraph (1), the Deputy Principal Clerk shall send a notice of the order
to the Registrar General for Scotland specifying—
  (a) the date of the adoption;
  (b) the name and address of the authority which granted the adoption;
  (c) the names of the adopter or adopters and of the adopted person as
       given in that petition;
  (d) the country in which the adoption was granted;
  (e) the country of which the adopted person is a national; and
  (f) the country in which the adopted person was born.

───────────

[1] R. 67.37 substituted by S.S.I. 2004 No. 52 (effective 1st March, 2004).

General note. The Court of Session has power to annul a Convention adoption order on the **67.37.1**
ground that it is contrary to public policy: Adoption (Scotland) Act, s. 47.

"petition". A petition is presented in the Outer House: r. 14.2(h). The petition must be in **67.37.2**

Form 14.4 in the official printed form: rr. 4.1 and 14.4. The petition must be signed by counsel or other person having a right of audience: r. 4.2; and see r. 1.3(1) (definition of "counsel" and "other person having a right of audience") and note 1.3.4.

The petitioner must lodge the petition with the required steps of process (r. 4.4).

A fee is payable on lodging the petition: see note 14.5.10.

67.37.3   *"send"*. Send includes deliver: r. 1.3(1).

Directions as to the status conferred by adoption

[1] **67.38.** An application under section 39(2A) of the Act of 1978 (application for direction as to status conferred by adoption) shall be made by petition.

---

[1] R. 67.38 substituted by S.S.I. 2004 No. 52 (effective 1st March 2004).

67.38.1   *General note.* The Court of Session has power to make a direction, in relation to a Convention adoption order in another country which is not a full adoption, that the child is not the legitimate child of the adopters, if it were more favourable to the child to make the direction: Act of 1978, s. 39(2A).

67.38.2   *"petition"*. A petition is presented in the Outer House: r. 14.2(h). The petition must be in Form 14.4 in the official printed form: rr. 4.1 and 14.4. The petition must be signed by counsel or other person having a right of audience: r. 4.2; and see r. 1.3(1) (definition of "counsel" and "other person having a right of audience") and note 1.3.4.

The petitioner must lodge the petition with the required steps of process (r. 4.4).

A fee is payable on lodging the petition: see note 14.5.10.

CHAPTER 68

APPLICATIONS UNDER THE SOLICITORS (SCOTLAND) ACT 1980

Application and interpretation of this Chapter

68.1.—(1) This Chapter applies to an application or appeal under the Solicitors (Scotland) Act 1980.

(2) In this Chapter—

"the Act of 1980" means the Solicitors (Scotland) Act 1980;

"the Council" means the Council of the Law Society of Scotland;

"the Discipline Tribunal" means the tribunal constituted under section 50 of the Act of 1980.

Applications and appeals under the Act of 1980

68.2.—(1) Except in the case of an application under paragraph 20 of Schedule 4 to the Act of 1980 (which shall be made by letter to the Deputy Principal Clerk), an application or appeal under the Act of 1980 shall be made by petition.

(2) An appeal under any of the following provisions of the Act of 1980 shall specify the date on which the decision appealed against was intimated to the petitioner:—
(a) section 16(2) (appeal in respect of issue of practising certificate);
(b) section 39A(8) (appeal against withdrawal of practising certificate);
(c) section 40(3) (appeal against decision to withdraw practising certificate or to refuse to terminate suspension);
(d) section 54(1) (appeal against decision of tribunal relating to discipline); and
(e) paragraph 3 of Schedule 2 (appeal in respect of restoration to roll of solicitors).

(3) An application under paragraph 5(4) of Schedule 3 to the Act of 1980 (application for order for return of documents) shall specify the date on which the notice was served on the petitioner.

(4) An application under section 54(2) of the Act of 1980 (application to vary or quash direction of the tribunal) shall specify the date on which the decision containing the direction or order was intimated to the petitioner.

Deriv. R.C.S. 1965, r. 2 substituted by S.I. 1992 No. 1422

"petition". The petition is presented to the Inner House: r. 14.3(b); and see r. 68.4(1). The **68.2.1** provisions for the lodging of documents in causes in the Inner House in r. 4.7 should be noted. On petitions generally, see Chap. 14.

Sch. 4, para. 20 of the Act of 1980. The Discipline Tribunal constituted under the Act of 1980 **68.2.1A** may make an award of expenses to or by the complainer or respondent. The person in whose favour an award is made may apply to the court (on production of a certificate from the clerk to the tribunal that there is no appeal or the appeal was dismissed or withdrawn) for a warrant authorising recovery of those expenses: Act of 1980, Sch. 4, para. 20.
By virtue of the amendment to r. 68.2(1) by A.S. (R.C.S.A. No. 4) (Miscellaneous) 1997 [S.I. 1997 No. 1050], that application is made by letter to the DPCS and not by petition.
The letter, a narrative of the findings of the tribunal, and the certificate are passed to the clerk of one of the Divisions of the Inner House. If all is in order an interlocutor is pronounced granting warrant for all lawful execution; accordingly, an extract is not required in order to do diligence. On the meaning of "all lawful execution", see note 7.10.2.

Section 16(2) of the Act of 1980. An appeal against a decision of the Council to refuse to issue a **68.2.2** practising certificate must be made within 14 days of notification of the decision: Act of 1980, s.16(2).

Section 39A(8) of the Act of 1980. An appeal against a decision of the Council to withdraw a **68.2.3** practising certificate where the solicitor has issued an account for professional fees and outlays which is grossly excessive must be made within 21 days of receiving written notice of the decision: Act of 1980, s.39A(8).

Section 40(3) of the Act of 1980. An appeal against a decision of the Council to withdraw a **68.2.4** practising certificate or to refuse to terminate a suspension from practice for failure to comply with account rules etc. must be made within 21 days after receiving written notice of the decision: Act of 1980, s.40(3).

Section 54 of the Act of 1980. A person aggrieved by a decision of the Discipline Tribunal may **68.2.5** appeal within 21 days of the date on which the decision was intimated to him: Act of 1980, s.54(1). Where the tribunal has directed its decision to take effect on the date of intimation, application can be made within 21 days to vary or quash that direction: Act of 1980, s.54(2).

Applications for admission as notary public

68.3.—(1) An application under section 57(2) of the Act of 1980 (application for admission as notary public) shall be made by either the Council on behalf of named persons seeking appointment as notaries public or the person seeking appointment as a notary public.
(2) The Council shall—
(a) nominate authorised representatives to administer the oath of the office of notary public;
(b) issue all commissions as notary public;

    (c) keep the register of notaries public; and

    (d) on request by a notary public, and on payment of such reasonable fee as the Council may impose, supply him with a duly certified and docquetted protocol book of ninety one folios.

Deriv. R.C.S. 1965, r. 3 substituted by S.I. 1992 No. 1422

68.3.1   *General note.* The petition for admission as a notary (an Inner House petition: r. 14.3(b)) may be made by the Council on behalf of a number of applicants or by the applicant. The pet-

[THE NEXT PAGE IS C 597]

ition may be combined with a petition to be admitted as a solicitor (also an Inner House petition: r. 14.3(b)). The provisions for lodging documents in causes in the Inner House in r. 4.7 should be noted.

Fee. The court fee for lodging the petition is payable on lodging. Where there is a combined petition for admission as a solicitor and notary, the fee for each is payable. For fee, see Court of Session etc. Fees Order 1997, Table of Fees, Pt I, C, item 3 and 4 [S.I. 1997 No. 688, as amended, pp. C1201 *et seq.*]. **68.3.2**

Intimation and service in causes under this Chapter

68.4.—(1) A petition to which this Chapter applies shall be brought before a Division of the Inner House in chambers, and the Division may, without hearing parties and subject to the following paragraphs, make such order for intimation and service as it thinks fit.

(2) In a cause under any of the following provisions of the Act of 1980, the court shall order service of the petition on the Council:—

  (a) section 16(1) (application following refusal of practising certificate to body corporate);

  (b) section 19(8) (appeal in respect of decision of Council in relation to suspension);

  (c) section 39A(8) (appeal against withdrawal of practising certificate);

  (d) section 40(3) (appeal against decision to withdraw practising certificate or to refuse to terminate suspension); and

  (e) paragraph 5(4) of Schedule 3 (application for order for return of documents).

(3) In an appeal under section 54(1) (appeal against decision of tribunal relating to discipline), or in an application under section 54(2) (application to vary or quash direction of the tribunal), of the Act of 1980, the court shall—

  (a) order service on the Discipline Tribunal and the Law Society of Scotland; and

  (b) ordain the Discipline Tribunal to lodge in process within the period for lodging answers—

    (i) the decision of the Discipline Tribunal in respect of which the appeal or application is made; and

    (ii) if available, the notes of evidence adduced before the Discipline Tribunal.

(4) In an application under any of the following provisions of the Act of 1980, the court shall order service of the petition on the respondent:—

  (a) section 41 (application for appointment of judicial factor);

  (b) paragraph 5(1) of Schedule 3 (application for order to produce documents); and

  (c) paragraph 12 of Schedule 4 (petition to cite witnesses for recovery of evidence).

(5) In an application under section 55(3) of the Act of 1980 (application for restoration to roll of solicitors), the court shall order service on the Discipline Tribunal and the Council.

Deriv. R.C.S. 1965, r. 4 substituted by S.I. 1992 No. 1422

General note. Petitions under this Chapter are usually dealt with by the First Division. Hearings in chambers are also in private. **68.4.1**

"intimation and service". No order is normally sought in the prayer, enrolled for or made by the court in a petition for admission as a notary or solicitor. See r. 14.7 and notes and Chap. 16, Pt I. Intimation is not usually made on the walls of the court except in petitions for admission. **68.4.2**

Procedure after order for intimation and service

68.5. The court shall, after an order for intimation and service under rule 68.4, proceed on the petition summarily in such manner as it thinks fit.

Deriv. R.C.S. 1965, r. 5 substituted by S.I. 1992 No. 1422

68.5.1   *General note.* Petitions are usually appointed to the Summar Roll.

Appeals under section 54(1) of the Act of 1980

68.6. In an appeal under section 54(1) of the Act of 1980 (appeal against decision of tribunal relating to discipline)—

(a)   the court may substitute any other punishment for that imposed by the decision appealed against, or make any order in relation to it which it thinks fit;

(b)   where the petitioner is a person or one of the persons who complained of the alleged professional misconduct of the solicitor, the court may order that person to give security for expenses (including the cost of extending the notes of evidence adduced before the Discipline Tribunal) as a condition of proceeding with the petition.

Deriv. R.C.S. 1965, r. 6 substituted by S.I. 1992 No. 1422

68.6.1   *General note.* It requires a very strong case before the court will interfere with an order (*i.e.* "sentence") of the tribunal following a finding of professional misconduct: *MacColl v. Council of the Law Society of Scotland* 1987 S.L.T. 524, 528G *per* L.P. Emslie.

68.6.2   *Expenses.* Where a solicitor is guilty of professional misconduct, the court may find him liable in any expenses involved in the proceedings before the court: Act of 1980, s.55(1)(e).

Remits for further inquiry

68.7.—(1) In an application or appeal under the Act of 1980, the court may remit to any person to make further inquiry into the facts, or to take further evidence and to report to the court.

(2) On completion of a report made under paragraph (1), the person to whom the remit was made shall send his report and three copies of it, and a copy of it for each party, to the Deputy Principal Clerk.

(3) On receipt of such a report, the Deputy Principal Clerk shall—

(a)   cause the report to be lodged in process; and

(b)   give written intimation to each party that this has been done and that he may uplift a copy of the report from process.

(4) After the lodging of such a report, any party may apply by motion for an order in respect of the report or for further procedure.

Deriv. R.C.S. 1965, r. 7 substituted by S.I. 1992 No. 1422

68.7.1   *General note.* The solicitors for the parties are personally responsible for the fees of a reporter and the solicitor for one party will be liable: r. 42.15.

68.7.2   *"send".* This includes deliver: r. 1.3(1) (definition of "send").

68.7.3   *"written intimation".* For methods, see r. 16.9.

68.7.4   *"motion".* For motions, see Chap. 23.

CHAPTER 69

ELECTION PETITIONS

Interpretation of this Chapter

[1] **69.1.** In this Chapter—

"the Act of 1983" means the Representation of the People Act 1983;

"election court" has the meaning assigned in section 123 of the Act of 1983;

"election petition" means a petition presented under Part III of the Act of 1983 or a petition presented under Part III of the Act of 1983 as applied and modified by article 85 of and Schedule 6 to the Scottish Parliament (Elections etc.) Order 1999; and any reference in this Chapter to an election petition shall be construed as a reference to a Scottish parliamentary election petition where it is a petition brought in relation to a Scottish parliamentary election; "region" means a region for the purposes of the Scotland Act 1998; and any reference in this Chapter to a constituency shall be construed as a reference to a constituency for the purposes of the said Act of 1998 where it is used in relation to a Scottish parliamentary election;

"Scottish parliamentary election" means an election for membership of the Scottish Parliament.

R. 69.1 amended by S.I. 1999 No. 787 (effective 11th March 1999).

General note. This Chapter is concerned with Parliamentary (including Scottish Parliamen- **69.1.1** tary) election petitions and European parliamentary election petitions (see note 69.1.3).

The Scottish Parliament (Election etc.) Order 1999 (S.I. 1999 No. 787) amends Chap. 69 so as to extend it to Scottish Parliamentary elections. The Order makes provision for the conduct of elections and return of members to the Scottish Parliament established by the Scotland Act 1998.

Rules 69.2 to 69.4, 69.8, 69.9, 69.18 to 69.20 and 69.25 are made under provisions in the Representation of the People Act 1983: see A.S. (R.C.S. 1994) 1994, Sched. 1 [S.I. 1994 No. 1443].

"election court". A Parliamentary election petition or European parliamentary election **69.1.2** petition is tried by two judges on the rota for the trial of such petitions: Act of 1983, s. 123(1). The judges are nominated by the Lord President: C.S.A. 1988, s. 44. The judges on the rota for the remainder of 2007 are Lords Osborne and Kingarth: Direction No.1 of 2007.

The election court has the same powers as a judge of the Court of Session presiding at a civil jury trial: Act of 1983, s. 123(2).

"election petition". This is a petition relating to a Parliamentary election or, by virtue of the **69.1.3** European Assembly Elections Regulations 1984 [S.I. 1984 No. 137], a European parliamentary election.

Form of election petitions
69.2.—(1) An election petition shall be in Form 69.2.

(2) Such a petition shall—
(a) specify the name, designation and address of—
    (i) each petitioner, and
    (ii) each person referred to as, or deemed to be, the respondent by virtue of section 121(2) of the Act of 1983; and
(b) set out in numbered paragraphs—
    (i) the title of the petitioner under section 121(1) of the Act of 1983 to present the petition;
    (ii) the proceedings at, and the result of, the election; and
    (iii) the facts relied on in support of the prayer of the petition.

Deriv. RCS 1965, r. 298 amended by S.I. 1979 No. 516 and 1985 No. 1426

General note. The petition must be presented within 21 days after the return made to the **69.2.1** Clerk of the Crown in Chancery: Act of 1983, s. 122(1).

"petition". The petition must be in Form 69.2 and comply with the requirements for the paper **69.2.2** used: r. 4.1. It must be signed by the petitioner: Act of 1983, s. 121(3).

The petitioner must lodge a process with the petition: r. 69.3. A fee is payable on lodging the petition: see note 69.3.4.

Title to present petition. A person who voted or had the right to vote, a person claiming to **69.2.3** have had a right to be elected at the election or a person alleging himself to have been a candidate at the election may present an election petition: Act of 1983, s. 121(1).

Presentation of petition
69.3. The election petition shall be lodged in the Petition Department with—

(a) a process;
(b) six copies of the petition; and
(c) a letter signed by or on behalf of the petitioner—
    (i) giving the name and address of a solicitor whom he authorises to act on his behalf or stating that he acts for himself, as the case may be; and
    (ii) specifying an address within Scotland at which notices addressed to him may be delivered.

Deriv. RCS 1965, r. 297(a) amended by S.I. 1979 No. 516
and r. 299(a) amended by S.I. 1991 No. 2483

69.3.1   *General note.* The petition must be presented within 21 days after the return made to the Clerk of the Crown in Chancery: Act of 1983, s. 122(1).

69.3.2   *"lodged in the Petition Department".* The petition may be lodged by post: P.N. No. 4 of 1994, paras 1, 6 and 8.

69.3.3   *"process".* For the steps of process to be lodged with the petition, see r. 4.4.

69.3.4   *Fee.* The court fee for the petition is payable on lodging. For fee, see Court of Session etc. Fees Order 1997, Table of Fees, Pt. I, E, item 1 [S.I. 1997 No. 688, as amended, pp. C1201 *et seq.*]. Certain persons are exempt from payment of fees: see 1997 Fees Order, art. 5 substituted by S.S.I. 2002 No. 270. A fee exemption certificate must be lodged in process: see P.N. No.1 of 2002.

    Where the petitioner is legally represented, the fee may be debited under a credit scheme introduced on 1st April 1976 by P.N. No. 4 of 1976 to the account (if one is kept or permitted) of the agent by the court cashier, and an account will be rendered weekly by the court cashier's office to the agent for all court fees due that week for immediate settlement. Party litigants, and agents not operating the scheme, must pay (by cash, cheque or postal order) on each occasion a fee is due at the time of lodging at the counter at the Petition Department.

Security for expenses

69.4.—(1) On presentation of an election petition, the petitioner shall apply by motion for—
(a) an order for intimation and service of the petition within such period as the court thinks fit after the giving of security,
(b) for an order for the respondent to lodge any objections in writing under section 136(4) of the Act of 1983 (objections to form of security) within such period as the court thinks fit, and
(c) the fixing of the amount of security for expenses;
and the petition shall be placed forthwith before the Lord Ordinary or the vacation judge, in court or in chambers, who shall fix the security to be given.

(2) A motion under paragraph (1) shall not be intimated to any person.

(3) Where the security to be given by the petitioner under section 136 of the Act of 1983 is given in whole or in part by bond of caution, the bond shall be in Form 69.4.

Deriv. RCS 1965, r. 299A inserted by S.I. 1985 No. 1426 (r. 69.4(1))
and r. 300 amended by S.I. 1985 No. 1426 (r. 69.4(3))

69.4.1   *"intimation and service".* On intimation and service of petitions generally, see r. 14.7. Note the provisions of r. 69.5.

69.4.2   *"security for expenses".* The security for expenses is a sum not exceeding £5,000: Act of 1983, s. 136(2) as amended by the Representation of the People Act 1985, Sched. 4, para. 48.
    On finding and lodging caution, see Chap. 33.

Service and intimation of election petition

69.5.—[1] (1) On serving the election petition on the respondent under subsection (3) of section 136 of the Act of 1983, the petitioner shall intimate a copy of each of the documents mentioned in that subsection to—
(a) the Lord Advocate; and
(b) the Advocate General for Scotland.

(2) The notice of presentation of the petition mentioned in section 136(3) of the Act of 1983 shall be in Form 69.5.

(3) Within five days after serving the petition under section 136 of the Act of 1983, the petitioner shall lodge in process an execution copy of the election petition containing the certificate of service and a copy of the notice mentioned in that subsection which was served on the respondent.

Deriv. RCS 1965, r. 303 amended by S.I. 1985 No. 1426

---

[1] R. 69.5(1) amended by S.I. 1999 No. 1386 (effective 19th May 1999).

General note. An election petition no longer has to be served within five days after **69.5.1** presentation: Act of 1983, s.136(3) as amended by the Representation of the People Act 1985, Sched. 4, para. 48. As all the periods specified in the Act of 1983, and in this Chapter, for the doing of something in relation to an election petition are short, it is unlikely that the court would stipulate a period of notice of 21 days as in an ordinary petition.

Documents to be served with election petition. These are the notice of presentation of the **69.5.2** petition in Form 69.5 and the notice of the amount of caution: Act of 1983, s.136(3).

"execution copy". The documents required as evidence of service (see note 16.1.5) are **69.5.3** attached (stitched in) to an execution copy of the principal writ: r. 16.1(4). A walling certificate is not required: P.N. No. 7 of 1994, para. 4.

Objection to form of security

69.6.—(1) Where the respondent makes an objection under section 136(4) of the Act of 1983 (objection to form of security), he shall—

(a) set out in writing the grounds of the objection;

(b) lodge the objection in process; and

(c) intimate a copy of the objection to the petitioner.

(2) As soon as possible after the lodging of an objection under paragraph (1), the Keeper of the Rolls shall—

(a) fix a diet for a hearing on the objections before one of the judges on the rota for the trial of election petitions or the vacation judge; and

(b) give written intimation of the time and place of the diet to the parties.

(3) The period within which the petitioner may, under section 136(7) of the Act of 1983, remove the objection shall be such period from the date of the decision on the objection as the court thinks fit.

Deriv. RCS 1965, r. 304(b) (r. 69.6(1)(a) and (b)),
r. 304(c) (r. 69.6(1)(c)),
r. 305 (r. 69.6(2)) and r. 306(c)(part) (r. 69.6(3))

General note. No form of objection is prescribed. It does not have to comply with r. 15.2. The **69.6.1** document itself must comply with the requirements for paper used: r. 4.1.

"intimate". For methods, see r. 16.7.   **69.6.2**

"written intimation". For methods, see r. 16.9.   **69.6.3**

Consequences of failure to give security etc.

69.7. If no security is given, or an objection to a security is allowed and not removed, the respondent may apply by motion to have the prayer of the petition refused.

General note. If no security is given or objection to it is allowed and not removed, no further **69.7.1** proceedings shall be had on the petition: Act of 1983, s.136(8).

"motion". For motions, see Chap. 23. See also rr. 69.29 and 69.30 on intimation of motions in **69.7.2** an election petition.

List of election petitions

69.8.—(1) In preparing the list of election petitions in terms of section 138(1) of the Act of 1983, the Deputy Principal Clerk shall insert the names of the solicitors, if any, acting for the petitioner and respondent, and the addresses, if any, to which any notices may be sent.

(2) The list of election petitions may be inspected in the Petition Department at any time during its normal office hours.

Deriv. RCS 1965, r. 307 amended by S.I. 1979 No. 516 and 1985 No. 1426

Time and place of trial

69.9.—(1) The time and place of the trial of an election petition shall be fixed by the Keeper of the Rolls, who shall give written intimation of the date of the trial by post to—

    (a) the parties;
    (b) the Lord Advocate;
² {(ba) the Advocate General of Scotland;
¹   (c) the returning officer for the relevant constituency or, as the case may be, region; and
    (d) the House of Commons shorthand writer.
¹ (2) On receipt of intimation given under paragraph (1), the returning officer shall forthwith publish the date of the diet of trial in the constituency or, as the case may be, region to which it relates.

Deriv. RCS 1965, r. 308 amended by S.I. 1979 No. 516 and 1985 No. 1426

---

¹ R. 69.9(1)(c) and (2) amended by S.I. 1999 No. 787 (effective 11th March 1999).
² R. 69.9(1)(ba) inserted by S.I. 1999 No. 1386 (effective 19th May 1999).

69.9.1   *General note.* The trial is in open court without a jury: Act of 1983, s.139(1). It may be held anywhere in Scotland. Notice of the trial diet must be given at least 14 days before: Act of 1983, s.139(1).

    At the end of the trial the judges report to the Speaker of the House of Commons in the case of a Parliamentary election (Act of 1983, s.144(2)) and to the Secretary of State in the case of a European election.

69.9.2   *"written intimation".* For methods, see r. 16.9.

Postponement of trial

69.10.—(1) The election court or any of the judges on the rota for the trial of election petitions, may, at its or his own instance or on the motion of a party, postpone the trial of a petition to such day as may be specified.

¹ (2) Written intimation of such postponement shall be given by the Keeper of the Rolls to the returning officer who shall forthwith publish the postponement and its new date in the constituency or, as the case may be, region.

Deriv. RCS 1965, r. 312

---

¹ R. 69.10(2) amended by S.I. 1996 No. 787 (effective 11th March 1999).

69.10.1   *"written intimation".* For methods, see r. 16.9.

Procedure where seat claimed

69.11.—(1) Where a petitioner claims the seat for an unsuccessful candidate, alleging that he had a majority of lawful votes, the party complaining of, and the party defending, the return, not less than six days before the date of the trial, shall each—

   (a) lodge in process a list of the voters intended to be objected to, and of
        the objections to each voter; and
[1] (b) intimate a copy of that list to—
        (i) every other party;
        (ii) the Lord Advocate; and
        (iii) the Advocate General for Scotland.
   (2) No evidence shall be allowed to be given against any vote or in support
of any objection which is not specified in the list, except by leave of the
election court or, on a motion heard before the date of the trial, of any of the
judges on the rota for the trial of election petitions, on such terms as to
amendment of the list, postponement of the trial and payment of expenses as
may be ordered.

Deriv. RCS 1965, r. 310 amended by S.I. 1985 No. 1426

---

[1] R. 69.11(1)(b) amended by S.I. 1999 No. 1386 (effective 19th May 1999).

"not less than six days before". There must be six clear days.   69.11.1

"lodge in process". The list is lodged as a step of process (r. 1.3(1) (definition of "step of   69.11.2
process")). On lodging steps of process, see r. 4.4. The list may be lodged by post: P.N. No. 4 of
1994, paras 1 and 8; and see note 4.4.10.

"intimate". For methods, see r. 16.7.   69.11.3

Evidence under section 139(5) of the Act of 1983

69.12.—(1) Where the respondent intends to give evidence permitted
under section 139(5) of the Act of 1983 (evidence to prove person not duly
elected), he shall, not less than six days before the date of the trial—
   (a) lodge in process a list of the objections to the election on which he
        intends to rely; and
[1] (b) intimate a copy of that list to—
        (i) every other party;
        (ii) the Lord Advocate; and
        (iii) the Advocate General for Scotland.
   (2) No evidence shall be allowed to be given on behalf of the respondent in
support of any objection to the return not specified in the list, except with
leave of the election court or, on a motion heard before the date of the trial,
of any of the judges on the rota for the trial of election petitions, on such
terms as to amendment of the list, postponement of the trial and payment of
expenses as may be ordered.

Deriv. RCS 1965, r. 311 amended by S.I. 1985 No. 1426

---

[1] R. 69.11(1)(b) amended by S.I. 1999 No. 1386 (effective 19th May 1999).

"not less than six days before". There must be six clear days.   69.12.1

"lodge in process". The list is lodged as a step of process (r. 1.3(1) (definition of "step of   69.12.2
process")). On lodging steps of process, see r. 4.4. The list may be lodged by post: P.N. No. 4 of
1994, paras 1 and 8; and see note 4.4.10.

"intimate". For methods, see r. 16.7.   69.12.3

Lodging of statement of evidence to be led

69.13.—(1) Subject to paragraph (2), any party shall, not less than six days
before the date of the trial, lodge in process a statement of the matters on
which he intends to lead evidence.

[1] (2) Before lodging such a statement in process, the party proposing to lodge it shall intimate a copy of the statement to—
    (a) every other party;
    (b) the Lord Advocate; and
    (c) the Advocate General for Scotland.

Deriv. RCS 1965, r. 313 amended by S.I. 1985 No. 1426

---

[1] R. 69.13(2) amended by S.I. 1999 No. 1386 (effective 19th May 1999).

69.13.1   *"not less than six days before"*. There must be six clear days.

69.13.2   *"intimate"*. For methods, see r. 16.7.

Evidence at trial
69.14.—(1) No evidence shall be led at the trial of an election petition other than matters contained in—
    (a) the list lodged under rule 69.11 (procedure where seat claimed) or 69.12 (evidence under section 139(5) of the Act of 1983),
    (b) the statement lodged under rule 69.13 (statement of evidence to be led), or
    (c) matters which have been sufficiently set out in the petition,
except with the leave of the election court or one of the judges on the rota for the trial of election petitions, on such conditions as to postponement of the trial, payment of expenses or otherwise, as may be ordered.
    (2) The admissibility of any evidence sought to be led on the matters referred to in paragraph (1) shall be within the discretion of the election court.

Deriv. RCS 1965, r. 314

Warrant to cite witnesses
69.15. The warrant for the citation of a witness to the trial of an election petition shall be granted on the motion of any party and shall be in Form 69.15.

Deriv. RCS 1965, r. 315

69.15.1   *General note.* A judge of the election court may require any person who appears to him to have been concerned in the election to appear as a witness and be examined by the court: Act of 1983, s.140(2) and (3).
    Witnesses cannot object to a question at the trial on the ground of incrimination or privilege, but the answer is not admissible in criminal proceedings except perjury: Act of 1983, s.141.

69.15.2   *"motion"*. For motions, see Chap. 23. See also rr. 69.29 and 69.30 on intimation of motions in election petitions.

Clerk of court at trial
69.16. At an election court held for the trial of an election petition, a clerk of session nominated by the Principal Clerk and appointed by the court shall discharge the duties of clerk of court of the election court.

Deriv. RCS 1965, r. 317 amended by S.I. 1979 No. 516

Expenses of witnesses
69.17.—(1) The prescribed officer for the purposes of section 143(1) of the Act of 1983 shall be the clerk of session appointed to act as clerk of court under rule 69.16.
    (2) The expenses of a witness permitted under section 143(1) of the Act of 1983 shall be ascertained by the clerk of court.
    (3) The expenses allowed under section 143(1) of the Act of 1983 shall, in the first instance, be paid by the party adducing that witness.

Deriv. RCS 1965, r. 316

General note. The reasonable expenses of a person appearing to give evidence on the scale for **69.17.1** civil actions before the Court of Session (see r. 42.16, Table of Fees, Chap. II) may be allowed by a certificate of the election court or the prescribed officer (the clerk of the election court): Act of 1983, s.143(1).

The expenses of a witness called by the court under s.140(2) of the Act of 1983 are part of the expenses of providing the election court: Act of 1983, s.143(2).

Applications for special case

69.18. An application under section 146(1) of the Act of 1983 for a special case, shall be made by motion to the Inner House or the vacation judge.

Deriv. RCS 1965, r. 318(1) amended by S.I. 1985 No. 426

General note. If it appears that the case raised by the petition can be conveniently stated as a **69.18.1** special case, this may be ordered: Act of 1983, s.146(1). The procedure in Chap. 41, Pt II will apply.

"motion". For motions, see Chap. 23. See also rr. 69.29 and 69.30 on intimation of motions in **69.18.2** election petitions.

Applications for leave to withdraw election petitions

69.19.—(1) A notice of intention to withdraw an election petition under section 147(2) of the Act of 1983 shall be in Form 69.19–A.

(2) A copy of such notice shall be intimated by the petitioners to—
(a) the respondent;
(b) the Lord Advocate;
² (ba) the Advocate General for Scotland;
¹ (c) the returning officer for the relevant constituency or, as the case may be, region; and
(d) the Deputy Principal Clerk.

(3) On receipt of a notice under paragraph (2), the returning officer shall publish it in the constituency to which it relates.

(4) An application for leave to withdraw an election petition shall—
(a) be in Form 69.19–B;
(b) state the ground on which the application to withdraw is made;
(c) be signed by the person making the application and by the consenters, if any, or by their respective solicitors; and
(d) be lodged in the process of the election petition.

Deriv. RCS 1965, r. 320 amended by S.I. 1985 No. 1426 (r. 69.19(1), (2) and (3)), and r. 321 (r. 69.19(4))

---

¹ R. 69.19(2)(c) amended by S.I. 1999 No. 787 (effective 11th March 1999).
² R. 69.19(2)(ba) inserted by S.I. 1999 No. 1386 (effective 19th May 1999).

General note. If there is more than one petitioner, all must consent: Act of 1983, s.147(3). The **69.19.1** petitioner is liable to the respondent for expenses: Act of 1983, s.147(4).

An agreement, terms or an undertaking to withdraw a petition in consideration of payment, or of the seat being vacated at any time or of the withdrawal of another election petition, is an offence: Act of 1983, s.149.

"intimated". For methods, see r. 16.7.   **69.19.2**

"leave to withdraw". Affidavits are required from all parties and their solicitors and the **69.19.3** election agent, unless on cause shown an affidavit is dispensed with (Act of 1983, s.148(1)), that no agreement, terms or undertaking has been given for withdrawal: Act of 1983, s.148(2).

The election court reports to the Speaker of the House of Commons in the case of a Parliamentary election (Act of 1983, s.151) or the Secretary of State in the case of a European election.

"lodged in the process". The application for leave is lodged as a step of process (r. 1.3(1) **69.19.4** (definition of "step of process")). On lodging steps of process, see r. 4.4. The list may be lodged by post: P.N. No. 4 of 1994, paras 1 and 8; and see note 4.4.10.

Applications to be substituted as petitioner on withdrawal

69.20.—(1) A person who seeks to apply under section 150(1) of the Act of 1983 to be substituted as a petitioner, shall, within five days after the date on which the notice of intention to withdraw has been given under section 147(2) of the Act of 1983 and rule 69.19 (applications for leave to withdraw election petitions), give notice in writing signed by him or on his behalf to the Deputy Principal Clerk of his intention to apply, at the hearing of the application for leave to withdraw, to be substituted as the petitioner.

(2) A copy of the notice given under paragraph (1) shall be intimated by the applicant to—

    (a) the respondent;

    (b) the Lord Advocate;

[1](ba) the Advocate General for Scotland; and

    (c) the returning officer for the relevant constituency.

(3) Any informality in such a notice shall not defeat an application to be substituted as the petitioner if it is made at the hearing of the application to withdraw, subject to such order as to postponement of that hearing and expenses as the election court thinks fit.

Deriv. RCS 1965, r. 322

—————

[1] R. 69.2(2)(ba) inserted by S.I. 1999 No. 1386 (effective 19th May 1999).

69.20.1   *"intimated"*. For methods, see r. 16.7.

Hearing of applications for leave to withdraw

69.21.—(1) Subject to paragraph (2), the time and place for hearing an application for leave to withdraw an election petition shall be fixed by one of the judges on the rota for the trial of election petitions or by the vacation judge, who shall hear and determine the application unless he considers that the application should be determined by the Inner House.

(2) The time fixed under paragraph (1) shall not be earlier than seven days after the expiry of the period specified in rule 69.20.

(3) The Keeper of the Rolls shall give written intimation of the diet fixed under paragraph (1) to—

    (a) the petitioner;

    (b) the respondent;

    (c) the Lord Advocate;

[1] (ca) the Advocate General for Scotland;

    (d) the returning officer for the relevant constituency; and

    (e) to any person who has given notice under rule 69.20 of his intention to apply to be substituted as the petitioner.

Deriv. RCS 1965, r. 324

—————

[1] R. 69(21)(3)(ca) inserted by S.I. 1999 No. 1386 (effective 19th May 1999).

69.21.1   *"not earlier than seven days after"*. There must be seven clear days.

69.21.2   *"written intimation"*. For methods, see r. 16.9.

Security of substituted petitioner

69.22.—(1) The period within which security shall be given on behalf of a substituted petitioner before he proceeds with the petition shall be five days after the order of substitution.

(2) The substituted petitioner shall lodge the letter referred to in rule 69.3(c) (name and address of solicitor, etc.) within five days after the order of substitution.

Deriv. RCS 1965, r. 323

General note. Where there has been an agreement, terms or an undertaking to withdraw a **69.22.1** petition in consideration of payment, or of the seat being vacated at any time or of the withdrawal of another election petition, the election court may order the original security to be the security for the substituted petitioner: Act of 1983, s.150(2).

Death of petitioner

69.23.—(1) In the event of the death of the petitioner or the surviving petitioner, the notice for the purpose of section 152(3) of the Act of 1983 (notice of abatement of petition by death) shall be intimated in Form 69.23 by the solicitor acting for the petitioner, the respondent, the returning officer or any other person interested to whose knowledge the death of the petitioner shall come, to, as the case may be—

(a) the respondent;
[1] (b) the Lord Advocate;
[2] (ba) the Advocate General for Scotland;
(c) the returning officer for the relevant constituency or, as the case may be, region; and
(d) the Deputy Principal Clerk.

[1] (2) The returning officer shall, on receipt of such a notice, or, where he is giving notice under paragraph (1), on intimating such notice to those persons mentioned in that paragraph, publish the notice in the constituency or, as the case may be, region to which it relates.

Deriv. RCS 1965, r. 325 amended by S.I. 1985 No. 1426

---

[1] R. 69.23(1)(c) and (2) amended by S.I. 1999 No. 787 (effective 11th March 1999).
[2] R. 69.23(1)(ba) inserted by S.I. 1999 No. 1386 (effective 19th May 1999).

General note. Abatement occurs on the death of a sole petitioner or of the survivor of several **69.23.1** petitioners: Act of 1983, s.152(1).

"intimated". For methods, see r. 16.7.   **69.23.2**

Applications to be substituted on death of petitioner

69.24.—(1) An application to be substituted as a petitioner on the death of the petitioner or surviving petitioner shall be made by motion within five days after the publication of the notice.

(2) A motion under paragraph (1) shall be intimated to—
(a) the respondent;
(b) the Lord Advocate;
[2] (ba) the Advocate General for Scotland; and
[1] (c) the returning officer for the relevant constituency or, as the case may be, region where he is not a respondent.

Deriv. RCS 1965, r. 326

---

[1] R. 69.24(2)(c) amended by S.I. 1999 No. 787 (effective 11th March 1999).
[2] R. 69.24(2)(ba) inserted by S.I. 1999 No. 1386 (effective 19th May 1999).

"motion". For motions, see Chap. 23. See also rr. 69.29 and 69.30 on intimation of motions in **69.24.1** election petitions.

"intimated". For methods, see r. 16.7.   **69.24.2**

Notice that respondent does not oppose

69.25.—(1) A notice, for the purposes of section 153(1) of the Act of 1983, by a respondent other than a returning officer, that he does not intend to oppose an election petition shall be—

(a) signed by him; and
(b) lodged in process not less than six days before the date of the trial.
    (2) Where a respondent lodges a notice under paragraph (1), he shall forthwith intimate a copy of it to—
(a) the petitioner;
(b) any other respondent;
(c) the Lord Advocate;
[1] (ca)the Advocate General for Scotland; and
(d) the returning officer for the relevant constituency.
    (3) On receipt of a notice under paragraph (1), the returning officer shall publish it in the constituency to which it relates.

Deriv. RCS 1965, r. 327 amended by S.I. 1985 No. 1426

———————

[1] R. 69.25(2)(ca) inserted by S.I. 1999 No. 1386 (effective 19th May 1999).

69.25.1   *"lodged in process"*. The notice that a respondent does not oppose the petition is lodged as a step of process (r. 1.3(1) (definition of "step of process")). On lodging steps of process, see r. 4.4. The list may be lodged by post: P.N. No. 4 of 1994, paras 1 and 8; and see note 4.4.10.

69.25.2   *"not less than six days before"*. There must be six clear days.

Death[1], peerage or resignation of respondent
    69.26.—(1) Where, for the purposes of section 153(1) of the Act of 1983—
(a) a respondent other than a returning officer dies,
(b) in the case of a parliamentary election, a respondent other than a returning officer is summoned to Parliament as a Peer of Great Britain,
(c) a respondent other than a returning officer has vacated his seat following a resolution by the House of Commons, or
[1] (d) a respondent resigns or otherwise ceases to be a Member of the Scottish Parliament,
the agent for the respondent shall give notice of that fact in the constituency to which the election petition relates.
    (2) Such a notice shall be published in at least one newspaper circulating in the constituency, and by intimating a copy of the notice, signed by him to—
(a) the petitioner;
(b) any other respondent;
(c) the Lord Advocate;
[2] (ca) the Advocate General for Scotland;
(d) the returning officer for the relevant constituency; and
(e) the Deputy Principal Clerk.

Deriv. RCS 1965, r. 328 amended by S.I. 1979 No. 516 and 1985 No. 1426

———————

[1] Heading and r. 69.26(1) amended by S.I. 1999 No. 787 (effective 11th March 1999).
[2] R. 69.26(2)(ca) inserted by S.I. 1999 No. 1386 (effective 19th May 1999).

69.26.1   *General note.* A judge of the election court reports to the Speaker of the House of Commons in the case of a Parliamentary election (Act of 1983, s.153(4)) or the Secretary of State in the case of a European election.

69.26.2   *"intimating"*. For methods, see r. 16.7.

Applications to be admitted as respondent
    69.27. The period of time within which a person may apply to be admitted as a respondent under section 153 of the Act of 1983 shall be—

    (a) five days after the notice is intimated under rule 69.25 (notice that respondent does not oppose);

[1] (b) 10 days after the notice is intimated under rule 69.26 (death, peerage or resignation of respondent); or

    (c) such other period as the court thinks fit.

Deriv. RCS 1965, r. 329 amended by S.I. 1985 No. 1426

---

[1] R. 69.27(b) amended by S.I. 1999 No. 787 (effective 11th March 1999).

Expenses in election petitions

69.28. Where any expenses are awarded by the election court in the course of proceedings under the Act of 1983, such an award shall be deemed equivalent to a finding of expenses in the Court of Session.

Deriv. RCS 1965, r. 330

Motions in election petitions

69.29.—(1) Subject to any other provision in this Chapter or the Act of 1983, all applications shall be dealt with by motion.

(2) Subject to the provisions of this Chapter, Chapter 23 (motions) shall apply to a motion in an election petition.

(3) A motion in an election petition shall be intimated to—

    (a) the Lord Advocate;

[2](aa) the Advocate General for Scotland; and

[1] (b) the returning officer for the relevant constituency or, as the case may be, region.

Deriv. RCS 1965, r. 309 (r. 69.29(1))

---

[1] R. 69.29(3)(b) amended by S.I. 1999 No. 787 (effective 11th March 1999).
[2] R. 69.29(3)(aa) inserted by S.I. 1999 No. 1386 (effective 19th May 1999).

Intimation to Lord Advocate

69.30. All applications to the court in an election petition other than a motion under rule 69.4(1) (security for expenses) shall be intimated to—

    (a) the Lord Advocate; and

    (b) the Advocate General for Scotland;

and the Lord Advocate and the Advocate General for Scotland shall be entitled to appear or be represented at the hearing of that application.

---

[1] R. 69.3 amended by S.I. 1999 No. 1386 (effective 19th May 1999).

Evidence of publication by returning officer

69.31.—(1) Where a returning officer publishes a notice in accordance with a provision in this Chapter or an order of the election court, he shall forthwith send to the Deputy Principal Clerk a letter—

    (a) certifying that the appropriate notice has been published; and

    (b) detailing the manner in which the publication has been made.

(2) Where publication has been made by inserting a notice in a newspaper or other publication, the letter under paragraph (1) shall be accompanied by—

    (a) a copy of the newspaper or other publication containing the notice; or

(b) a certificate of publication by the publisher stating the date of publication and the text of the notice.

CHAPTER 70

APPLICATIONS UNDER THE CHILD ABDUCTION AND CUSTODY ACT 1985

PART I

GENERAL PROVISIONS

Interpretation of this Chapter
¹ **70.1.** In this Chapter—
"the Act of 1985" means the Child Abduction and Custody Act 1985;
"the European Convention" means the convention defined in section 12(1) of the Act of 1985 and as set out in Schedule 2 to the Act of 1985;
"the Hague Convention" means the convention defined in section 1(1) of the Act of 1985 and as set out in Schedule 1 to the Act of 1985;
"relevant authority" means—
    (a) in the United Kingdom, a sheriff court, a children's hearing within the meaning of Part III of the Social Work (Scotland) Act 1968, the High Court, a county court or magistrates' court in England and Wales, the High Court, a county court or magistrates' court in Northern Ireland, or the Secretary of State, as the case may be; or
    (b) in a relevant territory, the appropriate authority or court within that territory;
"relevant territory" means a territory outside the United Kingdom to which the Act of 1985 extends by virtue of an Order in Council made under section 28(1) of that Act or in relation to which provision is made by an Order in Council under section 28(2) of that Act.

Translations of documents (r. 70.2)   **C 609**

Deriv. R.C.S. 1965, r. 260H(2) inserted by S.I. 1986 No. 1955

---

¹ R. 70.1 amended by S.I. 1996 No. 1756 (effective 5th August 1996).

General note. Pts. I and II of this Chapter are made under s. 10 of the Act of 1985 as well as **70.1.1**
under s. 5 of the C.S.A. 1988. Parts I and III are made under s. 24 of the Act of 1985 as well as s.
5 of the C.S.A. 1988: see A.S. (R.C.S. 1994) 1994, Sched. 1 [S.I. 1994 No. 1443]. Unless the
context otherwise requires, words and expressions used in this Chapter which are also used in
the Act of 1985 have the same meaning as in that Act.

"relevant territory". Under s. 28(1) of the Act of 1985 any provisions of the Act may be **70.1.2**
extended to the British Islands and colonies by an Order in Council. No such Order in Council
has been made.
S.28(2) of the Act of 1985 has effect only in the UK and provides that for the purpose of the
law of the UK certain things done in the British Islands or colonies in respect of which an Order
in Council has been made have the same effect as if done in the UK. S.28(2) would apply
whether the relevant territory enacted its own legislation to give effect to the Hague or
European Conventions. So far only the Isle of Man has enacted its own legislation and the only
Order in Council is in respect of the Isle of Man under s. 28(2) of the Act.
The Child Abduction and Custody Act 1985 (Isle of Man) Order 1994 [S.I. 1994 No. 2799]
provides that references in the Act of 1985 to orders made, proceedings brought or other things
done under the Hague and European conventions in the UK have effect as if made, brought or
done, as the case may be, in the Isle of Man. The Isle of Man has enacted its own legislation to
give effect to the Hague and European Conventions, the Child Custody Act 1987. The
"appropriate court" in the Isle of Man is the High Court of Justice of the Isle of Man.
The Child Abduction and Custody (Falkland Islands) Order 1996 [S.I. 1996 No. 3156]
applies, as modified by the Order, ss. 15, 24A, 25(1) and (2), 26, 27 and Scheds. 1 to 3 of the Act
of 1985 to the Falklands Islands.

Translations of documents
70.2. Where any document lodged in process in a cause to which this
Chapter applies is in a language other than English, there shall be lodged
with that document a translation into English certified as correct by the
translator; and the certificate shall include his full name, address and
qualifications.

Deriv. R.C.S. 1965, r. 260J(6), and r. 260K(9), both inserted by S.I. 1986 No. 1955

Applications for certified copy or extract
70.3.—(1) An application for a certified copy or extract of a decree or any
other interlocutor relating to a child, in respect of whom the applicant
wishes to apply under the Hague Convention or the European Convention
in another Contracting State, shall be made by letter to the Deputy Principal
Clerk.
(2) A certified copy or extract issued on an application under paragraph
(1) shall be supplied free of charge.

Deriv. R.C.S. 1965, r. 260L(1)

Disclosure of information
70.4. Where the court pronounces an interlocutor under section 24A of
the Act of 1985 (order to a person to disclose information to the court as to
a child's whereabouts), it may order that person to appear before it or to
lodge an affidavit.

Deriv. R.C.S. 1965, r. 260L(2)

General note. S. 24A of the Act of 1985 was inserted by s. 67(4) of the Family Law Act 1986. **70.4.1**
A person is not excused from complying with an order to disclose information on the ground of

incrimination of that person or his or her spouse, but a statement or admission is not admissible in evidence in criminal proceedings for an offence except perjury: Act of 1985, s. 24A(2).

The court has always had power to take whatever action was necessary to make an interlocutor effective including ordering the hearing of evidence from any witness who may have information which would assist in the recovery of a child: *Abusaif v. Abusaif* 1984 S.L.T. 90, 91 *per* L.P. Emslie.

PART II

INTERNATIONAL CHILD ABDUCTION (THE HAGUE CONVENTION)

Form of applications under this Part

70.5.—[2,4] (1) Subject to rule 70.16 (warrant for intimation on a child), an application for the return of a child under the Hague Convention shall be made by petition and—

    (a) shall include averments in relation to—

        (i) the identity of the petitioner and the person alleged to have removed or retained the child;

        (ii) the identity of the child and his date of birth;

        (iii) the whereabouts or suspected whereabouts of the child;

        (iv) the date on which the child is alleged to have been wrongfully removed or retained;

        (v) the grounds on which the petition is based; and

        (vi) any civil cause in dependence before any other court or authority in respect of the child, or any proceedings mentioned in section 9 of the Act of 1985 relating to the merits of the rights of custody of the child in or before a relevant authority;

    (b) there shall be produced with the petition and lodged as a production a certified or authorised copy of any relevant decision or agreement; and

[2] (c) there shall be lodged with the petition the evidence by affidavits of any witnesses and any documentary evidence, whether originals or copies initially, in support of the petition.

[2,3] (2) An application for organising or protecting rights of access granted by any court of a contracting party to the Hague Convention, or for securing respect for the conditions to which the exercise of such rights of access is subject shall be made by petition and—

    (a) shall include averments in relation to—

        (i) the identity of the petitioner;

        (ii) the identity of the child and his date of birth;

        (iii) the parents or guardians of the child;

        (iv) the whereabouts of the child;

        (v) the factual and legal grounds on which access is sought; and

        (vi) any civil cause in dependence before any other court or authority in respect of the child, or any proceedings mentioned in section 9 of the Act of 1985 relating to the merits of the rights of custody of the child in or before a relevant authority;

[1] (b) there shall be produced with the petition and lodged as a production a certified copy of any relevant decision or agreement; and

[2] (c) there shall be lodged with the petition the evidence by affidavits of any witnesses and any documentary evidence, whether originals or copies initially, in support of the petition.

[2] (3) An application under section 8 of the Act of 1985 (application for declarator that removal or retention of child was wrongful) shall be made by petition and—

    (a) shall include averments in relation to—

        (i) the identity of the petitioner and of the person who is alleged to have removed or retained the child;

    (ii) the identity of the child and his date of birth;

    (iii) the whereabouts or suspected whereabouts of the child;

    (iv) the date on which the child is alleged to have been wrongfully removed or retained;

    (v) the proceedings which gave custody to the petitioner; and

    (vi) the proceedings under the Hague Convention in relation to which the petition is necessary;

  (b) there shall be produced with the petition any relevant document; and

2 (c) there shall be lodged with the petition the evidence by affidavits of any witnesses and any documentary evidence, whether originals or copies initially, in support of the petition.

Deriv. R.C.S. 1965, r. 260J(1) inserted by S.I. 1986 No. 1955 and amended by S.I. 1991 No. 1157 (r. 70.5(1)); and r. 260J(2) and (3) inserted by S.I. 1986 No. 1955 (r. 70.5(2) and (3))

---

[1] R. 70.5(2)(b) amended by S.I. 1994 No. 2901 (effective 5th December 1994).

[2] R. 70.5(1), (2) and (3) amended by S.I. 1996 No. 1756 (effective 5th August 1996).

[3] R. 70.5(2) amended by S.S.I. 2001 No. 305, para. 15 (effective 18th September 2001).

[4] R. 70(5)(1) amended by S.S.I. 2005 No. 135, (effective 2nd March 2005).

General note. The U.K. has ratified the Hague Convention on the Civil Aspects of **70.5.1** International Child Abduction 1980 (Cmnd. 8155 (1982)). The convention is implemented by the Act of 1985 and is set out in Sched. 1 to that Act.

The convention applies to rights of custody which arise by operation of law, a judicial or administrative decision, or by agreement having legal effect: Act of 1985, Sched. 1, Art. 3. It also applies to rights of access. It applies to a child under the age of 16 years: Act of 1985, Sched. 1, Art. 4.

The intention of the convention is the immediate and summary return of an abducted child to the requesting country: *MacMillan v. MacMillan* 1989 S.C. 53, 60. Its provisions are intended as provisions supportive of existing rights: *Donofrio v. Burrell,* 2000 S.L.T. 1051, 1057H per Lord Prosser.

"Subject to rule 70.16". The Council Regulation (E,C,) No. 2201/2203 of 27th November **70.5.1A** 2003 concerning jurisdiction and enforcement of judgments in matrimonial matters and matters of parental responsibility (new Brussels II) applies between Member States of the E.U except Denmark. Where an application is made under the Hague Convention to which Pt. II of Chap. 70 applies, and the child is habitually resident in a Member State of the E.U., certain requirements of the Council Regulation apply where that child has been removed to or retained in another Member State. These include: (a) the child must be given an opportunity to be heard unless inappropriate because of his age or immaturity, (b) the court deals with the case in six weeks, (c) the court cannot refuse to return the child under art. 13(b) of the Hague Convention (see 1985 Act, Sched. 1, Art 13(b) (grave risk)) if adequate arrangements have been made to secure protection on return, and (d) the court cannot refuse to return the child unless the person requesting return has been given an opportunity to be heard: art. 11 of the Council Regulation.

It should be noted that the Council Regulation does not itself provide a regime for child abduction. A Member State retains its own jurisdiction while a child is habitually resident there until the child acquires an habitual residence in another Member State: art. 10. If the Hague Convention is applicable, that vehicle will be used subject to the Council Regulation requirements.

"petition". A petition is presented in the Outer House: r. 14.2(h). The petition must be in **70.5.2** Form 14.4 in the official printed form: rr. 4.1 and 14.4. The petition must be signed by counsel or other person having a right of audience: r. 4.2; and see r. 1.3(1) (definition of "counsel" and "other person having a right of audience") and note 1.3.4.

The petitioner must lodge the petition with the required steps of process (r. 4.4). A fee is payable on lodging the petition: see note 14.5.10.

On petitions generally, see Chap. 14.

Hague Convention country. A Contracting State to which the Hague Convention applies **70.5.3** between it and the U.K. and the dates on which the convention came into force between them are specified in Orders in Council: Act of 1985, s. 2.

The countries to which the convention currently applies are listed in the Child Abduction and Custody (Parties to Conventions) Order 1986 [S.I. 1986 No. 1159], Sched. 1 as substituted by the Child Abduction and Custody (Parties to Conventions) (Amendment) Order 2005 [S.I. 2005 No. 1260]. The countries (with the dates of coming into force in brackets) are as follows:—

Argentina (1st June 1991)
Australia (Australian States and mainland Territories—1st January 1987)
Austria (1st October 1988)
The Bahamas (1st January 1994)
Belarus (1st September 2003)
Belgium (1st May 1999)
Belize (1st October 1989)
Bosnia and Herzegovina (7th April 1992)
Brazil (1st March 2005)
Burkina Faso (1st August 1992)
Canada:
 Ontario (1st August 1986)
 New Brunswick (1st August 1986)
 British Columbia (1st August 1986)
 Manitoba (1st August 1986)
 Nova Scotia (1st August 1986)
 Newfoundland (1st August 1986)
 Prince Edward Island (1st August 1986)
 Quebec (1st August 1986)
 Yukon Territory (1st August 1986)
 Saskatchewan (1st November 1986)
 Alberta (1st February 1987)
 Northwest Territories (1st April 1988)
Chile (1st May 1994)
China:
 Hong Kong Special Administrative Region (1st September 1997)
 Macau Special Administrative Region (1st March 1999)
Colombia (1st March 1996)
Croatia (1st December 1991)
Cyprus (1st February 1995)
Czech Republic (1st March 1998)
Denmark (1st July 1991)
Ecuador (1st April 1992)
Estonia (1st October 2003)
Fiji (1st October 2003)
Finland (1st August 1994)
France (1st August 1986)
Georgia (1st October 1997)
Germany (1st December 1990)

Greece (1st June 1993)
Honduras (1st March 1994)
Hungary (1st September 1986)
Iceland (1st November 1996)
Republic of Ireland (1st October 1991)
Israel (1st December 1991)
Italy (1st May 1995)
Latvia (1st October 2003)
Lithuania (1st March 2005)
Luxembourg (1st January 1987)
Macau SAR, China (1st March 1999)
Macedonia (1st December 1991)
Malta (1st March 2002)
Mauritius (1st June 1993)
Mexico (1st September 1991)
Monaco (1st February 1993)
Netherlands (1st September 1990)
New Zealand (1st August 1991)
Norway (1st April 1989)
Panama (1st May 1994)
Peru (1st October 2003)
Poland (1st November 1992)
Portugal (1st August 1986)
Macau (1st March 1999)
Romania (1st February 1993)
St Kitts and Nevis (1st August 1994)
Serbia and Montenegro (1st December 1991)
Slovakia (1st February 2001)
Slovenia (1st June 1994)
South Africa (1st October 1997)
Spain (1st September 1987)
Sweden (1st June 1989)
Switzerland (1st August 1986)
Turkey (1st August 2001)
Turkmenistan (1st March 1998)
Venezuela (1st January 1997)
United States (1st July 1988)
Venezuela (1st January 1997)
Uruguay (1st October 2003)
Uzbekistan (1st October 2003)
Yugoslavia (1st December 1991)
Zimbabwe (1st July 1995)

The Act and the convention do not apply to a removal or retention of a child committed before the convention comes into force in relation to a particular country: *Kilgour v. Kilgour* 1987 S.C. 55. "Retention" means an initial act not a continuing retention, so that it would not apply to retaining a child after the convention came into force who was removed before it came into force: *Kilgour*, above.

The common law applies in respect of a country to which the convention does not apply: see note 70.5.5.

70.5.4   *Application for the return of a child.* The removal or retention of a child is wrongful where it is in breach of custody rights of a person under the law of the country in which the child was habitually resident before the removal or retention and those rights were exercised at the time of the removal or retention: Act of 1985, Sched. 1, Art. 3. Removal and retention are mutually exclusive concepts, and removal or retention does not mean removal or retention out of the care of the parent having custody rights but removal or retention out of the jurisdiction of the courts of the state of a child's habitual residence: *In re H (Minors) (Abduction: Custody Rights)* [1991] 2 A.C. 476, 500 *per* Lord Brandon of Oakbrook; and see *Findlay v. Findlay* 1994 S.L.T. 709. A right of access is not within the meaning of "rights of custody" in Art. 3: *Pirrie v. Sawacki* 1997 S.C.L.R. 59. Following the coming into force of the Children (Scotland) Act 1995, a parent not having a residence order but who has, or has not lost, parental rights (other than merely a right of contact) will have a right of custody order under Art. 3. Note the provisions in s. 2 of the

1995 Act about wrongful removal from the U.K. of a child habitually resident in Scotland.

The general policy of the Hague Convention, which the court has to bear in mind, is to achieve the return forthwith of children wrongfully rendered or retained to the State of their habitual residence which State would normally become the jurisdiction in which questions of custody and access would be determined: *Singh v. Singh* 1998 S.C. 68.

It is not a pre-condition of an application under s. 8 of the Act of 1985 to have the removal of a child declared wrongful that a request must have been made under Art. 15 of the Hague Convention by the judicial or administrative authority of a contracting state: *A.J. v. F.J.* [2005] CSIH 36, 29th April 2005, 2005 G.W.D. 15-251 (Second Div.).

An habitual residence is one enjoyed voluntarily with a settled intention that it should continue for some time; in the case of a child this will be chosen by his parents and, where his parents separate, cannot be changed by one parent without the consent of the other: *Dickson v. Dickson* 1990 S.C.L.R. 692, 703B *per* L.P. Hope; and see *Zenel v. Haddow* 1993 S.C. 612, 616F (where the authorities are referred to by Lord Marnoch), *Findlay v. Findlay (No. 2)* 1995 S.L.T. 492. There is no minimum period necessary in order to establish the acquisition of a new habitual residence: *Cameron v. Cameron* 1996 S.C. 17. In that case the opinion was expressed that a person can have only one habitual residence at any one time. The word "settled" as an element of habitual residence relates to one's purpose in living where one does and not to settlement in the sense of permanent or long-term residence, because habitual residence might be only for a limited period: *Moran v. Moran*, 1997 S.L.T. 541.

"Custody rights" are those which arise by operation of law, a judicial or administrative decision, or by agreement having legal effect: Act of 1985, Sched. 1, Art. 3; and see, *e.g. McKiver v. McKiver* 1995 S.L.T. 790. They include rights of contact by virtue of the fact that s. 2(3) and (6) of the Children (Scotland) Act 1995 confers on the contact parent the right to grant or withhold consent to the child's removal from the UK: *A.J. v. F.J.*, above.

The expression "rights relating to the care of the person of the child" in Art. 5 (custody rights) does not include the rights of a parent with access rights when the child is not in that parent's actual care: *Seroka v. Bellah* 1995 S.L.T. 204. In that case Lord Prosser at p. 210I–L doubted whether a court having power to deal with custody could be said to have rights of custody: *cf.* England in *B v. B* [1993] Fam. 32.

A wrongful removal or retention in breach of custody rights means less than full legal determination of custody rights and whether they have been breached, and the requirements of Art. 3 of Sched. 1 may be satisfied where removal is not challenged or seriously challenged as wrongful or if the removal was *prima facie* wrongful: *Perrin v. Perrin* 1994 S.C. 45. A court acquires rights of custody when an application for custody and access is made to it, and removal of a child from the jurisdiction of such a court even though only access had by then been dealt with: *O v. O*, 2002 S.C. 430 (OH).

Subject to Art. 13, a child must be returned forthwith if a period of less than one year has elapsed from the date of the wrongful removal or retention; and the child must also be returned after a year has elapsed unless the child is settled in its new environment: Act of 1985, Sched. 1, Art. 12. Where the lapse of time after the expiry of one year is short, the quality of evidence relied on to establish settlement has to be good: *Perrin*, above, at p. 51F. The concept of settlement appears to have two elements, a physical element relating to a community and an environment and an emotional element denoting security and stability: *Perrin*, above, at p. 51H. On the issue of settlement, the proper question is not just a balancing exercise between the interests of the child and the requirement of the convention but whether the child was so settled in the new environment that the court would be justified in disregarding an otherwise mandatory requirement to have the child returned: *Soucie v. Soucie* 1995 S.L.T. 414.

The court is not bound to return a child if the respondent establishes (a) that the person having care of the child was not actually exercising the custody rights or consented or acquiesced in the removal or retention, or (b) there is a grave risk that the child's return would expose the child to physical or psychological harm or otherwise place the child in an intolerable situation: Act of 1985, Sched. 1, Art. 13. Only in the clearest of cases should the court exercise this discretion: *Taylor v. Ford* 1993 S.L.T. 654, 658B *per* Temp. Judge Horsburgh, Q.C. In relation to ground (a), consent to removal of a child does not require to be connected in time to the actual removal: *Zenel v. Haddow* 1993 S.C. 612, 624G–A *per* Lord Allanbridge, and 628H *per* Lord Mayfield; Lord Morton of Shuna, dissenting at p. 629F–B, was of the opinion that the consent must relate to the particular act of removal. A person does not cease to exercise custody rights simply because he or she is in hospital: *S v. S*, 2003 S.L.T. 344; or ill: *A.J. v. F.J.*, above. The onus is on the parent who asserts consent to removal to prove that it was: *T v. T*, 2003 S.L.T. 1316 (First Div.) In relation to ground (b), one is concerned with exposure to harm as a consequence of return and not an exposure to harm which might emerge at a future time: *McCarthy v. McCarthy* 1994 S.L.T. 743. If there is a grave risk about the child's return it is not for the court to speculate whether arrangements can be made to obviate the risk as this is contrary to the spirit of the convention for the immediate and summary return of the child: *MacMillan v. MacMillan* 1989 S.C. 53. In *Cameron v. Cameron (No. 2)* 1997 S.L.T. 206 it was held that, while returning a child might result in increasing the risk of psychological damage, it was not established that the return would present a grave risk of exposure to the severe degree required by art. 13. The duty to take into account the social background of the child does not mean that there has to be a social background report: *Viola v. Viola* 1988 S.L.T. 7.

The court may also refuse to order the return of the child if the child objects to being returned and has attained an age and degree of understanding at which it is appropriate to take account of his views: Act of 1985, Sched. 1, Art. 13; the word "objects" is not to be construed narrowly: *Urness v. Minto* 1994 S.C. 249 (preference to remain in Scotland was objection to return to USA). In *Cameron*, above, it was held that, though the eldest child was articulate and confident, there was no basis for attributing to her a maturity greater than her seven years and she had not therefore attained the age or degree of maturity at which her views would be taken into account. The factors of objection and maturity do not merely open the door to an exercise of the court's discretion but are themselves factors to be taken into account in exercising that discretion; and also the court has to bear in mind the general policy of the convention: *Singh v. Singh* 1998 S.C. 68. There are difficulties in interviewing a child on this issue, and some of the difficulties and points to be covered are dealt with in *W v. W*, 2003 S.L.T. 1253, 1259A–G, paras. [29]–[31] (First Div.); *cf M, Ptnr*, 2005 S.L.T. 2 (OH).

The country to which the child has been taken cannot decide on the merits of the rights of custody until it has been determined that the child is not to be returned or the application under the convention is not lodged within a reasonable time: Act of 1985, Sched. 1, Art. 16.

70.5.5   *Common law.* The common law applies where the Hague Convention does not. A decree for custody of a court furth of the U.K. will be recognised here if made by the court of the country where the child was habitually resident: Family Law Act 1986, s. 26. The foreign order will, however, only be given grave consideration and will not be automatically or blindly enforced, the court treating the child's welfare as the first and paramount consideration: see *Campins v. Campins* 1979 S.L.T.(Notes) 41; *Sinclair v. Sinclair* 1988 S.L.T. 87. In England the principles of the Hague Convention are applied in a non-Convention case provided that the courts of the country of the child's habitual residence apply principles acceptable to the English courts: *Re S (Minors) (Abduction)* [1994] 1 F.L.R. 297.

A decree for custody of a court in the U.K. furth of Scotland will be recognised and have effect in Scotland if the court had jurisdiction to make it, and it can be enforced here if registered in the Court of Session: Family Law Act 1986, ss. 25 and 27; and see Chap. 71 for registration and enforcement of such decrees.

70.5.6   *"certified or authorised copy of any relevant decision".* A decision of a judicial or administrative authority furth of the U.K. may be proved by an authenticated copy: Act of 1985, s. 7.

70.5.7   *"relevant authority".* See r. 70.1.

70.5.8   *"evidence of witnesses by affidavits and any documentary evidence".* This is a new provision introduced by A.S. (R.C.S.A. No. 3) (Miscellaneous) 1996 [S.I. 1996 No. 1756] to expedite the determination of such cases (on which, see further note 70.6.20).

The rule is that the affidavits and documentary evidence must be lodged with the petition: r. 70.5(2)(c) and (3)(c). There may be circumstances in which it is not possible to lodge these documents with the petition, *e.g.* where the petition has to be lodged as a matter of urgency for the purpose of seeking an interim order. In such a case the court should be asked to dispense with the requirement to lodge the documents with the petition under r. 2.1. The court should, however, fix a period within which such documents must be lodged thereafter.

An affidavit should be in the form of a statement of evidence written in the first person. The affidavit should contain evidence in support of, and expanding on, the averments in the pleadings. It should be sworn or affirmed and signed by the deponent before any person who may competently take an oath. Such a person includes a notary, a justice of the peace, a sheriff or any judge (or in England a commissioner for oaths (includes any barrister or solicitor)). The person taking the oath or affirmation should also sign the affidavit. Witnesses are unnecessary. And see the definition of affidavit in r. 1.3(1).

Affidavits are lodged as steps of process and may be lodged by post: P.N. No. 4 of 1994, paras 1 and 8; and see note 4.4.10. They must also be served, with any documentary evidence, with the petition on the party to whom the petition is served: r. 70.6(2).

Where there are contradictions between affidavits, and no other evidence to support a conclusion on way or the other, no conclusion can be drawn by the court: *D v. D*, 2002 S.C. 33, 37D (Extra Div.).

In relation to children, it should be noted that in giving oral evidence a child under 12 is admonished to tell the truth, a child between 12 and 14 is sworn or admonished at the judge's discretion and a child over 14 is usually sworn. A child under the age of 14 should not normally swear an affidavit for two reasons: first, he is too young to be sworn (and the judge has no means of assessing the matter himself); and secondly, if the proceedings relate to him, his views should be ascertained in some other way (*e.g.* the appointment of a curator *ad litem*) so as to avoid the child being forced to take sides by one of the parties in a dispute about him. The court may have to ascertain the views of the child for the purposes of Art. 13(2) of Sched. 1 to the Act of 1985 (child objecting to being returned).

Applications with respect to access to a child. Questions of access may arise "under" the **70.5.9** Hague Convention, although there may be some application that may be so different from the original order as to be essentially a new one, the convention no longer being in point: see *Donofrio v. Burrell,* 2000 S.L.T. 1051 (Extra Div.). Doubts expressed in *Donofrio* about the use of the phrase "application for access to a child under the Hague Convention" formerly used in r. 70.5(2) have been addressed by substituting words used in Art. 21 of the Convention: A.S. (R.C.A. No. 4) (Miscellaneous) 2001 [S.S.I. 2001 No. 305].

It has been suggested in *Donofrio, per* Lord Prosser at p.1057J, that the need for the special provisions for applications for access under r. 70.5(2) should be reconsidered. The convention is concerned with urgent action to maintain the status quo on a short-term basis. Applications for access do not call for unusual expedition. The convention does not force a party to invoke it. Furthermore, r. 70.5(2) creates a procedure different from that in Chap. 49 for dealing with applications for access and is unhelpful to the satisfactory conduct of such applications. Lord Prosser's request was not taken up in A.S. (R.C.S.A. No.4) (Miscellaneous) 2001 [S.S.I. 2001 No. 305].

[1] *Period of notice, service of causes and hearings under this Part*
   70.6.—(1) Subject to rule 14.6(2), the period of notice for lodging answers to a petition to which rule 70.5 applies shall be four days.
   [1,4] (2) Subject to rule 70.16 (intimation of notice on child), such a petition, and a copy of any affidavit and documentary evidence lodged with it, shall be served on—
   (a) the person alleged to have brought the child into the United Kingdom;
   (b) the person with whom the child is presumed to be;
   (c) any parent or guardian of the child if he or she is within the United Kingdom, or a relevant territory and not otherwise a party;
   [3] (d) the chief executive of the local authority, and for the area in which the child resides and the Principal Reporter; and
   (e) any other person who may have an interest in the child.
   [1] (3) The first order under rule 14.5 (first order in petitions) in a petition to which rule 70.5 applies shall specify a date within seven days after the expiry of the period of notice for a first hearing to determine the further progress of the petition.
   [2] (4) A respondent shall lodge in process, and send a copy to the petitioner of, the evidence by affidavits of any witnesses and any documentary evidence, whether originals or copies initially, in support of his answers to the petition at least 3 days before the first hearing fixed under paragraph (3).
   [2,4] (5) Subject to rule 70.17 (views of the child), at the first hearing fixed under paragraph (3), the court—
   (a) shall determine to what extent, if any, further evidence by affidavit is required, by whom and in regard to what matters, and by what date any such affidavit should be lodged;
   (b) may, on special cause shown, direct that a particular matter should be the subject of oral evidence in lieu of further, or in addition to, affidavit evidence; and
   (c) may, if no further evidence is required, determine the petition at the first hearing or, if further evidence is required, shall give directions as to the period within which a second hearing shall be held to determine the petition.

Deriv. R.C.S. 1965, r. 260J(4) inserted by S.I. 1986 No. 1955, and r. 260J(5) inserted by S.I. 1986 No. 1955 and amended by S.I. 1991 No. 1157 (r. 70.6(1) and (2))

---

[1] R. 70.6(2) and (3) and heading amended by S.I. 1996 No. 1756 (effective 5th August 1996).
[2] R. 70.6(4) and (5) inserted by S.I. 1996 No. 1756 (effective 5th August 1996).
[3] R. 70.6(2)(d) amended by S.I. 1998 No. 890 (effective 21st April 1998).
[4] R. 70(6)(2) and r. 70(6)(5) amended by S.S.I. 2005 No. 135 (effective 2nd March 2005).

70.6.1   *"served"*. For service, see Chap. 16, Pt. I.

70.6.1A   *"Subject to rule 70.16"* and *"Subject to rule 70.17"*. Where a child habitually resident in a Member State of the E.U. has been removed to or retained in another Member State, the requirements of the Council Regulation No. 2201/2003 about giving the child an opportunity to be heard will apply: see art. 11 of the Council Regulation and note 70.5.1A. Intimation is required on the child unless inappropriate (see r. 70.16) and a form sent for the child to complete if he wishes (r. 70.17).

70.6.2   *First and second hearings.* R. 70.6(3) is designed to achieve expedition. Art. 11(1) of the Hague Convention requires expedition. If the court has not reached a decision within six weeks of the commencement of the proceedings a request may be made for a statement of reasons for the delay: Act of 1985, Sched. 1, Art. 11(2). The Court of Session has been criticised for the length of time it takes to make decisions (rarely within the six weeks) and for its inability to accept the concept of affidavit evidence.

A new procedure has, therefore, been introduced by A.S. (R.C.S.A. No. 3) (Miscellaneous) 1996 [S.I. 1996 No. 1756] following recommendations of the Cullen Report on the Business of the Outer House (1995). Affidavits must be lodged by the petitioner with the petition (r. 70 5(2)(c) or (3)(c)) and by the respondent with his answers (r. 70.6(4)). At a first hearing under r. 70.6(5), the court will determine, at its own instance or at the request of a party, whether and to what extent any further affidavit evidence is required or whether oral evidence is necessary in lieu of further, or in addition to, affidavit evidence. If further oral evidence is required at the second hearing, the interlocutor appointing that hearing must grant warrant for the citation of witnesses.

The court may determine the petition at the first hearing if it considers it has enough material before it to reach a decision. Parties must be prepared for that eventuality.

Where a second hearing is ordered, the court must, in giving directions for that hearing under r. 70.6(5)(c), fix a period to comply (if possible) with the six weeks deadline in Art. 11(2).

In England, it has been held that proceedings under the Hague Convention are summary in nature, that there was no right to give oral evidence and that there was a danger if oral evidence were generally admitted it would become impossible to deal with such cases expeditiously: *Re A.F. (A Minor) (Abduction)* [1992] 1 F.C.R. 269. In that case it was decided that oral evidence should be used sparingly; where the issue had to be decided on disputed non-oral evidence, the judge had to see if there was extraneous evidence in support of one side; evidence had to be compelling before the judge was entitled to reject sworn evidence of a deponent or, alternatively, the evidence in the affidavit might be so inherently improbable that he was entitled to reject it; and if there were no grounds for rejecting the written evidence of either side, the applicant would have failed to establish his case.

70.6.2A   *"evidence of witnesses by affidavits and any documentary evidence"*. This is a new provision introduced by A.S. (R.C.S.A. No. 3) (Miscellaneous) 1996 [S.I. 1996 No. 1756] to expedite the determination of such cases (on which, see note 70.6.2).

On affidavits, see note 70.5.8.

70.6.3   *Fee.* The court fee for each of the hearings to determine further procedure and the full hearing is payable by each party for every 30 minutes or part thereof. For fee, see Court of Session etc. Fees Order 1997, Table of Fees, Pt. I, C, item 18 [S.I. 1997 No. 688, as amended, pp. C 1201 *et seq.*]. Certain persons are exempt from payment of fees: see 1997 Fees Order, art. 5 substituted by S.S.I. 2002 No. 270. A fee exemption certificate must be lodged in process: see P.N. No.1 of 2002.

Where the petitioner is legally represented, the fee may be debited under a credit scheme introduced on 1st April 1976 by P.N. No. 4 of 1976 to the account (if one is kept or permitted) of the agent by the court cashier, and an account will be rendered weekly by the court cashier's office to the agent for all court fees due that week for immediate settlement. An agent not on the credit scheme will have an account opened for the purpose of lodging the fee: P.N. No. 2 of 1995. A debit slip and a copy of the court hearing time sheet will be delivered to the agent's box or sent by DX or post.

A party litigant must pay (by cash, cheque or postal order) to the clerk of court at the end of the hearing or, if the hearing lasts more than a day, at the end of each day: P.N. No. 2 of 1995.

A receipt will be issued. The assistant clerk of session will acknowledge receipt of the sum received from the clerk of court on the Minute of Proceedings.

"relevant territory". See r. 70.1 and note 70.1.2.   **70.6.4**

Notice of other proceedings

70.7.—(1) Where a petition is presented under paragraph (1) of rule 70.5 and there are proceedings mentioned in section 9 of the Act of 1985 relating to the merits of the rights of custody of the child depending in or before a relevant authority, the court shall give written intimation of the petition and, in due course of the outcome of the petition, to that relevant authority.

(2) Where the court receives a notice equivalent to that under paragraph (1) from a relevant authority, all proceedings in any cause mentioned in section 9 of the Act of 1985 relating to the merits of the rights of custody of the child shall be sisted by the court until the dismissal of the proceedings in that other court under the Hague Convention; and the Deputy Principal Clerk shall give written intimation to each party of the sist and of any such dismissal.

Deriv. R.C.S. 1965, r. 260J(7) and (8) inserted by S.I. 1986 No. 1955

General note. A decision on the merits of rights of custody (as defined by s. 9 of the Act of **70.7.1** 1985) cannot be taken in the country to which the child has been wrongfully taken until it has been decided that the child is not to be returned or the application for return of the child is not lodged within a reasonable time: Act of 1985, Sched. 1, Art. 16.

"written intimation". For methods, see r. 16.9.   **70.7.2**

Transfer of causes

70.8.—[1] (1) At any stage of a cause mentioned in paragraph (1) of rule 70.5, the court may, at its own instance or on the motion of any party, pronounce an interlocutor transmitting the cause to the High Court in England and Wales or Northern Ireland, or the appropriate court of a relevant territory, as the case may be.

(2) Where a cause is transferred under paragraph (1), the Deputy Principal Clerk shall—

[1] (a) transmit the process to the appropriate officer of the High Court in England and Wales or Northern Ireland, or the appropriate court of a relevant territory, as the case may be;

(b) give written intimation of such transfer to each party; and

(c) certify on the interlocutor sheet that such written intimation has been given.

(3) Where a cause is transferred under paragraph (1), the question of expenses shall not be determined by the court, but shall be at the discretion of the court to which the cause is transferred.

[1] (4) Where such a cause is transferred to the court from the High Court in England and Wales or Northern Ireland, or the appropriate court of a relevant territory—

(a) the Deputy Principal Clerk shall, on receipt of the order transferring the cause and any documents in the cause, give written intimation to each party of the transfer;

(b) the cause shall be deemed to have been commenced by petition; and

(c) the Deputy Principal Clerk shall, within two sederunt days of the receipt of it, cause it to be put out on the By Order Roll before the Lord Ordinary.

Deriv. R.C.S. 1965, r. 260J(9) to (12) inserted by S.I. 1986 No. 1955

---

[1] R. 70.8(1), (2)(a) and (4) amended by S.I. 1996 No. 1756 (effective 5th August 1996).

70.8.1   *General note.* Transfer of an application will arise if the child has moved from Scotland to another jurisdiction in the U.K. (or was never here) or from another jurisdiction in the U.K. to Scotland and saves time and the expense of raising fresh proceedings.

70.8.2   *"written intimation".* For methods, see r. 16.9.

70.8.3   *"relevant territory".* See r. 70.1 and note 70.1.2.

PART III

RECOGNITION AND ENFORCEMENT OF CUSTODY DECISIONS
(THE EUROPEAN CONVENTION)

Form of applications under this Part

70.9.—(1) An application under any of the following provisions shall be made by petition:—

(a) section 15 of the Act of 1985 (application to declare a decree for custody not to be recognised);

(b) section 16 of the Act of 1985 (application for registration of custody decision); and

(c) section 18 of the Act of 1985 (application for enforcement of custody decision).

(2) An application under section 17(4) of the Act of 1985 (application for variation or revocation of registered decision), shall be made by note in the process of the petition for registration.

(3) An application under section 23(2) of the Act of 1985 (application in custody proceedings for declarator that removal of a child was unlawful), shall be made—

(a) by minute in the process of a cause depending before the court commenced by summons; or

(b) by note in the process of a cause depending before the court commenced by petition.

[1] (4) In an application mentioned in this rule—

(a) the petition, minute or note, as the case may be, shall include averments in relation to—

(i) the identity of the petitioner, minuter or noter, as the case may be, and his interest in the cause;

(ii) the identity of the child and his date of birth;

(iii) the parents or guardians of the child;

(iv) the order which is required to be registered, enforced, declared unlawful, declared not recognised, varied or revoked, as the case may be;

(v) the whereabouts or suspected whereabouts of the child; and

(vi) any civil cause in dependence before any other court or authority in respect of the child, or any proceedings specified in section 20(2) of the Act of 1985 in dependence in or before a relevant authority;

(b) there shall be produced with the petition, minute or note, as the case may be—

(i) a certified or authorised copy of any decision to be registered or enforced;

(ii) where a decision to be registered was given in the absence of the person against whom the decision was made or in the absence of his legal representative, a document which establishes (subject to Article 9(1)(a) of the European Convention) that that person was duly served with the document which instituted the original proceedings;

(iii) a certificate or affidavit to the effect that any decision to be registered is enforceable in accordance with the law of the State in which the decision was made; and

    (iv) any other relevant document; and
  (c) there shall be lodged with the petition, minute or note, as the case may be, the evidence by affidavits of any witnesses and any documentary evidence, whether originals or copies initially, in support of the petition, minute or note.

Deriv. R.C.S. 1965, r. 260K(1) to (5) inserted by S.I. 1986 No. 1955

---

[1] R. 70.9(4) amended by S.I. 1996 No. 1756 (effective 5th August 1996).

General note. The Act of 1985 implements the European Convention on the Recognition and Enforcement of Decisions Concerning Custody of Children 1980 (Cmnd. 8281 (1981)). The convention is set out in Sched. 2 to the Act.   **70.9.1**

A decision concerning custody means a decision in so far as it relates to the care of the person of a child including the right to decide on the place of his residence or access to him: Act of 1985, Sched. 2, Art. 1(c). The convention applies to a child under the age of 16 years: Act of 1985, Sched. 2, Art. 1(a).

A decision relating to custody given in a Contracting State shall be recognised and enforceable in another Contracting State (Act of 1985, Sched. 2, Art. 7), but it is not enforceable in Scotland unless it has been registered in the Court of Session (Act of 1985, ss. 15 and 16).

Jurisdiction. The jurisdiction of the court to deal with applications under the European Convention is subject to the rule that in relations between member states of the E.U. the Council Regulation (EC) No. 2201/2003 of 27th November 2003 concerning jurisdiction and enforcement of judgments in matrimonial matters and matters of parental responsibility (new Brussels II) takes precedence: 1985 Act, s. 12(3) amended by the European Community (Matrimonial and Parental Responsibility Jurisdiction and Judgments (Scotland) Regulations 2005 [S.S.I. 2005 No. 42]; and art. 60 of the Council Regulation. This replaces Council Regulation 1347/2000 of 29th May 2000 (Brussels II) and the 1985 Act s. 12(3) as inserted by S.S.I. 2000 No.36. The primary ground under the Council Regulation 2201/2003 for a Member State to make decisions about parental responsibilities is habitual residence of the child in that Member State at the time the court in that state is seized of the matter: art. 8, but see arts. 9, 10 and 12.   **70.9.1A**

For recognition and enforcement of decisions relating to parental responsibility (including custody and access) under the Council Regulation No 2001/2003, see Chap. 62, Pt. XI, rr. 62.67 to 62.80.

"petition". A petition is presented in the Outer House: r. 14.2(h). The petition must be in Form 14.4 in the official printed form: rr. 4.1 and 14.4. The petition must be signed by counsel or other person having a right of audience: r. 4.2; and see r. 1.3(1) (definition of "counsel" and "other person having a right of audience") and note 1.3.4.   **70.9.2**

The petitioner must lodge the petition with the required steps of process (r. 4.4). A fee is payable on lodging the petition: see note 14.5.10.

On petitions generally, see Chap. 14.

European Convention country. A Contracting State to which the European Convention applies between it and the U.K. and the dates on which the convention came into force between them are specified in Orders in Council: Act of 1985, s. 13.   **70.9.3**

The countries to which the convention currently applies are listed in the Child Abduction and Custody (Parties to Conventions) Order 1986 [S.I. 1986 No. 1159], Sched. 2 as substituted by the Child Abduction and Custody (Parties to Conventions) (Amendment) Order 2003 [S.I. 2003 No. 1260]. The countries (with the dates of coming into force in brackets) are as follows:—

Austria (1st August 1986)	Iceland (1st November 1996)
Belgium (1st August 1986)	Republic of Ireland (1st October 1991)
Bulgaria (1st October 2003)	Italy (1st June 1995)
Cyprus (1st October 1986)	Latvia (1st August 2002)
Czech Republic (1st July 2000)	Liechtenstein (1st August 1997)
Denmark (1st August 1991)	Lithuania (1st May 2003)
Estonia (1st September 2001)	Luxembourg (1st August 1986)
Finland (1st August 1994)	Macedonia (1st March 2003)
France (1st August 1986)	Malta (1st February 2000)
Germany (1st February 1991)	Moldova (1st May 2004)
Greece (1st July 1993)	Netherlands (1st September 1990)
Hungary (1st June 2004)	Norway (1st May 1989)

Poland (1st March 1996)*
Portugal (1st August 1986)
Romania (1st September 2004)
Serbia and Montenegro (1st May 2002)
Slovakia (1st September 2001)

Spain (1st August 1986)
Sweden (1st July 1989)
Switzerland (1st August 1986)
Turkey (1st June 2000)

* Poland appeared in Sched. 2 to the 1986 Order by virtue of the Child Abduction and Custody (Parties to Conventions) (Amendment) Order 1996 [S.I. 1996 No. 269] on the European Convention coming into force as between that country and the U.K. on 1st March 1996, but was omitted in error from the amendment orders S.I. 1996 Nos. 2595 and 2874. It reappeared in S.I. 1997 No. 1747.

70.9.4   *Recognition and enforcement of custody orders.* A custody order of a Contracting State will be recognised unless declared not recognised by the court on an application to it: Act of 1985, s. 15(2). To be enforced here the foreign order must be registered in the Court of Session: Act of 1985, s. 15(2). An application for enforcement must be granted unless a ground in s. 16(4) is established: these are (a) the grounds specified in Sched. 2, Art. 9 or 10 (see, *e.g. Campins-Coll, Petr.* 1988 S.C. 305), (b) the decision is not enforceable in the Contracting State and is not a decision to which Art. 12 (no enforceable decision there when child removed) applies, or (c) an application under Pt. I of the Act of 1985 (international child abduction under the Hague Convention) is pending.

70.9.5   *"minute".* For applications by minute, see r. 15.1.

70.9.6   *"note".* For applications by note, see r. 15.2.

70.9.7   *"depending", "in dependence".* A cause is depending from the time it is commenced (*i.e.* from the time an action is served or a first order in a petition is made) until final decree, whereas a cause is in dependence until final extract. For the meaning of commenced, see note 13.4.4 (action) or 14.6.1 (petition). For the meaning of final decree, see note 4.15.2(2). For the meaning of final extract, see note 7.1.2(2).

70.9.8   *"relevant authority".* See r. 70.1.

70.9.9   *"evidence of witnesses by affidavits and any documentary evidence".* This is a new provision introduced by A.S. (R.C.S.A. No. 3) (Miscellaneous) 1996 [S.I. 1996 No. 1756] to expedite the determination of such cases (on which see further note 70.6.20).
   The rule is that the affidavits and documentary evidence must be lodged with the petition: r. 70.9(4)(c). There may be circumstances in which it is not possible to lodge these documents with the petition, e.g. where the petition has to be lodged as a matter of urgency for the purpose of seeking an interim order. In such a case the court should be asked to dispense with the requirement to lodge the documents with the petition under r. 2.1. The court should, however, fix a period within which such documents must be lodged thereafter.
   An affidavit should be in the form of a statement of evidence written in the first person. The affidavit should contain evidence in support of, and expanding on, the averments in the pleadings. It should be sworn or affirmed and signed by the deponent before any person who may competently take an oath. Such a person includes a notary, a justice of the peace, a sheriff or any judge (or in England a commissioner for oaths (includes, any barrister or solicitor). The person taking the oath or affirmation should also sign the affidavit. Witnesses are unnecessary. And see the definition of affidavit in r. 1.3(1).
   Affidavits are lodged as step of process and may be lodged by post: P.N. No. 4 of 1994, paras. 1 and 8; and see note 4.4.10. They must also be served, with any documentary evidence, with the petition on the party to whom the petition is served: r. 70.6(2).
   In relation to children, it should be noted that in giving oral evidence a child under 12 is admonished to tell the truth, a child between 12 and 14 is sworn or admonished at the judge's discretion and a child over 14 is usually sworn. A child under the age of 14 should not normally swear an affidavit for two reasons: first, he is too young to be sworn and the judge has no means of assessing the matter himself; and secondly, if the proceedings relate to him, his views should be ascertained in some other way (*e.g.* the appointment of a curator *ad litem*) so as to avoid the child being forced to take sides by one of the parties in a dispute about him. The court may have to obtain the child's views in relation to an application under s. 16 of the Act of 1985 (registration of decisions) by virtue of Art. 15(1)(a) of Sched. 2 to that Act.

[THE NEXT PAGE IS C 615]

[1] *Period of notice, service of causes and hearings under this Part*

70.10.—(1) Subject to rule 14.6(2), the period of notice for lodging answers in a petition to which rule 70.9 applies shall be four days.

[1] (2) Such a petition, and a copy of any affidavit and documentary evidence lodged with it, shall be served on—

(a) the person alleged to have brought the child into, or removed the child from, the United Kingdom, or a relevant territory, as the case may be;

(b) the person with whom the child is presumed to be in the United Kingdom or a relevant territory;

(c) the mother and father of the child if he or she is within the United Kingdom, or a relevant territory, and not otherwise a party;

[3] (d) the chief executive of the local authority, and for the area in which the child resides and the Principal Reporter; and

(e) any other person who may have an interest in the child.

[1] (3) The first order under rule 14.5 (first order in petitions) in a petition to which rule 70.9 applies shall specify a date within seven days after the expiry of the period of notice for a first hearing to determine the further progress of the petition.

[2] (4) A respondent shall lodge in process, and send a copy to the petitioner of, the evidence by affidavits of any witnesses and any documentary evidence, whether originals or copies initially, in support of his answers to the petition to which rule 70.9 applies at least 3 days before the first hearing fixed under paragraph (3).

(5) At the first hearing fixed under paragraph (3), the court—

(a) shall determine to what extent, if any, further evidence by affidavit is required, by whom and in regard to what matters, and by what date any such affidavit should be lodged;

(b) may, on special cause shown, direct that a particular matter should be the subject of oral evidence in lieu of further, or in addition to, affidavit evidence; and

(c) may, if no further evidence is required, determine the petition at the first hearing or, if further evidence is required, shall give directions as to the period within which a second hearing shall be held to determine the petition.

Deriv. R.C.S. 1965, r. 260K(6) inserted by S.I. 1986 No. 1955 (r. 70.10(1)); and r. 260K(8) inserted by S.I. 1986 No. 1955 and amended by S.I. 1991 No. 1157 (r. 70.10(2))

---

[1] R. 70.9(2) and (3) and heading amended by S.I. 1996 No. 1756 (effective 5th August 1996).
[2] R. 70.9(4) and (5) inserted by S.I. 1996 No. 1756 (effective 5th August 1996).
[3] R. 70.10(2)(d) amended by S.I. 1998 No. 890 (effective 21st April 1998).

"served". For service, see Chap. 16, Pt I. **70.10.1**

First and second hearings. R. 70.10(3) is designed to achieve expedition in relation to **70.10.2** applications under ss.15, 16 and 18 of the Act of 1985 (which relate to recognition and enforcement of European custody decisions). The Court of Session has been criticised for the length of time it takes to make decisions and for its inability to accept the concept of affidavit evidence.

A new procedure has, therefore, been introduced by A.S. (R.C.S.A. No. 3) (Miscellaneous) 1996 [S.I. 1996 No. 1756] following recommendations of the Cullen Report on the Business of the Outer House (1995). Affidavits must be lodged by the petitioner with the petition (r. 70 5(2)(c) or (3)(c)) and by the respondent with his answers (r. 70.6(4)). At a first hearing under r. 70.6(5), the court will determine, at its own instance or at the request of a party, whether and to what extent any further affidavit evidence is required or whether oral evidence is necessary in lieu of further, or in addition to, affidavit evidence. If further oral evidence is required at the second hearing, the interlocutor appointing that hearing must grant warrant for the citation of witnesses.

This court may determine the petition at the first hearing if it considers it has enough material before it to reach a decision. Parties must be prepared for that eventuality.

In England, it has been held that proceedings under the Hague Convention are summary in nature, that there was no right to give oral evidence and that there was a danger if oral evidence were generally admitted it would become impossible to deal with such cases expeditiously: *Re A.F. (A Minor) (Abduction)* [1992] 1 F.C.R. 269. In that case it was decided that oral evidence should be used sparingly; where the issue had to be decided on disputed non-oral evidence, the judge had to see if there was extraneous evidence in support of one side; evidence had to be compelling before the judge was entitled to reject sworn evidence of a deponent or, alternatively, the evidence in the affidavit might be so inherently improbable that he was entitled to reject it; and if there were no grounds for rejecting the written evidence of either side, the applicant would have failed to establish his case.

70.10.2A   *"evidence of witnesses by affidavits and any documentary evidence".* This is a new provision introduced by A.S. (R.C.S.A. No. 3) (Miscellaneous) 1996 [S.I. 1996 No. 1756] to expedite the determination of such cases (on which, see note 70.10.2).

On affidavits, see note 70.9.9.

70.10.3   *Fee.* The court fee for each of the hearings to determine further procedure and the full hearing is payable by each party for every 30 minutes or part thereof. For fee, see Court of Session etc. Fees Order 1997, Table of Fees, Pt I, C, item 18 [S.I. 1997 No. 688, as amended, pp. C1201 *et seq.*]. Certain persons are exempt from payment of fees: see 1997 Fees Order, art.5 substituted by S.S.I. 2002 No. 270. A fee exemption certificate must be lodged in process: see P.N. No.1 of 2002.

Where the petitioner is legally represented, the fee may be debited under a credit scheme introduced on 1st April 1976 by P.N. No. 4 of 1976 to the account (if one is kept or permitted) of the agent by the court cashier, and an account will be rendered weekly by the court cashier's office to the agent for all court fees due that week for immediate settlement. An agent not on the credit scheme will have an account opened for the purpose of lodging the fee: P.N. No. 2 of 1995. A debit slip and a copy of the court hearing time sheet will be delivered to the agent's box or sent by DX or post.

A party litigant must pay (by cash, cheque or postal order) to the clerk of court at the end of the hearing or, if the hearing lasts more than a day, at the end of each day: P.N. No. 2 of 1995. A receipt will be issued. The assistant clerk of session will acknowledge receipt of the sum received from the clerk of court on the Minute of Proceedings.

70.10.4   *"relevant territory".* See r. 70.1 and note 70.1.2.

Registration
70.11. Where the court pronounces an interlocutor ordering registration under section 16 of the Act of 1985, the Deputy Principal Clerk shall record that interlocutor in a register of decisions pronounced under that Act.

Deriv. R.C.S. 1965, r. 260K(10) inserted by S.I. 1986 No. 1955

Other proceedings
70.12.—(1) Where a petition is presented under section 16 (application for registration and enforcement of custody decision), or section 18 (application for enforcement of a custody decision), of the Act of 1985 and there are proceedings mentioned in section 20(2) of that Act depending or such proceedings are commenced after the petition has been presented—
  (a) the petitioner shall inform the court by including averments or lodging an affidavit, as the case may be, to that effect containing a concise statement of the nature of those proceedings; and
  (b) the court shall give written intimation of the petition and, in due course of the outcome of the petition, to the relevant authority.
[1] (2) Where the court receives a notice equivalent to that under paragraph (1)(b) from the High Court in England and Wales or Northern Ireland, or the appropriate court of a relevant territory, the Deputy Principal Clerk shall give written intimation to each party to any cause which is one mentioned in section 20(2) of the Act of 1985.

Deriv. R.C.S. 1965, r. 260K(11) and (12) inserted by S.I. 1986 No. 1955

---

[1] R. 70.12(2) amended by S.I. 1996 No. 1756 (effective 5th August 1996)

General note. Proceedings mentioned in s. 20(2) of the Act of 1985 which are pending may not   **70.12.1**
be determined after an application has been made for registration of a custody decision (other
than a decision relating to rights of access), or such a decision is registered, and the decision was
made before the proceedings which are pending unless the application for registration has been
refused: Act of 1985, s. 20(1).

"depending". A cause is depending from the time it is commenced (*i.e.* from the time an action is   **70.12.2**
served or a first order in a petition is made) until final decree, whereas a cause is in dependence
until final extract. For the meaning of commenced, see note 13.4.4 (action) or 14.6.1 (petition). For
the meaning of final decree, see note 4.15.2(2). For the meaning of final extract, see note 7.1.2(2).

"written intimation". For methods, see r. 16.9.   **70.12.3**

"relevant territory". See r. 70.1 and note 70.1.2.   **70.12.4**

Transfers

70.13.—[1] (1) At any stage of a cause mentioned in rule 70.9, the court
may, at its own instance or on the motion of any party, pronounce an
interlocutor transferring the cause to the High Court in England and Wales
or Northern Ireland, or the appropriate court of a relevant territory, as the
case may be.

(2) Where a cause is transferred under paragraph (1), the Deputy
Principal Clerk shall forthwith—
[1] (a) transmit the process to the appropriate officer of the High Court in
England and Wales or Northern Ireland, or the appropriate court of
a relevant territory, as the case may be;
  (b) give written intimation of such transfer to each party; and
  (c) certify on the interlocutor sheet that such written intimation has been
given.

(3) Where a cause is transferred under paragraph (1), the question of
expenses shall not be determined by the court, but shall be at the discretion
of the court to which the case is transferred.

[1] (4) Where such a cause is transferred to the court from the High Court in
England and Wales or Northern Ireland, or the appropriate court of a
relevant territory—
  (a) the Deputy Principal Clerk shall, on receipt of the order transferring
the cause and any papers in the cause, give written intimation to the
parties of the transfer;
  (b) the cause shall be deemed to have been commenced by petition; and
  (c) the Deputy Principal Clerk shall, within two days of the receipt of it,
cause it to be put out on the By Order Roll before the Lord Ordinary.

Deriv. R.C.S. 1965, r. 260K(13) to (16) inserted by S.I. 1986 No. 1955

---

[1] R. 70.13(1), (2)(a) and (4) amended by S.I. 1996 No. 1756 (effective 5th August 1996).

General note. Transfer of an application will arise if the child has moved from Scotland to   **70.13.1**
another jurisdiction in the UK (or was never here) or from another jurisdiction in the UK to
Scotland and saves time and the expense of raising fresh proceedings.

"written intimation". For methods, see r. 16.9.   **70.13.2**

"relevant territory". See r. 70.1 and note 70.1.2.   **70.13.3**

Variation and revocation of registered decision

70.14.—(1) Where a decision registered under section 16 of the Act of
1985 is varied or revoked by an authority in the Contracting State in which
the decision was made, the court shall—
  (a) on cancelling the registration of a decision which it has been notified
has been revoked, give written intimation of that cancellation to—
    (i) the person appearing to the court to have actual custody of the
child;
    (ii) the petitioner in the petition for registration; and
    (iii) any other party to that petition; and

   (b) on being notified of the variation of a decision, give written
       intimation to—
       (i) the person having custody in fact of the child; and
       (ii) any party to the petition for registration of the decision, of the
            variation.
   (2) Any person to whom intimation of a variation has been given under
paragraph (1)(b) may apply by note for the purpose of making
representations before the registration is varied.
   (3) An application under section 17(4) of the Act of 1985 (application to
cancel or vary registration) shall be made by note.

Deriv. R.C.S. 1965, r. 260(17) and (18) inserted by S.I. 1986 No. 1955

70.14.1   *"written intimation".* For methods, see r. 16.9.

70.14.2   *"note".* For applications by note, see r. 15.2.

¹ PART IV

APPLICATIONS UNDER THE HAGUE CONVENTION WHERE THE COUNCIL
REGULATION APPLIES

Application and interpretation of this Part
   ¹ **70.15**—(1) This Part applies to petitions under rule 70.5(1) (applications
for the return of a child) under the Hague Convention where the Council
Regulation (E.C.) No. 2201/2003 of 27th November 2003 on jurisdiction
and the recognition and enforcement of judgments in matrimonial matters
and matters of parental responsibility applies(a).
   (2) In this Part—
       "the Council Regulation" means Council Regulation (E.C.) No. 2201/
          2003 of 27th November 2003 concerning jurisdiction and the
          recognition and enforcement of judgments in matrimonial matters
          and matters of parental responsibility;
       "central authority" means a central authority designated under Article
          53 of the Council Regulation;
       "the Hague Convention" means the Convention defined in section 1(1)
          of the Child Abduction and Custody Act 1985(b) and as set out in
          Schedule 1 to that Act;
       "Member State" has the same meaning as in Article 2(3) of the Council
          Regulation;
       "wrongful removal or retention" has the same meaning as in Article
          2(11) of the Council Regulation.

---

¹ Pt. IV and r. 70.15 inserted by S.S.I. 2005 No. 135 (effective 2nd March 2005). Pt. IIA
    renumbered as Pt IV by S.S.I. 2005 No. 268 (effective 7th June 2005).

70.15.1   *General note.* Art. 61 of the Council Regulation 2201/2003 provides that the Council
Regulation applies in addition to the Hague Convention of 25th October 1980, in an application
to which the Hague Convention applies, where the child has his habitually residence on the
territory of a Member State.
   The Council Regulation (E.C.) No. 2201/2203 of 27th November 2003 concerning
jurisdiction and enforcement of judgments in matrimonial matters and matters of parental
responsibility (new Brussels II) applies between Member States of the E.U except Denmark.
Where an application is made under the Hague Convention to which Pt. II of Chap. 70 applies,
and the child is habitually resident in a Member State of the E.U., certain requirements of the
Council Regulation apply where that child has been removed to or retained in another Member
State. These include: (a) the child must be given an opportunity to be heard unless inappropriate
because of his age or immaturity, (b) the court deals with the case in six weeks, (c) the court
cannot refuse to return the child under art. 13(b) of the Hague Convention (see 1985 Act, Sched.
1, Art. 13(b) (grave risk)) if adequate arrangements have been made to secure protection on

return, and (d) the court cannot refuse to return the child unless the person requesting return has been given an opportunity to be heard: art. 11 of the Council Regulation.

It should be noted that the Council Regulation does not itself provide a regime for child abduction. A Member State retains its own jurisdiction while a child is habitually resident there until the child acquires an habitual residence in another Member State: art. 10. If the Hague Convention is applicable, that vehicle will be used subject to the Council Regulation requirements.

Intimation on child

[1] **70.16.**—(1) In a petition under rule 70.5(1) (application for the return of a child) where the Council Regulation applies, the petitioner shall insert a warrant for intimation to the child to whom the petition relates, if not a party to the petition.

(2) Where paragraph (1) applies a copy of the petition shall not be intimated to the child but a notice of intimation in Form 49.8—N(c) shall be intimated.

(3) Where a petitioner considers that a warrant for intimation to a child under paragraph (1) is inappropriate, he shall—

(a) apply by motion to dispense with intimation to that child; and

(b) include in the petition averments setting out the reasons why such intimation is inappropriate,

and the court may dispense with such intimation or make such other order as it thinks fit.

---

[1] Rule 70.16 inserted by S.S.I. 2005 No. 135 (effective 2nd March 2005).

"where the Council Regulation applies". See note 70.15.1.   **70.16.1**

Intimation on a warrant to intimate. For methods, see Chap. 16, r. 16.8.   **70.17.2**

"motion". For motions, see Chap. 23.   **70.17.3**

Views of child

[1] **70.17.**—(1) In an application under rule 70.5(1) (application for the return of a child) where the Council Regulation applies and the child has—

(a) returned Form 49.8–N (form of notice of intimation to a child), or

(b) otherwise indicated to the court a wish to express views on a matter affecting him,

the court shall not grant any order unless an opportunity has been given for the views of that child to be obtained or heard.

(2) Where a child has indicated his wish to express his views, the court shall order such steps to be taken as it considers appropriate to ascertain the views of that child.

(3) The court shall not grant an order in a petition under rule 70.5(1) (return of a child) affecting a child who has indicated his wish to express his views, unless due weight has been given by the court to the views expressed by that child, having regard to his age and maturity.

---

[1] Rule 70.17 inserted by S.S.I. 2005 No. 135 (effective 2nd March 2005).

"where the Council Regulation applies". See note 70.15.1.   **70.17.1**

Views of the child. The child may express views in the form 49.8–N or intimate that he would like someone else to do so for him.   **70.17.2**

Steps to ascertain views of child. The court may, e.g., appoint someone (e.g. a curator *ad litem* or a reporter) to take the child's views.   **70.17.3**

Continuations

[1] **70.18.** In an application under rule 70.5(1) (application for the return of the child), where the Council Regulation applies, the court may allow a continuation of the hearing for a period not exceeding 7 days or to the first

suitable court date thereafter but any further continuations shall only be allowed on special cause shown.

_____

[1] Rule 70.18 inserted by S.S.I. 2005 No. 135 (effective 2nd March 2005).

Recording of hearings under Article 12 of the Hague Convention
[1] **70.19.**—(1) Any hearing on an application for the return of a child under rule 70.5(1) and Article 12 of the Hague Convention, where the Council Regulation applies, shall be recorded by—
  (a) a shorthand writer to whom the oath de fidelis administratione officii has been administered on his appointment as a shorthand writer in the Court of Session; or
  (b) tape recording or other mechanical means approved by the Lord President.
(2) The record of the hearing shall include—
  (a) any objection taken to a question or to the line of evidence;
  (b) any submission made in relation to such an objection; and
  (c) the ruling of the court in relation to the objection and submission.
(3) A transcript of the record of the hearing shall be made only where an order is made under Article 13 of the Hague Convention refusing to order the return of a child in an application where the Council Regulation applies.
(4) The transcript of the record of the hearing shall be certified as a faithful record of the hearing by—
  (a) the shorthand writer or shorthand writers, if more than one, who recorded the hearing; or
  (b) where the hearing was recorded by tape recording or other mechanical means, the person who transcribed the record.
(5) The court may make such alterations to the transcript of the record of the hearing as appear to it to be necessary after hearing parties; and, where such alterations are made, the Lord Ordinary shall authenticate the alterations.

_____

[1] Rule 70.19 inserted by S.S.I. 2005 No. 135 (effective 2nd March 2005) and amended by S.S.I. 2006 No. 83 (effective 17th March 2006).

70.19.1   *"where the Council Regulation applies".* See note 70.15.1.

70.19.1   *Evidence at a hearing.* The Hague Convention and r. 70.6 do not envisage that oral evidence will necessarily be required: see note 70.6.2. Art. 11(6) of the Council Regulation 2201/2003 requires a transcript of the hearing to be sent to the court where the child is habitually resident where the court dealing with the application for return of the child makes an order for non-return under art. 13 of the Hague Convention (in Sched. 1 to the 1985 Act). The requirement is not limited to cases where there is evidence. There is no requirement for a transcript to be sent where the court orders return of the child.

Order under Article 13 of the Hague Convention
[1] **70.20.** Where an order is made under Article 13 of the Hague Convention refusing to order the return of a child in an application under rule 70.5(1) where the Council Regulation applies, the Deputy Principal Clerk shall transmit a copy of the order and a transcript of the proceedings to the central authority of the Member State where the child was habitually resident immediately before the wrongful removal or retention.

_____

[1] Rule 70.20 inserted by S.S.I. 2005 No. 135 (effective 2nd March 2005).

70.20.1   *General note.* See note 70.19.2.

CHAPTER 71

[1] REGISTRATION AND ENFORCEMENT OF PART I ORDERS UNDER THE FAMILY
LAW ACT 1986

Interpretation of this Chapter

[1] **71.1.** In this Chapter—

"the Act of 1986" means the Family Law Act 1986;

"appropriate court" means the High Court in England and Wales or the High Court in Northern Ireland or, in relation to a specified dependent territory, the corresponding court in that territory, as the case may be;

[1] "Part I order" has the meaning assigned in section 32 of the Act of 1986;

"proper officer" means the Secretary of the principal registry of the Family Division of the High Court in England and Wales or the Master (care and protection) of the High Court in Northern Ireland or, in relation to a specified dependent territory, the corresponding officer of the appropriate court in that territory, as the case may be;

[1] "register" means the Part I orders register kept under rule 71.2;

"specified dependent territory" means a dependent territory specified in an Order in Council made under section 43 of the Act of 1986.

Deriv. R.C.S. 1965, r. 260P(1) inserted by S.I. 1988 No. 615

---

[1] Chap. heading and r. 71.1 amended by S.I. 1997 No. 795 (effective 1st April 1997).

General note. The Act of 1986 gives effect to the recommendations of the English and Scottish **71.1.1** Law Commissions in their joint report on Custody of Children—Jurisdiction and Enforcement within the United Kingdom (Scot. Law Com. No. 91).

Part I of the Act of 1986 lays down jurisdictional rules for making what were formerly called custody orders (and are now referred to as Part I orders which include custody, access, residence and contact orders) in the UK. In general, a court has jurisdiction to make a Part I order other than in matrimonial proceedings (divorce, nullity or separation: Act of 1986, s. 18(1)) if the child is habitually resident in its jurisdiction, is present there and not habitually resident elsewhere in the UK, or in an emergency. The question of habitual residence is one of fact and not legal right: *Rellis v. Hart* 1993 S.L.T. 738.

Under Ch.V of Pt I of the Act of 1986, a Part I order made by a court in any part of the UK with respect to a child under the age of 16 years shall be recognised (except in relation to a provision as to the means of enforcement) in any other part of the UK as having the same effect as if it had been made in that other part as if the court in that other part had had jurisdiction to make it: Act of 1986, s. 25(1). The order is enforceable in that other part of the UK if registered there under s. 27 of the Act: Act of 1986, s. 25(3). Chap. 71 of the R.C.S. 1994 provides for registration of Court of Session Part I orders elsewhere in the UK (rr. 71.3 and 71.4) and registration and enforcement of Part I orders made elsewhere in the UK in Scotland (rr. 71.5 and 71.7), and for cancellation and variation of registered Part I orders (r. 71.6).

The Act of 1986 has not, apparently, affected the limited protective jurisdiction of the Court

of Session to refuse to give effect to a custody order of a foreign court which the Court of Session may always exercise if it is satisfied that enforcement of the foreign decree would result in physical or moral injury to the child: *Woodcock v. Woodcock* 1990 S.C. 266, 273.

"specified dependent territory". The only Order in Council specifying a dependent territory is **71.1.2** the Family Law Act 1986 (Dependent Territories) Order 1991 [S.I. 1991 No. 1723]. The only dependent territory specified is the Isle of Man.

Part I orders register

71.2.—[1] (1) The Deputy Principal Clerk shall maintain a register to be called the Part I orders register for the purposes of Chapter V of Part I of the Act of 1986.

[1] (2) In Part I of the register there shall be recorded applications for registration of a Part I order in another part of the United Kingdom; and in Part II of the register there shall be recorded Part I orders registered for enforcement in Scotland.

(3) The register may be inspected by—
   (a) the person who applied for registration; and
   (b) any other person who satisfies the Deputy Principal Clerk that he has an interest to do so.

Deriv. R.C.S. 1965, r.260Q inserted by S.I. 1988 No. 615 and amended by S.I. 1991 No. 2483 (r.71.2(1) and (2)), and r.260X(3) inserted by S.I. 1988 No. 615 (r.71.2(3))

---

[1] R. 71.2(1) and (2) and heading amended by S.I. 1997 No. 795 (effective 1st April 1997).

[1] Applications for registration of Part I orders in another court

71.3.—[1] (1) An application under section 27 of the Act of 1986 to register a Part I order made by the Court of Session in an appropriate court shall be made by letter to the Deputy Principal Clerk.

[1] (2) An application under paragraph (1) shall be accompanied by—
   (a) a copy of the letter of application;
   (b) an affidavit by the applicant;
   (c) a copy of that affidavit;
   (d) a certified copy of the interlocutor of the Part I order;
   (e) a certified copy of the interlocutor of any variation which is in force in respect of the Part I order; and
   (f) any other document relevant to the application and a copy of it.

(3) An affidavit required under this rule shall set out—
   (a) the name and address of the applicant and his right under the Part I order;
   (b) the name and date of birth of the child in respect of whom the Part I order was made, the present whereabouts or suspected whereabouts of the child and the name of any person with whom he is alleged to be;
   (c) the name and address of any other person who has an interest in the Part I order;
   (d) whether the custody order is to be registered in England and Wales, Northern Ireland or a specified dependent territory, and the court in which it is to be registered;
   (e) whether the Part I order is in force;
   (f) whether the Part I order is already registered and, if so, where it is registered; and

(g) details of any order known to the applicant which affects the child and is in force in the jurisdiction in which the Part I order is to be registered.

[1] (4) Where the Deputy Principal Clerk refuses to send an application under this rule to the appropriate court on the ground that the Part I order is no longer in force, he shall give written intimation to the applicant; and the applicant shall have the right to have the application brought before the Lord Ordinary for determination.

[1] (5) The Deputy Principal Clerk shall retain the letter of application under this rule and any documents which accompany it and which are not transmitted to the appropriate court under section 27(3) of the Act of 1986.

Deriv. R.C.S. 1965, r. 260R inserted by S.I. 1988 No. 615 and amended by S.I. 1990 No. 2118 and 1991 No. 2483

[1] R. 71.3(1)–(4) and heading amended by S.I. 1997 No. 795 (effective 1st April 1997).

General note. S. 27 of the Act of 1986 provides for applications for registration of Part I orders **71.3.1** of the Court of Session in another part of the UK, and r. 71.3 is made under that section (A.S. (R.C.S. 1994) 1994, Sched. 1 [S.I. 1994 No. 1443]).

Unless the Deputy Principal Clerk considers that the Part I order of the Court of Session is no longer in force he shall, on receiving the application, send to the appropriate court in which it is to be registered, a certified copy of the order, particulars of any variation of it, a copy of the application and any accompanying documents: Act of 1986, s.27(3). On receiving these documents, the appropriate court shall register the order: Act of 1986, s.27(4).

"Part I order". For meaning, see ss.1(1) and 32 of the Act of 1986. **71.3.2**

Transmission of applications for registration
71.4.—[1] (1) Where the Deputy Principal Clerk is satisfied that the Part I order is in force, he shall send the documents mentioned in section 27(3) of the Act of 1986 to the proper officer of the court in which the Part I order is to be registered.

[1] (2) For the purposes of section 27(3)(b) of the Act of 1986, the prescribed particulars of any variation which is in force in respect of a Part I order shall be a certified copy of the interlocutor of any such variation.

[1] (3) On sending an application under paragraph (1), the Deputy Principal Clerk shall make an entry in Part I of the register recording the date and particulars of the application and the Part I order.

[1] (4) On receiving notification from a proper officer of an appropriate court that the Part I order has been registered in that court under section 27(4) of the Act of 1986, the Deputy Principal Clerk shall record the date of registration in Part I of the register.

Deriv. R.C.S. 1965, r. 260S inserted by S.I. 1988 No. 615

[1] R. 71.4(1)–(4) amended by S.I. 1997 No. 795 (effective 1st April 1997).

General note. S. 27 of the Act of 1986 provides for registration elsewhere in the UK of Part I **71.4.1** orders made by the Court of Session.

"Part I order". For meaning, see ss.1(1) and 32 of the Act of 1986. **71.4.2**

[1] *Registration of Part I orders from another court*
71.5.—(1) The prescribed officer under section 27(4) of the Act of 1986 shall be the Deputy Principal Clerk.

[1] (2) Where the Deputy Principal Clerk receives a certified copy of a Part I order from a court for registration under section 27(4) of the Act of 1986, he shall enter the following particulars in Part II of the register:—

(a) the name and address of the applicant and his interest under the Part I order;

(b) a brief description of the nature of the Part I order, its date and the court which made it; and

(c) the name and whereabouts or suspected whereabouts of the child who is the subject of the Part I order, his date of birth and the date on which he will attain the age of 16 years.

[1] (3) On registering the Part I order, the Deputy Principal Clerk shall—

(a) retain the application and the documents which accompanied it; and

(b) give written intimation to—

    (i) the court from which he received the application, and

    (ii) the applicant who applied for registration,

that the Part I order has been registered.

[1] (4) Where the Deputy Principal Clerk gives written intimation to an applicant under paragraph (3), he shall state the date when the registration of the Part I order will automatically cease to have effect on the child attaining the age of 16 years.

Deriv. R.C.S. 1965, r. 260T inserted by S.I. 1988 No. 615 and amended by S.I. 1990 No. 2118

---

[1] R. 71.5(2)–(4) and heading amended by S.I. 1997 No. 795 (effective 1st April 1997).

71.5.1   *General note.* S. 27 of the Act of 1986 provides for registration of Part I orders made by a court elsewhere in the UK in Scotland (in the Court of Session).

On receiving a certified copy of the Part I order, particulars of any variation of it, a copy of the application and any accompanying documents, the Deputy Principal Clerk shall register the order: Act of 1986, s.27(4).

Once registered, the order can be enforced (excluding provisions as to the means of enforcement) under s.29 of the Act of 1986: see r. 71.7.

71.5.2   *"written intimation".* For methods, see r. 16.9.

71.5.3   *"Part I order".* For meaning, see ss.1(1) and 32 of the Act of 1986.

[1] *Cancellation or variation of registered Part I orders*
71.6.—[1] (1) Where the Court of Session revokes, recalls or varies a Part I order which it has made, the Deputy Principal Clerk, on being informed by the party who applied for the revocation, recall or variation that the Part I order has been registered in an appropriate court, shall—

(a) send a certified copy of the interlocutor of the revocation, recall or variation, as the case may be, to the proper officer of the court in which the Part I order is registered;

(b) record the transmission of the certified copy of that interlocutor in Part I of the register; and

(c) record the revocation, recall or variation, as the case may be, in Part I of the register.

[1] (2) On receiving notification from the proper officer of the court in which the Part I order is registered that he has amended his record, the Deputy Principal Clerk shall record the fact that the amendment has been made in Part II of the register.

[1] (3) Where the Deputy Principal Clerk receives a certified copy of an order which revokes, recalls or varies a Part I order registered in the Court of Session from an appropriate court, he shall—

(a) note the change and its date in Part II of the register; and

(b) give written intimation to—

    (i) the court from which he received the certified copy of the order which revokes, recalls or varies, as the case may be, the Part I order,

    (ii) the person who applied for registration of the Part I order, and

    (iii) the person, if different, who applied for the revocation, recall or variation, as the case may be, of the Part I order,

that he has amended the register.

[1] (4) An application to the Court of Session under section 28(2) of the Act of 1986 to cancel all or a part of the registration of a Part I order which it has registered shall be made by petition and shall be served on—
  (a) the person who applied for registration, if he is not the petitioner; and
  (b) any other interested person.
  [1] (5) Where, under section 28(2) of the Act of 1986, the court cancels all or a part of the registration of a Part I order which it has registered, the Deputy Principal Clerk shall—
  (a) note the cancellation and its date in Part II of the register; and
  (b) give written intimation to—
     (i) the court which made the Part I order;
     (ii) the person who applied for registration; and
     (iii) the person, if different, who applied for cancellation of the Part I order.

Deriv. R.C.S. 1965, r. 260U inserted by S.I. 1988 No. 615 and amended by S.I. 1990 No. 2118

---

[1] R. 71.6(1)–(5) and heading amended by S.I. 1997 No. 795 (effective 1st April 1997).

General note. A Part I order may be revoked, recalled or varied by a court in the country in **71.6.1** which it was originally made (not necessarily the court which made the order). Where the Court of Session makes such an order, notice must be given to the appropriate court where the order is registered: Act of 1986, s.28(1); and r. 71.6(1) to (3) is made under that subsection (A.S. (R.C.S. 1994) 1994, Sched. 1 [S.I. 1994 No. 1443]).

The Court of Session can cancel or vary a Part I order registered with it where the order has ceased to have effect in the part of the U.K. where it was made, other than by revocation, recall or variation (*e.g.* superseded by a later order by any U.K. court having jurisdiction), or as the result of an order in proceedings furth of the U.K.: Act of 1986, s.28(2). The application is made by petition: r. 71.6(4).

"written intimation". For methods, see r. 16.9.   **71.6.2**

"petition". A petition is presented in the Outer House: r. 14.2(h). The petition must be in **71.6.3** Form 14.4 in the official printed form: rr. 4.1 and 14.4. The petition must be signed by counsel or other person having a right of audience: r. 4.2; and see r. 1.3(1) (definition of "counsel" and "other person having a right of audience") and note 1.3.4.

The petitioner must lodge the petition with the required steps of process (r. 4.4). A fee is payable on lodging the petition: see note 14.5.10.
On petitions generally, see Chap. 14.

"served". For methods of service, see Chap. 16, Pt I.   **71.6.4**

"Part I order". For meaning, see ss.1(1) and 32 of the Act of 1986.   **71.6.5**

[1] *Enforcement of registered Part I orders in Scotland*
71.7.—[1] (1) An application under section s.29(1) of the Act of 1986 to enforce a Part I order registered in the Court of Session shall be made by petition.
  (2) Where the petitioner in an application under paragraph (1) is not the person who applied for registration of the Part I order, the petition shall be served on that person.

Deriv. R.C.S. 1965, r. 260V inserted by S.I. 1988 No. 615

---

[1] R. 71.7(1) and heading amended by S.I. 1997 No. 795 (effective 1st April 1997).

General note. Once registered in the Court of Session a custody order from another part of **71.7.1** the U.K. may be enforced (excluding provisions as to the means of enforcement) under s.29 of the Act of 1986: *i.e.* the court can exercise powers it would have had if it had made the custody order itself. The court can also make interim orders pending determination of the application for enforcement.

The court should not normally make an order for enforcement without giving the respondent an opportunity to be heard: *Woodcock v. Woodcock* 1990 S.C. 267.

The provisions for sist of enforcement proceedings in s.30 of the Act of 1986 should be noted: see r. 71.8. There are also provisions for dismissal of enforcement proceedings in s.31 of the Act of 1986 (and see r. 71.8).

71.7.2 *"petition".* A petition is presented in the Outer House: r. 14.2(h). The petition must be in Form 14.4 in the official printed form: rr. 4.1 and 14.4. The petition must be signed by counsel or other person having a right of audience: r. 4.2; and see r. 1.3(1) (definition of "counsel" and "other person having a right of audience") and note 1.3.4.

On petitions generally, see Chap. 14.

The petitioner must lodge the petition with the required steps of process (r. 4.4). A fee is payable on lodging the petition: see note 14.5.10.

71.7.3 *"served".* For methods of service, see Chap. 16, Pt I.

71.7.4 *"Part I order".* For meaning, see ss.1(1) and 32 of the Act of 1986.

Application to sist or refuse enforcement proceedings

71.8.—[1] (1) An application under section 30(1) of the Act of 1986 to sist enforcement proceedings, or under section 31(1) or (2), of the Act of 1986 to dismiss a petition for enforcement of a Part I order, shall be made by lodging answers at any time in the process of the petition for enforcement; and the answers shall be served on every other party and, if he is not a party, the applicant for registration of the Part I order.

(2) An application under section 30(3) of the Act of 1986 (recall of sist of enforcement proceedings) shall be made by motion.

(3) Where the court pronounces an interlocutor under section 30(2) or (3) or section 31(3) of the Act of 1986, the Deputy Principal Clerk shall—

(a) make an entry in Part II of the register noting the terms of the interlocutor and the date; and

(b) give written intimation to—

(i) the person who applied for registration where he was not a party to the application under section 30(1) or section 31(1) or (2) of the Act of 1986; and

(ii) the court from which the application for registration was received,

of the terms of the interlocutor.

Deriv. R.C.S. 1965, r. 260W inserted by S.I. 1988 No. 615

---

[1] R. 71.8(1) amended by S.I. 1997 No. 795 (effective 1st April 1997).

71.8.1 *General note.* The court may sist enforcement proceedings on application by any person having an interest on the ground that he has taken or intends to take other proceedings in the U.K. or elsewhere as a result of which the order may cease to have effect or have a different effect; and the court may recall the sist where there has been unreasonable delay in prosecuting those other proceedings or those proceedings have been concluded and the registered order remains in force: Act of 1986, s.30.

The intention of s.30 of the Act of 1986 is not to provide an open-ended observation to sist enforcement proceedings simply on the criteria relevant to an application for interim custody; the main issue to be considered is whether special circumstances have been established which are sufficient to justify a failure to comply with the primary purpose of the legislation (to ensure enforcement of the original order): *Cook v. Blackley* 1997 S.C. 45.

Enforcement proceedings may be dismissed on the application of a person having an interest on the ground that the custody order has ceased to have effect in the part of the U.K. where it was made or as a result of proceedings furth of the U.K.: Act of 1986, s.31.

71.8.2 *"answers".* For form and procedure, see r. 18.3.

71.8.3 *"motion".* For motions, see Chap. 23.

71.8.4 *"Part I order".* For meaning, see ss.1(1) and 32 of the Act of 1986.

Orders for disclosure of information

71.9. Where the court makes an order under section 33(1) of the Act of 1986 (order on person to disclose information as to child's whereabouts), it may ordain the person against whom the order was made to appear before it or to lodge an affidavit.

Deriv. R.C.S. 1965, r. 260X(1) inserted by S.I. 1988 No. 615

71.9.1 *General note.* The court has always had power to take whatever action was necessary to make an interlocutor effective including ordering the hearing of evidence from any witness who may have information which would assist in the recovery of a child: *Abusaif v. Abusaif* 1984 S.L.T. 90, 91 *per* L.P. Emslie.

The statutory provision in s. 33 of the Act of 1986 confirms the common law power including the power to order disclosure whether the order was made by a U.K. court or a court furth of the U.K. A person is not excused from complying with an order to disclose information on the ground of incrimination of that person or his or her spouse, but a statement or admission is not admissible in evidence in criminal proceedings for an offence except perjury: Act of 1986, s. 33(2).

Applications for interdict under section 35(3) of the Act of 1986

71.10. An application by a person mentioned in section 35(4)(b) or (c) of the Act of 1986 for interdict or interim interdict under section 35(3) of the Act of 1986 (prohibition of removal of child from United Kingdom) shall be made—

(a) by note in the process of a petition depending before the court to which this Chapter applies; or

(b) where there is no such depending process, by petition.

Deriv. R.C.S. 1965, r. 260X(2) inserted by S.I. 1988 No. 615

General note. Persons who may apply for interdict to restrict the removal of a child from the **71.10.1** jurisdiction of the court are a guardian or a person who wishes to obtain custody or care of the child: Act of 1986, s. 35(4)(b) and (c) as amended by the Age of Legal Capacity (Scotland) Act 1991, Sched. 1, para. 47.

"note". For applications by note, see r. 15.2. **71.10.2**

"petition". A petition is presented in the Outer House: r. 14.2(h). The petition must be in **71.10.3** Form 14.4 in the official printed form: rr. 4.1 and 14.4. The petition must be signed by counsel or other person having a right of audience: r. 4.2; and see r. 1.3(1) (definition of "counsel" and "other person having a right of audience") and note 1.3.4.

The petitioner must lodge the petition with the required steps of process (r. 4.4). A fee is payable on lodging the petition: see note 14.5.10.

On petitions generally, see Chap. 14.

"the EC Regulation" means Council Regulation (EC) 1346/2000 of 29th May 2000 on **71.10.4** insolvency proceedings.

CHAPTER 72

BANKRUPTCY (SCOTLAND) ACT 1985

Interpretation of this Chapter

72.1.—[1] (1) In this Chapter—

"the Act of 1985" means the Bankruptcy (Scotland) Act 1985; and

"the EC Regulation" means Council Regulation (EC) 1346/2000 of 29th May 2000 on insolvency proceedings.

(2) Unless the context otherwise requires, words and expressions used in this Chapter which are also used in the Act of 1985 have the same meaning as in that Act.

---

[1] Rule 72.1 amended by S.S.I. 2004 No. 514 (effective 30th November 2004) and then substituted by S.S.I. 2005 No. 268 (effective 7th June, 2005).

General note. The Act of 1985 repealed, subject to some minor re-enactments, the Bankruptcy **72.1.1** (Scotland) Act 1913 and largely gave effect to the proposals of the Scottish Law Commission Report on Bankruptcy and Related Aspects of Insolvency (Scot. Law Com. No. 68). The main changes effected by the Act of 1985 include: the introduction of an interim trustee who, as well as a permanent trustee, must be appointed in every case; the debtor may obtain an automatic discharge after the expiry of three years from the date of sequestration; the introduction of the "protected trust deed"; the introduction of a modified procedure, and payment of the trustee's remuneration and outlays from public funds, in cases where the debtor's assets are likely to be insufficient to pay a dividend ("small asset" cases); and the introduction of power conferred on the sheriff to cure defects in procedure. The effect of this last change has been to reduce the number of petitions to the *nobile officium* arising out of the bankruptcy process.

The Bankruptcy (Scotland) Act 1993 alters the personal insolvency regime introduced by the Act of 1985. In particular, the 1993 Act restricts the circumstances in which a trustee under a trust deed or the debtor himself may petition for sequestration; the Accountant in Bankruptcy may become the interim or permanent trustee in small asset cases (by a procedure known as "summary administration"); and the procedure for making a trust deed protected has been amended.

72.1.2 *Jurisdiction.* The grounds of jurisdiction are set out in s. 9 of the Act of 1985. The usual ground is the habitual residence of the debtor within Scotland in the year immediately preceding the presentation of the petition. An established place of business may also found jurisdiction. Bankruptcy proceedings are excluded from the C.J.J.A. 1982: Scheds 1 and 3C, Art. 1 (1968 Brussels and Lugano Conventions) and Sched. 9, para. 4 (jurisdiction of Scottish courts).

72.1.3 *Transitional provisions.* The Bankruptcy (Scotland) Act 1913 governs petitions presented before 1st April 1986, though some provisions of the Act of 1985, such as automatic discharge of the debtor (s. 54) and the power to cure defects (s. 63(1)), apply to such petitions. Some parts of the 1993 Act (namely ss. 8, 9, 12 and, insofar as they relate to s. 11(5), paras 22(5), 23, and 31(4) and (5) of Sched. 1 of the Act of 1985) came into force when the Act was passed (on 18th February 1993). The rest of the Act was brought into force on 1st April 1993: Bankruptcy (Scotland) Act 1993 Commencement and Savings Order [S.I. 1993 No. 438].

Application of the EU Regulation

[1] **72.1A.** A petition for sequestration to which section 12 of the Act of 1985 (petition for sequestration of debtor's estate) applies shall include averments stating—

(a) whether the EC Regulation applies; and

(b) if so, whether the proceedings are main proceedings or territorial proceedings.

---

[1] Rule 72.1A inserted by S.S.I. 2005 No. 268 (effective 7th June, 2005).

72.1A.1 *General note.* Section 12 of the 1985 Act is the general provision for the award of sequestration where a petition is presented by a debtor or creditor or trustee under a trust deed.

The importance of stating whether the E.U. Council Regulation 1346/2000 applies is this. Under that Regulation, courts of a Member State within which the centre of a debtor's main interests is situated have jurisdiction to open insolvency proceedings (these are referred to as the main insolvency proceedings): Art. 3(1). The courts of another Member State have jurisdiction to open insolvency proceedings (called "territorial insolvency proceedings) only if the debtor possesses an establishment (defined in art. 2(h)) within the territory of that other Member State; and in that case those proceedings affect only those assets in that territory: Art. 3(2)

First order in petitions for sequestration

72.2. A petition for sequestration to which subsection (2) of section 12 of the Act of 1985 (petition for sequestration of debtor's estate by creditor or trustee) applies shall, on being presented, be brought before the Lord Ordinary in court or in chambers for an order for a warrant to cite the debtor as required by that subsection.

Deriv. R.C.S. 1965, r. 189(a)(vii) amended by S.I. 1986 No. 514

72.2.1 *"petition".* A petition is presented in the Outer House: r. 14.2(h). The petition must be in Form 14.4 in the official printed form: rr. 4.1 and 14.4. The petition may be signed by the petitioner for his own sequestration, counsel or other person having a right of audience, or an agent: r. 4.2; and see r. 1.3(1) (definition of "counsel", "other person having a right of audience" and "agent") and note 1.3.4.

The petitioner must lodge the petition with the required steps of process (r. 4.4). A fee is payable on lodging the petition: see note 14.5.10.

Petitioners should also note the requirement in s. 5(6) of the Act of 1985 (as amended) to send a copy of the petition to the Accountant in Bankruptcy on the date of the presentation of the petition: *Mowbray v. Valentine* 1998 S.C. 424.

On petitions generally, see Chap. 14.

"on being presented". A petition is presented when it is received by the clerk of court (*i.e.* in **72.2.2**
the Petition Department): Act of 1985, s. 73(6) as inserted by the 1993 Act, Sched. 1, para. 7.
This is consistent with a case decided under the 1913 Act, in which the court held that, for the
purpose of determining the four month period within which the apparent insolvency (then more
attractively known as 'notour bankruptcy') of the debtor must have been constituted, the
petition was presented on the date when the petition was lodged in the Petition Department and
not the date when it was first brought before a Lord Ordinary: *Burgh of Millport, Petrs* 1974
S.L.T. (Notes) 23.

"creditor". A creditor must be a qualified creditor, being a creditor to whom at the date of the **72.2.3**
presentation of the petition the debtor owes debts (whether liquid or illiquid) amounting to not
less than £1,500: Act of 1985, s. 5(4) (amended by s. 3(3) of the 1993 Act (inserting the figure of
£1,500)) and s. 73(1). It has been held that a creditor is a qualified one if the total amount due,
including interest and expenses, is over the statutory limit, notwithstanding the fact that the
principal owed is under the statutory limit: *Arthur v. H.M. Advocate* 1993 J.C. 244; and *Arthur
v. The SMT Sales & Services Co. Ltd* 1999 S.C. 109 (First Div.). It has been further held that
legal expenses and sheriff officers' expenses, once incurred, constitute expenses of diligence
which are properly regarded as part of the sum owed (meaning of "principal" in Sched. 5, para.
1(1)) for the purposes of meeting the prescribed statutory limit for qualifying creditors: *Arthur*,
above. Accordingly, in *Arthur*, above the creditor was held to be a qualifying creditor where the
amount of principal and interest owed was less than the then prescribed limit for a qualifying
creditor but where the addition of legal and sheriff officers' expenses that limit was exceeded. A
creditor is always free to charge for less than the amount due: *Lord Advocate v. Mackenzie* 1993
S.C.L.R. 153 (interest omitted from charge). In the case of a petitioning creditor, the apparent
insolvency of the debtor must have been constituted within four months of the presentation of
the petition. The four month period does not run when a charge by which the apparent
insolvency of the debtor was constituted is suspended: *United Dominions Trust Ltd v. Dickson*
1983 S.L.T. 572.
    In addition to producing an oath in the prescribed form (Form 2 of the Bankruptcy
(Scotland) Regulations 1985 [S.I. 1985 No. 1925], as required by s. 11(1) of the Act of 1985), the
petitioning creditor must show that he is a qualified creditor and that the debtor is apparently
insolvent: Act of 1985, s. 11(5). The latter is usually evidenced by an execution of charge (*e.g.* as
in *Lord Advocate v. Mackenzie*, above) or a statutory demand (*e.g.* as in *Lord Advocate v.
Thomson* 1995 S.L.T. 56 where sequestration refused on other grounds). In *Waverley Vintners
Ltd v. Matthews* 1991 G.W.D. 19–1130 the sheriff principal used the dispensing power under s.
63(1) of the Act of 1985 to permit the production of a photostat of the lost original of the sheriff
clerk's certificate that the charge had been duly displayed on the walls of court for the days of
charge. Neither an execution of charge nor a statutory demand can be used as *prima facie*
evidence of the debt owed to the petitioning creditor as well as evidence of the debtor's apparent
insolvency. It is doubtful whether a statutory demand emanating from the same source as the
creditors' oath can itself vouch the debt (*Scott v. Scott* (1847) 9 D. 1347, 1352, *per* L.J.-C. Hope,
cited with approval in *Lord Advocate v. Thomson*, above); it is only an assertion that a debt is
due: *Lord Advocate v. Thomson*, above. An extract decree is sufficient evidence of the debt: *Lord
Advocate v. Mackenzie*, above. See *Scott*, above, for discussion of what constitutes a "voucher".
The court has treated as *pro non scripto* an incorrect reference in an oath to a charge, as evidence
of the debt itself, and awarded sequestration where the creditor had produced other evidence of
the debt (extract decree): *Lord Advocate v. Mackenzie*, above.
    The failure of a creditor to lodge the oath in the prescribed form for petition for sequestration
is a failure capable of being cured by an exercise of power conferred on the sheriff under s. 63 of
the Act of 1985: *Bell v. McMillan*, 1999 S.L.T. 947.
    It should be noted that the requirements of the form of statutory demand in Form 1 of the
1985 Regulations must be strictly complied with: *Lord Advocate v. Thomson*, above (note (f) not
fully complied with).

"trustee". Under the Act of 1985 it became common for a debtor to arrange his own **72.2.4**
sequestration by granting a trust deed for the behoof of his creditors and relying on the power
of his trustee to petition for sequestration (the 'trust deed route'). The competency of
sequestration by this route was upheld in *Archer Car Sales (Airdrie) Ltd v. Gregory's Tr.* 1993
S.L.T. 223. The advantage was that if an interim trustee reported to the statutory meeting of
creditors that the debtor's assets were unlikely to be sufficient to pay a dividend, then, after the
appointment of the interim trustee as the permanent trustee, public funds were available to meet
the interim and permanent trustees' outlays and remuneration. The large and unanticipated call
on public funds caused by the trust deed route to sequestration led to the reforms introduced by
the 1993 Act. In the main, the 1993 Act restricts the ability of the debtor to arrange his own
sequestration by this route. The trustee under a trust deed may now petition for sequestration
only if the conditions of s. 5(2C) of the Act of 1985 are met and the court is satisfied that the

trustee's averments are true (s. 12(3) of the Act of 1985 substituted by s. 4(4) of the 1993 Act). The grounds on which the debtor may directly petition for his own sequestration have also been restricted: s. 5(2B) Act of 1985, inserted by the 1993 Act, s. 3(2).

72.2.5   *"warrant to cite"*. The prayer of the petition should crave warrant to cite the debtor to appear before the court at a fixed diet (P.N. 16th July 1987, introduced after observations by Lord Prosser in *Royal Bank of Scotland plc v. W.G.M. & C. Forbes* 1988 S.L.T. 931), rather than to enter appearance, as was the practice under the 1913 Act, and after, until the practice note. The fixed diet should be not less than six nor more than 14 days after the date of citation: Act of 1985, s. 12(2). It is the practice of the court to fix the date for the first Thursday after the expiry of 14 days from the date of the first deliverance. Any request for an earlier diet should be made within 24 hours of presenting the petition.

If sequestration is subsequently granted, the effective date for the start of the sequestration, for the purpose of vesting of property in the trustee and calculating a host of other time-limits under the Act of 1985, is the date of the first deliverance of the court, being the date on which, in a petition by a person other than the debtor, the court granted warrant to cite the debtor: Act of 1985, s. 12(4)(b)(i) substituted by the 1993 Act, s. 4(5). Where there are successive warrants to cite, *e.g.* because attempts at service may have been unsuccessful, the effective date is still the date on which the first warrant was granted: Act of 1985, s. 12(4)(b)(ii) substituted by the 1993 Act, s. 4(5). This clarifies the doubt which had arisen under the Act of 1985, confirms the decisions in *Arthur v. H.M. Advocate* 1994 S.L.T. 244 and *MacDonald's Tr. v. MacDonald* 1992 S.L.T. (Sh. Ct.) 25 (Sheriff Principal Hay) and supersedes *Campbell v. Sheriff* 1991 S.L.T. (Sh. Ct.) 37. The case of *Arthur*, above, was followed in *Sutherland v. Inland Revenue Commissioners*, 1999 S.C. 104. Where the debtor petitions for his own sequestration, the effective date is the date when sequestration is awarded: s. 12(4)(a), substituted by s. 4(5) of the 1993 Act. It is not competent for the sheriff to change the effective date of sequestration: *Accountant in Bankruptcy v. Allans of Gillock* 1991 S.L.T. 765.

72.2.6   *"debtor"*. Debtor includes an entity whose estate may be sequestrated by virtue of s. 6 of the Act of 1985, a deceased debtor or his executor or a person entitled to be appointed as executor to a deceased debtor. In terms of that section, entities whose estates, whether belonging to or held for or jointly by the members, may be sequestrated include a trust (for the debts incurred by it), a partnership (including a dissolved partnership), a body corporate or an unincorporated body, and a limited partnership (including a dissolved limited partnership) within the meaning of the Limited Partnerships Act 1907. It is not competent to sequestrate the estate of a company registered under the Companies Acts: Act of 1985, s. 6(2).

It is not competent to sequestrate in a single petition and as a single 'estate' the separate estates of a partnership and its partners: *Royal Bank of Scotland v. J. & J. Messenger* 1991 S.L.T. 492. It is also generally not competent to sequestrate jointly the estates of more than one debtor as, *e.g.* happened in *Campbell v. Dunbar* 1989 S.L.T. (Sh. Ct.) 29 (single petition for sequestration of estates of husband and wife who were not in partnership or other form of business). Petitions for the sequestration of the separate estates of a partnership and an individual partner thereof may be combined if both the partnership and that partner, as an individual, are apparently insolvent: Act of 1985, s. 6(5). It is good practice, though not essential (*Maclean's Tr., Noter* 1992 G.W.D. 15–842), in a petition concerning a partnership and individual partners to aver the status of debtors who are partners. It is competent to sequestrate one of several co-obligants in respect of a debt due jointly and severally by them: *e.g. Wright v. Tennent Caledonian Breweries Ltd* 1991 S.L.T. 823.

On a petition by a creditor the court must, on being satisfied of certain matters, award sequestration forthwith under s. 12(3) of the 1985 Act unless the debtor forthwith pays or satisfies or produces written evidence of payment or satisfaction of, or gives or shows that there is sufficient security for payment of the debt: 1985 Act, s. 12(3A). It has been held, in *Advocate General v. Zaoui*, 2001 S.C. 448, 456D, para. 19, (OH) that "forthwith" does not mean immediately, and that though such cause for not awarding sequestration must be shown at that hearing, there might be a brief deferment or continuation lasting no more than a few days.

Declaration regarding an approved debt payment programme

[1] **72.2A.** The petitioner shall lodge with the petition a declaration or declarations by the petitioner and any concurring creditors in Form 72.2A confirming that the debtor has not entered into an approved debt payment programme or that the debts founded on in the petition are in respect of credit as defined in regulation 35(1)(b) of the 2004 Regulations.

---

[1]   Rule 72.2A inserted by S.S.I. 2004 No. 514 (effective 30th November 2004).

General note. Under reg. 35 of the Debt Arrangement Scheme (Scotland) Regulations 2004, **72.2A.1**
where a creditor gives credit in an approved debt payment programme (other than credit
specified in para. 35(1)(b)), it is not competent in a petition for sequestration of the debtor's
estate to found on that credit as long as the programme is approved. Hence the declaration
required by r. 72.2A.

Notice of concurrent proceedings

72.3. A person seeking to bring to the attention of the court a fact referred
to in section 10(1) of the Act of 1985 (concurrent proceedings for
sequestration or analogous remedy) shall do so by motion in the process
of the petition which may be affected.

General note. This is a new rule consistent with the introduction of an obligation, imposed by **72.3.1**
s. 10 of the Act of 1985, requiring the debtor, petitioner or concurring creditor to advise the
court of any concurrent proceedings or analogous remedies of which he is, or becomes, aware
during the course of the sequestration proceedings. Such a provision better enables the court to
regulate competing proceedings. In its Report on Bankruptcy and related Aspects of Insolvency
and Liquidation (No. 68), the Scottish Law Commission recommended the imposition of this
new duty in order to minimise the risk of concurrent proceedings or the making of more than
one award: see para. 3.42 and paras 6.24–31 of the Report for fuller discussion. Because of the
nature of the rules on jurisdiction, it is possible for sequestration to be awarded in both the
sheriff court and the Court of Session (*e.g. P. & W. Duncan, Petrs.* 1936 S.L.T. 162; *Fletcher v.
Anderson* (1883) 10 R. 835) or in more than one sheriff court. The obligation on the debtor is
designed to prevent abuses whereby the debtor petitions for, and obtains, his own sequestration
before the expiry of the induciae of a creditor's petition (*e.g.* as in *Fletcher*, above, and *Barns
Graham v. Bowie* (1903) 5 F. 1230). The debtor's failure to disclose this information is a criminal
offence; the failure to disclose such information by another petitioner or petitioning creditor
may render that petitioner liable for the expenses of the sequestration process: Act of 1985, s.
10(2).

The court may allow the petition for sequestration to proceed, or may sist or dismiss it: Act of
1985, s. 10(4). Relevant considerations in the court's exercise of its discretion include "what in
the interests of the creditors is the most convenient and least expensive mode of procedure":
Fletcher, above, *per* L.P. Inglis at p.837. This may also be a reason to combine the separate
sequestrations of a partnership and its partners: *P. & W. Duncan*, above.

"concurrent proceedings". These include the award of another petition for the sequestration **72.3.2**
of the debtor's estate, or the appointment of a judicial factor on the debtor's estate granted by
the court or sheriff court, including the sheriff court which granted the instant sequestration
(Act of 1985, s. 10(1)(a) and (b)) as well as analogous remedies. Concurrent proceedings also
include a petition for the winding-up of the debtor under Pt. IV or VI of the Insolvency Act
1986 or under s. 72 of the Financial Services Act 1986 or an application for an analogous
remedy.

The existence of a prior and subsisting sequestration will not necessarily bar the award of a
second sequestration, as multiple awards are competent (*Millar v. Drummond* 1919 2 S.L.T. 68),
albeit undesirable (*Barns Graham v. Bowie* (1903) 5 F. 1230). For a recent example of the award
of a second sequestration of an undischarged bankrupt under a subsisting sequestration, see
Campbell v. Cranshee 1990 S.L.T. (Sh. Ct.) 96 (second petition based on a different christian
name for the debtor, who habitually used two such names).

"analogous remedy". This is defined as an order under the Bankruptcy Act 1914, the **72.3.3**
Insolvency Act 1985 or under s. 112 of the County Courts Act 1984: Act of 1985, s. 10(5).

Applications for transfer or remit of sequestration

72.4.—(1) An application under section 15(2) (transfer of sequestration
from one sheriff to another), or section 63(3)(b) (application for a direction
to remit an application under section 63(1)), of the Act of 1985 from the
sheriff to the court shall be made—
  (a) where sequestration has been awarded by the court, by motion; or
  (b) where sequestration has been awarded by the sheriff, by petition.

(2) The applicant under section 15(2) of the Act of 1985 shall intimate such motion to or serve such petition on—
(a) the debtor;
(b) any person who was a petitioner or concurred in the petition for sequestration;
(c) the interim trustee or permanent trustee;
(d) the Accountant in Bankruptcy; and
(e) the sheriff clerk.
(3) A copy of the application under section 63(1) of the Act of 1985 (application to sheriff to cure defects in procedure), certified by the sheriff clerk, shall be lodged with any application under section 63(3)(b) of that Act.
(4) Where the court has determined an application under section 15(2) or section 63(3)(b) of the Act of 1985, the applicant shall intimate a certified copy of the interlocutor of the court forthwith to—
(a) the sheriff clerk; and
(b) the Accountant in Bankruptcy.
(5) Where the court grants an application under section 15(2) of the Act of 1985, the sheriff clerk shall, on receipt of a certified copy of the interlocutor of the court, transmit those parts of the sequestration process in his custody to the sheriff clerk of the sheriff court specified in the interlocutor.
(6) Where the court grants an application under section 63(3)(b) of the Act of 1985, the sheriff clerk shall, on receipt of a certified copy of the interlocutor of the court, transmit the application under section 63(1) of that Act, and those parts of the sequestration process in his custody, to the Deputy Principal Clerk.
(7) Where the court has determined the matters raised by the application under section 63(1) of the Act of 1985—
(a) the applicant under section 63(3)(b) of that Act shall intimate a certified copy of the interlocutor of the court forthwith to—
(i) the sheriff clerk; and
(ii) the Accountant in Bankruptcy; and
(b) the Deputy Principal Clerk shall transmit the parts of process transmitted to him under paragraph (6) to the sheriff clerk.

"transfer". This involves transfer of the sequestration process from one sheriff court to   **72.4.1** another or from the sheriff court to which a sequestration has been remitted from the court to another sheriff court.

"direction to remit an application under s.63(1)". Any person "having an interest" may apply   **72.4.2** to the court to have an application under s.63(1) of the Act of 1985 relating to a sequestration depending before the sheriff court remitted to the Court of Session: Act of 1985, s.63(3)(b). A person having an interest may apply to the sheriff court in which the sequestration is depending for remit, or the sheriff may at his own instance remit, to the court: Act of 1985, s.63(3)(a).

The power conferred on a sheriff by s.63(1) of the Act of 1985 to cure defects in procedure (by waiving a failure to comply with any requirement of the Act or any regulations made thereunder or by making an order to enable a thing to be done) should obviate the need for a separate petition to the *nobile officium*, as was necessary before April 1, 1986. The objective of s.63 is "to prevent the sensible progress of a sequestration from being hampered by irregularities which are purely technical when equitable considerations require otherwise": *Pattison v. Halliday* 1991 S.L.T. 645, 648 *per* Lord Caplan. There are, however, limits on the powers exercisable under s.63(1). A sheriff cannot, in the purported exercise of the power under s.63(1), pronounce an *ultra vires* order: *Accountant in Bankruptcy v. Allans of Gillock Ltd* 1991 S.L.T. 765 (attempt to alter the effective date of sequestration).

Examples of the exercise of the power under s.63(1) of the Act of 1985 include: waiving the failure to seek separate sequestrations in respect of the separate estates of a partnership and its individual partners (*Royal Bank of Scotland v. J. & J. Messenger* 1991 S.L.T. 492); waiving the failure to produce the original, instead of a photostat copy, of the sheriff clerk's certificate that a charge was displayed on the walls of court for the days of charge (*Waverley Vintners Ltd v. Matthews* 1991 G.W.D. 19–1130); allowing a trustee's non-timeous application under s.54 of the Act of 1985 to defer the debtor's discharge and ordering *interim* deferment (*Pattison*, above) although the court has also refused to exercise the power to defer a trustee's similar application in *Whittaker's Tr. v. Whittaker* 1993 G.W.D. 30–1857 (prejudice to debtor, who was pursuing a claim for solatium, outweighed possible prejudice to her creditors).

Petitions to the *nobile officium* may still be appropriate where, for example, through an unforeseen circumstance a person is denied a remedy afforded by the Act: *Wright v. Tennent Caledonian Breweries Ltd* 1991 S.L.T. 823 (debtor unable to petition for recall within the 10 week time limit prescribed by the Act, as sequestration itself had only been awarded after the expiry of that period); *cf. Brown v. Middlemas of Kelso Ltd*, 1994 S.L.T. 1352.

72.4.3   *"motion"*. For motions, see Chap. 23.

72.4.4   *"where sequestration has been awarded"*. It is only competent to move such a motion or present such a petition once sequestration has been awarded: Act of 1985, s.15(1) and (2).

72.4.5   *"petition"*. A petition is presented in the Outer House: r. 14.2(h). The petition must be in Form 14.4 in the official printed form: rr. 4.1 and 14.4. The petition must be signed by counsel or other person having a right of audience: r. 4.2; and see r. 1.3(1) (definition of "counsel" and "other person having a right of audience") and note 1.3.4.

The petitioner must lodge the petition with the required steps of process (r. 4.4). A fee is payable on lodging the petition: see note 14.5.10.

On petitions generally, see Chap. 14.

72.4.6   *"intimate"*. For methods, see r. 16.7.

72.4.7   *"service"*. For methods, see Chap. 16, Pt I.

72.4.8   *"determined an application under section 15(2) or section 63(3)(b)"*. Once the court has determined an application the sequestration will be remitted back to the sheriff court. In *Pattison v. Halliday* 1991 S.L.T. 645 the court, after waiving the trustee's failure to apply timeously for deferment of the debtor's discharge under s.63 of the Act of 1985, remitted the sequestration back to the sheriff court to determine the application for deferment.

Holding of sederunt book by Accountant in Bankruptcy

72.5. The Accountant in Bankruptcy shall hold the sederunt book for a period of at least six months from the date he receives it from the permanent trustee by virtue of section 57(1) of the Act of 1985 and—

   (a)   shall make it available for public inspection during office hours; and

   (b)   may allow such extracts to be made of entries in the sederunt book by such persons as he thinks fit.

Deriv. R.C.S. 1965, r. 201B inserted by S.I. 1986 No. 514

72.5.1   *"sederunt book"*. This means the sederunt book maintained under s.3(1)(e) of the Act of 1985: Act of 1985, s.73(1). There is no prescribed form for the sederunt book. Inspection of it is governed by s.2 of the Act of 1985. A permanent, but not an interim, trustee keeps a sederunt book. The Act of 1985 prescribes that the following be entered into the sederunt book: (1) copies of any order or decree of the court, such as the recall or refusal to recall an award of sequestration (s.17(8)(b)), any order protecting the occupancy rights of a non-entitled spouse (s.17(8)(b)), the permanent trustee's act and warrant (s.25(6)), any decree pronounced on a challenge of a gratuitous alienation or unfair preference affecting the sequestrated estate (s.34(9) or s.36(7) respectively), a decree recalling an order for payment of a capital sum on divorce (s.35(3)), an order deferring the debtor's discharge (s.54(7)(b)), any decision of a court curing any defects in procedure (s.63(4)), a decree arbitral (s.65(3)); and (2) accounts, reports and minutes produced by or to the permanent trustee, such as copies of the interim trustee's audited accounts and the Accountant's determination thereon (s.26(3)(b)(ii)), a record of the sequestration process prior to the confirmation of the election of the permanent trustee (s.26(5)), a certificate of discharge of the interim trustee, an inventory and valuation of the debtor's estate (s.38(1)(b)), the record of the debtor's examination (if any) (s.47(6)), the permanent trustee's adjudication on creditors' claims (s.49(5)), the decision of a sheriff in an appeal by the debtor or any creditor in relation to the acceptance or rejection of any claim (s.49(6)), the permanent trustee's audited accounts, the scheme of division and the final determination of his outlays and remuneration (s.53(10)), a record of a compromise of any claim (s.65(3)), recommendations, determinations and decrees in the process of a discharge on a compromise (Sched. 4), the minutes of the creditors' meetings (Sched. 6, para. 7(3)), the minutes of the commissioners' meeting (Sched. 6, paras 20 and 21) or a minute signed without a meeting (Sched. 6, para. 23), a reference to the grant of a certificate of discharge of a permanent trustee (s.57(6)).

After the final division of the debtor's estate, the permanent trustee sends the sederunt book to the Accountant in Bankruptcy: Act of 1985, s.57(1)(b).

Prescribed forms

72.6.—(1) The register of insolvencies kept by the Accountant in Bankruptcy under section 1A(1)(b) of the Act of 1985 shall contain the information required in Form 72.6–A.

(2) An undertaking by the interim trustee under section 2(3)(c) of the Act of 1985 shall be in Form 72.6–B.

(3) The memorandum to be sent by a permanent trustee to the Keeper of the Register of Inhibitions and Adjudications under section 14(4) of the Act of 1985 shall be in Form 72.6–C.

(4) A notice by a trustee under a trust deed for creditors to be recorded in the Register of Inhibitions and Adjudications under paragraph 2(1) of Schedule 5 to the Act of 1985 (registration of notice of inhibition) shall be in Form 72.6–D.

(5) A notice under paragraph 2(2) of Schedule 5 to the Act of 1985 recalling a notice registered under paragraph 2(1) of that Schedule shall be in Form 72.6–E.

Deriv. R.C.S. 1965, r. 201A inserted by S.I. 1986 No. 514 and amended by S.I. 1993 No. 899

"register of insolvencies". The maintenance of this register is one of several duties incumbent **72.6.1** on the Accountant in Bankruptcy, the others being the supervision of those involved in the sequestration process and the reporting of any alleged offences to the Lord Advocate. The register contains particulars of sequestrated estates and protected trust deeds. The content of the register is prescribed in Form 72.6–A.

"an undertaking by the interim trustee". In the regime introduced under the Act of 1985, an **72.6.2** interim and permanent trustee was to be appointed in every case. In petitions presented by creditors and trustees acting under a trust deed an interim trustee could be appointed, on cause shown, before an award of sequestration was made (s.13(1)), otherwise an interim trustee was appointed at the time sequestration was awarded (or as soon as may be thereafter (s.13(1)). Under the procedure now obtaining under the Bankruptcy (Scotland) Act 1993, the interim trustee will be either the person nominated by the petitioner, provided certain specified conditions are met, or the Accountant in Bankruptcy. The Accountant in Bankruptcy will become the interim trustee in all cases where the petitioner's nominee is unable to comply with the specified conditions (s.2 of the Act of 1985, substituted by s.2 of the 1993 Act). One of those conditions is the obligation on the person nominated to be the interim trustee to give a written undertaking that he will act as interim trustee and, if no permanent trustee is elected, as permanent trustee: s.2(3)(c) of the Act of 1985, substituted by the 1993 Act, s.2. The purpose of the undertaking is to prevent the interim trustee resigning if he discovers that there are insufficient assets to pay his fees and outlays.

"memorandum" by permanent trustee under s.14(4). Sending this memorandum will extend **72.6.3** for a further three years the effect of the original recording of the certified copy of the relevant court order, namely as an inhibition and a citation in an adjudication of the debtor's heritable estate from the date of sequestration: Act of 1985, s.14(4), amended by the 1993 Act, Sched. 1, para. 3. The effect can be continued for a subsequent three-year period by the recording of a fresh memorandum before the expiry of the current three-year period. A trustee need not send such a memorandum, as was required under the Act of 1985; and this should save unnecessary expense. Where the debtor has heritable estate and there is a reasonable prospect of that estate producing equity for the benefit of the creditors, the trustee should send such a memorandum to the Keeper of the Register of Inhibitions and Adjudications.

"notice" by trustee under a trust deed under para. 2(1) of Sched. 5. The effect of recording **72.6.4** such a notice by a trustee under a trust deed for creditors is as if letters of inhibition were recorded against the debtor in that register. This was a new provision introduced by the Act of 1985 as part of the protected trust deed procedure: Act of 1985, Sched. 5, para. 2. Letters of inhibition render the debtor's heritable subject litigious for five years (Conveyancing (Scotland) Act 1924, s.44(3)(a)) and strike at any future voluntary act of the debtor having the effect of disponing or burdening his heritable property.

"notice" by trustee under a trust deed under para. 2(2) of Sched. 5. The trustee has power, **72.6.5** once the debtor's estate has been finally distributed among his creditors or the trust deed has otherwise ceased to be operative, to record a notice recalling the notice (having the effect of letters of inhibition) recorded under para. 2(1) of Sched. 5 to the Act of 1985.

CHAPTER 73

RECTIFICATION OF DOCUMENTS

Application of this Chapter
73.1. This Chapter applies to an application under section 8 of the Law Reform (Miscellaneous Provisions) (Scotland) Act 1985 (rectification of defectively expressed documents).

73.1.1 *General note.* S.8 of the Law Reform (Miscellaneous Provisions) (Scotland) Act 1985 introduced a remedy not previously available where the expression of an agreement or other document is defective. Formerly, if the defect were patent it might be corrected by a favourable construction; but if latent, decree of reduction would have had to be sought: see *North British Insurance Co. v. Tunnock and Fraser* (1864) 3 M. 1; *Anderson v. Lambie* 1954 S.C.(HL) 43, 61 *per* Lord Reid; *Hudson v. St John* 1977 S.C. 255; *cf. Krupp v. Menzies* 1907 S.C. 903. s.8 of the 1985 Act makes no distinction between patent and latent defects and modifies the rule that parole evidence could not be led to contradict express terms of a written document: *Huewind Ltd v. Clydesdale Bank plc* 1995 S.L.T. 392.

S.8 of the 1985 Act implements the recommendations of the Scottish Law Commission's Report on Rectification of Contractual and Other Documents (Scot. Law Com. No. 79).

73.1.2 *Rectification of documents.* By s.8 of the Law Reform (Miscellaneous Provisions) (Scotland) Act 1985 a document, other than one of a testamentary nature, (a) intended to express or give effect to an agreement which fails to express accurately the common intention of the parties when made or (b) intended to create, transfer, vary or renounce a right which fails to express accurately the intention of the grantor when executed, may be rectified in any manner to give effect to the intention. Any document which would otherwise fall within (a) or (b) above and is defective as a consequence of the defect in the original document may also be rectified by the court at its own instance or on application to it. Proceedings for rectification are not by definition adversarial, a petitioner is not seeking a right against another but asking the court to provide a remedy which only the court can provide; and a petitioner cannot, for example, erect a case on a plea of personal bar: *Bank of Scotland v. Brunswick Developments (1987) Ltd* 1997 S.C. 226, 231B and 232I *per* L.P. Rodger. The remedy is discretionary: *Norwich Union Life Insurance Society v. Tanap Investments VK Ltd (in liquidation) (No. 3)* 1998 S.C.L.R. 627.

On what the court has to be satisfied for a case, and what must be averred to make the case relevant, under s.8(1)(a) of the 1985 Act, see *Shaw v. William Grant (Minerals) Ltd* 1989 S.L.T. 121; see also *Huewind Ltd v. Clydesdale Bank plc* 1995 S.L.T. 392. It is essential to aver that there is an antecedent agreement from which the parties' common intention can be inferred: *George Thompson Services Ltd v. Moore* 1993 S.L.T. 634.

The phrase "express accurately" covers a range of inaccuracies from errors of expression to errors of omission: *Bank of Scotland v. Graham's Tr.* 1992 S.C. 79, 88 *per* L.P. Hope. Ground (b) in s.8 of the 1985 Act extends to a mistake relating to the identity of the grantor of a document: *Bank of Scotland v. Brunswick Developments (1987) Ltd* 1995 S.C. 272. The grantor is the person who executed it if he is not the same person as that in whose name it was executed; it is the intention of the person who signs the document at the date it is executed which is in issue when rectification is sought: *Bank of Scotland v. Brunswick Developments*, above *per* L.P. Hope at p. 278G. For some doubts on the meaning of "grantor" given in that case, see observations of L.P. Rodger and Lord Marnoch in the sequel to that case reported in 1997 S.C. 226, 232C and 236I. In *Norwich Union Life Insurance Society v. Tanap Investments VK Ltd (in liquidation) (No. 3)* 1998 S.C.L.R. 627, the court rejected as too narrow an attempt to limit the application of ss.8 and 9 by reference to a class of error (document failed totally to reflect prior agreement). The court further observed that where parties joined issue on the facts that it would only be in the clearest case that the court could say in advance of proof that the scale or scope and character of amendments proposed went beyond the discretionary power of the court. Rectification might be justified where a document fails to adopt what might by then have become the only way of giving effect to an initial agreement expressed in broad terms: *Norwich Union Life Insurance Society v. Tanap Investments VK Ltd (in liquidation) (No.2)* 2000 S.L.T. 819, 2000 S.C. 515 (Extra Div.).

The phrase "common intention" does not simply mean a shared intention that certain words regardless of their meaning should be inserted into a contract, but that there should be a common intention as to the subject-matter of the agreement and its intended impact on the contract: *Belhaven Brewery Co. v. Swift* 1996 S.L.T.(Sh.Ct) 127, 131L–132A, *per* Sheriff Principal Nicholson, Q.C.

A document may only be rectified where the court is satisfied (a) that the interests of a person, who has acted or refrained from acting in reliance on the terms of the document or on the title sheet of an interest in the Land Register, would not be adversely affected to a material extent or (b) that that person has consented: 1985 Act, s.9. A party who has obtained a decree of rectification relating to an interest in land on the Land Register may, in order to implement that decree, have to apply to the Keeper of the Register for rectification under s.9 of the Land Registration (Scotland) Act 1979 as do those who hold a decree of reduction affecting a registered interest: *Short's Tr. v. Keeper of the Registers of Scotland* 1994 S.C. 122, aff'd 1996 S.C.(HL) 14.

It is doubtful whether a document can be rectified *vis-a-vis* one party but not another: *Belhaven Brewery Co.*, above, at p. 132E.

It is not incompetent to seek an order for rectification which is an alternative to, but inconsistent with, the primary remedy sought in the same action: *Norwich Union Life Insurance Society v. Tanap Investments VK Ltd (in liquidation) (No. 1)* 1998 S.L.T. 623.

The standard of proof is on a balance of probabilities: *Rehman v. Ahmad* 1993 S.L.T. 741 distinguishing *Anderson v. Lambie* 1954 S.C.(HL) 43 (see p. 62 *per* Lord Reid and p. 69 *per* Lord Keith of Avonholm). But the presumption that a written document embodies the agreement of the parties is a strong one, and the observations in *Anderson*, above, are pertinent: *Rehman*, above, *per* Lord Penrose at p. 746C.

Jurisdiction. The court may have jurisdiction by virtue of para. 13 of Sched. 9 to the C.J.J.A. **73.1.3**
1982 (proceedings where no decree sought against a person) or, *e.g.* under r. 1 (domicile), r. 2(2) (contract), r. 2(9) (declarator of rights), r. 3 (consumer contracts), r. 4(1)(c) (exclusive jurisdiction *re* public registers), r. 5 (prorogation) of Sched. 8 to the C.J.J.A. 1982 (jurisdiction of Scottish courts), or on the equivalent grounds in Sched. 1 or 3C to the C.J.J.A. 1982. On jurisdiction generally, see notes 13.2.6 to 13.2.15.

Preventive diligence. In a cause with a prayer or conclusion for rectification there is the **73.1.4**
possibility of preventive diligence in security by means of registration of a notice of the prayer or conclusion: Conveyancing (Scotland) Act 1924, s.44(2) (as amended by the Law Reform (Miscellaneous Provisions) (Scotland) Act 1985, Sched. 2, para. 6).

Form of applications
73.2.—(1) Subject to paragraph (2), an application to which this Chapter applies shall be made by petition.
[1] (2) An application to which this Chapter applies may be made—
[2](a) in an action to which Chapter 47 (commercial actions) applies, by summons or by a conclusion ancillary to other conclusions in the summons or in a counterclaim; or
[2](b) in any other action, by a conclusion in a summons or in a counterclaim.

Deriv. RCS 1965, r. 189(xxxi) inserted by S.I. 1987 No. 2160

---

[1] R. 73.2(2) amended by S.I. 1994 No. 2310 (effective 20th September 1994)
[2] R.73.2(2)(a) and (b) as amended by S.S.I. 2000 No. 66, para. 2(8) (effective 7th April 2000).

General note. R. 73.2(1) restates the general rule that any applications to the court under any **73.2.1**
enactment which is not in a depending cause shall be made by petition to the Outer House: r. 14.2(h). The purpose of this Chapter and this rule is also to allow an application

under s. 8 of the Law Reform (Miscellaneous Provisions) (Scotland) Act 1985 to be made by a conclusion ancillary to other conclusions in a summons or in a counterclaim. The converse, seeking declarator in a petition for rectification, is not competent: *Renyana-Stah Anstalt v. MacGregor*, 2001 S.L.T. 1247 (OH).

On rectification, see notes to r. 73.1.

"petition". A petition under this Chapter is presented to the Outer House: r. 14.2(h). The **73.2.2** petition must be in Form 14.4 in the official printed form: rr. 4.1 and 14.4. The petition must be signed by counsel or other person having a right of audience: r. 4.2; and see r. 1.3(1) (definition of "counsel" and "other person having a right of audience") and note 1.3.4.

The petitioner must lodge the petition with the required steps of process (r. 4.4). A fee is payable on lodging the petition: see note 14.5.10.

On petitions generally, see Chap. 14.

Conclusion(s) ancillary to other conclusions in a summons or in a counterclaim. A dispute as to **73.2.3** the terms of an agreement may arise in a wide variety of litigation. A pursuer in an action concerning the terms of a written agreement may seek rectification of the agreement as part of the same process.

Where rectification is sought in a dispute to which the definition of commercial action in r. 47.1(2) would apply, that remedy may be sought by bringing an action by summons which is a commercial action either for that remedy alone or as ancillary to other remedies sought: r. 73.2(2)(a). This provision enables a (commercial) action to be brought for rectification alone, as otherwise the remedy would have to be sought by petition.

It is not incompetent to conclude for rectification of a document as a conclusion alternative to a principal conclusion of declarator that a document has a specific effect: *Norwich Union Life Insurance Society v. Tanap Investments VK Ltd (in liquidation) (No. 1)* 1998 S.L.T. 623.

For actions generally, see Chap. 13.

Counterclaims. A defender may seek rectification of a deed in a counterclaim by virtue of, and **73.2.4** subject to the conditions of, r. 25.1(1). In *Euan Wallace & Partners v. Westscot Homes plc* 2000 S.L.T. 327, 331F-G Lord Macfadyen noted that there was believed to be some doubt as to whether rectification could be sought in a counterclaim and expressed the opinion (without reference to the first sentence of this note) that the effect of r. 73.2(2)(a) read with r. 25.1(1)(a) was that it was competent. Inspite of both these comments it was somehow thought necessary to spell it out in an amendment to r. 73.2(2) by A.S. (R.C.S.A.) (Miscellaneous) 2000 [S.S.I. 2000 No. 66]. Apparently neither Lord Macfadyen nor the annotation to this rule is regarded as sufficiently authoritative.

CHAPTER 74

COMPANIES

PART I

GENERAL PROVISIONS

Application and interpretation of this Chapter
   74.1.—(1) This Chapter applies to causes under—
 [1] (a) the Insolvency Act 1986; and
    (b) the Company Directors Disqualification Act 1986; and
 [3] (c) Chapter 3 of Part 3 of the Energy Act 2004.
 [2] (2) In this Chapter—
    "the Act of 1986" means the Insolvency Act 1986;
    [3] "the Act of 2004" means the Energy Act 2004;
    "the Insolvency Rules" means the Insolvency (Scotland) Rules 1986;
    [3] "the Energy Administration Rules" means the Energy Administration
        (Scotland) Rules 2006;
    "the EC Regulation" means Council Regulation (EC) 1346/2000 of
        29th May 2000 on insolvency proceedings;
    [3] "non GB company" shall have the meaning assigned in section 171 of
        the Act of 2004;
    "registered office" means—
        (i)   the place specified in the statement of the company delivered to
              the registrar of companies under section 10 of the Companies

Act 1985 as the intended place of its registered office on incorporation, or

(ii)   where notice has been given by the company to the registrar of companies under section 287 of the Companies Act 1985 of a change of registered office, the place specified in the last such notice.

[4] (3) Unless the context otherwise requires, words and expressions used in this Chapter which are also used in the Act of 1986, Chapter 3 of Part 3 of the Act of 2004, the Insolvency Rules or the Energy Administration Rules have the same meaning as in those Acts or Rules, as the case may be.

Deriv. R.C.S. 1965, r. 202(1) (part) and (2) substituted by S.I. 1986 No. 2298 (r. 74.1(2) and (3))

---

[1] Rule 74.1(1)(a) amended by S.I. 1996 No. 1756 (effective 5th August 1996).
[2] Rule 74.1(2) amended by S.S.I. 2003 No. 385 (effective 15th September 2003).
[3] Rule 74.1(1)(c) and definitions inserted by S.S.I. 2006 No. 83 (effective 17th March 2006).
[4] Rule 74.1(3) substituted by S.S.I. 2006 No. 83 (effective 17th March 2006).

74.1.1   *Co-operation between courts.* s. 426(1) of the Act of 1986 provides that an order made by a court in any part of the UK in exercise of its jurisdiction in relation to insolvency law shall be enforced in any other part of the UK. S.426(2) provides that nothing in subsection (1) requires a court to enforce any such order in relation to property in that other part of the UK. No statutory provision is made for the means of enforcement. The order would be enforced by a petition to the insolvency judge for an appropriate order to enforce it.

S. 426(4) of the Act of 1986 provides that courts having jurisdiction in relation to insolvency law in the UK shall assist courts having corresponding jurisdiction in any other part of the UK or any relevant country or territory. For this purpose a request may be made to a court by any other such court to apply the insolvency law applicable by either court: Act of 1986, s. 426(5). A request is made by petition by a party to the proceedings before that court.

Orders have been made by statutory instrument in respect of a "relevant country or territory" in s. 426 of the Act of 1986. These are the Co-operation of Insolvency Courts (Designation of Relevant Countries and Territories) Order 1986 [S.I. 1986 No. 2123] and the Co-operation of Insolvency Courts (Designation of Relevant Countries) Order 1996 [S.I. 1996 No. 253]. The countries and territories are listed below (unless otherwise specified in brackets the relevant S.I. is that of 1986):

Anguilla	Republic of Ireland
Australia	Malaysia (S.I. 1996 No. 253)
The Bahamas	Montserrat
Bermuda	New Zealand
Botswana	St Helena
Canada	South Africa (S.I. 1996 No. 253)
Cayman Islands	Turks and Caicos Islands
Falkland Islands	Tuvalu
Gibraltar	Virgin Islands
Hong Kong	

Proceedings before insolvency judge

[1] **74.2.** All proceedings in the Outer House in a cause under or by virtue of the Act of 1986, the Company Directors Disqualification Act 1986 or Chapter 3 of Part 3 of the Act of 2004, shall be brought before a judge of the court nominated by the Lord President as the insolvency judge or, where the insolvency judge is not available, any other judge of the court (including the vacation judge): and "insolvency judge" shall be construed accordingly.

Deriv. R.C.S. 1965, r. 202(1) (part) substituted by S.I. 1986 No. 2298 and r. 218Q(2) (part) inserted by S.I. 1986 No. 2298

---

[4] Rule 74.2 substituted by S.S.I. 2006 No. 83 (effective 17th March 2006).

74.2.1   *"insolvency judge"*. The insolvency judge is appointed in part by virtue of s. 121(1) of the Act of 1986 which provides for the court by A.S. to provide for proceedings for winding up to be heard by one of the Lords Ordinary.

The current insolvency judges are Lords Eassie, Reed, Clarke and Drummond Young.

"vacation judge". The powers of the vacation judge are limited by r. 11.1.   **74.2.2**

Notices and reports, etc., sent to the court

[1] **74.3.** Where, under the Act of 1986, the Act of 2004, the Insolvency Rules or the Energy Administration Rules—

(a) notice of a fact is to be given to the court,

(b) a report is to be made, or sent, to the court, or

(c) any other document is to be sent to the court,

it shall be sent to the Deputy Principal Clerk who shall cause it to be lodged in the process to which it relates.

Deriv. R.C.S. 1965, r. 218S inserted by S.I. 1986 No. 2298

---

[4] Rule 74.3 substituted by S.S.I. 2006 No. 83 (effective 17th March 2006).

"report". A report may be lodged to assist the court in deciding, *inter alia*, whether the **74.3.1** appointment of an administrator is expedient (see Insolvency Rules, r. 2.2) or whether a petition for the reduction of capital under s. 135 of the Companies Act 1985 should be granted. A report may be lodged by an inspector appointed to investigate a company's officers under Pt. XIV of the 1985 Act, or by a nominee for the purposes of a voluntary arrangement under Pt. I of the Act of 1986.

"sent". This includes deliver: r. 1.3(1) (definition of "send").   **74.3.2**

"document". This may include, *e.g.* minutes of a meeting of members or directors (which are **74.3.3** *prima facie* evidence that the meeting was duly held and convened and that the proceedings recorded took place: 1985 Act, s. 382(4)). See also the probative effect, accorded by s. 5(1) of the Civil Evidence (Scotland) Act 1988, to all memoranda, articles and minutes of meetings, if duly docqueted with a certificate by an officer (usually the secretary) of the company.

PART II

COMPANY VOLUNTARY ARRANGEMENTS

Lodging of nominee's report (company not in liquidation etc.)

74.4.—[1] (1) This rule applies where the company is not being wound up by the court and is not in administration.

(2) A report of a nominee submitted to the court under section 2(2) of the Act of 1986 (procedure where nominee is not the liquidator or administrator) shall be—

(a) lodged, with a covering letter, in the Petition Department;

(b) marked by the clerk of session receiving it with the date on which it is received; and

(c) placed before the insolvency judge for consideration of any direction which he may make under section 3(1) of that Act (which relates to the summoning of meetings).

(3) An application by a nominee to extend the time within which he may submit his report under section 2(2) of the Act of 1986 shall be made by letter addressed to the Deputy Principal Clerk who shall—

(a) place the letter before the insolvency judge for determination;

(b) intimate that determination by a written reply; and

(c) attach the letter, and a copy of the reply, to the nominee's report when it is subsequently lodged.

Deriv. R.C.S. 1965, r. 203(1) to (5) substituted by S.I. 1986 No. 2298

---

[1] R. 74.4(1) amended by S.S.I. 2003 No. 385 (effective 15th September 2003).

General note. Voluntary arrangements were introduced by Part I of the Act of 1986 as a **74.4.1** 74.4.1 simplified alternative to the cumbersome procedure for schemes of arrangement prescribed in s. 425 of the Companies Act 1985 but which would nonetheless be binding on the company's creditors. The purpose of proceeding by way of a voluntary arrangement is to enable an insolvent or near insolvent company to involve an independent person, who must be an insolvency practitioner, to convene a meeting of the company's creditors for the purpose of approving "a composition in satisfaction of [the company's] debts or a scheme of arrangement of its affairs": Act of 1986, s. 1(1). The proposal for a voluntary arrangement may be made by the directors of a company to which an administrator or liquidator has not been appointed: Act of 1986, s. 1(1). It is probably sufficient for this purpose that the proposal is made by a resolution of the board of directors (by analogy with *Re Equiticorp International plc* [1989] B.C.L.C. 597 (concerning the presentation of a petition for administration)) rather than by all of the directors (*Re Instrumentation Electrical Services Ltd* [1988] B.C.L.C. 550). A proposal for a voluntary arrangement may also be made by an administrator or a liquidator where an administration order is in force or where the company is being wound up: Act of 1986, s. 1(3); see r. 74.5 and note 74.5.1.

Directors proposing a voluntary arrangement must give notice of the proposal to a "nominee", who must also be given a copy of the proposal and a statement of the company's affairs: Act of 1986, s. 2(3). The nominee must be an insolvency practitioner: Act of 1986, s. 1(2). If the nominee agrees to act, he must docquet the notice and return it to the company forthwith: Insolvency Rules, r. 1.4. The purpose of supplying the prescribed information is to enable an independent person to form a view, on the basis of sufficient information, as to the feasibility of the proposal. The Insolvency Rules prescribe what information must be contained in the proposal (r. 1.3) and statement of affairs (r. 1.5). The nominee has powers to require the directors to give him certain additional information or to give him access to the company's accounts and records: Insolvency Rules, r. 1.6. It is on the basis of this information that the nominee makes his report to the court, which must be made within 28 days of notice of the proposal (or such longer period as the court may allow): Act of 1986, s. 2(2). In his report the nominee states whether meetings of the company and its creditors should be summoned to consider the proposal and, if such meetings should be summoned, the proposed dates, times and places of those meetings: Act of 1986, s. 2(2). Where the nominee is of the view that meetings should be summoned, the nominee shall (unless the court otherwise directs) summon those meetings on the specified dates and at the specified times and places: Act of 1986, s. 3(1). The Insolvency Rules prescribe the persons to whom notice of the meetings must be given (in the case of creditors' meetings, this requires notice to be given to all creditors specified in the statement of affairs and all other creditors of whose claims and addresses the nominee is aware: Act of 1986, s. 3(2)) as well as the contents of those notices (which must include a copy of the proposal and a copy of the statement of affairs or a summary thereof): Insolvency Rules, r. 1.9.

Lodging of nominee's report (company in liquidation etc.)
74.5.—[1] (1) This rule applies where the company is being wound up by the court or is in administration.

(2) In this rule, "process" means the process of the petition under section 9 (petition for administration order), or section 124 (petition to wind up a company), of the Act of 1986, as the case may be.

(3) A report of a nominee submitted to the court under section 2(2) of the Act of 1986 (procedure where nominee is not the liquidator or administrator) shall be—

(a) lodged in process; and
(b) placed before the insolvency judge for consideration of any direction which he may make under section 3(1) of that Act.

(4) An application by a nominee to extend the time within which he may submit his report under section 2(2) of the Act of 1986 shall be made by letter addressed to the Deputy Principal Clerk who shall—

(a) place the letter before the insolvency judge for determination;
(b) intimate that determination by a written reply; and
(c) lodge the letter, and a copy of the reply, in the process of the petition to which it relates.

Deriv. R.C.S. 1965, r. 204(1) to (5) substituted by S.I. 1986 No. 2298

---

[1] R. 74.5(1) amended by S.S.I. 2003 No. 385 (effective 15th September 2003).

74.5.1 *General note.* For an explanation of the purpose of a voluntary arrangement and the role of the nominee, see note 74.4.1. A proposal for a voluntary arrangement may also be made by an administrator or liquidator, as the case may be, where an administration order is in force in respect of the company or where the company is being wound up: Act of 1986, s. 1(3). Where the proposal is made by the administrator or liquidator, and where the administrator or liquidator is himself to act as nominee, no report is made to the court by him. The nominee, however, is still required to summon the meetings and to send out the prescribed notices to the prescribed persons. In addition, the proposal by the directors must also contain a list of the names and addresses of the company's preferential creditors, together with details of their claims. Where a proposal for a voluntary arrangement is made by an administrator or liquidator, but another insolvency practitioner is to act as nominee, the administrator or liquidator must give notice to the intended nominee, and must provide him with the same prescribed information (*i.e.* the proposal and statement of affairs) as is required of directors: Insolvency Rules, r. 1.12.

"lodged in process", "lodge the letter, and a copy of the reply, in the process". The report of the **74.5.2** nominee, and any application by him to extend the time for lodging it, are lodged in process as steps of process (r. 1.3(1) (definition of "step of process")). On lodging steps of process, see r. 4.4. The documents may be lodged by post: P.N. No. 4 of 1994, paras. 1 and 8; and see note 4.4.10.

Inspection of nominee's report

74.6. A person who states in a letter addressed to the Deputy Principal Clerk that he is a creditor, member or director of the company or his agent, may, on payment of the appropriate fee, inspect the nominee's report lodged under rule 74.4(2) (company not in liquidation etc.) or 74.5(3) (company in liquidation etc.), as the case may be.

Deriv. R.C.S. 1965, r. 203(6) and r. 204(6) substituted by S.I. 1986 No. 2298

Nominee's report. For an explanation of the contents of the nominee's report, and the **74.6.1** purpose for which the nominee is appointed, see note 74.4.1.

Fee. No fee is laid down in the Court of Session Fees etc. Order 1984 [S.I. 1984 No. 256, **74.6.2** Table substituted by S.I. 1993 No. 427].

Report of meetings to approve arrangement

74.7. The report of the result of a meeting to be sent to the court under section 4(6) of the Act of 1986 shall be sent to the Deputy Principal Clerk who shall lodge it—
   (a) in a case to which rule 74.4 (lodging of nominee's report (company not in liquidation etc.)) applies, with the nominee's report lodged under that rule; or
   (b) in a case to which rule 74.5 (lodging of nominee's report (company in liquidation etc.)) applies, in process as defined by paragraph (2) of that rule.

Deriv. R.C.S. 1965, r. 206 substituted by S.I. 1986 No. 2298

General note. The report of the meetings to consider the voluntary arrangement summoned **74.7.1** under s. 3 of the Act of 1986 is sent to the court. If the company is in liquidation or subject to an administration order, the court has to decide what to do with the winding up or the administration order: Act of 1986, s. 5.
The meetings of the creditors of the company and of the company are summoned by the nominee (Act of 1986, s. 3(1) or, where the administrator or liquidator himself acts as nominee, by that person (s. 3(2) of that Act). The purpose of the meetings is to decide whether to accept the proposed voluntary arrangement (with or without modifications): Act of 1986, s. 4(1). A meeting cannot approve any proposal or modification which adversely affects the rights of secured or preferential creditors without first securing the concurrence of the affected creditor: Act of 1986, s. 4(3) and (4). Meetings are conducted in accordance with the Insolvency Rules: s. 4(5). Within four days of the conclusion of each of the creditors' and company's meetings the chairman of the meeting is required to lodge in court a report of the results of the meeting to the court. He must also give notice of the results of the meeting to all persons who received notice of the meeting. It should be noted that, subject to a challenge under s. 6 of the Act of 1986, the court has itself no involvement in relation to the approval of the arrangement. The approval by each of the meetings of the proposed voluntary arrangement with the same modifications or without modifications

takes effect as if made by the company at the creditors' meeting and binds every person who, in accordance with the insolvency rules, had notice of and was entitled to vote at the meeting: Act of 1986, s. 5. The approval of the arrangement may be challenged on the basis of some material irregularity or as being unfairly prejudicial to the interest of a creditor, member or contributory of the company: Act of 1986, s. 6(1). Any challenge, however, must be brought within 28 days of the day on which each report was lodged with the court: Act of 1986, s. 6(3).

74.7.2   *"sent"*. This includes deliver: r. 1.3(1) (definition of "send").

Abstracts of supervisor's receipts and payments and notices of completion of arrangement

74.8. An abstract of receipts and payments prepared by a supervisor and sent to the court under rule 1.21(2) of the Insolvency Rules or a notice of completion of the arrangement (and a copy of the supervisor's report) to be sent to the court under rule 1.23(3) of those Rules shall be sent to the Deputy Principal Clerk who shall cause it to be lodged—

   (a) in a case to which rule 74.4 (lodging of nominee's report (company not in liquidation etc.)) applies, with the nominee's report lodged under that rule; or

   (b) in a case to which rule 74.5 (lodging of nominee's report (company in liquidation etc.)) applies, in process as defined by paragraph (2) of that rule.

Deriv. R.C.S. 1965, r. 207 substituted by S.I. 1986 No. 2298

74.8.1   *General note.* The supervisor of the voluntary arrangement (see Act of 1986, s. 7(2)) must send a copy of the abstracts of receipts and payments at least once every 12 months to the court: Insolvency Rules, r. 1.21. The court may dispense with the requirement to send copies to members of the company (Insolvency Rules, r. 1.21(2) and (5)(a)) or to vary the dates on which the obligation arises (Insolvency Rules, r. 1.21(5)(b)).

    The person responsible for carrying out the voluntary arrangement, once it takes effect, is known as the supervisor (Act of 1986, s. 7(2)) and is normally the nominee.

74.8.2   *"sent"*. This includes deliver: r. 1.3(1) (definition of "send").

Form of other applications

74.9.—(1) An application to which this rule applies shall be made—

[1] (a) where the company is not being wound up by the court and is not in administration, by petition; or

[1] (b) where the company is being wound up by the court or is in administration, by note in the process to which it relates.

   (2) This rule applies to an application under—

   (a) section 2(4) of the Act of 1986 (for the replacement of a nominee);

   (b) section 6 of that Act (to challenge a decision made in relation to an arrangement);

   (c) section 7(3) of that Act (to challenge the actings of a supervisor);

   (d) section 7(4)(a) of that Act (by a supervisor for directions);

   (e) section 7(5) of that Act (for the appointment of a supervisor);

   (f) rule 1.21(5) of the Insolvency Rules (to dispense with sending abstracts or reports or to vary the dates on which the obligation to send abstracts or reports arises);

   (g) rule 1.23(4) of those Rules (to extend the period for sending a notice of implementation of arrangement or report); or

   (h) any other provision in the Act of 1986 or the Insolvency Rules relating to company voluntary arrangements not mentioned in this Part.

Deriv. R.C.S. 1965, r. 205, and r. 208, both substituted by S.I. 1986 No. 2298

---

[1] R. 74.9(1)(a) and (b) amended by S.S.I. 2003 No. 385 (effective 15th September 2003).

74.9.1   *General note.* While part of the purpose of introducing voluntary arrangements was to keep the expense and formality of the court's role to a minimum, provision is made in the Act of 1986 and in the Insolvency Rules for application to be made by the court. Where there is no administration order in force in relation to the company or where the company is not being wound up, such an application must be made by petition. Where, however, one of those insolvency regimes is in place, any application must be made by note in that existing process.

The Act of 1986 provides for two circumstances where application may be made to the court prior to the taking effect of a voluntary arrangement. The first is under s. 2(4) of the Act of 1986 to replace a nominee who has failed to submit the initial report relating to the suitability and viability of the proposed arrangement. The second is a challenge to the approval of any scheme, which must be brought within 28 days of the lodging in court of the report of the chairman of the meeting (as required by s. 4(6)): Act of 1986, s. 6(3). The grounds of challenge are that there has been some material irregularity at or in relation to either of the creditors' or company's meetings or that the arrangement approved at such meetings unfairly prejudices the interest of a creditor, member or contributory of the company: Act of 1986, s. 6(1).

Once an arrangement has taken effect, applications may be made by a supervisor (for directions under s. 7(4)(a) of the Act of 1986), for the appointment of a supervisor (under s. 7(5)) or in relation to the actings of a supervisor (s. 7(3)). The supervisor, who usually acted as the nominee prior to the approval of the arrangement, is the person responsible for carrying out the voluntary arrangement: Act of 1986, s. 7(2).

"petition". A petition is presented in the Outer House: r. 14.2(h). The petition must be in **74.9.2** Form 14.4 in the official printed form: rr. 4.1 and 14.4. The petition must be signed by counsel or other person having a right of audience: r. 4.2; and see r. 1.3(1) (definition of "counsel" and "other person having a right of audience") and note 1.3.4.

The petitioner must lodge the petition with the required steps of process (r. 4.4) and any documents founded on or adopted (r. 27.1(1)). A fee is payable on lodging the petition: see note 14.5.10.

On petitions generally, see Chap. 14.

"note". For applications by note, see r. 15.2.   **74.9.3**

PART III

[1] ADMINISTRATION PROCEDURE

_____

[1] Pt. III heading amended by S.S.I. 2003 No. 385 (effective 15th September 2003).

Form of petition in administration procedure

74.10.—[3] (1) In this Part, "the petition" means a petition under section 9 of, or section 8 of and Schedule B1 to, the Act of 1986 (petition for administration order), or section 156 of the Act of 2004 (petition for energy administration order).

(2) The petition shall include averments in relation to—

(a) the petitioner and the capacity in which he presents the petition, if other than the company;

(b) whether it is believed that the company is, or is likely to become, unable to pay its debts and the grounds of that belief;

[2,3] (c) in the case of a petition under the Act of 1986, how the making of that order will achieve—

(i) any of the purposes specified in section 8(3) of the Act of 1986; or

(ii) an objective specified in paragraph 3 of Schedule B1 to the Act of 1986;

(d) the company's financial position specifying, so far as known, assets and liabilities, including contingent and prospective liabilities;

[3] (e) any security known or believed to be held by creditors of the company, whether in any case the security confers power on the holder to appoint a receiver or an administrator, and whether a receiver or an administrator, as the case may be, has been appointed;

[1] (f) so far as known to the petitioner, whether any steps have been taken for the winding up of the company;

[2,3] (g) other matters which, in the opinion of the petitioner, will assist the court in deciding whether to grant an order in respect of an administration or energy administrator, as the case may be;

² (h) [*Omitted by S.S.I. 2006 No. 83 (effective 17ᵗʰ March 2006)*].

²,³ (i) the name and address of the person proposed to be appointed, and his qualification to act, as administrator or energy administrator, as the case may be; and

²,³ (j) in the case of a petition under the Act of 1986, whether—
    (i) the EC Regulation applies; and
    (ii) if so, whether the proceedings are main proceedings or territorial proceedings.

⁴ (k) whether the Secretary of State has certified the case as one in which he considers it would be appropriate for him to petition under section 124A of the Act of 1986 (petition for winding up on grounds of public interest);

⁴ (l) so far as is known to the petitioner in a petition for an energy administration order, whether any steps have been taken for an administration order under Schedule B1 to the Act of 1986;

⁴ (m) whether a protected energy company in a petition for an energy administration order is a non GB company.

(3) [*Omitted by S.S.I. 2006 No. 83 (effective 17ᵗʰ March 2006)*].

Deriv. R.C.S. 1965, r. 209(1), (3) and (4) substituted by S.I. 1986 No. 2298

---

¹ Rule 74.10(2)(f) amended by S.I. 1994 No. 2901 (minor correction).
² Rule 74.10(2)(c), (g), (h), (i) and heading amended by, and r. 74.10(2)(j) inserted by, S.S.I. 2003 No. 385 (effective 15th September 2003).
³ Rule 74.10(1), (2)(c), (e), (f), (g), (h), (i), (j) amended by S.S.I. 2006 No. 83 (effective 17ᵗʰ March 2006).
⁴ Rule 74.10(2), (k), (l) and (m) inserted by S.S.I. 2006 No. 83 (effective 17ᵗʰ March 2006).

74.10.1 *General note.* A petition for an administration under the Act of 1986 order may be presented by a company, its directors or creditors (Act of 1986, s. 9(1)) and may be granted, where the company is or is likely to become unable to pay its debts, in order to achieve the survival of the company, the approval of a voluntary arrangement, the sanctioning of a compromise or arrangement or a more advantageous realisation of the company's assets than would be effected on a winding up: Act of 1986, s. 8. Certain others may petition where the company is authorised to carry on business under the Financial Services Act 1986 (s. 28 or 33(1)(b)), or the Bank of England may petition in relation to a company under the Banking Act 1987: Act of 1986, s. 9(1). An interim order under s. 9(4) or (5) of the Act of 1986 is not an administration order under s. 8: *Secretary of State for Trade and Industry v. Palmer* 1994 S.C. 707.

A petition by the directors should be supported by a resolution of the directors: *In re Equiticorp International plc* [1989] 1 W.L.R. 1010.

The court must be satisfied that there is a real prospect rather than probability of the purpose of the order being achieved: *In re Harris Simons Construction Ltd* [1989] 1 W.L.R. 368; *Re Rowbotham Baxter Ltd* [1990] B.C.L.C. 397. The presentation of a petition for an administration order on *ex parte* statements at short notice, when the court does not have the advantage of adversarial argument to draw its attention to points weighing for or against the ground of the petition, has been discouraged in England: *Re Rowbotham Baxter Ltd*, above, approved in *Cornhill Insurance plc v. Cornhill Financial Services Ltd* [1992] B.C.C. 818, 856F–H per Dillon L.J.

It is not appropriate when considering approval of the scheme to carry out an examination of the forecasts or assumptions on which the administrator and his advisors reached their conclusions on the validity of the scheme: *Re Olympia & York Canary Wharf Holdings Ltd* [1993] B.C.C. 866.

The petition freezes the position of creditors. On being granted any petition for winding up is dismissed (Act of 1986, s. 11(1)(a)) and an administrative receiver must vacate office (Act of 1986, s. 11(1)(b)). No proceedings may be commenced except with consent of the administrator or with leave of the court. On the granting of leave, see the guidance laid down in *In re Atlantic Computer Systems plc (No. 1)* [1992] Chap. 505; and see, *e.g. Scottish Exhibition Centre Ltd v. Mirestop Ltd* 1993 S.L.T. 1034. On the meaning of "proceedings", see *Air Ecosse Ltd v. Civil Aviation Authority* 1987 S.C. 285 (application for air route licences does not constitute proceedings), *In re Barrow Borough Transport Ltd* [1990] Chap. 227 (application for extension of time to register a charge not proceedings), *Carr v. British International Helicopters Ltd* [1993] B.C.C. 855 (redundant employee's application to industrial tribunal was "proceedings", but it would only be in rare circumstances that the administrator's consent would be required) and *Scottish Exhibition Centre Ltd v. Mirestop (in Administration)* 1996 S.L.T. 8 (service of notice of irritancy on appointment of interim administrators by landlords did not constitute "other legal process" and leave of the court not, therefore, required). In *Re Olympia & York Canary Wharf Ltd* [1993] B.C.C. 154, 157D, Millet J. stated that "legal process", used in s. 11(3)(d) of the Act of 1986, means a process which requires the assistance of the court and does not extend to the service of a contractual notice, whether or not the service of such a notice is a precondition to the bringing of legal proceedings. Millet J. refused to follow Harman J. in *Exchange Travel Ltd v. Triton Property plc* [1991] B.C.C. 341.

Differences in the law of landlord's remedies between Scotland and England may lead to leave being required in one jurisdiction where it is not required in the other. In *Exchange Travel Ltd*, above peaceful re-entry by a landlord was held to be enforcing a security requiring leave under s. 11(3)(d) of the Act of 1986. Irritancy is not, in Scotland, regarded as a security and, therefore, leave under that provision would not be required (and was not sought in *Scottish Exhibition Centre Ltd*, above).

The requirements of the Insolvency Rules should be noted.

Jurisdiction. The court having jurisdiction is the court having jurisdiction to wind up the **74.10.2** company: Act of 1986, s. 251 and the Companies Act 1985, s. 744; Company Directors Disqualification Act 1986, s. 2(2). The C.J.J.A. 1982 does not apply: C.J.J.A. 1982, Scheds. 1 and 3C, Art. 1 (1968 Brussels and Lugano Conventions) Sched. 5, para. 1 (inter-UK jurisdiction) and Sched. 9, para. 4 (jurisdiction of Scottish courts).

"petition". A petition is presented in the Outer House: r. 14.2(h). The petition must be in **74.10.3** Form 14.4 in the official printed form: rr. 4.1 and 14.4. The petition must be signed by counsel or other person having a right of audience: r. 4.2; and see r. 1.3(1) (definition of "counsel" and "other person having a right of audience") and note 1.3.4.

The petitioner must lodge the petition with the required steps of process (r. 4.4) and any documents founded on or adopted (r. 27.1(1)). A fee is payable on lodging the petition: see note 14.5.10.

On petitions generally, see Chap. 14.

Interim administrator. The court may appoint an interim administrator until the petition is **74.10.4** 74.10.4 determined. It is not necessary to specify his powers under the Act of 1986. The interim administrator must be an insolvency practitioner and the petition should state that the proposed interim administrator is such. Averments in support of the application for an interim administrator should be included in the petition. Only an individual may be an insolvency practitioner, and he must have the requisite authorisation and have in force caution for the proper performance of his duties: Act of 1986, s. 390; and see the Insolvency Practitioners Regulations 1986 [S.I. 1986 No. 1995] as amended. It is not necessary for the insolvency practitioner to lodge his bond of caution in process before taking up his appointment and the court will not nowadays order this to be done.

Interim orders
[1,2] **74.10A.**—(1) On making an interim order under paragraph 13(1)(d) of Schedule B1 to the Act of 1986 or section 157(1)(d) of the Act of 2004 the Lord Ordinary shall fix a hearing on the By Order Roll for a date after the expiry of the period of notice mentioned in rule 14.6 (period of notice for lodging answers).

(2) At the hearing under paragraph (1) the Lord Ordinary shall make such order as to further procedure as he thinks fit.

----

[1] Rule 74.10A inserted by S.S.I. 2005 No. 268 (effective 7th June, 2005).
[2] Rule 74.10A(1) amended by S.S.I. 2006 No. 83 (effective 17th March 2006).

General note. Sched. B1 to the Insolvency Act 1986, inserted by the Enterprise Act 2002, **74.10A.1** makes provision for administration. One of the things the court may do on an application for an administration order is make an interim order under para. 13(1)(d) of Sched. B1. An interim order may, in particular, restrict the exercise of a power by a director or the company or confer discretion on the court or an insolvency practitioner.

Notice of petition
74.11. Where—
[1] (a) the petition is to be served on a person mentioned in rule 2.3 of the Insolvency Rules, and

(b) by virtue of paragraph (2) of that rule, notice requires to be given to that person,

it shall be sufficient for the petitioner, where such notice and service is to be executed by post, to enclose the statutory notice and a copy of the petition in one envelope and to certify the giving of such notice and the execution of such service by one certificate.

or,

[2] (c) the petition and a notice are to be served on a person mentioned in section 156(2)(a) to (c) of the Act of 2004 (notice of application for energy administration order) or rule 5(1) of the Energy Administration Rules.

Deriv. R.C.S. 1965, r. 210 substituted by S.I. 1986 No. 2298

---

[1] Rule 74.11(a) amended by S.S.I. 2003 No. 385 (effective 15th September 2003).
[2] Rule 74.11(c) inserted by S.S.I. 2006 No. 83 (effective 17th March 2006).

Report of proposals of administrator

74.12.—(1) A report of the meeting to approve the proposals of the administrator to be sent to the court under section 24(4) of the Act of 1986 shall be sent to the Deputy Principal Clerk of Session, who shall—

(a) cause it to be lodged in the process of the petition to which it relates; and

(b) give written intimation to the parties of the receipt and lodging of the report.

(2) Where a report under section 24(4) of the Act of 1986 discloses that the meeting has declined to approve the proposals of the administrator, the Keeper of the Rolls shall put the cause out on the By Order Roll for determination by the insolvency judge for any order he may make under section 24(5) of that Act.

Deriv. R.C.S. 1965, r. 212 substituted by S.I. 1986 No. 2298

74.12.1   *General note.* Where the meeting of creditors declines to approve the administrator's proposals for achieving the object of the administration order, the court may discharge the order or make any other order: Act of 1986, s. 24(5).

74.12.2   *"sent".* This includes deliver: r. 1.3(1) (definition of "send").

Report of administrator's proposals: Schedule B1 to the Act of 1986

[1] **74.13.**—(1) Paragraph (2) shall apply where a report under paragraphs 53(2) or 54(6) of Schedule B1 to the Act of 1986 discloses a failure to approve, or to approve a revision of, an administrator's proposals.

(2) The Deputy Principal Clerk shall fix a hearing for determination by the insolvency judge of any order that may be made under paragraph 55(2) of Schedule B1 to the Act of 1986.

Deriv. R.C.S. 1965, r. 213 substituted by S.I. 1986 No. 2298

---

[1] Rule 74.13 substituted by S.S.I. 2003 No. 385 (effective 15th September 2003).

74.13.1   *General note.* A copy of the abstract of receipts and payments of the administrator must be sent to the court within two months after six months from the date of his appointment and every six months thereafter, and two months after he ceases to be administrator: Insolvency Rules, r. 2.17. The two-month period may be extended by the court: Insolvency Rules, r. 2.17(2); and see r. 74.14.

74.13.2   *"sent".* This includes deliver: r. 1.3(1) (definition of "send").

Time and date of lodging in an administration or energy administration
[1] **74.14.**—(1) The time and date of lodging of a notice or document relating to an administration under the Act of 1986 or the Insolvency Rules, or an energy administration under the Act of 2004 or the Energy Administration Rules, shall be noted by the Deputy Principal Clerk upon the notice or document.

(2) Subject to any provision in the Insolvency Rules or the Energy Administration Rules, as the case may be—

(a) where the time of lodging of a notice or document cannot be ascertained by the Deputy Principal Clerk, the notice or document shall be deemed to be lodged at 10 a.m. on the date of lodging; and

(b) where a notice or document under paragraph (1) is delivered on any day other than a business day, the date of lodging shall be the first business day after such delivery.

Deriv. R.C.S. 1965, r. 211(2) substituted by S.I. 1986 No. 2298

---

[1] Rule 74.14 substituted by S.S.I. 2006 No. 83 (effective 17th March 2006).

Applications during an administration or energy administration
[1] **74.15.** An application or appeal under any provision of the Act of 1986, the Insolvency Rules, the Act of 2004 or the Energy Administration Rules during an administration or energy administration, as the case may be, shall be—

(a) where no previous application or appeal has been made, by petition; or

(b) where a petition for an order in respect of an administration, or energy administration, as the case may be, has been lodged, by note in the process of that petition.

Deriv. R.C.S. 1965, r. 211(1) substituted by S.I. 1986 No. 2298 (r. 7415(1)) and r. 211(3) and (4) inserted by S.I. 1991 No. 1157 (r. 74.15(3) and (4))

---

[1] Rule 74.15 substituted by S.S.I. 2006 No. 83 (effective 17th March 2006).

Applications for directions. On an application for directions by an administrator under s. 15(2) of the Act of 1986, see *Re Maxwell Communications plc (No. 3)* [1993] B.C.C. 369. **74.15.1**

Discharge of administrator. On a successful application to postpone release of an administrator, see *Re Sibec Developments Ltd* [1993] B.C.C. 148; *Re Exchange Travel (Holdings) Ltd* [1992] B.C.C. 954; and see *Re Olympia & York Canary Wharf Holdings Ltd* [1993] B.C.C. 866. **74.15.2**

"note". For applications by note, see 4.15.2. **74.15.3**

PART IV

RECEIVERS

Interpretation of this Part
74.16. In this Part, "the petition" means a petition under section 54(1) of the Act of 1986 (petition to appoint a receiver).

Petition to appoint a receiver
74.17. The petition shall include averments in relation to—

(a) any floating charge and the property over which it is secured;

[1] (b) so far as known to the petitioner, whether any application for an order in respect of an administration has been made, or an administrator has been appointed in respect of the company;

(c) other matters which, in the opinion of the petitioner, will assist the court in deciding whether to appoint a receiver; and

(d) the name and address of the person proposed to be appointed, and his qualification to act, as receiver.

Deriv. R.C.S. 1965, r. 214(3) substituted by S.I. 1986 No. 2298

---

[1] R. 74.17(b) amended by S.S.I. 2003 No. 385 (effective 15th September 2003).

74.17.1   *General note.* The holder of a floating charge over all or part of the property of a company may apply to the court to appoint a receiver or, where the charge attaches to the whole or substantially the whole of the company's property, an administrative receiver, of such property as is subject to the charge on the occurrence of an event under the charge which entitles the holder to make the appointment or where the court is satisfied that the position of the holder would be prejudiced if the appointment were not made or on a ground specified in s. 52(1)(a)–(c) (Act of 1986, s. 52(2)): Act of 1986, ss. 51(2) and 251. Appointments by the court are not common because the floating charge holder can appoint a receiver without a court order on the occurrence of an event which under the charge entitled him to do so or an event in s. 52(1)(a)–(d): Act of 1986, s. 52(1).

The words in s. 462(1) of the Companies Act 1985, "property and undertaking" of a company, over which it may grant a floating charge, are unqualified and are intended to allow the widest scope for the creation of floating charges. Accordingly, a floating charge which has crystallised (*e.g.* on the appointment of a receiver) attached to and created a priority over heritable subjects in respect of which the company had granted and delivered a disposition but which had not been recorded by the disponee by the date of the crystallisation: *Sharp v. Thomson* 1995 S.C. 455.

74.17.2   *Jurisdiction.* The court having jurisdiction is the court having jurisdiction to wind up the company: Act of 1986, s. 251 and the Companies Act 1985, s. 744. The C.J.J.A. 1982 does not apply: C.J.J.A. 1982, Scheds 1 and 3C, Art. 1 (1968 Brussels and Lugano Conventions), Sched. 5, para. 1 (inter-UK jurisdiction) and Sched. 9, para. 4 (jurisdiction of Scottish courts).

74.17.3   *"petition".* A petition is presented in the Outer House: r. 14.2(h). The petition must be in Form 14.4 in the official printed form: rr. 4.1 and 14.4. The petition must be signed by counsel or other person having a right of audience: r. 4.2; and see r. 1.3(1) (definition of "counsel" and "other person having a right of audience") and note 1.3.4.

The petitioner must lodge the petition with the required steps of process (r. 4.4) and any documents founded on or adopted (r. 27.1(1)). A fee is payable on lodging the petition: see note 14.5.10.

On petitions generally, see Chap. 14.

74.17.4   *Receiver.* The receiver must be an insolvency practitioner: Act of 1986, s. 230(4). The petition should state that the proposed receiver is such. Only an individual may be an insolvency practitioner, and he must have the requisite authorisation and have in force caution for the proper performance of his duties: Act of 1986, s. 390; and see the Insolvency Practitioners Regulations 1986 [S.I. 1986 No. 1995] as amended. It is not necessary for the insolvency practitioner to lodge his bond of caution in process before taking up his appointment and the court will not nowadays order this to be done.

Intimation, service and advertisement under this Part

74.18.—(1) Unless the court otherwise directs, the order under rule 14.5 (first order in petitions) for intimation, service and advertisement of the petition shall include a requirement—

(a) to serve the petition—

(i) on the company; and

(ii) where an application for an administration order has been presented, on that applicant and any respondent to that application; and

(b) to advertise the petition forthwith—

(i) once in the Edinburgh Gazette; and

(ii) once in one or more of such newspapers as the court shall direct.

(2) Subject to rule 14.6(2) (application to shorten or extend the period of notice), the period of notice for lodging answers to the petition shall be eight days.

(3) An advertisement under paragraph (1) shall include—
(a) the name and address of the petitioner;
(b) the name and address of the agent for the petitioner;
(c) the date on which the petition was presented;
(d) the nature of the order sought;
(e) the period of notice for lodging answers; and
(f) a statement that any person who intends to appear in the petition must lodge answers within the period of notice.

Deriv. R.C.S. 1965, r. 215(1), (2) and (6) to (8) substituted by S.I. 1986 No. 2298

"intimation and service". See generally, r. 14.7.   **74.18.1**

"serve". For methods, see Chap. 16, Pt. I.   **74.18.2**

"answers". See r. 18.3.   **74.18.3**

Form of other applications and appeals
74.19.—(1) An application under—
(a) section 61(1) of the Act of 1986 (by a receiver for authority to dispose of property or an interest in property),
(b) section 62 of that Act (for removal of a receiver),
(c) section 63(1) of that Act (by a receiver for directions),
(d) section 69(1) of that Act (to enforce the receiver's duty to make returns etc.), or
(e) any other provision of that Act or the Insolvency Rules relating to receivers not mentioned in this Part,
shall, where the court has appointed the receiver, be made by note or, in any other case, by petition.
(2) An appeal against a decision of a receiver as to expenses of submitting a statement of affairs under rule 3.3(2) of the Insolvency Rules shall, where the receiver was appointed by the court, be made by note or in any other case, by petition.
(3) An application by a receiver—
(a) under section 67(1) or (2) of the Act of 1986 (to extend the time for sending a report),
(b) under rule 3.9(2) of the Insolvency Rules (to extend the time for sending an abstract of his receipts and payments),
shall, where the court has appointed the receiver, be made by motion or, in any other case, by petition.

Deriv. R.C.S. 1965, r. 216 substituted by S.I. 1986 No. 2298

Applications by receiver for directions. For recent examples of applications by receivers for **74.19.1**
directions, see *Scottish & Newcastle plc, Petrs* 1994 S.L.T. 1140 (whether certain heritable
subjects remained the property of the company at the date of the appointment of the receiver
notwithstanding the omission to register an instrument of alteration or a memorandum of
satisfaction under ss. 466 and 419, respectively, of the Companies Act 1985 and for declarator
that the receiver was a receiver and not an administrative receiver); *McKillop v. Tayside R.C.*
1994 S.C.L.R. 746 (whether receiver personally liable for local authority rates); *Turner v. Inland
Revenue Commissioners* 1994 S.L.T. 811 (whether Inland Revenue entitled to set off sums due to
the company against ordinary debts rather than pro rata against ordinary and preferential debts
due by the company to the Inland Revenue); *Powdrill v. Watson, Re Leyland DAF Ltd, Re
Ferranti International plc* [1995] 2 All E.R. 65 (H.L.) (whether administrative receivers had
"adopted" employees' contracts of employment for the purposes of s. 44(1)(b) of the Act of
1986).
The court has a discretion under s. 63(1) of the Act of 1986 whether or not to give the
directions sought: *McKillop,* above. In *Jamieson & Ors, Petrs* 1997 S.C. 195 (Extra Div.),
unreported, the court declined to give a direction under s. 63(1) of 1986 Act. In that case, in
anticipation of a large number of claims against receivers by employees whose contracts had
been adopted subsequent to the appointment of a receiver, a number of insolvency practitioners
sought a direction from the court compelling any such claimants to follow a specified procedure.

74.19.2 *"petition"*. A petition is presented in the Outer House: r. 14.2(h). The petition must be in Form 14.4 in the official printed form: rr. 4.1 and 14.4. The petition must be signed by counsel or other person having a right of audience: r. 4.2; and see r. 1.3(1) (definition of "counsel" and "other person having a right of audience") and note 1.3.4.

The petitioner must lodge the petition with the required steps of process (r. 4.4) and any documents founded on or adopted (r. 27.1(1)). A fee is payable on lodging the petition: see note 14.5.10.

On petitions generally, see Chap. 14.

74.19.3 *"note"*. For applications by note, see r. 15.2.

PART V

WINDING UP OF COMPANIES

Interpretation of this Part
74.20. In this Part, "the petition" means a petition under section 124 of the Act of 1986 (petition to wind up a company).

Petition to wind up a company
74.21.—(1) The petition shall include averments in relation to—
(a) the petitioner, if other than the company, and his title to present the petition;
(b) in respect of the company—
    (i) its current and any previous registered name;
    (ii) the address of its registered office, and any previous such address within six months immediately before the presentation of the petition so far as known to the petitioner;
    (iii) a statement of the nature of its business and objects, the amount of its capital (nominal and issued) indicating what part

is called up, paid up or credited as paid up, and the amount of the assets of the company so far as known to the petitioner;
(c) whether, to the knowledge of the petitioner, a receiver has been appointed in respect of any part of the property of the company or a liquidator has been appointed for the voluntary winding up of the company;
(d) the grounds on which the petition proceeds; and
(e) the name and address of the person proposed to be appointed, and his qualification to act, as interim liquidator.

Deriv. R.C.S. 1965, r. 217(3) substituted by S.I. 1986 No. 2298

General note. An application to wind up a company may be made by the company, its **74.21.1** directors, a creditor or contributory, or the Secretary of State in certain circumstances: Act of 1986, s.124. It may also be applied for by an administrative receiver: Act of 1986, Sched. 2, para. 21.

A contributory presenting a petition for the winding up of a company must demonstrate interest as well as complying with the relevant statutory qualifications: *O'Conner v. Atlantis Fisheries Ltd*, 27th January 1998, unreported (1998 G.W.D. 8–359).

Jurisdiction. The Court of Session has jurisdiction to wind up a company registered in **74.21.2** Scotland: Act of 1986, s.120(1). The sheriff court has concurrent jurisdiction where the share capital paid up or credited does not exceed £120,000. The C.J.J.A. 1982 does not apply: C.J.J.A. 1982, Scheds 1 and 3C, Art. 1, Sched. 5, para. 1 and Sched. 9, para. 4.

"petition". A petition is presented in the Outer House: r. 14.2(h). The petition must be in **74.21.3** Form 14.4 in the official printed form: rr. 4.1 and 14.4. The petition must be signed by counsel or other person having a right of audience: r. 4.2; and see r. 1.3(1) (definition of "counsel" and "other person having a right of audience") and note 1.3.4.

The petitioner must lodge the petition with the required steps of process (r. 4.4) and any documents founded on or adopted (r. 27.1(1)). A fee is payable on lodging the petition: see note 14.5.10.

On petitions generally, see Chap. 14.

"grounds on which the petition proceeds". The various grounds are set out in s.122 of the Act **74.21.4** of 1986. The Secretary of State may petition on grounds of public interest: Act of 1986, s.124A inserted by the Companies Act 1989, s.60(3). For a recent example of a successful petition at the instance of the Secretary of State on the ground of it being just and equitable in the public interest to wind up a company, see *Secretary of State for Trade and Industry v. Hasta International Ltd* 1998 S.L.T. 73 (pyramid selling constituting an illegal lottery).

Winding up a company under s.122(1)(f) (company unable to pay its debts). A petition on this ground presented by a creditor in respect of a debt which is due and unpaid will not normally be allowed to proceed if the existence of the petitioning creditor's alleged debt is *bona fide* disputed by the company on reasonable and substantial grounds. A petition for winding up is not a legitimate means of seeking to enforce payment of a debt which is *bona fide* in dispute: *Stonegate Securities Ltd v. Gregory* [1980] 1 Ch. 576, 579, *per* Buckley, L.J. It would be open to the court to sist the petition to enable the petitioner to constitute the debt in a separate process. A creditor petitioning to wind up a company on the ground that it is just and equitable to do so (under s.122(1)(g)) will also require to establish that he is a creditor, either actual, contingent or prospective, of the company within the meaning of s.124 of the Act of 1986. If there is a *bona fide* dispute as to whether the petitioner is a creditor and has *locus standi* to present the petition, this issue would normally be dealt with by the court before enquiry into the merits of the application: *Rocks v. Brae Hotel (Shetland) Ltd* 1997 S.L.T. 474.

Winding up a company under s.122(1)(g) (just and equitable). A creditor petitioning to wind up a company on the ground that it is just and equitable to do so does not need to have demanded payment before the petition is presented: *Macdonald v. North of Scotland Bank* 1942 S.C. 369, 375 *per* L.J.-C. Cooper.

"interim liquidator". An interim liquidator is appointed by the court on the making of the **74.21.5** winding-up order and he holds office until the liquidator is appointed: Act of 1986, s.138. He must be an insolvency practitioner and the petition must state that he is one. Normally the provisional liquidator is appointed interim liquidator.

"provisional liquidator". See r. 74.25 on an application for a provisional liquidator. The **74.21.6** averments required are set out in r. 74.25(2). He must be an insolvency practitioner, and it must be stated in the petition that he is one. There must be averments in support of the application in the petition. The provisional liquidator may be appointed before the winding-up order: Act of 1986, s.135(2). The application is usually made in the winding-up petition.

Cause must be shown for the appointment of a provisional liquidator: *Levy v. Napier* 1962 S.C. 468; *Teague, Petr* 1985 S.L.T. 469. Appearance at a motion for such an appointment will be required.

74.21.7   *Insolvency practitioner.* Only an individual may be an insolvency practitioner; he must have the required authorisation and have in force caution for the proper performance of his duties: Act of 1986, s.390(1), (2) and (3); and see the Insolvency Practitioners Regulations 1986 [S.I. 1986 No. 1995]. It is not necessary for an insolvency practitioner to lodge his bond of caution in process before taking up his appointment and the court will not nowadays order this to be done.

74.21.8   *Date of presentation of petition.* This is the date of presentation in the Petition Department. A winding up commences at the date of presentation of the petition: Act of 1986, s.129(2). The presentation interrupts the running of the prescriptive periods (Prescription and Limitations (Scotland) Act 1973, s.9) and is important in considering gratuitous alienations or unfair preferences: Act of 1986, ss.242 and 243. The date of the interlocutor granting the winding-up order is, however, the relevant date in considering the effect of the winding up on diligence: Act of 1986, s.185.

Intimation, service and advertisement under this Part

74.22.—(1) Unless the court otherwise directs, the order under rule 14.5 (first order in petitions) for intimation, service and advertisement of the petition shall include a requirement—
  (a) to serve the petition—
      (i) where the petitioner is not the company, on the company;
      (ii) where the company is being wound up voluntarily and a liquidator has been appointed, on the liquidator; and
      (iii) where a receiver or administrator has been appointed, on the receiver or administrator, as the case may be;
  (b) where the company is an authorised institution or former authorised institution within the meaning assigned in section 106(1) of the Banking Act 1987 and the petitioner is not the Bank of England, to serve the petition on the Bank of England; and
  (c) to advertise the petition forthwith—
      (i) once in the Edinburgh Gazette; and
      (ii) once in one or more of such newspapers as the court shall direct.
(2) Subject to rule 14.6(2) (application to shorten or extend the period of notice), the period of notice for lodging answers to the petition shall be eight days.
(3) An advertisement under paragraph (1) shall include—
  (a) the name and address of the petitioner and, where the petitioner is the company, its registered office;
  (b) the name and address of the agent for the petitioner;
  (c) the date on which the petition was presented;
  (d) the nature of the order sought;
  (e) where a provisional liquidator has been appointed by the court, his name, address and the date of his appointment;
  (f) the period of notice for lodging answers; and
  (g) a statement that any person who intends to appear in the petition must lodge answers within the period of notice.

Deriv. R.C.S. 1965, r. 218(2) and (6) to (8) substituted by S.I. 1986 No. 2298

74.22.1   *General note.* A caveat may have been lodged against a winding-up petition. If so the caveator will be notified by the Keeper of the Rolls and a hearing arranged for the motion for the first order at which appearance will be required and the caveator may be heard. On caveats, and procedure where caveats are lodged, see Chap. 5.

74.22.2   *"intimation and service".* See r. 14.7. On methods of service, see Chap. 16, Pt I.

74.22.3   *"advertised".* The advertisement in a newspaper or notice in the Gazettes should be headed with the cause reference number followed by a heading containing the name of the company.

74.22.4   *"period of notice".* See r. 14.6.

"provisional liquidator". Cause must be shown for the appointment of a provisional **74.22.5**
liquidator: *Levy v. Napier* 1962 S.C. 468; *Teague, Petr* 1985 S.L.T. 469. Appearance at a motion
for such an appointment will be required.
   See further notes 74.21.6 and 74.21.7.

Lodging execution copy of petition. After intimation, service and advertisement, the period of **74.22.6**
notice having expired, the execution copy of the petition (see r. 16.1(4) and note 16.1.6) must be
lodged in process before further procedure is permitted.

Remits from one court to another

74.23.—(1) An application under section 120(3)(a)(i) of the Act of 1986
(application for remit of petition to a sheriff court) shall be made by motion.
   (2) An application under—
    (a) section 120(3)(a)(ii) of the Act of 1986 (application for remit of
       petition from a sheriff court to the court), or
    (b) section 120(3)(b) of that Act (application for remit of petition from
       one sheriff court to another),
shall be made by petition.

Deriv. R.C.S. 1965, r. 218B inserted by S.I. 1986 No. 2298

General note. The court may, if it thinks it expedient having regard to the amount of the **74.23.1**
company's assets, remit a winding-up petition to the sheriff court or require a petition presented
in the sheriff court to be remitted to the Court of Session or another sheriff court: Act of 1986, s.
120(3)(*a*).

"motion". For motions, see Chap. 23.   **74.23.2**

"petition". A petition is presented in the Outer House: r. 14.2(*h*). The petition must be in **74.23.3**
Form 14.4 in the official printed form: rr. 4.1 and 14.4. The petition must be signed by counsel
or other person having a right of audience: r. 4.2; and see r. 1.3(1) (definition of "counsel" and
"other person having a right of audience") and note 1.3.4.
   The petitioner must lodge the petition with the required steps of process (r. 4.4). A fee is
payable on lodging the petition: see note 14.5.10.
   On petitions generally, see Chap. 14.

Substitution of creditor or contributory for petitioner

74.24.—(1) Where a petitioner in the petition—
    (*a*) is subsequently found not entitled to present the petition,
    (*b*) fails to make intimation, service and advertisement as directed by the
       court,
    (*c*) moves or consents to withdraw the petition or to allow it to be
       dismissed or refused,
    (*d*) fails to appear when the petition is called for hearing, or
    (*e*) appears, but does not move for an order in terms of the prayer of the
       petition,
the court may, on such terms as it thinks fit, sist as petitioner in place of the
original petitioner any creditor or contributory who, in the opinion of the
court, is entitled to present the petition.
  [1] (1A) Where a member State liquidator has been appointed in main
proceedings in relation to the company, without prejudice to paragraph (1)
the court may, on such terms as it thinks fit, substitute the member State
liquidator as petitioner, where he is desirous of prosecuting the petition.
   (2) An application by a creditor or a contributory to be sisted under
paragraph (1)—
    (*a*) may be made at any time before the petition is dismissed or refused,
       and
    (*b*) shall be made by note;
and, if necessary, the court may continue the petition for a specified period
to allow a note to be presented.

---

[1] R. 74.24(1A) inserted by SSI 2003/385 (effective 15th September 2003).

74.24.1   *General note.* A creditor may be a contingent or prospective creditor: Act of 1986, s. 124(1). A "contingent creditor" means a creditor in respect of a debt which may become due, and a "prospective creditor" means a creditor in respect of a debt which will become due.

A contributory (on the meaning of which, see s. 79 of the Act of 1986) may only be a petitioner, except where the number of members falls below two, if some of the shares in respect of which he is a contributory were originally allotted to him or have been held by him and registered in his name for at least six months during the 18 months before the commencement of the winding up or devolved to him on the death of the previous holder: Act of 1986, s. 124(2).

In the circumstances specified in r. 74.24(1), a creditor or contributory may be sisted in room of an original petitioner.

74.24.2   *"note".* For applications by note, see r. 15.2.

Provisional liquidator

74.25.—(1) An application to appoint a provisional liquidator under section 135 of the Act of 1986 may be made—

    (*a*) by the petitioner, in the prayer of the petition or, if made after the petition has been presented, by note; or

[1] (*b*) by a creditor or contributory of the company, the company, the Secretary of State, a member State liquidator appointed in main proceedings or a person entitled under any enactment to present a petition, by note.

(2) The application mentioned in paragraph (1) shall include averments in relation to—

    (*a*) the grounds for the appointment of the provisional liquidator;

    (*b*) the name and address of the person proposed to be appointed, and his qualification to act, as provisional liquidator; and

    (*c*) whether, to the knowledge of the applicant, an administrator has been appointed to the company or a receiver has been appointed in respect of any part of its property or a liquidator has been appointed voluntarily to wind it up.

(3) Where the court decides to appoint a provisional liquidator—

    (*a*) it shall pronounce an interlocutor making the appointment and specifying the functions to be carried out by him in relation to the affairs of the company; and

    (*b*) the applicant shall forthwith send a certified copy of such interlocutor to the person appointed.

(4) On receiving a certified copy of an interlocutor pronounced under paragraph (3), the provisional liquidator shall intimate his appointment forthwith—

(*a*) once in the Edinburgh Gazette; and
(*b*) once in one or more of such newspapers as the court has directed.
(5) An application for the discharge of a provisional liquidator shall be made by note.

Deriv. R.C.S. 1965, r. 218E inserted by S.I. 1986 No. 2298

---

[1] R. 74.25(1)(b) amended by S.S.I. 2003 No. 385 (effective 15th September 2003).

General note. An application for a provisional liquidator is usually made in the winding-up **74.25.1** petition; if not, it is made by note: see r. 74.25(1).

The averments required are set out in r. 74.25(2). The provisional liquidator must be an insolvency practitioner, and it must be stated in the petition that he is one. Only an individual may be an insolvency practitioner; he must have the required authorisation and have in force caution for the proper performance of his duties: Act of 1986, s. 390(1), (2) and (3); and see the Insolvency Practitioners Regulations 1986 [S.I. 1986 No. 1995]. It is not necessary for an insolvency practitioner to lodge his bond of caution in process before taking up his appointment and the court will not nowadays order this to be done.

The provisional liquidator may be appointed before the winding-up order: Act of 1986, s. 135(2).

Cause must be shown for the appointment of a provisional liquidator: *Levy v. Napier* 1962 S.C. 468; *Teague, Petr.* 1985 S.L.T. 469. Appearance at a motion for such an appointment will be required.

The purpose of seeking appointment of a provisional liquidator is for him to take custody of, and preserve, the assets of the company between the time of his appointment and the appointment of the liquidator. The public interest in a thorough investigation of the company's affairs, especially of a company carrying on investment business, may justify the appointment of a provisional liquidator notwithstanding that it might be cheaper to proceed with a members' voluntary winding up already under way: *Securities Investment Board v. Lancashire and Yorkshire Portfolio Management Ltd* [1992] B.C.C. 381. For an unsuccessful attempt to appoint an additional provisional liquidator, see *Re Bank of Credit and Commerce International S.A.* [1992] B.C.C. 83.

Where the company is not the petitioner it will only get notice of an application to appoint a provisional liquidator in a petition to wind it up if it has lodged a caveat. On caveats, see Chap. 5.

On appointment, as well as the notifications to be made by him under r. 74.25(4), the provisional liquidator must notify the Registrar of Companies, the company and any receiver: Insolvency Rules, r. 4.2(1).

In relation to the remuneration and expenses of a provisional liquidator, the words "Without prejudice to any order of the court as to expenses" in r. 4.5(3) of the Insolvency Rules recognise the discretion of the court to order that the remuneration and expenses might form part of the expenses of the case and to order which party was to bear that cost: *Graham v. John Tullis & Son (Plastics) Ltd* 1991 S.C. 302.

"contributory". A contributory is, generally, a registered member or shareholder of the **74.25.1A** company. It has been held competent for the trustee on the sequestrated estate of a bankrupt member to be able to petition for the winding up of the company, notwithstanding that the trustee has not taken steps to register himself as the holder of the bankrupt's shareholding: *Cumming's Tr. v. Glenrinnes Farms Ltd* 1993 S.L.T. 904.

Powers of provisional liquidator. These may be restricted (s. 135(5) of the Act of 1986) and are **74.25.2** usually limited in the first instance to those in Pt. II of Sched. 4 (power to bring or defend any action or other legal proceedings and to carry on the business of the company as may be necessary for its beneficial winding up): Act of 1986, Sched. 4, paras. 4 and 5.

"note". For applications by note, see r. 15.2.   **74.25.3**

Intimation in Edinburgh Gazette and newspapers. The advertisement in a newspaper or notice **74.25.4** in the Gazette should be headed with the cause reference number followed by a heading containing the name of the company.

The provisional liquidator must advertise his appointment without delay, as this is an obligation imposed on him as an officer of the court. In *International Factors v. Ves Voltech Electronic Services Ltd* 1994 S.L.T. (Sh. Ct.) 40, Sheriff Principal Hay disapproved of the practice of provisional liquidators in delaying, in some cases, to advertise their appointment. While there may be sound commercial reasons making advertisement inappropriate, the provisional liquidator must apply to the court immediately for dispensation of this requirement.

74.25.5 *Discharge of provisional liquidator.* The provisional liquidator may be removed from office only by order of the court: Act of 1986, s. 172(2). He may be removed, *e.g.* if he fails to maintain his caution: Insolvency Rules, r. 4.4(1).

If a decision to remove him is reclaimed, the provisional liquidator remains in office until the reclaiming motion is determined: *Levy* 1963 S.C. 46.

Appointment of a liquidator

74.26.—(1) Where the court pronounces an interlocutor appointing a liquidator—

    (a) the Deputy Principal Clerk shall send a certified copy of that interlocutor to the liquidator;

    (b) the court may, for the purposes of rule 4.18(4) of the Insolvency Rules (liquidator to give notice of appointment), give such direction as it thinks fit as to advertisement of such appointment.

(2) An application to appoint a liquidator under section 139(4) of the Act of 1986 shall be made by note.

Deriv. R.C.S. 1965, r. 218D, and r. 218H, both inserted by S.I. 1986 No. 2298

74.26.1 *General note.* For most purposes the winding up dates from presentation of the petition for winding up: Act of 1986, s. 129(2).

When a winding-up order is made the court appoints an interim liquidator who summons separate meetings of creditors and contributories to choose a liquidator: Act of 1986, s. 138(1) to (4).

The court may appoint a liquidator (a) where no liquidator is appointed by the meetings of creditors and contributories (Act of 1986, s. 138(5)); (b) where different persons are nominated by the creditors and contributories, on the application of the contributories within seven days of the creditors' nomination (Act of 1986, s. 139(4)); (c) on the discharge of an administration order (Act of 1986, s. 140(1)); or (d) where a winding-up order is made at a time when there is a supervisor of a voluntary arrangement, in which case the court may appoint the supervisor (Act of 1986, s. 140(2)).

The liquidator has the powers in Sched. 4 to the Act of 1986. A liquidator requires the sanction of the court or of the liquidation committee for the exercise of powers enumerated in Pts I and II of that Schedule: Act of 1986, s. 167(1). No such sanction is required for the exercise of the powers set out in Pt. III of that Schedule. A sale of the company's heritage is an example of one of the powers exercisable without sanction: *Duff v. Armour* 1990 G.W.D. 22–1212. While the power to bring or defend actions and other legal proceedings requires sanction, being a power within Pt. II of the Schedule, the requirement for sanction only applies to actions and proceedings brought in the name and on behalf of the company (*i.e.* where the company must be a party). This does not preclude actions by the liquidator alone, *e.g.* under s. 242 of the Act of 1986 (challenging gratuitous alienations, as in *Dyer v. Hyslop* 1994 S.C.L.R. 171 or in *Thomson v. M.B. Trustees Ltd* 1994 G.W.D. 32–1894) or under s. 243 of the Act of 1986 (challenging unfair preferences, as in *Nicoll v. Steelpress (Supplies) Ltd* 1993 S.L.T. 533), although such actions may in fact run in the name of both the liquidator and the company (*e.g.* challenging a gratuitous alienation, as in *Lafferty Construction Ltd v. McCombe* 1994 S.L.T. 858). It is thought that a liquidator's failure to obtain prior sanction will not invalidate the proceedings brought but may expose the liquidator to personal liability in expenses: *Dublin City Distillery (Great Brunswick Street, Dublin) v. Doherty* [1914] A.C. 823; *Dyer*, above. A liquidator's liability in expenses against him "as liquidator" is limited to the available funds of the company: *Dyer v. Craiglaw Developments Ltd*, 29th October 1998, unreported.

The liquidator may seek the directions of the court: *Liquidator of Upper Clyde Shipbuilders Ltd* 1975 S.L.T. 39 *per* Lord Grieve.

74.26.2 *"send".* This includes deliver: r. 1.3(1) (definition of "send").

74.26.3 *"note".* For applications by note, see r. 15.2.

Applications and appeals in relation to a statement of affairs

74.27.—(1) An application under section 131(5) of the Act of 1986 for—

    (a) release from an obligation imposed under section 131(1) or (2) of that Act, or

    (b) an extension of time for the submission of a statement of affairs,

shall be made by note.

(2) A note under paragraph (1) shall be served on the liquidator or provisional liquidator, as the case may be, who may lodge—

(a) answers to the note; or
(b) a report on any matters which he considers should be drawn to the attention of the court.

(3) Where the liquidator or provisional liquidator lodges a report under paragraph (2), he shall forthwith send a copy of it to the noter.

(4) Where the liquidator or the provisional liquidator does not appear at any hearing on the note, a certified copy of the interlocutor disposing of the note shall be sent to him forthwith by the noter.

(5) An appeal under rule 4.9(6) of the Insolvency Rules (appeal against refusal by liquidator of allowance towards expenses of preparing statement of affairs) shall be made by note.

Deriv. R.C.S. 1965, r. 218F inserted by S.I. 1986 No. 2298

General note. The liquidator or provisional liquidator may require officers of the company or **74.27.1** others who are or were connected with the company to prepare a statement of affairs of the company: Act of 1986, s. 131(1). He may release a person from the obligation to do so, or extend the time for doing so; but if the (provisional) liquidator refuses to exercise either power the court may exercise it: Act of 1986, s. 131(5).

An application may be made to the court against the liquidator's refusal to grant an allowance to a person required to prepare a statement of affairs who cannot prepare it himself: Insolvency Rules, r. 4.9(6).

"note". For applications by note, see r. 15.2.   **74.27.2**

"answers". For form and procedure, see r. 18.3.   **74.27.3**

"send". This includes deliver: r. 1.3(1) (definition of "send").   **74.27.4**

Appeals against adjudication of claims

74.28.—(1) An appeal under section 49(6) of the Bankruptcy (Scotland) Act 1985 as applied by rule 4.16 of the Insolvency Rules (appeal by a creditor or contributory of the company against a decision of the liquidator), shall be made by note.

(2) A note under paragraph (1) shall be served on the liquidator.

(3) On such a note being served on him, the liquidator shall send the claim in question, and a copy of his adjudication, forthwith to the Deputy Principal Clerk who shall cause them to be lodged in process.

(4) After the note has been disposed of, the Deputy Principal Clerk shall return the claim and the adjudication to the liquidator with a copy of the interlocutor disposing of the note.

Deriv. R.C.S. 1965, r. 218G inserted by S.I. 1986 No. 2298

General note. At the beginning of every meeting of creditors the liquidator has to accept or **74.28.1** reject each creditor's claim in so far as it relates to voting at a meeting: Bankruptcy (Scotland) Act 1985, s. 49(1). When funds are available for payment of dividends in respect of an accounting period the liquidator must accept or reject each creditor's claim to be entitled to a dividend: 1985 Act, s. 49(2). A creditor dissatisfied with a decision on a claim to vote may appeal to the court within two weeks of the decision, or on a claim to entitlement to a dividend not later than two weeks before the end of the accounting period: 1985 Act, s. 49(6).

Where the liquidator rejects a claim for damages the proper course is to bring an ordinary action rather than to appeal the liquidator's decision: *Crawford v. McCulloch* 1909 S.C. 1063; *Knoll Spinning Co. Ltd v. Brown* 1977 S.C. 291.

"note". For applications by note, see r. 15.2.   **74.28.2**

"send". This includes deliver: r. 1.3(1) (definition of "send").   **74.28.3**

Removal of liquidator

74.29. An application by a creditor of the company for an order—
(a) under section 171(3) of the Act of 1986 (order directing a liquidator to summon a meeting of creditors for the purpose of removing him), or

(b) under section 172 of that Act (order for removal of a liquidator), shall be made by note.

Deriv. R.C.S. 1965, r. 218J inserted by S.I. 1986 No. 2298

74.29.1   *General note.* A liquidator may be removed from office by the court or a general meeting of creditors: Act of 1986, s. 172(2); Insolvency Rules, rr. 4.23 and 4.26. A provisional liquidator may only be removed by the court: Act of 1985, s. 172(2).

    In *Geddes, Petr.*, 2006 S.L.T. 664, Lord Drummond Young held that the procedures contemplated by rules 4.28 and 4.29 of the Insolvency (Scotland) Rules 1986 for a liquidator seeking to be removed and replaced were unsatisfactory, and the procedure adopted in English cases such as *Re. Equity Nominees Ltd,* [2002] BCC 84, could competently be followed where the court had statutory power to remove a liquidator and a common law power to appoint a replacement.

74.29.2   *"note".* For applications by note, see r. 15.2.

Application in relation to remuneration of liquidator

74.30.—(1) An application—
- (a) by a liquidator under rule 4.34 of the Insolvency Rules (application to increase remuneration), or
- (b) by a creditor of the company under rule 4.35 of those Rules (application to reduce liquidator's remuneration),

shall be made by note.

(2) A note under paragraph (1)(b) shall be served on the liquidator.

Deriv. R.C.S. 1965, r. 218K inserted by S.I. 1986 No. 2298

74.30.1   *General note.* The liquidator may make a claim to the liquidation committee for outlays and remuneration: Act of 1986, s. 172(6); Insolvency Rules, r. 4.28(3). He may request an increase of the remuneration fixed by resolution of the creditors: Insolvency Rules, r. 4.28(4).

    An application by a creditor to reduce the remuneration must be by one or more creditors representing at least 25 per cent by value of creditors: Insolvency Rules, r. 4.35.

74.30.2   *"note".* For applications by note, see r. 15.2.

Applications under section 176A of the Act of 1986

[1] **74.30A.**—(1) An application by a liquidator, administrator or receiver under section 176A of the Act of 1986 shall be—
- (a) where there is no existing process in relation to any liquidation, administration or receivership, by petition; or
- (b) where a process exists in relation to any liquidation, administration or receivership, by note in that process.

(2) The Deputy Principal Clerk shall—
- (a) after the lodging of any petition or note fix a hearing for the insolvency judge to consider an application under paragraph (1); and
- (b) give notice of the hearing fixed under paragraph (2)(a) to the petitioner or noter.

(3) The petitioner or noter shall not be required to give notice to any person of the hearing fixed under paragraph (2)(a), unless the insolvency judge directs otherwise.

-----

[1] Rule 74.30A inserted by S.S.I. 2003 No. 385 (effective 15th September 2003).

Application to appoint a special manager

74.31.—(1) An application under section 177 of the Act of 1986 (application for the appointment of a special manager) shall be made by note.

(2) A bond of caution certified by the noter under rule 4.70(4) of the Insolvency Rules shall be sent to the Petition Department by the noter.

(3) After the Deputy Principal Clerk has satisfied himself as to the sufficiency of caution under rule 33.7(1) of these Rules, the clerk of session

shall issue to the person appointed to be special manager a certified copy of the interlocutor appointing him.

(4) A special manager may, before the expiry of the period for finding caution, apply to the insolvency judge for an extension of that period.

Deriv. R.C.S. 1965, r. 218L(1) and (3) to (5) inserted by S.I. 1986 No. 2298

General note. Where a provisional liquidator is appointed or a company is in liquidation, the   **74.31.1**
court may appoint a special manager of a part or the whole of the business or property of the company: Act of 1986, s. 177. The application must be supported by a report setting out the reasons for the appointment and the estimated value of the assets concerned: Insolvency Rules, r. 4.69(1) and (2).

The order of the court appointing the special manager must specify the period of appointment, whether for a specified period, until the occurrence of an event or until further order of the court: Insolvency Rules, r. 4.69(3).

A special manager must find caution: Act of 1986, s. 177(5)(a); Insolvency Rules, r. 4.70.

"note". For applications by note, see r. 15.2.   **74.31.2**

Other applications

74.32.—(1) An application under the Act of 1986 or any subordinate legislation made under that Act, or Part VII of the Companies Act 1989, in relation to a winding up by the court not mentioned in this Part shall—

(a) if made by a party to the petition, be made by motion; or

(b) in any other case, be made by note.

(2) At the hearing of a motion under paragraph (1)(a), the court may order that the application be made by note; and, in such a case, shall make an order for the lodging of answers to the note in process within such period as it thinks fit.

Deriv. R.C.S. 1965, r. 218M inserted by S.I. 1986 No. 2298 and amended by S.I. 1991 No. 1157

"motion". For motions, see Chap. 23.   **74.32.1**

"note". For applications by note, see r. 15.2.   **74.32.2**
There are a large number of applications arising out of or incidental to a liquidation which may be made by the liquidator or by other persons and for which these Rules make no separate provision. Examples are noted in the following paragraphs.

Once a winding up order has been pronounced or a provisional liquidator has been appointed, leave of the court is required under s. 130 of the Act of 1986 to proceed with or commence an action against a company. For an example of a successful note by a creditor for leave to raise proceedings against a company in liquidation, see: *Canon (Scotland) Business Machines Ltd v. G.A. Business Systems Ltd (in liquidation)* 1993 S.L.T. 387.

S. 212 of the Insolvency Act 1986 makes provision for a summary procedure against a delinquent director or other officer of the company. The purpose of bringing an application under s. 212 is to examine into the conduct of any person who is or has been an officer of the company, or who has acted as liquidator, administrator, or administrative receiver of the company, or who has been concerned or taken part in the promotion, formation or management of a company, and who has misapplied, retained or become accountable for the company's money or other property or who has been guilty of misfeasance or breach of duty in relation to the company. After examination, the court may compel the person in respect of whom the application was made to repay, restore or account for the money or property (with interest at such rate as the court thinks just), or to contribute such sum to the company's assets by way of compensation as the court thinks just. An application may be made by a liquidator, official receiver, or by any creditor or contributory of the company. For an example of a successful application, and observations of the Lord President (Hope) on pleadings appropriate to such an application, see *Blin v. Johnstone* 1988 S.C. 63. An application under s. 212 should not be used as a means to gather information, for which separate provision is made in ss. 236 and 237 of the Act of 1986: *Gray v. Davidson* 1991 S.L.T. (Sh. Ct.) 61. Further observations on the summary nature of an application under this section may be found in the note of Sheriff Kelbie in *Datastor Technology Ltd v. Baston*, 28th April 1994 (reported in part in the commentary to *Ross v. Davy* 1996 S.C.L.R. 369).

The liquidator, too, may apply by note, for example, to seek an order that the winding up of the company proceed jointly with the sequestration of the estates of one of the company's directors (*Taylor, Noter* 1993 S.L.T. 375) or for exoneration and discharge (although there is no express statutory provision for this) during the course of a winding up which was continuing (*Brown v. Dickson* 1995 S.L.T. 354).

Replacement liquidators

[1] **74.32A.**—(1) This rule applies where—

  (a) a person has been appointed by the court as a liquidator in respect of a petition; and

  (b) that person dies or otherwise ceases to be able to act as liquidator; and

  (c) an application is made to the court for the appointment of a replacement liquidator.

(2) An application mentioned in paragraph (1)(c) may include a list of other petitions in which the liquidator has been appointed by the court and in respect of which the appointment of the same replacement liquidator is sought.

(3) In an interlocutor appointing a replacement liquidator in respect of an application under paragraph (2), the court may—

  (a) order the replacement liquidator to be appointed in any or all of the petitions listed;

  (b) direct that a copy of the interlocutor be put in the process or processes of that petition or those petitions, as the case may be; and

  (c) make such orders as it thinks fit for the intimation and advertisement of such appointment.

---

[1] Rule 74.32A inserted by S.S.I. 2006 No. 83 (effective 17th March 2006).

PART VI

DISQUALIFICATION OF COMPANY DIRECTORS

Applications in relation to disqualification orders or undertakings

[1] **74.33.** An application—

  (a) under section 3(2) of the Company Directors Disqualification Act 1986 (for disqualification for persistent breaches of companies legislation),

  (b) under section 6(1) of that Act (to disqualify unfit directors of insolvent companies),

  (c) under section 8 of that Act (for disqualification of unfit director after investigation of a company),

[2] (ca) under section 8A of that Act (variation or cessation of disqualification undertaking),

  (d) under section 11(1) of that Act (for leave by an undischarged bankrupt to be concerned in a company),

  (e) for leave under that Act, or

  (f) by the Secretary of State under rule 4(2) of the Insolvent Companies (Reports on Conduct of Directors) (No. 2) (Scotland) Rules 1986 (application for direction to comply with requirements to furnish information etc.),

shall be made by petition.

Deriv. R.C.S. 1965, r. 218N(1) inserted by S.I. 1986 No. 2298

---

[1] Rule 74.33 amended by S.S.I. 2005 No. 521 (effective 21st October, 2005).
[2] Rule 74.33(ca) inserted by S.S.I. 2005 No. 521 (effective 21st October, 2005).

74.33.1   *General note.* A person may be disqualified on a number of grounds from being a director, liquidator, administrator, receiver, manager or in any way concerned with the promotion, formation or management of a company for a specified period without the leave of the court: Company Directors Disqualification Act 1986, s. 1(1). The Act of 1986 was intended for the protection of the public and was not a purely penal statute: *Re Jaymar Management* [1990] B.C.C. 303. The provisions of the Act of 1986 fall to be construed accordingly: *Secretary of State for Trade and Industry v. Lovat* 1996 S.L.T. 124.

(A) Grounds for disqualification. The grounds for disqualification fall into three categories: (1) disqualification for misconduct in connection with a company, (2) disqualification for unfitness and (3) other reasons for disqualification. Specific grounds in category (1) include cases where the person against whom an order is sought (a) has been convicted of an indictable offence in connection with the company (s.2 of the 1986 Act); (b) has committed persistent breaches of the companies legislation relating to the filing of returns, accounts, notices or other documents at Companies House (ss.3 and 5 of the 1986 Act); and (c) has participated in fraudulent trading (s.458 of the Companies Act 1985) or other fraud or breach of duty as a director which comes to light in the course of a winding up (s.4 of the 1986 Act). The fact that the person concerned has been or may be made criminally liable for his actings as a director does not preclude the making of an order for disqualification: s.1(4) of the 1986 Act. Category (2) relates generally to cases where, by reason of a person's conduct as a director, he shows himself to be unfit to be concerned with the management of a company. In all cases where it falls to a court to determine whether a person is unfit, the court shall have regard to the matters in Pt I of Sched. 1 to the 1986 Act and, where the company of which the person concerned was a director has become insolvent, the court shall also have regard to the matters in Part II of Sched. 1. The court has taken into account the conduct of a person after he ceased to be a director: *Re Godwin Warren Control Systems plc* [1992] B.C.C. 557. Included in category (3) are cases (a) where the person concerned was an undischarged bankrupt while acting as a director (s.11 of the 1986 Act) and (b) where the court makes a declaration under s.213 (wrongful trading) or s.214 (fraudulent trading) of the Insolvency Act 1986 that a person is liable to make a contribution to a company's assets it may also, whether or not application for such an order has been made, make an order for disqualification: s.10 of the 1986 Act.

Where the ground is conduct which makes a person unfit to be concerned in the management of a company and he is or has been a director of an insolvent company, the court must disqualify: 1986 Act, s.6. Only the Secretary of State may make an application under s.6: 1986 Act, s.7(1)(a); and see *Re NP Engineering and Security Products Ltd* [1995] 2 B.C.L.C. 585 (action brought by official receiver incompetent).

In exceptional circumstances an English court has stayed proceedings for disqualification where medical evidence established that it would be hazardous and difficult for the respondent director to embark on a trial lasting several weeks and where the director gave an undertaking not to act as a director or be concerned with the management of a company without leave of the court: *Re Homes Assured Corp. plc* [1996] B.C.C. 297.

To be unfit the director must be guilty of a serious failure to perform the duties of a director attendant on the privilege of trading through a company with limited liability: *Re Bath Glass Ltd* [1988] B.C.L.C. 329. A "breach of commercial morality" is one of several judicial formulations of unfitness. It is not a prerequisite to a finding of unfitness that the person concerned benefited from his misconduct: *Re Stanford Services Ltd* [1987] B.C.L.C. 607. A "marked degree of incompetence", even in the absence of dishonesty, will justify an order for disqualification: *In re Sevenoaks Stationers (Retail) Ltd* [1991] Ch. 164. In *In re Continental Assurance Co. of London, The Times*, 2nd July 1996, it was held that a failure to read the company's accounts and to appreciate that loans lacking any commercial justification had been made to the detriment of the company's creditors constituted "gross incompetence" to justify an order. A person does not escape liability by reason of his reliance on other directors to manage the financial affairs of the company: *Re City Investment Centres Ltd* [1992] B.C.L.C. 956. Each director has a responsibility to ensure proper control of the company's finances is maintained notwithstanding that one of their number has been appointed to have particular responsibility for the company's financial affairs: *Secretary of State for Trade and Industry v. Brown* 1995 S.L.T. 550. Directors who take advantage of limited liability must conduct their companies with due regard for the ordinary standards of commercial morality. They must observe the safeguards laid down by Parliament for the benefit of others who have dealings with their companies, including the proper maintenance, preparation and filing of books and accounts: *Re Swift Ltd*; *Secretary of State for Trade and Industry v. Ettinger* [1993] B.C.C. 312. A blatant disregard by a director for important aspects of accountability, such as complying with the requirements of the Companies Act 1985 for lodging of accounts, will itself be sufficient to attract a disqualification order: *Secretary of State for Trade and Industry v. Ettinger*, above; a dispute with the company's auditors over their fees did not justify such a failure: *Re Ward Sherrad Ltd* [1996] B.C.C. 418. Actings which are indicative of breaches of commercial probity on the part of a director include drawing a salary inappropriate for a company in distress, receiving a remuneration package out of proportion to the company's trading success and financial health, or taking unwarranted risks with creditors' money and trading at the expense of monies due to the Crown: *Synthetic*

Technology Ltd [1993] B.C.C. 549. Unfitness involves questions of fact: *Secretary of State for Trade and Industry v. Queen* 1998 S.L.T. 735 (Ex. Div.).

Under s.7(3) of the Rehabilitation of Offenders Act 1974, a court may have regard to a spent conviction in considering whether a person is unfit to be a director of a company. The provisions of s.4(3) of the 1974 Act (excluding consideration or disclosure of spent convictions) do not apply to a judicial authority: *Secretary of State for Trade and Industry v. Queen* 1998 S.L.T. 735 (Ex. Div.).

(B) Time limit for application. Except with leave of the court, an application to the court for an order under s.6 of the 1986 Act shall not be made after the end of two years beginning with the date on which the company became insolvent: 1986 Act, s.7(2). A company is deemed, for the purposes of calculating the start of the two year period, to have become insolvent (a) when the company goes into liquidation at a time when its liabilities exceeds it assets, (b) when an administration order is made in relation to the company or (c) when an administrative receiver of the company is appointed: 1986 Act, s.6(2). In the case of a voluntary winding up, the winding up commences on the date the resolution to wind up the company was passed: s.129(1) of the Insolvency Act 1986. A winding up by the court commences on the date the petition is presented to the court: s.129(2) of that Act. For the purposes of calculating the two year period within which a disqualification order must be sought, an administration order means an order under s.8 of the Insolvency Act 1986 and not an interim order under s.9 of that Act: *Secretary of State for Trade and Industry v. Palmer* 1994 S.C. 707. The date of the appointment of a receiver by the holder of a floating charge, from which the two year period begins to run, is the date on which the receiver receives the instrument of appointment: Insolvency Act 1986, s.53(6)(a). The receiver's docquet on that instrument of appointment is conclusive as to the date of his appointment: *Secretary of State for Trade and Industry v. Houston* 1994 S.L.T. 775, construing s.53(6) of the Insolvency Act 1986. In the case of an appointment of a receiver by the court, under s.51(2) of that Act, the two year period runs from the date of the presentation of the petition. Where there is more than one event triggering the deemed insolvency of the company, it would appear to be the case that the two year period runs from the date of the earlier event: *Official Receiver v. Nixon, The Times*, 16th December 1990. The date of the application for a disqualification order, for the purposes of determining whether that application is timeous, is the date of the presentation of the petition, not the subsequent date of the service on the respondent of that petition: *Secretary of State for Trade and Industry v. Normand* 1994 S.L.T. 1249, following *Secretary of State for Trade and Industry v. Josolyne* 1990 S.L.T.(Sh.Ct.) 48.

In considering whether to grant the Secretary of State leave to apply for a disqualification order outwith the two year statutory period under s.7(2) of the 1986 Act, the court will have regard to (a) the length of the delay (including the delay within the two year time limit for commencing proceedings), (b) the reason for the delay, (c) the strength of the case against the director, and (d) the degree of prejudice caused to the director by the delay: *Re Probe Data Systems Ltd (No. 3), Secretary of State for Trade and Industry v. Desai* [1992] B.C.L.C. 405, 416 per Scott L.J. Leave is likely to be refused where no good explanation is adduced by the Secretary of State for the delay in bringing proceedings: *Secretary of State for Trade and Industry v. Morral* [1996] B.C.C. 299. However, the adequacy of any explanation does not itself constitute a threshold test in respect of the granting of leave, but is one of the factors to be considered in the light of all the circumstances: *Secretary of State for Trade and Industry v. Davies, The Times*, 7th June 1996.

The requirement in s.16 of the 1986 Act to give not less than 10 days' notice to the person against whom a disqualification order is to be sought is directory, not mandatory; and, accordingly, an application for an order for which less than 10 days' notice had been given was not incompetent: *Secretary of State for Trade and Industry v. Lovat* 1997 S.L.T. 124; *Secretary of State for Trade and Industry v. Langridge* [1991] Ch. 402.

(C) Period of disqualification. Following its predilection for guidelines, the Court of Appeal in England has issued guidelines for periods of disqualification under s.6: *In re Sevenoaks Stationers (Retail) Ltd* [1991] Ch. 164. The Scottish courts have adopted and applied the guidelines in that case: see, *e.g. Secretary of State for Trade and Industry v. Marshall* 1994 G.W.D. 19–1151; *Secretary of State for Trade and Industry v. Aitken* 1994 G.W.D. 19–1152; *Secretary of State for Trade and Industry v. Brown* 1995 S.L.T. 550; *Secretary of State for Trade and Industry v. Palfreman* 1995 S.L.T. 156; *Secretary of State for Trade and Industry v. Henderson* 1995 G.W.D. 21–1159. When considering whether and for how long to make a disqualification order a court is entitled to look at specific instances of misconduct: *Secretary of State for Trade and Industry v. McTigue, The Times*, 10th July 1996. For the purpose of fixing an appropriate period under s.6, no consideration is to be given by the court to the period between the failure of the company and the making of any order: *Secretary of State for Trade and Industry v. Arif, The Times*, 25th March 1996.

(D) Procedure. The court may be satisfied without evidence in an unopposed application. In cases where a respondent has entered the process only to contest the length, not the making of, any disqualification order, it is not uncommon for the parties to agree the relevant facts by joint minute, *e.g.* as was done in *Secretary of State for Trade and Industry v Brown*, above. Affidavits sworn by accountants but containing mainly hearsay, advocacy and submissions rather than expert opinion have been struck out as irrelevant and oppressive: *Re Oakfame Construction Ltd* [1996] B.C.C. 67.

The court may order the director subject to proceedings under s.6 of the 1986 Act to pay part or all of the costs or expenses of the Secretary of State: *Re Pamstock Ltd* [1996] B.C.C. 341 (order for director to pay one-half of Secretary of State's costs, where every possible matter for complaint had been put forward, without real regard for circumstances or merits of the complaint, and which lengthened the hearing).

(E) Leave to continue to be concerned with the company. The person who has been, or is being, disqualified, however, may apply to the court for leave to be a director, administrator, liquidator of the company, or a receiver or manager of the company's property, or otherwise concerned with the company: s.1(1) of the 1986 Act. In considering whether or not to grant leave the court will have regard to the public interest in securing adequate protection from any real risk of bad management and whether there is a need for leave to be granted in the interests of the company: *Re Cargo Agency Ltd* [1992] B.C.C. 388. For an example of the court disqualifying a person from being a director under s.6 of the 1986 Act but, at the same time, granting leave for him to remain a director of another company, see *Secretary of State for Trade and Industry v Brown* 1995 S.L.T. 550. The court may, as a condition of granting such leave, impose conditions such as requiring the appointment of an independent director to the board of the company in respect of which leave to be a director is being granted: *Secretary of State for Trade and Industry v Palfreman*, above.

(F) Jurisdiction. The court having jurisdiction in an application under s.6 of the 1986 Act is, in the case of a company being wound up by the court, or a company in relation to which an administration order is in force, the court by which the winding-up order was made or by which the administration order was made: s.6(3)(a) and (c) of the 1986 Act. In relation to a company being wound up voluntarily, application for a disqualification order may be made to any court having jurisdiction to wind up the company: s.6(3)(b) of the 1986 Act. In any other case, the court to which application may be made includes the Court of Session. The date of the application for a disqualification order is the relevant date for determining jurisdiction. Where, therefore, a winding-up order was pronounced by a court subsequent to the appointment of a receiver, it is the court which has pronounced the winding up which had jurisdiction (*Secretary of State for Trade and Industry v Barnett*, 1998 S.L.T. 63, notwithstanding that another court (*i.e.* the Court of Session) would have had jurisdiction on the basis of s.6(3)(d) prior to the pronouncement of the winding-up order, or would have had concurrent jurisdiction in a winding up by the court. On jurisdiction in a winding up by the court, see 74.21.2.

Applications for leave. A person disqualified may seek leave of the court to do something from **74.33.2** which he is disqualified: Company Directors Disqualification Act 1986, ss.1(1) and 17.

For a recent example of the grant of leave to a person to remain as director of two companies associated with a third insolvent company in respect of which that person was being disqualified, see *Secretary of State for Trade and Industry v Palfreman* 1995 S.L.T. 156.

The phrase "leave of the court" has been interpreted in England as empowering the court to grant leave on conditions providing adequate protection from the danger legislated against. With some hesitation, but for reasons of comity in the application of a UK statute, Lord Johnston followed this interpretation in *Palfreman*, above. Typically, these conditions may require, for a person seeking to be appointed or to remain as a director, the appointment of an independent director or requirements ensuring financial accountability, or both. In *Palfreman*, above, the court imposed the condition that an independent director be appointed to the two companies of which the court granted leave to the respondent to remain as a director. In *Re Chatmore Ltd* [1990] B.C.L.C. 673, the court imposed the condition that the board of the company on which the disqualified person was to be granted leave to remain as a director was to hold monthly board meetings attended by the company's auditors.

For an example of the court's refusal of leave, see *Re Cargo Agency Ltd* [1992] B.C.L.C. 686.

An application for leave is required where the person disqualified wishes to act as a director of another company. There must be a real need in the interests of the company for leave to be granted: *Secretary of State for Trade and Industry v Brown* 1995 S.L.T. 550 following *Re Cargo Agency Ltd*, above. In addition, if leave is to be granted, steps must be taken to ensure the adequate protection of the public from the risk of bad management. Such steps can include the management of the company's accounts on a day-to-day basis, management by or the appointment of independent directors to the board of the company, or the transfer of a balancing shareholding to one or more of the independent directors: see, *e.g. Secretary of State for Trade and Industry v Brown*, above (leave for director to continue to be director of one company as there was no real risk of bad management of that company and his expertise was of great materiality to it).

74.33.3   *"petition"*. A petition is presented in the Outer House: r.14.2(h). The petition must be in Form 14.4 in the official printed form: rr.4.1 and 14.4. The petition must be signed by counsel or other person having a right of audience: r.4.2; and see r.1.3(1) (definition of "counsel" and "other person having a right of audience") and note 1.3.4.

The petitioner must lodge the petition with the required steps of process (r.4.4) and any documents founded on or adopted (r.27.1(1)). A fee is payable on lodging the petition: see note 14.5.10.

On petitions generally, see Ch.14.

Intimation, service and advertisement under this Part

74.34.—(1) Rule 74.22, except paragraphs (1)(c) and (2) of that rule, shall apply to the intimation, service and advertisement of a petition referred to in rule 74.33 (applications in relation to disqualification orders) as it applies to a petition under that rule.

[1] (2) A petition presented under rule 74.33 shall be intimated—

  (a) to the Secretary of State for Trade and Industry; or

(b) where a petition is presented under rule 74.33(ca) and the disqualification undertaking was given under section 9B of the Company Directors Disqualification Act 1986 (competition undertaking), to the Office of Fair Trading or any specified regulator which has accepted the undertaking, as the case may be;

unless the petition is presented by that person or body.

Deriv. R.C.S. 1965, r.218N(3) substituted by S.I. 1990 No. 705

---

[1] Rule 74.34(2) substituted by S.S.I. 2005 No. 521 (effective 21st October, 2005).

General note. The applicant for a disqualification order must give not less than 10 days' notice of intention to apply for the order to the person against whom the order is sought: Company Directors Disqualification Act 1986, s.16(1).   **74.34.1**

CHAPTER 75

[1] APPLICATIONS RELATING TO FINANCIAL SERVICES

PART I

APPLICATIONS UNDER THE FINANCIAL SERVICES ACT 1986

[1] *Application and interpretation of this Part*
[1] **75.1.**—(1) This Part applies to an application, under the Financial Services Act 1986, mentioned in rule 75.2.
(2) In this Part—
  "the Act of 1986" means the Financial Services Act 1986.
  "designated agency" has the meaning assigned in section 114(3) of the Act of 1986.

Deriv. R.C.S. 1965, r.260M inserted by S.I. 1987 No. 2160 (r.75.1(2))

Chap. heading, and r.75.1 and heading, amended by S.I. 1996 No. 1756 (effective 5th August 1996).

"designated agency". A number of the functions of the Secretary of State have been transferred to the Securities and Investments Board Ltd (currently the only designated agency): see the Financial Services Act 1986 (Delegation) Order 1987 [S.I. 1987 No. 942], the Financial Services Act 1986 (Delegation) (No.2) Order 1988 [S.I. 1988 No. 738], the Financial Services Act 1986 (Delegation) Order 1991 [S.I. 1991 No. 200] and the Financial Services Act 1986 (Delegation) (No.2) Order 1991 [S.I. 1991 No. 1256].   **75.1.1**

Form of applications under the Act of 1986
75.2.—(1) An application under any of the following provisions of the Act of 1986 shall be made by petition:—
  (a) sections 6, 61, 71(1), 91(4), 104(4), 131(8) and 184(8) (applications by Secretary of State or designated agency for interdict or restitution);
  (b) sections 12, 20, 37(8) and 39(8) (applications by Secretary of State or designated agency for compliance orders);
  (c) section 93 (applications by Secretary of State or designated agency to remove or replace a manager or trustee or to wind up a unit trust scheme); and
  (d) Schedule 11—
    (i) paragraph 6(1) (applications by the Friendly Societies Commission for compliance orders);
    (ii) paragraph 7(4) (applications by recognised self regulating organisations to set aside a direction);
    (iii) paragraph 22 (applications by the Friendly Societies Commission for interdict or to remedy a contravention); and

(iv) paragraph 23(1) so far as it modifies section 61 as applied by section 71(1) (applications by the Friendly Societies Commission for interdict or restitution).

(2) Certification by inspectors or the court by virtue of section 94(3), or under section 178(1), of the Act of 1986 shall be made by petition.

Deriv. R.C.S. 1965, r.260N(1) and (2) inserted by S.I. 1987 No. 2160

75.2.1   *"petition"*. A petition under this Chapter is presented to the Outer House: r.14.2(h). The petition must be in Form 14.4 in the official printed form: rr.4.1 and 14.4. The petition must be signed by counsel or other person having a right of audience: r.4.2; and see r.1.3(1) (definition of "counsel" and "other person having a right of audience") and note 1.3.4.

The petitioner must lodge the petition with the required steps of process (r.4.4). A fee is payable on lodging the petition: see note 14.5.10.

On petitions generally, see Ch.14.

Intimation and service
75.3. An order under any of the following provisions of the Act of 1986 shall only be made following intimation and service of the petition to the person against whom the order is to be made:—
   (a) section 6 (interdict and restitution orders);
   (b) section 61 (interdict and restitution orders);
   (c) section 71(1) (orders in respect of breach of prohibition or requirement);
   (d) section 91(4) (orders in respect of contravention of a direction);
   (e) section 104(4) (orders in respect of contravention of a requirement);
   (f) section 131(8) (orders in respect of contravention of restrictions on promotion of contracts of insurance);
   (g) section 184(8) (orders in respect of contravention of notice of restriction of investment or insurance business); and
   (h) paragraph 22 of Schedule 11 (interdict of regulated friendly society).

Deriv. R.C.S. 1965, r.260N(3) inserted by S.I. 1987 No. 2160

75.3.1   *"intimation and service"*. See r.14.7 and Ch.16, Pt I.

Questions relating to interpretation of rules or regulations
75.4. Where a question of the interpretation of any of the rules or regulations referred to in section 61(1)(a) of the Act of 1986 arises in a petition under this rule, the Secretary of State, a designated agency, or any person referred to in section 61(1)(a)(iv) of that Act, and not already a party in the cause, shall be given the opportunity to make representations to the court by lodging answers to the petition.

Deriv. R.C.S. 1965, r.260N(4) inserted by S.I. 1986 No. 2160

75.4.1   *"answers"*. On form and procedure for answers, see r.18.3.

[1] *PART II*

APPLICATIONS UNDER THE UNCERTIFICATED SECURITIES REGULATIONS *1995*

Interpretation of this Part
[1] **75.5.** In this Part—
   "operator" has the meaning assigned in regulation 3(1) of the Regulations of 1995;
   "the Regulations of 1995" means the Uncertificated Securities Regulations 1995.

[1] Pt II and r.75.5 inserted by S.I. 1996 No. 1756 (effective 5th August 1996).

General note. Part II of this Chapter (inserted by A.S. (R.C.S.A. No. 3) (Miscellaneous) 1996   **75.5.1**
(S.I. 1996 No. 1756) extends and adapts the provisions of Pt. I to applications under the
Uncertificated Securities Regulations 1995 (S.I. 1995/3272). The regulations provide a paperless
system of share transfer replacing share certificates with a computer-loaded system. This system
replaces the unsuccessful TAURUS system, and it is expected that CREST will apply for
approval as an operator.

"operator". The powers of the Treasury under the Regulations of 1995 have been delegated to   **75.5.2**
the Securities and Investments Board. No person has yet been approved as operator, though
applications for approval have been received.

Form of applications under the Regulations of 1995
[1] **75.6.** An application under regulation 8 (application by Secretary of
State for compliance order), or regulation 9 (application by Secretary of
State for interdict or restitution), of the Regulations of 1995 shall be made
by petition.

[1] R. 75.6 inserted by S.I. 1996 No. 1756 (effective 5th August 1996).

"petition". A petition under this Chapter is presented to the Outer House: r. 14.2(h). The   **75.6.1**
petition must be in the Form 14.4 in the official printed form: rr. 4.1 and 14.4. The petition must
be signed by counsel or other person having a right of audience: r. 4.2; and see r. 1.3(1)
(definition of "counsel" and "other person having a right of audience) and note 1.3.4.
   The petitioner must lodge the petition with the required steps of process (r. 4.4). A fee is
payable on lodging the petition: see note 14.5.10.
   On petitions generally, see Chap. 14.

Intimation and service
[1] **75.7.** An order under regulation 9 of the Regulations of 1995 shall only
be made following intimation and service of the petition—
   (a) on the person against whom the order is to be made; and
   (b) on the operator.

[1] R. 75.7 inserted by S.I. 1996 No. 1756 (effective 5th August 1996).

"intimation and service". See r. 14.7 and Chap. 16, Pt. I.   **75.7.1**

Questions relating to interpretation of rules of an operator
[1] **75.8.** Where a question of the interpretation of any of the rules of an
operator referred to in regulation 9(1)(a) of the Regulations of 1995 arises in
a petition under this rule, the Secretary of State and the operator, if not
already parties, shall be given the opportunity to make representations to
the court by lodging answers to the petition.

[1] R. 75.8 inserted by S.I. 1996 No. 1756 (effective 5th August 1996).

"answers". On form and procedure for answers, see r. 18.3.   **75.8.1**

CHAPTER 76

CAUSES IN RELATION TO CONFISCATION OF PROCEEDS OF CRIME

[1] *Part I*

CAUSES UNDER THE PROCEEDS OF CRIME (SCOTLAND) ACT 1995

Interpretation of this Part
   [1] **76.1.** In this Part—
      "the Act of 1995" means the Proceeds of Crime (Scotland) Act 1995;
      "administrator" means the person appointed under paragraph 1(1) of
         Schedule 1 to the Act of 1995;
      "restraint order" has the meaning assigned in section 49(1) of the Act
         of 1995.

Deriv. R.C.S. 1965, r. 201C inserted by S.I. 1990 No. 705

---

[1] Part I heading and r. 76.1 amended by S.I. 1996 No. 2168 (consolidating enactment).

76.1.1   *"restraint order".* This means an order interdicting the person in respect of whom it is made
from dealing with his realisable property, or that person and any person named in the order
who appears to have received from that person an implicative gift (see s. 6 of the Act of 1995)
from dealing with their own, or the other's, realisable property, whenever that property was
acquired and whether described in the order or not: Act of 1995 (c. 43), s. 28.

Disapplication of certain rules to this Part
76.2. The following rules shall not apply to a petition or note mentioned in this Part:—

rule 14.5	(first order in petitions),
rule 14.6(1)	(period of notice for lodging answers),
rule 14.7	(intimation and service of petitions),
rule 14.9	(unopposed petitions).

Applications for restraint orders
76.3.—[1] (1) An application under section 28(1) of the Act of 1995 (application for restraint order) shall be made by petition.

(2) Where the court pronounces an interlocutor making a restraint order, the Lord Advocate shall serve a certified copy of that interlocutor on every person named in the interlocutor as restrained by the order.

[2] (3) Where the application is made under the said section as applied by article 4 of the Confiscation of the Proceeds of Crime (Designated Countries and Territories) (Scotland) Order 1999 (application in relation to certain external confiscation orders etc.) or by article 4 of the Criminal Justice (International Co-operation) Act 1990 (Enforcement of Overseas Forfeiture Orders) (Scotland) Order 1999 (application in relation to certain external forfeiture orders etc.), there shall be appended to the petition a certificate in conformity with paragraph (b) of subsection (3) of the section as so applied by the article in question; but that certificate, as so appended, shall not include a statement of information or belief with the sources and grounds thereof if the prayer includes an application for a direction under that paragraph.

[2] (4) Where the court grants the prayer of the petition in an application such as is mentioned in paragraph (3) but declines to make such direction as is so mentioned, the petitioner shall forthwith lodge in process, as an addendum to the certificate which was appended to the petition, a statement of information or belief with the sources and grounds thereof.

Deriv. RCS 1965, r. 201E(1) (r. 76.3(1)), and r. 201F(2) (r. 76.3(2)), both inserted by S.I. 1990 No. 705

---

[1] R. 76.3(1) amended by S.I. 1996 No. 2168 (consolidating enactment).
[2] R. 76.3(3) and (4) inserted by S.I. 1999 No. 1220 (effective 1st May 1999).

General note. A restraint order may be applied for by the prosecutor where "proceedings have **76.3.1** been instituted" (defined in s.49(6)) for an offence to which Part I of the Act applies (any offence "which has been prosecuted" subject to one exception), the proceedings have not been concluded and either a confiscation order has been made or it appears that in the event of conviction there are reasonable grounds for thinking that a confiscation order may be made: Act of 1995, s.29(1). The apparent dichotomy between proceedings which have been instituted and an offence which has been prosecuted, which would frustrate the intentions of Parliament, has been resolved by adopting a workable interpretation where the intention of Parliament was that a restraint order might be pronounced immediately following the institution of proceedings: *Carnegie v. McKechnie* 1999 S.L.T. 536. Accordingly, a petition may be presented at any time after a suspect has had a petition charging him intimated to him or a complaint served on him even where no indictment has yet been served: *Carnegie* 1999 S.L.T. 536, above.

A restraint order may interdict any named person from dealing with his realisable property, or that or another named person who has received a gift from that person or an implicative gift from dealing with their own or that other's realisable property; or interdict any named person from dealing with any property which is or is liable to be the subject of a suspended forfeiture order: Act of 1995, s.28(1). On gifts, see ss.5 and 6 of the Act of 1995; and on suspended forfeiture orders, see s.21 of the Act of 1995.

Section 28 of the Act of 1995 is modified by Sched. 3 to the Confiscation of the Proceeds of Crime (Designated Countries and Territories) (Scotland) Order 1999 [S.I. 1999 No. 673] and by Sched. 3 to the Criminal Justice (International Co-operation) Act 1990 (Enforcement of Overseas Forfeiture Orders) (Scotland) Order 1999 [S.I. 1999 No. 675]. For the purposes of these orders (see art. 4 of each Order), s.28(3)(b) of the Act of 1995, as modified, requires a restraint order to be supported by a certificate giving certain particulars (including grounds for believing that an external confiscation order may be made in proceedings instituted or to be instituted in the designated country) and that it may, unless the court directs, a statement of information or belief with the sources and grounds thereof.

76.3.2 *"petition"*. A petition is presented in the Outer House: r. 14.2(h). The petition must be in Form 14.4 in the official printed form: rr. 4.1 and 14.4. The petition must be signed by counsel or other person having a right of audience: r. 4.2; and see r. 1.3(1) (definition of "counsel" and "other person having a right of audience") and note 1.3.4.

The petitioner must lodge the petition with the required steps of process (r. 4.4). A fee is payable on lodging the petition: see note 14.5.10.

On petitions generally, see Chap. 14.

76.3.3 *"certified copy of that interlocutor"*. A copy of the interlocutor must be prepared (handwritten or typed) by the party. It is checked by the clerk of session at the appropriate department, certified a true copy and stamped with the court stamp. A fee is payable: see Court of Session Fees etc. Order 1997, Table of Fees, Pt IV, J, item 2 (S.I. 1997 No. 688, as amended, pp. C 1201 *et seq.*). Certain persons are exempt from payment of fees: see 1997 Fees Order, art.5 substituted by S.S.I. 2002 No. 270. A fee exemption certificate must be lodged in process: see P.N. No.1 of 2002.

Applications in relation to protective measures

[1] **76.4.**—(1) An application under any of the following provisions of the Act of 1995 shall be made by note in the process containing the interlocutor making the restraint order to which the application relates:—

(a) section 29(4) or (5) (recall of restraint order in relation to realisable property);

(b) section 30(3) or (4) (recall of restraint order in relation to forfeitable property);

(c) section 31(1) (variation or recall of restraint order);

(d) section 32(5) (recall or restriction of inhibition);

(e) section 33(4) (recall or restriction of arrestment).

(2) In respect of an application by note under paragraph (1) by a person having an interest for an order under section 31(1)(b) of the Act of 1995—

(a) the note shall be lodged in process within 21 days after service of the restraint order on that person; and

(b) subject to rule 14.6(2) (application to shorten or extend the period of notice), the period of notice for lodging answers to the note shall be 14 days.

[2] (3) An application under section 31(1)(a) of the Act of 1995 to extend a restraint order shall not be intimated, served or advertised before the application is granted.

[2] (4) An application by the Lord Advocate under section 32(1) or 33(1) of the Act of 1995 by the Lord Advocate for warrant for arrestment or inhibition may be made—

(a) in the prayer of the petition under section 28(1) of that Act; or

(b) if made after the petition has been presented, by motion which shall not be intimated.

(5) An application under section 32(1)(a) (recall, loosing or restriction of inhibition), or section 33(2) (recall, loosing or restriction of arrestment) of the Act of 1995 to loose, restrict or recall an arrestment or to recall an inhibition shall be made by motion.

(6) An application under section 28(8) of the Act of 1995 (interdict) may be made—

[2] (a) in the prayer of the petition under section 28(1) of that Act; or

(b) if made after the petition has been presented, by note in the process of that petition.

(7) An application by note under paragraph (6)(b) shall not be intimated, served or advertised before the application is granted.

[3] (7A) Where the court, having pronounced an interlocutor making a restraint order, interdicts a person not subject to that order from dealing with the property affected by it while it is in force, the Lord Advocate shall so intimate to that person.

(8) Where the court pronounces an interlocutor granting an application mentioned in paragraph (3) or (4), the Lord Advocate shall serve a certified copy of that interlocutor on the persons affected by it.

[3] (9) At the time at which he complies with section 31(6) of the Act of 1995 (informing of persons interdicted in relation to a restraint order that the order is recalled), the clerk of court (or as the case may be the Deputy Principal Clerk) shall record in the process when and how the person in question was so informed.

Deriv. RCS 1965, r. 201G(1) (r. 76.4(1)), r. 201F(2) (r. 76.4(2)), r. 201G(4) (r. 76.4(3)), r. 201G(5) (r. 76.4(4)), and r. 201G(6) (r. 76.4(6)), all inserted by S.I. 1990 No. 705

---

[1] R. 76.4 amended by S.I. 1996 No. 2168 (consolidating enactment).
[2] R. 76.4(3), (4) and (6)(a) amended by S.I. 1999 No. 1220 (effective 1st May 1999).
[3] R. 76.4(7A) and (9) inserted by S.I. 1999 No. 1220 (effective 1st May 1999).

"note". For applications by note, see r. 15.2.   **76.4.1**

"within 21 days". The date from which the period is calculated is not counted. Where the last **76.4.2** day falls on a Saturday or Sunday or a public holiday on which the Office of Court is closed, the next available day is allowed: r. 1.3(7). For office hours and public holidays, see note 3.1.2.

"answers". For form and procedure, see r. 18.3.   **76.4.3**

"motion". For motions, see Chap. 23.   **76.4.4**

"certified copy of that interlocutor". A copy of the interlocutor must be prepared (handwritten **76.4.5** or typed) by the party. It is checked by the clerk of session at the appropriate department, certified a true copy and stamped with the court stamp. A fee is payable: see Court of Session Fees etc. Order 1984, Table of Fees, Pt IV, J, item 2 (S.I. 1984 No. 256, Table as amended, pp. **C** 1202 *et seq.*).

Applications for compensation

[1] **76.5.** An application under section 17 (compensation) of the Act of 1995 shall be made by petition.

Deriv. RCS 1965, r. 201G(7) inserted by S.I. 1990 No. 705

---

[1] R. 76.5 and heading amending by S.I. 1996 No. 2168 (consolidating enactment).

Section 17 of the Act of 1995. Compensation may be payable to a person who held realisable **76.5.1** property (including a person to whom an implicative gift was made by the person in respect of whom a confiscation order was made) and who suffered substantial loss and damage as a result of the exercise of powers under Pt I of the Act of 1995: Act of 1995, s.17.

"petition". A petition is presented in the Outer House: r.14.2(h). The petition must be in **76.5.2** Form 14.4 in the official printed form: rr.4.1 and 14.4. The petition must be signed by counsel or other person having a right of audience: r.4.2; and see r.1.3(1) (definition of "counsel" and "other person having a right of audience") and note 1.3.4.

The petitioner must lodge the petition with the required steps of process (r.4.4). A fee is payable on lodging the petition: see note 14.5.10.

On petitions generally, see Chap. 14.

Applications for disclosure of information by government departments

[1] **76.6.** An application under section 20 of the Act of 1995 (disclosure of information held by government departments) may be made—

- (a) by petition;
- (b) where there is a restraint order in force, by note in the process of the petition for that restraint order; or
- (c) where an administrator has been appointed, by note in the process of the petition to appoint him.

Deriv. R.C.S. 1965, r.201G(8) inserted by S.I. 1990 No. 705

---

[1] R.76.6 amended by S.I. 1996 No. 2168 (consolidating enactment).

General note. The court may, on the application of the Lord Advocate, order material in **76.6.1** possession of an authorised government department to be produced to the court which would facilitate the powers of the court in relation to restraint orders, the appointment of an administrator etc., or the realisation of property: Act of 1995, s.20. The court may order disclosure to other persons, *e.g.* the administrator.

"petition". A petition is presented in the Outer House: r.14.2(h). The petition must be in **76.6.2** Form 14.4 in the official printed form: rr.4.1 and 14.4. The petition must be signed by counsel or other person having a right of audience: r.4.2; and see r.1.3(1) (definition of "counsel" and "other person having a right of audience") and note 1.3.4.

The petitioner must lodge the petition with the required steps of process (r.4.4). A fee is payable on lodging the petition: see note 14.5.10.

On petitions generally, see Chap. 14.

"note". For applications by note, see r.15.2. **76.6.3**

Applications for appointment of administrators

[1] **76.7.**—(1) An application under paragraph 1(1) of Schedule 1 to the Act of 1995 (appointment of administrators) shall be made—

- (a) where a restraint order has been made, by note in the process of the petition for that restraint order; or
- (b) in any other case, by petition.

(2) The notification to be made by the clerk of court under paragraph 1(3)(a) of Schedule 1 to the Act of 1995 shall be made by intimation of a certified copy of the interlocutor to the person required to give possession of property to an administrator.

Deriv. R.C.S. 1965, r.201H inserted by S.I. 1990 No. 705

---

[1] R.76.7 amended by S.I. 1996 No. 2168 (consolidating enactment).

General note. An administrator may be appointed to manage property affected by a restraint **76.7.1** order or to realise property where a confiscation order has been made, and the court may require a person having possession of the property to give it up to the administrator: Act of 1995, Sch. 1, para.1(1). The functions of the administrator are set out in para.2(1) of Sch.1 to the Act of 1995.

76.7.2   *"notification by the clerk of court"*. This is notification to persons concerned of a requirement to give up property to the administrator.

76.7.3   *"note"*. For applications by note, see r.15.2.

76.7.4   *"petition"*. A petition is presented in the Outer House: r.14.2(h). The petition must be in Form 14.4 in the official printed form: rr.4.1 and 14.4. The petition must be signed by counsel or other person having a right of audience: r.4.2; and see r.1.3(1) (definition of "counsel" and "other person having a right of audience") and note 1.3.4.
    The petitioner must lodge the petition with the required steps of process (r.4.4). A fee is payable on lodging the petition: see note 14.5.10.
    On petitions generally, see Chap. 14.

76.7.5   *"certified copy of the interlocutor"*. A copy of the interlocutor must be prepared (handwritten or typed) by the party. It is checked by the clerk of session at the appropriate department, certified a true copy and stamped with the court stamp. A fee is payable: see Court of Session Fees etc. Order 1984, Table of Fees, Pt IV, J, item 2 (S.I. 1984 No. 256, Table as amended, pp. C 1202 *et seq.*).

Incidental applications in an administration

[1] **76.8.**—(1) An application under any of the following provisions of Schedule 1 to the Act of 1995 shall be made by note in the process of the petition for appointment of the administrator:—
    (a) paragraph 1(1) with respect to an application after appointment of an administrator to require a person to give property to him;
    (b) paragraph 1(4) (making or altering a requirement or removal of administrator);
    (c) paragraph 1(5) (appointment of new administrator on death, resignation or removal of administrator);
    (d) paragraph 2(1)(n) (directions as to functions of administrator); and
    (e) paragraph 4 (directions for application of proceeds).
    (2) An application under any of the following provisions of Schedule 1 to the Act of 1995 shall be made in the prayer of the petition for appointment of an administrator under paragraph 1 of that Schedule or, if made after the petition has been presented, by note in that process:—
    [2] (a) paragraph 2(1)(o) (special powers of administrator);
    (b) paragraph 2(3) (vesting of property in administrator); and
    [3] (c) paragraph 12 (orders to facilitate the realisation of property).

Deriv. R.C.S. 1965, r.201J inserted by S.I. 1990 No. 705

---

[1] R.76.8 amended by S.I. 1996 No. 2168 (consolidating enactment).

[2] R.76.8(2)(a) amended by S.I. 1994 No. 2901 (minor correction).

[3] R.76.8(2)(c) amended by S.I. 1998 No. 890 (effective 21st April, 1998).

76.8.1   *"note"*. For applications by note, see r.15.2.

Requirements where order to facilitate realisation of property considered

[1] **76.9.** Where the court considers making an order under paragraph 12(1) of Schedule 1 to the Act of 1995 (order to facilitate the realisation of property)—
    (a) the court shall fix a date for a hearing on the Motion Roll in the first instance; and
    (b) the petitioner or noter, as the case may be, shall serve a notice in Form 76.9 on any person who has an interest in the property.

Deriv. R.C.S. 1965, r.201K(2) inserted by S.I. 1990 No. 705

---

[1] R.76.9 amended by S.I. 1996 No. 2168 (consolidating enactment).

Documents for Accountant of Court

76.10.—(1) A person who has lodged any document in the process of an application for the appointment of an administrator shall forthwith send a copy of that document to the Accountant of Court.

(2) The clerk of session in the Petition Department shall transmit to the Accountant of Court any part of the process as the Accountant of Court may request in relation to an administration which is in dependence before the court unless such part of the process is, at the time of request, required by the court.

Deriv. R.C.S. 1965, r. 201L inserted by S.I. 1990 No. 705

General note. The Accountant of Court is responsible for supervising administrators **76.10.1** appointed under para. 5 of Sched. 1 of the Act of 1995.

"send". This includes deliver: r. 1.3(1) (definition of "send").   **76.10.2**

"in dependence". A cause is depending from the time it is commenced (*i.e.* from the time an **76.10.3** action is served or a first order in a petition is made) until final decree, whereas a cause is in dependence until final extract. For the meaning of commenced, see note 14.6.1. For the meaning of final decree, see note 4.15.2(2). For the meaning of final extract, see note 7.1.2(2).

Procedure for finding caution

76.11.—(1) Rule 61.9 (finding caution in judicial factories), except paragraph (4), shall, with the necessary modifications, apply to the finding of caution by an administrator under this Part as it applies to the finding of caution by a judicial factor.

(2) A certified copy of the interlocutor appointing an administrator shall not be issued by a clerk of session until the Accountant of Court has given written intimation to the Petition Department that caution has been found or other security given.

Deriv. R.C.S. 1965, r. 201M inserted by S.I. 1990 No. 705 (r. 76.11(2))

General note. It is for the Accountant of Court to impose any conditions as to caution as he **76.11.1** thinks fit: Act of 1995, Sched. 1, para. 1(8). The procedure for finding caution is the same as that for a judicial factor under r. 61.9.

"written intimation". For methods, see r. 16.9.   **76.11.2**

Administrator's title to act

76.12. An administrator shall not be entitled to act until he has obtained a certified copy of the interlocutor appointing him.

Duties of administrator

76.13.—(1) The administrator shall, as soon as possible, but within three months after the date of his appointment, lodge with the Accountant of Court—

(a) an inventory of the property in respect of which he has been appointed;

(b) all vouchers, securities, and other documents which are in his possession; and

(c) a statement of that property which he has in his possession or intends to realise.

(2) An administrator shall maintain accounts of his intromissions with the property in his charge and shall, subject to paragraph (3)—

(a) within six months after the date of his appointment, and

(b) at six monthly intervals after the first account during the subsistence of his appointment,

lodge with the Accountant of Court an account of his intromissions in such form, with such supporting vouchers and other documents, as the Accountant of Court may require.

(3) The Accountant of Court may waive the lodging of an account where the administrator certifies that there have been no intromissions during a particular accounting period.

Deriv. R.C.S. 1965, r. 201N inserted by S.I. 1990 No. 705

State of funds and scheme of division
76.14.—(1) The administrator shall—
[1] (a) where there are funds available for division, prepare a state of funds after application of sums in accordance with paragraph 4(2) of Schedule 1 to the Act of 1995 and a scheme of division amongst those who held property which has been realised under that Act and lodge them and all relevant documents with the Accountant of Court; or
  (b) where there are no funds available for division, prepare a state of funds only and lodge it with the Accountant of Court, and give to the Accountant of Court such explanations as he shall require.
(2) The Accountant of Court shall—
  (a) make a written report on the state of funds and any scheme of division including such observations as he considers appropriate for consideration by the Lord Ordinary; and
  (b) return the state of funds and any scheme of division to the administrator with his report.
(3) The administrator shall, on receiving the report of the Accountant of Court—
  (a) lodge in process the report, the state of funds and any scheme of division;
  (b) intimate a copy of it to the Lord Advocate; and
[1] (c) intimate to each person who held property which has been realised under the Act of 1995 a notice stating—
    (i) that the state of funds and scheme of division or the state of funds only, as the case may be, and the report of the Accountant of Court, have been lodged in process;
    (ii) the amount for which that person has been ranked, and whether he is to be paid in full, or by a dividend, and the amount of it, or that no funds are available for payment.

Deriv. R.C.S. 1965, r. 201P inserted by S.I. 1990 No. 705

---

[1] R. 76.14(1)(a) and (3)(c) amended by S.I. 1996 No. 2168 (consolidating enactment).

76.14.1   *"lodge in process"*. The report is lodged as a step of process (r. 1.3(1) (definition of "step of process")). On lodging steps of process, see r. 4.4. The list may be lodged by post: P.N. No. 4 of 1994, paras. 1 and 8; and see note 4.4.10.

76.14.2   *"intimate"*. For methods, see r. 16.7.

Objections to scheme of division
76.15.—[1] (1) A person wishing to be heard by the court in relation to the distribution of property under paragraph 4(3) of Schedule 1 to the Act of 1995 shall lodge a note of objection in the process to which the scheme of division relates within 21 days of the date of the notice intimated under rule 76.14(3)(c).
(2) After the period for lodging a note of objection has expired and no note of objection has been lodged, the administrator may apply by motion for approval of the scheme of division and state of funds, or the state of funds only, as the case may be.
(3) After the period for lodging a note of objection has expired and a note of objection has been lodged, the Lord Ordinary shall dispose of such objection after hearing any objector and the administrator and making such inquiry as he thinks fit.

(4) If any objection is sustained to any extent, the necessary alterations shall be made to the state of funds and any scheme of division and shall be approved by the Lord Ordinary.

Deriv. R.C.S. 1965, r. 201Q inserted by S.I. 1990 No. 705

---

[1] R. 76.15(1) amended by S.I. 1996 No. 2168 (consolidating enactment).

"note of objection". A note of objection does not have to be signed: r. 4.2(9)(f). R. 15.2 **76.15.1** (applications by note) does not apply: r. 15.2(4)(b).

"motion". For motions, see Chap. 23.   **76.15.2**

Application for discharge of administrator

76.16.—(1) Where the scheme of division is approved by the court and the administrator has paid, delivered or conveyed to the persons entitled the sums or receipts allocated to them in the scheme, the administrator may apply for his discharge.

[1] (2) An application for discharge of the administrator shall be made by note in the process of the application under paragraph 1(1) Schedule 1 to the Act of 1995.

Deriv.

---

[1] R. 76.16(2) amended by S.I. 1996 No. 2168 (consolidating enactment)

"note". For applications by note, see r. 15.2.   **76.16.1**

Appeals against determination of outlays and remuneration

76.17.—[1] (1) An appeal under paragraph 6(2) of Schedule 1 to the Act of 1995 (appeal against a determination by the Accountant of Court), shall be made by note in the process in which the administrator was appointed.

(2) Where a note is lodged under paragraph (1), the Keeper of the Rolls shall put the cause out on the By Order Roll on the first available day for a hearing before the Lord Ordinary.

Deriv. R.C.S. 1965, r. 201R inserted by S.I. 1990 No. 705

---

[1] R. 76.17 amended by S.I. 1996 No. 2168 (consolidating enactment).

General note. An appeal under para. 6(2) of Sched. 1 to the Act of 1995 is an appeal in **76.17.1** relation to an audit of the administrator's accounts by the Accountant of Court.

"note". For applications by note, see r. 15.2.   **76.17.2**

Remits from High Court of Justiciary
76.18. *Revoked by S.I. 1996 No. 2168.*

PART II

[1] APPLICATIONS UNDER THE PREVENTION OF TERRORISM (TEMPORARY PROVISIONS) ACT 1989 OR THE ORDER OF 1995

Application and interpretation of this Part
[1,2] **76.19.** In this Part—
"the Act of 1989" means the Prevention of Terrorism (Temporary Provisions) Act 1989;
"administrator" shall be construed in accordance with paragraph 11(1)(b) of Schedule 4 to the Act of 1989;

"the Order of 1995" means the Prevention of Terrorism (Temporary Provisions) Act 1989 (Enforcement of External Orders) Order 1995;

"restraint order" means an order made under paragraph 13(1) of Schedule 4 to the Act of 1989.

Deriv. R.C.S. 1965, r. 201S inserted by S.I. 1991 No. 1183

---

[1] Pt. II heading and r. 76.19 amended by S.I. 1996 No. 2168 (effective September 23, 1996).
[2] R. 76.19 amended by S.I. 1994 No. 2901 (clerical error).

76.19.1   *General note.* This Part deals with applications to the court where a forfeiture order has been made under s.13 of the 1989 Act or could be made by a court in Scotland, or where the procurator fiscal proposes to apply for such an order. In relation to applications for restraint orders and incidental applications in respect of which an external forfeiture order or an order elsewhere in the U.K. has been made or in respect of which such an order could be made, see r. 62.54. An external forfeiture order is an order made in a country or territory designated under art. 3 of, and specified in Sched. 2 to, the Prevention of Terrorism (Temporary Provisions) Act 1989 (Enforcement of External Orders) 1995 (S.I. 1995 No. 760).

The Act of 1989 has been replaced by the Terrorism Act 2000. The relevant provisions of that Act came fully into force on 15th February 2001: Terrorism Act 2000 (Commencement No.3) Order 2001 [S.I. 2001 No.421]. Accordingly, in relation to forfeiture and restraint orders made after that date, Chap.84 will apply.

76.19.2   *"restraint order".* The Court of Session may prohibit any person specified in the order from dealing in any property in respect of which a forfeiture order has been made or could be made in proceedings for, or where the procurator fiscal proposes to apply for a warrant to arrest and commit a person suspected of, an offence under Pt. III of the Act of 1989 (financial assistance for terrorism): Act of 1989, Sched. 4, para. 13(1).

Disapplication of certain rules to this Part

76.20. The following rules shall not apply to a petition or note mentioned in this Part:—

rule 14.5(1) (first order in petitions),

rule 14.6(1) (period of notice for lodging answers),

rule 14.7(1) (intimation and service of petitions),

rule 14.9(1) (unopposed petitions).

Applications for restraint orders

76.21.—(1) An application under paragraph 14(1) of Schedule 4 to the Act of 1989 (restraint order) shall be made by petition.

(2) Where the court pronounces an interlocutor making a restraint order, the Lord Advocate shall serve a certified copy of that interlocutor on every person named in the interlocutor as restrained by the order.

Deriv. R.C.S. 1965, r. 201T(1) (r. 76.21(1)), and r. 201U(1) (r. 76.21(2)), both inserted by S.I. 1991 No. 1183

76.21.1   *General note.* Application for a restraint order is made by the Lord Advocate and may be applied for *ex parte* in chambers (and presumably in private): Act of 1989, Sched. 4, para. 14(1).

76.21.2   *"petition".* A petition is presented in the Outer House: r. 14.2(h). The petition must be in Form 14.4 in the official printed form: rr. 4.1 and 14.4. The petition must be signed by counsel or other person having a right of audience: r. 4.2; and see r. 1.3(1) (definition of "counsel" and "other person having a right of audience") and note 1.3.4.

The petitioner must lodge the petition with the required steps of process (r. 4.4). A fee is payable on lodging the petition: see note 14.5.10.

On petitions generally, see Chap. 14.

"certified copy of that interlocutor". A copy of the interlocutor must be prepared **76.21.3**
(handwritten or typed) by the party. It is checked by the clerk of session at the appropriate
department, certified a true copy and stamped with the court stamp. A fee is payable: see Court
of Session Fees etc. Order 1984, Table of Fees, Pt. IV, J, item 2 (S.I. 1984 No. 256, Table as
amended, pp. **C** 1202 *et seq*).

Applications in relation to protective measures

76.22.—(1) An application under any of the following provisions of
Schedule 4 to the Act of 1989 shall be made by note in the process
containing the interlocutor making the restraint order to which the
application relates—
  (a) paragraph 13(4) (discharge of a restraint order);
  (b) paragraph 14(2) (variation or recall of restraint order); and
  (c) paragraph 14(3) (recall of restraint order).
  [1] (2) Subject to rule 14.6(2) (application to shorten or extend the period of
notice), the period of notice for lodging answers to a note under paragraph
(1)(b) of this rule by any person affected by a restraint order shall be 14
days.
  [2] (3) An application under paragraph 16(1) of Schedule 4 to the Act of
1989 (warrant for inhibition), or 16A(1) (warrant for arrestment), may be
made—
  (a) in the prayer of the petition under paragraph 13(1) of Schedule 4 to
the Act of 1989; or
  (b) if made after the petition has been presented, by motion which shall
not be intimated.
  [2] (4) Any of the following applications under Schedule 4 to the Act of
1989 shall be made by motion—
  (a) an application to recall, loose or restrict an inhibition under
paragraph 16(2)(a);
  (b) an application under paragraph 16(6)(a) (recall or restriction of
inhibition);
  (c) an application to recall, loose or restrict an arrestment under
paragraph 16A(2); or
  (d) an application under paragraph 16A(4) (recall or restriction of
arrestment).

Deriv. R.C.S. 1965, r. 201V(1) to (4) inserted by S.I. 1991 No. 1183

_____

[1] R. 76.22(2) amended by S.I. 1996 No. 2168 (minor correction).

[2] R. 76.22(3) and (4) amended by S.I. 1996 No. 2168 (consolidating enactment).

"period of notice". On period of notice generally, see r. 14.6. **76.22.1**

"note". For applications by note, see r. 15.2. **76.22.2**

"motion". For motions, see Chap. 23. **76.22.3**

Applications for compensation

76.23. An application under paragraph 17(1) of Schedule 4 to the Act of
1989 (compensation) shall be made by petition.

Deriv. R.C.S. 1965, r. 201V(5) inserted by S.I. 1991 No. 1183

_____

General note. Compensation may be payable to a person who had an interest in property **76.23.1**
which was the subject of a forfeiture or restraint order where there was serious default on the
part of a person in the investigation or prosecution of the offence concerned and the applicant
has suffered loss in consequence of anything done in relation to the property: Act of 1989,
Sched. 4, para. 17(1) and (3).

76.23.2   *"petition"*. A petition is presented in the Outer House: r. 14.2(h). The petition must be in Form 14.4 in the official printed form: rr. 4.1 and 14.4. The petition must be signed by counsel or other person having a right of audience: r. 4.2; and see r. 1.3(1) (definition of "counsel" and "other erson having a right of audience") and note 1.3.4.

The petitioner must lodge the petition with the required steps of process (r. 4.4). A fee is payable on lodging the petition: see note 14.5.10.

On petitions generally, see Chap. 14.

Powers and duties of administrator

76.24.—(1) Subject to any condition or exception specified by the court, an administrator appointed under paragraph 11(1)(b) of Schedule 4 to the Act of 1989—

(a) may take possession of the property in respect of which he has been appointed and of any document which—

    (i) is in the possession or control of the person in whom the property is vested; and

    (ii) relates to the property;

(b) may have access to, and copy, any document relating to the property and not in such possession or control as is mentioned in sub-paragraph (a);

(c) may bring, defend or continue any legal proceedings relating to the property;

(d) may borrow money in so far as it is necessary to do so to safeguard the property and may for the purposes of such borrowing create a security over any part of the property;

(e) may, if the administrator considers that to do so would be beneficial for the management and the realisation of theproperty, enter into any contract, or execute any deed, with respect to the property;

(f) may effect or maintain insurance policies with respect to the property;

(g) may, where the person in whom the property is vested has not completed title to any of the property, complete title to it: provided that completion of title in the name of the person in whom the property is vested shall not validate by accretion any unperfected right in favour of any person other than the administrator;

(h) may sell (but not to himself or an associate of his) the property and redeem any obligation secured on that property;

(i) may discharge any of his functions through agents or employees: provided that the administrator shall be personally liable to meet the fees and expenses of any such agents or employees out of such remuneration as is payable to the administrator by virtue of paragraph 12(2) and (3) of Schedule 4 to the Act of 1989;

(j) may take such professional advice as he considers necessary for the proper discharge of his functions;

(k) may at any time apply to the court for directions with respect to the exercise of his powers and duties;

(l) may exercise any power conferred on him by the court whether such power was conferred at the time of his appointment or on his subsequent application to the court; and

(m) may do anything incidental to the above powers and duties.

(2) Subject to the proviso to sub-paragraph (g) of paragraph (1)—

(a) a person dealing with an administrator in good faith and for value shall not require to determine whether the administrator is acting within the powers mentioned in that sub-paragraph; and

(b) the validity of any title shall not be challengeable by reason only of the administrator having acted outwith those powers.

(3) The exercise of a power mentioned in any of sub-paragraphs (c) to (h) of paragraph (1) shall be in the name of the person in whom the property is vested.

Deriv. R.C.S. 1965, r. 201W inserted by S.I. 1991 No. 1183

General note. A criminal court may make a forfeiture order under s. 13(2), (3) or (4) of the Act **76.24.1** of 1989 where a person is guilty of an offence under s. 9, 10 or 11 of that Act (financial assistance for terrorism). Where that court does so it may make an order appointing an administrator to take possession of property to which the forfeiture order applies: Act of 1989, Sched. 4, para. 11. R. 76.24 is made under Sched. 4, para. 11(2).

An administrator is subject to the supervision of the Accountant of Court: Act of 1989, Sched. 4, para. 12(3).

There is no provision, as there is in para. 1(8) of Sched. 1 to of the Act of 1995, for the finding of caution.

Duties of administrator in relation to accounts

76.25.—(1) The administrator shall, as soon as possible, but within three months after the date of his appointment, lodge with the Accountant of Court—
  (a) an inventory of the property in respect of which he has been appointed;
  (b) all land certificates, title deeds, vouchers and other documents which relate to that property and are in his possession; and
  (c) a statement of the property which he has in his possession or intends to realise.

(2) An administrator shall maintain accounts of his intromissions with the property in his charge and shall—
  (a) lodge an account of his intromissions with the Accountant of Court in such form as the Accountant of Court may require—
    (i) six months after the date of his appointment; and
    (ii) at six monthly intervals after the first account during the subsistence of his appointment, unless the Accountant of Court agrees to waive the lodging of an account where the administrator certifies that there have been no intromissions during a particular accounting period; and
  (b) lodge, with the account of his intromissions, all such supporting vouchers and other documents as the Accountant of Court may require.

Deriv. R.C.S. 1965, r. 201X inserted by S.I. 1991 No. 1183

Money received by administrator

76.26.—(1) Subject to paragraph (2), any money received by an administrator in the exercise of his powers and duties shall be deposited by him in an appropriate bank or institution, in the name of the person in whom the property is vested.

(2) The administrator may, at any time, retain in his hands a sum of money not exceeding £200.

(3) In paragraph (1), "appropriate bank or institution" means the Bank of England, an institution authorised under the Banking Act 1987 or a person for the time being specified in Schedule 2 to that Act.

Deriv. R.C.S. 1965, r. 201Y inserted by S.I. 1991 No. 1183

PART III

[1] APPLICATIONS UNDER THE PROCEEDS OF CRIME ACT 2002, THE OVERSEAS FORFEITURE ORDER OF 2005 AND THE POCA ORDER OF 2005

Interpretation and application of this Part

[1] **76.27.**—(1) In this Part—
  (a) "the Act of 2002" means the Proceeds of Crime Act 2002;
  (b) "the Overseas Forfeiture Order of 2005" means the Criminal Justice

(International Co-operation) Act 1990 (Enforcement of Overseas Forfeiture Orders) Order 2005;
(c) "the POCA Order of 2005" means the Proceeds of Crime Act 2002 (External Requests and Orders) Order 2005;
(d) "external order" has the meaning given in section 447(2) of the Act of 2002;
(e) references to an administrator are to an administrator appointed under section 125(1) or 128(3) of the Act of 2002, article 10(1) or 18(2) of the Overseas Forfeiture Order of 2005 or article 63(1) or 73(2) of the POCA Order of 2005.
(2) This Part applies to applications under—
(a) Parts 3 and 5 of the Act of 2002;
(b) Part 8 of the Act of 2002 in relation to property that is the subject of a civil recovery investigation;
(c) the Overseas Forfeiture Order of 2005 except article 13 (application to give effect to external forfeiture orders) and article 16 (registration of external orders);
(d) Parts 3 and 5 of the POCA Order of 2005 except article 66 (application to give effect to external orders) and article 69 (registration of external orders).

---

[1] Pt. III and r. 76.27 inserted by S.S.I. 2003 No. 222 (effective 28th March 2003, heading to Pt. III and r. 76.27 substituted by S.S.I. 2005 No. 663 (effective 31st December 2005).

76.27.1 *General note.* The Proceeds of Crime Act 2002 provides newprocedures for the confiscation (in criminal proceedings) and civil recovery of the proceeds of crime. Civil recovery under Pt. 5 of the Act of 2002 may be pursued by the Scottish Ministers (via the Civil Recovery Unit (CRU)), generally after any criminal procedure has been used (whether or not successful). Under s.244 of the Act of 2002 proceedings may be taken against any person who the CRU thinks holds recoverable property and the proceedings may be served on anyone the CRU thinks holds any associated property (as defined in s.245): see r.76.36 for procedure. An interim administration order may be applied for to detain, obtain custody of or preserve property and to appoint an interim administrator. The order prohibits any person to whose property the order applies from dealing with the property. A recovery order under s.266 may subsequently be made, in respect of property the court is satisfied is recoverable property, vesting the property in the trustee for civil recovery. Where the CRU is making civil recovery investigations, it may seek a disclosure order requiring any person to provide specified information or documents or answer questions relevant to the investigation: see r.76.37 for procedure.

Proceedings under Pt 5 of the 2002 Act do not involve a criminal penalty in the sense in art. 7(1) of ECHR: *The Scottish Minister v. McGuffie*, 2006 S.L.T. 1166 (Extra Div.).

In relation to a criminal investigation of an offence, there may be civil proceedings for restraint orders interdicting any person from dealing with any realizable property where it is believed that the alleged offender has benefited from his criminal conduct and there is evidence not available at the time of the confiscation order that the amount of that benefit exceeds the amount confiscated: see r.76.28 for procedure.

76.27.1 *"Parts, 3, 5 and 8 of the Act of 2002".* Part 3 is concerned with confiscation through the criminal process (confiscation orders under s.92) and restraint orders (under s.120) to interdict dealing with realizable property, together with administration of it, through a civil process as an adjunct to criminal investigation or proceedings. Part 5 is concerned with civil recovery of the proceeds of crime. Part 8 deals with investigations, and so far as the Court of Session is concerned, this means disclosure orders.

Restraint and administration orders
[1] **76.28.**—(1) An application under the following provisions shall be made by petition:—
(a) section 121(1) of the Act of 2002 (restraint orders);
(b) section 125(1) of the Act of 2002 (management administrators);
(c) section 128(2) of the Act of 2002 (enforcement administrators);
(d) article 6(1) of the Overseas Forfeiture Order of 2005 (restraint orders);
(e) article 10(1) of the Overseas Forfeiture Order of 2005 (management administrators);

   (f) article 18(2) of the Overseas Forfeiture Order of 2005 (enforcement administrators);

   (g) article 59(1) of the POCA Order of 2005 (restraint orders);

   (h) article 63(1) of the POCA Order of 2005 (management administrators); and

   (i) article 73(2) of the POCA Order of 2005 (enforcement administrators).

(2) An application under the following provisions shall be made by note in process:—

   (a) section 121(5) of the Act of 2002 (recall and variation of restraint orders);

   (b) section 134(2) of the Act of 2002 (protection of persons affected);

   (c) section 140(1)(b) of the Act of 2002 (variation or discharge of confiscation orders);

   (d) article 6(4) of the Overseas Forfeiture Order of 2005 (recall or variation of restraint orders);

   (e) article 22(2) of the Overseas Forfeiture Order of 2005 (protection of persons affected);

   (f) article 59(4) (recall or variation of restraint orders) of the POCA Order of 2005;

   (g) article 81(2) (protection of persons affected) of the POCA Order of 2005.

(3) An application under the following provisions shall be made by motion—

   (a) section 123(1) and (7) of the Act of 2002 (inhibition of property affected by restraint order);

   (b) section 124(1) and (6) of the Act of 2002 (arrestment of property affected by restraint order);

   (c) section 135(1) of the Act of 2002 (recall and variation of order appointing administrator);

   (d) article 8(1) and (7) of the Overseas Forfeiture Order of 2005 (inhibition of property affected by restraint order);

   (e) article 9(1) and (6) of the Overseas Forfeiture Order of 2005 (arrestment of property affected by restraint order);

   (f) article 23(1) of the Overseas Forfeiture Order of 2005 (recall and variation of order appointing administrator);

   (g) article 61(1) and (7) of the POCA Order of 2005 (inhibition of property affected by restraint order);

   (h) article 62(1) and (6) of the POCA Order of 2005 (arrestment of property affected by restraint order; and

   (i) article 82(1) of the POCA Order of 2005 (recall and variation of order appointing administrator).

(4) Before granting an application under the following provisions, the court may dispense with, postpone or order intimation to be made to such persons as it thinks fit:—

   (a) section 121(1) of the Act of 2002 (restraint orders);

   (b) section 123(1) of the Act of 2002 (inhibition of property affected by restraint order);

   (c) section 124(1) of the Act of 2002 (arrestment of property affected by restraint order);

   (d) article 6(1) of the Overseas Forfeiture Order in Council of 2005 (restraint orders);

   (e) article 8(1) of the Overseas Forfeiture Order of 2005 (inhibition of property affected by restraint order);

   (f) article 9(1) of the Overseas Forfeiture Order of 2005 (arrestment of property affected by restraint order);

   (g) article 59(1) of the POCA Order of 2005 (restraint orders);

   (h) article 61(1) of the POCA Order of 2005 (inhibition of property affected by restraint order); and

(i) article 62(1) of the POCA Order of 2005 (arrestment of property affected by restraint order).

---

[1] Rule 76.28 inserted by S.S.I. 2003 No. 222 (effective 28th March 2003), amended by S.S.I. 2004 No. 331 and substituted by S.S.I. 2005 No. 663 (effective 31st December 2005).

76.28.1   *General note.* A restraint order interdicting a person from dealing with any realizable property under s.120 of the Act of 2002 may be sought in support of (criminal) confiscation proceedings. The order may be recalled or varied. Inhibition and arrestment may be sought; management administrators may be appointed to manage the property and subsequently an enforcement administrator may be appointed.

A restraint order is a temporary measure, to prevent dissipation of assets by a respondent, until the court is in a position to make, if satisfied, a confiscation or forfeiture order. A restraint order ought, from the moment it is granted *ex parte*, to contain a proviso for reasonable living expenses, unless good reason is shown why this should not be done; it is generally appropriate to set a limit on the amount; it covers payment of ordinary debts as they fall due; it should be policed by appropriate arrangements as referred to (but not specified) by Lord Hamilton in *Hansen v. H.M. Advocate,* [2005] HCJAC 33, para. [12], 4th March 2005; and while the court cannot, under s. 120(3)(a) of the Act of 2002, allow the respondent to pay his legal expenses of defending the criminal case, the court may allow him to incur legal expenses in connection with the restraint order: *H.M. Advocate v. M,* 2005 S.L.T. 203 (OH), *per* Lord Glennie.

76.28.2   *"petition".* A petition is presented in the Outer House: r.14.2(h). The petition must be in Form 14.4 in the official printed form: rr.4.1 and 14.4. The petition must be signed by counsel or other person having a right of audience: r.4.2; and see r.1.3(1) (definition of "counsel" and "other person having a right of audience") and note 1.3.4.

The petitioner must lodge the petition with the required steps of process (r.4.4). A fee is payable on lodging the petition: see note 14.5.10.

On petitions generally, see Chap. 14.

76.28.3   *"note".* For applications by note, see r.15.2.

76.28.4   *"motion".* For motions, see Chap. 23.

76.28.5   *"intimation".* For methods, see r.16.8.

Documents for Accountant of Court

[1] **76.29.**—(1) A person who has lodged any document in the process of an application for the appointment of an administrator shall forthwith send a copy of that document to the Accountant of Court.

(2) The clerk of session in the Petition department shall transmit to the Accountant of Court any part of the process as the Accountant of Court may request in relation to an administration which is in dependence before the court unless such part of the process is, at the time of request, required by the court.

---

[1] Rule 76.29 inserted by S.S.I. 2003 No. 222 (effective 28th March, 2003) and as amended by S.S.I. 2004 No. 331 (effective 6th August 2004).

76.29.1   *General note.* The Accountant of Court has to be sent documents relating to the administrator because he supervises the administrator. An administrator may not exercise certain powers without the consent of the Accountant of Court: Act of 2002, Sched. 3, para. 4.

76.29.2   *"process".* For the process, see Chap. 4.

76.29.3   *"send".* This includes deliver: r. 1.3(1).

Procedure for fixing and finding caution

[1] **76.30.**—(1) Rule 61.9 (finding caution in judicial factories) shall, with the necessary modifications, apply to the finding of caution by an administrator under this Part as it applies to the finding of caution by a judicial factor.

(2) A certified copy of the interlocutor appointing an administrator shall not be issued by a clerk of session until the Accountant of Court has given

written intimation to the Petition Department that caution has been found or other security given.

---

[1] Rule 76.30 inserted by S.S.I. 2003 No. 222 (effective 28th March, 2003) and as amended by S.S.I. 2004 No. 331 (effective 6th August 2004).

General note. One of the dangers of applying another rule in this way is that it is not always clear what the modifications should be. Rule 61.9(2) applies r. 33.3 (further time for caution), but an administrator to whom r. 76.30 applies will seek any further time to pay under r. 76.31(2).   **76.30.1**

"caution". On the meaning of caution, see note 33.1.1.   **76.30.2**
Usually caution will be in the form of a bond of caution (r. 33.4(1)(a)), or it may be any other method of security approved by the court (r. 33.4(2)). Where caution is by bond of caution the bond may be by (a) an insurance company authorized to conduct such business (see r. 33.5); or (b) any other person, in which case the court must satisfy itself as to the sufficiency of the caution. The form of all bonds must comply with r. 37.6. A bond of caution must be sent to the Accountant of Court (together with a copy): r. 61.9(5). See further, note 61.9.2.

"certified copy interlocutor". A CCI is a copy of the interlocutor prepared by the party seeking the CCI, stamped and signed by a clerk of session in the General Department.   **76.30.3**

"written intimation". For methods, see r. 16.9.   **76.30.4**

Time for finding caution

[1] **76.31.**—(1) Where the time within which caution is to be found is not stipulated in the interlocutor appointing the administrator, the time allowed for finding caution shall be, subject to paragraph (2) of this rule, limited to one calendar month from the date of the interlocutor.

(2) The court may, on application made before the expiry of the period for finding caution, and, on cause shown, allow further time for finding caution.

---

[1] Rule 76.31 inserted by S.S.I. 2003 No. 222 (effective 28th March, 2003) and as amended by S.S.I. 2004 No. 331 (effective 6th August 2004).

General note. Although r. 76.30 applies r. 61.9 for finding caution, r. 61.9(2), which deals with the period for finding caution (which is in the discretion of the court) and with further time to pay, clearly does not apply here. Rule 76.31 applies instead.   **76.31.1**

Administrator's title to act

76.32. An administrator shall not be entitled to act until he has obtained a certified copy of the interlocutor appointing him.

---

[1] Rule 76.32 inserted by S.S.I. 2003 No. 222 (effective 28th March, 2003) and as amended by S.S.I. 2004 No. 331 (effective 6th August 2004).

Accounts

[1] **76.33.**—(1) An administrator shall maintain accounts of his intromissions with the property in his charge and shall, subject to paragraph (2)—
  (a) within six months after the date of his appointment; and
  (b) at six monthly intervals after the first account during the subsistence of his appointment,
lodge with the Accountant of Court an account of his intromissions in such form, with such supporting vouchers and other documents, as the Accountant of Court may require.

(2) The Accountant of Court may waive the lodging of an account where the administrator certifies that there have been no intromissions during a particular accounting period.

---

[1] Rule 76.33 inserted by S.S.I. 2003 No. 222 (effective 28th March, 2003) and as amended by S.S.I. 2004 No. 331 (effective 6th August 2004).

Application for discharge of administrator

76.34. An application to the court for the discharge of an administrator shall be made by minute in the process of the application in which the administrator was appointed.

---

[1] Rule 76.34 inserted by S.S.I. 2003 No. 222 (effective 28th March, 2003) and amended by S.S.I. 2004 No. 331 (effective 6th August 2004).

76.34.1   *"minute".* For applications by minute, see r. 15.1.

Appeals against determination of outlays and remuneration

[1]**76.35.**—[2] (1) An appeal under—

    (a) paragraph 9(1) of Schedule 3 to the Act of 2002 (appeal against a determination by the Accountant of Court);

    (b) paragraph 9(1) of Schedule 1 to the Overseas Forfeiture Order of 2005 (appeal against a determination by the Accountant of Court); or

    (c) paragraph 9(1) of Schedule 1 to the POCA Order of 2005 (appeal against a determination by the Accountant of Court),

shall be made by note in the process in which the administrator was appointed.

(2) Where a note is lodged under paragraph (1), the Keeper of the Rolls shall put the cause out on the By Order Roll on the first available day for a hearing before the Lord Ordinary.

---

[1] Rule 76.35 inserted by S.S.I. 2003 No. 222 (effective March 28, 2003) and amended by S.S.I. 2004 No. 331 (effective 6th August 2004).

[2] Rule 76.35(1) substituted by S.S.I. 2005 No. 663 (effective 31st December 2005).

76.35.1   *General note.* An administrator may appeal against the determination of the Accountant of Court as to remuneration and expenses not later than two weeks after the issuing of the determination: Act of 2002, Sched. 3, para. 9(1).

76.35.2   *"note".* For applications by note, see r. 15.2.

CIVIL RECOVERY PROCEEDINGS

Applications

[1]**76.36.**—(1) An application for a recovery order under section 244(1) of the Act of 2002 (proceedings for recovery orders in Scotland) or article 144(1) of the POCA Order of 2005 (proceedings for a recovery order pursuant to the registration of an external order) shall be made by petition.

(2) There shall be produced with a petition in respect of an application under article 144 of the POCA Order of 2005 a copy of the external order which is sought to be registered.

(3) Where the court grants an application under article 144 of the POCA Order of 2005 the Deputy Principal Clerk shall enter the external order in the register of orders under the POCA Order of 2005.

(4) An application for a prohibitory property order under section 255A(1) of the Act of 2002 or article 161(1) of the POCA Order of 2005 or for an interim administration order under section 256(1) of the Act of 2002 or article 67(1) of the POCA Order of 2005 shall be made—

    (a) if the application is made before the enforcement authority has commenced proceedings for a recovery order, by petition; or

    (b) if it is made after the enforcement authority has commenced such proceedings, by note in process.

(5) An application under the following provisions shall be made by note in process:—

(a) section 260(1) of the Act of 2002 (supervision of interim administrator);

(b) section 283(1) of the Act of 2002 (compensation);

(c) article 171(1) of the POCA Order of 2005 (supervision of interim administrator); and

(d) article 194(1) of the POCA Order of 2005 (compensation).

(6) An application under the following provisions shall be made by motion:—

(a) section 255E(1) and (6) of the Act of 2002 (arrestment of property affected by prohibitory property order);

(b) section 255F(1) and (6) of the Act of 2002 (inhibition of property affected by prohibitory property order);

(c) section 258(1) and (7) of the Act of 2002 (inhibition of property affected by interim administration order);

(d) section 265(1) and (7) of the Act of 2002 (arrestment of property affected by interim administration order);

(e) article 165(1) and (6) of the POCA Order of 2005 (arrestment of property affected by prohibitory property order);

(f) article 166(1) and (6) of the POCA Order of 2005 (inhibition of property affected by prohibitory property order);

(g) article 169(1) and (7) of the POCA Order of 2005 (inhibition of property affected by interim administration order); and

(h) article 176(1) and (7) of the POCA Order of 2005 (arrestment of property affected by interim administration order).

(7) An application under the following provisions shall be made by motion by any party having an interest:—

(a) sections 255B(1) and 260(3) of the Act of 2002 (variation and recall of order);

(b) articles 162(1) and 171(3) of the POCA Order of 2005 (variation and recall of order).

(8) At the hearing of a motion under paragraph (7) the court may order that the application be made by note; and, in such a case, shall make an order for the lodging of answers to the note in process within such period as the court thinks fit.

(9) Before granting an application under the following provisions, the court may dispense with, postpone or order intimation to be made to such persons as it thinks fit:—

(a) section 255E(1) and (6) of the Act of 2002;

(b) section 255F(1) and (6) of the Act of 2002;

(c) section 258(1) and (7) of the Act of 2002;

(d) section 265 (1) and (7) of the Act of 2002;

(e) article 165(1) and (6) of the POCA Order of 2005;

(f) article 166(1) and (6) of the POCA Order of 2005;

(g) article 169(1) and (7) of the POCA Order of 2005; and

(h) article 176(1) and (7) of the POCA Order of 2005.

---

[1] Rule 76.36 inserted by S.S.I. 2003 No. 222 (effective 28th March, 2003), amended by S.S.I. 2004 No. 331 and substituted by S.S.I. 2005 No. 663 (effective 31st December 2005).

General note. Once (criminal) confiscation proceedings have been concluded, abandoned or **76.36.1** not commenced, there may be civil proceedings for the recovery by a recovery order of recoverable property in the Court of Session: Act of 2002, s. 244(1). When a recovery order is made it vests the property in the trustee for civil recovery: Act of 2002, s. 266. Property obtained through unlawful conduct (defined in s. 241) is recoverable property: Act of 2002, s. 304. Such property which has been disposed of may be followed into the hands of a person who has acquired it. Property which represents the original recoverable property is also recoverable property (s. 305(1)), property obtained in place of the recoverable property is recoverable property (s. 305(2)) and property which represents original recoverable property may be followed into the hands of a person who has acquired it (s. 305(3)). Accrued profits are recoverable property: Act of 2002, s. 307. There are exemptions: Act of 2002, ss. 308 and 309. Property may be inhibited (s. 258) or arrested (s. 265).

It was held in *The Scottish Ministers v. McGuffie,* 2006 S.L.T. 401 (OH) that recovery of assets under Pt. 5 of the Act of 2002 was not a criminal penalty within the meaning of Art. 7 of the ECHR.

76.36.2   *"petition".* A petition is presented in the Outer House: r. 14.2(h). The petition must be in Form 14.4 in the official printed form: rr. 4.1 and 14.4. The petition must be signed by counsel or other person having a right of audience: r. 4.2; and see r. 1.3(1) (definition of "counsel" and "other person having a right of audience") and note 1.3.4.

The petitioner must lodge the petition with the required steps of process (r. 4.4). A fee is payable on lodging the petition: see note 14.5.10.

On petitions generally, see Chap. 14.

76.36.3   *Interim recovery order.* No mention is made in r. 76.36 of an application for an interim recovery order under s. 246 of the 2002 Act. Such an application is for the detention, custody or preservation of property and for the appointment of an interim receiver to secure the property. Such an application may be made without notice to anyone if it would prejudice a recovery order.

An application for an interim recovery order may be made in the petition for a recovery order. It is perhaps unlikely that an application would be made after a petition for a recovery order as "notice" would by then have been given; but if it were necessary, it is not clear whether the application would be by note or motion. The normal petition practice would be by note.

76.36.4   *"note".* For applications by note, see r. 15.2.

76.36.5   *"motion".* For motions, see Chap. 23.

76.36.6   *"intimation".* For intimation, see rr. 16.7 and 16.8.

CIVIL RECOVERY INVESTIGATIONS

Disclosure orders

[1] **76.37.**—(1) An application under section 391(1) (disclosure orders) shall be by petition.

(2) Before the court grants an application referred to in paragraph (1), the court may dispense with, postpone or order intimation to be made to such persons as it thinks fit.

(3) An application under section 396(4) of that Act (supplementary) shall by motion.

---

[1] Rule 76.37 inserted by S.S.I. 2003 No. 222 (effective 28th March, 2003) and amended by S.S.I. 2004 No. 331 (effective 6th August 2004).

76.37.1   *General note.* In a (criminal) confiscation investigation, the Lord Advocate, or in a civil recovery investigation the Scottish Ministers (the CRU), may apply to the Court of Session for a disclosure order. The application must state that the person specified in the application is subject to a confiscation investigation or that property specified in the application is subject to a civil recovery investigation.

A disclosure order may be sought authorizing notice in writing to a person requiring that person to answer questions, provide specified information, or produce documents, or documents of a description, specified in the notice, relevant to the investigation.

Such orders will usually be sought after other powers, such as production orders, have been tried. It may be necessary to consider whether convention rights under ECHR are affected.

"petition". A petition is presented in the Outer House: r.14.2(h). The petition must be in Form   **76.37.2**
14.4 in the official printed form: rr.4.1 and 14.4. The petition must be signed by counsel or other
person having a right of audience: r.4.2; and see r.1.3(1) (definition of "counsel" and "other
person having a right of audience") and note 1.3.4.

The petitioner must lodge the petition with the required steps of process (r.4.4). A fee is
payable on lodging the petition: see note 14.5.10.

On petitions generally, see Ch.14.

"intimation". For intimation, see rr.16.7 and 16.8.   **76.37.3**

"motion". For motions, see Ch.23.   **76.37.4**

CO-OPERATION

Co-operation

[1] **76.38.**—(1) In this rule "the Order of 2002" means The Proceeds of
Crime Act 2002 (Enforcement in different parts of the United Kingdom)
Order 2002.

(2) An application for registration under paragraph 11 of the Order of
2002 shall be by petition.

(3) Before the court grants an application referred to in paragraph (2), the
court may dispense with, postpone or order intimation to be made to such
persons as it thinks fit

(4) Where the Court makes an order under paragraph 11 of the Order of
2002, the Deputy Principal Clerk of Session shall—

  (a) register the order; and

  (b) send a copy of the order to any person affected by it.

(5) An order referred to in the foregoing paragraph shall be final and shall
not be subject to review.

---

[1] Rule 76.38 inserted by S.S.I. 2003 No. 222 (effective 28th March, 2003) and amended by
S.S.I. 2004 No. 331 (effective 6th August 2004).

General note. An English, Welsh or Northern Ireland receivership order or restraint order   **76.38.1**
under the 2002 Act may be registered under art. 11 of the Proceeds of Crime Act 2002
(Enforcement in different parts of the United Kingdom) Order 2002 for the purpose of
enforcement.

Where an application is made, the Court of Session must direct that the order is registered in
the Court of Session. The court may make such order as is appropriate to ensure that the
"foreign" order is effective or to assist a receiver to exercise his functions.

In r.76.38, the reference to "paragraph 11" of the Order of 2002 should be a reference to
"article 11" (Orders in Council have articles and not paragraphs).

"petition". A petition is presented in the Outer House: r.14.2(h). The petition must be in Form   **76.38.2**
14.4 in the official printed form: rr.4.1 and 14.4. The petition must be signed by counsel or other
person having a right of audience: r.4.2; and see r.1.3(1) (definition of "counsel" and "other
person having a right of audience") and note 1.3.4.

The petitioner must lodge the petition with the required steps of process (r.4.4). A fee is
payable on lodging the petition: see note 14.5.10.

On petitions generally, see Ch.14.

"intimation". For intimation, see rr.16.7 and 16.8.   **76.38.3**

"send". This includes deliver: see r.1.3(1).   **76.38.4**

"final and shall not be subject to review". This means that the decision may not be reclaimed   **76.38.5**
against.

CHAPTER 77

SUMMARY TRIALS

Application of this Chapter
77.1. This Chapter applies to a petition under section 26 of the Act of 1988 (summary trials).

General note. First introduced in R.C.S. 1934, Chap. IV, r. 40 (A.S. Rules of Court [S.I. **77.1.1** 1934 No. 772]), summary trial procedure was originally authorised by s. 10 of the A.J.A. 1933 and re-enacted in s. 26 of the C.S.A. 1988. The purpose of a summary trial is to provide a procedure for the speedy determination of a dispute by a particular Lord Ordinary where parties agree the questions of fact or law to be determined. The procedure provides a process of arbitration without having to pay for the services of the appointed arbiter. Unfortunately, the procedure has been infrequently used. The reasons for this are believed to include (*a*) that the procedure may be held in public or be reported in the law reports and (*b*) that there is no right of appeal. In fact r. 77.4(3) provides for hearings in chambers (and presumably in private), and even in ordinary arbitrations a right of appeal may be restricted under s. 3 of the Administration of Justice (Scotland) Act 1972 or, if arbitration is adopted under the UNCITRAL Model Law on International Commercial Arbitration, the award may only be set aside on very limited grounds of form and validity but not on the merits (see Law Reform (Miscellaneous Provisions) (Scotland) Act 1990, s. 66 and Sched. 7, Art. 34). A difficulty with the procedure is, where the dispute is one of law only, getting parties to agree the facts to be included in the petition. Equally, where parties disagree on certain facts it may be difficult for parties to delineate disputed facts expressly. Furthermore, while contracts may provide for arbitration they rarely provide for summary trial.

The summary trial process has advantages over arbitration in providing a quick cheap form of adjudication by a judge of parties' choice. It is expressly provided in s. 26(3) of the C.S.A. 1988 that a summary trial shall be disposed of with as little delay as possible and where the parties agreed on the facts, must be begun to be heard within six weeks of the interlocutor appointing a hearing: r. 77.4(3)(*a*).

The only limit to the use of the summary trial is that it cannot be used to decide a dispute or question which affects the status of any person: C.S.A. 1988, s. 26(4); and see note 77.7.2.

A depending action may be transferred to summary trial procedure: C.S.A. 1988, s. 26(2) and r. 77.11.

Jurisdiction. Since parties must agree to summary trial, jurisdiction will be prorogated, **77.1.2** except in those cases where, under the C.J.J.A. 1982, another court has jurisdiction under Arts. 12 (agreement on jurisdiction in insurance matters), 15 (agreement on jurisdiction in consumer contracts) or 16 (exclusive jurisdiction) in Scheds. 1 and 3C, Arts. 15 and 16 of Sched. 4 (inter-UK jurisdiction), or r. 4 (exclusive jurisdiction) of Sched. 8 (jurisdiction of Scottish Courts). On prorogation, see C.J.J.A. 1982, Scheds. 1, 3C and 4, Art. 17 and Sched. 8, r. 5. See notes 13.2.7 to 13.2.15.

Disapplication of certain rules to this Chapter
77.2. The following rules shall not apply to a petition under this Chapter:—
  14.5 (first order in petitions),
  14.6 (period of notice for lodging answers),
  14.7 (intimation and service of petitions),
  14.8 (procedure where answers lodged),
  14.9 (unopposed petitions).

General note. The procedure in an ordinary petition does not apply to a summary trial **77.2.1** which is presented by all parties by agreement.

Form of petition
77.3. A petition for a summary trial shall contain—
  (*a*) a concise narrative in numbered paragraphs of the facts or circumstances in relation to which the dispute or question arises;
  (*b*) where the parties are agreed on the facts—
    (i) a statement to that effect; and
    (ii) a note of the questions which have arisen between them;

    (*c*)   where the parties are not agreed on the facts—
        (i)   a statement to that effect;
        (ii)   specification of the facts which are in dispute; and
        (iii)   a note of any further questions which may arise when the dispute of fact has been determined, or a reservation of such questions; and
    (*d*)   a prayer that the dispute or question be referred to a particular Lord Ordinary for his determination.

Deriv. R.C.S. 1965, r. 231(*a*) and (*b*)

77.3.1   *Form of petition.* The general provisions in r. 14.3 apply, subject to the special rules in r. 77.3. Parties should be styled "First Party", "Second Party", etc. The petition should be signed by counsel or other person having a right of audience for each party. r. 4.2(3).
    For actions transferred to summary trial procedure, see r. 77.11

77.3.2   *"dispute or question".* This is any dispute or question, regardless of value, including the minimum limit for a pecuniary action in the Court of Session (currently £1,500: Sheriff Courts (Scotland) Act 1907, s. 7 amended by the Sheriff Courts (Scotland) Act 1971 (Privative Jurisdiction and Summary Cause) Order 1988 [S.I. 1988 No. 1993]), which does not affect the status of any person: C.S.A. 1988 s. 26(4). On disputes or questions which affect the status of persons, see note 77.7.2.

Presentation to Lord Ordinary

    77.4.—(1) The petition shall be placed before the Lord Ordinary named in the petition on the earliest available day but, subject to paragraph (2), within seven days after the date of presentation of the petition.
    (2) Where the last day of the period specified in paragraph (1) falls in vacation without the petition having been brought before the Lord Ordinary, the petition shall be placed before the Lord Ordinary on the first sederunt day of the following term.
    (3) On the petition being placed before the Lord Ordinary, he shall—
    (*a*)   where it appears that the parties are agreed on the facts, appoint the cause to be heard before him, in court or in chambers, on a date within six weeks (excluding days in vacation) after the date of the interlocutor appointing the hearing;
    (*b*)   where it appears that the parties are not agreed on the facts, appoint a proof to be taken before him in court or in chambers.
    (4) The Lord Ordinary may take any hearing or proof, or any continuation of such hearing or proof, during session or vacation.

Deriv. R.C.S. 1965, r. 231(*d*)(part) substituted by S.I. 1967 No. 387 (r. 77.4(1)),
r. 231(*d*)(part) substituted by S.I. 1967 No. 387 (r. 77.4(2)), r. 231(*e*) substituted by S.I. 1976
No. 387 (r. 77.4(3)), and r. 231(*f*) (r. 77.4(4))

77.4.1   *Vacation or recess.* See note 11.1.2. The Lord Ordinary may only begin to consider the petition on a sederunt day during session: r. 77.4(2). The first consideration of the petition will usually be a motion by the parties on presentation of the petition for hearing or proof. A hearing or proof may be begun or continued in session, vacation or recess: r. 77.4(4).

77.4.2   *Hearing or proof.* The hearing or proof may be in open court or in chambers: r. 77.4(3); and see *e.g. McGeachy v. Standard Life Assurance Co.* 1972 S.C. 145. Where the parties are agreed on the facts, the hearing must begin within six weeks (excluding vacation) after the date of the interlocutor appointing the hearing: r. 77.4(3)(*a*). In such a case, because of any difficulty in ensuring the availability of the nominated judge, parties should consult the Keeper of the Rolls before presenting the petition to discuss a date for the hearing and check the availability of the judge.
    A hearing is appointed where the parties are agreed on the facts; a proof where they are not: r. 77.4(3). Procedure is determined by the parties with consent of the judge or by him if the parties are not agreed. Evidence at a proof is not recorded unless agreed to be: r. 77.6. On the distinction between hearings and proofs, see note 14.8.6. On proofs generally, see Chap. 36.

Procedure in summary trials

77.5. Subject to any other provision in this Chapter, the petition shall follow such procedure as the parties may, with the consent of the Lord Ordinary, agree, or, failing such agreement, as the Lord Ordinary shall direct.

Deriv. R.C.S. 1965, r. 231(j)

General note. Before presenting a petition for a summary trial parties should try to agree **77.5.1**
how the petition will proceed.

Recording of evidence at proof

77.6. The evidence led at a proof allowed under rule 77.4(3)(*b*) shall not be recorded, unless the parties so agree.

Deriv. R.C.S. 1965, r. 231(g)

Recording of evidence. If parties are agreed that evidence led should be recorded the **77.6.1**
general rule on recording of evidence applies: see r. 36.11.

Reports to Inner House

77.7.—(1) If at any stage of the cause it appears to the Lord Ordinary that the determination of the petition may affect the status of any person, the Lord Ordinary shall report the matter to the Inner House in accordance with Chapter 34.

(2) On receiving a report under paragraph (1), the Lord President may appoint the parties to show cause before a Division of the Inner House why the petition should proceed under section 26 of the Act of 1988; and the Inner House shall, after hearing parties and subject to any conditions as it thinks fit, direct that the petition shall proceed or refuse the prayer of the petition.

Deriv. R.C.S. 1965, r. 231(h)

General note. R. 77.7 is without prejudice to Chap. 34 which provides that a Lord Ordinary **77.7.1**
may at any stage report a cause on any incidental matter arising out of it to the Inner House
for a ruling: r. 34.1(1). In a summary trial if there is a question whether the determination of
the petition may affect the status of any person the Lord Ordinary must report the matter to
the Inner House: r. 77.7(1). The decision of the Inner House on the question raised in the
report is final: r. 34.3(2). If the petition would clearly affect status, the Lord Ordinary need
not report the matter and shall refuse the petition.

"status of any person". S. 26(4) of the C.S.A. 1988 provides that summary trial procedure **77.7.2**
applies to any dispute or question not affecting the status of any person which might competently be the subject of any cause in the Outer House. Status means political status such as
citizenship or nationality; or civil status such as marriage, legitimacy (present or past), parentage, domicile, separation, adoption, bankruptcy or liquidation. Apart from the above
(except adoption), R.C.S. 1965, r. 231(*o*) (amended by A.S. (R.C.A. No. 3) (Presumption of
Death) 1978 [S.I. 1978 No. 161]) provided that a question affecting status for the purposes of
s. 10 of the A.J.A. 1933 (repealed and re-enacted in s. 26(4) of the C.S.A. 1988) included a
question which could be the subject of or might depend on the decision in actions for aliment
not depending on contractual obligation, for custody of children or actions which raised questions of capacity of a person; although these actions do not *per se* raise questions of status.
There is, however, no power in the C.S.A. 1988 to state in the rules what is included in the
meaning of "status of any person", and R.C.S. 1965, r. 231(*o*) has not, therefore, been re-enacted. The word "person" includes a corporate or unincorporated body: Interpretation Act
1978, Sched. 1.

Disposal of petitions

77.8. Any decision of the Lord Ordinary shall be given effect to in an interlocutor and he may—

    (*a*) pronounce any interlocutor which he thinks fit to enable his decision to be carried into effect; and

    (*b*) dispose of all questions of expenses.

Deriv. R.C.S. 1965, r. 231(*h*)

Finality of interlocutors
77.9. An interlocutor of the Lord Ordinary shall be final, binding only on the parties to the petition, and shall not be subject to review.

Deriv. R.C.S. 1965, r. 231(*l*)

77.9.1   *Finality of interlocutors.* No interlocutor in a summary trial pronounced by the Lord Ordinary may be reclaimed: r. 77.9. An interlocutor pronounced by the Inner House on a report is also final and not appealable to the House of Lords: r. 34.3(2).

Transfer to another Lord Ordinary
77.10.—(1) In the event of the death, disability or absence of the Lord Ordinary before the petition has been determined, the petitioners may lodge a joint minute in Form 77.10 in process for the cause to be referred to another Lord Ordinary named in that minute.
(2) On such a minute being lodged in process, the cause shall be transferred to the Lord Ordinary named in that minute who shall take up the procedure at the point which had been reached by his predecessor.
(3) The Lord Ordinary to whom the cause is transferred under paragraph (2) may re-hear the evidence of any witness heard by his predecessor.

Deriv. R.C.S. 1965, r. 231(*m*)

77.10.1   *"lodge in process".* The joint minute is lodged as a step of process (r. 1.3(1) (definition of "step of process")). On lodging steps of process, see r. 4.4. The list may be lodged by post: P.N. No. 4 of 1994, paras. 1 and 8; and see note 4.4.10.

77.10.2   *Re-hearing of evidence.* This will be necessary if the parties are not using a shorthand writer to record the evidence. R. 77.6 on the recording of evidence should be noted.

Agreement to adopt summary trial procedure in action in dependence
77.11.—(1) Where the parties to an action propose to adopt summary trial procedure by virtue of section 26(2) of the Act of 1988 (agreement to adopt summary trial procedure in action in dependence), they shall lodge in the process of the action a joint minute in Form 77.11.
(2) On such a joint minute being lodged in process, the Lord Ordinary shall pronounce an interlocutor directing that the action shall proceed as a summary trial.
(3) On an interlocutor being pronounced under paragraph (2), rules 77.3 to 77.10 shall, with the necessary modifications and the following modifications, apply to the further procedure in the action:—
   (*a*) subject to sub-paragraph (*b*) of this paragraph, in rule 77.4, for the word "petition" there shall be substituted the words "record or other pleading"; and
   (*b*) in rule 77.4(1), for the words "date of presentation of the petition" there shall be substituted the words "date of the interlocutor pronounced under rule 77.11(2)".

Deriv. R.C.S. 1965, r. 231(*n*)

77.11.1   *General note.* S. 26(2) of the C.S.A. 1988 allows an action not affecting the status of any person to be transferred to summary trial procedure. This provision is rarely used.
        An action affecting the status of any person may not be transferred to summary trial procedure: C.S.A. 1988, s. 26(2). For what affects status, see note 77.7.2.

77.11.2   *"action in dependence".* An action means a cause initiated by summons: C.S.A. 1988, s. 51. An action is depending from the time it is commenced (*i.e.* from the time it is served) until final decree, whereas an action is in dependence until final extract. For the meaning of "commenced", see note 13.4.4. For the meaning of final decree, see note 4.15.2(2). For the meaning of final extract, see note 7.1.2(2). S. 26(2) of the C.S.A. 1988 probably should refer to a "depending" action.

CHAPTER 78

SPECIAL CASES UNDER SECTION 27 OF COURT OF SESSION ACT 1988

Application of this Chapter
78.1. This Chapter applies to a special case under section 27 of the Act of 1988.

General note. The special case introduced by s.63 of the C.S.A. 1868 (now s.27 of the C.S.A. **78.1.1** 1988) is neither a summons nor a petition.

A special case is a contract binding on the parties to a certain statement of facts: *Aytoun v. Aytoun* 1939 S.C. 162

Where (*a*) any persons interested personally or in a fiduciary or official capacity, (*b*) in a decision of a question of law, (*c*) are agreed on the facts, and (*d*) are in dispute only on the law applicable to those facts, they may, without raising proceedings, or at any stage of any proceedings, present a special case to the Inner House for an opinion or judgment: C.S.A. 1988, s.27(1). The case must be signed by counsel. Parties may exclude appeal to the House of Lords.

After the instance, the case consists of four parts—the statement of who the parties are (called first party, second party, etc.), the statement of agreed facts, the contentions for each party, and the questions of law for the opinion or judgment of the Inner House.

All persons interested should be parties: *Mackie's Trs. v. Martins* (1875) 2 R. 621. They must have a patrimonial interest in the subject-matter: *Aberdeen Varieties Ltd v. James F. Donald (Aberdeen Cinemas) Ltd* 1940 S.C.(H.L.) 52. Agreement on the facts, including foreign law, is essential: see *e.g. Campbell's Trs. v. Campbell* (1903) 5 F. 366, 373 *per* Lord Kinnear. It is not essential, but it may be convenient, that the question(s) of law are in such form as can be answered yes or no. The question of law must be one which could be raised in another formal process (*e.g.* an action of declarator): *Ramsbotham v. Scottish American Investment Co. Ltd* (1891) 18 R. 558; *Turner's Trs. v. Turner* 1943 S.C. 389. The question of law must not be premature, hypothetical or academic: *Aberdeen Varieties Ltd*, above, *per* Viscount Simon L.C., at p. 54; *Turner's Trs.*, above. If the question of law is one which can competently be tried in the sheriff court, a special case can only be presented to the Inner House if the value of the subject-matter exceeds the privative limit of the sheriff court (currently £1,500: Sheriff Courts (Scotland) Act 1907, s.7 and S.I. 1988 No. 1993): *Bruce* (1889) 17 R. 276. There must be a contradictor: *Mackinnon's Trs. v. McNeill* (1897) 24 R. 981; *Turner's Trs.*, above. A party may, however, be entitled to an answer to a particular question (in his favour) if other parties do not present an argument against: *Shetland Salmon Farmers v. Crown Estate Commissioners* 1991 S.L.T. 166 (but *Turner's Trs.*, above, was not cited).

Lodging and hearing of special case
78.2.—(1) A special case shall be lodged with a process in the General Department.

(2) A special case shall, without appearance, be put out for hearing in the Summar Roll before the Inner House.

Deriv. R.C.S. 1965, r. 265(a) (r. 78.2(1)) and r. 265(b) (r. 78.2(2))

"special case lodged with a process". The special case should comply with the requirements for **78.2.1** size and quality of paper, etc., in r. 4.1. For the essential documents for a process, see r. 4.4.

Summar Roll. Once appointed to the Summar Roll a diet is fixed by the Keeper of the Rolls in **78.2.2** accordance with r. 6.3 after parties have sent him Form 6.3 duly completed. The case will be heard by a Division of the Inner House, usually consisting of three judges rather than four nowadays.

In case of difficulty, importance or equal division of the Division of the Inner House hearing the special case, a larger court may hear the case: C.S.A. 1988, s.27(2).

Fee. The court fee for each party (up to a maximum fee) is payable on lodging the special **78.2.3** case. For fee, see Court of Session etc. Fees Order 1997, Table of Fees, Pt I, B, item 8 [S.I. 1997 No. 688, as amended, pp. **C** 1201 *et seq.*]. Certain persons are exempt from payment of fees: see 1997 Fees Order, art.5 substituted by S.S.I. 2002 No. 270. A fee exemption certificate must be lodged in process: see P.N. No.1 of 2002.

Where a party is legally represented, the fee may be debited under a credit scheme introduced on 1st April 1976 by P.N. No. 4 of 1976 to the account (if one is kept or permitted) of the agent by the court cashier, and an account will be rendered weekly by the court cashier's office to the agent for all court fees due that week for immediate settlement. Party litigants and agents not operating the scheme must pay (by cash, cheque or postal order) on each occasion a fee is due at the time of lodging at the counter at the General Department.

The court fee for the hearing on the Summar Roll is payable by each party for every 30 minutes or part thereof. For fee, see Court of Session etc. Fees Order 1984, Table of Fees, Pt I, B, item 14 [S.I. 1984 No. 256, Table as amended, pp. C 1202 *et seq.*]. The fee may be debited under a credit scheme introduced on 1st April 1976 by P.N. No. 4 of 1976 to the account (if one is kept or permitted) of the agent by the court cashier, and an account will be rendered weekly by the court cashier's office to the agent for all court fees due that week for immediate settlement. An agent not on the credit scheme will have an account opened for the purpose of lodging the fee: P.N. No. 2 of 1995. A debit slip and a copy of the court hearing time sheet will be delivered to the agent's box or sent by DX or post.

A party litigant must pay cash to the clerk of court at the end of the hearing or, if the hearing lasts more than a day, at the end of each day: P.N. No. 2 of 1995. A receipt will be issued. The assistant clerk of session will acknowledge receipt of the sum received from the clerk of court on the Minute of Proceedings.

Amendment of case
78.3.—(1) A special case may be amended by consent of the parties.

(2) Where parties seek to amend a special case, any one of them may apply by motion for leave to amend of consent.

Deriv. R.C.S. 1965, r. 265(c) inserted by S.I. 1984 No. 472

Appointment of curator ad litem *to party* incapax
78.4.—(1) Where a party to a special case is *incapax* by reason of nonage, insanity or otherwise, it shall be the duty of the other parties (which duty may be performed by any of them), on the lodging of the special case under rule 78.2(1), to apply by motion for the appointment of a curator *ad litem* to such *incapax*.

(2) A curator *ad litem* appointed under paragraph (1) shall be given all necessary information and facilities by the other parties to enable him to perform his duties.

(3) Where a curator *ad litem* is satisfied that the special case is fully and accurately stated in relation to the interests of the *incapax*, he may sign it as curator *ad litem*.

(4) Where a curator *ad litem* is not given all necessary information and facilities by the other parties, or is not satisfied that the special case is fully and accurately stated in relation to the interest of the *incapax*, he shall report the position to the Inner House which may then recall his appointment and dispose of the special case as it thinks fit.

(5) An award of expenses—
(a) may not be made against a curator *ad litem*; and
(b) may be made in favour of a curator *ad litem* as the court thinks fit.

Deriv. R.C.S. 1965, r. 266

78.4.1   *General note*. The court may refuse to appoint a curator *ad litem* if the interest of the person concerned is adequately represented by another party: *Macdonald's Trs. v. Medhurst* 1915 S.C. 879 (mental illness). But in *Aytoun v. Aytoun* 1939 S.C. 162 (a case involving nonage), the appointment was insisted on because the special case would not be binding on a child.

78.4.2   *"motion"*. For motions, see Chap. 23.

CHAPTER 79

APPLICATIONS UNDER THE ACCESS TO HEALTH RECORDS ACT 1990

Application and interpretation of this Chapter
79.1.—(1) This Chapter applies to an application under section 8(1) of the Access to Health Records Act 1990 (application for order for holder of health record to comply with requirement of the Act).

(2) In this Chapter—
"the Act of 1990" means the Access to Health Records Act 1990;
"the Regulations" means the Access to Health Records (Steps to Secure
Compliance and Complaints Procedures) (Scotland) Regulations 1991;
"complaint" means a written notice of complaint under regulation 3 or 4 of
the Regulations;
"report" means a report under regulation 6 of the Regulations.

Deriv. R.C.S. 1965, r. 260Y(1) and (2) inserted by S.I. 1991 No. 2652

General note. Under the Data Protection Act 1984 (now the Data Protection Act 1998) patients **79.1.1**
are entitled to access to computerised health records. Under the Act of 1990 they are entitled to
access to written health records (but not to information to which the 1984 Act applies).

A patient's right of access to health records is not unrestricted. Access may be denied if it is in
the patient's best interests to do so, *e.g.* because disclosure would be detrimental to the patient's
health: Act of 1990, s.3(2); and see, in England, *R. v. Mid Glamorgan Family Health Services
Authority ex parte Martin* [1995] 1 All E.R. 356.

Form of applications, etc.
79.2.—(1) An application under section 8(1) of the Act of 1990 shall be
made by petition.
(2) A petition under paragraph (1) shall state those steps prescribed in the
Regulations which have been taken to secure compliance with the Act of
1990.
(3) On presentation of the petition, there shall be lodged in process as
productions—
  (a) a copy of the application under section 3 (access to health record) or
      section 6 (correction of inaccurate health record), as the case may be,
      of the Act of 1990;
  (b) a copy of the complaint; and
  (c) if applicable, a copy of the report.

Deriv. R.C.S. 1965, r. 260Y(3) and (5) inserted by S.I. 1991 No. 2652 (r. 79.2(1) and (3))

General note. This rule is made in part under s.8(1) of the Act of 1990. **79.2.1**
Where the holder of a health record has failed to comply with a requirement of the Act of
1990 and the applicant has taken all steps to secure compliance as may be prescribed by
regulations, the court may order the holder of the record to comply with the requirement: Act of
1990, s.8(1) and (2).

The requirements include a requirement that the patient (or certain others on his behalf) may
inspect the record and have it explained on application by him (Act of 1990, s.3) and to have a
correction made to it on application by him (Act of 1990, s.6). The steps to be taken by the
applicant are to apply to the holder in writing to see the record or have it corrected, as the case
may be, and to have made a complaint under the Regulations that the holder of the record has
failed to comply to which he has received a reply or to which there has been no response within
three months from the date of the complaint: 1991 Regulations, reg. 2.

The court may see the record; but, pending determination of the application to the court, the
applicant may not see it: Act of 1990, s.8(4).

"petition". A petition is presented in the Outer House: r. 14.2(h). The petition must be in **79.2.2**
Form 14.4 in the official printed form: rr. 4.1 and 14.4. The petition must be signed by counsel
or other person having a right of audience: r. 4.2; and see r. 1.3(1) (definition of "counsel" and
"other person having a right of audience") and note 1.3.4.

The petitioner must lodge the petition with the required steps of process (r. 4.4). A fee is
payable on lodging the petition: see note 14.5.10.

On petitions generally, see Chap. 14.

"lodged in process as productions". See r. 4.5. **79.2.3**

"a copy of the application". The application to the holder of the health record must be in **79.2.4**
writing: Act of 1990, s.11.

"complaint". Written notice of the complaint must be given to the appropriate Health Board **79.2.5**
within three months of the application to the holder: 1991 Regulations, regs 3(2) and 5.

Release 63: January 2002

79.2.6   *"copy of the report".* The holder of the health record is supposed to report to the applicant his response to the complaint within three months from the date of the complaint. A copy will only be available if he has reported.

Time-limit for applications
    79.3. An application under section 8(1) of the Act of 1990 may not be made unless the petition is presented—
    (a) where the applicant has received a report, within one year of the date after the report; or
    (b) where the applicant has not received a report, within 18 months after the date of the complaint.

Deriv. R.C.S. 1965, r. 260Y(4) inserted by S.I. 1991 No. 2652

79.3.1   *"within one year", "within 18 months".* The date from which the period is calculated is not counted. Where the last day falls on a Saturday or Sunday or a public holiday on which the Office of Court is closed, the next available day is allowed: r. 1.3(7). For office hours and public holidays, see note 3.1.2.

CHAPTER 80

APPLICATIONS IN RESPECT OF QUALIFIED CONVEYANCERS AND EXECUTRY PRACTITIONERS

Application and interpretation of this Chapter
    80.1.—(1) This Chapter applies to an application made under the Law Reform (Miscellaneous Provisions) (Scotland) Act 1990 in respect of a qualified conveyancer or executry practitioner.
    (2) In this Chapter, "the Act of 1990" means the Law Reform (Miscellaneous Provisions) (Scotland) Act 1990.
    (3) The expressions "the Board", "executry practitioner" and "qualified conveyancer" have the meanings assigned respectively in section 23 of the Act of 1990.

80.1.1   *General note.* In 1992 the Scottish Conveyancing and Executry Services Board, set up under s.16 of the Act of 1990 to regulate the provision of conveyancing and executry services by persons other than solicitors or unqualified persons under s.32(2) of the Solicitors (Scotland) Act 1980, was suspended. The reason was that the Government considered it was unlikely that the housing market would generate many opportunities for qualified conveyancers in the short term: see 1992 S.L.T. (News) 283. The Board did not grant any applications before it was suspended.
    The Board's suspension was lifted, and it opened for registration of qualifying conveyancers and executry practitioners, in early 1997.

Applications and appeals in respect of qualified conveyancers and executry practitioners
    80.2.—(1) Subject to paragraph (4), an application under any of the following provisions of the Act of 1990 shall be made by petition—
    (a) section 17(6) (application following refusal to register as qualified conveyancer);
    (b) section 18(7) (application following refusal to register as executry practitioner);
    (c) section 20(7) (application for order to require practitioner to comply with direction);
    (d) section 20(11)(b) (application following review of certain decisions of Board following misconduct etc.);
    (e) section 21(5) (application following direction relating to assets);
    (f) section 21(7) (application to secure compliance with direction);
    (g) section 21(10) (application by the Board for interdict); and
    (h) paragraph 20 of Schedule 1 (application for order to produce documents).

(2) An application under section 17(6), 18(7) or 20(11)(*b*) of the Act of 1990 shall state the date on which the outcome of the review was intimated to the petitioner.

(3) An application under section 21(5) of the Act of 1990 shall state the date on which the direction was received by the petitioner.

(4) An application for leave under section 21(10) of the Act of 1990 shall be made by motion.

"petition". A petition is presented in the Outer House: r.15.2(h). The petition must be in Form **80.2.1** 14.4 in the official printed form: rr.4.1 and 14.4. The petition must be signed by counsel or other person having a right of audience: r.4.2; and see r.1.3(1) (definition of "counsel" and "other person having a right of audience") and note 1.3.4.

The petitioner must lodge the petition with the required steps of process (r.4.4). A fee is payable on lodging the petition: see note 14.5.10.

On petitions generally, see Chap. 14.

"motion". For motions, see Chap. 23.   **80.2.2**

Deriv. R.C.S. 1965, r. 9 substituted by S.I. 1992 No. 1422

Intimation and service in petitions under this Chapter

80.3.—(1) A petition to which this Chapter applies shall be brought before a Division of the Inner House in chambers, and the Division may, without hearing parties and subject to the following paragraphs, make such order for intimation and service as it thinks fit.

(2) In an application under any of the following provisions of the Act of 1990, the court shall order service of the petition on the Board—
- (a) section 17(6) (application in respect of review of refusal to register as qualified conveyancer);
- (b) section 18(7) (application following review of refusal to register as executry practitioner);
- (c) section 20(11)(b) (application following review of certain decisions of the Board following misconduct etc.); and
- (d) section 21(5) (application following direction relating to assets).

(3) In an application under any of the following provisions of the Act of 1990, the court shall order service of the petition on the executry practitioner or qualified conveyancer, as the case may be—
- (a) section 20(7) (application for order to require practitioner to comply with directions);
- (b) section 21(7) (application to secure compliance with direction); and
- (c) paragraph 20 of Schedule 1 (application for order to produce documents).

(4) In an application under section 21(10) of the Act of 1990 (application by the Board for interdict), the court shall order service of the petition on the executry or qualified practitioner, as the case may be, and on the bank, building society or other deposit holder.

Deriv. R.C.S. 1965, r. 10 substituted by S.I. 1992 No. 1422

"intimation". On intimation, see r.16.8.

"service". On service, see Chap. 16.

Procedure after order for intimation and service

80.4. The court shall, after an order for intimation and service under rule 80.3, proceed on the petition summarily in such manner as it thinks fit.

Deriv. R.C.S. 1965, r. 11 substituted by S.I. 1992 No. 1422

Remit for further inquiry in petitions under this Chapter

80.5.—(1) In a petition to which this Chapter applies, the court may remit to any person to make further inquiry into the facts, or to take further evidence and to report to the court.

(2) On completion of a report made under paragraph (1), the person to whom the remit was made shall send his report and three copies of it, and a copy of it for each party, to the Deputy Principal Clerk.

(3) On receipt of such a report, the Deputy Principal Clerk shall—
- (a) cause the report to be lodged in process; and
- (b) give written intimation to each party that this has been done and that he may uplift a copy of the report from process.

(4) After the lodging of such a report, any party may apply by motion for an order in respect of the report or for further procedure.

Deriv. R.C.S. 1965, r. 11B substituted by S.I. 1992 No. 1422 (r. 80.5(1))

"written intimation". For methods, see r.16.9.

[1] CHAPTER 81

APPLICATIONS FOR PARENTAL ORDERS UNDER THE HUMAN FERTILISATION AND EMBRYOLOGY ACT 1990

Application and interpretation of this Chapter
[1] **81.1.**—(1) This Chapter applies to applications for parental orders under section 30 of the Human Fertilisation and Embryology Act 1990.

(2) In this Chapter, unless the context otherwise requires—

"the Act of 1978" means the Adoption (Scotland) Act 1978;

"the Act of 1990" means the Human Fertilisation and Embryology Act 1990;

"Her Majesty's Forces" means the Royal Navy, the regular armed forces as defined in section 225 of the Army Act 1955, the regular air force as defined in section 223 of the Air Force Act 1955 and the Queen Alexandra's Royal Naval Nursing Services;

"the Regulations" means the Parental Orders (Human Fertilisation and Embryology) (Scotland) Regulations 1994.

---

[1] Chap. 81 and r. 81.1 inserted by S.I. 1994 No. 2806 (effective 1st November 1994).

General note. This Chapter is made under s. 59 of the Adoption (Scotland) Act 1978 as applied and modified by para. 15 of Sched. 1 to the Parental Orders (Human Fertilisation and Embryology) (Scotland) Regulations 1994 [S.I. 1994 No. 2804], and was inserted by A.S. (R.C.S. 1994 Amendment No. 2) (Human Fertilisation and Embryology (Parental Orders) 1994 [S.I. 1994 No. 2806]). The Regulations apply, as modified, provisions of the 1978 Act to parental orders; and the rules in this Chapter are based on the Adoption Rules in Pt. III of Chap. 67. This Chapter should be read with the Regulations and the Guidance Notes on the Regulations issued by the Scottish Office Home and Health Department.

The Act of 1990 gives effect to the Warnock Report on Human Fertilisation and Embryology (Cmnd. 9314 (1984)). The Act is concerned with regulating infertility treatments (artificial insemination by donor, egg donation, embryo donation, *in vitro* fertilisation) which involve human gametes (unfertilised male sperm or female egg cells) and with regulating the using or keeping of human embryos outside a woman's body. This Chapter is concerned with applications for parental orders under s. 30 of the Act of 1990 which came into force on 1.11.94 (Human Fertilisation and Embryology Act 1990 (Commencement No. 5) Order 1994 [S.I. 1994 No. 1776]).

Under s. 30 of the Act of 1990 provision is made for a married couple (and only a married couple) to obtain a parental order in respect of a child within six months of the child's birth if the child was carried by a woman other than the wife of the couple as a result of placing in her an embryo or sperm and eggs or her artificial insemination, and the gametes of the husband or wife of the couple or both were used to bring about the creation of the embryo. The child must live with the married couple at least one of whom must be domiciled in a part of the U.K., the Channel Islands or the Isle of Man: Act of 1990, s. 30(3) and (4). The father of the child, where he is not the husband of the couple, and the woman who carried the child, must agree to the parental order: Act of 1990, s. 30(5).

Disapplication of certain rules to this Chapter
[1] **81.2.** Unless otherwise provided in this Chapter, the following rules shall not apply to a petition or note to which this Chapter applies:—

rule 14.5 (first order in petitions),

rule 14.6(1)(*d*) (period of notice for lodging answers where service by advertisement),

rule 14.7 (intimation and service of petitions),

rule 14.8 (procedure where answers lodged),

rule 14.9 (unopposed petitions).

---

[1] R. 81.2 inserted by S.I. 1994 No. 2806 (effective 1st November 1994).

General note. The primary consideration in a parental order is the need to safeguard and **81.2.1**
promote the welfare of the child: Act of 1978, s.6 as modified and applied by the 1994
Regulations, Sched. 1, para. 2. The rules therefore provide an expedited procedure to which
certain ordinary petition rules (listed in this rule) do not apply.

Confidentiality of documents in process

[1] **81.3.** Unless the court otherwise directs, in any cause to which this
Chapter applies—
  (a) any document lodged in process, including a report by a reporting
      officer or a curator *ad litem*, shall be treated as confidential and open
      only to the court, the parties, the reporting officer and the curator *ad
      litem*; and
  (b) a reporting officer or curator *ad litem* shall treat any information
      obtained by him in relation to the cause as confidential, and shall not
      disclose any such information to any person unless it is necessary for
      the proper execution of his duties.

---

[1] R. 81.3 inserted by S.I. 1994 No. 2806 (effective 1st November 1994).

General note. Confidentiality is necessary to ensure that a person is not reluctant to provide **81.3.1**
relevant information. All documents in process are confidential, not just the various reports.
The court may order non-disclosure of a document to a person, even a party where appropriate.

Inspection and borrowing of documents. Writs (defined in r. 1.3(1)) and certain documents **81.3.2**
may not be borrowed from process, although a person interested (such as those mentioned in
r. 67.3) may inspect them: r. 4.11. A party who is an individual may be given access (*i.e.* allowed
to inspect) to a document: r. 67.3(2).

Selection of reporting officer or curator ad litem

[1] **81.4.** Where the court appoints a reporting officer or a curator *ad litem*
and there is an established panel of persons from whom the appointment
may be made, the reporting officer or curator *ad litem* shall be selected from
that panel unless the court considers that it would be appropriate to appoint
a person who is not on the panel.

---

[1] R. 81.4 inserted by S.I. 1994 No. 2806 and substituted by S.I. 1997 No. 854 (effective 1st April
1997).

General note. The court is not obliged to appoint a curator *ad litem* or a reporting officer from **81.4.1**
the panel established under the Curators ad Litem and Reporting Officers (Panels) (Scotland)
Regulations 1984 [S.I. 1984/566], if it considers it appropriate to appoint someone not on the
panel.
  S. 58(1) of the Act of 1978 as modified and applied by the 1994 Regulations, Sched. 1, para. 14
specifies the general duties of the curator *ad litem* as being to safeguard the interests of the child
in the proceedings, and of the reporting officer as being to witness agreements to parental
orders and to perform such other duties as may be prescribed by rules. On the appointment of a
reporting officer, see r. 81.10(1)(a); on the duties of the reporting officer, see r. 81.11(1). On the
appointment of a curator *ad litem*, see r. 81.10(1)(b); on the duties of a curator *ad litem*, see
r. 81.11(2).
  The court may appoint the same person to be both reporting officer and curator *ad litem*: Act
of 1978, s.58(2) as modified and applied by the 1994 Regulations, Sched. 1, para. 14.

The Panel. A local authority (a regional or islands council) is required to establish a panel for **81.4.2**
its own area after consultation with the sheriff principal for the area of suitably qualified and
experienced persons under the Curators ad Litem and Reporting Officers (Panels) (Scotland)
Regulations 1984 [S.I. 1984/566]. Panels may include social workers, solicitors and advocates.
  The expenses of a reporting officer or curator *ad litem* appointed in a particular case from the
panel are paid for by the local authority: 1984 Regulations, reg. 10 as substituted by the Curators
ad Litem and Reporting Officers (Panels) (Scotland) Amendment Regulations 1985 [S.I.
1985/1556]. Local authorities have laid down their own scales. Where additional fees or
expenses are claimed these may be met by the local authority; but if not, the balance could be

claimed from the petitioner on an order for expenses being obtained from the sheriff under r. 81.7.

A person appointed to the panel takes the oath *de fideli administratione* on his appointment to the panel.

81.4.3 *Persons not on the panel.* The court may where it considers it appropriate appoint a person to be reporting officer or curator *ad litem* who is not on the panel of the local authority established under the Curators ad Litem and Reporting Officers (Panels) (Scotland) Regulations 1984 [S.I. 1984/566]. Where this happens the local authority will not pay the fee of the person appointed, and the fee will usually be the responsibility of the petitioner. The court may make any order it thinks fit in relation to expenses including those of a reporting officer or curator *ad litem*: r. 81.7.

A person not on the panel appointed to be a curator *ad litem* must take the oath *de fideli administratione* on his appointment.

Form of agreements to parental order

[1] **81.5.**—(1) An agreement for the purposes of section 30(5) of the Act of 1990 (agreement to parental order by a father who is not the husband of the female petitioner or by the woman who carried the child) shall be in Form 81.5.

(2) An agreement referred to in this rule which is executed furth of Scotland shall be witnessed—

  (a) where it is executed in England, Wales or Northern Ireland, by a justice of the peace or commissioner for oaths;

  (b) where it is executed furth of the United Kingdom—

    (i) in the case of a person who is serving in Her Majesty's Forces, by an officer holding a commission in those forces; or

    (ii) by a British consular official or any person authorised, by the law of the country where the agreement is executed, to administer an oath for any legal purpose.

---

[1] R. 81.5 inserted by S.I. 1994 No. 2806 (effective 1st November 1994).

81.5.1 *General note.* Where the agreement is executed in Scotland it should be witnessed by the reporting officer: r. 81.11(1)(c). Where the agreement is executed outside Scotland it should be witnessed in accordance with r. 81.5(2).

By virtue of s.81 of the Solicitors Act 1974 every solicitor who holds a practising certificate in England and Wales has the power of a commissioner for oaths under the Commissioners for Oaths Acts 1889 and 1891. The power was extended to public notaries (members of the Incorporated Company of Scriveners) within their jurisdiction by s.65 of the Administration of Justice Act 1985. Under s.113 of the Courts and Legal Services Act 1990, the power was extended to authorised persons and general notaries in England and Wales. An "authorised person" is an authorised advocate or litigator other than a solicitor, or a member of a body prescribed by the Lord Chancellor. From 1st August 1995 legal executives who are fellows of the Institute of Legal Executives may act as commissioners for oaths in England and Wales. Every such solicitor, notary or authorised person has the right to use the title "Commissioner for Oaths" and should use that title (although a solicitor may accidentally omit to do so).

An agreement witnessed in accordance with Form 81.5 is sufficient evidence without further proof of signature of the person by whom it was executed: Act of 1978, s.55(1) as modified and applied by the 1994 Regulations, Sched. 1, para. 11.

Orders for evidence

[1] **81.6.**—(1) In a cause to which this Chapter applies, the court may, before determining the cause, order—

  (a) production of further documents (including affidavits); or

  (b) parole evidence.

(2) A party may apply by motion for the evidence of a person to be received in evidence by affidavit; and the court may make such order as it thinks fit.

---

[1] R. 81.6 inserted by S.I. 1994 No. 2806 (effective 1st November 1994).

81.6.1 *"affidavits".* The affidavit should be in the form of a statement of evidence written in the first person. The affidavit should contain evidence in support of, and expanding on, the averments in the petition. It should be sworn and signed by the deponent before any person who may competently take an oath. Such a person includes a notary public, a justice of the peace, a sheriff, or any judge. The person taking the oath should also sign the affidavit. Witnesses are unnecessary. And see definition of affidavit in r. 1.3(1).

Expenses
[1] **81.7.** In a cause to which this Chapter applies, the court may make such order as to expenses, including the expenses of a reporting officer, a curator *ad litem*, or any other person who attended a hearing, as it thinks fit.

---

[1] R. 81.7 inserted by S.I. 1994 No. 2806 (effective 1st November 1994).

General note. In relation to the expenses of a reporting officer and curator *ad litem*, note that **81.7.1** the fees of such persons appointed from a panel established under the Curators ad Litem and Reporting Officers (Panels) (Scotland) Regulations 1984 [S.I. 1984/566] are paid for by the local authority; but not if the person appointed is not on the panel, in which case the petitioner will normally be responsible for the fee.

Protection of identity of petitioners
[1] **81.8.**—(1) Where a married couple, who seek to apply for a parental order, wish to prevent their identity being disclosed to any person whose agreement is required under section 30(5) of the Act of 1990 (agreement to parental order by a father who is not the husband of the female petitioner or by the woman who carried the child), they may, before presenting a petition, apply by letter to the Deputy Principal Clerk for a serial number to be assigned to them.

(2) On receipt of such a letter, the Deputy Principal Clerk shall assign a serial number to the applicants and shall enter a note of it opposite the names of the applicants in a register of serial numbers.

(3) Where a serial number has been assigned under paragraph (2)—

(a) the record of the serial number and the persons to whom it applies shall be treated as confidential and disclosed only to the court;

(b) any agreement under section 30(5) of the Act of 1990 shall not name or design the petitioners but shall refer to them by means of the serial number; and

(c) it shall be used to name or design the petitioners for all purposes connected with the petition.

---

[1] R. 81.8 inserted by S.I. 1994 No. 2806 (effective 1st November 1994).

General note. An application for a serial number to prevent disclosure of the identity of the **81.8.1** petitioner may be made, *e.g.* to prevent disclosure to a person such as the father or woman who carried the child (whose agreement is required under s.30(5) of the Act of 1990).

The letter should be addressed to the Deputy Principal Clerk of Session, Court of Session, 2 Parliament Square, Edinburgh EH1 1RQ.

Applications for parental order
[1] **81.9.**—(1) An application for a parental order shall be made by petition in Form 81.9.

(2) On presentation of the petition, there shall be lodged in process as productions—

(a) an extract or a certified copy of any entry in the register of births relating to the birth of the child;

(b) extracts or certified copies of any entries in the register of births relating to the birth of each of the petitioners; and

(c) an extract or a certified copy of any entry in the register of marriages relating to the marriage of the petitioners.

---

[1] R. 81.9 inserted by S.I. 1994 No. 2806 (effective 1st November 1994).

81.9.1   *Jurisdiction.* The court has jurisdiction if the child is in its jurisdiction: Act of 1990, s.30(8)(b).

81.9.2   *"petition".* A petition for a parental order is presented in the Outer House: r. 14.2(h). The petition must be in Form 81.9 in the official printed form: rr. 4.1 and 14.4. The petition must be signed by counsel or other person having a right of audience: r. 4.2; and see r. 1.3(1) (definitions of "counsel" and "other person having a right of audience") and note 1.3.4.

The petitioner must lodge the petition with the required steps of process (r. 4.4) and the productions required by r. 81.9(2) and any others (including those founded on or adopted (r. 27.1)) with an inventory of productions (r. 4.5). Other productions which should be lodged include the agreement of the father of the child where he is not the husband petitioner and the woman who carried the child: Act of 1990, s.30(5).

A fee is payable on lodging the petition: see note 14.5.10.

Appointment of reporting officer and curator ad litem

[1] **81.10.**—(1) On presentation of the petition, the court shall appoint—

(a) a reporting officer; and

(b) a curator *ad litem* where it appears desirable in order to safeguard the interests of the child.

(2) Where a curator *ad litem* is appointed under paragraph (1) and is not also the reporting officer, the court may order the reporting officer to make available to the curator *ad litem* any report or information in relation to the child.

(3) A married couple may, before presenting the petition, apply by letter to the Deputy Principal Clerk for the appointment of a reporting officer.

(4) An application under paragraph (3) shall—

(a) set out the reasons for which the appointment is sought;

(b) not require to be intimated to any person;

(c) be accompanied by an interlocutor sheet; and

(d) be placed by the Deputy Principal Clerk before the Lord Ordinary for his decision.

(5) The Deputy Principal Clerk shall give written intimation to the applicant under paragraph (3) of the decision of the Lord Ordinary.

(6) The decision of the Lord Ordinary on an application under paragraph (3) shall be final and not subject to review.

(7) The letter and the interlocutor sheet in an application under paragraph (3) shall be kept in the Petition Department and subsequently placed in the process of the petition.

---

[1] R. 81.10 inserted by S.I. 1994 No. 2806 (effective 1st November 1994).

81.10.1   *Appointment of reporting officer and curator ad litem.* A reporting officer must be appointed. A curator *ad litem* may be appointed where it appears desirable (r. 81.10(1)(b)). It is probable that a curator *ad litem* would be desirable in every case. The court will usually appoint a person from a panel established by the local authority under the Curators ad Litem and Reporting Officers (Panels) (Scotland) Regulations 1984 [S.I. 1984/566], but may appoint someone not on the panel where appropriate. The court may appoint the same person to be both reporting officer and curator *ad litem*: Act of 1978, s.58(2) as modified and applied by the 1994 Regulations, Sched. 1, para. 14. See further, r. 81.4 and notes.

Appointment of a reporting officer may be sought before the petition is presented, for example, where a person whose agreement is required is going abroad: r. 81.10(3)–(7).

The general duties of a reporting officer are to witness agreements to and to perform such other duties as may be prescribed by rules: Act of 1978, s.58(1) as modified and applied by the 1994 Regulations, Sched. 1, para. 14. The general duty of the curator *ad litem* is to safeguard the interests of the child: Act of 1978, s.58(1) as modified and applied by the 1994 Regulations, Sched. 1, para. 14; and see r. 81.11.

81.10.2   *"final and not subject to review".* The decision of the Lord Ordinary may not be reclaimed against.

Duties of reporting officer and curator ad litem

[1] **81.11.**—(1) A reporting officer appointed under rule 81.10(1)(a) shall, where appropriate—

(a) inquire into the facts and circumstances averred in the petition;

(b) ascertain whether the conditions in subsections (2) to (7) of section 30 of the Act of 1990 have been satisfied;

(c) witness any execution in Scotland of any agreement in Form 81.5 under section 30(5) of the Act of 1990 (agreement to parental order by a father who is not the husband of the female petitioner or by the woman who carried the child), and investigate whether the agreement is given freely, unconditionally and with full understanding of what is involved;

(d) where a person whose agreement is required is furth of Scotland, confirm his views in writing, ensure that any agreement under section 30(5) of the Act of 1990 is witnessed in accordance with rule 81.5(2) and investigate whether the agreement is given freely, unconditionally and with full understanding of what is involved;

[2] (e) ensure that each person whose agreement is required understands that in agreeing to the parental order he is giving up all future claims to the child and that all parental responsibilities and parental rights will vest in the petitioners;

(f) investigate whether there are any other persons with a relevant interest and whether they should be informed of the petition;

(g) ascertain from any person whose agreement is required and who can be found whether alternatives to a parental order have been discussed with him;

(h) ensure that any person whose agreement is required is aware of the date (if known) of the hearing to determine the application if he wishes to appear, and confirm that any such person understands that he may withdraw his agreement at any time before a parental order is made;

(i) draw to the attention of the court any matter which may be of assistance; and

(j) prepare a report in relation to the exercise of his duties within such period as the court may specify.

(2) A curator *ad litem* appointed under rule 81.10(1)(b) shall—

(a) safeguard generally the interests of the child;

(b) inquire, so far as he considers necessary, into the facts and circumstances averred in the petition;

(c) ascertain whether any money or other benefit has been received or agreed upon which is prohibited by section 30(7) of the Act of 1990 (prohibition on gift or receipt of money or other benefit);

[2] (d) establish that the petitioners understand that the nature and effect of a parental order is to transfer the parental responsibilities and parental rights in relation to the child to the petitioners and make them responsible for the maintenance and upbringing of the child;

[2] (e) ascertain whether the proposed parental order is likely to safeguard and promote the welfare of the child throughout his life;

(f) ascertain whether it may be in the interests of the child that the court should make a parental order subject to particular conditions including the making of special provision for the child;

(g) perform such other duties as appear to him to be necessary or as the court may require; and

(h) prepare a report in relation to the exercise of his duties within such period as the court may specify.

(3) The reporting officer shall, on completion of his report, send to the Deputy Principal Clerk—

(a) the report and a copy of it for each party; and

(b) any agreement for the purposes of section 30(5) of the Act of 1990.

(4) The curator *ad litem* shall, on completion of his report, send the report, and a copy of it for each party, to the Deputy Principal Clerk.

---

[1] R. 81.11 inserted by S.I. 1994 No. 2806 (effective 1st November 1994).
[2] R. 81.11(1)(e), (2)(d) and (e) amended by S.I. 1997 No. 854 (effective 1st April 1997).

81.11.1   *General note.* The duties of the reporting officer are largely administrative. The duties of the curator *ad litem* are to provide the court with evidence of the history of the child, the current situation and prospects of the married couple seeking the parental order.

The amendments to r. 81.11 by A.S. (R.C.S.A. No. 3) (Human Fertilisation and Embryology) 1997 [S.I. 1997 No. 854] do not apply to applications for parental orders made before 1st April 1997.

81.11.2   *"send".* This includes deliver: r. 1.3(1) (definition of "send").

81.11.3   *Lodging of reports etc.* A report by the reporting officer and the agreements of the father of the child if he is not the husband petitioner and the woman who carried the child, and any report of a curator *ad litem*, are, on receipt of them by the Deputy Principal Clerk, lodged in process as a step in process: r. 81.12(1) and r. 1.3(1) (definition of "step of process").

Hearing
[1] **81.12.**—(1) On receipt of the reports referred to in rule 81.11, the Deputy Principal Clerk shall—
   (a) cause the reports and any other documents to be lodged in process;
   (b) give written intimation to each party of the lodging of those documents and make them available to each party; and
   (c) within 7 days thereafter, cause—
      (i) the petition to be put out on the By Order Roll before the Lord Ordinary; and
      (ii) written intimation of the date of the hearing on the By Order Roll to be given to each party.
(2) At the hearing on the By Order Roll, the court—
   (a) shall pronounce an interlocutor appointing the petition to a hearing to determine the petition; and
   (b) may, in such interlocutor—
      (i) order any person whose agreement is required to be given to attend the hearing;
      (ii) order intimation of the date of the hearing to any person not mentioned in paragraph (3)(a), (b) or (c); and
      (iii) order the reporting officer or curator *ad litem* to perform additional duties to assist the court in determining the petition.
(3) The petitioners shall intimate the date of the hearing ordered under paragraph (2)(a) in Form 81.12 to—
   (a) every person whose whereabouts are known to them and whose agreement is required to be given;
   (b) the reporting officer appointed under rule 81.10(1)(a);
   (c) any curator *ad litem* appointed under rule 81.10(1)(b); and
   (d) any person on whom intimation has been ordered under paragraph (2)(b)(ii).
(4) At the hearing ordered under paragraph (2)(a)—
   (a) the petitioners, the reporting officer and, where one has been appointed, the curator *ad litem* shall, if required by the court, appear and may be represented;
   (b) any person required by the court to attend the hearing shall appear and may be represented;
   (c) any other person to whom intimation was made under paragraph (3)(a) or (d) may appear or be represented.

---

[1] R. 81.12 inserted by S.I. 1994 No. 2806 (effective 1st November 1994).

"party". The petitioner is a party. A person objecting to a petition becomes a party **81.12.1** (respondent) on lodging answers: see r. 14.8 and note 14.8.1.

"written intimation". For methods, see r. 16.9. **81.12.2**

"make available". Unless the court otherwise orders, parties may borrow the reports and **81.12.3** other documents lodged in process.

By Order Roll hearing. The purpose of this hearing is to enable the court (a) to clarify the **81.12.4** issues to be resolved at the (full) hearing and (b) to determine the form of the (full) hearing. Parties should be clear before the By Order Roll hearing what has to be resolved and what form the (full) hearing should take. If oral evidence is required there must be an interlocutor allowing proof and the citing of witnesses.

The (full) hearing could take the form of a procedure roll discussion or a proof (or proof before answer). The interlocutor should state, *inter alia*, the form of the hearing.

"intimation", *"intimate"*. For methods, see r. 16.7. **81.12.5**

Hearing to determine the petition. The (full) hearing could take the form of a procedure roll **81.12.6** discussion or a proof (or proof before answer). If oral evidence is required there must have been an interlocutor pronounced allowing proof and the citing of witnesses.

Privacy of hearings. Any hearing is heard in private unless the court otherwise directs: Act of **81.12.7** 1978, s.57 as modified and applied by the 1994 Regulations, Sched. 1, para. 13.

Representation. A person appearing may be represented by counsel or other person having a **81.12.8** right of audience (on the meaning of which, see definitions of "counsel" and "other person having a right of audience" in r. 1.3(1)).

Fee. The court fee for the full hearing is payable by each party for every 30 minutes or part **81.12.9** thereof. For fee, see Court of Session etc. Fees Order 1984, Table of Fees, Pt I, C, item 17 (or as appropriate) [S.I. 1984 No. 256, Table as amended, pp. C1202 *et seq.*]. The fee may be debited under a credit scheme introduced on 1st April 1976 by P.N. No. 4 of 1976 to the account (if one is kept or permitted) of the agent by the court cashier, and an account will be rendered weekly by the court cashier's office to the agent for all court fees due that week for immediate settlement. An agent not on the credit scheme will have an account opened for the purpose of lodging the fee: P.N. No. 2 of 1995. A debit slip and a copy of the court hearing time sheet will be delivered to the agent's box or sent by DX or post.

A party litigant must pay cash to the clerk of court at the end of the hearing or, if the hearing lasts more than a day, at the end of each day: P.N. No. 2 of 1995. A receipt will be issued. The assistant clerk of session will acknowledge receipt of the sum received from the clerk of court on the Minute of Proceedings.

No court fee is payable for the By Order Roll hearing under r. 81.12(1)(c)(i).

Supervision by or committal to care of local authority
81.13. [Revoked by S.I. 1997 No. 854.]

General note. The revocation of r. 81.13 by A.S. (R.C.S.A. No. 3) (Human Fertilisation and **81.13.1** Embryology) 1997 [S.I. 1997 No. 854] does not apply in relation to applications for parental orders before 1st April 1997.

Applications for return, removal or prohibition of removal of child
[1] **81.14.**—(1) An application under section 29 of the Act of 1978, as modified and applied in relation to applications for parental orders by Schedule 1 to the Regulations (order to return a child to, or not to remove a child from, the care of the applicants), in relation to a breach of section 27(1) of that Act as so modified and applied (restrictions on removal of child where application for parental order pending), or under section 27(1) of that Act as so modified and applied for leave to remove a child, shall be made by note in the process of the petition for a parental order to which it relates.

(2) Subject to paragraph (3), rule 81.2 (disapplication of certain rules to this Chapter) shall not apply to an application mentioned in paragraph (1) of this rule.

(3) An application mentioned in paragraph (1) shall not be intimated on the walls of the court or advertised.

---

[1] R. 81.14 inserted by S.I. 1994 No. 2806 (effective 1st November 1994).

81.14.1   *General note.* An application by a person, from whose care a child has been removed in breach of s.27(1) of the Act of 1978 or who has reasonable grounds for suspecting another person is intending to remove the child, may be made to the court for an order to return the child or to prohibit the removal of the child, as the case may be: Act of 1978, s.29 as modified and applied by the 1994 Regulations, Sched. 1, para. 7.

81.14.2   *Section 27(1) of the Act of 1978.* Where an application for a parental order is pending, the person who is the father or mother of the child by virtue of s.27 or 28 of the Act of 1990 may not remove the child against the will of the person with whom the child has his home except with leave of the court: Act of 1978, s.27(1) as modified and applied by the 1994 Regulations, Sched. 1, para. 6.

81.14.3   *"note".* For form of note, see r. 15.2 and notes. A fee is payable, by a person not already a party to the cause first entering the process, on lodging a note: see note 15.2.4. The note does not have to be intimated on the walls of court or advertised: r. 81.14(3).

Applications to amend, or revoke a direction in, a parental order

[1] **81.15.**—(1) An application under paragraph 3(1) of Schedule 1 to the Act of 1978, as modified and applied in relation to parental orders by Schedule 1 to the Regulations (amendment, or revocation of a direction in, a parental order), shall be made by petition.

(2) Subject to paragraph (3), rule 81.2 (disapplication of certain rules to this Chapter) shall not apply to an application mentioned in paragraph (1) of this rule.

(3) An application mentioned in paragraph (1) shall not be intimated on the walls of the court or advertised.

---

[1] R. 81.15 inserted by S.I. 1994 No. 2806 (effective 1st November 1994).

81.15.1   *General note.* An application by the husband and wife who applied for the parental order may be made to amend the order in respect of a new name given to the child but must be made within one year of the order: Act of 1978, Sched. 1, para. 4(1)(a) as modified and applied by the 1994 Regulations, Sched. 1, para. 18. The court may amend a parental order by correcting any errors in its particulars, or to revoke a direction for the marking of an entry in the register of births or the Parental Order Register, at any time: Act of 1978, Sched. 1, para. 4(1) as modified and applied by the 1994 Regulations, Sched. 1, para. 18.

81.15.2   *Jurisdiction.* The court has jurisdiction only if it made the parental order sought to be amended or revoked: Act of 1978, Sched. 1, para. 4 as modified and applied by the 1990 Regulations, Sched. 1, para. 18.

81.15.3   *"petition".* A petition is presented in the Outer House: r. 14.2(h). The petition must be in Form 14.4 in the official printed form: rr. 4.1 and 14.4. The petition must be signed by counsel or other person having a right of audience: r. 4.2; and see r. 1.3(1) (definitions of "counsel" and "other person having a right of audience"), and note 1.3.4.

The petitioner must lodge the petition with the required steps of process (r. 4.4) and the productions required by r. 81.9(2) and any others (including those founded on or adopted (r. 27.1)) with an inventory of productions (r. 4.5).

A fee is payable on lodging the petition: see note 14.5.10.

The ordinary petition rules apply to a petition under r. 81.15 except that it is not intimated on the walls of court or advertised: r. 81.15(3).

Registration of certified copy interlocutor

[1] **81.16.** On the court pronouncing an interlocutor making—

(a) a parental order,

(b) an amendment to, or revocation of a direction in, a parental order, or

(c) a revocation of a parental order,

the clerk of court shall send a certified copy of that interlocutor to the Registrar General for Scotland in a sealed envelope marked "confidential".

---

[1] R. 81.16 inserted by S.I. 1994 No. 2806 (effective 1st November 1994).

Registrar General for Scotland. This is the Registrar General of Births, Marriages and Deaths **81.16.1** for Scotland; Act of 1978, s.65(1). He maintains the Parental Order Register in which the parental order is registered: Act of 1978, s.45 as modified and applied by the 1994 Regulations, Sched. 1, para. 10.

"send". This includes deliver: r. 1.3(1) (definition of "send").   **81.16.2**

Extract of order
[1] **81.17.** An extract of a parental order shall not be issued except by order of the court on an application to it—
  (a) where there is a petition for the parental order depending before the court, by motion in that process; or
  (b) where there is no such petition depending before the court, by petition.

___

[1] R. 81.17 inserted by S.I. 1994 No. 2806 (effective 1st November 1994).

General note. The primary evidence that a parental order has been made is the entry in the **81.17.1** Parental Order Register which is not open to inspection except by order of the court or a sheriff: Act of 1978, s.45(5) as modified and applied by the 1994 Regulations, Sched. 1, para. 10. An extract of the court's interlocutor granting the order would not be so confidential and is not, therefore, normally available.

"depending". A cause is depending from the time it is commenced (*i.e.* from the time the first **81.17.2** order in the petition is made) until final decree, whereas a cause is in dependence until final extract. For the meaning of commenced, see note 14.6.1. For the meaning of final decree, see note 4.15.2(2). For the meaning of final extract, see note 7.1.2(2).

"motion". For motions, see Chap. 23.   **81.17.3**

"petition". A petition for an extract is presented in the Outer House: r. 14.2(h). The petition **81.17.4** must be in Form 14.4 in the official printed form: rr. 4.1 and 14.4. The petition must be signed by counsel or other person having a right of audience: r. 4.2; and see r. 1.3(1) (definitions of "counsel" and "other person having a right of audience"), and note 1.3.4.
  The petitioner must lodge the petition with the required steps of process (r. 4.4) and the productions required by r. 81.9(2) and any others (including those founded on or adopted (r. 27.1)) with an inventory of productions (r. 4.5).
  A fee is payable on lodging the petition: see note 14.5.10.

Procedure after intimation to Registrar General or issue of extract
[1] **81.18.**—(1) After a certified copy of an interlocutor mentioned in rule 81.16 has been sent to the Registrar General for Scotland, the clerk of court or the Extractor, as the case may be, shall—
  (a) place the whole process in an envelope bearing only—
    (i) the name of the petitioners;
    (ii) the full name of the child to whom the process relates; and
    (iii) the date of the order; and
  (b) seal the envelope and mark it "confidential".
  (2) No person shall open a process referred to in paragraph (1) or inspect its contents within 100 years after the date of the parental order except—
  [2] (a) the person in respect of whom the parental order was made after he has reached the age of 16 years;
  (b) any other person or body entitled under section 45(5) of the Act of 1978, as modified and applied in relation to parental orders and applications for such orders by Schedule 1 to the Regulations, to access to the registers and books kept under section 45(4) of that Act, as so modified and applied, with the written authority of the person in respect of whom the parental order was made;
  (c) by order of the court on an application made by petition presented by another court or authority (whether within the United Kingdom or not) having the power to make a parental order for the purpose of obtaining information in connection with an application to it for such an order;

(d) by order of the court on an application made by petition presented by any person; and

(e) a person who is authorised in writing by the Secretary of State to obtain information from the process for the purpose of research designed to improve the working of human fertilisation and embryology law and practice.

---

[1] R. 81.18 inserted by S.I. 1994 No. 2806 (effective 1st November 1994).
[2] R. 81.18(2)(a) amended by S.I. 1997 No. 854 (effective 1st April 1997).

81.18.1   *General note.* The purpose of r. 81.18 is to maintain confidentiality of the process and of a parental order in respect of a child during his lifetime.

After five years a process is transmitted from the Court of Session to the Keeper of the Records: r. 9.1.

The amendment to r. 81.18(2)(a) by A.S. (R.C.S.A. No. 3) (Human Fertilisation and Embryology) 1997 [S.I. 1997 No. 854] reducing the age from 17 to 16 years does not apply to applications for parental orders made before 1st April 1997.

81.18.2   *Registrar General for Scotland.* See note 81.17.1.

Chapter 82

The Human Rights Act 1998

Application and interpretation
[1] **82.1**—(1) This Chapter deals with various matters relating to the Human Rights Act 1998.

(2) In this Chapter—
   "the 1998 Act" means the Human Rights Act 1998;
   "declaration of incompatibility" has the meaning given by section 4 of the 1998 Act.

---

[1] Chap. 82 and r.82.1 inserted by S.S.I. 2000 No.316 (effective from 2nd October 2000).

82.1.1   *General note.* This Chapter deals with two matters arising out of the Human Rights Act 1998, which came into force on 2nd October 2000. The first is concerned with evidence of judgments (r. 82.2) and the second is concerned with declarations of incompatibility (rr. 82.3 and 82.4).

Evidence of judgments etc
[1] **82.2**—(1) Evidence of any judgment, decision, declaration or opinion of which account has to be taken by the court under section 2 of the 1998 Act shall be given by reference to any authoritative and complete report of the said judgment, decision, declaration or opinion and may be given in any manner.

(2) Evidence given in accordance with paragraph (1) shall be sufficient evidence of that judgment, decision, declaration or opinion.

---

[1] R.82.2 inserted by S.S.I. 2000 No.316 (effective from 2nd October 2000).

82.2.1   *General note.* This rule is concerned with the citation of judgments, decisions and opinions of the European Court of Human Rights, the European Commission of Human Rights and the Committee of Ministers.

Section 2 of the 1998 Act provides that the court must take account the decisions of the above bodies insofar as relevant. For some reason it has been thought to be necessary to provide for authorised citation of such decisions. Rule 82.2 provides for citation of authoritative and complete reports, but does not indicate what is authoritative or how purported authorisation is established. Presumably a report in a law report series such as E.H.R.R. hardly requires authorisation. A copy of a judgment stamped with a certificate of the judgment of the body concerned will not doubt be regarded as prima facie authoritative.

Declaration of incompatibility

[1] **82.3**—[2] (1) Where in any proceedings a party seeks a declaration of incompatibility or the court is considering whether to make such a declaration at its own instance—

(a) notice in Form 82.3-A shall be given as soon as reasonably practicable to such persons as the Lord President may from time to time direct—

   (i) by the party seeking the declaration; or

   (ii) by the clerk of court,

as the case may be, provided that there shall be no requirement to give such notice to a party or to the representative of a party; and

(b) where notice is given by the party seeking the declaration, the party shall lodge a certificate of notification in process.

(2) Where any—

(a) Minister of the Crown (or person nominated by him);

(b) member of the Scottish Executive;

(c) Northern Ireland Minister;

(d) Northern Ireland department,

wishes to be joined as a party to proceedings in relation to which the Crown is entitled to receive notice under section 5 of the 1998 Act he or, as the case may be, it shall serve notice in Form 82.3–B to that effect on the Deputy Principal Clerk of Session and shall serve a copy of the notice on all other parties to the proceedings.

----

[1] Rule 82.3 inserted by S.S.I. 2000 No.316 (effective 2nd October 2000).

[2] Rule 82.3(1) substituted by S.S.I. 2006 No. 83 (effective 17th March 2006).

General Note. This rule provides for the giving of notice under s. 5 of the 1998 Act. Where the court is considering whether to make a declaration of incompatibility, the Crown is entitled to notice of it: 1998 Act, s. 5(1). Where s. 5(1) applies, any of those "agents of the Crown" listed in r. 82.3(2) (which repeats the list in s. 5(2) of the 1998 Act) is entitled to be joined as a party: 1998 Act, s. 5(2).   **82.3.1**

Notice should be given to the Crown as early in the proceedings as possible: see *R v. A (No. 2)* [2001] 2 W.L.R. 1562 (HL); *Gunn v. Newman*, 2001 S.L.T. 776, 779G.

The purpose of intervention under s. 5(2) of the 1998 Act is not confined simply to arguing whether the court should make a declarator, but enables the Crown to address the court on the objects and purposes of the legislation in question and on any other matters which may be relevant: *R v. A (No. 2)*, above, *per* Lord Hope of Craighead.

"declaration of incompatibility". A declaration (*sic*) of incompatibility may be made (a) under s.4(2) of the 1998 Act where a provision of primary legislation is incompatible with a Convention right or (b) under s. 4(4) of the 1998 Act where a provision of subordinate legislation is incompatible with a Convention right and the primary legislation under which it is made prevents removal of the incompatibility. "Primary legislation" means Acts of the U.K. Parliament, Orders in Council and U.K. statutory instruments bringing them into force or amending them: 1998 Act, s. 21(1).   **82.3.2**

Such a declarator does not affect the validity, operation or enforcement of the provision declared incompatible and is not binding on the parties: 1998 Act, s. 4(6).

A "Convention right" means a right in the European Convention of Human Rights mentioned in s. 1(1) of the 1998 Act.

"as the lord President may from time to time direct". The current direction is No. 1 of 2005. Notice is to be given to the Solicitor to the Advocate-General and the Solicitor to the Scottish Executive.   **82.3.3**

"serve". For service, see Chap. 16.   **82.3.4**

[1] **82.4** Within 14 days after the date of service of the notice under rule 82.3(2), the person serving the notice shall lodge a minute in the proceedings in Form 82.4 and shall serve a copy of that minute on all other parties to the proceedings.

----

[1] Rule 82.4 inserted by S.S.I. 2000 No.316 (effective 2nd October 2000).

82.4.1 *"within 14 days"*. The date from which the period is calculated is not counted. Where the last day falls on Saturday or Sunday or a public holiday on which the Office of Court is closed, the next available day is allowed: r. 13(7). For office hours and public holidays, see note 3.1.2.

82.4.2 *"serve"*. For service, see Chap. 16.

82.5 The court may fix a diet for a hearing on the question of incompatibility as a separate hearing from any other hearing in the proceedings and may sist the proceedings if it considers it necessary to do so while the question of incompatibility is being determined.

---

[1] Rule 82.5 inserted by S.S.I. 2000 No. 316 (effective 2nd October 2000).

CHAPTER 83

APPLICATIONS FOR PURPOSES OF INVESTIGATIONS ORDERED PURSUANT TO ARTICLE 14 OF REGULATION 17 OF THE COUNCIL OF THE EUROPEAN COMMUNITIES

[*Chapter 83 revoked by S.S.I. 2005 No. 193, effective April 1, 2005.*]

[1] CHAPTER 84

APPLICATION UNDER THE TERRORISM ACT 2000

Interpretation of this Chapter
[1] **84.1** In this Chapter—
  "the Act of 2000" means the Terrorism Act 2000;
  "administrator" shall be construed in accordance with paragraph 16(1)(b) of Schedule 4 to the Act of 2000; and
  "restraint order" means an order under paragraph 18(1) of Schedule 4 to the Act of 2000.

---

[1] Chap. 84 and r. 84.1 inserted by S.S.I. 2001 No. 494 (effective 22nd December 2001).

General note. This Chapter deals with applications to the court where a forfeiture order has **84.1.1** been made by a criminal court under s. 23 of the Act of 2000 or could be made by a court in Scotland, or where the procurator fiscal proposes to apply for such an order. In relation to applications for restraint orders and incidental applications in respect of which an external forfeiture order has been made or in respect of which such an order could be made, see r. 62.54. An external forfeiture order is an order made in a country or territory designated under art. 3 of, and specified in Sched. 2 to the Prevention of Terrorism (Temporary Provisions) Act 1989 (Enforcement of External Orders) 1995 [S.I. 1995 No.760].
  The Act of 2000, the relevant provisions of which came fully into force on 15th February 2001 by virtue of the Terrorism Act 2000 (commencement No.3) Order 2001 [S.I. 2001 No.421] replaces the provisions in the Prevention of Terrorism (temporary Provisions) Act 1989.

"restraint order". The Court of Session may prohibit any person specified in the order from **84.1.2** dealing with any property in respect of which a forfeiture order has been made or could be made in proceedings for an offence under ss. 15 to 18 of the Act of 2000.

Form of application. An application to the court for a restrain order under para. 18(1) of **84.1.3** Sched. 4 to the Act of 2000 will be by petition to the Outer House: r. 14.2(h). The petition must be in Form 14.4 in the official printed form: rr. 4.1 and 14.4. The petition must be signed by counsel or other person having a right of audience: r. 4.2; and see r. 1.3(1) (definition of "counsel" and "other person having a right of audience") and note 1.3.4.
  The petitioner must lodge the petition with the required steps of process: r. 4.4. A fee is payable on lodging the petition: see note 14.5.10. On petitions generally, see Chap. 14.
  Unlike the provisions of Pt. II of Chap76 (applications under the Prevention of Terrorism (Temporary Provisions) Act 1989, there has been no disapplication of rr. 14.5 to 14.9 in Chap. 84.

Power and duties of administrator
[1] **84.2**—(1) Subject to any condition or exception specified by the court, an administrator appointed under paragraph 16(1)(b) of Schedule 4 to the Act of 2000—

(a) may take possession of the property in respect of which he has been appointed and of any document which—
   (i) is in the possession or control of the person in whom the property is vested; and
   (ii) relates to the property;

(b) may have access to, and copy, any document relating to the property and not in such possession or control as is mentioned in sub-paragraph (a);

(c) may bring, defend or continue any legal proceedings relating to the property;

(d) may borrow money in so far as it is necessary to do so to safeguard the property and may for the purposes of such borrowing create a security over any part of the property;

(e) may, if the administrator considers that to do so would be beneficial for the management and the realisation of the property, enter into any contract, or execute any deed, with respect to the property;

(f) may effect or maintain insurance policies with respect to the property;

(g) may, where the person in whom the property is vested has not completed title to any of the property, complete title to it: provided that completion of title in the name of the person in whom the property is vested shall not validate by accretion any unperfected right in favour of any person other than the administrator;

(h) may sell (but not to himself or an associate of his) the property and redeem any obligation secured on that property;

(i) may discharge any of his functions through agents or employees: provided that the administrator shall be personally liable to meet the fees and expenses of any such agents or employees out of such remuneration as is payable to the administrator by virtue of paragraph 17(2) of Schedule 4 to the Act of 2000;

(j) may take such professional advice as he considers necessary for the proper discharge of his functions;

(k) may at any time apply to the court for directions with respect to the exercise of his powers and duties;

(l) may exercise any power conferred on him by the court whether such power was conferred at the time of his appointment or on his subsequent application to the court; and

(m) may do anything incidental to the above powers and duties.

(2) Subject to the proviso to sub-paragraph (g) of paragraph (1)—

(a) a person dealing with an administrator in good faith and for value shall not require to determine whether the administrator is acting within the powers mentioned in that sub-paragraph; and

(b) the validity of any title shall not be challengeable by reason only of the administrator having acted outwith those powers.

(3) The exercise of a power mentioned in any of sub-paragraphs (c) to (h) of paragraph (1) shall be in the name of the person in whom the property is vested.

---

[1] R. 84.2 inserted by S.S.I. 2001 No. 494 (effective 22nd December 2001).

84.2.1   *General note.* A criminal court may make a forfeiture order under s. 23 of the Act of 2000 where a person is guilty of an offence under ss. 15 to 18 of that Act (financial assistance for terrorism). Where that court does so it may make an order appointing an administrator to take possession of property to which the forfeiture order applies: Act of 2000, Sched. 4, para16(1)(b). Rule 84.2 is made under para. 17(1) of Sched. 4 which gives the Court of Session power to provide for the powers and duties of an administrator.

An administrator is subject to the supervision of the Accountant of Court: Act of 2000, Sched. 4, para. 17(3).

There is no provision, as there is in para. 1(8) of Sched. 1 to the Act of 1995, for the finding of caution.

Applications for variation or recall of restraint order

[1] **84.3**—(1) An application under paragraph 19(2) (recall or variation of restraint order) of Schedule 4 to the Act of 2000 shall be made by note in the process containing the interlocutor making the restraint order to which the application relates.

(2) Subject to rule 14.6(2) (application to shorten or extend the period of notice), the period of notice for lodging answers to a note under paragraph (1) of this rule by any person affected by a restraint order shall be 14 days.

---

[1] R. 84.3 inserted by S.S.I. 2001 No. 494 (effective 22nd December 2001).

"note". For applications by note, see r. 15.2.   **84.3.1**

"period of notice". On period of notice generally, see r. 14.6.   **84.3.2**

[1] CHAPTER 85

APPLICATIONS UNDER THE PROTECTION FROM ABUSE (SCOTLAND) ACT 2001

Interpretation of this Chapter

[1] **85.1.** In this Chapter—
"the Act of 2001" means the Protection from Abuse (Scotland) Act 2001;
"documents" includes documents in electronic form; and
"interdict" includes interim interdict.

---

[1] Chap. 85 and r. 85.1 inserted by S.S.I. 2002 No. 514 (effective 1st December 2002).

General note. The Protection from Abuse (Scotland) Act 2001 extends the scope of the law on **85.1.1**
protection that began with the Matrimonial Homes (Family Protection) (Scotland) Act 1981.
That Act applies only to married couples or a man and a woman cohabiting as man and wife;
and is concerned with occupancy rights in the matrimonial home. The Act of 2001 follows a
report in 2000 on a Proposal for a Protection from Abuse Bill (JH/00/R9 SP Paper 221). What
the Act of 2001 does is simply allow for a power of arrest to be attached to interdicts.
The Act of 2001 allows any natural person, who is applying for or who has applied for an
interdict for protection from abuse, to apply for a power of arrest to be attached to the interdict
or interim interdict.

"Abuse". Abuse is defined in s. 7 of the Act of 2001 as including "violence, harassment, **85.1.2**
threatening conduct, and any other conduct giving rise, or likely to give rise, to physical or
mental injury, fear, alarm or distress"; and "conduct" includes speech or presence in a specified
place or area.

"documents". The word "document" has been defined in R.C.S. 1994 by reference to the **85.1.3**
inclusive definition in s. 9 of the Civil Evidence (Scotland) Act 1988: see r. 1.3(1). The word
includes documents in electronic form: Act of 2001, s. 7.

"interdict". References to interdict in this chapter include interim interdict. In the Act of 2001, **85.1.4**
interdict also includes interim interdict: Act of 2001, s. 7.
Interdict prohibits reasonably apprehended future breaches of duty by one person to another:
Inverurie Magistrates v. Sorrie, 1956 S.C. 175.
On interdict, see further note 60.1.1(2). On interim interdict, see further note 60.3.2.

Attachment of power of arrest to interdict

[1] **85.2.**—(1) An application under section 1(1) of the 2001 Act (application for attachment of power of arrest to interdict)—

(a) shall be made by a conclusion of the summons, the prayer of the petition, the defences, answers or counterclaim in which the interdict to which it relates is applied for, or, if made after the application for interdict, by motion in the process of the action in which the interdict was sought; and

(b) shall be intimated to the person against whom the interdict is sought or obtained.

[2] (2) Where the court attaches a power of arrest under section 1(2) or (1A) of the Act of 2001 (order attaching power of arrest) the following documents shall be served along with the power of arrest in accordance with section 2(1) of the Act of 2001 (documents to be served along with power of arrest)—

(a) a copy of the application for interdict;

(b) a copy of the interlocutor granting interdict; and

(c) where the application to attach a power of arrest was made after the interdict was granted, a copy of the certificate of service of the interdict.

(3) After the power of arrest has been served, the following documents shall be delivered by the person who obtained the power to the chief constable in accordance with section 3(1) of the Act of 2001 (notification to the police)—

(a) a copy of the application for interdict;

(b) a copy of the interlocutor granting interdict;

(c) a copy of the certificate of service of the interdict; and

(d) where the application to attach a power of arrest was made after the interdict was granted—

(i) a copy of the application for the power of arrest;

(ii) a copy of the interlocutor granting it; and

(iii) a copy of the certificate of service of the power of arrest and the documents that required to be served along with it in accordance with section 2(1) of the Act of 2001.

---

[1] Rule 85.2 inserted by S.S.I. 2002 No. 514 (effective 1st December 2002).
[2] Rule 85.2(2) amended by S.S.I. 2006 No. 206 (effective 4th May 2006).

85.2.1   *General note.* The power to attach a power of arrest is given in s. 1(1) of the Act of 2001. The power may be attached to an interdict from abuse granted in any proceedings.

85.2.2   *"conclusion of the summons".* On conclusions, see r. 13.2(2) and note 13.2.3.

85.2.3   *"prayer of the petition".* See r. 14.4(2)(b) and note 14.4.8, and Chap. 60.

85.2.4   *"defences"; "answers".* See Chap. 18. With the exception of defences in family actions (see r. 49.31(2)), defences and answers do not have conclusions in which an interdict can be applied for.

85.2.5   *"counterclaim".* See Chap. 25. The power of arrest will be a conclusion in the counterclaim.

85.2.6   *"motion".* See Chap. 23.

85.2.7   *"intimated".* The reference to intimation in r. 85.2(1)(b) is otiose. The application for a power of arrest will be intimated by being included in the writ, minute of amendment or motion which itself requires service or intimation.

85.2.8   *"power of arrest".* The power to attach a power of arrest is given in s. 1(1) of the Act of 2001. It must be applied for; and the person applying must be a natural person: Act of 2001, s. 7. The court cannot attach a power of arrest to an interdict unless—

(a) the interdicted person has been given an opportunity to be heard (thus it cannot be granted on an *ex parte* application for interim interdict);

(b) the interdicted person would not also be subject to a power of arrest under the Matrimonial Homes (Family Protection) (Scotland) Act 1981; and

(c) the power is necessary to protect the applicant from *a* risk of abuse in breach of *that* interdict (the provision does not specify a *substantial* risk).

In relation to (c) above, regard must be had to art. 5 of the ECHR (right to liberty) and art. 8 (right to private life).

The power of arrest must be for a specified period not exceeding three years, though that may be extended: Act of 2001, ss. 1(3) and 2(3).

Having the power of arrest attached to an interdict means that a constable may arrest the interdicted person without warrant if the constable: (a) has reasonable grounds to suspect that person of being in breach of the interdict; and (b) considers that there would be a risk of abuse or further abuse if not arrested: Act of 2001, s. 4(1).

Section 4 of the Act of 2001 lays down what must happen on arrest and what the arrestee must be told.

Service of power of arrest. A power of arrest has effect only when it has been served on the **85.2.9** interdicted person along with such documents as may be prescribed: Act of 2001, s. 2(1). Rule 85.2(2) prescribes the additional documents to be served as a copy of: (a) the application for the interdict; (b) the interlocutor granting it; and (c) where the power of arrest was applied for after the interdict (in most cases in fact, following an interim interdict), the certificate of service of the interdict.

For service, see Chap. 16. For certificate of service, see r. 161(3) and note 16.1.5.

Notification to police. Under s. 3(1) of the Act of 2001, the interdictor must notify the chief **85.2.10** constable of the police area in which the interdict has effect (that may be more than one police area) by delivering the prescribed documents to him. Rule 85.2(3) prescribes these documents as a copy of: (a) the application for interdict; (b) the interlocutor granting it; (c) the certificate of service; and (d) if separate, the power of arrest, the interlocutor granting it and the certificate of its service.

The power of arrest has effect whether or not the chief constable is notified by receipt of these documents: Act of 2001, s. 2(1). If the police are not aware of the power of arrest of course, they cannot act; but they may be aware of it independently of the s. 3 notification.

Extension or recall of power of arrest

[1] **85.3.**—(1) An application under section 2(3) (extension of duration of power of arrest) or section 2(7) (recall of power of arrest) of the Act of 2001 shall be made by minute in the process of the action in which the power of arrest was attached.

(2) Where the court extends the duration of, or recalls, a power of arrest, the person who obtained the extension or recall must deliver a copy of the interlocutor granting the extension or recall in accordance with section 3(1) of the Act of 2001.

---

[1] R. 85.3 inserted by S.S.I. 2002 No. 514 (effective 1st December 2002).

General note. A power of arrest ceases to have effect: (a) on the date it expires; (b) when **85.3.1** recalled; or (c) when the interdict is varied or recalled: Act of 2001, s. 2(2).

The power may be extended if (i) the interdicted person has had an opportunity to be heard and (ii) the extension is necessary to protect the interdicter from a risk of abuse in breach of that interdict: Act of 2001, s. 2(3). There may be more than one extension: Act of 2001, s. 2(6). An extension has effect only when served on the interdicted person: Act of 2001, s. 2(5)(b).

The power of arrest must be recalled on application of the interdictor or interdicted person if it is no longer necessary to protect the interdictor from abuse in breach of the interdict: Act of 2001, s. 2(7).

On extension of the power, the notification procedure under s. 3 of the Act of 2001 must be followed: r. 85.3(2) which in turn brings in r. 85.2(3) (notification to police). With regard to notification to the police on recall, see r. 85.4.

Rule 85.3 provides that the procedure for applications for extension or recall of the power of arrest is by minute.

"minute". The procedure for extension or recall of a power of arrest is by minute in the **85.3.2** process of the cause in which it was obtained: r. 85.3(2).

For procedure by minute, see r. 15.1.

Documents to be delivered to chief constable in relation to recall or variation of interdict

[1] **85.4.** Where an interdict to which a power of arrest has been attached under section 1(2) of the Act of 2001 is varied or recalled, the person who obtained the variation or recall must deliver a copy of the interlocutor varying or recalling the interdict in accordance with section 3(1) of that Act.

---

[1] Rule 85.4 inserted by S.S.I. 2002 No. 514 (effective 1st December 2002).

85.4.1 *General note.* Where a power of arrest is varied or recalled on an application under s. 2 of the Act of 2001, the interdictor must follow the notification procedure under s. 3(1), which in turn brings in the provisions of r. 85.2(3) specifying what documents must be notified to the chief constable.

Certificate of delivery of documents to chief constable

[1] **85.5.** Where a person is in any circumstances required to comply with section 3(1) of the Act of 2001, he shall, after such compliance, lodge in process a certificate of delivery in Form 85.5.

---

[1] Rule 85.5 inserted by S.S.I. 2002 No. 514 (effective 1st December 2002).

85.5.1 *"lodge in process a certificate of delivery".* The certificate of delivery is lodged in process as a step of process (r. 1.3(1) (definition of "step of process")). On lodging a step of process, see rr. 4.4–4.6.

Form 85.5, the form of certificate, simply certifies that the documents to be delivered to the chief constable (see r. 85.2(3)) have been delivered.

[1] CHAPTER 86

APPLICATIONS UNDER SECTION 28, 28A, 62, 62A, 63, 65G OR 65H OF THE COMPETITION ACT 1998

Application and interpretation of this Chapter

[1] **86.1.**—(1) This Chapter applies to applications for warrants under section 28, 28A, 62, 62A, 63, 65G or 65H of the Competition Act 1998.

(2) In this Chapter, "the Act of 1998" means the Competition Act 1998.

(3) Words and expressions used in this Chapter and in the Act of 1998 shall have the meanings given in the Act of 1998.

---

[1] Chap. 86 and r. 86.1 inserted by S.S.I. 2004 No. 331 (effective 6th August 2004).

86.1.1 *General note.* Under the sections of the Competition Act 1998 mentioned in r. 86.1, the Office of Fair Trading may seek a warrant to enter premises to look for documents in relation to investigations.

Sections 28A, 62A, 65G and 65H were inserted in the 1998 Act by the Competition Act 1998 and Other Enactments (Amendment) Regulations 2004 [S.I. 2004 No. 1261].

Disapplication of certain rules to this Chapter

[1] **86.2.** The following rules shall not apply to a petition to which this Chapter applies—

rule 4.3 (lodging of processes),
rule 4.4 (steps of process),
rule 4.5(1)(b) (copy inventory of productions to be sent to other parties),
rule 4.6 (intimation of steps of process),
rule 4.11 (documents not to be borrowed),
rule 4.12 (borrowing and returning documents),
rule 14.4 (form of petitions),
rule 14.5 (first order in petitions),

rule 14.6 (period of notice for lodging answers),
rule 14.7 (intimation and service of petitions),
rule 14.8 (procedure where answers lodged),
rule 14.9 (unopposed petitions).

---

[1] Rule 86.2 inserted by S.S.I. 2004 No. 331 (effective 6th August 2004).

Applications for warrants
[1] **86.3.**—(1) An application for a warrant under section 28, 28A, 62, 62A, 63, 65G or 65H of the Act of 1998 shall be made by petition in Form 86.3.
(2) The petition shall state—
(a) the address or other identification of the premises which are intended to be the subject of the warrant;
(b) the name of the occupier of those premises;
(c) the section of the Act of 1998 under which the application is being made;
(d) the subject matter of the investigation to which the application relates;
(e) a statement of the grounds for the application; and
(f) a prayer indicating the warrant sought.
(3) There shall be lodged with the petition—
(a) a draft warrant;
(b) a signed witness statement in support of the application;
(c) the written authorisation of the OFT containing the name of the officer who it is intended will be the named officer;
(d) in the case of an application under section 62, 62A or 63 of the Act of 1998, the written authorisations of the European Commission containing the names of any of its officials and other persons authorised by it for any of the purposes set out in section 62(10), 62A(12) or 63(10) of the Act of 1998 as applicable who it is intended will accompany the named officer in executing the warrant; and
(e) the written authorisation of the OFT containing the names of any other person who it is intended will accompany the named officer in executing the warrant.
(4) On lodging the petition, the petitioner shall provide the Deputy Principal Clerk with the draft warrant in electronic form compatible with the software used by the court.
(5) The petition and any documents lodged, sent or retained under these Rules in connection with the petition shall be treated as confidential and open only to the court unless the Lord Ordinary otherwise directs.

---

[1] Rule 86.3 inserted by S.S.I. 2004 No. 331 (effective 6th August 2004).

"petition". A petition under this Chapter is presented to the Outer House: r. 14.2(h). The **86.3.1** petition must be in Form 86.3 in the official printed form (r. 4.1). The petition must be signed by counsel or other person having a right of audience: r. 4.2; and see r. 1.3(1) (definition of "counsel" and "other person having a right of audience") and note 1.3.4.
The petitioner must lodge the petition with the required steps of process (r. 4.4). A fee is payable on lodging the petition: see note 14.5.10.
On petitions generally, see Chap. 14.

Hearing of petition
[1] **86.4.**—(1) On the lodging of the petition, the Keeper of the Rolls shall appoint the petition to a hearing to determine the petition.
(2) The petition shall be heard and determined in private unless the Lord Ordinary otherwise directs.

---

[1] Rule 86.4 inserted by S.S.I. 2004 No. 331 (effective 6th August 2004).

Form of warrants
[1] **86.5.**—(1) A warrant issued under section 28, 28A, 62, 62A, 63, 65G or 65H of the Act of 1998 shall indicate—
  (a) the address or other identification of the premises subject to the warrant;
  (b) the names of the named officer and any other persons authorised by the warrant to accompany the named officer in executing the warrant;
  (c) the date on which the warrant was issued; and
  (d) that the warrant continues in force until the end of the period of one month beginning with the day on which it is issued.
  (2) Subject to paragraph (3), a warrant issued under section 28, 28A, 62, 62A, 63, 65G or 65H of the Act of 1998 may be borrowed by the petitioner.
  (3) The petitioner shall give a receipt for any warrant borrowed under paragraph (2) and shall return the warrant to the Deputy Principal Clerk by the end of the period of one month referred to in paragraph (1)(d).
  (4) Where a warrant is borrowed under paragraph (2), a certified copy of a warrant issued under section 28, 28A, 62, 62A, 63, 65G or 65H of the Act of 1998 shall be retained by the Deputy Principal Clerk.

---

[1] Rule 86.5 inserted by S.S.I. 2004 No. 331 (effective 6th August 2004).

Service of copy petition and interlocutor
[1] **86.6.** Within 7 days after the date of first execution of a warrant which has been issued by the court under section 28, 28A, 62, 62A, 63, 65G or 65H of the Act of 1998, the petitioner shall serve on the occupier of the premises which are the subject of the warrant and such other persons as may be specified by the court in the interlocutor granting the prayer of the petition—
  (a) a copy of the petition; and
  (b) a certified copy of the interlocutor granting the prayer of the petition.

---

[1] Rule 86.6 inserted by S.S.I. 2004 No. 331 (effective 6th August 2004).

86.6.1 *"Within 7 days after"*. The date from which the period is calculated is not counted.

86.6.2 *"serve"*. For methods, see Chap. 16, Pt. I.

86.6.3 *"certified copy of the interlocutor"*. A certified copy interlocutor (a CCI) is obtained by a party presenting a copy of the interlocutor to a clerk of session at the relevant department. The clerk certifies and stamps it with the court stamp.

[1] CHAPTER 87

CAUSES RELATING TO ARTICLES 81 AND 82 OF THE TREATY ESTABLISHING THE EUROPEAN COMMUNITY

Intimation of actions to the Office of Fair Trading
[1] **87.1.**—(1) In this rule—
    "the Treaty" means the Treaty establishing the European Community;
    "the OFT" means the Office of Fair Trading.
  (2) In an action where an issue under Article 81 or 82 of the Treaty is raised:—
  (a) by the pursuer or petitioner in the summons or petition;
  (b) by the defender or respondent in the defences or answers; or
  (c) by any party in the pleadings;
intimation of the action shall be given to the OFT by the party raising the issue, by a notice of intimation in Form 87.1.

(3) Where the issue under Article 81 or 82 of the Treaty is raised in the summons or petition, a warrant for intimation shall be inserted in the summons or petition in the following terms: "Warrant to intimate to the Office of Fair Trading".

(4) Where the issue under Article 81 or 82 of the Treaty is raised in defences, answers or in any other part of the pleadings, the party raising the issue shall apply by motion for an order for intimation to the OFT.

(5) A certified copy of an interlocutor granting a motion under paragraph (4) shall be sufficient authority for the party to intimate by notice in Form 87.1.

(6) The notice of intimation shall be served on the OFT within such period as the court shall specify in the interlocutor allowing intimation.

(7) There shall be attached to the notice of intimation—
(a) a copy of the pleadings (including any adjustments and amendments);
(b) a copy of the interlocutor allowing intimation of the notice; and
(c) where the pleadings have not been amended in accordance with a minute of amendment, a copy of that minute.

---

[1] Chap. 87 and r. 87.1 inserted by S.S.I. 2004 No. 514 (effective 30th November 2004).

General note. Chap. 87 was inserted by A.S. (R.C.S.A. No. 6 (Miscellaneous) 2004 [S.S.I. **87.1.1** 2004 No.514].

"Article 81 or 82". Art. 81 relates to the prohibition of agreements affecting trade between **87.1.1** Member States which prevent, restrict or distort competition.
Art. 82 relates to abuse of a dominant position with the common market.

Office of Fair Trading (OFT). Intimation is required to the OFT because the Director **87.1.3** General of Fair Trading has responsibilities in relation to competition laws.

"intimation". The method of intimation will be that provided for in r. 16.8. **87.1.4**

"motion". For motions, see Chap. 23. **87.1.5**

[1] CHAPTER 88

CIVIL MATTERS INVOLVING PARENTAL RESPONSIBILITIES UNDER THE COUNCIL REGULATION

Interpretation
[1,2] **88.1.** In this Chapter—
"the Council Regulation" means Council Regulation (E.C.) No. 2201/2003 of 27th November 2003 concerning jurisdiction and the recognition and enforcement of judgments in matrimonial matters and matters of parental responsibility;
[3] "foreign court" means a court in a Member State other than the United Kingdom
"parental responsibility" has the same meaning as in Article 2(7) of the Council Regulation;
"Member State" has the same meaning as in Article 2(3) of the Council Regulation.

---

[1] Chap. 88 and r. 88.1 inserted by S.S.I. 2005 No. 135 (effective 2nd March 2005).
[2] Rule 88.1 amended (definition of "requesting court" omitted) by S.S.I. 2006 No. 83 (effective 17th March 2006).
[3] Rule 88.1 definition inserted by S.S.I. 2006 No. 83 (effective 17th March 2006).

General note. The Council Regulation No. 2201/2003 (new Brussels II) replaces Council **88.1.1** Regulation No 1347/2000 (for which there was no special provision in the RCS 1994). It deals with jurisdiction as well as recognition and enforcement of judgments in matrimonial matters and matters of parental responsibility.

Matrimonial matters and matters of parental responsibility with which the new Council Regulation is concerned are defined in art. 1 as (a) divorce, legal separation, annulment; and (b) attribution, exercise, delegation, restriction or termination of parental responsibility (which includes custody, access, guardianship, curatorship and similar institutions, designation and functions of a person or body over a child's person or property or representing or assisting a child, placement in a foster family or institution, and protection of a child's property).

The term "child" is not defined in the Regulation.

The Regulation applies to Member States of the E.U. except Denmark.

The primary ground of jurisdiction is habitual residence. Art. 15 of the Council Regulation provides that a court having jurisdiction in a case of parental responsibilities may, if it considers that a court of another Member State with which a child has a particular connection would be better placed to hear the case, request a court of that other Member State to assume jurisdiction.

Transfer of cases involving matters of parental responsibility

[1] **88.2.** Where the court receives a request under Article 15(1) (request for transfer to court better placed to hear the case) or an application under Article 15(2)(c) (application for transfer of case involving parental responsibilities to foreign court) of the Council Regulation, the request or application, as the case may be, shall—

(a) contain a detailed statement on the particular connection the child is considered to have with either Scotland or the Member State of the foreign court;

(b) contain the full name, designation and address of all the parties to the action involving parental responsibilities, including any Scottish agent instructed to represent any of the parties;

(c) in the case of a request under Article 15(1), be accompanied by any order of the foreign court confirming that at least one of the parties has accepted the request;

(d) be accompanied by any other documents considered by the foreign court to be relevant to the action involving parental responsibilities including any papers forming part of the process in the foreign court.

---

[1] Rule 88.2 inserted by S.S.I. 2005 No. 135 (effective 2nd March 2005) and substituted by by S.S.I. 2006 No. 83 (effective 17th March 2006).

88.2.1   *General note.* Art. 15(1) of the Council Regulation provides that a court having jurisdiction in a case of parental responsibilities may, if it considers that a court of another Member State with which a child has a particular connection would be better placed to hear the case, request a court of that other Member State to assume jurisdiction.

The request is made directly by one court to another under art. 15(1)(b). A request by a court in another Member State to the Court of Session will be dealt with by the Deputy Principal Clerk under Chap. 88. A time limit may be set by the requesting court. It should be noted that a court in another Member State may invite parties to make a request to the other court to assume jurisdiction: such a case is not dealt with under Chap. 88. One assumes that a petition or action, as appropriate, will be initiated in respect of the particular parental responsibility.

Under art. 15(2)(a) or (c) a party or a court in one Member State with which a child has a particular connection may apply to the court in another Member State exercising jurisdiction. This is in effect an application to request the latter court to decline jurisdiction.

Transfers where proceedings ongoing in the sheriff court

[1,2] **88.3.**—(1) Where an application under Article 15(2)(c) of the Council Regulation (application for transfer of case involving parental responsibilities to foreign court) is received and states that proceedings involving the same parties and matters involving parental responsibility are ongoing in a sheriff court, the Deputy Principal Clerk shall, within four days after the application is received, transmit the application to the sheriff clerk of the sheriff court specified in the application.

(2) When transmitting an application under paragraph (1) the Deputy Principal Clerk shall give written intimation of the transmission to—

(a) the parties; and

(b) to the foreign court.

(3) Failure by the Deputy Principal Clerk to comply with paragraph (2) shall not affect the validity of a transfer under paragraph (1).

---

[1] Rule 88.3 inserted by S.S.I. 2005 No. 135 (effective 2nd March 2005).
[2] Rule 88.3 amended by S.S.I. 2006 No. 83 (effective 17th March 2006).

General note. The application to decline jurisdiction arises out of art. 15(2)(a) or (c) of the Council Regulation. Under art. 15(2)(a) or (c) a party or a court in one Member State with which a child has a particular connection may apply to the court in another Member State exercising jurisdiction.   **88.3.1**

"written intimation". For methods, see r. 16.9.   **88.3.2**

Translations of documents
[1] **88.4.** Where any document received under rule 88.2 (transfer of cases involving matters of parental responsibility) is in a language other than English, there shall be lodged with that document a translation into English certified as correct by the translator; and the certificate shall include his full name, address and qualifications.

---

[1] Rule 88.4 inserted by S.S.I. 2005 No. 135 (effective 2nd March 2005).

Requests to accept transfer from a court in another Member State
[1] **88.5.**—(1) A request to the court to accept jurisdiction of an action involving parental responsibilities under rule 88.2 (request to transfer a case) shall be lodged with a summons in Form 13.2-A(a).

(2) When the summons lodged under paragraph (1) is signetted the pursuer shall request the Keeper of the Rolls to allocate a hearing within 14 days of the signetting, to determine whether the court will accept jurisdiction in the action.

(3) On allocation of the date of the hearing the pursuer shall serve a copy of the summons on the defender and at the same time intimate the date and time of the hearing on the defender by serving on him a notice in Form 88.5 (form of notice of intimation of a hearing to determine jurisdiction), not less than 7 days before the date of the hearing.

(4) The pursuer shall lodge a certificate of intimation in Form 16.2 (certificate of intimation furth of United Kingdom), 16.3 (certificate of service by messenger-at-arms) or 16.4 (certificate of service by post), as appropriate, at least 2 days before the date of the hearing.

[2] (5) Where the court orders that it will accept jurisdiction of an action after a hearing under paragraph (2) the Deputy Principal Clerk shall, within seven days, send a copy of the interlocutor to the foreign court.

---

[1] Rule 88.5 inserted by S.S.I. 2005 No. 135 (effective 2nd March 2005).
[2] Rule 88.5(5) amended by S.S.I. 2006 No. 83 (effective 17th March 2006).

General note. This rule is badly drafted. It cannot be intended to apply where it is the foreign court making the request to the Court of Session to accept jurisdiction. A foreign court can hardly be expected to lodge a summons in the Court of Session as well as making a request under r. 88.2. It can only be intended to apply where the foreign court has invited the parties to request the Court of Session to accept jurisdiction under art. 15(1)(a) of the Council Regulation. Rule 88.5, however, refers to a request under r. 88.2; but the only request under that rule is a request by a court of another Member State under art. 15(1)(b) and not a party under art. 15(1)(a).   **88.5.1**

"summons". See Chap. 13.   **88.5.1**

"serve". On service, see Chap. 16, Pt. I.   **88.5.3**

88.5.4   *"intimate".* For methods, see r. 16.7.

[2] *Application for transfer of case involving parental responsibilities to foreign court*

[1,2] **88.6.** Where an application under Article 15(2)(c) of the Council Regulation (application for transfer of case involving parental responsibilities to foreign court) is received the Deputy Principal Clerk shall—

    (a) on receipt of the application and any accompanying documents, give written intimation of the application to each party to the action and to any Scottish agents identified in the application as being instructed to represent any of the parties; and

    (b) within two sederunt days of receipt of the application, cause it to be put out on the By Order Roll before the Lord Ordinary.

----

[1] Rule 88.6 inserted by S.S.I. 2005 No. 135 (effective 2nd March 2005).
[2] Rule 88.6 and heading amended by S.S.I. 2006 No. 83 (effective 17th March 2006).

88.6.1   *General note.* The application to decline jurisdiction arises out of art. 15(2)(a) or (c) of the Council Regulation. Under art. 15(2)(a) or (c) a party or a court in one Member State with which a child has a particular connection may apply to the court in another Member State exercising jurisdiction.

Placement of child in another Member State

[1] **88.7.**—(1) Where the court requires to obtain the consent of a competent authority in another Member State to the placement of a child under Article 56 of the Council Regulation it shall send a request in Form 88.7 and any other documents it considers to be relevant to the Scottish central authority for transmission to the central authority in the other Member State.

    (2) In this rule "central authority" means an authority designated under Article 53 of the Council Regulation.

----

[1] Rule 88.7 inserted by S.S.I. 2006 No. 83 (effective 17th March 2006).

[1] CHAPTER 89

PREVENTION OF TERRORISM ACT 2005

Interpretation and application of this Chapter

[1] **89.1.**—(1) In this Chapter—

"the Act of 2005" means the Prevention of Terrorism Act 2005;

"control order proceedings" has the same meaning as in section 11(6) of the Act of 2005;

"controlled person" has the same meaning as in section 15(1) of the Act of 2005 but, where the context so requires, also means an individual against whom the Secretary of State is proposing to make a non-derogating control order or an individual against whom a derogating control order is sought under section 4(1) of the Act of 2005;

"derogating control order" has the same meaning as in section 15(1) of the Act of 2005;

"non-derogating control order" has the same meaning as in section 15(1) of the Act of 2005;

"relevant appeal proceedings" has the same meaning as in paragraph 1(2) of the Schedule to the Act of 2005;

"relevant material" has the same meaning as in paragraph 4(5) of the Schedule to the Act of 2005;

"relevant party" has the same meaning as in paragraph 11 of the Schedule to the Act of 2005; and "special representative" means a person appointed under paragraph 7 of the Schedule to the Act of 2005.

(2) This Chapter applies to control order proceedings and relevant appeal proceedings.

_____

[1] Chap. 89 and r. 89.1 inserted by S.S.I. 2005 No. 153 (effective 16th March 2005).

General note. The Prevention of Terrorism Act 2005 provides for the imposition of control **89.1.1** orders. A control order is an order against an individual that imposes obligations on him for purposes connected with protecting members of the public from a risk of terrorism: Act of 2005, s. 1(1). The obligations that may be imposed are obligations that are necessary for purposes connected with preventing or restricting involvement by that individual in terrorism-related activity (defined in s. 1(9)): Act of 2005, s. 1(3). There is a long list of obligations that may be included in a control order.

A control order may be made (a) by the Secretary of State where the obligations imposed are not incompatible with the right to liberty under art. 5 of the ECHR, or (b) only by the court where the obligations include derogating obligations. The former is called a non-derogating control order and lasts for 12 months unless renewed. A control order imposed by the court containing derogating obligations is called a derogating control order and lasts for six months unless revoked, ceases under s. 6 or is renewed. A derogating obligation is one that is incompatible with the right to liberty under art. 5 of the ECHR but is of a description of obligations which, for the purposes of the designation of a designated derogation, is set out in a designation order under s. 14(1) of the Human Rights Act 1998. Art. 15 of the ECHR gives a country the power to derogate from the Convention (but not arts. 2, 3, 4(1), 7 or Protocol 6) "in time of war or other public emergency threatening the life of the nation to the extent strictly required for the exigencies of the situation". Section 14 of the 1998 Act provides that a "designated derogation" means a derogation from art 5(3) (being brought promptly before a court and tried in reasonable time) or any other derogation designated in an order by the Secretary of State. The derogation from art. 5(3) is in Sched. 3 to the 1998 Act and is in respect of the Prevention of Terrorism (Temporary Provisions) Act 1989.

Control orders: petitions
[1] **89.2.**—(1) The following shall be made by lodging a petition with the Deputy Principal Clerk:—

> an application under section 3(1)(a) of the Act of 2005 for permission to make a non-derogating control order,
> a reference under section 3(3)(a) of the Act of 2005 of a non-derogating control order,
> an application under section 4(1) of the Act of 2005 for the making of a derogating control order.

(2) The following rules shall not apply to the petition:—

> rule 4.3 (lodging of processes),
> rule 4.4 (steps of process),
> rule 4.5(1)(b) (copy inventory of productions to be sent to other parties),
> rule 4.6 (intimation of steps of process),
> rule 4.11 (documents not to be borrowed),
> rule 4.12 (borrowing and returning documents),
> rule 14.5 (first order in petitions),
> rule 14.6 (period of notice for lodging answers),
> rule 14.7 (intimation and service of petitions),
> rule 14.8 (procedure where answers lodged),
> rule 14.9 (unopposed petitions).

(3) Subject to rule 89.7 (permission not to disclose relevant material etc.), the petition shall include, in numbered paragraphs, statements of reasons—

> (a) to support the making of the control order; and
> (b) for imposing each of the obligations under the control order.

(4) Subject to rule 89.7, there shall be lodged with the petition—

> (a) the productions of the Secretary of State;
> (b) in the case of an application under section 3(1)(a) for permission to make a non-derogating control order, a copy of the proposed control order;

    (c) in the case of a reference under section 3(3)(a) of the Act of 2005 of a non-derogating control order, a copy of the control order; and

    (d) in the case of an application under section 4(1) of the Act of 2005 for the making of a derogating control order against an individual, a draft of the control order sought.

    (5) Subject to rule 89.7, at the same time that the petition is lodged, a copy of the petition and copies of the productions and documents mentioned in paragraph (4) shall be served by the Secretary of State on the controlled person.

---

[1] Rule 89.2 inserted by S.S.I. 2005 No. 153 (effective 16th March 2005).

89.2.1   *Permission to make a non-derogating control order.* The Secretary of State has to have the permission of the court to make a non-derogating control order unless the order contains a statement that the urgency of the case required the order to be made without permission or it was made in certain circumstances before 14th March 2005: Act of 2005, s. 3(1)(a).

    On the meaning of a non-derogating control order, see note 89.1.1.

89.2.2   *"a reference under section 3(3)(a)".* Where the Secretary of State makes a non-derogating control order without the permission of the court, he must immediately refer the order to the court to consider if the order was obviously flawed: Act of 2005, s. 3(3). The court must consider the reference within seven days of the making of the order: Act of 2005, s. 3(4).

On the meaning of a non-derogating control order, see note 89.1.1.

"derogating order". On the meaning of a derogating order, see note 89.1.1.   **89.2.3**

"petition". A petition is presented to the Outer House: r. 14.2(h). The petition must be in **89.2.4** Form 86.3 in the official printed form (r. 4.1). The petition must be signed by counsel or other person having a right of audience: r. 4.2; and see r. 1.3(1) (definition of "counsel" and "other person having a right of audience") and note 1.3.4.

The petitioner must lodge the petition with the required steps of process (r. 4.4). A fee is payable on lodging the petition: see note 14.5.10.

On petitions generally, see Chap. 14.

Productions. The documents referred to in r. 62.69(2)(a)–(c) are those required by art. 30(3). **89.2.5** On productions and the lodging of them, see r. 4.5 and note 4.5.2.

"served". On service, see Chap. 16, Pt. I.   **89.2.6**

Preliminary hearings and initial diets

[1] **89.3.**—(1) On receipt of a petition under rule 89.2 (control orders: petitions), the Deputy Principal Clerk shall—

(a) in the case of an application under section 3(1)(a) for permission to make a non-derogating control order or a reference under section 3(3)(a) of the Act of 2005 of a non-derogating control order, allocate an initial diet for the court's consideration to begin; and

(b) in the case of an application under section 4(1) of the Act of 2005 for a derogating control order, allocate a preliminary hearing under section 4(1)(a) of the Act of 2005.

(2) The Deputy Principal Clerk shall notify the date and time of a preliminary hearing to the Secretary of State and, unless the Lord Ordinary orders otherwise, shall use reasonable endeavours to notify the date and time of that hearing to the controlled person and any special representative.

(3) The fact that the controlled person or any special representative has not received notification of the preliminary hearing shall not affect the holding of that hearing.

(4) The Deputy Principal Clerk shall notify the date and time of an initial diet to the Secretary of State and, unless the Lord Ordinary orders otherwise, the controlled person and any special representative.

(5) The controlled person shall, not later than the date of the preliminary hearing or initial diet, lodge with the Deputy Principal Clerk and serve on the Secretary of State a copy of any answers and productions that are to be founded upon by the controlled person at the preliminary hearing or initial diet.

(6) Where a special representative is appointed for the purposes of a preliminary hearing or initial diet, he shall lodge with the Deputy Principal Clerk and serve on the Secretary of State a copy of any answers that are to be founded upon by the special representative at the preliminary hearing or initial diet.

(7) At a preliminary hearing or initial diet, the parties present shall state their proposals for further procedure in respect of any hearing in pursuance of directions under section 3(2)(c), (6)(b) or (c) or any full hearing under section 4(1)(b) of the Act of 2005, and the interlocutor of the Lord Ordinary giving directions for the carrying out of any such hearing shall include such order for further procedure as he thinks fit, subject, where applicable, to section 3(7) of the Act of 2005.

(8) Where a preliminary hearing or initial diet has been held in the absence of the controlled person the Deputy Principal Clerk shall serve a copy of the interlocutor of the Lord Ordinary on that person.

---

[1] Rule 89.3 inserted by S.S.I. 2005 No. 153 (effective 16th March 2005).

89.3.1   *General note.* On application to the court, which must be made by the Secretary of State, for a derogating control order, there must first be an immediate preliminary hearing to determine whether to make an order that includes derogating obligations: Act of 2005, s. 4(1)(a). The preliminary hearing may be held in the absence of the individual in question, without his having had notice of the application and without his having had the opportunity to make any representations to the court: Act of 2005, s. 4(2). If the court makes a control order at that stage, it must give directions for the holding of a full hearing to determine whether to confirm the order: Act of 2005, s. 4(1)(b).

89.3.2   *"serve".* On service, see Chap. 16, Pt. I.

Applications for renewal, revocation or modification of derogating control orders
[1] **89.4.**—(1) An application—
   (a) under section 4(9) of the Act of 2005 for the renewal of a derogating control order; or
   (b) under section 7(4) of the Act of 2005 for the revocation of a derogating control order or for the modification of obligations imposed by such an order,
shall be made by note.

(2) A note referred to in paragraph (1) shall be lodged with the Deputy Principal Clerk.

---

[1] Rule 89.4 inserted by S.S.I. 2005 No. 153 (effective 16th March 2005).

89.4.1   *"note".* On applications by note, see r. 15.2.

Appeals relating to non-derogating orders
[1] **89.5.**—(1) Subject to paragraphs (2), (3) and (4) and to the modifications set out in rule 41.43 (application of Parts II and III to Part X), Part III of Chapter 41 (appeals to Lord Ordinary under statute) shall apply to appeals under section 10 (appeals relating to non-derogating control orders) of the Act of 2005.

(2) An appeal under section 10 of the Act of 2005 shall be lodged with the Deputy Principal Clerk and served on the Secretary of State within 28 days after the date on which the controlled person received notice of—
   (a) the control order that is the subject of the appeal, or
   (b) the decision by the Secretary of State on an application for the revocation of the control order, or the modification of an obligation imposed by the control order.

[3] (3) In a case where the Secretary of State has failed to determine an application for the revocation of the control order, or for the modification of an obligation imposed by such an order, any appeal under section 10 of the Act of 2005 shall be lodged—
   (a) no earlier than 28 days before; and
   (b) no later than 42 days after,
the date on which the application was made.

---

[1] Rule 89.5 inserted by S.S.I. 2005 No. 153 (effective 16th March 2005).
[2] Rule 89.5(3) substituted by S.S.I. 2005 No. 193 (effective 1st April 2005).

89.5.1   *General note.* The ground of appeal relating to a non-derogating control order is that the Secretary of State's decision is flawed.

Appeals against determinations of the court in relation to control orders may only be made on a point of law: Act of 2005, s. 11(3). There is, however, no appeal except by the Secretary of State, against a decision on an application for permission to impose a non-derogating control order under s. 3(1)(a) or a reference under s. 3(3)(a) (where the control order has been made without permission).

89.5.2   *"28 days after", "42 days after".* The day from which the calculation is made is not included. Where the last day falls on a Saturday or Sunday or a public holiday on which the Office of

Court is closed, the next available day is allowed: r. 1.3(7). For office hours and public holidays, see note 3.1.2.

Appointment of special representatives

[1] **89.6.**—(1) Subject to paragraph (2), the Secretary of State shall, upon—
  (a) making any application or reference under the Act of 2005;
  (b) making any motion in respect of control order proceedings or relevant appeal proceedings; or
  (c) being served with a note of appeal, reclaiming motion or other application in respect of control order proceedings or relevant appeal proceedings,
give notice to the Advocate General.
  (2) Paragraph (1) applies unless—
  (a) the Secretary of State does not intend to—
      (i) oppose the appeal, reclaiming motion or other application; or
      (ii) make an application under rule 89.7 (permission not to disclose relevant material etc.); or
  (b) a special representative has already been appointed to represent the interests of the controlled person in the proceedings.
  (3) Where notice is given to the Advocate General under paragraph (1), the Advocate General may appoint a special representative to represent the interests of the controlled person in the proceedings.
  (4) Where there are any control order proceedings or relevant appeal proceedings but no special representative has been appointed, the controlled person or the Secretary of State may at any time request the Advocate General to appoint a special representative.
  (5) On the appointment of any special representative, the Advocate General shall intimate the name of the special representative the Deputy Principal Clerk in writing.
  (6) The special representative may address the court in any control order proceedings or relevant appeal proceedings from which the controlled person is excluded.

---

[1] Rule 89.6 inserted by S.S.I. 2005 No. 153 (effective 16th March 2005).

"special representative". Under para. 7 of the Schedule to the Act of 2005, a special **89.6.1** representative may be appointed by the Advocate General to represent the interests of a relevant party to control order proceedings or appeals. Such a person will be required where there is to be non-disclosure of relevant material.

Special representatives: further provisions

[1] **89.6A.**—(1) A special representative upon whom relevant material has been served under rule 89.7(5)(a) shall not communicate about the proceedings or any matter connected with the proceedings except in accordance with this rule or with the authority of the court.
  (2) The special representative may, without the authority of the court, communicate about the proceedings with—
  (a) the court;
  (b) the Secretary of State, or any person acting for him;
  (c) the Advocate General, or any person acting for him;
  (d) any other person, except for the relevant party or his legal representative, with whom it is necessary for administrative purposes for him to communicate about matters not connected with the substance of the proceedings.
  (3) The special representative may apply by motion for authority to communicate with the relevant party or his legal representative or with any other person about the proceedings or a matter connected to the proceedings.
  (4) A notice of opposition to a motion under paragraph (3) shall be intimated to the special representative and the relevant party.

(5) The relevant party shall not communicate with a special representative upon whom relevant material has been served under rule 89.7(5) other than through a legal representative in writing.

(6) The special representative may, without the authority of the court, send a written acknowledgement of receipt of a communication under paragraph (5).

_____

[1] Rule 89.6A inserted by S.S.I. 2007 No. 7, para. 16 (effective 26th February 2007).

89.6A.1   *General note.* On "special representative", see note 89.6.1.

89.6A.2   *"motion".* On motions, see Chap. 23.

Permission not to disclose relevant material etc.
[1] **89.7.**—(1) Subject to paragraph (2), the Secretary of State shall lodge as productions all relevant material.

(2) The Secretary of State may apply by motion for permission not to disclose relevant material.

(3) The Secretary of State shall not require to disclose to the controlled person any relevant material which is the subject of an application under paragraph (2).

[2] (4) Subject to paragraph (4A), the Secretary of State shall not rely upon any relevant material which is the subject of an application under paragraph (2) unless a special representative has been appointed.

(4A) Paragraph (4) shall not apply in respect of a preliminary hearing or an initial diet where the court has ordered the Deputy Principal Clerk not to notify the controlled person of the date and time of the preliminary hearing or, as the case may be, initial diet.

(5) Where the Secretary of State makes an application under paragraph (2) and a special representative has been appointed, he shall lodge with the Deputy Principal Clerk and serve on the special representative—
 (a) the relevant material;
 (b) a statement of the reasons for the application for permission not to disclose the relevant material; and
 (c) if and to the extent that it is possible to do so without disclosing information contrary to the public interest, a summary of the relevant material which can be served on the controlled person.

_____

[1] Rule 89.7 inserted by S.S.I. 2005 No. 153 (effective 16th March 2005).
[2] Rule 89.7(4) substituted and (4A) inserted by S.S.I. 2007 No. 7, para. 17 (effective 26th February 2007).

89.7.1   *General note.* Rule 89.7 provides for applications by the Secretary of State for permission not to disclose relevant material. That rule does not indicate what power the court is exercising or what test it should apply. Rules 89.7 and 89.8 are made under para. 4 of the Schedule to the 2005 Act. Para. 4(3)(d) provides that rules of court must secure that the court is required to give permission for material not to be disclosed where it considers that the disclosure of the material would be contrary to the public interest. Rule 89.8(4), however, does provide that that is the test for granting permission not to disclose material

89.7.2   *Productions.* On productions and the lodging of them, see r. 4.5 and note 4.5.2.

89.7.3   *"motion".* For motions, see Chap. 23.

89.7.4   *"special representative".* See note 89.6.1.

Applications for permission not to disclose relevant material: further provisions
[1] **89.8.**—(1) On the making of an application under rule 89.7(2) (permission not to disclose relevant material etc.), the court shall, unless paragraph (2) applies, direct the Deputy Principal Clerk to allocate a diet for a hearing of the application and the Deputy Principal Clerk shall intimate that date and

time in writing to the Secretary of State and to any special representative appointed under rule 89.6 (appointment of special representatives).

(2) This paragraph applies where—

(a) the special representative gives notice that he does not oppose an application under rule 89.7(2);

(b) the court has previously considered an application by the Secretary of State for prohibition of disclosure of the same or substantially the same matters, and is satisfied that it would be just to prohibit disclosure without a hearing; or

(c) the Secretary of State and the special representative consent to the court deciding the issue without a hearing.

(3) An application under rule 89.7(2) shall be considered in the absence of the controlled person and his legal representative.

(4) The court shall grant an application under rule 89.7(2) where it considers that the disclosure of the relevant material would be contrary to the public interest.

(5) On granting an application under rule 89.7(2), the court shall order the Secretary of State to serve upon the controlled person, a copy of the summary lodged under rule 89.7(5)(c) unless the court considers that the summary contains information or other material the disclosure of which would be contrary to the public interest.

(6) In a case where the Secretary of State elects not to disclose the relevant material or (as the case may be) not to provide the summary, the court may—

(a) if it considers that the relevant material or anything that is required to be summarised might be of assistance to a relevant party in relation to a matter under consideration by the court, order that the matter is withdrawn from consideration by the court;

(b) in any other case, the court shall ensure that the Secretary of State does not rely in the proceedings on the material or (as the case may be) on what is required to be summarised.

---

[1] Rule 89.8 inserted by S.S.I. 2005 No. 153 (effective 16th March 2005) and amended by S.S.I. 2007 No. 7, para. 18 (effective 26th February 2007).

"special representative". See note 89.6.1.   **89.8.1**

"serve". For service, see Chap. 16, Pt. I.   **89.8.2**

Anonymity
[1] **89.9.** The Secretary of State or the controlled person may apply for an order requiring anonymity for the controlled person—

(a) in control order proceedings or relevant appeal proceedings, by motion;

(b) where there are no control order proceedings or relevant appeal proceedings, by lodging a petition with the Deputy principal Clerk.

---

[1] Rule 89.9 inserted by S.S.I. 2005 No. 153 (effective 16th March 2005).

General note. Anonymity. Para. 5 of the Schedule to the Act of 2005 gives the court power to **89.9.1**
make rules for anonymity.

Exclusion from diets or hearings etc.
[1] **89.10.**—(1) If the court considers it necessary for the controlled person and his legal representative, or any other relevant party, to be excluded from a diet or hearing or part of diet or a hearing to secure that information is not disclosed contrary to the public interest, it shall—

(a) make an order in that respect; and

(b) conduct the diet or hearing, or that part of it from which the controlled person and his legal representative are excluded, in private.

(2) The court may otherwise order a diet or hearing to be conducted in private if it thinks fit.

(3) When the court issues an opinion in any proceedings to which this Chapter applies, the court may withhold any or part of its reasons if and to the extent that it is not possible to give reasons without disclosing information contrary to the public interest.

(4) Where an opinion of the court does not include the full reasons for its decision—

(a) the court shall prepare a separate opinion including those reasons; and

(b) the Deputy Principal Clerk shall serve that separate opinion on the Secretary of State and the special representative.

---

[1] Rule 89.10 inserted by S.S.I. 2005 No. 153 (effective 16th March 2005).

89.10.1   *"serve".* For service, see Chap. 16, Pt. I.

Recording of control order proceedings

[1] **89.11.**—(1) Control order proceedings shall be recorded by—

(a) a shorthand writer to whom the oath de fideli administratione officii has been administered on his appointment as a shorthand writer in the Court of Session; or

(b) tape recording or other mechanical means approved by the Lord President.

(2) The record of the proceedings shall include—

(a) any objection to a question or line of evidence;

(b) any submission made in relation to such an objection; and

(c) the ruling of the court in relation to the objection and submission.

(3) A transcript of the record of the proceedings shall only be made on the direction of the court and shall be subject to such order as to the cost of the transcript as the court thinks fit.

(4) The transcript of the record of the proceedings shall be certified as a faithful record of the proceedings by—

(a) the shorthand writer or shorthand writers, if more than one, who recorded the evidence; or

(b) where the evidence was recorded by tape recording or other mechanical means, the person who transcribed the record.

(5) The court may make such alterations to the transcript of the record of the proceedings as appear to it to be necessary after hearing the parties; and where such alterations are made, the court shall authenticate the alterations.

---

[1] Rule 89.11 inserted by S.S.I. 2005 No. 153 (effective 16th March 2005).

[1] CHAPTER 90

FREEDOM OF INFORMATION

Applications

[1] **90.1.**—(1) In this rule—

"the Act of 2000" means the Freedom of Information Act 2000; and

"the Act of 2002" means the Freedom of Information (Scotland) Act 2002.

(2) An application under section 54(3) of the Act of 2000 or section 53(3) of the Act of 2002 for the court to deal with a public authority as if it had committed a contempt of court shall be by petition.

(3) There shall be attached to a petition mentioned in paragraph (2)—

(a) where the application is under the Act of 2000, a certificate under section 54(1) of that Act (certificate by Information Commissioner of failure to comply with notice);

(b) where the application is under the Act of 2002, a certificate under section 53(1) of that Act (certificate by Scottish Information Commissioner of failure to comply with notice).

---

[1] Chap. 90 and r. 90.1 inserted by S.S.I. 2005 No. 193 (effective 1st April, 2005).

Freedom of Information Act 2000. Under s. 50 of the Act of 2000 a person may apply to the **90.1.1** Information Commissioner (formerly the Data Protection Commissioner) for a decision as to whether a request for information to a public authority (defined in s. 3(1)) has been dealt with in accordance with Pt. I of the Act of 2000. When he has dealt with the application he may serve a decision notice (s. 50(3)). In dealing with the application the Commissioner may require information from the public authority by serving an information notice on it (s. 51); and if the Commissioner is satisfied that a public authority has failed to comply with a requirement of Pt. I, he may serve an enforcement notice on it (s. 52).

If a public authority fails to comply with a decision notice, information notice or enforcement notice, the Commissioner may certify in writing to the court that the public authority has failed to comply with the notice and the court may inquire into the matter: Act of 2000, s. 54.

Freedom of Information (Scotland) Act 2002. Under s. 47 of the Act of 20002 a person **90.1.2** dissatisfied, with a notice by a Scottish public authority on an application for review of its actions and decisions on a request for information or with the failure to give such a notice, may apply to the Scottish Information Commissioner for a decision as to whether a request for information to a public authority (defined in s. 3(1)) has been dealt with in accordance with Pt. I of the Act of 2002. When he has dealt with the application he may serve a decision notice (s. 49(5)). In dealing with the application the Commissioner may require information from the public authority by serving an information notice on it (s. 50); and if the Commissioner is satisfied that a public authority has failed to comply with a requirement of Pt. I, he may serve an enforcement notice on it (s. 51).

If a public authority fails to comply with a decision notice, information notice or enforcement notice, the Commissioner may certify in writing to the court that the public authority has failed to comply with the notice and the court may inquire into the matter: Act of 2000, s. 53.

"application under s. 54(3) of the Act of 2000 or section 53(3) of the Act of 2002". Neither **90.1.3** provision in fact provides for an application to the court. These provisions provide for an inquiry by the court on the Commissioner certifying to the court that there has been a failure to comply (see further notes 90.1.1 and 90.1.2). There is no known procedure in our courts for certifying to the court in this way. One is hardly surprised that the UK Parliament is ignorant of our civil procedure, but one would be entitled to expect that the Scottish Parliament should inform itself of that fact.

In effect what has to be done, and what r. 90.1(2) is striving to achieve, is that the certification is brought to the court's attention by petition. The rule is silent as to who presents the petition: it is presumably the Commissioner.

"petition". A petition is presented to the Outer House: r. 14.2(h). The petition must be in **90.1.4** Form 86.3 in the official printed form (r. 4.1). The petition must be signed by counsel or other person having a right of audience: r. 4.2; and see r. 1.3(1) (definition of "counsel" and "other person having a right of audience") and note 1.3.4.

The petitioner must lodge the petition with the required steps of process (r. 4.4). A fee is payable on lodging the petition: see note 14.5.10.

On petitions generally, see Chap. 14.

[1] CHAPTER 91

GENDER RECOGNITION ACT 2004

Interpretation of this Chapter
[1] **91.1.** In this Chapter—
  "the Act of 2004" means the Gender Recognition Act 2004;
  "full gender recognition certificate" has same meaning as in section 25 of the Act of 2004; and
  "Gender Recognition Panel" is to be construed in accordance with Schedule 1 to the Act of 2004.

---

[1] Chap. 91 and r. 91.1 inserted by S.S.I. 2005 No. 193 (effective 1st April, 2005).

91.1.1 *Reference under section 8 of the Gender Recognition Act 2004.* If the Secretary of State considers that the grant of an application under s. 1(1) (for a gender recognition certificate), 5(1) (issue of a full gender recognition certificate by a court) or 6(1) (corrected certificate) of the Act of 2004 has been secured by fraud, he may refer the case to the Court of Session.

91.1.2 *"petition".* A petition is presented to the Outer House: r. 14.2(h). The petition must be in Form 86.3 in the official printed form (r. 4.1). The petition must be signed by counsel or other person having a right of audience: r. 4.2; and see r. 1.3(1) (definition of "counsel" and "other person having a right of audience") and note 1.3.4.

The petitioner must lodge the petition with the required steps of process (r. 4.4). A fee is payable on lodging the petition: see note 14.5.10.

On petitions generally, see Chap. 14.

References by Secretary of State

[1] **91.2.**—(1) A reference by the Secretary of State under section 8(5) of the Act of 2004 shall be made by petition.

(2) Where the court quashes a decision by the Gender Recognition Panel to grant an application for a gender recognition certificate under section 1(1) or section 5(2), the Deputy Principal Clerk shall send a certified copy of the interlocutor to the Registrar General for Scotland.

---

[1] Rule 91.2 inserted by S.S.I. 2005 No. 193 (effective 1st April, 2005).

[1] CHAPTER 92

INQUIRIES ACT 2005

Applications

[1] **92.1.**—(1) In this rule "the Act of 2005" means the Inquiries Act 2005.

(2) An application under section 36(2) of the Act of 2005 for the court to make such order by way of enforcement, or otherwise as it could make if the matter had arisen in proceedings before the court, shall be by petition.

(3) There shall be attached to a petition mentioned in paragraph (2) a certificate under section 36(1) of the Act of 2005 (certificate by chairman of inquiry or Minister).

---

[1] Chap. 92 and r. 92.1 inserted by S.S.I. 2005 No. 521 (effective 21st October 2005).

92.1.1 *General note.* The Inquiries Act 2005 is supposed to provide a complete statutory framework for public inquiries about matters of public concern set up by government ministers. It repeals the Tribunals of Inquiries (Evidence) Act 1921.

Restrictions on attendance or disclosure of evidence or documents may be imposed by the chairman (s. 19); and a person may be required to attend by the chairman (s. 21). Under s. 36 of the Act of 2005 the chairman or the Minister may certify to the court that a person has failed to comply or threatens to do so.

92.1.2 *"application under section 36(2) of the Act of 2005".* This provision does not in fact provides for an application to the court. It provides for an inquiry by the court on the chairman or Minister certifying to the court that there has been a failure to comply or a threat not to do so (see further notes 92.1.1). There is no known procedure in our courts for certifying to the court in this way.

In effect what has to be done, and what r. 92.1(2) is striving to achieve, is that the certification is brought to the court's attention by petition. The rule is silent as to who presents the petition: it is presumably the chairman of the inquiry or the Minister.

92.1.3 *"petition".* A petition is presented to the Outer House: r. 14.2(h). The petition must be in Form 86.3 in the official printed form (r. 4.1). The petition must be signed by counsel or other person having a right of audience: r. 4.2; and see r. 1.3(1) (definition of "counsel" and "other person having a right of audience") and note 1.3.4.

The petitioner must lodge the petition with the required steps of process (r. 4.4). A fee is payable on lodging the petition: see note 14.5.10.

On petitions generally, see Chap. 14.

[1] CHAPTER 93

LIVE LINKS

Application for live link

[1] **93.1.**—(1) On cause shown, a party may apply by motion for authority for the whole or part of—

(a) the evidence of a witness or the party to be given; or

(b) a submission to be made,

through a live link.

(2) in paragraph (1)—

"witness" means a person who has been or may be cited to appear before the court as a witness;

"submission" means any oral submission which would otherwise be made to the court by the party or his representative in person including an oral submission in support of a motion;

"live link" means a live television link or such other arrangement as may be specified in the motion by which the witness, party or representative, as the case may be, is able to be seen and heard in the proceedings or heard in the proceedings and is able to see and hear or hear the proceedings while at a place which is outside the courtroom.

---

[1] Chap. 93 and r.93.1 inserted by S.S.I. 2007 No. 7 (effective from 29th January 2007).

General note. Chap. 93 was inserted as a stand alone chapter because it applies not only to the **93.1.1** evidence of a witness at a proof but also to submissions made in any form of proceedings before the court.

"motion". For motions, see Chap. 23.   **93.1.2**

Rule 1.4   APPENDIX

Rule 5.2(1)   FORM 5.2

Form of caveat

CAVEAT

for

[A.B.] (*designation and address**)

Should any application be made to the court for (*specify the nature of the application(s) to which the caveat is to apply*) against .... [*or* by [C.D.] (*designation and address*)], it is requested that intimation be made to the undernoted before any order is pronounced.

(*Signed*)
[A.B.]
[*or* Solicitor [*or* Agent for [A.B.]]

Caveator's telephone number
(only when caveat not lodged by a solicitor) ....

Particulars of solicitor or person having a right to conduct the litigation.

Name ....

Address ....

Tel. No. ....

Reference ....

Out of hours contacts

Name and telephone number **1** ....
Name and telephone number **2** ....

*Where appropriate state whether the caveat is lodged in an individual capacity, a specified representative capacity (*e.g.* as trustee of a named trust) or both such capacities. Where appropriate, state also the nature of the caveator's interest (*e.g.* shareholder; debenture holder).

Rule 7.1(3) [1] FORM 7.1

Form of application to Extractor for extract of a decree

EXTRACT NUMBER:

IN THE COURT OF SESSION

NOTE TO EXTRACTOR

A. Full name of case ....
.... Pursuer

against

....
.... Defender

Case number ....

Date and nature of interlocutor to be extracted ....
....

N.B. Where there is more than one interlocutor of a given date please be specific or alternatively produce a copy

Firm requesting extract ....

Signature of requesting solicitor ....

Date of request ....

B. (To be completed by Extracts Department)

Date sent to typing ....

Date returned ....

Date sent for amendment ....

Date returned ....

Date of extract ....

Date issued ....

Signature for receipt of process ....

Date of receipt ....

_____

[1] Form 7.1 amended by S.I. 1996 No. 1756 (effective 5th August 1996).

Rule 7.6   [1] FORM 7.6

Form of statement of accumulated sum to be lodged with application for extract of decree of adjudication

IN THE COURT OF SESSION

STATEMENT OF ACCUMULATED SUM

in the cause

[A.B.] (*designation and address*)

Pursuer

against

[C.D.] (*designation and address*)

Defender

Amount of principal sum contained in decree dated	£
Interest thereon from to (days)	£
Penalty	£
Expenses of process (of action of constitution)	£
Dues of Extract	£
Total accumulated sum	£

(*Signed*)

(*Name of firm*)

[Solicitor for pursuer *or as the case may be*] (*Address*)

---

[1] Form 7.6 amended by S.I. 1997 No. 1050 (minor amendment effective 6th April 1997).

Rule 13.2(1)   [1] FORM 13.2–A

Form of summons and backing
(*First page*)

[*Insert the Royal Arms in Scotland*]

(*This space will contain the cause reference number assigned to the summons on being presented for signeting and registration*)

IN THE COURT OF SESSION

SUMMONS

in the cause

[A.B.] (*designation and address*), Pursuer

against

[C.D.] (*designation and address*), Defender

Elizabeth II, by the Grace of God, of the United Kingdom of Great Britain and Northern Ireland and of Her other Realms and Territories, Queen, Head of the Commonwealth, Defender of the Faith, to [C.D.].

By this summons, the pursuer craves the Lords of our Council and Session to pronounce a decree against you in terms of the conclusions appended to this summons. If you have any good reason why such decree should not be pronounced, you must enter appearance at the Office of Court, Court of Session, 2 Parliament Square, Edinburgh EH1 1RQ, within three days after the date of the calling of the summons in court. The summons shall not call in court earlier than [21] days after the date of service on you of this summons. Be warned that, if appearance is not entered on your behalf, the pursuer may obtain decree against you in your absence.

This summons is warrant for intimation to (*name and address and reason for intimation as set out in the rule of the Rules of the Court of Session 1994 requiring intimation*).

Given under our Signet at Edinburgh on (*date*)

(*Signed*)

(*Name and address of or agent for pursuer*)

Warrant for diligence

This summons is warrant for [arrestment to found jurisdiction] [arrestment *in rem* of (*details of ship or cargo*)] [arrestment on the dependence of the action] [inhibition on the dependence of the action] [dismantling (*details of ship*)].

(*Signed*)

Lord

Date: (*date*)

(*Next page—back of first page and following pages*)

(*State the conclusions, followed by the condescendence and pleas-in-law.*)

(*Backing of summons*)

(*This space will contain the cause reference number assigned to the summons on being presented for signeting and registration*)

IN THE COURT OF SESSION

Summons

in the cause

[A.B.],   Pursuer

against

[C.D.],   Defender

Action of (*nature of action as in the appropriate heading, if any, of the forms of conclusion shown in Form 13.2–B*).

(*Name of firm of agent for pursuer*)

[1] Form 13.2–A amended by S.I. 1994 No. 2901 and S.S.I. 2004 No. 537.

Rule 13.2(2)   [1] FORM 13.2–B

Principal forms of conclusion

(1) *Action for payment.* For payment to the pursuer by the defender [jointly and severally, or severally, *or otherwise as may be appropriate*] of the sum of (*amount in words and figures*) with interest at the rate of   per cent a year from (*date*) until payment.

(2) *Action of damages.* For payment to the pursuer by the defender of the sum of (*amount in words and figures*) with interest at the rate of   per cent a year from (*date*) until payment.

(3) *Action of reduction*. For production and reduction of (*specify deed to be set aside*).

(4) *Action of declarator*. For declarator (*state declarator sought*).

(5) *Action of count, reckoning and payment*. For count and reckoning with the pursuer for the defender's intromissions with (*describe fund or estate*) and for payment to the pursuer by the defender of the balance found due to him, or otherwise of the sum of (*amount in words and figures*).

(6) *Action of proving the tenor*. For declarator that (*describe the lost deed*) was of the tenor following (*set out the terms of the lost deed*), and that the decree to be pronounced herein shall be equivalent to the original deed.

(7) *Action of multiplepoinding and exoneration*. For distribution of (*describe the fund in medio*) among the claimants found entitled to it, and exoneration of (*name of the holder of the fund*).

(8) *Action of furthcoming*. For payment to the pursuer by the arrestee of:—
   (*a*) the sum of (*amount in words and figures*); or
   (*b*) whichever is the lesser of:—
      (i) such sum as may be owing by the arrestee to (*name of debtor*) and has been arrested in his hands by the pursuer; and
      (ii) such sum as shall satisfy the pursuer in (*specify principal sum due and interest, in terms of the decree constituting the debt or otherwise, and expenses of the action in which that decree was obtained*).

or

For delivery to the pursuer or to such person as the court may appoint of the moveables belonging to or owing by the arrestee to (*name of the common debtor*) and arrested in his hands by the pursuer; and for warrant for the sale of such moveables under such conditions as may be directed; and for furthcoming and payment to the pursuer of the proceeds thereof, or at least of so much thereof as shall satisfy the pursuer in (i) the payment of the expenses of and incidental to the sale, and (ii) (*specify principal sum due and interest, in terms of the decree constituting the debt or otherwise, and expenses of the action in which that decree was obtained*).

(9) *Admiralty action* in rem. For declarator that the pursuer has a lien over the (*name of ship*) for the sum of   in respect of (*state the basis of the lien, as e.g. the collision—giving date*); and for declarator that the lien of the pursuer to the extent of the sum (*amount in words and figures*) of   with interest at   per cent a year from (*date*) to (*date*) is preferable to the right of all others having or pretending to have rights in the said ship and for warrant to sell the (*name of ship*) on the lien being declared, and to apply the proceeds in satisfaction of the lien in or towards payment of the said sum of   and interest.

(10) *Action of declarator of marriage*. For declarator that the pursuer and defender were lawfully married to one another by (*specify mode in which marriage was contracted, e.g.,* (*a*) interchange of consent *de praesenti* (*time and place*), (*b*) cohabitation by habit and repute (*time and place*) *or* (*c*) promise (*time*) *subsequente copula* at (*time and place*)).

(11) *Action of declarator of nullity of marriage*. For declarator that a pretended marriage between the pursuer and defender at (*place*) on (*date*) is null by reason of (*specify ground of nullity, e.g.,* (*a*) the pursuer's or defender's impotency, (*b*) the parties being within the forbidden degrees, (*c*) the defender being married to someone else, (*d*) nonage of one of the parties, *or* (*e*) insanity of one of the parties at the date of the marriage).

(12) *Action of declarator of (non-) parentage*. For declarator that (*name and address*) is [*or* was] [not] the son [or daughter] of (*name and address*).

(13) *Action of separation*. For separation of the defender from the pursuer on the ground of [the adultery of the defender] [the behaviour of the defender] [the desertion of the defender and non-cohabitation during a period of two years or more] [non-cohabitation for a period of two years or more and the defender's consent to the granting of decree of separation] [non-cohabitation for a period of five years or more].

(14) *Action of divorce.* For divorce of the defender from the pursuer in respect that the marriage has broken down irretrievably by reason of [the adultery of the defender] [the behaviour of the defender] [the desertion of the defender and non-cohabitation during a period of two years or more] [non-cohabitation for two years or more and the defender's consent to decree of divorce] [non-cohabitation for five years or more].

(15) *Conclusion for capital sum and periodical allowance.* For payment by the defender to the pursuer of (1) a capital sum of (*amount in words and figures*) with interest at the rate of   per cent a year from the date of decree to follow hereon until payment; and (2) a periodical allowance of (*amount in words and figures*) per week [or month] payable until the date three years after the date of decree to follow hereon [*or* until the remarriage or death of the pursuer, if sooner, *or as the case may be*].

(16) *Action of putting to silence.* For decree ordaining the defender to desist from asserting that he [*or* she] is the husband [*or* wife *or* child *or other relative*] of the pursuer, and putting him [*or her*] to silence.

(17) *Conclusion for custody of children.* For custody of (*name of child or children*), the child[ren] of the marriage under the age of sixteen years; and for payment by the defender to the pursuer of (*amount of aliment in words and figures*) as aliment for each [*or* the] child while in the custody of the pursuer and under the age of eighteen years.

(18) *Action for salvage.* For payment to the pursuer by the defender of the sum of (*amount in words and figures*) for salvage services performed by the pursuer to the vessel (*name of ship*) on (*date*) or for such an amount of salvage as to the court may seem just [(*or in the case of a summons for apportionment*), for payment to the pursuer of an equitable proportion of the sum of (*amount in words and figures*)]. (*Refer to any agreement under which the total amount of the salvage award was fixed.*)

(19) *Action of implement.* For decree ordaining the defender (*specify the order craved and such alternative conclusions as may be appropriate*).

(20) *Adjudication for debt.* For adjudication of the heritable property of the defender, that is to say, All and Whole (*insert conveyancing description of subjects*) from the defender to the pursuer; and that for payment to the pursuer of the principal sum, interest and expenses of process and of extract [*or as the case may be*] contained in a decree (*detail particulars of decree in pursuer's favour*); According as the same shall extend when accumulated at the date of decree to follow hereon and of the interest of the accumulated sum at the rate of   per cent a year during the non-redemption of the said heritable property, and the expenses of the infeftment to follow on the decree of adjudication with interest   at the rate of   per cent a year from the date of disbursing the same during the non-redemption.

[*Or in the case of heritable securities.* For adjudication of a [standard security] [bond and disposition in security] (*describe the security*) and of the subjects contained in the [standard security] [bond], that is to say, All and Whole (*insert conveyancing description of subjects*) from the defender to the pursuer for payment of (*describe debts*), during the non-redemption of the said lands and others].

(21) *Adjudication in implement.* For adjudication from the defender of All and Whole (*insert conveyancing description of subjects*) and all rights of the defender therein and the rents thereof from and after (*date of entry under missives*) in implement of missives of sale dated   between the defender and the pursuer and for declarator that the said lands and others belong to the pursuer and his heirs and assignees; and for decree ordaining the defender to free and relieve the said lands and others of all burdens and incumbrances affecting them, of all feuduties, and public and other burdens affecting the said lands at and preceding the pursuer's term of entry, or otherwise for payment of the sum of (*amount in words and figures*) or such sum as may be required for that purpose.

(22) *Declarator and division or sale.* For declarator that the pursuer is entitled to insist in an action of division or sale of All and Whole (*insert conveyancing description of subjects*); and for division of those subjects between the pursuer and the defender, or if division of those subjects is found to be impracticable or inexpedient for declarator that those subjects should be sold and the proceeds divided between the pursuer and the defender, and for warrant to sell accordingly; and for allocation of the expenses of the sale and of this process between the pursuer and the defender.

(23) *Maills and duties under Heritable Securities Act 1894.* For declarator that the pursuer has right to the rents, maills and duties of the subjects and others specified in the bond and disposition in security for   , granted by   in favour of   dated   and recorded in the   register or at least so much of those rents, maills and duties as will satisfy and pay the pursuer the principal sum of *(amount in words and figures)*, with interest at the rate of   per cent a year from the   day of   until payment together with £   liquidate penalty and termly failures, all as specified and contained in the said bond and disposition in security dated and recorded as aforesaid.

(24) *Poinding of the ground.* (a) *Against debtor in possession.* For warrant to poind and distrain all moveable goods and effects poindable or distrainable belonging to the defender which are or shall happen to be on the ground of the lands and others described and contained in the [standard security] [bond and disposition in security] [*or where the action proceeds on a real burden*, the disposition or other writ by which it is constituted] aftermentioned, that is to say, All and Whole *(insert conveyancing description of subjects)*: And for payment thereof to the pursuer of the amount of the principal sum of *(amount in words and figures)* together with £   liquidate penalty and termly failures, with interest on said principal sum from *(date)* until payment and in all time coming during the non-redemption conform to [standard security] [bond and disposition in security] dated   and [recorded in the Division of the General Register of Sasines applicable to the county of   ] [registered in the Land Register] both days of   granted by the defender in favour of the pursuer [*or where the pursuer is not the original security holder*, in favour of   and to which the pursuer has now right in virtue of *(describe title)*].

(b) *Against debtor and tenants.* For warrant to poind and distrain all moveable goods and effects poindable or distrainable of the defender [C.D.] principal debtor, [and of the defender[s] [E.F.] [and G.H.] his tenant[s] or possessor[s] of the lands and others aftermentioned which are or shall happen to be on the grounds of those lands and others described and contained in the [standard security] [bond and disposition in security] aftermentioned, that is to say, All and Whole *(insert description of subjects sufficient to identify them)* but in so far as relates to the said tenants and possessors to the amount only of the respective rents due or that may become due by them and for payment thereof to the pursuer to the amount of the principal sum of *(amount in words and figures)* with £   liquidate penalty and termly failures specified and contained in the bond and disposition in security dated   and [recorded in the Division of the General Register of Sasines applicable to the county of   ] [registered in the Land Register] the   [both days] of   granted by the defender [C.D.] in favour of the pursuer, with interest from the term of   and in all time coming during the not redemption.

---

[1] Form 13.2–B amended by S.I. 1994 No. 2901 (clerical error).

Rule 13.7(1)   FORM 13.7

Form of citation of defender

CITATION

Date: *(date of posting or other method of service)*

To: *(name and address of defender)*

IN HER MAJESTY'S NAME AND AUTHORITY, I, *(name of agent)*, solicitor [*or* person having a right to conduct the litigation], for *(name of pursuer)* [*or* *(name of messenger-at-arms)*, messenger-at-arms], serve the attached summons on you.

The summons contains a claim made by *(name of pursuer)* against you in the Court of Session, Edinburgh.

If you intend to deny the claim you must: (1) enter appearance at the Office of Court, Court of Session, 2 Parliament Square, Edinburgh EH1 1RQ within three days after the date on which the summons calls in court; and (2) subsequently lodge defences within seven days afterthe date on which the summons calls in court as required by the Rules of the Court of Session 1994. The summons will not call in court earlier than [21] days after the date of service on you of the summons. The date of service is the date stated at the top of this citation unless service has been by post in which case the date of service is the day after that date.

Release 34: 8 November 1994

If you do not enter appearance and lodge defences the court may make an order against you.

IF YOU ARE UNCERTAIN ABOUT THE EFFECT OF THIS CITATION, you should consult a solicitor, Citizens Advice Bureau or other local advice agency or adviser immediately.

(*Signed*)

Messenger-at-arms
[*or* Solicitor [*or* Agent] for pursuer]
(*Address*)

Rule 13.12(1)   [1] FORM 13.12

Form of notice of intimation to person holding a heritable security in an action relating to heritable property

Date: (*date of posting or other method of intimation*)

To: (*name and address of security holder*)

TAKE NOTICE

(*Name and address of pursuer*) has brought an action against (*name and address of defender*). The action relates to heritable property over which you are believed to hold a heritable security. A copy of the summons in the action is attached.

You may apply to the court by minute for leave to lodge defences in the action. You must do so at the Office of Court, Court of Session, 2 Parliament Square, Edinburgh EH1 1RQ within [21] days after the date of intimation to you of the summons [*or if the warrant for intimation is executed before calling of the summons*, within [7] days after the summons calls in court. The summons will not call in court earlier than [21] days after the date of intimation to you of the summons]. The date of intimation is the date stated at the top of this notice unless intimation has been made by post in which case the date of intimation is the day after that date.

IF YOU ARE UNCERTAIN ABOUT THE EFFECT OF THIS NOTICE, you should consult a solicitor, Citizens Advice Bureau or other local advice agency or adviser immediately.

(*Signed*)

Messenger-at-arms
[*or* Solicitor [*or* Agent] for pursuer]
(*Address*)

---

[1] Form 13.12 amended by S.I. 1994 No. 2901 (minor correction).

Rule 14.4(1)   [1] FORM 14.4

Form of petition

[*Insert the Royal Arms in Scotland*]

(*This space will contain the cause reference number assigned to the petition on being lodged*)

UNTO THE RIGHT HONOURABLE THE LORDS OF COUNCIL AND SESSION

The Petition of [A.B.] (*name, designation and address of petitioner*)

HUMBLY SHEWETH:—

1. That (*here set out in this and following numbered paragraphs the facts and circumstances which form the grounds of petition*).

MAY IT THEREFORE please your Lordships
to (insert prayer)

According to Justice, etc.

(*Signed*)

(*Backing of petition*)

┌─────────────────────┐
│   │
│   │
│   │
│   │
└─────────────────────┘

(*This space will contain the cause reference number assigned to the petition on being lodged*)

The Petition

of

[A.B.]

for

(*here describe shortly the nature or object of the petition*).

(*Name of firm of agent for petitioner*)

———

[1] Form 14.4 amended by S.I. 1994 No. 2901.

Rule 14.7(2)   FORM 14.7

Form of citation in petition

CITATION

Date: (*date of posting or other method of service*)

To: (*name and address of person on whom petition served*)

IN HER MAJESTY'S NAME AND AUTHORITY, and in the name and authority of Lord (*name*), I, (*name of agent*), solicitor [*or* person having a right to conduct the litigation], for (*name of pursuer*) [*or* (*name of messenger-at-arms*), messenger-at-arms], serve the attached petition and interlocutor of the court on you.

The interlocutor requires you, if so advised, to lodge answers to the petition.

If you intend to lodge answers to the petition you must lodge them at the Office of Court, Court of Session, 2 Parliament Square, Edinburgh EH1 1RQ within [21] days after the date of service on you of the petition. The date of service is the date stated at the top of this citation unless service has been by post in which case the date of service is the day after that date.

IF YOU ARE UNCERTAIN ABOUT THE EFFECT OF THIS CITATION, you should consult a solicitor, Citizens Advice Bureau or other local advice agency or adviser immediately.

(*Signed*)

Messenger-at-arms
[*or* Solicitor [*or* Agent] for petitioner]
(*Address*)

Rule 15.1(4)   FORM 15.1

Form of notice of minute

Date: (*date of posting or other method of service or intimation*)

To: (*name and address*)

TAKE NOTICE

(*Name of minuter*) has lodged the attached Minute in the process of an action in the Court of Session in which (*name*) is the pursuer and (*name*) is the defender. By virtue of an order of [Lord (*name*) in] the Court of Session dated (*date*) you may lodge answers at the Office of Court, Court of Session, 2 Parliament Square, Edinburgh EH1 1RQ within [21] days after the date of service on [*or* intimation to] you of the Minute. The date of service or intimation is the date stated at the top of this notice unless service or intimation has been by post in which case the date of service or intimation is the day after that date.

IF YOU ARE UNCERTAIN ABOUT THE EFFECT OF THIS NOTICE, you should consult a solicitor, Citizens Advice Bureau or other local advice agency or adviser immediately.

(*Signed*)

Messenger-at-arms
[*or* Solicitor [*or* Agent] for minuter]
(*Address*)

Rule 15.2(3)   FORM 15.2

Form of notice of Note

Date: (*date of posting or other method of service or intimation*)

To: (*name and address*)

TAKE NOTICE

(*Name of noter*) has lodged the attached Note in the process of a petition in the Court of Session in which (*name*) is the petitioner [and (*name*) is the respondent]. By virtue of an order of [Lord (*name*) in] the Court of Session dated (*date*) you may lodge answers to the Note at the Office of Court, Court of Session, 2 Parliament Square, Edinburgh EH1 1RQ within [21] days after the date of service on [*or* intimation to] you of the Note. The date of service or intimation is the date stated at the top of this notice unless service or intimation has been by post in which case the date of service or intimation is the day after that date.

IF YOU ARE UNCERTAIN ABOUT THE EFFECT OF THIS NOTICE, you should consult a solicitor, Citizens Advice Bureau or other local advice agency or adviser immediately.

(*Signed*)

Messenger-at-arms
[*or* Solicitor [*or* Agent] for noter]
(*Address*)

Rule 16.2(5)(b) FORM 16.2

Form of certificate of personal service or intimation on a warrant on person furth of United Kingdom

CERTIFICATE OF PERSONAL SERVICE [*OR* INTIMATION] FURTH OF UNITED KINGDOM

I, (*name*) pursuer [*or* authorised agent of the pursuer], certify that I served [*or* intimated] this summons [or other document (*specify*) on [*or* to] (*name of defender or other person on whom served or to whom intimated*) by (*state method of service*) at (*place and country*), being a method of service [*or* intimation] permitted in that country, on (*date*).

I did this in the presence of (*name, occupation and address of witness*).

(*Signed*)

Pursuer [*or* Authorised agent of pursuer] (*Address*)

(*Signed*)
Witness

Rule 16.3(1)(b) FORM 16.3

Form of certificate of service or intimation on a warrant by messenger-at-arms

CERTIFICATE OF SERVICE [*OR* INTIMATION]

I, (*name*) Messenger-at-Arms, certify that I served [*or* intimated] this summons [*or other document (specify)*] [and a citation] [*or* and a notice of intimation] on [*or* to] (*name of defender or other person on whom served or to whom intimated*)—

* by leaving it and a citation [*or* notice] with (*name of defender or other person*) at (*place*) at (*time*) on (*date*).

* by leaving it and a citation [*or* notice] with (*name and occupation of person with whom left*) at (*place*) on (*date*). (*Specify that enquiry made and that reasonable grounds exist for believing that the person on whom service is to be made or to whom intimation is to be given resides at the place but is not available.*)

* by depositing it and a citation [*or* notice] in (*place*) on (*date*). (*Specify that enquiry made and that reasonable grounds exist for believing that the person on whom service is to be made or to whom intimation is to be given resides at the place but is not available.*)

* by leaving it and a citation [*or* notice] with (*name and occupation of person with whom left*) at (*place of business*) on (*date*). (*Specify that enquiry made and that reasonable grounds exist for believing that the person on whom service is to be made or to whom intimation is to be given carries on business at the place.*)

* by depositing it and a citation [*or* notice] at (*place of business*) on (*date*). (*Specify that enquiry made and that reasonable grounds exist for believing that the person on whom service is to be made or to whom intimation is to be given carries on business at the place.*)

* by leaving it and a citation [*or* notice] at (*registered office or place of business*) on (*date*), in the hands of (*name of person*).

* by leaving [*or* depositing] it and a citation [*or* notice] at (*registered office, official address or place of business*) on (*date*) in such a way that it was likely to come to the attention of (*name of defender or other person on whom served or to whom intimated*). (*Specify how left.*)

I did this in the presence of (*name, occupation and address of witness*).

(*Signed*)

Messenger-at-Arms
(*Address*)

(*Signed*)
Witness

*Delete where not applicable.

Rule 16.4(4)(b)   FORM 16.4

Form of certificate of service, or intimation on a warrant, by post

CERTIFICATE OF SERVICE [*OR* INTIMATION] BY POST

I, (*name and designation*), certify that I served [*or* intimated] this summons (*or other document* (*specify*)) on [*or* to] (*name of defender or other person on whom served*) by posting a copy of it with a citation [*or* notice] attached, to that person between (*time*) and (*time*) on (*date*) at (*name of post office*) post office in a registered envelope [*or* recorded delivery envelope] addressed as follows:— (*address*). The post office receipt [*or* certificate of posting] is attached to this certificate.

(*Signed*)

Solicitor [*or* Agent] for pursuer [*or* other party]
[*or* Messenger-at-Arms]

(*Address*)

Rule 16.5(3)(a)   [1] FORM 16.5

Form of citation by advertisement

IN THE COURT OF SESSION

in the cause

[A.B.] (*designation and address*)

Pursuer

against

[C.D.]

Defender

An action has been brought in the Court of Session, Edinburgh, [Scotland,] by [A.B.], pursuer. [A.B.] calls as a defender [C.D.] whose last known address was (*address*). If [C.D.] wishes to challenge the jurisdiction of the court or to defend the action, he [*or* she [*or* it] [*or* they]] should contact the Deputy Principal Clerk of Session, Court of Session, Parliament Square, Edinburgh EH1 1RQ (Telephone 031–225 2595) immediately and in any event by not later than six months from the date of publication of this advertisement.

(*Signed*)

Solicitor [*or* Agent] for pursuer
(*Address*)

---

[1] Form 16.5 amended by S.I. 1998 No. 890.

Rule 16.7(2)(a)   [1] FORM 16.7

Form of certificate of intimation of a document

I, (*name and designation*), certify that I intimated (*specify document*) to (*name of person to whom intimation made*) [with a copy of the interlocutor of Lord (*name*) dated (*date*) a copy of which is attached] on (*date*).

(*Signed*)

Solicitor [*or* Agent] for pursuer
[*or as the case may be*]
(*Address*)

---

[1] Form 16.7 amended by S.I. 1996 No. 2168 (minor correction).

Rule 16.15(1)(a)   [1] FORM 16.15–A

Form of schedule of arrestment to found jurisdiction

SCHEDULE OF ARRESTMENT TO FOUND JURISDICTION

Date: (*date of execution*)

Time: (*time arrestment executed*)

To: (*name and address of arrestee*)

IN HER MAJESTY'S NAME AND AUTHORITY, I, (*name*), Messenger-at-Arms, by virtue of a summons containing a warrant for arrestment to found jurisdiction, at the instance of (*name and address of pursuer*) against (*name and address of defender*) and signeted on (*date*), arrest to found jurisdiction against (*name of defender*) in your hands: (i) the sum of (*amount*), more or less, due by you to (*name of defender*) or to any other person on his [*or* her] [*or* its] [*or* their] behalf; and (ii) all moveable subjects in your hands and belonging or pertaining to (*name of defender*).

This I do in the presence of (*name, occupation and address of witness*).

(*Signed*)

Messenger-at-Arms
(*Address*)

NOTE

(*Do not use this note where arrestment to found jurisdiction is combined with arrestment on the dependence in one schedule.*)

This schedule arrests in your hands debts due by you to the defender mentioned in the schedule and goods and other moveables held by you on his behalf. It does so solely for the purpose of establishing the jurisdiction of the Court of Session over the defender.

IF YOU ARE UNCERTAIN ABOUT THE EFFECT OF THIS DOCUMENT, you should consult a solicitor, Citizens Advice Bureau or other local advice agency or adviser immediately.

---

[1] Form 16.15–A substituted by S.I. 1998 No. 2637 (effective 1st December 1998).

Rule 16.15(1)(a)(ii)   [1] FORM 16.15–AA

Form of schedule of arrestment of ship to found jurisdiction

SCHEDULE OF ARRESTMENT OF SHIP TO FOUND JURISDICTION

Date: (*date of execution*)

Time: (*time arrestment executed*)

IN HER MAJESTY'S NAME AND AUTHORITY, I, (*name*), Messenger-at-Arms, by virtue of a summons containing a warrant for arrestment which to found jurisdiction, at the instance of (*name and address of pursuer*) against (*name and address of defender*) and signeted on (*date*), arrest to found jurisdiction against (*name of defender*) the ship (*name*) presently lying in (*describe location*) and belonging to the defender.

This I do in the presence of (*name, occupation and address of witness*).

(*Signed*)

Messenger-at-Arms
(*Address*)

NOTE

You should consult your legal adviser about the effect of this arrestment.

(The name, address and twenty-four hour contact telephone number of the agent for the party on whose behalf the arrestment was executed are to be inserted here.)

   (*Name of agent*)

   (*Address*)

   (*Telephone number*).

------

[1] Form 16.15–AA inserted by S.I. 1998 No. 2367 (effective 1st December 1998).

Rule 16.15(1)(b) and (e)   [1] FORM 16.15–B

Form of schedule of arrestment on the dependence

SCHEDULE OF ARRESTMENT ON THE DEPENDENCE

Date: (*date of execution*)

Time: (*time arrestment executed*)

To: (*name and address of arrestee*)

IN HER MAJESTY'S NAME AND AUTHORITY, I, (*name*), Messenger-at-Arms, by virtue of—

   * a summons containing a warrant for arrestment on the dependence of the action at the instance of (*name and address of pursuer*) against (*name and address of defender*) signeted on (*date*),

   * a counterclaim containing a warrant which has been granted for arrestment on the dependence of the claim by (*name and address of creditor*) against (*name and address of debtor*) and dated (*date of warrant*),

   * an order of [Lord (*name*) in] the Court of Session dated (*date of order*) granting warrant [for arrestment on the dependence of the action raised at the instance of (*name and address of pursuer*) against (*name and address of defender*)] [or for arrestment on the dependence of the claim in the counterclaim [*or* third party notice] by (*name and address of creditor*) against (*name and address of debtor*)] [*or* to arrest in the petition of (*name and address of petitioner*) against (*name and address of respondent*)],

arrest in your hands (i) the sum of (*amount*), more or less, due by you to (*defender's name*) [*or name and address of common debtor if common debtor is not the defender*] or to any other person on his [*or* her] [*or* its] [*or* their] behalf; and (ii) all moveable things in your hands belonging or pertaining to the said (*name of common debtor*), to remain in your hands under arrestment until they are made forthcoming to (*name of pursuer*) [*or name and address of creditor if he is not the pursuer*] or until further order of the court.

This I do in the presence of (*name, occupation and address of witness*).

(*Signed*)

Messenger-at-Arms
(*Address*)

NOTE

This schedule arrests in your hands (i) debts due by you to (*name of common debtor*); and (ii) goods and other moveables held by you for him. **You should not pay any debts to him or hand over any goods or other moveables to him without taking legal advice.**

IF YOU ARE UNCERTAIN ABOUT THE EFFECT OF THIS DOCUMENT, you should consult a solicitor, Citizens Advice Bureau or other local advice agency or adviser immediately.

*Delete where not applicable.

---

[1] Form 16.15–B substituted by S.I. 1998 No. 2637 (effective 1st December 1998).

Rule 16.15(1)(e)(ii)   [1] FORM 16.15–BB

Form of schedule of arrestment of ship on the dependence

SCHEDULE OF ARRESTMENT OF SHIP ON THE DEPENDENCE

Date: (*date of execution*)

Time: (*time arrestment executed*)

IN HER MAJESTY'S NAME AND AUTHORITY, I, (*name*), Messenger-at-Arms, by virtue of—

* a summons containing a warrant for arrestment on the dependence of the action at the instance of (*name and address of pursuer*) against (*name and address of defender*) signeted on (*date*),

* a counterclaim containing a warrant which has been granted for arrestment on the dependence of the claim by (*name and address of creditor*) against (*name and address of debtor*) and dated (*date of warrant*),

* an order of [Lord (*name*) in] the Court of Session dated (*date of order*) granting warrant [for arrestment on the dependence of the action raised at the instance of (*name and address of pursuer*) against (*name and address of defender*)] [*or* for arrestment on the dependence of the claim in the counterclaim [*or* third party notice] by (*name and address of creditor*) against (*name and address of debtor*) [*or* to arrest in the petition of (*name and address of petitioner*) against (*name and address of respondent*)],

arrest the ship (*name of ship*) presently lying in (*describe current location e.g. the port of X*) to remain in that (*more precisely if required*) under arrestment on the dependence of the action [*or* claim] until further order of the court.

This I do in the presence of (*name, occupation and address of witness*).

(*Signed*)

Messenger-at-Arms
(*Address*)

NOTE

You should consult your legal adviser about the effect of this arrestment.

(The name, address and twenty-four hour contact telephone number of the agent for the party on whose behalf the arrestment was executed are to be inserted here.)

(*Name of agent*)

(*Address*)

(*Telephone number*),

*Delete where not applicable.

---

[1] Form 16.15–BB inserted by S.I. 1998 No. 2637 (effective 1st December 1998).

Rule 16.15(1)(c)   [1] FORM 16.15–C

Form of schedule of arrestment in rem of ship, cargo or other maritime res to enforce maritime hypothec or lien

SCHEDULE OF ARRESTMENT *IN REM* IN ADMIRALTY ACTION *IN REM*

Date: (*date of execution*)

Time: (*time arrestment executed*)

IN HER MAJESTY'S NAME AND AUTHORITY, I, (*name*), Messenger-at-Arms, by virtue of a summons containing a warrant for arrestment *in rem* of the ship (*name of ship*) [*or* cargo (*describe*)] [*or other maritime res (describe)*] in an Admiralty action *in rem* at the instance of (*name and address of pursuer*) against (*name and address of defender*) and signeted on (*date*), arrest the ship (*name*) presently lying in (*describe current location e.g. the port of X*) with her float, boats, furniture, appurtenances and apparelling [*or cargo*] [*or other maritime res*] (*describe location*)], to remain in that (*specify more precisely if required*) under arrestment *in rem* until they are sold or until this arrestment is recalled or other order of the court.

This I do in the presence of (*name, occupation and address of witness*).

(*Signed*)

Messenger-at-Arms
(*Address*)

NOTE

You should consult your legal adviser about the effect of this arrestment.

(The name, address and twenty-four hour contact telephone number of the agent for the party on whose behalf the arrestment was executed are to be inserted here.)

(*Name of agent*)

(*Address*)

(*Telephone number*)

---

¹ Form 16.15–C substituted by S.I. 1998 No. 2637 (effective 1st December 1998).

Rule 16.15(1)(d)   ¹ Form 16.15–D

Form of schedule of arrestment in rem of ship to enforce non-pecuniary claim

SCHEDULE OF ARRESTMENT *IN REM* OF SHIP UNDER THE ADMINISTRATION
OF JUSTICE ACT 1956, SECTION 47(3)(b)

Date: (*date of execution*)

Time: (*time arrestment executed*)

IN HER MAJESTY'S NAME AND AUTHORITY, I, (*name*), Messenger-at-Arms, by virtue
of—

* an order of Lord (*name*) in the Court of Session dated (*date of order*) granting warrant
for arrestment *in rem* under section 47(3)(b) of the Administration of Justice Act 1956
of the ship (*name of ship*) in an action,

* a summons containing a warrant for arrestment *in rem* under section 47(3)(b) of the
Administration of Justice Act 1956 of the ship (*name of ship*),

at the instance of (*name and address of pursuer*) against (*name and address of defender*)
and signeted on (*date*), arrest the [ship] [*or* vessel] (*name*) presently lying in (*describe
current location e.g. the port of X*) with her float, boats, furniture, appurtenances and
apparelling to remain in that place (*specify more precisely if required*) under arrestment
in rem until this arrestment is recalled or other order of the court.

This I do in the presence of (*name, occupation and address of witness*).

(*Signed*)

Messenger-at-Arms
(*Address*)

NOTE

You should consult your legal adviser about the effect of this arrestment.

(The name, address and twenty-four hour contact telephone number of the agent for the
party on whose behalf the arrestment was executed are to be inserted here.)

(*Name of agent*)

(*Address*)

(*Telephone number*)

*Delete where not applicable.

¹ Form 16.15–D substituted by S.I. 1998 No. 2637 (effective 1st December 1998).

[NEXT TEXT PAGE IS C 687]

Rule 16.15(1)(f)   FORM 16.15–E

Form of schedule of arrestment in execution

SCHEDULE OF ARRESTMENT IN EXECUTION

Date: *(date of execution)*

To: *(name and address of arrestee)*

IN HER MAJESTY'S NAME AND AUTHORITY, I, *(name)*, Messenger-at-Arms, by virtue of an extract decree of the Court of Session dated *(date)* [*or* an extract of a document *(describe deed)* registered for execution on *(date)* in the Books of Council and Session] and extracted on *(date)* obtained at the instance of *(name of party arresting)* arrest in your hands (i) the sum of *(amount)*, more or less, due by you to *(common debtor's name and designation)* or to any other person on his [*or* her] [*or* its] [*or* their] behalf; and (ii) all moveable things in your hands and belonging or pertaining to the *(common debtor's name)*, to remain in your hands under arrestment until the *(name of party arresting)* has been paid *(amount)* in terms of the extract decree [*or* extract of the document registered in the Books of Council and Session].

This I do in the presence of *(name, occupation and address of witness)*.

                                    (Signed)

                                    Messenger-at-Arms

                                    (Address)

                                    (Signed)

                                    Witness

NOTE

This schedule arrests in your hands (i) debts due by you to *(common debtor's name)*; and (ii) goods and other moveables held by you for him. **You should not pay any debts to him or hand over any goods or other moveables to him without taking legal advice.**

This schedule may be used to arrest a ship or its cargo. If it is, you should consult your legal adviser about the effect of it.

IF YOU ARE UNCERTAIN ABOUT THE EFFECT OF THIS DOCUMENT, you should consult a solicitor, Citizens Advice Bureau or other local advice agency or adviser immediately.

Rule 16.15(1)(h)   FORM 16.15–F

Form of schedule of inhibition

SCHEDULE OF INHIBITION

Date: *(date of execution)*

To: *(name and address of person on whom served)*

IN HER MAJESTY'S NAME AND AUTHORITY, I *(name)*, Messenger-at-Arms, by virtue of—

* a warrant contained in a Court of Session summons,

* a warrant contained in letters of inhibition signeted at Edinburgh on *(date)*,

* an order of Lord *(name)* in the Court of Session granted on *(date)*,

a copy of which is attached, inhibit you from selling, disposing of, burdening or otherwise affecting your land and other heritable property to the prejudice of *(name and address of person entitled to inhibit)*.

This I do in the presence of *(name, occupation and address of witness)*.

                                    (Signed)

                                    Messenger-at-Arms

                                    (Address)

NOTE

This document forbids you from disposing of or dealing with any land or buildings in Scotland in which you have an interest without a further order from the court.

If you are in the course of or are contemplating a transaction which affects any land or building in Scotland in which you have an interest you should tell your solicitor immediately about this document.

Release 51: February 1999

IF YOU ARE UNCERTAIN ABOUT THE EFFECT OF THIS DOCUMENT, you should consult a solicitor, Citizens Advice Bureau or other local advice agency or adviser immediately.

*Delete where not applicable.

Rule 16.15(1)(i)   FORM 16.15–G

Form of charge for payment of money

CHARGE FOR PAYMENT OF MONEY

[A.B.] (*designation and address*)

Pursuer

against

[C.D.] (*designation and address*)

Defender

Date: (*date of execution*)

To: (*name and address of debtor*)

On (*date*) a decree against you was granted in the Court of Session for payment of a sum of money in the above action [*or give details of other document upon which charge proceeds such as a document registered for execution in the Books of Council and Session*].

The decree [*or* warrant for execution of the document mentioned above] was extracted on (*date*).

IN HER MAJESTY'S NAME AND AUTHORITY, I, (*name*), Messenger-at-Arms, by virtue of the extract decree, charge you to pay the total sum due as set out below [together with any further interest] within 14 [*or* 28] days after the date of this charge to (*name and address of person to whom payment to be made*).

If you do not pay this sum within 14 [*or* 28] days you are liable to have further action taken against you including arrestment of your earnings and the poinding and sale of articles belonging to you without further notice. You are also liable to be sequestrated (declared bankrupt).

This charge is executed on you today by me by (*state method of execution*) in the presence of (*name, occupation and address of witness*).

(*Signed*)

Messenger-at-Arms
(*Address*)

(*Signed*)

Witness

The sum now due by you is:–	
Principal sum	£
Interest to date*	£
Expenses	£
TOTAL OF ABOVE	£
Less paid to account	£
SUB TOTAL	£
Agent's fee	£
Expenses of messenger-at-arms:–	
Charge fee	£
Travelling	£
Witness fee	£
Other outlays in connection with service of charge (*specify*)	£
TOTAL SUM DUE	£

* Note.   Interest on the principal sum will continue to run until the date of payment.

IF YOU ARE UNCERTAIN ABOUT THE EFFECT OF THIS DOCUMENT, you should consult a solicitor, Citizens Advice Bureau or other local advice agency or adviser immediately.

Rule 16.15(1)   FORM 16.15–H

Form of certificate of execution of arrestment or inhibition

CERTIFICATE OF EXECUTION

I, (*name*), Messenger-at-Arms, certify that I executed (*specify the kind of arrestment or inhibition, whether on the dependence of an action, counterclaim or third party notice, whether on the authority of an interlocutor (specify), on letters of arrestment or inhibition or in execution of a decree (specify)*), [obtained] at the instance of (*name and address of party arresting or inhibiting*) against (*name and address of common debtor or person inhibited*) on (*name of person on whom executed*)—

* by leaving the schedule of [arrestment] [inhibition] with (*name of defender or other person*) at (*place*) on (*date*).

* by leaving the schedule of [arrestment] [inhibition] with (*name and occupation of person with whom left*) at (*place*) on (*date*). (*Specify that enquiry made and that reasonable grounds exist for believing that the person on whom service is to be made resides at the place but is not available.*)

* by depositing the schedule of [arrestment] [inhibition] in (*place*) on (*date*). (*Specify that enquiry made and that reasonable grounds exist for believing that the person on whom service is to be made resides at the place but is not available.*)

* by leaving the schedule of [arrestment] [inhibition] with (*name and occupation of person with whom left*) at (*place of business*) on (*date*). (*Specify that enquiry made and that reasonable grounds exist for believing that the person on whom service is to be made carries on business at the place.*)

* by depositing the schedule of [arrestment] [inhibition] at (*place of business*) on (*date*). (*Specify that enquiry made and that reasonable grounds exist for believing that the person on whom service is to be made carries on business at the place.*)

* by leaving the schedule of [arrestment] [inhibition] at (*registered office or place of business*) on (*date*), in the hands of (*name of person*).

* by leaving [*or* depositing] the schedule of [arrestment] [inhibition] at (*registered office, official address or place of business*) on (*date*) in such a way that it was likely to come to the attention of (*name of defender or other person on whom served*). (*Specify how left.*)

* edictally by leaving the schedule of [arrestment] [inhibition] with (*name and occupation of person with whom left*) at the office of the Extractor of the Court of Session, Parliament Square, Edinburgh on (*date*) and sending a copy of the schedule by registered post [*or* first class recorded delivery service] to (*name and address of residence, registered office, official address or place of business or such last known place*) on (*date*).

I did this in the presence of (*name, occupation and address of witness*).

(*Signed*)

Messenger-at-Arms
(*Address*)

(*Signed*)

Witness

*Delete where not applicable.

Rule 16.15(1)(a)(ii)   ¹ FORM 16.15–HH

Form of certificate of arrestment of ship to found jurisdiction

CERTIFICATE OF EXECUTION OF ARRESTMENT OF SHIP TO FOUND JURISDICTION

I, (*name*), Messenger-at-Arms, certify that I, by virtue of a summons containing a warrant for arrestment to found jurisdiction, executed an arrestment of the ship (*name*) at the instance of (*name and address of pursuer*) against (*name and address of defender*) by affixing the schedule of arrestment to the mainmast [*or as the case may be*] of the ship (*name*) and marked the initials ER above that affixed schedule at (*place*) on (*date*).

I did this in the presence of (*name, occupation and address of witness*).

> (*Signed*)
>
> Messenger-at-Arms
> (*Address*)
>
> (*Signed*)
> Witness

---

[1] Form 16.15–HH inserted by S.I. 1998 No. 2637 (effective 1st December 1998).

Rule 16.15(1)(c) and (d)   Form 16.15–I

Form of certificate of execution of arrestment of ship or cargo *in rem*

CERTIFICATE OF EXECUTION OF ARRESTMENT OF SHIP [*OR* CARGO] *IN REM*

I, (*name*), Messenger-at-Arms, certify that I executed an arrestment *in rem* of the ship [*or* vessel] (*name*) [*or* cargo (*describe*)] by virtue of a summons [*or* interlocutor of Lord (*name*) dated (*date*)] at the instance of (*name and address of pursuer*) against (*name and address of defender*) by affixing the schedule of arrestment to the mainmast [*or as the case may be*] of the ship [*or* vessel] [*or in the case of cargo landed or transhipped* on (*name*) as custodian for the time being of the cargo [*or* as harbourmaster of the harbour where the cargo lies]] [and delivering a copy of the schedule of arrestment and of this certificate to (*name*) the master of the ship [*or as the case may be*] at (*place*) on (*date*).
I did this in the presence of (*name, occupation and address of witness*).

> (*Signed*)
>
> Messenger-at-Arms
> (*Address*)
>
> (*Signed*)
> Witness

Rule 16.15(1)(e)   Form 16.15–J

Form of certificate of execution of arrestment of ship or cargo on the dependence

CERTIFICATE OF EXECUTION OF ARRESTMENT OF SHIP [*OR* CARGO] ON THE DEPENDENCE

I, (*name*), Messenger-at-Arms, certify that I executed an arrestment on the dependence of the ship [*or* vessel] (*name*) [*or* cargo (*describe*)] by virtue of a summons [*or* counterclaim] [*or* interlocutor of Lord (*name*) dated (*date*)] at the instance of (*name and address of pursuer*) against (*name and address of defender*) by affixing the schedule of arrestment to the mainmast [*or as the case may be*] of the ship [*or* vessel] (*name*) and marked the initials ER above the same [*or* by (*state method of service*)] at (*place*) on (*date*).

I did this in the presence of (*name, occupation and address of witness*).

> (*Signed*)
>
> Messenger-at-Arms
> (*Address*)
>
> (*Signed*)
> Witness

Rule 16.15(1)(i)   Form 16.15–K

Form of certificate of execution of charge for payment

CERTIFICATE OF EXECUTION OF CHARGE FOR PAYMENT

Date: (*date of service*)

I, (*name*), Messenger-at-Arms, certify that, by virtue of the attached extract of a decree of the Court of Session at the instance of [A.B.] against [C.D.] [*or* of a document registered for execution in the Books of Council and Session], I charged [C.D.] to pay the sum[s] of money, principal, interest and expenses stated in the extract [*or* to implement and perform the obligation[s] stated in the extract] [*or* both to pay the sum[s] of money, principal, interest and expenses] [*add where there are other debtors in the extract*, so far as incumbent upon him] to [A.B.] within [   ] days after the date of the charge.

I did this—

* by leaving the charge and a copy of the extract decree [*or* document registered for execution in the Books of Council and Session] with (*name of person charged*) at (*place*) on (*date*).

* by leaving the charge and a copy of the extract decree [*or* document registered for execution in the Books of Council and Session] with (*name and occupation of person with whom left*) at (*place*) on (*date*). (*Specify that enquiry made and that reasonable grounds exist for believing that the person charged resides at the place but is not available.*)

* by depositing the charge and a copy of the extract decree [*or* document registered for execution in the Books of Council and Session] in (*place*) and (*date*). (*Specify that enquiry made and that reasonable grounds exist for believing that the person charged resides at the place but is not available.*)

* by leaving the charge and a copy of the extract decree [*or* document registered for execution in the Books of Council and Session] with (*name and designation of person with whom left*) at (*place of business*) on (*date*). (*Specify that enquiry made and that reasonable grounds exist for believing that the person charged carries on business at the place.*)

* by depositing the charge and a copy of the extract decree [*or* document registered for execution in the Books of Council and Session] at (*place of business*) on (*date*). (*Specify that enquiry made and that reasonable grounds exist for believing that the person charged carries on business at the place.*)

* by leaving the charge and a copy of the extract decree [*or* document registered for execution in the Books of Council and Session] at (*registered office or place of business*] on (*date*) in the hands of (*name of person*).

* by leaving [*or* depositing] the charge and a copy of the extract decree [*or* document registered for execution in the Books of Council and Session] at (*registered office, official address or place of business*) on (*date*) in such a way that it was likely to come to the attention of (*name of person charged*). (*Specify how left.*)

I did this in the presence of (*name, occupation and address of witness*).

(*Signed*)

Messenger-at-Arms
(*Address*)

(*Signed*)

Witness

*Delete where not applicable.

Rule 23.2(2)   Form 23.2

Form of motion

PART I   Sheet 1 of .... sheets

(To be completed where motion enrolled by post or fax only)

Name of pursuer/petitioner* ....

Name of first defender/respondent* ....

Name and nature of petition (*e.g.* John Smith's curatory) ....
....

Court case number .... Date of last interlocutor ....

Is case due in court during the next seven days? Yes/No*

(If Yes, state reason)

PART II

Name of firm enrolling motion ....

Agent for .... Ref No. ....

Rutland Exchange No. .... Town ....

Tel. No. .... FAX No. ....

Date of enrolment of motion ....

Has motion been intimated? Yes/No* If yes, give date ....

THE MOTION IS (state terms of motion; if necessary, use a separate sheet):–

REASON FOR MOTION (state reason if reason required) by Practice Note of 10th December 1986; if necessary, use a separate sheet):–

* Delete as appropriate

PART III

MOTION SLIP – General Department only

Name of case† .... v. ....
Name of firm ....

† *e.g.* John Smith v. John Brown.

Rule 23.4(1)   FORM 23.4

Form of opposition to motion

PART I   Sheet 1 of ....sheets

(To be completed where motion opposed by
post or fax only)

Name of pursuer/petitioner* ....
Name of first defender/respondent* ....
Name of firm notifying opposition ....

PART II

Agent for ....   Ref No. ....
Rutland Exchange No. ....   Town ....
Tel. No. ....   FAX No. ....
Date of notice of opposition ....
Date opposition intimated ....
Nature and effective date of enrolment of motion to be opposed ....
....

* Delete as appropriate.

PART II

OPPOSITION SLIP–General Department only

Name of case .... v. ....
Name of firm ....

† *e.g.* John Smith v. John Brown.

Rule 23.5   FORM 23.5

Form of consent to motion

Sheet 1 of .... sheets

Name of pursuer/petitioner* ....

Name of first defender/respondent* ....

Name of firm notifying consent ....

Agent for .... Ref No. ....

Rutland Exchange No. .... Town ....

Tel. No. .... FAX No. ....

Date of notice of consent ....

Date consent intimated ....

Nature and effective date of enrolment of motion consented to ....

....

* Delete as appropriate.

Rule 24.3(2)   FORM 24.3

Form of notice to additional or substitute party

Date: (*date of posting or other method of service*)

To: (*name and address of party*)

TAKE NOTICE

(*Name and address of pursuer*) has raised an action against (*name and address of defender*) in the Court of Session, Edinburgh. By order of the court, dated (*date*), your name has been added [*or* substituted] as a party to the action. A copy of the summons [*or other principal writ or record*] in the action, as amended, is attached. If you intend to deny the claim made in the summons [*or as the case may be*] you must lodge defences [*or* answers] at the Office of Court, Court of Session, 2 Parliament Square, Edinburgh EH1 1RQ within [21] days after the date of service on you of the summons. The date of service is the date stated at the top of this notice unless service has been by post in which case the date of service is the date after that date.

If you do not lodge defences [*or* answers], the court may make an order against you.

IF YOU ARE UNCERTAIN ABOUT THE EFFECT OF THIS NOTICE, you should consult a solicitor, Citizens Advice Bureau or other local advice agency or adviser immediately.

(*Signed*)

Messenger-at-Arms
[*or* Solicitor [*or* Agent] for pursuer]
(*Address*)

Rule 25A.5   [1] FORM 25A.5

Form of intimation to a relevant authority of a devolution issue raised in civil proceedings

To: (*name and address of relevant authority*)

1. You are given notice that an action has been raised in the Court of Session which includes a conclusion or prayer in respect of a devolution issue. A copy of the pleadings in the case (*as adjusted*) is enclosed.

2. If you wish to take part as a party to the proceedings in so far as they relate to a devolution issue you must lodge with the Deputy Principal Clerk of Session, Court of Session, 2 Parliament Square, Edinburgh EH1 1RQ a notice in writing stating that you intend to take part as a party in the proceedings. The notice must be lodged within 14 days of (*insert date on which intimation was given*).

Date (*insert date*)

                                            (*Signed*)

                                            Solicitor for
                                            Pursuer/Defender/Petitioner/Respondent

[1] Form 25A.5 inserted by S.I. 1999 No. 1345.

Rule 25A.12   [1] FORM 25A.12

Form of intimation to a relevant authority that the court is considering making an order under [section 102 of the Scotland Act 1998/section 81 of the Northern Ireland Act 1998/ section 110 of the Government of Wales Act 1998]

To: (*name and address of relevant authority*)

1. You are given notice that in an action raised in the Court of Session, the court has decided [that an Act/provision of an Act of the Scottish Parliament is not within the legislative competence of the Parliament] [a member of the Scottish Executive does not have the power to make, confirm or approve a provision of subordinate legislation he has purported to make, confirm or approve]. A copy of the relevant opinion/interlocutor is enclosed.

2. The court is considering whether to make an order [removing or limiting the retrospective effect of the decision/suspending the effect of the decision to allow the defect to be corrected].

3. If you wish to take part as a party to the proceedings so far as they relate to the making of the order mentioned in paragraph 2 you must lodge with the Deputy Principal Clerk of Session, Court of Session, 2 Parliament Square, Edinburgh EH1 1RQ a notice in writing stating that you intend to take part as a party in the proceedings. The notice must be lodged within 7 days of (*date on which intimation was given*).

Date (*insert date*)

                                            (*Signed*)

                                            Deputy Principal Clerk of Session.

[1] Form 25A.12 inserted by S.I. 1999 No. 1345.

Rule 26.1(1)   [1] FORM 26.1–A

Form of third party notice

THIRD PARTY NOTICE

in the cause

[A.B.] (*designation and address*), Pursuer

and

[C.D.] (*designation and address*), Defender

and

[E.F.] (*designation and address*), Third Party

Date: (*date of posting or other method of service*)

To: (*name and address of [E.F.]*)

TAKE NOTICE

(*Name and address of pursuer*), pursuer, has raised an action against (*name and address of defender*), defender, in the Court of Session, Edinburgh. In the action the pursuer claims from the defender (*amount*) as damages for (*short explanation of basis of claim*) [*or as the case may be*]. A copy of the summons and defence [*or* record] in the action is attached.

The defender admits [*or* denies] liability to the pursuer. The defender claims that [if he is liable to the pursuer] you are obliged to relieve him [partially] of his liability. He claims this because (*short explanation of basis of right of contribution, relief or indemnity*). This is explained more fully in the attached defences [*or* record].

or

The defender denies liability for the claim made by the pursuer. He states that you alone [*or* you along with *names and addresses*] are liable to the pursuer for that claim. This is explained more fully in the attached defences [*or* record].

or

The defender denies liability for the claim made by the pursuer [*or* admits liability in part for the claim made by the pursuer, but disputes the amount of that claim]. He maintains, however, that if he is liable to the pursuers [for any amount], you are jointly liable [*or* jointly and severally liable] with him to the pursuer. This is explained more fully in the attached defences [*or* record].

(*or otherwise as the case may be*)

Accordingly, on (*date*) [Lord (*name*) in] the Court of Session ordered this notice to be served on you. If you dispute the claim by the pursuer against the defender, or the defender's claim against you, you must lodge answers at the Office of Court, 2 Parliament Square, Edinburgh EH1 1RQ. You must do so within [21] days after the date of service on you of this notice. The date of service is the date stated at the top of this notice unless service has been by post in which case the date of service is the day after that date.

If you do not lodge answers, the court may make an order against you.

IF YOU ARE UNCERTAIN ABOUT THE EFFECT OF THIS NOTICE, you should consult a solicitor, Citizens Advice Bureau or other local advice agency or adviser immediately.

(*Signed*)

Messenger-at-Arms
[*or* Solicitor [*or* Agent] for defender]
(*Address*)

---

[1] Form 26.1–A amended by S.I. 1994 No. 2901 (clerical error).

Rule 26.1(2)   FORM 26.1–B

Form of third party notice by pursuer

THIRD PARTY NOTICE BY PURSUER

in the cause

[A.B.] (*designation and address*), Pursuer

and

[C.D.] (*designation and address*), Defender

and

[E.F.] (*designation and address*), Third Party

Date: (*date of posting or other method of service*)

To: (*name and address of* [E.F.])

TAKE NOTICE

(*Name and address of pursuer*), pursuer, has raised an action against (*name and address of defender*), defender, in the Court of Session, Edinburgh. In the action the pursuer claims from the defender (*amount*) as damages for (*short explanation of basis of claim*) [*or as the case may be*]. The defender has made a counterclaim against the pursuer for (*amount*) as damages for (*short explanation of basis of counterclaim*) [*or as the case may be*]. A copy of the answers, defences and counterclaim [*or* record] in the action is attached.

The pursuer admits [*or* denies] liability to the defender for the counterclaim. However, the pursuer claims that [if he is liable to the defender] you are obliged to relieve him [partially] of his liability. He claims this because (*short explanation of basis of right of contribution, relief or indemnity*). This is explained more fully in the attached defences [*or* record].

[*or otherwise as the case may be*]

Accordingly, on (*date*) [Lord (*name*) in] the Court of Session ordered this notice to be served on you. If you dispute the defender's claim against the pursuer, or the pursuer's claim against you, you must lodge answers at the Office of Court, 2 Parliament Square, Edinburgh EH1 1RQ. You must do so within [21] days after the date of service on you of this notice. The date of service is the date stated at the top of this notice unless service has been by post in which case the date of service is the day after that date.

If you do not lodge answers, the court may make an order against you.

IF YOU ARE UNCERTAIN ABOUT THE EFFECT OF THIS NOTICE, you should consult a solicitor, Citizens Advice Bureau or other local advice agency or adviser immediately.

(*Signed*)

Messenger-at-Arms
[*or* Solicitor [*or* Agent] for pursuer]
(*Address*)

Rule 26.1(2)   FORM 26.1–C

Form of third party notice by third party

THIRD PARTY NOTICE BY THIRD PARTY

in the cause

[A.B.] (*designation and address*), Pursuer

and

[C.D.] (*designation and address*), Defender

and

[E.F.] (*designation and address*), Third Party

Date: (*date of posting or other method of service*)

To: (*name and address of* [*E.F.*])

TAKE NOTICE

(*Name and address of pursuer*), pursuer, has raised an action against (*name and address of defender*), defender, in the Court of Session, Edinburgh. In the action the pursuer claims from the defender (*amount*) as damages for (*short explanation of basis of claim*) [*or as the case may be*]. The defender has made a counterclaim against the pursuer for (*amount*) as damages for (*short explanation of basis of counterclaim*) [*or as the case may be*].

The defender [*or pursuer*] claims that [E.F.] is obliged to relieve him [partially] of his liability (if any) to the pursuer [*or the defender*] [*or as the case may be*]. [E.F.] admits [*or denies*] liability to do so. [E.F.], however, claims that [if he is liable to the defender [*or the pursuer*] you are obliged to relieve him [partially] of his liability. He claims this because (*short explanation of basis of right of contribution, relief or indemnity*) [*or as the case may be*].

This is explained more fully in the attached answers, defences [and counterclaim] and answers [*or record*].

Accordingly, on (*date*) [Lord (*name*) in] the Court of Session ordered this notice to be served on you. If you dispute the claim of the pursuer against the defender [*or the counterclaim of the defender against the pursuer*] [*or* [E.F.'s] liability to relieve [*or as the case may be*] the defender [*or the pursuer*]] [*or* [E.F.'s] claim against you], you must lodge answers at the Office of Court, 2 Parliament Square, Edinburgh EH1 1RQ. You must do so within [21] days after the date of service on you of this notice. The date of service is the date stated at the top of this notice unless service has been by post in which case the date of service is the day after that date.

If you do not lodge answers, the court may make an order against you.

IF YOU ARE UNCERTAIN ABOUT THE EFFECT OF THIS NOTICE, you should consult a solicitor, Citizens Advice Bureau or other local advice agency or adviser immediately.

(*Signed*)

Messenger-at-Arms
[*or* Solicitor [*or* Agent] for pursuer]
(*Address*)

Form of notice of intimation to party whose agent has withdrawn

Cause Reference No.   (*insert reference*)

IN THE COURT OF SESSION

in the cause

[A.B.] (*designation and address*)

Pursuer [*or* Petitioner]

against

[C.D.] (*designation and address*)

Defender [*or* Respondent]

Date: (*date of posting or other method of service*)

To: (*name and address of party whose agent has withdrawn*)

TAKE NOTICE

The court has been informed that your solicitor [*or* agent] has withdrawn from acting on your behalf in this cause.

In accordance with the interlocutor pronounced by [Lord (*name*) in] the Court of Session on (*date*) you must inform the Deputy Principal Clerk of Session within 14 days after the service of this notice whether you intend to insist in your action [*or* defences *or as the case may be*]. The date of service is the date stated at the top of this notice unless service has been by post in which case the date of service is the day after that date.

You should contact the Deputy Principal Clerk immediately to inform him what you intend to do. You must write to him at the Court of Session, 2 Parliament Square, Edinburgh EH1 1RQ quoting the name of the cause and the cause reference number at the top of this notice. You should also use the form attached to this notice.

If you do not write to the Deputy Principal Clerk and inform him what you intend to do the court may make an order or a finding or both against you as mentioned in the interlocutor referred to above.

IF YOU ARE UNCERTAIN ABOUT THE EFFECT OF THIS NOTICE, you should consult a solicitor, Citizens Advice Bureau or other local advice agency or adviser immediately.

(*Signed*)

Solicitor [*or* Agent]
(*Address*)

Appendix

(Form to be sent with Form 30.2)

Cause Reference No.

IN THE COURT OF SESSION

in the cause

[A.B.] *(designation and address)*

Pursuer [*or* Petitioner]

against

[C.D.] *(designation and address)*

Defender [*or* Respondent]

To the Deputy Principal Clerk of Session

* I am insisting * in the above cause/* in my defences to the above cause/* in my answers to the above cause. My new solicitor's name and address is:—

* I am NOT insisting in the above cause/* in my defences to the above cause/* in my answers to the above cause.

(Signed)

Pursuer*/Petitioner*/Defender*/Respondent*

* Delete whatever is not applicable.

This form is to be returned to the Deputy Principal Clerk of Session, 2 Parliament Square, Edinburgh EH1 1RQ.

Release 44: 28 April 1997

Rule 33.12(4) FORM 33.12

Form of book to be kept by the Accountant of Court under section 4 of the Court of Session Consignations (Scotland) Act 1895

No.	Date of Consignation.	By whom and Cause in which Consignation made.	Office mark.	Bank.	Date of Lodging in Bank.	Sum Consigned.	Deposits withdrawn from Bank.			Date of Payment.	Signature of Persons receiving Payment.	Date of Warrant.
							Principal.	Interest.	Total.			

Rule 35.3(1) [1] FORM 35.3–A

Form of order of court and certificate in optional procedure for recovery of documents

ORDER BY THE COURT OF SESSION

In the Cause (Cause Reference No.   )

in which

[A.B.] *(designation and address)*

Pursuer [*or* Petitioner]

against

[C.D.] *(designation and address)*

Defender [*or* Respondent]

Date: *(date of posting or other method of service)*

To: *(name and address of party or parties or named third party haver, from whom the documents are sought to be recovered)*

1. You are hereby required to produce to the agent for the Pursuer [*or as the case may be*], *(name and address of agents)* **within seven days** of the service on you of this Order—

    (a) this Order which must be produced intact;

    (b) the certificate below duly dated and signed by you; and

    (c) all documents in your possession falling within the enclosed specification and a list or inventory of such documents signed by you relating to this Order and your certificate.

2. Subject to note (1) below, you may produce these documents either by sending them by registered post or by the first class recorded delivery service or registered postal packet, or by hand to the address above.

(Signature and business address of the agent for the party in whose favour commission and diligence has been granted.)

NOTES

    (1) If you claim that any of the documents produced by you are **confidential**, you must still produce such documents but may place them in a separate sealed packet by themselves, marked "confidential". In that event they should NOT be sent to the address above, they must be delivered or sent by post as above provided to the **Deputy Principal Clerk of Session, 2 Parliament Square, Edinburgh, EH1 1RQ**.

(2) The documents will be considered by the parties to the action and they may or may not be lodged in the court process. A written receipt will be given or sent to you by the party recovering the documents, who may thereafter allow them to be inspected by the other parties. The party in whose possession the documents are will be responsible for their safekeeping.

(3) Parties are obliged by rules of court to return the documents to you when their purpose with the documents is finished. If they do not do so, you will be entitled to apply to the court, under rule 35.3(9) of the Rules of the Court of Session 1994, for an order to have this done and you may apply for an award of the expenses incurred in doing so. Further information about this can be obtained from the General Department, Court of Session, 2 Parliament Square, Edinburgh EH1 1RQ (Tel. 0131–225 2595).

Certificate

(*Date*)

I hereby certify with reference to the above order of the Court of Session in the cause (*cause reference number*) and the enclosed specification of documents, served on me and marked respectively X and Y:—

(1) That the documents which are produced and which are listed in the enclosed inventory signed by me and marked Z, are all the documents in my possession falling within the specification.

or

That I have no documents in my possession falling within the specification.

(2) That, to the best of my knowledge and belief, there are in existence other documents falling within the specification, but not in my possession. These documents are as follows:— (*describe them by reference to the descriptions of documents in the specification*). They were last seen by me on or about (*date*), at (*place*), in the hands of (*name and address of the person*).

or

That I know of the existence of no documents in the possession of any person, other than myself, which fall within the specification.

(*Signed*)

(*Name and address*)

---

[1] Form 35.3 substituted by S.I. 1996 No. 2168.

Rule 35.3(4)(a)   [1] FORM 35.3–B

Form of intimation to Deputy Principal Clerk of Session and other parties of documents recovered under optional procedure

In the Cause (Cause Reference No.   )

[A.B.] (*designation and address*)

Pursuer [*or* Petitioner]

against

[C.D.] (*designation and address*)

Defender [*or* Respondent]

The undernoted document[s] was [were] recovered from (*name, and address of haver*) on (*date of receipt*) under order of the court dated (*date of interlocutor authorising commission and diligence*) in so far as it relates to the specification of documents No.   of Process.

Document[s] received:— (*identify each*).

(*Signature, name and business address of the agent for the party in whose favour commission and diligence has been granted*)

Date:

---

[1] Form 35.3–B inserted by S.I. 1996 No. 2168.

Rule 35.3(4)(b)   [1] Form 35.3–C

Form of receipt to haver for documents recovered under optional procedure

In the Cause (Cause Reference No.   )

[A.B.] (*designation and address*)

Pursuer [*or* Petitioner]

against

[C.D.] (*designation and address*)

Defender [*or* Respondent]

The document[s] noted below, being recovered by order of the Court of Session dated (*date of interlocutor authorising commission and diligence*) in so far as it relates to the specification of documents No.   of Process, have been recovered from (*name and address of haver*).

Document[s] received:— (*identify each*).

> (*Signature, name and business address of the agent for the party in whose favour commission and diligence has been granted*)

Date:

_____

[1] Form 35.3–C inserted by S.I. 1996 No. 2168.

Rule 35.3(6)(b)   [1] Form 35.3–D

Form of receipt from party other than party who originally recovered documents under optional procedure

In the Cause (Cause Reference No.   )

[A.B.] (*designation and address*)

Pursuer [*or* Petitioner]

against

[C.D.] (*designation and address*)

Defender [*or* Respondent]

I acknowledge receipt of the undernoted document[s] received from you and recovered under order of the Court of Session dated (*date of interlocutor authorising commission and diligence*).

Documents received:— (*identify each*).

> (*Signature, name and business address of the agent for the party receiving documents*)

Date:

_____

[1] Form 35.3–D inserted by S.I. 1996 No. 2168.

Rule 35.3A(3)   [1] FORM 35.3A–A

Form of order of court and certificate in optional procedure for recovery of documents— party litigant cases

ORDER BY THE COURT OF SESSION

In the Cause (Cause Reference No.   )

[A.B.] (*designation and address*)

Pursuer [*or* Petitioner]

against

[C.D.] (*designation and address*)

Defender [*or* Respondent]

Date: (*date of posting or other method of service*)

To: (*name and address of party or parties or named third party haver, from whom the documents are sought to be recovered*)

You are hereby required to produce to the Deputy Principal Clerk of Session, 2 Parliament Square, Edinburgh EH1 1RQ **within seven days** of the date of service on you of this Order—
- (a) this Order which must be produced intact;
- (b) the certificate below duly dated and signed by you; and
- (c) all documents in your possession falling within the enclosed specification and a list or inventory of such documents signed by you relating to this Order and your certificate.

You may produce these documents either by lodging them at the Office of the Court of Session at the address below or by sending them by registered post or by the first class recorded delivery service or registered postal packet, addressed to the **Deputy Principal Clerk of Session, 2 Parliament Square, Edinburgh EH1 1RQ.**

(*Signature, name and business
address of the agent for the
party in whose favour commission and
diligence has been granted*)

NOTES

(1) If you claim that any of the documents produced by you are **confidential**, you must still produce such documents but may place them in a separate sealed packet by themselves, marked "confidential".

(2) The documents will be considered by the parties to the action and they may or may not be lodged in the court process. If they are not so lodged they will be returned to you by the Deputy Principal Clerk. The party in whose possession the documents are will be responsible for their safekeeping.

(3) Parties are obliged by rules of court to return the documents to you when their purpose with the documents is finished. If they do not do so, you will be entitled to apply to the court, under rule 35.3A(11) of the Rules of the Court of Session 1994 for an order to have this done and you may apply for an award of the expenses incurred in doing so. Further information about this can be obtained from the General Department, Court of Session, 2 Parliament Square, Edinburgh EH1 1RQ (Tel. 0131–225 2595).

Certificate

(*Date*)

I hereby certify with reference to the above order of the Court of Session in the cause (*cause reference number*) and the enclosed specification of documents, served on me and marked respectively X and Y:—

(1) That the documents which are produced and which are listed in the enclosed inventory signed by me and marked Z, are all the documents in my possession falling within the specification.

or

That I have no documents in my possession falling within the specification.

(2) That, to the best of my knowledge and belief, there are in existence other documents falling within the specification, but not in my possession. These documents are as follows:— (*describe them by reference to the descriptions of documents in the specification*). They were last seen by me on or about (*date*), at (*place*), in the hands of (*name and address of the person*).

or

That I know of the existence of no documents in the possession of any person, other than myself, which fall within the specification.

(*Signed*)

(*Name and address*)

---

[1] Form 35.3A–A inserted by S.I. 1996 No. 2168.

Rule 35.4(3)   [1] FORM 35.4–A

Form of citation of haver to commission for recovery of documents

CITATION OF HAVER

Date: (*date of posting or other method of service*)

To: (*name and address of haver*)

(*Name and address of pursuer*) has raised an action against (*name and address of defender*) [*or* has presented a petition*] in the Court of Session, Edinburgh. In the cause, (*name of party seeking to execute commission and diligence*) applied for a commission and diligence for the recovery of documents described in the attached specification. [A copy of the pleadings in the action is also attached.] On (*date of order*) [Lord (*name*) in] the Court of Session granted the application. The commission has been fixed before (*name of commissioner*) for (*date*) at (*time*). It will take place at (*place*).

By virtue of the order mentioned above, I hereby require you to attend the commission and to produce all documents which are in your possession and which fall within the specification and, if you are aware of any other documents within the specification, to declare where they may be.

IF YOU DO NOT ATTEND, A WARRANT MAY BE GRANTED FOR YOUR ARREST.

IF YOU ARE UNCERTAIN ABOUT THE EFFECT OF THIS NOTICE, you should consult a solicitor, Citizens Advice Bureau or other local advice agency or adviser immediately.

(*Signed*)

Messenger-at-Arms
[or Solicitor [*or* Agent] for (*name of party seeking to execute commission and diligence*)]
(*Address*)

---

[1] Form 35.4–A amended by S.I. 1994 No. 2901 (minor correction).

Appendix

Form of certificate of citation of haver to appear at commission

CERTIFICATE OF CITATION OF HAVER

I, (*name and designation*), certify that I cited (*name of haver*) to appear at a commission for the recovery of documents by posting a citation in Form 35.4–A to him [*or* her] between

[THE NEXT PAGE IS C 701]

(*time*) and (*time*) on (*date*) at (*name of post office*) post office in a registered envelope [*or* recorded delivery envelope] addressed as follows:— (*address*). The post office receipt [*or* certificate of posting*] is attached to this certificate.

(*Signed*)

Messenger-at-Arms
[*or* Solicitor [*or* Agent] for pursuer
[*or other party*]]
(*Address*)

Rule 35.4(4)(b)   FORM 35.4–C

Form of certificate of citation of haver personally to appear at commission

CERTIFICATE OF CITATION PERSONALLY

I, (*name*), Messenger-at-Arms, certify that, on the authority of the interlocutor of the Court of Session (*date*), I cited (*name of haver*) to appear at the commission for the recovery of documents personally by leaving the citation in Form 35.4–A with him [*or* her] at (*place*) on (*date*).

I did this in the presence of (*name, occupation and address of witness*).

(*Signed*)

Messenger-at-Arms
(*Address*)

(*Signed*)

Witness

Rule 35.4(8)(b) and 35.11(8)(b)   FORM 35.4–D

Form of oath for haver or witness at commission

I swear by Almighty God that I will tell the truth, the whole truth and nothing but the truth.

Rule 35.4(8)(b) and 35.11(8)(b)   FORM 35.4–E

Form of affirmation for haver or witness at commission

I solemnly, sincerely and truly declare and affirm that I will tell the truth, the whole truth and nothing but the truth.

Rule 35.11(5)   FORM 35.11–A

Form of citation of witness to commission to take his evidence

CITATION OF WITNESS

Date: (*date of posting or other method of service*)

To: (*name and address of witness*)

(*Name and address of pursuer or as the case may be*) has raised an action against (*name and address of defender*) [*or* has presented a petition] in the Court of Session, Edinburgh. In the cause, (*name of party seeking to execute commission to take the evidence of the witness*) applied for a commission to take your evidence. On (*date of order*) [Lord (*name*) in] the Court of Session granted the application. The commission has been fixed before (*name of commissioner*) for (*date*) at (*time*). It will take place at (*place*).

By virtue of the order mentioned above, I hereby require you to attend the commission to give evidence.

IF YOU DO NOT ATTEND, A WARRANT MAY BE GRANTED FOR YOUR ARREST.

(*Signed*)

Messenger-at-Arms
[*or* Solicitor [*or* Agent] for (*name of party seeking to execute commission*)]
(*Address*)

Rule 35.11(6)(a)   FORM 35.11–B

Form of certificate of citation of witness to appear at commission

CERTIFICATE OF CITATION OF WITNESS

I, (*name and designation*), certify that I cited (*name of witness*) to appear to give evidence at a commission by posting a citation in Form 35.11–A to him [*or* her] between (*time*) and (*time*) on (*date*) at (*name of post office*) post office in a registered envelope [*or* recorded delivery envelope] addressed as follows:— (*address*). The post office receipt [*or* certificate of posting] is attached to this certificate.

(*Signed*)

Messenger-at-Arms
[*or* Solicitor [*or* Agent] for pursuer
[*or* other party]]
(*Address*)

Rule 35.11(6)(b)   FORM 35.11–C

Form of certificate of citation of witness personally at commission to give evidence

CERTIFICATE OF CITATION PERSONALLY

I, (*name*), Messenger-at-Arms, certify that, on the authority of the interlocutor of the Court of Session (*date*), I cited (*name of witness*) to appear to give evidence at a commission personally by leaving the citation in Form 35.11–A with him [*or* her] at (*place*) on (*date*).

I did this in the presence of (*name, occupation and address of witness*).

(*Signed*)

Messenger-at-Arms
(*Address*)

(*Signed*)

Witness

Rule 35.15(3)   [1] Form 35.15–A

Form of minute for letter of request

IN THE COURT OF SESSION

MINUTE

for

[A.B.] (*designation and address*)

in the cause [*or* in the petition of]

[A.B.] (*designation and address*), Pursuer [*or* Petitioner]

against

[C.D.] (*designation and address*), Defender [*or* Respondent]

(*Name of counsel or other person having a right of audience*) for the Minuter states to the court that the evidence specified in the proposed letter of request lodged with this Minute is required for the purpose of this cause and prays the court to issue a letter of request in terms of the proposed letter of request to (*specify the court or tribunal having power to obtain evidence*) to obtain the evidence so specified.

(*Signed by counsel or other person having a right of audience*)

————————

[1] Form 35.15–A amended by S.I. 1997 No. 1050 (minor amendment, effective 6th April 1997).

Rule 35.15(3)   Form 35.15–B

Form of letter of request

(*Items to be included in all letters of request*)

1. Sender   (*identity & address*) ....
   ....
   ....

2. Central authority of the   (*identity & address*) ....
   ....

3. Person to whom the executed request is   (*identity & address*) ....
   to be returned   ....
   ....

4. The undersigned applicant has the
   honour to submit the following request:

5. a. Requesting judicial authority   (*identity & address*) ....
   ....
   ....

   b. To the competent authority   (*the requested State*) ....
   ....

6. Names and addresses of the parties and
   their representatives

   a. Pursuer   ....
   ....

   b. Defender   ....
   ....

   c. Other parties   ....
   ....

7. Nature and purpose of the proceedings   ....
   and summary of the facts   ....
   ....

8. Evidence to be obtained or other judicial act to be performed

....
....
....

(Items to be completed where applicable)

9. Identity and address of any person to be examined

....
....

10. Questions to be put to the persons to be examined or statement of the subject matter about which they are to be examined

[*or see attached list*] ....
....
....
....

11. Documents or other property to be inspected

(specify whether it is to be produced, copied, valued, etc.) ....
....
....

12. Any requirement that the evidence be given on oath or affirmation and any special form be used

(in the event that the evidence cannot be taken in the manner requested, specify whether it is to be taken in such manner as provided by local law for the formal taking of evidence) ....
....
....

13. Special methods or procedure to be followed

....
....

14. Request for notification of the time and place for the execution of the request and identity and address of any person to be notified

....
....
....

15. Request for attendance or participation of judicial personnel of the requesting authority at the execution of the letter of request

....

16. Specification of privilege or duty to refuse to give evidence under the law of the State of origin

....
....
....

17. The fees and expenses incurred will be borne by

(identity & address) ....
....
....

(Items to be included in all letters of request)

18. Date of request, signature and seal of the requesting authority

....
....
....

Rule 35.16(3)   [1] FORM 35.16–A

Form of minute for request to take evidence

IN THE COURT OF SESSION

MINUTE

for

[A.B.] (*or* [C.D.]) (*designation and address*)

in the cause [*or* in the petition of]

[A.B.] (*designation and address*), Pursuer [*or* Petitioner]

against

[C.D.] (*designation and address*), Defender [*or* Respondent]

(*Name of counsel or other person having a right of audience*) for the Minuter states to the court that the evidence specified in the proposed request lodged with this Minute is required for the purpose of this cause and prays the court to issue a request in terms of the proposed request to (*specify the court or tribunal having power to obtain evidence*) to obtain the evidence so specified.

(*Signed by counsel or other person having a right of audience*)

Rule 35.16(8)   FORM 35.16–B

Form of notice to person in another Member State of intention to seek to take direct evidence

Date: (*date of posting or other method of intimation*)

To: (*name and address of person to give evidence*)

You are a witness for the pursuer [*or* petitioner] [*or* defender] [*or* respondent] in the case raised by [*or* to be raised by] (*name*) against (*name*).

The pursuer [*or* petitioner] [*or* defender] [*or* respondent] has requested that evidence be taken directly from you by means of (*specify the communications technology to be used*) from the (*name of the requested court*) to the Court of Session.

This evidence can only be taken directly from you if you agree to give evidence in this way. If you do not agree to give evidence directly the pursuer [*or* petitioner] [*or* defender] [*or* respondent] may apply for a request to have evidence taken from you in (*name of requested court*) without the means of (*specify the communications technology*).

Please return the enclosed response form to the Deputy Principal Clerk of Session within 14 days after the date of this notice stated at the top of this notice.

Rule 35.16(8)   FORM 35.16–C

Form of response form to be completed and returned to requesting court by witness

WITNESS RESPONSE FORM

To: Deputy Principal Clerk of Session, Court of Session, Parliament House, Edinburgh, EH1 1RQ

From: (*name to be printed by person serving the notice*)

Date: (*date*)

I, (*name and address of witness to be completed by person serving the notice*), have received the notice seeking my agreement to have evidence taken directly from me as a witness for the pursuer [*or* petitioner] [*or* defender] [*or* respondent] in the Court of Session case raised by (*or* to be raised by) (*name of pursuer or petitioner*) against (*name of defender or respondent*) at (*person sending notice to specify the court*) by means of (*person serving notice to specify communications technology to be used*).

I confirm that I agree to voluntarily attend at (*person sending notice to specify the court*) to have evidence taken directly from me in this case.*

I confirm that I do not agree to voluntarily attend at (*person sending notice to specify the court*) to have evidence taken directly from me in this case.*

(**Please delete as appropriate*)

(*Signature of witness*)

---

[1] Inserted by SSI 2004/514, Art.2(8) (effective November 30, 2004).

Form of citation of witness to proof or jury trial

Date: (*insert date of service of citation*)

(*Name and address of pursuer or as the case may be*) has raised an action against (*name and address of defender*) [*or* has presented a petition] in the Court of Session, Edinburgh.

A proof [*or* jury trial] has been fixed. It will commence on (*date*) at (*time*) at the Court of Session, Parliament Square, Edinburgh. By virtue of an order made by [Lord (*name*) in] the Court of Session on (*date*), I, (*name*), Solicitor [*or* Agent] for (*name of party citing witness*) [*or* Messenger-at-Arms] on the instructions of (*name of agent on whose behalf citation executed*) hereby require you to attend the proof [*or* jury trial] as a witness for the pursuer [*or as the case may be*].

You must appear at the proof [*or* jury trial] on the date and at the time mentioned above and be prepared to give evidence at any time during the continuation of the proof [*or* jury trial].

[NEXT TEXT PAGE IS C 705]

IF YOU DO NOT APPEAR, A WARRANT MAY BE GRANTED FOR YOUR ARREST.

(*Signed*)

Messenger-at-Arms
[*or* Solicitor [*or* Agent] for (*name of party citing witness*)]
(*Address*)

Please read the notes attached and bring this citation with you when you come to the court.

NOTES

1. What must I do?

The attached document requires you to appear as a witness in the case mentioned in it.

It obliges you to attend at the Court of Session at the time and on the date mentioned. The hearing will start on that date and may continue on the following days. Because it is difficult to estimate how long it will take to hear the evidence of other witnesses, you cannot be given a precise time when you will be called to give evidence. The solicitor for the party who has called you as a witness may, however, be able to arrange to give you some indication of when you are likely to be required.

You should not bring a child under the age of 14 years with you to court unless he or she is to give evidence. You should make arrangements to have the child looked after while you are at the court.

2. Where is the court?

The Court of Session is behind St. Giles Cathedral, High Street, Edinburgh. Parking in central Edinburgh can be very difficult. If you are coming by car you should allow plenty of time to find a parking space.

3. What do I do when I get to court?

When you arrive at the Court of Session, you should enter by the main door, Door 11. You should inform the receptionist of the name of the case. You will be told where you should go. There are signs throughout the building indicating the routes and various courts and other facilities.

You should wait there until you are contacted by the solicitor for the party who cited you.

4. How long will I have to wait?

It is not possible to say how long you will require to wait before being asked to give evidence. The representative of the party who cited you will keep you advised of the situation; but you should note that you may have to stay all day. You may wish to bring a newspaper or magazine to read while you wait.

The court usually sits between 10am and 4pm, rising for lunch normally between 1pm and 2pm. There are occasions, however, when the court may sit after 4pm or may rise later for lunch, in order, for example, to complete an important part of the evidence. You will be advised when you may go for lunch and when you must return.

5. What facilities are available?

The court's restaurant is open between 9.00am and 3.00pm, and provides light refreshments as well as lunches. You should speak to the solicitor who cited you about the arrangements for going to the restaurant. You should not go to the restaurant without telling the representative of the party who cited you. Newspapers are also available for purchase there.

There are toilets in witness rooms and other locations throughout the building. If there is not a toilet in your immediate vicinity, a security guard will direct you to the nearest one.

6. What will happen when I am called to give evidence?

A court officer (the macer) will call you into court when you are to give evidence. You will give evidence from a witness box near the front of the courtroom. The judge will ask you to repeat the oath. If you wish to affirm instead of taking the oath, it is a good idea to tell the macer or the solicitor for the party who has called you in advance.

You will be asked questions by the advocate representing the party who has called you as a witness. Then the advocate or advocates for the other party or parties may ask you questions. Finally, the first advocate will have an opportunity to ask you further questions.

You must answer all the questions truthfully and honestly to the best of your ability.

A witness normally gives evidence standing in the witness box. If you find it difficult to stand for a long period, you should ask if you may sit down.

7. Who will be in court?

The judge will be seated on the bench. The shorthand writer or stenographer will be seated between the judge and you. The clerk of court sits at a table below the judge. The advocates will be sitting facing the judge, and solicitors, parties and their representatives will be sitting behind the advocates. The Press and members of the public may also be in court. If the case is tried by a jury, there will be twelve jurors sitting in a jury box opposite you.

8. Will I be compensated?

You do not get paid for giving evidence. You are entitled to some payment for out-of-pocket travelling and subsistence expenses. You should keep any receipts for these expenses and give them to the representative of the party who has called you. If you lose earnings, or need to pay someone else to do your job, you can be paid some compensation, subject to certain limits. These payments are the responsibility of the party who has called you as a witness and his representative. It is *not* the responsibility of the court.

9. If I wish to complain, how do I do so?

There are leaflets available at the reception desk at the entrance which contain the complaints procedures in relation to the services provided by (1) court staff, (2) solicitors and (3) the legal profession generally. If you have a complaint, please bring it to the attention of the appropriate person referred to in the leaflet.

---

[1] Form 36.2–A amended by S.I. 1994 No. 2901.

Rule 36.2(3)(*a*)   Form 36.2–B

Form of certificate of citation of witness to appear at proof or jury trial

CERTIFICATE OF CITATION OF WITNESS

I, (*name and designation*), certify that I cited (*name of witness*) to appear at the proof [*or* jury trial] on (*date*) by posting a citation in Form 36.2–A to him [*or* her] between (*time*) and (*time*) on (*date*) at (*name of post office*) post office in a registered envelope [*or* recorded delivery envelope] addressed as follows:—(*address*). The post office receipt [*or* certificate of posting] is attached to this certificate.

(*Signed*)

Messenger-at-Arms
[*or* Solicitor [*or* Agent] for pursuer
[*or other party*]]
(*Address*)

And YOU the said sheriff clerk or your...... from the List, with a copy of the list of the citation of the jurors to the .... Principal Clerk of Session, 2 Parliament Square, Edinburgh.

Rule 36.2(3)(b)   FORM 36.2–C

Form of certificate of citation of witness personally at proof or jury trial

CERTIFICATE OF CITATION PERSONALLY

I, (*name*), Messenger-at-Arms, certify that, on the authority of the interlocutor of the Court of Session (*date*), I cited (*name of witness*) to appear at the proof [*or* jury trial] on (*date*) personally by leaving the citation in Form 36.2–A with him [*or* her] at (*place*) on (*date*).

I did this in the presence of (*name, occupation and address of witness*).

(*Signed*)

Messenger-at-Arms
(*Address*)

(*Signed*)

Witness

Rule 36.10   FORM 36.10–A

Form of oath for witness

I swear by Almighty God that I will tell the truth, the whole truth and nothing but the truth.

Rule 36.10   FORM 36.10–B

Form of affirmation for witness

I solemnly, sincerely and truly declare and affirm that I will tell the truth, the whole truth and nothing but the truth.

Rule 37.2(3)   [1] FORM 37.2–A

Form of jury precept

JURY PRECEPT

_____

THE RIGHT HONOURABLE THE LORDS OF COUNCIL AND SESSION

To the Sheriff Principal and Sheriffs of Lothian and Borders, and to the sheriff clerk, Edinburgh or his deputes:

YOU are hereby authorised and required in terms of the statutes relating to the summoning of jurors to attach hereto a list of thirty six names and addresses of equal numbers of men and women, qualified to serve as jurors, living within the sheriff court districts of Edinburgh, Linlithgow and Haddington,

and YOU the said sheriff clerk or your depute shall cite the jurors to compear within the Parliament House at Edinburgh on the day of   at ten o'clock forenoon, with continuation of days, to try the matters at issue in the cause

then to be tried in the Court of Session;

Release 40: 1 July 1996

And YOU the said sheriff clerk or your depute shall return the List, with a certificate under your hand of the citation of the jurors, to the Deputy Principal Clerk of Session, 2 Parliament Square, Edinburgh EH1 1RQ, on or before the   day of

                                                                    Assistant Clerk of Session
                                                                                (*Date*)

TO The SHERIFF PRINCIPAL and
    Sheriffs of Lothian and Borders

                and

The SHERIFF CLERK, Edinburgh

---

[1] Form 37.2–A amended by S.I. 1996 No. 1756 (effective 5th August 1996).

Rule 37.2(5)   [1] FORM 37.2–B

[Form of citation of juror]

COURT OF SESSION JUROR'S CITATION

Citation Number:Date:

To:Time:

Place:

Name of case:

You are cited to attend personally on the date and at the time and place stated above, and on such succeeding days as may be necessary to serve, if required, as a juror. If you fail to attend, you will be liable to the penalty prescribed by Law.

Sheriff Clerk Depute

Please read the enclosed leaflets carefully BEFORE attending court for selection.

Expenses: Claims for loss of earnings and/or expenses should be made at the end of your jury service. You will be provided with an envelope for return of the completed form, and payment will be made by crossed cheque to your home address, seven to ten days from receipt of the claim.

YOU MUST BRING THIS CITATION WITH YOU TO COURT

If you wish to apply for exemption or excusal from jury service, please complete this form and return it as soon as possible to: **Deputy Principal Clerk of Session, Court of Session, 2 Parliament Square, Edinburgh EH1 1RQ.**

DECLARATION: *Please state why you are applying for exemption or excusal from jury service:*

[ ] **Age:**   I am .... years of age. My date of birth is ....

[ ] **Occupation:** I am employed as .... and therefore statutorily exempt from service.

[ ] **Medical Condition:**   I am medically unfit for jury service and enclose a medical certificate from my doctor.

[ ] **Special Reason:**   ....

N.B. *Should you be excused from jury service on this occasion, a further juror's citation may be sent out to you within twelve months.*

I declare that the foregoing information is correct and acknowledge that I may be asked for proof of any statement made above.

Signature .... Date ....

If you have any queries telephone **0131 225 2595.** *Please quote citation number and date of attendance.*

Unfortunately there are no facilities for car parking at or near the court.

CERTIFICATE OF LOSS OF EARNINGS OR PAYMENT TO SUBSTITUTE/CHILDMINDER
(OR LOSS OF NATIONAL INSURANCE BENEFIT)

I certify that for each day M ....
is required by the Court for Jury Service a *deduction/charge of £.................. per day
(.................. hours @ .... per hour) will be made from his/her* (earnings/benefit/service supplied)

Name and Address of Employer/Substitute/Childminder or Local Office where benefit is received
....

Date .... Signature ....

OFFICIAL USE ONLY
*(delete as applicable)

	Allowed	No. of days	Total
TRAVELLING	£ p		£ p
By public transport			
(a) Say whether rail, bus &c			
(b) Daily return fare £			
In own car, &c			
(a) Car, m/cycle &c? .... Engine capacity .... c.c.			
(b) Daily mileage (round trip)			
(c) Could you have travelled by public transport? *YES/NO			
If YES indicate how much time was saved by using your own vehicle			
SUBSISTENCE			
On the days on which the court has NOT provided meals for you, have you necessarily incurred expenses on subsistence? *YES/NO			
If YES. give number of hours, including travelling time you were away from your home or place of business. (If you attended Court on more than one day, show the number of hours for each day)			
LOSS OF EARNINGS (only refundable if certified above)			
Will you suffer any loss of earnings as a result of your attendance for jury service? *YES/NO			
If YES, please state			
(a) your occupation			
(b) daily or hourly rate (or equivalent) £			
(c) number of days and half-days lost			
Have you paid any person to act as a substitute for you during your attendance for jury service (*e.g.* at your place of employment, or to look after your children &c)? *YES/NO			
If YES, please state			
(a) capacity in which paid substitute employed			
(b) his/her daily or hourly rate £			
(c) number of days and half-days paid substitute employed			
I DECLARE that to the best of my knowledge and belief the particulars in the foregoing claim are correct			
TOTALS			
.... Signature of Claimant			

FOR OFFICIAL USE ONLY	RECEIVED the sum of
CERTIFIED CORRECT	£ ....
AUTHORISED FOR PAYMENT	(Signature) ....
DATE	(Date) ....

---

[1] Form 37.2–B amended by S.S.I. 2005 No. 193 (effective 1st April 2005).

Rule 37.6(1)   FORM 37.6–A

Form of oath for jurors

The jurors shall raise their right hands and the clerk of court shall ask them:—

"Do you swear by Almighty God that you will well and truly try the issue and give a true verdict according to the evidence?"

The jurors shall reply:

"I do".

Rule 37.6(2)   FORM 37.6–B

Form of affirmation for jurors

The juror shall repeat after the clerk of court:—

"I solemnly, sincerely and truly declare and affirm that I will well and truly try the issue and give a true verdict according to the evidence".

Rule 38.6(1)   FORM 38.6

Form of reclaiming motion to be written on Form 23.2

On behalf of the pursuer [*or as the case may be*], for review by the Inner House of the interlocutor of (*date*) of the Lord Ordinary.

Form of application for leave to appeal

IN THE COURT OF SESSION

APPLICATION

for

LEAVE TO APPEAL

under (*specify provision of enactment under which application is made*)

by

[A.B.] (*designation and address*)

Applicant

against

Decision of [*or* Refusal of leave to appeal]

(*name of court or tribunal*)

1. That on (*date*) the (*name of court or tribunal*) refused the application of the applicant for leave to appeal to the Court of Session against its decision of (*date*) refusing [*or* decided] (*briefly describe decision*). A copy of the decision of the (*name of court or tribunal*) [and of the decision refusing leave to appeal] is [*or* are] produced with this application.

2. That the reasons given by the (*name of court or tribunal*) for refusing leave to appeal are (*specify*) [*or* are set out in the copy of its decision produced with this application].

3. That the reasons given by the (*name of court or tribunal*) for its decision (*date*) against which leave to appeal is sought are (*specify*) [*or* are set out in the copy of the decision produced with this application].

4. That the grounds on which the applicant seeks leave to appeal [against the refusal of leave to appeal] to the Court of Session are as follows:—(*set out the grounds in numbered sub-paragraphs*).

5. That the grounds on which the applicant seeks to appeal against the decision of the (*name of court or tribunal*) of (*date*) are as follows:—(*set out the grounds in numbered sub-paragraphs*).

6. That this application is made under (*specify provision of enactment*) and rule 40.2(2) [*or* 41.2(3)] of the Rules of the Court of Session 1994.

IN RESPECT WHEREOF

(*Signed by counsel or other person having a right of audience*)

Rule 40.4(2) [1] FORM 40.4

Form of marking appeal from inferior court

The pursuer [*or* defender *or as the case may be*] appeals to the Court of Session.

(*Signed*)

Pursuer [*or as the case may be*]
[*or* Solicitor [*or* Agent] for pursuer
[*or as the case may be*]], Appellant

---

[1] Form 40.4 amended by S.I. 1996 No. 2587 (rule reference).

Rule 40.9(5)(a)   FORM 40.9

Form of certification by Deputy Principal Clerk on retransmitting abandoned appeal

(*Date*)   Retransmitted in respect of the abandonment of the appeal.

(*Signed*)

Deputy Principal Clerk of Session

Rule 41.9(1)   FORM 41.9

Form of case in appeal under statute to the Court of Session

CASE

for

OPINION OF THE COURT OF SESSION

under

(*State provision in enactment under which appeal is made*)

appeal by

[A.B.] (*designation and address*)

Appellant

against

[C.D.] (*designation and address*)

Respondent

I [*or* We] found the following facts admitted or proved:—

(*Set out in numbered paragraphs the facts admitted or proved*)

NOTE

(*Set out the basis on which the tribunal found the facts admitted or proved and the reasoning of the decision appealed against*)

The question(s) of law for the opinion of the court is [*or* are]:—

(*Set out the questions in numbered paragraphs*)

This case stated by [*me*]

(*Signed*)

(*Name*)

APPENDIX

(*Here append any documents referred to in the case necessary for the understanding of the case.*)

Rule 41.14(2)   FORM 41.14

Form of certification by Deputy Principal Clerk on retransmitting abandoned appeal

(*Date*).   Retransmitted in respect of the abandonment of the appeal.

(*Signed*)

Deputy Principal Clerk of Session

Form of appeal in appeal under statute to the Court of Session

APPEAL

to

THE COURT OF SESSION

under

(*State provision in enactment under which appeal is made*)

by

[A.B.] (*designation and address*)

Appellant

against

A decision [*or as the case may be*] of (*name of tribunal*)
dated (*date*) communicated to the appellant on (*date*)

The decision [*or as the case may be*] of (*name of tribunal*) dated (*date*) is in the following terms [*or where a lengthy or reasoned decision is appealed against, is appended to this appeal*].

The appellant appeals against the foregoing decision [*or as the case may be*] on the following grounds.

GROUNDS OF APPEAL

(*State the grounds of appeal in numbered paragraphs*)

(*Signed*)

Appellant
[*or Solicitor* [*or Agent*] for appellant]

APPENDIX

(*Here set out lengthy or reasoned decision appealed against*)

Rule 41.48   ¹ FORM 41.48

Form of petition in application under section 103A(1) of the Nationality, Immigration and Asylum Act 2002 for an order requiring the Asylum and Immigration Tribunal to reconsider a decision

UNTO THE RIGHT HONOURABLE THE LORDS OF COUNCIL AND SESSION

PETITION

of

[A.B.] (*designation and address*)

for

reconsideration of a decision by the Asylum and Immigration Tribunal

HUMBLY SHEWETH:–

1. That the petitioner is (*state designation, title and interest of petitioner*).

2. That on (*date*) the Asylum and Immigration Tribunal decided that (*specify decision to be reconsidered*).

3. That it is declared the Asylum and Immigration Tribunal that made the said decision on (*specify date on which decision was made*) consisted of less than three legally qualified members.

4. That the petitioner seeks an order requiring the Asylum and Immigration Tribunal to reconsider its decision.

(*State briefly the facts in support of the grounds for reconsideration in numbered paragraphs*).

5. (*State briefly in numbered paragraphs the legal argument(s) with reference to enactments or judicial authority on which it is intended to rely*).

MAY IT THEREFORE please your Lordships to order the Asylum and Immigration Tribunal to reconsider its decision and (*insert any additional orders sought*).

> According to Justice etc.
>
> (*Signed by counsel or other person having a right of audience*)

---

[1] Form 41.47 substituted by 41.48 when inserted by S.S.I. 2005 No. 198 (effective 4th April, 2005) and substituted by S.S.I. 2007 No. 283 (effective 2nd May 2007).

Rule 41.52   [1] FORM 41.52

Form of citation in petition under section 103A of the Nationality, Immigration and Asylum Act 2002

CITATION

Date: (*date of posting or other method of service*)

To: (*name and address of person on whom petition served*)

IN HER MAJESTY'S NAME AND AUTHORITY, and in the name and authority of Lord (*name*), I, (*name of agent*), solicitor [*or* person having a right to conduct the litigation], for (*name of petitioner*) [*or* (*name of messenger-at-arms*), messenger-at-arms], serve the attached petition and interlocutor of the court on you.

The interlocutor requires you to lodge written submissions on the petition.

If you intend to lodge written submissions to the petition you must lodge them at the Office of Court, Court of Session, 2 Parliament Square, Edinburgh EH1 1RQ within (*specify number of days*) days after the date of service on you of the petition. The date of service is the date stated at the top of this citation unless service has been by post in which case the date of service is the day after that date.

IF YOU ARE UNCERTAIN ABOUT THE EFFECT OF THIS CITATION, you should consult a solicitor, Citizens Advice Bureau or other local advice agency or adviser immediately.

> (*Signed*)
>
> Messenger-at-arms
>
> [Solicitor [*or* Agent] for petitioner]
>
> (*Address*).

---

[1] Form 41.52 inserted by S.S.I. 2005 No. 198 (effective 4th April, 2005) and substituted by S.S.I. 2007 No. 283 (effective 2nd May 2007).

Rule 41.56   [1] FORM 41.56

Form of reference on a preliminary point under an ACAS Scheme

UNTO THE RIGHT HONOURABLE

THE LORDS OF COUNCIL AND SESSION

REFERENCE ON A PRELIMINARY POINT

Under

(specify the ACAS Scheme under which the reference is being made)

by

[A.B.] *(address)*

Arbitrator in the case of

[C.D.] *(address)* against [E.F.] *(address)*

[or by

[C.D] *(address)* and [E.F.] (address) parties in a case in which [A.B.] *(address)*

is the arbitrator]

(Here state in numbered paragraphs the facts and circumstances out of which the reference arises and set out the question for answer by the court)

———

[1] Form 41.56 inserted by S.S.I. 2004 No. 331 (effective 6th August 2004).

Rule 42.7(5)(c)   FORM 42.7

Form of notice to client intimating diet of taxation of solicitors' account

To: *(name and address)*

Date: *(date of posting)*

(Name of solicitors), Applicant v. [C.D.], respondent

Cause reference number:

1. We enclose a copy of the solicitors' account in respect of which we seek payment.

2. The court has, in terms of the enclosed interlocutor, remitted the account to the Auditor of the Court of Session for taxation (assessment).

3. The taxation hearing will take place at the office of the Auditor of the Court of Session, Parliament House, 2 Parliament Square, Edinburgh on *(date and time)*.

4. If you wish to object to any part of the account you must appear or be represented at the taxation hearing.

5. You will lose any right to object to the account if you do not appear or are not represented at the taxation hearing.

(Signed)

Solicitor
(Address)

IF YOU ARE UNCERTAIN ABOUT THE EFFECT OF THIS NOTICE, you should consult a solicitor, Citizens Advice Bureau or other local advice agency or adviser immediately.

Rule 43.1A(1)   [1] Form 43.1A

Form of draft interlocutor granting authority to raise action based on clinical negligence as an ordinary action

[*To be inserted on the first page of the summons*]

Authority

The Lord Ordinary, having considered the application of the pursuer [and having heard counsel thereon], being satisfied that although this is a personal injuries action, there are exceptional reasons for not following the procedure in Chapter 43 of the Rules of the Court of Session 1994 such as would justify the granting of a motion under rule 43.5(1) (application to have action withdrawn from personal injuries procedure) grants authority for the cause to proceed as an ordinary action.

(*Signed*)

Lord/Lady

Date: (*date*)

---

[1] Form 43.1A inserted by the Act of Sederunt (Rules of the Court of Session Amendment No. 4) (Personal Injuries Actions etc.) 2007, para. 2 (effective 2nd May 2007).

[1] Form 43.2–A

Form of summons and backing in personal injuries action

[*Insert the Royal Arms in Scotland*]

(*This space will contain the cause reference number assigned to the summons on being presented for signeting and registration*)

IN THE COURT OF SESSION

SUMMONS

(Personal injuries action)

[A.B.] (*designation and address*), Pursuer

against

[C.D.] (*designation and address*), Defender

Elizabeth II, by the Grace of God, of the United Kingdom of Great Britain and Northern Ireland and of Her other Realms and Territories, Queen, Head of the Commonwealth, Defender of the Faith, to [C.D.].

By this summons, the pursuer craves the Lords of our Council and Session to pronounce a decree against you in terms of the conclusions appended to this summons. If you have any good reason why such decree should not be pronounced, you must enter appearance at the Office of Court, Court of Session, 2 Parliament Square, Edinburgh EH1 1RQ, within three days after the date of the calling of the summons in court. The summons shall not call in court earlier than (*enter period of notice*) days after it has been served on you. **Be warned that, if appearance is not entered on your behalf, the pursuer may obtain decree against you in your absence.**

This summons is warrant for intimation to (*name and address and reason for intimation as set out in the rule of the Rules of the Court of Session 1994 requiring intimation*).

Given under our Signet at Edinburgh on (*date*).

(*Signed*)

(*Name and address of or agent for pursuer*)

[*Back of first page*]

CONCLUSIONS

FIRST. For payment by the defender to the pursuer of the sum of (*amount of sum in words and figures*).

SECOND. [*enter only if a claim for provisional damages is sought in terms of rule 43.2(2)*] For payment by the defender to the pursuer of (*enter amount in words and figures*) of provisional damages.

THIRD. For the expenses of the action

STATEMENT OF CLAIM

1. The pursuer is (*state designation, address, occupation and date of birth of pursuer*). [*In an action arising out of the death of a relative state designation of the deceased and relation to the pursuer*].

2. The defender is (*state designation, address and occupation of defender*).

3. The court has jurisdiction to hear this claim against the defender because (*state briefly ground of jurisdiction*).

4. (*State briefly the facts necessary to establish the claim*).

5. (*State briefly the personal injuries suffered and the heads of claim. Give names and addresses of medical practitioners and hospitals or other institutions in which the person injured received treatment*).

6. (*State whether claim based on fault at common law or breach of statutory duty; if breach of statutory duty, state provision of enactment*).

IN RESPECT WHEREOF

(*Signed*)

Solicitor [or Agent] for the pursuer
(*address and solicitor/agent's reference number*)

(*Backing of summons*)

(*This space will contain the cause reference number assigned to the summons on being presented for signeting and registration*)

---

[1] Form 43.2–A substituted by S.S.I. 2004 No. 291 (effective 29th June 2004).

[1] FORM 43.2–B

Form of order of court for recovery of documents in personal injuries action

IN THE COURT OF SESSION

In the Cause (Cause Reference No.)

SPECIFICATION OF DOCUMENTS

[A.B.] (*designation and address*)

Pursuer

against

[C.D.] (*designation and address*)

Defender

Date: (*date of posting or other method of service*)

To: (*name and address of party or parties from whom the following documents are sought to be recovered*)

You are hereby required to produce to the agent for the pursuer within seven days of the service on you of this Order:—

[*Insert such of the following calls as are required.*]

    1. All books, medical records, reports, charts, X-rays, notes and other documents of (*specify the name of each medical practitioner or general practitioner practice named in summons in accordance with rule 43.2(1)(b)*), and relating to the pursuer [*or, as the case may be*, the deceased], in order that excerpts may be taken therefrom at the sight of the Commissioner of all entries showing or tending to show the nature, extent and cause of the pursuer's [*or, as the case may be*, the deceased's] injuries when he intended his doctor on or after (*specify date*) and the treatment received by him since that date.

    2. All books, medical records, reports, charts, X-rays, notes and other documents of (*specify, in separate calls, the name of each hospital or other institution named in summons in accordance with rule 43.2(1)(b)*), and relating to the pursuer [or, *as the case may be*, the deceased], in order that excerpts may be taken therefrom at the sight of the Commissioner of all entries showing or tending to show the nature, extent and cause of all injuries from which the pursuer [*or, as the case may be*, the deceased] was suffering when he was admitted to that institution on or about (*specify date*), the treatment received by him since that date and his certificate of discharge, if any.

    3. The medical records and capability assessments held by the defender's occupational health department relating to the pursuer [*or, as the case may be*, the deceased], except insofar as prepared for or in contemplation of litigation, in order that excerpts may be taken therefrom at the sight of the Commissioner of all entries showing or tending to show the nature and extent of any injuries, symptoms and condition from which the pursuer [*or as the case may be*, the deceased] was suffering and the nature of any assessment and diagnosis made thereof on or subsequent to (*specify date*).

    4. All wage books, cash books, wage sheets, computer records and other earnings information relating to the pursuer (*or, as the case may be*, the deceased) (N.I. Number (*specify number*)) held by or on behalf of (*specify employer*), for the period (*specify dates commencing not earlier than 26 weeks prior to the date of the accident or the first date of relevant absence, as the case may be*) in order that excerpts may be taken therefrom at the sight of the Commissioner of all entries showing or tending to show:—
    (a) the pursuer's [*or, as the case may be*, the deceased's] earnings, both gross and net of income tax and employee National Insurance Contributions, over the said period;

(b) the period or periods of the pursuer's [*or, as the case may be*, the deceased's] absence from employment over the said period and the reason for absence;

(c) details of any increases in the rate paid over the period (*specify dates*) and the dates on which any such increases took effect;

(d) the effective date of, the reasons for and the terms (including any terms relative to any pension entitlement) of the termination of the pursuer's [*or, as the case may be*, the deceased's] employment;

(e) the nature and extent of contributions (if any) to any occupational pension scheme made by the pursuer [*or, as the case may be*, the deceased] and his employer;

(f) the pursuer's present entitlement (if any) to occupational pension and the manner in which said entitlement is calculated.

5. All accident reports, memoranda or other written communications made to the defender or anyone on his behalf by an employee of the defender who was present at or about the time at which the pursuer [*or, as the case may be*, the deceased] sustained the injuries in respect of which the summons in this cause was issued and relevant to the matters contained in the statement of claim.

6. Any risk assessment current at the time of the accident referred to in the summons or at the time of the circumstances referred to in the summons giving rise to the cause of action (as the case may be) undertaken by or on behalf of the defender for the purpose of regulation 3 of the Management of Health and Safety at Work Regulations 1992 and subsequently regulation 3 of the Management of Health and Safety at Work Regulations 1999 [*or* (*specify the regulations or other legislative provision under which the risk assessment is required*)] in order that excerpts may be taken therefrom at the sight of the Commissioner of all entries relating to the risks posed to workers [*or* (*specify the matters set out in the statement of claim to which the risk assessment relates*)].

7. Failing principals, drafts, copies or duplicates of the above or any of them.

(*Signature, name and business address of the agent for the pursuer.*)

NOTES

(1) The documents recovered will be considered by the parties to the action and they may or may not be lodged in the court process. A written receipt will be given or sent to you by the pursuer, who may thereafter allow them to be inspected by the other parties. The party in whose possession the documents are will be responsible for their safekeeping.

(2) Parties are obliged by the rules of court to return the documents to you when their purpose with the documents is finished. If they do not, you will be entitled to apply to the court, under rule 35.3(9) of the Rules of the Court of Session 1994, for an order to have this done and you may apply for an award of expenses incurred in doing so. Further information about this can be obtained from the General Department, Court of Session, 2 Parliament Square, Edinburgh EH1 1RQ (Tel. 0131-225-2595).

(3) If you claim that any of the documents produced by you are **confidential**, you must still produce such documents but may place them in a separate sealed packet by themselves, marked "CONFIDENTIAL". In that event they must be delivered or sent by post to the **Deputy Principal Clerk of Session, 2 Parliament Square, Edinburgh, EH1 1RQ**. Any party who wishes to open the sealed packet must apply to the court by motion. A party who makes such an application must intimate the motion to you.

(4) Subject to paragraph (3) above, you may produce these documents by sending them by registered post or by the first class recorded delivery service or registered postal packet, or by hand to (*name and address of the agent for the pursuer*).

CERTIFICATE

(*Date*)

I hereby certify with reference to the above order of the Court of Session in the cause (*cause reference number*) and the enclosed specification of documents, served on me and market respectively X and Y:—

(1) That the documents which are produced and which are listed in the enclosed inventory signed by me and marked Z, are all the documents in my possession falling within the specification,

or

That I have no documents in my possession falling within the specification.

(2) That, to the best of my knowledge and belief, there are in existence other documents falling within the specification, but not in my possession. These documents are as follows:— (*describe them by reference to the descriptions of documents in the specification*). They were last seen by me on or about (*date*), at (*place*), in the hands of (*name and address of the person*),

or

That I know of the existence of no documents in the possession of any person, other than myself, which fall within the specification.

(*Signed*)

(*Name and address*)

---

[1] Form 43.2–B substituted by S.S.I. 2004 No. 291 (effective 29th June 2004) and amended by S.S.I. 2007 No. 282 (effective 2nd May 2007).

[1] FORM 43.3

Form of citation of defender

CITATION

Date: (*date of posting or other method of service*)

To: [C.D.] (*address of defender*)

IN HER MAJESTY'S NAME AND AUTHORITY, I, (*name of agent*), solicitor [or person having a right to conduct the litigation), for (*name of pursuer*) [or (*name of messenger-at-arms*), Messenger-at arms], serve the attached summons on you.

The summons contains a claim for reparation for personal injuries [or for reparation arising from the death of (*name of the deceased*) from personal injuries] made by (*name of pursuer*) against you in the Court of Session, Edinburgh.

If you intend to deny this claim you must: (1) enter appearance at the Office of Court, Court of Session, 2 Parliament Square, EDINBURGH, EH1 1RQ, within three days after (the date on which the summons calls in court); and (2) subsequently lodge defences within seven days after (*the date on which the summons calls in court*). The summons will not call in court earlier than (*enter period of notice*) days after it has been served on you. The date of service is the date stated at the top of this citation unless service has been by post in which case the date of service is the day after that date.

If you do not enter appearance and lodge defences, the court may make an order against you.

IF YOU ARE UNCERTAIN ABOUT THE EFFECT OF THIS NOTICE, you should consult a solicitor, Citizens Advice Bureau or other local advice agency or adviser immediately.

(*Signed*)

Messenger-at-Arms
[*or* Solicitor [*or* Agent] for pursuer(s)]
(*Address*)

---

[1] Form 43.3 substituted by S.S.I. 2002 No. 570 (effective 1st April 2003).

[1] FORM 43.6

Form of timetable order

IN THE COURT OF SESSION

TIMETABLE ORDER

In the cause

[A.B.]

Pursuer

against

[C.D.]

Defender

This order has effect as if it were an interlocutor of the court signed by the Lord Ordinary.

1. The diet allocated for the trial of this action will begin on (*date*). Subject to any variation under rule 43.7, this order requires the parties to undertake the conduct of this action within the periods specified in paragraphs 2 to 9 below.

2. Any motion under rule 26.1 (third party notice) shall be made by (date).

3. Where the pursuer has obtained a commission and diligence for the recovery of documents by virtue of rule 43.4, the pursuer shall serve an order under rule 35.3 not later than (date).

4. The pursuer shall lodge a statement of valuation of claim under rule 43.8(2) not later than (date).

5. For the purposes of rule 43.6(1)(b)(iii), the adjustment period shall end on (date).

6. The pursuer shall lodge a record no later than (date).

7. The defender [and any third party convened in the action] shall lodge a statement of valuation of claim under rule 43.9(2) not later than (date).

8. Not later than (date) parties shall lodge list of witnesses and productions.

9. Not later than (date) the pursuer shall lodge a pre-trial minute under rule 43.10(2).

_____

[1] Form 43.6 inserted by S.S.I. 2002 No. 570 (effective 1st April 2003).

Appendix

[1] FORM 43.9

Form of Statement of Valuation of Claim

Head of claim	Components	Valuation
Solatium	Past	£x
	Future	£x
Interest on past *solatium*	Percentage applied to past solatium State percentage rate	£x
Past wage loss	Date from which wage loss claimed (....) Date to which wage loss Claimed (....) Rate of net wage loss (per week, per month or per annum)	£x
Interest on past wage loss	Percentage applied to past wage loss (*State percentage rate*)	£x
Future wage loss	Multiplier (....) Multiplicand (showing how calculated) Discount factor applied (if appropriate) Or specify any other method of calculation	£x
Past services	Date from which services claimed (....) Date to which services claimed (....) Nature of services (....) Person by whom services provided (....) Hours per week services provided (....)	

Head of claim	Components	Valuation
	Net hourly rate claimed	£x
	(....)	
	Total amount claimed	
	(....)	
	Interest	
Future loss of capacity to provide personal services	Multiplier	
	(....)	
	Multiplicand (showing how calculated	£x
Needs and other expenses	One off	£x
	Multiplier	
	(....)	
	Multiplicand	£x
	Interest	
Any other heads as appropriate (specify)		

[1] Form 43.9 inserted by S.S.I. 2002 No. 570 (effective 1st April 2003) and amended by S.S.I. 2007 No. 282 (effective 2nd May 2007).

[1] FORM 43.10

Minute of Pre-Trial Meeting

IN THE COURT OF SESSION

Joint Minute of Pre-Trial Meeting

in the cause

[A.B.]

Pursuer

against

[C.D.]

Defender

[GH] for the Pursuer and

[IJ] for the Defenders hereby state to the court:-

(1) That the pre-trial meeting was held in this case at [ ] on [ ].

(2) That the following persons were present:-

 (*State names and designations of persons attending meeting*)

(2A) That the following persons were available to provide instructions by telephone—

 (*State names and designations of persons available to provide instructions by telephone*).

(3) That the persons present discussed settlement of the action.

(4) That the following questions were addressed:-

Section 1

		Yes	No
1.	Is the diet of proof or trial still required		
2.	If the answer to question 1 is "yes", does the defender admit liability? (If "no", complete section 2) If yes, does the defender plead contributory negligence? If yes, is the degree of contributory negligence agreed? If yes, state % degree of fault attributed to the pursuer		
3.	If the answer to question 1 is "yes", is the quantum" of damages agreed? (If "no", complete section 3)		

Section 2

[To be inserted only if the proof or trial is still required.]

It is estimated that the hearing will last days.

N.B. If the estimate is more or less than the 4 days then this should be brought to the attention of the Keeper. This may affect prioritisation of the case.

During the course of the pre-trial meeting, the pursuer called on the defender to agree certain facts, questions of law and matters of evidence.

Those calls, and the defender's responses, are as follows:-

Call	*Response*	
	Admitted	Denied
1.		
2.		
3.		
4.		

During the course of the pre-trial meeting, the defender called on the pursuer to agree certain facts, questions of law and matters of evidence.

Those calls, and the pursuer's responses, are as follows:-

Call	*Response*	
	Admitted	Denied
1.		
2.		
3.		
4.		

Quantum of Damages

Please indicate where agreement has been reached on an element of damages.

Head of claim	Components	Not agreed	Agreed at
Solatium	Past Future		
Interest on past *solatium*	Percentage applied to past *solatium* (*State percentage*)		
Past wage loss	Date from which wage loss claimed Date to which wage loss claimed Rate of net wage loss (per week, per month or per annum)		
Interest on past wage loss			
Future wage loss	Multiplier Multiplicand (showing how calculated)		
Past necessary services	Date from which services claimed Date to which services claimed Hours per week services provided Net hourly rate claimed		
Past personal services			
Interest on past necessary services			
Future necessary services	Multiplier Multiplicand (showing how calculated)		
Future personal services	Multiplier Multiplicand (showing how calculated)		

Head of claim	Components	Not agreed	Agreed at
Needs and other expenses	One off		
	Multiplier		
	Multiplicand (showing how calculated)		
Any other heads as appropriate (specify)			

IN RESPECT WHEREOF

(*Signed by counsel/solicitor advocate for each party*)

---

[1] Form 43.10 inserted by S.S.I. 2002 No. 570 (effective 1st April 2003) and amended by S.S.I. 2007 No. 282 (effective 2nd May 2007).

[1] FORM 43.12

---

[1] Form 43.12 revoked by S.S.I. 2002 No. 570 (effective 1st April 2003).

[1] FORM 43.13–A

Form of conclusion for application for an award of further damages

For payment to the pursuer by the defender of the sum (*amount in words and figures*) as further damages.

---

[1] Form 43.13–A substituted by S.S.I. 2002 No. 570 (effective 1st April 2003).

[1] FORM 43.13–B

Form of notice of application for further damages

Date: (*date of posting or other method of service*)

To: (*name and address of persons on whom served*)

TAKE NOTICE

(Pursuer's name and address), pursuer, raised an action against (defender's name and address), defender, in the Court of Session.

In the action, [Lord (name)] in the Court of Session on (date) made an award of provisional damages in favour of the pursuer against you [or (party's name)]. [The court specified that the pursuer may apply for an award of further damages at any time before (date).] The pursuer has applied by minute for an award of further damages against you [or (party's name)]. A copy of the minute is [and the summons in the action are] attached. You may lodge answers to the minute within [21] days after the date of service on you of the minute at the Office of Court, Court of Session, 2 Parliament Square, Edinburgh EH1 1RQ. The date of service is the date stated at the top of this notice unless service has been made by post in which case the date of service is the day after that date.

IF YOU ARE UNCERTAIN ABOUT THE EFFECT OF THIS NOTICE, you should consult a solicitor, Citizens Advice Bureau or other local advice agency or adviser immediately.

(*Signed*)

Messenger-at-Arms
[*or* Solicitor [*or* Agent] for pursuer]
(*Address*)

_____

[1] Form 43.13–B substituted by S.S.I. 2002 No. 570 (effective 1st April 2003).

[1] FORM 43.15

Form of notice of intimation to connected person in an action for damages

Date: (*date of posting or other method of intimation*)

To: (*name and address of connected person*)

TAKE NOTICE

(*Names and addresses of all pursuers*) have raised an action against (*names and addresses of all defenders*) in the Court of Session, Edinburgh. The action relates to the death of (*name and last address of deceased*) [or the personal injuries from which (*name and last address of deceased*) died].

You are believed to have a right to sue arising from his [or her] death. If this is the case, you are entitled to be added as an additional pursuer in the action. A copy of the summons in the action is attached.

You may apply to the court to be added as a pursuer after the date of intimation to you of the summons [or if the warrant for intimation is executed at the same time as citation of the defender, within seven days after the date on which the summons calls in the court. The summons may not call in Court earlier than (*enter period of notice*) days after the date of intimation to you of the summons. The date of intimation is the date stated at the top of this notice unless intimation has been made by post in which case the date of intimation is the day after that date.

If you do not apply to be added as an additional pursuer and subsequently bring a separate action, under rule 43.20 of the Rules of the Court of Session 1994 you may not be awarded the expenses of that action in the event of your being successful.

[It is proposed to apply to the court for authority to dispense with intimation to the person(s) mentioned in paragraph (number of paragraph) of the statement attached to the summons. The whereabouts of such person(s) are not known. If you know of that person (or any of those persons], you should inform the Deputy Principal Clerk of Session, Court of Session, Parliament Square, Edinburgh EH1 1RQ (Telephone 0131-225-2595)].

IF YOU ARE UNCERTAIN ABOUT THE EFFECT OF THIS NOTICE, you should consult a solicitor, Citizens Advice Bureau or other local advice agency or adviser immediately.

(*Signed*)

Messenger-at-Arms
[*or* Solicitor [*or* Agent] for pursuer(s)]
(*Address*)

_____

[1] Form 43.15 inserted by S.S.I. 2002 No. 570 (effective 1st April 2003).

Form of notice of intimation to connected person in an action for damages

Date: *(date of posting or other method of intimation)*

To: *(name and address of connected person)*

TAKE NOTICE

(Names and addresses of all pursuers) have raised an action against *(names and addresses of all defenders)* in the Court of Session, Edinburgh. The action relates to the death of *(name and last address of deceased)* [*or* the personal injuries from which *(name and last address of deceased)* died]. You are believed to have a right to sue arising from his [*or* her] death. If this is the case, you are entitled to be added as an additional pursuer in the action. A copy of the summons in the action is attached.

You may apply to the court to be added as a pursuer after the date of intimation to you of the summons [*or if the warrant for intimation is executed at the same time as citation of the defender,* within 7 days after the date on which the summons calls in court. The summons may not call in court earlier than [21] days after the date of intimation to you of the summons]. The date of intimation is the date stated at the top of this notice unless intimation has been made by post in which case the date of intimation is the day after that date.

If you make such an application you must give notice of your application to all the parties to the action.

If you do not apply to be added as an additional pursuer and subsequently bring a separate action, under rule 43.7 of the Rules of the Court of Session 1994 you may not be awarded the expenses of that action in the event of your being successful.

[It is proposed to apply to the court for authority to dispense with intimation to the person(s) mentioned in article *(number of article)* of the condescendence attached to the summons. The whereabouts of such person(s) are not known. If you know of that person [*or* any of those persons], you should inform the Deputy Principal Clerk of Session, Court of Session, Parliament Square, Edinburgh EH1 1RQ (Telephone: 031-225 2595)].

You are advised that although periods of 7 and 21 days are mentioned above, this does not mean that your right to be connected to the action will remain if the period of time, following the events which caused the death or personal injuries, within which the law would have allowed you to raise an action based on the events expires earlier.

IF YOU ARE UNCERTAIN ABOUT THE EFFECT OF THIS NOTICE, you should consult a solicitor, Citizens Advice Bureau or other local advice agency or adviser immediately.

                                           (Signed)

                                           Messenger-at-Arms
                                           [*or* Solicitor [*or* Agent] for pursuer]
                                           (Address)

----

[1] Form 43.3 as reproduced here (as amended by S.I. 1994 No. 2901 and S.S.I. 2001 No. 305) was revoked by S.S.I. 2002 No. 570 (effective 1st April 2003).

Form of conclusion for application for provisional damages

For payment to the pursuer by the defender of the sum of *(amount in words and figures)* as provisional damages.

_____

[1] Form 43.12 as reproduced here was revoked by S.S.I. 2002 No. 570 (effective 1st April 2003).

Rule 43.13(1)(a)   [1] (OLD) FORM 43.13–A

Form of conclusion for application for an award of further damages

For payment to the pursuer by the defender of the sum of *(amount in words and figures)* as further damages.

_____

[1] Form 43.13–A as reproduced here was revoked by S.S.I. 2002 No. 570 (effective 1st April 2003).

Rule 43.13(3)   [1] (OLD) FORM 43.13–B

Form of notice of application for further damages

Date: *(date of posting or other method of intimation)*

To: *(name and address of person on whom served)*

TAKE NOTICE

(Pursuer's name and address), pursuer, raised an action against *(defender's name and address)*, defender, in the Court of Session.

In the action, [Lord *(name)* in] the Court of Session on *(date)* made an award of provisional damages in favour of the pursuer against you [*or (party's name)*]. [The court specified that the pursuer may apply for an award of further damages at any time before *(date)*]. The pursuer has applied by minute for an award of further damages against you [*or (party's name)*]. A copy of the minute is [and the summons in the action are] attached. You may lodge answers to the minute within [21] days after the date of service on you of the minute at the Office of Court, Court of Session, 2 Parliament Square, Edinburgh EH1 1RQ. The date of service is the date stated at the top of this notice unless service has been made by post in which case the date of service is the day after that date.

IF YOU ARE UNCERTAIN ABOUT THE EFFECT OF THIS NOTICE, you should consult a solicitor, Citizens Advice Bureau or other local advice agency or adviser immediately.

                    (Signed)

                    Messenger-at-Arms
                    [*or* Solicitor [*or* Agent] for pursuer]
                    (Address)

_____

[1] Form 43.13–B as reproduced here (as amended by S.I. 1994 No. 2901) was revoked by S.S.I. 2002 No. 570 (effective 1st April 2003).

Appendix

Form of action in an action for reparation (optional procedure)

IN THE COURT OF SESSION

SUMMONS

(Action for Reparation (Optional Procedure))

[A.B.] *(designation of address)*, Pursuer

against

[C.D.] *(designation and address)*, Defender

[*Address, Charge and warrants as in Form 13.2–A*]

[*Back of first page*]

CONCLUSIONS

FIRST. For payment by the defender to the pursuer of the sum of (£) STERLING, or such other greater or smaller sum as to the court shall seem proper, with interest, at the rate of interest in rule 7.7 of the Rules of the Court of Session 1994 applicable at the date of decree [*or as the case may be*], from the date of decree to follow hereon until payment.

SECOND. For the expenses of the action.

[*Next page*]

CONDESCENDENCE

I. The pursuer is *(state date of birth; in an action for personal injuries, state occupation and relation to defender; or, in an action arising out of the death of a relative, state relation to the deceased)*. The defender is *(state occupation)*.

II. *(State, in accordance with R.C.S. 1994, r. 13.2(4), the ground of jurisdiction and, where relevant, the domicile of the defender, whether there is an agreement prorogating the jurisdiction of the court and whether there are proceedings involving the same cause of action in subsistence between the parties)*.

[III. *In the case of an action arising out of the death of a relative. The deceased was (state dates of birth, marriage and death, occupation and relation to defender)*].

[IV]. *(In numbered articles, each new part of the averments in a separate article, state briefly the facts relied on as causing the accident or death)*.

[[V]. *In the case of fault at common law. The accident [or death of the deceased] was caused by the fault and negligence of the defender at common law. The defender was in breach of his duty to take reasonable care for the safety of the pursuer [or the deceased or as may be (no other specification of particular duties or breaches is normally required)]*].

[[VI]. *In the case of breach of statutory duty. Further and in any event the [or The] accident [or death of the deceased] was caused by the breach by the defender of a statutory duty. The defender was in breach of the duty imposed on him by (state provision of enactment; no other specification of the duty or breach is normally required)]*].

[VII]. As a result of the accident [*or* the death of the deceased] the pursuer suffered loss, injury and damage. *(State briefly, in an action for personal injuries, the injuries sustained and consequent damage suffered, loss of past and/or future earnings, any other relevant loss and whether credit is to be given for any National Insurance benefits received; or, in an action for death of a relative, the loss of society, loss of support and earnings of the deceased; and specify every medical practitioner from whom, and hospital and other institution, in which, the pursuer or the deceased received treatment in respect of the injuries or disease to which the action relates.)*

[VIII]. The defender has been called upon to make reparation to the pursuer but delays or refuses to do so.

Old

PLEAS-IN-LAW

1. The pursuer having suffered loss, injury and damage through the fault and negligence [and] [*or* breach of statutory duty] of the defender is entitled to reparation therefor from him.

2. The sum sued for being a resonable estimate of the loss, injury and damage sustained by the pursuer, decree therefor should be pronounced in that sum.

IN RESPECT WHEREOF

(*Signed*)

Messenger-at-Arms
[*or* Solicitor [*or* Agent] for pursuer]
(*Address*)

---

[1] Form 43.18 as reproduced here was revoked by S.S.I. 2002 No. 570 (effective 1st April 2003).

Rule 44.2(1)   [1] FORM 44.2–A

Form of notice to debtor under the Debtors (Scotland) Act 1987 about time to pay directions

(*Cause reference number*)

IN THE COURT OF SESSION

in the cause

[A.B.] (*designation and address*)

Pursuer

against

[C.D.] (*designation and address*)

Defender

To: (*name of defender to whom notice is directed*)

YOUR RIGHTS UNDER THE DEBTORS (SCOTLAND) ACT 1987

The purpose of this notice is to advise you of your rights under the Debtors (Scotland) Act 1987.

The Act gives you a right to apply to the court for a "time to pay direction" directing that any sum of money you are ordered to pay to the pursuer (which may include interest and court expenses) shall be by instalments or deferred lump sum (that is by one total payment by a specified date).

In addition, when making a time to pay direction the court may recall or restrict an arrestment made in connection with the action or debt (*e.g.* your bank account may have been arrested freezing the money in it).

If you admit that the sum claimed by the pursuer is due but you wish to apply for a time to pay direction you should read on. If you do not admit the sum claimed by the pursuer is due, DO NOT complete the attached application but consult a solicitor IMMEDIATELY about defending the action.

HOW TO APPLY FOR A TIME TO PAY DIRECTION WHEN CLAIM ADMITTED AND YOU DO NOT WANT TO DEFEND THE ACTION

1. Attached to this notice is an application for a time to pay direction and for recall or restriction of an arrestment, if appropriate. If you want to make an application you should complete and lodge the completed application with the court on or before the date given below. No court fee is payable when lodging the application.

2. Before completing the application please read carefully the notes attached to this notice. In the event of difficulty you may contact the General Department in the Office of Court of the Court of Session, 2 Parliament Square, Edinburgh EH1 1RQ (Telephone 031–225 2595).

3. The date by which you must return the application form is (*insert date*).

HOW TO COMPLETE THE APPLICATION FOR A TIME TO PAY DIRECTION

PLEASE WRITE IN INK USING BLOCK CAPITALS

PART A of the application will have been completed in advance by the pursuer and gives details of the pursuer and you as the defender.

PART B. If you wish to offer instalments enter the amount and tick the appropriate box at B3(1).

If you wish to offer to pay the full sum due in one deferred payment enter the date at which you offer to pay at B3(2).

PART C. You should give full details of your financial position in the appropriate boxes.

PART D. If you wish the court, when making the time to pay direction, to recall or restrict an arrestment made in connection with the action then enter the appropriate details about what has been arrested and the place and date of the arrestment at D5, and attach the Schedule of Arrestment (*i.e.* the formal document which told you of the arrestment of your assets) or a copy of it. You should then complete D6 by deleting the words which do not apply.

Sign the application where indicated and send to the court. Retain the copy summons and this notice as you may need them at a later stage. You should ensure that your application arrives at the court before the date specified in paragraph 3 of the application for a time to pay direction.

WHAT WILL HAPPEN NEXT

If the pursuer does not accept your offer a hearing will be fixed and the pursuer will advise you in writing of the date and time.

If the pursuer accepts your offer, then a copy of the court order for payment (called an extract decree) will be served on you by the pursuer advising when payment of instalments should commence or by what date payment is to be made and to whom payments should be sent.

IF YOU ARE UNCERTAIN ABOUT THE EFFECT OF THIS NOTICE, you should consult a solicitor, Citizens Advice Bureau or other local advice agency or adviser immediately.

----

[1] Form 44.2–A amended by S.I. 1994 No. 2901 (minor correction) and S.I. 1997 No. 1050 (minor amendment, effective 6th April 1997).

Rules 44.2(1), 44.3(1) and 44.4(1)   ¹ FORM 44.2–B

Form of application for a time to pay direction

(Cause reference number)

IN THE COURT OF SESSION

APPLICATION FOR A TIME TO PAY DIRECTION

Under the Debtors (Scotland) Act 1987

by

PART A*   ....
....
....
.... **Defender**

*This section must be
completed by pursuer   In an action raised by
before service

....
....
....
.... **Pursuer(s)**

This application must be sent to the court on or before

PART B   1. I am the defender in the action brought by the above named pursuer[s].
          2. I admit the claim and apply to the court for a time to pay direction.
          3. I offer (1) To pay by instalments of £ ....

*Tick one box only.
Delete whichever is
not appropriate   EACH... WEEK [ ]   * FORTNIGHT [ ]   * MONTH [ ]

          or   (2) To pay the sum ordered in one payment by

(Insert date)   ....19......

PART C   4. My financial position is as follows:—
*Tick one box only

My outgoings are: My income is:

Weekly*   Fortnightly*   Monthly*   Weekly*   Fortnightly*   Monthly*

[ ]   [ ]   [ ]   [ ]   [ ]   [ ]

Rent/House purchase loan	£		Wages/Pensions	£
Heating	£		Social Security	£
Food	£		Other (specify)	£
HP, etc	£			
Other	£			
Total	£		Total	£

Release 34: 8 November 1994

Here list all capital, if any (e.g. value of house, amount in bank/building society accounts, shares or other investments):

Here list any outstanding debts:

PART D *Delete if not applicable	5. *I seek to have recalled or restricted an arrestment of which the details are as follows (Please state, and attach Schedule of Arrestment or a copy):–
	6. This application is made under the Debtors (Scotland) Act 1987. Therefore I ask the court: (a) to make a time to pay direction; and

*Delete if not
applicable. State
the restriction
wanted
	*(b) to recall the above arrestment; or
	  *(c) to restrict the above arrestment:–
	    (*state the restriction sought*)

Signed ....
Defender

Date .... 19.....

This application should be sent to the Deputy Principal Clerk of Session, Court of Session, 2 Parliament Square, Edinburgh EH1 1RQ.

---

[1] Form 44.2–B amended by S.I. 1994 No. 2901 (minor corrections).

Rule 44.3(4)   [1] **FORM 44.3**

Form of notice of application for decree and objection to application for time to pay direction made by defender

(*Cause reference number*)

IN THE COURT OF SESSION

SUMMONS

[A.B.] (*designation and address*)

Pursuer

against

[C.D.] (*designation and address*)

Defender

To: (*name of defender to whom notice is directed*)

THIS NOTICE tells you that the pursuer—
   (*a*) intends to apply for decree against you; and
   (*b*) objects to all or part of your application for a time to pay direction.

I,   , the solicitor for the pursuer give you notice:—

   (1) That on (*date of proposed enrolment of motion*) I shall enrol the following motion in the above action against you and that this will come before the court on (*date and time*):—

(*insert terms of motion*)

(2) That the pursuer objects to the application which you have made for—

a time to pay direction,*
recall or restriction of an arrestment made against you,*

and will ask the court not to grant your application for the following reasons—

(set out reasons in numbered paragraphs)

You have the right to attend the hearing on *(date motion will come before the court)* and make any further points in answer to the pursuer's objections.

If you do not wish to attend court, you may reply to the pursuer's objections to your application in a letter addressed to the Deputy Principal Clerk of Session, 2 Parliament Square, Edinburgh EH1 1RQ. This letter must reach him by *(insert date before the day on which the motion will come before the court)*. The court will consider this letter at the hearing of the pursuer's motion and objection.

If you do not attend court and you wish to know the outcome of the hearing before you receive formal notice of the decree you should contact the General Department of the Court of Session, 2 Parliament Square, Edinburgh EH1 1RQ (Telephone: 031–225 2595).

IF YOU ARE UNCERTAIN ABOUT THE EFFECT OF THIS NOTICE, you should consult a solicitor, Citizens Advice Bureau or other local advice agency or adviser immediately.

(Signed)

Solicitor for pursuer

Date   19

* Delete whichever is not applicable.

---

[1] Form 44.3 amended by S.I. 1994 No. 2901 (minor corrections).

Rule 45A.2(2)   [1] **FORM 45A.2**

Form of citation of unnamed occupiers

IN THE COURT OF SESSION

in the cause

[A.B.] *(designation and address)*

Pursuer

against

The occupier[s] of *(address)*

Defender[s]

An action has been brought in the Court of Session, Edinburgh, by [A.B.], pursuer. [A.B.] calls as a defender the occupier[s] of the property at *(address)*. If the occupier[s] [*or* any of them] wish[es] to challenge the jurisdiction of the court or to defend the action, he [*or* she [*or* it] [*or* they]] should contact the Deputy Principal Clerk of Session, Court of Session, Parliament Square, Edinburgh EH1 1RQ (Telephone 0131 225 2595) immediately and in any event by *(date on which period of notice expires)*.

(Signed)

Solicitor [or Agent] for pursuer
(Address)

---

[1] Form 45A.2 inserted by S.I. 1996 No. 2168.
Release 42: 14 November 1996

Rule 46.6(5) and (6)   FORM 46.6

Form of preliminary act in ship collision action

In the action in which

is Pursuer

and

is Defender

Preliminary Act

for

Pursuer [*or* Defender]

Preliminary Act

for

Pursuer [*or* Defender]

(1) (*State the names of the vessels which came into collision, their ports of registry, and the names of their masters.*)

(2) (*State the date and time of the collision.*)

(3) (*State the place of the collision.*)

(4) (*State the direction and force of the wind.*)
(5) (*State the state of the weather.*)

(6) (*State the state, direction and force of the tidal or other current.*)

(7) (*State the magnetic course steered and speed through the water of the vessel when the other vessel was first seen or immediately before any measures were taken with reference to her presence, whichever was the earlier.*)

(8) (*State the lights (if any) carried by the vessel.*)

(9) (*State the distance and bearing of the other vessel if and when her echo was first observed by radar.*)

(10) (*State the distance, bearing and approximate heading of the other vessel when first seen.*)

(11) (*State what light or combination of lights (if any) of the other vessel when first seen.*)

(12) (*State what other lights or combinations of lights (if any) of the other vessel were subsequently seen, before the collision, and when.*)

(13) (*State what alterations (if any) were made to the course and speed of the vessel after the earlier of the two times referred to in paragraph (7) up to the time of the collision, and when, and what measures (if any), other than alterations of course and speed, were taken to avoid the collision and when.*)

(14) (*State the parts of each vessel which first came into contact and the approximate angle between the two vessels at the moment of contact.*)

(15) (*State what sound signals (if any) were given, and when.*)

(16) (*State what sound signals (if any) were heard from the other vessel and when.*)

(*Signed by counsel or Agent*)

(*Dated*)

Rule 46.9(4)   FORM 46.9

Intimation to the International Oil Pollution Compensation Fund

Date: (*date of posting or other method of intimation*)

To: The International Oil Pollution Compensation Fund
         (*address*)

TAKE NOTICE

(*Pursuer's name and address*), pursuer, has brought an action against (*defender's name and address*), defender, in the Court of Session, Edinburgh. A copy of the summons in the action is attached. In the action the court may make an order which is binding on you.

You may apply to the court by minute for leave to lodge defences to the action. You must do so at the Office of Court, Court of Session, 2 Parliament Square, Edinburgh EH1 1RQ within 21 days after the date of intimation to you of the summons [*or if the warrant for intimation is executed before calling of the summons*, within seven days after the summons calls in court. The summons will not call in court earlier than [21] days after the date of intimation to you of the summons]. The date of intimation is the date stated at the top of this notice unless intimation has been made by post in which case the date of intimation is the day after the date.

(*Signed*)

Messenger-at-Arms
[*or* Solicitor [*or* Agent] for pursuer]
(*Address*)

[THE NEXT PAGE IS C 725]

Rule 49.8(3)(a)   [1] FORM 49.8–A

Form of notice of intimation to children and next of kin in family action where address of defender is not known

Date: (*date of posting or other method of intimation*)

To: (*name and address as in warrant for intimation*)

TAKE NOTICE

(*Pursuer's name and address*), pursuer, has brought an action against (*name of defender*), defender, your father [*or* mother, *or* brother *or other relative as the case may be*] in the Court of Session, Edinburgh. A copy of the summons in the action is attached. The address of (*name of defender*) is not known. If you know of his [*or* her] present address you should immediately inform the Deputy Principal Clerk of Session, 2 Parliament Square, Edinburgh EH1 1RQ (Telephone: 031–225 2595).

In any event you may apply to the court by minute for leave to become a party to the action. You must do so at the Office of Court, Court of Session, 2 Parliament Square, Edinburgh EH1 1RQ within [21] days after the date of intimation to you of the summons [*or if the warrant for intimation is executed before calling of the summons*, within seven days after the summons calls in court. The summons will not call in court earlier than [21] days after the date of intimation to you of the summons]. The date of intimation is the date stated at the top of this notice unless intimation has been made by post in which case the date of intimation is the day after that date.

IF YOU ARE UNCERTAIN ABOUT THE EFFECT OF THIS NOTICE, you should consult a solicitor, Citizens Advice Bureau or other local advice agency or adviser immediately.

                         (*Signed*)

                         Messenger-at-Arms
                         [*or* Solicitor [*or* Agent] for pursuer]
                         (*Address*)

---

[1] Form 49.8–A amended by S.I. 1994 No. 2901 (minor correction).

Rule 49.8(3)(b)   [1] FORM 49.8–B

Form of notice of intimation to person with whom defender is alleged to have committed adultery

Date: (*date of posting or other method of intimation*)

To: (*name and address as in warrant for intimation*)

TAKE NOTICE

(*Pursuer's name and address*), pursuer, has brought an action against (*defender's name and address*), defender, in the Court of Session, Edinburgh. A copy of the summons in the action is attached. It contains an allegation that the defender has committed adultery with you.

You may apply to the court by minute for leave to become a party to the action. You must do so at the Office of Court, Court of Session, 2 Parliament Square, Edinburgh EH1 1RQ within [21] days after the date of intimation to you of the summons [*or if the warrant for intimation is executed before calling of the summons*, within seven days after the summons calls in court. The summons will not call in court earlier than [21] days after the date of intimation to you of the summons]. The date of intimation is the date stated at the top of this notice unless intimation has been made by post in which case the date of intimation is the day after that date.

IF YOU ARE UNCERTAIN ABOUT THE EFFECT OF THIS NOTICE, you should consult a solicitor, Citizens Advice Bureau or other local advice agency or adviser immediately.

(*Signed*)

Messenger-at-Arms
[*or* Solicitor [*or* Agent] for pursuer]
(*Address*)

---

[1] Form 49.8–B amended by S.I. 1994 No. 2901 (minor correction).

Rule 49.8(3)(*c*)   [1] FORM 49.8–C

Form of notice of intimation to relatives and curator *bonis* in family action where defender suffers from mental disorder

Date: (*date of posting or other method of intimation*)

To: (*name and address as in warrant*)

TAKE NOTICE

(*Pursuer's name and address*), pursuer, has brought an action against (*defender's name and address*), defender, your father [*or* mother, *or* brother *or* other relative as the case may be or* ward] in the Court of Session, Edinburgh. A copy of the summons in the action is attached.

You may apply to the court by minute for leave to become a party to the action. You must do so at the Office of Court, Court of Session, 2 Parliament Square, Edinburgh EH1 1RQ within [21] days after the date of intimation to you of the summons [*or if the warrant for intimation is executed before calling of the summons*, within seven days after the summons calls in court. The summons will not call in court earlier than [21] days after the date of intimation to you of the summons]. The date of intimation is the date stated at the top of this notice unless intimation has been made by post in which case the date of intimation is the day after that date.

IF YOU ARE UNCERTAIN ABOUT THE EFFECT OF THIS NOTICE, you should consult a solicitor, Citizens Advice Bureau or other local advice agency or adviser immediately.

(*Signed*)

Messenger-at-Arms
[*or* Solicitor [*or* Agent] for pursuer]
(*Address*)

---

[1] Form 49.8–C amended by S.I. 1994 No. 2901 (minor correction).

Rule 49.8(3)(*d*)   [1] FORM 49.8–D

Form of notice of intimation to additional spouse of either party in proceedings relating to polygamous marriage

Date: (*date of posting or other method of intimation*)

To: (*name and address as in warrant for intimation*)

TAKE NOTICE

(*Pursuer's name and address*), pursuer, has brought an action against (*defender's name and address*), defender, in the Court of Session, Edinburgh. A copy of the summons in the action is attached. (*Party's name*) is believed to be your spouse.

You may apply to the court by minute for leave to become a party to the action. You must do so at the Office of Court, Court of Session, 2 Parliament Square, Edinburgh EH1 1RQ within [21] days after the date of intimation to you of the summons [*or if the warrant for intimation is executed before calling of the summons*, within seven days after the summons calls in court. The summons will not call in court earlier than [21] days after the date of intimation to you of the summons]. The date of intimation is the date stated at the top of this notice unless intimation has been made by post in which case the date of intimation is the day after that date.

IF YOU ARE UNCERTAIN ABOUT THE EFFECT OF THIS NOTICE, you should consult a solicitor, Citizens Advice Bureau or other local advice agency or adviser immediately.

(*Signed*)

Messenger-at-Arms
[*or* Solicitor [*or* Agent] for pursuer]
(*Address*)

---

[1] Form 49.8–D amended by S.I. 1994 No. 2901 (minor correction).

Rule 49.8(3)(e)   [1] FORM 49.8–E

Form of notice to local authority or other person who may be liable to maintain a child

Date: (*date of posting or other method of intimation*)

To: (*name and address as in warrant for intimation*)

TAKE NOTICE

(*Pursuer's name and address*), pursuer, has brought an action against (*defender's name and address*), defender, in the Court of Session, Edinburgh. The pursuer seeks an order under section 11 of the Children (Scotland) Act 1995 in respect of (*child's name and address*), a child in your care [*or* liable to be maintained by you]. A copy of the summons in the action is attached.

You may apply to the court by minute to become a party to the action. You must do so at the Office of Court, Court of Session, 2 Parliament Square, Edinburgh EH1 1RQ within [21] days after the date of intimation to you of the summons [*or if the warrant for intimation is executed before calling of the summons*, within seven days after the summons calls in court. The summons will not call in court earlier than [21] days after the date of intimation to you of the summons]. The date of intimation is the date stated at the top of this notice unless intimation has been made by post in which case the date of intimation is the day after that date.

IF YOU ARE UNCERTAIN ABOUT THE EFFECT OF THIS NOTICE, you should consult a solicitor, Citizens Advice Bureau or other local advice agency or adviser immediately.

(*Signed*)

Messenger-at-Arms
[*or* Solicitor [*or* Agent] for pursuer]
(*Address*)

---

[1] Form 49.8–E amended by S.I. 1994 No. 2901 (minor correction) and S.I. 1996 No. 2587.

Rule 49.8(3)(f)   [1] FORM 49.8–F

Form of notice of intimation to person who in fact exercises care or control

Date: (*date of posting or other method of intimation*)

To: (*name and address as in warrant for intimation*)

TAKE NOTICE

(*Pursuer's name and address*), pursuer, has brought an action against (*defender's name and address*), defender, in the Court of Session, Edinburgh. The pursuer seeks an order under section 11 of the Children (Scotland) Act 1995 in respect of (*child's name and address*), a child at present in your care or control. A copy of the summons in the action is attached.

You may apply to the court by minute to become a party to the action. You must do so at the Office of Court, Court of Session, 2 Parliament Square, Edinburgh EH1 1RQ within [21] days after the date of intimation to you of the summons [*or if the warrant for intimation is executed before calling of the summons*, within seven days after the summons calls in court. The summons will not call in court earlier than [21] days after the date of intimation to you of the summons]. The date of intimation is the date stated at the top of this notice unless intimation has been made by post in which case the date of intimation is the day after that date.

IF YOU ARE UNCERTAIN ABOUT THE EFFECT OF THIS NOTICE, you should consult a solicitor, Citizens Advice Bureau or other local advice agency or adviser immediately.

(*Signed*)

Messenger-at-Arms
[*or* Solicitor [*or* Agent] for pursuer]
(*Address*)

_____

[1] Form 49.8–F amended by S.I. 1994 No. 2901 (minor correction) and S.I. 1996 No. 2587.

Rule 49.8(3)(g)   [1] FORM 49.8–G

Form of notice of intimation to parent or guardian in family action for a section 11 order

Date: (*date of posting or other method of intimation*)

To: (*name and address as in warrant for intimation*)

TAKE NOTICE

(*Pursuer's name and address*), pursuer, has brought an action against (*defender's name and address*), defender, in the Court of Session, Edinburgh. The pursuer is seeking a section 11 order in respect of the child (*child's name and address*). A copy of the summons in the action is attached.

If you wish to oppose this action, and oppose the granting to the pursuer of a section 11 order in respect of the child, you may apply to the court by minute to become a party to the action. You must do so at the Office of Court, Court of Session, 2 Parliament Square, Edinburgh EH1 1RQ within [21] days after the date of intimation to you of the summons [*or if the warrant for intimation is executed before calling of the summons*, within 7 days after the summons calls in court. The summons will not call in court earlier than [21] days after the date of intimation to you of the summons]. The date of intimation is the date stated at the top of this notice unless intimation has been made by post in which case the date of intimation is the day after that date.

IF YOU ARE UNCERTAIN ABOUT THE EFFECT OF THIS NOTICE, you should consult a solicitor, Citizens Advice Bureau or other local advice agency or adviser immediately.

(*Signed*)

Messenger-at-Arms
[*or* Solicitor [*or* Agent] for pursuer]
(*Address*)

_____

[1] Form 49.8–G substituted by S.I. 1996 No. 2587.

Rules 49.8(3)(h), 49.8(4) and 49.11   [1] FORM 49.8–H

Form of notice of intimation to local authority in family action by non-parent for a residence order in respect of a child

Date: (*date of posting or other method of intimation*)

To: (*name and address as in warrant for intimation*)

TAKE NOTICE

(*Pursuer's name and address*), pursuer, has brought an action against (*defender's name and address*), defender, in the Court of Session, Edinburgh. The pursuer is seeking a residence order in respect of the child (*name and address of child*). A copy of the summons in the action is attached.

You are requested to submit to the court a report on all the circumstances of the child and on the proposed arrangements for the care and upbringing of the child without delay. On completion of the report please send it, with a copy for each party, to the Deputy Principal Clerk of Session, Court of Session, 2 Parliament Square, Edinburgh EH1 1RQ.

(*Signed*)

Messenger-at-Arms
[*or* Solicitor [*or* Agent] for pursuer]
(*Address*)

On completion of the report please send it, with a copy for each party, to the Deputy Principal Clerk of Session, Court of Session, 2 Parliament Square, Edinburgh EH1 1RQ.

(*Signed*)

Messenger-at-Arms
[*or* Solicitor [*or* Agent] for pursuer]
(*Address*)

----

[1] Form 49.8–H substituted by S.I. 1996 No. 2587.

Rule 49.8(3)(j)   [1] FORM 49.8–J

Form of notice of intimation to person whose consent is necessary or has an interest as heritable creditor in the transfer of property

Date: (*date of posting or other method of intimation*)

To: (*name and address as in warrant for intimation*)

[THE NEXT PAGE IS C 731]

TAKE NOTICE

(*Pursuer's name and address*), pursuer, has brought an action against (*defender's name and address*), defender, in the Court of Session, Edinburgh. A copy of the summons in the action is attached. The pursuer has applied for an order under section 8 of the Family Law (Scotland) Act 1985 to have the ownership of the property at (*address of property*) transferred to his [*or* her] name. [Your consent is necessary for the proposed transfer.]

You may apply to the court by minute to become a party to the action. You must do so at the Office of Court, Court of Session, 2 Parliament Square, Edinburgh EH1 1RQ within [21] days after the date of intimation to you of the summons [*or if the warrant for intimation is executed before calling of the summons*, within seven days after the summons calls in court. The summons will not call in court earlier than [21] days after the date of intimation to you of the summons]. The date of intimation is the date stated at the top of this notice unless intimation has been made by post in which case the date of intimation is the day after that date.

IF YOU ARE UNCERTAIN ABOUT THE EFFECT OF THIS NOTICE, you should consult a solicitor, Citizens Advice Bureau or other local advice agency or adviser immediately.

(*Signed*)

Messenger-at-Arms
[*or* Solicitor [*or* Agent] for pursuer]
(*Address*)

---

[1] Form 49.8–J amended by S.I. 1994 No. 2901 (minor correction).

Rule 49.8(3)(*k*)   [1] FORM 49.8–K

Form of notice of intimation to third party transferee or other person having an interest in the transfer of property

Date: (*date of posting or other method of intimation*)

To: (*name and address as in warrant for intimation*)

TAKE NOTICE

(*Pursuer's name and address*), pursuer, has brought an action against (*defender's name and address*), defender, in the Court of Session, Edinburgh. A copy of the summons in the action is attached. The pursuer has applied for an order under section 18 of the Family Law (Scotland) Act 1985 affecting your property at (*address*).

You may apply to the court by minute to become a party to the action. You must do so at the Office of Court, Court of Session, 2 Parliament Square, Edinburgh EH1 1RQ within [21] days after the date of intimation to you of the summons [*or if the warrant for intimation is executed before calling of the summons*, within seven days after the summons calls in court. The summons will not call in court earlier than [21] days after the date of intimation to you of the summons]. The date of intimation is the date stated at the top of this notice unless intimation has been made by post in which case the date of intimation is the day after that date.

IF YOU ARE UNCERTAIN ABOUT THE EFFECT OF THIS NOTICE, you should consult a solicitor, Citizens Advice Bureau or other local advice agency or adviser immediately.

(*Signed*)

Messenger-at-Arms
[*or* Solicitor [*or* Agent] for pursuer]
(*Address*)

---

[1] Form 49.8–K amended by S.I. 1994 No. 2901 (minor correction).

Rule 49.8(3)(*l***)**   [1] FORM 49.8–L

Form of notice of intimation to third party or other person having an interest in an application under the Matrimonial Homes (Family Protection) (Scotland) Act 1981

Date: (*date of posting or other method of intimation*)

To: (*name and address as in warrant for intimation*)

TAKE NOTICE

(*Pursuer's name and address*), pursuer, has brought an action against (*defender's name and address*), defender, in the Court of Session, Edinburgh. A copy of the summons in the action is attached. In the action, the court may make an order affecting occupancy rights in property at (*address of property*) in which you have an interest.

You may apply to the court by minute to become a party to the action. You must do so at the Office of Court, Court of Session, 2 Parliament Square, Edinburgh EH1 1RQ within [21] days after the date of intimation to you of the summons [*or if the warrant for intimation is executed before calling of the summons*, within seven days after the summons calls in court. The summons will not call in court earlier than [21] days after the date of intimation to you of the summons]. The date of intimation is the date stated at the top of this notice unless intimation has been made by post in which case the date of intimation is the day after that date.

IF YOU ARE UNCERTAIN ABOUT THE EFFECT OF THIS NOTICE, you should consult a solicitor, Citizens Advice Bureau or other local advice agency or adviser immediately.

                              (*Signed*)

                              Messenger-at-Arms
                              [*or* Solicitor [*or* Agent] for pursuer]
                              (*Address*)

---

[1] Form 49.8–L amended by S.I. 1994 No. 2901 (minor correction).

Rule 49.8(3)(m)   [1] FORM 49.8–M

Form of notice of intimation to person responsible for pension arrangement in relation to order for payment in respect of pension lump sum under section 12A of the Family Law (Scotland) Act 1985

Date: (*date of posting or other method of intimation*)

To: (*name and address as in warrant for intimation*)

TAKE NOTICE

(*Pursuer's name and address*), pursuer, has brought an action against (*defender's name and address*), defender, in the Court of Session, Edinburgh. A copy of the summons in the action is attached. The pursuer has applied for an order under section 8 of the Family Law (Scotland) Act 1985 for a capital sum in circumstances where the matrimonial [*or* family] property includes rights in a pension arrangement under which a lump sum is payable. The relevant pension arrangement is (*give details, including number, if known*).

You may apply to the court by minute to become a party to the action. You must do so at the Office of Court, Court of Session, 2 Parliament Square, Edinburgh EH1 1RQ within [21] days after the date of intimation to you of the summons [*or if the warrant for intimation is executed before calling of the summons*, within seven days after the summons calls in court. The summons will not call in court earlier than [21] days after the date of intimation to you of the summons]. The date of intimation is the date stated at the top of this notice unless intimation has been made by post in which case the date of intimation is the day after that date.

IF YOU ARE UNCERTAIN ABOUT THE EFFECT OF THIS NOTICE, you should consult a solicitor, Citizens Advice Bureau or other local advice agency or adviser immediately.

(Signed)

Messenger-at-Arms
[*or* Solicitor [*or* Agent] for pursuer]
(Address)

---

[1] Form 49.8–M inserted by S.I. 1996 No. 1756 (effective 5th August 1996) and amended by S.S.I. 2005 No. 632 (effective 8th December 2005).

Rule 49.8(3)(m)   [1] FORM 49.8–MA

Form of notice of intimation to person responsible for pension arrangement in relation to application for pension sharing order under section 8(1)(baa) of the Family Law (Scotland) Act 1985

Date: *(date of posting or other method of intimation)*.

To: *(name and address as in warrant for intimation)*.

TAKE NOTICE

(Pursuer's name and address), pursuer, has brought an action against *(defender's name and address)*, defender, in the Court of Session, Edinburgh. A copy of the summons in the action is attached. The pursuer has applied for a pension sharing order under section 8(1)(baa) of the Family Law (Scotland) Act 1985. The relevant pension arrangement is *(insert details, including number, if known)*.

You may apply to the court by minute to become a party to the action. You must do so at the Office of Court, Court of Session, 2 Parliament Square, Edinburgh EH1 1RQ within [21] days after the date of intimation to you of the summons [*or if the warrant for intimation is executed before calling of the summons*, within seven days after the summons calls in court. The summons will not call in court earlier than [21] days after the date of intimation to you of the summons]. The date of intimation is the date stated at the top of this notice unless intimation has been made by post in which case the date of intimation is the day after that date.

IF YOU ARE UNCERTAIN ABOUT THE EFFECT OF THIS NOTICE, you should consult a solicitor, Citizens Advice Bureau or other local advice agency or adviser immediately.

(Signed)

Messenger-at-Arms
[*or* Solicitor [*or* Agent] for pursuer]
(Address)

---

[1] Form 49.8-MA inserted by S.S.I. 2000 No. 412 (effective 1st December 2000).

Rule 49.8(7) and Rule 70.16   [1] FORM 49.8–N

Form of notice of intimation to a child of a family action in which an order under section 11 of the Children (Scotland) Act 1995 or Article 12 of the Hague Convention when regulated by Council Regulation (E.C.) No. 2201/2003 of 27th November 2003, is sought

Court Ref. No.

PART 1

THIS PART MUST BE COMPLETED BY THE PURSUER'S SOLICITOR IN LANGUAGE THAT A CHILD IS CAPABLE OF UNDERSTANDING

To: (*name and address of child*)

The court has been asked by your father [*or mother, or (other relative or person as the case may be)*] to decide (*insert appropriate wording to explain section 11 or Article 12 order[s] sought*).

If you want to tell the court your views, you should complete Part 2 of this form and return it to the court in the envelope provided by (*insert date*). This envelope does not need a stamp.

If you return the form, it will be given to the court. The judge may wish to speak to you, and may ask you to come and see him or her.

IF YOU DO NOT UNDERSTAND THIS FORM OR IF YOU WANT HELP TO COMPLETE IT you may get help from a SOLICITOR or you may contact the SCOTTISH CHILD LAW CENTRE ON the FREE ADVICE TELEPHONE LINE ON 0800 328 8970

PART 2

IF YOU WISH THE COURT TO KNOW YOUR VIEWS ABOUT YOUR FUTURE YOU SHOULD COMPLETE THIS PART OF THE FORM

To: Deputy Principal Clerk of Session   Court Ref. No.

From (*insert name of child*)

1. Do you want the court to know what your views are about your future?

YES   NO
☐   ☐
Please tick

2. Would you like someone else to tll the court what your views are about your future?

YES   NO
☐   ☐
Please tick

If YES, please write this person's name and address below:

Name:

Address:

3. Would you like to write to the court to give your views about your future?

YES   NO
☐   ☐
Please tick

If YES, please write your views below. You may continue on a separate piece of paper.

Thank you for taking the time to respond. Please now return the form and any separate piece of paper in the envelope provided.

---

[1] Form 49.8–N substituted by S.S.I. 2005 No. 135, para.3 (effective 2nd March 2005).

FORM 49.8-O

Rule 49.8(3)(m)

Form of notice of intimation to third party or person having an interest in an application under Chapter 3 or 4 of Part 3 of the Civil Partnership Act 2004

Date: (*date of posting or other method of intimation*)

To: (*name and address as in warrant for intimation*)

TAKE NOTICE

(*Pursuer's name and address*), pursuer, has brought an action against (*defender's name and address*), defender, in the Court of Session, Edinburgh. A copy of the summons in the action is attached. In the action, the court may make an order affecting occupancy rights in property at (*address of property*) in which you have an interest.

You may apply to the court by minute to become a party to the action. You must do so at the Office of Court, Court of Session, 2 Parliament Square, Edinburgh EH1 1RQ within [21] days after the date of intimation to you of the summons [*or if the warrant for intimation is executed before the calling of the summons,* within seven days after the summons calls in court. The summons will not call in court earlier than [21] days after the date of intimation to you of the summons]. The date of intimation is the date situated at the top of this notice unless intimation has been made by post in which case the date of intimation is the day after that date.

IF YOU ARE UNCERTAIN ABOUT THE EFFECT OF THIS NOTICE, you should consult a solicitor, Citizens Advice Bureau or other local advice agency or adviser immediately.

(*Signed*)

Messenger-at-Arms

[*or* Solicitor [*or* Agent] for pursuer]

(*Address*)

---

[1] Form 49.8–O inserted by S.S.I. 2005 No. 632 (effective 8th December 2005).

Rule 49.8(3)(o)   FORM 49.8–P

Form of intimation for financial provision on intestacy under section 29(2) of the Family Law (Scotland) Act 2006

Date: (*date of posting or other method of intimation*)

To: (*name and address as in warrant for intimation*)

(*Pursuer's name and address*), pursuer, has brought an action against (*defender's name and address*), defender, in the Court of Session, Edinburgh. A copy of the summons in the action is attached. The pursuer is seeking an order for financial provision on intestacy under section 29(2) of the Family Law (Scotland) Act 2006.

You may apply by minute to become a party to the action. You must do so at the Office of Court, Court of Session, 2 Parliament Square, Edinburgh, EH1 1RQ within [21] days after the date of intimation to you of the summons [*or if the warrant for intimation is executed before the calling of the summons,* within seven days after the summons calls in court. The summons will not call in court earlier than [21] days after the date of intimation to you of the summons]. The date of intimation is the date situation at the top of this notice unless intimation has been made by post in which case the date of intimation is the day after that date.

IF YOU ARE UNCERTAIN ABOUT THE EFFECT OF THIS NOTICE, you should consult a solicitor, Citizens Advice Bureau or other local advice agency or adviser immediately.

> *(Signed)*
>
> Messenger-at-Arms
>
> [*or* Solicitor [*or* Agent] for pursuer]
>
> *(Address)*

---

[2] Form 49.8–P inserted by S.S.I. 2006 No. 206 (effective 4th May 2006).

Rule 49.9(3)　　　　　　　　　　　　[1] FORM 49.9

Form of notice of intimation to person with whom a relevant association is alleged to have occurred

Date:　　*(date of posting or other method of intimation)*

To:　　*(name and address as in warrant for intimation)*

TAKE NOTICE

(*Pursuer's name and address*), pursuer, has brought an action against (*defender's name and address*), defender, in the Court of Session, Edinburgh. A copy of the summons in the action is attached. (*Defender's name*) is alleged to have had a relevant association with you as mentioned in the summons.

You may apply to the court by minute to become a party to the action in order to dispute the truth of the allegations made about you. You must do so at the Office of Court, Court of Session, 2 Parliament Square, Edinburgh EH1 1RQ within [21] days after the date of intimation to you of the summons [*or if the warrant for intimation is executed before calling of the summons*, within seven days after the summons calls in court. The summons will not call in court earlier than [21] days after the date of intimation to you of the summons]. The date of intimation is the date stated at the top of this notice unless intimation has been made by post in which case the date of intimation is the day after that date.

IF YOU ARE UNCERTAIN ABOUT THE EFFECT OF THIS NOTICE, you should consult a solicitor, Citizens Advice Bureau or other local advice agency or adviser immediately.

> *(Signed)*
>
> Messenger-at-Arms
> [*or* Solicitor [*or* Agent] for pursuer]
> *(Address)*

---

[1] Form 49.9 amended by S.I. 1994 No. 2901 (minor correction).

Rule 49.13(1)(b)　　　　　　　　　FORM 49.13–A

Form of request for medical officer of hospital or similar institution

Date:　　*(date of posting or other method of intimation)*

To:　　*(name and address)*

TAKE NOTICE

(*Pursuer's name and address*), pursuer, has brought an action against (*defender's name and address*), defender, in the Court of Session, Edinburgh. A copy of the summons in the action and citation [and a notice [and form of consent] under rule 49.14(1) [*or* rule 49.14A(1)] of the Rules of the Court of Session 1994] are attached.

Please deliver it personally to (*name of defender*) and explain the content or meaning of it to him [*or* her] unless you are satisfied that an explanation would be dangerous to his [*or* her] health. If you are so satisfied you must certify that this is the case and give your reasons on the attached certificate. Thereafter please complete the attached certificate and return it to me in the enclosed stamped addressed envelope.

(*Signed*)

Messenger-at-Arms
[*or* Solicitor [*or* Agent] for pursuer]
(*Address*)

---

[1] Form 49.13–A amended by S.S.I. 2005 No. 632 (effective 8th December 2005).

Rule 49.13(1)(b)(iii) and (2)   [1] Form 49.13–B

Form of certificate by medical officer or hospital or similar institution

IN THE COURT OF SESSION

†(*Cause reference number*)

in the cause

†[A.B.] (*designation and address*)

Pursuer

against

†[C.D.] (*designation and address*)

Defender

I, (*name of medical officer*), hereby certify as follows:—

1. I have received a copy summons in the action of (*pursuer's name*) against (*defender's name*). The defender is under my care at (*address*).

*2. On (*date*) I personally delivered the copy summons to the defender and explained to him [*or* her] its contents.

*2. I have not delivered the copy summons to the defender nor have I explained its contents. My reasons are:—

Signature   ....

Name   ....

Address   ....

....

....

....

Date   ....

†To be completed by or on behalf of the pursuer.
*Medical officer to delete as appropriate.

---

[1] Form 49.13–B amended by S.I. 1997 No. 1050 (minor amendment, effective 6th April 1997).

Rule 49.14(1)(a)(i)   [1] Form 49.14–A

Form of notice to defender where it is stated that he consents to decree of divorce

Date: (*date of posting or other method of service*)

To: (*name and address of defender in summons*)

TAKE NOTICE

(*Pursuer's name and address*), pursuer, has brought an action against you in the Court of Session, Edinburgh. The pursuer seeks divorce from you. A copy of the summons in the action is attached.

1. The summons states that you consent to a decree of divorce. If you do consent your husband [*or* wife] will obtain a decree of divorce if he shows that you have not cohabited with him [*or* her] at any time during a continuous period of one year after marriage and immediately before this action.

2. If your husband [*or* wife] obtains a decree of divorce, the consequences may be as follows:—
    (a) you may lose your rights of inheritance in your wife's [*or* husband's] property;

(b) you may lose the right to any pensions which depends on the marriage continuing or on your being left as a widow (the State widow's pension will not be payable to you when your husband dies);

(c) apart from these consequences there may be others depending on your particular circumstances.

3. If you consent to the grant of decree of divorce, you are still entitled to apply to the court:—

(a) to make financial or other provision for you by making an order under the Family Law (Scotland) Act 1985;

(b) to make an order under section 11 of the Children (Scotland) Act 1995 or for maintenance in respect of any child of the marriage, or any child accepted as such, who is under 16 years of age.

In order to make such an application you must lodge defences to the action seeking any such order. If you wish to do this you should consult a solicitor.

4. If after considering the above you wish to consent to decree of divorce, you should complete and sign the attached notice of consent form, and send it to:—

The Deputy Principal Clerk of Session
2 Parliament Square
Edinburgh EH1 1RQ

You may do so within [21] days after the date of service on you of the summons [*or if service is executed before calling of the summons*, within seven days after the summons calls in court. The summons will not call in court earlier than [21] days after the date of service on you of the summons]. The date of service is the date stated at the top of this notice unless service has been made by post in which case the date of service is the day after that date.

5. If after consent you wish to withdraw your consent, you must immediately inform the Deputy Principal Clerk of Session at the above address in writing. Please state the name of the court action in your letter.

IF YOU ARE UNCERTAIN ABOUT THE EFFECT OF THIS NOTICE, you should consult a solicitor, Citizens Advice Bureau or other local advice agency or adviser immediately.

(*Signed*)

Messenger-at-Arms
[*or* Solicitor [*or* Agent] for pursuer]
(*Address*)

---

[1] Form 49.14–A amended by S.I. 1994 No. 2901 (minor correction), S.I. 1996 No. 2587 and S.S.I. 2006 No. 206 (effective 4th May 2006).

Rules **49.14(1)(a)(i) and 49.19(1)**   Form 49.14–B

Form of notice of consent in action of divorce under section 1(2)(d) of the Divorce (Scotland) Act 1976

NOTICE OF CONSENT TO DIVORCE

I have received a copy of the summons in the court action raised against me by (*pursuer's name and address*).

I understand that it states that I consent to the granting of decree of divorce in this action.

I have considered the consequences of my consent.

I consent to the granting of decree of divorce in this action.

Signature ....

Name (in Block Capitals) ....

Address ....

....

....

....

Date ....

Signature of Witness ....

Name (in Block Capitals) ....

Address ....

....

....

....

Occupation ....

Rule 49.14(1)(a)(ii)   [1] FORM 49.14–C

Form of notice to defender where it is stated that he consents to decree of separation

Date: (*date of posting or other method of service*)

To: (*name and address of defender in summons*)

TAKE NOTICE

(*Pursuer's name and address*), pursuer, has brought an action against you, defender, in the Court of Session, Edinburgh. The pursuer seeks separation from you. A copy of the summons in the action is attached.

1. The summons states that you consent to the grant of a decree of separation. If you consent your husband [*or* wife] will obtain a decree of separation if he shows that you have not cohabited with him [*or* her] at any time during a continuous period of one year after marriage and immediately before this action.

2. If your husband obtains a decree of separation, the consequences may be as follows:—
   (a) you will be obliged to live apart from your husband [*or* wife] but the marriage will continue to exist;
   [(b) your husband will continue to have a legal obligation to support you and his children;]
   [(b) *or* (c)] apart from the above there may be other consequences applicable to you depending on your particular circumstances.

3. If you consent to the grant of a decree of separation, you are still entitled to apply to the court:—
   (a) for an order under section 11 of the Children (Scotland) Act 1995 for maintenance in respect of any child of the marriage, or any child accepted as such, who is under 16 years of age.
   (b) for payment of aliment by your husband [*or* wife] to you.

In order to make such an application you must lodge defences to the action seeking any such order. If you wish to do this you should consult a solicitor.

4. If after considering the above you wish to consent to decree, please complete the attached notice of consent form, and send it to:—

> The Deputy Principal Clerk of Session
> 2 Parliament Square
> Edinburgh EH1 1RQ

You may do so at the Office of Court, Court of Session, 2 Parliament Square, Edinburgh EH1 1RQ within [21] days after the date of service on you of the summons [*or if service is executed before calling of the summons*, within seven days after the summons calls in court. The summons will not call in court earlier than [21] days after the date of service on you of the summons]. The date of service is the date stated at the top of this notice unless service has been made by post in which case the date of service is the day after that date.

5. If after consent you wish to withdraw your consent, you must immediately inform the Deputy Principal Clerk of Session at the above address in writing. Please state the name of the court action in your letter.

IF YOU ARE UNCERTAIN ABOUT THE EFFECT OF THIS NOTICE, you should consult a solicitor, Citizens Advice Bureau or other local advice agency or adviser immediately.

> (*Signed*)

> Messenger-at-Arms
> [*or* Solicitor [*or* Agent] for pursuer]
> (*Address*)

---

[1] Form 49.14–C amended by S.I. 1994 No. 2901 (minor correction), S.I. 1996 No. 2587 and S.S.I. 2006 No. 206 (effective 4th May 2006).

Rules 49.14(1)(a)(ii) and 49.19(1)   FORM 49.14–D

Form of notice of consent in action of separation under section 1(2)(d) of the Divorce (Scotland) Act 1976

NOTICE OF CONSENT TO SEPARATION

I have received a copy of the summons in the court action raised against me by (*pursuer's name and address*).

I understand that it states that I consent to the granting of decree of separation in this action.

I have considered the consequences of my consent.

I consent to the granting of decree of separation in this action.

Signature ....

Name (in Block Capitals) ....

Address ....

....

....

Date ....

Signature of Witness ....

Name (in Block Capitals) ....

Address ....

....

....

Occupation ....

Rule 49.14(1)(b)(i) [1] FORM 49.14–E

Form of notice to defender in an action of divorce where it is stated there has been two years non-cohabitation

Date: (*date of posting or other method of service*)

To: (*name and address of defender in summons*)

TAKE NOTICE

(*Pursuer's name and address*), pursuer, has brought an action against you, defender, in the Court of Session, Edinburgh. The pursuer seeks divorce from you. A copy of the summons in the action is attached.

1. The summons states that you have not cohabited with the pursuer at any time during a continuous period of two years after marriage and immediately before this action. If the pursuer establishes this as a fact the pursuer will obtain a decree of divorce.

2. If the pursuer obtains a decree of divorce, the consequences may be as follows:—
    (a) you may lose your rights of inheritance in your wife's [*or* husband's] property;
    (b) you may lose the right to any pensions which depends on the marriage continuing or on your being left as a widow (the State widow's pension will not be payable to you when your husband dies);
    (c) apart from these consequences there may be others depending on your particular circumstances.

3. If you consent to the grant of decree of divorce, you are nevertheless entitled to apply to the court:—
    (a) to make financial or other provision for you by making an order under the Family Law (Scotland) Act 1985;
    (b) to make an order under section 11 of the Children (Scotland) Act 1995 for maintenance in respect of any child of the marriage, or any child accepted as such, who is under 16 years of age.

In order to make such an application you must lodge defences to the action seeking any such order. If you wish to do this you should consult a solicitor.

If you lodge defences, you may do so at the Office of Court, Court of Session, 2 Parliament Square, Edinburgh EH1 1RQ within [21] days after the date of service on you of the summons [*or if service is executed before calling of the summons*, within seven days after the summons calls in court. The summons will not call in court earlier than [21] days after the date of service on you of the summons]. The date of service is the date stated at the top of this notice unless service has been made by post in which case the date of service is the day after that date.

IF YOU ARE UNCERTAIN ABOUT THE EFFECT OF THIS NOTICE, you should consult a solicitor, Citizens Advice Bureau or other local advice agency or adviser immediately.

(*Signed*)

Messenger-at-Arms
[*or* Solicitor [*or* Agent] for pursuer]
(*Address*)

---

[1] Form 49.14–E amended by S.I. 1994 No. 2901 (minor correction), S.I. 1996 No. 2587 and S.S.I. 2006 No. 206 (effective 4th May 2006).

Rule 49.14(1)(b)(ii) [1] FORM 49.14–F

Form of notice to defender in an action of separation where it is stated there has been two years non-cohabitation

Date: (*date of posting or other method of service*)

To: (*name and address of defender in summons*)

TAKE NOTICE

(*Pursuer's name and address*), pursuer, has raised an action against you, defender, in the Court of Session, Edinburgh. The pursuer seeks separation from you. A copy of the summons in the action is attached.

1. The summons states that you have not cohabited with the pursuer at any time during a continuous period of two years after marriage and immediately before this action. If the pursuer establishes this as a fact and the court is satisfied that there are justified grounds for the decree, the pursuer will obtain a decree of separation.

2. If the pursuer obtains a decree of separation, the consequences may be as follows:—
   (a) you may be obliged to live apart from your husband [*or* wife] but the marriage will continue to exist;
   [(b) your husband will continue to have a legal obligation to support you and his children;]
   [(b) *or* (c)] apart from the above there may be other consequences applicable to you depending on your particular circumstances.

3. If you consent to the granting of a decree of separation, you are still entitled to apply to the court:—
   [(a)] for an order under section 11 of the Children (Scotland) Act 1995 for maintenance in respect of any child of the marriage, or any child accepted as such, who is under 16 years of age;
   [(b)] for payment of aliment by your husband [*or* wife] to you].

4. In order to make such an application you must lodge defences to the action. If you wish to do this you should consult a solicitor.

If you lodge defences, you must do so at the Office of Court, Court of Session, 2 Parliament Square, Edinburgh EH1 1RQ within [21] days after the date of service on you of the summons [*or if service is executed before calling of the summons*, within seven days after the summons calls in court. The summons will not call in court earlier than [21] days after the date of service on you of the summons]. The date of service is the date stated at the top of this notice unless service has been made by post in which case the date of service is the day after that date.

IF YOU ARE UNCERTAIN ABOUT THE EFFECT OF THIS NOTICE, you should consult a solicitor, Citizens Advice Bureau or other local advice agency or adviser immediately.

(*Signed*)

Messenger-at-Arms
[*or* Solicitor [*or* Agent] for pursuer]
(*Address*)

---

[1] Form 49.14–F amended by S.I. 1994 No. 2901 (minor correction), S.I. 1996 No. 2587 and S.S.I. 2006 No. 206 (effective 4th May 2006).

Rule 49.14(1)(c)   [1] Form 49.14–G

Form of notice to defender in action of divorce where an interim gender recognition certificate has been issued

Date: (*date of posting or other method of service*)

To: (*name and address of defender in summons*)

TAKE NOTICE

(*Pursuer's name and address*), pursuer, has raised an action against you, defender, in the Court of Session, Edinburgh. The pursuer seeks divorce from you. A copy of the summons in the action is attached.

1. The summons states that an interim gender recognition certificate has been issued to you [*or* the pursuer]. If the pursuer establishes this as a matter of fact the pursuer will obtain a decree of divorce.

2. If the pursuer obtains a decree of divorce, the consequences may be as follows—
(a) you may lose your rights of inheritance in your wife's [*or* husband's] property;
(b) you may lose the right to any pensions which depend on the marriage continuing or on you being left a widow;
(c) apart from these consequences there may be others depending on your particular circumstances.

3. If the pursuer is entitled to a decree of divorce, you are nevertheless entitled to apply to the court—
(a) to make financial or other provision for you by making an order under the Family Law (Scotland) Act 1985;
(b) to make an order under section 11 of the Children (Scotland) Act 1995 for maintenance in respect of any child of the marriage, or any child accepted as such, who is under 16 years of age.

In order to make such an application you must lodge defences to the action seeking any such order. If you wish to do this you should consult a solicitor.

If you lodge defences, you may do so at the Office of Court, Court of Session, 2 Parliament Square, Edinburgh EH1 1RQ within [21] days after the date of service on you of the summons [*or if service is executed before calling of the summons*, within seven days after the summons calls in court. The summons will not call in court earlier than [21] days after the date of service on you of the summons]. The date of service is the date stated at the top of this notice unless service has been made by post in which case the date of service is the day after that date.

IF YOU ARE UNCERTAIN ABOUT THE EFFECT OF THIS NOTICE, you should consult a solicitor, Citizens Advice Bureau or other local advice agency or adviser immediately.

(*Signed*)
Messenger-at-Arms
[*or* Solicitor [*or* Agent] for pursuer]
(*Address*)

---

[1] Form 49.14–G inserted by S.S.I. 2005 No. 193 (effective 1st April, 2005).

[1] FORM 49.14A–A

Rule 49.14A(1)(i)

Form of notice to defender where it is stated that he consents to decree of dissolution of civil partnership

Date: (*date of posting or other method of service*)

To: (*name and address of defender in summons*)

(*Pursuer's name and address*), pursuer, has brought an action against you in the Court of Session, Edinburgh. The pursuer seeks dissolution of your civil partnership. A copy of the summons in the action is attached.

1. The summons states that you consent to a decree of dissolution of your civil partnership. If you do consent your civil partner will obtain a decree of dissolution of your civil partnership if he [*or* she] shows that you have not cohabited with him [*or* her] at any time during a continuous period of one year after the registration of your civil partnership and immediately before this action.

2. If the pursuer obtains a decree of dissolution of your civil partnership, the consequences may be as follows:—

(a) you may lose your rights of inheritance in your civil partner's property;
(b) you may lose the right to any pensions which depends on the civil partnership continuing or on your civil partner dying;
(c) apart from these consequences there may be others depending on your particular circumstances.

3. If you consent to the grant of decree of dissolution of your civil partnership, you are still entitled to apply to the court—

(a) to make financial or other provision for you by making an order under the Family Law (Scotland) Act 1985;
(b) to make an order under section 11 of the Children (Scotland) Act 1995 or for maintenance in respect of any child of the family, or any child accepted as such, who is under 16 years of age.

In order to make such an application you must lodge defences to the action seeking any such order. If you wish to do this you should consult a solicitor.

4. If after considering the above you wish to consent to decree of dissolution of your civil partnership, you should complete and sign the attached notice of consent form, and send it to—

> The Deputy Principal Clerk of Session
> 2 Parliament Square
> Edinburgh EH1 1RQ

You may do so within [21] days after the date of service on you of the summons [*or if service is executed before calling of the summons*, within seven days after the summons calls in court. The summons will not call in court earlier than [21] days after the date of service on you of the summons]. The date of service is the date stated at the top of this notice unless service has been made by post in which case the date of service is the day after that date.

5. If after consent you wish to withdraw your consent, you must immediately inform the Deputy Principal Clerk of Session at the above address in writing. Please state the name of court action in your letter.

IF YOU ARE CERTAIN ABOUT THE EFFECT OF THIS NOTICE, you should consult a solicitor, Citizens Advice Bureau or other local advice agency of adviser immediately.

> (*Signed*)
>
> Messenger-at-Arms
>
> [*or* Solicitor [*or* Agent] for pursuer]
>
> (*Address*)

---

[1] Form 49.14A–A inserted by S.S.I. 2005 No. 632 (effective 8th December 2005) and S.S.I. 2006 No. 206 (effective 4th May 2006).

[1] FORM 49.14A–B

Rule 49.14A(1)(i)

**Form of notice of consent in action of dissolution of a civil partnership under
section 117(3)(c) of the Civil Partnership Act 2004**

NOTICE OF CONSENT TO DISSOLUTION OF CIVIL PARTNERSHIP

I have received a copy of the summons in the court action raised against me by (*pursuer's name
and address*).

I understand that it states that I consent to the granting of decree of dissolution of my civil
partnership in this action.

I consent to the granting of decree of dissolution of my civil partnership in this action.

Signature ....

Name (in Block Capitals) ....

Address ....

....

....

....

Date ....

Signature of Witness ....

Name (in Block Capitals) ....

Address ....

....

....

....

Occupation ....

[1] Form 49.14A–B inserted by S.S.I. 2005 No. 632 (effective 8th December 2005).

Rule 49.14A(1)(a)(ii)

Form of notice to defender where it is stated that he consents to decree of separation of civil partners

Date: (*date of posting or other method of service*)

To: (*name and address of defender in summons*)

(*Pursuer's name and address*), pursuer, has brought an action against you in the Court of Session, Edinburgh. The pursuer seeks separation from you. A copy of the summons in the action is attached.

1. The summons states that you consent to a decree of separation. If you do consent your civil partner will obtain a decree of separation if he [*or* she] shows that you have not cohabited with him [*or* her] at any time during a continuous period of one year after the registration of your civil partnership and immediately before this action.

2. If the pursuer obtains a decree of separation, the consequences may be as follows:–

     (a)   you may be obliged to live apart from your civil partner but the civil partnership will continue to exist;

     (b)   your civil partner may continue to have a legal obligation to support you and any children of the family;

     (c)   apart from the above there may be other consequences applicable to you depending on your particular circumstances.

3. If you consent to the grant of decree of separation, you are still entitled to apply to the court—

     (a)   for an order under section 11 of the Children (Scotland) Act 1995 for maintenance in respect of any child of the family, or any child accepted as such, who is under 16 years of age;

     (b)   for payment of aliment by your civil partner to you.

In order to make such an application you must lodge defences to the action seeking any such order If you wish to do this you should consult a solicitor.

4. If after considering the above you wish to consent to decree of separation, you should complete and sign the attached notice of consent form, and send it to—

     The Deputy Principal Clerk of Session
     2 Parliament Square
     Edinburgh EH1 1RQ

You may do so within [21] days after the date of service on you of the summons [*or if service is executed before calling of the summons*, within seven days after the summons calls in court. The summons will not call in court earlier than [21] days after the date of service on you of the summons]. The date of service is the date stated at the top of this notice unless service has been made by post in which case the date of service is the day after that date.

5. If after consent you wish to withdraw your consent, you must immediately inform the Deputy Principal Clerk of Session at the above address in writing. Please state the name of court action in your letter.

IF YOU ARE UNCERTAIN ABOUT THE EFFECT OF THIS NOTICE, you should consult a solicitor, Citizens Advice Bureau or other local advice agency or adviser immediately.

     (*Signed*)

     Messenger-at-Arms

     [*or* Solicitor [*or* Agent] for pursuer]

     (*Address*)

---

[1]   Form 49.14A–C inserted by S.S.I. 2005 No. 632 (effective 8th December 2005) and S.S.I. 2006 No. 206 (effective 4th May 2006).

¹ FORM 49.14A–D

Rule 49.14A(1)(a)(ii)

Form of notice of consent in action of separation of civil partners under section 117(3)(c) of the Civil Partnership Act 2004

NOTICE OF CONSENT TO SEPARATION OF CIVIL PARTNERS

I have received a copy of the summons in the court action raised against me by (*pursuer's name and address*).

I understand that it states that I consent to the granting of decree of dissolution of my civil partnership in this action.

I consent to the granting of decree of dissolution of my civil partnership in this action.

Signature ....

Name (in Block Capitals) ....

Address ....

....

....

....

Date ....

Signature of Witness ....

Name (in Block Capitals) ....

Address ....

....

....

Occupation ....

_____

¹ Form 49.14A-D inserted by S.S.I. 2005 No. 632 (effective 8th December 2005).

[1] FORM 49.14A–E

Rule 49.14A(1)(b)(i)

Form of notice to defender in an action of dissolution of civil partnership under section 117(3)(d) of the Civil Partnership Act 2004

Date: (*date of posting or other method of service*)

To: (*name and address of defender in summons*)

(*Pursuer's name and address*), pursuer, has brought an action against you in the Court of Session. Edinburgh. The pursuer seeks dissolution of your civil partnership. A copy of the summons in the action is attached.

1. The summons states that you have not cohabited with the pursuer at any time during a continuous period of two years after the registration of your civil partnership and immediately before this action. If the pursuer establishes this as a fact the pursner will obtain a decree of dissolution of your civil partnership.

2. If the pursuer obtains a decree of dissolution of your civil partnership, the consequences may be as follows:—

    (a) you may lose your rights of inheritance in your civil partner's property;

    (b) you may lose the right to any pensions which depends on the civil partnership continuing or on your civil partner dying;

    (c) apart from these consequences there may be others depending on your particular circumstances.

3. If you consent to the grant of decree of dissolution of your civil partnership, you are still entitled to apply to the court—

    (a) to make financial or other provision for you by making an order under the Family Law (Scotland) Act 1985;

    (b) to make an order under section 11 of the Children (Scotland) Act 1995 or for maintenance in respect of any child of the family, or any child accepted as such, who is under 16 years of age.

In order to make such an application you must lodge defences to the action seeking any such order If you wish to do this you should consult a solicitor.

If you lodge defences, you may do so at the Offices of Court, Court of Session, 2 Parliament Square, Edinburgh EH1 1RQ within [21] days after the date of service on you of the summons [*or if service is executed before calling of the summons*, within seven days after the summons calls in court. The summons will not call in court earlier than [21] days after the date of service on you of the summons]. The date of service is the date stated at the top of this notice unless service has been made by post in which case the date of service is the day after that date.

IF YOU ARE UNCERTAIN ABOUT THE EFFECT OF THIS NOTICE, you should consult a solicitor, Citizens Advice Bureau or other local advice agency or adviser immediately.

                  (*Signed*)

                  Messenger-at-Arms

                  [*or* Solicitor [*or* Agent] for pursuer]

                  (*Address*)

---

[1] Form 49.14A–E inserted by S.S.I. 2005 No. 632 (effective 8th December 2005) and S.S.I. 2006 No. 206 (effective 4th May 2006).

Rule 49.14A(i)(b)(ii)

Form of notice to defender in an action of separation of civil partners on grounds under section 117(3)(d) of the Civil Partnership Act 2004

Date: (*date of posting or other method of service*)

To: (*name and address of defender in summons*)

(*Pursuer's name and address*), pursuer, has brought an action against you in the Court of Session, Edinburgh. The pursuer seeks separation from you. A copy of the summons in the action is attached.

1. The summons states that you have not cohabited with him the pursuer at any time during a continuous period of two years after the registration of your civil partnership and immediately before this action. If the pursuer establishes this as a fact and the court is satisfied that there are justified grounds for the decree the pursuer will obtain a decree of separation.

2. If the pursuer obtains a decree of separation, the consequences may be as follows:–

   (a) you may be obliged to live apart from your civil partner but the civil partnership will continue to exist;

   (b) your civil partner may continue to have a legal obligation to support you and any children of the family;

   (c) apart from the above there may be other consequences applicable to you depending on your particular circumstances.

3. If you consent to the grant of decree of separation, you are still entitled to apply to the court—

   (a) for an order under section 11 of the Children (Scotland) Act 1995 for maintenance in respect of any child of the family, or any child accepted as such, who is under 16 years of age;

   (b) for payment of aliment by your civil partner to you.

4. In order to make such an application you must lodge defences to the action. If you wish to do this you should consult a solicitor.

If you lodge defences, you must do so at the Office of Court, Court of Session, 2 Parliament Square, Edinburgh EH1 1RQ within [21] days after the date of service on you of the summons [*or if service is executed before calling of the summons*, within seven days after the summons calls in court. The summons will not call in court earlier than [21] days after the date of service on you of the summons]. The date of service is the date stated at the top of this notice unless service has been made by post in which case the date of service is the day after that date.

IF YOU ARE UNCERTAIN ABOUT THE EFFECT OF THIS NOTICE, you should consult a solicitor, Citizens Advice Bureau or other local advice agency or adviser immediately.

(*Signed*)

Messenger-at-Arms

[*or* Solicitor [*or* Agent] for pursuer]

(*Address*)

───────────

[1] Form 49.14A–F inserted by S.S.I. 2005 No. 632 (effective 8th December 2005) and S.S.I. 2006 No. 206 (effective 4th May 2006).

Rule 49.14A(1)(c)
[1] FORM 49.14A–G

Form of notice to defender in action of dissolution of civil partnership on grounds under section 117(2)(b) of the Civil Partnership Act 2004

Date: (*date of posting or other method of service*)

To: (*name and address of defender in summons*)

(*Pursuer's name and address*), pursuer, has brought an action against you in the Court of Session, Edinburgh. The pursuer seeks dissolution of your civil partnership. A copy of the summons in the action is attached.

1. The summons states that an interim gender recognition certificate has been issued to you [*or* your civil partner] after the date of registration of your civil partnership. If the pursuer establishes this as a fact the pursuer will obtain a decree of dissolution of your civil partnership.

2. If the pursuer obtains a decree of dissolution of your civil partnership, the consequences may be as follows:–

   (a) you may lose your rights of inheritance in your civil partner's property;

   (b) you may lose the right to any pensions which depends on the civil partnership continuing or on your civil partner dying;

   (c) apart from these consequences there may be others depending on your particular circumstances.

3. If you consent to the grant of decree of dissolution of your civil partnership, you are still entitled to apply to the court–

   (a) to make financial or other provision for you by making an order under the Family Law (Scotland) Act 1985;

   (b) to make an order under section 11 of the Children (Scotland) Act 1995 or for maintenance in respect of any child of the family, or any child accepted as such, who is under 16 years of age.

4. In order to make such an application you must lodge defences to the action. If you wish to do this you should consult a solicitor.

5. If you lodge defences, you must do so at the Offices of Court, Court of Session, 2 Parliament Square, Edinburgh EH1 1RQ within [21] days after the date of service on you of the summons [*or if service is executed before calling of the summons*, within seven days after the summons calls in court. The summons will not call in court earlier than [21] days after the date of service on you of the summons]. The date of service is the date stated at the top of this notice unless service has been made by post in which case the date of service is the day after that date.

---

[1] Form 49.14A–G inserted by S.S.I. 2005 No. 632 (effective 8th December 2005).

Rule 49.29(1)
[1] FORM 49.29–A

Form of minute for decree in undefended family action

(*Name of counsel*) for the pursuer having considered the evidence contained in the affidavits and the other documents as specified in the attached schedule and being satisfied that on this evidence a motion for decree in terms of the conclusions of the summons [*or in such restricted terms as may be appropriate*] may properly be made, moves the court accordingly.

IN RESPECT WHEREOF

(*Signature of counsel or other person having a right of audience*)

SCHEDULE
(list of numbered documents)

---

[1] Form 49.29–A amended by S.I. 1994 No. 2901.

Rule 49.29(2)(b)   Form 49.29–B

Form of official card to be completed when decree sought in undefended family action

C	UNDEFENDED FAMILY ACTION DECREE SLIP (Use Block Capitals Only)	FOR COURT USE ONLY DISPOSAL
PURSUER .... (Christian names or forenames and surname only)		LORD .... DATE.......
v		DATE......
DEFENDER .... (Christian names or forenames and surname only)		DATE......
COUNSEL .... (or other person having a right of audience)		DATE......
SOLICITOR		DATE......

Rule 49.70(1) and (2) and 49.71G(1)   Form 49.70

[*Omitted by S.S.I. 2006 No. 206 (effective 4th May 2006)*]

Rule 49.73(1)   [1] Form 49.73–A

Under the Divorce (Scotland) Act 1976, Section 1(2)(d)
Simplified Procedure

Court of Session
Extracts Department (SP)
Parliament House
Edinburgh EH1 1RQ

Tel: 031–225 2595

APPLICATION FOR DIVORCE (WITH CONSENT OF OTHER PARTY TO THE MARRIAGE)
HUSBAND AND WIFE HAVING LIVED APART FOR AT LEAST ONE YEAR

Before completing this form, you should have read the leaflet entitled "Do it yourself Divorce", which explains the circumstances in which a divorce may be sought by that method. If the simplified procedure appears to suit your circumstances, you may use this form to apply for divorce.

Below you will find directions designed to assist you with your application. Please follow them carefully. In the event of difficulty, you may contact the Court's Divorce Section at the above address, or any Sheriff Clerk's Office or Citizens Advice Bureau.

Directions for making Application

WRITE IN INK, USING BLOCK CAPITALS

Application
(Part 1)

1. Complete and sign Part 1 of the form (pages 3–7), paying particular attention to the notes opposite each section.

Consent of
Husband/Wife
(Part 2)

2. When you have filled in Part 1 of the form, attach the (blue) Instruction Sheet SP3 to it and send both documents to your husband/wife for completion of the consent at Part 2 (page 9).

   NOTE: If your husband/wife does NOT complete and sign the form of consent, your application cannot proceed further under the simplified procedure. In that event, if you still wish to obtain a divorce, you should consult a solicitor.

Affidavit
(Part 3)

3. When the application has been returned to you with the Consent (Part 2) duly completed and signed, you should then take the form to a Justice of the Peace, Notary Public, Commissioner for Oaths or other duly authorised person so that your affidavit in Part 3 (page 10) can be completed and sworn.

Returning
completed
Application
Form to
court

4. When directions 1–3 above have all been carried out, your application is now ready to be sent to the court. With it you must enclose:—

   (i) Your marriage certificate (the document headed "Extract of an entry in a Register of Marriages"), which will be returned to you in due course, and

   (ii) Either   a cheque or postal order for the sum of £[40] in respect of the court fee, crossed and made payable to "Court of Session",

   or   a completed form SP15, claiming exemption from the court fee.

5. Receipt of your application will be promptly acknowledged. Should you wish to withdraw the application for any reason, please contact the court immediately.

THE NOTES ON THIS AND THE FOLLOWING PAGES ARE DESIGNED TO ASSIST YOU. PLEASE READ THEM CAREFULLY BEFORE COMPLETING EACH SECTION OF THE FORM.

Notes on Sections 1 and 2 opposite

(i) The names entered in Sections 1 and 2 opposite must be those shown on your marriage certificate. If you are known by another name which does not appear on that certificate, please write that name in brackets.

(ii) The surname given for a wife must be her present married name. Her maiden name and any names from previous marriages should be entered in the space for other names.

(iii) Home addresses should be given where these are known. The court is required by law to serve a copy of this application on your husband/wife.

Note on Section 3 opposite

"Domiciled" means that the person concerned regards Scotland as his/her permanent home and intends to live permanently in Scotland in the foreseeable future.

"the Council Regulation" means Council Regulation (EC) No. 2201/2003 of 27th November 2003 concerning jurisdiction and the recognition and enforcement of judgments in matrimonial matters and in matters of parental responsibility (O.J. No L. 338, 23.12.2003, p.1)

[1] The list of Contracting States is found in section 12(5)(b) of the Domicile and Matrimonial Proceedings Act 1973. As at 26th February 2007 the Contracting States are: Belgium, Cyprus, Czech Republic, Germany, Greece, Spain, Estonia, France, Hungary, Ireland, Italy, Latvia, Lithuania, Luxembourg, Malta, Netherlands, Austria, Poland, Portugal, Slovak Republic, Slovenia, Finland, Sweden and the United Kingdom.

---

[1] Form 49.73A amended by S.S.I. 2007 No. 7, para. 20 (effective 26th February 2007).

Notes on Section 4 opposite

You will be able to obtain these details from your marriage certificate (extract entry in the register of marriages) which must accompany this application form, when you send it to the court.

A photocopy of the marriage certificate will NOT be accepted. If you cannot find the original, you should apply for an official copy to:
  General Register Office (Scotland), Registration Section, New Register House, Edinburgh EH1 3YT, or the office where the marriage was registered.
stating both husband's and wife's full names, and the date and place of the marriage.

(Note that the Registrar will charge a fee for this service.)

[1] **PART 1**

WRITE IN INK, USING BLOCK CAPITALS

1.
NAME AND ADDRESS OF APPLICANT

Surname ....   Other name(s) ....
                                                         in full
Present ....
Address ....   Daytime
                                                         Telephone
                                                         Number
                                                         (if any) ....

2.
NAME AND ADDRESS OF HUSBAND/WIFE

Surname ....   Other name(s) ....
                                                         in full
Present ....
Address ....   Daytime
                                                         Telephone
                                                         Number
                                                         (if any) ....

3.
JURISDICTION

Please indicate with a tick ( ) in the appropriate box or boxes which of the following apply:

PART A

(i)   My spouse and I are habitually resident in Scotland   ☐

(ii)   My spouse and I were last habitually resident in Scotland, and one of us still resides there   ☐

(iii)   My spouse is habitually resident in Scotland   ☐

(iv)   I am habitually resident in Scotland having resided there for at least a year immediately before this application was made   ☐

(v)   I am habitually resident in Scotland having resided there for at least six months immediately before this application was made and am domiciled in Scotland   ☐

(vi)   My spouse and I are domiciled in Scotland   ☐

Part B applies where the defender is not a national of a Contracting State (other than the UK or Ireland) or domiciled in Ireland

PART B

(i)   I am domiciled in Scotland   ☐

(ii)   My spouse is domiciled in Scotland   ☐

AND

(iii)   No court of a Contracting State has jurisdiction under the Council Regulation   ☐

4.
DETAILS OF PRESENT MARRIAGE

Place of Marriage: .... (Registration District)

Date of Marriage:
               Day .... Month .... Year ....

Notes on Section 5 opposite

You and your husband/wife must have lived apart from each other for a continuous period of at least one year after the date of your marriage and immediately before the date of this application.

This minimum period of one year's separation is extended if you and your husband/wife have lived together again for **not more than six months in all** during that one year period. For example, if you lived together for three months in total during the one year period, then you should not complete this application until one year and three months have elapsed from the date of your original separation.

Notes on Section 6 opposite

Is there a reasonable chance that your can still settle the differences with your husband/wife and resume normal married life?

Are you satisfied that there is now no possibility of the marriage succeeding?

Note on Section 7 opposite

If your husband/wife is not prepared to sign the form of consent at Part 2 of this application, you will not obtain a divorce by this method.

Note on Section 9 opposite

"Children of the marriage" includes any adopted children and/or children accepted into the family.

---

[1] Amended by S.S.I. 2004 No. 52

PART 1 (continued)

5.
PERIOD OF SEPARATION

  (i) Please state the date on which you ceased to live with your husband/wife. (If more than 1½ years, just give the month and year)   Day .... Month .... Year ....

  (ii) Have you lived with your husband/wife since that date?
         (Tick box which applies)   YES   NO

  (iii) If yes, for how long in total did you live together before finally separating again?   ....Months

---

6.
RECONCILIATION

Is there any reasonable prospect of reconciliation with your husband/wife?
(Tick box which applies)   YES   NO

Do you consider that the marriage has broken down irretrievably?
(Tick box which applies)   YES   NO

7.
CONSENT

Does your husband/wife consent to a divorce being granted?   *(Tick box which applies)*   YES   NO

8.
MENTAL DISABILITY

Is your husband/wife incapable of managing
his/her affairs because of a mental disorder
(mental illness, personality disorder or
learning disability)

YES   NO

                  (Tick box which applies)   (If yes, give details)

9.
CHILDREN

Are there any children of the marriage under
the age of 16?   *(Tick box which applies)*

YES   NO

10.
OTHER COURT ACTIONS

Are your aware of any other court actions
currently proceeding in any country (including Scotland) which may affect your
marriage?

YES   NO

                  (Tick box which applies)   (If yes, give details)

10A.
REMARRIAGE

[*Omitted by S.S.I. 2007 No. 7, para. 20 (effective 26th February 2007).*]

Notes on Section 11 opposite

No claim can be made in this form of divorce application for payment to you of a periodical allowance (*i.e.* regular payment of money weekly, monthly,[1] etc.,[2] for your maintenance) or a capital sum (*i.e.* lump sum). If you wish to make such a claim, you should consult a solicitor.

    NOTE: While it may be possible to obtain an order for periodical allowance after divorce, the right to payment of a capital sum is lost once decree of divorce is granted.

[1] No application can be made in this form of divorce application for postponement of decree under section 3A of the Divorce (Scotland) Act 1976. On an application under that section, the court may postpone the grant of decree of divorce if it is satisfied that:
- (a) the applicant is prevented from entering into a religious marriage by virtue of a requirement of the religion of that marriage; and
- (b) the other party can act so as to remove or enable or contribute to the removal of, the impediment which prevents that marriage.

    As at 26th February 2007 "religious marriage" for the purposes of section 3A of the Divorce (Scotland) Act 1976 means a marriage solemnised by a celebrant of any Hebrew congregation (i.e. a Jewish marriage) (S.S.I. 2006/253).

    If you wish to make such an application you should consult a solicitor or Citizens' Advice Bureau.

11.
DECLARATION AND REQUEST FOR DIVORCE

I confirm that the facts stated in Sections 1–10 above apply to my marriage.

I do NOT ask the court to make any financial awards in connection with this application.

[1] I do NOT ask the court to postpone the grant of decree under section 3A of the Divorce (Scotland) Act 1976.

I request the court to grant decree of divorce from my husband/wife.

....
          (Date)   (Signature)

IMPORTANT—Part 1 MUST be completed, signed and dated before sending the application
form to your husband/wife.

_____

[1] Form 49.73A, Pt. 1 amended by S.S.I. 2007 No. 7, para. 20 (effective 26th February 2007).

NOTES ON COMPLETING PART 2 OPPOSITE (Page 9)

_____

1. Read over carefully PART 1 (pages 3–7) of this application, which has already been
    completed by your husband/wife.

2. **Financial Provisions**

    Please note that in Section 11 of Part 1, the Application states that he/she does NOT claim
    any financial awards by way of periodical allowance or capital sum. You also are required
    to state (items (c) and (d) opposite) that you make no claim upon the Applicant for
    payment of a periodical allowance or capital sum.

    Note: While it may be possible to obtain an order for **periodical allowance** after
              divorce, the right to payment of a **capital sum** is lost once decree of divorce is
              granted.

[1] 2A. **Postponement of decree**

    Please note that no application can be made in this form of divorce application for
    postponement of decree under section 3A of the Divorce (Scotland) Act 1976. On an
    application under that section, the court may postpone the grant of decree of divorce if it is
    satisfied that:
      (a) the applicant is prevented from entering into a religious marriage by virtue of a
           requirement of the religion of that marriage; and
      (b) the other party can act so as to remove or enable or contribute to the removal of,
           the impediment which prevents that marriage.
    As at 26th February 2007 "religious marriage" for the purposes of section 3A of the
    Divorce (Scotland) Act 1976 means a marriage solemnised by a celebrant of any Hebrew
    congregation (i.e. a Jewish marriage) (S.S.I. 2006/253).
    In Section 11 of Part 1, the Applicant states that he/she does not apply for postponement of
    decree under section 3A of the Divorce (Scotland) Act 1976. You are also required to state
    (item (f) opposite) that you make no such application.

3. **Warning**

    Divorce may result in the loss to you of property rights (*e.g.* the right to succeed to the
    Applicant's estate on his/her death) or the right, where appropriate, to a widow's pension.

    (If you are in any doubt about signing this form of consent you should consult a solicitor.)

_____

[1] Inserted by S.S.I. 2007 No. 7, para. 20 (effective 26th February 2007).

[1] **PART 2**

CONSENT BY APPLICANT'S HUSBAND/WIFE TO DIVORCE

_____

**NOTE: Before completing this Part of the form,
        please read Part 1 and the notes opposite (page 8).**

I, ...
      (Full names, in BLOCK letters, of Applicant's husband/wife)

residing at

....

     (Address, also in BLOCK letters)

....

....

HEREBY STATE THAT

    (a)   I have read Part 1 of this application;

    (b)   The Applicant has lived apart from me a continuous period of 1 year immediately preceding the date of the application (Section 11 of Part 1);

    (c)   I do not ask the court to make any order for payment to me by the Applicant of a periodical allowance (*i.e.* a regular payment of money weekly or monthly, etc., for maintenance);

    (d)   I do not ask the court to make any order for payment to me by the Applicant of a capital sum (*i.e.* a lump sum payment);

    (e)   I understand that divorce may result in the loss to me of property rights and

    (f)   I do not ask the court to postpone the grant of decree under section 3A of the Divorce (Scotland) Act 1976; and

    (g)   **I CONSENT TO DECREE OF DIVORCE BEING GRANTED IN RESPECT OF THIS APPLICATION.**

....

          (Date)   (Signature)

NOTE: You may withdraw your consent, even after giving it, at any time before divorce is granted by the court. Should you wish to do so, you must immediately advise:—

The Court of Session
Extracts Department (SP)
Parliament House
Edinburgh EH1 1RQ

—————

[1] Form 49.73A, Pt. 2 amended by S.S.I. 2007 No. 7, para. 20 (effective 26th February 2007).

PART 3

APPLICANT'S AFFIDAVIT

To be completed only after Parts 1 and 2 have been signed and dated.

I, (*insert Applicant's full name*) ....

residing at (*insert Applicant's present home address*) ....

....

Town ....   Country ....

SWEAR that to the best of my knowledge and belief:

    (1) the facts stated in Part 1 of this Application are true; and

    (2) the signature in Part 2 of this Application is that of my *husband/wife.

Signature of Applicant ....

SWORN at (Place) ....

this .... day of ....19 ....

before me (full name) ....

(full address) ....

....

....

To be completed
by Justice of Peace,
Notary Public or
Commissioner for
Oaths

Signature ....

*Justice of Peace/*Notary Public/*Commissioner for Oaths

*Delete where not applicable.

---

[1] Form 49.73–A amended by S.S.I. 2004 No. 52 and S.S.I. 2005 No. 632 and S.S.I. 2006 No. 206 (effective 4th May 2006).

Rule 49.73(2)   [1,2] FORM 49.73–B

Under the Divorce (Scotland) Act 1976, Section 1(2)(e)
Simplified Procedure

Court of Session
Extracts Department (SP)
Parliament House
Edinburgh EH1 1RQ

Tel: 031–225 2595

APPLICATION FOR DIVORCE
HUSBAND AND WIFE HAVING LIVED APART FOR AT LEAST TWO YEARS

Before completing this form, you should have read the leaflet entitled "Do it yourself Divorce", which explains the circumstances in which a divorce may be sought by that method. If the simplified procedure appears to suit your circumstances, you may use this form to apply for divorce.

Below you will find directions designed to assist you with your application. Please follow them carefully. In the event of difficulty, you may contact the Court's Divorce Section at the above address, or any Sheriff Clerk's Office or Citizens Advice Bureau.

Directions for making Application

WRITE IN INK, USING BLOCK CAPITALS

Application   1. Complete and sign Part 1 of the form (pages 3–7), paying particular
(Part 1)   attention to the notes opposite each section.

Affidavit   2. When you have completed Part 1, you should take the form to a Justice of
(Part 2)   the Peace, Notary Public, Commissioner for Oaths or other duly
                    authorised person so that your affidavit in Part 2 (page 8) can be
                    completed and sworn.

Returning   3. When directions 1 and 2 above have all been carried out, your application
completed   is now ready to be sent to the court. With it you must
Application   enclose:—
Form to court

Release 90: March 2007

(i) Your marriage certificate (the document headed "Extract of an entry in a Register of Marriages"), which will be returned to you in due course. Check the notes on page 2 to see if you also need to obtain a letter from the General Register Office stating that there is no record that your spouse has divorced you.

(ii) Either   a cheque or postal order for the court fee of £[40] crossed and made payable to "Court of Session",

or   a completed form SP15, claiming exemption from the court fee.

4.   Receipt of your application will be promptly acknowledged. Should you wish to withdraw the application for any reason, please contact the court immediately.

THE NOTES ON THIS AND FOLLOWING PAGES ARE DESIGNED TO ASSIST YOU. PLEASE READ THEM CAREFULLY BEFORE COMPLETING EACH SECTION OF THE FORM.

Notes on Sections 1 and 2 opposite

(i) The names entered in Sections 1 and 2 opposite must be those on your marriage certificate. If you are known by another name which does not appear on that certificate, please write that name in brackets.

(ii) The surname given for a wife must be her present married name. Her maiden name and any names from previous marriages should be entered in the space for other names.

(iii) Home addresses should be given where these are known. The court is required by law to serve a copy of this application on your husband/wife.

Note on Section 3 opposite

If the address of your husband/wife is NOT known or cannot reasonably be ascertained, please enter "not known" in this section; you must take all reasonable steps to find out where your husband/wife is living and state on a separate sheet what steps you have taken and attach it to this form. Then proceed to Section 4.

N.B. The statement must be signed.

Notes on Section 4 opposite

In the event that the address of your husband/wife is unknown to you, the court is required by law to intimate a copy of this application to:

(i) ONE of the next-of-kin of your husband/wife. ("Next-of-kin" does not include yourself or any children of the marriage for the purposes of this application.)

(ii) ALL children of your marriage aged 16 years or over, whether or not they live with you.

When entering the details of the next-of-kin, if any, please state his or her relationship to your husband/wife (i.e.—"mother", "father", "brother", "sister", etc.)

If you do not know the identity or whereabouts of any of the next-of-kin of your husband/wife, or the whereabouts of any of the children of your marriage, please enter "not known" where appropriate.

LETTER FROM GENERAL REGISTER OFFICE. If you do not know the address of your spouse and you were married in Scotland, you must obtain a letter from the General Register Office stating that there is no record that your spouse has divorced you. The letter must be issued not more than one month before the date of posting this application to the court. If you require to obtain a letter you should apply to:

General Register Office (Scotland), Registration Branch, New Register House, Edinburgh, EH1 3YT, stating both husband's and wife's full names, the date and place of your marriage and requesting that a search be made to confirm that there is no record that your husband/wife has divorce you. (Note – a fee will be charged for this service).

The requirement to obtain a letter from the General Register Office does not apply if you were married outwith Scotland.

PART 1

WRITE IN INK, USING BLOCK CAPITALS

1.
NAME AND ADDRESS OF APPLICANT

Surname ....

Present
Address ....

....

Other
name(s) ....
in full ....

Daytime
Telephone
Number
(if any) ....

2.
NAME OF HUSBAND/WIFE

Surname ....

Other
name(s) ....
in full

3.
ADDRESS OF HUSBAND/WIFE (if the address of your husband/wife is not known, please enter "not known" and proceed to Section 4)

Present
Address ....

....

Daytime
Telephone
Number
(if any) ....

4.
Only complete this section if you do not know the present address of your husband/wife

NEXT-OF-KIN

Name ....

Relationship
to your
husband/wife ....

Address ....

....

....

CHILDREN OF THE MARRIAGE

Names and dates of birth

....

....

....

Addresses

....

....

....

....

....

If sufficient space is not available here to list all the children of the marriage, please continue on a separate sheet and attach to this form.

Note on Section 5 opposite

"Domiciled" means that the person concerned regards Scotland as his/her permanent home and intends to live permanently in Scotland in the foreseeable future.

"the Council Regulation" means Council Regulation (EC) No. 2201/2003 of 27th November 2003 concerning jurisdiction and the recognition and enforcement of judgments in matrimonial matters and in matters of parental responsibility (O.J. No L. 338, 23.12.2003, p.1)

The list of Contracting States is found in section 12(5)(b) of the Domicile and Matrimonial Proceedings Act 1973. As at 26th February 2007 the Contracting States are: Belgium, Cyprus, Czech Republic, Germany, Greece, Spain, Estonia, France, Hungary, Ireland, Italy, Latvia, Lithuania, Luxembourg, Malta, Netherlands, Austria, Poland, Portugal, Slovak Republic, Slovenia, Finland, Sweden and the United Kingdom.

Notes on Section 6 opposite

You will be able to obtain these details from your marriage certificate (extract entry in a register of marriages), which must accompany this application form when you send it to the court.

A photocopy of the marriage certificate will NOT be accepted.

Notes on Section 7 opposite

You and your husband/wife must have lived apart from each other for a continuous period of at least 2 years and after the date of your marriage and immediately before the date of this application.

This minimum period of 2 years separation is extended if you and your husband/wife have lived together again for **not more than 6 months in all** during that 2 year period. For example, if you lived together for 3 months in total during the 2 years period, then you should not complete this application until 2 years and 3 months have elapsed from the date of your original separation.

Notes on Section 8 opposite

Is there a reasonable chance that you can still settle the differences with your husband/wife and resume normal married life?

Are you satisfied that there is now no possibility of the marriage succeeding?

[1] **PART 1 (continued)**

5.
JURISDICTION

Please indicate with a tick ( ) in the appropriate box or boxes which of the following apply:

PART A

(i)   My spouse and I are habitually resident in
        Scotland   ☐

(ii)   My spouse and I were last habitually resident in
        Scotland, and one of us still resides there   ☐

(iii)   My spouse is habitually resident in Scotland   ☐

(iv)   I am habitually resident in Scotland having
        resided there for at least a year immediately   ☐
        before this application was made

(v)   I am habitually resident in Scotland having
        resided there for at least six months immediately
        before this application was made and am   ☐
        domiciled in Scotland

(vi)   My spouse and I are domiciled in Scotland   ☐

**Part B applies where the defender is not a national of a Contracting State (other than the UK or
Ireland) or domiciled in Ireland**

PART B

(i)   I am domiciled in Scotland   ☐

(ii)   My spouse is domiciled in Scotland   ☐

AND

(iii)   No court of a Contracting State has jurisdiction   ☐
        under the Council Regulation

6.
DETAILS OF PRESENT MARRIAGE

Place of Marriage: .... (Registration District)

Date of Marriage:

        Day .... Month .... Year ....

7.
PERIOD OF SEPARATION

(i)   Please state the date on which you
        ceased to live with your husband/
        wife. (If more than 2½ years, just
        give the month and year)   Day .... Month .... Year ....

(ii)   Have you lived with your husband/   ☐ YES   ☐ NO
        wife since that date?
                (*Tick box which applies*)

(iii)   If yes, for how long in total did you
        live together before finally separat-
        ing again?   ....Months

8.
RECONCILIATION

Is there any reasonable prospect of reconcili-   ☐ YES   ☐ NO
ation with your husband/wife?
                (*Tick box which applies*)

Do you consider that the marriage has   ☐ YES   ☐ NO
broken down irretrievably?
                (*Tick box which applies*

Note on Section 10 opposite

"Children of the marriage" includes any adopted children and/or children accepted into the family.

Notes on Section 12 opposite

No claim can be made in this form of divorce application for payment to you of a periodical allowance (*i.e.* regular payment of money weekly, monthly, etc., for your maintenance) or a capital sum (*i.e.* lump sum). If you wish to make such a claim, you should consult a solicitor.

NOTE: While it may be possible to obtain an order for periodical allowance after divorce, the right to payment of a capital sum is lost once decree of divorce is granted.

No application can be made in this form of divorce application for postponement of decree under section 3A of the Divorce (Scotland) Act 1976. On an application under that section, the court may postpone the grant of decree of divorce if it is satisfied that:

(a) the applicant is prevented from entering into a religious marriage by virtue of a requirement of the religion of that marriage; and

(b) the other party can act so as to remove or enable or contribute to the removal of, the impediment which prevents that marriage.

As at 26th February 2007 "religious marriage" for the purposes of section 3A of the Divorce (Scotland) Act 1976 means a marriage solemnised by a celebrant of any Hebrew congregation (i.e. a Jewish marriage) (S.S.I. 2006/253).

If you wish to make such an application you should consult a solicitor or Citizens' Advice Bureau.

PART 1 (continued)

9.
MENTAL DISABILITY

As far as you are aware is your husband/wife incapable of managing his/her affairs because of a mental disorder (whether mental illness, personality disorder or learning disability)?

☐ YES   ☐ NO

(If yes, give details below)

10.
CHILDREN

Are there any children of the marriage under the age of 16?   (*Tick box which applies*)

☐ YES   ☐ NO

11.
OTHER COURT ACTIONS

Are you aware of any other court actions currently proceeding in any country (including Scotland) which may affect your marriage

☐ YES   ☐ NO

(Tick box which applies)   (If yes, give details below)

11A.
REMARRIAGE

[*Omitted by S.S.I. 2007 No. 7, para. 20 (effective 26th February 2007).*]

12.
DECLARATION AND REQUEST FOR DIVORCE

I confirm that the facts stated in Sections 1–11 above apply to my marriage.

I do not ask the court to make any financial award in connection with this application.

I do NOT ask the court to postpone the grant of decree under section 3A of the Divorce (Scotland) Act 1976.

I request the court to grant decree of divorce from my husband/wife.

....

        (Date)   (Signature of Applicant)

PART 2

APPLICANT'S AFFIDAVIT

To be completed only after Part 1 has been signed and dated.

I, (*insert Applicant's full name*) ....

residing at (*insert Applicant's present home address*) ....

....

Town .... Country ....

Swear that to the best of my knowledge and belief the facts stated in Part 1 of this Application are true.

Signature of Applicant ....

	SWORN at (Place) ....
	this .... day of ....19 ......
	before me (full name) ....
To be completed	(full address) ....
by Justice of Peace,	....
Notary Public or	....
Commissioner for	
Oaths	
	Signature ....
	*Justice of Peace/*Notary Public/*Commissioner for Oaths
	*Delete where not applicable.

[1] Form 49.73–B amended by S.I. 1994 No. 2901 (clerical error), S.S.I. 2004 No. 52 and S.S.I. 2005 No. 632 and S.S.I. 2006 No. 206 (effective 4th May 2006).
[2] Form 49.73B amended by S.S.I. 2007 No. 7, para. 20 (effective 26th February 2007).

Rule 49.73   [1,2] FORM 49.73C

Under the Divorce (Scotland) Act 1976, section 1(1)(b) Simplified Procedure

Court of Session
Extracts Department (SP)
Parliament House
Edinburgh
EH1 1RQ

APPLICATION FOR DIVORCE

ISSUE OF INTERIM GENDER RECOGNITION CERTIFICATE

> Before completing this form, you should have read the leaflet entitled "Do it yourself Divorce" which explains the circumstances in which a divorce may be sought by that method. If the simplified procedure appears to suit your circumstances, you may use this form to apply for divorce.

> Below you will find directions designed to assist you with your application. Please follow them carefully. In the event of difficulty, you may contact the Court's Extracts Department at the above address, or any Sheriff Clerk's Office or Citizen's Advice Bureau.

Direction for making Application

WRITE IN INK, USING BLOCK CAPITALS

Application (Part 1)	1. Complete and sign Part 1 of the form (pages 3–7), paying particular attention to the notes opposite each section.
Affidavit	2. When you have completed Part 1, you should take the form to a Justice of the Peace, Notary Public, Commissioner for Oaths or other duly authorised person so that your affidavit in Part 2 (page 8) can be completed and sworn.
Returning completed Application Form to court	3. When directions 1 and 2 above have all been carried out, your application is now ready to be sent to the court. With it you must enclose:–

(i) your marriage certificate (the document headed "Extract of an entry in a Register of Marriages"), which will be returned to you in due course. Check the notes on page 2 to see if you also need to obtain a letter from the General Register Office stating that there is no record that your spouse has divorced you;
(ii) either a cheque or postal order in respect of the court fee, crossed and made payable to "Scottish Court Service" or a completed form SP15, claiming exemption from the court fee.
(iii) the interim gender recognition certificate or a certified copy of it.
4. Receipt of your application will be promptly acknowledged. Should you wish to withdraw the application for any reason, please contact the court immediately.

THE NOTES ON THIS AND THE FOLLOWING PAGES ARE DESIGNED TO ASSIST YOU. PLEASE READ THEM CAREFULLY BEFORE COMPLETING EACH SECTION OF THE FORM.

Notes on Sections 1 and 2 opposite

(i)   The names entered in sections 1 and 2 opposite must be those shown on your marriage certificate. If you are known by another name which does not appear on that extract, please write that name in brackets.

(ii)   The surname given for a wife must be her present married name. Her maiden name and any names from previous marriages should be entered in the space for other names.

(iii) Home addresses should be given where these are known. The court is required by law to serve a copy of this application on your husband/wife.

Note on Section 3 opposite

If the address of your husband/wife is NOT known or cannot reasonably be ascertained, please enter "not known" in this section; you must take all reasonable steps to find out where your husband/wife is living and state on a separate sheet what steps you have taken and attach it to this form then proceed to section 4.

N.B. The statement must be signed

Notes on Section 4 opposite

In the event that the address of your husband/wife is unknown to you, the court is required by law to intimate a copy of this application to:

> (i)   ONE of the next-of-kin of your husband/wife. ("Next-of-kin" does not include yourself or any children of the marriage for the purposes of this application.)

> (ii) All children of your marriage aged 16 years or over, whether or not they live with you.

When entering details of next-of-kin, if any, please state his or her relationship to your husband/ wife (i.e.—"mother", "father", "brother", "sister", etc.)

If you do not know the identity or whereabouts of any of the next-of-kin of your husband/wife, or the whereabouts of any children of your marriage, please enter "not known" where appropriate.

LETTER FROM GENERAL REGISTER OFFICE. If you do not know the address of your spouse and you were married in Scotland, you must obtain a letter from the General Register Office stating that there is no record that your spouse has divorced you. The letter must be issued not more than one month before the date of posting this application to the court. If you require to obtain a letter you should apply to:

> General Register Office (Scotland), Registration Branch, New Register House,
> Edinburgh, EH1 3YT,

stating both husband's and wife's full names, the date and place of your marriage and requesting that a search be made to confirm that there is no record that your husband/wife has divorce you. (Note – a fee will be charged for this service).

The requirement to obtain a letter from the General Register Office does not apply if you were married outwith Scotland.

PART 1
WRITE IN INK, USING BLOCK CAPITALS

1. NAME AND ADDRESS OF APPLICANT

Surname ....

Other name(s) in full ....

Present Address ....

....

....

Daytime telephone number (if any) ....

2. NAME OF HUSBAND/WIFE

Surname ....

Other name(s) in full ....

3. ADDRESS OF HUSBAND/WIFE (if the address of your husband/wife is not known, please enter "not known" and proceed to Section 4)

Present Address ....

....

Daytime telephone number (if any) ....

4. Only complete this section if you do not know the present address of your husband/wife

NEXT-OF-KIN

Name ....   Address ....

....

....

Relationship to your
husband/wife ....

CHILDREN OF THE FAMILY

Names and dates of birth   Addresses

....

....

....

....

....

....

If sufficient space is not available here to list all the children of the marriage, please continue on a separate sheet and attach to this form.

Notes on Section 5 opposite

"Domiciled" means that the person concerned regards Scotland as his/her permanent home and intends to live permanently in Scotland in the foreseeable future.

"the Council Regulation" means Council Regulation (EC) No. 2201/2003 of 27th November 2003 concerning jurisdiction and the recognition and enforcement of judgments in matrimonial matters and in matters of parental responsibility (O.J. No. L. 338, 23.12.2003, p.1)

The list of Contracting States is found in section 12(5)(b) of the Domicile and Matrimonial Proceedings Act 1973. As at 26th February 2007 the Contracting States are: Belgium, Cyprus, Czech Republic, Germany, Greece, Spain, Estonia, France, Hungary, Ireland, Italy, Latvia, Lithuania, Luxembourg, Malta, Netherlands, Austria, Poland, Portugal, Slovak Republic, Slovenia, Finland, Sweden and the United Kingdom.

Notes on Section 6 opposite

You will be able to obtain these details from your marriage certificate, which must accompany this application form when you send it to the court.

A photocopy of the marriage certificate will NOT be accepted.

PART 1 (continued)

---

5. JURISDICTION

Please indicate with a tick (✓) in the appropriate box or boxes which of the following apply:

PART A

    (i)   My spouse and I are habitually resident in Scotland   ☐

    (ii)   My spouse and I were last habitually resident in Scotland, and one of us still resides there   ☐

    (iii)   My spouse is habitually resident in Scotland   ☐

    (iv)   I am habitually resident in Scotland having resided there for at least a year immediately before this application was made   ☐

(v)   I am habitually resident in Scotland having resided there for at least six months immediately before this application was made and am domiciled in Scotland

(vi)   My spouse and I are domiciled in Scotland

Part B applies where the defender is not a national of a Contracting State (other than the UK or Ireland) or domiciled in Ireland

PART B

(i)   I am domiciled in Scotland

(ii)   My spouse is domiciled in Scotland

AND

(iii)   No Court of a Contracting State has jurisdiction under the Council Regulation

6. DETAILS OF PRESENT MARRIAGE

Place of Marriage .... (Registration District)

Date of Marriage: Day .... month .... year ....

7. DETAILS OF ISSUE OF INTERIM GENDER RECOGNITION CERTIFICATE

(i) Please state whether the interim gender recognition certificate has been issued to you or your husband/wife.

(ii) Please state the date the interim gender recognition certificate was issued.   Day .... Month .... Year ....

Note on Section 9 opposite

"Children of the marriage" includes any adopted children and/or children accepted into the family.

Notes on Section 11 opposite

No claim can be made in this form of divorce application for payment to you of a periodical allowance (*i.e.* regular payment of money, weekly, monthly etc. for your maintenance) or a capital sum (*i.e.* lump sum). If you wish to make such a claim, you should consult a solicitor.

NOTE: While it may be possible to obtain an order for periodical allowance after divorce, the right to payment of a capital sum is lost once decree of divorce is granted.

No application can be made in this form of divorce application for postponement of decree under section 3A of the Divorce (Scotland) Act 1976. On an application under that section, the court may postpone the grant of decree of divorce if it is satisfied that:

    (a) the applicant is prevented from entering into a religious marriage by virtue of a requirement of the religion of that marriage; and

    (b) the other party can act so as to remove or enable or contribute to the removal of, the impediment which prevents that marriage.

As at 26th February 2007 "religious marriage" for the purposes of section 3A of the Divorce (Scotland) Act 1976 means a marriage solemnised by a celebrant of any Hebrew congregation (i.e. a Jewish marriage) (S.S.I. 2006/253).

If you wish to make such an application you should consult a solicitor or Citizens' Advice Bureau.

PART 1 (continued)

8. MENTAL DISABILITY

As far as you are aware is your husband/wife   YES   NO
incapable of managing his/her affairs because
of a mental disorder (whether mental illness,
personality disorder or learning disability

(*Tick box which applies*)

9. CHILDREN   YES   NO

Are there any children of the marriage under
the age of 16?
(*Tick box which applies*)

10. OTHER COURT ACTIONS   YES   NO

Are you aware of any court actions currently
proceeding in any country (including
Scotland) which may affect your marriage?
(If yes, give details)
(*Tick box which applies*)

11. DECLARATION AND REQUEST FOR DIVORCE

I confirm that the facts stated in Sections 1–10 above apply to my marriage.

I do not ask the court to make any financial awards in connection with this application.

I do not ask the court to postpone the grant of decree under section 3A of the Divorce (Scotland) Act 1976.

I request the court to grant decree of divorce from my husband/wife.

....

(Date)   (Signature of Applicant)

PART 2

APPLICANT'S AFFIDAVIT

To be completed only after Part 1 has been signed and dated.

1, (*Insert Applicant's full name*) ....

residing at (*insert Applicant's present home address*) ....

....

Town ....Country ....

SWEAR that to the best of my knowledge and belief the facts stated in Part 1 of this Application are true.

Signature of Applicant ....

SWORN at (*insert place*) ....

To be completed by
Justice of the Peace,
Notary Public or
Commissioner for
Oaths

this ....day of ....20 ....

before me (*insert full name*) ....

(*insert full address*) ....

....

....

Signature ....

*Justice of the Peace/Notary Public/Commissioner for Oaths

*Delete as appropriate

------

[1] Form 49.73C inserted by S.S.I. 2005 No. 632 (effective 8th December 2005) and S.S.I. 2006 No. 206 (effective 4th May 2006).
[2] Form 49.73C amended by S.S.I. 2007 No. 7, para. 20 (effective 26th February 2007).

Rule 49.76(3)   [1,2] FORM 49.76–A

Form of citation in simplified divorce application under section 1(2)(d) of the Divorce (Scotland) Act 1976

CITATION

Date: (*Date of posting or other method of service*)

To: ....

....

APPLICATION FOR DIVORCE (WITH CONSENT OF OTHER PARTY TO THE MARRIAGE), HUSBAND AND WIFE HAVING LIVED APART FOR AT LEAST ONE YEAR

You are hereby served with an application by your husband [*or* wife] which asks the court to grant a decree of divorce.

If you wish to oppose the granting of such a decree, you should put your reasons in writing and send your letter to the address shown below. Your letter must reach the court by (*insert date on which period of notice expires*).

(*Signed*)

....
Deputy Principal Clerk of Session
[*or* authorised clerk of session]
[*or* Messenger-at-Arms
(*Address*)]

IMPORTANT NOTE. If you wish to exercise your right to claim a financial award, or if you wish to apply for postponement of decree under section 3A of the Divorce (Scotland) Act 1976 (postponement of decree of divorce where impediment to religious remarriage exists), you should immediately advise the court that you oppose the application for that reason, and thereafter consult a solicitor.

Court of Session
Extracts Department (SP)
Parliament House Edinburgh EH1 1RQ
Tel: 031–225 2595

---

[1] Form 49.76–A amended by S.S.I. 2006 No. 206 (effective 4th May 2006).
[2] Form 49.76–A amended by S.S.I. 2007 No. 7, para. 20 (effective 26th February 2007).

Rule 49.76(3)   [1] FORM 49.76–B

Form of citation in simplified divorce application under section 1(2)(e) of the Divorce (Scotland) Act 1976

CITATION

Date: (*Date of posting or other method of service*)

To: ....
        ....
        ....

APPLICATION FOR DIVORCE, HUSBAND AND WIFE HAVING LIVED APART FOR AT LEAST TWO YEARS

Your husband [*or* wife] has applied to the court for divorce on the ground that the marriage has broken down irretrievably because you and (s)he have lived apart for a period of at least two years.

A copy of the application is hereby served on you.

1. Please note:—
    (a) that the court may not make a financial award under this procedure and that your husband [*or* wife] is making no claim against you for payment of a periodical allowance (*i.e.* regular payment of money weekly, monthly, etc., for his [*or* her] maintenance) or a capital sum (*i.e.* lump sum);
    (b) that no application may be made under this procedure for postponement of decree under section 3A of the Divorce (Scotland) Act 1976 (postponement of decree where impediment to religious remarriage exists).

2. Divorce may result in the loss to you of property rights (*e.g.* the right to succeed to the applicant's estate on his/her death) or the right, where appropriate, to a widow's pension.

3. If you wish to oppose the granting of a divorce, you should put your reasons in writing and send your letter to the address shown below. Your letter must reach the court by (*insert date on which period of time expires*).

4. In the event of the divorce being granted, you will be sent a copy of the extract decree. (Should you change your address before receiving the copy extract decree, please notify the court immediately.)

(*Signed*)

Deputy Principal Clerk of Session
[*or* authorised clerk of session]
[*or* Messenger-at-Arms
(*Address*)]

IMPORTANT NOTE. If you wish to exercise your right to claim a financial award, or if you wish to apply for postponement of decree under section 3A of the Divorce (Scotland) Act 1976 (postponement of decree of divorce where impediment to religious remarriage exists), you should immediately advise the court that you oppose the application for that reason, and thereafter consult a solicitor.

Court of Session
Extracts Department (SP)
Parliament House Edinburgh EH1 1RQ
Tel: 031–225 2595

_____

[1] Form 49.76–B amended by S.S.I. 2006 No. 206 (effective 4th May 2006) and by S.S.I. 2007 No. 7, para. 20 (effective 26th February 2007).

Rule 49.76   [1] FORM 49.76–BA

Form of citation in simplified divorce application under section 1(1)(b) of the Divorce (Scotland) Act 1976

CITATION

Date: (*Date of posting or other method of service*)

To: ....

          ....

          ....

APPLICATION FOR DIVORCE. INTERIM GENDER RECOGNITION CERTIFICATE ISSUED TO HUSBAND/WIFE AFTER MARRIAGE

Your husband [*or* wife] has applied to the court for divorce on the ground that an interim gender recognition certificate has been issued to you or your husband [*or* wife] after your marriage.

A copy of the application is hereby served on you.

1. Please note that the court may not make a financial award under this procedure and that your husband [*or* wife] is making no claim against you for payment of a periodical allowance (*i.e.* regular payment of money weekly, monthly, etc., for his [*or* her] maintenance or a capital sum (*i.e.* lump sum);

2. Dissolution of your marriage may result in the loss to you of property rights (*e.g.* the right to succeed to the applicant's estate on his/her death) or the right, where appropriate, to a pension.

2A. Please note that no application may be made under this procedure for postponement of decree under section 3A of the Divorce (Scotland) Act 1976 (postponement of decree where impediment to religious remarriage exists).

3. If you wish to oppose the granting of a divorce, you should put your reasons in writing and send your letter to the address shown below. Your letter must reach the court by (*insert date on which period of notice expires*).

4. In the event of the divorce being granted, you will be sent a copy of the extract decree. (Should you change your address before receiving the copy extract decree, please notify the court immediately.)

(*Signed*)

Deputy Principal Clerk of Session

[*or* authorised clerk of session]

[*or* Messenger-at-Arms]

(*Address*)

IMPORTANT NOTE. If you wish to exercise your right to claim a financial award you should immediately advise the court that you oppose the application for that reason, and thereafter consult a solicitor.

Court of Session
Extracts Department (SP)
Parliament House
Edinburgh EH1 1RQ
Tel: 0131–225–2595

---

[1] Form 49.76–BA inserted by S.S.I. 2005 No. 632 (effective 8th December 2005) and amended by S.S.I. 2007 No. 7, para. 20 (effective 26th February 2007).

Rule 49.76(4)　　　　　　　　　　[1] FORM 49.76–C

Form of intimation to child or next-of-kin in simplified divorce application under section 1(2)(e) or (1)(b) of the Divorce (Scotland) Act 1976

CITATION

Date:　(*Date of posting or other method of service*)

To:　　..

　　　..

　　　..

APPLICATION FOR DIVORCE. HUSBAND AND WIFE HAVING LIVED APART FOR AT LEAST TWO YEARS OR ISSUE OF INTERIM GENDER RECOGNITION CERTIFICATE AFTER REGISTRATION OF THE CIVIL PARTNERSHIP

.................................(Applicant) v ....(Respondent)

TAKE NOTICE

1. In the above application, a copy of which is enclosed, the applicant has indicated that you are the (*state relationship*) of (*name of respondent*) whose present address is not known to the applicant.

2. Should you know the present address of your (*state relationship*) or how he [*or* she] may be contacted, you are requested to give this information at once in writing to—

Court of Session
Extracts Department (SP)
Parliament House
Edinburgh EH1 1RQ
Tel: 0131-225-2595

This will enable the court to inform the respondent that the application has been made.

3. If you are unable to provide the above information, and/or you wish for your own interest to oppose the application for divorce, you should write to the above address by (*insert date on which period of time expires*).

(*Signed*)

Deputy Principal Clerk of Session

[*or* authorised clerk of session]

[*or* Messenger-at-Arms]

(*Address*)

---

[1] Form 49.76-C substituted by S.S.I. 2005 No. 632 (effective 8th December 2005) and S.S.I. 2006 No. 206 (effective 4th May 2006)

Rule 49.76(5)   FORM 49.76–D

Form of certificate of service of simplified divorce application

CERTIFICATE OF SERVICE [*or* INTIMATION]

I, (*name*), Deputy Principal Clerk of Session [*or clerk of session authorised by him*], certify that I served [*or* intimated] this simplified divorce application by (*name of applicant*) on [*or* to] (*name of person on whom service executed or to whom intimation given*) by posting it with a citation [*or* notice of intimation] in Form (*number of form*) to that person between (*time*) and (*time*) or (*date*) at (*name of post office*) in a registered envelope [*or* recorded delivery envelope] addressed as follows:— (*address*). The Post Office receipt [*or* certificate of posting] is attached to this certificate.

(*Signed*)

Deputy Principal Clerk of Session
[*or* authorised clerk of session]
[*or* Messenger-at-Arms
(*Address*)]

(*Signed*)

Witness]

Rule 49.76(5)   FORM 49.76–E

Form of certificate of service of simplified divorce application by messenger-at-arms

CERTIFICATE OF SERVICE [*OR* INTIMATION]

I, (*name*), Messenger-at-Arms, certify that I served [*or* intimated] this simplified divorce application [and a notice of intimation] on [*or* to] (*name of person on whom served or to whom intimated*)—

*   by leaving it and a citation [*or* notice] with (*name of person*) at (*place*) at (*time*) or (*date*).

*   by leaving it and a citation [*or* notice] with (*name and occupation of person with whom left*) at (*place*) on (*date*). (*Specify that enquiry made and that reasonable grounds exist for believing that the person on whom service is to be made or to whom intimation is to be given resides at the place but is not available.*)

*   by depositing it and a citation [*or* notice] in (*place*) on (*date*). (*Specify that enquiry made and that reasonable grounds exist for believing that the person on whom service is to be made or to whom intimation is to be given resides at the place but is not available.*)

*   by leaving it and a citation [*or* notice] with (*name and occupation of person with whom left*) at (*place of business*) on (*date*). (*Specify that enquiry made and that reasonable grounds exist for believing that the person on whom service is to be made or to whom intimation is to be given carries on business at the place.*)

*   by depositing it and a citation [*or* notice] at (*place of business*) on (*date*). (*Specify that enquiry made and that reasonable grounds exist for believing that the person on whom service is to be made or to whom intimation is to be given carries on business at the place.*)

*   by leaving it and a citation [*or* notice] at (*registered office or place of business*) on (*date*), in the hands of (*name of person*).

*   by leaving [*or* depositing] it and a citation [*or* notice] at (*registered office, official address or place of business*) on (*date*) in such a way that it was likely to come to the attention of (*name of person on whom served or to whom intimated*). (*Specify how left.*)

I did this in the presence of (*name, occupation and address of witness*).

(*Signed*)

Messenger-at-Arms
(*Address*)]

(*Signed*)

Witness

* Delete where not applicable.

FORM 49.80B–A

Rule 49.8B(1)

Form of simplified dissolution of civil partnership application under section 117(3)(c) of the Civil Partnership Act 2004

Court of Session
Extracts Department (SP)
Parliament House
Edinburgh EH1 1RQ

APPLICATION FOR DISSOLUTION OF A CIVIL PARTNERSHIP WITH CONSENT OF OTHER PARTY TO THE CIVIL PARTNERSHIP (CIVIL PARTNERS HAVING LIVED APART FOR AT LEAST ONE YEAR)

Before completing this form, you should have read the leaflet entitled "Do it yourself Dissolution", which explains the circumstances in which a dissolution of a civil partnership may be sought by this method. If the simplified procedure appears to suit your circumstances, you may use this form to apply for dissolution of your civil partnership.

Below you will find directions designed to assist you with your application. Please follow them carefully. In the event of difficulty, you may contact the Court's Extracts Department at the above address, or any Sheriff Clerk's Office or Citizen's Advice Bureau.

Directions for making Application

WRITE IN INK, USING BLOCK CAPITALS

Application
(Part 1)

1. Complete and sign Part 1 of the form (pages 3–7), paying particular attention to the notes opposite each section.

Consent of
civil partner
(Part 2)

2. When you have filled in Part 1 of the form, attach the (blue) Instruction Sheet SP3 to it and send both documents to your civil partner for completion of the consent at Part 2 (page 9).

NOTE: If your civil partner does NOT complete and sign the form of consent, your application cannot proceed further under the simplified procedure. In that event, if you still wish to obtain a dissolution of your civil partnership, you should consult a solicitor.

Affidavit
(Part 3)

3. When the application has been returned to you with the Consent (Part 2) duly completed and signed, you should then take the form to a Justice of the Peace, Notary Public, Commissioner for Oaths or other duly authorised person so that your affidavit at Part 3 (page 10) can be completed and sworn.

Returning
completed
Application
Form to court

4. When directions 1–3 above have been carried out, your application is now ready to be sent to the court. With it you must enclose:
(i) an extract of the registration of your civil partnership in the civil partnership register (the document headed "Extract of an entry in the Register of Civil Partnerships"), which will be returned to you in due course, or an equivalent document, and
(ii) Either a cheque or postal order in respect of the court fee, crossed and made payable to "the Scottish Court Service", or a completed form SP15, claiming exemption from the court fee.
5. Receipt of your application will be promptly acknowledged. Should you wish to withdraw the application for any reason, please contact the court immediately.

THE NOTES ON THIS AND THE FOLLOWING PAGES ARE DESIGNED TO ASSIST YOU. PLEASE READ THEM CAREFULLY BEFORE COMPLETING EACH SECTION OF THE FORM.

Notes on Sections 1 and 2 opposite

(i)   The names entered in sections 1 and 2 opposite must be those shown on your extract of registration of civil partnership. If you are known by another name which does not appear on that extract, please write the name in brackets.

(ii)   The surname given for a female civil partner must be her maiden surname. Any names from previous marriages should be entered in the space for other names.

(iii)   Home address should be given where these are known. The court is required by law to serve a copy of this application on your civil partner.

Note on Section 3 opposite

"Domiciled" means that the person concerned regards Scotland as his/her permanent home and intends to live permanently in Scotland in the foreseeable future.

Notes on Section 4 opposite

You will be able to obtain these details from your extract of registration of civil partnership which must accompany this application form, when you send it to the court.

A photocopy of the extract of registration of civil partnership will NOT be accepted. If you cannot find the original you should apply for an official copy to:

General Register Office (Scotland), Registration Section, New Register House, Edinburgh, EH1 3YT, or the office where the civil partnership was registered.

stating both civil partner's full names, and the date an place of registration of the civil partnership.

(Note that the Registrar will charge a fee for this service.)

Release 90: March 2007

PART 1

WRITE IN INK, USING BLOCK CAPITALS

---

1. NAME AND ADDRESS OF APPLICANT

Surname ....   Other name(s)
Present   in full ....
Address ....
....   Daytime telephone number (if
                                                                  any) ....

---

2. NAME AND ADDRESS OF CIVIL PARTNER

Surname ....   Other name(s)
Present   in full ....
Address ....
....   Daytime telephone number (if
                                                                  any) ....

3. JURISDICTION

Please indicate with a tick (√) in the appropriate box or boxes which of the following apply:

PART A

    (i)   My civil partner and I are habitually resident in Scotland   ☐

    (ii)   My civil partner and I were last habitually resident in
         Scotland, and one of us still resides there   ☐

    (iii) My civil partner is habitually resident in Scotland   ☐

    (iv) I am habitually resident in Scotland having resident there
         for at least a year immediately before this application was
         made   ☐

    (v)   I am habitually resident in Scotland having resided there for
         at least six months immediately before this application was
         made and am domiciled in Scotland   ☐

If you have ticked one of the boxes in Part A, you do not have to complete Part B or C. You should complete either Part B or Part C if you have not ticked any of the boxes in Part A

PART B

    (i)   No court has, or is recognised as having, jurisdiction under regulations made under section 219 of the Civil Partnership Act 2004

    AND

    (ii)   I am domiciled in Scotland

    (iii) My civil partner is domiciled in Scotland

PART C

    (i)   My civil partner and I are registered civil partners of each other in Scotland

    AND

    (ii)   No court has, or is recognised as having jurisdiction under regulations made under section 219 of the Civil Partnership Act 2004

    AND

    (iii) It is in the interests of justice for the Court of Session to assume jurisdiction in the case. (Please give reasons below).

4. DETAILS OF PRESENT CIVIL PARTNERSHIP

Place of Registration of Civil Partnership ....(Registration District)

Date of Registration of Civil Partnership: Day .... month .... year ....

Notes on Section 5 opposite

You and your civil partner must have lived apart from each other for a continuous period of at least one year after the date of registration of your civil partnership and immediately before the date of this application.

This minimum period of one year's separation is extended if you and your civil partner have lived together again for **not more than six months in all** during that one year period. For example, if you lived together for three months in total during the one year period, then you should not complete this application until one year and three months have elapsed from the date of your original separation.

Notes on Section 6 opposite

Is there a reasonable chance that you can still settle the differences with your civil partner and resume normal family life?

Are you satisfied that there is now no possibility of the civil partnership succeeding?

Notes on Section 7 opposite

If your civil partner is not prepared to sign the form of consent at Part 2 of this application you will not obtain a dissolution of your civil partnership by this method.

Note on Section 9 opposite

"Children of the family" includes any children accepted into the family.

5. PERIOD OF SEPARATION

(i) Please state the date on which you ceased to live with your civil partner. (If more than 1 year, just give the month and year)   Day .Month Year

(ii) Have you lived with your civil partner since that date?   YES [   ]   NO [   ]
(*Tick box which applies*)

(iii) If yes, for how long in total did you live together before finally separating again?   ....months

6. RECONCILIATION

Is there any reasonable prospect of reconciliation with your civil partner?   YES [   ]   NO [   ]
(*Tick box which applies*)

Do you consider that the civil partnership has broken down irretrievably?   YES [   ]   NO [   ]
(*Tick box which applies*)

7. CONSENT

Does your civil partner consent to a dissolution of the civil partnership being granted?   YES [   ]   NO [   ]
(*Tick box which applies*)

8. MENTAL DISABILITY

Is your civil partner incapable of managing his/her affairs because of a mental disorder (whether mental illness, personality disorder or learning disability? (If yes, give details)

YES ☐   NO ☐

(Tick box which applies)

9. CHILDREN

Are there any children of the family under the age of 16?

YES ☐   NO ☐

(Tick box which applies)

10. OTHER COURT ACTIONS

Are you aware of any court actions currently proceeding in any country (including Scotland) which may affect your civil partnership? (If yes, give details)

YES ☐   NO ☐

(Tick box which applies)

Notes on Section 11 opposite

No claim can be made in this form of dissolution application for payment to you of a periodical allowance (*i.e.* regular payment of money weekly, monthly, etc. for your maintenance) or a capital sum (*i.e.* lump sum). If you wish to make such a claim, you should consult a solicitor.

NOTE: While it may be possible to obtain an order for periodical allowance after dissolution of a civil partnership, the right to payment of a capital sum is lost once decree of dissolution is granted.

11. REQUEST FOR DISSOLUTION OF THE CIVIL PARTNERSHIP AND DISCLAIMER OF FINANCIAL PROVISION

I confirm that the facts stated in Sections 1–10 above apply to my civil partnership.

I do NOT ask the court to make any financial awards in connection with this application.

I request the court to grant decree of dissolution of my civil partnership.

....

        (Date)   (Signature)

IMPORTANT

Part 1 MUST be completed, signed and dated before sending the application form to your civil partner.

NOTES ON COMPLETING PART 2 OPPOSITE (page 9)

1.   Read over carefully PART 1 (pages 3–7) of this application, which has already been completed by your civil partner.

2. Financial Provisions

Please note that in section 11 of Part 1, the Applicant states that he/she does NOT claim any financial awards by way of periodical allowance or capital sum. You also are required to state (items (c) and (d) opposite) that you make no claim upon the Applicant for payment of a periodical allowance or capital sum.

> **Note**: While it may be possible to obtain an order for **periodical allowance** after dissolution of a civil partnership, the right to payment of a **capital sum** is lost once decree of dissolution is granted.

3. Warning

Dissolution of your civil partnership may result in the loss to you of property rights (*e.g.* the right to succeed to the Applicant's estate on his/her death) or the right, where appropriate, to a pension.

(If you are in any doubt about signing the form of consent you should consult a solicitor.)

PART 2

CONSENT BY APPLICANT'S CIVIL PARTNER TO DISSOLUTION OF CIVIL PARTNERSHIP

NOTE: Before completing this part of the form, please read the notes opposite (page 8)

I, ...

     (Full name, in BLOCK letters, of Applicant's civil partner)

residing at ....

....

....

     (Address, also in BLOCK letters)

HEREBY STATE THAT

(a) I have read Part 1 of this application;

(b) the Applicant has lived apart from me for a continuous period of one year immediately preceding the date of the application (Section 11 of Part 1);

(c) I do not ask the court to make any order for payment to me by the Applicant of a periodical allowance (*i.e.* a regular payment of money weekly or monthly, etc., for maintenance);

(d) I do not ask the court to make any order for payment to me by the Applicant of a capital sum (i.e. a lump sum payment);

(e) I understand that dissolution of my civil partnership may result in the loss to me of property rights; and

(f) **I CONSENT TO DECREE OF DISSOLUTION BEING GRANTED IN RESPECT OF THIS APPLICATION**

....

       (Date)   *(Signature)*

NOTE: You may withdraw your consent, even after giving it, at any time before the dissolution of the civil partnership is granted by the court. Should you wish to do so, you must immediately advise—

The Court of Session
Extracts Department (SP)
Parliament House
Edinburgh EH1 1RQ

PART 3

APPLICANT'S AFFIDAVIT

To be completed only after Parts 1 and 2 have been signed and dated.

I, (*insert Applicant's full name*) ....

residing at (*insert Applicant's present home address*) ....

....

Town .... Country ....

SWEAR that to the best of my knowledge and belief:

(1)   the facts stated in Part 1 of this Application are true; and

(2)   the signature in Part 2 of this application is that of my civil partner.

Signature of Applicant ....

                SWORN at (*insert place*) ....

To be completed by   this ....day of ....20 ....
Justice of the Peace,
Notary Public or   before me (*insert full name*) ....
Commissioner for
Oaths   (*insert full address*) ....

               ....

               Signature ....

               *Justice of the Peace/Notary Public/Commissioner for Oaths

               *Delete as appropriate

---

[1] Form 49.80B–A inserted by S.S.I. 2005 No. 632 (effective 8th December 2005) and S.S.I. 2006 No. 206 (effective 4th May 2006)

C 762/18

Appendix

FORM 49.80B–B

Rule 49.80B(2)

Form of simplified dissolution of civil partnership application under section 117(3)(d) of the Civil Partnership Act 2004

Court of Session
Extracts Department (SP)
Parliament House
Edinburgh EH1 1RQ

APPLICATION FOR DISSOLUTION OF A CIVIL PARTNERSHIP

(CIVIL PARTNERS HAVING LIVED APART FOR AT LEAST TWO YEARS)

Before completing this form, you should have read the leaflet entitled "Do it yourself Dissolution", which explains the circumstances in which a dissolution of a civil partnership may be sought by this method. If the simplified procedure appears to suit your circumstances, you may use this form to apply for dissolution of your civil partnership.

Below you will find directions designed to assist you with your application. Please follow them carefully. In the event of difficulty, you may contact the Court's Extracts Department at the above address, or any Sheriff Clerk's Office or Citizen's Advice Bureau.

Directions for making Application

WRITE IN INK, USING BLOCK CAPITALS

Application (Part 1)
1. Complete and sign Part 1 of the form (pages 3–7), paying particular attention to the notes opposite each section.

Affidavit (Part 2)
2. When you have completed Part 1, you should then take the form to a Justice of the Peace, Notary Public, Commissioner for Oaths or other duly authorised person so that your affidavit at Part 2 (page 8) can be completed and sworn.

Returning completed Application Form to court
3. When directions 1 and 2 above have been carried out, your application is now ready to be sent to the court. With it you must enclose:
(i) an extract of the registration of your civil partnership in the civil partnership register (the document headed "Extract of an entry in the Register of Civil Partnerships"), which will be returned to you in due course, or an equivalent document. Check the Notes on page 2 to see if you also need to obtain a letter from General Register Office stating that there is no record of your civil partner having dissolved the civil partnership; and
(ii) Either a cheque or postal order in respect of the court fee, crossed and made payable to "Scottish Court Service",
or a completed form SP15, claiming exemption from the court fee.
4. Receipt of your application will be promptly acknowledged. Should you wish to withdraw the application for any reason, please contact the court immediately.

THE NOTES ON THIS AND THE FOLLOWING PAGES ARE DESIGNED TO ASSIST YOU. PLEASE READ THEM CAREFULLY BEFORE COMPLETING EACH SECTION OF THE FORM.

Notes on Sections 1 and 2 opposite

(i)   The names entered in sections 1 and 2 opposite must be those shown on your extract of registration of civil partnership. If you are known by another name which does not appear on that extract, please write the name in brackets.

(ii) The surname given for a female civil partner must be her maiden surname. Any names from previous marriages should be entered in the space for other names.

(iii) Home address should be given where these are known. The court is required by law to serve a copy of this application on your civil partner.

Note on Section 3 opposite

If the address of your civil partner is NOT known or cannot reasonably be ascertained, please enter "not known" in this section; you must take all reasonable steps to find out where your civil partner is living and state on a separate sheet what steps you have taken and attach it to this form. then proceed to section 4.

N.B. The statement must be signed

Notes on Section 4 opposite

In the event that the address of your civil partner is unknown to you, the court is required by law to intimate a copy of this application to:

(i)   ONE of the next-of-kin of your civil partner. ("Next-of-kin" does not include yourself or any children of the family for the purposes of this application.)

(ii) All children of the family aged 16 years or over, whether or not they live with you.

When entering details of next-of-kin, if any, please state his or her relationship to your civil partner (i.e.—"mother", "father", "brother", "sister", etc.)

If you do not know the identity or whereabouts of any of the next-of-kin of your civil partner, or the whereabouts of any children of the family, please enter "not known" where appropriate.

LETTER FROM GENERAL REGISTER OFFICE. If you do not know the address of your civil partner and your civil partnership was registered in Scotland, you must obtain a letter from the General Register Office stating that there is no record that your civil partner has had your civil partnership dissolved. The letter must be issued not more than one month before the date of posting this application to the court. If you require to obtain a letter you should apply to:

General Register Office (Scotland), Registration Branch, New Register House, Edinburgh, EH1 3YT,

stating both civil partners' full names, the date and place of registration of your civil partnership and requesting that a search be made to confirm that there is no record that your civil partner has had your civil partnership dissolved. (Note – a fee will be charged for this service).

The requirement to obtain a letter from the General Register Office does not apply if your civil partnership was registered outwith Scotland.

WRITE IN INK, USING BLOCK CAPITALS

1. NAME AND ADDRESS OF APPLICANT

Surname ....
Present
Address ....

....

Other name(s)
in full ....

Daytime telephone number (if
any) ....

2. NAME OF CIVIL PARTNER

Surname ....

Other name(s)
in full ....

3. ADDRESS OF CIVIL PARTNER (if the address of your civil partner is not known, please enter "not known" and proceed to Section 4)

Present
Address ....

....

Daytime telephone number (if
any) ....

4. Only complete this section if you do not know the present address of your civil partner

NEXT-OF-KIN

Name ....

Address ....

....

....

Relationship to your civil
partner ....

CHILDREN OF THE FAMILY

Names and dates of birth   Addresses

....

....

....

....

....

....

If sufficient space is not available here to list all the children of the family, please continue on a separate sheet and attach to this form.

Notes on Section 5 opposite

"Domiciled" means that the person concerned regards Scotland as his/her permanent home and intends to live permanently in Scotland in the foreseeable future.

Notes on Section 6 opposite

You will be able to obtain these details from your extract of the registration of your civil partnership, which must accompany this application form when you send it to the court.

A photocopy of the extract of registration of the civil partnership will NOT be accepted.

Notes on Section 7 opposite

You and your civil partner must have lived apart from each other for continuous period of at least 2 years and after the date of registration of your civil partnership and immediately before the date of this application.

This minimum period of 2 years separation is extended if you and your civil partner have lived together again for **not more than 6 months in all** during that 2 year period. For example, if you have lived together for 3 months in total during the 2 year period, then you should not complete this application until 2 years and 3 months have elapsed from the date of your original separation.

Notes on Section 8 opposite

Is there a reasonable chance that you can still settle the differences with your civil partner and resume normal family life?

Are you satisfied that there is now no possibility of the civil partnership succeeding?

PART 1 (continued)

5. **JURISDICTION**

Please indicate with a tick (✓) in the appropriate box or boxes which of the following apply:

PART A

    (i)   My civil partner and I are habitually resident in Scotland   ☐

    (ii) My civil partner and I were last habitually resident in   ☐
          Scotland, and one of us still resides there

    (iii) My civil partner is habitually resident in Scotland   ☐

    (iv) I am habitually resident in Scotland having resided there   ☐
          for at least a year immediately before this application was
          made

    (v) I am habitually resident in Scotland having resided there   ☐
          for at least six months immediately before this application
          was made and am domiciled in Scotland

If you have ticked one of the boxes in Part A, you do not have to complete Part B or C. You should complete either Part B or Part C if you have not ticked any of the boxes in Part A

PART B

    (i)   No court has, or is recognised as having, jurisdiction under   ☐
          regulations made under section 219 of the Civil Partnership
          Act 2004

    AND

    (ii) I am domiciled in Scotland   ☐

    (iii) My civil partner is domiciled in Scotland   ☐

PART C

    (i)   My civil partner and I are registered civil partners of each   ☐
          other in Scotland

    AND

    (ii) No court has, or is recognised as having jurisdiction under   ☐
          regulations made under section 219 of the Civil Partnership
          Act 2004

Form 49.80B–B   **C 762/23**

6. DETAILS OF PRESENT CIVIL PARTNERSHIP

Place of Registration of Civil Partnership .... (Registration District)

Date of Registration of Civil Partnership: Day .... month ....year

7. PERIOD OF SEPARATION

(i) Please state the date on which you ceased to live with your civil partner. (If more than 2 1/2 years, just give the month and year)   Day . . . Month . . . Year . . .

(ii) Have you lived with your civil partner since that date?
(*Tick box which applies*)   YES ☐   NO ☐

8. RECONCILIATION
Is there any reasonable prospect of reconciliation with your civil partner?
(*Tick box which applies*)   YES ☐   NO ☐

Do you consider that the civil partnership has broken down irretrievably?
(*Tick box which applies*)   YES ☐   NO ☐

Note on Section 10 opposite

"Children of the family" includes any children accepted into the family.

Notes on Section 12 opposite

No claim can be made in this form of dissolution application for payment to you of a periodical allowance (*i.e.* regular payment of money, weekly, monthly etc. for your maintenance) or a capital sum (*i.e.* lump sum). If you wish to make such a claim, you should consult a solicitor.

NOTE: While it may be possible to obtain an order for periodical allowance after dissolution of your civil partnership, the right to payment of a capital sum is lost once decree of dissolution is granted.

PART 1 (continued)

9. MENTAL DISABILITY
As far as you are aware is your civil partner
incapable of managing his/her affairs because
of a mental disorder (whether mental illness,
personality disorder or learning disability) (If
yes, give details)

YES [ ]   NO [ ]

(*Tick box which applies*)

10. CHILDREN
Are there any children of the family under the age
of 16?

YES [ ]   NO [ ]

(*Tick box which applies*)

11. OTHER COURT ACTIONS
Are you aware of any court actions currently
proceeding in any country (including Scotland)
which may affect your civil partnership?

YES [ ]   NO [ ]

(If yes, give details)
(*Tick box which applies*)

12. DECLARATION AND REQUEST FOR DISSOLUTION OF CIVIL PARTNERSHIP

I confirm that the facts stated in Sections 1–11 above apply to my civil partnership.

I do not ask the court to make any financial awards in connection with this application.

I request the court to grant decree of dissolution of my civil partnership.

....

(*Date*)   (*Signature of Applicant*)

PART 2

APPLICANT'S AFFIDAVIT

To be completed only after Part 1 has been signed and dated.

I, (*Insert Applicant's full name*) ....

residing at (*insert Applicant's present home address*) ....

....

Town ....Country ....

SWEAR that to the best of my knowledge and belief the facts stated in Part 1 of this Application are true.

Signature of Applicant ....

	SWORN at (*insert place*) ....
To be completed by Justice of the Peace, Notary Public or Commissioner for Oaths	this .... day of .... 20 ....
	before me (*insert full name*) ....
	(*insert full address*) ....
	....
	....
	Signature ....
	*Justice of the Peace/Notary Public/Commissioner for Oaths
	*Delete as appropriate

-----

[1] Form 49.80B-B inserted by S.S.I. 2005 No. 632 (effective 8th December 2005) and S.S.I. 2006 No. 206 (effective 4th May 2006) and amended by S.S.I. 2007 No. 7, para. 20 (effective 26th February 2007).

Appendix

Rule 49.80B(3)

Form of simplified dissolution of civil partnership application under section 117(2)(b) of the Civil Partnership Act 2004

Court of Session
Extracts Department (SP)
Parliament House
Edinburgh EH1 1RQ

APPLICATION FOR DISSOLUTION OF A CIVIL PARTNERSHIP

(ISSUE OF INTERIM GENDER RECOGNITION CERTIFICATE)

Before completing this form, you should have read the leaflet entitled "Do it yourself Dissolution", which explains the circumstances in which a dissolution of a civil partnership may be sought by this method. If the simplified procedure appears to suit your circumstances, you may use this form to apply for dissolution of your civil partnership.

Below you will find directions designed to assist you with your application. Please follow them carefully. In the event of difficulty, you may contact the Court's Extracts Department at the above address, or any Sheriff Clerk's Office or Citizen's Advice Bureau.

Directions for making Application

WRITE IN INK, USING BLOCK CAPITALS

Application (Part 1)	1. Complete and sign Part 1 of the form (pages 3–7), paying particular attention to the notes opposite each section.
Affidavit (Part 2)	2. When you have completed Part 1, you should then take the form to a Justice of the Peace, Notary Public, Commissioner for Oaths or other duly authorised person so that your affidavit at Part 2 (page 8) can be completed and sworn.
Returning completed Application Form to court	3. When directions 1 and 2 above have been carried out, your application is now ready to be sent to the court. With it you must enclose:

(i) an extract of the registration of your civil partnership in the civil partnership register (the document headed "Extract of an entry in the Register of Civil Partnerships"), which will be returned to you in due course, or an equivalent document. Check the Notes on page 2 to see if you also need to obtain a letter from General Register Office stating that there is no record of your civil partner having dissolved the civil partnership;

(ii) the interim gender recognition certificate or a certified copy of it; and

(iii) Either a cheque or postal order in respect of the court fee, crossed and made payable to "Scottish Court Service",

or a completed form SP15, claiming exemption from the court fee.

4. Receipt of your application will be promptly acknowledged. Should you wish to withdraw the application for any reason, please contact the court immediately.

The surname given for a female civil partner must be her maiden surname. Any names from previous marriages should be entered in the space for other names.

THE NOTES ON THIS AND TEH FOLLOWING PAGES ARE DESIGNED TO ASSIST YOU. PLEASE READ THEM CAREFULLY BEFORE COMPLETING EACH SECTION OF THE FORM.

Notes on Sections 1 and 2 opposite

(i) The names entered in sections 1 and 2 opposite must be those shown on your extract of registration of civil partnership. If you are known by another name which does not appear on that extract, please write the name in brackets.

(ii) The surname given for a female civil partner must be her maiden surname. Any names from previous marriages should be entered in the space for other names.

(iii) Home address should be given where these are known. The court is required by law to serve a copy of this application on your civil partner.

Note on Section 3 opposite

If the address of your civil partner is NOT known or cannot reasonably be ascertained, please enter "not known" in this section; you must take all reasonable steps to find out where your civil partner is living and state on a separate sheet what steps you have taken and attach it to this form, then proceed to section 4.

N.B. The statement must be signed.

Notes on Section 4 opposite

In the event that the address of your civil partner is unknown to you, the court is required by law to intimate a copy of this application to:

(i) ONE of the next-of-kin of your civil partner. ("Next-of-kin" does not include yourself or any children of the family for the purposes of this application.)

(ii) All children of the family aged 16 years or over, whether or not they live with you.

When entering details of next-of-kin, if any, please state his or her relationship to your civil partner (i.e.—"mother", "father", "brother", "sister", etc.)

If you do not know the identity or whereabouts of any of the next-of-kin of your civil partner, or the whereabouts of any children of the family, please enter "not known" where appropriate.

LETTER FROM GENERAL REGISTER OFFICE. If you do not know the address of your civil partner and your civil partnership was registered in Scotland, you must obtain a letter from the General Register Office stating that there is no record that your civil partner has had your civil partnership dissolved. The letter must be issued not more than one month before the date of posting this application to the court. If you require to obtain a letter you should apply to:

General Register Office (Scotland), Registration Branch, New Register House, Edinburgh, EH1 3YT,

stating both civil partners' full names, the date and place of registration of your civil partnership and requesting that a search be made to confirm that there is no record that your civil partner has had your civil partnership dissolved. (Note – a fee will be charged for this service).

The requirement to obtain a letter from the General Register Office does not apply if your civil partnership was registered outwith Scotland.

PART 1

WRITE IN INK, USING BLOCK CAPITALS

1. NAME AND ADDRESS OF APPLICANT

Surname...

Present

Address...

Other name(s)

in full...

Daytime telephone number (if

any)..

2. NAME OF CIVIL PARTNER

Surname..

Other name(s)

in full..

3. ADDRESS OF CIVIL PARTNER (if the address of your civil partner is not known, please enter "not known" and proceed to Section 4)

Present

Address..

Daytime telephone number (if

any)..

....

4. Only complete this section if you do not know the present address of your civil partner

NEXT-OF-KIN

Name...

Address...

....

....

Relationship to your civil

partner..

PART 1 (continued)

CHILDREN OF THE FAMILY

Names and dates of birth   Addresses

....
                                            ....
....
                                            ....
....
                                            ....

If sufficient space is not available here to list all the children of the family, please continue on a separate sheet and attach to this form.

Notes on Section 5 opposite

"Domiciled" means that the person concerned regards Scotland as his/her permanent home and intends to live permanently in Scotland in the foreseeable future.

Notes on Section 6 opposite

You will be able to obtain these details from your extract of the registration of your civil partnership, which must accompany this application form when you send it to the court.

A photocopy of the extract of registration of the civil partnership will NOT be accepted.

5. JURISDICTION

Please indicate with a tick (√) in the appropriate box or boxes which of the following apply:

PART A

(i)   My civil partner and I are habitually resident in Scotland   ☐

(ii)   My civil partner and I were last habitually resident in Scotland, and one of us still resides there   ☐

(iii) My civil partner is habitually resident in Scotland   ☐

(iv)   I am habitually resident in Scotland having resided there for at least a year immediately before this application was made   ☐

(v)   I am habitually resident in Scotland having resided there for at least six months immediately before this application was made and am domiciled in Scotland   ☐

If you have ticked one of the boxes in Part A, you do not have to complete Part B or C. You should complete either Part B or Part C if you have not ticked any of the boxes in Part A

PART B

(i) No court has, or is recognised as having, jurisdiction under regulations made under section 219 of the Civil Partnership Act 2004

AND

(ii) I am domiciled in Scotland

(iii) My civil partner is domiciled in Scotland

PART C

(i) My civil partner and I are registered civil partners of each other in Scotland

AND

(ii) No court has, or is recognised as having jurisdiction under regulations made under section 219 of the Civil Partnership Act 2004

AND

(iii) It is in the interests of justice for the Court of Session to assume jurisdiction in the case. (Please give reasons below).

6. DETAILS OF PRESENT CIVIL PARTNERSHIP

Place of Registration of Civil Partnership.............................(Registration District)

Date of Registration of Civil Partnership: Day............month..........year..............

PART 1 (continued)

---

7. DETAILS OF ISSUE OF INTERIM GENDER RECOGNITION CERTIFICATE
(i) Please state whether the interim gender
recognition certificate has been issued to you or
your civil partner.

(ii) Please state the date the interim gender
recognition certificate was issued   Day...................Month..................Year

---

Note on Section 9 opposite

"Children of the family" includes any children accepted into the family.

Notes on Section 11 opposite

No claim can be made in this form of dissolution application for payment to you of a periodical
allowance (*i.e.* regular payment of money, weekly, monthly etc. for your maintenance) or a
capital sum (*i.e.* lump sum). If you wish to make such a claim, you should consult a solicitor.

**NOTE: While it may be possible to obtain an order for periodical allowance after dissolution of
your civil partnership, the right to payment of a capital sum is lost once decree of dissolution is
granted.**

8. MENTAL DISABILITY   YES ☐   NO ☐
As far as you are are aware is your civil partner
incapable of managing his/her affairs because of
a mental disorder (whether mental illness,
personality disorder or learning disability)
 (If yes, give details)
(Tick box which applies)

---

9. CHILDREN   YES ☐   NO ☐
Are there any children of the family under the
age of 16?
(Tick box which applies)

Release 90: March 2007

10. OTHER COURT ACTIONS   YES ☐   NO ☐

Are you aware of any court actions currently
proceeding in any country (including Scotland)
which may affect your civil partnership?
(If yes, give details)
(*Tick box which applies*)

---

11. DECLARATION AND REQUEST FOR DISSOLUTION OF CIVIL PARTNERSHIP

I confirm that the facts stated in Sections 1–10 above apply to my civil partnership.

I do not ask the court to make any financial awards in connection with this application.

I request the court to grant decree of dissolution of my civil partnership.

....

        (Date)   (Signature of Applicant)

PART 2

APPLICANT'S AFFIDAVIT

To be completed only after Part 1 has been signed and dated.

I, (*Insert Applicant's full name*) ....

residing at (*insert Applicant's present home address*) ....

....

Town ....Country ....

SWEAR that to the best of my knowledge and belief the facts stated in Part 1 of this
Application are true.

Signature of Applicant ....

                      SWORN at (*insert place*) ....

To be completed by   this ....day of .... 20 ....
Justice of the Peace,
Notary Public or   before me (*insert full name*) ....
Commissioner for   (*insert full address*) ....
Oaths

                     ....

                     ....

                     Signature ....

                     *Justice of the Peace/Notary Public/Commissioner for Oaths

                     *Delete as appropriate

---

[1] Form 49.80B-C inserted by S.S.I. 2005 No. 632 (effective 8th December 2005) and S.S.I. 2006
No. 206 (effective 4th May 2006) and amended by S.S.I. 2007 No. 7, para. 20 (effective 26th
February 2007).

Rule 49.80E(3)   [1] FORM 49.80E–A

Form of citation in simplified dissolution of civil partnership application under section 117(3)(c) of the Civil Partnership Act 2004

CITATION

Date: (*Date of posting or other method of service*)

To: ....

....

....

APPLICATION FOR DISSOLUTION OF A CIVIL PARTNERSHIP (WITH CONSENT OF OTHER PARTY TO THE CIVIL PARTNERSHIP) CIVIL PARTNERS HAVING LIVED APART FOR AT LEAST ONE YEARS

You are barely served with an application by your civil partner which asks the court to grant a decree of dissolution of your civil partnership.

If you wish to oppose the granting of such a decree, you should put your reasons in writing and send your letter to the address shown below. Your letter must reach the court by (*insert date on which period of notice expires*).

(*Signed*)

Deputy Principal Clerk of Session

[*or* authorised clerk of session]

[*or* Messenger-at-Arms]

(*Address*)

IMPORTANT NOTE. If you wish to exercise your right to claim a financial award you should immediately advise the court that you oppose the application for that reason, and thereafter consult a solicitor.

Court of Session
Extracts Department (SP)
Parliament House
Edinburgh EH1 1RQ
Tel: 0131–225–2595

---

[1] Form 49.80E-A inserted by S.S.I. 2005 No. 632 (effective 8th December 2005) and S.S.I. 2006 No. 206 (effective 4th May 2006).

Form of citation in simplified dissolution of civil partnership application under section 117(3)(d) of the Civil Partnership Act 2004

CITATION

Date: (*Date of posting or other method of service*)

To: ....

....

....

APPLICATION FOR DISSOLUTION OF A CIVIL PARTNERSHIP. CIVIL PARTNERS HAVING LIVED APART FOR AT LEAST TWO YEARS

Your civil partner has applied to the court for a decree of dissolution of your civil partnership on the ground your civil partnership has broken down irretrievably because you and (s)he have lived apart for a period of at least two years.

A copy of the application is hereby served on you.

1. Please note—

    (a) that the court may not make a financial award under this procedure and that your civil partner is making no claim against you for payment of a periodical allowance (*i.e.* regular payment of money weekly, monthly, etc., for this *or* her] maintenance or a capital sum (*i.e.* lump sum);

2. Dissolution of your civil partnership may result in the loss to you of property rights (*e.g.* the right to succeed to the applicant's estate on his/her death) or the right, where appropriate, to a pension.

3. If you wish to oppose the granting of such a dissolution of your civil partnership, you should put your reasons in writing and send your letter to the address shown below. Your letter must reach the court by (*insert date on which period of notice expires*).

4. In the event of the dissolution of your civil partnership being granted, you will be sent a copy of the extract decree. (Should you change your address before receiving the copy extract decree, please notify the court immediately.)

(*Signed*)

Deputy Principal Clerk of Session

[*or* authorised clerk of session]

[*or* Messenger-at-Arms]

(*Address*)

IMPORTANT NOTE. If you wish to exercise your right to claim a financial award you should immediately advise the court that you oppose the application for that reason, and thereafter consult a solicitor.

Court of Session
Extracts Department (SP)
Parliament House
Edinburgh EH1 1RQ
Tel: 0131–225–2595

---

[1] Form 49.80E-B inserted by S.S.I. 2005 No. 632 (effective 8th December 2005) and S.S.I. 2006 No. 206 (effective 4th May 2006).

Rule 49.80E(3)   [1] FORM 49.80E–C

Form of citation in simplified dissolution of civil partnership application under section 117(2)(b) of the Civil Partnership Act 2004

CITATION

Date: (*Date of posting or other method of service*)

To: ....

         ....

         ....

APPLICATION FOR DISSOLUTION OF A CIVIL PARTNERSHIP. INTERIM GENDER RECOGNITION CERTIFICATE ISSUED TO ONE OF THE CIVIL PARTNERS AFTER REGISTRATION OF THE CIVIL PARTNERSHIP.

Your civil partner has applied to the court for a decree of dissolution of your civil partnership on the ground that an interim gender recognition certificate has been issued to you or your civil partner after your civil partnership was registered.

A copy of the application is hereby served on you.

1. Please note that the court may not make a financial award under this procedure and that your civil partner is making no claim against you for payment of a periodical allowance (*i.e.* regular payment of money weekly, monthly, etc., for his [*or* her] maintenance or a capital sum (*i.e.* lump sum);

2. Dissolution of your civil partnership may result in the loss to you of property rights (*e.g.* the right to succeed to the applicant's estate on his/her death) or the right, where appropriate, to a pension.

3. If you wish to oppose the granting of such a dissolution of your civil partnership, you should put your reasons in writing and send your letter to the address shown below. Your letter must reach the court by (*insert date on which period of notice expires*).

4. In the event of the dissolution of your civil partnership being granted, you will be sent a copy of the extract decree. (Should you change your address before receiving the copy extract decree, please notify the court immediately.)

(*Signed*)

Deputy Principal Clerk of Session

[*or* authorised clerk of session]

[*or* Messenger-at-Arms]

(*Address*)

IMPORTANT NOTE. If you wish to exercise your right to claim a financial award you should immediately advise the court that you oppose the application for that reason, and thereafter consult a solicitor.

Court of Session
Extracts Department (SP)
Parliament House
Edinburgh EH1 1RQ
Tel: 0131–225–2595

----

[1] Form 49.80E–C inserted by S.S.I. 2005 No. 632 (effective 8th December 2005).

Form of intimation to child or next-of-kin in simplified dissolution of civil partnership application under section 117(3)(d) or 117(2)(b) of the Civil Partnership Act 2004

CITATION

Date: (*Date of posting or other method of service*)

To: ....

....

....

APPLICATION FOR DISSOLUTION OF A CIVIL PARTNERSHIP. CIVIL PARTNERS HAVING LIVED APART FOR AT LEAST TWO YEARS OR ISSUE OF INTERIM GENDER RECOGNITION CERTIFICATE AFTER REGISTRATION OF THE CIVIL PARTNERSHIP

.... (Applicant) v .... (Respondent)

TAKE NOTICE

1. In the above application, a copy of which is enclosed, the applicant has indicated that you are the (*state relationship*) of (*name of respondent*) whose present address is not known to the applicant.

2. Should you know the present address of your (*state relationship*) or how he [*or* she] may be contacted, you are requested to give this information at once in writing to—

Court of Session
Extracts Department (SP)
Parliament House
Edinburgh EH1 1RQ
Tel: 0131–225–2595

This will enable the court to inform the respondent that the application has been made.

3. If you are unable to provide the above information, and/or you wish for your own interest to oppose the application for dissolution of the civil partnership, you should write to the above address by (*insert date on which period of time expires*).

(*Signed*)

Deputy Principal Clerk of Session

[*or* authorised clerk of session]

[*or* Messenger-at-Arms]

(*Address*)

---

[1] Form 49.80E–D inserted by SSI 2005/632 (effective 8th December 2005) and S.S.I. 2006 No. 206 (effective 4th May 2006).

Rule 49.780E(5)   [1] FORM 49.80E–E

Form of certificate of service of simplified dissolution application

CERTIFICATE OF SERVICE [*or* INTIMATION]

I, (*name*), Deputy Principal Clerk of Session [*or clerk of session authorised by him*], certify that I served [*or* intimated] this simplified dissolution application by (*name of applicant*) on [*or to*] (*name of person on whom service executed or to whom intimation given*) by posting it with a citation [*or* notice of intimation] in Form (*number of form*) to that person between (*time*) and (*time*) on (*date*) at (*name of post office*) in a registered envelope [*or* recorded delivery envelope] address as follows:-(*address*). The Post Office receipt [*or* certificate of posting] is attached to this certificate.

(*Signed*)

Deputy Principal Clerk of Session

[*or* authorised clerk of session]

[*or* Messenger-at-Arms]

(*Address*)

(*Signed*)

Witness

---

[1] Form 49.80E–E inserted by SSI 2005/632 (effective 8th December 2005).

Rule 49.780E(5)   [1] FORM 49.80E–F

Form of certificate of service of simplified dissolution application by messenger-at-arms

CERTIFICATE OF SERVICE [*or* INTIMATION]

I, (*name*), Messenger-at-Arms, certify that I served [*or* intimated] this simplified dissolution application [and notice of intimation] on [*or to*] (*name of person on whom served or to whom intimated*)—

- by leaving it and a citation [*or* notice] with (*name of person*) at (*place*) at (*time*) on (*date*).

- by leaving it and a citation [*or* notice] with (*name and occupation of person with whom left*) at (*place*) on (*date*). (*Specify that enquiry made and that reasonable grounds exist for believing that the person on whom service is to be made or to whom intimation is to be given resident the place but is not available*).

- by depositing it and a citation [*or* notice] in (*place*) on (*date*). (*Specify that enquiry made and that reasonable grounds exist for believing that the person on whom service is to be made or to whom intimation is to be given resident the place but is not available*).

- by leaving it and a citation [*or* notice] with (*name and occupation of person with whom left*) at (*place of business*) on (*date*). (*Specify that enquiry made and that reasonable grounds exist for believing that the person on whom service is to be made or to whom intimation is to be given resident the place but is not available*).

- by depositing it and a citation [*or* notice] at (*place of business*) on (*date*). (*Specify that enquiry made and that reasonable grounds exist for believing that the person on whom service is to be made or to whom intimation is to be given resident the place but is not available*).

- by leaving it and a citation [*or* notice] at (*registered office or place of business*) on (*date*), in the hands of (*name of person*).

- by leaving [*or* depositing] it and a citation [*or* notice] at (*registered office, official address or place of business*) on (*date*), in such a way as it was likely to come to the attention of (*name of person on whom served or to whom intimated*). (*Specify how left*).

I did this in the presence of (*name, occupation and address of witness*).

(*Signed*)

Messenger-at-Arms

(*Address*)

(*Signed*)

Witness

---

[1] Form 49.80E–F inserted by SSI 2005/632 (effective 8th December 2005).

Rule 49.83   Form 49.83–A

Form of certificate relating to the making of a maintenance assessment under the Child Support Act 1991

I, Deputy Principal Clerk of Session, certify that notification has been received from the Secretary of State under section 10 of the Child Support Act 1991 of the making of a maintenance assessment under that Act which supersedes the decree [*or* order] granted on (*date*) in relation to aliment for (*name(s) of child(ren)*) with effect from (*date*).

(*Signed*)

Deputy Principal Clerk of Session

Date:

Rule 49.83   Form 49.83–B

Form of certificate relating to the cancellation or ceasing to have effect of a maintenance assessment under the Child Support Act 1991

I, Deputy Principal Clerk of Session, certify that notification has been received from the Secretary of State under section 10 of the Child Support Act 1991 that the maintenance assessment made on (*date*) has been cancelled [*or* ceased to have effect] on (*date*).

(*Signed*)

Deputy Principal Clerk of Session

Date:

Rule 49.84(1)   Form 49.84–A

Form of certificate endorsed on extract order for aliment affected by maintenance assessment

A maintenance assessment having been made under the Child Support Act 1991 on (*date*), this order, in so far as it relates to the making or securing of periodical payments to or for the benefit of (*name(s) of child(ren)*), ceases to have effect from (*date two days after the date on which the maintenance assessment was made*).

Rule 49.84(2)   Form 49.84–B

Form of certificate endorsed on extract order for aliment on maintenance assessment being cancelled or ceasing to have effect

The jurisdiction of the child support officer under the Child Support Act 1991 having terminated on (*date*), this order, in so far as it relates to (*name(s) of child(ren)*), again shall have effect as from (*date of termination of child support officer's jurisdiction*).

Rule 50.2(3)   FORM 50.2–A

Form of citation by advertisement on action of declarator of death under section 1(1) of the Presumption of Death (Scotland) Act 1977

IN THE COURT OF SESSION

in the cause

[A.B.] *(designation and address)*

                                                                    Pursuer

against

[C.D.]

                                                                    Defender

An action has been brought in the Court of Session, Edinburgh, by [A.B.], pursuer, to declare that [C.D.], defender, whose last known address was *(address)*, is dead. Any person having an interest may apply to the court by minute to defend the action or to seek an order under section 2 of the Presumption of Death (Scotland) Act 1977. If you wish to apply to the court you must do so by *(date on which period of notice expires)* at the Office of Court, Court of Session, 2 Parliament Square, Edinburgh EH1 1RQ.

                                        (Signed)

                                        Solicitor [*or* Agent] for pursuer
                                        (Address)

Rule 50.2(5)   [1] FORM 50.2–B

Form of notice of intimation in an action of declarator of death under section 1(1) of the Presumption of Death (Scotland) Act 1977

Date: *(date of posting or other method of intimation)*

To: *(name and address as in warrant for intimation)*

An action has been brought in the Court of Session, Edinburgh requesting the court to declare that *(name and last known address of missing person)* is dead. A copy of the summons is attached.

You may apply to the court by minute for leave to state defences to the action or to seek a determination or appointment under section 2 of the Presumption of Death (Scotland) Act 1977 which is not sought by the pursuer. You must do so at the Office of Court, Court of Session, 2 Parliament Square, Edinburgh EH1 1RQ within [21] days after the date of intimation to you of the summons [*or if the warrant for intimation is executed before calling of the summons*, within seven days after the summons calls in court. The summons will not call in court earlier than [21] days after the date of intimation to you of the summons). The date of intimation is the date stated at the top of this notice unless intimation has been made by post in which case the date of intimation is the day after that date.

If you do not wish to lodge defences to this action but you have information which you consider may be of value to the court in this matter, you may write to the court with any such information by addressing your correspondence to the Deputy Principal Clerk of Session, 2 Parliament Square, Edinburgh EH1 1RQ.

IF YOU ARE UNCERTAIN ABOUT THE EFFECT OF THIS NOTICE, you should consult a solicitor, Citizens Advice Bureau or other local advice agency or adviser immediately.

                                        (Signed)

                                        Messenger-at-Arms
                                        [*or* Solicitor [*or* Agent]
                                        for pursuer]
                                        (Address)

_____

[1] Form 50.2–B amended by S.I. 1994 No. 2901 (minor correction).

Rule 51.5(3) FORM 51.5

Form of advertisement for objections and claims in action of multiplepoinding

IN THE COURT OF SESSION

in the cause

[A.B.] (*designation and address*)
Pursuer and Real [*or* Nominal] Raiser

against

[C.D.] (*designation and address*)
and Others

Defenders

An action of multiplepoinding has been brought in the Court of Session, Edinburgh by [A.B.], pursuer, in respect of (*briefly describe nature of the fund in medio*). On (*date*) Lord (*name*) ordered advertisement for objections and claims. Any person who wishes to object to the condescendence of the fund must do so by lodging defences, and any person who wishes to make a claim on the fund must do so by lodging a condescendence and claim, by (*date on which period of notice expires*) at the Office of Court, Court Session, 2 Parliament Square, Edinburgh EH1 1RQ.

(*Signed*)

[Solicitor [*or* Agent] for pursuer]
(*Address*)

Rule 53.2(3) FORM 53.2

Form of notice of intimation to clerk of inferior court or tribunal in action of reduction

Date: (*date of posting or other method of intimation*)

To: (*designation of clerk of court or tribunal in warrant for intimation*)

TAKE NOTICE

(*Pursuer's name and address*), pursuer, has brought an action in the Court of Session, Edinburgh against (*name and address of defender*), defender, seeking reduction of (*specify document*) pronounced by you. A copy of the summons is attached.

(*Signed*)

Messenger-at-Arms
[*or* Solicitor [*or* Agent] for pursuer]
(*Address*)

Rule 58.6(1)   FORM 58.6

Form of petition in application for judicial review

UNTO THE RIGHT HONOURABLE
THE LORDS OF COUNCIL AND SESSION

PETITION

of

[A.B.] (*designation and address*)

for

Judicial review of (*state briefly matter sought to be reviewed*) by [C.D.]

HUMBLY SHEWETH:—

1. That the petitioner is (*state designation, title and interest of petitioner*). The respondent is (*state designation and relation of respondent to matter to be reviewed*). [The following persons may have an interest   ].

2. That on (*date*) the respondent (*specify act, decision or omission to be reviewed*).

3. That the petitioner seeks (*state remedies sought (final and interim) including damages or restitution*). The petitioner craves the court to pronounce such further order, decrees or orders (including an order for expenses) as may seem to the court to be just and reasonable in all the circumstances of the case.

4. That the petitioner challenges the decision [*or* act *or* omission] of the respondent on the following ground(s).

5. (*State shortly (in this and following numbered paragraphs) facts in support of the ground(s) of challenge.*)

[6]. (*State briefly (in numbered paragraphs) the legal argument with reference to enactments or judicial authority on which it is intended to rely.*)

PLEA(S)-IN-LAW

(*Specify pleas-in-law relating to each ground of challenge and remedy sought*)

                                    According to Justice etc.
                                    (*Signed by counsel or other person having
                                    a right of audience*)

SCHEDULE FOR SERVICE

Respondent(s) on whom service is sought in common form
Respondent(s) on whom service is sought by advertisement.
Interested parties on whom service is sought in common form
Interested parties on whom service is sought by advertisement.

SCHEDULE OF DOCUMENTS

(*Specify documents founded on: R.C.S. 1994, r. 58.6(2)*)

Appendix

[1] Form 58.8A

Form of Minute of Intervention

APPLICATION

for

LEAVE TO INTERVENE

in the

PUBLIC INTEREST

in the cause

[A.B.] (*designation and address*)

Petitioner [*or* Appellant]

Against

[C.D.] (*designation and address*)

Defender] *or* Respondent]

[*Here set out briefly:*
  (a) *the name and description of the applicant;*
  (b) *any issue in the proceedings which the applicant wishes to address and the applicant's reasons for believing that any such issue raises a matter of public interest;*
  (c) *the propositions to be advanced by the applicant and the applicant's reasons for believing that they are relevant to the proceedings and that they will assist the Court.*]

---

[1] Form 58.8A inserted by S.S.I. 2000 No. 317 (as 58.8) and renumbered as 58.8A by S.S.I. 2004 No. 52.

Rule 59.1(1)(a)   FORM 59.1–A

Form of letters of arrestment

IN THE COURT OF SESSION

Application of (*applicant's name*) for Letters of Arrestment

My Lords of Council and Session—

1. In a (*describe deed*) dated (*date*), (*common debtor's name, designation and address*) bound himself [*or* herself *or* themselves *or* itself] to pay to (*applicant's name, designation and address*) (1) (*amount of principal sum in words and figures*) and (2) interest on that amount at (*rate*) from (*date*) until payment [*or as the case may be*]. These amounts [*or amount in words and figures*] remain(s) unpaid.

2. The (*short reference to deed*) was registered for execution in your Lordships' Books of Council and Session on (*date*). An extract of it is produced with this application [*or as the case may be*].

3. The applicant, therefore, requests your Lordships to grant warrant to arrest the sum of (*amount*) more or less due and all moveable things in the hands of any person who is debtor to or has the moveable things of (*name, designation and address of common debtor*) in his possession.

According to Justice etc.

(*Signed*)

Solicitor [*or* Agent] for applicant
(*Address*)

Warrant to arrest granted in accordance with the above application.

Date:

(*Signed*)

Depute [*or* Assistant] Clerk of Session
(*Signet*)

Rule 59.1(1)(b) [1] FORM 59.1–B

Form of letters of inhibition where decree granted or foreign judgment registered for execution

IN THE COURT OF SESSION

Application of (*applicant's name*) for Letters of Inhibition

My Lords of Council and Session—

1. (*Applicant's name, designation and address*), the applicant (*or specify*), raised an action in (*specify court*) against (*defender's name, designation and address*). In the action, decree was granted on (*date*) against (*defender's name*) to pay to the applicant (*or specify*) (1) (*amount of principal sum in words and figures*), (2) interest on that amount at (*rate*) from (*date*) until payment, and (3) the expenses of the action [being (*amount in words and figures*)]. These amounts [*or amount in words and figures*] remain(s) unpaid. [The decree was registered for execution in your Lordships' Books of Council and Session on (*date*) following a warrant to register for execution granted by your Lordships' court.]

2. An extract of the decree [*or* decree of registration in the Books of Council and Session or an original, official or certified copy document having the same force and effect as an extract of a decree of the Court of Session] dated at (*place and date*) is produced with this application.

---

[1] Form 59.1–B amended by S.I. 1996 No. 1756 (effective 5th August 1996) and by S.S.I. 2004 No. 331 (effective 6th August 2004).

3. The applicant, therefore, requests your Lordships to grant warrant to inhibit (*defender's name*).

According to Justice etc.

(*Signed*)

Solicitor [*or* Agent] for applicant
(*Address*)

Warrant to inhibit granted in accordance with the above application.

Date:

(*Signed*)

Depute [*or* Assistant] Clerk of Session
(*Signet*)

Rule 59.1(1)(c)   [1] FORM 59.1–C

Form of letters of inhibition on deed registered for execution

IN THE COURT OF SESSION

Application of (*applicant's name*) for Letters of Inhibition

My Lords of Council and Session—

1. In a (*describe deed*) dated (*date*), (*debtor's name, designation and address*) bound himself [*or* herself *or* themselves *or* itself] to pay to (*applicant's name, designation and address*) (1) (*amount of principal sum in words and figures*), and (2) interest on that amount at (*rate*) from (*date*) until payment. These amounts [*or amount in words and figures*] remain(s) unpaid.

2. The (*short reference to deed*) was registered for execution in your Lordships' Books of Council and Session [*or* books of the sheriff court at (*name of court*)] on (*date*). An extract of it is produced with this application.

3. The applicant, therefore, requests your Lordships to grant warrant to inhibit (*debtor's name*).

According to Justice etc.

(*Signed*)

Solicitor [*or* Agent] for applicant
(*Address*)

Warrant to inhibit granted in accordance with the above application.

Date:

(*Signed*)

Depute [*or* Assistant] Clerk of Session
(*Signet*)

---

[1] Form 59.1–C amended by S.I. 1996 No. 1756 (effective 5th August 1996).

        [1] FORM 59.1–D

Form of letters of inhibition on dependence of action in sheriff court

IN THE COURT OF SESSION

Application of (*applicant's name*) for Letters of Inhibition

My Lords of Council and Session—

1. (*Applicant's name, designation and address*), the applicant, has raised an action in (*name of sheriff court*) Sheriff Court against (*defender's name, designation and address*). The initial writ in the action was warranted on (*date*) and served on (*date*). In the action, the applicant requests the court to order (*defender's name*) to pay to the applicant (1) (*amount of principal sum in words and figures*), (2) interest on that amount at (*rate*) from (*date*) until payment, and (3) the expenses of the action.

2. The initial writ with the warrant and execution is produced with this application.

3. The applicant, therefore, requests your Lordships to grant warrant to inhibit (*defender's name*).

                         According to Justice etc.

                         (*Signed*)

                         Lord

Warrant to inhibit granted in accordance with the above application.

Date:

                         (*Signed*)

                         Lord
                         (*Signet*)

---

[1] Form 59.1–D amended by S.S.I. 2004 No. 537.

        [1] FORM 59.1–E

Form of letters of inhibition in respect of future or contingent debt

IN THE COURT OF SESSION

Application of (*applicant's name*) for Letters of Inhibition

My Lords of Council and Session—

1. In a (*describe deed*) dated (*date*), (*debtor's name, designation and address*) bound himself [or herself **or** themselves **or** itself] to pay to (*applicant's name, designation and address*), (*amount in words and figures and date when, or circumstances in which, amount falls due*).

2. The deed is not yet liquid but the debtor is [*specify* vergens ad inopiam *or* in meditatione fugae *or other similar grounds*].

3. A copy of the deed is produced with this application.

4. The applicant, therefore, requests your Lordships to grant warrant to inhibit (*debtor's name*).

                         According to Justice etc.
                         (*Signed*)
                         Solicitor   [*or*   Agent]   for   applicant
                         (*Address*)

Warrant to inhibit granted in accordance with the above application.

Date:

(Signed)

Lord
(Signet)

_____

[1] Form 59.1–E inserted by S.I. 1998 No. 890.

Rule 59(1)(f)   [1] FORM 59.1–F

Form of letters of inhibition on contract for transfer of heritable property

IN THE COURT OF SESSION

Application of [A.B.] *(insert name of applicant)* for Letters of Inhibition

My Lords of Council and Session—

1. In a *[specify nature of contract]* dated *(insert date)* [C.D.] *(insert name and address of other party to contract)* bound himself *(or herself or themselves or itself)* to convey to [A.B.] *(insert name and address of applicant)* the heritable property known as *(insert description of property)* with entry as at *(insert date of entry)*. The *[contract]* is produced with this application.

2. The applicant is apprehensive that the said [C.D.] may grant a disposition of the said property in favour of a third party in breach of the said [C.D.]ís obligation to the applicant under the *[contract]*.

3. The applicant therefore requests your Lordships to grant warrant to inhibit the said [C.D.].

According to Justice etc.

(Signed)

Solicitor *[or* Agent] for applicant

(Address)

Warrant to inhibit granted in accordance with the above application.

Date:

(Signed)

Depute *[or* Assistant] Clerk of Session
(Signet)

_____

[1] Form 59.1–F inserted by S.S.I. 1999 No. 109.

Rule 61.2(2)   [1] FORM 61.2

Form of petition under section 9(5)(a) of the Act of 1995 for appointment of a judicial factor

UNTO THE RIGHT HONOURABLE THE LORDS OF COUNCIL AND SESSION

PETITION

of

The Accountant of Court

Under section 9(5)(a) of the Children (Scotland) Act 1995 for the appointment of a judicial factor to [C.D.] (*name of child as in birth certificate*)

HUMBLY SHEWETH:—

1. That an application has been made to the petitioner under section 9(2) or (3) of the Children (Scotland) Act 1995 for a direction as to the administration of the property of [C.D.] [*name and address of child*].

2. That [C.D.] [*name of child*] was born on [*date of birth of child*].

3. That the property is of the following description [*description of property*].

4. That the propertyís value is not less than [*minimum value of property*].

5. That the property is for the time being held by [*name, address and designation of person holding property owned by or due to the child*].

6. That for the following reason[s] the appointment of a judicial factor is more appropriate than the making of a direction under paragraph (b) or (c) of section 9(5) of the Children (Scotland) Act 1995; that is to say [*statement of reason[s]*].

MAY IT THEREFORE please your Lordships to appoint (*name and address of proposed judicial factor*), or such other person as the court shall think proper, to be judicial factor to [*name and address of child*] to administer, in terms of section 9(5)(a) of the Children (Scotland) Act 1995, the property owned by or due to the child, as described at paragraph 4 above.

According to Justice etc.

(*Signed*)

Accountant of Court

---

[1] Form 61.2 inserted by S.I. 1997 No. 1720.

Rule 61.5(2)   FORM 61.5–A

Form of advertisement of petition for appointment of judicial factor

(*Cause reference number*)

PETITION FOR APPOINTMENT OF CURATOR *BONIS* [or other judicial factor] TO [C.D.]

NOTICE is hereby given to all persons having an interest that application has been made to the Court of Session by [A.B.] (*designation and address*) for the appointment of [E.F.] (*designation and address*) as curator *bonis* [*or other judicial factor*] to [C.D.] (*last known address*).

Any person having an interest may lodge answers to the petition. Answers must be lodged at the Office of Court, Court of Session, 2 Parliament Square, Edinburgh EH1 1RQ within [21] days after the date of this notice.

(*Name*)

Judicial Factor to [C.D.]
[*or* Solicitor [*or* Agent] for petitioner]
(*Address*)

Rule 61.5(2)   FORM 61.5–B

Form of advertisement of petition for discharge of judicial factor

(*Cause reference number*)

PETITION FOR DISCHARGE OF CURATOR *BONIS* [or other judicial factor] TO [C.D.]

NOTICE is hereby given to all persons having an interest that application has been made to the Court of Session by [E.F.] (*designation and address*) as curator *bonis* [or other judical factor] to [C.D.] (*last known address*) for discharge from his office [or otherwise as the case may be].

Any person having an interest may lodge answers to the petition. Answers must be lodged at the Office of Court, Court of Session, 2 Parliament Square, Edinburgh EH1 1RQ within [21] days after the date of this notice.

(*Name*)

Judicial Factor to [C.D.]
[*or* Solicitor [*or* Agent] for petitioner]
(*Address*)

Rule 61.18(a)   FORM 61.18

Form of notice in the Edinburgh Gazette of application for appointment of judicial factor on estate of deceased person

(*Cause reference number*)

PETITION FOR APPOINTMENT OF JUDICIAL FACTOR ON THE ESTATE OF [C.D.]

To the creditors of any persons interested in the estate of the deceased (*name and last known address*).

NOTICE is hereby given that:—

1. An application under section 11A of the Judicial Factors (Scotland) Act 1889 has been presented to the Court of Session by [A.B.] (*address*), a creditor [or creditors] of the deceased [or having an interest in the succession of the deceased], the deceased having left no settlement appointing trustees or other parties having power to manage his estate [or the trustees under the deceased's settlement having refused to act], for the appointment of a judicial factor to the estate of the deceased (*name*).

2. Any person having an interest in the estate of the deceased may lodge answers to the petition. Answers must be lodged at the Office of Court, Court of Session, 2 Parliament Square, Edinburgh EH1 1RQ within [21] days after the date of this notice [or otherwise in terms of the first order].

(*Name*)

Petitioner
[*or* Solicitor [*or* Agent] for the petitioner]
(*Address*)

Rule 61.20(1)   FORM 61.20

Form of notice in the Edinburgh Gazette and appropriate newspaper calling for claims

(*Cause reference number*)

JUDICIAL FACTORY ON THE ESTATE OF [C.D.]

To the creditors and other persons interested in the estate of the deceased (*name and last known address*).

NOTICE is hereby given that [E.F.] (*designation and address*), having been appointed by the Court of Session on (*date of appointment*) as judicial factor on the estate of the deceased [C.D.] under section 11A of the Judicial Factors (Scotland) Act 1889, requires all the lawful creditors of the deceased [C.D.] and other persons interested in his estate, to lodge with the judicial factor, within four months after the date of this notice—

    (*a*) a statement of their claims as creditors of the deceased, or as otherwise interested in his estate, and

    (*b*) vouchers or other written evidence as they may have to found on in support of their claims,

so that the claims may be considered and reported on by the judicial factor.

                              (*Name*)

                              Judicial factor
                              [*or* Solicitor [*or* Agent] for the judicial factor]
                              (*Address*)

Rule 61.25(1)(*c*)   FORM 61.25

Form of notice in the Edinburgh Gazette on lodging statement of funds and schemes of division

(*Cause reference number*)

JUDICIAL FACTORY ON THE ESTATE OF [C.D.]

To the creditors of and persons interested in the succession to the estate of the deceased (*name and last known address*).

NOTICE is hereby given by [E.F.] (*designation and address*), judicial factor on the estate of the deceased [C.D.], that he has prepared and lodged in the Court of Session a state of funds and [first] scheme of division of the estate, to be considered and approved by the court.

                              (*Name*)

                              Judicial factor
                              [*or* Solicitor [*or* Agent] for the judicial factor]
                              (*Address*)

Rule 61.31(2)   [1] FORM 61.31

Form of notice where application for discharge is made to Accountant of Court

Date: (*insert date of posting or other method of intimation*)

To: (*name and address of cautioner or person with interest*)

TAKE NOTICE that A.B. (*address*) curator *bonis* [*or other judicial factor*] to [*or* on the estate of] C.D. (*address*) has applied to the Accountant of Court for a certificate of discharge.

The audited accounts of the judicial factory are available for inspection at the office of the Accountant of Court, 2 Parliament Square, Edinburgh EH1 1RQ.

Representations relating to the application must be made in writing and lodged with the Accountant of Court within [21] days after the date of intimation to you of this notice. The date of intimation is the date stated at the top of this notice unless intimation was given by post in which case the date of intimation is the day after that date.

IF YOU ARE UNCERTAIN ABOUT THE EFFECT OF THIS NOTICE, you should consult a solicitor, Citizens Advice Bureau or other local advice agency or adviser immediately.

(*Signed*)

Curator *bonis* to [C.D.]
(*or* Solicitor [*or* Agent] for [E.F.]
Curator *bonis* to [C.D.]]

---

[1] Form 61.31 amended by S.I. 1994 No. 2901 (minor correction).

Rule 61.33(2)(a)   Form 61.33

Form of notice in the Edinburgh Gazette of application for appointment of judicial factor on estate of deceased person

(*Cause reference number*)

PETITION FOR DISCHARGE OF JUDICIAL FACTOR ON THE ESTATE OF [C.D.]

To the creditors of and other persons interested in the succession to the estate of the deceased (*name and last known address*).

NOTICE is hereby given that [E.F.] (*address*), judicial factor on the estate of the deceased [C.D.], has presented a petition to the Court of Session for discharge from the office of judicial factor.

Any person having an interest may lodge answers to the petition. Answers must be lodged at the Office of Court, Court of Session, 2 Parliament Square, Edinburgh EH1 1RQ within [21] days after the date of this notice [*or otherwise in terms of the first order in the petition for discharge*].

(*Name*)

Judicial factor
[*or* Solicitor [*or* Agent] for petitioner]
(*Address*)

Rule 62.2(1)(b)   Form 62.2

Form of certificate of currency conversion

IN THE COURT OF SESSION

in the

Application of

(*name, designation and address of applicant(s)*)

under the Civil Jurisdiction and Judgments Act 1982 for   registration of a judgment [*or other document*] of the (*name of court*) of (*date of judgment*) in the cause (*name of pursuer*) against (*name of defender*).

In a terms of a certificate dated at (*place*) on (*date*) the sterling equivalent of (*a*) the principal sum is (£ . p); (*b*) the interest thereon is (£ . p); and (*c*) the expenses is (£ . p) at the rate of exchange prevailing at that date.

Date:

(*Signed*)

Depute [*or* Assistant] Clerk of Session

Rule 62.9   [1] FORM 62.9

Form of notice to judgment debtor of registration of judgment under the Administration of Justice Act 1920 or the Foreign Judgments (Reciprocal Enforcement) Act 1933

IN THE COURT OF SESSION

in the PETITION of

[A.B.] (*designation and address*)

Petitioner

for

Registration of a judgment of (*name of court*)
dated (*date*)

under

section 9 of the Administration of Justice Act 1920
[*or* section 2 of the Foreign Judgments (Reciprocal Enforcement) Act 1933]

Date: (*date of posting or other method of service*)

To: (*name of judgment debtor*)

TAKE NOTICE

That a judgment (*give details*) has been registered in the register of judgments of the Books of Council and Session on (*date*) on the application of the petitioner in the above petition.

If you intend to apply to the court to have the judgment set aside you must do so by note on or before (*insert date court has fixed under R.C.S. 1994, r. 62.7(2)*). You must lodge the note in the process of the above petition in the Petition Department, Court of Session, 2 Parliament Square, Edinburgh EH1 1RQ.

IF YOU ARE UNCERTAIN ABOUT THE EFFECT OF THIS NOTICE you should consult a solicitor, Citizens Advice Bureau or other local advice agency or adviser immediately.

(*Signed*)

Messenger-at-Arms
[*or* Solicitor [*or* Agent] for petitioner]
(*Address*)

---

[1] Form 62.9 amended by S.I. 1994 No. 2901 (minor correction).

Rule 62.11(2)   FORM 62.11

Form of certificate to be appended to copy of judgment certified under section 10 of the Administration of Justice Act 1920 or the Foreign Judgments (Reciprocal Enforcement) Act 1933

I, Deputy Principal Clerk of Session, certify that the foregoing extract decree is a true copy of a judgment obtained in the Court of Session. This certificate is issued in accordance with section 10 of the Administration of Justice Act 1920 [*or* Foreign Judgments (Reciprocal Enforcement) Act 1933] and in obedience to an interlocutor of Lord (*name*) dated (*date*).

Date:

(*Signed*)

Deputy Principal Clerk of Session
(*Stamp*)

Rule 62.16   FORM 62.16

Form of notice of registration of award under the Arbitration (International Investments Disputes) Act 1966

REGISTRATION OF AWARD UNDER THE ARBITRATION (INTERNATIONAL INVESTMENTS DISPUTES) ACT 1966

Date: (*date of posting or other method of service*)

To: (*name and address of person on whom service executed*)

TAKE NOTICE

That on (*date*) [Lord (*name*) in] the Court of Session, Edinburgh granted warrant for the registration of (*identify award to be registered*) on the application of (*name and address of petitioner*).

The above award was registered in the Books of Council and Session on (*date*) for execution (enforcement). An application will be made to the Keeper of the Registers of Scotland for an extract of the registered award with warrant for execution.

(*Signed*)

Messenger-at-Arms
[*or* Solicitor [*or* Agent] for petitioner]
(*Address*)

Rule 62.28   [1] FORM 62.28

Form of petition for registration of a judgment under section 4 of the Civil Jurisdiction and Judgments Act 1982 or under Article 38, Article 57 or Article 58 of the Council Regulation

UNTO THE RIGHT HONOURABLE THE LORDS OF COUNCIL AND SESSION

PETITION

of

[A.B.] (*designation and address*)

under the Civil Jurisdiction and Judgments Act 1982 [*or* under Council Regulation (E.C.) No. 44/2001 of 22nd December 2000 on jurisdiction and the recognition and enforcement of judgments in civil and commercial matters]

for registration of

a judgment [*or* authentic instrument *or* court settlement] [of the (*name of court*)]

dated the   day of

HUMBLY SHEWETH:—

1. That this petition is presented by (*name*) to register a judgment [*or authentic instrument or court settlement*] [of the (*name of court*) of (*date of judgment*)].

2. That in the cause in which the judgment [*or as the case may be*] was pronounced, A.B. was pursuer [*or defender or (as the case may be*) and [C.D.] was defender [*or pursuer or as the case may be*].

3. That the petitioner is a party having an interest to enforce the judgment [*or as the case may be*] because (*state reasons*).

4. That this petition is supported by the affidavit of (*name of deponent*) and the documents produced with it.

5. That the petitioner seeks warrant to register the judgment [*or as the case may be*] [and for decree in terms thereof] [and for decree to be pronounced in the following or such other terms as to the court may seem proper:— (*state terms in which decree is to be pronounced in accordance with Scots law*)].

6. That the petitioner seeks the authority of the court to execute the protective measure[s] of (*state measures*), for the following reasons (*state reasons*).

7. That this petition is made under section 4 of, and Article 31 [*or 50*] of the Convention in Schedule 1 [*or 3C*] to, the Civil Jurisdiction and Judgments Act 1982 [*or under Article 38 [or 57 or 58*] of Council Regulation (E.C.) No. 44/2001 of 22 December 2000 on jurisdiction and the recognition and enforcement of judgments in civil and commercial matters] and rule 62.28 of the Rules of the Court of Session 1994.

> According to Justice etc.
>
> (*Signed*)
>
> Petitioner
>
> [*or Solicitor [or Agent] for petitioner*]
>
> (*Address of solicitor or agent*)
>
> [*or counsel or other person having a right of audience*]

---

[1] Form 62.28 substituted by S.S.I. 2004 No. 52.

Rule 62.33   [1] FORM 62.33

Form of notice of decree and warrant for registration of a judgment under section 4 of the Civil Jurisdiction and Judgments Act 1982 or under Article 38, Article 57 or Article 58 of the Council Regulation

IN THE COURT OF SESSION

in the

PETITION

of

[A.B.] (*designation and address*)

under section 4 of the Civil Jurisdiction and Judgments Act 1982 [*or under Article 38 [or 57 or 58*] of Council Regulation (E.C.) No. 22/2002 of 22nd December 2000 on jurisdiction and the recognition and enforcement of judgments in civil and commercial mattters]

Date: (*date of posting or other method of service*)

To: (*name of person against whom judgment was given and decree and warrant granted*).

TAKE NOTICE

That an interlocutor dated the   day of   , a certified copy of which is attached, was pronounced at the Court of Session granting decree and warrant for registration of the judgment [*or as the case may be*] [of the (*name of court*)] dated the   day of   , for (*state briefly the terms of the judgment*).

You have the right to appeal to a Lord Ordinary in the Outer House of the Court of Session, Parliament Square, Edinburgh EH1 1RQ against the interlocutor granting decree and warrant for registration within one month [*or* two months *as the case may be*] after the date of service of this notice upon you. The date of service is the date stated at the top of this notice unless service has been executed by post in which case the notice of service is the day after that date.

An appeal must be by motion enrolled in the process of the petition.

The registered judgment and decree of the Court of Session may not be enforced in Scotland until the expiry of the period within which you may appeal and any appeal has been disposed of.

Intimation of an appeal should be made to the petitioner, [A.B.], at the following address for service in Scotland:—

(*Signed*)

Messenger-at-Arms
[*or* Petitioner [*or* Solicitor [*or*
Agent] for petitioner]]
(*Address*)

---

[1] Form 62.33 substituted by S.I. 2004 No. 52 (effective 1st March, 2004).

Rule 62.38(1)   FORM 62.38

Form of petition for registration of a judgment under paragraph 5 of Schedule 7 to the Civil Jurisdiction and Judgments Act 1982

UNTO THE RIGHT HONOURABLE THE LORDS OF COUNCIL AND SESSION

PETITION

of

[A.B.] (*designation and address*)

under the Civil Jurisdiction and Judgments Act 1982

for registration of

a judgment of the (*name of court*)

dated the   day of

HUMBLY SHEWETH:—

1. That this petition is presented by (*name*) to register a judgment [*or decision or other order*] of the (*name of court*) of (*date of judgment*).

2. That in the cause in which the judgment [*or decision or other order*] was pronounced [A.B.] was plaintiff [*or defendant or as the case may be*] and [C.D.] was defendant [*or plaintiff or as the case may be*].

3. That the petitioner is a party having an interest to enforce the judgment [*or decision or other order*] because (*state reasons*).

4. That the petitioner believes and avers that the usual [*or* last known] address of the (*state party liable in execution*) is (*state address*).

5. That the petitioner seeks warrant to register the judgment [and for decree in terms thereof] [and for decree to be pronounced in the following or such other terms as to the court may seem proper:— (*state terms in which decree is to be pronounced in accordance with Scots law*)].

6. That this petition is made under paragraph 5(1) of Schedule 7 to the Civil Jurisdiction and

Judgments Act 1982 and rule 62.38 of the Rules of the Court of Session 1994.

According to Justice etc.

(*Signed*)

Petitioner
[*or* Solicitor [*or* Agent] for petitioner]
(*Address of solicitor or agent*)

[*or counsel or other person having a right of audience*]

Rule 62.40(1)(*a*)   [1] Form 62.40–A

Form of certificate under section 12 of the Civil Jurisdiction and Judgments Act 1982 of a judgment given by the court or a court settlement

IN THE COURT OF SESSION

CERTIFICATE

under the Civil Jurisdiction and Judgments Act 1982

in the cause

[*or in the petition of*]

[A.B.] (*designation and address*)

Pursuer [*or* Petitioner]

against

[C.D.] (*designation and address*)

Defender [*or* Respondent]

I,   , a Deputy Principal Clerk of the Court Session, do hereby certify—

1. That the summons [*or* petition], brought [*or* presented] by the pursuer [*or* petitioner] [A.B.] was executed by citation of the defender [C.D.] served on him [*or* was served on the respondent [C.D.]] on the   day of   by (*state method of service*).

2. That in the summons [*or* petition] the pursuer, sought [payment of the sum of £   in respect of (*state briefly the nature of the claim*)] [and (*state other conclusions of the summons or orders sought in the prayer of petition*)].

3. [That the defender [C.D.] entered appearance on the   day of   ] [and lodged defences on the   day of   [*or* That the defender [C.D.] did not enter appearance].

4. That the pursuer [*or* petitioner] obtained decree [*or other order*] against the defender [*or* respondent] in the Court of Session for [payment of the sum of £   ] [or *state briefly the terms of the interlocutor or opinion of the court*] [and *state briefly other conclusions of the summons or orders sought in the prayer of the petition granted*] with the expenses of the cause in the sum of £   , all in terms of the certified copy interlocutor [and joint minute] attached.

5. That [no] objection to the jurisdiction of the court has been made [on the grounds that   ].

6. That the decree [in terms of the joint minute] includes interest at the rate of   per cent a year on the total of the sum of £   and expenses of £   from the   day of   until payment.

7. That the interlocutor containing the decree [*or other order or settlement*] has been served on the defender.

8. That the time for reclaiming (appealing) against the interlocutor has expired [and no reclaiming motion (appeal) has been enrolled within that time] [*or* and a reclaiming motion (appeal) having been enrolled within that time, has [not] been finally disposed of].

9. That enforcement of the decree has not for the time being been suspended and the time available for its enforcement has not expired.

10. That the whole pleadings of the parties are contained in the Closed Record [*or* summons *or* petition], a copy of which is attached.

11. That this certificate is issued under section 12 of the Civil Jurisdiction and Judgments Act 1982 and rule 62.40(1) of the Rules of the Court of Session 1994.

Dated the   day of

                    (*Signed*)

                    Deputy Principal Clerk of Session

---

[1] Form 62.40–A amended by S.I. 1994 No. 2901 (clerical error) and S.I. 1997 No. 1050 (minor amendment, effective 6th April 1997).

Form of certificate by Keeper of the Registers of writ registered for execution in the Books of Council and Session for registration under Article 50 of Schedule 1 or 3C to the Civil Jurisdiction and Judgments Act 1982

REGISTERS OF SCOTLAND

CERTIFICATE

under the Civil Jurisdiction and Judgments Act 1982

of

Deed [*or other writ*]

between

[A.B.] (*address*)

and

[C.D.] (*address*)

registered for execution in the Books of Council and Session

I,   , the Keeper of the Registers of Scotland, and as such, Keeper of the Register of Deeds, Bonds, Protests, Judgments and other writs registered for execution in the Books of Council and Session, do hereby certify—

1. That [A.B.] registered in the Books of Council and Session on the   day of   for execution against [C.D.] a (*describe writ and state terms of writ for which enforcement is to be sought*).

2. That the extract of the deed [*or other writ*] attached hereto is a true copy of the deed [*or other writ*] registered for execution by [A.B.].

[3. That the deed [*or other writ*] carries interest at the rate of   per cent a year from the   day of   until payment].

[4. That enforcement of the deed] [*or other writ*] has not for the time being been suspended and that the time available for its enforcement has not expired.

5. That the certificate is issued under Article 50 of Schedule 1 [*or* 3C] to the Civil Jurisdiction and Judgments Act 1982 and rule 62.40(3) of the Rules of the Court of Session 1994.

Dated the   day of

(*Signed*)

Keeper of the Registers of Scotland

Rule 62.41(1)   [1] FORM 62.41–A

**Form of certificate of money provisions in an interlocutor for registration under Schedule 6
to the Civil Jurisdiction and Judgments Act 1982**

IN THE COURT OF SESSION

CERTIFICATE

under the Civil Jurisdiction and Judgments Act 1982

in the cause

[*or* in the petition of]

[A.B.] (*designation and address*)

Pursuer [*or* Petitioner]

against

[C.D.] (*designation and address*)

Defender [*or* Respondent]

I,   , a Deputy Principal Clerk of the Court Session, do hereby certify—

1. That the pursuer A.B. obtained decree [*or other order*] against the defender [C.D.] on
the   day of   in the Court of Session for payment of the sum of £   in respect
of (*state briefly the nature of the claim and terms of the interlocutor*) with the sum of £   as
expenses.

2. That the interlocutor granting decree [*or other order*] was obtained on the grounds (*state
grounds briefly*).

3. That the decree [*or other order*] carries interest at the rate of   per cent a year on the total
of the sum of £   and expenses of £   from the   day of   until payment.

4. That the time for reclaiming (appealing) against the interlocutor has expired [and no
reclaiming motion (appeal) has been enrolled within that time] [and a reclaiming motion
(appeal) having been enrolled within that time, has been finally disposed of].

5. That enforcement of the decree [*or other order*] has not for the time being been suspended
and the time available for its enforcement has not expired.

Dated the   day of   .

(*Signed*)

Deputy Principal Clerk of Session

---

[1] Form 62.41–A amended by S.I. 1997 No. 1050 (minor amendment, effective 6th April 1997).

Form of certificate by Keeper of the Registers of money provisions in a writ registered for execution in the Books of Council and Session for registration under Schedule 6 to the Civil Jurisdiction and Judgments Act 1982

REGISTERS OF SCOTLAND

CERTIFICATE

under the Civil Jurisdiction and Judgments Act 1982

of

Deed [*or other writ*]

between

[A.B.] (*address*)

and

[C.D.] (*address*)

registered for execution in the Books of Council and Session

I,   , the Keeper of the Registers of Scotland, and as such, Keeper of the Register of Deeds, Bonds, Protests, Judgments and other writs registered for execution in the Books of Council and Session, do hereby certify—

1. That [A.B.] registered in the Books of Council and Session on the   day of   for execution against [C.D.] a (*describe writ and state terms of money provision in writ for which enforcement is to be sought*).

2. That the money provision in the deed [*or other writ*] carries interest at the rate of   per cent a year from the   day of   until payment.

3. That enforcement of the deed [*or other writ*] has not for the time being been suspended and that the time available for its enforcement has not expired.

4. That this certificate is issued under paragraph 4(1) of Schedule 6 to the Civil Jurisdiction and Judgments Act 1982 and rule 62.41(3) of the Rules of the Court of Session 1994.

Dated the   day of

(*Signed*)

Keeper of the Registers of Scotland

Rule 62.42(1)   [1] FORM 62.42–A

Form of certificate of non-money provisions in an interlocutor for registration under Schedule 7 to the Civil Jurisdiction and Judgments Act 1982

IN THE COURT OF SESSION

CERTIFICATE

under the Civil Jurisdiction and Judgments Act 1982

in the cause

[*or* in the PETITION of]

[A.B.] (*designation and address*)

Pursuer [*or* Petitioner]

against

[C.D.] (*designation and address*)

Defender [*or* Respondent]

I,   , a Deputy Principal Clerk of the Court Session, do hereby certify—

1. That the copy of the interlocutor attached hereto is a true copy of the decree [*or other order*] obtained in the Court of Session [and that the copy of the opinion of the court attached hereto is a true copy thereof] and is issued in accordance with section 18 of the Civil Jurisdiction and Judgments Act 1982.

2. That the time for reclaiming (appealing) against the interlocutor has expired [and no reclaiming motion (appeal) has been enrolled within that time] [and a reclaiming motion (appeal) having been enrolled within that time has been finally disposed of].

3. That enforcement of the decree [*or other order*] has not for the time being been suspended and the time available for its enforcement has not expired.

4. That this certificate is issued under paragraph 4(1)(b) of Schedule 7 to the Civil Jurisdiction and Judgments Act 1982 and rule 62.42(1) of the Rules of the Court of Session 1994.

Dated the   day of   .

(*Signed*)

Deputy Principal Clerk of Session

---

[1] Form 62.42–A amended by S.I. 1994 No. 2901 (clerical error) and S.I. 1997 No. 1050 (minor amendment, effective 6th April 1997).

Rule 62.42(4)   FORM 62.42–B

Form of certificate by Keeper of the Registers of non-money provisions in a writ registered for execution in the Books of Council and Session for registration under Schedule 7 to the Civil Jurisdiction and Judgments Act 1982

REGISTERS OF SCOTLAND

CERTIFICATE

under the Civil Jurisdiction and Judgments Act 1982

of

Deed [*or other writ*]

between

[A.B.] (*address*)

and

[C.D.] (*address*)

registered for execution in the Books of Council and Session

I,   , the Keeper of the Registers of Scotland, and as such, Keeper of the Register of Deeds, Bonds, Protests, Judgments and other writs registered for execution in the Books of Council and Session, do hereby certify—

1. That the extract of the deed [*or other writ*] attached hereto is a true copy of the deed [*or other writ*] registered for execution by [A.B.] and is issued in accordance with section 18 of the Civil Jurisdiction and Judgments Act 1982.

2. That enforcement of the deed [*or other writ*] has not for the time being been suspended and that the time available for its enforcement has not expired.

3. That this certificate is issued under paragraph 4(1)(b) of Schedule 7 to the Civil Jurisdiction and Judgments Act 1982 and rule 62.42(4) of the Rules of the Court of Session 1994.

Dated the   day of

(*Signed*)

Keeper of the Registers of Scotland

Form of notice of decree and warrant for registration of an order under the Criminal Justice (Scotland) Act 1987, the Criminal Justice Act 1988 or the Prevention of Terrorism (Temporary Provisions) Act 1989

IN THE COURT OF SESSION

in the

PETITION

of

[A.B.] (*designation and address*)

under section 28 [or 30A] of the Criminal

Justice (Scotland) Act 1987

[*or* section 90 of the Criminal Justice Act 1988]

[*or* paragraph 19(2) of Schedule 4 to the Prevention of Terrorism (Temporary Provisions) Act 1989]

for

registration of an order of

(*name of court*)

Dated the   day of

To: (*name of person against whom the order was made and decree and warrant for registration granted*)

TAKE NOTICE

An interlocutor dated the   day of   , a certified copy of which is attached, was pronounced in the Court of Session granting decree and warrant for registration in the Court of Session [and for registration in the Register of Judgments of the Books of Council and Session] of the order of the (*name of court*) dated the   day of   that (*briefly describe order*).

The order was registered in the Court of Session on (*date*).

[The order was registered in the Register of Judgments of the Books of Council and Session on (*date*) and an extract of the registered order and decree with warrant for execution has been issued by the Keeper of the Registers. Diligence in execution of the order may now be taken against you to enforce the order.]

Dated this   day of   .

(*Signed*)

Messenger-at-Arms
[*or* Petitioner] [*or* Solicitor
[*or* Agent] for petitioner]
(*Address*)

Rule 62.65 [1] FORM 62.65

Form of notice of registration of decision under a relevant instrument

REGISTRATION OF A DECISION (*or as the case may be*) UNDER THE
(*specify the relevant instrument*)

Date: (*date of posting or other method of service*)

To: (*name and address of person on whom service executed*)

TAKE NOTICE

That on (*date*) [Lord (*name*) in] the Court of Session, Edinburgh granted warrant for the registration of (*identify decision to be registered*) on the application of (*name and address of petitioner*).

The above award was registered in the Books of Council and Session on (*date*) for execution (i.e. enforcement). An application will be made to the Keeper of the Registers of Scotland for an extract of the registered award with warrant for execution.

(*Signed*)

Solicitor [*or* Agent] for petitioner
(*Address*)

---

[1] Form 62.65 inserted by S.I. 1996 No. 2168.

Rule 62.69(1) [1] FORM 62.69

Form of petition for enforcement of a judgment under Article 28 of the Council Regulation

UNTO THE RIGHT HONOURABLE THE LORDS OF COUNCIL AND SESSION

PETITION

of

[A.B.] (*designation and address*)

under Council Regulation (E.C.) No. 2201/2003 of 27th November 2003 on jurisdiction and the recognition and enforcement of judgments in matrimonial matters and matters of parental responsibility

for registration of

a judgment [*or* authentic instrument *or* enforceable agreement][of the (*name of court*)]

dated the   day of

HUMBLY SHEWETH:—

   1. That this petition is presented by [A.B.] to register a judgment [*or (as the case may be)*][of the (*name of court*)] of (*date of judgment or as the case may be*).

   2. That in the cause in which the judgment [*or (as the case may be)*] was pronounced, [A.B.] was pursuer [*or* defender *or (as the case may be)*] and [C.D.] was defender [*or* pursuer *or (as the case may be)*].

   3. That the petitioner is a party having an interest to enforce the judgment [*or (as the case may be)*] because (*state reasons*).

4. That this petition is supported by the affidavit of (*name of deponent*) and the documents produced with it.

5. That the petitioner seeks warrants to register the judgment [*or (as the case may be)*] [and for decree in terms thereof] [*or and for decree to be pronounced in the following or such other terms as to the court seem proper:—(state terms in which decree is to be pronounced in accordance with Scots law)*].

6. That the petition is made under Article 28 of the Council Regulation (E.C.) No. 2201/2003 of 27th November 2003 on jurisdiction and the recognition and enforcement of judgments in matrimonial matters and matters of parental responsibility and rule 62.69 of the Rules of the Court of Session 1994 [*or (as the case may be)*].

According to Justice etc.

(*Signed*)

Petitioner

[*or* Solicitor [*or* Agent] for petitioner]

[*Address of solicitor or agent*]

[*or counsel or other person having a right of audience*].

---

[1] Form 62.69 inserted by S.S.I. 2005 No. 135 (effective 8th December 2005).

Rule 62.73   FORM 62.73

Form of notice of decree and warrant for registration of a judgment under Article 28 of the Council Regulation

IN THE COURT OF SESSION

in the

PETITION of

[A.B.] (*designation and address*)

under Council Regulation (E.C.) No. 2201/2003 of 27th November 2003 on jurisdiction and the recognition and enforcement of judgments in matrimonial matters and matters of parental responsibility

for registration of

a judgment [*or* authentic instrument *or* enforceable agreement][of the (*name of court*)]

dated the   day of

Date: (*date of posting or other method of service*)

To: (*name of person against whom judgment was given and decree and warrant granted*)

TAKE NOTICE

That an interlocutor dated the   day of   , a certified copy of which is attached, was pronounced at the Court of Session granting decree and warrant for registration of the judgment [*or (as the case may be)*] [of the (*name of court*) dated the   day of   , for (*state briefly the terms of the judgment*).

You have the right to appeal to a Lord Ordinary in the Outer House of the Court of Session, Parliament Square, Edinburgh, EH1 1RQ against the interlocutor granting decree and warrant for registration within one month [*or* two months (*as the case may be*)] after the date of service of this notice upon you. The date of service is the date stated at the top of this notice unless service has been executed by post in which case the date of service is the day after that date.

An appeal must be by motion enrolled in the process of the petition.

The registered judgment and decree of the Court of Session may not be enforced in Scotland until the expiry of the period within which you may appeal and any appeal has been disposed of.

Intimation of an appeal should be made to the petitioner, [A.B.], at the following address for service in Scotland:—(*specify address*)

(*Signed*)

Messenger-at-Arms

[*or* Petitioner [*or* Solicitor [*or* Agent] for Petitioner]] (*Address*)

---

[1] Forms 62.69 and 62.73 inserted by S.S.I. 2005 No. 135, para.3 (effective 2nd March 2005).

[1] FORM 64.6

Form of order of court in procedure for recovery of documents under Chapter 64

ORDER BY THE COURT OF SESSION

In the Petition

of

[A.B.] (*designation and address*)

Petitioner

against

[C.D.] (*designation and address*)

Respondent

Date: (*date of interlocutor*)

To: (*name and address of party or parties or named third party haver, from whom the documents and other property are sought to be recovered*)

THE COURT having heard Counsel and being satisfied that it is appropriate to make an order under section 1 of the Administration of Justice (Scotland) Act 1972:

APPOINTS the Petition to be intimated on the walls of the court in common form and to be served upon the person(s) named and designed in the Petition;

APPOINTS (*name and designation of Commissioner*) to be Commissioner of the court;

GRANTS commission and diligence;

ORDERS the Commissioner to explain to the haver on executing the order—
(1) the meaning and effect of the order;
(2) that the haver may be entitled to claim that certain of the documents and other property are confidential or privileged;
(3) that the haver has a right to seek legal or other professional advice of his choice;
and to give the haver a copy of the Notice in Form 64–B of the Rules of Court.

GRANTS warrant to and authorises the said Commissioner, whether the haver has allowed entry or not—
(1) to enter, between the hours of 9am and 5pm on Monday to Friday, (*or, where the court has*

found cause shown under rule 64.11(1), otherwise specify the time) the premises at (*address of premises*) and any other place in Scotland owned or occupied by the haver at which it appears to the Commissioner that any of the items set out in the statement of facts in the application to the court (the "listed items") may be located;

(2) unless the haver is taking legal or other professional advice on the question of having the order varied—

    (a) to search for and take all other steps which he considers necessary to take possession of or preserve (*specify the listed items*); and

    (b) to take possession of and to preserve all or any of the listed items and to consign them with the Deputy Principal Clerk of Session to be held by him pending the further orders of the court; and for that purpose,

ORDERS the haver or his servants or agents to allow the Commissioner, any person whom the Commissioner considers necessary to assist him, and the Petitioner's representatives to enter the premises named in the order and, unless the haver has sought legal or other professional advice on the question of having the order varied, to allow them—

(1) to search for the listed items and take such other steps as the Commissioner considers it is reasonable to take to execute the order;

(2) to provide access to information stored on any computer owned or used by him by supplying or providing the means to overcome any and all security mechanisms inhibiting access thereto;

(3) to allow the Commissioner, any person whom the Commissioner considers necessary to assist him, and the Petitioner's representatives to remain in the premises until such time as the search is complete, including allowing them to continue the search on subsequent days if necessary;

(4) to inform the Commissioner immediately of the whereabouts of the listed items;

(5) to provide the Commissioner with a list of the names and addresses of everyone who has supplied him with any of the listed items and of the names and addresses of everyone to whom he has given any of the listed items;

and not to destroy, conceal or tamper with any of the listed items except in accordance with the terms of this order;

FURTHER AUTHORISES (*specify the representatives*) to be the sole representatives of the Petitioner to accompany the Commissioner for the purpose of identification of the said documents and other property.

SCHEDULE TO THE ORDER OF THE COURT

Undertakings given by Petitioner

The Petitioner has given the following undertakings—

1. That he will comply with any order of the court as to payment of compensation if it is subsequently discovered that the order, or the implementation of the order, has caused loss to the respondent or, where the respondent is not the haver, to the haver.

2. That he will bring within a reasonable time of the execution of the order any proceedings which he decides to bring.

3. That he will not, without leave of the court, use any information, documents or other property obtained as a result of the order, except for the purpose of any proceedings which he decides to bring and to which the order relates.

(*or as modified under rule 64.4*)

---

[1] Form 64.6 inserted by S.S.I. 2000 No. 319 as 64.–A and renumbered by S.S.I. 2004 No. 52.

[1] FORM 64.9

Notice to accompany order of the court when served by Commissioner

IMPORTANT

NOTICE TO PERSON ON WHOM THIS ORDER IS SERVED

1. This order orders you to allow the person appointed and named in the order as Commissioner to enter your premises to search for, examine and remove or copy the items mentioned in the order.
2. It also allows entry to the premises to any person appointed and named in the order as a representative of the person who has been granted the order and to any person accompanying the Commissioner to assist him.
3. No-one else is given authority to enter the premises.
4. You should read the order immediately.
5. You have the right to seek legal or other professional advice of your choice and you are advised to do so as soon as possible.
6. Consultation under paragraph 5 will not prevent the Commissioner from entering your premises for the purposes mentioned in paragraph 1 but if the purpose of your seeking advice is to help you to decide if you should ask the court to vary the order he will not be able to search the premises.
7. The Commissioner is obliged to explain the meaning and effect of the order to you.
8. He is also obliged to explain to you that you are entitled to claim that the items, or some of them, are protected as confidential or privileged.
9. You are entitled to ask the court to vary the order provided that—
you take steps to do so at once; and
you allow the Commissioner, any person appointed as a representative of the person who has been granted the order and any person accompanying the Commissioner to assist him, to enter the premises—but not to start the search—meantime.
10. The Commissioner and the people mentioned as representatives or assistants have a right to enter the premises even if you refuse to allow them to do so, unless—
  you are female and alone in the premises and there is no female with the Commissioner (where the Commissioner is not herself female), in which case they have no right to enter the premises; the Commissioner serves the order before 9am or after 5pm on a weekday or at any time on a Saturday or Sunday (except where the court has specifically allowed this, which will be stated in the order);
in which cases you should refuse to allow entry.
11. You are entitled to insist that there is no-one (or no-one other than X) present who could gain commercially from anything which might be read or seen on your premises.
12. You are required to hand over to the Commissioner any of the items mentioned in the order which are in your possession.
13. You may be found liable for contempt of court if you refuse to comply with the order.

---

[1] Form 64.9 inserted by S.S.I. 2000 No. 319 as 64.-B and renumbered by S.S.I. 2000 No. 52.

Rule 65.3(1A)   [1,2] FORM 65.3

Form of reference to the European Court

REQUEST

for

PRELIMINARY RULING

of

THE COURT OF JUSTICE OF THE EUROPEAN COMMUNITIES

from

THE COURT OF SESSION IN SCOTLAND

in the cause

[A.B.] (*designation and address*)

Pursuer [*or* Petitioner *or* Appellant]

against

[C.D.] (*designation and address*)

Defender [*or* Respondent]

[Here set out a clear and succinct statement of the case giving rise to the request for the ruling of the European Court in order to enable the European Court to consider and understand the issues of Community law raised and to enable governments of Member States and other interested parties to submit observations. The statement of the case should include:

(a)   *particulars of the parties;*
(b)   *the history of the dispute between the parties;*
(c)   *the history of the proceedings;*
(d)   *the relevant facts as agreed by the parties or found by the court or, failing such agreement or finding, the contentions of the parties on such facts;*
(e)   *the nature of the issues of law and fact between the parties;*
(f)   *the Scots law, so far as is relevant;*
(g)   *the Treaty provisions or other acts, instruments or rules of Community law concerned; and*
(h)   *an explanation of why the reference is being made.]*

The preliminary ruling of the Court of Justice of the European Communities is accordingly requested on the following questions:

1, 2, *etc. [Here set out the questions on which the ruling is sought, identifying the Treaty provisions or other acts, instruments or rules of Community law concerned.]*

Dated the   day of   19   .".

NOTES

---

[1] Form 65.3 inserted by S.I. 1999 No. 1281.
[2] Annex to Form 65.3 omitted by S.S.I. 2005 No. 521 (effective 21st October, 2005).

Form of agreement of a parent or guardian to an adoption order or an order under section 49 of the Adoption (Scotland) Act 1978 (to be used except where Form 67.5–F is appropriate)

IN THE COURT OF SESSION

in the PETITION of

[A.B.] *(designation and address)*

[*or serial number where one has been assigned*]

for

an Adoption Order under the Adoption (Scotland) Act 1978

[*or an Order under section 49(1) of the Adoption (Scotland) Act 1978*]

in respect of

[E.F.] *(address)*

I,　　　　　　, of *(address)* being a parent [*or* guardian] of the child, [E.F.], hereby state—

(1) That I understand that the effect of an adoption order [*or* an order under section 49 of the Adoption (Scotland) Act 1978] will be to deprive me permanently of the parental responsibilities and parental rights relating to the child and to vest them in the petitioner; and in particular I understand that, if an order is made, I shall have no right to see or get in touch with the child or to have him [*or* her] returned to me.

(2) That I understand that the court cannot make an adoption order [*or* an order under section 49 of the 1978 Act] in relation to the child, unless the child is free for adoption, without the agreement of each parent or guardian of the child unless the court dispenses with an agreement on the ground that the person concerned—

(a) is not known, cannot be found or is incapable of giving agreement;

(b) is withholding agreement unreasonably;

(c) has persistently failed, without reasonable cause, to fulfil one or other of the following parental responsibilities in relation to the child—

　(i) the responsibility to safeguard and promote the child's health, development and welfare; or

　(ii) if the child is not living with him, the responsibility to maintain personal relations and direct contact with the child on a regular basis; or

(d) has seriously ill-treated the child, whose reintegration into the same household as the parent or guardian is, because of the serious ill-treatment or for other reasons, unlikely.

(3) That I also understand that when the hearing on the petition to determine the application for an adoption order [*or* an order under section 49 of the 1978 Act] in relation to the child is heard, this document may be used as evidence of my agreement to the making of the order unless I inform the court that I no longer agree.

(4) That I hereby freely, and with full understanding of what is involved, agree unconditionally to the making of an adoption order [*or* an order under section 49 of the 1978 Act] in relation to the child in this petition.

[(5) That I have not received or given any payment or reward for, or in consideration of, the adoption of the child, for any agreement to the making of an adoption order or placing the child for adoption with any person or making any arrangements for the adoption of the child, other than a payment to an adoption agency for their expenses incurred in connection with the adoption.]

(Signed by parent or guardian)

This agreement was signed by　　　　　　before me at　　　　　　on the　　　　day of　　　　.

(Signed)

(Designation)

(Address)

---

¹ Form 67.5–A amended by S.I. 1997 No. 853 (effective 1st April 1997).
Release 44: 28 April 1997

Rule 67.5(1)(c) [1] FORM 67.5–B

Form of agreement of a parent or guardian to an adoption order in a petition for an order freeing a child for adoption under section 18 of the Adoption (Scotland) Act 1978

IN THE COURT OF SESSION

in the PETITION of

[A.B.] *(designation and address)*

for

an Order freeing the child [E.F.] for adoption under
section 18 of the Adoption (Scotland) Act 1978

I, , of *(address)* being a parent [*or* guardian] of the child, [E.F.], hereby state—

(1) That I understand that the effect of an adoption order would be to deprive me permanently of the parental responsibilities and parental rights relating to the child and to vest them in the adopters; and that if and when an adoption order is made, I shall have no right to see or get in touch with the child or to have him [*or* her] returned to me.

(2) That I understand that the court cannot make an order freeing a child for adoption without the agreement of each parent or guardian of the child to the making of an adoption order, unless the court dispenses with an agreement on the ground that the person concerned—
   (a) is not known, cannot be found or is incapable of giving agreement;
   (b) is withholding agreement unreasonably;
   (c) has persistently failed, without reasonable cause, to fulfil one or other of the following parental responsibilities in relation to the child—
      (i) the responsibility to safeguard and promote the child's health, development and welfare; or
      (ii) if the child is not living with him, the responsibility to maintain personal relations and direct contact with the child on a regular basis; or
   (d) has seriously ill-treated the child, whose reintegration into the same household as the parent or guardian is, because of the serious ill-treatment or for other reasons, unlikely.

(3) That I also understand that when the hearing on the petition to determine the application for an order freeing the child for adoption is heard, this document may be used as evidence of my agreement to the making of an adoption order unless I inform the court that I no longer agree.

(4) That I freely, and with full understanding of what is involved, agree unconditionally to the making of an adoption order.

(5) [That I have been given an opportunity of making a declaration that I prefer not to be involved in future questions concerning the adoption of the child. I understand that if I make such a declaration I will not be told when the child has been adopted or whether he has been placed for adoption. I also understand that I will not be able to apply for a revocation of the order freeing the child for adoption if I make such a declaration. I hereby declare freely, and with full understanding of what is involved, that I do not wish to be involved in future questions concerning the adoption of the child.] [*or* That I have been given an opportunity of making a declaration that I prefer not to be involved in future questions concerning the adoption of the child, and the effect of making such a declaration has been explained to me. I do not wish to make such declaration.]

[(6) That I have not received or given any payment or reward for, or in consideration of, the adoption of the child, for any agreement to the making of an adoption or consent to the making of an application for an order freeing the child for adoption, for placing the child for adoption with any person or making any arrangements for adoption of the child, other than a payment to an adoption agency for their expenses incurred in connection with the adoption.]

(Signed by parent or guardian)

This agreement was signed by before me at on the day of

(Signed)

(Designation)

(Address)

[1] Form 67.5–B amended by S.I. 1997 No. 853 (effective 1st April 1997).

Rule 67.5(2)(a)   FORM 67.5–C

Form of consent of a child to an order for his adoption or to an order under section 49 of the Adoption (Scotland) Act 1978

IN THE COURT OF SESSION

in the PETITION of

[A.B.] (*designation and address*)

for

An Adoption Order under the Adoption (Scotland) Act 1978

[*or* an Order under section 49(1) of the Adoption (Scotland) Act 1978]

in respect of

[E.F.] (*address*)

I,   , of (*address*) being a child and the child in respect of whom the petition for an order for my adoption [*or* an order under section 49 of the Adoption (Scotland) Act 1978] is presented, hereby state—

(1) That I understand that an order for my adoption [*or* an order under section 49 of the 1978 Act] cannot be made without my consent. The effect of my consent has been explained to me.

(2) That I also understand that, when the hearing on the petition to determine the application for an adoption order [*or* an order under section 49 of the 1978 Act] is heard, this document may be used as evidence of my consent to the making of an order for my adoption [*or* an order under section 49 of the 1978 Act] by the petitioner unless I inform the court that I no longer consent.

(3) That I, with full understanding of what it involves, consent to the making of an order for my adoption [*or* an order under section 49 of the 1978 Act] by the petitioner.

(*Signed by the child*)

This consent was signed by   before me at   on the   day of   .

(*Signed*)

(*Designation*)

(*Address*)

Rule 67.5(2)(b)   Form 67.5–D

Form of consent of a parent or guardian to petition for an order freeing a child for adoption under section 18 of the Adoption (Scotland) Act 1978

IN THE COURT OF SESSION

in the PETITION of

[A.B.] (*designation and address*)

for

An order freeing the child [E.F.] for adoption
under section 18 of the Adoption (Scotland) Act 1978

I,   , of (*address*) being a parent [*or* guardian] of the child [E.F.], hereby state—

(1) That I consent to the petition of [A.B.], an adoption agency, for an order freeing the child for adoption.

(2) That I understand that the petitioner cannot apply to the court for an order freeing the child for adoption without the consent of a parent or guardian, unless the petitioner is applying for dispensation of the agreement of each parent or guardian of the child and the child is in the care of the petitioner.

(Signed by parent or guardian)

This consent was signed by   before me at   on the   day of

(Signed)

(Designation)

(Address)

Rule 67.5(2)(c)   Form 67.5–E

Form of consent of a child to petition for an order freeing him for adoption under section 18 of the Adoption (Scotland) Act 1978

IN THE COURT OF SESSION

in the PETITION of

[A.B.] (*designation and address*)

for

An order freeing the child [E.F.] for adoption
under section 18 of the Adoption (Scotland) Act 1978

I,   , of (*address*) being a child and the child in respect of whom the petition for an order freeing me for adoption is presented, hereby state—

(1) That I understand that an order freeing me for adoption cannot be made without my consent. The effect of my consent has been explained to me.

(2) That I also understand that, when the hearing on the petition to determine the application for an order freeing me for adoption is heard, this document may be used as evidence of my consent to the making of an order freeing me for adoption unless I inform the court that I no longer consent.

(3) That I, with full understanding of what it involves, consent to the making of an order freeing me for adoption.

(4) That I understand, if an order is made freeing me for adoption and a petition for my adoption is subsequently presented to the court, that my consent to any order for my adoption will still be required to be obtained.

(Signed by the child)

This consent was signed by   before me at   on the   day of   .

(Signed)

(Designation)

(Address)

Rule 67.5(1)(a)   [1] FORM 67.5–F

Form of agreement of a natural parent to an adoption order made, by virtue of section 15(1)(aa) of the Adoption (Scotland) Act 1978, on the application of their spouse

IN THE COURT OF SESSION

in the PETITION of

[A.B.] *(designation and address)*

(or serial number where one has been assigned)

for

an Adoption Order under the Adoption (Scotland) Act 1978

in respect of

[E.F.] *(address)*

I,   , of *(address)* being a parent of the child, [E.F.], hereby state—

(1) That I understand that the effect of an adoption order will be to vest the parental responsibilities and parental rights in relation to the child in my spouse though it will not extinguish my own parental responsibilities and parental rights.

(2) That I understand that the court cannot grant this application in relation to the child without my agreement (unless the court dispenses with that agreement).

(3) That I also understand that when the hearing on the petition to determine the application for an adoption order in relation to the child is heard, this document may be used as evidence of my agreement to the making of the order unless I inform the court that I no longer agree.

(4) That I hereby freely, and with full understanding of what is involved, agree unconditionally to the making of an adoption order in relation to the child in this petition.

[(5) That I have not received or given any payment or reward for, or in consideration of, the adoption of the child, for any agreement to the making of an adoption order or the making of any arrangements for the adoption of the child, other than a payment to an adoption agency for their expenses incurred in connection with the adoption.]

(Signed by parent)

[This agreement was signed by   before me at   on the   day of

(Signed)

(Designation)

(Address)   .].

---

[1] Form 67.5–F inserted by S.I. 1997 No. 853 (effective 1st April 1997).
Release 44: 28 April 1997

Rule 67.12(1)   [1] FORM 67.12–A

Form of declaration by parent or guardian under section 18(6) or 19(4) of the Adoption (Scotland) Act 1978

IN THE COURT OF SESSION

in the PETITION of

[A.B.] *(designation and address)*

for

An order freeing the child [E.F.] for adoption
under section 18 of the Adoption (Scotland) Act 1978

I,   , of *(address)* being a parent [*or* guardian] of the child [E.F.], hereby state—

(1) That I declare that I prefer not to be involved in future questions concerning the adoption of [E.F.].

(2) [*Where the declaration is made under section 18(6)*: That this declaration and its effect has been explained to me by the reporting officer appointed by the court] [*or where the declaration is made under section 19(4)*: That this declaration and its effect has been explained to me by the adoption agency *(insert name)*].

                                     (Signed by parent or guardian)

This declaration was signed by   before me at   on the   day of   .

                                     (Signed)

                                   (Designation)

                                   (Address)

---

[1] Form 67.12–A amended by S.I. 1997 No. 853 (effective 1st April 1997).

Rule 67.12(1)   [1] FORM 67.12–B

Form of withdrawal of declaration under section 86(6) or 19(4) of the Adoption (Scotland) Act 1978 of preference not to be involved

IN THE COURT OF SESSION

in the PETITION of

[A.B.] *(designation and address)*

for

An order freeing the child [E.F.] for adoption

under section 18 of the Adoption (Scotland) Act 1978

I,   , of *(address)* being *(state relationship to child)* of the child [E.F.], hereby withdraw the declaration dated *(insert date of declaration)* that I prefer not to be involved in future questions concerning the adoption of [E.F.].

Dated the   day of   .

                                   (Signed by relevant parent).

---

[1] Form 67.12–B inserted by S.I. 1997 No. 853 (effective 1st April 1997).

Form of notice of hearing to determine application for an order freeing a child for adoption

IN THE COURT OF SESSION

in the

PETITION

of

[A.B.] (*designation and address*)

for

An order freeing the child [E.F.] for adoption under
section 18 of the Adoption (Scotland) Act 1978

Date: (*date of posting or other method of intimation*)

To: (*name and address*)

TAKE NOTICE

1. That the hearing on the petition to determine the application for an order freeing the child, [E.F.], for adoption will come before the Lord Ordinary in the Court of Session, Parliament Square, Edinburgh on the   day of   , at   o'clock forenoon and that you may then appear and be heard personally or by counsel or other person having a right of audience on the question whether an order freeing the child for adoption should be made.

2. That you are [not] obliged to attend the hearing [unless you wish to do so].

3. That, while the petition is pending, a parent or guardian of the child who did not consent to the making of the application must not, except with the leave of the court, remove the child from the actual custody of the person with whom the child has his home against the will of that person.

[4. That the court has been requested to dispense with your agreement to the making of an adoption order on the ground[s] that   .]

(*Signed*)

Messenger-at-Arms
[*or* Solicitor [*or* Agent] for petitioner]
(*Address*)

Rule 67.15(4) [1] FORM 67.15

Form of notice of hearing of an application for the revocation of an order freeing a child for adoption

IN THE COURT OF SESSION

in the

NOTE

by

[C.D.] (*designation and address*)

for

Revocation of an order freeing the child [E.F.] for adoption

Date: (*date of posting or other method of intimation*)

To: (*name and address*)

TAKE NOTICE

1. That the hearing on the Note to determine the application for revocation of an order freeing the child [E.F.] for adoption will come before the Lord Ordinary in the Court of Session, Parliament House, Edinburgh on the   day of   , at   o'clock forenoon and that you may then appear and be heard personally or by counsel or other person having a right of audience on the question whether the order freeing the child for adoption should be revoked.

2. That you are [not] obliged to attend the hearing [unless you wish to do so].

(*Signed*)

Messenger-at-Arms
[*or* Solicitor [*or* Agent] for noter]
(*Address*)

---

[1] Form 67.15 amended by S.I. 1994 No. 2901.

Rules 67.22 and 67.35   [1,2] FORM 67.22

Form of petition for adoption order or an order under section 49(1) of the Adoption (Scotland) Act 1978

UNTO THE RIGHT HONOURABLE THE LORDS OF COUNCIL AND SESSION

PETITION

of

[A.B.] (*designation and address*)

[*or serial number where one has been assigned on application*]

Petitioner

for

An Adoption Order

under the Adoption (Scotland) Act 1978

[*or* an Order under section 49(1) of the Adoption (Scotland) Act 1978]

[*or* a Convention Adoption Order under the Adoption (Scotland) Act 1978]

in respect of

[E.F.] (*name as in birth certificate,*
or name by which child is ordinarily known, and address)

HUMBLY SHEWETH:—

1. That the petitioner wishes to adopt the child, [E.F.], under the provisions of the Adoption (Scotland) Act 1978.

2. That the petitioner is domiciled in   and resides at   .

3. That the occupation of the petitioner is   .

4. That the petitioner is married [*or* unmarried], a widow [*or* a widower] (*if married, state whether spouse resides with or apart from, the petitioner*).

5. That the petitioner is   years of age.

6. That the petitioner has resident with him the following persons, namely,

7. That the petitioner [and his spouse] is [*or* are respectively] related to the child as follows:— [*or* that the petitioner [and his spouse] is not [*or* are not, nor is either of them] related to the child].

8. That the child—
    (a) is male [*or* female];
    (b) is unmarried;
    (c) is a child of (*name of mother*) [*and name of father, if known*];
    (d) is of British [*or*   ] nationality;
    (e) is   years of age, having been born on the   day of
        at   in (*local government area*) [*or* at   in (*country or territory outwith United Kingdom*)];
    (f) has had his home with the petitioner since (*day, month and year*);
    [(g) has the following guardian[s], namely (*name[s] and address[es]*);]
    [(h) has the following judicial factor, namely (*name and address*);] and
    (i) is entitled to the following property, namely,

[9. *Where the child was not placed for adoption*. That a medical report on the health of the child is produced.]

[10. That the child is free for adoption under section 18 of the 1978 Act. A certified copy interlocutor of the (*name of court*) dated the   day of   , is produced. The interlocutor freeing the child for adoption has not been revoked under section 20 of the 1978 Act. In terms of that interlocutor the parental responsibilities and parental rights relating to the child were transferred to (*name of adoption agency*). [The parental rights and duties relating to the child were transferred to (*name of adoption agency*) by interlocutor of (*name of court*) under section 21 of the 1978 Act on the   day of   . A certified copy of that interlocutor is produced.].]

[11. That the child is in the care of   who has [*or* have] the parental responsibilities and parental rights in respect of the child.]

[12. That (*name*) of (*address*) is liable to pay aliment to the child by interlocutor of the (*name of court*) [*or* by an agreement of (*names of parties to agreement*)] dated the   day of   .]

[13. That the petitioner believes and avers that (*name(s)*) is [*or* are] willing to agree to the making of an adoption order [*or* an order under section 49 of the 1978 Act] in favour of the petitioner.]

[14. That the petitioner desires the court to dispense with the agreement of (*name(s)*) on the ground[s] that   .]

[15. That the petitioner believes and avers that the child, being a minor, consents to the making of an adoption order [*or* an order under section 49(1) of the 1978 Act] in favour of the petitioner. [*Or* That the petitioners desire the court to dispense with the consent of the child on the ground that he is incapable of giving his consent because (*state reason*)   .]]

16. That the child has lived with the petitioner continuously since the   day of   19 . [He has accordingly had his home with the petitioner during the preceding five years.]

[17. That on the   day of   19 the child was placed with the petitioner for adoption by (*name of adoption agency*) [*or* received into the custody of the petitioner in the following circumstances   ].]

[18. That the petitioner notified the (*name of local authority*) on the   day of   19 of his intention to petition for an adoption order [*or* an order under section 49 of the 1978 Act] in respect of the child.]

[19. That the child has not been the subject of an adoption order or of a petition for an adoption order [save that (*state order and petition if any*)].]

[20. That the petitioner is prepared to undertake, if an adoption order [*or* an order under section 49 of the 1978 Act] is made in this petition, to make the following provision for the child   .]

[21. That the petitioner has not received or agreed to receive and no person has made or agreed to make or give to the petitioner any payment or reward in consideration of the adoption of the child [except as follows].]

[22. That the petitioner intends to adopt the child under the law of [*or* within] (*state country*) which is the country of the domicile of the petitioner. [The petitioner wishes to remove the child from Great Britain for the purpose of adoption.]]

[22A. That each parent or guardian of the child has consented under section 20(1) (advance consent to adoption: England and Wales) of the Adoption and Children Act 2002 and has not withdrawn consent.]

[22B. That by notice under section 20(4)(a) (notice that information about application for adoption order not required: England and Wales) of the Adoption and Children Act 2002 (*name of parent or guardian*) [and (*name of parent or guardian*)] stated that he [*or* she *or* they] did not wish to be informed of any application for an adoption order and that statement has not been withdrawn.]

[22C. That the child has been placed for adoption by an adoption agency within the meaning of section 2(1) (adoption agencies in England and Wales) of the Adoption and Children Act 2002 with the petitioner(s) and the child was placed for adoption under section 19(1) (placing children with parental consent: England and Wales) of that Act with the consent of each parent or guardian and the consent of the mother was given when the child was at least six weeks old [*or* under an order made under section 21(1) (placement orders: England and Wales) of that Act and the child was at least six weeks old when that order was made]].

23. That this petition is presented under the provisions of the Adoption (Scotland) Act 1978, and rule 67.22 of the Rules of the Court of Session 1994.

> MAY IT THEREFORE please your Lordships to dispense with intimation and to order notice of this petition to be served by registered or recorded delivery, letter post or otherwise on such person or persons as your Lordships may think proper; and to appoint a reporting officer, and, if necessary, a curator *ad litem* to the child sought to be adopted, and direct him [*or* them] to report; and thereafter, on resuming consideration hereof, together with the report by the reporting officer, and that of the curator *ad litem* if one is appointed, pronounce an interlocutor authorising the petitioner to adopt the child [*or* transferring to the petitioner the parental responsibilities and parental rights relating to the child under section 49 of the Adoption (Scotland) Act 1978], [E.F.], in terms of the Adoption (Scotland) Act 1978, on such terms and conditions, if any, as your Lordships may think fit; and to direct the Registrar General for Scotland to make an entry regarding the adoption [*or* order under section 49 of the 1978 Act] in the Adopted Children Register in the form prescribed by him, giving the name[s]   as the Christian [*or* forename[s]] and   as the surname of the child in that form; and, further, upon proof to the satisfaction of your Lordships in the course of the proceedings to follow hereon, to find that the child was born on the   day of   in the year   and is identical with the child to whom an entry numbered   and made on the   day of   in the year   , in the register of births for the registration district of   in the country of   relates; and to direct the Registrar General to cause such birth entry to be marked with the word "Adopted" [*or* "Proposed Foreign Adoption"] [and (*inserted only where the child was born in Scotland*) to include the above-mentioned date of birth in the entry recording the adoption in the manner indicated in that form]; and to pronounce such other or further orders or directions upon such matters, including the expenses of this petition, as your Lordships may think fit.

ACCORDING TO JUSTICE ETC.

(*Signed*)
Solicitor [*or* Agent] for the petitioner
(*Address of solicitor or agent*)

[*or counsel or other person having a right of audience*]

---

[1] Form 67.22 amended by S.I. 1997 No. 853 (effective 1st April 1997).
[2] Form 67.22 amended by S.S.I. 2007 No. 7, para. 20 (effective 26th February 2007).

Rule 67.23(1)(a)   FORM 67.23

Form of notice to adoption agency or local authority of presenting a petition for an adoption order or for an order under section 49 of the Adoption (Scotland) Act 1978

IN THE COURT OF SESSION

in the

PETITION

of

[A.B.] (*designation and address*)

for

An adoption order [*or* an order under section 49 of the
Adoption (Scotland) Act 1978] in respect of the child [E.F.]

Date: (*insert date of posting or other method of intimation*)
To: (*name and address*)

TAKE NOTICE

1. That the petitioner has presented a petition to the Court of Session for an adoption order [*or* an order under section 49 of the Adoption (Scotland) Act 1978] in respect of the child [E.F.].

2. That the petition relates to a child who was placed for adoption by you on the   day of   [*or* was not placed for adoption].

3. That you are required under section 23 [*or where notice has been given under section 22(1)*, you were notified on the   day of   that you were required [*or where notice has not been given under section 22(1)*, you are required] under section 22(1)] of the 1978 Act to submit to the court a report including the matters mentioned in rule 67.21(1) of the Rules of the Court of Session 1994.

4. That on completion of your report you are required under rule 67.21(2) of the Rules of the Court of Session 1994 to send the report and a copy of it for each party to the Deputy Principal Clerk of Session, Court of Session, Parliament Square, Edinburgh EH1 1RQ, and to send a copy to (*name and address*), the reporting officer [and a copy to (*name and address*), the curator *ad litem* to the child [E.F.]] in this petition.

(*Signed*)

Messenger-at-Arms
[*or* Solicitor [*or* Agent] for petitioner]
(*Address*)

Rule 67.25(3)   FORM 67.25

**Form of notice of hearing of application for an adoption order or an order
under section 49 of the Adoption (Scotland) Act 1978**

IN THE COURT OF SESSION

in the

PETITION

of

[A.B.] (*designation and address*)

for

An adoption order [*or* an order under section 49 of the
Adoption (Scotland) Act 1978] in respect of the child [E.F.]

Date: (*insert date of posting or other method of intimation*)

To: (*name and address*)

TAKE NOTICE

1. That the hearing on the petition to determine the application for an adoption order [*or* an order under section 49 of the Adoption (Scotland) Act 1978] will come before the Lord Ordinary in the Court of Session, Parliament House, Edinburgh on the   day of   , at   o'clock and that you may then appear and be heard personally or by counsel or other person having a right of audience on the question whether an adoption order [*or* an order under section 49 of the 1978 Act] should be made.

2. That you are [not] obliged to attend the hearing [unless you wish to do so].
Release 52: May 1999

3. That, while the petition is pending, a parent or guardian of the child who has agreed to the making of an order must not, except with the leave of the court, remove the child from the actual custody of the petitioner.

[4. That the petition states that the child has had his home with the petitioner for the five years preceding the presentation of the petition and accordingly, if that is correct, no person is entitled, against the will of the petitioner, to remove the child from the actual custody of the petitioner except with the leave of the court or under authority conferred by any enactment or on the arrest of the child.]

[5. That the court has been requested to dispense with your agreement to the making of an order on the ground[s] that   .]

(*Signed*)

Messenger-at-Arms
[*or* Solicitor [*or* Agent] for petitioner]
(*Address*)

Rule 69.2(1)   [1] FORM 69.2

Form of Parliamentary, European Parliamentary or Scottish Parliamentary election petition

IN THE ELECTION COURT

PETITION

under the Representation of the People Act 1983

of

[A.B.] [and [C.D.]] (*designation and address*)

Petitioner[s]

against

[E.F.] (*designation and address*), as the member
whose election or return is complained of

First Respondent

and

[G.H.] (*designation and address*), the returning officer

Second Respondent

in respect of

The election for (*place*) held on   day of

HUMBLY SHEWETH:—

1. That the [first named] petitioner voted [*or* had a right to vote, *as the case may be*] as an elector at the above election [*or* claims to have had a right to be elected or returned at the above election, *or* was a candidate at the above election, *as the case may be*]. The second named petitioner (*here state in like manner the right of each petitioner*).

2. That the election was held on the   day of   , when [A.B.] and [C.D.] (*name them*) were candidates, and the returning officer has returned [A.B.] (*name*) as being duly elected.

3. That (*state the facts on which the petitioners rely in this and following numbered paragraphs*).

[4.] That the petition is presented under the Representation of the People Act 1983 and rule 69.2 of the Rules of the Court of Session 1994.

> MAY IT THEREFORE please the court to determine that [E.F.] was not duly elected or returned, and that the election was void [*or* that [A.B. [*or* C.D.]] was duly elected, and ought to have been returned, *or as the case may be*].

According to Justice etc.

(*Signed*)

---

[1] Heading to Form 69.2 amended by S.I. 1999 No. 787.

Rule 69.4(3)   [1] FORM 69.4

Form of bond of caution in election petition

BOND OF CAUTION

Representation of the People Act 1983

We, [I.J.] and [K.L.] (*names and designations*), considering that a petition has been presented by [A.B.], complaining of an undue return (*or* undue election *as the case may be*) of [E.F.] as a member to serve in Parliament for the constituency of   [*or* representative to the European Parliament for (*name of constituency*) *or* Member of the Scottish Parliament for (*name of constituency or region*)] on the   day of   , and that by section 136 of the Representation of the People Act 1983, it is provided that security for the payment of all costs, charges, and expenses that may become payable by the petitioner in terms of the Act, shall, on presentation of such petition, be given on behalf of the petitioners, to the amount of £   ; and that by rule 69.4(3) of the Rules of the Court of Session 1994 for the trial of election petitions, under the Act, it is prescribed that the security so to be given on behalf of the petitioners may be by lodging a bond of caution, in terms of the Act; and seeing that we, the said parties, are willing to grant such bond, therefore we, the said parties, as cautioners, sureties, and full debtors for and with [A.B.], petitioner, do hereby bind and oblige ourselves conjunctly and severally, and our respective heirs, executors, and successors whomsoever, that [A.B.], petitioner, shall make payment of all costs, charges, and expenses that may become payable by him to any person or persons, by virtue of any decree to be pronounced in the petition; and that to the amount of £   sterling, with one-fifth part more of liquidate penalty in case of failure; and we consent to the registration hereof for execution. IN WITNESS WHEREOF, etc.

---

[1] Form 69.4 amended by S.I. 1999 No. 787.

Rule 69.5(2)   [1] FORM 69.5

Form of notice of the presentation of an election petition and of the nature of the proposed security

Representation of the People Act 1983

Date: (*insert date of posting or other method of intimation*)

To: (*name and address*)

TAKE NOTICE

(1) That, under the Representation of the People Act 1983 and rule 69.3 of the Rules of the Court of Session 1994, a petition has been presented to the Court of Session, Edinburgh touching the election of a Member of Parliament [*or* representative to the European Parliament *or* Member of the Scottish Parliament] for the (*place*), of which petition the foregoing is a full copy, and that you are named therein as a respondent.

(2) That the security which has been given in terms of section 136 of the above Act is in the form of a bond of caution to the amount of £   granted by [A.B.] and [C.D.] (*names, designations and addresses*) *or* by consignation of £   in the Bank of   . If you desire to object to the above bond of caution in terms of section 136(4) of the above Act, you may do so within [14] days of the date of this notice by lodging the objection in writing in the Petition Department, Court of Session, 2 Parliament Square, Edinburgh EH1 1RQ and sending or delivering a full copy of it to me at the following address (*address*).

(*Signed*)

Petitioner
[*or* Solicitor [*or* Agent] for petitioner]
(*Address*)

---

[1] Form 69.5 amended by S.I. 1999 No. 787.

Rule 69.15   [1] FORM 69.15

Form of warrant to cite witnesses in election petition

Representation of the People Act 1983

(*place and date*)

Having considered the motion for the petitioner [*or* respondent], grants warrant to all officers of the law for citing   (*name them*), to attend the Election Court, for the trial of the election petition to be held at   within (*name court-house*) on the   day of   , at   o'clock forenoon [*or* forthwith, *as the case may be*], to be severally examined as witnesses in the petition, and to attend the Election Court until their examination shall have been completed.

(*Signed*)

Judge of the Election Court

---

[1] Form number amended by S.I. 1994 No. 2901 (clerical error).

Rule 69.19(1)   FORM 69.19–A

Form of notice of intention to withdraw election petition

Representation of the People Act 1983

In the Election Petition for   in which   is petitioner and   is respondent.

Date: (*insert date of posting or other method of intimation*)

To: (*name and address*)

TAKE NOTICE

(1) That the above petitioner has, on the   day of   , lodged at the office of the Deputy Principal Clerk of Session notice of application to withdraw his petition, of which the following is a copy:— (*Set it out*)

(2) That under section 150 of the Representation of the People Act 1983 and rule 69.20 of the Rules of the Court of Session 1994, any person who might have been a petitioner, in respect of the election, may, within five days after publication of this Notice give notice in writing, signed by him or on his behalf, to the said Deputy Principal Clerk of Session, 2 Parliament Square, Edinburgh EH1 1RQ, of his intention to apply at the hearing to be substituted for the petitioner.

(*Signed*)

Petitioner
[*or* Solicitor [*or* Agent] for petitioner]
(*Address*)

Rule 69.19(4)   [1] FORM 69.19–B

Form of application for leave to withdraw election petition

Representation of the People Act 1983

Parliamentary [*or* European
Parliament[1] *or* Scottish Parliament] constituency [*or* region] of

IN THE ELECTION COURT

APPLICATION TO WITHDRAW

by

[A.B.] [and [C.D.]] (*designation and addresses*)

Petitioner[s]

in the PETITION of

[A.B.] [and [C.D.]] (*designation and addresses*)

Petitioner

against

[E.F.] (*designation and address*)

First Respondent

[G.H.] (*designation and address*)

Second Respondent

The petitioner [A.B.], with the consent of the petitioner [C.D.], applies for leave to withdraw his petition on the following grounds: (*state grounds in numbered paragraphs*), and prays that a day may be appointed for hearing his application.
Dated the   day of

(*To be signed by the applicant and con-senter, if any, or their respective solicitors, who shall each append to their signatures a statement of whether they sign as or on behalf of an applicant or a consenter.*)

---

[1] Form 69.19–B amended by S.I. 1999 No. 787.

Rule 69.23(1)   FORM 69.23

Form of notice of abatement of petition by death of petitioner

Representation of the People Act 1983

Constituency of

The election for (*place*) held on   day of

The election petition presented by [A.B. [and [C.D.]] (*designations and addresses*) against [E.F.] (*designation and address*), the member whose election or action is complained of, has been abated by the death of [A.B.] the [surviving] petitioner.

Any person who might have been a petitioner in respect of this election may apply by motion in the Election Court, Court of Session, 2 Parliament Square, Edinburgh EH1 1RQ within [14] days after the date of this notice to be substituted as a petitioner.

Date (*insert date*):

(*Signed*)

Rule 72.2A   [1]FORM 72.2A

Form of declaration regarding debt payment programme

IN THE COURT OF SESSION

in the PETITION of

[A.B.] (*designation and address*)

for

the sequestration of the estate of (*name and address of debtor*)

At   on the   day of

I, (*name of person making the declaration*) am the petitioner and debtor [*or* petitioner and creditor] [*or* a concurring creditor] in the petition for the sequestration of (*name of debtor*)] and I hereby state-

that the debt[s] founded upon in the petition for sequestration of the estates of (*name of debtor*) is [*or* are] not debt[s] subject to an approved debt payment programme under section 2 of the Debt Arrangement and Attachments (Scotland) Act 2002.

[*or*]

that although the debtor (*name of debtor*) is subject to an approved debt payment programme under section 2 of the Debt Arrangement and Attachment (Scotland) Act 2002 the debt[s] founded on in the petition for sequestration is [*or* are] in relation to credit given to the debtor in terms of Regulation 35(1)(b) of the Debt Arrangement Scheme (Scotland) Regulations 2004.

(*Signed by person making the declaration*)

(*Designation*)

(*Address*)

---

[1] Inserted by S.S.I. 2004 No.514 (effective 30th November 2004).

Rule 72.6(1)   FORM 72.6–A

Information to be contained in the Register of Insolvencies

A. Sequestrations

Name of debtor

Debtor's residence and his principal place of business (if any) at date of sequestration or date of death

Date of death in case of deceased debtor

Occupation of debtor

Name and address of petitioner for sequestration

Court by which sequestration awarded

Sheriff court to which sequestration remitted (where applicable)

Date of first order

Date of award of sequestration

Date of recall of sequestration (where applicable)

Date certificate for summary administration of sequestration of debtor's estate granted (where applicable)

Date certificate for summary administration of sequestration of debtor's estate withdrawn (where applicable)

Name and address of interim trustee and date of appointment

Level of debt when interim trustee's statement of debtor's affairs is produced

Level of assets when interim trustee's statement of debtor's affairs is produced

Name and address of permanent trustee and date of confirmation of appointment

Date of debtor's discharge and whether on composition or by operation of law

Date of interim trustee's discharge

Date of permanent trustee's discharge

B. Protected Trust Deeds for Creditors

Name and address of granter of trust deed

Name and address of trustee under the deed

Date (or dates) of execution of deed

Date on which copy deed and certificate of accession were registered

Date of registration of statement indicating how the estate was realised and distributed and certificate to the effect that the distribution was in accordance with the trust deed

Date of trustee's discharge

Date of registration of copy of order of court that non-acceding creditor is not bound by trustee's discharge

C 800/2

Rule 72.6(2)   FORM 72.6–B

Form of undertaking required by section 2(3)(c) of the Bankruptcy (Scotland) Act 1985

I, (*insert name, designation and address*), a qualified insolvency practitioner undertake, if appointed by the court to do so:—

     (a) to act as interim trustee in the sequestration of (*insert full name and address of debtor*); and

     (b) to act as permanent trustee in the sequestration where no permanent trustee is elected.

Date (*insert date*)

           (*Signed*)

           Qualified insolvency practitioner

Rule 72.6(3)   FORM 72.6–C

Form of memorandum by permanent trustee to be recorded in the Register of Inhibitions and Adjudications under section 14(4) of the Bankruptcy (Scotland) Act 1985

From: (*name, designation and address of permanent trustee*) trustee in the sequestration of (*full name and address of debtor*).

To: The Keeper of the Register of Inhibitions and Adjudications.

A certified copy of the court order of (*date*) awarding sequestration in respect of (*full name and address of debtor*) was recorded in your Register on (*date*).

Please record this memorandum to renew the effect of that recording for a further period of three years from the date of presentment of this memorandum.

Date (*insert date*)

           (*Signed*)

           Permanent trustee
           [*or* Solicitor [*or* Agent] for permanent trustee]

Rule 72.6(4)   FORM 72.6–D

Form of notice of inhibition by trustee under trust deed to be recorded in the Register of Inhibitions and Adjudications under paragraph 2(1) of Schedule 5 to the Bankruptcy (Scotland) Act 1985

A trust deed within the meaning of the Bankruptcy (Scotland) Act 1985 has been granted by (*full name and address of debtor*) and delivered to (*name, designation and address of permanent trustee*) as trustee acting under the trust deed.

Under the trust deed the estate of (*full name of debtor*) has been conveyed to (*name of permanent trustee*) as trustee for the benefit of the creditors generally of (*full name of debtor*).

Date (*insert date*)

           (*Signed*)

           Permanent trustee
           [*or* Solicitor [*or* Agent] for permanent trustee]

Rule 72.6(5)   FORM 72.6–E

Form of notice of recall of inhibition to be recorded in the Register of Inhibitions and Adjudications under paragraph 2(2) of Schedule 5 to the Bankruptcy (Scotland) Act 1985

The notice by (*name, designation and address of permanent trustee*) as trustee under a trust deed within the meaning of the Bankruptcy (Scotland) Act 1985 for creditors generally of (*full name and address of debtor*) recorded on (*date*) is now recalled.

Date (*insert date*)

(*Signed*)

Permanent trustee
[*or* Solicitor [*or* Agent] for permanent trustee]

Rule 76.9   [1,2] FORM 76.9

Form of notice to person with interest in property subject to an application for an order under paragraph 12 of Schedule 1 to the Proceeds of Crime (Scotland) Act 1995

(*Cause reference number*)

IN THE COURT OF SESSION

in the

PETITION [*or* NOTE]

of

[A.B.] (*designation and address*)

for an order under paragraph 12 of Schedule 1 to the Proceeds of Crime (Scotland) Act 1995

in respect of the estates of [C.D.] (*address*)

Date: (*date of posting or other method of service*)

To: (*name and address of person on whom notice is to be served*)

This Notice—
   (a) gives you warning that an application has been made to the Court of Session for an order which may affect your interest in property; and
   (b) informs you that you have an opportunity to appear and make representations to the court before the application is determined.

TAKE NOTICE

1. That on (*date*) in the High Court of Justiciary at (*place*) a confiscation order was made under section 1 of the Proceeds of Crime (Scotland) Act 1995 in respect of [C.D.] (*address*).

2. That on (*date*) the administrator appointed under paragraph 1(1)(a) of Schedule 1 to the Act of 1995 on (*date*) was empowered to realise property belonging to [C.D.].

or

2. That on (*date*) the administrator was appointed under paragraph 1(1)(b) of Schedule 1 to the Act of 1995 on (*date*) to realise property belonging to [C.D.].

3. That application has been made by petition [*or* note] for an order under paragraph 12 of Schedule 1 to the Act of 1995 (*here set out briefly the nature of the order sought*). A copy of the petition [*or* note] is attached.

4. That you have the right to appear before the court in person or by counsel or other person having a right of audience and make such representations as you may have in respect of the order applied for. The court has fixed (*insert day and date fixed for hearing the application*) at 10 a.m. in the Court of Session, 2 Parliament Square, Edinburgh as the time when you should appear to do this.

5. That if you do not appear or are not represented on the above date, the order applied for may be made in your absence.

IF YOU ARE UNCERTAIN ABOUT THE EFFECT OF THIS NOTICE, you should consult a Solicitor, Citizens Advice Bureau or other local advice agency or adviser immediately.

(*Signed*)

Messenger-at-Arms
[*or* Solicitor [*or* Agent] for petitioner [*or* noter]]
(*Address*)

---

[1] Form 76.9 amended by S.I. 1994 No. 2901 (minor correction).
[2] Form 76.9 amended by S.I. 1996 No. 2168 (consolidating enactment).

Rule 77.10(1)   FORM 77.10

Form of joint minute to transfer summary trial petition to another Lord Ordinary because of death, disability or absence

IN THE COURT OF SESSION

JOINT MINUTE

for the Parties

in the PETITION of

[A.B.] and [C.D.] (*designations and addresses*)

Petitioners

[E.F.] and [G.H.] for the parties concur in craving the court that the cause shall be remitted to Lord (*name*) for determination by him because of the death [*or* disability *or* absence] of Lord (*name*).

IN RESPECT WHEREOF

(*Signed by counsel or other person having a right of audience*)

Rule 77.11(1)   [1] FORM 77.11

Form of joint minute to adopt summary trial procedure in action in dependence

IN THE COURT OF SESSION

JOINT MINUTE

for the Parties

in the cause

[A.B.] *(designation and address)*

Pursuer

against

[C.D.] *(designation and address)*

Defender

[E.F.] and [G.H.] for the parties concur in craving the court that the cause shall be remitted to Lord *(name)* for determination by him under section 26 of the Court of Session Act 1988.

IN RESPECT WHEREOF

(Signed by counsel or other person having a right of audience)

---

[1] Form 77.11 amended by S.I. 1997 No. 1050 (minor amendment, effective 6th April 1997).

Rule 81.5(1)   [1,2] FORM 81.5

Form of agreement under section 30(5) of the Human Fertilisation and Embryology Act 1990

IN THE COURT OF SESSION

in the PETITION of

[A.B.] *(designation and address)*

and

[C.D.] *(designation and address)*
[*or serial number where one has been assigned*]

for

A Parental Order under the Human Fertilisation and
Embryology Act 1990

in respect of

[E.F.] *(name as in birth certificate)*

I, (*name and address*) being the father of the child by virtue of section 28 of the Human Fertilisation and Embryology Act 1990 [*or otherwise*] [*or* the woman who carried the child] hereby state—

(1) That I understand that the effect of the parental order for which application has been made will be to deprive me permanently of parental responsibilities and parental rights relating to the child and to vest them in the petitioners; and, in particular, I understand that, if an order is made, I shall have no right to see or get in touch with the child or to have him [*or* her] returned to me.

(2) That I understand that the court cannot make a parental order in relation to the child without my agreement and the agreement of the woman who carried the child [*or* the father of the child, where he is not one of the petitioners] unless the court dispenses with an agreement on the ground that the person concerned cannot be found or is incapable of giving agreement.

(3) That I understand that when the hearing of the petition to determine the application for a parental order in relation to the child is heard, this document may be used as evidence of my agreement to the making of the order unless I inform the court that I no longer agree.

(4) That I freely, and with full understanding of what is involved, agree unconditionally to the making of a parental order in relation to the child.

(5) That I have not received or given any money or benefit, other than for expenses reasonably incurred, for or in consideration of—
 (a) the making of a parental order,
 (b) the execution of this agreement,
 (c) the handing over of the child to the petitioners, or
 (d) the making of any arrangements with a view to the making of a parental order,
[other than (*state any money or other benefit given or received by authority of the court and specify such authority*)].

I have signed this agreement at (*place of signing*) on the   day of   .

 (*Signed by father of the child or woman who carried the child*)

This agreement was signed by   before me at   on the day of   .

 (*Signed*)

 Reporting Officer
 [*or* Witness
 (*full name and address*)]

---

[1] Form 81.5 inserted by S.I. 1994 No. 2806 (effective 1st November 1994).
[2] Form 81.5, para. (1) amended by S.I. 1997 No. 854 (effective 1st April 1997).

Rule 81.9(1)   [1] FORM 81.9

Form of petition for parental order under section 30 of the Human Fertilisation and Embryology Act 1990

UNTO THE RIGHT HONOURABLE THE LORDS OF COUNCIL AND SESSION

PETITION

of

[A.B.] *(designation and address)*

and

[C.D.] *(designation and address)*
[*or serial number where one has been assigned*]

Petitioners

for

A parental order under section 30 of the Human
Fertilisation and Embryology Act 1990

in respect of

[E.F.] *(name as in birth certificate)*

HUMBLY SHEWETH:—

1. That the petitioners are married to each other, are domiciled in Scotland and reside at (*state full address*).

2. That the petitioners are respectively   and   years of age.

3. That (*state name of child the subject of the petition*) is male [*or* female] and is   months old having been born on   at   .

4. That the child was received into the home of the petitioners on   .

5. That the child was carried by a woman other than the female petitioner as the result of the placing in her of an embryo [*or* the placing in her of sperm and eggs] [*or* her artificial insemination].

6. That the gametes of (*state which petitioner or if both state both petitioners*) were used to bring about the creation of the embryo of the child.

7. That the child is not the subject of any other pending or completed court proceedings (*if the child is so subject give full details*)—

[8. That (*state full name and address of the father of the child*), who is not the male petitioner, is the father of the child by virtue of section 28 of the Human Fertilisation and Embryology Act 1990 [*or otherwise*] and has freely and with full understanding of what is involved, agreed unconditionally to the making of the order sought.]

[[9.] That (*state full name and address of the woman who carried the child*), is the woman who carried the child and has freely and with full understanding of what is involved, agreed unconditionally to the making of the order sought.]

[10.] That no money or benefit, other than for expenses reasonably incurred, has been given or received by the petitioners for or in consideration of—

(a) the making of the order sought,
(b) any agreement required for the making of the order sought,
(c) the handing over of the child to the petitioners, or
(d) the making of any arrangements with a view to the making of the order,
[other than (*state any money or other benefit given or received by authority of the court and specify such authority*)].

[[11.] That the father of the child [and] [*or*] [the woman who carried the child] cannot be found (*state the efforts which have been made to find the person(s) concerned*) [*or* is [*or* are] incapable of giving agreement by reason of (*state reasons*)].]

MAY IT THEREFORE please your Lordships to dispense with intimation and to order notice of the petition to be served on such person or persons as the court thinks fit; to appoint a reporting officer and, if necessary, curator *ad litem*, to the child and direct them to report; [to dispense with the agreement of [the father of the child] [and] [*or*] [the woman who carried the child] [who cannot be found] [who is [*or* are] incapable of giving agreement];] on resuming consideration of this petition and the report by the reporting officer and the curator *ad litem*, if one is appointed, to make a parental order in their favour under section 30 of the Human Fertilisation and Embryology Act 1990 in respect of the child; to direct the Registrar General for Scotland to make an entry regarding the parental order in the Parental Order Register in the form prescribed by him giving   as the forename(s) and   as the surname of the child; and on proof to the satisfaction of the court in the course of the proceedings to follow hereon, to find that the child was born on the   day of   in the year   and is identical with the child to whom an entry numbered   and made on the   day of   in the year   , in the register of births for the registration district of   relates; and to direct the Registrar General for Scotland to cause such birth entry to be marked with the words "Parental Order" and to include the above mentioned date of birth in the entry recording the parental order in the manner indicated in that form; to pronounce such other or further orders or directions upon such matters, including the expenses of this petition, as the court thinks fit.

ACCORDING TO JUSTICE ETC.

(*Signed*)

Solicitor [*or* Agent] for petitioners
(*Address*)

[*or* (*Signed*)
Counsel or other person having a right of audience]

---

[1] Form 81.9 inserted by S.I. 1994 No. 2806 (effective 1st November 1994).

Form of intimation of hearing of application for a parental order under section 30 of the Human Fertilisation and Embryology Act 1990

IN THE COURT OF SESSION

in the

PETITION

of

[A.B.] (*designation and address*)

and

[C.D.] (*designation and address*)
[*or serial number where one has been assigned*]

for

A Parental Order under section 30 of the Human
Fertilisation and Embryology Act 1990

in respect of

[E.F.] (*name as in birth certificate*)

Date: (*date of posting or other method of intimation*)

To: (*name and address*)

TAKE NOTICE

1. That the hearing on this petition to determine the application for a parental order will come before the Lord Ordinary in the Court of Session, Parliament House, Edinburgh on the   day of   , at   o'clock and that you may then appear and be heard personally or by counsel or other person having a right of audience on the question whether a parental order should be made.

2. That you are [*not*] obliged to attend the hearing [unless you wish to do so].

3. That while the petition is pending you must not, except with the leave of the court, remove the child from the custody of the petitioners.

[4. That the court has been requested to dispense with your agreement to the making of an order on the ground[s] that (*specify ground(s)*).]

(*Signed*)

Messenger-at-Arms
[*or* Solicitor [*or* Agent] for petitioners]
(*Address*)

---

[1] Form 81.12 inserted by S.I. 1994 No. 2806 (effective 1st November 1994).

[1] FORM 82.3–A

Form of notice to Crown under section 5(1) of the Human Rights Act 1998

IN THE COURT OF SESSION

in causa

[A.B.] (*designation and address*)

Pursuer [*or* Petitioner]

against

[C.D.] (*designation and address*)

Defender [*or* Respondent]

Date: (*date of posting or other method of service*)

To: (*specify Minister or other person on whom notice is to be served*)

TAKE NOTICE

That the court is considering whether or not to [*Or*: That (*specify party*) is seeking that the court] make a declaration under section (*specify section 4(2), in relation to primary legislation or section 4(4) in relation to subordinate legislation*) of the Human Rights Act 1998 that (*specify the primary or subordinate legislation which is the subject of the proposed declaration*) is incompatible with (*specify the Convention right*) for the following reasons:

(*set out the reasons in summary*).

You may apply to become a party to the proceedings. If you wish to do so you should notify the Deputy Principal Clerk of Session in Form 82.3–B.

(Signed)

Deputy Principal Clerk of Session

[*or* Solicitor [*or* Agent] for (*specify*)]

---

[1] Form 82.3–A inserted by S.S.I. 2000 No. 316 and amended by S.S.I. 2004 No. 52 and amended by S.S.I. 2006 No. 83 (effective 17th March 2006).

[1] FORM 82.3–B

Form of notice to court under section 5(2) of the Human Rights Act 1998

IN THE COURT OF SESSION

in causa

[A.B.] (*designation and address*)

Pursuer [*or* Petitioner]

against

[C.D.] (*designation and address*)

Defender [*or* Respondent]

To the Deputy Principal Clerk of Session

The (*specify Minister or other person*) intends to join as a party to these proceedings.

(Signed)

Solicitor for (*specify Minister or other person*)
(*Address*)

---

[1] Form 82.3–B inserted by S.S.I. 2000 No. 316 (effective 2nd October 2000) and amended by S.S.I. 2004 No. 52.

Rule 82.4   [1] FORM 82.4

Form of minute under rule 82.4

IN THE COURT OF SESSION

MINUTE

By

[E.F.], (designation and address)

Minuter

in causa

[A.B.], (designation and address)

Pursuer [*or* Petitioner]

against

[C.D., (designation and address)

Defender [*or* Respondent]

1. The Minuter lodged a Notice under section 5(2) of the Human Rights Act 1998 on (*date*).

2. The position of the Minuter as to the proposed declaration of incompatibility is as follows—

(*here specify the position of the Minuter including where appropriate a summary of any facts on which the Minuter proposes to rely, of any propositions of law which the Minuter proposes to advance and of any argument which the Minuter proposes to make*)

(Signed)

Solicitor for (*specify Minister or other person*)

---

[1] Form 82.4 inserted by S.S.I. 2000 No. 316 and substituted by S.S.I. 2006 No. 83 (effective 17th March 2006).

Rule 85.5   [1] FORM 85.5

Form of certificate of delivery of documents to chief constable

(*Insert place and date*) I,   hereby certify that upon the   day of   I duly delivered to (*insert name and address*) chief constable of (*insert name of constabulary*) (*insert details of the documents delivered*). This I did by (*state method of delivery*).

(Signed)

Solicitor/sheriff officer
(add designation and business address)

[1] Form 85.5 inserted by S.S.I. 2002 No. 514.

Rule 86.3(1)   [1]FORM 86.3

Form of petition under section 28, 28A, 62, 62A, 63, 65G or 65H of the Competition Act 1998

UNTO THE RIGHT HONOURABLE

THE LORDS OF COUNCIL AND SESSION

PETITION

of

THE OFFICE OF FAIR TRADING ("THE OFT"), (*address*)

Petitioner

for a warrant under

section 28 [*or section 28A or section 62 or section 62A or section 63 or section 65G or section 65H*] of the Competition Act 1998

in respect of

(*insert name and address or as the case may be*)

HUMBLY SHEWETH:—

1. That (*here set out in this and the following numbered paragraphs the matters mentioned in rule 86.3.(2)*).

MAY IT THEREFORE please your Lordships to (*insert prayer*)

According to Justice, etc.

(Signed)

[1] Form 86.3 inserted by S.S.I. 2004 No. 331 (effective 6th August 2004).

Rule 87.1(2)   [1] FORM 87.1

Form of notice of intimation to the Office of Fair Trading

Date: (*date of posting or other method of intimation*)

To: The Office of Fair Trading

TAKE NOTICE

(*Name and address of pursuer or defender*) has brought an action against [*or* has defended an action brought by] (*name and address of defender or pursuer*) [*or* (*name and address of petitioner or respondent*) has raised a petition [*or* responded to a petition raised by] (*name and address of respondent or petitioner*)]. The action raises issues under Article 81 or 82 of the Treaty establishing the European Community. A copy of the summons [*or* petition] is [*or* pleadings and interlocutor allowing intimation are] attached.

You may apply to the court by motion for leave to be sisted as a party in the action. You must do so at the Office of Court, Court of Session, 2 Parliament Square, Edinburgh, EH1 1RQ within [21] days after the date of intimation to you of this notice [*or if the warrant for intimation is executed before the calling of the summons*, within [7] days after the summons calls in court. The summons will not call in court earlier than [21] days after the date of intimation to you of the summons]. The date of intimation is the date stated at the top of this notice unless intimation has been made by post in which case the date of intimation is the day after that date.

(*Signed*)

Messenger-at-arms

[*or* Solicitor [*or* Agent] for Pursuer [*or* Petitioner *or* Defender *or* Respondent]]

(*Address*)

---

[1] Form 87.1 inserted by S.S.I. 2004 No. 514, Art.2(8) (effective 30th November 2004).

Rule 88.5(3)   FORM 88.5

Form of notice of intimation of a hearing to determine jurisdiction under Article 15 of Council Regulation (E.C.) No. 2201/2003 of 27th November 2003

Date: (*date of posting or other method of intimation*)

To: (*name and address*)

TAKE NOTICE

(*Name and address of pursuer*) has lodged a summons in the Court of Session against (*name and address of defender*).

The parties are presently engaged in proceedings involving matters of parental responsibility in (*specify court in other Member State where proceedings are ongoing*) and a request has been made to the Court of Session to accept jurisdiction of these proceedings and for the action to be dealt with in the Court of Session.

A hearing has been fixed on (*date*) at (*time*) within the Court of Session to determine the issue of jurisdiction.

You may appear or be represented by a person having a right of audience before the Court of Session at the hearing.

You or your representative will be asked whether you agree to jurisdiction being accepted by the Court of Session and the proceedings involving matters of parental responsibility being dealt with in the Court of Session.

If you do not appear or are not represented at the hearing the court may decide whether to accept jurisdiction in your absence.

(*Signed*)

Solicitor [*or* Agent] for Pursuer

[*or as the case may be*]

(*Address*)

---

[1]Form 88.5 inserted by S.S.I. 2005 No. 135, para.3 (effective 2nd March 2005).

Rule 88.7(1)   [1] FORM 88.7

Form of request for consent to placement of child under Article 56 of Council Regulation (E.C.) No. 2201/2003 of 27th November 2003

Date: (*date of request*)

To: (*to be inserted by Scottish Central Authority*)

The Court of Session has jurisdiction in matters of parental responsibility under the Council Regulation (E.C.) No. 2201/2003 of 27th November 2003 in respect of (*name and address of child*). The court is contemplating the placement of (*name of child*) in (*name and address of institution*) [*or* with (*name and address of foster family*)] and requests your consent to the placement in accordance with Article 56 of Council Regulation.

(*Signed*)

Deputy Principal Clerk of Session

N.B. To be sent to: Scottish Central Authority,
                        Civil Justice and International Division,
                        2nd Floor West,
                        St Andrew's House,
                        Regent Road,
                        Edinburgh,
                        EH1 3DG.

Paragraph 3(1)   SCHEDULE 3

AMENDMENT TO ENACTMENT

Presumption of Death (Scotland) Act 1977 (c.27)

In section 4(3) of the Presumption of Death (Scotland) Act 1977 (person having an interest seeking determination or appointment in application for variation order), for the words "lodge a minute", substitute the words "make an application to the court".

Paragraph 3(2) SCHEDULE 4

ENACTMENTS REPEALED

Year of Session and Chapter	Short title	Extent of repeal	Rules of the Court of Session 1994
c.10 (S.)	Citation Act 1540	The whole Act	r. 16.1
c.21 (S.)	Citation Act 1693	The whole Act	Ch. 16
6 Geo. 4, c.120	Court of Session Act 1825	Section 53	r. 16.12(4)
1 & 2 Vict., c.114	Debtors (Scotland) Act 1838	Sections 16, 18 and 20	r. 13.6(c) r. 3.5(4) r. 13.11
31 & 32 Vict., c.100	Court of Session Act 1868	Section 39	r. 29.1(2)(b)
31 & 32 Vict., c.101	Titles to Land Consolidation Act 1868	Section 158 and Schedule QQ	r. 13.11 r. 59.1
45 & 46 Vict., c.77	Citation Amendment (Scotland) Act 1882	Sections 3, 4 (1) to (4), 5 and 6 and Schedules 1 and 2 in their application to any cause or proceedings in the Court of Session	4. 16.4
57 & 58 Vict., c.40	Nautical Assessors (Scotland) Act 1894	Sections 2, 3 4 and 5 in their application to the Court of Session	r. 12.1(3) r.12.8 r. 12.5 r. 12.9
58 & 59 Vict., c.19	Court of Session Consignations (Scotland) Act 1895	In section 3, the words from ", and the Clerk of Court" to "such Clerk"	r. 35.11(2)

Paragraph 3(3) SCHEDULE 5

ACTS OF SEDERUNT REVOKED

Statutory Instrument Year and Number	Title of Act of Sederunt	Extent of Revocation
1949/1896	Act of Sederunt (Court of Session Jury Trials) 1949	The whole of the Act of Sederunt
1964/1901	Act of Sederunt (Rules of Court Amendment No.5)	The whole of the Act of Sederunt
1965/321	Act of Sederunt (Rules of Court, consolidation and amendment) 1965	The whole of the Act of Sederunt
1965/1090	Act of Sederunt (Rules of Court Amendment No.1) 1965	The whole of the Act of Sederunt
1965/1266	Act of Sederunt (Rules of Court Amendment No.2) 1965	The whole of the Act of Sederunt
1965/1405	Act of Sederunt (Rules of Court Amendment No.3) 1965	The whole of the Act of Sederunt
1966/335	Act of Sederunt (Rules of Court Amendment No.1) 1966	The whole of the Act of Sederunt
1966/868	Act of Sederunt (Rules of Court Amendment No.2) 1966	The whole of the Act of Sederunt
1966/1283	Act of Sederunt (Rules of Court Amendment No.3) 1966	The whole of the Act of Sederunt
1966/1531	Act of Sederunt (Rules of Court Amendment No.4) 1966	The whole of the Act of Sederunt
1966/1620	Act of Sederunt (Rules of Court Amendment No.5) 1966	The whole of the Act of Sederunt
1967/387	Act of Sederunt (Rules of Court Amendment No.1) 1967	The whole of the Act of Sederunt

Statutory Instrument Year and Number	Title of Act of Sederunt	Extent of Revocation
1967/487	Act of Sederunt (Appointment of Judicial Factors and Rules of Court Amendment No.2) 1967	Paragraphs 5, 6, 7 and 8
1967/1090	Act of Sederunt (Rules of Court Amendment No.3) 1967	The whole of the Act of Sederunt
1967/1789	Act of Sederunt (Rules of Court Amendment No.4) 1967	The whole of the Act of Sederunt
1968/1016	Act of Sederunt (Rules of Court Amendment No.1) 1968	The whole of the Act of Sederunt
1968/1122	Act of Sederunt (Form of Extract Decree of Divorce) 1968	The whole of the Act of Sederunt
1968/1150	Act of Sederunt (Rules of Court Amendment No.2) 1968	The whole of the Act of Sederunt
1968/1602	Act of Sederunt (Rules of Court Amendment No.3) 1968	The whole of the Act of Sederunt
1968/1759	Act of Sederunt (Rules of Court Amendment No.4) 1968	The whole of the Act of Sederunt
1968/1760	Act of Sederunt (Rules of Court Amendment No.5) 1968	The whole of the Act of Sederunt
1969/474	Act of Sederunt (Rules of Court Amendment No.1) 1969	The whole of the Act of Sederunt
1969/475	Act of Sederunt (Rules of Court Amendment No.2) 1969	The whole of the Act of Sederunt
1969/1702	Act of Sederunt (Rules of Court Amendment No.3) 1969	The whole of the Act of Sederunt
1969/1703	Act of Sederunt (Rules of Court Amendment No.4) 1969	The whole of the Act of Sederunt
1969/1819	Act of Sederunt (Rules of Court Amendment No.5) 1969	The whole of the Act of Sederunt
1970/96	Act of Sederunt (Rules of Court Amendment No.1) 1970	The whole of the Act of Sederunt
1970/134	Act of Sederunt (Rules of Court Amendment No.2) 1970	The whole of the Act of Sederunt
1970/682	Act of Sederunt (Rules of Court Amendment No.3) 1970	The whole of the Act of Sederunt
1970/1058	Act of Sederunt (Rules of Court Amendment No.4) 1970	The whole of the Act of Sederunt
1970/1746	Act of Sederunt (Rules of Court Amendment No.5) 1970	The whole of the Act of Sederunt
1971/66	Act of Sederunt (Rules of Court Amendment No.1) 1971	The whole of the Act of Sederunt
1971/201	Act of Sederunt (Rules of Court Amendment No.1) (Alteration of Operative Date) 1971	The whole of the Act of Sederunt
1971/202	Act of Sederunt (Rules of Court Amendment No.2) 1971	The whole of the Act of Sederunt
1971/203	Act of Sederunt (Rules of Court Amendment No.3) 1971	The whole of the Act of Sederunt
1971/265	Act of Sederunt (Rules of Court Amendment No.4) 1971	The whole of the Act of Sederunt
1971/1161	Act of Sederunt (Rules of Court Amendment No.5) 1971	The whole of the Act of Sederunt
1971/198	Act of Sederunt (Rules of Court Amendment No.5) 1970 (Alteration of Fees to Shorthand Writers) 1971	The whole of the Act of Sederunt
1971/1162	Act of Sederunt (Rules of Court Amendment No.6) 1971	The whole of the Act of Sederunt
1971/1165	Act of Sederunt (Edictal Citations, Commissary Petitions and Petitions of Service) 1971	Paragraph 1
1971/1215	Act of Sederunt (Rules of Court Amendment No.7) 1971	The whole of the Act of Sederunt
1971/1714	Act of Sederunt (Rules of Court Amendment No.8) 1971	The whole of the Act of Sederunt

Statutory Instrument Year and Number	Title of Act of Sederunt	Extent of Revocation
1971/1797	Act of Sederunt (Rules of Court Amendment No.9) 1971	The whole of the Act of Sederunt
1971/1809	Act of Sederunt (Rules of Court Amendment No.10) 1971	The whole of the Act of Sederunt
1972/164	Act of Sederunt (Rules of Court Amendment No.1) 1972	The whole of the Act of Sederunt
1972/1530	Act of Sederunt (Rules of Court Amendment No.2) 1972	The whole of the Act of Sederunt
1972/1672	Act of Sederunt (Rules of Court Amendment No. 3) 1972 (Alteration of Fees to Shorthand Writers) 1972	The whole of the Act of Sederunt
1972/1835	Act of Sederunt (Rules of Court Amendment No.4) 1972	The whole of the Act of Sederunt
1972/1981	Act of Sederunt (Rules of Court Amendment No.5) 1972	The whole of the Act of Sederunt
1972/1982	Act of Sederunt (Rules of Court Amendment No.6) 1972	The whole of the Act of Sederunt
1972/2021	Act of Sederunt (Rules of Court Amendment No.7) 1972	The whole of the Act of Sederunt
1972/2022	Act of Sederunt (Rules of Court Amendment No.8) 1972	The whole of the Act of Sederunt
1973/145	Act of Sederunt (Rules of Court Amendment No.1) 1973	The whole of the Act of Sederunt
1973/360	Act of Sederunt (Rules of Court Amendment No.2) 1973	The whole of the Act of Sederunt
1973/540	Act of Sederunt (Rules of Court Amendment No.3) 1973	The whole of the Act of Sederunt
1973/541	Act of Sederunt (Rules of Court Amendment No.4) 1973	The whole of the Act of Sederunt
1973/984	Act of Sederunt (Rules of Court Amendment No.5 1973) (Alteration of fees to Shorthand Writers) 1973	The whole of the Act of Sederunt
1973/1991	Act of Sederunt (Rules of Court Amendment No.6) 1973	The whole of the Act of Sederunt
1974/845	Act of Sederunt (Rules of Court Amendment) 1974	The whole of the Act of Sederunt
1974/945	Act of Sederunt (Rules of Court Amendment No.2) 1974	The whole of the Act of Sederunt
1974/946	Act of Sederunt (Rules of Court Amendment No.3) 1974	The whole of the Act of Sederunt
1974/1603	Act of Sederunt (Rules of Court Amendment No.4) 1974	The whole of the Act of Sederunt
1974/1628	Act of Sederunt (Rules of Court Amendment No.5) (Alteration of Fees to Shorthand Writers) 1974	The whole of the Act of Sederunt
1974/1686	Act of Sederunt (Rules of Court Amendment No.6) 1974	The whole of the Act of Sederunt
1974/2090	Act of Sederunt (Rules of Court Amendment No.7) 1974	The whole of the Act of Sederunt
1975/89	Act of Sederunt (Rules of Court Amendment) 1975	The whole of the Act of Sederunt
1975/1106	Act of Sederunt (Rules of Court Amendment No.2) 1975	The whole of the Act of Sederunt
1975/1585	Act of Sederunt (Rules of Court Amendment No.3) (Alteration of Fees to Shorthand Writers) 1975	The whole of the Act of Sederunt
1976/137	Act of Sederunt (Rules of Court Amendment) 1976	The whole of the Act of Sederunt
1976/282	Act of Sederunt (Rules of Court Amendment No.2) 1976	The whole of the Act of Sederunt
1976/372	Act of Sederunt (Rules of Court Amendment No.3) (Alteration of Fees to Shorthand Writers) 1976	The whole of the Act of Sederunt

Acts of Sederunt revoked

Statutory Instrument Year and Number	Title of Act of Sederunt	Extent of Revocation
1976/745	Act of Sederunt (Rules of Court Amendment No.4) (Transmission of Records) 1976	The whole of the Act of Sederunt
1976/779	Act of Sederunt (Rules of Court Amendment No.5) (Appeals under Social Security Acts) 1976	The whole of the Act of Sederunt
1976/847	Act of Sederunt (Rules of Court Amendment No.6) (Appeals under Consumer Credit Act 1974) 1976	The whole of the Act of Sederunt
1976/867	Act of Sederunt (Rules of Court Amendment No.7) (Solicitor's Admission Fees) 1976	The whole of the Act of Sederunt
1976/1605	Act of Sederunt (Rules of Court Amendment No.9) (Alteration of Fees to Shorthand Writers No. 2) 1976	The whole of the Act of Sederunt
1976/1849	Act of Sederunt (Rules of Court Amendment No.10) (Revenue Appeals) 1976	The whole of the Act of Sederunt
1976/1994	Act of Sederunt (Rules of Court Amendment No.11) (Consistorial Actions) 1976	The whole of the Act of Sederunt
1976/2196	Act of Sederunt (Rules of Court Amendment No.13) (Medical Witnesses' Fees) 1976	The whole of the Act of Sederunt
1976/2197	Act of Sederunt (Rules of Court Amendment No.14) (Third Party Procedure) 1976	The whole of the Act of Sederunt
1977/472	Act of Sederunt (Rules of Court Amendment No.2) (Adoption Proceedings) 1977	The whole of the Act of Sederunt
1977/974	Act of Sederunt (Rules of Court Amendment No.3) (Applications under Companies and Insolvency Acts 1976) 1977	The whole of the Act of Sederunt
1977/978	Act of Sederunt (Rules of Court Amendment No.4) (Shorthand Writers' Fees) 1977	The whole of the Act of Sederunt
1977/1621	Act of Sederunt (Rules of Court Amendment No.5) (Miscellaneous Amendments) 1977	The whole of the Act of Sederunt
1978/106	Act of Sederunt (Rules of Court Amendment No.1) (Consistorial Causes) 1978	The whole of the Act of Sederunt
1978/161	Act of Sederunt (Rules of Court Amendment No.3) (Presumption of Death) 1978	The whole of the Act of Sederunt
1978/690	Act of Sederunt (Rules of Court Amendment No.4) (Commercial Causes) 1978	The whole of the Act of Sederunt
1978/799	Act of Sederunt (Rules of Court Amendment No.5) (Depute Clerks of Session) 1978	The whole of the Act of Sederunt
1978/925	Act of Sederunt (Rules of Court Amendment No.6) (Shorthand Writers' Fees) 1978	The whole of the Act of Sederunt
1978/955	Act of Sederunt (Rules of Court Amendment No.8) (Patent Rules) 1978	The whole of the Act of Sederunt
1978/1373	Act of Sederunt (Rules of Court Amendment No.9) (Convention Adoption Rules) 1978	The whole of the Act of Sederunt
1978/1804	Act of Sederunt (Rules of Court Amendment No.10) (Induciae) 1978	The whole of the Act of Sederunt
1979/516	Act of Sederunt (Rules of Court Amendment No.2) (European Assembly Election Petitions) 1979	The whole of the Act of Sederunt
1979/670	Act of Sederunt (Rules of Court Amendment No.3) (International Oil Pollution Compensation Fund) 1979	The whole of the Act of Sederunt
1979/1033	Act of Sederunt (Rules of Court Amendment No.4) (Shorthand Writers' Fees) 1979	The whole of the Act of Sederunt
1979/1410	Act of Sederunt (Rules of Court Amendment No.5) 1979	The whole of the Act of Sederunt
1980/290	Act of Sederunt (Rules of Court Amendment No.1) (Adoption Proceedings) 1980	The whole of the Act of Sederunt
1980/891	Act of Sederunt (Rules of Court Amendment No.3) (Protection of Trading Interests Act 1980) 1980	The whole of the Act of Sederunt

Statutory Instrument Year and Number	Title of Act of Sederunt	Extent of Revocation
1980/892	Act of Sederunt (Rules of Court Amendment No.4) (Applications under section 85 of Fair Trading Act 1973) 1980	The whole of the Act of Sederunt
1980/909	Act of Sederunt (Rules of Court Amendment No.5) (Witnesses' Fees) 1980	The whole of the Act of Sederunt
1980/1016	Act of Sederunt (Rules of Court Amendment No.6) (Shorthand Writers' Fees) 1980	The whole of the Act of Sederunt
1980/1144	Act of Sederunt (Rules of Court Amendment No.7) (Miscellaneous Amendments) 1980	The whole of the Act of Sederunt
1980/1754	Act of Sederunt (Rules of Court Amendment No.8) (Leave to appeal and appeals from Social Security Commissioners) 1980	The whole of the Act of Sederunt
1980/1801	Act of Sederunt (Rules of Court Amendment No.9) (Remits from Sheriff Court) 1980	The whole of the Act of Sederunt
1981/1137	Act of Sederunt (Rules of Court Amendment No.3) (Shorthand Writers' Fees) 1981	The whole of the Act of Sederunt
1982/654	Act of Sederunt (Rules of Court Amendment No.3) (Court Fees) 1982	The whole of the Act of Sederunt
1982/804	Act of Sederunt (Rules of Court Amendment No.4) (Shorthand Writers' Fees) 1982	The whole of the Act of Sederunt
1982/1381	Act of Sederunt (Rules of Court Amendment No.5) (Applications under Matrimonial Homes (Family Protection) (Scotland) Act 1981) 1982	The whole of the Act of Sederunt
1982/1679	Act of Sederunt (Rules of Court Amendment No.6) (Simplified Divorce Procedure) 1982	The whole of the Act of Sederunt
1982/1723	Act of Sederunt (Rules of Court Amendment No.7) (Witnesses' Fees) 1982	The whole of the Act of Sederunt
1982/1824	Act of Sederunt (Rules of Court Amendment No.8) (Court Fees in Simplified Divorce Procedure) 1982	The whole of the Act of Sederunt
1982/1825	Act of Sederunt (Rules of Court Amendment No.9) (Miscellaneous Amendments) 1982	The whole of the Act of Sederunt
1983/397	Act of Sederunt (Rules of Court Amendment No.1) (Appeals under Social Security Acts) 1983	The whole of the Act of Sederunt
1983/398	Act of Sederunt (Rules of Court Amendment No.2) (Interest in Decrees or Extracts) 1983	The whole of the Act of Sederunt
1983/656	Act of Sederunt (Rules of Court Amendment No.3) (Letters of Request) 1983	The whole of the Act of Sederunt
1983/826	Act of Sederunt (Rules of Court Amendment No.4) (Taxation of Accounts) 1983	The whole of the Act of Sederunt
1983/1210	Act of Sederunt (Rules of Court Amendment No.6) (Simplified Divorce Procedure) 1983	The whole of the Act of Sederunt
1983/1642	Act of Sederunt (Rules of Court Amendment No.7) (Shorthand Writers' Fees) 1983	The whole of the Act of Sederunt
1984/235	Act of Sederunt (Rules of Court Amendment No.1) (Court Fees) 1984	The whole of the Act of Sederunt
1984/472	Act of Sederunt (Rules of Court Amendment No.2) (Miscellaneous) 1984	The whole of the Act of Sederunt
1984/499	Act of Sederunt (Rules of Court Amendment No.3) (Summary Decree and Other Amendments) 1984	The whole of the Act of Sederunt
1984/919	Act of Sederunt (Amendment of Rules of Court No.4) (Provisional Damages) 1984	The whole of the Act of Sederunt
1984/920	Act of Sederunt (Amendment of Rules of Court No.5) (Intimation in fatal accident cases) 1984	The whole of the Act of Sederunt
1984/997	Act of Sederunt (Rules of Court Amendment No.6) (Adoption Proceedings) 1984	The whole of the Act of Sederunt
1984/1133	Act of Sederunt (Rules of Court Amendment No.8) (Shorthand Writers' Fees) 1984	The whole of the Act of Sederunt

Statutory Instrument Year and Number	Title of Act of Sederunt	Extent of Revocation
1985/227	Act of Sederunt (Rules of Court Amendment No.1) (Optional Procedure in Certain Actions of Reparation) 1985	The whole of the Act of Sederunt
1985/500	Act of Sederunt (Rules of Court Amendment No.2) (Judicial Review) 1985	The whole of the Act of Sederunt
1985/760	Act of Sederunt (Rules of Court Amendment No.4) (Shorthand Writers' Fees) 1985	The whole of the Act of Sederunt
1985/1178	Act of Sederunt (Rules of Court Amendment No.5) (Interest in Decrees or Extracts) 1985	The whole of the Act of Sederunt
1985/1426	Act of Sederunt (Rules of Court Amendment No.6) (Election Petitions) 1985	The whole of the Act of Sederunt
1985/1600	Act of Sederunt (Rules of Court Amendment No.7) (Miscellaneous Amendments) 1985	The whole of the Act of Sederunt
1986/514	Act of Sederunt (Rules of Court Amendment No.1) (Bankruptcy Forms) 1986	The whole of the Act of Sederunt
1986/515	Act of Sederunt (Rules of Court Amendment No.2) (Custody of Children) 1986	The whole of the Act of Sederunt
1986/694	Act of Sederunt (Rules of Court Amendment No.3) (Companies and Insolvency) 1986	The whole of the Act of Sederunt
1986/799	Act of Sederunt (Rules of Court Amendment No.4) (Liner Conferences) 1986	The whole of the Act of Sederunt
1986/967	Act of Sederunt (Rules of Court Amendment No.5) (Solicitors' Fees) 1986	The whole of the Act of Sederunt
1986/1128	Act of Sederunt (Rules of Court Amendment No.6) (Shorthand Writers' Fees) 1986	The whole of the Act of Sederunt
1986/1231	Act of Sederunt (Rules of Court Amendment No.7) (Consistorial Causes) 1986	The whole of the Act of Sederunt
1986/1937	Act of Sederunt (Rules of Court Amendment No.8) (Miscellaneous) 1986	The whole of the Act of Sederunt
1986/1941	Act of Sederunt (Rules of Court Amendment No.9) (Jurisdiction and Enforcement) 1986	The whole of the Act of Sederunt
1986/1955	Act of Sederunt (Rules of Court Amendment No.10) (Miscellaneous Amendments) 1986	The whole of the Act of Sederunt
1986/2298	Act of Sederunt (Rules of Court Amendment No.11) (Companies) 1986	The whole of the Act of Sederunt
1987/12	Act of Sederunt (Rules of Court Amendment No.1) (Drug Trafficking) 1987	The whole of the Act of Sederunt
1987/871	Act of Sederunt (Rules of Court Amendment No.2) (Solicitors' Fees) 1987	The whole of the Act of Sederunt
1987/1079	Act of Sederunt (Rules of Court Amendment No.3) (Shorthand Writers' Fees) 1987	The whole of the Act of Sederunt
1987/1206	Act of Sederunt (Rules of Court Amendment No.4) (Miscellaneous) 1987	The whole of the Act of Sederunt
1987/2160	Act of Sederunt (Rules of Court Amendment No.5) (Miscellaneous) 1987	The whole of the Act of Sederunt
1988/615	Act of Sederunt (Rules of the Court of Session Amendment No.1) (Family Law) 1988	The whole of the Act of Sederunt
1988/684	Act of Sederunt (Rules of the Court of Session Amendment No.2) (Solicitors' Fees) 1988	The whole of the Act of Sederunt
1988/1032	Act of Sederunt (Rules of the Court of Session Amendment No.3) (Shorthand Writers' Fees) 1988	The whole of the Act of Sederunt
1988/1521	Act of Sederunt (Rules of the Court of Session Amendment No.4) (Commercial Actions) 1988	The whole of the Act of Sederunt
1988/2059	Act of Sederunt (Form of charge for payment) 1988	The whole of the Act of Sederunt in its application to the Court of Session
1988/2060	Act of Sederunt (Rules of the Court of Session Amendment No.5) (Time to pay directions) 1988	The whole of the Act of Sederunt

Statutory Instrument Year and Number	Title of Act of Sederunt	Extent of Revocation
1989/435	Act of Sederunt (Rules of the Court of Session Amendment No.1) (Written Statements) 1989	The whole of the Act of Sederunt
1989/445	Act of Sederunt (Rules of the Court of Session Amendment No.2) (Solicitors' Fees) 1989	The whole of the Act of Sederunt
1989/778	Act of Sederunt (Rules of Court of Session Amendment No.3) Shorthand Writers' Fees) 1989	The whole of the Act of Sederunt
1990/705	Act of Sederunt (Rules of Court of Session Amendment No.1) (Miscellaneous) 1990	The whole of the Act of Sederunt
1990/717	Act of Sederunt (Rules of Court of the Session Amendment No.2) (Solicitors' Fees) 1990	The whole of the Act of Sederunt
1990/798	Act of Sederunt (Rules of Court of the Session Amendment No.3) (Shorthand Writers' Fees) 1990	The whole of the Act of Sederunt
1990/1262	Act of Sederunt (Rules of Court of the Session Amendment No.4) (Solicitors' Fees) 1990	The whole of the Act of Sederunt
1991/272	Act of Sederunt (Rules of the Court of Session Amendment No.1) (Fees of Solicitors) 1991	The whole of the Act of Sederunt
1991/1157	Act of Sederunt (Rules of the Court of Session Amendment No.2) (Miscellaneous) 1991	The whole of the Act of Sederunt
1991/846	Act of Sederunt (Rules of the Court of Session Amendment No.3) (Solicitors' Fees) 1991	The whole of the Act of Sederunt
1991/1158	Act of Sederunt (Rules of the Court of Session Amendment No.4) (Shorthand Writers' Fees) 1991	The whole of the Act of Sederunt
1991/1183	Act of Sederunt (Rules of the Court of Session Amendment No.5) (Prevention of Terrorism) 1991	The whole of the Act of Sederunt
1991/1621	Act of Sederunt (Rules of the Court of Session Amendment No.7) (Patents Rules) 1991	The whole of the Act of Sederunt
1991/1915	Act of Sederunt (Rules of the Court of Session Amendment No.8) (Discharge of Judicial Factors) 1991	The whole of the Act of Sederunt
1991/2213	Act of Sederunt (Rules of the Court of Session Amendment No.9) (International Commercial Arbitration) 1991	The whole of the Act of Sederunt
1991/2483	Act of Sederunt (Rules of the Court of Session Amendment No.10) (Miscellaneous) 1991	The whole of the Act of Sederunt
1991/2652	Act of Sederunt (Rules of the Court of Session Amendment No.11) (Applications under the Access to Health Records Act 1990) 1991	The whole of the Act of Sederunt
1992/88	Act of Sederunt (Rules of the Court of Session Amendment) (Optional Procedure and Miscellaneous) 1992	The whole of the Act of Sederunt
1992/894	Act of Sederunt (Rules of the Court of Session Amendment No.2) (Solicitors' Fees) 1992	The whole of the Act of Sederunt
1992/1433	Act of Sederunt (Rules of the Court of Session Amendment No.3) (Taxation of Accounts) 1992	The whole of the Act of Sederunt
1992/1422	Act of Sederunt (Rules of the Court of Session Amendment No.4) (Solicitors, Notaries Public, Qualified Conveyancers and Executry Practitioners) 1992	The whole of the Act of Sederunt
1992/1533	Act of Sederunt (Rules of the Court of Session Amendment No.5) (Public Trusts) 1992	The whole of the Act of Sederunt
1992/1905	Act of Sederunt (Rules of the Court of Session Amendment No.6) (Shorthand Writers' Fees) 1992	The whole of the Act of Sederunt
1992/1906	Act of Sederunt (Rules of the Court of Session Amendment No.7) (Witnesses' Fees) 1992	The whole of the Act of Sederunt

Statutory Instrument Year and Number	Title of Act of Sederunt	Extent of Revocation
1992/1898	Act of Sederunt (Rules of the Court of Session Amendment No.8) (Fees of Solicitors in Speculative Actions) 1992	The whole of the Act of Sederunt
1992/2289	Act of Sederunt (Rules of the Court of Session Amendment No.9) (Miscellaneous) 1992	The whole of the Act of Sederunt
1993/770	Act of Sederunt (Rules of the Court of Session Amendment) (Interest in Decrees and Extracts) 1993	The Whole of the Act of Sederunt
1993/899	Act of Sederunt (Rules of the Court of Session Amendment) (Register of Insolvencies) 1993	The whole of the Act of Sederunt
1993/900	Act of Sederunt (Rules of the Court of Session Amendment No.2) (Fees of Solicitors) 1993	The whole of the Act of Sederunt
1993/1357	Act of Sederunt (Rules of the Court of Session Amendment No.3) (Shorthand Writers' Fees) 1993	The whole of the Act of Sederunt
1994/1139	Act of Sederunt (Rules of the Court of Session Amendment No.1) (Fees of Solicitors) 1994	The whole of the Act of Sederunt
1994/1140	Act of Sederunt (Rules of the Court of Session Amendment No.2) (Shorthand Writers' Fees) 1994	The whole of the Act of Sederunt

[THE NEXT PAGE IS C1001]

¹ Other Acts of Sederunt

NOTE
¹ The Acts of Sederunt reprinted in this section are those relating to the Court of Session which have not been placed in one of the other subject Divisions in *Parliament House Book*. An alphabetical list of all Acts of Sederunt in *Parliament House Book* can be found in the Indices section at the front of Volumes 1, 3, 4 and 5.

Re-allocation of Deficiency of Stipend caused by Surrenders

(S.R. & O. 1925 No. 1060)

[15th July 1925]

Whereas it is provided by the Church of Scotland (Property and Endowments) Act 1925, section 41, that section 106 of the Court of Session (Scotland) Act 1868, (which relates to Acts of Sederunt), shall, for the purposes of Acts of Sederunt relating to the Court of Teinds, have effect as if references to that Act in the section included reference to the Church of Scotland (Property and Endowments) Act 1925, and whereas it is, *inter alia*, enacted by the said Court of Session (Scotland) Act 1868, section 106, that the Court of Session may from time to time make such regulations by Act of Sederunt for altering the course of proceeding thereinbefore prescribed in respect to the matters to which that Act relates, and whereas it is provided in paragraph 8 of the Sixth Schedule of the said Church of Scotland (Property and Endowments) Act 1925, that in certain cases the deficiency of stipend caused by a surrender shall be re-allocated among the heritors in the parish (if any) who have unexhausted teinds not yet allocated for stipend, the Lords of Council and Session hereby enact and declare that:—

1. Any claim under said paragraph 8 of the Sixth Schedule to have a deficiency of stipend re-allocated among those heritors in the parish (if any) who have unexhausted teinds not yet allocated for stipend shall be disposed of either in a depending process of locality relative to the said parish or in the proceedings for adjustment of the teind roll thereof.

2. The notification which the Clerk of Teinds is required by said paragraph 8 to make to the common agent of the heritors shall be given in such depending process or in the proceedings for adjustment of the teind roll, as the case may be.

3. In the application of paragraph 8 to the case of a depending process of locality it shall not be necessary for the Clerk of Teinds to issue any certificate specifying the amounts of stipend payable by the heritors whose teinds are affected by the re-allocation. Said re-allocation shall be made in the interim or final locality, as the case may be.

Procedure under Section 10 of the Church of Scotland (Property and Endowments) Act 1925, and the Fourth Schedule to the said Act, and for other Purposes

(S.R. & O. 1925 No. 1062)

[17th July 1925]

The Lords of Council and Session, in pursuance of the powers vested in them by the Church of Scotland (Property and Endowments) Act 1925, do hereby repeal Book H, Chapter ii, of the codifying Act of Sederunt without prejudice to any application for augmentation competently made before the passing of the said Act, or to anything following on such application or done therein, and enact and declare as follows:—

Sittings of Teind Court.—1. *That the Court of the Commissioners for Teinds shall meet once a fortnight on Friday during the sitting of the Court of Session at such hours as shall be convenient.*

AUGMENTATION, MODIFICATION, AND LOCALITY

Applications under section 10, the Church of Scotland (Property and Endowments) Act 1925
1. Applications under section 10 may be made by way of summons to the Court of Teinds. The pursuer shall state in the summons as accurately as he can the date when the last application for an augmentation was made, the number of chalders modified in stipend by the court, the value of same (including any allowance for furnishing communion elements), calculated in accordance with the provisions of the Fourth Schedule of the statute, and the surplus teinds which the pursuer believes to be available to allow of augmentation in terms of the statute, and may be in the form of Schedule A hereto annexed.

Citation and Notice
2.—(*a*) As soon as a summons of modification and locality is raised and signeted, it shall be competent to the pursuer to cite the titulars and tacksmen of the teinds, heritors, and liferenters, and all others having, or pretending to have, interest in the teinds of the parish, by a notice in writing affixed to the most patent door of the church, by the clerk of the kirk session or a police constable stating that the minister of the parish has raised a summons of modification and locality of his stipend which will be called in court on   , being the   day of next to come, not being less than six weeks after the date of the notice; and such clerk or constable shall return a certificate, subscribed by himself and two witnesses, that such notice has been affixed by him.
(*b*) The pursuer shall also cause notice to be inserted two several days in the *Scotsman* newspaper, and in a newspaper circulating in the county in which the parish referred to in such notice is situated, that he has raised a summons of modification and locality which will be called in court on   , being the   day of   , not being less than six weeks from the date of the first advertisement.
(*c*) The mode of citation and the *induciae* above mentioned shall be deemed sufficient although one or more of the defenders shall be a pupil or minor out of the kingdom at the time such citation shall be given.

Citation of Crown
3. When it is necessary to call the Lord Advocate on behalf of His Majesty or of the Crown, or any public department, he shall be cited upon the *induciae* of six weeks.

Certificates and Executions of Citation
4. Such certificate by the clerk or constable, with the notices in the newspapers above mentioned or certificate by the pursuer's agents of the due appearance in the requisite newspapers of such notices, and execution of citation to the Lord Advocate, shall be held as sufficient citation to all parties.

Death of a Defender
5. When any of the defenders die during the dependence of the process, his heir may be called by a diligence in the manner and upon the *induciae*

hitherto used; but such diligence may be executed either by a messenger-at-arms or a constable or under the provision of the Citation Amendment (Scotland) Act 1882.

Wakening of Process

6. When it is necessary to waken a process, it must be done by a summons or by a minute of wakening, in which all parties having interest must be called in the same manner, and on the same *induciae* as in the original process.

Note of Stipend and Rental to be Lodged

7. The pursuer of every process of modification and locality shall, as soon as the summons is signeted, lodge with the clerk of court a note, stating the amount of the stipend, distinguishing how much is paid in money, and how much in victual, and in what species of victual, and the measure by which it is paid; and also stating the amount of the communion elements. The pursuer must also, at the same time, produce a rental of the parish, distinguishing the rent of each heritor.

First Enrolment

8. As soon as the summons is called in court the pursuer may enrol it in the Teind Motion Roll of the Lord Ordinary; and all concerned will be allowed to see the summons and writings therewith produced in the clerk's hands for fourteen days.

Second Enrolment

9. After the elapse of the time for seeing, the pursuer may enrol the cause for a remit to the clerk to report whether there are any surplus teinds in the parish.

Third Enrolment

10. When the clerk's report is prepared, the pursuer may enrol the cause to consider same and thereupon—

(*a*) If the clerk has reported that there appear to be no surplus teinds in the parish the Lord Ordinary may either pronounce a decree accordingly, or ordain the pursuer to lodge a condescendence giving detailed particulars of the surplus teinds in the parish alleged in the summons to be available for an augmentation in terms of the statute.

(*b*) If it shall appear that there are surplus teinds in the parish the Lord Ordinary shall find in general terms accordingly, and, at the same time, shall ordain the heritors or their agents to meet for the purpose of naming a person to be suggested to the Lord Ordinary as common agent for conducting the locality, and a short notice of this interlocutor shall be inserted in the *Scotsman* newspaper, and in a newspaper circulating in the county in which the parish referred to in said notice is situated, the expense thereof to be paid by the common agent out of the general fund (unless in any case the appointment of a common agent shall be dispensed with by the Lord Ordinary); and shall further ordain the heritors to produce their rights to their teinds, if they any have, in the hands of the clerk within a time to be specified in the interlocutor, not being less than three months from the date thereof; with certification that after the elapse of that time, a remit shall be made to the clerk to prepare a scheme of locality either according to the rental lodged by the pursuer in case no rights are produced, or according to the State of Teinds lodged by the common agent (or by the heritors, as the case may be) as to the rights and interests which are produced by the heritors.

(*c*) The Lord Ordinary may pronounce such other or further order as shall seem to him to be necessary or expedient.

Agent for Party may not be Common Agent
11. No person who is agent for the minister or titular, or for any heritor in the parish, shall be appointed common agent.

Common Agent to prepare State of Teinds
12. The common agent, after his nomination has been confirmed by the court (or the heritors, as the case may be), on the expiry of the time specified within which the heritors shall produce their rights to their teinds, shall prepare and lodge a State of Teinds.

Preparation of Locality before the Lord Ordinary
13. After the elapse of the time for the heritors producing their rights to their teinds, a remit shall be made to the clerk to prepare a scheme of locality, either according to the rental lodged by the pursuer, in case no rights are produced, or according to the State of Teinds lodged by the common agent (or by the heritors, as the case may be), in terms of section 10 of the statute; and this scheme so prepared shall immediately be approved by the Lord Ordinary as an interim scheme, according to which the minister's stipend shall be paid, until a final locality shall be settled, and the minister furnished by the common agent (or by the heritors, as the case may be) with an extracted decree, at the expense of the heritors, and for which he is entitled to take credit in his account.

Preparation and Approval of Rectified Locality
14. If it shall appear, at any period or periods, that, under an interim locality, prepared and approved of in terms of the foresaid provisions, the minister is unable through surrender of teinds or other causes affecting its efficacy to operate payment to any considerable extent of the stipend awarded to him, then and in that case it shall be competent to the Lord Ordinary, on the motion of the minister or other party interested, to appoint a new interim scheme of locality to be prepared, and also a state of arrears remaining due from the causes before specified, to be made up; and when the said rectified locality and state of arrears shall be approved of, the Lord Ordinary shall give decreet for the arrears, and the rectified locality shall subsist as a new interim rule of payment of the stipend then current, and until it be set aside by any other rule which may afterwards be granted, on cause shewn.

Heritors' Motion for Rectified Locality
15. Under the reservation after provided as to expenses, it shall be competent to any heritor or heritors, the state of whose teinds has been materially altered by decreets of valuation, or by other circumstances, which may have occurred subsequent to the approval of an interim scheme, to apply for a rectification of the locality, giving effect to the new or corrected State of Teinds; and when the rectified locality shall be approved of by the Lord Ordinary as a new rule of payment, he shall, at the same time, appoint a state of arrears to be prepared, if the state of the process and the interests of the parties render this necessary, with power to give him decreet for the same.

New Interim Scheme on Account of Surrenders
16. Where any new interim scheme or schemes shall be rendered necessary by surrenders, or by production of rights made by heritors, or by any other unexpected emergency occurring subsequent to the previous interim scheme or schemes, it shall be competent to the Lord Ordinary to lay the expense of the new interim scheme and state of arrears, or such part thereof as may appear proper, on the party whose surrender, or productions or proceedings as aforesaid, shall make such new interim scheme necessary, unless such heritor or heritors shall be able to instruct a reason-

able cause to the contrary to the satisfaction of the Lord Ordinary; in which last case the expense shall be defrayed by the common agent (if any).

Preparation of Final Locality
17. That as soon as proceedings with regard to the interim locality are concluded, a scheme of a final locality shall be forthwith prepared, and the common agent shall distribute copies of this state and scheme among the agents for the heritors, as soon as may be after such state and scheme are prepared; and no new scheme shall thereafter be received, except upon payment of such expenses as may be occasioned by such new production, to be modified by the Lord Ordinary.

Disposal of Objections to Final Locality
18. After the foresaid state and scheme shall have been distributed among the heritors, the Lord Ordinary shall ordain objections thereto to be given in by any of the heritors who think themselves aggrieved by the proposed mode of allocation; and the Lord Ordinary may either hear parties *viva voce* upon such objections, and the answers that may be made thereto at the bar; or he may, if he shall see cause, allow all concerned to give in written answers to such objections within such time as he shall think &proper to appoint, and shall thereafter proceed, in so far as regards any application for prorogating the time for giving in papers, in the manner directed by section 12 of the Court of Session Act 1825[1].

NOTE
[1] Now repealed: see the Court of Session Act 1988 (c. 36), Sched. 2, Pts. I and III.

Review of Lord Ordinary's Judgment
19. When the Lord Ordinary has pronounced a judgment, other than a finding or decree as to surplus teinds, it may be reviewed by the Division to which the cause belongs by giving in a note, which must be lodged within twenty-one days after the date of the judgment complained of, and the procedure on that note shall be the same as in reviewing judgments of a Lord Ordinary in the Court of Session.

Form of Extract of Decreets of Locality and Warrants of Charge
20. Decreets of locality and warrants of charge shall be issued, in the form and to the effect of the schedules B and C respectively hereto annexed, as nearly as the circumstances of each case may admit of: Reserving always right to parties so advised, to take full extracts, according to the ancient form, when they require the same, in terms of the statute; Provided also, that the dues of extract in whatever form the same may be given out, shall be charged in precise conformity with the statute.

SCHEDULES REFERRED TO

SCHEDULE A

[1] *Summons of Modification and Locality*

GEORGE THE FIFTH, ETC.—Whereas it is humbly meant and shewn to us by our lovite(s), The Reverend (*name*), the present Minister of the Parish of   in the Presbytery of   and County of   ,—*Pursuer*; That the last application for an augmentation of the stipend of this parish was made on (*being the date of the signeting of the summons*): That the augmentation then granted was   chalders in addition to the then old stipend and allowance for furnishing the communion elements, making the amount of the present stipend, as last modified by the Court of Teinds,   chalders, with £   for furnishing the communion elements (*or as the case may be*), which modified stipend was found, in the Decree of Locality following upon said modification to be equivalent to (B   F   P   L   ) of meal, (B   F   P   L   ) of barley and £   of money sterling, inclusive of the allowance for communion elements (*state precisely the totals of the different kinds of victual and of the money*): That the value thereof, converted into money according to the provisions of the Fourth Schedule of the [Church of Scotland (Property and Endowments) Act 1925][2] is £   : That after deducting the said sum of £   there are, according to the State of Teinds in the last locality process (*or otherwise as the pursuer may specifically condescend*), surplus teinds in the parish amounting to £   or thereby available for an augmentation of the pursuer's stipend: That the following are the whole parties whom it is necessary to call as defenders in the present action, *videlicet*:—(*Here insert the names and designations of the defenders, specifying the characters in which they are called*): THEREFORE the Lords of our Council and Session, Commissioners appointed for Plantation of Kirks and Valuation of Teinds, per the Lord Ordinary in Teind causes, OUGHT and SHOULD find that there are surplus teinds in the parish available for an augmentation of the pursuer's stipend in accordance with the provisions of section 10 of the last-mentioned Act, and OUGHT and SHOULD modify, settle and appoint a constant local stipend, with the allowance for furnishing communion elements, to the pursuer and his successors in right of the emoluments of the cure of said parish, and establish and proportion a locality of the same; and DECERN for payment thereof to the pursuer and his successors in right of the emoluments of the cure of said parish against the heritors, titulars, tacksmen, and others, intromitters with the rents and teinds of the said parish, and that at the terms following, *videlicet*:—the money stipend and allowance for furnishing the communion elements at Whitsunday and Martinmas yearly, by equal portions, and the value of the victual money according to the highest fiars' prices of the same in the county of   between Yule and Candlemas yearly, after the separation of the crop from the ground, or as soon thereafter as the said fiars' prices shall have been struck, beginning the first payment thereof at Whitsunday (*next*) for one-half of the said money, and the other half at Martinmas thereafter, and the value of the victual betwixt Yule and Candlemas (*next*) or as soon thereafter as the said fiars' prices shall have been struck for crop and year   ; and so forth, yearly and termly thereafter, in all time coming; and for the greater expedition the pursuer is willing to refer the verity of the rental of the parish herewith produced to the heritors' oaths *simpliciter*, instead of all further probation; and in case of any of the said defenders appearing and occasioning unnecessary expense to the pursuer in the process to follow hereon, such defender or defenders OUGHT and SHOULD be DECERNED and ORDAINED, by decree foresaid, to make payment to the pursuer of the sum of £100 sterling, or of such other sum as our said Lords shall modify, as the expenses of the process to follow hereon, besides the dues of extract, conform to the[2] [Acts of Parliament thereanent] of Parliament, writs libelled, laws, and daily practice of Scotland, used and observed in the like cases, as is alleged.—OUR WILL IS HEREFORE, and we charge you that on sight hereof ye pass, and in our name and authority lawfully SUMMON, WARN, AND CHARGE the defenders, personally or at their respective dwelling-places, if within Scotland upon six days' warning, and if in Orkney or Shetland upon forty days' warning, and if furth of Scotland by delivering a copy hereof at the office of the Keeper of the Record of Edictal Citations at Edinburgh, in terms of the statute and Act of Sederunt thereanent, and that upon sixty days' warning; and the tutors and curators or other guardians of such of the defenders as are minors, if they any have, for their interest, also at the said office of the Keeper of the Record of Edictal Citations at Edinburgh, on the same *induciœ* as the minors themselves, or by the notices and in the forms prescribed by the Statute 15 & 16 Geo. 5, c. 33, and relative Acts of Sederunt, and that upon six weeks' warning; and all others having or pretending to have interest in the said matter, to compear before our said Lords Commissioners for Plantation of Kirks and Valuation of Teinds, at Edinburgh, or where they may then happen to be for the time, the   day of   Nineteen hundred and in the hour of cause, with continuation of days, to answer at the instance of the pursuer in the matter libelled: That is to say, the defenders to hear and see the premises verified and proven, and decree and sentence pronounced, conform to the conclusions above written, in all points, or else to allege a reasonable cause in the contrary, with certification as effeirs.—According to Justice, as ye shall answer to us thereupon: Which to do we commit to you and each of you full power by these our letters, delivering them by you duly executed and endorsed again to the bearer.—Given under our signet at Edinburgh, the   day of   in the   year of our reign, 19   .

(*To be signed by the Clerk of Teinds.*)

NOTES

[1] N.B. When the Church of Scotland General Trustees are the Pursuers or the Pursuer's stipend has been standardised, this form may be applied *mutatis mutandis*.

[2] Substituted by S.I. 1925 No. 1063.

SCHEDULE B

[1] *Form of Extract Decreet of Modification and Locality*

At Edinburgh, the   day of   Sitting in judgment, the Lords of Council and Session, Commissioners appointed for Plantation of Kirks and Valuation of Teinds, in the process of Modification and Locality raised and pursued at the instance of the Reverend-   Minister of the Gospel, of the Parish of   against the Officers of State, as representing His Majesty, for the interest of the Crown, and also against the whole Heritors, Titulars, Tacksmen, Liferenters, and others, intromitters with the Rents and Teinds of the said Parish, modified, decerned, and ordained, and hereby modify, decern, and ordain the constant Stipend and Provision of the Kirk and Parish of   to have been for crop, and year Nineteen hundred and   yearly, since and in time coming, such a quantity of Victual, half Meal, half Barley, in Imperialy Weight and Measure, as shall be equal to   Chalders of the late Standard Weight and Measure of Scotland, payable in Money, according to the highest fiars' prices of the County annually, with-   chalders of augmentation payable in money according to the Standard Value in terms of the Church of Scotland (Property and Endowments) Act 1925 (or with the sum of £   sterling of augmentation in terms of the Church of Scotland (Property and Endowments) Act 1925, being the amount of the surplus teinds in the parish available to meet *pro tanto* the statutory augmentation of   chalders), and that for Stipend, with   Sterling for furnishing the Communion Elements, payable the money stipend and allowance for communion elements at Whitsunday and Martinmas yealy by equal portions, and the victual betwixt Yule and Candlemas yearly after the separation of the crop from the ground or as soon thereafter as the Fiars' Prices of the County of   shall be struck. Which Modified Stipend, and Modification for furnishing the Communion Elements, the said Lords decern and ordain to be yearly paid to the said Kirk and Parish, by the Titulars and Tacksmen of the Teinds, Heritors, and Possessors of the Lands and others, intromitters with the Rents and Teinds of the said Parish, out of the first and readiest of the Teinds, parsonage and vicarage, of the same, conform to the Division and Locality following, viz. (*the Locality to be taken in here in figures and then say*), beginning the first term's payment thereof, for the said crop and year Nineteen hundred and   , as at the term of Whitsunday, Nineteen hundred and   as regards the money stipend and communion elements, and as regards the victual stipend betwixt Yule and Candlemas, after the separation of the crop from the ground, or as soon thereafter as the fiars' prices of the County are struck; and so forth yearly and termly in all time coming. The said Lords, as Commissioners foresaid, also decerned and ordained, and hereby decern and ordain, the whole Heritors of the said Parish, to make payment to   Common Agent in the process of their respective shares of the sum of £   sterling, being the amount of the account of the taxed expenses incurred by him in obtaining the Decreet of Locality; As also of their respective shares of the sum of £   sterling, being the expense of Extracting this Decreet and proportioning the Expenses among the Heritors, including therein Two pounds sterling, of fee-fund dues; making in whole £   sterling, and that in proportion to their several Teind Rentals in Process, and Scheme of Division made up and certified by the Clerk as relative hereto. And the said Lords of Council and Session, Commissioners foresaid, Grant Warrant to Messengers-at-Arms, in His Majesty's Name and Authority, to charge the Titulars and Tacksmen of the Teinds, Heritors, Feuars, Farmorers, Wadsetters, Liferenters, Factors, Chamberlains, Tenants, Occupiers, and Possessors of the Lands and others, intromitters with the Rents and Teinds of the said Parish of   Defenders, personally, or at their respective dwelling-places, if within Scotland, and if furth thereof, by delivery of a Copy of Charge at the Office of the Keeper of Edictal Citations at Edinburgh, to make payment of the foresaid Stipend and Communion Element Money, each of them for his or her own part and portion thereof, conform to the Division and Locality above set down, and that at the terms of payment above expressed,—in terms and to the effect contained in the Decreet of Locality and Extract above written, and here held as repeated *brevitatis causa*: as also of their respective proportions of the foresaid sums of Expenses and Dues of Extract, conform to the Scheme of Division above referred to; and that to the Reverend   , Pursuer, and his successors in right of the emoluments of the cure of said parish, and to the said Common Agent, respectively, within ten days if within Scotland, and if furth thereof, within sixty days after they are respectively charged to that effect, under the pain of Poinding, the terms of payment of said Stipend being always first come and bygone; And also Grant Warrant to Arrest the foresaid Defenders' readiest Goods, Gear, Debts, and sums of Money, in payment and satisfaction of their respective portions of Stipend and Communion Element Money, and also of their respective proportions of the Expenses foresaid, and Dues of Extract; And if the said Defenders fail to obey the said Charge, then after the said Charge is elapsed, to Poind their readiest Goods, Gear, Debts, and other effects; and if needful for effecting the said Poinding Grant Warrant to Open all shut and lockfast places, in form as effeirs.

Release 33: 15 August 1994

NOTE
[1] N.B. When the Church of Scotland General Trustees are the Pursuers or the Pursuer's stipend has been standardised, this form may be applied *mutatis mutandis*.

SCHEDULE C

Form of Warrant of Charge in terms of the Debtors (Scotland) Act 1838, ss.1 and 8

And the said Lords, as Commissioners foresaid, Grant Warrant to Messengers-at-Arms, in His Majesty's name and authority, to charge the foresaid titulars and tacksmen of Teinds, Heritors, Feuars, Farmorers, Wadsetters, Liferenters, Factors, Chamberlains, Tenants, Occupiers, and Possessors of the Lands and other intromitters with the Rents and Teinds of the said Parish of   personally, or at their respective dwelling-places, if within Scotland, or if furth thereof, by delivering a Copy of Charge at the Office of the Keeper of the Record of Edictal Citations at Edinburgh, to make payment of the foresaid Stipend and Communion Element Money, each of them for his or her own part and portion thereof, conform to the Division and Locality inserted in the great decerniture of the foregoing Decreet, and that at the terms of payment therein the victual betwixt Yule and Candlemas yearly after the separation of the crop above written, and here referred to, and held as repeated *brevitatis causa*; and that to the Reverend   now Minister of the Parish of   within ten days, if within Scotland, and if furth thereof, within sixty days after they are respectively charged to that effect, under pain of Poinding, the terms of payment being always first come and bygone; And also Grant Warrant to Arrest the foresaid Defenders' readiest Goods, Gear, Debts, and sums of Money, in payment and satisfaction of their respective portions of the aforesaid Stipend and Communion Element Money; and if the said Defenders fail to obey the said Charge, then after the said Charge is elapsed, to Poind their readiest Goods, Gear, and other effects; and if needful for effecting the said Poinding, Grant Warrant to Open all shut and lockfast places, in form as effeirs.—Given at Edinburgh, the   day of   One thousand nine hundred and

Procedure relating to the Preparation, Issuing, Adjustment, and Custody of Teind Rolls under the Church of Scotland (Property and Endowments) Act 1925

(S.R. & O. 1925 No. 1063)

[28th October 1925]

The Lords of Council and Session, in pursuance of the powers vested in them by the Church of Scotland (Property and Endowments) Act 1925, enact and declare as follows, viz.:—

1. A teind roll of a parish shall be prepared on application to the Court of Teinds by Petition at the instance of the Church of Scotland General Trustees.

2. The Petition may be presented at any time after the date of standardisation of the stipend of the parish provided that:
   (a) a final decree of locality following upon any application for an augmentation of stipend under section 10 of the foresaid Act has been pronounced; or
   (b) the time within which proceedings under section 10(2) of the foresaid Act may be taken has expired; or
   (c) the General Trustees state in the Petition that it is not intended to make any application under section 10 of the foresaid Act.

3. The Petition may be in the form of the Schedule hereto annexed.

4. All petitions shall be enrolled in the Teind Motion Roll of the Lord Ordinary for an order for intimation. It shall be sufficient intimation to all parties concerned that a copy of the Petition be affixed to the most patent door of the church of the parish to which the application applies on two successive Sundays before the diet of public worship on each of these days, and a notice intimating the Petition be inserted in the *Scotsman* newspaper, and in a newspaper circulating in the county in which the parish referred to in said notice is situated, once a week for two successive weeks in each of such newspapers, provided always that the Lord Ordinary may make such other or further order regarding intimation as he may consider to be necessary or expedient in the circumstances of the case.

5. After the period of intimation ordered by the Lord Ordinary has expired, the Petition may be enrolled for an order as follows, viz.:—

    (a) *If a state of teinds has been lodged with the Clerk of Teinds by the titulars or heritors,* for a remit to the Clerk to prepare a teind roll.

    (b) *If no state of teinds has been so lodged* (and unless an application under paragraph 6 hereof shall be granted), for an order on the heritors to meet and choose a common agent, and to lodge a state of teinds within a time to be specified in such order, and upon such state of teinds being lodged for a remit to the Clerk to prepare a teind roll.

6. On enrolment under paragraph 5 hereof, the petitioners or any heritor or titular may apply by motion to dispense with the appointment of a common agent and also (if the circumstances justify that course) with the preparation and lodging by the heritors of a state of teinds.

7. In any case in which application is made to dispense with the appointment by the heritors of a common agent the Lord Ordinary may by interlocutor make such orders with regard to the conduct of the process as he may think just and expedient, and may require as a condition of granting the application that the party applying shall make such provision as to the court may appear just and sufficient for the payment of the fee fund dues, including the expense of preparing the teind roll.

8. In any case in which the preparation and lodging of a state of teinds by the heritors is dispensed with, the Lord Ordinary shall remit to the Clerk of Teinds to prepare and lodge a teind roll according to the state of the teinds as disclosed in the last locality process.

9. The procedure for the appointment of a common agent shall be the same *mutatis mutandis* as for the appointment of a common agent in a process of locality.

10. After the teind roll has been prepared the clerk shall print and report the same to the Lord Ordinary, who shall take the roll into consideration and shall make such order as he shall think fit with respect to intimation of the roll by advertisement or on the church door or otherwise (including where necessary an order on the heritors for the appointment of a common agent in the event of such appointment having been formerly dispensed with).

11. The teind roll shall be retained in the hands of the clerk subject to inspection by any party interested, and shall not be lent or given out to any person whatsoever. But after the Lord Ordinary has made an order for intimation printed copies may be supplied to the common agent for distribution among the heritors, and where there is no common agent to any heritor who applies.

12. The Lord Ordinary shall either hear parties *viva voce* upon such objections as may be lodged within eighteen months after the order for intimation of the teind roll, and upon any answers that may be made thereto at the Bar; or he may, if he shall see cause, allow all concerned to give in written answers to such objections within such time as he shall think proper to appoint, and shall thereafter proceed, in so far as regards any application for prorogating the time for giving in papers, in the manner directed by section 12 of the Court of Session Act 1825[1].

NOTE

[1] Now repealed: see the Court of Session Act 1988 (c. 36), Sched. 2, Pts. I and III.

13. After (*a*) the objections (if any) to the teind roll have been disposed of by the Court, and (*b*) any extrajudicial surrenders of teind made before the passing of the said Church of Scotland (Property and Endowments) Act 1925, have been intimated, and evidence thereof produced, to the clerk (which shall be done before the expiry of six months after the date of the order for intimation of the teind roll), and (*c*) any surrenders of teind made in accordance with the provisions of the Sixth Schedule of the said Church of Scotland (Property and Endowments) Act 1925, have become effectual, and (*d*) intimation has been received by the clerk claiming that the deficiency of stipend caused by such surrenders shall be reallocated among the heritors in the parish who have unexhausted teinds not yet allocated for stipend, and (*e*) objections, if any, of any heritor to such reallocation have been disposed of by the Lord Ordinary, a remit shall be made to the clerk to amend the roll, and if, in virtue of the amendments, the Lord Ordinary shall deem it necessary, he may order the clerk to reprint the roll as amended before declaring the roll to be final.

14. After the Lord Ordinary has by interlocutor declared the roll to be final he shall, where a common agent has been appointed, direct that an account of the expenses incurred to the common agent be lodged in process, and when lodged remit the same to the auditor to tax and report; and after approving of such report, shall grant decree against the heritors in favour of the common agent for the taxed amount of the expenses as approved, and for the expense of extracting the decree and proportioning the same in accordance with a scheme of apportionment thereof prepared by the clerk in terms of the provisions of section 11 (3) of the said Church of Scotland (Property and Endowments) Act 1925.

15. Except in the cases specified in the said Church of Scotland (Property and Endowments) Act 1925, in which the finding or judgment of the Lord Ordinary is declared to be final, any judgment of the Lord Ordinary may be submitted to review by the Division to which the cause belongs by giving in a Note, which must be lodged within twenty-one days after the date of the finding or judgment complained of, and the procedure on that Note shall be the same as in reviewing judgments of a Lord Ordinary in the Court of Session.

16. The clerk shall, on receiving notice of any change of ownership of the lands contained in one entry in the teind roll in respect of which lands a standard charge has been constituted in accordance with the provisions of section 12 of the said Church of Scotland (Property and Endowments) Act 1925, insert in the teind roll the name of the new proprietor as stated in said notice; such notice may be in the form of Schedule A annexed to the Conveyancing (Scotland) Act 1874, provided always that notice of change of ownership of part only of an entry in the teind roll shall be given effect to by the clerk only where the provisions of section 13 of the said Church of Scotland (Property and Endowments) Act 1925, are complied with in said notice.

17. Where a standard charge has been constituted on the lands of any heritor in terms of the provisions of section 12 of the said Church of Scotland (Property and Endowments) Act 1925, and the same has been redeemed in accordance with the provisions of that section, or where a stipend exigible from the teinds of any lands of a heritor has been redeemed in accordance with the provisions of section 14 of the last-mentioned Act, the clerk shall, on receiving notice in writing of such redemption signed on behalf of the General Trustees and the owner of the lands the standard charge on which has been redeemed, or of the lands the stipend in respect whereof has been redeemed, make an entry to that effect in the teind roll.

18. An excerpt from a teind roll of any entry or entries therein certified by the Clerk of Teinds shall be received in any Court of Law as sufficient evidence of such entry or entries.

SCHEDULE REFERRED TO

UNTO THE RIGHT HONOURABLE

THE LORDS OF COUNCIL AND SESSION,
COMMISSIONERS FOR THE PLANTATION OF KIRKS AND VALUATION OF
TEINDS,

THE
PETITION
OF
THE CHURCH OF SCOTLAND GENERAL TRUSTEES, incorporated by the Church of
Scotland (General Trustees) Order 1921;

Humbly sheweth,—

THAT by the Church of Scotland (Property and Endowments) Act 1925, section 11, it is provided, *inter alia*, that "There shall be prepared by the Clerk of Teinds for every parish in Scotland a Teind Roll specifying in sterling money (*a*) the total teind of that parish; and (*b*) the amount of that total applicable to the lands of each heritor; and (*c*) the value of the whole stipend payable to the minister, so far as payable out of teinds, including vicarage teinds payable as stipend and surrendered teinds so payable; and (*d*) the proportion of that value payable by each heritor in the parish."

That the stipend[s] of the Minister[s] of the [United] Parish[es] of [   ] in the Presbytery of [   ] and County [or Counties] of [   ], became standardised within the meaning of the foresaid Act as at the term of Martinmas 19[   ], in consequence of the [death, resignation or translation of the Minister, or intimation in terms of section 4 of the said Act by the Minister to the petitioners of his election, or notification in terms of section 5 of said Act by the petitioners to the Minister and other parties mentioned in the said section—*the particulars and dates should be shortly stated*].

That the final augmentation in terms of section 10 of said Act has been localled upon the heritors conform to Decree of Locality made final on [*give date*]: *or* That no proceedings are to be taken to obtain an augmentation under section 10 of said Act: *or* That the Lord Ordinary has pronounced a finding that there is no surplus teind in the parish available for an augmentation under section 10 of said Act: *or* That the time within which proceedings under section 10 (2) of the foresaid Act may be taken has expired.

That in these circumstances the preparation of a Teind Roll of the Parish[es] of [   ] should now be proceeded with in terms of section 11 of the said Act.

May it therefore please your Lordships to appoint this Petition to be intimated to all parties concerned by affixing a copy thereof to the most patent door of the church of the said parish[es] on two successive Sundays before the diet of public worship on each of these days, and by inserting a short notice thereof in the Scotsman newspaper and in [another newspaper circulating in the county in which the said parish[es] [are] situated] *once a week for two successive weeks, or in such other or further form and manner as to your Lordships may seem proper; to appoint the heritors of the said parish[es] of   to meet and choose a common agent; to appoint said heritors to lodge a State of Teinds; to remit to the Clerk of Teinds to prepare a Teind Roll in terms of said Act 15 & 16 Geo. 5, c. 33, and upon the Teind Roll being reported to your Lordships, and after considering the same with any Objections and any Answers thereto and along with any Surrenders of Teinds that may be duly made, to adjust and complete said Roll, and to declare the same to be a Final Teind Roll.*

According to Justice, etc.

Intimation of Decrees registered in the Books of Council and Session pursuant to the Indian and Colonial Divorce Jurisdiction Act 1926

(S.R. & O. 1927 No. 1054)

[1st November 1927]

The Lords of Council and Session, considering that by section 1, subsection 3 of the Indian and Colonial Divorce Act, it is enacted that:—
On production of a Certificate purporting to be signed by the proper officer of the High Court in India by which Decree of Divorce is made, the decree shall, if the parties to the marriage are domiciled in Scotland, be registered in the Books of Council and Session and upon such registration shall as from the date of registration, have the same force and effect, and proceedings may be taken thereunder as if it had been a decree made by the Court of Session on that date on which it was made by the High Court in India
do hereby enact and declare that it shall be the duty of the Keeper of the Register of Deeds in the Books of Council and Session on the registration of any such Decree to supply an Extract of same to the Registrar General and that without fee.

Amending the Four Acts of Sederunt dated 10th July 1811, and the Act of Sederunt dated 18th February 1916, anent the Various Public Registers of Scotland, and making Further Regulations thereanent

(S.R. & O. 1934 No. 97)

[2nd February 1934]

The Lords of Council and Session considering that by four Acts of Sederunt of date 10th July 1811, it was *inter alia* provided that the various Minute Books and Registers therein referred to should be written in books issued and marked to the Keepers of the said Minute Books and Registers by the Lord Clerk Register or the Deputy Clerk Register, and that by the Lord Clerk Register (Scotland) Act 1879, s.6, it was provided that the Deputy Clerk Register should have the whole rights, authorities, privileges and duties in regard to the Public Registers, Records or Rolls of Scotland theretofore vested in the Lord Clerk Register. And considering that the foresaid Acts of Sederunt contained certain regulations and directions regarding the quality of paper, the number of lines and the numbers of words to be written on each page of the books to be issued and marked as aforesaid and that by an Act of Sederunt of date 18th February 1916 it was *inter alia* provided that the Deputy Clerk Register should have power to vary these regulations and directions from time to time as might be necessary, and that after the date of the passing of that Act the regulations and directions to be observed by the Keepers of the various Registers should be such as might from time to time be set forth on the title page of the volumes to be marked and issued to them as aforesaid. And considering that it was further declared that if at any time thereafter it should be necessary, in order to facilitate new methods of framing all or any of the various Registers, the books to be marked and issued as aforesaid might be so marked and issued in an unbound form or otherwise as the Deputy Clerk Register might direct. And further considering that by the Reorganisation of Offices (Scotland) Act 1928, s. 5 (1), it was provided that the whole powers and duties of the Deputy Clerk Register should be transferred to and vested in the Keeper of the Registers and Records of Scotland.
And now seeing that it is expedient that a photographic process of copy-

ing writs should be substituted for typing in the Department of the Registers and Records of Scotland and that this process does not permit of the issuing of marked volumes in conformity with the practice enjoined by the foresaid Acts of Sederunt, the Lords hereby enact and enjoin that after the date of the passing of this Act a photographic process of copying writs may be introduced in substitution for typing under such conditions and subject to such regulations and at such time or times as the Keeper of the Registers and Records may deem expedient, and that thereafter it shall not be necessary to issue marked volumes in conformity with the said practice, except to the Town Clerks of those Burghs in which the Burgh Registers have not been discontinued, and to Sheriff Clerks for the Register of Deeds in the Sheriff Court Books.

And the Lords do further declare that if, after the introduction of a photographic process, any writ presented for registration be found unsuitable for the process, owing to its illegibility or inconvenient size or for any other reason, the Keeper of the Registers and Records may cause such writ to be typed in the manner heretofore in use, and the copy of the writ so typed shall form part of the Record in the same way as a copy of a writ reproduced by the photographic process.

And the Lords do further enact that the photographic record of the various Registers, along with the record of any writ or writs typed as aforesaid, shall be made up into bound volumes of such a size and form as may be found convenient, which volumes shall be authenticated on the first and last pages thereof by the signature of the Keeper of the Registers and Records, and shall be open to the lieges at such times and under such conditions as are at present applicable to the Public Records as hitherto framed and preserved in H.M. General Register House, or at such other times and under such other conditions as may be prescribed.

And the Lords further enact that if at any time difficulties emerge which, in the opinion of the Keeper of the Registers and Records, might constitute a danger to the safety or accessibility of the Public Registers, it shall be the duty of the said Keeper to report the same to the Lords of Council and Session.

Edictal Citations, Commissary Petitions and Petitions of Service

(S.I. 1971 No. 1165)

[16th July 1971]

The Lords of Council and Session, by virtue of the powers conferred upon them by sections 16 and 34 of the Administration of Justice (Scotland) Act 1933 and section 22 of the Succession (Scotland) Act 1964 and of all other powers competent to them in that behalf, do hereby enact and declare as follows:—

1. [Revoked by S.I. 1994 No. 1443.]

2.—(1) The provisions of section 4 of the Confirmation and Probate Act 1858, in so far as they prescribe procedure in petitions for the appointment of an executor, shall no longer apply.

(2) Every petition for the appointment of an executor shall be intimated by the Sheriff Clerk affixing a full copy of the petition on the door of the Sheriff Court house or in some conspicuous place of the Court or of the office of the Sheriff Clerk, in such manner as the Sheriff shall direct.

3.—(1) The provisions of section 30 of the Titles to Land Consolidation (Scotland) Act 1868, as saved by section 37 of the Succession (Scotland) Act 1964, in so far as they prescribe procedure in petitions of service, shall no longer apply.

(2) A petition presented to the Sheriff of Chancery for general service, where the domicile of the deceased is known and was within Scotland, shall not proceed until the Sheriff Clerk of Chancery shall have received official notice from the sheriff clerk of the county of the domicile of the person deceased that publication has been made in such county, and such publication shall be effected by affixing an abstract of the petition on the door of the sheriff court house or in some conspicuous place of the court or of the office of the sheriff clerk, in such manner as the sheriff of the county shall direct.

(3) A petition presented to the Sheriff of Chancery for Special Service or a petition presented to the Sheriff of Chancery under section 10 of the Conveyancing (Scotland) Act 1874, shall not proceed until the Sheriff Clerk of Chancery shall have received official notice (i) from the sheriff clerk of the county or of each of the counties in which the lands are situated that publication has been made in such county or in each such county as the case may be, and either (ii) where the domicile of the deceased is known and was within Scotland, from the sheriff clerk of the county of the domicile of the person deceased that publication has been made in such county, or (iii) where the domicile of the deceased is furth of Scotland or is unknown, from the sheriff clerk of the Lothians and Peebles at Edinburgh that publication has been made at Edinburgh; and each such publication shall be effected by affixing an abstract of the petition on the door of the sheriff court house or in some conspicuous place of the court or of the office of the sheriff clerk, in such manner as the sheriff of the county or counties shall direct.

(4) A petition presented to the Sheriff of Chancery for General Service, where the domicile of the deceased was furth of Scotland or where such domicile is unknown and the person deceased died more than ten years prior to the presentation of the petition, shall not proceed until the Sheriff Clerk of Chancery shall have received official notice from the Sheriff Clerk of the Lothians and Peebles at Edinburgh that publication has been made at Edinburgh, and such publication shall be effected by affixing an abstract of the petition on the door of the sheriff court house or in some conspicuous place of the court or of the office of the sheriff clerk, in such manner as the Sheriff of the Lothians and Peebles shall direct.

(5) In each such petition as aforesaid, no further publication shall be necessary.

4. This Act of Sederunt may be cited as the Act of Sederunt (Edictal Citations, Commissary Petitions and Petitions of Service) 1971, and shall come into operation on 16th August 1971.

Expenses of Party Litigants

(S.I. 1976 No. 1606)

[28th September 1976]

The Lords of Council and Session, under and by virtue of the powers conferred upon them by section 16 of the Administration of Justice (Scotland) Act 1933, section 32 of the Sheriff Courts (Scotland) Act 1971, and section 1 of the Litigants in Person (Costs and Expenses) Act 1975, and of all other powers competent to them in that behalf, do hereby enact and declare:—

Citation, commencement and interpretation
    1.—(1) This Act of Sederunt may be cited as the Act of Sederunt (Expenses of Party Litigants) 1976 and shall come into operation on 1st October 1976.

(2) The Interpretation Act 1889 shall apply for the interpretation of this Act of Sederunt as it applies for the interpretation of an Act of Parliament.

Expenses allowable to party litigants
[1] **2.**—(1) Where in any proceedings in the Court of Session or the sheriff court, any expenses of a party litigant are ordered to be paid by any other party to the proceedings or in any other way, the auditor may, subject to the following provisions of this Rule, allow as expenses such sums as appear to the auditor to be reasonable having regard to all the circumstances in respect of—

(*a*) work done which was reasonably required in connection with the cause, up to the maximum of two-thirds of the sum allowable to a solicitor for that work under the table of fees for solicitors in judicial proceedings; and

(*b*) outlays reasonably incurred for the proper conduct of the cause.

(2) Without prejudice to the generality of paragraph (1) above, the circumstances to which the auditor shall have regard in determining what sum, if any, to allow in respect of any work done, shall include—

(*a*) the nature of the work;

(*b*) the time taken and the time reasonably required to do the work;

(*c*) the amount of time spent in respect of which there is no loss of earnings;

(*d*) the amount of any earnings lost during the time required to do the work;

(*e*) the importance of the cause to the party litigant;

(*f*) the complexity of the issues involved in the cause.

(3) In this Rule—

(*a*) the word "auditor" includes any person taxing or otherwise determining a claim for expenses incurred in any proceedings in the Court of Session or in the sheriff court;

(*b*) the expression "remunerative time" in relation to a litigant, means time when he is earning or would have been earning but for work done in or in connection with proceedings in court;

(*c*) the expression "leisure time" in relation to a litigant, means time other than remunerative time.

(*d*) the expression "table of fees for solicitors in judicial proceedings" means—

(i) in relation to a cause in the Court of Session, the table of fees in Rule 347 of the Rules of Court in force at the time the work is done; and

(ii) in relation to an ordinary action in the Sheriff Court, the table of fees in Schedule 2 to the Act of Sederunt (Alteration of Sheriff Court Fees) 1971 in force at the time the work is done.

NOTE
[1] As amended by S.I. 1983 No. 1438. For table of fees, see now Chapter 42 of the Rules of the Court of Session 1994, or Sched. 1 to the Act of Sederunt (Fees of Solicitors in the Sheriff Court) (Amendment and further Provisions) 1993, as amended.

Messengers-at-Arms and Sheriff Officers Rules 1991

(S.I. 1991 No. 1397)

[15th July 1991]

ARRANGEMENT OF RULES

PART I

INTRODUCTORY

27.   Appeals
28.   Suspension under particular rules

The Lords of Council and Session, under and by virtue of the powers conferred on them by section 75 of the Debtors (Scotland) Act 1987 and of all other powers enabling them in that behalf, do hereby enact and declare:—

PART I

INTRODUCTORY

Citation, commencement and revocation
1.—(1) This Act of Sederunt may be cited as the Act of Sederunt (Messengers-at-Arms and Sheriff Officers Rules) 1991 and shall come into force on 15th July 1991.

(2) The Act of Sederunt (Messengers-at-Arms and Sheriff Officers Rules) 1988 is hereby revoked.

(3) This Act of Sederunt shall be inserted in the Books of Sederunt.

Interpretation
2.—[1] (1) In this Act of Sederunt unless the context otherwise requires
    "the Act of 1987" means the Debtors (Scotland) Act 1987;
    "committee of examiners" means the committee appointed under rule
        6(1) below;
    "Lyon Clerk" means the Lyon Clerk and Keeper of the Records;
    "Lord Lyon" means the Lord Lyon King of Arms;
    "Lord President" means the Lord President of the Court of Session;
    "nominated sheriff clerk" means a sheriff clerk nominated by the
        Secretary of State for the purposes of this Act of Sederunt;
    "Policy" means, except in Schedule 2, the single document referred to
        in rule 9(2) below;
    "sheriff clerk" means the sheriff clerk of the sheriff court in which the
        application for a commission as a sheriff officer was granted; and
    "the Society" means the Society of Messengers-at-Arms and Sheriff
        Officers.

(2) A reference to a specified form in this Act of Sederunt means the forms so specified in Schedule 1 to this Act of Sederunt or a form substantially to the same effect with such variation as circumstances may require.

NOTE
[1] As amended by S.I. 1998 No. 2636, r. 2 (effective December 1, 1998).

PART II

QUALIFICATIONS, TRAINING AND EXAMINATIONS

Qualification as officer of court

3.—(1) Subject to paragraph (3) below, a person may not be an officer of court unless—

 (a) he has attained the age of 20 years;

 (b) he is not over the age of 70 years.

 (c) subject to rule 5(2) below, he has undergone a period of training for three years with a person who is in practice as an officer of court;

 (d) the officer of court with whom he has undergone a period of training has issued a certificate stating that the period of training has been completed satisfactorily;

 (e) within five years before applying for a commission as a sheriff officer, he has passed all such examinations as may be required by the committee of examiners; and

 (f) he has attained the educational standard determined by the committee of examiners.

(2) An officer of court shall retire from practice as an officer of court on attaining the age of 70 years.

(3) Paragraph (1) of this rule shall not apply to a person who was in practice as an officer of court on 30th November 1988.

(4) Paragraph (2) of this rule shall not apply to a person who was—

 (a) in practice as an officer of court, and

 (b) aged 70 years or over,

on 30th November 1988.

Qualification as messenger-at-arms

4.—(1) A sheriff officer may not become a messenger-at-arms unless—

 (a) subject to paragraph (2) below, he has been in practice as a sheriff officer for a period of not less than two years; and

 (b) within five years before applying to the Court of Session for recommendation for appointment as a messenger-at-arms, he has passed all such examinations as may be required by the committee of examiners.

(2) The Court of Session may, in an application to which rule 7 below applies, on special cause shown, reduce the period of practice required under paragraph (1)(a) above.

Training

5.—(1) An officer of court shall be responsible for the training required by rule 3(1)(c) above of any person whom he employs for the purpose of becoming an officer of court.

(2) The sheriff principal of the sheriffdom to whom an application for a first commission as a sheriff officer under rule 8(1) below is made may, having regard to the previous experience of the applicant, on the written application of that person, reduce the period of training to a period of not less than one year.

Examinations

6.—(1) The Society shall appoint a committee of examiners to examine any person who seeks to apply to become an officer of court.

(2) The committee of examiners shall consist of not more than five persons of whom—

 (a) not more than three shall be members of the Society nominated by the Society;

 (b) one shall be a solicitor nominated by the Law Society of Scotland; and

(c) one shall not be a member of the Society but shall be nominated by the Society, in consultation with the sheriffs principal and approved by the Lord President.

(3) The committee of examiners, in consultation with the Society, shall be responsible for—

(a) determining the educational standard required of candidates;

(b) setting examination papers; and

(c) regulating and fixing fees for examinations.

PART III

APPLICATIONS FOR COMMISSION

Applications for recommendation for commission as messenger-at-arms

7.—(1) An application by a sheriff officer for recommendation for a commission as a messenger-at-arms under section 77(1) of the Act of 1987 shall be by petition presented to the Outer House of the Court of Session in Form 1 and signed by the petitioner or his solicitor.

(2) There shall be lodged with a petition under paragraph (1) above—

(a) an inventory of productions;

(b) a copy of the entry in the Register of Births relating to the petitioner;

(c) a certificate from the Society that the petitioner has passed such examinations as may be required by the committee of examiners; and

(d) a certificate from another officer of court stating the period that the petitioner has been in practice as a sheriff officer.

(3) A petition under paragraph (1) above shall not require a process and shall not be intimated on the walls of court, served or advertised.

(4) Where the court grants the prayer of such a petition, the clerk of the Petition Department of the Court of Session shall send a copy of the petition, with interlocutor granting the prayer written on it, to the Lyon Clerk.

[1] (5) Subject to rule 11(10) below, the Lord Lyon shall not issue a commission to a sheriff officer as a messenger-at-arms until the sheriff officer has lodged with the Lyon Clerk—

(a) a copy letter of receipt of a premium receipt issued by a nominated sheriff clerk in terms of rule 10(3) below; and

(b) such further evidence as the Lord Lyon may require that the Policy in respect of which the premium receipt was issued is in force and applies to the commission of the sheriff officer as a messenger-at-arms.

(6) When the Lord Lyon issues a sheriff officer with a commission as a messenger-at-arms under section 77(1) of the Act of 1987, he shall administer to him the oath or declaration of allegiance to the Sovereign and the oath or declaration *de fideli administratione officii.*

(7) A commission as a messenger-at-arms shall cease to have effect when the holder of it attains the age of 70 years.

(8) Paragraph (7) of this rule shall not apply to a person who was—

(a) in practice as a messenger-at-arms, and

(b) aged 70 years or over,

on 30th November 1988.

NOTE
[1]As amended by S.I. 1998 No. 2636, r. 2 (effective December 1, 1998).

Application for commission as sheriff officer

8.—(1) An application by a person for a commission as a sheriff officer in a particular sheriffdom or a particular district of a sheriffdom shall be by initial writ in a summary application in Form 2 to the sheriff principal in such sheriff court as the sheriff principal shall direct and shall be signed by the applicant or his solicitor.

(2) There shall be lodged with an initial writ under paragraph (1) of this rule—

(a) an inventory of productions;

(b) a copy of the entry in the Register of Births relating to the applicant;

(c) the certificate required by rule 3(1)(d) above;

(d) a certificate from the Society to the effect that the applicant has passed such examinations as may be required by the committee of examiners; and

(e) two references of good character.

(3) An application under paragraph (1) above shall not be served but shall be ordered to be—

(a) intimated on the walls of every sheriff court in the sheriffdom or district of the sheriffdom for which appointment as a sheriff officer is sought; and

(b) advertised once in Form 3 in such newspapers circulating in the sheriffdom as the sheriff principal shall require.

(4) A person who intends to object to such an application shall lodge answers to the application with the sheriff clerk within 30 days from the date of such intimation and advertisement.

(5) Where the sheriff principal is satisfied that the applicant is suitably qualified, and is a fit and proper person, to be a sheriff officer, he may grant to the applicant a commission as sheriff officer in his sheriffdom or a district within that sheriffdom.

(6) Subject to paragraph (7) and rule 11(11) below the sheriff principal shall not issue a commission to a sheriff officer until the sheriff officer has sent to the sheriff principal—

(a) the Policy required under rule 9 below; or

(b) evidence satisfactory to the sheriff principal that the sheriff officer is covered by an existing Policy,

together with such further evidence as the sheriff principal may require that the Policy is in force and applies to the sheriff officer.

[1] (7) In the application of paragraph (6) above in a case where the sheriff officer already holds a commission as a sheriff officer, it shall be sufficient for the sheriff officer to send to the sheriff principal—

(a) a copy letter of receipt of a premium receipt, issued by the nominated sheriff clerk under rule 10(3) below; and

(b) such further evidence as the sheriff principal may require that the Policy in respect of which the premium was issued is in force and applies to the commission of the sheriff officer in his sheriffdom.

(8) When the sheriff principal issues a commission to a sheriff officer he, or a sheriff, shall administer to the sheriff officer the oath or declaration *de fideli administratione officii*.

(9) Where a person intends to apply to be a sheriff officer in more than one sheriffdom, he shall make a summary application under paragraph (1) of this rule in each sheriffdom in which he seeks to be appointed as sheriff officer.

(10) Where a sheriff officer is issued with a further commission as a sheriff officer in a sheriffdom other than the sheriffdom in which he first obtained a commission, he shall intimate a copy of his subsequent commission, certified by the sheriff clerk, to the sheriff principal of each sheriffdom in which he already holds a commission as a sheriff officer.

(11) Where a messenger-at-arms is issued with a further commission as a sheriff officer he shall intimate a copy of that commission, certified by the sheriff clerk, to the Lord Lyon.

(12) A commission as a sheriff officer shall cease to have effect when the holder of it attains the age of 70 years.

(13) Paragraph (12) of this rule shall not apply to a person who was—

(a) in practice as a sheriff officer, and

(b) aged 70 years or over,

on 30th November 1988.

NOTE
¹As amended by S.I. 1998 No. 2636, r.2 (effective December 1, 1998).

PART IV

THE POLICY

Caution and professional indemnity insurance
9.—(1) An officer of court and any partnership of officers of court shall be
covered by—
  (a) a bond of caution to the value of not less than £50,000 in respect of
each claim covering each commission held by each officer of court to
whom the bond of caution applies as sheriff officer and, where
applicable, as a messenger-at-arms, and
  (b) a policy of professional indemnity insurance for not less than
£100,000 in respect of each claim—
    (i) in the case of an officer of court, covering each commission held
by him as a sheriff officer and, where applicable, as a messenger-
at-arms, and any employee of the officer of court; and
    (ii) in the case of a partnership of officers of court, covering the firm,
any partner of the firm in respect of each commission held by
him as a sheriff officer and, where applicable, as a messenger-at-
arms, and any employee of the firm.
  (2) The bond of caution and policy of professional indemnity insurance
required under paragraph (1) above shall be incorporated in a single
document and shall be—
  (a) in such terms as may be approved by the sheriffs principal and the
Lord Lyon;
² (b) obtained from a person who may give a bond of caution or other
security under rule 33.5 of the Rules of the Court of Session;
  (c) renewed annually.

NOTES
  ¹ As amended by S.S.I. 2000 No. 30, para.2(2) (effective March 11, 2000).
  ² Substituted by S.S.I. 2005 No. 199 (effective April 14, 2005).

Renewals of policy
  10.—² (1) Each year every officer of court shall, within 30 days after the
expiry of the current Policy, lodge, in accordance with the following
paragraphs of this rule, a premium receipt from a person referred to in rule
9(2)(b) above stating that he is covered by a Policy in accordance with rule 9
above.
  (2) There shall be sent to the sheriff principal of the sheriffdom in which
the first current commission of the officer of court as a sheriff was granted—
  (a) the premium receipt referred to in paragraph (1) above; and
  (b) such further evidence as the sheriff principal may require that the
Policy in respect of which the premium receipt was issued is in force
and applies to the sheriff officer.
  ¹ (3) On being satisfied as to the premium receipt and any further evidence
sent to him under paragraph (2) above, the sheriff principal shall cause the
premium receipt to be lodged with the nominated sheriff clerk who shall
issue to the officer of court a letter of receipt of such premium receipt and
such copy letters of receipt as may reasonably be required by the officer of
court.
  ¹ (4) Where an officer of court holds a commission as a sheriff officer in
more than one sheriffdom, he shall send to the sheriff principal of every
sheriffdom in which he holds a commission (other than the first current
commission)—
  (a) a copy letter of receipt of such a premium receipt issued by the
nominated sheriff clerk; and

(b) such further evidence as the sheriff principal may require that the
Policy in respect of which the premium receipt was issued is in force
and applies to the commission of the sheriff officer in his sheriffdom.

[1] (5) Where an officer of court is also a messenger-at-arms, he shall send
to the Lyon Clerk—

(a) a copy letter of receipt of such a premium receipt issued by the
nominated sheriff clerk in respect of his commission as a sheriff
officer; and

(b) such further evidence as the Lord Lyon may require that the Policy in
respect of which the premium receipt was issued is in force and applies
to the commission of the officer of court as a messenger-at-arms.

(6) Where an officer of court fails to lodge a premium receipt under
paragraph (1) above—

(a) in respect of any commission as a sheriff officer, the sheriff principal
may suspend the officer of court from practice as a sheriff officer; and

(b) where applicable, in respect of his commission as a messenger-at-
arms, a Lord Ordinary may, following a report sent to the Deputy
Principal Clerk of Session by the Lyon Clerk, suspend the officer of
court from practice as a messenger-at-arms.

(7) Where an officer of court has been suspended under paragraph (6)
above, and subsequently lodges a premium receipt under paragraph (1)
above, the sheriff principal and, where applicable, in respect of his
commission as a messenger-at-arms a Lord Ordinary may recall his
suspension.

NOTES
[1] As amended by S.I. 1998 No. 2636, r.2 (effective December 1, 1998).
[2] As amended by S.S.I. 2005 No. 199 (effective April 14, 2005).

Transitional provisions
    11.—(1) This rule applies to officers of court who are in practice on the
date on which this Act of Sederunt comes into force.

[1] (2) In this rule—

(a) "the operative date" means the date on which this Act of Sederunt
comes into force;

(b) "the compliance date" in respect of an officer of court means
whichever shall first occur of—

(i) the date on which the bond of caution in respect of that officer of
court current on the operative date expires;

(ii) where more than one bond of caution is current in respect of that
officer of court on the operative date, the date on which the first
such bond expires;

(iii) the date on which the policy of professional indemnity insurance
current in respect of that officer of court on the operative date
expires; and

(iv) where more than one such policy of professional indemnity
insurance is current in respect of that officer of court on the
operative date, the date on which the first such policy expires;
and

(c) "the prescribed documents" means—

(i) a copy letter of receipt issued by a nominated sheriff clerk in
respect of the bond of caution required under paragraph 1 of
Schedule 2; and

(ii) a copy letter of receipt issued by a nominated sheriff clerk in
respect of a copy premium receipt from an insurance company
for the policy of professional indemnity insurance required under
paragraph 2 of Schedule 2.

(3) Within 30 days of the compliance date an officer of court shall send a
Policy, together with such further evidence as the sheriff principal may

require that the Policy is in force and applies to the officer of court, to the sheriff principal of the sheriffdom in which his first current commission as a sheriff officer was granted.

(4) On being satisfied as to the Policy and any further evidence furnished under paragraph (3) above, the sheriff principal shall cause the Policy and any such further evidence to be transmitted to the regional sheriff clerk who shall issue to the officer of court a letter of receipt of the Policy and such copy letters of receipt as may reasonably be required by the officer of court.

[1] (5) Where an officer of court holds a commission as a sheriff officer in more than one sheriffdom, he shall send to the sheriff principal of every sheriffdom in which he holds a commission (other than the first current commission)—

(a) a copy letter of receipt of the Policy issued by the nominated sheriff clerk under paragraph (4) above; and

(b) such further evidence as the sheriff principal may require that the Policy is in force and applies to the commission of the sheriff officer in his sheriffdom.

[1] (6) Where an officer of court is also a messenger-at-arms, he shall send to the Lyon Clerk—

(a) a copy letter of receipt of the Policy issued by the nominated sheriff clerk in respect of his commission as a sheriff officer; and

(b) such further evidence as the Lord Lyon may require that the Policy is in force and applies to the commission of the officer of court as a messenger-at-arms.

(7) Where an officer of court fails to lodge a Policy under paragraph (3) above—

(a) in respect of any commission as a sheriff officer, the sheriff principal may suspend the officer of court from practice as a sheriff officer; and

(b) where applicable, in respect of his commission as a messenger-at-arms, a Lord Ordinary may, following a report sent to the Deputy Principal Clerk of Session by the Lyon Clerk, suspend the officer of court from practice as a messenger-at-arms.

(8) Where an officer of court has been suspended under paragraph (7) above and subsequently lodges a Policy under paragraph (3) above the sheriff principal and, where applicable, in respect of his commission as a messenger-at-arms, a Lord Ordinary may recall his suspension.

(9) Until the compliance date, an officer of court shall comply with Schedule 2 to this Act of Sederunt.

(10) Where an officer of court—

(a) applies for recommendation for a commission as a messenger-at-arms; and

(b) the prayer of the petition under rule 7(1) above is granted before the compliance date in respect of that officer of court,

notwithstanding rule 7(5) above, the Lord Lyon shall not issue a commission to that officer of court as a messenger-at-arms until that officer of court has lodged with the Lyon Clerk

(i) the prescribed documents; or

(ii) the copy letter of receipt and further evidence referred to in rule 7(5) above.

(11) Where an officer of court—

(a) applies for a commission as a sheriff officer in a particular sheriffdom or a particular district of a sheriffdom, and

(b) his application is granted before the compliance date in respect of that officer of court,

notwithstanding rules 8(6) and 8(7) above, the sheriff principal shall not issue a commission to the officer of court in respect of that sheriffdom or district until the officer of court has sent to the sheriff principal

(i) the prescribed documents; or

(ii) the copy letter of receipt and further evidence referred to in rule 8(7) above.

NOTE
¹ As amended by S.I. 1998 No. 2636, r. 2 (effective December 1, 1998).

PART V

ACCOUNTS

Officers of court to keep accounts

12. Every officer of court shall keep—
    (a) written books and accounts, separately in respect of each client creditor, to show all monies collected by him from the creditor's debtor; and
    (b) a separate bank account in respect of client creditors.

Accountant's certificate

13.—(1) Every officer of court shall deliver annually to every sheriff principal from whom he holds a commission and, if he is a messenger-at-arms, to the Lyon Clerk a certificate by an accountant within six months of the end of his accounting year in respect of that year.

(2) Such a certificate shall state that in the opinion of the accountant satisfactory accounts have been kept in accordance with rule 12 above.

(3) In order to enable an accountant to grant such a certificate, every officer of court shall make available to the accountant such books and accounts as the accountant may reasonably require.

(4) If, after making the examination referred to in paragraph (3) above, it appears to the accountant that he is not able to sign such a certificate, he shall prepare a report giving his reasons.

(5) Where an accountant prepares a report under paragraph (4) above, he shall send a copy of it—
    (a) in the case of a sheriff officer, to every sheriff principal who has granted a commission to the sheriff officer;
    (b) in the case of a messenger-at-arms, to the Lyon Clerk; and
    (c) to the officer of court concerned.

(6) In this rule, "an accountant" means an accountant in public practice as a professional accountant who is a member of one of more of the following bodies:—
    (a) the Institute of Chartered Accountants of Scotland;
    (b) the Institute of Chartered Accountants in England and Wales;
    (c) the Institute of Chartered Accountants in Ireland; and
    (d) the Chartered Association of Certified Accountants.

(7) Where an officer of court fails to deliver to the sheriff principal or the Lyon Clerk a certificate by an accountant under paragraph (1) above—
    (a) in respect of his commission as a sheriff officer, the sheriff principal may suspend the officer of court from practice as a sheriff officer; and
    (b) where applicable, in respect of his commission as a messenger-at-arms, a Lord Ordinary may, following a report sent to the Deputy Principal Clerk of Session by the Lyon Clerk, suspend the officer of court from practice as a messenger-at-arms.

(8) Where an officer of court has been suspended under paragraph (7) above and subsequently lodges a certificate by an accountant under paragraph (1) above, the sheriff principal and, where applicable, in respect of his commission as a messenger-at-arms, a Lord Ordinary may recall his suspension.

PART VI

OFFICIAL FUNCTIONS AND EXTRA-OFFICIAL ACTIVITIES

Official functions

14.—(1) Without prejudice to rule 16 in the First Schedule to the Sheriff Courts (Scotland) Act 1907, rule 11 of the Act of Sederunt (Summary

Cause Rules, Sheriff Court) 1976, section 91(2) of the Act of 1987, and any functions under any other enactment, an officer of court may exercise the following official functions—

> (a) subject to paragraph (2) below, collect any debt constituted by decree or recoverable by summary warrant;
>
> (b) execute diligence; or
>
> (c) execute a citation or serve any document required under any legal process, in any place in respect of which he holds a commission as an officer of court.

(2) A debt constituted by decree or recoverable by summary warrant may be collected—

> (a) in the case of a decree or summary warrant of the sheriff court, by a sheriff officer; or
>
> (b) in the case of a decree or summary warrant of the Court of Session, by a messenger-at-arms.

(3) Without prejudice to rule 16 in the First Schedule to the Sheriff Courts (Scotland) Act 1907, rule 11 of the Act of Sederunt (Summary Cause Rules, Sheriff Court) 1976, section 91(2) of the Act of 1987, and any functions under any other enactment, a person who holds a commission as a sheriff officer may practise as a sheriff officer only in the sheriffdom or district of a sheriffdom in respect of which he has been granted a commission under rule 8(5) above.

(4) An officer of court may refuse to execute a citation, serve any document required under any legal process or execute diligence where—

> (a) the prescribed, or reasonable, expenses have not been tendered to him or secured by or on behalf of the person instructing him; or
>
> (b) it is not reasonably practicable for him to carry out his instructions and this has been intimated forthwith on receipt of the instructions to the person instructing him.

(5) An officer of court may not—

> (a) form a company within the meaning of section 735(1) of the Companies Act 1985 for the purpose of exercising any of his official functions; or
>
> (b) exercise any of his official functions as an employee of a company within the meaning of section 735(1) of the Companies Act 1985.

Extra-official activities

15.—(1) Subject to paragraph (2) below, the extra-official activities of an officer of court may include—

> (a) collection for remuneration of any debt not constituted by decree where authorised to do so under rule 16 below; or
>
> (b) in the absence of any statutory provision to the contrary, service on a person for remuneration of any notice which is required to be served under any enactment.

(2) An officer of court who performs an extra-official activity under paragraph (1) above shall not state or imply that he is acting in his capacity as an officer of court.

(3) An officer of court may not be—

> (a) an auctioneer with his own auction room;
>
> (b) an elected or appointed member of a public or local authority;
>
> (c) a house factor;
>
> (d) a member of the Faculty of Advocates;
>
> (e) a member of the Law Society of Scotland;
>
> (f) a member of the United Kingdom, or European, Parliament;
>
> (g) a money lender; or
>
> (h) a police officer.

Applications for authorisation to collect debts not constituted by decree

16.—(1) A sheriff principal may, on the application of a sheriff officer who has his principal place of business in the sheriffdom and holds a com-

(*b*) in the case of a messenger-at-arms, to the Lyon Clerk.
[1] (4) An officer of court shall give notice of the dates of his accounting year and of the renewal date in each year of the Policy currently in force in respect of each commission held by him as an officer of court—

(*a*) in the case of a sheriff officer, to the nominated sheriff clerk of each sheriffdom in which he holds a commission as a sheriff officer; and

(*b*) in the case of a messenger-at-arms, to the Lyon Clerk.

NOTE
[1] As amended by S.I. 1998 No. 2636, r. 2 (effective December 1, 1998).

PART VIII

REPORTS AND INVESTIGATIONS OF CONDUCT OF OFFICERS OF COURT

Reports and complaints
19.—(1) A copy of a report prepared under section 78(3) of the Act of 1987 in respect of a messenger-at-arms shall be sent to the Deputy Principal Clerk of Session who shall put the copy report before a judge nominated by the Lord President.

(2) Where a judge of the Court of Session or a sheriff principal has reason to believe that an officer of court may have been guilty of misconduct as provided in section 79(1)(*c*) of the Act of 1987, he shall put the allegation in writing.

(3) A report or complaint under section 79(1)(*b*)(i) of the Act of 1987 in respect of a messenger-at-arms shall be sent to the Deputy Principal Clerk of Session who shall put the report or complaint, as the case may be, before the judge nominated under section 79(2) of that Act.

Opportunity to officer of court to reply to allegation of misconduct
20. Where a report or complaint under section 79(1)(*a*) or (*b*), or a complaint under section 79(1)(*c*), of the Act of 1987 has been made, the judge nominated under section 79(2) of that Act or the sheriff principal, as the case may be, shall cause a copy of the report or complaint to be sent to the officer of court about whom an allegation of misconduct has been made together with a letter requesting him to reply within 14 days admitting, denying or giving an explanation of the alleged misconduct.

PART IX

DISCIPLINARY PROCEEDINGS

Disciplinary proceedings against messengers-at-arms
21.—(1) Disciplinary proceedings under section 79(3)(*a*) of the Act of 1987 against a messenger-at-arms shall be by petition presented to the Outer House of the Court of Session in which the messenger-at-arms complained against shall be made the respondent.

[1,2] (2) Subject to the following provisions of this rule, the Rules of the Court of Session which make provision as respects proceedings by way of petition to the Outer House of the Court of Session shall apply to a petition under this rule.

(3) A petition under paragraph (1) above shall include—

(*a*) averments specifying—
  (i) the alleged misconduct;
  (ii) the facts established by the investigation under section 79(2) of the Act of 1987 alleged to be the probable cause of misconduct; and

(*b*) a prayer praying the Lords of Council and Session to order—
  (i) service of the petition on the respondent;
  (ii) the respondent to lodge answers within 21 days from the date of service;
  (iii) intimation of the petition to the Lord Advocate;

(iv) a date for a hearing for further procedure; and

(v) in the event of the respondent being found guilty of misconduct, such order under section 80(5) of the Act of 1987, if any, as the court considers appropriate.

(4) When making the first order for service and intimation, the Lord Ordinary shall fix a date for a hearing for further procedure; and the petitioner shall intimate that date to the respondent and the Lord Advocate.

NOTE

[1] See now the Rules of the Court of Session 1994, Chap. 14.

[2] As amended by S.S.I. 2000 No. 30, para. 2(3) (effective March 11, 2000).

Procedure in proceedings against messengers-at-arms

22.—(1) this rule applies to a petition under rule 21 above.

(2) Subject to the following provisions of this rule, the Lord Ordinary shall determine the procedure to be followed in such a petition.

(3) Where the respondent fails to appear or be represented at the hearing for further procedure, the Lord Ordinary may grant the prayer of the petition.

(4) Where a further hearing or a proof is ordered, the petitioner shall fix a date with the Keeper of the Rolls of the Court of Session, and the Keeper of the Rolls shall fix an early date.

(5) Where a proof is fixed—

(a) the interlocutor allowing the proof shall be sufficient warrant for the citation of witnesses on not less than seven days' notice; and

(b) the parties may agree to dispense with the services of a shorthand writer.

(6) After a hearing on the question whether there was misconduct by the respondent, the Lord Ordinary may give his decision orally or make avizandum and issue his decision in writing at a later date.

(7) Where the Lord Ordinary pronounces an interlocutor under paragraph (3) or (6) above, or issues his decision in writing under paragraph (6), the clerk of court shall send a copy of the interlocutor or a copy of the decision, as the case may be, to the respondent.

(8) Where the respondent is found guilty of misconduct after a hearing to determine that matter, the court shall make no order under section 80(5) of the Act of 1987 without first giving the respondent an opportunity to be heard, or to make representations in writing, in mitigation.

(9) A hearing of a petition under section 79(3)(a) of the Act of 1987 shall be held in public unless—

(a) the respondent requests that it be held in private; or

(b) the judge considers that it would be prejudicial to the interests of justice if the hearing were not held, in whole or in part, in private.

(10) Where—

(a) a fine is imposed on the respondent, the clerk of court shall intimate details of the fine to the Lord Advocate;

(b) an order is made for repayment under section 80(5)(d) of the Act of 1987, the clerk of court shall intimate the order to the person to whom repayment is to be made; and

(c) an order is made under section 80(1), (4) or (8)(b) of the Act of 1987, the clerk of court shall intimate the order to the company from which the Policy currently in force in respect of the respondent was obtained.

(11) The warrant attached to an extract of a decree for payment of a fine shall be in the following terms:—"and the Lords grant warrant for all lawful execution hereon".

Disciplinary proceedings against sheriff officers

23.—(1) Disciplinary proceedings under section 79(3)(a) of the Act of 1987 against a sheriff officer shall be by initial writ in a summary application, to the sheriff principal who appointed the solicitor under section 79(2) of the Act of 1987 to investigate, in which the sheriff officer complained against shall be made the respondent.

(2) An application under paragraph (1) above shall include—

(a) averments specifying—
  (i) the alleged misconduct;
  (ii) the facts established by the investigation under section 79(2) of the Act of 1987 alleged to be the probable cause of misconduct; and

(b) a crave seeking the sheriff principal to order—
  (i) service of the application on the respondent;
  (ii) the respondent to lodge defences within 14 days from the date of service;
  (iii) intimation of the application to the Lord Advocate;
  (iv) a date for a hearing for further procedure; and
  (v) in the event of the respondent being found guilty of misconduct, such order under section 80(7) of the Act of 1987, if any, as the court considers appropriate.

(3) When making the first order for service and intimation, the sheriff principal shall fix a date for a hearing for further procedure; and the applicant shall intimate that date to the respondent and the Lord Advocate.

Procedure in proceedings against sheriff officers

24.—(1) This rule applies to an application under rule 23 above.

(2) Subject to the following provisions of this rule, the sheriff principal shall determine the procedure to be followed in such an application.

(3) Where the respondent fails to appear or to be represented at the hearing for further procedure, the sheriff principal may grant the crave of the application.

(4) Where a proof is fixed—

(a) the interlocutor allowing the proof shall be sufficient warrant for the citation of witnesses on not less than seven days' notice; and

(b) the parties may agree to dispense with the services of a shorthand writer.

(5) After a hearing on the question whether there was misconduct by the respondent, the sheriff principal may give his decision orally or make avizandum and issue his decision in writing at a later date.

(6) Where the sheriff principal pronounces an interlocutor under paragraph (3) or (5) above, or issues his decision in writing under paragraph (5), the clerk of court shall send a copy of the interlocutor or a copy of the decision, as the case may be, to the respondent.

(7) Where the respondent is found guilty of misconduct after a hearing to determine that matter, the court shall make no order under section 80(7) of the Act of 1987 without first giving the respondent an opportunity to be heard, or to make representations in writing, in mitigation.

(8) A hearing of an application under section 79(3)(a) of the Act of 1987 shall be held in public unless—

(a) the respondent requests that it be held in private; or

(b) the sheriff principal considers that it would be prejudicial to the interests of justice if the hearing were not held, in whole or in part, in private.

(9) Where—

(a) a fine is imposed on the respondent, the sheriff clerk shall intimate details of the fine to the Lord Advocate;

(b) an order is made for repayment under section 80(7)(b) of the Act of 1987, the clerk of court shall intimate the order to the person to whom repayment is to be made; and

(c) an order is made under section 80(2), (6) or (8)(b) or 81(3) of the Act of 1987, the clerk of court shall intimate the order to the company from which the Policy currently in force in respect of the respondent was obtained.

(10) The warrant attached to an extract of a decree for payment of a fine shall be in the following terms:—"and the Sheriff Principal grants warrant for all lawful execution hereon".

Remits of disciplinary proceedings
25. Where it is considered appropriate in the circumstances of a particular case, disciplinary proceedings may be remitted—
(a) by the Court of Session, to a sheriff principal to report; or
(b) by a sheriff principal, to another sheriff principal.

Opportunity to officer of court to make representations where order considered under section 80(1) and (2) of the Act of 1987
26. Where the Court of Session under section 80(1), or a sheriff principal under section 80(2), of the Act of 1987 considers making an order under one of these subsections, the Court of Session or the sheriff principal, as the case may be—
(a) shall give the officer of court an opportunity to make representations orally or in writing; and
(b) may ordain the officer of court to appear,
before making such an order.

Appeals
27.—(1) An appeal from Lord Ordinary or sheriff principal to the Inner House of the Court of Session under section 82 of the Act of 1987 shall be made within 21 days of the date of the decision appealed against.
[1,2] (2) Subject to paragraph (1) above, chapter 38 of the Rules of the Court of Session shall apply to an appeal from a Lord Ordinary under section 82 of the Act of 1987 and chapter 40 of the Rules of the Court of Session shall apply to an appeal from a sheriff principal under section 82 of the Act of 1987.

NOTE
[1] See now the Rules of the Court of Session 1994, rules 41.19 to 41.21.
[2] As amended by S.S.I. 2000 No. 30, para. 2(4) (effective March 11, 2000).

Suspension under particular rules
28.—(1) Where the sheriff principal suspends an officer of court from practice as a sheriff officer under rule 10(6)(a), 11(7)(a) or 13(7)(a) above, he shall cause intimation to be made—
(a) to every other sheriff principal from whom the sheriff officer holds a commission as a sheriff officer; and
(b) where the sheriff officer is also a messenger-at-arms, to the Deputy Principal Clerk of Session and the Lord Lyon.
(2) Where the Court of Session suspends an officer of court from practice as a messenger-at-arms under rule 10(6)(b), 11(7)(b) or 13(7)(b) above, it shall cause intimation to be made to the Lord Lyon, who shall cause intimation thereof to be made to every sheriff principal from whom the officer of court holds commission as a sheriff officer.
(3) Where a sheriff principal receives intimation under paragraph (1)(a) or (2) above, he may suspend the officer of court from practice as a sheriff officer.
(4) Where the Deputy Principal Clerk of Session receives intimation under paragraph (1)(b) above, he shall place the intimation before a Lord Ordinary, who may suspend the officer of court from practice as a messenger-at-arms.
(5) Where, after an officer of court has been suspended under rule 10(6), 11(7) or 13(7) above, that officer of court subsequently lodges the premium receipt, Policy or certificate, as the case may be, the regional sheriff clerk of the sheriffdom in which the officer of court's first current commission as a

sheriff officer was granted shall intimate that fact to—
- (*a*) every other sheriff principal from whom the officer of court holds a commission as a sheriff officer; and
- (*b*) where the sheriff officer is also a messenger-at-arms, to the Deputy Principal Clerk of Session and the Lord Lyon,

and each sheriff principal and, where applicable, in respect of his commission as a messenger-at-arms, a Lord Ordinary, may recall his suspension.

PART X

MISCELLANEOUS

Mandate to recover debt in diligence

29. Instructions to an officer of court to execute diligence in execution shall, unless the contrary intention is expressed, include a mandate to recover payment for, or on account of, any debt in respect of which the diligence is executed.

Dealings in goods attached or sold by virtue of diligence

[1] **30.** An officer of court shall not—

(*a*) himself or through an agent, purchase any goods attached or sold by virtue of a diligence in which he has acted in course of one of his official functions;

(*b*) share with the creditor any goods of a debtor or the proceeds of sale of such goods adjudged to the creditor of the debtor by virtue of diligence in which the officer of court has acted in course of one of his official functions; or

(*c*) share with the purchaser any profit made by the purchaser in re-selling any goods bought at a sale carried out by virtue of diligence in which the officer of court has acted in course of one of his official functions.

NOTE

[1] As amended by the Act of Sederunt (Debt Arrangement and Attachment (Scotland) Act 2002) 2002 (SSI 2002/560), art.4, Sch.3, para.3 (effective December 30, 2002).

Official identity card

31. An officer of court shall forthwith upon ceasing to practise as an officer of court deliver the official identity card issued to him under section 86 of the Act of 1987 to the person from whom he holds his commission.

SCHEDULE 1

FORMS

Rule 7(1)   FORM 1

Form of petition to the Court of Session for recommendation for a commission as a messenger-at-arms

UNTO THE RIGHT HONOURABLE
THE LORDS OF COUNCIL AND SESSION

PETITION

[AB] (*address*)

for

Recommendation for a commission as a messenger-at-arms

HUMBLY SHEWETH

1. That the petitioner was born on   and is a sheriff officer.

2. That the first current [or only] commission of the petitioner as a sheriff officer was granted by the sheriff principal of (*name of sheriffdom*) at (*name of court*) on (*insert date*).

3. That the petitioner has been in practice as a sheriff officer for a period of years. [The

petitioner seeks to have the period of practice required under rule 4(1)(*a*) of the Messengers-at-Arms and Sheriff Officers Rules 1991 reduced from two years to (*state period*). He does so on the following grounds, namely (*state grounds*).]

4. That the petitioner holds a certificate from the Society of Messengers-at-Arms and Sheriff Officers that he has passed the examinations of that Society.

5. That the petitioner has not been convicted of any offence [except (*state any convictions which are not spent convictions by virtue of the Rehabilitation of Offenders Act 1974*)].

6. That the petitioner is a fit and proper person to be granted a commission as a messenger-at-arms and makes this application for a recommendation to the Lord Lyon King of Arms for a commission as a messenger-at-arms.

7. That this petition is presented under section 77(1) of the Debtors (Scotland) Act 1987 and rule 7 [or rules 4(2) and 7] of the Messengers-at-Arms and Sheriff Officers Rules 1991.

MAY IT THEREFORE please your Lordships [to reduce the period of practice required under rule 4(1)(a) of the Messengers-at-Arms and Sheriff Officers Rules 1991 for two years to (*insert period*) and] to recommend the petitioner to the Lord Lyon King of Arms for a commission as a messenger-at-arms; or to do otherwise in the premises as to your Lordships shall seem proper.

ACCORDING TO JUSTICE, &c

Rule 8(1)   FORM 2

Form of initial writ in summary application to the sheriff principal for a commission as a sheriff officer

SHERIFFDOM OF   AT

INITIAL WRIT

in causa

[AB] (*address*)

Applicant

for

A commission as a sheriff officer

The applicant craves the court to grant to him a commission as a sheriff officer in the [(*name of district(s)*) district of the] sheriffdom of (*name of sheriffdom*).

CONDESCENDENCE

1. The applicant was born on

2. The applicant has [or proposes to have] a principal place of business [or is to be employed] at (*insert address*). [He has (an)other place(s) of business at (*insert address(es)*).] [The applicant holds a commission as a sheriff officer in the following sheriffdom(s) [or districts of sheriffdoms]]. [He holds a commission as a messenger-at-arms.

3. The applicant has undergone a period of training with [CD], sheriff officer, (*insert business address*) for a period of   years. [The period of training was reduced to   year(s) by the sheriff principal on (date). A [certified] copy of the relevant interlocutor is produced].

4. The applicant holds a certificate of completion of training issued by [CD]. He also holds a certificate from the Society of Messengers-at-Arms and Sheriff Officers that he has passed the examination of that Society.

5. The applicant is of good character as endorsed by the two character references produced. The applicant has not been convicted of any offence [except (state any convictions which are not spent convictions by virtue of the Rehabilitation of Offenders Act 1974)].

6. The applicant is a fit and proper person to hold a commission as a sheriff officer in the sheriffdom [of (*insert name of district*) district of the sheriffdom] and makes this application for a commission.

7. This application is made under rule 8 of the Messengers-at-Arms and Sheriff Officers Rules 1991.

PLEA-IN-LAW

The applicant being a fit and proper person to hold a commission as a sheriff officer, the application should be granted as craved.

IN RESPECT WHEREOF

Applicant [or EF
(*insert business address*)
Solicitor for applicant]

Rule 8(3)(b)   Form 3

Notice of advertisement in newspaper of application for commission as a sheriff officer

APPLICATION by [AB]

for

COMMISSION AS A SHERIFF OFFICER

NOTICE is hereby given that application has been made to the sheriff principal of (*name of sheriffdom*) at (*name of court*) by [AB] (*address or business address*) for a commission as a sheriff officer in (*name of sheriffdom or district of sheriffdom*). The sheriff principal, by inter-locutor (*insert date*), ordered any person who wishes to object to the application of [AB] to lodge answers to the application with the sheriff clerk at (*name and address of court*) within 30 days from the date of this notice.

(*name and address of solicitor*)
Solicitor for applicant

SCHEDULE 2

Transitional Provisions

Bonds of caution

1.—(1) An officer of court shall be covered by a bond of caution in the form set out in sub-paragraph (2) of this paragraph to the value of £50,000 from a company on the list of guarantee companies approved by the Lord President under rule 200(*e*)(iv) of the Rules of the Court of Session in respect of any commission held by him as—

(a) a sheriff officer; and

(b) where applicable, a messenger-at-arms,

and the bond of caution shall be renewed annually.

(2) The form referred to in sub-paragraph (1) of this paragraph is as follows—

BOND OF CAUTION

We, (*name of cautioner*), having a registered office at (*insert address*), hereby BIND and OBLIGE ourselves and our whole funds and property as cautioner and surety for the period from   to   ; for (*name and address of officer of court*) as OFFICER OF COURT that he shall faithfully, truly and honestly use and exercise the duties of the office of OFFICER OF COURT to ALL and SUNDRY without fear and favour upon payment of his reasonable expenses and if he fails to execute these duties, we shall incur whatsoever damages, interest and expenses any person shall happen to sustain through the dishonest, illegal or fraudulent actions or omissions of (*name of officer of court*). I, (*name of officer of court*), as principal, do hereby BIND and OBLIGE myself, my heirs, executors and successors and we, (*name of cautioner*), as cautioner, do hereby BIND and OBLIGE ourselves jointly and severally to pay and make good the same to any person interested and wronged by declaring that the obligation on us, the cautioner, is (in accordance with [paragraph 1 of Schedule 2 [rule 9] of the Messengers-at-Arms and Sheriff Officers Rules [1991] [1988]) restricted to, and shall not exceed the sum of, £50,000.

We, (*name of cautioner*) accordingly, hereby BIND and OBLIGE ourselves, within the aforementioned limits of the cautionary obligation, for the damages, interest and expenses any such person shall sustain hereby:

And we consent to the registration hereof for preservation and execution: IN WITNESS WHEREOF.

Policies of professional indemnity insurance
2.—(1) An officer and any partnership of officers of court shall be covered by a policy of professional indemnity insurance from an insurance company to a minimum limit of £100,000 in respect of—
    (a) the officer of court in respect of any commission as—
        (i) a sheriff officer; and
        (ii) where applicable, a messenger-at-arms;
    (b) the partnership of officers of court in respect of the firm; and
    (c) the partnership of officers of court in respect of its employees,
and the policy shall be renewed annually.
    (2) Every policy of professional indemnity insurance shall be in such terms as may be approved by the sheriffs principal and the Lord Lyon.

Solicitor's Right of Audience 1993

(S.I. 1993 No. 1215)

[29th April 1993]

The Lords of Council and Session, under and by virtue of the powers conferred on them by sections 5 and 48 of the Court of Session Act 1988 and of all other powers enabling them in that behalf, do hereby enact and declare:

Citation and commencement
1.—(1) This Act of Sederunt may be cited as the Act of Sederunt (Solicitor's Right of Audience) 1993 and shall come into force on 12th May 1993.
    (2) This Act of Sederunt shall be inserted in the Books of Sederunt.

Interpretation
2. In this Act of Sederunt—
    "the President" means the President of the Society for the time being, in his capacity as an office bearer of the Society;
    "a right of audience by virtue of section 25A of the Solicitors (Scotland) Act 1980" means a right of audience in, on the one hand, the Court of Session, the House of Lords and the Judicial Committee of the Privy Council or, on the other hand, the High Court of Justiciary; and
    "the Society" means the Law Society of Scotland established under the Solicitors (Scotland) Act 1980.

Right of audience
3. The President shall have a right of audience in the Outer House of the Court of Session for the purpose only of introducing to the court solicitors who have acquired a right of audience by virtue of section 25A of the Solicitors (Scotland) Act 1980 and inviting the Lord Ordinary to administer the appropriate declaration.

[THE NEXT PAGE IS C 1201]

Court Fees
Court of Session etc. Fees Order 1997

(S.I. 1997 No. 688)

[March 4, 1997]

The Secretary of State, in exercise of the powers conferred on him by section 2 of the Courts of Law Fees (Scotland) Act 1895 and of all other powers enabling him in that behalf, and with the concurrence of the Treasury, hereby makes the following order:—

Citation and commencement
1. This order may be cited as the Court of Session etc. Fees Order 1997 and shall come into force on 1st April 1997.

Interpretation
2.—(1) In this order—
"Office of Court" has the same meaning as in rule 3.1(1) of the Rules of Court;
"Rules of Court" mean the Rules of the Court of Session 1994;
"Table of Fees" means the Table of Fees specified in Schedule 1 to this order.
(2) For the purposes of any reference in this order to a party—
  (a) except in relation to a special case, a set of persons with the same interest, for whom one and the same first paper is or has been lodged, shall be treated as a single party; and
  (b) in relation to a special case, each person or set of persons who appear as one of the separate parties to the case shall be treated as a party.

Offices to which order applies and officers to whom fees are payable
3.—(1) This order shall regulate the fees payable in the Office of Court, the office of the accountant of court and the office of the auditor of the Court of Session.
(2) The fees regulated by this order shall be payable—
  (a) in relation to the Office of Court, to the Principal Clerk of Session or any officer acting for him;
  (b) in relation to the office of the accountant of court, to the accountant of court or any officer acting for him; and
  (c) in relation to the office of the auditor of the Court of Session, to the auditor of the Court of Session or any officer acting for him.

Fees payable
4.—1 (1) Subject to paragraph (2) and articles 5, 5A and 5B below, the fees payable in respect of the matters specified in column 1 of the Table of Fees shall be the fees specified in relation to those matters in column 2 of that table (the fees previously payable being shown in column 3 of that table).
(2) No fees shall be payable by a debtor in connection with any proceedings under the Debtors (Scotland) Act 1987.

NOTE
  1 As amended by S.I. 1999 No. 755, art. 2 (effective April 1, 1999).

Exemption of certain persons from fees
  1 **5.** A fee regulated by this Order shall not be payable by a person—

(a) who is in receipt of income support, working families' tax credit or disabled person's tax credit under Part VII of the Social Security Contributions and Benefits Act 1992;

(b) who is in receipt of an income-based jobseeker's allowance (payable under the Jobseekers Act 1995);

(c) who is in receipt of civil legal aid within the meaning of section 13(2) of the Legal Aid (Scotland) Act 1986 in respect of the matter in the Table of Fees in connection with which the fee is payable;

(d) where the fee is payable in connection with a simplified divorce application and the person is in receipt of advice and assistance from a solicitor under the Legal Aid (Scotland) 1986 in respect of that application; or

(e) where the person's solicitor is undertaking work in relation to the matter in the Table of Fees in connection with which the fee is payable on the basis of any regulations made under section 36 of the Legal Aid (Scotland) Act 1986 providing for legal aid in a matter of special urgency.

NOTE
[1] Substituted by the Court of Session etc. Fees Amendment Order 2002 (SSI 2002/270), art.2(2) (effective July 1, 2002).

Exemption of certain motions from fees
[1] **5A.**—(1) This article applies to motions which are enrolled in the process of the cause or made orally at the bar in accordance with rule 23.2 of the Rules of Court (enrolment of motions).

(2) The fees specified in items B23 and C22 of the Table of Fees shall not be payable in respect of motions which operate solely so as to activate further steps of procedure and any opposition to such motions.

(3) Without prejudice to the generality of paragraph (2) above, motions which are exempt from the payment of fees include motions under the following rules of the Rules of Court—

(a) rule 19.1 (decrees in absence);
(b) rule 22.3(5)(a) (closing record);
(c) rule 36.13 (death, disability, retiral, etc. of Lord Ordinary);
(d) rules 37.1(2)(b), 37.1(6) and 37.1(7) (applications for jury trial);
(e) rule 37.10 (application of verdicts);
(f) rule 38.17(1) (orders for hearing);
(g) rule 40.7(3) (procedure following transmission of appeal process);
(h) rule 40.11(1)(a) (early disposal of appeal) but only insofar as the motion relates to rule 40.7A (required application for early disposal of appeal against interlocutor other than final judgment);
(i) rule 40.15(1) (orders for hearing of appeal);
(j) rule 41.15(1) (motions for hearing of appeals); and
(k) rule 41.22(1) (motion for further procedure).

NOTE
[1] Inserted by S.I. 1999 No. 755, art. 2 (effective April 1, 1999).

Calculation of fees payable
[1] **5B.**—(1) Subject to article 5A above, the fees specified in items B23 and C22 of the Table of Fees shall be payable in addition to those fees which are specified in items B2, B6 and C5 of the Table of Fees.

(2) The fees specified in items B23 and C22 of the Table of Fees shall not be payable in addition to those fees which are specified in items B9, B10 and B13 and C10, C13 and C14 of the Table of Fees.

NOTE
[1] Inserted by S.I. 1999 No. 755, art. 2 (effective April 1, 1999).

Revocations
6. The orders specified in Schedule 2 to this order are hereby revoked.

Article 4   SCHEDULE

[1] TABLE OF FEES

Column 1 *(Matters)*	Column 2 *(Fee payable)*	Column 3 *(Fee formerly payable)*
PART I—FEES IN THE CENTRAL OFFICE OF THE COURT		
A. SIGNETING		
Signeting of any writ or summons, if attendance is necessary outwith the normal office hours	£62.00	*£57.00*
B. GENERAL DEPARTMENT		
1. Appeal, summons, or other writ or step by which any cause or proceeding, other than a family action, is originated in either the Inner or Outer House—fee (to comprehend signeting in normal office hours)	£106.00	*£97.00*
2. Defences, answers or other writ (including a joint minute) or step in process or enrolment or opposition to a motion in a pending process by which a party other than an originating party first makes an appearance in a course or proceeding other than a family action	£106.00	*£97.00*
3. Writ by which a family action is originated (other than a simplified divorce application)—inclusive fee (to comprehend signeting within normal office hours and, if applicable, issue to the pursuer of an extract in terms of item G5(a) of this Table, and to the defender, if appropriate, of a duplicate thereof)	£81.00	*£74.00*
4. Simplified divorce application (inclusive of all procedure other than that specified in item B5 of this Table)	£62.00	*£57.00*
5. In relation to a simplified divorce application, citation of any persons under rule 16.1(1)(a)(i), (ii) or (iii), as applied by rule 49.76, of the Rules of Court, or intimation to any person or persons under rule 16.1(1)(a)(i), (ii) or (iii), as applied by rule 49.76, of those Rules, where such intimation is required.	£41.00	*£38.00*
6. Defences, answers or other writ (including a joint minute) or step in process or enrolment of or opposition to a motion in a pending process by which a party other than an originating party first makes appearance in a family action	£81.00	*£74.00*
7. Fee for initial lodging of affidavits in a family action where proof by affidavit evidence has been allowed	£35.00	*£32.00*
8. Special case—		
For each party	£53.00	*£49.00*
Maximum fee payable per case	£215.00	*£197.00*
9. Application by minute or motion for variation of an order in a family action	£19.00	*£17.00*
10. Answers or opposition to an application under item B9 of this Table	£19.00	*£17.00*
11. Letter of request to a foreign court	£27.00	*£25.00*
12. Citation of each jury, to include outlays incurred in citing and countermanding—payable on receipt of instruments for issue of precept	£149.00	*£137.00*
13. Reclaiming motion—fee payable by party enrolling motion	£106.00	*£97.00*

Release 70: May 2003

Column 1 (*Matters*)	Column 2 (*Fee payable*)	Column 3 (*Fee formerly payable*)
14. Closed record—fee payable by each party on the lodging of the closed record or, where no closed record is lodged, when mode of enquiry is determined	£53.00	£49.00
15. Allowing proof, etc.—fee payable by each party on diet of proof, jury trial, procedure roll or summar roll hearing being allowed	£28.00	£26.00
16. Proof or Procedure Roll—fee payable by each party appearing at the hearing for every 30 minutes or part thereof	£16.00	£13.00
17. Summar Roll—fee payable by each party appearing at the hearing for every 30 minutes or part thereof	£33.00	£26.00
18. Jury Trial—fee payable by each party appearing at the trial for every 30 minutes or part thereof	£16.00	£13.00
19. Outer House hearing other than items B16, B18, B21 and B24 of this Table—fee payable by each party appearing at the hearing for every 30 minutes or part thereof	£16.00	£13.00
20. Inner House hearing other than items B17, B22 and B24 of this Table—fee payable by each party appearing at the hearing for every 30 minutes or part thereof	£33.00	£26.00
21. Motion Roll hearing—fee payable by each party appearing at the hearing after first 30 minutes—for every 30 minutes or part thereof	£16.00	£13.00
22. Single Bills hearing—fee payable by each party appearing at the hearing after first 30 minutes—for every 30 minutes or part thereof	£33.00	£26.00
23. Fee payable by any party enrolling a motion or making a motion orally at the bar and any party opposing any such motion	£27.00	£25.00
24. Hearing out of hours—fee payable by each party appearing at the hearing for every 30 minutes or part thereof	£33.00	£26.00
C. PETITION DEPARTMENT		
1. Petition of whatever nature presented to Inner or Outer House other than a petition under item C3 or C4 of this Table, whether in respect of the first or any subsequent step of process, and any application for registration or recognition of a judgment under the Civil Jurisdiction and Judgments Act 1982	£106.00	£97.00
2. Additional fee payable when a petition in terms of item C1 of this Table is presented outwith normal office hours	£62.00	£57.00
3. Petition to be admitted as a notary public: For each applicant	£80.00	£73.00
4. Petition to be admitted as a solicitor: For each applicant	£80.00	£73.00
5. Answers, objection or other writ (including a joint minute) or step in process or enrolment or opposition to a motion in a pending process by which a party other than an originating party first makes appearance in a proceeding to which item C1 of this Table applies	£106.00	£97.00
6. Caveat	£27.00	£25.00
7. Fiat	£27.00	£25.00
8. Registering official copies of orders of courts in England and Wales or Northern Ireland	£10.00	£9.00
9. Issue of an abbreviate in sequestration	£10.00	£9.00

Column 1 *(Matters)*	Column 2 *(Fee payable)*	Column 3 *(Fee formerly payable)*
10. Reclaiming motion—fee payable by party enrolling motion	£106.00	*£97.00*
11. Closed record—fee payable by each party on the lodging of the closed record or, when no closed record is lodged, when mode of enquiry is determined	£53.00	*£49.00*
12. Allowing proof, etc.—fee payable by each party on diet of proof, procedure roll, summar roll or judicial review hearing being allowed	£28.00	*£26.00*
13. Application by minute or motion for variation of an order in a petition for custody, aliment or access	£20.00	*£18.00*
14. Answers or opposition to a motion under item C13 of this Table	£20.00	*£18.00*
15. Registering orders for enforcement under section 426 of the Insolvency Act 1986	£10.00	*£9.00*
16. Proof or Procedure Roll—fee payable by each party appearing at the hearing for every 30 minutes or part thereof	£16.00	*£13.00*
17. Summar Roll—fee payable by each party appearing at the hearing for every 30 minutes or part thereof	£33.00	*£26.00*
18. Outer House hearing other than items C16, C20 and C23 of this Table—fee payable by each party appearing at the hearing for every 30 minutes or part thereof	£16.00	*£13.00*
19. Inner House hearing other than items C17, C21 and C23 of this Table—fee payable by each party appearing at the hearing for every 30 minutes or part thereof	£33.00	*£26.00*
20. Motion Roll Hearing—fee payable by each party appearing at the hearing after first 30 minutes—for every 30 minutes or part thereof	£16.00	*£13.00*
21. Single Bills hearing—fee payable by each party appearing at the hearing after first 30 minutes—for every 30 minutes or part thereof	£33.00	*£26.00*
22. Fee payable by any party enrolling a motion or making a motion orally at the bar; and any party opposing any such motion	£27.00	*£25.00*
23. Hearing out of hours—fee payable by each party appearing at the hearing for every 30 minutes or part thereof	£33.00	*£26.00*
D. COURT FOR HEARING APPEALS RELATING TO THE REGISTRATION OF ELECTORS		
Appeal—inclusive fee	£106.00	*£97.00*
E. ELECTION COURT		
1 Parliamentary election petition	£106.00	*£97.00*
2. Statement of matters	£10.00	*£9.00*
3. Any other petition, application, answers or objections submitted to the court	£27.00	*£25.00*
4. Certificate of judgement	£27.00	*£25.00*
F. LANDS VALUATION APPEAL COURT		
1. Appeal—inclusive fee	£106.00	*£97.00*
2. Answers—inclusive fee	£106.00	*£97.00*
G. EXTRACTS DEPARTMENT		
1. Extract decree following upon a summons, petition or appeal, or after protestation of a note, and whether in absence or otherwise	£29.00	*£27.00*
2. Extract of admission as a solicitor	£26.00	*£24.00*

Column 1 (Matters)	Column 2 (Fee payable)	Column 3 (Fee formerly payable)
3. Extract of protestation	£26.00	*£24.00*
4. Certificate under the Civil Jurisdiction and Judgments Act 1982	£26.00	*£24.00*
5. Documentation evidencing divorce, nullity or dissolution of marriage:		
(a) Extract from Consistorial Register of Decrees of decree pronounced on or after 23rd September 1975 if not issued in terms of item B3 or B4 of this Table	£15.00	*£14.00*
(b) Certificate of divorce in decree pronounced prior to 23rd September 1975	£15.00	*£14.00*
(c) Certified copy interlocutor in decree pronounced prior to 23rd September 1975	£15.00	*£14.00*
6. Extract from the Register of Acts and Decrees—per sheet or part thereof	£15.00	*£14.00*
7. Sealing and certifying any document for exhibition in a foreign jurisdiction or otherwise	£15.00	*£14.00*
8. Acknowledgement of receipt of a notice under section 19(6) or 21(2) of the Conveyancing and Feudal Reform (Scotland) Act 1970	£26.00	*£24.00*
9. Acknowledgement of receipt of an offer under section 9 of the Conveyancing Amendment (Scotland) Act 1938	£26.00	*£24.00*

PART II—FEES IN THE OFFICE OF THE ACCOUNTANT OF COURT

H. OFFICE OF THE ACCOUNTANT OF COURT

I. In Factories and Curatories

1. For registering case and receiving and delivering up bond of caution—		
in Court of Session appointments	£26.00	*£24.00*
in Sheriff Court appointments	£17.00	*£16.00*
2. For examining factor's inventory—0.333% of the value of the estate as disclosed		
minimum fee payable	£19.00	*£17.00*
maximum fee payable	£469.00	*£430.00*
3. For auditing each account—		
basic fee	£10.00	*£9.00*
additional percentage fee on the factor's commission as fixed (or what would have been the factor's full commission if chargeable or fully allowed)	17.5%	*17.5%*
4. For reporting *re* discharge, special powers or on other special matters	£32.00 to £144.00	*£29.00 to £132.00*
5. For granting consent in terms of section 2(4) of the Trusts (Scotland) Act 1961 and rule 61.14 of the Rules of Court	£76.00	*£70.00*
6. For report on scheme of division—		
basic fee	£17.00	*£16.00*
additional fee for each £1,000 (excluding the first £1,000) or part thereof of value of estate to be divided	£10.00	*£9.00*
maximum fee payable	£328.00	*£301.00*
7. For certificate under seal	£19.00	*£17.00*

II. In Consignations

8. For lodging consignation	£14.00	*£13.00*
9. For producing or delivering up—		
basic fee	£14.00	*£13.00*
additional fee for every £100 or part thereof uplifted	£1.00	*£1.00*
maximum fee payable	£49.00	*£45.00*

Column 1 (*Matters*)	Column 2 (*Fee payable*)	Column 3 (*Fee formerly* *payable*)
III. Liquidations		
10. For uplifting bond of caution	£4.00	£4.00

PART III—FEES IN THE OFFICE OF THE AUDITOR OF THE COURT OF SESSION

I. OFFICE OF THE AUDITOR OF THE COURT OF SESSION

1. Taxing accounts of expenses incurred in judicial proceedings (including proceedings in the High Court of Justiciary) remitted to the Auditor of the Court of Session for taxation:

(a) Auditor's fee on lodging account for taxation	£30.00	£12.00
(b) Auditor's fee for taxing accounts for expenses etc.		
(i) up to £400	£16.00	£12.00
(ii) for every additional £100 or part thereof	£4.00	£4.00

Note: fee to be determined by the Auditor of the Court of Session on amount of account as submitted

2. Fee for assessing account remitted to the Auditor to determine whether an additional fee should be paid — £200.00

3. Fee for cancellation of diet of taxation—

(a) where written notice of cancellation received within three working days of diet, half of fee that would have been payable under item I1(b) of this Table

(b) where written notice of cancellation received on the working day before or the day of the diet, three-quarters of fee that would have been payable under item I1(b) of this Table

PART IV—FEES COMMON TO ALL OFFICES

J. MISCELLANEOUS

1. Certified copy of proceedings for appeal to the House of Lords	£106.00	£97.00
2. Certifying of any other document (plus copying charges if necessary)	£10.00	£9.00
3. Recording, engrossing, extracting or copying-all documents:		
(a) By manuscript or typescript (exclusive of search fee)— for each page or part thereof	£7.00	
(b) By copying by any other means (exclusive of search fee)— for each page	£0.30	
4. Searches—for any search of records or archives:		
(a) For first half hour of time taken	£10.00	£9.00
(b) For more than one half hour up to a maximum of two hours	£26.00	£24.00
(c) For each half hour or part thereof in excess of two hours	£7.00	£6.00
(d) Correspondence fee where applicable	£7.00	£6.00
5. Captions:		
(a) Marking caption when ordered	£5.00	£5.00
(b) Warrant for caption when issued	£5.00	£5.00
6. Rolls of Court—annual subscription fee per copy including delivery	£687.00	£630.00

NOTE
[1] Substituted by the Court of Session etc. Fees Amendment Order 2002 (SSI 2002/270), art.2(3) (effective July 1, 2002).
Release 70: May 2003

REVOCATIONS

Orders revoked	Reference
The Court of Session etc. Fees Order 1984	S.I. 1984/256
The Court of Session etc. Fees Amendment Order 1985	S.I. 1985/826
The Court of Session etc. Fees Amendment (No. 2) Order 1988	S.I. 1988/969
The Court of Session etc. Fees Amendment (No. 3) Order 1988	S.I. 1988/1892
The Court of Session etc. Fees Amendment Order 1996	S.I. 1996/514

Act of Sederunt (Rules of the Court of Session Amendment) (Fees of Solicitors, Shorthand Writers and Witnesses) 2002

(SSI 2002/301)

[June 18, 2002]

The Lords of Council and Session, under and by virtue of the powers conferred upon them by section 5 of the Court of Session Act 1988 and of all other powers enabling them in that behalf, do hereby enact and declare:

Citation and commencement
    1.—(1) This Act of Sederunt may be cited as the Act of Sederunt (Rules of the Court of Session Amendment) (Fees of Solicitors, Shorthand Writers and Witnesses) 2002 and shall come into force on 1st July 2002.
    (2) This Act of Sederunt shall be inserted in the Books of Sederunt.

Increase in fees of solicitors and shorthand writers
    2.—(1) The Table of Fees in rule 42.16(3) of the Rules of the Court of Session shall be amended in accordance with the following sub-paragraph.
    (2) In the provisions mentioned in column 1 of Schedule 1 to this Act of Sederunt, for the amounts specified in column 2 of that Schedule, there shall be substituted the amounts specified in column 3.

Fees of witnesses
    3. Schedule 2 to this Act of Sederunt shall have effect to regulate the fees charged and outlays incurred, by a witness in civil proceedings in the Court of Session.

Saving and revocation
    4.—(1) Paragraphs 2 and 3 shall not affect fees chargeable for work done, or outlays incurred before 1 July 2002.
    (2) Chapter II of the Table of Fees set out in rule 42.16(3) of the Act of Sederunt (Rules of the Court of Session) 1994 is revoked, but shall continue to have effect in respect of fees chargeable and outlays incurred before the date on which this Act of Sederunt comes into force.

SCHEDULE 1

[*Omitted.*]

SCHEDULE 2

WITNESSES' FEES

1. Skilled Persons
Where it is necessary to employ a skilled person to make investigation in order to qualify that person to report and/or give evidence in any action, charges for such investigations and for attendance at any hearing in the action shall be allowed at a rate which the Auditor of Court shall determine is fair and reasonable.

2. Witnesses
A person who is cited to give evidence and in consequence incurs financial loss shall be allowed reimbursement, being such reasonable sum as the Auditor may determine to have been reasonably and necessarily incurred by the witness, but not exceeding £400 per day.

3. Travelling Allowance
In respect of any witness there shall be allowed a travelling allowance, being such sum as the Auditor may determine to have been reasonably and necessarily incurred by the witness in the travelling from and to the witnesses' residence or place of business and the Court.

4. Subsistence Allowance
In respect of any witness there shall be allowed a subsistence allowance, being such sum as the Auditor may determine to have been reasonably incurred by the witness for the extra cost of subsistence during the witnesses' absence from the witnesses' home or place of business for the purpose of giving evidence, and where the witness reasonably requires to stay overnight, for the reasonable cost of board and lodging.

5. Value Added Tax
Where any witness is a taxable person in terms of the Value Added Tax Act 1983, the amount of value added tax may be added by the witness to the witnesses' note of fee, and may be paid to the witness by the Solicitor.

6. Receipts and Vouchers
Receipts and detailed vouchers for all payments claimed in respect of a witness shall be produced to the party found liable in expenses, prior to the taxation of the Account of Expenses, and to the Auditor, if the Auditor requires.

7. Account of fees of Witnesses
The fees charged for any witness shall be stated in the Account of Expenses in a lump sum and the details of the charges shall be entered in a separate schedule appended to the Account as follows:

Name and designation	Where from	Days charged	Rate per day	Travelling and Subsistence allowance	Total	Taxed off

Directions

No. 3 of 1994

Productions which May be Sent by Facsimile Transmission

I, the Lord President of the Court of Session, under and by virtue of the powers conferred on me by rule 23.2(4)(*a*)(iv) (documents which may be transmitted by facsimile) of the Rules of the Court of Session 1994, hereby make the following direction:

1. A production may not be sent to the court and lodged in process by facsimile transmission except as permitted under this direction.

2. Subject to paragraph 3 below, where a motion mentioned in column 1 of the following table is enrolled by facsimile transmission, a document mentioned in column 2 of that table which is to be referred to solely in support of the motion may be sent by facsimile transmission with an Inventory of Productions.

TABLE

Column 1	Column 2 Supporting document
1. Assessment of liability for expenses under or by virtue of the Legal Aid (Scotland) Act 1967 or the Legal Aid (Scotland) Act 1986	Minute of assessment
2. Commission to take evidence of witness	Medical certificate
3. Interim aliment	Wage certificate etc.
4. To open confidential envelope	Copy of letter of intimation of motion to haver
5. Loosing, restriction or recall of arrestment or recall of inhibition	Copy of letter of intimation of motion

3. Where—
(*a*) a motion to which paragraph 2 applies is opposed, or
(*b*) the court requests,
the original of a document transmitted under paragraph 1 above shall be lodged in process as a production.

4. This direction shall come into force on 5th September 1994.

28th June 1994

No. 4 of 1994

Motions

I, the Lord President of the Court of Session, under and by virtue of the powers conferred on me by rule 23.4(1)(*a*) (day and time for lodging notices of opposition to witness) and rule 23.6(1) (day and publication and hearing of motions) of the Rules of the Court of Session 1994, hereby make the following direction:—

1. This direction does not apply to a motion under any of the following rules:

    rule 23.8 (motions by pursuer before calling or petitioner before first order);

    rule 23.9 (motions where caveat lodged);

    rule 23.10 (motions by defender or other person before calling).

2. Where, after calling, a motion is enrolled during a term, the provisions of the following timetable shall apply.

TIMETABLE

Time for enrolment	Latest time for opposition	Day of publication in the rolls	Day of court hearing
Monday 4 p.m.	Tuesday 12.30 p.m.	Tuesday	Wednesday
Tuesday 4 p.m.	Wednesday 12.30 p.m.	Wednesday	Thursday
Wednesday 4 p.m.	Thursday 12.30 p.m.	Thursday	Friday
Thursday 4 p.m.	Monday 12.30 p.m.	Monday	Tuesday
Friday 4 p.m.	Monday 12.30 p.m.	Monday	Tuesday

4. Where a motion is enrolled in session outwith a term or in vacation, the timetable in paragraph 2 above shall apply subject to the following provisions:—

    (*a*) there shall be no publication in the rolls of the motion; and

    (*b*) where a motion enrolled in a cause in the Inner House is one which—

        (i) may not be heard by the Lord Ordinary or the vacation judge; and

        (ii) the day for hearing the motion would fall outwith a term or in vacation,

the motion should be put out for hearing in the Single Bills on the earliest available day in the following term of the court.

5. This direction shall come into force on 5th September 1994.

28th June 1994

No. 5 of 1994

Judges for Election Court

I, the Lord President of the Court of Session, under and by virtue of the power conferred on me by section 44 of the Court of Session Act 1988, do hereby make the following direction—

1. The judges to be placed on the rota for the trial of parliamentary election petitions under Part III of the Representation of the People Act 1983 for the remainder of 1994 and for 1995 shall be the Honourable Lord Morison and the Honourable Lord Sutherland.

2. Direction No. 2 of 1989 (Rota of Judges for Election Court) is hereby revoked.

1st October 1994

Motions in Commercial Actions

I, the Lord President of the Court of Session, under and by virtue of the powers conferred on me by rule 23.6(1) of the Rules of the Court of Session 1994 (day of publication and hearing of motions), hereby make the following direction:

1. This direction applies to a motion enrolled in an action within the meaning of rule 47.1(2) (definition of commercial action). It is intended to ensure that the substantive business scheduled to begin at 10 a.m. is not interrupted or delayed.

2. Direction No. 4 of 1994 (Motions) shall apply to such a motion subject to the following paragraph.

3. Any opposed motion, or a motion requiring explanation, will be put out for hearing at a date and time convenient to the court and, where possible, to the parties. Where a motion is opposed or otherwise starred, the clerk of court will fix a date for hearing and give intimation of that date to the parties. Urgent motions will be dealt with on a priority basis.

4. This direction shall come into force on 10 July 1995.

30th June 1995

No. 4 of 1999

The Advocate General for Scotland

I, the Lord President of the Court of Session, under and by virtue of the powers conferred on me by rule 1.4 of the Rules of the Court of Session 1994, hereby make the following direction:—

When appearing in the Court of Session, the Advocate General for Scotland shall be entitled to sit at the table within the Bar, immediately below the Bench at the left hand side of the Chair.

19th May 1999

No. 2 of 2000

Rota of Judges for Election Court

I, the Lord President of the Court of Session, under and by virtue of the power conferred on me by section 44 of the Court of Session Act 1988(a), do hereby make the following direction —

1. The judges to be placed on the rota for the trial of parliamentary election petitions under Part III of the Representation of the People Act 1983(b) for the remainder of 2000 shall be the Honourable Lord Kirkwood and the Honourable Lord Milligan.

2. Direction No 2 of 1997 (Rota of Judges for Election Court) is hereby revoked.

29th February 2000

Direction

No. 2 of 2004

Sittings of the Court of Session for the Legal Years 2004/2005; 2005/2006; and 2006/2007

I, the Lord President of the Court of Session, under and by virtue of the powers conferred on me by rules 10.1, 10.2(2), 10.3 and 10.4 of the Rules of the Court of Session 1994 hereby make the following direction—

Revocation of previous direction

1. Direction No. 1 of 2004 (sittings of the Court of Session for the legal years 2004/5; 2005/6; and 2006/7) is hereby revoked.

Sessions of court

2. Subject to paragraph 4 below, the court shall be in session from—
  (a) Saturday 18th September 2004 to Monday 26th September 2005 ("legal year 2004/2005");
  (b) Tuesday 27th September 2005 to Monday 25th September 2006 ("legal year 2005/2006"); and
  (c) Tuesday 26th September 2006 to Monday 24th September 2007 ("legal year 2006/2007").

Terms of court

3.—(1) The terms of the court for the legal year 2004/2005 shall be as follows—
  (a) winter term – Tuesday 21st September 2004 to Friday 17th December 2004;
  (b) spring term – Thursday 6th January 2005 to Friday 18th March 2005; and
  (c) summer term – Tuesday 19th April 2005 to Friday 15th July 2005.
  (2) The terms of the court for the legal year 2005/2006 shall be as follows—
  (a) winter term – Tuesday 27th September 2005 to Friday 23rd December 2005;
  (b) spring term – Thursday 5th January 2006 to Friday 24th March 2006; and
  (c) summer term – Tuesday 25th April 2006 to Friday 14th July 2006.
  (3) The terms of the court for the legal year 2006/2007 shall be as follows—
  (a) winter term – Tuesday 26th September 2006 to Friday 22nd December 2006;
  (b) spring term – Thursday 4th January 2007 to Friday 23rd March 2007; and
  (c) summer term – Tuesday 24th April 2007 to Friday 13th July 2007.

Vacation

4.—(1) The court shall be in vacation from—
  (a) Saturday 18th December 2004 to Wednesday 5th January 2005;
  (b) Saturday 24th December 2005 to Wednesday 4th January 2006; and
  (c) Saturday 23rd December 2006 to Wednesday 3rd January 2007.
  (2) Each Thursday during the periods mentioned in sub-paragraph (1) shall be a sederunt day.

Public holidays

5.—(1) Subject to rule 10.3(3) of the Rules of the Court of Session 1994, no Division, Lord Ordinary or Vacation Judge shall sit during the public holidays specified in sub-paragraphs (2) to (4).

(2) The public holidays for the legal year 2004/2005 shall be as follows—
the afternoon of Friday 24th December 2004;
Monday 27th December 2004;
Tuesday 28th December 2004;
Monday 3rd January 2005;
Tuesday 4th January 2005;
Friday 25th March 2005 (Good Friday);
Monday 28th March 2005 (Easter Monday);
Monday 18th April 2005 (Spring Holiday);
Monday 2nd May 2005 (May Day Holiday);
Monday 23rd May 2005 (Victoria Day Holiday); and
Monday 19th September 2005 (Autumn Holiday).

(3) The public holidays for the legal year 2005/2006 shall be as follows—
the afternoon of Friday 23rd December 2005;
Monday 26th December 2005;
Tuesday 27th December 2005;
Monday 2nd January 2006;
Tuesday 3rd January 2006;
Monday 10th April 2006 (Spring Holiday);
Friday 14th April 2006 (Good Friday);
Monday 17th April 2006 (Easter Monday);
Monday 1st May 2006 (May Day Holiday);
Monday 22nd May 2006 (Victoria Day Holiday); and
Monday 18th September 2006 (Autumn Holiday).

(4) The public holidays for the legal year 2006/2007 shall be as follows—
the afternoon of Friday 22nd December 2006;
Monday 25th December 2006;
Tuesday 26th December 2006;
Monday 1st January 2007;
Tuesday 2nd January 2007;
Friday 6th April 2007 (Good Friday);
Monday 9th April 2007 (Easter Monday);
Monday 16th April 2007 (Spring Holiday);
Monday 7th May 2007 (May Day Holiday);
Monday 21st May 2007 (Victoria Day Holiday); and
Monday 17th September 2007 (Autumn Holiday).

Court hours

6. In term, the court shall normally sit between the following hours, with an appropriate adjournment for luncheon—
(a) Inner House – 10.30 am and 4.00 pm; and
(b) Outer House – 10.00 am and 4.00 pm

17th March 2004

Direction

No.1 of 2005

Human Rights Act 1998: declarations of incompatibility

I, the Lord President of the Court of Session, under and by virtue of the power conferred on me by rule 82.3 of the Rules of the Court of Session 1994, hereby make the following direction—

1. Direction No.2 of 2003 (intimation to the Crown in proceedings where the court is considering whether to make a declaration of incompatibility) is hereby revoked.

2. Where in any proceedings the court is considering whether to make a declaration of incompatibility within the meaning of section 4 of the Human Rights Act 1998, notice in Form 82.3–A of the Rules of the Court of Session 1994 shall be given to the following—

    (a) Solicitor to the Advocate General for Scotland,
        Victoria Quay,
        Edinburgh,
        EH6 6QQ

    (b) Solicitor to the Scottish Executive,
        Victoria Quay,
        Edinburgh,
        EH6 6QQ

13th April 2005

No. 2 of 2005

Rota for trial of parliamentary election petitions

I, the Lord President of the Court of Session, under and by virtue of the power conferred on me by section 44 of the Court of Session Act 1988, hereby make the following direction—

The judges to be placed on the rota for the trial of parliamentary election petitions under Part III of the Representation of the People Act 1983 for the remainder of 2005 shall be the Right Honourable Lord Osborne and the Right Honourable Lord Abernethy.

26th May 2005

No. 3 of 2005

Motions in certain insolvency and companies actions

I, the Lord President of the Court of Session, under and by virtue of the power conferred on me by rule 23.6 of the Rules of the Court of Session 1994, hereby make the following direction—

1. This direction applies to a motion enrolled in—

    (a) proceedings in the Outer House in a cause under or by virtue of the Insolvency Act 1986 or the Company Directors Disqualification Act 1986; and

    (b) proceedings in the Outer House in a cause under or by virtue of section 136 (application to court for order of confirmation) or section 425 (power of company to compromise with creditors and members) of the Companies Act 1985.

2. This direction is intended to ensure that the substantive business scheduled to begin at 10 a.m. is not interrupted or delayed.

3. Direction No.4 of 1994 (motions) shall apply to such a motion subject to the following paragraph.

4. Any opposed motion, or a motion requiring explanation, will be put out for hearing at a date and time convenient to the court and, where possible, to the parties. Where a motion is opposed or otherwise starred, the clerk of court will fix a date for hearing and give intimation of that date to the parties. Urgent motions will be dealt with on a priority basis.

5. This direction shall come into force on 1st July 2005.

26th May 2005

No. 2 of 2006

Sittings of the Court of Session for the Legal Years 2007/2008; 2008/2009; and 2009/2010

I, the Lord President of the Court of Session, under and by virtue of the powers conferred on me by rules 10.1, 10.2(2), 10.3 and 10.4 of the Rules of the Court of Session 1994 hereby make the following direction—

Revocation of previous direction

1. Direction No. 1 of 2006 (sittings of the Court of Session for the legal years 2007/2008; 2008/2009; and 2009/2010) is hereby revoked.

Sessions of court

2. Subject to paragraph 4 below, the court shall be in session from—
   (a) Tuesday 25th September 2007 to Monday 22nd September 2008 ("legal year 2007/2008");
   (b) Tuesday 23rd September 2008 to Monday 21st September 2009 ("legal year 2008/2009"); and
   (c) Tuesday 22nd September 2009 to Monday 20th September 2010 ("legal year 2009/2010").

Terms of court

3.—(1) The terms of the court for the legal year 2007/2008 shall be as follows—
  (a) winter term—Tuesday 25th September 2007 to Friday 21st December 2007;
  (b) spring term—Friday 4th January 2008 to Thursday 20th March 2008; and
  (c) summer term—Tuesday 22nd April 2008 to Friday 11th July 2008.
(2) The terms of the court for the legal year 2008/2009 shall be as follows—
  (a) winter term—Tuesday 23rd September 2008 to Friday 19th December 2008;
  (b) spring term—Tuesday 6th January 2009 to Friday 20th March 2009; and
  (c) summer term—Tuesday 21st April 2009 to Friday 10th July 2009.
(3) The terms of the court for the legal year 2009/2010 shall be as follows—
  (a) winter term—Tuesday 22nd September 2009 to Friday 18th December 2009;
  (b) spring term—Wednesday 6th January 2010 to Friday 26th March 2010; and
  (c) summer term—Monday 26th April 2010 to Friday 16th July 2010.

Vacation

4.—(1) The court shall be in vacation from—
  (a) Saturday 22nd December 2007 to Thursday 3rd January 2008;
  (b) Saturday 20th December 2008 to Monday 5th January 2009; and
  (c) Saturday 19th December 2009 to Tuesday 5th January 2010.
(2) Each Thursday during the periods mentioned in sub-paragraph (1) shall be a sederunt day.

Public holidays

5.—(1) Subject to rule 10.3(3) of the Rules of the Court of Session 1994, no Division, Lord Ordinary or Vacation Judge shall sit during the public holidays specified in sub-paragraphs (2) to (4).
(2) The public holidays for the legal year 2007/2008 shall be as follows—
  the afternoon of Monday 24th December 2007;
  Tuesday 25th December 2007;
  Wednesday 26th December 2007;
  Tuesday 1st January 2008;
  Wednesday 2nd January 2008;
  Friday 21st March 2008 (Good Friday);
  Monday 24th March 2008 (Easter Monday);
  Monday 21st April 2008 (Spring Holiday);
  Monday 5th May 2008 (May Day Holiday);
  Monday 19th May 2008 (Victoria Day Holiday); and
  Monday 15th September 2008 (Autumn Holiday).
(3) The public holidays for the legal year 2008/2009 shall be as follows—
  the afternoon of Wednesday 24th December 2008;
  Thursday 25th December 2008;
  Friday 26th December 2008;
  Thursday 1st January 2009;
  Friday 2nd January 2009;
  Friday 10th April 2009 (Good Friday);
  Monday 13th April 2009 (Easter Monday);
  Monday 20th April 2009 (Spring Holiday);
  Monday 4th May 2009 (May Day Holiday);
  Monday 18th May 2009 (Victoria Day Holiday); and
  Monday 21st September 2009 (Autumn Holiday).

(4) The public holidays for the legal year 2009/2010 shall be as follows—
the afternoon of Thursday 24th December 2009;
Friday 25th December 2009;
Monday 28th December 2009;
Friday 1st January 2010;
Monday 4th January 2010;
Friday 2nd April 2010 (Good Friday);
Monday 5th April 2010 (Easter Monday);
Monday 19th April 2010 (Spring Holiday);
Monday 3rd May 2010 (May Day Holiday);
Monday 17th May 2010 (Victoria Day Holiday); and
Monday 20th September 2010 (Autumn Holiday).

Court hours

6. In term, the court shall normally sit between the following hours, with an appropriate adjournment for luncheon—
  (a) Inner House—10.30 am and 4.00 pm; and
  (b) Outer House—10.00 am and 4.00 pm.

November 2006

[NEXT TEXT PAGE IS C 2001]

Practice Notes

23rd July 1952

Designation of Defender in Divorce Summonses

Cases have been occurring in which Divorce Summonses have designed the defender as "at present a prisoner in" a named prison. This designation enters the Minute Book and if, as frequently happens after a long interval, a certificate or extract is required of the decree of divorce, the designation will re-appear. It is suggested to solicitors that, subject to suitable arrangements being made to secure that service is duly made, it is undesirable that the instance of the Summons should needlessly place on permanent record the fact that the defender was at the time temporarily in custody.

16th April 1953

Lodging Certificate of Search for Declarator of Marriage

A case having occurred in which two decrees of declarator of marriage were pronounced relating to the same irregular marriage, the parties having lost touch with each other, arrangements have been made that in all such cases the Registrar General will be prepared on application to state whether a previous declarator has been granted and recorded in his Registers, and a letter from him certifying the result of his search should be lodged in process before the proof.

28th September 1956

Copies of Entries in Register of Births

It has been arranged that photostatic copies of entries in the Register of Births will be treated by the court as equivalent to the principals. In Scotland, applications for such photostatic copies should be made to the Registrar General of Births, Deaths and Marriages for Scotland, who holds duplicate originals of all entries, but in England where the system is different, applications should be made to the local Registrars.

15th November 1957

Care of Hospital Reports and X-rays

The attention of all members of the legal profession is drawn to complaints which have been received from hospital boards regarding the condition in which hospital reports and X-ray plates, produced for use in the courts, have been returned to hospitals on the termination of proceedings. It is reported that X-ray plates in particular have been returned so folded and cracked that their value has been most seriously affected when the condition of the patient has required further examination of the plates.

It is hoped that in future the greatest care will be used in dealing with such productions, especially in guarding them from damage during transmission.

6th June 1968

Soul and Conscience Medical Certificates

It shall no longer be necessary, in connection with any action pending before the Court of Session, that a medical certificate should bear the words "on soul and conscience."

6th June 1968

Report under Section 11(1) of the Matrimonial Proceedings (Children) Act 1958

An Officer who has furnished a Report to the Court under subsection (1) of section 11 of the Matrimonial Proceedings (Children) Act 1958 shall not be cited as a witness unless, in terms of subsection (4) of said section, the Court, on consideration of such a Report, either *ex proprio motu* or on the application of any person interested requires the person who furnished the Report to appear and be examined on oath regarding any matter dealt with in the Report, and such person may be examined or cross-examined accordingly.

18th July 1969

Fee Fund Dues on Account of Expenses

With effect from 1st August 1969, the amount of the Fee Fund Dues which are payable when lodging an Account of Expenses in process should not be included as an outlay in the Account. The sum paid for these Fee Fund Dues will be added to the total amount of the Account by the Auditor.

14th May 1970

Right of Reply at Conclusion of Proof

This Note is issued to confirm the practice that it is in the discretion of the Lord Ordinary to grant a right of reply to the defender's speech made at the conclusion of a proof.

14th December 1972

Availability of Medical Records for Party's Medical Attendant

Medical records required for the purposes of a court action should at all times be available to a party's medical attendant.[1] With effect from this date it will be the duty of the solicitor concerned immediately on receipt by him of such records to furnish the medical attendant with a copy thereof. If medical records are received by the court marked "confidential" it will be the duty of the solicitor concerned immediately to enrol a motion to have the envelope containing such records opened up and, if the court admits the same, to transmit a copy thereof without delay to the medical attendant.

NOTE
[1] "Medical attendant" means "general practitioner." The practice note does not refer to hospital records.

14th April 1973

[1] **Office of Auditor of Court of Session:**
Value added tax; Taxation of expenses in (1) Civil proceedings; (2) Criminal proceedings and (3) General business

NOTE
[1] As amended by P.N. No. 9 of 1994, with effect from 5th September 1994.

R.C.S. 1994, r. 42.12(1), authorises solicitors to make an addition to fees, where appropriate, of such amount as is equal to the amount of value added tax.

Value added tax was introduced by the Finance Act 1972. Every taxable person as defined by the Act must be registered and in general terms (and subject to the exceptions set out in the Act) whenever a taxable person supplies goods or services in the United Kingdom in the course of business a liability to tax arises.

Responsibility for making a charge for VAT in a proper case and for accounting to Customs and Excise for the proper amount of VAT is solely that of the registered person concerned.

The following directions will apply to all accounts lodged for taxation which include any charge for work done or services rendered on or after 1st April 1973, namely:—

1. *Registered Number*

The registered number allocated by Customs and Excise to every person registered under the Act must appear in a prominent place at the head of every Account of Expenses, Business Accounts, Note of Fee, account or voucher on which VAT is claimed or chargeable.

2. *Action before Taxation*

(a) If there is a possibility of a dispute as to whether any person claiming expenses is a taxable person or whether any service in respect of which a charge is proposed to be made in the account is zero rated or exempt, reference should be made to Customs and Excise, and wherever possible, a statement produced on taxation.

(b) Where VAT is claimed by a person who is engaged in business and the expenses of the proceedings to be submitted for taxation are chargeable as an expense of that business, then (unless the paying party agrees the basis on which VAT is claimed) a certificate must be produced on taxation that the receiving party is not entitled to recover, or is only entitled to recover a stated proportion of, the VAT claimed on such expenses as input tax in his VAT account with Customs and Excise. A form of certificate to be given by the Solicitor or accountant for the party receiving expenses is set out in the schedule hereto.

3. *Form of Accounts*

The form of accounts in practice will require amendment as follows:—

(a) *Apportionment*
The account must be divided into separate parts so as to show the work done on a day to day basis before and from 1st April 1973. Wherever a lump sum charge has been made for work, only part of which was performed by 31st March 1973, the lump sum or scale fee must also be apportioned.

(b) *Disbursements*
(i) VAT attributable to any disbursement must be shown stating it has been paid. This will consist of the VAT which has been paid at the time

when the account is drawn and an amount in respect of any unpaid disbursement. These amounts may be shown in the disbursement column immediately below the disbursement to which it relates.

(ii) Posts and incidents should be charged with VAT even though they bear no tax when the Solicitor incurs them.

It is otherwise where the disbursement is normally charged as a specific disbursement to the client, *e.g.* the cost of travel by public transport on a specific journey for a particular client. Taxi fares, however, are subject to VAT.

The end of the account must show the total for VAT including the VAT on the fees and posts.

The fee fund dues on Auditor's fee will be calculated on the total of profit fees and disbursements as lodged without the VAT thereon.

(c) *Legal Aid*

In legal aid cases the account must be drawn so as to show the total VAT on counsel's fees as a separate item from the VAT on profit costs and other disbursements and must take account of the fact that VAT will only be payable on 90 per cent of the solicitor profit fees and counsel's fees (see para. 7 below).

4. *Tax Invoice in Judicial Proceedings*

The taxed account is always retained in process so that where a Solicitor waives his Solicitor and own client expenses and accepts the taxed expenses payable by the unsuccessful party in settlement it will be necessary for a short statement as to the amount of the taxed expenses and the VAT thereon to be prepared for use as the tax invoice.

5. *Vouchers*

Where receipted accounts for disbursement made by the solicitor or his client are retained as tax invoices a photostat copy of any such receipted account may be produced and will be accepted as sufficient evidence of payment when disbursements are vouched.

6. *Rate of VAT*

The rate of VAT which will be applied on taxation will be the rate at that date, save in respect of disbursements which have been paid when the rate will be the rate at the date of payment. Should there be a change in the rate applied on taxation between the date of taxation and the signing of the report of taxation, any interested party may apply for the taxation to be varied so as to take account of any increase or reduction in the amount of tax payable. Once the report of taxation has been signed no variation will be possible.

7. *Calculation of VAT Recoverable by a Legally Aided Party*

VAT will not be recoverable on the 10 per cent of the solicitor's fees and counsel's fees which is retained by the legal aid fund. Accordingly, the recoverable VAT must be calculated on 90 per cent of the Solicitor's fees and 90 per cent of counsel's fees. This will not apply to other disbursements, which are paid in full by the legal aid fund.

8. *Auditor's Reports*

In non legal aid cases the total VAT allowed will be shown as a separate item. In legal aid cases the VAT on counsel's fees will be shown separately from the remaining VAT.

9. *Posts and Incidents*

Posts and incidents must be shown separately at the different rates in operation before and after 1st April 1973. Posts and incidents are not chargeable on the 10 per cent increase in fees for VAT.

10. *Fee Fund Dues and Auditor's Fees*

The sums payable as fee fund dues on an account of expenses or as Auditor's fees should not be added to the account. The appropriate sum will be added to the account by the Auditor. When it is impossible to ascertain the correct sum payable as fee fund dues when lodging an account in process (*e.g.* where an additional fee is allowed under the Rules of Court 347(*d*)) arrangements may be made for the fee fund stamps to be affixed to the account after taxation.

11. *Witnesses' Expenses*

In cases where it is impossible, because of the incidence of VAT for witnesses to incur accounts for subsistence at or below the levels prescribed by the Act of Sederunt (Rules of Court Amendment No. 5) 1970, such higher sums may be allowed as the Auditor may determine as having been reasonably incurred.

SCHEDULE

FORM OF CERTIFICATE

Address:
Date:

To: The Auditor of the Court of Session
A. *v.* B.C. Ltd
With reference to the pending taxation of the defender's   (or as the case may be) fees and disbursements herein which are payable by the pursuer, or   (as the case may be) we the undersigned as   (solicitors to) (the auditors of) the above-named defender   (or as the case may be) company, hereby certify that the defender   (or as the case may be) company on the basis of its last completed VAT return would   (not be entitled to recover) (be entitled to recover only   per cent of the) value added tax on such fees and disbursements, as input tax pursuant to s. 3 of the Finance Act 1972.

(Signed)...
Solicitor/Auditor, to/or (Defender) ....
Registered No. ....

17th December 1974

Summons Served on Soldiers in Northern Ireland

A case arose recently where a copy Summons was posted to a member of Her Majesty's Forces whose address was a private billet in Northern Ireland. The envelope containing the copy Summons revealed his name, rank and number. In future, such information should be excluded from the address on the envelope, and the recipient should be addressed as if he were a private citizen. Where the address of the barracks to which the recipient is attached is known, any document should be sent there rather than to his private billet.

No. 2 of 1976

Reporters in Petitions to Sanction a Scheme of Arrangement

Petition for sanction of schemes of arrangement under section 206 of the Companies Act 1948:—solicitors are advised that when they enrol a motion for a first order in such a petition they may at the same time enrol a separate motion of the same date for the appointment by the court of a reporter for the process. The person so appointed will be the same person to whom the court will ultimately remit the petition for report.

No. 4 of 1976

Fee Fund Dues

As solicitors will be aware, the Court of Session (Scotland) (Fees) Order 1976, made on 10th February 1976, enacted that as from 1st April 1976 all fees payable to the Court of Session will cease to be collected in stamps. It is recognised that the payment of many individual fees, whether by cheques or by cash, would present some inconvenience to practitioners and that even the physical transmission of funds would create security difficulties. It has accordingly been decided that the general interest would best be served by the introduction of a credit system, and the following arrangements will therefore apply as from 1st April 1976.

1. There will be a central cashier's office for the Court of Session which will in the meantime be situated in room J15.

2. No cash will be handed over in either the general or petition departments in respect of any fee which is payable there. Instead, any fee due to be paid in either of these departments by any solicitor will be debited by the cashier to the account of the appropriate firm. This will include fees due in respect of requests for certified copy interlocutors.

3. A statement of account will thereafter be rendered to the appropriate firm weekly. This statement will show both the details of the individual items and the total due, and will be for immediate settlement which may be made by a single payment at the office of the cashier during business hours.

4. It is an essential feature of the scheme that all accounts be settled promptly and it is hoped that solicitors will co-operate with the departments in this respect.

5. The credit scheme will not in the meantime apply to payments falling to be made in the office of the extractor, in the opinions room, and in the teinds and the justiciary offices.

6. During the period from 1st April to 2nd May (when on the latter date the Court of Session will assume the duties of the signeting office) signeting dues will be payable in cash.

No. 3 of 1977

Reconciliation in Breakdown of Marriages

1. The attention of practitioners is drawn to the provisions of section 2 of the Divorce (Scotland) Act 1976, and to the long title.

2. The provisions of section 2 are designed to facilitate and encourage the reconciliation of estranged spouses who are, or may become, involved in a consistorial action. By enacting those provisions, Parliament has

emphasised the importance of exploring the possibility of effecting a reconciliation between the parties to a marriage which has not broken down irretrievably. Central and local government agencies have likewise sanctioned this policy by giving assistance in cash or in kind to voluntary organisations concerned with marriage counselling.

3. Experience shows that once an action has been raised, it is usually too late for the parties to attempt to effect a reconciliation, and it is not expected that the court will be frequently requested, or be in a position, to exercise the powers conferred on it by section 2(1) of the Act (power to continue an action to enable attempts to be made to effect a reconciliation). In these circumstances, in order to promote the success of the legislative policy, legal practitioners who are consulted about marital problems with a view to consistorial proceedings should try to identify, at as early a stage as possible, those cases in which the parties might benefit from the expert advice and guidance of a marriage counsellor, and in those cases should encourage the parties to seek such advice and guidance.

4. There are a number of voluntary organisations, some of them denominational, concerned with marriage counselling who have branch offices in Scotland. Direct liaison or referral by a solicitor will often not present any difficulty, but advice concerning the appropriate organisation may usually be obtained from the local citizens' advice bureau or social work department.

11th March 1977

No. 4 of 1977

Value Added Tax; Taxation of Expenses in (1) Civil Proceedings; (2) Criminal Proceedings; and (3) General Business

The Auditor refers to the above practice note.[1] Accounts are being lodged for taxation which do not conform to the directions or to the Act of Sederunt dated 28th February 1973. Solicitors are therefore requested to comply in order to save unnecessary time both in the auditor's office and at taxations.

For the guidance of solicitors it is explained that where the recoverable expenses of a legally aided party are paid by the Law Society of Scotland out of the legal aid fund without taxation, value added tax is not recoverable on the 10 per cent of solicitors' fees and counsel's fees which is retained by the legal aid fund. Attention is directed to paragraph 3(c) (forms of accounts) and paragraph 7 (calculation of VAT) in the above practice note.

An example of an abstract where a dual taxation has been carried out by the Auditor in any of the circumstances likely to be encountered is appended for reference.

NOTE
[1] See Practice Note of 14th April 1973.

Abstract Party & Party, Legal Aid Fund—Pre- and Post-Legal Aid

TAXED OFF		LEGAL AID FUND			PARTY & PARTY		
P. & P.	L.A.	VAT	Disbs.	Fees and Posts	VAT	Disbs.	Fees and Posts
£10.00	PRE LEGAL AID—POST VAT						
	£00.00				£0.80	£30.00	£60.00
	Taxed Off						10.00
							50.00
	Add 30% to 1/9/76						15.00
							65.00
	Add VAT on Solicitors' Fees and Posts						5.20
							70.20
	Add Disbursements						30.00
							£100.20
	Add VAT on Disbursements						80
							101.00
	Add Fee Fund Dues						2.00
							£103.00

LEGAL AID—POST VAT

£10.00	£0.72	£20.00	£4.04	£65.00		

£15.00 Taxed Off		£35.00	£140.00
		15.00	10.00
		20.00	130.00
Add VAT on 90% Solicitors' Fees and Posts		1.44	9.36
Add disbursements		21.44	139.36
		20.00	65.00
		41.44	204.36
Add VAT on Disbursements		0.72	4.04
		42.16	208.40
Add Fee Fund Dues		1.00	4.00
TOTAL		£43.16	£212.40

LEGAL AID ABSTRACT

Solicitors Fees and Posts	£150.00
VAT on 90%	10.80
Counsel's Fees	55.00
VAT on 90%	3.96
Disbursements	35.00
VAT on 100%	0.80
TOTAL	£255.56

21st March 1985

Form of Extracts in Decrees of Divorce

The attention of solicitors is drawn to the fact that as the result of the recent extension of word processing facilities in the Court of Session now available to the Extracts Department, the form of extract in decrees of divorce will include (a) the divorce, (b) decrees for custody, access, aliment, periodical allowance, capital sum and expenses and (c) decrees for interdict and orders under the Matrimonial Homes (Family Protection) (Scotland) Act 1981.

10th December 1986

Hearing of Motions

[1] 1. All unopposed motions enrolled for hearing in the Outer House, other than those referred to in paragraph 9, shall *not*, in the first instance, require the appearance of counsel.

NOTE
[1] As amended by P.N. No. 6 of 1994 with effect from 5th September 1994.

Categories of unopposed motions
2. (1) Those motions which are according to present practice unstarred shall continue to be enrolled in the same manner as hitherto. (2) Those motions of a procedural nature, which have hitherto required the appearance of counsel, shall be dealt with by the clerk of court. (3) Those motions which have hitherto required the appearance of counsel and which will require to receive judicial consideration shall be dealt with by the judge in chambers.

Information to be supplied to the court

3. (1) Written reasons or explanations shall be incorporated in or produced as a paper apart along with motions categorised in paras. 2(2) and 2(3) and any relevant documentary evidence produced therewith where appropriate. (2) Details of the motions in the category referred to in para. 2(2), and illustrations of the information required, are set forth in appendix I to this practice note. (3) Similar details in respect of para. 2(3) are set forth in appendix II to this practice note. Details in this appendix are not exhaustive but practitioners should apply the principles illustrated therein to any motion which is not covered thereby.

Procedure in respect of disposal of motions

4. In regard to motions referred to in paras. 2(1) and 2(2) the following procedures shall apply: (1) Where the clerk of court is satisfied that any such motion may be granted he shall prepare and sign the appropriate interlocutor (subject to the provisions of Rule of Court 93A). (2) Where the clerk of court is not satisfied with the motion as enrolled, he shall either (a) where there is a defect of a technical nature (*e.g.* specification for the recovery of documents for which there is no call on record) which cannot be remedied immediately, drop the motion; or (b) consult with the practitioner to obtain any additional information which would allow the motion to be granted in full or in such restricted terms as may be agreed. (3) Where the clerk of court after such consultation is still not so satisfied, he shall either (a) of consent, drop the motion; or (b) arrange that the motion be put out starred in order that counsel may be heard thereon.

5. In regard to motions referred to in para. 2(3), the following procedures shall apply: (1) On receipt of such a motion, the terms thereof and any documentation relative thereto shall be examined by the clerk of court for any obvious errors or omissions. (2) Where any such error or omission is discovered, the clerk of court shall consult with the practitioner to obtain further information. (3) Where the clerk of court, with or without such consultation, is satisfied with the terms of and any documentation relative to such a motion, he shall present the papers to the Lord Ordinary in chambers. (4) After consideration of such papers the Lord Ordinary shall either (a) grant the motion in full; (b) grant the motion in such restricted terms as may be agreed after further consultation between the clerk of court and the practitioner; (c) of consent drop the motion; or (d) direct that the motion be put out starred in order that counsel may be heard thereon.

6. Where the Lord Ordinary has directed that a motion is to be put out starred in terms of paras. 4(3)(b) or 5(4)(d), the clerk of court, in consultation with the practitioner, shall arrange for such appearance in the motion roll on a mutually convenient date.

7. To facilitate consultation referred to in paras. 4 and 5 hereof, all motions shall include the name of the individual practitioner with whom contact should be made by the clerk of court.

8. Where, by 12.30 p.m. on the day the motion appears on the rolls, either (a) the clerk of court has been unable to consult with the practitioner through the absence of the individual or someone authorised to deputise for him; or (b) such additional information as has been sought is not available to the clerk of court, the clerk of court may drop the motion.

9. The present practice in regard to the appearance of counsel in (i) motions before calling; (ii) orders before service of a petition (which do not appear in the motion roll); and (iii) motions for interim orders under the Matrimonial Homes (Family Protection) (Scotland) Act 1981, shall continue to apply in the meantime.

N.B.

1. Practitioners who encounter problems in regard to the new procedure are requested to communicate with either of the deputy principal clerks, . . . who will be monitoring the procedure.

2. In an effort to ensure that motions are properly enrolled, the following are published as examples of motions and relative information which would be acceptable to the court. (1) "On behalf of the pursuer to allow a further continuation of the period of adjustment for four weeks in respect that extensive adjustments were received from the defenders two days ago and further advice now has to be obtained from pursuer's expert witness." (2) "On behalf of the pursuer for interim custody of the child . . . and for interim aliment for said child at the rate of . . . in respect of (1) the averments contained in articles 4 and 5 of the condescendence and (2) [where appropriate] the other factors narrated in paper apart 'A' annexed hereto."

Appendix I

Column 1	Column 2
Dispensation with service or intimation (or further service any document).	Reason for dispensation to be stated. Any previous executions of service or intimation to be lodged with this motion.
Second sist for legal aid.	Reason for application to be stated.
[1]Late documents (except late closed records).	Reason for the delay on lodging the document to be stated.
Commission to take evidence.	Reason for the taking of the evidence on commission to be stated. Where appropriate any supporting documents such as medical or birth certificates to be lodged.
Application for authority to print a record on minute and answers or on petition and answers (as adjusted where appropriate) which is not made of consent.	Adjustments should be shown on principal documents to enable clerk of court to decide whether the expense of printing a record is necessary.
Continuation of adjustment period or restoration of cause to adjustment roll.	Reason for further continuation of adjustment or resoration to the roll to be stated. Any adjustments made to date should be shown on either an adjusted copy of the open record or, in the case of minute and answers, on the principal documents.
Lost step in process.	Explanation of the likely fate of the lost step of process and efforts made to try and trace same to be stated.
To allow a parole consistorial proof (other than nullity).	Reason why affidavit procedure inappropriate to be stated.
To discharge diet of proof or jury trial.	Reason for discharge to be stated, with provision for expenses.
Recall of arrestment/inhibition (by party who has arrested/inhibited).	Reason for recall to be stated. (As a party is entitled to recall any diligence no reason is really necessary other than why it requires to be done by motion as opposed to extrajudicially.)
Prorogation of time for lodging documents outwith time ordered by interlocutor or imposed by Rule of Court.	Reason why time limit cannot be complied with to be stated.
Prorogation of time for finding caution.	Reason why time limit cannot be complied with to be stated.
First order in judicial review (not accompanied by a motion for an interim order therein).	(As the only matter in contention at this stage is the date of the first hearing—which can be arranged between keeper and clerk, as is indeed the practice—there would seem to be no necessity for agents to supply further information.)

[1] NOTE
As amended by Practice Note No. 5 of 1991.

Appendix II

Column 1	Column 2
Interim custody and aliment (and variation thereof).	Up to date information on custody arrangements and the financial circumstances of the parties to be submitted along with the motion. Where information regarding the financial position of the other party is not available or cannot be obtained an appropriate explanation should be made in the motion sheet and the most recent information should be produced. (To enable the court to exercise its discretion in respect of any award of aliment the motion should include the phrase "or such other lesser sum as to the court shall seem proper".)
Interim access (and variation thereof).	Details of the arrangements for access should be provided with the motion sheet.
Assessment of liability for expenses under s. 2 (6) (e) of Legal Aid (Scotland) Act 1967.	Motion to be accompanied by statement of parties' income and expenditure (either wage certificates or a certificate of earnings) and a statement of estimated expenses.
Recall of arrestment/inhibition (by party other than party who arrested/inhibited).	Copy letter of intimation confirming that the other party has received intimation of the motion to be produced, with provision for expenses.
To open "confidential" envelope recovered under specification.	Reason as to why contents are relevant to be stated. Copy letter of intimation to havers to be produced.
Appointment ad interim of curator/factor after service of petition.	Reason for application to be stated.
Appointment of provisional/official liquidator.	Statement of assets of the company to be included.
Of new for appointment of curator/factor.	Reason why caution not found timeously to be included.
For award of sequestration	Name of proposed interim trustee to be included.
For appointment of a curator ad litem.	Reason for the appointment to be included. Where necessary, relevant medical certificate to be produced.
[1]Late closed records	Reasons for delay to be stated.

Note. The [fifth last to second last] items in this appendix could well be added to appendix I were it not for the fact that the interlocutors would still require the signature of the judge.

NOTE
[1] As inserted by Practice Note No. 5 of 1991.

27th March 1987

Publication of Adjustment Rolls

As from the commencement of the summer session of the court the practice whereby causes due to call in the adjustment roll and continued adjustment roll are published in the rolls of court on the preceding Friday and Monday will cease, and the following practice will be introduced in place thereof:—

1. A list of causes calling in the adjustment roll on any Wednesday will be published on that day with a note of the date to which the adjustment of record has been continued prefixed thereto.
2. A list of causes due to call in the continued adjustment roll on any Wednesday will be published on the preceding Friday.

To facilitate identification of causes in each of the aforementioned lists the names of the solicitors for parties will be shown.

No. 1 of 1987

Bankruptcy Procedure

With effect from Monday, 20th July 1987, a new procedure will commence in accordance with s. 12(2) of the Bankruptcy (Scotland) Act 1985 for the citation of debtors in sequestration proceedings at the instance of a creditor or a trustee acting under a trust deed. The procedure for ordering a respondent to enter appearance in a sequestration process will no longer apply and the court will now fix a date for the debtor to appear when issuing the first deliverance in the sequestration.

After presentation of the petition, the court on granting a first deliverance citing the debtor shall fix a hearing for a date more than 14 days from the date of the first deliverance. Any request for an earlier diet should be made within 24 hours of the presentation of the petition.

One day a week will be fixed for the hearing of orders for sequestration (not the first deliverance which can be dealt with on any date) and that will be on a Thursday of each week. Counsel will be required to appear at that hearing to move for the sequestration order in anticipation of an appearance by a debtor. The new procedure will also require the petitioner's counsel to make a motion at the bar for sequestration as no motion will now be enrolled in the motion sheet for an award of sequestration.

16th July 1987

Notice: 3rd December 1987

Opinions

Following representations from interested individuals and bodies a working group examined and reported on the proposal that judges' opinions should be prepared and published to a common style. One of the recommendations, since approved by the Lord President, was that the names of local correspondents be included on the backing of the opinion and thereafter published with the report of the case. This information is only available if Edinburgh solicitors include the details on the backing of the record. Practitioners are requested to provide these details with immediate effect, as agreed at the recent meeting of the Joint Committee of Legal Societies in Edinburgh and Midlothian.

Notice: 11th December 1987

Solicitors' References on Principal Writ

With a view to improving communication between court staff and solicitors in a cause, solicitors are requested to provide their reference on the backing of their principal writ. It would also be of considerable assistance in this regard if the respective references of solicitors were shown on any closed record lodged in process.

No. 4 of 1987

Names of Counsel in the Rolls

1. From 5th January 1988, where particulars of any cause set down for hearing are published in the rolls of court, the name(s) of counsel in the cause will not be shown.

2. With regard to the motion roll, notwithstanding the provision in Rule of Court 93(*b*), the solicitor or his representative shall, when enrolling a motion in any cause, hand to the clerk a slip containing the names of the parties and the title of his firm abbreviated to the first two names thereof, where appropriate.

3. In consequence of the foregoing, and in order to facilitate communication between counsel in a cause solicitors, when instructing counsel for any proof, jury trials or debate, should provide him/her where possible with the name of counsel for the other party or parties.

11th December 1987

No. 2 of 1988

Copies of Petitions for Advocates' Library

Solicitors are reminded that, in addition to the provisions of Rule of Court 200, a copy of any petition presented to the Outer House should be lodged, at the same time as the principal petition, for the use of the Advocates' Library.

2nd March 1988

No. 4 of 1988

Fee Fund Dues

From 1st July 1988, a Kalamazoo System of receipting/debiting will be introduced in all offices of the Court of Session and High Court of Justiciary. Solicitors will be issued with an individual receipt/debit slip for every first paper or document lodged, or for enrolment or opposition to a motion by which a party, other than the originating party, first makes appearance in a cause or proceeding.

Paragraph B11 makes provision for charging to each party of a fee in respect of the lodging of a closed record. In addition to the receipt/debit slip issued to the party lodging the closed record, a receipt/debit slip will also be issued to each other party to the cause. This will be deposited in the appropriate solicitors' box outside the General Department. Where no box is available it will be mailed directly to the party concerned or their representative.

The credit system introduced on 1st April 1976 and detailed in Practice Note No. 4 of 1976, will continue to operate as before. Please note that payments falling to be made in the office of the Extractor, and in the Teinds and Justiciary offices will continue to be excluded from the credit scheme.

30th June 1988

Notice: 1st July 1988

Further to Practice Note No. 4 of 1988 a list of standard abbreviations for use with the Kalamazoo System has been devised. These abbreviations will be contained on the receipt/debit slip issued and also on the principal credit account rendered for payment by the cashier each month.

A/C EXPS	Accounts of Expenses
ANS	Answers
CAV	Caveat
CCI	Certified Copy Interlocutor
CERT FEE	Certification Fee
C/R	Closed Record
DEFS	Defences
EXT	Extract Abbreviate
FIAT	Fiat
FIRST APP	First Appearance into process, other than by originating party
HOL	Certification of proceedings for Appeal to House of Lords
J/M	Joint Minute
J/P	Jury Precept
LOR	Letter of Request
LVA	Lands Valuation Appeal
MAD	Minute after Decree
M/E	Minute of Election
NOTE	Note
OBJ	Objections
OHF	Out of hours fee
OP	Opinion
PH	Photocopying
PROT	Protestation
R/M	Reclaiming Motion
SCA	Sheriff Court Appeal
SP/C	Special Case
ST/C	Stated Case
S/S	Signet and Summons
TEIND	Teind

Notice: 7th March 1990

Agents are reminded of the importance of notifying the keeper's office of any motion likely to take longer than 20 minutes. There have been a number of recent instances where either no prior notification has been given to this office or the estimate given is so wildly at variance with the eventual duration as to imply that no thought was given to the original estimate. On a number of occasions this has caused unacceptable delays in the commencement of proofs where, had proper notification been given, the matter could have been dealt with by another judge at a later stage in the morning.

No. 2 of 1990

Ex Tempore Judgments

For the avoidance of doubt it is confirmed that where the court issues an *ex tempore* judgment the interlocutor resulting therefrom will be signed and dated on the day that judgment is delivered and not at the date of the issue of the opinion. The reclaiming days will commence on the date of issue of the interlocutor and not on the date of issue of the opinion.

31st May 1990

No. 3 of 1991

Procedure Roll

[*Revoked by P.N. No. 2 of 2004*]

No. 4 of 1991

Advance Copies of Opinions

Practitioners are reminded that the only purpose of the informal practice under which advance copies of opinions are provided to them, is to allow them to prepare, in consultation with counsel, motions for expenses, leave to reclaim, etc., with a view to minimising the court time required for the advising of the opinion.

It is a condition of this practice that neither the opinion itself nor any indication of the contents thereof should be revealed to any other person, including any party to the action involved, in advance of the date of the advising.

There have been a number of instances where this requirement of confidentiality has been breached. Any further breaches may lead to this practice being withdrawn and a return to the system by which opinions were issued only on the day on which they were to be advised.

1st May 1991

No. 5 of 1991

Late Closed Records

1. As a result of two recent surveys, the court is concerned at the high incidence of motions to allow closed records to be received late, and in particular, at the lengthy delays in lodging many of these records.

2. Consequently, notwithstanding the terms of the Practice Note of 10th December 1986, and as from 14th May 1991, all motions to allow a closed record to be received late shall be dealt with by a judge who, if he is not satisfied with the explanation given for the lateness of the record, shall direct that the motion be put out starred.

3. The terms of said Practice Note are amended as follows:
   (*a*) the words "(except late closed records)" are added to the third item in Column 1 of Appendix I; and
   (*b*) the words "late closed records—reasons for delay to be stated" are added as a new item in Appendix II.

4. Practitioners are reminded that the court has a discretion in regard to the expenses of any appearance necessary to dispose of such motions.

9th May 1991

No. 7 of 1991

Reclaiming Motions

1. Practitioners are reminded that, when enrolling a reclaiming motion in a case in respect of which no opinion has been issued, they should advise the depute clerk

(a) that a reclaiming motion has been enrolled, and

(b) that an opinion is required.

2. Further, and as from this date, when enrolling a reclaiming motion where a matter likely to be at issue at the hearing of the reclaiming motion is not covered by an opinion already in process (*e.g.* the disposal of expenses following upon the appearance of judgment) practitioners will require

(a) to indicate in the motion sheet the particular matter which is not so covered, and

(b) advise the depute clerk that an opinion is required thereon.

20th June 1991

No. 1 of 1992

Judicial Review of Decision of Adjudicator Appointed under Section 12 of the Immigration Act 1971

1. Practitioners are advised that, where a decision of an adjudicator appointed under section 12 of the Immigration Act 1971 is subject to an application for judicial review in terms of Rule of Court 260B, the adjudicator should not be called as a respondent in the petition but he should receive intimation thereof as a person who may have an interest.

2. In any such petition, the Home Secretary should be called as respondent.

9th January 1992

No. 2 of 1992

Short Notice Inner House Diets

From time to time tentative offers are made by the Keeper of the Rolls of diets in the Inner House of which it has been agreed that short notice may be given. It should be understood, however, that no such offer is to be taken as being confirmed as a fixed diet until written notice of the diet has been issued by the Keeper.

22nd July 1992

Notice: 6th August 1992

Television in the Courts

The Lord President has issued the following directions about the practice which will be followed in regard to requests by the broadcasting authorities for permission to televise proceedings in the Court of Session and the High Court of Justiciary.

(*a*) The rule hitherto has been that television cameras are not allowed within the precincts of the court. While the absolute nature of the rule makes it easy to apply, it is an impediment to the making of programmes of an educational or documentary nature and to the use of television in other cases where there would be no risk to the administration of justice.

(*b*) In future the criterion will be whether the presence of television cameras in the court would be without risk to the administration of justice.

(*c*) In view of the risks to the administration of justice the televising of current proceedings in criminal cases at first instance will not be permitted under any circumstances.

(*d*) Civil proofs at first instance do not normally involve juries, but the risks inherent in the televising of current proceedings while witnesses are giving their evidence justify the same practice here as in the case of criminal trials.

(*e*) Subject to satisfactory arrangements about the placing of cameras and to there being no additional lighting, which would make conditions in the court room intolerable, the televising of current proceedings at the appellate level in both civil and criminal cases may be undertaken with the approval of the presiding Judge and subject to such conditions as he may impose.

(*f*) Subject to the same conditions, ceremonies held in a court room may also be televised for the purpose of news broadcasting.

(*g*) The taking of television pictures, without sound, of Judges on the Bench—as a replacement for the still photographs currently in use—will be permitted with the consent of the Judge concerned.

(*h*) Requests from television companies for permission to film proceedings, including proceedings at first instance, for the purpose of showing educational or documentary programmes at a later date will be favourably considered. But such filming may be done only with the consent of all parties involved in the proceedings, and it will be subject to approval by the presiding Judge of the final product before it is televised.

No. 3 of 1992

Form of Address of Female Judges

The fact that a woman will shortly for the first time be sitting as a temporary judge in the Court of Session makes it necessary for the Lord President to give guidance as to the way in which woman judges should be addressed in this court.

The office which she will hold will be that of a Temporary Lord Ordinary, since that is the term in the statute: Court of Session Act 1988, section 2(5). All interlocutors issued by a woman temporary judge will therefore refer to her as "The Temporary Lord Ordinary". She should, however, be addressed as "my Lady" or "your Ladyship" when she is sitting on the bench.

The same form of address should be followed when she is sitting as a temporary judge in the High Court, although by statute she will be sitting as a Temporary Lord Commissioner of Justiciary: Criminal Procedure (Scotland) Act 1975, section 113(1).

12th November 1992

No. 4 of 1992

Liquidations—Early Dissolution

1. An application for early dissolution under section 204 of the Insolvency Act 1986 shall be made by letter addressed to the Deputy Principal Clerk of Session.

2. On receipt of an application, the Deputy Principal Clerk of Session shall transmit the process to the Auditor of Court who shall obtain from the liquidator sufficient information to enable him to report to the court on whether or not in his opinion:

(*a*) the company may be dissolved,

(*b*) the liquidator be exonerated and discharged, and

(*c*) the liquidator be allowed to retain any remaining funds as remuneration.

3. A report lodged in terms of paragraph 2 above shall be placed before the court in chambers and an order pronounced in terms of the report, or otherwise as the court shall think fit.

3rd December 1992

No. 6 of 1992

Short Notice Inner House Diets

Practitioners are advised that the Keeper of the Rolls may now issue peremptory diets in certain sheriff court and statutory appeals where the hearing has been assessed as being of not more than two days' duration. A minimum of two working days' notice of such diets will be given.

A notice will be published periodically in the Rolls of Court advising practitioners of the cases which may be called in under this procedure. The fact that a later diet has already been allocated in any such case will not preclude the issue of a short notice diet.

23rd December 1992

No. 2 of 1993

Bankruptcy—Sequestration of Estate of Debtors

1. The Practice Note of 27th March 1986 dealing with certain bankruptcy matters is hereby revoked.

2. In order to satisfy the court that the provision of section 5(6) of the Bankruptcy (Scotland) Act 1985 as amended by section 3(5) of the Bankruptcy (Scotland) Act 1993 (copy of petition for sequestration to be sent to Accountant of Court) has been complied with, a solicitor will require to append to the execution copy of a petition for sequestration a certificate giving notice to the court of the date on which a copy of the petition was sent to the Accountant in Bankruptcy. Such a certificate must be signed by the solicitor concerned.

16th September 1993

No. 3 of 1993

Office of the Auditor of the Court of Session

Consolidated Guidance Notes for Taxation of Accounts

General

1.1 These Guidance Notes are issued with a view to facilitating the conduct of taxations and minimising the necessity of holding continued diets.

1.2 These Guidance Notes will apply to judicial accounts lodged for taxation on or after 4th October 1993.

1.3 The Auditor will not delay consideration of an account to await subsequent production of documentation or information which is required for the taxation of an account.

Lodging of accounts of expenses

2.1 Not later than 10 days prior to the lodging of an account of expenses for taxation the receiving party shall intimate a copy of it to the paying party, unless exceptional circumstances necessitate that a shorter period of intimation be given.

2.2 The account lodged for taxation shall have prefixed to it copies of every interlocutor which contains a remit to the Auditor, so far as relevant to any items contained in the account.

2.3 When an account of expenses is lodged for taxation it shall be accompanied by a note stating (1) the name and current address of the paying party, or his solicitor and the latter's file reference (2) the date on which a copy of the account was intimated to the paying party and (3) the estimated duration of the taxation when it is considered that more than half an hour will be required.

Fixing diet of taxation—contra-account

3.1 On receipt of the process and the account the Auditor will assign a diet of taxation for the earliest available date.

3.2 If the paying party has an outstanding award of expenses the account for these should be lodged forthwith to be dealt with at the same diet.

Points of objection

4.1 The paying party shall not later than three working days prior to the diet of taxation intimate to the Auditor, and the receiving party, specific points of objection, setting out the item objected to and stating concisely the nature and ground of objection in each case.

4.2 At the diet of taxation it will be expected that only those items so specified will be raised.

Papers and vouchers to be available at diet

5. There will be available at the diet of taxation the following:

(*a*) all precognitions and reports charged for in the account, notes by counsel, documents showing adjustments, letters of instruction to counsel and experts, all solicitors' correspondence, attendance notes, and other papers necessary, to support the entries in the account;

(*b*) fee notes detailing the work done by counsel; and

(*c*) receipts and detailed vouchers (unless previously exhibited to, and agreed with each paying party) for all sums stated to have been paid giving full details of the services rendered and the time expended and unit rate of charge.

Numbering of vouchers

6. To facilitate the progress of the taxation the supporting documentation is to be arranged and presented in chronological order and appropriately numbered to correspond to the relevant item in the account.

Schedule of witnesses' expenses

7. The fees and expenses charged for witnesses are to be set out in a separate schedule to the account in the form prescribed by paragraph 11 of Chapter II of the Table of Fees of Solicitors in the Court of Session, and the total thereof stated in the body of the account in a lump sum.

Representation at diet

8.1 The Auditor from time to time receives intimation, frequently just prior to the diet of taxation, that the solicitors for the paying party are without instructions to appear at the diet.

8.2 As a cause in which expenses have been awarded is still before the court until the Auditor's report on the taxed account has been lodged, the solicitors who acted for the paying party have a responsibility to inform their client immediately on receiving notification of the diet of taxation, which is peremptory, of the date, time and place of it, so that the client can intimate timeously any points of objection and thereafter attend personally, or be represented, at the diet.

8.3 The Auditor will proceed with the taxation of an account on the basis that such notification has been given to the client timeously.

Taxation at an agreed amount

9. In the event of parties reaching agreement as to the amount of expenses for which the paying party is to be found liable and the receiving party wishing an Auditor's report thereon, the Auditor requires to have consent in writing of the paying party specifying (1) the agreed amount of expenses and (2) to what extent the fee fund dues, which are calculated on the amount of the account lodged for taxation, are to be added to the agreed amount.

Value added tax

10. Where applicable the certificate required by Practice Note dated 14th April 1973 is to be available at the diet of taxation.

30th September 1993

No. 1 of 1994

Note of Objections to Auditor's Report

As from this date, practitioners are advised that, when attending at the office of the Keeper of the Rolls to fix a diet for a hearing on a note of objections to a report by the Auditor of Court, they will require to indicate whether or not the diet should be assigned to a particular judge and, if so, the reason for it.

10th March 1994

No. 2 of 1994

Judicial Factors—Caution

1. Practitioners are reminded that a judicial factor (*a*) is an officer of court and (*b*) requires to obtain a certified copy interlocutor of his/her appointment *without delay*.
2. As a certified copy interlocutor is not issued until the judicial factor finds caution, the practitioner before presenting a petition for appointment should reach agreement with the nominees as to whose responsibility it will be to arrange caution.
3. If such responsibility lies with the nominee then the practitioner should advise the nominee of his/her appointment within 24 hours thereof and the nominee should proceed to find caution without delay.
4. If such responsibility lies with the practitioner then the practitioner should proceed to find caution without delay.
5. The foregoing is of particular importance where such an appointment is made *ad interim*.

26th May 1994

No. 3 of 1994

Revocation of Previous Practice Notes

1. The practice notes listed in the Schedule to this Practice Note are hereby revoked.
2. This practice note comes into force on the day that the new Rules of the Court of Session in the Act of Sederunt (Rules of the Court of Session) 1994 [S.I. 1994 No. 1443] come into force, that is to say, on 5th September 1994.

28th June 1994

SCHEDULE

PRACTICE NOTES REVOKED BY PARAGRAPH 1 OF THIS PRACTICE NOTE

28th January 1955	(Jury trials)
11th January 1957	(Motions)
7th May 1959	(Appeals to the House of Lords)
16th November 1961	(Walling)
20th March 1962	(Motions to ordain party to lodge account of expenses)
26th October 1962	(Lodging copies of closed record)
28th June 1963	(Lodging of issues and counter-issues)
26th November 1963	(Late lodging of closed record)
15th July 1964	(Copies of productions for use of the court)
10th March 1966	(Up to date marriage certificate in certain consistorial actions)

1st June 1967	(By Order (Adjustment) Roll)
18th July 1968	(Extract decree of divorce)
16th December 1968	(Adjustment Roll)
13th November 1969	(Motions relating to interim custody and aliment; appeals and remits from inferior courts; remits to reporters in consistorial causes)
3rd December 1969	(Hearings for petitions under the Trusts (Scotland) Act 1961)
16th January 1970	(Modification of expenses against assisted persons)
20th February 1970	(By Order (Adjustment) Roll)
31st March 1970	(Vacation Court)
14th May 1970	(Bond of caution)
2nd March 1972	(Shorthand writer to record objections)
5th May 1972	(Procedure Roll)
4th January 1973	(Consistorial causes)
23rd November 1973	(By Order (Adjustment) Roll)
9th July 1974	(Fees and expenses of reporters in matters affecting children)
21st November 1974	(Fixing undefended proofs)
29th May 1975	(Proof forms)
29th May 1975	(Diets of proof and hearing)
No. 1 of 1976	(Fixing proofs in consistorial actions)
No. 5 of 1976	(Motion roll)
No. 6 of 1976	Defended consistorial causes – 4 January 1973
No. 1 of 1977	(Diets of undefended proof in consistorial actions)
No. 2 of 1977	(Applications for undefended proofs in consistorial actions)
3rd January 1980	(Inclusive fees in undefended divorce actions)
9th July 1980	Extracts Department Regulations
30th October 1980	Remits to local authorities in consistorial causes
26th March 1981	(Amendment of pleadings in reclaiming motions)
10th February 1983	(Curator *ad litem* in consistorial actions)
15th September 1983	(Return of medical records to Health Boards)
21st February 1986	(Applications for fiats)
6th November 1986	Applications for leave to appeal from Employment Appeal Tribunal
No. 2 of 1987	Fixing and Allocation of Diets of Proof etc.
No. 3 of 1987	Fixing and allocation of diets of procedure roll hearings
No. 1 of 1988	Children: supervision of access arrangements by social work department
No. 3 of 1988	Fee fund dues
Notice 22nd September 1988	(Average waiting times for hearings)
No. 7 of 1988	Registration and enforcement of money judgments under s.4 of the Civil Jurisdiction and Judgments Act 1982
No. 1 of 1989	Enrolment of motions
No. 2 of 1989	Appendix in reclaiming motions and appeals from sheriff court
No. 1 of 1990	Fixing and Allocation of Diets – Form 64
Notice 22nd March 1990	Commissions to take evidence and/or recover documents
No. 6 of 1991	Warrants for diligence on the dependence of consistorial causes
No. 8 of 1991	Transaction of business by post or facsimile
No. 5 of 1992	Intimation on the walls of court
No. 1 of 1993	Optional prodecure – List of witnesses – Rule of Court 188L

No. 4 of 1994

Transaction of Business by Post or Facsimile

Lodging documents by post

1. A step of process or a production may be lodged by post.

Fees

2.—(1) Where any item of business transacted by post requires payment of a fee, a cheque for the appropriate fee must be enclosed with the item, unless the person seeking to transact that item of business is an agent who holds a Court of Session account.

(2) No item of business which requires payment of a fee may be transacted by facsimile unless the person seeking to transact that item of business is an agent who holds a Court of Session account.

Signeting

3.—(1) A summons accompanied by the process, or an application for letters of arrestment or inhibition accompanied by relevant supporting documents, may be lodged for signeting by post.

(2) If the summons or letters are in order—
 (a) the summons, or
 (b) the letters of arrestment or inhibition and the relevant supporting documents,
duly signeted will be returned by post to the sender.

(3) If there is a defect of a kind which cannot be remedied by a telephone call from the Signet Officer—
 (a) the summons and process, or
 (b) the application for letters of arrestment or inhibition and the relevant supporting documents,
will be returned by post to the sender with a letter stating the reasons for their return.

Calling of summons

4.—(1) Where a summons is lodged for calling by post, there shall be enclosed with the summons (which shall have the certificate of service attached) the calling slip required by R.C.S. 1994, r. 13.13(4).

(2) If the summons is accepted for calling, the clerk of session will advise the agent by letter of the calling date.

(3) If there is a defect of a kind which may be dealt with by telephone, the clerk of session will telephone the agent for the pursuer. If the defect cannot be remedied by telephone the summons will be returned to the agent by post with a letter stating the reasons.

Entering appearance by post or facsimile

5.—(1) Appearance in an action under R.C.S. 1994, r. 17.1(1) may be made by post or facsimile.

(2) Where appearance is entered on behalf of a defender to an action by post or by facsimile, details of the cause reference number, parties to the action, date of calling and the names of counsel and agent(s) representing the defender (and in multi-defender cases which defender they represent) must be received in the General Department not later than 4pm on the last day for entering appearance.

Petitions and notes—warrant for intimation and service

6.—(1) Where a petition or note is lodged by post, it shall be accompanied by any motion, which is required under R.C.S. 1994 to be enrolled, in accordance with R.C.S. 1994, r. 23.2 (enrolment of motions).

(2) Where an interlocutor pronounced following the procedure in sub-paragraph (1) above contains a warrant for intimation and service of the petition or note, a copy of the interlocutor will be transmitted by post to the agent who lodged the petition or note.

Walling of petitions and notes
7. Where a petition or note requires to be intimated on the walls of court, a copy of the first page of the petition or note may be transmitted by post or by facsimile to the Petition Department which will arrange for the petition or note to be walled.

Lodging of steps of process and productions by post
8.—(1) Productions lodged in process shall be numbered as sub-numbers of the number of process assigned to the inventory of productions (*e.g.* in an inventory of productions no. 15 of process, production 1 will be no. 15/1 of process; production 2 will be no. 15/2 of process; etc.).
(2) A step of process or inventory of productions sent by post, must—
  (*a*) be received in the Office of Court not later than the last day for lodging it; and
  (*b*) if intimated, be marked accordingly.
(3) When a solicitor proposes to lodge an inventory of productions and accompanying productions by post, he must—
  (*a*) contact the appropriate section of the General Department or the Petition Department, as the case may be, to ascertain from the clerk of session the relevant number of process; and
  (*b*) write the relevant number of process and the cause reference number on the inventory of productions and each production.
(4) Where a motion is required to be enrolled in respect of the lodgment of any document by post, the motion shall be sent with the document in accordance with paragraph 9 below.

Enrolment of motions by post or facsimile transmission
9.—(1) A motion or notice of opposition to a motion enrolled by post or facsimile transmission shall be accompanied by—
  (*a*) any paper apart required under paragraph 3 of Practice Note 10 December 1986 (Hearing of Motions); and
  (*b*) any relevant document or step of process which may be transmitted with it in terms of this Practice Note or Direction No. 3 of 1994 (productions which may be sent by facsimile transmission).
(2) A motion or notice of opposition to a motion may be transmitted at any time of the day but must be received in the Office of Court at such time as shall comply with the latest times for enrolment and opposition set out in the table to Direction No. 4 of 1994 (Motions).

Cause reference numbers
10. Practitioners should ascertain from the General or Petition Department, as the case may be, the cause reference number of existing cases before enrolling a motion or lodging a document. The cause reference number is shown at the top of the summons returned for service in terms of paragraph 3(2) above or the copy interlocutor transmitted in terms of paragraph 6(2) above and should be noted for future use.

Transactions by facsimile transmission
11.—(1) Practitioners who intend to conduct business by facsimile transmission are reminded that fax machines can receive messages outwith the hours during which business is normally conducted. It follows, therefore, that there may be advantage in transmitting a message in the evening for the following day rather than waiting until the following day when the line may be busier.

(2) Practitioners who intend to conduct business by facsimile transmission should ensure that appropriate arrangements are made to deal expeditiously with fax transmissions from the Court of Session (*e.g.* returned motions).

(3) It is unnecessary to send a hard copy of a fax message sent in terms of this Practice Note.

(4) The following are the fax numbers to be used for transacting business under this Practice Note:
  (*a*) General Department 031–225 5496; and
  (*b*) Petition Department 031–225 7233.

Date of commencement of this Practice Note
12. This Practice Note shall come into force on 5th September 1994.

28th June 1994

No. 5 of 1994

Fixing and Allocation of Proofs etc.

1. Copies of Form 6.2 (form for information for fixing diets in Outer House) and Form 6.3 (form for information for fixing diets in Inner House) to be sent to the Keeper of the Rolls under R.C.S. 1994, r. 6.2(6) and r. 6.3(2) respectively may be obtained from the Keeper's Office.

2.—(1) Where there is an estimate that the length of a proof, jury trial or hearing will be not more than four days, the Keeper of the Rolls will normally allocate a diet of the length sought.

(2) Where there is an estimate that the length of a proof, jury trial or hearing will be more than four days or there is substantial variation in the estimates given by the parties, the Keeper of the Rolls will communicate with parties with a view to ascertaining a better estimate and fixing a diet.

3. This Practice Note comes into force on 5th September 1994.

28th June 1994

No. 6 of 1994

Hearing of Motions

1. For paragraph 1 of the Practice Note of 10th December 1986 (Hearing of Motions) there shall be substituted the following paragraph:
  "1. All unopposed motions enrolled for hearing in the Outer House, other than those referred to in paragraph 9, shall *not*, in the first instance, require the appearance of counsel."

2. This Practice Note comes into force on 5th September 1994.

28th June 1994

No. 7 of 1994

Intimation on the Walls of Court

1.—(1) The information required for intimation of the presentation of a petition, note or other application on the walls of court must include (*a*) the nature of the application, (*b*) the name and address of the applicant, (*c*) the general purpose of the application and (*d*) the name of the solicitor for the petitioner, or noter or other applicant.

(2) If the above information appears on the first page of the petition, note or other application, a copy of that page will be sufficient. If not, a separate typed slip must be prepared.

2. In accordance with paragraph 7 of the Practice Note No. 4 of 1994 (transaction of business by post or facsimile) a copy of the first page of the petition, note or other application may be sent by post or facsimile transmission to the Petition Department. Where a separate typed slip is required, it may also be sent by such means.

3. On the day on which an interlocutor is pronounced ordering intimation on the walls of court of the petition, note or other application, as the case may be, a clerk of session in the Petition Department will be responsible for the walling of the petition, note or other application on the notice board at the entrance to the box corridor from the reception area at door 11.

4. A walling certificate shall not be required to be attached to the execution copy of a petition, note or other application or any certificate or intimation.

5. This Practice Note comes into force on 5th September 1994.

28th June 1994

No. 8 of 1994

Exchange of Lists of Witnesses

1. Subject to the provisions in R.C.S. 1994, Chapter 43, Part V (optional procedure in certain actions of damages) and Chapter 47 (commercial actions), not later than 28 days before the diet fixed for a proof or jury trial, each party shall—
  (*a*) give written intimation to every other party of a list containing the name, occupation (if known) and address of each person whom he intends to call as a witness; and
  (*b*) lodge a copy of that list in process.

2. A party who seeks to call as a witness a person not on his list intimated under paragraph (1) may do so subject to such conditions, if any, as the court thinks fit.

3. This Practice Note comes into force on 5th September 1994.

28th June 1994

No. 9 of 1994

Value Added Tax in Accounts for Expenses

1. For the first paragraph of the preamble to the Practice Note 14th April 1973 (Office of Auditor of Court of Session: Value added tax, etc.), there shall be substituted the following paragraph:—
  "R.C.S. 1994, r. 42.12(1) (Value added tax) authorises solicitors to make an addition to fees, where appropriate, of such amount as is equal to the amount of value added tax."

2. This Practice Note comes into force on 5th September 1994.

28th June 1994

No. 10 of 1994

Revocations

The following Practice Notes are hereby revoked with effect from 5th September 1994:
No. 3 of 1976 (signeting of summonses)
27th March 1986 (procedure for minutes of amendment).

12th August 1994

No. 11 of 1994

Petitions for the Appointment of Tutor Dative

As from this date, a petition for the appointment of a tutor dative will require to seek service in common form on the Mental Welfare Commission for Scotland, 25 Drumsheugh Gardens, Edinburgh EH3 7RB.

18th August 1994

[Notice: 18th August 1994]

Agents are asked to note, pending the introduction of the Rules of the Court of Session 1994, on 5th September 1994, that with effect from Monday 22nd August 1994, all processes in relation to appeals from inferior courts shall in the first instance be lodged in the Signet Office, within the General Department, and not the Petition Department as has been the practice previously.

Agents are also asked to note that with effect from Monday 22nd August 1994, all processes at the instance of the Royal Bank of Scotland and the Bank of Scotland shall be transferred to Section P–Z of the General Department and shall cease to be held on Section A–C.

No. 12 of 1994

Commercial Actions

[Revoked by P.N. No. 6 of 2004]

No. 1 of 1995

Early Disposal of Reclaiming Motions and Appeals

1. Where a motion for early disposal under R.C.S. 1994, 38.13 or 40.11 is appropriate, the rule is available for the purpose of obtaining (a) an order for an early date for the hearing of the reclaiming motion or appeal on the Summar Roll or (b) determination of the reclaiming motion or appeal in the Single Bills.

2. Where the party seeking early disposal wishes to obtain an order for an early date for the hearing of the reclaiming motion or appeal on the Summar

Roll, he should make this clear in his motion by enrolling for early disposal of the reclaiming motion or appeal *and* for an order for an early date for the hearing on the Summar Roll.

3. Where the party seeking early disposal wishes to have the cause determined in the Single Bills, he should make this clear in his motion by enrolling for early disposal of the reclaiming motion or appeal *and* for its determination in the Single Bills.

4. A motion under paragraph 2 or 3 will be starred and will require the appearance of counsel or other person having a right of audience. The court will wish to know parties' estimate of the duration of the hearing to determine the reclaiming motion for appeal, as the case may be.

19th January 1995

No. 2 of 1995

Court of Session etc. Fees Amendment Order 1994

The Court of Session etc. Fees Amendment Order 1994 which comes into effect on 1st February 1995 introduces at items B14, B15, B16, B17, B18, C16, C17, C18 and C19, fees in respect of certain "hearings".

Solicitors who currently hold a Supreme Courts' account will have the fees invoiced to them at the end of the hearing under the existing procedure for these accounts.

For solicitors who do not have a Supreme Courts' account, an account will be opened in their name for the purposes of levying hearing fees. They will be invoiced each month for the fees incurred in all actions where a hearing has taken place during the preceding month. Payment will be required within 14 days of receipt of the invoice.

In order that solicitors can monitor the fee which is charged, a copy of the Court calculation will be transmitted to solicitors at the conclusion of each hearing along with the requisite debit slip when the fee is debited to their account.

Party litigants who incur a fee for a hearing will require to pay the appropriate fee to the Clerk of Court, in the case of a hearing of up to one day's duration, at the end of the hearing. In the case of hearings lasting more than one day they will require to pay the fee at the end of each day of the hearing. The exact amount payable should be ascertained from the Clerk of Court. Details of the appropriate fees can be obtained from the Offices of Court.

31st January 1995

No. 3 of 1995

Applications for Additional Fee Remitted to the Auditor

Where an application for an additional fee has been remitted to the Auditor in terms of R.C.S. 1994, r. 42.14(2)(b), there shall be lodged with the account of expenses a full statement of reasons in support of the particular factors which are considered justify the allowance of an additional fee.

A copy of the statement must accompany the intimation copy account of expenses under R.C.S. 1994, r. 42.1(2)(b).

31st January 1995

Notice (*sic*)

[P.N. No. 1 of 1996]

Consignation

With effect from June 3, 1995 the present practice of lodging funds on consignation receipt shall cease. All moneys consigned under orders of court, or otherwise, in the name of the Accountant of Court shall be placed on special deposit account, which will be held solely by The Royal Bank of Scotland plc, North Bridge branch, Edinburgh. Special deposit accounts will continue to afford to the court maximum flexibility in the partial release of funds but attract a higher rate of interest than that previously earned by consignation receipt.

Moneys may be lodged (a) at the branch concerned, (b) at any bank or branch and transferred through the bank's credit transfer system, or, in exceptional circumstances (c) with the Accountant of Court (registration department).

Funds currently consigned on receipt will be transferred into special deposit accounts by the Accountant of Court as soon as is reasonably practicable. No action by a solicitor will be required.

30th May 1996

Notice (*sic*)

[P.N. No. 2 of 1996]

Daily call over of cases

1. With effect from June 18, 1996 a representative from each agent will be required to attend jointly the office of the Keeper of the Rolls between 10 am–10.20 am each day in relation to those cases awaiting allocation to court that day as proofs or procedure rolls.

2. The keeper, or a member of his staff, will require to be informed of those cases in which discussions with a view to settlement are current or imminent.

3. The keeper, or a member of his staff, may require agents or their representatives, to re-attend at intervals throughout the day.

13th June 1996

Notice (*sic*)

[P.N. No. 3 of 1996]

Hearings for Judicial Review

With effect from Friday 5th July 1996 when fixing diets of hearing for judicial review etc, a full copy of the petition will be required by the Keeper's office.

4th July 1996

No. 4 of 1996

Starred Motions

1. With effect from 24th September 1996 any motion enrolled which is expected to be starred and to require 10 minutes or more duration on the motion roll will require to have the relevant duration marked on the motion slip.

2. Any agent or party who opposes a previously enrolled motion will require to mark upon the opposition slip the expected duration of hearing upon the motion roll.

3. A Lord Ordinary who has been allocated substantive business (for example a proof) may be allocated, in normal circumstances, no more than three opposed motions, each estimated to require no more than 10 minutes. Allowance will be made for such other number of starred motions or other interlocutory work as can be accommodated within the time available up to 10.30 am.

4. All other starred motions, and those motions which are likely to take more than 10 minutes, will: (a) be allocated to a judge assigned to that category of business; (b) be published for disposal in groups allocated to a specific period of one half hour between the hours of 10.00 am and 1.00 pm and those remaining thereafter, published for disposal not before 2.00 pm; (c) be considered in the order printed upon the roll unless the court otherwise allows.

15th August 1996

No. 5 of 1996

Counsel's Fees for Settled or Discharged Cases

Rule 42.10(1) of R.C.S. 1994, in regard to fees of solicitors, states that only such expenses as are reasonable for conducting the cause in a proper manner shall be allowed. In the light of Lord Osborne's observations in *Gorrie's Executrix v. Ciba Geigy Ltd*, 26th June 1996, the question has arisen whether a solicitor is nevertheless entitled to include in his account the fee charged by counsel, in accordance with paragraph 5.12 of the Guide to the Professional Conduct of Advocates, where he has been instructed for a case which has subsequently settled or the diet in which has been discharged.

The solicitor should continue to include this fee in his account for consideration at taxation by the Auditor where it was reasonable for the solicitor, in order to conduct the cause in a proper manner, to instruct counsel in order to retain his services for the proof or other hearing in the case. It will then be for the Auditor to consider, having regard to the factors mentioned in paragraph 5.12 of the Guide, whether the fee charged by counsel is appropriate to the circumstances.

26th September 1996

No. 6 of 1996

Notes of Argument

[Revoked by P.N. No. 2 of 2004]

No. 7 of 1996

Opposition to Motions

For an experimental period, where a party seeks to oppose a motion he shall, at the same time, notwithstanding the terms of Rule of Court 23.4, include therein, and in the intimation thereof, a brief statement of the extent and basis of said opposition.

To facilitate this, a party enrolling a motion on or after 25th November 1996 should, notwithstanding the terms of Rule of Court 23.3(3) and subject to the exceptions contained therein, intimate the motion so that the intimation reaches the other party not later than 12.30 pm two days before its enrolment.

Further, where a motion for recovery of documents under a specification is opposed, the Court will expect Counsel for parties to have discussed the call or calls in question with a view to resolving the matters in issue before appearing in Court. Counsel should be in a position to tell the Court that this has taken place.

5th November 1996

Notice (*sic*)

Reclaiming motions—merits/expenses

1. It has become apparent that practitioners are unsure about the proper time limits for enrolling a reclaiming motion against an interlocutor disposing of the whole merits of the cause.

2. In the recent (as yet unreported) case of *Dingley v. Chief Constable, Strathclyde Police*, 6th December 1996 [1996 G.W.D. 2–49], the court, under reference to rules 38.3, 38.8(1) and 38.8(2) of the Rules of the Court of Session, indicated that, where there is an interlocutor disposing of the merits but continuing the cause on the question of expenses, a party *must* reclaim that interlocutor within the period of 21 days set down in rule 38.3(2), even though that interlocutor is followed by an interlocutor at a later date disposing of the question of expenses.

6th February 1997

Notice (*sic*)

[Recording of proceedings]

[Revoked by P.N. No. 4 of 2004]

P.N. No. 1 of 1997

Royal Arms in Scotland

The attention of practitioners is drawn to the fact that it is permissible for them to reproduce a facsimile of the Royal Arms in Scotland on a principal petition or principal summons.

5th June 1997

Notice (*sic*)

[General Department Sections]

With effect from Monday 9 June 1997 there will be a slight alteration to the alphabetical divisions between the sections in the General Department. The three sections will be: A–F; G–Mac; Mad–Z.

(undated)

No. 2 of 1997

Flat, boxed Process

For an experimental period commencing on 23 September 1997 Rules of Court (*sic*) 4.1, 4.3, 4.4 and 4.5 will not apply.
In lieu thereof the following will apply:—

(1) **Form, size etc. of documents forming the process [in lieu of Rule 4.1]**
 (a) In an action or petition the principal writ or other writ bringing a cause before the court shall be in the appropriate or prescribed form; it and all steps of process, except motion sheets, shall be completed in writing, transcript or print on durable quality paper of A4 size and shall be backed and securely fastened with a two-piece filing clip.
 (b) Motion sheets shall be in A4 size and consist of a backing sheet and two-piece filing clip.

(2) **Steps of process [in lieu of Rule 4.4]**
 (a) The process shall include the following steps enumerated thus:—
  (1) the principal writ;
  (2) certified copy principal writ;
  (3) the interlocutor sheets;
  (4) a motion sheet;
  (5) a minute of proceedings;
  (6)   (number reserved for pursuer's productions)
  (7)   (number reserved for defender's productions)
  Ø an inventory of process
 (b) A step of process referred to in paragraph 2(a) above other than the principal writ, certified copy writ and motion sheet writ shall contain at least 2 pages.
 (c) A step of process shall be assigned a number corresponding to (a) above where appropriate or another number consecutive thereto and said number shall be marked on the backing along with the cause reference number and recorded in the inventory of process.

(3) **Lodging of process [in lieu of Rule 4.3]**
 (a) A process shall be lodged in every cause commenced by summons or petition when—
  (i) in the case of a summons, the summons is presented for signetting; and
  (ii) in the case of a petition, the petition is presented to the Petition Department.
 (b) (i) Subject to (b)(ii) below, a black process box shall be lodged by the agent for the pursuer or petitioner
   — along with the Open Record prescribed by rule of court 22.1 in a cause commenced by summons or

    — within 3 days of answers having been intimated in a cause commenced by petition.

  (ii) A red process box shall be lodged by the agent for the pursuer

    — within 3 days of defences having been intimated in a Commercial Action or

    — along with the Open Record prescribed by rule of court 22.1 in any cause relating to Intellectual Property.

 (c) A process box shall conform to the following specification:

   (i) of durable plastic with secure fastener;

   (ii) depth 245 mm × width 60 mm × height 330 mm

  (iii) with space for names of parties and a finger hole on its spine.

(4) Productions [in lieu of Rule 4.5]

 (a) On each occasion a production is lodged in process:

   (i) an inventory of productions shall be lodged in process; and

   (ii) a copy of the inventory of productions shall be sent to every other party.

 (b) A production shall be:

   (i) marked with a number of process with the cause reference number assigned to the principal writ; and

   (ii) if consisting of more than one sheet, securely fastened together.

 (c) Productions should be numbered as follows:

   (i) where there is only one pursuer, all pursuer's productions will be assigned number 6 of process and will be numbered consecutively thereafter *e.g.* 6/1–6/x;

   (ii) where there is only one defender, all defender's productions will be assigned number 7 and will be numbered consecutively thereafter *e.g.* 7/1–7/x;

  (iii) where there are further pursuers/defenders another number of process will be assigned to each and productions should be enumerated as at (i) and (ii) above.

10th July 1997

Notice (*sic*)

[Issuing of Judgments]

Practitioners may wish to note that, in future, unless a judge orders otherwise, all judgments of the Court of Session will be issued in what is currently referred to as "vacation style" *i.e.* without the necessity of the attendance of counsel or solicitor.

As at present, clerks will give agents notice of the date an opinion will be issued. Where possible, this notice will be given at least 2 days prior to the date of the opinion. Opinions may be collected on or after the date of issue, from the Opinions desk, within opening hours, upon payment of the prescribed fee.

Where the opinion does not address the matter of expenses a motion therefor should be enrolled as soon as practicably possible. Unless opposed, or starred by the court, motions for expenses will be dealt with by the appropriate judge in chambers.

The names of cases in which opinion have been issued will continue to be published in the rolls of court.

4th September 1997

No. 3 of 1997

Schedule of Damages etc.

On or after 6 October 1997, in all cases to which the Social Security (Recovery of Benefits) Act 1997 applies, seeking decree (except where that decree is sought of consent, for instance, as the result of a Joint Minute) should lodge in process a schedule of damages stating the amount of any compensation which is claimed in respect of the relevant period under any of the headings in Column 1 of Schedule 2 of the Act.

For the avoidance of doubt it should be noted that this requirement will apply not only to final decrees after proof or jury trial but to decrees in absence, decrees by default, summary decrees, interim decrees and decrees for provisional damages.

Issues in cases where the jury trial will take place on or after 6 October 1997 should be drafted in such a way as to ensure that the provisions of the Act can be applied to the jury's verdict.

24th September 1997

No. 4 of 1997

Notes of Argument

[Revoked by P.N. No. 2 of 2004]

No. 1 of 1999

Limitation Actions

In any limitation action raised in pursuance of the Merchant Shipping (Oil Pollution) Act 1971:—
  (1) any order for advertisement for condescendence and claims to be lodged and the time limit for lodging them shall be as directed by the court;
  (2) any order for the lodging of objections to said condescendence and claims, and the time limit for lodging them shall be as directed by the court;
  (3) any order for adjustment to the condescendence and claims and objections thereto, shall be applied for by motion, and shall be for such period as may be directed by the court;
  (4) within two weeks of the lodging of objections, or after the expiry of any period of adjustment, the condescendence and claim, and objections thereto, shall be put out by order to determine further procedure;
  (5) where the condescendence and claim are based upon any existing payment action in this court no further steps in that action shall be taken. All steps of process in that payment action, the pleadings, productions, minute of proceedings, opinions and interlocutors all as at the date of lodging the condescendence and claim in the limitation action shall become steps of process etc. in the limitation action.

15th May 1999

Notice (*sic*)

Opinions

The present system for issuing opinions in the Court of Session is being modified.

The opinions will continue to be issued formally at 10am on the day of advising and will be available for collection by the media at that time. The court will, however, send an advance copy by email to the parties' Edinburgh agents' central mail box before 9.30am on the day of issue. This copy will be provided on a confidential basis so that agents will be in a position to inform their clients of the decision when it is formally issued at 10am.

If, in a particular case, it is more convenient for an agent to receive the opinion in hard copy, the agent should inform the opinions desk in advance and arrangements will be made for the hard copy to be available, on the same confidential basis, at 9.30am in the petition department.

No change is being made to the system for issuing opinions in the High Court.

If you do not receive the emailed opinion please contact supremecourts@ scotcourts.gov.uk, or telephone 0131 240 6772.

28th May 2001

No. 1 of 2001

Allocation of Diets in the Outer House

As recommended in Lord Cullen's Review of Business in the Outer House, the Keeper of the Rolls consults a senior Lord Ordinary before making the weekly allocation of cases to the judges sitting in the Outer House.

In order to further improve this arrangement, practitioners are invited to inform the Keeper of the Rolls, in writing no later than 12 noon on the Friday of the week preceding the diet, of any factors they consider may have a bearing on setting the priority of their case.

Any information received will be placed with the papers considered by a senior Lord Ordinary.

31st July 2001

No.2 of 2001

Entering appearance by email

(1) For an experimental period appearance in an action under the Rules of the Court of Session 1994, rule 17.1(1) may be made electronic by email.

(2) Where appearance is entered on behalf of a defender to an action by email, details of the cause reference number, parties to the action, date of calling and the names of counsel and agent(s) representing the defender (and in multi-defender cases which defender they represent) must be sent to the following email address: supreme.courts@scot-courts.gov.uk not later than 4pm on the last day for entering appearance.

(3) Appearance in an action may still be made by post, facsimile or attendance at the public counter.

(4) This practice note shall come into force with immediate effect.

31st July 2001

No. 1 of 2002

Exemptions from payment of fees

The following guidance note has been issued by the depute in charge in relation to applications for exemption from payment of court fees in the Court of Session:

Background

The Court of Session etc Fees Amendment Order 2002 (S.S.I. 2002 No. 270) came into force on 1st July 2002. It extended the fee exemption provision previously available only for simplified divorce applications, to all fees regulated by the order with the exception of those for commissary and criminal complaints. To adequately monitor and police the use of exemption claims the former fee exemption certificate has been adjusted for use from 1 July 2002. In addition, a fee exemption slip has been produced which is used to certify the continuing need for fee exemption for example on enrolling a motion. Copies of these forms can be accessed on the Scottish Court Service web site (www.scot courts.gov.uk) under "New Rules". The order does not prescribe that fee exemption applies retrospectively. Parties can only be treated as "fee exempt" on receipt by the court of a fee exemption certificate.

The procedures to be followed in the Court of Session

1. Summons and petition proceedings
   (a) An action is lodged for signet/first order accompanied by a fee exemption certificate. The form may be signed by the applicant personally or by a solicitor on their behalf. We cannot accept a faxed exemption certificate. Verification or proof of eligibility will periodically be sought by this office to comply with audit requirements.
   (b) The same procedure requires to be followed on the lodgment of defences, answers to a petition etc (ie the lodgment of a document by which a party enters a process).
   (c) The exemption certificate is lodged as a part of process and marked as such in the inventory.
   (d) Our computerised records will reflect the fact that a party is "fee exempt". The process requires to be marked (FE) by the solicitors (or runners) to reflect this.
   (e) A white sticker will be attached to the front of the process indicating the presence of a fee exemption certificate, showing which party is exempt and the nature of their exemption. This quickly identifies such cases to all those who come into contact with the process.

It may be that entitlement to exemption arises part way through proceedings. On receipt of an exemption certificate the court will carry out the procedures set out above.

The detailed exemption form need only be lodged at the outset of the proceedings or entitlement unless there has been a change of circumstances, in which case a fresh application should be lodged. The benefits office and/ or legal aid reference numbers must be completed as appropriate.

The marking on parts of process (FE) is an administrative step, which will greatly assist the processing of business, but has no legal significance. (AP) is marked on a process when a legal aid certificate is lodged in process. This is in compliance with rule 3 of the Act of Sederunt (Legal Aid Rules) 1987 and of course carries with it special significance in relation to awards of expenses. It may be that parties will be described as (FE) (AP) but the two are not mutually exclusive. A party may be (FE) but not be in receipt of legal aid.

2. Enrolling and opposing motions
In every case where fee exemption continues to be claimed, parties enrolling (or opposing) a motion will require to lodge an exemption slip which certifies that there has been no change in circumstances detailed in the original exemption form. This can be signed by the applicant personally or by a solicitor on their behalf. This document may be faxed to the court along with a motion or opposition.

3. Lodging of closed records, court time and the allowance of proofs etc
There are a number of occasions when fees are payable by all parties to an action such as those for lodging closed records, fees arising out of court time and the allowance of proof etc. It will not be necessary for parties to provide a continuing exemption slip for these fees in isolation. However, in relation to closed records, these are accompanied by a motion in terms of RCS, rule 22.3 (5), seeking the allowance of a mode of proof or appointment to the by

order (adjustment) roll. Therefore an exemption slip will be sought for the accompanying motion in accordance with para 2 above.

4. Change in circumstances

If circumstances prevail which result in the entitlement to exemption no longer applying, the court must be notified in writing at the earliest possible opportunity. The letter will be recorded in the inventory, and the process marked accordingly. The onus is on the party seeking exemption or the solicitor on their behalf, to inform the court of any material change of circumstances affecting eligibility.

No. 2 of 2002

Petitions relating to the distribution of estates of deceased Lloyd's names

[Revoked by P.N. No. 1 of 2006]

No. 2 of 2003

Personal injuries actions

The following notes are designed to explain how the Courts will approach the application and interpretation of the new rules for personal injuries actions. For the most part, they are arranged by reference to the rules in the Act of Sederunt. Practitioners may find it helpful to refer to the Report of Working Party chaired by Lord Coulsfield, issued in 1998 and to the Supplementary Report issued in 2002, both of which are available on the Scottish Courts Website www.scotcourts.gov.uk.

Rule 43.1 Application and interpretation

Personal injuries actions are defined as actions of damages for or arising from personal injuries or the death of a person from personal injuries and personal injuries are defined as including any disease or impairment, physical or mental. It is not intended that actions of defamation or any actions which are not, in ordinary parlance, concerned with personal injuries should be covered by these rules. Any such actions are likely to be transferred to the ordinary roll if they are raised under Chapter 43.

Rule 43.2 Summons and pleadings

The question of pleadings was discussed in the original Working Party Report and in the Supplementary Report on pleadings. In the original report it was pointed out that, in the past, it had proved difficult to restrict pleadings even though it had for very many years been the rule that pleadings should be short and simple. It was therefore emphasised that for the purposes of these rules pleadings should be kept to a basic minimum. The Working Party stated:

"The discussions in the Working Party tended to the conclusion that, realistically speaking, what it is required in most cases in relation to liability is the briefest description of the events on which the claim is based, together with a brief indication of the ground of fault alleged and a specific reference to any statutory provision which may be founded upon."

In the Supplementary Report, it was stated that the Committee remained of the view that the approach of the Working Party was correct, notwithstanding some observations which had been made upon it. The Committee stated:

"Essentially, therefore, we agree that what is necessary is a method of pleading which encourages brevity and simplicity and discourages technicality and artificiality."

Rule 43.4   Specification and recovery of documents

Specifications for recovery of medical records should not be intimated to the Lord Advocate. The specification should be sent directly to haver.

The question has been raised as to the action to be taken if documents are not returned after the pursuer has finished with them. Any such situation is dealt with under the existing rules applicable to ordinary procedure, namely that application may be made to the Court for an order requiring the pursuer to return the documents.

Rule 43.5   Applications to dispense with timetable
  (a) Motions

In general, the rules as to motions are those which apply in ordinary actions. Certain motions will be placed before a judge and may be granted, in accordance with existing practice, if sufficient information is before the judge in writing. It should, however, be noted that motions for sist, for removal of the case to the ordinary roll and for the alteration of a timetable will not be granted, even if made of consent, unless information to justify them, in accordance with the terms of the rules, is before the judge. Such motions will be starred if there is objection to them or if there is insufficient material placed before the judge to satisfy the requirements of the rules.

  (b) Dispensing with the timetable

It should be noted that a motion to dispense with the timetable is to be made within 28 days. This rule is intended to be strictly observed. Further, it should be noted that it is not to be granted unless there are exceptional reasons, and that an interlocutor granting or refusing a motion under this rule may be reclaimed against only with leave of the Court within fourteen days. It should be understood that if a case is regarded as suitable for the procedure under this Chapter (that is, if a motion for removal to the ordinary roll is not made or not granted) a motion to extend a period of time under the timetable (Rule 43.8) is most unlikely to be granted.

  (c) Sist

It should be noted that the timetable is set from the lodging of defences. Wherever possible, an application for sist should be made before or at the lodging of defences in order to avoid the issue of a timetable which may later require to be changed. It is provided in the rules that a sist will be for a fixed period, and the Court will take account of all the circumstances of the case in fixing the period and, whenever possible, will avoid any delay to any timetable which may have been issued.

The Court will expect parties to consider at the earliest possible stage whether they may require to make an application to the Scottish Legal Aid Board, such as in respect of sanction for an expert witness or for work of an unusual nature. Delay in making an application for legal aid or in applying for a sist, may lead to the motion being refused. Generally, the Court will expect parties to adhere to guidance issued by the Scottish Legal Aid Board.

Rule 43.6   Allocation of diets and timetable
  (a) Timetable

This rule provides for the issue of a timetable. The rules do not set out specific periods to be entered in the timetable for most purposes. The periods which will be followed, so far as possible, will from time to time be prescribed by the Lord President. The table in the Appendix to this Note incorporates the periods which, as at the date of issuing of this Practice Note, it is envisaged will be so prescribed.

A party who is concerned that a step of procedure has not been complied with timeously, or that a party is not complying with the spirit of the procedures, and that failure is threatening to cause delay to or prejudice the settlement of the action, should:

- if the matter relates to a stage in the timetable, approach the Keeper of the Rolls with a view to having the case put out By Order; or

- if the matter is outwith the control of the timetable, enrol a motion to bring it before the court.

(b) Third Party Notices

The timetable provides a limited period for the service of third party notices. Parties should be aware that this period, like other periods in the timetable, will be strictly insisted on. If timeous application is not made, any question of third party involvement may require to be raised in a separate action.

(c) Productions

Where any productions are sought to be lodged late, permission will be granted only by the Court and subject to such order, in particular as to expenses, as the Court may consider appropriate.

(d) Order for further procedure

Rule 43.6(5) deals with the making of an order for further procedure after the lodging of a record. It should be stressed, consistently with what has been already said in regard to written pleadings, that it is anticipated that an order for inquiry will be made at this stage. If the defender does not agree with the pursuer's motion, he should oppose it. If a party seeks a debate then full notice of the grounds will require to be given in writing. In particular, if the specification of the pursuers' case is criticised, details of the averments which ought to be made and which have not been made should be included in the grounds for the motion so that the pursuer may have an opportunity to consider whether to meet any such objections in advance of the hearing of the motion. A motion for Procedure Roll will not be granted lightly. Normally any question of specification will be dealt with on the motion roll hearing.

Where a party enrols for jury trial, where practicable the diet assigned in the original timetable will, where practicable, be adhered to. A party opposing such a motion will be expected to specify fully, in the notice of opposition, the grounds on which the motion is opposed.

A party seeking inquiry who estimates that the allocation of four days is not appropriate should communicate with the Keeper with a view to the making of any necessary additional arrangements.

Rule 43.7   By Order hearings

Where under the rules any matter is put out to be heard By Order, the hearing is to take place and parties are to be represented even if, for example, any document not timeously lodged or any step not timeously taken has been lodged or taken prior the hearing. The object of this requirement is to enable the Court to insist upon, and consider, any explanation for failure to act timeously.

Rule 43.8   Motions for variation of timetable

Reference has been made earlier with regard to motions to dispense with the timetable (R.43.5(2)). Rule 43.8(1) deals with motions to vary the timetable. Variation may be by either extension or acceleration. Such motions should be made as soon as the timetable has been issued. Motions for extension are most unlikely to be granted. However, the Court would look with considerable sympathy on any application for acceleration of the timetable where the pursuer has a life expectancy which does not exceed the duration of the timetable that has been issued by the Keeper.

A motion to vary the timetable should give full details of the grounds on which the motion is based and where relevant be accompanied by supporting medical evidence. Any party opposing such an application will be required to demonstrate that their opposition is well founded. When hearing the motion the judge will give such directions as he or she considers appropriate.

Rule 43.9 Statements of valuation of claim

The statements of valuation required by this rule are not binding upon the parties who make them. It is, however, intended that these statements should reflect a real assessment of the value of the claim and accordingly it will be open to either party to found upon the making of its own statement of valuation or upon that of the other party.

Parties' attention is drawn to the terms of rule 43.9(7), which provides for either the dismissal of the action or an award of expenses where a statement of valuation is not lodged timeously.

Rule 43.10 Pre-trial meetings

The object of the rule is to ensure that a pre-trial meeting takes place in accordance with the recommendations of the Working Party. The Working Party stressed that in order to be of value the meeting must be a real meeting, that is a meeting conducted by the legal advisers who are in charge of the conduct of the case, along with each of the parties or someone who has the complete authority to act on behalf of a party at the time. The Working Party stopped short of laying down formal requirements for the meeting since to do so would possibly interfere with the professional requirements of the parties' advisers. Accordingly the Working Party was prepared to contemplate that meetings might be carried out, for example, by video conferencing. It should however be understood that it is the obligation of each party to take all such steps as are necessary to comply with the letter and the spirit of the rule. Similarly, the obligation to sign a minute of the meeting is placed upon counsel or solicitor-advocate acting in the case. It has to be clearly understood that in signing such a minute the signatory is accepting responsibility to the Court for the conduct of the meeting and the recording of what took place at it.

Electronic Communication

It is already the case that under Practice Note 2 of 2001 parties may enter appearance by e-mail. Generally parties are encouraged to supply the necessary references and addresses when entering appearance to make it practicable to utilise electronic communication to the maximum practicable effect.

14 March 2003

APPENDIX

Stage in proceedings	Date
Motion for 3rd party notices, additional defenders to be lodged by	(defences + 28 days)
Commission under rule 43,4 to be executed by	(defences + 28 days)
Motion to withdraw from this procedure and appoint to Ordinary Roll to be lodged by	(defences + 28 days)
Pursuers valuation to be lodged by	(defences + 8 weeks)
Adjustment period ends on	(defences + 8 weeks)
Record to be lodged and motion enrolled for proof or jury trial by	(defences + 10 weeks)
Defenders valuation to be lodged by	(defences + 16 weeks)
Productions/ lists of witnesses to be lodged by	(proof – 8 weeks)
Pre-trial minute to be lodged by to be lodged by	(proof – 21 days)

Diet of proof/jury trial	Defences + 12 months*

* This date may be adjusted to reflect periods of Vacation and loading at the discretion of the Keeper of the Roll with the approval of the Lord President

No. 3 of 2003

Accelerated diets in personal injuries actions on the ordinary roll

As from 1st April 2003 new procedures for the disposal of personal injuries actions will come into force (SSI 2002 No. 570). Under Rule 43.8 a party may apply to the court for a variation of the timetable and an accelerated diet of proof or jury trial.

Practitioners are reminded that in any personal injuries actions which have been raised under the existing procedures or transferred to the ordinary roll, it is possible for a party to seek an early or accelerated diet of proof or jury trial, where there is good reason for doing so. The Keeper intends to review diets of proof and jury trial which have been fixed for dates later than 31 October 2003, with a view to identifying any cases in which the diets ought to be accelerated by the Court on its own initiative. Applications by parties for an early or accelerated diet should be made to the Keeper of the Rolls and intimated to the other parties.

When he deems it appropriate, the Keeper of the Rolls will consult with parties before dealing with such applications. In the event of any continuing issue as to whether an application for an accelerated diet should be granted, the case will be put out By Order for the determination of further procedure. If an accelerated diet is fixed for a date to which any party objects, it is open to that party to enrol a motion seeking to have the diet discharged and a further diet fixed.

14th March 2003

No. 1 of 2004

Affidavits in Family Actions

1. The Practice Note dated 11 April 1978 is hereby revoked.
2. The Practice Note set out in the Appendix is approved by me and shall have immediate effect in the Court of Session.

1st June 2004

APPENDIX

Affidavits in Family Actions

When affidavits may be lodged
1. Once the period within which a notice of intention to defend (in the Sheriff Court) or defences (in the Court of Session) require to be lodged has expired, without such defences having been lodged, affidavits may be prepared and lodged without any order of court.

Person before whom sworn or affirmed

2. An affidavit is admissible if it is sworn (or affirmed) before a notary public, justice of the peace, or any person having authority to administer oaths for the place where the affidavit is sworn, such as a commissioner for oaths or a British diplomatic officer or consul abroad. A solicitor acting for such a party to the action may act in a notarial capacity when an affidavit is sworn. Any person before whom an affidavit is sworn (referred to below as "the notary") must observe all the normal rules in this connection and must satisfy himself or herself as to the capacity of the witness to swear an affidavit.

Importance of affidavits

3. The witness should be made to appreciate the importance of the affidavit and that the affidavit constitutes his or her evidence in the case. The possible consequences of giving false evidence should be explained to the witness. Before the witness signs the affidavit he or she must have read it or the notary must have read it over to the witness.

Oaths or affirmation

4. The witness must be placed on oath or must affirm.

Form and signature of the affidavit

5. The document should be on A4 paper. The affidavit should commence with the words "At   the   day of   20 , in the presence of I   having been solemnly sworn/having affirmed give evidence as follows:". The affidavit should be drafted in the first person and should take the form of numbered paragraphs. The full name, age, address and occupation of the witness should be given in the first paragraph. The affidavit should end with the words "All of which is the truth as I shall answer to God" or "All of which is affirmed by me to be true", as appropriate. Any blanks in the affidavit must be filled in. Any insertion, deletion or other amendment to the affidavit requires to be initialled by the witness and the notary. Each page must be signed by both the witness and the notary. It is not necessary for the affidavit to be sealed by the notary.

Drafting the affidavit

6. An affidavit should be based on a reliable and full precognition of the witness.

7. The drafter of an affidavit should provide himself or herself, before drawing it, with an up to date copy of the pleadings, a copy of the appropriate precognition and the relative productions. The affidavit should be drawn up so as to follow the averments in the pleadings to the extent that these are within the knowledge of that particular witness and in the same order.

8. Affidavits should be expressed in the words of the person whose affidavit it is, should be accurate as to the date of the affidavit and should not consist of a repetition of passages in the pleadings. It should be clear from the terms of the affidavit whether the witness is speaking from his or her own knowledge, as when the witness was present and saw what happened, or whether the witness is relying on what he or she was told by a particular person.

Productions

9. Productions already lodged in process must be borrowed up, and put to the party or to the witness who refers to them in his or her affidavit. Each production will require to be referred to in the affidavit by its number of process and must be docqueted and signed by the witness and the notary. If a production has not yet been lodged when the affidavit is sworn, it will require to be identified by the witness in the affidavit, should be docqueted

with regard to the affidavit and signed by the witness and the notary. It must then be lodged as a production. Some productions will necessarily be docqueted with regard to more than one affidavit.

10. In consent cases, the defender's written consent form will have to be put to the pursuer in his or her affidavit, and be identified, docqueted and signed in the same way as other productions.

11. In adultery cases, photographs of both the pursuer and the defender may require to be produced, put to the appropriate witnesses and be identified, docqueted and signed in the manner already described.

Date of affidavit

12. All affidavits lodged must be of recent date. This factor is particularly important in cases involving children, cases in which financial craves are involved and in any other circumstances where the evidence of a witness or circumstances to which the witness speaks are liable to change through the passage of time. The notary must take particular care in such cases to ensure that the affidavit evidence as to such matters is correct as at the time the affidavit is sworn. Affidavits relating to the welfare of children which have been sworn more than three months prior to lodging a minute for decree are likely to be rejected by the court as out of date.

Applications relating to parental responsibilities and rights (See RCS 49.28, OCR 33.28)

13. In actions in which an application in terms of section 11 of the Children (Scotland) Act 1995 is before the court not fewer than two affidavits dealing with the welfare of the child(ren) should be provided, at least one of them from a person who is neither a parent nor a party to the action. These affidavits should present the court with a full picture of the arrangements for the care of the child(ren) along the lines set out in paragraph 15, adapted to suit the circumstances of the particular case. The affidavits should set out the reasons why it is better that the section 11 order be made than not. The pursuer's affidavit should deal fully with the arrangements which have been made for their care, so far as within his or her knowledge. If the pursuer cannot give substantial evidence as to that it is likely to be necessary to obtain such evidence from the person who is responsible for their care.

14. In actions of divorce, judicial separation or nullity of marriage in which there are children of the marriage or children treated by the parties as a child of the family but in which no order in terms of section 11 of the Children (Scotland) Act 1995 is sought, the court, in terms of section 12, requires to consider whether to exercise the powers set out in section 11 or 54 of that Act in light of the information before it as to the arrangements for the child(ren)'s upbringing. Information accordingly requires to be before the court as to these arrangements. As a minimum, the affidavits of the witnesses should include the information set out in paragraph 15 (a) to (e) below.

15. An affidavit dealing with the arrangements for the care of children should, where relevant, include the following:
   (a) the qualifications of the witness, if not a parent, to speak about the child; how often, and in what circumstances the witness normally sees the child;
   (b) the ability of those with whom the child lives to provide proper care for him or her;
   (c) observations as to the relationship between the child and the other members of the household, the child's general appearance, interests, state of health and well-being;
   (d) a description of the home conditions in which the child lives;
   (e) the arrangements for contact between the child and any parent (and siblings) who do not live in the same household as the child;

(f) information about the school the child attends; whether the child attends school regularly; and

(g) details of child care arrangements during working hours, including the arrangements for such care outwith school hours.

Affidavit relating to disclosure of the whereabouts of children

16. An affidavit sworn or affirmed in compliance with an order to disclose the whereabouts of children (in terms of the Family Law Act 1986, section 33 and RCS 49.24 or OCR 33.23) will require to be drafted in such a way as to meet the requirements of the court in the circumstances of the particular case. The form of the affidavit should be as above.

Financial and other ancillary craves

17. Affidavit evidence in support of financial craves is necessary in an undefended action. (See *Ali v Ali* 2001 SLT 602). Where financial craves are involved, the evidence should be as full, accurate and up-to-date as possible. If the evidence is insufficient the court may require supplementary evidence to be provided. If, after an affidavit has been sworn and the solicitor concerned has parted with it, a material change of circumstances occurs before decree has been granted the court must be informed forthwith. A further affidavit may have to be sworn.

18. The pursuer should give evidence as to his or own financial position at the date of the affidavit. Where the pursuer gives evidence in an affidavit as to the financial position of the defender, the affidavit should state the date, as precisely as possible, at which the information was valid. The court must be provided with information which is as up-to-date as possible as to the defender's ability to pay the sums the pursuer is seeking. Where the pursuer cannot obtain recent information as to the defender's means the affidavit should state that that is the case but should contain as much material information relating to the defender's means as possible. If the pursuer is unable to provide sufficient evidence to justify the orders concluded for or craved in full, in the minute for decree, after the words "in terms of conclusion(s)/crave(s) (number(s)...) of the summons/initial writ", there may be added words such as "or such other such sum (or sums) as the court may think proper".

19. Where the pursuer has concluded for or craved a capital sum, an order for the sale of the matrimonial home, a periodical allowance, interdict or expenses, for example, and in the minute for decree does not seek decree for one or more of these, the reasons for that should be given in his or her affidavit.

Joint minutes

20. When parties record their agreement in a joint minute as to how financial and other ancillary conclusions or craves should be dealt with by the court, the pursuer's affidavit should refer to the joint minute and indicate that he or she is content that the agreement set out in it should be given effect.

Minute for decree

21. The minute for decree must be signed by counsel or by a solicitor who has examined the affidavits and other documents. That counsel or solicitor takes responsibility therefor, whether or not he or she is the person who drew the summons, initial writ or affidavits. The minute for decree should not be signed seeking decree of divorce, separation or declarator of marriage or nullity of marriage unless the evidence consists of or includes evidence other than that of a party to the marriage (or alleged or purported marriage). [Civil Evidence (Scotland) Act 1988, section 8(3), *Taylor v Taylor* 2001 SCLR 16].

No.2 of 2004

Procedure Roll

1. The following practice notes are hereby revoked:

26th April 1991 (No.3 of 1991)	Procedure Roll
30th October (No.6 of 1996)	Notes of Argument
12th December 1997 (No.4 of 1997)	Notes of Argument.

2. Practitioners are reminded that the court expects that, on the closing of the record, discussions will take place between parties about the future procedure in the cause with particular regard to the resolution of points at issue without recourse to a hearing on the Procedure Roll.

3. The court may, in determining any question of expenses arising out of a hearing on the Procedure Roll, take into account the extent to which parties have complied with paragraph 2 above.

6th August 2004

No.3 of 2004

Pleas-in-Law in personal injuries actions

1. Summonses, defences, and all other pleadings in personal injuries actions to which Chapter 43 of the Rules of Court applies should not contain pleas-in-law. Pleadings not complying with this Practice Note will not be accepted by the General Department. Defenders who wish to include in their pleadings an outline of their propositions in law should do so be inserting a brief summary of those propositions in the last answer of the defences.

2. For the avoidance of doubt, those defences containing pleas-in-law which have already been accepted by the General Department prior to the issue of this Practice Note will be permitted to continue in that form.

3rd September 2004

No.4 of 2004

Revocation

The following Practice Note is hereby revoked with effect from 12th November 2004:
6th March 1997 (recording of proceedings).

12th November 2004

No.5 of 2004

Form of Opinions and Neutral Citation

Form of opinions
With effect from 1 January 2005 all opinions in the Court of Session will be issued with single spacing, paragraph numbering but no page numbers.

In courts consisting of more than one judge the paragraph numbering will continue sequentially through each opinion and will not start again at the beginning of the second or any subsequent opinion. Indented paragraphs will not be given a number.

Neutral citation of cases

With effect from 1 January 2005 a form of neutral citation will be introduced in the Court of Session. A unique number will be given by the Deputy Principal Clerk of Session to opinions issued by the Court of Session. Opinions will be numbered in the following way:

Court of Session, Outer House: [2005] CSOH 1 (2, 3 etc.)
Court of Session, Inner House: [2005] CSIH 1 (2, 3 etc.)

Under these new arrangements any particular paragraph of the case to be referred to will be cited in square brackets at the end of the neutral citation as follows:

Smith v Brown [2005] CSOH 1.

The neutral citation will be the official number attributed to the opinion by the court and must always be used on at least the first occasion when the case is cited and referred to in any later opinion. Once the case is reported the neutral citation will appear in front of the citation from the law report series.

Citation of cases in court

It is permissible to cite a case reported in a series of reports by means of a copy of a reproduction of the opinion in electronic form that has been authorised by the publisher of the relevant series, provided that the report is presented to the court in an easily legible form and that the advocate presenting the report is satisfied that it has been reproduced in an accurate form from the data source. In any case of doubt the court will rely on the printed text of the report unless the editor of the report has certified that the electronic version is more accurate because it corrects an error in an earlier printed text of the report. For the avoidance of doubt, the Court of Session requires that where a case has been reported in Session Cases it must be cited from that source. Other series of reports may only be used when a case is not reported in Session Cases.

16th November 2004

No.6 of 2004

Commercial Actions

Application and interpretation of Chapter 47: R.C.S. 1994, r. 47.1

1. The actions to which the rules apply are intended to comprise all actions arising out of or concerned with any relationship of a commercial or business nature, whether contractual or not, and to include, but not to be limited to—

the construction of a commercial or mercantile document,
the sale or hire purchase of goods,
the export or import of merchandise,
the carriage of goods by land, air or sea,
insurance,
banking,
the provision of financial services,
mercantile agency,
mercantile usage or a custom of trade,
a building, engineering or construction contract,
a commercial lease.

Some Admiralty actions *in personam,* such as actions relating to or arising out of bills of lading, may also be suitable for treatment of commercial actions if they do not require the special facilities of Admiralty procedure in relation to defenders whose names are not known.

Commercial judge: R.C.S. 1994, r. 47.2

2. The commercial judge may hear and determine a commercial action when the court is in session or in vacation: rule 10.7.

Election of procedure: R.C.S. 1994, r. 47.3

3.—(1) The initial pleadings in a commercial action are expected to be in an abbreviated form: the purpose of the pleadings is to give notice of the essential elements of the case to the court and the other parties to the action. Compliance with the requirements of paragraph 11 of the practice note will enable the essential elements of the case to be presented in the pleadings in succinct form. Where damages are sought, a summary statement of the claim or a statement in the form of an account will normally be sufficient. Where it is sought to obtain from the court a decision only on the construction of a document, it is permissible for the summons to contain an appropriate conclusion without a condescendence or pleas-in-law. The conclusion in such a case should specify the document, the construction of which is in dispute and conclude for the construction contended for.

(2) Rule 47.3(3) is intended to require a party to produce with its summons the "core" or essential documents to establish the contract or transaction with which the cause is concerned. Under rule 27.1(1)(a) documents founded on or adopted as incorporated in a summons must be lodged at the time the summons is lodged for calling.

(3) When the summons is lodged for signetting, a commercial action registration form (Form CA 1), copies of which are available from the General Department, must be completed, lodged in process and a copy served with the summons.

Disapplication of certain rules: R.C.S. 1994, r. 47.4

4. The ordinary rules of the Rules of the Court of Session 1994 apply to a commercial action to which Chapter 47 applies except insofar as specifically excluded under rule 47.4 or which are excluded by implication because of a provision in Chapter 47.

Procedure in commercial actions: R.C.S. 1994 r. 47.5

5. The procedure in, and progress of, a commercial action is under the direct control of the commercial judge. He will take a proactive approach.

Defences: R.C.S. 1994 r. 47.6

6.—(1) In the first instance detailed averments are not required in the defences any more than in the summons and it is not necessary that each allegation should be admitted or denied provided that the extent of the dispute is reasonably well identified. One of the objectives of the procedure is to make the extent of written pleadings subject to the control of the court. Compliance with the requirements of paragraph 11 of this practice note will enable the essential elements of the defence to be presented in the defences in succinct form.

(2) Under rule 27(1)(1)(b), documents founded on or adopted as incorporated in defence must be lodged at the time the defences are lodged.

(3) Defences must be lodged within 7 days after the summons is lodged for calling: rule 18.1(1).

(4) The defenders must complete a commercial action registration form (Form CA1) and lodge it in process, or complete the process copy, with the information required.

Counterclaims and Third Party Notices: R.C.S. 1994, r. 47.7.

7. No counterclaim or the bringing in of a third party may be pursued without an order from the commercial judge.

Commercial Roll: R.C.S. 1994, r. 47.8

8. In the Outer House, an action, and all proceedings in it, in which an election has been made to adopt the procedure in Chapter 47 for commercial actions or which has been transferred under rule 47.10 to be dealt with as a commercial action, shall be heard and determined on the Commercial Roll.

Withdrawal of action from Commercial Roll: R.C.S. 1994, r. 47.9

9. The object of rule 47.9 is to enable cases which are unsuitable for the commercial procedure to be removed from the Commercial Roll, but it should be understood that the commercial procedure is not to be regarded as limited to cases which are straightforward or simple or as excluding cases which involve the investigation of difficult and complicated facts.

Transfer of actions to Commercial Roll: R.C.S. 1994, r. 4 7.10

10.—(1) An ordinary action which has not been brought as a commercial action under rule 47.3(1) may be transferred to the Commercial Roll as a commercial action on application by motion by any party (including the pursuer) to the commercial judge if it is an action within the meaning of a commercial action in rule 47.1(2).

(2) An interlocutor granting or refusing a motion to transfer an action to the Commercial Roll may be reclaimed against only with leave of the commercial judge within 14 days after the date of the interlocutor: rule 38.4(6).

Pre-action communication

11.—(1) Before a commercial action is commenced it is important that, save in exceptional cases, the matters in dispute should have been discussed and focused in pre-litigation communications between the prospective parties' legal advisers. This is because the commercial action procedure is intended for cases in which there is a real dispute between the parties which requires to be resolved by judicial decision, rather than other means; and because the procedure functions best if issues have been investigated and ventilated prior to the raising of the action.

(2) It is therefore expected that, before a commercial action has begun, the solicitors acting for the pursuers will have:
  (i) fully set out in correspondence to the intended defender the nature of the claim and the factual and legal grounds on which it proceeds;
  (ii) supplied to the intended defender copies of any documents relied upon; and
  (iii) where the issue sought to be litigated is one for which expert evidence is necessary, obtained and disclosed, to the intended defender, the expert's report.

For their part, solicitors acting for the defender are expected to respond to such pre-litigation communications by setting out the defender's position in substantial terms; and by disclosing any document or expert's report upon which the defender relies. To that response the solicitors for the pursuers are expected to give a considered and reasoned reply. Both parties may wish to consider whether all or some of the dispute may be amenable to some form of alternative dispute resolution.

(3) Saving cases involving an element of urgency, actions should not be raised using the commercial procedure, until the nature and extent of the dispute between the parties has been the subject of careful discussion between the parties and/or their representatives and the action can be said to be truly necessary.

Preliminary hearing on Commercial Roll: R.C.S. 1994 R. 47.11

12.—(1) The preliminary hearing will normally be conducted on the basis that the provisions of paragraph 11 in relation to pre-action communication have been complied with. The preliminary hearing, and any continuations thereof, are not designed to give parties the opportunity to formulate their claim and response thereto.

(2) Parties should lodge, prior to the preliminary hearing, and for consideration at the preliminary hearing all correspondence and other documents which set out their respective material contentions of fact and law which show their compliance with the provisions of paragraph 11. These provisions are supplementary to the provisions of rule 47.3(3).

(3) Where it appears to the court that the need to grant any request for a continuation of a preliminary hearing is brought about by a failure to comply with the provisions of paragraph 11, this may result in the party responsible for any such failure having the expenses of the continued hearing awarded against him on an agent/client basis. Apart from that possible disposal, motions for continuations of the preliminary hearings which are sought simply to enable information to be obtained, which could and should have been obtained, prior to the preliminary hearing, may be refused.

(4) At the preliminary hearing the parties should be in a position to lodge a document setting out in concise form the issues which they contend require judicial determination. The statement of issues should, where possible, be set out in an agreed document.

(5) In applying rule 47.11(3), the court will expect to set realistic time limits; but once established those time limits will be expected to be achieved and extension will only be granted in certain circumstances. This emphasises the importance of ensuring that parties at the preliminary hearing are in a position to explain fully what will be required. Since it is part of the administration of commercial causes that wherever possible a commercial action should at all stages be heard before the same judge, it is important to avoid repeated appearances of the action on the commercial roll. For that reason it is necessary to try to give the court accurate information in order to enable the appropriate time limits for a particular case to be established in the manner which is both realistic and does not prejudice the overall requirement that commercial actions should be dealt with expeditiously.

Procedural Hearing on Commercial Roll: R.C.S. 1994, r. 47.12

13.—(1) The procedural hearing is also an important hearing at which parties will be expected to be in a position to discuss realistically the issues involved in the action and the method of disposing of them. It should normally be expected that by the time of the procedural hearing the parties' positions will have been ascertained and identified and that all prospects for settlement have been fully discussed. In consequence it is expected that, once a case has passed beyond the stage of a procedural hearing, it will not settle.

(2) This is one of the ways in which it is sought to meet the problem of ensuring that the judge is in the position to deal realistically with the procedure which he cannot do unless he is given information on which to proceed.

(3) Rule 47.12(2) is the kernel of the procedures and it is intended to enable the court to direct what is really to happen.

Debates: R.C.S. 1994, r. 47.13

14. A debate in a commercial action is not heard on the Procedure Roll but on the Commercial Roll. The provisions of Chapter 28 of the R.C.S. 1994 (Procedure Roll), however, do apply to a debate in a commercial action.

Pre-Proof By Order Hearing

15. When a proof, or proof before answer, has been allowed, the court will normally also fix a pre-proof by order hearing to take place in advance of the proof diet. The general purpose of such a hearing is to ascertain the parties' state of preparation for the proof hearing and to review the estimated duration of that hearing.

Without prejudice to the foregoing generality, the following matters will be dealt with at the pre-proof by order hearing:

(1) Consideration of any joint minute of admissions, agreed by the parties, which should be lodged no later than two days prior to the pre-proof by order hearing.

(2) A review of the documents, or other productions which the parties at the time of the pre-proof by order hearing consider will be relied upon at the proof hearing. Any such document should be lodged no later than two days prior to the pre-proof by order hearing.

(3) The up-to-date position with regard to any expert reports which are to be relied upon by the parties will be reviewed. The parties should be in a position to advise the court of what consultation, if any, has taken place between their respective experts with a view to reaching agreement about any points held in common and what matters remain truly in dispute between them.

(4) Where a proof before answer has been allowed, parties should *produce,* for consideration, at the pre-proof by order hearing, a statement of legal arguments and lists of authorities which they may seek to rely on at the diet of proof before answer, insofar as these have not already been lodged.

Lodging of productions: R.C.S. 1994, r. 47.14

16. Before any proof or other hearing at which reference is to be made to documents, parties shall, as well as lodging their productions, prepare for the use of the court a working bundle in which the documents are arranged chronologically or in another appropriate order without multiple copies of the same document.

Hearings for further procedure: R.C.S. 1994, r. 47.15

17. The commercial judge or a party may have a commercial action put out for a hearing other than a preliminary or procedural hearing to deal with a procedural or other matter which has arisen for which provision has not been made.

Failure to comply with rule or order of commercial judge: R.C.S. 1994, r. 47.16

18. The purpose of this rule is to provide for discipline to ensure effective supervision of case management.

General

19.—(1) Arrangements will be made to ensure that (save in exceptional circumstances) at all appearances of an action in the commercial roll the same judge shall preside. Parties are expected to arrange that counsel, or solicitors having rights of audience responsible for the conduct of the case, and authorised to take any necessary decision on questions both of substance and procedure, are available and appear at any calling in the commercial roll.

(2) Where any pleadings or other documents are to be adjusted, the party proposing adjustment shall do so by preparing a new copy of the document as adjusted in which the new material is indicated by underlining, side-lining, a difference in typeface, or other means.

(3) An interlocutor pronounced on the commercial roll, other than a final interlocutor, may be reclaimed against only with leave of the commercial judge within 14 days after the date of the interlocutor: rule 38.4(7).

Revocation of previous practice note

20.1. The Practice Note No.12 of 1994 (commercial actions) is hereby revoked.

29th November 2004

No. 7 of 2004

Procedure Roll Diets

With effect from 1st January 2005, a party seeking the discharge of a procedure roll diet which has been allocated under rule 6.2(4) will require to make an application by motion for discharge of that diet and further (specified) procedure.

Accordingly, the practice of discharging such diets following a telephone call or other informal request, will cease. The intention is that this will reduce delays arising while causes remain appointed to the procedure roll without fixed or allocated diets.

16th December 2004

No. 1 of 2005

Applications under Section 103A of the Nationality and Immigration and Asylum Act 2002

1. This Practice Note shall come into force on 4 April 2005.
2. A petition on relation to which paragraph 30 of Schedule 2 to the Asylum and Immigration (Treatment of Claimants, etc.) Act 2004 has effect shall be lodged at the following address—
Asylum and Immigration Tribunal
Field House,
P.O. Box 6987,
Leicester,
LE1 6ZX.

24th March 2005

No. 1 of 2006

Petitions by Executors of Underwriting Members of Lloyd's of London

1. This practice note has effect from 17th March 2006.
2. The purpose of this practice note is to provide guidance in respect of applications to which Rule 63.6A of the Rules of the Court of Session applies[1]

Reinsurance
3. It is anticipated that Rule 63.6A will only apply where the liabilities of the estate in respect of syndicates of which the deceased was a member—
    (a) for years of account before and including 1992, have been reinsured (whether directly or indirectly) into the Equitas Group; and
    (b) for years of account from and including 1993, have arisen from membership of syndicates in respect of which any liability will be met by the Central Funds at Lloyd's or which is otherwise reinsured or the subject of indemnity (such as by being protected by an Estate Protection Plan covered by Centrewrite Ltd. or by EXEAT insurance cover provided by Centrewrite Ltd).

Remit to a reporter

4. In accordance with the opinion of the Inner House in the Petitions of James Crosby Chisholm *(Pardoe's Executor) and Others [2005] CSIH 82*, in general it will be sufficient that the remit to a reporter on an application under rule 63.6A(2)(a) covers—

(a) identification of the insurance business underwritten by the deceased;
(b) confirmation from the documentation produced by the petitioners of the reinsurance cover taken or other indemnity;
(c) where relevant, an assessment of the current position of the Equitas Group from the most recently available reports; and
(d) where relevant, confirmation in documentary form that the Lloyd's Central Fund remains available to meet prospectively valid claims by a relevant policy holder or that there is available some other suitable reinsurance or indemnity in respect of such claims.

Revocation

5. Practice Note No. 2 of 2002 (petitions relating to the distribution of estates of deceased Lloyd's names) is hereby revoked.

10th March 2006

NOTE
[1] Rule 63.6A was inserted by S.S.I. 2006 No. 83.

No. 2 of 2006

Specifications for Recovery of Medical Records

1. This practice note has effect from 1st November 2006.
2. For the purpose of rule 35.2(3)(c), the court no longer considers it necessary for a copy of a specification for the recovery of medical records to be intimated to the Lord Advocate.
3. The Practice Note of 1950 in respect of the recovery of hospital records (1950 S.L.T. 87) is revoked.

19th October 2006

No. 1 of 2007

Personal Injuries Actions: Expert Evidence

1. Under Rule 43.6 of the Rules of the Court of Session, parties in Personal Injuries Actions are required to lodge in process any productions on which they intend to rely in accordance with the timetable issued by the Keeper of the Rolls, generally 8 weeks before the diet of proof or jury trial.
2. Practitioners are reminded of the principles of early disclosure of evidence underlying the procedures set out in Chapter 43 with a view to facilitating early settlement. The practice whereby parties delay disclosure of expert reports until the last minute is to be discouraged. Parties will be expected to lodge in process, within a reasonable time after receipt, all expert reports on which they intend to rely, whether in relation to liability or quantum. Failure to do so without reasonable cause may have a consequence in expenses.

16th January 2007

[NEXT TEXT PAGE IS C 2501]

INDEX

References in **bold type** are to a rule in the R.C.S. 1994; (references in ordinary type are to annotations.)

Assessors—*cont.*
 leading of skilled witnesses, **12.7(2), (3), (4)**
  where nautical assessor summoned,
   12.7(1), 12.7.2, 12.7.3
 may be summoned by the court to assist at
  a proof or hearing, **12.1(1)**
 motion to summon, **12.3,** 12.3.1–12.3.4
 nautical, **12.5(2)(3),** 12.5.3
 note of questions submitted to, **12.8,** 12.8.1
 number of, to be summoned, **12.6,** 12.6.1
 parties to be heard where court summons
  of its own motion, **12.1(2)**
 remuneration of, **12.9,** 12.2.1, 12.2.2
  treated as expenses in the cause, **12.9,** 12.9.1
 selection of, **12.5,** 12.5.1
 where inappropriate, 12.1.3
Assisted persons
 modification of expenses awarded against,
  42.6, 42.6.1
Asylum, See **Immigration**
Attachment
 Warrant for execution for, 7.10.2
Auditor of the Court of Session
 disallowance of expenses of motion by, **23.12**
 disallowance of expenses by, 42.5.2
 duties of, **3.7,** 3.7.1
  at diet of taxation, 42.2.1, 42.2.3, 42.2.4
 interpretation, **1.3(1)**
 objections to report, 42.4, 42.4.1–42.4.4
  note of objection, **4.2(9)(f),** 42.4.1–42.4.2
 powers of taxation, 42.3.1–42.3.6
 report of taxation, 42.3.1–42.3.6
Authorities
 proper citation of, 28.1.16, 36.11.2(17)
 where not cited by counsel, 28.1.13

Bankers' books
 commission and diligence for recovery of,
  35.2.16
Bankruptcy
 Accountant in Bankruptcy,
  as interim trustee, 72.6.2
  holding of sederunt book by, **72.5,** 72.5.1
  register of insolvencies kept by, **72.6(1),**
   72.6.1
 Approved debt arrangement scheme,
  declaration of approved debt payment
  programme, **72.2A,** 72.2A1
 Bankruptcy (Scotland) Acts 1985 and 1993,
  commencement and transitional
  provisions, 72.1.3
  general effect of, 72.1.1
 bankrupt, title to sue, 13.2.2(D)(4)
 Council Regulation (EC) 1346/2000, effect
  on jurisdiction, 72.1A.1
 debtor, definition of, 72.2.6
 interpretation of rules, **72.1**
 jurisdiction, 72.1A.1, 72.1.2
 petition, 72.2.1
 sederunt book, **72.5,** 72.5.1
 sequestration,
  apparent insolvency, evidence of, 72.2.3
  applications for transfer or remit of, **72.4,**
   72.4.1, 72.4.4
  curing of defects in procedure, 72.4.2

Bankruptcy—*cont.*
 sequestration—*cont.*
  direction to remit application to cure
   defects, 72.4.2, 72.4.8
  effective date of, 72.2.5
  petition, by debtor, 72.2.6
  petition, first order in, **72.2**
  petition, presentation of, 72.2.2
  petition to *nobile officium*, where
   appropriate, 72.4.2
  qualified creditor, 72.2.3
  warrant to cite debtor, **72.2,** 72.2.5
 trustee, 72.2.4
  interim trustee, 72.6.2
  memorandum to extend effect of original
   order, **72.6(3),** 72.6.3
  under trust deed, notice to be recorded
   by, **72.6(4),** 72.6.4
  recall of, **72.6(5),** 72.6.5
  under trust deed, when may petition for
   sequestration, 72.2.4
Best evidence
 rule of, 36.11.2(14)
Bilateral Convention countries
 jurisdiction in actions concerning, 13.2.12,
  13.2.14, 13.2.15
 service in, 16.2.5
Blood tests
 medical examinations and, 35.2.6A
Bond of caution. See Caution
Borrowing
 before extract, each party to borrow
  productions, **7.4(b)**
 before extract, steps of processes borrowed
  to be returned, **7.4(a)**
 court may ordain a party to return a
  document borrowed, **4.12(6)**
 finally extracted processes not borrowable,
  4.13
 keeper of the records, no document may be
  borrowed from, **9.2(2)**
 of documents, **4.11, 4.12(1)**
 of productions by defender on entering
  appearance, **17.1(3)**
 principal copy of a report ordered by court
  not borrowable, **4.11(3)(f)**
 return of documents borrowed, **4.12(2), (3),
  (4), (5), (6)**
 steps of process not borrowable, **4.11(3)**
Brussels Convention countries
 jurisdiction in actions concerning, 13.2.12,
  13.2.14, 13.2.15
 service in, 16.2.4
By Order (Adjustment) Roll
 appointment of cause to, **22.3(5)(b),** 22.3.12
 expenses of, 22.3.15
By Order Roll
 decree by default for failure to attend,
  20.1(1)(a)
 Form 6.2, failure to complete, **6.2(8), (9),
  (10)**
 Form 6.3, failure to complete, **6.3(4), (5), (6)**
 in Inner House before hearing on Summar
  Roll, **6.3**

[NEXT TEXT PAGE IS C 2511]

C 2510/2

Interlocutor—*cont.*
    summoning assessors only pronounced
        subject to condition of consignation of
        assessors' fees, **12.2**
    unsigned, extract of, is void, **4.15(5), 4.16(6)**
International child abduction. See **Child**
    abduction
International Oil Pollution Compensation Fund
    explanation of, 46.9.1
    intimation to, **46.9**
Internet
    opinions of the court available on, 4.15.7,
        4.16.4
Interrogatories. See **Commission and diligence**
Intimation. See also **Written intimation**
    acceptance of, **16.10**, 16.10.1, 16.10.2
    by advertisement, **16.7(1)**
    by Keeper of the Rolls of diet of proof or
        jury trial, **6.2(12)(a)**
    by Keeper of the Rolls of hearing on
        Summar Roll, **6.3(8)**
    by messenger-at-arms, **16.7(1)**
    challenging irregularity in, 16.11.1
    dispensing with, in a petition, **14.4(6),
        14.5(2)**, 14.4.8, 14.5.5, 14.7.1
    dispensing with period of notice, **16.10**,
        16.10.1
    form of certificate of, **16.7(2)**
    furth of United Kingdom, **16.7(1)**
    methods and manner of, **16.7**, 16.7.1,
        16.7.2, **16.8, 16.9**
    not to be made, of application by Lord
        Advocate to extend restraint order
        against proceeds of crime, **76.4(3)**
    of actions relating to heritable property,
        13.12, 13.12.1–13.12.2
    of application to be sisted as party, **31.1(2)**
    of documents, **16.7**, 16.7.1, 16.7.2
    of intention to proceed by party whose
        agent has withdrawn, **30.2(1)**
    of lodging steps of process, **4.6**, 4.6.1
    of motion, **23.3**
    of motion by defender or other person
        before calling to pursuer by Deputy
        Principal Clerk, **23.10(1)**
    of motion for recovery of document or for
        order under Administration of Justice
        (Scotland) Act 1972 s.1, **35.2(3)**, 35.2.14
    of motion to lead skilled witnesses where
        assessor summoned, **12.7(4)(b)**
    of motion to open up sealed packet where
        confidentiality claimed, **35.8(3)**
    of motion to summon an assessor, **12.3(1)(b)**
    of petition, **14.7, 16.7, 16.8**
    of receipt of process transmitted from
        sheriff court, **32.3**
    of summons, 13.6.6, **13.7**, 13.7.1
    of withdrawal of agent, **30.1**, 30.1.1
    on a warrant, **16.8**, 16.8.1
    to a party is sufficient if made to the agent
        acting for that party, **1.3(5)**
    to the pursuer that appearance has been
        entered, **17.1(2)**
    warrant for, in summons, **13.6(d)**

Issues. See **Jury trial**
    proof or jury trial, 28.1.8
    special cause for refusing, 28.1.8(B)

Joint minute
    in extra-judicial settlement, 36.11.7(1)
Judgments
    issuing of, 4.15.7, 4.16.4
    on the internet, 4.15.7, 4.16.4
Judicial factor
    Accountant of Court,
        application to, for discharge of, **61.31**,
            61.31.1–61.31.5
        appeal against decision of, **61.32**,
            61.32.1, 61.32.2
        caution, fixing of by, **61.9(3)**, 61.9.5
        caution, increase of by, **61.9(4), (7)**,
            61.9.5
        certificate by, that caution found, **61.9(6)**
        documents lodged to be copied to, **61.6(1)**
        duties of, 61.6.2, **61.7**, 61.7.1, **61.12**,
            61.12.1, **61.13(3), (8)**, 61.14.1,
            61.15(4)
        intimation to, of petition or note, **61.5(1)**
        parts of process to be transmitted to on
            request, **61.6(2)**
        remission or modification of penal
            interest incurred, **61.12**
        report of, lodging, 61.25.1
        transmission of process to, for fixing and
            finding caution, **61.8**
    application for appointment on estate of
        missing person, **50.7**
    application for consent under Trusts
        (Scotland) Act 1961 s.2(3), **61.14**,
        61.14.1–61.14.5
    application for official certified copy
        interlocutor of the appointment of,
        7.11(1)(a)
    application for special powers under Trusts
        (Scotland) Act 1921 s.5, **61.15**,
        61.15.1–61.15.8
    application to encroach on capital, **61.13**,
        61.13.1–61.13.6, 61.14.1
    intimation of, **61.13(5)–(7)**
    objection to, **61.13(9)**
    appointment of, 61.1.2, 61.1.3
    advertisement of petition, **61.5(2), (3)**,
        61.5.2
    application for by petition, **61.2**, 61.2.1
    as curator *bonis*, 61.1.2(1)
    as factor *loco absentis*, 61.1.2(2)
    as factor
        on common property, 61.1.2(9)
        on company estate, 61.1.2(7)
        on damages payable to child,
            61.1.2(10)
        on estate of deceased person, 61.1.2(5),
            61.16.1
        on partnership estate, 61.1.2(6)
        on solicitor's estate, 61.1.2(8)
        on trust estate, 61.1.2(3)
    pending litigation on heritable or
        moveable property, 61.1.2(11)
    as guardian to child, 61.1.2(4)

Jury trial—*cont.*
note of exceptions, **37.7(2),** 37.7.1
certification of, **37.7(3)**
notices of non-admission, **37.4**

Jury trial—*cont.*
notices to admit, **37.4**
objections to opinion or direction in,
37.4.2(4)

Lodging—*cont.*

of copies of pleadings for use of assessors, **12.4**

of defences, **19.2(3)(a), (6), 18.1(2)**

of document in Inner House causes, **4.7(1), (2)**

of records, **22.3(2)(b), 22.1(1)(b)**

of summons for calling, **13.13(3),(4)**

productions, **4.5**

prorogation of time for, **4.9(2)**

receipt of documents, **4.10**

refusal of clerk of session to accept copy of a document, **4.8**

step of process, **4.6**

where the Office of Court is closed on last day for, **1.3(7)**

Lord Advocate

as defender in action of proving the tenor, **52.1(b)**

as pursuer in action of declarator of death, 50.1.4

in actions of declarators of nullity of marriage or divorce, 49.15.4

intimation to, of motion for recovery of documents, 35.2.14

title to sue and be sued on behalf of Crown, 13.2.2(D)(12)

Lord Justice-Clerk

cannot act as vacation judge, **10.5(1)**

power to make directions in absence of Lord President, **1.3(3)**

Lord Ordinary

argument not presented to, 38.16.8

death, disability or absence of, before determination of summary trial, **77.10**, 77.10.1–77.10.2

death, disability or retirement during proof, **36.13**, 36.13.1

decision final and not subject to review, 38.2.2

determination of refusal to sign warrant for arrestment or inhibition, **59.1(3)**, 59.1.4

for commission for examination of witness, **35.11(3)(b)**

grant or refusal of leave to reclaim, **38.5(6)**, 38.5.3

in adoption order, 67.23.4

in allowing more than one skilled witness where assessor summoned, **12.7(3)**, 12.7.4

in appeal from Accountant of Court on determination of application of discharge of judicial factor, **61.32(5)**

in summary trial, **77.9**, 77.9.1

on application for inhibition or arrestment in claim for aliment or financial provision, **59.1(5)**, 59.1.4

on application to dispense with preliminary act in Admiralty action, **46.7(8)**

on motion for recovery of evidence before calling of summons, **35.2(5)**

on request for leave to proceed without signature of document, **4.2(5)**

Lord Ordinary—*cont.*

decision final and not subject to review—*cont.*

on sufficiency of stamp duty on document adduced in evidence, **36.12**

to appoint action to be commercial action, **47.7(3)**

to shorten or extend period of notice before service, **13.4(3)(b)**, 13.4.9

to shorten or extend period of notice in petition, **14.6(3)**

to withdraw commercial action from commercial action procedure, **47.6(3)**

declinature of jurisdiction by, 13.2.19

determination of refusal to send application for registration of United Kingdom custody order, **71.3(4)**

determination of refusal to sign warrant for arrestment or inhibition, **59.1(3)**, 59.1.4

dismissing or refusing cause called on procedure roll, **28.1(1)**

in Exchequer causes, 48.1.1, 48.1.2

interlocutor pronounced by another judge, **48.1(3)**

may hear such a cause during vacation, **10.6**, 10.6.1

proceedings before, **48.1(1), (2)**

Inner House interfering with decision of, 38.16.7

issues, authentication of, by, **37.1(9),(10)**

judgment, of, 36.11.2(13)

where authorities not cited by counsel, 28.1.13, 36.11.2(13)

jurors, excusal from jury service, **37.3(2)**, 37.3.4

jury trial,

authentication of issues for, **37.1(9), (10)**

leave to reclaim from, **38,4, 38.5**

excused from obedience to interlocutor by, **38.5(7)**, 38.5.4

motion for further procedure in process transmitted from sheriff court disposed of by, **32.4(3)**

motion outwith term before, **23.7(1),(4),(5)**

motions by pursuer before calling or petitioner before first order, **23.8(1)(a)**

motions in chambers, 23.6.4, **23.8(1)(a)**, 23.8.3, **23.9(a)**, 23.9.3

motions in court, 23.6.4, **23.8(1)(a)**, 23.8.3, **23.9(a)**, 23.9.3

motions in Outer House causes before, **23.6(3)**

note of objection to Auditor's report, 42.4.11

opinion of, 36.11.2(13)

powers outwith term, 10.4.3

reclaiming against interlocutor of, **38.2(a)**

discretion of, 49.46.5

report to Inner House, **34.1–34.3**, 34.1.1–34.1.2

duty to report, where question of status may arise in summary trial, **77.7(1)**, 77.7.1

Motions—*cont.*
duration of, 23.2.18
enrolment, **23.2(1)(b)**, 23.2.1–23.2.18
  at the bar, **23.2(1)(a)**, 23.2.2
  by fax, **23.2(2)(c), (4)**, 23.2.3
  by lodging, **23.2(2)(a)**, 23.2.3
  by post, **23.2(2)(b)**, 23.2.3
expenses, **23.12**, 23.12.1–23.12.2
fax, by, **23.2(2)(c)**
  unsuitable for, **23.2(4)(c)**, 23.2.10
  which may not be enrolled by, **23.2(4)**
fees, 23.2.6, 23.2.19
  hearing, 23.6.6
  variation of order in consistorial cause,
    for, 23.2.19
form of, 23.2.4
granting of, conditions for, 23.13.1–23.13.2
hearing, generally, **23.6**, 23.6.1
  appearance by solicitors, 23.14.1
  date of, 23.6.2
  in chambers, 23.6.4, **23.8(1)(a)**, 23.8.3,
    23.9(a), 23.9.3, **23.10(2)(a)**, 23.10.3
  in court, 23.6.4, **23.8(1)(a)**, 23.8.3, 23.8.4,
    23.9(a), 23.9.3, **23.10(2)(a)**, 23.10.3
Inner House,
  reports to, from Lord Ordinary, **34.1(1)**
  unopposed starred, 23.2.17(2)
  unopposed unstarred, 23.2.17(1)
intimation, written, **23.3**, 23.3.1–23.3.4
  consent to shorter period of, **23.3(3)(a)**
  extending period of, **23.3(3)(c)**
  of opposition to, **23.4(4), (5)**
  period of, **23.3(3)**, 23.3.3
  shortening period of, **23.3(3)(c)**
  statement of written intimation, **23.3(5)**,
    23.3.4
  where not required, **23.3(2)**
Keeper of the Rolls,
  fixing hearing of motions by defender of
    other person before calling, **23.10(2)**
  motions by pursuer before calling or
    petitioner before first order,
    23.8(1)(a)
motion sheet, 23.2.11
  not borrowable, **4.11(3)**
opposition to, **23.4**, 23.4.1
  by fax, **23.4(1)(c)**
  by lodging, **23.4(1)(a)**
  by post, **23.4(1)(b)**
  procedure, 23.4.2–23.4.8
order of calling outwith term or in
  vacation, **23.7(5)**
Outer House,
  starred unopposed, 23.2.16
  unstarred unopposed, 23.2.15
outwith term, **23.7**, 23.7.1–23.7.3
parties, 23.1.1
post, which may not be enrolled by, **23.2(3)**
publication, 23.6.3
  not required, **23.8(1)(b)**
  outwith term or in vacation, **23.7(4)**
requiring appearance, 23.2.12, 23.2.14,
  23.2.16, 23.7.3
solicitor's right of audience in, **23.14**

Motions—*cont.*
starred, **23.2(7), 23.4(6)**, 23.2.14
  appearance required where, **23.2(7)**
  opposed, where, **23.4(6)**
statutory applications in depending
  process, **23.11**, 23.11.1–23.11.2
step of process, 23.2.8
vacation, **23.7**, 23.7.1–23.7.3
wakening a cause, 23.3.1
written intimation, **23.3**
  statement of, **23.3(5)**, 23.3.4
  where not required, **23.3(2)**
Multiplepoinding
advertisement,
  for objections to condescendence and
    claims, **51.5**, 51.5.1–51.5.3
  of dependence of action, **51.8**, 51.8.1,
    51.8.2, **51.9**
  lodging copy of, **51.9**
certificate by officer of Inland Revenue, **8.1**
certificate of intimation,
  lodging of, **51.9**, 51.9.2
challenge by claimant to any other claim,
  51.12.6
claim, failure to lodge timeously, **51.11**,
  51.11.1, 51.11.3
late claimant, 51.2.4, 51.11.1
claim for ranking, 51.6.3
claim upon fund *in medio* by holder, 51.3.6
competition of claims, 51.12.2
conclusions (by holder of fund), 51.2.3
condescendence,
  approval of, **51.7(3)(a)**, 51.7.3, 51.10.1
  claimant, of, **51.6(4)**, 51.6.2–51.6.5
  fund *in medio*, **51.3**, 51.3.1–51.3.8
  lodging of, 51.4.4
  objections to, **51.6(4)**, 51.5.1–51.5.3
  purpose of, 51.3.4
consignation of fund, **51.10**, 51.10.4
decree for aught yet seen, 51.13.2
decree for payment, **51.13**, 51.13.1
  preconditions for, **51.13(1)**
  warrants to be included in, where fund in
    medio consigned into court, **51.13(2)**
defences, lodging of, **51.6(1), (4)**, 51.6.1–
  51.6.6
defender, **51.2(2)**, 51.2.4, 51.2.6
defender and real raiser, 51.2.3, 51.3.2
document of debt, lodging of, **51.6(3)**,
  51.6.5
effect of raising action, 51.2.8
exoneration and discharge,
  generally, 51.2.3
  of holder, **51.10(2)**, 51.10.5, **51.15**,
    51.15.1, 51.15.2
expenses,
  not to be decerned for, when payable out
    of fund *in medio*, **51.12(3)**
  of holder of the fund, 51.10.3
  payment by late claimant, 51.11.3
  taxation of accounts of, before decree for
    payment, **51.13(1)**
final interlocutor, 51.7.3

Suspension and liberation—*cont.*
petition for—*cont.*
on detention by immigration officer,
60.1.1(3)
procedure where answers lodged, **60.5,**
60.5.1–60.5.6
reduction, in action of, **53.1**

Tape recordings
of evidence at proof, **36.11,** 36.11.1
Taxation of accounts
additional fee, **42.14,** 42.14.1–42.14.2
factors to be taken into account,
42.14(3), (4), 42.14.2
content and form of account, 42.1.3, **42.9**
copy of account sent to paying party,
42.3(2), 42.3.5
counsel, employment of, 42.10.2
diet of taxation, **42.2,** 42.2.1
fixing and intimation, **42.2(1)**
production of vouchers etc., **42.2(2),**
42.2.3
expenses,
disallowance by Auditor, **42.5(2),** 42.5.2
generally, 42.1.2
modification of, by court, **42.5(1),** 42.5.1
modification of, by court where assisted
person found liable, **42.6(1),** 42.6.1
time limit for application, **42.6(2)**
fee for lodging account, 42.1.9
fee for taxing account, 42.2.5
interlocutor, final,
dealing with expenses, 42.1.6
form of, where expenses found due,
42.1(1)
intimation of account, **42.1(3),** 42.1.7
late lodging, **42.1(2)(a), (aa),** 42.1.5
lodging of account of expenses, **42.1(2),**
42.1.4, 42.1.5
time limit, **42.1(2)**
motion for approval of report, 42.3.6
objections to account,
failure to intimate, **42.2(1B),** 42.2.4
points of, **42.2(1A),** 42.4.4
time-table for, **42.2(1A),** 42.2.4
relief from failure to lodge or intimate,
42.2(1C), 42.2.4
objections to report, **42.4,** 42.4.1–42.4.4
hearing on, **42.4(4), (5),** 42.4.10, 42.4.11
lodging of note of, **42.4(1),** 42.4.3, 42.4.4
procedure after lodging of minute by
Auditor, **42.4(3),** 42.4.9
reclaiming against decision of Lord
Ordinary on, **38.4(5),** 38.4.6, 42.4.11
outlays, interest on, 7.7.3
powers of Auditor, 42.3.1–42.3.6
remit to Auditor, **42.1(1)(a),** 42.1.1–42.1.9
report of taxation by Auditor, **42.3(1),** 42.3.1
not borrowable, 42.3.1
responsibility of Auditor, **3.7**
solicitor's account to own client, **42.7,**
42.7.1–42.7.6
criteria for Auditor on taxation, **42.7(6)**
form of account, **42.7(3)**
objections to report, **42.7(8)**

Taxation of accounts—*cont.*
solicitor's account to own client—*cont.*
procedure on receipt of intimation of diet
of taxation, **42.7(5)**
report of taxation, **42.7(7)**
transmission of process,
from Auditor, **42.3(1)(b),** 42.3.2–42.3.4
to Auditor, 42.1.8
Taxes
money under control of court, **8.1, 8.2,**
8.1.1
certificate of Inland Revenue, **8.1(2),**
8.1.2
money consigned with Accountant of
Court, **8.1(c),** 8.1.1
Teind Court, 3.6.1
clerk of teinds, 3.6.4
jurisdiction, 3.6.2
procedure, 3.6.3
Teind Office
clerk of teinds, **3.6**
Tenders
acceptance of, 36.11.8(4)
damages in personal injuries, 7.7.3, 43.12.4,
43.18.4
expenses in, 36.11.8(2)
expenses where tender not accepted,
36.11.8(5)
form of, 36.11.8(1)
generally, 36.11.8
interest in, 7.7.7
plurality of parties, 36.11.8(6)
Williamson tenders, 36.11.8(8)
Third party procedure
adjustment of pleadings in, **26.7(2)**
answers to notice, **26.5,** 26.5.1
failure to lodge, **26.6,** 26.6.1
fee for, 26.5.2
form and lodging of, **26.5,** 26.5.1
procedure following, **26.7,** 26.7.1–
26.7.6
time limits, 26.7.1
applications for third party notice, **26.1,**
26.1.1
by defender, **26.1(1)**
by pursuer, **26.1(2)(a)**
by third party, **26.1(2)(b)**
averments, **26.2(1), (2),** 26.2.1
defender,
right of contribution, 26.1.4(1)
right of indemnity, 26.1.4(3)
right of relief, 26.1.4(2)
title and interest, 26.1.4
expenses of abandonment against third
party, **29.1(2)(a)**
granting of order by court, 26.1.1
grounds for, **26.1(1),** 26.1.1–26.1.6
history and purpose, 26.1.1
jurisdiction, 26.1.2
jury trial, loss of right to, 26.1.8
making up open record in, **26.7(1)**
motion for third party notice, **26.2**
procedure after answers, **26.7,** 26.7.1–
26.7.6
proof of claim, **26.7(3),** 26.7.4

C 2554